Equatorial Scale 1:80 000 000 THE WO

S7-00

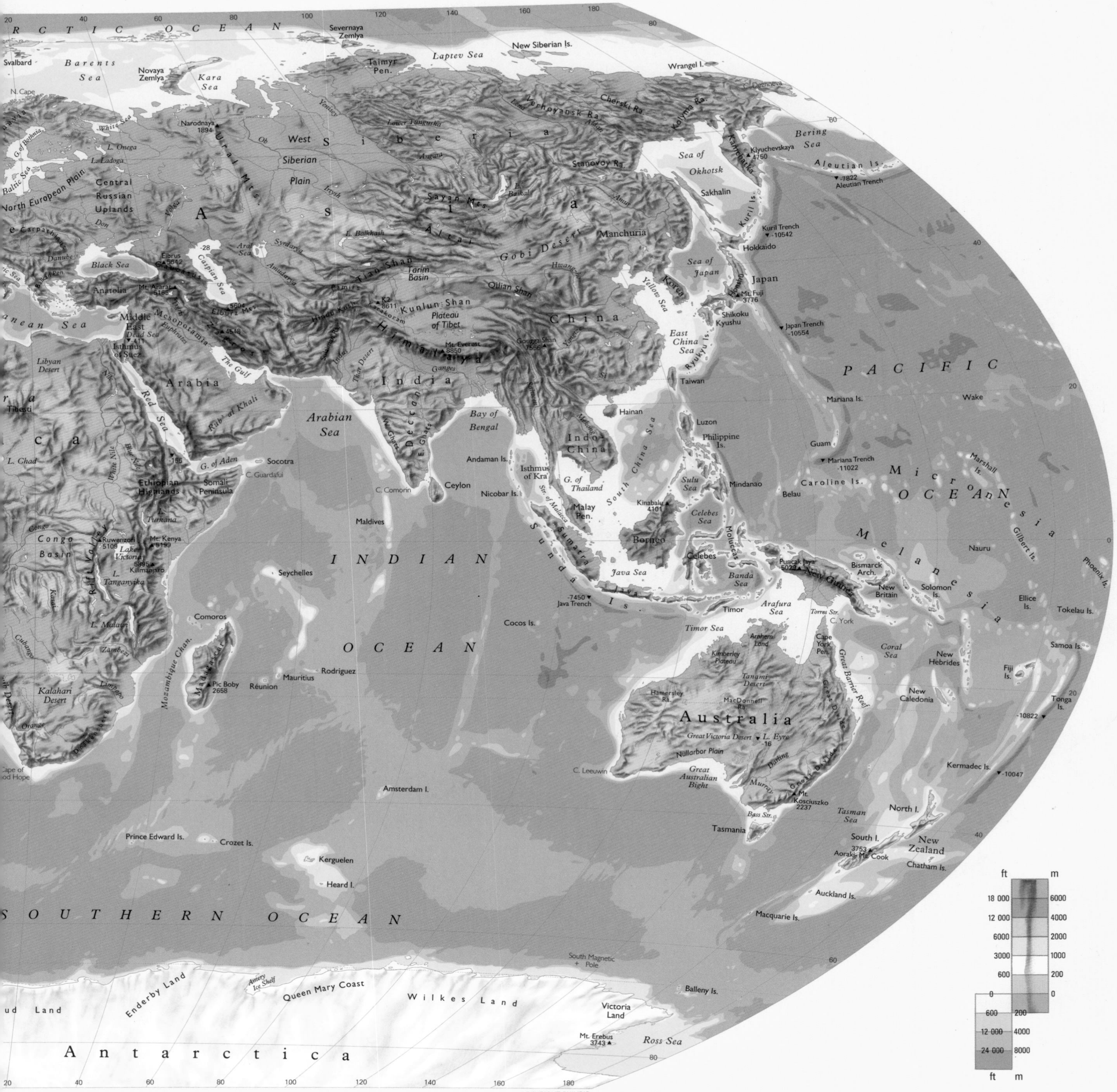

PHILIP'S

GREAT WORLD ATLAS

PHILIP'S
GREAT WORLD ATLAS

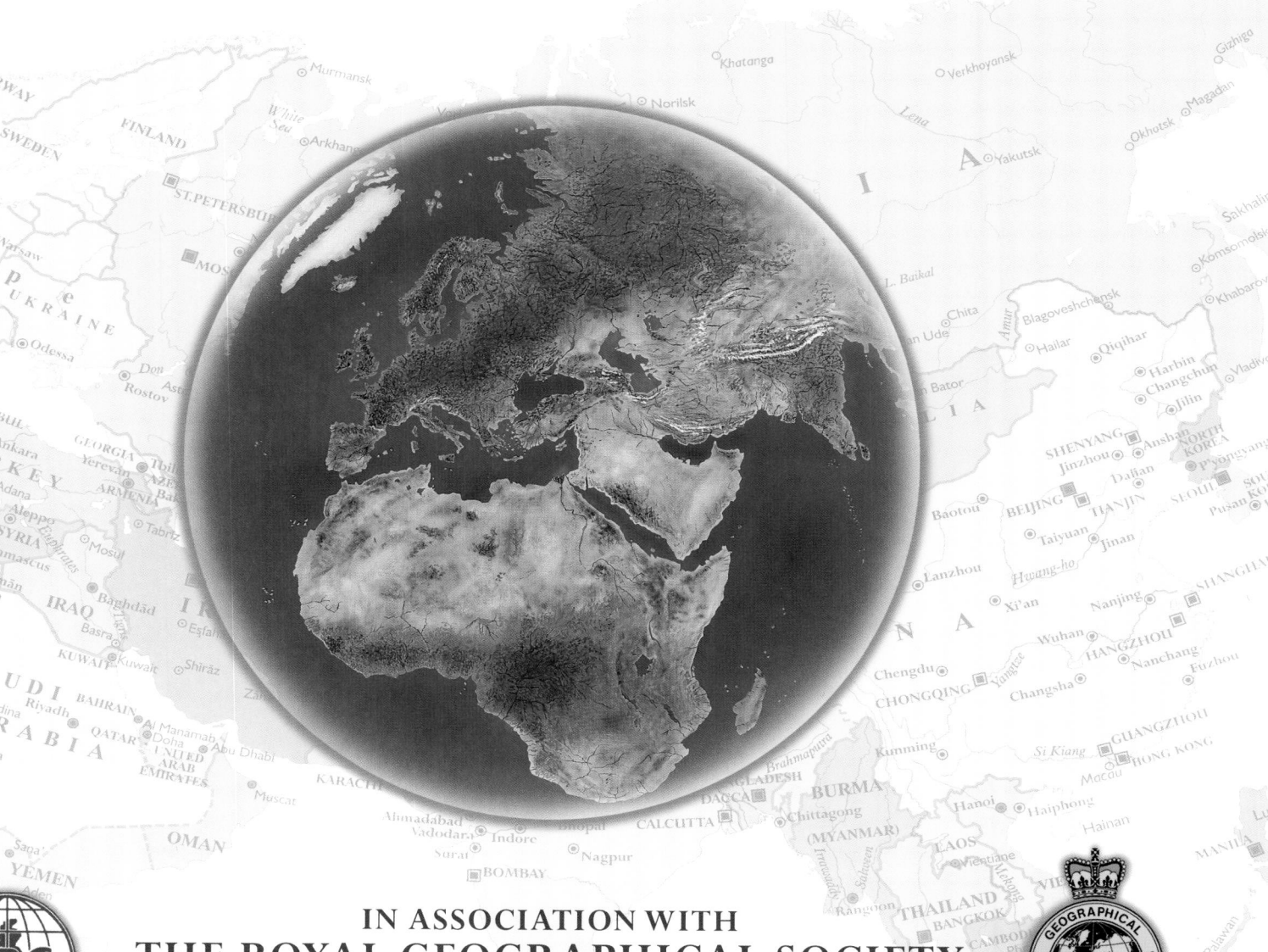

IN ASSOCIATION WITH
THE ROYAL GEOGRAPHICAL SOCIETY
WITH THE INSTITUTE OF BRITISH GEOGRAPHERS

Specialist Geography Consultants

Philip's is grateful to the following people for acting as specialist geography consultants on the 'Introduction to World Geography' front section:

Professor D. Brunsden, Kings College, University of London, UK

Dr C. Clarke, Oxford University, UK

Professor P. Haggett, University of Bristol, UK

Professor M-L. Hsu, University of Minnesota, Minnesota, USA

Professor K. McLachlan, Geopolitical and International Boundaries Research Centre, School of Oriental and African Studies, University of London, UK

Professor M. Monmonier, Syracuse University, New York, USA

Professor M. J. Tooley, University of St Andrews, UK

Dr T. Unwin, Royal Holloway, University of London, UK

Philip's would also like to thank:

Keith Lye

Robin Scagell

Dr I. S. Evans, Durham University, UK

Dr Andrew Tatham, The Royal Geographical Society

Images of Earth (pages XVII–XXXII)
All satellite images in this section courtesy of NPA Group Limited, Edenbridge, UK
(www.satmaps.com)

Introduction to World Geography
Picture Acknowledgements
Courtesy of NPA Group, Edenbridge, UK 9, 48
Science Photo Library /Earth Satellite Corporation 20
NASA/GSFC 22 bottom left and bottom right

Illustrations
Stefan Chabluk
William Donohoe
Bernard Thornton Artists /Steve Seymour

Star charts
John Cox and Richard Monkhouse

Cartography by Philip's

Published in Great Britain in 2003
by Philip's,
a division of Octopus Publishing Group Ltd,
2–4 Heron Quays, London E14 4JP

Copyright © 2003 Philip's

ISBN 0–540–08232–5

A CIP catalogue record for this book is available from the British Library.

Printed in Spain

Details of other Philip's titles and services can be found on our website at:
www.philips-maps.co.uk

Philip's World Atlases are published in association with The Royal Geographical Society (with The Institute of British Geographers).

The Society was founded in 1830 and given a Royal Charter in 1859 for 'the advancement of geographical science'. It holds historical collections of national and international importance, many of which relate to the Society's association with and support for scientific exploration and research from the 19th century onwards. It was pivotal in establishing geography as a teaching and research discipline in British universities close to the turn of the century, and has played a key role in geographical and environmental education ever since.

Today the Society is a leading world centre for geographical learning – supporting education, teaching, research and expeditions, and promoting public understanding of the subject.

The Society welcomes those interested in geography as members. For further information, please visit the website at: www.rgs.org

Philip's World Maps

The reference maps which form the main body of this atlas have been prepared in accordance with the highest standards of international cartography to provide an accurate and detailed representation of the Earth. The scales and projections used have been carefully chosen to give balanced coverage of the world, while emphasizing the most densely populated and economically significant regions. A hallmark of Philip's mapping is the use of hill shading and relief colouring to create a graphic impression of landforms: this makes the maps exceptionally easy to read. However, knowledge of the key features employed in the construction and presentation of the maps will enable the reader to derive the fullest benefit from the atlas.

Map Sequence

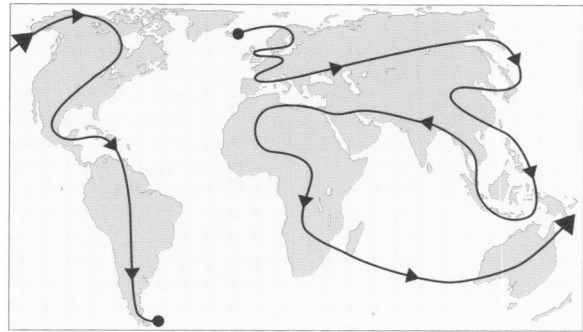

The atlas covers the Earth continent by continent: first Europe; then its land neighbour Asia (mapped north before south, in a clockwise sequence); then Africa, Australia and Oceania, North America and South America. This is the classic arrangement adopted by most cartographers since the 16th century. For each continent, there are maps at a variety of scales. First, physical relief and political maps of the whole continent; then a series of larger-scale maps of the regions within the continent, each followed, where required, by still larger-scale maps of the most important or densely populated areas. The governing principle is that by turning the pages of the atlas, the reader moves steadily from north to south through each continent, with each map overlapping its neighbours.

Map Presentation

With very few exceptions (for example, for the Arctic and Antarctic), the maps are drawn with north at the top, regardless of whether they are presented upright or sideways on the page. In the borders will be found the map title; a locator diagram showing the area covered; continuation arrows showing the page numbers for maps of adjacent areas; the scale; the projection used; the degrees of latitude and longitude; and the letters and figures used in the index for locating place names and geographical features. Physical relief maps also have a height reference panel identifying the colours used for each layer of contouring.

Map Symbols

Each map contains a vast amount of detail which can only be conveyed clearly and accurately by the use of symbols. Points and circles of varying sizes locate and identify the relative importance of towns and cities; different styles of type are employed for administrative, geographical and regional place names to aid identification. A variety of pictorial symbols denote landforms such as glaciers, marshes and coral reefs, and man-made structures including roads, railways, airports and canals. International borders are shown by red lines. Where neighbouring countries are in dispute, for example in parts of the Middle East, the maps show the *de facto* boundary between nations, regardless of the legal or historical situation. The symbols are explained on the first page of the World Maps section of the atlas.

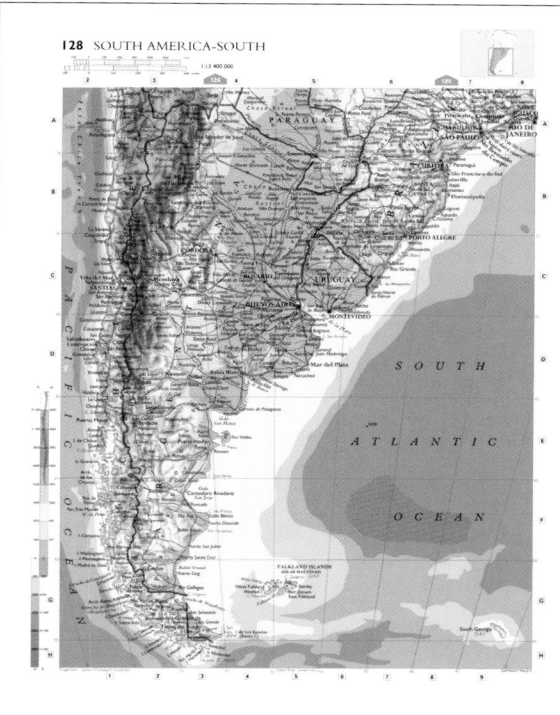

Map Scales

1:16 000 000
1 inch = 252 statute miles

The scale of each map is given in the numerical form known as the 'representative fraction'. The first figure is always one, signifying one unit of distance on the map; the second figure, usually in millions, is the number by which the map unit must be multiplied to give the equivalent distance on the Earth's surface. Calculations can easily be made in centimetres and kilometres, by dividing the Earth units figure by 100 000 (i.e. deleting the last five 0s). Thus 1:1 000 000 means 1 cm = 10 km. The calculation for inches and miles is more laborious, but 1 000 000 divided by 63 360 (the number of inches in a mile) shows that 1:1 000 000 means approximately 1 inch = 16 miles. The table below provides distance equivalents for scales down to 1:50 000 000.

LARGE SCALE		
1:1 000 000	1 cm = 10 km	1 inch = 16 miles
1:2 500 000	1 cm = 25 km	1 inch = 39.5 miles
1:5 000 000	1 cm = 50 km	1 inch = 79 miles
1:6 000 000	1 cm = 60 km	1 inch = 95 miles
1:8 000 000	1 cm = 80 km	1 inch = 126 miles
1:10 000 000	1 cm = 100 km	1 inch = 158 miles
1:15 000 000	1 cm = 150 km	1 inch = 237 miles
1:20 000 000	1 cm = 200 km	1 inch = 316 miles
1:50 000 000	1 cm = 500 km	1 inch = 790 miles

SMALL SCALE

Measuring Distances

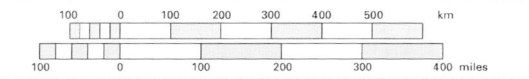

Although each map is accompanied by a scale bar, distances cannot always be measured with confidence because of the distortions involved in portraying the curved surface of the Earth on a flat page. As a general rule, the larger the map scale, the more accurate and reliable will be the distance measured. On small-scale maps, such as those of the world and of entire continents, measurement may only be accurate along the 'standard parallels', or central axes, and should not be attempted without considering the map projection.

Map Projections

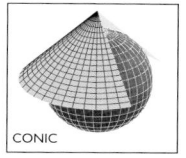  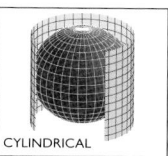

Unlike a globe, no flat map can give a true scale representation of the world in terms of area, shape and position of every region. Each of the numerous systems that have been devised for projecting the curved surface of the Earth on to a flat page involves the sacrifice of accuracy in one or more of these elements. The variations in shape and position of landmasses such as Alaska, Greenland and Australia, for example, can be quite dramatic when different projections are compared.

For this atlas, the guiding principle has been to select projections that involve the least distortion of size and distance. The projection used for each map is noted in the border. Most fall into one of three categories – conic, azimuthal or cylindrical – whose basic concepts are shown above. Each involves plotting the forms of the Earth's surface on a grid of latitude and longitude lines, which may be shown as parallels, curves or radiating spokes.

Latitude and Longitude

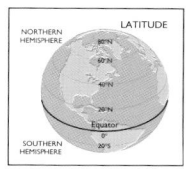 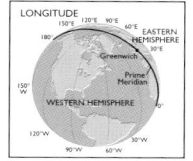 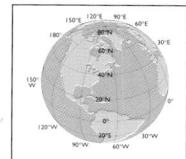

Accurate positioning of individual points on the Earth's surface is made possible by reference to the geometrical system of latitude and longitude. Latitude *parallels* are drawn west–east around the Earth and numbered by degrees north and south of the Equator, which is designated 0° of latitude. Longitude *meridians* are drawn north–south and numbered by degrees east and west of the *prime meridian*, 0° of longitude, which passes through Greenwich in England. By referring to these co-ordinates and their subdivisions of minutes (1/60th of a degree) and seconds (1/60th of a minute), any place on Earth can be located to within a few hundred metres. Latitude and longitude are indicated by blue lines on the maps; they are straight or curved according to the projection employed. Reference to these lines is the easiest way of determining the relative positions of places on different maps, and for plotting compass directions.

Name Forms

For ease of reference, both English and local name forms appear in the atlas. Oceans, seas and countries are shown in English throughout the atlas; country names may be abbreviated to their commonly accepted form (for example, Germany, not The Federal Republic of Germany). Conventional English forms are also used for place names on the smaller-scale maps of the continents. However, local name forms are used on all large-scale and regional maps, with the English form given in brackets only for important cities – the large-scale map of Russia and Central Asia thus shows Moskva (Moscow). For countries which do not use a Roman script, place names have been transcribed according to the systems adopted by the British and US Geographic Names Authorities. For China, the Pin Yin system has been used, with some more widely known forms appearing in brackets, as with Beijing (Peking). Both the English and local names appear in the index, the English form being cross-referenced to the local form.

Contents

World Statistics

Countries	X
Cities	XI
Distances	XII
Climate	XIII
Physical Dimensions	XIV–XV
Regions in the News	XVI

Images of Earth

San Francisco, USA	XVII
Grand Canyon, USA	XVIII
Chicago, USA	XIX
Niagara Falls, USA/Canada	XX
New York, USA	XXI
Washington, DC, USA	XXII
Miami, USA	XXIII
River Amazon, Brazil	XXIV
Buenos Aires, Argentina	XXV
London, UK	XXVI
IJsselmeer, Netherlands	XXVII
Cairo, Egypt	XXVIII
Western Cape, South Africa	XXIX
Shanghai, China	XXX
Tokyo, Japan	XXXI
Sydney, Australia	XXXII

Introduction to World Geography

The Universe	2–3
The Solar System	4–5
Time and Motion	6–7
Oceans	8–9
Geology	10–11
Landforms	12–13
Atmosphere and Weather	14–15
Climate	16–17
Water and Vegetation	18–19
The Natural Environment	20–21
People and the Environment	22–23
Population	24–25
Cities	26–27
The Human Family	28–29
Conflict and Co-operation	30–31
Agriculture	32–33
Energy	34–35
Minerals	36–37
Manufacturing	38–39
Trade	40–41
Health	42–43
Wealth	44–45
Standards of Living	46–47

World Maps

Map Symbols	1
The World: Political 1:80 000 000	2–3
Arctic Ocean 1:29 400 000	4
Antarctica 1:29 400 000	5

Europe

Europe: Physical 1:16 800 000	6
Europe: Political 1:16 800 000	7
Scandinavia 1:4 200 000 Iceland 1: 4 200 000	8–9

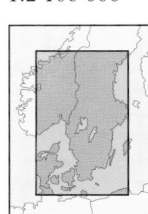

Denmark and Southern Sweden 1:2 100 000	10–11

Ireland 1:1 700 000	12

Scotland 1:1 700 000	13

England and Wales 14–15
1:1 700 000

British Isles 16
1:4 200 000

Netherlands, Belgium and Luxembourg 17
1:2 100 000

Northern France 18–19
1:2 100 000

Southern France 20–21
1:2 100 000

Central Europe 22–23
1:4 200 000

Germany and Switzerland 24–25
1:2 100 000

Austria, Czech Republic and Slovak Republic 26–27
1:2 100 000

Hungary, Romania and the Lower Danube 28–29
1:2 100 000

Poland and the Southern Baltic 30–31
1:2 100 000

Baltic States, Belarus and Ukraine 32–33
1:4 200 000

The Volga Basin and the Caucasus 34–35
1:4 200 000

Western Spain and Portugal 36–37
1:2 100 000

Eastern Spain 38–39
1:2 100 000

Northern Italy, Slovenia and Croatia 40–41
1:2 100 000

Southern Italy 42–43
1:2 100 000

Serbia and Montenegro, Bulgaria and Northern Greece 44–45
1:2 100 000

Southern Greece and Western Turkey 46–47
1:2 100 000

The Balearics, the Canaries and Madeira 48
1:840 000 / 1:1 680 000

Malta, Crete, Corfu, Rhodes and Cyprus 49
1:840 000 / 1:1 090 000

Asia

Asia: Physical   50
1:42 000 000

Asia: Political   51
1:42 000 000

Russia and Central Asia   52–53
1:16 800 000

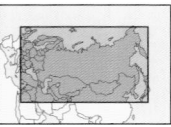

Japan   54–55
1:4 200 000

Northern China and Korea   56–57
1:5 000 000

Southern China   58–59
1:5 000 000

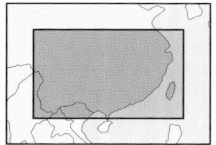

China   60
1:16 800 000

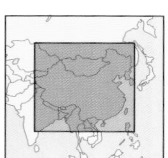

The Philippines   61
1:6 300 000

Indonesia and the Philippines   62–63
1:10 500 000
Java and Madura 1:6 300 000
Bali 1:1 700 000

Mainland South-east Asia   64–65
1:5 000 000
Ko Phuket 1:840 000
Ko Samui 1:840 000
Pinang 1:840 000
Singapore 1:840 000

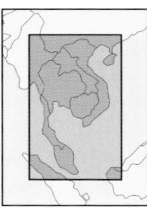

South Asia   66–67
1:8 400 000

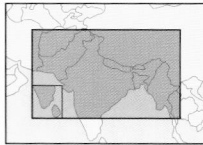

Northern India and Nepal   68–69
1:5 000 000
Jammu and Kashmir 1:5 000 000

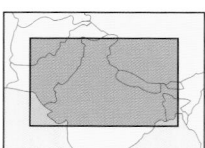

The Middle East   70–71
1:5 900 000

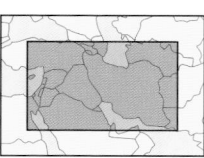

Turkey and Transcaucasia   72–73
1:4 200 000

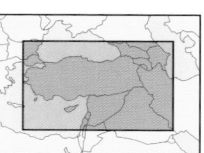

The Near East   74
1:2 100 000

Arabia and the Horn of Africa   75
1:12 600 000

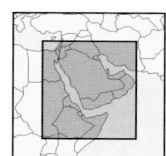

Africa

Africa: Physical   76
1:35 300 000

Africa: Political   77
1:35 300 000

Northern Africa   78–79
1:12 600 000

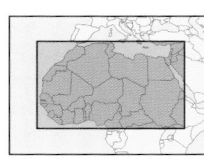

The Nile Valley   80–81
1:6 700 000
The Nile Delta 1:3 400 000

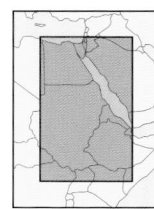

West Africa   82–83
1:6 700 000

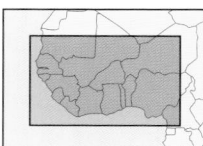

Central and Southern Africa   84–85
1:12 600 000

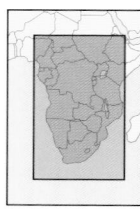

East Africa   86–87
1:6 700 000

Southern Africa   88–89
1:6 700 000

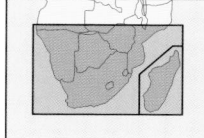

Australia and Oceania

**Australia and Oceania:
Physical and Political**   **90**
1:42 000 000

New Zealand   **91**
1:5 000 000
Samoan Islands 1:10 100 000
Fiji and Tonga 1:10 100 000

Western Australia   **92–93**
1:6 700 000

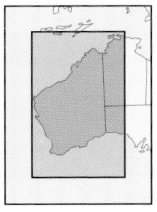

Eastern Australia   **94–95**
1:6 700 000
Whitsunday Islands 1:2 100 000

Pacific Ocean   **96–97**
1:45 400 000

North America

North America: Physical   **98**
1:29 400 000

North America: Political   **99**
1:29 400 000

Canada   **100–101**
1:12 600 000
Alaska 1:25 200 000

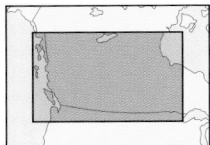

Western Canada   **102–103**
1:5 900 000

Eastern Canada   **104–105**
1:5 900 000

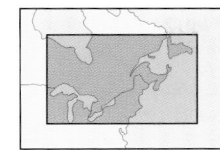

United States   **106–107**
1:10 100 000
Hawaii 1:8 400 000

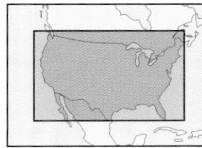

Western United States   **108–109**
1:5 000 000

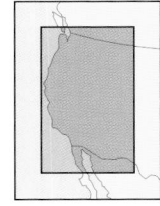

**Central and Southern
California and
Western Washington**   **110–111**
1:2 100 000

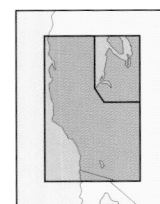

Middle United States   **112–113**
1:5 000 000

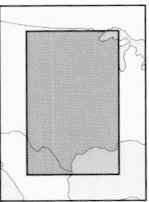

Eastern United States   **114–115**
1:5 000 000

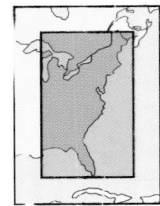

**North-eastern United
States**   **116–117**
1:2 100 000

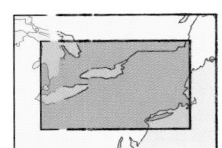

Mexico   **118–119**
1:6 700 000

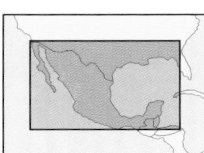

**Central America and
the West Indies**   **120–121**
1:6 700 000
Jamaica 1:2 500 000
Guadeloupe 1:1 700 000
Martinique 1:1 700 000
Puerto Rico 1:2 500 000
Virgin Islands 1:1 700 000
St Lucia 1:840 000
Barbados 1:840 000

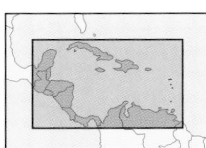

South America

South America: Physical   **122**
1:29 400 000

South America: Political   **123**
1:29 400 000

South America – North   **124–125**
1:13 400 000
Trinidad and Tobago 1:2 100 000

Central South America   **126–127**
1:6 700 000

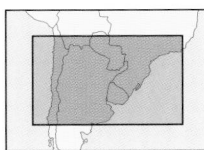

South America – South   **128**
1:13 400 000

Index to
World Maps   **129–224**

World Statistics: Countries

This alphabetical list includes all the countries and territories of the world. If a territory is not completely independent, the country it is associated with is named. The area figures give the total area of land, inland water and ice.

The population figures are 2002 estimates. The annual income is the Gross Domestic Product per capita[†] in US dollars. The figures are the latest available, usually 2001 estimates.

Country/Territory	Area km² Thousands	Area miles² Thousands	Population Thousands	Capital	Annual Income US $
Afghanistan	652	252	27,756	Kabul	800
Albania	28.8	11.1	3,545	Tirana	3,800
Algeria	2,382	920	32,278	Algiers	5,600
American Samoa (US)	0.2	0.08	69	Pago Pago	8,000
Andorra	0.45	0.17	68	Andorra La Vella	19,000
Angola	1,247	481	10,593	Luanda	1,330
Anguilla (UK)	0.1	0.04	12	The Valley	8,600
Antigua & Barbuda	0.44	0.17	67	St John's	10,000
Argentina	2,767	1,068	37,813	Buenos Aires	12,000
Armenia	29.8	11.5	3,330	Yerevan	3,350
Aruba (Netherlands)	0.19	0.07	70	Oranjestad	28,000
Australia	7,687	2,968	19,547	Canberra	24,000
Austria	83.9	32.4	8,170	Vienna	27,000
Azerbaijan	86.6	33.4	7,798	Baku	3,100
Azores (Portugal)	2.2	0.87	234	Ponta Delgada	12,600
Bahamas	13.9	5.4	301	Nassau	16,800
Bahrain	0.68	0.26	656	Manama	13,000
Bangladesh	144	56	133,377	Dhaka	1,750
Barbados	0.43	0.17	277	Bridgetown	14,500
Belarus	207.6	80.1	10,335	Minsk	8,200
Belgium	30.5	11.8	10,275	Brussels	26,100
Belize	23	8.9	263	Belmopan	3,250
Benin	113	43	6,788	Porto-Novo	1,040
Bermuda (UK)	0.05	0.02	64	Hamilton	34,800
Bhutan	47	18.1	2,094	Thimphu	1,200
Bolivia	1,099	424	8,445	La Paz/Sucre	2,600
Bosnia-Herzegovina	51	20	3,964	Sarajevo	1,800
Botswana	582	225	1,591	Gaborone	7,800
Brazil	8,512	3,286	176,030	Brasília	7,400
Brunei	5.8	2.2	351	Bandar Seri Begawan	18,000
Bulgaria	111	43	7,621	Sofia	6,200
Burkina Faso	274	106	12,603	Ouagadougou	1,040
Burma (= Myanmar)	677	261	42,238	Rangoon	1,500
Burundi	27.8	10.7	6,373	Bujumbura	600
Cambodia	181	70	12,775	Phnom Penh	1,500
Cameroon	475	184	16,185	Yaoundé	1,700
Canada	9,976	3,852	31,902	Ottawa	27,700
Canary Is. (Spain)	7.3	2.8	1,694	Las Palmas/Santa Cruz	18,200
Cape Verde Is.	4	1.6	409	Praia	1,500
Cayman Is. (UK)	0.26	0.1	36	George Town	30,000
Central African Republic	623	241	3,643	Bangui	1,300
Chad	1,284	496	8,997	Ndjaména	1,030
Chile	757	292	15,499	Santiago	10,000
China	9,597	3,705	1,284,304	Beijing	4,300
Colombia	1,139	440	41,008	Bogotá	6,300
Comoros	2.2	0.86	614	Moroni	710
Congo	342	132	2,958	Brazzaville	900
Congo (Dem. Rep. of the)	2,345	905	55,225	Kinshasa	590
Cook Is. (NZ)	0.24	0.09	21	Avarua	5,000
Costa Rica	51.1	19.7	3,835	San José	8,500
Croatia	56.5	21.8	4,391	Zagreb	8,300
Cuba	111	43	11,224	Havana	2,300
Cyprus	9.3	3.6	767	Nicosia	11,500
Czech Republic	78.9	30.4	10,257	Prague	14,400
Denmark	43.1	16.6	5,369	Copenhagen	28,000
Djibouti	23.2	9	473	Djibouti	1,400
Dominica	0.75	0.29	70	Roseau	3,700
Dominican Republic	48.7	18.8	8,722	Santo Domingo	5,800
East Timor	14.9	5.7	953	Dili	500
Ecuador	284	109	13,447	Quito	3,000
Egypt	1,001	387	70,712	Cairo	3,700
El Salvador	21	8.1	6,354	San Salvador	4,600
Equatorial Guinea	28.1	10.8	498	Malabo	2,100
Eritrea	94	36	4,466	Asmara	740
Estonia	44.7	17.3	1,416	Tallinn	10,000
Ethiopia	1,128	436	67,673	Addis Ababa	700
Faroe Is. (Denmark)	1.4	0.54	46	Tórshavn	20,000
Fiji	18.3	7.1	856	Suva	5,200
Finland	338	131	5,184	Helsinki	25,800
France	552	213	59,766	Paris	25,400
French Guiana (France)	90	34.7	182	Cayenne	6,000
French Polynesia (France)	4	1.5	258	Papeete	5,000
Gabon	268	103	1,233	Libreville	5,500
Gambia, The	11.3	4.4	1,456	Banjul	1,770
Gaza Strip (OPT)*	0.36	0.14	1,226	–	630
Georgia	69.7	26.9	4,961	Tbilisi	3,100
Germany	357	138	83,252	Berlin	26,200
Ghana	239	92	20,244	Accra	1,980
Gibraltar (UK)	0.007	0.003	28	Gibraltar Town	17,500
Greece	132	51	10,645	Athens	17,900
Greenland (Denmark)	2,176	840	56	Nuuk (Godthåb)	20,000
Grenada	0.34	0.13	89	St George's	4,750
Guadeloupe (France)	1.7	0.66	436	Basse-Terre	9,000
Guam (US)	0.55	0.21	161	Agana	21,000
Guatemala	109	42	13,314	Guatemala City	3,700
Guinea	246	95	7,775	Conakry	1,970
Guinea-Bissau	36.1	13.9	1,345	Bissau	900
Guyana	215	83	698	Georgetown	3,600
Haiti	27.8	10.7	7,064	Port-au-Prince	1,700
Honduras	112	43	6,561	Tegucigalpa	2,600
Hong Kong (China)	1.1	0.4	7,303	–	25,000
Hungary	93	35.9	10,075	Budapest	12,000
Iceland	103	40	279	Reykjavik	24,800
India	3,288	1,269	1,045,845	New Delhi	2,500
Indonesia	1,890	730	231,328	Jakarta	3,000
Iran	1,648	636	66,623	Tehran	6,400
Iraq	438	169	24,002	Baghdad	2,500
Ireland	70.3	27.1	3,883	Dublin	27,300
Israel	20.6	7.96	6,030	Jerusalem	20,000
Italy	301	116	57,716	Rome	24,300
Ivory Coast (= Côte d'Ivoire)	322	125	16,805	Yamoussoukro	1,550
Jamaica	11	4.2	2,680	Kingston	3,700
Japan	378	146	126,975	Tokyo	27,200
Jordan	89.2	34.4	5,307	Amman	4,200
Kazakhstan	2,717	1,049	16,742	Astana	5,900
Kenya	580	224	31,139	Nairobi	1,000
Kiribati	0.72	0.28	96	Tarawa	840
Korea, North	121	47	22,224	Pyŏngyang	1,000
Korea, South	99	38.2	48,324	Seoul	18,000
Kuwait	17.8	6.9	2,112	Kuwait City	15,100
Kyrgyzstan	198.5	76.6	4,822	Bishkek	2,800
Laos	237	91	5,777	Vientiane	1,630
Latvia	65	25	2,367	Riga	7,800
Lebanon	10.4	4	3,678	Beirut	5,200
Lesotho	30.4	11.7	2,208	Maseru	2,450
Liberia	111	43	3,288	Monrovia	1,100
Libya	1,760	679	5,369	Tripoli	7,600
Liechtenstein	0.16	0.06	33	Vaduz	23,000
Lithuania	65.2	25.2	3,601	Vilnius	7,600
Luxembourg	2.6	1	449	Luxembourg	43,400
Macau (China)	0.02	0.006	462	–	17,600
Macedonia (FYROM)	25.7	9.9	2,055	Skopje	4,400
Madagascar	587	227	16,473	Antananarivo	870
Madeira (Portugal)	0.81	0.31	241	Funchal	16,800
Malawi	118	46	10,702	Lilongwe	660
Malaysia	330	127	22,662	Kuala Lumpur/Putrajaya	9,000
Maldives	0.3	0.12	320	Malé	3,870
Mali	1,240	479	11,340	Bamako	840
Malta	0.32	0.12	397	Valletta	15,000
Marshall Is.	0.18	0.07	74	Dalap-Uliga-Darrit	1,600
Martinique (France)	1.1	0.42	422	Fort-de-France	11,000
Mauritania	1,030	398	2,829	Nouakchott	1,800
Mauritius	2	0.72	1,200	Port Louis	10,800
Mayotte (France)	0.37	0.14	171	Mamoundzou	600
Mexico	1,958	756	103,400	Mexico City	9,000
Micronesia, Fed. States of	0.7	0.27	136	Palikir	2,000
Moldova	33.7	13	4,435	Chişinău	2,550
Monaco	0.002	0.001	32	Monaco	27,000
Mongolia	1,567	605	2,694	Ulan Bator	1,770
Montserrat (UK)	0.1	0.04	8	Plymouth	2,400
Morocco	447	172	31,168	Rabat	3,700
Mozambique	802	309	19,608	Maputo	900
Namibia	825	318	1,821	Windhoek	4,500
Nauru	0.02	0.008	12	Yaren District	5,000
Nepal	141	54	25,874	Katmandu	1,400
Netherlands	41.5	16	16,068	Amsterdam/The Hague	25,800
Netherlands Antilles (Neths)	0.99	0.38	214	Willemstad	11,400
New Caledonia (France)	18.6	7.2	208	Nouméa	15,000
New Zealand	269	104	3,908	Wellington	19,500
Nicaragua	130	50	5,024	Managua	2,500
Niger	1,267	489	10,640	Niamey	820
Nigeria	924	357	129,935	Abuja	840
Northern Mariana Is. (US)	0.48	0.18	77	Saipan	12,500
Norway	324	125	4,525	Oslo	30,800
Oman	212	82	2,713	Muscat	8,200
Pakistan	796	307	147,663	Islamabad	2,100
Palau	0.46	0.18	19	Koror	9,000
Panama	77.1	29.8	2,882	Panamá	5,900
Papua New Guinea	463	179	5,172	Port Moresby	2,400
Paraguay	407	157	5,884	Asunción	4,600
Peru	1,285	496	27,950	Lima	4,800
Philippines	300	116	84,526	Manila	4,000
Poland	313	121	38,625	Warsaw	8,800
Portugal	92.4	35.7	9,609	Lisbon	17,300
Puerto Rico (US)	9	3.5	3,958	San Juan	11,200
Qatar	11	4.2	793	Doha	21,200
Réunion (France)	2.5	0.97	744	St-Denis	4,800
Romania	238	92	22,318	Bucharest	6,800
Russia	17,075	6,592	144,979	Moscow	8,300
Rwanda	26.3	10.2	7,398	Kigali	1,000
St Kitts & Nevis	0.36	0.14	39	Basseterre	8,700
St Lucia	0.62	0.24	160	Castries	4,400
St Vincent & Grenadines	0.39	0.15	116	Kingstown	2,900
Samoa	2.8	1.1	179	Apia	3,500
San Marino	0.06	0.02	28	San Marino	34,600
São Tomé & Príncipe	0.96	0.37	170	São Tomé	1,200
Saudi Arabia	2,150	830	23,513	Riyadh	10,600
Senegal	197	76	10,590	Dakar	1,580
Serbia & Montenegro	102.3	39.5	10,657	Belgrade	2,250
Seychelles	0.46	0.18	80	Victoria	7,600
Sierra Leone	71.7	27.7	5,615	Freetown	500
Singapore	0.62	0.24	4,453	Singapore	24,700
Slovak Republic	49	18.9	5,422	Bratislava	11,500
Slovenia	20.3	7.8	1,933	Ljubljana	16,000
Solomon Is.	28.9	11.2	495	Honiara	1,700
Somalia	638	246	7,753	Mogadishu	550
South Africa	1,220	471	43,648	C. Town/Pretoria/Bloem.	9,400
Spain	505	195	38,383	Madrid	18,900
Sri Lanka	65.6	25.3	19,577	Colombo	3,250
Sudan	2,506	967	37,090	Khartoum	1,360
Suriname	163	63	436	Paramaribo	3,500
Swaziland	17.4	6.7	1,124	Mbabane	4,200
Sweden	450	174	8,877	Stockholm	24,700
Switzerland	41.3	15.9	7,302	Bern	31,100
Syria	185	71	17,156	Damascus	3,200
Taiwan	36	13.9	22,548	Taipei	17,200
Tajikistan	143.1	55.2	6,720	Dushanbe	1,140
Tanzania	945	365	37,188	Dodoma	610
Thailand	513	198	62,354	Bangkok	6,600
Togo	56.8	21.9	5,286	Lomé	1,500
Tonga	0.75	0.29	106	Nuku'alofa	2,200
Trinidad & Tobago	5.1	2	1,164	Port of Spain	9,000
Tunisia	164	63	9,816	Tunis	6,600
Turkey	779	301	67,309	Ankara	6,700
Turkmenistan	488.1	188.5	4,689	Ashkhabad	4,700
Turks & Caicos Is. (UK)	0.43	0.17	19	Cockburn Town	7,300
Tuvalu	0.03	0.01	11	Fongafale	1,100
Uganda	236	91	24,699	Kampala	1,200
Ukraine	603.7	233.1	48,396	Kiev	4,200
United Arab Emirates	83.6	32.3	2,446	Abu Dhabi	21,100
United Kingdom	243.3	94	59,778	London	24,700
United States of America	9,373	3,619	280,562	Washington, DC	36,300
Uruguay	177	68	3,387	Montevideo	9,200
Uzbekistan	447.4	172.7	25,563	Tashkent	2,500
Vanuatu	12.2	4.7	196	Port-Vila	1,300
Vatican City	0.0004	0.0002	1	Vatican City	N/A
Venezuela	912	352	24,288	Caracas	6,100
Vietnam	332	127	81,098	Hanoi	2,100
Virgin Is. (UK)	0.15	0.06	21	Road Town	16,000
Virgin Is. (US)	0.34	0.13	123	Charlotte Amalie	15,000
Wallis & Futuna Is. (France)	0.2	0.08	16	Mata-Utu	2,000
West Bank (OPT)*	5.86	2.26	2,164	–	1,000
Western Sahara	266	103	256	El Aaiún	N/A
Yemen	528	204	18,701	Sana	820
Zambia	753	291	9,959	Lusaka	870
Zimbabwe	391	151	11,377	Harare	2,450

*OPT = Occupied Palestinian Territory   N/A = Not Available

[†] Gross Domestic Product per capita has been measured using the purchasing power parity method. This enables comparisons to be made between countries through their purchasing power (in US dollars), showing real price levels of goods and services rather than using currency exchange rates.

World Statistics: Cities

This list shows the principal cities with more than 500,000 inhabitants (only cities with more than 1 million inhabitants are included for Brazil, China, India, Indonesia, Japan and Russia). The figures are taken from the most recent census or estimate available, and as far as possible are the population of the metropolitan area, e.g. greater New York, Mexico or Paris. All the figures are in thousands. Local name forms have been used for the smaller cities (e.g. Kraków).

AFGHANISTAN
Kabul 1,565
ALGERIA
Algiers 1,722
Oran 664
ANGOLA
Luanda 2,250
ARGENTINA
Buenos Aires 10,990
Córdoba 1,198
Rosario 1,096
Mendoza 775
La Plata 640
San Miguel de
 Tucumán 622
Mar del Plata 520
ARMENIA
Yerevan 1,256
AUSTRALIA
Sydney 4,041
Melbourne 3,417
Brisbane 1,601
Perth 1,364
Adelaide 1,093
AUSTRIA
Vienna 1,560
AZERBAIJAN
Baku 1,713
BANGLADESH
Dhaka 7,832
Chittagong 2,041
Khulna 877
Rajshahi 517
BELARUS
Minsk 1,717
Homyel 502
BELGIUM
Brussels 948
BENIN
Cotonou 537
BOLIVIA
La Paz 1,126
Santa Cruz 767
BOSNIA-HERZEGOVINA
Sarajevo 526
BRAZIL
São Paulo 10,434
Rio de Janeiro 5,858
Salvador 2,443
Belo Horizonte 2,239
Fortaleza 2,141
Brasília 2,051
Curitiba 1,587
Recife 1,423
Manaus 1,406
Pôrto Alegre 1,361
Belém 1,281
Goiânia 1,093
Guarulhos 1,073
BULGARIA
Sofia 1,139
BURKINA FASO
Ouagadougou 690
BURMA (MYANMAR)
Rangoon 2,513
Mandalay 533
CAMBODIA
Phnom Penh 570
CAMEROON
Douala 1,200
Yaoundé 800
CANADA
Toronto 4,881
Montréal 3,511
Vancouver 2,079
Ottawa-Hull 1,107
Calgary 972
Edmonton 957
Québec 693
Winnipeg 685
Hamilton 681
CENTRAL AFRICAN
 REPUBLIC
Bangui 553
CHAD
Ndjaména 530
CHILE
Santiago 4,691
CHINA
Shanghai 15,082
Beijing 12,362
Tianjin 10,687
Hong Kong (SAR)* 6,502
Chongqing 3,870
Shenyang 3,762
Wuhan 3,520
Guangzhou 3,114

Harbin 2,505
Nanjing 2,211
Xi'an 2,115
Chengdu 1,933
Dalian 1,855
Changchun 1,810
Jinan 1,660
Taiyuan 1,642
Qingdao 1,584
Zibo 1,346
Zhengzhou 1,324
Lanzhou 1,296
Anshan 1,252
Fushun 1,246
Kunming 1,242
Changsha 1,198
Hangzhou 1,185
Nanchang 1,169
Shijiazhuang 1,159
Guiyang 1,131
Ürümqi 1,130
Jilin 1,118
Tangshan 1,110
Qiqihar 1,104
Baotou 1,033
COLOMBIA
Bogotá 6,005
Cali 1,986
Medellín 1,971
Barranquilla 1,158
Cartagena 813
Cúcuta 589
Bucaramanga 508
CONGO
Brazzaville 938
Pointe-Noire 576
CONGO (DEM. REP.)
Kinshasa 2,664
Lubumbashi 565
CROATIA
Zagreb 868
CUBA
Havana 2,204
CZECH REPUBLIC
Prague 1,203
DENMARK
Copenhagen 1,362
DOMINICAN REPUBLIC
Santo Domingo 2,135
Stgo. de los
 Caballeros 691
ECUADOR
Guayaquil 2,070
Quito 1,574
EGYPT
Cairo 6,800
Alexandria 3,339
El Gîza 2,222
Shubra el Kheima 871
EL SALVADOR
San Salvador 1,522
ETHIOPIA
Addis Ababa 2,316
FINLAND
Helsinki 532
FRANCE
Paris 11,175
Lyons 1,648
Marseilles 1,516
Lille 1,143
Toulouse 965
Nice 933
Bordeaux 925
Nantes 711
Strasbourg 612
Toulon 565
Douai 553
Rennes 521
Rouen 518
Grenoble 515
GEORGIA
Tbilisi 1,253
GERMANY
Berlin 3,426
Hamburg 1,705
Munich 1,206
Cologne 964
Frankfurt 644
Essen 609
Dortmund 595
Stuttgart 585
Düsseldorf 571
Bremen 547
Duisburg 529
Hanover 521
GHANA
Accra 1,781

GREECE
Athens 3,097
GUATEMALA
Guatemala 1,167
GUINEA
Conakry 1,508
HAITI
Port-au-Prince 885
HONDURAS
Tegucigalpa 814
HUNGARY
Budapest 1,885
INDIA
Mumbai (Bombay) 16,368
Kolkata (Calcutta) 13,217
Delhi 12,791
Chennai (Madras) 6,425
Bangalore 5,687
Hyderabad 5,534
Ahmadabad 4,519
Pune 3,756
Surat 2,811
Kanpur 2,690
Jaipur 2,324
Lucknow 2,267
Nagpur 2,123
Patna 1,707
Indore 1,639
Vadodara 1,492
Bhopal 1,455
Coimbatore 1,446
Ludhiana 1,395
Cochin 1,355
Vishakhapatnam 1,329
Agra 1,321
Varanasi 1,212
Madurai 1,195
Meerut 1,167
Nasik 1,152
Jabalpur 1,117
Jamshedpur 1,102
Asansol 1,090
Faridabad 1,055
Allahabad 1,050
Amritsar 1,011
Vijayawada 1,011
Rajkot 1,002
INDONESIA
Jakarta 11,500
Surabaya 2,701
Bandung 2,368
Medan 1,910
Semarang 1,366
Palembang 1,352
Tangerang 1,198
Ujung Pandang 1,092
IRAN
Tehran 6,759
Mashhad 1,887
Esfahan 1,266
Tabriz 1,191
Shiraz 1,053
Karaj 941
Ahvaz 805
Qom 778
Bakhtaran 693
IRAQ
Baghdad 3,841
As Sulaymaniyah 952
Arbil 770
Al Mawsil 664
Al Kazimiyah 521
IRELAND
Dublin 1,024
ISRAEL
Tel Aviv-Yafo 1,880
Jerusalem 591
ITALY
Rome 2,654
Milan 1,306
Naples 1,050
Turin 923
Palermo 689
Genoa 659
IVORY COAST
Abidjan 2,500
JAMAICA
Kingston 644
JAPAN
Tokyo 17,950
Yokohama 3,427
Osaka 2,599
Nagoya 2,171
Sapporo 1,822
Kobe 1,494
Kyoto 1,468
Fukuoka 1,341

Kawasaki 1,250
Hiroshima 1,126
Kitakyushu 1,011
Sendai 1,008
JORDAN
Amman 1,752
KAZAKHSTAN
Almaty 1,151
Qaraghandy 574
KENYA
Nairobi 2,000
Mombasa 600
KOREA, NORTH
Pyŏngyang 2,741
Hamhung 710
Chŏngjin 583
KOREA, SOUTH
Seoul 10,231
Pusan 3,814
Taegu 2,449
Inch'on 2,308
Taejŏn 1,272
Kwangju 1,258
Ulsan 967
Sŏngnam 869
Puch'on 779
Suwŏn 756
Anyang 590
Chŏnju 563
Chŏngju 531
Ansan 510
P'ohang 509
KYRGYZSTAN
Bishkek 589
LAOS
Vientiane 532
LATVIA
Riga 811
LEBANON
Beirut 1,500
Tripoli 500
LIBERIA
Monrovia 962
LIBYA
Tripoli 960
LITHUANIA
Vilnius 580
MACEDONIA
Skopje 541
MADAGASCAR
Antananarivo 1,053
MALAYSIA
Kuala Lumpur 1,145
MALI
Bamako 810
MAURITANIA
Nouakchott 735
MEXICO
Mexico City 15,643
Guadalajara 2,847
Monterrey 2,522
Puebla 1,055
León 872
Ciudad Juárez 798
Tijuana 743
Culiacán 602
Mexicali 602
Acapulco 592
Mérida 557
Chihuahua 530
San Luis Potosí 526
Aguascalientés 506
MOLDOVA
Chişinău 658
MONGOLIA
Ulan Bator 673
MOROCCO
Casablanca 2,943
Rabat-Salé 1,220
Marrakesh 602
Fès 564
MOZAMBIQUE
Maputo 2,000
NEPAL
Katmandu 535
NETHERLANDS
Amsterdam 1,115
Rotterdam 1,086
The Hague 700
Utrecht 557
NEW ZEALAND
Auckland 1,090
NICARAGUA
Managua 864
NIGERIA
Lagos 10,287
Ibadan 1,432

Ogbomosho 730
Kano 674
NORWAY
Oslo 502
PAKISTAN
Karachi 9,269
Lahore 5,064
Faisalabad 1,977
Rawalpindi 1,406
Multan 1,182
Hyderabad 1,151
Gujranwala 1,125
Peshawar 988
Quetta 560
Islamabad 525
PARAGUAY
Asunción 945
PERU
Lima 6,601
Arequipa 620
Trujillo 509
PHILIPPINES
Manila 8,594
Quezon City 1,989
Caloocan 1,023
Davao 1,009
Cebu 662
Zamboanga 511
POLAND
Warsaw 1,626
Lódz 815
Kraków 740
Wroclaw 641
Poznań 580
PORTUGAL
Lisbon 2,561
Oporto 1,174
ROMANIA
Bucharest 2,028
RUSSIA
Moscow 8,405
St Petersburg 4,216
Nizhniy Novgorod 1,371
Novosibirsk 1,367
Yekaterinburg 1,275
Samara 1,170
Omsk 1,158
Kazan 1,085
Chelyabinsk 1,084
Ufa 1,082
Perm 1,025
Rostov 1,023
Volgograd 1,005
SAUDI ARABIA
Riyadh 1,800
Jedda 1,500
Mecca 630
SENEGAL
Dakar 1,905
SERBIA &
 MONTENEGRO
Belgrade 1,598
SIERRA LEONE
Freetown 505
SINGAPORE
Singapore 3,866
SOMALIA
Mogadishu 997
SOUTH AFRICA
Cape Town 2,350
Johannesburg 1,196
Durban 1,137
Pretoria 1,080
Port Elizabeth 853
Vanderbijlpark-
 Vereeniging 774
Soweto 597
Sasolburg 540
SPAIN
Madrid 3,030
Barcelona 1,615
Valencia 763
Sevilla 720
Zaragoza 608
Málaga 532
SRI LANKA
Colombo 1,863
SUDAN
Omdurman 1,271
Khartoum 925
Khartoum North 701
SWEDEN
Stockholm 727
SWITZERLAND
Zürich 733
SYRIA
Aleppo 1,813

Damascus 1,394
Homs 659
TAIWAN
T'aipei 2,596
Kaohsiung 1,435
T'aichung 858
T'ainan 708
Panch'iao 539
TAJIKISTAN
Dushanbe 524
TANZANIA
Dar-es-Salaam 1,361
THAILAND
Bangkok 7,507
TOGO
Lomé 590
TUNISIA
Tunis 1,827
TURKEY
Istanbul 8,506
Ankara 3,294
Izmir 2,554
Bursa 1,485
Adana 1,273
Konya 1,140
Mersin (Içel) 956
Gaziantep 867
Antalya 867
Kayseri 862
Diyarbakir 833
Urfa 785
Manisa 696
Kocaeli 629
Antalya 591
Samsun 590
Kahramanmaras 551
Balikesir 538
Eskisehir 519
Erzurum 512
Malatya 510
TURKMENISTAN
Ashkhabad 536
UGANDA
Kampala 954
UKRAINE
Kiev 2,621
Kharkov 1,521
Dnepropetrovsk 1,122
Donetsk 1,065
Odessa 1,027
Zaporizhzhya 863
Lviv 794
Kryvyy Rih 720
Mykolayiv 518
Mariupol 500
UNITED ARAB EMIRATES
Abu Dhabi 928
Dubai 674
UNITED KINGDOM
London 8,089
Birmingham 2,373
Manchester 2,353
Liverpool 852
Glasgow 832
Sheffield 661
Nottingham 649
Newcastle 617
Bristol 552
Leeds 529
UNITED STATES
New York 21,200
Los Angeles 16,374
Chicago-Gary 9,158
Washington-
 Baltimore 7,608
San Francisco-
 San Jose 7,039
Philadelphia-
 Atlantic City 6,188
Boston-Worcester 5,819
Detroit-Flint 5,456
Dallas-Fort Worth 5,222
Houston-Galveston 4,670
Atlanta 4,112
Miami-
 Fort Lauderdale 3,876
Seattle-Tacoma 3,554
Phoenix-Mesa 3,252
Minneapolis-St Paul 2,969
Cleveland-Akron 2,946
San Diego 2,814
St Louis 2,604
Denver-Boulder 2,582
San Juan 2,450
Tampa-
 St Petersburg 2,396
Pittsburgh 2,359

Portland-Salem 2,265
Cincinnati-Hamilton 1,979
Sacramento-Yolo 1,797
Kansas City 1,776
Milwaukee-Racine 1,690
Orlando 1,645
Indianapolis 1,607
San Antonio 1,592
Norfolk-
 Virginia Beach-
 Newport News 1,570
Las Vegas 1,563
Columbus, OH 1,540
Charlotte-Gastonia 1,499
New Orleans 1,338
Salt Lake City 1,334
Greensboro-
 Winston Salem-
 High Point 1,252
Austin-San Marcos 1,250
Nashville 1,231
Providence-
 Fall River 1,189
Raleigh-Durham 1,188
Hartford 1,183
Buffalo-
 Niagara Falls 1,170
Memphis 1,136
West Palm Beach 1,131
Jacksonville, FL 1,100
Rochester 1,098
Grand Rapids 1,089
Oklahoma City 1,083
Louisville 1,026
Richmond-
 Petersburg 997
Greenville 962
Dayton-Springfield 951
Fresno 923
Birmingham 921
Honolulu 876
Albany-Schenectady 876
Tucson 844
Tulsa 803
Syracuse 732
Omaha 717
Albuquerque 713
Knoxville 687
El Paso 680
Bakersfield 662
Allentown 638
Harrisburg 629
Scranton 625
Toledo 618
Baton Rouge 603
Youngstown-Warren 595
Springfield, MA 592
Sarasota 590
Little Rock 584
McAllen 569
Stockton-Lodi 564
Charleston 549
Wichita 545
Mobile 540
Columbia, SC 537
Colorado Springs 517
Fort Wayne 502
URUGUAY
Montevideo 1,379
UZBEKISTAN
Tashkent 2,118
VENEZUELA
Caracas 1,975
Maracaibo 1,706
Valencia 1,263
Barquisimeto 811
Ciudad Guayana 642
VIETNAM
Ho Chi Minh City 4,322
Hanoi 3,056
Haiphong 783
YEMEN
Sana' 972
Aden 562
ZAMBIA
Lusaka 982
ZIMBABWE
Harare 1,189
Bulawayo 622

* SAR = Special
 Administrative
 Region of China

World Statistics: Distances

The table shows air distances in miles and kilometres between 30 major cities. Known as 'Great Circle' distances, these measure the shortest routes between the cities, which aircraft use wherever possible. The maps show the world centred on six cities, and illustrate, for example, why direct flights from Japan to northern America and Europe are across the Arctic regions. The maps have been constructed on an Azimuthal Equidistant projection, on which all distances measured through the centre point are true to scale. The red lines are drawn at 5,000, 10,000 and 15,000 km from the central city.

Upper-right triangle = miles; lower-left triangle = km; diagonal = city.

	Beijing	Bombay (Mumbai)	Buenos Aires	Cairo	Calcutta (Kolkata)	Caracas	Chicago	Hong Kong	Honolulu	Johannesburg	Lagos	London	Los Angeles	Mexico City	Moscow	Nairobi	New York	Paris	Rio de Janeiro	Rome	Singapore	Sydney	Tokyo	Wellington
Beijing		2956	11972	4688	2031	8947	6588	1220	5070	7276	7119	5057	6251	7742	3600	5727	6828	5106	10773	5049	2783	5561	1304	6700
Bombay (Mumbai)	4757		9275	2706	1034	9024	8048	2683	8024	4334	4730	4467	8700	9728	3126	2816	7793	4356	8332	3837	2432	6313	4189	7686
Buenos Aires	19268	14925		7341	10268	3167	5599	11481	7558	5025	4919	6917	6122	4591	8374	6463	5298	6867	1214	6929	9867	7332	11410	6202
Cairo	7544	4355	11814		3541	6340	6127	5064	8838	3894	2432	2180	7580	7687	1803	2197	5605	1994	6149	1325	5137	8959	5947	10268
Calcutta (Kolkata)	3269	1664	16524	5699		9609	7978	1653	7048	5256	5727	4946	8152	9494	3438	3839	7921	4883	9366	4486	1800	5678	3195	7055
Caracas	14399	14522	5096	10203	15464		2502	10166	6009	6847	4810	4664	3612	2228	6175	7173	2131	4738	2825	5196	11407	9534	8801	8154
Chicago	10603	12953	9011	3206	12839	4027		7783	4247	8689	5973	3949	1742	1694	4971	8005	711	4132	5311	4809	9369	9243	6299	8358
Hong Kong	1963	4317	18478	8150	2659	16360	12526		5543	6669	7360	5980	7232	8775	4439	5453	8047	5984	11001	5769	1615	4582	1786	5857
Honolulu	8160	12914	12164	14223	11343	9670	6836	8921		11934	10133	7228	2558	3781	7036	10739	4958	7437	8290	8026	6721	5075	3854	4669
Johannesburg	11710	6974	8088	6267	8459	11019	13984	10732	19206		2799	5637	10362	9063	5692	1818	7979	5426	4420	4811	5381	6860	8418	7308
Lagos	11457	7612	7916	3915	9216	7741	9612	11845	16308	4505		3118	7713	6879	3886	2366	5268	2929	3750	2510	6925	9643	8376	9973
London	8138	7190	11131	3508	7961	7507	6356	9623	11632	9071	5017		5442	5552	1552	4237	3463	212	5778	889	6743	10558	5942	11691
Los Angeles	10060	14000	9852	12200	13120	5812	2804	11639	4117	16676	12414	8758		1549	6070	9659	2446	5645	6310	6331	8776	7502	5475	6719
Mexico City	12460	15656	7389	12372	15280	3586	2726	14122	6085	14585	11071	8936	2493		6664	9207	2090	5717	4780	6365	10321	8058	7024	6897
Moscow	5794	5031	13477	2902	5534	9938	8000	7144	11323	9161	6254	2498	9769	10724		3942	4666	1545	7184	1477	5237	9008	4651	10283
Nairobi	9216	4532	10402	3536	6179	11544	12883	8776	17282	2927	3807	6819	15544	14818	6344		7358	4029	5548	3350	4635	7552	6996	8490
New York	10988	12541	8526	9020	12747	3430	1145	12950	7980	12841	8477	5572	3936	3264	7510	11842		3626	4832	4280	9531	9935	6741	8951
Paris	8217	7010	11051	3210	7858	7625	6650	9630	11968	8732	4714	342	9085	9200	2486	6485	5836		5708	687	6671	10539	6038	11798
Rio de Janeiro	17338	13409	1953	9896	15073	4546	8547	17704	13342	7113	6035	9299	10155	7693	11562	8928	7777	9187		5725	9763	8389	11551	7367
Rome	8126	6175	11151	2133	7219	8363	7739	9284	12916	7743	4039	1431	10188	10243	2376	5391	6888	1105	9214		6229	10143	6127	11523
Singapore	4478	3914	15879	8267	2897	18359	15078	2599	10816	8660	11145	10852	14123	16610	8428	7460	15339	10737	15712	10025		3915	3306	5298
Sydney	8949	10160	11800	14418	9138	15343	14875	7374	8168	11040	15519	16992	12073	12969	14497	12153	15989	16962	13501	16324	6300		4861	1383
Tokyo	2099	6742	18362	9571	5141	14164	10137	2874	6202	13547	13480	9562	8811	11304	7485	11260	10849	9718	18589	9861	5321	7823		5762
Wellington	10782	12370	9981	16524	11354	13122	13451	9427	7513	11761	16050	18814	10814	11100	16549	13664	14405	18987	11855	18545	8526	2226	9273	

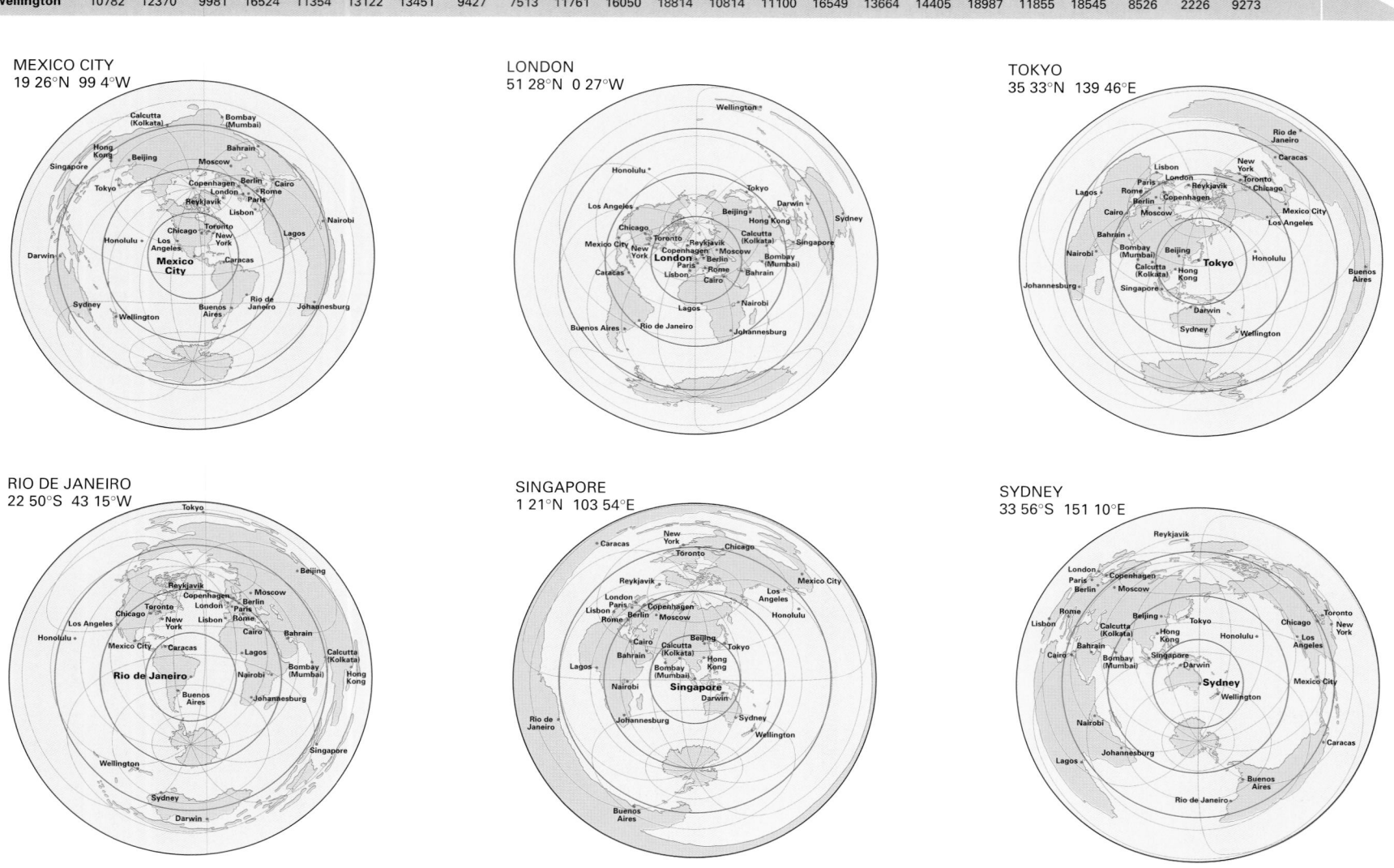

MEXICO CITY 19 26°N 99 4°W

LONDON 51 28°N 0 27°W

TOKYO 35 33°N 139 46°E

RIO DE JANEIRO 22 50°S 43 15°W

SINGAPORE 1 21°N 103 54°E

SYDNEY 33 56°S 151 10°E

World Statistics: Climate

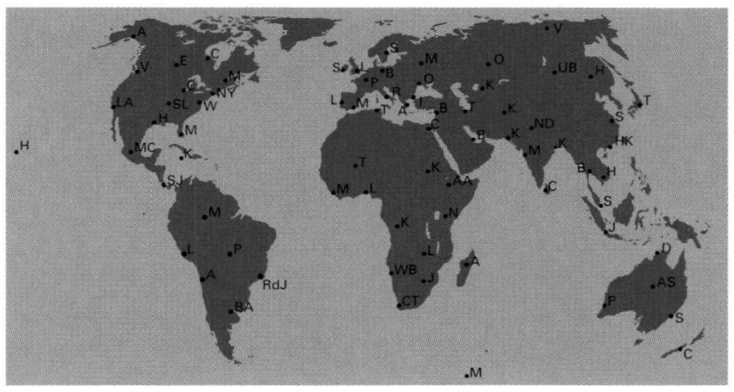

Rainfall and temperature figures are provided for more than 70 cities around the world. As climate is affected by altitude, the height of each city is shown in metres beneath its name. For each location, the top row of figures shows the total rainfall or snow in millimetres, and the bottom row the average temperature in degrees Celsius; the total annual rainfall and average annual temperature are at the end of the rows.

EUROPE

	Jan.	Feb.	Mar.	Apr.	May	June	July	Aug.	Sept.	Oct.	Nov.	Dec.	Year
Athens, Greece	62	37	37	23	23	14	6	7	15	51	56	71	402
107 m	10	10	12	16	20	25	28	28	24	20	15	11	18
Berlin, Germany	46	40	33	42	49	65	73	69	48	49	46	43	603
55 m	−1	0	4	9	14	17	19	18	15	9	5	1	9
Istanbul, Turkey	109	92	72	46	38	34	34	30	58	81	103	119	816
14 m	5	6	7	11	16	20	23	23	20	16	12	8	14
Lisbon, Portugal	111	76	109	54	44	16	3	4	33	62	93	103	708
77 m	11	12	14	16	17	20	22	23	21	18	14	12	17
London, UK	54	40	37	37	46	45	57	59	49	57	64	48	593
5 m	4	5	7	9	12	16	18	17	15	11	8	5	11
Málaga, Spain	61	51	62	46	26	5	1	3	29	64	64	62	474
33 m	12	13	16	17	19	29	25	26	23	20	16	13	18
Moscow, Russia	39	38	36	37	53	58	88	71	58	45	47	54	624
156 m	−13	−10	−4	6	13	16	18	17	12	6	−1	−7	4
Odesa, Ukraine	57	62	30	21	34	34	42	37	37	13	35	71	473
64 m	−3	−1	2	9	15	20	22	22	18	12	9	1	10
Paris, France	56	46	35	42	57	54	59	64	55	50	51	50	619
75 m	3	4	8	11	15	18	20	19	17	12	7	4	12
Rome, Italy	71	62	57	51	46	37	15	21	63	99	129	93	744
17 m	8	9	11	14	18	22	25	25	22	17	13	10	16
Shannon, Irish Republic	94	67	56	53	61	57	77	79	86	86	96	117	929
2 m	5	5	7	9	12	14	16	16	14	11	8	6	10
Stockholm, Sweden	43	30	25	31	34	45	61	76	60	48	53	48	554
44 m	−3	−3	−1	5	10	15	18	17	12	7	3	0	7

ASIA

	Jan.	Feb.	Mar.	Apr.	May	June	July	Aug.	Sept.	Oct.	Nov.	Dec.	Year
Bahrain	8	18	13	8	<3	0	0	0	0	0	18	18	81
5 m	17	18	21	25	29	32	33	34	31	28	24	19	26
Bangkok, Thailand	8	20	36	58	198	160	160	175	305	206	66	5	1,397
2 m	26	28	29	30	29	29	28	28	28	28	26	25	28
Beirut, Lebanon	191	158	94	53	18	3	<3	<3	5	51	132	185	892
34 m	14	14	16	18	22	24	27	28	26	24	19	16	21
Colombo, Sri Lanka	89	69	147	231	371	224	135	109	160	348	315	147	2,365
7 m	26	26	27	28	28	27	27	27	27	27	26	26	27
Harbin, China	6	5	10	23	43	94	112	104	46	33	8	5	488
160 m	−18	−15	−5	6	13	19	22	21	14	4	−6	−16	3
Ho Chi Minh, Vietnam	15	3	13	43	221	330	315	269	335	269	114	56	1,984
9 m	26	27	29	30	29	28	28	28	27	27	27	26	28
Hong Kong, China	33	46	74	137	292	394	381	361	257	114	43	31	2,162
33 m	16	15	18	22	26	28	28	28	27	25	21	18	23
Jakarta, Indonesia	300	300	211	147	114	97	64	43	66	112	142	203	1,798
8 m	26	26	27	27	27	27	27	27	27	27	27	26	27
Kabul, Afghanistan	31	36	94	102	20	5	3	3	<3	15	20	10	338
1,815 m	−3	−1	6	13	18	22	25	24	20	14	7	3	12
Karachi, Pakistan	13	10	8	3	3	18	81	41	13	<3	3	5	196
4 m	19	20	24	28	30	31	30	29	28	28	24	20	26
Kazalinsk, Kazakhstan	10	10	13	13	15	5	5	8	8	10	13	15	125
63 m	−12	−11	−3	6	18	23	25	23	16	8	−1	−7	7
Kolkata (Calcutta), India	10	31	36	43	140	297	325	328	252	114	20	5	1,600
6 m	20	22	27	30	30	30	29	29	29	28	23	19	26
Mumbai (Bombay), India	3	3	3	<3	18	485	617	340	264	64	13	3	1,809
11 m	24	24	26	28	30	29	27	27	27	28	27	26	27
New Delhi, India	23	18	13	8	13	74	180	172	117	10	3	10	640
218 m	14	17	23	28	33	34	31	30	29	26	20	15	25
Omsk, Russia	15	8	8	13	31	51	51	51	28	25	18	20	318
85 m	−22	−19	−12	−1	10	16	18	16	10	1	−11	−18	−1
Shanghai, China	48	58	84	94	94	180	147	142	130	71	51	36	1,135
7 m	4	5	9	14	20	24	28	28	23	19	12	7	16
Singapore	252	173	193	188	173	173	170	196	178	208	254	257	2,413
10 m	26	27	28	28	28	28	28	27	27	27	27	27	27
Tehran, Iran	46	38	46	36	13	3	3	3	3	8	20	31	246
1,220 m	2	5	9	16	21	26	30	29	25	18	12	6	17
Tokyo, Japan	48	74	107	135	147	165	142	152	234	208	97	56	1,565
6 m	3	4	7	13	17	21	25	26	23	17	11	6	14
Ulan Bator, Mongolia	<3	<3	3	5	10	28	76	51	23	5	5	3	208
1,325 m	−26	−21	−13	−1	6	14	16	14	8	−1	−13	−22	−3
Verkhoyansk, Russia	5	5	3	5	8	23	28	25	13	8	8	5	134
100 m	−50	−45	−32	−15	0	12	14	9	2	−15	−38	−48	−17

AFRICA

	Jan.	Feb.	Mar.	Apr.	May	June	July	Aug.	Sept.	Oct.	Nov.	Dec.	Year
Addis Ababa, Ethiopia	<3	3	25	135	213	201	206	239	102	28	<3	0	1,151
2,450 m	19	20	20	20	19	18	18	19	21	22	21	20	20
Antananarivo, Madagas.	300	279	178	53	18	8	8	10	18	61	135	287	1,356
1,372 m	21	21	21	19	18	15	14	15	17	19	21	21	19
Cairo, Egypt	5	5	5	3	3	<3	0	0	<3	<3	3	5	28
116 m	13	15	18	21	25	28	28	28	26	24	20	15	22
Cape Town, S. Africa	15	8	18	48	79	84	89	66	43	31	18	10	508
17 m	21	21	20	17	14	13	12	13	14	16	18	19	17
Johannesburg, S. Africa	114	109	89	38	25	8	8	8	23	56	107	125	709
1,665 m	20	20	18	16	13	10	11	13	16	18	19	20	16
Khartoum, Sudan	<3	<3	<3	<3	3	8	53	71	18	5	<3	0	158
390 m	24	25	28	31	33	34	32	31	32	32	28	25	29
Kinshasa, Congo (D.R.)	135	145	196	196	158	8	3	3	31	119	221	142	1,354
325 m	26	26	27	27	26	24	23	24	25	26	26	26	25
Lagos, Nigeria	28	46	102	150	269	460	279	64	140	206	69	25	1,836
3 m	27	28	29	28	28	26	26	25	26	26	28	28	27
Lusaka, Zambia	231	191	142	18	3	<3	<3	0	<3	10	91	150	836
1,277 m	21	22	21	21	19	16	16	18	22	24	23	22	21
Monrovia, Liberia	31	56	97	216	516	973	996	373	744	772	236	130	5,138
23 m	26	26	27	27	26	25	24	25	25	25	26	26	26
Nairobi, Kenya	38	64	125	211	158	46	15	23	31	53	109	86	958
1,820 m	19	19	19	19	18	16	16	16	18	19	18	18	18
Timbuktu, Mali	<3	<3	3	<3	5	23	79	81	38	3	<3	<3	231
301 m	22	24	28	32	34	35	32	30	32	31	28	23	29
Tunis, Tunisia	64	51	41	36	18	8	3	8	33	51	48	61	419
66 m	10	11	13	16	19	23	26	27	25	20	16	11	18
Walvis Bay, Namibia	<3	5	8	3	3	<3	<3	3	<3	<3	<3	<3	23
7 m	19	19	19	18	17	16	15	14	14	15	17	18	18

AUSTRALIA, NEW ZEALAND AND ANTARCTICA

	Jan.	Feb.	Mar.	Apr.	May	June	July	Aug.	Sept.	Oct.	Nov.	Dec.	Year
Alice Springs, Australia	43	33	28	10	15	13	8	8	8	18	31	38	252
579 m	29	28	25	20	15	12	12	14	18	23	26	28	21
Christchurch, N. Zealand	56	43	48	48	66	66	69	48	46	43	48	56	638
10 m	16	16	14	12	9	6	6	7	9	12	14	16	11
Darwin, Australia	386	312	254	97	15	3	<3	3	13	51	119	239	1,491
30 m	29	29	29	29	28	26	25	26	28	29	30	29	28
Mawson, Antarctica	11	30	20	10	44	180	4	40	3	20	0	0	362
14 m	0	−5	−10	−14	−15	−16	−18	−18	−19	−13	−5	−1	−11
Perth, Australia	8	10	20	43	130	180	170	149	86	56	20	13	881
60 m	23	23	22	19	16	14	13	13	15	16	19	22	18
Sydney, Australia	89	102	127	135	127	117	117	76	73	71	73	73	1,181
42 m	22	22	21	18	15	13	12	13	15	18	19	21	17

NORTH AMERICA

	Jan.	Feb.	Mar.	Apr.	May	June	July	Aug.	Sept.	Oct.	Nov.	Dec.	Year
Anchorage, Alaska, USA	20	18	15	10	13	18	41	66	66	56	25	23	371
40 m	−11	−8	−5	2	7	12	14	13	9	2	−5	−11	2
Chicago, Illinois, USA	51	51	66	71	86	89	84	81	79	66	61	51	836
251 m	−4	−3	2	9	14	20	23	22	19	12	5	−1	10
Churchill, Man., Canada	15	13	18	23	32	44	46	58	51	43	39	21	402
13 m	−28	−26	−20	−10	−2	6	12	11	5	−2	−12	−22	−7
Edmonton, Alta., Canada	25	19	19	22	43	77	89	78	39	17	16	25	466
676 m	−15	−10	−5	4	11	15	17	16	11	6	−4	−10	3
Honolulu, Hawaii, USA	104	66	79	48	25	18	23	28	36	48	64	104	643
12 m	23	18	19	20	22	24	25	26	26	24	22	19	22
Houston, Texas, USA	89	76	84	91	119	117	99	99	104	94	89	109	1,171
12 m	12	13	17	21	24	27	28	29	26	22	16	12	21
Kingston, Jamaica	23	15	23	31	102	89	38	91	99	180	74	36	800
34 m	25	25	25	26	26	28	28	28	27	27	26	26	26
Los Angeles, Calif., USA	79	76	71	25	10	3	<3	<3	5	15	31	66	381
95 m	13	14	14	16	17	19	21	22	21	18	16	14	17
Mexico City, Mexico	13	5	10	20	53	119	170	152	130	51	18	8	747
2,309 m	12	13	16	18	19	19	17	18	18	16	14	13	16
Miami, Florida, USA	71	53	64	81	173	178	155	160	203	234	71	51	1,516
8 m	20	20	22	23	25	27	28	28	27	25	22	21	24
Montréal, Que., Canada	72	65	74	74	66	82	90	92	88	76	81	87	946
57 m	−10	−9	−3	−6	13	18	21	20	15	9	2	−7	6
New York City, NY, USA	94	97	91	81	81	84	107	109	86	89	76	91	1,092
96 m	−1	−1	3	10	16	20	23	23	21	15	7	2	11
St Louis, Mo., USA	58	64	89	97	114	114	89	86	81	74	71	64	1,001
173 m	0	1	7	13	19	24	26	26	22	15	8	2	14
San José, Costa Rica	15	5	20	46	229	241	211	241	305	300	145	41	1,798
1,146 m	19	19	21	21	22	21	21	21	21	20	20	19	20
Vancouver, BC, Canada	154	115	101	60	52	45	32	41	67	114	150	182	1,113
14 m	3	5	6	9	12	15	17	17	14	10	6	4	10
Washington, DC, USA	86	76	91	84	94	99	112	109	94	74	66	79	1,064
22 m	1	2	7	12	18	23	25	24	20	14	8	3	13

SOUTH AMERICA

	Jan.	Feb.	Mar.	Apr.	May	June	July	Aug.	Sept.	Oct.	Nov.	Dec.	Year
Antofagasta, Chile	0	0	0	<3	<3	3	5	3	<3	3	<3	0	13
94 m	21	21	20	18	16	15	14	14	15	16	18	19	17
Buenos Aires, Argentina	79	71	109	89	76	61	56	61	79	86	84	99	950
27 m	23	23	21	17	13	9	10	11	13	15	19	22	16
Lima, Peru	3	<3	<3	<3	5	5	8	8	8	3	3	<3	41
120 m	23	24	24	22	19	17	17	16	17	18	19	21	20
Manaus, Brazil	249	231	262	221	170	84	58	38	46	107	142	203	1,811
44 m	28	28	28	27	28	28	28	28	29	29	29	28	28
Paraná, Brazil	287	236	239	102	13	<3	3	5	28	127	231	310	1,582
260 m	23	23	23	23	23	21	21	22	24	24	24	23	23
Rio de Janeiro, Brazil	125	122	130	107	79	53	41	43	66	79	104	137	1,082
61 m	26	26	25	24	22	21	21	21	21	22	23	25	23

World Statistics: Physical Dimensions

Each topic list is divided into continents and within a continent the items are listed in order of size. The order of the continents is the same as in the atlas, beginning with Europe and ending with South America. The bottom part of many of the lists is selective in order to give examples from as many different countries as possible. The world top ten are shown in square brackets; in the case of mountains this has not been done because the world top 30 are all in Asia. The figures are rounded as appropriate.

WORLD, CONTINENTS, OCEANS

THE WORLD	km²	miles²	%
The World	509,450,000	196,672,000	–
Land	149,450,000	57,688,000	29.3
Water	360,000,000	138,984,000	70.7
Asia	44,500,000	17,177,000	29.8
Africa	30,302,000	11,697,000	20.3
North America	24,241,000	9,357,000	16.2
South America	17,793,000	6,868,000	11.9
Antarctica	14,100,000	5,443,000	9.4
Europe	9,957,000	3,843,000	6.7
Australia and Oceania	8,557,000	3,303,000	5.7
Pacific Ocean	179,679,000	69,356,000	49.9
Atlantic Ocean	92,373,000	35,657,000	25.7
Indian Ocean	73,917,000	28,532,000	20.5
Arctic Ocean	14,090,000	5,439,000	3.9

SEAS

PACIFIC	km²	miles²
South China Sea	2,974,600	1,148,500
Bering Sea	2,268,000	875,000
Sea of Okhotsk	1,528,000	590,000
East China and Yellow	1,249,000	482,000
Sea of Japan	1,008,000	389,000
Gulf of California	162,000	62,500
Bass Strait	75,000	29,000

ATLANTIC	km²	miles²
Caribbean Sea	2,766,000	1,068,000
Mediterranean Sea	2,516,000	971,000
Gulf of Mexico	1,543,000	596,000
Hudson Bay	1,232,000	476,000
North Sea	575,000	223,000
Black Sea	462,000	178,000
Baltic Sea	422,170	163,000
Gulf of St Lawrence	238,000	92,000

INDIAN	km²	miles²
Red Sea	438,000	169,000
The Gulf	239,000	92,000

MOUNTAINS

EUROPE		m	ft
Elbrus	Russia	5,642	18,510
Mont Blanc	France/Italy	4,807	15,771
Monte Rosa	Italy/Switzerland	4,634	15,203
Dom	Switzerland	4,545	14,911
Liskamm	Switzerland	4,527	14,852
Weisshorn	Switzerland	4,505	14,780
Taschorn	Switzerland	4,490	14,730
Matterhorn/Cervino	Italy/Switz.	4,478	14,691
Mont Maudit	France/Italy	4,465	14,649
Dent Blanche	Switzerland	4,356	14,291
Nadelhorn	Switzerland	4,327	14,196
Grandes Jorasses	France/Italy	4,208	13,806
Jungfrau	Switzerland	4,158	13,642
Barre des Ecrins	France	4,103	13,461
Gran Paradiso	Italy	4,061	13,323
Piz Bernina	Italy/Switzerland	4,049	13,284
Eiger	Switzerland	3,970	13,025
Monte Viso	Italy	3,841	12,602
Grossglockner	Austria	3,797	12,457
Wildspitze	Austria	3,772	12,382
Monte Disgrazia	Italy	3,678	12,066
Mulhacén	Spain	3,478	11,411
Pico de Aneto	Spain	3,404	11,168
Marmolada	Italy	3,342	10,964
Etna	Italy	3,340	10,958
Punta del'Argentera	Italy	3,297	10,817
Zugspitze	Germany	2,962	9,718
Musala	Bulgaria	2,925	9,596
Olympus	Greece	2,917	9,570
Triglav	Slovenia	2,863	9,393
Monte Cinto	France (Corsica)	2,710	8,891
Gerlachovka	Slovak Republic	2,655	8,711
Torre de Cerrado	Spain	2,648	8,688
Galdhöpiggen	Norway	2,468	8,100
Hvannadalshnúkur	Iceland	2,119	6,952
Kebnekaise	Sweden	2,117	6,946
Ben Nevis	UK	1,343	4,406

ASIA		m	ft
Everest	China/Nepal	8,850	29,035
K2 (Godwin Austen)	China/Kashmir	8,611	28,251
Kanchenjunga	India/Nepal	8,598	28,208
Lhotse	China/Nepal	8,516	27,939
Makalu	China/Nepal	8,481	27,824
Cho Oyu	China/Nepal	8,201	26,906
Dhaulagiri	Nepal	8,172	26,811
Manaslu	Nepal	8,156	26,758
Nanga Parbat	Kashmir	8,126	26,660
Annapurna	Nepal	8,078	26,502
Gasherbrum	China/Kashmir	8,068	26,469
Broad Peak	China/Kashmir	8,051	26,414
Xixabangma	China	8,012	26,286
Kangbachen	India/Nepal	7,902	25,925
Jannu	India/Nepal	7,902	25,925
Gayachung Kang	Nepal	7,897	25,909
Himalchuli	Nepal	7,893	25,896
Disteghil Sar	Kashmir	7,885	25,869
Nuptse	Nepal	7,879	25,849
Khunyang Chhish	Kashmir	7,852	25,761
Masherbrum	Kashmir	7,821	25,659
Nanda Devi	India	7,817	25,646
Rakaposhi	Kashmir	7,788	25,551
Batura	Kashmir	7,785	25,541
Namche Barwa	China	7,756	25,446
Kamet	India	7,756	25,446
Soltoro Kangri	Kashmir	7,742	25,400
Gurla Mandhata	China	7,728	25,354
Trivor	Pakistan	7,720	25,328
Kongur Shan	China	7,719	25,324
Tirich Mir	Pakistan	7,690	25,229
K'ula Shan	Bhutan/China	7,543	24,747
Pik Kommunizma	Tajikistan	7,495	24,590
Demavend	Iran	5,604	18,386
Ararat	Turkey	5,165	16,945
Gunong Kinabalu	Malaysia (Borneo)	4,101	13,455
Yu Shan	Taiwan	3,997	13,113
Fuji-San	Japan	3,776	12,388

AFRICA		m	ft
Kilimanjaro	Tanzania	5,895	19,340
Mt Kenya	Kenya	5,199	17,057
Ruwenzori (Margherita)	Uganda/Congo (D.R.)	5,109	16,762
Ras Dashan	Ethiopia	4,620	15,157
Meru	Tanzania	4,565	14,977
Karisimbi	Rwanda/Congo (D.R.)	4,507	14,787
Mt Elgon	Kenya/Uganda	4,321	14,176
Batu	Ethiopia	4,307	14,130
Guna	Ethiopia	4,231	13,882
Toubkal	Morocco	4,165	13,665
Irhil Mgoun	Morocco	4,071	13,356
Mt Cameroon	Cameroon	4,070	13,353
Amba Ferit	Ethiopia	3,875	13,042
Pico del Teide	Spain (Tenerife)	3,718	12,198
Thabana Ntlenyana	Lesotho	3,482	11,424
Emi Koussi	Chad	3,415	11,204
Mt aux Sources	Lesotho/S. Africa	3,282	10,768
Mt Piton	Réunion	3,069	10,069

OCEANIA		m	ft
Puncak Jaya	Indonesia	5,030	16,503
Puncak Trikora	Indonesia	4,750	15,584
Puncak Mandala	Indonesia	4,702	15,427
Mt Wilhelm	Papua NG	4,508	14,790
Mauna Kea	USA (Hawaii)	4,205	13,796
Mauna Loa	USA (Hawaii)	4,169	13,681
Mt Cook (Aoraki)	New Zealand	3,753	12,313
Mt Balbi	Solomon Is.	2,439	8,002
Orohena	Tahiti	2,241	7,352
Mt Kosciuszko	Australia	2,237	7,339

NORTH AMERICA		m	ft
Mt McKinley (Denali)	USA (Alaska)	6,194	20,321
Mt Logan	Canada	5,959	19,551
Pico de Orizaba	Mexico	5,610	18,405
Mt St Elias	USA/Canada	5,489	18,008
Popocatepetl	Mexico	5,452	17,887
Mt Foraker	USA (Alaska)	5,304	17,401
Ixtaccihuatl	Mexico	5,286	17,342
Lucania	Canada	5,227	17,149
Mt Steele	Canada	5,073	16,644
Mt Bona	USA (Alaska)	5,005	16,420
Mt Blackburn	USA (Alaska)	4,996	16,391
Mt Sanford	USA (Alaska)	4,940	16,207
Mt Wood	Canada	4,848	15,905
Nevado de Toluca	Mexico	4,670	15,321

NORTH AMERICA (continued)		m	ft
Mt Fairweather	USA (Alaska)	4,663	15,298
Mt Hunter	USA (Alaska)	4,442	14,573
Mt Whitney	USA	4,418	14,495
Mt Elbert	USA	4,399	14,432
Mt Harvard	USA	4,395	14,419
Mt Rainier	USA	4,392	14,409
Blanca Peak	USA	4,372	14,344
Longs Peak	USA	4,345	14,255
Tajumulco	Guatemala	4,220	13,845
Grand Teton	USA	4,197	13,770
Mt Waddington	Canada	3,994	13,104
Mt Robson	Canada	3,954	12,972
Chirripó Grande	Costa Rica	3,837	12,589
Pico Duarte	Dominican Rep.	3,175	10,417

SOUTH AMERICA		m	ft
Aconcagua	Argentina	6,962	22,841
Bonete	Argentina	6,872	22,546
Ojos del Salado	Argentina/Chile	6,863	22,516
Pissis	Argentina	6,779	22,241
Mercedario	Argentina/Chile	6,770	22,211
Huascaran	Peru	6,768	22,204
Llullaillaco	Argentina/Chile	6,723	22,057
Nudo de Cachi	Argentina	6,720	22,047
Yerupaja	Peru	6,632	21,758
N. de Tres Cruces	Argentina/Chile	6,620	21,719
Incahuasi	Argentina/Chile	6,601	21,654
Cerro Galan	Argentina	6,600	21,654
Tupungato	Argentina/Chile	6,570	21,555
Sajama	Bolivia	6,542	21,463
Illimani	Bolivia	6,485	21,276
Coropuna	Peru	6,425	21,079
Ausangate	Peru	6,384	20,945
Cerro del Toro	Argentina	6,380	20,932
Siula Grande	Peru	6,356	20,853
Chimborazo	Ecuador	6,267	20,561
Alpamayo	Peru	5,947	19,511
Cotapaxi	Ecuador	5,896	19,344
Pico Colon	Colombia	5,800	19,029
Pico Bolivar	Venezuela	5,007	16,427

ANTARCTICA	m	ft
Vinson Massif	4,897	16,066
Mt Kirkpatrick	4,528	14,855
Mt Markham	4,349	14,268

OCEAN DEPTHS

ATLANTIC OCEAN	m	ft	
Puerto Rico (Milwaukee) Deep	9,220	30,249	[7]
Cayman Trench	7,680	25,197	[10]
Gulf of Mexico	5,203	17,070	
Mediterranean Sea	5,121	16,801	
Black Sea	2,211	7,254	
North Sea	660	2,165	
Baltic Sea	463	1,519	
Hudson Bay	258	846	

INDIAN OCEAN	m	ft
Java Trench	7,450	24,442
Red Sea	2,635	8,454
Persian Gulf	73	239

PACIFIC OCEAN	m	ft	
Mariana Trench	11,022	36,161	[1]
Tonga Trench	10,882	35,702	[2]
Japan Trench	10,554	34,626	[3]
Kuril Trench	10,542	34,587	[4]
Mindanao Trench	10,497	34,439	[5]
Kermadec Trench	10,047	32,962	[6]
Peru–Chile Trench	8,050	26,410	[8]
Aleutian Trench	7,822	25,662	[9]

ARCTIC OCEAN	m	ft
Molloy Deep	5,608	18,399

LAND LOWS

THE WORLD		m	ft
Dead Sea	Asia	−411	−1,348
Lake Assal	Africa	−156	−512
Death Valley	N. America	−86	−282
Valdés Peninsula	S. America	−40	−131
Caspian Sea	Europe	−28	−92
Lake Eyre North	Oceania	−16	−52

RIVERS

EUROPE
		km	miles	
Volga	Caspian Sea	3,700	2,300	
Danube	Black Sea	2,850	1,770	
Ural	Caspian Sea	2,535	1,575	
Dnepr (Dnipro)	Black Sea	2,285	1,420	
Kama	Volga	2,030	1,260	
Don	Black Sea	1,990	1,240	
Petchora	Arctic Ocean	1,790	1,110	
Oka	Volga	1,480	920	
Belaya	Kama	1,420	880	
Dnister (Dniester)	Black Sea	1,400	870	
Vyatka	Kama	1,370	850	
Rhine	North Sea	1,320	820	
N. Dvina	Arctic Ocean	1,290	800	
Desna	Dnepr (Dnipro)	1,190	740	
Elbe	North Sea	1,145	710	
Wisla	Baltic Sea	1,090	675	
Loire	Atlantic Ocean	1,020	635	

ASIA
		km	miles	
Yangtze	Pacific Ocean	6,380	3,960	[3]
Yenisey–Angara	Arctic Ocean	5,550	3,445	[5]
Huang He	Pacific Ocean	5,464	3,395	[6]
Ob–Irtysh	Arctic Ocean	5,410	3,360	[7]
Mekong	Pacific Ocean	4,500	2,795	[9]
Amur	Pacific Ocean	4,400	2,730	[10]
Lena	Arctic Ocean	4,400	2,730	
Irtysh	Ob	4,250	2,640	
Yenisey	Arctic Ocean	4,090	2,540	
Ob	Arctic Ocean	3,680	2,285	
Indus	Indian Ocean	3,100	1,925	
Brahmaputra	Indian Ocean	2,900	1,800	
Syrdarya	Aral Sea	2,860	1,775	
Salween	Indian Ocean	2,800	1,740	
Euphrates	Indian Ocean	2,700	1,675	
Vilyuy	Lena	2,650	1,645	
Kolyma	Arctic Ocean	2,600	1,615	
Amudarya	Aral Sea	2,540	1,575	
Ural	Caspian Sea	2,535	1,575	
Ganges	Indian Ocean	2,510	1,560	
Si Kiang	Pacific Ocean	2,100	1,305	
Irrawaddy	Indian Ocean	2,010	1,250	
Tarim–Yarkand	Lop Nor	2,000	1,240	
Tigris	Indian Ocean	1,900	1,180	

AFRICA
		km	miles	
Nile	Mediterranean	6,670	4,140	[1]
Congo	Atlantic Ocean	4,670	2,900	[8]
Niger	Atlantic Ocean	4,180	2,595	
Zambezi	Indian Ocean	3,540	2,200	
Oubangi/Uele	Congo (D.R.)	2,250	1,400	
Kasai	Congo (D.R.)	1,950	1,210	
Shaballe	Indian Ocean	1,930	1,200	
Orange	Atlantic Ocean	1,860	1,155	
Cubango	Okavango Delta	1,800	1,120	
Limpopo	Indian Ocean	1,600	995	
Senegal	Atlantic Ocean	1,600	995	
Volta	Atlantic Ocean	1,500	930	

AUSTRALIA
		km	miles	
Murray–Darling	Indian Ocean	3,750	2,330	
Darling	Murray	3,070	1,905	
Murray	Indian Ocean	2,575	1,600	
Murrumbidgee	Murray	1,690	1,050	

NORTH AMERICA
		km	miles	
Mississippi–Missouri	Gulf of Mexico	6,020	3,740	[4]
Mackenzie	Arctic Ocean	4,240	2,630	
Mississippi	Gulf of Mexico	3,780	2,350	
Missouri	Mississippi	3,780	2,350	
Yukon	Pacific Ocean	3,185	1,980	
Rio Grande	Gulf of Mexico	3,030	1,880	
Arkansas	Mississippi	2,340	1,450	
Colorado	Pacific Ocean	2,330	1,445	
Red	Mississippi	2,040	1,270	
Columbia	Pacific Ocean	1,950	1,210	
Saskatchewan	Lake Winnipeg	1,940	1,205	
Snake	Columbia	1,670	1,040	
Churchill	Hudson Bay	1,600	990	
Ohio	Mississippi	1,580	980	
Brazos	Gulf of Mexico	1,400	870	
St Lawrence	Atlantic Ocean	1,170	730	

SOUTH AMERICA
		km	miles	
Amazon	Atlantic Ocean	6,450	4,010	[2]
Paraná–Plate	Atlantic Ocean	4,500	2,800	
Purus	Amazon	3,350	2,080	
Madeira	Amazon	3,200	1,990	
São Francisco	Atlantic Ocean	2,900	1,800	
Paraná	Plate	2,800	1,740	

SOUTH AMERICA (continued)
		km	miles	
Tocantins	Atlantic Ocean	2,750	1,710	
Paraguay	Paraná	2,550	1,580	
Orinoco	Atlantic Ocean	2,500	1,550	
Pilcomayo	Paraná	2,500	1,550	
Araguaia	Tocantins	2,250	1,400	
Juruá	Amazon	2,000	1,240	
Xingu	Amazon	1,980	1,230	
Ucayali	Amazon	1,900	1,180	
Maranón	Amazon	1,600	990	
Uruguay	Plate	1,600	990	

LAKES

EUROPE
		km²	miles²	
Lake Ladoga	Russia	17,700	6,800	
Lake Onega	Russia	9,700	3,700	
Saimaa system	Finland	8,000	3,100	
Vänern	Sweden	5,500	2,100	
Rybinskoye Res.	Russia	4,700	1,800	

ASIA
		km²	miles²	
Caspian Sea	Asia	371,800	143,550	[1]
Lake Baykal	Russia	30,500	11,780	[8]
Aral Sea	Kazakh./Uzbekistan	28,687	11,086	[10]
Tonlé Sap	Cambodia	20,000	7,700	
Lake Balqash	Kazakhstan	18,500	7,100	
Lake Dongting	China	12,000	4,600	
Lake Ysyk	Kyrgyzstan	6,200	2,400	
Lake Orumiyeh	Iran	5,900	2,300	
Lake Koko	China	5,700	2,200	
Lake Poyang	China	5,000	1,900	
Lake Khanka	China/Russia	4,400	1,700	
Lake Van	Turkey	3,500	1,400	

AFRICA
		km²	miles²	
Lake Victoria	E. Africa	68,000	26,000	[3]
Lake Tanganyika	C. Africa	33,000	13,000	[6]
Lake Malawi/Nyasa	E. Africa	29,600	11,430	[9]
Lake Chad	C. Africa	25,000	9,700	
Lake Turkana	Ethiopia/Kenya	8,500	3,300	
Lake Volta	Ghana	8,500	3,300	
Lake Bangweulu	Zambia	8,000	3,100	
Lake Rukwa	Tanzania	7,000	2,700	
Lake Mai-Ndombe	Congo (D.R.)	6,500	2,500	
Lake Kariba	Zam./Zimbabwe	5,300	2,000	
Lake Albert	Ug./Congo (D.R.)	5,300	2,000	
Lake Nasser	Egypt/Sudan	5,200	2,000	
Lake Mweru	Zam./Congo (D.R.)	4,900	1,900	
Lake Cabora Bassa	Mozambique	4,500	1,700	
Lake Kyoga	Uganda	4,400	1,700	
Lake Tana	Ethiopia	3,630	1,400	

AUSTRALIA
		km²	miles²	
Lake Eyre	Australia	8,900	3,400	
Lake Torrens	Australia	5,800	2,200	
Lake Gairdner	Australia	4,800	1,900	

NORTH AMERICA
		km²	miles²	
Lake Superior	Canada/USA	82,350	31,800	[2]
Lake Huron	Canada/USA	59,600	23,010	[4]
Lake Michigan	USA	58,000	22,400	[5]
Great Bear Lake	Canada	31,800	12,280	[7]
Great Slave Lake	Canada	28,500	11,000	
Lake Erie	Canada/USA	25,700	9,900	
Lake Winnipeg	Canada	24,400	9,400	
Lake Ontario	Canada/USA	19,500	7,500	
Lake Nicaragua	Nicaragua	8,200	3,200	
Lake Athabasca	Canada	8,100	3,100	
Smallwood Reservoir	Canada	6,530	2,520	
Reindeer Lake	Canada	6,400	2,500	
Nettilling Lake	Canada	5,500	2,100	
Lake Winnipegosis	Canada	5,400	2,100	

SOUTH AMERICA
		km²	miles²	
Lake Titicaca	Bolivia/Peru	8,300	3,200	
Lake Poopo	Bolivia	2,800	1,100	

ISLANDS

EUROPE
		km²	miles²	
Great Britain	UK	229,880	88,700	[8]
Iceland	Atlantic Ocean	103,000	39,800	
Ireland	Ireland/UK	84,400	32,600	
Novaya Zemlya (N.)	Russia	48,200	18,600	
W. Spitzbergen	Norway	39,000	15,100	
Novaya Zemlya (S.)	Russia	33,200	12,800	
Sicily	Italy	25,500	9,800	
Sardinia	Italy	24,000	9,300	
N. E. Spitzbergen	Norway	15,000	5,600	

EUROPE (continued)
		km²	miles²	
Corsica	France	8,700	3,400	
Crete	Greece	8,350	3,200	
Zealand	Denmark	6,850	2,600	

ASIA
		km²	miles²	
Borneo	S. E. Asia	744,360	287,400	[3]
Sumatra	Indonesia	473,600	182,860	[6]
Honshu	Japan	230,500	88,980	[7]
Sulawesi (Celebes)	Indonesia	189,000	73,000	
Java	Indonesia	126,700	48,900	
Luzon	Philippines	104,700	40,400	
Mindanao	Philippines	101,500	39,200	
Hokkaido	Japan	78,400	30,300	
Sakhalin	Russia	74,060	28,600	
Sri Lanka	Indian Ocean	65,600	25,300	
Taiwan	Pacific Ocean	36,000	13,900	
Kyushu	Japan	35,700	13,800	
Hainan	China	34,000	13,100	
Timor	Indonesia	33,600	13,000	
Shikoku	Japan	18,800	7,300	
Halmahera	Indonesia	18,000	6,900	
Ceram	Indonesia	17,150	6,600	
Sumbawa	Indonesia	15,450	6,000	
Flores	Indonesia	15,200	5,900	
Samar	Philippines	13,100	5,100	
Negros	Philippines	12,700	4,900	
Bangka	Indonesia	12,000	4,600	
Palawan	Philippines	12,000	4,600	
Panay	Philippines	11,500	4,400	
Sumba	Indonesia	11,100	4,300	
Mindoro	Philippines	9,750	3,800	

AFRICA
		km²	miles²	
Madagascar	Indian Ocean	587,040	226,660	[4]
Socotra	Indian Ocean	3,600	1,400	
Réunion	Indian Ocean	2,500	965	
Tenerife	Atlantic Ocean	2,350	900	
Mauritius	Indian Ocean	1,865	720	

OCEANIA
		km²	miles²	
New Guinea	Indon./Papua NG	821,030	317,000	[2]
New Zealand (S.)	Pacific Ocean	150,500	58,100	
New Zealand (N.)	Pacific Ocean	114,700	44,300	
Tasmania	Australia	67,800	26,200	
New Britain	Papua NG	37,800	14,600	
New Caledonia	Pacific Ocean	19,100	7,400	
Viti Levu	Fiji	10,500	4,100	
Hawaii	Pacific Ocean	10,450	4,000	
Bougainville	Papua NG	9,600	3,700	
Guadalcanal	Solomon Is.	6,500	2,500	
Vanua Levu	Fiji	5,550	2,100	
New Ireland	Papua NG	3,200	1,200	

NORTH AMERICA
		km²	miles²	
Greenland	Atlantic Ocean	2,175,600	839,800	[1]
Baffin Is.	Canada	508,000	196,100	[5]
Victoria Is.	Canada	212,200	81,900	[9]
Ellesmere Is.	Canada	212,000	81,800	[10]
Cuba	Caribbean Sea	110,860	42,800	
Newfoundland	Canada	110,680	42,700	
Hispaniola	Dom. Rep./Haiti	76,200	29,400	
Banks Is.	Canada	67,000	25,900	
Devon Is.	Canada	54,500	21,000	
Melville Is.	Canada	42,400	16,400	
Vancouver Is.	Canada	32,150	12,400	
Somerset Is.	Canada	24,300	9,400	
Jamaica	Caribbean Sea	11,400	4,400	
Puerto Rico	Atlantic Ocean	8,900	3,400	
Cape Breton Is.	Canada	4,000	1,500	

SOUTH AMERICA
		km²	miles²	
Tierra del Fuego	Arg./Chile	47,000	18,100	
Falkland Is. (East)	Atlantic Ocean	6,800	2,600	
South Georgia	Atlantic Ocean	4,200	1,600	
Galapagos (Isabela)	Pacific Ocean	2,250	870	

World: Regions in the News

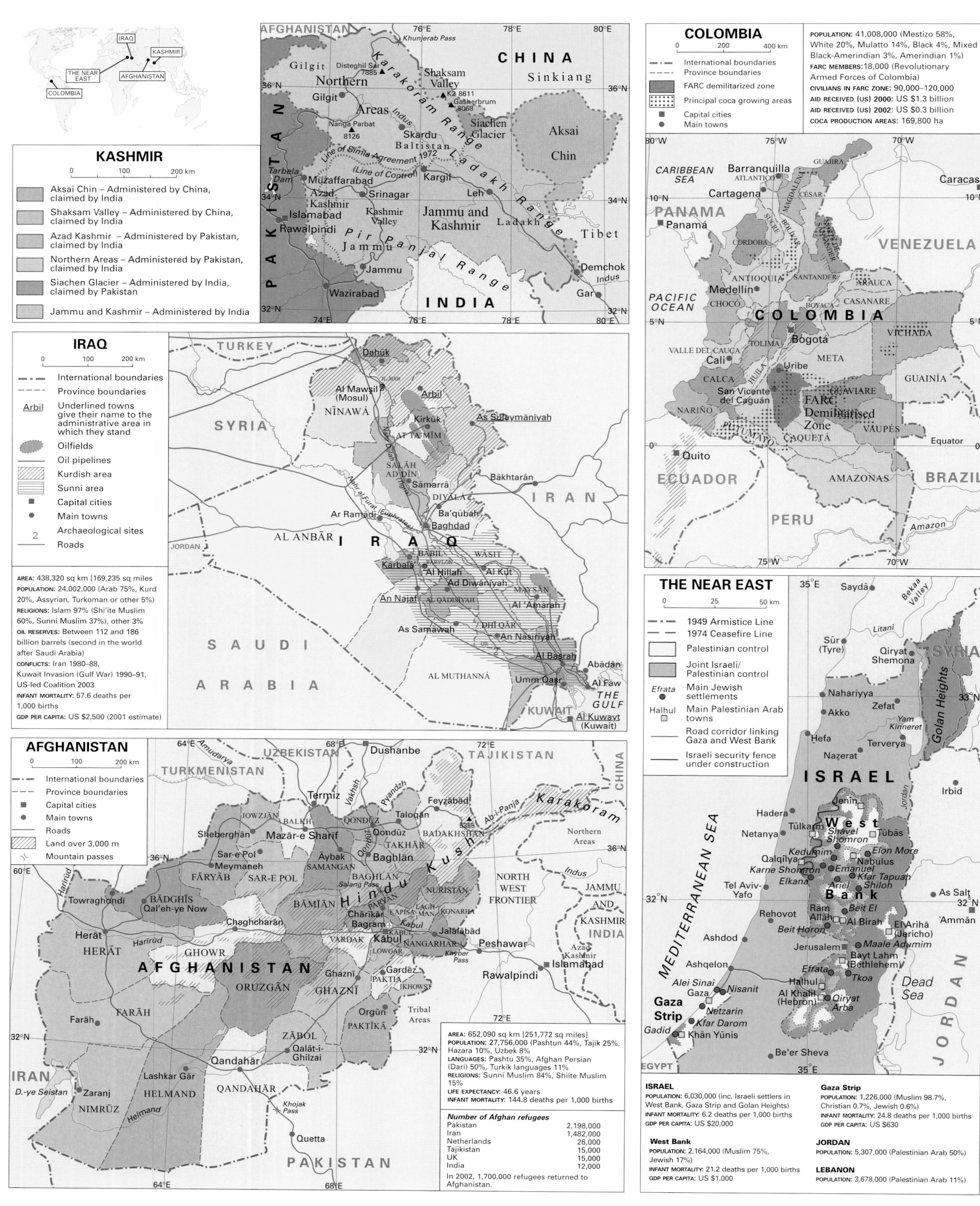

KASHMIR

0   100   200 km

- Aksai Chin – Administered by China, claimed by India
- Shaksam Valley – Administered by China, claimed by India
- Azad Kashmir – Administered by Pakistan, claimed by India
- Northern Areas – Administered by Pakistan, claimed by India
- Siachen Glacier – Administered by India, claimed by Pakistan
- Jammu and Kashmir – Administered by India

IRAQ

0   100   200 km

- International boundaries
- Province boundaries
- Arbil   Underlined towns give their name to the administrative area in which they stand
- Oilfields
- Oil pipelines
- Kurdish area
- Sunni area
- Capital cities
- Main towns
- 2   Archaeological sites
- Roads

AREA: 438,320 sq km [169,235 sq miles]
POPULATION: 24,002,000 (Arab 75%, Kurd 20%, Assyrian, Turkoman or other 5%)
RELIGIONS: Islam 97% (Shi'ite Muslim 60%, Sunni Muslim 37%), other 3%
OIL RESERVES: Between 112 and 186 billion barrels (second in the world after Saudi Arabia)
CONFLICTS: Iran 1980–88, Kuwait Invasion (Gulf War) 1990–91, US-led Coalition 2003
INFANT MORTALITY: 57.6 deaths per 1,000 births
GDP PER CAPITA: US $2,500 (2001 estimate)

AFGHANISTAN

0   100   200 km

- International boundaries
- Province boundaries
- Capital cities
- Main towns
- Roads
- Land over 3,000 m
- Mountain passes

AREA: 652,090 sq km [251,772 sq miles]
POPULATION: 27,756,000 (Pashtun 44%, Tajik 25%, Hazara 10%, Uzbek 8%)
LANGUAGES: Pashtu 35%, Afghan Persian (Dari) 50%, Turkik languages 11%
RELIGIONS: Sunni Muslim 84%, Shiite Muslim 15%
LIFE EXPECTANCY: 46.6 years
INFANT MORTALITY: 144.8 deaths per 1,000 births

Number of Afghan refugees

Pakistan	2,198,000
Iran	1,482,000
Netherlands	26,000
Tajikistan	15,000
UK	15,000
India	12,000

In 2002, 1,700,000 refugees returned to Afghanistan.

COLOMBIA

0   200   400 km

- International boundaries
- Province boundaries
- FARC demilitarized zone
- Principal coca growing areas
- Capital cities
- Main towns

POPULATION: 41,008,000 (Mestizo 58%, White 20%, Mulatto 14%, Mixed Black-Amerindian 3%, Amerindian 1%)
FARC MEMBERS: 18,000 (Revolutionary Armed Forces of Colombia)
CIVILIANS IN FARC ZONE: 90,000–120,000
AID RECEIVED (US) 2000: US $1.3 billion
AID RECEIVED (US) 2002: US $0.3 billion
COCA PRODUCTION AREAS: 169,800 ha

THE NEAR EAST

0   25   50 km

- 1949 Armistice Line
- 1974 Ceasefire Line
- Palestinian control
- Joint Israeli/Palestinian control
- Efrata   Main Jewish settlements
- Halhul   Main Palestinian Arab towns
- Road corridor linking Gaza and West Bank
- Israeli security fence under construction

ISRAEL
POPULATION: 6,030,000 (inc. Israeli settlers in West Bank, Gaza Strip and Golan Heights)
INFANT MORTALITY: 6.2 deaths per 1,000 births
GDP PER CAPITA: US $20,000

West Bank
POPULATION: 2,164,000 (Muslim 75%, Jewish 17%)
INFANT MORTALITY: 21.2 deaths per 1,000 births
GDP PER CAPITA: US $1,000

Gaza Strip
POPULATION: 1,226,000 (Muslim 98.7%, Christian 0.7%, Jewish 0.6%)
INFANT MORTALITY: 24.8 deaths per 1,000 births
GDP PER CAPITA: US $630

JORDAN
POPULATION: 5,307,000 (Palestinian Arab 50%)

LEBANON
POPULATION: 3,678,000 (Palestinian Arab 11%)

Images of Earth

– SAN FRANCISCO, USA –

The whole of the 'Bay Area' is shown: hilly San Francisco is at the top end of the southern peninsula, with the Golden Gate Bridge connecting it to Sausalito to the north. Alcatraz Island, former home of the infamous prison, can be seen as a small light area to the east of the bridge. On the opposite shore, connected by the double-decker Bay Bridge, are Oakland and Berkeley, while at the southern end of the Bay is the city of San Jose.

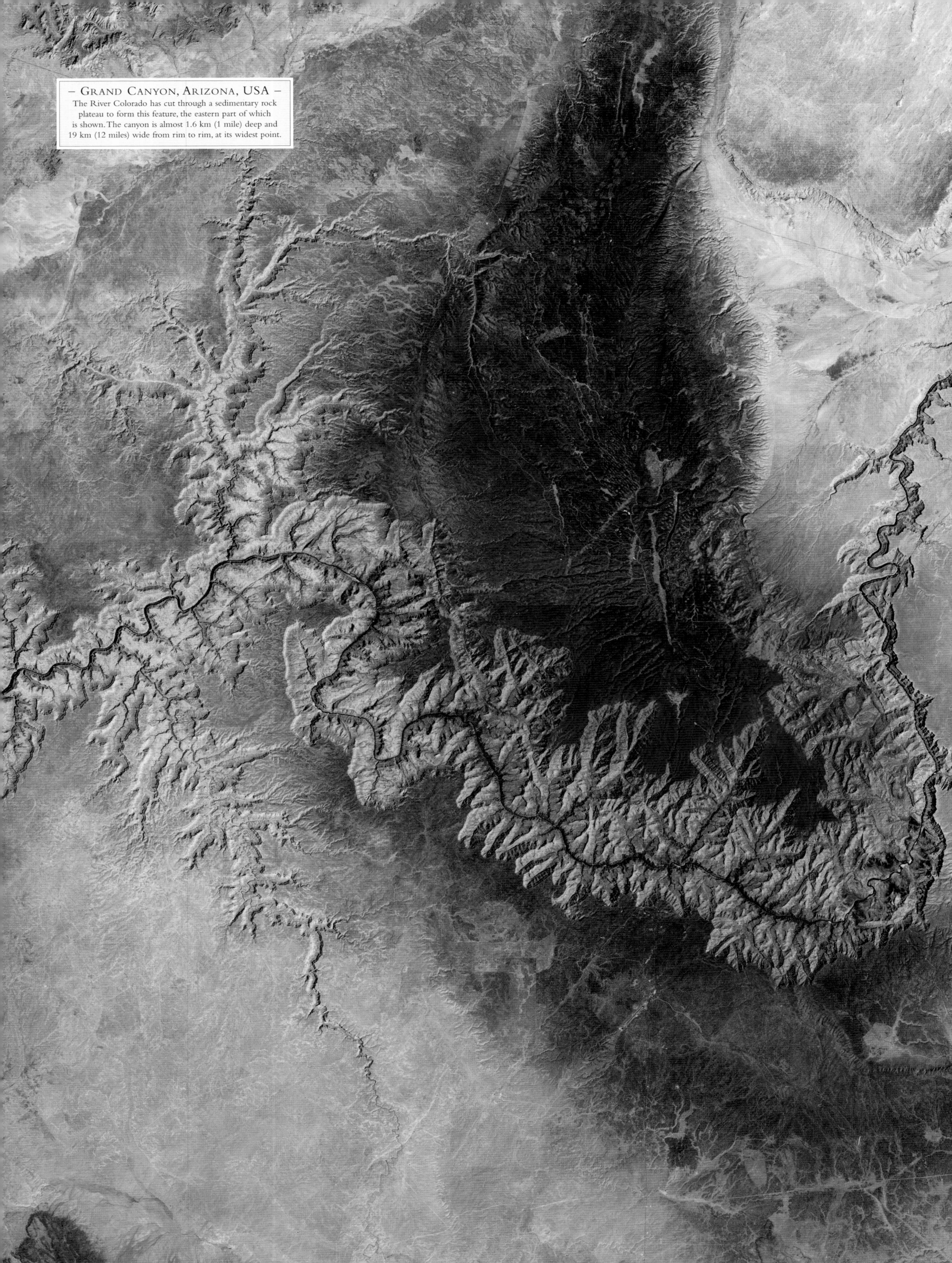

- GRAND CANYON, ARIZONA, USA -
The River Colorado has cut through a sedimentary rock
plateau to form this feature, the eastern part of which
is shown. The canyon is almost 1.6 km (1 mile) deep and
19 km (12 miles) wide from rim to rim, at its widest point.

- CHICAGO, ILLINOIS, USA -
This image shows the entire urban area of greater Chicago,
which is situated on the south-western shore of Lake
Michigan. The runway pattern of the second busiest airport
in the world, O'Hare International, can be clearly seen
towards the top of the image.

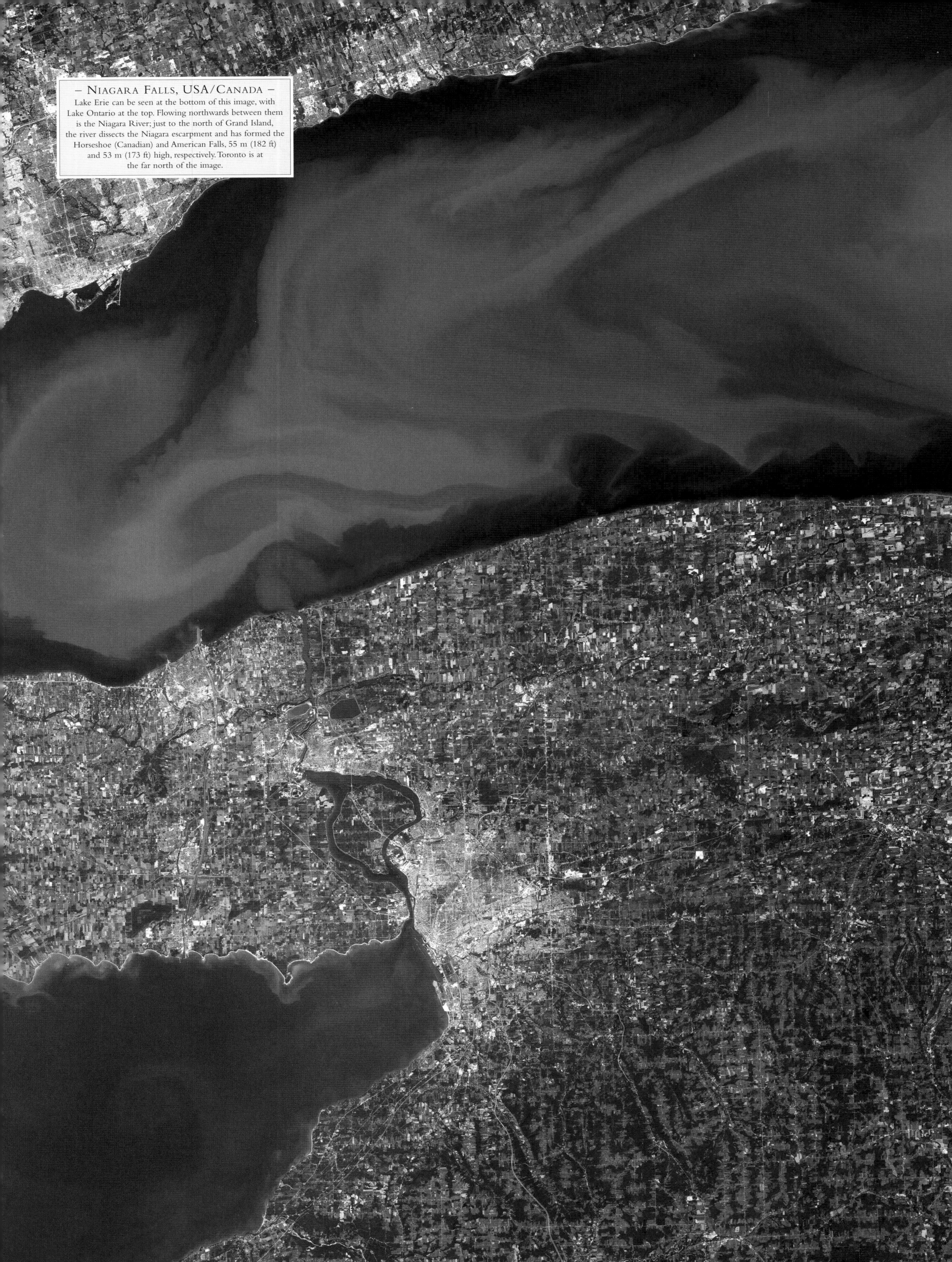

Lake Erie can be seen at the bottom of this image, with Lake Ontario at the top. Flowing northwards between them is the Niagara River; just to the north of Grand Island, the river dissects the Niagara escarpment and has formed the Horseshoe (Canadian) and American Falls, 55 m (182 ft) and 53 m (173 ft) high, respectively. Toronto is at the far north of the image.

— NEW YORK, USA —

This image covers most of the largest urban area in
the USA, which has a population of over 20 million people.
Flowing from the north, the Hudson River divides the two
cities of New York (to the east) and New Jersey (to the west).
Towards its mouth on the east bank lies Manhattan Island,
with Central Park clearly visible. Below this is the end of
Long Island, which is connected by bridge to
Staten Island, to the west.

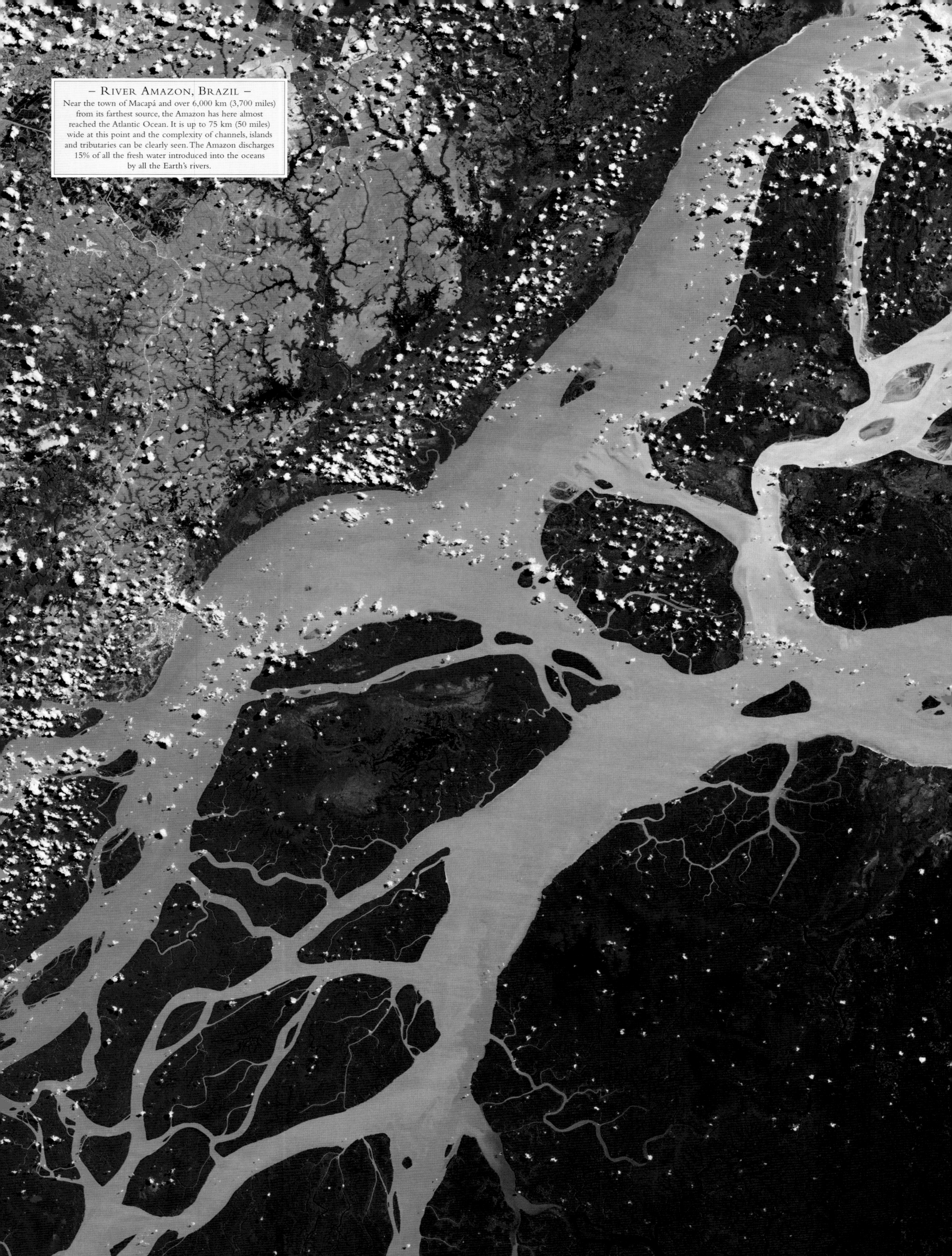

Near the town of Macapá and over 6,000 km (3,700 miles)
from its farthest source, the Amazon has here almost
reached the Atlantic Ocean. It is up to 75 km (50 miles)
wide at this point and the complexity of channels, islands
and tributaries can be clearly seen. The Amazon discharges
15% of all the fresh water introduced into the oceans
by all the Earth's rivers.

— LONDON, UNITED KINGDOM —
The whole area of Greater London is shown here, including
Heathrow Airport at far left. The River Thames stands out,
as do the former London docks and the reservoirs in the
River Lea valley to the north-east. Despite having a
population in excess of 8 million people, there are still many
open spaces and parks around the city centre.

— IJSSELMEER, NETHERLANDS —
This unique feature was created in the 13th century when
the sea breached a protective sand bar, flooding all the
low-lying land. The remnants of the bar can still be seen
as the chain of Frisian Islands at the top of the image.
Reclamation on a large scale started in 1932 with the
completion of the causeway in the north. Since then four
'polders' have been drained and reclaimed. The city of
Amsterdam is situated at bottom left.

– Cairo, Egypt –

The largest city in Africa with almost 10 million inhabitants, Cairo evolved on the eastern bank of the River Nile, near its delta. This image clearly shows the differences between the arid desert areas to the south-east and south-west, the fertile lands of the Nile flood plain, and the urban area itself. The shadows of the Pyramids on the Giza Plateau can be seen on the left-hand edge of the cultivated area, below where the road crosses it.

— WESTERN CAPE, SOUTH AFRICA —
Cape Town sits to the bottom left of this image, with
the Cape Peninsula running south-east to the Cape of
Good Hope. Inland from the fertile coastal plain, where most
of South Africa's wine is produced, is the rugged interior
of the Great Karoo where parallel mountain ranges are
dissected by river valleys.

— TOKYO, JAPAN —

At the head of Tokyo Bay, the city, with its satellites of
Kawasaki and Yokohama, forms one of the world's most
densely populated areas with over 26 million people. Owing
to the shortage of space, much development has taken place
on areas reclaimed from the sea. One of these is Haneda
International Airport, whose runway pattern is clearly
visible at the mouth of the Tama River. The Tokyo Bay
bridge/tunnel projects into the Bay from the eastern shore.

— SYDNEY, AUSTRALIA —

Sydney, the largest city in Australia, was founded at the
end of the 18th century on the north shore of Botany Bay,
the southern of the two enclosed bays shown here. The
runways of the international airport project into this, and to
the north, on the south shore of Sydney Harbour, the
shadows of the skyscrapers in the central business district
can be seen, with the Sydney Harbour Bridge beyond.

INTRODUCTION TO WORLD GEOGRAPHY

THE UNIVERSE	2	WATER AND VEGETATION	18	AGRICULTURE	32
THE SOLAR SYSTEM	4	THE NATURAL ENVIRONMENT	20	ENERGY	34
TIME AND MOTION	6	PEOPLE		MINERALS	36
OCEANS	8	AND THE ENVIRONMENT	22	MANUFACTURING	38
GEOLOGY	10	POPULATION	24	TRADE	40
LANDFORMS	12	CITIES	26	HEALTH	42
ATMOSPHERE AND WEATHER	14	THE HUMAN FAMILY	28	WEALTH	44
CLIMATE	16	CONFLICT AND CO-OPERATION	30	STANDARDS OF LIVING	46

THE UNIVERSE

For more information:
4 Orbits of the planets
Planetary data

About 13.7 billion years ago, time and space began with the most colossal explosion in cosmic history: the so-called 'Big Bang' that is believed to have initiated the universe. According to current theory, in the first millionth of a second of its existence it expanded from a dimensionless point of infinite mass and density into a fireball about 30 billion kilometres across; and it has been expanding ever since.

It took almost a million years for the primal fireball to cool enough for atoms to form. They were mostly hydrogen, still the most abundant material in the universe. But the new matter was not evenly distributed around the young universe, and a few billion years later atoms in relatively dense regions began to cling together under the influence of gravity, forming distinct masses of gas separated by vast expanses of empty space. To begin with, these first proto-galaxies were dark places: the universe had cooled. But gravitational attraction continued, condensing matter into coherent lumps inside the galactic gas clouds. About 3 billion years later, some of these masses had contracted so much that internal pressure produced the high temperatures necessary to bring about nuclear fusion: the first stars were born.

There were several generations of stars, each feeding on the wreckage of its extinct predecessors as well as the original galactic gas swirls. With each new generation, progressively larger atoms were forged in stellar furnaces and the galaxy's range of elements, once restricted to hydrogen, grew larger. About 9 billion years after the Big Bang, a star formed on the outskirts of our galaxy with enough matter left over to create a retinue of planets. Nearly 5 billion years after that human beings evolved.

The Sun is one of more than 100 billion stars in the home galaxy alone. Our galaxy, in turn, forms part of a local group of approximately 30 similar structures, some much larger than our own; there are at least 100 billion other galaxies in the universe as a whole. The most distant ever observed, a highly energetic galactic core known only as quasar PC 1247 +3406, lies about 12 billion light-years away.

Life of a Star

For most of its existence, a star produces energy by the nuclear fusion of hydrogen into helium at its core. The duration of this hydrogen-burning period – known as the main sequence – depends on the star's mass; the greater the mass, the higher the core temperatures and the sooner the star's supply of hydrogen is exhausted. Dim, dwarf stars consume their hydrogen slowly, eking it out over 1,000 billion years or more. The Sun, like other stars of its mass, should spend about 10 billion years on the main sequence; since it was formed less than 5 billion years ago, it still has half its life left.

Once all a star's core hydrogen has been fused into helium, nuclear activity moves outwards into layers of unconsumed hydrogen. For a time, energy production sharply increases: the star grows hotter and expands enormously, turning into a so-called red giant. Its energy output will increase a thousandfold, and it will swell to a hundred times its present diameter.

After a few hundred million years, helium in the core will become sufficiently compressed to initiate a new cycle of nuclear fusion: from helium to carbon. The star will contract somewhat, before beginning its last expansion, in the Sun's case engulfing the Earth and perhaps Mars. In this bloated condition, the Sun's outer layers will break off into space, leaving a tiny inner core, mainly of carbon, that shrinks progressively under the force of its own gravity: dwarf stars can attain a density more than 10,000 times that of normal matter, with crushing surface gravities to match. Gradually, the nuclear fires will die down, and the Sun will reach its terminal stage: a black dwarf, emitting insignificant amounts of energy.

However, stars more massive than the Sun may undergo another transformation. The additional mass allows gravitational collapse to continue indefinitely: eventually, all the star's remaining matter shrinks to a point, and its density approaches infinity – a state that will not permit even subatomic structures to survive.

The star has become a black hole: an anomalous 'singularity' in the fabric of space and time. Although vast coruscations of radiation will be emitted by any matter falling into its grasp, the singularity itself has an escape velocity that exceeds the speed of light, and nothing can ever be released from it. Within the boundaries of the black hole, the laws of physics are suspended, but no physicist can ever observe the extraordinary events that may occur.

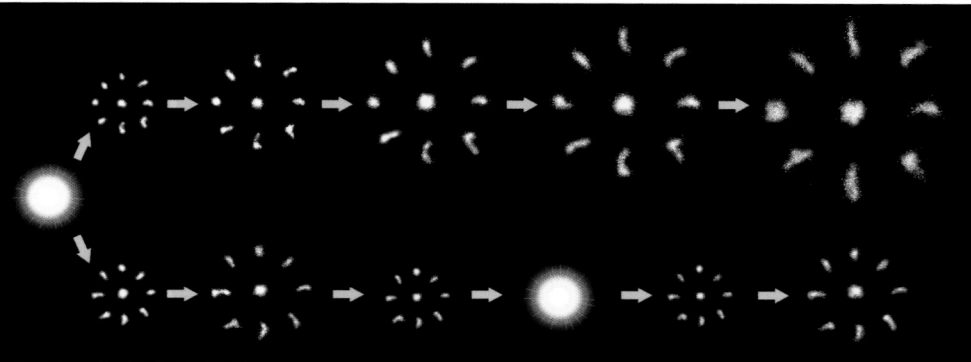

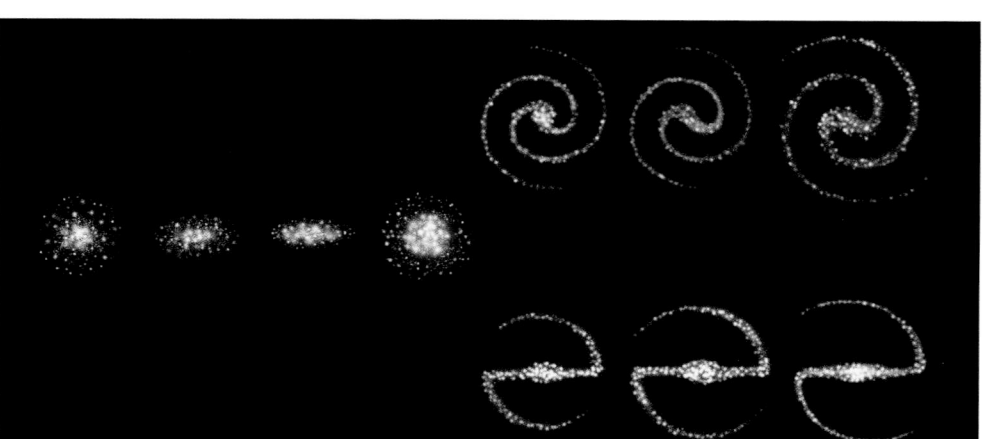

The End of the Universe

The likely fate of the universe is disputed. One theory (*top left*) dictates that the expansion begun at the time of the Big Bang will continue 'indefinitely', with ageing galaxies moving further and further apart in an immense, dark graveyard. Alternatively, gravity may overcome the expansion (*bottom left*). Galaxies will fall back together until everything is again concentrated at a single point, followed by a new Big Bang and a new expansion, in an endlessly repeated cycle.

The first theory is supported by the amount of visible matter in the universe; the second assumes there is enough dark material to bring about the gravitational collapse.

Galactic Structures

Many of the universe's 100 billion galaxies show clear structural patterns, originally classified by the American astronomer Edwin Hubble in 1925. Spiral galaxies like our own (*top row*) have a central, almost spherical bulge and a surrounding disk composed of spiral arms. Barred spirals (*bottom row*) have a central bar of stars across the nucleus, with spiral arms trailing from the ends of the bar. Elliptical galaxies (*far left*) have a uniform appearance, ranging from a flattened disk to a near sphere. So-called SO galaxies (*left row, right*) have a central bulge, but no spiral arms. Most galaxies, however, have no obvious structure at all.

Galaxies also vary enormously in size, from dwarfs only 2,000 light-years across to great assemblies of stars 80 or more times larger.

The Home Galaxy

The Sun and its planets are located in one of the spiral arms, a little less than 28,000 light-years from the galactic centre and orbiting around it in a period of 200 million years. The centre is invisible from the Earth, masked by vast, light-absorbing clouds of interstellar dust. The Galaxy is probably around 12 billion years old and, like other spiral galaxies, has three distinct regions. The central bulge is about 30,000 light-years in diameter. The disk in which the Sun is located is not much more than 1,000 light-years thick, but 100,000 light-years from end to end. Around the Galaxy is the halo, a spherical zone 300,000 light-years across, studded with globular star clusters and sprinkled with individual suns.

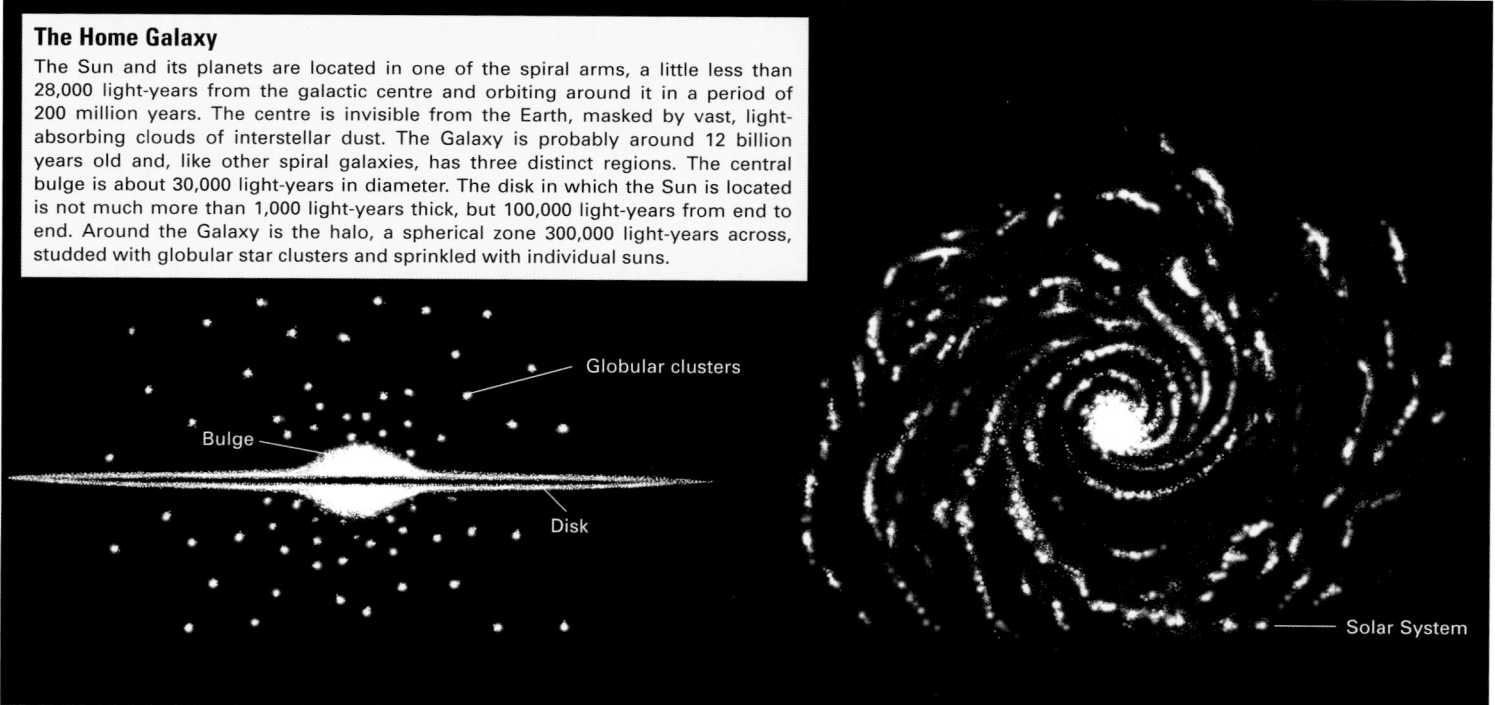

Globular clusters

Bulge

Disk

Solar System

Star Charts

Star charts are drawn as projections of a vast, hollow sphere with the observer in the middle. Each circle below represents slightly more than one hemisphere, centred on the north and south celestial poles respectively – projections of the Earth's poles in the heavens. At the present era, the north pole is marked by the star Polaris; the south pole has no such convenient reference point.

Astronomical co-ordinates are normally given in terms of 'Right Ascension' for longitude and 'Declination' for latitude or altitude. Since the stars appear to rotate around the Earth once every 24 hours, Right Ascension is measured eastwards – anticlockwise – in hours and minutes and is marked around the edge of the map. One hour is equivalent to 15 angular degrees; zero on the scale is the point at which the Sun crosses the celestial equator at the spring equinox, known to astronomers as the First Point in Aries. Unlike the Sun, stars always rise and set at the same point on the horizon. Declination measures (in degrees) a star's angular distance above or below the celestial equator and is marked on the vertical line.

To use the maps, first choose the one for your hemisphere and hold it with the month at the bottom. The stars in the lower part of the map are then due south (or north, in the southern hemisphere) at about 1 AM local time, not allowing for summer or daylight saving time. Their exact position above the horizon depends on your latitude. The closer to the Equator you live, the higher in the sky these stars will appear. Some additional stars from the map for the other hemisphere will be visible in the lower sky.

Stars near the top of the map will be below the opposite horizon at this date and time but will be visible at other times of the night and year. The sky appears to move anticlockwise around the celestial pole during the course of the day (clockwise in the southern hemisphere), so the same stars will be visible at 11 PM a month earlier.

NORTHERN HEAVENS

SOUTHERN HEAVENS

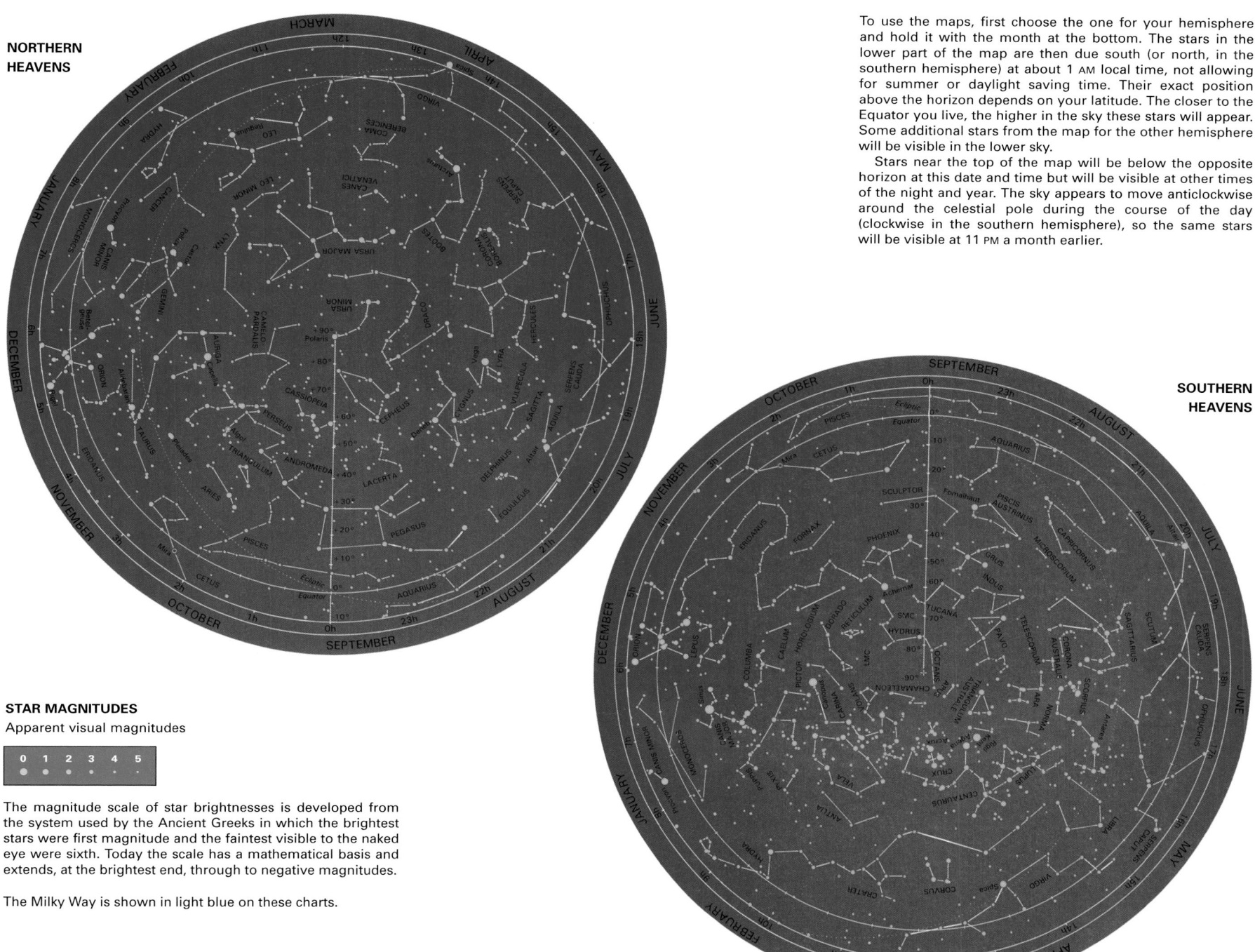

STAR MAGNITUDES

Apparent visual magnitudes

0	1	2	3	4	5

The magnitude scale of star brightnesses is developed from the system used by the Ancient Greeks in which the brightest stars were first magnitude and the faintest visible to the naked eye were sixth. Today the scale has a mathematical basis and extends, at the brightest end, through to negative magnitudes.

The Milky Way is shown in light blue on these charts.

THE NEAREST STARS

The 20 nearest stars, excluding the Sun, with their distance from Earth in light-years*

Proxima Centauri	4.25	Many of the nearest stars, like
Alpha Centauri A	4.3	Alpha Centauri A and B, are
Alpha Centauri B	4.3	doubles, orbiting about the
Barnard's Star	6.0	common centre of gravity
Wolf 359	7.8	and to all intents and
Lalande 21185	8.3	purposes equidistant from
Sirius A	8.7	Earth. Many of them are dim
Sirius B	8.7	objects, with no name other
UV Ceti A	8.7	than the designation given
UV Ceti B	8.7	by the astronomers who
Ross 154	9.4	investigated them. However,
Ross 248	10.3	they include Sirius, the
Epsilon Eridani	10.7	brightest star in the sky,
Ross 128	10.9	and Procyon, the seventh
61 Cygni A	11.1	brightest. Both are far larger
61 Cygni B	11.1	than the Sun; of the nearest
Epsilon Indi	11.2	stars, only Epsilon Eridani is
Groombridge 34A	11.2	similar in size and luminosity.
Groombridge 34B	11.2	
L789-6	11.2	* A light-year equals approx.
Procyon A	11.4	9,500,000,000,000 kilometres
Procyon B	11.4	

THE CONSTELLATIONS

The constellations and their English names

Andromeda	Andromeda	Circinus	Compasses	Lacerta	Lizard	Piscis Austrinus	Southern Fish
Antlia	Air Pump	Columba	Dove	Leo	Lion	Puppis	Ship's Stern
Apus	Bird of Paradise	Coma Berenices	Berenice's Hair	Leo Minor	Little Lion	Pyxis	Mariner's Compass
Aquarius	Water Carrier	Corona Australis	Southern Crown	Lepus	Hare	Reticulum	Net
Aquila	Eagle	Corona Borealis	Northern Crown	Libra	Scales	Sagitta	Arrow
Ara	Altar	Corvus	Crow	Lupus	Wolf	Sagittarius	Archer
Aries	Ram	Crater	Cup	Lynx	Lynx	Scorpius	Scorpion
Auriga	Charioteer	Crux	Southern Cross	Lyra	Lyre	Sculptor	Sculptor
Boötes	Herdsman	Cygnus	Swan	Mensa	Table	Scutum	Shield
Caelum	Chisel	Delphinus	Dolphin	Microscopium	Microscope	Serpens	Serpent
Camelopardalis	Giraffe	Dorado	Swordfish	Monoceros	Unicorn	Sextans	Sextant
Cancer	Crab	Draco	Dragon	Musca	Fly	Taurus	Bull
Canes Venatici	Hunting Dogs	Equuleus	Little Horse	Norma	Level	Telescopium	Telescope
Canis Major	Great Dog	Eridanus	Eridanus	Octans	Octant	Triangulum	Triangle
Canis Minor	Little Dog	Fornax	Furnace	Ophiuchus	Serpent Bearer	Triangulum Australe	Southern Triangle
Capricornus	Goat	Gemini	Twins	Orion	Orion	Tucana	Toucan
Carina	Keel	Grus	Crane	Pavo	Peacock	Ursa Major	Great Bear
Cassiopeia	Cassiopeia	Hercules	Hercules	Pegasus	Winged Horse	Ursa Minor	Little Bear
Centaurus	Centaur	Horologium	Clock	Perseus	Perseus	Vela	Sails
Cepheus	Cepheus	Hydra	Water Snake	Phoenix	Phoenix	Virgo	Virgin
Cetus	Whale	Hydrus	Sea Serpent	Pictor	Easel	Volans	Flying Fish
Chamaeleon	Chameleon	Indus	Indian	Pisces	Fishes	Vulpecula	Fox

THE SOLAR SYSTEM

For more information:
2 The Home Galaxy
6 The seasons
  Day and night
7 The Moon

Lying 28,000 light-years from the centre of one of billions of galaxies that comprise the observable universe, our Solar System contains nine planets and their moons, innumerable asteroids and comets, and a miscellany of dust and gas, all tethered by the immense gravitational field of the Sun, the middling-sized star whose thermonuclear furnaces provide them all with heat and light. The Solar System was formed about 4,600 million years ago, when a spinning cloud of gas, mostly hydrogen but seeded with other, heavier elements, condensed enough to ignite a nuclear reaction and create a star. The Sun still accounts for almost 99.9% of the system's total mass; one planet, Jupiter, contains most of the remainder.

By composition as well as distance, the planetary array divides quite neatly in two: an inner system of four small, solid planets, including the Earth, and an outer system, from Jupiter to Neptune, of four much larger planets composed of lighter materials, such as gas, liquid and ice. Between the two groups lies a scattering of rocky asteroids, perhaps as many as 400,000. They may be debris left over from the inner Solar System's formation. The outermost planet, Pluto, may simply be the largest of a number of bodies composed of rock and ice orbiting beyond Neptune, similarly left over from the formation of the outer Solar System.

By the 1990s, however, the Solar System also included some newer anomalies: several thousand spacecraft. Most were in orbit around the Earth, but some had probed far and wide around the system. The valuable information beamed back by these robotic investigators has transformed our knowledge of our celestial environment.

Much of the early history of science is the story of people trying to make sense of the errant points of light that were all they knew of the planets. Now, men have themselves stood on the Earth's Moon; probes have landed on Mars and Venus, and orbiting radars have mapped far distant landscapes with astonishing accuracy. In the 1980s, the US Voyager probes skimmed all four major planets of the outer system, bringing new revelations with each close approach. Only Pluto, inscrutably distant in an orbit that takes it 50 times the Earth's distance from the Sun, remains unvisited by our messengers.

Orbits of the Planets

The planets of the Solar System and their orbits, showing the relative position of each planet at the vernal equinox of 1992.

Orbits are drawn to exact scale, but with the Sun and planets greatly enlarged for clarity. The Solar System is shown from the viewpoint of an observer a few light-hours distant in the direction of the constellation Hercules. Seen from such a position, above the plane of the ecliptic, all the planets revolve about the Sun in an anticlockwise direction. The perspective view exaggerates the elliptical form of all the planetary orbits: only Pluto and Mercury follow paths that deviate noticeably from circularity. Near perihelion – its closest approach to the Sun – Pluto actually passes inside the orbit of Neptune, an event that last occurred in 1983. Pluto did not regain its station as the Sun's outermost planet until February 1999.

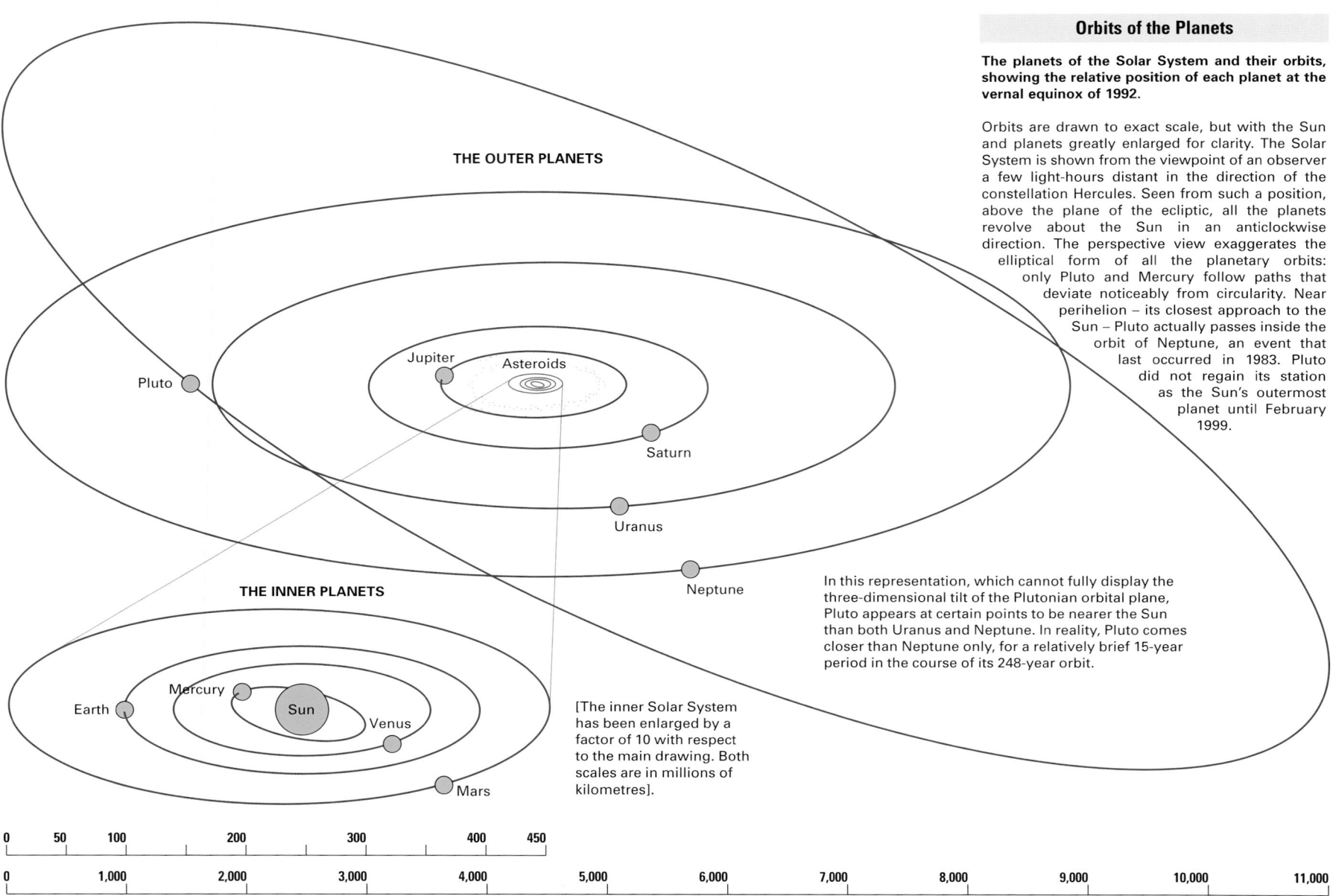

THE OUTER PLANETS

Pluto

Jupiter

Asteroids

Saturn

Uranus

Neptune

THE INNER PLANETS

Mercury

Earth

Sun

Venus

Mars

In this representation, which cannot fully display the three-dimensional tilt of the Plutonian orbital plane, Pluto appears at certain points to be nearer the Sun than both Uranus and Neptune. In reality, Pluto comes closer than Neptune only, for a relatively brief 15-year period in the course of its 248-year orbit.

[The inner Solar System has been enlarged by a factor of 10 with respect to the main drawing. Both scales are in millions of kilometres].

```
0    50   100      200       300       400   450
0        1,000    2,000     3,000     4,000      5,000      6,000      7,000      8,000      9,000      10,000     11,000
```

Planetary Data

	Mean distance from Sun (million km)	Mass (Earth = 1)	Period of orbit (Earth days/years)	Period of rotation (Earth days)	Equatorial diameter (km)	Average density (water = 1)	Surface gravity (Earth = 1)	Escape velocity (km/sec)	Number of known satellites
Sun	–	332,946	–	25.4	1,392,000	1.41	27.9	617.5	–
Mercury	57.9	0.055	87.97d	58.67	4,878	5.44	0.38	4.25	0
Venus	108.2	0.815	224.7d	243.00	12,104	5.25	0.90	10.36	0
Earth	149.6	1.0	365.3d	1.00	12,756	5.52	1.00	11.18	1
Mars	227.9	0.11	687.0d	1.028	6,794	3.94	0.38	5.03	2
Jupiter	778	317.9	11.86y	0.411	143,884	1.33	2.64	59.60	60
Saturn	1,427	95.2	29.46y	0.427	120,536	0.71	1.16	35.60	31
Uranus	2,870	14.6	84.01y	0.748	51,118	1.27	0.79	21.10	21
Neptune	4,497	17.2	164.8y	0.710	50,538	1.77	0.98	24.60	11
Pluto	5,900	0.002	247.7y	6.39	2,324	2.02	0.06	1.20	1

Planetary days are given in sidereal time – that is, with respect to the stars rather than the Sun. Most of the information in the table was confirmed by spacecraft and often obtained from photographs and other data transmitted back to the Earth. In the case of Pluto, however, only Earthbound observations have been made, and no spacecraft will encounter it until well into the 21st century. Given the planet's small size and great distance, figures for its diameter and rotation period have only recently been confirmed.

Pluto is not massive enough to account for the perturbations in the orbits of Uranus and Neptune that led to its discovery in 1930, but it is now widely believed that these perturbations can be explained away as observational errors made by the earlier observers.

The Planets

Mercury is the closest planet to the Sun and hence the fastest-moving. It is very hot, with a cratered, wrinkled surface very similar to that of Earth's Moon. It is small and has no gravity, hence there is no significant atmosphere.

Venus has much the same physical dimensions as Earth. Its dense atmosphere is composed of 97% CO_2 resulting in a runaway greenhouse effect that makes the Venusian surface, at 477°C, the hottest of all the planets in the Solar System. Radar mapping shows the land to be relatively level, with volcanic regions whose sulphurous discharges explain the sulphuric-acid rains reported by soft-landing space probes before they succumbed to Venus' fierce climate.

Earth seen from space is easily the most beautiful of the inner planets; it is also, and more objectively, the largest, as well as the only home of known life. Living things are the main reason why the Earth is able to retain a substantial proportion of corrosive and highly reactive oxygen in its atmosphere, a state of affairs that contradicts the laws of chemical equilibrium; the oxygen in turn supports the life that constantly regenerates it.

Mars, smaller and cooler than the Earth, is nevertheless the most likely planet other than Earth where life may have formed. Vast water channels show that it was once warmer and wetter; there may still be traces of former simple life forms, though whether life could thrive in its current cold, dry and thin atmosphere is doubtful. The ice caps are mainly frozen carbon dioxide, though data from NASA's probe, Mars Odyssey, launched in 2001, suggests that vast reservoirs of water ice may lie a few centimetres beneath the surface over much of the planet. But the surface itself is a dustbowl, where occasional storms whirl dust high into the atmosphere.

Jupiter masses almost three times as much as all the other planets combined; had it scooped up rather more matter during its formation, it might have evolved into a small companion star for the Sun. The planet is mostly gas, under intense pressure in the lower atmosphere above a core of fiercely compressed hydrogen and helium. The upper layers form strikingly-coloured rotating belts, the outward sign of the intense storms created by Jupiter's rapid diurnal rotation. Close approaches by spacecraft have shown an orbiting ring system and discovered several previously unknown moons: Jupiter has at least 60 moons, though many are extremely small.

Saturn is structurally similar to Jupiter, rotating fast enough to produce an obvious bulge at its equator. It is composed of 89% hydrogen and 11% helium, and has wind velocities in the outer atmosphere of 500 metres per second. Ever since the invention of the telescope, however, Saturn's rings have been the feature that has attracted most observers. Voyager probes in 1980 and 1981 sent back detailed pictures that showed them to be composed of thousands of separate ringlets, each in turn made up of tiny icy particles.

Uranus was unknown to the ancients. Although it is faintly visible to the naked eye, it was not discovered until 1781. Its interior is largely water, with an atmosphere of hydrogen, helium and some methane, which gives the planet its blue-green colour. Observations in 1977 suggested the presence of a faint ring system, amply confirmed when Voyager 2 swung past the planet in 1986.

Neptune is always more than 4,000 million km from Earth, and despite its diameter of over 50,000 km, it can only be seen by telescope. Its 1846 discovery was the result of mathematical predictions by astronomers seeking to explain irregularities in the orbit of Uranus, but until Voyager 2 closed with the planet in 1989, very little was known of it. Like Uranus, it has a ring system; recent observations have revealed a total of 11 moons.

Pluto is the most mysterious of the solar planets, if only because even the most powerful telescopes can scarcely resolve it from a point of light to a disk. It was discovered as recently as 1930, as the result (like Neptune) of perturbations in the orbits of the two then outermost planets. Its small size, as well as its eccentric and highly tilted orbit, has led to suggestions that it is a former satellite of Neptune, somehow liberated from its primary. In 1978 Pluto was found to have a moon of its own, Charon, apparently half the size of Pluto itself.

Mean distance from the Sun in million kilometres (not to scale)

Mercury

57.9 Mercury

Venus

108.2 Venus

Earth

149.6 Earth

Mars

227.9 Mars

Jupiter

778 Jupiter

Saturn

1,427 Saturn

Uranus

2,870 Uranus

Neptune

4,497 Neptune

Pluto

5,900 Pluto

Diagram not drawn to scale

TIME AND MOTION

For more information:
4 Orbits of the planets
9 Ocean currents
14 Circulation of the air
16 Climate

The basic unit of time measurement is the day, that is, one rotation of the Earth on its axis. Our present calendar is based on the solar year of 365.24 days, the time taken by the Earth to orbit the Sun.

Calendars based on the movements of the Sun and Moon have been used since ancient times. The average length of the year, according to the Julian Calendar introduced by Julius Caesar, was about 11 minutes too long. The cumulative error was rectified in 1582 by the Gregorian Calendar, when Pope Gregory XIII decreed that the day following 4 October was 15 October, and in that century years did not count as leap years unless they were divisible by 400. England finally adopted the reformed calendar in 1752, when it was 11 days behind the European mainland.

The rotation of the Earth on its axis causes day and night. Because the Earth rotates through 360° every 24 hours, the world is divided into 24 time zones centred on lines of longitude at 15° longitude.

The tilt of the Earth's axis, also called the obliquity of the ecliptic, accounts for the seasons which are so familiar in the middle latitudes. But geological evidence shows that, over long periods of time, climates change, and the advances and retreats of the ice during the Pleistocene Ice Age may have been caused by regular variations in the Earth's tilt, its orbit around the Sun, and changes in the season when it is closest to the Sun (perihelion).

Earth Data

Aphelion (maximum distance from Sun): 152,007,016 km

Perihelion (minimum distance from Sun): 147,000,830 km

Angle of tilt (obliquity of the ecliptic): 23° 27' 08"

Length of year – solar tropical (equinox to equinox): 365.24 days

Length of year: 365 days, 5 hours, 48 minutes, 46 seconds of mean solar time

Superficial area: 510,000,000 sq km

Land surface: 149,000,000 sq km (29.2%)

Water surface: 361,000,000 sq km (70.8%)

Equatorial circumference: 40,077 km

Polar circumference: 40,009 km

Equatorial diameter: 12,756.8 km

Polar diameter: 12,713.8 km

Equatorial radius: 6,378.4 km

Polar radius: 6,356.9 km

Volume of the Earth: 1,083,230 × 10^6 cu km

Mass of the Earth: 5.9 × 10^21 tonnes

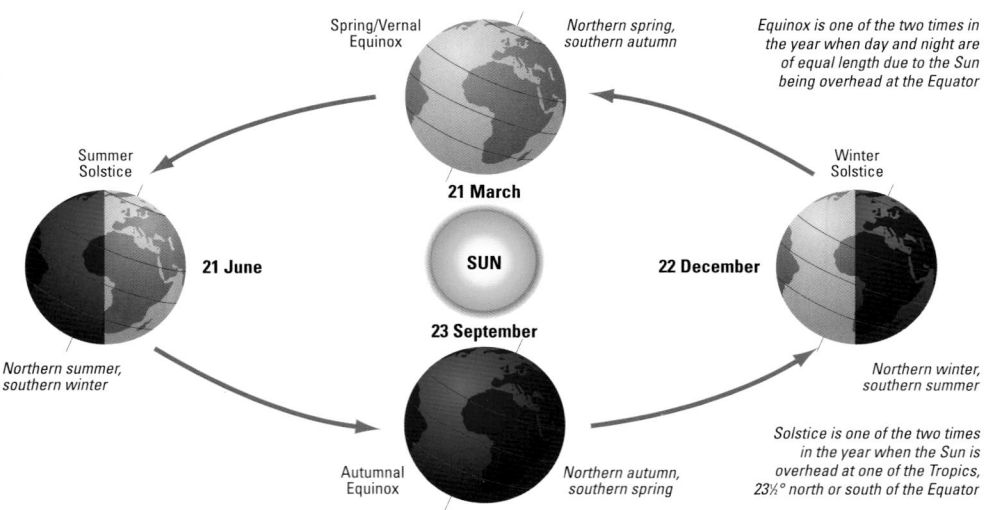

The Seasons

Seasons occur because the Earth's axis is tilted at an angle of approximately 23½°. When the northern hemisphere is tilted to a maximum extent towards the Sun, on 21 June, the Sun is overhead at the Tropic of Cancer (latitude 23½° North). This is midsummer, or the summer solstice, in the northern hemisphere.

On 22 or 23 September, the Sun is overhead at the Equator, and day and night are of equal length throughout the world. This is the autumnal equinox in the northern hemisphere. On 21 or 22 December, the Sun is overhead at the Tropic of Capricorn (23½° South), the winter solstice in the northern hemisphere. The overhead Sun then tracks north until, on 21 March, it is overhead at the Equator. This is the spring (vernal) equinox in the northern hemisphere.

In the southern hemisphere, the seasons are the reverse of those in the north.

Day and Night

The Sun appears to rise in the east, reach its highest point at noon, and then set in the west, to be followed by night. In reality, it is not the Sun that is moving but the Earth rotating from west to east. The moment when the Sun's upper limb first appears above the horizon is termed sunrise; the moment when the Sun's upper limb disappears below the horizon is sunset.

At the summer solstice in the northern hemisphere (21 June), the Arctic has total daylight and the Antarctic total darkness. The opposite occurs at the winter solstice (21 or 22 December). At the Equator, the length of day and night are almost equal all year.

The Sun's Path

The diagrams on the right illustrate the apparent path of the Sun at (A) the Equator, (B) in mid-latitude (45°), (C) at the Arctic Circle (66½°), and (D) at the North Pole, where there are six months of continuous daylight and six months of continuous night.

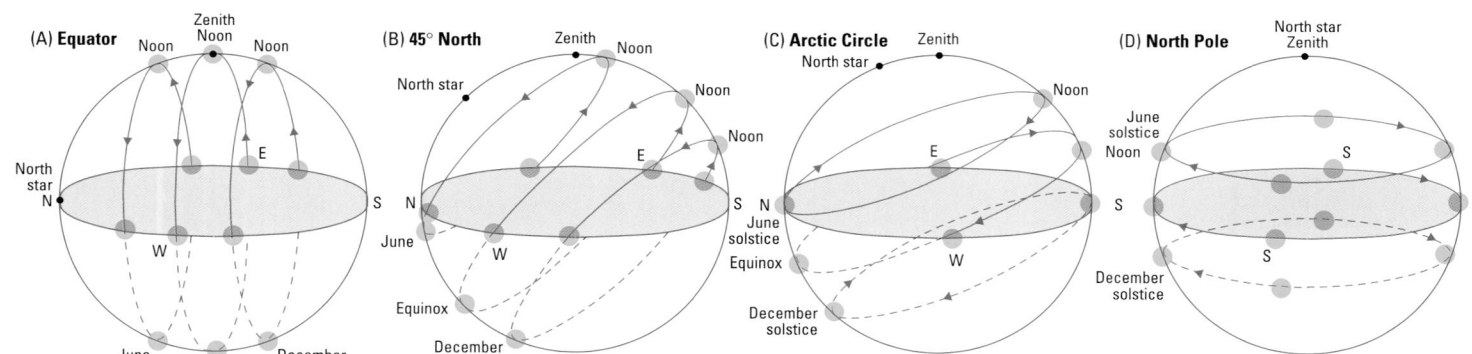

Sunrise and Sunset

The term equinox comes from two Latin words meaning 'equal night'. At the spring and autumnal equinoxes, the Sun is vertically overhead at the Equator and all places on Earth have 12 hours of darkness and 12 hours of daylight. The graphs showing sunrise and sunset show that these occasions occur on 21 March and on 22 or 23 September. The graphs also show that, because the Sun remains high in the sky throughout the year, the length of the day and night at the Equator remain roughly the same throughout the year, with sunrise occurring around 6 AM and sunset at around 6 PM. The further north or south one travels, the greater the difference between the number of hours of daylight and darkness. For example, the graph (*right*) shows that at latitude 60°N sunrise varies from just after 9 AM in midwinter (on 22 or 23 December) to about 2.30 AM in midsummer (around the summer solstice on 21 June). By contrast, the second graph (*far right*) shows that sunset at latitude 60°N occurs at about 2.45 PM in midwinter and 9.20 PM in midsummer.

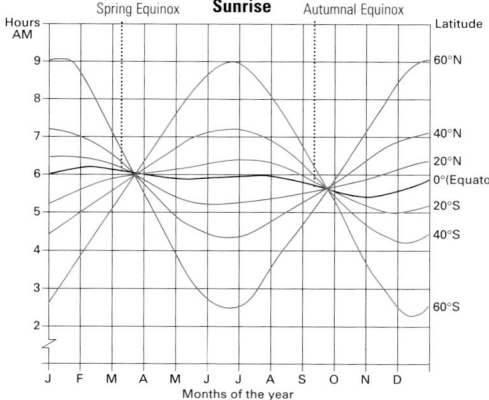

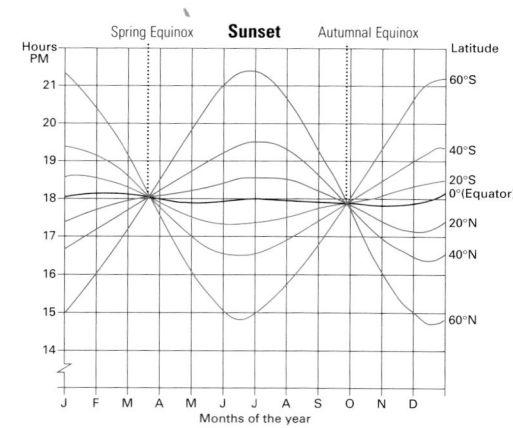

The Moon

The Moon rotates more slowly than the Earth, making one complete turn on its axis in just over 27 days. Since this corresponds to its period of revolution around the Earth, the Moon always presents the same hemisphere or face to us, and we never see 'the dark side'. The interval between one full Moon and the next (and between new Moons) is about 29½ days – a lunar month. The apparent changes in the shape of the Moon are caused by its changing position in relation to the Earth; like the planets, it produces no light of its own and shines only by reflecting the rays of the Sun.

Phases of the Moon

Distance from Earth: 356,410 km – 406,685 km; Mean diameter: 3,475.1 km;
Mass: approximately 1/81 that of Earth; Surface gravity: one-sixth of Earth's;
Daily range of temperature at lunar equator: 200°C; Average orbital speed: 3,683 km/h

New Moon	Crescent	First quarter	Gibbous	Full Moon	Gibbous	Last quarter	Crescent	New Moon

Moon Data

Distance from Earth
The Moon orbits at a mean distance of 384,199.1 km, at an average speed of 3,683 km/h in relation to the Earth.

Size and mass
The average diameter of the Moon is 3,475.1 km. It is 400 times smaller than the Sun but is about 400 times closer to the Earth, so we see them as the same size. The Moon has a mass of $7,348 \times 10^{19}$ tonnes, with a density 3.344 times that of water.

Visibility
Only 59% of the Moon's surface is directly visible from Earth. Reflected light takes 1.25 seconds to reach Earth – compared to 8 minutes 27.3 seconds for light to reach us from the Sun.

Temperature
With the Sun overhead, the temperature on the lunar equator can reach 117.2°C [243°F]. At night it can sink to −162.7°C [−261°F].

Eclipses

When the Moon passes between the Sun and the Earth it causes a partial eclipse of the Sun (1) if the Earth passes through the Moon's outer shadow (P), or a total eclipse (2) if the inner cone shadow crosses the Earth's surface. In a lunar eclipse, the Earth's shadow crosses the Moon and, again, provides either a partial or total eclipse.

Eclipses of the Sun and the Moon do not occur every month because of the 5° difference between the plane of the Moon's orbit and the plane in which the Earth moves. In the 1990s only 14 lunar eclipses were possible, for example, seven partial and seven total; each was visible only from certain, and variable, parts of the world. The same period witnessed 13 solar eclipses – six partial (or annular) and seven total.

Partial eclipse (1)

Solar eclipse

Lunar eclipse

Total eclipse (2)

Time Zones

The Earth rotates through 360° in 24 hours, and so moves 15° every hour. The world is divided into 24 standard time zones, each centred on lines of longitude at 15° intervals. At the centre of the first zone is the Prime meridian or Greenwich meridian. All places to the west of Greenwich are one hour behind for every 15° of longitude; places to the east are ahead by one hour for every 15°. When it is 12 noon at the Greenwich meridian, 180° east it is midnight of the same day – while 180° west the day is just beginning. To overcome this, the International Date Line was established, approximately following the 180° meridian. Thus, if you travelled eastwards from Japan (140°E) to Samoa (170°W), you would pass from Sunday night into Sunday morning.

Tides

The daily rise and fall of the ocean's tides are the result of the gravitational pull of the Moon and that of the Sun, though the effect of the latter is only 46.6% as strong as that of the Moon. This effect is greatest on the hemisphere facing the Moon and causes a tidal 'bulge'. When the Sun, Earth and Moon are in line, tide-raising forces are at a maximum and Spring tides occur: high tide reaches the highest values, and low tide falls to low levels. When lunar and solar forces are least coincidental with the Sun and Moon at an angle (near the Moon's first and third quarters), Neap tides occur, which have a small tidal range.

Spring tide

Neap tide

Spring tide

New Moon

Last quarter

Full Moon

Gravitational pull by the Sun

Neap tide

First quarter

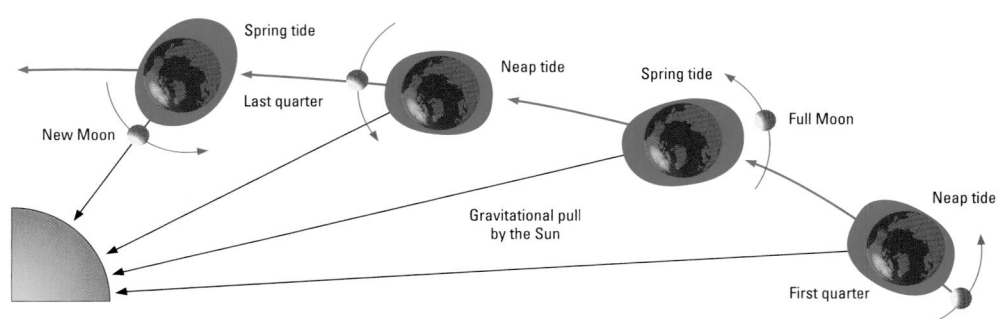

10   Hours slow or fast of UT or Co-ordinated Universal Time

Zones using UT (GMT)

Zones slow of UT (GMT)

International boundaries

Zones fast of UT (GMT)

Half-hour zones

Time zone boundaries

International Date Line

Actual Solar Time when time at Greenwich is 12:00 (noon)

Note: Certain of the above time zones are affected by the incidence of 'Summer Time' in countries where it is adopted.

Projection: Mercator

OCEANS

For more information:

7 Tides
10 The spreading Earth
14 Atmosphere
18 Hydrological cycle
   Water distribution
19 Watersheds
23 Water pollution
41 Shipping

Seawater

The chemical composition of the sea, by percentage, excluding the elements of water itself

Chloride (Cl) 55.04%
Sodium (Na) 30.61%
Sulphate (SO₄) 7.69%
Magnesium (Mg) 3.69%
Calcium (Ca) 1.16%
Potassium (K) 1.10%
Bicarbonate (HCO₃) 0.41%
Bromide (Br) 0.19%
Boric Acid (H₃BO₃) 0.07%
Strontium (Sr) 0.04%
Fluoride (Fl) 0.003%
Lithium (Li) .... trace
Rubidium (Rb) .... trace
Phosphorus (P) .... trace
Iodine (I) .... trace
Barium (Ba) .... trace
Arsenic (As) .... trace
Caesium (Cs) .... trace

Eleven constituents account for over 99% of the salt content of seawater, but seawater also contains virtually every other element. In natural conditions, its composition is broadly consistent across the world's seas and oceans; but in coastal areas, especially, variations are sometimes substantial. The oceans are about 35 parts water to one part salt.

Atoll Building

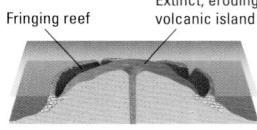

Volcano rises from ocean floor

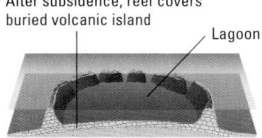

Fringing reef — Extinct, eroding volcanic island

After subsidence, reef covers buried volcanic island — Lagoon

A coral atoll usually begins existence as a bare volcanic peak, thrusting above the surface of the ocean. A colony of coral – organisms with calcium carbonate skeletons – forms itself in the shallow water around the peak. The volcano is eroded and slowly sinks, leaving the coral forming a ring of hard limestone around its remnant. In time, the barrier reef of an atoll is all that remains.

The last 40 years have been described as the 'Space Age', but another exciting and perhaps even more important area of discovery, proceeding at the same time, has been the exploration of 'inner space', namely the oceans which cover more than 70% of our planet. The study of the ocean floor and oceanic islands has revealed features that help to explain how continents move, and how the movements are related to earthquakes and volcanic activity.

Manned submersibles have established that life exists even in the deepest trenches, where the pressure reaches 1,000 atmospheres, the equivalent of the force of one tonne bearing down on every square centimetre. Further exploration in the pitch-black environment of the ocean ridges has revealed strange forms of marine life around scalding hot vents. The creatures include giant tubeworms, blind shrimps, and bacteria, some of which are genetically very different from any other known life forms. In 1996, an analysis of one microorganism revealed that at least half of its 1,700 or so genes were hitherto unknown. This environment, which is based on chemicals, not sunlight, may resemble the places where life on Earth first began.

Another vital area of contemporary research concerns the interactions between the oceans and the atmosphere, as exemplified in the El Niño–Southern Oscillation (ENSO), and the bearing that these have on climatic change.

Most geographers divide the world's ocean waters into four areas: the Pacific, Atlantic, Indian and Arctic oceans. The most active zone in the oceans is the sunlit upper layer, where the water is moved around by wind-blown currents. It is the home of most sea life and acts as a membrane through which the ocean breathes,

Life in the Oceans

An imaginary profile of the typical coastal and oceanic zones is shown, with a selection of the life forms that might occur in the water off the Pacific Coast of Central America. The animals illustrated are not drawn to scale as the range of sizes is too great. Most marine life is confined to the first 200 metres, the upper sunlit (photic) zone, where sunlight can still penetrate. Plant and animal plankton, the basis of life in the ocean, occur in great quantities in all zones.

In the pelagic environment (open sea), vertical gradients, including those of light, temperature and salinity, determine the distribution of organisms. From the tidal zone at the coastline, the continental shelf, geologically still part of the continental landmass, drops gently to about 200 metres – the sunlit zone. At the end of the shelf, the seabed falls away in the steeper angle of the continental slope. The subsequent descent to the deep ocean floor, known as the continental rise, is more gentle, with gradients between 1 in 100 and 1 in 700 until the abyssal plains and hills between 2,500 and 6,000 metres below the surface.

The deep sea floor contains seamounts, some of which are capped by coral reefs, ocean ridges, the longest mountain chains on Earth, and deep ocean trenches, especially in the Pacific Ocean where six trenches reach depths of more than 10,000 metres, including the 11,022-metre deep Mariana Trench.

Each of these zones contains a distinctive community of species adapted to the different conditions of salinity, temperature and light intensity. Indeed, a few organisms have been found even in the abyssal darkness of the great ocean trenches.

absorbing great quantities of carbon dioxide and partly exchanging it for oxygen.

As the depth increases, so light fades and temperatures fall until just before 1,000 metres where there is a marked temperature change at the thermocline, the boundary between the warm surface zone and the cold deep zone. Below the thermocline, slow currents are caused by density differences between bodies of water with varying temperatures and salinity.

The El Niño Phenomenon

The importance of the ocean–atmosphere interaction is nowhere more dramatically demonstrated than in the El Niño phenomenon of the southern Pacific Ocean.

Under normal conditions, called La Niña, surface water flows eastwards from South America (see diagram right, top) under the influence of trade winds. Near the coast, cold, nutrient-rich water (dark blue) rises to the surface and spreads westwards. In the western Pacific, sea surface temperatures reach 28°C or more and warm air rises, creating a low-pressure air system and causing heavy rains. The rising air spreads out and some of it descends over South America and the eastern Pacific, creating a high-pressure air system from which winds blow westwards. This rotating system is called a Walker Circulation Cell.

An El Niño event, also called an El Niño–Southern Oscillation cycle, or ENSO cycle, is characterized by a reversal of currents, whereby the eastwards-moving South Equatorial Current extends much further to the east and the trade winds weaken. The upwelling of cold water off South America is greatly reduced and surface water temperatures rise, causing a drastic reduction in fish life. The heaviest rainfall is over the eastern Pacific, while South-east Asia is drier than usual. Warm air rises in the east, spreads out, and descends in the western Pacific, which becomes a high-pressure area, as shown on the second diagram (right, below).

During an intense El Niño, such as in 1982–3 when sea temperatures in the eastern Pacific rose by 6°C, the effects of the current and wind reversals affect the weather around the world. In Australia and South-east Asia, the monsoon rainfall is reduced, while in 1983–4, a severe drought occurred in the Sahel, south of the Sahara, and also in southern Africa. The south-east coast of the United States also suffered storms and heavy rainfall, and even Europe experienced changes in weather patterns, possibly as a result of consequent changes in the course of the jet stream.

Scientists have found evidence that the frequency of the El Niño event, which normally occurs every two to seven years, may have increased in recent years with warm conditions persisting in the eastern Pacific from 1990 until mid-1995, an unprecedented length of time during the 114 years for which data exist. Another intense El Niño occurred in 1997–8, with resultant freak weather conditions across the entire Pacific region. Scientists do not know the causes of the El Niño event, though some researchers are investigating possible connections between major volcanic eruptions in the tropical Pacific region, the ENSO cycle and atmospheric circulation.

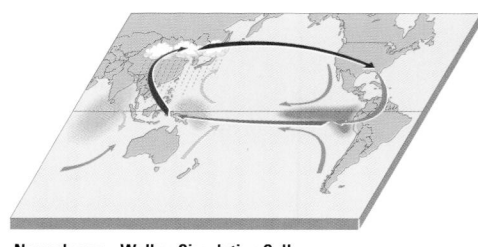

Normal year – Walker Circulation Cell

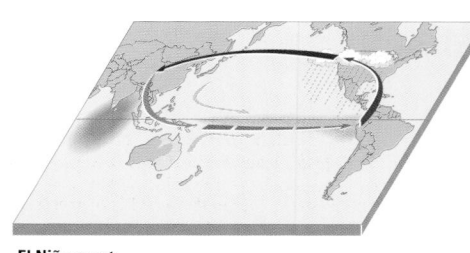

El Niño event

Ocean Currents

Moving immense quantities of energy as well as billions of tonnes of water every hour, the ocean currents are a vital part of the great heat engine that drives the Earth's climate. They themselves are produced by a twofold mechanism. At the surface, winds push huge masses of water before them; in the deep ocean, below an abrupt temperature gradient that separates the churning surface waters from the still depths, density variations cause slow vertical movements.

The pattern of circulation of the great surface currents is determined by the displacement known as the Coriolis effect. As the Earth turns beneath a moving object – whether it is a tennis ball or a vast mass of water – it appears to be deflected to one side. The deflection is most obvious near the Equator, where the Earth's surface is spinning eastwards at 1,700 km/h; currents moving polewards are curved clockwise in the northern hemisphere and anti-clockwise in the southern.

The result is a system of spinning circles known as gyres. Warm currents move constantly from the Equator towards the poles, while cold water moves in the reverse direction. In this way, ocean currents act like a thermostat, helping to regulate temperatures around the world.

Depending on the annual movements of the prevailing wind belts, some currents on or near the Equator may reverse their direction in the course of the year, a variation on which Asia's monsoon rains depend and whose occasional failure has brought disaster to millions of people.

JANUARY CURRENTS AND TEMPERATURES
(Northern Hemisphere: winter)

ACTUAL SURFACE TEMPERATURE

°C
30
20
10
0
-10
-20
-30
-40

OCEAN CURRENTS
Cold | Warm | Speed (knots)
Less than 0.5
0.5 – 1.0
Over 1.0

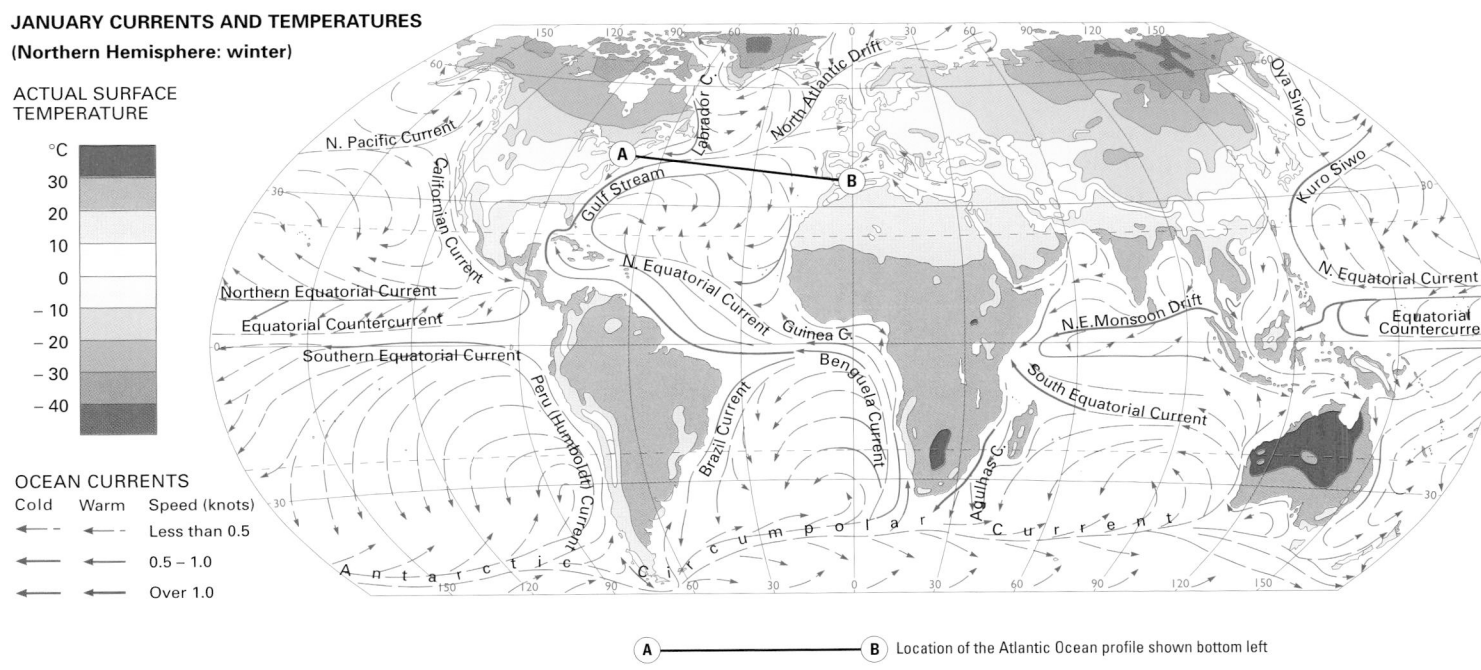

A ———————————— B Location of the Atlantic Ocean profile shown bottom left

JULY CURRENTS AND TEMPERATURES
(Northern Hemisphere: summer)

ACTUAL SURFACE TEMPERATURE

°C
30
20
10
0
-10

OCEAN CURRENTS
Cold | Warm | Speed (knots)
Less than 0.5
0.5 – 1.0
Over 1.0

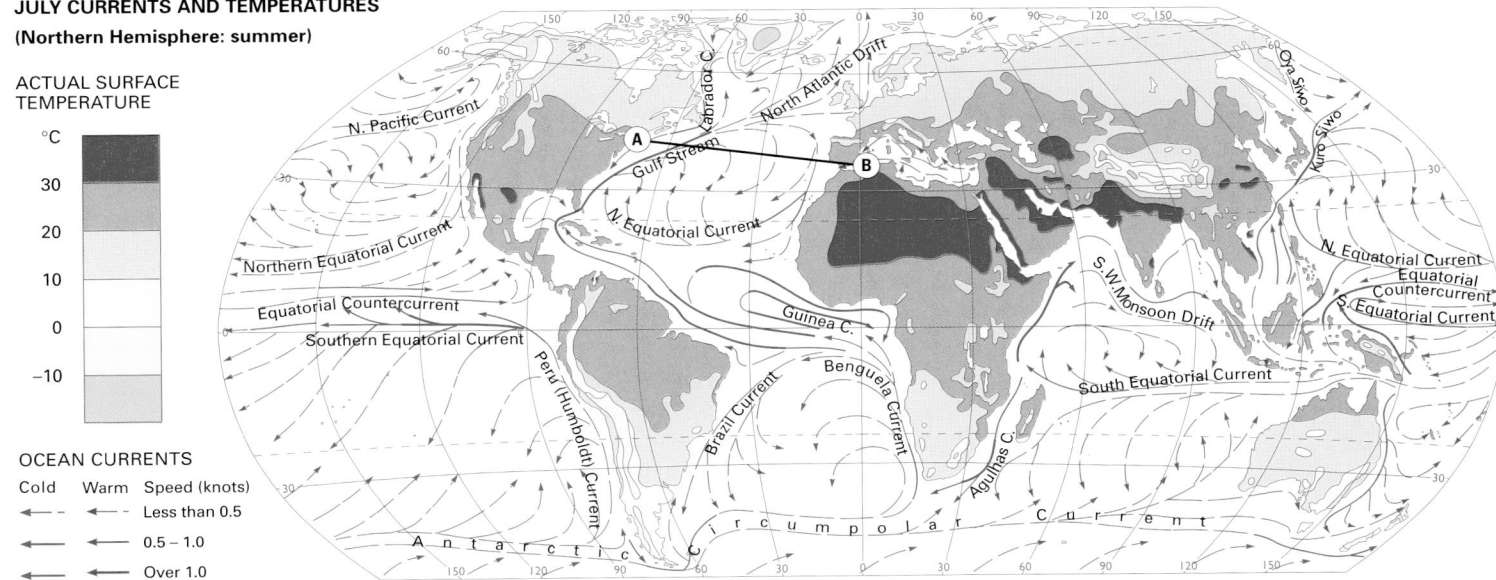

Topography of the Ocean Floor

Profile of the Atlantic Ocean

The deep ocean floor was once believed to be flat, but maps compiled from readings made by sonar equipment show that it is no more uniform than the surface of the continents. The profile (*below*) shows some of the features on the Atlantic Ocean floor between Massachusetts in North America and Gibraltar (*for location of profile, see maps above*). Around the continents are shallow continental shelves composed of rocks which are less dense than the underlying oceanic crust. The continents end at the top of the steep continental slope, which descends to the abyss via the continental rise, made up of sediments washed down from the continental shelves. The abyss contains large plains overlain by oozes, but the plains are broken by volcanic seamounts and guyots (flat-topped seamounts), a few of which reach the surface as islands. The other main feature is the Mid-Atlantic Ridge, through which runs a rift valley where new crustal rock is being formed as the plates on either side move apart.

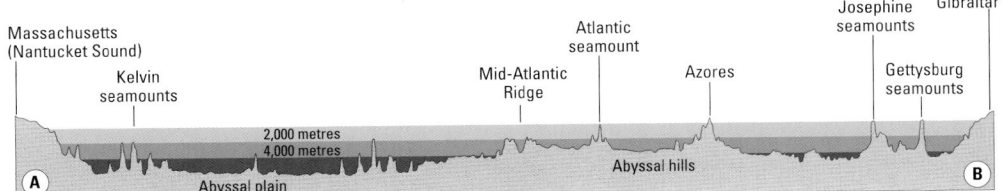

Topography of the ocean floor around Australia

In the image on the right, land areas are shown in grey, with shaded relief. The colours represent sea depth, with red representing the shallowest areas, through yellow and green to dark blue (the deepest). The data for the sea topography are from the Seasat radar satellite. The deep blue area in the upper left is the Java Trench which forms the boundary between the Indian-Australian plate and the Eurasian plate. In the top right, the New Guinea trench, which has a maximum depth of 9,103 metres, forms the border of the Indian-Australian and Pacific plates. Alongside the trenches are volcanic islands formed from magma, created as the edge of the Indian-Australian plate is subducted and melted.

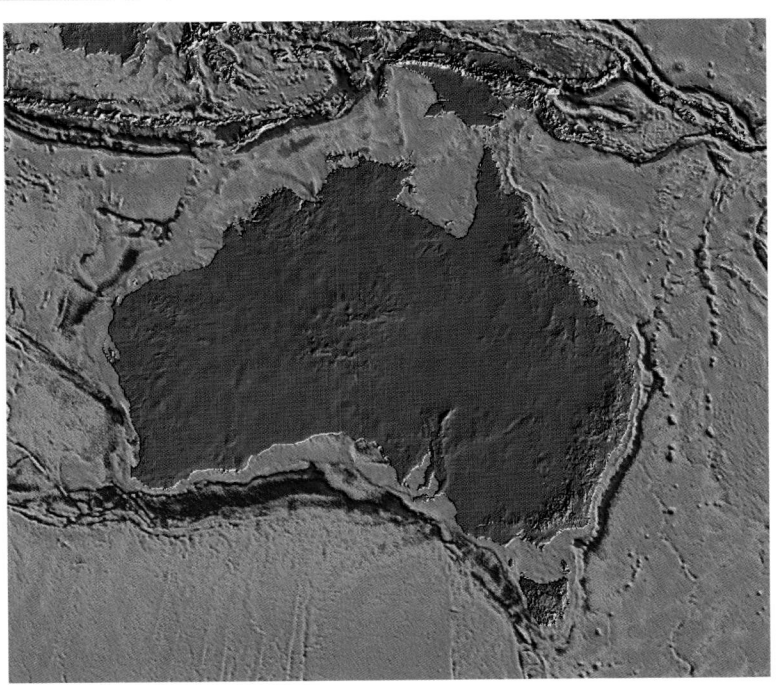

Geology of the Earth

For more information:

12 Types of rock
   Mountain building
13 Surface processes
21 The carbon cycle
36 Minerals

Every year, earthquakes and volcanic eruptions cause much destruction throughout the world. Such phenomena were once thought to be unconnected, but since the late 1960s, scientists have understood that these events are surface manifestations of the tremendous forces operating in the Earth's interior that are slowly but constantly changing the face of our planet.

The Earth is divided into three zones. The crust, a brittle, low-density zone, overlies the dense mantle. Separating the crust from the mantle is a distinct boundary called the Mohorovičić (or Moho) discontinuity. Enclosed by the mantle is the Earth's core, which consists mainly of iron and nickel.

Temperatures inside the Earth range from about 870°C in the upper mantle to perhaps 5,000°C in the core. Heat creates convection currents in a semi-molten part of the mantle called the asthenosphere. Above the asthenosphere is the lithosphere, a solid layer about 70 km thick, consisting of the crust and part of the mantle. The lithosphere is divided into rigid plates, moved around by the currents in the asthenosphere, a process named plate tectonics.

The Earth was formed around 4.6 billion years ago. Lighter elements floated towards the surface, where they formed crustal rocks. The oldest rocks so far discovered are about 4 billion years old, while the oldest fossils occur in rocks formed around 3.5 billion years ago. An explosion of life occurred at the start of the Cambrian period, 570 million years ago. The fossil record since the start of the Cambrian has enabled scientists to piece together the story of life on Earth.

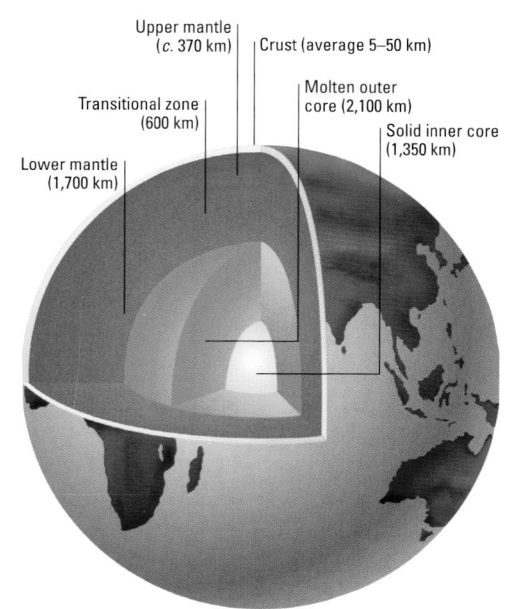

Upper mantle (c. 370 km)
Crust (average 5–50 km)
Transitional zone (600 km)
Molten outer core (2,100 km)
Lower mantle (1,700 km)
Solid inner core (1,350 km)

Plate Tectonics

In the early 20th century, the German scientist Alfred Wegener and others noticed similarities between the shapes of the continents. From a study of rocks and fossils in widely separated continents, they suggested that the continents had once been joined together and that somehow they had drifted apart. But no one knew of a mechanism that might cause continents to drift. However, in the 1950s and 1960s, evidence from studies of the ocean floor suggested that the low-density continents rest on huge slow-moving plates.

Sea-floor spreading in the Indian Ocean and continental plate collision

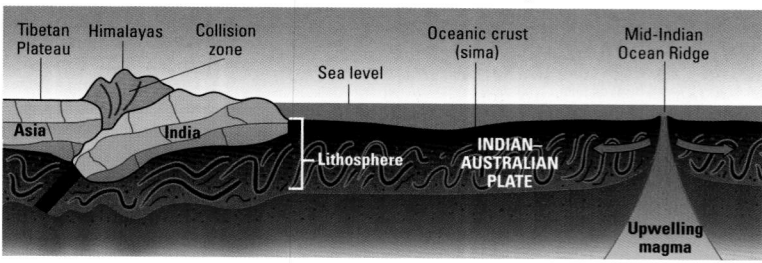

Tibetan Plateau | Himalayas | Collision zone | Oceanic crust (sima) | Mid-Indian Ocean Ridge
Sea level
Asia | India | Lithosphere | INDIAN-AUSTRALIAN PLATE | Upwelling magma

Sea-floor spreading in the Atlantic Ocean and plate collision

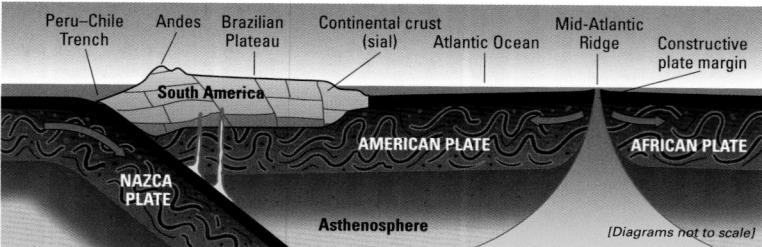

Peru–Chile Trench | Andes | Brazilian Plateau | Continental crust (sial) | Atlantic Ocean | Mid-Atlantic Ridge | Constructive plate margin
South America
NAZCA PLATE | AMERICAN PLATE | AFRICAN PLATE
Asthenosphere | [Diagrams not to scale]

The huge ridges that run through the oceans represent boundaries between plates. Here plates are diverging at rates of 20–41 mm a year. Molten magma from the mantle rises along a central rift valley to form new crustal rock. These ocean ridges, which are active zones where earthquakes and volcanic eruptions are common, are called constructive plate margins. Destructive plate margins, which occur when two plates converge, are marked by deep ocean trenches as one plate is forced under the other. The descending plate is melted to produce the magma that fuels volcanoes alongside the trenches. Movements of descending plates are often sudden and violent, triggering earthquakes in overlying continental areas. Where two continents collide, their margins are buckled up to form fold mountain ranges. A third type of plate margin, the transform fault, is not illustrated above. Along these plate margins, such as California's San Andreas fault, plates are moving parallel to each other.

The debate about plate tectonics is not over. Questions still arise as to why some active volcanoes lie far from plate margins, and why major earthquakes occur in mid-plate areas.

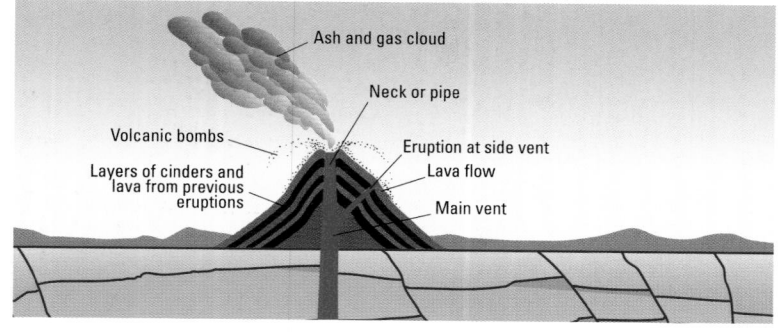

Ash and gas cloud
Neck or pipe
Volcanic bombs
Eruption at side vent
Layers of cinders and lava from previous eruptions
Lava flow
Main vent

Continental Drift

In 1915, Alfred Wegener produced a series of world maps proposing that, around 200 million years ago, the continents had been joined together in a supercontinent which he called Pangaea. This landmass started to break up about 180 million years ago and the parts drifted to their present positions. The arrows on the present-day world map (*below*) shows that the continents are still on the move.

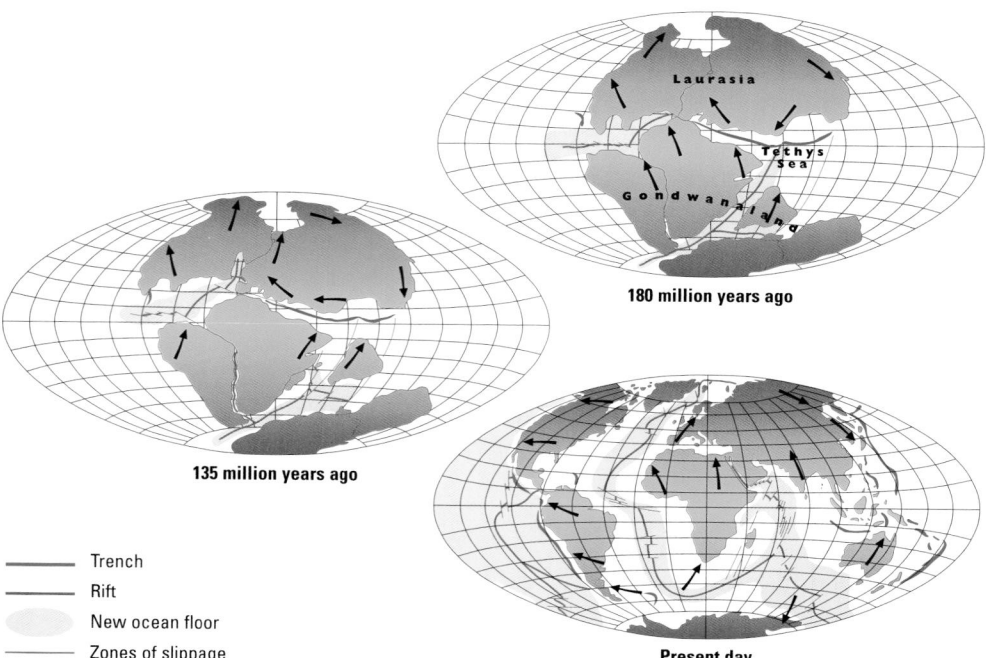

Laurasia
Tethys Sea
Gondwanaland
180 million years ago

135 million years ago

Trench
Rift
New ocean floor
Zones of slippage

Present day

Distribution of Volcanoes

Volcanoes occur when hot liquefied rock beneath the Earth's crust is pushed up by pressure to the surface as molten lava. There are some 550 known active volcanoes, around 20 of which are erupting at any one time.

- Submarine volcanoes
- ▲ Land volcanoes active since 1700
- — Boundaries of tectonic plates

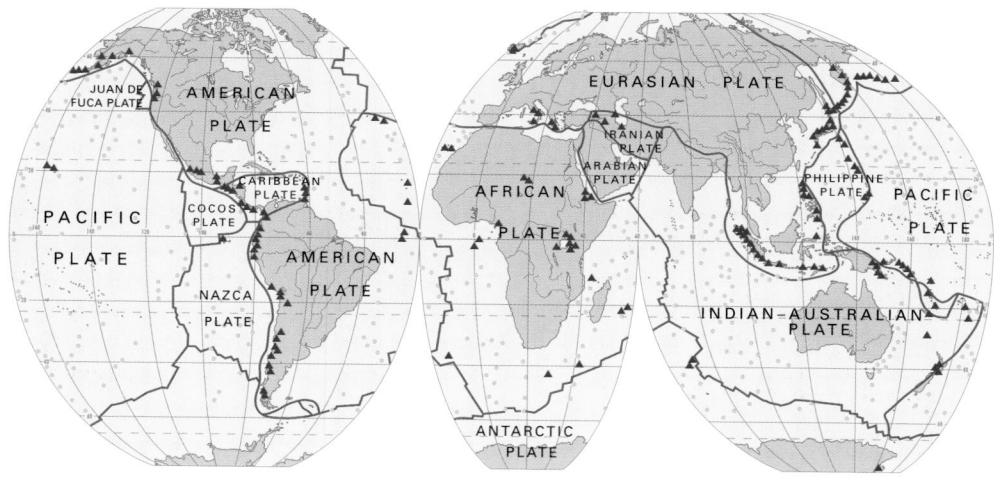

JUAN DE FUCA PLATE | AMERICAN PLATE | EURASIAN PLATE
CARIBBEAN PLATE | IRANIAN PLATE | ARABIAN PLATE | PHILIPPINE PLATE
PACIFIC PLATE | COCOS PLATE | AFRICAN PLATE | PACIFIC PLATE
NAZCA PLATE | AMERICAN PLATE | INDIAN-AUSTRALIAN PLATE
ANTARCTIC PLATE

Geological Time

Time, in millions of years before the present, is shown on a sliding scale, greatly compressed in the distant past.

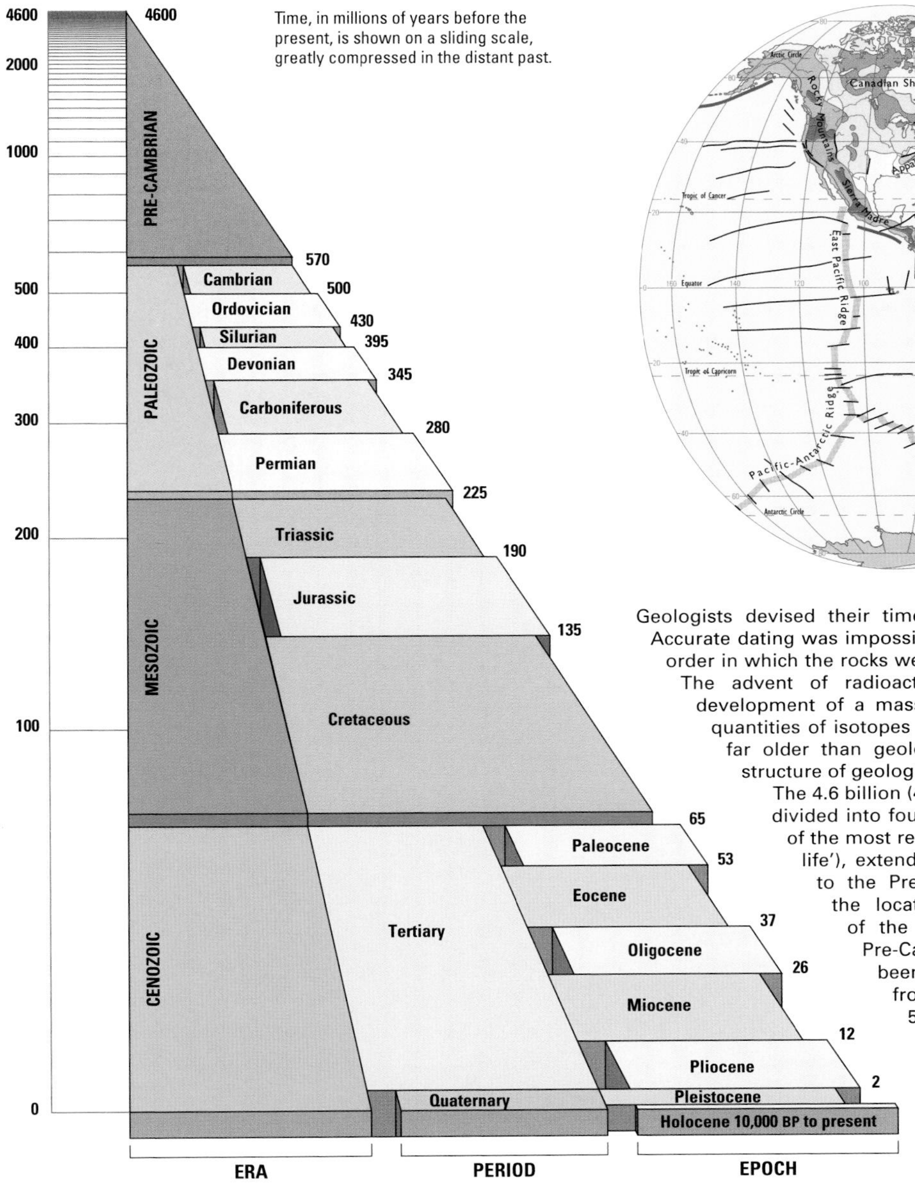

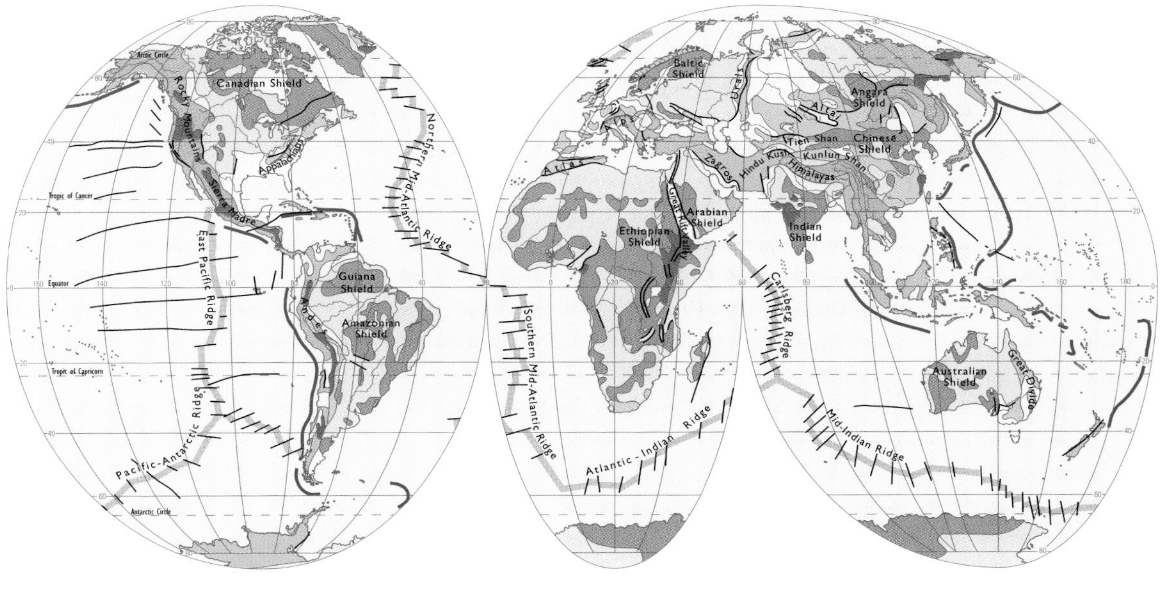

ERA	PERIOD	EPOCH
PRE-CAMBRIAN		
PALEOZOIC	Cambrian 570	
	Ordovician 500	
	Silurian 430	
	Devonian 395	
	Carboniferous 345	
	Permian 280	
MESOZOIC	Triassic 225	
	Jurassic 190	
	Cretaceous 135	
CENOZOIC	Tertiary	Paleocene 65
		Eocene 53
		Oligocene 37
		Miocene 26
		Pliocene 12
	Quaternary	Pleistocene 2
		Holocene 10,000 BP to present

(Scale in millions of years: 4600, 2000, 1000, 500, 400, 300, 200, 100, 0)

Geologists devised their timescale on the basis of relative, not calendar, ages. Accurate dating was impossible and estimates were often bitterly disputed, but the order in which the rocks were formed could be deduced from careful observation. The advent of radioactive dating – culminating in the 1950s with the development of a mass spectrometer capable of accurately measuring tiny quantities of isotopes – appears to have settled the arguments. The Earth is far older than geologists first imagined, but their painstakingly-created structure of geological time has withstood the advent of high technology.

The 4.6 billion (4,600 million) years since the formation of the Earth are divided into four great eras, further split into periods and, in the case of the most recent era, epochs. The present era is the Cenozoic ('new life'), extending backwards through 'middle life' and 'ancient life' to the Pre-Cambrian, named after the Latin word for Wales, the location of some of the earliest known fossils. Most of the Earth's geological history is encompassed by the Pre-Cambrian: though traces of ancient life have since been found, it was largely the proliferation of fossils from the beginning of the Paleozoic era onwards, some 570 million years ago, which first allowed precise subdivisions to be made.

Like the Cambrian, most are named after regions exemplifying a period's geology. Others – such as the Carboniferous ('coal-bearing') or the Cretaceous ('chalk-bearing') – are more directly descriptive.

Legend:
- Pre-Cambrian shields
- Sedimentary cover on Pre-Cambrian shields
- Paleozoic (Caledonian and Hercynian) folding
- Sedimentary cover on Paleozoic folding
- Mesozoic folding
- Sedimentary cover on Mesozoic folding
- Cenozoic (Alpine) folding
- Sedimentary cover on Cenozoic folding
- Intensive Mesozoic and Cenozoic vulcanism
- Principal faults
- Oceanic marginal troughs
- Mid-oceanic ridges
- Overthrust faults

Earthquakes

Earthquake magnitude is usually rated according to either the Richter or the Modified Mercalli scale, both devised by seismologists in the 1930s. The Richter scale measures absolute earthquake power with mathematical precision: each step upwards represents a tenfold increase in the amplitude of the shockwave. Theoretically, there is no upper limit, but the largest earthquakes measured have been rated at between 8.8 and 8.9. The 12-point Mercalli scale, based on observed effects, is often more meaningful, ranging from I (earthquakes noticed only by seismographs) to XII (total destruction); intermediate points include V (people awakened at night; unstable objects overturned), VII (collapse of ordinary buildings; chimneys and monuments fall), and IX (conspicuous cracks in ground; serious damage to reservoirs).

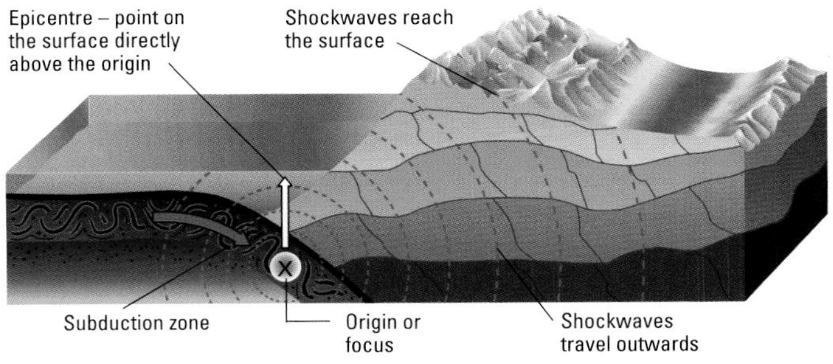

Epicentre – point on the surface directly above the origin

Shockwaves reach the surface

Subduction zone

Origin or focus

Shockwaves travel outwards

Legend:
- Mobile land areas
- Submarine zones of mobile land areas
- Stable land platforms
- Submarine extensions of land platforms
- Mid-oceanic volcanic ridges
- Oceanic platforms
- 1976 Principal earthquakes and dates (since 1900)

Earthquakes are a series of rapid vibrations originating from the slipping or faulting of parts of the Earth's crust when stresses within build up to breaking point. They usually happen at depths varying from 8 km to 30 km. Severe earthquakes cause extensive damage when they take place in populated areas, destroying structures and severing communications. Most initial loss of life occurs due to secondary causes such as falling masonry, fires and flooding.

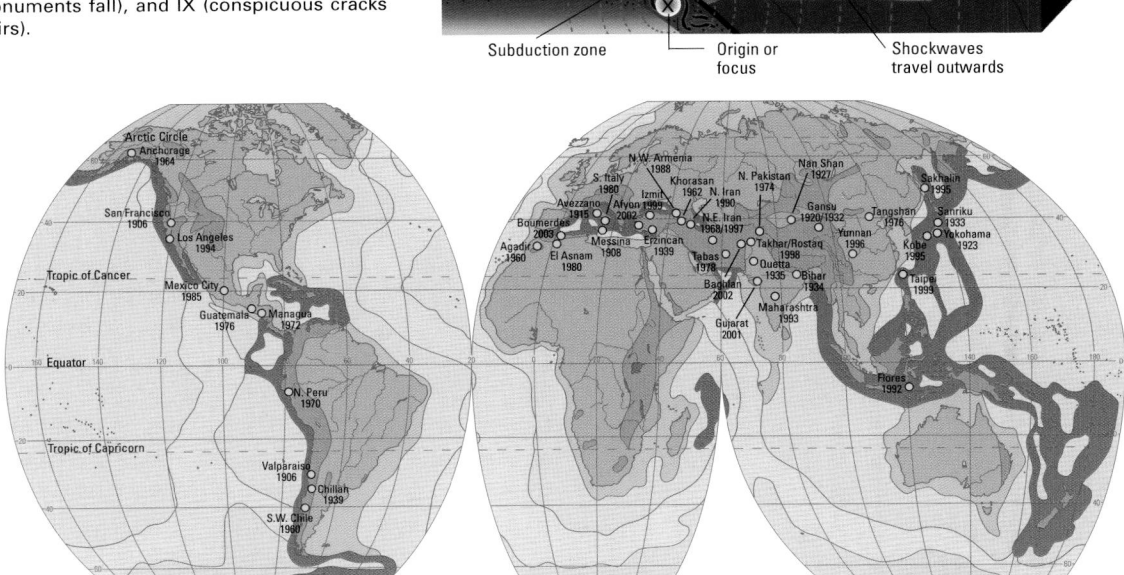

Notable Earthquakes Since 1900

Year	Location	Mag.	Deaths
1906	San Francisco, USA	7.7	3,000
1906	Valparaiso, Chile	8.6	22,000
1908	Messina, Italy	7.5	83,000
1915	Avezzano, Italy	7.5	30,000
1920	Gansu (Kansu), China	8.6	180,000
1923	Yokohama, Japan	8.3	143,000
1927	Nan Shan, China	8.3	200,000
1932	Gansu (Kansu), China	7.6	70,000
1933	Sanriku, Japan	8.9	2,990
1934	Bihar, India/Nepal	8.4	10,700
1935	Quetta, India*	7.5	60,000
1939	Chillan, Chile	8.3	28,000
1939	Erzincan, Turkey	7.9	30,000
1960	S. W. Chile	9.5	2,200
1960	Agadir, Morocco	5.8	12,000
1962	Khorasan, Iran	7.1	12,230
1964	Anchorage, USA	9.2	125
1968	N. E. Iran	7.4	12,000
1970	N. Peru	7.7	66,794
1972	Managua, Nicaragua	6.2	5,000
1974	N. Pakistan	6.3	5,200
1976	Guatemala	7.5	22,778
1976	Tangshan, China	8.2	255,000
1978	Tabas, Iran	7.7	25,000
1980	El Asnam, Algeria	7.3	20,000
1980	S. Italy	7.2	4,800
1985	Mexico City, Mexico	8.1	4,200
1988	N.W. Armenia	6.8	55,000
1990	N. Iran	7.7	36,000
1992	Flores, Indonesia	6.8	1,895
1993	Maharashtra, India	6.4	30,000
1994	Los Angeles, USA	6.6	51
1995	Kobe, Japan	7.2	5,000
1995	Sakhalin Is., Russia	7.5	2,000
1996	Yunnan, China	7.0	240
1997	N. E. Iran	7.1	2,400
1998	Takhar, Afghanistan	6.1	4,200
1998	Rostaq, Afghanistan	7.0	5,000
1999	Izmit, Turkey	7.4	15,000
1999	Taipei, Taiwan	7.6	1,700
2001	Gujarat, India	7.7	14,000
2002	Afyon, Turkey	6.5	44
2002	Baghlan, Afghanistan	6.1	1,000
2003	Boumerdes, Algeria	6.8	2,200

The most devastating quake ever was at Shaanxi (Shenshi) province, central China, on 3 January 1556, when an estimated 830,000 people were killed.

* now Pakistan

LANDFORMS

For more information:

8 Oceans
10 The Earth's structure
   Plate tectonics
   Volcanoes
11 Geological time
18 Hydrological cycle
37 Structural regions

The theory of plate tectonics has offered new insights as to how the Earth works, elucidating mysteries concerning continental drift, volcanic eruptions and earthquakes. It has also contributed to our understanding of how plate collisions can squeeze up layers of sediments on seabeds into fold mountain ranges, such as the Himalayas.

Yet even as mountains rise, natural forces are wearing them away. In hot, dry climates, mechanical weathering, a result of rapid temperature changes, causes the outer layers of rocks to peel away, while, in cold mountain regions, boulders are prised apart when water freezes in cracks in rocks. Chemical weathering is responsible for hollowing out limestone caves and decomposing granites.

Climatic conditions have a great bearing on the principal agent of erosion in any particular area. Running water is most important in moist temperate regions. In cold regions, ice is the major agent of erosion, and in many mountain ranges, U-shaped valleys are evidence of the erosive power of valley glaciers. Ice sheets moulded much of the Earth's surface during the Ice Ages, the most recent of which, in the northern hemisphere, ended only 10,000 years ago. Polar climates also shape the scenery of the periglacial areas that border bodies of ice. Such areas are subject to constant freeze-thaw action, which creates such features as pingos (domed mounds).

Climatic change has also affected many of the landforms in hot deserts, which were shaped by running water at a time when the deserts enjoyed much wetter climates. However, the major agent of erosion in deserts today is wind-blown sand, which erodes rock strata to form mushroom-shaped rocks and caves.

The surface of the Earth is under constant assault from tectonic processes and the agents of erosion. The products of erosion, fragments of rock such as sand, are deposited to form sedimentary rocks. Metamorphic rocks are created when igneous or sedimentary rocks are buried and metamorphosed by heat and pressure. Eventually the rocks are recycled to form magma, which rises upwards to start the rock cycle all over again.

The Rock Cycle

James Hutton first proposed the rock cycle in the late 1700s after he observed the slow but steady effects of erosion.

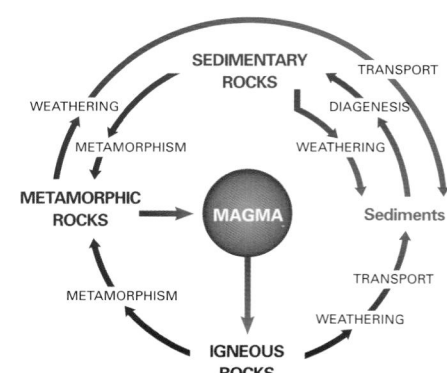

Rocks are divided into three types, according to the way in which they are formed:

Igneous rocks, including granite and basalt, are formed when magma cools inside the Earth's crust or on the surface.

Metamorphic rocks, such as slate, marble and quartzite, are formed below the Earth's surface by the compression or baking of existing rocks.

Sedimentary rocks, like sandstone and limestone, are formed on the surface of the Earth from the remains of living organisms and eroded fragments of older rocks.

Mountain Building

Mountains are formed when pressures on the Earth's crust caused by continental drift become so intense that the surface buckles or cracks. This happens where oceanic crust is subducted by continental crust or, more dramatically, where two tectonic plates collide: the Rockies, Andes, Alps, Urals and Himalayas resulted from such impacts. These are all known as fold mountains because they were formed by the compression of the rocks, forcing the surface to bend and fold like a crumpled rug. The Himalayas are formed from the folded former sediments of the Tethys Sea, which was trapped in the collision zone between the Indian–Australian and Eurasian plates.

The other main mountain-building process occurs when the crust fractures to create faults, allowing rock to be forced upwards in large blocks; or when the pressure of magma within the crust forces the surface to bulge into a dome, or erupts to form a volcano. Large mountain ranges may reveal a combination of these features; the Alps, for example, have been compressed so violently that the folds are fragmented by numerous faults and intrusions of molten igneous rock.

Over millions of years, even the greatest mountain ranges can be reduced by the agents of erosion (especially rivers) to a low, rugged landscape known as a peneplain.

Types of faults: Faults occur where the crust is being stretched or compressed so violently that the rock strata break in a horizontal or vertical movement. They are classified by the direction in which the blocks of rock have moved. A normal fault results when a vertical movement causes the surface to break apart; compression causes a reverse fault. Horizontal movement causes shearing, known as a strike-slip fault. When the rock breaks in two places, the central block may be pushed up in a horst fault, or sink (creating a rift valley) in a graben fault.

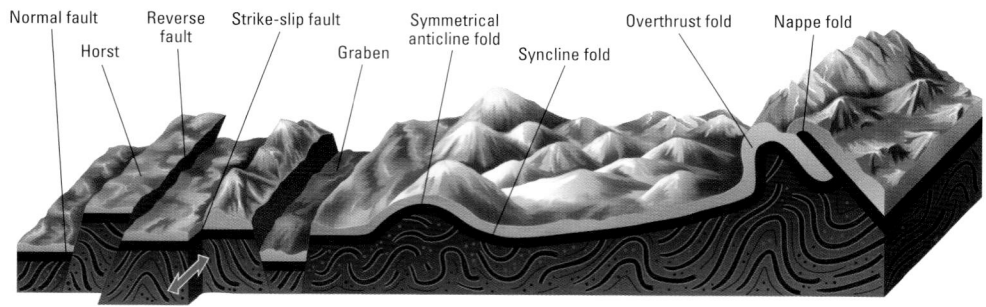

Types of fold: Folds occur when rock strata are squeezed and compressed. They are common, therefore, at destructive plate margins and where plates have collided, forcing the rocks to buckle into mountain ranges. Geographers give different names to the degrees of fold that result from continuing pressure on the rock. A simple fold may be symmetric, with even slopes on either side, but as the pressure builds up, one slope becomes steeper and the fold becomes asymmetric. Later, the ridge or 'anticline' at the top of the fold may slide over the lower ground or 'syncline' to form a recumbent fold. Eventually, the rock strata may break under the pressure to form an overthrust and finally a nappe fold.

Annual Fluctuations for Selected Glaciers

Glacier name and location	Change in mass balance 1970–90
Wolverine, USA	+2,320
Storglaciaren, Sweden	−120
Djankuat, Russia	−1,890
Grasubreen, Norway	−2,530
Ürümqi, China	−3,828
Golubin, Kyrgyzstan	−7,105
Gries, Switzerland	−10,600
Careser, Italy	−11,610
Abramov, Tajikistan	−13,700
Sarennes, France	−15,020
Place, Canada	−15,175

The mass balance is defined as the difference between glacier accumulation and ablation (melting), and is expressed as water equivalent in millimetres. A minus indicates a reduction in the depth or length of a glacier. As can be seen from this geographically diverse selection, glaciers are retreating in many areas worldwide. The most dramatic and serious example of this phenomenon is the continuing distintegration of several large Antarctic ice-shelves.

The extent to which glacial retreat is due to global warming, or to longer term climatic fluctuations, remains a matter for debate.

Continental Glaciation

Many landforms in the northern hemisphere were shaped by ice sheets and meltwater during the Pleistocene Ice Age, which began about 2 million years ago. During the Ice Age, the ice sheets periodically advanced and retreated. The first map (*below left*) shows the ice cover at its greatest extent about 200,000 years BP (before the present), when it covered about 30% of the land surface, as compared with 10% today.

About 18,000 years BP, the ice covered most of Canada and extended as far south as the Bristol Channel in England. Around the ice sheets, land areas experienced periglacial conditions.

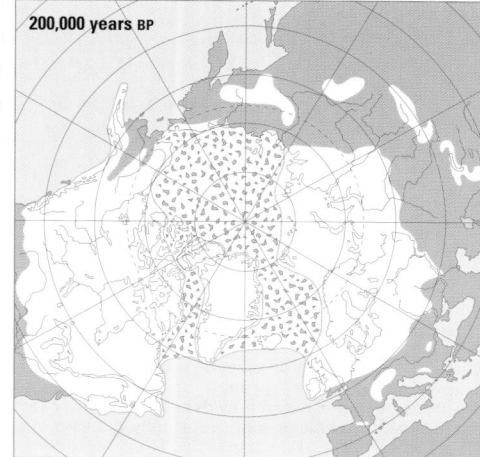

200,000 years BP

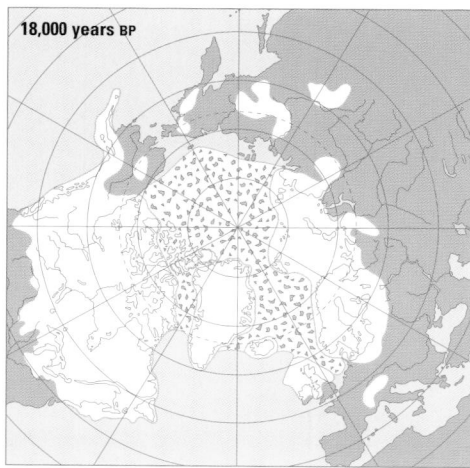

18,000 years BP

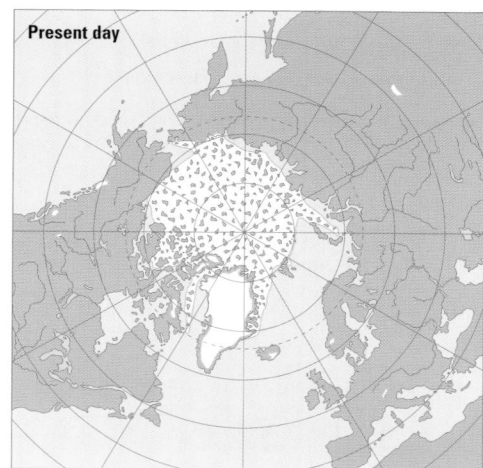

Present day

Natural Landforms

Natural landforms reflect the influence of plate tectonics through mountain-building and the generation of new rocks from the interior, together with the agents of erosion: running water, ice, winds and coastal waves. Over millions of years, mountains are gradually eroded, producing landforms that reflect the major forces that have been at work, as well as the underlying geology, the climatic conditions, which often vary over time, and the vegetation cover. The stylized diagram (*below*) shows some major natural landforms found in the mid-latitudes.

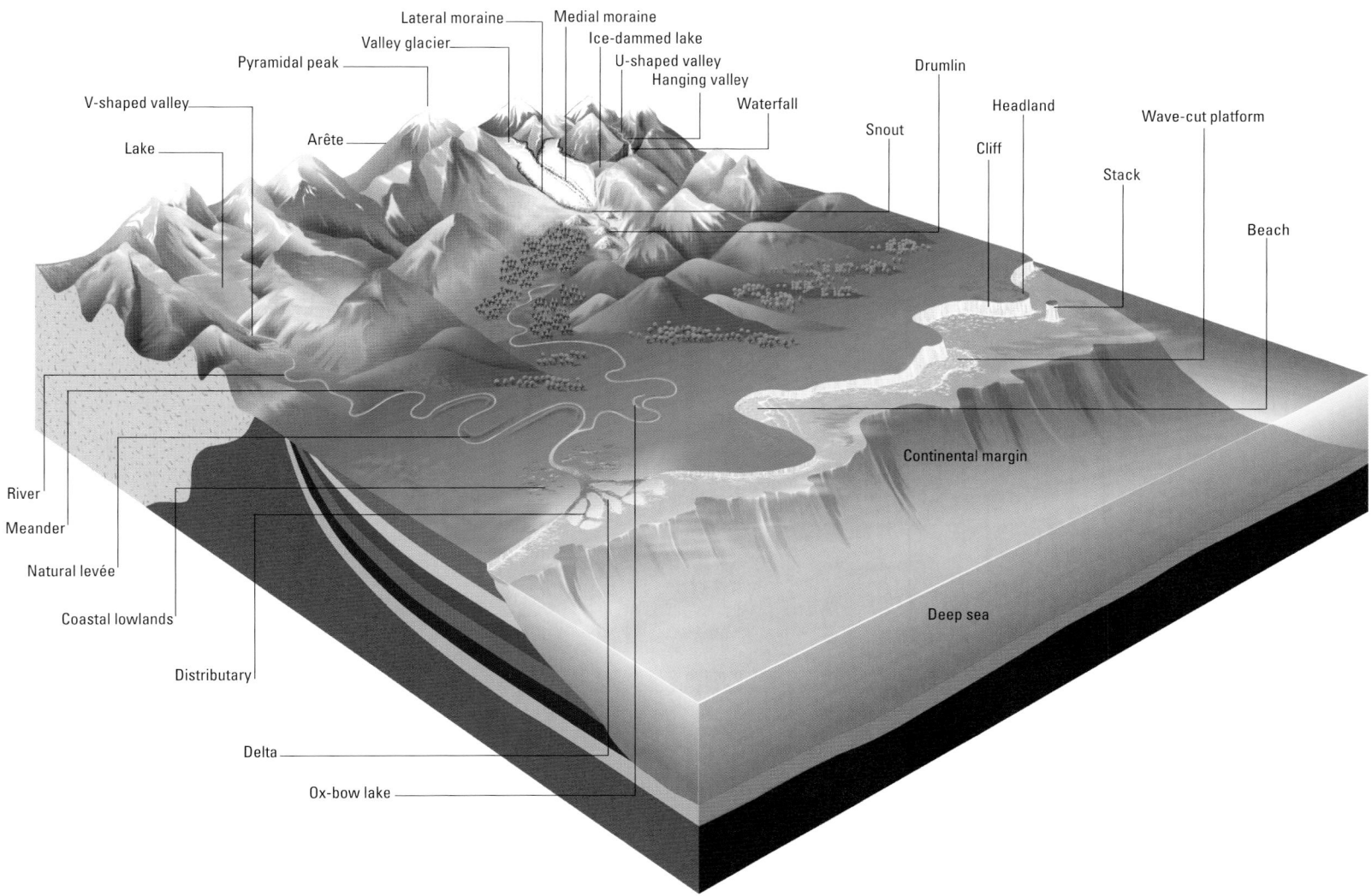

Desert Landforms

Deserts are defined as places with an average annual precipitation of 250 mm per year, though places with a higher rainfall and a high evaporation rate may also qualify as deserts. The three types of desert landforms are known by their Arabic names, a reflection of the fact that the Sahara in North Africa is the world's largest desert. Sand desert, called erg, covers about one-fifth of the world's deserts. The rest is divided between hammada (areas of bare rock) and reg (broad plains covered by loose gravel or pebbles).

The shapes of dunes in sand deserts reflect the character of local winds. Where winds are constant in direction, the sand often piles up in crescent-shaped dunes, called barchans. Barchans are constantly on the move and their forward march, unless halted by vegetation, may overwhelm settlements at oases. Seif dunes, named after the Arabic word for 'sword', are long ridges of sand that lie parallel to the direction of the wind, but where winds are variable, the sand sheets are often featureless.

Wind-blown sand is an effective agent of erosion, but because of the weight of sand grains, this type of erosion is confined to within 2 metres of the land surface, creating caves and mushroom-shaped rocks.

In assessing desert landforms, it is important to remember that other processes were at work in the past when the climate was very different from today. For example, cave paintings suggest that the Sahara had a much wetter climate after the end of the Ice Age and only began to dry up after about 5000 BC. However, human action, including overgrazing and the cutting down of trees for firewood, can turn a grassland region into desert – a process known as desertification.

Erg

Hammada

Reg

Surface Processes

Catastrophic changes to landforms are periodically caused by such phenomena as avalanches, landslides and volcanic eruptions, but most of the processes that shape the Earth's surface operate extremely slowly in human terms. One estimate, based on a study of landforms in the United States, suggests that, on average, 1 metre of land is removed from the entire surface of the country every 29,500 years. However, the terrain and the climate have a great effect on the erosion rate. For example, on cold plains, such as the Hudson Bay lowlands, the rate drops to around 1 metre for every 154,200 years, while in wet, tropical mountain areas, the rate may reach 1 metre for every 1,300 years.

Chemical weathering is at its greatest in warm, humid regions, while mechanical weathering, or the physical break-up of rocks, predominates in cold mountain or hot desert regions. The most familiar type of chemical weathering is caused by the reaction of rainwater containing dissolved carbon dioxide on limestone. This leads to the creation of labyrinthine cave networks dissolved by groundwater. Mechanical weathering includes frost action, while in hot deserts, rapid temperature changes cause the outer layers of rocks to expand and contract until they crack and peel away, a process called exfoliation.

The most important product of weathering is soil, which consists of rock fragments and humus, the decayed remains of plants and animals, together with living organisms, including vast numbers of micro-organisms. Soils vary in character according to the climate, ranging from the heavily leached, red laterite soils of wet tropical areas to the fertile, brown soils of dry grasslands. Soils are important because they support plants, which in turn anchor the soil and act as a protection against erosion. Soil erosion is greatest on sloping land because the steeper the slope, the greater the tendency for the soil to creep or flow downhill. The degree of movement of soil and rock downhill under the influence of gravity, called mass wasting, depends on a slope's stability. The stability may be disturbed by earthquakes or by heavy rain (water acts as a lubricant and increases the weight of the overlying material), which may trigger flows, slides or large falls of rock.

Running water is probably the world's leading agent of erosion and transportation. The energy of a river depends on several factors, including its velocity and volume, and its erosive power is at its peak when it is in full flood, sweeping soil, pebbles and even boulders along its course, cutting downwards into the bedrock or widening its valley. Sea waves also exert tremendous erosive power during storms, when they hurl pebbles and large rocks against the shore, undercutting cliffs and hollowing out caves. Headlands are often attacked on both sides, forming caves, then a natural arch and eventually an isolated stack.

Glacier ice forms in mountain hollows, called cirques, and spills out to form valley glaciers, which transport rocks shattered by frost action. As a glacier moves, rocks embedded in the base and sides scrape away bedrock, eroding steep-sided, flat-bottomed, U-shaped valleys. Evidence of past glaciation in mountain regions includes cirques, knife-edged ridges, or arêtes, and pyramidal peaks, or horns.

Geologists once considered that landforms evolved from 'young', newly uplifted mountainous areas, through a 'mature' hilly stage, to an 'old age' stage when the land was reduced to an almost flat plain, or peneplain. This theory, called the 'cycle of erosion', fell into disuse when it became evident that so many factors, including the effects of plate tectonics and climatic change, constantly interrupt the cycle, which takes no account of the highly complex interactions that shape the surface of our planet.

THE ATMOSPHERE

For more information:
9 Ocean currents
17 Beaufort wind scale
Climate change
Monsoon
21 Solar energy
Greenhouse effect
22 Greenhouse power
23 Acid rain

The atmosphere is a meteor shield, a radiation deflector, a thermal blanket and a source of chemical energy for the Earth's diverse life forms. Five-sixths of its mass is in the lowest layer, the troposphere, which ranges in thickness from 18 to 10 km between the Equator and the poles. Powered by the Sun, the air is always on the move, flowing generally from high- to low-pressure areas. The troposphere is the layer where virtually all weather phenomena, including clouds, precipitation and winds, occur. Above the troposphere is the stratosphere, which contains the important ozone layer and extends to about 50 km above the Earth's surface. Beyond 100 km, atmospheric density is lower than most laboratory vacuums.

Structure of the Atmosphere

600 km — Hubble Space Telescope — pressure 10^{-20} mb

exosphere

400 km — International Space Station — 10^{-22} mb

350 km

300 km — Space Shuttle — 10^{-16} mb

250 km

thermosphere

200 km — 10^{-10} mb

aurorae

150 km

mesosphere

100 km — meteor trails — 10^{-3} mb

50 km — ozone layer

stratosphere

10 km — Concorde — 10^{3} mb

troposphere

Mount Everest 8,850 m

Circulation of the Air

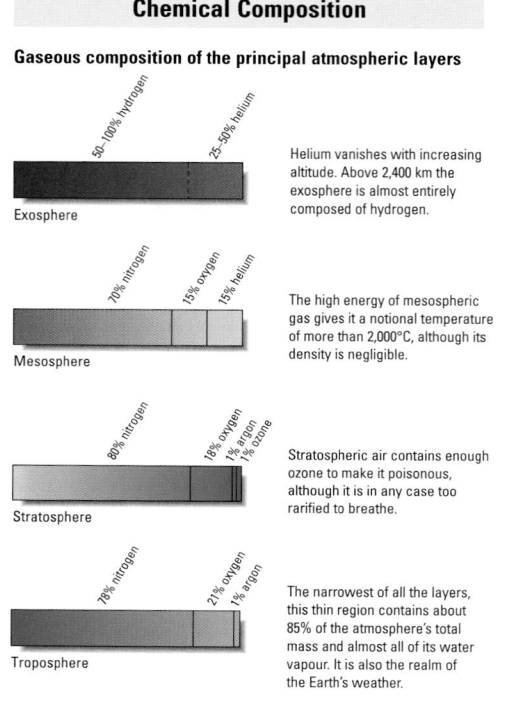

N
3
FRONTAL RAIN
60° — EASTERLY WINDS
SOUTH-WESTERLY WINDS
2
30° — NORTH-EASTERLY TRADES
1
0° — DOLDRUMS — ITCZ — CONVECTIONAL THUNDERSTORM
SOUTH-EASTERLY TRADES
1
30° — NORTH-WESTERLY WINDS
2
60° — EASTERLY WINDS
3
S — FRONTAL RAIN

Chemical Composition

Gaseous composition of the principal atmospheric layers

50–100% hydrogen | 25–50% helium

Exosphere

Helium vanishes with increasing altitude. Above 2,400 km the exosphere is almost entirely composed of hydrogen.

70% nitrogen | 15% oxygen | 15% helium

Mesosphere

The high energy of mesospheric gas gives it a notional temperature of more than 2,000°C, although its density is negligible.

80% nitrogen | 18% oxygen | 1% argon | 1% ozone

Stratosphere

Stratospheric air contains enough ozone to make it poisonous, although it is in any case too rarified to breathe.

78% nitrogen | 21% oxygen | 1% argon

Troposphere

The narrowest of all the layers, this thin region contains about 85% of the atmosphere's total mass and almost all of its water vapour. It is also the realm of the Earth's weather.

High pressure
Low pressure
Warm air
Cold air
Surface winds
Clouds

1 Hadley Cell
2 Ferrel Cell
3 Polar Cell

ITCZ Intertropical convergence zone

Frontal Systems

Depressions, or cyclones, form along the polar front where dense polar easterlies meet warm subtropical westerlies. Depressions occur when warm air flows into waves in the polar front, while cold air flows in behind it, creating rotating air systems that bring changeable weather. Along the warm front (the boundary on the ground between the warm and cold air), the warm air flows upwards over the cold air, producing a sequence of clouds which help forecasters to predict a depression's advance. Along the cold front, the advancing cold air forces warm air to rise steeply. Towering cumulonimbus clouds form in the rising air. When the cold front overtakes the warm front, the warm air is pushed above ground level to form an occluded front. Cloud and rain persist along occlusions until temperatures equalize, the air mixes, and the depression dies out.

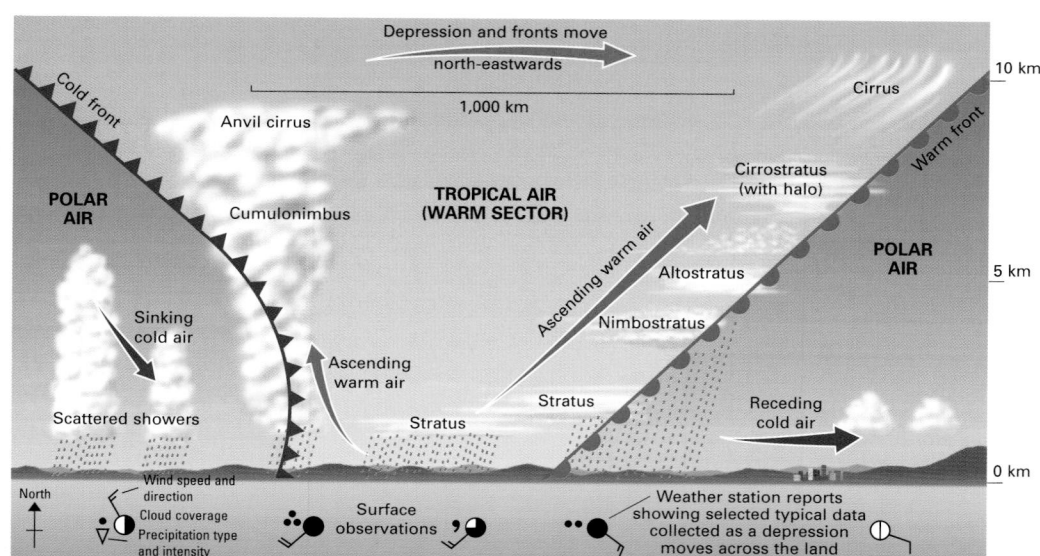

Depression and fronts move north-eastwards
10 km
Cirrus
Cold front
Anvil cirrus
1,000 km
Warm front
Cirrostratus (with halo)
POLAR AIR
Cumulonimbus
TROPICAL AIR (WARM SECTOR)
Ascending warm air
5 km
Altostratus
POLAR AIR
Sinking cold air
Ascending warm air
Nimbostratus
Stratus
Scattered showers
Stratus
Receding cold air
0 km

North
Wind speed and direction
Cloud coverage
Precipitation type and intensity
Surface observations
Weather station reports showing selected typical data collected as a depression moves across the land

Air Masses

Air masses are bodies of air whose characteristics are broadly the same over a large area.
Around the Equator, where the Sun's heat creates
relatively high surface temperatures, warm air
rises to create a zone of low pressure called the
doldrums. The air cools and finally spreads out
towards the poles. Around latitudes 30° north
and south, the air sinks back to the surface,
becoming warmer as it descends and creating
zones of high pressure called the horse latitudes.

The high- and low-pressure zones are both
areas of comparative calm, but between them lie
the prevailing trade wind belts. Air also flows
north and south from the high-pressure horse
latitudes and these airflows meet up with cold,
dense air flowing from the poles along the polar
front. This basic circulatory system is complicated
by the Coriolis effect, brought about by the
spinning Earth. Because of the Coriolis effect,
the prevailing winds do not flow directly
north–south but are deflected to the right in the
northern hemisphere and to the left in the southern. Along the polar front, depressions form
where the polar easterlies meet the westerlies.

The first classification of clouds was developed by a London chemist, Luke Howard, in
1803, and it was later modified by the World
Meteorological Organization. The main types are
divided into three groups according to their
altitude, and into subgroups according to their
shape, which vary from hairlike filaments (cirrus),
heaps or piles (cumulus), and layers (stratus).
Each cloud carries some kind of message, though
not always a clear one, to weather forecasters.

Classification of Clouds

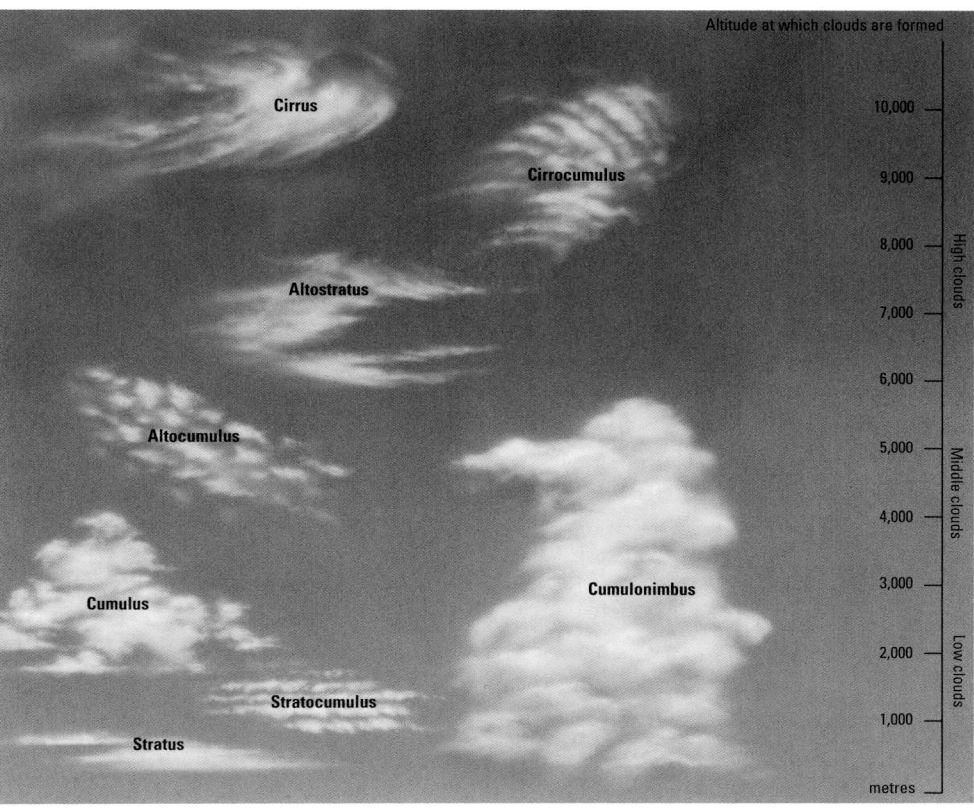

Clouds form when damp,
usually rising, air is cooled.
Thus they form when a
wind rises to cross hills or
mountains; when a mass
of air rises over, or is pushed
up by, another mass of
denser air; or when local
heating of the ground causes
convection currents.

The types of clouds are
classified according to
altitude as high, middle
or low. The high ones,
composed of ice crystals,
are cirrus, cirrostratus and
cirrocumulus. The middle
clouds are altostratus, a grey
or bluish striated, fibrous or
uniform sheet producing light
drizzle, and altocumulus, a
thicker and fluffier version
of cirrocumulus.

Low clouds include nimbo-
stratus, a dark grey layer that
brings rain or snow; cumulus,
a detached heap, dark at the
base; stratus, which forms
dull, overcast skies at low
levels; and stratocumulus,
which consists of fluffy
greyish-white layers.

Cumulonimbus, associated
with storms and rains, heavy
and dense with a flat base
and a high, fluffy outline,
can be tall enough to occupy
middle as well as low
altitudes.

Pressure and Surface Winds

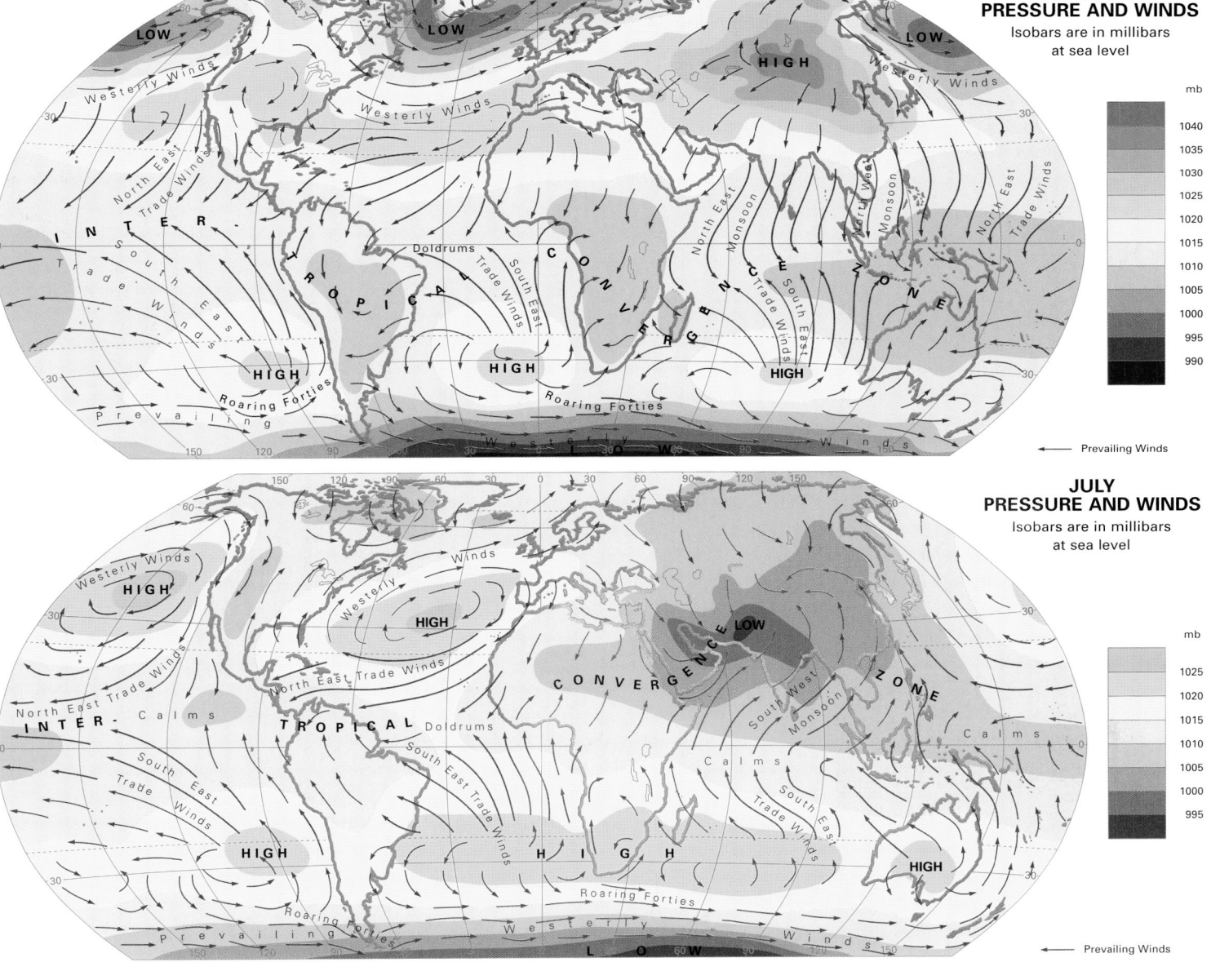

Climate Records

Pressure and winds

Highest barometric pressure:
Agata, Siberia, 1,083.8 mb
at altitude 262 m [862 ft],
31 December 1968.

Lowest barometric pressure:
Typhoon Tip, 480 km
[300 mi] west of Guam,
Pacific Ocean, 870 mb,
12 October 1979.

**Highest recorded wind
speed**: Mt Washington, New
Hampshire, USA, 371 km/h
[231 mph], 12 April 1934.
This is three times as strong
as hurricane force on the
Beaufort Scale.

Windiest place:
Commonwealth Bay,
George V Coast, Antarctica,
where gales frequently reach
over 320 km/h [200 mph].

Worst recorded storm:
Bangladesh (then East
Pakistan) cyclone*,
13 November 1970 – over
300,000 dead or missing. The
1991 cyclone, Bangladesh's
and the world's second worst
in terms of loss of life, killed
an estimated 138,000 people.

Worst recorded tornado:
Missouri/Illinois/Indiana,
USA, 18 March 1925 – 792
deaths. The tornado was
only 275 m [300 yds] wide.

*Tropical cyclones are
known as hurricanes in
Central and North America,
as typhoons in the Far East,
and as willy-willies in
northern Australia.*

CLIMATE

For more information:
9 Ocean currents
14 Circulation of the air
15 Classification of clouds
   Pressure and winds
18 Hydrological cycle
19 Natural vegetation
21 Greenhouse effect
22 Global warming

Weather is the day-to-day or hour-to-hour condition of the air, while climate is weather in the long term, the seasonal pattern of hot and cold, wet and dry, averaged over a long period. Most classifications of climate are based on a system developed by a Russian meteorologist, Vladimir Köppen, in the early 19th century. Using a code based on letters and a classification centred on two main features, temperature and precipitation, he identified five main climatic types: tropical (A), dry (B), warm temperate (C), cold temperate (D), and polar (E). A highland mountain climate (H) was added later to account for the variety of altitudinal climatic zones on high mountains. Each of these main regions was then further subdivided.

Latitude is a major factor in determining climate, but other factors add to the complexity. They include the differential heating of land and sea, the distance from the sea, the effect of mountains on winds, and the influence of ocean currents. For example, New York City, Naples and the Gobi Desert share almost the same latitude, but their climates are very different.

Climates are not indefinitely stable. During the last Ice Age, the Earth underwent alternating cold periods, called glacials, separated by warm interglacials. The Milankovich theory suggests such cycles may be caused by variations in the Earth's path around the Sun, changing from almost circular to elliptical every 95,000 years, and variations in the Earth's tilt from 21.5° to 24.5° every 42,000 years. Another factor is that the Earth is now closest to the Sun in the middle of winter in the northern hemisphere and furthest away in summer. But 12,000 years ago, at the height of the last glacial period, the northern winter fell with the Sun at its most distant.

Studies of these cycles suggest that we are now in an interglacial with a new glacial period on the way. However, many scientists believe that global warming, largely a result of burning fossil fuels and deforestation, may be occurring much faster than the great, slow cycles of the Solar System.

Tropical rainy climates
All mean monthly temperatures above 18°C.

Af	Rainforest climate
Am	Monsoon climate
Aw	Savanna climate

Dry climates
Low rainfall combined with a wide range of temperatures

| BS | Steppe climate |
| BW | Desert climate |

Warm temperate rainy climates
The mean temperature is below 18°C but above –3°C and that of the warmest month is over 10°C.

Cw	Dry winter climate
Cs	Dry summer climate
Cf	Climate with no dry season

Cold temperate rainy climates
The mean temperature of the coldest month is below –3°C but that of the warmest month is still over 10°C.

| Dw | Dry winter climate |
| Df | Climate with no dry season |

Polar climates
The mean temperature of the warmest month is below 10°C, giving permanently frozen subsoil.

| ET | Tundra climate |

The mean temperature of the warmest month is below 0°C, giving permanent ice and snow.

| EF | Polar climate |

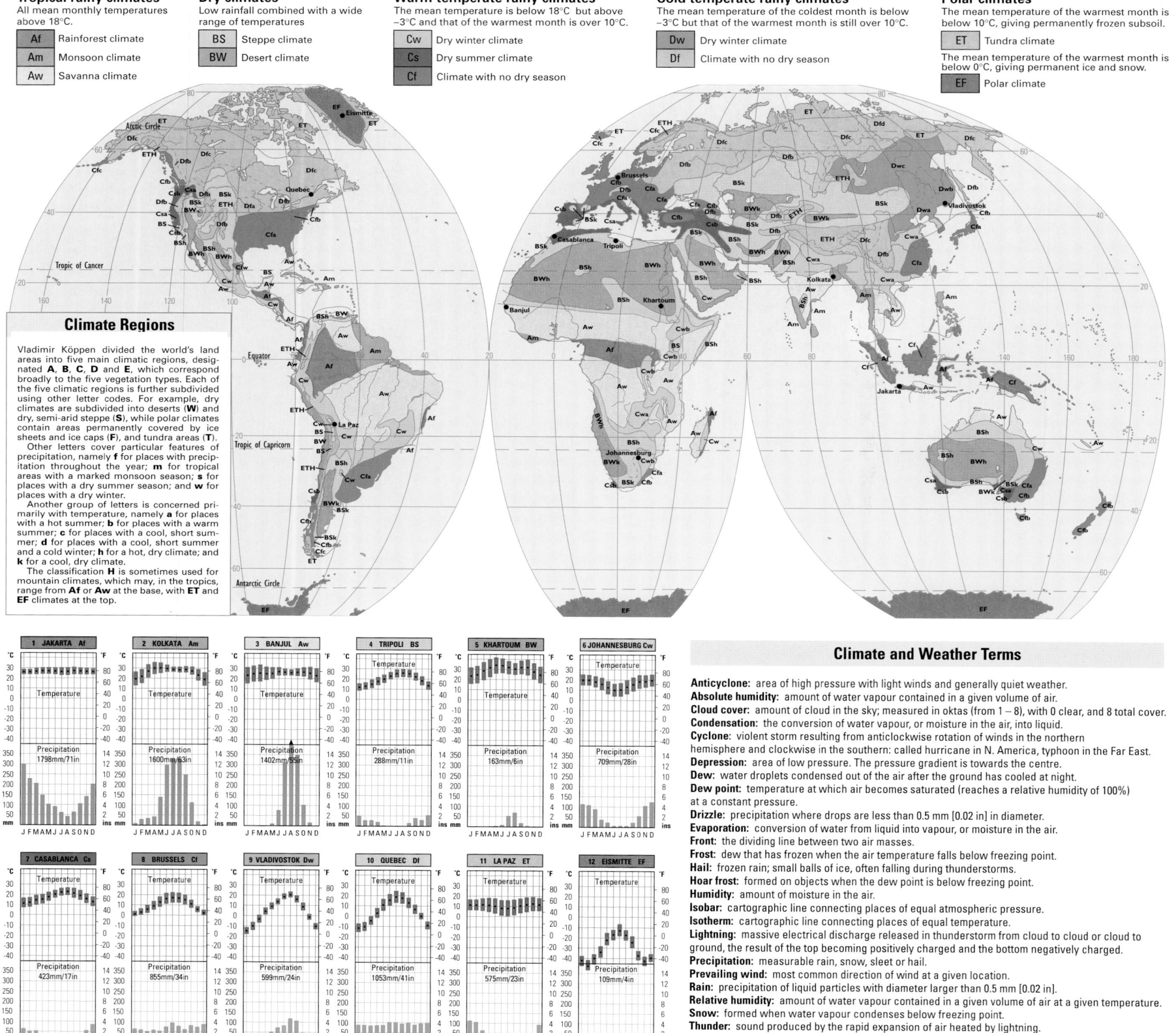

Climate Regions

Vladimir Köppen divided the world's land areas into five main climatic regions, designated **A, B, C, D** and **E**, which correspond broadly to the five vegetation types. Each of the five climatic regions is further subdivided using other letter codes. For example, dry climates are subdivided into deserts (**W**) and dry, semi-arid steppe (**S**), while polar climates contain areas permanently covered by ice sheets and ice caps (**F**), and tundra areas (**T**).

Other letters cover particular features of precipitation, namely **f** for places with precipitation throughout the year; **m** for tropical areas with a marked monsoon season; **s** for places with a dry summer season; and **w** for places with a dry winter.

Another group of letters is concerned primarily with temperature, namely **a** for places with a hot summer; **b** for places with a warm summer; **c** for places with a cool, short summer; **d** for places with a cool, short summer and a cold winter; **h** for a hot, dry climate; and **k** for a cool, dry climate.

The classification **H** is sometimes used for mountain climates, which may, in the tropics, range from **Af** or **Aw** at the base, with **ET** and **EF** climates at the top.

Climate and Weather Terms

Anticyclone: area of high pressure with light winds and generally quiet weather.
Absolute humidity: amount of water vapour contained in a given volume of air.
Cloud cover: amount of cloud in the sky; measured in oktas (from 1 – 8), with 0 clear, and 8 total cover.
Condensation: the conversion of water vapour, or moisture in the air, into liquid.
Cyclone: violent storm resulting from anticlockwise rotation of winds in the northern hemisphere and clockwise in the southern: called hurricane in N. America, typhoon in the Far East.
Depression: area of low pressure. The pressure gradient is towards the centre.
Dew: water droplets condensed out of the air after the ground has cooled at night.
Dew point: temperature at which air becomes saturated (reaches a relative humidity of 100%) at a constant pressure.
Drizzle: precipitation where drops are less than 0.5 mm [0.02 in] in diameter.
Evaporation: conversion of water from liquid into vapour, or moisture in the air.
Front: the dividing line between two air masses.
Frost: dew that has frozen when the air temperature falls below freezing point.
Hail: frozen rain; small balls of ice, often falling during thunderstorms.
Hoar frost: formed on objects when the dew point is below freezing point.
Humidity: amount of moisture in the air.
Isobar: cartographic line connecting places of equal atmospheric pressure.
Isotherm: cartographic line connecting places of equal temperature.
Lightning: massive electrical discharge released in thunderstorm from cloud to cloud or cloud to ground, the result of the top becoming positively charged and the bottom negatively charged.
Precipitation: measurable rain, snow, sleet or hail.
Prevailing wind: most common direction of wind at a given location.
Rain: precipitation of liquid particles with diameter larger than 0.5 mm [0.02 in].
Relative humidity: amount of water vapour contained in a given volume of air at a given temperature.
Snow: formed when water vapour condenses below freezing point.
Thunder: sound produced by the rapid expansion of air heated by lightning.
Tornado: severe funnel-shaped storm that twists as hot air spins vertically (waterspout at sea).
Whirlwind: rapidly rotating column of air, only a few metres across, made visible by dust.

Climate Change

Human factors, such as the emission of greenhouse gases through the burning of fossil fuels and deforestation, have contributed to global warming. The histogram (*below*) shows in blue the average global temperatures from 1860 (when sufficient observations became available for global averages to be calculated) to 1996. The red line is a 10-year running average. Overall, there is an upwards trend, particularly so since the 1970s, when global warming became a matter of concern in scientific circles. The large year-to-year changes indicate the Earth's natural climatic variability and the influence of such factors as major volcanic eruptions.

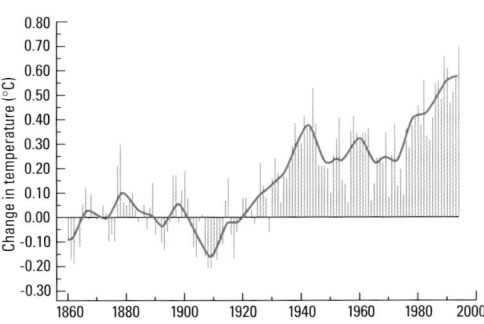

Data from the Hadley Centre for Climate Research and Prediction

The Monsoon

Monsoon is the term given to the seasonal reversal of wind direction, most noticeably in South-east Asia. It results from a combination of factors: the extreme heating and cooling of large landmasses in relation to the less marked changes in temperature of the adjacent seas; the northwards movement of the Intertropical Convergence Zone (ITCZ); and the effect of the Himalayas on the circulation of the air.

In early March, which normally marks the end of the subcontinent's cool season and the start of the hot season, winds blow outwards from the mainland. But as the overhead Sun and the ITCZ move northwards, the land is intensely heated, and a low-pressure system develops. The south-east trade winds, which are drawn across the Equator, change direction and are sucked into the interior to become south-westerly winds, bringing heavy rain. By November, the overhead Sun and the ITCZ have again moved southwards and the wind directions are again reversed. Cool winds blow from the Asian interior to the sea, losing any moisture on the Himalayas before descending to the coast.

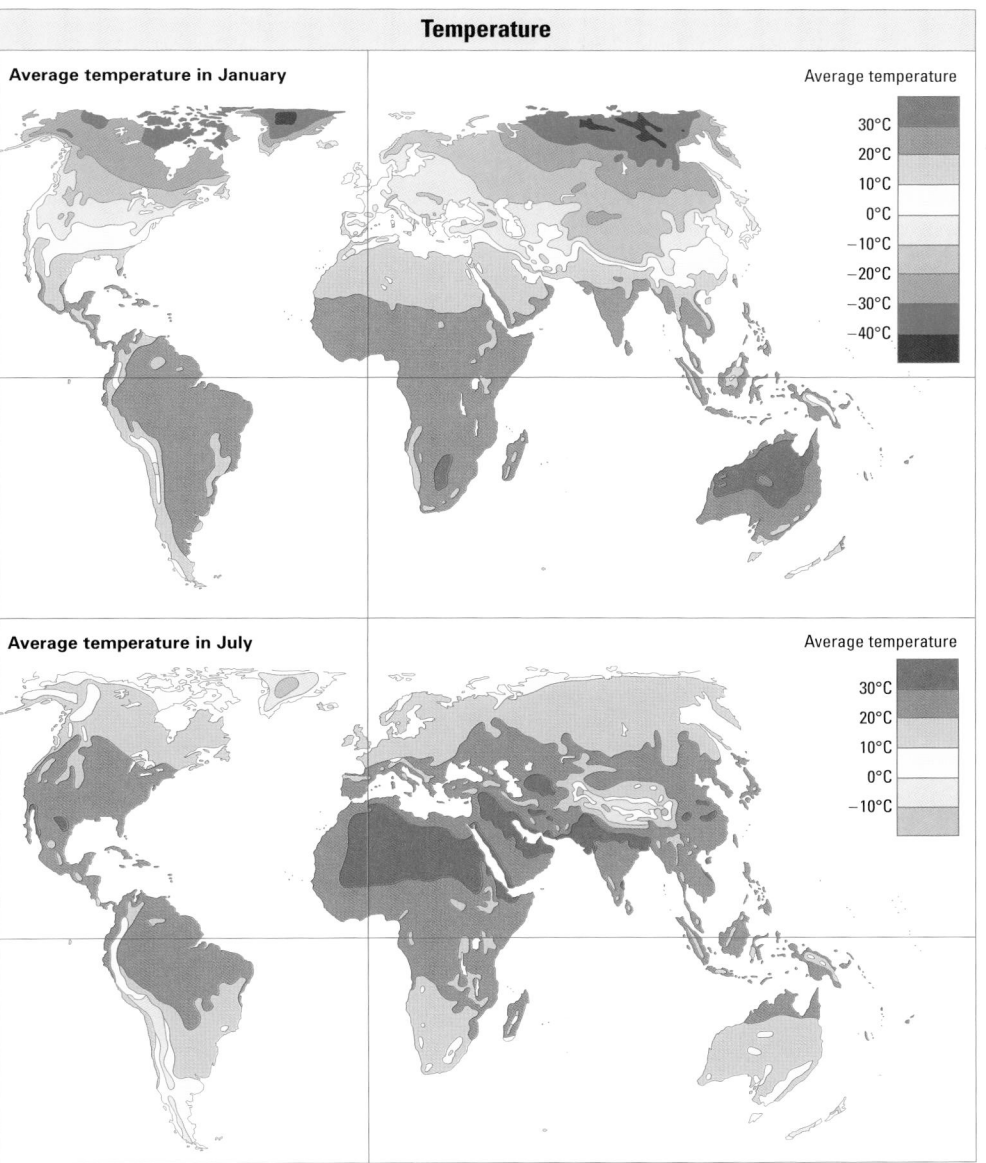

Average temperature in January

Average temperature

30°C / 20°C / 10°C / 0°C / –10°C / –20°C / –30°C / –40°C

Average temperature in July

Average temperature

30°C / 20°C / 10°C / 0°C / –10°C

Precipitation

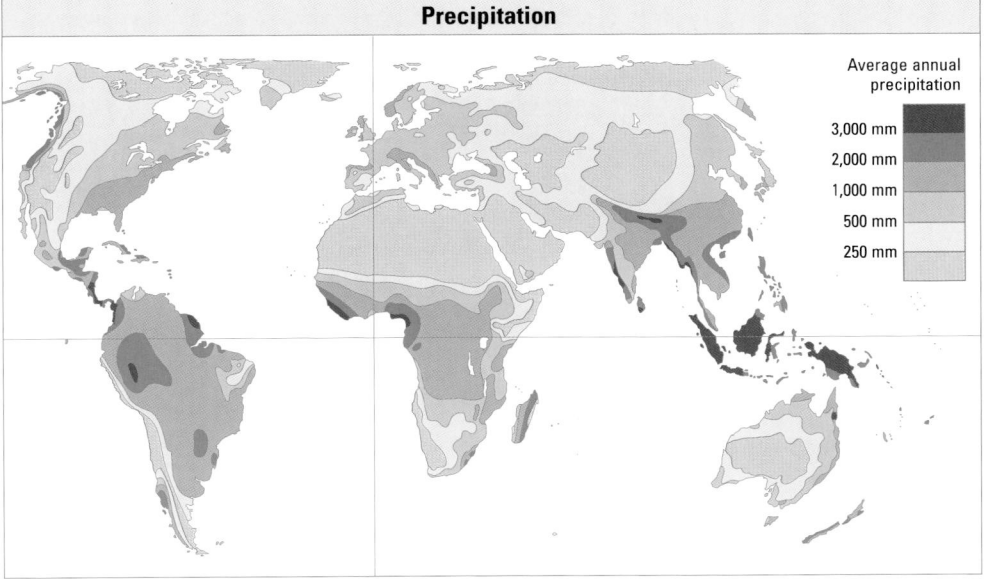

Average annual precipitation

3,000 mm / 2,000 mm / 1,000 mm / 500 mm / 250 mm

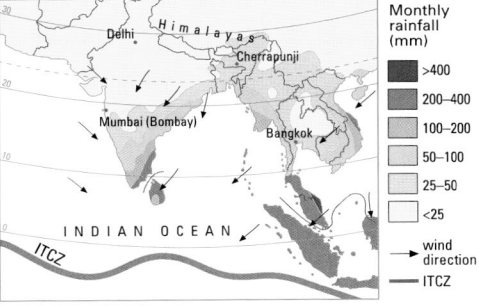

Monthly rainfall (mm)

>400 / 200–400 / 100–200 / 50–100 / 25–50 / <25

— wind direction
— ITCZ

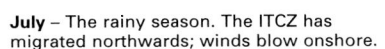

March – Start of the hot, dry season. The ITCZ is over the southern Indian Ocean.

July – The rainy season. The ITCZ has migrated northwards; winds blow onshore.

November – The ITCZ has returned south. The offshore winds are cool and dry.

Climate Records

Temperature

Highest recorded temperature: Al Aziziyah, Libya, 58°C [136.4°F], 13 September 1922.

Highest mean annual temperature: Dallol, Ethiopia, 34.4°C [94°F], 1960–6.

Longest heatwave: Marble Bar, W. Australia, 162 days over 38°C [100°F], 23 October 1923 to 7 April 1924.

Lowest recorded temperature (outside poles): Verkhoyansk, Siberia, –68°C [–90°F], 6 February 1933. Verkhoyansk also registered the greatest annual range of temperature: –70°C to 37°C [–94°F to 98°F].

Lowest mean annual temperature: Polus Nedostupnosti, Pole of Cold, Antarctica, –57.8°C [–72°F].

Precipitation

Driest place: Calama, N. Chile: no recorded rainfall in 400 years to 1971.

Wettest place (average): Tututendo, Colombia: mean annual rainfall 11,770 mm [463.4 in].

Wettest place (12 months): Cherrapunji, Meghalaya, N.E. India, 26,470 mm [1,040 in], August 1860 to August 1861. Cherrapunji also holds the record for rainfall in one month: 2,930 mm [115 in], July 1861. (*See maps below.*)

Wettest place (24 hours): Cilaos, Réunion, Indian Ocean, 1,870 mm [73.6 in], 15–16 March 1952.

Heaviest hailstones: Gopalganj, Bangladesh, up to 1.02 kg [2.25 lb], 14 April 1986 (killed 92 people).

Heaviest snowfall (continuous): Bessans, Savoie, France, 1,730 mm [68 in] in 19 hours, 5–6 April 1969.

Heaviest snowfall (season/year): Paradise Ranger Station, Mt Rainier, Washington, USA, 31,102 mm [1,224.5 in], 19 February 1971 to 18 February 1972.

WATER AND VEGETATION

For more information:

12 Rivers and glaciers
14 Types of
    precipitation
20 Biodiversity

Without the hydrological cycle, whereby water is constantly recycled between the oceans, the atmosphere and the land, the continents would be barren. Precipitation enables plants to grow and soils to form, creating the world's natural vegetation regions and the ecosystems that support animal life. Running water also plays a major role in shaping landforms. Yet in many parts of the world, people do not have safe water to drink and suffer from diseases caused by water-borne organisms and pollution. In 2002, an estimated 1 billion people lacked access to safe water and 2.6 billion lacked basic sanitation.

UN experts argue that the world demand for water is increasing at about twice the rate of population growth. They have predicted that, by 2025, half of the world's population will face water shortages. This could lead to conflict and even boundary wars, especially because 300 major rivers cross national frontiers and access to their water is likely to be disputed.

The Hydrological Cycle

The world's water balance is regulated by the constant recycling of water between the oceans, atmosphere and land. The movement of water between these three reservoirs is known as the hydrological cycle. The oceans play a vital role in the hydrological cycle: 74% of the total precipitation falls over the oceans and 84% of the total evaporation comes from the oceans. Water vapour in the atmosphere circulates around the planet, transporting energy as well as the water itself. When the vapour cools, it falls as rain or snow. The whole cycle is driven by the Sun.

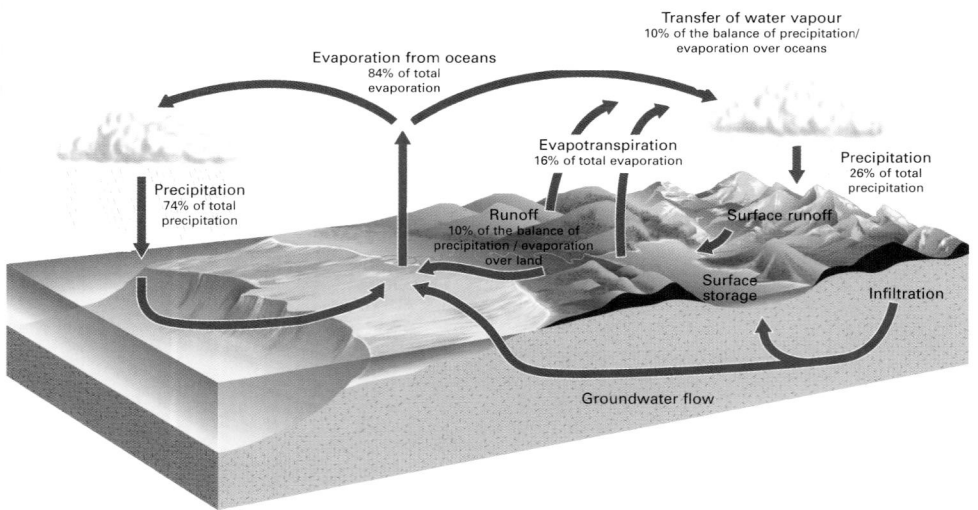

Water Distribution

The distribution of planetary water, by percentage. Oceans and ice caps together account for more than 99% of the total; the breakdown of the remainder is estimated.

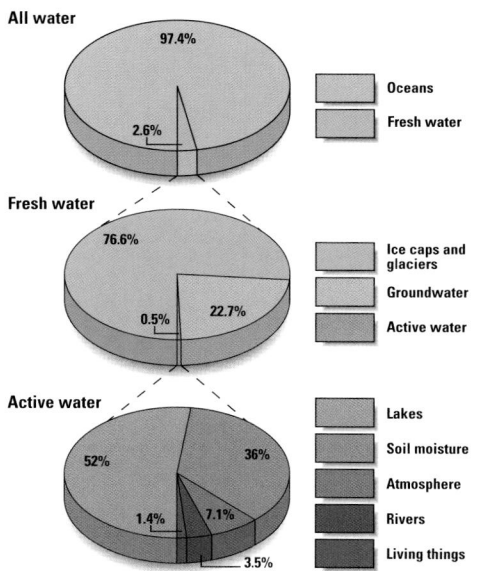

All water
- 97.4% Oceans
- 2.6% Fresh water

Fresh water
- 76.6% Ice caps and glaciers
- 0.5% Groundwater
- 22.7% Active water

Active water
- 52% Lakes
- 36% Soil moisture
- 1.4% Atmosphere
- 7.1% Rivers
- 3.5% Living things

Almost all the world's water is 3,000 million years old, and all of it cycles endlessly through the hydrosphere, though at different rates. Water vapour circulates over days, even hours; deep ocean water circulates over millennia; and ice-cap water remains solid for millions of years.

Water Utilization

The percentage breakdown of water usage by sector, selected countries (latest available year)

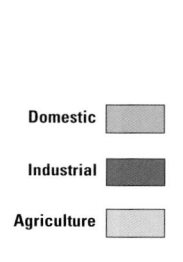

Domestic
Industrial
Agriculture

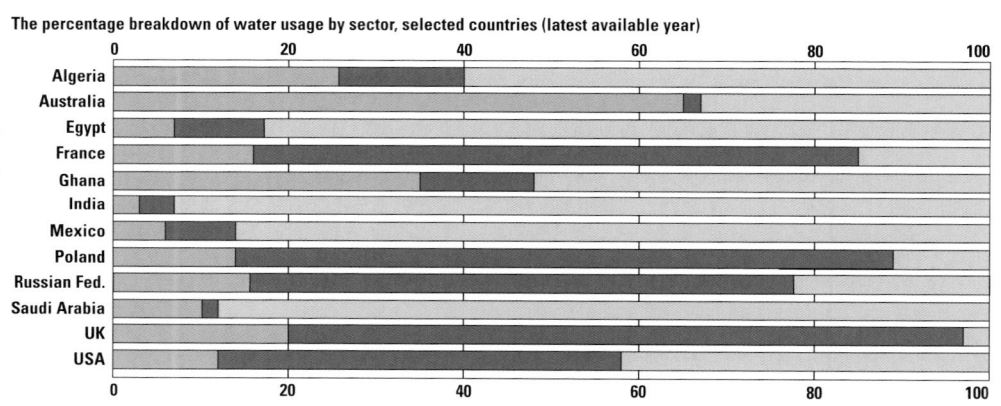

Algeria
Australia
Egypt
France
Ghana
India
Mexico
Poland
Russian Fed.
Saudi Arabia
UK
USA

Water Runoff

Annual freshwater runoff by continent in cubic kilometres

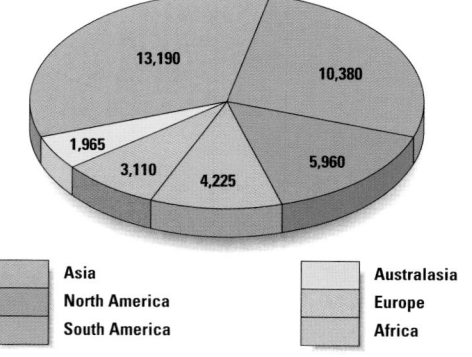

- 13,190
- 10,380
- 1,965
- 3,110
- 4,225
- 5,960

- Asia
- North America
- South America
- Australasia
- Europe
- Africa

Water Supply

Percentage of total population with access to safe drinking water (2000)

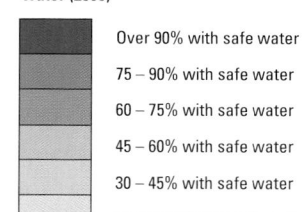

- Over 90% with safe water
- 75 – 90% with safe water
- 60 – 75% with safe water
- 45 – 60% with safe water
- 30 – 45% with safe water
- Under 30% with safe water

△ Under 80 litres average per capita daily
   water consumption

▲ Over 320 litres average per capita daily
   water consumption

80 litres of water a day is considered necessary for a reasonable quality of life

Least well-provided countries

Afghanistan	13%	Cambodia	30%
Ethiopia	24%	Mauritania	37%
Chad	27%	Angola	38%
Sierra Leone	28%	Oman	39%

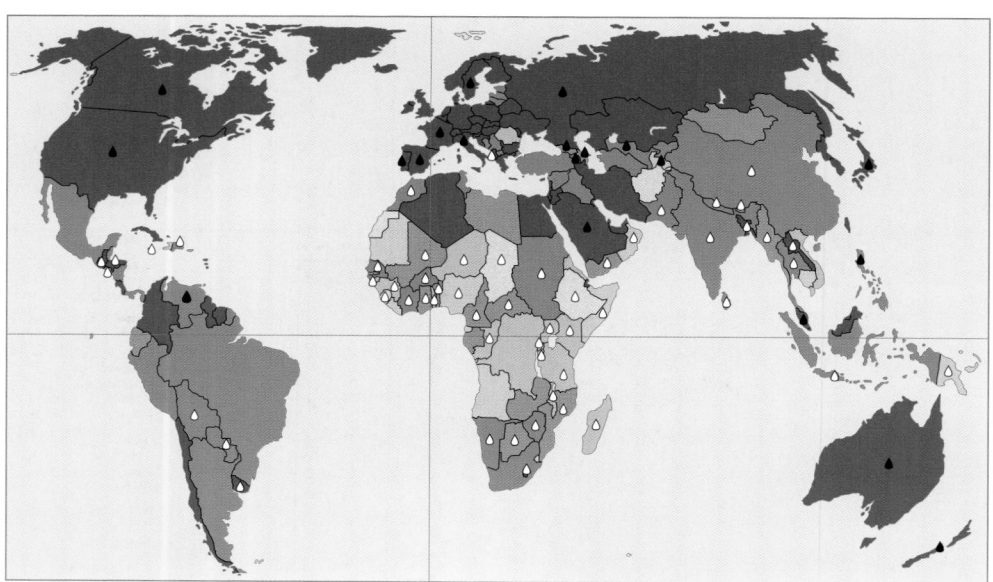

Watersheds

The world's major rivers; the rank of the world's 20 longest is shown in square brackets, led by the Nile and the Amazon.

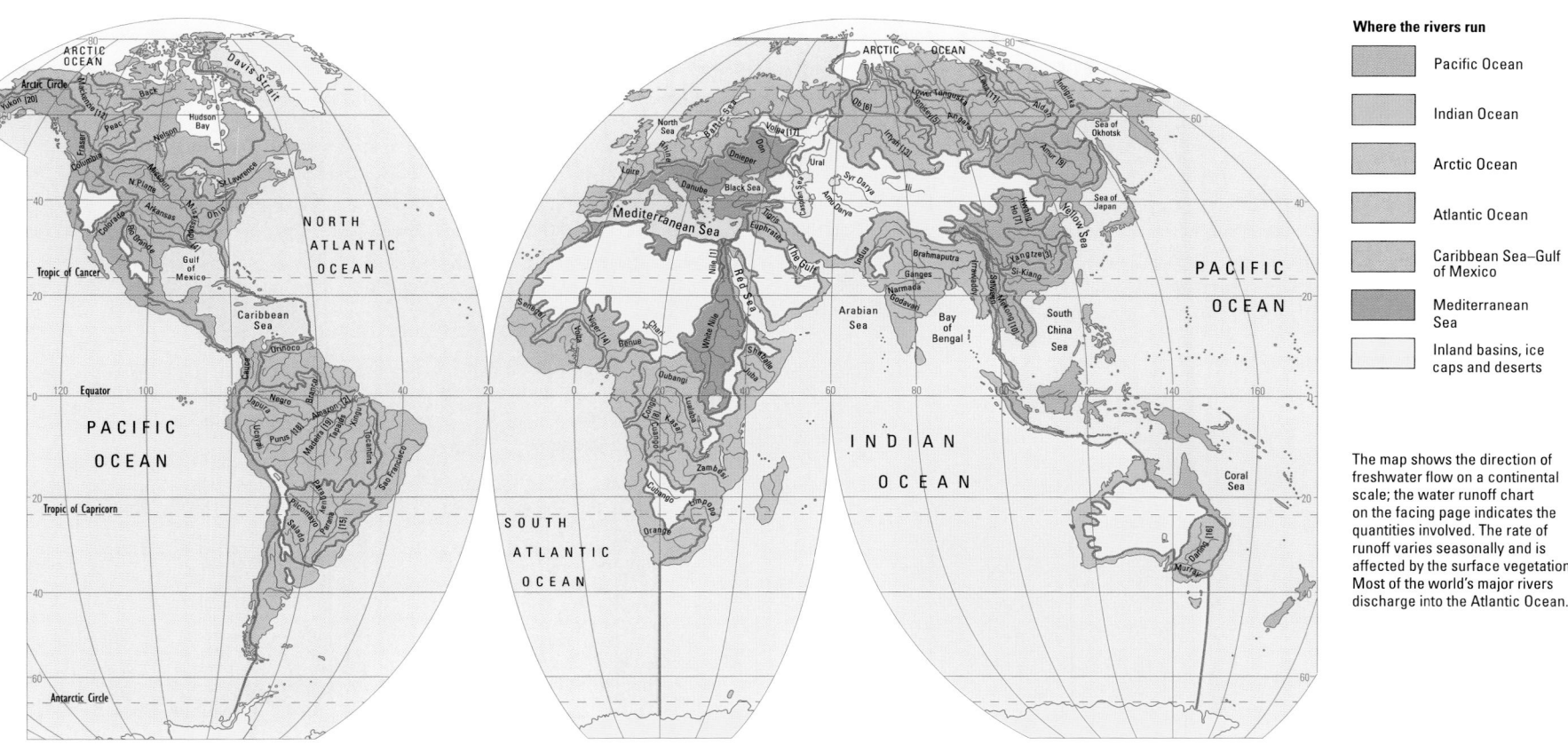

Where the rivers run

- Pacific Ocean
- Indian Ocean
- Arctic Ocean
- Atlantic Ocean
- Caribbean Sea–Gulf of Mexico
- Mediterranean Sea
- Inland basins, ice caps and deserts

The map shows the direction of freshwater flow on a continental scale; the water runoff chart on the facing page indicates the quantities involved. The rate of runoff varies seasonally and is affected by the surface vegetation. Most of the world's major rivers discharge into the Atlantic Ocean.

Annual Sediment Yield

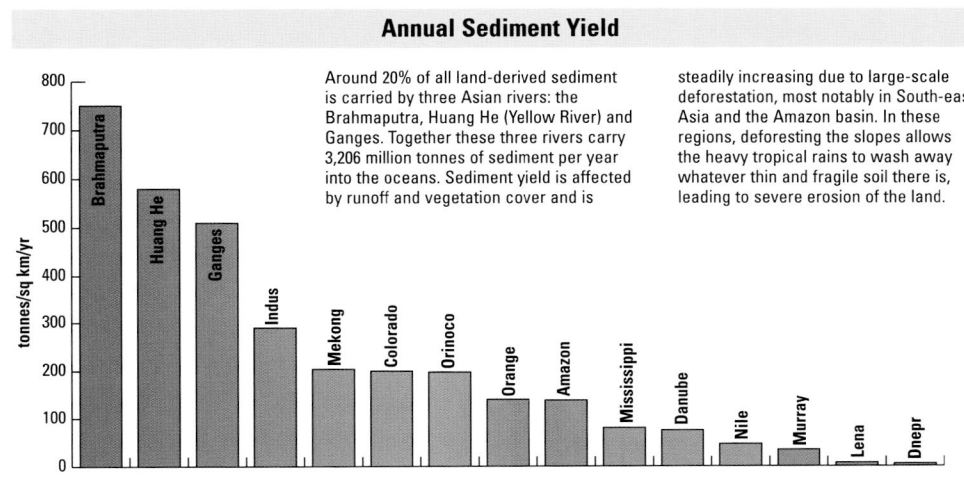

Around 20% of all land-derived sediment is carried by three Asian rivers: the Brahmaputra, Huang He (Yellow River) and Ganges. Together these three rivers carry 3,206 million tonnes of sediment per year into the oceans. Sediment yield is affected by runoff and vegetation cover and is steadily increasing due to large-scale deforestation, most notably in South-east Asia and the Amazon basin. In these regions, deforesting the slopes allows the heavy tropical rains to wash away whatever thin and fragile soil there is, leading to severe erosion of the land.

Land Use by Continent

The proportion of productive land has reached its upper limit in Europe, and in Asia more than 80% of potential cropland is already under cultivation.

- Forest
- Permanent pasture and rough grazing
- Permanent crops and plantations
- Arable
- Non-productive

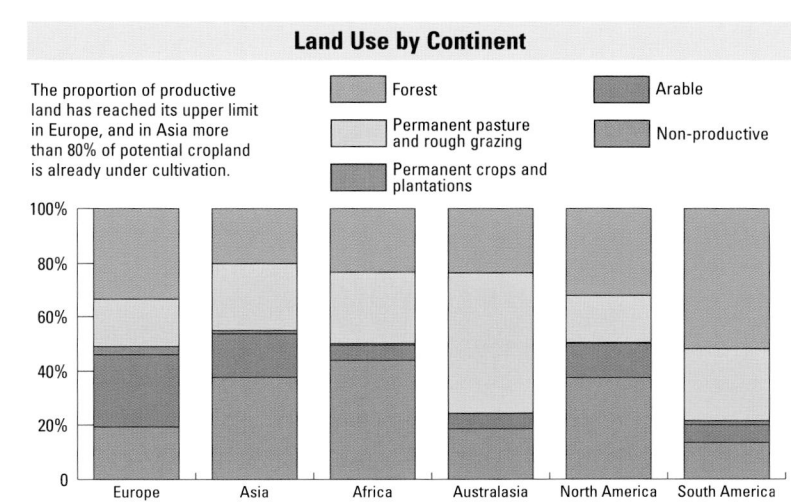

Natural Vegetation

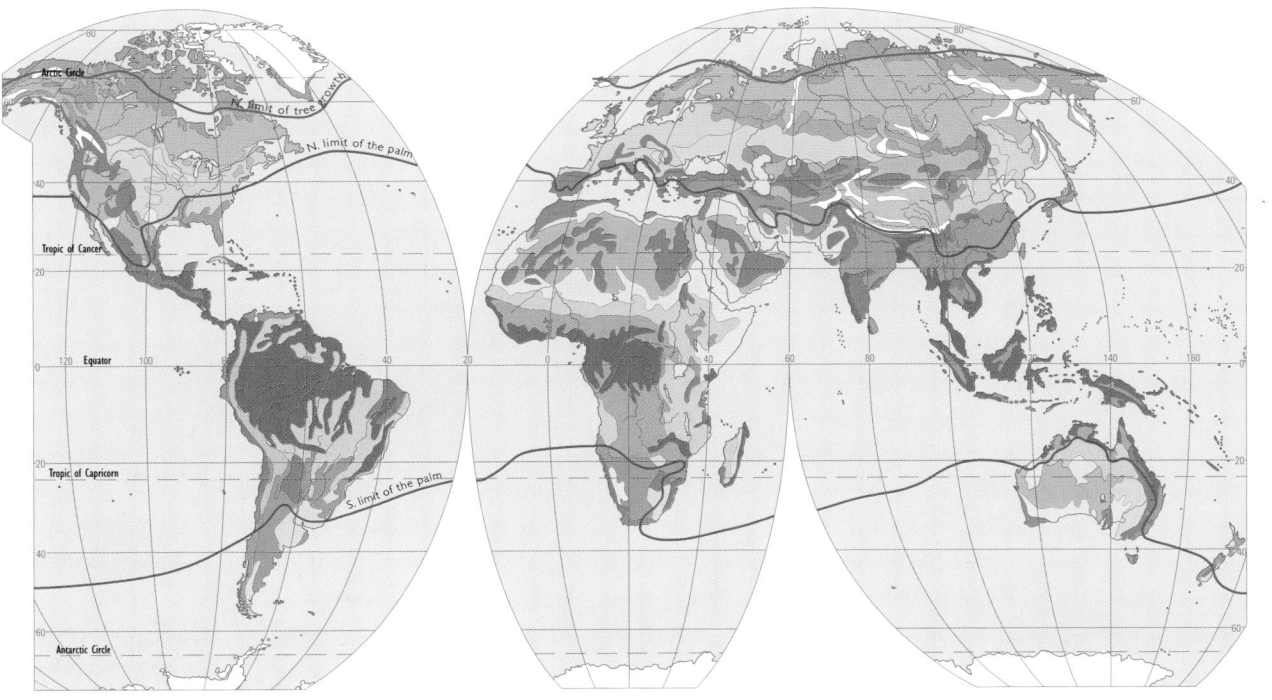

- Tropical rainforest
- Subtropical and temperate rainforest
- Monsoon woodland and open jungle
- Subtropical and temperate woodland, scrub and bush
- Tropical savanna, with low trees and bush
- Tropical savanna and grasslands
- Dry semi-desert, with shrub and grass
- Desert shrub
- Desert
- Dry steppe and shrub
- Temperate grasslands, prairie and steppe
- Mediterranean hardwood forest and scrub
- Temperate deciduous forest and meadow
- Temperate deciduous and coniferous forest
- Northern coniferous forest (taiga)
- Mountainous forest, mainly coniferous
- High plateau steppe and tundra
- Arctic tundra
- Polar and mountainous ice desert

The map illustrates the natural 'climax vegetation' of a region, as dictated by its climate and topography. In most cases, human agricultural activity has drastically altered the vegetation pattern. Western Europe, for example, lost most of its broadleaf forest many centuries ago, while elsewhere irrigation has turned some natural semi-desert into productive land. The various vegetation regions support different kinds of animals and, in an undisturbed state, they are highly developed biological communities, or biomes.

The blue line on the map represents the northern limit of tree growth, and the red lines indicate the northern and southern limits of palm growth.

THE NATURAL ENVIRONMENT

For more information:
8 Oceans
14 Atmosphere
19 Natural vegetation
22 Carbon dioxide
Greenhouse power
Global warming
23 Acid rain
Desertification
Deforestation
Water pollution

Recent discoveries of life forms in some of the world's most hostile environments, such as around the black smokers along the ocean ridges, prepared the way for the announcement by NASA scientists in 1996 that they had found microfossils in a Martian meteorite. But other scientists were sceptical, believing them to be natural mineral structures and not evidence of extraterrestrial life.

Until further evidence is available, the Earth remains the only planet where we know for sure that life exists. According to the fossil record, life on Earth appeared at least 3,500 million years ago. Since then, it has evolved from its primitive beginnings to its modern biodiversity, including millions of plants, animals and micro-organisms. Living organisms have not only adapted to the environ-ment but they have also changed their environment to suit themselves. For example, the Earth's early atmosphere contained little oxygen but the emergence of multi-celled, oxygen-producing algae, around 2,000 million years ago, led to the creation of an oxygen-rich atmosphere. This enabled land animals to populate the ancient continents.

The amount of the greenhouse gas carbon dioxide in the atmosphere would steadily increase from its present 0.03% were it not for plants. Without them, the Earth's atmos-phere would, in a few million years, be similar to that of Venus, where surface temperatures reach 477°C. The Earth has evolved into a complex control system, sensing and reacting to changes and tending always to maintain the balance it has achieved.

Much discussion has centred on how that balance changes. Only recently, scientists were suggesting that we may be living in an interglacial stage of the Pleistocene Ice Age. From the 1980s, however, predictions of future climates have concentrated more on global warming, caused by pollution which has led to an increase in greenhouse gases in the atmosphere. Interference in the natural cycles that control the environment may have consequences that are hard to predict.

Furthermore, we are currently experienc-ing a period of mass extinction of species, causing a rapid reduction in our planet's biodiversity. In 2002, a report by the Inter-national Union for the Conservation of Nature listed 11,167 organisms facing extinction. This was 121 more than in 2000.

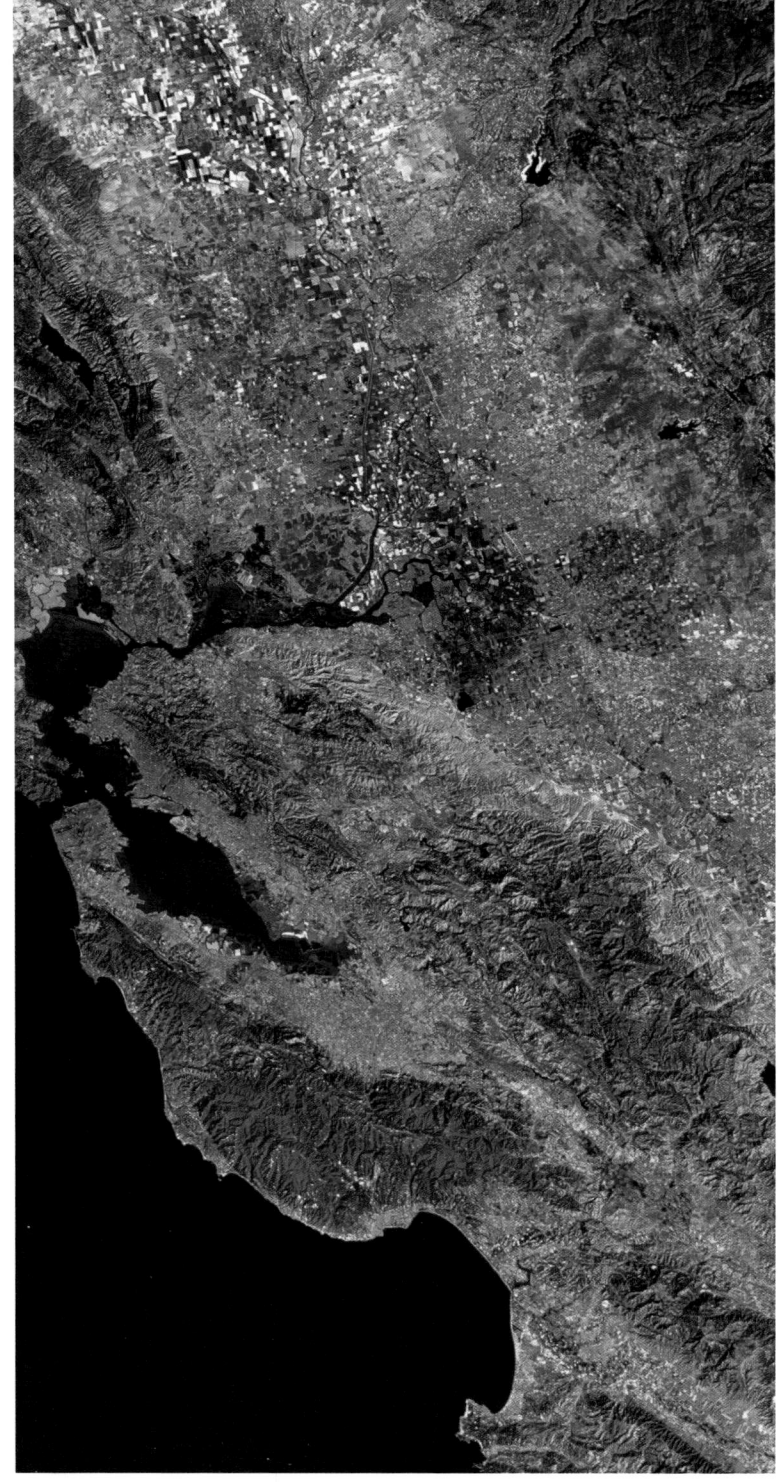

Biodiversity in California

The photograph (*left*) is a false-colour satellite image of central California in the south-western United States. The large inlet of the Pacific Ocean is San Francisco Bay. San Francisco lies just below the entrance to the bay, with Oakland on the far side and San Jose to the south-east. California, nicknamed the Golden State, is the third largest state in the United States and the most populous.

Because of its varied terrain and climate, California has a wide range of diverse habitats within a relatively small area. East of the forested Coast Ranges (the grey and red areas just inland from the bay) lies the fertile Central Valley, which appears as a red and blue chequerboard. The Sierra Nevada is the red area in the top right-hand corner. In the north-west and south-west of the state (*not shown here*) lie parts of the Basin and Range region, much of which is desert. It includes Death Valley, which contains the country's lowest point on land at 86 m below sea level.

Forests cover about 40% of California and they include bristlecone pines, thought to be the oldest living things on Earth, together with coastal red-woods, the world's tallest trees. Wildlife is still abundant, though some species, such as the rare California condor, are on the endangered list.

The state has achieved much to protect its biodiversity. It contains eight of the 56 national parks in the United States. Two of them, Death Valley and Joshua Tree, were designated national parks as recently as 1994, as part of a conservation measure, including the protection of large areas of wilderness in the deserts.

California has vast resources and, were it a separate nation, it would rank among the world's ten most productive in terms of the total value of its goods and services. This means that, like the United States as a whole, it has resources, which many developing countries lack, to finance conservation measures. For example, the World Conservation Union reported in 1996 that 8% of mammals were threatened in the United States, as compared with 32% in the Philippines and 44% in Madagascar, two countries where habitat destruction has been on a large scale.

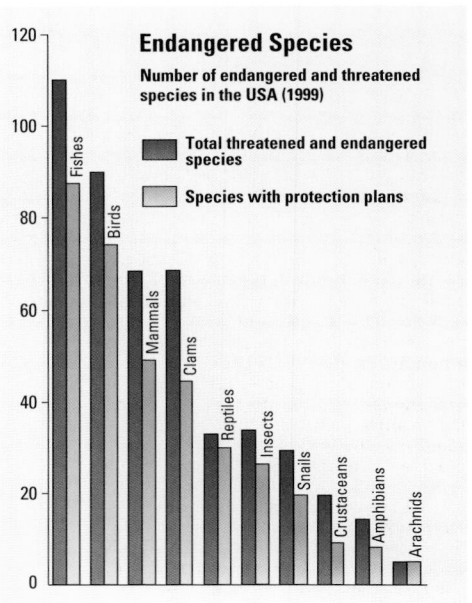

Endangered Species

Number of endangered and threatened species in the USA (1999)

- Total threatened and endangered species
- Species with protection plans

(Categories shown: Fishes, Birds, Mammals, Clams, Reptiles, Insects, Snails, Crustaceans, Amphibians, Arachnids)

Threatened Mammals

Percentage of mammal species classified as threatened (2002)
Many scientists believe we are currently experiencing a period of mass extinction of species rivalling five other periods in the past half a billion years. Among the most threatened mammals are elephants, primates and rhinoceroses.

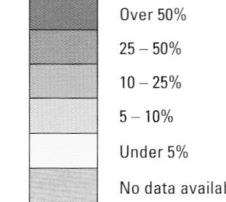

Over 50%
25 – 50%
10 – 25%
5 – 10%
Under 5%
No data available

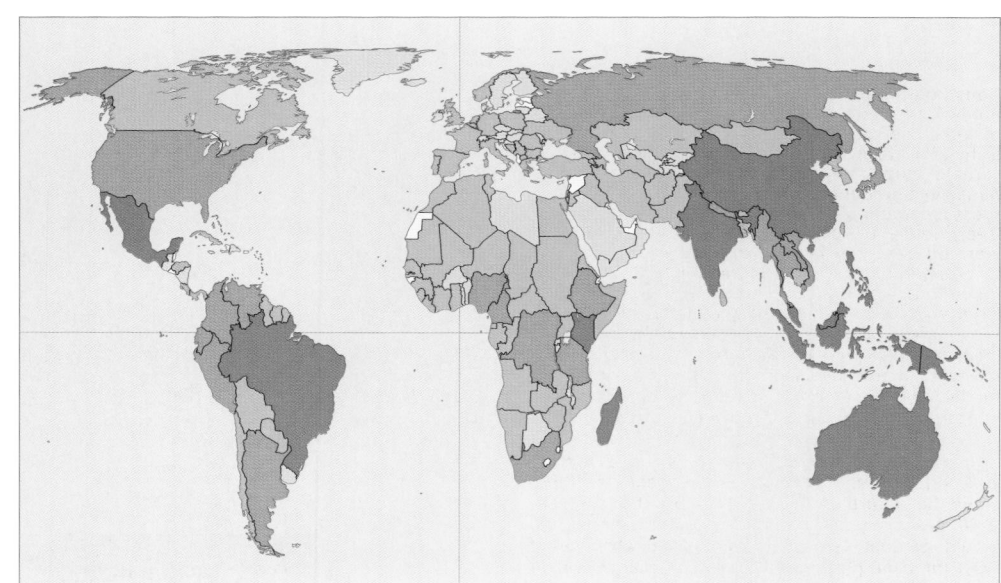

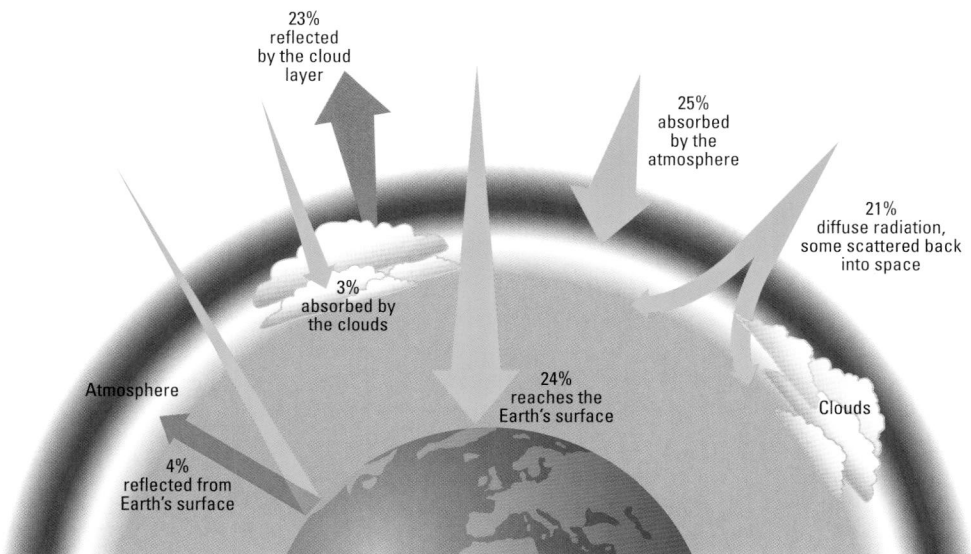

23% reflected by the cloud layer

25% absorbed by the atmosphere

21% diffuse radiation, some scattered back into space

3% absorbed by the clouds

Atmosphere

24% reaches the Earth's surface

Clouds

4% reflected from Earth's surface

The Earth's Energy Balance

Apart from a modest quantity of internal heat from its molten core, the Earth receives all of its energy from the Sun. If the planet is to remain at a constant temperature, it must reradiate exactly as much energy as it receives. Even a minute surplus would lead to a warmer Earth, a deficit to a cooler one. The temperature at which thermal equilibrium is reached depends on a multitude of interconnected factors. Two of the most important are the relative brightness of the Earth – its index of reflectivity, called the 'albedo' – and the heat-trapping capacity of the atmosphere – the celebrated 'greenhouse effect' (*see below*).

Because the Sun is very hot, most of its energy arrives in the form of relatively short-wave radiation: the shorter the waves, the more energy they carry. Some of the incoming energy is reflected straight back into space, exactly as it arrived; some is absorbed by the atmosphere on its way towards the surface; some is absorbed by the Earth itself. Absorbed energy heats the Earth and its atmosphere alike. But since its temperature is very much lower than that of the Sun, the outgoing energy is emitted at much longer infrared wavelengths. Some of the outgoing radiation escapes directly into outer space; some of it is reabsorbed by the atmosphere. Atmospheric energy eventually finds its way back into space, too, after a complex series of interactions. These include the air movements we call the weather and, almost incidentally, the maintenance of life on Earth.

This diagram (*left*) does not attempt to illustrate the actual mechanisms of heat exchange, but gives a reasonable account (in percentages) of what happens to 100 energy 'units'. Short-wave radiation is shown in yellow, long-wave in orange.

The Carbon Cycle

Most of the constituents of the atmosphere are kept in constant balance by complex cycles in which life plays an essential and indeed a dominant part. The control of carbon dioxide, which if left to its own devices would be the dominant atmospheric gas, is possibly the most important, although since all the Earth's biological and geophysical cycles interact and interlock, it is hard to separate them even in theory and quite impossible in practice.

The Earth has a huge supply of carbon, only a small quantity of which is in the form of carbon dioxide. Of that, around 98% is dissolved in the sea; the fraction circulating in the air amounts to only 340 parts per million of the atmosphere, where its capacity as a greenhouse gas is the key regulator of the planetary temperature. In turn, life regulates the regulator, keeping carbon dioxide concentrations below danger level.

If all life were to vanish from the Earth tomorrow, the atmosphere would begin the process of change immediately, although it might take several million years to achieve a new, inorganic stability. First, the oxygen content would begin to fall away; with no more assistance than a little solar radiation, a few electrical storms and its own high chemical potential, oxygen would steadily combine with atmospheric nitrogen and volcanic outgassing. In doing so, it would yield sufficient acid to react with carbonaceous rocks such as limestone, releasing carbon dioxide. Once carbon dioxide levels exceeded about 1%, its greenhouse power would increase disproportionately. Rising temperatures – well above the boiling point of water – would speed chemical reactions; in time, the Earth's atmosphere would consist of little more than carbon dioxide and superheated water vapour.

Living things, however, circulate carbon. They do so first by simply existing: after all, the carbon atom is the basic building block of living matter.

pool of CO_2 in atmosphere

combustion   photosynthesis

respiration   respiration   respiration

CO_2

CO_2

decay organisms

respiration

death

carbonification, gradual production of fossil fuels

death

decay organisms

peat

coal

oil and gas

During life, plants absorb carbon dioxide from the atmosphere and, along with various chemicals, as soluble salts from the soil, incorporating the carbon into their structure – leaves and trunks in the case of land plants, shells in the case of plankton and the tiny creatures that feed on it. The oxygen thereby freed is added to the atmosphere, at least for a time. The carbon is returned to circulation when the plants die or is passed up the food chain to the herbivores, and then to the carnivores that feed on them. As organisms at each of these trophic levels die, they decay, releasing the carbon, which then combines once more with the oxygen released during life. However, a small proportion of carbon, about one part in 1,000, is removed almost permanently, buried beneath mud on land or at sea, sinking as dead matter to the ocean floor. In time, it is slowly compressed into sedimentary rocks such as limestone and chalk.

But in the evolution of the Earth, nothing is quite permanent. On an even longer timescale, the planet's crustal movements force new rock upwards in mid-ocean ridges. Limestone deposits are moved, and sea levels change; ancient carboniferous rocks are exposed to weathering, and a little of their carbon is released to be fixed in turn by the current generation of plants.

The carbon cycle has continued quietly for an immensely long time, and without gross disturbance there is no reason why it would not continue almost indefinitely in the future. However, human beings have found a way to release fixed carbon at a rate far faster than existing global systems can re-circulate it. The fossil fuels – coal, oil, gas and peat deposits – represent the work of millions of years of carbon accumulation; but it has taken only a few human generations of high-energy scavenging to endanger the entire complex regulatory cycle.

The Greenhouse Effect

Constituting less than 1% of the atmosphere, the natural greenhouse gases (water vapour, carbon dioxide, methane, nitrous oxide and ozone) have a hugely disproportionate effect on the Earth's climate, and even its habitability. Like the glass panes in a greenhouse, the gases are transparent to most incoming short-wave radiation, which passes freely to heat the planet beneath. But when the warmed Earth retransmits that energy, in the form of longer-wave infrared radiation, the gases function as an opaque shield preventing some of it from escaping, so that the planetary surface (like the interior of a greenhouse) stays relatively hot.

Over the last 150 years, there has been a gradual increase in the levels of greenhouse gases (with the exception of water vapour, which remains a constant in the system). These increases are causing alarm – global warming associated with a runaway greenhouse effect could bring disaster – and, what is more, predictions suggest that there could be a further rise of 1.5–4.5°C by the year 2100. A serious reduction in the greenhouse gases would be just as damaging; a total absence of CO_2, for example, would leave the planet with a temperature roughly 33°C colder than at present.

N.B. The thickness of the Earth's atmosphere is proportionately much thinner than the peel of an apple.

Sun

Less heat escapes into space

Outgoing long-wave radiation (infared) is radiated back into space

Increased greenhouse gases means that more long-wave radiation is reflected back to Earth

Atmosphere

The atmosphere of the Earth gets hotter as more heat is trapped

Increased greenhouse gases act as a shield to long-wave radiation

Incoming short-wave radiation (ultraviolet) reaches the surface of the Earth

PEOPLE AND THE ENVIRONMENT

For more information:
8 Oceans
14 Atmosphere
16 Climate
21 Greenhouse effect
27 Urban pollution

In 1996, the Intergovernmental Panel on Climate Change issued a report stating that 'The balance of evidence suggests a discernible human influence on global climate through emissions of carbon dioxide and other greenhouse gases.' The report acknowledged that average global temperatures have risen by about 0.5°C since the mid-19th century, though there were still reasons for caution on attributing this entirely to actions taken by humans.

Human interference with nature is nothing new, at least since people turned from hunting and gathering to agriculture more than 10,000 years ago. At first, human actions seemed to have no ill effects because the systems that regulate the global environment were able to absorb damage. But from the late 18th century, the Industrial Revolution and the population explosion have caused massive pollution that threatens to overwhelm the Earth's ability to cope.

The 20th century experienced many disasters, including the dumping of industrial wastes in rivers and seas, accidents at nuclear power stations, and the creation of acid rain through the release of sulphur dioxides and nitrous oxides by the burning of fossil fuels. The release of greenhouse gases are held to be the main reason for global warming, while CFCs (chlorofluorocarbons) have damaged the ozone layer in the stratosphere, the planet's screen against ultraviolet radiation.

In December 1998, an international conference in Kyoto, Japan, reached an agreement to reduce the emission of greenhouse gases by 5.2% by 2012. But, in the early 21st century, the USA, which produces about a third of all emissions, opposed the Kyoto protocol.

Global warming will lead to melting ice sheets and the flooding of fertile coastal plains. Computer models suggest that it might affect ocean currents so that northwestern Europe, which owes its mild climate to the Gulf Stream, could expect bitterly cold winters. Some models have suggested that cloud cover could increase, reflecting more solar energy back into space and thus start a new Ice Age.

In many tropical areas, deforestation is making productive land barren, while in the dry grasslands bordering deserts, the removal of plant cover is causing desertification. But human ingenuity can respond to this crisis in planet management.

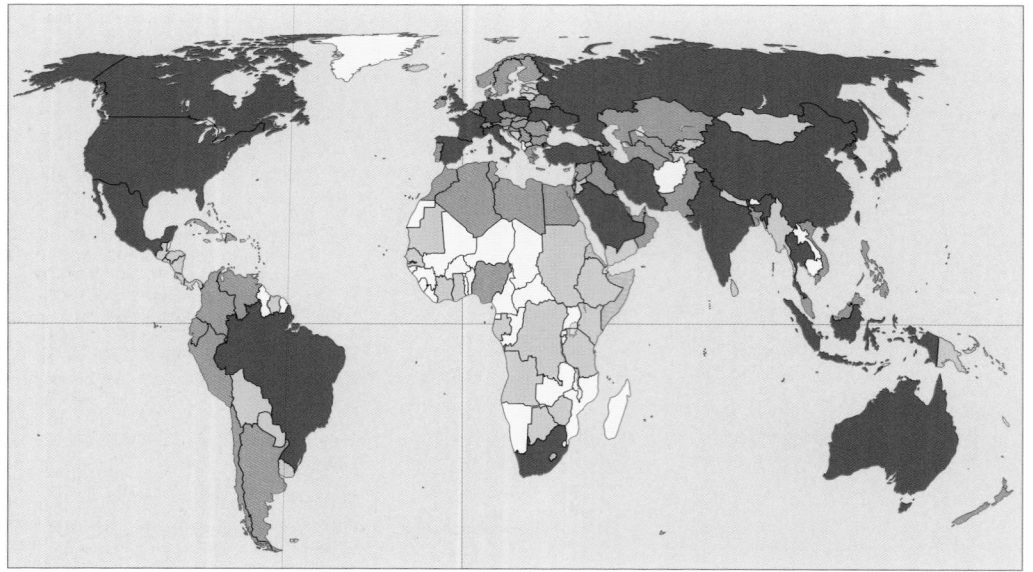

Global Warming

Carbon dioxide emissions in tonnes (1998)

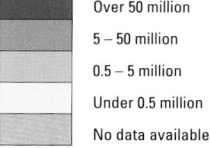

- Over 50 million
- 5 – 50 million
- 0.5 – 5 million
- Under 0.5 million
- No data available

High atmospheric concentrations of heat-absorbing gases appear to be causing a rise in average temperatures worldwide – up to 1.5°C [3°F] by the year 2020, according to some estimates. Global warming is likely to bring about a rise in sea levels that may flood some of the world's densely populated coastal areas.

Evidence of global warming is attributed mainly to the Greenhouse Effect, caused by the emission of certain gases, notably carbon dioxide (CO_2), into the atmosphere since the start of the Industrial Revolution. At first, much of the CO_2 was absorbed by the oceans. However, the vast increase in fuel combustion since 1950 has led CO_2 content in the atmosphere to increase gradually from 280 parts per million to more than 370 parts per million by 2002. Despite international action to control emissions of some greenhouse gases, CO_2 levels are still rising.

Greenhouse Power

Relative contributions to the Greenhouse Effect by the major heat-absorbing gases in the atmosphere

The chart combines greenhouse potency and volume. Carbon dioxide has a greenhouse potential of only 1, but its concentration of 350 parts per million makes it predominate. CFC 12, with 25,000 times the absorption capacity of CO_2, is present only as 0.00044 ppm.

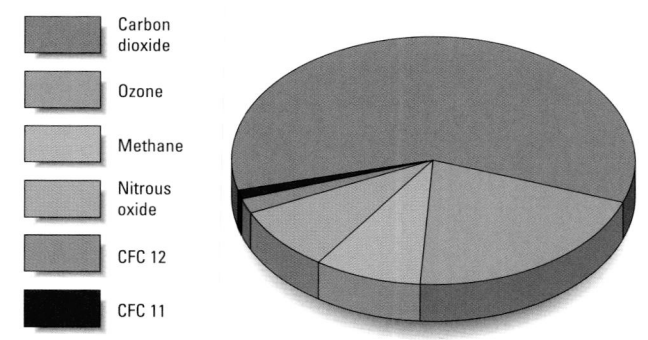

- Carbon dioxide
- Ozone
- Methane
- Nitrous oxide
- CFC 12
- CFC 11

Carbon Dioxide

Estimated percentage share of total world CO_2 emissions (2000)

USA, China, Russia, Japan, India, Germany, Canada, UK

Temperature Rise

The rise in average temperatures caused by carbon dioxide and other greenhouse gases, assuming present trends continue (1960–2020)

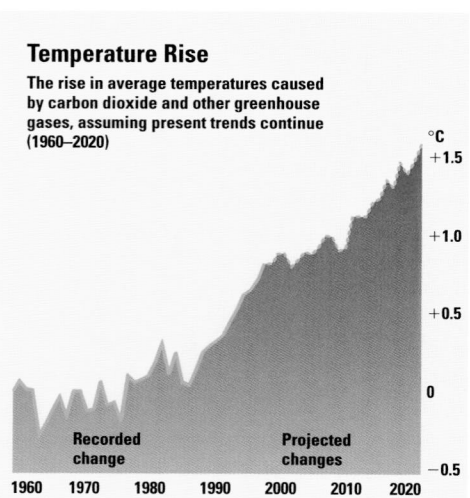

Recorded change

Projected changes

1960 1970 1980 1990 2000 2010 2020

The Thinning Ozone Layer

Total atmospheric ozone concentration in the southern and northern hemispheres (Dobson Units, 2000)

In 1985, scientists working in Antarctica discovered a thinning of the ozone layer, commonly known as an 'ozone hole'. This caused immediate alarm because the ozone layer absorbs most of the Sun's dangerous ultraviolet radiation, which is believed to cause an increase in skin cancer, cataracts and damage to the immune system. Since 1985, ozone depletion has increased and, by 2002, the ozone hole over the South Pole was estimated to be three times as large as the USA. The false-colour images (*right*) show the total atmospheric ozone concentration in the southern hemisphere (in September 2000) and the northern hemisphere (in March 2000) with the ozone hole clearly identifiable at the centre. The data is from the Tiros Ozone Vertical Sounder, an instrument on the American TIROS weather satellite. The colours represent the ozone concentration in Dobson Units (DU). Scientists agree that ozone depletion is caused by CFCs, a group of manufactured chemicals used in air conditioning systems and refrigerators. In a 1987 treaty most industrial nations agreed to phase out CFCs and a complete ban on most CFCs was agreed after the end of 1995. However, scientists believe that the chemicals will remain in the atmosphere for 50 to 100 years. As a result, ozone depletion will continue for many years.

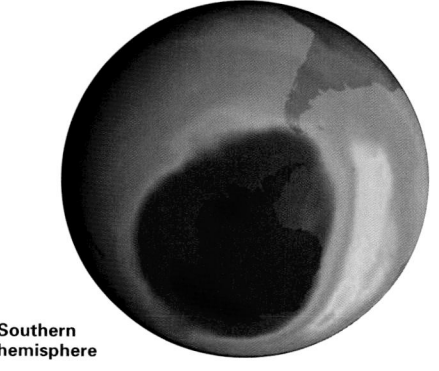

Southern hemisphere

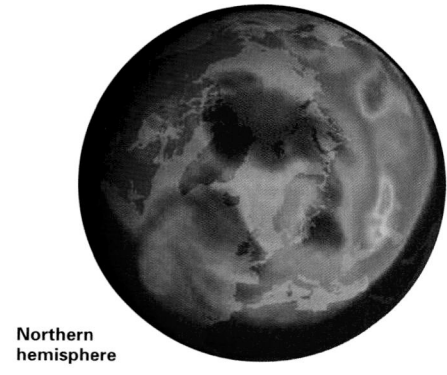

Northern hemisphere

World Pollution

Acid rain and sources of acidic emissions (latest available year)

Acid rain is caused by high levels of sulphur and nitrogen in the atmosphere. They combine with water vapour and oxygen to form acids (H_2SO_4 and HNO_3) which fall as precipitation.

 Regions where sulphur and nitrogen oxides are released in high concentrations, mainly from fossil fuel combustion

• Major cities with high levels of air pollution (including nitrogen and sulphur emissions)

Areas of heavy acid deposition

pH numbers indicate acidity, decreasing from a neutral 7. Normal rain, slightly acid from dissolved carbon dioxide, never exceeds a pH of 5.6.

pH less than 4.0 (most acidic)

pH 4.0 to 4.5

pH 4.5 to 5.0

Areas where acid rain is a potential problem

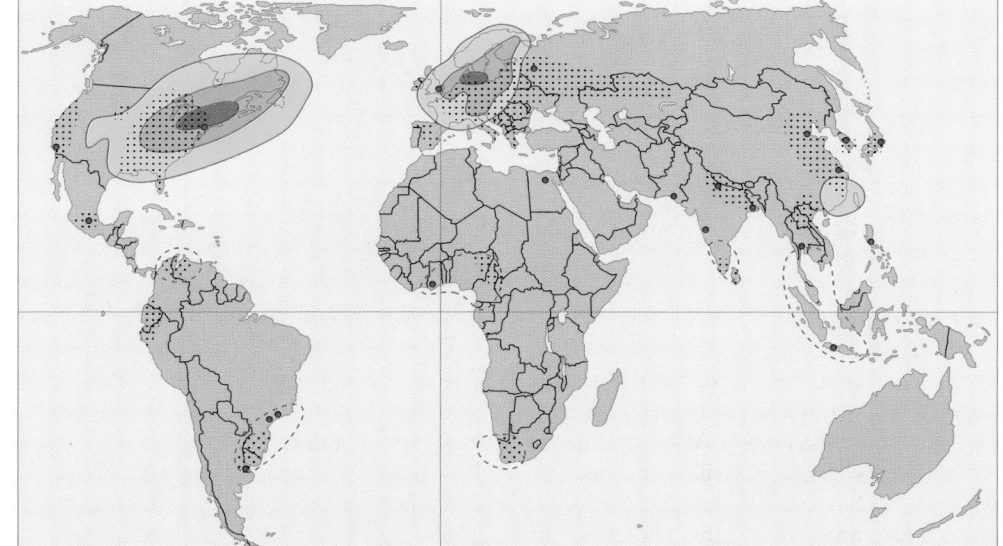

Desertification

 Existing deserts

Areas with a high risk of desertification

Areas with a moderate risk of desertification

Former areas of rainforest

Existing rainforest

Deforestation

Thousands of hectares of forest cleared annually, tropical countries surveyed 1981–85, 1987–90 and 1990–5. Loss as a percentage of remaining stocks is shown in figures on each column.

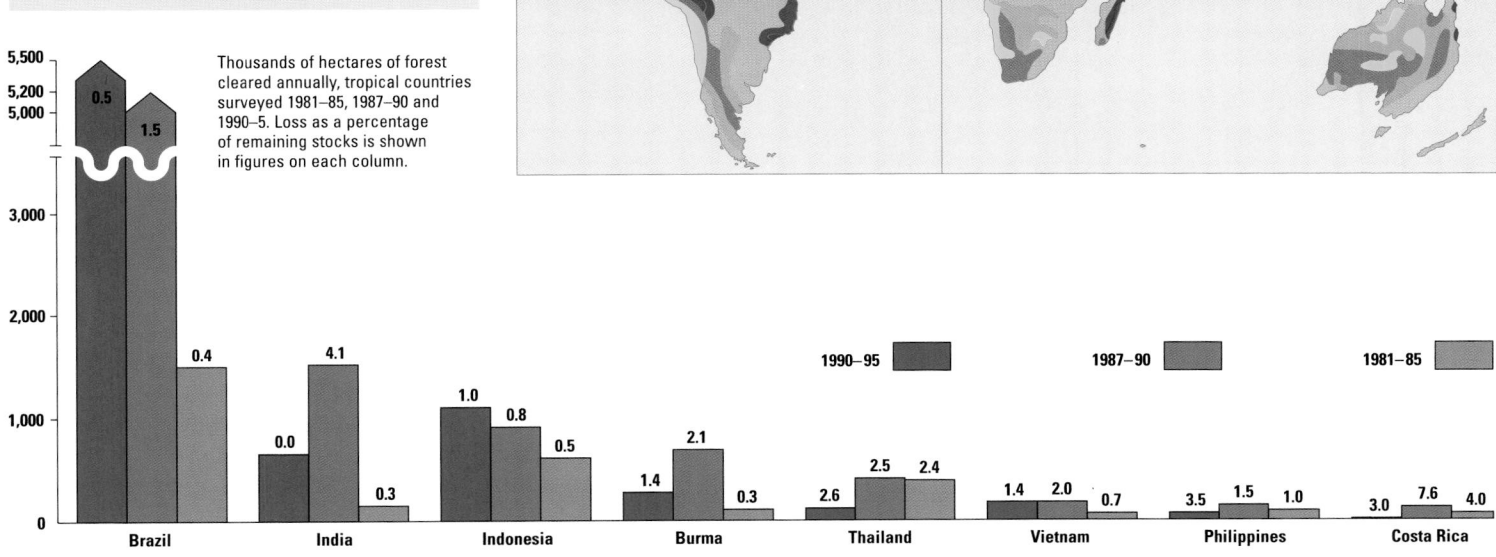

■ 1990–95   ■ 1987–90   ■ 1981–85

Brazil	India	Indonesia	Burma	Thailand	Vietnam	Philippines	Costa Rica
0.5 / 1.5 / 0.4	0.0 / 4.1 / 0.3	1.0 / 0.8 / 0.5	1.4 / 2.1 / 0.3	2.6 / 2.5 / 2.4	1.4 / 2.0 / 0.7	3.5 / 1.5 / 1.0	3.0 / 7.6 / 4.0

Water Pollution

 Severely polluted sea areas and lakes

Polluted sea areas and lakes

Areas of frequent oil pollution by shipping

◤ Major oil tanker spills

▲ Major oil rig blow-outs

▼ Offshore dumpsites for industrial and municipal waste

— Severely polluted rivers and estuaries

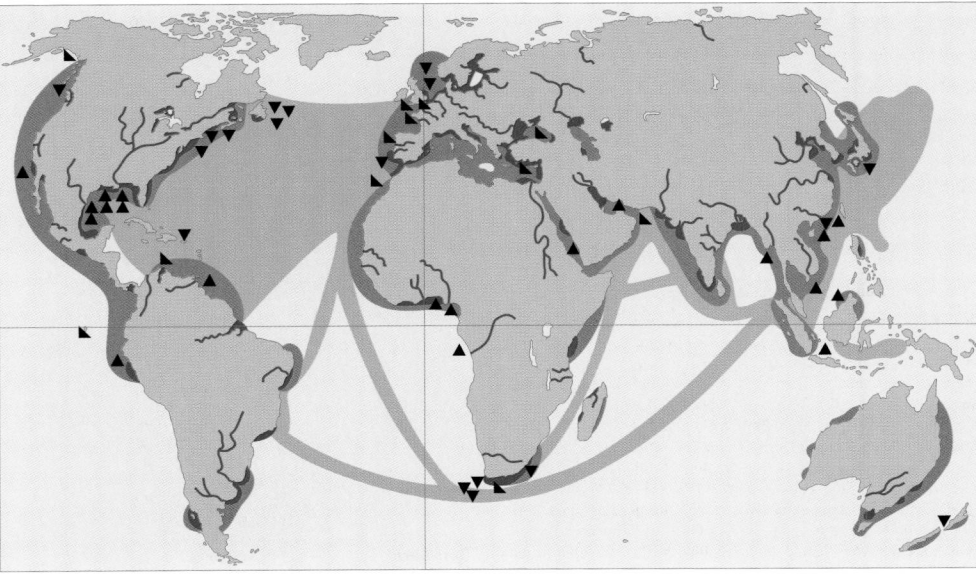

Antarctica

The vast Antarctic ice sheet, containing some 70% of the Earth's fresh water, plays a crucial role in the circulation of the atmosphere and oceans, and hence in determining the planetary climate. The frozen southern continent is also the last remaining wilderness – the largest area to remain free from human colonization.

Ever since Amundsen and Scott raced for the South Pole in 1911, various countries have pressed territorial claims over sections of Antarctica, spurred in recent years by its known and suspected mineral wealth: enough iron ore to supply the world at present levels for 200 years, large oil reserves and, probably, the biggest coal deposits on Earth.

However, the 1961 Antarctic Treaty set aside the area for peaceful uses only, guaranteeing freedom of scientific investigation, banning waste disposal and nuclear testing, and suspending the issue of territorial rights. By 1990, the original 12 signatories had grown to 25, with a further 15 nations granted observer status in subsequent deliberations. However, the Treaty itself was threatened by wrangles between different countries, government agencies and international pressure groups.

Finally, in July 1991, the belated agreement of the UK and the USA assured unanimity on a new accord to ban all mineral exploration for a further 50 years. The ban can only be rescinded if all the present signatories, plus a majority of any future adherents, agree. While the treaty has always lacked a formal mechanism for enforcement, it is firmly underwritten by public concern generated by the efforts of environmental pressure groups such as Greenpeace, which has been foremost in the campaign to have Antarctica declared a 'World Park'.

However, from the mid-1990s, the continent appeared to be under threat from global warming, which some scientists believe was the cause of the break-up of ice shelves along the Antarctic peninsula. Rising temperatures have also disturbed the breeding patterns of Adelie penguins.

In December 2002, oil slicks from the 77,000-tonne *Prestige* tanker, which broke up off Spain, caused environmental damage to the north coast of Spain and, in 2003, to the south-west coast of France. This was a small incident by comparison with some earlier events, such as the collision between the *Atlantic Empress* and the *Aegean Captain* in July 1979. This was the worst tanker incident ever. It polluted the Caribbean with 1,890,000 barrels of crude oil. Oil spills, however, declined in the 1980s, from a peak of 750,000 tonnes in 1979 to less than 50,000 tonnes in 1990. The most notorious spill of that period – when the *Exxon Valdez* ran aground in Prince William Sound, Alaska, in March 1989 – released only 267,000 barrels, a relatively small amount when compared with the 2,500,000 barrels spilled during the Gulf War of 1991. Oil spillage, poisoned rivers, and domestic sewage have in recent years badly contaminated parts of the oceans.

POPULATION

For more information:

26 Urbanization of the Earth

Urban population

27 Largest cities

33 Food and population

44 Wealth and population

In 8000 BC, following the development of agriculture, the world had an estimated population of 8 million and by AD 1000 it was about 300 million. The onset of the Industrial Revolution in the late 18th century led to a population explosion. The 1,000 million mark was passed by 1850, it doubled by the 1920s, and doubled again to 4,000 million by 1975.

In the 1990s, UN demographers estimated that the world's population, which passed the 6 billion mark in 1999, would reach 8.9 billion by 2050 and only level out in 2200, at a peak of around 11 billion. However, in the early 21st century, after the rate of population growth had shown signs of decline, the Institute for Applied Systems Analysis, suggested that the world's population might peak at about 9 billion in 2070. Whatever the global projections, everyone agreed that the greatest population growth will be in the developing countries.

The developing world includes what the World Bank (2001) describes as low-income economies (average per capita GNP of US $420), lower-middle-income economies (average per capita GNP of US $1,200) and upper-middle-income economies (average per capita GNP of US $4,870). Most developing countries are in Africa, Asia and Latin America. The developed world, made up of high-income, industrialized economies (average per capita GNP of US $26,440), contains Australasia, most of Europe and North America, and Japan.

In developing countries, a high proportion of the population is young and so these countries face high expenditure on education and health. In developed countries, the population pyramids are becoming top-heavy, with increasingly ageing populations.

Most Crowded Nations

Population per square kilometre (2002 est.)

1.	Monaco	16,000
2.	Singapore	7,182
3.	Vatican City	2,500
4.	Malta	1,241
5.	Maldives	1,067
6.	Bahrain	965
7.	Bangladesh	926
8.	Barbados	644
9.	Taiwan	626
10.	Nauru	600

Least Crowded Nations

Population per square kilometre (2002 est.)

1.	Mongolia	1.7
2.	Namibia	2.2
3.	Australia	2.5
4.	Suriname	2.7
5.	Iceland	2.7
6.	Botswana	2.7
7.	Mauritania	2.7
8.	Libya	3.0
9.	Canada	3.2
10.	Guyana	3.2

Largest Nations

The world's most populous nations, in millions (2002 est.)

1.	China	1,284
2.	India	1,046
3.	USA	281
4.	Indonesia	231
5.	Brazil	176
6.	Pakistan	148
7.	Russia	145
8.	Bangladesh	133
9.	Nigeria	130
10.	Japan	127
11.	Mexico	103
12.	Philippines	85
13.	Germany	83
14.	Vietnam	81
15.	Egypt	71
16.	Ethiopia	68
17.	Turkey	67
18.	Iran	67
19.	Thailand	62
20.	UK	60
21.	France	60
22.	Italy	58
23.	Congo (Dem.Rep.)	55
24.	Ukraine	48
25.	South Korea	48

Population Density

Inhabitants per square kilometre

- Over 200
- 100 – 200
- 50 – 100
- 25 – 50
- 6 – 25
- 3 – 6
- 1 – 3
- Under 1

Urban population

- ■ Over 10,000,000
- ● 5,000,000 – 10,000,000
- • 1,000,000 – 5,000,000

Places marked are conurbations, not city limits; San Francisco itself, for example, has an official population of less than a million.

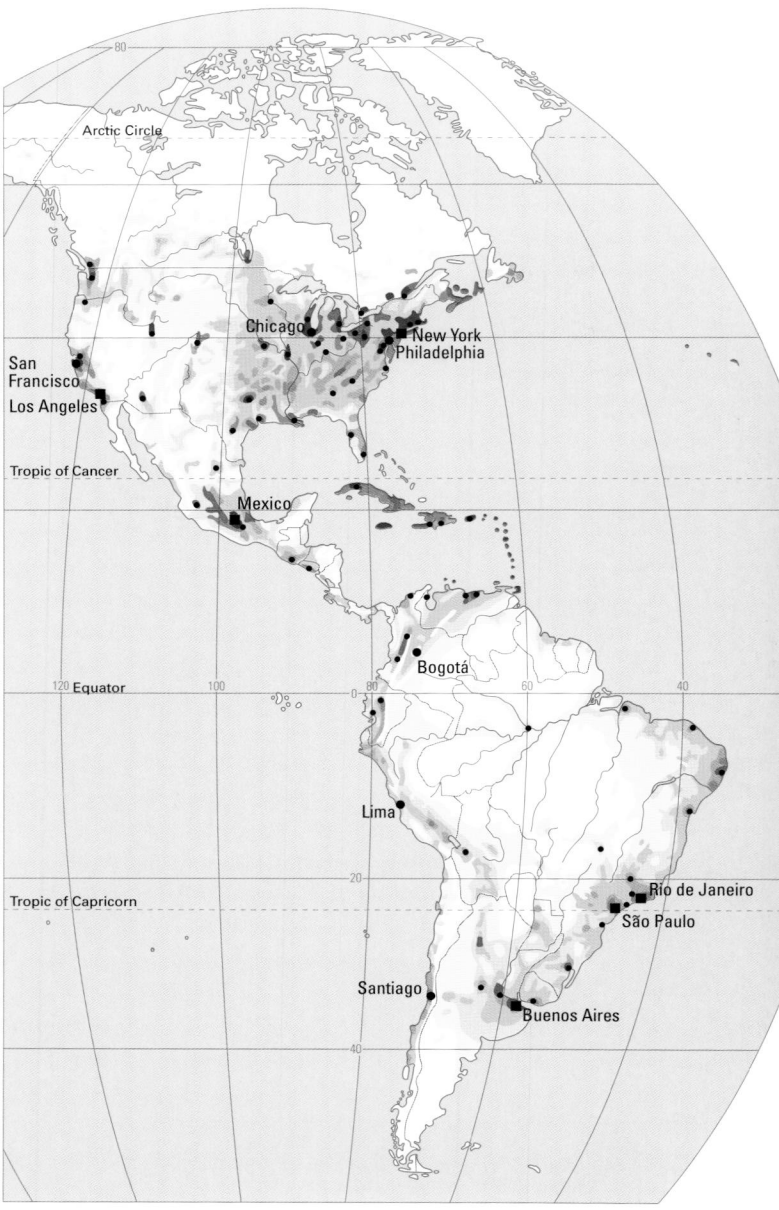

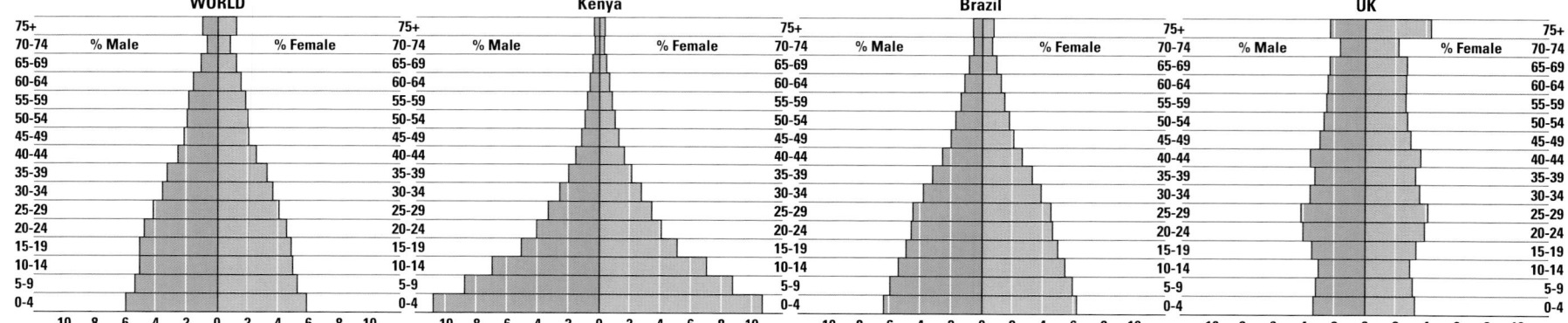

WORLD / Kenya / Brazil / UK population pyramids, age groups 0-4 through 75+, % Male and % Female, scale 10 8 6 4 2 0 2 4 6 8 10

Rates of Growth

The world population doubled between 1950 and 1990. Small rates of population growth led to dramatic increases over two or three generations. The table below translates annual percentage growth into the number of years required to double a population.

% change	Doubling time
0.5	139.0
1.0	69.7
1.5	46.6
2.0	35.0
2.5	28.1
3.0	23.4
3.5	20.1
4.0	17.7

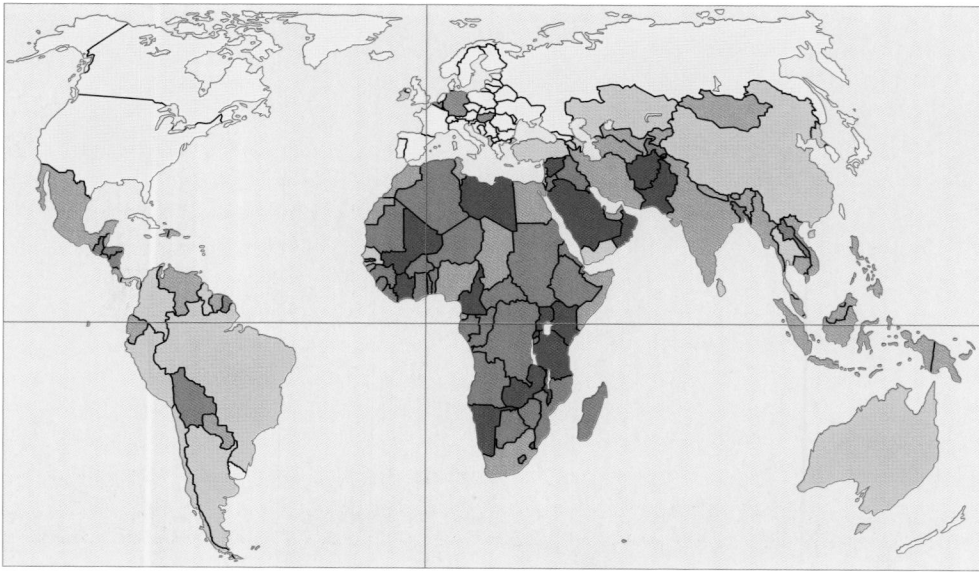

Population Change 1990–2000

The population change for the years 1990–2000

- Over 40% population gain
- 30 – 40% population gain
- 20 – 30% population gain
- 10 – 20% population gain
- 0 – 10% population gain
- No change or population loss

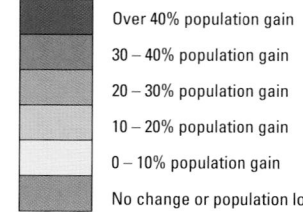

Top 5 countries		Bottom 5 countries	
Kuwait	+75.9%	Belgium	–0.1%
Namibia	+62.5%	Hungary	–0.2%
Afghanistan	+60.1%	Grenada	–2.4%
Mali	+55.5%	Germany	–3.2%
Tanzania	+54.6%	Tonga	–3.2%

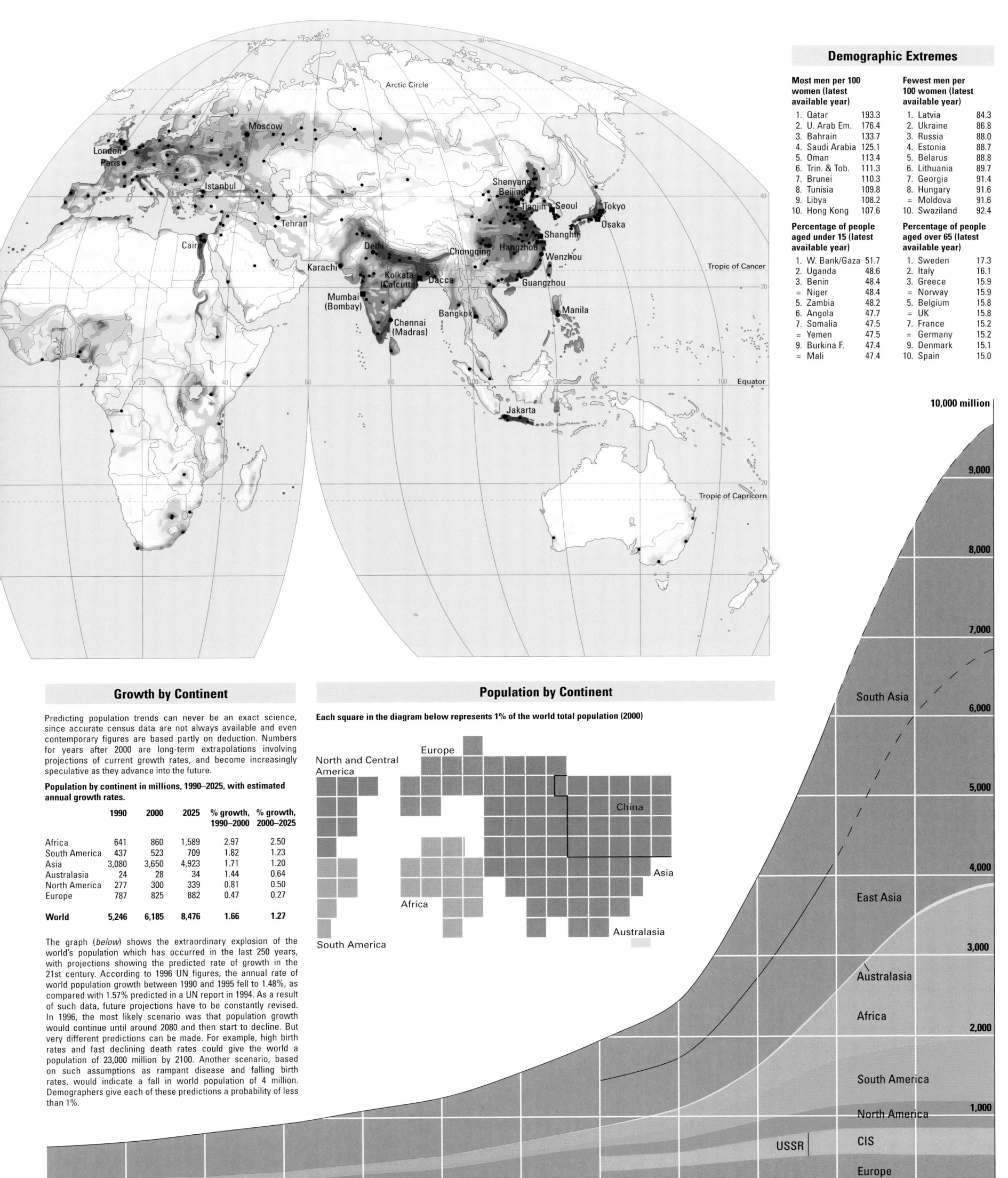

Demographic Extremes

Most men per 100 women (latest available year)		Fewest men per 100 women (latest available year)	
1. Qatar	193.3	1. Latvia	84.3
2. U. Arab Em.	176.4	2. Ukraine	86.8
3. Bahrain	133.7	3. Russia	88.0
4. Saudi Arabia	125.1	4. Estonia	88.7
5. Oman	113.4	5. Belarus	88.8
6. Trin. & Tob.	111.3	6. Lithuania	89.7
7. Brunei	110.3	7. Georgia	91.4
8. Tunisia	109.8	8. Hungary	91.6
9. Libya	108.2	= Moldova	91.6
10. Hong Kong	107.6	10. Swaziland	92.4

Percentage of people aged under 15 (latest available year)		Percentage of people aged over 65 (latest available year)	
1. W. Bank/Gaza	51.7	1. Sweden	17.3
2. Uganda	48.6	2. Italy	16.1
3. Benin	48.4	3. Greece	15.9
= Niger	48.4	= Norway	15.9
5. Zambia	48.2	5. Belgium	15.8
6. Angola	47.7	= UK	15.8
7. Somalia	47.5	7. France	15.2
= Yemen	47.5	= Germany	15.2
9. Burkina F.	47.4	9. Denmark	15.1
= Mali	47.4	10. Spain	15.0

Growth by Continent

Predicting population trends can never be an exact science, since accurate census data are not always available and even contemporary figures are based partly on deduction. Numbers for years after 2000 are long-term extrapolations involving projections of current growth rates, and become increasingly speculative as they advance into the future.

Population by continent in millions, 1990–2025, with estimated annual growth rates.

	1990	2000	2025	% growth, 1990–2000	% growth, 2000–2025
Africa	641	860	1,589	2.97	2.50
South America	437	523	709	1.82	1.23
Asia	3,080	3,650	4,923	1.71	1.20
Australasia	24	28	34	1.44	0.64
North America	277	300	339	0.81	0.50
Europe	787	825	882	0.47	0.27
World	**5,246**	**6,185**	**8,476**	**1.66**	**1.27**

The graph (*below*) shows the extraordinary explosion of the world's population which has occurred in the last 250 years, with projections showing the predicted rate of growth in the 21st century. According to 1996 UN figures, the annual rate of world population growth between 1990 and 1995 fell to 1.48%, as compared with 1.57% predicted in a UN report in 1994. As a result of such data, future projections have to be constantly revised. In 1996, the most likely scenario was that population growth would continue until around 2080 and then start to decline. But very different predictions can be made. For example, high birth rates and fast declining death rates could give the world a population of 23,000 million by 2100. Another scenario, based on such assumptions as rampant disease and falling birth rates, would indicate a fall in world population of 4 million. Demographers give each of these predictions a probability of less than 1%.

Population by Continent

Each square in the diagram below represents 1% of the world total population (2000)

North and Central America

Europe

China

Asia

Africa

South America

Australasia

10,000 million

9,000

8,000

7,000

South Asia

6,000

5,000

East Asia

4,000

3,000

Australasia

Africa

2,000

South America

North America

1,000

USSR | CIS

Europe

1750 1775 1800 1825 1850 1875 1900 1925 1950 1975 2000 2025 2050

CITIES

For more information:
18 Water supply
24 Population density
41 The great ports

Following the development of agriculture more than 10,000 years ago, people began to live in farming villages. Around 5,500 years ago, the world's first cities appeared in the lower Tigris and Euphrates valleys in Mesopotamia. Cities were founded in Ancient Egypt around 5,000 years ago and in China around 3,600 years ago. By contrast with the villages, most people in the early cities were not engaged in farming. Instead, they worked in craft industries, in government services, in religion and in trade. The cities became centres of early civilizations and, through trade, their influence spread far and wide. However, they were dependent on the surrounding farming communities for their food and other materials.

In 1750, prior to the start of the Industrial Revolution, barely 3% of the world's population lived in urban areas. By 1850, London and Paris had more than a million people, and, by 1900, 14% of the world's population lived in cities. By 1950, the world had 83 cities with more than a million people, and by 1996, there were 280. By 2015, experts predict that there will be more than 500. New York City was the only city with a population in excess of 10 million in 1950; by 2015 the experts predict 27 such cities worldwide, the majority located in the developing world.

However, predictions have to be constantly revised in the light of new data. For example, in the late 1990s, UN demographers calculated that urban areas then accounted for 50% of the world's population. But after much lower census figures emerged for many cities in the early 21st century, the UN demographers had to push back the date when half of the world's population would be living in cities to 2007.

Urbanization is greatest in industrialized countries. For example, in 2000, 77.2% of the people in the United States lived in urban areas. However, in low-income countries, which contained nearly 60% of the world's population in the late 1990s, only 28% lived in urban areas.

The rapid rate of urbanization has created many social problems, especially in cities which have been unable to provide enough jobs and services for the new arrivals. Many of the new city dwellers come from rural areas and take time to adjust to urban life and employment possibilities.

A typical city in a developing country contains millions of people living, often illegally, in shanty towns (or 'informal settlements'), while thousands live on the streets. Yet many of these shanty towns are healthier than the industrial cities of 19th-century Europe and North America. Indeed, surveys have shown that the migrants to the cities in developing countries are less likely to face poverty than they are in rural areas, while benefiting from greater access to healthcare services and education.

Modern cities face many problems, including pollution, crime and unemployment. Yet, given competent central and local government, they are capable of generating the wealth they need to solve them, as well as making a major contribution to the economy.

The Urbanization of the Earth

City-building, 1850–2000; each white spot represents a city of at least 1 million inhabitants.

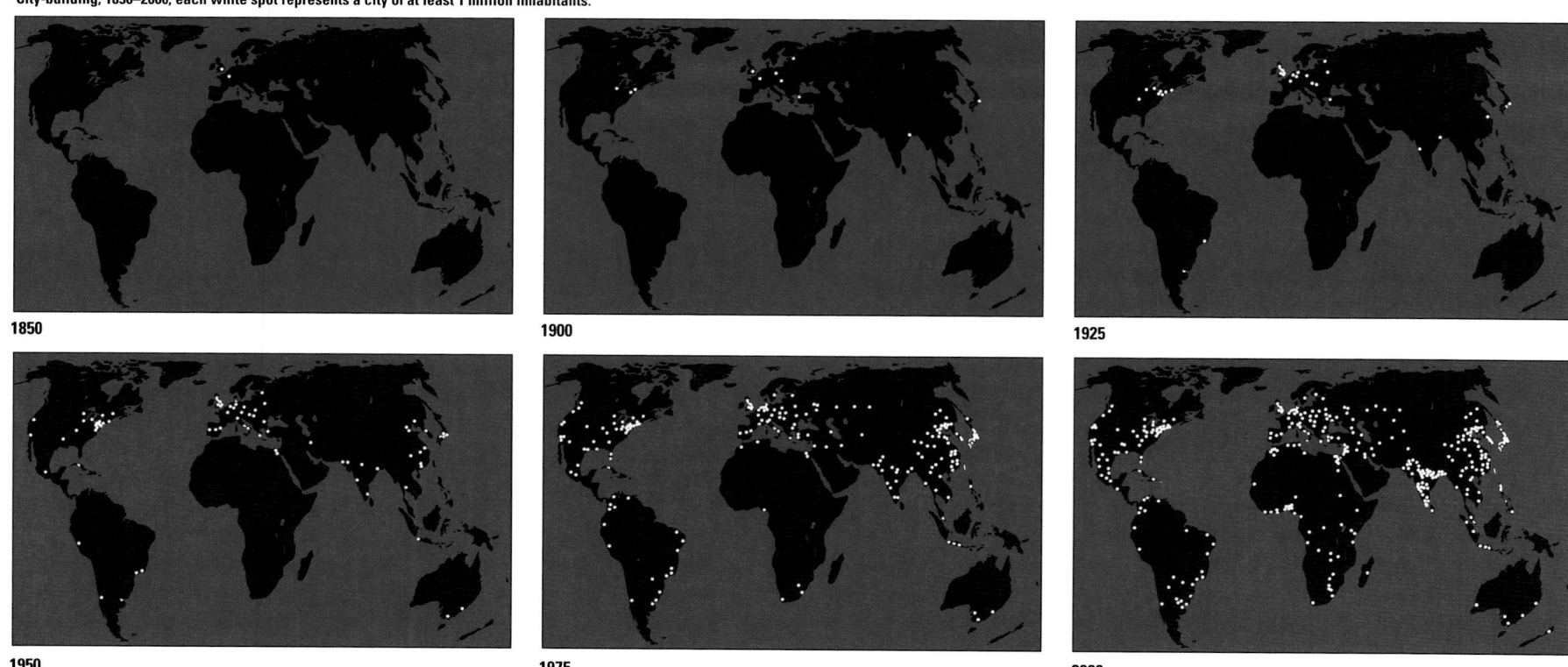

1850 1900 1925
1950 1975 2000

Urban Population

Percentage of total population living in towns and cities (2000)

Most urbanized

Belgium	97%
W. Sahara	96%
Singapore	93%
UAE	93%
Iceland	93%

Over 80%	
60 – 80%	
40 – 60%	
20 – 40%	
Under 20%	

Least urbanized

Rwanda	6%
Bhutan	7%
East Timor	7%
Burundi	9%
Nepal	11%

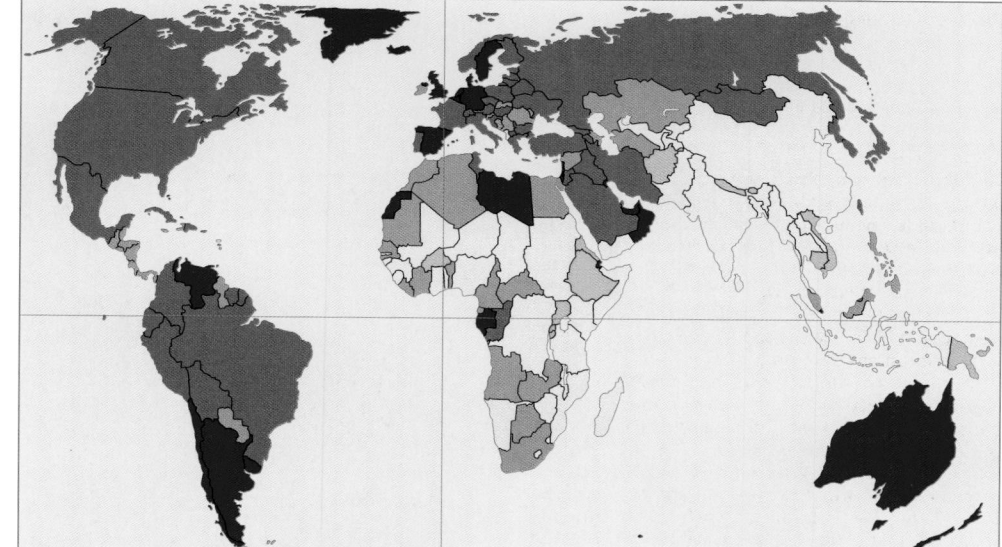

Expanding Cities

The growth of some of the world's largest cities in millions, 1950–2015.
Comparisons of city populations over time are problematic due to changes in the definition of the city limits.
These figures attempt to take such changes into consideration. The figure for London is the metropolitan region.

■ 1950   ■ 2015

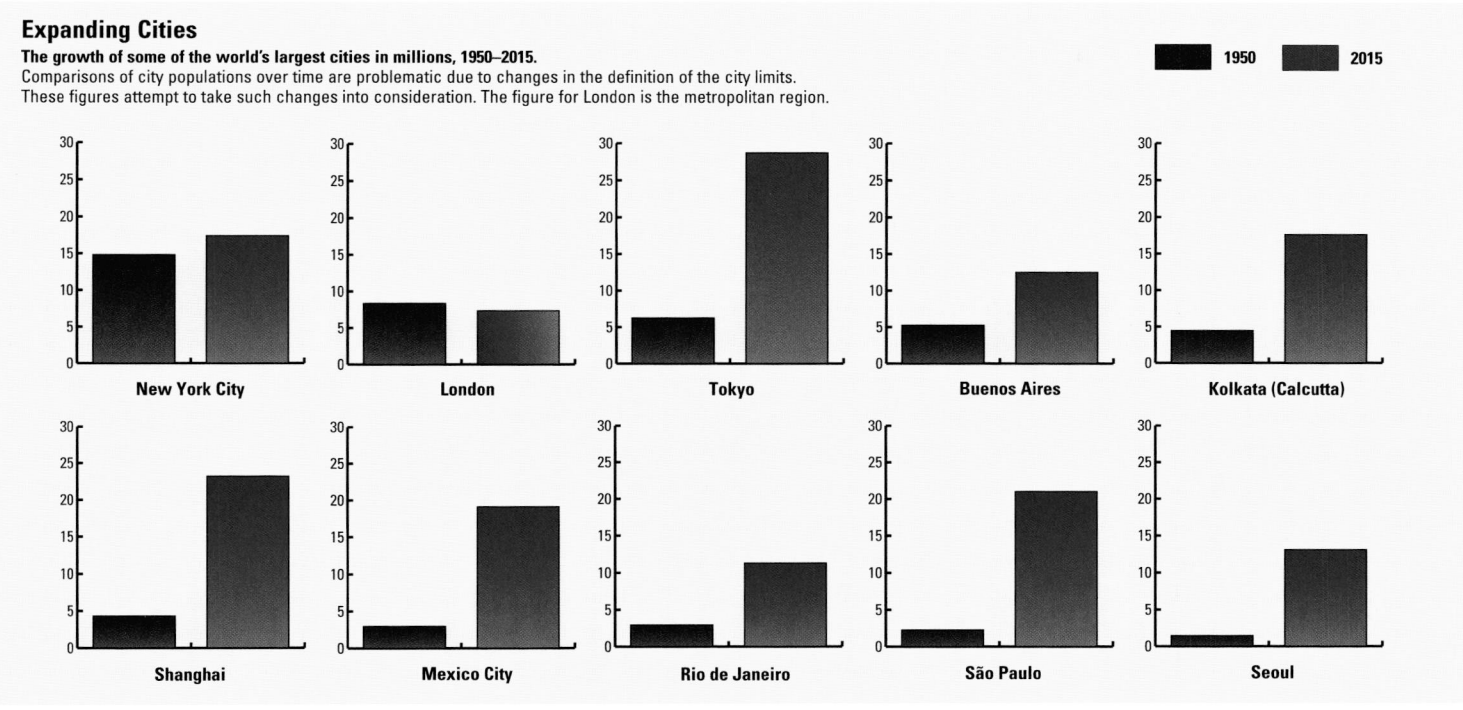

The graphs show the projected growth of megacities between 1950 and 2015. New York City, the world's largest city in 1950, reached a peak in 1970, but it has experienced periods of negative growth. London's population also declined between 1970 and 1985, before resuming a modest rate of increase. In both cases, the divergence from world trends is explained in part by counting methods. Each lies at the centre of a great agglomeration, and definitions of the 'city limits' may vary over time. Also, in developing countries, many areas around the megacities, which are counted as urban, are rural in character. The rates of city population growth in developing countries have also often been over-estimated. For example, it was once predicted that Kolkata (Calcutta) would have a population of 40 million by the late 1990s. The reason why many estimates have proven incorrect is partly explained by a new trend, namely that rapid urban growth is now greatest, in some regions, in the smaller cities. For example, the main expansion in West Bengal is no longer in Kolkata (Calcutta), but in a rash of small cities across the state.

Cities in Danger

In mid-2002, a 'brown haze', 3 km [2 mi] high, covered much of southern Asia. Caused mainly by the burning of coal and biomass, it caused respiratory diseases and deaths. Alarm concerning urban air pollution had been expressed much earlier, but controls since the 1980s had proved difficult to enforce and expensive to install.

Those taking part in the United Nations' Global Environment Monitoring System (*see right*) frequently show dangerous levels of pollutants ranging from soot to sulphur dioxide and photo-chemical smog; air in the majority of cities without such sampling equipment is likely to be at least as bad. Traffic, a major source of air pollution worldwide, loses Thailand's workforce 44 working days each year.

Urban Air Pollution

The world's most polluted cities: number of days each year when sulphur dioxide levels exceeded the WHO threshold of 150 micrograms per cubic metre (averaged over 4 to 15 years, 1970s – 1980s)

Sulphur dioxide is the main pollutant associated with industrial cities. According to the World Health Organization, more than seven days in a year above 150 µg per cubic metre bring a serious risk of respiratory disease: at least 600 million people live in urban areas where SO_2 concentrations regularly reach damaging levels.

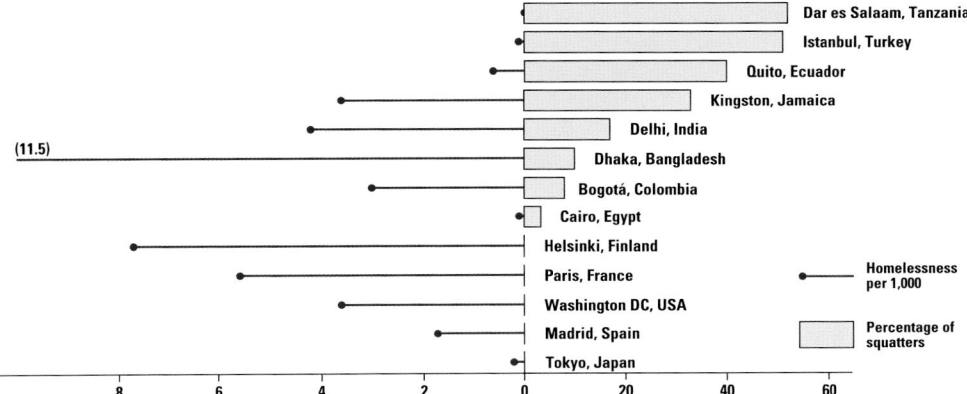

Urban Housing Needs

Proportion of the population living in squatter settlements and the number of homeless per thousand, for selected cities.

Urbanization in most developing countries has been proceeding so rapidly that local governments have been unable to provide the necessary services and housing. In some cities, many people find their homes in squatter settlements, frequently without power, water and sanitation. Yet these communities are often a dynamic part of the city's economy, while their inhabitants sometimes take all kinds of initiatives, including the setting up of their own local government and self-help associations. Some of the world's richest cities also have a homeless underclass, although calculating the numbers of people involved is problematic. Yet it is the case that homelessness and unemployment are currently affecting an increasing number of people in the developed world.

Largest Cities

Early in the 21st century for the first time in history, the majority of the world's population will live in cities. Below is a list of all the cities with more than 10 million inhabitants, based on estimates for the year 2015.

1.	Tokyo–Yokohama	28.7
2.	Mumbai (Bombay)	27.4
3.	Lagos	24.1
4.	Shanghai	23.2
5.	Jakarta	21.5
6.	São Paulo	21.0
7.	Karachi	20.6
8.	Beijing	19.6
9.	Dhaka	19.2
10.	Mexico City	19.1
11.	Kolkata (Calcutta)	17.6
12.	Delhi	17.5
13.	New York City	17.4
14.	Tianjin	17.1
15.	Manila	14.9
16.	Cairo	14.7
17.	Los Angeles	14.5
18.	Seoul	13.1
19.	Buenos Aires	12.5
20.	Istanbul	12.1
21.	Rio de Janeiro	11.3
22.	Lahore	10.9
23.	Hyderabad	10.6
24.	Bangkok	10.4
25.	Osaka	10.2
26.	Lima	10.1
27.	Tehran	10.0

City populations are based on urban agglomerations rather than legal city limits. In some cases where two adjacent cities have merged into one concentration, such as Tokyo–Yokohama, they have been regarded as a single unit.

Urban Advantages

Despite overcrowding and poor housing, living standards in the developing world's cities are almost invariably better than in the surrounding countryside. Resources – financial, material and administrative – are concentrated in the towns, which are usually also the centres of political activity and pressure. Governments – frequently unstable, and rarely established on a solid democratic base – are usually more responsive to urban discontent than rural misery.

In many countries, especially in Africa, food prices are kept artificially low, appeasing the underemployed urban masses at the expense of agricultural development. The imbalance encourages further citywards migration, helping to account for the astonishing rate of post-1950 urbanization and putting great strain on the ability of many nations to provide even modest improvements for their people.

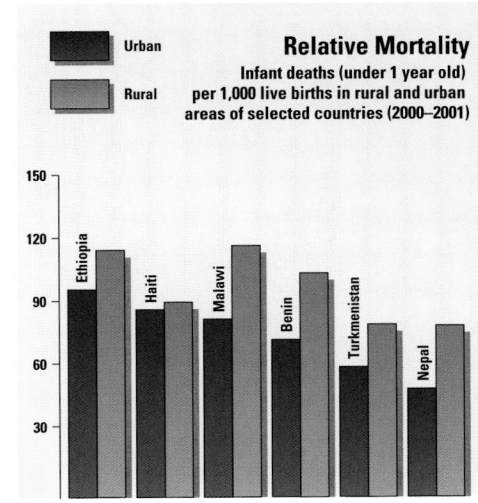

Relative Mortality
Infant deaths (under 1 year old) per 1,000 live births in rural and urban areas of selected countries (2000–2001)

■ Urban   ■ Rural

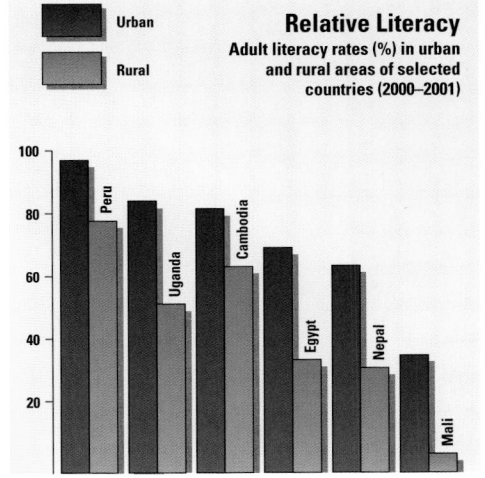

Relative Literacy
Adult literacy rates (%) in urban and rural areas of selected countries (2000–2001)

■ Urban   ■ Rural

CARTOGRAPHY BY PHILIP'S. COPYRIGHT PHILIP'S.

27

THE HUMAN FAMILY

For more information:
24 Population density
30 The world's refugees
   War since 1945
31 United Nations
   International
   organizations

Racial, language and religious differences have led to appalling acts of inhumanity throughout history. Yet strictly speaking, all human beings belong to one species, *Homo sapiens*, which has no subspecies. The differences between the three racial types which most people identify – namely Caucasoid, Mongoloid and Negroid – reflect not so much evolutionary differences as long periods of separation.

Migration has recently mingled the various groups to an unprecedented extent, and most nations now have some degree of racial mixing. For example, the United States has often been called a melting pot, because of the large numbers of people from various geographical locations which make up the population. The country has

no official language but, until recently, English was spoken by the vast majority of the people. But in recent years, some of the immigrants from Mexico, Cuba and other parts of Latin America have not learned English and speak only Spanish. This development disturbs those Americans who believe that the use of English binds the nation together, and several states have passed laws stating that English is their only official language.

Language is fundamental to human culture and any particular language is almost the definition of that particular culture. Because definitions of languages vary, estimates of the total number range from 3,000 to 6,000, although most are spoken by only a few people. The world's languages

are grouped into families, the largest of which are the Indo-European and Sino-Tibetan. Chinese, a Sino-Tibetan language, is spoken by more people as a first language than any other. English, an Indo-European tongue, ranks second, but it is the leading international language, because so many people speak it as their second tongue.

Like language, religion encourages cohesion in single human groups and it satisfies a deep human need by assigning people a place in a divinely ordered world. Religion is a way in which a culture can express its individuality. For example, the rise of Islamic fundamentalism in the late 20th century was partly an expression of resentment that secular Western values were being imposed on Muslims.

World Migration

The greatest voluntary migration was the colonization of North America by 30–35 million European settlers during the 19th century. The greatest forced migration involved 9–11 million Africans taken as slaves to America between 1550 and 1860. The migrations shown on the map below are mostly international, as population movements within borders are not usually recorded. Many of the statistics are necessarily estimates as so many refugees and migrant workers enter countries illegally and unrecorded. Emigrants may have a variety of motives for leaving, thus making it difficult to distinguish between voluntary and involuntary migrations.

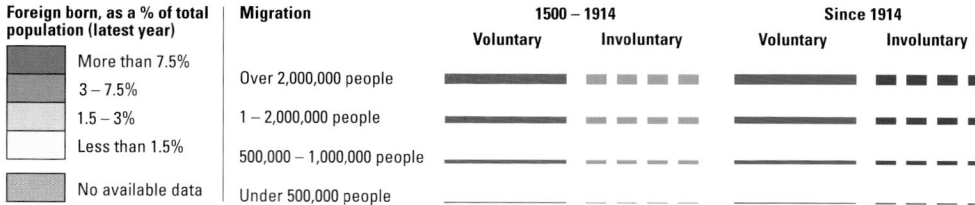

Foreign born, as a % of total population (latest year)
More than 7.5%
3 – 7.5%
1.5 – 3%
Less than 1.5%
No available data

Migration
Over 2,000,000 people
1 – 2,000,000 people
500,000 – 1,000,000 people
Under 500,000 people

1500 – 1914: Voluntary / Involuntary
Since 1914: Voluntary / Involuntary

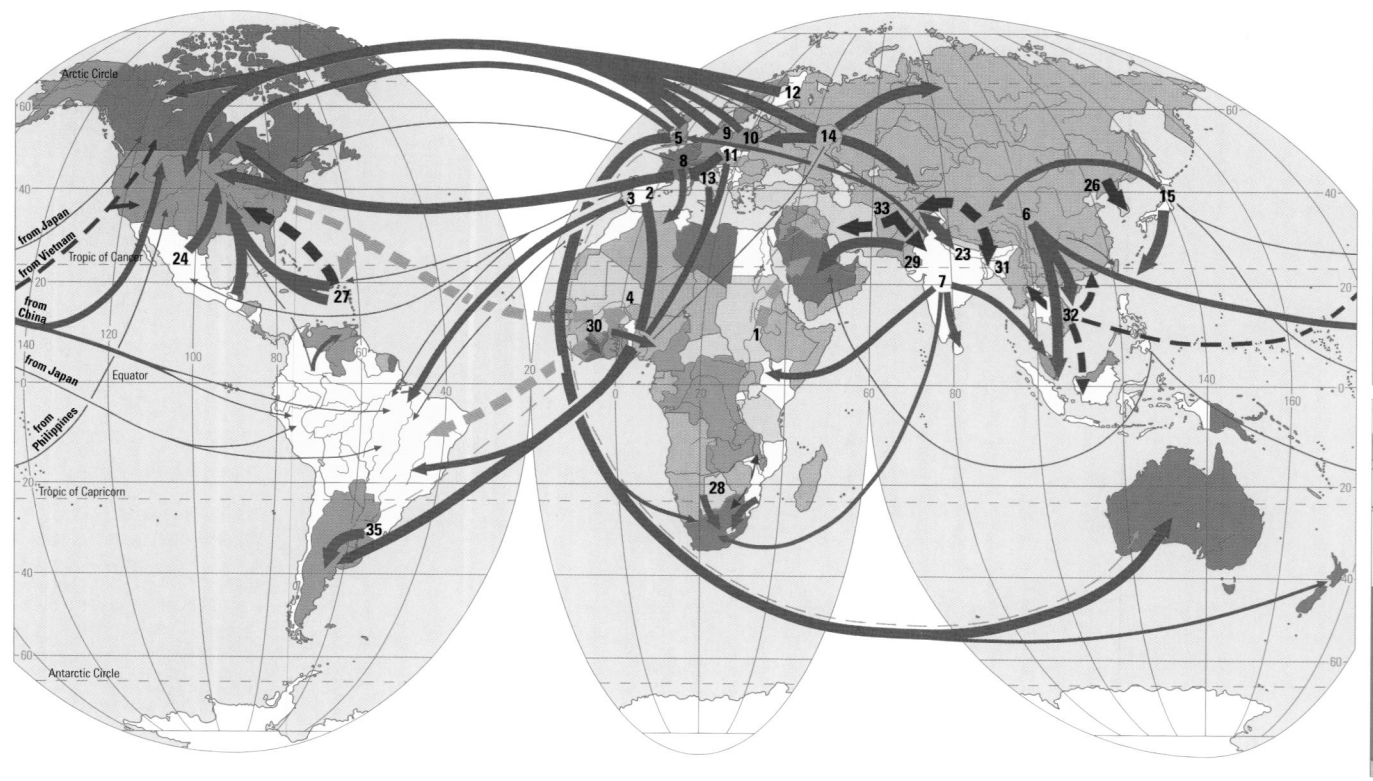

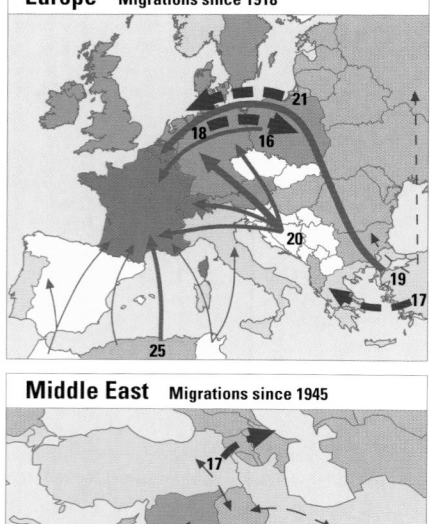

Europe — Migrations since 1918

Middle East — Migrations since 1945

Building the USA

US Immigration, 1920 and 2000

For decades the USA was the magnet that attracted millions of immigrants, notably from Central and Eastern Europe, the flow peaking in the early years of the 20th century. By the mid-1990s the proportion of immigrants had increased again to pre-World War II rates, reaching almost 10% by 2000. However, the balance of origin had swung from Europe to Latin America and Asia, as the graphs below indicate.

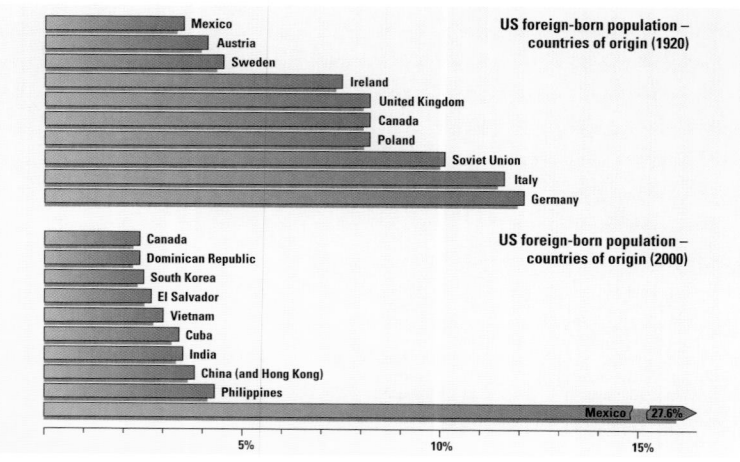

US foreign-born population – countries of origin (1920)
Mexico, Austria, Sweden, Ireland, United Kingdom, Canada, Poland, Soviet Union, Italy, Germany

US foreign-born population – countries of origin (2000)
Canada, Dominican Republic, South Korea, El Salvador, Vietnam, Cuba, India, China (and Hong Kong), Philippines, Mexico (27.6%)

Major world migrations since 1500 (over 1 million people)

1. North and East African slaves to Arabia (4.3m) 1500–1900
2. Spanish to South and Central America (2.3m) 1530–1914
3. Portuguese to Brazil (1.4m) 1530–1914
4. West African slaves to South America (4.6m) 1550–1860
    to Caribbean (4m) 1580–1860
    to North/Central America (1m) 1650–1820
5. British and Irish to North America (13.5m) 1620–1914
    to Australasia and
    South Africa (3m) 1790–1914
6. Chinese to South-east Asia (22m) 1820–1914
    to North America (1m) 1880–1914
7. Indian migrant workers (3m) 1850–1914
8. French to North Africa (1.5m) 1850–1914
9. Germans to North America (5m) .1850–1914
10. Poles to North America (3.6m) 1850–1914
11. Austro-Hungarians to North America (3.2m) 1850–1914
    to Western Europe (3.4m) 1850–1914
    to South America (1.8m) 1850–1914
12. Scandinavians to North America (2.7m) 1850–1914
13. Italians to North America (5m) 1860–1914
    to South America (3.7m) 1860–1914
14. Russians to North America (2.2m) 1880–1914
    to Western Europe (2.2m) 1880–1914
    to Siberia (6m) .1880–1914
    to Central Asia (4m) 1880–1914
15. Japanese to Eastern Asia, South-east Asia
    and America (8m) 1900–1914
16. Poles to Western Europe (1m) 1920–1940
17. Greeks and Armenians from Turkey (1.6m) 1922–1923
18. European Jews to extermination camps (5m) 1940–1944
19. Turks to Western Europe (1.9m) .1940–
20. Yugoslavs to Western Europe (2m) 1940–
21. Germans to Western Europe (9.8m) 1945–1947
22. Palestinian refugees (2m) 1947–
23. Indian and Pakistani refugees (15m) 1947
24. Mexicans to North America (9m) 1950–
25. North Africans to Western Europe (1.1m) 1950–
26. Korean refugees (5m) 1950–1954
27. Latin Americans and West Indians to
    North America (4.7m) 1960–
28. Migrant workers to South Africa (1.5m) 1960–
29. Indians and Pakistanis to The Gulf (2.4m) 1970–
30. Migrant workers to Nigeria and Ivory Coast (3m) 1970–
31. Bangladeshi and Pakistani refugees (2m) 1972
32. Vietnamese and Cambodian refugees (1.5m) 1975–
33. Afghan refugees (6.1m) 1979–
34. Egyptians to The Gulf and Libya (2.9m) 1980–
35. Migrant workers to Argentina (2m) 1980–
36. Mozambique refugees (1.7m) 1985–
37. Yugoslav/Balkan refugees (1.7m) 1992–
38. Rwanda/Burundi refugees (2.6m) 1994–

Predominant Languages

INDO-EUROPEAN FAMILY
- **1** Balto-Slavic group (incl. Russian, Ukrainian)
- **2** Germanic group (incl. English, German)
- **3** Celtic group
- **4** Greek
- **5** Albanian
- **6** Iranian group
- **7** Armenian
- **8** Romance group (incl. Spanish, Portuguese, French, Italian)
- **9** Indo-Aryan group (incl. Hindi, Bengali, Urdu, Punjabi, Marathi)
- **10** CAUCASIAN FAMILY

AFRO-ASIATIC FAMILY
- **11** Semitic group (incl. Arabic)
- **12** Kushitic group
- **13** Berber group
- **14** KHOISAN FAMILY
- **15** NIGER-CONGO FAMILY
- **16** NILO-SAHARAN FAMILY
- **17** URALIC FAMILY

ALTAIC FAMILY
- **18** Turkic group (incl. Turkish)
- **19** Mongolian group
- **20** Tungus-Manchu group
- **21** Japanese and Korean

SINO-TIBETAN FAMILY
- **22** Sinitic (Chinese) languages (incl. Mandarin, Wu, Yue)
- **23** Tibetic-Burmic languages
- **24** TAI FAMILY

AUSTRO-ASIATIC FAMILY
- **25** Mon-Khmer group
- **26** Munda group
- **27** Vietnamese
- **28** DRAVIDIAN FAMILY (incl. Telugu, Tamil)
- **29** AUSTRONESIAN FAMILY (incl. Malay-Indonesian, Javanese)
- **30** OTHER LANGUAGES

First-language speakers, in millions (1999)	
Mandarin Chinese	885m
Spanish	332m
English	322m
Bengali	189m
Hindi	182m
Portuguese	170m
Russian	170m
Japanese	125m
German	98m
Wu Chinese	77m
Javanese	76m
Korean	75m
French	72m
Vietnamese	68m
Yue Chinese	66m
Marathi	65m
Tamil	63m
Turkish	59m
Urdu	58m

Languages form a kind of tree of development, splitting from a few ancient proto-tongues into branches that have grown apart and further divided with the passage of time. English and Hindi, for example, both belong to the great Indo-European family, although the relationship is only apparent after much analysis and comparison with non-Indo-European languages such as Chinese or Arabic; Hindi is part of the Indo-Aryan subgroup, whereas English is a member of Indo-European's Germanic branch; French, another Indo-European tongue, traces its descent through the Latin, or Romance, branch. A few languages – Basque is one example – have no apparent links with any other, living or dead. Most modern languages, of course, have acquired enormous quantities of vocabulary from each other.

Distribution of Living Languages

The figures refer to the number of languages currently in use in the regions shown.

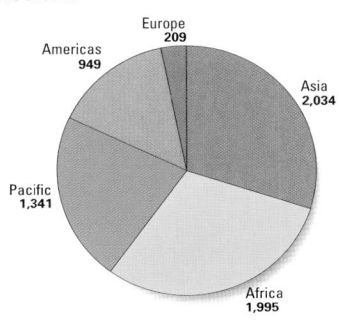

- Europe 209
- Americas 949
- Asia 2,034
- Pacific 1,341
- Africa 1,995

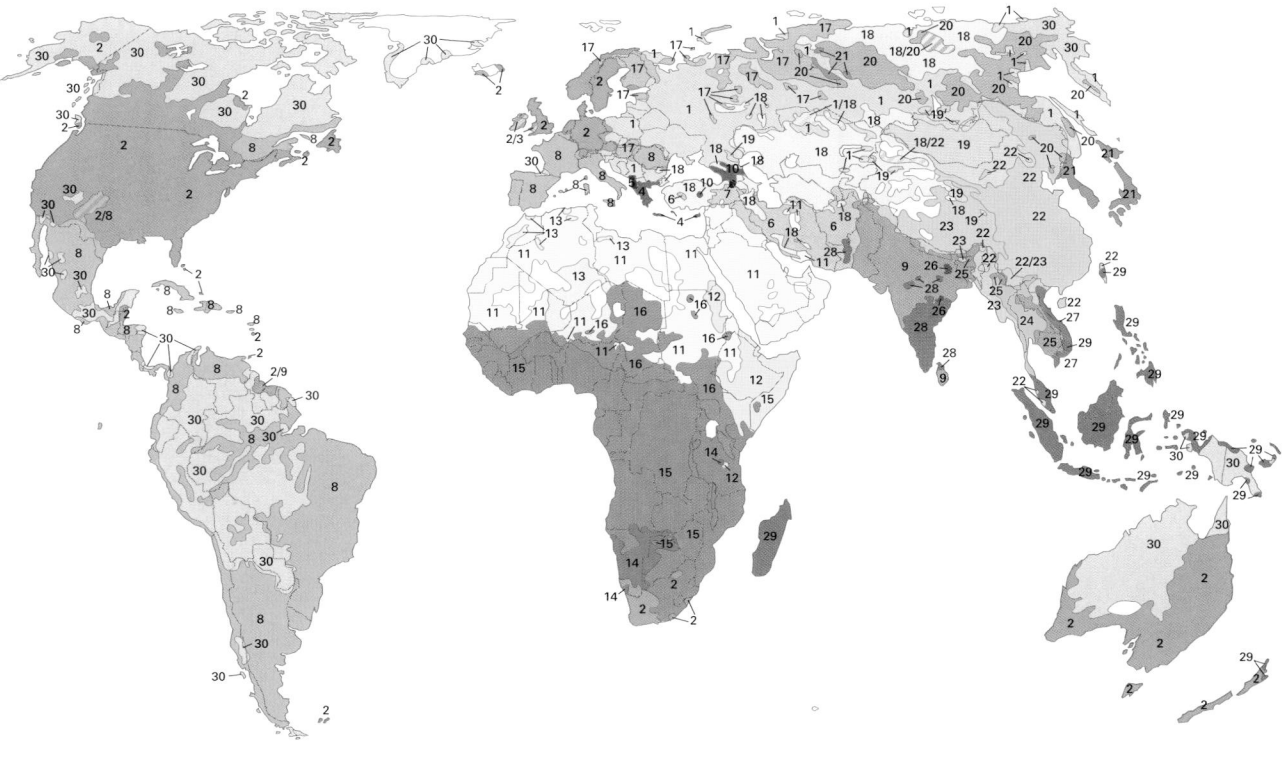

Predominant Religions

- ▲ Roman Catholicism
- Orthodox and other Eastern Churches
- • Protestantism
- Sunni Islam
- Shia Islam
- Buddhism
- Hinduism
- Confucianism
- ★ Judaism
- Shintoism
- Tribal Religions

Religions are not as easily mapped as the physical contours of the land. Divisions are often blurred and frequently overlapping: most nations include people of many different faiths – or no faith at all. Some religions, like Islam and Christianity, have proselytes worldwide; others, like Hinduism and Confucianism, are restricted to a particular area, though modern migrations have taken some Indians and Chinese very far from their cultural origins. It is also difficult to show the degree to which religion controls daily life: Christian Western Europe, for example, is now far less dominated by its religion than are the Islamic nations of the Middle East. Similarly, figures for the major faiths' adherents make no distinction between nominal believers enrolled at birth and those for whom religion is a vital part of existence.

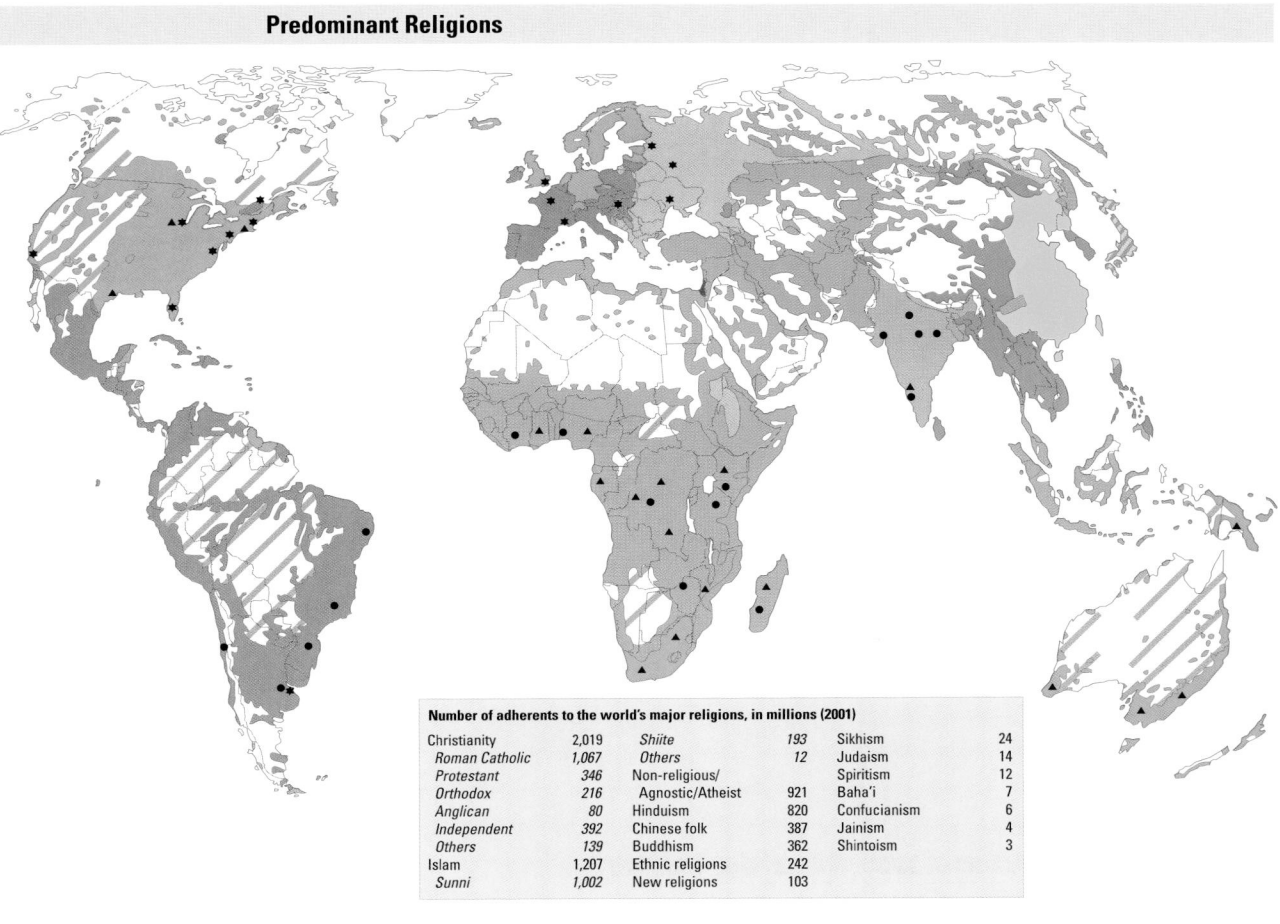

Number of adherents to the world's major religions, in millions (2001)					
Christianity	2,019	Shiite	193	Sikhism	24
Roman Catholic	1,067	Others	12	Judaism	14
Protestant	346	Non-religious/		Spiritism	12
Orthodox	216	Agnostic/Atheist	921	Baha'i	7
Anglican	80	Hinduism	820	Confucianism	6
Independent	392	Chinese folk	387	Jainism	4
Others	139	Buddhism	362	Shintoism	3
Islam	1,207	Ethnic religions	242		
Sunni	1,002	New religions	103		

CARTOGRAPHY BY PHILIP'S. COPYRIGHT PHILIP'S

CONFLICT AND CO-OPERATION

For more information:
28 Migration
29 Religion

The 20th century witnessed two world wars, followed by a Cold War which several times threatened to erupt into a third world war, fought with nuclear weapons. The Cold War was marked by a great number of conflicts. Some were colonial wars, as the empires of the first half of the century fell apart, some were border wars, and some were civil wars. All the wars have caused great suffering among civilians, many of whom were forced to join the ranks of the world's refugees.

In the late 1980s, many people hoped that the end of the Cold War, following the collapse of Communist regimes in the former Soviet Union and Eastern Europe, would herald a new era of international stability. Instead, old ethnic and religious antagonisms surfaced in many areas, leading to civil war in such places as Chechenia, in Russia, and the former Yugoslavia. Nationalist rivalries, suppressed under Communist rule, replaced ideological factors as the major cause of conflict.

War is a very human activity, with no real equivalent in any other species. Yet humans also function well when they co-operate. Evolution has made this so. Hunter-gatherers in co-operative bands were far more effective than animals that prowled. Agriculture, urbanization and industrialization all depend on the ability of humans to co-operate.

The creation of the United Nations in 1945 held out hope that the world's nations, tired of war, would have the means to control humanity's aggressive instincts. Although the UN lacks the power to halt conflicts, it has often helped to achieve negotiation. Economic pressures have led to another kind of co-operation, the creation of common markets and economic unions, such as ASEAN in South-east Asia, the European Union and NAFTA in North America.

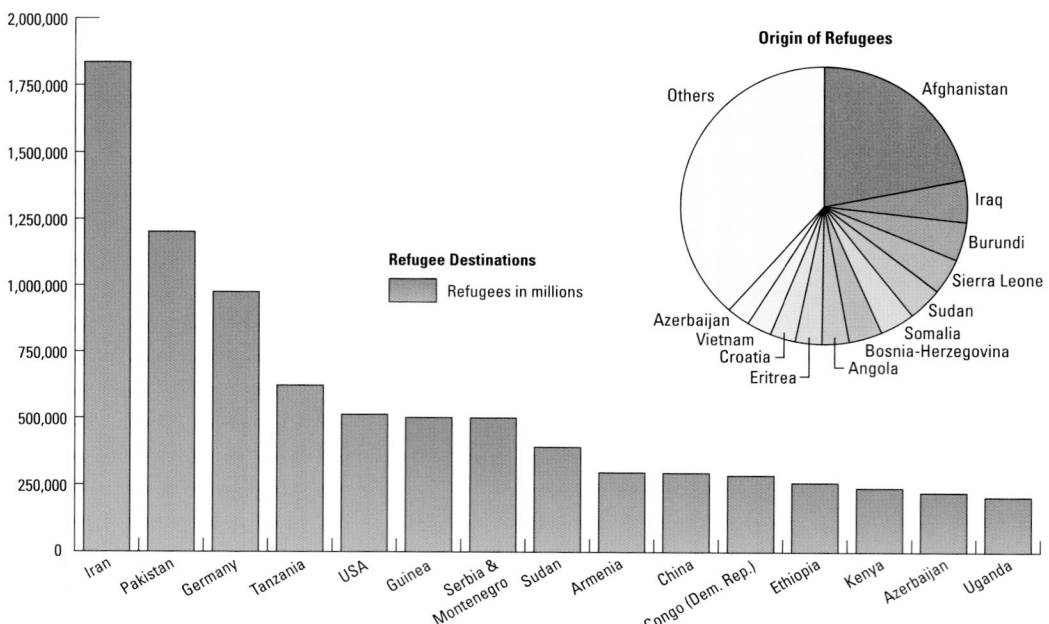

The World's Refugees

Refugees by host nation (bar-chart, left) and by nation of origin (pie-chart, left) (2000). The source is the United Nations High Commission for Refugees (UNHCR). The 3.2 million Palestinian refugees living in Jordan, Syria, Lebanon, Gaza and the West Bank fall under the mandate of United Nations Relief and Works Agency (UNRWA) and are not included on the graphs.

The pie-chart shows the origins of the world's refugees, while the bar-chart below shows their destinations. According to the United Nations High Commission for Refugees (UNHCR) in 2000 there were 12.1 million refugees. However, the UNHCR definition of a refugee, 'a person who has left or remains outside their own country because they have a well-founded fear of persecution, or because their safety is threatened by events seriously disturbing public order', does not include people who are in a refugee-like situation but who have not been formally recognized. In 2000, there were a further 5.3 million people who were internally displaced, and a total 'population of concern' 21.1 million people, worldwide.

All but a few who cross international boundaries seek asylum in neighbouring countries, which are often the least equipped to deal with them. Lacking any rights or power, they frequently become an unwelcome burden to their hosts. Usually, the best any refugee can hope for is rudimentary food and shelter in temporary camps. Many Palestinians have been forced to live in camps since 1948.

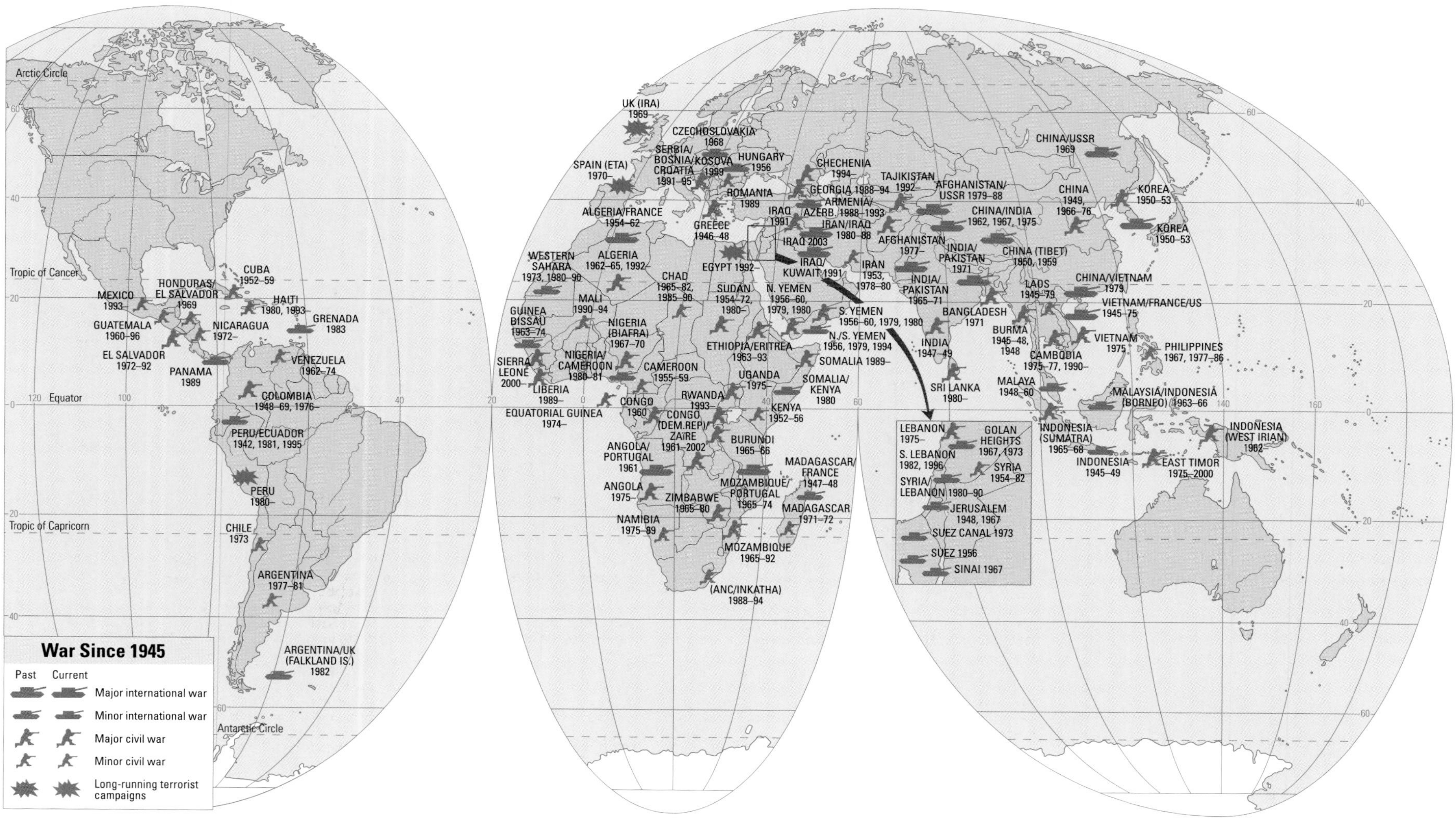

War Since 1945

Past	Current	
		Major international war
		Minor international war
		Major civil war
		Minor civil war
		Long-running terrorist campaigns

United Nations

The United Nations Organization was born as World War II drew to its conclusion. Six years of strife had strengthened the world's desire for peace, but an effective international organization was needed to help achieve it. That body would replace the League of Nations which, since its inception in 1920, had failed to curb the aggression of at least some of its member nations. At the United Nations Conference on International Organization held in San Francisco, the United Nations Charter was drawn up. Ratified by the Security Council and signed by the 51 original members, it came into effect on 24 October 1945.

The Charter set out the aims of the organization: to maintain peace and security, and develop friendly relations between nations; to achieve international co-operation in solving economic, social, cultural and humanitarian problems; to promote respect for human rights and fundamental freedoms; and to harmonize the activities of nations in order to achieve these common goals.

The United Nations has five principal organs :

The General Assembly
The forum at which member nations discuss moral and political issues affecting world development, peace and security meets annually in September, under a newly-elected President whose tenure lasts one year. Any member can bring business to the agenda, and each member nation has one vote.

The Security Council
A legislative and executive body, the Security Council is the primary instrument for establishing and maintaining international peace by attempting to settle disputes between nations. It has the power to dispatch UN forces, and member nations undertake to provide armed forces, assistance and facilities. The Security Council has ten temporary members elected by the General Assembly for two-year terms, and five permanent members – China, France, Russia, UK and USA.

The Economic and Social Council
By far the largest United Nations executive, the Council operates as a conduit between the General Assembly and the many United Nations agencies it instructs to implement Assembly decisions, and whose work it co-ordinates. The Council also commissions studies on economic conditions, collects data and makes recommendations to the Assembly.

The Secretariat
This is the staff of the United Nations, and its task is to administer the policies and programmes of the UN and its organs, and assist and advise the Head of the Secretariat, the Secretary-General – a full-time, non-political appointment made by the General Assembly.

The Trusteeship Council
This no longer administers any of the original 11 trust territories as they are all now independent.

The International Court of Justice (the World Court)
The World Court is the judicial organ of the United Nations. It deals only with United Nations disputes and all members are subject to its jurisdiction. There are 15 judges, elected for nine-year terms by the General Assembly and the Security Council.

The social and humanitarian operations of the UN include:
United Nations Development Programme (UNDP) Plans and funds projects to help developing countries make better use of their resources.
United Nations International Childrens' Fund (UNICEF) Created at the General Assembly's first session in 1945 to help children in the aftermath of World War II, it now provides basic health care and aid worldwide.
Food and Agriculture Organization (FAO) Aims to raise living standards and nutrition levels in rural areas by improving food production and distribution.
United Nations Educational, Scientific and Cultural Organization (UNESCO) Promotes international co-operation through broader and better education.
World Health Organization (WHO) Promotes and provides for better health care, public and environmental health and medical research.

United Nations agencies are involved in many aspects of international trade, safety and security:
International Maritime Organization (IMO) Promotes unity amongst merchant shipping, especially in regard to safety, marine pollution and standardization.
International Labour Organization (ILO) Seeks to improve labour conditions and promote productive employment to raise living standards.
World Meteorological Organization (WMO) Promotes co-operation in weather observation, reporting and forecasting.
World Trade Organization (WTO) On 1 January 1995 the WTO replaced GATT. It advocates a common code of conduct and its aim is the liberalization of world trade.
Disarmament Commission Considers and makes recommendations to the General Assembly on disarmament issues.
International Atomic Energy Agency (IAEA) Fosters development of peaceful uses for nuclear energy and establishes safety standards.

The **World Bank** comprises three United Nations agencies:
International Monetary Fund (IMF) Cultivates international monetary co-operation and expansion of trade.
International Bank for Reconstruction and Development (IBRD) Provides funds and technical assistance to developing countries.
International Finance Corporation (IFC) Encourages the growth of productive private enterprise in less developed countries.

Membership There are two independent states which are not members of the UN – Taiwan and Vatican City. Official languages are Chinese, English, French, Russian, Spanish and Arabic.
Funding The UN regular budget for 2002 was US $1.3 billion. Contributions are assessed by the members' ability to pay, with the maximum 22% of the total (USA's share), the minimum 0.01%. The 15-country EU pays over 37% of the budget.
Peacekeeping The UN has been involved in 54 peacekeeping operations worldwide since 1948.

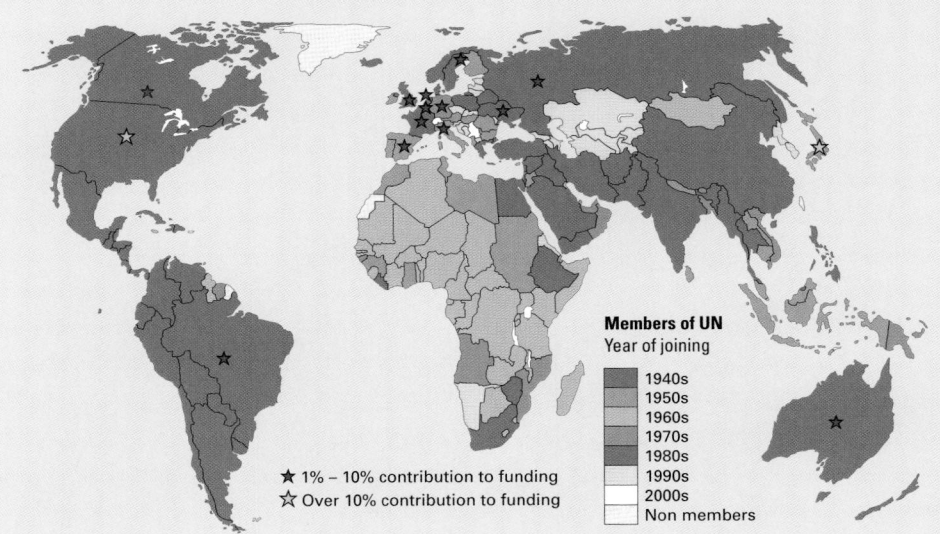

Members of UN
Year of joining

★ 1% – 10% contribution to funding
☆ Over 10% contribution to funding

- 1940s
- 1950s
- 1960s
- 1970s
- 1980s
- 1990s
- 2000s
- Non members

Military Spending

Military expenditure as a % of GDP (2000)

1. Eritrea	22.9%	14. Turkey	4.9%
2. Angola	21.2%	15. Singapore	4.8%
3. Saudi Arabia	11.6%	16. Zimbabwe	4.8%
4. Oman	9.7%	17. Sri Lanka	4.5%
5. Jordan	9.5%	18. Pakistan	4.5%
6. Ethiopia	9.4%	19. Djibouti	4.4%
7. Kuwait	8.2%	20. Armenia	4.4%
8. Israel	8.0%	21. Morocco	4.2%
9. Brunei	7.6%	22. Bahrain	4.0%
10. Syria	5.5%	23. Russia	4.0%
11. Burundi	5.4%	24. Turkmenistan	3.8%
12. Yemen	5.2%	25. Iran	3.8%
13. Greece	4.9%	26. Botswana	3.7%

It is worth noting that the total amount of expenditure varies considerably depending on the size of the economy, so that although the percentages show the importance given to military spending within each country, they give no idea as to the total expenditure. In 2001, for example, the USA spent a total of US $281 billion, Russia US $44 billion, France US $40 billion, Japan US $38.5 billion, and the UK US $37 billion. In 2001, the USA also provided the most military assistance worldwide, providing US $3.5 billion.

The period 1987–98 saw a decline in global military spending which generated what the United Nations Development Programme termed a 'peace dividend'. Between 1998–2001, however, global expenditure increased by 7.4%. Unfortunately, there is no clear link between reduced military spending and enhanced expenditure on human development. Moreover, the poorest regions of the world (notably sub-Saharan Africa) failed to contain their military spending and, in some cases, it increased.

International Organizations

OAS · EFTA · EU · AU · COLOMBO PLAN

★ G8

OECD · ACP · OPEC · CIS

NATO · LAIA · ARAB LEAGUE · COMMONWEALTH · ASEAN

ACP African-Caribbean-Pacific (formed in 1963). Members enjoy economic ties with the EU.
ARAB LEAGUE (1945) Aims to promote economic, social, political and military co-operation.
ASEAN Association of South-east Asian Nations (formed in 1967). Cambodia joined in 1999.
AU The African Union was set up in 2002, taking over from the Organization of African Unity (1963). It has 53 members. Working languages are Arabic, English, French and Portuguese.
CIS The Commonwealth of Independent States (formed in 1991) comprises the countries of the former Soviet Union except for Estonia, Latvia and Lithuania.
COLOMBO PLAN (formed in 1951) Its 25 members aim to promote economic and social development in Asia and the Pacific.
COMMONWEALTH The Commonwealth of Nations evolved from the British Empire; it comprises 16 nations recognizing the British monarch as head of state, 32 republics and 5 indigenous monarchies, giving a total of 53. Nigeria was suspended in 1995, but reinstated in 1999.
EFTA European Free Trade Organization (founded 1960). Since Austria, Finland, Portugal and Sweden left to join the EU, it has four members: Iceland, Liechtenstein, Norway and Switzerland.
EU The European Union evolved from the European Community (EC) in 1993. The original body, the European Coal and Steel Community (ECSC), was created in 1951 following the signing of the Treaty of Paris. The 15 members of the EU – Austria, Belgium, Denmark, Finland, France, Germany, Greece, Ireland, Italy, Luxembourg, Netherlands, Portugal, Spain, Sweden and the UK – aim to integrate economies and co-ordinate social development. In 2002, the EU invited ten countries – Cyprus, the Czech Republic, Estonia, Hungary, Latvia, Lithuania, Malta, Poland, the Slovak Republic and Slovenia – to join the organization on 1 May 2004.
LAIA The Latin American Integration Association (formed in 1980) superceded the Latin American Free Trade Association formed in 1961. Its aim is to promote freer regional trade.
NATO North Atlantic Treaty Organization (formed in 1949). It continues despite the winding up of the Warsaw Pact in 1991. The Czech Rep., Hungary and Poland were the latest to join in 1999.
OAS Organization of American States (formed in 1948). It aims to promote social and economic co-operation between countries in the developed North America and developing Latin America.
OECD Organization for Economic Co-operation and Development (formed in 1961). It comprises 29 major free-market economies. The 'G8' is its 'inner group' of leading industrial nations, comprising Canada, France, Germany, Italy, Japan, Russia, UK and the USA.
OPEC Organization of Petroleum Exporting Countries (formed in 1960). It controls about three-quarters of the world's oil supply. Gabon formally withdrew from OPEC in August 1996.

AGRICULTURE

For more information:
16 Climate regions
17 Temperature and precipitation
18 Water utilization
19 Natural vegetation
   Land use by continent
38 Division of employment

When harvests are bad and world grain reserves fall, an old debate is revived, namely whether the population explosion will cause major food crises in the 21st century.

Experts estimate that 3 billion tonnes of cereals will be needed to feed the world's population in 25 years' time, as compared with 1.9 billion tonnes at present. To expand food production to this extent, some argue, will place great strain on the environment.

Other experts argue that there should be no food crises. World grain production tripled between 1950 and 1990, largely as a result of the Green Revolution, during which genetically improved, high-yield varieties of maize, rice and wheat, the world's three leading staple crops, were developed. These new varieties have helped many developing countries to achieve food surpluses and prevent widespread starvation. However, some people oppose the use of genetically modified crops. In 2002, with severe droughts causing starvation, Zambia and Zimbabwe refused large maize donations from the USA because they might be genetically modified.

The only region of the world which seems likely to suffer food shortages in the 21st century is sub-Saharan Africa, where in the late 1990s the average daily calorie intake was 6% less than what was needed and where the population is expected to double in 20 years. Improved land management and a huge increase in global trade, especially in food distribution, is necessary if sub-Saharan Africans are not to go hungry.

The development of agriculture more than 10,000 years ago transformed human existence more than any other major advance. By supporting larger populations, it led to the growth of early civilizations and later it sustained people in the industrial cities which sprang up in the 19th century.

Today, agricultural production varies a great deal between the developed world, where it is highly mechanized and employs few people, such as 2% of the workforce in the United States, and the developing world, such as sub-Saharan Africa, where it employs 66% of the workforce. Many Africans are engaged in subsistence farming, providing the basic needs of their families but not contributing to the national economy. Much of Africa also suffers from economic mismanagement, as well as civil war and corruption.

Political problems have also affected food production in other parts of the world. The former USSR had much excellent farmland, but the failure of the collectives and state farms to maintain sufficiently high levels of production helped to bring about the collapse of Communism.

Farmers are under great pressure not only to maintain high levels of production but to increase them. However, the cultivation of marginal areas is one of the prime causes of soil erosion and desertification.

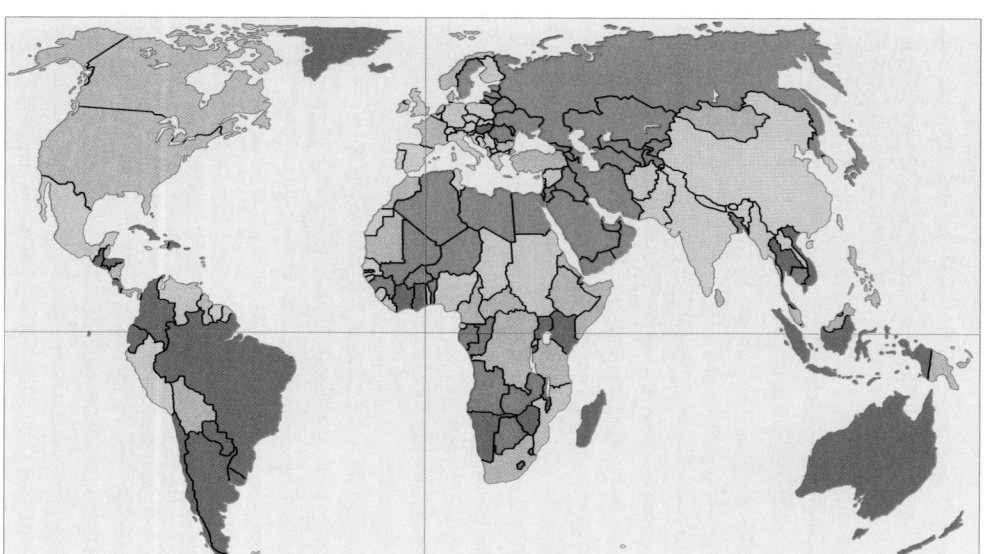

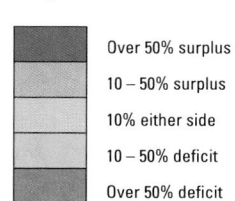

Self-sufficiency in Food

Balance of trade in food products as a percentage of total trade in food products – S.I.T.C. Classes 0, 1 and 4 (latest available year)

- Over 50% surplus
- 10 – 50% surplus
- 10% either side
- 10 – 50% deficit
- Over 50% deficit

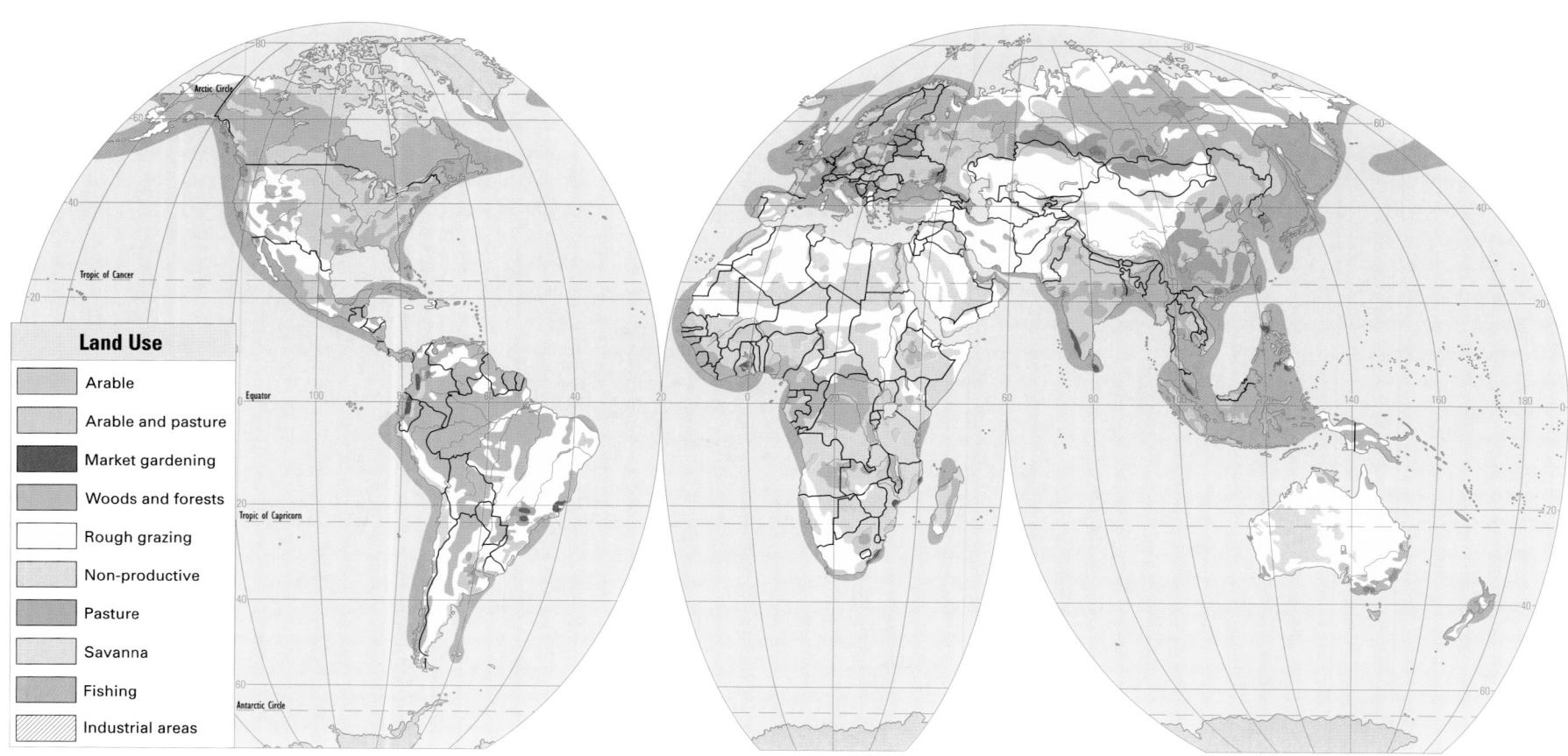

Land Use

- Arable
- Arable and pasture
- Market gardening
- Woods and forests
- Rough grazing
- Non-productive
- Pasture
- Savanna
- Fishing
- Industrial areas

Staple Crops

Wheat: Grown in a range of climates, with most varieties – including the highest-quality bread wheats – requiring temperate conditions. Mainly used in baking, it is also used for pasta and breakfast cereals.

China 18.9% | India 12.7% | USA 11.0% | France 5.7% | Russia 5.1% | Canada 4.6%

World total (2000): 576,317,000 tonnes

Maize: Originating in the New World and still an important human food in Africa and Latin America, in the developed world it is processed into breakfast cereals, oil, starches and adhesives. It is also used for animal feed.

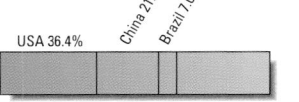

USA 36.4% | China 21.8% | Brazil 7.0%

World total (2000): 590,791,000 tonnes

Oats: Most widely used to feed livestock, but eaten by humans as oatmeal or porridge. Oats have a beneficial effect on the cardiovascular system, and human consumption is likely to increase.

Russia 29.7% | Canada 9.9% | USA 8.2% | Australia 6.7% | Germany 5.6%

World total (2000): 25,953,000 tonnes

Millet: The name covers a number of small-grained cereals, members of the grass family with a short growing season. Used to produce flour, meal and animal feed, and fermented to make beer, especially in Africa.

India 33.2% | Nigeria 18.3% | China 16.1% | Niger 6.4%

World total (2000): 27,255,000 tonnes

Rice: Thrives on the high humidity and temperatures of the Far East, where it is the traditional staple food of half the human race. Usually grown standing in water, rice responds well to continuous cultivation, with three or four crops annually.

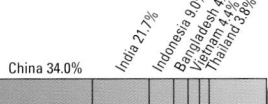

China 34.0% | India 21.7% | Indonesia 9.1% | Bangladesh 9.0% | Vietnam 4.4% | Thailand 3.6%

World total (2000): 598,852,000 tonnes

Potatoes: The most important of the edible tubers, potatoes grow in well-watered, temperate areas. Weight for weight less nutritious than grain, they are a human staple as well as an important animal feed.

China 16.0% | Russia 14.0% | Poland 8.7% | USA 6.3% | Ukraine 5.2%

World total (2000): 311,288,000 tonnes

Soya: Beans from soya bushes (soybeans) are very high (30–40%) in protein. Most are processed into oil and proprietary protein foods. Consumption since 1950 has tripled, mainly due to the health-conscious developed world.

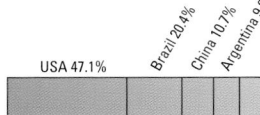

USA 47.1% | Brazil 20.4% | China 10.7% | Argentina 9.6%

World total (2000): 161,993,000 tonnes

Cassava: A tropical shrub that needs high rainfall (over 1,000 mm annually) and a 10–30 month growing season to produce its large, edible tubers. Used as flour by humans, as cattle feed and in industrial starches.

Nigeria 19.2% | Brazil 15.6% | Thailand 11.1% | Congo (D.R.) 10.7% | Indonesia 9.4% | Ghana 4.2%

World total (2000): 172,737,000 tonnes

Sugars

Sugar cane: Confined to tropical regions, cane sugar accounts for the bulk of international trade in sugar. Most is produced as a foodstuff, but some countries, notably Brazil and South Africa, distil sugar cane to make motor fuels.

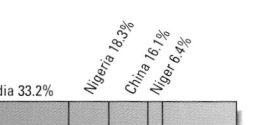

Brazil 26.0% | India 22.2% | China 6.0% | Thailand 5.0% | Pakistan 4.0% | Mexico 3.6%

World total (2000): 1,278,093,000 tonnes

Sugar beet: Closely related to the beetroot, sugar beet's yield after processing is indistinguishable from cane sugar. It is replacing sugar-cane imports in Europe, to the detriment of the developing countries that rely on it as a major cash crop.

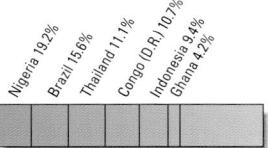

France 11.5% | Ukraine 11.2% | Germany 9.8% | USA 9.6% | Italy 7.2% | Poland 5.0% | Turkey 4.2%

World total (2000): 244,780,000 tonnes

Cereals are grasses with starchy, edible seeds; every important civilization has depended on them as a source of food. The major cereal grains contain about 10% protein and 75% carbohydrate. Grain contributes more than any other group of foods to the energy and protein content of the human diet. Starchy tuber crops or root crops are second in importance after cereals as staple foods; easily cultivated, they provide high yields for little effort.

Food and Population

Comparison of food production and population by continent
The left column indicates the % of world food production and the right shows population in proportion.

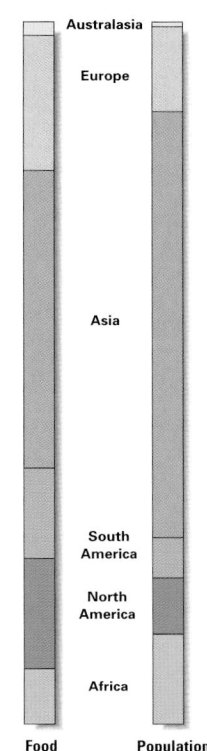

Australasia
Europe
Asia
South America
North America
Africa

Food | Population

Agricultural Population

Percentage of the total population dependent on agriculture for their livelihood (2000)

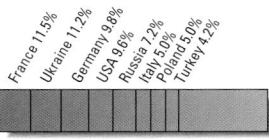

- Over 75% dependent
- 50 – 75% dependent
- 25 – 50% dependent
- 10 – 25% dependent
- Under 10% dependent

Top 5 countries

Bhutan 93.7%
Nepal 93.0%
Burkina Faso 92.3%
Burundi 90.4%
Rwanda 90.3%

Bottom 5 countries

Singapore 0.1%
Brunei 0.7%
Bahrain 1.0%
Kuwait 1.1%
Qatar 1.3%

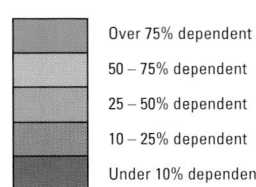

Animal Products

Traditionally, food animals subsisted on land unsuitable for cultivation, supporting agricultural production with their fertilizing dung. But free-ranging animals grow slowly and yield less meat than those more intensively reared; the demands of urban markets in the developed world have encouraged the growth of factory-like production methods. A large proportion of staple crops, especially cereals, are fed to animals, an inefficient way to produce protein but one likely to continue as long as people value meat and dairy products in their diet.

Cheese: Least perishable of all dairy products, cheese is milk fermented with selected bacterial strains to produce a foodstuff with a potentially immense range of flavours and textures. The vast majority of cheeses are made from cow's milk, although sheep and goat cheeses are highly prized.

USA 23.5% | France 10.8% | Germany 9.6% | Italy 6.0% | Netherlands 4.6%

World total (2000): 16,045,000 tonnes

Beef and Veal: Most beef and veal is reared for home markets, and the top five producers are also the biggest consumers. The USA produces nearly a quarter of the world's beef and eats even more.

USA 21.7% | Brazil 8.6% | China 8.5% | Russia 5.3% | Argentina 4.6% | France 3.6%

World total (2000): 57,170,000 tonnes

Milk: Many human groups, including most Asians, find raw milk indigestible after infancy, and it is often only the starting point for other dairy products such as butter, cheese and yoghurt. Most world production comes from cows, but sheep's milk and goats' milk are also important.

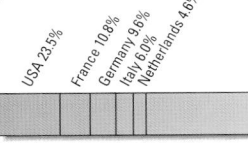

USA 15.2% | Russia 8.4% | India 6.9% | Germany 6.0% | France 5.5% | Ukraine 5.0% | Brazil 3.7%

World total (2000): 2,504,000 tonnes

Butter: A traditional source of vitamin A as well as calories, butter has lost much popularity in the developed world for health reasons, although it remains a valuable food. Most butter from India, the world's largest producer, is clarified into ghee, which has religious as well as nutritional importance.

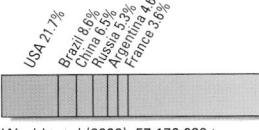

India 19.0% | USA 8.9% | Germany 7.2% | France 7.1% | Russia 6.2% | Pakistan 5.5% | New Zealand 4.6%

World total (2000): 7,049,000 tonnes

Pork: Although pork is forbidden to many millions, notably Muslims, on religious grounds, more is produced than any other meat in the world, mainly because it is the cheapest. It accounts for about 90% of China's meat output, although per capita meat consumption is relatively low.

China 45.1% | USA 9.7% | France 4.9% | Germany 4.3% | Russia 3.4%

World total (2000): 90,909,000 tonnes

Crisis in Africa

Each year 40 million people, almost half of whom are children, die from starvation and related diseases. In 2000, 600 million people worldwide were estimated to be suffering from malnutrition. Africa suffers from more natural disasters than any other continent; pests such as locusts destroy crops, and tropical storms and floods ruin harvests. Famines periodically affect parts of Africa causing widespread hardship, even though enough food is produced worldwide to feed everyone. One major phenomenon that affects the weather over tropical and subtropical regions areas around the world is called El Niño. It occurs when there is unusual warming in the tropical eastern Pacific Ocean, causing changes in the wind and pressure systems. Normal years are called La Niña (*see page 8, The El Niño Phenomenon*). El Niño years included 1973–4, 1982–3, 1986–7, 1992, 1997–8, and 2002.

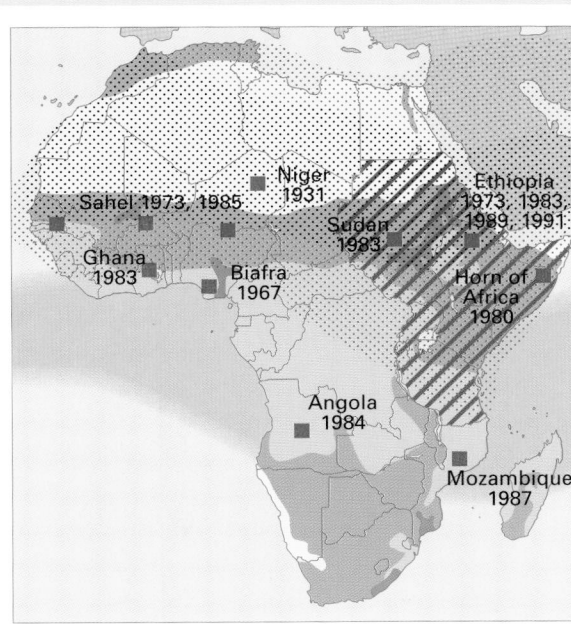

Ocean areas affected by El Niño and La Niña temperature fluctuations

Crop Failure

- Areas liable to periodic crop failure
- Areas where crop failures are rare
- Desert

Desert Locusts

- Areas liable to invasions by desert locusts
- Areas affected by 1993 swarm of desert locusts

Countries affected by four years of continuous drought 1996–2000

Areas liable to flood

■ Major famines since 1900 (with dates)

CARTOGRAPHY BY PHILIP'S. COPYRIGHT PHILIP'S

ENERGY

For more information:
22 Carbon dioxide
   Greenhouse power
   CO$_2$ producers
   Global warming
23 Water pollution
41 World shipping

Every year, the world's energy consumption is about the equivalent of what would come from burning 9,000 million tonnes of oil (9,000 MtOe) – a 20-fold increase since 1850. Two-fifths of this total actually comes from burning oil and most of the rest comes from coal and natural gas.

The oil crises in the 1970s precipitated concern over dependence on finite fossil fuels as the primary source of energy, and growing environmental awareness has added impetus to the search for alternative energy resources.

Fossil fuel combustion damages the environment through the release of gases and particulate matter, but two other major sources of energy, hydroelectricity and nuclear power, are also controversial. For example, hydroelectricity production involves flooding large areas to create reservoirs, while nuclear power stations generate dangerous radioactive wastes and can cause major disasters. Significantly, by 2002, five European countries – Belgium, Germany, the Netherlands, Spain and Sweden – had plans to

phase out the use of nuclear energy.

Alternative energy resources may soon provide a much larger proportion of the world's energy consumption, especially in developing countries. Solar and wind energy may become important in such countries as China and India, while tidal, wave and geothermal energy all have potential in appropriate areas. Experts have calculated that solar power could, in theory, supply between five and ten times the present electricity supply of developing countries.

Conversions

For historical reasons, oil is still traded in barrels. The weight and volume equivalents shown below are all based on average density 'Arabian light' crude oil, and should be considered approximate.

The energy equivalents given for a tonne of oil are also somewhat imprecise: oil and coal of different qualities will have varying energy contents, a fact usually reflected in their price on world markets.

1 barrel:
0.136 tonnes
159 litres
35 Imperial gallons
42 US gallons

1 tonne:
7.33 barrels
1,185 litres
256 Imperial gallons
261 US gallons

1 tonne oil:
1.5 tonnes hard coal
3.0 tonnes lignite
12,000 kWh

1 gallon (Imperial):
227,42 cubic inches
1.201 US gallons
4,546 litres

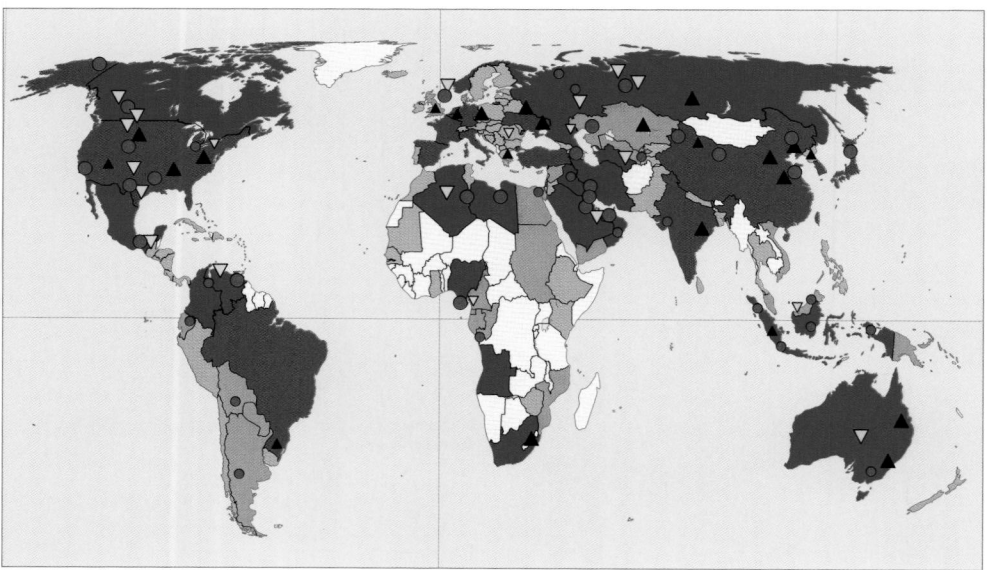

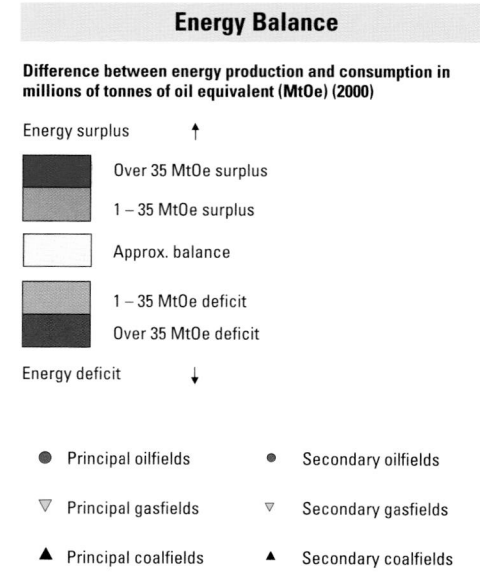

Energy Balance

Difference between energy production and consumption in millions of tonnes of oil equivalent (MtOe) (2000)

Energy surplus ↑

- Over 35 MtOe surplus
- 1 – 35 MtOe surplus
- Approx. balance
- 1 – 35 MtOe deficit
- Over 35 MtOe deficit

Energy deficit ↓

- ● Principal oilfields
- ● Secondary oilfields
- ▽ Principal gasfields
- ▽ Secondary gasfields
- ▲ Principal coalfields
- ▲ Secondary coalfields

World Energy Consumption

Energy consumed by world regions, measured in million tonnes of oil equivalent in 2001. Total world consumption was 9,125 MtOe. Only energy from oil, gas, coal, nuclear and hydroelectric sources are included. Excluded are fuels such as wood, peat, animal waste, wind, solar and geothermal which, though important in some countries, are unreliably documented in terms of consumption statistics.

Oil   Gas   Coal   Nuclear   Hydro

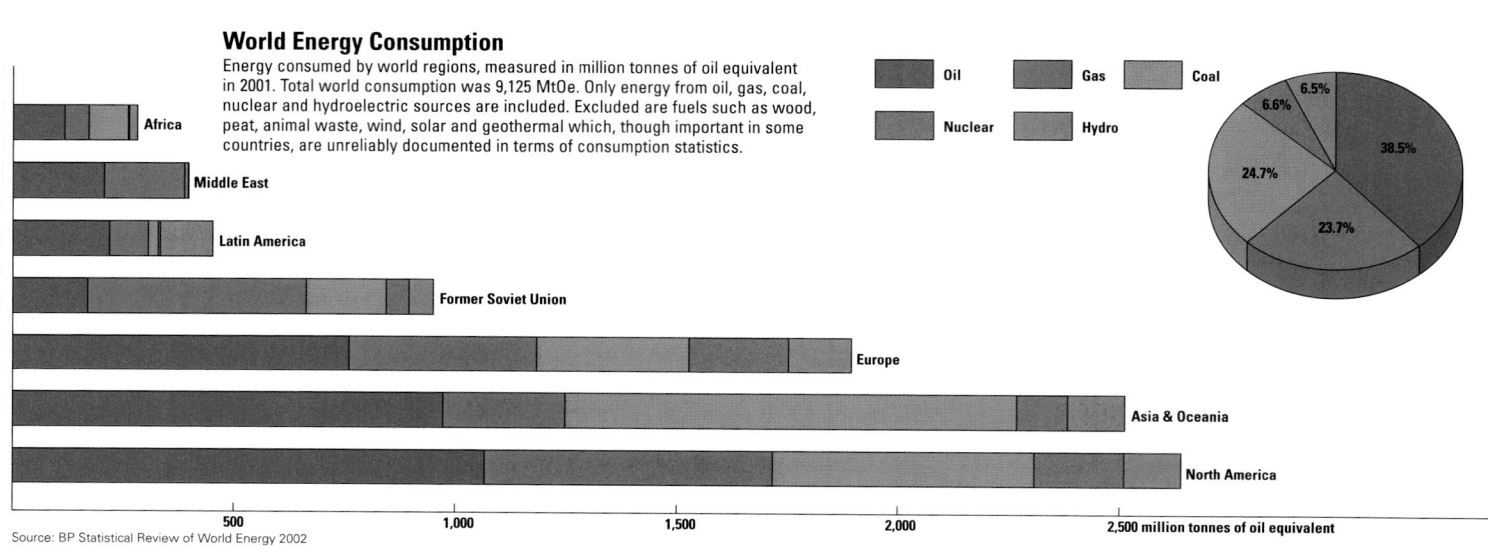

Source: BP Statistical Review of World Energy 2002

Africa
Middle East
Latin America
Former Soviet Union
Europe
Asia & Oceania
North America

500   1,000   1,500   2,000   2,500 million tonnes of oil equivalent

6.5%
6.6%
24.7%
38.5%
23.7%

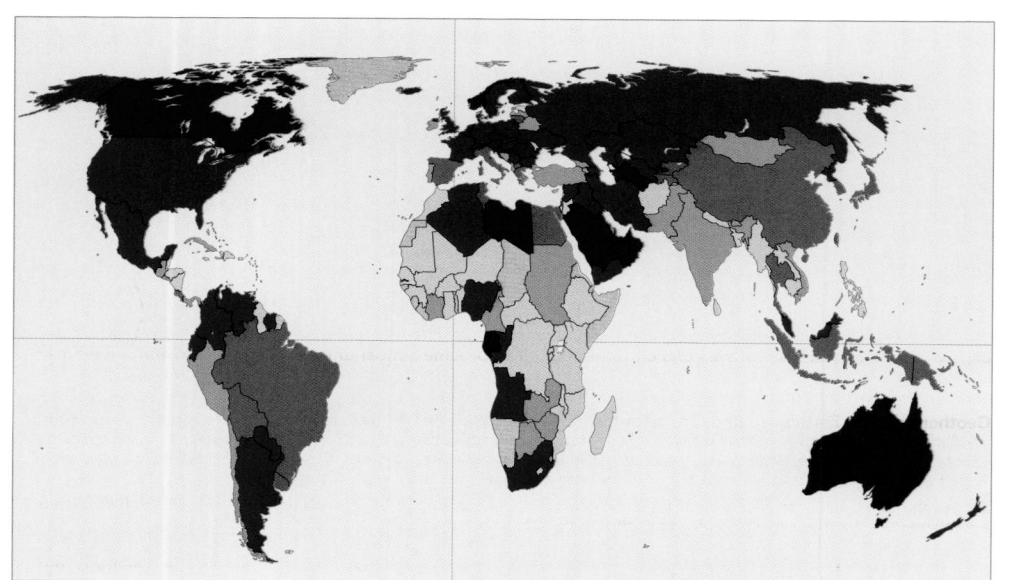

Energy Production

Energy production in tonnes of oil equivalent per capita (2000)

- Over 10
- 1 – 10
- 0.5 – 1
- 0.1 – 0.5
- Under 0.1
- No data available

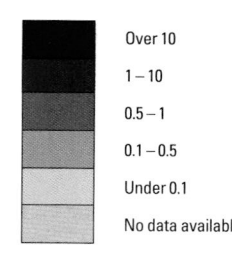

In developing countries traditional fuels are still very important. These so-called biomass fuels include wood, charcoal and dried dung. The pie-chart (*right*) highlights the importance of biomass in terms of energy consumption in Nigeria. Collecting fuelwood can be a time-consuming task, sometimes taking all day.

Nigeria

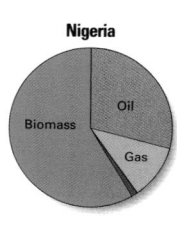

Oil
Gas
Biomass

Oil Movements

Major world movements of oil in millions of tonnes (2001)

1. Middle East to Asia (not China or Japan)	.316.7
2. Middle East to Japan	.208.8
3. Former Soviet Union to Europe	.181.2
4. Middle East to Europe	.176.2
5. Middle East to USA	.138.0
6. South and Central America to USA	.126.3
7. North Africa to Europe	.96.9
8. Canada to USA	.88.0
9. Mexico to USA	.70.8
10. West Africa to USA	.68.1
11. Europe to USA	.46.2
12. Middle East to Africa	.41.0
13. West Africa to Asia (not China or Japan)	.36.9
14. West Africa to Europe	.34.9
15. Middle East to China	.34.2
16. Asia (not China) to Japan	.34.2

Total world imports . . . . .2,159,300,000 tonnes

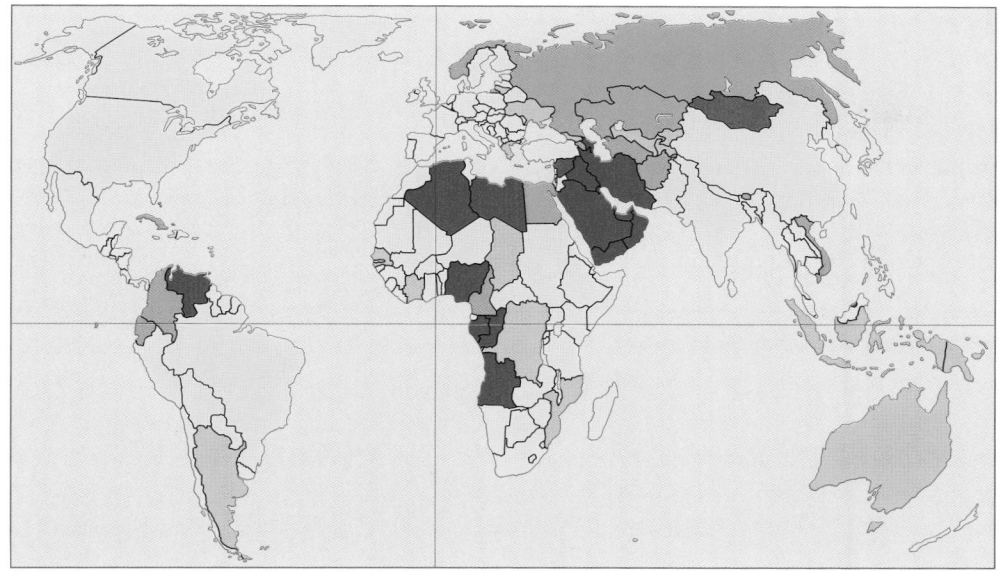

Fuel Exports

Fuels as a percentage of total value of exports (1999)

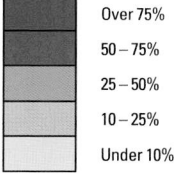

- Over 75%
- 50 – 75%
- 25 – 50%
- 10 – 25%
- Under 10%

In the 1970s, oil exports became a political issue when OPEC sought to increase the influence of developing countries in world affairs by raising oil prices and restricting production. But its power was short-lived, following a fall in demand for oil in the 1980s, due to an increase in energy efficiency and development of alternative resources.

World Coal Reserves

World coal reserves (including lignite) by region and country, thousand million tonnes (2001)

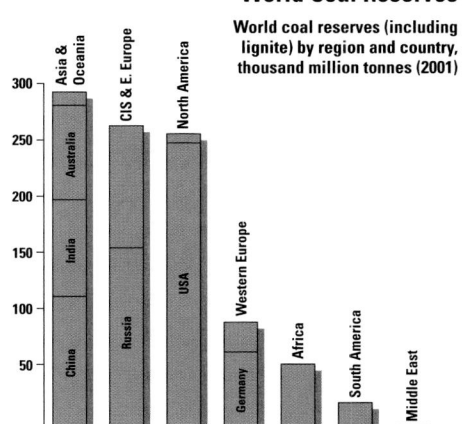

World Gas Reserves

World natural gas reserves by region and country, thousand million tonnes of oil equivalent (2001)

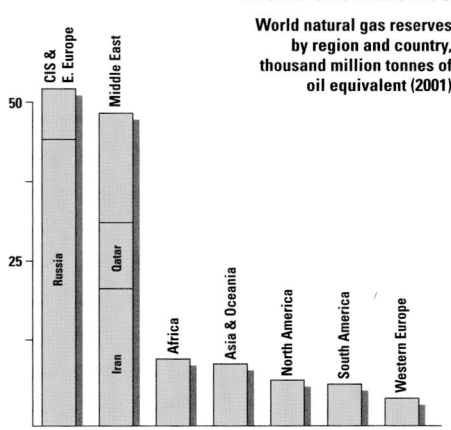

World Oil Reserves

World oil reserves by region and country, thousand million tonnes (2001)

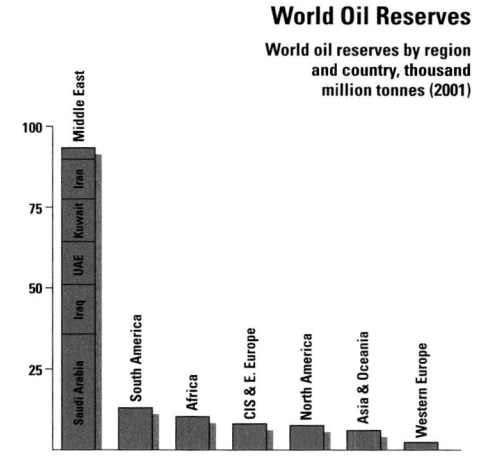

Nuclear Power

Major producers by percentage of world total (2000) and by percentage of domestic electricity generation (1999)

Country	% of world total production	Country	% of nuclear as proportion of domestic electricity
1. USA	.30.5%	1. Lithuania	.76.1%
2. France	.15.7%	2. France	.75.1%
3. Japan	.12.6%	3. Belgium	.58.2%
4. Germany	.6.7%	4. Slovak Rep.	.47.5%
5. Russia	.4.6%	5. Sweden	.44.2%
6. South Korea	.4.1%	6. Ukraine	.41.6%
7. UK	.3.8%	7. Bulgaria	.41.4%
8. Canada	.2.9%	8. South Korea	.39.1%
9. Ukraine	.2.8%	9. Hungary	.38.1%
= Sweden	.2.8%	10. Slovenia	.35.9%

Although the 1980s were a bad time for the nuclear power industry (major projects ran over budget and fears of long-term environmental damage were heavily reinforced by the 1986 disaster at Chernobyl), the industry picked up in the early 1990s. Whilst the number of reactors is still increasing, however, orders for new plants have shrunk. In 1997, the Swedish government began to decommission the country's 12 nuclear power plants.

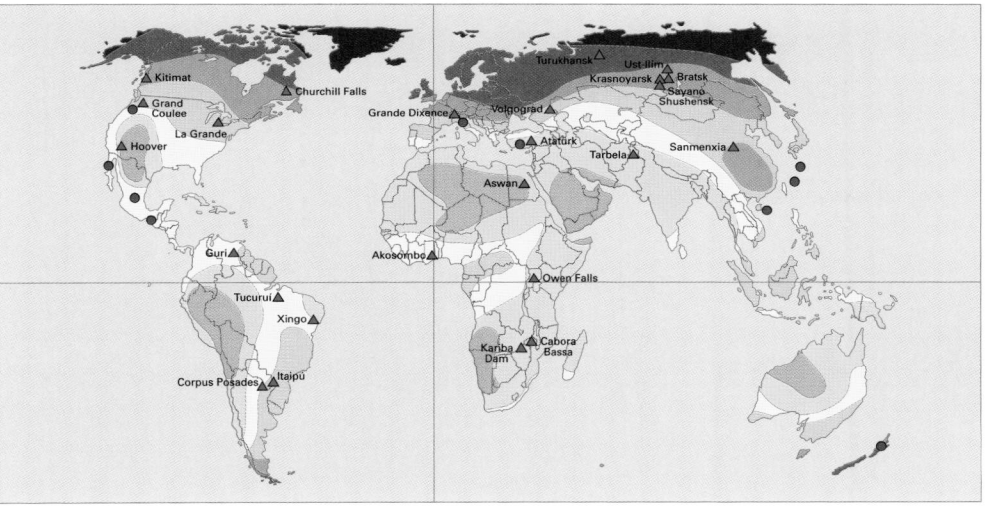

Renewable Energy

Average annual solar irradiance in kWh/m², with selected major hydroelectric and geothermal power stations

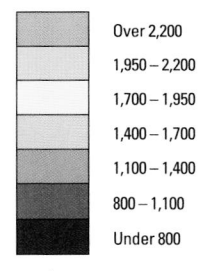

- Over 2,200
- 1,950 – 2,200
- 1,700 – 1,950
- 1,400 – 1,700
- 1,100 – 1,400
- 800 – 1,100
- Under 800

▲ Hydroelectric plants

● Geothermal plants

Hydroelectricity

Major producers by percentage of world total (2000) and by percentage of domestic electricity generation (1999)

Country	% of world total production	Country	% of hydroelectric as proportion of domestic electricity
1. Canada	.13.1%	1. Bhutan	.99.9%
2. USA	.12.0%	2. Paraguay	.99.8%
3. Brazil	.11.1%	= Zambia	.99.8%
4. China	.8.5%	4. Norway	.99.1%
5. Russia	.6.1%	5. Ethiopia	.98.1%
6. Norway	.4.6%	6. Congo (Rep. Dem.)	.97.9%
7. Japan	.3.3%	7. Tajikistan	.97.8%
8. India	.3.1%	8. Cameroon	.97.3%
9. France	.2.8%	9. Albania	.97.2%
10. Sweden	.2.7%	= Laos	.97.2%

Countries heavily reliant on hydroelectricity are usually small and non-industrial: a high proportion of hydroelectric power more often reflects a modest energy budget than vast hydroelectric resources. The USA, for instance, produces only 8.5% of its power requirements from hydroelectricity; yet that 8.5% amounts to more than three times the hydropower generated by most of Africa.

Alternative Energy Resources

Solar: Each year the Sun bestows upon the Earth almost a million times as much energy as is locked up in all the planet's oil reserves, but only an insignificant fraction is trapped and used commercially. In a few installations around the world, mirrors focus the Sun's rays on to boilers, whose steam generates electricity by spinning turbines.

Wind: Caused by uneven heating of the Earth, winds are themselves a form of solar energy. Windmills have been long used for wind power; recent models, often arranged in banks on wind-swept high ground or off coastlines, usually generate electricity. Wind-power figures are given in the table (*right*) – it is the world's fastest growing energy source. In 2002, Germany, the USA, Spain and Denmark produced nearly 16,000 MW.

Tidal: The energy from tides is potentially enormous, although only a few installations have so far been built to exploit it. In theory at least, waves and currents could also provide almost unimaginable power, and the thermal differences in the ocean depths are another huge well of potential energy. But work on extracting it is still at the experimental stage.

Geothermal: The Earth's temperature rises by 1°C for every 30 metres descent, with much steeper temperature gradients in geologically active areas. El Salvador, for example, produces 39% of its electricity from geothermal power stations, whilst the USA is the world's leading producer. Some of the oldest and most successful applications are in Iceland, where 86% of all households are heated by geothermal energy.

Biomass: The oldest of human fuels ranges from animal dung, still burned in cooking fires in much of North Africa and elsewhere, to sugar-cane plantations feeding high-technology distilleries to produce ethanol for motor-vehicle engines. In Brazil and South Africa, plant ethanol provides up to 25% of motor fuel. Throughout the developing world, most biomass energy comes from firewood: although accurate figures are impossible to obtain, it may yield as much as 10% of the world's total energy consumption.

Wind Power

World wind energy generating capacity, in megawatts

1980	.10
1982	.90
1984	.600
1986	.1,270
1988	.1,580
1989	.1,730
1990	.1,930
1991	.2,170
1992	.2,510
1993	.3,050
1994	.3,710
1995	.4,820
1996	.6,115
1997	.7,630
1998	.9,600

Wind power is the fastest growing source of energy. Between 1998 and 2002, world production more than doubled.

Minerals

For more information:
10 Geology
39 Patterns of production
41 World shipping

The use of metals played a vital part in the evolving technologies of early peoples. Copper first came into use around 10,000 years ago, bronze about 5,000 years ago, and iron 3,300 years ago. In the early stages of the Industrial Revolution, the location of coal, iron ore and water power usually determined the location of new industries. But due to continuing improvements in transport, including oil pipelines, industries can now be located almost anywhere.

Minerals are distributed unevenly and some industrial countries, lacking their own mineral resources, import most of the raw materials they need. Some imports come from mineral-rich countries, such as Australia, but others come from developing countries, especially in Africa and South America.

Most of the developing countries export unprocessed ores, losing out on the much higher revenues gained from exporting metals.

Most minerals come from land deposits, because undersea deposits, with the exception of oil reserves under the continental shelves, have been regarded as inaccessible. But shortages of terrestrial minerals may one day encourage exploitation of the ocean floor.

Mineral Exports

Exports of mine and quarry products as a percentage of total value of exports (2000)

- Over 60%
- 30 – 60%
- 15 – 30%
- 1 – 15%
- Under 1%
- No data available

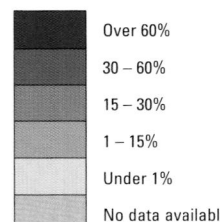

Uranium

In its pure state, uranium is an immensely heavy, white metal; but although spent uranium is employed as projectiles in anti-missile cannons, where its mass ensures a lethal punch, its main use is as a fuel in nuclear reactors, and in nuclear weaponry. Uranium is very scarce: the main source is the rare ore pitchblende, which itself contains only 0.2% uranium oxide. Only a minute fraction of that is the radioactive U^{235} isotope, though so-called breeder reactors can transmute the more common U^{238} into highly radioactive plutonium.

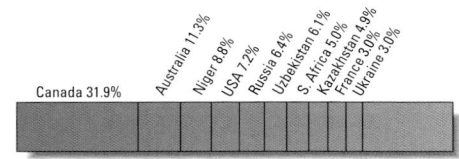

Canada 31.9% | Australia 11.3% | Niger 9.8% | USA 7.2% | Russia 6.4% | Uzbekistan 6.1% | S. Africa 5.0% | Kazakhstan 4.9% | France 3.0% | Ukraine 3.0%

World total (2000): 34,746 tonnes

Metals

* Figures for aluminium are for refined metal; all other figures refer to ore production.

The world's leading producers of aluminium ore (bauxite) in 2000 were as follows:

1. Australia 38.6%
2. Guinea 11.8%
3. Brazil 10.4%
4. Jamaica 8.8%
5. China 6.3%
6. India 4.9%
7. Venezuela 3.5%
8. Suriname 3.1%
9. Russia 3.1%
10. Guyana 2.6%

The figures shown above are in stark contrast to the figures showing aluminium production on the right. Australia, for example, produces 38.6% of the world's bauxite but only 5.9% of the aluminium metal. Guinea and Jamaica account for over 20% of the bauxite mined but have no smelters and export virtually all of it to countries like the USA and Canada.

Diamond

Most of the world's diamond is found in kimberlite, or 'blue ground', a basic peridotite rock; erosion may wash the diamond from its kimberlite matrix and deposit it with sand or gravel on river beds. Only a small proportion of the world's diamond, the most flawless, is cut into gemstones – 'diamonds'; most is used in industry, where the material's remarkable hardness and abrasion resistance finds a use in cutting tools, drills and dies. Australia produced 31.6% of the world's total in 2000. The other main producers are the Democratic Republic of the Congo (24.7%), Russia (20%), South Africa (10.5%) and Botswana (8.5%). Natural diamonds now account for less than 10% of all industrial diamond output. Synthetic diamond production in centres such as Ireland, Japan, Russia and the USA far exceeds it.

Aluminium: Produced mainly from its oxide, bauxite, which yields 25% of its weight in aluminium. The cost of refining and production is often too high for producer-countries to bear, so bauxite is largely exported. Lightweight and corrosion resistant, aluminium alloys are widely used in aircraft, vehicles, cans and packaging.

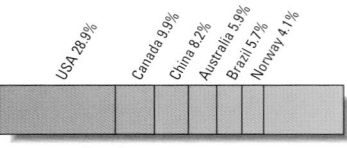

USA 28.9% | Canada 9.9% | China 8.2% | Australia 5.9% | Brazil 5.7% | Norway 4.1%

World total (2000): 23,900,000 tonnes *

Lead: A soft metal, obtained mainly from galena (lead sulphide), which occurs in veins associated with iron, zinc and silver sulphides. Its use in vehicle batteries accounts for the USA's prime consumer status; lead is also made into sheeting and piping. Its use as an additive to paints and petrol is decreasing.

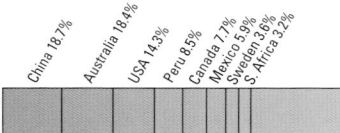

China 18.7% | Australia 18.4% | USA 14.3% | Peru 8.5% | Canada 7.7% | Mexico 5.9% | Sweden 3.6% | S. Africa 2.9%

World total (2000): 2,980,000 tonnes *

Tin: Soft, pliable and non-toxic, used to coat 'tin' (tin-plated steel) cans, in the manufacture of foils and in alloys. The principal tin-bearing mineral is cassiterite (SnO_2), found in ore formed from molten rock. Producers and refiners were hit by a price collapse in 1991.

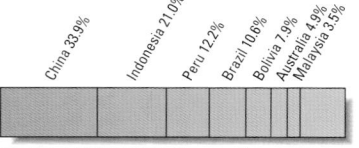

China 33.9% | Indonesia 21.0% | Peru 12.2% | Brazil 10.6% | Bolivia 7.9% | Australia 4.9% | Malaysia 3.5%

World total (2000): 200,000 tonnes *

Gold: Regarded for centuries as the most valuable metal in the world and used to make coins, gold is still recognized as the monetary standard. A soft metal, it is alloyed to make jewellery; the electronics industry values its corrosion resistance and conductivity.

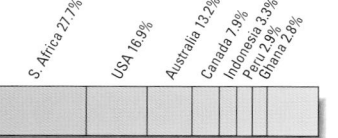

S. Africa 27.7% | USA 16.9% | Australia 13.2% | Canada 7.9% | Indonesia 3.3% | Peru 2.9% | Ghana 2.8%

World total (2000): 2,445 tonnes *

Copper: Derived from low-yielding sulphide ores, copper is an important export for several developing countries. An excellent conductor of heat and electricity, it forms part of most electrical items, and is used in the manufacture of brass and bronze. Major importers include Japan and Germany.

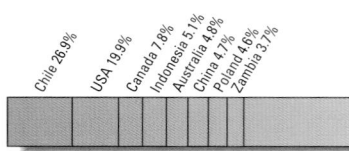

Chile 26.8% | USA 10.9% | Canada 7.8% | Indonesia 5.1% | Australia 4.8% | China 4.7% | Poland 4.6% | Zambia 3.7%

World total (2000): 12,900,000 tonnes *

Mercury: The only metal that is liquid at normal temperatures, most is derived from its sulphide, cinnabar, found only in small quantities in volcanic areas. Apart from its value in thermometers and other instruments, most mercury production is used in anti-fungal and anti-fouling preparations, and to make detonators.

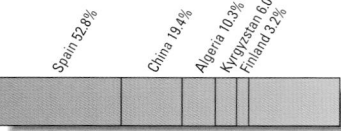

Spain 52.8% | China 19.4% | Algeria 10.3% | Kyrgyzstan 6.0% | Finland 3.2%

World total (2000): 1,800 tonnes *

Zinc: Often found in association with lead ores, zinc is highly resistant to corrosion, and about 40% of the refined metal is used to plate sheet steel, particularly vehicle bodies – a process known as galvanizing. Zinc is also used in dry batteries, paints and dyes.

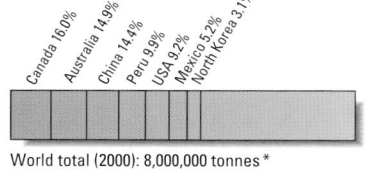

Canada 16.0% | Australia 14.9% | China 14.4% | Peru 9.9% | USA 9.2% | Mexico 5.2% | North Korea 3.1%

World total (2000): 8,000,000 tonnes *

Silver: Most silver comes from ores mined and processed for other metals (including lead and copper). Pure or alloyed with harder metals, it is used for jewellery and ornaments. Industrial use includes dentistry, electronics, photography and as a chemical catalyst.

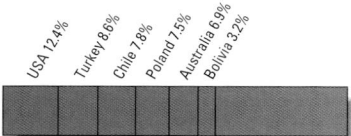

USA 12.4% | Turkey 8.6% | Chile 7.8% | Poland 7.5% | Australia 6.9% | Bolivia 3.2%

World total (2000): 17,900 tonnes *

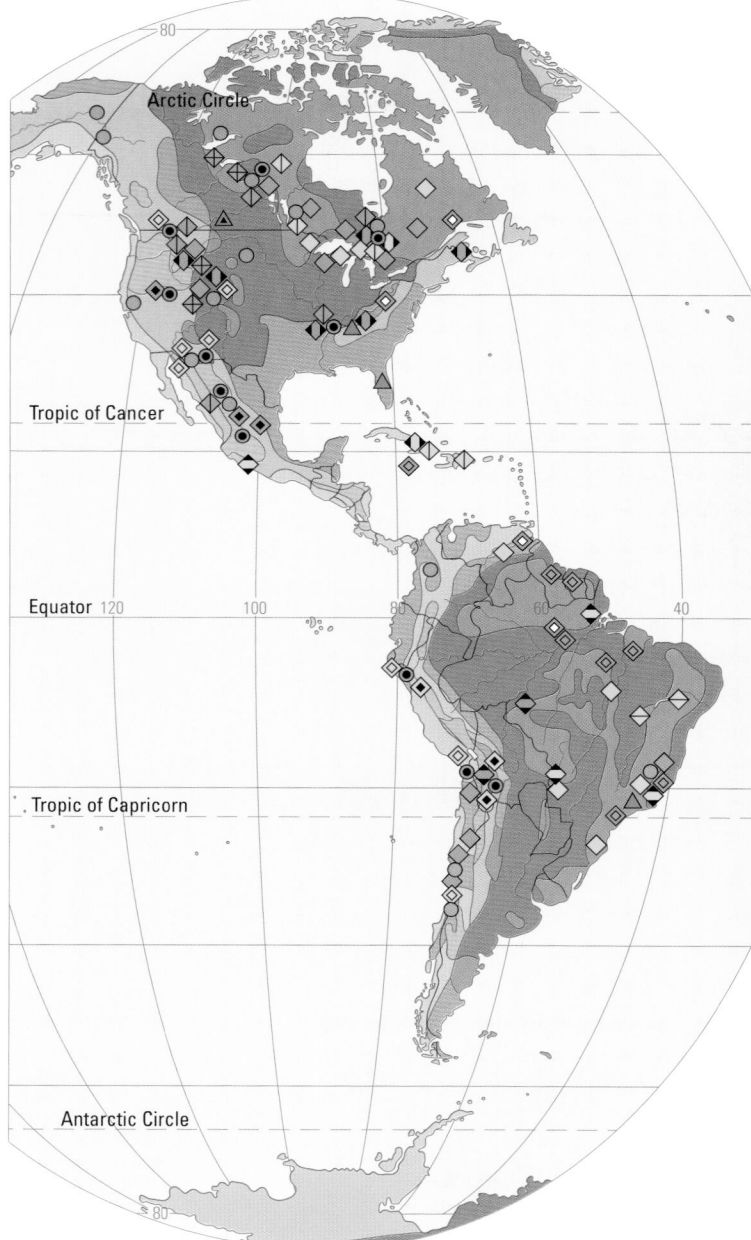

Strategic Minerals

Ever since the art of high-temperature smelting was discovered, some time in the second millennium BC, iron has been by far the most important metal known to man. The earliest iron ploughs transformed primitive agriculture and led to the first human population explosion, while iron weapons – or the lack of them – ensured the rise or fall of entire cultures.

Widely distributed around the world, iron ores usually contain 25–60% iron; blast furnaces process the raw product into pig-iron, which is then alloyed with carbon and other minerals to produce steels of various qualities. From the time of the Industrial Revolution, steel has been almost literally the backbone of modern civilization, the prime structural material on which all else is built.

Iron smelting usually developed close to the sources of ore and, later, to the coalfields that fuelled the furnaces. Today, most ore comes from a few richly-endowed locations where large-scale mining is possible. Iron and steel plants are generally built at coastal sites so that giant ore carriers, which account for a sizeable proportion of the world's merchant fleet, can easily discharge their cargoes.

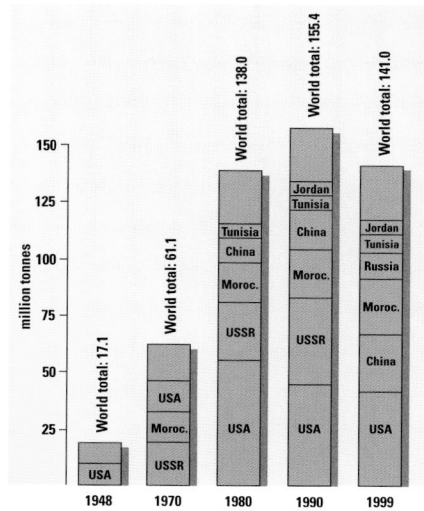

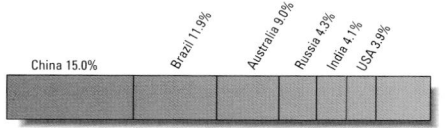

World total production of iron ore (2000): 1,010,000,000 tonnes

World production of phosphates in millions of tonnes (1999): Phosphate production is vital to the economies of several small countries. Nauru, for example, is heavily dependent on phosphate exports – the island has one of the world's richest deposits. In 1999, 500,000 tonnes were mined, employing 1,000 people. In Togo, earnings from phosphate exports have superseded all agricultural exports.

Percentage of total world phosphate production (1999)

1. USA	28.8%	7. Brazil	2.9%
2. China	17.8%	8. Israel	2.9%
3. Morocco	17.0%	9. South Africa	2.1%
4. Russia	7.9%	10. Syria	1.5%
5. Tunisia	5.7%	11. Senegal	1.3%
6. Jordan	4.3%	12. India	1.2%

World production of pig-iron (2000): All countries with an annual output of more than 1 million tonnes are shown

Total world production: 571 million tonnes

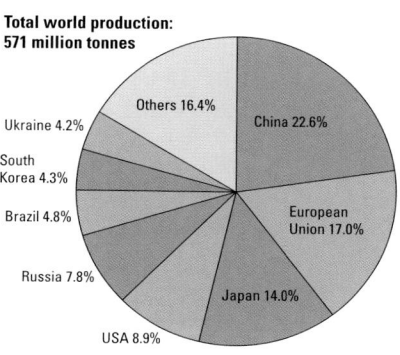

Manganese: In its pure state, manganese is a hard, brittle metal. Alloyed with chrome, iron and nickel, it produces abrasion-resistant steels; manganese-aluminium alloys are light but tough. Found in batteries and inks, manganese is also used in glass production. Manganese ores are frequently found in the same location as sedimentary iron ores. Pyrolusite (MnO_2) and psilomelane are the main economically-exploitable sources.

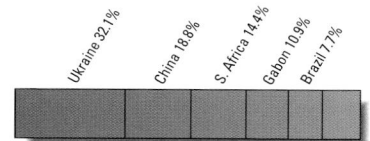

World total (2000): 7,450,000 tonnes (metal content)

Chromium: Most of the world's chromium production is alloyed with iron and other metals to produce steels with various different properties. Combined with iron, nickel, cobalt and tungsten, chromium produces an exceptionally hard steel, resistant to heat; chrome steels are used for many household items where utility must be matched with appearance – cutlery, for example. Chromium is also used in the production of refractory bricks, and its salts for tanning and dyeing leather and cloth.

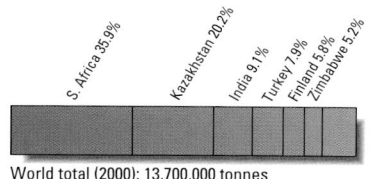

World total (2000): 13,700,000 tonnes

Nickel: Combined with chrome and iron, nickel produces stainless and high-strength steels; similar alloys go to make magnets and electrical heating elements. Nickel combined with copper is widely used to make coins; cupro-nickel alloy is very resistant to corrosion. Its ores yield only modest quantities of nickel – 0.5% to 3.0% – but also contain copper, iron and small amounts of precious metals. Japan, USA, UK, Germany and France are the principal importers.

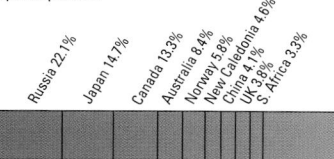

World total (2000): 1,230,000 tonnes

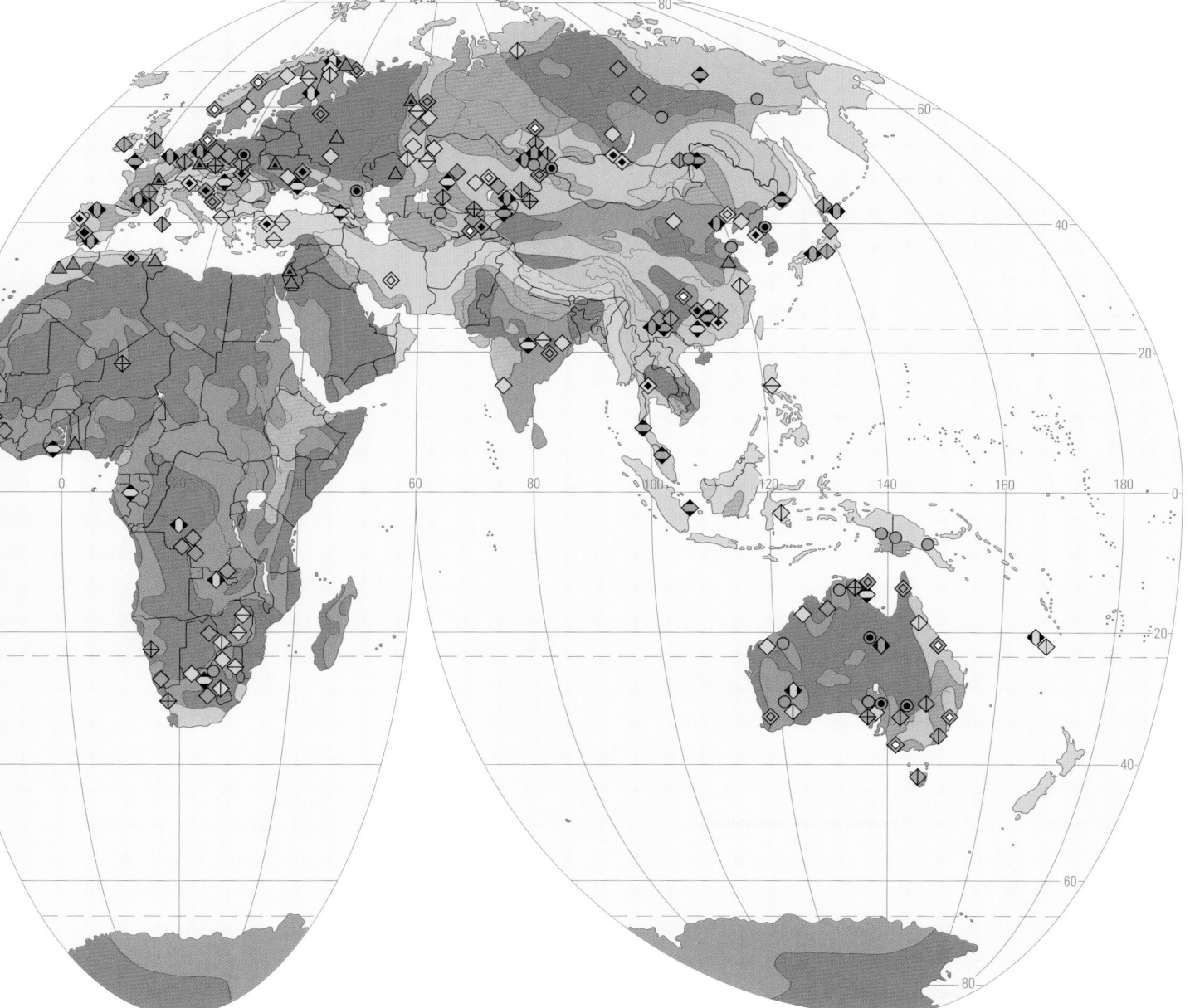

Distribution of Minerals

Structural Regions

- Pre-Cambrian shields
- Sedimentary cover on Pre-Cambrian shields
- Paleozoic (Caledonian and Hercynian) folding
- Sedimentary cover on Paleozoic folding
- Mesozoic folding
- Sedimentary cover on Mesozoic folding
- Cenozoic (Alpine) folding
- Sedimentary cover on Cenozoic folding
- Intensive Mesozoic and Cenozoic vulcanism

Distribution

Iron and ferro-alloys
- Chrome
- Cobalt
- Iron Ore
- Manganese
- Molybdenum
- Nickel Ore
- Tungsten

Non-ferrous metals
- Bauxite (Aluminium)
- Copper
- Lead
- Mercury
- Tin
- Zinc
- Uranium

Precious metals and stones
- Diamonds
- Gold
- Silver

Fertilizers
- Phosphates
- Potash

MANUFACTURING

For more information:
18 Water utilization
32 Land use and economy
36 Mineral production
37 Iron and ferro-alloys
40 Trading nations
 Major exports
 Traded products

The Industrial Revolution which began in Britain in the late 18th century, represented a major technological advance in the evolution of human society. It enabled a group of countries to become prosperous by replacing expensive human labour with increasingly sophisticated machinery. In economic terms, manufacturing is the transformation of raw materials, energy, labour and machines into finished goods, which have a higher value than the various elements used in production.

The economies of countries can be compared by reference to their per capita Gross National Products (or per capita GNPs), namely, the total value of goods and services produced in a country in a year, divided by the population.

The industrialized, or developed, countries accounted for 15% of the world's population in 2000 with an average per capita GNP of more than US $25,000. On the other hand, low-income developing countries, with small industrial sectors, accounted for 34% of the world's population. Their per capita GNPs are less than $755, with some as low as $200.

Kenya, with its low-income economy, had a per capita GNP in 2000 of US $350. Agriculture employs 19% of the people, industry 18% and services 64%. The main industries are the processing of agricultural imports and import substitution (making such necessities as cement, footwear and textiles). Heavy industry plays only a small part. By contrast, Germany had a per capita GNP in 2000 of $25,120. Agriculture employs only 2% of the population, with 30% in industry and 68% in services. Germany's industrial sector differs greatly from Kenya's, with its emphasis on vehicles, machinery, chemicals and electronics.

Since the 1970s, some former developing countries in eastern Asia achieved rapid economic growth through industrialization. Despite setbacks in the late 1990s, they demonstrated that a developing industrial sector can transform an economy, which starts off with certain advantages, such as low labour costs. But economic success also depends on such factors as education to provide skills, and regulations that attract foreign investors. China, whose economy grew by more than 9% per year between 1989 and 2002, satisfies many of these criteria, though its record on human rights leaves much to be desired.

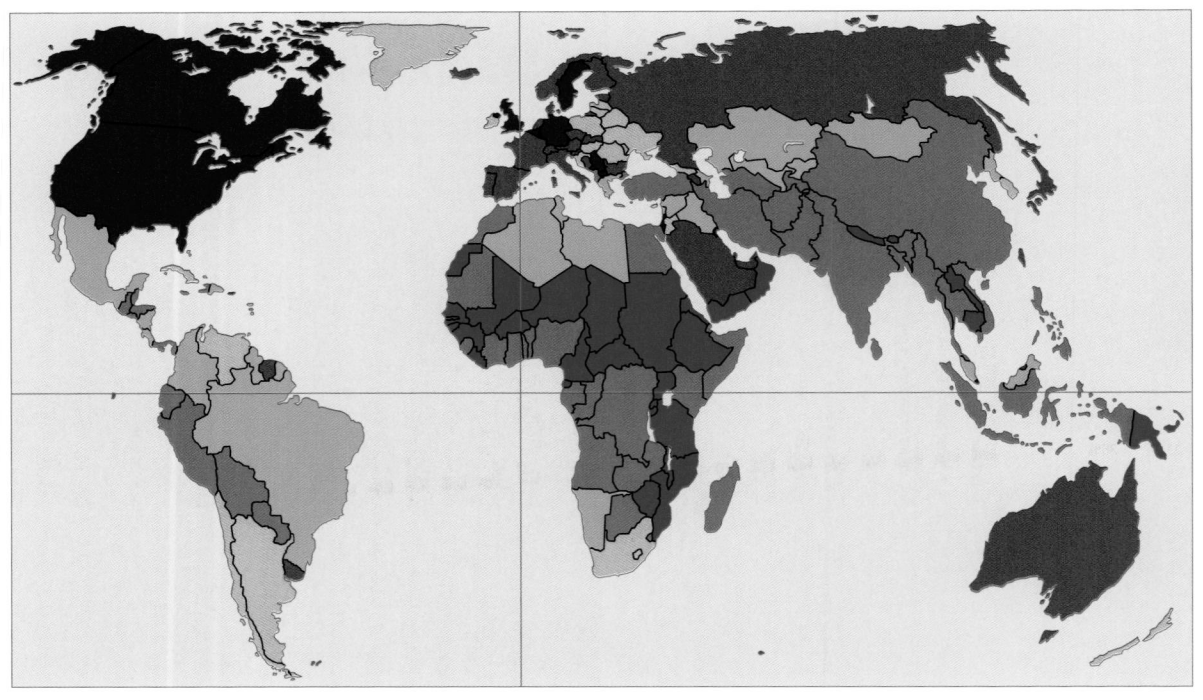

Employment

The number of workers employed in manufacturing for every 100 workers engaged in agriculture (latest available year)

Under 10 / 10 – 50 / 50 – 100 — Mainly agricultural countries
100 – 200 / 200 – 500 / Over 500 — Mainly industrial countries

Selected countries (latest available year)

Singapore	8,860
UK	1,270
Belgium	820
Germany	800
Kuwait	767
Bahrain	660
USA	657
Israel	633

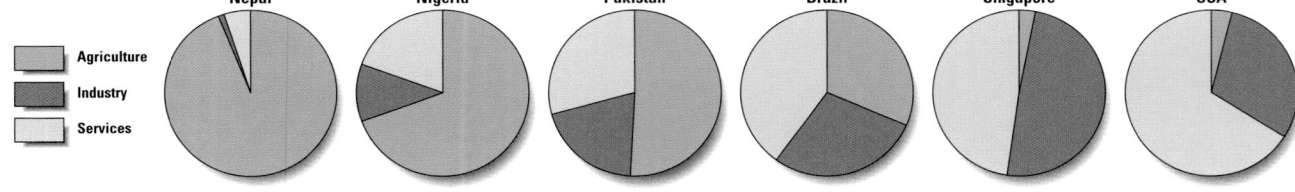

Agriculture / Industry / Services

Nepal — Nigeria — Pakistan — Brazil — Singapore — USA

Division of Employment

Distribution of workers between agriculture, industry and services, selected countries (latest available year)

The six countries selected illustrate the usual stages of economic development, from dependence on agriculture through industrial growth to the expansion of the service sector.

The Workforce

Percentages of men and women between 15 and 64 in employment, selected countries (latest available year)

The figures include employees and the self-employed, who in developing countries are often subsistence farmers. People in full-time education are excluded. Because of the population age structure in developing countries, the employed population has to support a far larger number of non-workers than its industrial equivalent. For example, more than 52% of Kenya's people are under 15, an age group that makes up less than a tenth of the UK population.

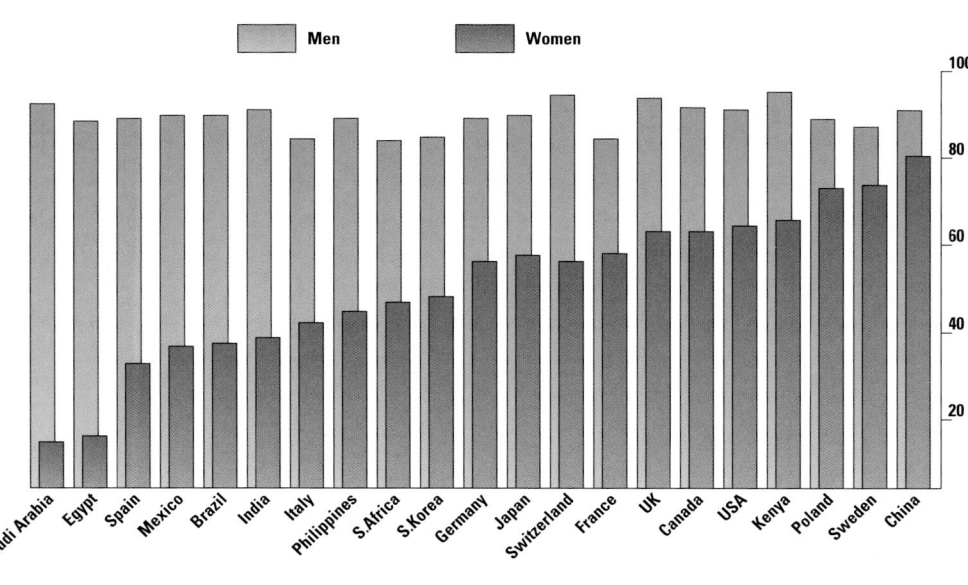

Men / Women

Saudi Arabia, Egypt, Spain, Mexico, Brazil, India, Italy, Philippines, S.Africa, S.Korea, Germany, Japan, Switzerland, France, UK, Canada, USA, Kenya, Poland, Sweden, China

Wealth Creation

The Gross National Income (GNI) of the world's largest economies, US $ million (2001)

1.	USA	9,900,724	21.	Austria	194,463
2.	Japan	4,574,164	22.	Hong Kong	176,157
3.	Germany	1,947,951	23.	Turkey	168,335
4.	UK	1,451,442	24.	Denmark	166,345
5.	France	1,377,389	25.	Poland	163,907
6.	China	1,130,984	26.	Norway	160,577
7.	Italy	1,123,478	27.	Saudi Arabia	149,932
8.	Canada	661,881	28.	Indonesia	144,731
9.	Spain	586,874	29.	South Africa	125,486
10.	Mexico	550,456	30.	Greece	124,553
11.	Brazil	528,503	31.	Finland	124,171
12.	India	474,323	32.	Thailand	120,871
13.	South Korea	447,698	33.	Venezuela	117,169
14.	Netherlands	385,401	34.	Iran	112,855
15.	Australia	383,291	35.	Portugal	109,156
16.	Switzerland	266,503	36.	Israel	104,128
17.	Argentina	260,994	37.	Egypt	99,406
18.	Russia	253,413	38.	Singapore	99,404
19.	Belgium	239,779	39.	Ireland	88,385
20.	Sweden	225,894	40.	Malaysia	86,510

Patterns of Production

Breakdown of industrial output by value, selected countries (latest available year)

	Food & agric. products	Textiles & clothing	Machinery & transport	Chemicals	Other
Algeria	26%	20%	11%	1%	41%
Argentina	24%	10%	16%	12%	37%
Australia	18%	7%	21%	8%	45%
Austria	17%	8%	25%	6%	43%
Belgium	19%	8%	23%	13%	36%
Brazil	15%	12%	24%	9%	40%
Burkina Faso	62%	18%	2%	1%	17%
Canada	15%	7%	25%	9%	44%
Denmark	22%	6%	23%	10%	39%
Egypt	20%	27%	13%	10%	31%
Finland	13%	6%	24%	7%	50%
France	18%	7%	33%	9%	33%
Germany	12%	5%	38%	10%	36%
Greece	20%	22%	14%	7%	38%
Hungary	6%	11%	37%	11%	35%
India	11%	16%	26%	15%	32%
Indonesia	23%	11%	10%	10%	47%
Iran	13%	22%	22%	7%	36%
Ireland	28%	7%	20%	15%	28%
Israel	13%	10%	28%	8%	42%
Italy	7%	13%	32%	10%	38%
Japan	10%	6%	38%	10%	37%
Kenya	35%	12%	14%	9%	29%
Malaysia	21%	5%	23%	14%	37%
Mexico	24%	12%	14%	12%	39%
Netherlands	19%	4%	28%	11%	38%
New Zealand	26%	10%	16%	6%	43%
Norway	21%	3%	26%	7%	44%
Pakistan	34%	21%	8%	12%	25%
Philippines	40%	7%	7%	10%	35%
Poland	15%	16%	30%	6%	33%
Portugal	17%	22%	16%	8%	38%
Singapore	6%	5%	46%	8%	36%
South Africa	14%	8%	17%	11%	49%
South Korea	15%	17%	24%	9%	35%
Spain	17%	9%	22%	9%	43%
Sweden	10%	2%	35%	8%	44%
Thailand	30%	17%	14%	6%	33%
Turkey	20%	14%	15%	8%	43%
UK	14%	6%	32%	11%	36%
USA	12%	5%	35%	10%	38%
Venezuela	23%	8%	9%	11%	49%

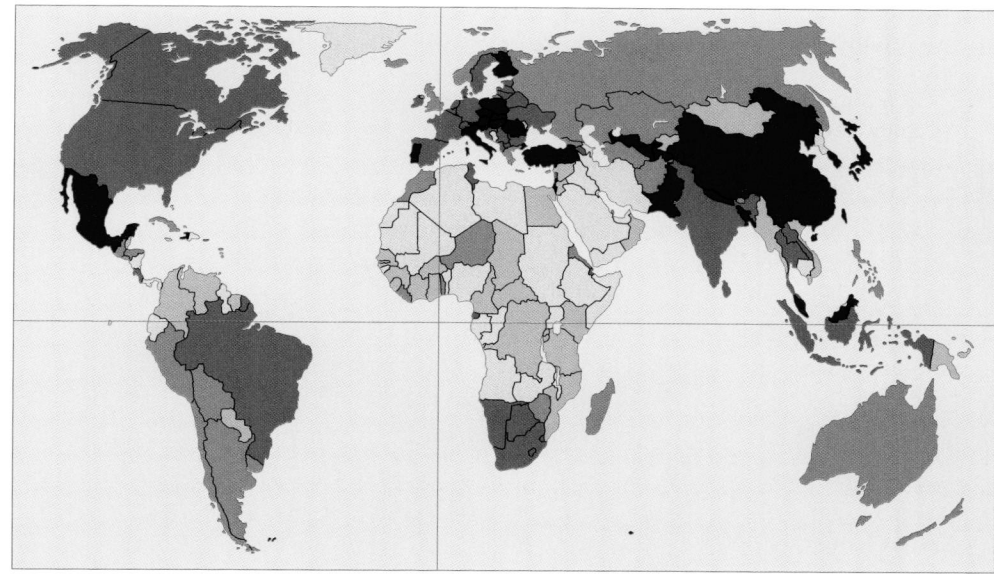

Industry and Trade

Manufactured goods (including machinery and transport) as a percentage of total exports (1999)

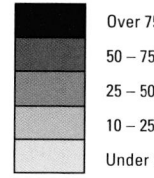

■	Over 75%
■	50 – 75%
■	25 – 50%
■	10 – 25%
■	Under 10%

Countries most dependent on the export of manufactured goods

Malta	91%
Bangladesh	90%
China	90%
Japan	88%
South Korea	83%
Luxembourg	83%
Pakistan	83%

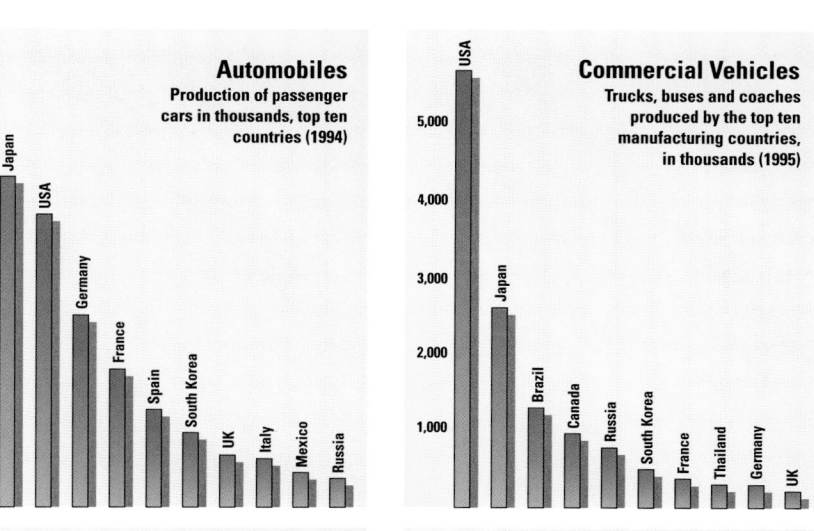

Automobiles
Production of passenger cars in thousands, top ten countries (1994)

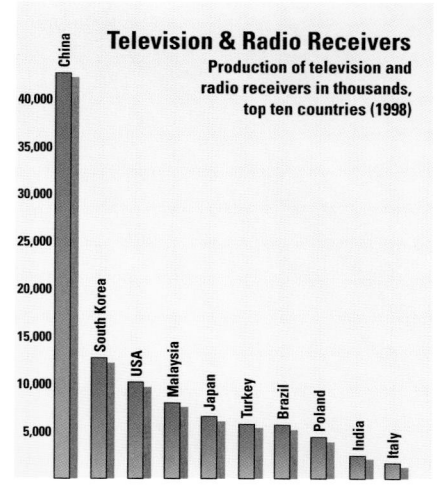

Commercial Vehicles
Trucks, buses and coaches produced by the top ten manufacturing countries, in thousands (1995)

Television & Radio Receivers
Production of television and radio receivers in thousands, top ten countries (1998)

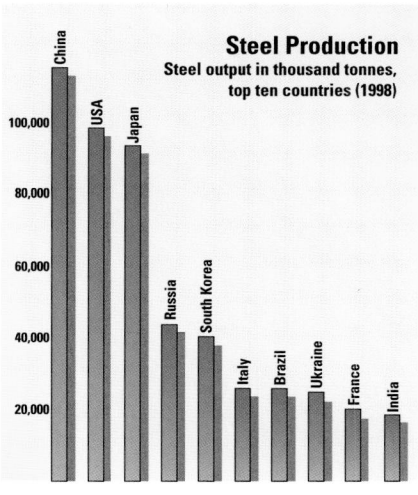

Steel Production
Steel output in thousand tonnes, top ten countries (1998)

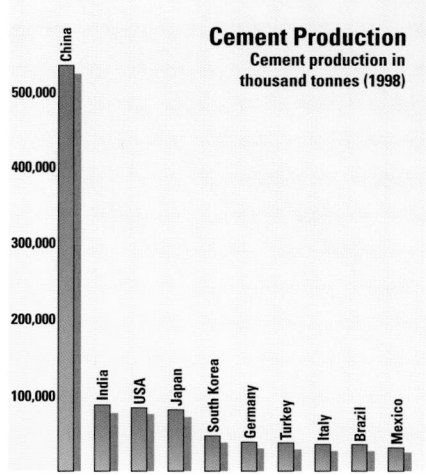

Cement Production
Cement production in thousand tonnes (1998)

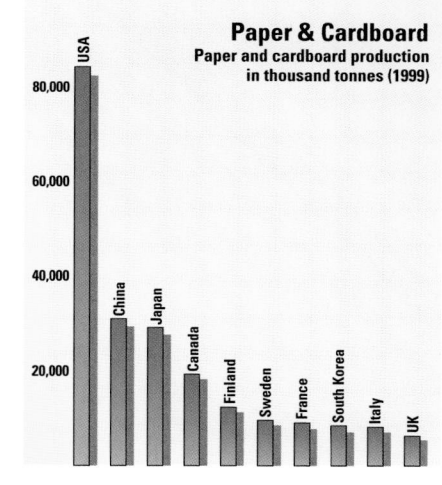

Paper & Cardboard
Paper and cardboard production in thousand tonnes (1999)

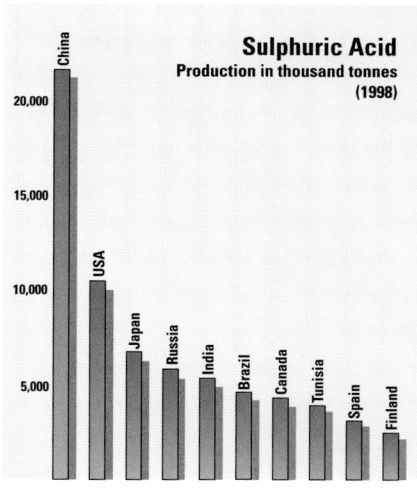

Sulphuric Acid
Production in thousand tonnes (1998)

Industrial Output

Industrial output (mining, manufacturing, construction, energy and water production), US $ billion (latest available year)

1.	Japan	1,941	21.	Sweden	73
2.	USA	1,808	22.	Saudi Arabia	67
3.	Germany	780	=	Thailand	67
4.	France	415	24.	Mexico	65
5.	UK	354	25.	Turkey	51
6.	Italy	337	26.	Denmark	50
7.	China	335	27.	Finland	46
8.	Brazil	255	=	Poland	46
9.	South Korea	196	29.	Norway	44
10.	Spain	187	30.	Malaysia	37
11.	Canada	174	=	Portugal	37
12.	Russia	131	32.	Ukraine	34
13.	Netherlands	107	33.	Greece	33
14.	Australia	98	34.	Singapore	30
15.	Switzerland	96	35.	Venezuela	29
16.	India	94	=	Israel	29
17.	Argentina	87	37.	Chile	24
18.	Belgium	83	=	Colombia	24
=	Indonesia	83	=	Hong Kong	24
20.	Austria	79	=	Philippines	24

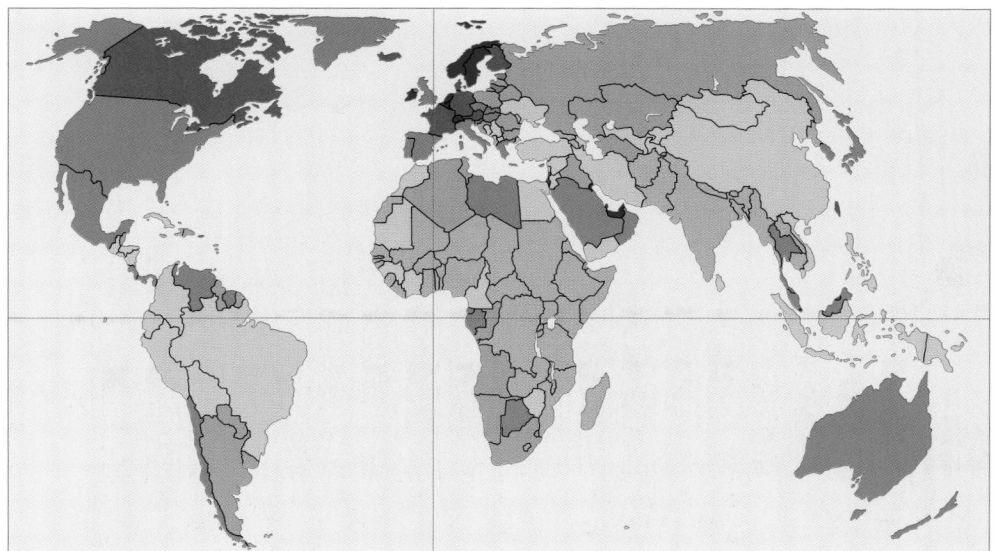

Exports Per Capita

Value of exports in US $, divided by total population (2000)

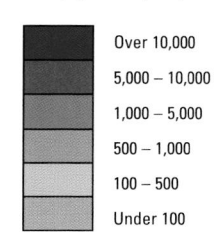

■	Over 10,000
■	5,000 – 10,000
■	1,000 – 5,000
■	500 – 1,000
■	100 – 500
■	Under 100

[UK 4,728] [USA 2,791]

Highest per capita

Kuwait	113,614
Liechtenstein	78,848
Singapore	31,860
Aruba (Neths)	31,429
Hong Kong (China)	28,290
Ireland	19,136

TRADE

For more information:

31 International organizations
35 Fuel exports
   Movements of oil
36 Mineral exports
39 Industry and trade
   Exports per capita
45 Tourism

Trade played a vital role in the growth of early civilizations and it was later a spur to European exploration and colonization. The colonial powers grew rich by exporting cheap manufactures, such as clothing and footwear, while obtaining primary products from their colonies.

From the late 19th century to the early 1950s, as transport technology improved, primary products, especially oil in the later stages of this period, dominated world

trade. However, since that time, manufactures have become the chief commodities in world trade, which is dominated by the industrialized countries. Nearly half of all world trade flows between the developed market economies of the European Union, the United States and Japan, although a number of Asian economies, notably China, Malaysia, Singapore, South Korea, Taiwan and Thailand, increased their share in the 1990s.

China's remarkable economic growth meant that, by 2002, it had overtaken Japan to become the fourth biggest exporter to the United States. China's low production costs, especially its cheap labour, was estimated to be one-twentieth of those of Japan, making its high-quality exports highly competitive in price. Growth in world trade is regarded as a sign of economic health, as is a favourable balance of trade (or trade surplus) in any country.

World Trade

Percentage share of total world exports by value (2000)

- Over 5% of world trade
- 2.5 – 5% of world trade
- 1 – 2.5% of world trade
- 0.25 – 1% of world trade
- 0.1 – 0.25% of world trade
- Under 0.1% of world trade
- No data available

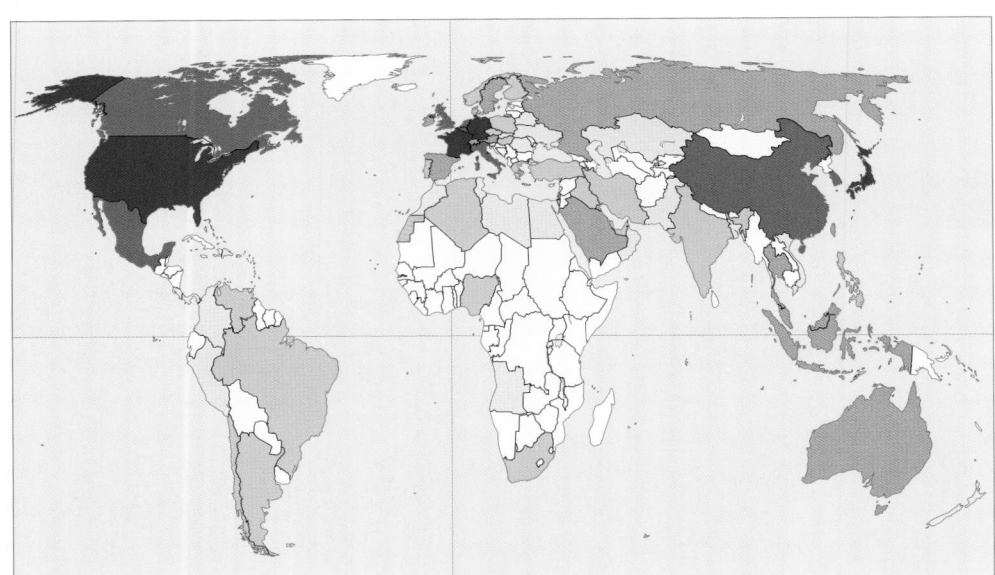

The Main Trading Nations

The imports and exports of the top ten trading nations as a percentage of world trade (2001). Each country's trade in manufactured goods is shown in dark blue.

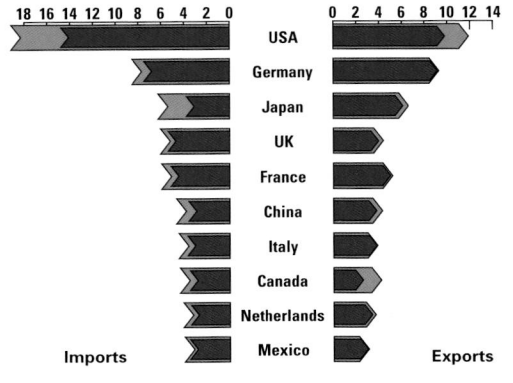

USA, Germany, Japan, UK, France, China, Italy, Canada, Netherlands, Mexico

Imports — Exports

Dependence on Trade

Exports as a percentage of GDP (2001)

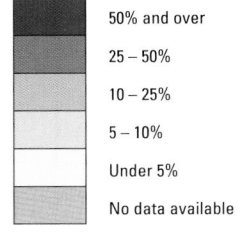

- 50% and over
- 25 – 50%
- 10 – 25%
- 5 – 10%
- Under 5%
- No data available

Major Exports

Leading manufactured items and their exporters (2000)

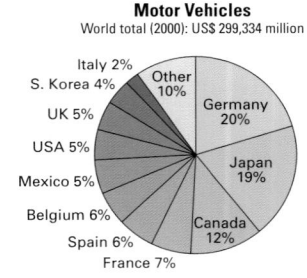

Motor Vehicles
World total (2000): US$ 299,334 million

Germany 20%, Japan 19%, Canada 12%, France 7%, Spain 6%, Belgium 6%, Mexico 5%, USA 5%, UK 5%, S. Korea 4%, Italy 2%, Other 10%

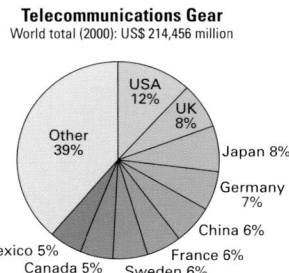

Telecommunications Gear
World total (2000): US$ 214,456 million

USA 12%, UK 8%, Japan 8%, Germany 7%, China 6%, France 6%, Sweden 6%, Canada 5%, Mexico 5%, Other 39%

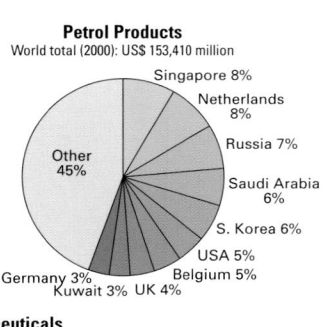

Petrol Products
World total (2000): US$ 153,410 million

Singapore 8%, Netherlands 8%, Russia 7%, Saudi Arabia 6%, S. Korea 6%, USA 5%, Belgium 5%, UK 4%, Kuwait 3%, Germany 3%, Other 45%

Computers
World total (2000): US$ 182,866 million

USA 17%, Singapore 11%, Netherlands 8%, Japan 8%, UK 8%, China 6%, S. Korea 5%, Mexico 5%, Other 33%

Electrical Components
World total (2000): US$ 274,240 million

Thailand 17%, Hungary 16%, Portugal 13%, Ireland 9%, Japan 6%, Kuwait 6%, China 6%, Germany 6%, Other 23%

Pharmaceuticals
World total (2000): US$ 107,334 million

USA 12%, Germany 12%, UK 10%, Switzerland 10%, France 10%, Belgium 6%, Italy 6%, Other 34%

Traded Products

Major manufactures traded by value, in millions of US $ (2000)

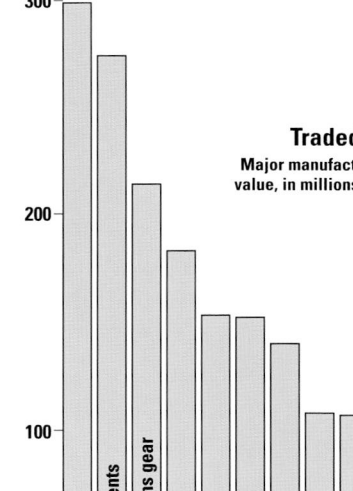

Motor vehicles, Electrical components, Telecommunications gear, Computers, Petrol products, Machine parts, Vehicle parts, Aircraft, Pharmaceuticals, Electrical machinery

World Shipping

While ocean passenger traffic is nowadays relatively modest, sea transport still carries most of the world's trade. Oil and bulk carriers make up the majority of the world fleet, although the general cargo category is the fastest growing. Two innovations have revolutionized sea transport. The first is the development of the roll-on/roll-off (Ro-Ro) method where lorries or even trains loaded with freight are driven straight on to the ship, thus saving time. The second is containerization in which goods are packed into containers (the dimensions of which are fixed) at the factory, driven to the port and loaded on board by specialist machinery.

Almost 30% of world shipping sails under a 'flag of convenience', whereby owners take advantage of low taxes by registering their vessels in a foreign country the ships will never see, notably Panama and Liberia.

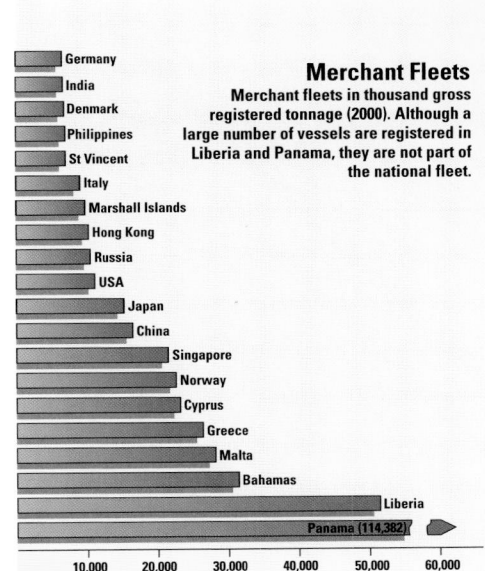

Merchant Fleets
Merchant fleets in thousand gross registered tonnage (2000). Although a large number of vessels are registered in Liberia and Panama, they are not part of the national fleet.

Trade in Primary Products

Primary products (excluding fuels, metals and minerals) as a percentage of total export value (2000)

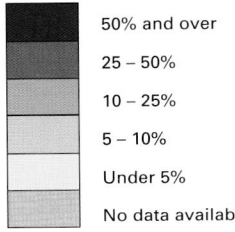

- 50% and over
- 25 – 50%
- 10 – 25%
- 5 – 10%
- Under 5%
- No data available

Primary products are raw materials or partly processed products which form the basis for manufacturing. They are the necessary requirements of industries and include agricultural products, minerals and timber, as well as many semi-manufactured goods such as cotton, which has been spun but not woven, wood pulp or flour. Many developed countries have few natural resources and rely on imports for the majority of their primary products. The countries of South-east Asia export hardwoods to the rest of the world, whilst many South American countries are heavily dependent on coffee exports.

Balance of Trade

Value of exports in proportion to the value of imports (2000)

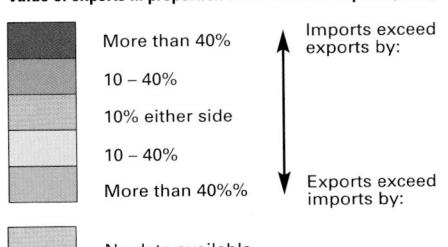

- More than 40%
- 10 – 40%
- 10% either side
- 10 – 40%
- More than 40%%

Imports exceed exports by: ↑
Exports exceed imports by: ↓

- No data available

The total world trade balance should amount to zero, since exports must equal imports on a global scale. In practice, at least $100 billion in exports go unrecorded, leaving the world with an apparent deficit and many countries in a better position than public accounting reveals. However, a favourable trade balance is not necessarily a sign of prosperity: many poorer countries must maintain a high surplus in order to service debts, and do so by restricting imports below the levels needed to sustain successful economies.

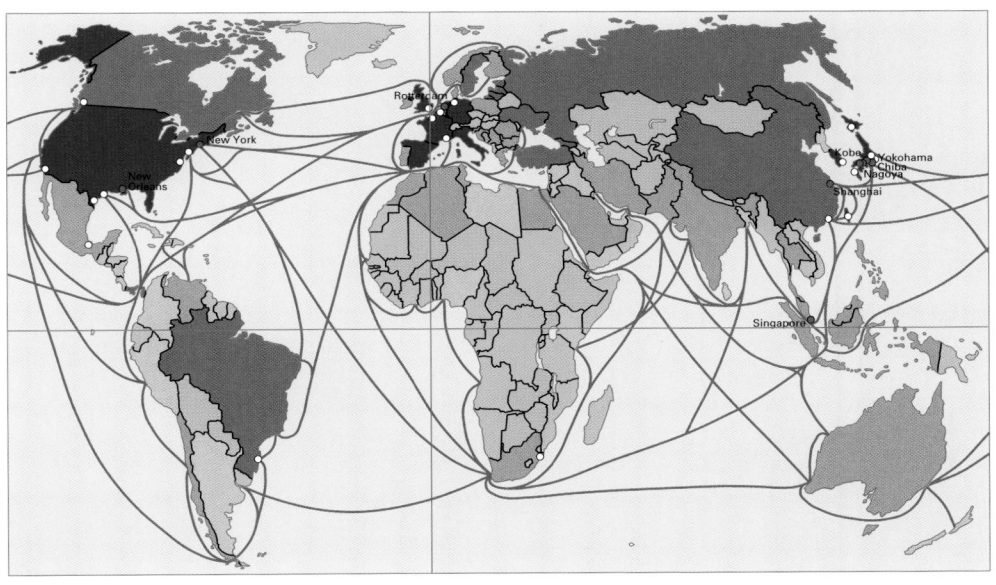

Types of Vessels
World merchant fleet by type of vessel and deadweight tonnage (2000)

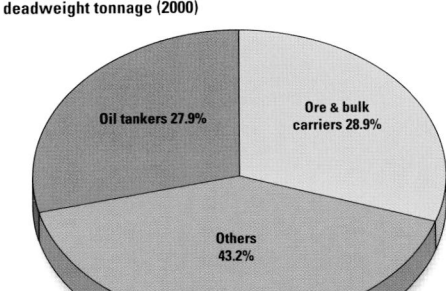

- Oil tankers 27.9%
- Ore & bulk carriers 28.9%
- Others 43.2%

The Great Ports
Total cargo traffic, in million tonnes (2000)

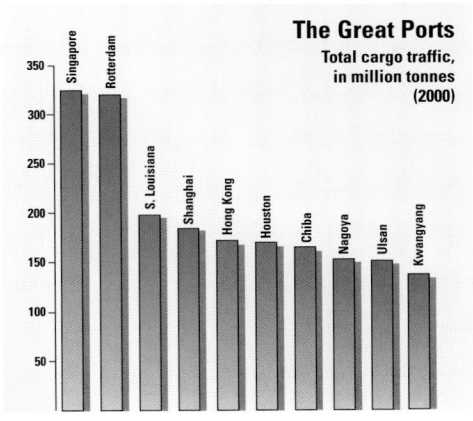

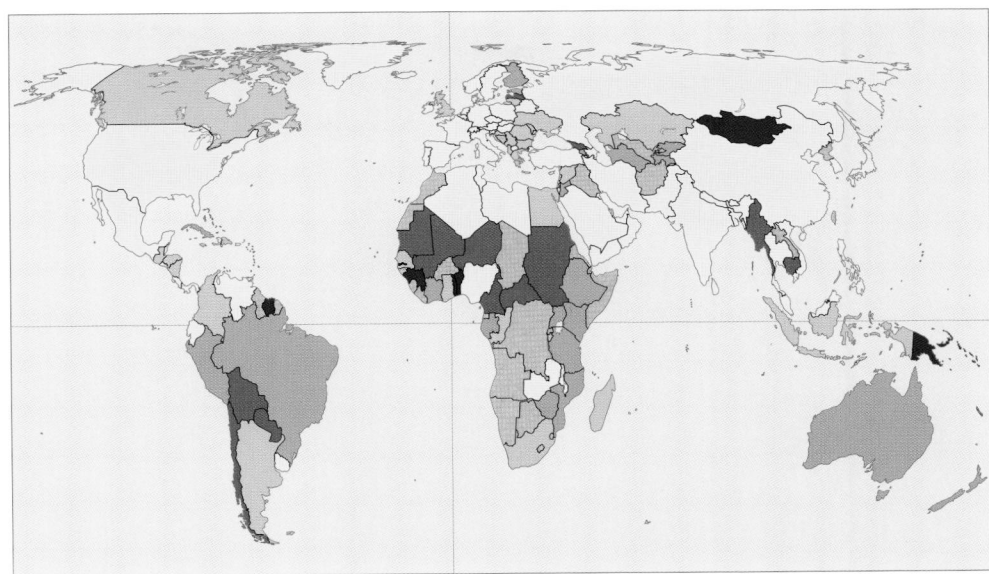

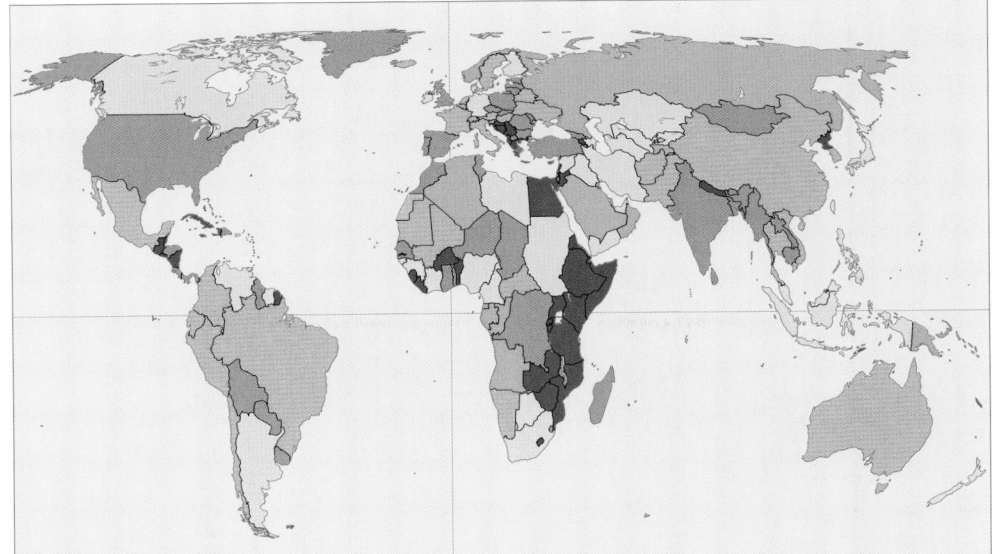

Freight

Freight unloaded in millions of tonnes (latest available year)

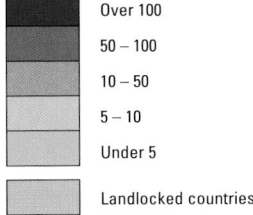

- Over 100
- 50 – 100
- 10 – 50
- 5 – 10
- Under 5
- Landlocked countries

Major seaports
- ● Over 100 million tonnes per year
- ○ 50 – 100 million tonnes per year
- —— Major shipping routes

Air Freight

Trends in air freight in million tonne-km*, selected countries (1995–9)

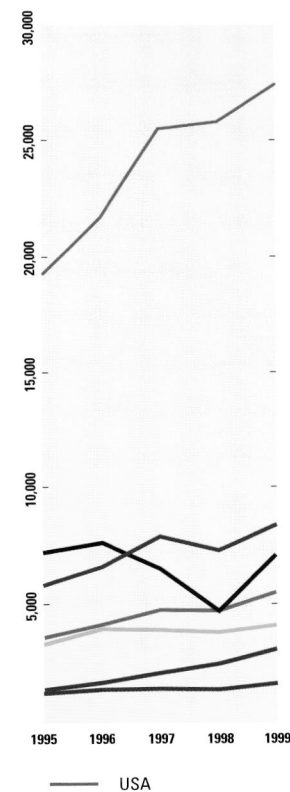

- USA
- South Korea
- UK
- Singapore
- Netherlands
- China
- Malaysia

* Equivalent to million tonnes of air freight flown over 1 million kilometres per year.

Air transport is important to countries of considerable size; where ground terrain is difficult; when crossing short stretches of sea; and where goods are of high value, light in weight or perishable. The deregulation of airlines (in the USA since 1978 and the EU in 1993) has led to increased competition and lower fares.

41

HEALTH

For more information:
18 Water supply
27 Urban pollution
    Urban advantages
33 Crisis in Africa
    Food and population
47 Distribution of
    spending

Until the late 1990s, when the full extent of the AIDS crisis emerged, average life expectancies at birth were rising almost everywhere. By 2000, they ranged from 78 years in high income economies to 47 in sub-Saharan Africa. These figures represented an enormous advance on the situation in 1880, when citizens of Berlin had an estimated life expectancy of 30 years.

The ravages of AIDS have been greatest in southern Africa. One of the worst affected countries is Botswana, where nearly 40% of the adult population were thought to be infected by 2002. In Botswana, life expectancies were expected to fall to 27 years in 2010 instead of an original estimate of 74 years. However, in much of the world, average life expectancies are still increasing. The rises are attributed to improvements in agriculture and, hence, nutrition, as well as health education, an increase in sanitation and the quality of drinking water, together with advances in medicine.

Besides AIDS, the people of the developing world are subject to another affliction – malnutrition. Below, the map on this page shows that in most of Africa, Asia and Latin America, the average daily calorie supply per person is so low as to cause malnutrition. (The daily requirement rated adequate by the World Health Organization is between 2,300 and 2,500 calories per day.) Malnutrition is a serious condition. For example, among pregnant women it causes high rates of child mortality.

Deficiency diseases occur when people do not have a balanced diet. Protein deficiency causes stunting and kwashiorkor, which can be fatal, especially among young children, while vitamin deficiencies cause such illnesses as beri beri, pellagra, scurvy and rickets. Iron deficiency causes anaemia, while a lack of iodine causes mental retardation. A UN report in the early 1990s reported that iodine deficiency affected 458 million women worldwide, as compared with 238 million men. Women's nutritional problems are especially acute in southern Asia. For example, the UN report stated that 88% of pregnant women in India were anaemic, as compared with 15% in developed countries.

Infectious diseases in association, directly or indirectly, with deficient diets, continue to affect people in developing countries, especially the countries in the low human development category, where only 32% of the people have access to sanitation and 68% to safe water supplies.

Around the turn of the century, a WHO report stated that infectious diseases cause over 16 million deaths a year. Most of the victims are young and otherwise fit people in developing countries. The major killers are AIDS, cholera, dysentery, malaria, measles, pneumonia, respiratory infections, tuberculosis and typhoid. Many of these diseases are preventable and, according to the United Nations Children's Fund, an investment of US $25,000 million per year, about half of the money spent annually on cigarettes in Europe alone, would have saved the lives of all the children who currently die from avoidable diseases.

Infectious diseases are much less important as causes of death in developed countries, where cancer and circulatory diseases, such as atherosclerosis and hypertension, which cause strokes and heart attacks, are the most common causes of fatality. Because these diseases tend to kill older people, they are relatively less important in developing countries where people have shorter lifespans.

Harmful habits are also generally practiced more by the rich than the poor. For example, smoking is an important cause of death in developed countries, though, curiously, the Japanese, with an average life expectancy of 81 years in 2000, are among the highest tobacco consumers. Similarly, high alcohol consumption, although it has bad effects on health, does not seem to affect longevity. The leading consumers, the French, had a life expectancy of 79 years in 2000.

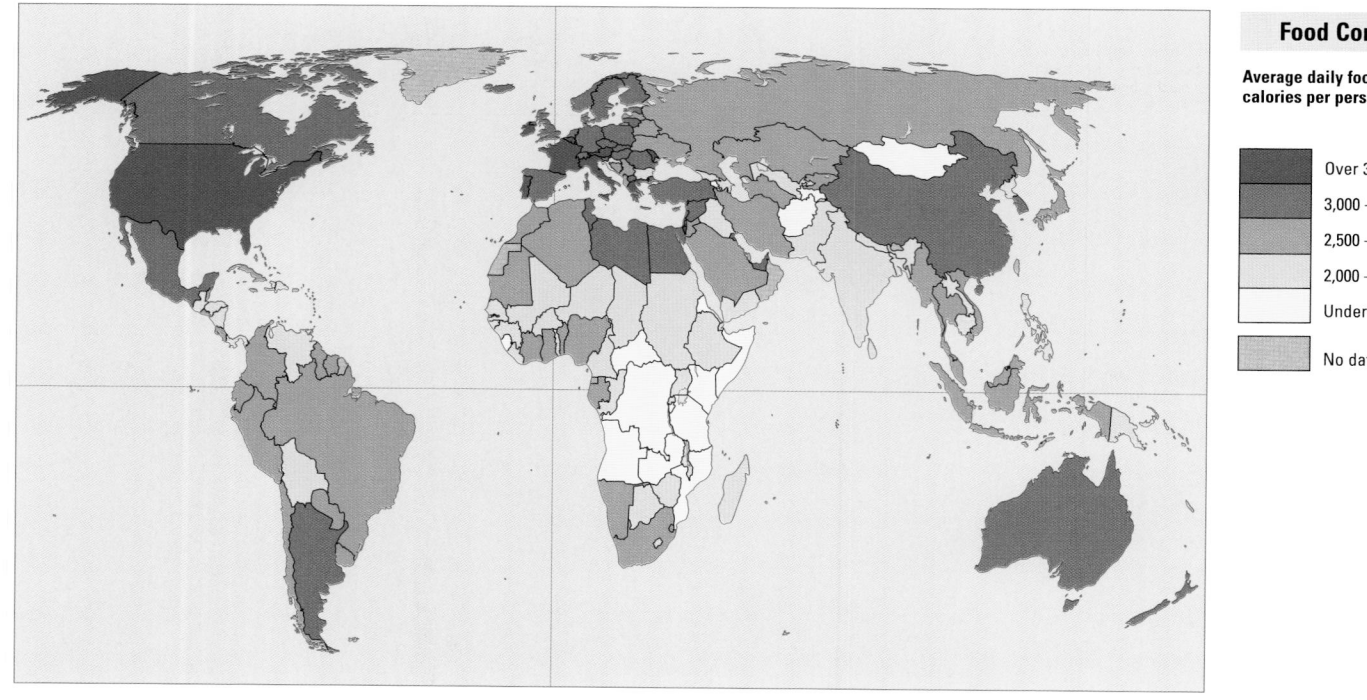

Food Consumption

Average daily food intake in calories per person (2000)

- Over 3,500 calories
- 3,000 – 3,500 calories
- 2,500 – 3,000 calories
- 2,000 – 2,500 calories
- Under 2,000 calories
- No data available

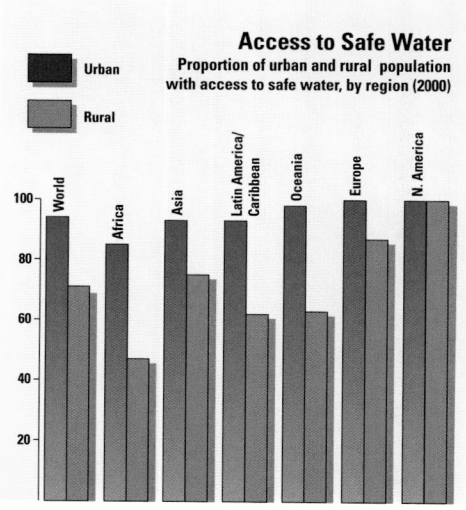

Access to Safe Water
Proportion of urban and rural population with access to safe water, by region (2000)

Urban
Rural

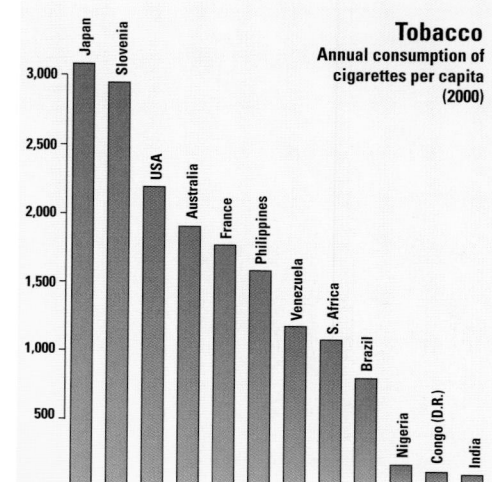

Tobacco
Annual consumption of cigarettes per capita (2000)

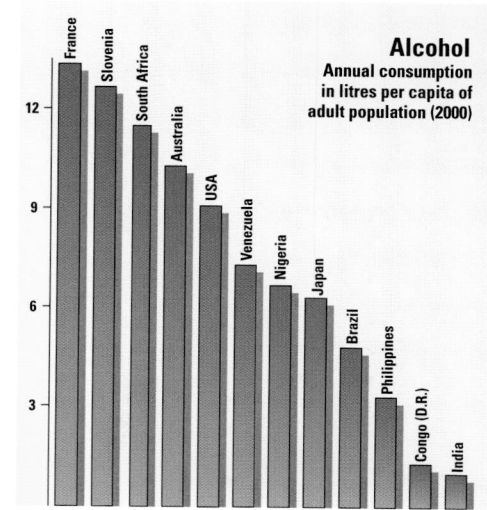

Alcohol
Annual consumption in litres per capita of adult population (2000)

Life Expectancy

Years of life expectancy at birth, selected countries (1997)

The chart shows combined data for both sexes. On average, women live longer than men worldwide, even in developing countries with high maternal mortality rates. Overall, life expectancy is steadily rising, though the difference between rich and poor nations remains dramatic.

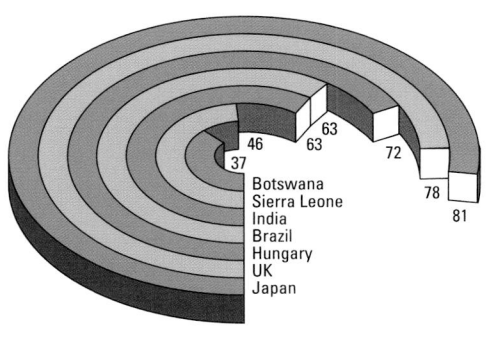

46
63
63
72
37
78
81

Botswana
Sierra Leone
India
Brazil
Hungary
UK
Japan

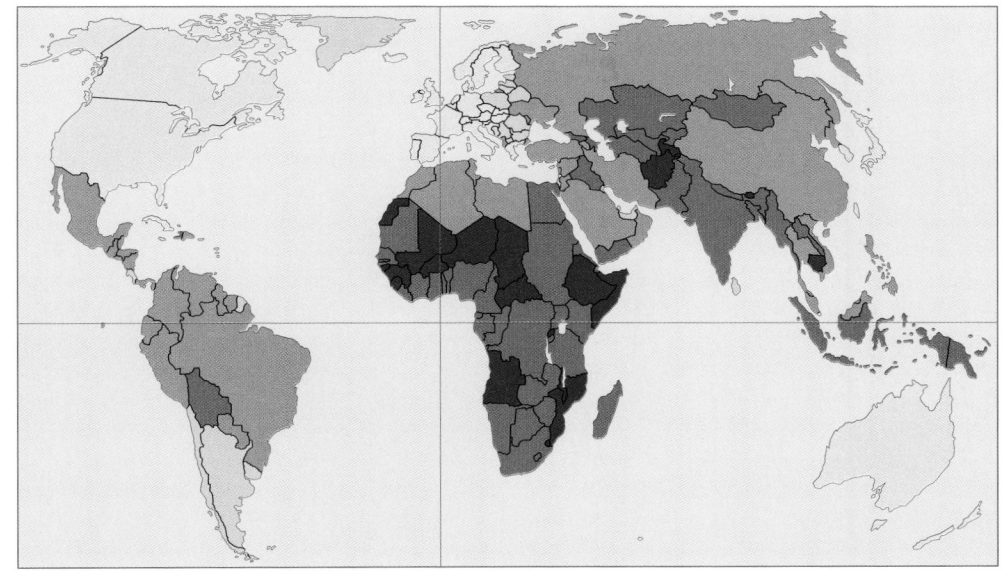

Infant Mortality

Number of babies who died under the age of one, per 1,000 births (2000)

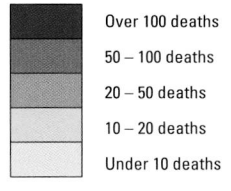

Over 100 deaths
50 – 100 deaths
20 – 50 deaths
10 – 20 deaths
Under 10 deaths

Highest infant mortality

Afghanistan . . . . .137 deaths
Western Sahara . . . . . .134 deaths
Malawi . . . . .131 deaths

Lowest infant mortality

Iceland . . . . .5 deaths
Finland . . . . .4 deaths
Japan . . . . .4 deaths

Expenditure on Health

Public health expenditure per capita, in US $ (1998)

Countries with the highest spending		Countries with the lowest spending	
USA	$4,271	Mozambique	$8
Switzerland	$3,857	Tanzania	$8
Norway	$3,182	Sierra Leone	$8
Denmark	$2,785	Indonesia	$8
Luxembourg	$2,731	Chad	$7
Iceland	$2,701	Laos	$6
Germany	$2,697	Niger	$5
France	$2,288	Madagascar	$5
Japan	$2,243	Burundi	$5
Netherlands	$2,173	Ethiopia	$4

The allocation of limited funds for health care in developing countries is rarely evenly spread – the quality of treatment can vary enormously from place to place within the same country. Urban dwellers tend to have much better access to health provisions than those living in rural areas.

Medical Provision

Doctors per 100,000 population, selected countries (2000)

Although the ratio of people to doctors gives a good approximation of a country's health provision, it is not an absolute indicator. Raw numbers may mask inefficiency and other weaknesses: the high proportion of physicians in Hungary, for example, has not prevented infant mortality rates more than twice as high as in the United Kingdom.

The definition of a doctor also varies from nation to nation. As well as registered medical practitioners, it may include trained medical assistants – an especially important category in developing countries, where they provide many of the same services as fully qualified physicians, including simple operations.

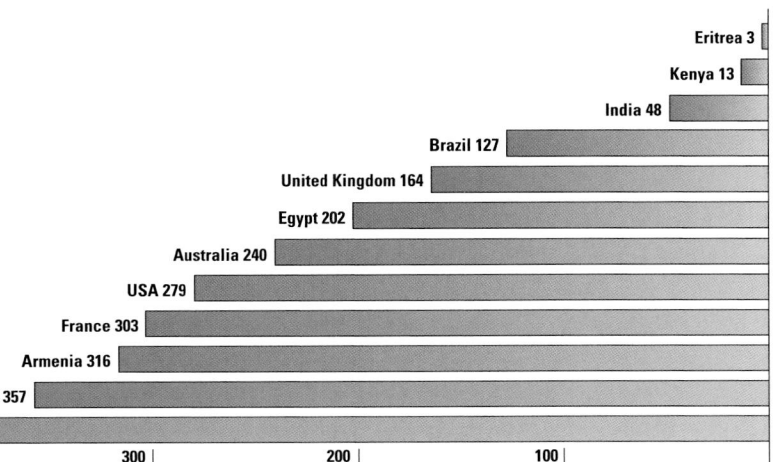

Eritrea 3
Kenya 13
India 48
Brazil 127
United Kingdom 164
Egypt 202
Australia 240
USA 279
France 303
Armenia 316
Hungary 357
Italy 554

600   500   400   300   200   100

The Aids Crisis

The Acquired Immune Deficiency Syndrome (AIDS) was first identified in 1981 when American doctors found otherwise healthy young men succumbing to rare infections. By 1984 the cause had been traced to the Human Immunodeficiency Virus (HIV) which can remain dormant for many years and perhaps indefinitely: only half of those known to carry the virus in 1981 had developed AIDS ten years later.

In Western countries in the 1990s, most AIDS deaths were among male homosexuals or needle-sharing drug-users. However, the disease is spreading fastest among heterosexual men and women, which is its usual vector in the developing world where most of its victims live.

In 2002, 25 million people had already died of AIDS and another 42 million were infected with the HIV virus. Around 30 million of them live in Africa. In some southern African countries, more than a third of the population carries the virus. In South Africa, which has the largest number of HIV infections, about 6 million people were expected to die of the disease between 2002 and 2012.

Most people who die of AIDS are young. AIDS also has other serious consequences. A report by UNAIDS and UNICEF stated that the number of children orphaned by AIDS rose threefold between 1996 and 2002, reaching an all-time high of 13.4 million.

Causes of Death

■ Accidents, poisoning and violence   ■ Metabolic disorders

■ Respiratory and digestive diseases   ■ Cancers

■ Nervous and circulatory diseases   ■ Infectious and parasitic diseases

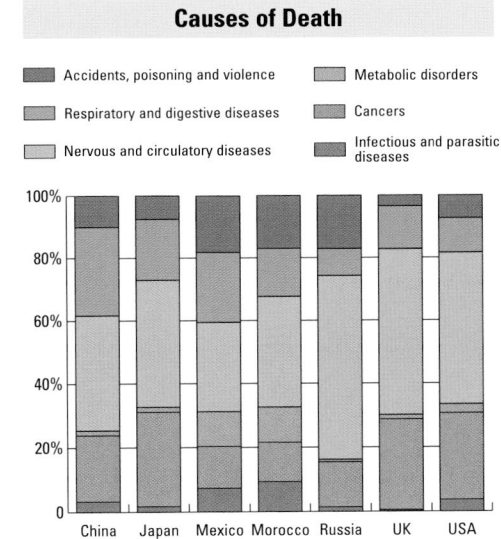

100%
80%
60%
40%
20%
0

China   Japan   Mexico   Morocco   Russia   UK   USA

Circulatory Disease in Europe

Diseases of the circulatory system per 100,000 people (latest available year)

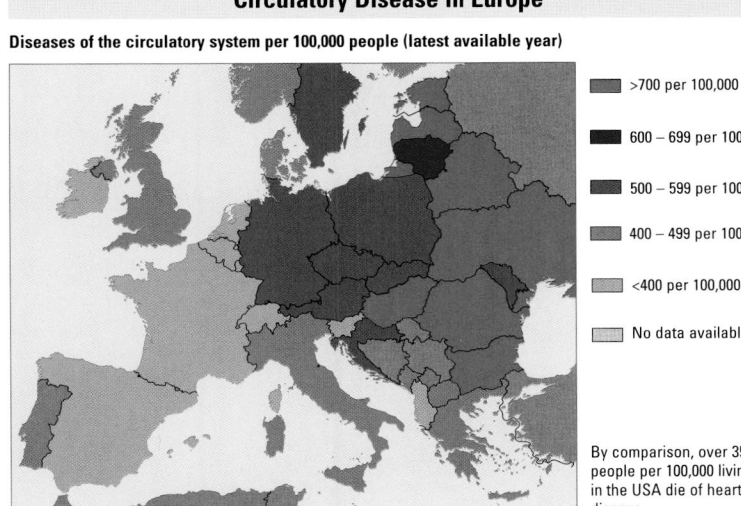

■ >700 per 100,000
■ 600 – 699 per 100,000
■ 500 – 599 per 100,000
■ 400 – 499 per 100,000
▨ <400 per 100,000
▨ No data available

By comparison, over 354 people per 100,000 living in the USA die of heart disease.

AIDS

Cases reported in 1999

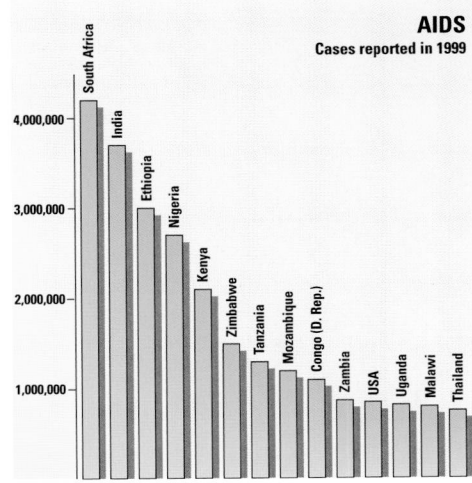

South Africa
India
Ethiopia
Nigeria
Kenya
Zimbabwe
Tanzania
Mozambique
Congo (D. Rep.)
Zambia
USA
Uganda
Malawi
Thailand

4,000,000
3,000,000
2,000,000
1,000,000

Sanitation

Percentage of the population with access to sanitation services, selected countries (latest available year)

■ Urban
■ Rural

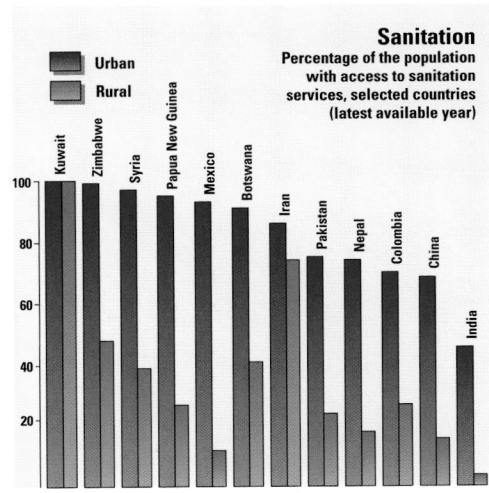

Kuwait
Zimbabwe
Syria
Papua New Guinea
Mexico
Botswana
Iran
Pakistan
Nepal
Colombia
China
India

100
80
60
40
20

Malaria

Cases of malaria per 100,000 people exposed to malaria-infected environments, selected countries* (latest available year)

*** data are not available for Africa where 80% of malaria cases occur**

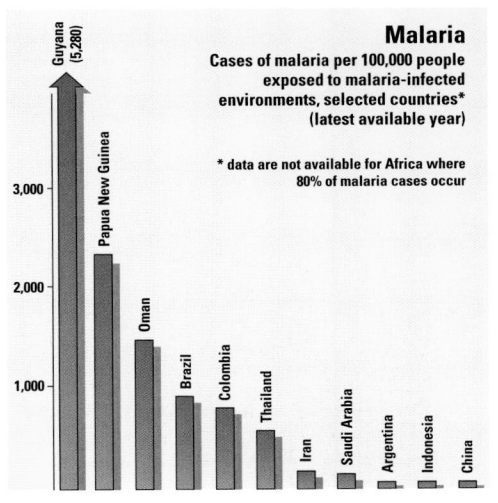

Guyana (5,280)

Papua New Guinea
Oman
Brazil
Colombia
Thailand
Iran
Saudi Arabia
Argentina
Indonesia
China

3,000
2,000
1,000

Infectious and parasitic diseases, such as malaria, which claimed 2.5 million lives in 2002, remain a scourge in the developing countries. Respiratory infections and injury also claim more lives in developing countries, which lack the drugs and the medical personnel to deal with them. Developing countries lack the basic services taken for granted in developed nations. For example, in rural Africa in 2000, only 49% of the population had access to sanitation and 44% to safe water, with the situation being worse in rural areas. By contrast, circulatory diseases and cancer are the main causes of death in the rich, industrialized countries. For example, in the UK in the 1990s, circulatory diseases, which cause heart attacks and strokes, accounted for nearly half the deaths, with cancer accounting for nearly a quarter.

WEALTH

For more information:
38 Wealth creation
39 Industrial power
   Exports per capita
40 World trade
   Major exports
41 Balance of trade
47 Distribution of spending
   Distribution of income

Perhaps the most glaring differences in the world today are those between the rich and the poor. The World Bank divides countries into three main groups based on average economic production expressed in terms of per capita GNP (Gross National Product). They are the low-income economies, including most African countries and much of Asia; the middle-income economies, including most of Latin America and most of the former USSR; and the high-income economies of Canada, the United States, Western Europe, Japan and Australia.

Per capita GNPs are a measure of the total goods and services produced by a country divided by the population, and then converted into US dollars at official exchange rates. They are useful indicators of a country's prosperity, though, like all statistics, they must be treated with care. For example, the prices for goods and services in China are far cheaper than they are in the United States. China's per capita GNP in 2000 was $840 (as compared with $34,100 in the USA), but the PPP (Purchasing Power Parity) estimate of China's per capita GNP was considerably higher at $3,920. Another problem with per capita GNPs is that they are averages, which often conceal wide internal variations.

The pattern of poverty varies from region to region. In Latin America, much progress has been made through industrialization, though startling inequalities still exist between rich and poor. China and other countries in eastern Asia, including South Korea and Taiwan, have followed Japan's example in pursuing export-led industrial policies. The success of China's Special Economic Zones, where foreign investment is encouraged, has led to a huge rise in China's per capita GNP.

Solutions to poverty in Africa are much harder to find because of its high population growth, civil wars, natural disasters and high inflation rates. Although Africa receives more aid than any other continent, aid is only a partial solution. Much aid has been wasted on overambitious projects, in the servicing of huge national debts, or lost by inexperienced or corrupt governments. One initiative in some African countries has been to improve the infrastructure and develop tourism, creating employment and providing much-needed foreign currency. But tourism alone cannot solve the problems of under-development.

The International Monetary Fund and the World Bank argue that real economic progress in Africa will be achieved only when African countries create market-friendly economies that encourage trade through export-led manufacturing, while at the same time strictly controlling public spending on welfare, the civil service and other areas.

Continental Shares

Shares of population and of wealth (GNP) by continent

These generalized continental figures show the startling difference between rich and poor but mask the successes or failures of individual countries. Japan, for example, with less than 4% of Asia's population, produces almost 70% of the continent's output. Within countries, the difference between rich and poor can also be startling. In Brazil, for example, the richest 20% of the population own 60% of the wealth.

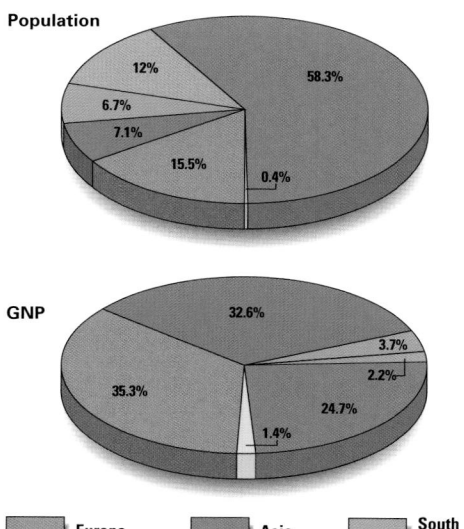

Population

GNP

| Europe | Asia | South America |
| Australia | Africa | North America |

Currencies

Currency units of the world's most powerful economies

1. USA: US dollar ($, US $) = 100 cents
2. Japan: Yen (Y, ¥) = 100 sen
3. EU: euro = 100 cents
4. UK: Pound sterling (£) = 100 pence
5. Canada: Canadian dollar (C$, Can$) = 100 cents
6. China: Renminbi yuan (RMBY, $, Y) = 10 jiao = 100 fen
7. Brazil: Cruzeiro real (BRC) = 100 centavos
8. India: Indian rupee (Re, Rs) = 100 paisa
9. Australia: Australian dollar ($A) = 100 cents
10. Switzerland: Swiss franc (SFr, SwF) = 100 centimes
11. South Korea: Won (W) = 100 chon
12. Sweden: Swedish krona (SKr) = 100 ore
13. Mexico: Mexican peso (Mex$) = 100 centavos
14. Denmark: Danish krone (DKr) = 100 øre
15. Norway: Norwegian krone (NKr) = 100 øre
16. Saudi Arabia: Riyal (SAR, SRI$) = 100 halalah
17. Indonesia: Rupiah (Rp) = 100 sen
18. South Africa: Rand (R) = 100 cents

On 1 January 2002, three years after the launch of Europe's single currency, euro banknotes and coins were brought into circulation in the 12 member states of the European Union that had adopted the euro. Their former national currencies remained in dual circulation with the euro until the end of February 2002.
The 12 countries in the euro area are: Austria, Belgium, Germany, Greece, Finland, France, Ireland, Italy, Luxembourg, the Netherlands, Portugal and Spain.

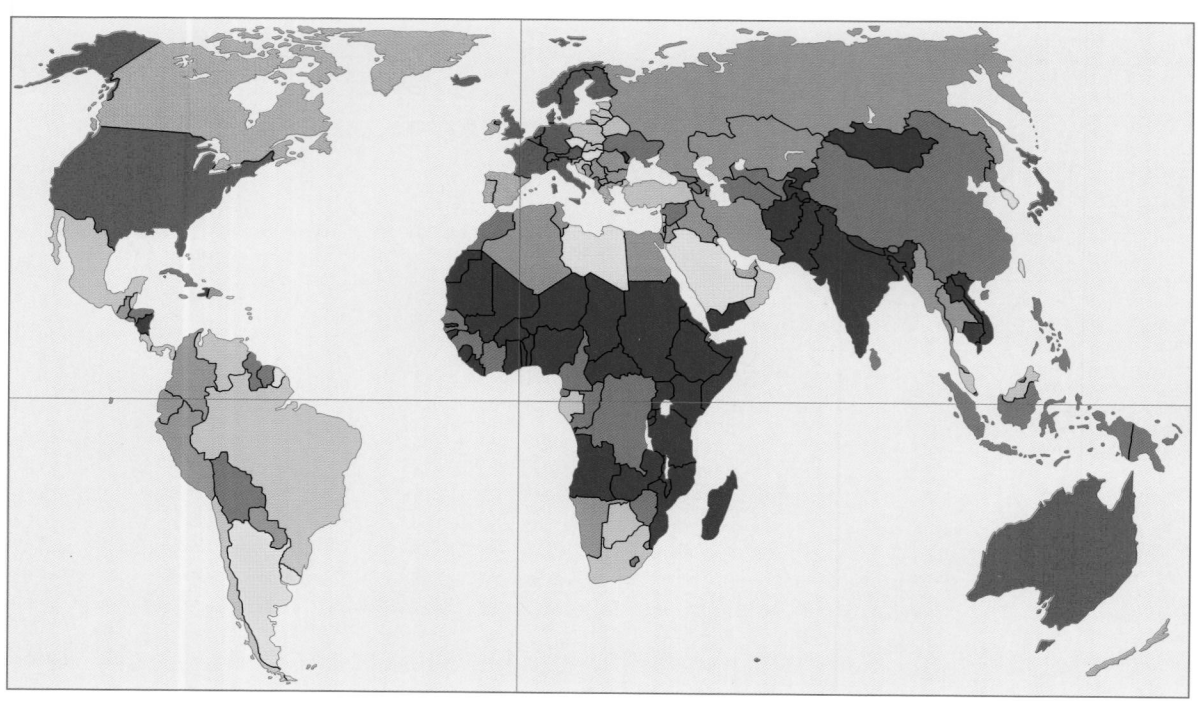

Levels of Income

Gross National Income per capita: the value of total production divided by the population (2000)

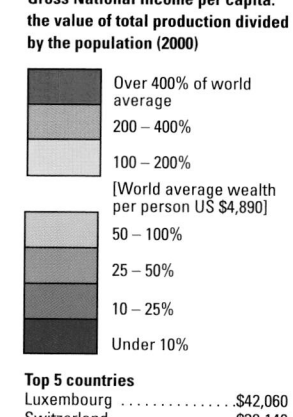

- Over 400% of world average
- 200 – 400%
- 100 – 200%
  [World average wealth per person US $4,890]
- 50 – 100%
- 25 – 50%
- 10 – 25%
- Under 10%

Top 5 countries
Luxembourg $42,060
Switzerland $38,140
Japan $35,620
Norway $34,530
Bermuda $34,470

Bottom 5 countries
Ethiopia $100
Burundi $110
Sierra Leone $130
Eritrea $170
Malawi $170

Indicators

The gap between the world's rich and poor is now so great that it is difficult to illustrate on a single graph. Within each income group (as defined by the World Bank), however, comparisons have some meaning. The wealth gap in many developing countries, though, is wide, with a small, rich class and a large, impoverished majority, while many high-income countries contain an underclass of unemployed and homeless people.

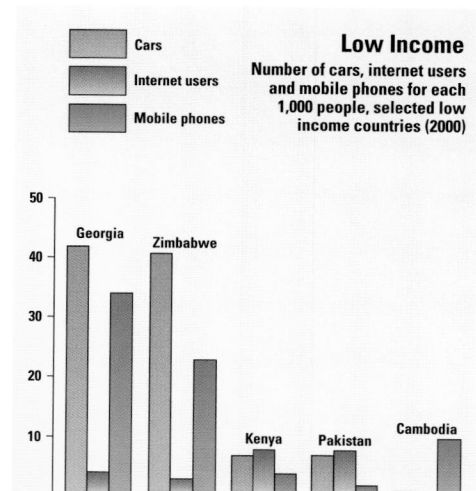

Cars / Internet users / Mobile phones

High Income — Number of cars, internet users and mobile phones for each 1,000 people, selected high income countries (2000)

USA, UK, Japan, New Zealand, Qatar

Middle Income — Number of cars, internet users and mobile phones for each 1,000 people, selected middle income countries (2000)

Russia, Mexico, Egypt, Jordan, Albania

Low Income — Number of cars, internet users and mobile phones for each 1,000 people, selected low income countries (2000)

Georgia, Zimbabwe, Kenya, Pakistan, Cambodia

World Tourism

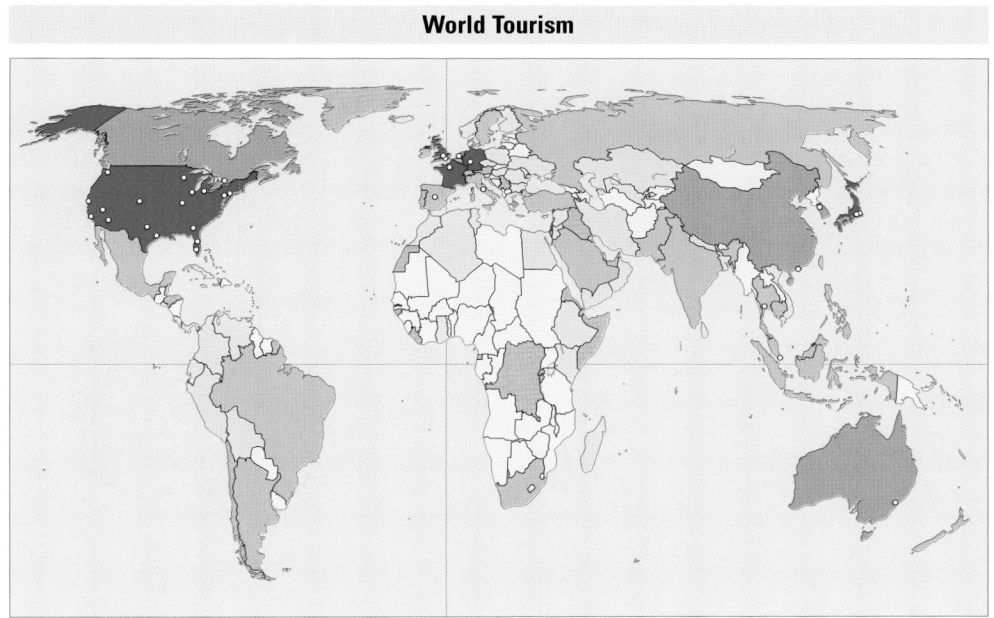

Passenger km flown (the number of passengers multiplied by the distance flown from the airport of origin) (1999)

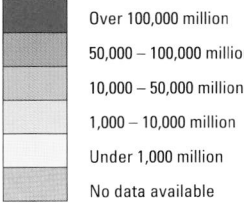

- Over 100,000 million
- 50,000 – 100,000 million
- 10,000 – 50,000 million
- 1,000 – 10,000 million
- Under 1,000 million
- No data available

○ Major airports (handling over 25 million passengers in 2001)

Leisure and tourism is the world's second largest industry in terms of revenue generated. Small economies in attractive areas are often completely dominated by tourism: in some Caribbean islands, tourist spending provides over 90% of the total income and is the biggest foreign exchange earner. In cash terms the USA is the world leader: its 2000 earnings exceeded US $82 billion, though that sum amounted to approximately 0.9% of its total GDP. Of the 51 million visitors to the USA, 29% came from Canada and 20% from Mexico. Germany spends the most on overseas tourism; this amounts to over US $50,000 million. The next biggest spenders are the USA, Japan and the UK.

The world's busiest airport in terms of total number of passengers is Atlanta (75.9 million passengers in 2000); the busiest international airport is London's Heathrow.

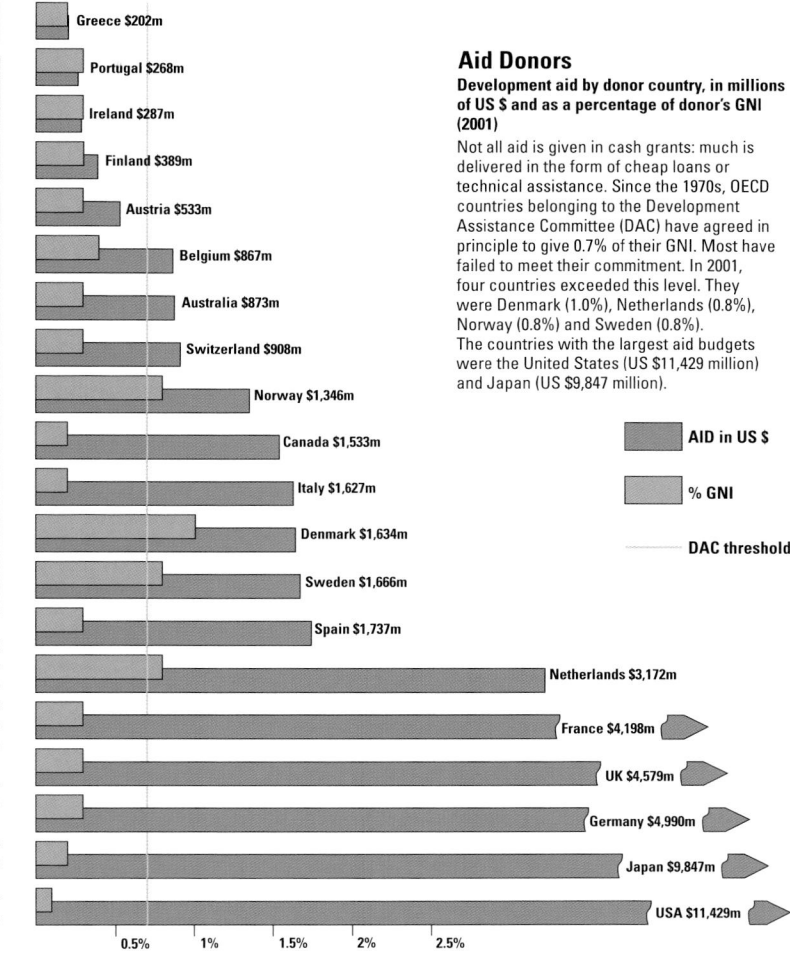

Aid Donors

Development aid by donor country, in millions of US $ and as a percentage of donor's GNI (2001)

Not all aid is given in cash grants: much is delivered in the form of cheap loans or technical assistance. Since the 1970s, OECD countries belonging to the Development Assistance Committee (DAC) have agreed in principle to give 0.7% of their GNI. Most have failed to meet their commitment. In 2001, four countries exceeded this level. They were Denmark (1.0%), Netherlands (0.8%), Norway (0.8%) and Sweden (0.8%). The countries with the largest aid budgets were the United States (US $11,429 million) and Japan (US $9,847 million).

- AID in US $
- % GNI
- DAC threshold

Greece $202m
Portugal $268m
Ireland $287m
Finland $389m
Austria $533m
Belgium $867m
Australia $873m
Switzerland $908m
Norway $1,346m
Canada $1,533m
Italy $1,627m
Denmark $1,634m
Sweden $1,666m
Spain $1,737m
Netherlands $3,172m
France $4,198m
UK $4,579m
Germany $4,990m
Japan $9,847m
USA $11,429m

0.5% 1% 1.5% 2% 2.5%

State Finance

Inflation rates, shown on the map (*right*) are an index of a country's financial stability and usually of its prosperity. Annual inflation rates above 20% are usually marked by slow or even negative growth of the GNP. Above 50%, it becomes hyperinflation and an economy is reeling. In the late 1980s and early 1990s, many high-income countries had to contend with annual inflation rates of 10% or more, while Japan, the growth leader, had an average inflation rate of 1.3% between 1985 and 1994.

The per capita GNI figures listed below are useful indicators of economic success or failure, but they do not account for living costs. Nor do they reveal the gaps between the rich and poor within countries.

Market-friendly policies, including low taxes and state spending, liberal trade policies and a welcome for foreign investors, are major factors in countries that have enjoyed rapid economic growth since 1980. For example, the setting up of Special Economic Zones in eastern China has led to a spectacular rise in the per capita GNP. Other successful countries included South Korea and Singapore, although an Asian market crash in 1997 temporarily halted the dramatic economic expansion of these countries.

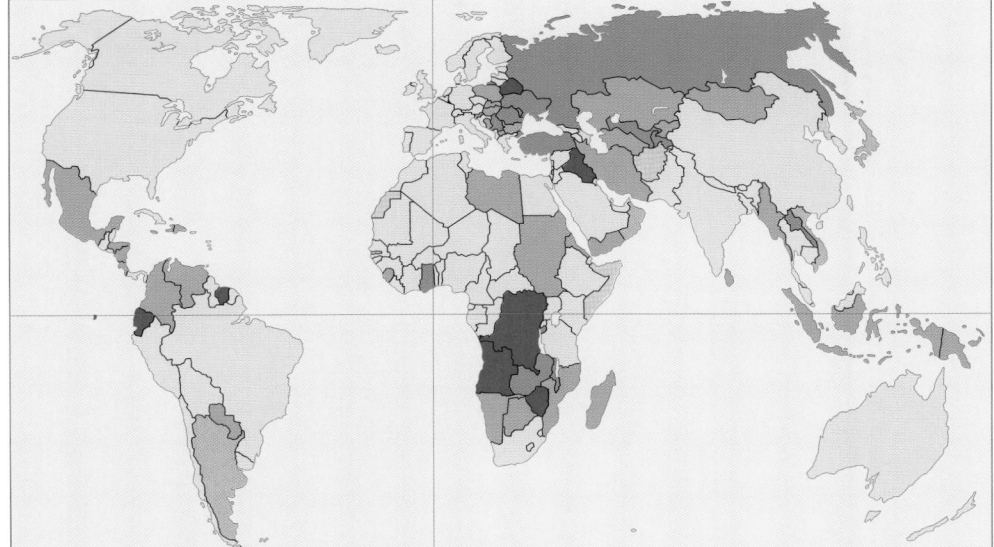

Inflation

Average annual rate of inflation (2000)

- Over 50%
- 20 – 50%
- 7.5 – 20%
- 1 – 7.5%
- Negative inflation
- No data available

Highest average inflation
Congo (Dem. Rep.) 1,423%
Angola 740%
Turkmenistan............................. 407%

Lowest average inflation
Antigua and Barbuda .... –11.5%
Argentina* .... –3.1%
Bahrain...................................... –0.1%

* During 2002, Argentina experienced a sharp rise in inflation which is not reflected on this map.

The Wealth Gap

The world's richest and poorest countries, by Gross National Income per capita in US $ (2001)

1. Luxembourg	41,770	1. Ethiopia	100
2. Switzerland	36,970	2. Burundi	100
3. Japan	35,990	3. Sierra Leone	140
4. Norway	35,530	4. Guinea-Bissau	160
5. USA	34,870	5. Tajikistan	170
6. Denmark	31,090	6. Niger	170
7. Iceland	28,880	7. Malawi	170
8. Sweden	25,400	8. Eritrea	190
9. UK	24,230	9. Chad	200
10. Netherlands	24,040	10. Mozambique	210
11. Finland	23,940	11. Mali	210
12. Austria	23,940	12. Burkina Faso	210
13. Germany	23,700	13. Rwanda	220
14. Belgium	23,340	14. Nepal	250
15. Ireland	23,060	15. Madagascar	260
16. France	22,690	16. Togo	270
17. Canada	21,340	17. Tanzania	270
18. Australia	19,770	18. Central African Rep.	270
19. Italy	19,470	19. Cambodia	270
20. Spain	14,860	20. Uganda	280

GNI per capita is calculated by dividing a country's Gross National Income by its total population.

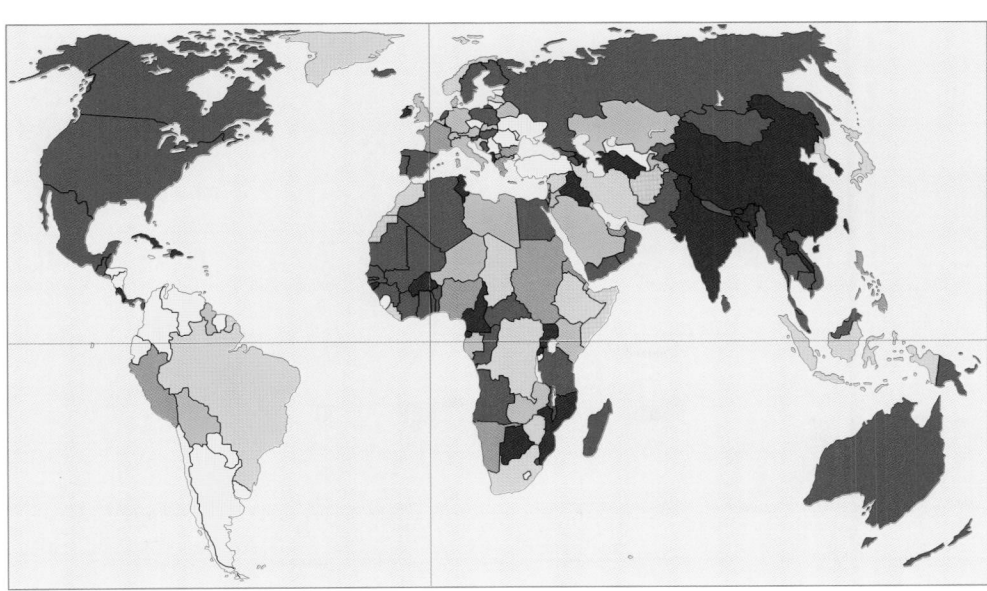
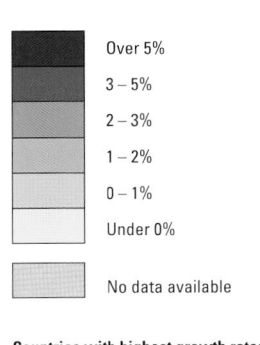

Growth in GNI

GNI per capita annual growth rate (1998–9)

- Over 5%
- 3 – 5%
- 2 – 3%
- 1 – 2%
- 0 – 1%
- Under 0%
- No data available

Countries with highest growth rates
Equatorial Guinea 15.0%
Mozambique 10.0%
Palau 10.0%
South Korea 10.0%
Guinea-Bissau 9.5%

STANDARDS OF LIVING

For more information:
18 Water supply
24 Population density
27 Urban pollution
    Squatter settlements
    Urban advantages
30 World's refugees
    War since 1945
38 Employment
    The workforce
43 Life expectancy
    Infant mortality
45 The wealth gap
    Aid donors

Wealth is a basic factor in determining standards of living. Everywhere, the rich have more of everything, including higher average life expectancies, while the poor have to spend most of their income on basic human needs, such as food and clothing. Yet poverty and wealth are relative terms. Slum dwellers living on social security in an industrial society feel their poverty acutely, but they have far more resources than an average African living in a rural area.

In 1990 the United Nations Development Programme published its first Human Development Index (HDI), an attempt to construct a comparative scale by which a simplified form of well-being might be measured. The HDI, expressed as a value between 0 and 0.999, combines figures for life expectancy and literacy with a wealth scale, based on Purchasing Power Parity. The world's countries are divided into three groups, those with a high HDI (0.800 and above); those with a medium HDI (0.500 to 0.799); and those with a low HDI (below 0.500).

In 2002, Norway was top in the world rankings and Sierra Leone was bottom. In fact, of the 36 countries with a low HDI, 29 were from Africa, 6 from Asia, plus Haiti from the Caribbean. Besides having low per capita GNPs, the average life expectancy in these countries was 59 years, while the adult literacy rate was 58%. By comparison, the average life expectancy at birth in countries in the high HDI group was 78 years, while the literacy rate was 98%.

Comparisons between countries with similar per capita GNPs reveal the effects of government actions. For example, the World Bank classifies both India and China as low-income economies, but India's HDI at 0.577 is much lower than that of China, at 0.726. This reflects not only China's economic progress in the 1980s and 1990s, but also differences in average life expectancies (63 years in India and 70 years in China), and adult literacy rates (52% in India and 82% in China).

Disparities in standards of living exist not only between countries but also between individuals, groups and regions within countries. For example, income distribution figures for 1995 show that, in the United States, the poorest 20% of households received less than 4% of the income.

Other contrasts exist in developing countries between rural communities, where incomes are low and basic services are often in short supply, and urban areas, where even those living in slums are generally better off than their rural neighbours. Other striking differences exist between men and women. For example, while adult literacy rates for men and women living in developed countries are more or less the same, large differences exist in many developing countries. In 2001, in countries in the lowest HDI category, only 64% of women were literate, as compared with 73% of men.

Female education is a factor in population control, especially as women's fertility rates appear to fall in direct proportion to the amount of secondary education they receive. This point was acknowledged in 1994 by the UN Population Fund, which defined four main objectives relating to women and population control. They were: the reduction of maternal, infant and child mortality; better education, especially for girls; universal access to reproductive health services; and gender equality.

Statistical analysis presents many problems of interpretation, especially when trying to define such intangible factors as a sense of well-being. For example, education helps create wealth; but are rich countries wealthy because their people are well educated, or are they well educated because they are rich?

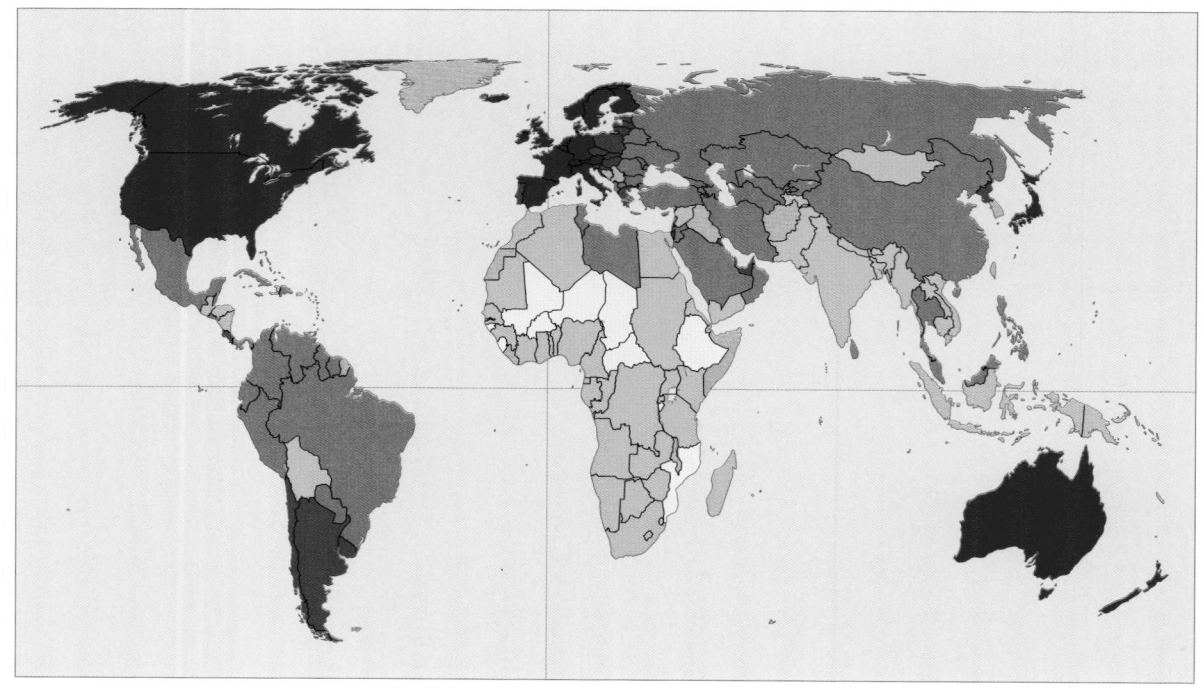

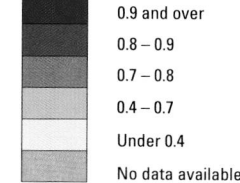

Human Development Index

The Human Development Index (HDI), calculated by the UN Development Programme (UNDP), gives a value to countries using indicators of life expectancy, education and standards of living in 2000. Higher values show more developed countries.

- 0.9 and over
- 0.8 – 0.9
- 0.7 – 0.8
- 0.4 – 0.7
- Under 0.4
- No data available

Highest values
Norway 0.942
Sweden 0.941
Canada 0.940
USA 0.939
Belgium 0.939

Lowest values
Sierra Leone 0.275
Niger 0.277
Burundi 0.313
Mozambique 0.322
Burkina Faso 0.325

Education

The developing countries made great efforts in the 1970s and 1980s to bring at least a basic education to their people. Primary school enrolments rose above 60% in all but the poorest nations. Figures often include teenagers or young adults, however, and there are still an estimated 300 million children worldwide who receive no schooling at all. A lack of resources has restricted the development of secondary and higher education. Most primary school education is free in the poorer countries, but fees are often paid for secondary and higher education, thus heightening the differences between rich and poor.

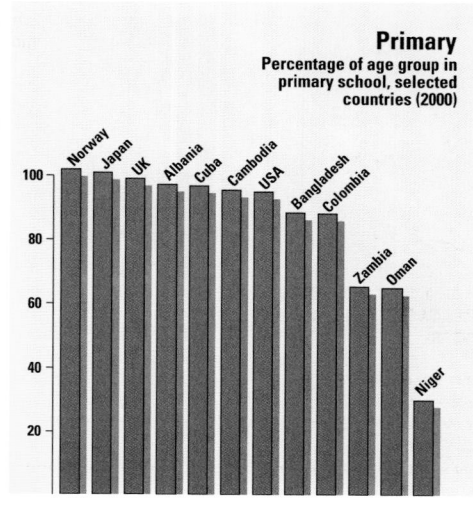

Primary
Percentage of age group in primary school, selected countries (2000)

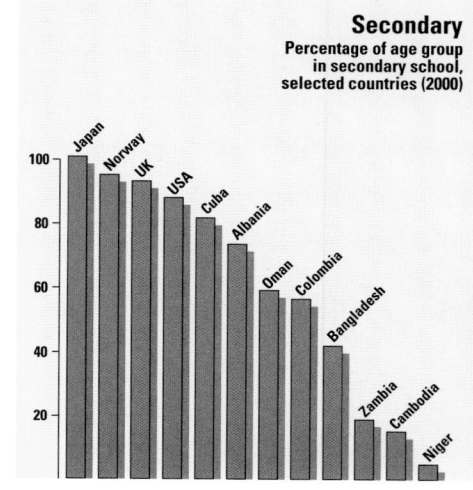

Secondary
Percentage of age group in secondary school, selected countries (2000)

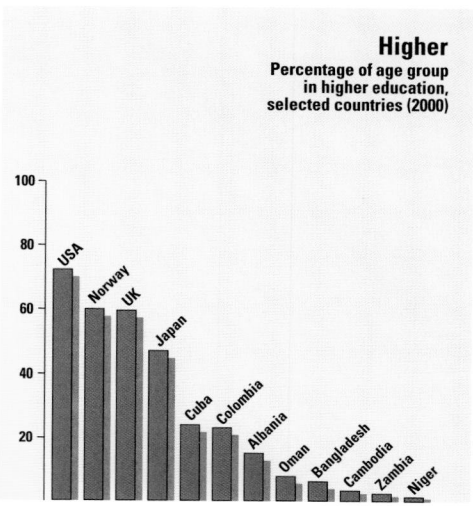

Higher
Percentage of age group in higher education, selected countries (2000)

Distribution of Spending

Percentage share of household spending (latest available year)

A high proportion of the average income of households in developing nations is spent on basic needs such as food and clothing. In most Western countries food and clothing account for less than 25% of expenditure.

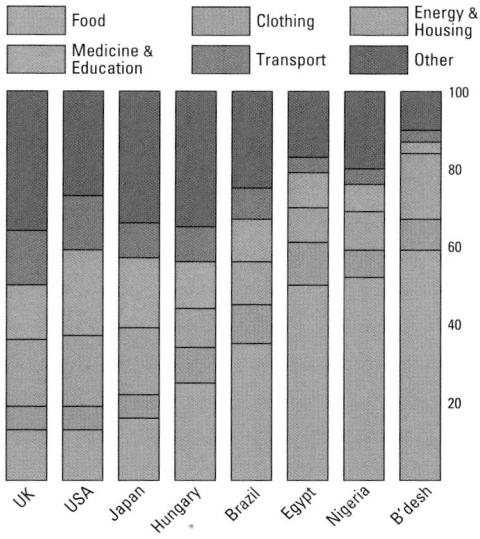

Distribution of Income

Percentage share of household income from poorest fifth to richest fifth, selected countries (latest available year)

The graph (*below*) shows that wealth is not distributed evenly throughout the population of the six countries. In every country worldwide the richest 20% of the population have a disproportionately high percentage of the income. This disparity between rich and poor is nowhere more pronounced than in Brazil, where the richest 20% of the population have over 60% of the income. The poorest 20%, on the other hand, have less than 5%.

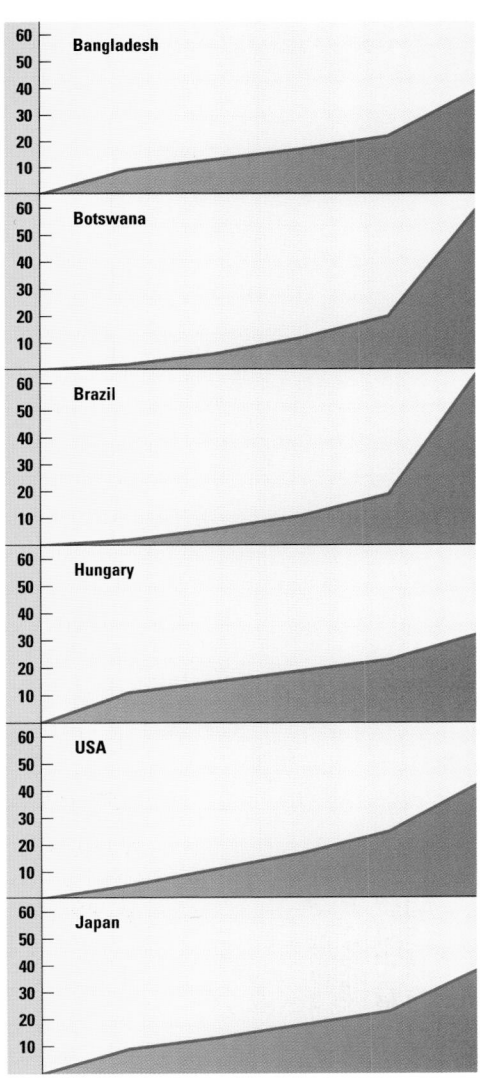

Fertility and Education

Fertility rates compared with female education, selected countries (1995–2000)

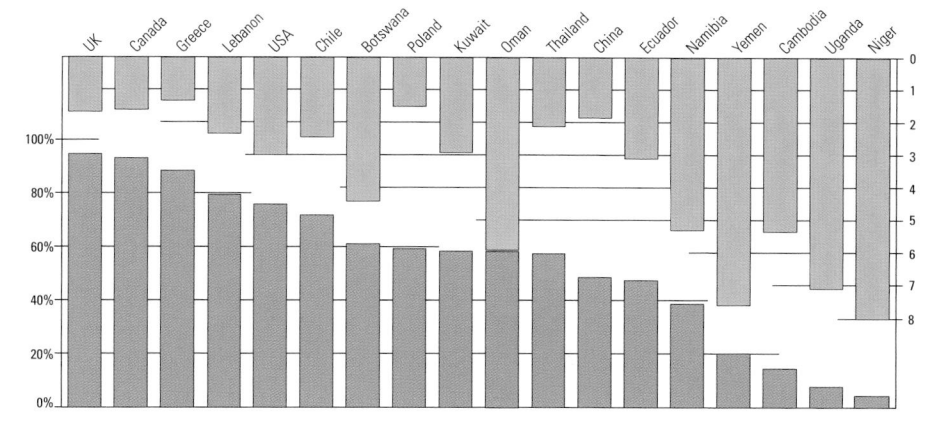

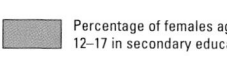
Fertility rate: average number of children borne per woman

Percentage of females aged 12–17 in secondary education

Access to secondary education is closely linked to low fertility rates in developed countries. By contrast, in many developing countries, women's lives are dominated by agriculture, or they lack access to secondary and higher education for cultural reasons, as in Muslim countries. Such disparities are reflected in women's parliamentary representation which is only one-seventh that of men, despite the emergence of such figures as Mrs Indira Gandhi, India's former prime minister. Female wages are also, on average, only two-thirds of those of men.

Gender Development Index

The Gender Development Index (GDI) shows economic and social differences between men and women by using various UNDP indicators (2002). Countries with higher values of GDI have more equality between men and women.

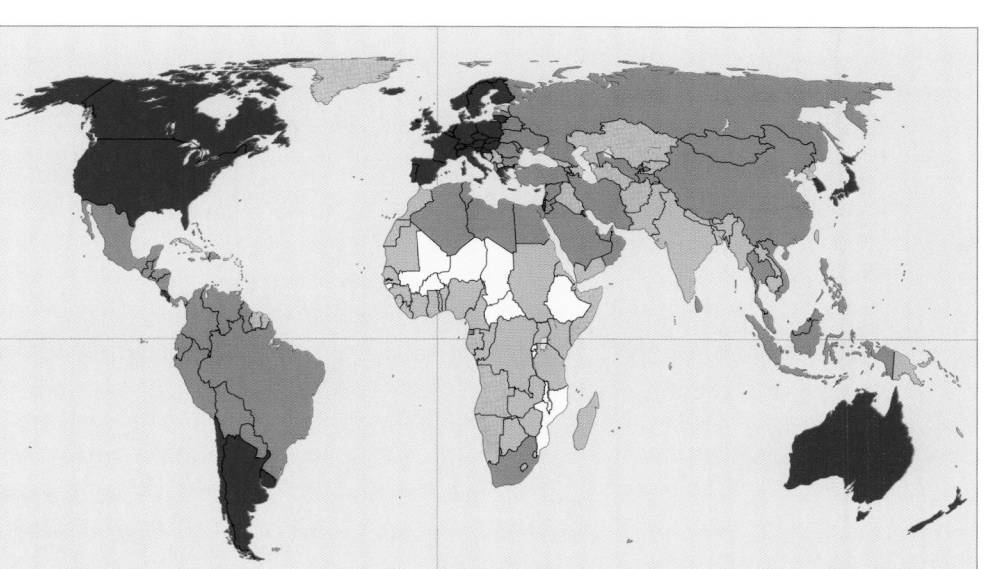

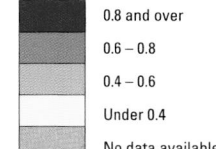
- 0.8 and over
- 0.6 – 0.8
- 0.4 – 0.6
- Under 0.4
- No data available

Highest values

Norway	.0.941
Australia	.0.938
Canada	.0.938
USA	.0.937

Lowest values

Niger	.0.263
Burundi	.0.306
Mozambique	.0.307
Burkina Faso	.0.312

Car Ownership

Proportion of the world's vehicles, by region

North America
Western Europe
Asia
E.Europe & CIS
Others

TOTAL = 312 million vehicles

Motor cars per 100 people

Lebanon	73.1
Brunei	57.5
Italy	56.8
Luxembourg	56.1
USA	51.8

Standards of Living in the USA by Race, Age and Region

A comparison of measures of income and education, by selected characteristics (2001–2)

Median income per household (US $), by age and region	Per capita income (US $), by race and Hispanic origin of householder	Percentage of persons aged 25 and over who have completed High School, by race or origin
15–24 years 28,196		
25–34 years 45,086	ALL RACES 22,851	ALL RACES 1975 .... 62.5
35–44 years 53,320	White 24,127	2001 .... 84.1
45–54 years 58,045	Black 14,953	White 1975 .... 64.5
55–64 years 45,864	Asian and Pacific Is. .. 24,277	2001 .... 84.4
65 years and over 23,118	Hispanic (any race) 13,003	Black 1975 .... 42.5
		2001 .... 78.7
North-east 45,716	The poorest 20% of households	Hispanic 1975 .... 37.9
Mid-west 43,834	received just 3.6% of the	2001 .... 57.0
South 38,904	income, whereas the richest	
West 45,687	20% received 48.2%.	

Regional Inequality in Italy

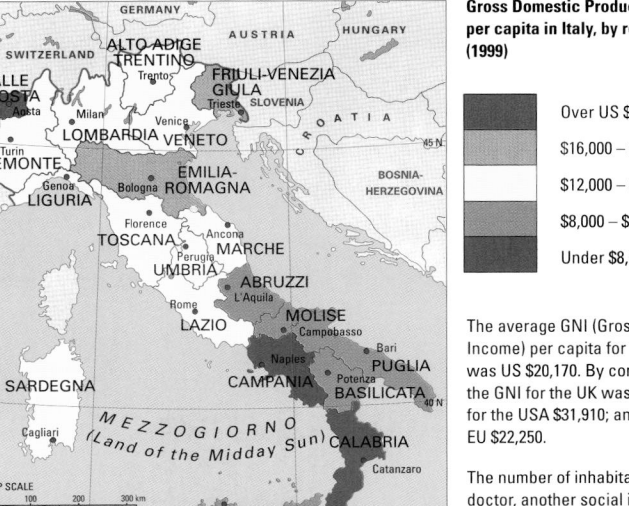

Gross Domestic Product (GDP) per capita in Italy, by region (1999)

- Over US $20,000
- $16,000 – $19,999
- $12,000 – $15,999
- $8,000 – $11,999
- Under $8,000

The average GNI (Gross National Income) per capita for Italy was US $20,170. By comparison, the GNI for the UK was $23,590; for the USA $31,910; and for the EU $22,250.

The number of inhabitants per doctor, another social indicator, varies from less than 500 in the north-west of Italy to over 800 in the far south (the *Mezzogiorno*), with a national average of 607.

The southern part of Italy, known as the *Mezzogiorno* (or 'Land of the midday sun'), has been described as the poorest part of the European Union. It is identifiable on the map (*left*) as all the regions with a GDP per capita of less than US $12,000 (including the two islands of Sicily and Sardinia), plus Abruzzi whose capital is L'Aquila.

The *Mezzogiorno* region suffers from a lack of mineral and energy resources, industry, commerce, services and skilled labour. As a result, standards of living in the region are well below the rest of Italy and Europe. Employment is predominantly agricultural and small-scale.

The north of Italy accounts for 60% of the population but 80% of the GDP, whereas the *Mezzogiorno* accounts for 40% of the population and only 20% of the GDP. Manpower surpluses in the south led to emigration to other parts of Europe and the Americas. It has also led, especially in the last 50 years, to inter-regional migration from the islands and the southern mainland to the north. The main regions attracting migrants were the north-west – the prosperous Liguria–Piedmont–Lombardy triangle with its great industrial cities of Genoa, Milan and Turin – and the Venetia region in the north-east. As a result, the north has experienced much higher population growth rates than the rest of Italy.

In 1996 the Northern League, one of Italy's political parties, exploited the regional differences by declaring the north to be the independent 'Republic of Padania'. However, only a small minority of northerners supports secession.

WORLD
MAPS

SETTLEMENTS

■ **PARIS**   ◉ **Rotterdam**   ◉ **Livorno**   ◎ **Brugge**   ◉ Exeter   ○ Torremolinos   ○ Oberammergau   ○ Thira

Settlement symbols and type styles vary according to the scale of each map and indicate the importance
of towns on the map rather than specific population figures

● Vaduz   Capital cities have red infills   ∴   Ruins or Archaeological Sites

⬠   Urban Agglomerations   Wells in Desert

ADMINISTRATION

────── International Boundaries   ·········· Internal Boundaries   **PERU**   Country Names

- - - - - International Boundaries   ⬓ National Parks   KENT   Administrative
(Undefined or Disputed)   Area Names

International boundaries show the *de facto* situation where there are rival claims to territory

COMMUNICATIONS

────── Motorways, Freeways   ────── Principal Railways   LHR ✈ Principal Airports
and Expressways

────── Principal Roads   - - - - Railways   ✈ Other Airports
Under Construction

────── Other Roads   ────── Other Railways   ·········· Principal Canals

⊣-⊢ Road Tunnels   ⊣-⊢ Railway Tunnels   ⤫ Passes

PHYSICAL FEATURES

────── Perennial Streams   ◌ Intermittent Lakes   ▲ 8850 Elevations in metres

- - - - Intermittent Streams   ◌ Swamps and Marshes   ▼ 8500 Sea Depths in metres

◯ Perennial Lakes   ▨ Permanent Ice   *1134* Height of Lake Surface
and Glaciers   Above Sea Level in metres

ELEVATION AND DEPTH TINTS

Height of Land above Sea Level   Land Below Sea Level   Depth of Sea

in metres   6000 4000 3000 2000 1500 1000 400 200   0
                                                                          6000 12 000 15 000 18 000 24 000   in feet

in feet   18 000 12 000 9000 6000 4500 3000 1200 600
                                                              0   200 2000 4000 5000 6000 8000   in metres

Some of the maps have different contours to highlight and clarify the principal relief features

Equatorial Scale 1:80 000 000

Projection: *Hammer Equal Area*

Hanoi ● Capital Cities

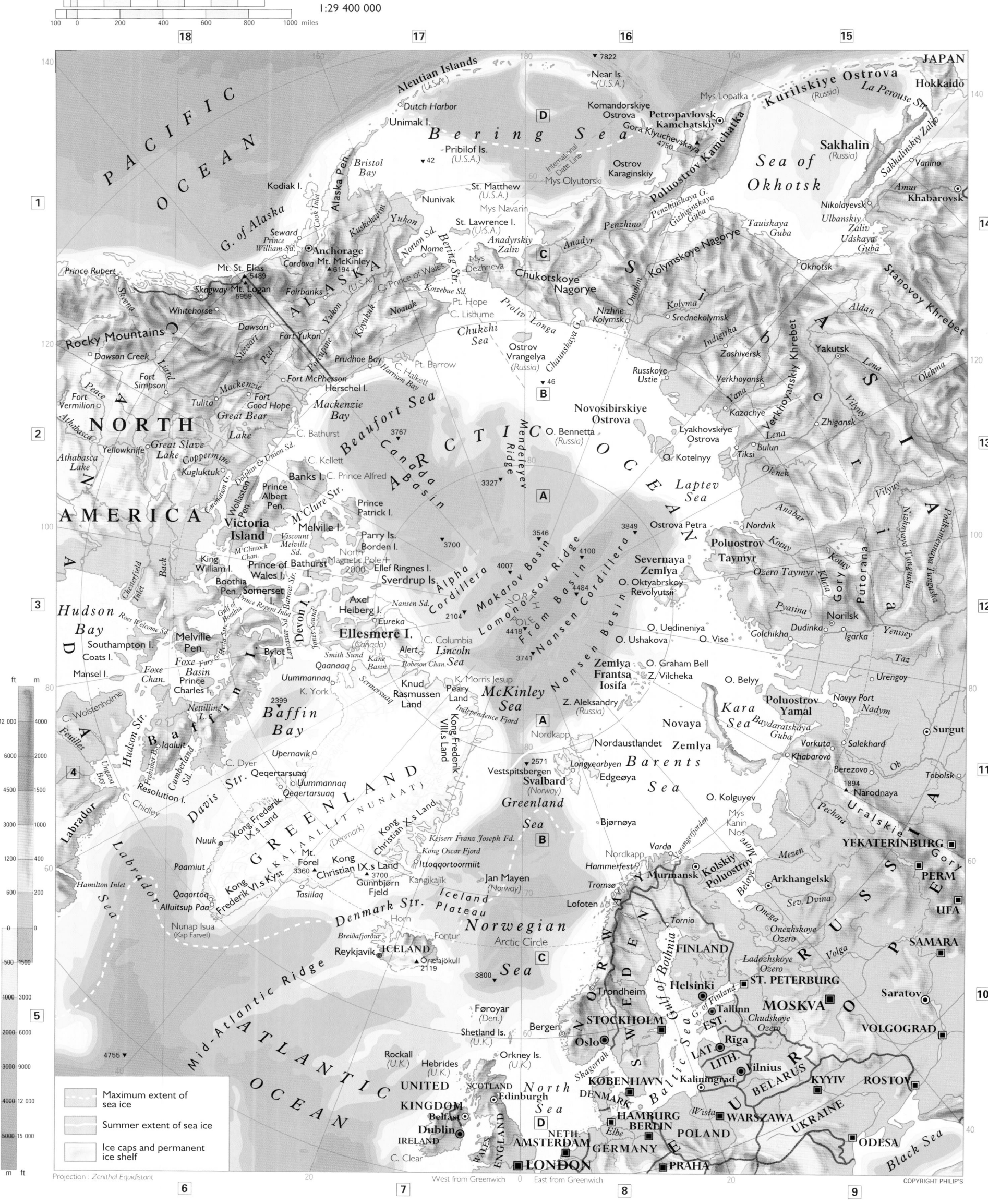

1:29 400 000

Maximum extent of sea ice

Summer extent of sea ice

Ice caps and permanent ice shelf

Projection : Zenithal Equidistant

COPYRIGHT PHILIP'S

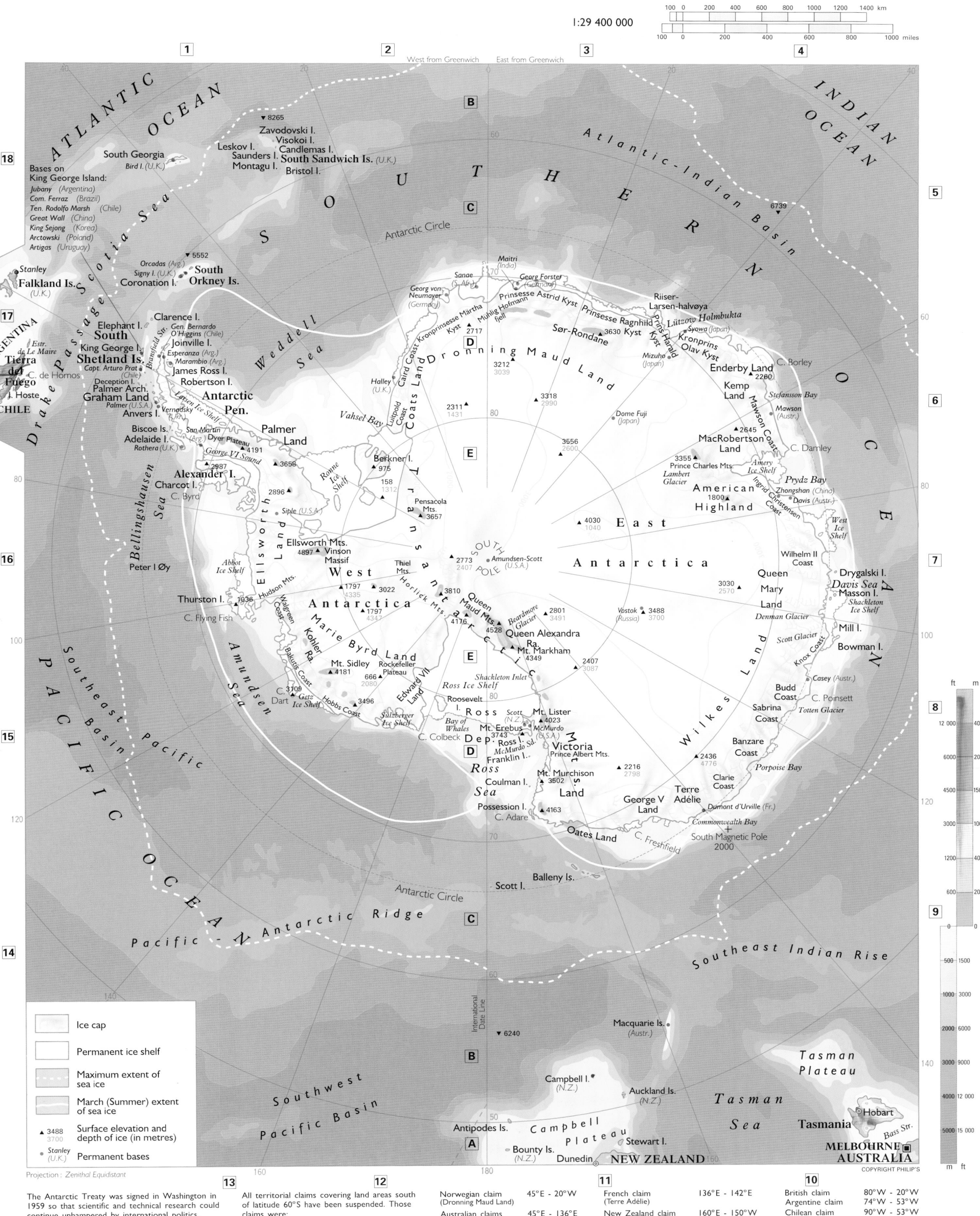

1:29 400 000

| 100 | 0 | 200 | 400 | 600 | 800 | 1000 | 1200 | 1400 km |

| 100 | 0 | 200 | 400 | 600 | 800 | 1000 miles |

Legend:

- Ice cap
- Permanent ice shelf
- Maximum extent of sea ice
- March (Summer) extent of sea ice
- ▲ 3488 / 3700 — Surface elevation and depth of ice (in metres)
- Stanley (U.K.) Permanent bases

Projection: Zenithal Equidistant

The Antarctic Treaty was signed in Washington in 1959 so that scientific and technical research could continue unhampered by international politics.

All territorial claims covering land areas south of latitude 60°S have been suspended. Those claims were:

Norwegian claim (Dronning Maud Land)	45°E – 20°W
Australian claims	45°E – 136°E / 142°E – 160°E
French claim (Terre Adélie)	136°E – 142°E
New Zealand claim (Ross Dependency)	160°E – 150°W
British claim	80°W – 20°W
Argentine claim	74°W – 53°W
Chilean claim	90°W – 53°W

Bases on King George Island:
Jubany (Argentina)
Com. Ferraz (Brazil)
Ten. Rodolfo Marsh (Chile)
Great Wall (China)
King Sejong (Korea)
Arctowski (Poland)
Artigas (Uruguay)

COPYRIGHT PHILIP'S

1:16 800 000

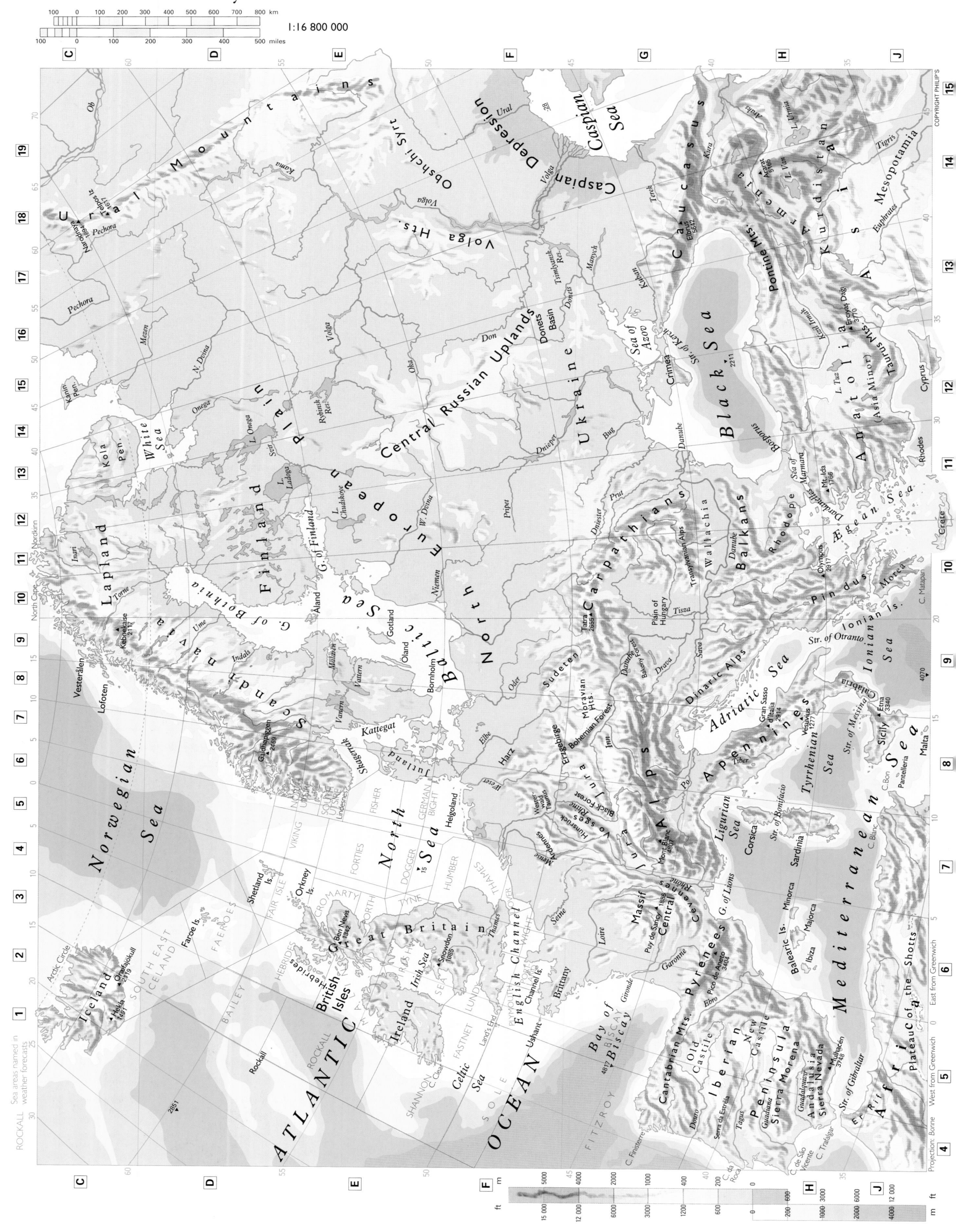

COPYRIGHT PHILIPS

Projection: Bonne

1:16 800 000

100 0 100 200 300 400 500 600 700 800 km

100 0 100 200 300 400 500 miles

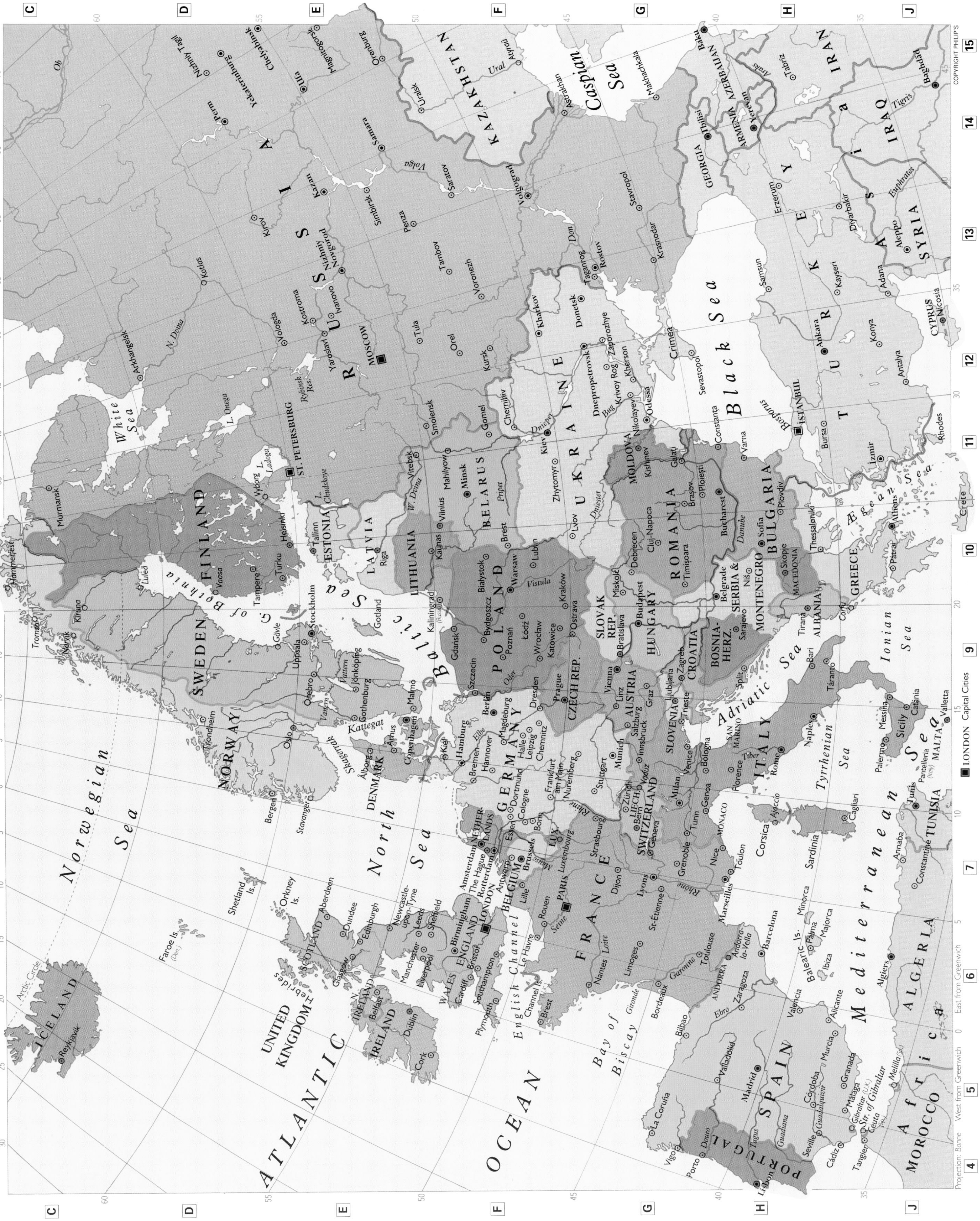
ICELAND
Reykjavík
Norwegian Sea
NORWAY
SWEDEN
FINLAND
ESTONIA
LATVIA
LITHUANIA
BELARUS
UKRAINE
MOLDOVA
ROMANIA
BULGARIA
GREECE
ALBANIA
MACEDONIA
SERBIA & MONTENEGRO
BOSNIA-HERZ.
CROATIA
SLOVENIA
HUNGARY
SLOVAK REP.
CZECH REP.
POLAND
GERMANY
DENMARK
NETHER-LANDS
BELGIUM
LUX.
FRANCE
SWITZERLAND
AUSTRIA
ITALY
SPAIN
PORTUGAL
UNITED KINGDOM
IRELAND
RUSSIA
KAZAKHSTAN
GEORGIA
ARMENIA
AZERBAIJAN
TURKEY
SYRIA
IRAQ
IRAN
CYPRUS
MOROCCO
ALGERIA
TUNISIA
Africa
ATLANTIC OCEAN
North Sea
Baltic Sea
Black Sea
Caspian Sea
Mediterranean Sea
Adriatic Sea
Ionian Sea
Tyrrhenian Sea
Aegean Sea
Bay of Biscay
English Channel
White Sea
G. of Bothnia
LONDON
PARIS
MOSCOW
ST. PETERSBURG
ISTANBUL
LONDON Capital Cities
Projection: Bonne
West from Greenwich
East from Greenwich
COPYRIGHT PHILIP'S

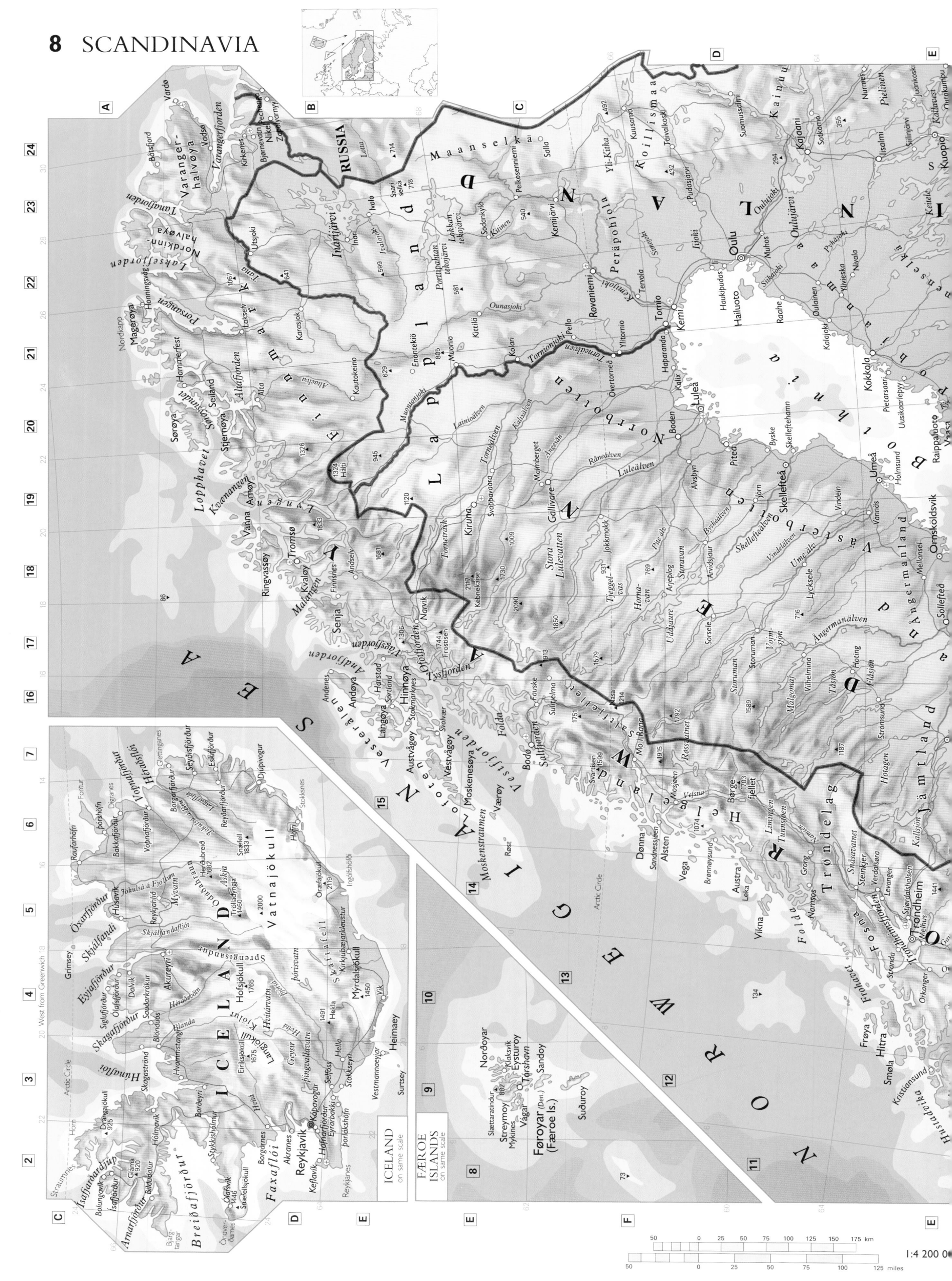

ICELAND
on same scale

FÆROE
ISLANDS
on same scale

1:4 200 000

50   0   25   50   75   100 125 150 175 km

50   0   25   50   75   100 125 miles

Map of southern Scandinavia and northern Germany (Denmark, southern Sweden, northern Poland and Germany).

POLAND

GERMANY

DENMARK

BALTIC SEA

Kattegat

Skagerrak

ÖSTERGÖTLANDS

JÖNKÖPINGS LÄN

KALMAR LÄN

KRONOBERGS LÄN

BLEKINGE LÄN

HALLANDS LÄN

SKÅNE LÄN

VÄSTRA GÖTALANDS LÄN

Bohuslän

Dalsland

Götaland

Småland

Gotland (Sweden)

Öland (Sweden)

Bornholm (Denmark)

Göteborg · Borås · Jönköping · Linköping · Norrköping · Kalmar · Växjö · Karlskrona · Kristianstad · Helsingborg · Lund · Malmö · Visby

København · Roskilde · Odense · Århus · Ålborg · Esbjerg · Kolding · Vejle · Randers · Horsens

NORDJYLLANDS AMT · VIBORG AMT · RINGKØBING AMT · ÅRHUS AMT · VEJLE AMT · RIBE AMT · SØNDERJYLLANDS AMT · FYNS AMT · VESTSJÆLLANDS AMT · STORSTRØMS AMT · FREDERIKSBORGS AMT · KØBENHAVNS AMT · ROSKILDE AMT · BORNHOLMS AMT

Jylland · Fyn · Sjælland · Lolland · Falster · Langeland · Als

Flensburg · Kiel · Eckernförde · Husum · Sylt · Föhr

Slupsk · Łeba · Ustka · Lębork

National Parks

1:1 700 000

10 0 10 20 30 40 50 60 70 80 km
10 0 10 20 30 40 50 miles

SCOTLAND
Kintyre
Mull of Oa
Brodick Arran
Campbeltown
Mull of Kintyre
Ailsa Craig
Firth of Clyde

ATLANTIC OCEAN

Inishtrahull
Tory I.
Malin Hd.
Horn Hd.
Sheep Haven
Lough Swilly
Fanad Hd.
Malin Pen.
Cardonagh
Moville
Inishowen Pen.
Portstewart Portrush
Giants Causeway
Rathlin I.
Fair Hd.
Ballycastle
North Channel
Mts of Antrim
Cairnryan
Stranraer
Portpatrick

Bloody Foreland
Buncrana
L. Foyle
Coleraine
Limavady
Ballymoney
554 Garron Pt.
GLENARIFF
Trostan
L. Ryan

Inishfree B.
Gweedore Errigal 752
The Rosses
Derryveagh Mts
GLENVEAGH
Rathmelton
Letterkenny
Londonderry
LONDONDERRY
Ballymena
Larne
Portpatrick

Aran I.
Crohy Hd.
683
Lifford Strabane
Sion Mills
Sawel Mt. 683
Spertin Mts
Roe Bann
Ballymoney
Randalstown Ballyclare
NORTHERN
Donaghadee
Newtownards

Gweebarra B.
Dawros Hd.
Glenties
DONEGAL
Lavagh More 676
Castlederg
Newtownstewart
Moyle
TYRONE
Magherafelt
Cookstown
Moneymore
Coalisland
Lough
Neagh
Antrim
Newtownabbey
Belfast L.
Belfast
Lisburn
Bangor
Comber
Strangford L.
Ards Pen.

Rossan Pt.
601 Slieve League
Donegal
Omagh
Dungannon
Craigavon
Lurgan
Portadown
Lagan
Banbridge
Tandragee
DOWN
Ballynahinch
Portaferry
Ballyquintin Pt.

Killybegs
St. John's Pt.
Ballyshannon
Bundoran
Erne
Lower L. Erne
Irvinestown
Enniskillen
Dromore
Clones
Monaghan
Armagh
Middletown
Keady
Newry
Mourne Mts
577 Slieve Gullion
852 Slieve Donard
Newcastle
St. John's Pt.
Dundrum B.

Donegal Bay
Downpatrick Hd.
FERMANAGH
Upper Erne
Belturbet
Annalee
Castleblaney
Cootehill
Warrenpoint
Greenore
Kilkeel
Carlingford L.

Broad Haven
Erris Hd.
Killala B.
Sligo Bay
Sligo
Collooney
L. Allen
MONAGHAN
Dundalk
Carlingford L.

Mullet Pen.
Belmullet
380
Killala
Ballina
Dromore West
544
S Gamph
Ballymote
L. Arrow
LEITRIM
Leitrim
Carrickmacross
Kingscourt
Ardee
LOUTH
Dundalk Bay

Inishkea North
Inishkea South
Blacksod Bay
Slieve
SLIGO
Charlestown
Boyle
Carrick-on-Shannon
CAVAN
L. Gowna
L. Sheelin
Oldcastle
Ceanannus Mor (Kells)
Blackwater
Dunleer
Clogher Hd.

Achill Hd.
672
Achill I.
Corraun Pen.
MAYO
Newport
Castlebar
Swinford
Knock
Ballaghaderreen
ROSCOMMON
Castlerea
Granard
L. Gowna
Cavan
Kingscourt
MEATH
An Uaimh (Navan)
Drogheda
Balbriggan

Clare I.
Clew Bay
Westport
765 Croagh Patrick
Mweelrea 819
Ballinrobe
Ballyhaunis
Claremorris
Castlerea
Roscommon
LONGFORD
Longford
Castlepollard
Boyne
Trim
Rush
Lambay I.

Inishturk
Killary Harbour
Inishbofin
Inishshark
Connemara
CONNEMARA
Lough Mask
Tuam
Lough Ree
IRELAND
WESTMEATH
Mullingar
Athboy
Swords
DUB
Malahide
Howth Hd.
DUBLIN

Slyne Hd.
Clifden
Lough Corrib
Oughterard
GALWAY
Athenry
Ballinasloe
Athlone
Moate
Royal Canal
Leinster
Maynooth
Dun Laoghaire

Bertraghboy B.
Kilkieran B.
Galway
Galway Bay
Black Hd.
Loughrea
Shannon
Suck
Clara
Grand Canal
Edenderry
Bog of Allen
KILDARE
Droichead Nua
Naas
Clondalkin
Bray
Greystones
123

Aran Is.
Inishmore
Inishmaan
Inisheer
BURREN
Gort
368
Slieve Aughty
Portumna
Birr
Tullamore
OFFALY
Portarlington
Kildare
Monasterevin
Port Laoise
Athy
Kippure 754
WICKLOW
WICKLOW MTS.

Cliffs of Moher
Hags Hd.
Liscannor Bay
Ennistimon
Lough Derg
Roscrea
Mountmellick
Slieve Bloom
529 Arderin
Mountrath
Wicklow
Lugnaquillia 926
Wicklow Hd.

Mal Bay
Mutton I.
Tulla
CLARE
Ennis
Killaloe
Nenagh
Templemore
LAOIS
Durrow
Carlow
Tullow
Shillelagh
Aughrim
Arklow

Loop Hd.
Kilkee
Kilrush
Shannon Airport
Sixmilebridge
694 Keeper Hill
Thurles
Kilkenny
KILKENNY
796 Mt. Leinster
Bunclody
Gorey
Mizen Hd.

Mouth of the Shannon
Kerry Hd.
Ballybunion
Foynes
LIMERICK
Limerick
Rathkeale
TIPPERARY
Golden Vale
Tipperary
Cashel
Callan
Muine Bheag
Cahore Pt.

Brandon B.
Smerwick Harbour
953 Brandon Mt.
Slieve Mish 853
Tralee
Listowel
Feale
Newcastle West
Kilfinnane
Galtymore 920
Galty Mts.
Caher
Slievenamon 722
Clonmel
Carrick-on-Suir
New Ross
WEXFORD
Enniscorthy
Wexford Harbour
Rosslare

Great Blasket I.
Dingle
KERRY
Maine
Newmarket
Kanturk
Buttevant
Mitchelstown
Fermoy
Knockmealdown Mts. 795
Comeragh Mts. 792
Waterford
Tramore
Rosslare Harbour
Greenore Pt.
Carnsore Pt.

Inishvickillane
Dingle Bay
Killorglin
Killarney
L. Leane
646
Macgillycuddy's Reeks
Mallow
Blackwater
WATERFORD
Lismore
Dungarvan
Tramore B.
Waterford Harbour
Hook Hd.
Saltee Is.

Valencia I.
Cahirceveen
Carrauntoohil 1041
KILLARNEY
Kenmare
Boggeragh Mts.
CORK
Blarney
Cork
Youghal
Cobh
Youghal B.
St. David's Hd.
St. David's
WALES

Puffin I.
Great Skellig
707
Caha Mts.
Lee
Macroom
Passage West
Crosshaven
Cork Harbour
Dungarvan Harbour
St. Brides Bay
115

Ballinskelligs B.
Scariff I.
Kenmare River
686
Glengarriff
Dunmanway
Bandon
Bandon
Kinsale
Old Head of Kinsale
St. George's Channel

Dursey I.
Castletown Bearhaven
Bear I.
Bantry
Bantry Bay
Clonakilty
Crow Hd.
Dunmanus B.
Skull
Clonakilty B.
Galley Hd.

Mizen Hd.
Long I.
Baltimore
Sherkin I.
Skibbereen
C. Clear
Clear I.
Fastnet Rock

CELTIC SEA

IRISH SEA

ft m
1500 500
600 200
300 100
0 0
50 150
100 300
200 600
500 1500
1000 3000
2000 6000
m ft

Projection: Lambert's Conformal Conic
West from Greenwich
COPYRIGHT PHILIP'S

National Parks

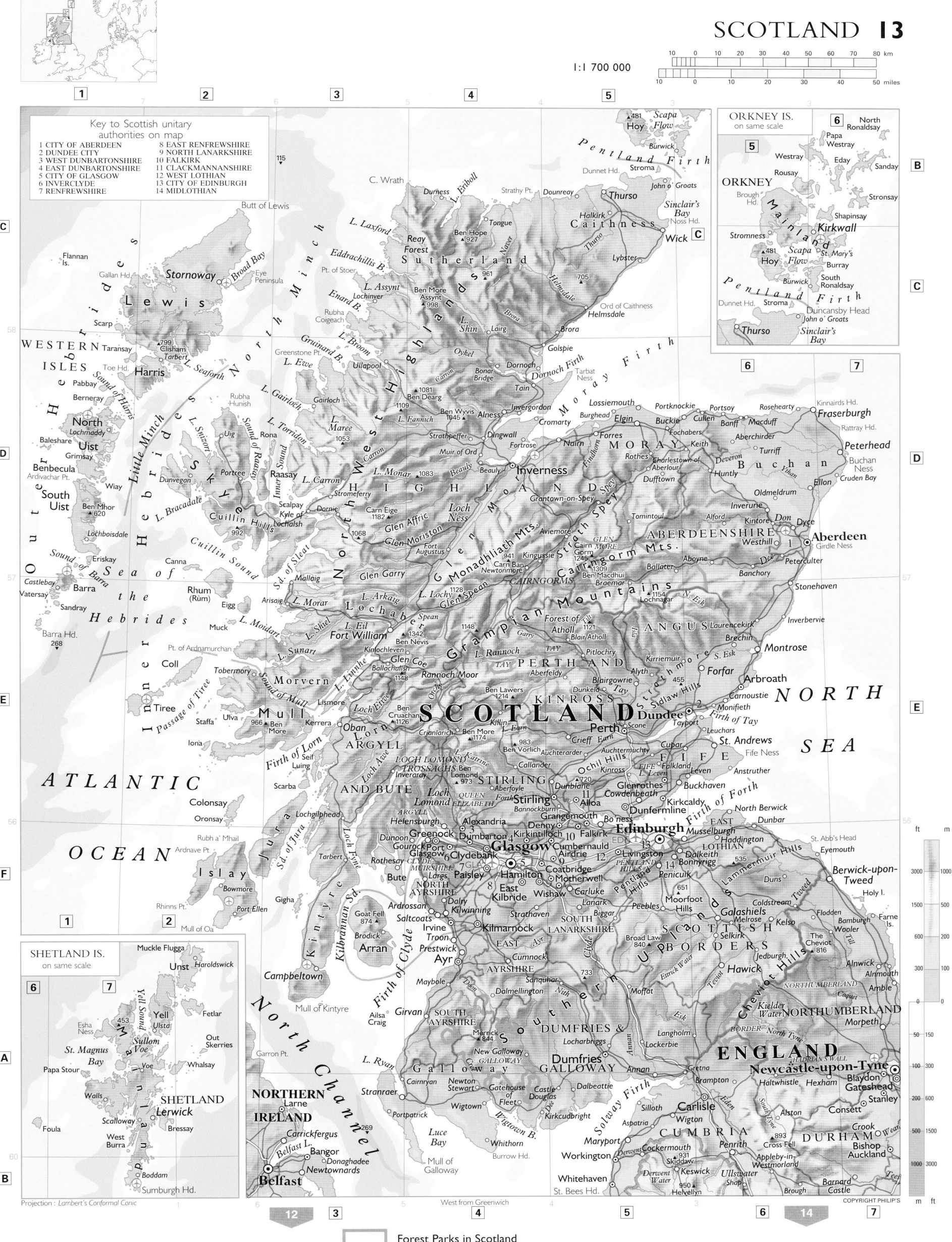

1:1 700 000

10   0   10   20   30   40   50   60   70   80 km
10   0   10   20   30   40   50 miles

Key to Scottish unitary authorities on map

1 CITY OF ABERDEEN
2 DUNDEE CITY
3 WEST DUNBARTONSHIRE
4 EAST DUNBARTONSHIRE
5 CITY OF GLASGOW
6 INVERCLYDE
7 RENFREWSHIRE
8 EAST RENFREWSHIRE
9 NORTH LANARKSHIRE
10 FALKIRK
11 CLACKMANNANSHIRE
12 WEST LOTHIAN
13 CITY OF EDINBURGH
14 MIDLOTHIAN

ORKNEY IS.
on same scale

ORKNEY

SHETLAND IS.
on same scale

Projection : Lambert's Conformal Conic

COPYRIGHT PHILIP'S

Forest Parks in Scotland

10 0 10 20 30 40 50 60 70 80 km

1:1 700 000

10 0 10 20 30 40 50 miles

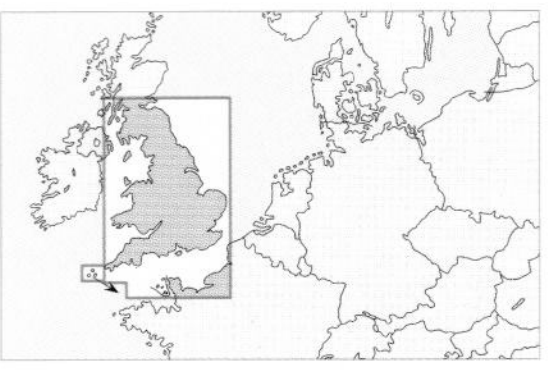

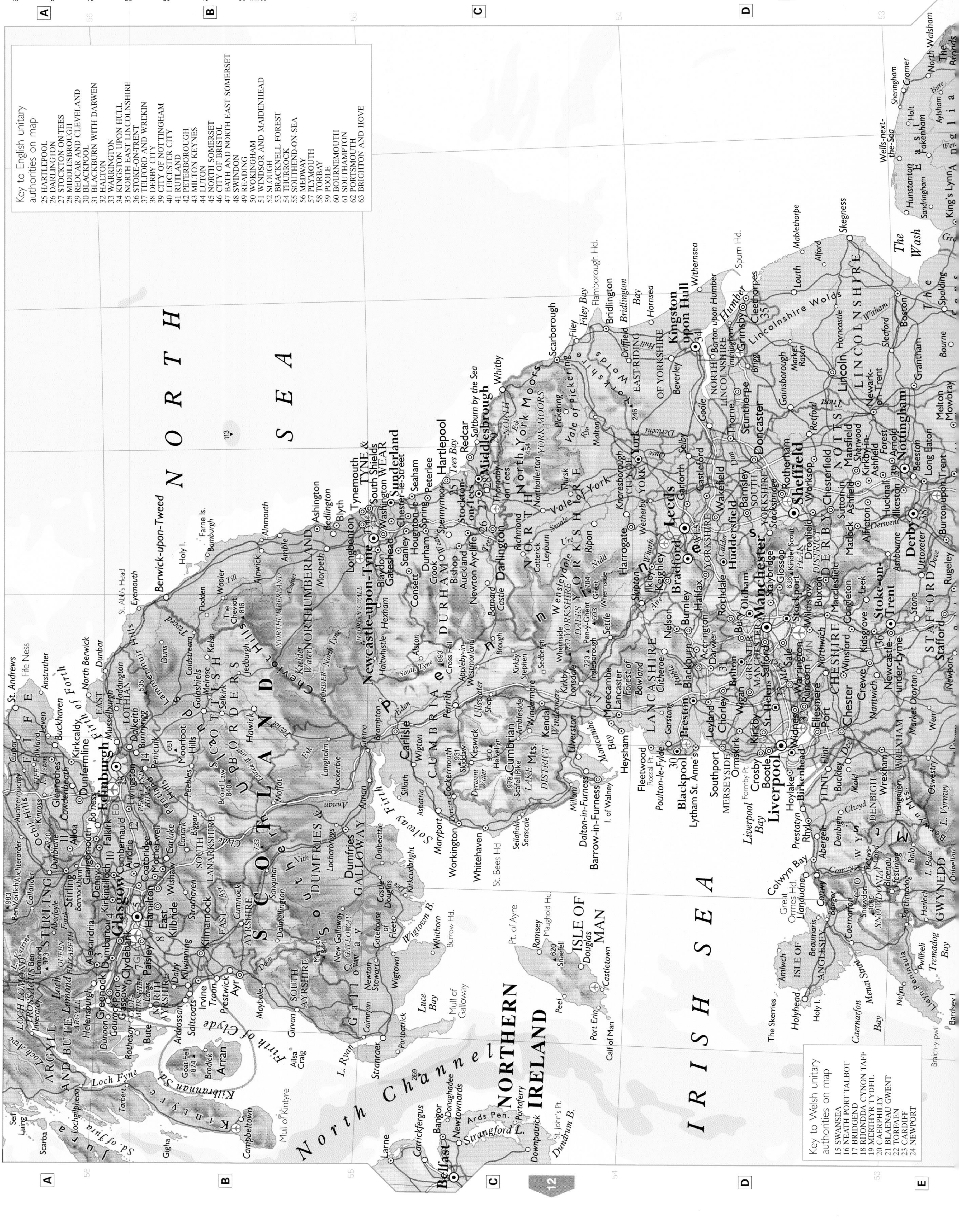

Key to English unitary authorities on map
25 HARTLEPOOL
26 DARLINGTON
27 STOCKTON-ON-TEES
28 MIDDLESBROUGH
29 REDCAR AND CLEVELAND
30 BLACKPOOL
31 BLACKBURN WITH DARWEN
32 HALTON
33 WARRINGTON
34 KINGSTON UPON HULL
35 NORTH EAST LINCOLNSHIRE
36 STOKE-ON-TRENT
37 TELFORD AND WREKIN
38 DERBY CITY
39 CITY OF NOTTINGHAM
40 LEICESTER CITY
41 RUTLAND
42 PETERBOROUGH
43 MILTON KEYNES
44 LUTON
45 NORTH SOMERSET
46 CITY OF BRISTOL
47 BATH AND NORTH EAST SOMERSET
48 SWINDON
49 READING
50 WOKINGHAM
51 WINDSOR AND MAIDENHEAD
52 SLOUGH
53 BRACKNELL FOREST
54 THURROCK
55 SOUTHEND-ON-SEA
56 MEDWAY
57 PLYMOUTH
58 TORBAY
59 POOLE
60 BOURNEMOUTH
61 SOUTHAMPTON
62 PORTSMOUTH
63 BRIGHTON AND HOVE
Key to Welsh unitary authorities on map
15 SWANSEA
16 NEATH PORT TALBOT
17 BRIDGEND
18 RHONDDA CYNON TAFF
19 MERTHYR TYDFIL
20 CAERPHILLY
21 BLAENAU GWENT
22 TORFAEN
23 CARDIFF
24 NEWPORT
NORTH SEA
IRISH SEA
North Channel
SCOTLAND
NORTHERN IRELAND
ISLE OF MAN
Edinburgh
Glasgow
Newcastle-upon-Tyne
Sunderland
Middlesbrough
Leeds
Bradford
Sheffield
Manchester
Liverpool
Kingston upon Hull
Nottingham
Derby
Stoke-on-Trent
Lincoln
Belfast

FRANCE

HAUTE-NORMANDIE

SEINE-MARITIME

CALVADOS

MANCHE

CHANNEL ISLANDS (U.K.)

Guernsey

Jersey

Alderney

Herm Sark

ENGLISH CHANNEL

Bristol Channel

Cardigan Bay

WALES

ENGLAND

CEREDIGION

POWYS

PEMBROKESHIRE

CARMARTHENSHIRE

SHROPSHIRE

HEREFORD

WORCESTER

GLOUCS

GLAMORGAN

VALE OF GLAMORGAN

SOMERSET

DEVON

CORNWALL

DORSET

WILTSHIRE

HANTS

WEST SUSSEX

EAST SUSSEX

KENT

SURREY

BERKSHIRE

OXFORDSHIRE

BUCKS

HERTS

BEDFORD

NORTHANTS

WARWICK

LEICS

CAMBRIDGE

NORFOLK

SUFFOLK

ESSEX

LONDON

ISLE OF WIGHT

Baie de la Seine

Strait of Dover

National Parks in England and Wales

Forest Parks in Scotland

ISLES OF SCILLY on same scale

Isles of Scilly

St. Mary's

Projection: Lambert's Conformal Conic

COPYRIGHT PHILIP'S

East from Greenwich

West from Greenwich

50 25 0 25 50 75 100 125 150 175 km
50 0 25 50 75 100 125 miles

1:4 200 000

ft m

ATLANTIC OCEAN

NORTH SEA

IRISH SEA

CELTIC SEA

NORTH CHANNEL

Shetland Is.
Yell · Unst · Fetlar
Foula · Mainland · Lerwick
Fair Isle

Orkney Is.
Westray · Sanday · Stronsay
Mainland · Kirkwall
Hoy · South Ronaldsay

Pentland Firth

C. Wrath
Lewis · Stornoway
St. Kilda
Harris
Outer Hebrides
North Uist · Benbecula
South Uist
Barra

Thurso · Wick · Helmsdale
Ullapool · Lairg · Golspie
North West Highlands
North Minch
Tain · Dingwall · Nairn · Elgin · Buckie · Banff · Fraserburgh · Peterhead
Inverness · Huntly · Inverurie
Moray Firth
Aviemore · Aberdeen
Glen More · L. Ness
Skye · Fort William · Ben Nevis 1342
Inner Hebrides
Sea of the Hebrides
Rhum · Eigg · Coll
Tobermory · Tiree
Mull · Oban
Colonsay
Jura · Islay
L. Awe · L. Lomond · Stirling · Perth · St. Andrews
L. Fyne · Dumbarton · Glenrothes · Kirkcaldy · Dunbar
Greenock · Paisley · GLASGOW · Edinburgh
Campbeltown · East Kilbride · Hamilton · Galashiels · Berwick-upon-Tweed
Arran · Irvine · Kilmarnock · Jedburgh
Ayr · Southern Uplands · Hawick · Cheviot Hills · Alnwick

SCOTLAND
GRAMPIAN MTS.
Forfar · Arbroath · Montrose
Dundee

Malin Hd.
Buncrana · Coleraine · Larne
Aran I. · Letterkenny · Londonderry · Ballymena · Antrim · Bangor
Donegal · Lifford · Omagh · NORTHERN IRELAND
Bundoran · Lower L. Erne · Lough Neagh · Belfast
Ballina · Enniskillen · Clones · Portadown · Lurgan · Armagh · Newry
Sligo · Leitrim · Cavan · Castleblaney
Castlebar · L. Conn · Dundalk

Mull of Galloway
Stranraer · Kirkcudbright · Dumfries · Annan · Carlisle · Hexham · Newcastle-upon-Tyne
Workington · Whitehaven · South Shields · Sunderland
Douglas · I. of Man · Cumbrian Mts. · Durham · Hartlepool
Barrow-in-Furness · Lancaster · Darlington · Middlesbrough · Stockton-on-Tees · Redcar
Scarborough
Bridlington

UNITED KINGDOM

IRELAND
Westport · Roscommon · Longford
Lough Mask · Lough Corrib · Athlone · Lough Ree · Mullingar
Connemara · Galway · Ballinasloe · Tullamore · Boyne
Galway B. · Aran Is. · Ceanannus Mor · Drogheda
Ennis · Birr · DUBLIN · Dun Laoghaire · Bray
Limerick · Nenagh · Port Laoise · Athy · Carlow · Wicklow Mts. · Arklow
Shannon · Listowel · Tipperary · Thurles · Kilkenny · Wexford · Rosslare
Tralee · Clonmel · Carrick-on-Suir
Dingle · Killarney · Waterford · Dungarvan
Carrauntoohill 1041 · Macgillycuddy's Reeks · Cork · Youghal
Valencia I. · Bandon · Cóbh
C. Clear · Bantry · Kinsale

Blackpool · Keighley · Harrogate · York · Beverley · Kingston upon Hull
Preston · Burnley · Leeds · Bradford
Blackburn · Halifax · Huddersfield · Barnsley · Doncaster · Scunthorpe · Grimsby
Bolton · Rochdale · Rotherham · Lincoln · Louth
Anglesey · Liverpool · Manchester · Oldham · Sheffield · Skegness
Holyhead · Warrington · Stockport · Chesterfield · Mansfield · Boston · The Wash
Bangor · Colwyn Bay · Crewe · Derby · Nottingham · Grantham · King's Lynn · Cromer
Pwllheli · Wrexham · Stoke-on-Trent · Stafford · Telford · Norwich · Great Yarmouth
Snowdon 1085 · Cambrian Mts. · Shrewsbury · ENGLAND · Lowestoft
Cardigan Bay · Welshpool · Nuneaton · Leicester · Corby · Peterborough · Thetford
Aberystwyth · BIRMINGHAM · Coventry · Rugby · Northampton · Ely · Bury St. Edmunds
WALES · Worcester · Redditch · Cambridge · Ipswich
Carmarthen · Brecon 886 · Hereford · Leamington Spa · Bedford · Felixstowe · Harwich
Merthyr Tydfil · Gloucester · Cheltenham · Milton Keynes · Stevenage · Colchester · Chelmsford
Llanelli · Neath · Cwmbran · Oxford · Hemel Hempstead · Luton · Harlow
Swansea · Rhondda · Cardiff · Bristol · Swindon · High Wycombe · Watford · Basildon · Southend-on-Sea
Port Talbot · Barry · Newbury · Slough · LONDON · Chatham · Margate
Bristol Channel · Weston-super-Mare · Bath · Reading · Reigate · Canterbury · Dover
Barnstaple · Salisbury · Basingstoke · Guildford · Crawley · Maidstone · Folkestone
Exmoor · Taunton · Winchester · Fareham · Hastings · Eastbourne
Bude · Yeovil · Southampton · Havant · Brighton · Worthing
Exeter · Bournemouth · Portsmouth · Isle of Wight · Worthing
Dartmoor 618 · Poole · Newport · Weymouth
Newquay · Torbay · English Channel
Truro · St. Austell · Plymouth
Land's End · Falmouth · Penzance
Isles of Scilly

NORWAY
Bergen · Osøyro · Stord · Bømlo · Leir · Haugesund · Koparvik · Åkrahamn · Stavanger · Sandnes · Bryne · Nærbø

NETHERLANDS
's-Gravenhage (Den Haag) · Haarlem · Den Helder
Hoek van Holland · ROTTERDAM · Dordrecht · Alkmaar

BELGIUM
Vlissingen · Zeebrugge · Oostende · Antwerpen · Mechelen
Brugge · Gent · BRUSSEL (Bruxelles)
Dunkerque · St-Omer · Tourcoing · Lille · Tournai
Calais · Béthune · Roubaix · Valenciennes · Cambrai
Gris-Nez · Boulogne-sur-Mer · Bruay-la-Buissière · Lens · Villeneuve d'Ascq
Le Touquet-Paris-Plage · Arras · St. Quentin
Abbeville · Amiens · PICARDIE
FRANCE
Le Tréport · Dieppe · Fécamp · Rouen · Laon
C. de la Hague · Pte. de Barfleur · Le Havre · Bolbec · Elbeuf
Alderney · St. Peter Port · Cherbourg · Valognes · Pays de Caux
Guernsey · Bayeux · Trouville-sur-Mer · Lisieux
Channel Is. (U.K.) · St. Helier · Jersey · Caen · Seine · Cotentin

Projection: Conical with two standard parallels

West from Greenwich

East from Greenwich
COPYRIGHT PHILIP'S

1:2 100 000

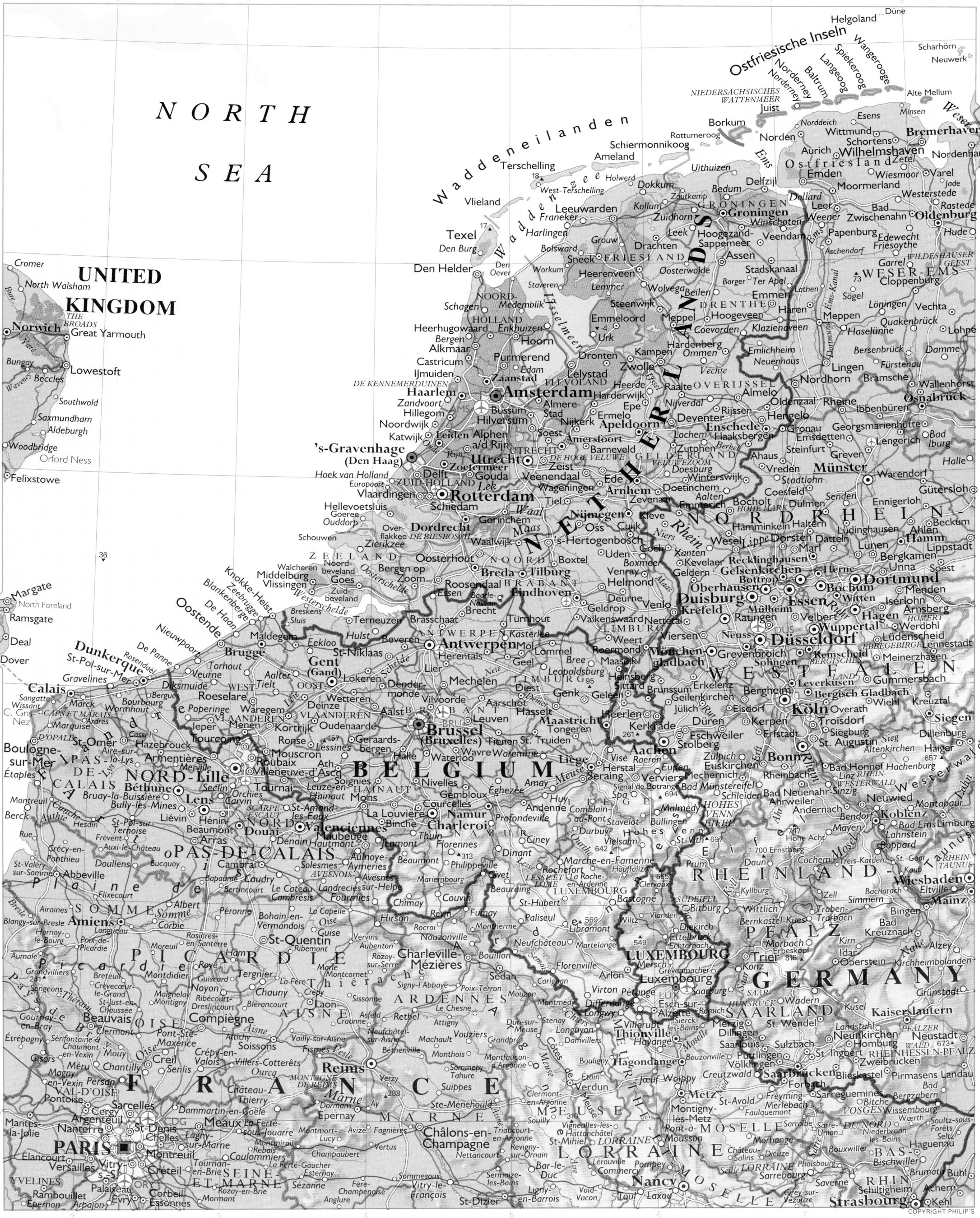

NORTH SEA

UNITED KINGDOM

NETHERLANDS

BELGIUM

GERMANY

LUXEMBOURG

FRANCE

NORDRHEIN-WESTFALEN

RHEINLAND-PFALZ

SAARLAND

Amsterdam
's-Gravenhage (Den Haag)
Rotterdam
Utrecht
Groningen
Leeuwarden
Haarlem
Antwerpen
Brussel (Bruxelles)
Gent (Gand)
Brugge
Luxembourg
Lille
Reims
Paris
Nancy
Strasbourg
Köln
Düsseldorf
Dortmund
Essen
Duisburg
Münster
Bonn
Aachen
Wiesbaden
Mainz
Kaiserslautern
Saarbrücken
Trier
Koblenz

Underlined towns give their name to the administrative area in which they stand.

National Parks

COPYRIGHT PHILIP'S

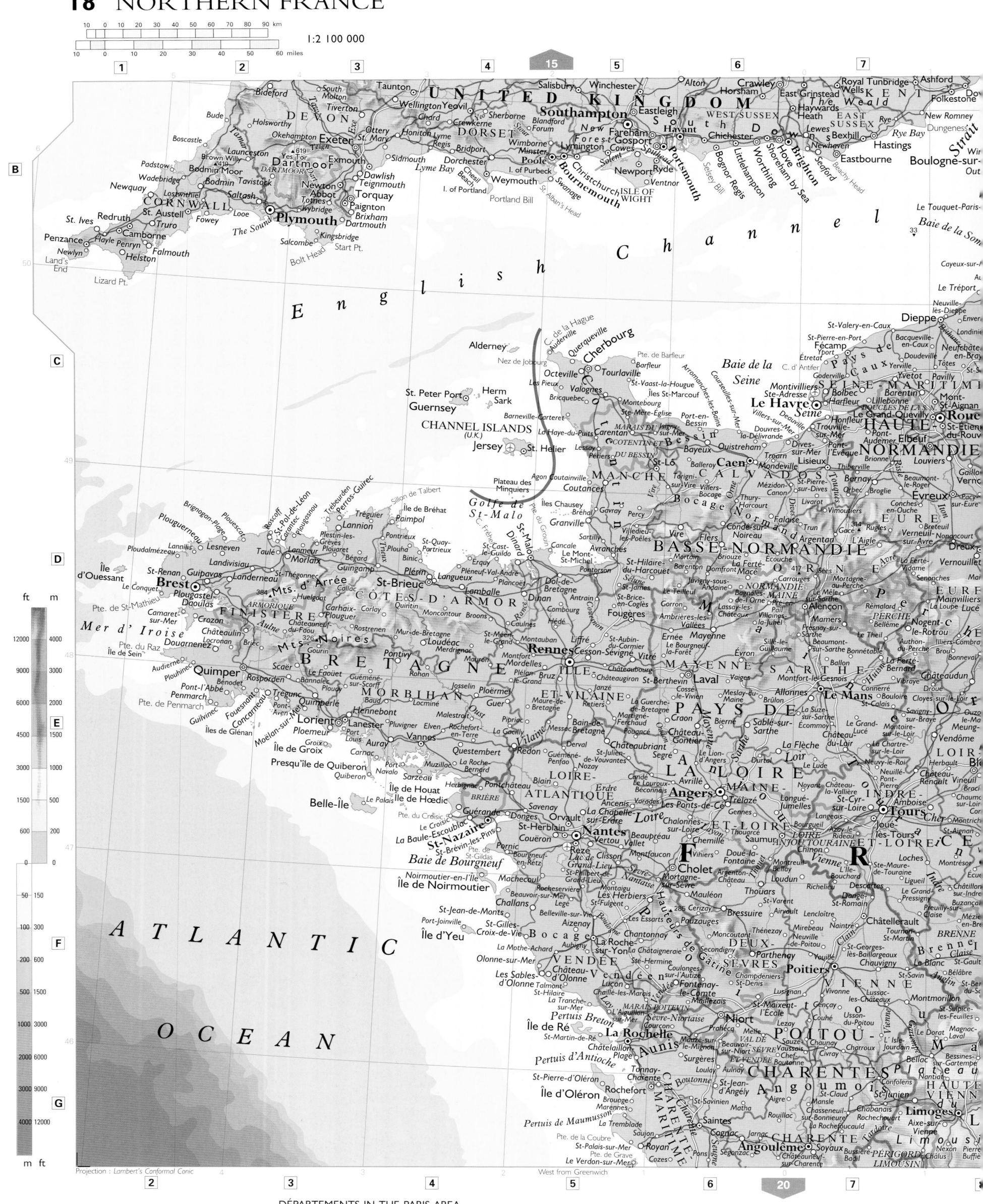

1:2 100 000

10 0 10 20 30 40 50 60 70 80 90 km

10 0 10 20 30 40 50 60 miles

Projection : Lambert's Conformal Conic

West from Greenwich

DÉPARTEMENTS IN THE PARIS AREA
1 Ville de Paris   3 Val-de-Marne
2 Seine-St-Denis   4 Hauts-de-Seine

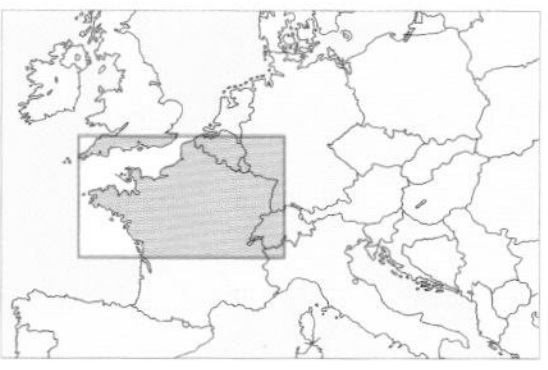

DE-LES

BELGIUM

GERMANY

LUXEMBOURG

SAARLAND

PICARDIE

ARDENNES

NORD

PAS-DE-CALAIS

SOMME

AISNE

CHAMPAGNE-ARDENNE

LORRAINE

ALSACE

VOSGES

PARIS

SEINE-ET-MARNE

ÎLE-DE-FRANCE

ESSONNE

LOIRET

YONNE

HAUTE-MARNE

BOURGOGNE

CÔTE-D'OR

FRANCHE-COMTÉ

HAUTE-SAÔNE

DOUBS

JURA

NIÈVRE

FRANCE

BOURBONNAIS

CREUSE

LIMOUSIN

PUY-DE-DÔME

RHÔNE-ALPES

HAUTE-SAVOIE

SAVOIE

SWITZERLAND

ITALY

VAUD

VALAIS

East from Greenwich

COPYRIGHT PHILIP'S

Underlined towns give their name to the administrative area in which they stand.

National Parks

Regional Nature Parks in France

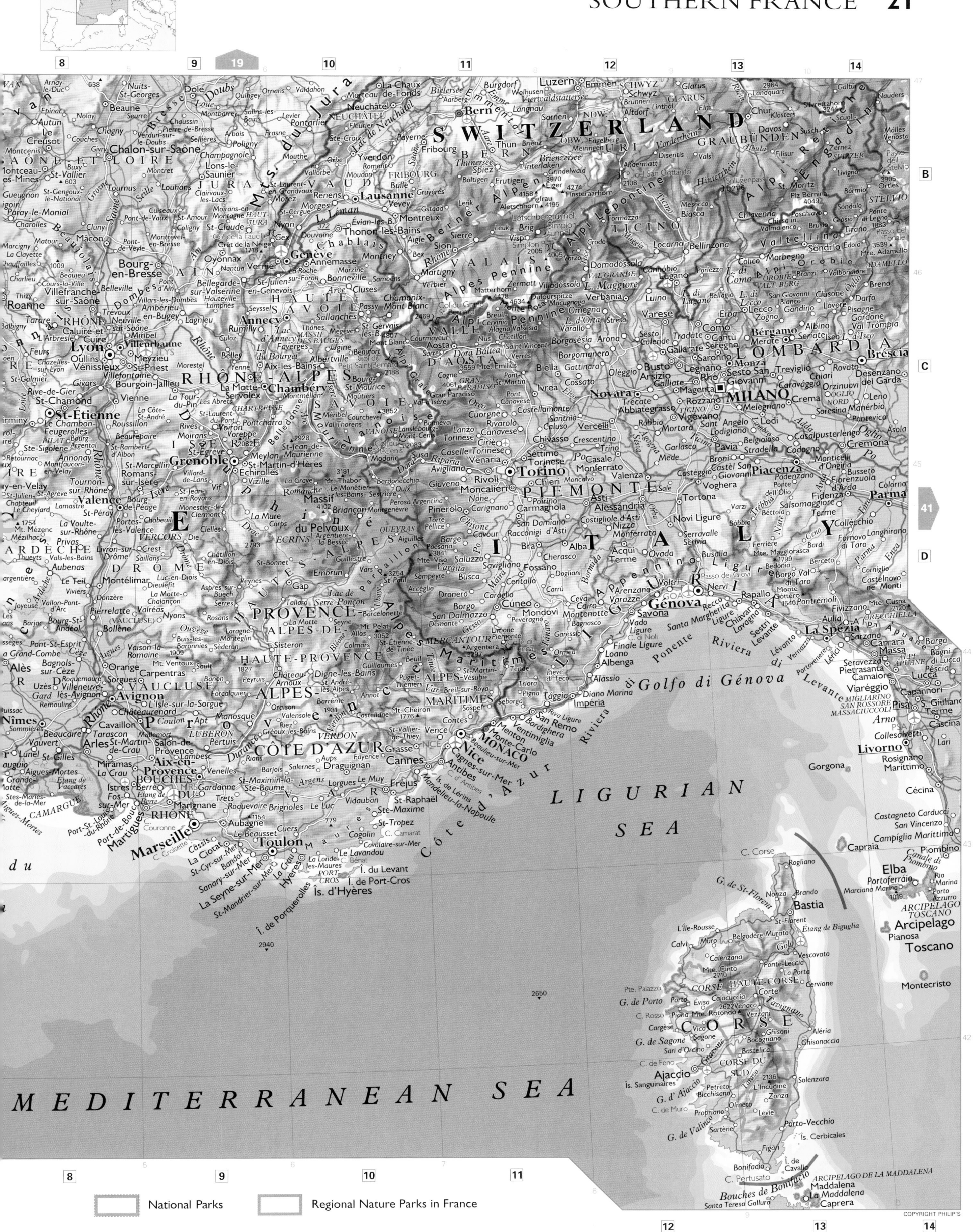

National Parks   Regional Nature Parks in France

COPYRIGHT PHILIP'S

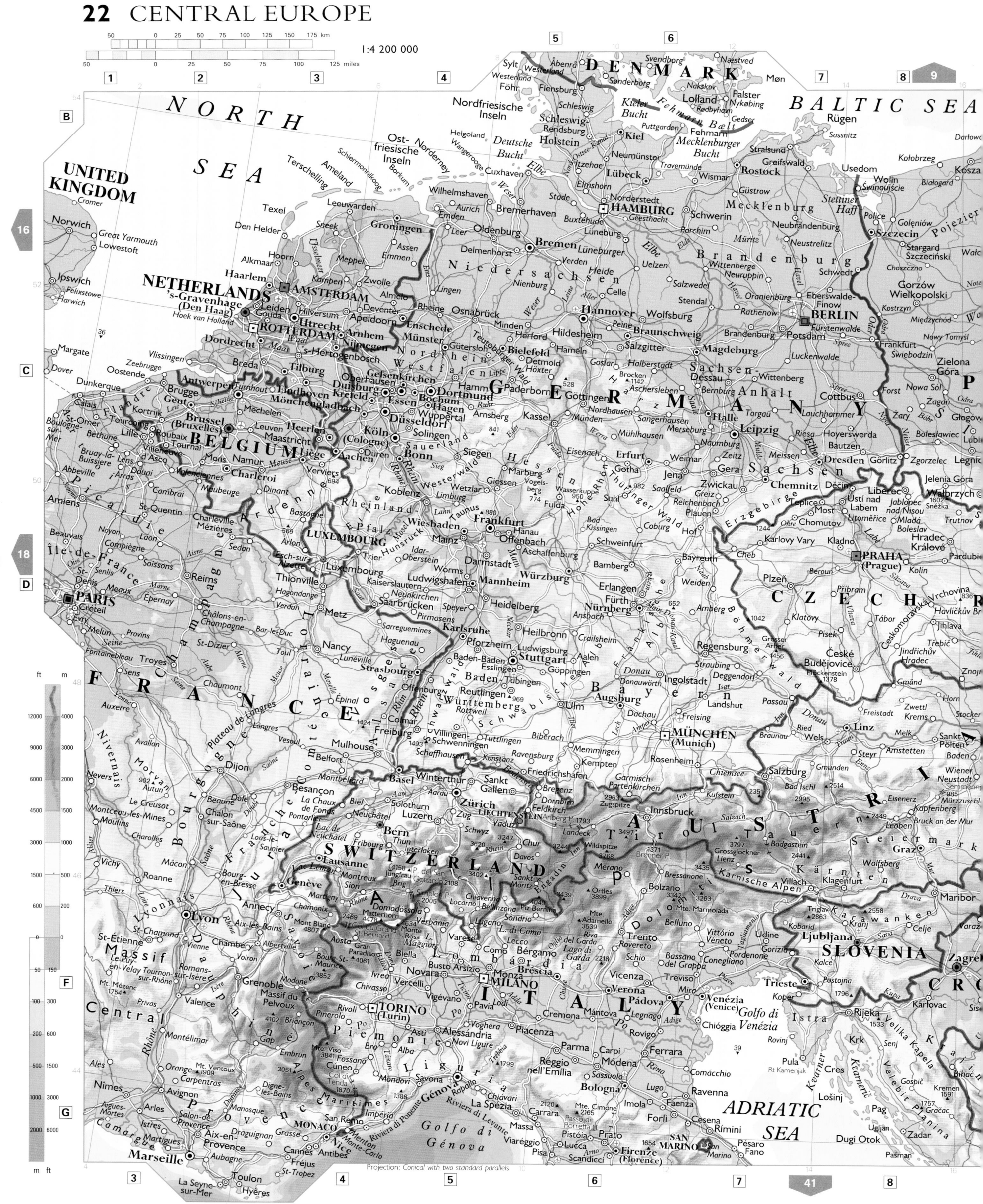

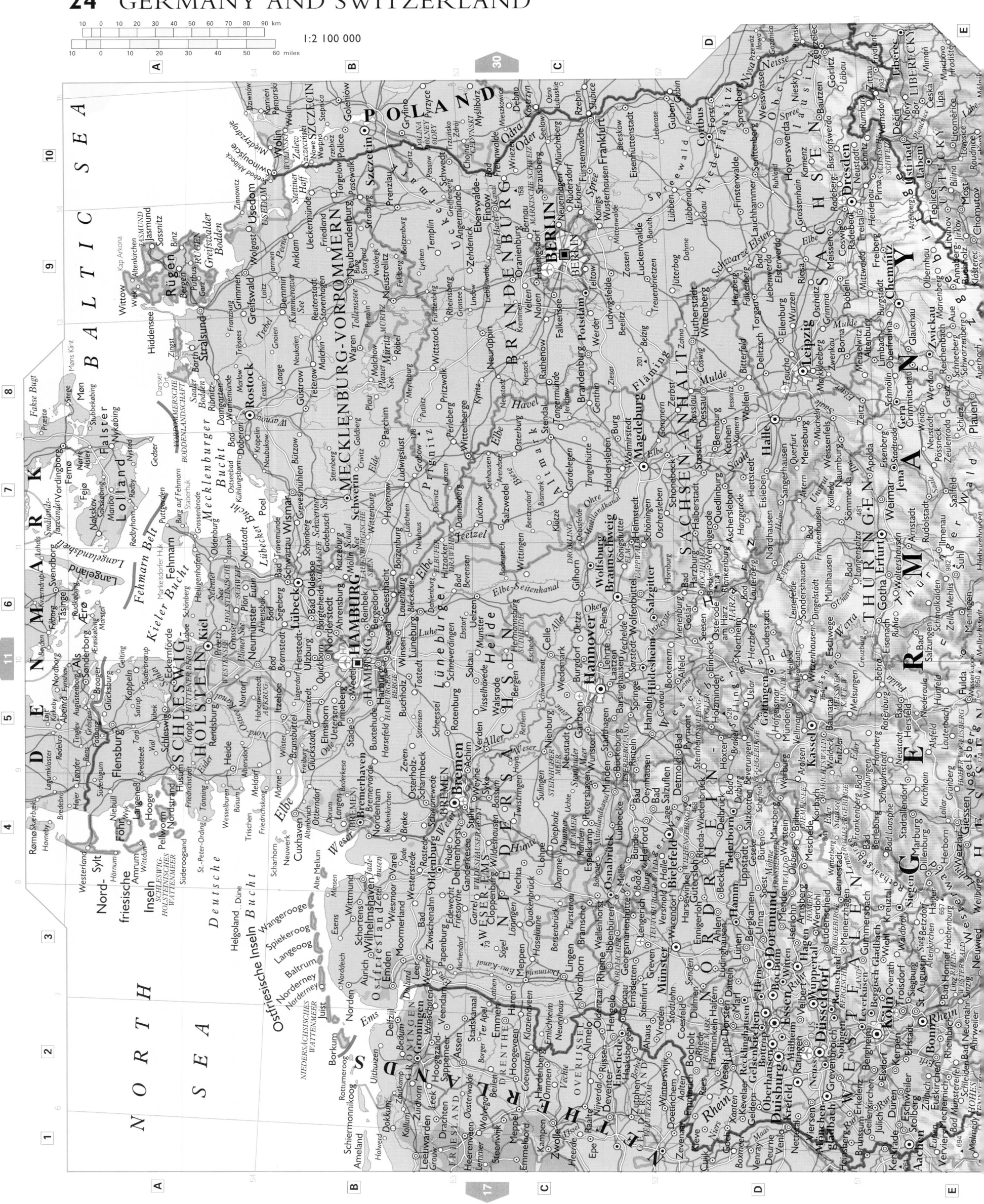

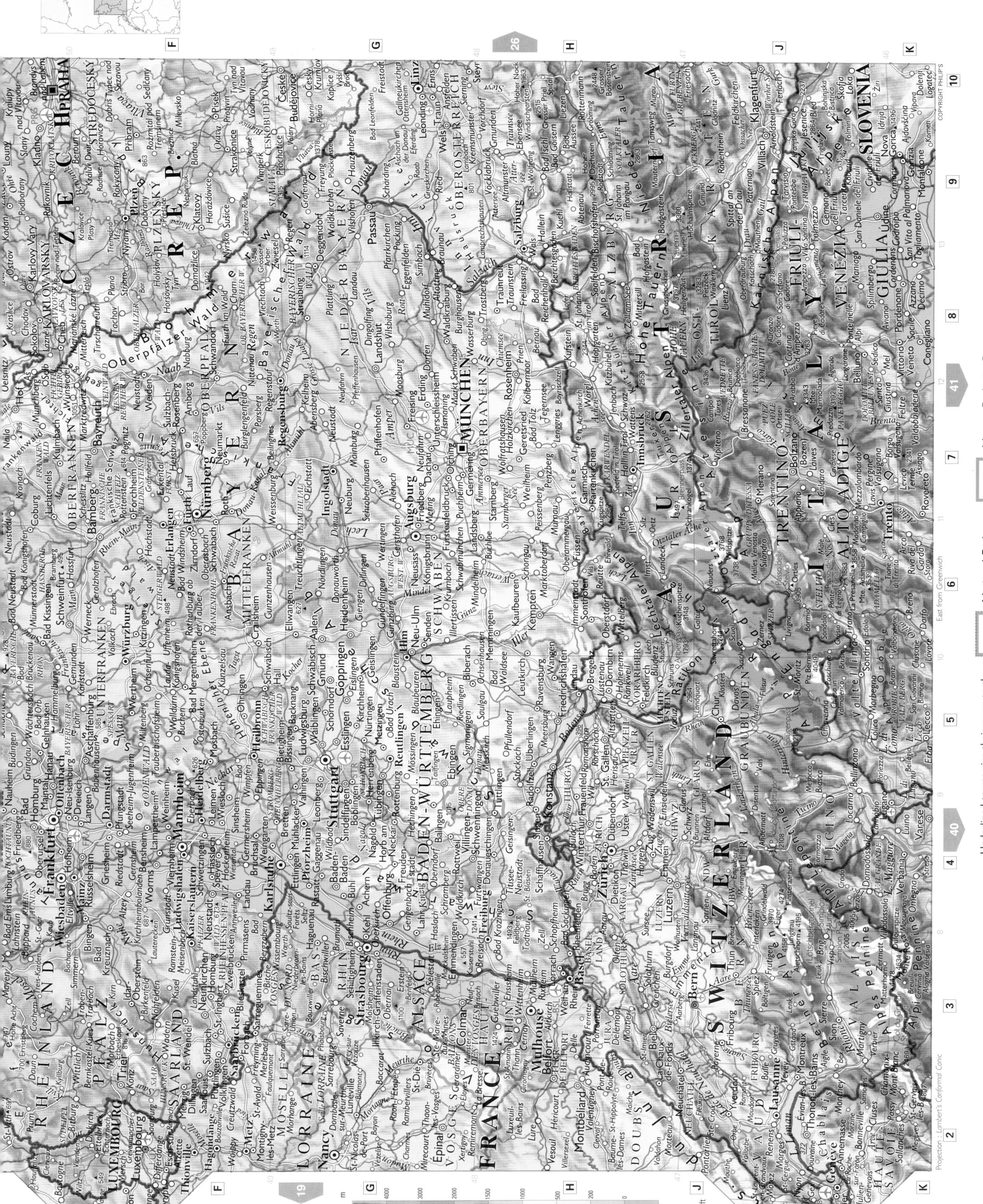

Nature Parks in Germany

National Parks

Underlined towns give their name to the administrative area in which they stand.

Projection : Lambert's Conformal Conic

East from Greenwich

1:2 100 000

Projection : Lambert's Conformal Conic

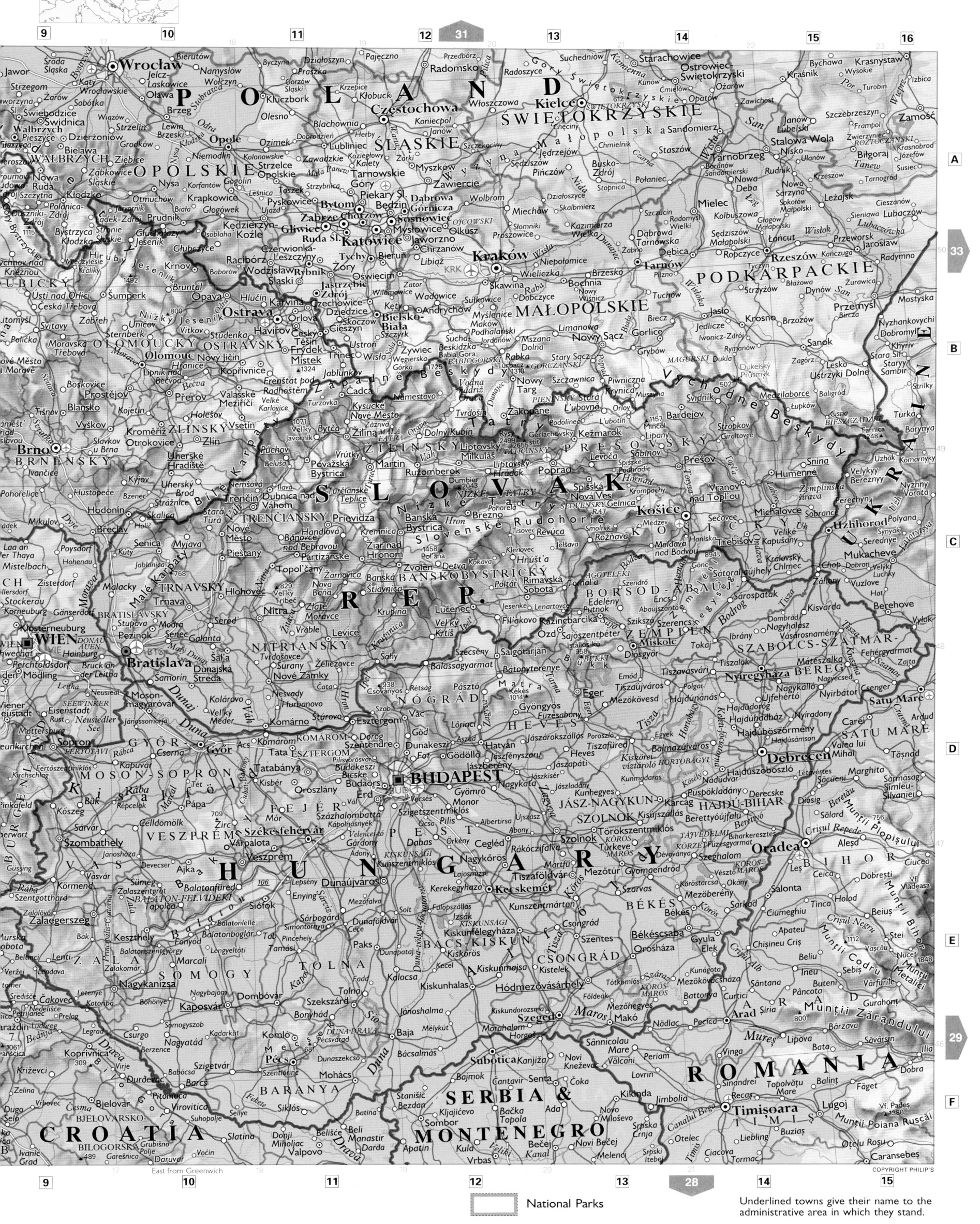

National Parks

Underlined towns give their name to the
administrative area in which they stand.

East from Greenwich

COPYRIGHT PHILIP'S

1:2 100 000

Administrative divisions in Croatia:
1 Brodsko-Posavska   5 Osječko-Baranjska   9 Vukovarsko-Srijemska
2 Koprivničko-Križevačka   6 Požeško-Slavonska
4 Medimurska   8 Virovitičko-Podravska

Inter-entity boundaries as agreed
at the 1995 Dayton Peace Agreement

East from Greenwich

Underlined towns give their name to the
administrative area in which they stand.

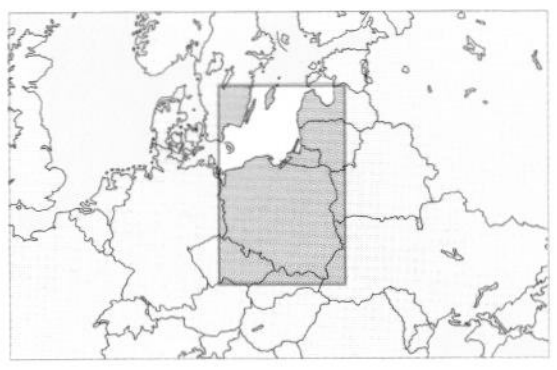

10 0 10 20 30 40 50 60 70 80 90 km
10 0 10 20 30 40 50 60 miles

1:2 100 000

Gulf of Riga

LATVIA

LITHUANIA

Irbes saurums (Kura kurk)

S W E D E N

Gotland (Sweden)

GOTLANDS LÄN

Öland (Sweden)

KALMAR

SMÅLAND

JÖNKÖPINGS LÄN

BLEKINGE LÄN

B A L T I C S E A

Bornholm (Denmark)
BORNHOLMS AMT.

Hanöbukten

Bornholmsgattet

KALININGRAD (Russia)

Kaliningrad

WARMIŃSKO-MAZURSKIE

Mazury

POMORSKIE

Pomorze

ZACHODNIO-POMORSKIE

Zatoka Gdańska

Gdańsk

Gdynia

Sopot

Wisła

Riga
Jūrmala
Jelgava
Šiauliai
Kaunas
Marijampolė
Hrodna
Alytus
Klaipėda
Liepāja
Ventspils
Tukums
Talsi
Kuldīga
Saldus
Dobele
Mažeikiai
Telšiai
Plungė
Tauragė
Neringa
Elbląg
Malbork
Olsztyn
Koszalin
Słupsk
Szczecin
Świnoujście

Kuršių Neringa
Kuršskaja Zalic
Kurshskaya Kosa

Nemunas / Neman

Wisła
Zalew Wiślany

Underlined towns give their name to the administrative area in which they stand.

National Parks

East from Greenwich

Projection: Lambert's Conformal Conic

COPYRIGHT PHILIP'S

1:4 200 000

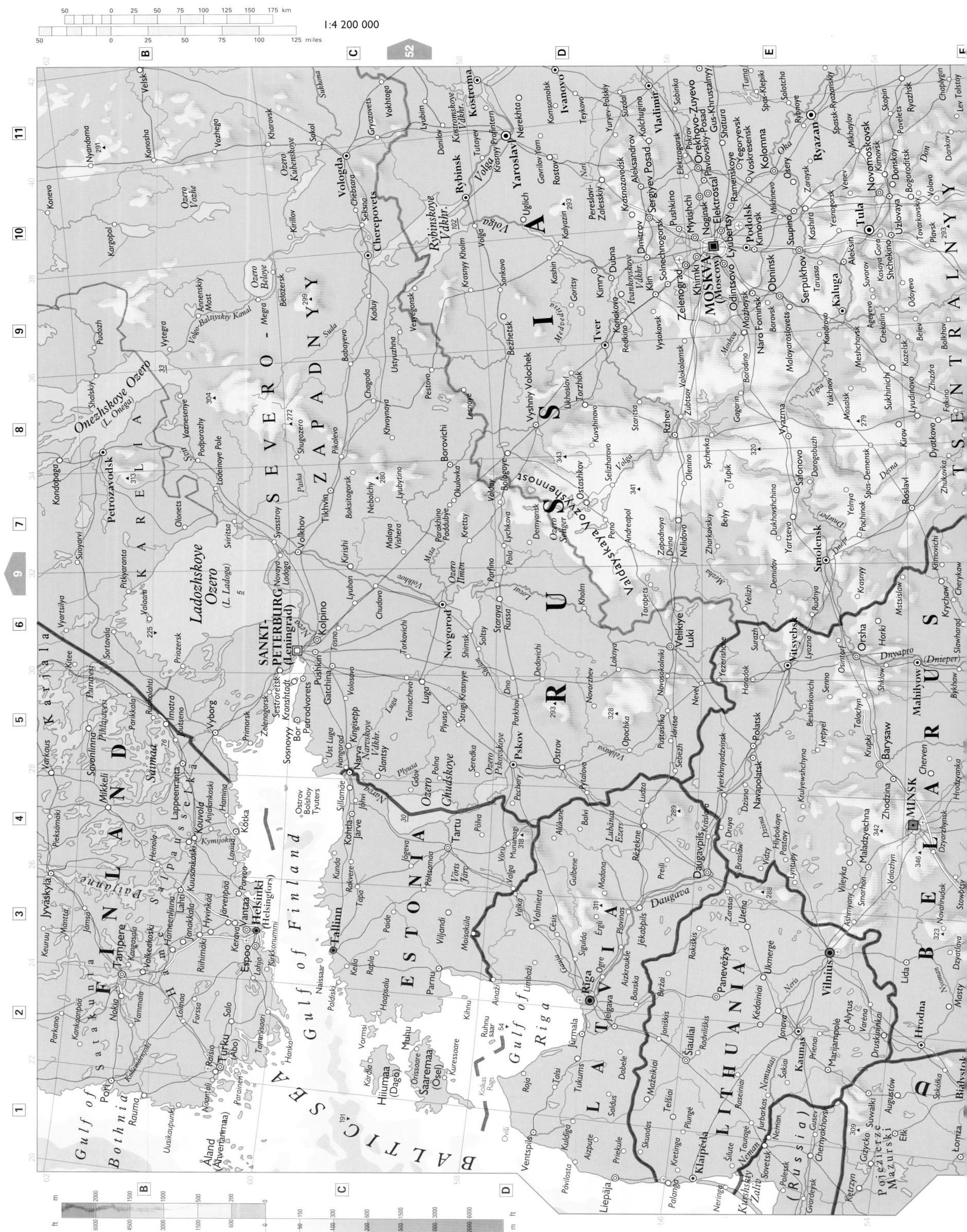

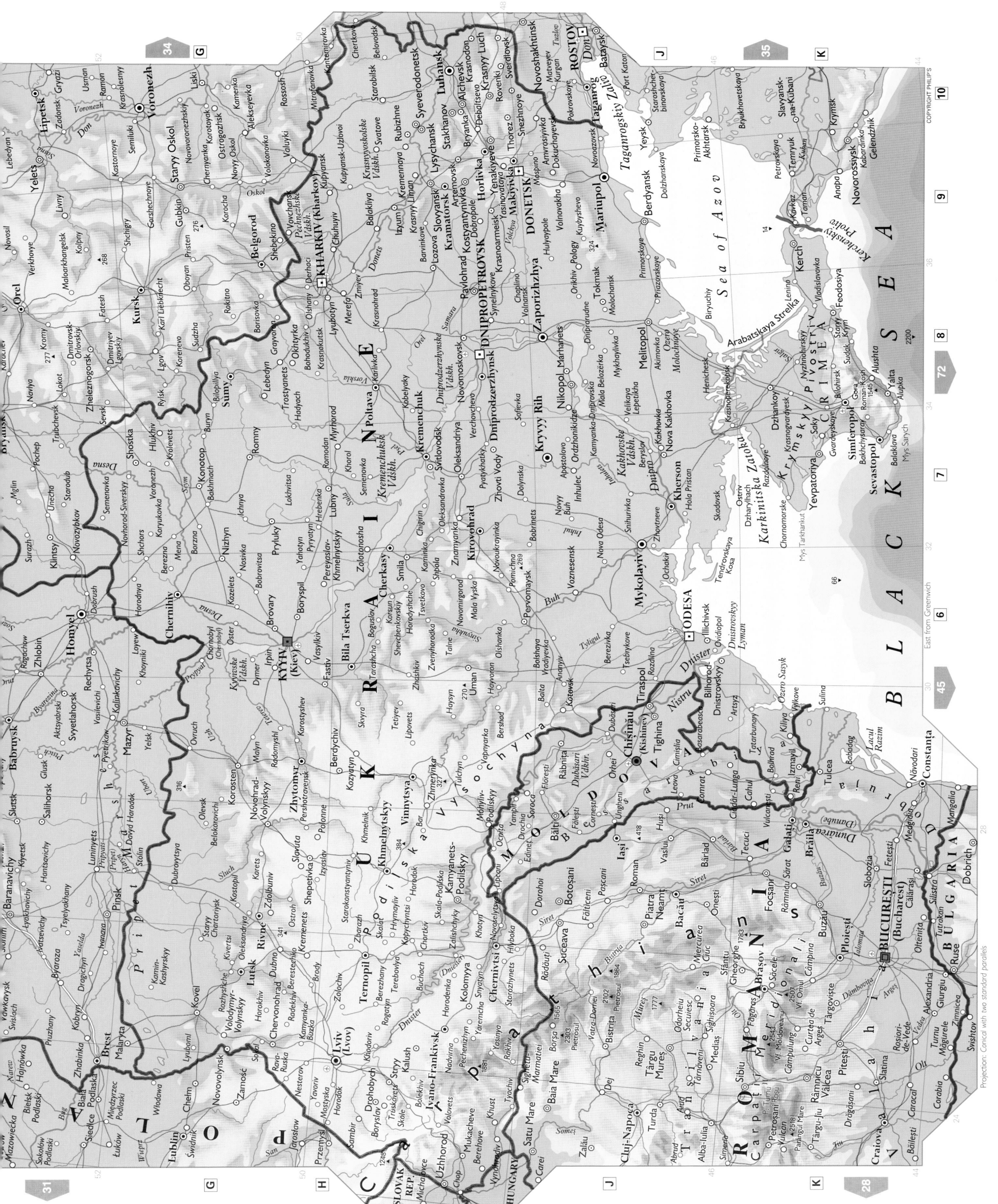

Projection: Conical with two standard parallels

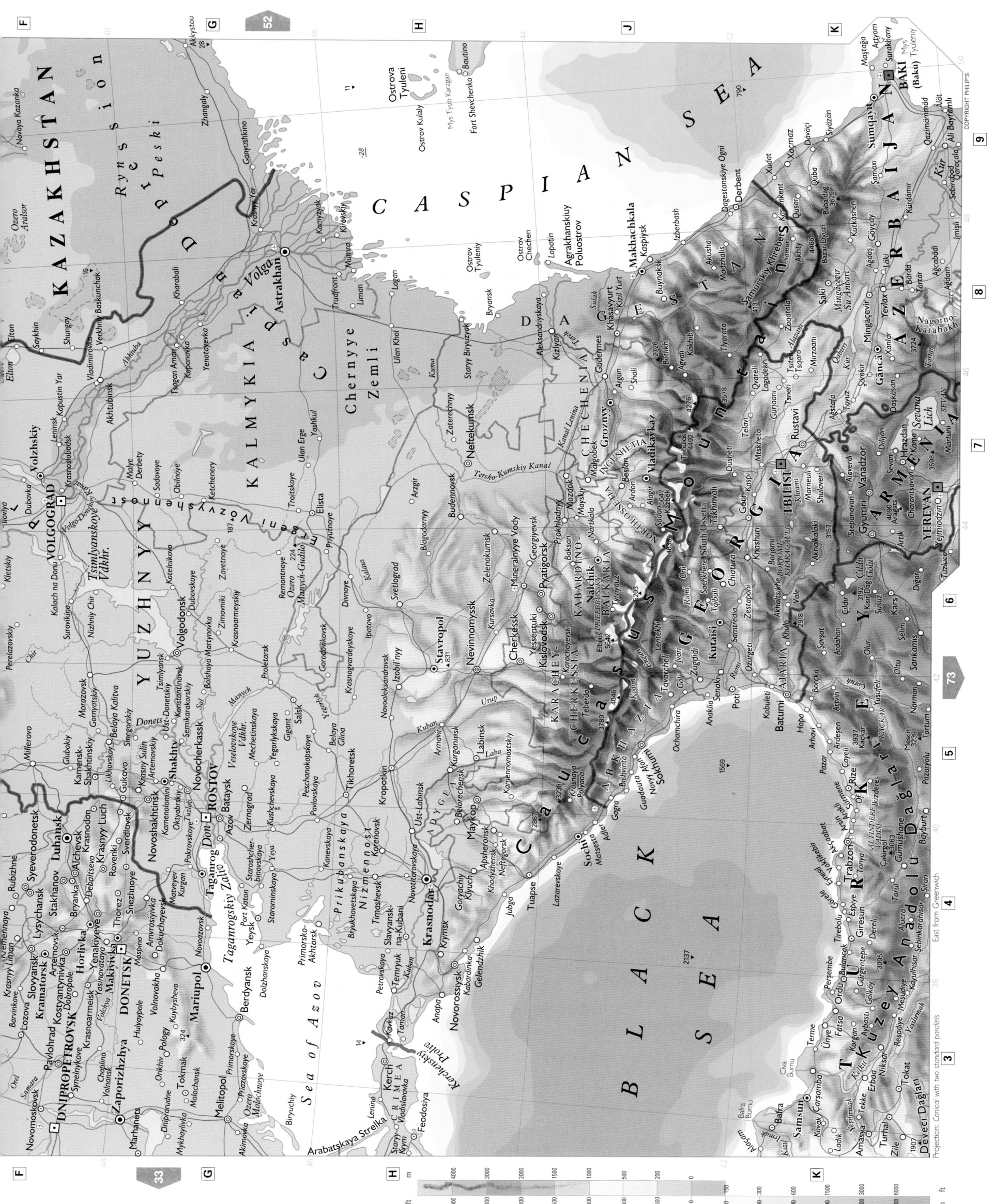

CASPIAN SEA

BLACK SEA

Sea of Azov

KAZAKHSTAN

AZERBAIJAN

ARMENIA

GEORGIA

DAGESTAN

CHECHENIA

KALMYKIA

KAZAKHSTAN

Projection: Conical with two standard parallels

East from Greenwich

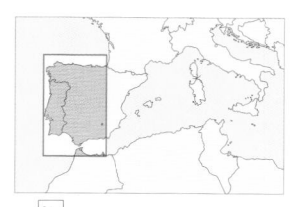

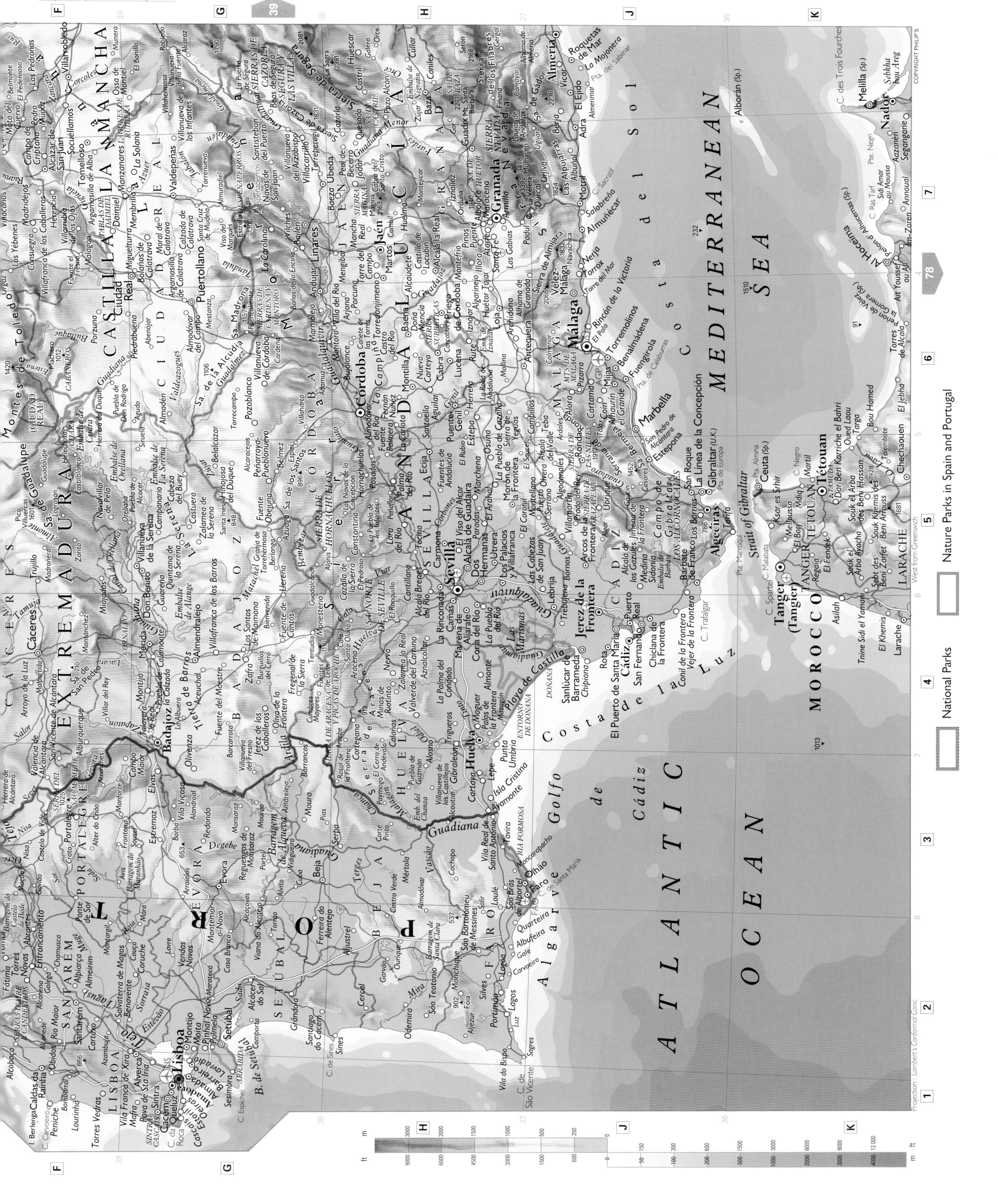
ATLANTIC OCEAN
MEDITERRANEAN SEA
Golfo de Cádiz
Costa de la Luz
Costa del Sol
Strait of Gibraltar
PORTUGAL
EXTREMADURA
CASTILLA-LA MANCHA
ANDALUCÍA
MOROCCO
Lisboa
Sevilla
Córdoba
Granada
Málaga
Cádiz
Huelva
Badajoz
Cáceres
Gibraltar (U.K.)
Ceuta (Sp.)
Tanger (Tangier)
Tétouan
National Parks
Nature Parks in Spain and Portugal
Projection: Lambert's Conformal Conic
COPYRIGHT PHILIP'S

MEDITERRANEAN SEA

National Parks

Nature Parks in Spain

Projection: Lambert's Conformal Conic

National Parks

Underlined towns give their name to the administrative area in which they stand

Administrative divisions in Croatia:

Brodsko-Posavska		4 Medimurska		8 Viroviticˇko-Podravska	
Koprivnicˇko-Krizˇevacˇka		6 Pozˇesˇko-Slavonska		10 Zagreba cˇka	
Krapinsko-Zagorska		7 Varazˇdinska			

Nature Parks in Italy

Inter-entity boundaries as agreed
at the 1995 Dayton Peace Agreement

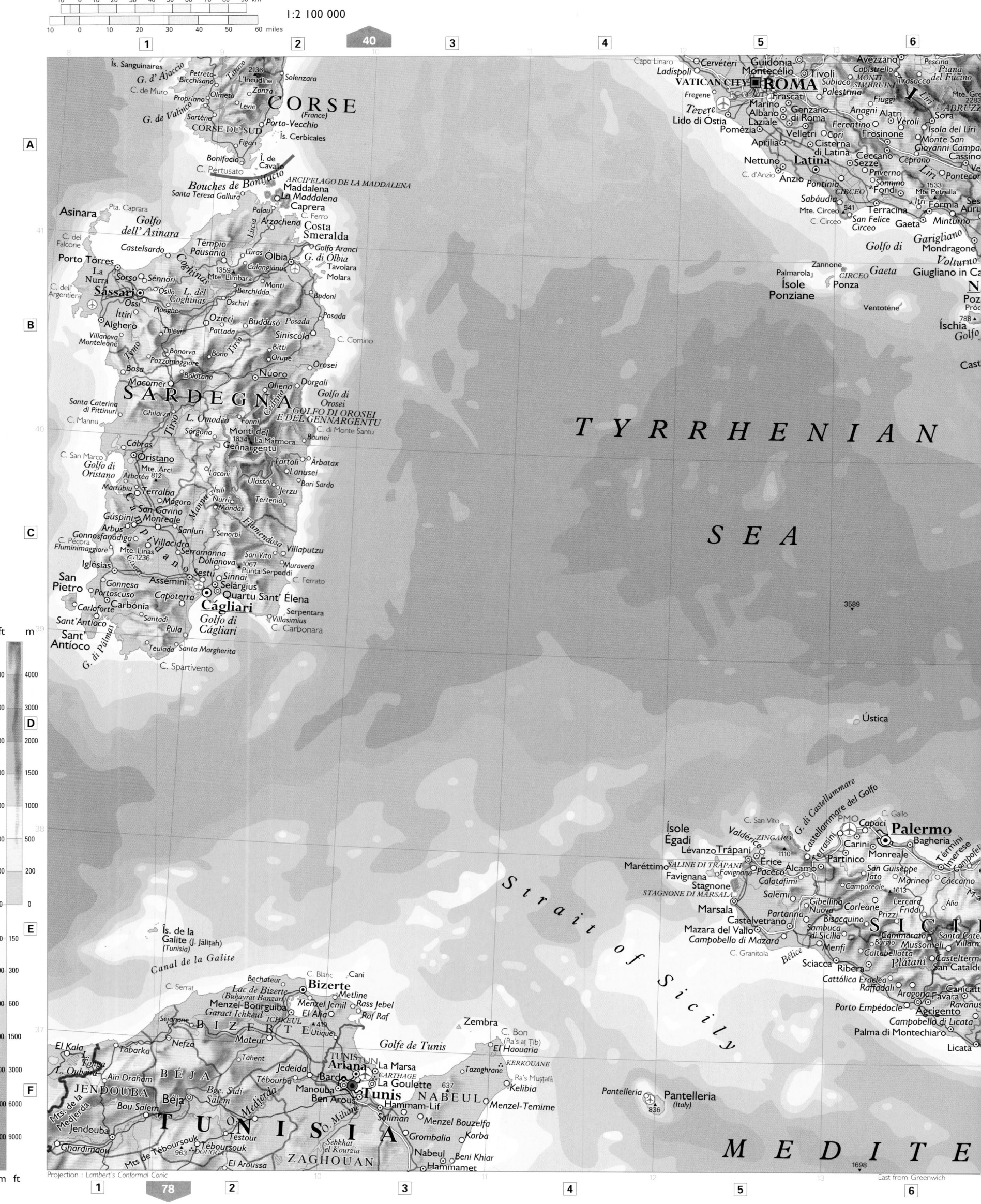

1:2 100 000

TYRRHENIAN SEA

CORSE
(France)

SARDEGNA

TUNISIA

Strait of Sicily

SICILI

Palermo

ROMA
VATICAN CITY

MEDITE

East from Greenwich

Nature Parks in Italy

National Parks

Underlined towns give their name to the administrative area in which they stand.

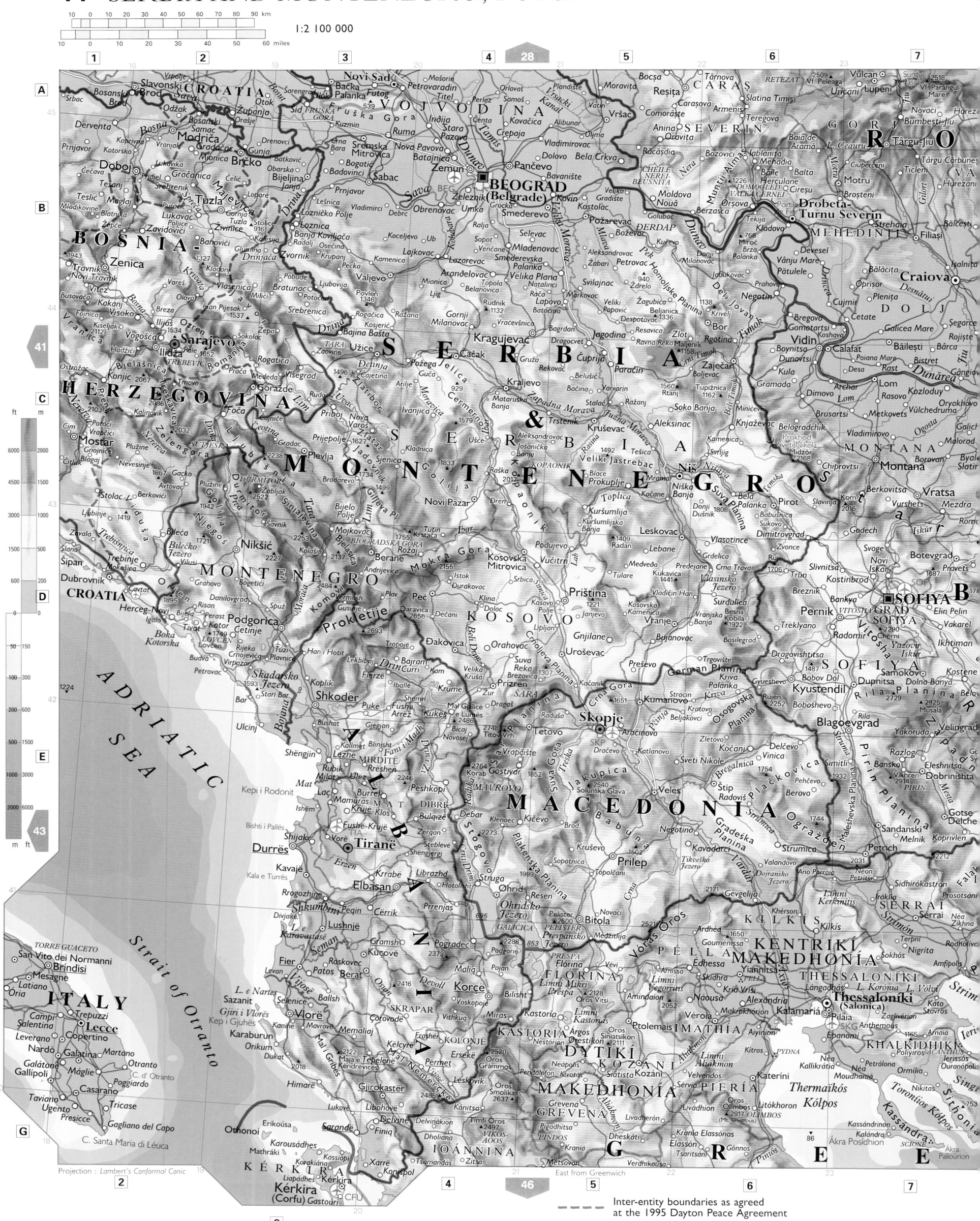

1:2 100 000

Projection : Lambert's Conformal Conic

East from Greenwich

Inter-entity boundaries as agreed
at the 1995 Dayton Peace Agreement

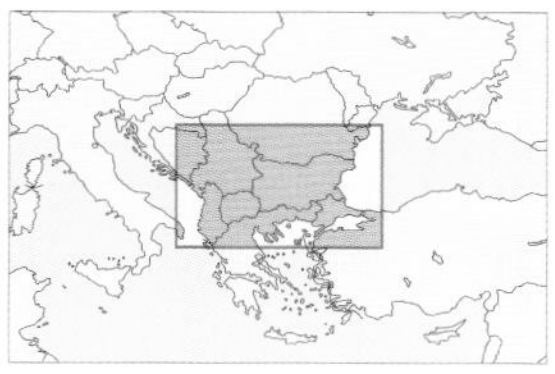

BLACK SEA

BULGARIA

ROMANIA

TURKEY

Major towns and cities: Galaţi, Brăila, Buzău, Ploieşti, Piteşti, Râmnicu Vâlcea, BUCUREŞTI (Bucharest), Giurgiu, Slobozia, Călăraşi, Silistra, Constanţa, Mangalia, Dobrich, Varna, Burgas, Ruse, Pleven, Veliko Tûrnovo, Gabrovo, Shumen, Razgrad, Sliven, Stara Zagora, Yambol, Kazanlûk, Plovdiv, Pazardzhik, Asenovgrad, Dimitrovgrad, Haskovo, Kûrdzhali, Smolyan, Edirne, Kırklareli, Lüleburgaz, Tekirdağ, Çorlu, İSTANBUL, Üsküdar, Kartal, Gebze, Bursa, İnegöl, Gemlik, Bandırma, Çanakkale, Xánthi, Komotini, Kaválla, Alexandroúpolis, Samothráki, Thásos, Límnos

Marmara Denizi (Sea of Marmara)

Thrakikón Pélagos

ANATOLIKÍ MAKEDHONÍA KAI THRÁKI

RODÓPI

ÉVROS

Underlined towns give their name to the administrative area in which they stand.

National Parks

COPYRIGHT PHILIP'S

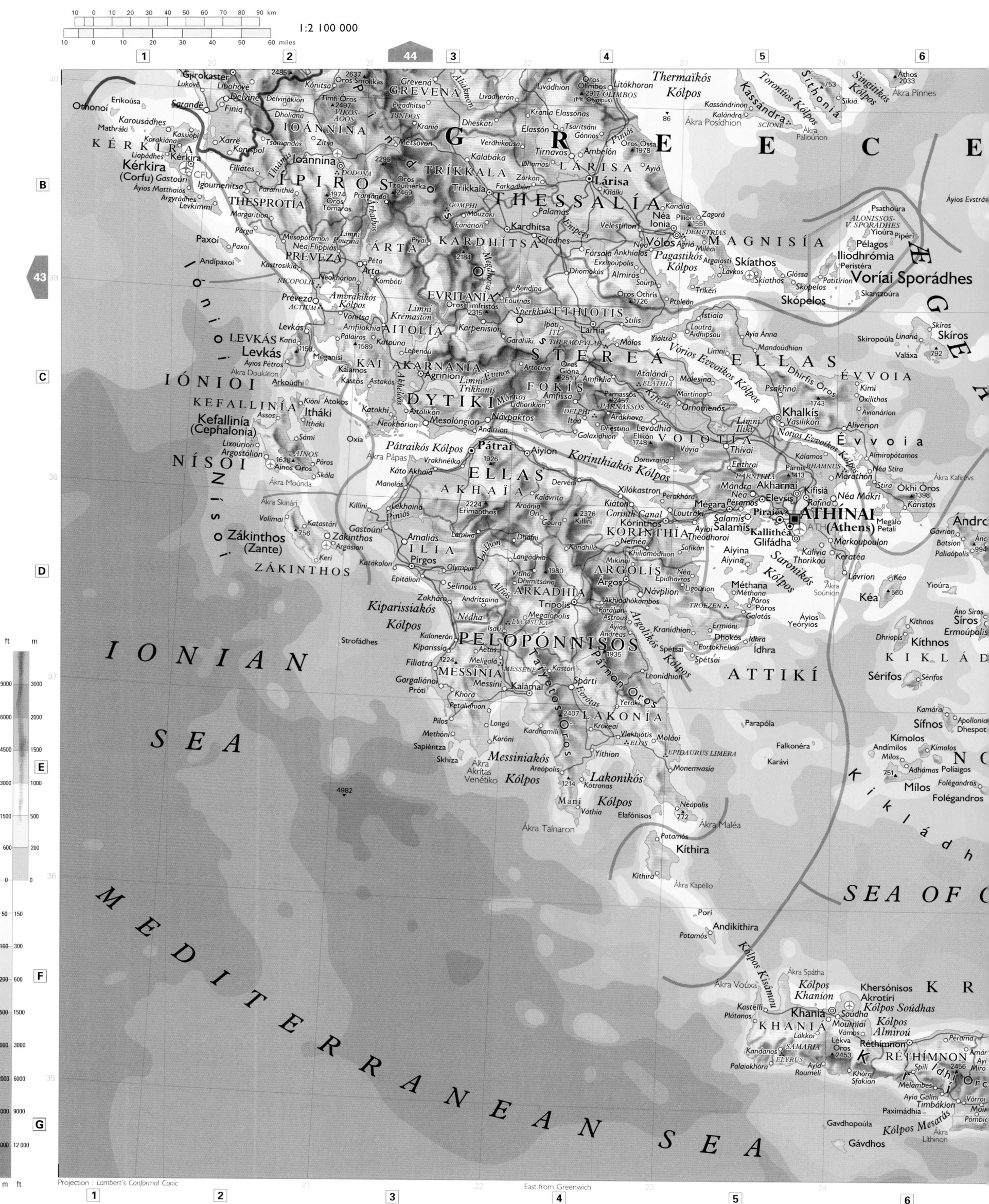

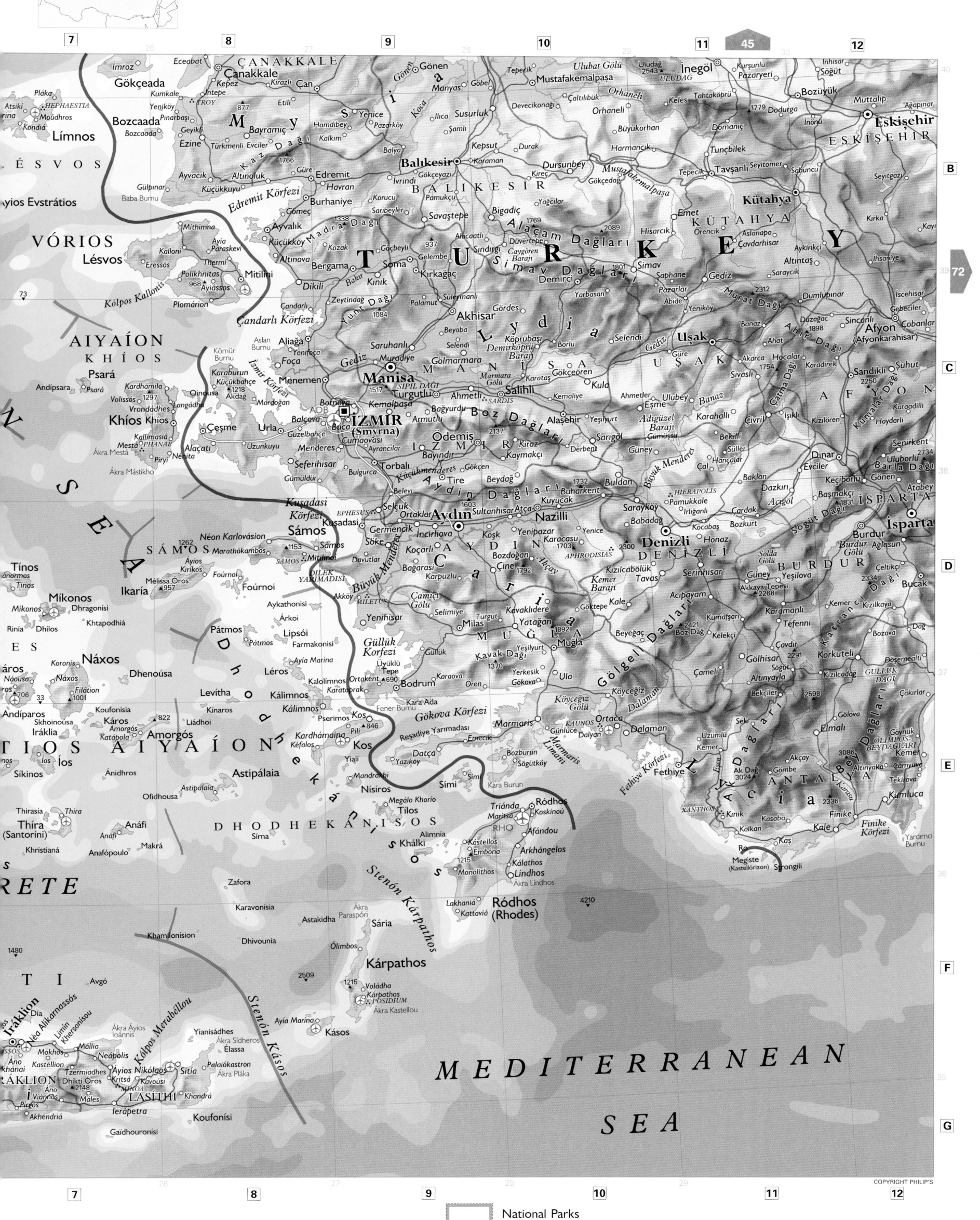

National Parks

Madeira

Canary Islands

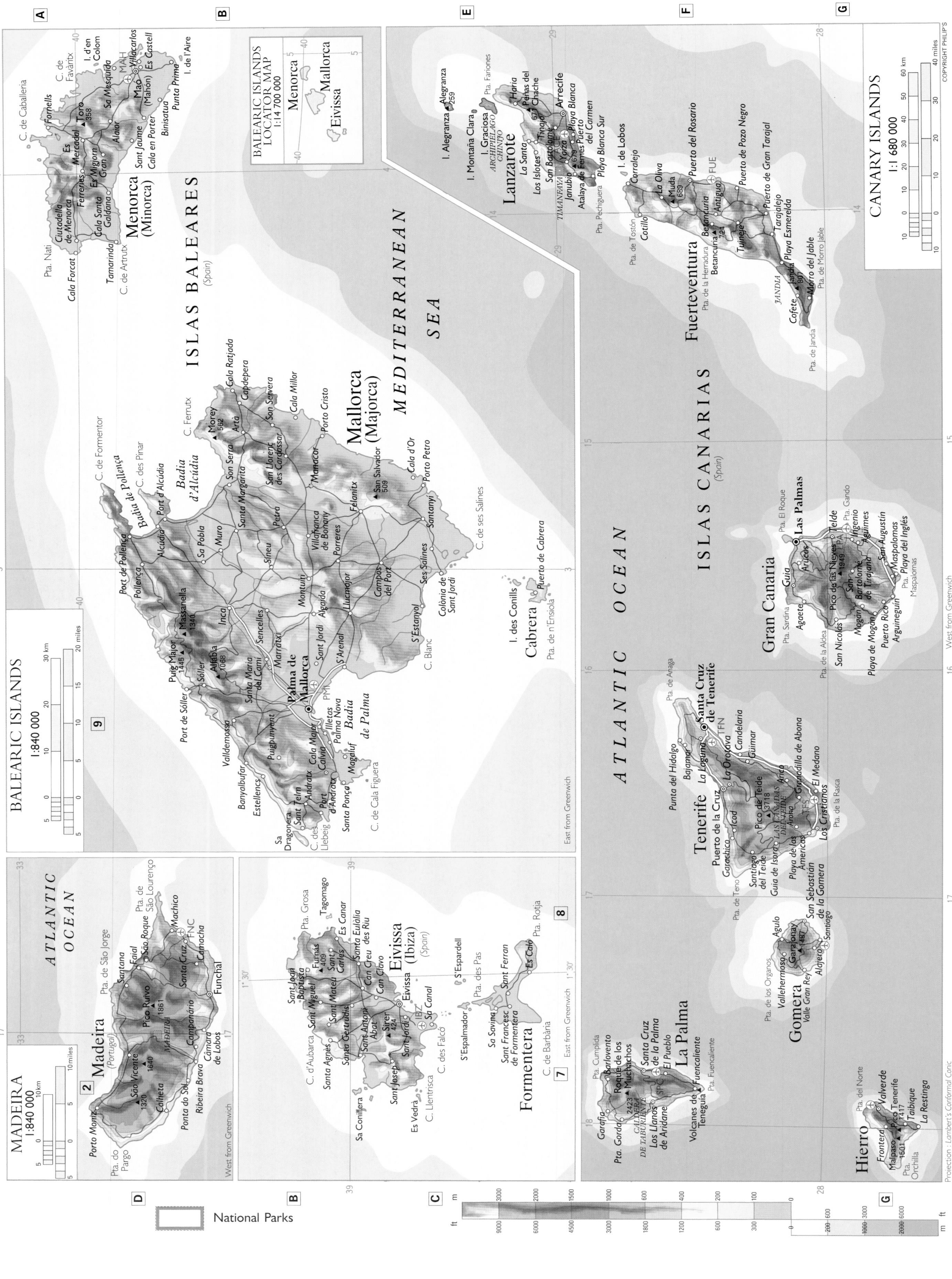

Balearic Islands

BALEARIC ISLANDS LOCATOR MAP
1:14 700 000
Menorca
Mallorca
Eivissa

Menorca (Minorca)
C. de Cavalleria
Fornells
Ciutadella de Menorca
Ferreries
Es Mercadal
Alaior
Maó (Mahón)
MAH
Sa Mesquida
Es Castell
Villacarlos
I. de l'Aire
Punta Prima
Binisafua
Cala en Porter
Sant Jaume
Cala Santa Galdana
Toro 358
Pta. Nati
Pta. de Artrutx
Tamarinda
C. de Favàritx
I. d'en Colom

ISLAS BALEARES (Spain)

MEDITERRANEAN SEA

Mallorca (Majorca)
C. de Formentor
C. de Pollença
Port de Pollença
Pollença
C. des Pinar
Alcúdia
Badia de Pollença
Badia d'Alcúdia
Port d'Alcúdia
Sa Pobla
Muro
Santa Margarita
Morey 562
Artà
Cala Ratjada
Capdepera
Son Servera
Cala Millor
Son Serra
San Llorenç des Cardassar
Porto Cristo
Manacor
C. Ferrutx
Inca
Sineu
Petra
Felanitx
San Salvador 509
Cala d'Or
Porto Petro
Villafranca de Bonany
Puig Major 1445
Alfabia 1068
Massanella 1340
Sóller
Port de Sóller
Valldemossa
Banyalbufar
Estellencs
Sa Dragonera
C. de Tramuntana
Andratx
Port d'Andratx
Sant Telm
Santa Ponça
C. de Cala Figuera
Santa Maria del Camí
Marratxí
Santa Eugènia
Sencelles
Montuïri
Algaida
Porreres
Llucmajor
Campos del Port
Ses Salines
S'Estanyol
Colònia de Sant Jordi
Palma de Mallorca
PM
S'Arenal
Sant Jordi
Magaluf
Palma Nova
Illetas
Cala Major
C. Blanc
C. de ses Salines
Puigpunyent
Badia de Palma
Puerto de Cabrera
Cabrera
I. des Conills
Pta. de n'Ensiola

Lanzarote
I. Alegranza
Alegranza 259
I. Montaña Clara
I. Graciosa
ARCHIPIÉLAGO CHINIJO
Haria
Peñas del Chache 671
Arrecife
La Santa
San Bartolomé
Los Islotes
Tinajo
Puerto del Carmen
Playa Blanca
Tías
Janubio
Atalaya de Femés 609
Playa Blanca Sur
TIMANFAYA
Pta. Pechiguera
I. de Lobos

Fuerteventura
Corralejo
La Oliva
Cotillo
Puerto del Rosario
FUE
Muda 689
Betancuria 724
Pta. de Toston
Pta. de la Herradura
Antigua
Puerto de Pozo Negro
Tuineje
Tarajalejo
Puerto de Gran Tarajal
Gran Tarajal
JANDÍA
Pájara
Cofete
Jable Playa Esmerelda
807
Morro del Jable
Pta. de Morro Jable
Pta. de Jandía

CANARY ISLANDS
1:1 680 000

ATLANTIC OCEAN

ISLAS CANARIAS (Spain)

Gran Canaria
Las Palmas
Pta. El Roque
Pta. Sardina
Guía
Agaete
Arucas
Telde
Pico de las Nieves 1949
Teror
San Mateo
Ingenio
Agüimes
San Agustín
San Nicolás
Mogán
Pta. de la Aldea
Puerto Rico
Tejeda
Playa de Mogán
Arguineguín
Maspalomas
Playa del Inglés
Pta. de Maspalomas

Tenerife
Pta. de Anaga
Santa Cruz de Tenerife
La Laguna
TFN
Tacoronte
La Orotava
Puerto de la Cruz
Candelaria
Güimar
Punta del Hidalgo
Bajamar
Icod
Garachico
Pico de Teide 3718
LAS CAÑADAS DEL TEIDE
Arico
Arafo
Granadilla de Abona
El Médano
Pta. de Teno
Guía de Isora
Santiago del Teide
Playa de las Américas
Los Cristianos
Pta. de la Rasca

Gomera
San Sebastián de la Gomera
Agulo
Vallehermoso
Garajonay 1487
Santiago
Hermigua
Alajeró
Valle Gran Rey
Pta. de los Órganos

La Palma
Santa Cruz de la Palma
SPC
Garafía
Barlovento
Roque de los Muchachos 2423
Los Llanos de Aridane
El Pueblo
CALDERA DE TABURIENTE
Volcanes de Teneguía
Pta. Cumplida
Pta. Gorda
Fuencaliente
Pta. Fuencaliente

Hierro
Valverde
Frontera
Pico de Tenerife 1417
Taibíque
La Restinga
Pta. del Norte
Malpaso 1501
Pta. Orchilla

MADEIRA
1:840 000

ATLANTIC OCEAN

Madeira (Portugal)
Pta. de São Lourenço
Pta. de São Jorge
Santana
Faial
São Roque
Machico
Camacha
Santa Cruz
FNC
Funchal
Pico Ruivo 1861
Pico Arieiro
Campanário
Câmara de Lobos
Ribeira Brava
Ponta do Sol
São Vicente 1640
Colheta
Porto Moniz
Pta. do Pargo
Pta. de São Jorge

Eivissa (Ibiza) (Spain)
Pta. Grossa
Tagomago
Es Canar
Santa Eulalia
Pta. des Riu
Sant Joan Baptista
Sant Miquel
Es Canar
Portinatx 409
Sant Carles
Can Cirer
Santa Gertrudis
Sant Mateu
Sant Antoni Abat
Sant Josep
Sant Jordi
Sa Talaia 424
Sant Francesc
Eivissa
IBZ
C. d'Aubarca
Santa Agnès
Es Vedrà
C. Llentrisca
Sa Conillera
Formentera
S'Espalmador
S'Espardell
Sa Savina
Sant Francesc de Formentera
Es Caló
Es Pujols
Sant Ferran
Pta. Rotja
C. de Barbaria
Sa Canal
C. des Falcó

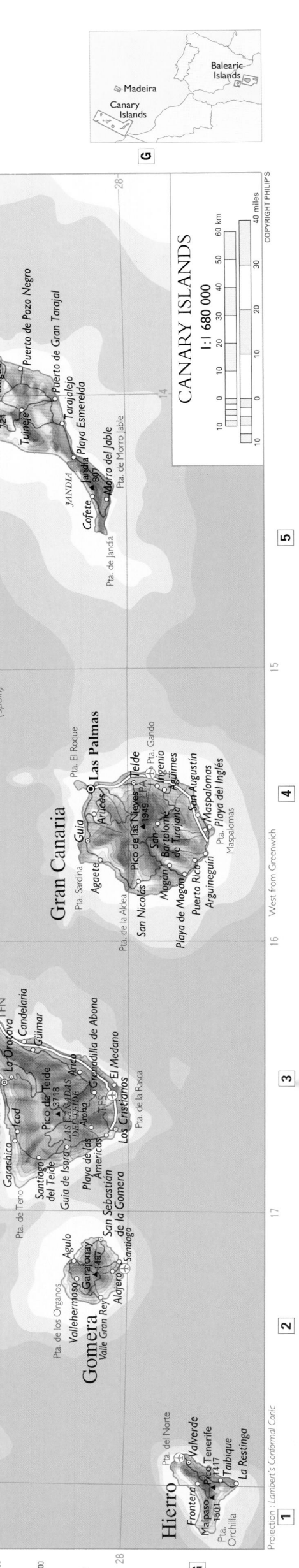

Projection: Lambert's Conformal Conic

COPYRIGHT PHILIP'S

National Parks

Corfu
Malta
Rhodes
Crete
Cyprus

CRETE
1:1 090 000
Kríti (Crete)
(Greece)
SEA OF CRETE
MEDITERRANEAN SEA
KHANIÁ
RÉTHIMNON
IRÁKLION
LASÍTHI
Iráklion
Khaniá
Réthimnon
Gávdhos
CYPRUS
1:1 090 000
MEDITERRANEAN SEA
Nicosia (Lefkosia)
Famagusta (Ammochostos)
Famagusta Bay
Larnaca
Larnaca Bay
Limassol
Paphos
Morphou Bay
Troodos
MALTA
1:840 000
GOZO
MALTA
Valletta
MEDITERRANEAN SEA
CORFU
1:840 000
Kérkira (Corfu)
(Greece)
IONIAN SEA
ALBANIA
GREECE
RHODES
1:840 000
Ródhos (Rhodes)
(Greece)
ÆGEAN SEA
MEDITERRANEAN SEA
Ródhos
Projection: Lambert's Conformal Conic
East from Greenwich
COPYRIGHT PHILIP'S

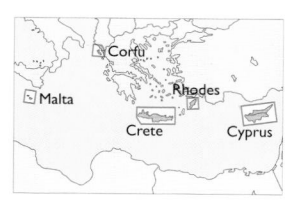

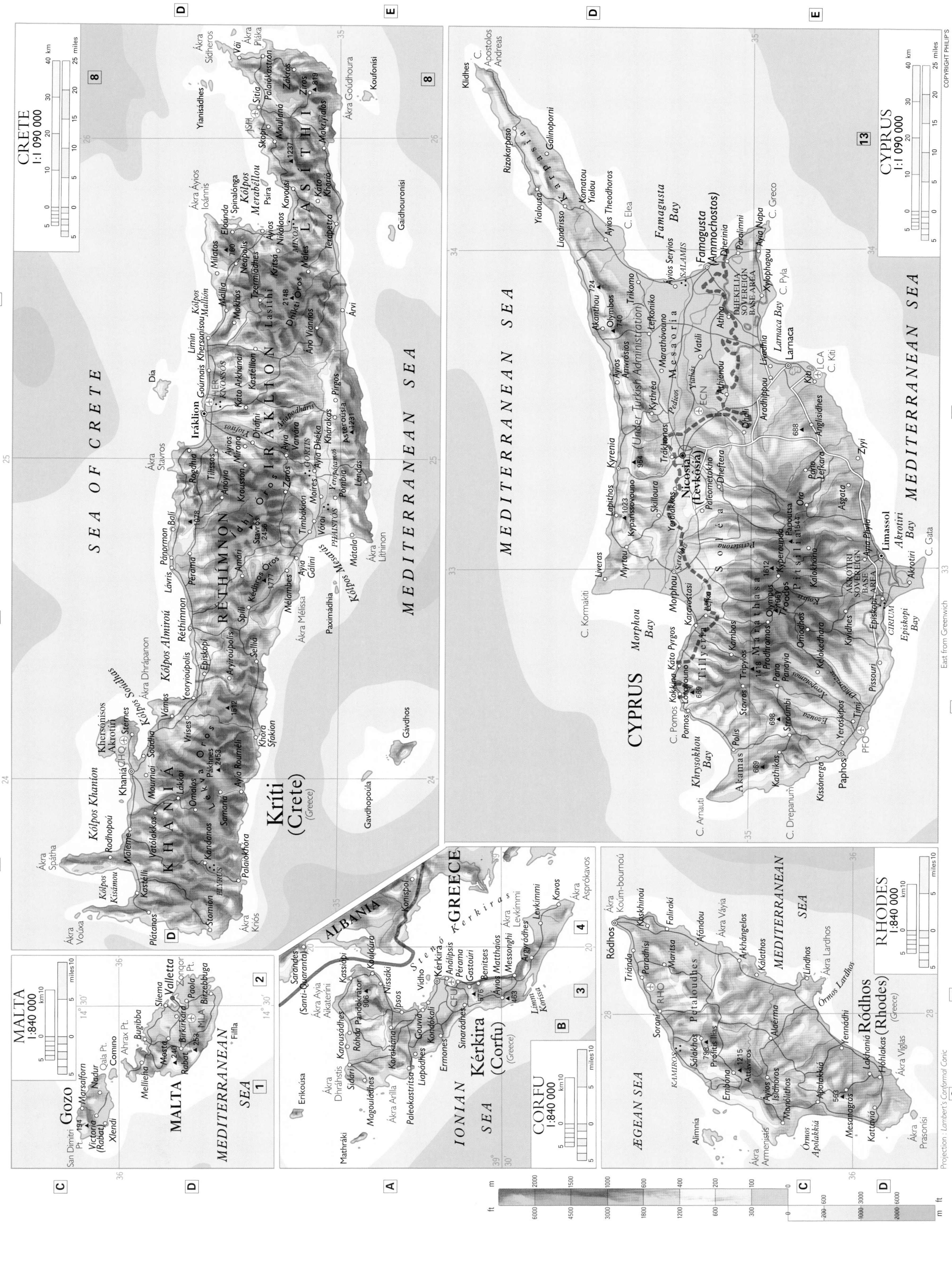

500 0 250 500 750 1000 1250 1500 1750 km

1:42 000 000

500 0 250 500 750 1000 1250 miles

Projection: Bonne

m 4000 3000 2000 1000 500 200 0 200 · 600 1000 3000 2000 6000 4000 12 000 6000 18 000 8000 24 000

ft 12 000 9000 6000 3000 1500 600 0 ft

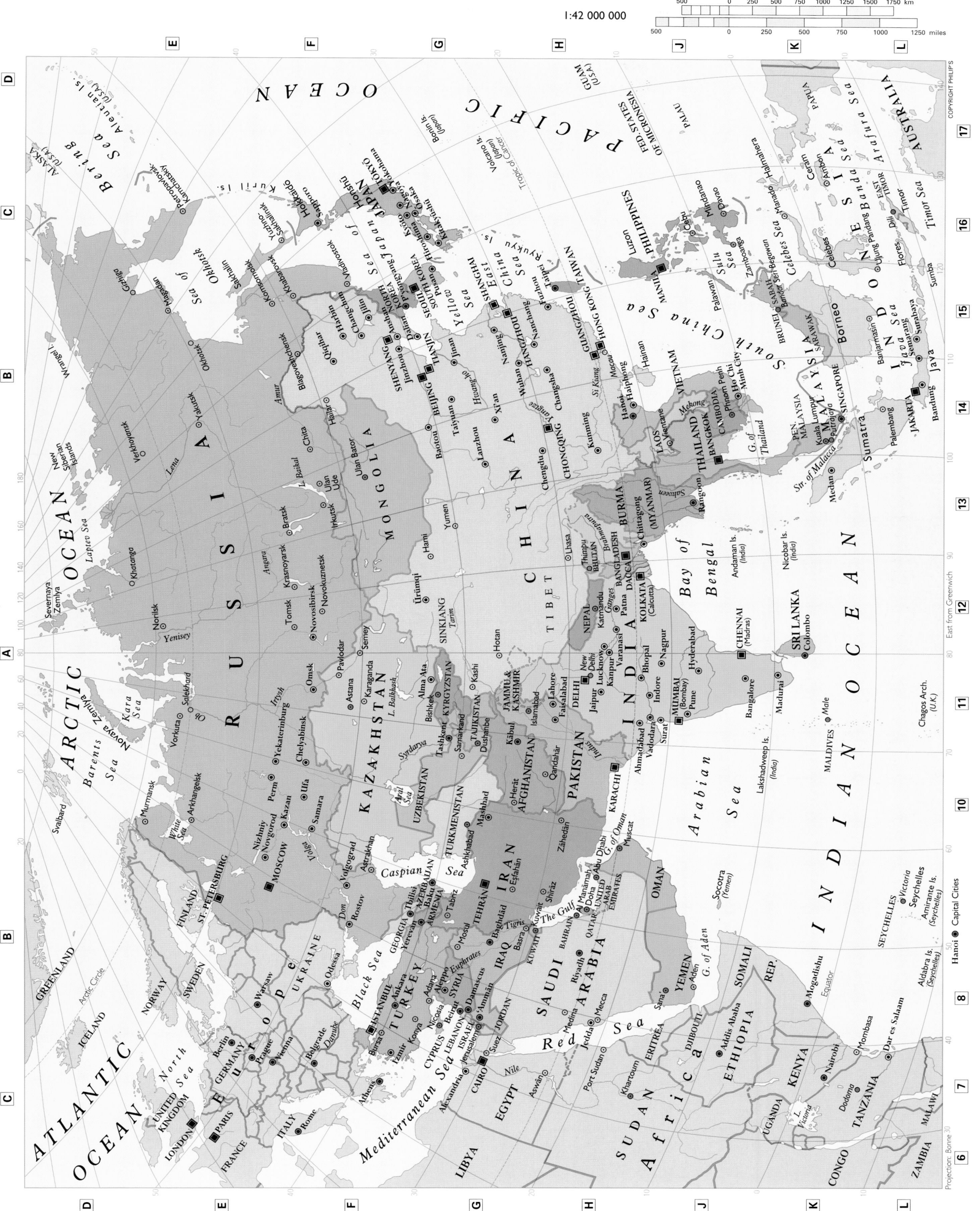

1:42 000 000

COPYRIGHT PHILIP'S

Projection: Bonne

RUSSIA
1 Adygea
2 Karachey-Cherkessia
3 Kabardino-Balkaria
4 North Ossetia
5 Ingushetia
6 Chechenia
7 Dagestan
8 Mordvinia
9 Chuvashia
10 Mari El
11 Tatarstan
12 Udmurtia
13 Khakassia

AZERBAIJAN
14 Naxçıvan

GEORGIA
15 Ajaria
16 Abkhazia

UKRAINE
17 Crimea

Projection: Conical Orthomorphic with two standard parallels

East from Greenwich

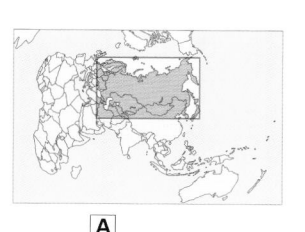

COPYRIGHT PHILIP'S

50 0 25 50 75 100 125 150 175 km

50 0 25 50 75 100 125 miles

1:4 200 000

SEA OF OKHOTSK

Ostrov Kunashir

Nemuro-Kaikyō

Shiretoko-Misaki
Rausu-Dake 1661
Abashiri-Wan
Abashiri
Shari
Nakashibetsu
Nakashibetsu
Akkeshi
Kushiro
Nemuro

Sakhalin

La Perouse Strait
(Sōya-Kaikyō)

Sōya-Misaki

Wakkanai
RISHIRI-
REBUN-
SAROBETSU
Rebun-Tō
Rishin-Tō

Ōmu
Mombetsu
Yūbetsu
Engaru
Kitami
Tokoro-Gawa
Shibecha
Kushiro

Esashi

Otoineppu
Teshio-Gawa
Kitami-Sammyaku
Asahidake 2290
DAISETSU-ZAN
Sammyaku
Tokachi-Dake
2077
Obihiro
Tokachi-Gawa
Hiroo

Emmo-Misaki

TŌHOKU

Teshio
Embetsu
Haboro
Shibetsu
Nayoro
Fukagawa
Akabira
Ashibetsu
Furano
Bibai
Iwamizawa
Yūbari
Oiwake

Obihiro
Tokachi-Dake
Hidaka-Sammyaku
Urakawa
Samani

HOKKAIDŌ

HOKKAIDO

Rumoi
Ōtaru
(Otaru-Wan)
Ishikari-Wan
Ōtaru
Ishikari
SAPPORO
Ebetsu
SHIKOTSU
TŌYA
Chitose
Tomakomai

Ōyubari

Atsuta

Iwanai
Suttsu
Toya-Ko
Uchiura-Wan
Muroran
Noboribetsu
Shiraoi

Kamui-Misaki

Setana
Yakumo
Mori

Hakodate
Tsugaru-Kaikyō

Esan-Misaki

Esashi
Okushiri-Tō

Matsumae
Shiragami-Misaki

Shioya-Zaki

Ōma
Shiriya-Zaki
Mutsu
Mutsu-Wan
Ōhata

Henashi-Misaki

Misawa
Hachinohe

Hakkōda
Aomori
AOMORI
Towada
Kazuno
Kuji

Ajigasawa
ŌU
Hirosaki
Ōdate
Towada-Ko
Kosaka

Oga-Hantō
Gosyogawara

Noshiro
Takanosu

Miyako

RIKUCHŪ-
KAIGAN

Morioka
IWATE
Iwate-San
2041
KITAKAMI

Tono
Kamaishi
Ōtsuchi
Kesennuma
Ishinomaki
Sendai-Wan
SENDAI
Shiogama

Akita
AKITA
Honjo
Ōgata
CHŌKAI-SAN 2236
Yokote
Yuzawa
Kuriko-mi-eki
Kitakami
Ichinoseki

Sakata
Tsuruoka
YAMAGATA
Shinjo
Yamagata
Sendai
Shiogama

Murakami

BANDAI
ŌYAMA
Bandai-San
Aizu-Wakamatsu
Fukushima
Abukuma-Gawa
Soma
Haramachi

Niigata
Nishi
Nagaoka
Karino
Aizu

Ryōtsu
Sado
CHŪBU
Aikawa

Honshū

OF

JAPAN

(EAST SEA)

SEA

Svetlaya

Amgu
Velikaya Kema
Terney
Plastun

Sikhote-Alin

1745

Dalnegorsk
Rudnaja Pristan

Krasnorechenskiy
Lifudzin
Kavalerovo
Olga

Bikin
Lesopilnoye
Bikin
Boli
Dalnerechensk

Margaritovo

Dongfanghong
Muling He
Hulin
Lesozavodsk
Ussurka
Ariadnoye
Kirovskiy
Gornyy
1855
Lazo

Valentin

Preobrazheniye

RUSSIA

HEILONGJIANG

CHINA

Hegang
Songhua Jiang
Jiamusi
Huanan
Qitaihe
Boli
Linkou

Fujin

Spassk
Dalniy
Yakovlevka
Asenev
Suchan
Nakhodka

Wusuli Jiang

Shuangyashan

Mishan

Jixi

Hulin
Novokachalinsk
Lake
Khanka
Kamen-
Rybolov
Pogranichny
Suiyang
Suifenhe

Kameran-
Rybolov
Libovts
Marizovka
Razdolnoye
Artem
Ussuriysk
Dunayo
VLADIVOSTOK
Zaliv
Petra Velikogo

Trudovoye

JILIN

1498
Hunchun
Kraskino
Khasan

Unggi

Najin

Chŏngjin

NORTH
KOREA

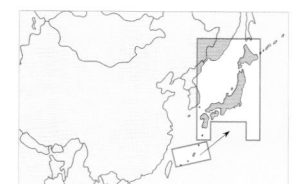

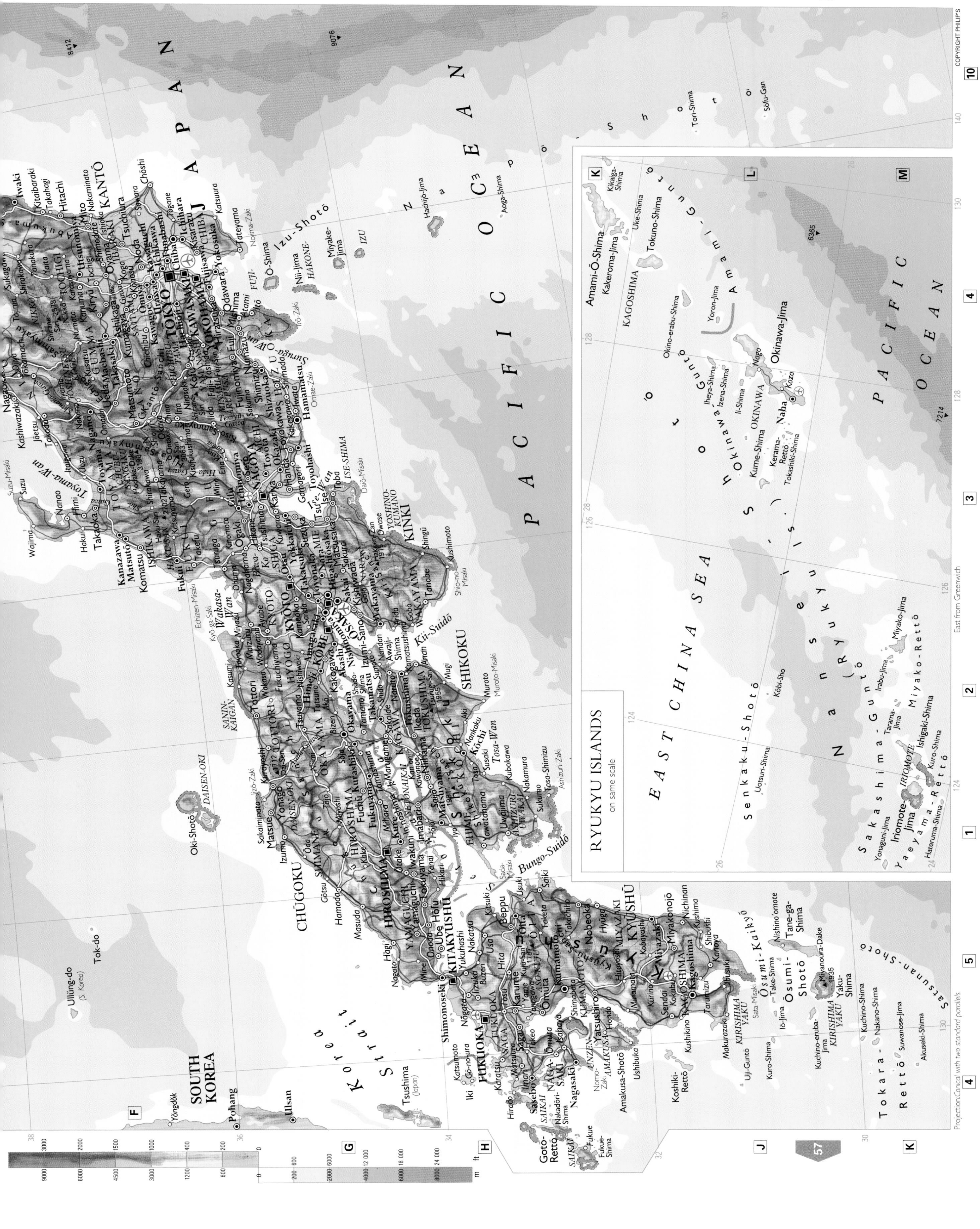
P A C I F I C   O C E A N
EAST CHINA SEA
RYUKYU ISLANDS
on same scale
SOUTH KOREA
Korea Strait
TOKYO
YOKOHAMA
KAWASAKI
NAGOYA
KYOTO
OSAKA
KOBE
HIROSHIMA
KITAKYUSHU
FUKUOKA
SHIKOKU
KYŪSHŪ
CHŪGOKU
KINKI
KANTŌ
Tsushima
Oki-Shotō
Ōsumi-Shotō
Tokara-Rettō
Izu-Shotō
Amami-Ō-Shima
Okinawa-Jima
Naha
Miyako-Rettō
Yaeyama-Rettō
Senkaku-Shotō
Nansei-Shotō (Ryukyu-Rettō)
Projection: Conical with two standard parallels
East from Greenwich
COPYRIGHT PHILIP'S

57

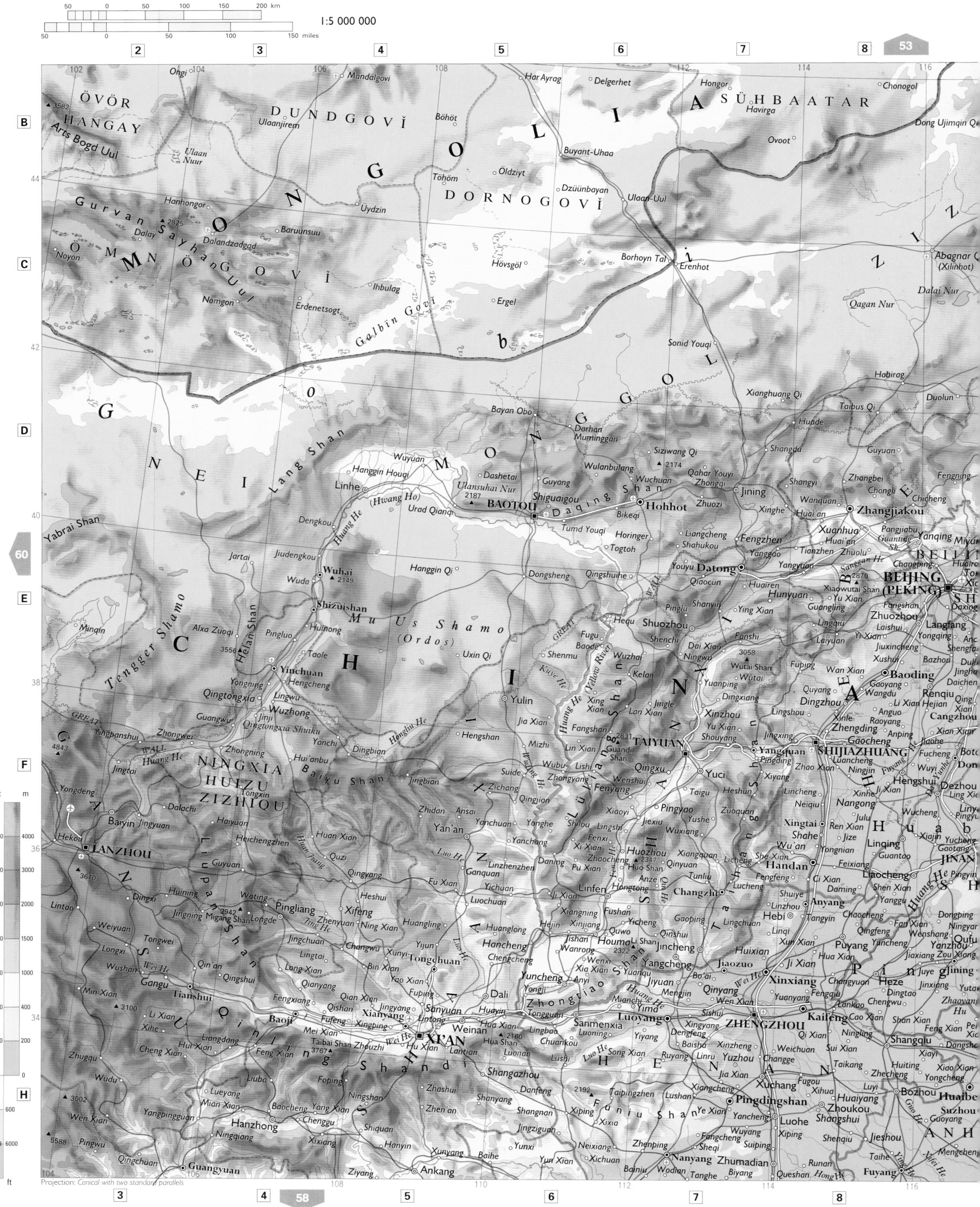

1:5 000 000

Projection: Conical with two standard parallels

B

44

C

42

D

55

40

E

SEA OF

JAPAN

(EAST SEA)

38

F

36

G

34

H

East from Greenwich

COPYRIGHT PHILIP'S

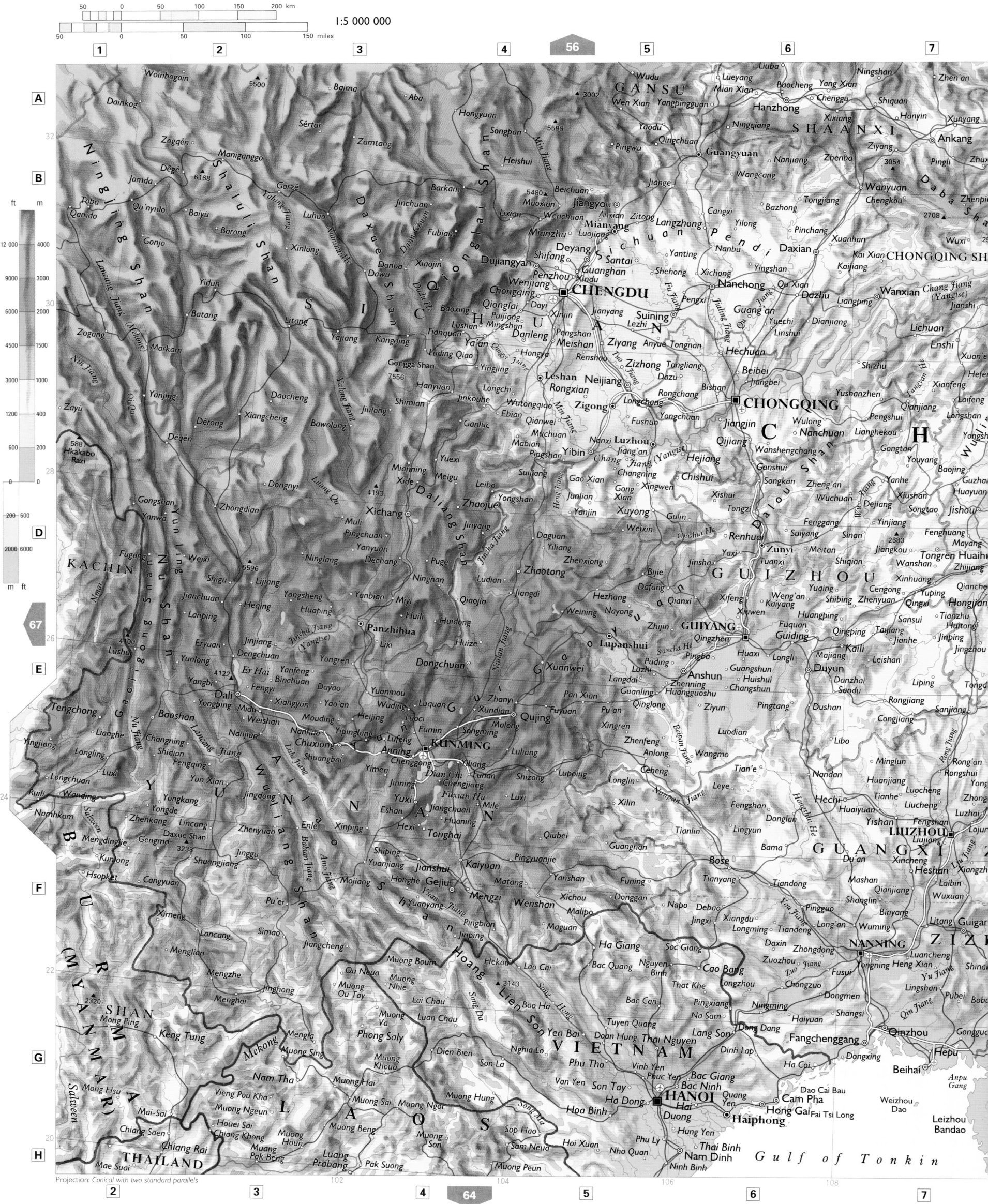

Projection: Conical with two standard parallels

8
9
10
57
11
12
13
14
A
B
C
D
E
F
G
H
HENAN
JIANGSU
ANHUI
HUBEI
HUNAN
JIANGXI
ZHEJIANG
FUJIAN
GUANGDONG
GUANGXI ZHUANGZU
TAIWAN
SHANGHAI SHI
WUHAN
NANJING
SHANGHAI
HANGZHOU
CHANGSHA
NANCHANG
FUZHOU
GUANGZHOU
HONG KONG (XIANGGANG)
T'AIPEI
KAOHSIUNG
Shangnan
Xiping
Xixia
Fangcheng
Wuyang
Xiping
Shenqiu
Jieshou
Mengcheng
Guzhen
Hongze Hu
Xinghua
Dongtai
Jingziguan
Yun Xian
Neixiang
Zhenping
Nanyang
Sheqi
Zhumadian
Suiping
Runan
Taihe
Fuyang
Madian
Huaiyuan
Bengbu
Huainan
Fengyang
Mingguang
Gaoyou Hu
Gaoyou
Hai'an
Rugao
Rudong
Xichuan
Danjiangkou Shuiku
Wadian
Tanghe
Biyang
Queshan
Xincai
Yingshang
Fengtai
Shou Xian
Dingyuan
Tianchang
Yangzhou
Taizhou
Jiangyan
Shiyan
Bainiu
Dengzhou
Xinye
Zhengyang
Huaibin
Xi Xian
Zhengyangguan
Changfeng
Lai'an
Luhe
Yizheng
Jiangdu
Yangzhong
Taixing
Nantong
Danjiangkou
Laohekou
Minggang
Huai He
Huoqiu
Wabu Hu
Chuzhou
Pukou
Zhenjiang
Jingjiang
Jiangyin
Haimen
Qidong
Chang Jiang (Yangtze)
Chongming Dao
Zhushan
Gucheng
Zaoyang
Tongbai
Luoshan
Xinyang
Huangchuan
Gushi
Chengxi Hu
Chengdong Hu
Hefei
Zhegao
Jiangning
Jurong
Danyang
Changzhou
Chongming
Changshu
Fang Xian
Bookang
Xiangfan
Shennongjia
Nanzhang
Suizhou
Guangshui
Shangcheng
Lu'an
Feixi
Chao Hu
Chaohu
He Xian
Ma'anshan
Lishui
Jintan
Wuxi
Kunshan
Jiading
Baoshan
Nanhui
Yicheng
Dahong Shan
Maping
Dawu
Jinzhai
Huoshan
Shucheng
Wuwei
Wuhu
Gaochun
Yixing
Liyang
Suzhou
Qingpu
Wujiang
Tai Hu
Jiashan
Songjiang
Jinshan
Xuejiaping
Xiemahe
Fengle
Jing Shan
Anlu
Hong'an
Dabie Shan
Yuexi
Tongcheng
Lujiang
Fangchang
Nanyi Hu
Langxi
Changxing
Guangde
Huzhou
Jiaxing
Pinghu
Xingshan
Yangping
Zhongxiang
Yunmeng
Xiaogan
Macheng
Tongling
Datong
Nanling
Xuanzhou
Xinfeng
Ningguo
Anji
Tongxiang
Haining
Haiyan
Hangzhou Wan
Dai Shan
Daishan
Daqu Shan
Three Gorges Dam
Yuan'an
Jingmen
Jingshan
Yingcheng
Huangpi
Luotian
Gaohebu
Zongyang
Guichi
Qingyang
Jing Xian
Chongde
Shangyu
Cixi
Zhoushan
Zhoushan Dao
Putuo
Yichang
Dangyang
Tianmen
Hankou
Hanchuan
Xinzhou
Tuanfeng
Yingshan
Qianshan
Anqing
Taiping
Jingde
Qianyang
Lin'an
Yuyao
Zhenhai
Taohua Dao
Changyang
Zhijiang
Shayang
Jiangling
Caidian
Hanyang
Jinkou
Xishui
Taihu
Huaining
Dongliu
Changhua
Xiaoshan
Shaoxing
Ningbo
Fenghua
Liuheng Dao
Wufeng
Zhicheng
Songzi
Shashi
Qianjiang
Xiantao
Paizhou
Huangshi
Ezhou
Qichun
Wangjiang
Susong
Shitai
Yi Xian
She Xian
Fuyang
Zhuji
Shengzhou
Xiangshan
Gong'an
Haoxue
Hong Hu
Jiayu
Daye
Meichuan
Huangmei
Dongzhi
Pengze
Qimen
Huangshan
Tonglu
Fuchun Jiang
Xinchang
Ninghai
Nanping
Shimen
Jianli
Honghu
Xianning
Yangxin
Wuxue
Jiujiang
Hukou
Shimenjie
Xiuning
Chun'an
Meicheng
Jiande
Pujiang
Tiantai
Niutou Shan
Li Xian
Jinshi
Shishou
Huarong
Linxiang
Puqi
Ruichang
Mufu Shan
Lu Shan
De'an
Fuliang
Jingdezhen
Wuyuan
Shouchang
Yiwu
Dongyang
Sanmen
Sangzhi
Li Shui
Cili
Linli
Anxiang
Nan Xian
Yueyang
Tongcheng
Wuning
Duchang
Xiu Shui
Poyang Hu
Kaihua
Longyou
Lanxi
Jinhua
Tangxi
Anwen
Linhai
Changde
Dongting Hu
Xiushui
Yongxiu
Leping
Changshan
Quzhou
Wuyi
Yongkang
Xianju
Jiaojiang
Taizhou Liedao
Dayong
Hanshou
Yuanjiang
Pingjiang
Jing'an
Anyi
Boyang
Dexing
Yushan
Jiangshan
Jinyun
Huangyan
Wenling
Yuan Jiang
Taoyuan
Zi Shui
Miluo
Jiuling Shan
Fengxin
Xinjian
Nanchang
Wannian
Hengfeng
Shangrao
Suichang
Lishui
Yongjia
Yuhuan
Yuhuan Dao
Xiongyin
Tonggu
Gan Jiang
Yiyang
Yanshan
Guangfeng
Xiping
Qingtian
Yueqing
Yuanling
Anhua
Wangcheng
Yifeng
Gao'an
Jinxian
Yingtan
Guixi
Xin Jiang
Yunhe
Wenzhou
Dongtou
Ningxiang
Shanggao
Fengcheng
Dongxiang
Yujiang
Longquan
Hexi
Xiang Jiang
Liuyang
Zhangshu
Linchuan
Jinxi
Pucheng
Wencheng
Rui'an
Meichengzhen
Wanzai
Xinyu
Chongren
Wuyishan
Qingyuan
Pinyang
Nanji Shan
Chenxi
Xupu
Xiangtan
Zhuzhou
Yichun
Fenyi
Xingan
Zixi
Wuyi Shan
Songxi
Taishun
Cangnan
Xinhua
Loudi
Shaoshan
Liling
Xiajiang
Guangze
Shouning
Fuding
Lengshuijiang
Lianyuan
Xiangxiang
Pingxiang
Gaokeng
Yihuang
Nancheng
Jianyang
Zhenghe
Zherong
Le'an
Shaowu
Shuiji
Zhouning
Fu'an
Shuangfeng
Anfu
Gujiang
Yongfeng
Lichuan
Pingnan
Sansha
Xinshao
Shaodong
Hengshan
Wugong Shan
Lianhua
Ji'an
Jishui
Xinfeng
Nanfeng
Jian'ou
Xiapu
Qianyang
Longhui
Shaoyang
You Xian
Yongxin
Taining
Shunchang
Ningde
Dongkou
Shaoyang
Hengyang
Chaling
Xincheng
Taihe
Guangchang
Jianning
Jiangle
Nanping
Gutian
Fuying Dao
Xuefeng Shan
Qidong
Anren
Ninggang
Jinggangshan
Luoxiao Shan
Wugang
Huangyangsi
Qiyang
Lei Shui
Ling Xian
Wan'an
Ningdu
Xingguo
Mingxi
Sha Xian
Sha Xi
Min Jiang
Minqing
Luoyuan
Lianjiang
Matsu Tao (Taiwan)
Lengshuitan
Xiang Jiang
Changning
Leiyang
Shicheng
Sanming
Youxi
Fuzhou
Changle
Xinning
Dong'an
Yongzhou
Yongxing
Suichuan
Longkou
Ninghua
Qingliu
Minhou
Yongtai
Fuqing
Ziyuan
Guidong
Shadi
Yudu
Ruijin
Changting
Yong'an
Datian
Haitan Dao
Pingtan
Quanzhou
Xintian
Zixing
Ganzhou
Shangyou
Liancheng
Hanjiang
Xingan
Guiyang
Jiahe
Chenzhou
Chongyi
Nankang
Huichang
Maiyuan
Dehua
Xianyou
Putian
Xinghua Wan
Nanri Dao
Yizhang
Nan Ling
Rucheng
Dayu
Xinfeng
Anyuan
Ting Jiang
Zhangping
Yongchun
Anxi
Hui'an
Taiwan Strait
Guanyang
Guilin
Dao Xian
Lanshan
Linwu
Nanxiong
Wuping
Longyan
Nanan
Quanzhou
Jiangyong
Jianghua
Lechang
Renhua
Xunwu
Shanghang
Hua'an
Tong'an
Jinjiang
Shishi
Gongcheng
Fuchuan
Lianzhou
Shixing
Longnan
Dingnan
Jiaoling
Yongding
Changtai
Zhangzhou
Xiamen
Chinmen (Quemoy)
Chinmen Tao (Taiwan)
Pingle
Lianshan
Ruyuan
Shaoguan
Quannan
Pingyuan
Heping
Meizhou
Nanjing
Pinghe
Longhai
Zhangpu
Zhongshan
He Xian
Yangshan
Wengcheng
Lianping
Dabu
Han Jiang
Zhaoping
Yingde
Wengyuan
Longchuan
Xingning
Yunxiao
Dongshan
Zhao'an
Huaiji
Xinfeng
Xinfengjiang Shuiku
Huacheng
Fengshun
Raoping
Fogang
Longmen
Dong Jiang
Heyuan
Chaozhou
Chenghai
Nan'ao
Tropic of Cancer
Nanfeng
Qingyuan
Bei Jiang
Jieyang
Wuzhou
Guangning
Conghua
Zijin
Puning
Shantou
Xun Jiang
Fengkai
Sihui
Huadu
Zengcheng
Chaoyang
Haimen
Gui Jiang
Teng Xian
Cangwu
Xi Jiang
Hekou
Boluo
Huizhou
Haifeng
Lufeng
Huilai
Yunan
Deqing
Zhaoqing
Sanshui
Gaoyao
Foshan
Shilong
Panyu
Dongguan
Huidong
Shanwei
Honghai Wan
Rong Xian
Cenxi
Yunkai Dashan
Yunfu
Jiujiang
Shunde
Xiaolan
Shenzhen
Yulin
Luoding
Xinxing
Jiangmen
Zhongshan
Kowloon
Kaiping
Xinhui
Zhuhai
Tsuen Wan
Luchuan
Enping
Taishan
Doumen
Macau
Zhu Jiang
Dangan Liedao
Xinyi
Yangchun
Chixi
Gaolan Dao
Gaozhou
Yangjiang
Huazhou
Maoming
Dianbai
Shangchuan Dao
Xiachuan Dao
Hailing Dao
Wuchuan
Diancheng
Lianjiang
Suixi
Zhanjiang
Leizhou
Donghai Dao
Naozhou Dao
Leizhou Wan
Xuwen
Hai'an
Tanshui
Chilung
T'aoyüan
Chungli
Panch'iao
Hsinchu
Ilan
Chuhsi
Yüanli
Miaoli
T'uch'ang
Lotung
Tachia
T'aichung
Tailuko
Fengyüan
Changhua
Lukang
Yüanlin
Hualien
Erhlin
Nantou
Fenglin
Makung
P'enghu
Ch'üntou (Pescadores) (Taiwan)
Tounan
Yunlin
Alishan
Pekang
Chiai
Yü Shan
Paiho
Yuli
P'otzu
Hsinying
Chiali
Ch'ishan
Kuanshan
T'ainan
T'aitung
Chungyang Shanmo
Fengshan
Lü-Tao
P'ingtung
Fangliao
Tawu
Fengkang
Hengchun
Hungt'ou Hsü
Maopi T'ou
Oluanpi
Luzon Strait
Dongsha Dao (Pratas I.) (China)
SOUTH CHINA SEA
2393
1636
1834
1810
1474
1596
1794
1725
2120
1963
1629
1510
2164
1703
3931
3997
112
114
116
118
120
122
32
30
28
26
24
22
20
East from Greenwich
COPYRIGHT PHILIP'S
8
9
10
11
61
12
13

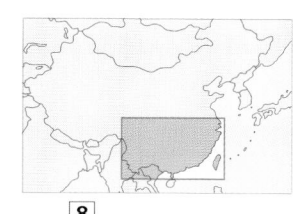

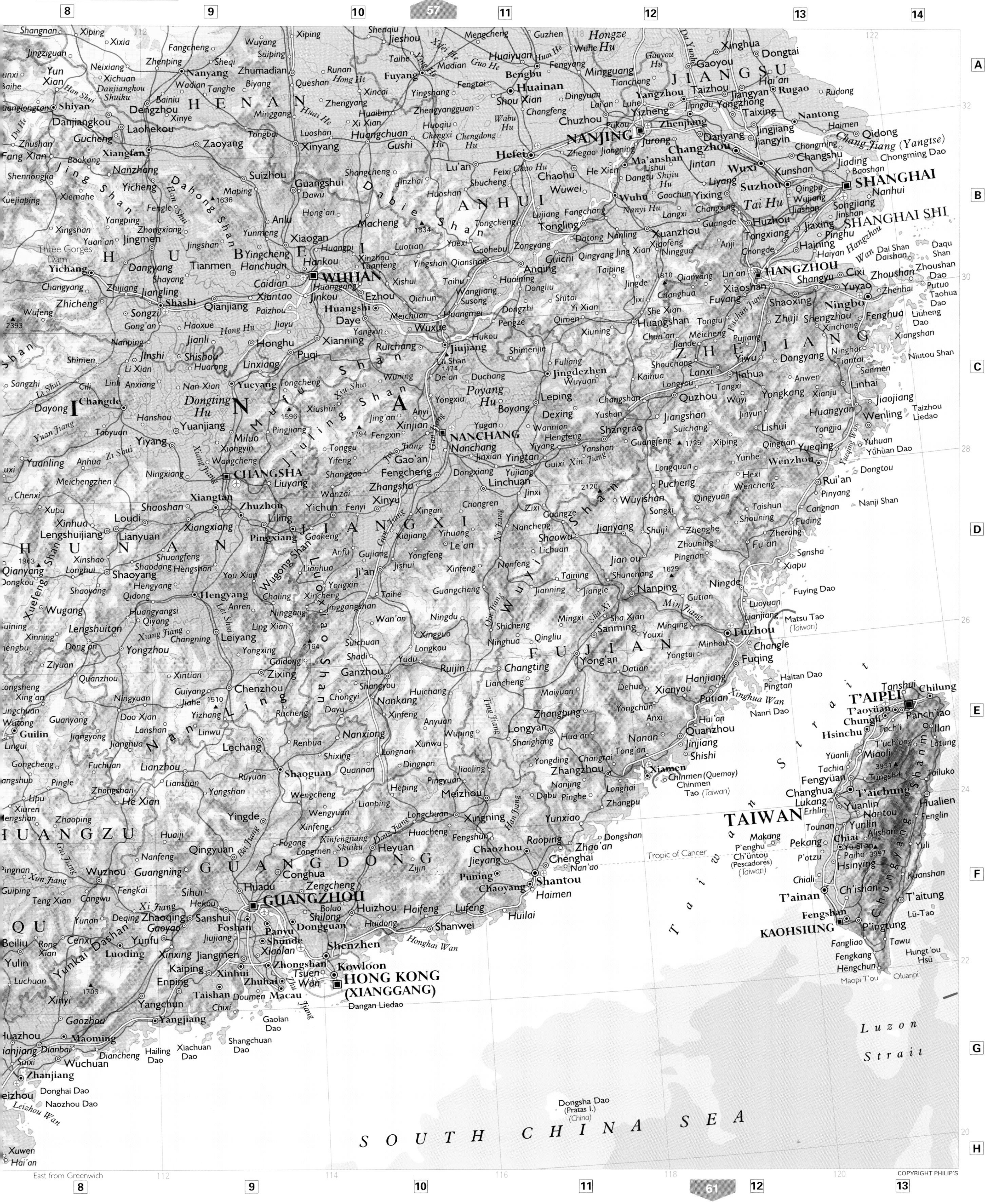

1:16 800 000

100 0 100 200 300 400 500 600 700 800 km
100 0 100 200 300 400 500 miles

COPYRIGHT PHILIP'S

East from Greenwich

Projection: Borne

RUSSIA

MONGOLIA

NEI MONGOL ZIZHIQU

KAZAKHSTAN

KYRGYZSTAN

XINJIANG UYGUR ZIZHIQU

XIZANG ZIZHIQU (TIBET)

QINGHAI

GANSU

SICHUAN

YUNNAN

GUIZHOU

GUANGXI ZHUANGZU ZIZHIQU

GUANGDONG

HAINAN

HUNAN

HUBEI

HENAN

SHAANXI

SHANXI

HEBEI

SHANDONG

JIANGSU

ANHUI

ZHEJIANG

JIANGXI

FUJIAN

NINGXIA HUIZU ZIZHIQU

LIAONING

JILIN

HEILONGJIANG

NORTH KOREA

SOUTH KOREA

JAPAN

TAIWAN (FORMOSA)

PHILIPPINES

VIETNAM

LAOS

THAILAND (SIAM)

BURMA (MYANMAR)

BANGLADESH

INDIA

NEPAL

BHUTAN

JAMMU & KASHMIR

KAZAKHSTAN

BEIJING (PEKING)
TIANJIN
SHANGHAI
HONG KONG
MACAU

YELLOW SEA
EAST CHINA SEA
SOUTH CHINA SEA
BAY OF BENGAL

Tropic of Cancer

Tarim Pendi
Taklamakan Shamo

Kunlun Shan
Tien Shan
Altai Shan

Qaidam Pendi

Gobi Desert

Huang He

Chang Jiang

K2 8611

Mt Everest 8850

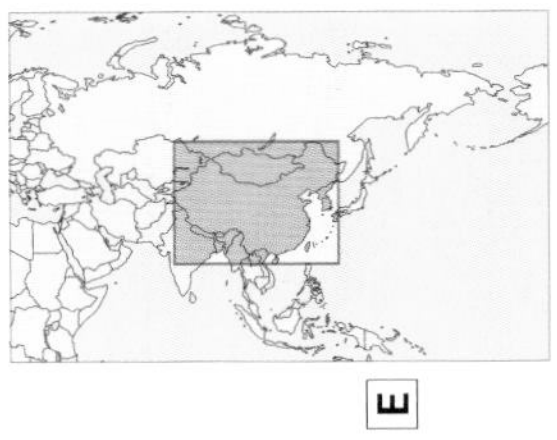

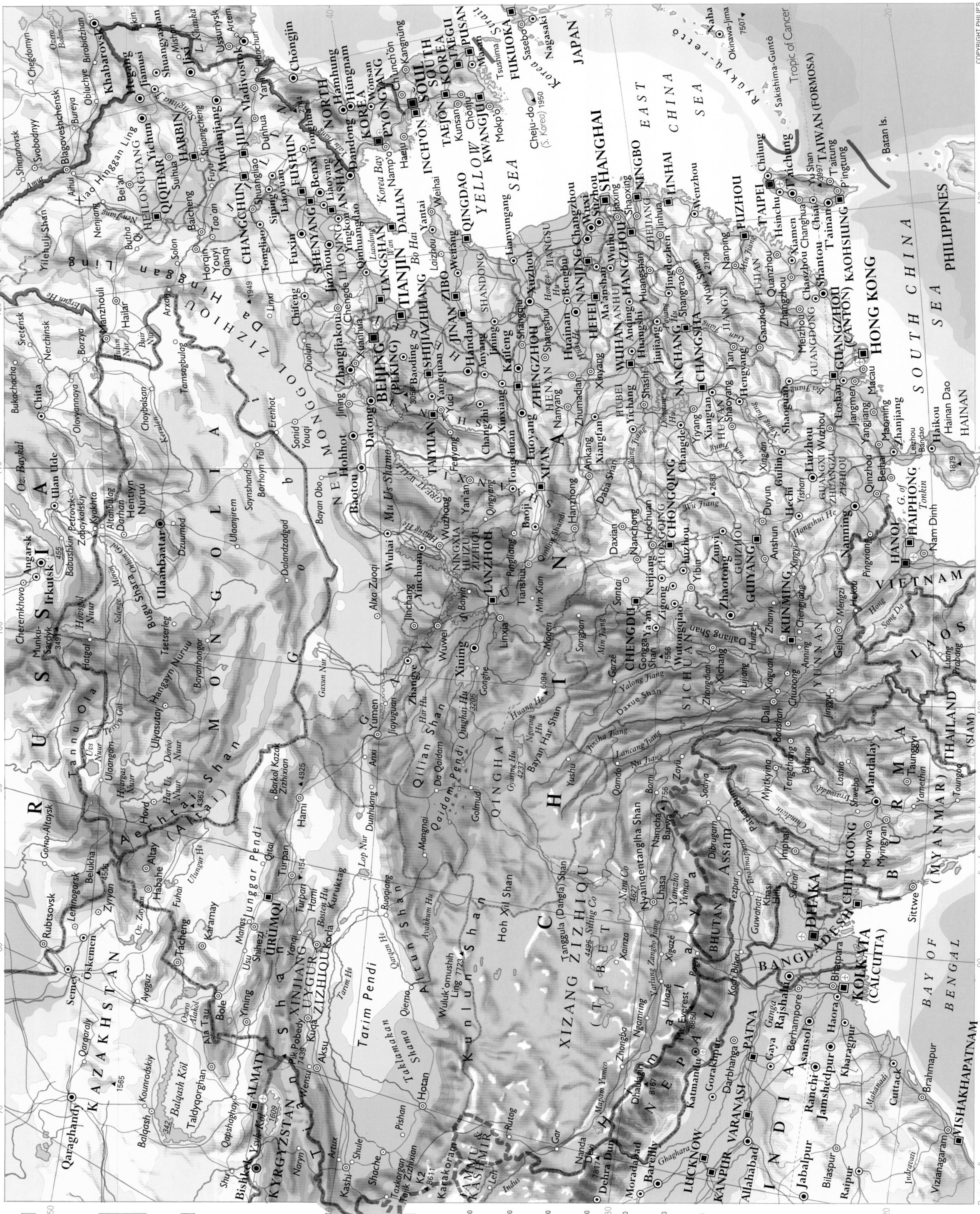

1:6 300 000

50 0 100 150 200 250 300 km
50 0 50 100 150 200 miles

A

Dongsha Dao
(China)

Itbayat I.
Batan Is.
Batan I.

P A C I F I C

B

Balintang Channel

Calayan I.
Babuyan I.

Dalupiri I. Babuyan
Islands
Fuga I. Camiguin I.

Mayraira Pt.
Babuyan Channel

O C E A N

Bacarra Claveria Santa Ana
Bangui Gonzaga
San Nicolas Laoag Kabugao Aparri
Batac Gattaran

Cabugao 2360 Tuao Tuguegarao
Bangued

Vigan Santa Lubuagan Mt. Cresta
Maria Roxas 1685
Candon Bontoc Ilagan Palanan Pt.
San Matteo Palanan
Balaoan MT. Santiago **Luzon**
Tagudin DATA Cordon
San Fernando Mt. Pulog Solano
Lingayen 2928 Bayombong C. San Ildefonso *PHILIPPINE*
Bolinao HUNDRED Baguio Mt. Anacuao
Alaminos ISLANDS Rosario 1852
Lingayen Dagupan Baler Bay
Gulf San Manuel San Jose Baler
San Carlos Bayambang San Jose
Santa Cruz Moncada Cuyapo *SEA*
Masinloc Camiling Victoria AURORA MEMORIAL
Iba 2037 La Tarlac Cabanatuan Dingalan
Concepcion Paz Gapan
Angeles Polillo Str.
1780 Mt. Pinatubo San Fernando **PHILIPPINES**
San Antonio Malabon Polillo Is.
Olongapo **Caloocan** Patnanongan I.
Orani *Manila* **Quezon City** Jomalig I.
Bataan *Bay* **MANILA**
Mariveles **Pasay** Santa Cruz Lamon Bay
Cavite Alabat I. Paracale
Dasmariñas Lucban Labo
Tagaytay L. de Bay Lucena Daet
Nasugbu San Atimonan Pandan
Balayan Pablo QUEZON Calauag Viga Catanduanes
Lemery Lipa Lucena BICOL Calabanga San Andres
Batangas Lopez 1976 Virac
Lubang Verde I. Pass Catanauan Mt. Isarog Lagonoy Gulf
Is. Lobo Tayabas Bay Naga Rapu Rapu I.
C. Calavite Boac Nabua 2421
Calapan Marin- Iriga Tabaco
Mamburao Victoria duque Ligao Mayon Vol.
Mindoro LAKE Teblas Strait Legazpi Sorsogon
NAUJAN Burias I. San Bernardino Str.
Sablayan Mt. Baco Pinamalayan Donsol Gubat
Bongabong 2487 *SIBUYAN* Magallanes Laoag
APO REEF Bulan Mondragon
San Jose Roxas Tablas I. Romblon Ticao I. Irosin Allen Gamay
Busuanga I. Odiongan Sibuyan I. Catarman Atcheve
Culion I. *SEA* Aroroy Masbate Calbayog Oras
Linapacan Str. Pandan Placer Catbalogan Parañas **Samar**
Linapacan I. Calamian Masbate Catbalogan Santa
Group Kalibo Milagros *VISAYAN* Bilinan I. Caibiran Rita Borongan
Taytay Cuyo Is. Roxas Dao Pilar *SEA* Calubian Basey Llorente
Cuyo Tibiao 2117 Sara Bantayan Carigara General MacArthur
Cuyo West Pass San Jose **Panay** Ajuy Passi Palompon **Leyte** Guiuan
Bugasong Pototan Cadiz Bogo Ormoc
Cuyo East Pass Silay Sagay Tuburan Camotes Is. Dulag Homonhon I.
Iloilo Victorias Danao Baybay Leyte Gulf
Palawan Guimaras Jordan San Carlos Camotes Abuyog
ST PAUL Hinigaran La Carlota CENTRAL CEBU Sogod Sagay San Juan Str. Dinagat I.
1593 Binalbagan 2460 **Mandaue** *Sea* Bato Siargao I.
Dumaran I. Himamaylan **Cebu** Maasin Surigao Str. 10 497
Irahuan Honda Bay Kabankalan Carcar Panaon I. Placer
Puerto Princesa Sipalay Bais Argao Bohol I. Surigao Bucas Grande I.
Cagayan Is. Tanjay *SABAH* Tagbilaran Carrascal
Negros Hinoba-an Dumaguete *IKATUNA* Cabadbaran L. Lanuza
Bayawan Oslob **BOHOL** 2012 Mainit Tandag
Siaton Siquijor I. Talisayan Nasipit Tago
Zamboanguita Camiguin I. **Butuan** Marihatag
SULU Dipolog Dapitan Cabadbaran *SEA* Esperanza Bayugan Lianga
TUBBATAHA Iligan Balingasag Hinatuan
Mt. Mantalingajan REEFS Manukan Bay Alubijid Talacogan Bislig
2085 Oroquieta Opol 2938 MT. Malaybalay
SEA Sindangan Ozamiz **Cagayan de Oro** Bunawan
C. Buliluyan Labason MALINDANG **Iligan** Malaybalay Cateel
Bugsuk I. Liloy Tubod Marawi City Baganga
Balabac I. Kabasalan Pagadian L. Lanao **Mindanao**
Balabac Strait Siocon Malabang 2815 Tagum Panabo
Balambangan Cagayan Sulu I. Margosatubig Parang Midsayap Pantukan Manay
Banggi Ilana Pikit Mt. Apo Mati
Kudat Sibuca Bay Cotabato 2954 **Davao**
Senaja Jembongan *Sibuguey* Datu Piang Digos Davao San Isidro
Langkon Suba Talan *Bay* Talayan Gulf
Tenghilan Turtle Is. Kalamansig Lebak Koronadal C. San Agustin
Kota Belud **Zamboanga** *Moro Gulf* Malita
G. Kinabalu Pilas Basilan Str. 2083 **General**
Kota 4101 Group Isabela Palimbang **Santos**
Kinabalu Pangutaran Basilan I. Kiamba
Papar Group Lamitan Tinaca Pt.
Melalap **MALAYSIA** Jolo Sarangani Is.
Keningau Group Samales Group
SABAH Parang *CELEBES*
Tambunan Jolo Talipao
Kuamut Pata I. Tapul *SEA*
Sandakan Siasi I. Group
Langkon Tawi-tawi *INDONESIA* Kep. Talaud
Silam Group Sulu Archipelago
Borneo Sibutu Group

SOUTH CHINA SEA

MINDORO STRAIT

SULU SEA

Mindanao Trench

ft m
9000 3000
6000 2000
4500 1500
3000 1000
1200 400
600 200
0 0
200 600
4000 12 000
8000 24 000
m ft

Projection: Lambert's Conformal Conic
East from Greenwich
COPYRIGHT PHILIP'S

National Parks

1:10 500 000

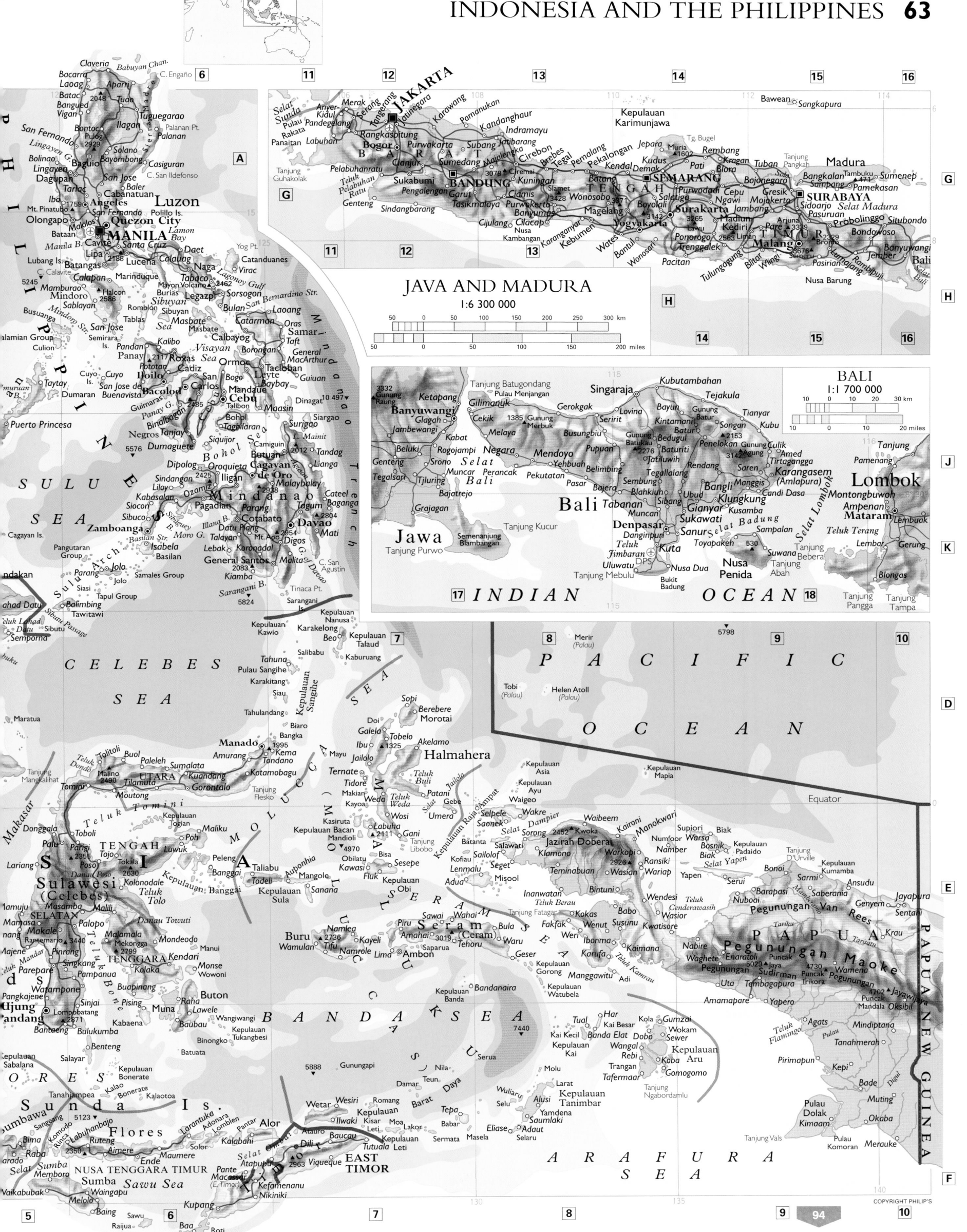

JAVA AND MADURA

1:6 300 000

50   0   50   100   150   200   250   300 km

50   0   50   100   150   200 miles

BALI

1:1 700 000

10   0   10   20   30 km

10   0   10   20 miles

COPYRIGHT PHILIP'S

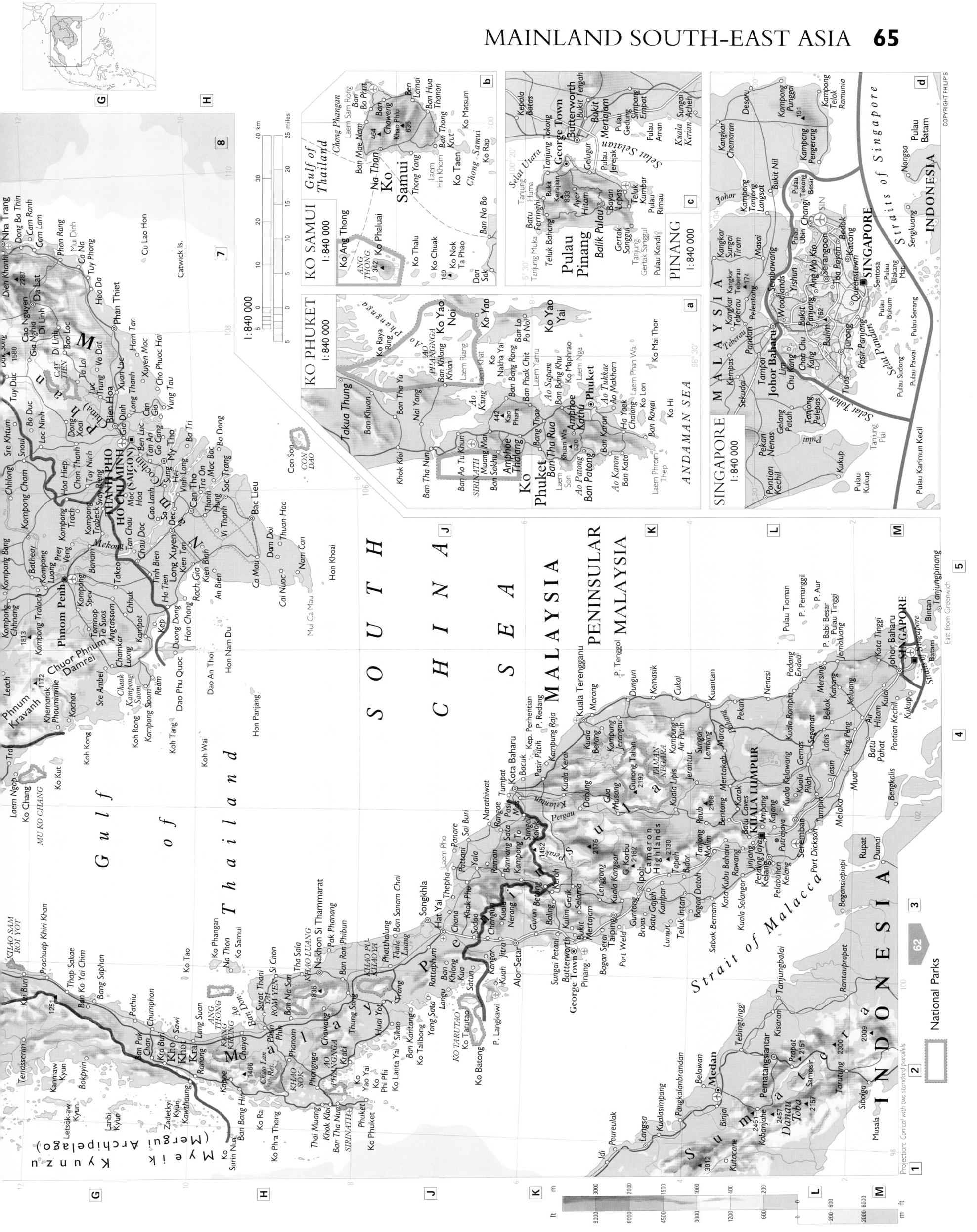

1:8 400 000

Continuation Southwards
on same scale

Projection: *Conical* with two standard parallels

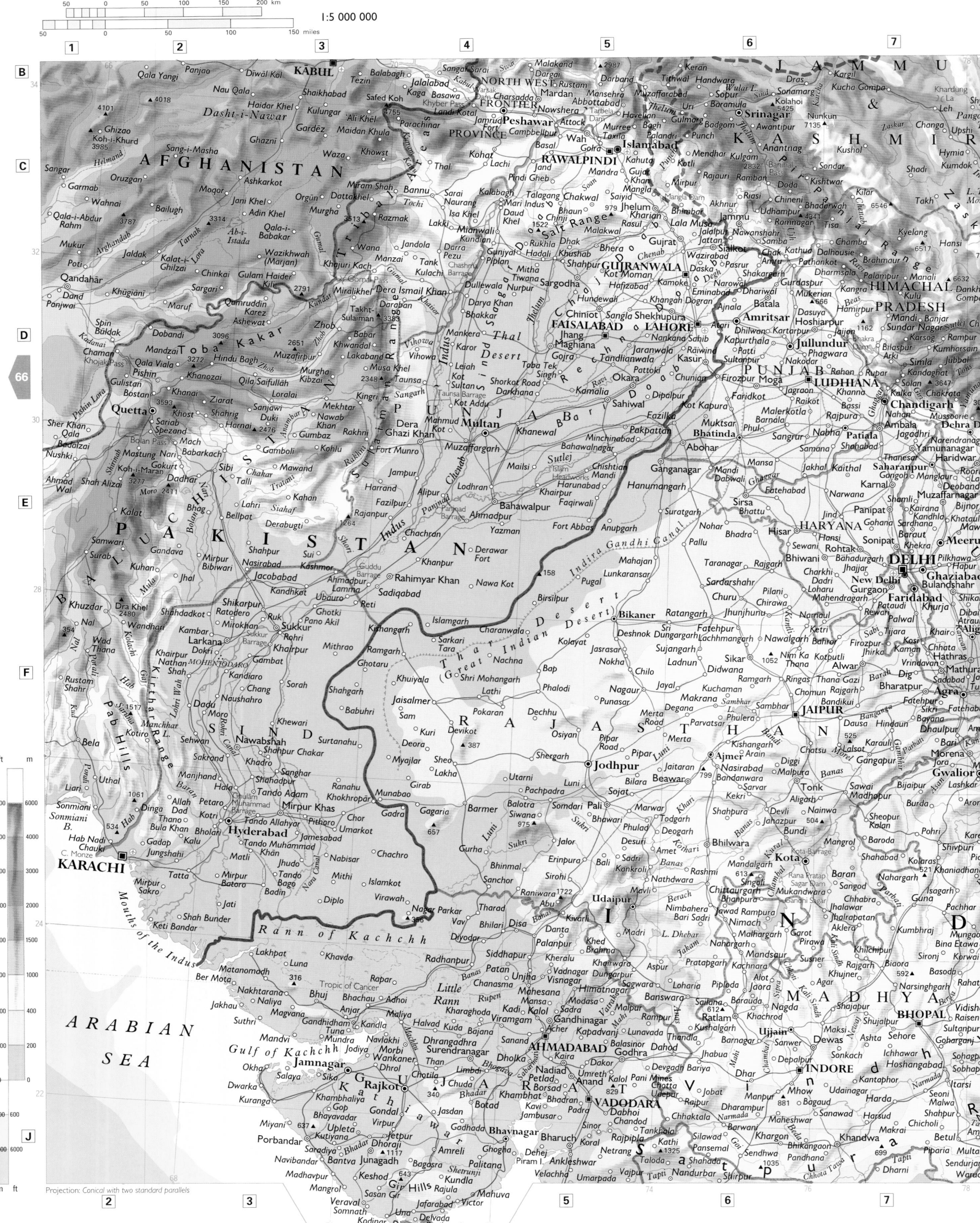

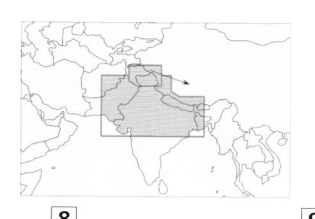

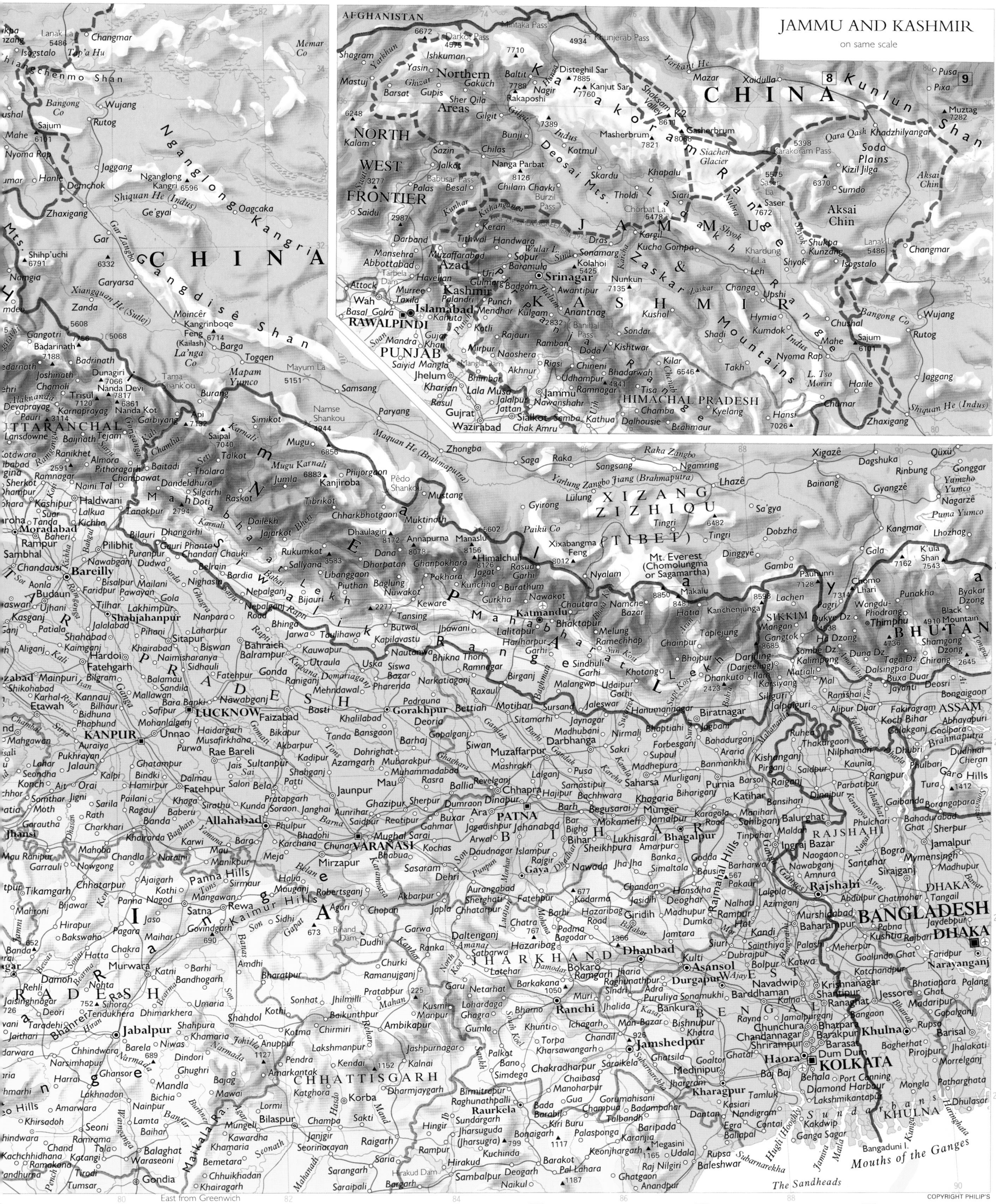

JAMMU AND KASHMIR
on same scale

1:5 900 000

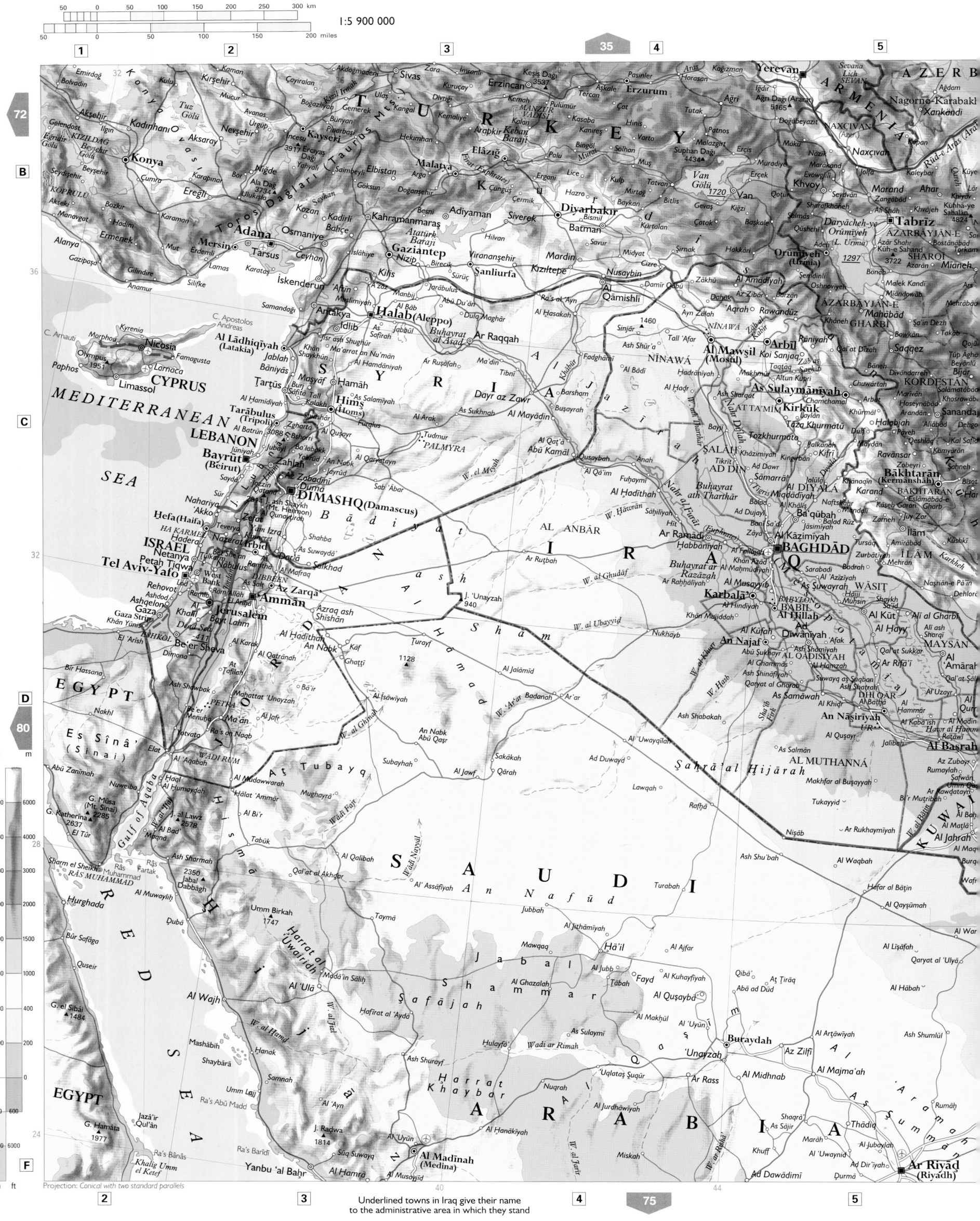

Projection: Conical with two standard parallels

6
7
8
9
10
B
C
D
E
F
66
TURKMENISTAN
Kara Kum
Kopet Dagh
CASPIAN SEA
BAKI (Baku)
Türkmenbashi
Khrebet Bolshoy Balkhan 1880
Nebitdag
Gazanjyk
Cheleken Yarymadasy
Ostrov Ogurchinskiy
Ashgabat
Chärjew
Amudarya
Mary
Bayramaly
Yoloten
Murgab
Tejen
Dushak
Serakhs
Sarakhs
Mashhad
Kashaf
Neyshābūr
Sabzevār
Bojnūrd
Qūchān
Kūh-e Bīnālūd 3314
GOLESTĀN
Gorgān
Gonbad-e Kāvūs
Bandar-e Torkeman
Reshteh-ye Kūhhā-ye Alborz
MĀZANDARĀN
Sārī
Bābol
Āmol
Qā'emshahr
Behshahr
Damāvand
TEHRĀN
Karaj
Eslāmshahr
Rey
Varāmīn
Qazvīn
QAZVĪN
GĪLĀN
Rasht
Bandar-e Anzalī
Lāhījān
Ardabīl
Astara
Länkäran
SEMNĀN
Semnān
Dāmghān
Shāhrūd
Qom
QOM
Kāshān
Arāk
Dasht-e Kavīr
Daryācheh-ye Namak
IRAN
KHORĀSĀN
Torbat-e Ḩeydārīyeh
Torbat-e Jām
Kāshmar
Kūh-e Sorkh 3020
Gonābād
Ferdows
Bīrjand
Tabas
Dasht-e Lūt
Eşfahān
EŞFAHĀN
Najafābād
Khomeynī Shahr
Shahr-e Kord
CHAHĀR MAḨALL VA BAKHTĪĀRĪ
Yazd
YAZD
Kūh-e Zard 4548
Dezfūl
Shūshtar
Masjed Soleymān
Ahvāz
KHUZESTĀN
Ābādān
Khorramshahr
Bandar-e Ma'shur
Bandar-e Emām Khomeynī
Shatt al Arab
Khorramābād
Borūjerd
Malāyer
Zagros
Kūh-e Dīnār 4431
KOHKĪLŪYEH VA BŪYER AḨMADĪ
Yāsūj
Shīrāz
FĀRS
Persepolis
Daryācheh-ye Tashk
Neyrīz
Jahrom
Kerman
KERMĀN
Kūh-e Hazārān 4419
Rafsanjān
Sīrjān
Bam
Kūh-e Jebāl Bārez 3962
Namakzār-e Shahdād
Kūh-e Bazmān 3489
Zāhedān
SĪSTĀN VA BALŪCHESTĀN
Zābol
Daryācheh-ye Sīstān
Hāmūn-e Jaz Mūrīān
Īrānshahr
Kūh-e Taftān 4042
Khāsh
Chāh Bahār
Makran
Kūhhā-ye Bashākerd
HORMOZGĀN
Bandar-e Abbās
Qeshm
Str. of Hormuz
Bandar-e Lengeh
Būshehr
BŪSHEHR
Kāzerūn
AFGHANISTAN
Herāt
HERĀT
Safīd Kūh
FARĀH
Farāh
Shīndand
Dasht-e Khāsh
Daryācheh-ye Namakzār
NĪMRŪZ
Dasht-e Mārgow
Gowd-e Zirreh
PAKISTAN
Hāmūn-i-Mashkel
Al Kuwayt (Kuwait)
Būbiyān
Mīnā' al Aḩmadī
Al Khafji
THE GULF
Ad Dammām
Az Zahrān (Dhahran)
Al Qaţīf
Al Jubayl
Ra's Tannūrah
Al Manāmah
BAHRAIN
Al Hufūf
Al Mubarraz
Ad Dawḩah (Doha)
QATAR
Dukhān
Al Jāfūrah
UNITED ARAB EMIRATES
Abū Ẓaby (Abu Dhabi)
Dubayy (Dubai)
Ash Shāriqah (Sharjah)
Umm al Qaywayn
Ra's al Khaymah
Al Fujayrah
Al Ayn
OMAN
Ṣuḩār
Al Khābūra
Ra's Musandam (Oman)
Gulf of Oman
Al Ḩajar al Gharbī
Tropic of Cancer
East from Greenwich
COPYRIGHT PHILIP'S

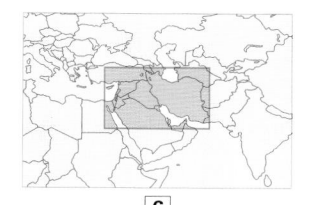

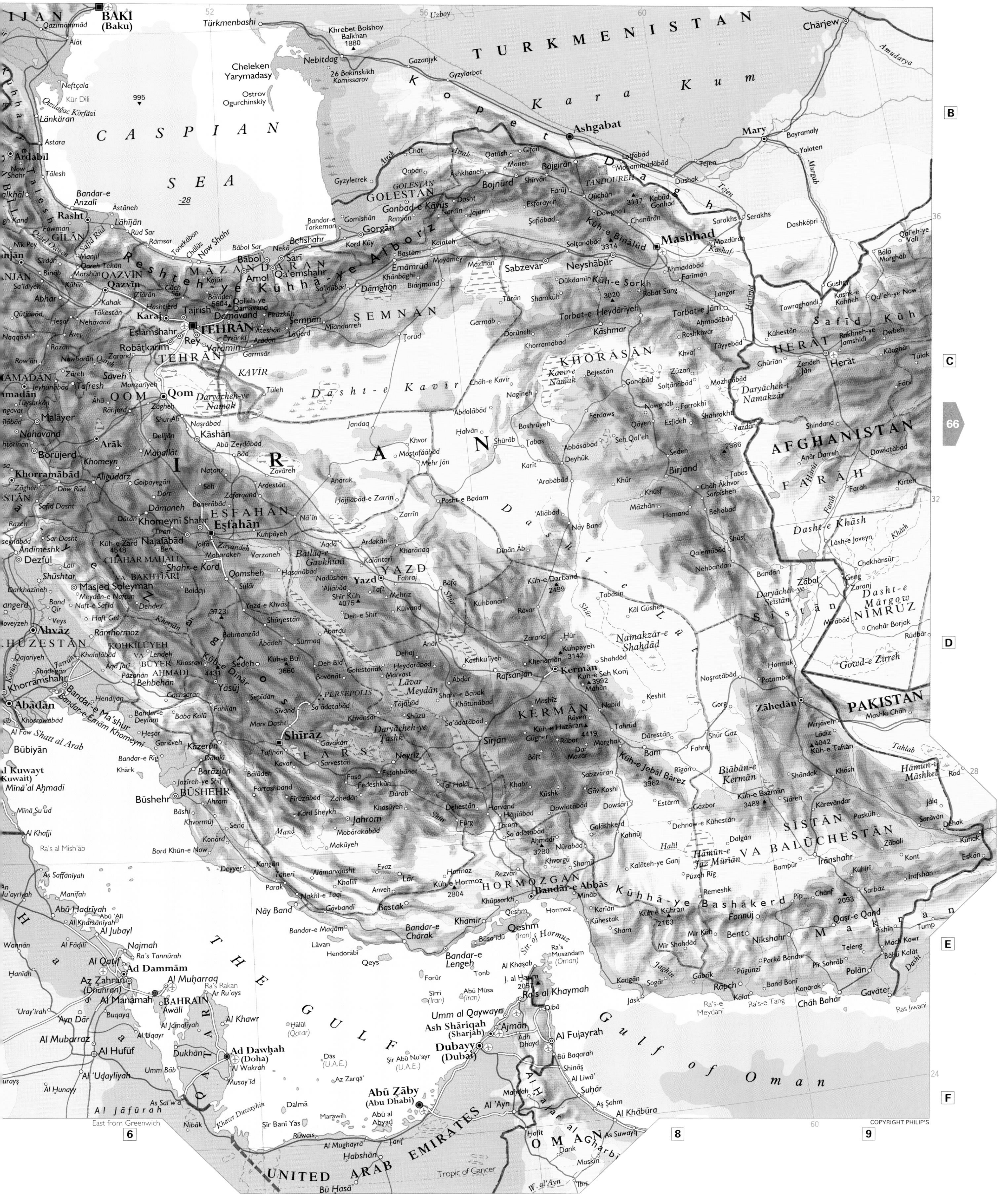

50   0 25 50 75 100 125 150 175 km

1: 4 200 000

50   0   25   50   75   100   125 miles

| 1 | | 2 | | 3 | | 4 | 33 | 5 | | 6 | | 7 |

BULGARIA

B L A C K   S E A

Stara Zagora
Aytos
Yambol
Burgas
Nos Emine
1830
2206

Elkhovo
Michurin
Arda
1018
Kırklareli
Edirne
İğneada Burnu
Demirköy
Kilimli
Kerempe Burnu
İnce Burun
Sinop

Orestías
Pınarhisar
Vize
Saray
Çerkezköy
Zonguldak
Amasra
Kurucaşile
Cide
İnebolu
Abana
Ayancık
Gerze

Hayrabolu
Lüleburgaz
Babaeski
Uzunköprü
Muratlı
Çorlu
Çatalca
İstanbul Boğazı
(Bosporus)
Kozlu
Ereğli
Karasu
Devrek
Karabük
Safranbolu
Daday
Kastamonu
Taşköprü
Duraçan
Küre Dağları
1670
Boyabat
Alaçam
Bafra
Civa Burnu

Ipsala
Keşan
Malkara
Tekirdağ
Büyükçekmece
Silivri
İSTANBUL
Şile
Kandıra
Sakarya
(Adapazarı)
Akçakoca
Düzce
Bolu
Gerede
Araç
Çankırı
İskilip
Osmancık
Merzifon
Samsun
Terme
Ünye
Fatsa
Persen

Saros Körfezi
(Dardanelles)
Marmara
Marmara
Denizi
(Sea of Marmara)
Kartal
Kocaeli (İzmit)
Gebze
Darıca
Yalova
Orhangazi
Gölcük
Sapanca
Akyazı
Mudurnu
Göynük
Seben
Kızılcahamam
Çubuk
Kızılırmak
Çorum
Mecitözü
Amasya
Turhal
Tokat
Erbaa
Niksar
Reşadiye Mesu

Thrace
1600
Samothráki
Gökçeada
Ecéabat
Çanakkale Boğazı
Biga
Karabiga
Bandırma
Kuş Gölü
Gönen
Mustafakemalpaşa
Ulubat Gölü
İznik Gölü
Yenişehir
İznik
Bilecik
Söğüt
Bozüyük
Sarıyar Barajı
Nallıhan
Beypazarı
Ayaş
Sincan
Kalecik
Delice
Yozgat
Sorgun
Akdağmadeni
Yıldızeli
Sivas
2802

TROY
Ezine
Bayramıç
1766
Yenice
Susurluk
BURSA
Orhaneli
Uludağ
2543
İnegöl
Domaniç
Eskişehir
Sakarya
Tavşanlı
Kütahya
Polatlı
ANKARA
Gölbaşı
Elmadağ
Bâlâ
Kırıkkale
Keskin
Kaman
Kırşehir
Yerköy
Boğazlıyan
Sarıkaya
Çayıralan
Gemerek
Kangal

Edremit Körfezi
Ayvacık
Balya
Bigadiç
Alaçam Dağları
2089
Emet
Seyitgazi
Mihalıççık
Sivrihisar
Kırka
Hoymana
Yeniçe
Kulu
Hirfanlı Barajı
Mucur
Hacıbektaş
Ortaköy
Nevşehir
Kayseri
Bünyan
Talas
Pınarbaşı
2235
Ak Dağ
Teçer Dağ

Mitilini
Bergama
Soma
Kınık
Demirci
Simav
Gediz
Uşak
Banaz
Afyon (Afyonkarahisar)
Emirdağ
Yunak
Sülüklü
Tuz Gölü
899
Şereflikoçhisar
Aksaray
Gülçayır
GÖREME
3370
Tomarza
Gürün
Darende
Açca

Lésvos
968
Khíos
Foça
Karaburun
Manisa
Akhisar
Salihli
Alaşehir
Kula
Sarıgöl
Çivril
Bolvadin
Eber Gölü
Çay
Akşehir Gölü
Akşehir
Sarayönü
Kadınhanı
Derinkuyu
Yeşilhisar
Bakırdağı
Saimbeyli
Afşin
Elbistan

Khíos
1297
Çeşme
Urla
İZMİR (Smyrna)
Menemen
Turgutlu
SARDIS
Boz Dağ
2137
Ödemiş
Ulubey
Dinar
Senirkent
Yalvaç
Eğridir
Gölü
Ilgın
Konya
Obruk
Konya Ovası
Yahyalı
Göksun
Doğanşehir

Seferihisar
Selçuk
Tire
Bayındır
Nazilli
Buldan
Çal
Uluborlu
Eğridir
Gelendost
Beyşehir
Çumra
Karapınar
Bor
Niğde
3734
Feke
Gürün

Sámos
EPHESUS
Kuşadası
Söke
Aydın
Büyük Menderes
İncirliova
Karacasu
Denizli
Sarayköy
Çardak
Burdur
Gölü
Isparta
Beyşehir Gölü
2980
116
Ereğli
Ulukışla
3488
Pozantı
Kozan
Kadirli
Türkoğlu
Yavuzeli

Ikaria
1153
MILETUS
Milas
Güllük
Muğla
Bozdoğan
Çine
Tavas
Acıgöl
Burdur
Ağlasun
Sütçüler
Bozkır
2464
Karaman
Ayrancı
Karaisalı
3430
Seyhan Barajı
İmamoğlu
Osmaniye
Gaziantep
Nizip

Pátmos
Fournoi
Kálimnos
Kos
Bodrum
Ören
Gökova Körfezi
Göktepe Dağları
Köyceğiz
2421
Boz Dağ
2598
Tefenni
Bucak
Korkuteli
Seydişehir
Suğla Gölü
Pozantı
Pisidia
3024
3070
Antalya
Serik
Aspendos
Hadım
Göksu
Mut
Seyhan
Tarsus
Adana
Ceyhan
Bahçe
İslâhiye

Astipálaia
Dhodhekánisos
Sími
Tilos
Datça
Bozburun
Marmaris
Ortaca
Dalaman
Dalaman Dağı
Fethiye
Elmalı
Ak Dağ
Bey Dağları
Kemer
Kumluca
Finike
Antalya Körfezi
Manavgat
Alanya
2339
Gülnar
Silifke
Erdemli
Mersin (İçel)
Seyhan Yumurtalık
Dörtyol
İskenderun Körfezi
Kırıkhan
A'zâz
Al Bâb

GREECE
Ródhos (Rhodes)
1215
Lindhos
4210
Kárpathos
1215
Kásos
Kalkan
Kaş
Megiste
Yardımcı Burnu
Gazipaşa
Anamur
Anamur Burnu
İncekum Burnu
Karataş
Uluçınar
Belen
Hınzır Burnu
1735
Antakya
Reyhanlı
Kilis
HALAB (Aleppo)
As Safîrah

Xanthos
Lycia
Pamphylia
Toros Dağları
Cilicia
İskenderun
Samandağı
Harbiye
İdlib
Jisr ash Shughûr
Ma'arrat an Nu'mân

47

CYPRUS
Rizokarpaso
C. Apostolos Andreas
Morphou
Kyrenia
Nicosia
Famagusta
Polis
Olympus
1951
Troodos
Larnaca
Paphos
Episkopi
Limassol
Al Lâdhiqîyah (Latakia)
Jablah
Khân Shaykhûn
Bâniyâs
1385
Hamâh
As Salamîyah
Maşyâf
Himş (Homs)
Shinshar
Furqlus
SYRIA

M E D I T E R R A N E A N   S E A

2775
Tartûs
Burj Sâfîtâ
Tall Kalakh
Al Hamidîyah
Tarâbulus (Tripoli)
Al Batrûn
Zgharta
3088
Bsharrî
Al Qusayr
Al Qaryatayn

LEBANON
Jubayl
Ba'labakk
An Nabk
BAYRÛT (Beirut)
Zahlah
Jûniyah
Şaydâ
Az Zabdânî
Az Zahlah
Yabrûd
Jayrûd
Sab'
Dûma
DIMASHQ (Damascus)
Al Qatana
Jaramanah
B

Şûr
Naharîyya
'Akko
Qiryat Shemona
2814
Ash Shaykh
Qunaytirah
Izra
Shahba
As Suwaydâ'
1800

ISRAEL
Hefa (Haifa)
Teverya
Yam Kinneret
Dar'â
Buşra ash Shâm
Salkhad
Hadera
Nazerat
Netanya
Nâblus
As Salt
1247
Irbid
Al Mafraq
Az Zarqâ
JORDAN

Tel Aviv-Yafo
West Bank
Rehovot
Ashdod
Ramla
El 'Arîsh
AMMÂN
Ashqelon
Jerusalem

Projection: Conical with two standard parallels

| 80 | 3 | | 4 | | 5 | 74 | 7 |

Division between Greeks and Turks
in Cyprus; Turks to the North.

6

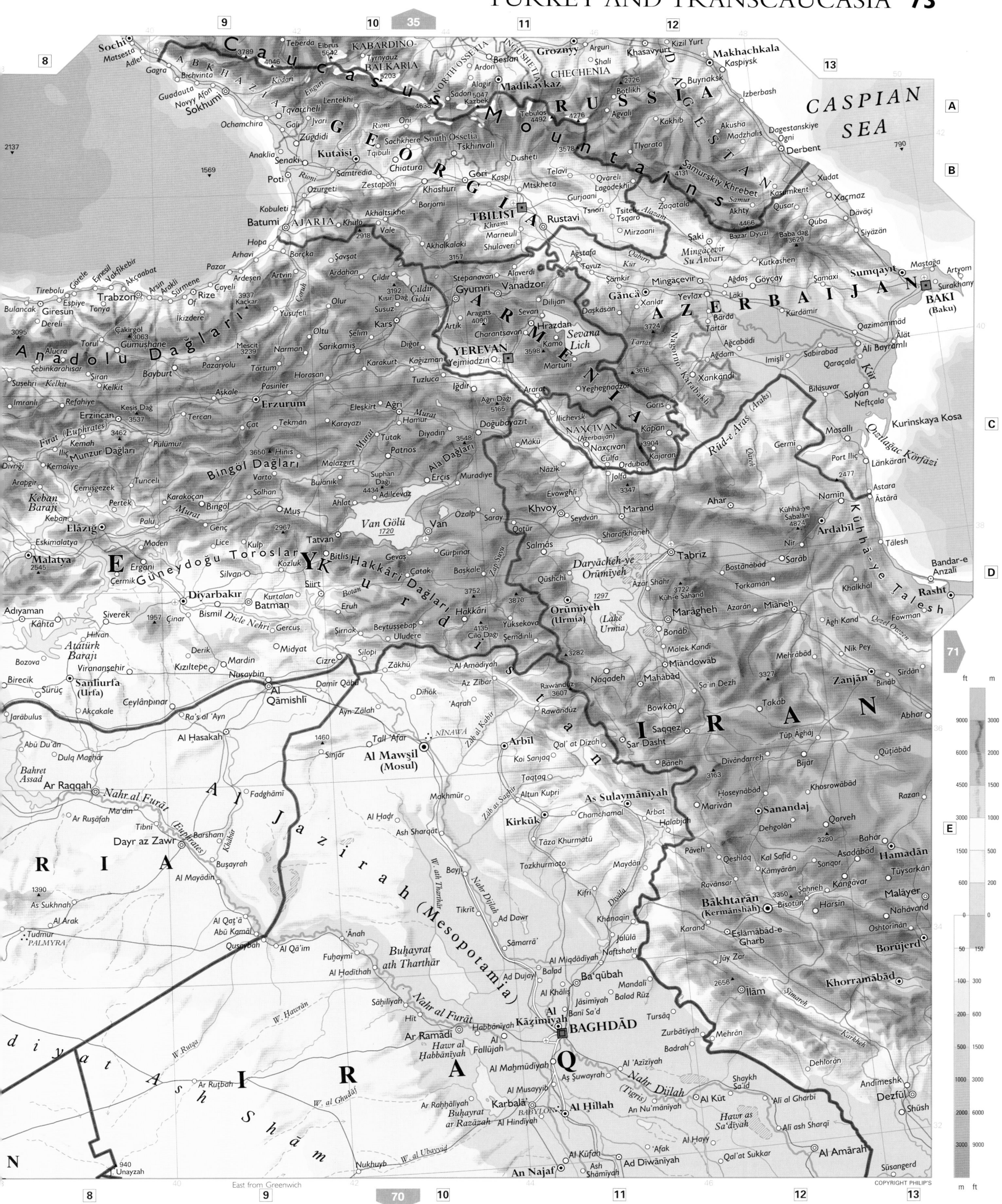

10 0 10 20 30 40 50 60 70 80 100 km

1:2 100 000

10 0 10 20 30 40 50 60 miles

CYPRUS

Paphos
Episkopi
Episkopi Bay
Limassol
Akrotiri Bay
C. Gata

M E D I T E R R A N E A N

S E A

Hims (Homs)
Shinshār
Furqlus
Al Ḥamīdīyah
Tall Kalakh
Halba
Al Quṣayr
ASH SHAMĀL
Al Hirmil
Al Qaryatayn
Al Minā'
Tarābulus **Ṭarābulus** (Tripoli)
Zgharta
Qurnat as Sawdā' ▲3088
Bsharri
Al Buṛayj
Al Batrūn
Al Labwah ▲2464
Jubayl
Qartābā
▲2616
An Nabk
Bi'r Ghadīr
Ibrāhīm
Ba'labakk
Yabrūd

SYRIA

Jūniyah
Bikfayyā
▲2628
J. Sannīn
Sirghāyā
Khān Abū Shāmat
BAYRŪT (Beirut)
'Alayh
Zahlah
Dumayr
Ash Shuwayfāt
Hawsh Mūssā
Ad Dāmūr
JABAL LUBNĀN
Az Zabadānī
Qartābā
LEBANON
▲1942 J. al Bārūk
Baradá
Dūmā
Khān Abū Shāmat
Saydā (Sidon)
Darayyā
DIMASHQ (Damascus)
Jazzīn
J. ash Shaykh (Mt. Hermon) ▲2814
Qaṭanā
Al Hājānah
An Nabaṭīyah at Tahta
Marj 'Uyūn
Al Kiswah
DIMASHQ
AL JANŪB
Al Khiyām
Burāq
Sūr (Tyre)
Qiryat Shemona
▲1197
Al Qunayṭirah
As Sanamayn
Nahariyya
Me'ona
Golan Heights
Ar Rafīd
DAR'Ā
'Akko (Acre)
Mifraz Hefa
HAZAFON
Zefat
Shahbā
Qiryat Yam
Karmi'el
Yam Kinneret
Fiq
Shaykh Miskīn
Izra
AS SUWAYDĀ
Hefa (Haifa)
Qiryat Ata
Teverya (Tiberias)
▲-210
Saham al Jawlān
Dar'ā
▲1800
As Suwaydā
Dāliyat el Karmel
HA KARMEL
Nazerat (Nazareth)
Yarmūk
Ṭayyiba
IRBID
Ar Ramthā
J. ad Durūz
Salah
TEL MEGIDDO
Afula
Bet She'an
Irbid
Buṣrá ash Shām
Salkhad
Malaḥ
Umm el Fahm
Jenin
▲1247 'Ajlūn
CAESAREA
Shōmrōn
AJLŪN
Umm ad Darāj
Hadera
Hanna-Karkur
Ṭūbās
JARASH Jarash
Al Mafraq
Umm al Qiṭṭayn
ISRAEL
Tulkarm
SAMARIA
JIBBEEN
Netanya
HAMERKAZ
Nābulus
N. az Zarqā'
Herzliyya
Kefar Sava
AL MAFRAQ
Benē Beraq
Petah Tiqwa
W. el Fār'ah
SHILO
Tel Aviv-Yafo
Ramat Gan
AL BALQĀ
Bat Yam
Az Zarqā
Rishon le Ziyyon
West Bank
As Salt
Wādī as Sīr
Lod
Rām Allāh
Karama
Yavne
Ramla
Rehovot
El Arīḥā (Jericho)
▲-289
'AMMĀN
Nā'ūr
Azraq ash Shīshān
Ashdod
El Arīḥā
AMMĀN
AZ ZARQĀ
Qiryat Mal'akhi
Bet Shemesh
Jerusalem (Yerushalayim) (Al Quds)
Ma'daba
Ashqelon
Qiryat Gat
Bayt Laḥm (Bethlehem)
MA'DĀBA
'AMMĀN
TEL LAKHISH
Al Khalīl (Hebron)
Gaza
N. Shiqma
Az Zāhirīyah
W. al Haydān
Dhībān
Gaza Strip
Sederot
Khān Yūnis
Rafah
N. Besor
ESHKOL
Be'er Sheva (Beersheba)
Dead Sea
Arad
▲1305
Al Karak
Sedom
AL KARAK
Al Mazār
Bûr Sa'îd (Port Said)
Bûr Fu'ād
Rās Burūn
Sabkhet el Bardawil
El 'Arîsh
Bir el 'Abd
Bor Mashash
Dimona
▲-333
W. Al Ghadaf
Al Hadithah
Qanṭara es Suweis
Khalîg el Tîna
HADAROM
W. al Hasā
Rōmâni
Bir el Garārât
Bir el Abd
W. al 'Arîsh
Qezi'ot
Sedé Boqér
JORDAN
Al Qatrānah
Bir el Duweidar
Bir Qaṭia
Bir Kaseiba
Birein
W. Bā'ir
El Qantara
Bir el Jafir
Muweilih
SHAMĀL SĪNÎ
Mizpe Ramon
AT ṬAFĪLAH
Bā'ir
Wâhid
Bir Madkûr
El Quşeima
At Ṭafīlah
J. ash Shawmari ▲1072
ISMÂ'ÎLÎYA
Ṭalâta
Bir el Mâlhi
Bir Hasana
Hanegev
▲-121
▲1736
Al Jafr
Qa'el Jafr
Ismâ'îlîya
Khamsa
El Buheirat el Murrat el Kubra (Bitter Lakes)
G.Yi 'Allaq ▲1094
Bir Beiḍa
Njil
Mahattat 'Unayzah
PETRA
Gineifa
Bir el Thamâda
W. el Brûk
W. Qurâya
El 'Agrûd
N. Paran
Wādī Mūsa
MA'ĀN
E G Y P T
Mamarr Mitlâ
Bir Gebeil Hisn
W. Mahashim
Ma'ān
Bir el Mârî
El Suweis (Suez)
Bûr Taufîq
N. Hiyyon
Ra's an Naqb ▲1435
SAUDI
Adabiya
Uyûn Mûsa
E S S Î N Â' (Sinai)
Nakhl
W. el Aqaba
El Kuntilla
Yotvata
Mahattat ash Shīdīyah
Ghubbet el Bûs
G. el Kabrit ▲948
'Ain Sudr
'En 'Avrona
Bir Abu Muhammad
El Thamad
▲1592
Wādī Rum
A R A B I A
Bir Abu Sandûq
El Wabeira
JANŪB SĪNÎ
Gebel el Tih
Bir el Biarât
Elat
▲1754
Baṭn al Ghûl
At Tubayq
El Suweis ▲1272
Rās Matarma
W. Abu Ga'da
Bir el Heisi
Al 'Aqabah
Rum
Bir Ṭâba
Haql
Al Mudawwarah
EL SUWEIS
Bir Wuseit
▲1165
Gulf of Aqaba
AL 'AQABAH

ft m
9000 3000
6000 2000
4500 1500
3000 1000
1200 400
600 200
0
200 600
2000 6000
m ft

Projection: Polyconic

East from Greenwich

COPYRIGHT PHILIP'S

= = = 1974 Cease Fire Lines

▭ National Parks

1:12 600 000

100   0   100   200   300   400   500   600 km
100   0   100   200   300   400 miles

LEBANON
BAYRŪT (BEIRUT)
SYRIA
DIMASHQ (DAMASCUS)
ISRAEL
Tel Aviv-Yafo
Ashdod
Jerusalem
Bûr Sa'îd (Port Said) Strip
Qanâ es Suweis
Ismâ'iliya
El Suweis (Suez)
Khalîg es Suweis
Elat
Es Sinâ'
G. Mûsa 2637
Tabûk
Al Muwaylih
Hurghada
Bûr Safâga
EGYPT
Qena
Quseir
El Uqsur
Idfû
Kôm Ombo
Aswân
Sadd el Ali
Buheirat en Naser
Ras Bânâs
Bîr Shalatein
Halaib
Ras Hadarba
Wadi Halfa
Kosha
3rd Cataract
Delgo
Dongola
4th Cataract
Kareima
Berber
Ed Debba
Atbara
Wad Hamid
6th Cataract
Shendî
Omdurmân
El Khartûm (Khartoum)
Kassalâ
El Gezira
Kôstî
Umm Ruwaba
Wad Medanî
Gedaref
Ed Dueim
Ed Damazin
SUDAN
Malakâl
Sobat
Sûdd
Bahr el Gebel
Pibor Post
Bôr
Tali Post
Mongalla
Juba
Kapoeta
Yei
Arua
Gulu
Lira
Moroto
Murchison Falls
Pakwach
UGANDA
L. Albert
Masindi
L. Kyoga
Mbale
Soroti
Kitale
KENYA
Lodwar
South Horn
L. Turkana
Mega
El Wak
Moyale
Marsabit
Wajir
Dif
Bardera
Bur Acaba
Baidoa
Dolo
Lugh Ganana
Belet Uen
El Dere
Sinadogo
Obbia
Merca
MUQDISHO (MOGADISHU)
Wabi Scebeli
Gimba
Ferfer
Negele
Dila
L. Abaya
L. Shamo
Arba Minch
Kibre Mengist
Yirga Alem
Goba
Mt. Batu 4307
Awasa
Shashemene
Ginir
Kebri Dehar
Imi
Jima
Ziway
Asela
Nazret
Awash
Harer
Jijiga
Dire Dawa
Hargeisa
Burao
Las Anod
Garoe
Gardo
Bender Beila
Eil
Ras Hafun
Dante
El Gal
Erigavo
Bosaso
Ras Asir
Karin
Berbera
Zeila
Djibouti
DJIBOUTI
Tadjoura
Dikhil
L. Abbé
Dese
Debre Markos
Bure
Bahir Dar
Debre Tabor
Lalibela
Gonder
L. Tana
ADDIS ABEBA
Debre Zeyit
Nekemte
Dembidolo
Gore
Metu
ETHIOPIA
Ras Dashen 4620
Mekele
Adigrat
Adwa
Aksum
Akordat
Asmera
Massawa
Zula
Adarama
Karora
Nakfa
ERITREA
Danakil Desert
Aseb
Bab el Mandeb
Al Mukhâ
Al' Adan (Aden)
Gulf of Aden
Abd al Kûrî
Bereda
Hadiboh
Socotra (Yemen)
Ta'izz
Sana'
Al Hudaydah
Kamaran
Al Luhayyah
Jîzân
Farasân
Abhâ
Najrân
Khamir
YEMEN
Nisâb
Al Mukallâ
Shaqrâ
Ahwar
Sayhût
Ras Fartak
Hadramawt
Shibâm
Zufâr
Salâlah
Mirbât
J. Khurîyâ Murîyâ
Ras al Madrakah
Khalîj Masîrah
Masîrah
Khalûf
Sûr
Ras al Hadd
Masqat
Matrah
Nazwâ
Al 'Ayn
Suhâr
OMAN
Gulf of Oman
Ash Shâriqah (Sharjah)
Dubayy (Dubai)
Abû Zaby (Abu Dhabi)
UNITED ARAB EMIRATES
Ra's al-Khaymah
Ra's Musandam (Oman)
Str. of Hormuz
Gâbrik
Bampûr
Bandar-e Abbas
Qeshm
Khamir
Bûshehr
Deyyer
Jahrom
Neyriz
Bam
Zâhedân
Daryâcheh-ye Seistan
Zâbol
Farâh
AFGHANISTAN
Birjand
Khvor
Yazd
Kermân
Shîrâz
Kâzerûn
Esfahân
IRAN
Dasht-e Lut
Dash-e Kavir
PERSEPOLIS
The Gulf
Al Kuwayt
KUWAIT
Hafar al Bâtin
J. Khârk
Bûbiyân
Al Basrah
Âbâdân
Khorrâmshahr
Al Amârah
Ahvâz
Kûhhâ-ye Zâgros
BAGHDAD
Karbalâ
An Najaf
An Nâsiriyah
Rafhâ
Al Qatîf
Ad Dammâm
BAHRAIN
Al Manâmah
QATAR
Al Dawhah (Doha)
Al Mubarraz
Al Hufûf
Harad
Al 'Ubaylah
Rub' al Khâlî (Empty Quarter)
Laylâ
As Sulayyil
AR RIYÂD (RIYADH)
SAUDI ARABIA
Buraydah
'Unayzah
Hâ'il
An Nafûd
Al Jawf
IRAQ
Al 'Irâq
Mesopotamia
El 'Irâq
Nahr Dijlah
Nahr al Furât
Ar Rutbah
Jabal ad Durûz 1801
JORDAN
Bâdiyat ash Shâm
AMMAN
Ma'ân
Al 'Aqabah
RED SEA
Hijâz
Al Wajh
Yanbu 'al Bahr
Al Madînah
Rābigh
Al Lîth
JIDDAH (JEDDA)
Muhammad Qol 2259
MAKKAH (Mecca)
At Tâ'if 2565
Turabah
Asîr
Bûr Sûdân
Suakin
Trinkitat
Sinkat
Haiya
Tropic of Cancer
Es Sahrâ en Nûbîya
INDIAN OCEAN
SOMALI REP.
Ogaden
Genale
Scebeli
Wabi Scebeli
Galcaio
Obbia

ft   m
12 000   4000
9000   3000
6000   2000
4500   1500
3000   1000
1200   400
600   200
0   0
200   600
1000   3000
2000   6000
4000   12 000
m   ft

Projection: Sanson-Flamsteed's Sinusoidal
East from Greenwich
COPYRIGHT PHILIP'S

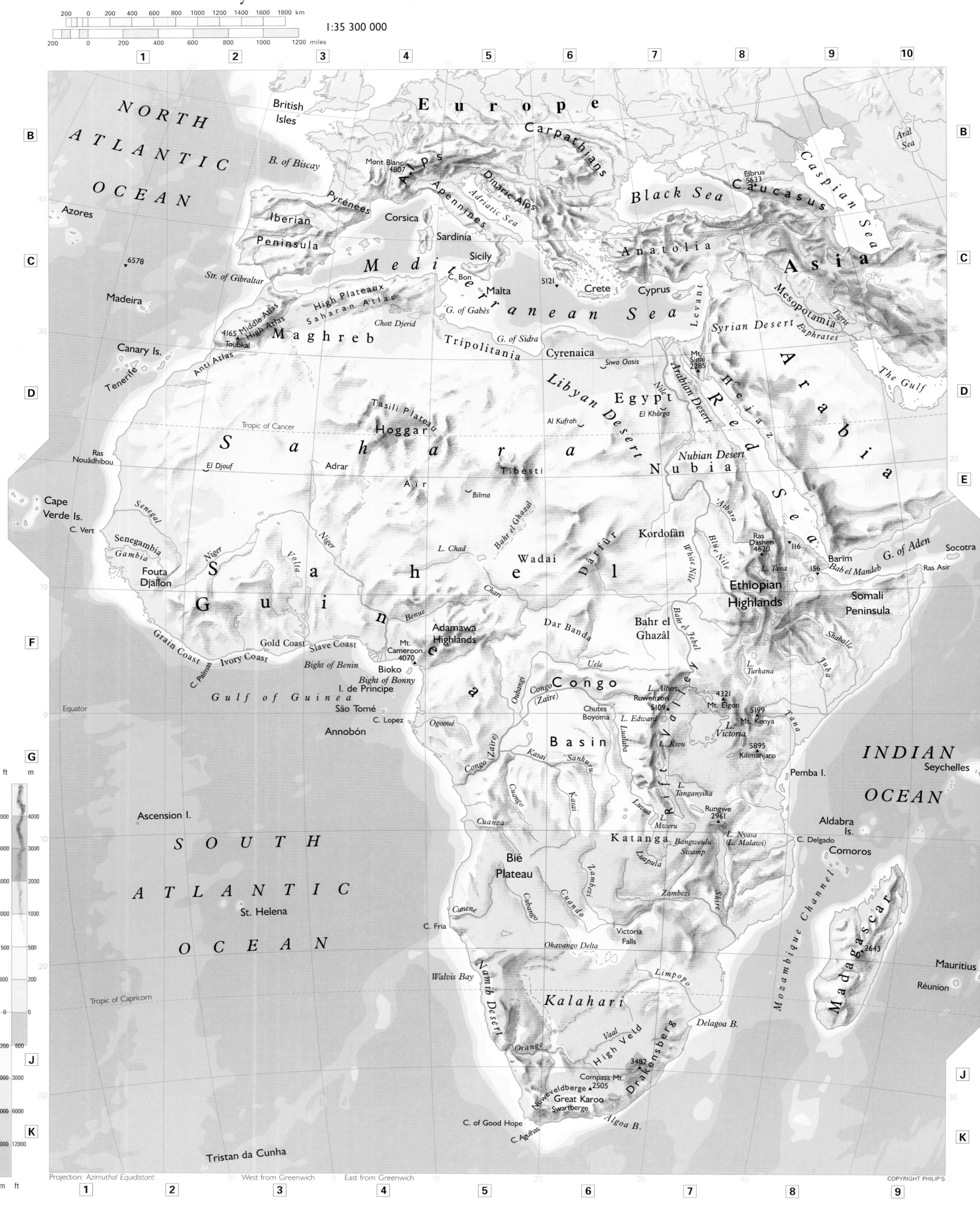

1:35 300 000

Projection: Azimuthal Equidistant

COPYRIGHT PHILIP'S

1:35 300 000

200 0 200 400 600 800 1000 1200 1400 1600 1800 km
200 0 200 400 600 800 1000 1200 miles

Projection: Azimuthal Equidistant

West from Greenwich   East from Greenwich

COPYRIGHT PHILIP'S

● Dakar   Capital Cities

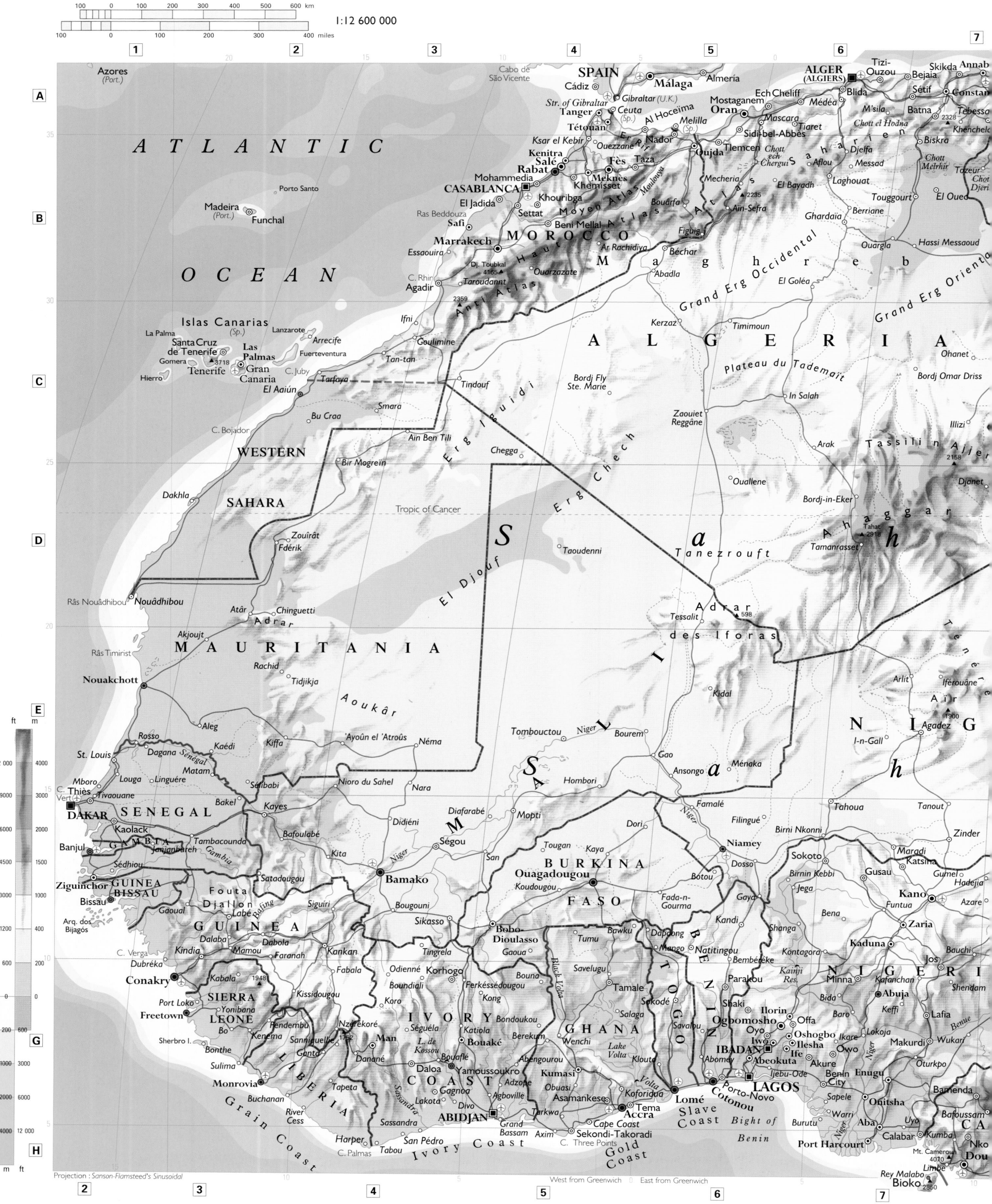

100 0 100 200 300 400 500 600 km
1:12 600 000
100 0 100 200 300 400 miles

Projection : Sanson-Flamsteed's Sinusoidal

West from Greenwich   East from Greenwich

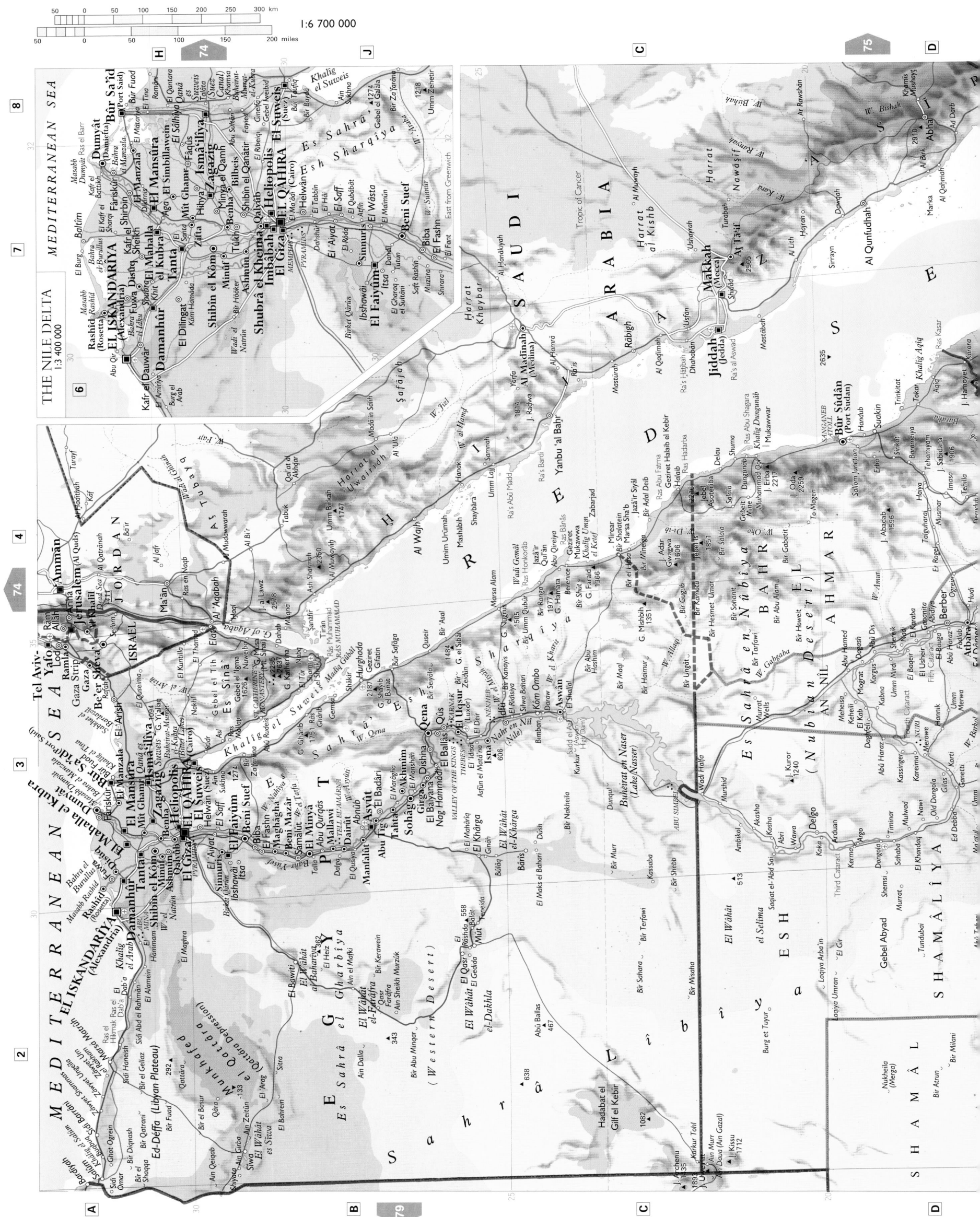

1:6 700 000

THE NILE DELTA
1:3 400 000

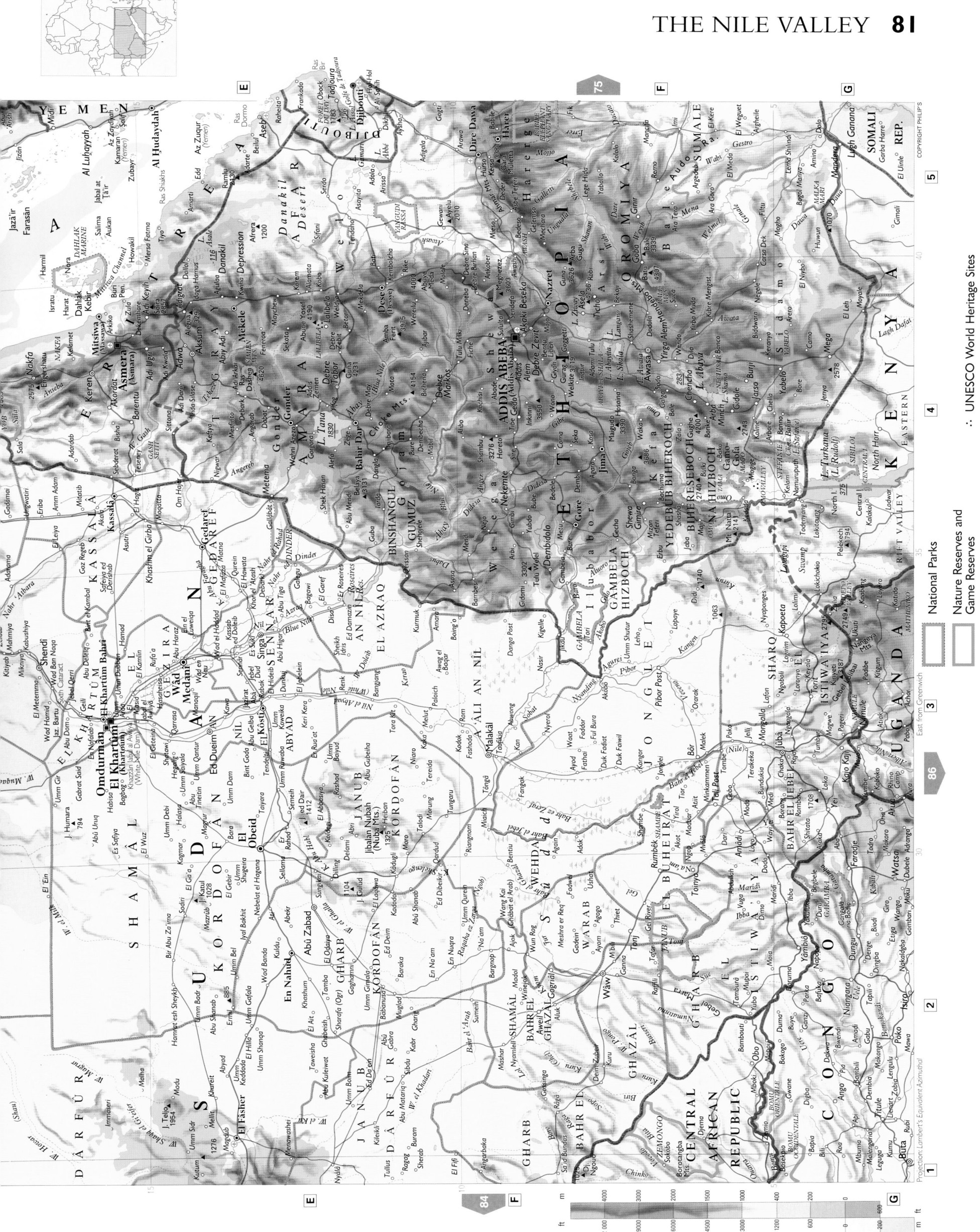

:: UNESCO World Heritage Sites

National Parks

Nature Reserves and
Game Reserves

Projection: Lambert's Equivalent Azimuthal

East from Greenwich

50 0 50 100 150 200 250 300 km
1:6 700 000
50 0 50 100 150 200 miles

1   **2**   78   **3**

BANC
D'ARGUIN
Et Tîdra
Ras Tïmïris
Nouâmghâr

S A H A

Oujeft

Akjoujt

Bennichchâb

Ouâlâta
MAURITANIA

Tidjikja 420
Gâneb Tîchît
Akreijit
Aratâne
Araouane

Azao...

Bou Djébéha

Dayet en
Naharat

In-Tébri

TOMBOUCTOU
(Timbuktu)
L. Faguibine
Koriouomé
Diré
Kabara
Niafounké
Sarèyamou
Sébi
Sarafêré
Ngorkou
Bamba
Maoundé
DOUENTZ

Nouakchott

Boutilimit
T r a r z a
Mederdra

Sebkhet
Te-n-Dghâmcha

Rosso Dagana
Ross Béchio
DJOUDJ
Podor
Bogué
Kiffa
'Ayoûn el 'Atroûs
Néma
Timbedgha

Aleg Mâl
Moudjeria

Magta Lahjar

Boûmdeïd

A o u k â r

Togba
Tâmchekket
Kobenni
Boulou
Guirel
Lêré
Akka
Ouro-Ndia
Korienzé

L. Débo
L. Korarou

M a c i n a
791

Tenenkou
Mopti
Bandiagara
Gangafa...

Sénégal
St. Louis
LANGUE
DE BARBARIE
Richard
Thille-
Boubacar
N'Dioum
Mbagne
Kaédi
Mbout
Séllbabi
Maghama
Ould Yenjé
409
Nioro du
Sahel
Baikal
Karounga
Goumbou
Nara
Nampala
Akor
Sokolo
Diorua
Koro
Douentz

L. de Guiers
Dagana
NDIAEL
Toll
Tilogne
Matam
Séméé
Bakel
Ambidédi
Kidira
Kayes
Koniakari
Diémo
Mourdiah
Doubabougou
Niono
Manimpé
Diafarabé
Ké-Macina
Say
Niga
Sarro
Djenné
Diallassagou
Bankas
Koro

Louga
Yang-Yang
Linguère
Vallée
du Ferlo
FERLO-
NORD
Ouro Sogui
Harr
Bouli
Kirane
Yélimané
Diôka
Sandar
Dilly
Goumbou
Diora
Sansanding
Niga
Sofara

Mboro
Koki
Dahrâ
Darou-Mousti
Tiel
FERLO-
SUD
Fété Bowé
Kanel
Koussané
Maréna
Diongoi
Kalabana
Didiéni
Maréna
Sagala
Ségou
Douna
Tomian
Goursi

C. Vert
Thiès
DAKAR
Rufisque
Diourbel
Mbour
Fatick
Gossas
Khombole
Touba
Bambey
Vélingara
Sine
Mbaba
Mérinaghène
Koungheul
Mboune
Koussanar
Bala
Goudiry
Naye
584
Séfeto
Dinanko
Kayes
Didiéni
Nossombougou
Tamani
Barouéli
Bla
Mpésoba
Réo
Dédougou
Louta
Tougan
Nouna
Benena
Barani
BU...

Joal Fadiout
Foundiougne
Kaolack
Nioro du Rip
Kaffrine
Koumpentoum
Kuntaur
Maka
Koussanar
Bafoulabé
BADINKO
BOUCLE DU
BAOULE
Diala
Kourouninkoto
Fasso
Madina
Kolokani
Banamba
Santiguila
Kimparana
Yorosso
Koutiala
Sikasso
Karangana
Sanaba
Karo
Koudougou

Saloum
Missirah
Gambia
Banjul
GAMBIA
Brikama
DELTA
DU SALOUM
KLANG
WEST
Janjanbureh
Basse
Santa-Su
Vélingara
Dialakoto
Maka
Kedougou
Gourbassi
Kourouba
Toukoto
FINA
Kangaré
Sido
Massigui
Bougouni
Kolondiéba
Zégoua
Banfora
Sidéradougou
Nako
Lawra

Dioloulou
Bignona
Sédhiou
Kolda
Patine Kouka
BADIAR
Saraya
Kéniéba
Kita
Sébékoro
Sirakoro
Kati
BAMAKO
Dioila
Klé
Sangasso
Koumbou
Sara
Ouarkoye
Busie
Wa

Casamance
C. Skiring
Diembéring
Kabrousse
Sao
Domingos
ZIGUINCHOR
Farim
Colina do Norte
Nova
Lamego
Kounkana
Youkounkoun
Faléa
Mali
1537
M. du
Tamgué
Tamba-
Dabatou
952
Kourémalé
Kangaba
Dialakoro
Koumankou
Koloko
Karangana
Faramana
Kouroumba
Sara
Boromo
Sili

Teixeira Pinto
Cacheu
Bissorã
Bafatá
Xime
Fulacunda
Xitole
Kifaya
Timbo
Yambering
Gaoual
Fatoya
Biramféro
Siguiri
Yanfolila
Sokolo
820
Kadiolo
Sindou
Yendéré
Niangoloko
Dangouadougou
Kampti
Hamél...
Ouessa

GUINEA-
BISSAU
Arquipélago dos Bijagós
Ilha Uno
Bissau
São João
Bolama
Bubaque
Buba
Mampatá
Caravela
Roxa
Orango
Catio
Tombankóna
Boké
Fodécontéa
Bembaya
Kamsar
Victoria
1425
Dalaba
Télimélé
Pita
F o u t a
Labé
Djallon
Dinguiraye
Niandan
Dabola
Bissikrima
Kouroussa
Mandiana
Manankoro
Foulalaba
Tingrela
Kolia
Kouto
Téhini
Wangolodougou
Bania
Savia
Larabanga
Bole
Batie

C. Verga
Dubréka
Kindia
1124
NORTHERN
Fria
Boffa
Coyah
Kolenté
Balia
OUTAMBA-
KILIMI
Mamou
Kaba
HAUT
NIGER
Dabola
Dalaba
Diabakania
Diariguila
Faranah
Soro
Kankan
Tintioulé
Kalankalan
Manankoro
Maninian
Goulia
Madinani
Niébo
Kong
Dikodougou
Niango
Dabakala
Nassian
BUI
741
Bamboi

Conakry
Îles de Los
Forécariah
Kambia
FALABA
Falaba
Mongo
Kabala
Nianforando
Douako
Moribaya
Fabala
Odienné
Boundiali
914
Sirasso
Korhogo
Tafiré
Koro
Ferkéssédougou
Bouna
COMOE
Niangbo
Katiola
Satama
Soukoura
Tabagné
Bondoukou
Bole

Kindia
Port Loko
Lungi
Airport
Pepel
Marampa
Makeni
Bumbuna
Mabonto
Kayima
Yende
Millimou
Konsankoro
1504
Nionsamoridougou
Borotou
Morondo
Séguéla
Béoumi
Prikro
M'bahiakro
Kouadou
Ouellé
Sampa
Wenchi
Berekum

SIERRA
Freetown
Waterloo
Banana Is.
Yawri
Bay
Turtle Is.
Sherbro I.
Rokupr
Sefadu
Magburaka
Kailahun
Guékédou
Macenta
Beyla
Touba
Sarhala
Mankono
Botro
Goutafla
Zuénoula
Daoukro
Arrah
M'batto
Bongouanou
Anoumaba
Agnibilékrou
Asafo
Sunyan...

WESTERN
SOUTHERN
Bonthe
Moyamba
Yonibana
Marampa
Bo
Kenema
Gelehun
Segbwema
Pendembu
Irié
Nzébéla
Gouéké
Lola
Biankouma
Man
Fakobli
MONT SANGBE
MONT PEKO
Vavoua
Séguéla
Sakassou
Sinfra
Toumodi
Dimbokro
Abengourou
Bibiani
Sefwi
Bekwai

LEONE
Waterloo
Shenge
Mano
Mano
River
Pujehun
Zimi
Bomi
Hills
Gbarnga
Ganta
(Gompa)
Zouan
Hounien
Danané
Bangolo
Duékoué
Gregbeu
Guiberoua
Gagnoa
Lakota
Divo
Tiassalé
Abidjan
Dabou
Grand Bassam

Sulima
Robertsport
L. Piso
CAPE
MOUNT
Whiteplains
Brewerville
Monrovia
Paynesville
Marshall
Buchanan
Trade Town
River Cess
Arthington
Salala
Kakata
Coreysburg
Edina
Tchien
Toulepleu
Taï
Soubré
Guéyo
Issia
Oumé
Gagnoa
Moronou
Rubino
Adzopé
Agboville
Anyama
Aboisso
Grand Bassam
Assini
Port-
Bouët

A T L A N T I C
O C E A N

SAPO
SEHNKWEHN
Greenville
Nyaake
(Webo)
San Pédro
TAÏ
914
GAVALLA
Sassandra
L. de
Buyo
L. de
Tiadio
Bandama Rouge
Lagune
Ébrié
Vridi
Lag...

Grain Coast
Nana Kru
Grand Cess
Garawe
Cape
Palmas
Harper
Tabou
Grand Béréby
Ivory Coast
6363

G U L F

ft m
12 000 4000
9000 3000
6000 2000
4500 1500
3000 1000
1200 400
600 200
0 0
200 600
2000 6000
4000 12 000
6000 18 000
m ft

Projection : Lambert's Equivalent Azimuthal

West from Greenwich

1   **2**   **3**   **4**

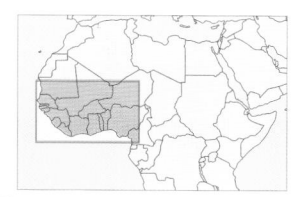

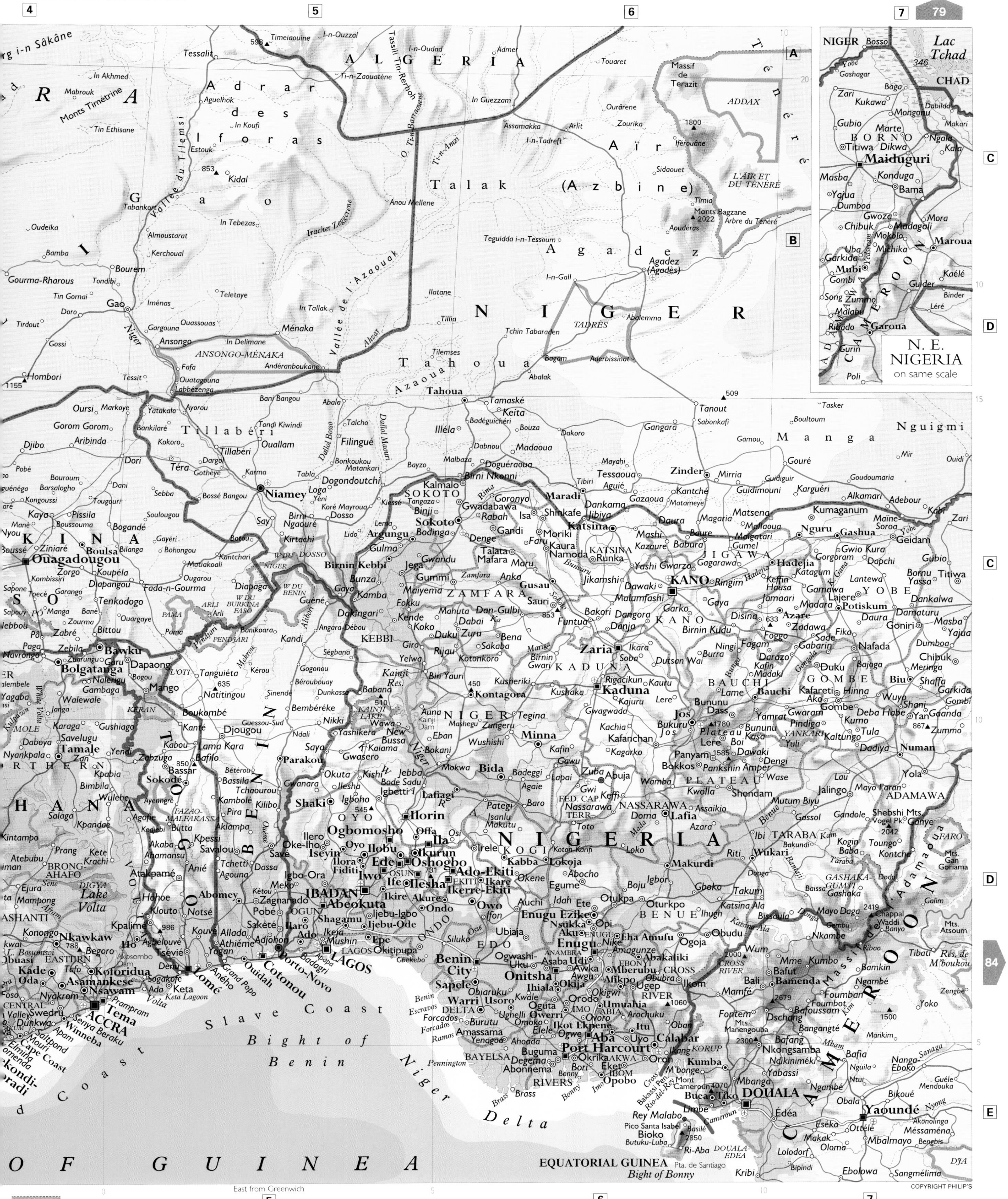

79

N. E.
NIGERIA
on same scale

84

National Parks

Nature Reserves and
Game Reserves

∴ UNESCO World Heritage Sites

East from Greenwich

COPYRIGHT PHILIP'S

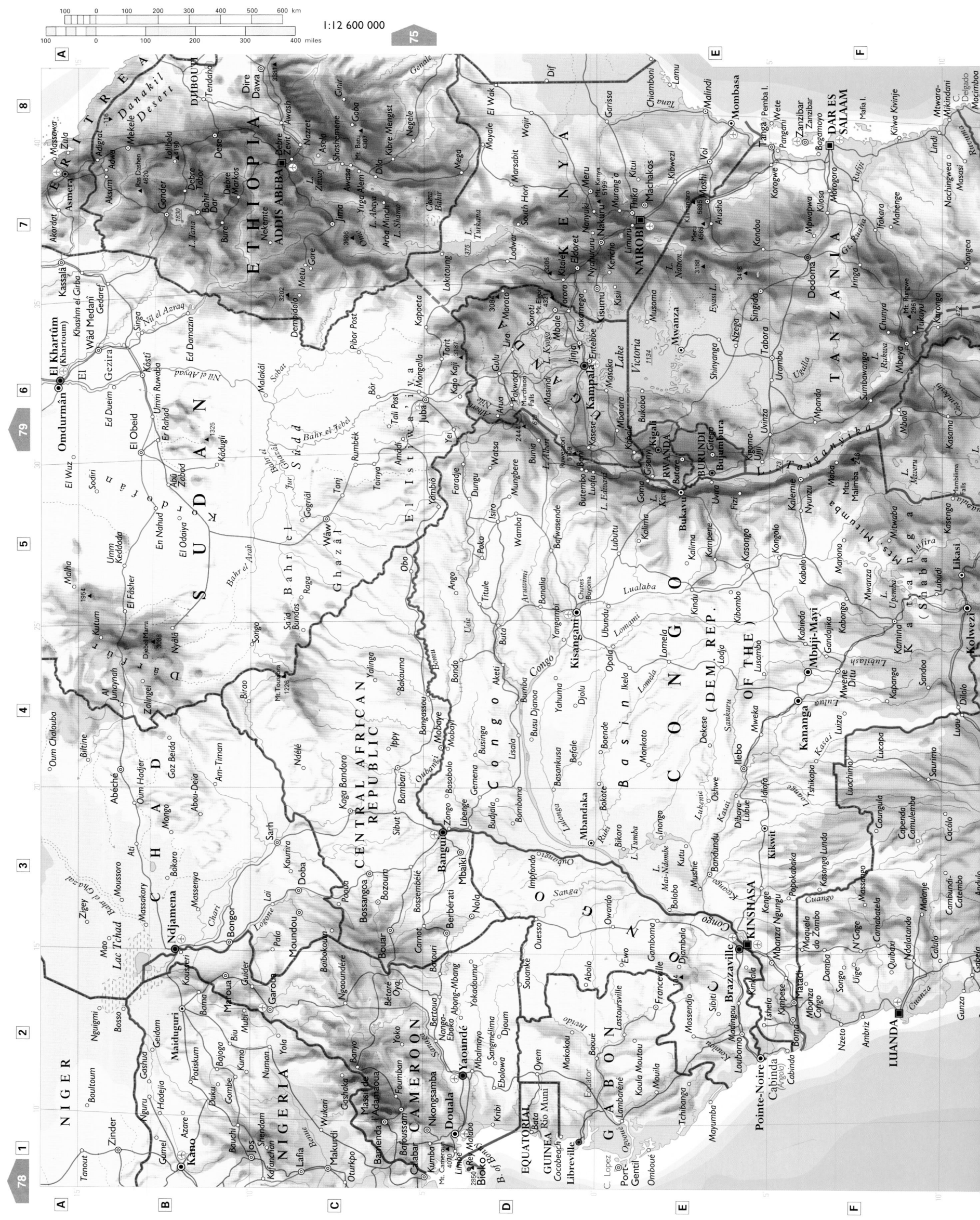

ATLANTIC OCEAN
INDIAN OCEAN
MADAGASCAR
on same scale
ANGOLA
ZAMBIA
MALAWI
MOZAMBIQUE
ZIMBABWE
BOTSWANA
NAMIBIA
SOUTH AFRICA
LESOTHO
SWAZILAND
Kalahari
Namib Desert
Skeleton Coast
Caprivi Strip
L. Nyasa (L. Malawi)
Lusaka
HARARE
PRETORIA
JOHANNESBURG
MAPUTO
CAPE TOWN
DURBAN
Port Elizabeth
East London
Bloemfontein
Kimberley
Windhoek
Walvis Bay
Lüderitz
Gaborone
Bulawayo
Beira
Blantyre
Lilongwe
Ndola
Kitwe
Lubumbashi
Huambo
Lobito
Benguela
Namibe
Lubango
Antananarivo
Toamasina
Mahajanga
Fianarantsoa
Toliara
Taolanaro
Antsiranana
Mayotte (Fr.)
Is. Glorieuses (Réunion)
Bassas da India (Réunion)
Île Europa (Réunion)
Cape of Good Hope
Cape Agulhas
Tropic of Capricorn
East from Greenwich
Projection: Sanson-Flamsteed's Sinusoidal
COPYRIGHT PHILIPS
G
H
J
K
L
M
1
2
3
4
5
6
7
8
9
10
m
ft
4000
3000
2000
1500
1000
400
200
0
200
600
1000
2000
3000
4000
12 000
9000
6000
4500
3000
1200
600
0
600
3000
6000
12 000

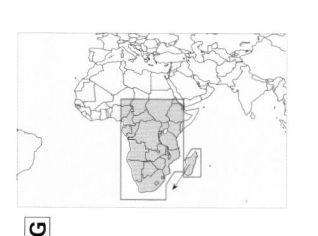

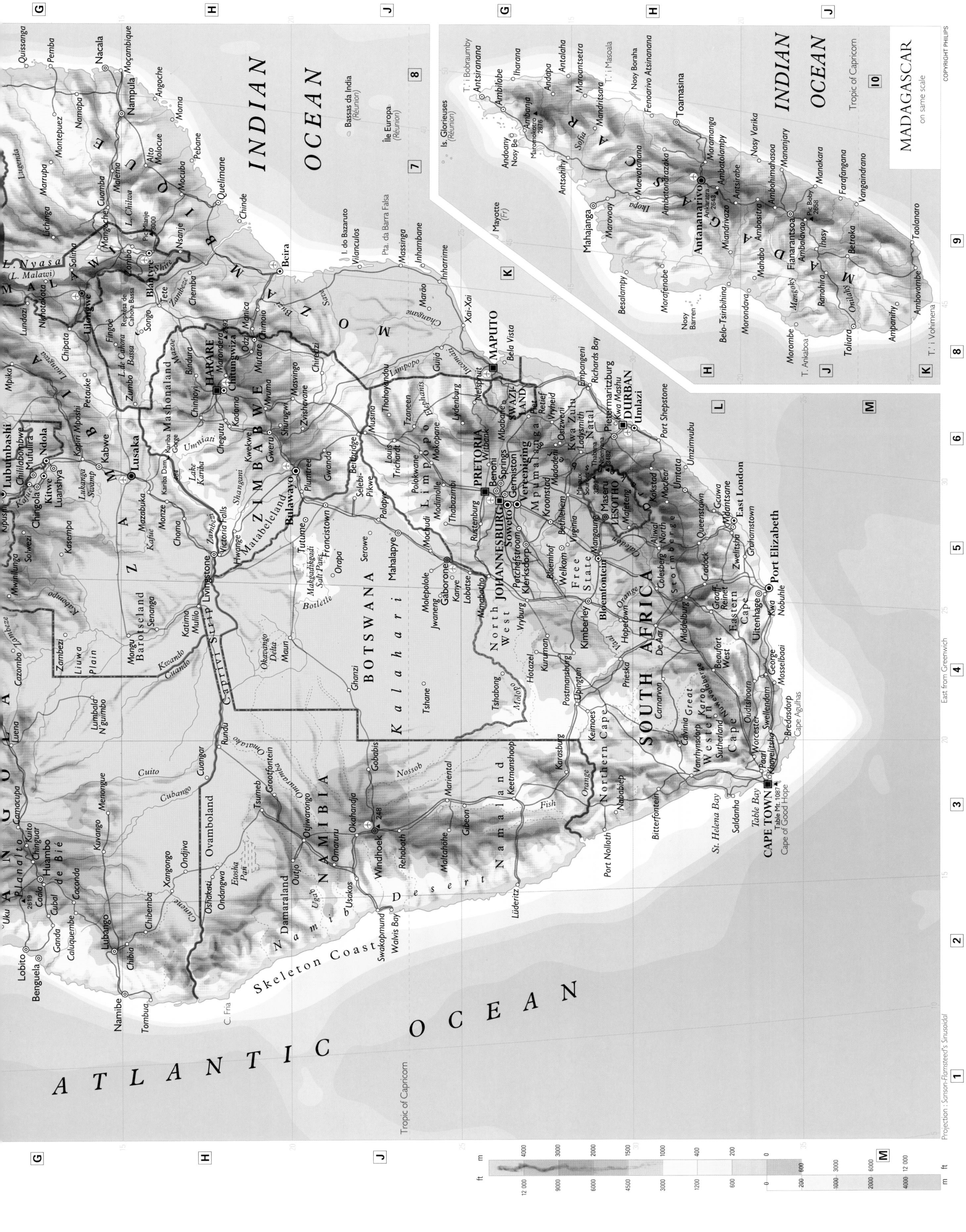

1:6 700 000

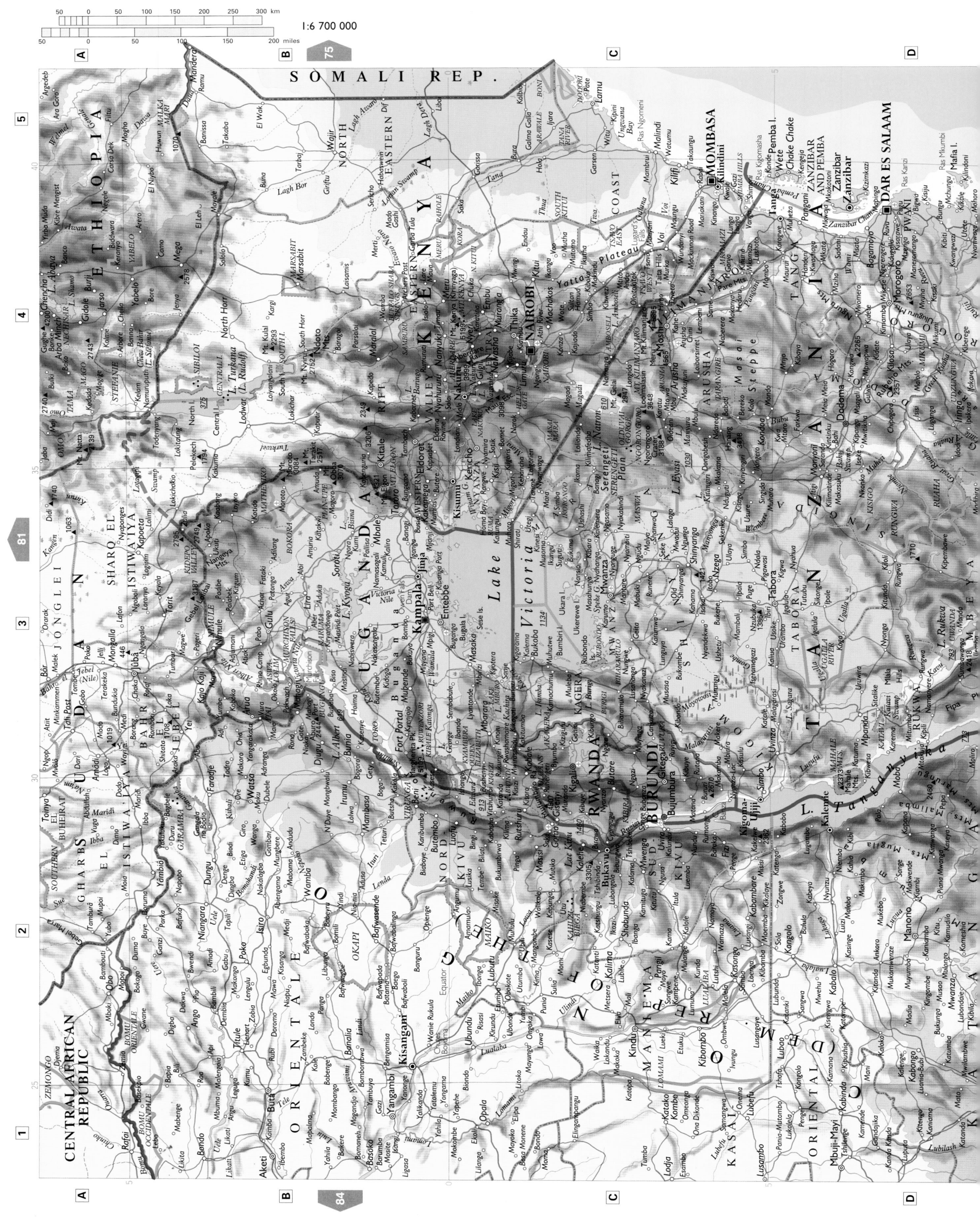

INDIAN OCEAN
ZAMBIA
MALAWI
MOZAMBIQUE
ZIMBABWE
BOTSWANA
SOUTH AFRICA
NAMIBIA
ANGOLA
L. Nyasa / Malawi
Lusaka
Harare
Bulawayo
Lilongwe
Blantyre
Beira
Lubumbashi
National Parks
Nature Reserves and Game Reserves
UNESCO World Heritage Sites
Projection: Lambert's Equivalent Azimuthal
East from Greenwich
COPYRIGHT PHILIP'S
85
88
89

m
ft
4000
12 000
3000
9000
2000
6000
1500
4500
1000
3000
400
1200
200
600
0
0
200
600
2000
6000

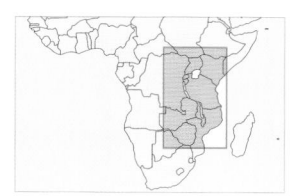

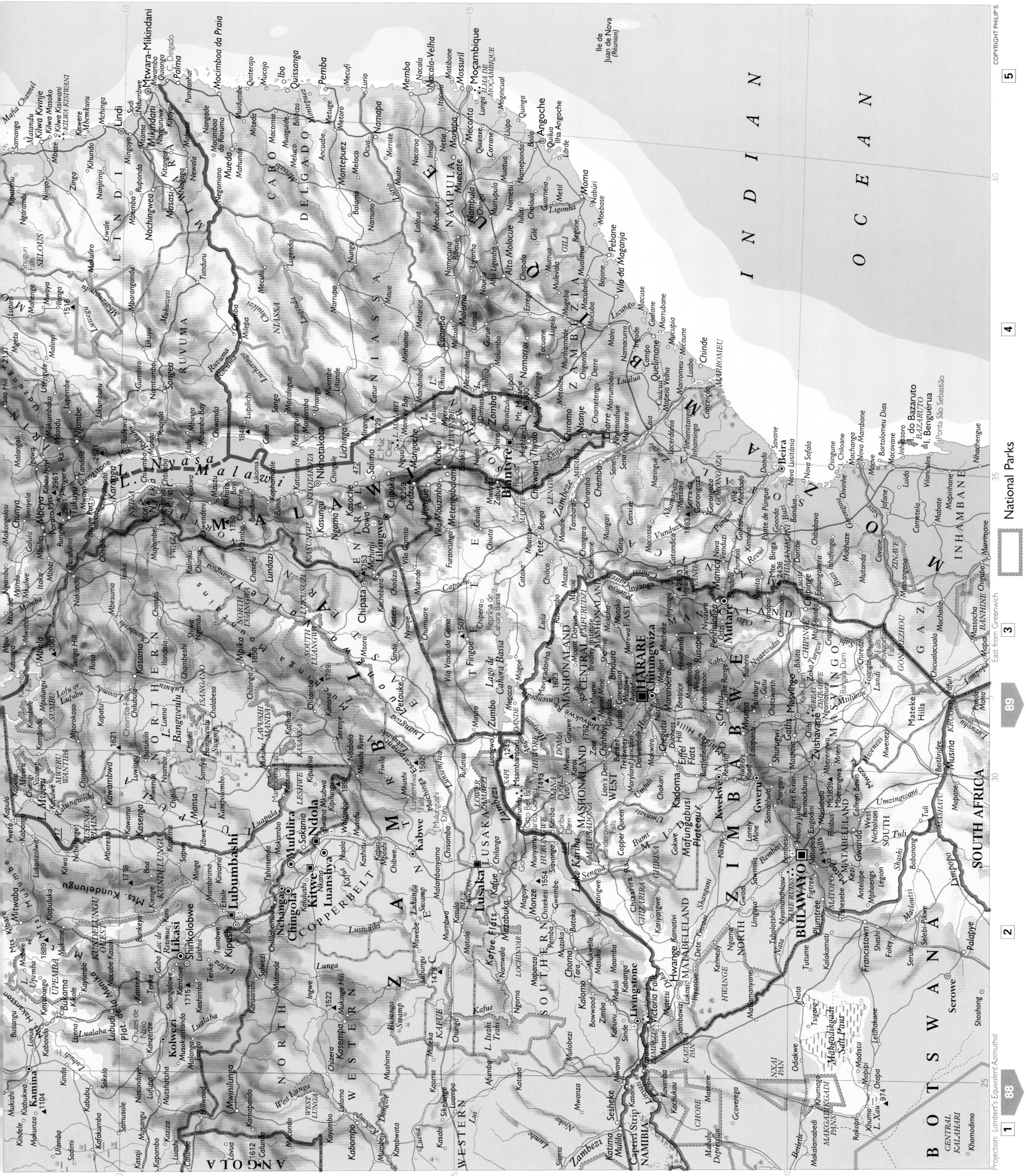

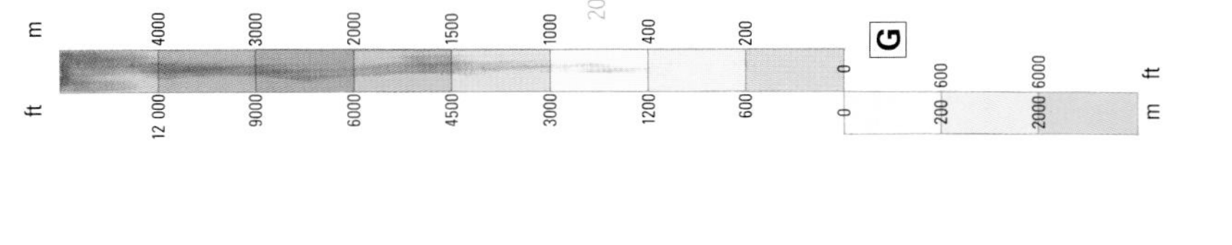

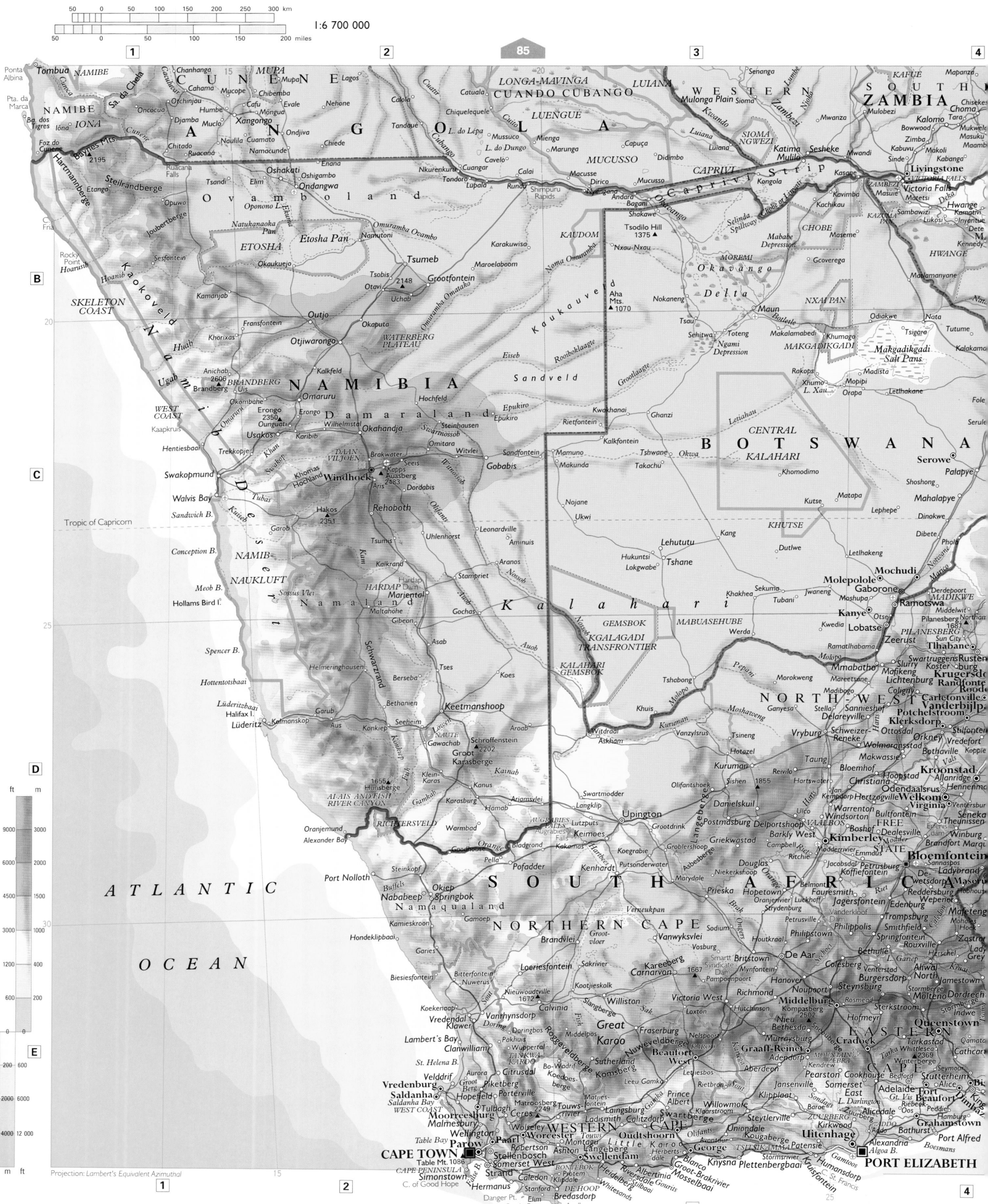

National Parks

Nature Reserves and Game Reserves

△∴ UNESCO World Heritage Sites

MADAGASCAR

on same scale

COPYRIGHT PHILIP'S

East from Greenwich

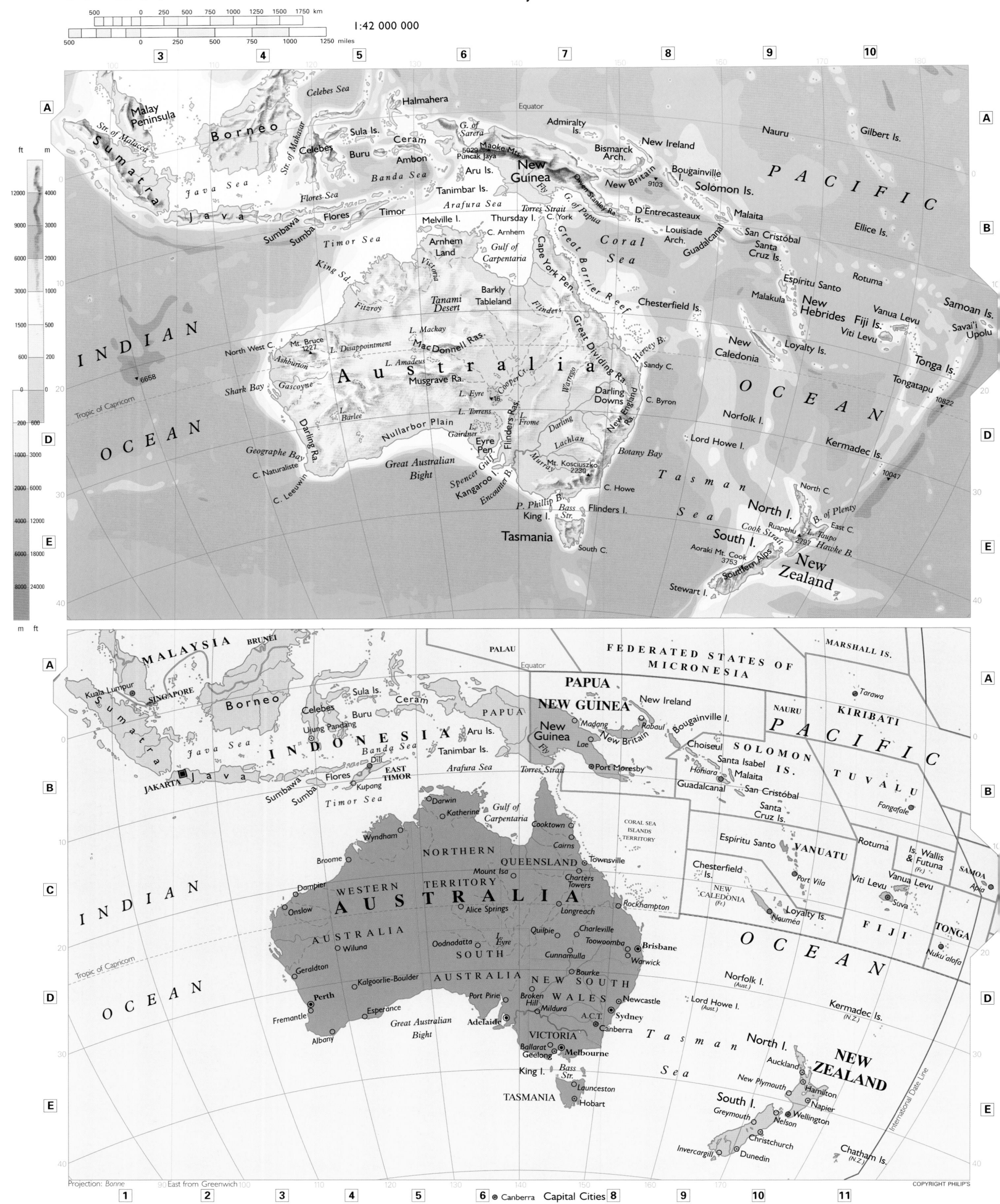

1:42 000 000

Projection: *Bonne*

90 East from Greenwich 100

6 ● Canberra Capital Cities

COPYRIGHT PHILIP'S

1:5 000 000

50   0   50   100   150   200 km
50   0   50   100   150 miles

F · G · H · J · K · L · M

North Island

C. Reinga
C. Maria van Diemen
North C.
Houhora Heads
Rangaunu B.
Doubtless B.
Mangonui
Whangaroa Harb.
Ahipara B.
Kaitaia
Tauroa Pt.
Okaihau
B. of Islands
C. Brett
Rawene
Hokianga Harbour
Opua
Hikurangi
Whangarei
Whangarei Harb.
Bream Hd.
Donnelly's Crossing
Waipu
Bream B.
Dargaville
Little Barrier I.
Great Barrier I.
Warkworth
C. Rodney
C. Colville
Cuvier I.
Kaipara Harbour
Helensville
Hauraki Gulf
Coromandel
Whitianga
Takapuna
AUCKLAND
Manukau
Papakura
Thames
Waiuku
Pukekohe
Mayor I.
Waiuku
Mercer
Paeroa
Waihi
Tauranga Harb.
Waikato
Huntly
Te Aroha
White I.   C. Runaway
Raglan
Morrinsville
Mount Maunganui
Bay of Plenty
Hamilton
Tauranga
Te Puke
Cambridge
Kawhia Harbour
Te Awamutu
Whakatane
East C.
Otorohanga
Putaruru
Kawerau
Opotiki
Raukumara Ra.
Mokau
Te Kuiti
Rotorua
Taneatua
Hikurangi 1753
Mokau
Mokai
L. Tarawera
Murupara
Motu
Waipiro
North Taranaki Bight
Ongarue
Wairakei
Rotoma
UREWERA
Tolaga Bay
Waitara
Taumarunui
Taupo
L. Taupo
Waikaremoana
Ormond
New Plymouth
WHANGANUI
Whangamomona
Turangi
Gisborne
Inglewood
Mt. Taranaki
EGMONT
Ruapehu 2797
Kaimanawa Mts.
Nuhaka
Poverty Bay
C. Egmont
2518
Stratford
Ohakune
TONGARIRO
Wairoa
Waikokopu
Opunake
Eltham
Raetihi
Waiouru
Mahia Pen.
Kapuni
Hawera
Taihape
Ruahine Ra.
Bay View
Hawke Bay
South Taranaki Bight
Waverley
Mangaweka
Napier
Patea
Marton
Hunterville
Hastings
Wanganui
Halcombe
Waipawa
Feilding
Danevirke
Palmerston North
Woodville
Waipukurau
Bulls
Foxton
Pahiatua
C. Turnagain
Shannon
Otaki
Levin
Eketahuna
Paraparaumu
Masterton
Kapiti I.
Pelorus Sd.
Carterton
Upper Hutt
Greytown
Featherston
Martinborough
Petone
L. Wairarapa
Lower Hutt
Eastbourne
WELLINGTON
Cook Strait

South Island

C. Farewell
Golden B.
D'Urville I.
Collingwood
ABEL TASMAN
Takaka
Tasman B.
KAHURANGI
Tasman Mts.
Motueka
Karamea
Nelson
Havelock
Picton
Karamea Bight
Tadmor
Richmond
Blenheim
Seddonville
NELSON LAKES
Wakefield
Granity
Murchison
2885 Tapuaenuku
Seddon
Westport
Lyell
Inangahua
Ward
Matiri Ra.
L. Rotoiti
PAPAROA
Reefton
Mt. Travers 2338
Kaikoura
Spenser Mts.
Blackball
Lewis Pass
Clarence
Runanga
Stillwater
Hanmer Springs
Greymouth
L. Brunner
Jacksons
ARTHUR'S PASS
Waiau
Kumara
Waikari
Hurunui
Culverden
Hokitika
Arthur's Pass
Waipara
Ross
Amberley
Oxford
Kaiapoi
Pegasus Bay
Abut Hd.
Coleridge
Springfield
New Brighton
Whitecliffs
Riccarton
Christchurch
WESTLAND
Aoraki
Mt. Cook
Lincoln
Lyttelton
Westland Bight
3753
MOUNT COOK
Methven
Banks Pen.
Jackson B.
Okuru
Mount Cook
Staveley
Akaroa
Haast
L. Tekapo
Fairlie
Canterbury Plains
Little River
Southbridge
Rakaia
Rakaia
MOUNT ASPIRING
Mt. Aspiring 3027
L. Pukaki
Temuka
Ashburton
Milford Sd.
Mt. Earnslaw 2818
L. Ohau
Timaru
Ashburton Bight
Sutherland Falls
Wanaka L.
Hakataramea
St. Andrews
Bligh Sound
Wanaka
George Sound
Arrowtown
Cromwell
Kurow
Waimate
Queenstown
Wakatipu
Tokarahi
Oamaru
Secretary I.
Te Anau Kingston
Alexandra
Naseby
Maheno
Doubtful Sd.
Clyde
Kakanui Mts.
Hampden
FIORDLAND
L. Te Anau
Eyre Mts.
Roxburgh
Danback
Breaksea Sd.
Manapouri
Garvie Mts.
Waikouaiti
Palmerston
Resolution I.
L. Manapouri
Umbrella Mts.
Mosgiel
Port Chalmers
Dusky Sd.
Mossburn
Waipahi
Otago Harbour
Lawrence
Saunders C.
Lumsden
Fairfield
Dunedin
Preservation Inlet
Chalky Inlet
Clifden
Ohai
Edievale
Milton
Te Waewae B.
Tuatapere
Nightcaps
Kelso
Tapanui
Kaitangata
Winton
Clinton
Orepuki
Hedgehope
Mataura
Owaka
Riverton
Gore
Wyndham
Nugget Pt.
Invercargill
South Invercargill
Tokanui
Tahakopa
Bluff
Ruapuke I.
Foveaux Str.
Halfmoon Bay
Stewart I.
Southwest C.
Port Pegasus

TASMAN SEA

PACIFIC OCEAN

Southern Alps
Westland Bight
Southland
Otago
Canterbury Plains

Projection: Conical with two standard parallels
East from Greenwich
National Parks

SAMOAN ISLANDS
1:10 100 000

SAMOA
Savai'i
Apia
Upolu
AMERICAN SAMOA
Pago Pago
Tutuila
West from Greenwich

A · B

12 · 13 · 14

Wallis & Futuna (Fr.)
Futuna

FIJI
Yasawa Group
Labasa
Vanua Levu
Thikombia
Niuafo'ou (Tonga)
Taveuni
Vanua Balavu
Lautoka
Koro
Nandi
1323
Levuka
Ovalau
Viti Levu
Gau
Lau Group
Suva
Koro Sea
Lakeba
Moala
Kandavu
Vatoa
Vava'u
Tofua
TONGA (Friendly Is.)
Tongatapu
Nuku'alofa

FIJI AND TONGA
1:10 100 000

50   0   50   100   150   200 km
50   0   50   100   150 miles

West from Greenwich

B · C · D · E

7 · 8 · 9 · 10 · 11

COPYRIGHT PHILIP'S

ft   m
9000   3000
6000   2000
3000   1000
1200   600
600   200
0   0
200   600
2000   6000
4000   12000
6000   18000
m   ft

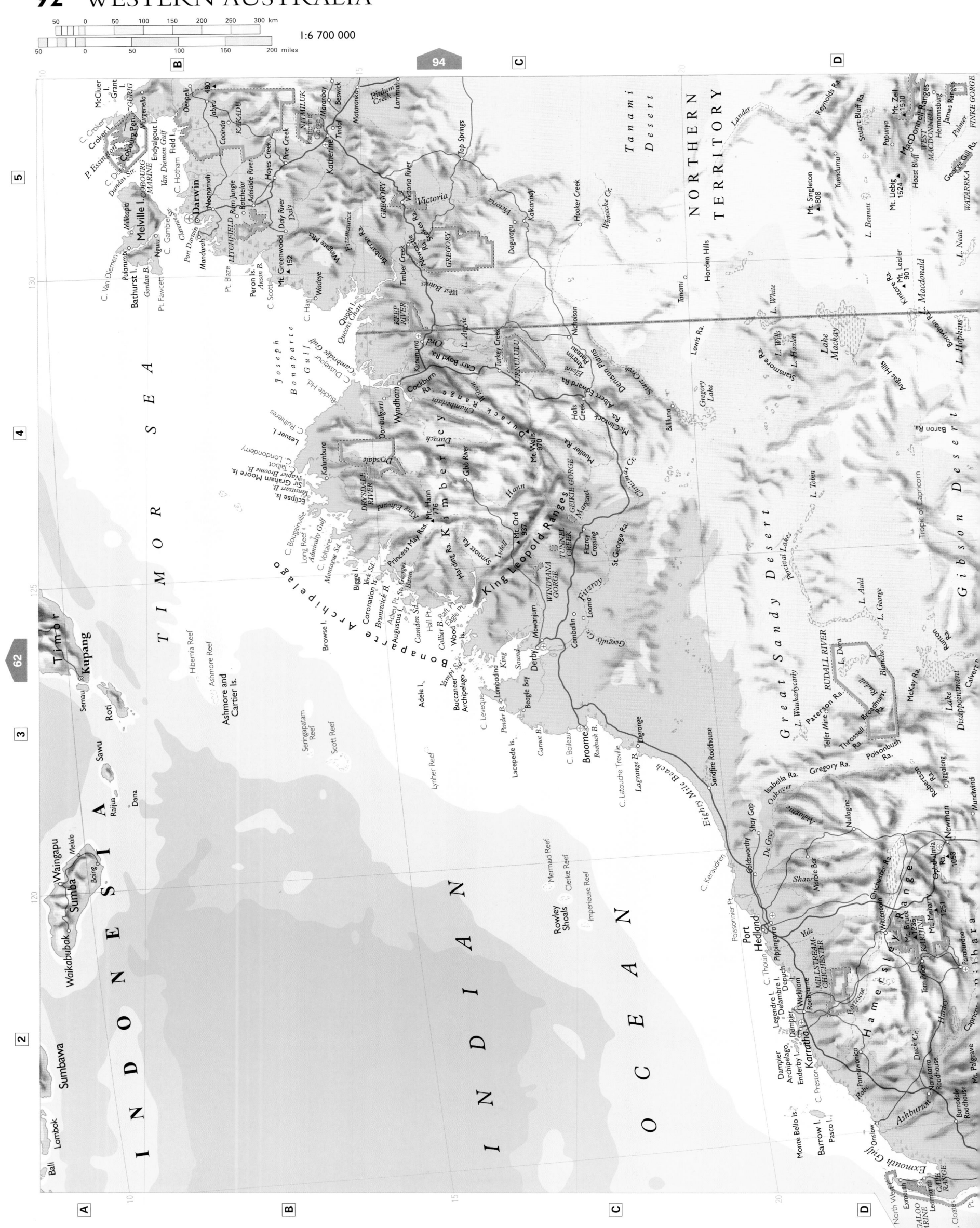

WESTERN AUSTRALIA

SOUTH AUSTRALIA

INDIAN OCEAN

SOUTHERN OCEAN

Great Australian Bight

Great Victoria Desert

Nullarbor Plain

Hampton Tableland

Projection : Bonne

East from Greenwich

National Parks

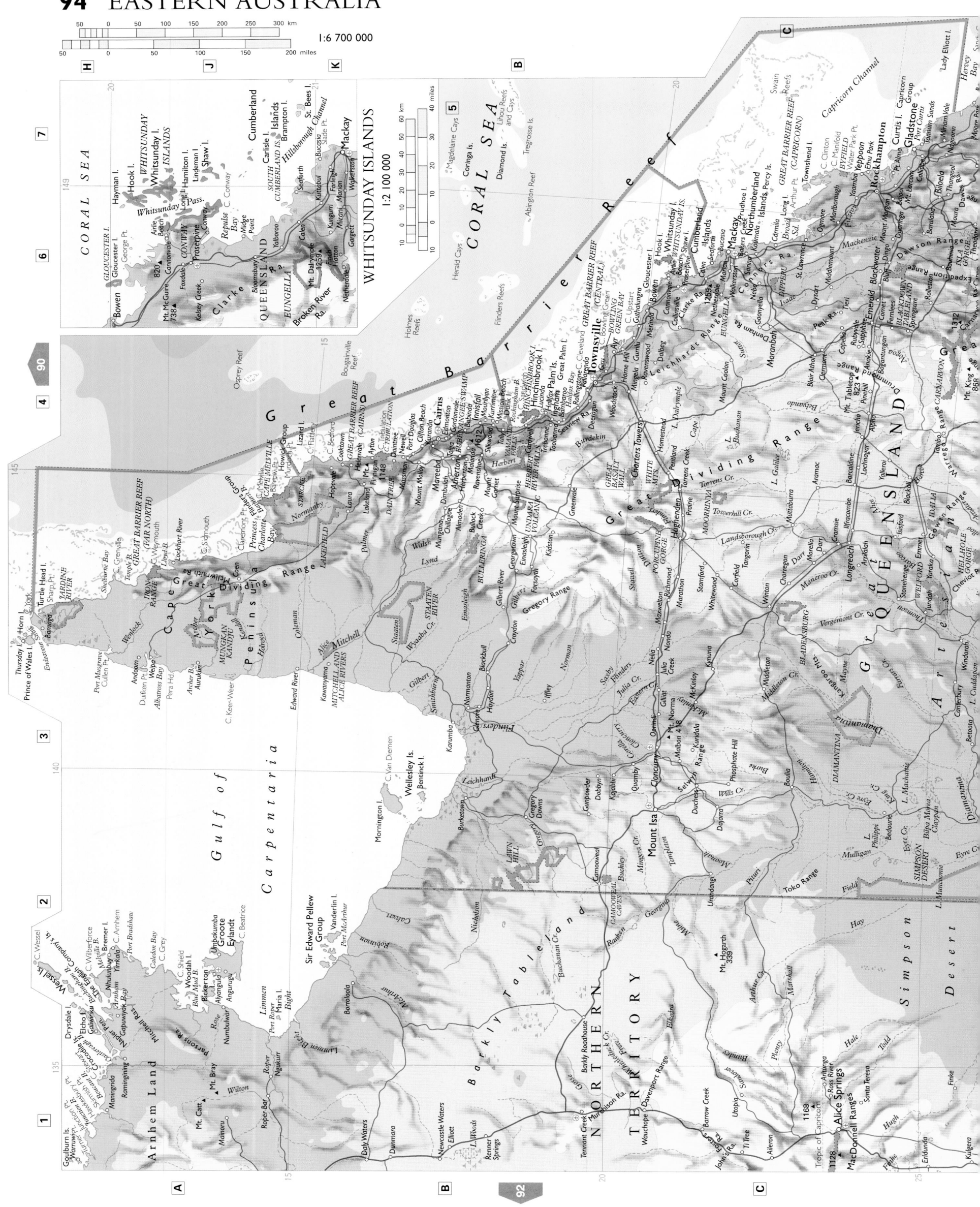

COPYRIGHT PHILIP'S

Major labels

QUEENSLAND

NEW SOUTH WALES

SOUTH AUSTRALIA

VICTORIA

TASMANIA

AUSTRALIAN CAPITAL TERRITORY

TASMAN SEA

Bass Strait

Great Dividing Range

Darling Downs

Barrier Range

Flinders Ranges

Gammon Ranges

Grampians

Gippsland

Cities and towns

BRISBANE • Gold Coast • Tweed Heads • Ipswich • Toowoomba • Warwick • Maryborough • Hervey Bay • Bundaberg • Gympie • Nambour • Caloundra • Redcliffe • Beenleigh • Nerang • Ballina • Byron Bay • Evans Head • Grafton • Coffs Harbour • Nambucca Heads • Kempsey • Port Macquarie • Taree • Tuncurry-Forster • Newcastle • Raymond Terrace • Maitland • Cessnock • Gosford • SYDNEY • Windsor • Penrith • Campbelltown • Katoomba • Lithgow • Wollongong • Shellharbour • Kiama • Nowra-Bomaderry • Ulladulla • Batemans Bay • Bega • Armidale • Tamworth • Gunnedah • Narrabri • Moree • Inverell • Glen Innes • Dubbo • Orange • Bathurst • Mudgee • Parkes • Forbes • Cowra • Young • Goulburn • CANBERRA • Queanbeyan • Cooma • Wagga Wagga • Albury • Wodonga • Griffith • Leeton • Narrandera • Hay • Deniliquin • Broken Hill • Mildura • Swan Hill • Echuca • Shepparton • Bendigo • Ballarat • Geelong • MELBOURNE • Dandenong • Frankston • Mornington • Sale • Bairnsdale • Traralgon • Moe • Morwell • Warrnambool • Mount Gambier • Portland • Hamilton • Horsham • Stawell • ADELAIDE • Elizabeth • Gawler • Murray Bridge • Port Augusta • Port Pirie • Whyalla • Port Lincoln • Kadina • Victor Harbor • Hobart • Launceston • Devonport • Burnie • Queenstown

King Island • Flinders Island • Kangaroo I. • Furneaux Group • Cape Barren I.

Lake Eyre (North) • Lake Eyre (South) • Lake Torrens • Lake Gairdner • Lake Frome • Lake Blanche • Lake Gregory • Lake Callabonna

Murray River • Darling River • Murrumbidgee River • Lachlan River • Cooper Cr. • Warrego

Spencer Gulf • Gulf St. Vincent • Encounter Bay • Coorong

National Parks

on same scale

Projection Bonne

East from Greenwich

m 4500 3000 1500 1000 600 400 200 0
ft
ft 12 000 6000 2000 0 200 500 m

RUSSIA

Yekaterinburg
Tomsk
Novosibirsk
Ob
Lena
Irkutsk
Oz. Baykal
Chita
Amur
Okhotsk
Sea of Okhotsk
Bering Sea
Poluostrov Kamchatka

MOSKVA
Volga
Astana
(Aqmola)
Semey

KAZAKHSTAN
Aral Sea
Balqash Köl
Altay
MONGOLIA
Ulaanbaatar
Changchun
Blagoveshchensk
Khabarovsk
Harbin
Sakhalin
La Pérouse Str.
Kurilskiye Ostrova
(Russia)
Kuril Trench
Petropavlovsk
-Kamchatskiy
Komandorskiye
Ostrova
(Russia)
Near Is.
(U.S.A.)
Andreanof Is.
(U.S.A.)
7822
Aleutian Trench

Almaty
Toshkent
Ürümqi
KYRGYZSTAN
TAJIKISTAN
AFGHANISTAN
Kabul
Srinagar
PAKISTAN
Lahore
DELHI
Kanpur

CHINA
Kunlun Shan
XIZANG
Lanzhou
Xi'an
Lhasa
Himalaya
8850
Mt. Everest
NEPAL
Ganga
Brahmaputra
KOLKATA
(Calcutta)
DHAKA
BANGLADESH
Irrawaddy
Salween
Mandalay
BURMA
Rangoon

BEIJING
TIANJIN
Taiyuan
Huang He
SHENYANG
NORTH
KOREA
SOUTH
KOREA
Dalian
SÖUL
Qingdao
Yellow Sea
Kitakyūshū
Kyūshū
Shikoku

CHONGQING
Nanjing
Wuhan
Chang Jiang
Changsha
SHANGHAI
HANGZHOU
East China Sea

Kunming
Fuzhou
GUANGZHOU
Taipei
TAIWAN
Macau
HONG KONG
Ryūkyū-rettō
(Japan)

Vladivostok
Sapporo
Hakodate
Sea of Japan
Nagoya
Kyōto
Osaka
Fuji-San
3776
TOKYO
Yokohama
JAPAN
Sendai
10,542
10,554
Japan Trench
South Honshu Ridge

Midway Is.
(U.S.A.)
Hawaiian
Lisianski I.
(U.S.A.)

Ogasawara Gunto
(Japan)
Minami-Tori-Shima
(Japan)
Kazan-Rettō
(Japan)
Emperor Seamount Chain
Marcus Necker Ridge
Wake I. (U.S.A.)
International Dateline Ridge

Hyderabad
INDIA
CHENNAI
(Madras)
SRI LANKA
Colombo

THAILAND
BANGKOK
CAMBODIA
Phnom Penh
VIETNAM
Hanoi
LAOS
Mekong
Bay of Bengal
Nicobar Is.
(India)
Andaman Is.
(India)
G. of Thailand
Thanh Pho
Ho Chi Minh
South China Sea
Hainan
C. Engano
Luzon
Paracel Is.
MANILA
PHILIPPINES
Mindoro
Samar
Palawan
10,497
Mindanao
Mindanao Trench

NORTHERN
MARIANAS
(U.S.A.)
Saipan
GUAM
(U.S.A.)
11,022
Mariana Trench
Yap
Koror
PALAU
Caroline Is.
Truk
MARSHALL IS.
Bikini
Atoll
Enewetak
Atoll
Micronesia
Pohnpei
Palikir
Jaluit I.
Dalap-Uliga-
Darrit
Butaritari

P
A

MALAYSIA
Sulu Sea
Celebes Sea
BRUNEI
SABAH
Kuala Lumpur
PEN. MALAYSIA
Sarawak
SINGAPORE
Sumatera
Sunda Islands
Palembang
Java Sea
JAKARTA
Ujung Pandang
INDONESIA
Borneo
Sulawesi
Halmahera
Buru
Seram
Maluku
Banda Sea
Puncak Jaya
5029
PAPUA
Celebes Sea
4101

FEDERATED STATES
OF MICRONESIA
Melanesia
PAPUA NEW GUINEA
Admiralty Is.
New Ireland
Bismarck Arch.
New Britain
Rabaul
Bougainville
New Guinea
Lae
SOLOMON IS.
NAURU
Tarawa
Gilbert Is.
Banaba
Butaritari

KOROR
PALAU
Howland I. (U.S.)
Baker I. (U.S.)
Phoenix Is.
Abariringa
Enderbury
K
I
N

Jawa
Surabaya
Bali
Sumbawa
Sumba
Flores Sea
Flores
Timor
EAST TIMOR
Arafura Sea
Torres Strait
C. York
7440
Port Moresby
Honiara
Guadalcanal
Santa Cruz I.
9165

Fongafale
TUVALU
Tokelau Is.
(N.Z.)
Rotuma
Is. Wallis
& Futuna
(Fr.)
SAMOA
Apia

Christmas I.
(Austral.)
Cocos Is.
(Austral.)
C. Arnhem
Darwin
Gulf of Carpentaria
Broome
North West C.
Cairns
Townsville
Mount Isa
Louisiade
Arch.
Coral Sea
Great Barrier Reef
VANUATU
Is. Chesterfield
Espíritu Santo
Port Vila
7570
NEW
CALEDONIA
(Fr.)
Nouméa
Is. Loyauté
Vanua Levu
Viti Levu
Suva
FIJI
Nuku'alofa
TONGA
Lord Howe Ridge
Howe

INDIAN
OCEAN

Geraldton
Perth
Albany
Great Australian Bight
L. Eyre
Alice Springs
AUSTRALIA
Darling
Murray
Rockhampton
Brisbane
Sydney
Canberra
Mt. Kosciuszko
2237
Adelaide
Melbourne
Bass Str.
Tasmania
Hobart
Norfolk I.
(Austral.)
Lord Howe I. (Austral.)
Tasman Sea
NEW
ZEALAND
Auckland
Cook Strait
Wellington
Aoraki Mt. Cook
3753
Christchurch
Chatham Is.
(N.Z.)
Dunedin
Invercargill
Kermadec Is.
(N.Z.)
Kermadec Trench
10,047
10,822
Tonga Trench

Nouvelle Amsterdam
(Fr.)
I. St. Paul (Fr.)
Is. Crozet
(Fr.)
Kerguelen
(Fr.)
Heard I.
(Austral.)
Mid-Indian Ridge
Southwest Indian Ridge
Bounty Is.
(N.Z.)
Antipodes Is.
(N.Z.)
Auckland Is.
(N.Z.)
Campbell I.
(N.Z.)
Macquarie Is.
(Austral.)

ft	m
12 000	4000
9000	3000
6000	2000
3000	1000
1500	500
600	200
0	0
200	600
1000	3000
2000	6000
4000	12 000
6000	18 000
8000	24 000
m	ft

Projection: Mollweide's Homolographic   East from Greenwich

Arctic Circle

ALASKA
(U.S.A.)
Anchorage
5959

Bristol Bay

Gulf of Alaska

Juneau

Is. (U.S.A.)

Prince of Wales I.
(U.S.A.) Prince Rupert
Queen Charlotte Is.
(Canada)

ROCKY

CANADA

Edmonton

L. Winnipeg

Newfoundland

NORTH

Calgary
Regina
Winnipeg

Vancouver
Vancouver I.
Victoria
Seattle
Portland
Boise

L. Superior

Québec
St. Lawrence
St. John's

Minneapolis
Missouri
L. Huron
L. Michigan
Toronto
Detroit
L. Ontario
L. Erie
Buffalo

Montréal
Ottawa
Boston

ATLANTIC

C. Mendocino

6741

Salt Lake
City
Denver

CHICAGO
Pittsburgh
Cincinnati

NEW YORK
PHILADELPHIA
Baltimore
Washington D.C.

Sacramento

UNITED STATES

Kansas City
St. Louis

SAN FRANCISCO

4418

Oklahoma City
Memphis

Atlanta
C. Hatteras

LOS ANGELES
San Diego

Phoenix
Dallas

Houston

Bermuda
(U.K.)

Ciudad
Juárez

San Antonio

New
Orleans

Jacksonville

Sargasso Sea

OCEAN

Guadalupe
(Mex.)

Baja California

Gulf of Mexico
Monterrey

Miami

BAHAMAS

Tropic of Cancer

Honolulu
Oahu
4205
HAWAIIAN IS.
(U.S.A.)
Hawaii

C. San Lucas

MEXICO

La Habana

CUBA

West Indies

E

Johnston I.
(U.S.A.)

an Ridge

Guadalajara

Puebla

Mérida

Canal de Yucatán

JAMAICA
Kingston

HAITI

7680
9200
DOMINICAN REP.

Leeward
Is.

CIFIC

Is. Revilla Gigedo
(Mex.)

Acapulco

5610

BELIZE
GUATEMALA
Guatemala
San Salvador
EL SALVADOR

HONDURAS

NICARAGUA
Managua

Caribbean Sea

PUERTO
RICO
(U.S.A.)

BARBADOS

Palmyra Is.
(U.S.A.)

I. Clipperton
(Fr.)

COSTA
RICA

San José

Colón Panamá

Barranquilla

Windward Is.

Maracaibo

Caracas

Teraina
Tabuaeran
Kiritimati

POLY

North West Christmas I. Ridge

PANAMA

I. del Coco
(Costa Rica)

Medellín

Orinoco

VENEZUELA

Jarvis I.
(U.S.A.)

CEAN

Equator

I. de Malpelo
(Colombia)

Bogotá
Cali
COLOMBIA

Galápagos
(Ecuador)

Quito
ECUADOR

Malden I.
Starbuck I.

Guayaquil

Amazonas

IBATI

Line Is.

Iquitos

BRAZIL

Tongareva

Pukapuka
Manihiki

MER.
AMOA
U.S.A.

Vostok I.
Caroline I.
(Millennium I.)
Flint I.

Is. Marquises

East Pacific Ridge

C. Pariñas

Trujillo

Suwarrow Is.

Is. de la
Société

Tuamotu

6369

PERU

Niue
(N.Z.)

Cook Is.
(N.Z.)

Papeete Tahiti

Is. Tuamotu

LIMA

Cuzco

Austral

Seamount Chain

FRENCH POLYNESIA

L. Titicaca
Nevada Ancohuma
6550

Rarotonga

Is. Tubuai

Mururoa

6866

Arequipa

Peru-
Arica

La Paz
BOLIVIA

Tropic of Capricorn

Ducie I.

Iquique
Chile

Antofagasta

PARAGUAY

Rapa

Pitcairn I.
(U.K.)

Sala-y-Gómez
(Chile)

San Felix
(Chile)

San Ambrosio
(Chile)

8050
Trench

San Miguel
de Tucumán

Asunción

I. de Pascua
(Chile)

Pôrto
Alegre

Arch. de
Juan Fernández
(Chile)

Aconcagua
6962

Córdoba

Valparaíso

Rosario

URUGUAY

Pacific-Antarctic Ridge

Chile Rise

SANTIAGO
Concepción

BUENOS
AIRES

Montevideo

Río de la Plata

ARGENTINA

SOUTH

Patagonia

ATLANTIC

6212

OCEAN

Punta Arenas

Est. de Magallanes
Tierra del Fuego

C. de Hornos

Falkland Is.
(U.K.)

South Georgia
(U.K.)

100 0 200 400 600 800 1000 1200 1400 km
1:29 400 000
100 0 200 400 600 800 1000 miles

Projection: Bonne

West from Greenwich

COPYRIGHT PHILIP'S

1:29 400 000

100 0 200 400 600 800 1000 1200 1400 km
100 0 200 400 600 800 1000 miles

B   A   B

C   RUSSIA   ARCTIC   OCEAN   GREENLAND   ICELAND   C
Asia   International Date Line   Denmark Strait   Reykjavik

Bering Strait   Beaufort   Queen Elizabeth Is.   (Denmark)

Bering Sea   Sea   Ellesmere I.

St. Lawrence   Baffin Bay

Yukon   ALASKA   Victoria I.   Baffin Island   Davis Strait   D
(U.S.A.)   Porcupine   NUNAVUT   Nuuk

Fairbanks   YUKON   NORTHWEST   Cape Farewell

Anchorage   TERRITORY   Mackenzie   Great Bear L.

Kodiak I.   Gulf of Alaska   Whitehorse   Hudson Strait

Juneau   TERRITORIES   Yellowknife   Back   Hudson   E

Liard   Great Slave L.   Dubawnt   Bay   NEWFOUNDLAND &
Skeena   BRITISH   CANADA   LABRADOR   St. John's
COLUMBIA   Peace   Lake   Athabasca   Eastmain   St-Pierre et Miquelon (Fr.)
Fraser   ALBERTA   Athabasca   QUÉBEC   PRINCE EDWARD I.

Edmonton   SASKATCHEWAN   Churchill   Nelson   St. Lawrence   Charlottetown
Victoria   Vancouver   Calgary   MANITOBA   NEW   NOVA SCOTIA
Saskatchewan   L. Winnipeg   ONTARIO   Québec   Fredericton   Halifax
Regina   BRUNSWICK   MAINE   C. Sable
WASHINGTON   Winnipeg   L. Superior   Ottawa   Montréal   Augusta   40
Olympia   Seattle   L. Huron   Toronto   VER.   Concord
Portland   MONTANA   Missouri   MINNESOTA   L. Ontario   Buffalo   N.H.   Boston
Salem   Columbia   Helena   Bismarck   WISCONSIN   MICHIGAN   Detroit   NEW YORK   Hartford   Providence
OREGON   IDAHO   NORTH DAKOTA   Minneapolis   Madison   Lansing   Cleveland   Erie   CT.   R.I.   F
Boise   Snake   SOUTH   Milwaukee   L. Michigan   Toledo   PA.   Pittsburgh   PHILADELPHIA
WYOMING   DAKOTA   IOWA   CHICAGO   OHIO   Columbus   Baltimore   NEW YORK CITY
Salt Lake   Cheyenne   NEBRASKA   Lincoln   ILLINOIS   INDIANA   Cincinnati   Washington D.C.   MD.
Sacramento   City   Denver   Springfield   Indianapolis   W.V.   Richmond
San Francisco   Carson City   NEVADA   UTAH   Kansas City   St.   KENTUCKY   VIRGINIA   Raleigh   Bermuda (U.K.)
San Jose   Las Vegas   COLORADO   KANSAS   Topeka   Louis   MISSOURI   Nashville   NORTH   Charlotte   NORTH
Santa Fe   OKLAHOMA   TENNESSEE   CAROLINA   ATLANTIC
LOS ANGELES   CALIFORNIA   ARIZONA   NEW MEXICO   Albuquerque   Oklahoma City   ARKANSAS   Memphis   Columbia   Charleston   OCEAN
San Diego   Phoenix   Little Rock   Birmingham   SOUTH   G
Tucson   El Paso   Dallas   MISSISSIPPI   Jackson   Atlanta   CAROLINA
Guadalupe (Mex.)   Rio Grande   TEXAS   GEORGIA   Montgomery   Jacksonville
PACIFIC   Austin   Baton   ALABAMA   Tallahassee   FLORIDA
Hermosillo   Houston   Rouge   New   Tampa   Miami
OCEAN   LOUISIANA   Orleans   Nassau   BAHAMAS
Tropic of Cancer   Gulf of Mexico   Florida Str.   Turks & Caicos Is. (U.K.)
Culiacan   Monterrey   Havana   CUBA   DOMINICAN   San Juan
Guadalupe   MÉXICO   Cayman Is. (U.K.)   REP.   PUERTO RICO (U.S.A.)
Revilla Gigedo Is. (Mex.)   Mérida   HAITI   Santo   H
Guadalajara   MÉXICO   JAMAICA   Port-au-Prince   Domingo
Puebla   Kingston   Caribbean Sea
Acapulco   Belmopan   BELIZE
Maracaibo
GUATEMALA   HONDURAS   NICARAGUA   Barranquilla   VENEZUELA   J
Guatemala   Tegucigalpa   Managua   L. Nicaragua
San Salvador   EL SALVADOR   COSTA   San José   South
Panama   America
RICA   PANAMA   COLOMBIA
Medellín   COPYRIGHT PHILIP'S

Projection: Bonne

7   MÉXICO Capital Cities   8   120   110   West from Greenwich   100   9   10   90   11   80   12

1:12 600 000

Projection : Bonne

ALASKA
1:25 200 000

B

Devon I.
Lancaster Sound
Brodeur
Peninsula
Arctic Bay
Nanisivik
Borden
Pen.
Bylot I.
Eclipse
Sd.
Pond Inlet
Clyde River
C. Adair
2136
Baffin Bay
Nunavik
Uummannaq
Qeqertarsuaq
Qeqertarsuaq
Ilulissat
Qasigiannguit
Ammassalik
GREENLAND
(KALAALLIT NUNAAT)
(Denmark)
Kong Frederik VI's Kyst
Gulf
of
Boothia
Fury and Hecla Str.
Igloolik
C. Raper
Home B.
Qikiqtarjuaq
C. Dyer
2591
Cumberland
Peninsula
Panghirtung
Hoare B.
C. Mercy
Qeqertarsuaq
Sisimiut
Kangerlussuaq
Maniitsoq
2850
Simpson
Pen.
Kugaaruk
Hall Beach
Melville
Peninsula
Foxe
Basin
Prince
Charles
I.
Air
Force
Nettilling L.
Amadjuak
L.
C. Dorchester
Cumberland Sd.
Nuuk
Arsuk
Qeqertarsuatsiaat
Paamiut
Qaqortoq
Alluitsup Paa
Nanortalik
Rae Isthmus
Repulse
Bay
N U N A V U T
Foxe
Pen.
Cape Dorset
Meta
Iqaluit
Hall
Peninsula
Incognita
Kimmirut
Frobisher Bay
Peninsula
Resolution I.
Qikiqtarjuaq
Nunap Isua
Circle
Chesterfield Inlet
Southampton
I.
Coral
Harbour
Bell
Pen.
Coats
I.
Nottingham
I.
Salisbury
I.
Hudson   Strait
Ivujivik
Salluit
Quaqtaq
Akpatok I.
C. Chidley
Labrador
Sea
3809
Wager B.
Mansel
I.
Kangiqsujuaq
Kangirsuk
1652
Kangiqsualujjuaq
Hebron
Péninsule
Arnaud
Puvirnituq
L. Payne
d'Ungava
Ungava Bay
Kuujjuaq
Nain
ATLANTIC
Hudson
Ottawa Is.
257
Inukjuak
Feuilles
Mélèzes
George
Baleine
Koksoak
Hopedale
C. Harrison
Rigolet
Cartwright
Port Hope Simpson
Belle Isle
50
Bay
Sleeper Is.
King George Is.
Sanikiluaq
Baker's
Dozen
Is.
Belcher Is.
L. à l'Eau
Claire
L. Minto
L. Bienville
Caniapiscau
Schefferville
Smallwood
Res.
North West River
Happy Valley
Goose Bay
NEWFOUNDLAND &
C. Bauld
St-Anthony
C. Tatnam
Peawanuck
Winisk
C. Henrietta
Maria
Kuujjuarapik
Grande Baleine
Kanaaupscow
La Grande
Esker
Churchill
Falls
Churchill
St-Augustin
LABRADOR
Str. of Belle Isle
Notre Dame B.
Bonavista
Trinity B.
D
Big
Trout L.
Severn
Pte. Louis
XIV
Chisasibi
James Bay
Akimiski I.
Wemindji
Eastmain
L. à
Claire
Fermont
Labrador
City
Ashuanipi
1135
Gagnon
Q U É B E C
Rés.
Manicouagan
Moisie
Romaine
Natashquan
St-Augustin
Havre-
St-Pierre
Sept-Îles
Natashquan
î. d'Anticosti
814
Deer
Lake
Grand Falls
Windsor
Corner Brook
Stephenville
Lewisporte
Gander
Carbonear
St. John's
Marystown
Placentia
C. Race
Newfoundland
D
O C E A N
TARIO
Attawapiskat
Attawapiskat
Fort Albany
Charlton
Albany
Moosonee
Nottaway
Rupert
Eastmain
L. Albanel
L.
Mistassini
Chibougamau
Baie-Comeau
St. Lawrence
Matane
Gaspé
Pén. de la
Gaspésie
Port-Cartier
Gulf of
St. Lawrence
Cabot Str.
Ray
C. North
St-PIERRE
et
MIQUELON
(Fr)
Channel-Port
aux Basques
Albany
L. St. Joseph
Nakina
Hearst
Kapuskasing
Kenogami
L. Matagami
Harricana
Matagami
Dolbeau-
Mistassini
Rés. Gouin
L. St-Jean
Chicoutimi
Rimouski
Campbellton
Chatham
Bathurst
Charlottetown
PR. EDWARD I.
Cape Breton I.
Glace Bay
Sydney
Port Hawkesbury
Sable I.
(Nova Scotia)
L.
Nipigon
Greenstone
Nipigon
Marathon
Oba
Kirkland
Lake
Rouyn-
Noranda
Val-d'Or
Amos
Ahitibi L.
Roberval
Jonquière
Lévis
1190
Grand Falls
Woodstock
NEW
BRUNSWICK
Moncton
Summerside
Northumberland Str.
Amherst
Antigonish
New Glasgow
Thunder Bay
Chapleau
Wawa
New
Liskeard
Cochrane
Timmins
La Tuque
Rés.
Cabonga
Mont-
Laurier
Shawinigan
Trois-Rivières
Québec
St-Hyacinthe
Sherbrooke
Fredericton
MAINE
Saint
John
Kentville
Truro
Dartmouth
Halifax
6309
Houghton
183
Sault Ste.
Marie
Elliot
Lake
Sudbury
North
Bay
L. Nipissing
Pembroke
Joliette
Granby
Montpelier
Bangor
Augusta
B. of Fundy
Digby
Bridgewater
Liverpool
40
ES
Marquette
Ironwood
Manistique
Sault Ste.
Marie
Manitoulin
I.
Georgian
Bay
Parry
Sound
Huntsville
Ottawa
MONTRÉAL
Hull
Cornwall
Burlington
VERMONT
NEW
HAMPSHIRE
Concord
Lewiston
Portland
Yarmouth
C. Sable
M'CHIGAN
Rhinelander
Escanaba
Menominee
Wausau
Petoskey
Traverse City
Cadillac
Barrie
Owen Sound
Peterborough
Kingston
Belleville
Oshawa
Manchester
MASS.
Boston
C. Cod
E
ONSIN
Appleton
Sheboygan
Green
Bay
Lake
Huron
TORONTO
L. Ontario
Hamilton
Syracuse
Albany
Springfield
Providence
R.I.
Milwaukee
Madison
Racine
Kenosha
Grand
Rapids
Saginaw
Flint
Lansing
London
Kitchener
Niagara
Falls
Rochester
Buffalo
NEW   YORK
Elmira
Binghamton
Hartford
CONN.
New Haven
Bridgeport
NEW YORK
Rockford
CHICAGO
DETROIT
Gary
South Bend
Sarnia
Windsor
Toledo
174
L. Erie
Erie
CLEVELAND
Cleveland
Jamestown
Scranton
Newark
N.J.
Trenton
Allentown
ILLINOIS
INDIANA
OHIO
PENNSYLVANIA

West from Greenwich

COPYRIGHT PHILIP'S

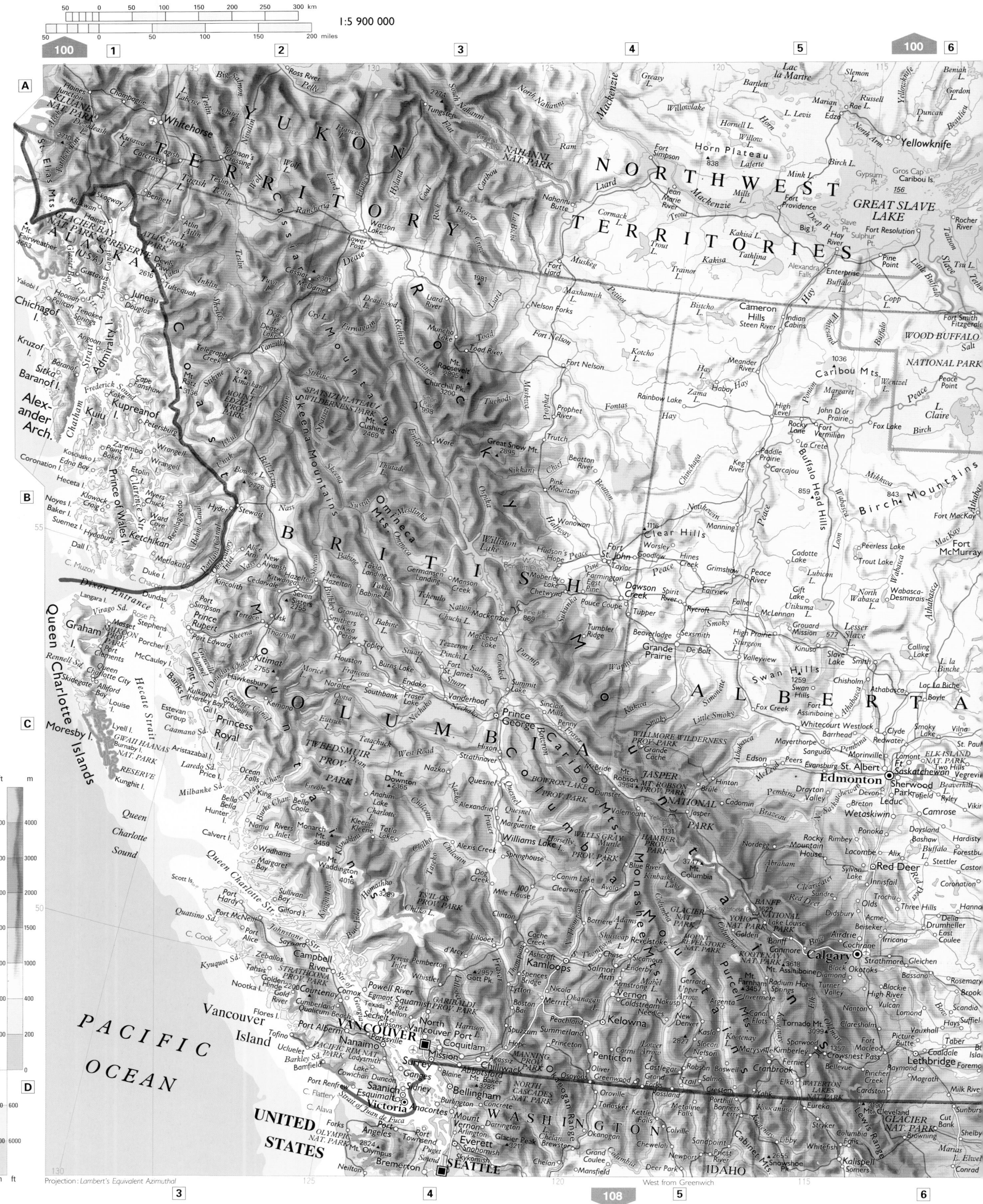

1:5 900 000

PACIFIC OCEAN

YUKON TERRITORY

NORTHWEST TERRITORIES

BRITISH COLUMBIA

ALBERTA

ALASKA (U.S.A.)

UNITED STATES

WASHINGTON

IDAHO

Queen Charlotte Islands

Vancouver Island

GREAT SLAVE LAKE

WOOD BUFFALO NATIONAL PARK

Edmonton

Calgary

Red Deer

Seattle

Vancouver

Victoria

Whitehorse

Yellowknife

Projection: Lambert's Equivalent Azimuthal

West from Greenwich

National Parks

COPYRIGHT PHILIP'S

1:5 900 000

National Parks

101

6   7   8   9

LABRADOR SEA

A

NEWFOUNDLAND &

B

Labrador

LABRADOR

Newfoundland

50

C

QUÉBEC

Plateau de la Côte Nord

Î. d'Anticosti

GULF OF ST. LAWRENCE

Long Range Mts.

St-Pierre et Miquelon (France)

Cabot Strait

NEW BRUNSWICK

PRINCE EDWARD ISLAND

Cape Breton Island

45

NOVA SCOTIA

MAINE

Bay of Fundy

ATLANTIC

Sable I. (Nova Scotia)

OCEAN

N. HAMPSHIRE

BOSTON

UNITED STATES

MASS.

West from Greenwich

70   65   60

6   7   8

COPYRIGHT PHILIP'S

Selected place names: Nain, Hopedale, Postville, Davis Inlet, Makkovik, Cartwright, Happy Valley-Goose Bay, Churchill Falls, Labrador City, Wabush, Schefferville, Sept-Îles, Port-Cartier, Gaspé, Rimouski, Matane, Corner Brook, Stephenville, Channel-Port aux Basques, Grand Falls, Windsor, Gander, St. John's, Mt. Pearl, Charlottetown, Summerside, Moncton, Fredericton, Saint John, Sydney, Glace Bay, Louisbourg, Truro, Halifax, Dartmouth, Yarmouth, Lunenburg, Quebéc, Lévis, Sherbrooke, Chicoutimi, Jonquière, Bangor, Augusta, Portland, Manchester, Concord, Lowell, Worcester, Quincy, Brockton

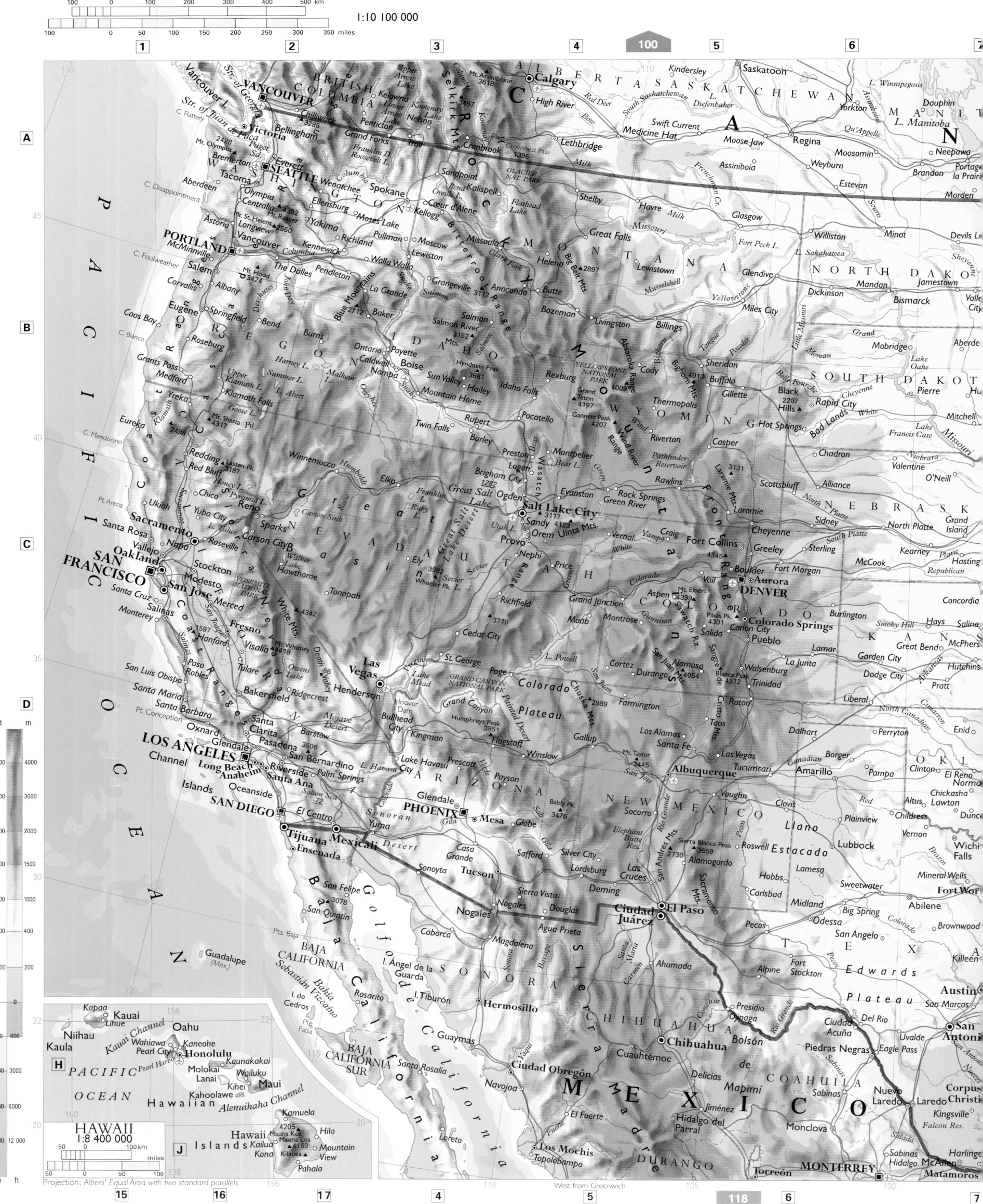

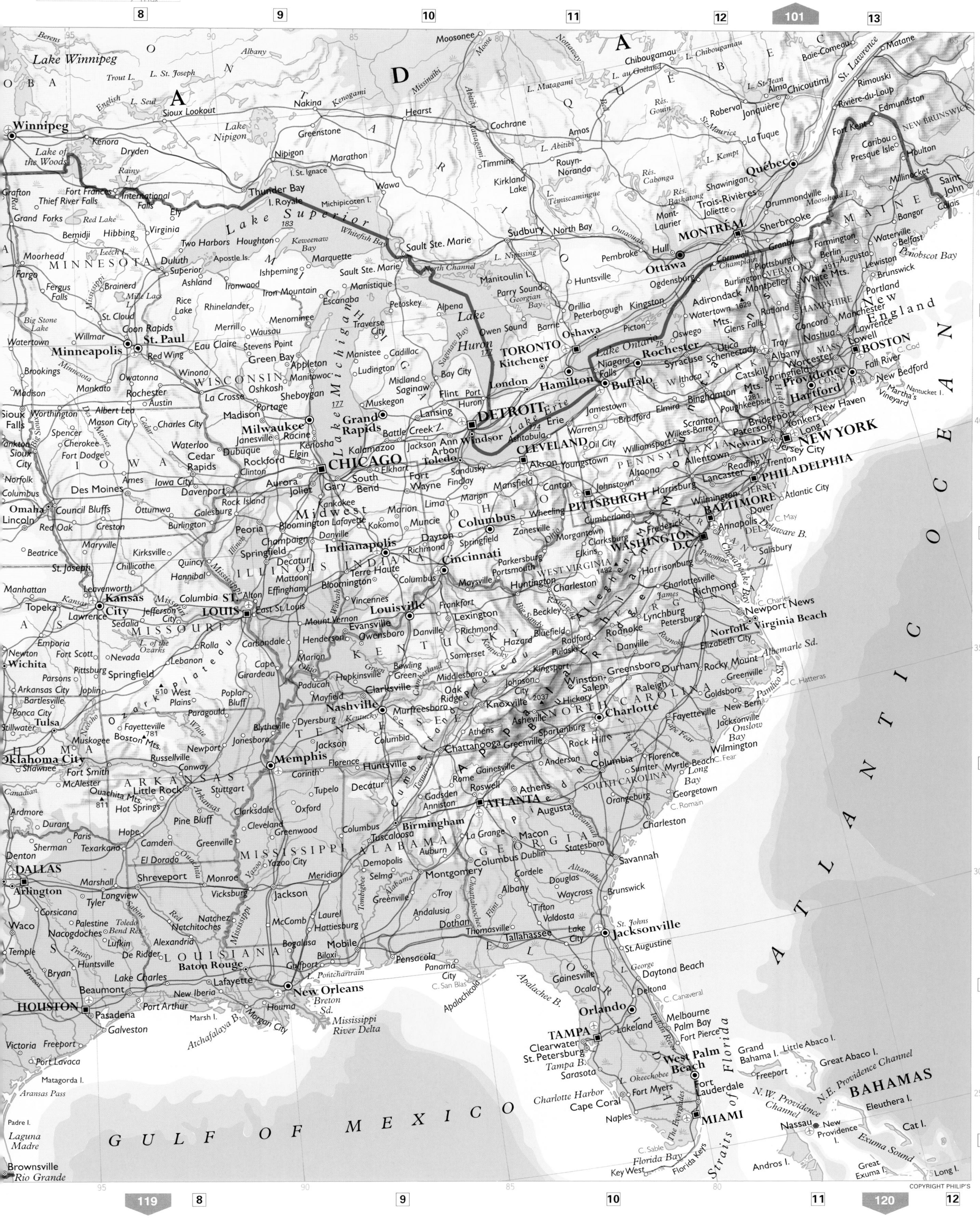

1:5 000 000

50 0 50 100 150 200 km
50 0 50 100 150 miles

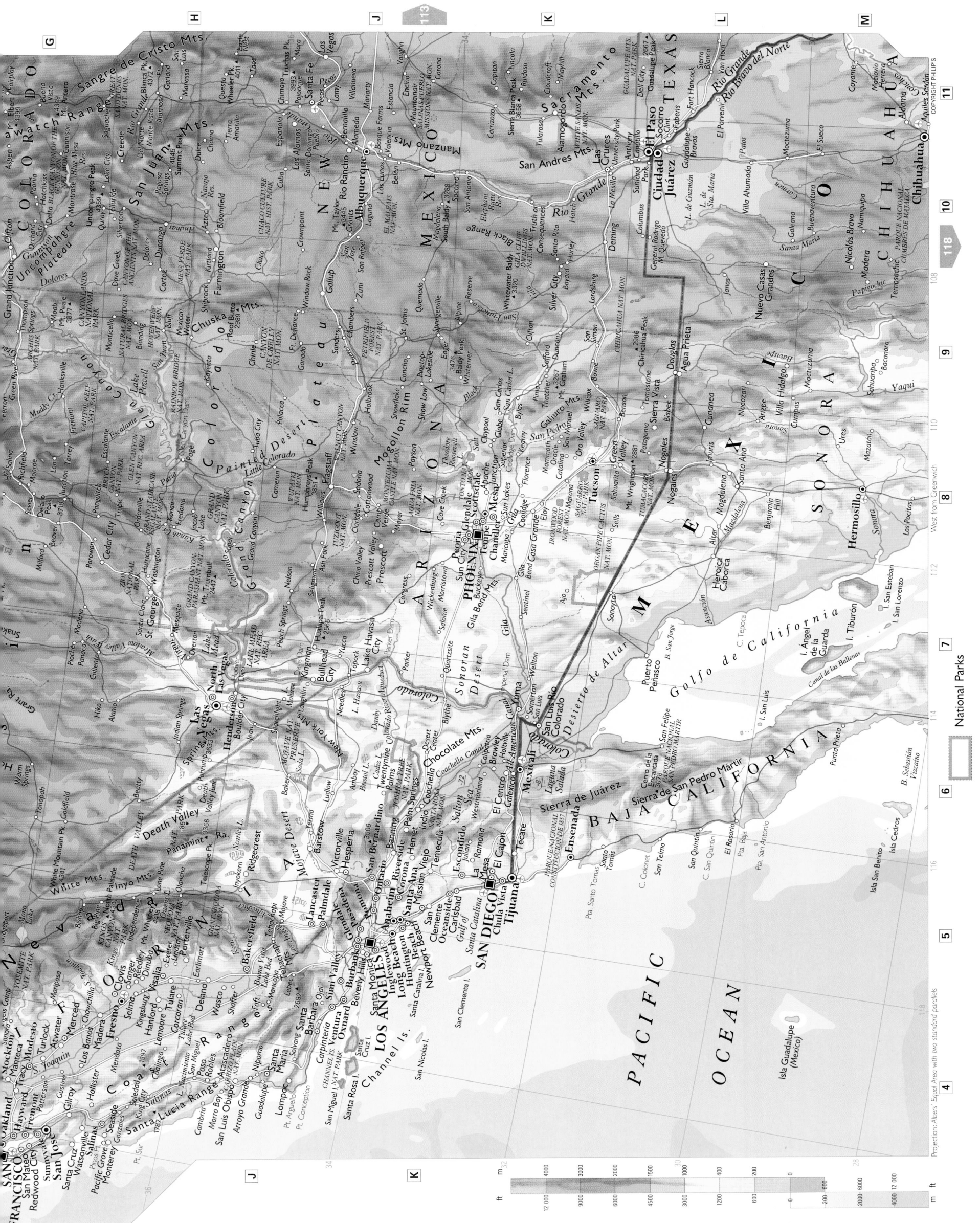

1:2 100 000

WESTERN WASHINGTON REGION
on same scale

PACIFIC OCEAN

National Parks

Projection: Bonne

West from Greenwich

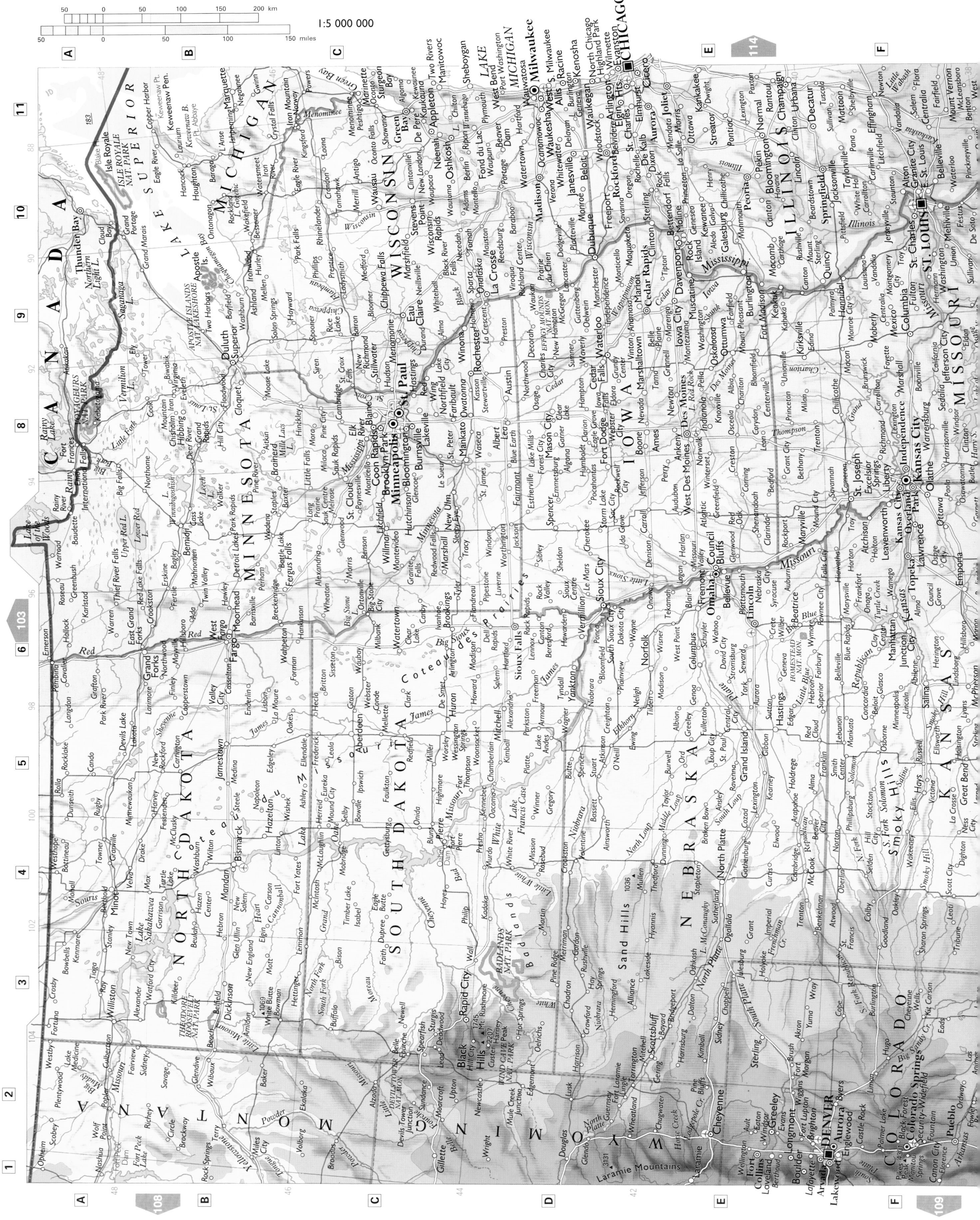

50 0 50 100 150 200 km
50 0 50 100 150 miles

1:5 000 000

CANADA

LAKE SUPERIOR

MICHIGAN

WISCONSIN

MINNESOTA

NORTH DAKOTA

SOUTH DAKOTA

NEBRASKA

KANSAS

IOWA

MISSOURI

ILLINOIS

WYOMING

COLORADO

LAKE MICHIGAN

CHICAGO
Milwaukee
Madison
Duluth
St. Paul
Minneapolis
Fargo
Bismarck
Rapid City
Sioux Falls
Sioux City
Omaha
Lincoln
Council Bluffs
Des Moines
Cedar Rapids
Davenport
Dubuque
Rockford
Peoria
Springfield
St. Louis
Kansas City
St. Joseph
Topeka
Denver
Colorado Springs
Pueblo
Cheyenne

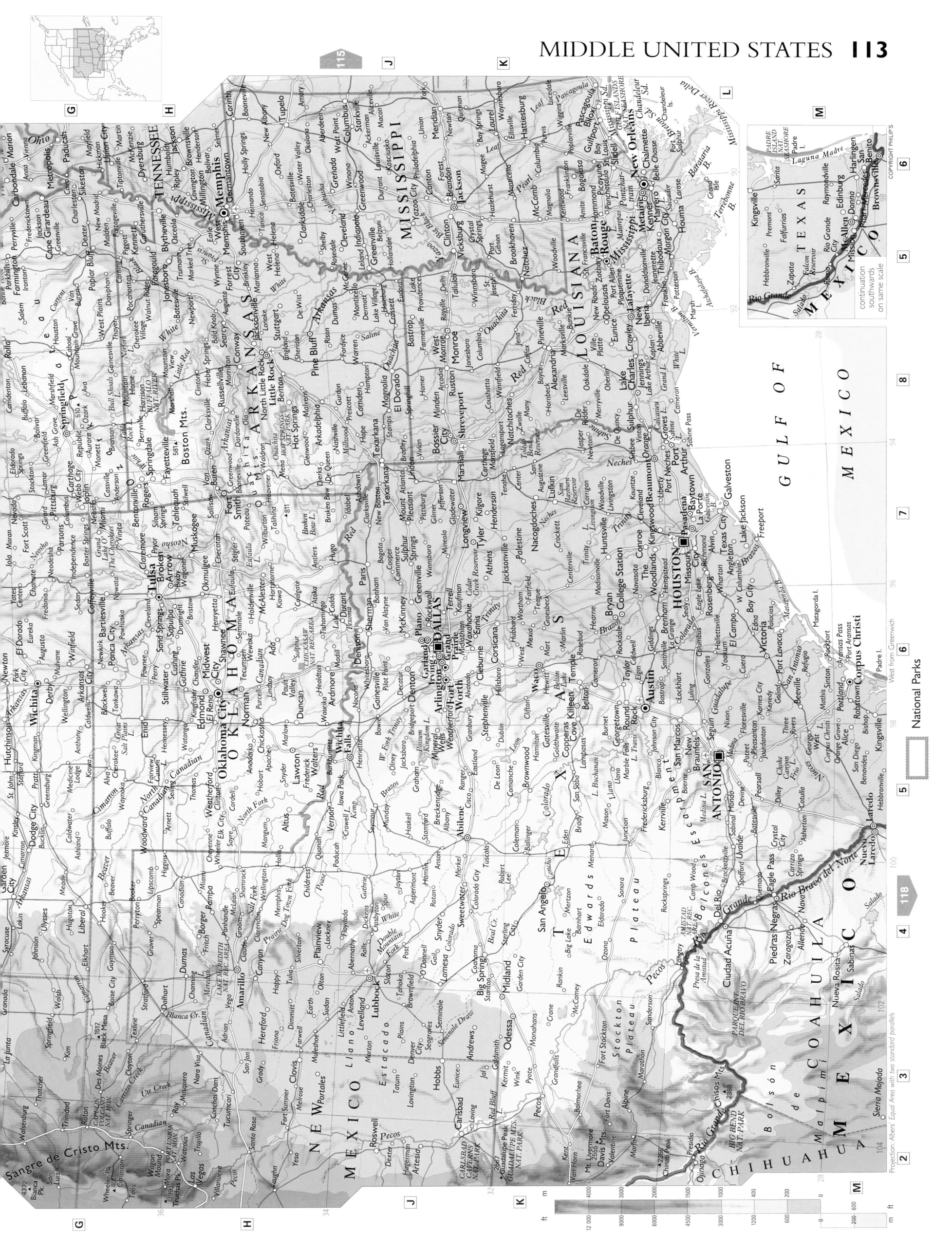

National Parks

1:5 000 000

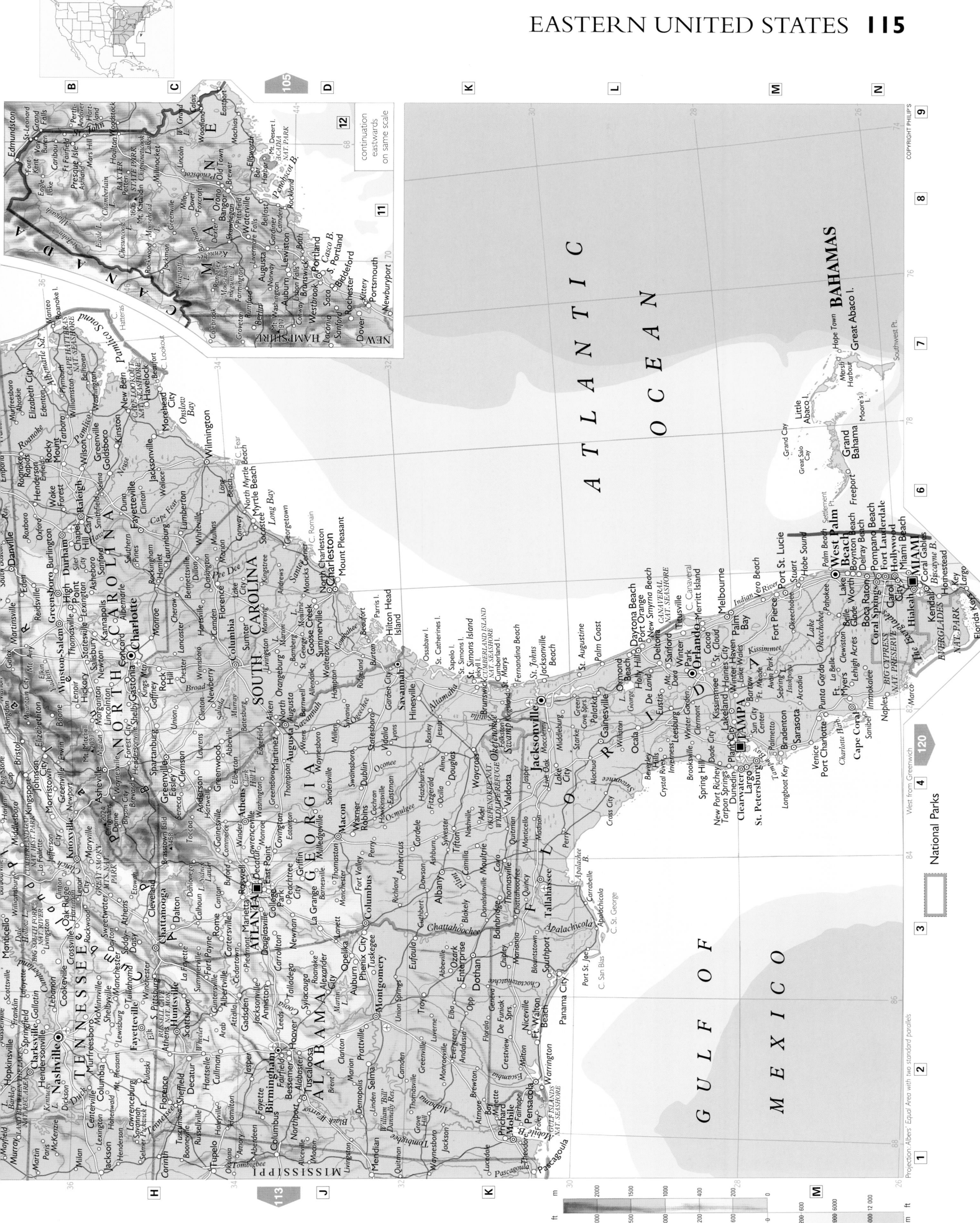

ATLANTIC OCEAN

GULF OF MEXICO

BAHAMAS

continuation eastwards on same scale

National Parks

Projection: Albers Equal Area with two standard parallels

West from Greenwich

COPYRIGHT PHILIP'S

1:2 100 000

National Parks

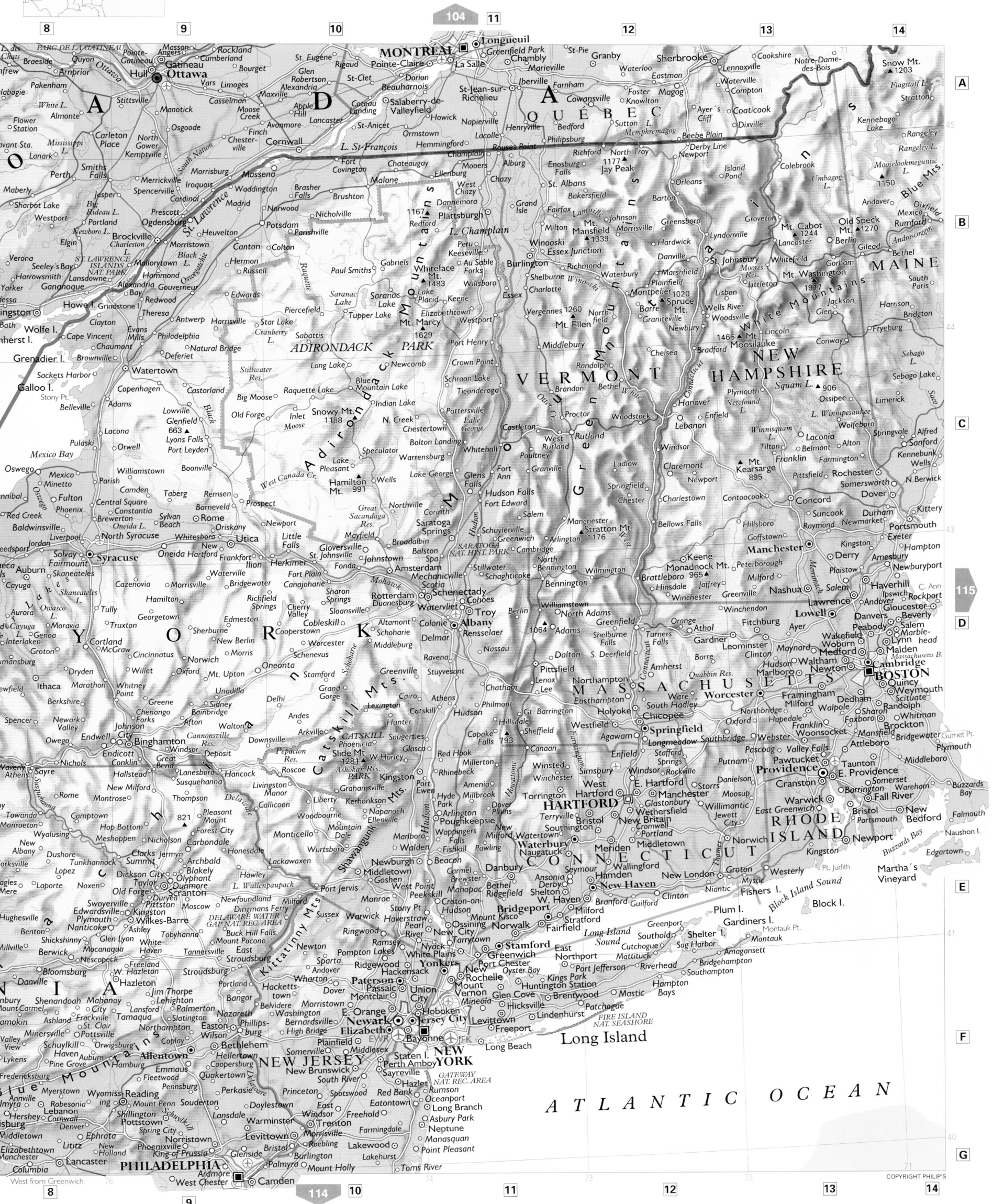

Projection: Bi-polar oblique Conical Orthomorphic

West from Greenwich

National Parks

State names in Central Mexico

1 DISTRITO FEDERAL   5 MÉXICO
2 AGUASCALIENTES   6 MORELOS
3 GUANAJUATO   7 QUERÉTARO
4 HIDALGO   8 TLAXCALA

5   6   7   8

A

B

C

D

E

GULF OF MEXICO

Golfo de Campeche

UNITED STATES

TEXAS

ARKANSAS

LOUISIANA

MISSISSIPPI

ALABAMA

GEORGIA

FLORIDA

Wichita Falls
Denison
Sherman
Paris
Camden
Greenville
Tuscaloosa
Opelika
Columbus
McRae

Denton
Greenville
Texarkana
El Dorado
Meridian
Selma
Phenix City
Montgomery
Americus
Cordele

FORT WORTH
DALLAS
Marshall
Monroe
Vicksburg
Jackson
Troy
Albany
Tifton
Waycross

Ranger
Abilene
Cleburne
Longview
Tyler
Shreveport
Tallulah
Natchez
McComb
Bogalusa
Dothan
Flomaton
Chattahoochee
Valdosta

Brownwood
Hillsboro
Corsicana
Palestine
Nacogdoches
Alexandria
Baton Rouge
Hattiesburg
Laurel
MOBILE
Pensacola
Panama City
Tallahassee
Lake City

Waco
Jewett
Lufkin
Sam Rayburn Reservoir
Hammond
Gulfport
Biloxi
Mobile Bay
C. San Blas
Apalachee Bay

Temple
Bryan
Huntsville
College Station
Lake Charles
Lafayette
NEW ORLEANS
Breton Sd.
Suwannee

Austin
Navasota
Beaumont
Port Arthur
L. Pontchartrain
Terrebonne Bay
Mississippi River Delta

SAN ANTONIO
Rosenberg
HOUSTON
Galveston
Atchafalaya Bay
Clearwater

Dilley
Victoria

Alice
Corpus Christi
PADRE ISLAND NAT. SEASHORE

Laredo
Kingsville
Nuevo Laredo
Zapata

Nuevo Guerrero
Camargo
McAllen
Harlingen
Brownsville
Laguna Madre

Reynosa
Matamoros
Valle Hermoso
Santa Teresa
Laguna Madre

Montemorelos
Mendez
San Fernando

Linares
Villagrán
Santander Jiménez
La Pesca
Soto la Marina
Pta. Jerez

Ciudad Victoria
Aldama

Ciudad Mante
Altamira
Ciudad Madero
Tampico
L. de Tamiahua
C. Rojo

Cárdenas Valles
Pánuco
Ozuluama
Magozal
Tantoyuca

Tempoal
Tamazunchale
Chicontepec
Tuxpan

Zimapán
Zacualtipán
Poza Rica
Papantla
Nautla
Misantla

San Juan del Río
Huichapan
Pachuca
Huauchinango
Tulancingo
Teziutlán

Tula
El Oro
Zumpango
TEOTIHUACAN
Xalapa
ZEMPOALA

Toluca
MEXICO
Apizaco
Veracruz

PUEBLA
Pico de Orizaba
Alvarado
Tlacotalpan

Cuernavaca
Orizaba
Córdoba
San Andrés Tuxtla
Frontera

Taxco
Tehuacán
Cosamaloapan
Paraíso
Comalcalco

Iguala
Chilapa
Acatlán
Tierra Blanca
Tres Valles
Acayucan
Coatzacoalcos
Minatitlán
Cárdenas
Villahermosa

Chilpancingo
Huajuapan
Asunción Nochixtlán
San Juan Bautista Valle Nacional
TABASCO
Macuspana

Tlaxiaco
Oaxaca
Ixtepec
Juchitán
Istmo de Tehuantepec

Acapulco
Ometepec
Ejutla
Tehuantepec
Arriaga
Tonalá

Pinotepa Nacional
Jamiltepec
Pochutla
Salina Cruz
CHIAPAS
Tapachula

Golfo de Tehuantepec

Dzilam de Bravo
Río Lagartos
El Cuyo
Isla Mujeres
C. Catoche
Cancún

Progreso
Motul
Temax
Tizimín
Puerto Morelos

Mérida
YUCATÁN
Valladolid
COBA
Cozumel
Isla Cozumel

Maxcanú
Ticul
Peto
TULUM

Tenabo
Tekax
UXMAL
Vigía Chico
B. de la Ascensión
SIAN KA'AN
B. del Espíritu Santo

Campeche
Hopelchén
Felipe Carrillo Puerto
QUINTANA ROO
Banco Chinchorro

Champotón
Chenkán
Bacalar
Chetumal
B. de Chetumal

Ciudad del Carmen
L. de Términos
Escárcega
Corozal
Ambergris Cay

PANTANOS DE CENTLA
CAMPECHE
CALAKMUL
Orange Walk
San Pedro

Palizada
Balancán
Tenosique
BELIZE CITY
Belmopan

PALENQUE
BELIZE

GUATEMALA

HONDURAS

Tropic of Cancer

CUBA
Canal de Yucatán

COPYRIGHT PHILIP'S

AMAS

ATLANTIC OCEAN

PUERTO RICO
1:2 500 000
PUERTO RICO (U.S.A.)

ATLANTIC OCEAN

Pta. Agujereada
Isabela
Aguadilla
Arecibo
Barceloneta
Manati
Vega Baja
Bayamón
SAN JUAN
SJU
Rio Grande
Carolina
Dewey
Mayagüez
San Sebastian
Adjuntas
Utuado
Cordillera Central
Cerro de Punta 1338
Caguas
Sierra de Luquillo
Fajardo
Pta. Puerca
Culebra
Vieques
Esperanza
San German
Uroyan Mts.
Yauco
Cayey
Coamo
Humacao
Yabucoa
Pta. Aguila
Guanica
Ponce
Guayama
I. Caja de Muertos

VIRGIN ISLANDS
1:1 700 000
Ruffing Pt.
The Settlement
East Pt.
Anegada
Virgin Islands (U.K.)
Jost Van Dyke I.
Hans Lollik I.
Great Camanoe
Guana I.
Beef
Virgin Gorda
Spanish Town
Tortola 521
Road Town
Charlotte Amalie
Cruz Bay
St. Thomas I.
St. John I.
VIRGIN IS.
Peter I.

ST. LUCIA
1:840 000
Cap Point
Pte. Hardy
Gros Islet
Esperance Bay
Castries
Marquis
Babonneau
L'Anse la Raye
Canaries
Millet
Dennery
Soufrière
Mt. Gimie 950
Trou Gras Pt.
Soufrière Bay
Petit Piton 750
Micoud
Gros Piton Pt.
Gros Piton 796
Vierge Pt.
Choiseul
Laborie
Vieux Fort
C. Moule à Chique
ST. LUCIA

BARBADOS
1:840 000
ATLANTIC OCEAN
Crabhill
North Point
Fustic
Spring Hall
Boscobelle
Portland
245
Bellplaine
Speightstown
Bathsheba
BARBADOS
Westmoreland
Alleynes Bay
Mt. Hillaby 340
Hillcrest
Martin's Bay
Holetown
Jackson
Bridgefield
Massiah Street
Black Rock
Ellerton
Six Cross Roads
Ragged Pt.
Bridgetown
Ivy
Edey
The Crane
Carlisle Bay
Oistins
St. Martins
Worthing
Oistins Bay
BGI
Chancery Lane
South Point

Arthur's Town
The Bight
Cat I.
San Salvador I.
Conception I.
Rum Cay
Long I.
Tropic of Cancer
Sandy Cay
Clarence Town
Samana Cay
Crooked I. Passage
Crooked I.
Plana Cays
Albert Town
Snug Corner
Mayaguana I.
Cay Verde
Acklins I.
Mira por vos Cay
Caicos Passage
Turks & Caicos (U.K.)
Cay Santa Domingo
Hogsty Reef
Little Inagua I.
Caicos Is.
Cockburn Town
Turks Is.
Lake Rose
Great Inagua I.
INAGUA
Matthew Town
Banes
Antilla
Moa
Mayari
Baracoa
Pta. de Maisi
Î. de la Tortue
Monte Cristi
LA ISABELA
Santiago de los Caballeros
Milwaukee Deep 9200
Puerto Rico Trench
Guantanamo
Maisi
Cap-Haïtien
Puerto Plata
San Francisco de Macorís
Nagua
Samana
GUANTANAMO BAY (U.S.A)
Paso de los Vientos (Windward Passage)
Jean Rabel
Port-de-Paix
Cord. La Vega
Sabana de la Mar
Cap-à-Foux
G. de la Gonâve
Gonaïves
3175
La Vega
Sánchez
Hinche
Pico Duarte
Hato Mayor
C. Engaño
Jérémie
Î. de la Gonâve
St-Marc
ARMANDO BERMUDEZ
HAITISES
Bayamón
SAN JUAN
Dame Marie
PORT-AU-PRINCE
HAITI
DOMINICAN REP.
San Pedro de Macorís
Higüey
Aguadilla
Arecibo
Carolina
Fajardo
Navassa I. (U.S.A)
Massif de la Hotte
Petit Goâve
2280
L. Enriquillo
San Juan
SIERRA DE NEIBA
Bani
SANTO DOMINGO
La Romana
Mayagüez
Ponce
1338
Caguas
Road Town
Anegada
Virgin Gorda
Virgin Is.
Sombrero (U.K.)
Les Cayes
Aquin
Î. à Vache
Jacmel
SIERRA DE BAORUCO
Agua de Horcón
San Cristóbal
B. de Yuma
ESTE
Guayama
St. Thomas
Charlotte Amalie
Virgin Is. (U.S.A.)
Anguilla (U.K.)
St.-Martin
St.-Barthélemy (Fr.)
Pointe-à-Gravois
Barahona
Compostela
Pedernales
Isla Mona (U.S.A.)
PUERTO RICO (U.S.A.)
Frederiksted
St. Croix (U.S.A.)
Christiansted
St. Eustatius (Neth.)
St. Maarten (Neth.)
Saba (Neth.)
Barbuda
I. Beata
C. Beata
Hispaniola
St. Kitts & Nevis
Basseterre
Redonda
Nevis
ANTIGUA & BARBUDA
St. John's
Antigua
Montserrat (U.K.)
Antilles
Guadeloupe Passage
Ste.-Rose
Moule
La Désirade
GUADELOUPE (Fr.)
1467
Pointe-à-Pitre
Marie-Galante (Fr.)
Basse-Terre
Grand-Bourg
I. de Aves (Venezuela)
I. des Saintes (Fr.)
Dominica Passage
Portsmouth
1447
MORNE TROIS PITONS
Roseau
DOMINICA
Martinique Passage
Mt. Pelée 1397
Ste.-Marie
Le François
Fort-de-France
Rivière-Pilote
MARTINIQUE (Fr.)
St. Lucia Channel
Castries
850
ST. LUCIA
Soufrière
St. Vincent Passage
Soufrière 1234
St. Vincent
Speightstown
Kingstown
Bridgetown
BARBADOS
Hillsborough
Grenadines
ST. VINCENT & THE GRENADINES
St. George's
GRENADA
I. Blanquilla (Ven.)
Is. Los Hermanos (Ven.)

CARIBBEAN SEA

Lesser Antilles

Leeward Islands

Windward Islands

COLOMBIA

Pta. Gallinas
Oranjestad
Aruba (Neth.)
Curaçao
NETH. ANTILLES
Bonaire
ARC. LOS ROQUES
I. Orchila (Ven.)
Pta. Espada
MACURIA
C. San Román
Pen. de Paraguaná
Willemstad
Is. Las Aves (Ven.)
Is. Los Roques (Ven.)
I. Los Testigos (Ven.)
Tobago
Scarborough
Santa Marta
Ríohacha
Uribia
Golfo de Venezuela
Punto Fijo
MEDANOS DE CORO
Puerto Cumarebo
NUEVA ESPARTA
I. de Margarita
Porlamar
La Asunción
Galera Point
BARRAN-QUILLA
Soledad
GUAJIRA
Punta Cardón
La Vela de Coro
CUEVA DE LA QUEBRADA DEL TORO
HENRI PITTIER
Maiquetía
La Guaira
CARACAS
VARGAS
Carúpano
Rio Caribe
Güiria
Port of Spain
Arima
Rio Claro
Trinidad
ATLÁNTICO
Fundación
Valledupar
San Rafael
Coro
La Concepción
Cabimas
FALCÓN
Mene de Mauroa
Tucacas
Puerto Cabello
Maracay
Los Teques
Ocumare del Tuy
Cumaná
Barcelona
SUCRE
Caripito
Maturín
TRINIDAD & TOBAGO
San Fernando
Serpent's Mouth
El Carmen
Ciénaga
SIERRA NEVADA DE STA. MARTA
5800
Ciudad Ojeda
Machiques
Lago de Maracaibo
Barquisimeto
LARA
Carora
YARACUY
San Felipe
Valencia
CARABOBO
MIRANDA
Villa de Cura
San Juan de los Morros
Higuerote
Puerto La Cruz
Anaco
Cantaura
El Tigre
MONAGAS
DELTA AMACURO
Tucupita
Calabozo
Valle de la Pascua
Santa María de Ipire
Pariaguan
MAGDALENA
ZULIA
Trujillo
TRUJILLO
Guanare
PORTUGUESA
GUÁRICO
El Baúl
ANZOÁTEGUI
Soledad
El Pao
Sierra Imataca
Ciudad Guayana
El Barco
CÉSAR
Mompós
Plato
Zambrano
Magangué
El Banco
Betijoque
Acarigua
Cojedes
San Carlos
NORTE DE SANTANDER
Valera
MÉRIDA
Barinas
BARINAS
Libertad
Guárico
Orinoco
Caicara
Ciudad Bolívar
Upata
El Callao
Tumeremo
Ocaña
Cúcuta
TÁCHIRA
San Cristóbal
Barinas
Ciudad Bolivia
San Fernando de Apure
APURE
Embalse de Guri
Guasipati
SANTANDER
COLOMBIA
VENEZUELA

West from Greenwich

National Parks

COPYRIGHT PHILIP'S

100 0 200 400 600 800 1000 1200 1400 km

1:29 400 000

100 0 200 400 600 800 1000 miles

1 **2** **3** **4** **5** **6** **7**

Projection: Lambert's Azimuthal Equal Area

COPYRIGHT PHILIP'S

1:29 400 000

100 0   200   400   600   800   1000 1200 1400 km

100 0   200   400   600   800   1000 miles

COPYRIGHT PHILIP'S

■ LIMA   Capital Cities

West from Greenwich

1:13 400 000

Projection: Sanson-Flamsteed's Sinusoidal

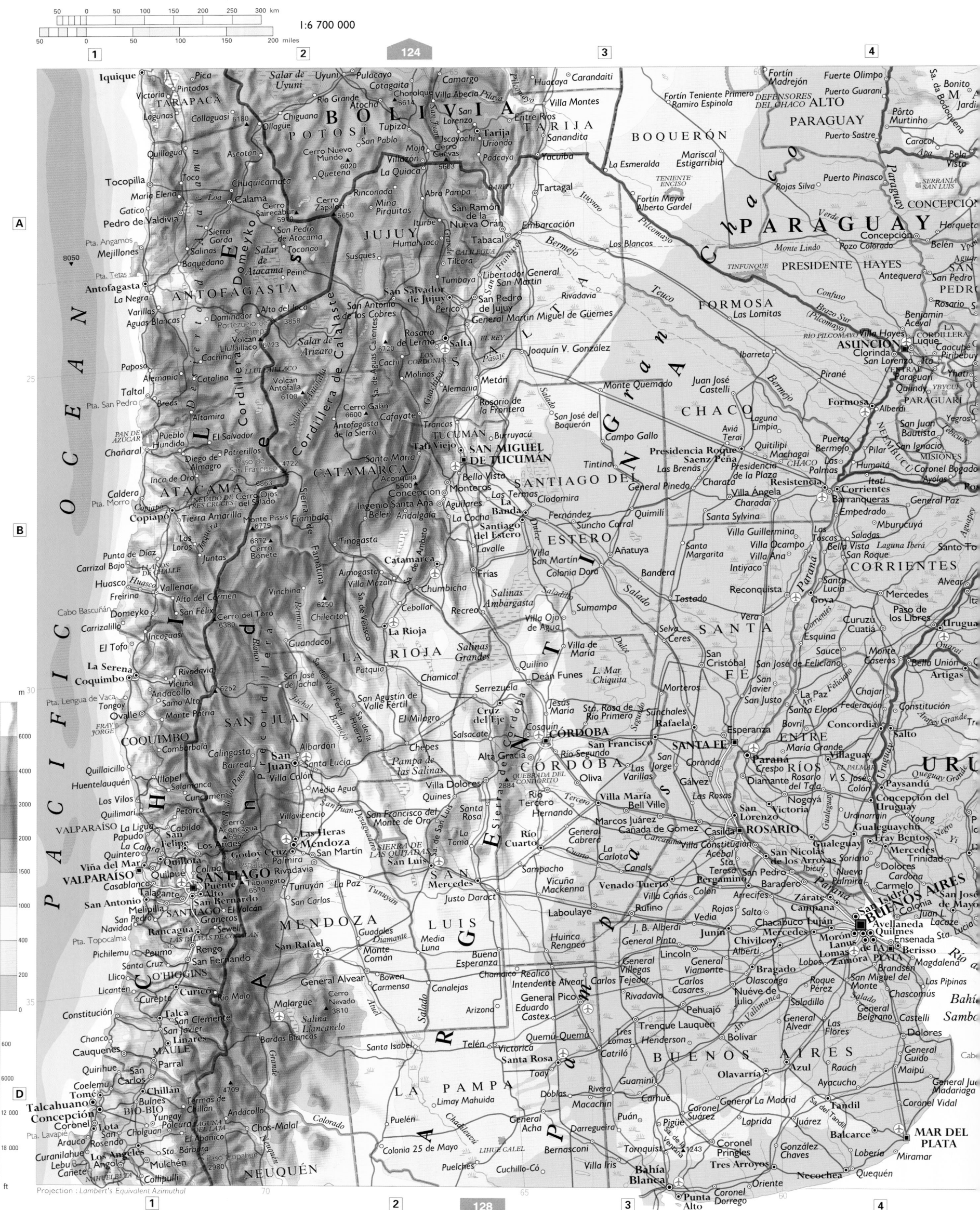

MATO GROSSO DO SUL

Sidrolândia
Nioaque
Guia Lopes da Laguna
Maracaju
Dourados
Nova Alvorada do Sul
Rio Brilhante
Ponta Porã
Pedro Juan Caballero
Amambai
Amambai
Naviraí
Mundo Novo
Salto del Guairá
Guaíra

Três Lagoas
Xavantina
Mirandópolis
Andradina
Araçatuba
Tietê
Mirassol
Olímpia
São José do Rio Prêto
Batatais
Passos
Oliveira
Conselheiro Lafaiete
Congonhas
Nova Lima
BELO HORIZONTE
Itabirito
Ouro Prêto
Ponte Nova
VITÓRIA
Itaquari
Vila Velha
Guarapari

Panorama
Adamantina
Tupã
Biriguí
Bebedouro
Catanduva
São Sebastião do Paraíso
Campo Belo
Três Pontas
Lavras
São João del Rei
Barbacena
Caxambu
Cataguases
Muriaé
Carangola
Alegre
Castelo
Cachoeiro de Itapemirim

Presidente Epitácio
Presidente Prudente
Paraguaçu Paulista
Santo Anastácio
Marília
Garça
Jaú
São Carlos
Rio Claro
Limeira
Piracicaba
Mococa
Casa Branca
Alfenas
Varginha
Pouso Alegre
Juiz de Fora
Leopoldina
Ubá
Barbacena
Itaperuna
Cambuci
Guarus
CAMPOS

São Paulo state label: SÃO PAULO

BRAZIL

PARANÁ

Londrina
Maringá
Apucarana
Ponta Grossa
CURITIBA

SANTA CATARINA

Blumenau
Florianópolis

RIO GRANDE DO SUL

Caxias do Sul
PORTO ALEGRE
Pelotas
Rio Grande

URUGUAY

MONTEVIDEO

Tropic of Capricorn

ATLANTIC

OCEAN

5304 ▼

☐ National Parks

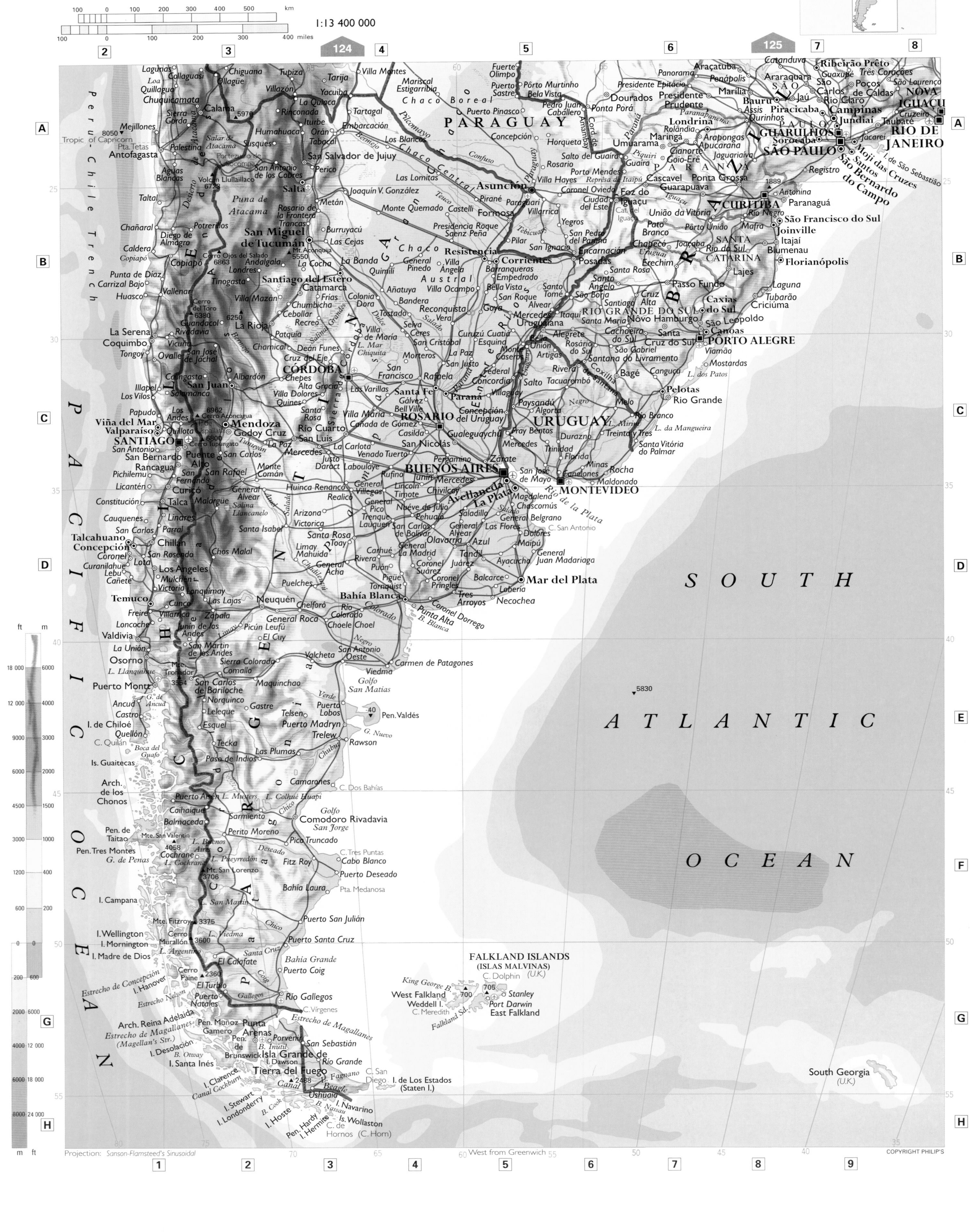

1:13 400 000

100   0   100   200   300   400   500   km
100   100   200   300   400 miles

124   125

PARAGUAY

PARANÁ

RIO GRANDE DO SUL

URUGUAY

BRASIL

SÃO PAULO

CÓRDOBA

ROSARIO

BUENOS AIRES

MONTEVIDEO

SANTIAGO

Mendoza

RIO DE JANEIRO

NOVA IGUAÇU

CURITIBA

PÔRTO ALEGRE

Mar del Plata

Bahía Blanca

Puna de Atacama

Desierto de Atacama

Tropic of Capricorn

Peru–Chile Trench

P A C I F I C   O C E A N

A N D E S

P A T A G O N I A

S O U T H

A T L A N T I C

O C E A N

FALKLAND ISLANDS (ISLAS MALVINAS) (U.K.)

West Falkland   East Falkland   Stanley   Port Darwin

South Georgia (U.K.)

Estrecho de Magallanes (Magellan's Str.)

Tierra del Fuego

Ushuaia

C. de Hornos (C. Horn)

ft   m
18 000   6000
12 000   4000
9000   3000
6000   2000
4500   1500
3000   1000
1200   400
600   200
0   0
200   600
2000   6000
4000   12 000
6000   18 000
8000   24 000
m   ft

INDEX TO WORLD MAPS

How to use the index

The index contains the names of all the principal places and features shown on the World Maps. Each name is followed by an additional entry in italics giving the country or region within which it is located. The alphabetical order of names composed of two or more words is governed primarily by the first word and then by the second. This is an example of the rule:

Mīr Kūh, *Iran*	**71 E8**	26 22N 58 55 E
Mīr Shahdād, *Iran*	**71 E8**	26 15N 58 29 E
Mira, *Italy*	**41 C9**	45 26N 12 8 E
Mira por vos Cay, *Bahamas*	**121 B5**	22 9N 74 30W
Miraj, *India*	**66 L9**	16 50N 74 45 E

Physical features composed of a proper name (Erie) and a description (Lake) are positioned alphabetically by the proper name. The description is positioned after the proper name and is usually abbreviated:

Erie, L., *N. Amer.*	**116 D4**	42 15N 81 0W

Where a description forms part of a settlement or administrative name however, it is always written in full and put in its true alphabetic position:

Mount Isa, *Australia*	**94 C2**	20 42 S 139 26 E

Names beginning with M' and Mc are indexed as if they were spelled Mac. Names beginning St. are alphabetized under Saint, but Sankt, Sint, Sant', Santa and San are all spelt in full and are alphabetized accordingly. If the same place name occurs two or more times in the index and all are in the same country, each is followed by the name of the administrative subdivision in which it is located.

The number in bold type which follows each name in the index refers to the number of the map page where that feature or place will be found. This is usually the largest scale at which the place or feature appears.

The letter and figure which are in bold type immediately after the page number give the grid square on the map page, within which the feature is situated. The letter represents the latitude and the figure the longitude. A lower case letter immediately after the page number refers to an inset map on that page.

In some cases the feature itself may fall within the specified square, while the name is outside. This is usually the case only with features which are larger than a grid square.

The geographical co-ordinates which follow the letter-figure references give the latitude and longitude of each place. The first co-ordinate indicates latitude – the distance north or south of the Equator. The second co-ordinate indicates longitude – the distance east or west of the Greenwich Meridian. Both latitude and longitude are measured in degrees and minutes (there are 60 minutes in a degree).

The latitude is followed by N(orth) or S(outh) and the longitude by E(ast) or W(est).

Rivers are indexed to their mouths or confluences, and carry the symbol � after their names. The following symbols are also used in the index: ■ country, ☑ overseas territory or dependency, ☐ first order administrative area, △ national park, ◠ other park (provincial park, nature reserve or game reserve), ✈ (LHR) principal airport (and location identifier).

How to pronounce place names

English-speaking people usually have no difficulty in reading and pronouncing correctly English place names. However, foreign place name pronunciations may present many problems. Such problems can be minimised by following some simple rules. However, these rules cannot be applied to all situations, and there will be many exceptions.

1. In general, stress each syllable equally, unless your experience suggests otherwise.
2. Pronounce the letter 'a' as a broad 'a' as in 'arm'.
3. Pronounce the letter 'e' as a short 'e' as in 'elm'.
4. Pronounce the letter 'i' as a cross between a short 'i' and long 'e', as the two 'i's in 'California'.
5. Pronounce the letter 'o' as an intermediate 'o' as in 'soft'.
6. Pronounce the letter 'u' as an intermediate 'u' as in 'sure'.
7. Pronounce consonants hard, except in the Romance-language areas where 'g's are likely to be pronounced softly like 'j' in 'jam'; 'j' itself may be pronounced as 'y'; and 'x's may be pronounced as 'h'.
8. For names in mainland China, pronounce 'q' like the 'ch' in 'chin', 'x' like the 'sh' in 'she', 'zh' like the 'j' in 'jam', and 'z' as if it were spelled 'dz'. In general pronounce 'a' as in 'father', 'e' as in 'but', 'i' as in 'keep', 'o' as in 'or', and 'u' as in 'rule'.

Moreover, English has no diacritical marks (accent and pronunciation signs), although some languages do. The following is a brief and general guide to the pronunciation of those most frequently used in the principal Western European languages.

		Pronunciation as in
French	é	day and shows that the e is to be pronounced; e.g. Orléans.
	è	mare
	î	used over any vowel and does not affect pronunciation; shows contraction of the name, usually omission of 's' following a vowel.
	ç	's' before 'a', 'o' and 'u'.
	ë, ï, ü	over 'e', 'i' and 'u' when they are used with another vowel and shows that each is to be pronounced.
German	ä	fate
	ö	fur
	ü	no English equivalent; like French 'tu'
Italian	à, é	over vowels and indicates stress.
Portuguese	ã, õ	vowels pronounced nasally.
	ç	boss
	á	shows stress
	ô	shows that a vowel has an 'i' or 'u' sound combined with it.
Spanish	ñ	canyon
	ü	pronounced as w and separately from adjoining vowels.
	á	usually indicates that this is a stressed vowel.

Abbreviations

A.C.T. – Australian Capital Territory
A.R. – Autonomous Region
Afghan. – Afghanistan
Afr. – Africa
Ala. – Alabama
Alta. – Alberta
Amer. – America(n)
Arch. – Archipelago
Ariz. – Arizona
Ark. – Arkansas
Atl. Oc. – Atlantic Ocean
B. – Baie, Bahía, Bay, Bucht, Bugt
B.C. – British Columbia
Bangla. – Bangladesh
Barr. – Barrage
Bos.-H. – Bosnia-Herzegovina
C. – Cabo, Cap, Cape, Coast
C.A.R. – Central African Republic
C. Prov. – Cape Province
Calif. – California
Cat. – Catarata
Cent. – Central
Chan. – Channel
Colo. – Colorado
Conn. – Connecticut
Cord. – Cordillera
Cr. – Creek
Czech. – Czech Republic
D.C. – District of Columbia
Del. – Delaware
Dem. – Democratic
Dep. – Dependency
Des. – Desert
Dét. – Détroit
Dist. – District
Dj. – Djebel
Domin. – Dominica
Dom. Rep. – Dominican Republic

E. – East
E. Salv. – El Salvador
Eq. Guin. – Equatorial Guinea
Est. – Estrecho
Falk. Is. – Falkland Is.
Fd. – Fjord
Fla. – Florida
Fr. – French
G. – Golfe, Golfo, Gulf, Guba, Gebel
Ga. – Georgia
Gt. – Great, Greater
Guinea-Biss. – Guinea-Bissau
H.K. – Hong Kong
H.P. – Himachal Pradesh
Hants. – Hampshire
Harb. – Harbor, Harbour
Hd. – Head
Hts. – Heights
I.(s). – Île, Ilha, Insel, Isla, Island, Isle
Ill. – Illinois
Ind. – Indiana
Ind. Oc. – Indian Ocean
Ivory C. – Ivory Coast
J. – Jabal, Jebel
Jaz. – Jazīrah
Junc. – Junction
K. – Kap, Kapp
Kans. – Kansas
Kep. – Kepulauan
Ky. – Kentucky
L. – Lac, Lacul, Lago, Lagoa, Lake, Limni, Loch, Lough
La. – Louisiana
Ld. – Land
Liech. – Liechtenstein
Lux. – Luxembourg
Mad. P. – Madhya Pradesh

Madag. – Madagascar
Man. – Manitoba
Mass. – Massachusetts
Md. – Maryland
Me. – Maine
Medit. S. – Mediterranean Sea
Mich. – Michigan
Minn. – Minnesota
Miss. – Mississippi
Mo. – Missouri
Mont. – Montana
Mozam. – Mozambique
Mt.(s) – Mont, Montaña, Mountain
Mte. – Monte
Mti. – Monti
N. – Nord, Norte, North, Northern, Nouveau
N.B. – New Brunswick
N.C. – North Carolina
N. Cal. – New Caledonia
N. Dak. – North Dakota
N.H. – New Hampshire
N.I. – North Island
N.J. – New Jersey
N. Mex. – New Mexico
N.S. – Nova Scotia
N.S.W. – New South Wales
N.W.T. – North West Territory
N.Y. – New York
N.Z. – New Zealand
Nac. – Nacional
Nat. – National
Nebr. – Nebraska
Neths. – Netherlands
Nev. – Nevada
Nfld. – Newfoundland
Nic. – Nicaragua
O. – Oued, Ouadi
Occ. – Occidentale

Okla. – Oklahoma
Ont. – Ontario
Or. – Orientale
Oreg. – Oregon
Os. – Ostrov
Oz. – Ozero
P. – Pass, Passo, Pasul, Pulau
P.E.I. – Prince Edward Island
Pa. – Pennsylvania
Pac. Oc. – Pacific Ocean
Papua N.G. – Papua New Guinea
Pass. – Passage
Peg. – Pegunungan
Pen. – Peninsula, Péninsule
Phil. – Philippines
Pk. – Peak
Plat. – Plateau
Prov. – Province, Provincial
Pt. – Point
Pta. – Ponta, Punta
Pte. – Pointe
Qué. – Québec
Queens. – Queensland
R. – Rio, River
R.I. – Rhode Island
Ra. – Range
Raj. – Rajasthan
Recr. – Recreational, Récréatif
Reg. – Region
Rep. – Republic
Res. – Reserve, Reservoir
Rhld-Pfz. – Rheinland-Pfalz
S. – South, Southern, Sur
Si. Arabia – Saudi Arabia
S.C. – South Carolina
S. Dak. – South Dakota
S.I. – South Island
S. Leone – Sierra Leone
Sa. – Serra, Sierra

Sask. – Saskatchewan
Scot. – Scotland
Sd. – Sound
Serbia & M. – Serbia & Montenegro
Sev. – Severnaya
Sib. – Siberia
Sprs. – Springs
St. – Saint
Sta. – Santa
Ste. – Sainte
Sto. – Santo
Str. – Strait, Stretto
Switz. – Switzerland
Tas. – Tasmania
Tenn. – Tennessee
Terr. – Territory, Territoire
Tex. – Texas
Tg. – Tanjung
Trin. & Tob. – Trinidad & Tobago
U.A.E. – United Arab Emirates
U.K. – United Kingdom
U.S.A. – United States of America
Ut. P. – Uttar Pradesh
Va. – Virginia
Vdkhr. – Vodokhranilishche
Vdskh. – Vodoskhovyshche
Vf. – Vírful
Vic. – Victoria
Vol. – Volcano
Vt. – Vermont
W. – Wadi, West
W. Va. – West Virginia
Wall. & F. Is. – Wallis and Futuna Is.
Wash. – Washington
Wis. – Wisconsin
Wlkp. – Wielkopolski
Wyo. – Wyoming
Yorks. – Yorkshire

A

A 'Âli an Nîl □, Sudan 81 F3 9 30N 33 0 E
A Baña, Spain 36 C2 42 58N 8 46W
A Cañiza, Spain 36 C2 42 13N 8 16W
A Coruña, Spain 36 B2 43 20N 8 25W
A Estrada, Spain 36 C2 42 43N 8 27W
A Fonsagrada, Spain 36 B3 43 8N 7 4W
A Guarda, Spain 36 D2 41 56N 8 52W
A Gudiña, Spain 36 C3 42 4N 7 8W
A Rúa, Spain 36 C3 42 24N 7 6W
Aachen, Germany 24 E2 50 45N 6 6 E
Aalborg = Ålborg, Denmark 11 G3 57 2N 9 54 E
Aalen, Germany 25 G6 48 51N 10 6 E
Aalst, Belgium 17 D4 50 56N 4 2 E
Aalten, Neths. 17 C6 51 56N 6 35 E
Aalter, Belgium 17 C3 51 5N 3 28 E
Äänekoski, Finland 9 E21 62 36N 25 44 E
Aarau, Switz. 25 H4 47 23N 8 4 E
Aarberg, Switz. 25 H3 47 2N 7 16 E
Aare ➙, Switz. 25 H4 47 33N 8 14 E
Aargau □, Switz. 25 H4 47 26N 8 10 E
Aarhus = Århus, Denmark 11 H4 56 8N 10 11 E
Aarschot, Belgium 17 D4 50 59N 4 49 E
Aba, China 58 A3 32 59N 101 42 E
Aba, Dem. Rep. of the Congo 86 B3 3 58N 30 17 E
Aba, Nigeria 83 D6 5 10N 7 19 E
Âbâ, Jazîrat, Sudan 81 E3 13 30N 32 31 E
Abadab, J., Sudan 80 D4 18 54N 35 56 E
Ābādān, Iran 71 D6 30 22N 48 20 E
Abade, Ethiopia 81 F4 9 22N 38 3 E
Ābādeh, Iran 71 D7 31 8N 52 40 E
Abadin, Spain 36 B3 43 21N 7 29W
Abadla, Algeria 78 B5 31 2N 2 45W
Abaetetuba, Brazil 125 D9 1 40 S 48 50W
Abagnar Qi, China 56 C9 43 52N 116 2 E
Abah, Tanjung, Indonesia 63 K18 8 46 S 115 38 E
Abai, Paraguay 127 B4 25 58 S 55 54W
Abak, Nigeria 83 E6 4 58N 7 50 E
Abakaliki, Nigeria 83 D6 6 22N 8 2 E
Abakan, Russia 53 D10 53 40N 91 10 E
Abala, Niger 83 C5 14 56N 3 22 E
Abalak, Niger 83 B6 15 22N 6 21 E
Abalemma, Niger 83 B6 16 12N 7 50 E
Abana, Turkey 72 B6 41 59N 34 1 E
Abancay, Peru 124 F4 13 35 S 72 55W
Abano Terme, Italy 41 C8 45 22N 11 46 E
Abarán, Spain 39 G3 38 12N 1 23W
Abariringa, Kiribati 96 H10 2 50 S 171 40W
Abarqū, Iran 71 D7 31 10N 53 20 E
Abashiri, Japan 54 B12 44 0N 144 15 E
Abashiri-Wan, Japan 54 C12 44 0N 144 30 E
Abaújszántó, Hungary 28 B6 48 16N 21 12 E
Abava ➙, Latvia 30 A8 57 6N 21 54 E
Ābay = Nîl el Azraq ➙, Sudan 81 D3 15 38N 32 31 E
Abay, Kazakhstan 52 E8 49 38N 72 53 E
Abaya, L., Ethiopia 81 F4 6 30N 37 50 E
Abayita-Shala Lakes △, Ethiopia 81 F4 7 40N 38 37 E
Abaza, Russia 52 D9 52 39N 90 6 E
Abbadia di Fiastra ⌓, Italy 41 E10 43 12N 13 24 E
Abbadia San Salvatore, Italy 41 F8 42 53N 11 41 E
'Abbāsābād, Iran 71 C8 33 34N 58 23 E
Abbay = Nîl el Azraq ➙, Sudan 81 D3 15 38N 32 31 E
Abbaye, Pt., U.S.A. 114 B1 46 58N 88 8W
Abbé, L., Ethiopia 81 E5 11 8N 41 47 E
Abbeville, France 19 B8 50 6N 1 49 E
Abbeville, Ala., U.S.A. 115 K3 31 34N 85 15W
Abbeville, La., U.S.A. 113 L8 29 58N 92 8W
Abbeville, S.C., U.S.A. 115 H4 34 11N 82 23W
Abbiategrasso, Italy 40 C5 45 24N 8 54 E
Abbot Ice Shelf, Antarctica 5 D16 73 0 S 92 0W
Abbottabad, Pakistan 68 B5 34 10N 73 15 E
Abd al Kūrī, Yemen 75 E5 12 5N 52 20 E
Ābdar, Iran 71 D7 30 16N 55 19 E
'Abdolābād, Iran 71 C8 34 12N 56 30 E
Abdulpur, Bangla. 69 G13 24 15N 88 59 E
Abéché, Chad 79 F10 13 50N 20 35 E
Abejar, Spain 38 D2 41 48N 2 47W
Abekr, Sudan 81 E2 12 45N 28 50 E
Abel Tasman △, N.Z. 91 J4 40 59 S 173 3 E
Abengourou, Ivory C. 82 D4 6 42N 3 27W
Abenójar, Spain 37 G6 38 53N 4 21W
Åbenrå, Denmark 11 J3 55 3N 9 25 E
Abensberg, Germany 25 G7 48 48N 11 51 E
Abeokuta, Nigeria 83 D5 7 3N 3 19 E
Aber, Uganda 86 B3 2 12N 32 25 E
Aberaeron, U.K. 15 E3 52 15N 4 15W
Aberayron = Aberaeron, U.K. 15 E3 52 15N 4 15W
Aberchirder, U.K. 13 D6 57 34N 2 37W
Abercorn, Australia 95 D5 25 12 S 151 5 E
Aberdare, U.K. 15 F4 51 43N 3 27W
Aberdare △, Kenya 86 C4 0 22 S 36 44 E
Aberdare Ra., Kenya 86 C4 0 15 S 36 50 E
Aberdeen, Australia 95 E5 32 9 S 150 56 E
Aberdeen, Canada 103 C7 52 20N 106 8W
Aberdeen, S. Africa 88 E3 32 28 S 24 2 E
Aberdeen, U.K. 13 D6 57 9N 2 5W
Aberdeen, Ala., U.S.A. 115 J1 33 49N 88 33W
Aberdeen, Idaho, U.S.A. 108 E7 42 57N 112 50W
Aberdeen, Md., U.S.A. 114 F7 39 31N 76 10W
Aberdeen, S. Dak., U.S.A. 112 C5 45 28N 98 29W
Aberdeen, Wash., U.S.A. 110 D3 46 59N 123 50W
Aberdeen, City of □, U.K. 13 D6 57 10N 2 10W
Aberdeenshire □, U.K. 13 D6 57 17N 2 36W
Aberdovey = Aberdyfi, U.K. 15 E3 52 33N 4 3W
Aberdyfi, U.K. 15 E3 52 33N 4 3W
Aberfeldy, U.K. 13 E5 56 37N 3 51W
Aberfoyle, U.K. 13 E4 56 11N 4 23W
Abergavenny, U.K. 15 F4 51 49N 3 1W
Abergele, U.K. 14 D4 53 17N 3 35W
Abernathy, U.S.A. 113 J4 33 50N 101 51W
Abert, L., U.S.A. 108 E3 42 38N 120 14W
Aberystwyth, U.K. 15 E3 52 25N 4 5W
Abhā, Si. Arabia 75 D3 18 0N 42 34 E
Abhar, Iran 71 B6 36 9N 49 13 E
Abhayapuri, India 69 F14 26 24N 90 38 E
Abia □, Nigeria 83 D6 5 30N 7 35 E
Abide, Turkey 47 C11 38 55N 29 20 E
Abidiya, Sudan 80 D3 18 18N 34 3 E
Abidjan, Ivory C. 82 D4 5 26N 3 58W
Abilene, Kans., U.S.A. 112 F6 38 55N 97 13W
Abilene, Tex., U.S.A. 113 J5 32 28N 99 43W
Abingdon, U.K. 15 F6 51 40N 1 17W
Abingdon, U.S.A. 115 G5 36 43N 81 59W
Abington Reef, Australia 94 B4 18 0 S 149 35 E
Abitau ➙, Canada 103 B7 59 53N 109 3W
Abitibi ➙, Canada 104 B3 51 3N 80 55W
Abitibi, L., Canada 104 C4 48 40N 79 40W
Abiy Adi, Ethiopia 81 E4 13 39N 39 3 E
Abkhaz Republic = Abkhazia □, Georgia 35 J5 43 12N 41 5 E
Abkhazia □, Georgia 35 J5 43 12N 41 5 E
Abminga, Australia 95 D1 26 8 S 134 51 E
Abnûb, Egypt 80 B3 27 18N 31 4 E
Åbo = Turku, Finland 9 F20 60 30N 22 19 E
Abocho, Nigeria 83 D6 7 35N 6 56 E
Abohar, India 68 D6 30 10N 74 10 E
Aboisso, Ivory C. 82 D4 5 30N 3 5W
Abomey, Benin 83 D5 7 10N 2 5 E
Abong-Mbang, Cameroon 84 D2 4 0N 13 8 E
Abonnema, Nigeria 83 E6 4 41N 6 49 E
Abony, Hungary 28 C5 47 12N 20 3 E
Aboso, Ghana 82 D4 5 23N 1 57W
Abou-Deïa, Chad 79 F9 11 20N 19 20 E
Aboyne, U.K. 13 D6 57 4N 2 47W
Abra Pampa, Argentina 126 A2 22 43 S 65 42W
Abraham L., Canada 102 C5 52 15N 116 35W
Abrantes, Portugal 37 F2 39 24N 8 7W
Abreojos, Pta., Mexico 118 B2 26 50N 113 40W
Abri, Esh Shamâliya, Sudan 80 C3 20 50N 30 27 E
Abri, Janub Kordofân, Sudan 81 E3 11 40N 30 21 E
Abrolhos, Banka, Brazil 122 E7 18 0 S 38 0W
Abrud, Romania 28 D8 46 19N 23 5 E
Abruzzo □, Italy 41 F10 42 15N 14 0 E
Absaroka Range, U.S.A. 108 D9 44 45N 109 50W
Abtenau, Austria 26 D6 47 33N 13 21 E
Abu, India 68 G5 24 41N 72 50 E
Abū al Abyad, U.A.E. 71 E7 24 11N 53 50 E
Abū al Khaṣīb, Iraq 71 D6 30 25N 48 0 E
Abū 'Alī, Si. Arabia 71 E6 27 20N 49 27 E
Abū 'Alī ➙, Lebanon 74 A4 34 25N 35 50 E
Abu Ballas, Egypt 80 C2 24 26N 27 36 E
Abu Deleiq, Sudan 81 D3 15 57N 33 48 E
Abu Dhabi = Abū Ẓāby, U.A.E. 71 E7 24 28N 54 22 E
Abu Dis, Sudan 80 D3 19 12N 33 38 E
Abu Dom, Sudan 81 D3 16 18N 32 25 E
Abū Du'ān, Syria 70 B3 36 25N 38 15 E
Abu el Gairi, W. ➙, Egypt 74 F2 29 35N 33 30 E
Abu Fatma, Ras, Sudan 80 C4 22 25N 36 25 E
Abu Gabra, Sudan 81 E2 11 2N 26 50 E
Abu Ga'da, W. ➙, Egypt 74 F1 29 15N 32 53 E
Abu Gelba, Sudan 81 E3 13 11N 31 52 E
Abu Gubeiha, Sudan 81 E3 11 30N 31 15 E
Abu Habl, Khawr ➙, Sudan 81 E3 12 37N 31 0 E
Abū Ḥadrīyah, Si. Arabia 71 E6 27 20N 48 58 E
Abu Hamed, Sudan 80 D3 19 32N 33 13 E
Abu Haraz, An Nîl el Azraq, Sudan 80 D3 18 1N 33 58 E
Abu Haraz, El Gezira, Sudan 81 E3 14 35N 33 30 E
Abu Haraz, Esh Shamâliya, Sudan 80 D3 19 8N 32 18 E
Abu Higar, Sudan 81 E3 12 50N 33 59 E
Abū Kamāl, Syria 70 C4 34 30N 41 0 E
Abu Kuleiwat, Sudan 81 E2 12 20N 26 0 E
Abū Madd, Ra's, Si. Arabia 70 E3 24 50N 37 7 E
Abu Matariq, Sudan 81 E2 10 59N 26 9 E
Abu Mendi, Ethiopia 81 E4 11 48N 35 42 E
Abū Mūsā, U.A.E. 71 E7 25 52N 55 3 E
Abū Qaṣr, Si. Arabia 70 D3 30 21N 38 34 E
Abu Qir, Egypt 80 H7 31 18N 30 0 E
Abu Qireiya, Egypt 80 C4 24 5N 35 28 E
Abu Qurqâs, Egypt 80 B3 28 1N 30 44 E
Abu Shagara, Ras, Sudan 80 C4 21 4N 37 19 E
Abu Shanab, Sudan 81 E2 13 58N 27 49 E
Abu Simbel, Egypt 80 C3 22 18N 31 40 E
Abū Şukhayr, Iraq 70 D5 31 54N 44 30 E
Abu Sultân, Egypt 80 H8 30 24N 32 21 E
Abu Tabari, Sudan 80 D2 17 32N 28 32 E
Abu Tig, Egypt 80 B3 27 4N 31 15 E
Abu Tiga, Sudan 81 E3 12 47N 34 12 E
Abu Tineitin, Sudan 81 E3 14 24N 31 1 E
Abu Uruq, Sudan 81 D3 15 52N 30 25 E
Abu Zabad, Sudan 81 E2 12 25N 29 10 E
Abū Ẓāby, U.A.E. 71 E7 24 28N 54 22 E
Abū Zeydābād, Iran 71 C6 33 54N 51 45 E
Abuja, Nigeria 83 D6 9 5N 7 32 E
Abukuma-Gawa ➙, Japan 54 E10 38 6N 140 52 E
Abukuma-Sammyaku, Japan 54 F10 37 30N 140 45 E
Abunã, Brazil 124 E5 9 40 S 65 20W
Abunã ➙, Brazil 124 E5 9 41 S 65 20W
Abune Yosef, Ethiopia 81 E4 12 5N 39 12 E
Aburo, Dem. Rep. of the Congo 86 B3 2 4N 30 53 E
Abut Hd., N.Z. 91 K3 43 7 S 170 15 E
Abuye Meda, Ethiopia 81 E4 10 30N 39 49 E
Abwong, Sudan 81 F3 9 2N 32 14 E
Åby, Sweden 11 F10 58 40N 16 10 E
Aby, Lagune, Ivory C. 82 D4 5 15N 3 14W
Abyad, Sudan 81 E2 13 47N 26 24 E
Åbybro, Denmark 11 G3 57 10N 9 44 E
Acadia △, U.S.A. 115 C11 44 20N 68 13W
Açailândia, Brazil 125 D9 4 57 S 47 0W
Acajutla, El Salv. 120 D2 13 36N 89 50W
Acámbaro, Mexico 118 D4 20 0N 100 40W
Acanthus, Greece 44 F7 40 27N 23 47 E
Acaponeta, Mexico 118 C3 22 30N 105 20W
Acapulco, Mexico 119 D5 16 51N 99 56W
Acarai, Serra, Brazil 124 C7 1 50N 57 50W
Acarigua, Venezuela 124 B5 9 33N 69 12W
Acatlán, Mexico 119 D5 18 10N 98 3W
Acayucan, Mexico 119 D6 17 59N 94 58W
Accéglio, Italy 40 D4 44 28N 7 0 E
Accomac, U.S.A. 114 G8 37 43N 75 40W
Accous, France 20 E3 43 0N 0 36W
Accra, Ghana 83 D4 5 35N 0 6W
Accrington, U.K. 14 D5 53 45N 2 22W
Acebal, Argentina 126 C3 33 20 S 60 50W
Aceh □, Indonesia 62 D1 4 15N 97 30 E
Acerra, Italy 43 B7 40 57N 14 22 E
Aceuchal, Spain 37 G4 38 39N 6 30W
Achalpur, India 66 J10 21 22N 77 32 E
Acheng, China 57 B14 45 30N 126 58 E
Achenkirch, Austria 26 D4 47 32N 11 45 E
Achensee, Austria 26 D4 47 26N 11 45 E
Acher, India 68 H5 23 10N 72 32 E
Achern, Germany 25 G4 48 37N 8 4 E
Achill Hd., Ireland 12 C1 53 58N 10 15W
Achill I., Ireland 12 C1 53 58N 10 1W
Achim, Germany 24 B5 53 1N 9 3 E
Achinsk, Russia 53 D10 56 20N 90 20 E
Acıgöl, Turkey 47 D11 37 50N 29 50 E
Acıpayam, Turkey 47 D11 37 26N 29 22 E
Acireale, Italy 43 E8 37 37N 15 10 E
Ackerman, U.S.A. 113 J10 33 19N 89 11W
Acklins I., Bahamas 121 B5 22 30N 74 0W
Acme, Canada 102 C6 51 33N 113 30W
Acme, U.S.A. 116 F5 40 8N 79 26W
Aconcagua, Cerro, Argentina 126 C2 32 39 S 70 0W
Aconquija, Mt., Argentina 126 B2 27 0 S 66 0W
Açores, Is. dos, Atl. Oc. 78 A1 38 0N 27 0W
Acornhoek, S. Africa 89 C5 24 37 S 31 2 E
Acquapendente, Italy 41 F8 42 44N 11 52 E
Acquasanta Terme, Italy 41 F10 42 46N 13 24 E
Acquasparta, Italy 41 F9 42 41N 12 33 E
Acquaviva delle Fonti, Italy 43 B9 40 54N 16 50 E
Ácqui Terme, Italy 40 D5 44 41N 8 28 E
Acraman, L., Australia 95 E2 32 2 S 135 23 E
Acre = 'Akko, Israel 74 C4 32 55N 35 4 E
Acre □, Brazil 124 E4 9 1 S 71 0W
Acre ➙, Brazil 124 E5 8 45 S 67 22W
Acri, Italy 43 C9 39 29N 16 23 E
Acs, Hungary 28 C3 47 42N 18 2 E
Actium, Greece 46 C2 38 57N 20 45 E
Acton, Canada 116 C4 43 38N 80 3W
Acuña, Mexico 118 B4 29 18N 100 55W
Ad Dammām, Si. Arabia 71 E6 26 20N 50 5 E
Ad Dāmūr, Lebanon 74 B4 33 44N 35 27 E
Ad Dawādimī, Si. Arabia 70 E5 24 35N 44 15 E
Ad Dawḥah, Qatar 71 E6 25 15N 51 35 E
Ad Dawr, Iraq 70 C4 34 27N 43 47 E
Ad Dir'īyah, Si. Arabia 70 E5 24 44N 46 35 E
Ad Dīwānīyah, Iraq 70 D5 32 0N 45 0 E
Ad Dujayl, Iraq 70 C5 33 51N 44 14 E
Ad Duwayd, Si. Arabia 70 D4 30 15N 42 17 E
Ada, Ghana 83 D5 5 44N 0 40 E
Ada, Serbia & M. 28 E5 45 49N 20 9 E
Ada, Minn., U.S.A. 112 B6 47 18N 96 31W
Ada, Okla., U.S.A. 113 H6 34 46N 96 41W
Adabiya, Egypt 74 F1 29 53N 32 28 E
Adair, C., Canada 101 A12 71 30N 71 34W
Adaja ➙, Spain 36 D6 41 32N 4 52W
Adak I., U.S.A. 100 C2 51 45N 176 45W
Adamaoua, Massif de l', Cameroon 83 D7 7 20N 12 20 E
Adamawa □, Nigeria 83 D7 9 20N 12 30 E
Adamawa Highlands = Adamaoua, Massif de l', Cameroon 83 D7 7 20N 12 20 E
Adamello ⌓, Italy 40 B7 46 4N 10 28 E
Adamello, Mte., Italy 40 B7 46 9N 10 30 E
Adami Tulu, Ethiopia 81 F4 7 53N 38 41 E
Adaminaby, Australia 95 F4 36 0 S 148 45 E
Adams, Mass., U.S.A. 117 D11 42 38N 73 7W
Adams, N.Y., U.S.A. 117 C8 43 49N 76 1W
Adams, Wis., U.S.A. 112 D10 43 57N 89 49W
Adams, Mt., U.S.A. 110 D5 46 12N 121 30W
Adam's Bridge, Sri Lanka 66 Q11 9 15N 79 40 E
Adams L., Canada 102 C5 51 10N 119 40W
Adam's Peak, Sri Lanka 66 R12 6 48N 80 30 E
Adamuz, Spain 37 G6 38 2N 4 32W
Adana, Turkey 70 B2 37 0N 35 16 E
Adanero, Spain 36 E6 40 56N 4 36W
Adapazarı = Sakarya, Turkey 72 B4 40 48N 30 25 E
Adar Gwagwa, J., Sudan 80 C4 22 15N 35 20 E
Adarama, Sudan 81 D3 17 10N 34 52 E
Adare, C., Antarctica 5 D11 71 0 S 171 0 E
Adarte, Eritrea 81 E5 13 18N 42 8 E
Adaut, Indonesia 63 F8 8 8 S 131 7 E
Adavale, Australia 95 D3 25 52 S 144 32 E
Adda ➙, Italy 40 C6 45 8N 9 53 E
Addis Ababa = Addis Abeba, Ethiopia 81 F4 9 2N 38 42 E
Addis Abeba, Ethiopia 81 F4 9 2N 38 42 E
Addis Alem, Ethiopia 81 F4 9 0N 38 17 E
Addis Zemen, Ethiopia 81 E4 12 7N 37 47 E
Addison, U.S.A. 116 D7 42 1N 77 14W
Addo, S. Africa 88 E4 33 32 S 25 45 E
Addo △, S. Africa 88 E4 33 30 S 25 50 E
Adebour, Niger 83 C7 13 17N 11 50 E
Ādeh, Iran 70 B5 37 42N 45 11 E
Adel, U.S.A. 115 K4 31 8N 83 25W
Adelaide, Australia 95 E2 34 52 S 138 30 E
Adelaide, Bahamas 120 A4 25 4N 77 31W
Adelaide, S. Africa 88 E4 32 42 S 26 20 E
Adelaide I., Antarctica 5 C17 67 15 S 68 30W
Adelaide Pen., Canada 100 B10 68 15N 97 30W
Adelaide River, Australia 92 B5 13 15 S 131 7 E
Adelanto, U.S.A. 111 L9 34 35N 117 22W
Adele I., Australia 92 C3 15 32 S 123 9 E
Adélie, Terre, Antarctica 5 C10 68 0 S 140 0 E
Adelie Land = Adélie, Terre, Antarctica 5 C10 68 0 S 140 0 E
Adelsk, Belarus 30 E10 53 24N 23 47 E
Ademuz, Spain 38 E3 40 5N 1 13W
Aden = Al 'Adan, Yemen 75 E4 12 45N 45 0 E
Aden, G. of, Asia 75 E4 12 30N 47 30 E
Adendorp, S. Africa 88 E3 32 15 S 24 30 E
Aderbissinat, Niger 83 B6 15 34N 7 54 E
Adh Dhayd, U.A.E. 71 E7 25 17N 55 53 E
Adhoi, India 68 H4 23 26N 70 32 E
Adi, Indonesia 63 E8 4 15 S 133 30 E
Adi Arkai, Ethiopia 81 E4 13 35N 37 57 E
Adi Daro, Ethiopia 81 E4 14 20N 38 14 E
Adi Keyih, Eritrea 81 E4 14 51N 39 22 E
Adi Kwala, Eritrea 81 E4 14 38N 38 48 E
Adi Ugri, Eritrea 81 E4 14 58N 38 48 E
Adieu, C., Australia 93 F5 32 0 S 132 10 E
Adieu Pt., Australia 92 C3 15 14 S 124 35 E
Adigala, Ethiopia 81 E5 10 24N 42 15 E
Adige ➙, Italy 41 C9 45 9N 12 20 E
Adigrat, Ethiopia 81 E4 14 20N 39 26 E
Adıgüzel Barajı, Turkey 47 C11 38 13N 29 14 E
Adilabad, India 66 K11 19 33N 78 20 E
Adilcevaz, Turkey 73 C10 38 47N 42 43 E
Adirondack ⌓, U.S.A. 117 C10 44 0N 74 20W
Adirondack Mts., U.S.A. 117 C10 44 0N 74 0W
Adis Abeba = Addis Abeba, Ethiopia 81 F4 9 2N 38 42 E
Adıyaman, Turkey 73 D8 37 45N 38 16 E
Adjohon, Benin 83 D5 6 41N 2 32 E
Adjud, Romania 29 D12 46 7N 27 10 E
Adjumani, Uganda 86 B3 3 20N 31 50 E
Adjuntas, Puerto Rico 121 d 18 10N 66 43W
Adlavik Is., Canada 105 B8 55 0N 58 40W
Adler, Russia 35 J4 43 28N 39 52 E
Admer, Algeria 83 A6 20 21N 5 27 E
Admiralty G., Australia 92 B4 14 20 S 125 55 E
Admiralty I., U.S.A. 102 B2 57 30N 134 30W
Admiralty Is., Papua N. G. 96 H6 2 0 S 147 0 E
Adnan Menderes, İzmir ✈ (ADB), Turkey 47 C9 38 23N 27 6 E
Ado, Nigeria 83 D5 6 36N 2 56 E
Ado-Ekiti, Nigeria 83 D6 7 38N 5 12 E
Adok, Sudan 81 F3 8 10N 30 20 E
Adola, Ethiopia 81 E5 11 14N 41 44 E
Adonara, Indonesia 63 F6 8 15 S 123 5 E
Adoni, India 66 M10 15 33N 77 18 E
Adony, Hungary 28 C3 47 6N 18 52 E
Adour ➙, France 20 E2 43 32N 1 32W
Adra, India 69 H12 23 30N 86 42 E
Adra, Spain 37 J7 36 43N 3 3W
Adrano, Italy 43 E7 37 40N 14 50 E
Adrar, Mauritania 78 D3 20 30N 7 30 E
Adrar des Iforas, Algeria 78 C5 27 51N 0 11 E
Ádria, Italy 41 C9 45 3N 12 3 E
Adrian, Mich., U.S.A. 114 E3 41 54N 84 2W
Adrian, Tex., U.S.A. 113 H3 35 16N 102 40W
Adriatic Sea, Medit. S. 6 G9 43 0N 16 0 E
Adua, Indonesia 63 E7 1 45 S 129 50 E
Adwa, Ethiopia 81 E4 14 15N 38 52 E
Adygea □, Russia 35 H5 45 0N 40 0 E
Adzhar Republic = Ajaria □, Georgia 35 K6 41 30N 42 0 E
Adzopé, Ivory C. 82 D4 6 7N 3 49W
Ægean Sea, Medit. S. 47 C7 38 30N 25 0 E
Aerhtai Shan, Mongolia 60 B4 46 40N 92 45 E
Ærø, Denmark 11 K4 54 52N 10 25 E
Ærøskøbing, Denmark 11 K4 54 53N 10 24 E
Aëtós, Greece 46 D3 37 15N 21 50 E
'Afak, Iraq 70 C5 32 4N 45 15 E
Afándou, Greece 49 C10 36 18N 28 12 E
Afar □, Ethiopia 81 E5 12 0N 41 0 E
Afghanistan ■, Asia 66 C4 33 0N 65 0 E
Afikpo, Nigeria 83 D6 5 53N 7 54 E
Aflou, Algeria 78 B6 34 7N 2 3 E
Afragóla, Italy 43 B7 40 55N 14 18 E
Afram ➙, Ghana 83 D4 7 0N 0 52W
Afrera, Ethiopia 81 E5 13 16N 41 5 E
Africa 76 E6 10 0N 20 0 E
'Afrīn, Syria 70 B3 36 32N 36 50 E
Afşin, Turkey 72 C7 38 14N 36 55 E
Afton, N.Y., U.S.A. 117 D9 42 14N 75 32W
Afton, Wyo., U.S.A. 108 E8 42 44N 110 56W
Afuá, Brazil 125 D8 0 15 S 50 20W
'Afula, Israel 74 C4 32 37N 35 17 E
Afyon, Turkey 47 C12 38 45N 30 33 E
Afyon □, Turkey 47 C12 38 25N 30 30 E
Afyonkarahisar = Afyon, Turkey 47 C12 38 45N 30 33 E
Aga, Egypt 80 H7 30 55N 31 10 E
Agadès = Agadez, Niger 83 B6 16 58N 7 59 E
Agadez, Niger 83 B6 16 58N 7 59 E
Agadir, Morocco 78 B4 30 28N 9 55W
Agaete, Canary Is. 48 F4 28 6N 15 43W
Agaie, Nigeria 83 D6 9 1N 6 18 E
Again, Sudan 81 F2 8 28N 29 55 E
Agalega Is., Mauritius 3 E12 11 0 S 57 0 E
Ağapınar, Turkey 47 B12 39 48N 30 47 E
Agar, India 68 H7 23 40N 76 2 E
Agaro, Ethiopia 81 F4 7 50N 36 38 E
Agartala, India 67 H17 23 50N 91 23 E
Agăş, Romania 29 D11 46 28N 26 15 E
Agassiz, Canada 102 D4 49 14N 121 46W
Agats, Indonesia 63 F9 5 33 S 138 0 E
Agawam, U.S.A. 117 D12 42 5N 72 37W
Agbélouvé, Togo 83 D5 6 35N 1 14 E
Agboville, Ivory C. 82 D4 5 55N 4 15W
Ağcabädi, Azerbaijan 35 K8 40 5N 47 27 E
Ağdam, Azerbaijan 35 L8 40 0N 46 58 E
Ağdaş, Azerbaijan 35 K8 40 44N 47 22 E
Agde, France 20 E7 43 19N 3 28 E
Agde, C. d', France 20 E7 43 16N 3 28 E
Agdzhabedi = Ağcabädi, Azerbaijan 35 K8 40 5N 47 27 E
Agen, France 20 D4 44 12N 0 38 E
Agerbæk, Denmark 11 J2 55 36N 8 48 E
Agersø, Denmark 11 J5 55 13N 11 12 E
Ageyevo, Russia 32 E9 54 10N 36 27 E
Aggteleki △, Hungary 28 B5 48 27N 20 36 E
Āgh Kand, Iran 71 B6 37 15N 48 4 E
Aghireşu, Romania 29 D8 46 53N 23 15 E
Aginskoye, Russia 53 D12 51 6N 114 32 E
Ağlasun, Turkey 47 D12 37 39N 30 31 E
Agly ➙, France 20 F7 42 46N 3 3 E
Agnew, Australia 93 E3 28 1 S 120 31 E
Agnibilékrou, Ivory C. 82 D4 7 10N 3 11W
Agnita, Romania 29 E9 45 59N 24 40 E
Agnone, Italy 41 G11 41 48N 14 22 E
Agofie, Ghana 83 D5 8 27N 0 15 E
Agogna ➙, Italy 40 C5 45 4N 8 54 E
Agogo, Sudan 81 F2 7 50N 28 45 E
Agön, Sweden 10 C11 61 34N 17 23 E
Agon Coutainville, France 18 C5 49 2N 1 34W
Ágordo, Italy 41 B9 46 18N 12 2 E
Agori, India 69 G10 24 33N 82 57 E
Agouna, Benin 83 D5 7 39N 1 47 E
Agout ➙, France 20 E5 43 47N 1 41 E
Agra, India 68 F7 27 17N 77 58 E
Agrakhanskiuy Poluostrov, Russia 35 J8 43 42N 47 36 E
Agramunt, Spain 38 D6 41 48N 1 6 E
Agreda, Spain 38 D3 41 51N 1 55W
Ağri, Turkey 73 C10 39 44N 43 3 E
Agri ➙, Italy 43 B9 40 13N 16 44 E
Ağrı Dağı, Turkey 70 B5 39 50N 44 15 E
Ağri Karakose = Ağri, Turkey 73 C10 39 44N 43 3 E
Agriá, Greece 46 B5 39 20N 23 1 E
Agrigento, Italy 42 E6 37 19N 13 34 E
Agrínion, Greece 46 C3 38 37N 21 27 E
Agrópoli, Italy 43 B7 40 21N 14 59 E
Ağstafa, Azerbaijan 35 K7 41 7N 45 27 E
Agua Caliente, Baja Calif., Mexico 111 N10 32 29N 116 59W
Agua Caliente, Sinaloa, Mexico 118 B3 26 30N 108 20W
Agua Caliente Springs, U.S.A. 111 N10 32 56N 116 19W
Água Clara, Brazil 125 H8 20 25 S 52 45W
Agua Fria ⌓, U.S.A. 109 J8 34 14N 112 0W
Agua Hechicero, Mexico 111 N10 32 26N 116 14W
Agua Prieta, Mexico 118 A3 31 20N 109 32W
Aguadilla, Puerto Rico 121 d 18 26N 67 10W
Aguadulce, Panama 120 E3 8 15N 80 32W
Aguanga, U.S.A. 111 M10 33 27N 116 51W
Aguanish, Canada 105 B7 50 14N 62 2W
Aguanus ➙, Canada 105 B7 50 13N 62 5W
Aguapey ➙, Argentina 126 B4 29 7 S 56 36W
Aguaray Guazú ➙, Paraguay 126 A4 24 47 S 57 19W
Aguarico ➙, Ecuador 124 D3 0 59 S 75 11W
Aguaro-Guariquito △, Venezuela 121 E6 8 20N 66 35W
Aguas ➙, Spain 38 D4 41 20N 0 30W
Aguas Blancas, Chile 126 A2 24 15 S 69 55W
Aguas Calientes, Sierra de, Argentina 126 B2 25 26 S 66 40W
Aguascalientes, Mexico 118 C4 21 53N 102 12W
Aguascalientes □, Mexico 118 C4 22 0N 102 20W
Agudo, Spain 37 G6 38 59N 4 52W
Águeda, Portugal 36 E2 40 34N 8 27W
Agueda ➙, Spain 36 D4 41 2N 6 56W
Aguelhok, Mali 83 B5 19 29N 0 52 E
Aguié, Niger 83 C6 13 31N 7 46 E
Aguila, Punta, Puerto Rico 121 d 17 57N 67 13W
Aguilafuente, Spain 36 D6 41 13N 4 7W
Aguilar, Spain 37 H6 37 31N 4 40W
Aguilar de Campóo, Spain 36 C6 42 47N 4 15W
Aguilares, Argentina 126 B2 27 26 S 65 35W
Aguilas, Spain 39 H3 37 23N 1 35W
Agüimes, Canary Is. 48 G4 27 58N 15 27W
Aguja, C. de la, Colombia 122 B3 11 18N 74 12W
Agujereada, Pta., Puerto Rico 121 d 18 30N 67 8W
Agulaa, Ethiopia 81 E4 13 40N 39 40 E
Agulhas, C., S. Africa 88 E3 34 52 S 20 0 E
Agulo, Canary Is. 48 F2 28 11N 17 12W
Agung, Gunung, Indonesia 63 J18 8 20 S 115 28 E
Agur, Uganda 86 B3 2 28N 32 55 E
Agusan ➙, Phil. 61 G6 9 0N 125 30 E
Ağva, Turkey 45 E13 41 8N 29 51 E
Agvali, Russia 35 J8 42 36N 46 8 E
Aha Mts., Botswana 88 B3 19 45 S 21 0 E
Ahaggar, Algeria 78 D7 23 0N 6 30 E
Ahamansu, Ghana 83 D5 7 38N 0 35 E
Ahar, Iran 70 B5 38 35N 47 0 E
Ahat, Turkey 47 C11 38 39N 29 47 E
Ahaus, Germany 24 C2 52 4N 7 0 E
Ahipara B., N.Z. 91 F4 35 5 S 173 5 E
Ahir Dağı, Turkey 47 C12 38 45N 30 10 E
Ahiri, India 66 K12 19 30N 80 0 E
Ahlat, Turkey 73 C10 38 45N 42 29 E
Ahlen, Germany 24 D3 51 45N 7 53 E
Ahmad Wal, Pakistan 68 E1 29 18N 65 58 E
Ahmadabad, India 68 H5 23 0N 72 40 E
Aḩmadābād, Khorāsān, Iran 71 C9 35 3N 60 50 E
Aḩmadābād, Khorāsān, Iran 71 C8 35 49N 59 42 E
Aḩmadī, Iran 71 E8 27 56N 56 42 E
Ahmadnagar, India 66 K9 19 7N 74 46 E
Ahmadpur, Pakistan 68 E4 29 12N 71 10 E
Ahmadpur Lamma, Pakistan 68 E4 28 19N 70 3 E
Ahmar, Ethiopia 81 F5 9 20N 41 15 E
Ahmedabad = Ahmadabad, India 68 H5 23 0N 72 40 E
Ahmednagar = Ahmadnagar, India 66 K9 19 7N 74 46 E
Ahmetbey, Turkey 45 E11 41 26N 27 34 E
Ahmetler, Turkey 47 C11 38 28N 29 5 E
Ahmetli, Turkey 47 C9 38 32N 27 57 E
Ahoada, Nigeria 83 D6 5 8N 6 36 E
Ahome, Mexico 118 B3 25 55N 109 11W
Ahoskie, U.S.A. 115 G7 36 17N 76 59W
Ahr ➙, Germany 24 E3 50 32N 7 16 E
Ahram, Iran 71 D6 28 52N 51 16 E
Ahrax Pt., Malta 49 D1 36 0N 14 22 E
Ahrensbök, Germany 24 A6 54 2N 10 35 E
Ahrensburg, Germany 24 B6 53 40N 10 13 E
Āhū, Iran 71 C6 34 33N 50 2 E
Ahuachapán, El Salv. 120 D2 13 54N 89 52W
Ahun, France 19 F9 46 4N 2 5 E
Åhus, Sweden 11 J8 55 56N 14 18 E
Ahvāz, Iran 71 D6 31 20N 48 40 E
Ahvenanmaa, Finland 9 F19 60 15N 20 0 E
Aḩwar, Yemen 75 E4 13 30N 46 40 E
Ahzar ➙, Mali 83 B5 15 30N 3 20 E
Ai ➙, India 69 F14 26 26N 90 44 E
Ai-Ais, Namibia 88 D2 27 54 S 17 59 E
Ai-Ais and Fish River Canyon △, Namibia 88 C2 24 45 S 17 15 E
Aichach, Germany 25 G7 48 27N 11 8 E
Aichi □, Japan 55 G8 35 0N 137 15 E
Aigle, Switz. 25 J2 46 18N 6 58 E
Aignay-le-Duc, France 19 E11 47 40N 4 43 E
Aigoual, Mt., France 20 D7 44 8N 3 35 E
Aigre, France 20 C4 45 54N 0 1 E
Aigua, Uruguay 127 C5 34 13 S 54 46W
Aigueperse, France 19 F10 46 3N 3 13 E
Aigues ➙, France 21 D8 44 7N 4 43 E
Aigues-Mortes, France 21 E8 43 35N 4 12 E
Aigues-Mortes, G. d', France 21 E8 43 31N 4 3 E
Aigües Tortes y Lago San Mauricio △, Spain 38 C4 42 38N 0 31W
Aiguilles, France 21 D10 44 47N 6 51 E
Aiguillon, France 20 D4 44 18N 0 21 E
Aigurande, France 19 F8 46 27N 1 49 E
Aihui, China 60 A7 50 10N 127 30 E
Aija, Peru 124 E3 9 50 S 77 45W
Aikawa, Japan 54 E9 38 2N 138 15 E
Aiken, U.S.A. 115 J5 33 34N 81 43W
Ailao Shan, China 58 F3 24 0N 101 20 E
Aileron, Australia 94 C1 22 39 S 133 20 E
Aillant-sur-Tholon, France 19 E10 47 52N 3 20 E
Aillik, Canada 105 A8 55 11N 59 18W
Ailsa Craig, U.K. 13 F3 55 15N 5 6W
Aim, Russia 53 D14 59 0N 133 55 E
Aimere, Indonesia 63 F6 8 45 S 121 3 E
Aimogasta, Argentina 126 B2 28 33 S 66 50W
Ain □, France 19 F12 46 5N 5 20 E
Ain ➙, France 21 C9 45 45N 5 11 E
Aïn Ben Tili, Mauritania 78 C4 25 59N 9 27W
Ain Dalla, Egypt 80 B2 27 20N 27 23 E
Ain el Mafki, Egypt 80 B2 27 30N 28 15 E
Ain Girba, Egypt 80 B2 29 20N 25 14 E
Ain Murr, Sudan 80 C2 21 50N 25 9 E
Ain Qeiqab, Egypt 80 B1 29 42N 24 55 E
Aïn Sefra, Algeria 78 B5 32 47N 0 37W
Ain Sheikh Murzûk, Egypt 80 B2 26 47N 27 45 E
Ain Sudr, Egypt 74 F2 29 50N 33 6 E
Ain Sukhna, Egypt 80 J8 29 32N 32 20 E
Ain Zeitûn, Egypt 80 B2 29 10N 25 48 E
Ainaži, Latvia 9 H21 57 50N 24 24 E
Aínos Óros, Greece 46 C2 38 9N 20 40 E
Ainsworth, U.S.A. 112 D5 42 33N 99 52W

Aiquile, Bolivia ...... 124 G5 18 10 S 65 10W
Aïr, Niger ...... 83 B6 18 30N 8 0 E
Air Force I., Canada .. 101 B12 67 58N 74 5W
Air Hitam, Malaysia .. 65 M4 1 55N 103 11 E
Airaines, France ...... 19 C5 49 58N 1 55 E
Airdrie, Canada 102 C6 51 18N 114 2W
Airdrie, U.K. 13 F5 55 52N 3 57W
Aire →, France ...... 19 C11 49 18N 4 49 E
Aire →, U.K. 14 D7 53 43N 0 55W
Aire, I. de l', France .. 48 B11 39 48N 4 16 E
Aire-sur-la-Lys, France 19 B9 50 37N 2 22 E
Aire-sur-l'Adour, France 20 E3 43 42N 0 15W
Airlie Beach, Australia 94 J6 20 16 S 148 43 E
Airvault, France 18 F6 46 50N 0 8W
Aisch →, Germany .... 25 F6 49 46N 10 51 E
Aisne □, France ...... 19 C10 49 42N 3 40 E
Aisne →, France ...... 19 C9 49 26N 2 50 E
Ait, India ...... 69 G8 25 54N 79 14 E
Aitana, Sierra de, Spain 39 G4 38 35N 0 24W
Aitkin, U.S.A. 112 B8 46 32N 93 42W
Aitolía kai Akarnanía □,
  Greece ...... 46 C3 38 45N 21 18 E
Aitolikón, Greece ...... 46 C3 38 26N 21 21 E
Aiud, Romania ...... 29 D8 46 19N 23 44 E
Aix-en-Provence, France 21 E9 43 32N 5 27 E
Aix-la-Chapelle =
  Aachen, Germany .. 24 E2 50 45N 6 6 E
Aix-les-Bains, France . 21 C9 45 41N 5 53 E
Aixe-sur-Vienne, France 20 C5 45 47N 1 9 E
Aíyina, Greece ...... 46 D5 37 45N 23 26 E
Aiyínion, Greece ...... 44 F6 40 28N 22 28 E
Aíyion, Greece ...... 46 C4 38 15N 22 5 E
Aizawl, India ...... 67 H18 23 40N 92 44 E
Aizenay, France 18 F5 46 44N 1 38W
Aizkraukle, Latvia .... 9 H21 56 36N 25 11 E
Aizpute, Latvia ...... 9 H19 56 43N 21 40 E
Aizuwakamatsu, Japan 54 F9 37 30N 139 56 E
Ajaccio, France ...... 21 G12 41 55N 8 40 E
Ajaccio, G. d', France . 21 G12 41 52N 8 40 E
Ajai △, Uganda ...... 86 B3 2 52N 31 16 E
Ajaigarh, India ...... 69 G9 24 52N 80 16 E
Ajalpan, Mexico 119 D5 18 22N 97 15W
Ajanta Ra., India ...... 66 J9 20 28N 75 50 E
Ajari Rep. = Ajaria □,
  Georgia ...... 35 K6 41 30N 42 0 E
Ajaria □, Georgia ...... 35 K6 41 30N 42 0 E
Ajax, Canada 116 C5 43 50N 79 1W
Ajdâbiyâ, Libya ...... 79 B10 30 54N 20 4 E
Ajdovščina, Slovenia .. 41 C10 45 54N 13 54 E
Ajibar, Ethiopia ...... 81 E4 10 35N 38 36 E
Ajka, Hungary ...... 28 C2 47 4N 17 31 E
'Ajlūn, Jordan ...... 74 C4 32 18N 35 47 E
'Ajlūn □, Jordan ...... 74 C4 32 18N 35 47 E
'Ajmān, U.A.E. ...... 71 E7 25 25N 55 30 E
Ajmer, India ...... 68 F6 26 28N 74 37 E
Ajnala, India ...... 68 D6 31 50N 74 48 E
Ajo, U.S.A. 109 K7 32 22N 112 52W
Ajo, C. de, Spain 36 B7 43 31N 3 35W
Ajok, Sudan ...... 81 F2 9 15N 28 28 E
Ajuy, Phil. ...... 61 F5 11 10N 123 1 E
Ak Dağ, Turkey ...... 47 E11 36 30N 29 32 E
Ak Dağları, Muğla,
  Turkey ...... 47 E11 36 30N 29 30 E
Ak Dağları, Sivas,
  Turkey ...... 72 C7 39 32N 36 12 E
Akaba, Togo ...... 83 D5 8 10N 1 2 E
Akabira, Japan ...... 54 C11 43 33N 142 5 E
Akagera △, Rwanda .. 86 C3 1 31 S 30 33 E
Akaki Beseka, Ethiopia 81 F4 8 55N 38 45 E
Akala, Sudan ...... 81 D4 15 39N 36 13 E
Akamas □, Cyprus .... 49 D11 35 3N 32 18 E
Akan △, Japan ...... 54 C12 43 20N 144 20 E
Akanthou, Cyprus .... 49 D12 35 22N 33 45 E
Akarca, Turkey ...... 47 C11 38 35N 29 35 E
Akaroa, N.Z. ...... 91 K4 43 49 S 172 59 E
Akasha, Sudan ...... 80 C3 21 10N 30 32 E
Akashi, Japan ...... 55 G7 34 45N 134 58 E
Akbarpur, Bihar, India 69 G10 24 39N 83 58 E
Akbarpur, Ut. P., India 69 F10 26 25N 82 32 E
Akçaabat, Turkey ...... 73 B8 41 1N 39 34 E
Akçadağ, Turkey ...... 72 C7 38 27N 37 43 E
Akçakale, Turkey ...... 73 D8 36 41N 38 56 E
Akçakoca, Turkey ...... 72 B4 41 5N 31 8 E
Akçaova, Turkey ...... 45 E13 41 3N 29 47 E
Akçay, Turkey ...... 47 E11 36 36N 29 4 E
Akçay →, Turkey ...... 47 D10 37 50N 28 15 E
Akdağ, Turkey ...... 47 C8 38 33N 30 0 E
Akdağmadeni, Turkey . 72 C6 39 39N 35 53 E
Akelamo, Indonesia ... 63 D7 1 35N 129 40 E
Åkers styckebruk,
  Sweden ...... 10 E11 59 15N 17 5 E
Åkersberga, Sweden ... 10 E12 59 29N 18 18 E
Aketi, Dem. Rep. of
  the Congo ...... 84 D4 2 38N 23 47 E
Akhaïa □, Greece ...... 46 C3 38 5N 21 45 E
Akhalkalaki, Georgia .. 35 K6 41 27N 43 25 E
Akhaltsikhe, Georgia .. 35 K6 41 40N 43 0 E
Akharnaí, Greece ...... 46 C5 38 5N 23 44 E
Akhelóös →, Greece .. 46 C3 38 19N 21 7 E
Akhisar, Turkey ...... 47 C9 38 56N 27 48 E
Akhladhókambos,
  Greece ...... 46 D4 37 31N 22 35 E
Akhmím, Egypt ...... 80 B3 26 31N 31 47 E
Akhnur, India ...... 69 C6 32 52N 74 45 E
Akhtopol, Bulgaria .... 45 D11 42 6N 27 56 E
Akhtuba →, Russia ... 35 G8 47 41N 46 55 E
Akhtubinsk, Russia .... 35 F8 48 13N 46 7 E
Akhty, Russia ...... 35 K8 41 30N 47 45 E
Akhtyrka = Okhtyrka,
  Ukraine ...... 33 G8 50 25N 35 0 E
Aki, Japan ...... 55 H6 33 30N 133 54 E
Akimiski I., Canada ... 104 B3 52 50N 81 30W
Akimovka, Ukraine .... 33 J8 46 44N 35 0 E
Åkirkeby, Denmark .... 11 J8 55 4N 14 55 E
Akita, Japan ...... 54 E10 39 45N 140 7 E
Akita □, Japan ...... 54 E10 39 40N 140 30 E
Akjoujt, Mauritania ... 82 B2 19 45N 14 15W
Akka, Mali 82 B4 15 24N 4 11W
Akkaya Tepesi, Turkey 47 D11 37 25N 29 34 E
Akkeshi, Japan ...... 54 C12 43 2N 144 51 E
'Akko, Israel ...... 74 C4 32 55N 35 4 E
Akköy, Turkey ...... 47 D9 37 29N 27 15 E
Aklampa, Benin ...... 83 D5 8 15N 2 10 E
Aklavik, Canada 100 B6 68 12N 135 0W
Aklera, India ...... 68 G7 24 26N 76 32 E
Akmené, Lithuania .... 9 H20 56 15N 22 45 E
Akmenrags, Latvia .... 30 B8 56 50N 21 0 E
Akmonte = Almonte,
  Spain 37 H4 37 13N 6 38W
Ako, Nigeria ...... 83 C7 10 19N 10 48 E
Akobo, Sudan ...... 81 F3 7 47N 33 1 E
Akobo →, Ethiopia .... 81 F3 7 48N 33 3 E
Akola, India ...... 66 J10 20 42N 77 2 E
Akonolinga, Cameroon 83 E7 3 50N 12 18 E
Akor, Mali 82 C3 14 59N 6 58W

Akordat, Eritrea ...... 81 D4 15 30N 37 40 E
Akosombo Dam, Ghana 83 D5 6 20N 0 5 E
Akot, Sudan ...... 81 F3 6 31N 30 9 E
Akoupé, Ivory C. 82 D4 6 23N 3 54W
Akpatok I., Canada 101 B13 60 25N 68 8W
Åkrahamn, Norway .... 9 G11 59 15N 5 10 E
Akranes, Iceland 8 D2 64 19N 22 5W
Akreïjit, Mauritania ... 82 B3 18 19N 9 11W
Akrítas Venétiko, Ákra,
  Greece ...... 46 E3 36 43N 21 54 E
Akron, Colo., U.S.A. .. 112 E3 40 10N 103 13W
Akron, Ohio, U.S.A. .. 116 E3 41 5N 81 31W
Akrotiri, Cyprus ...... 49 E11 34 36N 32 57 E
Akrotiri, Ákra, Greece 45 F9 40 26N 25 27 E
Akrotiri Bay, Cyprus .. 49 E12 34 35N 33 10 E
Aksai Chin, China ..... 69 B8 35 15N 79 55 E
Aksaray, Turkey ...... 70 B2 38 25N 34 2 E
Aksay, Kazakhstan .... 52 D6 51 11N 53 0 E
Akşehir, Turkey ...... 72 C4 38 18N 31 30 E
Akşehir Gölü, Turkey . 72 C4 38 30N 31 25 E
Akstafa = Ağstafa,
  Azerbaijan ...... 35 K7 41 7N 45 27 E
Aksu, China ...... 60 B3 41 5N 80 10 E
Aksu →, Turkey ...... 72 D4 36 52N 30 57 E
Aksum, Ethiopia ...... 81 E4 14 5N 38 40 E
Aktash, Russia ...... 34 C11 55 2N 52 3 E
Aktogay, Kazakhstan .. 52 E8 46 57N 79 40 E
Aktsyabrski, Belarus .. 33 F5 52 38N 28 53 E
Aktyubinsk = Aqtöbe,
  Kazakhstan ...... 52 D6 50 17N 57 10 E
Aku, Nigeria ...... 83 D6 6 40N 7 18 E
Akure, Nigeria ...... 83 D6 7 15N 5 5 E
Akureyri, Iceland 8 D4 65 40N 18 6W
Akuseki-Shima, Japan . 55 K4 29 27N 129 37 E
Akusha, Russia ...... 35 J8 42 18N 47 30 E
Akwa-Ibom □, Nigeria 83 E6 4 30N 7 30 E
Akyab = Sittwe, Burma 67 J18 20 18N 92 45 E
Akyazı, Turkey ...... 72 B4 40 40N 30 38 E
Al 'Adan, Yemen ...... 75 E4 12 45N 45 0 E
Al Aḥsā = Hasa □,
  Si. Arabia ...... 71 E6 25 50N 49 0 E
Al Ajfar, Si. Arabia ... 70 E4 27 26N 43 0 E
Al Amādīyah, Iraq .... 70 B4 37 5N 43 30 E
Al 'Amārah, Iraq ...... 70 D5 31 55N 47 15 E
Al 'Aqabah, Jordan ... 74 F4 29 31N 35 0 E
Al 'Aqabah □, Jordan . 74 F4 29 30N 35 0 E
Al Arak, Syria ...... 70 C3 34 38N 38 35 E
Al 'Aramah, Si. Arabia 70 E5 25 30N 46 0 E
Al 'Arṭāwīyah,
  Si. Arabia ...... 70 E5 26 31N 45 20 E
Al 'Āṣimah =
  'Ammān □, Jordan .. 74 D5 31 40N 36 30 E
Al 'Assāfīyah, Si. Arabia 70 D3 28 17N 38 59 E
Al 'Ayn, Si. Arabia ... 70 E3 25 4N 38 6 E
Al 'Ayn, U.A.E. ...... 71 E7 24 15N 55 45 E
Al 'Azīzīyah, Iraq ..... 70 C5 32 54N 45 4 E
Al Bāb, Syria ...... 70 B3 36 23N 37 29 E
Al Bad', Si. Arabia ... 70 D2 28 28N 35 1 E
Al Bādī, Iraq ...... 70 C4 35 56N 41 32 E
Al Baḥral Mayyit =
  Dead Sea, Asia ...... 74 D4 31 30N 35 30 E
Al Balqā' □, Jordan ... 74 C4 32 5N 35 45 E
Al Bārūk, J., Lebanon . 74 B4 33 39N 35 40 E
Al Baṣrah, Iraq ...... 70 D5 30 30N 47 50 E
Al Baṭḥā, Iraq ...... 70 D5 31 6N 45 53 E
Al Batrūn, Lebanon ... 74 A4 34 15N 35 40 E
Al Baydā, Libya ...... 79 B10 32 50N 21 44 E
Al Biqā, Lebanon ..... 74 A5 34 10N 36 10 E
Al Bi'r, Si. Arabia .... 70 D3 28 51N 36 16 E
Al Burayj, Syria ...... 74 A5 34 15N 36 46 E
Al Faḍilī, Si. Arabia ... 71 E6 26 58N 49 10 E
Al Fallūjah, Iraq ...... 70 C4 33 20N 43 55 E
Al Fāw, Iraq ...... 71 D6 30 0N 48 30 E
Al Fujayrah, U.A.E. ... 71 E8 25 7N 56 18 E
Al Ghadaf, W. →,
  Jordan ...... 74 D5 31 26N 36 43 E
Al Ghammās, Iraq .... 70 D5 31 45N 44 37 E
Al Ghazālah, Si. Arabia 70 E4 26 48N 41 19 E
Al Ḥadīthah, Iraq ..... 70 C4 34 0N 41 13 E
Al Ḥadīthah, Si. Arabia 70 D4 31 28N 37 8 E
Al Ḥaḍr, Iraq ...... 70 C4 35 35N 42 44 E
Al Hājānah, Syria ..... 74 B5 33 20N 36 33 E
Al Hajar al Gharbī,
  Oman ...... 71 E8 24 10N 56 15 E
Al Ḥamad, Si. Arabia . 70 D3 31 30N 39 30 E
Al Hamdāniyah, Syria . 70 C3 35 25N 36 50 E
Al Ḥamīdīyah, Syria .. 74 A4 34 42N 35 57 E
Al Ḥammār, Iraq ...... 70 D5 30 57N 46 51 E
Al Ḥamrā', Si. Arabia . 70 E3 24 2N 38 55 E
Al Ḥamzah, Iraq ...... 70 D5 31 43N 44 58 E
Al Ḥanākīyah,
  Si. Arabia ...... 70 E4 24 51N 40 31 E
Al Ḥarīr, W. →, Syria . 74 C4 32 44N 35 59 E
Al Ḥasā →, Jordan ... 74 D4 31 4N 35 29 E
Al Hasakah, Syria ..... 70 B4 36 35N 40 45 E
Al Ḥaydān, W. →,
  Jordan ...... 74 D4 31 29N 35 34 E
Al Ḥayy, Iraq ...... 70 C5 32 5N 46 5 E
Al Ḥijarah, Asia ...... 70 D4 30 0N 44 0 E
Al Ḥillah, Iraq ...... 70 C5 32 30N 44 25 E
Al Ḥillah, Si. Arabia .. 75 B4 23 35N 46 50 E
Al Ḥindīyah, Iraq ..... 70 C5 32 30N 44 10 E
Al Hirmil, Lebanon ... 74 A5 34 26N 36 24 E
Al Hoceïma, Morocco . 78 A5 35 8N 3 58W
Al Ḥudaydah, Yemen . 75 E3 14 50N 43 0 E
Al Ḥufūf, Si. Arabia ... 71 E6 25 25N 49 45 E
Al Ḥumaydah,
  Si. Arabia ...... 70 D2 29 14N 34 56 E
Al Ḥunayy, Si. Arabia . 71 E6 25 58N 48 45 E
Al Iskandarīyah,
  Si. Arabia ...... 70 D3 30 43N 37 59 E
Al Jafr, Jordan ...... 74 E5 30 18N 36 14 E
Al Jāfūrah, Si. Arabia . 71 E7 25 0N 50 15 E
Al Jaghbūb, Libya ..... 79 C10 29 42N 24 38 E
Al Jahrah, Kuwait ..... 70 D5 29 25N 47 40 E
Al Jamalīyah, Qatar ... 71 E6 25 37N 51 5 E
Al Janūb □, Lebanon .. 74 B4 33 20N 35 20 E
Al Jawf, Libya ...... 79 D10 24 10N 23 24 E
Al Jazirah, Iraq ...... 70 C5 33 30N 44 0 E
Al Jithāmīyah,
  Si. Arabia ...... 70 E4 27 41N 41 43 E
Al Jubayl, Si. Arabia .. 71 E6 27 0N 49 50 E
Al Jubb, Si. Arabia .... 70 E4 27 11N 42 17 E
Al Junaynah, Sudan ... 79 F10 13 27N 22 45 E
Al Kabā'ish, Iraq ...... 70 D5 30 58N 47 0 E
Al Karak, Jordan ...... 74 D4 31 11N 35 42 E
Al Karak □, Jordan ... 74 E5 31 0N 36 0 E
Al Kāẓimīyah, Iraq .... 70 C5 33 22N 44 18 E
Al Khābūra, Oman .... 71 F8 23 57N 57 5 E
Al Khafji, Si. Arabia ... 71 E6 28 24N 48 29 E
Al Khalīl, West Bank .. 74 D4 31 32N 35 6 E
Al Khāliṣ, Iraq ...... 70 C5 33 49N 44 32 E
Al Kharsānīyah,
  Si. Arabia ...... 71 E6 27 13N 49 18 E

Al Khaṣab, Oman ..... 71 E8 26 14N 56 15 E
Al Khawr, Qatar ...... 71 E6 25 41N 51 30 E
Al Khiḍr, Iraq ...... 70 D5 31 12N 45 33 E
Al Khiyām, Lebanon .. 74 B4 33 20N 35 36 E
Al Khums, Libya ...... 79 B8 32 40N 14 17 E
Al Kiswah, Syria ...... 74 B5 33 23N 36 14 E
Al Kūfah, Iraq ...... 70 C5 32 2N 44 24 E
Al Kufrah, Libya ...... 79 D10 24 17N 23 15 E
Al Kuhayfiyah,
  Si. Arabia ...... 70 E4 27 12N 43 3 E
Al Kūt, Iraq ...... 70 C5 32 30N 46 0 E
Al Kuwayt, Kuwait .... 70 D5 29 30N 48 0 E
Al Labwah, Lebanon .. 74 A5 34 11N 36 20 E
Al Lādhiqīyah, Syria .. 70 C2 35 30N 35 45 E
Al Līth, Si. Arabia ..... 75 C3 20 9N 40 15 E
Al Liwā', Oman ...... 71 E8 24 31N 56 36 E
Al Luḥayyah, Yemen .. 75 D3 15 45N 42 40 E
Al Madīnah, Iraq ...... 70 D5 30 57N 47 16 E
Al Madīnah, Si. Arabia 70 E3 24 35N 39 52 E
Al Mafraq, Jordan .... 74 C5 32 17N 36 14 E
Al Mafraq □, Jordan .. 74 C5 32 17N 36 15 E
Al Maḥmūdīyah, Iraq . 70 C5 33 3N 44 21 E
Al Majma'ah, Si. Arabia 70 E5 25 57N 45 22 E
Al Makhruq, W. →,
  Jordan ...... 74 D6 31 28N 37 0 E
Al Makhūl, Si. Arabia . 70 E4 26 37N 42 39 E
Al Manāmah, Bahrain . 71 E6 26 10N 50 30 E
Al Maqwa', Kuwait ... 70 D5 29 10N 47 59 E
Al Marj, Libya ...... 79 B10 32 25N 20 30 E
Al Maṭlā, Kuwait ...... 70 D5 29 24N 47 40 E
Al Mawjib, W. →,
  Jordan ...... 74 D4 31 28N 35 36 E
Al Mawṣil, Iraq ...... 70 B4 36 15N 43 5 E
Al Mayādin, Syria ..... 70 C4 35 1N 40 27 E
Al Mazār, Jordan ...... 74 D4 31 4N 35 41 E
Al Midhnab, Si. Arabia 70 E5 25 50N 44 18 E
Al Minā', Lebanon .... 74 A4 34 24N 35 49 E
Al Miqdādīyah, Iraq .. 70 C5 34 0N 45 0 E
Al Mubarraz, Si. Arabia 71 E6 25 30N 49 40 E
Al Mudawwarah, Jordan 74 F5 29 19N 36 0 E
Al Mughayrā', U.A.E. . 71 E7 24 5N 53 32 E
Al Muḥarraq, Bahrain . 71 E6 26 15N 50 40 E
Al Mukallā, Yemen .... 75 E4 14 33N 49 2 E
Al Mukhā, Yemen ..... 75 E3 13 18N 43 15 E
Al Musayjīd, Si. Arabia 70 E3 24 5N 39 5 E
Al Musayyib, Iraq ..... 70 C5 32 49N 44 20 E
Al Muthanná □, Iraq .. 70 D5 30 30N 45 15 E
Al Muwayh, Si. Arabia 80 C5 22 41N 41 37 E
Al Muwayliḥ, Si. Arabia 70 E2 27 40N 35 30 E
Al Owuho = Otukpa,
  Nigeria ...... 83 D6 7 9N 7 41 E
Al Qādisīyah □, Iraq .. 70 D5 30 0N 45 0 E
Al Qā'im, Iraq ...... 70 C4 34 21N 41 7 E
Al Qalībah, Si. Arabia . 70 D3 28 24N 37 42 E
Al Qāmishlī, Syria ..... 70 B4 37 2N 41 14 E
Al Qaryatayn, Syria ... 74 A6 34 12N 37 13 E
Al Qaṣīm, Si. Arabia .. 70 E4 26 0N 43 0 E
Al Qaṭ'ā, Syria ...... 70 C4 35 20N 40 48 E
Al Qaṭīf, Si. Arabia ... 71 E6 26 35N 50 0 E
Al Qaṭrānah, Jordan .. 74 D5 31 12N 36 6 E
Al Qaṭrūn, Libya ...... 79 D9 24 56N 15 3 E
Al Qayṣūmah, Si. Arabia 70 D5 28 20N 46 7 E
Al Quds = Jerusalem,
  Israel ...... 74 D4 31 47N 35 10 E
Al Qunayṭirah, Syria .. 74 C4 32 55N 35 45 E
Al Qunfudhah,
  Si. Arabia ...... 80 D5 19 3N 41 4 E
Al Qurnah, Iraq ...... 70 D5 31 1N 47 25 E
Al Quṣayr, Iraq ...... 70 D5 30 39N 45 50 E
Al Quṣayr, Syria ...... 74 A5 34 31N 36 34 E
Al Qutayfah, Syria ..... 74 B5 33 44N 36 36 E
Al 'Ubaylah, Si. Arabia 75 C5 21 59N 50 57 E
Al 'Uḍayliyah,
  Si. Arabia ...... 71 E6 25 8N 49 18 E
Al 'Ulā, Si. Arabia ..... 70 E3 26 35N 38 0 E
Al 'Uqayr, Si. Arabia .. 71 E6 25 40N 50 15 E
Al 'Uwaynid, Si. Arabia 70 E5 24 50N 46 0 E
Al 'Uwayqīlah,
  Si. Arabia ...... 70 D4 30 30N 42 10 E
Al 'Uyūn, Ḥijāz,
  Si. Arabia ...... 70 E3 24 33N 39 35 E
Al 'Uyūn, Najd,
  Si. Arabia ...... 70 E4 26 30N 43 50 E
Al 'Uzayr, Iraq ...... 70 D5 31 19N 47 25 E
Al Wajh, Si. Arabia ... 70 E3 26 10N 36 30 E
Al Wakrah, Qatar ..... 71 E6 25 10N 51 40 E
Al Waqbah, Si. Arabia 70 D5 28 48N 45 33 E
Al Wari'āh, Si. Arabia . 70 E5 27 51N 47 25 E
Ala, Italy ...... 40 C8 45 45N 11 0 E
Ala Dağ, Turkey ...... 70 B2 37 44N 35 9 E
Ala Dağları, Turkey ... 73 C10 39 15N 43 33 E
Alabama □, U.S.A. 115 J2 33 0N 87 0W
Alabama →, U.S.A. ... 115 K2 31 8N 87 57W
Alabaster, U.S.A. 115 J2 33 15N 86 49W
Alaca, Turkey ...... 72 B6 40 10N 34 51 E
Alaçatı, Turkey ...... 47 C8 38 16N 26 22 E
Alachua, U.S.A. 115 L4 29 47N 82 30W
Alaejos, Spain 36 D5 41 18N 5 13W
Alaérma, Greece ...... 49 C9 36 9N 27 57 E
Alagir, Russia ...... 35 J7 43 3N 44 14 E
Alagna Valsésia, Italy . 40 C4 45 51N 7 56 E
Alagoa Grande, Brazil 125 E11 7 3 S 35 35W
Alagoas □, Brazil ...... 125 E11 9 0 S 36 0W
Alagoinhas, Brazil ..... 125 F11 12 7 S 38 20W
Alagón, Spain 38 D3 41 46N 1 12W
Alagón →, Spain 36 F4 39 44N 6 53W
Alaior, Spain ...... 38 B11 39 57N 4 8 E
Alajero, Canary Is. ... 48 F2 28 3N 17 13W
Alajuela, Costa Rica .. 120 D3 10 2N 84 8W
Alakamisy, Madag. .... 89 C8 21 19 S 47 14 E
Alaknanda →, India ... 69 D8 30 8N 78 36 E
Alakol, Ozero,
  Kazakhstan ...... 60 B3 46 0N 81 5 E
Alamarvdasht, Iran .... 71 E7 27 37N 52 59 E
Alamata, Ethiopia ..... 81 E4 12 25N 39 40 E
Alameda, Calif., U.S.A. 110 H4 37 46N 122 15W
Alameda, N. Mex.,
  U.S.A. 109 J10 35 11N 106 37W
Alaminos, Phil. ...... 61 C3 16 10N 119 59 E
Alamo, U.S.A. 111 J11 37 22N 115 10W
Alamo Crossing, U.S.A. 111 L13 34 16N 113 33W
Alamogordo, U.S.A. ... 109 K11 32 54N 105 57W
Alamos, Mexico 118 B3 27 0N 109 0W
Alamosa, U.S.A. 109 H11 37 28N 105 52W
Åland = Ahvenanmaa,
  Finland ...... 9 F19 60 15N 20 0 E
Ålands hav, Europe ... 9 F18 60 0N 19 30 E
Alange, Embalse d',
  Spain 37 G4 38 45N 6 18W
Alania = North
  Ossetia □, Russia ... 35 J7 43 30N 44 30 E

Alanís, Spain 37 G5 38 3N 5 43W
Alanya, Turkey ...... 70 B1 36 38N 32 0 E
Alaotra, Farihin',
  Madag. ...... 89 B8 17 30 S 48 30 E
Alapayevsk, Russia .... 52 D7 57 52N 61 42 E
Alappuzha = Alleppey,
  India ...... 66 Q10 9 30N 76 28 E
Alar del Rey, Spain ... 36 C6 42 38N 4 20W
Alaraz, Spain 36 E5 40 45N 5 17W
Alarcón, Embalse de,
  Spain 38 F2 39 36N 2 10W
Alaşehir, Turkey ...... 47 C10 38 23N 28 30 E
Alaska □, U.S.A. 100 C5 64 0N 154 0W
Alaska, G. of, Pac. Oc. 100 C5 58 0N 145 0W
Alaska Peninsula, U.S.A. 100 C4 56 0N 159 0W
Alaska Range, U.S.A. . 100 B4 62 50N 151 0W
Alássio, Italy ...... 40 E5 44 0N 8 10 E
Älät, Azerbaijan ...... 35 L9 39 58N 49 25 E
Alatri, Italy ...... 41 G10 41 43N 13 21 E
Alatyr, Russia ...... 34 C8 54 55N 46 35 E
Alatyr →, Russia ...... 34 C8 54 52N 46 36 E
Alausí, Ecuador ...... 124 D3 2 0 S 78 50W
Álava □, Spain 38 C2 42 48N 2 28W
Alava, C., U.S.A. 108 B1 48 10N 124 44W
Alaverdi, Armenia ..... 35 K7 41 15N 44 37 E
Alavo = Alavus, Finland 9 E20 62 35N 23 36 E
Alavus, Finland ...... 9 E20 62 35N 23 36 E
Alawoona, Australia ... 95 E3 34 45 S 140 30 E
Alazani →, Azerbaijan 35 K8 41 5N 46 40 E
Alba, Italy ...... 40 D5 44 42N 8 2 E
Alba □, Romania ...... 29 D8 46 10N 23 30 E
Alba Adriática, Italy .. 41 F10 42 50N 13 56 E
Alba de Tormes, Spain 36 E5 40 50N 5 30W
Alba-Iulia, Romania ... 29 D8 46 8N 23 39 E
Albac, Romania ...... 28 D7 46 28N 22 58 E
Albacete, Spain 39 F3 39 0N 1 50W
Albacete □, Spain 39 G3 38 50N 2 0W
Albacutya, L., Australia 95 F3 35 45 S 141 58 E
Albæk, Denmark ...... 11 G4 57 36N 10 25 E
Albæk Bugt, Denmark . 11 G4 57 35N 10 40 E
Albaida, Spain 39 G4 38 51N 0 31W
Albalate de las
  Nogueras, Spain 38 E2 40 22N 2 18W
Albalate del Arzobispo,
  Spain 38 D4 41 6N 0 31W
Albania ■, Europe .... 44 E4 41 0N 20 0 E
Albano Laziale, Italy .. 41 G9 41 44N 12 39 E
Albany, Australia ...... 93 G2 35 1 S 117 58 E
Albany, Ga., U.S.A. ... 115 K3 31 35N 84 10W
Albany, N.Y., U.S.A. .. 117 D11 42 39N 73 45W
Albany, Oreg., U.S.A. . 108 D2 44 38N 123 6W
Albany, Tex., U.S.A. .. 113 J5 32 44N 99 18W
Albany →, Canada ... 104 B3 52 17N 81 31W
Albardón, Argentina .. 126 C2 31 20 S 68 30W
Albarracín, Spain 38 E3 40 25N 1 26W
Albarracín, Sierra de,
  Spain 38 E3 40 30N 1 30W
Albatera, Spain 39 G4 38 11N 0 52W
Albatross B., Australia . 94 A3 12 45 S 141 30 E
Albegna →, Italy ...... 41 F8 42 30N 11 11 E
Albemarle, U.S.A. 115 H5 35 21N 80 11W
Albemarle Sd., U.S.A. . 115 H7 36 5N 76 0W
Albenga, Italy ...... 40 D5 44 3N 8 13 E
Alberche →, Spain 36 F6 39 58N 4 46W
Alberdi, Paraguay ..... 126 B4 26 14 S 58 20W
Albères, Mts., France . 20 F6 42 28N 2 56 E
Alberga, Sweden ...... 11 F10 58 44N 16 35 E
Alberga, The →,
  Australia ...... 95 D2 27 6 S 135 33 E
Albersdorf, Germany .. 24 A5 54 8N 9 17 E
Albert, France ...... 19 C9 50 0N 2 38 E
Albert, L., Africa ...... 86 B3 1 30N 31 0 E
Albert, L., Australia ... 95 F2 35 30 S 139 10 E
Albert Edward Ra.,
  Australia ...... 92 C4 18 17 S 127 57 E
Albert Lea, U.S.A. 112 D8 43 39N 93 22W
Albert Nile →, Uganda 86 B3 3 36N 32 2 E
Albert Town, Bahamas 121 B5 22 37N 74 33W
Alberta □, Canada 102 C6 54 40N 115 0W
Alberti, Argentina ..... 126 D3 35 1 S 60 16W
Albertinia, S. Africa ... 88 E3 34 11 S 21 34 E
Alberton, Canada 105 C7 46 50N 64 0W
Albertville, France ..... 21 C10 45 40N 6 22 E
Albertville, U.S.A. 115 H2 34 16N 86 13W
Albi, France ...... 20 E6 43 56N 2 9 E
Albia, U.S.A. 112 E8 41 2N 92 48W
Albina, Suriname 125 B8 5 37N 54 15W
Albina, Ponta, Angola 88 B1 15 52 S 11 44 E
Albino, Italy ...... 40 C6 45 46N 9 47 E
Albion, Mich., U.S.A. . 114 D3 42 15N 84 45W
Albion, Nebr., U.S.A. . 112 E5 41 42N 98 0W
Albion, Pa., U.S.A. 116 E4 41 53N 80 22W
Alböke, Sweden ...... 11 H10 56 57N 16 47 E
Albolote, Spain 37 H7 37 14N 3 39W
Alborán, Medit. S. 37 K7 35 57N 3 0W
Alborea, Spain 39 F3 39 17N 1 24W
Ålborg, Denmark ...... 11 G3 57 2N 9 54 E
Ålborg Bugt, Denmark 11 H4 56 50N 10 35 E
Alborz, Reshteh-ye
  Kūhhā-ye, Iran ...... 71 C7 36 0N 52 0 E
Albox, Spain 39 H2 37 23N 2 8W
Albufeira, Portugal 37 H2 37 5N 8 15W
Albula →, Switz. ...... 25 J5 46 38N 9 28 E
Albuñol, Spain 37 J7 36 48N 3 11W
Albuquerque, U.S.A. .. 109 J10 35 5N 106 39W
Albuquerque, Cayos de,
  Caribbean 120 D3 12 10N 81 50W
Alburg, U.S.A. 117 B11 44 59N 73 18W
Alburno, Mte., Italy ... 43 B8 40 33N 15 17 E
Alburquerque, Spain .. 37 F4 39 15N 6 59W
Albury = Albury-
  Wodonga, Australia . 95 F4 36 3 S 146 56 E
Albury-Wodonga,
  Australia ...... 95 F4 36 3 S 146 56 E
Alcácer do Sal, Portugal 37 G2 38 23N 8 9W
Alcáçovas, Portugal ... 37 G2 38 23N 8 9W
Alcalá de Chivert, Spain 38 E5 40 19N 0 13 E
Alcalá de Guadaira,
  Spain 37 H5 37 20N 5 50W
Alcalá de Henares,
  Spain 36 E7 40 28N 3 22W
Alcalá de los Gazules,
  Spain 37 J5 36 29N 5 43W
Alcalá del Júcar, Spain 39 F3 39 12N 1 26W
Alcalá del Río, Spain .. 37 H5 37 31N 5 59W
Alcalá del Valle, Spain 37 J5 36 54N 5 10W
Alcalá la Real, Spain .. 37 H7 37 27N 3 57W
Álcamo, Italy ...... 42 E5 37 59N 12 55 E
Alcanadre →, Spain ... 38 D4 41 43N 0 12W
Alcanar, Spain ...... 38 E5 40 33N 0 28 E

Alcanede, Portugal 37 F2 39 25N 8 49W
Alcanena, Portugal 37 F2 39 27N 8 40W
Alcañices, Spain 36 D4 41 41N 6 21W
Alcañiz, Spain 38 D4 41 2N 0 8W
Alcântara, Brazil ...... 125 D10 2 20 S 44 30W
Alcántara, Spain 36 F4 39 41N 6 57W
Alcántara, Embalse de,
  Spain 36 F4 39 44N 6 50W
Alcantarilla, Spain 39 H3 37 59N 1 12W
Alcaracejos, Spain 37 G6 38 24N 4 58W
Alcaraz, Spain 39 G2 38 40N 2 29W
Alcaraz, Sierra de, Spain 39 G2 38 40N 2 20W
Alcaudete, Spain 37 H6 37 35N 4 5W
Alcázar de San Juan,
  Spain 37 F7 39 24N 3 12W
Alchevsk, Ukraine ..... 33 H10 48 30N 38 45 E
Alcira = Alzira, Spain . 39 F4 39 9N 0 30W
Alcobaça, Portugal 37 F2 39 32N 9 0W
Alcobendas, Spain 36 E7 40 32N 3 38W
Alcolea del Pinar, Spain 38 D2 41 2N 2 28W
Alcora, Spain 38 E4 40 5N 0 14W
Alcorcón, Spain 36 E7 40 20N 3 50W
Alcoutim, Portugal 37 H3 37 25N 7 28W
Alcova, U.S.A. 108 E10 42 34N 106 43W
Alcoy, Spain 39 G4 38 43N 0 30W
Alcubierre, Sierra de,
  Spain 38 D4 41 45N 0 22W
Alcublas, Spain 38 F4 39 48N 0 43W
Alcúdia, Spain ...... 48 B10 39 51N 3 7 E
Alcúdia, B. d', Spain .. 48 B10 39 47N 3 15 E
Alcudia, Sierra de la,
  Spain 37 G6 38 34N 4 30W
Aldabra Is., Seychelles . 77 G8 9 22 S 46 28 E
Aldama, Mexico 119 C5 23 0N 98 4W
Aldan, Russia ...... 53 D13 58 40N 125 30 E
Aldan →, Russia ...... 53 C13 63 28N 129 35 E
Aldea, Pta. de la,
  Canary Is. 48 G4 28 0N 15 50W
Aldeburgh, U.K. ...... 15 E9 52 10N 1 37 E
Alder Pk., U.S.A. 110 K5 35 53N 121 22W
Alderney, U.K. 15 H5 49 42N 2 11W
Aldershot, U.K. 15 F7 51 15N 0 44W
Åled, Sweden ...... 11 H6 56 54N 12 49 E
Aledo, U.S.A. 112 E9 41 12N 90 45W
Alefa, Ethiopia ...... 81 E4 11 55N 36 55 E
Aleg, Mauritania 82 B2 17 3N 13 55W
Alegranza, Canary Is. . 48 E6 29 23N 13 32W
Alegranza, I., Canary Is. 48 E6 29 23N 13 32W
Alegre, Brazil ...... 127 A7 20 50 S 41 30W
Alegrete, Brazil ...... 127 B4 29 40 S 56 0W
Aleisk, Russia ...... 52 D9 52 40N 83 0 E
Aleksandriya =
  Oleksandriya,
  Kirovohrad, Ukraine 33 H7 48 42N 33 3 E
Aleksandriya =
  Oleksandriya, Rivne,
  Ukraine ...... 33 G4 50 37N 26 19 E
Aleksandriyskaya,
  Russia ...... 35 J8 43 58N 47 14 E
Aleksandrov, Russia ... 32 D10 56 23N 38 44 E
Aleksandrov Gay,
  Russia ...... 34 E9 50 9N 48 34 E
Aleksandrovac,
  Serbia & M. ...... 44 C5 43 28N 21 3 E
Aleksandrovac,
  Serbia & M. ...... 44 B5 44 28N 21 13 E
Aleksandrovka =
  Oleksandrovka,
  Ukraine ...... 33 H7 48 55N 32 20 E
Aleksandrovo, Bulgaria 45 C8 43 14N 24 51 E
Aleksandrovsk-
  Sakhalinskiy, Russia . 53 D15 50 50N 142 20 E
Aleksandrów Kujawski,
  Poland ...... 31 F5 52 53N 18 43 E
Aleksandrów Łódzki,
  Poland ...... 31 G6 51 49N 19 17 E
Aleksandry, Z., Russia . 4 A10 80 25N 48 0 E
Alekseyevka, Samara,
  Russia ...... 34 D10 52 35N 51 17 E
Alekseyevka, Voronezh,
  Russia ...... 33 G10 50 43N 38 40 E
Aleksin, Russia ...... 32 D9 54 31N 37 9 E
Aleksinac, Serbia & M. 44 C5 43 31N 21 42 E
Além Paraíba, Brazil .. 127 A7 21 52 S 42 41W
Alemania, Argentina .. 126 B2 25 40 S 65 30W
Alemania, Chile ...... 126 B2 25 10 S 69 55W
Alençon, France ...... 18 D7 48 27N 0 4 E
Alenquer, Brazil ...... 125 D8 1 56 S 54 46W
Alenuihaha Channel,
  U.S.A. 106 H17 20 30N 156 0W
Alépé, Ivory C. 82 D4 5 29N 3 40W
Aleppo = Ḥalab, Syria 70 B3 36 10N 37 15 E
Aléria, France ...... 21 F13 42 5N 9 26 E
Alert, Canada 4 A4 83 2N 60 0W
Alès, France ...... 21 D8 44 9N 4 5 E
Aleşd, Romania ...... 28 C7 47 3N 22 22 E
Alessándria, Italy ...... 40 D5 44 54N 8 37 E
Ålestrup, Denmark .... 11 H3 56 42N 9 29 E
Ålesund, Norway ...... 9 E12 62 28N 6 12 E
Alet-les-Bains, France . 20 F6 42 59N 2 14 E
Aletschhorn, Switz. ... 25 J4 46 28N 8 0 E
Aleutian Is., Pac. Oc. . 100 C2 52 0N 175 0W
Aleutian Trench,
  Pac. Oc. ...... 96 C10 48 0N 180 0 E
Alexander, U.S.A. 112 B3 47 51N 103 39W
Alexander, Mt.,
  Australia ...... 93 E3 28 58 S 120 16 E
Alexander Arch., U.S.A. 100 C6 56 0N 136 0W
Alexander Bay, S. Africa 88 D2 28 40 S 16 30 E
Alexander City, U.S.A. 115 J3 32 56N 85 58W
Alexander I., Antarctica 5 C17 69 0N 70 0W
Alexandra, Australia ... 95 F4 37 8 S 145 40 E
Alexandra, N.Z. ...... 91 L2 45 14 S 169 25 E
Alexandra Falls, Canada 102 A5 60 29N 116 18W
Alexandria = El
  Iskandarîya, Egypt .. 80 H7 31 13N 29 58 E
Alexandria, B.C.,
  Canada 102 C4 52 35N 122 27W
Alexandria, Ont.,
  Canada 117 A10 45 19N 74 38W
Alexandria, Romania .. 29 G10 43 57N 25 24 E
Alexandria, S. Africa .. 88 E4 33 38 S 26 28 E
Alexandria, U.K. 13 F4 55 59N 4 35W
Alexandria, La., U.S.A. 113 K8 31 18N 92 27W
Alexandria, Minn.,
  U.S.A. 112 C7 45 53N 95 22W
Alexandria, S. Dak.,
  U.S.A. 112 D6 43 39N 97 47W
Alexandria, Va., U.S.A. 114 F7 38 48N 77 3W
Alexandria Bay, U.S.A. 117 B9 44 20N 75 55W
Alexandrina, L.,
  Australia ...... 95 F2 35 25 S 139 10 E
Alexandroúpolis, Greece 45 F9 40 50N 25 54 E
Alexis →, Canada 105 B8 52 33N 56 8W
Alexis Creek, Canada . 102 C4 52 10N 123 20W
Alfabia, Spain ...... 48 B9 39 44N 2 44 E
Alfambra, Spain 38 E3 40 33N 1 5W

Alfândega da Fé,
Portugal **36 D4** 41 20N 6 59W
Alfaro, Spain **38 C3** 42 10N 1 50W
Alfatar, Bulgaria .... **45 C11** 43 59N 27 13 E
Alfaz del Pi, Spain ... **39 G4** 38 35N 0 9 E
Alfeld, Germany ..... **24 D5** 51 59N 9 50 E
Alfenas, Brazil ...... **127 A6** 21 20 S 46 10W
Alfiós →, Greece .... **46 D3** 37 40N 21 33 E
Alföld, Hungary ..... **28 D5** 46 30N 20 0 E
Alfonsine, Italy ...... **41 D9** 44 30N 12 3 E
Alford, Aberds., U.K. . **13 D6** 57 14N 2 41W
Alford, Lincs., U.K. .. **14 D8** 53 15N 0 10 E
Alfred, Maine, U.S.A. . **117 C14** 43 29N 70 43W
Alfred, N.Y., U.S.A. .. **116 D7** 42 16N 77 48W
Alfreton, U.K. **14 D6** 53 6N 1 24W
Alfta, Sweden .... **10 C10** 61 21N 16 4 E
Alga, Kazakhstan .... **52 E6** 49 53N 57 20 E
Algaida, Spain ...... **48 B9** 39 33N 2 53 E
Algar, Spain **37 J5** 36 40N 5 39W
Ålgård, Norway ..... **9 G11** 58 46N 5 53 E
Algarinejo, Spain **37 H6** 37 19N 4 9W
Algarve, Portugal ... **37 J2** 36 58N 8 20W
Algeciras, Spain **37 J5** 36 9N 5 28W
Algemesí, Spain **39 F4** 39 11N 0 27W
Alger, Algeria ...... **78 A6** 36 42N 3 8 E
Alger ✕ (ALG), Algeria **78 A6** 36 39N 3 13 E
Algeria ■, Africa .... **78 C6** 28 30N 2 0 E
Alghero, Italy .... **42 B1** 40 33N 8 19 E
Alghult, Sweden ..... **11 G9** 57 0N 15 35 E
Algiers = Alger, Algeria **78 A6** 36 42N 3 8 E
Algoa B., S. Africa ... **88 E4** 33 50 S 25 45 E
Algodonales, Spain .. **37 J5** 36 54N 5 24W
Algodor →, Spain ... **36 F7** 39 55N 3 53W
Algoma, U.S.A. **114 C2** 44 36N 87 26W
Algona, U.S.A. **112 D7** 43 4N 94 14W
Algonac, U.S.A. **116 D2** 42 37N 82 32W
Algonquin △, Canada **104 C4** 45 50N 78 30W
Algorta, Uruguay .... **128 C5** 32 25 S 57 23W
Alhama de Almería,
Spain **37 J8** 36 57N 2 34W
Alhama de Aragón,
Spain **38 D3** 41 18N 1 54W
Alhama de Granada,
Spain **37 H7** 37 0N 3 59W
Alhama de Murcia,
Spain **39 H3** 37 51N 1 25W
Alhambra, U.S.A. ... **111 L8** 34 8N 118 6W
Alhaurín el Grande,
Spain **37 J6** 36 39N 4 41W
Alhucemas = Al
Hoceima, Morocco . **78 A5** 35 8N 3 58W
'Alī al Gharbī, Iraq ... **70 C5** 32 30N 46 45 E
'Alī ash Sharqī, Iraq .. **70 C5** 32 7N 46 44 E
Āli Bayramlı,
Azerbaijan .... **35 L9** 39 59N 48 52 E
'Alī Khēl, Afghan. .... **68 C3** 33 57N 69 43 E
Ali Sahîh, Djibouti ... **81 E5** 11 10N 42 44 E
Alī Shāh, Iran ...... **70 B5** 38 9N 45 50 E
Ália, Italy .... **42 E6** 37 47N 13 43 E
'Alīābād, Khorāsān, Iran **71 C8** 32 30N 57 30 E
'Alīābād, Kordestān,
Iran .... **70 C5** 35 4N 46 58 E
'Alīābād, Yazd, Iran .. **71 D7** 31 41N 53 49 E
Aliaga, Spain **38 E4** 40 40N 0 42W
Aliağa, Turkey ...... **47 C8** 38 47N 26 59 E
Aliákmon →, Greece . **44 F6** 40 30N 22 36 E
Alibo, Ethiopia ...... **81 F4** 9 52N 37 5 E
Alibori →, Benin .... **83 C5** 11 56N 3 17 E
Alibunar, Serbia & M. . **28 E5** 45 5N 20 57 E
Alicante, Spain **39 G4** 38 23N 0 30W
Alicante □, Spain ... **39 G4** 38 30N 0 37W
Alicante ✕ (ALC),
Spain **39 G4** 38 14N 0 36W
Alice, S. Africa ..... **88 E4** 32 48 S 26 55 E
Alice, U.S.A. **113 M5** 27 45N 98 5W
Alice →, Queens.,
Australia .... **94 C3** 24 2 S 144 50 E
Alice →, Queens.,
Australia .... **94 B3** 15 35 S 142 20 E
Alice, Punta, Italy ... **43 C10** 39 24N 17 9 E
Alice Arm, Canada .. **102 B3** 55 29N 129 31W
Alice Springs, Australia **94 C1** 23 40 S 133 50 E
Alicedale, S. Africa .. **88 E4** 33 15 S 26 4 E
Aliceville, U.S.A. **115 J1** 33 8N 88 9W
Alicudi, Italy .... **43 D7** 38 33N 14 20 E
Aliganj, India ...... **69 F8** 27 30N 79 10 E
Aligarh, Raj., India .. **68 G7** 25 55N 76 15 E
Aligarh, Ut. P., India . **68 F8** 27 55N 78 10 E
Alīgūdarz, Iran ..... **71 C6** 33 25N 49 45 E
Alijó, Portugal **36 D3** 41 16N 7 27W
Alimnía, Greece ..... **49 C9** 36 16N 27 43 E
Alingsås, Sweden ... **11 G6** 57 56N 12 31 E
Alipur, Pakistan ..... **68 E4** 29 25N 70 55 E
Alipur Duar, India ... **67 F16** 26 30N 89 35 E
Aliquippa, U.S.A. ... **116 F4** 40 37N 80 15W
Alishan, Taiwan ..... **59 F13** 23 31N 120 48 E
Aliste →, Spain **36 D5** 41 34N 5 58W
Alitus = Alytus,
Lithuania .... **9 J21** 54 24N 24 3 E
Alivérion, Greece .... **46 C6** 38 24N 24 2 E
Aliwal North, S. Africa **88 E4** 30 45 S 26 45 E
Alix, Canada **102 C6** 52 24N 113 11W
Aljezur, Portugal **37 H2** 37 18N 8 49W
Aljustrel, Portugal ... **37 H2** 37 55N 8 10W
Alkamari, Niger ..... **83 C7** 13 27N 11 10 E
Alkmaar, Neths. .... **17 B4** 52 37N 4 45 E
All American Canal,
U.S.A. **109 K6** 32 45N 115 15W
Allada, Benin .... **83 D5** 6 41N 2 9 E
Allagash →, U.S.A. . **115 B11** 47 5N 69 3W
Allah Dad, Pakistan .. **68 G2** 25 38N 67 34 E
Allahabad, India .... **69 G9** 25 25N 81 58 E
Allan, Canada **103 C7** 51 53N 106 4W
Allanche, France .... **20 C6** 45 14N 2 57 E
Allanridge, S. Africa .. **88 D4** 27 45 S 26 40 E
Allaqi, Wadi →, Egypt **80 C3** 23 7N 32 47 E
Allariz, Spain **36 C3** 42 11N 7 50W
Allassac, France ..... **20 C5** 45 15N 1 29 E
Ålleberg, Sweden ... **11 F7** 58 8N 13 36 E
Allegany, U.S.A. **116 D6** 42 6N 78 30W
Allegheny →, U.S.A. **116 F5** 40 27N 80 1W
Allegheny Mts., U.S.A. **114 G6** 38 15N 80 10W
Allegheny Reservoir,
U.S.A. **116 E6** 41 50N 78 55W
Allègre, France ..... **20 C7** 45 12N 3 41 E
Allègre, Pte.,
Guadeloupe ...... **120 b** 16 22N 61 46W
Allen, Bog of, Ireland . **12 C5** 53 15N 7 0W
Allen, L., Ireland **12 B3** 54 8N 8 4W
Allendale, U.S.A. ... **115 J5** 33 1N 81 18W
Allende, Mexico **118 B4** 28 20N 100 50W
Allentown, U.S.A. ... **117 F9** 40 37N 75 29W
Allentsteig, Austria .. **26 C8** 48 41N 15 20 E
Alleppey, India ..... **66 Q10** 9 30N 76 28 E
Allepuz, Spain **38 E4** 40 29N 0 44W
Aller →, Germany ... **24 C5** 52 56N 9 12 E
Alleynes B., Barbados . **121 g** 13 13N 59 39W

Alliance, Nebr., U.S.A. **112 D3** 42 6N 102 52W
Alliance, Ohio, U.S.A. **116 F3** 40 55N 81 6W
Allier □, France ..... **19 F9** 46 25N 2 40 E
Allier →, France .... **19 F10** 46 57N 3 4 E
Alliford Bay, Canada . **102 C2** 53 12N 131 58W
Alligator Pond, Jamaica **120 a** 17 52N 77 34W
Allinge, Denmark .... **11 J8** 55 17N 14 50 E
Alliston = New
Tecumseth, Canada **116 B5** 44 9N 79 52W
Alloa, U.K. **13 E5** 56 7N 3 47W
Allones, France ..... **18 D8** 48 20N 1 40 E
Allora, Australia .... **95 D5** 28 2 S 152 0 E
Allos, France .... **21 D10** 44 15N 6 38 E
Alluitsup Paa,
Greenland **101 B15** 60 30N 45 35W
Alma, Canada **105 C5** 48 35N 71 40W
Alma, Ga., U.S.A. ... **115 K4** 31 33N 82 28W
Alma, Kans., U.S.A. .. **112 F6** 39 1N 96 17W
Alma, Mich., U.S.A. .. **114 D3** 43 23N 84 39W
Alma, Nebr., U.S.A. .. **112 E5** 40 6N 99 22W
Alma Ata = Almaty,
Kazakhstan ...... **52 E8** 43 15N 76 57 E
Almacelles, Spain ... **38 D5** 41 43N 0 27 E
Almada, Portugal **37 G1** 38 40N 9 9W
Almaden, Australia .. **94 B3** 17 22 S 144 40 E
Almadén, Spain **37 G6** 38 49N 4 52W
Almanor, L., U.S.A. .. **108 F3** 40 14N 121 9W
Almansa, Spain **39 G3** 38 51N 1 5W
Almanza, Spain **36 C5** 42 39N 5 3W
Almanzor, Pico, Spain **36 E5** 40 15N 5 18W
Almanzora →, Spain **39 H3** 37 14N 1 46W
Almaş, Munţii, Romania **28 F7** 44 49N 22 12 E
Almassora, Spain **38 F4** 39 57N 0 3W
Almaty, Kazakhstan .. **52 E8** 43 15N 76 57 E
Almazán, Spain **38 D2** 41 30N 2 30W
Almeirim, Brazil .... **125 D8** 1 30 S 52 34W
Almeirim, Portugal .. **37 F2** 39 12N 8 37W
Almelo, Neths. ...... **17 B6** 52 22N 6 42 E
Almenar de Soria, Spain **38 D2** 41 43N 2 12W
Almenara, Spain **38 F4** 39 46N 0 14W
Almenara, Sierra de la,
Spain **39 H3** 37 34N 1 32W
Almendra, Embalse de,
Spain **36 D4** 41 10N 6 5W
Almendralejo, Spain . **37 G4** 38 41N 6 26W
Almere-Stad, Neths. . **17 B5** 52 20N 5 15 E
Almería, Spain **37 J8** 36 52N 2 27W
Almería □, Spain ... **39 H2** 37 20N 2 20W
Almería, G. de, Spain **39 J2** 36 41N 2 28W
Almetyevsk, Russia .. **34 C11** 54 53N 52 20 E
Älmhult, Sweden .... **11 H8** 56 33N 14 8 E
Almirante, Panama .. **120 E3** 9 10N 82 30W
Almiropótamos, Greece **46 C6** 38 16N 24 11 E
Almirós, Greece ..... **46 B4** 39 11N 22 45 E
Almirou, Kólpos, Greece **49 D6** 35 23N 24 20 E
Almodôvar, Portugal . **37 H2** 37 31N 8 2W
Almodóvar del Campo,
Spain **37 G6** 38 43N 4 10W
Almodóvar del Río,
Spain **37 H5** 37 48N 5 1W
Almond, U.S.A. **116 D7** 42 19N 77 44W
Almont, U.S.A. **116 D1** 42 55N 83 3W
Almonte, Canada **117 A8** 45 14N 76 12W
Almonte →, Spain .. **37 H4** 37 13N 6 38W
Almora, India ...... **69 E8** 29 38N 79 40 E
Almoradí, Spain **39 G4** 38 7N 0 46W
Almorox, Spain **36 E6** 40 14N 4 24W
Almoustarat, Mali ... **83 B5** 17 35N 0 8 E
Älmsta, Sweden ..... **10 E12** 59 58N 18 50 E
Almudévar, Spain ... **38 C4** 42 3N 0 35W
Almuñécar, Spain ... **37 J7** 36 43N 3 41W
Almunge, Sweden ... **10 E12** 59 53N 18 3 E
Almuradiel, Spain ... **37 G7** 38 32N 3 28W
Alness, U.K. **13 D4** 57 41N 4 16W
Alnmouth, U.K. **14 B6** 55 24N 1 37W
Alnwick, U.K. **14 B6** 55 24N 1 42W
Aloi, Uganda .... **86 B3** 2 16N 33 10 E
Alon, Burma .... **67 H19** 22 12N 95 5 E
Alonissos-Vorfai
Sporades △, Greece **46 B6** 39 15N 24 5 E
Alor, Indonesia ..... **63 F6** 8 15 S 124 30 E
Alor Setar, Malaysia .. **65 J3** 6 7N 100 22 E
Alora, Spain **37 J6** 36 49N 4 46W
Alosno, Spain **37 H3** 37 33N 7 7W
Alot, India .... **68 H6** 23 56N 75 40 E
Aloysius, Mt., Australia **93 E4** 26 0 S 128 38 E
Alpaugh, U.S.A. **110 K7** 35 53N 119 29W
Alpe Apuane △, Italy **40 D7** 44 4N 10 15 E
Alpedrinha, Portugal . **36 E3** 40 6N 7 27W
Alpena, U.S.A. **114 C4** 45 4N 83 27W
Alpes-de-Haute-
Provence □, France **21 D10** 44 8N 6 10 E
Alpes-Maritimes □,
France .... **21 E11** 43 55N 7 10 E
Alpha, Australia .... **94 C4** 23 39 S 146 37 E
Alpha Cordillera, Arctic **4 A2** 84 0N 118 0W
Alphen aan den Rijn,
Neths. .... **17 B4** 52 7N 4 40 E
Alpiarça, Portugal ... **37 F2** 39 15N 8 35W
Alpine, Ariz., U.S.A. . **109 K9** 33 51N 109 9W
Alpine, Calif., U.S.A. . **111 N10** 32 50N 116 46W
Alpine, Tex., U.S.A. .. **113 K3** 30 22N 103 40W
Alps, Europe .... **6 F7** 46 30N 9 30 E
Alpu, Turkey .... **72 C4** 39 46N 30 58 E
Alqueta, Barragem do,
Portugal **37 G3** 38 20N 7 25W
Alrø, Denmark ...... **11 J4** 55 52N 10 5 E
Als, Denmark .... **11 K3** 54 59N 9 55 E
Alsace □, France .... **19 D14** 48 15N 7 25 E
Alsask, Canada **103 C7** 51 21N 109 59W
Alsasua, Spain **38 C2** 42 54N 2 10W
Alsek →, U.S.A. ... **102 B1** 59 10N 138 12W
Alsfeld, Germany ... **24 E5** 50 44N 9 16 E
Alsten, Norway ..... **8 D15** 65 58N 12 40 E
Alstermo, Sweden ... **11 H9** 56 58N 15 38 E
Alston, U.K. **14 C5** 54 49N 2 25W
Alta, Norway .... **8 B20** 69 57N 23 10 E
Alta, Sierra, Spain ... **38 E3** 40 31N 1 30W
Alta Gracia, Argentina **126 C3** 31 40 S 64 30W
Alta Sierra, U.S.A. ... **111 K8** 35 42N 118 33W
Altaelva →, Norway . **8 B20** 69 54N 23 17 E
Altafjorden, Norway . **8 A20** 70 5N 23 5 E
Altai = Aerhtai Shan,
Mongolia .... **60 B4** 46 40N 92 45 E
Altamaha →, U.S.A. **115 K5** 31 20N 81 20W
Altamira, Brazil ..... **125 D8** 3 12 S 52 10W
Altamira, Chile ..... **126 B2** 25 47 S 69 51W
Altamira, Mexico **119 C5** 22 24N 97 55W
Altamira, Cuevas de,
Spain **36 B6** 43 20N 4 5W
Altamont, U.S.A. ... **117 D10** 42 43N 74 3W
Altamura, Italy ..... **43 B9** 40 49N 16 33 E
Altanbulag, Mongolia **60 A5** 50 16N 106 30 E
Altar, Mexico **118 A2** 30 40N 111 50W
Altar, Desierto de,
Mexico **118 B2** 30 10N 112 0W
Altata, Mexico **118 C3** 24 30N 108 0W

Altavista, U.S.A. **114 G6** 37 6N 79 17W
Altay, China .... **60 B3** 47 48N 88 10 E
Altdorf, Switz. ...... **25 J4** 46 52N 8 36 E
Alte Mellum, Germany **24 B4** 53 45N 8 10 E
Altea, Spain **39 G4** 38 38N 0 2W
Altenberg, Germany . **24 E9** 50 45N 13 45 E
Altenbruch, Germany **24 B4** 53 49N 8 46 E
Altenburg, Germany . **24 E8** 50 59N 12 25 E
Altenkirchen,
Mecklenburg-Vorpommern,
Germany .... **24 A9** 54 38N 13 22 E
Altenkirchen, Rhld.-Pfz.,
Germany .... **24 E3** 50 41N 7 39 E
Altenmarkt, Austria .. **26 D7** 47 43N 14 39 E
Alter do Chão, Portugal **37 F3** 39 12N 7 40W
Altınoluk, Turkey .... **47 B8** 39 34N 26 45 E
Altınova, Turkey .... **47 B8** 39 12N 26 47 E
Altıntaş, Turkey ..... **47 B12** 39 4N 30 7 E
Altınyaka, Turkey ... **47 E12** 36 33N 30 20 E
Altınyayla, Turkey ... **47 D11** 37 0N 29 33 E
Altiplano, Bolivia ... **122 E4** 17 0 S 68 0W
Altkirch, France ..... **19 E14** 47 37N 7 15 E
Altmark, Germany ... **24 C7** 52 45N 11 30 E
Altmühl →, Germany **25 G7** 48 54N 11 52 E
Altmühltal △, Germany **25 G7** 48 54N 11 15 E
Altmunster, Austria .. **26 D6** 47 54N 13 45 E
Alto Adige = Trentino-
Alto Adige □, Italy . **41 B8** 46 30N 11 0 E
Alto Araguaia, Brazil . **125 G8** 17 15 S 53 20W
Alto Cuchumatanes =
Cuchumatanes, Sierra
de los, Guatemala . **120 C1** 15 35N 91 25W
Alto del Carmen, Chile **126 B1** 28 46 S 70 30W
Alto del Inca, Chile .. **126 A2** 24 10 S 68 10W
Alto Garda
Bresciano △, Italy . **40 C7** 45 42N 10 38 E
Alto Ligonha, Mozam. **87 F4** 15 30 S 38 11 E
Alto Molocue, Mozam. **87 F4** 15 50 S 37 35 E
Alto Paraguai □,
Paraguay .... **126 A4** 21 0 S 58 30W
Alto Paraná □,
Paraguay .... **127 B5** 25 30 S 54 50W
Alton, Canada **116 C4** 43 54N 80 5W
Alton, U.K. **15 F7** 51 9N 0 59W
Alton, Ill., U.S.A. **112 F9** 38 53N 90 11W
Alton, N.H., U.S.A. .. **117 C13** 43 27N 71 13W
Altona, Canada **103 D9** 49 6N 97 33W
Altoona, U.S.A. **116 F6** 40 31N 78 24W
Altötting, Germany .. **25 G8** 48 12N 12 39 E
Altstätten, Switz. .... **25 H5** 47 22N 9 33 E
Altun Kupri, Iraq .... **70 C5** 35 45N 44 9 E
Altun Shan, China ... **60 C3** 38 30N 88 0 E
Alturas, U.S.A. **108 F3** 41 29N 120 32W
Altus, U.S.A. **113 H5** 34 38N 99 20W
Alubijid, Phil. ...... **61 G6** 8 35N 124 29 E
Alucra, Turkey ...... **73 B8** 40 22N 38 47 E
Aluk, Sudan .... **81 F2** 8 25N 27 30 E
Alüksne, Latvia ..... **9 H22** 57 24N 27 3 E
Alunda, Sweden ..... **10 D12** 60 4N 18 5 E
Alunite, U.S.A. **111 K12** 35 59N 114 55W
Aluropo, Ethiopia ... **81 F3** 8 26N 33 24 E
Alupka, Ukraine ..... **33 K8** 44 23N 34 2 E
Alushta, Ukraine .... **33 K8** 44 40N 34 25 E
Alusi, Indonesia ..... **63 F8** 7 35 S 131 40 E
Alustante, Spain **38 E3** 40 36N 1 40W
Alva, U.S.A. **113 G5** 36 48N 98 40W
Alvaiázere, Portugal . **36 F2** 39 49N 8 23W
Ålvängen, Sweden ... **11 G6** 57 58N 12 8 E
Alvão △, Portugal ... **36 D3** 41 22N 7 48W
Alvarado, Mexico **119 D5** 18 40N 95 50W
Alvarado, U.S.A. **113 J6** 32 24N 97 13W
Alvaro Obregón, Presa,
Mexico **118 B3** 27 55N 109 52W
Älvdalen, Sweden ... **10 C8** 61 13N 14 4 E
Alvear, Argentina ... **126 B4** 29 5 S 56 30W
Alverca, Portugal **37 G1** 38 56N 9 1W
Alvesta, Sweden ..... **11 H8** 56 54N 14 35 E
Alvin, U.S.A. **113 L7** 29 26N 95 15W
Alvinston, Canada ... **116 D3** 42 49N 81 52W
Alvito, Portugal **37 G3** 38 15N 7 58W
Älvkarleby, Sweden .. **10 D11** 60 34N 17 26 E
Alvord Desert, U.S.A. **108 E4** 42 30N 118 25W
Älvros, Sweden ..... **10 B8** 62 3N 14 38 E
Älvsbyn, Sweden .... **8 D19** 65 40N 21 0 E
Alwar, India .... **68 F7** 27 38N 76 34 E
Alxa Zuoqi, China ... **56 E3** 38 50N 105 40 E
Alyangula, Australia . **94 A2** 13 55 S 136 30 E
Alyata = Älät,
Azerbaijan .... **35 L9** 39 58N 49 25 E
Alyth, U.K. **13 E5** 56 38N 3 13W
Alytus, Lithuania .... **9 J21** 54 24N 24 3 E
Alzada, U.S.A. **112 C2** 45 2N 104 25W
Alzey, Germany ..... **25 F4** 49 45N 8 7 E
Alzira, Spain **39 F4** 39 9N 0 30W
Am Timan, Chad .... **79 F10** 11 0N 20 10 E
Amadeus, L., Australia **93 D5** 24 54 S 131 0 E
Amadi, Dem. Rep. of
the Congo .... **86 B2** 3 40N 26 40 E
Amâdi, Sudan .... **81 F3** 5 29N 30 25 E
Amadjuak L., Canada **101 B12** 65 0N 71 8W
Amadora, Portugal .. **37 G1** 38 45N 9 13W
Amagansett, U.S.A. . **117 F12** 40 59N 72 9W
Amagasaki, Japan ... **55 G7** 34 42N 135 20 E
Amager, Denmark ... **11 J6** 55 37N 12 35 E
Amagunze, Nigeria .. **83 D6** 6 20N 7 40 E
Amahai, Indonesia ... **63 E7** 3 20 S 128 55 E
Amakusa-Shotō, Japan **55 H5** 32 15N 130 10 E
Åmål, Sweden ...... **10 E6** 59 3N 12 42 E
Amaliás, Greece ..... **46 D3** 37 47N 21 22 E
Amalner, India ...... **66 J9** 21 5N 75 5 E
Amamapare, Indonesia **63 E9** 4 53 S 136 38 E
Amambaí, Brazil .... **127 A4** 23 5 S 55 13W
Amambaí →, Brazil . **127 A5** 23 22 S 53 56W
Amambay □, Paraguay **127 A4** 23 0 S 56 0W
Amambay, Cordillera
de, S. Amer. ..... **127 A4** 20 0 S 55 45W
Amami-Guntō, Japan **55 L4** 27 16N 129 21 E
Amami-Ō-Shima, Japan **55 L4** 28 0N 129 0 E
Amaná, L., Brazil .... **124 D6** 2 35 S 64 40W
Amanat →, India .... **69 G11** 24 7N 84 4 E
Amanda Park, U.S.A. **110 C3** 47 28N 123 55W
Amangeldy, Kazakhstan **52 D7** 50 10N 65 10 E
Amantea, Italy ...... **43 C9** 39 8N 16 4 E
Amapá, Brazil **125 C8** 2 5N 50 50W
Amapá □, Brazil **125 C8** 1 40N 52 0W
Amara, Sudan .... **81 E3** 10 25N 34 10 E
Amara □, Ethiopia ... **81 E4** 10 50N 37 0 E
Amarante, Brazil .... **125 E10** 6 14 S 42 50W
Amarante, Portugal .. **36 D2** 41 16N 8 5W
Amaranth, Canada ... **103 C9** 50 36N 98 43W
Amareleja, Portugal . **37 G3** 38 12N 7 13W
Amargosa →, U.S.A. **111 J10** 36 14N 116 51W
Amargosa Range,
U.S.A. **111 J10** 36 20N 116 45W
Amári, Greece ...... **49 D6** 35 13N 24 40 E

Amarillo, U.S.A. **113 H4** 35 13N 101 50W
Amarkantak, India ... **69 H9** 22 40N 81 45 E
Amârna, Tell el', Sudan **80 B3** 27 38N 30 52 E
Amaro, Mte., Italy ... **41 F11** 42 5N 14 5 E
Amarpur, India ..... **69 G12** 25 5N 87 0 E
Amarti, Eritrea ...... **81 E5** 14 17N 41 6 E
Amarwara, India .... **69 H8** 22 18N 79 10 E
Amasra, Turkey ..... **72 B5** 41 45N 32 23 E
Amasya, Turkey ..... **72 B6** 40 40N 35 50 E
Amata, Australia .... **93 E5** 26 9 S 131 9 E
Amatikulu, S. Africa . **89 D5** 29 3 S 31 33 E
Amatitlán, Guatemala **120 D1** 14 29N 90 38W
Amatrice, Italy ..... **41 F10** 42 38N 13 17 E
Amay, Belgium ..... **17 D5** 50 33N 5 19 E
Amazon =
Amazonas →,
S. Amer. .... **125 D9** 0 5 S 50 0W
Amazonas □, Brazil . **124 E6** 5 0 S 65 0W
Amazonas →, S. Amer. **125 D9** 0 5 S 50 0W
Amba Ferit, Ethiopia . **81 E4** 10 55N 38 52 E
Ambah, India .... **68 F8** 26 43N 78 13 E
Ambahakily, Madag. . **89 C7** 21 36 S 43 41 E
Ambahita, Madag. ... **89 C8** 24 1 S 45 16 E
Ambala, India ...... **68 D7** 30 23N 76 56 E
Ambalavao, Madag. . **89 C8** 21 50 S 46 56 E
Ambanja, Madag. ... **89 A8** 13 40 S 48 27 E
Ambararata, Madag. . **89 B8** 15 3 S 48 33 E
Ambarchik, Russia ... **53 C17** 69 40N 162 20 E
Ambarijeby, Madag. . **89 A8** 14 56 S 47 41 E
Ambaro, Helodrano',
Madag. .... **89 A8** 13 23 S 48 38 E
Ambato, Ecuador .... **124 D3** 1 5 S 78 42W
Ambato, Sierra de,
Argentina .... **126 B2** 28 25 S 66 10W
Ambato Boeny, Madag. **89 B8** 16 28 S 46 43 E
Ambatofinandrahana,
Madag. .... **89 C8** 20 33 S 46 48 E
Ambatolampy, Madag. **89 B8** 19 20 S 47 35 E
Ambatomainty, Madag. **89 B8** 17 41 S 45 40 E
Ambatomanoina,
Madag. .... **89 B8** 18 18 S 47 37 E
Ambatondrazaka,
Madag. .... **89 B8** 17 55 S 48 28 E
Ambatosoratra, Madag. **89 B8** 17 37 S 48 31 E
Ambelón, Greece .... **46 B4** 39 45N 22 22 E
Ambenja, Madag. ... **89 B8** 15 17 S 46 58 E
Amberg, Germany ... **25 F7** 49 26N 11 52 E
Ambergris Cay, Belize **119 D7** 18 0N 88 0W
Ambérieu-en-Bugey,
France .... **21 C9** 45 57N 5 20 E
Amberley, N.Z. ..... **91 K4** 43 9 S 172 44 E
Ambert, France ..... **20 C7** 45 33N 3 44 E
Ambidédi, Mali **82 C2** 14 35N 11 47W
Ambikapur, India ... **69 H10** 23 15N 83 15 E
Ambikol, Sudan ..... **80 D3** 21 20N 30 50 E
Ambilobé, Madag. ... **89 A8** 13 10 S 49 3 E
Ambinanindrano,
Madag. .... **89 C8** 20 5 S 48 23 E
Ambinanitelo, Madag. **89 B8** 15 21 S 49 35 E
Ambinda, Madag. ... **89 B8** 16 25 S 45 52 E
Amble, U.K. **14 B6** 55 20N 1 36W
Ambleside, U.K. **14 C5** 54 26N 2 58W
Ambo, Peru .... **124 F3** 10 5 S 76 10W
Amboahangy, Madag. **89 C8** 24 15 S 46 22 E
Ambodifototra, Madag. **89 B8** 16 59 S 49 52 E
Ambodilazana, Madag. **89 B8** 18 6 S 49 10 E
Ambodiriana, Madag. **89 B8** 17 55 S 49 18 E
Ambohidratrimo,
Madag. .... **89 B8** 18 50 S 47 26 E
Ambohidray, Madag. **89 B8** 18 36 S 48 18 E
Ambohimahamasina,
Madag. .... **89 C8** 21 56 S 47 11 E
Ambohimahasoa,
Madag. .... **89 C8** 21 7 S 47 13 E
Ambohimanga, Madag. **89 C8** 20 52 S 47 36 E
Ambohimitombo,
Madag. .... **89 C8** 20 43 S 47 26 E
Ambohitra, Madag. .. **89 A8** 12 30 S 49 10 E
Amboise, France .... **18 E8** 47 24N 1 2 E
Ambon, Indonesia ... **63 E7** 3 43 S 128 12 E
Ambondro, Madag. .. **89 D8** 25 13 S 45 44 E
Amboseli □, Kenya .. **86 C4** 2 37 S 37 13 E
Amboseli, L., Kenya . **86 C4** 2 40 S 37 10 E
Ambovombe, Madag. **89 D8** 25 11 S 46 5 E
Amboy, U.S.A. **111 L11** 34 33N 115 45W
Amboyna Cay,
S. China Sea ..... **62 C4** 7 50N 112 50 E
Ambridge, U.S.A. ... **116 F4** 40 36N 80 14W
Ambriz, Angola ..... **84 F2** 7 48 S 13 8 E
Amchitka I., U.S.A. .. **100 C1** 51 32N 179 0 E
Amderma, Russia ... **52 C7** 69 45N 61 30 E
Amdhi, India .... **69 H9** 23 51N 81 27 E
Ameca, Mexico **118 C4** 20 30N 104 0W
Ameca →, Mexico .. **118 C3** 20 40N 105 15W
Amecameca, Mexico . **119 D5** 19 7N 98 46W
Ameland, Neths. .... **17 A5** 53 27N 5 45 E
Amélia, Italy .... **41 F9** 42 33N 12 25 E
Amendolara, Italy ... **43 C9** 39 57N 16 35 E
Amenia, U.S.A. **117 E11** 41 51N 73 33W
American Falls, U.S.A. **108 E7** 42 47N 112 51W
American Falls
Reservoir, U.S.A. . **108 E7** 42 47N 112 52W
American Fork, U.S.A. **108 F8** 40 23N 111 48W
American Highland,
Antarctica .... **5 D6** 73 0 S 75 0 E
American Samoa ☑,
Pac. Oc. .... **91 B13** 14 20 S 170 40W
Americana, Brazil ... **127 A6** 22 45 S 47 20W
Americus, U.S.A. **115 K3** 32 4N 84 14W
Amerigo Vespucci,
Firenze (FLR), Italy . **40 E8** 43 49N 11 13 E
Amersfoort, Neths. .. **17 B5** 52 9N 5 23 E
Amersfoort, S. Africa **89 D4** 26 59 S 29 53 E
Amery Ice Shelf,
Antarctica .... **5 C6** 69 30 S 72 0 E
Ames, U.S.A. **112 E8** 42 2N 93 37W
Ames, Spain **36 C2** 42 54N 8 38W
Amesbury, U.S.A. ... **117 D14** 42 51N 70 56W
Amet, India .... **68 G5** 25 18N 73 56 E
Amfíklia, Greece .... **46 C4** 38 38N 22 35 E
Amfilokhía, Greece .. **46 C3** 38 52N 21 9 E
Amfípolis, Greece ... **44 F7** 40 48N 23 52 E
Ámfissa, Greece ..... **46 C4** 38 32N 22 22 E
Amga, Russia .... **53 C14** 60 50N 132 0 E
Amga →, Russia .... **53 C14** 62 38N 134 32 E
Amgu, Russia .... **54 B8** 45 45N 137 15 E
Amgun →, Russia .. **53 D14** 52 56N 139 38 E
Amherst, Mass., U.S.A. **117 D12** 42 23N 72 31W
Amherst, N.Y., U.S.A. **116 D6** 42 59N 78 48W
Amherst, Ohio, U.S.A. **116 E2** 41 24N 82 14W
Amherstburg, Canada **104 D3** 42 6N 83 6W

Amidon, U.S.A. **112 B3** 46 29N 103 19W
Amiens, France ..... **19 C9** 49 54N 2 16 E
Amindaion, Greece .. **44 F5** 40 42N 21 42 E
Áminne, Sweden .... **11 G7** 57 7N 14 0 E
Amino, Ethiopia .... **81 G5** 4 25N 41 52 E
Aminuis, Namibia ... **88 C2** 23 43 S 19 21 E
Amirābād, Iran ..... **70 C5** 33 20N 46 16 E
Amirante Is., Seychelles **50 K9** 6 0 S 53 0 E
Amisk L., Canada ... **103 B8** 54 35N 102 15W
Amisk L., Canada ... **103 C8** 54 35N 102 15W
Amistad △, U.S.A. .. **113 L4** 29 32N 101 12W
Amistad, Presa de la,
Mexico **118 B4** 29 24N 101 0W
Amite, U.S.A. **113 K9** 30 44N 90 30W
Amla, India .... **68 J8** 21 56N 78 7 E
Amlapura =
Karangasem,
Indonesia .... **63 J18** 8 27 S 115 37 E
Amlia I., U.S.A. **100 C2** 52 4N 173 30W
Amlwch, U.K. **14 D3** 53 24N 4 20W
Amm Adam, Sudan .. **81 D4** 16 20N 36 1 E
'Ammān, Jordan .... **74 D4** 31 57N 35 52 E
'Ammān □, Jordan .. **74 D5** 31 40N 36 30 E
'Ammān ✕ (AMM),
Jordan .... **74 D5** 31 45N 36 2 E
Ammanford, U.K. ... **15 F4** 51 48N 3 59W
Ammassalik = Tasiilaq,
Greenland **4 C6** 65 40N 37 20W
Ammerån →, Sweden **10 A10** 63 9N 16 13 E
Ammersee, Germany **25 G7** 48 0N 11 7 E
Ammochostos =
Famagusta, Cyprus **49 D12** 35 8N 33 55 E
Ammon, U.S.A. **108 E8** 43 28N 111 58W
Amnat Charoen,
Thailand .... **64 E5** 15 51N 104 38 E
Amnura, Bangla. .... **69 G13** 24 37N 88 25 E
Amo Jiang →, China **58 F3** 23 0N 101 50 E
Āmol, Iran .... **71 B7** 36 23N 52 20 E
Amorgós, Greece ... **47 E7** 36 50N 25 57 E
Amory, U.S.A. **115 J1** 33 59N 88 29W
Amos, Canada **104 C4** 48 35N 78 5W
Åmot, Norway ...... **9 G13** 59 57N 9 54 E
Åmotfors, Sweden ... **10 E6** 59 47N 12 22 E
Amoy = Xiamen, China **59 E12** 24 25N 118 4 E
Ampanavoana, Madag. **89 B9** 15 41 S 50 22 E
Ampang, Malaysia .. **65 L3** 3 8N 101 45 E
Ampangalana,
Lakandranon',
Madag. .... **89 C8** 22 48 S 47 50 E
Ampanihy, Madag. .. **89 C7** 24 40 S 44 45 E
Amparafaravola,
Madag. .... **89 B8** 17 35 S 48 13 E
Ampasinambo, Madag. **89 C8** 20 31 S 48 0 E
Ampasindava,
Helodranon', Madag. **89 A8** 13 40 S 48 15 E
Ampasindava,
Saikanosy, Madag. . **89 A8** 13 42 S 47 55 E
Ampenan, Indonesia . **63 K18** 8 34 S 116 4 E
Amper, Nigeria ..... **83 D6** 9 25N 9 40 E
Amper →, Germany . **25 G7** 48 29N 11 55 E
Ampezzo, Italy ..... **41 B9** 46 25N 12 48 E
Amphoe Kathu,
Thailand .... **65 a** 7 55N 98 21 E
Amphoe Thalang,
Thailand .... **65 a** 8 1N 98 20 E
Ampitsikinana, Réunion **89 A8** 12 57 S 49 49 E
Ampombiantambo,
Madag. .... **89 A8** 12 42 S 48 57 E
Amposta, Spain ..... **38 E5** 40 43N 0 34 E
Ampotaka, Madag. .. **89 D7** 25 3 S 44 41 E
Ampoza, Madag. .... **89 C7** 22 20 S 44 44 E
Amqui, Canada **105 C6** 48 28N 67 27W
Amravati, India ..... **66 J10** 20 55N 77 45 E
Amreli, India .... **68 J4** 21 35N 71 17 E
Amritsar, India ..... **68 D6** 31 35N 74 57 E
Amroha, India ...... **69 E8** 28 53N 78 30 E
Amrum, Germany ... **24 A4** 54 38N 8 21 E
Amsterdam, Neths. .. **17 B4** 52 23N 4 54 E
Amsterdam, U.S.A. .. **117 D10** 42 56N 74 11W
Amsterdam ✕ (AMS),
Neths. .... **17 B4** 52 18N 4 45 E
Amsterdam, I. =
Nouvelle-Amsterdam,
Î., Ind. Oc. ...... **3 F13** 38 30 S 77 30 E
Amstetten, Austria .. **26 C7** 48 7N 14 51 E
Amudarya →,
Uzbekistan .... **52 E6** 43 58N 59 34 E
Amundsen Gulf, Canada **100 A7** 71 0N 124 0W
Amundsen-Scott,
Antarctica .... **5 E** 90 0 S 166 0 E
Amundsen Sea,
Antarctica .... **5 D15** 72 0 S 115 0W
Amungen, Sweden .. **10 C9** 61 10N 15 40 E
Amuntai, Indonesia . **62 E5** 2 28 S 115 25 E
Amur →, Russia .... **53 D15** 52 56N 141 10 E
Amur, W. →, Sudan **80 D3** 18 56N 33 34 E
Amurang, Indonesia . **63 D6** 1 5N 124 40 E
Amurrio, Spain **38 B1** 43 3N 3 0W
Amursk, Russia ..... **53 D14** 50 14N 136 54 E
Amyderya =
Amudarya →,
Uzbekistan .... **52 E6** 43 58N 59 34 E
Amvrosiyvka, Ukraine **33 J10** 47 43N 38 30 E
Amvrakikós Kólpos,
Greece .... **46 C2** 39 0N 20 55 E
An Anbār □, Iraq ... **70 C4** 33 25N 42 0 E
An Bien, Vietnam ... **65 H5** 9 45N 105 0 E
An Hoa, Vietnam ... **64 E7** 15 40N 108 5 E
An Nabatīyah at Tahta,
Lebanon .... **74 B4** 33 23N 35 27 E
An Nabk, Si. Arabia . **70 D3** 31 20N 37 20 E
An Nabk, Syria ..... **74 A5** 34 2N 36 44 E
An Nafūd, Si. Arabia . **70 D4** 28 15N 41 0 E
An Najaf, Iraq ...... **70 C5** 32 3N 44 15 E
An Nāşiriyah, Iraq ... **70 D5** 31 0N 46 15 E
An Nhon, Vietnam ... **64 F7** 13 55N 109 7 E
An Nîl □, Sudan .... **80 D3** 19 30N 33 0 E
An Nîl el Abyad □,
Sudan .... **81 E3** 14 0N 32 15 E
An Nîl el Azraq □,
Sudan .... **81 E3** 13 0N 34 30 E
An Nu'ayrīyah,
Si. Arabia .... **71 E6** 27 30N 48 30 E
An Nu'mānīyah, Iraq . **73 F11** 32 32N 45 25 E
An Nuwayb'ī, W. →,
Si. Arabia .... **74 F3** 29 18N 34 57 E
An Thoi, Dao, Vietnam **65 H4** 9 58N 104 0 E
An Uaimh, Ireland .. **12 C5** 53 39N 6 41W
Anabar →, Russia ... **53 B12** 73 8N 113 36 E
'Anabtā, West Bank .. **74 C4** 32 19N 35 7 E
Anaconda, U.S.A. ... **108 C7** 46 8N 112 57W
Anacortes, U.S.A. ... **110 B4** 48 30N 122 37W
Anacuao, Mt., Phil. .. **61 C4** 16 16N 121 53 E
Anadarko, U.S.A. ... **113 H5** 35 4N 98 15W
Anadia, Portugal **36 E2** 40 26N 8 27W
Anadolu, Turkey .... **72 C5** 39 0N 30 0 E

Anadyr, Russia .... **53 C18** 64 35N 177 20 E
Anadyr ➤, Russia .... **53 C18** 64 55N 176 5 E
Anadyrskiy Zaliv,
  Russia .... **53 C19** 64 0N 180 0 E
Anáfi, Greece .... **47 E7** 36 22N 25 48 E
Anafópoulo, Greece ... **47 E7** 36 17N 25 50 E
Anaga, Pta. de,
  Canary Is. **48 F3** 28 34N 16 9W
Anagni, Italy .... **41 G10** 41 44N 13 9 E
'Ānah, Iraq .... **70 C4** 34 25N 42 0 E
Anaheim, U.S.A. **111 M9** 33 50N 117 55W
Anahim Lake, Canada . **102 C3** 52 28N 125 18W
Anáhuac, Mexico **118 B4** 27 14N 100 9W
Anakapalle, India .... **67 L13** 17 42N 83 6 E
Anakie, Australia ..... **94 C4** 23 32 S 147 45 E
Anaklia, Georgia ..... **35 J5** 42 22N 41 35 E
Analalava, Madag. .... **89 A8** 14 35 S 48 0 E
Análipsis, Greece ..... **49 A3** 39 36N 19 55 E
Anambar ➤, Pakistan . **68 D3** 30 15N 68 50 E
Anambas, Kepulauan,
  Indonesia .... **62 D3** 3 20N 106 30 E
Anambas Is. =
  Anambas, Kepulauan,
  Indonesia .... **62 D3** 3 20N 106 30 E
Anambra □, Nigeria .. **83 D6** 6 20N 7 0 E
Anamosa, U.S.A. **112 D9** 42 7N 91 17W
Anamur, Turkey ...... **70 B2** 36 8N 32 58 E
Anamur Burnu, Turkey **72 D5** 36 2N 32 47 E
Anan, Japan .... **55 H7** 33 54N 134 40 E
Anand, India .... **68 H5** 22 32N 72 59 E
Anánes, Greece ...... **46 E6** 36 33N 24 9 E
Anantapur, India ..... **66 M10** 14 39N 77 42 E
Anantnag, India ..... **69 C6** 33 45N 75 10 E
Ananyiv, Ukraine ..... **33 J5** 47 44N 29 58 E
Anapa, Russia .... **33 K9** 44 55N 37 25 E
Anapodháris ➤, Greece **49 E7** 34 59N 25 20 E
Anápolis, Brazil ..... **125 G9** 16 15 S 48 50W
Anapu ➤, Brazil ..... **125 D8** 1 53 S 50 53W
Anár, Iran .... **71 D7** 30 55N 55 13 E
Anārak, Iran .... **71 C7** 33 25N 53 40 E
Anarisfjällen, Sweden . **10 A7** 63 6N 13 0 E
Anas ➤, India .... **68 H5** 23 26N 74 0 E
Anatolia = Anadolu,
  Turkey .... **72 C5** 39 0N 30 0 E
Anatsogno, Madag. ... **89 C7** 23 33 S 43 46 E
Añatuya, Argentina ... **126 B3** 28 20 S 62 50W
Anaunethna L., Canada **103 A8** 60 55N 104 25W
Anbyon, N. Korea .... **57 E14** 39 1N 127 35 E
Ancares, Sierra de,
  Spain **36 C4** 42 50N 6 40W
Ancaster, Canada **116 C5** 43 13N 79 59W
Ancenis, France **18 E5** 47 21N 1 10W
Anchor Bay, U.S.A. .. **110 G3** 38 48N 123 34W
Anchorage, U.S.A. ... **100 B5** 61 13N 149 54W
Anci, China .... **56 E9** 39 20N 116 40 E
Ancohuma, Nevado,
  Bolivia .... **124 G5** 16 0 S 68 50W
Ancón, Peru .... **124 F3** 11 50 S 77 10W
Ancona, Italy .... **41 E10** 43 38N 13 30 E
Ancud, Chile .... **128 E2** 42 0 S 73 50W
Ancud, G. de, Chile .. **128 E2** 42 0 S 73 0W
Ancy-le-Franc, France . **19 E11** 47 46N 4 10 E
Andacollo, Argentina . **126 D1** 37 10 S 70 42W
Andacollo, Chile ..... **126 C1** 30 14 S 71 6W
Andaingo, Madag. ... **89 B8** 18 12 S 48 17 E
Andalgalá, Argentina . **126 B2** 27 40 S 66 30W
Åndalsnes, Norway ... **9 E12** 62 35N 7 43 E
Andalucía □, Spain .. **37 H6** 37 35N 5 0W
Andalusia =
  Andalucía □, Spain . **37 H6** 37 35N 5 0W
Andalusia, U.S.A. **115 K2** 31 18N 86 29W
Andaman Is., Ind. Oc. **50 H13** 12 30N 92 45 E
Andaman Sea, Ind. Oc. **62 B1** 13 0N 96 0 E
Andamooka Opal
  Fields, Australia .... **95 E2** 30 27 S 137 9 E
Andapa, Madag. ..... **89 A8** 14 39 S 49 39 E
Andara, Namibia ..... **88 B3** 18 2 S 21 9 E
Andelot-Blancheville,
  France .... **19 D12** 48 15N 5 18 E
Andenes, Norway .... **8 B17** 69 19N 16 18 E
Andenne, Belgium .... **17 D5** 50 28N 5 5 E
Andéranboukane, Mali **83 B5** 15 26N 3 2 E
Andermatt, Switz. .... **25 J4** 46 38N 8 35 E
Andernach, Germany . **24 E3** 50 26N 7 24 E
Andernos-les-Bains,
  France **20 D2** 44 44N 1 6W
Anderslöv, Sweden ... **11 J7** 55 26N 13 19 E
Anderson, Alaska,
  U.S.A. **100 B5** 64 25N 149 15W
Anderson, Calif., U.S.A. **108 F2** 40 27N 122 18W
Anderson, Ind., U.S.A. **114 E3** 40 10N 85 41W
Anderson, Mo., U.S.A. **113 G7** 36 39N 94 27W
Anderson, S.C., U.S.A. **115 H4** 34 31N 82 39W
Anderson ➤, Canada . **100 B7** 69 42N 129 0W
Anderstorp, Sweden .. **11 G7** 57 19N 13 39 E
Andes, U.S.A. **117 D10** 42 12N 74 47W
Andes, Cord. de los,
  S. Amer. .... **124 H5** 20 0 S 68 0W
Andfjorden, Norway .. **8 B17** 69 10N 16 20 E
Andhra Pradesh □,
  India .... **66 L11** 18 0N 79 0 E
Andijon, Uzbekistan .. **52 E8** 41 10N 72 15 E
Andikíthira, Greece ... **46 F5** 35 52N 23 15 E
Andilamena, Madag. .. **89 B8** 17 1 S 48 35 E
Andimeshk, Iran ..... **71 C6** 32 27N 48 21 E
Andímilos, Greece ... **46 E6** 36 47N 24 12 E
Andíparos, Greece ... **47 D7** 37 0N 25 3 E
Andípaxoi, Greece ... **46 B2** 39 9N 20 13 E
Andípsara, Greece ... **47 C7** 38 30N 25 29 E
Andírrion, Greece .... **46 C3** 38 20N 21 46 E
Andizhan = Andijon,
  Uzbekistan .... **52 E8** 41 10N 72 15 E
Andoain, Spain **38 B2** 43 13N 2 1W
Andoany, Madag. .... **89 A8** 13 25 S 48 16 E
Andohahela △, Madag. **89 C8** 24 4 S 46 44 E
Andong, S. Korea .... **57 F15** 36 40N 128 43 E
Andongwei, China ... **57 G10** 35 6N 119 20 E
Andoom, Australia ... **94 A3** 12 25 S 141 53 E
Andorra, Spain ...... **38 E4** 40 59N 0 0 E
Andorra □, Europe .. **20 F5** 42 30N 1 30 E
Andorra La Vella,
  Andorra .... **20 F5** 42 31N 1 32 E
Andover, U.K. **15 F6** 51 12N 1 29W
Andover, Maine, U.S.A. **117 B14** 44 38N 70 45W
Andover, Mass., U.S.A. **117 D13** 42 40N 71 8W
Andover, N.J., U.S.A. . **117 F10** 40 59N 74 45W
Andover, N.Y., U.S.A. **116 D7** 42 10N 77 48W
Andover, Ohio, U.S.A. **116 E4** 41 36N 80 34W
Andøya, Norway ..... **8 B16** 69 10N 15 50 E
Andradina, Brazil .... **125 H8** 20 54 S 51 23W
Andramasina, Madag. . **89 B8** 19 11 S 47 35 E
Andranopasy, Madag. . **89 C7** 21 17 S 43 44 E
Andranovory, Madag. . **89 C7** 23 8 S 44 10 E
Andratx, Spain ...... **48 B9** 39 39N 2 25 E

Andreanof Is., U.S.A. . **100 C2** 51 30N 176 0W
Andreapol, Russia .... **32 D7** 56 40N 32 17 E
Andrews, S.C., U.S.A. **115 J6** 33 27N 79 34W
Andrews, Tex., U.S.A. **113 J3** 32 19N 102 33W
Andreyevka, Russia ... **34 D10** 52 19N 51 55 E
Ándria, Italy .... **43 A9** 41 13N 16 17 E
Andriamena, Madag. . **89 B8** 17 26 S 47 30 E
Andriandampy, Madag. **89 C8** 22 45 S 45 41 E
Andriba, Madag. ..... **89 B8** 17 30 S 46 58 E
Andrijevica, Serbia & M. **44 D3** 42 45N 19 48 E
Andringitra △, Madag. **89 C8** 22 13 S 46 5 E
Andritsaina, Greece .. **46 D3** 37 29N 21 52 E
Androka, Madag. .... **89 C7** 24 58 S 44 2 E
Ándros, Greece ...... **46 D6** 37 50N 24 57 E
Andros I., Bahamas .. **120 B4** 24 30N 78 0W
Andros Town, Bahamas **120 B4** 24 43N 77 47W
Androscoggin ➤,
  U.S.A. **117 C14** 43 58N 70 0W
Andrychów, Poland .. **31 J6** 49 51N 19 18 E
Andselv, Norway .... **8 B18** 69 4N 18 34 E
Andújar, Spain **37 G6** 38 3N 4 5W
Andulo, Angola ...... **84 G3** 11 25 S 16 45 E
Aneby, Sweden ...... **11 G8** 57 48N 14 49 E
Anegada I.,
  Br. Virgin Is. ...... **121 e** 18 45N 64 20W
Anegada Passage,
  W. Indies **121 C7** 18 15N 63 45W
Aného, Togo .... **83 D5** 6 12N 1 34 E
Anenni-Noi, Moldova . **29 D14** 46 53N 29 15 E
Aneto, Pico de, Spain **38 C5** 42 37N 0 40 E
Anfu, China .... **59 D10** 27 21N 114 40 E
Ang Mo Kio, Singapore **65 d** 1 23N 103 50 E
Ang Thong, Thailand . **64 E3** 14 35N 100 31 E
Ang Thong ➤, Thailand **64 E3** 14 47N 99 43 E
Ang Thong, Ko,
  Thailand .... **65 b** 9 37N 99 41 E
Angamos, Punta, Chile **126 A1** 23 1 S 70 32W
Angara ➤, Russia .... **53 D10** 58 5N 94 20 E
Angara-Débou, Benin . **83 C5** 11 19N 3 3 E
Angarab, Ethiopia ... **81 E4** 13 11N 37 7 E
Angarbaka, Sudan ... **81 F1** 9 44N 24 44 E
Angarsk, Russia ..... **53 D11** 52 30N 104 0 E
Angas Hills, Australia . **92 D4** 23 0 S 127 50 E
Angaston, Australia .. **95 E2** 34 30 S 139 8 E
Ånge, Sweden .... **10 B9** 62 31N 15 35 E
Ángel, Salto = Angel
  Falls, Venezuela ... **124 B6** 5 57N 62 30W
Ángel de la Guarda, I.,
  Mexico **118 B2** 29 30N 113 30W
Angel Falls, Venezuela **124 B6** 5 57N 62 30W
Angeles, Phil. .... **61 D4** 15 9N 120 33 E
Ängelholm, Sweden .. **11 H6** 56 15N 12 58 E
Angels Camp, U.S.A. . **110 G6** 38 4N 120 32W
Ängelsberg, Sweden .. **10 E10** 59 58N 16 0 E
Anger ➤, Ethiopia ... **81 F4** 9 37N 36 6 E
Angereb ➤, Ethiopia . **81 E4** 13 45N 36 40 E
Ångermanälven ➤,
  Sweden .... **10 B11** 62 40N 18 0 E
Ångermanland, Sweden **8 E18** 63 36N 17 45 E
Angermünde, Germany **24 B9** 53 1N 14 0 E
Angers, Canada **117 A9** 45 31N 75 29W
Angers, France **18 E6** 47 30N 0 35W
Angerville, France .... **19 D9** 48 19N 2 0 E
Ängesån ➤, Sweden . **8 C20** 66 16N 22 47 E
Angikuni L., Canada .. **103 A9** 62 12N 99 59W
Angkor, Cambodia ... **64 F4** 13 22N 103 50 E
Anglés, Spain .... **38 D7** 41 57N 2 38 E
Anglesey, Isle of □, U.K. **14 D3** 53 16N 4 18W
Anglet, France **20 E2** 43 29N 1 31W
Angleton, U.S.A. **113 L7** 29 10N 95 26W
Anglin ➤, France .... **20 B4** 46 42N 0 52 E
Anglisídhes, Cyprus .. **49 E12** 34 51N 33 27 E
Anglure, France ..... **19 D10** 48 35N 3 50 E
Angmagssalik =
  Tasiilaq, Greenland . **4 C6** 65 40N 37 20W
Ango, Dem. Rep. of
  the Congo .... **86 B2** 4 10N 26 5 E
Angoche, Mozam. ... **87 F4** 16 8 S 39 55 E
Angoche, I., Mozam. . **87 F4** 16 20 S 39 50 E
Angol, Chile .... **126 D1** 37 56 S 72 45W
Angola, Ind., U.S.A. . **114 E3** 41 38N 85 0W
Angola, N.Y., U.S.A. . **116 D5** 42 38N 79 2W
Angola ■, Africa .... **85 G3** 12 0 S 18 0 E
Angoulême, France .. **20 C4** 45 39N 0 10 E
Angoumois, France .. **20 C4** 45 50N 0 25 E
Angra dos Reis, Brazil **127 A7** 23 0 S 44 10W
Angrapa ➤, Russia .. **30 D8** 54 37N 21 54 E
Angren, Uzbekistan .. **52 E8** 41 1N 70 12 E
Angtassom, Cambodia **65 G5** 11 1N 104 41 E
Angu, Dem. Rep. of
  the Congo .... **86 B1** 3 23N 24 30 E
Anguang, China ..... **57 B12** 45 15N 123 45 E
Anguilla ☒, W. Indies **121 C7** 18 14N 63 5W
Anguo, China .... **56 E8** 38 28N 115 15 E
Angurugu, Australia .. **94 A2** 14 0 S 136 25 E
Angus □, U.K. **13 E6** 56 46N 2 56W
Angwa ➤, Zimbabwe **89 B5** 16 0 S 30 23 E
Anhandui ➤, Brazil .. **127 A5** 21 46 S 52 9W
Anholt, Denmark .... **11 H5** 56 42N 11 33 E
Anhua, China .... **59 C8** 28 23N 111 12 E
Anhui □, China ..... **59 B11** 32 0N 117 0 E
Anhwei = Anhui □,
  China .... **59 B11** 32 0N 117 0 E
Anichab, Namibia ... **88 C1** 21 0 S 14 46 E
Ánidhros, Greece .... **47 E7** 36 38N 25 43 E
Anié, Togo .... **83 D5** 7 42N 1 8 E
Animas ➤, U.S.A. ... **109 H9** 36 43N 108 13W
Anina, Romania ..... **28 E6** 45 6N 21 51 E
Aninoasa, Romania .. **29 F9** 44 47N 24 10 E
Anivorano, Madag. .. **89 B8** 18 44 S 48 58 E
Anjalankoski, Finland . **9 F22** 60 45N 26 51 E
Anjar, India .... **68 H4** 23 6N 70 10 E
Anjou, France **18 E6** 47 20N 0 15W
Anjozorobe, Madag. . **89 B8** 18 22 S 47 52 E
Anju, N. Korea ...... **57 E13** 39 36N 125 40 E
Anka, Nigeria .... **83 C6** 12 13N 5 58 E
Ankaboa, Tanjona,
  Madag. .... **89 C7** 21 58 S 43 20 E
Ankang, China ...... **56 H5** 32 40N 109 1 E
Ankara, Turkey ...... **72 C5** 39 57N 32 54 E
Ankarafantsika △,
  Madag. .... **89 B8** 16 8 S 47 5 E
Ankaramena, Madag. . **89 C8** 21 57 S 46 39 E
Ankaratra, Madag. ... **85 H9** 19 25 S 47 12 E
Ankarsrum, Sweden .. **11 G10** 57 41N 16 20 E
Ankasakasa, Madag. . **89 B7** 16 21 S 44 52 E
Ankavandra, Madag. . **89 B8** 18 46 S 45 18 E
Ankazoabo, Madag. . **89 C7** 22 18 S 44 31 E
Ankazobe, Madag. .. **89 B8** 18 20 S 47 10 E
Ankeny, U.S.A. **112 E8** 41 44N 93 36W
Ankilimalinika, Madag. **89 C7** 22 55 S 43 45 E
Ankilizato, Madag. ... **89 C8** 20 25 S 45 1 E
Ankisabe, Madag. ... **89 B8** 19 17 S 46 29 E
Anklam, Germany ... **24 B9** 53 51N 13 41 E
Ankober, Ethiopia ... **81 F4** 9 35N 39 40 E
Ankoro, Dem. Rep. of
  the Congo .... **86 D2** 6 45 S 26 55 E

Ankororoka, Madag. . **89 D8** 25 30 S 45 11 E
Anlong, China ...... **58 E5** 25 2N 105 27 E
Anlu, China .... **59 B9** 31 15N 113 45 E
Anmyon-do, S. Korea **57 F14** 36 25N 126 25 E
Ånn, Sweden .... **10 A6** 63 19N 12 33 E
Ann, C., U.S.A. **117 D14** 42 38N 70 35W
Ann Arbor, U.S.A. ... **114 D4** 42 17N 83 45W
Anna, Russia .... **34 E5** 51 28N 40 23 E
Anna, U.S.A. **113 G10** 37 28N 89 15W
Annaba, Algeria ..... **78 A7** 36 50N 7 46 E
Annaberg-Buchholz,
  Germany .... **24 E9** 50 34N 13 0 E
Annalee ➤, Ireland .. **12 B4** 54 2N 7 24W
Annam, Vietnam .... **64 E7** 16 0N 108 0 E
Annamitique, Chaîne,
  Asia .... **64 D6** 17 0N 106 0 E
Annan, U.K. **13 G5** 54 59N 3 16W
Annan ➤, U.K. **13 G5** 54 58N 3 16W
Annapolis, U.S.A. **114 F7** 38 59N 76 30W
Annapolis Royal,
  Canada **105 D6** 44 44N 65 32W
Annapurna, Nepal ... **69 E10** 28 34N 83 50 E
Annean, L., Australia . **93 E2** 26 54 S 118 14 E
Anneberg, Sweden .. **11 G8** 57 44N 14 49 E
Annecy, France ..... **21 C10** 45 55N 6 8 E
Annecy, Lac d', France **21 C10** 45 52N 6 10 E
Annemasse, France .. **19 F13** 46 12N 6 16 E
Annenskiy Most, Russia **32 B9** 60 45N 37 10 E
Anning, China ...... **58 E4** 24 55N 102 26 E
Anniston, U.S.A. **115 J3** 33 39N 85 50W
Annobón, Atl. Oc. ... **77 G4** 1 25 S 5 36 E
Annonay, France .... **21 C8** 45 15N 4 40 E
Annot, France ...... **21 E10** 43 58N 6 38 E
Annotto Bay, Jamaica **120 a** 18 17N 76 45W
Ånnsjön, Sweden ... **10 A6** 63 19N 12 34 E
Annville, U.S.A. **117 F8** 40 20N 76 31W
Áno Arkhánai, Greece **47 F7** 35 16N 25 11 E
Áno Porróia, Greece . **44 E7** 41 17N 23 2 E
Áno Síros, Greece ... **46 D6** 37 29N 24 56 E
Áno Viánnos, Greece **49 D7** 35 2N 25 21 E
Anorotsangana, Madag. **89 A8** 13 56 S 47 55 E
Anosibe, Madag. .... **89 B8** 19 26 S 48 13 E
Anou Mellene, Mali . **83 B5** 17 29N 0 33 E
Anoumaba, Ivory C. . **82 D4** 6 23N 4 38W
Anóyia, Greece ..... **49 D6** 35 16N 24 52 E
Anping, Hebei, China **56 E8** 38 15N 115 30 E
Anping, Liaoning, China **57 D12** 41 5N 123 30 E
Anpu Gang, China .. **58 G7** 21 25N 109 50 E
Anqing, China ...... **59 B11** 30 30N 117 3 E
Anqiu, China .... **57 F10** 36 25N 119 10 E
Anren, China .... **59 D9** 26 43N 113 18 E
Ansager, Denmark .. **11 J2** 55 43N 8 45 E
Ansai, China .... **56 F5** 36 50N 109 20 E
Ansbach, Germany .. **25 F6** 49 28N 10 34 E
Anseba ➤, Eritrea ... **81 D4** 16 0N 38 30 E
Anshan, China ...... **57 D12** 41 5N 122 58 E
Anshun, China ...... **58 D5** 26 18N 105 57 E
Ansião, Portugal .... **36 F2** 39 56N 8 27 E
Ansley, U.S.A. **112 E5** 41 18N 99 23W
Ansó, Spain **38 C3** 42 51N 0 48W
Ansoain, Spain **38 C3** 42 50N 1 38W
Anson, U.S.A. **113 J5** 32 45N 99 54W
Anson B., Australia .. **92 B5** 13 20 S 130 6 E
Ansongo, Mali ...... **83 B5** 15 25N 0 35 E
Ansonia, U.S.A. **117 E11** 41 21N 73 4W
Anstruther, U.K. **13 E6** 56 14N 2 41W
Ansudu, Indonesia .. **63 E9** 2 11 S 139 22 E
Antabamba, Peru .... **124 F4** 14 40 S 73 0W
Antakya, Turkey .... **70 B3** 36 14N 36 10 E
Antalya, Turkey ..... **72 D4** 36 52N 30 45 E
Antalya □, Turkey ... **47 E12** 36 30N 30 0 E
Antalya Körfezi, Turkey **72 D4** 36 15N 31 30 E
Antambohobe, Madag. **89 C8** 22 20 S 46 47 E
Antanambao-
  Manampotsy, Madag. **89 B8** 19 29 S 48 34 E
Antanambe, Madag. . **89 B8** 16 26 S 49 52 E
Antananarivo, Madag. **89 B8** 18 55 S 47 31 E
Antananarivo □, Madag. **89 B8** 19 0 S 47 0 E
Antanifotsy, Madag. . **89 B8** 19 39 S 47 19 E
Antanimbaribe, Madag. **89 C7** 21 30 S 44 48 E
Antanimora, Madag. . **89 C8** 24 49 S 45 40 E
Antarctic Pen.,
  Antarctica .... **5 C18** 67 0 S 60 0W
Antarctica .... **5 E3** 90 0 S 0 0W
Antelope, Zimbabwe . **87 G2** 21 2 S 28 31 E
Antequera, Paraguay . **126 A4** 24 8 S 57 7W
Antequera, Spain **37 H6** 37 5N 4 33W
Antero, Mt., U.S.A. . **109 G10** 38 41N 106 15W
Antevamena, Madag. **89 C7** 21 2 S 43 43 E
Anthemoús, Greece . **44 F7** 40 31N 23 15 E
Anthony, Kans., U.S.A. **113 G5** 37 9N 98 2W
Anthony, N. Mex.,
  U.S.A. **109 K10** 32 0N 106 36W
Anti Atlas, Morocco . **78 C4** 30 0N 8 30W
Anti-Lebanon = Ash
  Sharqi, Al Jabal,
  Lebanon .... **74 B5** 33 40N 36 10 E
Antibes, France ..... **21 E11** 43 34N 7 6 E
Antibes, C. d', France **21 E11** 43 31N 7 7 E
Anticosti, Î. d', Canada **105 C7** 49 30N 63 0W
Antifer, C. d', France . **18 C7** 49 41N 0 10 E
Antigo, U.S.A. **112 C10** 45 9N 89 9W
Antigonish, Canada .. **105 C7** 45 38N 61 58W
Antigua, Canary Is. .. **48 F5** 28 24N 14 1W
Antigua, Guatemala . **120 D1** 14 34N 90 41W
Antigua, W. Indies ... **121 C7** 17 0N 61 50W
Antigua & Barbuda ■,
  W. Indies **121 C7** 17 20N 61 48W
Antilla, Cuba **120 B4** 20 40N 75 50W
Antilles = West Indies,
  Cent. Amer. **121 D7** 15 0N 65 0W
Antioch, U.S.A. **110 G5** 38 1N 121 48W
Antioche, Pertuis d',
  France **20 B2** 46 6N 1 20W
Antioquia, Colombia . **124 B3** 6 40N 75 55W
Antipodes Is., Pac. Oc. **96 M9** 49 45 S 178 40 E
Antlers, U.S.A. **113 H7** 34 14N 95 37W
Antoetra, Madag. ... **89 C8** 20 46 S 47 20 E
Antofagasta, Chile ... **126 A1** 23 50 S 70 30W
Antofagasta □, Chile . **126 A2** 24 0 S 69 0W
Antofagasta de la Sierra,
  Argentina .... **126 B2** 26 5 S 67 20W
Antofalla, Argentina . **126 B2** 25 30 S 68 5W
Antofalla, Salar de,
  Argentina .... **126 B2** 25 40 S 67 45W
Anton, U.S.A. **113 J3** 33 49N 102 10W
Antongila, Helodrano,
  Madag. .... **89 B8** 15 30 S 49 50 E
Antonibé, Madag. ... **89 B8** 15 7 S 47 24 E
Antonibé, Presqu'île d',
  Madag. .... **89 A8** 14 55 S 47 20 E
Antonina, Brazil ..... **127 B6** 25 26 S 48 42W

Antrain, France **18 D5** 48 28N 1 30W
Antrim, U.K. **12 B5** 54 43N 6 14W
Antrim, U.S.A. **116 F3** 40 7N 81 21W
Antrim □, U.K. **12 B5** 54 56N 6 25W
Antrim, Mts. of, U.K. **12 A5** 55 3N 6 14W
Antrim Plateau,
  Australia .... **92 C4** 18 8 S 128 20 E
Antrodoco, Italy .... **41 F10** 42 25N 13 5 E
Antropovo, Russia ... **34 A6** 58 24N 43 6 E
Antsakabary, Madag. **89 B8** 15 3 S 48 56 E
Antsalova, Madag. ... **89 B7** 18 40 S 44 37 E
Antsenavolo, Madag. **89 C8** 21 24 S 48 3 E
Antsiafabositra, Madag. **89 B8** 17 18 S 46 57 E
Antsirabe,
  Antananarivo, Madag. **89 B8** 19 55 S 47 2 E
Antsirabe, Antsiranana,
  Madag. .... **89 A8** 14 0 S 49 59 E
Antsirabe, Mahajanga,
  Madag. .... **89 B8** 15 57 S 48 58 E
Antsiranana, Madag. . **89 A8** 12 25 S 49 20 E
Antsiranana □, Madag. **89 A8** 12 16 S 49 17 E
Antsohihy, Madag. .. **89 A8** 14 50 S 47 59 E
Antsohimbondrona
  Seranana, Madag. .. **89 A8** 13 7 S 48 48 E
Antu, China .... **57 C15** 42 30N 128 20 E
Antwerp = Antwerpen,
  Belgium .... **17 C4** 51 13N 4 25 E
Antwerp, U.S.A. **117 B9** 44 12N 75 37W
Antwerpen, Belgium . **17 C4** 51 13N 4 25 E
Antwerpen □, Belgium **17 C4** 51 15N 4 40 E
Anupgarh, India .... **68 E5** 29 10N 73 10 E
Anuppur, India ..... **69 H9** 23 6N 81 41 E
Anuradhapura,
  Sri Lanka .... **66 Q12** 8 22N 80 28 E
Anveh, Iran .... **71 E7** 27 23N 54 11 E
Anvers = Antwerpen,
  Belgium .... **17 C4** 51 13N 4 25 E
Anvers I., Antarctica . **5 C17** 64 30 S 63 40W
Anwen, China ...... **59 C13** 29 4N 120 26 E
Anxi, Fujian, China .. **59 E12** 25 2N 118 12 E
Anxi, Gansu, China .. **60 B4** 40 30N 95 43 E
Anxian, China ...... **58 B5** 31 40N 104 25 E
Anxiang, China ..... **59 C9** 29 27N 112 11 E
Anxious B., Australia . **95 E1** 33 24 S 134 45 E
Anyama, Ivory C. ... **82 D4** 5 30N 4 3W
Anyang, China ...... **56 F8** 36 5N 114 21 E
Anyer-Kidul, Indonesia **63 G11** 6 4 S 105 53 E
Anyi, Jiangxi, China .. **59 C10** 28 49N 115 25 E
Anyi, Shanxi, China .. **56 G6** 35 2N 111 2 E
Anyuan, China ...... **59 E10** 25 9N 115 21 E
Anyue, China .... **58 B5** 30 9N 105 50 E
Anza, U.S.A. **111 M10** 33 35N 116 39W
Anze, China .... **56 F7** 36 10N 112 12 E
Anzhero-Sudzhensk,
  Russia .... **52 D9** 56 10N 86 0 E
Ánzio, Italy .... **42 A5** 41 27N 12 37 E
Ao Makham, Thailand **65 a** 7 50N 98 24 E
Ao Phangnga △,
  Thailand .... **65 a** 8 10N 98 32 E
Aoga-Shima, Japan .. **55 H9** 32 28N 139 46 E
Aoiz, Spain **38 C3** 42 46N 1 22W
Aomen = Macau, China **59 F9** 22 12N 113 33 E
Aomori, Japan ...... **54 D10** 40 45N 140 45 E
Aomori □, Japan .... **54 D10** 40 45N 140 40 E
Aonla, India .... **69 E8** 28 16N 79 11 E
Aoraki Mount Cook,
  N.Z. .... **91 K3** 43 36 S 170 9 E
Aosta, Italy .... **40 C4** 45 45N 7 20 E
Aotearoa = New
  Zealand ■, Oceania **91 J6** 40 0 S 176 0 E
Aoudéras, Niger ..... **83 B6** 17 45N 8 20 E
Aoukâr, Mauritania . **82 B3** 17 40N 10 0W
Aozou, Couloir d', Chad **79 D9** 22 0N 19 0 E
Aozou Strip = Aozou,
  Couloir d', Chad ... **79 D9** 22 0N 19 0 E
Apa ➤, S. Amer. .... **126 A4** 22 6 S 58 2W
Apache, U.S.A. **113 H5** 34 54N 98 22W
Apache Junction, U.S.A. **109 K8** 33 25N 111 33W
Apalachee B., U.S.A. **115 L4** 30 0N 84 0W
Apalachicola, U.S.A. . **115 L3** 29 43N 84 59W
Apalachicola ➤, U.S.A. **115 L3** 29 43N 84 58W
Apam, Ghana **83 D4** 5 19N 0 42W
Apapa, Nigeria ..... **83 D5** 6 25N 3 25 E
Apaporis ➤, Colombia **124 D5** 1 23 S 69 25W
Aparados da Serra △,
  Brazil .... **127 B5** 29 10 S 50 8W
Aparri, Phil. .... **61 B4** 18 22N 121 38 E
Apateu, Romania .... **28 D6** 46 36N 21 47 E
Apatin, Serbia & M. . **28 E4** 45 40N 19 0 E
Apatity, Russia ...... **52 C4** 67 34N 33 22 E
Apatzingán, Mexico . **118 D4** 19 0N 102 20W
Apeldoorn, Neths. ... **17 B5** 52 13N 5 57 E
Apen, Germany ..... **24 B3** 53 13N 7 48 E
Apennines = Appennini,
  Italy .... **40 D7** 44 30N 10 0 E
Aphrodisias, Turkey . **47 D10** 37 42N 28 46 E
Apia, Samoa .... **91 A13** 13 50 S 171 50W
Apiacás, Serra dos,
  Brazil .... **124 E7** 9 50 S 57 0W
Apies ➤, S. Africa ... **89 D4** 25 15 S 28 8 E
Apizaco, Mexico **119 D5** 19 26N 98 9W
Aplao, Peru .... **124 G4** 16 0 S 72 40W
Apo, Mt., Phil. ..... **63 C7** 6 53N 125 14 E
Apolakkiá, Greece ... **49 C9** 36 5N 27 48 E
Apolakkiá, Órmos,
  Greece .... **49 C9** 36 5N 27 45 E
Apolda, Germany ... **24 D7** 51 2N 11 32 E
Apollonia, Greece ... **46 E6** 36 58N 24 43 E
Apolo, Bolivia ...... **124 F5** 14 30 S 68 30W
Aporé ➤, Brazil ..... **125 G8** 19 27 S 50 57W
Apostle Is., U.S.A. .. **112 B9** 47 0N 90 40W
Apóstoles, Argentina . **127 B4** 28 0 S 56 0W
Apostolos Andreas, C.,
  Cyprus .... **49 D13** 35 42N 34 35 E
Apostolovo, Ukraine . **33 J7** 47 39N 33 42 E
Apoteri, Guyana **124 C7** 4 2N 58 32W
Appalachian Mts.,
  U.S.A. **114 G6** 38 0N 80 0W
Äppelbo, Sweden ... **10 D8** 60 29N 14 1 E
Appennini, Italy ..... **40 D7** 44 30N 10 0 E
Appennino Ligure, Italy **40 D6** 44 30N 9 0 E
Appenzell-Ausser
  Rhoden □, Switz. .. **25 H5** 47 23N 9 23 E
Appenzell-Inner
  Rhoden □, Switz. .. **25 H5** 47 20N 9 25 E
Appiano, Italy ...... **41 B8** 46 28N 11 15 E
Apple Hill, Canada .. **117 A10** 45 13N 74 46W
Apple Valley, U.S.A. . **111 L9** 34 32N 117 14W
Appleby-in-
  Westmorland, U.K. . **14 C5** 54 35N 2 29W
Appledore, U.K. **15 F3** 51 3N 4 13W
Appleton, U.S.A. **114 C1** 44 16N 88 25W
Approuague ➤,
  Fr. Guiana **125 C8** 4 30N 51 57W
Apricena, Italy ...... **41 G12** 41 47N 15 27 E

Aprília, Italy .... **42 A5** 41 36N 12 39 E
Apsheronsk, Russia .. **35 H4** 44 28N 39 42 E
Apsley, Canada **116 B6** 44 45N 78 6W
Apt, France .... **21 E9** 43 53N 5 24 E
Apuane, Alpi, Italy ... **40 D7** 44 7N 10 14 E
Apucarana, Brazil ... **127 A5** 23 55 S 51 33W
Apulia = Púglia □, Italy **43 A9** 41 15N 16 15 E
Apure ➤, Venezuela . **124 B5** 7 37N 66 25W
Apurímac ➤, Peru ... **124 F4** 12 17 S 73 56W
Apuseni, Munții,
  Romania .... **28 D7** 46 30N 22 45 E
Āqā Jari, Iran .... **71 D6** 30 42N 49 50 E
Aqaba = Al 'Aqabah,
  Jordan .... **74 F4** 29 31N 35 0 E
Aqaba, G. of, Red Sea **70 D2** 28 15N 33 20 E
Aqabah = Al 'Aqabah,
  Jordan .... **74 F4** 29 31N 35 0 E
'Aqabah, Khalīj al =
  Aqaba, G. of, Red Sea **70 D2** 28 15N 33 20 E
'Aqdā, Iran .... **71 C7** 32 26N 53 37 E
Aqiq, Sudan .... **80 D4** 18 14N 38 12 E
Aqiq, Khalīg, Sudan . **80 D4** 18 20N 38 10 E
'Aqrah, Iraq .... **70 B4** 36 46N 43 45 E
Aqtaū, Kazakhstan .. **52 E6** 43 39N 51 12 E
Aqtöbe, Kazakhstan . **52 D6** 50 17N 57 10 E
Aquidauana, Brazil .. **125 H7** 20 30 S 55 50W
Aquiles Serdán, Mexico **118 B3** 28 37N 105 54W
Aquin, Haiti **121 C5** 18 16N 73 24W
Aquitaine □, France . **20 D3** 44 25N 0 30W
Ar Rachidiya = Er
  Rachidia, Morocco . **78 B5** 31 58N 4 20W
Ar Rafid, Syria ...... **74 C4** 32 57N 35 52 E
Ar Raḥḥālīyah, Iraq . **70 C4** 32 44N 43 23 E
Ar Ramādī, Iraq ..... **70 C4** 33 25N 43 20 E
Ar Ramthā, Jordan .. **74 C5** 32 34N 36 0 E
Ar Raqqah, Syria .... **70 C3** 35 59N 39 8 E
Ar Rass, Si. Arabia .. **70 E4** 25 50N 43 40 E
Ar Rawshān, Si. Arabia **80 C5** 20 2N 42 36 E
Ar Rifā'ī, Iraq .... **70 D5** 31 50N 46 10 E
Ar Riyāḍ, Si. Arabia . **70 E5** 24 41N 46 42 E
Ar Ru'ays, Qatar .... **71 E6** 26 8N 51 12 E
Ar Rukhaymiyah, Iraq **70 D5** 29 22N 45 38 E
Ar Ruṣāfah, Syria ... **70 C3** 35 45N 38 49 E
Ar Ruṭbah, Iraq ..... **70 C4** 33 0N 40 15 E
Ara, India .... **69 G11** 25 35N 84 32 E
Ara Goro, Ethiopia .. **81 F5** 5 48N 41 18 E
Ara Tera, Ethiopia .. **81 F5** 6 38N 40 57 E
Arab, U.S.A. **115 H2** 34 19N 86 30W
'Arab, Bahr el ➤,
  Sudan .... **81 F2** 9 0N 29 30 E
Arab, Khalīg el, Egypt **80 A2** 30 55N 29 0 E
Arab, Shatt al ➤, Asia **71 D6** 30 0N 48 31 E
'Araba, W. ➤, Egypt . **80 J8** 28 19N 33 31 E
'Arabābād, Iran ..... **71 C8** 33 2N 57 41 E
Araban, Turkey ..... **72 D7** 37 28N 37 44 E
Arabatskaya Strelka,
  Ukraine .... **33 K8** 45 40N 35 0 E
Arabba, Italy .... **41 B8** 46 30N 11 52 E
Arabia, Asia .... **50 G8** 25 0N 45 0 E
Arabian Desert = Es
  Sahrā' Esh Sharqīya,
  Egypt .... **80 B3** 27 30N 32 30 E
Arabian Gulf = Gulf,
  The, Asia .... **71 E6** 27 0N 50 0 E
Arabian Sea, Ind. Oc. **50 H10** 16 0N 65 0 E
Araç, Turkey .... **72 B5** 41 15N 33 21 E
Aracaju, Brazil ...... **125 F11** 10 55 S 37 4W
Aracati, Brazil ...... **125 D11** 4 30 S 37 44W
Araçatuba, Brazil ... **127 A5** 21 10 S 50 30W
Aracena, Spain **37 H4** 37 53N 6 38W
Aracena, Sierra de,
  Spain **37 H4** 37 50N 6 50W
Aračinovo, Macedonia **44 D5** 42 1N 21 34 E
Araçuaí, Brazil ...... **125 G10** 16 52 S 42 4W
'Arad, Israel .... **74 D4** 31 15N 35 12 E
Arad, Romania ..... **28 D6** 46 10N 21 20 E
Arad □, Romania ... **28 D6** 46 20N 22 0 E
Arādān, Iran .... **71 C7** 35 21N 52 30 E
Aradhippou, Cyprus . **49 E12** 34 57N 33 36 E
Arafura Sea, E. Indies **96 H5** 9 0 S 135 0 E
Aragats, Armenia ... **35 K7** 40 30N 44 15 E
Aragón □, Spain **38 D4** 41 25N 0 40W
Aragón ➤, Spain **38 C3** 42 13N 1 44W
Aragona, Italy ...... **42 E6** 37 24N 13 37 E
Araguacema, Brazil . **125 E9** 8 50 S 49 20W
Araguaia ➤, Brazil .. **125 E9** 5 21 S 48 41W
Araguaína, Brazil ... **125 E9** 7 12 S 48 12W
Araguari, Brazil ..... **125 G9** 18 38 S 48 11W
Araguari ➤, Brazil .. **125 C9** 1 15N 49 55W
Arain, India .... **68 F6** 26 27N 75 2 E
Arak, Algeria .... **78 C6** 25 20N 3 45 E
Arāk, Iran .... **71 C6** 34 0N 49 40 E
Araka, Sudan .... **81 G3** 4 20N 30 23 E
Arakan Coast, Burma **67 K19** 19 0N 94 0 E
Arakan Yoma, Burma **67 K19** 20 0N 94 40 E
Arákhova, Greece ... **46 C4** 38 28N 22 35 E
Arakli, Turkey ...... **73 B8** 41 6N 40 2 E
Araks = Aras, Rūd-e ➤,
  Asia .... **35 K9** 40 5N 48 29 E
Aral, Kazakhstan .... **52 E7** 46 41N 61 45 E
Aral Sea, Asia ...... **52 E7** 44 30N 60 0 E
Aral Tengizi = Aral Sea,
  Asia .... **52 E7** 44 30N 60 0 E
Aralsk = Aral,
  Kazakhstan .... **52 E7** 46 41N 61 45 E
Aralskoye More = Aral
  Sea, Asia .... **52 E7** 44 30N 60 0 E
Aralsor, Ozero,
  Kazakhstan .... **35 F9** 49 5N 48 12 E
Aramac, Australia ... **94 C4** 22 58 S 145 14 E
Aran I., Ireland **12 A3** 55 0N 8 30W
Aran Is., Ireland **12 C2** 53 6N 9 38W
Aranda de Duero, Spain **38 D7** 41 39N 3 42W
Arandān, Iran .... **70 C5** 35 23N 46 55 E
Arandelovac,
  Serbia & M. .... **44 B4** 44 18N 20 34 E
Aranjuez, Spain **36 E7** 40 1N 3 40W
Aranos, Namibia .... **88 C2** 24 9 S 19 7 E
Aransas Pass, U.S.A. **113 M6** 27 55N 97 9W
Aranyaprathet, Thailand **64 F4** 13 41N 102 30 E
Araouane, Mali **82 B4** 18 55N 3 30W
Arapahoe, U.S.A. ... **112 E5** 40 18N 99 54W
Arapey Grande ➤,
  Uruguay .... **126 C4** 30 55 S 57 49W
Arapgir, Turkey ..... **70 B3** 39 5N 38 30 E
Arapiraca, Brazil .... **125 E11** 9 45 S 36 39W
Arapongas, Brazil ... **127 A5** 23 29 S 51 28W
Ar'ar, Si. Arabia .... **70 D4** 30 59N 41 2 E
Araranguá, Brazil ... **127 B6** 29 0 S 49 30W
Araraquara, Brazil ... **125 H9** 21 50 S 48 0W
Ararás, Serra das, Brazil **127 B5** 25 0 S 53 10W
Ararat, Armenia .... **73 C11** 39 48N 44 30 E
Ararat, Australia .... **95 F3** 37 16 S 143 0 E
Ararat, Mt. = Ağri Dağı,
  Turkey .... **70 B5** 39 50N 44 15 E
Araria, India .... **69 F12** 26 9N 87 33 E
Araripe, Chapada do,
  Brazil .... **125 E11** 7 20 S 40 0W
Araruama, L. de, Brazil **127 A7** 22 53 S 42 12W

Aras, Rūd-e →, *Asia* .. **35 K9** 40 5N 48 29 E
Aratāne, *Mauritania* .. **82 B3** 18 24N 8 32W
Arauca, *Colombia* .. **124 B4** 7 0N 70 40W
Arauca →, *Venezuela* .. **124 B5** 7 24N 66 35W
Arauco, *Chile* .. **126 D1** 37 16 S 73 25W
Arawa, *Ethiopia* .. **81 F5** 9 57N 41 58 E
Arawale →, *Kenya* .. **86 C5** 1 24 S 40 9 E
Araxá, *Brazil* .. **125 G9** 19 35 S 46 55W
Araya, Pen. de,
Venezuela .. **124 A6** 10 40N 64 0W
Arba Gugu, *Ethiopia* .. **81 F5** 8 40N 40 15 E
Arba Minch, *Ethiopia* .. **81 F4** 6 0N 37 30 E
Arbat, *Iraq* .. **70 C5** 35 25N 45 35 E
Árbatax, *Italy* .. **42 C2** 39 56N 9 42 E
Arbi, *Ethiopia* .. **81 F4** 9 4N 35 7 E
Arbīl, *Iraq* .. **70 B5** 36 15N 44 5 E
Arboga, *Sweden* .. **10 E9** 59 24N 15 52 E
Arbois, *France* .. **19 F12** 46 55N 5 46 E
Arbore, *Ethiopia* .. **81 F4** 5 3N 36 50 E
Arboréa, *Italy* .. **42 C1** 39 46N 8 35 E
Arborfield, *Canada* .. **103 C8** 53 6N 103 39W
Arborg, *Canada* .. **103 C9** 50 54N 97 13W
Arbroath, *U.K.* .. **13 E5** 56 34N 2 35W
Arbuckle, *U.S.A.* .. **110 F4** 39 1N 122 3W
Arbus, *Italy* .. **42 C1** 39 30N 8 33 E
Arc →, *France* .. **21 C10** 45 34N 6 12 E
Arc-lès-Gray, *France* .. **19 E12** 47 28N 5 34 E
Arcachon, *France* .. **20 D2** 44 40N 1 10W
Arcachon, Bassin d',
France .. **20 D2** 44 42N 1 10W
Arcade, *Calif., U.S.A.* .. **111 L8** 34 2N 118 15W
Arcade, *N.Y., U.S.A.* .. **116 D6** 42 32N 78 25W
Arcadia, *Fla., U.S.A.* .. **115 M5** 27 13N 81 52W
Arcadia, *La., U.S.A.* .. **113 J8** 32 33N 92 55W
Arcadia, *Pa., U.S.A.* .. **116 F6** 40 47N 78 51W
Arcata, *U.S.A.* .. **108 F1** 40 52N 124 5W
Arcévia, *Italy* .. **41 E9** 43 30N 12 56 E
Archangel =
Arkhangelsk, *Russia* .. **52 C5** 64 38N 40 36 E
Archar, *Bulgaria* .. **44 C6** 43 50N 22 54 E
Archbald, *U.S.A.* .. **117 E9** 41 30N 75 32W
Archena, *Spain* .. **39 G3** 38 9N 1 16 E
Archer →, *Australia* .. **94 A3** 13 28 S 141 41 E
Archer B., *Australia* .. **94 A3** 13 20 S 141 30 E
Archer Bend =
Mungkan Kandju △,
Australia .. **94 A3** 13 35 S 142 52 E
Archers Post, *Kenya* .. **86 B4** 0 35N 37 35 E
Arches △, *U.S.A.* .. **109 G9** 38 45N 109 25W
Archidona, *Spain* .. **37 H6** 37 6N 4 22W
Archipel-de-Mingan △,
Canada .. **105 B7** 50 13N 63 10W
Archipiélago Chinijo △,
Canary Is. .. **48 E6** 29 20N 13 30W
Archipiélago Los
Roques △, *Venezuela* .. **121 D6** 11 50N 66 44W
Arci, Mte., *Italy* .. **42 C1** 39 47N 8 45 E
Arcidosso, *Italy* .. **41 F8** 42 52N 11 33 E
Arcipelago de la
Maddalena △, *Italy* .. **42 A2** 41 14N 9 24 E
Arcipelago Toscano △,
Italy .. **40 F7** 42 45N 10 15 E
Arcis-sur-Aube, *France* .. **19 D11** 48 32N 4 10 E
Arckaringa Cr. →,
Australia .. **95 D2** 28 10 S 135 22 E
Arco, *Italy* .. **40 C7** 45 55N 10 53 E
Arco, *U.S.A.* .. **108 E7** 43 38N 113 18W
Arcos de Jalón, *Spain* .. **38 D2** 41 12N 2 16W
Arcos de la Frontera,
Spain .. **37 J5** 36 45N 5 49W
Arcos de Valdevez,
Portugal .. **36 D2** 41 55N 8 22W
Arcot, *India* .. **66 N11** 12 53N 79 20 E
Arcozelo, *Portugal* .. **36 E3** 40 32N 7 47W
Arctic Bay, *Canada* .. **101 A11** 73 1N 85 7W
Arctic Ocean, *Arctic* .. **4 B18** 78 0N 160 0W
Arctic Red River =
Tsiigehtchic, *Canada* .. **100 B6** 67 15N 134 0W
Arctowski, *Antarctica* .. **5 C18** 62 30 S 58 0W
Arda →, *Bulgaria* .. **45 E10** 41 40N 26 30 E
Arda →, *Italy* .. **40 C7** 45 2N 10 2 E
Ardabīl, *Iran* .. **71 B6** 38 15N 48 18 E
Ardabīl □, *Iran* .. **71 B6** 38 15N 48 20 E
Ardahan, *Turkey* .. **73 B10** 41 7N 42 41 E
Ardakān = Sepīdān, *Iran* .. **71 D7** 30 20N 52 5 E
Ardakān, *Iran* .. **71 C7** 32 19N 53 59 E
Ardala, *Sweden* .. **11 F7** 58 22N 13 8 E
Ardales, *Spain* .. **37 J6** 36 53N 4 51W
Ardèche □, *France* .. **21 D8** 44 42N 4 16 E
Ardèche →, *France* .. **21 D8** 44 16N 4 39 E
Ardee, *Ireland* .. **12 C5** 53 52N 6 33W
Arden, *Canada* .. **116 B8** 44 43N 76 56W
Arden, *Denmark* .. **11 H3** 56 46N 9 52 E
Arden, *Calif., U.S.A.* .. **110 G5** 38 36N 121 33W
Arden, *Nev., U.S.A.* .. **111 J11** 36 1N 115 14W
Ardennes, *Belgium* .. **17 E5** 49 50N 5 5 E
Ardennes = Ardenne,
Belgium .. **17 E5** 49 50N 5 5 E
Ardennes □, *France* .. **19 C11** 49 35N 4 40 E
Ardentes, *France* .. **19 F8** 46 45N 1 50 E
Arderin, *Ireland* .. **12 C4** 53 2N 7 39W
Ardeşen, *Turkey* .. **73 B9** 41 12N 41 2 E
Ardestān, *Iran* .. **71 C7** 33 20N 52 25 E
Árdhas →, *Greece* .. **45 E10** 41 40N 26 30 E
Ardhéa, *Greece* .. **44 F6** 40 58N 22 3 E
Ardila →, *Portugal* .. **37 G3** 38 12N 7 28W
Ardino, *Bulgaria* .. **45 E9** 41 34N 25 9 E
Ardivachar Pt., *U.K.* .. **13 D1** 57 23N 7 26W
Ardlethan, *Australia* .. **95 E4** 34 22 S 146 53 E
Ardmore, *Okla., U.S.A.* .. **113 H6** 34 10N 97 8W
Ardmore, *Pa., U.S.A.* .. **117 G9** 39 58N 75 18W
Ardnamurchan, Pt. of,
U.K. .. **13 E2** 56 43N 6 14W
Ardnave Pt., *U.K.* .. **13 F2** 55 53N 6 20W
Ardon, *Russia* .. **35 J7** 43 10N 44 8 E
Ardore, *Italy* .. **43 D9** 38 11N 16 10 E
Ardres, *France* .. **19 B8** 50 50N 1 59 E
Ardrossan, *Australia* .. **95 E2** 34 26 S 137 53 E
Ardrossan, *U.K.* .. **12 F6** 55 39N 4 49W
Ards Pen., *U.K.* .. **12 B6** 54 33N 5 34W
Arduan, *Sudan* .. **80 D3** 19 54N 30 20 E
Ardud, *Romania* .. **28 C7** 47 37N 22 52 E
Åre, *Sweden* .. **10 A7** 63 22N 13 15 E
Arecibo, *Puerto Rico* .. **121 d** 18 29N 66 43W
Areia Branca, *Brazil* .. **125 E11** 5 0 S 37 0W
Arena, Pt., *U.S.A.* .. **110 G3** 38 57N 123 44W
Arenal, *Honduras* .. **120 C2** 15 21N 86 50W
Arenas = Las Arenas,
Spain .. **36 B6** 43 17N 4 50W
Arenas de San Pedro,
Spain .. **36 E5** 40 12N 5 5W
Arendal, *Norway* .. **9 G13** 58 28N 8 46 E
Arendsee, *Germany* .. **24 C7** 52 52N 11 27 E
Arenys de Mar, *Spain* .. **38 D7** 41 35N 2 33 E
Arenzano, *Italy* .. **40 D5** 44 24N 8 41 E
Areópolis, *Greece* .. **46 E4** 36 40N 22 22 E

Arequipa, *Peru* .. **124 G4** 16 20 S 71 30W
Arero, *Ethiopia* .. **81 G4** 4 41N 38 50 E
Arès, *France* .. **20 D2** 44 47N 1 8W
Arévalo, *Spain* .. **36 D6** 41 3N 4 43W
Arezzo, *Italy* .. **41 E8** 43 25N 11 53 E
Arga, *Turkey* .. **70 B3** 38 21N 37 59 E
Arga →, *Spain* .. **38 C3** 42 18N 1 47W
Argalastí, *Greece* .. **46 B5** 39 13N 23 13 E
Argamasilla de Alba,
Spain .. **37 F7** 39 8N 3 5W
Argamasilla de
Calatrava, *Spain* .. **37 G6** 38 44N 4 4W
Arganda, *Spain* .. **36 E7** 40 19N 3 26W
Arganil, *Portugal* .. **36 E2** 40 13N 8 3W
Argedeb, *Ethiopia* .. **81 F5** 6 11N 41 13 E
Argelès-Gazost, *France* .. **20 E3** 43 0N 0 6W
Argelès-sur-Mer, *France* .. **20 F7** 42 34N 3 1 E
Argens →, *France* .. **21 E10** 43 24N 6 44 E
Argent-sur-Sauldre,
France .. **19 E9** 47 33N 2 25 E
Argenta, *Canada* .. **102 C5** 50 11N 116 56W
Argenta, *Italy* .. **41 D8** 44 37N 11 50 E
Argentan, *France* .. **18 D6** 48 45N 0 1W
Argentário, Mte., *Italy* .. **41 F8** 42 24N 11 9 E
Argentat, *France* .. **20 C5** 45 6N 1 56 E
Argentera, *Italy* .. **40 D4** 44 12N 7 5 E
Argenteuil, *France* .. **19 D9** 48 57N 2 14 E
Argentia, *Canada* .. **105 C9** 47 18N 53 58W
Argentiera, C. dell', *Italy* .. **42 B1** 40 44N 8 8 E
Argentina ■, *S. Amer.* .. **128 D3** 35 0 S 66 0W
Argentine Basin,
S. Amer. .. **122 H5** 45 0 S 58 0W
Argentino, L., *Argentina* .. **128 G2** 50 10 S 73 0W
Argenton-Château,
France .. **18 F6** 46 59N 0 27W
Argenton-sur-Creuse,
France .. **19 F8** 46 36N 1 30 E
Argeş □, *Romania* .. **29 E9** 45 0N 24 45 E
Argeş →, *Romania* .. **29 F11** 44 5N 26 38 E
Arghandab →, *Afghan.* .. **68 D1** 31 30N 64 15 E
Argheile, *Ethiopia* .. **81 F5** 5 19N 42 4 E
Argo, *Sudan* .. **80 D3** 19 28N 30 30 E
Argolikós Kólpos,
Greece .. **46 D4** 37 20N 22 52 E
Argolís □, *Greece* .. **46 D4** 37 38N 22 50 E
Argonne, *France* .. **19 C12** 49 10N 5 0 E
Árgos, *Greece* .. **46 D4** 37 40N 22 43 E
Árgos Orestikón, *Greece* .. **44 F5** 40 27N 21 18 E
Argostólion, *Greece* .. **46 C2** 38 11N 20 29 E
Arguedas, *Spain* .. **38 C3** 42 11N 1 36W
Arguello, Pt., *U.S.A.* .. **111 L6** 34 35N 120 39W
Arguineguín, *Canary Is.* .. **48 G4** 27 46N 15 41W
Argun →, *Russia* .. **35 J7** 43 18N 45 52 E
Argun →, *Russia* .. **53 D13** 53 20N 121 28 E
Argungu, *Nigeria* .. **83 C5** 12 40N 4 31 E
Argus Pk., *U.S.A.* .. **111 K9** 35 52N 117 26W
Argyle, L., *Australia* .. **92 C4** 16 20 S 128 40 E
Argyll □, *U.K.* .. **13 E4** 56 6N 5 0W
Argyll & Bute □, *U.K.* .. **13 E3** 56 13N 5 28W
Arhavi, *Turkey* .. **73 B9** 41 21N 41 18 E
Århus, *Denmark* .. **11 H4** 56 8N 10 11 E
Århus
Amtskommune □,
Denmark .. **11 H4** 56 15N 10 15 E
Ariadnoye, *Russia* .. **54 B7** 45 8N 134 25 E
Ariamsvlei, *Namibia* .. **88 D2** 28 9 S 19 51 E
Ariano Irpino, *Italy* .. **43 A8** 41 9N 15 5 E
Aribinda, *Burkina Faso* .. **83 C4** 14 17N 0 52W
Arica, *Chile* .. **124 G4** 18 32 S 70 20W
Arica, *Colombia* .. **124 D4** 2 0 S 71 50W
Arico, *Canary Is.* .. **48 F3** 28 9N 16 29W
Arid, C., *Australia* .. **93 F3** 34 1 S 123 10 E
Arida, *Japan* .. **55 G7** 34 5N 135 8 E
Ariège □, *France* .. **20 F5** 42 56N 1 30 E
Ariège →, *France* .. **20 E5** 43 30N 1 25 E
Arieş →, *Romania* .. **29 D8** 46 24N 23 20 E
Arihā, *Israel* .. **80 A4** 31 51N 35 27 E
Arilje, *Serbia & M.* .. **44 C4** 43 44N 20 7 E
Arílla, Ákra, *Greece* .. **49 A3** 39 43N 19 39 E
Arima, *Trin. & Tob.* .. **121 D7** 10 38N 61 17W
Arinos →, *Brazil* .. **124 F7** 10 25 S 58 20W
Ario de Rosales, *Mexico* .. **118 D4** 19 12N 102 0W
Ariogala, *Lithuania* .. **9 J20** 55 16N 23 28 E
Aripo, Mt., *Trin. & Tob.* .. **125 K15** 10 45N 61 15W
Aripuanã, *Brazil* .. **124 E6** 9 25 S 60 30W
Aripuanã →, *Brazil* .. **124 E6** 5 7 S 60 25W
Ariquemes, *Brazil* .. **124 E6** 9 55 S 63 6W
Arisaig, *U.K.* .. **13 E3** 56 55N 5 51W
Arish, W. el →, *Egypt* .. **80 A3** 31 9N 33 49 E
Arissa, *Ethiopia* .. **81 E5** 11 10N 41 35 E
Aristazabal I., *Canada* .. **102 C3** 52 40N 129 10W
Arivonimamo, *Madag.* .. **89 B8** 19 1 S 47 11 E
Ariza, *Spain* .. **38 D2** 41 19N 2 3W
Arizaro, Salar de,
Argentina .. **126 A2** 24 40 S 67 50W
Arizona, *Argentina* .. **126 D2** 35 45 S 65 25W
Arizona □, *U.S.A.* .. **109 J8** 34 0N 112 0W
Arizpe, *Mexico* .. **118 A2** 30 20N 110 11W
Arjäng, *Sweden* .. **10 E6** 59 24N 12 8 E
Arjeplog, *Sweden* .. **8 D18** 66 3N 17 54 E
Arjeplouve = Arjeplog,
Sweden .. **8 D18** 66 3N 17 54 E
Arjona, *Colombia* .. **124 A3** 10 14N 75 22W
Arjona, *Spain* .. **37 H6** 37 56N 4 4W
Arjuna, *Indonesia* .. **63 G15** 7 49 S 112 34 E
Arka, *Russia* .. **53 C15** 60 15N 142 0 E
Arkadak, *Russia* .. **34 E6** 51 58N 43 30 E
Arkadelphia, *U.S.A.* .. **113 H8** 34 7N 93 4W
Arkadhía □, *Greece* .. **46 D4** 37 30N 22 20 E
Arkaig, L., *U.K.* .. **13 E3** 56 59N 5 10W
Arkalyk = Arqalyk,
Kazakhstan .. **52 D7** 50 13N 66 50 E
Arkansas □, *U.S.A.* .. **113 H8** 35 0N 92 30W
Arkansas →, *U.S.A.* .. **113 J9** 33 47N 91 4W
Arkansas City, *U.S.A.* .. **113 G6** 37 4N 97 2W
Arkaroola, *Australia* .. **95 E2** 30 20 S 139 22 E
Árkhangelos, *Greece* .. **49 C10** 36 13N 28 7 E
Arkhangelsk, *Russia* .. **52 C5** 64 38N 40 36 E
Arkhangelskoye, *Russia* .. **34 E5** 51 32N 40 58 E
Arki, *India* .. **68 D7** 31 9N 76 58 E
Arkiko, *Eritrea* .. **81 D4** 15 33N 39 30 E
Arklow, *Ireland* .. **12 D5** 52 48N 6 10W
Árkoi, *Greece* .. **47 D8** 37 24N 26 44 E
Arkona, Kap, *Germany* .. **24 A9** 54 41N 13 26 E
Arkösund, *Sweden* .. **11 F10** 58 29N 16 56 E
Arkoúdhi Nísis, *Greece* .. **46 C2** 38 33N 20 43 E
Arkport, *U.S.A.* .. **116 D7** 42 24N 77 42W
Arkticheskiy, Mys,
Russia .. **53 A10** 81 10N 95 0 E
Arkül, *Russia* .. **34 B10** 57 17N 50 0 E
Arkville, *U.S.A.* .. **117 D10** 42 9N 74 37W
Årla, *Sweden* .. **10 E10** 59 17N 16 40 E
Arlanc, *France* .. **20 C7** 45 25N 3 42 E
Arlanza →, *Spain* .. **36 C6** 42 6N 4 9W
Arlanzón →, *Spain* .. **36 C6** 42 3N 4 17W

Arlbergpass, *Austria* .. **26 D3** 47 9N 10 12 E
Arles, *France* .. **21 E8** 43 41N 4 40 E
Arli, *Burkina Faso* .. **83 C5** 11 35N 1 28 E
Arli △, *Burkina Faso* .. **83 C5** 11 35N 1 28 E
Arlington, *S. Africa* .. **89 D4** 28 1 S 27 53 E
Arlington, *N.Y., U.S.A.* .. **117 E11** 41 42N 73 54W
Arlington, *Oreg., U.S.A.* .. **108 D3** 45 43N 120 12W
Arlington, *S. Dak.,
U.S.A.* .. **112 C6** 44 22N 97 8W
Arlington, *Tex., U.S.A.* .. **113 J6** 32 44N 97 7W
Arlington, *Va., U.S.A.* .. **114 F7** 38 53N 77 7W
Arlington, *Vt., U.S.A.* .. **117 C11** 43 5N 73 9W
Arlington, *Wash., U.S.A.* .. **110 B4** 48 12N 122 8W
Arlington Heights,
U.S.A. .. **114 D2** 42 5N 87 59W
Arlit, *Niger* .. **78 E7** 19 0N 7 38 E
Arlon, *Belgium* .. **17 E5** 49 42N 5 49 E
Arltunga, *Australia* .. **94 C1** 23 26 S 134 41 E
Armagh, *U.K.* .. **12 B5** 54 21N 6 39W
Armagh □, *U.K.* .. **12 B5** 54 18N 6 37W
Armagnac, *France* .. **20 E4** 43 50N 0 10 E
Armançon →, *France* .. **19 E10** 47 59N 3 30 E
Armando Bermúdez △,
Dom. Rep. .. **121 C5** 19 3N 71 0W
Armavir, *Russia* .. **35 H5** 45 2N 41 7 E
Armenia, *Colombia* .. **124 C3** 4 35N 75 45W
Armenia ■, *Asia* .. **35 K7** 40 20N 45 0 E
Armeniş, *Romania* .. **28 E7** 45 13N 22 17 E
Armenistís, Ákra,
Greece .. **49 C9** 36 8N 27 42 E
Armentières, *France* .. **19 B9** 50 40N 2 50 E
Armidale, *Australia* .. **95 E5** 30 30 S 151 40 E
Armilla, *Spain* .. **37 H7** 37 9N 3 37W
Armórique △, *France* .. **18 D3** 48 22 N 3 30W
Armour, *U.S.A.* .. **112 D5** 43 19N 98 21W
Armstrong, *B.C.,
Canada* .. **102 C5** 50 25N 119 10W
Armstrong, *Ont.,
Canada* .. **104 B2** 50 18N 89 4W
Arnaía, *Greece* .. **45 F12** 40 31N 28 50 E
Arnaud →, *Canada* .. **101 B12** 59 59N 69 46W
Arnauti, C., *Cyprus* .. **49 D11** 35 6N 32 17 E
Arnay-le-Duc, *France* .. **19 E11** 47 10N 4 27 E
Arnedillo, *Spain* .. **38 C2** 42 13N 2 14W
Arnedo, *Spain* .. **38 C2** 42 12N 2 5W
Arnett, *U.S.A.* .. **113 G5** 36 8N 99 46W
Arnhem, *Neths.* .. **17 C5** 51 58N 5 55 E
Arnhem, C., *Australia* .. **94 A2** 12 20 S 137 30 E
Arnhem B., *Australia* .. **94 A2** 12 20 S 136 10 E
Arnhem Land, *Australia* .. **94 A1** 13 10 S 134 30 E
Arníssa, *Greece* .. **44 F5** 40 47N 21 49 E
Arno →, *Italy* .. **40 E7** 43 41N 10 17 E
Arno Bay, *Australia* .. **95 E2** 33 54 S 136 34 E
Arnold, *U.K.* .. **14 D6** 53 1N 1 7W
Arnold, *U.S.A.* .. **110 G6** 38 15N 120 20W
Arnoldstein, *Austria* .. **26 E6** 46 33N 13 43 E
Arnon →, *France* .. **19 E9** 47 13N 2 1 E
Arnot, *Canada* .. **103 B9** 55 56N 96 41W
Arnøy, *Norway* .. **8 A19** 70 9N 20 40 E
Arnprior, *Canada* .. **117 A8** 45 26N 76 21W
Arnsberg, *Germany* .. **24 D4** 51 24N 8 5 E
Arnsberger Wald △,
Germany .. **24 D4** 51 25N 8 5 E
Arnstadt, *Germany* .. **24 E6** 50 50N 10 56 E
Aroab, *Namibia* .. **88 D2** 26 41 S 19 39 E
Aroánia Óri, *Greece* .. **46 D4** 37 56N 22 12 E
Aroche, *Spain* .. **37 H4** 37 56N 6 57W
Arochuku, *Nigeria* .. **83 D6** 5 21N 7 54 E
Arolsen, *Germany* .. **24 D5** 51 23N 9 2 E
Aron →, *India* .. **68 G6** 25 57N 77 56 E
Arona, *Canary Is.* .. **48 F3** 28 6N 16 40W
Arona, *Italy* .. **40 C5** 45 46N 8 34 E
Aroroy, *Phil.* .. **61 E5** 12 31N 123 24 E
Arosa, Ría de, *Spain* .. **36 C2** 42 28N 8 57W
Arpajon, *France* .. **19 D9** 48 36N 2 15 E
Arpajon-sur-Cère,
France .. **20 D6** 44 53N 2 28 E
Arpaşu de Jos, *Romania* .. **29 E9** 45 47N 24 37 E
Arqalyk, *Kazakhstan* .. **52 D7** 50 13N 66 50 E
Arrah = Ara, *India* .. **69 G11** 25 35N 84 32 E
Arrah, *Ivory C.* .. **82 D4** 6 40N 3 58W
Arraiolos, *Portugal* .. **37 G3** 38 44N 7 59W
Arran, *U.K.* .. **13 F3** 55 34N 5 12W
Arras, *France* .. **19 B9** 50 17N 2 46 E
Arrasate, *Spain* .. **38 B2** 43 4N 2 30W
Arrats →, *France* .. **20 D4** 44 6N 0 52 E
Arreau, *France* .. **20 F4** 42 54N 0 22 E
Arrecife, *Canary Is.* .. **48 F6** 28 57N 13 37W
Arrecifes, *Argentina* .. **126 C3** 34 6 S 60 9W
Arrée, Mts. d', *France* .. **18 D3** 48 26N 3 55W
Arresø, *Denmark* .. **11 J6** 55 58N 12 6 E
Arriaga, *Chiapas,
Mexico* .. **119 D6** 16 15N 93 52W
Arriaga,
*San Luis Potosí,
Mexico* .. **118 C4** 21 55N 101 23W
Arribes del Duero △,
Spain .. **36 D4** 41 11N 6 36W
Arrilalah, *Australia* .. **94 C3** 23 43 S 143 54 E
Arrino, *Australia* .. **93 E2** 29 30 S 115 40 E
Arriondas, *Spain* .. **36 B5** 43 25N 5 11W
Arromanches-les-Bains,
France .. **18 C6** 49 20N 0 38W
Arronches, *Portugal* .. **37 F3** 39 8N 7 16W
Arros →, *France* .. **20 E3** 43 40N 0 2W
Arrow, L., *Ireland* .. **12 B3** 54 3N 8 19W
Arrowhead, L., *U.S.A.* .. **111 L9** 34 16N 117 10W
Arrowtown, *N.Z.* .. **91 L2** 44 57 S 168 50 E
Arroyo de la Luz, *Spain* .. **37 F4** 39 30N 6 38W
Arroyo Grande, *U.S.A.* .. **111 K6** 35 7N 120 35W
Års, *Denmark* .. **11 H3** 56 48N 9 30 E
Ars, *Iran* .. **70 B5** 37 9N 47 46 E
Ars-sur-Moselle, *France* .. **19 C13** 49 5N 6 4 E
Arsenault L., *Canada* .. **103 B7** 55 6N 108 32W
Arsenev, *Russia* .. **54 B6** 44 10N 133 15 E
Arsi, *Ethiopia* .. **81 C4** 7 45N 39 0 E
Arsiero, *Italy* .. **41 C8** 45 48N 11 21 E
Arsin, *Turkey* .. **73 B8** 41 3N 39 58 E
Arsk, *Russia* .. **34 B9** 56 10N 49 50 E
Årsunda, *Sweden* .. **10 D10** 60 31N 16 45 E
Arta, *Greece* .. **46 B3** 39 8N 21 2 E
Artà, *Spain* .. **48 B10** 39 41N 3 21 E
Arta □, *Greece* .. **46 B3** 39 15N 21 5 E
Arteaga, *Mexico* .. **118 D4** 18 50N 102 20W
Arteche, *Phil.* .. **61 E6** 12 17N 125 22 E
Artela, *Ethiopia* .. **81 F4** 8 0N 37 49 E
Artem = Artyom,
Azerbaijan .. **35 K10** 40 28N 50 20 E
Artem, *Russia* .. **54 C6** 43 22N 132 13 E
Artemovsk, *Russia* .. **53 D10** 54 45N 93 35 E
Artemovsk, *Ukraine* .. **33 H9** 48 35N 38 0 E
Artemovskiy, *Russia* .. **35 G5** 47 45N 40 16 E

Artenay, *France* .. **19 D8** 48 5N 1 50 E
Artern, *Germany* .. **24 D7** 51 22N 11 18 E
Artesa de Segre, *Spain* .. **38 D6** 41 54N 1 3 E
Artesia = Mosomane,
Botswana .. **88 C4** 24 2 S 26 19 E
Artesia, *U.S.A.* .. **113 J2** 32 51N 104 24W
Arthington, *Liberia* .. **82 D2** 6 35N 10 45W
Arthur, *Canada* .. **116 C4** 43 50N 80 32W
Arthur →, *Australia* .. **95 G3** 41 2 S 144 40 E
Arthur Cr. →, *Australia* .. **94 C2** 22 5 S 150 3 E
Arthur Pt., *Australia* .. **94 C5** 22 7 S 150 3 E
Arthur River, *Australia* .. **93 F2** 33 20 S 117 2 E
Arthur's Pass, *N.Z.* .. **91 K3** 42 54 S 171 35 E
Arthur's Pass △, *N.Z.* .. **91 K3** 42 53 S 171 42 E
Arthur's Town,
Bahamas .. **121 B4** 24 38N 75 42W
Artigas, *Antarctica* .. **5 C18** 62 30 S 58 0W
Artigas, *Uruguay* .. **126 C4** 30 20 S 56 30W
Artik, *Armenia* .. **35 K6** 40 38N 43 58 E
Artillery L., *Canada* .. **103 A7** 63 9N 107 52W
Artois, *France* .. **19 B9** 50 20N 2 30 E
Artotína, *Greece* .. **46 C4** 38 42N 22 2 E
Artrutx, C. de, *Spain* .. **48 B10** 39 55N 3 49 E
Artsyz, *Ukraine* .. **29 D14** 46 4N 29 26 E
Artvin, *Turkey* .. **73 B9** 41 14N 41 44 E
Artyom, *Azerbaijan* .. **35 K10** 40 28N 50 20 E
Aru, Kepulauan,
Indonesia .. **63 F8** 6 0 S 134 30 E
Aru Is. = Aru,
Kepulauan, *Indonesia* .. **63 F8** 6 0 S 134 30 E
Arua, *Uganda* .. **86 B3** 3 1N 30 58 E
Aruanã, *Brazil* .. **125 F8** 14 54 S 51 10W
Aruba ⵣ, *W. Indies* .. **121 D6** 12 30N 70 0W
Arucas, *Canary Is.* .. **48 F4** 28 7N 15 32W
Arudy, *France* .. **20 E3** 43 7N 0 28W
Arun →, *Nepal* .. **69 F12** 26 55N 87 10 E
Arun →, *U.K.* .. **15 G7** 50 49N 0 33W
Arunachal Pradesh □,
India .. **67 F19** 28 0N 95 0 E
Arusha, *Tanzania* .. **86 C4** 3 20 S 36 40 E
Arusha □, *Tanzania* .. **86 C4** 4 0 S 36 30 E
Arusha →, *Tanzania* .. **86 C4** 3 16 S 36 47 E
Arusha Chini, *Tanzania* .. **86 C4** 3 32 S 37 20 E
Aruwimi →, *Dem. Rep.
of the Congo* .. **86 B1** 1 13N 23 36 E
Arvada, *Colo., U.S.A.* .. **112 F2** 39 48N 105 5W
Arvada, *Wyo., U.S.A.* .. **108 D10** 44 39N 106 8W
Arve →, *France* .. **19 F13** 46 11N 6 8 E
Árvi, *Greece* .. **49 E7** 34 59N 25 28 E
Arviat, *Canada* .. **103 A10** 61 6N 93 59W
Arvidsjaur, *Sweden* .. **8 D18** 65 35N 19 10 E
Arvika, *Sweden* .. **10 E6** 59 40N 12 36 E
Arvin, *U.S.A.* .. **111 K8** 35 12N 118 50W
Arwal, *India* .. **69 G11** 25 15N 84 41 E
Arxan, *China* .. **60 B6** 47 11N 119 57 E
Åryd, *Sweden* .. **11 H8** 56 49N 14 59 E
Aryirádhes, *Greece* .. **49 B3** 39 27N 19 58 E
Aryiroúpolis, *Greece* .. **49 D6** 35 17N 24 20 E
Arys, *Kazakhstan* .. **52 E7** 42 26N 68 48 E
Arzachena, *Italy* .. **42 A2** 41 5N 9 23 E
Arzamas, *Russia* .. **34 C6** 55 27N 43 55 E
Arzgir, *Russia* .. **35 H7** 45 18N 44 23 E
Arzignano, *Italy* .. **41 C8** 45 31N 11 20 E
Arzúa, *Spain* .. **36 C2** 42 56N 8 9W
Aš, *Czech Rep.* .. **26 A5** 50 13N 12 12 E
Ås, *Sweden* .. **10 A8** 63 15N 14 34 E
As Pontes de García
Rodríguez, *Spain* .. **36 B3** 43 27N 7 50W
Aş Şafā, *Syria* .. **74 B6** 33 10N 37 0 E
Aş Saffāniyah,
Si. Arabia .. **71 E6** 27 55N 48 50 E
Aş Şafīrah, *Syria* .. **70 B3** 36 5N 37 21 E
Aş Şahm, *Oman* .. **71 E8** 24 10N 56 53 E
Aş Sājir, *Si. Arabia* .. **70 E5** 25 11N 44 36 E
Aş Salamīyah, *Syria* .. **70 C3** 35 1N 37 2 E
Aş Salmān, *Iraq* .. **70 D5** 30 30N 44 32 E
Aş Salt, *Jordan* .. **74 C4** 32 2N 35 43 E
Aş Sal'wa, *Qatar* .. **71 E6** 24 23N 50 50 E
Aş Samāwah, *Iraq* .. **70 D5** 31 15N 45 15 E
Aş Sanamayn, *Syria* .. **74 B5** 33 3N 36 10 E
Aş Sohar = Şuḩār,
Oman .. **71 E8** 24 20N 56 40 E
As Sukhnah, *Syria* .. **70 C3** 34 52N 38 52 E
Aş Sulaymānīyah, *Iraq* .. **70 C5** 35 35N 45 29 E
Aş Sulaymī, *Si. Arabia* .. **70 E4** 26 17N 41 21 E
Aş Sulayyil, *Si. Arabia* .. **75 C4** 20 27N 45 34 E
Aş Summān, *Si. Arabia* .. **70 E5** 25 0N 47 0 E
Aş Suwaydā, *Syria* .. **74 C5** 32 40N 36 30 E
Aş Suwaydā' □, *Syria* .. **74 C5** 32 45N 36 45 E
Aş Suwayq, *Oman* .. **71 F8** 23 51N 57 26 E
Aş Şuwayrah, *Iraq* .. **70 C5** 32 55N 45 0 E
Āsa, *Sweden* .. **11 G6** 57 21N 12 8 E
Asab, *Namibia* .. **88 D2** 25 30 S 18 0 E
Asaba, *Nigeria* .. **83 D6** 6 12N 6 38 E
Asad, Buḩayrat al, *Syria* .. **70 C3** 36 0N 38 15 E
Asadābād, *Iran* .. **71 C6** 34 47N 48 7 E
Asafo, *Ghana* .. **82 D4** 6 20N 2 40W
Asahi-Gawa →, *Japan* .. **55 G6** 34 36N 133 58 E
Asahigawa, *Japan* .. **54 C11** 43 46N 142 22 E
Asale, L., *Ethiopia* .. **81 E5** 14 0N 40 20 E
Asamankese, *Ghana* .. **83 D4** 5 50N 0 40W
Asan →, *India* .. **69 E8** 26 37N 78 24 E
Asansol, *India* .. **69 H12** 23 40N 87 1 E
Åsarna, *Sweden* .. **10 B8** 62 39N 14 22 E
Asayita, *Ethiopia* .. **81 E5** 11 33N 41 23 E
Asbe Teferi, *Ethiopia* .. **81 F5** 9 4N 40 49 E
Asbesberg, *S. Africa* .. **88 D3** 29 0 S 23 0 E
Asbestos, *Canada* .. **105 C5** 45 47N 71 58W
Asbury Park, *U.S.A.* .. **117 F10** 40 13N 74 1W
Ascea, *Italy* .. **43 B8** 40 8N 15 11 E
Ascensión, *Mexico* .. **118 A3** 31 6N 107 59W
Ascensión, B. de la,
Mexico .. **119 D7** 19 50N 87 20W
Ascension I., *Atl. Oc.* .. **77 G2** 7 57 S 14 23W
Aschach an der Donau,
Austria .. **26 C7** 48 22N 14 2 E
Aschaffenburg,
Germany .. **25 F5** 49 58N 9 6 E
Aschendorf, *Germany* .. **24 B3** 53 3N 7 19 E
Aschersleben, *Germany* .. **24 D7** 51 45N 11 29 E
Asciano, *Italy* .. **41 E8** 43 14N 11 33 E
Ascoli Piceno, *Italy* .. **41 F10** 42 51N 13 34 E
Ascoli Satriano, *Italy* .. **43 A8** 41 11N 15 32 E
Ascope, *Peru* .. **124 E3** 7 46 S 79 8W
Ascotán, *Chile* .. **126 A2** 21 45 S 68 17W
Aseb, *Eritrea* .. **81 E5** 13 0N 42 40 E
Åseda, *Sweden* .. **11 G9** 57 10N 15 20 E
Asela, *Ethiopia* .. **81 F4** 8 0N 39 0 E
Åsen, *Sweden* .. **10 C7** 61 17N 13 50 E
Asenovgrad, *Bulgaria* .. **45 D8** 42 1N 24 51 E
Aserradero, *Mexico* .. **118 C3** 23 40N 105 43W
Asfeld, *France* .. **19 C11** 49 27N 4 5 E
Asfūn el Matā'na, *Egypt* .. **80 B3** 25 26N 32 30 E
Asgata, *Cyprus* .. **49 E12** 34 46N 33 15 E
Ash Fork, *U.S.A.* .. **109 J7** 35 13N 112 29W
Ash Grove, *U.S.A.* .. **113 G8** 37 19N 93 35W
Ash Shabakah, *Iraq* .. **70 D4** 30 49N 43 39 E

Ash Shamāl □, *Lebanon* .. **74 A5** 34 25N 36 0 E
Ash Shāmīyah, *Iraq* .. **70 D5** 31 55N 44 35 E
Ash Shāriqah, *U.A.E.* .. **71 E7** 25 23N 55 26 E
Ash Sharmah, *Si. Arabia* .. **70 C4** 35 27N 43 16 E
Ash Sharqi, Al Jabal,
Lebanon .. **74 B5** 33 40N 36 10 E
Ash Shaṭrah, *Iraq* .. **70 D5** 31 30N 46 10 E
Ash Shawbak, *Jordan* .. **70 D2** 30 32N 35 34 E
Ash Shawmari, J.,
Jordan .. **74 E5** 30 35N 36 35 E
Ash Shināfīyah, *Iraq* .. **70 D5** 31 35N 44 39 E
Ash Shu'bah, *Si. Arabia* .. **70 D5** 28 54N 44 44 E
Ash Shumlūl, *Si. Arabia* .. **70 E5** 26 31N 47 20 E
Ash Shūr', *Iraq* .. **70 C4** 35 58N 43 13 E
Ash Shuwayfāt,
Lebanon .. **74 B4** 33 45N 35 30 E
Ashanti □, *Ghana* .. **83 D4** 7 30N 1 30W
Ashau, *Vietnam* .. **64 D6** 16 6N 107 22 E
Ashbourne, *U.K.* .. **14 D6** 53 2N 1 43W
Ashburn, *U.S.A.* .. **115 K4** 31 43N 83 39W
Ashburton, *N.Z.* .. **91 K3** 43 53 S 171 48 E
Ashburton →, *Australia* .. **92 D1** 21 40 S 114 56 E
Ashcroft, *Canada* .. **102 C4** 50 40N 121 20W
Ashdod, *Israel* .. **74 D3** 31 49N 34 35 E
Ashdown, *U.S.A.* .. **113 J7** 33 40N 94 8W
Asheboro, *U.S.A.* .. **115 H6** 35 43N 79 49W
Ashern, *Canada* .. **103 C9** 51 11N 98 21W
Asherton, *U.S.A.* .. **113 L5** 28 27N 99 46W
Asheville, *U.S.A.* .. **115 H4** 35 36N 82 33W
Ashewat, *Pakistan* .. **68 D3** 31 22N 68 32 E
Asheweig →, *Canada* .. **104 B2** 54 17N 87 12W
Ashford, *Australia* .. **95 D5** 29 15 S 151 3 E
Ashford, *U.K.* .. **15 F8** 51 8N 0 53 E
Ashgabat, *Turkmenistan* .. **52 F6** 38 0N 57 50 E
Ashibetsu, *Japan* .. **54 C11** 43 31N 142 11 E
Ashikaga, *Japan* .. **55 F9** 36 28N 139 29 E
Ashington, *U.K.* .. **14 B6** 55 11N 1 33W
Ashizuri-Uwakai △,
Japan .. **55 H6** 32 56N 132 32 E
Ashizuri-Zaki, *Japan* .. **55 H6** 32 44N 133 0 E
Ashkarkot, *Afghan.* .. **68 C2** 33 3N 67 58 E
Ashkhabad = Ashgabat,
Turkmenistan .. **52 F6** 38 0N 57 50 E
Āshkhāneh, *Iran* .. **71 B8** 37 26N 56 55 E
Ashland, *Kans., U.S.A.* .. **113 G5** 37 11N 99 46W
Ashland, *Ky., U.S.A.* .. **114 F4** 38 28N 82 38W
Ashland, *Mont., U.S.A.* .. **108 D10** 45 36N 106 16W
Ashland, *Ohio, U.S.A.* .. **116 F2** 40 52N 82 19W
Ashland, *Oreg., U.S.A.* .. **108 E2** 42 12N 122 43W
Ashland, *Pa., U.S.A.* .. **117 F8** 40 45N 76 22W
Ashland, *Va., U.S.A.* .. **114 G7** 37 46N 77 29W
Ashland, *Wis., U.S.A.* .. **112 B9** 46 35N 90 53W
Ashley, *N. Dak., U.S.A.* .. **112 B5** 46 2N 99 22W
Ashley, *Pa., U.S.A.* .. **117 E9** 41 12N 75 55W
Ashmore and Cartier Is.,
Ind. Oc. .. **92 B3** 12 15 S 123 0 E
Ashmore Reef, *Australia* .. **92 B3** 12 14 S 123 5 E
Ashmûn, *Egypt* .. **80 H7** 30 18N 30 55 E
Ashmyany, *Belarus* .. **9 J21** 54 26N 25 52 E
Ashokan Reservoir,
U.S.A. .. **117 E10** 41 56N 74 13W
Ashqelon, *Israel* .. **74 D3** 31 42N 34 35 E
Ashta, *India* .. **68 H7** 23 1N 76 43 E
Ashtabula, *U.S.A.* .. **116 E4** 41 52N 80 47W
Ashton, *S. Africa* .. **88 E3** 33 50 S 20 5 E
Ashton, *U.S.A.* .. **108 D8** 44 4N 111 27W
Ashuanipi, L., *Canada* .. **105 B6** 52 45N 66 15W
Ashuapmushuan →,
Canada .. **104 C5** 48 37N 72 20W
Ashville, *U.S.A.* .. **116 F6** 40 34N 78 33W
'Āşī →, *Asia* .. **72 D6** 36 3N 35 59 E
Asia, *Kepulauan,
Indonesia* .. **63 D8** 1 0N 131 13 E
Asiago, *Italy* .. **41 C8** 45 52N 11 30 E
Asifabad, *India* .. **66 K11** 19 20N 79 24 E
Asinara, *Italy* .. **42 A1** 41 4N 8 16 E
Asinara, G. dell', *Italy* .. **42 A1** 41 0N 8 30 E
Asino, *Russia* .. **52 D9** 57 0N 86 0 E
Asipovichy, *Belarus* .. **32 F5** 53 19N 28 33 E
'Asīr □, *Si. Arabia* .. **75 D3** 18 40N 42 30 E
Asir, Ras, *Somali Rep.* .. **75 E5** 11 55N 51 10 E
Aşkale, *Turkey* .. **73 C9** 39 55N 40 41 E
Askersund, *Sweden* .. **11 F8** 58 53N 14 55 E
Askham, *S. Africa* .. **88 D3** 26 59 S 20 47 E
Askim, *Norway* .. **9 G14** 59 35N 11 10 E
Askja, *Iceland* .. **8 D5** 65 3N 16 48W
Askøy, *Norway* .. **9 F11** 60 29N 5 10 E
Asl, *Egypt* .. **80 B3** 29 33N 32 44 E
Aslan Burnu, *Turkey* .. **47 C8** 38 44N 26 45 E
Aslanapa, *Turkey* .. **47 B11** 39 13N 29 52 E
Asmara = Asmera,
Eritrea .. **81 D4** 15 19N 38 55 E
Asmera, *Eritrea* .. **81 D4** 15 19N 38 55 E
Åsnæs, *Denmark* .. **11 J4** 55 40N 11 0 E
Åsnen, *Sweden* .. **11 H8** 56 37N 14 45 E
Aso Kuju △, *Japan* .. **55 H5** 32 53N 131 6 E
Åsola, *Italy* .. **40 C7** 45 13N 10 24 E
Asosa, *Ethiopia* .. **81 E3** 10 3N 34 32 E
Asoteriba, Jebel, *Sudan* .. **80 C4** 21 51N 36 30 E
Aspatria, *U.K.* .. **14 C4** 54 47N 3 19W
Aspe, *Spain* .. **39 G4** 38 20N 0 40W
Aspen, *U.S.A.* .. **109 G10** 39 11N 106 49W
Aspermont, *U.S.A.* .. **113 J4** 33 8N 100 14W
Aspet, *France* .. **20 E4** 43 1N 0 48 E
Aspiring, Mt., *N.Z.* .. **91 L2** 44 23 S 168 46 E
Aspres-sur-Buëch,
France .. **21 D9** 44 32N 5 44 E
Asprókavos, Ákra,
Greece .. **49 B4** 39 21N 20 6 E
Aspromonte △, *Italy* .. **43 D8** 38 9N 15 58 E
Aspur, *India* .. **68 H6** 23 58N 74 7 E
Asquith, *Canada* .. **103 C7** 52 8N 107 13W
Assab = Aseb, *Eritrea* .. **81 E5** 13 0N 42 40 E
Assâba, Massif de l',
Mauritania .. **82 B2** 16 10N 11 45W
Assagny △, *Ivory C.* .. **82 D3** 5 10N 4 48W
Assaikio, *Nigeria* .. **83 D6** 8 34N 8 55 E
Assal, L., *Djibouti* .. **81 E5** 11 40N 42 26 E
Assam □, *India* .. **67 G18** 26 0N 93 0 E
Assamakka, *Niger* .. **83 B6** 19 21N 5 38 E
Assateague Island
U.S.A. .. **114 F8** 38 15N 75 10W
Asse, *Belgium* .. **17 D4** 50 24N 4 10 E
Assémini, *Italy* .. **42 C1** 39 0N 6 35 E
Assen, *Neths.* .. **17 A6** 53 0N 6 35 E
Assens, *Denmark* .. **11 J3** 55 16N 9 55 E
Assini, *Ivory C.* .. **82 D4** 5 9N 3 17W
Assiniboia, *Canada* .. **103 D7** 49 40N 105 59W
Assiniboine →, *Canada* .. **103 D9** 49 53N 97 8W
Assiniboine, Mt.,
Canada .. **102 C5** 50 52N 115 39W
Assis, *Brazil* .. **127 A5** 22 40 S 50 20W
Assisi, *Italy* .. **41 E9** 43 4N 12 37 E

Ássos, Greece .... 46 C2 38 22N 20 33 E
Assynt, L., U.K. 13 C3 58 10N 5 3W
Astaffort, France ... 20 D4 44 4N 0 40 E
Astakidha, Greece ... 47 F8 35 53N 26 50 E
Astakós, Greece ..... 46 C3 38 32N 21 5 E
Astana, Kazakhstan .. 52 D8 51 10N 71 30 E
Ăstāneh, Iran .... 71 B6 37 17N 49 59 E
Astara, Azerbaijan .. 71 B6 38 30N 48 50 E
Ăstārā, Iran .... 73 C13 38 20N 48 52 E
Asterousia, Greece .. 49 E7 34 59N 25 3 E
Asti, Italy .... 40 D5 44 54N 8 12 E
Astipálaia, Greece .. 47 E8 36 32N 26 22 E
Astorga, Spain 36 C4 42 29N 6 8W
Astoria, U.S.A. 110 D3 46 11N 123 50W
Åstorp, Sweden ..... 11 H6 56 6N 12 55 E
Astrakhan, Russia ... 35 G9 46 25N 48 5 E
Astudillo, Spain 36 C6 42 12N 4 22W
Asturias □, Spain ... 36 B5 43 15N 6 0W
Asturias ✈ (OVD),
    Spain 36 B4 43 33N 6 3W
Asunción, Paraguay . 126 B4 25 10 S 57 30W
Asunción Nochixtlán,
    Mexico 119 D5 17 28N 97 14W
Ăsunden, Sweden ... 11 F9 58 0N 15 51 E
Asutri, Sudan .... 81 D4 15 25N 35 45 E
Aswa →, Uganda ... 86 B3 3 43N 31 55 E
Aswa-Lolim △, Uganda 86 B3 2 43N 31 35 E
Aswad, Ra's al,
    Si. Arabia .... 80 C4 21 20N 39 0 E
Aswân, Egypt .... 80 C3 24 4N 32 57 E
Aswân Dam = Sadd el
    Aali, Egypt ...... 80 C3 23 54N 32 54 E
Asyût, Egypt .... 80 C3 27 11N 31 4 E
Asyûti, Wadi →, Egypt 80 B3 27 11N 31 16 E
Aszód, Hungary .... 28 C4 47 39N 19 28 E
At Tafilah, Jordan .. 74 E4 30 45N 35 30 E
At Tafilah □, Jordan 74 E4 30 45N 35 30 E
Aţ Ţā'if, Si. Arabia . 75 C3 21 5N 40 27 E
At Ta'mīm □, Iraq .. 70 C5 35 30N 44 20 E
Aţ Ţirāq, Si. Arabia 70 E5 27 19N 44 33 E
Aţ Ţubayq, Si. Arabia 70 D3 29 30N 37 0 E
Atabey, Turkey ..... 47 D12 37 57N 30 39 E
Atacama, Desierto de,
    Chile .... 126 B2 24 0 S 69 20W
Atacama, Salar de, Chile 126 A2 23 30 S 68 20W
Atakpamé, Togo .... 83 D5 7 31N 1 13 E
Atalándi, Greece .... 46 C4 38 39N 22 58 E
Atalaya, Peru .... 124 F4 10 45 S 73 50W
Atalaya de Femes,
    Canary Is. 48 F6 28 56N 13 47W
Atami, Japan .... 55 G9 35 5N 139 4 E
Atapupu, E. Timor .. 63 F6 9 0 S 124 51 E
Atâr, Mauritania 78 D3 20 30N 13 5W
Atarfe, Spain 37 H7 37 13N 3 40W
Atari, Pakistan ..... 68 D6 30 56N 74 38 E
Atascadero, U.S.A. . 110 K6 35 29N 120 40W
Atasu, Kazakhstan .. 52 E8 48 30N 71 0 E

Atoka, U.S.A. 113 H6 34 23N 96 8W
Átokos Nisís, Greece 46 C2 38 28N 20 49 E
Atolia, U.S.A. 111 K9 35 19N 117 37W
Atrai →, Bangla. ... 69 G13 24 7N 89 22 E
Atrak = Atrek →,
    Turkmenistan .... 71 B8 37 35N 53 58 E
Åtran, Sweden ..... 11 G6 57 7N 12 57 E
Åtran →, Sweden .. 11 H6 56 53N 12 30 E
Atrauli, India ...... 68 E8 28 2N 78 20 E
Atrek →, Turkmenistan 71 B8 37 35N 53 58 E
Atri, Italy .... 41 F10 42 35N 13 58 E
Atsiki, Greece ...... 47 B7 39 56N 25 13 E
Atsoum, Mts.,
    Cameroon .... 83 D7 6 41N 12 57 E
Atsuta, Japan ...... 54 C10 43 24N 141 26 E
Attalla, U.S.A. 115 H2 34 1N 86 6W
Attapu, Laos .... 64 E6 14 48N 106 50 E
Attáviros, Greece ... 49 C9 36 12N 27 50 E
Attawapiskat, Canada 104 B3 52 56N 82 24W
Attawapiskat →,
    Canada 104 B3 52 57N 82 18W
Attawapiskat L., Canada 104 B2 52 18N 87 54W
Attersee, Austria ... 26 D6 47 55N 13 32 E
Attica, Ind., U.S.A. . 114 E2 40 18N 87 15W
Attica, Ohio, U.S.A. 116 E2 41 4N 82 53W
Attichy, France ..... 19 C10 49 25N 3 3 E
Attigny, France ..... 19 C11 49 28N 4 35 E
Attika = Attikí □,
    Greece .... 46 D5 37 10N 23 40 E
Attikamagen L., Canada 105 B6 55 0N 66 30W
Attikí □, Greece .... 46 D5 37 10N 23 40 E
Attleboro, U.S.A. ... 117 E13 41 57N 71 17W
Attock, Pakistan .... 68 C5 33 52N 72 20 E
Attopeu = Attapu, Laos 64 E6 14 48N 106 50 E
Attu I., U.S.A. ..... 100 C1 52 55N 172 55 E
Attur, India .... 66 P11 11 35N 78 30 E
Atuel →, Argentina . 126 D2 36 17 S 66 50W
Åtvidaberg, Sweden . 11 F10 58 12N 16 0 E
Atwater, U.S.A. 110 H6 37 21N 120 37W
Atwood, Canada 116 C3 43 40N 81 1W
Atwood, U.S.A. 112 F4 39 48N 101 3W
Atyraü, Kazakhstan . 52 E6 47 5N 52 0 E
Au Sable, U.S.A. ... 116 B1 44 25N 83 20W
Au Sable →, U.S.A. 114 C4 44 25N 83 20W
Au Sable Forks, U.S.A. 117 B11 44 27N 73 41W
Au Sable Pt., U.S.A. 116 B1 44 20N 83 20W
Aubagne, France ... 21 E9 43 17N 5 37 E
Aubarca, C. d', Spain 48 B7 39 4N 1 22 E
Aube □, France .... 19 D11 48 15N 4 10 E
Aube →, France ... 19 D10 48 34N 3 43 E
Aubenas, France ... 21 D8 44 37N 4 24 E
Aubenton, France .. 19 C11 49 50N 4 12 E
Auberry, U.S.A. 110 H7 37 7N 119 29W
Aubigny-sur-Nère,
    France .... 19 E9 47 30N 2 24 E
Aubin, France ...... 20 D6 44 33N 2 15 E
Aubrac, Mts. d', France 20 D7 44 40N 3 2 E
Auburn, Ala., U.S.A. 115 J3 32 36N 85 29W
Auburn, Calif., U.S.A. 110 G5 38 54N 121 4W
Auburn, Ind., U.S.A. 114 E3 41 22N 85 4W
Auburn, Maine, U.S.A. 115 C10 44 6N 70 14W
Auburn, N.Y., U.S.A. 117 D8 42 56N 76 34W
Auburn, Nebr., U.S.A. 112 E7 40 23N 95 51W
Auburn, Pa., U.S.A. 117 F8 40 36N 76 6W
Auburn, Wash., U.S.A. 110 C4 47 18N 122 14W
Auburn Ra., Australia 95 D5 25 15 S 150 30 E
Auburndale, U.S.A. . 115 L5 28 4N 81 48W
Aubusson, France .. 20 C6 45 57N 2 11 E
Auce, Latvia .... 30 B9 56 28N 22 53 E
Auch, France .... 20 E4 43 39N 0 36 E
Auchi, Nigeria ...... 83 D6 7 6N 6 13 E
Auchterarder, U.K. . 13 E5 56 18N 3 41W
Auchtermuchty, U.K. 13 E5 56 18N 3 13W
Auckland, N.Z. ..... 91 G5 36 52 S 174 46 E
Auckland Is., Pac. Oc. 96 N8 50 40 S 166 5 E
Aude □, France .... 20 E6 43 8N 2 28 E
Aude →, France ... 20 E7 43 13N 3 14 E
Auden, Canada 104 B2 50 14N 87 53W
Auderville, France .. 18 C5 49 43N 1 57W
Audierne, France ... 18 D2 48 1N 4 34W
Audincourt, France . 19 E13 47 30N 6 50 E
Audo Ra., Ethiopia . 81 F5 6 20N 41 50 E
Audubon, U.S.A. ... 112 E7 41 43N 94 56W
Aue, Germany ...... 24 E8 50 35N 12 41 E
Auerbach, Germany . 24 E8 50 30N 12 24 E
Augathella, Australia 95 D4 25 48 S 146 35 E
Aughnacloy, U.K. .. 12 B5 54 25N 6 59W
Augrabies Falls,
    S. Africa .... 88 D3 28 35 S 20 20 E
Augrabies Falls △,
    S. Africa .... 88 D3 28 40 S 20 22 E
Augsburg, Germany . 25 G6 48 25N 10 52 E
Augsburg-Westliche
    Wälder △, Germany 25 G6 48 20N 10 40 E
Augusta, Australia .. 93 F2 34 19 S 115 9 E
Augusta, Italy ...... 43 E8 37 13N 15 13 E
Augusta, Ark., U.S.A. 113 H9 35 17N 91 22W
Augusta, Ga., U.S.A. 115 J5 33 28N 81 58W
Augusta, Kans., U.S.A. 113 G6 37 41N 96 59W
Augusta, Maine, U.S.A. 101 D13 44 19N 69 47W
Augusta, Mont., U.S.A. 108 C7 47 30N 112 24W
Augustenborg, Denmark 11 K3 54 57N 9 53 E
Augustów, Poland .. 30 E9 53 51N 23 0 E
Augustus, Mt., Australia 93 D2 24 20 S 116 50 E
Augustus I., Australia 92 C3 15 20 S 124 30 E
Aukan, Eritrea ...... 81 D5 15 29N 40 50 E
Aukrug △, Germany . 24 A5 54 5N 9 45 E
Aukum, U.S.A. 110 G6 38 34N 120 43W
Auld, L., Australia .. 92 D3 22 25 S 123 50 E
Aulla, Italy .... 40 D6 44 12N 9 58 E
Aulnay, France 20 B3 46 2N 0 22W
Aulne →, France ... 18 D2 48 17N 4 16W
Aulnoye-Aymeries,
    France .... 19 B10 50 12N 3 50 E
Ault, France .... 18 B8 50 5N 1 26 E
Ault, U.S.A. 112 E2 40 35N 104 44W
Aulus-les-Bains, France 20 F5 42 49N 1 19 E
Aumale, France .... 19 C8 49 46N 1 46 E
Aumont-Aubrac, France 20 D7 44 43N 3 17 E
Auna, Nigeria ...... 83 C5 10 9N 4 42 E
Auning, Denmark .. 11 H4 56 26N 10 22 E
Aunis, France 20 B3 46 5N 0 50W
Auponhia, Indonesia 63 E7 1 58 S 125 27 E
Aups, France .... 21 E10 43 37N 6 15 E
Aur, Pulau, Malaysia 65 L5 2 35N 104 10 E
Auraiya, India ...... 69 F8 26 28N 79 33 E
Aurangabad, Bihar,
    India .... 69 G11 24 45N 84 18 E
Aurangabad,
    Maharashtra, India 66 K9 19 50N 75 23 E
Auray, France 18 E4 47 40N 2 59W
Aurich, Germany ... 24 B3 53 28N 7 28 E
Auronzo di Cadore, Italy 41 B9 46 33N 12 26 E
Aurora, Canada 116 C5 44 0N 79 28W
Aurora, S. Africa ... 88 E2 32 40 S 18 29 E
Aurora, Colo., U.S.A. 112 F2 39 44N 104 52W

Aurora, Ill., U.S.A. . 114 E1 41 45N 88 19W
Aurora, Mo., U.S.A. 113 G8 36 58N 93 43W
Aurora, N.Y., U.S.A. 117 D8 42 45N 76 42W
Aurora, Nebr., U.S.A. 112 E6 40 52N 98 0W
Aurora, Ohio, U.S.A. 116 E3 41 21N 81 20W
Aurukun, Australia .. 94 A3 13 20 S 141 45 E
Aus, Namibia .... 88 D2 26 35 S 16 12 E
Ausable →, Canada 116 C3 43 19N 81 46W
Auschwitz = Oświęcim,
    Poland .... 31 H6 50 2N 19 11 E
Austerlitz = Slavkov u
    Brna, Czech Rep. . 27 B9 49 10N 16 52 E
Austin, Minn., U.S.A. 112 D8 43 40N 92 58W
Austin, Nev., U.S.A. 108 G5 39 30N 117 4W
Austin, Pa., U.S.A. . 116 E6 41 38N 78 6W
Austin, Tex., U.S.A. 113 K6 30 17N 97 45W
Austin, L., Australia 93 E2 27 40 S 118 0 E
Austin I., Canada ... 103 A10 61 10N 94 0W
Austra, Norway .... 8 D14 65 8N 11 55 E
Austral Is. = Tubuai Is.,
    French Polynesia .. 97 K13 25 0 S 150 0W
Austral Seamount
    Chain, Pac. Oc. .. 97 K13 24 0 S 150 0W
Australia ■, Oceania 96 K5 23 0 S 135 0 E
Australian Capital
    Territory □, Australia 95 F4 35 30 S 149 0 E
Australind, Australia 93 F2 33 17 S 115 42 E
Austria ■, Europe .. 26 E7 47 0N 14 0 E
Austvågøy, Norway . 8 B16 68 20N 14 40 E
Auterive, France .... 20 E5 43 21N 1 29 E
Authie →, France .. 19 B8 50 22N 1 38 E
Authon-du-Perche,
    France .... 18 D7 48 12N 0 54 E
Autlán, Mexico 118 D4 19 40N 104 30W
Autun, France ...... 19 F11 46 58N 4 17 E
Auvergne □, France 20 C7 45 20N 3 15 E
Auvergne, Mts. d',
    France .... 20 C6 45 20N 2 55 E
Auvézère →, France 20 C4 45 12N 0 50 E
Auxerre, France .... 19 E10 47 48N 3 32 E
Auxi-le-Château, France 19 B9 50 15N 2 8 E
Auxonne, France ... 19 E12 47 10N 5 20 E
Ava, U.S.A. 113 G8 36 57N 92 40W
Avallon, France .... 19 E10 47 30N 3 53 E
Avalon, U.S.A. 111 M8 33 21N 118 20W
Avalon Pen., Canada 105 C9 47 30N 53 20W
Avanos, Turkey .... 70 B2 38 43N 34 51 E
Avaré, Brazil .... 127 A6 23 4 S 48 58W
Åvas, Greece .... 45 F9 40 57N 25 56 E
Avawatz Mts., U.S.A. 111 K10 35 40N 116 30W
Aveiro, Brazil ...... 125 D7 3 10 S 55 5W
Aveiro, Portugal 36 E2 40 37N 8 38W
Aveiro □, Portugal . 36 E2 40 40N 8 35W
Åvej, Iran .... 71 C6 35 40N 49 15 E
Avellaneda, Argentina 126 C4 34 50 S 58 10W
Avellino, Italy ...... 43 B7 40 54N 14 47 E
Avenal, U.S.A. 110 K6 36 0N 120 8W
Aversa, Italy .... 43 B7 40 58N 14 12 E
Avery, U.S.A. 108 C6 47 15N 115 49W
Aves, Is. las, Venezuela 121 D6 12 0N 67 30W
Avesnes-sur-Helpe,
    France .... 19 B10 50 8N 3 55 E
Avesnois □, France 19 B10 50 10N 3 45 E
Avesta, Sweden .... 10 D10 60 9N 16 10 E
Aveyron □, France . 20 D5 44 22N 2 45 E
Aveyron →, France 20 D5 44 5N 1 16 E
Avezzano, Italy ..... 41 F10 42 2N 13 25 E
Avgó, Greece .... 47 F7 35 33N 25 37 E
Aviá Terai, Argentina 126 B3 26 45 S 60 50W
Aviano, Italy .... 41 B9 46 4N 12 36 E
Aviemore, U.K. 13 D5 57 12N 3 50W
Avigliana, Italy ..... 40 C4 45 7N 7 23 E
Avigliano, Italy ..... 43 B8 40 44N 15 43 E
Avignon, France .... 21 E8 43 57N 4 50 E
Ávila, Spain 36 E6 40 39N 4 43W
Ávila □, Spain 36 E6 40 30N 5 0W
Ávila, Sierra de, Spain 36 E5 40 40N 5 15W
Avila Beach, U.S.A. 111 K6 35 11N 120 44W
Avilés, Spain 36 B5 43 35N 5 57W
Avintes, Portugal ... 36 D2 41 7N 8 33W
Avionárion, Greece . 46 C6 38 31N 24 8 E
Avis, U.S.A. 116 E7 41 11N 77 19W
Avisio →, Italy ..... 40 B8 46 7N 11 5 E
Avísio = Avis, Portugal 37 F3 39 4N 7 53W
Avize, France .... 19 D11 48 59N 4 1 E
Avlum, Denmark ... 11 H2 56 16N 8 47 E
Avoca →, Australia 95 F3 35 40 S 143 43 E
Avoca →, Ireland .. 12 D5 52 48N 6 10W
Avola, Canada 102 C5 51 45N 119 19W
Avola, Italy .... 43 F8 36 56N 15 7 E
Avon, U.S.A. 116 D7 42 55N 77 45W
Avon →, Australia . 93 F2 31 40 S 116 7 E
Avon →, Bristol, U.K. 15 F5 51 29N 2 41W
Avon →, Dorset, U.K. 15 G6 50 44N 1 46W
Avon →, Warks., U.K. 15 E5 52 0N 2 8W
Avon Park, U.S.A. . 115 M5 27 36N 81 31W
Avondale, Zimbabwe 87 F3 17 43 S 30 58 E
Avonlea, Canada ... 103 D8 50 0N 105 0W
Avonmore, Canada . 117 A10 45 10N 74 58W
Avonmouth, U.K. .. 15 F5 51 30N 2 42W
Avramov, Bulgaria . 45 D10 42 45N 26 38 E
Avranches, France .. 18 D5 48 40N 1 20W
Avre →, France .... 18 D8 48 47N 1 22 E
Avrig, Romania ..... 29 E9 45 43N 24 21 E
Avrillé, France 18 E6 47 30N 0 35W
Avtovac, Bos.-H. ... 44 C2 43 9N 18 35 E
Awag el Baqar, Sudan 81 E3 10 10N 33 10 E
A'waj →, Syria ..... 74 B5 33 23N 36 20 E
Awaji-Shima, Japan . 55 G7 34 30N 134 50 E
'Awālī, Bahrain ..... 71 E6 26 0N 50 30 E
Awantipur, India ... 69 C6 33 55N 75 3 E
Awasa, Ethiopia .... 81 F4 7 2N 38 28 E
Awasa, L., Ethiopia . 81 F4 7 0N 38 30 E
Awash, Ethiopia .... 81 F5 9 1N 40 10 E
Awash →, Ethiopia . 81 E5 11 45N 41 5 E
Awash △, Ethiopia . 81 F5 9 8N 40 0 E
Awaso, Ghana 82 D4 6 15N 2 22W
Awatere →, N.Z. ... 91 J5 41 37 S 174 10 E
Awbārī, Libya ...... 79 C8 26 46N 12 57 E
Awbārī, Idehan, Libya 79 C8 27 10N 11 30 E
Awe, L., U.K. 13 E3 56 17N 5 16W
Aweil, Sudan .... 81 F2 8 42N 27 20 E
Awgu, Nigeria ...... 83 D6 6 4N 7 24 E
Awjilah, Libya ...... 79 C10 29 8N 21 7 E
Awka, Nigeria ...... 83 D6 6 12N 7 5 E
Ax-les-Thermes, France 20 F5 42 44N 1 50 E
Axat, France .... 20 F6 42 48N 2 14 E
Axe →, U.K. 15 F5 50 42N 3 4W
Axel Heiberg I., Canada 98 A10 80 0N 90 0W
Axim, Ghana 82 E4 4 51N 2 15W
Axintele, Romania .. 29 F11 44 37N 26 47 E
Axiós →, Greece ... 44 F6 40 57N 22 35 E
Axminster, U.K. 15 G4 50 46N 3 0W

Axvall, Sweden ..... 11 F7 58 23N 13 34 E
Ay, France .... 19 C11 49 3N 4 0 E
Ayabaca, Peru ...... 124 D3 4 40 S 79 53W
Ayabe, Japan .... 55 G7 35 20N 135 20 E
Ayacucho, Argentina 126 D4 37 5 S 58 20W
Ayacucho, Peru ..... 124 F4 13 0 S 74 0W
Ayaguz, Kazakhstan 52 E9 48 10N 80 10 E
Ayamé, Ivory C. 82 D4 5 35N 3 9W
Ayamonte, Spain ... 37 H3 37 12N 7 24W
Ayan, Russia .... 53 D14 56 30N 138 16 E
Ayancık, Turkey .... 72 B6 41 57N 34 35 E
Ayas, Turkey .... 72 B5 40 2N 32 21 E
Ayaviri, Peru .... 124 F4 14 50 S 70 35W
Aybastı, Turkey .... 72 B7 40 41N 37 23 E
Aydın, Turkey ...... 72 D2 37 51N 27 51 E
Aydın □, Turkey ... 47 D9 37 50N 28 0 E
Aydın Dağları, Turkey 47 C9 38 10N 28 0 E
Ayelu, Ethiopia ..... 81 E5 10 5N 40 42 E
Ayenngré, Togo .... 83 D5 8 40N 1 1 E
Ayer, U.S.A. 117 D13 42 34N 71 35W
Ayer Hitam, Malaysia 65 c 5 24N 100 16 E
Ayerbe, Spain 38 C4 42 17N 0 41W
Ayer's Cliff, Canada 117 A12 45 10N 72 3W
Ayers Rock, Australia 93 E5 25 23 S 131 5 E
Ayiá, Greece .... 46 B4 39 43N 22 45 E
Ayia Aikateríni, Ákra,
    Greece .... 49 A3 39 50N 19 50 E
Ayía Ánna, Greece . 46 C5 38 52N 23 24 E
Ayía Dhéka, Greece 49 D6 35 3N 24 58 E
Ayía Gálini, Greece . 49 D6 35 6N 24 41 E
Ayía Marína, Kásos,
    Greece .... 47 F8 35 27N 26 53 E
Ayía Marína, Léros,
    Greece .... 47 D8 37 11N 26 48 E
Ayía Napa, Cyprus . 49 E13 34 59N 34 0 E
Ayía Paraskeví, Greece 47 B8 39 14N 26 21 E
Ayía Phyla, Cyprus . 49 E12 34 43N 33 1 E
Ayía Rouméli, Greece 46 F5 35 14N 23 58 E
Ayía Varvára, Greece 49 D7 35 8N 25 1 E
Ayiássos, Greece ... 47 B8 39 5N 26 23 E
Áyioi Theódhoroi,
    Greece .... 46 D5 37 55N 23 9 E
Áyion Óros □, Greece 45 F8 40 25N 24 6 E
Áyios Amvrósios,
    Cyprus .... 49 D12 35 20N 33 35 E
Áyios Andréas, Greece 46 D4 37 21N 22 45 E
Áyios Evstrátios, Greece 46 B6 39 34N 24 58 E
Áyios Ioánnis, Ákra,
    Greece .... 49 D7 35 20N 25 40 E
Áyios Isídhoros, Greece 49 C9 36 9N 27 51 E
Áyios Kiríkos, Greece 47 D8 37 34N 26 14 E
Áyios Matthaíos, Greece 49 B3 39 30N 19 47 E
Áyios Míronas, Greece 47 F7 35 15N 25 1 E
Áyios Nikólaos, Greece 49 D7 35 11N 25 41 E
Áyios Pétros, Greece 46 C2 38 40N 20 36 E
Áyios Seryios, Cyprus 49 D12 35 12N 33 53 E
Áyios Theodhoros,
    Cyprus .... 49 D13 35 22N 34 1 E
Áyios Yeóryios, Greece 46 D5 37 28N 23 57 E
Aykathonísi, Greece 47 D8 37 28N 27 0 E
Aykirikçi, Turkey ... 47 B12 39 8N 30 9 E
Aylesbury, U.K. 15 F7 51 49N 0 49W
Aylmer, Canada 116 D4 42 46N 80 59W
Aylmer, L., Canada . 100 B8 64 0N 110 8W
'Ayn, Wādī al, Oman 71 F7 22 15N 55 28 E
Ayn Dār, Si. Arabia 71 E7 25 55N 49 10 E
Ayn Zālah, Iraq .... 70 B4 36 45N 42 35 E
Ayna, Spain 39 G2 38 34N 2 3W
Ayod, Sudan .... 81 F3 8 7N 31 26 E
Ayolas, Paraguay ... 126 B4 27 10 S 56 59W
Ayom, Sudan .... 81 F2 7 49N 28 23 E
Ayora, Spain 39 F3 39 3N 1 3W
Ayon, Ostrov, Russia 53 C17 69 50N 169 0 E
Ayorou, Niger ...... 83 C5 14 53N 1 0 E
'Ayoûn el 'Atroûs,
    Mauritania 82 B3 16 38N 9 37W
Ayr, Australia ...... 94 B4 19 35 S 147 25 E
Ayr, Canada 116 C4 43 17N 80 27W
Ayr, U.K. 13 F4 55 28N 4 38W
Ayr →, U.K. 13 F4 55 28N 4 38W
Ayranci, Turkey .... 72 D5 37 21N 33 41 E
Ayrancılar, Turkey . 47 C9 38 15N 27 18 E
Ayre, Pt. of, U.K. .. 14 C3 54 25N 4 21W
Aysha, Ethiopia .... 81 E5 10 50N 42 23 E
Ayton, Australia .... 94 B4 15 56 S 145 22 E
Aytos, Bulgaria .... 45 D11 42 42N 27 16 E
Aytoska Planina,
    Bulgaria .... 45 D11 42 45N 27 30 E
Ayu, Kepulauan,
    Indonesia .... 63 D8 0 35N 131 5 E
Ayutla, Guatemala . 120 D1 14 40N 92 10W
Ayutla, Mexico 119 D5 16 58N 99 17W
Ayvacık, Turkey .... 72 C2 39 36N 26 24 E
Ayvalık, Turkey .... 47 B8 39 20N 26 46 E
Az Zabadānī, Syria . 74 B5 33 43N 36 5 E
Az Zāhiriyah,
    West Bank .... 74 D3 31 25N 34 58 E
Az Zahrān, Si. Arabia 71 E6 26 10N 50 7 E
Az Zarqā, Jordan ... 74 C5 32 5N 36 4 E
Az Zarqā', U.A.E. .. 71 E7 24 53N 53 4 E
Az Zarqā □, Jordan 74 C5 32 5N 36 4 E
Az Zāwiyah, Libya . 79 B8 32 52N 12 56 E
Az Zibār, Iraq ...... 70 B5 36 52N 44 4 E
Az Zilfi, Si. Arabia . 70 E5 26 12N 44 52 E
Az Zubayr, Iraq .... 70 D5 30 26N 47 40 E
Az Zuqur, Yemen .. 81 E5 14 0N 42 45 E
Azad Kashmir □,
    Pakistan .... 69 C5 33 50N 73 50 E
Azambuja, Portugal 37 F2 39 4N 8 51W
Azamgarh, India ... 69 F10 26 5N 83 13 E
Azángaro, Peru ..... 124 F4 14 55 S 70 13W
Azaouad, Mali ..... 82 B4 19 0N 3 0 E
Azaouak, Vallée de l',
    Mali .... 83 B5 15 50N 3 20 E
Azar Shahr, Iran ... 70 B5 37 45N 45 59 E
Azara, Nigeria ...... 83 D6 8 22N 9 12 E
Azärbayjan =
    Azerbaijan ■, Asia 35 K9 40 20N 48 0 E
Azärbāyjan-e Gharbī □,
    Iran .... 70 B5 37 0N 44 30 E
Azärbāyjan-e Sharqī □,
    Iran .... 70 B5 37 20N 47 0 E
Azare, Nigeria ...... 83 C7 11 55N 10 10 E
Azay-le-Rideau, France 18 E7 47 16N 0 30 E
Azazga, Algeria .... 83 A6 36 36N 4 22 E
Azbine = Aïr, Niger 83 B6 18 30N 8 0 E
Azerbaijan ■, Asia . 35 K9 40 20N 48 0 E
Azerbaijchan =
    Azerbaijan ■, Asia 35 K9 40 20N 48 0 E
Azezo, Ethiopia .... 81 E4 12 28N 37 15 E
Azimganj, India .... 69 G13 24 14N 88 16 E
Aznalcóllar, Spain .. 37 H4 37 32N 6 17W
Azogues, Ecuador .. 124 D3 2 35 S 78 0W

Azov, Russia .... 35 G4 47 3N 39 25 E
Azov, Sea of, Europe 33 J9 46 0N 36 30 E
Azovskoye More =
    Azov, Sea of, Europe 33 J9 46 0N 36 30 E
Azpeitia, Spain 38 B2 43 12N 2 19W
Azraq ash Shīshān,
    Jordan .... 74 D5 31 50N 36 49 E
Aztec, U.S.A. 109 H10 36 49N 107 59W
Azúa de Compostela,
    Dom. Rep. 121 C5 18 25N 70 44W
Azuaga, Spain 37 G5 38 16N 5 39W
Azuara, Spain 38 D4 41 15N 0 53W
Azuer →, Spain 37 F7 39 8N 3 36W
Azuero, Pen. de,
    Panama 120 E3 7 30N 80 30W
Azul, Argentina .... 126 D4 36 42 S 59 43W
Azusa, U.S.A. 111 L9 34 8N 117 52W

B

Ba Be △, Vietnam ... 64 A5 22 25N 105 37 E
Ba Don, Vietnam ... 64 D6 17 45N 106 26 E
Ba Dong, Vietnam . 65 H6 9 40N 106 33 E
Ba Ngoi = Cam Lam,
    Vietnam .... 65 G7 11 54N 109 10 E
Ba Tri, Vietnam .... 65 G6 10 2N 106 36 E
Ba Vì △, Vietnam ... 64 B5 21 1N 105 22 E
Ba Xian = Bazhou,
    China .... 56 E9 39 8N 116 22 E
Baa, Indonesia ..... 63 F6 10 50 S 123 0 E
Baamonde, Spain ... 36 B3 43 7N 7 44W
Baardheere = Bardera,
    Somali Rep. ..... 75 G3 2 20N 42 27 E
Baarle-Nassau, Belgium 17 C4 51 27N 4 56 E
Bab el Mandeb, Red Sea 75 E3 12 35N 43 25 E
Baba, Bulgaria ...... 44 D7 42 44N 23 59 E
Bābā, Koh-i-, Afghan. 66 B5 34 30N 67 0 E
Baba Burnu, Turkey 47 B8 39 29N 26 2 E
Baba dag, Azerbaijan 35 K9 41 0N 48 19 E
Bābā Kalū, Iran .... 71 D6 30 7N 50 49 E
Babadag, Romania .. 29 F13 44 53N 28 44 E
Babadağ, Turkey ... 47 D10 37 49N 28 52 E
Babaeski, Turkey ... 45 E11 41 26N 27 6 E
Babahoyo, Ecuador 124 D3 1 40 S 79 30W
Babai = Sarju →, India 69 F9 27 21N 81 23 E
Babana, Nigeria .... 83 C5 10 31N 3 46 E
Babanusa, Sudan ... 81 E2 11 20N 27 48 E
Babar, Indonesia ... 63 F7 8 0 S 129 30 E
Babar, Pakistan .... 68 D3 31 7N 69 32 E
Babarkach, Pakistan 68 E3 29 45N 68 0 E
Babayevo, Russia ... 32 C8 59 24N 35 55 E
Babb, U.S.A. 108 B7 48 51N 113 27W
Babenhausen, Germany 25 F4 49 57N 8 57 E
Bābeni, Romania ... 29 F9 44 59N 24 11 E
Baberu, India .... 69 G9 25 33N 80 43 E
Babi Besar, Pulau,
    Malaysia .... 65 L4 2 25N 103 59 E
Babia Gora, Europe . 31 J6 49 38N 19 38 E
Babian Jiang →, China 58 F3 22 55N 101 47 E
Babīl □, Iraq .... 70 C5 32 30N 44 30 E
Babile, Ethiopia .... 81 F5 9 16N 42 11 E
Babimost, Poland .. 31 F2 52 10N 15 49 E
Babinda, Australia .. 94 B4 17 20 S 145 56 E
Babine, Canada 102 B3 55 22N 126 37W
Babine →, Canada . 102 B3 55 45N 127 44W
Babine L., Canada .. 102 C3 54 48N 126 0W
Babiogórski △, Poland 31 J6 49 38N 19 38 E
Babo, Indonesia .... 63 E8 2 30 S 133 30 E
Babócsa, Hungary .. 28 D2 46 2N 17 21 E
Bābol, Iran .... 71 B7 36 40N 52 50 E
Bābol Sar, Iran ..... 71 B7 36 45N 52 45 E
Baborów, Poland ... 31 H5 50 7N 18 1 E
Babruysk, Belarus .. 33 F5 53 10N 29 15 E
Babuhri, India ...... 68 F3 26 49N 69 43 E
Babuna, Macedonia 44 E5 41 30N 21 40 E
Babura, Nigeria .... 83 C6 12 51N 8 59 E
Babusar Pass, Pakistan 69 B5 35 12N 73 59 E
Babushkin, Russia . 60 A5 51 40N 105 50 E
Babušnica, Serbia & M. 44 C6 43 7N 22 27 E
Babuyan Chan., Phil. 61 B4 18 40N 121 30 E
Babylon, Iraq ...... 70 C5 32 34N 44 22 E
Bač, Serbia & M. .. 28 E4 45 29N 19 17 E
Bac →, Moldova .. 29 D14 46 55N 29 26 E
Bac Giang, Vietnam 58 F5 22 38N 105 49 E
Bac Lieu, Vietnam . 65 H5 9 17N 105 43 E
Bac Ninh, Vietnam 58 F5 21 13N 106 4 E
Bac Phan, Vietnam 64 B5 22 0N 105 0 E
Bac Quang, Vietnam 58 F5 22 30N 104 48 E
Bacabal, Brazil ..... 125 D10 4 15 S 44 45W
Bacalar, Mexico 119 D7 18 50N 87 27W
Bacan, Kepulauan,
    Indonesia .... 63 E7 0 35 S 127 30 E
Bacarra, Phil. ...... 61 B4 18 15N 120 37 E
Bacău, Romania .... 29 D11 46 35N 26 55 E
Bacău □, Romania . 29 D11 46 30N 26 45 E
Baccarat, France ... 19 D13 48 28N 6 42 E
Bacerac, Mexico ... 118 A3 30 18N 108 50W
Băcești, Romania .. 29 D12 46 50N 27 11 E
Bach Long Vi, Dao,
    Vietnam .... 64 B6 20 10N 107 40 E
Bach Ma △, Vietnam 64 D6 16 11N 107 49 E
Bacharach, Germany 25 E3 50 3N 7 46 E
Bachhwara, India ... 69 G11 25 35N 85 54 E
Bachuma, Ethiopia . 81 F4 6 48N 35 53 E
Back →, Canada ... 100 B9 65 10N 104 0W
Bačka Palanka,
    Serbia & M. ..... 28 E4 45 17N 19 27 E
Bačka Topola,
    Serbia & M. ..... 28 E4 45 49N 19 39 E
Bäckebo, Sweden .. 11 H10 56 53N 16 4 E
Bäckefors, Sweden . 11 F6 58 48N 12 9 E
Backhammar, Sweden 10 E8 59 10N 14 11 E
Bački Petrovac,
    Serbia & M. ..... 28 E4 45 29N 19 32 E
Backnang, Germany 25 G5 48 56N 9 26 E
Baco, Mt., Phil. .... 61 E4 12 50N 121 20 E
Bacolod, Phil. ...... 61 F5 10 40N 122 57 E
Bacqueville-en-Caux,
    France .... 18 C8 49 47N 1 0 E
Bács-Kiskun □,
    Hungary .... 28 D4 46 43N 19 30 E
Bácsalmás, Hungary 28 D4 46 8N 19 17 E
Bacuag = Placer, Phil. 61 G6 9 36N 125 38 E
Bacuk, Malaysia .... 65 J4 6 4N 102 25 E
Bād, Iran .... 71 C7 33 41N 52 1 E
Bad →, U.S.A. 112 C4 44 21N 100 22W
Bad Aussee, Austria 26 D6 47 43N 13 45 E
Bad Axe, U.S.A. ... 116 C2 43 48N 83 0W
Bad Bergzabern,
    Germany .... 25 F3 49 6N 7 59 E
Bad Berleburg,
    Germany .... 24 D4 51 2N 8 26 E

Bad Bevensen, *Germany* . **24 B6** 53 5N 10 35 E
Bad Bramstedt, *Germany* . **24 B5** 53 55N 9 53 E
Bad Brückenau, *Germany* . **25 E5** 50 18N 9 47 E
Bad Doberan, *Germany* . **24 A7** 54 6N 11 53 E
Bad Driburg, *Germany* . **24 D5** 51 43N 9 1 E
Bad Ems, *Germany* . **25 E3** 50 20N 7 43 E
Bad Frankenhausen, *Germany* . **24 D7** 51 21N 11 5 E
Bad Freienwalde, *Germany* . **24 C10** 52 46N 14 1 E
Bad Goisern, *Austria* . **26 D6** 47 38N 13 38 E
Bad Harzburg, *Germany* . **24 D6** 51 52N 10 34 E
Bad Hersfeld, *Germany* . **24 D6** 47 17N 13 6 E
Bad Hofgastein, *Austria* . **26 D6** 47 17N 13 6 E
Bad Homburg, *Germany* . **25 E4** 50 13N 8 38 E
Bad Honnef, *Germany* . **24 E3** 50 38N 7 13 E
Bad Iburg, *Germany* . **24 C4** 52 10N 8 3 E
Bad Ischl, *Austria* . **26 D6** 47 44N 13 38 E
Bad Kissingen, *Germany* . **25 E6** 50 11N 10 4 E
Bad Königshofen, *Germany* . **25 E6** 50 17N 10 28 E
Bad Kreuznach, *Germany* . **25 F3** 49 50N 7 51 E
Bad Krozingen, *Germany* . **25 H3** 47 54N 7 42 E
Bad Laasphe, *Germany* **24 D4** 50 56N 8 25 E
Bad Lands, *U.S.A.* . **112 D3** 43 40N 102 10W
Bad Langensalza, *Germany* . **24 D6** 51 5N 10 38 E
Bad Lauterberg, *Germany* . **24 D6** 51 38N 10 28 E
Bad Leonfelden, *Austria* . **26 C7** 48 31N 14 18 E
Bad Liebenwerda, *Germany* . **24 D9** 51 31N 13 24 E
Bad Mergentheim, *Germany* . **25 F5** 49 28N 9 42 E
Bad Münstereifel, *Germany* . **24 E2** 50 33N 6 46 E
Bad Nauheim, *Germany* . **25 E4** 50 21N 8 43 E
Bad Neuenahr-Ahrweiler, *Germany* . **24 E3** 50 32N 7 5 E
Bad Neustadt, *Germany* . **25 E6** 50 18N 10 13 E
Bad Oeynhausen, *Germany* . **24 C4** 52 12N 8 46 E
Bad Oldesloe, *Germany* . **24 B6** 53 48N 10 22 E
Bad Orb, *Germany* . **25 E5** 50 12N 9 22 E
Bad Pyrmont, *Germany* . **24 D5** 51 59N 9 16 E
Bad Reichenhall, *Germany* . **25 H8** 47 43N 12 54 E
Bad Säckingen, *Germany* . **25 H3** 47 33N 7 56 E
Bad Salzuflen, *Germany* . **24 C4** 52 5N 8 45 E
Bad Salzungen, *Germany* . **24 E6** 50 48N 10 14 E
Bad Schwartau, *Germany* . **24 B6** 53 55N 10 41 E
Bad Segeberg, *Germany* . **24 B6** 53 56N 10 17 E
Bad St. Leonhard, *Austria* . **26 E7** 46 58N 14 47 E
Bad Tölz, *Germany* . **25 H7** 47 45N 11 34 E
Bad Urach, *Germany* . **25 G5** 48 29N 9 23 E
Bad Vöslau, *Austria* . **27 D9** 47 58N 16 12 E
Bad Waldsee, *Germany* . **25 H5** 47 55N 9 45 E
Bad Wildungen, *Germany* . **24 D5** 51 6N 9 7 E
Bad Wimpfen, *Germany* . **25 F5** 49 13N 9 11 E
Bad Windsheim, *Germany* . **25 F6** 49 36N 10 25 E
Bad Zwischenahn, *Germany* . **24 B4** 53 12N 8 1 E
Bada Barabil, *India* . **69 H11** 22 7N 85 24 E
Badagara, *India* . **66 P9** 11 35N 75 40 E
Badagri, *Nigeria* . **83 D5** 6 25N 2 55 E
Badajós, L., *Brazil* . **124 D6** 3 15 S 62 50W
Badajoz, *Spain* . **37 G4** 38 50N 6 59W
Badajoz □, *Spain* . **37 G4** 38 40N 6 30W
Badakhshān □, *Afghan.* . **66 A7** 36 30N 71 0 E
Badalona, *Spain* . **38 D7** 41 26N 2 15 E
Badalzai, *Afghan.* . **68 E1** 29 50N 65 35 E
Badampahar, *India* . **67 H15** 22 10N 86 10 E
Badanah, *Si. Arabia* . **70 D4** 30 58N 41 30 E
Badarinath, *India* . **69 D8** 30 45N 79 30 E
Badas, Kepulauan, *Indonesia* . **62 D3** 0 45N 107 5 E
Baddo →, *Pakistan* . **66 F4** 28 0N 64 20 E
Bade, *Indonesia* . **63 F9** 7 10 S 139 35 E
Badeggi, *Nigeria* . **83 D6** 9 1N 6 8 E
Baden, *Austria* . **27 C9** 48 1N 16 13 E
Baden, *Switz.* . **25 H4** 47 28N 8 18 E
Baden, *U.S.A.* . **116 F4** 40 38N 80 14W
Baden-Baden, *Germany* . **25 G4** 48 44N 8 13 E
Baden-Württemberg □, *Germany* . **25 G4** 48 20N 8 40 E
Badgastein, *Austria* . **26 D6** 47 7N 13 9 E
Badger, *Canada* . **105 C8** 49 0N 56 4W
Badger, *U.S.A.* . **110 J7** 36 38N 119 1W
Bādghīs □, *Afghan.* . **66 B3** 35 0N 63 0 E
Badgingarra △, *Australia* . **93 F2** 30 23 S 115 22 E
Badgom, *India* . **69 B6** 34 1N 74 45 E
Badia Polésine, *Italy* . **41 C8** 45 6N 11 29 E
Badiar △, *Guinea* . **82 C2** 13 37N 13 11W
Badin, *Pakistan* . **68 G3** 24 38N 68 54 E
Badinka △, *Mali* . **82 C3** 13 31N 9 8W
Badlands △, *U.S.A.* . **112 D3** 43 38N 102 56W
Badogo, *Mali* . **82 C3** 11 2N 8 13W
Badoumbé, *Mali* . **82 C2** 13 42N 10 15W
Badrah, *Iraq* . **70 C5** 33 6N 45 58 E
Badrinath, *India* . **69 D8** 30 44N 79 29 E
Badulla, *Sri Lanka* . **66 R12** 7 1N 81 7 E
Badung, Selat, *Indonesia* . **63 K18** 8 40 S 115 22 E
Baena, *Spain* . **37 H6** 37 37N 4 20W
Baeza, *Spain* . **37 H7** 37 57N 3 25W
Bafang, *Cameroon* . **83 D7** 5 9N 10 11 E
Bafatá, *Guinea-Biss.* . **82 C2** 12 8N 14 40W
Baffin B., *Canada* . **101 A13** 72 0N 64 0W
Baffin I., *Canada* . **101 B12** 68 0N 75 0W
Bafia, *Cameroon* . **83 E7** 4 40N 11 10 E
Bafilo, *Togo* . **83 D5** 9 22N 1 22 E
Bafing △, *Mali* . **82 C2** 13 49N 10 50W
Bafing →, *Mali* . **82 C2** 13 49N 10 50W
Bafliyūn, *Syria* . **70 B3** 36 37N 36 59 E
Bafoulabé, *Mali* . **82 C2** 13 50N 10 55W
Bafoussam, *Cameroon* . **83 D7** 5 28N 10 25 E
Bāfq, *Iran* . **71 D7** 31 40N 55 25 E
Bafra, *Turkey* . **72 B7** 41 34N 35 54 E
Bafra Burnu, *Turkey* . **72 B7** 41 45N 36 2 E
Bāft, *Iran* . **71 D8** 29 15N 56 38 E
Bafut, *Cameroon* . **83 D7** 6 6N 10 2 E
Bafwasende, *Dem. Rep. of the Congo* . **86 B2** 1 3N 27 5 E
Bagam, *Niger* . **83 B6** 15 43N 6 53 E
Bagamoyo, *Tanzania* . **86 D4** 6 28 S 38 55 E
Bagan Datoh, *Malaysia* . **65 L3** 3 59N 100 47 E

Bagan Serai, *Malaysia* . **65 K3** 5 1N 100 32 E
Baganga, *Phil.* . **61 H7** 7 34N 126 33 E
Bagani, *Namibia* . **88 B3** 18 7 S 21 41 E
Bagansiapiapi, *Indonesia* . **62 D2** 2 12N 100 50 E
Bagasra, *India* . **68 J4** 21 30N 71 0 E
Bagawi, *Sudan* . **81 E3** 12 20N 34 18 E
Bagbag, *Sudan* . **81 D3** 15 23N 31 30 E
Bagdad, *U.S.A.* . **111 L11** 34 35N 115 53W
Bagdarin, *Russia* . **53 D12** 54 26N 113 36 E
Bagé, *Brazil* . **127 C5** 31 20 S 54 15W
Bagenalstown = Muine Bheag, *Ireland* . **12 D5** 52 42N 6 58W
Baggs, *U.S.A.* . **108 F10** 41 2N 107 39W
Bagh, *Pakistan* . **69 C5** 33 59N 73 45 E
Baghain →, *India* . **69 G9** 25 32N 81 1 E
Baghdād, *Iraq* . **70 C5** 33 20N 44 30 E
Bagheria, *Italy* . **42 D6** 38 5N 13 30 E
Baghlān, *Afghan.* . **66 A6** 32 12N 68 46 E
Baghlān □, *Afghan.* . **66 B6** 36 0N 68 30 E
Bagley, *U.S.A.* . **112 B7** 47 32N 95 24W
Bagnara Cálabra, *Italy* . **43 D8** 38 17N 15 48 E
Bagnasco, *Italy* . **40 D5** 44 18N 8 2 E
Bagnères-de-Bigorre, *France* . **20 E4** 43 5N 0 9 E
Bagnères-de-Luchon, *France* . **20 F4** 42 47N 0 38 E
Bagni di Lucca, *Italy* . **40 D7** 44 1N 10 35 E
Bagno di Romagna, *Italy* . **41 E8** 43 50N 11 57 E
Bagnoles-de-l'Orne, *France* . **18 D6** 48 32N 0 25W
Bagnols-sur-Cèze, *France* . **21 D8** 44 10N 4 36 E
Bagnorégio, *Italy* . **41 F9** 42 37N 12 5 E
Bago = Pegu, *Burma* . **67 L20** 17 20N 96 29 E
Bagodar, *India* . **69 G11** 24 5N 85 52 E
Bagrationovsk, *Russia* . **9 J19** 54 23N 20 39 E
Bagrdan, *Serbia & M.* . **44 B5** 44 5N 21 11 E
Baguio, *Phil.* . **61 C4** 16 26N 120 34 E
Bağyurdu, *Turkey* . **47 C9** 38 25N 27 41 E
Bağzane, Monts, *Niger* . **83 B6** 17 43N 8 45 E
Bah, *India* . **69 F8** 26 53N 78 36 E
Bahabón de Esgueva, *Spain* . **36 D7** 41 52N 3 43W
Bahadurganj, *India* . **69 F12** 26 16N 87 49 E
Bahadurgarh, *India* . **68 E7** 28 40N 76 57 E
Bahama, Canal Viejo de, *W. Indies* . **120 B4** 22 10N 77 30W
Bahamas ■, *N. Amer.* . **121 B5** 24 0N 75 0W
Bahār, *Iran* . **73 E13** 34 54N 48 26 E
Baharampur, *India* . **69 G13** 24 2N 88 27 E
Baharîya, El Wâhât al, *Egypt* . **80 B2** 28 0N 28 50 E
Baharu Pandan = Pandan, *Malaysia* . **65 d** 1 32N 103 46 E
Bahawalnagar, *Pakistan* . **68 E5** 30 0N 73 15 E
Bahawalpur, *Pakistan* . **68 E4** 29 24N 71 40 E
Bahçe, *Turkey* . **72 D7** 37 13N 36 34 E
Bahçecik, *Turkey* . **45 F13** 40 41N 29 44 E
Baheri, *India* . **69 E8** 28 45N 79 34 E
Bahgul →, *India* . **69 F8** 27 45N 79 36 E
Bahi, *Tanzania* . **86 D4** 5 58 S 35 21 E
Bahi Swamp, *Tanzania* . **86 D4** 6 10 S 35 0 E
Bahía = Salvador, *Brazil* . **125 F11** 13 0 S 38 30W
Bahía □, *Brazil* . **125 F10** 12 0 S 42 0W
Bahía, Is. de la, *Honduras* . **120 C2** 16 45N 86 15W
Bahía Blanca, *Argentina* . **126 D3** 38 35 S 62 13W
Bahía de Caráquez, *Ecuador* . **124 D2** 0 40 S 80 27W
Bahía Honda, *Cuba* . **120 B3** 22 54N 83 10W
Bahía Laura, *Argentina* . **128 F3** 48 10 S 66 30W
Bahía Negra, *Paraguay* . **124 H7** 20 5 S 58 5W
Bahir Dar, *Ethiopia* . **81 E4** 11 37N 37 10 E
Bahmanzād, *Iran* . **71 D6** 31 15N 51 47 E
Bahr el Ahmar □, *Sudan* . **80 D4** 20 0N 35 0 E
Bahr el Ghazâl □, *Sudan* . **81 F2** 7 0N 28 0 E
Bahr el Jabal □, *Sudan* . **81 G3** 4 0N 31 0 E
Bahraich, *India* . **69 F9** 27 38N 81 37 E
Bahrain ■, *Asia* . **71 E6** 26 0N 50 35 E
Bahror, *India* . **68 F7** 27 51N 76 20 E
Bāhū Kalāt, *Iran* . **71 E9** 25 43N 61 25 E
Bai, *Mali* . **82 C4** 13 35N 3 28W
Bai Bung, Mui = Ca Mau, Mui, *Vietnam* . **65 H5** 8 38N 104 44 E
Bai Duc, *Vietnam* . **64 C5** 18 3N 105 49 E
Bai Thuong, *Vietnam* . **64 C5** 19 54N 105 23 E
Baia de Aramă, *Romania* . **28 E7** 45 0N 22 50 E
Baia Mare, *Romania* . **29 C8** 47 40N 23 35 E
Baia-Sprie, *Romania* . **29 C8** 47 41N 23 43 E
Baião, *Brazil* . **125 D9** 2 40 S 49 40W
Baibokoum, *Chad* . **79 G9** 7 46N 15 43 E
Báicoi, *Romania* . **29 E10** 45 3N 25 52 E
Baidoa, *Somali Rep.* . **75 G3** 3 8N 43 30 E
Baie-Comeau, *Canada* . **105 C6** 49 12N 68 10W
Baie-St-Paul, *Canada* . **105 C5** 47 28N 70 32W
Baie-Trinité, *Canada* . **105 C6** 49 25N 67 20W
Baie Verte, *Canada* . **105 C8** 49 55N 56 12W
Baignes-Ste-Radegonde, *France* . **20 C3** 45 23N 0 25W
Baigneux-les-Juifs, *France* . **19 E11** 47 31N 4 39 E
Baihar, *India* . **69 H9** 22 6N 80 33 E
Baihe, *China* . **56 H6** 32 50N 110 5 E
Baijnath, *India* . **69 E8** 29 55N 79 37 E
Baikal, L. = Baykal, Oz., *Russia* . **53 D11** 53 0N 108 0 E
Baikunthpur, *India* . **69 H10** 23 15N 82 33 E
Baile Atha Cliath = Dublin, *Ireland* . **12 C5** 53 21N 6 15W
Baile Govora, *Romania* . **29 E9** 45 5N 24 11 E
Bâile Herculane, *Romania* . **28 F7** 44 53N 22 26 E
Bâile Olănești, *Romania* . **29 E9** 45 12N 24 14 E
Bâile Tuşnad, *Romania* . **29 D10** 46 9N 25 51 E
Bailén, *Spain* . **37 G7** 38 8N 3 48W
Bâilești, *Romania* . **29 F8** 44 1N 23 20 E
Baima, *China* . **58 A3** 33 0N 100 26 E
Bain-de-Bretagne, *France* . **18 E5** 47 50N 1 40W
Bainbridge, Ga., *U.S.A.* . **115 K3** 30 55N 84 35W
Bainbridge, N.Y., *U.S.A.* . **117 D9** 42 18N 75 29W
Baing, *Indonesia* . **63 F6** 10 14 S 120 34 E
Bainiu, *China* . **56 H7** 32 50N 112 15 E
Baiona, *Spain* . **36 C2** 42 6N 8 52W
Baʿir, *Jordan* . **74 E5** 30 45N 36 55 E
Bairiki = Tarawa, *Kiribati* . **96 G9** 1 30N 173 0 E
Bairin Youqi, *China* . **57 C10** 43 30N 118 35 E
Bairin Zuoqi, *China* . **57 C10** 43 58N 119 15 E
Bairnsdale, *Australia* . **95 F4** 37 48 S 147 36 E
Bais, *Phil.* . **61 G5** 9 35N 123 7 E
Baisha, *China* . **56 G7** 34 20N 112 32 E
Baissa, *Nigeria* . **83 D7** 7 14N 10 38 E
Baitadi, *Nepal* . **69 E9** 29 35N 80 25 E

Baixa Limia-Sierra do Xurés △, *Spain* . **36 D2** 41 59N 8 2W
Baiyin, *China* . **56 F3** 36 45N 104 14 E
Baiyū, *China* . **58 B2** 31 16N 98 50 E
Baiyu Shan, *China* . **56 F4** 37 15N 107 30 E
Baiyuda, *Sudan* . **80 D3** 17 35N 32 7 E
Baj Baj, *India* . **69 H13** 22 30N 88 5 E
Baja, *Hungary* . **28 D3** 46 12N 18 59 E
Baja, Pta., *Mexico* . **118 B1** 29 50N 116 0W
Baja California, *Mexico* . **118 A1** 31 10N 115 12W
Baja California □, *Mexico* . **118 B2** 30 0N 115 0W
Baja California Sur □, *Mexico* . **118 B2** 25 50N 111 50W
Bajag, *India* . **69 H9** 22 40N 81 21 E
Bajamar, *Canary Is.* . **48 F3** 28 33N 16 20W
Bajana, *India* . **68 H4** 23 7N 71 49 E
Bajatrejo, *Indonesia* . **63 J17** 8 29 S 114 19 E
Bajera, *Indonesia* . **63 J18** 8 31 S 115 2 E
Bājgīrān, *Iran* . **71 B8** 37 36N 58 24 E
Bajimba, Mt., *Australia* . **95 D5** 29 17 S 152 6 E
Bajina Bašta, *Serbia & M.* . **44 C3** 43 58N 19 35 E
Bajmok, *Serbia & M.* . **28 E4** 45 57N 19 24 E
Bajo Nuevo, *Caribbean* . **120 C4** 15 40N 78 50W
Bajoga, *Nigeria* . **83 C7** 10 57N 11 20 E
Bajool, *Australia* . **94 C5** 23 40 S 150 35 E
Bak, *Hungary* . **28 D1** 46 43N 16 51 E
Bakar, *Croatia* . **41 C11** 45 18N 14 32 E
Bakasi, Pen., *Cameroon* . **83 E6** 4 42N 8 20 E
Bakel, *Senegal* . **82 C2** 14 56N 12 20W
Baker, Calif., *U.S.A.* . **111 K10** 35 16N 116 4W
Baker, Mont., *U.S.A.* . **112 B2** 46 22N 104 17W
Baker, L., *Canada* . **100 B10** 64 0N 96 0W
Baker, Mt., *U.S.A.* . **108 B3** 48 50N 121 49W
Baker City, *U.S.A.* . **108 D5** 44 47N 117 50W
Baker I., Pac. Oc. . **96 G10** 0 10N 176 35W
Baker I., *U.S.A.* . **102 B2** 55 20N 133 40W
Baker I., *Australia* . **93 E4** 26 54 S 126 5 E
Baker Lake, *Canada* . **100 B10** 64 20N 96 3W
Bakers Creek, *Australia* . **94 C4** 21 13 S 149 7 E
Bakers Dozen Is., *Canada* . **104 A4** 56 45N 78 45W
Bakersfield, Calif., *U.S.A.* . **111 K8** 35 23N 119 1W
Bakersfield, Vt., *U.S.A.* . **117 B12** 44 45N 72 48W
Bakhchysaray, *Ukraine* . **33 K7** 44 40N 33 45 E
Bakhmach, *Ukraine* . **33 G7** 51 10N 32 45 E
Bākhtarān, *Iran* . **70 C5** 34 23N 47 0 E
Bākhtarān □, *Iran* . **70 C5** 34 0N 46 30 E
Bakı, *Azerbaijan* . **35 K9** 40 29N 49 56 E
Bakır →, *Turkey* . **47 C9** 38 55N 27 0 E
Bakırdağı, *Turkey* . **72 C6** 38 13N 35 46 E
Bakkafjörður, *Iceland* . **8 C6** 66 2N 14 48W
Baklan, *Turkey* . **47 C11** 38 0N 29 36 E
Bako, *Ethiopia* . **81 F4** 5 51N 36 23 E
Bako, Ivory C. . **82 D3** 9 8N 7 40W
Bakouma, *C.A.R.* . **84 C4** 5 40N 22 56 E
Baksan, *Russia* . **35 J6** 43 42N 43 32 E
Bakswaho, *India* . **69 G8** 24 15N 79 18 E
Baku = Bakı, *Azerbaijan* . **35 K9** 40 29N 49 56 E
Bakundi, *Nigeria* . **83 D7** 8 2N 10 45 E
Bakutis Coast, *Antarctica* . **5 D15** 74 0 S 120 0W
Baky = Bakı, *Azerbaijan* . **35 K9** 40 29N 49 56 E
Bala, *Canada* . **116 A5** 45 1N 79 37W
Bala, *Senegal* . **82 C2** 14 1N 13 8W
Bâlâ, *Turkey* . **72 C5** 39 32N 33 6 E
Bala, *U.K.* . **14 E4** 52 54N 3 36W
Bala, L., *U.K.* . **14 E4** 52 53N 3 37W
Balabac I., *Phil.* . **62 C5** 8 0N 117 0 E
Balabac Str., E. Indies . **62 C5** 7 53N 117 5 E
Balabagh, *Afghan.* . **68 B4** 34 25N 70 12 E
Baʿalbak, *Lebanon* . **74 B5** 34 0N 36 10 E
Balabalangan, Kepulauan, *Indonesia* . **62 E5** 2 20 S 117 30 E
Bălăcița, *Romania* . **29 F8** 44 23N 23 8 E
Balad, *Iraq* . **70 C5** 34 1N 44 9 E
Balad Rūz, *Iraq* . **70 C5** 33 42N 45 5 E
Bālādeh, Fārs, *Iran* . **71 D6** 29 17N 51 56 E
Bālādeh, Māzandaran, *Iran* . **71 B6** 36 12N 51 48 E
Balaghat, *India* . **66 J12** 21 49N 80 12 E
Balaghat Ra., *India* . **66 K10** 18 50N 76 30 E
Balaguer, *Spain* . **38 D5** 41 50N 0 50 E
Balakhna, *Russia* . **34 B6** 56 25N 43 32 E
Balaklava, *Ukraine* . **33 K7** 44 30N 33 30 E
Balakliya, *Ukraine* . **33 H9** 49 28N 36 55 E
Balakovo, *Russia* . **34 D8** 52 4N 47 55 E
Balamau, *India* . **69 F9** 27 10N 80 21 E
Bālan, *Romania* . **29 D10** 46 39N 25 49 E
Balancán, *Mexico* . **119 D6** 17 48N 91 32W
Balanivka, *Ukraine* . **29 B14** 48 24N 29 24 E
Balashov, *Russia* . **34 E6** 51 30N 43 10 E
Balasinor, *India* . **68 H5** 22 57N 73 23 E
Balasore = Baleshwar, *India* . **67 J15** 21 35N 87 3 E
Balassagyarmat, *Hungary* . **28 B4** 48 4N 19 15 E
Balât, *Egypt* . **80 B2** 25 36N 29 19 E
Balaton, *Hungary* . **28 D2** 46 50N 17 40 E
Balaton-Felvidéki △, *Hungary* . **28 D2** 46 52N 17 30 E
Balatonboglár, *Hungary* . **28 D2** 46 46N 17 40 E
Balatonfüred, *Hungary* . **28 D2** 46 58N 17 54 E
Balatonszentgyörgy, *Hungary* . **28 D2** 46 41N 17 19 E
Balayan, *Phil.* . **61 E4** 13 57N 120 44 E
Balazote, *Spain* . **39 G2** 38 54N 2 9W
Balbieriškis, *Lithuania* . **9 J20** 54 30N 23 53 E
Balbigny, *France* . **21 C8** 45 49N 4 11 E
Balbina, Reprêsa de, *Brazil* . **124 D7** 2 0 S 59 30W
Balboa, *Panama* . **120 E4** 8 57N 79 34W
Balbriggan, *Ireland* . **12 C5** 53 37N 6 11W
Balcarce, *Argentina* . **126 D4** 38 0 S 58 10W
Balcarres, *Canada* . **103 C8** 50 50N 103 35W
Bălcești, *Romania* . **29 F8** 44 37N 23 57 E
Balchik, *Bulgaria* . **45 C12** 43 28N 28 11 E
Balclutha, *N.Z.* . **91 M2** 46 15 S 169 45 E
Balcones Escarpment, *U.S.A.* . **113 L5** 29 30N 99 15W
Balçova, *Turkey* . **47 C9** 38 22N 27 4 E
Bald Hd., *Australia* . **93 G2** 35 6 S 118 1 E
Bald I., *Australia* . **93 F2** 34 57 S 118 27 E
Bald Knob, *U.S.A.* . **113 H9** 35 19N 91 34W
Baldock L., *Canada* . **103 B9** 56 33N 97 57W
Baldwin, Mich., *U.S.A.* . **114 D3** 43 54N 85 51W
Baldwin, Pa., *U.S.A.* . **116 F5** 40 23N 79 58W
Baldwinsville, *U.S.A.* . **117 C8** 43 10N 76 20W
Baldy Mt., *U.S.A.* . **108 B9** 48 9N 109 39W
Baldy Peak, *U.S.A.* . **109 K9** 33 54N 109 34W
Bale, *Croatia* . **41 C10** 45 4N 13 46 E

Bale, *Ethiopia* . **81 F5** 6 57N 40 8 E
Bale, *Ethiopia* . **81 F5** 6 20N 41 30 E
Bale Mts. △, *Ethiopia* . **81 F4** 6 30N 39 52 E
Baleares, Is., *Spain* . **48 B10** 39 30N 3 0 E
Balearic Is. = Baleares, Is., *Spain* . **48 B10** 39 30N 3 0 E
Baleine = Whale →, *Canada* . **105 A6** 58 15N 67 40W
Baleine, Petite R. de la →, *Canada* . **104 A4** 56 0N 76 45W
Băleni, *Romania* . **29 E12** 45 48N 27 51 E
Baler, *Phil.* . **61 D4** 15 46N 121 34 E
Baler Bay, *Phil.* . **61 D4** 15 50N 121 35 E
Baleshare, *U.K.* . **13 D1** 57 31N 7 22W
Baleshwar, *India* . **67 J15** 21 35N 87 3 E
Balezino, *Russia* . **34 B11** 58 2N 53 6 E
Balfate, *Honduras* . **120 C2** 15 48N 86 25W
Bali, *Cameroon* . **83 D7** 5 54N 10 0 E
Balí, *Greece* . **49 D6** 35 25N 24 47 E
Bali, *India* . **68 G5** 25 11N 73 17 E
Bali □, *Indonesia* . **63 J18** 8 20 S 115 0 E
Bali, Selat, *Indonesia* . **63 J17** 8 18 S 114 25 E
Bali Sea, *Indonesia* . **63 J18** 8 0 S 115 0 E
Balia, S. Leone . **82 D2** 9 22N 11 1W
Baliapal, *India* . **69 J12** 21 40N 87 17 E
Baligród, *Poland* . **31 J9** 49 20N 22 17 E
Balik Pulau, *Malaysia* . **65 c** 5 21N 100 14 E
Balikeşir, *Turkey* . **47 B9** 39 39N 27 53 E
Balıkeşir □, *Turkey* . **47 B9** 39 45N 28 0 E
Balıkhçeşme, *Turkey* . **45 F11** 40 18N 27 5 E
Balikpapan, *Indonesia* . **62 E5** 1 10 S 116 55 E
Balimbing, *Phil.* . **63 C5** 5 5N 119 58 E
Baling, *Malaysia* . **65 K3** 5 41N 100 55 E
Balingen, *Germany* . **25 G4** 48 16N 8 51 E
Balintang Channel, *Phil.* . **61 B4** 19 49N 121 40 E
Balipara, *India* . **67 F18** 26 50N 92 45 E
Balkan Mts. = Stara Planina, *Bulgaria* . **44 C7** 43 15N 23 0 E
Balkhash = Balqash, *Kazakhstan* . **52 E8** 46 50N 74 50 E
Balkhash, Ozero = Balqash Köl, *Kazakhstan* . **52 E8** 46 0N 74 50 E
Balla, *Bangla.* . **67 G17** 24 10N 91 35 E
Ballachulish, *U.K.* . **13 E3** 56 41N 5 8W
Balladonia, *Australia* . **93 F3** 32 27 S 123 51 E
Ballarat, *Australia* . **95 F3** 37 33 S 143 50 E
Ballard, L., *Australia* . **93 E3** 29 20 S 120 40 E
Ballater, *U.K.* . **13 D5** 57 3N 3 3W
Ballé, *Mali* . **82 B3** 15 18N 8 33W
Ballena Gris = Ojo de Liebre △, *Mexico* . **118 B2** 27 50N 114 0W
Ballenas, Canal de, *Mexico* . **118 B2** 29 10N 113 45W
Balleny Is., *Antarctica* . **5 C11** 66 30 S 163 0 E
Balleroy, *France* . **18 C6** 49 11N 0 50W
Ballerup, *Denmark* . **11 J6** 55 44N 12 21 E
Balli, *Turkey* . **45 F11** 40 50N 27 3 E
Ballia, *India* . **69 G11** 25 46N 84 12 E
Ballina, *Australia* . **95 D5** 28 50 S 153 31 E
Ballina, *Ireland* . **12 B2** 54 7N 9 9W
Ballinasloe, *Ireland* . **12 C3** 53 20N 8 13W
Ballinger, *U.S.A.* . **113 K5** 31 45N 99 57W
Ballinrobe, *Ireland* . **12 C2** 53 38N 9 13W
Ballinskelligs B., *Ireland* . **12 E1** 51 48N 10 13W
Ballon, *France* . **18 D7** 48 10N 0 14 E
Ballons des Vosges △, *France* . **19 E14** 48 0N 7 0 E
Ballsh, *Albania* . **44 F3** 40 36N 19 44 E
Ballston Spa, *U.S.A.* . **117 D11** 43 0N 73 51W
Ballybunion, *Ireland* . **12 D2** 52 31N 9 40W
Ballycastle, *U.K.* . **12 A5** 55 12N 6 15W
Ballyclare, *U.K.* . **12 B5** 54 46N 6 0W
Ballyhaunis, *Ireland* . **12 C3** 53 46N 8 46W
Ballymena, *U.K.* . **12 B5** 54 52N 6 17W
Ballymoney, *U.K.* . **12 A5** 55 5N 6 31W
Ballymote, *Ireland* . **12 B3** 54 5N 8 31W
Ballynahinch, *U.K.* . **12 B6** 54 24N 5 54W
Ballyquintin Pt., *U.K.* . **12 B6** 54 20N 5 30W
Ballyshannon, *Ireland* . **12 B3** 54 30N 8 11W
Balmaceda, *Chile* . **128 F2** 46 0 S 71 50W
Balmaseda, *Spain* . **38 B1** 43 11N 3 12W
Balmazújváros, *Hungary* . **28 C6** 47 37N 21 21 E
Balmertown, *Canada* . **103 C10** 51 4N 93 41W
Balmoral, *Australia* . **95 F3** 37 15 S 141 48 E
Balmorhea, *U.S.A.* . **113 K3** 30 59N 103 45W
Balochistan = Baluchistan □, *Pakistan* . **66 F4** 27 30N 65 0 E
Balonne →, *Australia* . **95 D4** 28 47 S 147 56 E
Balotra, *India* . **68 G5** 25 50N 72 14 E
Balqash, *Kazakhstan* . **52 E8** 46 50N 74 50 E
Balqash Köl, *Kazakhstan* . **52 E8** 46 0N 74 50 E
Balrampur, *India* . **69 F10** 27 30N 82 20 E
Balranald, *Australia* . **95 E3** 34 38 S 143 33 E
Balş, *Romania* . **29 F9** 44 22N 24 5 E
Balsas, *Mexico* . **119 D5** 18 0N 99 40W
Balsas →, *Brazil* . **125 E9** 7 15 S 44 35W
Balsas →, *Mexico* . **118 D4** 17 55N 102 10W
Bålsta, *Sweden* . **10 E11** 59 35N 17 30 E
Balston Spa, *U.S.A.* . **117 D11** 43 0N 73 51W
Balta, *Romania* . **28 F7** 44 54N 22 38 E
Balta, *Ukraine* . **29 B14** 48 2N 29 45 E
Baltanás, *Spain* . **36 D6** 41 56N 4 15W
Bălți, *Moldova* . **29 C12** 47 48N 27 58 E
Baltic Sea, *Europe* . **9 H18** 57 0N 19 0 E
Baltîm, *Egypt* . **80 H7** 31 35N 31 10 E
Baltimore, *Ireland* . **12 E2** 51 29N 9 22W
Baltimore, Md., *U.S.A.* . **114 F7** 39 17N 76 37W
Baltimore, Ohio, *U.S.A.* . **116 G2** 39 51N 82 36W
Baltit, *Pakistan* . **69 A6** 36 15N 74 40 E
Baltiysk, *Russia* . **9 J18** 54 41N 19 58 E
Baltrum, *Germany* . **24 B3** 53 43N 7 24 E
Baluchistan □, *Pakistan* . **66 F4** 27 30N 65 0 E
Balurghat, *India* . **69 G13** 25 15N 88 44 E
Balvi, *Latvia* . **9 H22** 57 8N 27 15 E
Balya, *Turkey* . **47 B9** 39 44N 27 35 E
Bam, *Iran* . **71 D8** 29 7N 58 14 E
Bama, *China* . **58 E6** 24 8N 107 12 E
Bama, *Nigeria* . **83 C7** 11 33N 13 41 E
Bamaga, *Australia* . **94 A3** 10 50 S 142 25 E
Bamaji L., *Canada* . **104 B1** 51 9N 91 25W
Bamako, *Mali* . **82 C3** 12 34N 7 55W
Bamba, *Mali* . **83 B4** 17 5N 1 24W
Bambara Maoundé, *Mali* . **82 B4** 13 26N 4 3W
Bambari, *C.A.R.* . **84 C4** 5 40N 20 35 E
Bambaroo, *Australia* . **94 B4** 18 50 S 146 10 E
Bambaya, *Guinea* . **82 D2** 8 8N 11 16W
Bamberg, *Germany* . **25 F6** 49 54N 10 54 E
Bamberg, *U.S.A.* . **115 J5** 33 18N 81 2W
Bambesi, *Ethiopia* . **81 F3** 9 45N 34 40 E
Bambey, *Senegal* . **82 C1** 14 42N 16 28W

Bambili, *Dem. Rep. of the Congo* . **86 B2** 3 40N 26 0 E
Bamboi, *Ghana* . **82 D4** 8 13N 2 1W
Bamburgh, *U.K.* . **14 B6** 55 37N 1 43W
Bamenda, *Cameroon* . **83 D7** 5 57N 10 11 E
Bamfield, *Canada* . **102 D3** 48 45N 125 10W
Bāmīān □, *Afghan.* . **66 B5** 35 0N 67 0 E
Bamiancheng, *China* . **57 C13** 43 15N 124 2 E
Bamkin, *Cameroon* . **83 D7** 6 3N 11 27 E
Bampūr, *Iran* . **71 E9** 27 15N 60 21 E
Ban Ao Tu Khun, *Thailand* . **65 a** 8 9N 98 20 E
Ban Ban, *Laos* . **64 C4** 19 31N 103 30 E
Ban Bang Hin, *Thailand* . **65 H2** 9 32N 98 35 E
Ban Bang Khu, *Thailand* . **65 a** 7 57N 98 23 E
Ban Bang Rong, *Thailand* . **65 a** 8 3N 98 25 E
Ban Bo Phut, *Thailand* . **65 b** 9 33N 100 2 E
Ban Chaweng, *Thailand* . **65 b** 9 32N 100 3 E
Ban Chiang Klang, *Thailand* . **64 C3** 19 25N 100 55 E
Ban Chik, *Laos* . **64 D4** 17 15N 102 22 E
Ban Choho, *Thailand* . **64 E4** 15 2N 102 9 E
Ban Dan Lan Hoi, *Thailand* . **64 D2** 17 0N 99 35 E
Ban Don = Surat Thani, *Thailand* . **65 H2** 9 6N 99 20 E
Ban Don, *Vietnam* . **64 F6** 12 53N 107 48 E
Ban Don, Ao →, *Thailand* . **65 H2** 9 20N 99 25 E
Ban Dong, *Thailand* . **64 C3** 19 30N 100 59 E
Ban Hong, *Thailand* . **64 C2** 18 18N 98 50 E
Ban Hua Thanon, *Thailand* . **65 b** 9 26N 100 1 E
Ban Kaeng, *Thailand* . **64 D3** 17 29N 100 7 E
Ban Kantang, *Thailand* . **65 J2** 7 25N 99 31 E
Ban Karon, *Thailand* . **65 a** 7 51N 98 18 E
Ban Kata, *Thailand* . **65 a** 7 50N 98 18 E
Ban Keun, *Laos* . **64 C4** 18 22N 102 35 E
Ban Khai, *Thailand* . **64 F3** 12 46N 101 18 E
Ban Kheun, *Laos* . **64 B3** 20 13N 101 7 E
Ban Khlong Khian, *Thailand* . **65 a** 8 10N 98 26 E
Ban Khlong Kua, *Thailand* . **65 J3** 6 57N 100 8 E
Ban Khuan, *Thailand* . **65 a** 8 20N 98 25 E
Ban Khuan Mao, *Thailand* . **65 J2** 7 50N 99 37 E
Ban Ko Yai Chim, *Thailand* . **65 G2** 11 17N 99 26 E
Ban Kok, *Thailand* . **64 D4** 16 40N 103 40 E
Ban Laem, *Thailand* . **64 F2** 13 13N 99 59 E
Ban Lamai, *Thailand* . **65 b** 9 28N 100 3 E
Ban Lao Ngam, *Laos* . **64 E6** 15 28N 106 10 E
Ban Le Kathe, *Thailand* . **64 E2** 15 49N 98 53 E
Ban Lo Po Noi, *Thailand* . **65 a** 8 1N 98 34 E
Ban Mae Chedi, *Thailand* . **64 C2** 19 11N 99 31 E
Ban Mae Laeng, *Thailand* . **64 B2** 20 1N 99 17 E
Ban Mae Nam, *Thailand* . **65 b** 9 34N 100 0 E
Ban Mae Sariang, *Thailand* . **64 C1** 18 10N 97 56 E
Ban Mê Thuột = Buon Ma Thuot, *Vietnam* . **64 F7** 12 40N 108 3 E
Ban Mi, *Thailand* . **64 E3** 15 3N 100 32 E
Ban Muong Mo, *Laos* . **64 C4** 19 4N 103 58 E
Ban Na Bo, *Thailand* . **65 b** 9 19N 99 41 E
Ban Na Mo, *Laos* . **64 D5** 17 7N 105 40 E
Ban Na Tong, *Laos* . **64 B3** 20 56N 101 47 E
Ban Nam Bac, *Laos* . **64 B4** 20 38N 102 20 E
Ban Nam Ma, *Laos* . **64 A3** 22 2N 101 37 E
Ban Ngang, *Laos* . **64 E6** 15 59N 106 11 E
Ban Nong Bok, *Laos* . **64 D5** 17 5N 104 48 E
Ban Nong Boua, *Laos* . **64 E6** 15 40N 106 33 E
Ban Nong Pling, *Thailand* . **64 E3** 15 40N 100 10 E
Ban Pak Chan, *Thailand* . **65 G2** 10 32N 98 51 E
Ban Patong, *Thailand* . **65 a** 7 54N 98 18 E
Ban Phai, *Thailand* . **64 D4** 16 4N 102 44 E
Ban Phak Chit, *Thailand* . **65 a** 8 0N 98 24 E
Ban Pong, *Thailand* . **64 F2** 13 50N 99 55 E
Ban Rawai, *Thailand* . **65 a** 7 47N 98 20 E
Ban Ron Phibun, *Thailand* . **65 H2** 8 9N 99 51 E
Ban Sakhu, *Thailand* . **65 a** 8 4N 98 18 E
Ban Sanam Chai, *Thailand* . **65 J3** 7 33N 100 25 E
Ban Sangkha, *Thailand* . **64 E4** 14 37N 103 52 E
Ban Tak, *Thailand* . **64 D2** 17 2N 99 4 E
Ban Tako, *Thailand* . **64 E4** 14 5N 102 40 E
Ban Tha Dua, *Thailand* . **64 D2** 17 59N 98 39 E
Ban Tha Li, *Thailand* . **64 D3** 17 37N 101 25 E
Ban Tha Nun, *Thailand* . **65 a** 8 12N 98 18 E
Ban Tha Rua, *Thailand* . **65 a** 7 59N 98 22 E
Ban Tha Yu, *Thailand* . **65 a** 8 17N 98 22 E
Ban Thahine, *Laos* . **64 E5** 14 12N 105 33 E
Ban Thong Krut, *Thailand* . **65 b** 9 25N 99 57 E
Ban Xien Kok, *Laos* . **64 B3** 20 54N 100 39 E
Ban Yen Nhan, *Vietnam* . **64 B6** 20 57N 106 2 E
Banaba, *Kiribati* . **96 H8** 0 45 S 169 50 E
Banalia, *Dem. Rep. of the Congo* . **86 B2** 1 32N 25 5 E
Banam, *Cambodia* . **65 G5** 11 20N 105 17 E
Banamba, *Mali* . **82 C3** 13 29N 7 22W
Banana, I. do, *Brazil* . **82 D2** 7 31 S 15 0W
Bananal, I. do, *Brazil* . **125 F8** 11 30 S 50 30W
Banaras = Varanasi, *India* . **69 G10** 25 22N 83 0 E
Banas →, *Gujarat, India* . **68 H4** 23 45N 71 25 E
Banas →, Mad. P., *India* . **69 G9** 24 15N 81 30 E
Bânâs, Ras, *Egypt* . **80 C4** 23 57N 35 59 E
Banaz, *Turkey* . **47 C11** 38 46N 29 46 E
Banaz →, *Turkey* . **47 C11** 38 12N 29 41 E
Banbridge, *U.K.* . **12 B5** 54 22N 6 16W
Banbury, *U.K.* . **15 E6** 52 4N 1 20W
Banchory, *U.K.* . **13 D6** 57 3N 2 49W
Banco, *Ethiopia* . **81 F4** 6 12N 38 13 E
Bancroft, *Canada* . **116 A7** 45 3N 77 51W
Band Boni, *Iran* . **71 E8** 25 30N 59 33 E
Band Qīr, *Iran* . **71 D6** 31 39N 48 53 E
Banda, Ut. P., *India* . **69 G8** 25 30N 80 26 E
Banda, Kepulauan, *Indonesia* . **63 E7** 4 37 S 129 50 E
Banda Aceh, *Indonesia* . **62 C1** 5 35N 95 20 E
Banda Banda, Mt., *Australia* . **95 E5** 31 10 S 152 28 E
Banda Elat, *Indonesia* . **63 F8** 5 40 S 133 5 E
Banda Is. = Banda, Kepulauan, *Indonesia* . **63 E7** 4 37 S 129 50 E
Banda Sea, *Indonesia* . **63 F7** 6 0 S 130 0 E

Bandai-Asahi △, *Japan* **54 F10** 37 38N 140 5 E
Bandai-San, *Japan* **54 F10** 37 36N 140 4 E
Bandama →, *Ivory C.* **82 D3** 6 32N 4 30W
Bandama Blanc →, *Ivory C.* **82 D3** 6 55N 5 30W
Bandama Rouge →, *Ivory C.* **82 D4** 6 55N 5 30W
Bandān, *Iran* **71 D9** 31 23N 60 44 E
Bandanaira, *Indonesia* **63 E7** 4 32 S 129 54 E
Bandanwara, *India* **68 F6** 26 9N 74 38 E
Bandar = Machilipatnam, *India* **67 L12** 16 12N 81 8 E
Bandar-e Abbās, *Iran* **71 E8** 27 15N 56 15 E
Bandar-e Anzali, *Iran* **71 B6** 37 30N 49 30 E
Bandar-e Bushehr = Büshehr, *Iran* **71 D6** 28 55N 50 55 E
Bandar-e Chārak, *Iran* **71 E7** 26 45N 54 20 E
Bandar-e Deylam, *Iran* **71 D6** 30 5N 50 10 E
Bandar-e Emām Khomeynī, *Iran* **71 D6** 30 30N 49 5 E
Bandar-e Lengeh, *Iran* **71 E7** 26 35N 54 58 E
Bandar-e Maqām, *Iran* **71 E7** 26 56N 53 29 E
Bandar-e Ma'shur, *Iran* **71 D6** 30 35N 49 10 E
Bandar-e Rīg, *Iran* **71 D6** 29 29N 50 38 E
Bandar-e Torkeman, *Iran* **71 B7** 37 0N 54 10 E
Bandar Lampung = Tanjungkarang Telukbetung, *Indonesia* **62 F3** 5 20 S 105 10 E
Bandar Maharani = Muar, *Malaysia* **65 L4** 2 3N 102 34 E
Bandar Penggaram = Batu Pahat, *Malaysia* **65 M4** 1 50N 102 56 E
Bandar Seri Begawan, *Brunei* **62 C4** 4 52N 115 0 E
Bandar Sri Aman, *Malaysia* **62 D4** 1 15N 111 32 E
Bandawe, *Malawi* **87 E3** 11 58 S 34 5 E
Bande, *Spain* **36 C3** 42 3N 7 58W
Bandeira, Pico da, *Brazil* **127 A7** 20 26 S 41 47W
Bandera, *Argentina* **126 B3** 28 55 S 62 20W
Banderas, B. de, *Mexico* **118 C3** 20 40N 105 30W
Bandhogarh, *India* **69 H9** 23 40N 81 2 E
Bandi →, *India* **68 F6** 26 12N 75 47 E
Bandiagara, *Mali* **82 C4** 14 12N 3 29W
Bandikui, *India* **68 F7** 27 3N 76 34 E
Bandırma, *Turkey* **45 F11** 40 20N 28 0 E
Bandjarmasin = Banjarmasin, *Indonesia* **62 E4** 3 20 S 114 35 E
Bandol, *France* **21 E9** 43 8N 5 46 E
Bandon, *Ireland* **12 E3** 51 44N 8 44W
Bandon →, *Ireland* **12 E3** 51 43N 8 37W
Bandula, *Mozam.* **87 F3** 19 0 S 33 7 E
Bandundu, *Dem. Rep. of the Congo* **84 E3** 3 15 S 17 22 E
Bandung, *Indonesia* **63 G12** 6 54 S 107 36 E
Bané, *Burkina Faso* **83 C4** 11 42N 0 15W
Bǎneasa, *Romania* **29 E12** 45 56N 27 55 E
Bāneh, *Iran* **70 C5** 35 59N 45 53 E
Bañeres, *Spain* **39 G4** 38 44N 0 38W
Banes, *Cuba* **121 B4** 21 0N 75 42W
Banff, *Canada* **102 C5** 51 10N 115 34W
Banff, *U.K.* **13 D6** 57 40N 2 33W
Banff △, *Canada* **102 C5** 51 30N 116 15W
Banfora, *Burkina Faso* **82 C4** 10 40N 4 40W
Bang Fai →, *Laos* **64 D5** 16 57N 104 45 E
Bang Hieng →, *Laos* **64 D5** 16 10N 105 10 E
Bang Krathum, *Thailand* **64 D3** 16 34N 100 18 E
Bang Lamung, *Thailand* **64 F3** 13 3N 100 56 E
Bang Mun Nak, *Thailand* **64 D3** 16 2N 100 23 E
Bang Pa In, *Thailand* **64 E3** 14 14N 100 35 E
Bang Rakam, *Thailand* **64 D3** 16 45N 100 7 E
Bang Saphan, *Thailand* **65 G2** 11 14N 99 28 E
Bang Thao, *Thailand* **65 a** 7 59N 98 18 E
Banganduni I., *India* **69 J13** 21 34N 88 52 E
Bangala Dam, *Zimbabwe* **87 G3** 21 7 S 31 25 E
Bangalore, *India* **66 N10** 12 59N 77 40 E
Bangana →, *India* **68 F6** 27 6N 77 25 E
Bangangté, *Cameroon* **83 D7** 5 8N 10 32 E
Bangaon, *India* **69 H13** 23 0N 88 47 E
Bangassou, *C.A.R.* **84 D4** 4 55N 23 7 E
Banggai, *Indonesia* **63 E6** 1 34 S 123 30 E
Banggai, Kepulauan, *Indonesia* **63 E6** 1 40 S 123 30 E
Banggai Arch. = Banggai, Kepulauan, *Indonesia* **63 E6** 1 40 S 123 30 E
Banggi, *Malaysia* **62 C5** 7 17N 117 12 E
Banghāzī, *Libya* **79 B10** 32 11N 20 3 E
Bangjang, *Sudan* **81 E3** 11 23N 32 41 E
Bangka, *Sulawesi, Indonesia* **63 D7** 1 50N 125 5 E
Bangka, *Sumatera, Indonesia* **62 E3** 2 0 S 105 50 E
Bangka, Selat, *Indonesia* **62 E3** 2 30 S 105 50 E
Bangkalan, *Indonesia* **63 G15** 7 2 S 112 46 E
Bangkinang, *Indonesia* **62 D2** 0 18N 101 5 E
Bangko, *Indonesia* **62 E2** 2 5 S 102 9 E
Bangkok, *Thailand* **64 F3** 13 45N 100 35 E
Bangladesh ■, *Asia* **67 H17** 24 0N 90 0 E
Bangli, *Indonesia* **63 J18** 8 27 S 115 21 E
Bangolo, *Ivory C.* **82 D3** 7 1N 7 29W
Bangong Co, *India* **69 B8** 35 50N 79 20 E
Bangor, *Down, U.K.* **12 B6** 54 40N 5 40W
Bangor, *Gwynedd, U.K.* **14 D3** 53 14N 4 8W
Bangor, *Maine, U.S.A.* **101 D13** 44 48N 68 46W
Bangor, *Pa., U.S.A.* **117 F9** 40 52N 75 13W
Bangued, *Phil.* **61 C4** 17 40N 120 37 E
Bangui, *C.A.R.* **84 D3** 4 23N 18 35 E
Bangui, *Phil.* **61 B4** 18 32N 120 46 E
Banguru, *Dem. Rep. of the Congo* **86 B2** 0 30N 27 10 E
Bangweulu, L., *Zambia* **87 E3** 11 0 S 30 0 E
Bangweulu Swamp, *Zambia* **87 E3** 11 20 S 30 15 E
Banhine △, *Mozam.* **89 C5** 22 49 S 32 55 E
Bani, *Dom. Rep.* **121 C5** 18 16N 70 22W
Bani →, *Mali* **82 C4** 14 30N 4 12W
Bani Bangou, *Niger* **83 B5** 15 3N 2 42 E
Banī Sa'd, *Iraq* **70 C5** 33 34N 44 32 E
Bania, *Ivory C.* **82 D4** 9 4N 3 6W
Banihal Pass, *India* **69 C6** 33 30N 75 12 E
Banikoara, *Benin* **83 C5** 11 18N 2 26 E
Bāniyās, *Syria* **70 C3** 35 10N 36 0 E
Banja Luka, *Bos.-H.* **28 F7** 44 49N 17 11 E
Banjar, *India* **68 D7** 31 38N 77 21 E
Banjar →, *India* **69 H9** 22 36N 80 22 E
Banjarmasin, *Indonesia* **62 E4** 3 20 S 114 35 E
Banjul, *Gambia* **82 C1** 13 28N 16 40W
Banka, *India* **69 G12** 24 53N 86 55 E
Bankas, *Mali* **82 C4** 14 4N 3 31W
Bankeryd, *Sweden* **11 G8** 57 53N 14 6 E
Banket, *Zimbabwe* **87 F3** 17 27 S 30 19 E

Bankilaré, *Niger* **83 C5** 14 35N 0 44 E
Bankipore, *India* **67 G14** 25 35N 85 10 E
Banks I., *B.C., Canada* **102 C3** 53 20N 130 0 E
Banks I., N.W.T., Canada **100 A7** 73 15N 121 30W
Banks Pen., N.Z. **91 K4** 43 45 S 173 15 E
Banks Str., Australia **95 G4** 40 40 S 148 10 E
Bankura, *India* **69 H12** 23 11N 87 18 E
Banmankhi, *India* **69 G12** 25 53N 87 11 E
Bann →, Arm., U.K. **12 B5** 54 30N 6 31W
Bann →, L'derry., U.K. **12 A5** 55 8N 6 41W
Bannalec, *France* **18 E3** 47 57N 3 42W
Bannang Sata, *Thailand* **65 J3** 6 16N 101 16 E
Banning, U.S.A. **111 M10** 33 56N 116 53W
Banno, *Ethiopia* **81 G4** 4 51N 37 24 E
Bannockburn, *Canada* **116 B7** 44 39N 77 33W
Bannockburn, U.K. **13 E5** 56 5N 3 55W
Bannockburn, *Zimbabwe* **87 G2** 20 17 S 29 48 E
Bannu, *Pakistan* **66 C7** 33 0N 70 18 E
Bano, *India* **69 H11** 22 40N 84 55 E
Bañolas = Banyoles, *Spain* **38 C7** 42 16N 2 44 E
Banon, *France* **21 D9** 44 2N 5 38 E
Baños de la Encina, *Spain* **37 G7** 38 10N 3 46W
Baños de Molgas, *Spain* **36 C3** 42 15N 7 40W
Bánovce nad Bebravou, *Slovak Rep.* **27 C11** 48 44N 18 16 E
Banovići, *Bos.-H.* **28 F3** 44 25N 18 32 E
Bansgaon, *India* **69 F10** 26 33N 83 21 E
Banská Bystrica, *Slovak Rep.* **27 C12** 48 46N 19 14 E
Banská Štiavnica, *Slovak Rep.* **27 C11** 48 25N 18 55 E
Bansko, *Bulgaria* **44 E7** 41 52N 23 28 E
Banskobystrický □, *Slovak Rep.* **27 C12** 48 20N 19 0 E
Banswara, *India* **68 H6** 23 32N 74 24 E
Bantaeng, *Indonesia* **63 F5** 5 32 S 119 56 E
Bantaji, *Nigeria* **83 D7** 8 6N 10 15 E
Bantayan, *Phil.* **61 F5** 11 10N 123 43 E
Bantry, *Ireland* **12 E2** 51 41N 9 27W
Bantry B., *Ireland* **12 E2** 51 37N 9 44W
Bantul, *Indonesia* **63 G14** 7 55 S 110 19 E
Bantva, *India* **68 J4** 21 29N 70 12 E
Banya, *Bulgaria* **45 D8** 42 33N 24 50 E
Banyak, Kepulauan, *Indonesia* **62 D1** 2 10N 97 10 E
Banyalbufar, *Spain* **48 B9** 39 42N 2 31 E
Banyo, *Cameroon* **83 D7** 6 52N 11 45 E
Banyoles, *Spain* **38 C7** 42 16N 2 44 E
Banyuls-sur-Mer, *France* **20 F7** 42 28N 3 8 E
Banyumas, *Indonesia* **63 G13** 7 32 S 109 18 E
Banyuwangi, *Indonesia* **63 J17** 8 13 S 114 21 E
Banzare Coast, *Antarctica* **5 C9** 68 0 S 125 0 E
Bao Ha, *Vietnam* **58 F5** 22 11N 104 21 E
Bao Lac, *Vietnam* **64 A5** 22 57N 105 40 E
Bao Loc, *Vietnam* **65 G6** 11 32N 107 48 E
Bao'an = Shenzhen, *China* **59 F10** 22 32N 114 5 E
Baocheng, *China* **56 H4** 33 12N 106 56 E
Baode, *China* **56 E6** 39 1N 111 5 E
Baodi, *China* **57 E9** 39 38N 117 20 E
Baoding, *China* **56 E8** 38 50N 115 28 E
Baoji, *China* **56 G4** 34 20N 107 5 E
Baojing, *China* **58 C7** 28 45N 109 41 E
Baokang, *China* **59 B8** 31 54N 111 12 E
Baoshan, *Shanghai, China* **59 B13** 31 27N 121 26 E
Baoshan, *Yunnan, China* **58 E2** 25 10N 99 5 E
Baotou, *China* **56 D6** 40 32N 110 2 E
Baoxing, *China* **58 B4** 30 24N 102 50 E
Baoying, *China* **57 H10** 33 17N 119 20 E
Bap, *India* **68 F5** 27 23N 72 18 E
Bapatla, *India* **67 M12** 15 55N 80 30 E
Bapaume, *France* **19 B9** 50 7N 2 50 E
Ba'qūbah, *Iraq* **70 C5** 33 45N 44 50 E
Baquedano, *Chile* **126 A2** 23 20 S 69 52W
Bar, *Serbia & M.* **44 D3** 42 8N 19 6 E
Bar, *Ukraine* **33 H4** 49 4N 27 40 E
Bar Bigha, *India* **69 G11** 25 21N 85 47 E
Bar Harbor, U.S.A. **115 C11** 44 23N 68 13W
Bar-le-Duc, *France* **19 D12** 48 47N 5 10 E
Bar-sur-Aube, *France* **19 D11** 48 14N 4 40 E
Bar-sur-Seine, *France* **19 D11** 48 7N 4 20 E
Bara, *India* **69 G9** 25 16N 81 43 E
Bâra, *Romania* **29 C12** 47 2N 27 7 E
Bara Banki, *India* **69 F9** 26 55N 81 12 E
Barabai, *Indonesia* **62 E5** 2 32 S 115 34 E
Baraboo, U.S.A. **112 D10** 43 28N 89 45W
Baracoa, *Cuba* **121 B5** 20 20N 74 30W
Baradā →, *Syria* **74 B5** 33 33N 36 34 E
Baradero, *Argentina* **126 C4** 33 52 S 59 29W
Bārāganul, *Romania* **29 F12** 44 49N 27 31 E
Barah →, *India* **68 F6** 27 42N 77 5 E
Barahona, *Dom. Rep.* **121 C5** 18 13N 71 7W
Barahona, *Spain* **38 D2** 41 17N 2 39W
Barail Range, *India* **67 G18** 25 15N 93 20 E
Barajas, Madrid ✈ (MAD), *Spain* **36 E7** 40 26N 3 34W
Barakaldo, *Spain* **38 B2** 43 18N 2 59W
Barakar →, *India* **69 G12** 24 7N 86 14 E
Barakhola, *India* **67 G18** 25 0N 92 45 E
Barakot, *India* **69 J11** 21 33N 84 59 E
Barakpur, *India* **69 H13** 22 44N 88 30 E
Baralaba, *Australia* **94 C4** 24 13 S 149 50 E
Baralla, *Spain* **36 C3** 42 53N 7 15W
Baralzon L., *Canada* **103 B9** 60 0N 98 3W
Barameiya, *Sudan* **80 D4** 18 32N 36 38 E
Baramula, *India* **69 B6** 34 15N 74 20 E
Baran, *India* **68 G7** 25 9N 76 40 E
Baran →, *Pakistan* **68 G3** 25 13N 68 17 E
Barañain, *Spain* **38 C3** 42 48N 1 40W
Baranavichy, *Belarus* **33 F4** 53 10N 26 0 E
Barani, *Burkina Faso* **82 C4** 13 9N 3 51W
Baranof, U.S.A. **102 B2** 57 5N 134 50W
Baranof I., U.S.A. **100 C6** 57 0N 135 0W
Baranów Sandomierski, *Poland* **31 H8** 50 29N 21 30 E
Baranya □, *Hungary* **28 E3** 46 0N 18 15 E
Baraolt, *Romania* **29 D10** 46 5N 25 34 E
Barapasi, *Indonesia* **63 E9** 2 15 S 137 5 E
Barasat, *India* **69 H13** 22 46N 88 31 E
Barat Daya, Kepulauan, *Indonesia* **63 F7** 7 30 S 128 0 E
Barataria B., U.S.A. **113 L10** 29 20N 89 55W
Barauda, *India* **68 H6** 23 33N 75 15 E
Baraut, *India* **68 E7** 29 13N 77 7 E
Barbacena, *Brazil* **127 A7** 21 15 S 43 56W
Barbados ■, W. Indies **121 g** 13 10N 59 30W

Barban, *Croatia* **41 C11** 45 5N 14 2 E
Barbària, C. de, *Spain* **48 C7** 38 39N 1 24 E
Barbaros, *Turkey* **45 F11** 40 54N 27 27 E
Barbastro, *Spain* **38 C5** 42 2N 0 5 E
Barbate de Franco, *Spain* **37 J5** 36 13N 5 56W
Barberino di Mugello, *Italy* **41 E8** 44 0N 11 15 E
Barberton, S. Africa **89 D5** 25 42 S 31 2 E
Barberton, U.S.A. **116 E3** 41 0N 81 39W
Barbezieux-St-Hilaire, *France* **20 C3** 45 28N 0 9W
Barbonneau, St. Lucia **121 f** 13 59N 60 58W
Barbosa, *Colombia* **124 B4** 5 57N 73 37W
Barbourville, U.S.A. **115 G4** 36 52N 83 53W
Barbuda, W. Indies **121 C7** 17 30N 61 40W
Bârca, *Romania* **29 G8** 43 59N 23 36 E
Barcaldine, *Australia* **94 C4** 23 43 S 145 6 E
Barcarrota, *Spain* **37 G4** 38 31N 6 51W
Barcellona Pozzo di Gotto, *Italy* **43 D8** 38 9N 15 13 E
Barcelona, *Spain* **38 D7** 41 21N 2 10 E
Barcelona, *Venezuela* **124 A6** 10 10N 64 40W
Barcelona □, *Spain* **38 D7** 41 30N 2 0 E
Barceloneta, *Puerto Rico* **121 d** 18 27N 66 32W
Barcelonnette, *France* **21 D10** 44 23N 6 40 E
Barcelos, *Brazil* **124 D6** 1 0 S 63 0W
Barcin, *Poland* **31 F4** 52 52N 17 55 E
Barclayville, *Liberia* **82 E3** 4 48N 8 10W
Barcoo →, *Australia* **94 D3** 25 30 S 142 50 E
Barcs, *Hungary* **28 E2** 45 58N 17 28 E
Barczewo, *Poland* **30 E7** 53 50N 20 42 E
Bārda, *Azerbaijan* **35 K8** 40 25N 47 10 E
Bardaï, *Chad* **79 D9** 21 25N 17 0 E
Bardas Blancas, *Argentina* **126 D2** 35 49 S 69 45W
Bardawîl, Sabkhet el, *Egypt* **74 D2** 31 10N 33 15 E
Barddhaman, *India* **69 H12** 23 14N 87 39 E
Bardejov, *Slovak Rep.* **27 B14** 49 18N 21 15 E
Bardera, *Somali Rep.* **75 G3** 2 20N 42 27 E
Bardi, *Italy* **40 D6** 44 38N 9 44 E
Bardīyah, *Libya* **79 B10** 31 45N 25 5 E
Bardolino, *Italy* **40 C7** 45 33N 10 43 E
Bardonécchia, *Italy* **40 C3** 45 5N 6 42 E
Bardsey I., U.K. **14 E3** 52 45N 4 47W
Bardstown, U.S.A. **114 G3** 37 49N 85 28W
Bareilly, *India* **69 E8** 28 22N 79 27 E
Barela, *India* **69 H9** 23 6N 80 3 E
Barentin, *France* **18 C7** 49 33N 0 58 E
Barenton, *France* **18 D6** 48 38N 0 50W
Barents Sea, *Arctic* **50 B7** 73 0N 39 0 E
Barentu, *Eritrea* **81 D4** 15 2N 37 35 E
Barfleur, *France* **18 C5** 49 40N 1 17W
Barfleur, Pte. de, *France* **18 C5** 49 42N 1 16W
Barga, *Italy* **40 D7** 44 4N 10 29 E
Barge, *Italy* **40 D4** 44 43N 7 20 E
Bargnop, *Sudan* **81 F2** 9 32N 28 25 E
Bargteheide, *Germany* **24 B6** 53 44N 10 14 E
Barguzin, *Russia* **53 D11** 53 37N 109 37 E
Barh, *India* **69 G11** 25 29N 85 46 E
Barhaj, *India* **69 F10** 26 18N 83 44 E
Barharwa, *India* **69 G12** 24 52N 87 47 E
Barhi, *India* **69 G11** 24 15N 85 25 E
Bari, *India* **68 F7** 26 39N 77 39 E
Bari, *Italy* **43 A9** 41 8N 16 51 E
Bari Doab, *Pakistan* **68 D5** 30 20N 73 0 E
Bari Sadri, *India* **68 G6** 24 28N 74 30 E
Bari Sardo, *Italy* **42 C2** 39 50N 9 38 E
Barīdī, Ra's, Si. Arabia **70 E3** 24 17N 37 31 E
Barīm, *Yemen* **76 E8** 12 39N 43 25 E
Barinas, *Venezuela* **124 B4** 8 36N 70 15W
Baring, C., *Canada* **100 B8** 70 0N 117 30W
Baringo, L., *Kenya* **86 B4** 0 47N 36 16 E
Bârîs, *Egypt* **80 C3** 24 42N 30 31 E
Barisal, *Bangla.* **67 H17** 22 45N 90 20 E
Barisal □, *Bangla.* **67 H17** 22 40N 90 20 E
Barisan, Bukit, *Indonesia* **62 E2** 3 30 S 102 15 E
Barito →, *Indonesia* **62 E4** 4 0 S 114 50 E
Baritú △, *Argentina* **126 A3** 22 43 S 64 40W
Barjac, *France* **21 D8** 44 20N 4 22 E
Barjols, *France* **21 E10** 43 34N 6 2 E
Bark L., *Canada* **116 A7** 45 27N 77 51W
Barka = Baraka →, *Sudan* **80 D4** 18 13N 37 35 E
Barkakana, *India* **69 H11** 23 37N 85 29 E
Barkam, *China* **58 B4** 31 51N 102 28 E
Barker, U.S.A. **116 C6** 43 20N 78 33W
Barkley, L., U.S.A. **115 G2** 37 1N 88 14W
Barkley Sound, *Canada* **102 D3** 48 50N 125 10W
Barkly East, S. Africa **88 E4** 30 58 S 27 33 E
Barkly Roadhouse, *Australia* **94 B2** 19 52 S 135 50 E
Barkly Tableland, *Australia* **94 B2** 17 50 S 136 40 E
Barkly West, S. Africa **88 D3** 28 5 S 24 31 E
Barkol, Wadi →, *Sudan* **80 D3** 17 40N 32 0 E
Barla Dağı, *Turkey* **47 C12** 38 5N 30 40 E
Bârlad, *Romania* **29 D12** 46 15N 27 38 E
Bârlad →, *Romania* **29 E12** 45 38N 27 32 E
Barlee, L., *Australia* **93 E2** 29 15 S 119 30 E
Barlee, Mt., *Australia* **93 D4** 24 38 S 128 13 E
Barletta, *Italy* **43 A9** 41 19N 16 17 E
Barlinek, *Poland* **31 F2** 53 0N 15 15 E
Barlovento, *Canary Is.* **48 F2** 28 48N 17 48W
Barlow L., *Canada* **103 A8** 62 0N 103 0W
Barmedman, *Australia* **95 E4** 34 9 S 147 21 E
Barmer, *India* **68 G4** 25 45N 71 20 E
Barmera, *Australia* **95 E3** 34 15 S 140 28 E
Barmouth, U.K. **14 E3** 52 44N 4 4W
Barmstedt, *Germany* **24 B5** 53 47N 9 46 E
Barna →, *India* **69 G10** 25 21N 83 3 E
Barnagar, *India* **68 H6** 23 7N 75 19 E
Barnard Castle, U.K. **14 C6** 54 33N 1 55W
Barnaul, *Russia* **52 D9** 53 20N 83 40 E
Barnesville, U.S.A. **115 J3** 33 3N 84 9W
Barnet □, U.K. **15 F7** 51 38N 0 9W
Barneveld, Neths. **17 B5** 52 7N 5 36 E
Barneville-Cartevert, *France* **18 C5** 49 23N 1 46W
Barnhart, U.S.A. **113 K4** 31 8N 101 10W
Barnsley, U.K. **14 D6** 53 34N 1 27W
Barnstable □ = Bideford Bay, U.K. **15 F3** 51 5N 4 20W
Barnsville, U.S.A. **112 B6** 46 43N 96 28W
Barnwell, U.S.A. **115 J5** 33 15N 81 23W

Baro, *Nigeria* **83 D6** 8 35N 6 18 E
Baro →, *Ethiopia* **81 F3** 8 26N 33 13 E
Baroda = Vadodara, *India* **68 H5** 22 20N 73 10 E
Baroda, *India* **68 G7** 25 29N 76 35 E
Baroe, S. Africa **88 E3** 33 13 S 24 33 E
Barong, *China* **58 B2** 31 3N 99 20 E
Barotseland, *Zambia* **85 H4** 15 0 S 24 0 E
Barpeta, *India* **67 F17** 26 20N 91 10 E
Barqah, *Libya* **79 C10** 27 0N 22 0 E
Barques, Pt. Aux, U.S.A. **116 B2** 44 4N 82 58W
Barquísimeto, *Venezuela* **124 A5** 10 4N 69 19W
Barr, Ras el, *Egypt* **80 H7** 31 32N 31 50 E
Barr Smith Range, *Australia* **93 E3** 27 4 S 120 20 E
Barra, *Brazil* **125 F10** 11 5 S 43 10W
Barra, U.K. **13 E1** 57 0N 7 29W
Barra, Sd. of, U.K. **13 D1** 57 4N 7 25W
Barra de Navidad, *Mexico* **118 D4** 19 12N 104 41W
Barra do Corda, *Brazil* **125 E9** 5 30 S 45 10W
Barra do Piraí, *Brazil* **127 A7** 22 30 S 43 50W
Barra Falsa, Pta. da, *Mozam.* **89 C6** 22 58 S 35 37 E
Barra Hd., U.K. **13 E1** 56 47N 7 40W
Barra Mansa, *Brazil* **127 A7** 22 35 S 44 12W
Barraba, *Australia* **95 E5** 30 21 S 150 35 E
Barrackpur = Barakpur, *India* **69 H13** 22 44N 88 30 E
Barradale Roadhouse, *Australia* **92 D2** 22 42 S 114 58 E
Barrafranca, *Italy* **43 E7** 37 22N 14 12 E
Barraigh = Barra, U.K. **13 E1** 57 0N 7 29W
Barranca, Lima, Peru **124 F3** 10 45 S 77 50W
Barranca, Loreto, Peru **124 D3** 4 50 S 76 50W
Barranca del Cobre △, *Mexico* **118 B3** 27 18N 107 40W
Barrancabermeja, *Colombia* **124 B4** 7 0N 73 50W
Barrancas, *Venezuela* **124 B6** 8 55N 62 5W
Barrancos, *Portugal* **37 G4** 38 10N 6 58W
Barranqueras, *Argentina* **126 B4** 27 30 S 59 0W
Barranquilla, *Colombia* **124 A4** 11 0N 74 50W
Barraute, *Canada* **104 C4** 48 26N 77 38W
Barre, Mass., U.S.A. **117 D12** 42 25N 72 6W
Barre, Vt., U.S.A. **117 B12** 44 12N 72 30W
Barreal, *Argentina* **126 C2** 31 33 S 69 28W
Barreiras, *Brazil* **125 F10** 12 8 S 45 0W
Barreirinhas, *Brazil* **125 D10** 2 30 S 42 50W
Barreiro, *Portugal* **37 G1** 38 40N 9 6W
Barrême, *France* **21 E10** 43 57N 6 23 E
Barren, Nosy, *Madag.* **89 B7** 18 25 S 43 40 E
Barretos, *Brazil* **125 H9** 20 30 S 48 35W
Barrhead, *Canada* **102 C6** 54 10N 114 24W
Barrie, *Canada* **116 B5** 44 24N 79 40W
Barrier Ra., *Australia* **95 E3** 31 0 S 141 30 E
Barrière, *Canada* **102 C4** 51 12N 120 7W
Barrington, U.S.A. **117 E13** 41 44N 71 18W
Barrington L., *Canada* **103 B8** 56 55N 100 15W
Barrington Tops, *Australia* **95 E5** 32 6 S 151 28 E
Barringun, *Australia* **95 D4** 29 1 S 145 41 E
Barro do Garças, *Brazil* **125 G8** 15 54 S 52 16W
Barron, U.S.A. **112 C9** 45 24N 91 51W
Barrow, U.S.A. **100 A4** 71 18N 156 47W
Barrow →, Ireland **12 D5** 52 25N 6 58W
Barrow Creek, *Australia* **94 C1** 21 30 S 133 55 E
Barrow I., *Australia* **92 D2** 20 45 S 115 20 E
Barrow-in-Furness, U.K. **14 C4** 54 7N 3 14W
Barrow Pt., *Australia* **94 A3** 14 20 S 144 40 E
Barrow Pt., U.S.A. **98 B4** 71 10N 156 20W
Barrow Ra., *Australia* **93 E4** 26 0 S 127 40 E
Barrow Str., *Canada* **4 B3** 74 20N 95 0W
Barruecopardo, *Spain* **36 D4** 41 4N 6 40W
Barruelo de Santullán, *Spain* **36 C6** 42 54N 4 17W
Barry, U.K. **15 F4** 51 24N 3 16W
Barry's Bay, *Canada* **116 A7** 45 29N 77 41W
Barsalogho, *Burkina Faso* **83 C4** 13 25N 1 3W
Barsat, *Pakistan* **69 A5** 36 10N 72 45 E
Barsham, *Syria* **70 C4** 35 21N 40 33 E
Barsi, *India* **66 K9** 18 10N 75 50 E
Barsinghausen, *Germany* **24 C5** 52 18N 9 28 E
Barsoi, *India* **67 G15** 25 48N 87 57 E
Barstow, U.S.A. **111 L9** 34 54N 117 1W
Barth, *Germany* **24 A8** 54 22N 12 42 E
Barthélemy, Col, *Vietnam* **64 C5** 19 26N 104 6 E
Bartica, *Guyana* **124 B7** 6 25N 58 40W
Bartin, *Turkey* **72 B5** 41 38N 32 21 E
Bartlesville, U.S.A. **113 G7** 36 45N 95 59W
Bartlett, U.S.A. **110 J8** 36 29N 118 2W
Bartlett, L., *Canada* **102 A5** 63 5N 118 20W
Bartolomeu Dias, *Mozam.* **87 G4** 21 10 S 35 8 E
Barton, Australia **93 F5** 30 31 S 132 39 E
Barton upon Humber, U.K. **14 D7** 53 41N 0 25W
Bartoszyce, *Poland* **30 D7** 54 15N 20 55 E
Bartow, U.S.A. **115 M5** 27 54N 81 50W
Barú, Volcan, *Panama* **120 E3** 8 55N 82 35W
Barumba, Dem. Rep. of the Congo **86 B1** 1 3N 23 37 E
Baruth, *Germany* **24 C9** 52 3N 13 30 E
Baruunsuu, *Mongolia* **56 C3** 43 43N 105 35 E
Barvinkove, *Ukraine* **33 H9** 48 57N 37 0 E
Barwani, *India* **68 H6** 22 2N 74 57 E
Barwice, *Poland* **30 E3** 53 50N 16 25 E
Barysaw, *Belarus* **32 E5** 54 17N 28 28 E
Barysh, *Russia* **34 D8** 53 39N 47 8 E
Barzān, *Iraq* **70 B5** 36 55N 44 3 E
Bârzava, *Romania* **28 D6** 46 7N 21 59 E
Bas-Rhin □, *France* **19 D14** 48 40N 7 30 E
Başaid, Serbia & M. **28 E5** 45 38N 20 25 E
Bāsa'idū, *Iran* **71 E7** 26 35N 55 20 E
Basal, *Pakistan* **68 C5** 33 33N 72 13 E
Basankusa, Dem. Rep. of the Congo **84 D3** 1 5N 19 50 E
Basarabeasca, *Moldova* **29 D13** 46 21N 28 58 E
Basarabi, *Romania* **29 F13** 44 10N 28 26 E
Basarabia = Bessarabiya, *Moldova* **33 J5** 47 0N 28 10 E
Basauri, *Spain* **38 B2** 43 3N 2 53W
Bascuñán, C., Chile **126 B1** 28 52 S 71 35W
Basel, Switz. **25 H3** 47 35N 7 35 E
Basel-Euroairport ✈ (BSL), *Europe* **19 E14** 47 36N 7 33 E
Basel-Landschaft □, Switz. **25 H3** 47 26N 7 45 E
Basento →, *Italy* **43 B9** 40 20N 16 49 E
Bashākerd, Kūhhā-ye, *Iran* **71 E8** 26 42N 58 35 E

Bashaw, *Canada* **102 C6** 52 35N 112 58W
Bāshī, *Iran* **71 D6** 28 41N 51 4 E
Bashkir Republic = Bashkortostan □, Russia **52 D6** 54 0N 57 0 E
Bashkortostan □, Russia **52 D6** 54 0N 57 0 E
Bashtanka, *Ukraine* **29 E14** 45 46N 29 29 E
Basibasy, *Madag.* **89 C7** 22 10 S 43 40 E
Basilan I., Phil. **61 H5** 6 35N 122 0 E
Basilan Str., Phil. **61 H5** 6 50N 122 0 E
Basildon, U.K. **15 F8** 51 34N 0 28 E
Basile, Eq. Guin. **83 E6** 3 42N 8 48 E
Basilicata □, *Italy* **43 B9** 40 30N 16 0 E
Basim = Washim, *India* **66 J10** 20 3N 77 0 E
Basin, U.S.A. **108 D9** 44 23N 108 2W
Basingstoke, U.K. **15 F6** 51 15N 1 5W
Baška, *Croatia* **41 D11** 44 58N 14 45 E
Başkale, *Turkey* **73 C10** 38 5N 43 59 E
Baskatong, Rés., Canada **104 C4** 46 46N 75 50W
Basle = Basel, Switz. **25 H3** 47 35N 7 35 E
Başmakçı, *Turkey* **47 D12** 37 54N 30 1 E
Basoda, *India* **68 H7** 23 52N 77 54 E
Basoko, Dem. Rep. of the Congo **86 B1** 1 16N 23 40 E
Basque, Pays, *France* **20 E2** 43 15N 1 20W
Basque Provinces = País Vasco □, *Spain* **38 C2** 42 50N 2 45W
Basra = Al Başrah, *Iraq* **70 D5** 30 30N 47 50 E
Bass Str., *Australia* **95 F4** 39 15 S 146 30 E
Bassano, *Canada* **102 C6** 50 48N 112 20W
Bassano del Grappa, *Italy* **41 C8** 45 46N 11 44 E
Bassar, *Togo* **83 D5** 9 19N 0 57 E
Bassas da India, Ind. Oc. **85 J7** 22 0 S 39 0 E
Basse-Normandie □, *France* **18 D6** 48 45N 0 30W
Basse-Pointe, *Martinique* **120 c** 14 52N 61 8W
Basse Santa-Su, *Gambia* **82 C2** 13 13N 14 15W
Basse-Terre, *Guadeloupe* **120 b** 16 0N 61 44W
Basse Terre, Trin. & Tob. **125 K15** 10 7N 61 19W
Bassein, *Burma* **67 L19** 16 45N 94 30 E
Basses, Pte. des, *Guadeloupe* **120 b** 15 52N 61 17W
Basseterre, St. Kitts & Nevis **121 C7** 17 17N 62 43W
Bassett, U.S.A. **112 D5** 42 35N 99 32W
Bassigny, *France* **19 E12** 48 0N 5 30 E
Bassikounou, *Mauritania* **82 B3** 15 55N 6 1W
Bassila, *Benin* **83 D5** 9 1N 1 46 E
Bassum, *Germany* **24 C4** 52 50N 8 40 E
Båstad, *Sweden* **11 H6** 56 25N 12 51 E
Bastak, *Iran* **71 E7** 27 15N 54 25 E
Baştām, *Iran* **71 B7** 36 29N 55 4 E
Bastar, *India* **67 K12** 19 15N 81 40 E
Bastelica, *France* **21 F13** 42 0N 9 3 E
Basti, *India* **69 F10** 26 52N 82 55 E
Bastia, *France* **21 F13** 42 40N 9 30 E
Bastogne, *Belgium* **17 D5** 50 1N 5 43 E
Bastrop, La., U.S.A. **113 J9** 32 47N 91 55W
Bastrop, Tex., U.S.A. **113 K6** 30 7N 97 19W
Bat Yam, *Israel* **74 C3** 32 2N 34 44 E
Bata, Eq. Guin. **84 D1** 1 57N 9 50 E
Bata, *Romania* **28 D7** 46 1N 22 4 E
Bataan □, Phil. **61 D4** 14 40N 120 25 E
Batabanó, *Cuba* **120 B3** 22 40N 82 20W
Batabanó, G. de, *Cuba* **120 B3** 22 30N 82 30W
Batac, Phil. **61 B4** 18 3N 120 34 E
Batagai, *Russia* **53 C14** 67 38N 134 38 E
Batajnica, Serbia & M. **44 B4** 44 54N 20 17 E
Batak, *Bulgaria* **45 E8** 41 57N 24 12 E
Batala, *India* **68 D6** 31 48N 75 12 E
Batalha, *Portugal* **36 F2** 39 40N 8 50W
Batama, Dem. Rep. of the Congo **86 B2** 0 58N 26 33 E
Batamay, *Russia* **53 C13** 63 30N 129 15 E
Batang, *China* **58 B2** 30 1N 99 0 E
Batang, *Indonesia* **63 G13** 6 55 S 109 45 E
Batangas, Phil. **61 E4** 13 35N 121 10 E
Batanta, *Indonesia* **63 E8** 0 55 S 130 40 E
Batatais, *Brazil* **127 A6** 20 54 S 47 37W
Batavia, U.S.A. **116 D6** 43 0N 78 11W
Bataysk, *Russia* **33 J10** 47 3N 39 45 E
Batchelor, *Australia* **92 B5** 13 4 S 131 1 E
Batdambang, *Cambodia* **64 F4** 13 7N 103 12 E
Batemans B., *Australia* **95 F5** 35 40 S 150 12 E
Batemans Bay, *Australia* **95 F5** 35 44 S 150 11 E
Bates Ra., *Australia* **93 E3** 27 27 S 121 5 E
Batesburg-Leesville, U.S.A. **115 J5** 33 54N 81 33W
Batesville, Ark., U.S.A. **113 H9** 35 46N 91 39W
Batesville, Miss., U.S.A. **113 H10** 34 19N 89 57W
Batesville, Tex., U.S.A. **113 L5** 28 58N 99 37W
Bath, *Canada* **117 B8** 44 11N 76 47W
Bath, U.K. **15 F5** 51 23N 2 22W
Bath, Maine, U.S.A. **115 D11** 43 55N 69 49W
Bath, N.Y., U.S.A. **116 D7** 42 20N 77 19W
Bath & North East Somerset □, U.K. **15 F5** 51 21N 2 27W
Batheay, *Cambodia* **65 G5** 11 59N 104 57 E
Bathsheba, *Barbados* **121 g** 13 13N 59 31W
Bathurst, *Australia* **95 E4** 33 25 S 149 31 E
Bathurst, *Canada* **105 C6** 47 37N 65 43W
Bathurst, S. Africa **88 E4** 33 30 S 26 50 E
Bathurst, C., *Canada* **100 A7** 70 34N 128 0W
Bathurst B., *Australia* **94 A3** 14 16 S 144 25 E
Bathurst Harb., *Australia* **95 G4** 43 15 S 146 10 E
Bathurst I., *Australia* **92 B5** 11 30 S 130 10 E
Bathurst I., *Canada* **98 B9** 76 0N 100 30W
Bathurst Inlet, *Canada* **100 B9** 66 50N 108 1W
Bati, *Ethiopia* **81 E5** 11 10N 40 0 E
Batie, *Burkina Faso* **82 D4** 9 53N 2 53W
Batlow, *Australia* **95 F4** 35 31 S 148 9 E
Batman, *Turkey* **73 C9** 37 55N 41 5 E
Batna, *Algeria* **78 A7** 35 34N 6 15 E
Batobato = San Isidro, Phil. **61 H7** 6 48N 126 21 E
Batočina, Serbia & M. **44 B5** 44 7N 21 5 E
Batoka, *Zambia* **87 F2** 16 45 S 27 15 E
Baton Rouge, U.S.A. **113 K9** 30 27N 91 11W
Batong, Ko, *Thailand* **65 J2** 6 32N 99 12 E
Bátonyterenye, *Hungary* **28 C4** 47 59N 19 50 E
Batopilas, *Mexico* **118 B3** 27 0N 107 45W
Batouri, *Cameroon* **84 D2** 4 30N 14 25 E
Bátsfjord, *Norway* **8 A23** 70 38N 29 39 E
Battambang = Batdambang, *Cambodia* **64 F4** 13 7N 103 12 E
Batticaloa, Sri Lanka **66 R12** 7 43N 81 45 E
Battipáglia, *Italy* **43 B7** 40 37N 14 58 E
Battle, U.K. **15 G8** 50 55N 0 30 E
Battle →, *Canada* **103 C7** 52 43N 108 15W

Battle Creek, *U.S.A.* ... **114 D3** 42 19N 85 11W
Battle Ground, *U.S.A.* ... **110 E4** 45 47N 122 32W
Battle Harbour, *Canada* **105 B8** 52 16N 55 35W
Battle Lake, *U.S.A.* ... **112 B7** 46 17N 95 43W
Battle Mountain, *U.S.A.* **108 F5** 40 38N 116 56W
Battlefields, *Zimbabwe* **87 F2** 18 37 S 29 47 E
Battleford, *Canada* ... **103 C7** 52 45N 108 15W
Battonya, *Hungary* ... **28 D6** 46 16N 21 3 E
Batu, *Ethiopia* ... **81 F4** 6 55N 39 45 E
Batu, Kepulauan, *Indonesia* ... **62 E1** 0 30 S 98 25 E
Batu Caves, *Malaysia* **65 L3** 3 15N 101 40 E
Batu Ferringhi, *Malaysia* **65 c** 5 28N 100 15 E
Batu Gajah, *Malaysia* **65 K3** 4 28N 101 3 E
Batu Is. = Batu, Kepulauan, *Indonesia* **62 E1** 0 30 S 98 25 E
Batu Pahat, *Malaysia* **65 M4** 1 50N 102 56 E
Batuata, *Indonesia* ... **83 F6** 6 12 S 122 42 E
Batugondang, Tanjung, *Indonesia* **63 J17** 8 6 S 114 29 E
Batukau, Gunung, *Indonesia* **63 J18** 8 20 S 115 5 E
Batumi, *Georgia* ... **35 K5** 41 39N 41 44 E
Batur, *Indonesia* ... **63 J18** 8 15 S 115 20 E
Batur, Gunung, *Indonesia* **63 J18** 8 14 S 115 23 E
Baturaja, *Indonesia* ... **62 E2** 4 11 S 104 15 E
Baturité, *Brazil* ... **125 D11** 4 28 S 38 45W
Baturiti, *Indonesia* ... **63 J18** 8 19 S 115 11 E
Bau, *Malaysia* ... **62 D4** 1 25N 110 9 E
Baubau, *Indonesia* ... **63 F6** 5 25 S 122 38 E
Baucau, *E. Timor* ... **63 F7** 8 27 S 126 27 E
Bauchi, *Nigeria* ... **83 C6** 10 22N 9 48 E
Bauchi □, *Nigeria* ... **83 C7** 10 30N 10 0 E
Baud, *France* ... **18 E3** 47 52N 3 1W
Baudette, *U.S.A.* ... **112 A7** 48 43N 94 36W
Bauer, C., *Australia* ... **95 E1** 32 44 S 134 4 E
Bauhinia, *Australia* ... **94 C4** 24 35 S 149 18 E
Baukau = Baucau, *E. Timor* ... **63 F7** 8 27 S 126 27 E
Bauld, C., *Canada* ... **101 C14** 51 38N 55 26W
Baume-les-Dames, *France* ... **19 E13** 47 22N 6 22 E
Baunatal, *Germany* ... **24 D5** 51 14N 9 24 E
Baunei, *Italy* ... **42 B2** 40 2N 9 40 E
Baure, *Nigeria* ... **83 C6** 12 52N 8 50 E
Bauru, *Brazil* ... **127 A6** 22 10 S 49 0W
Bausi, *India* ... **69 G12** 24 48N 87 1 E
Bauska, *Latvia* ... **9 H21** 56 24N 24 15 E
Bautino, *Kazakhstan* ... **35 H10** 44 35N 50 14 E
Bautzen, *Germany* ... **24 D10** 51 10N 14 26 E
Bauya, *S. Leone* ... **82 D2** 8 12N 12 38W
Bavănăt, *Iran* ... **71 D7** 30 28N 53 27 E
Bavanište, *Serbia & M.* **28 F5** 44 49N 20 55 E
Bavaria = Bayern □, *Germany* ... **25 G7** 48 50N 12 0 E
Båven, *Sweden* ... **10 E10** 59 0N 16 56 E
Bavispe →, *Mexico* ... **118 B3** 29 30N 109 11W
Bawdwin, *Burma* ... **67 H20** 23 5N 97 20 E
Bawean, *Indonesia* ... **62 F4** 5 46 S 112 35 E
Bawku, *Ghana* ... **83 C4** 11 3N 0 19W
Bawlake, *Burma* ... **67 K20** 19 11N 97 21 E
Bawolung, *China* ... **58 C3** 28 50N 101 16 E
Baxley, *U.S.A.* ... **115 K4** 31 47N 82 21W
Baxoi, *China* ... **58 B1** 30 1N 96 50 E
Baxter, *U.S.A.* ... **112 B7** 46 21N 94 17W
Baxter Springs, *U.S.A.* **113 G7** 37 2N 94 44W
Baxter State △, *U.S.A.* **115 B11** 46 5N 68 57W
Bay, L. de, *Phil.* ... **61 D4** 14 20N 121 11 E
Bay City, *Mich., U.S.A.* **114 D4** 43 36N 83 54W
Bay City, *Tex., U.S.A.* **113 L7** 28 59N 95 58W
Bay Minette, *U.S.A.* ... **115 K2** 30 53N 87 46W
Bay Roberts, *Canada* **105 C9** 47 36N 53 16W
Bay St. Louis, *U.S.A.* **113 K10** 30 19N 89 20W
Bay Springs, *U.S.A.* ... **113 K10** 31 59N 89 17W
Bay View, *N.Z.* ... **91 H6** 39 25 S 176 50 E
Baya, *Dem. Rep. of the Congo* **87 E2** 11 53 S 27 25 E
Bayamo, *Cuba* ... **120 B4** 20 20N 76 40W
Bayamón, *Puerto Rico* **121 d** 18 24N 66 10W
Bayan Har Shan, *China* **60 C4** 34 0N 98 0 E
Bayan Hot = Alxa Zuoqi, *China* **56 E3** 38 50N 105 40 E
Bayan Lepas, *Malaysia* **65 c** 5 17N 100 12 E
Bayan Obo, *China* ... **56 D5** 41 52N 109 59 E
Bayan-Ovoo = Erdenetsogt, *Mongolia* ... **56 C4** 42 55N 106 5 E
Bayana, *India* ... **68 F7** 26 55N 77 18 E
Bayanaüyl, *Kazakhstan* **52 D8** 50 45N 75 45 E
Bayandalay, *Mongolia* **56 C2** 43 30N 103 29 E
Bayanhongor, *Mongolia* **60 B5** 46 8N 102 43 E
Bayard, *N. Mex., U.S.A.* **109 K9** 32 46N 108 8W
Bayard, *Nebr., U.S.A.* **112 E3** 41 45N 103 20W
Bayawan, *Phil.* ... **61 G5** 9 46N 122 45 E
Baybay, *Phil.* ... **61 F6** 10 40N 124 55 E
Bayburt, *Turkey* ... **73 B9** 40 15N 40 20 E
Baydhabo = Baidoa, *Somali Rep.* **75 G3** 3 8N 43 30 E
Bayelsa □, *Nigeria* ... **83 E6** 4 30N 6 0 E
Bayerische Alpen, *Germany* ... **25 H7** 47 35N 11 30 E
Bayerische Rhön △, *Germany* ... **25 E6** 50 15N 10 5 E
Bayerischer Spessart △, *Germany* ... **25 F6** 49 58N 10 15 E
Bayerischer Wald, *Germany* ... **25 G8** 48 56N 12 50 E
Bayern □, *Germany* ... **25 G7** 48 50N 12 0 E
Bayeux, *France* ... **18 C6** 49 17N 0 42W
Bayfield, *Canada* ... **116 C3** 43 34N 81 42W
Bayfield, *U.S.A.* ... **112 B9** 46 49N 90 49W
Bayındır, *Turkey* ... **47 C9** 38 13N 27 39 E
Bayjï, *Iraq* ... **70 C4** 35 0N 43 30 E
Baykal, Oz., *Russia* ... **53 D11** 53 0N 108 0 E
Baykan, *Turkey* ... **70 B4** 38 7N 41 44 E
Baykonur = Bayqongyr, *Kazakhstan* ... **52 E7** 47 48N 65 50 E
Baynes Mts., *Namibia* **88 B1** 17 15 S 13 0 E
Bayombong, *Phil.* ... **61 C4** 16 30N 121 10 E
Bayon, *France* ... **19 D13** 48 30N 6 20 E
Bayona = Baiona, *Spain* **36 C2** 42 6N 8 52W
Bayonne, *France* ... **20 E2** 43 30N 1 28W
Bayonne, *U.S.A.* ... **117 F10** 40 40N 74 7W
Bayovar, *Peru* ... **124 E2** 5 50 S 81 0W
Bayqongyr, *Kazakhstan* **52 E7** 47 48N 65 50 E
Bayram-Ali = Bayramaly, *Turkmenistan* **52 F7** 37 37N 62 10 E
Bayramaly, *Turkmenistan* **52 F7** 37 37N 62 10 E
Bayramiç, *Turkey* ... **47 B8** 39 48N 26 36 E
Bayreuth, *Germany* ... **25 F7** 49 56N 11 35 E
Bayrischzell, *Germany* **25 H8** 47 41N 12 0 E
Bayrūt, *Lebanon* ... **74 B4** 33 53N 35 31 E
Bays, L. of, *Canada* ... **116 A5** 45 15N 79 4W
Baysville, *Canada* ... **116 A5** 45 9N 79 7W

Bayt Lahm, *West Bank* **74 D4** 31 43N 35 12 E
Baytown, *U.S.A.* ... **113 L7** 29 43N 94 59W
Bayun, *Indonesia* ... **63 J18** 8 11 S 115 16 E
Bayzo, *Niger* ... **83 C5** 13 52N 4 35 E
Baza, *Spain* ... **37 H8** 37 30N 2 47W
Bazar Dyuzi, *Russia* ... **35 K8** 41 12N 47 50 E
Bazardüzü = Bazar Dyuzi, *Russia* ... **35 K8** 41 12N 47 50 E
Bazaruy Karabulak, *Russia* ... **34 D8** 52 20N 46 29 E
Bazarnyy Syzgan, *Russia* **34 D8** 53 45N 46 40 E
Bazaruto △, *Mozam.* **89 C6** 21 42 S 35 26 E
Bazaruto, I. do, *Mozam.* **89 C6** 21 40 S 35 28 E
Bazas, *France* ... **20 D3** 44 27N 0 13W
Bazhong, *China* ... **58 B6** 31 52N 106 46 E
Bazhou, *China* ... **56 E9** 39 8N 116 22 E
Bazmán, Küh-e, *Iran* **71 D9** 28 4N 60 1 E
Beach, *U.S.A.* ... **112 B3** 46 58N 104 0W
Beach City, *U.S.A.* ... **116 F3** 40 39N 81 35W
Beachport, *Australia* **95 F3** 37 29 S 140 0 E
Beachy Hd., *U.K.* ... **15 G8** 50 44N 0 15 E
Beacon, *Australia* ... **93 F2** 30 26 S 117 52 E
Beacon, *U.S.A.* ... **117 E11** 41 30N 73 58W
Beaconsfield, *Australia* **95 G4** 41 11 S 146 48 E
Beagle, Canal, *S. Amer.* **128 H3** 55 0 S 68 30W
Beagle Bay, *Australia* **92 C3** 16 58 S 122 40 E
Bealanana, *Madag.* ... **89 A8** 14 33 S 48 44 E
Beals Cr. →, *U.S.A.* ... **113 J4** 32 10N 100 51W
Beamsville, *Canada* ... **116 C5** 43 12N 79 28W
Bear →, *Calif., U.S.A.* **110 G5** 38 56N 121 36W
Bear →, *Utah, U.S.A.* **106 B4** 41 30N 112 8W
Béar, C., *France* ... **20 F7** 42 31N 3 8 E
Bear I., *Ireland* ... **12 E2** 51 38N 9 50W
Bear L., *Canada* ... **103 B9** 55 8N 96 0W
Bear L., *U.S.A.* ... **108 F8** 41 59N 111 21W
Beardmore, *Canada* **104 C2** 49 36N 87 57W
Beardmore Glacier, *Antarctica* **5 E11** 84 30 S 170 0 E
Beardstown, *U.S.A.* ... **112 F9** 40 1N 90 26W
Bearma →, *India* ... **69 G8** 24 20N 79 51 E
Béarn, *France* ... **20 E3** 43 20N 0 30W
Bearpaw Mts., *U.S.A.* **108 B9** 48 12N 109 30W
Bearskin Lake, *Canada* **104 B1** 53 58N 91 2W
Beas →, *India* ... **68 D6** 31 10N 74 59 E
Beas de Segura, *Spain* **37 G8** 38 15N 2 53W
Beasain, *Spain* ... **38 B2** 43 3N 2 11W
Beata, C., *Dom. Rep.* **121 C5** 17 40N 71 30W
Beata, I., *Dom. Rep.* **121 C5** 17 34N 71 31W
Beatrice, *U.S.A.* ... **112 E6** 40 16N 96 45W
Beatrice, *Zimbabwe* **87 F3** 18 15 S 30 55 E
Beatrice, C., *Australia* **94 A2** 14 20 S 136 55 E
Beatton →, *Canada* **102 B4** 56 15N 120 45W
Beatton River, *Canada* **102 B4** 57 26N 121 20W
Beatty, *U.S.A.* ... **110 J10** 36 54N 116 46W
Beaucaire, *France* ... **21 E8** 43 48N 4 39 E
Beauce, Plaine de la, *France* ... **19 D8** 48 10N 1 45 E
Beauceville, *Canada* **105 C5** 46 13N 70 46W
Beaudesert, *Australia* **95 D5** 27 59 S 153 0 E
Beaufort, *France* ... **21 C10** 45 44N 6 34 E
Beaufort, *Malaysia* ... **62 C5** 5 30N 115 40 E
Beaufort, *N.C., U.S.A.* **115 H7** 34 43N 76 40W
Beaufort, *S.C., U.S.A.* **115 J5** 32 26N 80 40W
Beaufort Sea, *Arctic* **98 B5** 72 0N 140 0W
Beaufort West, *S. Africa* **88 E3** 32 18 S 22 36 E
Beaugency, *France* ... **19 E8** 47 47N 1 38 E
Beauharnois, *Canada* **117 A11** 45 20N 73 52W
Beaujeu, *France* ... **19 F11** 46 10N 4 35 E
Beaujolais, *France* ... **19 F11** 46 0N 4 25 E
Beaulieu →, *Canada* **102 A6** 62 3N 113 11W
Beaulieu-sur-Dordogne, *France* ... **20 D5** 44 58N 1 50 E
Beaulieu-sur-Mer, *France* ... **21 E11** 43 42N 7 20 E
Beauly, *U.K.* ... **13 D4** 57 30N 4 28W
Beauly →, *U.K.* ... **13 D4** 57 29N 4 27W
Beaumaris, *U.K.* ... **14 D3** 53 16N 4 6W
Beaumont, *Belgium* **17 D4** 50 15N 4 14 E
Beaumont, *France* ... **20 D4** 44 45N 0 46 E
Beaumont, *U.S.A.* ... **113 K7** 30 5N 94 6W
Beaumont-de-Lomagne, *France* ... **20 E5** 43 53N 1 0 E
Beaumont-le-Roger, *France* ... **18 C7** 49 4N 0 47 E
Beaumont-sur-Sarthe, *France* ... **18 D7** 48 13N 0 8 E
Beaune, *France* ... **19 E11** 47 2N 4 50 E
Beaune-la-Rolande, *France* ... **19 D9** 48 4N 2 25 E
Beaupré, *Canada* ... **105 C5** 47 3N 70 54W
Beaupréau, *France* ... **18 E6** 47 12N 1 0W
Beauraing, *Belgium* ... **17 D4** 50 7N 4 57 E
Beaurepaire, *France* ... **21 C9** 45 22N 5 1 E
Beausejour, *Canada* **103 C9** 50 5N 96 35W
Beauvais, *France* ... **19 C9** 49 25N 2 8 E
Beauval, *Canada* ... **103 B7** 55 9N 107 37W
Beauvoir-sur-Mer, *France* ... **18 F4** 46 55N 2 2W
Beauvoir-sur-Niort, *France* ... **20 B3** 46 12N 0 30W
Beaver, *Okla., U.S.A.* **113 G4** 36 49N 100 31W
Beaver, *Pa., U.S.A.* ... **116 F4** 40 42N 80 19W
Beaver, *Utah, U.S.A.* **109 G7** 38 17N 112 38W
Beaver →, *B.C., Canada* **102 B4** 59 52N 124 20W
Beaver →, *Ont., Canada* **104 A2** 55 55N 87 48W
Beaver →, *Sask., Canada* **103 B7** 55 26N 107 45W
Beaver →, *U.S.A.* ... **113 G5** 36 35N 99 30W
Beaver City, *U.S.A.* ... **112 E5** 40 8N 99 50W
Beaver Creek, *Canada* **100 B5** 63 0N 141 0W
Beaver Dam, *U.S.A.* ... **112 D10** 43 28N 88 50W
Beaver Falls, *U.S.A.* ... **116 F4** 40 46N 80 20W
Beaver Hill L., *Canada* **103 C10** 54 5N 94 50W
Beaver I., *U.S.A.* ... **114 C3** 45 40N 85 33W
Beaverhill L., *Canada* **102 C6** 53 27N 112 32W
Beaverlodge, *Canada* **102 B5** 55 11N 119 29W
Beaverstone →, *Canada* **104 B2** 54 59N 89 25W
Beaverton, *Canada* ... **116 B5** 44 26N 79 9W
Beaverton, *U.S.A.* ... **110 E4** 45 29N 122 48W
Beawar, *India* ... **68 F6** 26 3N 74 18 E
Bebedouro, *Brazil* ... **127 A6** 21 0 S 48 25W
Bebera, Tanjung, *Indonesia* ... **63 K18** 8 44 S 115 51 E
Beboa, *Madag.* ... **89 B7** 17 22 S 44 33 E
Bebra, *Germany* ... **24 E5** 50 58N 9 48 E
Becan, *Mexico* ... **119 D7** 18 31N 89 28W
Beccles, *U.K.* ... **15 E9** 52 27N 1 35 E
Bečej, *Serbia & M.* ... **28 E5** 45 36N 20 3 E
Beceni, *Romania* ... **29 E11** 45 23N 26 48 E
Becerreá, *Spain* ... **36 C3** 42 51N 7 10W
Béchar, *Algeria* ... **78 B5** 31 38N 2 18W
Bechyně, *Czech Rep.* **26 B7** 49 17N 14 29 E
Beckley, *U.S.A.* ... **114 G5** 37 47N 81 11W
Beckum, *Germany* ... **24 D4** 51 45N 8 1 E
Beclean, *Romania* ... **29 C9** 47 11N 24 11 E
Bečov nad Teplou, *Czech Rep.* ... **26 A5** 50 5N 12 49 E

Bečva →, *Czech Rep.* **27 B10** 49 31N 17 20 E
Bédar, *Spain* ... **39 H3** 37 11N 1 59W
Bédarieux, *France* ... **20 E7** 43 37N 3 10 E
Beddouza, Ras, *Morocco* **78 B4** 32 33N 9 9W
Bedele, *Ethiopia* ... **81 F4** 8 31N 36 23 E
Bederkesa, *Germany* **24 B4** 53 37N 8 50 E
Bedeso, *Ethiopia* ... **81 F5** 9 58N 40 52 E
Bedford, *Canada* ... **117 A12** 45 7N 72 59W
Bedford, *S. Africa* ... **88 E4** 32 40 S 26 10 E
Bedford, *U.K.* ... **15 E7** 52 8N 0 28W
Bedford, *Ind., U.S.A.* **114 F2** 38 52N 86 29W
Bedford, *Iowa, U.S.A.* **112 E7** 40 40N 94 44W
Bedford, *Ohio, U.S.A.* **116 E3** 41 23N 81 32W
Bedford, *Pa., U.S.A.* **116 F6** 40 1N 78 30W
Bedford, *Va., U.S.A.* **114 G6** 37 20N 79 31W
Bedford, C., *Australia* **94 B4** 15 14 S 145 21 E
Bedfordshire □, *U.K.* **15 E7** 52 4N 0 28W
Będków, *Poland* ... **31 G6** 51 36N 19 44 E
Bednja →, *Croatia* ... **41 B13** 46 12N 16 25 E
Bednodemyanovsk, *Russia* ... **34 D6** 53 55N 43 15 E
Bedok, *Singapore* ... **65 d** 1 19N 103 56 E
Bedónia, *Italy* ... **40 D6** 44 30N 9 38 E
Bedourie, *Australia* ... **94 C2** 24 30 S 139 30 E
Bedum, *Neths.* ... **17 A6** 53 18N 6 36 E
Będzin, *Poland* ... **31 H6** 50 19N 19 7 E
Beebe Plain, *Canada* **117 A12** 45 1N 72 9W
Beech Creek, *U.S.A.* **116 E7** 41 5N 77 36W
Beef I., *Br. Virgin Is.* **121 e** 18 26N 64 30W
Beelitz, *Germany* ... **24 C8** 52 14N 12 58 E
Beenleigh, *Australia* **95 D5** 27 43 S 153 10 E
Be'er Menuha, *Israel* **70 D2** 30 19N 35 8 E
Be'er Sheva, *Israel* **74 D3** 31 15N 34 48 E
Beersheba = Be'er Sheva, *Israel* **74 D3** 31 15N 34 48 E
Beeskow, *Germany* ... **24 C10** 52 10N 14 15 E
Beestekraal, *S. Africa* **89 D4** 25 23 S 27 38 E
Beeston, *U.K.* ... **14 E6** 52 56N 1 14W
Beetzendorf, *Germany* **24 C7** 52 42N 11 6 E
Beeville, *U.S.A.* ... **113 L6** 28 24N 97 45W
Befale, *Dem. Rep. of the Congo* **84 D4** 0 25N 20 45 E
Befandriana, *Mahajanga, Madag.* **89 B8** 15 16 S 48 32 E
Befandriana, *Toliara, Madag.* **89 C7** 21 55 S 44 0 E
Befasy, *Madag.* ... **89 C7** 20 33 S 44 23 E
Befotaka, *Antsiranana, Madag.* **89 A8** 13 15 S 48 16 E
Befotaka, *Fianarantsoa, Madag.* **89 C8** 23 49 S 47 0 E
Bega, *Australia* ... **95 F4** 36 41 S 149 51 E
Bega, Canalul, *Romania* **28 E5** 45 37N 20 46 E
Bégard, *France* ... **18 D3** 48 38N 3 18W
Beğendik, *Turkey* ... **45 F10** 40 55N 26 34 E
Begoro, *Ghana* ... **83 D4** 6 23N 0 23W
Begusarai, *India* ... **69 G12** 25 24N 86 9 E
Behābād, *Iran* ... **71 C8** 32 24N 59 47 E
Behala, *India* ... **69 H13** 22 30N 88 20 E
Behara, *Madag.* ... **89 C8** 24 55 S 46 20 E
Behbehān, *Iran* ... **71 D6** 30 30N 50 15 E
Behm Canal, *U.S.A.* **102 B2** 55 10N 131 0W
Behshahr, *Iran* ... **72 D7** 36 45N 53 35 E
Bei Jiang →, *China* **59 F9** 23 2N 112 58 E
Bei'an, *China* ... **60 B7** 48 10N 126 20 E
Beibei, *China* ... **58 C6** 29 47N 106 22 E
Beichuan, *China* ... **58 B5** 31 55N 104 39 E
Beihai, *China* ... **58 G7** 21 28N 109 6 E
Beijing, *China* ... **56 E9** 39 55N 116 20 E
Beijing □, *China* ... **56 E9** 39 55N 116 20 E
Beilen, *Neths.* ... **17 B6** 52 52N 6 27 E
Beiliu, *China* ... **59 F8** 22 41N 110 21 E
Beilngries, *Germany* **25 F7** 49 2N 11 28 E
Beilpajah, *Australia* **95 E3** 32 54 S 143 52 E
Beilul, *Eritrea* ... **81 E5** 13 2N 42 20 E
Beinn na Faoghla = Benbecula, *U.K.* **13 D1** 57 26N 7 21W
Beipan Jiang →, *China* **58 E5** 25 7N 106 1 E
Beipiao, *China* ... **57 D11** 41 52N 120 32 E
Beira, *Mozam.* ... **87 F3** 19 50 S 34 52 E
Beirut = Bayrūt, *Lebanon* **74 B4** 33 53N 35 31 E
Beiseker, *Canada* ... **102 C6** 51 23N 113 32W
Beitaolaizhao, *China* **57 B13** 44 58N 125 58 E
Beitbridge, *Zimbabwe* **87 G3** 22 12 S 30 0 E
Beiuș, *Romania* ... **28 D7** 46 40N 22 21 E
Beizhen = Binzhou, *China* ... **57 F10** 37 20N 118 2 E
Beizhen, *China* ... **57 D11** 41 38N 121 54 E
Beizhengzhen, *China* **57 B12** 44 31N 123 30 E
Beja, *Portugal* ... **37 G3** 38 2N 7 53W
Béja, *Tunisia* ... **79 A7** 36 43N 9 12 E
Beja □, *Portugal* ... **37 H3** 37 55N 7 55W
Bejaïa, *Algeria* ... **78 A7** 36 42N 5 2 E
Béjar, *Spain* ... **36 E5** 40 23N 5 46W
Bejestān, *Iran* ... **71 C8** 34 30N 58 5 E
Bekaa Valley = Al Biqā, *Lebanon* **74 A5** 34 10N 36 10 E
Bekçiler, *Turkey* ... **47 E11** 36 56N 29 44 E
Békés, *Hungary* ... **28 D6** 46 47N 21 9 E
Békés □, *Hungary* ... **28 D6** 46 45N 21 0 E
Békéscsaba, *Hungary* **28 D6** 46 40N 21 5 E
Bekilli, *Turkey* ... **47 C11** 38 17N 29 27 E
Bekily, *Madag.* ... **89 C8** 24 13 S 45 19 E
Bekisopa, *Madag.* ... **89 C8** 21 40 S 45 54 E
Bekitro, *Madag.* ... **89 C8** 24 33 S 45 18 E
Bekodoka, *Madag.* ... **89 B8** 16 58 S 45 7 E
Bekoji, *Ethiopia* ... **81 F4** 7 40N 39 17 E
Bekok, *Malaysia* ... **65 L4** 2 20N 103 7 E
Bekopaka, *Madag.* ... **89 B7** 19 9 S 44 48 E
Bekuli, *Indonesia* ... **63 J17** 8 22 S 114 13 E
Bekwai, *Ghana* ... **83 D4** 6 30N 1 34W
Bela, *India* ... **69 G10** 25 50N 82 0 E
Bela, *Pakistan* ... **68 F2** 26 12N 66 20 E
Bela Bela, *S. Africa* ... **89 C4** 24 51 S 28 19 E
Bela Crkva, *Serbia & M.* **28 F6** 44 55N 21 27 E
Bela Palanka, *Serbia & M.* **44 C6** 43 13N 22 17 E
Bela Vista, *Brazil* ... **126 A4** 22 12 S 56 20W
Bela Vista, *Mozam.* **89 D5** 26 10 S 32 44 E
Bélábre, *France* ... **20 B5** 46 34N 1 8 E
Belalcázar, *Spain* ... **37 G5** 38 35N 5 10W
Belan →, *India* ... **69 G9** 24 2N 81 45 E
Belanovica, *Serbia & M.* **44 B5** 44 15N 20 23 E
Belarus ■, *Europe* ... **32 F4** 53 30N 27 0 E
Belau = Palau ■, *Pac. Oc.* **96 G5** 7 30N 134 30 E
Belavenona, *Madag.* **89 C8** 24 50 S 47 4 E
Belawan, *Indonesia* ... **62 D1** 3 33N 98 32 E
Belaya, *Ethiopia* ... **81 E4** 11 25N 36 8 E
Belaya Glina, *Russia* **35 G5** 46 5N 40 48 E
Belaya Kalitva, *Russia* **35 F5** 48 13N 40 50 E
Belaya Tserkov = Bila Tserkva, *Ukraine* **33 H5** 49 45N 30 10 E
Belcești, *Romania* ... **29 C12** 47 19N 27 7 E
Belchatów, *Poland* ... **31 G6** 51 21N 19 22 E

Belcher Is., *Canada* ... **104 A3** 56 15N 78 45W
Belchite, *Spain* ... **38 D4** 41 18N 0 43W
Belden, *U.S.A.* ... **110 E5** 40 2N 121 17W
Beled Weyne = Belet Uen, *Somali Rep.* **75 G4** 4 30N 45 5 E
Belém, *Brazil* ... **125 D9** 1 20 S 48 30W
Belén, *Argentina* ... **126 B2** 27 40 S 67 5W
Belén, *Paraguay* ... **126 A4** 23 30 S 57 6W
Belen, *U.S.A.* ... **109 J10** 34 40N 106 46W
Belene, *Bulgaria* ... **45 C9** 43 39N 25 10 E
Beleni, *Turkey* ... **72 D7** 36 31N 36 10 E
Bélesta, *France* ... **20 F5** 42 55N 1 56 E
Belet Uen, *Somali Rep.* **75 G4** 4 30N 45 5 E
Belev, *Russia* ... **32 F9** 53 50N 36 5 E
Belevi, *Turkey* ... **47 C9** 38 2N 27 24 E
Belfair, *U.S.A.* ... **110 C4** 47 27N 122 50W
Belfast, *S. Africa* ... **89 D5** 25 42 S 30 2 E
Belfast, *Maine, U.S.A.* **115 C11** 44 26N 69 1W
Belfast, *U.K.* ... **12 B6** 54 37N 5 56W
Belfast, *N.Y., U.S.A.* **116 D6** 42 21N 78 7W
Belfast L., *U.K.* ... **12 B6** 54 40N 5 50W
Belfield, *U.S.A.* ... **112 B3** 46 53N 103 12W
Belfort, *France* ... **19 E13** 47 38N 6 50 E
Belfort, Territoire de □, *France* ... **19 E13** 47 40N 6 55 E
Belfry, *U.S.A.* ... **108 D9** 45 9N 109 1W
Belgaum, *India* ... **66 M9** 15 55N 74 35 E
Belgioioso, *Italy* ... **40 C6** 45 10N 9 19 E
Belgium ■, *Europe* ... **17 D4** 50 30N 5 0 E
Belgodère, *France* ... **21 F13** 42 35N 9 1 E
Belgorod, *Russia* ... **33 G9** 50 35N 36 35 E
Belgorod-Dnestrovskiy = Bilhorod-Dnistrovskyy, *Ukraine* **33 J6** 46 11N 30 23 E
Belgrade = Beograd, *Serbia & M.* ... **44 B4** 44 50N 20 37 E
Belgrade, *U.S.A.* ... **108 D8** 45 47N 111 11W
Belhaven, *U.S.A.* ... **115 H7** 35 33N 76 37W
Beli Drim →, *Europe* **44 D4** 42 6N 20 25 E
Beli Manastir, *Croatia* **28 E3** 45 45N 18 36 E
Beli Timok →, *Serbia & M.* **44 C6** 43 53N 22 14 E
Bélice →, *Italy* ... **42 E5** 37 35N 12 55 E
Belimbing, *Indonesia* **63 J18** 8 24 S 115 2 E
Belinskiy, *Russia* ... **34 D6** 53 0N 43 25 E
Belinyu, *Indonesia* ... **62 E3** 1 35 S 105 50 E
Beliton Is. = Belitung, *Indonesia* ... **62 E3** 3 10 S 107 50 E
Belitung, *Indonesia* ... **62 E3** 3 10 S 107 50 E
Beliu, *Romania* ... **28 D6** 46 30N 22 0 E
Belize ■, *Cent. Amer.* **119 D7** 17 0N 88 30W
Belize City, *Belize* ... **119 D7** 17 25N 88 0W
Beljakovci, *Macedonia* **44 D5** 42 6N 21 59 E
Beljanica, *Serbia & M.* **44 B5** 44 8N 21 43 E
Belkovskiy, Ostrov, *Russia* **53 B14** 75 32N 135 44 E
Bell →, *Canada* ... **104 C4** 49 48N 77 38W
Bell I., *Canada* ... **105 B8** 50 46N 55 35W
Bell-Irving →, *Canada* **102 B3** 56 12N 129 5W
Bell Peninsula, *Canada* **101 B11** 63 50N 82 0W
Bell Ville, *Argentina* **126 C3** 32 40 S 62 40W
Bella, *Italy* ... **43 B8** 40 45N 15 32 E
Bella Bella, *Canada* **102 C3** 52 10N 128 10W
Bella Coola, *Canada* **102 C3** 52 25N 126 40W
Bella Unión, *Uruguay* **126 C4** 30 15 S 57 40W
Bella Vista, *Corrientes, Argentina* **126 B4** 28 33 S 59 0W
Bella Vista, *Tucuman, Argentina* **126 B2** 27 10 S 65 25W
Bellac, *France* ... **20 B5** 46 7N 1 3 E
Bellágio, *Italy* ... **40 C6** 45 59N 9 15 E
Bellaire, *U.S.A.* ... **116 F4** 40 1N 80 45W
Bellária, *Italy* ... **41 D9** 44 9N 12 28 E
Bellary, *India* ... **66 M10** 15 10N 76 56 E
Bellata, *Australia* ... **95 D4** 29 53 S 149 46 E
Belle-Chasse, *U.S.A.* **113 L10** 29 51N 89 59W
Belle Fourche, *U.S.A.* **112 C3** 44 40N 103 51W
Belle Fourche →, *U.S.A.* ... **112 C3** 44 26N 102 18W
Belle Glade, *U.S.A.* **115 M5** 26 41N 80 40W
Belle-Île, *France* ... **18 E3** 47 20N 3 10W
Belle Isle, *Canada* ... **105 B8** 51 57N 55 25W
Belle Isle, Str. of, *Canada* ... **105 B8** 51 30N 56 30W
Belle Plaine, *U.S.A.* **112 E8** 41 54N 92 17W
Belle Yella, *Liberia* **82 D3** 7 24N 10 0W
Belledonne, *France* **21 C10** 45 20N 6 10 E
Bellefontaine, *U.S.A.* **114 E4** 40 22N 83 46W
Bellefonte, *U.S.A.* ... **116 F7** 40 55N 77 47W
Bellegarde, *France* ... **19 F9** 47 59N 2 26 E
Bellegarde-en-Marche, *France* ... **20 C6** 45 59N 2 18 E
Bellegarde-sur-Valserine, *France* **19 F12** 46 4N 5 50 E
Bellême, *France* ... **18 D7** 48 22N 0 34 E
Belleoram, *Canada* ... **105 C8** 47 31N 55 25W
Belleplaine, *Barbados* **121 g** 13 15N 59 34W
Belleville, *Canada* ... **116 B7** 44 10N 77 23W
Belleville, *France* ... **19 F11** 46 7N 4 45 E
Belleville, *Ill., U.S.A.* **112 F10** 38 31N 89 59W
Belleville, *Kans., U.S.A.* **112 F6** 39 50N 97 38W
Belleville, *N.Y., U.S.A.* **117 C8** 43 46N 76 10W
Belleville-sur-Vie, *France* ... **18 F5** 46 46N 1 25W
Bellevue, *Canada* ... **102 D6** 49 35N 114 22W
Bellevue, *Idaho, U.S.A.* **108 E6** 43 28N 114 16W
Bellevue, *Nebr., U.S.A.* **112 E7** 41 8N 95 53W
Bellevue, *Ohio, U.S.A.* **116 E2** 41 17N 82 51W
Bellevue, *Wash., U.S.A.* **110 C4** 47 37N 122 12W
Belley, *France* ... **21 C9** 45 46N 5 41 E
Bellin = Kangirsuk, *Canada* **101 B13** 60 0N 70 0W
Bellingen, *Australia* ... **95 E5** 30 25 S 152 50 E
Bellingham, *U.S.A.* **110 B4** 48 46N 122 29W
Bellingshausen Sea, *Antarctica* **5 C17** 66 0 S 80 0W
Bellinzona, *Switz.* ... **25 J5** 46 11N 9 1 E
Bello, *Colombia* ... **124 B3** 6 20N 75 33W
Bellows Falls, *U.S.A.* **117 C12** 43 8N 72 27W
Bellpat, *Pakistan* ... **68 E3** 29 0N 68 5 E
Bellpuig d'Urgell, *Spain* **38 D6** 41 37N 1 1 E
Belluno, *Italy* ... **41 B9** 46 9N 12 13 E
Bellville, *U.S.A.* ... **113 L6** 29 57N 96 15W
Bellwood, *U.S.A.* ... **116 F6** 40 36N 78 20W
Bélmez, *Spain* ... **37 G5** 38 17N 5 17W
Belmont, *S. Africa* **88 D3** 29 28 S 24 22 E
Belmont, *Canada* ... **116 D3** 42 53N 81 5W
Belmont, *U.S.A.* ... **116 D6** 42 14N 78 2W
Belmonte, *Brazil* ... **125 G11** 16 0 S 39 0W
Belmonte, *Portugal* **36 E3** 40 21N 7 20W
Belmonte, *Spain* ... **39 F2** 39 34N 2 43W
Belmopan, *Belize* ... **119 D7** 17 18N 88 30W
Belmullet, *Ireland* ... **12 B2** 54 14N 9 58W
Belo Horizonte, *Brazil* **125 G10** 19 55 S 43 56W
Belo-sur-Mer, *Madag.* **89 C7** 20 42 S 44 0 E
Belo-Tsiribihina, *Madag.* **89 B7** 19 40 S 44 30 E

Belogorsk = Bilohirsk, *Ukraine* ... **33 K8** 45 3N 34 35 E
Belogorsk, *Russia* ... **53 D13** 51 0N 128 20 E
Belogradchik, *Bulgaria* **44 C6** 43 53N 22 42 E
Belogradets, *Bulgaria* **45 C11** 43 22N 27 18 E
Beloha, *Madag.* ... **89 D8** 25 10 S 45 3 E
Beloit, *Kans., U.S.A.* **112 F5** 39 28N 98 6W
Beloit, *Wis., U.S.A.* ... **112 D10** 42 31N 89 2W
Belokorovichi, *Ukraine* **33 G5** 51 7N 28 2 E
Belomorsk, *Russia* ... **52 C4** 64 35N 34 54 E
Belonia, *India* ... **67 H17** 23 15N 91 30 E
Belopolye = Bilopillya, *Ukraine* ... **33 G8** 51 14N 34 20 E
Belorechensk, *Russia* **35 H4** 44 46N 39 52 E
Belorussia = Belarus ■, *Europe* ... **32 F4** 53 30N 27 0 E
Beloslav, *Bulgaria* ... **45 C11** 43 13N 27 42 E
Belovo, *Bulgaria* ... **45 D8** 42 13N 24 1 E
Belovo, *Russia* ... **52 D9** 54 30N 86 0 E
Belovodsk, *Ukraine* **33 H10** 49 13N 39 36 E
Beloye, Ozero, *Russia* **32 B9** 60 10N 37 35 E
Beloye More, *Russia* **52 C4** 66 30N 38 0 E
Belozem, *Bulgaria* ... **45 D9** 42 12N 25 2 E
Belozersk, *Russia* ... **32 B9** 60 1N 37 45 E
Belpasso, *Italy* ... **43 E7** 37 35N 14 58 E
Belpre, *U.S.A.* ... **114 F5** 39 17N 81 34W
Belrain, *India* ... **69 E9** 28 23N 80 55 E
Belt, *U.S.A.* ... **108 C8** 47 23N 110 55W
Beltana, *Australia* ... **95 E2** 30 48 S 138 25 E
Belterra, *Brazil* ... **125 D8** 2 45 S 55 0W
Beltinci, *Slovenia* ... **41 B13** 46 37N 16 20 E
Belton, *U.S.A.* ... **113 K6** 31 3N 97 28W
Belton L., *U.S.A.* ... **113 K6** 31 8N 97 32W
Beltsy = Bălți, *Moldova* **29 C12** 47 48N 27 58 E
Belturbet, *Ireland* ... **12 B4** 54 6N 7 26W
Belukha, *Russia* ... **52 E9** 49 50N 86 50 E
Beluran, *Malaysia* ... **62 C5** 5 48N 117 35 E
Beluša, *Slovak Rep.* ... **27 B11** 49 5N 18 17 E
Belušić, *Serbia & M.* **44 C5** 43 50N 21 10 E
Belvedere Marittimo, *Italy* ... **43 C8** 39 37N 15 52 E
Belvès, *France* ... **20 D5** 44 46N 1 0 E
Belvidere, *Ill., U.S.A.* **112 D10** 42 15N 88 50W
Belvidere, *N.J., U.S.A.* **117 F9** 40 50N 75 5W
Belvis de la Jara, *Spain* **36 F6** 39 45N 4 57W
Belyando →, *Australia* **94 C4** 21 38 S 146 50 E
Belyy, *Russia* ... **32 E7** 55 49N 33 3 E
Belyy, Ostrov, *Russia* **52 B8** 73 30N 71 0 E
Belyy Yar, *Russia* ... **52 D9** 58 26N 84 39 E
Belz, *Ukraine* ... **31 H10** 50 23N 24 1 E
Belżec, *Poland* ... **31 H10** 50 23N 23 26 E
Belzig, *Germany* ... **24 C8** 52 8N 12 35 E
Belzoni, *U.S.A.* ... **113 J9** 33 11N 90 29W
Bełżyce, *Poland* ... **31 G9** 51 11N 22 17 E
Bemaraha, Lembalemban' i, *Madag.* **89 B7** 18 40 S 44 45 E
Bemarivo, *Madag.* **89 C7** 21 45 S 44 45 E
Bemarivo →, *Antsiranana, Madag.* **89 A9** 14 9 S 50 9 E
Bemarivo →, *Mahajanga, Madag.* **89 B8** 15 27 S 47 40 E
Bemavo, *Madag.* **89 C8** 21 33 S 45 25 E
Bembéréke, *Benin* **83 C5** 10 11N 2 43 E
Bembesi, *Zimbabwe* **87 G2** 20 0 S 28 58 E
Bembesi →, *Zimbabwe* **87 F2** 18 57 S 27 47 E
Bembézar →, *Spain* **37 H5** 37 45 S 5 13W
Bembibre, *Spain* **36 C4** 42 37N 6 25W
Bemetara, *India* **69 J9** 21 42N 81 32 E
Bemidji, *U.S.A.* **112 B7** 47 28N 94 53W
Bemolanga, *Madag.* **89 B8** 17 44 S 45 6 E
Ben, *Iran* **71 C6** 32 32N 50 45 E
Ben Cruachan, *U.K.* **13 E3** 56 26N 5 8W
Ben Dearg, *U.K.* **13 D4** 57 47N 4 56W
Ben En △, *Vietnam* **64 C5** 19 37N 105 30 E
Ben Hope, *U.K.* **13 C4** 58 25N 4 36W
Ben Lawers, *U.K.* **13 E4** 56 32N 4 14W
Ben Lomond, *N.S.W., Australia* **95 E5** 30 1 S 151 43 E
Ben Lomond, *Tas., Australia* **95 G4** 41 38 S 147 42 E
Ben Lomond, *U.K.* **13 E4** 56 11N 4 38W
Ben Lomond △, *Australia* **95 G4** 41 33 S 147 39 E
Ben Luc, *Vietnam* **65 G6** 10 39N 106 29 E
Ben Macdhui, *U.K.* **13 D5** 57 4N 3 40W
Ben Mhor, *U.K.* **13 D1** 57 15N 7 18W
Ben More, *Arg. & Bute, U.K.* **13 E2** 56 26N 6 1W
Ben More, *Stirl., U.K.* **13 E4** 56 23N 4 32W
Ben More Assynt, *U.K.* **13 C4** 58 8N 4 52W
Ben Nevis, *U.K.* **13 E3** 56 48N 5 1W
Ben Quang, *Vietnam* **64 D6** 17 3N 106 55 E
Ben Vorlich, *U.K.* **13 E4** 56 21N 4 14W
Ben Wyvis, *U.K.* **13 D4** 57 40N 4 35W
Bena, *Nigeria* **83 C6** 11 20N 5 50 E
Benalla, *Australia* **95 F4** 36 30 S 146 0 E
Benalmádena, *Spain* **37 J6** 36 36N 4 34W
Benares = Varanasi, *India* **69 G10** 25 22N 83 0 E
Bénat, C., *France* **21 E10** 43 5N 6 22 E
Benavente, *Portugal* **37 G2** 38 59N 8 49W
Benavente, *Spain* **36 C5** 42 2N 5 43W
Benavides, *U.S.A.* **113 M5** 27 36N 98 25W
Benavides de Órbigo, *Spain* **36 C5** 42 30N 5 54W
Benbecula, *U.K.* **13 D1** 57 26N 7 21W
Benbonyathe, *Australia* **95 E2** 30 25 S 139 11 E
Bend, *U.S.A.* **108 D3** 44 4N 121 19W
Bender Beila, *Somali Rep.* **75 F5** 9 30N 50 48 E
Bendery = Tighina, *Moldova* **29 D14** 46 50N 29 30 E
Bendigo, *Australia* **95 F3** 36 40 S 144 15 E
Bendorf, *Germany* **24 E3** 50 25N 7 35 E
Bene Beraq, *Israel* **74 C3** 32 6N 34 51 E
Bénéna, *Mali* **82 C4** 13 9N 4 17W
Benenitra, *Madag.* **89 C8** 23 27 S 45 5 E
Benešov, *Czech Rep.* **26 B7** 49 46N 14 41 E
Benevento, *Italy* **43 A7** 41 8N 14 45 E
Benfeld, *France* **19 D14** 48 22N 7 34 E
Benga, *Mozam.* **87 F3** 16 11 S 33 40 E
Bengal, Bay of, *Ind. Oc.* **67 M17** 15 0N 90 0 E
Bengalūru = Bangalore, *India* **66 N10** 12 59N 77 40 E
Bengbis, *Cameroon* **83 E7** 3 27N 12 36 E
Bengbu, *China* **57 H9** 32 58N 117 20 E
Benghazi = Banghāzī, *Libya* **79 B10** 32 11N 20 3 E
Bengkalis, *Indonesia* **62 D2** 1 30N 102 10 E
Bengkulu, *Indonesia* **62 E2** 3 50 S 102 12 E
Bengkulu □, *Indonesia* **62 E2** 3 48 S 102 16 E
Bengough, *Canada* **103 D7** 49 25N 105 10W
Benguela, *Angola* **85 G2** 12 37 S 13 25 E
Benguérua, I., *Mozam.* **89 C6** 21 58 S 35 28 E
Benha, *Egypt* **80 H7** 30 26N 31 8 E

Beni, Dem. Rep. of the Congo 86 B2 0 30N 29 27 E
Beni →, Bolivia 124 F5 10 23 S 65 24W
Beni Mazâr, Egypt 80 B3 28 32N 30 44 E
Beni Mellal, Morocco 78 B4 32 21N 6 21W
Beni Suef, Egypt 80 J7 29 5N 31 6 E
Beniah L., Canada 102 A6 63 23N 112 17W
Benicarló, Spain 38 E5 40 23N 0 23 E
Benicàssim, Spain 38 E5 40 3N 0 4 E
Benicia, U.S.A. 110 G4 38 3N 122 9W
Benidorm, Spain 39 G4 38 33N 0 9W
Benin ■, Africa 83 D5 10 0N 2 0 E
Benin →, Nigeria 83 D6 5 45N 5 0 E
Benin, Bight of, W. Afr. 83 E5 5 0N 3 0 E
Benin City, Nigeria 83 D6 6 20N 5 31 E
Benisa, Spain 39 G5 38 43N 0 3 E
Benitses, Greece 49 A3 39 32N 19 55 E
Benjamin Aceval, Paraguay 126 A4 24 58 S 57 34W
Benjamin Constant, Brazil 124 D4 4 40 S 70 15W
Benjamin Hill, Mexico 118 A2 30 10N 111 10W
Benkelman, U.S.A. 112 E4 40 3N 101 32W
Benkovac, Croatia 41 D12 44 2N 15 37 E
Bennett, Canada 102 B2 59 56N 134 53W
Bennetta, Ostrov, Russia 53 B15 76 21N 148 56 E
Bennettsville, U.S.A. 115 H6 34 37N 79 41W
Bennichchâb, Mauritania 82 B1 19 32N 15 12W
Bennington, N.H., U.S.A. 117 D11 43 0N 71 55W
Bennington, Vt., U.S.A. 117 D11 42 53N 73 12W
Bénodet, France 18 E2 47 53N 4 7W
Benoni, S. Africa 89 D4 26 11 S 28 18 E
Benque Viejo, Belize 119 D7 17 5N 89 8W
Bensheim, Germany 25 F4 49 40N 8 38 E
Benson, Ariz., U.S.A. 109 L8 31 58N 110 18W
Benson, Minn., U.S.A. 112 C7 45 19N 95 36W
Bent, Iran 71 E8 26 20N 59 31 E
Benteng, Indonesia 63 F6 6 10 S 120 30 E
Bentinck I., Australia 94 B2 17 3 S 139 35 E
Bentiu, Sudan 81 F2 9 10N 29 55 E
Bento Gonçalves, Brazil 127 B5 29 10 S 51 31W
Benton, Ark., U.S.A. 113 H8 34 34N 92 35W
Benton, Calif., U.S.A. 110 H8 37 48N 118 32W
Benton, Ill., U.S.A. 112 G10 38 0N 88 55W
Benton, Pa., U.S.A. 117 E8 41 12N 76 23W
Benton Harbor, U.S.A. 114 D2 42 6N 86 27W
Bentong, Malaysia 65 L3 3 31N 101 55 E
Bentonville, U.S.A. 113 G7 36 22N 94 13W
Bentu Liben, Ethiopia 81 F4 8 32N 38 21 E
Benue □, Nigeria 83 D6 7 20N 8 45 E
Benue →, Nigeria 83 D6 7 48N 6 46 E
Benxi, China 57 D12 41 20N 123 48 E
Beo, Indonesia 63 D7 4 25N 126 50 E
Beograd, Serbia & M. 44 B4 44 50N 20 37 E
Beograd ✈ (BEG), Serbia & M. 44 C4 44 49N 20 17 E
Beoumi, Ivory C. 82 D3 7 9N 5 28W
Bepan Jiang →, China 58 E6 24 55N 106 5 E
Beppu, Japan 55 H5 33 15N 131 30 E
Beqaa Valley = Al Biqâ, Lebanon 74 A5 34 10N 36 10 E
Ber Mota, India 68 H3 23 27N 68 34 E
Berach →, India 68 G6 25 15N 75 2 E
Beraketa, Madag. 89 C7 23 7 S 44 25 E
Berane, Serbia & M. 44 D3 42 51N 19 52 E
Berat, Albania 44 F3 40 43N 19 59 E
Berau, Teluk, Indonesia 63 E8 3 30 S 132 30 E
Beravina, Madag. 89 B8 18 10 S 45 14 E
Berber, Sudan 80 D3 18 0N 34 0 E
Berbera, Somali Rep. 75 E4 10 30N 45 2 E
Berbérati, C.A.R. 84 D3 4 15N 15 40 E
Berbice →, Guyana 124 B7 6 20N 57 32W
Berceto, Italy 40 D6 44 31N 9 51 E
Berchidda, Italy 42 B2 40 47N 9 10 E
Berchtesgaden, Germany 25 H8 47 38N 13 0 E
Berchtesgaden △, Germany 25 H8 47 34N 12 55 E
Berck, France 19 B8 50 25N 1 36 E
Berdichev = Berdychiv, Ukraine 33 H5 49 57N 28 30 E
Berdsk, Russia 52 D9 54 47N 83 2 E
Berdyansk, Ukraine 33 J9 46 45N 36 50 E
Berdychiv, Ukraine 33 H5 49 57N 28 30 E
Berea, U.S.A. 114 G3 37 34N 84 17W
Berebere, Indonesia 63 D7 2 25N 128 45 E
Bereda, Somali Rep. 75 E5 11 45N 51 0 E
Berehomet, Ukraine 29 B10 48 10N 25 19 E
Berehove, Ukraine 28 B7 48 15N 22 35 E
Berekum, Ghana 82 D4 7 29N 2 34W
Berenice, Egypt 80 C4 24 2N 35 25 E
Berens →, Canada 103 C9 52 25N 97 2W
Berens I., Canada 103 C9 52 18N 97 18W
Berens River, Canada 103 C9 52 25N 97 0W
Beresford, U.S.A. 112 D6 43 5N 96 47W
Berestechko, Ukraine 33 G3 50 22N 25 5 E
Bereşti, Romania 29 D12 46 6N 27 50 E
Beretău →, Romania 28 C6 47 10N 21 50 E
Berettyó →, Hungary 28 D6 46 59N 21 7 E
Berettyóújfalu, Hungary 28 C6 47 13N 21 33 E
Berevo, Mahajanga, Madag. 89 B7 17 14 S 44 17 E
Berevo, Toliara, Madag. 89 B7 19 44 S 44 58 E
Bereza = Byaroza, Belarus 33 F3 52 31N 24 51 E
Berezhany, Ukraine 33 H3 49 26N 24 58 E
Berezina = Byarezina →, Belarus 33 F6 52 33N 30 14 E
Berezivka, Ukraine 33 J6 47 14N 30 55 E
Berezna, Ukraine 33 G6 51 35N 31 46 E
Bereznik, Russia 52 C5 62 51N 42 40 E
Berezniki, Russia 52 C5 59 24N 56 46 E
Berezovo, Russia 52 C7 64 0N 65 0 E
Berezyne, Ukraine 29 D14 46 14N 29 12 E
Berga, Spain 38 C6 42 6N 1 48 E
Berga, Sweden 11 G10 57 14N 16 3 E
Bergama, Turkey 47 B9 39 8N 27 15 E
Bérgamo, Italy 40 C6 45 41N 9 43 E
Bergara, Spain 38 B2 43 6N 2 30W
Bergby, Sweden 10 D11 60 57N 17 2 E
Bergedorf, Germany 24 B6 53 28N 10 6 E
Bergeforsen, Sweden 10 B11 62 32N 17 23 E
Bergen, Mecklenburg-Vorpommern, Germany 24 A9 54 25N 13 25 E
Bergen, Niedersachsen, Germany 24 C5 52 49N 9 58 E
Bergen, Neths. 17 B4 52 40N 4 43 E
Bergen, Norway 9 F11 60 20N 5 20 E
Bergen op Zoom, Neths. 17 C4 51 28N 4 18 E
Bergerac, France 20 D4 44 51N 0 30 E
Bergheim, Germany 24 E2 50 57N 6 38 E
Bergholz, U.S.A. 116 F4 40 31N 80 53W

Bergisch Gladbach, Germany 17 D7 50 59N 7 8 E
Bergisches Land △, Germany 24 E3 51 0N 7 30 E
Bergkamen, Germany 24 D3 51 37N 7 38 E
Bergkvara, Sweden 11 H10 56 23N 16 5 E
Bergshamra, Sweden 10 E12 59 38N 18 37 E
Bergsjö, Sweden 10 C11 61 59N 17 3 E
Bergstrasse-Odenwald △, Germany 25 F1 49 45N 5 55 E
Bergues, France 19 B9 50 58N 2 24 E
Bergviken, Sweden 10 C10 61 15N 16 40 E
Bergville, S. Africa 89 D4 28 52 S 29 18 E
Berhala, Selat, Indonesia 62 E2 1 0 S 104 15 E
Berhampore = Baharampur, India 69 G13 24 2N 88 27 E
Berhampur = Brahmapur, India 67 K14 19 15N 84 54 E
Berheci →, Romania 29 E12 45 58N 27 28 E
Bering Sea, Pac. Oc. 100 C1 58 0N 171 0 E
Bering Strait, Pac. Oc. 100 B3 65 30N 169 0W
Beringovskiy, Russia 53 C18 63 3N 179 19 E
Berisso, Argentina 126 C4 34 56 S 57 50W
Berja, Spain 37 J8 36 50N 2 56W
Berkeley, U.S.A. 110 H4 37 52N 122 16W
Berkner I., Antarctica 5 D18 79 30 S 50 0W
Berkovitsa, Bulgaria 44 C7 43 16N 23 8 E
Berkshire, U.S.A. 117 D8 42 19N 76 11W
Berkshire Downs, U.K. 15 F6 51 33N 1 29W
Berlanga, Spain 37 G5 38 17N 5 50W
Berlenga, I., Portugal 37 F1 39 25N 9 30W
Berlin, Germany 24 C9 52 30N 13 25 E
Berlin, Md., U.S.A. 114 F8 38 20N 75 13W
Berlin, N.H., U.S.A. 117 B13 44 28N 71 11W
Berlin, N.Y., U.S.A. 117 D11 42 42N 73 23W
Berlin, Wis., U.S.A. 114 D1 43 58N 88 57W
Berlin □, Germany 24 C9 52 30N 13 20 E
Berlin L., U.S.A. 116 E4 41 3N 81 0W
Berlin Tegel ✈ (TXL), Germany 24 C9 52 35N 13 14 E
Bermeja, Sierra, Spain 37 J5 36 30N 5 11W
Bermejo →, Formosa, Argentina 126 B4 26 51 S 58 23W
Bermejo →, San Juan, Argentina 126 C2 32 30 S 67 30W
Bermen, L., Canada 105 B6 53 35N 68 55W
Bermeo, Spain 38 B2 43 25N 2 47W
Bermillo de Sayago, Spain 36 D4 41 22N 6 8W
Bermuda ☒, Atl. Oc. 98 F13 32 45N 65 0W
Bern, Switz. 25 J3 46 57N 7 28 E
Bern □, Switz. 25 J3 46 45N 7 40 E
Bernalda, Italy 43 B9 40 24N 16 41 E
Bernalillo, U.S.A. 109 J10 35 18N 106 33W
Bernardo de Irigoyen, Argentina 127 B5 26 15 S 53 40W
Bernardo O'Higgins □, Chile 126 C1 34 15 S 70 45W
Bernardsville, U.S.A. 117 F10 40 43N 74 34W
Bernasconi, Argentina 126 D3 37 55 S 63 44W
Bernau, Bayern, Germany 25 H8 47 47N 12 22 E
Bernau, Brandenburg, Germany 24 C9 52 40N 13 35 E
Bernay, France 18 C7 49 5N 0 35 E
Bernburg, Germany 24 D7 51 47N 11 44 E
Berndorf, Austria 26 D9 47 59N 16 1 E
Berne = Bern, Switz. 25 J3 46 57N 7 28 E
Berne = Bern □, Switz. 25 J3 46 45N 7 40 E
Berner Alpen, Switz. 25 J3 46 27N 7 35 E
Berneray, U.K. 13 D1 57 43N 7 11W
Bernier I., Australia 93 D1 24 50 S 113 12 E
Bernina, Piz, Switz. 25 J5 46 20N 9 54 E
Bernkastel-Kues, Germany 25 F3 49 55N 7 3 E
Beroroha, Madag. 89 C8 21 40 S 45 10 E
Bérouabay, Benin 83 C5 10 34N 2 46 E
Beroun, Czech Rep. 26 B7 49 57N 14 5 E
Berounka →, Czech Rep. 26 B7 50 0N 14 22 E
Berovo, Macedonia 44 E6 41 38N 22 51 E
Berre, Étang de, France 21 E9 43 27N 5 5 E
Berre-l'Étang, France 21 E9 43 27N 5 10 E
Berri, Australia 95 E3 34 14 S 140 35 E
Berriane, Algeria 78 B6 32 50N 3 46 E
Berry, Australia 95 E5 34 46 S 150 43 E
Berry, France 19 F8 46 50N 2 0 E
Berry Is., Bahamas 120 A4 25 40N 77 50W
Berryessa L., U.S.A. 110 G4 38 31N 122 6W
Berryville, U.S.A. 113 G8 36 22N 93 34W
Berseba, Namibia 88 D2 26 0 S 17 46 E
Bersenbrück, Germany 24 C3 52 34N 7 56 E
Bershad, Ukraine 29 B14 48 22N 29 31 E
Berthold, U.S.A. 112 A4 48 19N 101 44W
Berthoud, U.S.A. 112 E2 40 19N 105 5W
Bertincourt, France 19 B9 50 5N 2 58 E
Bertoua, Cameroon 84 D2 4 30N 13 45 E
Bertraghboy B., Ireland 12 C2 53 22N 9 54W
Berwick, U.S.A. 117 E8 41 3N 76 14W
Berwick-upon-Tweed, U.K. 14 B6 55 46N 2 0W
Berwyn Mts., U.K. 14 E4 52 54N 3 26W
Beryslav, Ukraine 33 J7 46 50N 33 30 E
Berzasca, Romania 28 F6 44 39N 21 58 E
Berzence, Hungary 28 D7 46 12N 17 11 E
Besal, Pakistan 69 B5 35 4N 73 56 E
Besalampy, Madag. 89 B7 16 43 S 44 29 E
Besançon, France 19 E13 47 15N 6 2 E
Besar, Indonesia 62 E5 2 40 S 116 0 E
Beshenkovichi, Belarus 32 E5 55 2N 29 29 E
Beška, Serbia & M. 28 E5 45 8N 20 6 E
Beslan, Russia 35 J7 43 15N 44 28 E
Besna Kobila, Serbia & M. 44 D6 42 31N 22 10 E
Besnard L., Canada 103 B7 55 25N 106 0W
Besni, Turkey 70 B3 37 41N 37 52 E
Besor, N. →, Egypt 74 D3 31 28N 34 22 E
Bessarabiya, Moldova 33 J5 47 0N 28 10 E
Bessarabka = Basarabeasca, Moldova 29 D13 46 21N 28 58 E
Bessèges, France 21 D8 44 18N 4 8 E
Bessemer, Ala., U.S.A. 115 J2 33 24N 86 58W
Bessemer, Mich., U.S.A. 112 B9 46 29N 90 3W
Bessemer, Pa., U.S.A. 116 F4 40 59N 80 30W
Bessin, France 18 C6 49 18N 1 0W
Bessines-sur-Gartempe, France 20 B5 46 6N 1 22 E
Beswick, Australia 92 B5 14 34 S 132 53 E
Bet She'an, Israel 74 C4 32 30N 35 30 E
Bet Shemesh, Israel 74 D3 31 44N 35 0 E
Betafo, Madag. 89 B8 19 50 S 46 51 E
Betancuria, Canary Is. 48 F5 28 25N 14 3W
Betanzos, Spain 36 B2 43 15N 8 12W
Bétaré Oya, Cameroon 84 C2 5 40N 14 5 E
Betatao, Madag. 89 B8 18 11 S 47 52 E

Bétera, Spain 39 F4 39 35N 0 28W
Bétérou, Benin 83 D5 9 12N 2 16 E
Bethal, S. Africa 89 D4 26 27 S 29 28 E
Bethanien, Namibia 88 D2 26 31 S 17 8 E
Bethany, Canada 116 B6 44 11N 78 34W
Bethany, U.S.A. 112 E7 40 16N 94 2W
Bethel, Alaska, U.S.A. 100 B3 60 48N 161 45W
Bethel, Conn., U.S.A. 117 E11 41 22N 73 25W
Bethel, Maine, U.S.A. 117 B14 44 25N 70 47W
Bethel, Vt., U.S.A. 117 C12 43 50N 72 38W
Bethel Park, U.S.A. 116 F4 40 20N 80 1W
Bethlehem = Bayt Lahm, West Bank 74 D4 31 43N 35 12 E
Bethlehem, S. Africa 89 D4 28 14 S 28 18 E
Bethlehem, U.S.A. 117 F9 40 37N 75 23W
Bethulie, S. Africa 88 E4 30 30 S 25 59 E
Béthune, France 19 B9 50 30N 2 38 E
Béthune →, France 18 C8 49 53N 1 4 E
Betioky, Madag. 89 C7 23 48 S 44 20 E
Betong, Thailand 65 K3 5 45N 101 5 E
Betoota, Australia 94 D3 25 45 S 140 42 E
Betor, Ethiopia 81 E4 11 37N 39 2 E
Betroka, Madag. 89 C8 23 16 S 46 0 E
Betsiamites, Canada 105 C6 48 56N 68 40W
Betsiamites →, Canada 105 C6 48 56N 68 38W
Betsiboka →, Madag. 89 B8 16 3 S 46 36 E
Bettendorf, U.S.A. 112 E9 41 32N 90 30W
Bettiah, India 69 F11 26 48N 84 33 E
Bettna, Sweden 11 F10 58 55N 16 38 E
Béttola, Italy 40 D6 44 47N 9 36 E
Betul, India 66 J10 21 58N 77 59 E
Betung, Malaysia 62 D4 1 24N 111 31 E
Betws-y-Coed, U.K. 14 D4 53 5N 3 48W
Betxi, Spain 38 F4 39 56N 0 12W
Betzdorf, Germany 24 E3 50 46N 7 52 E
Beuil, France 21 D10 44 6N 6 59 E
Beulah, Mich., U.S.A. 114 C2 44 38N 86 6W
Beulah, N. Dak., U.S.A. 112 B4 47 16N 101 47W
Beuvron →, France 18 E8 47 29N 1 15 E
Beveren, Belgium 17 C4 51 12N 4 16 E
Beverley, Australia 93 F2 32 9 S 116 56 E
Beverley, U.K. 14 D7 53 51N 0 26W
Beverley Hills, U.S.A. 115 L4 28 56N 82 28W
Beverly, U.S.A. 117 D14 42 33N 70 53W
Beverly Hills, U.S.A. 111 L8 34 4N 118 25W
Beverungen, Germany 24 D5 51 59N 9 22 E
Bevoalavo, Madag. 89 D7 25 13 S 45 26 E
Bewas →, India 69 H8 23 59N 79 21 E
Bex, Switz. 25 J3 46 15N 7 1 E
Bexhill, U.K. 15 G8 50 51N 0 29 E
Bey Dağları, Turkey 47 E12 36 38N 30 29 E
Beyānlū, Iran 70 C5 36 0N 47 51 E
Beyazköy, Turkey 45 E11 41 21N 27 42 E
Beyçayırı, Turkey 45 F10 40 15N 26 55 E
Beydağ, Turkey 47 C10 38 5N 28 13 E
Beyeğaç, Turkey 47 D10 37 14N 28 53 E
Beyin, Ghana 82 D4 5 1N 2 41W
Beykoz, Turkey 45 E13 41 8N 29 7 E
Beyla, Guinea 82 D3 8 30N 8 38W
Beynat, France 20 C5 45 8N 1 44 E
Beyneu, Kazakhstan 52 E6 45 18N 55 9 E
Beyoba, Turkey 47 C9 38 48N 27 47 E
Beyoğlu, Turkey 45 E12 41 2N 28 59 E
Beypazarı, Turkey 72 B4 40 10N 31 56 E
Beyşehir, Turkey 72 D4 37 41N 31 43 E
Beyşehir Gölü, Turkey 70 B1 37 41N 31 33 E
Beytüşşebap, Turkey 73 D10 37 35N 43 10 E
Bezdan, Serbia & M. 28 E3 45 50N 18 57 E
Bezhetsk, Russia 32 D9 57 47N 36 39 E
Béziers, France 20 E7 43 20N 3 12 E
Bezwada = Vijayawada, India 67 L12 16 31N 80 39 E
Bhabua, India 69 G10 25 3N 83 37 E
Bhachau, India 66 H7 23 20N 70 16 E
Bhadar →, Gujarat, India 68 H5 22 17N 72 20 E
Bhadar →, Gujarat, India 68 J3 21 27N 69 47 E
Bhadarwah, India 69 C6 32 58N 75 46 E
Bhadgaon = Bhaktapur, Nepal 69 F11 27 38N 85 24 E
Bhadohi, India 69 G10 25 25N 82 34 E
Bhadra, India 68 E6 29 8N 75 14 E
Bhadrakh, India 67 J15 21 10N 86 30 E
Bhadran, India 68 H5 22 19N 72 6 E
Bhadravati, India 66 N9 13 49N 75 40 E
Bhag, Pakistan 68 E2 29 2N 67 49 E
Bhagalpur, India 69 G12 25 10N 87 0 E
Bhagirathi →, Uttaranchal, India 69 D8 30 8N 78 35 E
Bhagirathi →, W. Bengal, India 69 H13 23 25N 88 23 E
Bhakkar, Pakistan 68 D4 31 40N 71 5 E
Bhakra Dam, India 68 D7 31 30N 76 45 E
Bhaktapur, Nepal 69 F11 27 38N 85 24 E
Bhamo, Burma 67 G20 24 15N 97 15 E
Bhandara, India 66 J11 21 5N 79 42 E
Bhanpura, India 68 G6 24 31N 75 44 E
Bhanrer Ra., India 69 H8 23 40N 79 45 E
Bhaptiahi, India 69 F12 26 19N 86 44 E
Bharat = India ■, Asia 66 K11 20 0N 78 0 E
Bharatpur, Chhattisgarh, India 69 H9 23 44N 81 46 E
Bharatpur, Raj., India 68 F7 27 15N 77 30 E
Bharno, India 69 H11 23 14N 84 53 E
Bharuch, India 66 J8 21 47N 73 0 E
Bhatinda, India 68 D6 30 15N 74 57 E
Bhatpara, India 69 H13 22 50N 88 25 E
Bhattu, India 68 E6 29 36N 75 19 E
Bhaun, Pakistan 68 C5 32 55N 72 40 E
Bhaunagar = Bhavnagar, India 68 J8 21 45N 72 10 E
Bhavnagar, India 68 J8 21 45N 72 10 E
Bhawari, India 68 G5 25 42N 73 4 E
Bhayavadar, India 68 J4 21 51N 70 15 E
Bhera, Pakistan 68 C5 32 29N 72 57 E
Bhikangaon, India 68 J6 21 52N 75 57 E
Bhilsa = Vidisha, India 68 H7 23 28N 77 53 E
Bhilwara, India 68 G6 25 25N 74 38 E
Bhima →, India 66 L10 16 25N 77 17 E
Bhimbar, Pakistan 69 C6 32 59N 74 3 E
Bhind, India 69 F8 26 30N 78 46 E
Bhinga, India 69 F9 27 43N 81 56 E
Bhinmal, India 68 G5 25 0N 72 15 E
Bhiwandi, India 66 K8 19 20N 73 0 E
Bhiwani, India 68 E7 28 50N 76 9 E
Bhogava →, India 68 H5 22 26N 72 20 E
Bhola, Bangla. 67 H17 22 45N 90 35 E
Bholari, Pakistan 68 G3 25 19N 68 1 E
Bhopal, India 68 H7 23 20N 77 30 E
Bhubaneshwar, India 67 J14 20 15N 85 50 E
Bhuj, India 68 H3 23 15N 69 49 E
Bhumiphol Res., Thailand 64 D2 17 20N 98 40 E
Bhusawal, India 66 J9 21 3N 75 46 E
Bhutan ■, Asia 67 F17 27 25N 90 30 E

Biafra, B. of = Bonny, Bight of, Africa 83 E6 3 30N 9 20 E
Biak, Indonesia 63 E9 1 10 S 136 6 E
Biała, Poland 31 H4 50 24N 17 40 E
Biała →, Poland 30 E2 26 31 S 17 8 E
Biała Piska, Poland 30 E9 53 37N 22 5 E
Biała Podlaska, Poland 31 F10 52 4N 23 6 E
Biała Rawska, Poland 31 G7 51 48N 20 29 E
Białogard, Poland 30 D2 54 2N 15 58 E
Białowieski △, Poland 31 F10 52 43N 23 50 E
Białobrzegi, Poland 31 G7 51 39N 20 57 E
Białogard, Poland 30 D2 54 2N 15 58 E
Białystok, Poland 31 E10 53 10N 23 10 E
Biancavilla, Italy 43 E7 37 38N 14 52 E
Bianco, Italy 43 D9 38 5N 16 9 E
Biankouma, Ivory C. 82 D3 7 50N 7 40W
Biaora, India 68 H7 23 56N 76 56 E
Biaro, Indonesia 63 D7 2 5N 125 26 E
Biarritz, France 20 E2 43 29N 1 33W
Bias, Indonesia 63 J18 8 24 S 115 36 E
Biasca, Switz. 25 J4 46 22N 8 58 E
Biba, Egypt 80 J7 28 55N 31 0 E
Bibai, Japan 54 C10 43 19N 141 52 E
Bibbiena, Italy 41 E8 43 42N 11 49 E
Bibby I., Canada 103 A10 61 55N 93 0W
Bibel, Spain 36 C3 42 7N 7 13W
Biberach, Germany 25 G5 48 5N 9 47 E
Bibiani, Ghana 82 D4 6 30N 2 8W
Bibungwa, Dem. Rep. of the Congo 86 C2 2 40 S 28 15 E
Bicaj, Albania 44 E4 41 59N 20 25 E
Bicaz, Romania 29 D11 46 53N 26 5 E
Bicazu Ardelean, Romania 29 D10 46 51N 25 56 E
Bíccari, Italy 43 A8 41 23N 15 12 E
Bicester, U.K. 15 F6 51 54N 1 9W
Bichena, Ethiopia 81 E4 10 28N 38 10 E
Bicheno, Australia 95 G4 41 52 S 148 18 E
Bichia, India 69 H9 22 5N 80 42 E
Bichvinta, Georgia 35 J5 43 9N 40 21 E
Bickerton I., Australia 94 A2 13 45 S 136 10 E
Bicske, Hungary 28 C3 47 29N 18 38 E
Bida, Nigeria 83 D6 9 3N 5 58 E
Bidar, India 66 L10 17 55N 77 35 E
Biddeford, U.S.A. 113 D10 43 30N 70 28W
Biddwara, Ethiopia 81 F4 5 11N 38 34 E
Bideford, U.K. 15 F3 51 1N 4 13W
Bideford Bay, U.K. 15 F3 51 5N 4 20W
Bidhuna, India 69 F8 26 49N 79 31 E
Bidor, Malaysia 65 K3 4 6N 101 15 E
Bie, Indonesia 10 E10 59 5N 16 12 E
Bié, Planalto de, Angola 85 G3 12 0 S 16 0 E
Bieber, U.S.A. 108 F3 41 7N 121 8W
Biebrza →, Poland 31 E9 53 13N 22 25 E
Biebrzański △, Poland 30 E9 53 36N 22 45 E
Biecz, Poland 31 J8 49 44N 21 15 E
Biel, Switz. 25 H3 47 8N 7 14 E
Bielawa, Poland 31 H3 50 43N 16 37 E
Bielefeld, Germany 24 C4 52 1N 8 33 E
Bielersee, Switz. 25 H3 47 6N 7 5 E
Biella, Italy 40 C5 45 34N 8 3 E
Bielsk Podlaski, Poland 31 F10 52 47N 23 12 E
Bielsko-Biała, Poland 31 J6 49 50N 19 2 E
Bien Hoa, Vietnam 65 G6 10 57N 106 49 E
Bienne = Biel, Switz. 25 H3 47 8N 7 14 E
Bienvenida, Spain 37 G4 38 18N 6 12W
Bienville, L., Canada 104 A5 55 5N 72 40W
Bierné, France 18 E6 47 48N 0 33W
Bierun, Poland 31 H6 50 6N 19 6 E
Bierutów, Poland 31 G4 51 7N 17 32 E
Biescas, Spain 38 C4 42 37N 0 20W
Biese →, Germany 24 C7 52 53N 11 46 E
Biesiesfontein, S. Africa 88 E2 30 57 S 17 58 E
Bieszczadzki △, Poland 31 J9 49 5N 22 43 E
Bietigheim-Bissingen, Germany 25 G5 48 58N 9 8 E
Bieżuń, Poland 31 F6 52 58N 19 54 E
Biferno →, Italy 41 G12 41 59N 15 2 E
Big →, Canada 105 B8 54 50N 58 55W
Big B. = Big, Canada 105 A7 55 43N 60 35W
Big Bear City, U.S.A. 111 L10 34 16N 116 51W
Big Bear Lake, U.S.A. 111 L10 34 15N 116 56W
Big Belt Mts., U.S.A. 108 C8 46 30N 111 25W
Big Bend, Swaziland 89 D5 26 50 S 31 58 E
Big Bend △, U.S.A. 113 L3 29 20N 103 5W
Big Black →, U.S.A. 113 K9 32 3N 91 4W
Big Blue →, U.S.A. 112 F6 39 35N 96 34W
Big Creek, U.S.A. 110 H7 37 11N 119 14W
Big Cypress △, U.S.A. 115 M5 26 0N 81 10W
Big Cypress Swamp, U.S.A. 115 M5 26 15N 81 30W
Big Falls, U.S.A. 112 A8 48 12N 93 48W
Big Fork →, U.S.A. 112 A8 48 31N 93 43W
Big Horn Mts. = Bighorn Mts., U.S.A. 108 D10 44 30N 107 30W
Big I., Canada 102 A5 61 7N 116 45W
Big Lake, U.S.A. 113 K4 31 12N 101 28W
Big Moose, U.S.A. 117 C10 43 49N 74 58W
Big Muddy Cr. →, U.S.A. 112 A2 48 8N 104 36W
Big Pine, U.S.A. 110 H8 37 10N 118 17W
Big Piney, U.S.A. 108 E8 42 32N 110 7W
Big Rapids, U.S.A. 114 D3 43 42N 85 29W
Big Rideau L., Canada 117 B8 44 40N 76 15W
Big River, Canada 103 C7 53 50N 107 0W
Big Run, U.S.A. 116 F6 40 57N 78 55W
Big Sable Pt., U.S.A. 114 C2 44 3N 86 1W
Big Salmon →, Canada 102 A2 61 52N 134 55W
Big Sandy, U.S.A. 108 B8 48 11N 110 7W
Big Sandy →, U.S.A. 114 F4 38 25N 82 36W
Big Sandy Cr. →, U.S.A. 112 F3 38 7N 102 29W
Big Sioux →, U.S.A. 112 D6 42 29N 96 27W
Big Spring, U.S.A. 113 J4 32 15N 101 28W
Big Stone City, U.S.A. 112 C6 45 18N 96 28W
Big Stone Gap, U.S.A. 115 G4 36 52N 82 47W
Big Stone L., U.S.A. 112 C6 45 30N 96 35W
Big Sur, U.S.A. 110 J5 36 15N 121 48W
Big Timber, U.S.A. 108 D9 45 50N 109 57W
Big Trout L., Canada 104 B2 53 40N 90 0W
Big Trout Lake, Canada 104 B2 53 45N 90 0W
Biğa, Turkey 45 F11 40 13N 27 14 E
Biga →, Turkey 45 F11 40 20N 27 14 E
Bigadiç, Turkey 47 B10 39 22N 28 7 E
Biganos, France 20 D3 44 39N 0 59W
Biggar, Canada 103 C7 52 4N 108 0W
Biggar, U.K. 13 F5 55 38N 3 32W
Bigge I., Australia 92 B4 14 35 S 125 10 E
Biggenden, Australia 95 D5 25 31 S 152 4 E
Biggleswade, U.K. 15 E7 52 5N 0 14W
Bighorn, U.S.A. 108 C10 46 10N 107 27W
Bighorn →, U.S.A. 108 C10 46 10N 107 28W

Bighorn Canyon △, U.S.A. 108 D9 45 10N 108 0W
Bighorn L., U.S.A. 108 D9 44 55N 108 15W
Bighorn Mts., U.S.A. 108 D10 44 30N 107 30W
Bignona, Senegal 82 C1 12 52N 16 14W
Bigorre, France 20 E4 43 10N 0 5 E
Bigstone L., Canada 103 C9 53 42N 95 44W
Biguglia, Étang de, France 21 F13 42 36N 9 29 E
Bigwa, Tanzania 86 D4 7 10 S 39 10 E
Bihać, Bos.-H. 41 D12 44 49N 15 57 E
Bihar, India 69 G11 25 5N 85 40 E
Bihar □, India 69 G12 25 0N 86 0 E
Biharamulo, Tanzania 86 C3 2 25 S 31 25 E
Biharamulo △, Tanzania 86 C3 2 15 S 31 20 E
Bihariganj, India 69 G12 25 44N 86 59 E
Biharkeresztes, Hungary 28 C6 47 8N 21 44 E
Bihor □, Romania 28 D7 47 0N 22 10 E
Bihor, Munţii, Romania 28 D7 46 29N 22 47 E
Bijagós, Arquipélago dos, Guinea-Biss. 82 C1 11 15N 16 10W
Bijaipur, India 68 F7 26 2N 77 20 E
Bijapur, Chhattisgarh, India 67 K12 18 50N 80 50 E
Bijapur, Karnataka, India 66 L9 16 50N 75 55 E
Bījār, Iran 70 C5 35 52N 47 35 E
Bijawar, India 69 G8 24 38N 79 30 E
Bijeljina, Bos.-H. 28 F4 44 46N 19 14 E
Bijelo Polje, Serbia & M. 44 C3 43 1N 19 45 E
Bijie, China 58 D5 27 20N 105 16 E
Bijnor, India 68 E8 29 27N 78 11 E
Bikaner, India 68 E5 28 2N 73 18 E
Bikapur, India 69 F10 26 30N 82 7 E
Bikeqi, China 56 D6 40 43N 111 20 E
Bikfayyā, Lebanon 74 B4 33 55N 35 41 E
Bikin, Russia 53 E14 46 50N 134 20 E
Bikin →, Russia 54 A7 46 51N 134 2 E
Bikini Atoll, Marshall Is. 96 F8 12 0N 167 30 E
Bikita, Zimbabwe 89 C5 20 6 S 31 41 E
Bikoué, Cameroon 83 E7 3 55N 11 50 E
Bila Tserkva, Ukraine 33 H6 49 45N 30 10 E
Bilanga, Burkina Faso 83 C4 12 40N 0 1W
Bilara, India 68 F5 26 14N 73 53 E
Bilaspur, Chhattisgarh, India 69 H10 22 2N 82 15 E
Bilaspur, Punjab, India 68 D7 31 19N 76 50 E
Bilāsuvar, Azerbaijan 73 C13 39 27N 48 32 E
Bilauk Taungdan, Thailand 64 F2 13 0N 99 0 E
Bilbao, Spain 38 B2 43 16N 2 56W
Bilbeis, Egypt 80 H7 30 25N 31 34 E
Bilbo = Bilbao, Spain 38 B2 43 16N 2 56W
Bilbor, Romania 29 C10 47 6N 25 30 E
Bilche-Zolote, Ukraine 29 B10 48 47N 25 53 E
Bilciureşti, Romania 29 F10 44 44N 25 48 E
Bildudalur, Iceland 8 D2 65 41N 23 36W
Bílé Karpaty, Europe 27 B11 49 5N 18 0 E
Bileća, Bos.-H. 44 D2 42 53N 18 27 E
Bilecik, Turkey 72 B4 40 5N 30 5 E
Bilgoraj, Poland 31 H9 50 33N 22 42 E
Bilgram, India 69 F9 27 11N 80 2 E
Bilhaur, India 69 F9 26 51N 80 5 E
Bilhorod-Dnistrovskyy, Ukraine 33 J6 46 11N 30 23 E
Bilibino, Russia 53 C17 68 3N 166 20 E
Bilibiza, Mozam. 87 E5 12 30 S 40 20 E
Bilisht, Albania 44 F5 40 37N 21 2 E
Billabong Roadhouse, Australia 93 E2 27 25 S 115 49 E
Billdal, Sweden 11 G5 57 35N 11 57 E
Billiluna, Australia 92 C4 19 37 S 127 41 E
Billings, U.S.A. 108 D9 45 47N 108 30W
Billiton Is. = Belitung, Indonesia 62 E3 3 10 S 107 50 E
Billsta, Sweden 10 A12 63 20N 18 28 E
Billund, Denmark 11 J3 55 44N 9 6 E
Bilma, Niger 79 E8 18 50N 13 30 E
Bilo Gora, Croatia 28 E2 45 53N 17 15 E
Biloela, Australia 94 C5 24 24 S 150 31 E
Bilohirsk, Ukraine 33 K8 45 3N 34 35 E
Bilopillya, Ukraine 33 G8 51 14N 34 14 E
Biloxi, U.S.A. 113 K10 30 24N 88 53W
Bilpa Morea Claypan, Australia 94 D3 25 0 S 140 0 E
Biltine, Chad 79 F10 14 40N 20 50 E
Bilyarsk, Russia 34 C10 54 58N 50 22 E
Bima, Indonesia 63 F5 8 22 S 118 49 E
Bimban, Egypt 80 C3 24 24N 32 54 E
Bimbila, Ghana 83 D5 8 54N 0 5 E
Bimini Is., Bahamas 120 A4 25 42N 79 25W
Bin Xian, Heilongjiang, China 57 B14 45 42N 127 32 E
Bin Xian, Shaanxi, China 56 G5 35 2N 108 4 E
Bin Yauri, Nigeria 83 C5 10 46N 4 45 E
Bina-Etawah, India 68 G8 24 13N 78 14 E
Bināb, Iran 71 B6 36 35N 48 41 E
Binalbagan, Phil. 61 F5 10 12N 122 50 E
Binalong, Australia 95 E4 34 40 S 148 39 E
Bīnālūd, Kūh-e, Iran 71 B8 36 30N 58 30 E
Binatang = Bintangor, Malaysia 62 D4 2 10N 111 40 E
Binche, Belgium 17 D4 50 26N 4 10 E
Binchuan, China 58 E3 25 42N 100 38 E
Binder, Chad 83 D7 9 56N 14 27 E
Bindki, India 69 F9 26 2N 80 36 E
Bindslev, Denmark 11 G4 57 35N 10 11 E
Bindura, Zimbabwe 87 F3 17 18 S 31 18 E
Binéfar, Spain 38 D5 41 51N 0 18 E
Bingara, Australia 95 D5 29 52 S 150 36 E
Bingen, Germany 25 F3 49 57N 7 55 E
Bingham, U.S.A. 115 C11 45 3N 69 53W
Binghamton, U.S.A. 117 D9 42 6N 75 55W
Bingöl, Turkey 70 B4 38 53N 40 29 E
Bingsjö, Sweden 10 C9 61 1N 15 39 E
Binh Dinh = An Nhon, Vietnam 64 F7 13 55N 109 7 E
Binh Khe, Vietnam 64 F7 13 57N 108 51 E
Binh Son, Vietnam 64 E7 15 20N 108 40 E
Binhai, China 57 G10 34 2N 119 49 E
Binic, France 18 D4 48 46N 2 50W
Binisatua, Spain 48 B11 39 50N 4 11 E
Binjai, Indonesia 62 D3 3 20N 98 30 E
Binji, Nigeria 83 C5 13 10N 4 55 E
Binnaway, Australia 95 E4 31 28 S 149 24 E
Binongko, Indonesia 63 F6 5 55 S 123 55 E
Binscarth, Canada 103 C8 50 37N 101 17W
Binshangul Gumuz □, Ethiopia 81 E4 10 0N 35 30 E
Bintan, Indonesia 62 D2 1 0N 104 0 E
Bintangor, Malaysia 62 D4 2 10N 111 40 E
Bintulu, Malaysia 62 D4 3 10N 113 0 E

Bintuni, Indonesia ..... **63 E8** 2 7 S 133 32 E
Binyang, China .... **58 F7** 23 12N 108 47 E
Binz, Germany .... **24 A9** 54 24N 13 35 E
Binzert = Bizerte,
  Tunisia .... **79 A7** 37 15N 9 50 E
Binzhou, China ...... **57 F10** 37 20N 118 2 E
Bío Bío □, Chile .... **126 D1** 37 35 S 72 0W
Biograd na Moru,
  Croatia .... **41 E12** 43 56N 15 29 E
Biogradska Gora △,
  Serbia & M. .... **44 D3** 42 55N 19 40 E
Bioko, Eq. Guin. .... **83 E6** 3 30N 8 40 E
Biokovo, Croatia ..... **41 E14** 43 23N 17 0 E
Bipindi, Cameroon .. **83 E7** 3 6N 10 30 E
Bir, India .... **66 K9** 19 4N 75 46 E
Bir, Ras, Djibouti ... **81 E5** 12 0N 43 20 E
Bîr Abu Hashim, Egypt **80 C3** 23 42N 34 6 E
Bîr Abu Minqar, Egypt **80 B2** 26 33N 27 33 E
Bîr Abu Muḥammad,
  Egypt .... **74 F3** 29 44N 34 14 E
Bi'r ad Dabbāghāt,
  Jordan .... **74 E4** 30 26N 35 32 E
Bîr Adal Deib, Sudan . **80 C4** 22 35N 36 10 E
Bi'r al Butayyihāt,
  Jordan .... **74 F4** 29 47N 35 20 E
Bi'r al Mārī, Jordan .. **74 E4** 30 4N 35 33 E
Bi'r al Qaṭṭār, Jordan . **74 F4** 29 47N 35 32 E
Bîr 'Asal, Egypt ..... **80 B3** 25 55N 34 20 E
Bîr Atrun, Sudan .... **80 D2** 18 15N 26 40 E
Bîr Beiḍa, Egypt .... **74 D2** 30 25N 34 29 E
Bîr Diqnash, Egypt .. **80 A2** 31 3N 25 23 E
Bîr el 'Abd, Egypt ... **74 D2** 31 2N 33 0 E
Bîr el Basur, Egypt .. **80 B2** 29 51N 25 49 E
Bîr el Biarât, Egypt .. **74 F3** 29 30N 34 43 E
Bîr el Duweidar, Egypt **74 E1** 30 56N 32 32 E
Bîr el Garârât, Egypt . **74 D2** 31 3N 33 34 E
Bîr el Gellaz, Egypt .. **80 A2** 30 50N 26 40 E
Bîr el Heisi, Egypt ... **74 F3** 29 22N 34 36 E
Bîr el Jafir, Egypt ... **74 E1** 30 50N 32 41 E
Bîr el Mâlḥi, Egypt .. **74 E2** 30 38N 33 19 E
Bîr el Shaqqa, Egypt . **80 A2** 30 54N 25 1 E
Bîr el Thamâda, Egypt **74 E2** 30 12N 33 27 E
Bîr Fuad, Egypt ..... **80 A2** 30 35N 26 28 E
Bîr Gebeil Ḥisn, Egypt **74 E2** 30 2N 33 18 E
Bi'r Ghaḍîr, Syria ... **74 A6** 34 6N 37 3 E
Bîr Haimur, Egypt ... **80 C3** 22 45N 33 40 E
Bîr Ḥasana, Egypt ... **74 E2** 30 29N 33 46 E
Bîr Hōöker, Egypt ... **80 H7** 30 22N 30 21 E
Bîr Kanayis, Egypt .. **80 C3** 24 59N 33 15 E
Bîr Kaseiba, Egypt .. **74 E2** 31 0N 33 17 E
Bîr Kerawein, Egypt . **80 B2** 27 10N 28 25 E
Bîr Lahfân, Egypt ... **74 E1** 30 44N 32 33 E
Bîr Madkûr, Egypt .. **74 E1** 30 2N 32 40 E
Bîr Maql, Egypt .... **80 C3** 23 7N 33 40 E
Bîr Mîneiga, Sudan .. **80 C4** 22 47N 35 12 E
Bîr Misaha, Egypt ... **80 C2** 22 13N 27 59 E
Bîr Mogreïn, Mauritania **78 C3** 25 10N 11 25 E
Bîr Murr, Egypt .... **80 C3** 23 28N 30 10 E
Bi'r Muṭribah, Kuwait **70 D5** 29 54N 47 17 E
Bîr Nakheila, Egypt .. **80 C3** 24 1N 30 50 E
Bîr Qaṭia, Egypt .... **74 E1** 30 58N 32 45 E
Bîr Qatrani, Egypt ... **80 A2** 30 55N 26 10 E
Bîr Ranga, Egypt .... **80 C4** 24 25N 35 15 E
Bîr Sahara, Egypt ... **80 C2** 22 54N 28 40 E
Bîr Seiyâla, Egypt ... **80 B3** 26 10N 33 50 E
Bîr Shalatein, Egypt .. **80 C4** 23 5N 35 25 E
Bîr Shebb, Egypt .... **80 C2** 22 25N 29 40 E
Bîr Shût, Egypt ..... **80 C3** 23 50N 35 15 E
Bîr Terfawi, Egypt ... **80 C2** 22 57N 28 55 E
Bîr Umm Qubûr, Egypt **80 C3** 24 35N 34 2 E
Bîr Ungât, Egypt .... **80 C3** 22 8N 33 48 E
Bîr Za'farâna, Egypt . **80 J8** 29 10N 32 40 E
Bîr Zeidûn, Egypt ... **80 B3** 25 45N 33 40 E
Biramféro, Guinea ... **82 C3** 11 40N 9 10W
Biratnagar, Nepal .... **69 F12** 26 27N 87 17 E
Birawa, Dem. Rep. of
  the Congo .... **86 C2** 2 20 S 28 48 E
Birch →, Canada **102 B6** 58 28N 112 17W
Birch Hills, Canada ... **103 C7** 52 59N 105 25W
Birch I., Canada **103 C9** 52 26N 99 54W
Birch L., N.W.T.,
  Canada **102 A5** 62 4N 116 33W
Birch L., Ont., Canada **104 B1** 51 23N 92 18W
Birch L., U.S.A. **102 B6** 57 30N 113 10W
Birch Mts., Canada .. **103 C8** 52 24N 101 6W
Birch River, Canada .. **103 C8** 52 24N 101 6W
Birchip, Australia .... **95 F3** 35 56 S 142 55 E
Birchiş, Romania .... **28 E7** 45 58N 22 9 E
Bird, Canada **103 B10** 56 30N 94 13W
Bird I. = Las Aves, Is.,
  W. Indies **121 C7** 15 45N 63 55W
Bird I., Antarctica ... **5 B1** 54 0 S 38 0W
Birdsville, Australia .. **94 D2** 25 51 S 139 20 E
Birdum Cr. →, Australia **92 C5** 15 14 S 133 0 E
Birecik, Turkey ..... **70 B3** 37 2N 38 0 E
Birein, Israel .... **74 E3** 30 50N 34 28 E
Bireuen, Indonesia .. **62 C1** 5 14N 96 39 E
Biri →, Sudan ...... **81 F2** 7 56N 26 33 E
Birifo, Gambia **82 C2** 13 30N 14 0W
Birigui, Brazil ...... **127 A5** 21 18 S 50 16W
Birjand, Iran .... **71 C8** 32 53N 59 13 E
Birkenfeld, Germany . **25 F3** 49 38N 7 9 E
Birkenhead, U.K. **14 D4** 53 23N 3 2W
Birkerød, Denmark .. **11 J6** 55 50N 12 25 E
Birket Qârûn, Egypt . **80 J7** 29 30N 30 40 E
Birkfeld, Austria .... **26 D8** 47 21N 15 45 E
Bîrlad = Bârlad,
  Romania .... **29 D12** 46 15N 27 38 E
Birmingham, U.K. ... **15 E6** 52 29N 1 52W
Birmingham, U.S.A. . **115 J2** 33 31N 86 48W
Birmingham
  International ✈
  (BHX), U.K. **15 E6** 52 26N 1 45W
Birmitrapur, India ... **67 H14** 22 24N 84 46 E
Birni Ngaouré, Niger . **83 C5** 13 5N 2 51 E
Birni Nkonni, Niger .. **83 C6** 13 55N 5 15 E
Birnin Gwari, Nigeria **83 C6** 11 0N 6 45 E
Birnin Kebbi, Nigeria **83 C5** 12 32N 4 12 E
Birnin Kudu, Nigeria . **83 C6** 11 30N 9 29 E
Birobidzhan, Russia .. **53 E14** 48 50N 132 50 E
Birr, Ireland **12 C4** 53 6N 7 54W
Birrie →, Australia .. **95 D4** 29 43 S 146 37 E
Birsilpur, India ..... **68 E5** 28 11N 72 15 E
Birsk, Russia .... **52 D6** 55 25N 55 55 E
Birštonas, Lithuania . **30 D11** 54 37N 24 2 E
Birtle, Canada **103 C8** 50 30N 101 5W
Birur, India .... **66 N9** 13 30N 75 55 E
Biryuchiy, Ukraine ... **33 J8** 46 10N 35 0 E
Biržai, Lithuania .... **9 H21** 56 11N 24 45 E
Birzebbuga, Malta ... **49 D2** 35 50N 14 32 E
Bisa, Indonesia ..... **63 E7** 1 15 S 127 28 E
Bisáccia, Italy ...... **43 A8** 41 1N 15 22 E
Bisacquino, Italy .... **42 E6** 37 42N 13 15 E
Bisalpur, India ..... **69 E8** 28 14N 79 48 E
Bisbee, U.S.A. **109 L9** 31 27N 109 55W
Biscarrosse, France .. **20 D2** 44 22N 1 10W
Biscarrosse et de
  Parentis, Étang de,
  France **20 D2** 44 21N 1 10W

Biscay, B. of, Atl. Oc. .. **6 F5** 45 0N 2 0W
Biscayne B., U.S.A. .. **115 N5** 25 40N 80 12W
Biscéglie, Italy ..... **43 A9** 41 14N 16 30 E
Bischheim, France ... **19 D14** 48 37N 7 46 E
Bischofshofen, Austria **26 D6** 47 26N 13 14 E
Bischofswerda, Germany **24 D10** 51 7N 14 10 E
Bischwiller, France .. **19 D14** 48 46N 7 50 E
Biscoe Is., Antarctica . **5 C17** 66 0 S 67 0W
Biscotasing, Canada . **104 C3** 47 18N 82 9W
Biševo, Croatia ..... **41 F13** 42 57N 16 3 E
Bisha, Eritrea ...... **81 D4** 15 30N 37 31 E
Bishah, W. →,
  Si. Arabia .... **80 C5** 21 24N 43 26 E
Bishan, China ...... **58 C6** 29 33N 106 12 E
Bishkek, Kyrgyzstan . **52 E8** 42 54N 74 46 E
Bishnupur, India .... **69 H12** 23 8N 87 20 E
Bisho, S. Africa ..... **89 E4** 32 50 S 27 23 E
Bishop, Calif., U.S.A. **110 H8** 37 22N 118 24W
Bishop, Tex., U.S.A. . **113 M6** 27 35N 97 48W
Bishop Auckland, U.K. **14 C6** 54 39N 1 40W
Bishop's Falls, Canada **105 C8** 49 2N 55 30W
Bishop's Stortford, U.K. **15 F8** 51 52N 0 10 E
Bisignano, Italy ..... **43 C9** 39 31N 16 17 E
Bisina, L., Uganda ... **86 B3** 1 38N 33 56 E
Biskra, Algeria ..... **78 B7** 34 50N 5 44 E
Biskupiec, Poland ... **30 E7** 53 53N 20 58 E
Bismarck, U.S.A. **112 B4** 46 48N 100 47W
Bismarck Arch.,
  Papua N. G. .... **96 H7** 2 30 S 150 0 E
Bismark, Germany ... **24 C7** 52 40N 11 33 E
Bismil, Turkey ..... **73 D9** 37 51N 40 40 E
Biso, Uganda .... **86 B3** 1 44N 31 26 E
Bison, U.S.A. **112 C3** 45 31N 102 28W
Bisotūn, Iran .... **70 C5** 34 23N 47 26 E
Bispgården, Sweden . **10 A10** 63 2N 16 40 E
Bissagos = Bijagós,
  Arquipélago dos,
  Guinea-Biss. **82 C1** 11 15N 16 10W
Bissau, Guinea-Biss. .. **82 C1** 11 45N 15 45W
Bissaula, Nigeria .... **83 D7** 7 0N 10 27 E
Bissikrima, Guinea ... **82 C2** 10 50N 10 58W
Bissorã, Guinea-Biss. . **82 C1** 12 16N 15 35W
Bistcho L., Canada .. **102 B5** 59 45N 118 50W
Bistreţ, Romania .... **29 G8** 43 54N 23 23 E
Bistrica = Ilirska-
  Bistrica, Slovenia ... **41 C11** 45 34N 14 14 E
Bistriţa, Romania ... **29 C9** 47 9N 24 35 E
Bistriţa →, Romania . **29 D11** 46 30N 26 57 E
Bistriţa Năsăud □,
  Romania .... **29 C9** 47 15N 24 30 E
Bistriţei, Munţii,
  Romania .... **29 C10** 47 15N 25 40 E
Biswan, India ...... **69 F9** 27 29N 81 2 E
Bisztynek, Poland ... **30 D7** 54 8N 20 53 E
Bitburg, Germany ... **25 F2** 49 58N 6 31 E
Bitche, France ...... **19 C14** 49 2N 7 25 E
Bithynia, Turkey .... **72 B4** 40 40N 31 0 E
Bitlis, Turkey ...... **70 B4** 38 20N 42 3 E
Bitola, Macedonia ... **44 E5** 41 1N 21 20 E
Bitolj = Bitola,
  Macedonia .... **44 E5** 41 1N 21 20 E
Bitonto, Italy ...... **43 A9** 41 6N 16 41 E
Bitter Creek, U.S.A. . **108 F9** 41 33N 108 33W
Bitter L. = Buheirat-
  Murrat-el-Kubra,
  Egypt .... **80 H8** 30 18N 32 26 E
Bitterfeld, Germany .. **24 D8** 51 37N 12 20 E
Bitterfontein, S. Africa **88 E2** 31 1 S 18 32 E
Bitterroot →, U.S.A. . **108 C6** 46 52N 114 7W
Bitterroot Range, U.S.A. **108 D6** 46 0N 114 20W
Bitterwater, U.S.A. .. **110 J6** 36 23N 121 0W
Bitti, Italy .... **42 B2** 40 29N 9 23 E
Bittou, Burkina Faso . **83 C4** 11 17N 0 18W
Biu, Nigeria .... **83 C7** 10 40N 12 3 E
Bivolari, Romania ... **29 C12** 47 31N 27 27 E
Bivolu, Vf., Romania . **29 C10** 47 16N 25 58 E
Biwa-Ko, Japan .... **55 G8** 35 15N 136 10 E
Biwabik, U.S.A. **112 B8** 47 32N 92 21W
Bixad, Romania .... **29 C8** 47 56N 23 28 E
Bixby, U.S.A. **113 H7** 35 57N 95 53W
Biyang, China ...... **56 H7** 32 38N 113 21 E
Biysk, Russia ...... **52 D9** 52 40N 85 0 E
Bizana, S. Africa .... **89 E4** 30 50 S 29 52 E
Bizen, Japan .... **55 G7** 34 43N 134 8 E
Bizerte, Tunisia .... **79 A7** 37 15N 9 50 E
Bjargtangar, Iceland . **8 D1** 65 30N 24 30W
Bjärnum, Sweden ... **11 H7** 56 17N 13 43 E
Bjästa, Sweden ..... **10 A12** 63 12N 18 29 E
Bjelasica, Serbia & M. **44 D3** 42 50N 19 40 E
Bjelašnica, Bos.-H. .. **28 G3** 43 43N 18 9 E
Bjelovar, Croatia .... **41 C13** 45 56N 16 49 E
Bjerringbro, Denmark **11 H3** 56 23N 9 39 E
Björbo, Sweden ..... **10 D8** 60 27N 14 44 E
Björklinge, Sweden .. **10 D11** 60 2N 17 33 E
Björneborg = Pori,
  Finland .... **9 F19** 61 29N 21 48 E
Björneborg, Sweden . **10 E8** 59 14N 14 16 E
Bjørnevatn, Norway . **8 B23** 69 40N 30 0 E
Bjørnøya, Arctic .... **4 B8** 74 30N 19 0 E
Bjursås, Sweden .... **10 D9** 60 44N 15 25 E
Bjuv, Sweden ...... **11 H6** 56 5N 12 55 E
Bła, Mali **82 C3** 12 56N 5 47W
Blace, Serbia & M. ... **44 C5** 43 18N 21 17 E
Blachownia, Poland . **31 H5** 50 49N 18 56 E
Black = Da →, Vietnam **58 G5** 21 15N 105 20 E
Black →, Canada ... **116 B5** 44 42N 79 19W
Black →, Ariz., U.S.A. **109 K8** 33 44N 110 13W
Black →, Ark., U.S.A. **113 H9** 35 38N 91 20W
Black →, Mich., U.S.A. **116 D2** 42 59N 82 27W
Black →, N.Y., U.S.A. **117 C8** 43 59N 76 4W
Black →, Wis., U.S.A. **112 D9** 43 57N 91 22W
Black Bay Pen., Canada **104 C2** 48 38N 88 21W
Black Birch L., Canada **103 B7** 56 53N 107 45W
Black Canyon of the
  Gunnison △, U.S.A. **109 G10** 38 40N 107 35W
Black Diamond, Canada **102 C6** 50 45N 114 14W
Black Duck →, Canada **104 A2** 56 51N 89 2W
Black Forest =
  Schwarzwald,
  Germany .... **25 G4** 48 30N 8 20 E
Black Forest, U.S.A. . **112 F2** 39 0N 104 43W
Black Hd., Ireland ... **12 C2** 53 9N 9 16W
Black Hills, U.S.A. .. **112 D3** 44 0N 103 45W
Black I., Canada **103 C9** 51 12N 96 30W
Black L., Canada **103 B7** 59 12N 105 15W
Black L., Mich., U.S.A. **114 C3** 45 28N 84 16W
Black L., N.Y., U.S.A. **117 B9** 44 31N 75 36W
Black Lake, Canada .. **103 B7** 59 11N 105 20W
Black Mesa, U.S.A. .. **113 G3** 36 58N 102 58W
Black Mt. = Mynydd Du,
  U.K. **15 F4** 51 52N 3 50W
Black Mts., U.K. **15 F4** 51 55N 3 7W
Black Range, U.S.A. . **109 K10** 33 15N 107 50W
Black River, Jamaica . **120 a** 18 0N 77 50W
Black River Falls, U.S.A. **112 C9** 44 18N 90 51W
Black Rock, Barbados . **121 g** 13 7N 59 37W
Black Sea, Eurasia ... **6 G12** 43 30N 35 0 E

Black Tickle, Canada . **105 B8** 53 28N 55 45W
Black Volta →, Africa **82 D4** 8 41N 1 33W
Black Warrior →,
  U.S.A. **115 J2** 32 32N 87 51W
Blackall, Australia ... **94 C4** 24 25 S 145 45 E
Blackball, N.Z. ..... **91 K3** 42 22 S 171 26 E
Blackbull, Australia .. **94 B3** 17 55 S 141 45 E
Blackburn, U.K. **14 D5** 53 45N 2 29W
Blackburn with
  Darwen □, U.K. ... **14 D5** 53 45N 2 29W
Blackdown Tableland △,
  Australia .... **94 C4** 23 52 S 149 8 E
Blackfoot, U.S.A. ... **108 E7** 43 11N 112 21W
Blackfoot →, U.S.A. . **108 C7** 46 52N 113 53W
Blackfoot River
  Reservoir, U.S.A. .. **108 E8** 43 0N 111 43W
Blackpool, U.K. **14 D4** 53 49N 3 3W
Blackpool □, U.K. ... **14 D4** 53 49N 3 3W
Blackriver, U.S.A. ... **116 B1** 44 46N 83 17W
Blacks Harbour, Canada **105 C6** 45 3N 66 49W
Blacksburg, U.S.A. .. **114 G5** 37 14N 80 25W
Blackstone, U.S.A. .. **114 G7** 37 4N 78 0W
Blackstone Ra.,
  Australia .... **93 E4** 26 0 S 128 30 E
Blackwater = West
  Road →, Canada .. **102 C4** 53 18N 122 53W
Blackwater, Australia . **94 C4** 23 35 S 148 53 E
Blackwater →, Meath,
  Ireland **12 C4** 53 39N 6 41W
Blackwater →,
  Waterford, Ireland . **12 D4** 52 4N 7 52W
Blackwater →, U.K. .. **12 B5** 54 31N 6 35W
Blackwell, U.S.A. ... **113 G6** 36 48N 97 17W
Blackwells Corner,
  U.S.A. **111 K7** 35 37N 119 47W
Bladensburg △,
  Australia .... **94 C3** 22 25 S 142 59 E
Blaenau Ffestiniog, U.K. **14 E4** 53 0N 3 56W
Blaenau Gwent □, U.K. **15 F4** 51 48N 3 12W
Blagaj, Bos.-H. ..... **44 C1** 43 16N 17 55 E
Blagnac, France .... **20 E5** 43 37N 1 23 E
Blagnac, Toulouse ✈
  (TLS), France ..... **20 E5** 43 37N 1 22 E
Blagodarnoye =
  Blagodarnyy, Russia **35 H6** 45 7N 43 37 E
Blagodarnyy, Russia . **35 H6** 45 7N 43 37 E
Blagoevgrad, Bulgaria **44 D7** 42 2N 23 5 E
Blagoveshchensk, Russia **53 D13** 50 20N 127 30 E
Blahkiuh, Indonesia . **63 J18** 8 31 S 115 12 E
Blain, France **18 E5** 47 29N 1 45W
Blain, U.S.A. **116 F7** 40 20N 77 31W
Blaine, Minn., U.S.A. . **112 C8** 45 10N 93 13W
Blaine, Wash., U.S.A. **110 B4** 48 59N 122 45W
Blaine Lake, Canada . **103 C7** 52 51N 106 52W
Blair, U.S.A. **112 E6** 41 33N 96 8W
Blair Athol, Australia . **94 C4** 22 42 S 147 31 E
Blair Atholl, U.K. ... **13 E5** 56 46N 3 50W
Blairgowrie, U.K. ... **13 E5** 56 35N 3 21W
Blairsden, U.S.A. ... **110 F6** 39 47N 120 37W
Blairsville, U.S.A. ... **116 F5** 40 26N 79 16W
Blaj, Romania ...... **29 D8** 46 10N 23 57 E
Blakang Mati, Pulau,
  Singapore .... **65 d** 1 15N 103 50 E
Blake Pt., U.S.A. ... **112 A10** 48 11N 88 25W
Blakely, Ga., U.S.A. . **115 K3** 31 23N 84 56W
Blakely, Pa., U.S.A. . **117 E9** 41 28N 75 37W
Blâmont, France .... **19 D13** 48 35N 6 50 E
Blanc, C., Spain .... **48 B9** 39 21N 2 51 E
Blanc, Mont, Europe . **21 C10** 45 48N 6 50 E
Blanc-Sablon, Canada **105 B8** 51 24N 57 12W
Blanca, Costa Rica .. **120 D2** 9 34N 85 8W
Blanca, B., Argentina . **128 D4** 39 10 S 61 30W
Blanca Peak, U.S.A. . **109 H11** 37 35N 105 29W
Blanche, C., Australia **95 E1** 33 1 S 134 9 E
Blanche, L., S. Austral.,
  Australia .... **95 D2** 29 15 S 139 40 E
Blanche, L., W. Austral.,
  Australia .... **92 D3** 22 25 S 123 17 E
Blanchisseuse,
  Trin. & Tob. **125 K15** 10 48N 61 18W
Blanco, S. Africa .... **88 E3** 33 55 S 22 23 E
Blanco, U.S.A. **113 K5** 30 6N 98 25W
Blanco →, Argentina . **126 C2** 30 20 S 68 42W
Blanco, C., Costa Rica **120 E2** 9 34N 85 8W
Blanco, C., U.S.A. ... **108 E1** 42 51N 124 34W
Blanda →, Iceland .. **8 D3** 65 37N 20 9W
Blandford Forum, U.K. **15 G5** 50 51N 2 9W
Blanding, U.S.A. **109 H9** 37 37N 109 29W
Blanes, Spain ...... **38 D7** 41 40N 2 48 E
Blangy-sur-Bresle,
  France .... **19 C8** 49 55N 1 37 E
Blanice →, Czech Rep. **26 B7** 49 10N 14 5 E
Blankaholm, Sweden **11 G10** 57 36N 16 31 E
Blankenberge, Belgium **17 C3** 51 20N 3 9 E
Blankenburg, Germany **24 D6** 51 47N 10 57 E
Blanquefort, France . **20 D3** 44 55N 0 38W
Blanquillo, Uruguay . **127 C4** 32 53 S 55 37W
Blansko, Czech Rep. . **27 B9** 49 22N 16 40 E
Blantyre, Malawi ... **87 F4** 15 45 S 35 0 E
Blarney, Ireland **12 E3** 51 56N 8 33W
Blasdell, U.S.A. **116 D6** 42 48N 78 50W
Błaszki, Poland .... **31 G5** 51 38N 18 30 E
Blatná, Czech Rep. .. **26 B6** 49 25N 13 52 E
Blato, Croatia ...... **41 F13** 42 56N 16 48 E
Blaubeuren, Germany **25 G5** 48 24N 9 46 E
Blaustein, Germany . **25 G5** 48 24N 9 53 E
Blåvands Huk, Denmark **11 J2** 55 33N 8 4 E
Blaydon, U.K. **14 C6** 54 58N 1 42W
Blaye, France **20 D3** 45 8N 0 40W
Blaye-les-Mines, France **20 D6** 44 1N 2 8 E
Blayney, Australia ... **95 E4** 33 32 S 149 14 E
Blaze, Pt., Australia .. **92 B5** 12 56 S 130 11 E
Błażowa, Poland ... **31 J9** 49 53N 22 7 E
Bleckede, Germany . **24 B6** 53 17N 10 43 E
Bled, Slovenia ...... **41 B11** 46 27N 14 7 E
Bleiburg, Austria .... **26 E7** 46 35N 14 49 E
Blejeşti, Romania ... **29 F10** 44 19N 25 27 E
Blekinge, Sweden ... **9 H16** 56 25N 15 20 E
Blekinge län □, Sweden **11 H9** 56 20N 15 20 E
Blenheim, Canada ... **116 D3** 42 20N 82 0W
Blenheim, N.Z. ..... **91 J4** 41 38 S 173 57 E
Bléone →, France .. **21 D10** 44 5N 6 0 E
Blérancourt, France . **19 C10** 49 31N 3 9 E
Bletchley, U.K. **15 F7** 51 59N 0 44W
Blida, Algeria ...... **78 A6** 36 30N 2 49 E
Blidö, Sweden ..... **10 E12** 59 37N 18 53 E
Blidsberg, Sweden .. **11 G7** 57 56N 13 30 E
Blieskastel, Germany **25 F3** 49 14N 7 12 E
Bligh Sound, N.Z. .. **91 L1** 44 47 S 167 32 E
Blind River, Canada . **104 C3** 46 10N 82 58W
Blinisht, Albania ... **44 E3** 41 52N 19 58 E
Bliss, Idaho, U.S.A. . **108 E6** 42 56N 114 57W
Bliss, N.Y., U.S.A. .. **116 D6** 42 34N 78 15W
Blissfield, U.S.A. ... **116 F3** 41 50N 83 52W
Blitar, Indonesia ... **63 H15** 8 5 S 112 11 E
Blitta, Togo .... **83 D5** 8 23N 1 6 E
Block I., U.S.A. **117 E13** 41 11N 71 35W

Block Island Sd., U.S.A. **117 E13** 41 15N 71 40W
Bloemfontein, S. Africa **88 D4** 29 6 S 26 7 E
Bloemhof, S. Africa . **88 D4** 27 38 S 25 32 E
Blois, France .... **18 E8** 47 35N 1 20 E
Blomskog, Sweden . **10 E6** 59 16N 12 2 E
Blomstermåla, Sweden **11 H10** 56 59N 16 21 E
Blönduós, Iceland .. **8 D3** 65 40N 20 12W
Blongas, Indonesia .. **63 K19** 8 53 S 116 2 E
Błonie, Poland ..... **31 F7** 52 12N 20 37 E
Bloodvein →, Canada **103 C9** 51 47N 96 43W
Bloody Foreland,
  Ireland **12 A3** 55 10N 8 17W
Bloomer, U.S.A. **112 C9** 45 6N 91 29W
Bloomfield, Canada . **116 C7** 43 59N 77 14W
Bloomfield, Iowa,
  U.S.A. **112 E8** 40 45N 92 25W
Bloomfield, N. Mex.,
  U.S.A. **109 H10** 36 43N 107 59W
Bloomfield, Nebr.,
  U.S.A. **112 D6** 42 36N 97 39W
Bloomington, Ill., U.S.A. **112 E10** 40 28N 89 0W
Bloomington, Ind.,
  U.S.A. **114 F2** 39 10N 86 32W
Bloomington, Minn.,
  U.S.A. **112 C8** 44 50N 93 17W
Bloomsburg, U.S.A. . **117 F8** 41 0N 76 27W
Bloomsbury, Australia **94 J6** 20 48 S 148 38 E
Blora, Indonesia **116 E7** 41 41N 77 4W
Blossburg, U.S.A. .. **116 E7** 41 41N 77 4W
Blouberg, S. Africa .. **89 C4** 23 8 S 28 59 E
Blountstown, U.S.A. . **115 K3** 30 27N 85 3W
Bludenz, Austria .... **26 D2** 47 10N 9 50 E
Blue Earth, U.S.A. .. **112 D8** 43 38N 94 6W
Blue Hole △, Belize . **120 C2** 17 24N 88 30W
Blue Lagoon △, Zambia **87 F2** 15 28 S 27 26 E
Blue Mesa Reservoir,
  U.S.A. **109 G10** 38 28N 107 20W
Blue Mountain Lake,
  U.S.A. **117 C10** 43 52N 74 30W
Blue Mountain Pk.,
  Jamaica .... **120 a** 18 3N 76 36W
Blue Mts., Jamaica .. **120 a** 18 3N 76 36W
Blue Mts., Maine, U.S.A. **117 B14** 44 50N 70 35W
Blue Mts., Oreg., U.S.A. **108 D4** 45 15N 119 0W
Blue Mts., Pa., U.S.A. **117 F8** 40 30N 76 30W
Blue Mud B., Australia **94 A2** 13 30 S 136 0 E
Blue Nile = Nîl el
  Azraq →, Sudan .. **81 D3** 15 38N 32 31 E
Blue Rapids, U.S.A. . **112 F6** 39 41N 96 39W
Blue Ridge Mts., U.S.A. **115 G5** 36 30N 80 15W
Blue River, Canada .. **102 C5** 52 6N 119 18W
Bluefield, U.S.A. ... **114 G5** 37 15N 81 17W
Bluefields, Nic. **120 D3** 12 20N 83 50W
Bluff, Australia ..... **94 C4** 23 35 S 149 4 E
Bluff, N.Z. .... **91 M2** 46 37 S 168 20 E
Bluff, U.S.A. **109 H9** 37 17N 109 33W
Bluff Knoll, Australia . **93 F2** 34 24 S 118 15 E
Bluff Pt., Australia ... **93 E1** 27 50 S 114 5 E
Bluffton, U.S.A. **114 E3** 40 44N 85 11W
Blumenau, Brazil ... **127 B6** 27 0 S 49 0W
Blunt, U.S.A. **112 C5** 44 31N 99 59W
Bly, U.S.A. **108 E3** 42 24N 121 3W
Blyde River Canyon △,
  S. Africa .... **89 C5** 24 37 S 31 2 E
Blyth, Canada **116 C3** 43 44N 81 26W
Blyth, U.K. **14 B6** 55 8N 1 31W
Blythe, U.S.A. **111 M12** 33 37N 114 36W
Blytheville, U.S.A. .. **113 H10** 35 56N 89 55W
Bo, S. Leone **82 D2** 7 55N 11 50W
Bo Duc, Vietnam ... **65 G6** 11 58N 106 50 E
Bo Hai, China ...... **57 E10** 39 0N 119 0 E
Bo Xian = Bozhou,
  China .... **56 H8** 33 55N 115 41 E
Boa Vista, Brazil **124 C6** 2 48N 60 30W
Boac, Phil. .... **61 E4** 13 27N 121 50 E
Boaco, Nic. **120 D2** 12 29N 85 35W
Bo'ai, China .... **56 G7** 35 10N 113 3 E
Boal, Spain **36 B4** 43 25N 6 49W
Boalsburg, U.S.A. .. **116 F7** 40 46N 77 47W
Boane, Mozam. .... **89 D5** 26 6 S 32 19 E
Boardman, U.S.A. .. **116 E4** 41 2N 80 40W
Bobadah, Australia .. **95 E4** 32 19 S 146 41 E
Bobai, China .... **58 F7** 22 17N 109 59 E
Bobbili, India ...... **67 K13** 18 35N 83 30 E
Bóbbio, Italy .... **40 D6** 44 46N 9 23 E
Bobcaygeon, Canada **116 B6** 44 33N 78 33W
Böblingen, Germany . **25 G5** 48 40N 9 1 E
Bobo-Dioulasso,
  Burkina Faso **82 C4** 11 8N 4 13W
Bobolice, Poland .... **30 E3** 53 58N 16 37 E
Boboshevo, Bulgaria **44 D7** 42 9N 23 0 E
Bobov Dol, Bulgaria **44 D6** 42 20N 22 59 E
Bóbr →, Poland .... **31 F2** 52 4N 15 4 E
Bobraomby, Tanjon' i,
  Madag. .... **89 A8** 12 40 S 49 10 E
Bobrinets, Ukraine .. **33 H6** 48 4N 32 5 E
Bobrov, Russia ..... **34 E5** 51 5N 40 2 E
Bobrovitsa, Ukraine . **33 G6** 50 45N 31 23 E
Bobruysk = Babruysk,
  Belarus .... **33 F5** 53 10N 29 15 E
Boby, Pic, Madag. .. **85 J9** 22 12 S 46 55 E
Boca de Drago,
  Venezuela **125 K15** 11 0N 61 50W
Bôca do Acre, Brazil . **124 E5** 8 50 S 67 27W
Boca Raton, U.S.A. . **115 M5** 26 21N 80 5W
Bocanda, Ivory C. .. **82 D4** 7 5N 4 31W
Bocas del Toro, Panama **120 E3** 9 15N 82 20W
Boceguillas, Spain .. **36 D7** 41 20N 3 39W
Bochnia, Poland .... **31 J7** 49 58N 20 27 E
Bocholt, Germany .. **24 D2** 51 50N 6 36 E
Bochum, Germany .. **24 D3** 51 28N 7 13 E
Bockenem, Germany **24 C6** 52 1N 10 8 E
Boćki, Poland ...... **31 F10** 52 39N 23 3 E
Bocognano, France . **21 F13** 42 5N 9 4 E
Bocoyna, Mexico ... **118 B3** 27 50N 107 30W
Bocşa, Romania .... **28 E6** 45 21N 21 47 E
Boda, Dalarna, Sweden **9 H16** 56 25N 15 20 E
Böda, Kalmar, Sweden **11 G11** 57 15N 17 3 E
Boda, Västernorrland,
  Sweden .... **10 B10** 62 52N 16 39 E
Bodafors, Sweden .. **11 G8** 57 48N 14 23 E
Bodaybo, Russia ... **53 D12** 57 50N 114 0 E
Boddam, U.K. **13 B7** 59 56N 1 17W
Boddington, Australia **93 F2** 32 50 S 116 30 E
Bode Sadu, Nigeria . **83 D5** 9 4N 4 48 E
Bodega Bay, U.S.A. . **110 G3** 38 20N 123 3W
Boden, Sweden ..... **8 D19** 65 50N 21 42 E
Bodensee, Europe .. **25 H5** 47 35N 9 25 E
Bodenteich, Germany **24 C6** 52 49N 10 42 E
Bodhan, India ...... **66 K10** 18 40N 77 44 E
Bodinga, Nigeria ... **83 C6** 12 58N 5 10 E
Bodmin, U.K. **15 G3** 50 28N 4 43W
Bodmin Moor, U.K. . **15 G3** 50 33N 4 36W
Bodø, Norway ..... **8 C16** 67 17N 14 24 E
Bodrog →, Hungary **28 B5** 48 11N 21 22 E
Bodrum, Turkey .... **47 D9** 37 3N 27 30 E

Bódva →, Hungary . **28 B5** 48 19N 20 45 E
Boën, France ...... **21 C8** 45 44N 4 1 E
Boende, Dem. Rep. of
  the Congo .... **84 E4** 0 24 S 21 12 E
Boerne, U.S.A. **113 L5** 29 47N 98 44W
Boesmans →, S. Africa **88 E4** 33 42 S 26 39 E
Boffa, Guinea **82 C2** 10 16N 14 3W
Bogalusa, U.S.A. ... **113 K10** 30 47N 89 52W
Bogan →, Australia . **95 E4** 30 20 S 146 55 E
Bogan Gate, Australia **95 E4** 33 7 S 147 49 E
Bogandé, Burkina Faso **83 C4** 13 2N 0 8W
Bogantungan, Australia **94 C4** 23 41 S 147 17 E
Bogata, U.S.A. **113 J7** 33 28N 95 13W
Bogatić, Serbia & M. **44 B3** 44 51N 19 30 E
Bogazkale, Turkey .. **72 B6** 40 2N 34 37 E
Boğazlıyan, Turkey . **72 C6** 39 11N 35 14 E
Bogen, Sweden ..... **10 D6** 60 4N 12 5 E
Bogense, Denmark .. **11 J4** 55 34N 10 5 E
Bogetići, Serbia & M. **44 D2** 42 41N 18 58 E
Boggabilla, Australia . **95 D5** 28 36 S 150 24 E
Boggabri, Australia .. **95 E5** 30 45 S 150 5 E
Boggeragh Mts., Ireland **12 D3** 52 2N 8 55W
Boglan = Solhan, Turkey **73 C9** 38 57N 41 3 E
Bognor Regis, U.K. . **15 G7** 50 47N 0 40W
Bogo, Phil. .... **61 F6** 11 3N 124 0 E
Bogodukhov, Ukraine **33 G8** 50 9N 35 33 E
Bogol Manya, Ethiopia **81 G5** 4 34N 41 29 E
Bogong, Mt., Australia **95 F4** 36 47 S 147 17 E
Bogor, Indonesia ... **63 G12** 6 36 S 106 48 E
Bogorodick, Russia . **34 F10** 53 47N 38 8 E
Bogorodsk, Russia .. **34 B6** 56 4N 43 30 E
Bogoso, Ghana **82 D4** 5 38N 2 3W
Bogotá, Colombia .. **124 C4** 4 34N 74 0W
Bogotol, Russia .... **52 D9** 56 15N 89 50 E
Bogou, Togo .... **83 C5** 10 40N 0 4 E
Bogra, Bangla. ..... **67 G16** 24 51N 89 22 E
Boguchany, Russia .. **53 D10** 58 40N 97 30 E
Boguchar, Russia ... **34 F5** 49 55N 40 32 E
Bogué, Mauritania .. **82 B2** 16 45N 14 10W
Boguslav, Ukraine .. **33 H6** 49 33N 30 56 E
Boguszów-Gorce,
  Poland .... **31 H3** 50 45N 16 12 E
Bohain-en-Vermandois,
  France .... **19 C10** 49 59N 3 28 E
Bohdan, Ukraine ... **29 B9** 48 2N 24 22 E
Bohemian Forest =
  Böhmerwald,
  Germany .... **25 F9** 49 8N 13 14 E
Bohinjska Bistrica,
  Slovenia .... **41 B11** 46 17N 14 1 E
Böhmerwald, Germany **25 F9** 49 8N 13 14 E
Bohmte, Germany .. **24 C4** 52 22N 8 19 E
Bohodukhiv, Ukraine **33 G8** 50 9N 35 33 E
Bohol, Phil. .... **61 G6** 9 50N 124 10 E
Bohol Sea, Phil. .... **61 G6** 9 0N 124 0 E
Bohongou,
  Burkina Faso ...... **83 C5** 12 30N 0 40 E
Böhönye, Hungary . **28 D2** 46 25N 17 28 E
Bohorodchany, Ukraine **29 B9** 48 48N 24 32 E
Bohuslän, Sweden .. **11 F5** 58 25N 12 0 E
Boi, Nigeria .... **83 D6** 9 35N 9 27 E
Boi, Pta. de, Brazil .. **127 A6** 23 55 S 45 15W
Boiaçu, Brazil ...... **124 D6** 0 27 S 61 46W
Boileau, C., Australia **92 C3** 17 40 S 122 7 E
Boing'o, Sudan ..... **81 F3** 9 58N 33 44 E
Boise, U.S.A. **108 E5** 43 37N 116 13W
Boise City, U.S.A. .. **113 G3** 36 44N 102 31W
Boissevain, Canada . **103 D8** 49 15N 100 5W
Bóite →, Italy ...... **41 B9** 46 5N 12 5 E
Boitzenburg, Germany **24 B9** 53 16N 13 35 E
Boizenburg, Germany **24 B6** 53 23N 10 43 E
Bojador, C., W. Sahara **78 C3** 26 0N 14 30W
Bojana →, Albania . **44 E3** 41 52N 19 22 E
Bojano, Italy .... **43 A7** 41 29N 14 29 E
Bojanowo, Poland .. **31 G3** 51 43N 16 42 E
Bøjden, Denmark .. **11 J4** 55 6N 10 7 E
Bojnūrd, Iran ...... **71 B8** 37 30N 57 20 E
Bojonegoro, Indonesia **63 G14** 7 11 S 111 54 E
Boju, Nigeria ...... **83 D6** 7 22 S 7 55 E
Boka, Serbia & M. .. **28 E5** 45 22N 20 52 E
Boka Kotorska,
  Serbia & M. .... **44 D2** 42 23N 18 32 E
Bokala, Ivory C. **82 D4** 8 31N 4 33W
Bokani, Nigeria .... **83 D6** 9 35N 5 10 E
Bokaro, India ...... **69 H11** 23 46N 85 55 E
Boké, Guinea **82 C2** 10 56N 14 17W
Bokhara →, Australia **95 D4** 29 55 S 146 42 E
Bokkos, Nigeria .... **83 D6** 9 17N 9 1 E
Boknafjorden, Norway **9 G11** 59 14N 5 40 E
Bokora △, Uganda .. **86 B3** 2 12N 34 1 E
Bokoro, Chad ...... **79 F9** 12 25N 17 14 E
Bokpyin, Burma .... **65 G2** 11 18N 98 42 E
Boksitogorsk, Russia **32 C7** 59 22N 33 50 E
Bol, Croatia .... **41 E13** 43 18N 16 38 E
Bolama, Guinea-Biss. **82 C1** 11 30N 15 30W
Bolan →, Pakistan .. **68 E2** 28 38N 67 42 E
Bolan Pass, Pakistan **66 E5** 29 50N 67 20 E
Bolaños →, Mexico . **118 C4** 21 14N 104 8W
Bolaños de Calatrava,
  Spain **37 G7** 38 54N 3 40W
Bolayır, Turkey ..... **45 F10** 40 31N 26 45 E
Bolbec, France ..... **18 C7** 49 30N 0 30 E
Boldăjî, Iran .... **71 D6** 31 56N 51 3 E
Boldeşti-Scăeni,
  Romania .... **29 E11** 45 3N 26 2 E
Bole, China .... **60 B3** 45 11N 81 37 E
Bole, Ethiopia ...... **81 F4** 6 36N 37 20 E
Bole, Ghana **82 D4** 9 2N 2 23W
Bolekhiv, Ukraine ... **33 H2** 49 0N 23 57 E
Bolesławiec, Poland . **31 G2** 51 17N 15 37 E
Bolgatanga, Ghana . **83 C4** 10 44N 0 53W
Bolgrad = Bolhrad,
  Ukraine .... **29 E13** 45 40N 28 32 E
Bolhrad, Ukraine ... **29 E13** 45 40N 28 32 E
Boli, China .... **57 B16** 45 46N 130 31 E
Bolinao, Phil. ...... **61 C3** 16 23N 119 54 E
Bolintin-Vale, Romania **29 F10** 44 27N 25 46 E
Bolívar, Argentina .. **126 D3** 36 15 S 60 53W
Bolívar, Mo., U.S.A. **113 G8** 37 37N 93 25W
Bolívar, N.Y., U.S.A. **116 D6** 42 4N 78 10W
Bolívar, Tenn., U.S.A. **113 H10** 35 12N 89 0W
Bolivia ■, S. Amer. .. **124 G6** 17 6 S 64 0W
Bolivian Plateau =
  Altiplano, Bolivia .. **122 E4** 17 0 S 68 0W
Boljevac, Serbia & M. **44 C5** 43 51N 21 58 E
Bolkhov, Russia .... **32 F9** 53 25N 36 0 E
Bolków, Poland .... **31 H3** 50 55N 16 6 E
Bollebygd, Sweden . **11 G6** 57 40N 12 35 E
Bollène, France ..... **21 D8** 44 18N 4 45 E
Bollnäs, Sweden ... **10 C10** 61 21N 16 24 E
Bollon, Australia ... **95 D4** 28 2 S 147 29 E
Bollstabruk, Sweden **10 B11** 63 1N 17 53 E
Bolmen, Sweden ... **11 H7** 56 55N 13 40 E
Bolobo, Dem. Rep. of
  the Congo .... **84 E3** 2 6 S 16 20 E
Bologna, Italy ...... **41 D8** 44 29N 11 20 E

Bologna ✈ (BLQ), *Italy* .. **41 D8** 44 34N 11 16 E
Bologoye, *Russia* .... **32 D8** 57 55N 34 5 E
Bolon, Ozero, *Russia* ... **60 B8** 49 50N 133 0 E
Bolonchenticul, *Mexico* **119 D7** 20 0N 89 49W
Bolótana, *Italy* .... **42 B1** 40 20N 8 52 E
Boloven, Cao Nguyen,
  Laos .... **64 E6** 15 10N 106 30 E
Bolpur, *India* .... **69 H12** 23 40N 87 45 E
Bolsena, *Italy* .... **41 F8** 42 39N 11 59 E
Bolsena, L. di, *Italy* .... **41 F8** 42 36N 11 56 E
Bolshakovo, *Russia* .... **30 D8** 54 53N 21 40 E
Bolshaya Chernigovka,
  Russia .... **34 D10** 52 6N 50 52 E
Bolshaya Glushitsa,
  Russia .... **34 D10** 52 28N 50 30 E
Bolshaya Martynovka,
  Russia .... **35 G5** 47 19N 41 37 E
Bolshaya Vradiyevka,
  Ukraine .... **33 J6** 47 50N 30 40 E
Bolshevik, Ostrov,
  Russia .... **53 B11** 78 30N 102 0 E
Bolshoy Anyuy ➤,
  Russia .... **53 C17** 68 30N 160 49 E
Bolshoy Begichev,
  Ostrov, *Russia* .. **53 B12** 74 20N 112 30 E
Bolshoy Kavkas =
  Caucasus Mountains,
  Eurasia .... **35 J7** 42 50N 44 0 E
Bolshoy Lyakhovskiy,
  Ostrov, *Russia* .. **53 B15** 73 35N 142 0 E
Bolshoy Tyuters, Ostrov,
  Russia .... **9 G22** 59 51N 27 13 E
Bolsward, *Neths.* ...... **17 A5** 53 3N 5 32 E
Bolt Head, *U.K.* **15 G4** 50 12N 3 48W
Boltaña, *Spain* .... **38 C5** 42 28N 0 4 E
Boltigen, *Switz.* .... **25 J3** 46 38N 7 24 E
Bolton, *Canada* **116 C5** 43 54N 79 45W
Bolton, *U.K.* **14 D5** 53 35N 2 26W
Bolton Landing, *U.S.A.* **117 C11** 43 32N 73 35W
Bolu, *Turkey* .... **72 B4** 40 45N 31 35 E
Bolungavík, *Iceland* **8 C2** 66 9N 23 15W
Boluo, *China* .... **59 F10** 23 3N 114 21 E
Bolvadin, *Turkey* ...... **70 B1** 38 45N 31 4 E
Bolzano, *Italy* .... **41 B8** 46 31N 11 22 E
Bom Jesus da Lapa,
  Brazil .... **125 F10** 13 15 S 43 25W
Boma, *Dem. Rep. of
  the Congo* .... **84 F2** 5 50 S 13 4 E
Bombala, *Australia* .... **95 F4** 36 56 S 149 15 E
Bombarral, *Portugal* **37 F1** 39 15N 9 9W
Bombay = Mumbai,
  India .... **66 K8** 18 55N 72 50 E
Bombedor, Pta.,
  Venezuela **125 L15** 9 53N 61 37W
Bomboma, *Dem. Rep. of
  the Congo* .... **84 D3** 2 25N 18 55 E
Bombombwa,
  *Dem. Rep. of
  the Congo* .... **86 B2** 1 40N 25 40 E
Bomi Hills, *Liberia* **82 D2** 7 1N 10 38W
Bomili, *Dem. Rep. of
  the Congo* .... **86 B2** 1 45N 27 5 E
Bømlo, *Norway* .... **9 G11** 59 37N 5 13 E
Bomokandi ➤,
  *Dem. Rep. of
  the Congo* .... **86 B2** 3 39N 26 8 E
Bomu ➤, *C.A.R.* ...... **84 D4** 4 40N 22 30 E
Bon, C., *Tunisia* .... **76 C5** 37 1N 11 2 E
Bon Sar Pa, *Vietnam* .. **64 F6** 12 24N 107 35 E
Bonāb, *Iran* .... **73 D12** 37 20N 46 4 E
Bonaigarh, *India* ..... **69 J11** 21 50N 84 57 E
Bonaire, *Neth. Ant.* .. **121 D6** 12 10N 68 15W
Bonampak, *Mexico* ... **119 D6** 16 44N 90 0W
Bonang, *Australia* ..... **95 F4** 37 11 S 148 41 E
Bonanza, *Nic.* **120 D3** 13 54N 84 35W
Bonaparte Arch.,
  Australia .... **92 B3** 14 0 S 124 30 E
Boñar, *Spain* **36 C5** 42 52N 5 19W
Bonar Bridge, *U.K.* **13 D4** 57 54N 4 20W
Bonasse, *Trin. & Tob.* **125 K15** 10 5N 61 54W
Bonaventure, *Canada* **105 C6** 48 5N 65 32W
Bonavista, *Canada* .. **105 C9** 48 40N 53 5W
Bonavista, C., *Canada* **105 C9** 48 42N 53 5W
Bonavista B., *Canada* **105 C9** 48 45N 53 25W
Bondeno, *Italy* .... **41 D8** 44 53N 11 25 E
Bondo, *Dem. Rep. of
  the Congo* .... **86 B1** 3 55N 23 53 E
Bondoukou, *Ivory C.* .. **82 D4** 8 2N 2 47W
Bondowoso, *Indonesia* **63 G15** 7 55 S 113 49 E
Bone, Teluk, *Indonesia* **63 E6** 4 10 S 120 50 E
Bonerate, *Indonesia* ... **63 F6** 7 25 S 121 5 E
Bonerate, Kepulauan,
  Indonesia .... **63 F6** 6 30 S 121 10 E
Bo'ness, *U.K.* **13 E5** 56 1N 3 37W
Bonete, Cerro,
  Argentina .... **126 B2** 27 55 S 68 40W
Bong Son = Hoai Nhon,
  Vietnam .... **64 E7** 14 28N 109 1 E
Bonga, *Ethiopia* ...... **81 F4** 7 15N 36 14 E
Bongabong, *Phil.* ..... **61 E4** 12 45N 121 29 E
Bongor, *Chad* .... **79 F9** 10 35N 15 20 E
Bongouanou, *Ivory C.* . **82 D4** 6 42N 4 15W
Bonham, *U.S.A.* **113 J6** 33 35N 96 11W
Boni, *Mali* **82 B4** 15 3N 2 10W
Boni = Kenya .... **86 C5** 1 35 S 41 18 E
Bonifacio, *France* .... **21 G13** 41 24N 9 10 E
Bonifacio, Bouches de,
  Medit. S. .... **42 A2** 41 12N 9 15 E
Bonin Is. = Ogasawara
  Gunto, *Pac. Oc.* .. **96 E6** 27 0N 142 0 E
Bonke, *Ethiopia* ...... **81 F4** 6 5N 37 16 E
Bonkoukou, *Niger* .... **83 C5** 14 0N 3 15 E
Bonn, *Germany* ...... **24 E3** 50 46N 7 6 E
Bonnat, *France* ...... **19 F8** 46 20N 1 54 E
Bonne Terre, *U.S.A.* .. **113 G9** 37 55N 90 33W
Bonners Ferry, *U.S.A.* **108 B5** 48 42N 116 19W
Bonnétable, *France* ... **18 D7** 48 11N 0 25 E
Bonneval, *France* ..... **21 C11** 45 37N 7 3 E
Bonneval-sur-Arc,
  France .... **18 D8** 48 11N 1 24 E
Bonneville, *France* .... **19 F13** 46 4N 6 24 E
Bonney, L., *Australia* .. **95 F3** 37 50 S 140 20 E
Bonnie Rock, *Australia* **93 F2** 30 29 S 118 22 E
Bonny, *Nigeria* .... **83 E6** 4 25N 7 13 E
Bonny ➤, *Nigeria* .... **83 E6** 4 20N 7 10 E
Bonny, Bight of, *Africa* **83 E6** 3 30N 9 20 E
Bonny-sur-Loire, *France* **19 E9** 47 33N 2 50 E
Bonnyrigg, *U.K.* **13 F5** 55 53N 3 6W
Bonnyville, *Canada* .. **103 C6** 54 20N 110 45W
Bono, *Italy* .... **42 B2** 40 25N 9 2 E
Bonoi, *Indonesia* ..... **63 E9** 1 45 S 137 41 E
Bonorva, *Italy* .... **42 B1** 40 25N 8 46 E
Bontang, *Indonesia* ... **62 D5** 0 10N 117 30 E
Bonthe, S. *Africa* ..... **88 E3** 34 5 S 20 28 E
Bonthe, *S. Leone* **82 D2** 7 30N 12 33W
Bontoc, *Phil.* .... **61 C4** 17 7N 120 58 E

Bonyeri, *Ghana* **82 D4** 5 1N 2 46W
Bonyhád, *Hungary* ... **28 D3** 46 18N 18 32 E
Bonython Ra., *Australia* **92 D4** 23 40 S 128 45 E
Bookabie, *Australia* .... **93 F5** 31 50 S 132 41 E
Booker, *U.S.A.* **113 G4** 36 27N 100 32W
Boola, *Guinea* .... **82 D3** 8 22N 8 41 E
Booligal, *Australia* ..... **95 E3** 33 58 S 144 53 E
Boonah, *Australia* ..... **95 D5** 27 58 S 152 41 E
Boone, Iowa, *U.S.A.* .. **112 D8** 42 4N 93 53W
Boone, N.C., *U.S.A.* .. **115 G5** 36 13N 81 41W
Booneville, Ark., *U.S.A.* **113 H8** 35 8N 93 55W
Booneville, Miss., *U.S.A.* **115 H1** 34 39N 88 34W
Boonville, Calif., *U.S.A.* **110 F3** 39 1N 123 22W
Boonville, Ind., *U.S.A.* **114 F2** 38 3N 87 16W
Boonville, Mo., *U.S.A.* **112 F8** 38 58N 92 44W
Boonville, N.Y., *U.S.A.* **117 C9** 43 29N 75 20W
Boorabbin △, *Australia* **93 F4** 31 30 S 129 57 E
Boorindal, *Australia* ... **95 E4** 30 22 S 146 11 E
Boorowa, *Australia* .... **95 E4** 34 28 S 148 44 E
Boosaaso = Bosaso,
  Somali Rep. ...... **75 E4** 11 12N 49 18 E
Boothia, Gulf of,
  Canada **101 A11** 71 0N 90 0W
Boothia Pen., *Canada* **100 A10** 71 0N 94 0W
Bootle, *U.K.* **14 D4** 53 28N 3 1W
Booué, *Gabon* .... **84 E2** 0 5 S 11 55 E
Boppard, *Germany* .... **25 E3** 50 13N 7 35 E
Boquete, *Panama* **120 E3** 8 46N 82 27W
Boquilla, Presa de la,
  Mexico **118 B3** 27 40N 105 30W
Boquillas del Carmen,
  Mexico **118 B4** 29 17N 102 53W
Bor, *Czech Rep.* ...... **26 B5** 49 41N 12 45 E
Bor, *Russia* .... **34 B7** 56 28N 43 59 E
Bor, *Serbia & M.* ..... **44 B6** 44 5N 22 7 E
Bôr, *Sudan* .... **81 F3** 6 10N 31 40 E
Bor, *Sweden* .... **11 G8** 57 9N 14 10 E
Bor, *Turkey* .... **72 D6** 37 54N 34 32 E
Bor Mashash, *Israel* ... **74 D3** 31 7N 34 50 E
Borah Peak, *U.S.A.* .. **108 D7** 44 8N 113 47W
Borang, *Sudan* .... **81 G3** 4 50N 30 59 E
Borås, *Sweden* .... **11 G6** 57 43N 12 56 E
Borāzjān, *Iran* .... **71 D6** 29 22N 51 10 E
Borba, *Brazil* .... **124 D7** 4 12 S 59 34W
Borba, *Portugal* **37 G3** 38 50N 7 26W
Borborema, Planalto da,
  Brazil .... **122 D7** 7 0 S 37 0W
Borcea, *Romania* ... **29 F12** 44 20N 27 45 E
Borçka, *Turkey* .... **73 B9** 41 25N 41 41 E
Bord Khūn-e Now, *Iran* **71 D6** 28 3N 51 28 E
Borda, C., *Australia* ... **95 F2** 35 45 S 136 34 E
Bordeaux, *France* **20 D3** 44 50N 0 36W
Bordeaux ✈ (BOD),
  France **20 D3** 44 50N 0 35W
Borden, *Australia* ..... **93 F2** 34 4 S 118 12 E
Borden-Carleton,
  Canada **105 C7** 46 18N 63 47W
Borden I., *Canada* **4 B2** 78 30N 111 30W
Borden Pen., *Canada* **101 A11** 73 0N 83 0W
Border Ranges △,
  Australia .... **95 D5** 28 24 S 152 56 E
Borders = Scottish
  Borders □, *U.K.* ... **13 F6** 55 35N 2 50W
Bordertown, *Australia* . **95 F3** 36 19 S 140 45 E
Bordeyri, *Iceland* **8 D3** 65 12N 21 6W
Bordighera, *Italy* ..... **40 E4** 43 46N 7 39 E
Bordj Fly Ste. Marie,
  Algeria **78 C5** 27 19N 2 32W
Bordj-in-Eker, *Algeria* . **78 D7** 24 9N 5 3 E
Bordj Omar Driss,
  Algeria .... **78 C7** 28 10N 6 40 E
Bore, *Ethiopia* .... **81 G4** 4 39N 37 39 E
Borehamwood, *U.K.* .. **15 F7** 51 40N 0 15W
Borek Wielkopolski,
  Poland .... **31 G4** 51 54N 17 11 E
Borensberg, *Sweden* .. **11 F9** 58 34N 15 17 E
Borgå = Porvoo, *Finland* **9 F21** 60 24N 25 40 E
Borgarfjörður, *Iceland* . **8 D7** 65 31N 13 49W
Borgarnes, *Iceland* **8 D3** 64 32N 21 55W
Børgefjellet, *Norway* .. **8 D15** 65 20N 13 45 E
Borger, *Neths.* .... **17 B6** 52 54N 6 44 E
Borger, *U.S.A.* **113 H4** 35 39N 101 24W
Borgholm, *Sweden* ... **11 H10** 56 52N 16 39 E
Bórgia, *Italy* .... **43 D9** 38 49N 16 30 E
Borgo San Dalmazzo,
  Italy .... **40 D4** 44 20N 7 30 E
Borgo San Lorenzo,
  Italy .... **41 E8** 43 57N 11 23 E
Borgo Val di Taro, *Italy* **40 D6** 44 29N 9 46 E
Borgo Valsugana, *Italy* **41 B8** 46 3N 11 27 E
Borgomanero, *Italy* ... **40 C5** 45 42N 8 28 E
Borgorose, *Italy* ..... **41 F10** 42 11N 13 13 E
Borgosésia, *Italy* ..... **40 C5** 45 43N 8 16 E
Borhoyn Tal, *Mongolia* **56 C6** 43 50N 111 58 E
Bori, *Nigeria* .... **83 E6** 4 42N 7 21 E
Borikhane, *Laos* ...... **64 C4** 18 33N 103 43 E
Borisoglebsk, *Russia* .. **34 E6** 51 27N 42 5 E
Borisov = Barysaw,
  Belarus .... **32 E5** 54 17N 28 28 E
Borisovka, *Russia* .... **33 G9** 50 36N 36 1 E
Borja, *Peru* .... **124 D3** 4 20 S 77 40W
Borja, *Spain* **38 D3** 41 48N 1 34W
Borjas Blancas = Les
  Borges Blanques,
  Spain .... **38 D5** 41 31N 0 52 E
Borjomi, *Georgia* .... **35 K6** 41 48N 43 28 E
Børkop, *Denmark* .... **11 J3** 55 39N 9 39 E
Borkou, *Chad* .... **79 E9** 18 15N 18 50 E
Borkum, *Germany* .... **24 B2** 53 34N 6 40 E
Borlänge, *Sweden* .... **10 D9** 60 29N 15 26 E
Borley, C., *Antarctica* . **5 C5** 66 15 S 52 30 E
Borlu, *Turkey* .... **47 C10** 38 44N 28 27 E
Bormida ➤, *Italy* ..... **40 D5** 44 23N 8 13 E
Bórmio, *Italy* .... **40 B7** 46 28N 10 22 E
Borna, *Germany* ..... **24 D8** 51 7N 12 29 E
Borne Sulinowo, *Poland* **30 E3** 53 32N 16 36 E
Borneo, E. Indies ..... **62 D5** 1 0N 115 0 E
Bornholm, *Denmark* .. **11 J8** 55 10N 15 0 E
Bornholms
  Amtskommune □,
  Denmark .... **11 J8** 55 5N 15 0 E
Bornholmsgattet,
  Europe .... **11 J8** 55 15N 14 20 E
Borno □, *Nigeria* ..... **83 C7** 11 30N 13 0 E
Bornos, *Spain* **37 J5** 36 48N 5 42W
Bornova, *Turkey* ..... **47 C9** 38 27N 27 14 E
Bornu Yassa, *Nigeria* . **83 C7** 12 14N 12 25 E
Boro ➤, *Sudan* ...... **81 F2** 8 52N 26 11 E
Borodino, *Russia* .... **32 E8** 55 31N 35 40 E
Borodino, *Ukraine* ... **29 D14** 46 18N 29 15 E
Borogontsy, *Russia* ... **53 C14** 62 42N 131 8 E
Boromo, *Burkina Faso* **82 C4** 11 45N 2 58W
Boron, *U.S.A.* **111 L9** 35 0N 117 39W
Borongan, *Phil.* ...... **61 F6** 11 37N 125 26 E
Borotangba Mts., *C.A.R.* **81 F2** 6 30N 25 0 E
Borotou, *Ivory C.* **82 D3** 8 46N 7 30W
Borovan, *Bulgaria* .... **44 C7** 43 27N 23 45 E

Borovichi, *Russia* ..... **32 C7** 58 25N 33 55 E
Borovsk, *Russia* ...... **32 E9** 55 12N 36 24 E
Borrby, *Sweden* ...... **11 J8** 55 27N 14 10 E
Borrego Springs, *U.S.A.* **111 M10** 33 15N 116 23W
Borriol, *Spain* **38 E4** 40 4N 0 4W
Borroloola, *Australia* .. **94 B2** 16 4 S 136 17 E
Borşa, *Cluj, Romania* .. **29 D8** 46 56N 23 40 E
Borşa, *Maramureş,
  Romania* .... **29 C9** 47 41N 24 50 E
Borsad, *India* .... **68 H5** 22 25N 72 54 E
Borsec, *Romania* ..... **29 D10** 46 57N 25 34 E
Borshchiv, *Ukraine* ... **29 B11** 48 48N 26 3 E
Borsod-Abaúj-
  Zemplén □, *Hungary* **28 B6** 48 20N 21 0 E
Bort-les-Orgues, *France* **20 C6** 45 24N 2 29 E
Borth, *U.K.* **15 E3** 52 29N 4 2W
Börtnan, *Sweden* ..... **10 B7** 62 45N 13 50 E
Borūjerd, *Iran* .... **71 C6** 33 55N 48 50 E
Borynya, *Ukraine* ..... **31 J10** 49 4N 23 0 E
Boryslav, *Ukraine* .... **31 J10** 49 18N 23 28 E
Boryspil, *Ukraine* ..... **33 G6** 50 21N 30 59 E
Borzhomi = Borjomi,
  Georgia .... **35 K6** 41 48N 43 28 E
Borzna, *Ukraine* ...... **33 G7** 51 18N 32 26 E
Borzya, *Russia* ...... **53 D12** 50 24N 116 31 E
Bosa, *Italy* .... **42 B1** 40 18N 8 30 E
Bosanska Dubica,
  Bos.-H. .... **41 C13** 45 10N 16 50 E
Bosanska Gradiška,
  Bos.-H. .... **28 E2** 45 10N 17 15 E
Bosanska Kostajnica,
  Bos.-H. .... **41 C13** 45 11N 16 33 E
Bosanska Krupa,
  Bos.-H. .... **41 D13** 44 53N 16 10 E
Bosanski Brod, *Bos.-H.* **28 E2** 45 10N 18 0 E
Bosanski Novi, *Bos.-H.* **41 C13** 45 2N 16 22 E
Bosanski Petrovac,
  Bos.-H. .... **41 D13** 44 12N 16 21 E
Bosanski Šamac, *Bos.-H.* **28 E3** 45 3N 18 29 E
Bosansko Grahovo,
  Bos.-H. .... **41 D13** 44 12N 16 26 E
Bosaso, *Somali Rep.* .. **75 E4** 11 12N 49 18 E
Boscastle, *U.K.* **15 G3** 50 41N 4 42W
Boscobelle, *Barbados* **121 g** 13 16N 59 34W
Bose, *China* .... **58 F6** 23 53N 106 35 E
Boshan, *China* .... **57 F9** 36 28N 117 49 E
Boshof, *S. Africa* ..... **88 D4** 28 31 S 25 13 E
Boshrūyeh, *Iran* ...... **71 C8** 33 55N 57 30 E
Bosilegrad, *Serbia & M.* **44 D6** 42 30N 22 27 E
Boskovice, *Czech Rep.* **27 B9** 49 29N 16 40 E
Bosna ➤, *Bos.-H.* .... **28 E3** 45 4N 18 29 E
Bosna i Hercegovina =
  Bosnia-
  Herzegovina ■,
  Europe .... **28 G2** 44 0N 18 0 E
Bosnia-Herzegovina ■,
  Europe .... **28 G2** 44 0N 18 0 E
Bosnik, *Indonesia* .... **63 E9** 1 5 S 136 10 E
Bosobolo, *Dem. Rep. of
  the Congo* .... **84 D3** 4 15N 19 50 E
Bosporus = Istanbul
  Boğazı, *Turkey* ... **45 E13** 41 10N 29 10 E
Bosque Farms, *U.S.A.* **109 J10** 34 53N 106 40W
Bossangoa, *C.A.R.* .... **84 C3** 6 35N 17 30 E
Bossé Bangou, *Niger* .. **83 C5** 13 20N 1 18 E
Bossier City, *U.S.A.* .. **113 J8** 32 31N 93 44W
Bosso, *Niger* .... **83 C7** 13 43N 13 19 E
Bosso, Dallol ➤, *Niger* **83 C5** 12 25N 2 50 E
Bostan, *Pakistan* ..... **68 D2** 30 26N 67 2 E
Bostānābād, *Iran* ..... **70 B5** 37 50N 46 50 E
Bosten Hu, *China* .... **60 B3** 41 55N 87 40 E
Boston, *U.K.* **14 E7** 52 59N 0 2W
Boston, *U.S.A.* **117 D13** 42 22N 71 4W
Boston Bar, *Canada* .. **102 D4** 49 52N 121 30W
Boston Mts., *U.S.A.* .. **113 H8** 35 42N 93 15W
Bosumtwi, L., *Ghana* .. **83 D4** 6 30N 1 25W
Bosut ➤, *Croatia* ..... **28 E3** 45 20N 18 45 E
Boswell, *Canada* **102 D5** 49 28N 116 45W
Boswell, *U.S.A.* **116 F5** 40 10N 79 2W
Botad, *India* .... **68 H4** 22 15N 71 40 E
Botan ➤, *Turkey* ..... **73 D10** 37 52N 42 9 E
Botev, *Bulgaria* ...... **45 D8** 42 44N 24 52 E
Botevgrad, *Bulgaria* .. **44 D7** 42 55N 23 47 E
Bothaville, *S. Africa* ... **88 D4** 27 23 S 26 34 E
Bothnia, G. of, *Europe* **8 E19** 62 0N 20 0 E
Bothwell, *Australia* .... **95 G4** 42 20 S 147 1 E
Bothwell, *Canada* **116 D3** 42 38N 81 52W
Boticas, *Portugal* **36 D3** 41 41N 7 40W
Botletle ➤, *Botswana* **88 C3** 20 10 S 23 15 E
Botlikh, *Russia* ...... **35 J8** 42 46N 46 11 E
Botna ➤, *Moldova* .. **29 D14** 46 43N 29 34 E
Botoroaga, *Romania* **29 F10** 44 8N 25 32 E
Botoşani, *Romania* ... **29 C11** 47 42N 26 41 E
Botoşani □, *Romania* . **29 C11** 47 50N 26 50 E
Botou, *Burkina Faso* .. **83 C5** 12 42N 1 59 E
Botricello, *Italy* ...... **43 D9** 38 56N 16 51 E
Botro, *Ivory C.* **82 D3** 7 51N 5 19W
Botswana ■, *Africa* ... **88 C3** 22 0 S 24 0 E
Bottineau, *U.S.A.* **112 A4** 48 50N 100 27W
Bottnaryd, *Sweden* ... **11 G7** 57 47N 13 50 E
Bottrop, *Germany* .... **17 C6** 51 31N 6 58 E
Botucatu, *Brazil* .... **127 A6** 22 55 S 48 30W
Botwood, *Canada* ... **105 C8** 49 6N 55 23W
Bou Djébéha, *Mali* ... **82 B4** 18 25N 2 45W
Bou Rjeïmât, *Mauritania* **82 B1** 19 0N 15 3W
Bouafié, *Ivory C.* **82 D3** 7 1N 5 47W
Bouaké, *Ivory C.* **82 D3** 7 40N 5 2W
Bouar, *C.A.R.* .... **84 C3** 6 0N 15 40 E
Bouârfa, *Morocco* **78 B5** 32 32N 1 58W
Boucaut B., *Australia* . **94 A1** 12 0 S 134 25 E
Bouches-du-Rhône □,
  France .... **21 E9** 43 37N 5 2 E
Boucle de Baoule △,
  Mali **82 C3** 13 53N 9 0W
Boucles de la Seine
  Normande △, *France* **18 C7** 49 32N 0 35 E
Bouctouche, *Canada* .. **105 C7** 46 30N 64 45W
Bougainville, C.,
  Australia .... **92 B4** 13 57 S 126 4 E
Bougainville I.,
  Papua N. G. ...... **96 H7** 6 0 S 155 0 E
Bougainville Reef,
  Australia .... **94 B4** 15 30 S 147 5 E
Bougie = Bejaïa, *Algeria* **78 A7** 36 42N 5 2 E
Bougouni, *Mali* **82 C3** 11 30N 7 20W
Bouillon, *Belgium* .... **17 E5** 49 44N 5 3 E
Boukombé, *Benin* ..... **83 C5** 10 13N 1 9 E
Boulal, *Mali* **82 B3** 15 8N 8 21W
Boulazac, *France* ..... **20 C4** 45 10N 0 47 E
Boulder, Colo., *U.S.A.* **112 E2** 40 1N 105 17W
Boulder, Mont., *U.S.A.* **108 C7** 46 14N 112 7W
Boulder City, *U.S.A.* . **111 K12** 35 59N 114 50W
Boulder Creek, *U.S.A.* **110 H4** 37 7N 122 7W
Boulder Dam = Hoover
  Dam, *U.S.A.* **111 K12** 36 1N 114 44W
Bouli, *Mauritania* **82 B2** 15 17N 12 18W

Boulia, *Australia* ..... **94 C2** 22 52 S 139 51 E
Bouligny, *France* ..... **19 C12** 49 17N 5 45 E
Boulogne ➤, *France* .. **18 E5** 47 12N 1 47W
Boulogne-sur-Gesse,
  France .... **20 E4** 43 18N 0 38 E
Boulogne-sur-Mer,
  France .... **19 B8** 50 42N 1 36 E
Bouloire, *France* ..... **18 E7** 47 59N 0 45 E
Boulouli, *Mali* **82 B3** 15 30N 9 25W
Boulsa, *Burkina Faso* .. **83 C4** 12 39N 0 34W
Boultoum, *Niger* ..... **83 C7** 14 45N 10 25 E
Boûmdeïd, *Mauritania* **82 B2** 17 25N 9 50W
Boun Neua, *Laos* ..... **64 B3** 21 38N 101 54 E
Boun Tai, *Laos* .... **64 B3** 21 23N 101 58 E
Bouna, *Ivory C.* **82 D4** 9 10N 3 0W
Boundary Peak, *U.S.A.* **110 H8** 37 51N 118 21W
Boundiali, *Ivory C.* ... **82 D3** 9 30N 6 20W
Bountiful, *U.S.A.* **108 F8** 40 53N 111 53W
Bounty Is., *Pac. Oc.* .. **96 M9** 48 0 S 178 30 E
Boura, *Mali* **82 C4** 11 55N 4 33W
Bourbon-Lancy, *France* **19 F10** 46 37N 3 45 E
Bourbon-l'Archambault,
  France .... **19 F10** 46 36N 3 4 E
Bourbonnais, *France* .. **19 F10** 46 28N 3 0 E
Bourbonne-les-Bains,
  France .... **19 E12** 47 54N 5 45 E
Bourbourg, *France* .... **19 B9** 50 56N 2 12 E
Bourdel L., *Canada* .. **104 A5** 56 43N 74 10W
Bourem, *Mali* **83 B4** 17 0N 0 24W
Bourg, *France* **20 C3** 45 3N 0 34W
Bourg-Argental, *France* **21 C8** 45 18N 4 32 E
Bourg-de-Péage, *France* **21 C9** 45 2N 5 3 E
Bourg-en-Bresse, *France* **19 F12** 46 13N 5 12 E
Bourg-Lastic, *France* .. **20 C6** 45 39N 2 35 E
Bourg-Madame, *France* **20 F5** 42 26N 1 55 E
Bourg-St-Andéol,
  France .... **21 D8** 44 23N 4 39 E
Bourg-St-Maurice,
  France .... **21 C10** 45 35N 6 46 E
Bourganeuf, *France* ... **20 C5** 45 57N 1 45 E
Bourges, *France* ...... **19 E9** 47 9N 2 25 E
Bourget, *Canada* **117 A9** 45 26N 75 9W
Bourgneuf, B. de, *France* **18 E4** 47 3N 2 10W
Bourgneuf-en-Retz,
  France **18 E5** 47 2N 1 58W
Bourgogne, *France* ... **19 F11** 47 0N 4 50 E
Bourgoin-Jallieu, *France* **21 C9** 45 36N 5 17 E
Bourgueil, *France* ..... **18 E7** 47 17N 0 10 E
Bourke, *Australia* ..... **95 E4** 30 8 S 145 55 E
Bourne, *U.K.* **15 E7** 52 47N 0 22W
Bournemouth, *U.K.* .. **15 G6** 50 43N 1 52W
Bournemouth □, *U.K.* **15 G6** 50 43N 1 52W
Bouroum, *Burkina Faso* **83 C4** 13 37N 0 39W
Bouse, *U.S.A.* **111 M13** 33 56N 114 0W
Boussac, *France* ...... **19 F9** 46 22N 2 13 E
Boussé, *Burkina Faso* . **83 C4** 12 39N 1 53W
Boussouma,
  Burkina Faso **83 C4** 12 52N 1 13W
Boutilimit, *Mauritania* **82 B2** 17 45N 14 40W
Boutonne ➤, *France* .. **20 C3** 45 54N 0 50W
Bouvet I. = Bouvetøya,
  Antarctica .... **3 G10** 54 26 S 3 24 E
Bouvetøya, *Antarctica* **3 G10** 54 26 S 3 24 E
Bouxwiller, *France* .. **19 D14** 48 49N 7 27 E
Bouza, *Niger* .... **83 C6** 14 25N 6 2 E
Bouzonville, *France* .. **19 C13** 49 17N 6 32 E
Bova Marina, *Italy* .... **43 E8** 37 56N 15 55 E
Bovalino Marina, *Italy* **43 D9** 38 10N 16 10 E
Bovec, *Slovenia* ..... **41 B10** 46 20N 13 33 E
Bovill, *U.S.A.* **108 C5** 46 51N 116 24W
Bovino, *Italy* .... **43 A8** 41 15N 15 20 E
Bovril, *Argentina* .... **126 C4** 31 21 S 59 26W
Bow ➤, *Canada* **102 C6** 49 57N 111 41W
Bow Island, *Canada* .. **102 D6** 49 50N 111 23W
Bowbells, *U.S.A.* **112 A3** 48 48N 102 15W
Bowdle, *U.S.A.* **112 C5** 45 27N 99 39W
Bowelling, *Australia* .. **93 F2** 33 25 S 116 30 E
Bowen, *Argentina* .... **126 D2** 35 0 S 67 31W
Bowen, *Australia* .... **94 J6** 20 0 S 148 16 E
Bowen Mts., *Australia* **95 F4** 37 0 S 147 50 E
Bowie, Ariz., *U.S.A.* . **109 K9** 32 19N 109 29W
Bowie, Tex., *U.S.A.* .. **113 J5** 33 34N 97 51W
Bowkān, *Iran* .... **70 B5** 36 31N 46 12 E
Bowland, Forest of, *U.K.* **14 D5** 54 0N 2 30W
Bowling Green, Ky.,
  U.S.A. **114 G2** 36 59N 86 27W
Bowling Green, Ohio,
  U.S.A. **114 E4** 41 23N 83 39W
Bowling Green, C.,
  Australia .... **94 B4** 19 19 S 147 25 E
Bowling Green Bay △,
  Australia .... **94 B4** 19 26 S 146 57 E
Bowman, *U.S.A.* **112 B3** 46 11N 103 24W
Bowman I., *Antarctica* **5 C8** 65 0 S 104 0 E
Bowmanville =
  Clarington, *Canada* **116 C6** 43 55N 78 41W
Bowmore, *U.K.* **13 F2** 55 45N 6 17W
Bowral, *Australia* ..... **95 E5** 34 26 S 150 27 E
Bowraville, *Australia* .. **95 E5** 30 37 S 152 52 E
Bowron ➤, *Canada* .. **102 C4** 54 3N 121 50W
Bowron Lake △, *Canada* **102 C4** 53 10N 121 5W
Bowser L., *Canada* .. **102 B3** 56 30N 129 30W
Bowsman, *Canada* ... **103 C8** 52 14N 101 12W
Bowwood, *Zambia* ... **87 F2** 17 5 S 26 20 E
Box Cr. ➤, *Australia* .. **95 E3** 34 10 S 143 50 E
Boxholm, *Sweden* .... **11 F9** 58 12N 15 3 E
Boxmeer, *Neths.* ..... **17 C5** 51 38N 5 56 E
Boxtel, *Neths.* .... **17 C5** 51 36N 5 20 E
Boyabat, *Turkey* ..... **72 B6** 41 28N 34 47 E
Boyalıca, *Turkey* ..... **45 F12** 40 32N 28 46 E
Boyang, *China* ...... **59 C11** 29 0N 116 38 E
Boyany, *Ukraine* ..... **29 B11** 48 17N 26 8 E
Boyce, *U.S.A.* **113 K8** 31 23N 92 40W
Boyd L., *Canada* **104 B4** 52 46N 76 42W
Boyle, *Canada* **102 C6** 54 35N 112 49W
Boyle, *Ireland* **12 C3** 53 59N 8 18W
Boyne ➤, *Ireland* **12 C5** 53 43N 6 15W
Boyne City, *U.S.A.* ... **114 C3** 45 13N 85 1W
Boynitsa, *Bulgaria* .... **44 C6** 43 58N 22 33 E
Boynton Beach, *U.S.A.* **115 M5** 26 32N 80 4W
Boyolali, *Indonesia* ... **63 G14** 7 32 S 110 35 E
Boyoma, Chutes,
  *Dem. Rep. of
  the Congo* .... **86 B2** 0 35N 25 23 E
Boysen Reservoir,
  U.S.A. **108 E9** 43 25N 108 11W
Boyuibe, *Bolivia* .... **124 G6** 20 25 S 63 17W
Boyup Brook, *Australia* **93 F2** 33 50 S 116 23 E
Boz Burun, *Turkey* ... **45 F12** 40 32N 28 46 E
Boz Dağ, *Turkey* ..... **47 D11** 37 18N 29 11 E
Boz Dağları, *Turkey* .. **47 C10** 38 20N 28 0 E
Bozan, *Turkey* ...... **47 C11** 39 44N 31 52 E
Bozburun, *Turkey* .... **47 E10** 36 43N 28 8 E
Bozcaada, *Turkey* .... **72 C2** 39 49N 26 3 E
Bozdoğan, *Turkey* ... **108 D8** 45 41N 111 2W
Bozeman, *U.S.A.* .... **47 D10** 37 40N 28 17 E

Boževac, *Serbia & M.* . **44 B5** 44 32N 21 24 E
Bozhou, *China* .... **56 H8** 33 55N 115 41 E
Bozkır, *Turkey* .... **72 D5** 37 11N 32 14 E
Bozkurt, *Turkey* ..... **47 D11** 37 50N 29 37 E
Bozouls, *France* ...... **20 D6** 44 28N 2 43 E
Bozoum, *C.A.R.* ..... **84 C3** 6 25N 16 35 E
Bozova, *Antalya, Turkey* **47 C12** 37 13N 30 18 E
Bozova, *Sanliurfa,
  Turkey* .... **73 D8** 37 21N 38 32 E
Bozovici, *Romania* ... **28 F7** 44 56N 22 0 E
Bozüyük, *Turkey* ..... **47 B12** 39 54N 30 3 E
Bra, *Italy* .... **40 D4** 44 42N 7 51 E
Braås, *Sweden* .... **11 G9** 57 4N 15 3 E
Brabant □, *Belgium* ... **17 D4** 50 46N 4 30 E
Brabant L., *Canada* .. **103 B8** 55 58N 103 43W
Brabrand, *Denmark* .. **11 H4** 56 9N 10 7 E
Brač, *Croatia* .... **41 E13** 43 20N 16 40 E
Bracadale, L., *U.K.* ... **13 D2** 57 20N 6 30W
Bracciano, *Italy* ...... **41 F9** 42 6N 12 10 E
Bracciano, L. di, *Italy* . **41 F9** 42 7N 12 14 E
Bracebridge, *Canada* **116 A5** 45 2N 79 19W
Brach, *Libya* .... **79 C8** 27 31N 14 20 E
Bracieux, *France* ..... **18 E8** 47 30N 1 30 E
Bräcke, *Sweden* ..... **10 B9** 62 45N 15 26 E
Brackettville, *U.S.A.* .. **113 L4** 29 19N 100 25W
Brački Kanal, *Croatia* **41 E13** 43 24N 16 40 E
Bracknell, *U.K.* **15 F7** 51 25N 0 43W
Bracknell Forest □, *U.K.* **15 F7** 51 25N 0 44W
Brad, *Romania* ...... **28 D7** 46 10N 22 50 E
Brádano ➤, *Italy* ..... **43 B9** 40 23N 16 51 E
Bradenton, *U.S.A.* ... **115 M4** 27 30N 82 34W
Bradford, *Canada* ... **116 B5** 44 7N 79 34W
Bradford, *U.K.* **14 D6** 53 47N 1 45W
Bradford, Pa., *U.S.A.* . **116 E6** 41 58N 78 38W
Bradford, Vt., *U.S.A.* **117 C12** 43 59N 72 9W
Bradley, Ark., *U.S.A.* . **113 J8** 33 6N 93 39W
Bradley, Calif., *U.S.A.* **110 K6** 35 52N 120 48W
Bradley Institute,
  Zimbabwe .... **87 F3** 17 7 S 31 25 E
Brady, *U.S.A.* **113 K5** 31 9N 99 20W
Brædstrup, *Denmark* .. **11 J3** 55 58N 9 37 E
Braeside, *Canada* ... **117 A8** 45 28N 76 24W
Braga, *Portugal* **36 D2** 41 35N 8 25W
Braga □, *Portugal* **36 D2** 41 30N 8 30W
Bragadiru, *Romania* .. **29 G10** 44 4N 26 31 E
Bragado, *Argentina* .. **126 D3** 35 2 S 60 27W
Bragança, *Brazil* .... **125 D9** 1 0 S 47 2W
Bragança, *Portugal* ... **36 D4** 41 48N 6 50W
Bragança □, *Portugal* **36 D4** 41 30N 6 45W
Bragança Paulista,
  Brazil .... **127 A6** 22 55 S 46 32W
Brahestad = Raahe,
  Finland .... **8 D21** 64 40N 24 28 E
Brahmanbaria, *Bangla.* **67 H17** 23 58N 91 15 E
Brahmani ➤, *India* ... **67 J15** 20 39N 86 46 E
Brahmapur, *India* .... **67 K14** 19 15N 84 54 E
Brahmaputra ➤, *Asia* **69 H13** 23 40N 90 35 E
Braich-y-pwll, *U.K.* ... **14 E3** 52 47N 4 46W
Braidwood, *Australia* .. **95 F4** 35 27 S 149 49 E
Brăila, *Romania* .... **29 E12** 45 19N 27 59 E
Brăila □, *Romania* ... **29 E12** 45 5N 27 30 E
Brainerd, *U.S.A.* **112 B7** 46 22N 94 12W
Braintree, *U.K.* ...... **15 F8** 51 53N 0 34 E
Braintree, *U.S.A.* ... **117 D14** 42 13N 71 0W
Brak ➤, *S. Africa* .... **88 D3** 29 35 S 22 55 E
Brake, *Germany* ..... **24 B4** 53 20N 8 28 E
Brakel, *Germany* ..... **24 D5** 51 42N 9 11 E
Bräkne-Hoby, *Sweden* **11 H9** 56 14N 15 6 E
Brakwater, *Namibia* .. **88 C2** 22 28 S 17 3 E
Brålanda, *Sweden* .... **11 F6** 58 34N 12 21 E
Bramberg,
  Denmark .... **11 J3** 55 31N 9 28 E
Bramming, *Denmark* . **11 J2** 55 28N 8 42 E
Brämön, *Sweden* ..... **10 B11** 62 14N 17 40 E
Brampton, *Canada* ... **116 C5** 43 45N 79 45W
Brampton, *U.K.* **14 C5** 54 57N 2 44W
Bramsche, *Germany* .. **24 C3** 52 24N 7 59 E
Bramton I., *Australia* .. **94 J7** 20 50 S 149 17 E
Branco ➤, *Brazil* .... **124 D6** 1 20 S 61 50W
Brandberg, *Namibia* .. **88 C1** 21 10 S 14 33 E
Brandberg △, *Namibia* **88 C1** 21 10 S 14 30 E
Brande, *Denmark* .... **11 J3** 55 57N 9 8 E
Brandenburg =
  Neubrandenburg,
  Germany .... **24 B9** 53 33N 13 15 E
Brandenburg, *Germany* **24 C8** 52 25N 12 33 E
Brandenburg □,
  Germany .... **24 C9** 52 50N 13 0 E
Brandfort, *S. Africa* ... **88 D4** 28 40 S 26 30 E
Brando, *France* ..... **21 F13** 42 47N 9 27 E
Brandon, *Canada* ... **103 D9** 49 50N 99 57W
Brandon, *U.S.A.* ... **117 C11** 43 48N 73 4W
Brandon B., *Ireland* ... **12 D1** 52 17N 10 8W
Brandon Mt., *Ireland* .. **12 D1** 52 15N 10 15W
Brandsen, *Argentina* .. **126 D4** 35 10 S 58 15W
Brandvlei, *S. Africa* ... **88 E3** 30 25 S 20 30 E
Brandýs nad Labem,
  Czech Rep. ...... **26 A7** 50 10N 14 40 E
Brăneşti, *Romania* ... **29 F11** 44 27N 26 20 E
Branford, *U.S.A.* **117 E12** 41 17N 72 49W
Braniewo, *Poland* .... **30 D6** 54 25N 19 50 E
Bransfield Str.,
  Antarctica .... **5 C18** 63 0 S 59 0W
Brańsk, *Poland* ...... **31 F9** 52 45N 22 50 E
Branson, *U.S.A.* **113 G8** 36 39N 93 13W
Brantford, *Canada* ... **116 C4** 43 10N 80 15W
Brantôme, *France* .... **20 C4** 45 22N 0 39 E
Branxholme, *Australia* **95 F3** 37 52 S 141 49 E
Branxton, *Australia* ... **95 E5** 32 38 S 151 21 E
Bras d'Or L., *Canada* . **105 C7** 45 50N 60 50W
Brasher Falls, *U.S.A.* **117 B10** 44 49N 74 47W
Brasil, Planalto, *Brazil* **122 E6** 18 0 S 46 30W
Brasiléia, *Brazil* ...... **124 F5** 11 0 S 68 45W
Brasília, *Brazil* .... **125 G9** 15 47 S 47 55W
Brasília Legal, *Brazil* .. **125 D7** 3 49 S 55 36W
Braslaw, *Belarus* ..... **9 J22** 55 38N 27 0 E
Braslovče, *Slovenia* .. **41 B12** 46 21N 15 3 E
Braşov, *Romania* .... **29 E10** 45 45N 25 15 E
Braşov □, *Romania* .. **29 E10** 45 45N 25 15 E
Brass, *Nigeria* .... **83 E6** 4 35N 6 14 E
Brass ➤, *Nigeria* ..... **83 E6** 4 15N 6 13 E
Brassac-les-Mines,
  France .... **20 C7** 45 24N 3 20 E
Brasschaat, *Belgium* .. **17 C4** 51 19N 4 27 E
Brassey, Banjaran,
  Malaysia .... **62 D5** 5 0N 117 15 E
Brassey Ra., *Australia* **93 E3** 25 8 S 122 15 E
Brasstown Bald, *U.S.A.* **115 H4** 34 53N 83 49W
Brastad, *Sweden* ..... **11 F5** 58 23N 11 30 E
Brastavățu, *Romania* . **29 G9** 43 55N 24 24 E
Bratan = Morozov,
  Bulgaria .... **45 D9** 42 30N 25 10 E
Brateş, *Romania* ..... **29 E11** 45 50N 28 5 E
Bratislava, *Slovak Rep.* **27 C10** 48 10N 17 7 E
Bratislava M.R.
  Stefanik ✈ (BTS),
  Slovak Rep. ...... **27 C10** 48 11N 17 9 E

Bratislavský □,
Slovak Rep. . . . . **27 C10** 48 15N 17 20 E
Bratsigovo, Bulgaria . . **45 D8** 42 1N 24 22 E
Bratsk, Russia . . . . . . **53 D11** 56 10N 101 30 E
Brattleboro, U.S.A. . . . **117 D12** 42 51N 72 34W
Bratunac, Bos.-H. . . . . **28 F4** 44 13N 19 21 E
Braunau, Austria . . . . **26 C6** 48 15N 13 3 E
Braunschweig, Germany **24 C6** 52 15N 10 31 E
Braunton, U.K. **15 F3** 51 7N 4 10W
Bravicea, Moldova . . . **29 C13** 47 22N 28 27 E
Bråviken, Sweden . . . . **11 F10** 58 38N 16 32 E
Bravo del Norte, Rio →,
= Grande, Rio →,
U.S.A. **113 N6** 25 58N 97 9W
Brawley, U.S.A. **111 N11** 32 59N 115 31W
Bray, Ireland **12 C5** 53 13N 6 7W
Bray, Mt., Australia . . **94 A1** 14 0 S 134 30 E
Bray-sur-Seine, France **19 D10** 48 25N 3 14 E
Brazeau →, Canada . . **102 C5** 52 55N 115 14W
Brazil, U.S.A. **114 F2** 39 32N 87 8W
Brazil ■, S. Amer. . . . **125 F9** 12 0 S 50 0W
Brazilian Highlands =
Brasil, Planalto, Brazil **122 E6** 18 0 S 46 30W
Brazo Sur →, S. Amer. **126 B4** 25 21 S 57 42W
Brazos →, U.S.A. **113 L7** 28 53N 95 23W
Brazzaville, Congo . . . **84 E3** 4 9 S 15 12 E
Brčko, Bos.-H. . . . . . . **28 F3** 44 54N 18 46 E
Brda →, Poland . . . . . . **31 E5** 53 8N 18 8 E
Brdy, Czech Rep. . . . . . **26 B6** 49 43N 13 55 E
Breaden, L., Australia . **93 E4** 25 51 S 125 28 E
Breaksea Sd., N.Z. . . . **91 L1** 45 35 S 166 35 E
Bream B., N.Z. . . . . . . **91 F5** 35 56 S 174 28 E
Bream Hd., N.Z. . . . . . **91 F5** 35 51 S 174 36 E
Breas, Chile . . . . **126 B1** 25 29 S 70 24W
Breaza, Romania . . . . **29 E10** 45 11N 25 40 E
Brebes, Indonesia . . . . **63 G13** 6 52 S 109 3 E
Brechin, Canada **116 B5** 44 32N 79 10W
Brechin, U.K. **13 E6** 56 44N 2 39W
Brecht, Belgium . . . . . **17 C4** 51 21N 4 38 E
Breckenridge, Colo.,
U.S.A. **108 G10** 39 29N 106 3W
Breckenridge, Minn.,
U.S.A. **112 B6** 46 16N 96 35W
Breckenridge, Tex.,
U.S.A. **113 J5** 32 45N 98 54W
Breckland, U.K. . . . . . **15 E8** 52 30N 0 40 E
Břeclav, Czech Rep. . . **27 C9** 48 46N 16 53 E
Brecon, U.K. **15 F4** 51 57N 3 23W
Brecon Beacons, U.K. . **15 F4** 51 53N 3 26W
Brecon Beacons △, U.K. **15 F4** 51 50N 3 30W
Breda, Neths. . . . . **17 C4** 51 35N 4 45 E
Bredaryd, Sweden . . . . **11 G7** 57 10N 13 45 E
Bredasdorp, S. Africa . **88 E3** 34 33 S 20 2 E
Bredebro, Denmark . . . **11 J2** 55 4N 8 50 E
Bredstedt, Germany . . **24 A4** 54 37N 8 57 E
Bree, Belgium . . . . **17 C5** 51 8N 5 35 E
Bregalnica →,
Macedonia . . . . **44 E6** 41 43N 22 9 E
Bregenz, Austria . . . . . **26 D2** 47 30N 9 45 E
Bregovo, Bulgaria . . . **44 B6** 44 9N 22 39 E
Bréhal, France **18 D5** 48 53N 1 30W
Bréhat, Î. de, France . . **18 D4** 48 51 S 3 0W
Breiðafjörður, Iceland . **8 D2** 65 15N 23 15W
Breil-sur-Roya, France **21 E11** 43 56N 7 31 E
Breisach, Germany . . . **25 G3** 48 1N 7 36 E
Brejo, Brazil . . . . **125 D10** 3 41 S 42 47W
Bremen, Germany . . . . **24 B4** 53 4N 8 47 E
Bremen □, Germany . . **24 B4** 53 4N 8 50 E
Bremer Bay, Australia . **93 F2** 34 21 S 119 20 E
Bremer I., Australia . . **94 A2** 12 5 S 136 45 E
Bremerhaven, Germany **24 B4** 53 33N 8 36 E
Bremerton, U.S.A. . . . **110 C4** 47 34N 122 38W
Bremervörde, Germany **24 B5** 53 29N 9 8 E
Brenes, Spain **37 H5** 37 32N 5 54W
Brenham, U.S.A. **113 K6** 30 10N 96 24W
Brenne, France . . . . . . **20 B5** 46 44N 1 14 E
Brenne →, France . . . . **20 B5** 46 40N 1 15 E
Brennerpass, Austria . . **26 D4** 47 2N 11 30 E
Breno, Italy . . . . **40 C7** 45 57N 10 18 E
Brent →, Italy **115 J2** 32 56N 87 10W
Brenta →, Italy . . . . . **41 C9** 45 11N 12 18 E
Brentwood, U.K. . . . . **15 F8** 51 37N 0 19 E
Brentwood, Calif.,
U.S.A. **110 H5** 37 56N 121 42W
Brentwood, N.Y., U.S.A. **117 F11** 40 47N 73 15W
Bréscia, Italy . . . . **40 C7** 45 33N 10 15 E
Breskens, Neths. . . . . . **17 C3** 51 23N 3 33 E
Breslau = Wrocław,
Poland . . . . **31 G4** 51 5N 17 5 E
Bresle →, France . . . . **18 B8** 50 4N 1 22 E
Bressanone, Italy . . . . **41 B8** 46 43N 11 39 E
Bressay, U.K. **13 A7** 60 9N 1 6W
Bresse, France . . . . . . **19 F12** 46 50N 5 10 E
Bressuire, France **18 F6** 46 51N 0 30W
Brest, Belarus . . . . . . **33 F2** 52 10N 23 40 E
Brest, France **18 D2** 48 24N 4 31W
Brest-Litovsk = Brest,
Belarus . . . . **33 F2** 52 10N 23 40 E
Bretagne □, France . . . **18 D3** 48 10N 3 0W
Breteuil, Romania . . . . **29 D11** 46 7N 26 18 E
Bretenoux, France . . . **20 D5** 44 54N 1 51 E
Breteuil, Eure, France . **18 D7** 48 50N 0 57 E
Breteuil, Oise, France . **19 C9** 49 38N 2 18 E
Breton, Canada **102 C6** 53 7N 114 28W
Breton, Pertuis, France **20 B2** 46 17N 1 25W
Breton Sd., U.S.A. . . . **113 L10** 29 35N 89 15W
Brett, C., N.Z. . . . . **91 F5** 35 10 S 174 20 E
Bretten, Germany . . . . **25 F4** 49 2N 8 42 E
Breuil-Cérvínia, Italy . **40 C4** 45 56N 7 38 E
Brevard, U.S.A. **115 H4** 35 14N 82 44W
Breves, Brazil . . . . **125 D8** 1 40 S 50 29W
Brewarrina, Australia . **95 E4** 30 0 S 146 51 E
Brewer, U.S.A. **115 C11** 44 48N 68 46W
Brewer, Mt., U.S.A. . . **110 J8** 36 44N 118 28W
Brewerville, Liberia . . **82 D2** 6 26N 10 47W
Brewster, N.Y., U.S.A. . **117 E11** 41 23N 73 37W
Brewster, Ohio, U.S.A. **116 F3** 40 43N 81 36W
Brewster, Wash., U.S.A. **108 B4** 48 6N 119 47W
Brewster, Kap =
Kangikajik, Greenland **4 B6** 70 7N 22 0W
Brewton, U.S.A. **115 K2** 31 7N 87 4W
Breyten, S. Africa . . . . **89 D5** 26 16 S 30 0 E
Breza, Bos.-H. . . . . . . **28 F3** 44 0N 18 10 E
Brežice, Slovenia . . . . **41 C12** 45 54N 15 35 E
Březnice, Czech Rep. . **26 B6** 49 32N 13 57 E
Breznik, Bulgaria . . . . **44 D6** 42 44N 22 55 E
Brezno, Slovak Rep. . . **27 C12** 48 50N 19 40 E
Brezoi, Romania . . . . . **29 E9** 45 21N 24 15 E
Brezovica, Serbia & M. **44 D5** 42 15N 21 3 E
Brezovo, Bulgaria . . . . **45 D9** 42 21N 25 5 E
Briançon, France . . . . **21 D10** 44 54N 6 39 E
Briare, France . . . . . . **19 E9** 47 38N 2 45 E
Briático, Italy . . . . . . **43 D9** 38 43N 16 2 E
Bribie I., Australia . . . **95 D5** 27 0 S 153 10 E
Bribri, Costa Rica **120 E3** 9 38N 82 50W
Briceni, Moldova . . . . **29 B12** 48 22N 27 6 E
Bricquebec, France . . . **18 C5** 49 28N 1 38W

Bridgefield, Barbados . **121 g** 13 9N 59 36W
Bridgehampton, U.S.A. **117 F12** 40 56N 72 19W
Bridgend, U.K. **15 F4** 51 30N 3 34W
Bridgend □, U.K. **15 F4** 51 36N 3 36W
Bridgeport, Calif.,
U.S.A. **110 G7** 38 15N 119 14W
Bridgeport, Conn.,
U.S.A. **117 E11** 41 11N 73 12W
Bridgeport, Nebr.,
U.S.A. **112 E3** 41 40N 103 6W
Bridgeport, Tex., U.S.A. **113 J6** 33 13N 97 45W
Bridger, U.S.A. **108 D9** 45 18N 108 55W
Bridgeton, U.S.A. **114 F8** 39 26N 75 14W
Bridgetown, Australia . **93 F2** 33 58 S 116 7 E
Bridgetown, Barbados . **121 g** 13 5N 59 30W
Bridgetown, Canada . . **105 D6** 44 55N 65 18W
Bridgewater, Canada . . **105 D7** 44 25N 64 31W
Bridgewater, Mass.,
U.S.A. **117 E14** 41 59N 70 58W
Bridgewater, N.Y.,
U.S.A. **117 D9** 42 53N 75 15W
Bridgewater, C.,
Australia . . . . **95 F3** 38 23 S 141 23 E
Bridgewater-
Gagebrook, Australia **95 G4** 42 44 S 147 14 E
Bridgnorth, U.K. **15 E5** 52 32N 2 25W
Bridgton, U.S.A. **117 B14** 44 3N 70 42W
Bridgwater, U.K. **15 F5** 51 8N 2 59W
Bridgwater B., U.K. . . **15 F4** 51 15N 3 15W
Bridlington, U.K. **14 C7** 54 5N 0 12W
Bridlington B., U.K. . . **14 C7** 54 4N 0 10W
Bridport, Australia . . . **95 G4** 40 59 S 147 23 E
Bridport, U.K. **15 G5** 50 44N 2 45W
Briec, France **18 D2** 48 6N 4 0W
Brienne-le-Château,
France . . . . **19 D11** 48 24N 4 30 E
Brienon-sur-Armançon,
France . . . . **19 E10** 47 59N 3 38 E
Brienz, Switz. . . . . . . **25 J4** 46 46N 8 2 E
Brienzersee, Switz. . . . **25 J3** 46 44N 7 53 E
Brière △, France **18 E4** 47 22N 2 13W
Brig, Switz. . . . . **25 J4** 46 18N 7 59 E
Brigg, U.K. **14 D7** 53 34N 0 28W
Brigham City, U.S.A. . **108 F7** 41 31N 112 1W
Bright, Australia . . . . . **95 F4** 36 42 S 146 56 E
Brighton, Australia . . . **95 F2** 35 5 S 138 30 E
Brighton, Canada **116 B7** 44 2N 77 44W
Brighton, Trin. & Tob. **125 K15** 10 13N 61 39W
Brighton, U.K. **15 G7** 50 49N 0 7W
Brighton, Colo., U.S.A. **112 F2** 39 59N 104 49W
Brighton, N.Y., U.S.A. **116 C7** 43 8N 77 34W
Brignogan-Plage, France **18 D2** 48 40N 4 20W
Brignoles, France . . . . **21 E10** 43 25N 6 5 E
Brihuega, Spain **38 E2** 40 45N 2 52W
Brikama, Gambia **82 C1** 13 15N 16 45W
Brilliant, U.S.A. **116 F4** 40 15N 80 39W
Brilon, Germany . . . . . **24 D4** 51 23N 8 35 E
Bríndisi, Italy . . . . **43 B10** 40 39N 17 55 E
Brinje, Croatia . . . . . . **41 D12** 44 59N 15 9 E
Brinkley, U.S.A. **113 H9** 34 53N 91 12W
Brinnon, U.S.A. **110 C4** 47 41N 122 54W
Brion, Î., Canada **105 C7** 47 46N 61 26W
Brionne, France . . . . . **18 C7** 49 11N 0 43 E
Brionski, Croatia . . . . **41 D10** 44 55N 13 45 E
Brioude, France . . . . . **20 C7** 45 18N 3 24 E
Briouze, France **18 D6** 48 42N 0 23W
Brisbane, Australia . . . **95 D5** 27 25 S 153 2 E
Brisbane →, Australia . **95 D5** 27 24 S 153 9 E
Brisighella, Italy . . . . **41 D8** 44 13N 11 46 E
Bristol, U.K. **15 F5** 51 26N 2 35W
Bristol, Conn., U.S.A. . **117 E12** 41 40N 72 57W
Bristol, Pa., U.S.A. . . . **117 F10** 40 6N 74 51W
Bristol, R.I., U.S.A. . . **117 E13** 41 40N 71 16W
Bristol, Tenn., U.S.A. . **115 G4** 36 36N 82 11W
Bristol, City of □, U.K. **15 F5** 51 27N 2 36W
Bristol B., U.S.A. **100 C4** 58 0N 160 0W
Bristol Channel, U.K. . **15 F3** 51 18N 4 30W
Bristol I., Antarctica . . **5 B1** 58 45 S 28 0W
Bristol L., U.S.A. **109 J5** 34 23N 116 50W
Bristow, U.S.A. **113 H6** 35 50N 96 23W
Britain = Great Britain,
Europe **6 E5** 54 0N 2 15W
British Columbia □,
Canada **102 C3** 55 0N 125 15W
British Indian Ocean
Terr. = Chagos
Arch. ⌀, Ind. Oc. . . . **50 K11** 6 0 S 72 0 E
British Isles, Europe . . **6 D4** 54 0N 4 0W
British Virgin Is. ⌀,
W. Indies . . . . **121 e** 18 30N 64 30W
Brits, S. Africa . . . . . . **89 D4** 25 37 S 27 48 E
Britstown, S. Africa . . **88 E3** 30 37 S 23 30 E
Britt, Canada **104 C3** 45 46N 80 34W
Brittany = Bretagne □,
France **18 D3** 48 10N 3 0W
Britton, U.S.A. **112 C6** 45 48N 97 45W
Brive-la-Gaillarde,
France . . . . **20 C5** 45 10N 1 32 E
Briviesca, Spain **36 C7** 42 32N 3 19W
Brixen = Bressanone,
Italy . . . . **41 B8** 46 43N 11 39 E
Brixham, U.K. **15 G4** 50 23N 3 31W
Brnaze, Croatia . . . . . **41 E13** 43 41N 16 40 E
Brnenský □, Czech Rep. **27 B9** 49 10N 16 40 E
Brno, Czech Rep. . . . . **27 B9** 49 10N 16 35 E
Broach = Bharuch, India **66 J8** 21 47N 73 0 E
Broad →, U.S.A. **115 J5** 34 1N 81 4W
Broad Arrow, Australia **93 F3** 30 23 S 121 15 E
Broad B., U.K. **13 C2** 58 14N 6 18W
Broad Haven, Ireland . **12 B2** 54 20N 9 55W
Broad Law, U.K. **13 F5** 55 30N 3 21W
Broad Sd., Australia . . **94 C4** 22 0 S 149 45 E
Broadalbin, U.S.A. . . . **117 C10** 43 4N 74 12W
Broadback →, Canada . **104 B4** 51 21N 78 52W
Broadhurst Ra.,
Australia . . . . **92 D3** 22 30 S 122 30 E
Broads △, U.K. . . . . . **15 E9** 52 45N 1 30 E
Broads, The, U.K. . . . . **14 E9** 52 45N 1 30 E
Broadus, U.S.A. **112 C2** 45 27N 105 25W
Broager, Denmark . . . . **11 K3** 54 53N 9 40 E
Broby, Sweden . . . . . . **11 H8** 56 15N 14 4 E
Brocēni, Latvia . . . . . **30 B9** 56 42N 22 35 E
Brochet, Canada **103 B8** 57 53N 101 40W
Brochet, L., Canada . . **103 B8** 58 36N 101 35W
Brocken, Germany . . . **24 D6** 51 47N 10 37 E
Brockport, U.S.A. **116 C7** 43 13N 77 56W
Brockton, U.S.A. **117 D13** 42 5N 71 1W
Brockville, Canada . . . **117 B9** 44 35N 75 41W
Brockway, Mont., U.S.A. **112 B2** 47 18N 105 45W
Brockway, Pa., U.S.A. . **116 E6** 41 15N 78 47W
Brocton, U.S.A. **116 D5** 42 23N 79 26W
Brod, Macedonia . . . . **44 E5** 41 32N 21 17 E
Brodarevo, Serbia & M. **44 C3** 43 14N 19 44 E
Brodeur Pen., Canada . **101 A11** 72 30N 88 10W
Brodhead, Mt., U.S.A. **116 E7** 41 39N 77 47W
Brodick, U.K. **13 F3** 55 35N 5 9W
Brodnica, Poland . . . . **31 E6** 53 15N 19 25 E

Brody, Ukraine . . . . . . **33 G3** 50 5N 25 10 E
Brogan, U.S.A. **108 D5** 44 15N 117 31W
Broglie, France . . . . . . **18 C7** 49 2N 0 30 E
Brok, Poland . . . . **31 F8** 52 43N 21 52 E
Broken Arrow, U.S.A. . **113 G7** 36 3N 95 48W
Broken Bow, Nebr.,
U.S.A. **112 E5** 41 24N 99 38W
Broken Bow, Okla.,
U.S.A. **113 H7** 34 2N 94 44W
Broken Bow Lake,
U.S.A. **113 H7** 34 9N 94 40W
Broken Hill, Australia . **95 E3** 31 58 S 141 29 E
Broken River Ra.,
Australia . . . . **94 K6** 21 0 S 148 22 E
Brokind, Sweden . . . . **11 F9** 58 13N 15 42 E
Bromley □, U.K. . . . . **15 F8** 51 24N 0 2 E
Bromo, Indonesia . . . . **63 G15** 7 55 S 112 55 E
Bromölla, Sweden . . . . **11 H8** 56 5N 14 28 E
Bromsgrove, U.K. **15 E5** 52 21N 2 2W
Brønderslev, Denmark . **11 G3** 57 16N 9 57 E
Brong-Ahafo □, Ghana **82 D4** 7 50N 2 0W
Broni, Italy . . . . **40 C6** 45 4N 9 16 E
Bronkhorstspruit,
S. Africa . . . . **89 D4** 25 46 S 28 45 E
Brønnøysund, Norway . **8 D15** 65 28N 12 14 E
Bronte, Italy . . . . **43 E7** 37 47N 14 50 E
Brook Park, U.S.A. . . . **116 E4** 41 24N 81 51W
Brookhaven, U.S.A. . . **113 K9** 31 35N 90 26W
Brookings, Oreg., U.S.A. **108 E1** 42 3N 124 17W
Brookings, S. Dak.,
U.S.A. **112 C6** 44 19N 96 48W
Brooklin, Canada **116 C6** 43 55N 78 55W
Brooklyn Park, U.S.A. **112 C8** 45 6N 93 23W
Brooks, Canada **102 C6** 50 35N 111 55W
Brooks Range, U.S.A. . **100 B5** 68 0N 152 0W
Brooksville, U.S.A. . . . **115 L4** 28 33N 82 23W
Brookton, Australia . . . **93 F2** 32 22 S 117 0 E
Brookville, U.S.A. . . . **116 E5** 41 10N 79 5W
Broom, L., U.K. **13 D3** 57 55N 5 15W
Broome, Australia . . . . **92 C3** 18 0 S 122 15 E
Broons, France **18 D4** 48 20N 2 16W
Brora, U.K. **13 C5** 58 0N 3 52W
Brora →, U.K. **13 C5** 58 0N 3 51W
Brørup, Denmark . . . . **11 J2** 55 29N 9 1 E
Brösarp, Sweden . . . . **11 J8** 55 43N 14 6 E
Brosna →, Ireland . . . **12 C4** 53 14N 7 58W
Broșteni, Mehedinți,
Romania . . . . **28 F7** 44 45N 22 59 E
Broșteni, Suceava,
Romania . . . . **29 C10** 47 14N 25 43 E
Brothers, U.S.A. **108 E3** 43 49N 120 36W
Brou, France . . . . **18 D8** 48 13N 1 11 E
Brouage, France **20 C2** 45 52N 1 4W
Brough, U.K. **14 C5** 54 32N 2 18W
Brough Hd., U.K. **13 B5** 59 8N 3 20W
Broughton Island =
Qikiqtarjuaq, Canada **101 B13** 67 33N 63 0W
Broumov, Czech Rep. . **27 A9** 50 35N 16 20 E
Broumy, Ukraine . . . . **33 G6** 50 34N 30 48 E
Brovst, Denmark . . . . **11 G3** 57 6N 9 31 E
Brown, L., Australia . . **93 F2** 31 5 S 118 15 E
Brown, Pt., Australia . . **95 E1** 32 32 S 133 50 E
Brown City, U.S.A. . . . **116 C2** 43 13N 82 59W
Brown Willy, U.K. . . . **15 G3** 50 35N 4 37W
Brownfield, U.S.A. . . . **113 J3** 33 11N 102 17W
Browning, U.S.A. **108 B7** 48 34N 113 1W
Brownsville, Oreg.,
U.S.A. **108 D2** 44 24N 122 59W
Brownsville, Pa., U.S.A. **116 F5** 40 1N 79 53W
Brownsville, Tenn.,
U.S.A. **113 H10** 35 36N 89 16W
Brownsville, Tex., U.S.A. **113 N6** 25 54N 97 30W
Brownville, U.S.A. . . . **117 C9** 44 0N 75 59W
Brownwood, U.S.A. . . **113 K5** 31 43N 98 59W
Browse I., Australia . . **92 B3** 14 7 S 123 33 E
Bruas, Malaysia . . . . . **65 K3** 4 30N 100 47 E
Bruay-la-Buissière,
France . . . . **19 B9** 50 29N 2 33 E
Bruce, Mt., Australia . . **92 D2** 22 37 S 118 8 E
Bruce Pen., Canada . . **116 B3** 45 0N 81 30W
Bruce Peninsula △,
Canada **116 A3** 45 14N 81 36W
Bruce Rock, Australia . **93 F2** 31 52 S 118 8 E
Bruche →, France . . . . **19 D14** 48 34N 7 43 E
Bruchsal, Germany . . . **25 F4** 49 7N 8 35 E
Bruck an der Leitha,
Austria . . . . **27 C9** 48 1N 16 47 E
Bruck an der Mur,
Austria . . . . **26 D8** 47 24N 15 16 E
Brue →, U.K. **15 F5** 51 13N 2 59W
Bruges = Brugge,
Belgium . . . . **17 C3** 51 13N 3 13 E
Brugg, Switz. . . . . **25 H4** 47 29N 8 11 E
Brugge, Belgium . . . . . **17 C3** 51 13N 3 13 E
Bruin, U.S.A. **116 E5** 41 3N 79 43W
Brûlé, Canada **102 C5** 53 15N 117 58W
Brûlon, France **18 E6** 47 58N 0 15W
Brumado, Brazil . . . . . **125 F10** 14 14 S 41 40W
Brumath, France . . . . . **19 D14** 48 43N 7 40 E
Brumunddal, Norway . **9 F14** 60 53N 10 56 E
Bruneau, U.S.A. **108 E6** 42 56N 115 48W
Bruneau →, U.S.A. . . **108 E6** 42 56N 115 57W
Bruneck = Brunico, Italy **41 B8** 46 48N 11 56 E
Brunei = Bandar Seri
Begawan, Brunei . . **62 C4** 4 52N 115 0 E
Brunei ■, Asia . . . . . . **62 D4** 4 50N 115 0 E
Brunflo, Sweden . . . . . **10 A8** 63 5N 14 50 E
Brunico, Italy . . . . **41 B8** 46 48N 11 56 E
Brunna, Sweden . . . . . **10 E11** 59 52N 17 25 E
Brunnen, Switz. . . . . . **25 J4** 46 59N 8 37 E
Brunner, L., N.Z. . . . . **91 K3** 42 37 S 171 27 E
Brunsbüttel, Germany . **24 B5** 53 53N 9 6 E
Brunssum, Neths. . . . . **17 D5** 50 57N 5 59 E
Brunswick =
Braunschweig,
Germany . . . . **24 C6** 52 15N 10 31 E
Brunswick, Ga., U.S.A. **115 K5** 31 10N 81 30W
Brunswick, Maine,
U.S.A. **115 D11** 43 55N 69 58W
Brunswick, Md., U.S.A. **114 F7** 39 19N 77 38W
Brunswick, Mo., U.S.A. **112 F8** 39 26N 93 8W
Brunswick, Ohio, U.S.A. **116 E3** 41 14N 81 51W
Brunswick, Pen. de,
Chile . . . . **128 G2** 53 30 S 71 30W
Brunswick B., Australia **92 C3** 15 15 S 124 50 E
Brunswick Junction,
Australia . . . . **93 F2** 33 15 S 115 50 E
Bruntál, Czech Rep. . . **27 A10** 49 59N 17 27 E
Bruny I., Australia . . . **95 G4** 43 20 S 147 15 E
Brus Laguna, Honduras **120 C3** 15 47N 84 35W
Brusartsi, Bulgaria . . . **44 C7** 43 40N 23 5 E
Brush, U.S.A. **112 E3** 40 15N 103 37W
Brushton, U.S.A. **117 B10** 44 50N 74 31W
Brusio, Switz. . . . . . . **25 J6** 46 14N 10 8 E
Brusque, Brazil . . . . . . **127 B6** 27 5 S 49 0W
Brussel, Belgium . . . . **17 D4** 50 51N 4 21 E
Brussel ✈ (BRU),
Belgium . . . . **17 D5** 50 54N 5 41 E

Brussels = Brussel,
Belgium . . . . **17 D4** 50 51N 4 21 E
Brussels, Canada **116 C3** 43 44N 81 15W
Brusy, Poland . . . . **30 E4** 53 53N 17 40 E
Bruthen, Australia . . . . **95 F4** 37 42 S 147 50 E
Bruxelles = Brussel,
Belgium . . . . **17 D4** 50 51N 4 21 E
Bruyères, France . . . . **19 D13** 48 10N 6 40 E
Bruz, France **18 D5** 48 1N 1 46W
Brwinów, Poland . . . . **31 F7** 52 9N 20 40 E
Bryagovo, Bulgaria . . . **45 E9** 41 58N 25 8 E
Bryan, Ohio, U.S.A. . . **114 E3** 41 28N 84 33W
Bryan, Tex., U.S.A. . . . **113 K6** 30 40N 96 22W
Bryan, Mt., Australia . . **95 E2** 33 30 S 139 0 E
Bryanka, Ukraine . . . . **33 H10** 48 32N 38 45 E
Bryansk, Bryansk,
Russia . . . . **33 F8** 53 13N 34 25 E
Bryansk, Dagestan,
Russia . . . . **35 H8** 44 20N 47 10 E
Bryanskoye = Bryansk,
Russia . . . . **35 H8** 44 20N 47 10 E
Bryce Canyon △, U.S.A. **109 H7** 37 30N 112 10W
Bryne, Norway . . . . . . **9 G11** 58 44N 5 38 E
Bryson City, U.S.A. . . **115 H4** 35 26N 83 27W
Bryukhovetskaya,
Russia . . . . **33 K10** 45 48N 39 0 E
Brza Palanka,
Serbia & M. . . . . . . **44 B6** 44 28N 22 27 E
Brzeg, Poland . . . . **31 H4** 50 52N 17 30 E
Brzeg Dolny, Poland . . **31 G3** 51 16N 16 41 E
Brześć Kujawski, Poland **31 F5** 52 36N 18 55 E
Brzesko, Poland . . . . . **31 J7** 49 59N 20 34 E
Brzeziny, Poland . . . . . **31 G6** 51 49N 19 42 E
Brzozów, Poland . . . . . **31 J9** 49 41N 22 3 E
Bsharri, Lebanon . . . . **74 A5** 34 15N 36 0 E
Bū Baqarah, U.A.E. . . **71 E8** 25 35N 56 25 E
Bu Craa, W. Sahara . . **78 C3** 26 45N 12 50W
Bū Ḥasā, U.A.E. . . . . **71 F7** 23 30N 53 20 E
Bua, Sweden . . . . **11 G6** 57 14N 12 7 E
Bua Yai, Thailand . . . . **64 E4** 15 33N 102 26 E
Buapinang, Indonesia . **63 E6** 4 40 S 121 30 E
Buba, Guinea-Biss. . . . **82 C2** 11 40N 14 59W
Bubanza, Burundi . . . . **86 C2** 3 6 S 29 23 E
Bubaque, Guinea-Biss. **82 C1** 11 16N 15 51W
Bube, Ethiopia . . . . . . **81 F4** 8 46N 35 48 E
Būbiyān, Kuwait . . . . **71 D6** 29 45N 48 15 E
Buca, Turkey . . . . **47 C9** 38 22N 27 11 E
Bucak, Turkey . . . . . . **47 D12** 37 28N 30 36 E
Bucaramanga, Colombia **124 B4** 7 0N 73 0W
Bucas Grande I., Phil. . **61 G6** 9 40N 125 57 E
Bucasia, Australia . . . . **94 K7** 21 2 S 149 10 E
Buccaneer Arch.,
Australia . . . . **92 C3** 16 7 S 123 20 E
Bucecea, Romania . . . . **29 C11** 47 47N 26 28 E
Bucegi △, Romania . . . **29 E10** 45 25N 25 27 E
Buchach, Ukraine . . . . **33 H3** 49 5N 25 25 E
Buchan, U.K. **13 D6** 57 32N 2 21W
Buchan Ness, U.K. . . . **13 D7** 57 29N 1 46W
Buchanan, Canada . . . **103 C8** 51 40N 102 45W
Buchanan, Liberia **82 D2** 5 57N 10 2W
Buchanan, L., Queens.,
Australia . . . . **94 C4** 21 35 S 145 52 E
Buchanan, L.,
W. Austral., Australia **93 E3** 25 33 S 123 2 E
Buchanan, L., U.S.A. . **113 K5** 30 45N 98 25W
Buchanan Cr. →,
Australia . . . . **94 B2** 19 13 S 136 33 E
Buchans, Canada **105 C8** 48 50N 56 52W
Bucharest = București,
Romania . . . . **29 F11** 44 27N 26 10 E
Buchen, Germany . . . . **25 F5** 49 32N 9 20 E
Buchholz, Germany . . **24 B5** 53 19N 9 52 E
Buchloe, Germany . . . **25 G6** 48 1N 10 44 E
Buchon, Pt., U.S.A. . . **110 K6** 35 15N 120 54W
Buciumi, Romania . . . **28 C8** 47 3N 23 1 E
Buck Hill Falls, U.S.A. **117 E9** 41 11N 75 16W
Bückeburg, Germany . **24 C5** 52 16N 9 7 E
Buckeye, U.S.A. **109 K7** 33 22N 112 35W
Buckeye Lake, U.S.A. . **116 F2** 39 55N 82 29W
Buckhannon, U.S.A. . . **114 F5** 39 0N 80 8W
Buckhaven, U.K. **13 E5** 56 11N 3 3W
Buckhorn L., Canada . . **116 B6** 44 29N 78 23W
Buckie, U.K. **13 D6** 57 41N 2 58W
Buckingham, Canada . **104 C4** 45 37N 75 24W
Buckingham, U.K. . . . **15 F7** 51 59N 0 57W
Buckingham B.,
Australia . . . . **94 A2** 12 10 S 135 40 E
Buckinghamshire □,
U.K. **15 F7** 51 53N 0 55W
Buckle Hd., Australia . **92 B4** 14 26 S 127 52 E
Buckleboo, Australia . . **95 E2** 32 54 S 136 12 E
Buckley, U.K. **14 D4** 53 10N 3 5W
Buckley →, Australia . **94 C2** 20 10 S 138 49 E
Bucklin, U.S.A. **113 G5** 37 33N 99 38W
Bucks L., U.S.A. **110 F5** 39 54N 121 12W
Bucquoy, France . . . . . **19 B9** 50 9N 2 43 E
Bucureșci, Romania . . **29 E8** 45 59N 22 51 E
București, Romania . . . **29 F11** 44 27N 26 10 E
București Otopeni ✈
(OTP), Romania . . . **45 B10** 44 30N 26 17 E
Bucyrus, U.S.A. **114 E4** 40 48N 82 59W
Budacu, Vf., Romania . **29 C10** 47 7N 25 41 E
Budalin, Burma . . . . . **67 H19** 22 20N 95 10 E
Budaörs, Hungary . . . **28 C3** 47 27N 18 58 E
Budapest, Hungary . . . **28 C3** 47 29N 19 5 E
Budapest ✈ (BUD),
Hungary . . . . **28 C4** 47 25N 19 12 E
Budaun, India . . . . **69 E8** 28 5N 79 10 E
Budd Coast, Antarctica **5 C8** 68 0 S 112 0 E
Buddusò, Italy . . . . . . **42 B2** 40 35N 9 15 E
Budești, Romania . . . . **29 F11** 44 13N 26 30 E
Budge Budge = Baj Baj,
India . . . . **69 H13** 22 30N 88 5 E
Budgewoi, Australia . . **95 E5** 33 13 S 151 34 E
Budia, Spain **38 E2** 40 38N 2 46W
Büdingen, Germany . . **25 E5** 50 16N 9 7 E
Budjala, Dem. Rep. of
the Congo . . . . **84 D3** 2 50N 19 40 E
Budoni, Italy . . . . **42 B2** 40 40N 9 45 E
Búdrio, Italy . . . . **41 D8** 44 32N 11 32 E
Budva, Serbia & M. . . **44 D2** 42 17N 18 50 E
Budzyń, Poland . . . . . **31 F3** 52 54N 16 59 E
Buea, Cameroon . . . . . **83 E6** 4 10N 9 9 E
Buellton, U.S.A. **111 L6** 34 37N 120 12W
Buena Esperanza,
Argentina . . . . **126 C2** 34 45 S 65 15W
Buena Park, U.S.A. . . . **111 M9** 33 52N 117 59W
Buena Vista, Colo.,
U.S.A. **109 G10** 38 51N 106 8W
Buena Vista, Va., U.S.A. **114 G6** 37 44N 79 21W
Buena Vista Lake Bed,
U.S.A. **111 K7** 35 12N 119 18W

Buenaventura,
Colombia **124 C3** 3 53N 77 4W
Buenaventura, Mexico . **118 B3** 29 50N 107 30W
Buendía, Embalse de,
Spain **38 E2** 40 25N 2 43W
Buenos Aires, Argentina **126 C4** 34 30 S 58 20W
Buenos Aires,
Costa Rica **120 E3** 9 10N 83 20W
Buenos Aires □,
Argentina . . . . **126 D4** 36 30 S 60 0W
Buenos Aires, L., Chile **128 F2** 46 35 S 72 30W
Buffalo, Mo., U.S.A. . . **113 G8** 37 39N 93 6W
Buffalo, N.Y., U.S.A. . **116 D6** 42 53N 78 53W
Buffalo, Okla., U.S.A. . **113 G5** 36 50N 99 38W
Buffalo, S. Dak., U.S.A. **112 C3** 45 35N 103 33W
Buffalo, Wyo., U.S.A. . **108 D10** 44 21N 106 42W
Buffalo →, Canada . . . **102 A5** 60 5N 115 5W
Buffalo →, Canada . . . **89 D5** 28 43 S 30 37 E
Buffalo Head Hills,
Canada **102 B5** 57 25N 115 55W
Buffalo L., Alta., Canada **102 C6** 52 27N 112 54W
Buffalo L., N.W.T.,
Canada **102 A5** 60 12N 115 25W
Buffalo Narrows,
Canada **103 B7** 55 51N 108 29W
Buffalo Springs △,
Kenya . . . . **86 B4** 0 32N 37 35 E
Buffels →, S. Africa . . **88 D2** 29 36 S 17 3 E
Buford, U.S.A. **115 H4** 34 10N 84 0W
Bug = Buh →, Ukraine **33 J6** 46 59N 31 58 E
Bug →, Poland . . . . . . **31 F8** 52 31N 21 5 E
Buga, Colombia **124 C3** 4 0N 76 15W
Bugala I., Uganda . . . . **86 C3** 0 40 S 32 20 E
Buganda, Uganda . . . . **86 C3** 0 0 31 30 E
Buganga, Uganda . . . . **86 C3** 0 3 S 32 0 E
Bugasong, Phil. . . . . . **61 F5** 11 3N 122 4 E
Bugeat, France . . . . . . **20 C5** 45 36N 1 55 E
Bugel, Tanjung,
Indonesia . . . . **63 G14** 6 26 S 111 3 E
Bugibba, Malta . . . . . **49 D1** 35 57N 14 25 E
Bugojno, Bos.-H. . . . . **28 F2** 44 2N 17 25 E
Bugsuk, Phil. . . . . **62 C5** 8 15N 117 15 E
Buguma, Nigeria . . . . **83 E6** 4 42N 6 55 E
Bugun Shara, Mongolia **60 B5** 49 0N 104 0 E
Bugungu △, Uganda . . **86 B3** 2 17N 31 50 E
Buguruslan, Russia . . . **52 D6** 53 39N 52 26 E
Buh →, Ukraine . . . . . **33 J6** 46 59N 31 58 E
Buharkent, Turkey . . . **47 D10** 37 58N 28 44 E
Buheirat-Murrat-el-
Kubra, Egypt . . . . . **80 H8** 30 18N 32 26 E
Buhera, Zimbabwe . . . **89 B5** 19 18 S 31 29 E
Bühl, Germany . . . . . . **25 G4** 48 40N 8 10 E
Buhl, U.S.A. **108 E6** 42 36N 114 46W
Buhuși, Romania . . . . **29 D11** 46 41N 26 45 E
Bui △, Ghana **82 D4** 8 21N 2 21W
Builth Wells, U.K. . . . **15 E4** 52 9N 3 25W
Buinsk, Russia . . . . . . **34 C9** 55 0N 48 18 E
Buir Nur, Mongolia . . **60 B6** 47 50N 117 42 E
Buis-les-Baronnies,
France . . . . **21 D9** 44 17N 5 16 E
Buitrago del Lozoya,
Spain **36 E7** 40 58N 3 38W
Bujalance, Spain **37 H6** 37 54N 4 23W
Bujanovac, Serbia & M. **44 D5** 42 28N 21 44 E
Bujaraloz, Spain **38 D4** 41 29N 0 10W
Buje, Croatia . . . . **41 C10** 45 24N 13 39 E
Bujumbura, Burundi . . **86 C2** 3 16 S 29 18 E
Būk, Hungary . . . . **28 C1** 47 22N 16 45 E
Buk, Poland . . . . **31 F3** 52 21N 16 30 E
Bukachacha, Russia . . **53 D12** 52 55N 116 50 E
Bukama, Dem. Rep. of
the Congo . . . . **87 D2** 9 10 S 25 50 E
Bukavu, Dem. Rep. of
the Congo . . . . **86 C2** 2 20 S 28 52 E
Bukene, Tanzania . . . . **86 C3** 4 15 S 32 48 E
Bukhara = Bukhoro,
Uzbekistan . . . . **52 F7** 39 48N 64 25 E
Bukhoro, Uzbekistan . **52 F7** 39 48N 64 25 E
Bukima, Tanzania . . . . **86 C3** 1 50 S 33 25 E
Bukit Badung, Indonesia **63 K18** 8 49 S 115 10 E
Bukit Kerajaan,
Malaysia . . . . **65 c** 5 25N 100 15 E
Bukit Mertajam,
Malaysia . . . . **65 c** 5 22N 100 28 E
Bukit Ni, Malaysia . . . **65 d** 1 22N 104 12 E
Bukit Panjang,
Singapore . . . . **65 d** 1 23N 103 46 E
Bukit Tengah, Indonesia **62 E2** 5 22N 100 25 E
Bukittinggi, Indonesia . **62 E2** 0 20 S 100 20 E
Bükk, Hungary . . . . . . **28 B5** 48 0N 20 30 E
Bükki △, Hungary . . . **28 B5** 48 0N 20 30 E
Bukoba, Tanzania . . . . **86 C3** 1 20 S 31 49 E
Bukum, Pulau,
Singapore . . . . **65 d** 1 14N 103 46 E
Bukuru, Nigeria . . . . . **83 D6** 9 42N 8 48 E
Bukuya, Uganda . . . . . **86 B3** 0 40N 31 52 E
Būl, Kuh-e, Iran . . . . . **71 D7** 30 48N 52 45 E
Bula, Guinea-Biss. . . . **82 C1** 12 7N 15 43W
Bula, Indonesia . . . . . **63 E8** 3 6 S 130 30 E
Bülach, Switz. . . . . . . **25 H4** 47 31N 8 32 E
Bulahdelah, Australia . **95 E5** 32 23 S 152 13 E
Bulan, Phil. . . . . **61 E5** 12 40N 123 52 E
Bulancak, Turkey . . . . **73 B8** 40 56N 38 14 E
Bulandshahr, India . . . **68 E7** 28 28N 77 51 E
Bulanık, Turkey . . . . . **73 C10** 39 4N 42 14 E
Bûlâq, Egypt . . . . **80 B3** 25 10N 30 38 E
Bulawayo, Zimbabwe . **87 G2** 20 7 S 28 32 E
Buldan, Turkey . . . . . . **47 C10** 38 2N 28 50 E
Bulgar, Russia . . . . . . **34 C9** 54 57N 49 4 E
Bulgaria ■, Europe . . . **45 D9** 42 35N 25 30 E
Bulgheria, Monte, Italy **43 B8** 40 4N 15 26 E
Bulgurca, Turkey . . . . **47 D9** 38 7N 27 4 E
Buli, Teluk, Indonesia . **63 D7** 0 48N 128 25 E
Buliluyan, C., Phil. . . . **61 G2** 8 20N 117 15 E
Bulim, Singapore . . . . **65 d** 1 22N 103 43 E
Bulki, Ethiopia . . . . . . **81 F4** 6 11N 36 31 E
Bulkley →, Canada . . . **102 B3** 55 15N 127 40W
Bull Shoals L., U.S.A. . **113 G8** 36 22N 92 35W
Bullaque →, Spain . . . **37 G6** 38 59N 4 17W
Bullas, Spain **39 G3** 38 2N 1 40W
Bulle, Switz. . . . . **25 J3** 46 37N 7 3 E
Bullenga →, Australia . **94 B3** 17 43 S 144 31 E
Bullhead City, U.S.A. . **111 K12** 35 8N 114 32W
Büllingen, Belgium . . . **17 D6** 50 25N 6 16 E
Bullock Creek, Australia **94 B3** 17 43 S 144 31 E
Bulloo →, Australia . . **95 D3** 28 43 S 142 30 E
Bulloo L., Australia . . **95 D3** 28 43 S 142 30 E
Bulls, N.Z. . . . . **91 J5** 40 10 S 175 24 E
Bully-les-Mines, France **19 B9** 50 27N 2 44 E
Bulnes, Chile . . . . **126 D1** 36 42 S 72 19W
Bulqizë, Albania . . . . . **44 E4** 41 30N 20 21 E
Bulsar = Valsad, India **66 J8** 20 40N 72 58 E
Bultfontein, S. Africa . **88 D4** 28 18 S 26 10 E
Bulukumba, Indonesia . **63 F6** 5 33 S 120 11 E
Bulun, Russia . . . . **53 B13** 70 37N 127 30 E
Bumba, Dem. Rep. of
the Congo . . . . **84 D4** 2 13N 22 30 E

Bumbeşti-Jiu, Romania ... 29 E8 45 10N 23 24 E
Bumbiri I., Tanzania .. 86 C3 1 40 S 31 55 E
Bumbuna, S. Leone .. 82 D2 9 2N 11 49 W
Bumhpa Bum, Burma .. 67 F20 26 51N 97 14 E
Bumi ➤, Zimbabwe ... 87 F2 17 0 S 28 20 E
Buna, Kenya ...... 86 B4 2 58N 39 30 E
Bunawan, Phil. ..... 61 G6 8 12N 125 57 E
Bunazi, Tanzania .... 86 C3 1 3 S 31 23 E
Bunbury, Australia ... 93 F2 33 20 S 115 35 E
Bunclody, Ireland ... 12 D5 52 39N 6 40W
Buncrana, Ireland ... 12 A4 55 8N 7 27W
Bundaberg, Australia .. 95 C5 24 54 S 152 22 E
Bünde, Germany .... 24 C4 52 11N 8 35 E
Bundey ➤, Australia .. 94 C2 21 46 S 135 37 E
Bundi, India ...... 68 G6 25 30N 75 35 E
Bundjalung △, Australia 95 D5 29 16 S 153 21 E
Bundoran, Ireland ... 12 B3 54 28N 8 16W
Bundukia, Sudan ... 81 F3 5 14N 30 55 E
Bung Kan, Thailand .. 64 C4 18 23N 103 37 E
Bunga ➤, Nigeria ... 83 C6 11 23N 9 56 E
Bungay, U.K. ..... 15 E9 52 27N 1 28 E
Bungil Cr. ➤, Australia 95 D4 27 5 S 149 5 E
Bungo-Suidō, Japan .. 55 H6 33 0N 132 15 E
Bungoma, Kenya .... 86 B3 0 34N 34 34 E
Bungotakada, Japan .. 55 H5 33 35N 131 25 E
Bungu, Tanzania .... 86 D4 7 35 S 39 0 E
Bunia, Dem. Rep. of
the Congo ...... 86 B3 1 35N 30 20 E
Bunji, Pakistan .... 69 B6 35 45N 74 40 E
Bunkie, U.S.A. 113 K8 30 57N 92 11W
Bunnell, U.S.A. 115 L5 29 28N 81 16W
Buñol, Spain 39 F4 39 25N 0 47W
Bunsuru, Nigeria ... 83 C5 13 0N 5 8 E
Buntok, Indonesia ... 62 E4 1 40 S 114 58 E
Bununu Dass, Nigeria . 83 C6 10 5N 9 31 E
Bununu Kasa, Nigeria . 83 D6 9 51N 9 32 E
Bunya Mts. △, Australia 95 D5 26 51 S 151 34 E
Bünyan, Turkey .... 72 C6 38 51N 35 51 E
Bunyu, Indonesia ... 62 D5 3 35N 117 50 E
Bunza, Nigeria .... 83 C5 12 8N 4 0 E
Buol, Indonesia .... 63 D6 1 15N 121 32 E
Buon Brieng, Vietnam . 64 F7 13 9N 108 12 E
Buon Ma Thuot,
Vietnam .... 64 F7 12 40N 108 3 E
Buong Long, Cambodia . 64 F6 13 44N 106 59 E
Buorkhaya, Mys, Russia 53 B14 71 50N 132 40 E
Buqayq, Si. Arabia .. 71 E6 26 0N 49 45 E
Buqbuq, Egypt ..... 80 A2 31 29N 25 29 E
Bur Acaba, Somali Rep. 75 G3 3 12N 44 20 E
Bûr Fuad, Egypt .... 80 H8 31 15N 32 20 E
Bûr Safâga, Egypt ... 70 E2 26 43N 33 57 E
Bûr Sa'îd, Egypt .... 80 H8 31 16N 32 18 E
Bûr Sûdân, Sudan ... 80 D4 19 32N 37 9 E
Bûr Taufiq, Egypt ... 80 J8 29 54N 32 32 E
Bura, Kenya ...... 86 C4 1 4 S 39 58 E
Burakin, Australia ... 93 F2 30 31 S 117 10 E
Buram, Sudan ..... 81 E2 10 51N 25 9 E
Burao, Somali Rep. .. 75 F4 9 32N 45 32 E
Burāq, Syria ...... 74 B5 33 11N 36 29 E
Buraydah, Si. Arabia . 70 E4 26 20N 43 59 E
Burbank, U.S.A. 111 L8 34 11N 118 19W
Burda, India ...... 68 G6 25 50N 77 35 E
Burdekin ➤, Australia . 94 B4 19 38 S 147 25 E
Burdur, Turkey .... 47 D12 37 45N 30 17 E
Burdur □, Turkey ... 47 D12 37 45N 30 10 E
Burdur Gölü, Turkey .. 47 D12 37 44N 30 10 E
Burdwan =
Barddhaman, India . 69 H12 23 14N 87 39 E
Bure, Gojam, Ethiopia . 81 E4 10 40N 37 4 E
Bure, Ilubabor, Ethiopia 81 F4 8 19N 35 8 E
Bure ➤, U.K. ..... 14 E9 52 38N 1 43 E
Büren, Germany .... 24 D4 51 33N 8 34 E
Bureya ➤, Russia ... 53 E13 49 27N 129 30 E
Burford, Canada 116 C4 43 7N 80 27W
Burg, Germany ..... 24 C7 52 16N 11 51 E
Burg auf Fehmarn,
Germany .... 24 A7 54 28N 11 9 E
Burg el Arab, Egypt .. 80 H6 30 54N 29 32 E
Burg et Tuyur, Sudan . 80 C2 20 55N 27 56 E
Burg Stargard, Germany 24 B9 53 29N 13 18 E
Burgas, Bulgaria ... 45 D11 42 33N 27 29 E
Burgas □, Bulgaria ... 45 D11 42 30N 26 50 E
Burgaski Zaliv, Bulgaria 45 D11 42 30N 27 39 E
Burgdorf, Germany .. 24 C6 52 27N 10 1 E
Burgdorf, Switz. ... 25 H3 47 3N 7 37 E
Burgenland □, Austria . 27 D9 47 20N 16 20 E
Burgeo, Canada 105 C8 47 37N 57 38W
Burgersdorp, S. Africa . 88 E4 31 0 S 26 20 E
Burges, Mt., Australia . 93 F3 30 50 S 121 5 E
Burghausen, Germany . 25 G8 48 9N 12 49 E
Burghead, U.K. 13 D5 57 43N 3 30W
Búrgio, Italy ...... 42 E6 37 36N 13 17 E
Burglengenfeld,
Germany .... 25 F8 49 12N 12 2 E
Burgohondo, Spain .. 36 E6 40 26N 4 47W
Burgos, Spain 36 C7 42 21N 3 41W
Burgos □, Spain ... 36 C7 42 21N 3 42W
Burgstädt, Germany .. 24 E8 50 54N 12 49 E
Burgsvik, Sweden ... 11 G12 57 3N 18 19 E
Burguillos del Cerro,
Spain 37 G4 38 23N 6 35W
Burgundy =
Bourgogne □, France 19 F11 47 0N 4 50 E
Burhaniye, Turkey ... 47 B8 39 30N 26 58 E
Burhanpur, India ... 66 J10 21 18N 76 14 E
Burhi Gandak ➤, India 69 G12 25 20N 86 37 E
Burhner ➤, India ... 69 H9 22 43N 80 31 E
Buri Peni, Eritrea ... 81 D4 15 25N 39 55 E
Burias I., Phil. .... 61 E5 12 55N 123 5 E
Burica, Pta., Costa Rica 120 E3 8 3N 82 51W
Burien, U.S.A. 110 C4 47 28N 122 21W
Burigi □, Tanzania .. 86 C3 2 20 S 31 6 E
Burigi, L., Tanzania .. 86 C3 2 5 S 31 22 E
Burin, Canada 105 C8 47 1N 55 14W
Buriram, Thailand ... 64 E4 15 0N 103 0 E
Burj Sāfita, Syria ... 70 C3 34 48N 36 7 E
Búrjassot, Spain ... 39 F4 39 31N 0 25W
Burkburnett, U.S.A. .. 113 H5 34 6N 98 34W
Burke ➤, Australia .. 94 C2 23 12 S 139 33 E
Burke Chan., Canada . 102 C3 52 10N 127 30W
Burketown, Australia . 94 B2 17 45 S 139 33 E
Burkina Faso ■, Africa 82 C4 12 0N 1 0W
Burk's Falls, Canada . 104 A5 45 37N 79 24W
Burlada, Spain 38 C3 42 49N 1 36W
Burleigh Falls, Canada 116 B6 44 33N 78 12W
Burley, U.S.A. 108 E7 42 32N 113 48W
Burlingame, U.S.A. .. 110 H4 37 35N 122 21W
Burlington, Canada .. 116 C5 43 18N 79 45W
Burlington, Colo.,
U.S.A. 112 F3 39 18N 102 16W
Burlington, Iowa, U.S.A. 112 E9 40 49N 91 14W
Burlington, Kans.,
U.S.A. 112 F7 38 12N 95 45W
Burlington, N.C., U.S.A. 115 G6 36 6N 79 26W
Burlington, N.J., U.S.A. 117 F10 40 4N 74 51W
Burlington, Vt., U.S.A. . 117 B11 44 29N 73 12W
Burlington, Wash.,
U.S.A. 110 B4 48 28N 122 20W

Burlington, Wis., U.S.A. 114 D1 42 41N 88 17W
Burlyu-Tyube,
Kazakhstan ..... 52 E8 46 30N 79 10 E
Burma ■, Asia ..... 67 J20 21 0N 96 30 E
Burnaby I., Canada .. 102 C2 52 25N 131 19W
Burnet, U.S.A. 113 K5 30 45N 98 14W
Burnham, U.S.A. ... 116 F7 40 38N 77 34W
Burnham-on-Sea, U.K. 15 F5 51 14N 3 0W
Burnie, Australia ... 95 G4 41 4 S 145 56 E
Burnley, U.K. 14 D5 53 47N 2 14W
Burns, U.S.A. 108 E4 43 35N 119 3W
Burns Lake, Canada .. 102 C3 54 20N 125 45W
Burnside ➤, Canada . 100 B9 66 51N 108 4W
Burnside, L., Australia 93 E3 25 22 S 123 0 E
Burnsville, U.S.A. ... 112 C8 44 47N 93 17W
Burnt L., Canada 105 B7 53 35N 64 4W
Burnt River, Canada . 116 B6 44 41N 78 42W
Burntwood ➤, Canada 103 B9 56 8N 96 34W
Burntwood L., Canada 103 B8 55 22N 100 26W
Burqān, Kuwait .... 70 D5 29 0N 47 57 E
Burra, Australia .... 95 E2 33 40 S 138 55 E
Burra, Nigeria ..... 83 C6 11 0N 8 56 E
Burray, U.K. 13 C6 58 51N 2 54W
Burrel, Albania .... 44 E4 41 36N 20 1 E
Burren △, Ireland ... 12 C3 53 1N 8 58W
Burren Junction,
Australia ...... 95 E4 30 7 S 148 59 E
Burriana, Spain 38 F4 39 50N 0 4W
Burrinjuck Res.,
Australia ...... 95 F4 35 0 S 148 36 E
Burro, Serranías del,
Mexico 118 B4 29 0N 102 0W
Burrow Hd., U.K. ... 13 G4 54 41N 4 24W
Burrum Coast △,
Australia ...... 95 D5 25 13 S 152 36 E
Burruyacú, Argentina . 126 B3 26 30 S 64 40W
Burry Port, U.K. 15 F3 51 41N 4 15W
Bursa, Turkey ..... 45 F13 40 15N 29 5 E
Burseryd, Sweden ... 11 G7 57 12N 13 17 E
Burstall, Canada 103 C7 50 39N 109 54W
Burton, Ohio, U.S.A. . 116 E3 41 28N 81 8W
Burton, S.C., U.S.A. .. 115 J5 32 25N 80 45W
Burton, L., Canada .. 104 B4 54 45N 78 20W
Burton upon Trent, U.K. 14 E6 52 48N 1 38W
Buru, Indonesia .... 63 E7 3 30 S 126 30 E
Burullus, Bahra el,
Egypt .... 80 H7 31 25N 31 0 E
Burun, Râs, Egypt ... 74 D2 31 14N 33 7 E
Burundi ■, Africa ... 86 C3 3 15 S 30 0 E
Bururi, Burundi .... 86 C2 3 57 S 29 37 E
Burutu, Nigeria .... 83 D6 5 20N 5 29 E
Burwell, U.S.A. 112 E5 41 47N 99 8W
Burwick, U.K. 13 C5 58 45N 2 58W
Bury, U.K. 14 D5 53 35N 2 17W
Bury St. Edmunds, U.K. 15 E8 52 15N 0 43 E
Buryatia □, Russia ... 53 D11 53 0N 110 0 E
Buryn, Ukraine ..... 33 G7 51 13N 33 50 E
Burzenin, Poland ... 31 G5 51 28N 18 47 E
Busalla, Italy ...... 40 D5 44 34N 8 57 E
Busango Swamp,
Zambia .... 87 E2 14 15 S 25 45 E
Buşayrah, Syria .... 70 C4 35 9N 40 26 E
Busca, Italy ...... 40 D4 44 31N 7 29 E
Bushat, Albania .... 44 E3 41 58N 19 34 E
Büshehr, Iran ..... 71 D6 28 55N 50 55 E
Büshehr □, Iran .... 71 D6 28 20N 51 45 E
Bushell, Canada 103 B7 59 31N 108 45W
Bushenyi, Uganda ... 86 C3 0 35 S 30 10 E
Bushire = Büshehr, Iran 71 D6 28 55N 50 55 E
Bushtyna, Ukraine ... 29 B8 48 3N 23 28 E
Busie, Ghana 82 C4 10 29N 2 22W
Businga, Dem. Rep. of
the Congo ...... 84 D4 3 16N 20 59 E
Busko-Zdrój, Poland . 31 H7 50 28N 20 42 E
Busovača, Bos.-H. ... 42 F7 44 6N 17 53 E
Buşra ash Shām, Syria . 74 C5 32 30N 36 25 E
Busselton, Australia .. 93 F2 33 42 S 115 15 E
Busseri ➤, Sudan ... 81 F2 7 41N 28 3 E
Busseto, Italy ..... 40 D7 44 59N 10 2 E
Bussière-Badil, France . 20 C4 45 39N 0 36 E
Bussolengo, Italy ... 40 C7 45 28N 10 51 E
Bussum, Neths. .... 17 B5 52 16N 5 10 E
Bușteni, Romania ... 29 E10 45 24N 25 32 E
Busto, C., Spain 36 B4 43 34N 6 28W
Busto Arsízio, Italy ... 40 C5 45 37N 8 51 E
Busu Djanoa, Dem. Rep.
of the Congo .... 84 D4 1 43N 21 23 E
Busuanga I., Phil. ... 61 E3 12 10N 120 0 E
Büsum, Germany ... 24 A4 54 7N 8 51 E
Busungbiu, Indonesia . 63 J17 8 16 S 114 58 E
Buta, Dem. Rep. of
the Congo ...... 86 B1 2 50N 24 53 E
Butare, Rwanda .... 86 C2 2 31 S 29 52 E
Butaritari, Kiribati ... 96 G9 3 30N 174 0 E
Bute, U.K. 13 F3 55 48N 5 2W
Bute Inlet, Canada ... 102 C4 50 40N 124 53W
Butemba, Uganda ... 86 B3 1 9N 31 37 E
Butembo, Dem. Rep. of
the Congo ...... 86 B2 0 9N 29 18 E
Buteni, Romania ... 28 D7 46 19N 22 7 E
Butera, Italy ...... 43 E7 37 11N 14 11 E
Butha Qi, China .... 60 B7 48 0N 122 32 E
Butiaba, Uganda ... 86 B3 1 50N 31 20 E
Butler, Mo., U.S.A. .. 112 F7 38 16N 94 20W
Butler, Pa., U.S.A. ... 116 F5 40 52N 79 54W
Buton, Indonesia ... 63 E6 5 0 S 122 45 E
Butte, Mont., U.S.A. . 108 C7 46 0N 112 32W
Butte, Nebr., U.S.A. .. 112 D5 42 58N 98 51W
Butte Creek ➤, U.S.A. 110 F5 39 12N 121 56W
Butterworth = Gcuwa,
S. Africa ...... 89 E4 32 20 S 28 11 E
Butterworth, Malaysia 65 c 5 24N 100 23 E
Buttevant, Ireland ... 12 D3 52 14N 8 40W
Buttfield, Mt., Australia 93 D4 24 45 S 128 9 E
Button B., Canada ... 103 B10 58 45N 94 23W
Buttonwillow, U.S.A. . 111 K7 35 24N 119 28W
Butty Hd., Australia .. 93 F3 33 54 S 121 39 E
Butuan, Phil. ...... 61 G6 8 57N 125 33 E
Butuku-Luba, Eq. Guin. 83 E6 3 29N 8 33 E
Butung = Buton,
Indonesia ...... 63 E6 5 0 S 122 45 E
Buturlinovka, Russia . 34 E5 50 50N 40 35 E
Butzbach, Germany .. 25 E4 50 25N 8 40 E
Bützow, Germany ... 24 B7 53 50N 11 58 E
Buur Hakaba = Bur
Acaba, Somali Rep. . 75 G3 3 12N 44 20 E
Buxa Duar, India ... 69 F13 27 45N 89 35 E
Buxar, India ...... 69 G10 25 34N 83 58 E
Buxtehude, Germany . 24 B5 53 28N 9 39 E
Buxton, U.K. 14 D6 53 16N 1 54W
Buxy, France ...... 19 F11 46 44N 4 40 E
Buy, Russia ...... 34 A5 58 28N 41 28 E
Buynaksk, Russia ... 35 J8 42 48N 47 7 E
Buyo, Ivory C. 82 D3 6 21N 7 5W
Buyo, L. de, Ivory C. . 82 D3 6 16N 7 10W

Büyük Menderes ➤,
Turkey .... 47 D9 37 28N 27 11 E
Büyükçekmece, Turkey 45 E12 41 2N 28 35 E
Büyükkarıştıran, Turkey 45 E11 41 18N 27 32 E
Büyükkemikli Burnu,
Turkey .... 45 F10 40 18N 26 14 E
Büyükkorhan, Turkey . 47 B10 39 46N 28 56 E
Büyükyoncalı, Turkey . 45 E11 41 25N 27 59 E
Buzançais, France ... 18 F8 46 54N 1 25 E
Buzau, Romania .... 29 E11 45 10N 26 50 E
Buzău □, Romania ... 29 E11 45 20N 26 30 E
Buzău ➤, Romania .. 29 E12 45 26N 27 44 E
Buzău, Pasul, Romania 29 E11 45 35N 26 12 E
Buzen, Japan ..... 55 H5 33 35N 131 5 E
Buzet, Croatia ..... 41 C10 45 24N 13 58 E
Buzi ➤, Mozam. .... 87 F3 19 50 S 34 43 E
Buziaş, Romania ... 28 E6 45 38N 21 36 E
Buzuluk, Russia .... 52 D6 52 48N 52 12 E
Buzuluk ➤, Russia .. 34 E6 50 15N 42 7 E
Buzzards B., U.S.A. .. 117 E14 41 45N 70 37W
Buzzards Bay, U.S.A. . 117 E14 41 44N 70 37W
Bwana Mkubwe,
Dem. Rep. of
the Congo ...... 87 E2 13 8 S 28 38 E
Bwindi △, Uganda ... 86 C2 1 2 S 29 42 E
Byala, Ruse, Bulgaria . 45 C9 43 28N 25 44 E
Byala, Varna, Bulgaria 45 C11 42 53N 27 55 E
Byala Slatina, Bulgaria 44 C7 43 26N 23 58 E
Byarezina ➤, Belarus . 33 F6 52 33N 30 14 E
Byaroza, Belarus .... 31 G9 52 31N 24 51 E
Bychawa, Poland ... 31 G9 51 1N 22 36 E
Byczyna, Poland .... 31 G5 51 7N 18 12 E
Bydgoszcz, Poland .. 31 E5 53 10N 18 0 E
Byelorussia = Belarus ■,
Europe .... 32 F4 53 30N 27 0 E
Byers, U.S.A. 112 F2 39 43N 104 14W
Byesville, U.S.A. ... 116 G3 39 58N 81 32W
Byfield △, Australia .. 94 C5 22 52 S 150 45 E
Byford, Australia ... 93 F2 32 15 S 116 0 E
Bykhaw, Belarus ... 32 F6 53 31N 30 14 E
Bykhov = Bykhaw,
Belarus .... 32 F6 53 31N 30 14 E
Bykovo, Russia .... 34 F7 49 50N 45 25 E
Bylas, U.S.A. 109 K8 33 8N 110 7W
Bylot, Canada 103 B10 58 25N 94 8W
Bylot I., Canada 101 A12 73 13N 78 34W
Byrd, C., Antarctica .. 5 C17 69 38 S 76 7W
Byrock, Australia ... 95 E4 30 40 S 146 27 E
Byron, C., Australia .. 95 D5 28 43 S 153 37 E
Byron Bay, Australia . 95 D5 28 43 S 153 37 E
Byrranga ➤, Russia .. 53 B11 75 0N 100 0 E
Byrranga Mts. =
Byrranga, Gory,
Russia .... 53 B11 75 0N 100 0 E
Byrum, Denmark ... 11 G5 57 16N 11 0 E
Byske, Sweden .... 8 D19 64 57N 21 11 E
Byskeälven ➤, Sweden 8 D19 64 57N 21 13 E
Bystrytsya, Ukraine .. 29 B9 48 27N 24 14 E
Bystrzyca ➤,
Dolnośląskie, Poland 31 G3 51 12N 16 55 E
Bystrzyca ➤, Lubelskie,
Poland .... 31 G9 51 21N 22 46 E
Bystrzyca Kłodzka,
Poland .... 31 H3 50 19N 16 39 E
Byča, Slovak Rep. ... 27 B11 49 13N 18 34 E
Bytkiv, Ukraine ..... 29 B9 48 38N 24 28 E
Bytom, Poland ..... 31 H5 50 25N 18 54 E
Bytom Odrzański,
Poland .... 31 G2 51 44N 15 48 E
Bytów, Poland ..... 30 D4 54 10N 17 30 E
Byumba, Rwanda ... 86 C3 1 35 S 30 4 E
Bzenec, Czech Rep. .. 27 C10 48 58N 17 18 E
Bzura ➤, Poland ... 31 F7 52 25N 20 15 E

C

Ca ➤, Vietnam ..... 64 C5 18 45N 105 45 E
Ca Mau, Vietnam ... 65 H5 9 7N 105 8 E
Ca Mau, Mui, Vietnam . 65 H5 8 38N 104 44 E
Ca Na, Vietnam .... 65 G7 11 20N 108 54 E
Caacupé, Paraguay .. 126 B4 25 23 S 57 5W
Caaguazú □, Paraguay 127 B4 25 5 S 55 31W
Caála, Angola ..... 85 G3 12 46 S 15 30 E
Caamaño Sd., Canada 102 C3 52 55N 129 25W
Caazapá, Paraguay .. 126 B4 26 8 S 56 19W
Caazapá □, Paraguay . 127 B4 26 10 S 56 0W
Cabadbaran, Phil. ... 61 G6 9 10N 125 38 E
Cabalian = San Juan,
Phil. .... 61 F6 10 16N 125 10 E
Caballeria, C. de, Spain 48 A11 40 5N 4 5 E
Cabana, Peru ...... 124 C2 8 25 S 78 5W
Cabanaconde, Peru .. 124 D3 15 40 S 71 59W
Cabañaquinta, Spain . 36 B5 43 11N 5 41W
Cabanatuan, Phil. ... 61 D4 15 30N 120 58 E
Cabañeros △, Spain .. 37 F6 39 18N 4 35W
Cabanes, Spain .... 38 E5 40 9N 0 2 E
Cabano, Canada 105 C6 47 40N 68 56W
Cabar, Croatia ..... 41 C11 45 36N 14 39 E
Cabazon, U.S.A. 111 M10 33 55N 116 47W
Cabedelo, Brazil .... 125 E12 7 0 S 34 50W
Cabeza del Buey, Spain 37 G5 38 44N 5 13W
Cabezón de la Sal, Spain 36 B6 43 18N 4 12W
Cabildo, Chile ..... 126 C1 32 30 S 71 5W
Cabimas, Venezuela . 124 A4 10 23N 71 25W
Cabinda, Angola ... 84 F2 5 33 S 12 11 E
Cabinda □, Angola .. 84 F2 5 0 S 12 30 E
Cabinet Mts., U.S.A. . 108 C6 48 0N 115 30W
Cabo Blanco, Argentina 128 F3 47 15 S 65 47W
Cabo de Gata-Níjar △,
Spain 39 J2 36 51N 2 6W
Cabo Frio, Brazil .... 127 A7 22 51 S 42 3W
Cabo Pantoja, Peru .. 124 D3 1 0 S 75 10W
Cabonga, Réservoir,
Canada 104 C4 47 20N 76 40W
Cabool, U.S.A. 113 G8 37 7N 92 6W
Caboolture, Australia . 95 D5 27 5 S 152 58 E
Cabora Bassa Dam =
Cahora Bassa,
Répresa de, Mozam. . 87 F3 15 20 S 32 50 E
Caborca, Mexico ... 118 A2 30 40N 112 10W
Cabot Hd., Canada .. 116 A3 45 14N 81 17W
Cabot Str., Canada .. 105 C8 47 15N 59 40W
Cabra, Spain 37 H6 37 30N 4 28W
Cabra del Santo Cristo,
Spain 37 H7 37 42N 3 16W
Cábras, Italy ...... 42 C1 39 56N 8 32 E
Cabrera □, Spain ... 48 B9 39 8N 2 57 E
Cabrera, Sierra, Spain . 36 C4 42 12N 6 40W
Cabri, Canada 103 C7 50 35N 108 25W
Cabriel ➤, Spain ... 39 F3 39 14N 1 3W
Cabugao, Phil. ..... 61 C4 17 48N 120 27 E
Cacabelos, Spain ... 36 C4 42 36N 6 44W

Caçador, Brazil ..... 127 B5 26 47 S 51 0W
Čačak, Serbia & M. .. 44 C4 43 54N 20 20 E
Caçapava do Sul, Brazil 127 C5 30 30 S 53 30W
Cáccamo, Italy ..... 42 E6 37 56N 13 40 E
Cacém, Portugal ... 37 G1 38 46N 9 18W
Cáceres, Brazil ..... 124 G7 16 5 S 57 40W
Cáceres, Spain 37 F4 39 26N 6 23W
Cáceres □, Spain ... 36 F5 39 45N 6 0W
Cache Bay, Canada .. 104 C4 46 22N 80 0W
Cache Cr. ➤, U.S.A. . 110 G5 38 42N 121 42W
Cache Creek, Canada . 102 C4 50 48N 121 19W
Cacheu, Guinea-Biss. . 82 C1 12 14N 16 8W
Cachi, Argentina ... 126 B2 25 5 S 66 10W
Cachinal de la Sierra,
Chile .... 126 A2 24 58 S 69 32W
Cachoeira, Brazil ... 125 F11 12 30 S 39 0W
Cachoeira do Sul, Brazil 127 C5 30 3 S 52 53W
Cachoeiro de
Itapemirim, Brazil .. 127 A7 20 51 S 41 7W
Cachopo, Portugal .. 37 H3 37 20N 7 49W
Cacine, Guinea-Biss. . 82 C1 11 8N 14 57W
Cacoal, Brazil ..... 124 F6 11 32 S 61 18W
Cacólo, Angola .... 84 G3 10 9 S 19 21 E
Caconda, Angola ... 85 G3 13 48 S 15 8 E
Caçu, Brazil ...... 125 E7 9 30 S 55 30W
Cader Idris, U.K. 15 E4 52 42N 3 53W
Cadereyta, Mexico .. 118 B5 25 36N 100 0W
Cadí, Sierra del, Spain 38 C6 42 17N 1 42 E
Cadí-Moixeró △, Spain 38 C6 42 19N 1 45 E
Cadibarrawirracanna, L.,
Australia ...... 95 D2 28 52 S 135 27 E
Cadillac, France 20 D3 44 38N 0 20W
Cadillac, U.S.A. 114 C3 44 15N 85 24W
Cádiz, Phil. ...... 61 F5 10 57N 123 15 E
Cádiz, Spain 37 J4 36 30N 6 20W
Cadiz, Calif., U.S.A. . 111 L11 34 30N 115 28W
Cadiz, Ohio, U.S.A. .. 116 F4 40 22N 81 0W
Cádiz □, Spain 37 J5 36 40N 5 45W
Cádiz, G. de, Spain .. 37 J3 36 40N 7 0W
Cadiz L., U.S.A. 109 J6 34 18N 115 24W
Cadney Park, Australia 95 D1 27 55 S 134 3 E
Cadomin, Canada ... 102 C5 53 2N 117 20W
Cadotte Lake, Canada 102 B5 56 26N 116 23W
Cadours, France .... 20 E5 43 44N 1 2 E
Cadoux, Australia ... 93 F2 30 46 S 117 7 E
Caen, France 18 C6 49 10N 0 22W
Caernarfon, U.K. ... 14 D3 53 8N 4 16W
Caernarfon B., U.K. .. 14 D3 53 4N 4 40W
Caernarvon =
Caernarfon, U.K. .. 14 D3 53 8N 4 16W
Caerphilly, U.K. 15 F4 51 35N 3 13W
Caerphilly □, U.K. ... 15 F4 51 37N 3 12W
Caesarea, Israel .... 74 C3 32 30N 34 53 E
Caetité, Brazil ..... 125 F10 13 50 S 42 32W
Cafayate, Argentina . 126 B2 26 2 S 66 0W
Cafu, Angola ..... 88 B2 16 30 S 15 8 E
Cagayan ➤, Phil. ... 61 B4 18 25N 121 42 E
Cagayan de Oro, Phil. 61 G6 8 30N 124 40 E
Cagayan Is., Phil. ... 61 G4 9 40N 121 16 E
Cagayan Sulu I., Phil. . 61 H3 7 1N 118 30 E
Cagli, Italy .... 41 E9 43 33N 12 39 E
Cágliari, Italy ...... 42 C2 39 13N 9 7 E
Cágliari, G. di, Italy .. 42 C2 39 8N 9 11 E
Cagnano Varano, Italy . 41 G12 41 49N 15 47 E
Cagnes-sur-Mer, France 21 E11 43 40N 7 9 E
Caguán ➤, Colombia . 124 D4 0 8 S 74 18W
Caguas, Puerto Rico . 121 d 18 14N 66 2W
Caha Mts., Ireland ... 12 E2 51 45N 9 40W
Cahama, Angola ... 88 B1 16 17 S 14 19 E
Caher, Ireland 12 D4 52 22N 7 56W
Caherciveen, Ireland . 12 E1 51 56N 10 14W
Cahora Bassa, L. de,
Mozam. .... 87 F3 15 35 S 32 0 E
Cahora Bassa, Répresa
de, Mozam. ..... 87 F3 15 20 S 32 50 E
Cahore Pt., Ireland .. 12 D5 52 33N 6 12W
Cahors, France .... 20 D5 44 27N 1 27 E
Cahul, Moldova .... 29 E13 45 50N 28 15 E
Cai Bau, Dao, Vietnam 58 G6 21 10N 107 27 E
Cai Nuoc, Vietnam .. 65 H5 8 56N 105 1 E
Caia, Mozam. ..... 87 F4 17 51 S 35 24 E
Caianda, Angola ... 87 E1 11 2 S 23 31 E
Caibarién, Cuba 120 B4 22 30N 79 30W
Caibiran, Phil. ..... 61 F6 11 34N 124 35 E
Caicara, Venezuela .. 124 B5 7 38N 66 10W
Caicó, Brazil ...... 125 E11 6 20 S 37 0W
Caicos Is.,
Turks & Caicos ... 121 B5 21 40N 71 40W
Caicos Passage,
W. Indies 121 B5 22 45N 72 45W
Caidian, China ..... 59 B10 30 35N 114 2 E
Căinari, Moldova ... 29 D14 46 41N 29 3 E
Caird Coast, Antarctica 5 D1 75 0 S 25 0W
Cairn Gorm, U.K. ... 13 D5 57 7N 3 39W
Cairngorm Mts., U.K. . 13 D5 57 6N 3 42W
Cairngorms △, U.K. .. 13 D5 57 10N 3 50W
Cairnryan, U.K. 13 G3 54 59N 5 1W
Cairns, Australia ... 94 B4 16 57 S 145 45 E
Cairns L., Canada ... 103 C10 51 42N 94 30W
Cairo = El Qâhira,
Egypt .... 80 H7 30 1N 31 14 E
Cairo, Ga., U.S.A. ... 115 K3 30 52N 84 13W
Cairo, Ill., U.S.A. ... 113 G10 37 0N 89 11W
Cairo Montenotte, Italy 40 D5 44 23N 8 16 E
Caithness, U.K. 13 C5 58 25N 3 35W
Caithness, Ord of, U.K. 13 C5 58 8N 3 36W
Caja de Muertos, I.,
Puerto Rico .... 121 d 17 54N 66 32W
Cajamarca, Peru ... 124 E3 7 5 S 78 28W
Cajarc, France ..... 20 D5 44 29N 1 50 E
Cajàzeiras, Brazil ... 125 E11 6 52 S 38 30W
Çajetina, Serbia & M. . 44 C3 43 47N 19 42 E
Çakırgol, Turkey .... 73 B8 40 33N 39 40 E
Çakırlar, Turkey .... 47 E12 36 32N 30 26 E
Čakovec, Croatia ... 41 B13 46 23N 16 26 E
Çal, Turkey .... 47 C11 38 9N 29 25 E
Cala ➤, Spain 37 H4 37 59N 6 21W
Cala, Spain 37 H4 37 38N 6 5W
Cala Cadolar, Punta
de = Rotja, Pta., Spain 39 G6 38 08N 1 35 E
Cala d'Or, Spain .... 48 B10 39 23N 3 14 E
Cala en Porter, Spain . 48 B11 39 52N 4 8 E
Cala Figuera, C. de,
Spain .... 48 B10 39 27N 2 31 E
Cala Forcat, Spain ... 48 B10 40 0N 3 47 E
Cala Major, Spain ... 48 B9 39 33N 2 37 E
Cala Mezquida = Sa
Mesquida, Spain .. 48 B11 39 55N 4 16 E
Cala Millor, Spain ... 48 B10 39 35N 3 22 E
Cala Ratjada, Spain .. 48 B10 39 43N 3 27 E
Cala Santa Galdana,
Spain .... 48 B10 39 56N 3 58 E

Calabar, Nigeria .... 83 E6 4 57N 8 20 E
Calabogie, Canada .. 117 A8 45 18N 76 43W
Calabozo, Venezuela . 124 B5 9 0N 67 28W
Calábria □, Italy ... 43 C9 39 0N 16 30 E
Calábria □, Italy ... 43 C9 39 6N 16 35 E
Calaburras, Pta. de,
Spain 37 J6 36 30N 4 38W
Calaceite, Spain .... 38 D5 41 1N 0 11 E
Calacuccia, France .. 21 F13 42 21N 9 1 E
Calafat, Romania ... 28 G7 43 58N 22 59 E
Calafate, Argentina .. 128 G2 50 19 S 72 15W
Calafell, Spain ..... 38 D6 41 11N 1 34 E
Calahorra, Spain ... 38 C3 42 18N 1 59W
Calais, France ..... 19 B8 50 57N 1 56 E
Calais, U.S.A. 115 C12 45 11N 67 17W
Calakmul ○, Mexico . 119 D7 18 14N 89 48W
Calalaste, Cord. de,
Argentina ...... 126 B2 25 0 S 67 0W
Calama, Brazil ..... 124 E6 8 0 S 62 50W
Calama, Chile ..... 126 A2 22 30 S 68 55W
Calamar, Colombia .. 124 A4 10 15N 74 55W
Calamian Group, Phil. 61 F3 11 50N 119 55 E
Calamocha, Spain ... 38 E3 40 50N 1 17W
Calamonte, Spain ... 37 G4 38 53N 6 23W
Călan, Romania .... 28 E7 45 44N 22 59 E
Calañas, Spain 37 H4 37 40N 6 53W
Calanda, Spain 38 E4 40 56N 0 15W
Calang, Indonesia .. 62 D1 4 37N 95 37 E
Calangiánus, Italy ... 42 B2 40 56N 9 11 E
Calapan, Phil. ..... 61 E4 13 25N 121 7 E
Calăraşi, Moldova .. 29 C13 47 16N 28 19 E
Călăraşi, Romania .. 29 F12 44 12N 27 20 E
Călăraşi □, Romania . 29 F12 44 10N 27 0 E
Calasparra, Spain ... 39 G3 38 14N 1 41W
Calatafimi, Italy .... 42 E5 37 55N 12 52 E
Calatayud, Spain ... 38 D3 41 20N 1 40W
Călățele, Romania .. 28 D8 46 46N 23 1 E
Calato = Kálathos,
Greece .... 47 E10 36 9N 28 8 E
Calauag, Phil. ..... 61 E5 13 55N 122 15 E
Calavà, C., Italy .... 43 D7 38 11N 14 55 E
Calavite, C., Phil. ... 61 E4 13 26N 120 20 E
Calayan, Phil. ..... 61 B4 19 16N 121 28 E
Calbayog, Phil. .... 61 E6 12 4N 124 38 E
Calca, Peru ...... 124 F4 13 22 S 72 0W
Calcasieu L., U.S.A. .. 113 L8 29 55N 93 18W
Calcutta = Kolkata,
India .... 69 H13 22 36N 88 24 E
Calcutta, U.S.A. 116 F4 40 40N 80 34W
Caldaro, Italy ..... 41 B8 46 25N 11 14 E
Caldas da Rainha,
Portugal 37 F1 39 24N 9 8W
Caldas de Reis, Spain . 36 C2 42 36N 8 39W
Calder ➤, U.K. 14 D6 53 44N 1 22W
Caldera, Chile ..... 126 B1 27 5 S 70 55W
Caldera de
Taburiente △,
Canary Is. 48 F2 28 43N 17 52W
Caldwell, Idaho, U.S.A. 108 E5 43 40N 116 41W
Caldwell, Kans., U.S.A. 113 G6 37 2N 97 37W
Caldwell, Tex., U.S.A. 113 K6 30 32N 96 42W
Caledon, S. Africa .. 88 E2 34 14 S 19 26 E
Caledon ➤, S. Africa . 88 E4 30 31 S 26 5 E
Caledon B., Australia . 94 A2 12 45 S 137 0 E
Caledonia, Canada .. 116 C5 43 7N 79 58W
Caledonia, U.S.A. ... 116 D7 42 58N 77 51W
Calella, Spain ..... 38 D7 41 37N 2 40 E
Calemba, Angola ... 88 B2 16 0 S 15 44 E
Calen, Australia ... 94 J6 20 56 S 148 48 E
Calenzana, France .. 21 F12 42 31N 8 51 E
Caletones, Chile .... 126 C1 34 6 S 70 27W
Calexico, U.S.A. 111 N11 32 40N 115 30W
Calf of Man, U.K. ... 14 C3 54 3N 4 48W
Calgary, Canada 102 C6 51 0N 114 10W
Calheta, Madeira ... 48 D2 32 44N 17 11W
Calhoun, U.S.A. 115 H3 34 30N 84 57W
Cali, Colombia 124 C3 3 25N 76 35W
Calicut, India ..... 66 P9 11 15N 75 43 E
Caliente, U.S.A. 109 H6 37 37N 114 31W
California, Mo., U.S.A. 112 F8 38 38N 92 34W
California, Pa., U.S.A. . 116 F5 40 4N 79 54W
California □, U.S.A. .. 110 H7 37 30N 119 30W
California, Baja, Mexico 118 A1 32 10N 115 12W
California, Baja, T.N. =
Baja California □,
Mexico 118 B2 30 0N 115 0W
California, Baja, T.S. =
Baja California Sur □,
Mexico 118 B2 25 50N 111 50W
California, G. de,
Mexico 118 B2 27 0N 111 0W
California City, U.S.A. 111 K9 35 10N 117 55W
California Hot Springs,
U.S.A. 111 K8 35 51N 118 41W
Calilegua △, Argentina 126 B3 23 36 S 64 50W
Călimăneşti, Romania 29 E9 45 14N 24 20 E
Călimani, Munții,
Romania ...... 29 C10 47 12N 25 0 E
Calingasta, Argentina 126 C2 31 15 S 69 30W
Calipatria, U.S.A. ... 111 M11 33 8N 115 31W
Calistoga, U.S.A. ... 110 G4 38 35N 122 35W
Calitri, Italy ...... 43 B8 40 54N 15 26 E
Calitzdorp, S. Africa . 88 E3 33 33 S 21 42 E
Callabonna, L., Australia 95 D3 29 40 S 140 5 E
Callac, France 18 D3 48 25N 3 27W
Callan, Ireland 12 D4 52 32N 7 24W
Callander, U.K. 13 E4 56 15N 4 13W
Callao, Peru ...... 124 F3 12 0 S 77 0W
Calles, Mexico 119 C5 23 2N 98 42W
Callicoon, U.S.A. ... 117 E9 41 46N 75 3W
Calling Lake, Canada . 102 B6 55 15N 113 12W
Calliope, Australia .. 94 C5 24 0 S 151 16 E
Callosa de Ensarriá,
Spain .... 39 G4 38 40N 0 8 E
Callosa de Segura, Spain 39 G4 38 7N 0 53W
Calne, U.K. 15 F6 51 26N 2 0W
Calola, Angola ..... 88 B2 16 25 S 17 48 E
Calolbon = San Andres,
Phil. .... 61 E6 13 36N 124 6 E
Calonge, Spain .... 38 D8 41 52N 3 5 E
Caloocan, Phil. .... 61 D4 14 39N 120 58 E
Caloré ➤, Italy .... 43 A7 41 11N 14 28 E
Caloundra, Australia . 95 D5 26 45 S 153 10 E
Calpe, Spain ...... 39 G5 38 39N 0 3 E
Calpella, U.S.A. 110 F3 39 14N 123 12W
Calpine, U.S.A. 110 F6 39 40N 120 27W
Caltagirone, Italy ... 43 E7 37 14N 14 31 E
Caltanissetta, Italy .. 43 E7 37 29N 14 4 E
Caltilibük, Turkey ... 45 G12 39 57N 28 36 E
Caluire-et-Cuire, France 19 G11 45 48N 4 52 E
Calulo, Angola ..... 84 G2 10 1 S 14 56 E
Caluso, Italy ...... 40 C4 45 18N 7 53 E
Calvados □, France .. 18 C6 49 5N 0 15W
Calvert ➤, Australia . 94 B2 16 17 S 137 44 E
Calvert I., Canada ... 102 C3 51 30N 128 0W

Calvert Ra., *Australia* . **92 D3** 24 0 S 122 30 E
Calvi, *France* .... **21 F12** 42 34N 8 45 E
Calviá, *Spain* .... **39 F7** 39 34N 2 31 E
Calvillo, *Mexico* **118 C4** 21 51N 102 43W
Calvinia, *S. Africa* ... **88 E2** 31 28 S 19 45 E
Calvo, Mte., *Italy* .... **41 G12** 41 44N 15 46 E
Calwa, *U.S.A.* **110 J7** 36 42N 119 46W
Calzada Almuradiel =
Almuradiel, *Spain* . **37 G7** 38 32N 3 28W
Calzada de Calatrava,
Spain **37 G7** 38 42N 3 46W
Cam →, *U.K.* .... **15 E8** 52 21N 0 16 E
Cam Lam, *Vietnam* ... **65 G7** 11 54N 109 10 E
Cam Pha, *Vietnam* ... **58 G6** 21 7N 107 18 E
Cam Ranh, *Vietnam* .. **65 G7** 11 54N 109 12 E
Cam Xuyen, *Vietnam* . **64 C6** 18 15N 106 0 E
Camabatela, *Angola* .. **84 F3** 8 20 S 15 26 E
Camacha, *Madeira* **48 D3** 32 41N 16 49W
Camacho, *Mexico* **118 C4** 24 25N 102 18W
Camacupa, *Angola* .... **85 G3** 11 58 S 17 22 E
Camagüey, *Cuba* **120 B4** 21 20N 78 0W
Camaiore, *Italy* ...... **40 E7** 43 56N 10 18 E
Camaná, *Peru* .... **124 G4** 16 30 S 72 50W
Camanche Reservoir,
U.S.A. **110 G6** 38 14N 121 1W
Camaquã, *Brazil* ..... **127 C5** 30 51 S 51 49W
Camaquã →, *Brazil* .. **127 C5** 31 17 S 51 47W
Câmara de Lobos,
Madeira **48 D3** 32 39N 16 59W
Camarat, C., *France* ... **21 E10** 43 12N 6 41 E
Camarès, *France* ..... **20 E6** 43 49N 2 53 E
Camaret-sur-Mer,
France **18 D2** 48 16N 4 37W
Camargo, *Mexico* **119 B5** 26 19N 98 50W
Camargue, *France* .... **21 E8** 43 34N 4 34 E
Camargue △, *France* .. **21 E8** 43 30N 4 40 E
Camarillo, *U.S.A.* **111 L7** 34 13N 119 2W
Camariñas, *Spain* **36 B1** 43 8N 9 12W
Camarón, C., *Honduras* **120 C2** 16 0N 85 5W
Camarones, *Argentina* . **128 E3** 44 50 S 65 40W
Camas, *Spain* **37 H4** 37 24N 6 2W
Camas, *U.S.A.* **110 E4** 45 35N 122 24W
Camas Valley, *U.S.A.* . **108 E2** 43 2N 123 40W
Camballin, *Australia* .. **92 C3** 17 59 S 124 12 E
Cambará = *Brazil* .... **127 A5** 23 2 S 50 5W
Cambay = Khambhat,
India .... **68 H5** 22 23N 72 33 E
Cambay, G. of =
Khambhat, G. of,
India .... **66 J8** 20 45N 72 30 E
Cambil, *Spain* **37 H7** 37 40N 3 33W
Cambo-les-Bains, *France* **20 E2** 43 22N 1 23W
Cambodia ■, *Asia* .... **64 F5** 12 15N 105 0 E
Camborne, *U.K.* **15 G2** 50 12N 5 19W
Cambrai, *France* ..... **19 B10** 50 11N 3 14 E
Cambre, *Spain* **36 B2** 43 17N 8 20W
Cambria, *U.S.A.* **110 K5** 35 34N 121 5W
Cambrian Mts., *U.K.* .. **15 E4** 52 3N 3 57W
Cambridge, *Canada* ... **116 C4** 43 23N 80 15W
Cambridge, *Jamaica* .. **120 a** 18 18N 77 54W
Cambridge, *N.Z.* ..... **91 G5** 37 54 S 175 29 E
Cambridge, *U.K.* ..... **15 E8** 52 12N 0 8 E
Cambridge, *Mass.*,
U.S.A. **117 D13** 42 22N 71 6W
Cambridge, *Minn.*,
U.S.A. **112 C8** 45 34N 93 13W
Cambridge, *N.Y., U.S.A.* **117 C11** 43 2N 73 22W
Cambridge, *Nebr.*,
U.S.A. **112 E4** 40 17N 100 10W
Cambridge, *Ohio*,
U.S.A. **116 F3** 40 2N 81 35W
Cambridge Bay =
Ikaluktutiak, *Canada* **100 B9** 69 10N 105 0W
Cambridge G., *Australia* **92 B4** 14 55 S 128 15 E
Cambridge Springs,
U.S.A. **116 E4** 41 48N 80 4W
Cambridgeshire □, *U.K.* **15 E7** 52 25N 0 7W
Cambrils, *Spain* ..... **38 D6** 41 8N 1 3 E
Cambuci, *Brazil* ..... **127 A7** 21 35 S 41 55W
Cambundi-Catembo,
Angola .... **84 G3** 10 10 S 17 35 E
Camden, *Ala., U.S.A.* . **115 K2** 31 59N 87 17W
Camden, *Ark., U.S.A.* . **113 J8** 33 35N 92 50W
Camden, *Maine, U.S.A.* **115 C11** 44 13N 69 4W
Camden, *N.J., U.S.A.* . **117 G9** 39 56N 75 7W
Camden, *N.Y., U.S.A.* . **117 C9** 43 20N 75 45W
Camden, *S.C., U.S.A.* . **115 H5** 34 16N 80 36W
Camden Sd., *Australia* . **92 C3** 15 27 S 124 25 E
Camdenton, *U.S.A.* ... **113 F8** 38 1N 92 45W
Camelford, *U.K.* **15 G3** 50 37N 4 42W
Cameron, *Ariz., U.S.A.* **109 J8** 35 53N 111 25W
Cameron, *La., U.S.A.* . **113 L8** 29 48N 93 20W
Cameron, *Mo., U.S.A.* . **112 F7** 39 44N 94 14W
Cameron, *Tex., U.S.A.* . **113 K6** 30 51N 96 59W
Cameron Highlands,
Malaysia .... **65 K3** 4 27N 101 22 E
Cameron Hills, *Canada* **102 B5** 59 48N 118 0W
Cameroon ■, *Africa* ... **79 G7** 6 0N 12 30 E
Camerota, *Italy* ...... **43 B8** 40 2N 15 22 E
Cameroun →,
Cameroon .... **83 E6** 4 0N 9 35 E
Cameroun, Mt.,
Cameroon .... **83 E6** 4 13N 9 10 E
Cametá, *Brazil* ...... **125 D9** 2 12 S 49 30W
Çamiçi Gölü, *Turkey* .. **47 D9** 37 29N 27 18 E
Camiguin □, *Phil.* .... **61 G6** 9 11N 124 42 E
Camiguin I., *Phil.* .... **61 B4** 18 56N 121 55 E
Camiling, *Phil.* ...... **61 D4** 15 42N 120 24 E
Camilla, *U.S.A.* **115 K3** 31 14N 84 12W
Caminha, *Portugal* ... **36 D2** 41 50N 8 50W
Camino, *U.S.A.* **110 G6** 38 44N 120 41W
Camira Creek, *Australia* **95 D5** 29 15 S 152 58 E
Cammal, *U.S.A.* **116 E7** 41 24N 77 28W
Cammarata, *Italy* .... **42 E6** 37 38N 13 38 E
Camocim, *Brazil* ..... **125 D10** 2 55 S 40 50W
Camooweal, *Australia* . **94 B2** 19 56 S 138 7 E
Camooweal Caves △,
Australia .... **94 C2** 20 1 S 138 11 E
Camopi, *Fr. Guiana* ... **125 C8** 3 12N 52 17W
Camotes Sea, *Phil.* ... **61 F6** 10 30N 124 15 E
Camotes Is., *Phil.* .... **61 F6** 10 40N 124 24 E
Camp Borden, *Canada* . **116 B5** 44 18N 79 56W
Camp Hill, *U.S.A.* **116 F8** 40 14N 76 55W
Camp Nelson, *U.S.A.* . **111 J8** 36 8N 118 39W
Camp Pendleton, *U.S.A.* **111 M9** 33 16N 117 23W
Camp Verde, *U.S.A.* .. **109 J8** 34 34N 111 51W
Camp Wood, *U.S.A.* .. **113 L5** 29 40N 100 1W
Campagna, *Italy* ..... **43 B8** 40 40N 15 6 E
Campana, *Argentina* .. **126 C4** 34 10 S 58 55W
Campana, I., *Chile* ... **128 F1** 48 20 S 75 20W
Campanário, *Madeira* . **48 D3** 32 39N 17 2W
Campanario, *Spain* ... **37 G5** 38 52N 5 36W
Campánia □, *Italy* .... **43 B7** 41 0N 14 30 E
Campbell, *S. Africa* ... **88 D3** 28 48 S 23 44 E

Campbell, *Calif., U.S.A.* **110 H5** 37 17N 121 57W
Campbell, *Ohio, U.S.A.* **116 E4** 41 5N 80 37W
Campbell I., *Pac. Oc.* . **96 N8** 52 30 S 169 0 E
Campbell L., *Canada* .. **103 A7** 63 14N 106 55W
Campbell River, *Canada* **102 C3** 50 5N 125 20W
Campbell Town,
Australia .... **95 G4** 41 52 S 147 30 E
Campbellford, *Canada* . **116 B7** 44 18N 77 48W
Campbellpur, *Pakistan* . **68 C5** 33 46N 72 26 E
Campbellsville, *U.S.A.* . **114 G3** 37 21N 85 20W
Campbellton, *Canada* . **105 C6** 47 57N 66 43W
Campbelltown, *Australia* **95 E5** 34 4 S 150 49 E
Campbeltown, *U.K.* ... **13 F3** 55 26N 5 36W
Campeche, *Mexico* ... **119 D6** 19 50N 90 32W
Campeche □, *Mexico* . **119 D6** 19 50N 90 32W
Campeche, Golfo de,
Mexico **119 D6** 19 30N 93 0W
Campello, *Spain* **39 G4** 38 26N 0 24W
Câmpeni, *Romania* ... **28 D8** 46 22N 23 3 E
Camperdown, *Australia* **95 F3** 38 14 S 143 9 E
Camperville, *Canada* .. **103 C8** 51 59N 100 9W
Campi Salentina, *Italy* . **43 B11** 40 22N 18 1 E
Câmpia Turzii, *Romania* **29 D8** 46 34N 23 53 E
Campidano, *Italy* ..... **42 C1** 39 30N 8 47 E
Campíglia Maríttima,
Italy .... **40 E7** 43 4N 10 37 E
Campillo de Altobuey,
Spain **39 F3** 39 36N 1 49W
Campillos, *Spain* **37 H6** 37 4N 4 51W
Câmpina, *Romania* ... **29 F10** 45 10N 25 45 E
Campina Grande, *Brazil* **125 E11** 7 20 S 35 47W
Campinas, *Brazil* ..... **127 A6** 22 50 S 47 0W
Campli, *Italy* .... **41 F10** 42 44N 13 41 E
Campo, *Spain* .... **38 C5** 42 25N 0 24 E
Campo de Criptana,
Spain **37 F7** 39 24N 3 7W
Campo de Gibraltar,
Spain **37 J5** 36 15N 5 25W
Campo Grande, *Brazil* . **125 H8** 20 25 S 54 40W
Campo Maior, *Brazil* . **125 D10** 4 50 S 42 12W
Campo Maior, *Portugal* **37 F3** 39 2N 7 7W
Campo Mourão, *Brazil* **127 A5** 24 3 S 52 22W
Campo Túres, *Italy* ... **41 B8** 46 53N 11 55 E
Campobasso, *Italy* .... **43 A7** 41 34N 14 39 E
Campobello di Licata,
Italy .... **42 E6** 37 15N 13 55 E
Campobello di Mazara,
Italy .... **42 E5** 37 38N 12 45 E
Campofelice di Roccella,
Italy .... **42 E6** 37 59N 13 53 E
Campomarino, *Italy* ... **41 G12** 41 57N 15 2 E
Camporeale, *Italy* .... **42 E6** 37 54N 13 6 E
Camporrobles, *Spain* . **38 F3** 39 39N 1 24W
Campos, *Brazil* ...... **127 A7** 21 50 S 41 20W
Campos Belos, *Brazil* . **125 F9** 13 10 S 47 3W
Campos del Port, *Spain* **48 B10** 39 26N 3 1 E
Campos Novos, *Brazil* . **127 B5** 27 21 S 51 50W
Camprodón, *Spain* ... **38 C7** 42 19N 2 23 E
Camptonville, *U.S.A.* . **110 F5** 39 27N 121 3W
Camptown, *U.S.A.* ... **117 E8** 41 44N 76 14W
Câmpulung, *Argeş,
Romania* .... **29 E10** 45 17N 25 3 E
Câmpulung, *Suceava,
Romania* .... **29 C10** 47 32N 25 30 E
Câmpuri, *Romania* ... **29 D11** 46 0N 26 50 E
Camrose, *Canada* **102 C6** 53 0N 112 50W
Camsell Portage,
Canada **103 B7** 59 37N 109 15W
Çamyuva, *Turkey* .... **47 E12** 36 30N 30 30 E
Çan, *Turkey* .... **45 F11** 40 2N 27 3 E
Can Clavo, *Spain* .... **48 C7** 38 57N 1 27 E
Can Creu, *Spain* ..... **48 C7** 38 58N 1 28 E
Can Gio, *Vietnam* .... **65 G6** 10 25N 106 58 E
Can Tho, *Vietnam* .... **65 G5** 10 2N 105 46 E
Canaan, *U.S.A.* **117 D11** 42 2N 73 20W
Canada ■, *N. Amer.* .. **100 C10** 60 0N 100 0W
Canada Basin, *Arctic* . **4 B18** 80 0N 145 0W
Cañada de Gómez,
Argentina .... **126 C3** 32 40 S 61 30W
Canadian, *U.S.A.* **113 H4** 35 55N 100 23W
Canadian →, *U.S.A.* .. **113 H7** 35 28N 95 3W
Canajoharie, *U.S.A.* .. **117 D10** 42 54N 74 35W
Çanakkale, *Turkey* ... **45 F10** 40 8N 26 24 E
Çanakkale □, *Turkey* . **45 F10** 40 10N 26 25 E
Çanakkale Boğazı,
Turkey .... **45 F10** 40 17N 26 32 E
Canal Flats, *Canada* .. **102 C5** 50 10N 115 48W
Canalejas, *Argentina* .. **126 D2** 35 15 S 66 34W
Canals, *Argentina* .... **126 C3** 33 35 S 62 53W
Canals, *Spain* **39 G4** 38 58N 0 35W
Canandaigua, *U.S.A.* . **116 D7** 42 54N 77 17W
Canandaigua L., *U.S.A.* **116 D7** 42 47N 77 19W
Cananea, *Mexico* **118 A2** 31 0N 110 20W
Canarias, Is., *Atl. Oc.* . **48 F4** 28 30N 16 0W
Canaries, *St. Lucia* ... **121 f** 13 55N 61 4W
Canarreos, Arch. de los,
Cuba **120 B3** 21 35N 81 40W
Canary Is. = Canarias,
Is., *Atl. Oc.* **48 F4** 28 30N 16 0W
Canaseraga, *U.S.A.* ... **116 D7** 42 27N 77 45W
Canatlán, *Mexico* **118 C4** 24 31N 104 47W
Canaveral △, *U.S.A.* . **115 L5** 28 28N 80 34W
Canaveral, C., *U.S.A.* . **115 L5** 28 27N 80 32W
Cañaveruelas, *Spain* .. **38 E2** 40 24N 2 38W
Canavieiras, *Brazil* ... **125 G11** 15 39 S 39 0W
Canberra, *Australia* ... **95 F4** 35 15 S 149 8 E
Canby, *Calif., U.S.A.* . **108 F3** 41 27N 120 52W
Canby, *Minn., U.S.A.* . **112 C6** 44 43N 96 16W
Canby, *Oreg., U.S.A.* . **110 E4** 45 16N 122 42W
Cancale, *France* **18 D5** 48 40N 1 50W
Canche →, *France* .... **19 B8** 50 31N 1 39 E
Cancún, *Mexico* **119 C7** 21 8N 86 44W
Candanchú, *Spain* **38 C4** 42 47N 0 32W
Çandarlı, *Turkey* .... **47 C8** 38 56N 26 56 E
Çandarlı Körfezi,
Turkey .... **47 C8** 38 52N 26 55 E
Candas, *Spain* **36 B5** 43 35N 5 45W
Candé, *France* **18 E5** 47 34N 1 2W
Candela, *Italy* .... **43 A8** 41 8N 15 31 E
Candelaria, *Argentina* . **127 B4** 27 29 S 55 44W
Candelaria, *Canary Is.* **48 F3** 28 22N 16 22W
Candelario △, *Spain* .. **36 E5** 40 27N 5 43W
Candeleda, *Spain* **36 E5** 40 10N 5 14W
Candelo, *Australia* ... **95 F4** 36 47 S 149 43 E
Candi Dasa, *Indonesia* **63 J18** 8 30 S 115 34 E
Candia = Iráklion,
Greece .... **49 D7** 35 20N 25 12 E
Candia, Sea of = Crete,
Sea of, *Greece* .... **47 E7** 36 0N 25 0 E
Candle L., *Canada* **103 C7** 53 50N 105 18W
Candlemas I., *Antarctica* **5 B1** 57 3 S 26 40W
Cando, *U.S.A.* **112 A5** 48 32N 99 12W
Candon, *Phil.* .... **61 C4** 17 12N 120 27 E
Canea = Khaniá, *Greece* **49 D6** 35 30N 24 4 E
Canelli, *Italy* .... **40 D5** 44 43N 8 17 E
Canelones, *Uruguay* .. **127 C4** 34 32 S 56 17W
Canet-Plage, *France* .. **20 F7** 42 41N 3 2 E

Cañete, *Chile* .... **126 D1** 37 50 S 73 30W
Cañete, *Peru* .... **124 F3** 13 8 S 76 30W
Cañete, *Spain* **38 E3** 40 3N 1 54W
Cañete de las Torres,
Spain **37 H6** 37 53N 4 19W
Cangas, *Spain* **36 C2** 42 16N 8 47W
Cangas de Narcea, *Spain* **36 B4** 43 10N 6 32W
Cangas de Onís, *Spain* . **36 B5** 43 21N 5 8W
Cangnan, *China* ...... **59 D13** 27 30N 120 23 E
Canguaretama, *Brazil* . **125 E11** 6 20 S 35 5W
Canguçu, *Brazil* ..... **127 C5** 31 22 S 52 43W
Canguçu, Serra do,
Brazil .... **127 C5** 31 20 S 52 40W
Cangwu, *China* ...... **59 F8** 23 25N 111 17 E
Cangxi, *China* .... **58 B5** 31 47N 105 59 E
Cangyuan, *China* ..... **58 F2** 23 12N 99 14 E
Cangzhou, *China* ..... **56 E9** 38 19N 116 52 E
Caniapiscau →, *Canada* **105 A6** 56 40N 69 30W
Caniapiscau, L. de,
Canada **105 B6** 54 10N 69 55W
Canicattì, *Italy* ...... **42 E6** 37 21N 13 51 E
Canicattini Bagni, *Italy* **43 E8** 37 2N 15 4 E
Caniles, *Spain* **37 H8** 37 26N 2 43W
Canim Lake, *Canada* .. **102 C4** 51 47N 120 54W
Canindeyu □, *Paraguay* **127 A5** 24 10 S 55 0W
Canino, *Italy* .... **41 F8** 42 34N 11 45 E
Canisteo, *U.S.A.* **116 D7** 42 16N 77 36W
Canisteo →, *U.S.A.* ... **116 D7** 42 7N 77 8W
Cañitas, *Mexico* **118 C4** 23 36N 102 43W
Cañizal, *Spain* **36 D5** 41 12N 5 22W
Canjáyar, *Spain* **37 H8** 37 1N 2 44W
Çankırı, *Turkey* ..... **72 B5** 40 40N 33 37 E
Cankuzo, *Burundi* .... **86 C3** 3 10 S 30 31 E
Canmore, *Canada* **102 C5** 51 7N 115 18W
Cann River, *Australia* . **95 F4** 37 35 S 149 7 E
Canna, *U.K.* **13 D2** 57 3N 6 33W
Cannanore, *India* ..... **66 P9** 11 53N 75 27 E
Cannes, *France* ...... **21 E11** 43 32N 7 1 E
Canning Town = Port
Canning, *India* .... **69 H13** 22 23N 88 40 E
Cannington, *Canada* .. **116 B5** 44 20N 79 2W
Cannóbio, *Italy* ...... **40 B5** 46 4N 8 42 E
Cannock, *U.K.* **15 E5** 52 41N 2 1W
Cannon Ball →, *U.S.A.* **112 B4** 46 20N 100 38W
Cannondale Mt.,
Australia .... **94 D4** 25 13 S 148 57 E
Cannonsville Reservoir,
U.S.A. **117 D9** 42 4N 75 22W
Cannonvale, *Australia* . **94 J6** 20 17 S 148 43 E
Canoas, *Brazil* ...... **127 B5** 29 56 S 51 11W
Canoe L., *Canada* **103 B7** 55 10N 108 15W
Canon City, *U.S.A.* ... **112 F2** 38 27N 105 14W
Cañon de Rio Blanco △,
Mexico **119 D5** 18 43N 97 15W
Cañón del Río Lobos △,
Spain **36 D7** 41 46N 3 28W
Cañón del Sumidero △,
Mexico **119 D5** 19 22N 96 24W
Canora, *Canada* **103 C8** 51 40N 102 30W
Canosa di Púglia, *Italy* **43 A9** 41 13N 16 4 E
Canowindra, *Australia* . **95 E4** 33 35 S 148 38 E
Canso, *Canada* **105 C7** 45 20N 61 0W
Cantabria □, *Spain* ... **36 B7** 43 10N 4 0W
Cantabria, Sierra de,
Spain **38 C2** 42 40N 2 30W
Cantabrian Mts. =
Cantábrica,
Cordillera, *Spain* .. **36 C5** 43 0N 5 10W
Cantábrica, Cordillera,
Spain **36 C5** 43 0N 5 10W
Cantal □, *France* ..... **20 C6** 45 5N 2 45 E
Cantal, Plomb du,
France .... **20 C6** 45 3N 2 45 E
Cantanhede, *Portugal* . **36 E2** 40 20N 8 36W
Cantavieja, *Spain* **38 E4** 40 31N 0 25W
Čantavir, *Serbia & M.* . **28 E4** 45 55N 19 46 E
Cantemir, *Moldova* ... **29 D13** 46 17N 28 14 E
Canterbury, *Australia* . **94 D3** 25 23 S 141 53 E
Canterbury, *U.K.* ..... **15 F9** 51 16N 1 6 E
Canterbury Bight, *N.Z.* **91 L3** 44 16 S 171 55 E
Canterbury Plains, *N.Z.* **91 K3** 43 55 S 171 22 E
Cantil, *U.S.A.* **111 K9** 35 18N 117 58W
Cantillana, *Spain* **37 H5** 37 36N 5 50W
Canton = Guangzhou,
China .... **59 F9** 23 5N 113 10 E
Canton, *Ga., U.S.A.* .. **115 H3** 34 14N 84 29W
Canton, *Ill., U.S.A.* ... **112 E9** 40 33N 90 2W
Canton, *Miss., U.S.A.* . **113 J9** 32 37N 90 2W
Canton, *Mo., U.S.A.* .. **112 E9** 40 8N 91 32W
Canton, *N.Y., U.S.A.* . **117 B9** 44 36N 75 10W
Canton, *Ohio, U.S.A.* . **116 F3** 40 48N 81 23W
Canton, *Pa., U.S.A.* ... **116 E8** 41 39N 76 51W
Canton, *S. Dak., U.S.A.* **112 D6** 43 18N 96 35W
Canton L., *U.S.A.* **113 G5** 36 6N 98 35W
Cantù, *Italy* .... **40 C6** 45 44N 9 8 E
Canudos, *Brazil* ..... **124 E7** 7 13 S 58 5W
Canumã →, *Brazil* .... **124 D7** 3 55 S 59 10W
Canutama, *Brazil* .... **124 E6** 6 30 S 64 20W
Canutillo, *U.S.A.* **109 L10** 31 55N 106 36W
Canvey, *U.K.* .... **15 F8** 51 31N 0 37 E
Canyon, *U.S.A.* **113 H4** 34 59N 101 55W
Canyon De Chelly △,
U.S.A. **109 H9** 36 10N 109 20W
Canyon of the
Ancients △, *U.S.A.* **109 H9** 37 30N 108 50W
Canyonlands △, *U.S.A.* **109 G9** 38 15N 110 0W
Canyonville, *U.S.A.* .. **108 E2** 42 56N 123 17W
Cao Bang, *Vietnam* ... **58 F6** 22 40N 106 15 E
Cao He →, *China* ..... **57 D13** 40 10N 124 32 E
Cao Lanh, *Vietnam* ... **65 G5** 10 27N 105 38 E
Cao Xian, *China* ..... **56 G8** 34 50N 115 35 E
Cáorle, *Italy* .... **41 C9** 45 36N 12 53 E
Cap-aux-Meules,
Canada **105 C7** 47 23N 61 52W
Cap-Chat, *Canada* **105 C6** 49 6N 66 40W
Cap-de-la-Madeleine,
Canada **104 C5** 46 22N 72 31W
Cap-Haïtien, *Haiti* ... **121 C5** 19 40N 72 20W
Cap Pt., *St. Lucia* .... **121 f** 14 7N 60 57W
Capac, *U.S.A.* **116 D1** 43 1N 82 56W
Capáccio, *Italy* ...... **43 B8** 40 25N 15 5 E
Capaci, *Italy* .... **42 D6** 38 10N 13 14 E
Capanaparo →,
Venezuela **124 B5** 7 1N 67 7W
Capánnori, *Italy* ..... **40 E7** 43 50N 10 34 E
Capbreton, *France* ... **20 E2** 43 39N 1 26W
Capdenac, *France* .... **20 D6** 44 34N 2 5 E
Capdepera, *Spain* .... **38 F8** 39 42N 3 26 E
Cape →, *Australia* .... **94 C4** 20 59 S 146 51 E
Cape Arid △, *Australia* **93 F3** 33 58 S 123 13 E
Cape Barren I.,
Australia .... **95 G4** 40 25 S 148 15 E
Cape Breton
Highlands △, *Canada* **105 C7** 46 50N 60 40W
Cape Breton I., *Canada* **105 C7** 46 0N 60 30W
Cape Charles, *U.S.A.* . **114 G8** 37 16N 76 1W
Cape Coast, *Ghana* ... **83 D4** 5 5N 1 15W

Cape Cod, *U.S.A.* **114 E10** 41 56N 70 6W
Cape Coral, *U.S.A.* ... **115 M5** 26 33N 81 57W
Cape Dorset, *Canada* . **101 B12** 64 14N 76 32W
Cape Fear →, *U.S.A.* . **115 H6** 33 53N 78 1W
Cape Girardeau, *U.S.A.* **113 G10** 37 19N 89 32W
Cape Hatteras, *U.S.A.* **115 H8** 35 30N 75 28W
Cape Lee △, *Australia* . **93 F3** 33 54 S 122 26 E
Cape Lookout △, *U.S.A.* **115 H7** 35 45N 76 25W
Cape May, *U.S.A.* **114 F8** 38 56N 74 56W
Cape May Point, *U.S.A.* **114 F8** 38 56N 74 58W
Cape Melville △,
Australia .... **94 A3** 14 26 S 144 28 E
Cape Mount △, *Liberia* **82 D2** 6 44N 11 24W
Cape Peninsula △,
S. Africa .... **88 E2** 34 20 S 18 28 E
Cape Range △, *Australia* **92 D1** 22 3 S 111 0 E
Cape Tormentine,
Canada **105 C7** 46 8N 63 47W
Cape Town, *S. Africa* . **88 E2** 33 55 S 18 22 E
Cape Tribulation △,
Australia .... **94 B4** 16 5 S 145 25 E
Cape Verde Is. ■,
Atl. Oc. **77 E1** 16 0N 24 0W
Cape Vincent, *U.S.A.* . **117 B8** 44 8N 76 20W
Cape York Peninsula,
Australia .... **94 A3** 12 0 S 142 30 E
Capela, *Brazil* .... **125 F11** 10 30 S 37 0W
Capella, *Australia* .... **94 C4** 23 2 S 148 1 E
Capendu, *France* ..... **20 E6** 43 11N 2 31 E
Capestang, *France* .... **20 E7** 43 20N 3 2 E
Capesterre, *Guadeloupe* **120 b** 15 53N 61 14W
Capesterre-Belle-Eau,
Guadeloupe ...... **120 b** 16 4N 61 36W
Capim →, *Brazil* ..... **125 D9** 1 40 S 47 47W
Capistrello, *Italy* ..... **41 G10** 41 57N 13 23 E
Capitan, *U.S.A.* **109 K11** 33 35N 105 35W
Capitán Arturo Prat,
Antarctica .... **5 C17** 63 0 S 61 0W
Capitol Reef △, *U.S.A.* **109 G8** 38 15N 111 10W
Capitola, *U.S.A.* **110 J5** 36 59N 121 57W
Capizzi, *Italy* .... **43 E7** 37 51N 14 29 E
Capoche →, *Mozam.* . **87 F3** 15 35 S 33 0 E
Capodíchino, Nápoli ✈
(NAP), *Italy* ...... **43 B7** 40 53N 14 16 E
Capoterra, *Italy* ..... **42 C1** 39 11N 8 58 E
Cappadocia, *Turkey* .. **72 C6** 39 0N 35 0 E
Capraia, *Italy* .... **40 E6** 43 2N 9 50 E
Caprara, Pta., *Italy* ... **42 A1** 41 7N 8 19 E
Caprarola, *Italy* ..... **41 F9** 42 19N 12 14 E
Capreol, *Canada* **104 C3** 46 43N 80 56W
Capri, *Italy* .... **43 B7** 40 33N 14 14 E
Capricorn Group,
Australia .... **94 C5** 23 30 S 151 55 E
Capricorn Ra., *Australia* **92 D2** 23 20 S 116 50 E
Caprino Veronese, *Italy* **40 C7** 45 36N 10 47 E
Caprivi Game △,
Namibia .... **88 B3** 17 55 S 22 37 E
Caprivi Strip, *Namibia* . **88 B3** 18 0 S 23 0 E
Caps et Marais
d'Opale △, *France* . **19 B9** 50 40N 2 0 E
Captain's Flat, *Australia* **95 F4** 35 35 S 149 27 E
Captieux, *France* **20 D3** 44 18N 0 16W
Capulin Volcano △,
U.S.A. **113 G3** 36 47N 103 58W
Caquetá →, *Colombia* . **124 D5** 1 15 S 69 15W
Caracal, *Romania* .... **29 F9** 44 8N 24 22 E
Caracas, *Venezuela* ... **124 A5** 10 30N 66 55W
Caracol,
*Mato Grosso do Sul,
Brazil* .... **126 A4** 22 18 S 57 1W
Caracol, *Piauí, Brazil* . **125 E10** 9 15 S 43 22W
Carágio, *Italy* .... **40 D4** 44 25N 7 26 E
Carajás, *Brazil* ...... **125 E8** 6 5 S 50 23W
Carajás, Serra dos,
Brazil .... **125 E8** 6 0 S 51 30W
Carangola, *Brazil* .... **127 A7** 20 44 S 42 5W
Caransebeş, *Romania* . **28 E7** 45 28N 22 18 E
Carantec, *France* **18 D3** 48 40N 3 55W
Caraquet, *Canada* **105 C6** 47 48N 64 57W
Caras, *Peru* .... **124 E3** 9 3 S 77 47W
Caraş Severin □,
Romania .... **28 E7** 45 10N 22 10 E
Caraşova, *Romania* ... **28 E6** 45 11N 21 51 E
Caratasca, L., *Honduras* **120 C3** 15 20N 83 40W
Caratinga, *Brazil* .... **125 G10** 19 50 S 42 10W
Caraúbas, *Brazil* ..... **125 E11** 5 43 S 37 33W
Caravaca de la Cruz,
Spain **39 G3** 38 8N 1 52W
Caravággio, *Italy* .... **40 C6** 45 30N 9 38 E
Caravela, *Guinea-Biss.* **82 C1** 11 30N 16 30W
Caravelas, *Brazil* .... **125 G11** 17 45 S 39 15W
Caraveli, *Peru* .... **124 G4** 15 45 S 73 25W
Caravelle, Presqu'île de
la, *Martinique* .... **120 c** 14 46N 60 48W
Caràzinho, *Brazil* .... **127 B5** 28 16 S 52 46W
Carballino = O
Carballiño, *Spain* .. **36 C2** 42 26N 8 5W
Carballo, *Spain* **36 B2** 43 13N 8 41W
Carberry, *Canada* **103 D9** 49 50N 99 25W
Carbó, *Mexico* **118 B2** 29 42N 110 58W
Carbonara, C., *Italy* .. **42 C2** 39 6N 9 31 E
Carbondale, *Colo.,
U.S.A.* **108 G10** 39 24N 107 13W
Carbondale, *Ill., U.S.A.* **113 G10** 37 44N 89 13W
Carbondale, *Pa., U.S.A.* **117 E9** 41 35N 75 30W
Carbonear, *Canada* ... **105 C9** 47 42N 53 13W
Carboneras, *Spain* ... **39 J3** 36 59N 1 53W
Carboneras de
Guadazón, *Spain* .. **38 F3** 39 54N 1 50W
Carbónia, *Italy* ...... **42 C1** 39 10N 8 30 E
Carcabuey, *Spain* **37 H6** 37 27N 4 17W
Carcagente =
Carcaixent, *Spain* . **39 F4** 39 8N 0 28W
Carcaixent, *Spain* **39 F4** 39 8N 0 28W
Carcajou, *Canada* **102 B5** 57 47N 117 6W
Carcar, *Phil.* .... **61 F5** 10 6N 123 38 E
Carcarana →, *Argentina* **126 C3** 32 27 S 60 48W
Carcasse, C., *Haiti* ... **121 C5** 18 30N 74 28W
Carcassonne, *France* . **20 E6** 43 13N 2 20 E
Carcross, *Canada* **102 A2** 60 13N 134 45W
Çardak, *Çanakkale,
Turkey* .... **45 F10** 40 22N 26 43 E
Çardak, *Denizli, Turkey* **47 D11** 37 49N 29 39 E
Cardamon Hills, *India* . **66 Q10** 9 30N 77 15 E
Cardeña, *Spain* **37 G6** 38 16N 4 20W
Cárdenas, *Cuba* **120 B3** 23 0N 81 30W
Cárdenas,
*San Luis Potosí,
Mexico* **119 C5** 22 0N 99 41W
Cárdenas, *Tabasco,
Mexico* **119 D6** 17 59N 93 21W
Cardiff, *U.K.* **15 F4** 51 29N 3 10W
Cardiff, *U.S.A.* **116 F7** 40 12N 77 12W
Cardiff-by-the-Sea,
U.S.A. **111 M9** 33 1N 117 17W

Cardigan, *U.K.* **15 E3** 52 5N 4 40W
Cardigan B., *U.K.* **15 E3** 52 30N 4 30W
Cardinal, *Canada* **117 B9** 44 47N 75 23W
Cardona, *Spain* ...... **38 D6** 41 56N 1 40 E
Cardona, *Uruguay* ... **126 C4** 33 53 S 57 18W
Cardoner →, *Spain* ... **38 D6** 41 41N 1 51 E
Cardoso, Ilha do, *Brazil* **127 B5** 25 8 S 47 58W
Cardston, *Canada* **102 D6** 49 15N 113 20W
Cardwell, *Australia* ... **94 B4** 18 14 S 146 2 E
Careen L., *Canada* **103 B7** 57 0N 108 11W
Carei, *Romania* ..... **28 C7** 47 40N 22 29 E
Careme = Ciremay,
Indonesia .... **63 G13** 6 55 S 108 27 E
Carentan, *France* **18 C5** 49 19N 1 15W
Carey, *U.S.A.* **108 E7** 43 19N 113 57W
Carey, L., *Australia* ... **93 E3** 29 0 S 122 15 E
Carey, L., *Canada* **103 A8** 62 12N 102 55W
Careysburg, *Liberia* .. **82 D2** 6 34N 10 30W
Cargèse, *France* ...... **21 F12** 42 7N 8 35 E
Carhaix-Plouguer,
France **18 D3** 48 18N 3 36W
Carhué, *Argentina* ... **126 D3** 37 10 S 62 50W
Caria, *Turkey* .... **47 D10** 37 20N 28 10 E
Cariacica, *Brazil* ..... **125 H10** 20 16 S 40 25W
Cariati, *Italy* .... **43 C9** 39 30N 16 57 E
Caribbean Sea,
W. Indies **121 D5** 15 0N 75 0W
Cariboo Mts., *Canada* . **102 C4** 53 0N 121 0W
Caribou, *U.S.A.* **115 B12** 46 52N 68 1W
Caribou →, *Man.,
Canada* **103 B10** 59 20N 94 44W
Caribou →, *N.W.T.,
Canada* **102 A3** 61 27N 125 45W
Caribou I., *Canada* ... **104 C2** 47 22N 85 49W
Caribou Is., *Canada* ... **102 A6** 61 55N 113 15W
Caribou L., *Man.,
Canada* **103 B9** 59 21N 96 10W
Caribou L., *Ont.,
Canada* **104 B2** 50 25N 89 5W
Caribou Mts., *Canada* . **102 B5** 59 12N 115 40W
Caribou River △,
Canada **103 B9** 59 35N 96 35W
Caribrod =
Dimitrovgrad,
Serbia & M. ..... **44 C6** 43 2N 22 48 E
Carichíc, *Mexico* **118 B3** 27 56N 107 3W
Carigara, *Phil.* ...... **61 F6** 11 18N 124 41 E
Carignan, *France* ..... **19 C12** 49 38N 5 10 E
Carignano, *Italy* ..... **40 D4** 44 55N 7 40 E
Carillo, *Mexico* **118 B4** 26 50N 103 55W
Carinda, *Australia* .... **95 E4** 30 28 S 147 41 E
Cariñena, *Spain* **38 D3** 41 20N 1 13W
Carinhanha, *Brazil* ... **125 F10** 14 15 S 44 46W
Carinhanha →, *Brazil* . **125 F10** 14 15 S 43 47W
Carini, *Italy* .... **42 D6** 38 8N 13 11 E
Cariño, *Spain* **36 B3** 43 45N 7 52W
Carínola, *Italy* .... **42 A6** 41 11N 13 58 E
Carinthia = Kärnten □,
Austria .... **26 E6** 46 52N 13 30 E
Caripito, *Venezuela* ... **124 A6** 10 8N 63 6W
Carlet, *Spain* **39 F4** 39 14N 0 31W
Carleton, Mt., *Canada* . **105 C6** 47 23N 66 53W
Carleton Place, *Canada* **117 A8** 45 8N 76 9W
Carletonville, *S. Africa* **88 D4** 26 23 S 27 22 E
Cârlibaba, *Romania* ... **29 C10** 47 35N 25 8 E
Carlin, *U.S.A.* **108 F5** 40 43N 116 7W
Carlingford L., *U.K.* ... **12 B5** 54 3N 6 9W
Carlinville, *U.S.A.* **112 F10** 39 17N 89 53W
Carlisle, *U.K.* **14 C5** 54 54N 2 56W
Carlisle, *U.S.A.* **116 F7** 40 12N 77 12W
Carlisle B., *Barbados* . **121 g** 13 5 S 59 37W
Carlisle I., *Australia* ... **94 J7** 20 49 S 149 18 E
Carlit, Pic, *France* .... **20 F5** 42 35N 1 55 E
Carloforte, *Italy* ..... **42 C1** 39 8N 8 18 E
Carlos Casares,
Argentina .... **126 D3** 35 32 S 61 20W
Carlos Tejedor,
Argentina .... **126 D3** 35 25 S 62 25W
Carlow, *Ireland* **12 D5** 52 50N 6 56W
Carlow □, *Ireland* **12 D5** 52 43N 6 50W
Carlsbad, *Calif., U.S.A.* **111 M9** 33 10N 117 21W
Carlsbad, *N. Mex.,
U.S.A.* **113 J2** 32 25N 104 14W
Carlsbad Caverns △,
U.S.A. **113 J2** 32 10N 104 35W
Carluke, *U.S.A.* **13 F5** 55 45N 3 50W
Carlyle, *Canada* **103 D8** 49 40N 102 20W
Carmacks, *Canada* ... **100 B6** 62 5N 136 16W
Carmagnola, *Italy* .... **40 D4** 44 51N 7 43 E
Carman, *Canada* **103 D9** 49 30N 98 0W
Carmarthen, *U.K.* **15 F3** 51 52N 4 19W
Carmarthen B., *U.K.* .. **15 F3** 51 40N 4 30W
Carmarthenshire □,
U.K. **15 F3** 51 55N 4 13W
Carmaux, *France* ..... **20 D6** 44 3N 2 10 E
Carmel, *U.S.A.* **117 E11** 41 26N 73 41W
Carmel-by-the-Sea,
U.S.A. **110 J5** 36 33N 121 55W
Carmel Valley, *U.S.A.* . **110 J5** 36 29N 121 43W
Carmelo, *Uruguay* ... **126 C4** 34 0 S 58 20W
Carmen, *Colombia* ... **124 B3** 9 43N 75 8W
Carmen, *Paraguay* ... **127 B4** 27 13 S 56 12W
Carmen →, *Mexico* ... **118 A3** 30 42N 106 29W
Carmen, I., *Mexico* ... **118 B2** 26 0N 111 20W
Carmen de Patagones,
Argentina .... **128 E4** 40 50 S 63 0W
Cármenes, *Spain* **36 C5** 42 58N 5 34W
Carmensa, *Argentina* . **126 D2** 35 15 S 67 40W
Carmi, *Canada* **102 D5** 49 36N 119 8W
Carmi, *U.S.A.* **114 F1** 38 5N 88 10W
Carmichael, *U.S.A.* ... **110 G5** 38 38N 121 19W
Carmila, *Australia* .... **94 C4** 21 55 S 149 24 E
Carmona, *Costa Rica* . **120 E2** 10 0N 85 15W
Carmona, *Spain* **37 H5** 37 28N 5 42W
Carn Ban, *U.K.* **13 D4** 57 7N 4 15W
Carn Eige, *U.K.* **13 D3** 57 17N 5 8W
Carnamah, *Australia* .. **93 E2** 29 41 S 115 53 E
Carnarvon, *Australia* .. **92 D1** 24 51 S 113 42 E
Carnarvon, *S. Africa* .. **88 E3** 30 56 S 22 8 E
Carnarvon △, *Australia* **94 C4** 24 54 S 148 2 E
Carnarvon Ra., *Queens.,
Australia* .... **94 D4** 25 15 S 148 30 E
Carnarvon Ra.,
W. Austral., Australia **93 E3** 25 20 S 120 45 E
Carnation, *U.S.A.* **110 C5** 47 39N 121 55W
Carndonagh, *Ireland* .. **12 A4** 55 16N 7 15W
Carnduff, *Canada* **103 D8** 49 10N 101 50W
Carnegie, *U.S.A.* **116 F4** 40 24N 80 5W
Carnegie, L., *Australia* . **93 E3** 26 5 S 122 30 E
Carnic Alps = Karnische
Alpen, *Europe* .... **26 E6** 46 36N 13 0 E
Carniche Alpi =
Karnische Alpen,
Europe .... **26 E6** 46 36N 13 0 E
Carnot, *C.A.R.* ...... **84 D3** 4 59N 15 56 E
Carnot, *Australia* .... **95 E2** 34 57 S 135 38 E
Carnot B., *Australia* .. **92 C3** 17 20 S 121 30 E

Carnoustie, *U.K.* **13 E6** 56 30N 2 42W
Carnsore Pt., *Ireland* .. **12 D5** 52 10N 6 22W
Caro, *U.S.A.* **114 D4** 43 29N 83 24W
Carol City, *U.S.A.* **115 N5** 25 56N 80 16W
Carolina, *Brazil* ...... **125 E9** 7 10 S 47 30W
Carolina, *Puerto Rico* . **121 d** 18 23N 65 58W
Carolina, *S. Africa* ... **89 D5** 26 5 S 30 6 E
Caroline I., *Kiribati* ... **97 H12** 9 58 S 150 13W
Caroline Is., *Micronesia* **96 G7** 8 0N 150 0 E
Caroni →, *Venezuela* ... **124 B6** 8 21N 62 43W
Caronie = Nébrodi,
  Monti, *Italy* .... **43 E7** 37 54N 14 35 E
Caroona, *Australia* .... **95 E5** 31 24 S 150 26 E
Carpathians, *Europe* .. **6 F10** 49 30N 21 0 E
Carpaţii Meridionali,
  Romania .... **29 E9** 45 30N 25 0 E
Carpentaria, G. of,
  Australia .... **94 A2** 14 0 S 139 0 E
Carpentras, *France* ... **21 D9** 44 3N 5 2 E
Carpi, *Italy* .... **40 D7** 44 47N 10 53 E
Cărpineni, *Moldova* ... **29 D13** 46 46N 28 22 E
Carpinteria, *U.S.A.* ... **111 L7** 34 24N 119 31W
Carpio, *Spain* **36 D5** 41 13N 5 7W
Carr Boyd Ra., *Australia* **92 C4** 16 15 S 128 35 E
Carrabelle, *U.S.A.* **115 L3** 29 51N 84 40W
Carral, *Spain* **36 B2** 43 14N 8 21W
Carranza, Presa V.,
  Mexico **118 B4** 27 20N 100 50W
Carrara, *Italy* .... **40 D7** 44 5N 10 6 E
Carrascal, *Phil.* ...... **61 G6** 9 22N 125 56 E
Carrascosa del Campo,
  Spain **38 E2** 40 2N 2 45W
Carrauntoohill, *Ireland* **12 D2** 52 0N 9 45W
Carrick-on-Shannon,
  Ireland **12 C3** 53 57N 8 5W
Carrick-on-Suir, *Ireland* **12 D4** 52 21N 7 24W
Carrickfergus, *U.K.* ... **12 B6** 54 43N 5 49W
Carrickmacross, *Ireland* **12 C5** 53 59N 6 43W
Carrieton, *Australia* ... **95 E2** 32 25 S 138 31 E
Carrión →, *Spain* **36 D6** 41 53N 4 32W
Carrión de los Condes,
  Spain **36 C6** 42 20N 4 37W
Carrizal Bajo, *Chile* ... **126 B1** 28 5 S 71 20W
Carrizalillo, *Chile* ..... **126 B1** 29 5 S 71 30W
Carrizo Cr. →, *U.S.A.* . **113 G3** 36 55N 103 55W
Carrizo Plain △, *U.S.A.* **110 K7** 35 12N 119 48W
Carrizo Springs, *U.S.A.* **113 L5** 28 31N 99 52W
Carrizozo, *U.S.A.* **109 K11** 33 38N 105 53W
Carroll, *U.S.A.* **112 D7** 42 4N 94 52W
Carrollton, *Ga., U.S.A.* **115 J3** 33 35N 85 5W
Carrollton, *Ill., U.S.A.* . **112 F9** 39 18N 90 24W
Carrollton, *Ky., U.S.A.* **114 F3** 38 41N 85 11W
Carrollton, *Mo., U.S.A.* **112 F8** 39 22N 93 30W
Carrollton, *Ohio, U.S.A.* **116 F3** 40 34N 81 5W
Carron →, *U.K.* **13 D4** 57 53N 4 22W
Carron, L., *U.K.* **13 D3** 57 22N 5 35W
Carrot →, *Canada* **103 C8** 53 50N 101 17W
Carrot River, *Canada* .. **103 C8** 53 17N 103 35W
Carrouges, *France* **18 B3** 48 34N 0 10W
Carrù, *Italy* .... **40 D4** 44 29N 7 52 E
Carruthers, *Canada* ... **103 C7** 52 52N 109 16W
Carsa Dek, *Ethiopia* ... **81 F4** 5 13N 39 50 E
Çarşamba, *Turkey* .... **72 B7** 41 11N 36 44 E
Carsóli, *Italy* .... **41 F10** 42 6N 13 5 E
Carson, *Calif., U.S.A.* . **111 M8** 33 48N 118 17W
Carson, *N. Dak., U.S.A.* **112 B4** 46 25N 101 34W
Carson →, *U.S.A.* **110 F8** 39 45N 118 40W
Carson City, *U.S.A.* ... **110 F7** 39 10N 119 46W
Carson Sink, *U.S.A.* ... **108 G4** 39 50N 118 25W
Cartagena, *Colombia* .. **124 A3** 10 25N 75 33W
Cartagena, *Spain* **39 H4** 37 38N 0 59W
Cartago, *Colombia* **124 C3** 4 45N 75 55W
Cartago, *Costa Rica* ... **120 E3** 9 50N 83 55W
Cártama, *Spain* **37 J6** 36 43N 4 39W
Cartaxo, *Portugal* **37 F2** 39 10N 8 47W
Cartaya, *Spain* **37 H3** 37 16N 7 9W
Cartersville, *U.S.A.* ... **115 H3** 34 10N 84 48W
Carterton, *N.Z.* ...... **91 J5** 41 2 S 175 31 E
Carthage, *Tunisia* ..... **42 F3** 36 50N 10 21 E
Carthage, *Ill., U.S.A.* .. **112 E9** 40 25N 91 8W
Carthage, *Mo., U.S.A.* . **113 G7** 37 11N 94 19W
Carthage, *N.Y., U.S.A.* **114 D8** 43 59N 75 37W
Carthage, *Tex., U.S.A.* **113 J7** 32 9N 94 20W
Cartier I., *Australia* ... **92 B3** 12 31 S 123 29 E
Cartwright, *Canada* **105 B8** 53 41N 56 58W
Caruaru, *Brazil* .... **125 E11** 8 15 S 35 55W
Carúpano, *Venezuela* .. **124 A6** 10 39N 63 15W
Caruthersville, *U.S.A.* .. **113 G10** 36 11N 89 39W
Carvin, *France* .... **19 B9** 50 30N 2 57 E
Carvoeiro, *Brazil* ..... **124 D6** 1 30 S 61 59W
Carvoeiro, C., *Portugal* **37 F1** 39 21N 9 24W
Cary, *U.S.A.* **115 H6** 35 47N 78 46W
Casa, Pas de la =
  Envalira, Port d',
  Europe .... **38 C6** 42 33N 1 43 E
Casa Branca, *Portugal* . **37 G2** 38 29N 8 12W
Casa Grande, *U.S.A.* .. **109 K8** 32 53N 111 45W
Casablanca, *Chile* ..... **126 C1** 33 20 S 71 25W
Casablanca, *Morocco* .. **78 B4** 33 36N 7 36W
Casacalenda, *Italy* ..... **41 G11** 41 44N 14 51 E
Casale Monferrato, *Italy* **40 C5** 45 8N 8 27 E
Casalmaggiore, *Italy* ... **40 D7** 44 59N 10 26 E
Casalpusterlengo, *Italy* . **40 C6** 45 11N 9 39 E
Casamance →, *Senegal* **82 C1** 12 33N 16 46W
Casarano, *Italy* .... **43 B11** 40 0N 18 10 E
Casares, *Spain* **37 J5** 36 27N 5 16W
Casas Ibáñez, *Spain* ... **39 F3** 39 17N 1 30W
Casasimarro, *Spain* **39 F2** 39 22N 2 3W
Casatejada, *Spain* **36 F5** 39 54N 5 40W
Casavieja, *Spain* **36 E6** 40 17N 4 46W
Cascada de
  Basaseachic △,
  Mexico **118 B3** 28 9N 108 15W
Cascade, *Idaho, U.S.A.* **108 D5** 44 31N 116 2W
Cascade, *Mont., U.S.A.* **108 C8** 47 16N 111 42W
Cascade Locks, *U.S.A.* **110 D5** 45 40N 121 54W
Cascade Ra., *U.S.A.* ... **110 D5** 47 0N 121 30W
Cascade Reservoir,
  U.S.A. **108 D5** 44 32N 116 3W
Cascais, *Portugal* **37 G1** 38 41N 9 25W
Cascavel, *Brazil* ...... **127 A5** 24 57 S 53 28W
Cáscina, *Italy* .... **40 E7** 43 41N 10 33 E
Casco B., *U.S.A.* **115 D10** 43 45N 70 0W
Caselle Torinese, *Italy* . **40 C4** 45 10N 7 39 E
Caserta, *Italy* .... **43 A7** 41 4N 14 20 E
Casey, *Antárctica* ..... **5 C8** 66 0 S 76 0 E
Caseyr, Raas = Asir,
  Ras, *Somali Rep.* .... **75 E5** 11 55N 51 10 E
Cashel, *Ireland* **12 D4** 52 30N 7 53W
Casiguran, *Phil.* ...... **61 C5** 16 22N 122 7 E
Casilda, *Argentina* .... **126 C3** 33 10 S 61 10W
Casimcea, *Romania* .... **29 F13** 44 45N 28 23 E
Casino, *Australia* ...... **95 D5** 28 52 S 153 3 E
Casiquiare →,
  Venezuela **124 C5** 2 1N 67 7W

Čáslav, *Czech Rep.* .... **26 B8** 49 54N 15 22 E
Casma, *Peru* .... **124 E3** 9 30 S 78 20W
Casmalia, *U.S.A.* **111 L6** 34 50N 120 32W
Cásola Valsénio, *Italy* .. **41 D8** 44 12N 11 40 E
Cásoli, *Italy* .... **41 F11** 42 7N 14 18 E
Caspe, *Spain* **38 D4** 41 14N 0 1W
Casper, *U.S.A.* **108 E10** 42 51N 106 19W
Caspian Depression,
  Eurasia .... **35 G9** 47 0N 48 0 E
Caspian Sea, *Eurasia* .. **52 E6** 43 0N 50 0 E
Cass Lake, *U.S.A.* **112 B7** 47 23N 94 37W
Cassà de la Selva, *Spain* **38 D7** 41 53N 2 52 E
Cassadaga, *U.S.A.* **116 D5** 42 20N 79 19W
Cassano allo Iónio, *Italy* **43 C9** 39 47N 16 20 E
Cassel, *France* .... **19 B9** 50 48N 2 30 E
Casselman, *Canada* **117 A9** 45 19N 75 5W
Casselton, *U.S.A.* **112 B6** 46 54N 97 13W
Cassiar, *Canada* **102 B3** 59 16N 129 40W
Cassiar Mts., *Canada* .. **102 B2** 59 30N 130 30W
Cassino, *Italy* .... **42 A6** 41 30N 13 49 E
Cassis, *France* .... **21 E9** 43 14N 5 32 E
Cassville, *U.S.A.* **113 G8** 36 41N 93 52W
Castagneto Carducci,
  Italy .... **40 E7** 43 9N 10 36 E
Castaic, *U.S.A.* **111 L8** 34 30N 118 38W
Castalia, *U.S.A.* **116 E2** 41 24N 82 49W
Castanhal, *Brazil* ...... **125 D9** 1 18 S 47 55W
Castara, *Trin. & Tob.* .. **125 J16** 11 17N 60 42W
Castéggio, *Italy* .... **40 C6** 45 0N 9 7 E
Castejón de Monegros,
  Spain **38 D4** 41 37N 0 15W
Castèl di Sangro, *Italy* . **41 G11** 41 47N 14 6 E
Castèl San Giovanni,
  Italy .... **40 C6** 45 4N 9 26 E
Castèl San Pietro Terme,
  Italy .... **41 D8** 44 24N 11 35 E
Castelbuono, *Italy* ..... **43 E7** 37 56N 14 5 E
Castelfidardo, *Italy* .... **41 E10** 43 28N 13 33 E
Castelfiorentino, *Italy* .. **40 E7** 43 36N 10 58 E
Castelfranco Emília,
  Italy .... **40 D8** 44 37N 11 3 E
Castelfranco Véneto,
  Italy .... **41 C8** 45 40N 11 55 E
Casteljaloux, *France* ... **20 D4** 44 19N 0 6 E
Castellabate, *Italy* ..... **43 B7** 40 17N 14 57 E
Castellammare, G. di,
  Italy .... **42 D5** 38 8N 12 54 E
Castellammare del
  Golfo, *Italy* .... **42 D5** 38 8N 12 53 E
Castellammare di Stábia,
  Italy .... **43 B7** 40 42N 14 29 E
Castellamonte, *Italy* ... **40 C4** 45 23N 7 42 E
Castellane, *France* ..... **21 E10** 43 50N 6 31 E
Castellaneta, *Italy* ..... **43 B9** 40 38N 16 56 E
Castelli, *Argentina* ..... **126 D4** 36 7 S 57 47W
Castelló de la Plana,
  Spain **38 F4** 39 58N 0 3W
Castellón de la Plana □,
  Spain **38 E4** 40 15N 0 5W
Castellote, *Spain* **38 E4** 40 48N 0 15W
Castelmáuro, *Italy* ..... **41 G11** 41 50N 14 43 E
Castelnau-de-Médoc,
  France **20 C3** 45 2N 0 48W
Castelnau-Magnoac,
  France .... **20 E4** 43 17N 0 31 E
Castelnaudary, *France* .. **20 E5** 43 20N 1 58 E
Castelnovo ne' Monti,
  Italy .... **40 D7** 44 26N 10 24 E
Castelnuovo di Val di
  Cécina, *Italy* .... **40 E7** 43 12N 10 59 E
Castelo, *Brazil* .... **127 A7** 20 33 S 41 14W
Castelo Branco,
  Portugal **36 F3** 39 50N 7 31W
Castelo Branco □,
  Portugal **36 F3** 39 52N 7 45W
Castelo de Paiva,
  Portugal **36 D2** 41 2N 8 16W
Castelo de Vide,
  Portugal **37 F3** 39 25N 7 27W
Castelsardo, *Italy* ...... **42 B1** 40 55N 8 43 E
Castelsarrasin, *France* .. **20 D5** 44 2N 1 7 E
Casteltérmini, *Italy* .... **42 E6** 37 32N 13 39 E
Castelvetrano, *Italy* .... **42 E5** 37 41N 12 47 E
Casterton, *Australia* .... **95 F3** 37 30 S 141 30 E
Castets, *France* **20 E2** 43 52N 1 6W
Castiglion Fiorentino,
  Italy .... **41 E8** 43 20N 11 55 E
Castiglione del Lago,
  Italy .... **41 E9** 43 7N 12 3 E
Castiglione della
  Pescáia, *Italy* ...... **40 F7** 42 46N 10 53 E
Castiglione delle
  Stiviere, *Italy* ...... **40 C7** 45 23N 10 29 E
Castilblanco, *Spain* **37 F5** 39 17N 5 5W
Castile, *U.S.A.* **116 D6** 42 38N 78 3W
Castilla, Playa de, *Spain* **37 J4** 37 0N 6 33W
Castilla-La Mancha □,
  Spain **6 H5** 39 30N 3 30W
Castilla y León □, *Spain* **36 D6** 42 0N 5 0W
Castillo de Locubín,
  Spain **37 H7** 37 32N 3 56W
Castillon-en-Couserans,
  France .... **20 F5** 42 56N 1 1 E
Castillonès, *France* .... **20 D4** 44 39N 0 37 E
Castillos, *Uruguay* ..... **127 C5** 34 12 S 53 52W
Castle Dale, *U.S.A.* **108 G8** 39 13N 111 1W
Castle Douglas, *U.K.* ... **13 G5** 54 56N 3 56W
Castle Rock, *Colo.,*
  U.S.A. **112 F2** 39 22N 104 51W
Castle Rock, *Wash.,*
  U.S.A. **110 D4** 46 17N 122 54W
Castlebar, *Ireland* **12 C2** 53 52N 9 18W
Castlebay, *U.K.* **13 E1** 56 57N 7 31W
Castleblaney, *Ireland* ... **12 B5** 54 7N 6 44W
Castlederg, *U.K.* **12 B4** 54 42N 7 35W
Castleford, *U.K.* **14 D6** 53 43N 1 21W
Castlegar, *Canada* **102 D5** 49 20N 117 40W
Castlemaine, *Australia* .. **95 F3** 37 2 S 144 12 E
Castlepollard, *Ireland* ... **12 C4** 53 41N 7 19W
Castlerea, *Ireland* **12 C3** 53 46N 8 29W
Castlereagh →,
  Australia .... **95 E4** 30 12 S 147 32 E
Castlereagh B., *Australia* **94 A2** 12 10 S 135 10 E
Castleton, *U.S.A.* **117 C11** 43 37N 73 11W
Castletown, *U.K.* **14 C3** 54 5N 4 38W
Castletown Bearhaven,
  Ireland **12 E2** 51 39N 9 55W
Castor, *Canada* **102 C6** 52 15N 111 50W
Castor →, *Canada* **104 B4** 53 24N 78 58W
Castorland, *U.S.A.* **117 C9** 43 53N 75 31W
Castres, *France* .... **20 E6** 43 37N 2 13 E
Castricum, *Neths.* ..... **17 B4** 52 33N 4 40 E
Castries, *St. Lucia* ..... **121 f** 14 2N 60 58W
Castril, *Spain* **37 H8** 37 48N 2 46W
Castro, *Brazil* .... **127 A6** 24 45 S 50 0W
Castro, *Chile* .... **128 E2** 42 30 S 73 50W
Castro Alves, *Brazil* .... **125 F11** 12 46 S 39 33W

Castro del Río, *Spain* .. **37 H6** 37 41N 4 29W
Castro-Urdiales, *Spain* . **36 B7** 43 23N 3 11W
Castro Verde, *Portugal* . **37 H2** 37 41N 8 4W
Castrojeriz, *Spain* **36 C6** 42 17N 4 9W
Castropol, *Spain* **36 B4** 43 32N 7 0W
Castroreale, *Italy* ...... **43 D8** 38 6N 15 12 E
Castrovíllari, *Italy* ..... **43 C9** 39 49N 16 12 E
Castroville, *U.S.A.* **110 J5** 36 46N 121 45W
Castuera, *Spain* **37 G5** 38 43N 5 37W
Çat, *Turkey* .... **73 C9** 39 40N 41 3 E
Cat Ba △, *Vietnam* .... **64 B6** 20 50N 107 3 E
Cat Ba, Dao, *Vietnam* .. **64 B6** 20 50N 107 0 E
Cat I., *Bahamas* **121 B4** 24 30N 75 30W
Cat L., *Canada* **104 B1** 51 40N 91 50W
Cat Lake, *Canada* **104 B1** 51 40N 91 50W
Cat Tien △, *Vietnam* ... **65 G6** 11 25N 107 17 E
Çata, *Slovak Rep.* ..... **27 D11** 47 58N 18 38 E
Catacamas, *Honduras* .. **120 D2** 14 54N 85 56W
Cataguases, *Brazil* ..... **127 A7** 21 23 S 42 39W
Çatak, *Turkey* .... **73 C10** 38 1N 43 8 E
Catalão, *Brazil* .... **125 G9** 18 10 S 47 57W
Catalca, *Turkey* .... **45 E12** 41 8N 28 27 E
Catalina, *Canada* **105 C9** 48 31N 53 4W
Catalina, *Chile* .... **126 B2** 25 13 S 69 43W
Catalina, *U.S.A.* **109 K8** 32 30N 110 50W
Catalonia = Cataluña □,
  Spain .... **38 D6** 41 40N 1 15 E
Cataluña □, *Spain* ..... **38 D6** 41 40N 1 15 E
Catamarca, *Argentina* .. **126 B2** 28 30 S 65 50W
Catamarca □, *Argentina* **126 B2** 27 0 S 65 50W
Catanauan, *Phil.* ...... **61 E5** 13 36N 122 19 E
Catanduanes □, *Phil.* .. **61 E6** 13 50N 124 20 E
Catanduva, *Brazil* ..... **127 A6** 21 5 S 48 58W
Catánia, *Italy* .... **43 E8** 37 30N 15 6 E
Catánia, G. di, *Italy* .... **43 E8** 37 24N 15 9 E
Catanzaro, *Italy* ...... **43 D9** 38 54N 16 35 E
Catarman, *Phil.* ...... **61 E6** 12 28N 124 35 E
Catatumbo-Bari △,
  Colombia **121 E5** 9 3N 73 12W
Catbalogan, *Phil.* ..... **61 E6** 11 46N 124 53 E
Cateel, *Phil.* .... **61 H7** 7 47N 126 24 E
Catembe, *Mozam.* ..... **89 D5** 26 0 S 32 33 E
Caterham, *U.K.* **15 F7** 51 15N 0 4W
Cathcart, *S. Africa* ..... **88 E4** 32 18 S 27 10 E
Cathlamet, *U.S.A.* **110 D3** 46 12N 123 23W
Catio, *Guinea-Biss.* **82 C1** 11 17N 15 15W
Catlettsburg, *U.S.A.* ... **114 F4** 38 25N 82 36W
Çatma Dağı, *Turkey* ... **47 C11** 38 25N 29 50 E
Catoche, C., *Mexico* ... **119 C7** 21 40N 87 8W
Cátria, Mte., *Italy* ..... **41 E9** 43 28N 12 42 E
Catril, *Argentina* ...... **126 D3** 36 26 S 63 24W
Catrimani, *Brazil* **124 C6** 0 27N 61 41W
Catrimani →, *Brazil* ... **124 C6** 0 28N 61 44W
Catskill, *U.S.A.* **117 D11** 42 14N 73 52W
Catskill Mts., *U.S.A.* ... **117 D10** 42 10N 74 25W
Catt, Mt., *Australia* .... **94 A1** 13 49 S 134 23 E
Cattaraugus, *U.S.A.* ... **116 D6** 42 22N 78 52W
Catterick, *U.K.* **14 C6** 54 23N 1 37W
Cáttólica, *Italy* .... **41 E9** 43 58N 12 44 E
Cáttólica Eraclea, *Italy* . **42 E6** 37 26N 13 24 E
Catuala, *Angola* ...... **88 B2** 16 25 S 19 2 E
Catuane, *Mozam.* ..... **89 D5** 26 48 S 32 18 E
Catur, *Mozam.* .... **87 E4** 13 45 S 35 30 E
Catwick Is., *Vietnam* ... **65 G7** 10 0N 109 0 E
Cauca →, *Colombia* ... **124 B4** 8 54N 74 28W
Caucaia, *Brazil* .... **125 D11** 3 40 S 38 35W
Caucasus Mountains,
  Eurasia .... **35 J7** 42 50N 44 0 E
Caudete, *Spain* **39 G3** 38 42N 1 2W
Caudry, *France* .... **19 B10** 50 7N 3 22 E
Caulnes, *France* **18 D4** 48 18N 2 10W
Caulónia, *Italy* .... **43 D9** 38 23N 16 24 E
Caungula, *Angola* ..... **84 F3** 8 26 S 18 38 E
Cauquenes, *Chile* ..... **126 D1** 36 0 S 72 22W
Caura →, *Venezuela* ... **124 B6** 7 38N 64 53W
Caúresi →, *Mozam.* ... **87 F3** 17 8 S 33 0 E
Căuşani, *Moldova* ..... **29 D14** 46 38N 29 25 E
Causapscal, *Canada* ... **105 C6** 48 19N 67 12W
Caussade, *France* ..... **20 D5** 44 10N 1 33 E
Causse-Méjean △,
  France .... **20 D7** 44 18N 3 42 E
Causses du Quercy △,
  France .... **20 D5** 44 35N 1 35 E
Cauterets, *France* **20 F3** 42 52N 0 8W
Cauvery →, *India* ..... **66 P11** 11 9N 78 52 E
Caux, Pays de, *France* . **18 C7** 49 38N 0 35 E
Cava de' Tirreni, *Italy* .. **43 B7** 40 42N 14 42 E
Cávado →, *Portugal* ... **36 D2** 41 32N 8 48W
Cavagrande del
  Cassibile △, *Italy* .... **43 F8** 36 58N 15 6 E
Cavaillon, *France* ..... **21 E9** 43 50N 5 2 E
Cavalaire-sur-Mer,
  France .... **21 E10** 43 10N 6 33 E
Cavalese, *Italy* .... **41 B8** 46 17N 11 27 E
Cavalier, *U.S.A.* **112 A6** 48 48N 97 37W
Cavalla = Cavally →,
  Africa **82 E3** 4 22N 7 32W
Cavallo, Î. de, *France* .. **21 G13** 41 22N 9 16 E
Cavally →, *Africa* **82 E3** 4 22N 7 32W
Cavan, *Ireland* **12 B4** 54 0N 7 22W
Cavan □, *Ireland* **12 C4** 54 1N 7 16W
Cavárzere, *Italy* ...... **41 C9** 45 8N 12 5 E
Çavdarhisar, *Turkey* ... **47 B11** 39 12N 29 37 E
Çavdır, *Turkey* .... **47 D11** 37 10N 29 42 E
Cave Creek, *U.S.A.* **109 K7** 33 50N 111 57W
Cavenagh Ra., *Australia* **93 E4** 26 12 S 127 55 E
Cavendish, *Australia* ... **95 F3** 37 31 S 142 2 E
Caviana, I., *Brazil* **125 C8** 0 10N 50 10W
Cavite, *Phil.* .... **61 D4** 14 29N 120 55 E
Cavnic, *Romania* ...... **29 C8** 47 35N 23 52 E
Cavour, *Italy* .... **40 D4** 44 47N 7 22 E
Cavtat, *Croatia* .... **44 D2** 42 35N 18 13 E
Cawndilla L., *Australia* .. **95 E3** 32 30 S 142 15 E
Cawnpore = Kanpur,
  India .... **69 F9** 26 28N 80 20 E
Caxias, *Brazil* .... **125 D10** 4 55 S 43 20W
Caxias do Sul, *Brazil* ... **127 B5** 29 10 S 51 10W
Çay, *Turkey* .... **72 C4** 38 35N 31 1 E
Cay Sal Bank, *Bahamas* **120 B4** 23 45N 80 0W
Cayambe, *Ecuador* **124 C3** 0 3N 78 8W
Çaycuma, *Turkey* ..... **72 B5** 41 25N 32 2 E
Cayenne, *Fr. Guiana* ... **125 B8** 5 5N 52 18W
Çayeli, *Turkey* .... **73 B9** 41 5N 40 45 E
Cayey, *Puerto Rico* .... **121 d** 18 7N 66 10W
Caygören Baraji, *Turkey* **47 B10** 39 15N 28 12 E
Çayiralan, *Turkey* ..... **72 C6** 39 17N 35 38 E
Caylus, *France* .... **20 D5** 44 15N 1 47 E
Cayman Brac,
  Cayman Is. **120 C4** 19 43N 79 49W
Cayman Is. ■, *W. Indies* **120 C3** 19 40N 80 30W
Cayman Trough,
  Caribbean **98 H11** 19 0N 81 0W
Cayo Romano, *Cuba* ... **120 B4** 22 0N 78 0W
Cayres, *France* .... **20 D7** 44 55N 3 48 E
Cayuga, *U.S.A.* **117 D8** 42 54N 76 44W
Cayuga L., *U.S.A.* **117 D8** 42 41N 76 41W

Cazalla de la Sierra,
  Spain **37 H5** 37 56N 5 45W
Căzăneşti, *Romania* ... **29 F12** 44 36N 27 3 E
Cazaubon, *France* **20 E3** 43 56N 0 3W
Cazaux et de Sanguinet,
  Étang de, *France* **20 D2** 44 29N 1 10W
Cazenovia, *U.S.A.* **117 D9** 42 56N 75 51W
Cazères, *France* ...... **20 E5** 43 13N 1 5 E
Cazin, *Bos.-H.* .... **41 D12** 44 57N 15 57 E
Čazma, *Croatia* .... **41 C13** 45 45N 16 39 E
Cazombo, *Angola* ..... **85 G4** 11 54 S 22 56 E
Cazorla, *Spain* **37 H7** 37 55N 3 2W
Cazorla, Sierra de, *Spain* **37 G8** 38 5N 2 55W
Cea →, *Spain* **36 C5** 42 0N 5 36W
Ceamurlia de Jos,
  Romania .... **29 F13** 44 43N 28 47 E
Ceanannus Mor, *Ireland* **12 C5** 53 44N 6 53W
Ceará = Fortaleza,
  Brazil .... **125 D11** 3 45 S 38 35W
Ceará □, *Brazil* .... **125 E11** 5 0 S 40 0W
Ceará Mirim, *Brazil* .... **125 E11** 5 38 S 35 25W
Ceauru, L., *Romania* ... **29 F8** 44 58N 23 11 E
Cebaco, I. de, *Panama* . **120 E3** 7 33N 81 9W
Cebollar, *Argentina* .... **126 B2** 29 10 S 66 35W
Cebollera, Sierra de,
  Spain **38 D2** 42 0N 2 30W
Cebreros, *Spain* **36 E6** 40 27N 4 28W
Cebu, *Phil.* .... **61 F5** 10 18N 123 54 E
Čečava, *Bos.-H.* ...... **28 F2** 44 42N 17 44 E
Ceccano, *Italy* .... **42 A6** 41 34N 13 20 E
Cece, *Hungary* .... **28 D3** 46 46N 18 39 E
Cechi, *Ivory C.* **82 D4** 6 15N 4 25W
Cecil Plains, *Australia* .. **95 D5** 27 30 S 151 11 E
Cécina, *Italy* .... **40 E7** 43 19N 10 31 E
Cécina →, *Italy* ...... **40 E7** 43 18N 10 29 E
Ceclavín, *Spain* **36 F4** 39 50N 6 45W
Cedar →, *U.S.A.* **112 E9** 41 17N 91 21W
Cedar City, *U.S.A.* **109 H7** 37 41N 113 4W
Cedar Creek Reservoir,
  U.S.A. **113 J6** 32 11N 96 4W
Cedar Falls, *Iowa,*
  U.S.A. **112 D8** 42 32N 92 27W
Cedar Falls, *Wash.,*
  U.S.A. **110 C5** 47 25N 121 45W
Cedar Key, *U.S.A.* **115 L4** 29 8N 83 2W
Cedar L., *Canada* **103 C9** 53 10N 100 0W
Cedar Rapids, *U.S.A.* .. **112 E9** 41 59N 91 40W
Cedartown, *U.S.A.* **115 H3** 34 1N 85 15W
Cedarvale, *Canada* **102 B3** 55 1N 128 22W
Cedarville, *S. Africa* ... **89 E4** 30 23 S 29 3 E
Cedeira, *Spain* **36 B2** 43 39N 8 2W
Cedral, *Mexico* **118 C4** 23 50N 100 42W
Cedrino →, *Italy* ..... **42 B2** 40 11N 9 24 E
Cedro, *Brazil* .... **125 E11** 6 34 S 39 3W
Cedros, I. de, *Mexico* .. **118 B1** 28 10N 115 20W
Cedros B., *Trin. & Tob.* **125 K15** 10 16N 61 54W
Ceduna, *Australia* ..... **95 E1** 32 7 S 133 46 E
Cedynia, *Poland* ...... **31 F1** 52 53N 14 12 E
Cée, *Spain* **36 C1** 42 57N 9 10W
Ceerigaabo = Erigavo,
  Somali Rep. .... **75 E4** 10 35N 47 20 E
Cefalù, *Italy* .... **43 D7** 38 2N 14 1 E
Cega →, *Spain* **36 D6** 41 33N 4 46W
Cegléd, *Hungary* ...... **28 C4** 47 11N 19 47 E
Céglie Messápico, *Italy* . **43 B10** 40 39N 17 31 E
Cehegín, *Spain* **39 G3** 38 6N 1 48W
Ceheng, *China* .... **58 E5** 24 58N 105 48 E
Cehu-Silvaniei, *Romania* **29 C8** 47 24N 23 9 E
Ceica, *Romania* ...... **28 D7** 46 53N 22 10 E
Ceira →, *Portugal* **36 E2** 40 8N 8 16W
Cekik, *Indonesia* ...... **63 J17** 8 12 S 114 27 E
Čelákovice, *Czech Rep.* **26 A7** 50 10N 14 46 E
Celano, *Italy* .... **41 F10** 42 5N 13 33 E
Celanova, *Spain* **36 C3** 42 9N 7 58W
Celaque △, *Honduras* .. **120 D2** 14 30N 88 43W
Celaya, *Mexico* **118 C4** 20 31N 100 37W
Celebes = Sulawesi,
  Indonesia .... **63 E6** 2 0 S 120 0 E
Celebes Sea, *Indonesia* **63 D6** 3 0N 123 0 E
Celic, *Bos.-H.* .... **28 F3** 44 43N 18 49 E
Celina, *U.S.A.* **114 E3** 40 33N 84 35W
Celinac, *Bos.-H.* ...... **28 F2** 44 44N 17 22 E
Celje, *Slovenia* .... **41 B12** 46 16N 15 18 E
Celldömölk, *Hungary* ... **28 C2** 47 16N 17 10 E
Celle, *Germany* .... **24 C6** 52 37N 10 4 E
Celorico da Beira,
  Portugal **36 E3** 40 38N 7 24W
Celtic Sea, *Atl. Oc.* **6 E4** 50 9N 9 34W
Çeltikçi, *Turkey* ...... **47 D12** 37 32N 30 29 E
Çemişgezek, *Turkey* ... **73 C8** 39 3N 38 56 E
Cenderwasih, Teluk,
  Indonesia .... **63 E9** 3 0 S 135 20 E
Cengong, *China* .... **58 D7** 27 13N 108 44 E
Ceno →, *Italy* .... **40 D7** 44 43N 10 5 E
Centallo, *Italy* .... **40 D4** 44 30N 7 35 E
Centelles, *Spain* ...... **38 D7** 41 50N 2 14 E
Center, *N. Dak., U.S.A.* **112 B4** 47 7N 101 18W
Center, *Tex., U.S.A.* ... **113 K7** 31 48N 94 11W
Centerburg, *U.S.A.* **116 F2** 40 18N 82 42W
Centerville, *Calif.,*
  U.S.A. **110 J7** 36 44N 119 30W
Centerville, *Iowa, U.S.A.* **112 E8** 40 44N 92 52W
Centerville, *Pa., U.S.A.* **116 F5** 40 3N 79 59W
Centerville, *Tenn.,*
  U.S.A. **115 H2** 35 47N 87 28W
Centerville, *Tex., U.S.A.* **113 K7** 31 16N 95 59W
Cento, *Italy* .... **41 D8** 44 43N 11 17 E
Central □, *Ghana* **83 D4** 5 30N 1 0W
Central □, *Kenya* ..... **86 C4** 0 30 S 37 30 E
Central □, *Malawi* ..... **87 E3** 13 30 S 33 30 E
Central □, *Zambia* .... **87 E2** 14 25 S 28 50 E
Central, Cordillera,
  Colombia **124 C4** 5 0N 75 0W
Central, Cordillera,
  Costa Rica **120 D3** 10 10N 84 5W
Central, Cordillera,
  Dom. Rep. **121 C5** 19 15N 71 0W
Central, Cordillera, *Phil.* **61 C4** 17 20N 120 57 E
Central, Cordillera,
  Puerto Rico .... **121 d** 18 8N 66 35W
Central African Rep. ■,
  Africa .... **79 G9** 7 0N 20 0 E
Central America,
  America **98 H11** 12 0N 85 0W
Central Butte, *Canada* .. **103 C7** 50 48N 106 31W
Central City, *Colo.,*
  U.S.A. **108 G11** 39 48N 105 31W
Central City, *Ky., U.S.A.* **114 G2** 37 18N 87 7W
Central City, *Nebr.,*
  U.S.A. **112 E6** 41 7N 98 0W
Central I., *Kenya* ..... **86 B4** 3 30N 36 0 E
Central Island △, *Kenya* **86 B4** 2 33N 36 1 E
Central Kalahari △,
  Botswana .... **88 C3** 22 36 S 23 58 E
Central Makran Range,
  Pakistan .... **66 F4** 26 30N 64 15 E

Central Patricia, *Canada* **104 B1** 51 30N 90 9W
Central Point, *U.S.A.* ... **108 E2** 42 23N 122 55W
Central Russian
  Uplands, *Europe* .... **6 E13** 54 0N 36 0 E
Central Siberian
  Plateau, *Asia* .... **50 C14** 65 0N 105 0 E
Central Square, *U.S.A.* . **117 C8** 43 17N 76 9W
Centralia, *Ill., U.S.A.* ... **112 F10** 38 32N 89 8W
Centralia, *Mo., U.S.A.* . **112 F8** 39 13N 92 8W
Centralia, *Wash., U.S.A.* **110 C4** 46 43N 122 58W
Cenxi, *China* .... **59 F8** 22 57N 110 57 E
Čeotina →, *Bos.-H.* .... **44 C2** 43 36N 18 50 E
Cephalonia = Kefalliniá,
  Greece .... **46 C2** 38 15N 20 30 E
Čepin, *Croatia* .... **28 E3** 45 32N 18 34 E
Ceprano, *Italy* .... **42 A6** 41 33N 13 31 E
Ceptura, *Romania* ..... **29 E11** 45 1N 26 21 E
Cepu, *Indonesia* ...... **63 G14** 7 9 S 111 35 E
Ceram = Seram,
  Indonesia .... **63 E7** 3 10 S 129 0 E
Ceram Sea = Seram Sea,
  Indonesia .... **63 E7** 2 30 S 128 30 E
Cerbère, *France* ...... **20 F7** 42 26N 3 10 E
Cerbicales, Îs., *France* .. **21 G13** 41 33N 9 22 E
Cercal, *Portugal* **37 H2** 37 48N 8 40W
Cerdaña, *Spain* .... **38 C6** 42 22N 1 35 E
Cère →, *France* ...... **20 D5** 44 55N 1 49 E
Cerea, *Italy* .... **41 C8** 45 12N 11 13 E
Ceredigion □, *U.K.* **15 E3** 52 16N 4 15W
Ceres, *Argentina* ...... **126 B3** 29 55 S 61 55W
Ceres, *S. Africa* ...... **88 E2** 33 21 S 19 18 E
Ceres, *U.S.A.* **110 H6** 37 35N 120 57W
Céret, *France* .... **20 F6** 42 30N 2 42 E
Cergy, *France* .... **19 C9** 49 2N 2 4 E
Cerignola, *Italy* .... **43 A8** 41 17N 15 53 E
Cerigo = Kíthira, *Greece* **46 E5** 36 8N 23 0 E
Cérilly, *France* .... **19 F9** 46 37N 2 50 E
Cerisiers, *France* ...... **19 D10** 48 8N 3 30 E
Cerizay, *France* **18 F6** 46 50N 0 40W
Çerkeş, *Turkey* ...... **72 B5** 40 49N 32 52 E
Çerkezköy, *Turkey* .... **45 E12** 41 17N 28 0 E
Cerknica, *Slovenia* .... **41 C11** 45 48N 14 21 E
Cerkovica, *Bulgaria* ... **45 C8** 43 41N 24 50 E
Cermeno, *Serbia & M.* .. **44 C4** 43 35N 20 25 E
Çermik, *Turkey* ...... **73 C8** 38 8N 39 26 E
Cerna, *Romania* ...... **29 E13** 45 4N 28 17 E
Cerna →, *Romania* ... **29 F8** 44 38N 23 58 E
Cernavodă, *Romania* ... **29 F13** 44 22N 28 3 E
Cernay, *France* .... **19 E14** 47 44N 7 10 E
Cernik, *Croatia* .... **28 E2** 45 17N 17 22 E
Cerralvo, I., *Mexico* ... **118 C3** 24 20N 109 45W
Cërrik, *Albania* .... **44 E3** 41 2N 19 58 E
Cerritos, *Mexico* **118 C4** 22 27N 100 20W
Cerro Chato, *Uruguay* .. **127 C4** 33 6 S 55 8W
Cerro Corá △, *Paraguay* **127 A4** 22 35 S 56 2W
Cerro el Copey △,
  Venezuela **121 D7** 10 59N 63 53W
Cerro Hoya △, *Panama* **120 E3** 7 17N 80 45W
Cerro Saroche △,
  Venezuela **121 D6** 10 8N 69 38W
Certaldo, *Italy* .... **40 E8** 43 33N 11 2 E
Cervaro →, *Italy* ...... **43 A8** 41 30N 15 52 E
Cervati, Monte, *Italy* ... **43 B8** 40 17N 15 29 E
Cervera, *Spain* .... **38 D6** 41 40N 1 16 E
Cervera de Pisuerga,
  Spain **36 C6** 42 51N 4 30W
Cervera del Río
  Alhama, *Spain* **38 C3** 42 2N 1 58W
Cervéteri, *Italy* .... **41 F9** 42 0N 12 6 E
Cérvia, *Italy* .... **41 D9** 44 15N 12 22 E
Cervignano del Friuli,
  Italy .... **41 C10** 45 49N 13 20 E
Cervinara, *Italy* ...... **43 A7** 41 1N 14 37 E
Cervione, *France* ..... **21 F13** 42 20N 9 29 E
Cervo, *Spain* **36 B3** 43 40N 7 24W
Cesarò, *Italy* .... **43 E7** 37 50N 14 38 E
Cesena, *Italy* .... **41 D9** 44 8N 12 15 E
Cesenático, *Italy* ..... **41 D9** 44 12N 12 24 E
Cēsis, *Latvia* .... **9 H21** 57 18N 25 15 E
Česká Lípa, *Czech Rep.* **26 A7** 50 45N 14 30 E
Česká Třebová,
  Czech Rep. .... **27 B9** 49 54N 16 27 E
České Budějovice,
  Czech Rep. .... **26 C7** 48 55N 14 25 E
České Velenice,
  Czech Rep. .... **26 C7** 48 45N 14 57 E
Českobudějovický □,
  Czech Rep. .... **26 B7** 49 10N 14 30 E
Českomoravská
  Vrchovina,
  Czech Rep. .... **26 B8** 49 30N 15 40 E
Český Brod, *Czech Rep.* **26 A7** 50 4N 14 52 E
Český Krumlov,
  Czech Rep. .... **26 C7** 48 43N 14 21 E
Český Těšín, *Czech Rep.* **27 B11** 49 45N 18 39 E
Çeşma, *Croatia* ...... **41 C13** 45 35N 16 29 E
Çeşme, *Turkey* .... **47 C8** 38 20N 26 23 E
Cessnock, *Australia* ... **95 E5** 32 50 S 151 21 E
Cesson-Sévigné, *France* **18 D5** 48 7N 1 36W
Cestas, *France* **20 D3** 44 44N 0 41W
Cestos →, *Liberia* **82 D3** 5 40N 9 10W
Cestos Sehnkwehn □,
  Liberia **82 D3** 5 40N 9 10W
Cetate, *Romania* ...... **28 F8** 44 7N 23 2 E
Cetin Grad, *Croatia* .... **41 C12** 45 9N 15 45 E
Cetina →, *Croatia* ..... **41 E13** 43 26N 16 42 E
Cetinje, *Serbia & M.* ... **44 D2** 42 23N 18 59 E
Cetraro, *Italy* .... **43 C8** 39 31N 15 55 E
Ceuta, *N. Afr.* **78 A4** 35 52N 5 18W
Ceva, *Italy* .... **40 D5** 44 23N 8 2 E
Cévennes, *France* ..... **20 D7** 44 10N 3 50 E
Cévennes △, *France* ... **70 B2** 37 4N 35 4 E
Ceyhan, *Turkey* ...... **20 D7** 44 10N 3 45 E
Ceyhan →, *Turkey* .... **72 D6** 36 38N 35 40 E
Ceylanpinar, *Turkey* ... **73 D9** 36 50N 40 2 E
Ceylon = Sri Lanka ■,
  Asia .... **66 R12** 7 30N 80 50 E
Cèze →, *France* ...... **21 D8** 44 6N 4 43 E
Cha-am, *Thailand* ..... **64 F2** 12 48N 99 58 E
Cha Pa, *Vietnam* ...... **64 A4** 22 20N 103 47 E
Chabanais, *France* .... **20 C4** 45 50N 0 48 E
Chabeuil, *France* ...... **21 D9** 44 54N 5 1 E
Chablais, *France* ...... **19 F13** 46 20N 6 36 E
Chablis, *France* ...... **19 E10** 47 47N 3 48 E
Chacabuco, *Argentina* . **126 C3** 34 40 S 60 27W
Chachapoyas, *Peru* .... **124 E3** 6 15 S 77 50W
Chachran, *Pakistan* .... **66 E7** 28 55N 70 30 E
Chachro, *Pakistan* .... **68 G4** 25 5N 70 15 E
Chaco □, *Argentina* ... **126 B4** 26 30 S 61 0W
Chaco □, *Paraguay* .... **126 B4** 26 30 S 60 0W
Chaco →, *U.S.A.* **109 H9** 36 46N 108 39W
Chaco Austral, *S. Amer.* **128 B4** 27 0 S 61 30W
Chaco Boreal, *S. Amer.* **124 H6** 22 0 S 60 0W
Chaco Central, *S. Amer.* **128 A4** 24 0 S 61 0W

Chaco Culture △, U.S.A. **109 H10** 36 3N 107 58W
Chacon, C., U.S.A. **102 C2** 54 42N 132 0W
Chad ■, Africa **79 F8** 15 0N 17 15 E
Chad, L. = Tchad, L., Chad **79 F8** 13 30N 14 30 E
Chadan, Russia **53 D10** 51 17N 91 35 E
Chadileuvú →, Argentina **126 D2** 37 46 S 66 0W
Chadiza, Zambia **87 E3** 14 45 S 32 27 E
Chadron, U.S.A. **112 D3** 42 50N 103 0W
Chadyr-Lunga = Ciadâr-Lunga, Moldova **29 D13** 46 3N 28 51 E
Chae Hom, Thailand **64 C2** 18 43N 99 35 E
Chae Son △, Thailand **64 C2** 18 42N 99 20 E
Chaem →, Thailand **64 C2** 18 11N 98 38 E
Chaeryŏng, N. Korea **57 E13** 38 24N 125 36 E
Chagai Hills = Chāh Gay Hills, Afghan. **66 E3** 29 30N 64 0 E
Chagda, Russia **53 D14** 58 45N 130 38 E
Chaghcharān, Afghan. **66 B4** 34 31N 65 15 E
Chagny, France **19 F11** 46 57N 4 45 E
Chagoda, Russia **32 C8** 59 10N 35 15 E
Chagos Arch. ☒, Ind. Oc. **50 K11** 6 0 S 72 0 E
Chagres △, Panama **120 E4** 9 33N 79 37W
Chagrin Falls, U.S.A. **116 E3** 41 26N 81 24W
Chaguanas, Trin. & Tob. **125 K15** 10 30N 61 26W
Chāh Ākhvor, Iran **71 C8** 32 41N 59 40 E
Chāh Bahar, Iran **71 E9** 25 20N 60 40 E
Chāh-e Kavīr, Iran **71 C8** 34 29N 56 52 E
Chāh Gay Hills, Afghan. **66 E3** 29 30N 64 0 E
Chahar Burjak, Afghan. **66 D3** 30 15N 62 0 E
Chahār Mahāll va Bakhtīarī □, Iran **71 C6** 32 0N 49 0 E
Chaibasa, India **67 H14** 22 42N 85 49 E
Chaillé-les-Marais, France **20 B2** 46 25N 1 2W
Chainat, Thailand **64 E3** 15 11N 100 8 E
Chaiya, Thailand **65 H2** 9 23N 99 14 E
Chaiyaphum, Thailand **64 E4** 15 48N 102 2 E
Chaj Doab, Pakistan **68 C5** 32 15N 73 0 E
Chajari, Argentina **126 C4** 30 42 S 58 0W
Chak Amru, Pakistan **68 C6** 32 22N 75 11 E
Chaka, Sudan **81 G3** 4 49N 31 14 E
Chakar →, Pakistan **68 E3** 29 29N 68 2 E
Chakari, Zimbabwe **89 B4** 18 5 S 29 51 E
Chake Chake, Tanzania **86 D4** 5 15 S 39 45 E
Chakhānsūr, Afghan. **66 D3** 31 10N 62 0 E
Chakonipau, L., Canada **105 A6** 56 18N 68 30W
Chakradharpur, India **69 H11** 22 45N 85 40 E
Chakrata, India **68 D7** 30 42N 77 51 E
Chakwal, Pakistan **68 C5** 32 56N 72 53 E
Chala, Peru **124 G4** 15 48 S 74 20W
Chalais, France **20 C4** 45 16N 0 3 E
Chalchihuites, Mexico **118 C4** 23 29N 103 53W
Chalcis = Khalkís, Greece **46 C5** 38 27N 23 42 E
Châlette-sur-Loing, France **19 D9** 48 1N 2 44 E
Chaleur B., Canada **105 C6** 47 55N 65 30W
Chalfant, U.S.A. **110 H8** 37 32N 118 21W
Chalhuanca, Peru **124 F4** 14 15 S 73 15W
Chalindrey, France **19 E12** 47 43N 5 26 E
Chaling, China **59 D9** 26 58N 113 30 E
Chalisgaon, India **66 J9** 20 30N 75 10 E
Chalk River, Canada **104 C4** 46 1N 77 27W
Chalky Inlet, N.Z. **91 M1** 46 3 S 166 31 E
Challans, France **18 F5** 46 50N 1 52W
Challapata, Bolivia **124 G5** 18 53 S 66 50W
Challis, U.S.A. **108 D6** 44 30N 114 14W
Chalmette, U.S.A. **113 L10** 29 56N 89 58W
Chalon-sur-Saône, France **19 F11** 46 48N 4 50 E
Chalonnes-sur-Loire, France **18 E6** 47 20N 0 45W
Châlons-en-Champagne, France **19 D11** 48 58N 4 20 E
Châlus, France **20 C4** 45 39N 0 58 E
Chālūs, Iran **71 B6** 36 38N 51 26 E
Cham, Germany **25 F8** 49 13N 12 39 E
Cham, Cu Lao, Vietnam **64 E7** 15 57N 108 30 E
Chama, U.S.A. **109 H10** 36 54N 106 35W
Chamaicó, Argentina **126 D3** 35 3 S 64 58W
Chaman, Pakistan **66 D5** 30 58N 66 25 E
Chamba, India **68 C7** 32 35N 76 10 E
Chamba, Tanzania **87 E4** 11 37 S 37 0 E
Chambal →, India **69 F8** 26 29N 79 15 E
Chamberlain, U.S.A. **112 D5** 43 49N 99 20W
Chamberlain →, Australia **92 C4** 15 30 S 127 54 E
Chamberlain L., U.S.A. **115 B11** 46 14N 69 19W
Chambers, U.S.A. **109 J9** 35 11N 109 26W
Chambersburg, U.S.A. **114 F7** 39 56N 77 40W
Chambéry, France **21 C9** 45 34N 5 55 E
Chambeshi →, Zambia **84 G6** 11 53 S 29 48 E
Chambly, Canada **117 A11** 45 27N 73 17W
Chambord, Canada **105 C5** 48 25N 72 6W
Chamboulive, France **20 C5** 45 26N 1 42 E
Chamchamal, Iraq **70 C5** 35 32N 44 50 E
Chamela, Mexico **118 D3** 19 32N 105 5W
Chamical, Argentina **126 C2** 30 22 S 66 27W
Chamkar Luong, Cambodia **65 G4** 11 0N 103 45 E
Chamoli, India **69 D8** 30 24N 79 21 E
Chamonix-Mont Blanc, France **21 C10** 45 55N 6 51 E
Champa, India **69 H10** 22 2N 82 43 E
Champagne, Canada **102 A1** 60 49N 136 30W
Champagne, France **19 D11** 48 40N 4 20 E
Champagnole, France **19 F12** 46 45N 5 55 E
Champaign, U.S.A. **114 E1** 40 7N 88 15W
Champassak, Laos **64 E5** 14 53N 105 52 E
Champaubert, France **19 D10** 48 50N 3 45 E
Champawat, India **69 E9** 29 20N 80 6 E
Champdeniers-St-Denis, France **20 B3** 46 29N 0 25W
Champdoré, L., Canada **105 A6** 55 55N 65 49W
Champeix, France **20 C7** 45 37N 3 8 E
Champion, U.S.A. **116 E4** 41 19N 80 51W
Champlain, U.S.A. **117 B11** 44 59N 73 27W
Champlain, L., U.S.A. **117 B11** 44 40N 73 20W
Champlitte, France **19 E12** 47 32N 5 31 E
Champotón, Mexico **119 D6** 19 20N 90 50W
Champua, India **69 H11** 22 5N 85 40 E
Chamusca, Portugal **37 F2** 39 21N 8 29W
Chana, Thailand **65 J3** 6 55N 100 44 E
Chañaral, Chile **126 B1** 26 23 S 70 40W
Chanārān, Iran **71 B8** 36 39N 59 6 E
Chanasma, India **68 H5** 23 44N 72 5 E
Chancery Lane, Barbados **121 g** 13 4N 59 30W
Chanco, Chile **126 D1** 35 44 S 72 32W
Chand, India **69 J8** 21 57N 79 7 E
Chandan, India **69 G12** 24 38N 86 40 E
Chandan Chauki, India **69 E9** 28 33N 80 47 E
Chandannagar, India **69 H13** 22 52N 88 24 E
Chandausi, India **69 E8** 28 27N 78 49 E
Chandeleur Is., U.S.A. **113 L10** 29 55N 88 57W
Chandeleur Sd., U.S.A. **113 L10** 29 55N 89 0W
Chandigarh, India **68 D7** 30 43N 76 47 E
Chandil, India **69 H12** 22 58N 86 3 E
Chandler, Australia **95 D1** 27 0 S 133 19 E
Chandler, Canada **105 C7** 48 18N 64 46W
Chandler, Ariz., U.S.A. **109 K8** 33 18N 111 50W
Chandler, Okla., U.S.A. **113 H6** 35 42N 96 53W
Chandod, India **68 J5** 21 59N 73 28 E
Chandpur, Bangla. **67 H17** 23 8N 90 45 E
Chandrapur, India **66 K11** 19 57N 79 25 E
Chānf, Iran **71 E9** 26 38N 60 29 E
Chang, Pakistan **68 F3** 26 59N 68 30 E
Chang, Ko, Thailand **65 F4** 12 0N 102 23 E
Ch'ang Chiang = Chang Jiang →, China **59 B13** 31 48N 121 10 E
Chang Jiang →, China **59 B13** 31 48N 121 10 E
Changa, India **69 C7** 33 53N 77 35 E
Changanacheri, India **66 Q10** 9 25N 76 31 E
Changane →, Mozam. **89 C5** 24 30 S 33 30 E
Changbai, China **57 D15** 41 25N 128 5 E
Changbai Shan, China **57 C15** 42 20N 129 0 E
Changchiak'ou = Zhangjiakou, China **56 D8** 40 48N 114 55 E
Ch'angchou = Changzhou, China **59 B12** 31 47N 119 58 E
Changchun, China **57 C13** 43 57N 125 17 E
Changchunling, China **57 B13** 45 18N 125 27 E
Changde, China **59 C8** 29 4N 111 35 E
Changdo-ri, N. Korea **57 E14** 38 30N 127 40 E
Changfeng, China **59 A11** 32 28N 117 10 E
Changhai = Shanghai, China **59 B13** 31 15N 121 26 E
Changhua, China **59 B12** 30 12N 119 12 E
Changhua, Taiwan **59 E13** 24 2N 120 30 E
Changhŭng, S. Korea **57 G14** 34 41N 126 52 E
Changhŭngni, N. Korea **57 D15** 40 24N 128 19 E
Changi, Singapore **65 d** 1 23N 103 59 E
Changi, Singapore ✕ (SIN), Singapore **65 M4** 1 23N 103 59 E
Changjiang, China **64 C7** 19 20N 108 55 E
Changjin, N. Korea **57 D14** 40 23N 127 15 E
Changjin-chŏsuji, N. Korea **57 D14** 40 30N 127 15 E
Changle, China **59 E12** 25 59N 119 27 E
Changli, China **57 E10** 39 40N 119 13 E
Changling, China **57 B12** 44 20N 123 58 E
Changlun, Malaysia **65 J3** 6 25N 100 26 E
Changning, Hunan, China **59 D9** 26 28N 112 22 E
Changning, Sichuan, China **58 C5** 28 40N 104 56 E
Changning, Yunnan, China **58 E2** 24 45N 99 30 E
Changping, China **56 D9** 40 14N 116 12 E
Changsha, China **59 C9** 28 12N 113 0 E
Changshan, China **59 C12** 28 55N 118 27 E
Changshu, China **59 B13** 31 38N 120 43 E
Changshun, China **58 D6** 26 3N 106 25 E
Changtai, China **59 E11** 24 35N 117 42 E
Changting, China **59 E11** 25 50N 116 22 E
Changwu, China **56 G4** 35 10N 107 45 E
Changxing, China **59 B12** 31 0N 119 55 E
Changyang, China **59 B8** 30 30N 111 10 E
Changyi, China **57 F10** 36 40N 119 30 E
Changyŏn, N. Korea **57 E13** 38 15N 125 6 E
Changyuan, China **56 G8** 35 15N 114 42 E
Changzhi, China **56 F7** 36 10N 113 6 E
Changzhou, China **59 B12** 31 47N 119 58 E
Chanhanga, Angola **88 B1** 16 0 S 14 8 E
Chania = Khaniá, Greece **49 D6** 35 30N 24 4 E
Chanlar = Xanlar, Azerbaijan **35 K8** 40 37N 46 12 E
Channapatna, India **66 N10** 12 40N 77 15 E
Channel Is., U.K. **15 H5** 49 19N 2 24W
Channel Is., U.S.A. **111 M7** 33 40N 119 15W
Channel Islands △, U.S.A. **111 L7** 34 0N 119 24W
Channel-Port aux Basques, Canada **105 C8** 47 30N 59 9W
Channel Tunnel, Europe **15 F9** 51 0N 1 30 E
Channing, U.S.A. **113 H3** 35 41N 102 20W
Chantada, Spain **36 C3** 42 36N 7 46W
Chanthaburi, Thailand **64 F4** 12 38N 102 12 E
Chantilly, France **19 C9** 49 12N 2 29 E
Chantonnay, France **18 F5** 46 40N 1 3W
Chantrey Inlet, Canada **100 B10** 67 48N 96 20W
Chanute, U.S.A. **113 G7** 37 41N 95 27W
Chanza →, Spain **37 H3** 37 32N 7 30W
Chao Hu, China **59 B11** 31 30N 117 30 E
Chao Phraya →, Thailand **64 F3** 13 32N 100 36 E
Chao Phraya Lowlands, Thailand **64 E3** 15 30N 100 0 E
Chaocheng, China **56 F8** 36 4N 115 37 E
Chaohu, China **59 B11** 31 38N 117 50 E
Chaoyang, Guangdong, China **59 F11** 23 17N 116 30 E
Chaoyang, Liaoning, China **57 D11** 41 35N 120 22 E
Chaozhou, China **59 F11** 23 42N 116 32 E
Chapais, Canada **104 C5** 49 47N 74 51W
Chapala, Mozam. **87 F4** 15 50 S 37 35 E
Chapala, L. de, Mexico **118 C4** 20 10N 103 20W
Chapayev, Kazakhstan **34 E10** 50 25N 51 10 E
Chapayevsk, Russia **34 D9** 53 0N 49 40 E
Chapecó, Brazil **127 B5** 27 14 S 52 41W
Chapel Hill, U.S.A. **115 H6** 35 55N 79 4W
Chapleau, Canada **104 C3** 47 50N 83 24W
Chaplin, Canada **103 C7** 50 28N 106 40W
Chaplin L., Canada **103 C7** 50 22N 106 36W
Chaplino, Ukraine **33 H9** 48 8N 36 15 E
Chaplygin, Russia **32 F11** 53 15N 40 0 E
Chappell, U.S.A. **112 E3** 41 6N 102 28W
Chapra = Chhapra, India **69 G11** 25 48N 84 44 E
Chara, Russia **53 D12** 56 54N 118 20 E
Charadai, Argentina **126 B4** 27 35 S 59 55W
Charagua, Bolivia **124 G6** 19 45 S 63 10W
Charambirá, Punta, Colombia **124 C3** 4 16N 77 32W
Charaña, Bolivia **124 G5** 17 30 S 69 25W
Charantsavan, Armenia **35 K7** 40 35N 44 41 E
Charanwala, India **68 F5** 27 51N 72 10 E
Charata, Argentina **126 B3** 27 13 S 61 14W
Charcas, Mexico **118 C4** 23 10N 101 20W
Charcot I., Antarctica **5 C17** 70 0 S 70 0W
Chard, U.K. **15 G5** 50 52N 2 58W
Chardon, U.S.A. **116 E3** 41 35N 81 12W
Chardzhou = Chärjew, Turkmenistan **52 F7** 39 6N 63 34 E
Charente □, France **20 C4** 45 50N 0 16 E
Charente →, France **20 C2** 45 57N 1 5W
Charente-Maritime □, France **20 C3** 45 45N 0 45W
Charenton-du-Cher, France **19 F9** 46 44N 2 39 E
Chari →, Chad **79 F8** 12 58N 14 31 E
Chārīkār, Afghan. **66 B6** 35 0N 69 10 E
Chariton →, U.S.A. **112 F8** 39 19N 92 58W
Chärjew, Turkmenistan **52 F7** 39 6N 63 34 E
Charkhari, India **69 G8** 25 24N 79 45 E
Charkhi Dadri, India **68 E7** 28 37N 76 17 E
Charleroi, Belgium **17 D4** 50 24N 4 27 E
Charleroi, U.S.A. **116 F5** 40 9N 79 57W
Charles, C., U.S.A. **114 G8** 37 7N 75 58W
Charles City, U.S.A. **112 D8** 43 4N 92 41W
Charles de Gaulle, Paris ✕ (CDG), France **19 D9** 49 0N 2 32 E
Charles L., Canada **103 B6** 59 50N 110 33W
Charles Town, U.S.A. **114 F7** 39 17N 77 52W
Charleston, Ill., U.S.A. **114 F1** 39 30N 88 10W
Charleston, Miss., U.S.A. **113 H9** 34 1N 90 4W
Charleston, Mo., U.S.A. **113 G10** 36 55N 89 21W
Charleston, S.C., U.S.A. **115 J6** 32 46N 79 56W
Charleston, W. Va., U.S.A. **114 F5** 38 21N 81 38W
Charleston L., Canada **117 B9** 44 32N 76 0W
Charleston Peak, U.S.A. **111 J11** 36 16N 115 42W
Charlestown, Ireland **12 C3** 53 58N 8 48W
Charlestown, S. Africa **89 D4** 27 26 S 29 53 E
Charlestown, Ind., U.S.A. **114 F3** 38 27N 85 40W
Charlestown, N.H., U.S.A. **117 C12** 43 14N 72 25W
Charlestown of Aberlour, U.K. **13 D5** 57 28N 3 14W
Charleville = Rath Luirc, Ireland **12 D3** 52 21N 8 40W
Charleville, Australia **95 D4** 26 24 S 146 15 E
Charleville-Mézières, France **19 C11** 49 44N 4 40 E
Charlevoix, U.S.A. **114 C3** 45 19N 85 16W
Charlieu, France **19 F11** 46 10N 4 10 E
Charlotte, Mich., U.S.A. **114 D3** 42 34N 84 50W
Charlotte, N.C., U.S.A. **115 H5** 35 13N 80 51W
Charlotte, Vt., U.S.A. **117 B11** 44 19N 73 14W
Charlotte Amalie, U.S. Virgin Is. **121 e** 18 21N 64 56W
Charlotte Harbor, U.S.A. **115 M4** 26 50N 82 10W
Charlotte L., Canada **102 C3** 52 12N 125 19W
Charlottenberg, Sweden **10 E6** 59 54N 12 17 E
Charlottesville, U.S.A. **114 F6** 38 2N 78 30W
Charlottetown, Nfld. & L., Canada **105 B8** 52 46N 56 7W
Charlottetown, P.E.I., Canada **105 C7** 46 14N 63 8W
Charlotteville, Trin. & Tob. **125 J16** 11 20N 60 33W
Charlton, Australia **95 F3** 36 16 S 143 24 E
Charlton, U.S.A. **112 E8** 40 59N 93 20W
Charlton I., Canada **104 B4** 52 0N 79 20W
Charmes, France **19 D13** 48 22N 6 17 E
Charny, Canada **105 C5** 46 43N 71 15W
Charnyany, Belarus **31 G11** 51 59N 24 12 E
Charolles, France **19 F11** 46 27N 4 16 E
Chârost, France **19 F9** 47 0N 2 7 E
Charre, Mozam. **87 F4** 17 13 S 35 10 E
Charroux, France **20 B4** 46 9N 0 25 E
Charsadda, Pakistan **68 B4** 34 7N 71 45 E
Charters Towers, Australia **94 C4** 20 5 S 146 13 E
Chartres, France **18 D8** 48 29N 1 30 E
Chartreuse ⌂, France **21 C9** 45 20N 5 42 E
Chascomús, Argentina **126 D4** 35 30 S 58 0W
Chasefu, Zambia **87 E3** 11 55 S 33 8 E
Chashma Barrage, Pakistan **68 C4** 32 27N 71 20 E
Chasseneuil-sur-Bonnieure, France **20 C4** 45 52N 0 29 E
Chāt, Iran **71 B7** 37 59N 55 16 E
Chatal Balkan = Udvoy Balkan, Bulgaria **45 D10** 42 50N 26 50 E
Château-Arnoux-St-Auban, France **21 D10** 44 6N 6 0 E
Château-Chinon, France **19 E10** 47 4N 3 56 E
Château-d'Olonne, France **20 B2** 46 30N 1 44W
Château-du-Loir, France **18 E7** 47 40N 0 25 E
Château-Gontier, France **18 E6** 47 50N 0 48W
Château-la-Vallière, France **18 E7** 47 30N 0 20 E
Château-Landon, France **19 D9** 48 8N 2 40 E
Château-Renard, France **19 E9** 47 56N 2 55 E
Château-Renault, France **18 E7** 47 36N 0 56 E
Château-Salins, France **19 D13** 48 50N 6 30 E
Château-Thierry, France **19 C10** 49 3N 3 20 E
Châteaubourg, France **18 D5** 48 7N 1 25W
Châteaubriant, France **18 E5** 47 43N 1 23W
Châteaudun, France **18 D8** 48 3N 1 20 E
Chateaugay, U.S.A. **117 B10** 44 56N 74 5W
Châteaugiron, France **18 D5** 48 3N 1 30W
Châteauguay, L., Canada **105 A5** 56 26N 70 3W
Châteaulin, France **18 D2** 48 11N 4 8W
Châteaumeillant, France **19 F9** 46 35N 2 12 E
Châteauneuf-du-Faou, France **18 D3** 48 11N 3 50W
Châteauneuf-sur-Charente, France **20 C3** 45 36N 0 3W
Châteauneuf-sur-Cher, France **19 F9** 46 52N 2 18 E
Châteauneuf-sur-Loire, France **19 E9** 47 52N 2 13 E
Châteaurenard, France **21 E8** 43 53N 4 51 E
Châteauroux, France **19 F8** 46 50N 1 40 E
Châteauvillain, France **19 D11** 48 2N 4 55 E
Châteaux, Pte. des, Guadeloupe **120 b** 16 15N 61 10W
Châtelaillon-Plage, France **20 B2** 46 5N 1 5W
Châtelguyon, France **20 C7** 45 55N 3 4 E
Châtellerault, France **18 F7** 46 50N 0 30 E
Châtelus-Malvaleix, France **19 F9** 46 18N 2 1 E
Chatham = Chatham-Kent, Canada **116 D2** 42 24N 82 11W
Chatham = Miramichi, Canada **105 C6** 47 2N 65 28W
Chatham, U.K. **15 F8** 51 22N 0 32 E
Chatham, U.S.A. **117 D11** 42 21N 73 36W
Chatham Is., Pac. Oc. **96 M10** 44 0 S 176 40W
Chatham-Kent, Canada **116 D2** 42 24N 82 11W
Châtillon, Italy **40 C4** 45 45N 7 37 E
Châtillon-Coligny, France **19 E9** 47 50N 2 51 E
Châtillon-en-Diois, France **21 D9** 44 41N 5 29 E
Châtillon-sur-Indre, France **18 F8** 46 59N 1 10 E
Châtillon-sur-Loire, France **19 E9** 47 35N 2 44 E
Châtillon-sur-Seine, France **19 E11** 47 50N 4 33 E
Chatmohar, Bangla. **69 G13** 24 15N 89 15 E
Chatra, India **69 G11** 24 12N 84 56 E
Chatrapur, India **67 K14** 19 22N 85 2 E
Chats, L. des, Canada **117 A8** 45 30N 76 20W
Chatsu, India **68 F6** 26 36N 75 57 E
Chatsworth, Canada **116 B4** 44 27N 80 54W
Chatsworth, Zimbabwe **87 F3** 19 38 S 31 13 E
Chāttagām = Chittagong, Bangla. **67 H17** 22 19N 91 48 E
Chattahoochee, U.S.A. **115 K3** 30 42N 84 51W
Chattahoochee →, U.S.A. **115 K3** 30 54N 84 57W
Chattanooga, U.S.A. **115 H3** 35 3N 85 19W
Chatteris, U.K. **15 E8** 52 28N 0 2 E
Chaturat, Thailand **64 E3** 15 40N 101 51 E
Chau Doc, Vietnam **65 G5** 10 42N 105 7 E
Chaudes-Aigues, France **20 D7** 44 51N 3 1 E
Chauffailles, France **19 F11** 46 13N 4 20 E
Chaukan Pass, Burma **67 F20** 27 0N 97 15 E
Chaumont, France **19 D12** 48 7N 5 8 E
Chaumont, U.S.A. **117 B8** 44 4N 76 8W
Chaumont-en-Vexin, France **19 C8** 49 16N 1 53 E
Chaumont-sur-Loire, France **18 E8** 47 29N 1 11 E
Chaunay, France **20 B4** 46 13N 0 9 E
Chaunskaya G., Russia **4 C16** 69 0N 169 0 E
Chauny, France **19 C10** 49 37N 3 12 E
Chausey, Is., France **18 D5** 48 52N 1 49W
Chaussin, France **19 F12** 46 59N 5 22 E
Chautauqua L., U.S.A. **116 D5** 42 10N 79 24W
Chauvigny, France **18 F7** 46 34N 0 39 E
Chauvin, Canada **103 C6** 52 45N 110 10W
Chavanges, France **19 D11** 48 30N 4 35 E
Chaves, Brazil **125 D9** 0 15 S 49 55W
Chaves, Portugal **36 D3** 41 45N 7 32W
Chawang, Thailand **65 H2** 8 25N 99 30 E
Chazelles-sur-Lyon, France **21 C8** 45 39N 4 22 E
Chazy, U.S.A. **117 B11** 44 53N 73 26W
Cheb, Czech Rep. **26 A5** 50 9N 12 28 E
Cheboksarskoye Vdkhr., Russia **34 B8** 56 13N 46 58 E
Cheboksary, Russia **34 B8** 56 8N 47 12 E
Cheboygan, U.S.A. **114 C3** 45 39N 84 29W
Chebsara, Russia **32 C10** 59 10N 38 59 E
Chech, Erg, Africa **78 D5** 25 0N 2 15W
Chechelnyk, Ukraine **29 B14** 48 13N 29 22 E
Chechen, Ostrov, Russia **35 H8** 43 59N 47 40 E
Chechenia □, Russia **35 J7** 43 30N 45 29 E
Checheno-Ingush Republic = Chechenia □, Russia **35 J7** 43 30N 45 29 E
Chechnya = Chechenia □, Russia **35 J7** 43 30N 45 29 E
Chech'ŏn, S. Korea **57 F15** 37 8N 128 12 E
Chęciny, Poland **31 H7** 50 46N 20 28 E
Checotah, U.S.A. **113 H7** 35 28N 95 31W
Chedabucto B., Canada **105 C7** 45 25N 61 8W
Cheduba I., Burma **67 K18** 18 45N 93 40 E
Cheepie, Australia **95 D4** 26 33 S 145 1 E
Chef-Boutonne, France **20 B3** 46 7N 0 4W
Chegdomyn, Russia **53 D14** 51 7N 133 1 E
Chegga, Mauritania **78 C4** 25 27N 5 40W
Chegutu, Zimbabwe **87 F3** 18 10 S 30 14 E
Chehalis, U.S.A. **110 D4** 46 40N 122 58W
Chehalis →, U.S.A. **110 D3** 46 57N 123 50W
Cheile Nerei-Beusnita △, Romania **28 F6** 44 56N 21 52 E
Cheiron, Mt., France **21 E10** 43 49N 6 58 E
Cheju do, S. Korea **57 H14** 33 29N 126 34 E
Chekalin, Russia **32 E9** 54 10N 36 10 E
Chekhovo, Russia **30 D7** 54 33N 20 43 E
Chekiang = Zhejiang □, China **59 C13** 29 0N 120 0 E
Chel = Kuru, Bahr el →, Sudan **81 F2** 8 10N 26 50 E
Chela, Sa. da, Angola **88 B1** 16 20 S 13 20 E
Chelan, U.S.A. **108 C4** 47 51N 120 1W
Chelan, L., U.S.A. **108 B3** 48 11N 120 30W
Cheleken, Turkmenistan **52 F6** 39 34N 53 16 E
Cheleken Yarymadasy, Turkmenistan **71 B7** 39 30N 53 15 E
Chelforó, Argentina **128 D3** 39 0 S 66 33W
Chelkar = Shalqar, Kazakhstan **52 E6** 47 48N 59 39 E
Chelkar Tengiz, Solonchak, Kazakhstan **52 E7** 48 5N 63 7 E
Chella, Ethiopia **81 F4** 5 0N 37 26 E
Chelles, France **19 D9** 48 52N 2 33 E
Chełm, Poland **31 G10** 51 8N 23 30 E
Chełmno, Poland **31 E5** 53 20N 18 30 E
Chelmsford, U.K. **15 F8** 51 44N 0 29 E
Chełmża, Poland **31 E5** 53 10N 18 39 E
Chelsea, U.S.A. **117 C12** 43 59N 72 27W
Cheltenham, U.K. **15 F5** 51 54N 2 4W
Chelva, Spain **38 F4** 39 45N 1 0W
Chelyabinsk, Russia **52 D7** 55 10N 61 24 E
Chelyuskin, C. = Chelyuskin, Mys, Russia **53 B11** 77 30N 103 0 E
Chelyuskin, Mys, Russia **53 B11** 77 30N 103 0 E
Chemainus, Canada **110 B3** 48 55N 123 42W
Chemba, Mozam. **85 H6** 17 9 S 34 53 E
Chembar = Belinskiy, Russia **34 D6** 53 0N 43 25 E
Chemillé, France **18 E6** 47 14N 0 45W
Chemnitz, Germany **24 E8** 50 51N 12 54 E
Chemult, U.S.A. **108 E3** 43 14N 121 47W
Chen, Gora, Russia **53 C15** 65 16N 141 50 E
Chenab →, Pakistan **68 D4** 30 23N 71 2 E
Chenango Forks, U.S.A. **117 D9** 42 15N 75 51W
Chencha, Ethiopia **81 F4** 6 15N 37 32 E
Chenchiang = Zhenjiang, China **59 A12** 32 11N 119 26 E
Cheney, U.S.A. **108 C5** 47 30N 117 35W
Cheng Xian, China **56 H3** 33 43N 105 42 E
Chengbu, China **59 D8** 26 18N 110 16 E
Chengcheng, China **56 G5** 35 8N 109 56 E
Chengchou = Zhengzhou, China **56 G7** 34 45N 113 34 E
Chengde, China **57 D9** 40 59N 117 58 E
Chengdong Hu, China **59 A11** 32 15N 116 20 E
Chengdu, China **58 B5** 30 38N 104 2 E
Chenggong, China **58 E4** 24 52N 102 56 E
Chenggu, China **56 H4** 33 10N 107 21 E
Chenghai, China **59 F11** 23 30N 116 42 E
Chengjiang, China **58 E4** 24 39N 103 0 E
Chengkou, China **58 B7** 31 54N 108 31 E
Ch'engmai, China **64 C7** 19 50N 109 58 E
Ch'engtu = Chengdu, China **58 B5** 30 38N 104 2 E
Chengwu, China **56 G8** 34 58N 115 50 E
Chengxi Hu, China **59 A11** 32 15N 116 10 E
Chengyang, China **57 F11** 36 18N 120 21 E
Chenjiagang, China **57 G10** 34 23N 119 47 E
Chenkán, Mexico **119 D6** 19 8N 90 58W
Chennai, India **66 N12** 13 8N 80 19 E
Chenôve, France **19 E12** 47 16N 5 1 E
Chenxi, China **59 C8** 28 2N 110 12 E
Chenzhou, China **59 E9** 25 47N 113 1 E
Cheo Reo, Vietnam **62 B3** 13 25N 108 28 E
Cheom Ksan, Cambodia **64 E5** 14 13N 104 56 E
Chepelare, Bulgaria **45 E8** 41 44N 24 40 E
Chepén, Peru **124 E3** 7 15 S 79 23W
Chepes, Argentina **126 C2** 31 20 S 66 35W
Chepo, Panama **120 E4** 9 10N 79 6W
Chepstow, U.K. **15 F5** 51 38N 2 41W
Chequamegon B., U.S.A. **112 B9** 46 40N 90 30W
Cher □, France **19 E9** 47 10N 2 30 E
Cher →, France **18 E7** 47 21N 0 29 E
Chéradi, Italy **43 B10** 40 27N 17 10 E
Cherasco, Italy **40 D4** 44 39N 7 51 E
Cheraw, U.S.A. **115 H6** 34 42N 79 53W
Cherbourg, France **18 C5** 49 39N 1 40W
Cherdakly, Russia **34 C9** 54 25N 48 50 E
Cherdyn, Russia **52 C6** 60 24N 56 29 E
Cheremkhovo, Russia **53 D11** 53 8N 103 1 E
Cherepanovo, Russia **52 D9** 54 15N 83 30 E
Cherepovets, Russia **32 C9** 59 5N 37 55 E
Chergui, Chott ech, Algeria **78 B6** 34 21N 0 25 E
Cherikov = Cherykaw, Belarus **32 F6** 53 32N 31 20 E
Cherkasy, Ukraine **33 H7** 49 27N 32 4 E
Cherkessk, Russia **35 H6** 44 15N 42 5 E
Cherlak, Russia **52 D8** 54 15N 74 55 E
Chernaya, Russia **53 B9** 70 30N 89 10 E
Chernelytsya, Ukraine **29 B10** 48 49N 25 26 E
Cherni, Bulgaria **44 D7** 42 35N 23 18 E
Chernigov = Chernihiv, Ukraine **33 G6** 51 28N 31 20 E
Chernihiv, Ukraine **33 G6** 51 28N 31 20 E
Chernivetska □, Ukraine **29 B10** 48 20N 26 0 E
Chernivtsi, Ukraine **29 B13** 48 32N 28 9 E
Chernivtsi, Ukraine **29 B10** 48 15N 25 52 E
Chernobyl = Chornobyl, Ukraine **33 G6** 51 20N 30 15 E
Chernogorsk, Russia **53 D10** 53 49N 91 18 E
Chernomorskoye = Chornomorske, Ukraine **33 K7** 45 31N 32 40 E
Chernovtsy = Chernivtsi, Ukraine **29 B10** 48 15N 25 52 E
Chernyakhovsk, Russia **9 J19** 54 36N 21 48 E
Chernyanka, Russia **33 G9** 50 56N 37 49 E
Chernysheyskiy, Russia **53 C12** 63 0N 112 30 E
Chernyye Zemli, Russia **35 H8** 46 10N 46 0 E
Cherokee, Iowa, U.S.A. **112 D7** 42 45N 95 33W
Cherokee, Okla., U.S.A. **113 G5** 36 45N 98 21W
Cherokee Village, U.S.A. **113 G9** 36 17N 91 30W
Cherokees, Grand Lake O' The, U.S.A. **113 G7** 36 28N 95 2W
Cherrapunji, India **67 G17** 25 17N 91 47 E
Cherry Valley, Calif., U.S.A. **111 M10** 33 59N 116 57W
Cherry Valley, N.Y., U.S.A. **117 D10** 42 48N 74 45W
Cherskiy, Russia **53 C17** 68 45N 161 18 E
Cherskogo Khrebet, Russia **53 C15** 65 0N 143 0 E
Chertkovo, Russia **33 H11** 49 25N 40 19 E
Cherven, Belarus **32 F5** 53 45N 28 28 E
Cherven-Bryag, Bulgaria **45 C8** 43 17N 24 7 E
Chervonoarmiyske, Ukraine **29 E13** 45 47N 28 44 E
Chervonohrad, Ukraine **33 G3** 50 25N 24 10 E
Cherwell →, U.K. **15 F6** 51 44N 1 14W
Cherykaw, Belarus **32 F6** 53 32N 31 20 E
Chesapeake, U.S.A. **114 G7** 36 50N 76 17W
Chesapeake B., U.S.A. **114 G7** 38 0N 76 10W
Cheshire □, U.K. **14 D5** 53 14N 2 30W
Cheshskaya Guba, Russia **52 C5** 67 20N 47 0 E
Cheshunt, U.K. **15 F7** 51 43N 0 1W
Chesil Beach, U.K. **15 G5** 50 37N 2 33W
Chesley, Canada **116 B3** 44 17N 81 5W
Cheste, Spain **39 F4** 39 30N 0 41W
Chester, U.K. **14 D5** 53 12N 2 53W
Chester, Calif., U.S.A. **108 F3** 40 19N 121 14W
Chester, Ill., U.S.A. **113 G10** 37 55N 89 49W
Chester, Mont., U.S.A. **108 B8** 48 31N 110 58W
Chester, Pa., U.S.A. **114 F8** 39 51N 75 22W
Chester, S.C., U.S.A. **115 H5** 34 43N 81 12W
Chester, Vt., U.S.A. **117 C12** 43 16N 72 36W
Chester, W. Va., U.S.A. **116 F4** 40 37N 80 34W
Chester-le-Street, U.K. **14 C6** 54 51N 1 34W
Chesterfield, U.K. **14 D6** 53 15N 1 25W
Chesterfield, Is., N. Cal. **96 J7** 19 52 S 158 15 E
Chesterfield Inlet, Canada **100 B10** 63 30N 90 45W
Chesterton Ra., Australia **95 D4** 25 30 S 147 27 E
Chesterton Range △, Australia **95 D4** 26 16 S 147 22 E
Chestertown, U.S.A. **117 C11** 43 40N 73 48W
Chesterville, Canada **117 A9** 45 6N 75 14W
Chestnut Ridge, U.S.A. **116 F5** 40 20N 79 10W
Chesuncook L., U.S.A. **115 C11** 46 0N 69 21W
Chéticamp, Canada **105 C7** 46 37N 60 59W
Chetrosu, Moldova **29 B12** 48 5N 27 54 E
Chetumal, Mexico **119 D7** 18 30N 88 20W
Chetumal, B. de, Mexico **119 D7** 18 40N 88 10W
Chetwynd, Canada **102 B4** 55 45N 121 36W
Chevanceaux, France **20 C3** 45 18N 0 14W
Cheviot, The, U.K. **14 B5** 55 29N 2 9W
Cheviot Hills, U.K. **14 B5** 55 20N 2 30W
Cheviot Ra., Australia **94 D3** 25 20 S 143 45 E
Chew Bahir, Ethiopia **81 G4** 4 40N 36 50 E
Chewelah, U.S.A. **108 B5** 48 17N 117 43W
Chewore △, Zimbabwe **87 F2** 16 0 S 29 52 E
Cheyenne, Okla., U.S.A. **113 H5** 35 37N 99 40W
Cheyenne, Wyo., U.S.A. **112 E2** 41 8N 104 49W
Cheyenne →, U.S.A. **112 C4** 44 41N 101 18W
Cheyenne Wells, U.S.A. **112 F3** 38 49N 102 21W
Cheyne B., Australia **93 F2** 34 35 S 118 50 E
Chhabra, India **68 G7** 24 40N 76 54 E
Chhaktala, India **68 H6** 22 6N 74 11 E
Chhapra, India **69 G11** 25 48N 84 44 E
Chhata, India **68 F7** 27 42N 77 30 E
Chhatarpur, Jharkhand, India **69 G11** 24 23N 84 11 E
Chhatarpur, Mad. P., India **69 G8** 24 55N 79 35 E
Chhattisgarh □, India **69 J10** 22 0N 82 0 E
Chhep, Cambodia **64 F5** 13 45N 105 24 E
Chhindwara, Mad. P., India **69 H8** 23 3N 79 29 E
Chhindwara, Mad. P., India **69 H8** 22 2N 78 59 E

Chhlong, Cambodia .... 65 F5 12 15N 105 58 E
Chhota Tawa →, India 68 H7 22 14N 76 36 E
Chhoti Kali Sindh →,
  India .... 68 G6 24 2N 75 31 E
Chhuikhadan, India .. 69 J9 21 32N 80 59 E
Chhuk, Cambodia .... 65 G5 10 46N 104 28 E
Chi →, Thailand ..... 64 E5 15 11N 104 43 E
Chiai, Taiwan .... 59 F13 23 29N 120 25 E
Chiali, Taiwan ...... 59 F13 23 10N 120 11 E
Chiamboni, Somali Rep. 84 E8 1 39 S 41 35 E
Chianciano Terme, Italy 41 E8 43 2N 11 49 E
Chiang Dao, Thailand . 64 C2 19 22N 98 58 E
Chiang Kham, Thailand 64 C3 19 32N 100 18 E
Chiang Khan, Thailand 64 D3 17 52N 101 36 E
Chiang Khong, Thailand 58 G3 20 17N 100 24 E
Chiang Mai, Thailand . 64 C2 18 47N 98 59 E
Chiang Rai, Thailand . 58 H2 19 52N 99 50 E
Chiang Saen, Thailand 58 G3 20 16N 100 5 E
Chianti, Italy .... 41 E8 43 32N 11 25 E
Chiapa →, Mexico ... 119 D6 16 42N 93 0W
Chiapa de Corzo,
  Mexico 119 D6 16 42N 93 0W
Chiapas □, Mexico ... 119 D6 17 0N 92 45W
Chiaramonte Gulfi, Italy 43 E7 37 2N 14 42 E
Chiaravalle, Italy .... 41 E10 43 36N 13 19 E
Chiaravalle Centrale,
  Italy .... 43 D9 38 41N 16 25 E
Chiari, Italy .... 40 C6 45 32N 9 56 E
Chiatura, Georgia ... 35 J6 42 15N 43 17 E
Chiautla, Mexico 119 D5 18 18N 98 34W
Chiávari, Italy ...... 40 D6 44 19N 9 19 E
Chiavenna, Italy ..... 40 B6 46 19N 9 24 E
Chiba, Japan .... 55 G10 35 30N 140 7 E
Chiba □, Japan ...... 55 G10 35 30N 140 20 E
Chibabava, Mozam. .. 89 C5 20 17 S 33 35 E
Chibemba, Cunene,
  Angola .... 85 H2 15 48 S 14 8 E
Chibemba, Huila,
  Angola .... 88 B2 16 20 S 15 20 E
Chibi, Zimbabwe .... 89 C5 20 18 S 30 25 E
Chibia, Angola ...... 85 H2 15 10 S 13 42 E
Chibougamau, Canada 104 C5 49 56N 74 24W
Chibougamau, L.,
  Canada 104 C5 49 50N 74 20W
Chibuk, Nigeria ..... 83 C7 10 52N 12 50 E
Chibuto, Mozam. .... 89 C5 24 40 S 33 33 E
Chic-Chocs, Mts.,
  Canada 105 C6 48 55N 66 0W
Chicacole = Srikakulam,
  India .... 67 K13 18 14N 83 58 E
Chicago, U.S.A. 114 E2 41 53N 87 38W
Chicago Heights, U.S.A. 114 E2 41 30N 87 38W
Chichagof I., U.S.A. .. 100 C6 57 30N 135 30W
Chichén-Itzá, Mexico . 119 C7 20 40N 88 36W
Chicheng, China ..... 56 D8 40 55N 115 55 E
Chichester, U.K. 15 G7 50 50N 0 47W
Chichester Ra., Australia 92 D2 22 12 S 119 15 E
Chichibu, Japan ..... 55 F9 35 59N 139 10 E
Chichibu-Tama △,
  Japan .... 55 G9 35 52N 138 42 E
Ch'ich'ihaerh = Qiqihar,
  China .... 53 E13 47 26N 124 0 E
Chicholi, India ...... 68 H8 22 1N 77 40 E
Chickasaw △, U.S.A. . 113 H6 34 26N 97 0W
Chickasha, U.S.A. ... 113 H6 35 2N 97 58W
Chiclana de la Frontera,
  Spain 37 J4 36 26N 6 9W
Chiclayo, Peru ...... 124 E3 6 42 S 79 50W
Chico, U.S.A. 110 F5 39 44N 121 50W
Chico →, Chubut,
  Argentina .... 128 E3 44 0 S 67 0W
Chico →, Santa Cruz,
  Argentina .... 128 G3 50 0 S 68 30W
Chicomo, Mozam. .... 89 C5 24 31 S 34 6 E
Chicomostoc, Mexico . 118 C4 22 28N 102 49W
Chicontepec, Mexico . 119 C5 20 58N 98 10W
Chicopee, U.S.A. 117 D12 42 9N 72 37W
Chicoutimi, Canada .. 105 C5 48 28N 71 5W
Chicualacuala, Mozam. 89 C5 22 6 S 31 42 E
Chidambaram, India . 66 P11 11 20N 79 45 E
Chidenguele, Mozam. . 89 C5 24 55 S 34 11 E
Chidley, C., Canada .. 101 B13 60 23N 64 26W
Chiducuane, Mozam. . 89 C5 24 35 S 34 25 E
Chiede, Angola ...... 88 B2 17 15 S 16 22 E
Chiefs Pt., Canada .. 116 B3 44 41N 81 18W
Chiem Ho, Vietnam .. 64 A5 22 12N 105 17 E
Chiemsee, Germany .. 25 H8 47 53N 12 28 E
Chiengi, Zambia ..... 87 D2 8 45 S 29 10 E
Chiengmai = Chiang
  Mai, Thailand .... 64 C2 18 47N 98 59 E
Chienti →, Italy ..... 41 E10 43 18N 13 45 E
Chieri, Italy .... 40 C4 45 1N 7 49 E
Chiers →, France .... 19 C11 49 39N 4 59 E
Chiesa in Valmalenco,
  Italy .... 40 B6 46 16N 9 51 E
Chiese →, Italy ...... 40 C7 45 8N 10 25 E
Chieti, Italy .... 41 F11 42 21N 14 10 E
Chifeng, China ...... 57 C10 42 18N 118 58 E
Chigirin, Ukraine .... 33 H7 49 4N 32 38 E
Chignecto B., Canada 105 C7 45 30N 64 40W
Chiguana, Bolivia .... 126 A2 21 0 S 67 58W
Chigwell, U.K. ...... 15 F8 51 37N 0 5 E
Chiha-ri, N. Korea ... 57 E14 38 40N 126 30 E
Chihli, G. of = Bo Hai,
  China .... 57 E10 39 0N 119 0 E
Chihuahua, Mexico .. 118 B3 28 40N 106 3W
Chihuahua □, Mexico 118 B3 28 40N 106 3W
Chiili = Shieli,
  Kazakhstan .... 52 E7 44 20N 66 15 E
Chik Bollapur, India . 66 N10 13 25N 77 45 E
Chikmagalur, India .. 66 N9 13 15N 75 45 E
Chikwawa, Malawi ... 87 F3 16 2 S 34 50 E
Chilac, Mexico 119 D5 18 20N 97 24W
Chilam Chavki, Pakistan 69 B6 35 5N 75 5 E
Chilanga, Zambia .... 87 F2 15 33 S 28 16 E
Chilapa, Mexico 119 D5 17 40N 99 11W
Chilas, Pakistan ..... 69 B6 35 25N 74 5 E
Chilaw, Sri Lanka .... 66 R11 7 30N 79 50 E
Chilcotin →, Canada . 102 C4 51 44N 122 23W
Childers, Australia ... 95 D5 25 15 S 152 17 E
Childress, U.S.A. 113 H4 34 25N 100 13W
Chile ■, S. Amer. .... 128 D2 35 0 S 72 0W
Chile Rise, Pac. Oc. .. 97 L18 38 0 S 92 0W
Chilecito, Argentina .. 126 B2 29 10 S 67 30W
Chilete, Peru .... 124 E3 7 10 S 78 50W
Chilia, Brațul →,
  Romania .... 29 E14 45 14N 29 42 E
Chililabombwe, Zambia 87 E2 12 18 S 27 43 E
Chilin = Jilin, China . 57 C14 43 44N 126 30 E
Chilka L., India ..... 67 K14 19 40N 85 25 E
Chilko →, Canada ... 102 C4 52 0N 123 40W
Chilko L., Canada ... 102 C4 51 20N 124 10W
Chillagoe, Australia .. 94 B3 17 7 S 144 33 E
Chillán, Chile .... 126 D1 36 40 S 72 10W
Chillicothe, Ill., U.S.A. 112 E10 40 55N 89 29W
Chillicothe, Mo., U.S.A. 112 F8 39 48N 93 33W
Chillicothe, Ohio, U.S.A. 114 F4 39 20N 82 59W

Chilliwack, Canada ... 102 D4 49 10N 121 54W
Chilo, Russia .... 68 F5 25 25N 73 32 E
Chiloane, I., Mozam. . 89 C5 20 40 S 34 55 E
Chiloé, I. de, Chile .. 128 E2 42 30 S 73 50W
Chilpancingo, Mexico 119 D5 17 30N 99 30W
Chiltern Hills, U.K. .. 15 F7 51 40N 0 53W
Chilton, U.S.A. 114 C1 44 2N 88 10W
Chilubi, Zambia ..... 87 E2 11 5 S 29 58 E
Chilubula, Zambia ... 87 E3 10 14 S 30 51 E
Chilumba, Malawi ... 87 E3 10 28 S 34 12 E
Chilung, Taiwan ..... 59 E13 25 3N 121 45 E
Chilwa, L., Malawi ... 87 F4 15 15 S 35 40 E
Chimaltitán, Mexico . 118 C4 21 46N 103 50W
Chimán, Panama 120 E4 8 45N 78 40W
Chimanimani,
  Zimbabwe .... 89 B5 19 48 S 32 52 E
Chimanimani △,
  Zimbabwe .... 87 F3 19 48 S 33 0 E
Chimay, Belgium .... 17 D4 50 3N 4 20 E
Chimayo, U.S.A. 109 H11 36 0N 105 56W
Chimbay, Uzbekistan . 52 E6 42 57N 59 47 E
Chimborazo, Ecuador 124 D3 1 29 S 78 55W
Chimbote, Peru ..... 124 E3 9 0 S 78 35W
Chimkent = Shymkent,
  Kazakhstan .... 52 E7 42 18N 69 36 E
Chimoio, Mozam. ... 87 F3 19 4 S 33 30 E
Chimpembe, Zambia . 87 D2 9 31 S 29 33 E
Chin □, Burma ...... 67 J18 22 0N 93 0 E
Chin Ling Shan =
  Qinling Shandi, China 56 H5 33 50N 108 10 E
China, Mexico 119 B5 25 40N 99 20W
China ■, Asia .... 60 D6 30 0N 110 0 E
China, Great Plain of,
  Asia .... 50 F15 35 0N 115 0 E
China Lake, U.S.A. .. 111 K9 35 44N 117 37W
Chinan = Jinan, China 56 F9 36 38N 117 1 E
Chinandega, Nic. 120 D2 12 35N 87 12W
Chinati Peak, U.S.A. . 113 L2 29 57N 104 29W
Chincha Alta, Peru .. 124 F3 13 25 S 76 7W
Chinchaga →, Canada 102 B5 58 53N 118 20W
Chinchilla, Australia . 95 D5 26 45 S 150 38 E
Chinchilla de Monte
  Aragón, Spain 39 G3 38 53N 1 40W
Chinchorro, Banco,
  Mexico 119 D7 18 35N 87 20W
Chinchou = Jinzhou,
  China .... 57 D11 41 5N 121 3 E
Chincoteague, U.S.A. . 114 G8 37 56N 75 23W
Chinde, Mozam. ..... 87 F4 18 35 S 36 30 E
Chindo, S. Korea .... 57 G14 34 28N 126 15 E
Chindwin →, Burma . 67 J19 21 26N 95 15 E
Chineni, India ...... 69 C6 33 2N 75 15 E
Chinga, Mozam. ..... 87 F4 15 13 S 38 35 E
Chingola, Zambia .... 87 E2 12 31 S 27 53 E
Chingole, Malawi .... 87 E3 13 4 S 34 17 E
Ch'ingtao = Qingdao,
  China .... 57 F11 36 5N 120 20 E
Chinguetti, Mauritania 78 D3 20 25N 12 24W
Chingune, Mozam. ... 89 C5 20 33 S 34 58 E
Chinhae, S. Korea ... 57 G15 35 9N 128 47 E
Chinhanguanine,
  Mozam. .... 89 D5 25 21 S 32 30 E
Chinhoyi, Zimbabwe . 87 F3 17 20 S 30 8 E
Chini, India .... 68 D8 31 32N 78 15 E
Chiniot, Pakistan .... 68 D5 31 45N 73 0 E
Chínipas, Mexico 118 B3 27 22N 108 32W
Chinji, Pakistan ..... 68 C5 32 42N 72 22 E
Chinju, S. Korea ..... 57 G15 35 12N 128 2 E
Chinle, U.S.A. 109 H9 36 9N 109 33W
Chinmen, Taiwan .... 59 E13 24 26N 118 19 E
Chinmen Tao, Taiwan 59 E12 24 27N 118 23 E
Chinnampo = Namp'o,
  N. Korea .... 57 E13 38 52N 125 10 E
Chino, Japan .... 55 G9 35 59N 138 9 E
Chino, U.S.A. 111 L9 34 1N 117 41W
Chino Valley, U.S.A. . 109 J7 34 45N 112 27W
Chinon, France ...... 18 E7 47 10N 0 15 E
Chinook, U.S.A. 108 B9 48 35N 109 14W
Chinsali, Zambia .... 87 E3 10 30 S 32 2 E
Chióggia, Italy ...... 41 C9 45 13N 12 17 E
Chíos = Khíos, Greece 47 C8 38 27N 26 9 E
Chipata, Zambia ..... 87 E3 13 38 S 32 28 E
Chipcerceni, Moldova 29 C13 47 31N 28 50 E
Chipinge, Zimbabwe . 87 G3 20 13 S 32 28 E
Chipinge △, Zimbabwe 87 G3 20 14 S 33 0 E
Chipiona, Spain 37 J4 36 44N 6 26W
Chipley, U.S.A. 115 K3 30 47N 85 32W
Chipman, Canada 105 C6 46 6N 65 53W
Chipoka, Malawi .... 87 E3 13 57 S 34 28 E
Chippenham, U.K. ... 15 F5 51 27N 2 6W
Chippewa →, U.S.A. . 112 C8 44 25N 92 5W
Chippewa Falls, U.S.A. 112 C9 44 56N 91 24W
Chipping Norton, U.K. 15 F6 51 56N 1 32W
Chiprovtsi, Bulgaria . 44 C6 43 24N 22 52 E
Chiputneticook Lakes,
  U.S.A. 115 C11 45 35N 67 35W
Chiquián, Peru ...... 124 F3 10 10 S 77 0W
Chiquibul △, Belize .. 120 C2 16 49N 88 52W
Chiquimula, Guatemala 120 D2 14 51N 89 37W
Chiquinquira, Colombia 124 B4 5 37N 73 50W
Chir →, Russia ...... 35 F6 48 30N 43 0 E
Chirala, India .... 66 M12 15 50N 80 26 E
Chiramba, Mozam. ... 87 F3 16 55 S 34 39 E
Chirawa, India ...... 68 E6 28 14N 75 42 E
Chirchiq, Uzbekistan . 52 E7 41 29N 69 35 E
Chiredzi, Zimbabwe . 89 C5 21 0 S 31 38 E
Chiricahua △, U.S.A. . 109 K9 32 0N 109 20W
Chiricahua Peak, U.S.A. 109 L9 31 51N 109 18W
Chiriquí, G. de, Panama 120 E3 8 0N 82 10W
Chiriquí, L. de, Panama 120 E3 9 10N 82 0W
Chirisa △, Zimbabwe . 87 F2 17 53 S 28 15 E
Chirivira Falls,
  Zimbabwe .... 87 G3 21 10 S 32 12 E
Chirmiri, India ...... 67 H13 23 15N 82 20 E
Chirnogi, Romania .. 29 F11 44 7N 26 32 E
Chirpan, Bulgaria ... 45 D9 42 10N 25 19 E
Chirripó Grande, Cerro,
  Costa Rica 120 E3 9 29N 83 29W
Chirundu, Zimbabwe 89 B4 16 3 S 28 50 E
Chisamba, Zambia ... 87 E2 14 55 S 28 5 E
Chisapani Garhi, Nepal 67 F14 27 30N 84 2 E
Chisasibi, Canada ... 104 B4 53 50N 79 0W
Ch'ishan, Taiwan .... 59 F13 22 52N 120 30 E
Chisholm, Canada ... 102 C6 54 55N 114 10W
Chisholm, U.S.A. 112 B8 47 29N 92 53W
Chishtian Mandi,
  Pakistan .... 68 E5 29 50N 72 55 E
Chishui, China ...... 58 C5 28 30N 105 42 E
Chishui He →, China 58 C5 28 40N 105 50 E
Chisimaio, Somali Rep. 77 G8 0 22 S 42 32 E
Chisimba Falls, Zambia 87 E3 10 12 S 30 56 E
Chișinău, Moldova ... 29 C13 47 2N 28 50 E
Chișineu Criș, Romania 28 D6 46 32N 21 37 E
Chisone →, Italy .... 40 D4 44 49N 7 25 E
Chisos Mts., U.S.A. .. 113 L3 29 5N 103 15W

Chistopol, Russia .... 34 C10 55 25N 50 38 E
Chita, Russia .... 53 D12 52 0N 113 35 E
Chitipa, Malawi ..... 87 D3 9 41 S 33 19 E
Chitose, Japan ...... 54 C10 42 49N 141 39 E
Chitral, Pakistan .... 66 B7 35 50N 71 56 E
Chitré, Panama 120 E3 7 59N 80 27W
Chittagong, Bangla. .. 67 H17 22 19N 91 48 E
Chittagong □, Bangla. 67 G17 24 5N 91 0 E
Chittaurgarh, India .. 68 G6 24 52N 74 38 E
Chittoor, India ...... 66 N11 13 15N 79 5 E
Chitungwiza, Zimbabwe 87 F3 18 0 S 31 6 E
Chiusi, Italy .... 41 E8 43 1N 11 57 E
Chiva, Spain 39 F4 39 27N 0 41W
Chivasso, Italy ...... 40 C4 45 11N 7 53 E
Chivhu, Zimbabwe ... 87 F3 19 2 S 30 52 E
Chivilcoy, Argentina . 126 C4 34 55 S 60 0W
Chiwanda, Tanzania . 87 E3 11 23 S 34 55 E
Chixi, China .... 59 G9 22 0N 112 58 E
Chizarira, Zimbabwe . 87 F2 17 36 S 27 45 E
Chizarira △, Zimbabwe 87 F2 17 44 S 27 52 E
Chizera, Zambia ..... 87 E2 13 10 S 25 0 E
Chkalov = Orenburg,
  Russia .... 52 D6 51 45N 55 6 E
Chkolovsk, Russia ... 34 B6 56 50N 43 10 E
Chloride, U.S.A. 111 K12 35 25N 114 12W
Chlumec nad Cidlinou,
  Czech Rep. .... 26 A8 50 9N 15 29 E
Chmielnik, Poland .. 31 H7 50 37N 20 43 E
Cho Bo, Vietnam .... 58 G5 20 46N 105 10 E
Cho-do, N. Korea .... 57 E13 38 30N 124 40 E
Cho Phuoc Hai, Vietnam 65 G6 10 26N 107 18 E
Choa Chu Kang,
  Singapore .... 65 d 1 22N 103 41 E
Choba, Kenya .... 86 B4 2 30N 38 5 E
Chobe △, Botswana .. 88 B4 18 37 S 24 23 E
Choch'iwŏn, S. Korea 57 F14 36 37N 127 18 E
Chociwel, Poland .... 30 E2 53 29N 15 21 E
Chocolate Mts., U.S.A. 111 M11 33 15N 115 15W
Choctawhatchee →,
  U.S.A. 115 K3 30 25N 86 8W
Chodecz, Poland .... 31 F6 52 24N 19 2 E
Chodov, Czech Rep. . 26 A5 50 15N 12 45 E
Chodzież, Poland .... 31 F3 52 58N 16 58 E
Choele Choel, Argentina 128 F3 39 11 S 65 40W
Choiseul, St. Lucia .. 121 f 13 47N 61 3W
Choix, Mexico 118 B3 26 40N 108 23W
Chojna, Poland ...... 31 F1 52 58N 14 25 E
Chojnice, Poland .... 30 E4 53 42N 17 32 E
Chojnów, Poland .... 31 G2 51 18N 15 58 E
Chōkai-San, Japan ... 54 E10 39 6N 140 3 E
Choke Canyon L.,
  U.S.A. 113 L5 28 30N 98 20W
Choke Mts., Ethiopia . 81 E4 11 18N 37 15 E
Chokurdakh, Russia . 53 B15 70 38N 147 55 E
Cholame, U.S.A. 110 K6 35 44N 120 18W
Cholet, France 18 E6 47 4N 0 52W
Cholguan, Chile ..... 126 D1 37 10 S 72 3W
Choluteca, Honduras . 120 D2 13 20N 87 14W
Choluteca →, Honduras 120 D2 13 0N 87 20W
Chom Bung, Thailand 64 F2 13 37N 99 36 E
Chom Thong, Thailand 64 C2 18 25N 98 41 E
Choma, Zambia ...... 87 F2 16 48 S 26 59 E
Chomolungma =
  Everest, Mt., Nepal 69 E12 28 5N 86 58 E
Chomun, India ...... 68 F6 27 15N 75 40 E
Chomutov, Czech Rep. 26 A6 50 28N 13 23 E
Chon Buri, Thailand . 64 F3 13 21N 101 1 E
Chon Thanh, Vietnam 65 G6 11 24N 106 36 E
Ch'onan, S. Korea ... 57 F14 36 48N 127 9 E
Chone, Ecuador ..... 124 D3 0 40 S 80 0W
Chong Kai, Cambodia 64 F4 13 57N 103 35 E
Chong Mek, Thailand 64 E5 15 10N 105 27 E
Chong Phangan,
  Thailand .... 65 b 9 39N 100 0 E
Chong Samui, Thailand 65 b 9 21N 99 50 E
Chongde, China ..... 59 B13 30 32N 120 26 E
Chŏngdo, S. Korea ... 57 G15 35 38N 128 42 E
Chŏngha, S. Korea ... 57 F15 36 12N 129 21 E
Chŏngjin, N. Korea .. 57 D15 41 47N 129 50 E
Chŏngju, S. Korea ... 57 F14 36 39N 127 27 E
Chŏngju, N. Korea ... 57 E13 39 40N 125 5 E
Chongli, China ...... 56 D8 40 58N 115 15 E
Chongming, China .. 59 B13 31 38N 121 23 E
Chongming Dao, China 59 B13 31 40N 121 30 E
Chongqing, Chongqing,
  China .... 58 C6 29 35N 106 25 E
Chongqing, Sichuan,
  China .... 58 C6 30 0N 108 0 E
Chongqing Shi □, China 58 C6 30 0N 108 0 E
Chongren, China .... 59 D11 27 46N 116 3 E
Chonguene, Mozam. . 89 C5 25 3 S 33 49 E
Chŏngup, S. Korea ... 57 G14 35 35N 126 50 E
Chongyi, China ...... 59 E10 25 45N 114 29 E
Chongzuo, China .... 58 F6 22 23N 107 20 E
Chŏnju, S. Korea .... 57 G14 35 50N 127 4 E
Chonos, Arch. de los,
  Chile .... 128 F2 45 0 S 75 0W
Chop, Ukraine ...... 33 H2 48 26N 22 12 E
Chopim →, Brazil ... 127 B5 25 35 S 53 5W
Chor, Pakistan ...... 68 G3 25 31N 69 46 E
Chorbat La, India ... 69 B7 34 42N 76 37 E
Chorley, U.K. 14 D5 53 39N 2 38W
Chorna, Ukraine .... 29 C14 47 36N 29 20 E
Chornobyl, Ukraine . 33 G6 51 20N 30 15 E
Chornomorske, Ukraine 33 K7 45 31N 32 40 E
Chorolque, Cerro,
  Bolivia .... 126 A2 20 59 S 66 5W
Choroszcz, Poland .. 31 E9 53 10N 22 59 E
Chorregon, Australia . 94 C3 22 40 S 143 32 E
Chorro el Indio △,
  Venezuela 121 E5 7 43N 72 9W
Chortkiv, Ukraine ... 33 H3 49 2N 25 46 E
Ch'orwon, S. Korea .. 57 E14 38 15N 127 10 E
Chorzele, Poland .... 31 E7 53 15N 20 55 E
Chorzów, Poland .... 31 H5 50 18N 18 57 E
Chos-Malal, Argentina 126 D1 37 20 S 70 15W
Ch'osan, N. Korea ... 57 D13 40 50N 125 47 E
Choszczno, Poland .. 31 E2 53 7N 15 25 E
Choteau, U.S.A. 108 C7 47 49N 112 11W
Chotěboř, Czech Rep. 26 B8 49 43N 15 40 E
Chotila, India .... 68 H4 22 23N 71 15 E
Chotta Udepur, India 68 H6 22 9N 74 1 E
Chowchilla, U.S.A. .. 110 H6 37 7N 120 16W
Choybalsan, Mongolia 60 B6 48 4N 114 30 E
Christchurch, N.Z. ... 91 K4 43 33 S 172 47 E
Christchurch, U.K. .. 15 G6 50 44N 1 47W
Christian I., Canada . 116 B4 44 50N 80 12W
Christiana, S. Africa . 88 D4 27 52 S 25 8 E
Christiansfeld, Denmark 11 J3 55 21N 9 29 E
Christiansted,
  U.S. Virgin Is. 121 C7 17 45N 64 42W
Christie B., Canada .. 103 A6 62 32N 111 10W
Christina →, Canada 103 B6 56 40N 111 3W
Christmas Cr. →,
  Australia .... 92 C4 18 29 S 125 23 E
Christmas I. =
  Kiritimati, Kiribati 97 G12 1 58N 157 27W

Christmas I., Ind. Oc. . 96 J2 10 30 S 105 40 E
Christopher L., Australia 93 D4 24 49 S 127 42 E
Chrudim, Czech Rep. 26 B8 49 58N 15 43 E
Chrzanów, Poland ... 31 H6 50 10N 19 21 E
Chtimba, Malawi .... 87 E3 10 35 S 34 13 E
Chū = Shū,
  Kazakhstan .... 52 E8 43 36N 73 42 E
Chu = Shū →,
  Kazakhstan .... 50 E10 45 0N 67 44 E
Chu →, Vietnam .... 64 C5 19 53N 105 45 E
Chu Lai, Vietnam ... 64 E7 15 28N 108 45 E
Chuak, Ko, Thailand . 65 b 9 39N 99 41 E
Ch'uanchou =
  Quanzhou, China . 59 E12 24 55N 118 34 E
Chuankou, China .... 56 G6 34 20N 110 59 E
Chubbuck, U.S.A. ... 108 E7 42 55N 112 28W
Chūbu □, Japan ..... 55 F8 36 45N 137 30 E
Chubu-Sangaku △,
  Japan .... 55 F8 36 30N 137 40 E
Chubut □, Argentina . 128 E3 43 20 S 65 5W
Chuchi L., Canada ... 102 B4 55 12N 124 30W
Chuda, India .... 68 H4 22 29N 71 41 E
Chudovo, Russia .... 32 C6 59 10N 31 41 E
Chudskoye, Ozero,
  Russia .... 9 G22 58 13N 27 30 E
Chūgoku □, Japan ... 55 G6 35 0N 133 0 E
Chūgoku-Sanchi, Japan 55 G6 35 0N 133 10 E
Chuguyev = Chuhuyiv,
  Ukraine .... 33 H9 49 55N 36 45 E
Chugwater, U.S.A. .. 112 E2 41 46N 104 50W
Chuhuyiv, Ukraine .. 33 H9 49 55N 36 45 E
Chukchi Sea, Russia . 53 C19 68 0N 175 0W
Chukotskoye Nagorye,
  Russia .... 53 C18 68 0N 175 0 E
Chula Vista, U.S.A. .. 111 N9 32 39N 117 5W
Chulucanas, Peru ... 124 E2 5 8 S 80 10W
Chulym →, Russia .. 52 D9 57 43N 83 51 E
Chum Phae, Thailand 64 D3 16 40N 102 6 E
Chum Saeng, Thailand 64 E3 15 55N 100 15 E
Chumar, India .... 69 C8 32 40N 78 35 E
Chumbicha, Argentina 126 B2 29 0 S 66 10W
Chumerna, Bulgaria . 45 D9 42 45N 25 55 E
Chumikan, Russia ... 53 D14 54 40N 135 10 E
Chumphon, Thailand 65 G2 10 35N 99 14 E
Chumuare, Mozam. . 87 E3 14 31 S 31 50 E
Chumunjin, S. Korea 57 F15 37 55N 127 44 E
Chuna →, Russia .... 53 D10 57 47N 94 37 E
Chun'an, China ...... 59 C12 29 35N 119 3 E
Ch'unch'ŏn, S. Korea 57 F14 37 58N 127 44 E
Chunchura, India ... 69 H13 22 53N 88 27 E
Chunga, Zambia .... 87 F2 15 0 S 26 2 E
Chunggang-ŭp, N. Korea 57 D14 41 48N 126 48 E
Chunghwa, N. Korea 57 E13 38 52N 125 47 E
Ch'ungju, S. Korea .. 57 F14 36 58N 127 58 E
Chungking =
  Chongqing, China 58 C6 29 35N 106 25 E
Chungli, Taiwan ..... 59 E13 24 57N 121 13 E
Ch'ungmu, S. Korea . 57 G15 34 50N 128 20 E
Chungt'iaoshan =
  Zhongtiao Shan,
  China .... 56 G6 35 0N 111 10 E
Chungyang Shanmo,
  Taiwan .... 59 F13 23 10N 121 0 E
Chunian, Pakistan ... 68 D6 30 57N 74 0 E
Chunya, Tanzania ... 87 D3 8 30 S 33 27 E
Chunyang, China .... 58 E5 23 38N 102 23 E
Chupara Pt.,
  Trin. & Tob. 125 K15 10 49N 61 22W
Chuquibamba, Peru . 124 G4 15 47 S 72 44W
Chuquicamata, Chile . 126 A2 22 15 S 69 0W
Chur, Switz. .... 25 J5 46 52N 9 32 E
Churachandpur, India 67 G18 24 20N 93 40 E
Church Stretton, U.K. 15 E5 52 32N 2 48W
Churchill, Canada ... 103 B10 58 47N 94 11W
Churchill →, Man.,
  Canada 103 B10 58 47N 94 12W
Churchill, C., Canada 103 B10 58 46N 93 12W
Churchill Falls, Canada 105 B7 53 36N 64 19W
Churchill L., Canada . 103 B7 55 55N 108 20W
Churchill Pk., Canada 102 B3 58 10N 125 10W
Churki, India .... 69 H10 23 50N 83 12 E
Churu, India .... 68 E6 28 20N 74 50 E
Churún →, Venezuela = Angel
  Falls, Venezuela .. 124 B6 5 57N 62 30W
Chushal, India ...... 69 C8 33 40N 78 40 E
Chuska Mts., U.S.A. . 109 H9 36 15N 108 50W
Chusovoy, Russia .... 52 D6 58 22N 57 50 E
Chute-aux-Outardes,
  Canada 105 C6 49 7N 68 24W
Chuuronjang, N. Korea 57 D15 41 35N 129 40 E
Chuvash Republic =
  Chuvashia □, Russia 34 C8 55 30N 47 0 E
Chuvashia □, Russia . 34 C8 55 30N 47 0 E
Chuwārtah, Iraq .... 70 C5 35 43N 45 34 E
Chuxiong, China .... 58 E3 25 2N 101 28 E
Chuy, Uruguay ...... 127 C5 33 41 S 53 27W
Chuzhou, China ..... 59 A12 32 19N 118 20 E
Chynadiyeve, Ukraine 28 B7 48 29N 22 56 E
Ci Xian, China ...... 56 F8 36 20N 114 25 E
Ciacova, Romania ... 28 E6 45 35N 21 10 E
Ciadâr-Lunga, Moldova 29 D13 46 3N 28 51 E
Ciamis, Indonesia ... 63 G13 7 20 S 108 21 E
Cianjur, Indonesia .. 63 G12 6 49 S 107 8 E
Cianorte, Brazil ..... 127 A5 23 37 S 52 37W
Cibola, U.S.A. 111 M12 33 17N 114 42W
Cicero, U.S.A. 114 E2 41 51N 87 45W
Cidacos →, Spain ... 38 C3 42 21N 1 38W
Cide, Turkey .... 72 B5 41 53N 33 1 E

Cibilia, Romania .... 29 E12 45 4N 27 4 E
Cilicia, Turkey ...... 72 D5 36 30N 33 40 E
Cill Chainnigh =
  Kilkenny, Ireland . 12 D4 52 39N 7 15W
Cilo Dağı, Turkey ... 73 D10 37 28N 43 55 E
Cima, U.S.A. 111 K11 35 14N 115 30W
Cimarron, Kans., U.S.A. 113 G4 37 48N 100 21W
Cimarron, N. Mex.,
  U.S.A. 113 G2 36 31N 104 55W
Cimarron →, U.S.A. . 113 G6 36 10N 96 17W
Cimișlia, Moldova ... 29 D13 46 34N 28 44 E
Cimone, Mte., Italy .. 40 D7 44 12N 10 42 E
Çınar, Turkey .... 73 D9 37 46N 40 19 E
Çınarcık, Turkey .... 45 F13 40 38N 29 9 E
Cinca →, Spain ..... 38 D5 41 26N 0 21 E
Cincar, Bos.-H. ...... 28 G2 43 55N 17 5 E
Cincinnati, U.S.A. ... 114 F3 39 6N 84 31W
Cincinnatus, U.S.A. . 117 D9 42 33N 75 54W
Çine, Turkey .... 47 D10 37 37N 28 2 E
Ciney, Belgium ...... 17 D5 50 18N 5 5 E
Cíngoli, Italy .... 41 E10 43 23N 13 10 E
Cinigiano, Italy ..... 41 F8 42 53N 11 24 E
Cinto, Mte., France . 21 F12 42 24N 8 54 E
Cintruénigo, Spain .. 38 C3 42 5N 1 49W
Ciocile, Romania .... 29 F12 44 49N 27 14 E
Ciolăneşti din Deal,
  Romania .... 29 F10 44 19N 25 5 E
Ciorani, Romania ... 29 F11 44 45N 26 25 E
Čiovo, Croatia ...... 41 E13 43 30N 16 17 E
Circeo, Mte., Italy ... 42 A6 41 14N 13 3 E
Çırçır, Turkey .... 72 C7 40 5N 36 47 E
Circle, Alaska, U.S.A. . 100 B5 65 50N 144 4W
Circle, Mont., U.S.A. . 112 B2 47 25N 105 35W
Circleville, U.S.A. ... 114 F4 39 36N 82 57W
Cirebon, Indonesia .. 63 G13 6 45 S 108 32 E
Ciremay, Indonesia .. 63 G13 6 55 S 108 27 E
Cirencester, U.K. 15 F6 51 43N 1 57W
Cireşu, Romania .... 28 F7 44 47N 22 31 E
Cirey-sur-Vezouze,
  France .... 19 D13 48 35N 6 57 E
Ciriè, Italy .... 40 C4 45 14N 7 36 E
Cirium, Cyprus ...... 49 E11 34 40N 32 53 E
Cirò, Italy .... 43 C10 39 23N 17 4 E
Cirò Marina, Italy ... 43 C10 39 22N 17 8 E
Ciron →, France 20 D3 44 36N 0 18W
Cisco, U.S.A. 113 J5 32 23N 98 59W
Cislău, Romania .... 29 E11 45 14N 26 20 E
Cisna, Poland .... 31 J9 49 12N 22 20 E
Cisnădie, Romania .. 29 E9 45 42N 24 9 E
Cisterna di Latina, Italy 42 A5 41 35N 12 49 E
Cisternino, Italy .... 43 B10 40 44N 17 25 E
Cistierna, Spain 36 C5 42 48N 5 7W
Citeli-Ckaro = Tsiteli-
  Tsqaro, Georgia .. 35 K8 41 33N 46 0 E
Citlaltépetl = Orizaba,
  Pico de, Mexico .. 119 D5 19 0N 97 20W
Citrus Heights, U.S.A. 110 G5 38 42N 121 17W
Citrusdal, S. Africa .. 88 E2 32 35 S 19 0 E
Città della Pieve, Italy 41 F9 42 57N 12 1 E
Città di Castello, Italy 41 E9 43 27N 12 14 E
Città Sant' Angelo, Italy 41 F11 42 32N 14 5 E
Cittadella, Italy ..... 41 C8 45 39N 11 47 E
Cittaducale, Italy .... 41 F9 42 24N 12 57 E
Cittanova, Italy ..... 43 D9 38 21N 16 5 E
Ciuc, Munții, Romania 29 D11 46 25N 26 5 E
Ciucaş, Vf., Romania 29 E10 45 31N 25 56 E
Ciucea, Romania .... 28 D7 46 57N 22 49 E
Ciuciulea, Moldova .. 29 C12 47 40N 27 29 E
Ciuciuleni, Moldova . 29 C13 47 2N 28 25 E
Ciudad Altamirano,
  Mexico 118 D4 18 20N 100 40W
Ciudad Bolívar,
  Venezuela 124 B6 8 5N 63 36W
Ciudad Camargo,
  Mexico 118 B3 27 41N 105 10W
Ciudad de Valles,
  Mexico 119 C5 22 0N 99 0W
Ciudad del Carmen,
  Mexico 119 D6 18 38N 91 50W
Ciudad del Este,
  Paraguay .... 127 B5 25 30 S 54 50W
Ciudad Delicias =
  Delicias, Mexico .. 118 B3 28 10N 105 30W
Ciudad Guayana,
  Venezuela 124 B6 8 0N 62 30W
Ciudad Guerrero,
  Mexico 118 B3 28 33N 107 28W
Ciudad Guzmán, Mexico 118 D4 19 40N 103 30W
Ciudad Juárez, Mexico 118 A3 31 40N 106 28W
Ciudad Madero, Mexico 119 C5 22 19N 97 50W
Ciudad Mante, Mexico 119 C5 22 50N 99 0W
Ciudad Obregón,
  Mexico 118 B3 27 28N 109 59W
Ciudad Real, Spain .. 37 G7 38 59N 3 55W
Ciudad Real □, Spain 37 G7 38 50N 4 0W
Ciudad Rodrigo, Spain 36 E4 40 35N 6 32W
Ciudad Victoria, Mexico 119 C5 23 41N 99 9W
Ciudadela, Spain .... 48 B10 40 0N 3 50 E
Ciulniţa, Romania ... 29 F12 44 26N 27 22 E
Ciumeghiu, Romania 28 D6 46 44N 21 35 E
Ciuperceni, Romania 28 F8 44 54N 23 4 E
Civa Burnu, Turkey .. 72 B7 41 30N 36 38 E
Cividale del Friuli, Italy 41 B10 46 6N 13 25 E
Civita Castellana, Italy 41 F9 42 17N 12 24 E
Civitanova Marche, Italy 41 E10 43 18N 13 44 E
Civitavécchia, Italy .. 41 F8 42 6N 11 48 E
Civray, France ...... 20 B4 46 10N 0 17 E
Çivril, Turkey .... 47 C11 38 20N 29 43 E
Cixerri →, Italy ..... 42 C1 39 17N 8 59 E
Cixi, China .... 59 B13 30 17N 121 9 E
Cizre, Turkey .... 70 B4 37 19N 42 10 E
Cizur Mayor, Spain . 38 C3 42 47N 1 41W
Clackmannanshire □,
  U.K. 13 E5 56 10N 3 43W
Clacton-on-Sea, U.K. 15 F9 51 47N 1 11 E
Clain →, France ..... 18 F7 46 47N 0 33 E
Claire, L., Canada ... 102 B6 58 35N 112 5W
Clairton, U.S.A. 116 F5 40 18N 79 53W
Clairvaux-les-Lacs,
  France .... 19 F12 46 35N 5 45 E
Claise →, France .... 20 B5 46 56N 0 42 E
Clallam Bay, U.S.A. . 110 B2 48 15N 124 16W
Clamecy, France .... 19 E10 47 28N 3 30 E
Clanton, U.S.A. 115 J2 32 51N 86 38W
Clanwilliam, S. Africa 88 E2 32 11 S 18 52 E
Clara, Ireland 12 C4 53 21N 7 37W
Claraville, U.S.A. ... 111 K8 35 24N 118 20W
Clare, Australia ..... 95 E2 33 50 S 138 37 E
Clare, U.S.A. 114 D3 43 49N 84 46W
Clare □, Ireland 12 D3 52 45N 9 0W
Clare →, Ireland 12 C2 53 20N 9 2W
Clare I., Ireland 12 C1 53 49N 10 0W
Claremont, Calif., U.S.A. 111 L9 34 6N 117 43W
Claremont, N.H., U.S.A. 117 C12 43 23N 72 20W
Claremont Pt., Australia 94 A3 14 1 S 143 41 E
Claremore, U.S.A. ... 113 G7 36 19N 95 36W
Claremorris, Ireland . 12 C3 53 45N 9 0W

Clarence →, *Australia* . **95 D5** 29 25 S 153 22 E
Clarence →, *N.Z.* . **91 K4** 43 0 S 173 56 E
Clarence, I., *Chile* . **128 G2** 54 0 S 72 0W
Clarence L., *Australia* . **5 C18** 61 10 S 54 0W
Clarence Str., *Australia* . **92 B5** 12 0 S 131 0 E
Clarence Town, *Bahamas* . **121 B5** 23 6N 74 59W
Clarendon, *Pa., U.S.A.* . **116 E5** 41 47N 79 6W
Clarendon, *Tex., U.S.A.* . **113 H4** 34 56N 100 53W
Clarenville-Shoal Harbour, *Canada* . **105 C9** 48 10N 54 1W
Claresholm, *Canada* . **102 D6** 50 2N 113 33W
Clarie Coast, *Antarctica* . **5 C9** 68 0 S 135 0 E
Clarinda, *U.S.A.* . **112 E7** 40 44N 95 2W
Clarington, *Canada* . **116 C6** 43 55N 78 41W
Clarion, *Iowa, U.S.A.* . **112 D8** 42 44N 93 44W
Clarion, *Pa., U.S.A.* . **116 E5** 41 13N 79 23W
Clarion →, *U.S.A.* . **116 E5** 41 7N 79 41W
Clarion Fracture Zone, *Pac. Oc.* . **98 H7** 20 0N 120 0W
Clark, *U.S.A.* . **112 C6** 44 53N 97 44W
Clark, Pt., *Canada* . **116 B3** 44 4N 81 45W
Clark Fork, *U.S.A.* . **108 B5** 48 9N 116 11W
Clark Fork →, *U.S.A.* . **108 B5** 48 9N 116 15W
Clarkdale, *U.S.A.* . **109 J7** 34 46N 112 3W
Clarke City, *Canada* . **105 B6** 50 12N 66 38W
Clarke I., *Australia* . **95 G4** 40 32 S 148 10 E
Clarke Ra., *Australia* . **94 J6** 20 40 S 148 30 E
Clark's Harbour, *Canada* . **105 D6** 43 25N 65 38W
Clarks Hill L., *U.S.A.* . **115 J4** 33 40N 82 12W
Clarks Summit, *U.S.A.* . **117 E9** 41 30N 75 42W
Clarksburg, *U.S.A.* . **114 F5** 39 17N 80 30W
Clarksdale, *U.S.A.* . **113 H9** 34 12N 90 35W
Clarksville, *Ark., U.S.A.* . **113 H8** 35 28N 93 28W
Clarksville, *Tenn., U.S.A.* . **115 G2** 36 32N 87 21W
Clarksville, *Tex., U.S.A.* . **113 J7** 33 37N 95 3W
Clatskanie, *U.S.A.* . **110 D3** 46 6N 123 12W
Claude, *U.S.A.* . **113 H4** 35 7N 101 22W
Claveria, *Phil.* . **61 B4** 18 37N 121 4 E
Clay, *U.S.A.* . **110 G5** 38 17N 121 10W
Clay Center, *U.S.A.* . **112 F6** 39 23N 97 8W
Claypool, *U.S.A.* . **109 K8** 33 25N 110 51W
Claysburg, *U.S.A.* . **116 F6** 40 17N 78 27W
Claysville, *U.S.A.* . **116 F4** 40 7N 80 25W
Clayton, *N. Mex., U.S.A.* . **113 G3** 36 27N 103 11W
Clayton, *N.Y., U.S.A.* . **117 B8** 44 14N 76 5W
Clear, C., *Ireland* . **12 E2** 51 25N 9 32W
Clear, L., *Canada* . **116 A7** 45 26N 77 12W
Clear Hills, *Canada* . **102 B5** 56 40N 119 30W
Clear I., *Ireland* . **12 E2** 51 26N 9 30W
Clear L., *U.S.A.* . **110 F4** 39 2N 122 47W
Clear Lake, *Iowa, U.S.A.* . **112 D8** 43 8N 93 23W
Clear Lake, *S. Dak., U.S.A.* . **112 C6** 44 45N 96 41W
Clear Lake Reservoir, *U.S.A.* . **108 F3** 41 56N 121 5W
Clearfield, *Pa., U.S.A.* . **116 E6** 41 2N 78 27W
Clearfield, *Utah, U.S.A.* . **108 F8** 41 7N 112 2W
Clearlake, *U.S.A.* . **108 G2** 38 57N 122 38W
Clearlake Highlands, *U.S.A.* . **110 G4** 38 57N 122 38W
Clearwater, *Canada* . **102 C4** 51 38N 120 2W
Clearwater, *U.S.A.* . **115 M4** 27 58N 82 48W
Clearwater →, *Alta., Canada* . **102 C6** 52 22N 114 57W
Clearwater →, *Alta., Canada* . **103 B6** 56 44N 111 23W
Clearwater L., *Canada* . **103 C9** 53 34N 99 49W
Clearwater Lake △, *Canada* . **103 C8** 54 0N 101 0W
Clearwater Mts., *U.S.A.* . **108 C6** 46 5N 115 20W
Clearwater River △, *Canada* . **103 B7** 56 55N 109 10W
Cleburne, *U.S.A.* . **113 J6** 32 21N 97 23W
Clee Hills, *U.K.* . **15 E5** 52 26N 2 35W
Cleethorpes, *U.K.* . **14 D7** 53 33N 0 3W
Cleeve Cloud, *U.K.* . **15 F6** 51 56N 2 0W
Clelles, *France* . **21 D9** 44 50N 5 38 E
Clemson, *U.S.A.* . **115 H4** 34 41N 82 50W
Clerke Reef, *Australia* . **92 C2** 17 22 S 119 20 E
Clermont, *Australia* . **94 C4** 22 49 S 147 39 E
Clermont, *France* . **19 C9** 49 23N 2 24 E
Clermont, *U.S.A.* . **115 L5** 28 33N 81 46W
Clermont-en-Argonne, *France* . **19 C12** 49 5N 5 4 E
Clermont-Ferrand, *France* . **20 C7** 45 46N 3 4 E
Clermont-l'Hérault, *France* . **20 E7** 43 38N 3 26 E
Clerval, *France* . **19 E13** 47 25N 6 30 E
Clervaux, *Lux.* . **17 D6** 50 4N 6 2 E
Cles, *Italy* . **40 B8** 46 22N 11 2 E
Clevedon, *U.K.* . **15 F5** 51 26N 2 52W
Cleveland, *Miss., U.S.A.* . **113 J9** 33 45N 90 43W
Cleveland, *Ohio, U.S.A.* . **116 E3** 41 30N 81 42W
Cleveland, *Okla., U.S.A.* . **113 G6** 36 19N 96 28W
Cleveland, *Tenn., U.S.A.* . **115 H3** 35 10N 84 53W
Cleveland, *Tex., U.S.A.* . **113 K7** 30 21N 95 5W
Cleveland, C., *Australia* . **94 B4** 19 11 S 147 1 E
Cleveland, Mt., *U.S.A.* . **108 B7** 48 56N 113 51W
Cleveland Heights, *U.S.A.* . **116 E3** 41 30N 81 34W
Clevelândia, *Brazil* . **127 B5** 26 24 S 52 23W
Clew B., *Ireland* . **12 C2** 53 50N 9 49W
Clewiston, *U.S.A.* . **115 M5** 26 45N 80 56W
Clifden, *Ireland* . **12 C1** 53 29N 10 1W
Clifden, *N.Z.* . **91 M1** 46 1 S 167 42 E
Cliffdell, *U.S.A.* . **110 D5** 46 56N 121 5W
Cliffy Hd., *Australia* . **93 G2** 35 1 S 116 29 E
Clifton, *Australia* . **95 D5** 27 59 S 151 53 E
Clifton, *Ariz., U.S.A.* . **109 K9** 33 3N 109 18W
Clifton, *Colo., U.S.A.* . **109 G9** 39 7N 108 25W
Clifton, *Tex., U.S.A.* . **113 K6** 31 47N 97 35W
Clifton Beach, *Australia* . **94 B4** 16 46 S 145 39 E
Climax, *Canada* . **103 D7** 49 10N 108 20W
Clinch →, *U.S.A.* . **115 H3** 35 53N 84 29W
Clingmans Dome, *U.S.A.* . **115 H4** 35 34N 83 30W
Clint, *U.S.A.* . **109 L10** 31 35N 106 14W
Clinton, *B.C., Canada* . **102 C4** 51 6N 121 35W
Clinton, *Ont., Canada* . **116 C3** 43 37N 81 32W
Clinton, *N.Z.* . **91 M2** 46 12 S 169 23 E
Clinton, *Ark., U.S.A.* . **113 H8** 35 36N 92 28W
Clinton, *Conn., U.S.A.* . **117 E12** 41 17N 72 32W
Clinton, *Ill., U.S.A.* . **112 E10** 40 9N 88 57W
Clinton, *Ind., U.S.A.* . **114 F2** 39 40N 87 24W
Clinton, *Iowa, U.S.A.* . **112 E9** 41 51N 90 12W
Clinton, *Mass., U.S.A.* . **117 D13** 42 25N 71 41W
Clinton, *Miss., U.S.A.* . **113 J9** 32 20N 90 20W
Clinton, *Mo., U.S.A.* . **112 F8** 38 22N 93 46W
Clinton, *N.C., U.S.A.* . **115 H6** 35 0N 78 22W
Clinton, *Okla., U.S.A.* . **113 H5** 35 31N 98 58W
Clinton, *Tenn., U.S.A.* . **115 G3** 36 6N 84 8W

Clinton, *Wash., U.S.A.* . **110 C4** 47 59N 122 21W
Clinton C., *Australia* . **94 C5** 22 30 S 150 45 E
Clinton Colden L., *Canada* . **100 B9** 63 58N 107 27W
Clintonville, *U.S.A.* . **112 C10** 44 37N 88 46W
Clipperton, I., *Pac. Oc.* . **97 F17** 10 18N 109 13W
Clisham, *U.K.* . **13 D2** 57 57N 6 49W
Clisson, *France* . **18 E5** 47 5N 1 16W
Clitheroe, *U.K.* . **14 D5** 53 53N 2 22W
Clo-oose, *Canada* . **110 B2** 48 39N 124 49W
Cloates, Pt., *Australia* . **92 D1** 22 43 S 113 40 E
Clocolan, *S. Africa* . **89 D4** 28 55 S 27 34 E
Clodomira, *Argentina* . **126 B3** 27 35 S 64 14W
Clogher Hd., *Ireland* . **12 C5** 53 48N 6 14W
Clonakilty, *Ireland* . **12 E3** 51 37N 8 53W
Clonakilty B., *Ireland* . **12 E3** 51 35N 8 51W
Cloncurry, *Australia* . **94 C3** 20 40 S 140 28 E
Cloncurry →, *Australia* . **94 B3** 18 37 S 140 40 E
Clondalkin, *Ireland* . **12 C5** 53 19N 6 25W
Clones, *Ireland* . **12 B4** 54 11N 7 15W
Clonmel, *Ireland* . **12 D4** 52 21N 7 42W
Cloppenburg, *Germany* . **24 C4** 52 51N 8 1 E
Cloquet, *U.S.A.* . **112 B8** 46 43N 92 28W
Clorinda, *Argentina* . **126 B4** 25 16 S 57 45W
Cloud Bay, *Canada* . **104 C2** 48 5N 89 26W
Cloud Peak, *U.S.A.* . **108 D10** 44 23N 107 11W
Cloudcroft, *U.S.A.* . **109 K11** 32 58N 105 45W
Cloverdale, *U.S.A.* . **110 G4** 38 48N 123 1W
Clovis, *Calif., U.S.A.* . **110 J7** 36 49N 119 42W
Clovis, *N. Mex., U.S.A.* . **113 H3** 34 24N 103 12W
Cloyes-sur-le-Loir, *France* . **18 E8** 48 0N 1 14 E
Cloyne, *Canada* . **116 B7** 44 49N 77 11W
Cluj □, *Romania* . **29 D8** 46 45 S 23 30 E
Cluj-Napoca, *Romania* . **29 D8** 46 47N 23 38 E
Clunes, *Australia* . **95 F3** 37 20 S 143 45 E
Cluny, *France* . **19 F11** 46 26N 4 38 E
Cluses, *France* . **19 F13** 46 5N 6 35 E
Clusone, *Italy* . **40 C6** 45 53N 9 57 E
Clutha →, *N.Z.* . **91 M2** 46 20 S 169 49 E
Clwyd →, *U.K.* . **14 D4** 53 19N 3 31W
Clyde, *Canada* . **102 C6** 54 9N 113 39W
Clyde, *N.Z.* . **91 L2** 45 12 S 169 20 E
Clyde, *U.S.A.* . **116 C8** 43 5N 76 52W
Clyde →, *U.K.* . **13 F4** 55 55N 4 30W
Clyde Muirshiel △, *U.K.* . **13 F4** 55 50N 4 40W
Clyde River, *Canada* . **101 A13** 70 30N 68 30W
Clydebank, *U.K.* . **13 F4** 55 54N 4 23W
Clymer, *N.Y., U.S.A.* . **116 D5** 42 1N 79 37W
Clymer, *Pa., U.S.A.* . **116 D5** 40 40N 79 1W
Ćmielów, *Poland* . **31 H8** 50 53N 21 31 E
Côa →, *Portugal* . **36 D3** 41 5N 7 6W
Coachella, *U.S.A.* . **111 M10** 33 41N 116 10W
Coachella Canal, *U.S.A.* . **111 N12** 32 43N 114 57W
Coahoma, *U.S.A.* . **113 J4** 32 18N 101 18W
Coahuayana →, *Mexico* . **118 D4** 18 41N 103 45W
Coahuila □, *Mexico* . **118 B4** 27 0N 103 0W
Coal →, *Canada* . **102 B3** 59 39N 126 57W
Coalane, *Mozam.* . **87 F4** 17 48 S 37 2 E
Coalcomán, *Mexico* . **118 D4** 18 40N 103 10W
Coaldale, *Canada* . **102 D6** 49 45N 112 35W
Coalgate, *U.S.A.* . **113 H6** 34 32N 96 13W
Coalinga, *U.S.A.* . **110 J6** 36 9N 120 21W
Coalisland, *U.K.* . **12 B5** 54 33N 6 42W
Coalville, *U.K.* . **14 E6** 52 44N 1 23W
Coalville, *U.S.A.* . **108 F8** 40 55N 111 24W
Coamo, *Puerto Rico* . **121 d** 18 5N 66 22W
Coari, *Brazil* . **124 D6** 4 8 S 63 7W
Coast □, *Kenya* . **86 C4** 2 40 S 39 45 E
Coast Mts., *Canada* . **102 C3** 55 0N 129 20W
Coast Ranges, *U.S.A.* . **110 G4** 39 0N 123 0W
Coatbridge, *U.K.* . **13 F4** 55 52N 4 6W
Coatepec, *Mexico* . **119 D5** 19 27N 96 58W
Coatepeque, *Guatemala* . **120 D1** 14 46N 91 55W
Coatesville, *U.S.A.* . **114 F8** 39 59N 75 50W
Coaticook, *Canada* . **117 A13** 45 10N 71 46W
Coats I., *Canada* . **101 B11** 62 30N 83 0W
Coats Land, *Antarctica* . **5 D1** 77 0 S 25 0W
Coatzacoalcos, *Mexico* . **119 D6** 18 7N 94 25W
Coba, *Mexico* . **119 C7** 20 31N 87 39W
Cobadin, *Romania* . **29 F13** 44 5N 28 13 E
Cobalt, *Canada* . **104 C4** 47 25N 79 42W
Cobán, *Guatemala* . **120 C1** 15 30N 90 21W
Cobanlar, *Turkey* . **47 C12** 38 41N 30 47 E
Cobar, *Australia* . **95 E4** 31 27 S 145 48 E
Cóbh, *Ireland* . **12 E3** 51 51N 8 17W
Cobija, *Bolivia* . **124 F5** 11 0 S 68 50W
Cobleskill, *U.S.A.* . **117 D10** 42 41N 74 29W
Coboconk, *Canada* . **116 B6** 44 39N 78 48W
Cobourg, *Canada* . **116 C6** 43 58N 78 10W
Cobourg □, *Australia* . **92 B5** 11 26 S 131 58 E
Cobourg Pen., *Australia* . **92 B5** 11 20 S 132 15 E
Cobram, *Australia* . **95 F4** 35 54 S 145 40 E
Cóbué, *Mozam.* . **87 E3** 12 0 S 34 58 E
Coburg, *Germany* . **25 E6** 50 15N 10 58 E
Coca, *Spain* . **36 D6** 41 13N 4 32W
Cocanada = Kakinada, *India* . **67 L13** 16 57N 82 11 E
Cocentaina, *Spain* . **39 G4** 38 45N 0 27W
Cochabamba, *Bolivia* . **124 G5** 17 26 S 66 10W
Cochem, *Germany* . **25 E3** 50 9N 7 9 E
Cochemane, *Mozam.* . **87 F3** 17 0 S 33 48 E
Cochin, *India* . **66 Q10** 9 58N 76 20 E
Cochin China = Nam-Phan, *Vietnam* . **65 G6** 10 30N 106 0 E
Cochran, *U.S.A.* . **115 J4** 32 23N 83 21W
Cochrane, *Alta., Canada* . **102 C6** 51 11N 114 30W
Cochrane, *Ont., Canada* . **104 C3** 49 0N 81 0W
Cochrane, *Chile* . **128 F2** 47 15 S 72 33W
Cochrane →, *Canada* . **103 B8** 59 0N 103 40W
Cochrane, L., *Chile* . **128 F2** 47 10 S 72 0W
Cochranton, *U.S.A.* . **116 E4** 41 31N 80 3W
Cockburn, *Australia* . **95 E3** 32 5 S 141 0 E
Cockburn, Canal, *Chile* . **128 G2** 54 30 S 72 0W
Cockburn I., *Canada* . **104 C3** 45 55N 83 22W
Cockburn Ra., *Australia* . **92 C4** 15 46 S 128 0 E
Cockermouth, *U.K.* . **14 C4** 54 40N 3 22W
Cocklebiddy, *Australia* . **93 F4** 32 0 S 126 3 E
Cockpit Country, The, *Jamaica* . **120 a** 18 15N 77 45W
Coco →, *Cent. Amer.* . **120 D3** 15 0N 83 8W
Coco, I. del, *Pac. Oc.* . **97 G19** 5 25N 87 55W
Cocoa, *U.S.A.* . **115 L5** 28 21N 80 44W
Cocobeach, *Gabon* . **84 D1** 0 59N 9 34 E
Cocora, *Romania* . **29 F12** 44 45N 27 3 E
Cocos, B. *Trin & Tob.* . **125 K15** 10 25N 61 2W
Cocos Is., *Ind. Oc.* . **96 J1** 12 10 S 96 55 E
Cod, C., *U.S.A.* . **114 D10** 42 5N 70 10W
Codajás, *Brazil* . **124 D6** 3 55 S 62 0W
Codigoro, *Italy* . **41 D9** 44 49N 12 8 E
Codlea, *Romania* . **29 E10** 45 43N 25 27 E
Codó, *Brazil* . **125 D10** 4 30 S 43 55W
Codogno, *Italy* . **40 C6** 45 9N 9 42 E
Codróipo, *Italy* . **41 C10** 45 58N 12 59 E
Codru, Munții, *Romania* . **28 D7** 46 30N 22 15 E
Cody, *U.S.A.* . **108 D9** 44 32N 109 3W

Coe Hill, *Canada* . **116 B7** 44 52N 77 50W
Coelemu, *Chile* . **126 D1** 36 30 S 72 48W
Coen, *Australia* . **94 A3** 13 52 S 143 12 E
Coesfeld, *Germany* . **24 D3** 51 56N 7 10 E
Cœur d'Alene, *U.S.A.* . **108 C5** 47 45N 116 51W
Cœur d'Alene L., *U.S.A.* . **108 C5** 47 32N 116 48W
Coevorden, *Neths.* . **17 B6** 52 40N 6 44 E
Coffeyville, *U.S.A.* . **113 G7** 37 2N 95 37W
Coffin B., *Australia* . **95 E2** 34 38 S 135 28 E
Coffin Bay, *Australia* . **95 E2** 34 37 S 135 29 E
Coffin Bay △, *Australia* . **95 E2** 34 34 S 135 19 E
Coffin Bay Peninsula, *Australia* . **95 E2** 34 32 S 135 15 E
Coffs Harbour, *Australia* . **95 E5** 30 16 S 153 5 E
Cofre de Perote △, *Mexico* . **119 D5** 19 29N 97 8W
Cofrentes, *Spain* . **39 F3** 39 13N 1 5W
Cogalnic →, *Moldova* . **29 E14** 45 49N 29 40 E
Cogealac, *Romania* . **29 F13** 44 36N 28 36 E
Coghinas →, *Italy* . **42 B1** 40 55N 8 48 E
Coghinas, L. del, *Italy* . **42 B2** 40 46N 9 3 E
Cognac, *France* . **20 C3** 45 41N 0 20W
Cogne, *Italy* . **21 E10** 45 35N 7 21 E
Cogolludo, *Spain* . **38 E1** 40 59N 3 10W
Cohocton, *U.S.A.* . **116 D7** 42 30N 77 30W
Cohocton →, *U.S.A.* . **116 D7** 42 9N 77 6W
Cohoes, *U.S.A.* . **117 D11** 42 46N 73 42W
Cohuna, *Australia* . **95 F3** 35 45 S 144 15 E
Coiba, I., *Panama* . **120 E3** 7 30N 81 40W
Coig →, *Argentina* . **128 G3** 51 0 S 69 10W
Coigeach, Rubha, *U.K.* . **13 C3** 58 6N 5 26W
Coihaique, *Chile* . **128 F2** 45 30 S 71 45W
Coimbatore, *India* . **66 P10** 11 2N 76 59 E
Coimbra, *Brazil* . **124 G7** 19 55 S 57 48W
Coimbra, *Portugal* . **36 E2** 40 15N 8 27W
Coimbra □, *Portugal* . **36 E2** 40 12N 8 25W
Coín, *Spain* . **37 J6** 36 40N 4 48W
Coipasa, Salar de, *Bolivia* . **124 G5** 19 26 S 68 9W
Cojimies, *Ecuador* . **124 C3** 0 20N 80 0W
Cojocna, *Romania* . **29 D8** 46 45 S 23 50 E
Cojutepeque, *El Salv.* . **120 D2** 13 41N 88 54W
Čoka, *Serbia & M.* . **28 E5** 45 57N 20 12 E
Cokeville, *U.S.A.* . **108 E8** 42 5N 110 57W
Colac, *Australia* . **95 F3** 38 21 S 143 35 E
Colatina, *Brazil* . **125 G10** 19 32 S 40 37W
Colbeck, C., *Antarctica* . **5 D13** 77 6 S 157 48W
Colborne, *Canada* . **116 C7** 44 0N 77 53W
Colby, *U.S.A.* . **112 F4** 39 24N 101 3W
Colchester, *U.K.* . **15 F8** 51 54N 0 55 E
Cold L., *Canada* . **103 C7** 54 33N 110 5W
Coldstream, *Canada* . **102 C5** 50 13N 119 11W
Coldstream, *U.K.* . **13 F6** 55 39N 2 15W
Coldwater, *Canada* . **116 B5** 44 42N 79 40W
Coldwater, *Kans., U.S.A.* . **113 G5** 37 16N 99 20W
Coldwater, *Mich., U.S.A.* . **114 E3** 41 57N 85 0W
Colebrook, *U.S.A.* . **117 B13** 44 54N 71 30W
Coleman, *U.S.A.* . **113 K5** 31 50N 99 26W
Coleman →, *Australia* . **94 B3** 15 6 S 141 38 E
Colenso, *S. Africa* . **89 D4** 28 44 S 29 50 E
Coleraine, *Australia* . **95 F3** 37 36 S 141 40 E
Coleraine, *U.K.* . **12 A5** 55 8N 6 41W
Coleridge, L., *N.Z.* . **91 K3** 43 17 S 171 30 E
Colesberg, *S. Africa* . **88 E4** 30 45 S 25 5 E
Coleville, *U.S.A.* . **110 G7** 38 34N 119 30W
Colfax, *Calif., U.S.A.* . **110 F6** 39 6N 120 57W
Colfax, *La., U.S.A.* . **113 K8** 31 31N 92 42W
Colfax, *Wash., U.S.A.* . **108 C5** 46 53N 117 22W
Colhué Huapi, L., *Argentina* . **128 F3** 45 30 S 69 0W
Colibași, *Moldova* . **29 E13** 45 43N 28 11 E
Colibași, *Romania* . **29 F9** 44 56N 24 54 E
Cólico, *Italy* . **40 B6** 46 8N 9 22 E
Coligny, *France* . **19 F12** 46 23N 5 21 E
Coligny, *S. Africa* . **89 D4** 26 17 S 26 15 E
Colima, *Mexico* . **118 D4** 19 14N 103 43W
Colima □, *Mexico* . **118 D4** 19 10N 103 40W
Colima, Nevado de, *Mexico* . **118 D4** 19 35N 103 45W
Colina, *Chile* . **126 C1** 33 13 S 70 45W
Colina do Norte, *Guinea-Biss.* . **82 C2** 12 28N 15 0W
Colinas, *Brazil* . **125 E10** 6 0 S 44 10W
Colindres, *Spain* . **36 B7** 43 24N 3 27W
Coll, *U.K.* . **13 E2** 56 39N 6 34W
Collaguasi, *Chile* . **126 A2** 21 5 S 68 45W
Collarada, Peña, *Spain* . **38 C4** 42 43N 0 29W
Collarenebri, *Australia* . **95 D4** 29 33 S 148 34 E
Colle di Val d'Elsa, *Italy* . **40 E8** 43 25N 11 7 E
Collécchio, *Italy* . **40 D7** 44 45N 10 13 E
Colleen Bawn, *Zimbabwe* . **87 G2** 21 0 S 29 12 E
College Park, *U.S.A.* . **115 J3** 33 40N 84 27W
College Station, *U.S.A.* . **113 K6** 30 37N 96 21W
Collesalvetti, *Italy* . **40 E7** 43 34N 10 27 E
Colli Euganei, *Italy* . **41 C8** 45 18N 11 43 E
Collie, *Australia* . **93 F2** 33 22 S 116 8 E
Collier B., *Australia* . **92 C3** 16 10 S 124 15 E
Collier Ra., *Australia* . **93 D2** 24 45 S 119 10 E
Collier Range △, *Australia* . **93 D2** 24 39 S 119 7 E
Collina, Passo di, *Italy* . **40 D7** 44 2N 10 56 E
Collingwood, *Canada* . **116 B4** 44 29 S 80 13W
Collingwood, *N.Z.* . **91 J4** 40 41 S 172 40 E
Collins, *Canada* . **104 B2** 50 17N 89 27W
Collinsville, *Australia* . **94 C4** 20 30 S 147 56 E
Collipulli, *Chile* . **126 D1** 37 55 S 72 30W
Collooney, *Ireland* . **12 B3** 54 11N 8 29W
Colmar, *France* . **19 D14** 48 5N 7 20 E
Colmars, *France* . **21 D10** 44 11N 6 39 E
Colmenar, *Spain* . **37 J6** 36 54N 4 20W
Colmenar de Oreja, *Spain* . **36 E7** 40 6N 3 25W
Colmenar Viejo, *Spain* . **36 E7** 40 39N 3 47W
Colo →, *Australia* . **95 E5** 33 25 S 150 52 E
Cologne = Köln, *Germany* . **24 E2** 50 56N 6 57 E
Colom, I. d'en, *Spain* . **48 B11** 39 58N 4 16 E
Coloma, *U.S.A.* . **110 G6** 38 48N 120 53W
Colomb-Béchar = Béchar, *Algeria* . **78 B5** 31 38N 2 18W
Colombey-les-Belles, *France* . **19 D12** 48 32N 5 54 E
Colombey-les-Deux-Églises, *France* . **19 D11** 48 13N 4 50 E
Colombia ■, *S. Amer.* . **124 C4** 3 45N 73 0W
Colombian Basin, *S. Amer.* . **98 H12** 14 0N 76 0W
Colombo, *Sri Lanka* . **66 R11** 6 56N 79 58 E
Colomiers, *France* . **20 E5** 43 37N 1 21 E
Colón, *Buenos Aires, Argentina* . **126 C3** 33 53 S 61 7W
Colón, *Entre Ríos, Argentina* . **126 C4** 32 12 S 58 10W
Colón, *Cuba* . **120 B3** 22 42N 80 54W

Colón, *Panama* . **120 E4** 9 20N 79 54W
Colón, Arch. de, *Ecuador* . **97 H18** 0 0 91 0W
Colònia de Sant Jordi, *Spain* . **48 B9** 39 19N 2 59 E
Colonia del Sacramento, *Uruguay* . **126 C4** 34 25 S 57 50W
Colonia Dora, *Argentina* . **126 B3** 28 34 S 62 59W
Colonial Beach, *U.S.A.* . **114 F7** 38 15N 76 58W
Colonie, *U.S.A.* . **117 D11** 42 43N 73 50W
Colonna, C., *Italy* . **43 C10** 39 2N 17 12 E
Colonsay, *Canada* . **103 C7** 51 59N 105 52W
Colonsay, *U.K.* . **13 E2** 56 5N 6 12W
Colorado □, *U.S.A.* . **109 G10** 39 30N 105 30W
Colorado →, *Argentina* . **128 D4** 39 50 S 62 8W
Colorado →, *N. Amer.* . **109 L6** 31 45N 114 40W
Colorado →, *U.S.A.* . **113 L7** 28 36N 95 59W
Colorado City, *U.S.A.* . **113 J4** 32 24N 100 52W
Colorado Plateau, *U.S.A.* . **109 H8** 37 0N 111 0W
Colorado River Aqueduct, *U.S.A.* . **111 L12** 34 17N 114 10W
Colorado Springs, *U.S.A.* . **112 F2** 38 50N 104 49W
Colorno, *Italy* . **40 D7** 44 56N 10 22 E
Colotlán, *Mexico* . **118 C4** 22 6N 103 16W
Colstrip, *U.S.A.* . **108 D10** 45 53N 106 38W
Colton, *U.S.A.* . **117 B10** 44 33N 74 56W
Columbia, *Ky., U.S.A.* . **114 G3** 37 6N 85 18W
Columbia, *La., U.S.A.* . **113 J8** 32 6N 92 5W
Columbia, *Miss., U.S.A.* . **113 K10** 31 15N 89 50W
Columbia, *Mo., U.S.A.* . **112 F8** 38 57N 92 20W
Columbia, *Pa., U.S.A.* . **117 F8** 40 2N 76 30W
Columbia, *S.C., U.S.A.* . **115 J5** 34 0N 81 2W
Columbia, *Tenn., U.S.A.* . **115 H2** 35 37N 87 2W
Columbia →, *N. Amer.* . **110 D2** 46 15N 124 5W
Columbia, C., *Canada* . **4 A4** 83 6N 69 57W
Columbia, District of □, *U.S.A.* . **114 F7** 38 55N 77 0W
Columbia, Mt., *Canada* . **102 C5** 52 8N 117 20W
Columbia Basin, *U.S.A.* . **108 C4** 46 45N 119 5W
Columbia Falls, *U.S.A.* . **108 B6** 48 23N 114 11W
Columbia Mts., *Canada* . **102 C5** 52 0N 119 0W
Columbia Plateau, *U.S.A.* . **108 D5** 44 0N 117 30W
Columbiana, *U.S.A.* . **116 F4** 40 53N 80 42W
Columbretes, Is., *Spain* . **38 F5** 39 50N 0 50 E
Columbus, *Ga., U.S.A.* . **115 J3** 32 28N 84 59W
Columbus, *Ind., U.S.A.* . **114 F3** 39 13N 85 55W
Columbus, *Kans., U.S.A.* . **113 G7** 37 10N 94 50W
Columbus, *Miss., U.S.A.* . **115 J1** 33 30N 88 25W
Columbus, *Mont., U.S.A.* . **108 D9** 45 38N 109 15W
Columbus, *N. Mex., U.S.A.* . **109 L10** 31 50N 107 38W
Columbus, *Nebr., U.S.A.* . **112 E6** 41 26N 97 22W
Columbus, *Ohio, U.S.A.* . **114 F4** 39 58N 83 0W
Columbus, *Tex., U.S.A.* . **113 L6** 29 42N 96 33W
Colunga, *Spain* . **36 B5** 43 29N 5 16W
Colusa, *U.S.A.* . **110 F4** 39 13N 122 1W
Colville, *U.S.A.* . **108 B5** 48 33N 117 54W
Colville →, *U.S.A.* . **100 A4** 70 25N 150 30W
Colville, C., *N.Z.* . **91 G5** 36 29 S 175 21 E
Colwood, *Canada* . **110 B3** 48 26N 123 29W
Colwyn Bay, *U.K.* . **14 D4** 53 18N 3 44W
Coma, *Ethiopia* . **81 F4** 8 29N 36 53 E
Comácchio, *Italy* . **41 D9** 44 42N 12 11 E
Comalcalco, *Mexico* . **119 D6** 18 16N 93 13W
Comallo, *Argentina* . **128 E2** 41 0 S 70 5W
Comana, *Romania* . **29 F11** 44 10N 26 10 E
Comanche, *U.S.A.* . **113 K5** 31 54N 98 36W
Comandante Ferraz, *Antarctica* . **5 C18** 62 30 S 58 0W
Comăneşti, *Romania* . **29 E11** 46 25N 26 26 E
Comarnic, *Romania* . **29 E10** 45 15N 25 38 E
Comayagua, *Honduras* . **120 D2** 14 25N 87 37W
Combahee →, *U.S.A.* . **115 J5** 32 30N 80 31W
Combarbalá, *Chile* . **126 C1** 31 11 S 71 2W
Combe Martin, *U.K.* . **15 F3** 51 12N 4 3W
Combeaufontaine, *France* . **19 E12** 47 38N 5 54 E
Comber, *Canada* . **116 D2** 42 14N 82 33W
Comber, *U.K.* . **12 B6** 54 33N 5 45W
Combermere, *Canada* . **116 A7** 45 22N 77 37W
Comblain-au-Pont, *Belgium* . **17 D5** 50 29N 5 35 E
Combourg, *France* . **18 D5** 48 25N 1 46W
Combrailles, *France* . **19 F9** 46 8N 2 8 E
Combronde, *France* . **20 C7** 45 58N 3 5 E
Comeragh Mts., *Ireland* . **12 D4** 52 18N 7 34W
Comet, *Australia* . **94 C4** 23 36 S 148 38 E
Comilla, *Bangla.* . **67 H17** 23 28N 91 10 E
Comino, *Malta* . **49 C1** 36 1N 14 20 E
Comino, C., *Italy* . **42 B2** 40 32N 9 49 E
Cómiso, *Italy* . **43 F7** 36 56N 14 37 E
Comitán, *Mexico* . **119 D6** 16 18N 92 9W
Commentry, *France* . **20 C6** 46 20N 2 46 E
Commerce, *Ga., U.S.A.* . **115 H4** 34 12N 83 28W
Commerce, *Tex., U.S.A.* . **113 J7** 33 15N 95 54W
Commercy, *France* . **19 D12** 48 43N 5 34 E
Committee B., *Canada* . **101 B11** 68 30N 86 30W
Commonwealth B., *Antarctica* . **5 C10** 67 0 S 144 0 E
Commoron Cr. →, *Australia* . **95 D5** 28 22 S 150 8 E
Communism Pk. = Kommunizma, Pik, *Tajikistan* . **52 F8** 39 0N 72 2 E
Como, *Italy* . **40 C6** 45 47N 9 5 E
Como, Lago di, *Italy* . **40 B6** 46 0N 9 11 E
Comodoro Rivadavia, *Argentina* . **128 F3** 45 50 S 67 40W
Comoé →, *Ivory C.* . **82 D4** 5 0N 3 5W
Comorâşte, *Romania* . **28 E6** 45 10N 21 35 E
Comorin, C., *India* . **66 Q10** 8 3N 77 40 E
Comoros ■, *Ind. Oc.* . **77 H8** 12 10 S 44 15 E
Comox, *Canada* . **102 D4** 49 42N 124 55W
Compiègne, *France* . **19 C9** 49 24N 2 50 E
Comporta, *Portugal* . **37 G2** 38 22N 8 46W
Compostela, *Mexico* . **118 C4** 21 15N 104 53W
Comprida, I., *Brazil* . **127 A6** 24 50 S 47 42W
Compton, *Canada* . **117 A13** 45 14N 71 49W
Compton, *U.S.A.* . **111 M8** 33 54N 118 13W
Comrat, *Moldova* . **29 D13** 46 18N 28 40 E
Comrie, *U.K.* . **13 E5** 56 22N 3 59W
Con Cuong, *Vietnam* . **64 C5** 19 2N 104 54 E
Con Dao △, *Vietnam* . **65 H6** 8 42N 106 35 E
Con Son, *Vietnam* . **65 H6** 8 41N 106 37 E
Conakry, *Guinea* . **82 D2** 9 29N 13 49W
Conara, *Australia* . **95 G4** 41 50 S 147 26 E
Concarneau, *France* . **18 E3** 47 52N 3 56W
Conceição, *Mozam.* . **87 F4** 18 47 S 36 7 E
Conceição da Barra, *Brazil* . **125 G11** 18 35 S 39 45W
Conceição do Araguaia, *Brazil* . **125 E9** 8 0 S 49 2W
Concepción, *Argentina* . **126 B2** 27 20 S 65 35W

Concepción, *Bolivia* . **124 G6** 16 15 S 62 8W
Concepción, *Chile* . **126 D1** 36 50 S 73 0W
Concepción, *Mexico* . **119 D6** 18 15N 90 5W
Concepción, *Paraguay* . **126 A4** 23 22 S 57 26W
Concepción □, *Chile* . **126 D1** 37 0 S 72 30W
Concepción →, *Mexico* . **118 A2** 30 32N 113 2W
Concepción, Est. de, *Chile* . **128 G2** 50 30 S 74 55W
Concepción, L., *Bolivia* . **124 G6** 17 20 S 61 20W
Concepción, Punta, *Mexico* . **118 B2** 26 55N 111 59W
Concepción del Oro, *Mexico* . **118 C4** 24 40N 101 30W
Concepción del Uruguay, *Argentina* . **126 C4** 32 35 S 58 20W
Conception, Pt., *U.S.A.* . **111 L6** 34 27N 120 28W
Conception B., *Canada* . **105 C9** 47 45N 53 0W
Conception B., *Namibia* . **88 C1** 23 55 S 14 22 E
Conception I., *Bahamas* . **121 B4** 23 52N 75 9W
Concession, *Zimbabwe* . **87 F3** 17 27 S 30 56 E
Conchas Dam, *U.S.A.* . **113 H2** 35 22N 104 11W
Conches-en-Ouche, *France* . **18 D7** 48 58N 0 56 E
Concho, *U.S.A.* . **109 J9** 34 28N 109 36W
Concho →, *U.S.A.* . **113 K5** 31 34N 99 43W
Conchos →, *Chihuahua, Mexico* . **118 B4** 29 32N 105 0W
Conchos →, *Tamaulipas, Mexico* . **119 B5** 25 9N 98 35W
Concord, *Calif., U.S.A.* . **110 H4** 37 59N 122 2W
Concord, *N.C., U.S.A.* . **115 H5** 35 25N 80 35W
Concord, *N.H., U.S.A.* . **117 C13** 43 12N 71 32W
Concordia, *Argentina* . **126 C4** 31 20 S 58 2W
Concórdia, *Brazil* . **124 D5** 4 36 S 66 36W
Concordia, *Mexico* . **118 C3** 23 18N 106 2W
Concordia, *U.S.A.* . **112 F6** 39 34N 97 40W
Concrete, *U.S.A.* . **108 B3** 48 32N 121 45W
Condamine, *Australia* . **95 D5** 26 56 S 150 9 E
Condat, *France* . **20 C6** 45 21N 2 46 E
Conde, *U.S.A.* . **112 C5** 45 9N 98 6W
Condé-sur-Noireau, *France* . **18 D6** 48 51N 0 33W
Condeúba, *Brazil* . **125 F10** 14 52 S 42 0W
Condobolin, *Australia* . **95 E4** 33 4 S 147 6 E
Condom, *France* . **20 E4** 43 57N 0 22 E
Condon, *U.S.A.* . **108 D3** 45 14N 120 11W
Conegliano, *Italy* . **41 C9** 45 53N 12 18 E
Conejera, I. = Conills, I. des, *Spain* . **48 B9** 39 11N 2 58 E
Conejos, *Mexico* . **118 B4** 26 14N 103 53W
Conero △, *Italy* . **41 E10** 43 32N 13 35 E
Confolens, *France* . **20 B4** 46 2N 0 40 E
Confuso →, *Paraguay* . **126 B4** 25 9 S 57 34W
Congaz, *Moldova* . **29 D13** 46 7N 28 36 E
Congjiang, *China* . **59 F9** 23 36N 113 31 E
Congleton, *U.K.* . **14 D5** 53 10N 2 13W
Congo (Brazzaville) = Congo ■, *Africa* . **84 E3** 1 0 S 16 0 E
Congo (Kinshasa) = Congo, Dem. Rep. of the ■, *Africa* . **84 E4** 3 0 S 23 0 E
Congo ■, *Africa* . **84 E3** 1 0 S 16 0 E
Congo →, *Africa* . **84 F2** 6 4 S 12 24 E
Congo, Dem. Rep. of the ■, *Africa* . **84 E4** 3 0 S 23 0 E
Congo Basin, *Africa* . **84 E4** 0 10 S 24 30 E
Congonhas, *Brazil* . **127 A7** 20 30 S 43 52W
Congress, *U.S.A.* . **109 J7** 34 9N 112 51W
Conil de la Frontera, *Spain* . **37 J4** 36 17N 6 10W
Conills, I. des, *Spain* . **48 B9** 39 11N 2 58 E
Coniston, *Canada* . **104 C3** 46 29N 80 51W
Conjeeveram = Kanchipuram, *India* . **66 N11** 12 52N 79 45 E
Conklin, *Canada* . **103 B6** 55 38N 111 5W
Conklin, *U.S.A.* . **117 D9** 42 2N 75 49W
Conn, L., *Ireland* . **12 B2** 54 3N 9 15W
Connacht □, *Ireland* . **12 C2** 53 43N 9 12W
Conneaut, *U.S.A.* . **116 E4** 41 57N 80 34W
Connecticut □, *U.S.A.* . **117 E12** 41 30N 72 45W
Connecticut →, *U.S.A.* . **117 E12** 41 16N 72 20W
Connell, *U.S.A.* . **108 C4** 46 40N 118 52W
Connellsville, *U.S.A.* . **116 F5** 40 1N 79 35W
Connemara, *Ireland* . **12 C2** 53 29N 9 45W
Connemara △, *Ireland* . **12 C2** 53 32N 9 52W
Connemaugh →, *U.S.A.* . **116 F5** 40 28N 79 19W
Connerré, *France* . **18 D7** 48 3N 0 30 E
Connersville, *U.S.A.* . **114 F3** 39 39N 85 8W
Connors Ra., *Australia* . **94 C4** 21 40 S 149 10 E
Conques, *France* . **20 D6** 44 36N 2 23 E
Conquest, *Canada* . **103 C7** 51 32N 107 14W
Conrad, *U.S.A.* . **108 B8** 48 10N 111 57W
Conran, C., *Australia* . **95 F4** 37 49 S 148 44 E
Conroe, *U.S.A.* . **113 K7** 30 19N 95 27W
Consecon, *Canada* . **116 C7** 44 0N 77 31W
Conselheiro Lafaiete, *Brazil* . **127 A7** 20 40 S 43 48W
Conselve, *Italy* . **41 C8** 45 14N 11 52 E
Consett, *U.K.* . **14 C6** 54 51N 1 50W
Consort, *Canada* . **103 C6** 52 1N 110 46W
Constance = Konstanz, *Germany* . **25 H5** 47 40N 9 10 E
Constance, L. = Bodensee, *Europe* . **25 H5** 47 35N 9 25 E
Constanţa, *Romania* . **29 F13** 44 14N 28 38 E
Constanţa □, *Romania* . **29 F13** 44 15N 28 15 E
Constantia, *U.S.A.* . **117 C8** 43 15N 76 1W
Constantina, *Spain* . **37 H5** 37 51N 5 40W
Constantine, *Algeria* . **78 A7** 36 25N 6 42 E
Constitución, *Chile* . **126 D1** 35 20 S 72 30W
Constitución, *Uruguay* . **126 C4** 31 0 S 57 50W
Constitucion de 1857 △, *Mexico* . **118 A1** 32 4N 115 55W
Consuegra, *Spain* . **37 F7** 39 28N 3 36W
Consul, *Canada* . **103 D7** 49 20N 109 30W
Contact, *U.S.A.* . **108 F6** 41 46N 114 45W
Contai, *India* . **69 J12** 21 54N 87 46 E
Contamana, *Peru* . **124 E4** 7 19 S 74 55W
Contarina, *Italy* . **41 C9** 45 1N 12 13 E
Contas →, *Brazil* . **125 F11** 14 17 S 39 1W
Contes, *France* . **21 E11** 43 49N 7 19 E
Contoocook, *U.S.A.* . **117 C13** 43 13N 71 45W
Contra Costa, *Mozam.* . **89 D5** 25 9 S 33 30 E
Contres, *France* . **18 E8** 47 24N 1 26 E
Contrexéville, *France* . **19 D12** 48 10N 5 53 E
Contwoyto L., *Canada* . **100 B8** 65 42N 110 50W
Conversano, *Italy* . **43 B10** 40 58N 17 7 E
Conway = Conwy, *U.K.* . **14 D4** 53 17N 3 50W
Conway = Conwy →, *U.K.* . **14 D4** 53 17N 3 50W
Conway, *Australia* . **94 J6** 20 24 S 148 41 E
Conway, *Ark., U.S.A.* . **113 H8** 35 5N 92 26W
Conway, *N.H., U.S.A.* . **117 C13** 43 59N 71 7W
Conway, *S.C., U.S.A.* . **115 J6** 33 51N 79 3W
Conway, C., *Australia* . **94 J6** 20 34 S 148 46 E
Conway, L., *Australia* . **95 D2** 28 17 S 135 35 E

Conwy, U.K. 14 D4 53 17N 3 50W
Conwy □, U.K. 14 D4 53 10N 3 44W
Conwy →, U.K. 14 D4 53 17N 3 50W
Coober Pedy, Australia 95 D1 29 1S 134 43 E
Cooch Behar = Koch
  Bihar, India 67 F16 26 22N 89 29 E
Cooinda, Australia 92 B5 13 15S 130 5 E
Cook, Australia 93 F5 30 37S 130 25 E
Cook, U.S.A. 112 B8 47 49N 92 39W
Cook, B., Chile 128 H3 55 10S 70 0W
Cook, C., Canada 102 C3 50 8N 127 55W
Cook, Mt. = Aoraki
  Mount Cook, N.Z. 91 K3 43 36S 170 9 E
Cook Inlet, U.S.A. 100 C4 60 0N 152 0W
Cook Is., Pac. Oc. 97 J12 17 0S 160 0W
Cook Strait, N.Z. 91 J5 41 15S 174 29 E
Cookeville, U.S.A. 115 G3 36 10N 85 30W
Cookhouse, S. Africa 88 E4 32 44S 25 47 E
Cookshire, Canada 117 A13 45 25N 71 38W
Cooksville, Canada 116 C5 43 36N 79 35W
Cooktown, Australia 94 B4 15 30S 145 16 E
Coolabah, Australia 95 E4 31 1S 146 43 E
Cooladdi, Australia 95 D4 26 37S 145 23 E
Coolah, Australia 95 E4 31 48S 149 41 E
Coolamon, Australia 95 E4 34 46S 147 8 E
Coolgardie, Australia 93 F3 30 55S 121 8 E
Coolidge, U.S.A. 109 K8 32 59N 111 31W
Coolidge Dam, U.S.A. 109 K8 33 0N 110 20W
Cooloola △, Australia 95 D5 26 13S 153 2 E
Cooma, Australia 95 F4 36 12S 149 8 E
Coon Rapids, U.S.A. 112 C8 45 9N 93 19W
Coonabarabran,
  Australia 95 E4 31 14S 149 18 E
Coonamble, Australia 95 E4 30 56S 148 27 E
Coonana, Australia 93 F3 31 0S 123 0 E
Coondapoor, India 66 N9 13 42N 74 40 E
Cooninie, L., Australia 95 D2 26 4S 139 59 E
Cooper →, U.S.A. 113 J7 33 23N 95 42W
Cooper Cr. →, Australia 95 D2 28 29S 137 46 E
Cooperstown, N. Dak.,
  U.S.A. 112 B5 47 27N 98 8W
Cooperstown, N.Y.,
  U.S.A. 117 D10 42 42N 74 56W
Coorabie, Australia 93 F5 31 54S 132 18 E
Coorong, The, Australia 95 F2 35 50S 139 20 E
Coorow, Australia 93 E2 29 53S 116 2 E
Cooroy, Australia 95 D5 26 22S 152 54 E
Coos Bay, U.S.A. 108 E1 43 22N 124 13W
Coosa →, U.S.A. 115 J2 32 30N 86 16W
Cootamundra, Australia 95 E4 34 36S 148 1 E
Cootehill, Ireland 12 B4 54 4N 7 5W
Copahue Paso,
  Argentina 126 D1 37 49S 71 8W
Copainalá, Mexico 119 D6 17 8N 93 11W
Copake Falls, U.S.A. 117 D11 42 7N 73 31W
Copalnic Mănăştur,
  Romania 29 C8 47 30N 23 41 E
Copán, Honduras 120 D2 14 50N 89 9W
Cope, U.S.A. 112 F3 39 40N 102 51W
Cope, C., Spain 39 H3 37 26N 1 28W
Copenhagen =
  København, Denmark 11 J6 55 41N 12 34 E
Copenhagen, U.S.A. 117 C9 43 54N 75 41W
Copertino, Italy 43 B11 40 16N 18 2 E
Copiapó, Chile 126 B1 27 30S 70 20W
Copiapó →, Chile 126 B1 27 19S 70 56W
Coplay, U.S.A. 117 F9 40 44N 75 29W
Copp L., Canada 102 A6 60 14N 114 40W
Copparo, Italy 41 D8 44 54N 11 49 E
Coppename →,
  Suriname 125 B7 5 48N 55 55W
Copper Harbor, U.S.A. 114 B2 47 28N 87 53W
Copper Queen,
  Zimbabwe 87 F2 17 29S 29 18 E
Copperas Cove, U.S.A. 113 K6 31 8N 97 54W
Copperbelt □, Zambia 87 E2 13 15S 27 30 E
Coppermine =
  Kugluktuk, Canada 100 B8 67 50N 115 5W
Coppermine →, Canada 100 B8 67 49N 116 4W
Copperopolis, U.S.A. 110 H6 37 58N 120 38W
Copşa Mică, Romania 29 D9 46 7N 24 15 E
Coquet →, U.K. 14 B6 55 20N 1 32W
Coquille, U.S.A. 108 E1 43 11N 124 11W
Coquimbo, Chile 126 C1 30 0S 71 20W
Coquimbo □, Chile 126 C1 31 0S 71 0W
Corabia, Romania 29 G9 43 48N 24 30 E
Coracora, Peru 124 G4 15 5S 73 45W
Coraki, Australia 95 D5 28 59S 153 17 E
Coral, U.S.A. 116 F5 40 29N 79 10W
Coral Gables, U.S.A. 115 N5 25 45N 80 16W
Coral Harbour, Canada 101 B11 64 8N 83 10W
Coral Sea, Pac. Oc. 96 J7 15 0S 150 0 E
Coral Springs, U.S.A. 115 M5 26 16N 80 13W
Coraopolis, U.S.A. 116 F4 40 31N 80 10W
Corato, Italy 43 A9 41 9N 16 25 E

Corbeil-Essonnes,
  France 19 D9 48 36N 2 26 E
Corbie, France 19 C9 49 54N 2 30 E
Corbières, France 20 F6 42 55N 2 35 E
Corbigny, France 19 E10 47 16N 3 40 E
Corbin, U.S.A. 114 G3 36 57N 84 6W
Corbones →, Spain 37 H5 37 36N 5 39W
Corby, Romania 29 F13 44 25N 28 39 E
Corby, U.K. 15 E7 52 30N 0 41W
Corcaigh = Cork, Ireland 12 E3 51 54N 8 29W
Corcoran, U.S.A. 110 J7 36 6N 119 33W
Corcovado △,
  Costa Rica 120 E3 8 33N 83 35W
Cordele, U.S.A. 115 K4 31 58N 83 47W
Cordell, U.S.A. 113 H5 35 17N 98 59W
Cordenòns, Italy 41 C9 45 59N 12 42 E
Cordes-sur-Ciel, France 20 D5 44 5N 1 57 E
Córdoba, Argentina 126 C3 31 20S 64 10W
Córdoba, Mexico 119 D5 18 50N 97 0W
Córdoba, Spain 37 H6 37 50N 4 50W
Córdoba □, Argentina 126 C3 31 22S 64 15W
Córdoba □, Spain 37 G6 38 5N 5 0W
Córdoba, Sierra de,
  Argentina 126 C3 31 10S 64 25W
Cordon, Phil. 61 C4 16 42N 121 32 E
Cordova, U.S.A. 100 B5 60 33N 145 45W
Corella, Spain 38 C3 42 7N 1 48W
Corella →, Australia 94 B3 19 34S 140 47 E
Corfield, Australia 94 C3 21 40S 143 21 E
Corfu = Kérkira, Greece 49 A3 39 38N 19 50 E
Corfu ✈ (CFU), Greece 46 B1 39 35N 19 54 E
Corfu, Str. of, Greece 49 A4 39 34N 20 0 E
Corgo = O Corgo, Spain 36 C3 42 56N 7 25W
Cori, Italy 42 A5 41 39N 12 55 E
Coria, Spain 36 F4 39 58N 6 33W
Coria del Río, Spain 37 H4 37 16N 6 3W
Corigliano Cálabro, Italy 43 C9 39 36N 16 31 E
Coringa Is., Australia 94 B4 16 58S 149 58 E
Corinth = Kórinthos,
  Greece 46 D4 37 56N 22 55 E
Corinth, Miss., U.S.A. 115 H1 34 56N 88 31W

Corinth, N.Y., U.S.A. 117 C11 43 15N 73 49W
Corinth, G. of =
  Korinthiakós Kólpos,
  Greece 46 C4 38 16N 22 30 E
Corinth Canal, Greece 46 D4 37 58N 23 0 E
Corinto, Brazil 125 G10 18 20S 44 30W
Corinto, Nic. 120 D2 12 30N 87 10W
Cork, Ireland 12 E3 51 54N 8 29W
Cork □, Ireland 12 E3 51 57N 8 40W
Cork Harbour, Ireland 12 E3 51 47N 8 16W
Corlay, France 18 D3 48 20N 3 5W
Corleone, Italy 42 E6 37 49N 13 18 E
Corleto Perticara, Italy 43 B9 40 23N 16 2 E
Çorlu, Turkey 45 E11 41 11N 27 49 E
Cormack L., Canada 102 A4 60 56N 121 37W
Cormòns, Italy 41 C10 45 58N 13 28 E
Cormorant, Canada 103 C8 54 14N 100 35W
Cormorant L., Canada 103 C8 54 15N 100 50W
Corn Is. = Maíz, Is. del,
  Nic. 120 D3 12 15N 83 4W
Cornalvo △, Spain 37 F4 39 1N 6 19W
Cornélio Procópio,
  Brazil 127 A5 23 7S 50 40W
Corner Brook, Canada 105 C8 48 57N 57 58W
Corneşti, Moldova 29 C13 47 21N 28 1 E
Corníglio, Italy 40 D7 44 29N 10 5 E
Corning, Ark., U.S.A. 113 G9 36 25N 90 35W
Corning, Calif., U.S.A. 108 G2 39 56N 122 11W
Corning, Iowa, U.S.A. 112 E7 40 59N 94 44W
Corning, N.Y., U.S.A. 116 D7 42 9N 77 3W
Corno Grande, Italy 41 F10 42 28N 13 34 E
Cornwall, Canada 117 A10 45 2N 74 44W
Cornwall, U.S.A. 117 F8 40 17N 76 25W
Cornwall □, U.K. 15 G3 50 26N 4 40W
Corny Pt., Australia 95 E2 34 55S 137 0 E
Coro, Venezuela 124 A5 11 25N 69 41W
Coroatá, Brazil 125 D10 4 8S 44 0W
Corocoro, Bolivia 124 G5 17 15S 68 28W
Coroico, Bolivia 124 G5 16 0S 67 50W
Coromandel, N.Z. 91 G5 36 45S 175 31 E
Coromandel Coast,
  India 66 N12 12 30N 81 0 E
Corona, Calif., U.S.A. 111 M9 33 53N 117 34W
Corona, N. Mex., U.S.A. 109 J11 34 15N 105 36W
Coronach, Canada 103 D7 49 7N 105 31W
Coronado, U.S.A. 111 N9 32 41N 117 11W
Coronado, B. de,
  Costa Rica 120 E3 9 0N 83 40W
Coronados, Is. los,
  U.S.A. 111 N9 32 25N 117 15W
Coronation, Canada 102 C6 52 5N 111 27W
Coronation Gulf,
  Canada 100 B8 68 25N 110 0W
Coronation I., Antarctica 5 C18 60 45S 46 0W
Coronation Is., Australia 92 B3 14 57S 124 55 E
Coronda, Argentina 126 C3 31 58S 60 56W
Coronel, Chile 126 D1 37 0S 73 10W
Coronel Bogado,
  Paraguay 126 B4 27 11S 56 18W
Coronel Dorrego,
  Argentina 126 D3 38 40S 61 10W
Coronel Oviedo,
  Paraguay 126 B4 25 24S 56 30W
Coronel Pringles,
  Argentina 126 D3 38 0S 61 30W
Coronel Suárez,
  Argentina 126 D3 37 30S 61 52W
Coronel Vidal,
  Argentina 126 D4 37 28S 57 45W
Coropuna, Nevado, Peru 124 G4 15 30S 72 41W
Corowa, Australia 95 F4 35 58S 146 21 E
Corozal, Belize 119 D7 18 23N 88 23W
Corozal, Trin. & Tob. 125 K15 10 24N 61 40W
Corps, France 21 D9 44 50N 5 56 E
Corpus, Argentina 127 B4 27 10S 55 30W
Corpus Christi, U.S.A. 113 M6 27 47N 97 24W
Corpus Christi, L.,
  U.S.A. 113 L6 28 2N 97 52W
Corral de Almaguer,
  Spain 36 F7 39 45N 3 10W
Corralejo, Canary Is. 48 F6 28 43N 13 53W
Corraun Pen., Ireland 12 C2 53 54N 9 54W
Corréggio, Italy 40 D7 44 46N 10 47 E
Corrib, L., Ireland 12 C2 53 27N 9 16W
Corridónia, Italy 41 E10 43 15N 13 30 E
Corrientes, Argentina 126 B4 27 30S 58 45W
Corrientes □, Argentina 126 B4 28 0S 57 0W
Corrientes →, Argentina 126 C4 30 42S 59 38W
Corrientes →, Peru 124 D4 3 43S 74 35W
Corrientes, C., Colombia 124 B3 5 30N 77 34W
Corrientes, C., Cuba 120 B3 21 43N 84 30W
Corrientes, C., Mexico 118 C3 20 25N 105 42W
Corrigan, U.S.A. 113 K7 31 0N 94 52W
Corrigin, Australia 93 F2 32 20S 117 53 E
Corry, U.S.A. 116 E5 41 55N 79 39W
Corse □, France 21 F13 42 14N 9 10 E
Corse □, France 21 G13 42 0N 9 0 E
Corse, C., France 21 E13 43 1N 9 25 E
Corse-du-Sud □, France 21 G13 41 45N 9 0 E
Corsica = Corse □,
  France 21 G13 42 0N 9 0 E
Corsicana, U.S.A. 113 J6 32 6N 96 28W
Corte, France 21 F13 42 19N 9 11 E
Corte Pinto, Portugal 37 H3 37 42N 7 29W
Cortegana, Spain 37 H4 37 54N 6 49W
Cortez, U.S.A. 109 H9 37 21N 108 35W
Cortina d'Ampezzo,
  Italy 41 B9 46 32N 12 8 E
Cortland, N.Y., U.S.A. 117 D8 42 36N 76 11W
Cortland, Ohio, U.S.A. 116 E4 41 20N 80 44W
Cortona, Italy 41 E8 43 16N 11 59 E
Coruche, Portugal 37 G2 38 57N 8 30W
Çoruh →, Turkey 35 K5 41 38N 41 38 E
Çorum, Turkey 72 B6 40 30N 34 57 E
Corumbá, Brazil 124 G7 19 0S 57 30W
Corund, Romania 29 D10 46 30N 25 13 E
Corunna = A Coruña,
  Spain 36 B2 43 20N 8 25W
Corvallis, U.S.A. 108 D2 44 34N 123 16W
Corvette, L. de la,
  Canada 104 B5 53 25N 74 3W
Corydon, U.S.A. 112 E8 40 46N 93 19W
Cosalá, Mexico 118 C3 24 28N 106 40W
Cosamaloapan, Mexico 119 D5 18 23N 95 50W
Cosenza, Italy 43 C9 39 18N 16 15 E
Coşereni, Romania 29 F11 44 38N 26 35 E
Coshocton, U.S.A. 116 F3 40 16N 81 51W
Cosmo Newberry,
  Australia 93 E3 28 0S 122 54 E
Cosne-Cours-sur-Loire,
  France 19 E9 47 24N 2 54 E

Coso Junction, U.S.A. 111 J9 36 3N 117 57W
Coso Pk., U.S.A. 111 J9 36 13N 117 44W
Cospeito, Spain 36 B3 43 12N 7 34W
Cosquín, Argentina 126 C3 31 15S 64 30W
Cossato, Italy 40 C5 45 34N 8 10 E
Cossé-le-Vivien, France 18 E6 47 57N 0 54W
Cosson →, France 18 E8 47 30N 1 15 E
Costa Blanca, Spain 39 G4 38 25N 0 10W
Costa Brava, Spain 38 D8 41 30N 3 0 E
Costa del Sol, Spain 37 J6 36 30N 4 30W
Costa Dorada, Spain 38 D6 41 12N 1 15 E
Costa Mesa, U.S.A. 111 M9 33 38N 117 55W
Costa Rica ■,
  Cent. Amer. 120 E3 10 0N 84 0W
Costa Smeralda, Italy 42 A2 41 5N 9 35 E
Costeşti, Romania 29 F9 44 40N 24 53 E
Costigliole d'Asti, Italy 40 D5 44 48N 8 11 E
Cosumnes →, U.S.A. 110 G5 38 16N 121 26W
Coswig, Sachsen,
  Germany 24 D9 51 7N 13 34 E
Coswig, Sachsen-Anhalt,
  Germany 24 D8 51 53N 12 27 E
Cotabato, Phil. 61 H6 7 14N 124 15 E
Cotagaita, Bolivia 126 A2 20 45S 65 40W
Côte d'Azur, France 21 E11 43 25N 7 10 E
Côte-d'Ivoire = Ivory
  Coast ■, Africa 82 D4 7 30N 5 0W
Côte d'Or, France 19 E11 47 10N 4 50 E
Côte-d'Or □, France 19 E11 47 30N 4 50 E
Coteau des Prairies,
  U.S.A. 112 C6 45 20N 97 50W
Coteau du Missouri,
  U.S.A. 112 B4 47 0N 100 0W
Cotentin, France 18 C5 49 15N 1 30W
Côtes-d'Armor □,
  France 18 D4 48 25N 2 40W
Côtes de Meuse, France 19 C12 49 15N 5 22 E
Côtes-du-Nord = Côtes-
  d'Armor □, France 18 D4 48 25N 2 40W
Cotiella, Spain 38 C5 42 31N 0 19 E
Cotillo, Canary Is. 48 F5 28 41N 14 1W
Cotiujeni, Moldova 29 C13 47 51N 28 33 E
Cotonou, Benin 83 D5 6 20N 2 25 E
Cotopaxi, Ecuador 124 D3 0 40S 78 30W
Cotronei, Italy 43 C9 39 9N 16 47 E
Cotswold Hills, U.K. 15 F5 51 42N 2 10W
Cottage Grove, U.S.A. 108 E2 43 48N 123 3W
Cottbus, Germany 24 D10 51 45N 14 20 E
Cottonwood, U.S.A. 109 J7 34 45N 112 1W
Cotulla, U.S.A. 113 L5 28 26N 99 14W
Coubre, Pte. de la,
  France 20 C2 45 42N 1 15W
Couches, France 19 F11 46 53N 4 30 E
Couço, Portugal 37 G2 38 59N 8 17W
Coudersport, U.S.A. 116 E6 41 46N 78 1W
Couëdic, C. du, Australia 95 F2 36 5S 136 40 E
Couëron, France 18 E5 47 13N 1 44W
Couesnon →, France 18 D5 48 38N 1 32W
Couhé, France 20 B4 46 17N 0 11 E
Coulanges-sur-Yonne,
  France 19 E10 47 31N 3 33 E
Coulee City, U.S.A. 108 C4 47 37N 119 17W
Coulman I., Antarctica 5 D11 73 35S 170 0 E
Coulommiers, France 19 D10 48 50N 3 3 E
Coulon →, France 21 E9 43 51N 5 6 E
Coulonge →, Canada 104 C4 45 52N 76 46W
Coulonges-sur-l'Autize,
  France 20 B3 46 29N 0 36W
Coulounieix-Chamiers,
  France 20 C4 45 11N 0 42 E
Coulterville, U.S.A. 110 H6 37 43N 120 12W
Council, U.S.A. 108 D5 44 44N 116 26W
Council Bluffs, U.S.A. 112 E7 41 16N 95 52W
Council Grove, U.S.A. 112 F6 38 40N 96 29W
Coupeville, U.S.A. 110 B4 48 13N 122 41W
Courantyne →, S. Amer. 124 B7 5 55N 57 5W
Courcelles, Belgium 17 D4 50 28N 4 22 E
Courchevel, France 21 C10 45 25N 6 36 E
Courçon, France 20 B3 46 15N 0 50W
Courmayeur, Italy 40 C3 45 47N 6 58 E
Couronne, C., France 21 E9 43 19N 5 3 E
Cours-la-Ville, France 19 F11 46 7N 4 19 E
Coursan, France 20 E7 43 14N 3 4 E
Courseulles-sur-Mer,
  France 18 C6 49 20N 0 29W
Courtenay, Canada 102 D4 49 45N 125 0W
Courtland, U.S.A. 110 G5 38 20N 121 34W
Courtrai = Kortrijk,
  Belgium 17 D3 50 50N 3 17 E
Courtright, Canada 116 D2 42 49N 82 28W
Coushatta, U.S.A. 113 J8 32 1N 93 21W
Coutances, France 18 C5 49 3N 1 28W
Coutras, France 20 C3 45 3N 0 8W
Coutts Crossing,
  Australia 95 D5 29 49S 152 55 E
Couva, Trin. & Tob. 125 K15 10 24N 61 30W
Couvin, Belgium 17 D4 50 3N 4 29 E
Covarrubias, Spain 36 C7 42 4N 3 31W
Covasna, Romania 29 E11 45 50N 26 10 E
Covasna □, Romania 29 E10 46 0N 26 0 E
Cove I., Canada 116 A3 45 17N 81 44W
Coventry, U.K. 15 E6 52 25N 1 28W
Covilhã, Portugal 36 E3 40 17N 7 31W
Covington, Ga., U.S.A. 115 J4 33 36N 83 51W
Covington, Ky., U.S.A. 114 F3 39 5N 84 31W
Covington, Okla., U.S.A. 113 G6 36 18N 97 35W
Covington, Tenn., U.S.A. 113 H10 35 34N 89 39W
Covington, Va., U.S.A. 114 G5 37 47N 79 59W
Cowal, L., Australia 95 E4 33 40S 147 25 E
Cowan, L., Australia 93 F3 31 45S 121 45 E
Cowan L., Canada 103 C7 54 0N 107 15W
Cowangie, Australia 95 F3 35 12S 141 26 E
Cowansville, Canada 117 A12 45 14N 72 46W
Coward Springs,
  Australia 95 D2 29 24S 136 49 E
Cowcowing Lakes,
  Australia 93 F2 30 55S 117 20 E
Cowdenbeath, U.K. 13 E5 56 7N 3 21W
Cowell, Australia 95 E2 33 39S 136 56 E
Cowes, U.K. 15 G6 50 45N 1 18W
Cowichan L., Canada 110 D4 48 53N 124 17W
Cowlitz →, U.S.A. 110 D4 46 6N 122 55W
Cowra, Australia 95 E4 33 49S 148 42 E
Cox, Spain 39 G4 38 8N 0 53W
Coxilha Grande, Brazil 127 B5 28 18S 51 30W
Coxim, Brazil 125 G8 18 30S 54 55W
Cox's Bazar, Bangla. 67 J17 21 26N 91 59 E
Coyote Wells, U.S.A. 111 N11 32 44N 115 58W
Coyuca de Benítez,
  Mexico 119 D4 17 1N 100 8W
Coyuca de Catalan,
  Mexico 118 D4 18 18N 100 41W
Cozad, U.S.A. 112 E5 40 52N 99 59W
Cozes, France 20 C3 45 34N 0 50W
Cozumel, Mexico 119 C7 20 31N 86 55W
Cozumel, Isla, Mexico 119 C7 20 30N 86 40W

Crabhill, Barbados 121 g 13 19N 59 38W
Cracow = Kraków,
  Poland 31 H6 50 4N 19 57 E
Cracow, Australia 95 D5 25 17S 150 17 E
Cradle Mt.-Lake St.
  Clair △, Australia 95 G4 41 49S 147 56 E
Cradock, Australia 95 E2 32 6S 138 31 E
Cradock, S. Africa 88 E4 32 8S 25 36 E
Craig, U.S.A. 108 F10 40 31N 107 33W
Craigavon, U.K. 12 B5 54 27N 6 23W
Craigmore, Zimbabwe 87 G3 20 28S 32 50 E
Craik, Canada 103 C7 51 3N 105 49W
Crailsheim, Germany 25 F6 49 8N 10 5 E
Craiova, Romania 29 F8 44 21N 23 48 E
Cramsie, Australia 94 C3 23 20S 144 15 E
Cranberry L., U.S.A. 117 B10 44 11N 74 50W
Cranberry Portage,
  Canada 103 C8 54 35N 101 23W
Cranbrook, Australia 93 F2 34 18S 117 33 E
Cranbrook, Canada 102 D5 49 30N 115 46W
Crandon, U.S.A. 112 C10 45 34N 88 54W
Crane, Oreg., U.S.A. 108 E4 43 25N 118 35W
Crane, Tex., U.S.A. 113 K3 31 24N 102 21W
Cranston, U.S.A. 117 E13 41 47N 71 26W
Craon, France 18 E6 47 50N 0 58W
Craonne, France 19 C10 49 27N 3 46 E
Craponne-sur-Arzon,
  France 20 C7 45 19N 3 51 E
Crasna, Romania 29 D12 46 32N 27 51 E
Crasna →, Romania 28 C7 47 44N 22 35 E
Crasnei, Munţii,
  Romania 29 C8 47 0N 23 20 E
Crater L., U.S.A. 108 E2 42 56N 122 6W
Crater Lake △, U.S.A. 108 E2 42 55N 122 10W
Craters of the Moon △,
  U.S.A. 108 E7 43 25N 113 30W
Crateús, Brazil 125 E10 5 10S 40 39W
Crati →, Italy 43 C9 39 43N 16 31 E
Crato, Brazil 125 E11 7 10S 39 25W
Crato, Portugal 37 F3 39 16N 7 39W
Craven, L., Canada 104 B4 54 20N 76 56W
Crawford, U.S.A. 112 D3 42 41N 103 25W
Crawfordsville, U.S.A. 114 E2 40 2N 86 54W
Crawley, U.K. 15 F7 51 7N 0 11W
Crazy Mts., U.S.A. 108 C8 46 12N 110 20W
Crean L., Canada 103 C7 54 5N 106 9W
Crécy-en-Ponthieu,
  France 19 B8 50 15N 1 53 E
Crediton, Canada 116 C3 43 17N 81 33W
Crediton, U.K. 15 G4 50 47N 3 40W
Cree →, Canada 103 B7 58 57N 105 47W
Cree →, U.K. 13 G4 54 55N 4 25W
Cree L., Canada 103 B7 57 30N 106 56W
Creede, U.S.A. 109 H10 37 51N 106 56W
Creekside, U.S.A. 116 F5 40 40N 79 11W
Creel, Mexico 118 B3 27 45N 107 38W
Creemore, Canada 116 B4 44 19N 80 6W
Creighton, Canada 103 C8 54 45N 101 54W
Creighton, U.S.A. 112 D6 42 28N 97 54W
Creil, France 19 C9 49 15N 2 29 E
Crema, Italy 40 C6 45 22N 9 41 E
Cremona, Italy 40 C7 45 7N 10 2 E
Crepaja, Serbia & M. 28 E5 45 1N 20 38 E
Crépy, France 19 C10 49 35N 3 32 E
Crépy-en-Valois, France 19 C9 49 14N 2 54 E
Cres, Croatia 41 D11 44 58N 14 25 E
Crescent City, U.S.A. 108 F1 41 45N 124 12W
Crescentino, Italy 40 C5 45 11N 8 7 E
Crespo, Argentina 126 C3 32 2S 60 19W
Cresson, U.S.A. 116 F6 40 28N 78 36W
Cresta, Mt., Phil. 61 C5 17 17N 122 6 E
Crestline, Calif., U.S.A. 111 L9 34 14N 117 18W
Crestline, Ohio, U.S.A. 116 F2 40 47N 82 44W
Creston, Canada 102 D5 49 10N 116 31W
Creston, Calif., U.S.A. 110 K6 35 32N 120 33W
Creston, Iowa, U.S.A. 112 E7 41 4N 94 22W
Crestview, Calif., U.S.A. 110 H8 37 46N 118 58W
Crestview, Fla., U.S.A. 115 K2 30 46N 86 34W
Crêt de la Neige, France 19 F12 46 16N 5 58 E
Crete = Kríti, Greece 49 D7 35 15N 25 0 E
Crete, U.S.A. 112 E6 40 38N 96 58W
Crete, Sea of, Greece 47 E7 36 0N 25 0 E
Créteil, France 19 D9 48 47N 2 28 E
Creus, C. de, Spain 38 C8 42 20N 3 19 E
Creuse □, France 19 F9 46 10N 2 0 E
Creuse →, France 20 B4 47 0N 0 34 E
Creutzwald, France 19 C13 49 12N 6 42 E
Creuzburg, Germany 24 D6 51 3N 10 14 E
Crèvecœur-le-Grand,
  France 19 C9 49 37N 2 5 E
Crevillente, Spain 39 G4 38 12N 0 48W
Crewe, U.K. 14 D5 53 6N 2 26W
Crewkerne, U.K. 15 G5 50 53N 2 48W
Crianlarich, U.K. 13 E4 56 24N 4 37W
Criciúma, Brazil 127 B6 28 40S 49 23W
Cricova, Moldova 29 C13 47 13N 29 10 E
Crieff, U.K. 13 E5 56 22N 3 50W
Crikvenica, Croatia 41 C11 45 11N 14 40 E
Crimea □, Ukraine 33 K8 45 30N 33 10 E
Crimean Pen. =
  Krymskyy Pivostriv,
  Ukraine 33 K8 45 0N 34 0 E
Crimmitschau, Germany 24 E8 50 48N 12 24 E
Cristuru Secuiesc,
  Romania 29 D10 46 17N 25 2 E
Crişul Alb →, Romania 28 D6 46 42N 21 17 E
Crişul Negru →,
  Romania 28 D6 46 42N 21 16 E
Crişul Repede →,
  Romania 28 D5 46 55N 20 59 E
Criuleni, Moldova 29 C14 47 13N 29 10 E
Crivitz, Germany 24 B7 53 34N 11 39 E
Crna →, Macedonia 44 E5 41 33N 21 59 E
Crna Gora =
  Montenegro □,
  Serbia & M. 44 D3 42 40N 19 20 E
Crna Gora, Macedonia 44 D5 42 10N 21 30 E
Crna Reka = Crna →,
  Macedonia 44 E5 41 33N 21 59 E
Crna Trava, Serbia & M. 44 D6 42 49N 22 19 E
Crni Drim →,
  Macedonia 44 E4 41 17N 20 40 E
Crni Timok →,
  Serbia & M. 44 C6 43 53N 22 15 E
Crnoljeva Planina,
  Serbia & M. 44 D5 42 20N 21 0 E
Črnomelj, Slovenia 41 C12 45 33N 15 10 E
Croagh Patrick, Ireland 12 C2 53 46N 9 40W
Croatia ■, Europe 41 C13 45 20N 16 0 E
Crocker, Banjaran,
  Malaysia 62 C5 5 40N 116 30 E
Crockett, U.S.A. 113 K7 31 19N 95 27W
Crocodile = Krokodil →,
  Mozam. 89 D5 25 14S 32 18 E
Crocodile Is., Australia 94 A1 12 3S 134 58 E
Crocq, France 20 C6 45 52N 2 21 E

Crodo, Italy 40 B5 46 13N 8 19 E
Crohy Hd., Ireland 12 B3 54 55N 8 26W
Croisette, C., France 21 E9 43 14N 5 22 E
Croisic, Pte. du, France 18 E4 47 19N 2 31W
Croix, L. La, Canada 104 C1 48 20N 92 15W
Croker, C., Australia 92 B5 10 58S 132 35 E
Croker, C., Canada 116 B4 44 58N 80 59W
Croker I., Australia 92 B5 11 12S 132 32 E
Cromarty, U.K. 13 D4 57 40N 4 2W
Cromer, U.K. 14 E9 52 56N 1 17 E
Cromwell, N.Z. 91 L2 45 3S 169 14 E
Cromwell, U.S.A. 117 E12 41 36N 72 39W
Cronat, France 19 F10 46 43N 3 40 E
Crook, U.K. 14 C6 54 43N 1 45W
Crooked →, Canada 102 C4 54 50N 122 54W
Crooked →, U.S.A. 108 D3 44 32N 121 16W
Crooked I., Bahamas 121 B5 22 50N 74 10W
Crooked Island Passage,
  Bahamas 121 B5 23 0N 74 30W
Crookston, Minn.,
  U.S.A. 112 B6 47 47N 96 37W
Crookston, Nebr., U.S.A. 112 D4 42 56N 100 45W
Crookwell, Australia 95 E4 34 28S 149 24 E
Cropane-Micone △,
  Italy 43 D9 38 31N 16 18 E
Crosby, U.K. 14 D4 53 30N 3 3W
Crosby, N. Dak., U.S.A. 112 A3 48 55N 103 18W
Crosby, Pa., U.S.A. 116 E6 41 45S 78 23W
Crosbyton, U.S.A. 113 J4 33 40N 101 14W
Crosía, Italy 43 C9 39 35N 16 45 E
Cross →, Nigeria 83 E6 4 42N 8 21 E
Cross City, U.S.A. 115 L4 29 38N 83 7W
Cross Fell, U.K. 14 C5 54 43N 2 28W
Cross L., Canada 103 C9 54 45N 97 30W
Cross Lake, Canada 103 C9 54 37N 97 47W
Cross River □, Nigeria 83 D6 6 0N 8 0 E
Cross River △, Nigeria 83 D6 5 50N 9 50 E
Cross Sound, U.S.A. 100 C6 58 0N 135 0W
Crossett, U.S.A. 113 J9 33 8N 91 58W
Crosshaven, Ireland 12 E3 51 47N 8 17W
Crossville, U.S.A. 115 G3 35 57N 85 2W
Croswell, U.S.A. 116 C2 43 16N 82 37W
Croton-on-Hudson,
  U.S.A. 117 E11 41 12N 73 55W
Crotone, Italy 43 C10 39 5N 17 8 E
Crow →, Canada 102 B4 59 41N 124 20W
Crow Agency, U.S.A. 108 D10 45 36N 107 28W
Crow Hd., Ireland 12 E1 51 35N 10 9W
Crowell, U.S.A. 113 J5 33 59N 99 43W
Crowley, U.S.A. 113 K8 30 13N 92 22W
Crowley, L., U.S.A. 110 H8 37 35N 118 42W
Crown Point, Ind.,
  U.S.A. 114 E2 41 25N 87 22W
Crown Point, N.Y.,
  U.S.A. 117 C11 43 57N 73 26W
Crown Pt., Trin. & Tob. 125 J16 11 18N 60 51W
Crownpoint, U.S.A. 109 J9 35 41N 108 9W
Crows Landing, U.S.A. 110 H5 37 23N 121 6W
Crows Nest, Australia 95 D5 27 16S 152 4 E
Crowsnest Pass, Canada 102 D6 49 40N 114 40W
Croydon, Australia 94 B3 18 13S 142 14 E
Croydon □, U.K. 15 F7 51 22N 0 5W
Crozet, Is., Ind. Oc. 3 G12 46 27S 52 0 E
Crozon, France 18 D2 48 15N 4 30W
Cruz, C., Cuba 120 C4 19 50N 77 50W
Cruz Alta, Brazil 127 B5 28 45S 53 40W
Cruz Bay, U.S. Virgin Is. 121 e 18 20N 64 48W
Cruz de Incio, Spain 36 C3 42 39N 7 21W
Cruz del Eje, Argentina 126 C3 30 45S 64 50W
Cruzeiro, Brazil 127 A7 22 33S 45 0W
Cruzeiro do Oeste,
  Brazil 127 A5 23 46S 53 4W
Cruzeiro do Sul, Brazil 124 E4 7 35S 72 35W
Cry L., Canada 102 B3 58 45N 129 0W
Crystal Bay, U.S.A. 110 F7 39 15N 120 0W
Crystal Brook, Australia 95 E2 33 21S 138 12 E
Crystal City, U.S.A. 113 L5 28 41N 99 50W
Crystal Falls, U.S.A. 114 B1 46 5N 88 20W
Crystal River, U.S.A. 115 L4 28 54N 82 35W
Crystal Springs, U.S.A. 113 K9 31 59N 90 21W
Csenger, Hungary 28 C7 47 50N 22 41 E
Csongrád, Hungary 28 D5 46 43N 20 12 E
Csongrád □, Hungary 28 D5 46 32N 20 15 E
Csorna, Hungary 28 C3 47 38N 17 18 E
Csurgo, Hungary 28 D2 46 16N 17 9 E
Cu Lao Hon, Vietnam 65 G7 10 54N 108 18 E
Cua Rao, Vietnam 64 C5 19 16N 104 27 E
Cuácua →, Mozam. 87 F4 17 54S 37 0 E
Cuamato, Angola 88 B2 17 2S 15 7 E
Cuamba, Mozam. 87 E4 14 45S 36 22 E
Cuando →, Angola 85 H4 17 30S 23 15 E
Cuando Cubango □,
  Angola 88 B3 16 25S 20 0 E
Cuangar, Angola 88 B2 17 36S 18 39 E
Cuango = Kwango →,
  Dem. Rep. of
  the Congo 84 E3 3 14S 17 22 E
Cuanza →, Angola 84 F2 9 21S 13 9 E
Cuarto →, Argentina 126 C3 33 25S 63 2W
Cuatrociénegas, Mexico 118 B4 26 59N 102 5W
Cuauhtémoc, Mexico 118 B3 28 25N 106 52W
Cuba, Portugal 37 G3 38 10N 7 54W
Cuba, N. Mex., U.S.A. 109 J10 36 1N 107 4W
Cuba, N.Y., U.S.A. 116 D6 42 13N 78 17W
Cuba ■, W. Indies 120 B4 22 0N 79 0W
Cubango →, Africa 88 B3 18 50S 22 25 E
Çubuk, Turkey 72 B5 40 14N 33 3 E
Cuc Phuong △, Vietnam 64 B5 20 17N 105 38 E
Cuchumatanes, Sierra de
  los, Guatemala 120 C1 15 35N 91 25W
Cuckfield, U.K. 15 F7 51 1N 0 8W
Cucuí, Brazil 124 C5 1 12N 66 50W
Cucurpe, Mexico 118 A2 30 20N 110 43W
Cúcuta, Colombia 124 B4 7 54N 72 31W
Cudalbi, Romania 29 E12 45 46N 27 41 E
Cuddalore, India 66 P11 11 46N 79 45 E
Cuddapah, India 66 M11 14 30N 78 47 E
Cuddapan, L., Australia 94 D3 25 45S 141 26 E
Cudillero, Spain 36 B4 43 33N 6 9W
Cue, Australia 93 E2 27 25S 117 54 E
Cuéllar, Spain 36 D6 41 23N 4 21W
Cuenca, Ecuador 124 D3 2 50S 79 9W
Cuenca, Spain 38 E2 40 5N 2 10W
Cuenca □, Spain 38 F3 40 0N 2 0W
Cuenca, Serranía de,
  Spain 38 F3 39 55N 1 50W
Cuenca Alta del
  Manzanares △, Spain 36 E7 40 40N 3 55W
Cuerdo del Pozo,
  Embalse de la, Spain 38 D2 41 51N 2 44W
Cuernavaca, Mexico 119 D5 18 55N 99 15W
Cuero, U.S.A. 113 L6 29 6N 97 17W
Cuers, France 21 E10 43 14N 6 5 E
Cueva de la Quebrada
  del Toro △, Venezuela 121 D6 10 46N 69 3W
Cuevas del Almanzora,
  Spain 39 H3 37 18N 1 58W

Cuevo, Bolivia .... **124 H6** 20 15 S 63 30W
Cugir, Romania ...... **29 E8** 45 48N 23 25 E
Cugnaux, France ..... **20 E5** 43 32N 1 20 E
Cuhai-Bakony →,
   Hungary .... **28 C2** 47 35N 17 54 E
Cuiabá, Brazil .... **125 G7** 15 30 S 56 0W
Cuiabá →, Brazil .... **125 G7** 17 5 S 56 36W
Cuijk, Neths. .... **17 C5** 51 44N 5 50 E
Cuilco, Guatemala ... **120 C1** 15 24N 91 58W
Cuillin Hills, U.K. ... **13 D2** 57 13 N 6 15W
Cuillin Sd., U.K. **13 D2** 57 4N 6 20W
Cuito →, Angola ..... **88 B3** 18 1 S 20 48 E
Cuitzeo, L. de, Mexico **118 D4** 19 55N 101 5W
Cujmir, Romania ..... **28 F7** 44 13N 22 57 E
Cukai, Malaysia ...... **65 K4** 4 13N 103 25 E
Culbertson, U.S.A. ... **112 A2** 48 9N 104 31W
Culcairn, Australia ... **95 F4** 35 41 S 147 3 E
Culebra, Isla de,
   Puerto Rico .... **121 d** 18 19N 65 18W
Culebra, Sierra de la,
   Spain **36 D4** 41 55N 6 20W
Culfa, Azerbaijan .... **73 C11** 38 57N 45 38 E
Culgoa →, Australia . **95 D4** 29 56 S 146 20 E
Culgoa Flood Plain △,
   Australia .... **95 D4** 28 58 S 147 5 E
Culiacán, Mexico **118 C3** 24 50N 107 23W
Culiacán →, Mexico .. **118 C3** 24 30N 107 42W
Culik, Indonesia ..... **63 J18** 8 21 S 115 37 E
Culion, Phil. .... **61 F4** 11 54N 119 58 E
Cúllar, Spain **37 H8** 37 35N 2 34W
Cullarin Ra., Australia **95 E4** 34 30 S 149 30 E
Cullen, U.K. **13 D6** 57 42N 2 49W
Cullen Pt., Australia . **94 A3** 11 57 S 141 54 E
Cullera, Spain **39 F4** 39 9N 0 17W
Cullman, U.S.A. **115 H2** 34 11N 86 51W
Cullompton, U.K. **15 G4** 50 51N 3 24W
Culoz, France .... **21 C9** 45 47N 5 46 E
Culpeper, U.S.A. **114 F7** 38 30N 78 0W
Culuene →, Brazil ... **125 F8** 12 56 S 52 51W
Culver, Pt., Australia . **93 F3** 32 54 S 124 43 E
Culverden, N.Z. ..... **91 K4** 42 47 S 172 49 E
Cumaná, Venezuela .. **124 A6** 10 30N 64 5W
Cumaovası, Turkey .. **47 C9** 38 15N 27 9 E
Cumberland, B.C.,
   Canada **102 D4** 49 40N 125 0W
Cumberland, Ont.,
   Canada **117 A9** 45 29N 75 24W
Cumberland, U.S.A. .. **114 F6** 39 39N 78 46W
Cumberland →, U.S.A. **115 G2** 36 15N 87 0W
Cumberland I., U.S.A. **115 G3** 36 57N 84 55W
Cumberland Gap △,
   U.S.A. **115 G4** 36 36N 83 40W
Cumberland Is.,
   Australia .... **94 J7** 20 35 S 149 10 E
Cumberland Island △,
   U.S.A. **115 K5** 30 12N 81 24W
Cumberland L., Canada **103 C8** 54 3N 102 18W
Cumberland Pen.,
   Canada **101 B13** 67 0N 64 0W
Cumberland Plateau,
   U.S.A. **115 H3** 36 0N 85 0W
Cumberland Sd., Canada **101 B13** 65 30N 66 0W
Cumbernauld, U.K. .. **13 F5** 55 57N 3 58W
Cumborah, Australia . **95 D4** 29 40 S 147 45 E
Cumbres de Majalca △,
   Mexico **118 B3** 28 52N 106 24W
Cumbres de
   Monterrey △, Mexico **118 B4** 25 40N 100 35W
Cumbres Mayores,
   Spain **37 G4** 38 4N 6 39W
Cumbria □, U.K. **14 C5** 54 42N 2 52W
Cumbrian Mts., U.K. . **14 C5** 54 30N 3 0W
Cumbum, India ...... **66 M11** 15 40N 79 10 E
Cuminá →, Brazil ... **125 D7** 1 30 S 56 0W
Cummings, Mt., U.S.A. **111 K8** 35 2N 118 34W
Cummins, Australia .. **95 E2** 34 16 S 135 43 E
Cumnock, Australia .. **95 E4** 32 59 S 148 46 E
Cumnock, U.K. **13 F4** 55 28N 4 17W
Cumpas, Mexico **118 B3** 30 0N 109 48W
Cumplida, Pta.,
   Canary Is. **48 F2** 28 50N 17 48W
Çumra, Turkey ...... **72 D5** 37 34N 32 45 E
Cunco, Chile .... **128 D2** 38 55 S 72 2W
Cucumén, Chile ..... **126 C1** 31 53 S 70 38W
Cunderdin, Australia . **93 F2** 31 37 S 117 12 E
Cunene →, Angola .. **88 B1** 17 20 S 11 50 E
Cúneo, Italy .... **40 D4** 44 23N 7 32 E
Çüngüş, Turkey ..... **70 B3** 38 13N 39 17 E
Cunillera, I. = Sa
   Conillera, Spain .... **48 C7** 38 59N 1 13 E
Cunlhat, France ..... **20 C7** 45 38N 3 32 E
Cunnamulla, Australia **95 D4** 28 2 S 145 38 E
Cuorgnè, Italy ...... **40 C4** 45 23N 7 39 E
Cupar, Canada **103 C8** 50 57N 104 10W
Cupar, U.K. **13 E5** 56 19N 3 1W
Cupcini, Moldova .... **29 B12** 48 6N 27 2 E
Cupica, G. de, Colombia **124 B3** 6 25N 77 30W
Čuprija, Serbia & M. .. **44 C5** 43 57N 21 26 E
Curaçao, Neth. Ant. .. **121 D6** 12 10N 69 0W
Curanilahue, Chile ... **126 D1** 37 29 S 73 28W
Curaray →, Peru .... **124 D4** 2 20 S 74 5W
Cure →, France ..... **19 E10** 47 40N 3 41 E
Curepto, Chile ...... **126 D1** 35 8 S 72 1W
Curiapo, Venezuela .. **124 B6** 8 33N 61 5W
Curicó, Chile .... **126 C1** 34 55 S 71 20W
Curinga, Italy .... **43 D9** 38 49N 16 19 E
Curitiba, Brazil ...... **127 B6** 25 20 S 49 10W
Curitibanos, Brazil ... **127 B5** 27 18 S 50 36W
Currabubula, Australia **95 E5** 31 16 S 150 44 E
Currais Novos, Brazil . **125 E11** 6 13 S 36 30W
Curralinho, Brazil .... **125 D9** 1 45 S 49 46W
Currant, U.S.A. **108 G6** 38 51N 115 32W
Currawinya △, Australia **95 D3** 28 55 S 144 27 E
Current →, U.S.A. .. **113 G9** 36 15N 90 55W
Currie, Australia ..... **95 F3** 39 56 S 143 53 E
Currie, U.S.A. **108 F6** 40 16N 114 45W
Curtea de Argeş,
   Romania .... **29 E9** 45 12N 24 42 E
Curtici, Romania .... **28 D6** 46 21N 21 18 E
Curtis, U.S.A. **112 E4** 40 38N 100 31W
Curtis Group, Australia **95 F4** 39 30 S 146 37 E
Curtis I., Australia ... **94 C5** 23 35 S 151 10 E
Curuápanema →, Brazil **125 D7** 2 25 S 55 2W
Curuçá, Brazil .... **125 D9** 0 43 S 47 50W
Curuguaty, Paraguay . **127 A4** 24 31 S 55 42W
Curup, Indonesia ..... **62 E2** 4 26 S 102 13 E
Cururupu, Brazil ..... **125 D10** 1 50 S 44 50W
Curuzú Cuatiá,
   Argentina .... **126 B4** 29 50 S 58 5W
Curvelo, Brazil ...... **125 G10** 18 45 S 44 27W
Cushing, U.S.A. **113 H6** 35 59N 96 46W
Cushing, Mt., Canada **102 B3** 57 35N 126 57W
Cusihuiriáchic, Mexico **118 B3** 28 14N 106 50W
Cusna, Mte., Italy ... **40 D7** 44 17N 10 23 E
Cusset, France ...... **19 F10** 46 8N 3 28 E

Custer, U.S.A. **112 D3** 43 46N 103 36W
Cut Bank, U.S.A. **108 B7** 48 38N 112 20W
Cutchogue, U.S.A. ... **117 E12** 41 1N 72 30W
Cuthbert, U.S.A. **115 K3** 31 46N 84 48W
Cutler, U.S.A. **110 J7** 36 31N 119 17W
Cutro, Italy .... **43 C9** 39 2N 16 59 E
Cuttaburra →, Australia **95 D3** 29 43 S 144 22 E
Cuttack, India .... **67 J14** 20 25N 85 57 E
Cuvier, C., Australia . **93 D1** 23 14 S 113 22 E
Cuvier I., N.Z. ...... **91 G5** 36 27 S 175 50 E
Cuxhaven, Germany . **24 B4** 53 51N 8 41 E
Cuyahoga Falls, U.S.A. **116 E3** 41 8N 81 29W
Cuyahoga Valley △,
   U.S.A. **116 E3** 41 15N 81 33W
Cuyapo, Phil. .... **61 D4** 15 46N 120 46 E
Cuyo, Phil. .... **61 F4** 10 50N 121 5 E
Cuyo East Pass, Phil. . **61 F4** 11 0N 121 0 E
Cuyo West Pass, Phil. **61 F4** 11 0N 120 30 E
Cuyuni →, Guyana .. **124 B7** 6 23N 58 41W
Cuzco, Bolivia ...... **124 H5** 20 0 S 66 50W
Cuzco, Peru .... **124 F4** 13 32 S 72 0W
Čvrsnica, Bos.-H. .... **28 G2** 43 36N 17 35 E
Cwmbran, U.K. **15 F4** 51 39N 3 2W
Cyangugu, Rwanda .. **86 C2** 2 29 S 28 54 E
Cybinka, Poland ..... **31 F1** 52 12N 14 46 E
Cyclades = Kikládhes,
   Greece .... **46 E6** 37 0N 24 30 E
Cygnet, Australia .... **95 G4** 43 8 S 147 1 E
Cynthiana, U.S.A. ... **114 F3** 38 23N 84 18W
Cypress Hills, Canada **103 D7** 49 40N 109 30W
Cypress Hills △, Canada **103 D7** 49 40N 109 30W
Cyprus ■, Asia ..... **49 E12** 35 0N 33 0 E
Cyrenaica, Libya .... **79 C10** 27 0N 23 0 E
Czaplinek, Poland ... **30 E3** 53 34N 16 14 E
Czar, Canada **103 C6** 52 27N 110 50W
Czarna →, Łódzkie,
   Poland .... **31 G6** 51 18N 19 55 E
Czarna →,
   Świętokrzyskie,
   Poland .... **31 H8** 50 28N 21 21 E
Czarna Białostocka,
   Poland .... **31 E10** 53 18N 23 17 E
Czarna Woda, Poland **30 E5** 53 51N 18 6 E
Czarne, Poland ...... **30 E3** 53 42N 16 58 E
Czarnków, Poland ... **31 F3** 52 55N 16 38 E
Czech Rep. ■, Europe **26 B8** 50 0N 15 0 E
Czechowice-Dziedzice,
   Poland .... **31 J5** 49 54N 18 59 E
Czempiń, Poland ..... **31 F3** 52 9N 16 43 E
Czeremcha, Poland .. **31 F10** 52 31N 23 21 E
Czerniejewo, Poland . **31 F4** 52 26N 17 30 E
Czersk, Poland ...... **30 E4** 53 46N 17 58 E
Czerwieńsk, Poland . **31 F2** 52 1N 15 23 E
Czerwionka-Leszczyny,
   Poland .... **31 H5** 50 7N 18 37 E
Częstochowa, Poland **31 H6** 50 49N 19 7 E
Człopa, Poland ...... **31 E3** 53 6N 16 6 E
Człuchów, Poland ... **30 E4** 53 41N 17 22 E
Czyżew-Osada, Poland **31 F9** 52 48N 22 19 E

D

Da →, Vietnam ...... **58 G5** 21 15N 105 20 E
Da Hinggan Ling, China **60 B7** 48 0N 121 0 E
Da Lat, Vietnam ..... **65 G7** 11 56N 108 25 E
Da Nang, Vietnam ... **64 D7** 16 4N 108 13 E
Da Qaidam, China ... **60 C4** 37 50N 95 15 E
Da Yunhe →, China . **57 G11** 34 25N 120 5 E
Da'an, China .... **57 B13** 45 30N 124 7 E
Daan Viljoen △,
   Namibia .... **88 C2** 22 2 S 16 45 E
Dab'a, Ras el, Egypt . **80 H6** 31 3N 28 31 E
Daba Shan, China ... **58 B7** 32 0N 109 0 E
Dabai, Nigeria .... **83 C6** 11 25N 5 15 E
Dabakala, Ivory C. ... **82 D4** 8 15N 4 20W
Dabas, Hungary ..... **28 C4** 47 11N 19 19 E
Dabat, Ethiopia ...... **81 E4** 12 58N 37 41 E
Dabbagh, Jabal,
   Si. Arabia .... **70 E2** 27 52N 35 45 E
Dabhoi, India .... **68 H5** 22 10N 73 20 E
Dąbie, Poland .... **31 F5** 52 5N 18 50 E
Dabie Shan, China ... **59 B10** 31 20N 115 20 E
Dabilda, Cameroon .. **83 C7** 12 45N 14 35 E
Dabnou, Niger ...... **83 C6** 14 10N 5 22 E
Dabo = Pasirkuning,
   Indonesia .... **62 E2** 0 30 S 104 33 E
Dabola, Guinea **82 C2** 10 50N 11 5W
Dabou, Ivory C. **82 D4** 5 20N 4 23W
Daboya, Ghana **83 D4** 9 30N 1 20W
Dabrowa, Belarus ... **31 F10** 52 55N 23 59 E
Dąbrowa Białostocka,
   Poland .... **30 E10** 53 40N 23 21 E
Dąbrowa Górnicza,
   Poland .... **31 H6** 50 15N 19 10 E
Dąbrowa Tarnowska,
   Poland .... **31 H7** 50 10N 20 59 E
Dabu, China .... **59 E11** 24 22N 116 41 E
Dabung, Malaysia ... **65 K4** 5 23N 102 1 E
Dabus →, Ethiopia .. **81 E4** 10 48N 35 10 E
Dacato →, Ethiopia . **81 F5** 7 25N 42 40 E
Dacca = Dhaka, Bangla. **69 H14** 23 43N 90 26 E
Dacca = Dhaka □,
   Bangla. .... **69 G14** 24 25N 90 25 E
Dachau, Germany ... **25 G7** 48 15N 11 26 E
Dachstein, Hoher,
   Austria .... **26 D6** 47 28N 13 35 E
Dačice, Czech Rep. .. **26 B8** 49 5N 15 26 E
Dadanawa, Guyana .. **124 C7** 2 50N 59 30W
Daday, Turkey .... **72 B5** 41 28N 33 27 E
Dade City, U.S.A. ... **115 L4** 28 22N 82 11W
Dadhar, Pakistan .... **68 E2** 29 28N 67 39 E
Dadiya, Nigeria ...... **83 D7** 9 35N 11 24 E
Dadra & Nagar
   Haveli □, India .... **66 J8** 20 5N 73 0 E
Dadri = Charkhi Dadri,
   India .... **68 E7** 28 37N 76 17 E
Dadu, Pakistan ...... **68 F2** 26 45N 67 45 E
Dadu He →, China .. **58 C4** 29 31N 103 46 E
Daet, Phil. .... **61 D5** 14 2N 122 55 E
Dağ, Turkey .... **47 D12** 37 12N 30 31 E
Dagana, Senegal **82 B1** 16 30N 15 35W
Dagash, Sudan ...... **80 D3** 19 19N 33 25 E
Dagestan □, Russia .. **35 J8** 42 30N 47 0 E
Dagestanskiye Ogni,
   Russia .... **35 J9** 42 6N 48 12 E
Daggett, U.S.A. **111 L10** 34 52N 116 52W
Daghestan Republic =
   Dagestan □, Russia . **35 J8** 42 30N 47 0 E
Daghfeli, Sudan ..... **80 D3** 19 18N 32 40 E
Dago = Hiiumaa,
   Estonia .... **9 G20** 58 50N 22 45 E

Dagu, China .... **57 E9** 38 59N 117 40 E
Daguan, China .... **58 D4** 27 43N 103 56 E
Dagupan, Phil. ...... **61 C4** 16 3N 120 20 E
Daguragu, Australia .. **92 C5** 17 33 S 130 30 E
Dahab, Egypt .... **80 B3** 28 31N 34 31 E
Dahlak I., Eritrea .... **81 D5** 15 50N 40 10 E
Dahlak Kebir, Eritrea **81 D5** 15 50N 40 10 E
Dahlenburg, Germany **24 B6** 53 11N 10 44 E
Dahlonega, U.S.A. ... **115 H4** 34 32N 83 59W
Dahme, Germany .... **24 D9** 51 52N 13 25 E
Dahod, India .... **68 H6** 22 50N 74 15 E
Dahong Shan, China . **59 B9** 31 25N 113 0 E
Dahra, Senegal **82 B1** 15 22N 15 30W
Dahshūr, Egypt ..... **80 J7** 29 55N 31 14 E
Dahūk, Iraq .... **70 B3** 36 50N 43 1 E
Dai Hao, Vietnam ... **64 C6** 18 1N 106 25 E
Dai-Sen, Japan ...... **55 G6** 35 22N 133 32 E
Dai Shan, China ..... **59 B14** 30 25N 122 10 E
Dai Xian, China ..... **56 E7** 39 4N 112 58 E
Daicheng, China ..... **56 E9** 38 42N 116 38 E
Daimiel, Spain **37 F7** 39 5N 3 35W
Daingean, Ireland **12 C4** 53 18N 7 17W
Dainkog, China ...... **58 A1** 32 30N 97 58 E
Daintree, Australia .. **94 B4** 16 20 S 145 20 E
Daintree →, Australia **94 B4** 16 8 S 145 2 E
Daiō-Misaki, Japan .. **55 G8** 34 15N 136 45 E
Dair, J. ed, Sudan ... **81 E3** 12 27N 30 42 E
Dairût, Egypt .... **80 B3** 27 34N 30 43 E
Daisen-Oki △, Japan . **55 G6** 35 23N 133 34 E
Daisetsu-Zan △, Japan **54 C11** 43 30N 142 57 E
Daisetsu-Zan △, Japan **54 C11** 43 30N 142 55 E
Dajarra, Australia ... **94 C2** 21 42 S 139 30 E
Dajin Chuan →, China **58 B3** 31 16N 101 59 E
Dak Dam, Cambodia . **64 F6** 12 20N 107 21 E
Dak Nhe, Vietnam ... **64 E6** 15 28N 107 48 E
Dak Pek, Vietnam ... **64 E6** 15 4N 107 44 E
Dak Song, Vietnam .. **65 F6** 12 19N 107 35 E
Dak Sui, Vietnam .... **64 E6** 14 55N 107 43 E
Dakar, Senegal **82 C1** 14 34N 17 29W
Dakhla, W. Sahara ... **78 D2** 23 50N 15 53W
Dakhla, El Wâhât el-,
   Egypt .... **80 B2** 25 30N 28 50 E
Dakingari, Nigeria ... **83 C5** 11 37N 4 1 E
Dakor, India .... **68 H5** 22 45N 73 11 E
Dakoro, Niger .... **83 C6** 14 31N 6 46 E
Dakota City, U.S.A. . **112 D6** 42 25N 96 25W
Dakovica, Serbia & M. **44 D4** 42 22N 20 26 E
Đakovo, Croatia ..... **28 E3** 45 19N 18 24 E
Dalaba, Guinea **82 C2** 10 47N 12 12W
Dalachi, China ...... **56 F3** 36 48N 105 0 E
Dalai Nur, China .... **56 C9** 43 20N 116 45 E
Dāläki, Iran .... **71 D6** 29 26N 51 17 E
Dalälven →, Sweden **10 D10** 60 12N 16 43 E
Dalaman, Turkey .... **47 E10** 36 41N 28 43 E
Dalaman →, Turkey . **47 E10** 36 41N 28 43 E
Dalandzadgad,
   Mongolia .... **56 C3** 43 27N 104 30 E
Dalap-Uliga-Darrit,
   Marshall Is. .... **96 G9** 7 7N 171 24 E
Dalarna, Sweden .... **10 D8** 61 0N 14 0 E
Dalarnas län □, Sweden **10 C8** 61 0N 14 15 E
Đälbandīn, Pakistan . **66 E4** 29 0N 64 23 E
Dalbeattie, U.K. **13 G5** 54 56N 3 50W
Dalbeg, Australia .... **94 C4** 20 16 S 147 18 E
Dalbosjön, Sweden .. **11 F6** 58 40N 12 45 E
Dalby, Australia ..... **95 D5** 27 10 S 151 17 E
Dalby, Sweden ...... **11 J7** 55 40N 13 22 E
Dalby Söderskog △,
   Sweden .... **11 J7** 55 41N 13 21 E
Dale, U.S.A. **114 F7** 38 38N 77 18W
Dale Hollow L., U.S.A. **115 G3** 36 32N 85 27W
Dalga, Egypt .... **80 B3** 27 39N 30 41 E
Dalgán, Iran .... **71 E8** 27 31N 59 19 E
Dalhart, U.S.A. **113 G3** 36 4N 102 31W
Dalhousie, Canada .. **105 C6** 48 5N 66 26W
Dalhousie, India .... **68 C6** 32 38N 75 58 E
Dali, Shaanxi, China . **56 G5** 34 48N 109 58 E
Dali, Yunnan, China . **58 E3** 25 40N 100 10 E
Dalian, China .... **57 E11** 38 50N 121 40 E
Daliang Shan, China . **58 D4** 28 0N 102 45 E
Daling He →, China . **57 D11** 40 55N 121 40 E
Dāliyat el Karmel, Israel **74 C4** 32 43N 35 2 E
Dalj, Croatia .... **28 E3** 45 29N 18 59 E
Dalkeith, U.K. **13 F5** 55 54N 3 4W
Dallas, Oreg., U.S.A. . **108 D2** 44 55N 123 19W
Dallas, Tex., U.S.A. .. **113 J6** 32 47N 96 49W
Dallol, Ethiopia ..... **81 E5** 14 14N 40 17 E
Dalmā, U.A.E. ...... **71 E7** 24 30N 52 20 E
Dalmacija, Croatia ... **41 E13** 43 20N 17 0 E
Dalmas, L., Canada .. **105 B5** 53 30N 71 50W
Dalmatia = Dalmacija,
   Croatia .... **41 E13** 43 20N 17 0 E
Dalmau, India .... **69 F9** 26 4N 81 2 E
Dalmellington, U.K. . **13 F4** 55 19N 4 23W
Dalnegorsk, Russia .. **53 E14** 44 32N 135 33 E
Dalnerechensk, Russia **53 E14** 45 50N 133 40 E
Dalnovostochnyy □,
   Russia .... **53 C14** 67 0N 140 0 E
Daloa, Ivory C. **82 D3** 7 0N 6 30W
Dalou Shan, China ... **58 C6** 28 0N 106 0 E
Dalry, U.K. **13 F4** 55 42N 4 43W
Dalrymple, L., Australia **94 C4** 20 40 S 147 0 E
Dalrymple, Mt.,
   Australia .... **94 K6** 21 1 S 148 39 E
Dals Långed, Sweden **11 F6** 58 56N 12 18 E
Dalsjöfors, Sweden .. **11 G7** 57 46N 13 5 E
Dalsland, Sweden ... **11 F6** 58 50N 12 15 E
Daltenganj, India .... **69 H11** 24 0N 84 4 E
Dalton, Ga., U.S.A. .. **115 H3** 34 46N 84 58W
Dalton, Mass., U.S.A. **117 D11** 42 28N 73 11W
Dalton, Nebr., U.S.A. **112 E3** 41 25N 102 58W
Dalton-in-Furness, U.K. **14 C4** 54 10N 3 11W
Dalupiri I., Phil. ..... **61 B4** 19 5N 121 12 E
Dalvík, Iceland **8 D4** 65 58N 18 32W
Dálvvadis = Jokkmokk,
   Sweden .... **8 C18** 66 35N 19 50 E
Dalwallinu, Australia . **93 F2** 30 17 S 116 40 E
Daly →, Australia ... **92 B5** 13 35 S 130 19 E
Daly City, U.S.A. **110 H4** 37 42N 122 28W
Daly L., Canada **103 B7** 56 32N 105 39W
Daly River, Australia . **92 B5** 13 46 S 130 42 E
Daly Waters, Australia **94 B1** 16 15 S 133 24 E
Dalyan, Turkey ...... **47 E10** 36 50N 28 39 E
Dam Doi, Vietnam .. **64 B6** 21 21N 107 36 E
Damachova, Belarus . **31 G10** 51 45N 24 32 E
Daman, India .... **66 J8** 20 25N 72 57 E
Dāmaneh, Iran ...... **71 C6** 33 1N 50 29 E
Damanhûr, Egypt ... **80 H7** 31 0N 30 30 E
Damant L., Canada .. **103 A7** 61 45N 105 5W
Damanzhuang, China **56 E9** 38 5N 116 35 E
Damar, Indonesia .... **63 F7** 7 7 S 128 40 E
Damaraland, Namibia **88 C2** 20 0 S 15 0 E
Damascus = Dimashq,
   Syria .... **74 B5** 33 30N 36 18 E
Damaturu, Nigeria ... **83 C7** 11 45N 11 55 E
Damāvand, Iran ..... **71 C7** 35 47N 52 0 E

Damāvand, Qolleh-ye,
   Iran .... **71 C7** 35 56N 52 10 E
Damba, Angola ...... **84 F3** 6 44 S 15 20 E
Dâmboviţa →, Romania **29 F10** 45 0N 25 30 E
Dâmboviţa □, Romania **29 F11** 44 12N 26 26 E
Dâmbovnic →,
   Romania .... **29 F10** 44 28N 25 18 E
Dame Marie, Haiti ... **121 C5** 18 36N 74 26W
Dāmghān, Iran ...... **71 B7** 36 10N 54 17 E
Dāmienesti, Romania **29 D11** 46 44N 26 59 E
Damietta = Dumyât,
   Egypt .... **80 H7** 31 24N 31 48 E
Daming, China ...... **56 F8** 36 15N 115 6 E
Damīr Qābū, Syria .. **70 B4** 36 58N 41 51 E
Dammam = Ad
   Dammām, Si. Arabia **71 E6** 26 20N 50 5 E
Dammarie-les-Lys,
   France .... **19 D9** 48 31N 2 39 E
Dammartin-en-Goële,
   France .... **19 C9** 49 3N 2 41 E
Damme, Germany ... **24 C4** 52 32N 8 11 E
Damoh, India .... **69 H8** 23 50N 79 28 E
Damodar →, India .. **69 H12** 23 17N 87 35 E
Dampier, Australia .. **92 D2** 20 41 S 116 42 E
Dampier, Selat,
   Indonesia .... **63 E8** 0 40 S 131 0 E
Dampier Arch.,
   Australia .... **92 D2** 20 38 S 116 32 E
Damrei, Chuor Phnum,
   Cambodia .... **65 G4** 11 30N 103 0 E
Damville, France .... **19 C12** 49 20N 5 21 E
Dan-Gulbi, Nigeria .. **83 C6** 11 40N 6 15 E
Dan Xian, China .... **64 C7** 19 31N 109 33 E
Dana, Indonesia ..... **63 F6** 11 0 S 122 52 E
Dana, L., Canada **104 B4** 50 53N 77 20W
Dana, Mt., U.S.A. ... **110 H7** 37 54N 119 12W
Danakil Desert,
   Ethiopia .... **81 E5** 12 45N 41 0 E
Danané, Ivory C. **82 D3** 7 16N 8 9W
Danao, Phil. .... **61 F6** 10 31N 124 1 E
Danau Poso, Indonesia **63 E6** 1 52 S 120 35 E
Danba, China .... **58 B3** 30 54N 101 48 E
Danbury, U.S.A. **117 E11** 41 24N 73 28W
Danby L., U.S.A. **109 J6** 34 13N 115 5W
Dand, Afghan. ...... **68 D1** 31 28N 65 32 E
Dandeldhura, Nepal . **69 E9** 29 20N 80 35 E
Dandeli, India .... **66 M9** 15 5N 74 30 E
Dandenong, Australia **95 F4** 38 0 S 145 15 E
Dandīl, Egypt .... **80 J7** 29 10N 31 2 E
Dandong, China ..... **57 D13** 40 10N 124 20 E
Danfeng, China ..... **56 H6** 33 45N 110 25 E
Dangan Liedao, China **59 F10** 22 0N 114 8 E
Dangé-St-Romain,
   France .... **20 B4** 46 56N 0 36 E
Dăngeni, Romania ... **29 C11** 47 51N 26 58 E
Danger Is. = Pukapuka,
   Cook Is. .... **97 J11** 10 53 S 165 49W
Danger Pt., S. Africa . **88 E2** 34 40 S 19 17 E
Danginpuri, Indonesia **63 K18** 8 40 S 115 13 E
Dangla, Ethiopia .... **81 E4** 11 18N 36 56 E
Dangla Shan = Tanggula
   Shan, China .... **60 C4** 32 40N 92 10 E
Dangora, Nigeria .... **83 C6** 11 30N 8 7 E
Dangrek, Phnom,
   Thailand .... **64 E5** 14 15N 105 0 E
Dangriga, Belize **119 D7** 17 0N 88 13W
Dangshan, China .... **56 G9** 34 27N 116 22 E
Dangtu, China ...... **59 B12** 31 32N 118 25 E
Dangyang, China .... **59 B8** 30 52N 111 44 E
Dani, Burkina Faso .. **83 C4** 13 43N 0 10W
Daniel, U.S.A. **108 E8** 42 52N 110 4W
Daniel's Harbour,
   Canada **105 B8** 50 13N 57 35W
Danielskuil, S. Africa **88 D3** 28 11 S 23 33 E
Danielson, U.S.A. ... **117 E13** 41 48N 71 53W
Danilov, Russia ..... **32 C11** 58 16N 40 13 E
Danilovgrad,
   Serbia & M. .... **44 D3** 42 38N 19 4 E
Danilovka, Russia ... **34 E7** 50 25N 44 12 E
Daning, China ...... **56 F6** 36 28N 110 45 E
Danja, Nigeria ...... **83 C6** 11 21N 7 30 E
Danjiangkou, China . **59 A8** 32 31N 111 30 E
Danjiangkou Shuiku,
   China .... **59 A8** 32 37N 111 30 E
Dank, Oman .... **71 F8** 23 33N 56 16 E
Dankalwa, Nigeria ... **83 C7** 11 52N 12 12 E
Dankama, Nigeria ... **83 C6** 13 20N 7 44 E
Dankhar Gompa, India **66 C11** 32 10N 78 10 E
Dankov, Russia ..... **32 F10** 53 20N 39 5 E
Danleng, China ..... **58 B4** 30 1N 103 31 E
Danlí, Honduras **120 D2** 14 4N 86 35W
Dannemora, U.S.A. . **117 B11** 44 43N 73 44W
Dannenberg, Germany **24 B7** 53 6N 11 5 E
Dannevirke, N.Z. .... **91 J6** 40 12 S 176 8 E
Dannhauser, S. Africa **89 D5** 28 0 S 30 3 E
Dansville, U.S.A. **116 D7** 42 34N 77 42W
Dantan, India .... **69 J12** 21 57N 87 20 E
Dante = Dunărea →,
   Europe .... **29 E14** 45 20N 29 40 E
Danvers, U.S.A. **117 D14** 42 34N 70 56W
Danville, Ill., U.S.A. . **114 E2** 40 8N 87 37W
Danville, Ky., U.S.A. **114 G3** 37 39N 84 46W
Danville, Pa., U.S.A. . **114 F8** 40 58N 76 37W
Danville, Va., U.S.A. . **115 G6** 36 36N 79 23W
Danville, Vt., U.S.A. . **117 B12** 44 25N 72 9W
Danyang, China ..... **59 B12** 32 0N 119 31 E
Danzhai, China ...... **58 D6** 26 11N 107 48 E
Danzig = Gdańsk,
   Poland .... **30 D5** 54 22N 18 40 E
Dao Xian, China ..... **59 E8** 25 36N 111 31 E
Daocheng, China .... **58 C3** 29 10N 100 10 E
Daoukro, Ivory C. ... **82 D4** 7 10N 3 58W
Dapaong, Togo ...... **83 C5** 12 10N 1 31 E
Dapchi, Nigeria ..... **83 C7** 12 30N 11 31 E
Dapitan, Phil. .... **61 G5** 8 30N 123 30 E
Daqing Shan, China . **56 D6** 40 40N 111 0 E
Daqu Shan, China ... **59 B14** 30 25N 122 20 E
Dar Banda, Africa ... **76 F6** 8 0N 23 0 E
Dar el Beida =
   Casablanca, Morocco **78 B4** 33 36N 7 36W
Dar es Salaam, Tanzania **86 D4** 6 50 S 39 12 E
Dar Mazār, Iran ..... **71 D8** 29 14N 57 20 E
Dar'ā, Syria .... **74 C5** 32 36N 36 7 E
Dar'ā □, Syria ...... **74 C5** 32 55N 36 10 E
Dārāb, Iran .... **71 D7** 28 50N 54 30 E
Daraban, Pakistan ... **68 D4** 31 44N 70 20 E
Dărăbani, Romania .. **29 B11** 48 10N 26 39 E
Daraina, Madag. .... **89 A8** 13 12 S 49 40 E
Daraj, Libya .... **79 B8** 30 10N 10 28 E
Daravica, Serbia & M. **44 D4** 42 32N 20 8 E
Daraw, Egypt .... **80 C3** 24 22N 32 51 E

Dārayyā, Syria ...... **74 B5** 33 28N 36 15 E
Darazo, Nigeria ..... **83 C7** 11 1N 10 24 E
Darband, Pakistan ... **68 B5** 34 20N 72 50 E
Darband, Kūh-e, Iran **71 D8** 31 34N 57 8 E
Darbhanga, India ... **69 F11** 26 15N 85 55 E
D'Arcy, Canada **102 C4** 50 27N 122 35W
Darda, Croatia ...... **28 E3** 45 40N 18 41 E
Dardanelle, Ark., U.S.A. **113 H8** 35 13N 93 9W
Dardanelle, Calif.,
   U.S.A. **110 G7** 38 20N 119 50W
Dardanelles =
   Çanakkale Boğazı,
   Turkey .... **45 F10** 40 17N 26 32 E
Dare →, Ethiopia ... **81 F5** 7 20N 42 11 E
Darende, Turkey .... **72 C7** 38 31N 37 30 E
Dārestān, Iran ...... **71 D8** 29 9N 58 42 E
Darfo, Italy .... **40 C7** 45 53N 10 11 E
Dârfûr, Sudan .... **79 F10** 13 40N 24 0 E
Dargai, Pakistan .... **68 B4** 34 25N 71 55 E
Dargan Ata,
   Turkmenistan ..... **52 E7** 40 29N 62 10 E
Dargaville, N.Z. ..... **91 F4** 35 57 S 173 52 E
Dargol, Niger .... **83 C5** 13 54N 1 22 E
Darhan, Mongolia ... **60 B5** 49 37N 106 21 E
Darhan Muminggan
   Lianheqi, China .... **56 D6** 41 40N 110 28 E
Dari, Sudan .... **81 F3** 5 48N 30 26 E
Darıca, Turkey ...... **72 B3** 40 45N 29 23 E
Darién, G. del, Panama **120 E4** 7 36N 77 57W
Darién, G. del,
   Colombia **124 B3** 9 0N 77 0W
Dariganga = Ovoot,
   Mongolia .... **56 B7** 45 21N 113 45 E
Darinskoye, Kazakhstan **34 E10** 51 20N 51 44 E
Darjeeling = Darjiling,
   India .... **69 F13** 27 3N 88 18 E
Darjiling, India ...... **69 F13** 27 3N 88 18 E
Darkan, Australia .... **93 F2** 33 20 S 116 43 E
Darkhana, Pakistan . **68 D5** 30 39N 72 11 E
Darkhazīneh, Iran ... **71 D6** 31 54N 48 39 E
Darkot Pass, Pakistan **69 A5** 36 45N 73 26 E
Darling →, Australia **95 E3** 34 4 S 141 54 E
Darling Downs,
   Australia .... **95 D5** 27 30 S 150 30 E
Darling Ra., Australia **93 F2** 32 30 S 116 0 E
Darlington, U.K. **14 C6** 54 32N 1 33W
Darlington, U.S.A. .. **115 H6** 34 18N 79 52W
Darlington □, U.K. .. **14 C6** 54 32N 1 33W
Darlington, L., S. Africa **88 E4** 33 10 S 25 9 E
Darlot, L., Australia . **93 E3** 27 48 S 121 35 E
Darłowo, Poland .... **30 D3** 54 25N 16 25 E
Dărmăneşti, Bacău,
   Romania .... **29 D11** 46 21N 26 33 E
Dărmăneşti, Suceava,
   Romania .... **29 C11** 47 44N 26 9 E
Darmstadt, Germany **25 F4** 49 51N 8 39 E
Darnah, Libya .... **79 B10** 32 45N 22 45 E
Darnall, S. Africa .... **89 D5** 29 23 S 31 18 E
Darney, France ...... **19 D13** 48 5N 6 2 E
Darnley, C., Antarctica **5 C6** 68 0 S 69 0 E
Darnley B., Canada .. **100 B7** 69 30N 123 30W
Daroca, Spain **38 D3** 41 9N 1 25W
Darou-Mousti, Senegal **82 B1** 15 3N 16 3W
Darr →, Australia ... **94 C3** 23 39 S 143 50 E
Darra Pezu, Pakistan **68 C4** 32 19N 70 44 E
Darreqeira, Argentina **126 D3** 37 42 S 63 10W
Darrington, U.S.A. .. **108 B3** 48 15N 121 36W
Darsser Ort, Germany **24 A8** 54 28N 12 32 E
Dart →, U.K. **15 G4** 50 24N 3 39W
Dart, C., Antarctica . **5 D14** 73 6 S 126 20W
Dartford, U.K. ...... **15 F8** 51 26N 0 13 E
Dartmoor, U.K. **15 G4** 50 38N 3 57W
Dartmoor △, U.K. ... **15 G4** 50 37N 3 59W
Dartmouth, Canada . **105 D7** 44 40N 63 30W
Dartmouth, U.K. **15 G4** 50 21N 3 36W
Dartmouth Res.,
   Australia .... **95 D4** 26 4 S 145 18 E
Dartuch, C. = Artrutx,
   C. de, Spain .... **48 B10** 39 55N 3 49 E
Daruvar, Croatia .... **28 E2** 45 35N 17 14 E
Darvaza, Turkmenistan **52 E6** 40 11N 58 24 E
Darvel, Teluk = Lahad
   Datu, Teluk, Malaysia **63 D5** 4 50N 118 20 E
Darwen, U.K. **14 D5** 53 42N 2 29W
Darwendale, Zimbabwe **89 B5** 17 41 S 30 33 E
Darwha, India .... **66 J10** 20 15N 77 45 E
Darwin, Australia ... **92 B5** 12 25 S 130 51 E
Darwin, U.S.A. **111 J9** 36 15N 117 35W
Darya Khan, Pakistan **68 D4** 31 48N 71 6 E
Daryoi Amu =
   Amudarya →,
   Uzbekistan .... **52 E6** 43 58N 59 34 E
Dās, U.A.E. .... **71 E7** 25 20N 53 30 E
Dashen, Ras, Ethiopia **81 E4** 13 8N 38 26 E
Dashetai, China ..... **56 D5** 41 0N 109 5 E
Dashhowuz,
   Turkmenistan ..... **52 E6** 41 49N 59 58 E
Dashköpri,
   Turkmenistan ..... **71 B9** 36 16N 62 8 E
Dasht, Iran .... **71 B8** 37 17N 56 7 E
Dasht →, Pakistan .. **66 G2** 25 10N 61 40 E
Daska, Pakistan ..... **68 C6** 32 20N 74 20 E
Daşkäsän, Azerbaijan **35 K7** 40 25N 46 0 E
Dassa, Benin .... **83 D5** 7 46N 2 14 E
Dasuya, India .... **68 D6** 31 49N 75 38 E
Datça, Turkey .... **47 E9** 36 46N 27 40 E
Datia, India .... **69 G8** 25 39N 78 27 E
Datian, China .... **59 E11** 25 40N 117 50 E
Datong, Shanxi, China **56 D7** 40 6N 113 18 E
Dattakhel, Pakistan . **68 C3** 32 54N 69 46 E
Datteln, Germany ... **24 D3** 51 39N 7 21 E
Datu, Tanjung,
   Indonesia .... **62 D3** 2 5N 109 39 E
Datu Piang, Phil. .... **61 H6** 7 2N 124 30 E
Datuk, Tanjong = Datu,
   Tanjung, Indonesia . **62 D3** 2 5N 109 39 E
Daua = Dawa →, Africa **81 G5** 4 11N 42 6 E
Daud Khel, Pakistan . **68 C4** 32 53N 71 34 E
Daudnagar, India .... **69 G11** 25 2N 84 24 E
Daugava →, Latvia . **9 H21** 57 4N 24 3 E
Daugavpils, Latvia .. **9 J22** 55 53N 26 32 E
Daulpur, India ...... **68 F7** 26 45N 77 59 E
Daun, Germany ...... **25 E2** 50 11N 6 50 E
Dauphin, Canada **103 C8** 51 9N 100 5W
Dauphin, U.S.A. **116 F8** 40 22N 76 56W
Dauphin L., Canada . **103 C9** 51 20N 99 45W
Dauphiné, France ... **21 C9** 45 15N 5 25 E
Daura, Borno, Nigeria **83 C7** 11 31N 11 24 E
Daura, Katsina, Nigeria **83 C6** 13 2N 8 21 E
Dăvăci, Azerbaijan .. **35 K9** 41 15N 48 57 E
Davangere, India .... **66 M9** 14 25N 75 55 E
Davao, Phil. .... **61 H6** 7 0N 125 40 E
Davao G., Phil. ..... **61 H6** 6 30N 125 48 E

Dāvar Panāh = Sarāvān,
  Iran .... 71 E9 27 25N 62 15 E
Davenport, Calif.,
  U.S.A. 110 H4 37 1N 122 12W
Davenport, Iowa, U.S.A. 112 E9 41 32N 90 35W
Davenport, Wash.,
  U.S.A. 108 C4 47 39N 118 9W
Davenport Ra.,
  Australia .... 94 C1 20 28 S 134 0 E
Daventry, U.K. 15 E6 52 16N 1 10W
David, Panama 120 E3 8 30N 82 30W
David City, U.S.A. .. 112 E6 41 15N 97 8W
David Gorodok =
  Davyd Haradok,
  Belarus .... 33 F4 52 4N 27 8 E
Davidson, Canada 103 C7 51 16N 105 59W
Davis, Antarctica ... 5 C6 68 34 S 77 55 E
Davis, Calif., U.S.A. 110 G5 38 33N 121 44W
Davis Dam, U.S.A. ... 111 K12 35 11N 114 34W
Davis Inlet, Canada . 105 A7 55 50N 60 59W
Davis Mts., U.S.A. .. 113 K2 30 50N 103 55W
Davis Sea, Antarctica 5 C7 66 0 S 92 0 E
Davis Str., N. Amer. . 101 B14 65 0N 58 0W
Davo →, Ivory C. 82 D3   5 0N   6 10W
Davos, Switz. .... 25 J5 46 48N   9 49 E
Davutlar, Turkey .... 47 D9 37 43N 27 17 E
Davy L., Canada 103 B7 58 53N 108 18W
Davyd Haradok, Belarus 33 F4 52 4N 27 8 E
Dawa →, Africa ...... 81 G5   4 11N 42 6 E
Dawaki, Bauchi, Nigeria 83 D6   9 25N   9 33 E
Dawaki, Kano, Nigeria 83 C6 12 5N   8 23 E
Dawei = Tavoy, Burma 64 E2 14 2N 98 12 E
Dawes Ra., Australia 94 C5 24 40 S 150 40 E
Dawlish, U.K. 15 G4 50 35N   3 28W
Dawna Ra., Burma ... 64 D2 16 30N 98 30 E
Dawros Hd., Ireland . 12 B3 54 50N   8 33W
Dawson, Canada 100 B6 64 10N 139 30W
Dawson, U.S.A. 115 K3 31 46N 84 27W
Dawson, I., Chile ... 128 G2 53 50 S 70 50W
Dawson B., Canada .. 103 C8 52 53N 100 49W
Dawson Creek, Canada 102 B4 55 45N 120 15W
Dawson Inlet, Canada 103 A10 61 50N 93 25W
Dawson Ra., Australia 94 C4 24 30 S 149 48 E
Dawu, Hubei, China . 59 B9 31 34N 114 7 E
Dawu, Sichuan, China 58 B3 30 55N 101 10 E
Dax, France 20 E2 43 44N   1 3W
Daxian, China .... 58 B6 31 15N 107 23 E
Daxin, China .... 58 F6 22 50N 107 11 E
Daxindian, China .... 57 F11 37 30N 120 50 E
Daxinggou, China ... 57 C15 43 25N 129 40 E
Daxue Shan, Sichuan,
  China .... 58 B3 30 30N 101 30 E
Daxue Shan, Yunnan,
  China .... 58 F2 23 42N 99 48 E
Dayao, China .... 58 E3 25 43N 101 20 E
Daye, China .... 59 B10 30 6N 114 58 E
Dayet en Naharat, Mali 82 B4 17 39N   3 10W
Dayi, China .... 58 B4 30 41N 103 29 E
Daylesford, Australia 95 F3 37 21 S 144 9 E
Dayong, China ...... 59 C8 29 11N 110 30 E
Dayr az Zawr, Syria . 70 C4 35 20N 40 5 E
Daysland, Canada ... 102 C6 52 50N 112 20W
Dayton, Nev., U.S.A. 110 F7 39 14N 119 36W
Dayton, Ohio, U.S.A. 114 F3 39 45N 84 12W
Dayton, Pa., U.S.A. . 116 F5 40 53N 79 15W
Dayton, Tenn., U.S.A. 115 H3 35 30N 85 1W
Dayton, Wash., U.S.A. 108 C4 46 19N 117 59W
Dayton, Wyo., U.S.A. 108 D10 44 53N 107 16W
Daytona Beach, U.S.A. 115 L5 29 13N 81 1W
Dayu, China .... 59 E10 25 24N 114 22 E
Dayville, U.S.A. 108 D4 44 28N 119 32W
Dazhu, China .... 58 B6 30 41N 107 15 E
Dazkırı, Turkey ..... 47 D11 37 57N 29 52 E
Dazu, China .... 58 C5 29 40N 105 42 E
De Aar, S. Africa .... 88 E3 30 39 S 24 0 E
De Biesbosch △, Neths. 17 C4 51 45N   4 48 E
De Funiak Springs,
  U.S.A. 115 K2 30 43N 86 7W
De Grey →, Australia 92 D2 20 12 S 119 13 E
De Haan, Belgium ... 17 C3 51 16N   3 2 E
De Hoge Veluwe △,
  Neths. .... 17 B5 52 5N   5 46 E
De Hoop △, S. Africa 88 E3 34 30 S 20 28 E
De Kalb, U.S.A. 112 E10 41 56N 88 46W
De Kennemerduinen △,
  Neths. .... 17 B4 52 27N   4 33 E
De Land, U.S.A. 115 L5 29 2N 81 18W
De Leon, U.S.A. 113 J5 32 7N 98 32W
De Panne, Belgium .. 17 C2 51 6N   2 34 E
De Pere, U.S.A. 114 C1 44 27N 88 4W
De Queen, U.S.A. ... 113 H7 34 2N 94 21W
De Quincy, U.S.A. .. 113 K8 30 27N 93 26W
De Ridder, U.S.A. ... 113 K8 30 51N 93 17W
De Smet, U.S.A. 112 C6 44 23N 97 33W
De Soto, U.S.A. 112 F9 38 8N 90 34W
De Tour Village, U.S.A. 114 C4 46 0N 83 56W
De Witt, U.S.A. 113 H9 34 18N 91 20W
Dead Sea, Asia ...... 74 D4 31 30N 35 30 E
Deadwood, U.S.A. ... 112 C3 44 23N 103 44W
Deadwood L., Canada 102 B3 59 10N 128 30W
Deal, U.K. .... 15 F9 51 13N   1 25 E
Deal I., Australia .... 95 F4 39 30 S 147 20 E
Dealesville, S. Africa . 88 D4 28 41 S 25 4 E
De'an, China .... 59 C10 29 21N 115 46 E
Dean →, Canada 102 C3 52 49N 126 58W
Dean, Forest of, U.K. 15 F5 51 45N   2 33W
Dean Chan., Canada . 102 C3 52 30N 127 15W
Deán Funes, Argentina 126 C3 30 20 S 64 20W
Dease →, Canada 102 B3 59 56N 128 32W
Dease L., Canada 102 B2 58 40N 130 5W
Dease Lake, Canada .. 102 B2 58 25N 130 6W
Death Valley, U.S.A. . 111 J10 36 15N 116 50W
Death Valley △, U.S.A. 111 J10 36 45N 117 15W
Death Valley Junction,
  U.S.A. 111 J10 36 20N 116 25W
Deauville, France .... 18 C7 49 23N   0 2 E
Deba, Spain 38 B2 43 18N   2 21W
Debaltsevo, Ukraine . 33 H10 48 22N 38 26 E
Debar, Macedonia ... 44 E4 41 31N 20 30 E
Debark, Ethiopia .... 81 E4 13 1N 37 48 E
Debre Sina, Ethiopia 81 F4 11 20N 37 25 E
Debre Tabor, Ethiopia 81 E4 11 50N 38 26 E
Debre Zebit, Ethiopia 81 E4 11 48N 38 30 E
Debre Zevit, Ethiopia 81 F4   8 50N 39 0 E
Debrecen, Hungary .. 28 C6 47 33N 21 42 E
Debrno, Poland ...... 30 D6 53 31N 17 14 E
Dečani, Serbia & M. . 44 D4 42 30N 20 18 E
Dechang, China ...... 58 D4 27 25N 102 11 E
Dechhu, India .... 68 F5 26 46N 72 20 E
Děčín, Czech Rep. ... 26 A7 50 47N 14 12 E
Decize, France ...... 19 F10 46 50N   3 28 E
Deckerville, U.S.A. .. 116 C2 43 32N 82 44W
Decollatura, Italy ... 43 C9 39 3N 16 21 E
Decorah, U.S.A. 112 D9 43 18N 91 48W
Deda, Romania ...... 29 D9 46 56N 24 50 E
Dédéagach =
  Alexandroúpolis,
  Greece .... 45 F9 40 50N 25 54 E
Deder, Ethiopia ..... 81 F5   9 19N 41 27 E
Dedham, U.S.A. 117 D13 42 15N 71 10W
Dédougou,
  Burkina Faso 82 C4 12 30N   3 25W
Dedovichi, Russia ... 32 D5 57 32N 29 56 E
Dedza, Malawi ...... 87 E3 14 20 S 34 20 E
Dee →, Aberds., U.K. 13 D6 57 9N   2 5W
Dee →, Dumf. & Gall.,
  U.K. 13 G4 54 51N   4 3W
Dee →, Wales, U.K. . 14 D4 53 22N   3 17W
Deep B., Canada 102 A5 61 15N 116 35W
Deepwater, Australia 95 D5 29 25 S 151 51 E
Deer →, Canada 103 B10 58 23N 94 13W
Deer L., Canada 103 C10 52 40N 94 20W
Deer Lake, Nfld. & L.,
  Canada 105 C8 49 11N 57 27W
Deer Lake, Ont.,
  Canada 103 C10 52 36N 94 20W
Deer Lodge, U.S.A. .. 108 C7 46 24N 112 44W
Deer Park, U.S.A. ... 108 C5 47 57N 117 28W
Deer River, U.S.A. .. 112 B8 47 20N 93 48W
Deeragun, Australia . 94 B4 19 16 S 146 33 E
Deerdepoort, S. Africa 88 C4 24 37 S 26 27 E
Deferiet, U.S.A. 117 B9 44 2N 75 41W
Defiance, U.S.A. 114 E3 41 17N 84 22W
Degana, India .... 68 F6 26 50N 74 20 E
Dêgê, China .... 58 B2 31 44N 98 39 E
Degebe →, Portugal . 37 G3 38 13N   7 29W
Degeberga, Sweden . 11 J8 55 51N 14 5 E
Dégelis, Canada 105 C6 47 30N 68 35W
Degema, Nigeria .... 83 E6   4 50N   6 48 E
Degerfors, Sweden .. 10 E8 59 15N 14 27 E
Degerhamn, Sweden . 11 H10 56 20N 16 24 E
Deggendorf, Germany 25 G8 48 50N 12 57 E
Degh →, Pakistan ... 68 D5 31 3N 73 21 E
Değirmendere, Turkey 45 F13 40 42N 29 47 E
Deh Bid, Iran .... 71 D7 30 39N 53 11 E
Deh-e Shīr, Iran .... 71 D7 31 29N 53 45 E
Dehaj, Iran .... 71 D7 30 42N 54 53 E
Dehak, Iran .... 71 E9 27 11N 62 37 E
Dehdez, Iran .... 71 D6 31 43N 50 17 E
Dehej, India .... 68 J5 21 44N 72 40 E
Dehestān, Iran ...... 71 D7 28 30N 55 35 E
Dehgolān, Iran ...... 70 C5 35 17N 47 25 E
Dehibat, Tunisia .... 79 B8 32 0N 10 47 E
Dehlorān, Iran ...... 70 C5 32 41N 47 16 E
Dehnow-e Kūhestān,
  Iran .... 71 E8 27 58N 58 32 E
Dehra Dun, India ... 68 D8 30 20N 78 4 E
Dehri, India .... 69 G11 24 50N 84 15 E
Dehua, China .... 59 E12 25 26N 118 14 E
Dehui, China .... 57 B13 44 30N 125 40 E
Deim Zubeir, Sudan . 81 F2   7 49N 26 16 E
Deinze, Belgium ..... 17 D3 50 59N   3 32 E
Dej, Romania .... 29 C8 47 10N 23 52 E
Deje, Sweden .... 10 E7 59 35N 13 29 E
Dejiang, China ...... 58 C7 28 18N 108 7 E
Deka →, Zimbabwe .. 88 B4 18 4 S 26 42 E
Dekemhare, Eritrea . 81 D4 15 6N 39 0 E
Dekese, Dem. Rep. of
  the Congo .... 84 E4   3 24 S 21 24 E
Del Mar, U.S.A. 111 N9 32 58N 117 16W
Del Norte, U.S.A. ... 109 H10 37 41N 106 21W
Del Rio, U.S.A. 113 L4 29 22N 100 54W
Delai, Sudan .... 80 D4 17 21N 36 6 E
Delambre I., Australia 92 D2 20 26 S 117 5 E
Delami, Sudan ...... 81 E3 11 38N 30 23 E
Delano, U.S.A. 111 K7 35 46N 119 15W
Delano Peak, U.S.A. . 109 G7 38 22N 112 22W
Delareyville, S. Africa 88 D4 26 41 S 25 26 E
Delaronde L., Canada 103 C7 54 30N 107 3W
Delavan, U.S.A. 112 D10 42 38N 88 39W
Delaware, U.S.A. 114 E4 40 18N 83 4W
Delaware □, U.S.A. .. 114 F8 39 0N 75 20W
Delaware →, U.S.A. . 117 G9 39 15N 75 20W
Delaware B., U.S.A. . 114 F8 39 0N 75 10W
Delaware Water Gap △,
  U.S.A. 117 E10 41 10N 74 55W
Delay →, Canada 105 A5 56 56N 71 28W
Delbrück, Germany . 24 D4 51 46N   8 34 E
Delčevo, Macedonia . 44 E6 41 58N 22 46 E
Delegate, Australia .. 95 F4 37 4 S 148 56 E
Delémont, Switz. .... 25 H3 47 22N   7 20 E
Delevan, U.S.A. 116 D6 42 29N 78 29W
Delft, Neths. .... 17 B4 52 1N   4 22 E
Delfzijl, Neths. ..... 17 A6 53 20N   6 55 E
Delgado, C., Mozam. 87 E5 10 45 S 40 40 E
Delgerhet, Mongolia 56 B6 45 50N 110 30 E
Delgo, Sudan .... 80 C3 20 6N 30 40 E
Delhi, Canada 116 D4 42 51N 80 30W
Delhi, India .... 68 E7 28 38N 77 17 E
Delhi □, India .... 68 E7 28 38N 77 17 E
Delhi, La., U.S.A. ... 113 J9 32 28N 91 30W
Delhi, N.Y., U.S.A. .. 117 D10 42 17N 74 55W
Deli Jovan, Serbia & M. 44 B6 44 13N 22 9 E
Delia, Canada 102 C6 51 38N 112 23W
Delice, Turkey ...... 72 C6 39 54N 34 2 E
Delicias, Mexico 118 B3 28 10N 105 30W
Delījān, Iran .... 71 C6 33 59N 50 40 E
Déline, Canada 100 B7 65 11N 123 25W
Delisle, Canada 103 C7 51 55N 107 8W
Delitzsch, Germany . 24 D8 51 32N 12 22 E
Dell City, U.S.A. 109 L11 31 56N 105 12W
Dell Rapids, U.S.A. . 112 D6 43 50N 96 43W
Delle, France .... 19 E14 47 30N   7 2 E
Delmar, U.S.A. 117 D11 42 37N 73 47W
Delmenhorst, Germany 24 B4 53 3N   8 37 E
Delnice, Croatia ..... 41 C11 45 23N 14 50 E
Delonga, Ostrova,
  Russia .... 53 B15 76 40N 149 20 E
Deloraine, Australia . 95 G4 41 30 S 146 40 E
Deloraine, Canada ... 103 D8 49 15N 100 29W
Delphi, Greece ...... 46 C4 38 28N 22 30 E
Delphi, U.S.A. 114 E2 40 36N 86 41W
Delphos, U.S.A. 114 E3 40 51N 84 21W
Delportshoop, S. Africa 88 D3 28 22 S 24 20 E
Delray Beach, U.S.A. 115 M5 26 28N 80 4W
Delsbo, Sweden ..... 10 C10 61 48N 16 32 E
Delta, Colo., U.S.A. . 109 G9 38 44N 108 4W
Delta, Utah, U.S.A. . 108 G7 39 21N 112 35W
Delta □, Nigeria .... 83 D6   5 30N   6 0 E
Delta del Ebro →, Spain 38 E5 40 43N   0 43 E
Delta del Po →, Italy 41 D9 44 50N 12 15 E
Delta du Saloum △,
  Senegal 82 C1 13 42N 16 43W
Delta Dunărea =
  Romania .... 29 E14 45 15N 29 25 E
Delta Junction, U.S.A. 100 B5 64 2N 145 44W
Deltona, U.S.A. 115 L5 28 54N 81 16W
Delungra, Australia . 95 D5 29 39 S 150 51 E
Delvada, India ...... 68 J4 20 46N 71 2 E
Delvinákion, Greece 46 B2 39 57N 20 32 E
Delvinë, Albania .... 44 G4 39 59N 20 6 E
Delyatyn, Ukraine .. 29 B9 48 32N 24 38 E
Demak, Indonesia ... 63 G14 6 53 S 110 38 E
Demanda, Sierra de la,
  Spain 38 C2 42 15N   3 0W
Demavend =
  Damāvand, Qolleh-ye,
  Iran .... 71 C7 35 56N 52 10 E
Dembecha, Ethiopia 81 E4 10 32N 37 30 E
Dembi, Ethiopia ..... 81 F4   8 5N 36 25 E
Dembia, Dem. Rep. of
  the Congo .... 86 B2   3 33N 25 48 E
Dembidolo, Ethiopia 81 F3   8 34N 34 50 E
Demchok, India ...... 69 C8 32 42N 79 29 E
Demer →, Belgium .. 17 D4 50 57N   4 42 E
Demetrias, Greece .. 46 B5 39 22N 23 1 E
Demidov, Russia .... 32 E6 55 16N 31 30 E
Deming, N. Mex., U.S.A. 109 K10 32 16N 107 46W
Deming, Wash., U.S.A. 110 B4 48 50N 122 13W
Demini →, Brazil ... 124 D6   0 46 S 62 56W
Demirci, Turkey .... 47 B10 39 2N 28 38 E
Demirköprü Baraji,
  Turkey .... 47 C10 38 42N 28 25 E
Demirköy, Turkey .. 45 E11 41 49N 27 45 E
Demmin, Germany .. 24 B9 53 54N 13 2 E
Demonte, Italy ...... 40 D4 44 19N   7 17 E
Demopolis, U.S.A. .. 115 J2 32 31N 87 50W
Dempo, Indonesia ... 62 E2   4 2 S 103 15 E
Demyansk, Russia ... 32 D7 57 40N 32 27 E
Den Burg, Neths. .... 17 A4 53 3N   4 47 E
Den Chai, Thailand . 64 D3 17 59N 100 4 E
Den Haag = 's-
  Gravenhage, Neths. 17 B4 52 7N   4 17 E
Den Helder, Neths. .. 17 B4 52 57N   4 45 E
Den Oever, Neths. ... 17 B5 52 56N   5 2 E
Denain, France ...... 19 B10 50 20N   3 22 E
Denair, U.S.A. 110 H6 37 32N 120 48W
Denau, Uzbekistan .. 52 F7 38 16N 67 54 E
Denbigh, Canada 116 A7 45 8N 77 15W
Denbigh, U.K. 14 D4 53 12N   3 25W
Denbighshire □, U.K. 14 D4 53 8N   3 22W
Dendang, Indonesia . 62 E3   3 7 S 107 56 E
Dendermonde, Belgium 17 C4 51 2N   4 7 E
Deneba, Ethiopia .... 81 F4   9 47N 39 10 E
Dengchuan, China ... 58 E3 25 59N 100 3 E
Denge, Nigeria ...... 83 C6 12 52N   5 21 E
Dengfeng, China .... 56 G7 34 25N 113 2 E
Dengi, Nigeria ...... 83 D6   9 25N   9 55 E
Dengkou, China ..... 56 D4 40 18N 106 55 E
Dengzhou, China .... 59 A9 32 34N 112 4 E
Denham, Australia .. 93 E1 25 56 S 113 31 E
Denham, Mt., Jamaica 120 a 18 13N 77 32W
Denham Ra., Australia 94 C4 21 55 S 147 46 E
Denham Sd., Australia 93 E1 25 45 S 113 15 E
Denholm, Canada 103 C7 52 39N 108 1W
Denia, Spain .... 39 G5 38 49N   0 8 E
Denial B., Australia . 95 E1 32 14 S 133 32 E
Deniliquin, Australia 95 F3 35 30 S 144 58 E
Denison, Iowa, U.S.A. 112 E7 42 1N 95 21W
Denison, Tex., U.S.A. 113 J6 33 45N 96 33W
Denison Plains,
  Australia .... 92 C4 18 35 S 128 0 E
Denizli, Turkey ..... 47 D11 37 42N 29 2 E
Denizli □, Turkey ... 47 D11 37 45N 29 5 E
Denman Glacier,
  Antarctica .... 5 C7 66 45 S 99 25 E
Denmark, Australia . 93 F2 34 59 S 117 25 E
Denmark ■, Europe . 11 J3 55 45N 10 0 E
Denmark Str., Atl. Oc. 4 C6 66 0N 30 0W
Dennery, St. Lucia .. 121 f 13 55N 60 54W
Dennison, U.S.A. ... 116 F3 40 24N 81 19W
Denny, U.K. 13 E5 56 1N   3 55W
Denpasar, Indonesia 63 K18 8 39 S 115 13 E
Denpasar ✈ (DPS),
  Indonesia .... 63 K18 8 44 S 115 10 E
Denton, Mont., U.S.A. 108 C9 47 19N 109 57W
Denton, Tex., U.S.A. 113 J6 33 13N 97 8W
D'Entrecasteaux △,
  Australia .... 93 F2 34 20 S 115 33 E
D'Entrecasteaux, Pt.,
  Australia .... 93 F2 34 50 S 115 57 E
Denu, Ghana .... 83 D5   6 4N   1 8 E
Denver, Colo., U.S.A. 112 F2 39 44N 104 59W
Denver, Pa., U.S.A. . 117 F8 40 14N 76 8W
Denver City, U.S.A. . 113 J3 32 58N 102 50W
Deoband, India ...... 68 E7 29 42N 77 43 E
Deogarh, India ...... 68 G5 25 32N 73 54 E
Deoghar, India ...... 69 G12 24 30N 86 42 E
Deolali, India .... 66 K8 19 58N 73 50 E
Deoli = Devli, India 68 G6 25 50N 75 20 E
Deoli, India .... 69 J8 20 38N 78 48 E
Deora, India .... 68 F4 26 22N 70 55 E
Deori, India .... 69 H8 23 24N 79 1 E
Deoria, India .... 69 F10 26 31N 83 48 E
Deosai Mts., Pakistan 69 B6 35 40N 75 0 E
Depalpur, India ..... 68 H6 22 51N 75 33 E
Deping, China .... 57 F9 37 25N 116 58 E
Deposit, U.S.A. 117 D9 42 4N 75 25W
Depuch I., Australia . 92 D2 20 37 S 117 44 E
Deputatskiy, Russia . 53 C14 69 18N 139 54 E
Dêqên, China .... 58 C2 28 34N 98 51 E
Deqing, China .... 59 F9 23 8N 111 42 E
Dera Ghazi Khan,
  Pakistan .... 68 D4 30 5N 70 43 E
Dera Ismail Khan,
  Pakistan .... 68 D4 31 50N 70 50 E
Derabugti, Pakistan . 68 E3 29 2N 69 9 E
Derawar Fort, Pakistan 68 E4 28 46N 71 20 E
Derbent, Russia ..... 35 J9 42 5N 48 15 E
Derby, Australia ..... 92 C3 17 18 S 123 38 E
Derby, U.K. 14 E6 52 56N   1 28W
Derby, Conn., U.S.A. 117 E11 41 19N 73 5W
Derby, Kans., U.S.A. 113 G6 37 33N 97 16W
Derby, N.Y., U.S.A. . 116 D6 42 41N 78 58W
Derby □, U.K. 14 E6 52 56N   1 28W
Derby Line, U.S.A. .. 117 B12 45 0N 72 6W
Derbyshire □, U.K. .. 14 D6 53 11N   1 38W
Đerdap △, Serbia & M. 44 B6 44 40N 22 23 E
Dereham, U.K. ...... 15 E8 52 41N   0 57 E
Derecske, Hungary .. 28 C6 47 20N 21 33 E
Dereham, U.K. ...... 15 E8 52 41N   0 57 E
Derecske, Hungary .. 28 C6 47 20N 21 33 E
Dereköy, Turkey .... 45 E11 41 53N 27 21 E
Dereli, Turkey ...... 73 B8 40 44N 38 26 E
Derg →, U.K. 12 B4 54 44N   7 26W
Derg, L., Ireland 12 D3 53 0N   8 20W
Dergachi = Derhaci,
  Ukraine .... 33 G9 50 9N 36 11 E
Dergaon, India ...... 67 F19 26 45N 94 0 E
Derhaci, Ukraine .... 33 G9 50 9N 36 11 E
Derik, Turkey .... 73 D9 37 21N 40 18 E
Derinkuyu, Turkey . 72 C6 38 22N 34 45 E
Dermantsi, Bulgaria 45 C8 43 8N 24 17 E
Dermott, U.S.A. 113 J9 33 32N 91 26W
Dêrong, China ...... 58 C2 28 44N 99 9 E
Derry = Londonderry,
  U.K. 12 B4 55 0N   7 20W
Derry = Londonderry □,
  U.K. 12 B4 55 0N   7 20W
Derry, N.H., U.S.A. . 117 D13 42 53N 71 19W
Derry, Pa., U.S.A. ... 116 F5 40 20N 79 18W
Derryveagh Mts.,
  Ireland 12 B3 54 56N   8 11W
Derudub, Sudan ..... 80 D4 17 31N 36 7 E
Derval, France 18 E5 47 40N   1 41W
Dervéni, Greece ..... 46 C4 38 8N 22 25 E
Derventa, Bos.-H. ... 28 F2 44 59N 17 55 E
Derwent →, Cumb.,
  U.K. 14 C4 54 39N   3 33W
Derwent →, Derby,
  U.K. 14 E6 52 57N   1 28W
Derwent →, N. Yorks.,
  U.K. 14 D7 53 45N   0 58W
Derwent Water, U.K. 14 C4 54 35N   3 9W
Des Moines, Iowa,
  U.S.A. 112 E8 41 35N 93 37W
Des Moines, N. Mex.,
  U.S.A. 113 G3 36 46N 103 50W
Des Moines →, U.S.A. 112 E9 40 23N 91 25W
Desa, Romania ...... 28 G8 43 52N 23 1 E
Desaguadero →,
  Argentina .... 126 C2 34 30 S 66 46W
Desaguadero →, Bolivia 124 G5 16 35 S 69 5W
Desantne, Ukraine .. 29 E14 45 34N 29 54 E
Desar, Malaysia ..... 65 d   1 31N 104 17 E
Descanso, Pta., Mexico 111 N9 32 21N 117 3W
Descartes, France ... 20 B4 46 59N   0 42 E
Deschaillons-sur-St-
  Laurent, Canada .. 105 C5 46 32N 72 7W
Deschambault L.,
  Canada 103 C8 54 50N 103 30W
Deschutes →, U.S.A. 108 D3 45 38N 120 55W
Dese, Ethiopia ...... 81 E4 11 5N 39 40 E
Deseado →, Argentina 128 F3 47 45 S 65 54W
Desenzano del Garda,
  Italy .... 40 C7 45 28N 10 32 E
Desert Center, U.S.A. 111 M11 33 43N 115 24W
Desert Hot Springs,
  U.S.A. 111 M10 33 58N 116 30W
Deshnok, India ...... 68 F5 27 48N 73 21 E
Desierto Central de Baja
  California △, Mexico 118 B2 29 40N 114 43W
Desna →, Ukraine ... 33 G6 50 33N 30 32 E
Desnătui →, Romania 29 G8 43 53N 23 35 E
Desolación, I., Chile . 128 G2 53 0 S 74 0W
Despeñaperros, Paso,
  Spain 37 G7 38 24N   3 30W
Despeñaperros, Paso,
  Spain 37 G7 38 24N   3 30W
Despotovac,
  Serbia & M. ...... 44 B5 44 6N 21 30 E
Dessau, Germany ... 24 D8 51 51N 12 14 E
Dessye = Dese, Ethiopia 81 E4 11 5N 39 40 E
D'Estrees B., Australia 95 F2 35 55 S 137 45 E
Desuri, India .... 68 G5 25 18N 73 35 E
Desvres, France ..... 19 B8 50 40N   1 48 E
Det Udom, Thailand 64 E5 14 54N 105 5 E
Deta, Romania ...... 28 E6 45 24N 21 13 E
Detinja →, Serbia & M. 44 C4 43 51N 20 0 E
Detmold, Germany .. 24 D4 51 56N   8 52 E
Detour, Pt., U.S.A. . 114 C2 45 40N 86 40W
Detroit, U.S.A. 116 D1 42 20N 83 3W
Detroit Lakes, U.S.A. 112 B7 46 49N 95 51W
Detva, Slovak Rep. .. 27 C12 48 34N 19 25 E
Deurne, Neths. ...... 17 C5 51 27N   5 49 E
Deutsch-
  Luxemburgischer △,
  Germany .... 25 F2 49 58N   6 12 E
Deutsche Bucht,
  Germany .... 24 A4 54 15N   8 0 E
Deutschlandsberg,
  Austria .... 26 E8 46 49N 15 14 E
Deux-Sèvres □, France 18 F6 46 35N   0 20W
Deva, Romania ...... 28 E7 45 53N 22 55 E
Devakottai, India ... 66 Q11 9 55N 78 45 E
Devaprayag, India .. 69 D8 30 13N 78 35 E
Dévaványa, Hungary 28 C5 47 2N 20 59 E
Deveci Dağları, Turkey 72 B7 40 6N 36 15 E
Devecikonağı, Turkey 45 G12 39 55N 28 34 E
Devecser, Hungary .. 28 C2 47 6N 17 26 E
Develi, Turkey ...... 72 C6 38 23N 35 29 E
Deventer, Neths. .... 17 B6 52 15N   6 10 E
Deveron →, U.K. 13 D6 57 41N   2 32W
Devesel, Romania ... 28 F7 44 28N 22 41 E
Devgadh Bariya, India 68 H5 22 40N 73 55 E
Devikot, India ...... 68 F4 26 42N 71 12 E
Devils Den, U.S.A. .. 110 K7 35 46N 119 58W
Devils Lake, U.S.A. . 112 A5 48 7N 98 52W
Devils Paw, Canada . 102 B2 58 47N 134 0W
Devils Postpile △,
  U.S.A. 110 H7 37 37N 119 5W
Devils Tower △, U.S.A. 112 C2 44 35N 104 43W
Devils Tower Junction,
  U.S.A. 112 C2 44 35N 104 43W
Devin, Bulgaria ..... 45 E8 41 44N 24 24 E
Devine, U.S.A. 113 L5 29 8N 98 54W
Devizes, U.K. 15 F6 51 22N   1 58W
Devli, India .... 68 G6 25 50N 75 20 E
Devnya, Bulgaria ... 45 C11 43 13N 27 33 E
Devoll →, Albania ... 44 F4 40 57N 20 15 E
Devon, Canada 102 C6 53 24N 113 44W
Devon □, U.K. 15 G4 50 50N   3 40W
Devon I., Canada 98 B11 75 10N 85 0W
Devonport, Australia 95 G4 41 10 S 146 22 E
Devonport, N.Z. .... 91 G5 36 49 S 174 49 E
Devrek, Turkey ..... 72 B4 41 7N 31 58 E
Devrekâni, Turkey .. 72 B5 41 33N 33 50 E
Devrez →, Turkey ... 72 B6 41 5N 34 24 E
Dewas, India .... 68 H7 22 59N 76 3 E
Dewetsdorp, S. Africa 88 D4 29 33 S 26 39 E
Dewey, Puerto Rico . 121 d 18 18N 65 18W
Dexing, China .... 59 C11 28 46N 117 30 E
Dexter, Maine, U.S.A. 115 C11 45 1N 69 18W
Dexter, Mo., U.S.A. . 113 G10 36 48N 89 57W
Dexter, N. Mex., U.S.A. 113 J2 33 12N 104 22W
Dey-Dey, L., Australia 93 E5 29 12 S 131 4 E
Deyang, China ...... 58 B5 31 3N 104 27 E
Deyhūk, Iran .... 71 C8 33 15N 57 30 E
Deyyer, Iran .... 71 E6 27 55N 51 55 E
Dezadeash L., Canada 102 A1 60 28N 136 58W
Dezfūl, Iran .... 71 C6 32 20N 48 30 E
Dezhneva, Mys, Russia 53 C19 66 5N 169 40W
Dezhou, China ...... 56 F9 37 26N 116 18 E
Dhadhar →, India ... 69 G11 24 56N 85 24 E
Dháfni, Kríti, Greece 49 D7 35 13N 25 3 E
Dháfni, Pelópónnisos,
  Greece .... 46 D4 37 48N 22 1 E
Dhahabān, Si. Arabia 80 C4 21 58N 39 3 E
Dhahiriya = Az
  Zāhirīyah, West Bank 74 D3 31 25N 34 58 E
Dhahran = Az Zahrān,
  Si. Arabia .... 71 E6 26 10N 50 7 E
Dhak, Pakistan ..... 68 C5 32 25N 72 20 E
Dhaka, Bangla. ..... 69 H14 23 43N 90 26 E
Dhaka □, Bangla. ... 69 G14 24 25N 90 25 E
Dhali, Cyprus .... 49 D12 35 1N 33 25 E
Dhamási, Greece .... 46 B4 39 43N 22 11 E
Dhampur, India ..... 69 E8 29 19N 78 33 E
Dhamtari, India ..... 67 J12 20 42N 81 35 E
Dhanbād, India ..... 69 H12 23 50N 86 30 E
Dhangarhi, Nepal ... 69 E12 28 55N 80 40 E
Dhankuta, Nepal .... 69 F12 26 55N 87 40 E
Dhar, India .... 68 H6 22 35N 75 26 E
Dharampur, India ... 68 H6 20 32N 73 17 E
Dharamsala =
  Dharmsala, India . 68 C7 32 16N 76 23 E
Dhariwal, India ..... 68 D6 31 57N 75 19 E
Dharla →, Bangla. .. 69 G13 25 46N 89 42 E
Dharmapuri, India .. 66 N11 12 10N 78 10 E
Dharmjaygarh, India 69 H10 22 28N 83 13 E
Dharmsala, India ... 68 C7 32 16N 76 23 E
Dharni, India .... 68 J7 21 33N 76 53 E
Dharwad, India ..... 66 M9 15 30N 75 4 E
Dhasan →, India .... 69 G8 24 58N 79 24 E
Dhaulagiri, Nepal ... 69 E10 28 39N 83 28 E
Dhebar, L., India ... 68 G6 24 10N 74 0 E
Dheftera, Cyprus ... 49 D12 35 5N 33 16 E
Dhenkanal, India ... 67 J14 20 45N 85 35 E
Dhenoúsa, Greece .. 47 D7 37 8N 25 48 E
Dherinia, Cyprus ... 49 D12 35 3N 33 57 E
Dheskáti, Greece .... 44 G5 39 55N 21 49 E
Dhespotikó, Greece . 46 E6 36 57N 24 58 E
Dhestina, Greece .... 46 C4 38 25N 22 31 E
Dhī Qār □, Iraq .... 70 D5 31 0N 46 15 E
Dhiarrizos →, Cyprus 49 E11 34 41N 32 34 E
Dhībān, Jordan ..... 74 D4 31 30N 35 46 E
Dhidhimótikhon, Greece 45 E10 41 22N 26 29 E
Dhíkti Óros, Greece 49 D7 35 8N 25 30 E
Dhilianáta, Greece .. 46 C2 38 15N 20 31 E
Dhílos, Greece ...... 47 D7 37 23N 25 15 E
Dhimarkhera, India . 69 H9 23 28N 80 22 E
Dhimitsána, Greece . 46 D4 37 36N 22 3 E
Dhírfis Óros, Greece 46 C5 38 40N 23 54 E
Dhodhekánisos, Greece 47 E8 36 35N 27 0 E
Dhodhekánisos □,
  Greece .... 47 E8 36 35N 27 0 E
Dhokós, Greece ..... 46 D5 37 20N 23 20 E
Dholiana, Greece ... 46 B2 39 54N 20 32 E
Dholka, India .... 68 H5 22 44N 72 29 E
Dhomokós, Greece .. 46 B4 39 10N 22 18 E
Dhoraji, India ...... 68 J4 21 45N 70 37 E
Dhoxáton, Greece .. 45 E8 41 9N 24 16 E
Dhragónisi, Greece . 47 D7 37 27N 25 29 E
Dhráhstis, Ákra, Greece 49 A3 39 48N 19 40 E
Dhrangadhra, India . 68 H4 22 59N 71 31 E
Dhrápanon, Ákra,
  Greece .... 49 D6 35 28N 24 14 E
Dhriopís, Greece .... 46 D6 37 20N 24 26 E
Dhrol, India .... 68 H4 22 33N 70 25 E
Dhuburi, India ...... 67 F16 26 2N 89 59 E
Dhule, India .... 66 J9 20 58N 74 50 E
Di-ib, W. →, Sudan . 80 C4 22 38N 36 6 E
Di Linh, Vietnam ... 65 G7 11 35N 108 4 E
Di Linh, Cao Nguyen,
  Vietnam .... 65 G7 11 30N 108 0 E
Día, Greece .... 49 D7 35 28N 25 14 E
Diabakania, Guinea . 82 C2 10 38N 10 58W
Diablo, Mt., U.S.A. . 110 H5 37 53N 121 56W
Diablo Range, U.S.A. 110 J5 37 20N 121 25W
Diafarabé, Mali 82 C4 14 9N   5 0W
Diala, Mali 82 C3 14 10N   9 58W
Dialakoto, Senegal .. 82 C2 13 21N 13 19W
Diallassagou, Mali .. 82 C4 13 47N   3 41W
Diamante, Argentina 126 C3 32 5 S 60 40W
Diamante, Italy ..... 43 C8 39 41N 15 49 E
Diamante →, Argentina 126 C2 34 30 S 66 46W
Diamantina, Brazil . 125 G10 18 17 S 43 40W
Diamantina →,
  Australia .... 95 D2 26 45 S 139 10 E
Diamantino, Brazil . 125 F7 14 30 S 56 30W
Diamond Bar, U.S.A. 111 L9 34 1N 117 48W
Diamond Harbour,
  India .... 69 H12 22 11N 88 14 E
Diamond Is., Australia 94 B5 17 25 S 151 5 E
Diamond Mts., U.S.A. 108 G6 39 50N 115 30W
Diamond Springs,
  U.S.A. 110 G6 38 42N 120 49W
Dian Chi, China ..... 58 E4 24 50N 102 43 E
Dianalund, Denmark 11 J5 55 32N 11 30 E
Dianbai, China ...... 59 G8 21 33N 111 4 E
Diancheng, China ... 59 G8 21 30N 111 4 E
Dianjiang, China .... 58 B6 30 24N 107 20 E
Diano Marina, Italy . 40 E5 43 54N   8 5 E
Dianra, Ivory C. 82 D3   8 45N   6 14W
Diapaga, Burkina Faso 83 C5 12 5N   1 46 E
Diapangou,
  Burkina Faso ..... 83 C5 12 5N   0 10 E
Diariguila, Guinea .. 82 C2 10 35N 10 2W
Diba, U.A.E. .... 71 E8 25 45N 56 16 E
Dibai, India .... 68 E8 28 13N 78 15 E
Dibaya-Lubue,
  Dem. Rep. of
  the Congo .... 84 E3   4 12 S 19 54 E
Dibben →, Jordan ... 74 C4 32 20N 35 45 E
Dibete, Botswana ... 88 C4 23 45 S 26 32 E
Dibrugarh, India .... 67 F19 27 29N 94 55 E
Dickens, U.S.A. 113 J4 33 37N 100 50W
Dickinson, U.S.A. ... 112 B3 46 53N 102 47W
Dickson = Dikson,
  Russia .... 52 B9 73 40N 80 5 E
Dickson, U.S.A. 115 G2 36 5N 87 23W
Dickson City, U.S.A. 117 E9 41 29N 75 40W
Dicle Nehri →, Turkey 73 D9 37 44N 41 10 E
Dicomano, Italy .... 41 E8 43 53N 11 31 E
Didesa, W. →, Ethiopia 81 E4 10 2N 35 32 E
Didi, Sudan .... 81 F3   5 18N 34 29 E
Didiéni, Mali 82 C3 13 53N   8 6W

Didsbury, Canada ... 102 C6 51 35N 114 10W
Didwana, India ... 68 F6 27 23N 74 36 E
Die, France ... 21 D9 44 47N 5 22 E
Diébougou, Burkina Faso ... 82 C4 11 0N 3 15W
Diecke, Guinea ... 82 D3 7 27N 8 54W
Diefenbaker, L., Canada 103 C7 51 0N 106 55W
Diego de Almagro, Chile 126 B1 26 22 S 70 3W
Diego Garcia, Ind. Oc. ... 3 E13 7 50 S 72 50 E
Diekirch, Lux. ... 17 E6 49 52N 6 10 E
Diéma, Mali ... 82 C3 14 32N 9 12W
Diembéring, Senegal ... 82 C1 12 29N 16 47W
Diemelsee △, Germany ... 24 A5 51 22N 8 48 16 E
Dien Ban, Vietnam ... 64 E7 15 53N 108 16 E
Dien Khanh, Vietnam ... 58 G4 21 20N 103 0 E
Dien Bien, Vietnam ... 65 F7 12 15N 109 6 E
Diepholz, Germany ... 24 C4 52 37N 8 22 E
Dieppe, France ... 18 C8 49 54N 1 4 E
Dierks, U.S.A. ... 113 H8 34 7N 94 1W
Diest, Belgium ... 17 D5 50 58N 5 4 E
Dietikon, Switz. ... 25 H4 47 24N 8 24 E
Dieulefit, France ... 21 D9 44 32N 5 4 E
Dieuze, France ... 19 D13 48 49N 6 43 E
Dif, Somali Rep. ... 75 G3 0 59N 40 58 E
Differdange, Lux. ... 17 E5 49 31N 5 54 E
Dig, India ... 68 F7 27 28N 77 20 E
Digba, Dem. Rep. of the Congo ... 86 B2 4 25N 25 48 E
Digby, Canada ... 105 D6 44 38N 65 50W
Diggi, India ... 68 F6 26 22N 75 26 E
Dighinala, Bangla. ... 67 H18 23 15N 92 5 E
Dighton, U.S.A. ... 112 F4 38 29N 100 28W
Digna, Mali ... 82 C3 14 48N 8 10W
Digne-les-Bains, France ... 21 D10 44 5N 6 12 E
Digoin, France ... 19 F11 46 29N 4 1 E
Digor, Turkey ... 73 B10 40 22N 43 25 E
Digos, Phil. ... 61 H6 6 45N 125 20 E
Digranes, Iceland ... 8 C6 66 4N 14 44W
Digul →, Indonesia ... 63 F9 7 7 S 138 42 E
Digya △, Ghana ... 83 D5 7 15N 0 5 E
Dihang = Brahmaputra →, Asia 69 H13 23 40N 90 35 E
Dijlah, Nahr →, Asia ... 70 D5 31 0N 47 25 E
Dijon, France ... 19 E12 47 20N 5 3 E
Dikhil, Djibouti ... 81 E5 11 8N 42 20 E
Dikili, Turkey ... 47 B8 39 4N 26 53 E
Dikirnis, Egypt ... 80 H7 31 6N 31 35 E
Dikkil = Dikhil, Djibouti ... 81 E5 11 8N 42 20 E
Dikodougou, Ivory C. ... 82 D3 9 4N 5 45W
Diksmuide, Belgium ... 17 C2 51 2N 2 52 E
Dikson, Russia ... 52 B9 73 40N 80 5 E
Dikwa, Nigeria ... 83 C7 12 4N 13 30 E
Dila, Ethiopia ... 81 F4 6 21N 38 22 E
Dilek Yarimadisi △, Turkey ... 47 D9 37 40N 27 10 E
Dili, E. Timor ... 63 F7 8 39 S 125 34 E
Dilijan, Armenia ... 35 K7 40 46N 44 57 E
Dilizhan = Dilijan, Armenia ... 35 K7 40 46N 44 57 E
Dilj, Croatia ... 28 E3 45 29N 18 1 E
Dillenburg, Germany ... 24 E4 50 43N 8 17 E
Dilley, U.S.A. ... 113 L5 28 40N 99 10W
Dilli = Delhi, India ... 68 E7 28 38N 77 17 E
Dilling, Sudan ... 81 E2 12 3N 29 35 E
Dillingen, Bayern, Germany ... 25 G6 48 36N 10 30 E
Dillingen, Saarland, Germany ... 25 F2 49 22N 6 43 E
Dillingham, U.S.A. ... 100 C4 59 3N 158 28W
Dillon, Canada ... 103 B7 55 56N 108 35W
Dillon, Mont., U.S.A. ... 108 D7 45 13N 112 38W
Dillon, S.C., U.S.A. ... 115 H6 34 25N 79 22W
Dillon →, Canada ... 103 B7 55 56N 108 56W
Dillsburg, U.S.A. ... 116 F7 40 7N 77 2W
Dilly, Mali ... 82 C3 15 1N 7 40W
Dilolo, Dem. Rep. of the Congo ... 84 G4 10 28 S 22 18 E
Dilove, Ukraine ... 29 C9 47 56N 24 11 E
Dimas, Mexico ... 118 C3 23 43N 106 47W
Dimashq, Syria ... 74 B5 33 30N 36 18 E
Dimashq □, Syria ... 74 B5 33 30N 36 30 E
Dimbaza, S. Africa ... 89 E4 32 50 S 27 14 E
Dimbokro, Ivory C. ... 82 D4 6 45N 4 46W
Dimboola, Australia ... 95 F3 36 28 S 142 7 E
Dîmbovița = Dâmbovița →, Romania ... 29 F11 44 12N 26 26 E
Dimbulah, Australia ... 94 B4 17 8 S 145 4 E
Dimitrovgrad, Bulgaria ... 45 D9 42 5N 25 35 E
Dimitrovgrad, Russia ... 34 C9 54 14N 49 39 E
Dimitrovo = Pernik, Bulgaria ... 44 D7 42 35N 23 2 E
Dimmitt, U.S.A. ... 113 H3 34 33N 102 19W
Dimo, Sudan ... 81 F2 5 19N 29 10 E
Dimona, Israel ... 74 D4 31 2N 35 1 E
Dimovo, Bulgaria ... 44 C6 43 43N 22 50 E
Dinagat, Phil. ... 61 F6 10 10N 125 40 E
Dinajpur, Bangla. ... 67 G16 25 33N 88 43 E
Dinan, France ... 18 D4 48 28N 2 2W
Dīnān Āb, Iran ... 71 C8 32 4N 56 49 E
Dinant, Belgium ... 17 D4 50 16N 4 55 E
Dinapur, India ... 69 G11 25 38N 85 5 E
Dinar, Turkey ... 47 C12 38 5N 30 10 E
Dīnār, Kūh-e, Iran ... 71 D6 30 42N 51 46 E
Dinara Planina, Croatia ... 41 D13 44 0N 16 30 E
Dinard, France ... 18 D4 48 38N 2 6W
Dinaric Alps = Dinara Planina, Croatia ... 41 D13 44 0N 16 30 E
Dindanko, Mali ... 82 C3 14 8N 9 30W
Dinder △, Sudan ... 81 E4 12 30N 35 10 E
Dinder, Nahr ed →, Sudan ... 81 E3 14 6N 33 40 E
Dindigul, India ... 66 P11 10 25N 78 0 E
Dindori, India ... 69 H9 22 57N 81 5 E
Ding Xian = Dingzhou, China ... 56 E8 38 30N 114 59 E
Dinga, Pakistan ... 68 G2 25 26N 67 10 E
Dingalan, Phil. ... 61 D4 15 18N 121 25 E
Dingbian, China ... 56 F4 37 35N 107 32 E
Dingelstädt, Germany ... 24 D6 51 18N 10 19 E
Dingle, Ireland ... 12 D1 52 9N 10 17W
Dingle, Sweden ... 11 F5 58 32N 11 35 E
Dingle B., Ireland ... 12 D1 52 3N 10 20W
Dingmans Ferry, U.S.A. ... 117 E10 41 13N 74 55W
Dingnan, China ... 59 E10 24 45N 115 0 E
Dingo, Australia ... 94 C4 23 38 S 149 19 E
Dingolfing, Germany ... 25 G8 48 37N 12 30 E
Dinguira, Mali ... 82 C2 14 11N 11 16W
Dinguiraye, Guinea ... 82 C2 11 18N 10 49W
Dingwall, U.K. ... 13 D4 57 36N 4 26W
Dingxi, China ... 56 G3 35 30N 104 33 E
Dingxiang, China ... 56 E7 38 30N 112 58 E
Dingyuan, China ... 59 A11 32 32N 117 40 E
Dingzhou, China ... 56 E8 38 30N 114 59 E

Dinh, Mui, Vietnam ... 65 G7 11 22N 109 1 E
Dinh Lap, Vietnam ... 58 G6 21 33N 107 6 E
Dinira △, Venezuela ... 121 E6 9 57N 70 6W
Dinokwe, Botswana ... 88 C4 23 29 S 26 37 E
Dinorwic, Canada ... 103 D10 49 41N 92 30W
Dinosaur △, Canada ... 102 C6 50 47N 111 30W
Dinosaur △, U.S.A. ... 108 F9 40 30N 108 45 E
Dinuba, U.S.A. ... 110 J7 36 32N 119 23W
Diö, Sweden ... 11 H8 56 37N 14 15 E
Dioila, Mali ... 82 C3 12 30N 6 50W
Dioka, Mali ... 82 C2 14 57N 10 4W
Diongoï, Mali ... 82 C3 14 38N 8 34W
Diósgyőr, Hungary ... 28 B5 48 7N 20 43 E
Diosig, Romania ... 28 C7 47 18N 22 2 E
Diougani, Mali ... 82 C4 14 19N 2 44W
Diouloulou, Senegal ... 82 C1 13 5N 16 38W
Dioura, Mali ... 82 C3 14 59N 5 12W
Diourbel, Senegal ... 82 C1 14 39N 16 12W
Dipalpur, Pakistan ... 68 D5 30 40N 73 39 E
Diplo, Pakistan ... 68 G3 24 35N 69 35 E
Dipolog, Phil. ... 61 G5 8 36N 123 20 E
Dipperu △, Australia ... 94 C4 21 56 S 148 42 E
Dir, Pakistan ... 66 B7 35 8N 71 59 E
Diré, Mali ... 82 B4 16 20N 3 25W
Diriamba, Nic. ... 120 D2 11 51N 86 19W
Dirk Hartog I., Australia ... 93 E1 25 50 S 113 5 E
Dirranbandi, Australia ... 95 D4 28 33 S 148 17 E
Disa, India ... 68 G5 24 18N 72 10 E
Disa, Sudan ... 81 E3 12 5N 34 15 E
Disappointment, C., U.S.A. ... 108 C2 46 18N 124 5W
Disappointment, L., Australia ... 92 D3 23 20 S 122 40 E
Disaster B., Australia ... 95 F4 37 15 S 149 58 E
Discovery B., Australia ... 95 F3 38 10 S 140 40 E
Disentis Muster, Switz. ... 25 J4 46 42N 8 50 E
Dishna, Egypt ... 80 B3 26 9N 32 32 E
Disina, Nigeria ... 83 C6 11 35N 9 50 E
Disko = Qeqertarsuaq, Greenland ... 101 B5 69 45N 53 30W
Disna = Dzisna →, Belarus ... 9 E22 55 34N 28 12 E
Diss, U.K. ... 15 E9 52 23N 1 7 E
Disteghil Sar, Pakistan ... 69 A6 36 20N 75 12 E
Distrito Federal □, Brazil ... 125 G9 15 45 S 47 45W
Distrito Federal □, Mexico ... 119 D5 19 15N 99 10W
Disûq, Egypt ... 80 H7 31 8N 30 35 E
Diu, India ... 68 J4 20 45N 70 58 E
Dīvāndarreh, Iran ... 70 C5 35 55N 47 2 E
Dives →, France ... 18 C6 49 18N 0 7W
Dives-sur-Mer, France ... 18 C6 49 18N 0 8W
Divichi = Däväçi, Azerbaijan ... 35 K9 41 15N 48 57 E
Divide, U.S.A. ... 108 D7 45 45N 112 45W
Dividing Ra., Australia ... 93 E2 27 45 S 116 0 E
Divinópolis, Brazil ... 125 H10 20 10 S 44 54W
Divjake, Albania ... 44 F3 41 0N 19 32 E
Divnoye, Russia ... 35 H6 45 55N 43 21 E
Divo, Ivory C. ... 82 D3 5 48N 5 15W
Divriği, Turkey ... 73 C8 39 22N 38 7 E
Dīwāl Kol, Afghan. ... 68 B2 34 23N 67 52 E
Dixie Mt., U.S.A. ... 110 F6 39 55N 120 16W
Dixon, Calif., U.S.A. ... 110 G5 38 27N 121 49W
Dixon, Ill., U.S.A. ... 112 E10 41 50N 89 29W
Dixon Entrance, U.S.A. ... 100 C6 54 30N 132 0W
Dixville, Canada ... 117 A13 45 4N 71 46W
Diyadin, Turkey ... 73 C10 39 33N 43 41 E
Diyālā □, Iraq ... 70 C5 33 45N 44 50 E
Diyālā →, Iraq ... 70 C5 33 14N 44 31 E
Diyarbakır, Turkey ... 70 B4 37 55N 40 18 E
Diyodar, India ... 68 G4 24 8N 71 50 E
Djakarta = Jakarta, Indonesia ... 63 G12 6 9 S 106 49 E
Djamba, Angola ... 88 B1 16 45 S 13 58 E
Djambala, Congo ... 84 E2 2 32 S 14 30 E
Djanet, Algeria ... 78 D7 24 35N 9 32 E
Djawa = Jawa, Indonesia ... 62 F3 7 0 S 110 0 E
Djelfa, Algeria ... 78 B6 34 40N 3 15 E
Djema, C.A.R. ... 86 A2 6 3N 25 15 E
Djenné, Mali ... 82 C4 14 0N 4 30W
Djerba, I. de, Tunisia ... 79 B8 33 50N 10 48 E
Djerid, Chott, Tunisia ... 78 B7 33 42N 8 30 E
Djibo, Burkina Faso ... 83 C4 14 9N 1 35W
Djibouti, Djibouti ... 81 E5 11 30N 43 5 E
Djibouti ■, Africa ... 81 E5 12 0N 43 0 E
Djolu, Dem. Rep. of the Congo ... 84 D4 0 35N 22 5 E
Djougou, Benin ... 83 D5 9 40N 1 45 E
Djoum, Cameroon ... 84 D2 2 41N 12 35 E
Djourab, Erg du, Chad ... 79 E9 16 40N 18 50 E
Djugu, Dem. Rep. of the Congo ... 86 B3 1 55N 30 35 E
Djúpivogur, Iceland ... 8 D6 64 39N 14 17W
Djurås, Sweden ... 10 D9 60 34N 15 8 E
Djuró △, Sweden ... 11 F7 58 52N 13 28 E
Djursland, Denmark ... 11 H4 56 27N 10 45 E
Dmitriya Lapteva, Proliv, Russia ... 53 B15 73 0N 140 0 E
Dmitriyev Lgovskiy, Russia ... 33 F8 52 10N 35 0 E
Dmitrov, Russia ... 32 D9 56 25N 37 32 E
Dmitrovsk-Orlovskiy, Russia ... 33 F8 52 29N 35 10 E
Dnepr = Dnipro →, Ukraine ... 33 J7 46 30N 32 18 E
Dneprodzerzhinsk = Dniprodzerzhynsk, Ukraine ... 33 H8 48 32N 34 37 E
Dneprodzerzhinskoye Vdkhr. = Dniprodzerzhynske Vdskh., Ukraine ... 33 H8 48 49N 34 8 E
Dnepropetrovsk = Dnipropetrovsk, Ukraine ... 33 H8 48 30N 35 0 E
Dneprorudnoye = Dniprorudne, Ukraine ... 33 J8 47 21N 34 58 E
Dnestr = Dnister →, Europe ... 33 J6 46 18N 30 17 E
Dnieper = Dnipro →, Ukraine ... 33 J7 46 30N 32 18 E
Dniester = Dnister →, Europe ... 33 J6 46 18N 30 17 E
Dnipro →, Ukraine ... 33 J7 46 30N 32 18 E
Dniprodzerzhynsk, Ukraine ... 33 H8 48 32N 34 37 E
Dniprodzerzhynske Vdskh., Ukraine ... 33 H8 48 49N 34 8 E
Dnipropetrovsk, Ukraine ... 33 H8 48 30N 35 0 E
Dniprorudne, Ukraine ... 33 J8 47 21N 34 58 E
Dnister →, Europe ... 33 J6 46 18N 30 17 E
Dnistrovskyy Lyman, Ukraine ... 33 J6 46 15N 30 17 E

Dno, Russia ... 32 D5 57 50N 29 58 E
Dnyapro = Dnipro →, Ukraine ... 33 J7 46 30N 32 18 E
Doaktown, Canada ... 105 C6 46 33N 66 8W
Doan Hung, Vietnam ... 58 G5 21 30N 105 10 E
Doany, Madag. ... 89 A8 14 21 S 49 30 E
Doba, Chad ... 79 G9 8 40N 16 50 E
Dobandi, Pakistan ... 68 D2 31 13N 66 50 E
Dobbiaco, Italy ... 41 B9 46 44N 12 14 E
Dobbyn, Australia ... 94 B3 19 44 S 140 2 E
Dobczyce, Poland ... 31 J7 49 52N 20 5 E
Dobele, Latvia ... 9 H20 56 37N 23 16 E
Dobele □, Latvia ... 30 B10 56 35N 23 5 E
Döbeln, Germany ... 24 D9 51 6N 13 7 E
Doberai, Jazirah, Indonesia ... 63 E8 1 25 S 133 0 E
Dobiegniew, Poland ... 31 F2 52 59N 15 45 E
Doblas, Argentina ... 126 D3 37 5 S 64 0W
Dobo, Indonesia ... 63 F8 5 45 S 134 15 E
Doboj, Bos.-H. ... 28 F3 44 46N 18 4 E
Dobra, Wielkopolskie, Poland ... 31 G5 51 55N 18 37 E
Dobra, Zachodnio-Pomorskie, Poland ... 30 E2 53 34N 15 20 E
Dobra, Dâmbovita, Romania ... 29 F10 44 52N 25 40 E
Dobra, Hunedoara, Romania ... 28 E7 45 54N 22 36 E
Dobre Miasto, Poland ... 30 E7 53 58N 20 26 E
Dobreşti, Romania ... 28 D7 46 51N 22 18 E
Dobrich, Bulgaria ... 45 C11 43 37N 27 49 E
Dobrinishta, Bulgaria ... 44 E7 41 49N 23 34 E
Dobrodzień, Poland ... 31 H5 50 45N 18 25 E
Döbrököz, Hungary ... 28 D3 46 26N 18 12 E
Dobromyl, Ukraine ... 31 J9 49 34N 22 46 E
Dobron, Ukraine ... 28 B7 48 25N 22 12 E
Dobropole, Ukraine ... 33 H9 48 25N 37 2 E
Dobrovolsk, Russia ... 30 D9 54 46N 22 31 E
Dobruja, Europe ... 29 F13 44 30N 28 15 E
Dobrush, Belarus ... 33 F6 52 25N 31 22 E
Dobrzany, Poland ... 30 E2 53 22N 15 25 E
Dobrzyń nad Wisłą, Poland ... 31 F6 52 39N 19 22 E
Doc, Mui, Vietnam ... 64 E6 17 58N 106 30 E
Docker River, Australia ... 93 D4 24 52 S 129 5 E
Docksta, Sweden ... 10 A12 63 3N 18 18 E
Doctor Arroyo, Mexico ... 118 C4 23 40N 100 11W
Doda, India ... 69 C6 33 10N 75 34 E
Doda, L., Canada ... 104 C4 49 25N 75 13W
Dodecanese = Dhodhekánisos, Greece ... 47 E8 36 35N 27 0 E
Dodge City, U.S.A. ... 113 G5 37 45N 100 1W
Dodge L., Canada ... 103 B7 59 50N 105 36W
Dodgeville, U.S.A. ... 112 D9 42 58N 90 8W
Dodo, Cameroon ... 83 D7 7 30N 12 3 E
Dodo, Sudan ... 81 F2 5 10N 29 57 E
Dodola, Ethiopia ... 81 F4 6 59N 39 11 E
Dodoma, Tanzania ... 86 D4 6 8 S 35 45 E
Dodoma □, Tanzania ... 86 D4 6 0 S 36 0 E
Dodona, Greece ... 46 B2 39 40N 20 46 E
Dodori □, Kenya ... 86 C5 1 55 S 41 7 E
Dodsland, Canada ... 103 C7 51 50N 108 45W
Dodson, U.S.A. ... 108 B9 48 24N 108 15W
Dodurga, Turkey ... 47 B11 39 49N 29 57 E
Doesburg, Neths. ... 17 B6 52 1N 6 9 E
Dog Creek, Canada ... 102 C4 51 35N 122 14W
Dog L., Man., Canada ... 103 C9 51 2N 98 31W
Dog L., Ont., Canada ... 104 C2 48 48N 89 30W
Doğanşehir, Turkey ... 72 C7 38 5N 37 53 E
Dogliani, Italy ... 40 D4 44 32N 7 56 E
Dogondoutchi, Niger ... 83 C5 13 38N 4 2 E
Dogran, Pakistan ... 68 D5 31 48N 73 35 E
Doğubayazıt, Turkey ... 70 B5 39 31N 44 5 E
Dogué?raoua, Niger ... 83 C6 14 0N 5 31 E
Doha = Ad Dawḥah, Qatar ... 71 E6 25 15N 51 35 E
Dohazari, Bangla. ... 67 H18 22 10N 92 5 E
Dohrighat, India ... 69 F10 26 16N 83 31 E
Doi, Indonesia ... 63 D7 2 14N 127 49 E
Doi Inthanon △, Thailand ... 64 C2 18 33N 98 34 E
Doi Khuntan △, Thailand ... 64 C2 18 33N 99 14 E
Doi Luang, Thailand ... 64 C3 18 30N 101 0 E
Doi Luang △, Thailand ... 64 C2 19 22N 99 35 E
Doi Saket, Thailand ... 64 C2 18 52N 99 9 E
Doi Suthep △, Thailand ... 64 C2 18 49N 98 53 E
Dois Irmãos, Sa., Brazil ... 125 E10 9 0 S 42 30W
Dojransko Jezero, Macedonia ... 44 E6 41 13N 22 44 E
Dokkum, Neths. ... 17 A5 53 20N 5 59 E
Dokri, Pakistan ... 68 F3 27 25N 68 7 E
Dokuchayevsk, Ukraine ... 33 J9 47 45N 37 40 E
Dol-de-Bretagne, France ... 18 D5 48 34N 1 47W
Dolac, Serbia & M. ... 44 D4 42 36N 20 36 E
Dolak, Pulau, Indonesia ... 63 F9 8 0 S 138 30 E
Dolbeau-Mistassini, Canada ... 105 C5 48 53N 72 14W
Dole, France ... 19 E12 47 7N 5 31 E
Doleib, Wadi →, Sudan ... 81 E3 12 10N 33 15 E
Dolenji Logatec, Slovenia ... 41 C11 45 56N 14 15 E
Dolgellau, U.K. ... 14 E4 52 45N 3 53W
Dolgelley = Dolgellau, U.K. ... 14 E4 52 45N 3 53W
Dolhasca, Romania ... 29 C11 47 26N 26 36 E
Dolianova, Italy ... 42 C2 39 22N 9 10 E
Dolinskaya = Dolynska, Ukraine ... 33 H7 48 6N 32 46 E
Dolj □, Romania ... 29 F8 44 10N 23 30 E
Dollard, Neths. ... 17 A7 53 20N 7 10 E
Dolna Banya, Bulgaria ... 44 D7 42 18N 23 44 E
Dolni Chiflik, Bulgaria ... 45 D11 42 59N 27 43 E
Dolní Dübník, Bulgaria ... 45 C8 43 24N 24 26 E
Dolnośląskie □, Poland ... 31 G3 51 10N 16 30 E
Dolný Kubín, Slovak Rep. ... 27 B12 49 12N 19 18 E
Dolo, Ethiopia ... 81 G5 4 11N 42 3 E
Dolo, Italy ... 41 C9 45 25N 12 5 E
Dolomites = Dolomiti, Italy ... 41 B8 46 23N 11 51 E
Dolomiti, Italy ... 41 B8 46 23N 11 51 E
Dolomiti Bellunesi △, Italy ... 41 B9 46 10N 12 5 E
Dolores, Argentina ... 126 D4 36 20 S 57 40W
Dolores, Uruguay ... 126 C4 33 34 S 58 15W
Dolores, U.S.A. ... 109 H9 37 28N 108 30W
Dolores →, U.S.A. ... 109 G9 38 49N 109 17W
Dolovo, Serbia & M. ... 28 E5 44 55N 20 52 E
Dolphin, C., Falk. Is. ... 128 G5 51 10 S 59 0W
Dolphin and Union Str., Canada ... 100 B8 69 5N 114 45W
Dolsk, Poland ... 31 G4 51 59N 17 3 E
Dolyna, Ukraine ... 29 B9 48 56N 24 2 E

Dolynska, Ukraine ... 33 H7 48 6N 32 46 E
Dolynske, Ukraine ... 29 C14 46 32N 29 55 E
Dolzhanskaya, Russia ... 33 J9 46 37N 37 48 E
Dom Pedrito, Brazil ... 127 C5 31 0 S 54 40W
Dom Pedro, Brazil ... 125 E10 5 21N 44 42W
Doma, Nigeria ... 83 D6 8 25N 8 18 E
Doma △, Zimbabwe ... 87 F3 16 28 S 30 12 E
Domaniç, Turkey ... 47 B11 39 48N 29 36 E
Domariaganj →, India ... 69 F10 26 17N 83 44 E
Domasi, Malawi ... 87 F15 15 15 S 35 22 E
Domažlice, Czech Rep. ... 26 B5 49 28N 12 58 E
Dombarovskiy, Russia ... 52 D6 50 46N 59 32 E
Dombås, Norway ... 9 E13 62 4N 9 8 E
Dombasle-sur-Meurthe, France ... 19 D13 48 38N 6 21 E
Dombes, France ... 21 C9 45 58N 5 0 E
Dombóvár, Hungary ... 28 D3 46 21N 18 9 E
Dombrád, Hungary ... 28 B5 48 13N 21 54 E
Dome Fuji, Antarctica ... 5 D5 77 20 S 39 45 E
Domel I. = Letsôk-aw Kyun, Burma ... 65 G2 11 30N 98 25 E
Domérat, France ... 19 F9 46 21N 2 32 E
Domeyko, Chile ... 126 B1 29 0 S 71 0W
Domeyko, Cordillera, Chile ... 126 A2 24 30 S 69 0W
Domfront, France ... 18 D6 48 37N 0 40W
Dominador, Chile ... 126 A2 24 21 S 69 20W
Dominica ■, W. Indies ... 121 C7 15 20N 61 20W
Dominica Passage, W. Indies ... 121 C7 15 10N 61 20W
Dominican Rep. ■, W. Indies ... 121 C5 19 0N 70 30W
Dömitz, Germany ... 24 B7 53 9N 11 16 E
Domme, France ... 20 D5 44 48N 1 12 E
Domneşti, Romania ... 29 E9 45 12N 24 50 E
Domodóssola, Italy ... 40 B5 46 7N 8 17 E
Domogled-Valea Cernei △, Romania ... 28 F7 44 52N 22 27 E
Dompaire, France ... 19 D13 48 14N 6 14 E
Dompierre-sur-Besbre, France ... 19 F10 46 31N 3 41 E
Dompim, Ghana ... 82 D4 5 10N 2 5W
Domrémy-la-Pucelle, France ... 19 D12 48 26N 5 40 E
Domville, Mt., Australia ... 95 D5 28 1 S 151 15 E
Domvraína, Greece ... 46 C4 38 15N 22 59 E
Domžale, Slovenia ... 41 B11 46 9N 14 35 E
Don →, Russia ... 33 J4 47 4N 39 18 E
Don →, Aberds., U.K. ... 13 D6 57 11N 2 5W
Don →, S. Yorks., U.K. ... 14 D7 53 41N 0 52W
Don, C., Australia ... 92 B5 11 18 S 131 46 E
Don Benito, Spain ... 37 G5 38 53N 5 51W
Don Figuero Mts., Jamaica ... 120 a 18 5N 77 36W
Don Sak, Thailand ... 65 b 9 18N 99 41 E
Dona Ana = Nhamaanda, Mozam. ... 87 F4 17 25 S 35 5 E
Doña Mencía, Spain ... 37 H6 37 33N 4 21W
Donaghadee, U.K. ... 12 B6 54 39N 5 33W
Donald, Australia ... 95 F3 36 23 S 143 0 E
Donaldsonville, U.S.A. ... 113 K9 30 6N 90 59W
Donalsonville, U.S.A. ... 115 K3 31 3N 84 53W
Donau = Dunărea →, Europe ... 29 E14 45 20N 29 40 E
Donau →, Austria ... 27 C10 48 10N 17 0 E
Donau Auen △, Austria ... 27 C9 48 8N 16 44 E
Donaueschingen, Germany ... 25 H4 47 56N 8 29 E
Donauwörth, Germany ... 25 G6 48 43N 10 47 E
Doncaster, U.K. ... 14 D6 53 32N 1 6W
Dondo, Mozam. ... 87 F3 19 33 S 34 46 E
Dondo, Teluk, Indonesia ... 63 D6 0 50N 120 30 E
Dondra Head, Sri Lanka ... 66 S12 5 55N 80 40 E
Dondușeni, Moldova ... 29 B12 48 14N 27 36 E
Donegal, Ireland ... 12 B3 54 39N 8 5W
Donegal □, Ireland ... 12 B4 54 53N 8 0W
Donegal B., Ireland ... 12 B3 54 31N 8 49W
Donets →, Russia ... 35 G5 47 33N 40 55 E
Donets Basin, Ukraine ... 6 F13 49 0N 38 0 E
Donetsk, Ukraine ... 33 J9 48 0N 37 45 E
Dong Ba Thin, Vietnam ... 65 F7 12 8N 109 13 E
Dong Dang, Vietnam ... 58 G6 21 54N 106 42 E
Dong Giam, Vietnam ... 64 C5 19 25N 105 31 E
Dong Ha, Vietnam ... 64 D6 16 55N 107 8 E
Dong Hene, Laos ... 64 D5 16 40N 105 18 E
Dong Hoi, Vietnam ... 64 D6 17 29N 106 36 E
Dong Jiang →, China ... 59 F10 23 6N 114 0 E
Dong Khe, Vietnam ... 64 A6 22 26N 106 27 E
Dong Ujimqin Qi, China ... 56 B9 45 32N 116 55 E
Dong Van, Vietnam ... 64 A5 23 16N 105 22 E
Dong Xoai, Vietnam ... 65 G6 11 32N 106 55 E
Donga, Nigeria ... 83 D7 7 45N 10 2 E
Donga →, Nigeria ... 83 D7 8 20N 9 58 E
Dong'an, China ... 59 D8 26 23N 111 12 E
Dongara, Australia ... 93 E1 29 14 S 114 57 E
Dongbei, China ... 53 E13 45 0N 125 0 E
Dongchuan, China ... 58 E4 26 8N 103 1 E
Dongfang, China ... 64 C7 18 50N 108 33 E
Dongfeng, China ... 57 C13 42 40N 125 34 E
Donggala, Indonesia ... 63 E5 0 30 S 119 40 E
Donggan, China ... 58 F5 23 52N 104 10 E
Donggou, China ... 57 E13 39 52N 124 10 E
Dongguan, China ... 59 F9 22 58N 113 44 E
Dongguang, China ... 56 F9 37 50N 116 30 E
Donghai Dao, China ... 59 G8 21 0N 110 15 E
Dongjingcheng, China ... 57 B15 44 0N 130 25 E
Dongkou, China ... 59 D8 27 0N 110 35 E
Donglan, China ... 58 E6 24 30N 107 21 E
Dongliu, China ... 59 B11 30 13N 116 54 E
Dongmen, China ... 58 F6 22 20N 107 48 E
Dongming, China ... 57 B16 44 2N 131 5 E
Dongnyi, China ... 58 C3 28 35N 100 15 E
Dongola, Sudan ... 80 D3 19 9N 30 22 E
Dongping, China ... 56 G9 35 55N 116 20 E
Dongsha Dao, China ... 59 G11 20 45N 116 43 E
Dongshan, China ... 59 F11 23 43N 117 30 E
Dongsheng, China ... 56 E6 39 50N 110 0 E
Dongtai, China ... 57 H11 32 51N 120 21 E
Dongting Hu, China ... 59 C9 29 18N 112 45 E
Dongxiang, China ... 59 C11 28 14N 116 34 E
Dongxing, China ... 58 G7 21 34N 108 0 E
Dongyang, China ... 59 C13 29 13N 120 15 E
Dongzhi, China ... 59 B11 30 12N 116 56 E
Donington, C., Australia ... 95 E2 34 45 S 136 0 E
Doniphan, U.S.A. ... 113 G9 36 37N 90 50W
Donja Stubica, Croatia ... 41 C12 45 59N 15 59 E
Donji Dušnik, Serbia & M. ... 44 C6 43 12N 22 5 E
Donji Miholjac, Croatia ... 28 E3 45 45N 18 10 E
Donji Milanovac, Serbia & M. ... 44 B6 44 28N 22 6 E
Donji Vakuf, Bos.-H. ... 28 F2 44 8N 17 24 E
Dønna, Norway ... 8 C15 66 6N 12 30 E
Donna, U.S.A. ... 113 M5 26 9N 98 4W
Donnaconna, Canada ... 105 C5 46 41N 71 41W

Donnelly's Crossing, N.Z. ... 91 F4 35 42 S 173 38 E
Donnybrook, Australia ... 93 F2 33 34 S 115 48 E
Donnybrook, S. Africa ... 89 D4 29 59 S 29 48 E
Donora, U.S.A. ... 116 F5 40 11N 79 52W
Donostia = Donostia-San Sebastián, Spain ... 38 B3 43 17N 1 58W
Donostia-San Sebastián, Spain ... 38 B3 43 17N 1 58W
Donskoy, Russia ... 32 F10 53 55N 38 15 E
Donsol, Phil. ... 61 E5 12 54N 123 36 E
Donzère, France ... 21 D8 44 28N 4 43 E
Donzy, France ... 19 E10 47 20N 3 6 E
Doon →, U.K. ... 13 F4 55 27N 4 39W
Dora Báltea →, Italy ... 40 C5 45 11N 8 3 E
Dora Ripária →, Italy ... 40 C4 45 5N 7 44 E
Doran L., Canada ... 103 A7 61 13N 108 6W
Dorchester, U.K. ... 15 G5 50 42N 2 27W
Dorchester, C., Canada ... 101 B12 65 27N 77 27W
Dordabis, Namibia ... 88 C2 22 52 S 17 38 E
Dordogne □, France ... 20 C4 45 5N 0 40 E
Dordogne →, France ... 20 C3 45 2N 0 36W
Dordrecht, Neths. ... 17 C4 51 48N 4 39 E
Dordrecht, S. Africa ... 88 E4 31 20 S 27 3 E
Dore →, France ... 20 C7 45 50N 3 35 E
Dore, Mts., France ... 20 C6 45 32N 2 50 E
Doré L., Canada ... 103 C7 54 46N 107 17W
Doré Lake, Canada ... 103 C7 54 38N 107 36W
Dorfen, Germany ... 25 G8 48 15N 12 8 E
Dorgali, Italy ... 42 B2 40 17N 9 35 E
Dori, Burkina Faso ... 83 C4 14 3N 0 2W
Doring →, S. Africa ... 88 E2 31 54 S 18 39 E
Doringbos, S. Africa ... 88 E2 31 59 S 19 16 E
Dorking, U.K. ... 15 F7 51 14N 0 19W
Dormaa-Ahenkro, Ghana ... 82 D4 7 15N 2 52W
Dormans, France ... 19 C10 49 4N 3 38 E
Dormo, Ras, Eritrea ... 81 E5 13 14N 42 35 E
Dornbirn, Austria ... 26 D2 47 25N 9 45 E
Dornești, Romania ... 29 C11 47 52N 26 1 E
Dornie, U.K. ... 13 D3 57 17N 5 31W
Dornoch, U.K. ... 13 D4 57 53N 4 2W
Dornoch Firth, U.K. ... 13 D4 57 51N 4 4W
Dornogovĭ □, Mongolia ... 56 C6 44 0N 110 0 E
Doro, Mali ... 83 B4 16 9N 0 51W
Dorog, Hungary ... 28 C3 47 42N 18 45 E
Dorogobuzh, Russia ... 32 E7 54 50N 33 18 E
Dorohoi, Romania ... 29 C11 47 56N 26 23 E
Döröö Nuur, Mongolia ... 60 B4 48 0N 93 0 E
Dorr, Iran ... 71 C6 33 17N 50 38 E
Dorre I., Australia ... 93 E1 25 13 S 113 12 E
Dorrigo, Australia ... 95 E5 30 20 S 152 44 E
Dorris, U.S.A. ... 108 F3 41 58N 121 55W
Dorset, Canada ... 116 A6 45 14N 78 54W
Dorset, U.S.A. ... 116 E4 41 40N 80 40W
Dorset □, U.K. ... 15 G5 50 45N 2 26W
Dorsten, Germany ... 24 D2 51 40N 6 58 E
Dortmund, Germany ... 24 D3 51 30N 7 28 E
Dortmund-Ems-Kanal →, Germany ... 24 D3 51 50N 7 26 E
Dörtyol, Turkey ... 72 D7 36 50N 36 13 E
Dorum, Germany ... 24 B4 53 41N 8 34 E
Doruma, Dem. Rep. of the Congo ... 86 B2 4 42N 27 33 E
Dorūneh, Iran ... 71 C8 35 10N 57 18 E
Dos Bahías, C., Argentina ... 128 E3 44 58 S 65 32W
Dos Hermanas, Spain ... 37 H5 37 16N 5 55W
Dos Palos, U.S.A. ... 110 J6 36 59N 120 37W
Dosso, Niger ... 83 C5 13 0N 3 13 E
Dosso □, Niger ... 83 C5 12 36N 2 36 E
Dothan, U.S.A. ... 115 K3 31 13N 85 24W
Doty, U.S.A. ... 110 C3 46 38N 123 17W
Douai, France ... 19 B10 50 21N 3 4 E
Douako, Guinea ... 82 D2 9 45N 10 8W
Douala, Cameroon ... 83 E6 4 0N 9 45 E
Douarnenez, France ... 18 D2 48 6N 4 21W
Doubabougou, Mali ... 82 C3 14 13N 7 59W
Double Island Pt., Australia ... 95 D5 25 56 S 153 11 E
Double Mountain Fork →, U.S.A. ... 113 J4 33 16N 100 0W
Doubrava →, Czech Rep. ... 26 A8 50 2N 15 20 E
Doubs □, France ... 19 E13 47 10N 6 20 E
Doubs →, France ... 19 F12 46 53N 5 1 E
Doubtful Sd., N.Z. ... 91 L1 45 20 S 166 49 E
Doubtless B., N.Z. ... 91 F4 34 55 S 173 26 E
Doudeville, France ... 18 C7 49 43N 0 47 E
Doué-la-Fontaine, France ... 18 E6 47 11N 0 16W
Douentza, Mali ... 82 C4 14 58N 2 48W
Douentza △, Mali ... 82 B4 15 40N 2 25W
Douglas, S. Africa ... 88 D3 29 4 S 23 46 E
Douglas, U.K. ... 14 C3 54 10N 4 28W
Douglas, Ariz., U.S.A. ... 109 L9 31 21N 109 33W
Douglas, Ga., U.S.A. ... 115 K4 31 31N 82 51W
Douglas, Wyo., U.S.A. ... 112 D2 42 45N 105 24W
Douglas Apsley △, Australia ... 95 G4 41 45 S 148 11 E
Douglas Chan., Canada ... 102 C3 53 40N 129 20W
Douglas Pt., Canada ... 116 B3 44 19N 81 37W
Douglasville, U.S.A. ... 115 J3 33 45N 84 45W
Doukáton, Ákra, Greece ... 46 C2 38 34N 20 33 E
Doulevant-le-Château, France ... 19 D11 48 23N 4 55 E
Doullens, France ... 19 B9 50 10N 2 20 E
Doumen, China ... 59 F9 22 10N 113 18 E
Douna, Mali ... 82 C3 13 13N 6 0W
Dounreay, U.K. ... 13 C5 58 35N 3 44W
Dourada, Serra, Brazil ... 125 F9 13 10 S 48 45W
Dourados, Brazil ... 127 A5 22 9 S 54 50W
Dourados →, Brazil ... 127 A5 21 58 S 54 18W
Dourados, Serra dos, Brazil ... 127 A5 23 30 S 53 30W

Dourdan, France ... 19 D9 48 30N 2 1 E
Douro →, Europe ... 36 D2 41 8N 8 40W
Douvaine, France ... 19 F13 46 19N 6 16 E
Douvres-la-Délivrande, France ... 18 C6 49 17N 0 23W
Douze →, France ... 20 E3 43 54N 0 30W
Dove →, U.K. ... 14 E6 52 51N 1 36W
Dove Creek, U.S.A. ... 109 H9 37 46N 108 54W
Dover, Australia ... 95 G4 43 18 S 147 2 E
Dover, U.K. ... 15 F9 51 7N 1 19 E
Dover, Del., U.S.A. ... 113 F8 39 10N 75 32W
Dover, N.H., U.S.A. ... 117 C14 43 12N 70 56W
Dover, N.J., U.S.A. ... 117 F10 40 53N 74 34W
Dover, Ohio, U.S.A. ... 116 F3 40 32N 81 29W
Dover, Pt. of, Australia ... 93 F4 32 32 S 125 32 E
Dover, Str. of, Europe ... 15 G9 51 0N 1 30 E
Dover-Foxcroft, U.S.A. ... 115 C11 45 11N 69 13W
Dover Plains, U.S.A. ... 117 E11 41 43N 73 35W
Dovey = Dyfi →, U.K. ... 15 E3 52 32N 4 3W

Dovhe, *Ukraine* ...... **29 B8** 48 22N 23 17 E
Dovrefjell, *Norway* ... **9 E13** 62 15N 9 33 E
Dow Rūd, *Iran* ...... **71 C6** 33 28N 49 4 E
Dowa, *Malawi* ...... **87 E3** 13 38S 33 58 E
Dowagiac, *U.S.A.* **114 E2** 41 59N 86 6W
Dowerin, *Australia* ... **93 F2** 31 12S 117 2 E
Dowgha'i, *Iran* ...... **71 B8** 36 54N 58 32 E
Dowlatābād, *Iran* .... **71 D8** 28 20N 56 40 E
Down □, *U.K.* **12 B5** 54 23N 6 2W
Downey, *Calif., U.S.A.* **111 M8** 33 56N 118 7W
Downey, *Idaho, U.S.A.* **108 E7** 42 26N 112 7W
Downham Market, *U.K.* **15 E8** 52 37N 0 23 E
Downieville, *U.S.A.* .. **110 F6** 39 34N 120 50W
Downpatrick, *U.K.* ... **12 B6** 54 20N 5 43W
Downpatrick Hd.,
Ireland **12 B2** 54 20N 9 21W
Downsville, *U.S.A.* ... **117 D10** 42 5N 74 50W
Downton, Mt., *Canada* **102 C4** 52 42N 124 52W
Dowsāri, *Iran* ...... **71 D8** 28 25N 57 59 E
Doyle, *U.S.A.* **110 E6** 40 2N 120 6W
Doylestown, *U.S.A.* .. **117 F9** 40 21N 75 10W
Dozois, Rés., *Canada* . **104 C4** 47 30N 77 5W
Dra Khel, *Pakistan* ... **68 F2** 27 58N 66 45 E
Drac →, *France* ..... **21 C9** 45 12S 5 42 E
Dračevo, *Macedonia* .. **44 E5** 41 56N 21 31 E
Drachten, *Neths.* ..... **17 A6** 53 7N 6 5 E
Drăgănești, *Moldova* . **29 C13** 47 43N 28 15 E
Drăgănești-Olt,
Romania .... **29 F9** 44 9N 24 32 E
Drăgănești-Vlașca,
Romania .... **29 F10** 44 5N 25 33 E
Dragaš, Serbia & M. ... **44 D4** 42 5N 20 41 E
Drăgășani, *Romania* .. **29 F9** 44 39N 24 17 E
Dragichyn, *Belarus* ... **33 F3** 52 15N 25 8 E
Dragoman, *Bulgaria* .. **44 C7** 43 58N 21 15 E
Dragon's Mouth = Boca
de Drago, *Venezuela* **125 K15** 11 0N 61 50W
Dragovishtitsa, *Bulgaria* **44 D6** 42 22N 22 39 E
Draguignan, *France* ... **21 E10** 43 32N 6 27 E
Drahove, *Ukraine* .... **29 B8** 48 14N 23 33 E
Drain, *U.S.A.* **108 E2** 43 40N 123 19W
Drake, *U.S.A.* **112 B4** 47 55N 100 23W
Drake Passage, S. Ocean **5 B17** 58 0S 68 0W
Drakensberg, S. Africa . **89 D4** 31 0S 28 0 E
Dráma, *Greece* ...... **45 E8** 41 9N 24 10 E
Dráma □, *Greece* .... **45 E8** 41 20N 24 0 E
Drammen, *Norway* ... **9 G14** 59 42N 10 12 E
Drangajökull, *Iceland* . **8 C2** 66 9N 22 15W
Dranov, Ostrov,
Romania .... **29 F14** 44 55N 29 30 E
Dras, *India* .... **69 B6** 34 25N 75 48 E
Drau = Drava →,
Croatia .... **28 E3** 45 33N 18 55 E
Drava →, *Croatia* ... **28 E3** 45 33N 18 55 E
Dravograd, *Slovenia* . **41 B12** 46 36N 15 5 E
Drawa →, *Poland* ... **31 F2** 52 52N 15 9 E
Drawieński △, *Poland* **31 E2** 53 13N 15 58 E
Drawno, *Poland* .... **31 E2** 53 13N 15 46 E
Drawsko Pomorskie,
Poland .... **30 E2** 53 35N 15 50 E
Drayton Valley, *Canada* **102 C6** 53 12N 114 58W
Dreieich, *Germany* ... **25 E4** 50 1N 8 41 E
Dren, Serbia & M. .... **44 C4** 43 8N 20 46 E
Drenthe □, *Neths.* ... **17 B6** 52 52N 6 40 E
Drepanum, C., *Cyprus* **49 E11** 34 54N 32 19 E
Dresden, *Canada* **116 D2** 42 35N 82 11W
Dresden, *Germany* ... **24 D9** 51 3N 13 44 E
Dreux, *France* ...... **18 D8** 48 44N 1 23 E
Drezdenko, *Poland* ... **31 F2** 52 50N 15 49 E
Driffield, *U.K.* **14 C7** 54 0N 0 26W
Driftwood, *U.S.A.* ... **116 E6** 41 20N 78 8W
Driggs, *U.S.A.* **108 E8** 43 44N 111 6W
Drin →, *Albania* .... **44 D3** 42 1N 19 38 E
Drin i Zi →, *Albania* . **44 E4** 41 37N 20 28 E
Drina →, Bos.-H. .... **44 B3** 44 53N 19 21 E
Drincea →, *Romania* . **28 F7** 44 20N 22 55 E
Drinjača →, Bos.-H. .. **28 F4** 44 15N 19 8 E
Drissa =
Vyerkhnyadzvinsk,
Belarus .... **32 E4** 55 45N 27 58 E
Drniš, *Croatia* ...... **41 E13** 43 51N 16 10 E
Drøbak, *Norway* .... **9 G14** 59 39N 10 39 E
Drobeta-Turnu Severin,
Romania .... **28 F7** 44 39N 22 41 E
Drobin, *Poland* ..... **31 F6** 52 42N 19 58 E
Drochia, *Moldova* ... **29 B12** 48 2N 27 48 E
Drogheda, *Ireland* ... **12 C5** 53 43N 6 22W
Drogichin = Dragichyn,
Belarus .... **33 F3** 52 15N 25 8 E
Drogobych =
Drohobych, *Ukraine* **31 J10** 49 20N 23 30 E
Drohiczyn, *Poland* ... **31 F9** 52 24N 22 39 E
Drohobych, *Ukraine* . **31 J10** 49 20N 23 30 E
Droichead Atha =
Drogheda, *Ireland* . **12 C5** 53 43N 6 22W
Droichead Nua, *Ireland* **12 C5** 53 11N 6 48W
Droitwich, *U.K.* **15 E5** 52 16N 2 8W
Drôme □, *France* ... **21 D9** 44 38N 5 15 E
Drôme →, *France* ... **21 D8** 44 46N 4 46 E
Dromedary, C.,
Australia .... **95 F5** 36 17S 150 10 E
Drömling △, *Germany* **24 C7** 52 29N 11 5 E
Dromore, *U.K.* **12 B4** 54 31N 7 28W
Dromore West, *Ireland* **12 B3** 54 15N 8 52W
Dronero, *Italy* ..... **40 D4** 44 28N 7 22 E
Dronfield, *U.K.* **14 D6** 53 19N 1 27W
Dronne →, *France* ... **20 C3** 45 2N 0 9W
Dronning Maud Land,
Antarctica .... **5 D3** 72 30S 12 0 E
Dronninglund, *Denmark* **11 G4** 57 10N 10 19 E
Dronten, *Neths.* ..... **17 B5** 52 32N 5 43 E
Dropt →, *France* **20 D3** 44 35N 0 6W
Drosendorf, *Austria* .. **26 C8** 48 52N 15 37 E
Droué, *France* ...... **18 D8** 48 3N 1 6 E
Drumbo, *Canada* **116 C4** 43 16N 80 35W
Drumheller, *Canada* .. **102 C6** 51 25N 112 40W
Drummond, *U.S.A.* .. **108 C7** 46 40N 113 9W
Drummond I., *U.S.A.* **114 C4** 46 1N 83 39W
Drummond Pt.,
Australia .... **95 E2** 34 9S 135 16 E
Drummond Ra.,
Australia .... **94 C4** 23 45S 147 10 E
Drummondville, *Canada* **104 C5** 45 55N 72 25W
Drumright, *U.S.A.* ... **113 H6** 35 59N 96 36W
Druskininkai, *Lithuania* **9 J20** 54 3N 23 58 E
Drut →, *Belarus* .... **33 F6** 53 8N 30 5 E
Druya, *Belarus* ...... **32 E4** 55 45N 27 28 E
Druzhba, *Bulgaria* ... **45 C12** 43 15N 28 1 E
Druzhina, *Russia* .... **53 C15** 68 14N 145 18 E
Drvar, Bos.-H. ...... **41 D13** 44 21N 16 23 E
Drvenik, *Croatia* .... **41 E13** 43 27N 16 3 E
Drwęca →, *Poland* .. **31 E5** 53 0N 18 42 E
Dry Harbour Mts.,
Jamaica .... **120 a** 18 19N 77 24W
Dry Tortugas, *U.S.A.* **120 B3** 24 38N 82 55W
Dryanovo, *Bulgaria* .. **45 D9** 42 59N 25 28 E
Dryden, *Canada* **103 D10** 49 47N 92 50W

Dryden, *U.S.A.* **117 D8** 42 30N 76 18W
Drygalski I., *Antarctica* **5 C7** 66 0S 92 0 E
Drysdale →, *Australia* **92 B4** 13 59S 126 51 E
Drysdale I., *Australia* . **94 A2** 11 41S 136 0 E
Drysdale River △,
Australia .... **92 B4** 14 56S 127 2 E
Drzewica, *Poland* .... **31 G7** 51 27N 20 29 E
Drzewiczka →, *Poland* **31 G7** 51 36N 20 36 E
Dschang, *Cameroon* .. **83 D7** 5 32N 10 3 E
Du Bois, *U.S.A.* **116 E6** 41 8N 78 46W
Du Gué →, *Canada* .. **104 A5** 57 21N 70 45W
Du He, *China* ...... **59 A8** 32 48N 110 40 E
Du Quoin, *U.S.A.* ... **112 G10** 38 1N 89 14W
Du'an, *China* ...... **58 F7** 23 59N 108 3 E
Duanesburg, *U.S.A.* .. **117 D10** 42 45N 74 11W
Duaringa, *Australia* .. **94 C4** 23 42S 149 42 E
Duarte, Pico, Dom. Rep. **121 D5** 19 2N 70 59W
Dubā, Si. Arabia ..... **70 E2** 27 10N 35 40 E
Dubai = Dubayy, U.A.E. **71 E7** 25 18N 55 20 E
Dubăsari, *Moldova* .. **29 C14** 47 15N 29 10 E
Dubăsari Vdkhr.,
Moldova .... **29 C13** 47 30N 29 0 E
Dubawnt →, *Canada* . **103 A8** 64 33N 100 6W
Dubawnt L., *Canada* . **103 A8** 63 8N 101 28W
Dubayy, U.A.E. ..... **71 E7** 25 18N 55 20 E
Dubbo, *Australia* .... **95 E4** 32 11S 148 35 E
Dubele, Dem. Rep. of
the *Congo* .... **86 B2** 2 56N 29 35 E
Dübendorf, *Switz.* ... **25 H4** 47 24N 8 37 E
Dubica, *Croatia* ..... **41 C13** 45 11N 16 48 E
Dublin, *Ireland* **12 C5** 53 21N 6 15W
Dublin, Ga., U.S.A. .. **115 J4** 32 32N 82 54W
Dublin, Tex., U.S.A. .. **113 J5** 32 5N 98 21W
Dublin □, *Ireland* ... **12 C5** 53 24N 6 15W
Dublin ✈ (DUB),
Ireland **12 C5** 53 26N 6 15W
Dubna, *Russia* ...... **32 D9** 56 44N 37 10 E
Dubnica nad Váhom,
Slovak Rep. .... **27 C11** 48 58N 18 11 E
Dubno, *Ukraine* ..... **33 G3** 50 25N 25 45 E
Dubois, *U.S.A.* **108 D7** 44 10N 112 14W
Dubossary = Dubăsari,
Moldova .... **29 C14** 47 15N 29 10 E
Dubossary Vdkhr. =
Dubăsari Vdkhr.,
Moldova .... **29 C13** 47 30N 29 0 E
Dubove, *Ukraine* .... **29 B8** 48 10N 23 53 E
Dubovka, *Russia* .... **35 F7** 49 5N 44 50 E
Dubovskoye, *Russia* . **35 G6** 47 28N 42 46 E
Dubrajpur, *India* .... **69 H12** 23 48N 87 25 E
Dubréka, *Guinea* **82 D2** 9 46N 13 31W
Dubrovitsa =
Dubrovytsya, *Ukraine* **33 G4** 51 31N 26 35 E
Dubrovnik, *Croatia* .. **44 D2** 42 39N 18 6 E
Dubrovytsya, *Ukraine* **33 G4** 51 31N 26 35 E
Dubuque, *U.S.A.* **112 D9** 42 30N 90 41W
Duchang, *China* ..... **59 C11** 29 18N 116 12 E
Duchesne, *U.S.A.* ... **108 F8** 40 10N 110 24W
Duchess, *Australia* ... **94 C2** 21 20S 139 50 E
Ducie I., Pac. Oc. **97 K15** 24 40S 124 48W
Duck →, *U.S.A.* **115 G2** 36 2N 87 52W
Duck Cr. →, *Australia* **92 D2** 22 37S 116 53 E
Duck Lake, *Canada* .. **103 C7** 52 50N 106 16W
Duck Mountain △,
Canada **103 C8** 51 45N 101 0W
Duckwall, Mt., U.S.A. **110 H6** 37 58N 120 7W
Duderstadt, *Germany* . **24 D6** 51 31N 10 15 E
Dudhi, *India* .... **67 G13** 24 15N 83 10 E
Dudinka, *Russia* .... **53 C9** 69 30N 86 13 E
Dudley, *U.K.* **15 E5** 52 31N 2 5W
Dudwa, *India* ...... **69 E9** 28 30N 80 41 E
Duékoué, Ivory C. ... **82 D3** 6 40N 7 15W
Dueñas, *Spain* **36 D6** 41 52N 4 33W
Duero = Douro →,
Europe **36 D2** 41 8N 8 40W
Dufftown, *U.K.* **13 D5** 57 27N 3 8W
Dufourspitz, *Switz.* .. **25 K3** 45 56N 7 52 E
Dūghī Kalā, *Afghan.* . **66 C3** 32 20N 62 50 E
Dugi Otok, *Croatia* .. **41 D11** 44 0N 15 3 E
Dugo Selo, *Croatia* .. **41 C13** 45 51N 16 18 E
Duifken Pt., *Australia* **94 A3** 12 33S 141 38 E
Duisburg, *Germany* .. **24 D2** 51 26N 6 45 E
Duiwelskloof, S. Africa **89 C5** 23 42S 30 10 E
Dujiangyan, *China* ... **58 B4** 31 2N 103 38 E
Duk Fadiat, *Sudan* ... **81 F3** 7 45N 31 25 E
Duk Faiwil, *Sudan* ... **81 F3** 7 30N 31 29 E
Dukat, *Albania* ..... **44 F3** 40 16N 19 32 E
Dükdamin, *Iran* .... **71 C8** 35 59N 57 43 E
Dukelský Průsmyk,
Slovak Rep. .... **27 B14** 49 25N 21 42 E
Dukhān, *Qatar* ..... **71 E6** 25 25N 50 50 E
Dukhovshchina, *Russia* **32 E7** 55 15N 32 27 E
Duki, *Pakistan* ..... **66 D6** 30 14N 68 25 E
Dukla, *Poland* ...... **31 J8** 49 30N 21 35 E
Duku, Bauchi, Nigeria **83 C6** 10 43N 10 43 E
Duku, Sokoto, Nigeria **83 C5** 11 11N 4 55 E
Dulag, *Phil.* .... **61 F6** 10 57N 125 2 E
Dulce, *U.S.A.* **109 H10** 36 56N 107 0W
Dulce →, *Argentina* . **126 C3** 30 32S 62 33W
Dulce, G., Costa Rica . **120 E3** 8 40N 83 20W
Dulf, *Iraq* .... **70 C5** 35 7N 45 51 E
Dŭlgopol, *Bulgaria* .. **45 C11** 43 3N 27 22 E
Dulit, Banjaran,
Malaysia .... **62 D4** 3 15N 114 30 E
Duliu, *China* .... **56 E9** 39 2N 116 55 E
Dullewala, *Pakistan* .. **68 D4** 31 50N 71 25 E
Dullstroom, S. Africa . **89 D5** 25 27S 30 7 E
Dülmen, *Germany* ... **24 D3** 51 49N 7 17 E
Dulovo, *Bulgaria* .... **45 C11** 43 48N 27 9 E
Duluth, *U.S.A.* **112 B8** 46 47N 92 6W
Dum Dum, *India* .... **69 H13** 22 39N 88 33 E
Dum Duma, *India* ... **67 F19** 27 40N 95 40 E
Dūmā, *Syria* .... **74 B5** 33 34N 36 24 E
Dumaguete, *Phil.* .... **61 G5** 9 17N 123 15 E
Dumai, *Indonesia* .... **62 D2** 1 35N 101 28 E
Dumaran, *Phil.* ..... **61 F3** 10 33N 119 50 E
Dumas, Ark., U.S.A. . **113 J9** 33 53N 91 29W
Dumas, Tex., U.S.A. . **113 H4** 35 52N 101 58W
Dumayr, *Syria* ..... **74 B5** 33 39N 36 42 E
Dumbarton, *U.K.* ... **13 F4** 55 57N 4 33W
Dumbier, Slovak Rep. . **27 C12** 48 56N 19 25 E
Dumbleyung, *Australia* **93 F2** 33 17S 117 42 E
Dumbrăveni, *Romania* **29 D9** 46 14N 24 34 E
Dumfries, *U.K.* **13 F5** 55 4N 3 37W
Dumfries &
Galloway □, U.K. . **13 F5** 55 9N 3 58W
Dumitrești, *Romania* . **29 E11** 45 33N 26 55 E
Dumka, *India* ...... **69 G12** 24 12N 87 15 E
Dumlupınar, *Turkey* . **47 C12** 38 50N 30 2 E
Dümmer, *Germany* .. **24 C4** 52 31N 8 21 E
Dümmer □, *Germany* **24 C4** 52 30N 8 21 E
Dumoine →, *Canada* . **104 C4** 46 13N 77 51W
Dumoine, L., *Canada* **104 C4** 46 55N 77 55W
Dumont d'Urville,
Antarctica .... **5 C10** 67 0S 110 0 E

Dumraon, *India* ..... **69 G11** 25 33N 84 8 E
Dumyât, *Egypt* ..... **80 H7** 31 24N 31 48 E
Dumyât, Masabb, Egypt **80 H7** 31 28N 31 51 E
Dún Dealgan =
Dundalk, *Ireland* .. **12 B5** 54 1N 6 24W
Dún Laoghaire, Ireland **12 C5** 53 17N 6 8W
Dun-sur-Auron, *France* **19 F9** 46 53N 2 33 E
Dun-sur-Meuse, *France* **19 C12** 49 23N 5 11 E
Duna = Dunărea →,
Europe .... **29 E14** 45 20N 29 40 E
Duna →, *Hungary* ... **28 E3** 45 51N 18 48 E
Duna-Drava △,
Hungary .... **28 D3** 46 15N 18 50 E
Duna-völgyi-főcsatorna,
Hungary .... **28 D4** 46 40N 19 14 E
Dunaföldvár, *Hungary* **28 D3** 46 50N 18 57 E
Dunagiri, *India* ..... **69 D8** 30 31N 79 52 E
Dunaj = Dunărea →,
Europe .... **29 E14** 45 20N 29 40 E
Dunaj →, Slovak Rep. **27 D11** 47 50N 18 50 E
Dunajec →, *Poland* .. **31 H7** 50 15N 20 44 E
Dunajská Streda,
Slovak Rep. .... **27 C10** 48 0N 17 37 E
Dunakeszi, *Hungary* . **28 C4** 47 37N 19 8 E
Dunapataj, *Hungary* . **28 D4** 46 39N 19 4 E
Dunărea →, *Europe* . **29 E14** 45 20N 29 40 E
Dunaszekcső, *Hungary* **28 D3** 46 6N 18 45 E
Dunaújváros, *Hungary* **28 D3** 46 58N 18 57 E
Dunav = Dunărea →,
Europe .... **29 E14** 45 20N 29 40 E
Dunavaţu de Jos,
Romania .... **29 F14** 44 59N 29 13 E
Dunavtsi, *Bulgaria* ... **44 C6** 43 57N 22 53 E
Dunay, *Russia* ...... **54 C6** 42 52N 132 22 E
Dunayivtsi, *Ukraine* . **29 B11** 48 54N 26 56 E
Dunback, N.Z. ...... **91 L3** 45 23S 170 36 E
Dunbar, *U.K.* **13 E6** 56 0N 2 31W
Dunblane, *U.K.* **13 E5** 56 11N 3 58W
Duncan, *Canada* **102 D4** 48 45N 123 40W
Duncan, Ariz., U.S.A. **109 K9** 32 43N 109 6W
Duncan, Okla., U.S.A. **113 H6** 34 30N 97 57W
Duncan, L., *Canada* .. **104 B4** 53 29N 77 58W
Duncan L., *Canada* .. **102 A6** 62 51N 113 58W
Duncan Town, Bahamas **120 B4** 22 15N 75 45W
Duncannon, *U.S.A.* .. **116 F7** 40 23N 77 2W
Duncansby Head, U.K. **13 C5** 58 38N 3 1W
Duncansville, *U.S.A.* . **116 F6** 40 25N 78 26W
Dundaga, *Latvia* .... **30 A9** 57 30N 22 21 E
Dundalk, *Canada* **116 B4** 44 10N 80 24W
Dundalk, *Ireland* **12 B5** 54 1N 6 24W
Dundalk, *U.S.A.* **114 F7** 39 16N 76 32W
Dundalk Bay, Ireland . **12 C5** 53 55N 6 15W
Dundas = Uummannaq,
Greenland **4 B4** 77 0N 69 0W
Dundas = Uummannaq,
Greenland **4 B5** 70 58N 52 0W
Dundas, *Canada* **116 C5** 43 17N 79 59W
Dundas, L., *Australia* **93 F3** 32 35S 121 50 E
Dundas I., *Canada* ... **102 C2** 54 30N 130 35W
Dundas Str., *Australia* **92 B5** 11 15S 131 35 E
Dundee, S. Africa .... **89 D5** 28 11S 30 15 E
Dundee, *U.K.* **13 E6** 56 28N 2 59W
Dundee, U.S.A. **116 D8** 42 32N 76 59W
Dundee City □, U.K. . **13 E6** 56 30N 2 58W
Dundgovĭ □, Mongolia **56 B4** 45 10N 106 0 E
Dundrum, *U.K.* **12 B6** 54 16N 5 52W
Dundrum B., U.K. ... **12 B6** 54 13N 5 47W
Dunedin, N.Z. ...... **91 L3** 45 50S 170 33 E
Dunedin, U.S.A. **115 L4** 28 1N 82 47W
Dunfermline, U.K. ... **13 E5** 56 5N 3 27W
Dungannon, *Canada* . **116 C3** 43 51N 81 36W
Dungannon, U.K. **12 B5** 54 31N 6 46W
Dungarpur, *India* .... **68 H5** 23 52N 73 45 E
Dungarvan, *Ireland* .. **12 D4** 52 5N 7 37W
Dungarvan Harbour,
Ireland **12 D4** 52 4N 7 35W
Dungeness, *U.K.* .... **15 G8** 50 54N 0 59 E
Dungo, L. do, Angola . **88 B2** 17 15S 19 0 E
Dungog, *Australia* ... **95 E5** 32 22S 151 46 E
Dungu, Dem. Rep. of
the *Congo* .... **86 B2** 3 40N 28 32 E
Dungun, *Malaysia* ... **65 K4** 4 45N 103 25 E
Dungunâb, *Sudan* ... **80 C4** 21 10N 37 9 E
Dungunâb, Khalîg,
Sudan .... **80 C4** 21 5N 37 12 E
Dunhua, *China* ..... **57 C15** 43 20N 128 14 E
Dunhuang, *China* .... **60 B4** 40 8N 94 36 E
Dunk I., *Australia* ... **94 B4** 17 59S 146 29 E
Dunkassa, Benin ..... **83 C5** 10 23N 3 10 E
Dunkeld, *Australia* ... **95 E4** 33 25S 149 29 E
Dunkeld, U.K. **13 E5** 56 34N 3 35W
Dunkerque, *France* .. **19 A9** 51 2N 2 20 E
Dunkery Beacon, U.K. **15 F4** 51 9N 3 36W
Dunkirk = Dunkerque,
France .... **19 A9** 51 2N 2 20 E
Dunkirk, *U.S.A.* **116 D5** 42 29N 79 20W
Dunkuj, *Sudan* ..... **81 E3** 12 50N 32 49 E
Dunkwa, Central, Ghana **82 D4** 6 0N 1 47W
Dunkwa, Central, Ghana **83 D4** 5 30N 1 0W
Dúnleary = Dún
Laoghaire, Ireland .. **12 C5** 53 17N 6 8W
Dunleer, *Ireland* **12 C5** 53 50N 6 24W
Dunmanus B., Ireland . **12 E2** 51 31N 9 50W
Dunmanway, Ireland . **12 E2** 51 43N 9 6W
Dunmara, *Australia* .. **94 B1** 16 42S 133 25 E
Dunmore, U.S.A. **117 E9** 41 25N 75 38W
Dunmore Hd., Ireland . **12 D1** 52 10N 10 35W
Dunmore Town,
Bahamas **120 A4** 25 30N 76 39W
Dunn, U.S.A. **115 H6** 35 19N 78 37W
Dunnellon, U.S.A. ... **115 L4** 29 3N 82 28W
Dunnet Hd., U.K. ... **13 C5** 58 40N 3 21W
Dunning, U.S.A. **112 E4** 41 50N 100 6W
Dunnville, *Canada* ... **116 D5** 42 54N 79 36W
Dunolly, *Australia* ... **95 F3** 36 51S 143 44 E
Dunoon, *U.K.* **13 F4** 55 57N 4 56W
Dunphy, U.S.A. **108 F5** 40 42N 116 31W
Dunqul, Egypt ...... **80 C3** 23 26N 31 37 E
Duns, *U.K.* **13 F6** 55 47N 2 20W
Dunseith, *U.S.A.* **112 A4** 48 50N 100 3W
Dunshaughlin, *Ireland* **12 C5** 53 31N 6 48W
Dunstable, U.K. **15 F7** 51 53N 0 32W
Dunstan Mts., N.Z. .. **91 L2** 44 53S 169 35 E
Dunster, *Canada* **102 C5** 53 8N 119 50W
Dunvegan, U.K. **13 D2** 57 27N 6 35W
Dunvegan L., *Canada* **103 A7** 60 8N 107 10W
Duolun, *China* ...... **56 C9** 42 12N 116 28 E
Duong Dong, *Vietnam* **65 G4** 10 13N 103 58 E
Dupree, *U.S.A.* **112 C4** 45 4N 101 35W
Dupuyer, U.S.A. **108 B7** 48 13N 112 30W
Duque de Caxias, Brazil **127 A7** 22 45S 43 19W
Durack →, *Australia* . **92 C4** 15 33S 127 52 E
Durack Ra., *Australia* **92 C4** 16 50S 127 40 E
Durağan, *Turkey* .... **72 B6** 41 25N 35 2 E
Durak, *Turkey* ...... **47 B10** 39 42N 28 17 E
Đurakovac, Serbia & M. **44 D4** 42 43N 20 29 E

Durance →, *France* .. **21 E8** 43 55N 4 45 E
Durand, *U.S.A.* **112 C9** 44 38N 91 58W
Durango, *Mexico* **118 C4** 24 3N 104 39W
Durango □, Mexico ... **118 C4** 25 0N 105 0W
Durango, *U.S.A.* **109 H10** 37 16N 107 53W
Durankulak, *Bulgaria* **45 C12** 43 41N 28 32 E
Durant, Miss., U.S.A. . **113 J10** 33 4N 89 51W
Durant, Okla., U.S.A. **113 J6** 33 59N 96 25W
Durazno, *Uruguay* ... **126 C4** 33 25S 56 31W
Durazzo = Durrës,
Albania .... **44 E3** 41 19N 19 28 E
Durban, *France* ..... **20 E7** 42 52N 2 49 E
Durban, S. Africa .... **89 D5** 29 49S 31 1 E
Durbuy, *Belgium* .... **17 D5** 50 21N 5 28 E
Dúrcal, *Spain* **37 J7** 36 59N 3 34W
Đurđevac, *Croatia* ... **28 D2** 46 2N 17 3 E
Düren, *Germany* .... **24 E2** 50 48N 6 29 E
Durg, *India* .... **67 J12** 21 15N 81 22 E
Durgapur, *India* ..... **69 H12** 23 30N 87 20 E
Durham, *Canada* **116 B4** 44 10N 80 49W
Durham, *U.K.* **14 C6** 54 47N 1 34W
Durham, Calif., U.S.A. **110 F5** 39 39N 121 48W
Durham, N.C., U.S.A. **115 H6** 35 59N 78 54W
Durham, N.H., U.S.A. **117 C14** 43 8N 70 56W
Durham □, U.K. **14 C6** 54 42N 1 45W
Durlești, *Moldova* ... **29 C13** 47 1N 28 46 E
Đurmanec, Serbia & M. **70 E5** 24 37N 46 8 E
Durmitor,
Serbia & M. ...... **44 C3** 43 15N 19 5 E
Durness, *U.K.* **13 C4** 58 34N 4 45W
Durrës, *Albania* ..... **44 E3** 41 19N 19 28 E
Durrow, *Ireland* **12 D4** 52 51N 7 24W
Dursey I., *Ireland* ... **12 E1** 51 36N 10 12W
Dursley, U.K. **15 F5** 51 40N 2 21W
Dursunbey, *Turkey* .. **47 B10** 39 35N 28 37 E
Durtal, *France* **18 E6** 47 40N 0 18W
Duru, Dem. Rep. of
the *Congo* .... **86 B2** 4 14N 28 50 E
Duru Gölü, Turkey ... **45 E12** 41 30N 27 40 E
Durusu, *Turkey* ..... **45 E12** 41 17N 28 41 E
Durūz, Jabal ad, Jordan **74 C5** 32 35N 36 40 E
D'Urville, Tanjung,
Indonesia .... **63 E9** 1 28S 137 54 E
D'Urville I., N.Z. .... **91 J4** 40 50S 173 55 E
Duryea, *U.S.A.* **117 E9** 41 20N 75 45W
Dûsh, *Egypt* .... **80 C3** 24 35N 30 41 E
Dushak, Turkmenistan **52 F7** 37 13N 60 1 E
Dushan, *China* ...... **58 E6** 25 48N 107 30 E
Dushanbe, Tajikistan . **52 F7** 38 33N 68 48 E
Dusheti, Georgia ..... **35 J7** 42 10N 44 42 E
Dushore, *U.S.A.* **117 E8** 41 31N 76 24W
Dusky Sd., N.Z. ..... **91 L1** 45 47S 166 30 E
Dussejour, C., Australia **92 B4** 14 45S 128 13 E
Düsseldorf, *Germany* **24 D2** 51 14N 6 47 E
Düsseldorf Rhein-
Ruhr ✈ (DUS),
Germany .... **24 D2** 51 17N 6 46 E
Dusznicki-Zdrój, Poland **31 H3** 50 24N 16 24 E
Dutch Harbor, U.S.A. **100 C3** 53 53N 166 32W
Dutlwe, *Botswana* ... **88 C3** 23 58S 23 46 E
Dutsan Wai, Nigeria . **83 C6** 10 50N 8 10 E
Dutton, *Canada* **116 D3** 42 39N 81 30W
Dutton →, *Australia* . **94 C3** 20 44S 143 10 E
Duved, *Sweden* ..... **10 A6** 63 23N 12 55 E
Düvertepe, *Turkey* .. **47 B10** 39 14N 28 27 E
Duwayhin, Khawr,
U.A.E. .... **71 E6** 24 20N 51 25 E
Duyun, *China* ...... **58 D6** 26 18N 107 29 E
Düzağaç, *Turkey* .... **47 C12** 38 48N 30 10 E
Düzce, *Turkey* ...... **72 B4** 40 50N 31 10 E
Dve Mogili, *Bulgaria* **45 C9** 43 35N 25 55 E
Dvina, Severnaya →,
Russia .... **52 C5** 64 32N 40 30 E
Dvinsk = Daugavpils,
Latvia .... **9 J22** 55 53N 26 32 E
Dvor, *Croatia* ...... **41 C13** 45 4N 16 22 E
Dvůr Králové nad
Labem, Czech Rep. . **26 A8** 50 27N 15 50 E
Dwarka, *India* ...... **68 H3** 22 18N 69 8 E
Dwellingup, *Australia* **93 F2** 32 43S 116 4 E
Dwight, *Canada* **116 A5** 45 20N 79 1W
Dwight, *U.S.A.* **114 E1** 41 5N 88 26W
Dyakovo, *Ukraine* ... **28 B7** 48 1N 23 0 E
Dyatkovo, *Russia* ... **32 F8** 53 40N 34 27 E
Dyatlovo = Dzyatlava,
Belarus .... **32 F3** 53 28N 25 28 E
Dyce, U.K. **13 D6** 57 13N 2 12W
Dyer, C., *Canada* ... **101 B13** 66 37N 61 16W
Dyer Bay, *Canada* ... **116 A3** 45 10N 81 20W
Dyer Plateau, Antarctica **5 D17** 70 45S 65 30W
Dyersburg, *U.S.A.* ... **113 G10** 36 3N 89 23W
Dyfi →, *U.K.* **15 E3** 52 32N 4 3W
Dyje →, Czech Rep. . **27 C9** 48 37N 16 56 E
Dymer, *Ukraine* ..... **33 G6** 50 47N 30 18 E
Dynów, *Poland* ..... **31 J9** 49 50N 22 11 E
Dysart, *Australia* .... **94 C4** 22 32S 148 23 E
Dyviziya, *Ukraine* ... **29 E14** 45 55N 29 59 E
Dzamin Üüd = Borhoyn
Tal, *Mongolia* ..... **56 C6** 43 50N 111 58 E
Dzerzhinsk, *Russia* ... **34 B6** 56 14N 43 30 E
Dzhalinda, *Russia* ... **53 D13** 53 26N 124 0 E
Dzhambul = Taraz,
Kazakhstan .... **52 E8** 42 54N 71 22 E
Dzhankoy, *Ukraine* . **33 K8** 45 40N 34 20 E
Dzhanybek, *Kazakhstan* **34 F8** 49 25N 46 50 E
Dzharylhach, Ostriv,
Ukraine .... **33 J7** 46 2N 32 55 E
Dzhezkazgan =
Zhezqazghan,
Kazakhstan .... **52 E7** 47 44N 67 40 E
Dzhizak = Jizzakh,
Uzbekistan .... **52 E7** 40 6N 67 50 E
Dzhugdzur, Khrebet,
Russia .... **53 D14** 57 30N 138 0 E
Dzhulynk, *Ukraine* .. **29 B14** 48 26N 29 45 E
Dzhvari = Jvari, Georgia **35 J6** 42 42N 42 4 E
Działdowo, *Poland* .. **31 E7** 53 15N 20 15 E
Działoszyce, *Poland* . **31 H7** 50 22N 20 20 E
Działoszyn, *Poland* .. **31 G5** 51 6N 18 50 E
Dzibilchaltún, Mexico . **119 C7** 21 5N 89 36W
Dzierzgoń, *Poland* ... **30 E6** 53 58N 19 20 E
Dzierżoniów, *Poland* . **31 H3** 50 45N 16 39 E
Dzilam de Bravo,
Mexico **119 C7** 21 24N 88 53W
Dzisna, *Belarus* ..... **32 E5** 55 34N 28 12 E
Dzisna →, *Belarus* .. **32 E5** 55 34N 28 12 E
Dziwnów, *Poland* ... **30 D1** 54 2N 14 45 E
Dzuumod, Mongolia . **60 B5** 47 45N 106 58 E
Dzyarzhynsk, *Belarus* **32 F4** 53 40N 27 1 E
Dzyatlava, *Belarus* ... **32 F3** 53 28N 25 28 E

E

E.C. Manning △,
Canada **102 D4** 49 5N 120 45W
Eabamet L., *Canada* . **104 B2** 51 30N 87 46W
Eads, *U.S.A.* **112 F3** 38 29N 102 47W
Eagar, *U.S.A.* **109 J9** 34 6N 109 17W
Eagle, Alaska, U.S.A. . **100 B5** 64 47N 141 12W
Eagle, Colo., U.S.A. .. **108 G10** 39 39N 106 50W
Eagle →, *Canada* **105 B8** 53 36N 57 26W
Eagle Butte, *U.S.A.* .. **112 C4** 45 0N 101 10W
Eagle Grove, U.S.A. . **112 D8** 42 40N 93 54W
Eagle L., *Canada* **103 D10** 49 42N 93 13W
Eagle L., Calif., U.S.A. **108 F3** 40 39N 120 45W
Eagle L., Maine, U.S.A. **115 B11** 46 20N 69 22W
Eagle Lake, *Canada* .. **116 A6** 45 8N 78 29W
Eagle Lake, Maine,
U.S.A. **115 B11** 47 3N 68 36W
Eagle Lake, Tex., U.S.A. **113 L6** 29 35N 96 20W
Eagle Mountain, U.S.A. **111 M11** 33 49N 115 27W
Eagle Nest, *U.S.A.* .. **109 H11** 36 33N 105 16W
Eagle Pass, *U.S.A.* .. **113 L4** 28 43N 100 30W
Eagle Pk., *U.S.A.* ... **110 G7** 38 10N 119 25W
Eagle Pt., *Australia* .. **92 C3** 16 11S 124 23 E
Eagle River, Mich.,
U.S.A. **114 B1** 47 24N 88 18W
Eagle River, Wis.,
U.S.A. **112 C10** 45 55N 89 15W
Eaglehawk, *Australia* **95 F3** 36 44S 144 15 E
Eagles Mere, *U.S.A.* . **117 E8** 41 25N 76 33W
Ealing, *U.K.* **15 F7** 51 31N 0 19W
Ear Falls, *Canada* ... **103 C10** 50 38N 93 13W
Earle, *U.S.A.* **113 H9** 35 16N 90 28W
Earlimart, U.S.A. **111 K7** 35 53N 119 16W
Earn →, *U.K.* **13 E5** 56 21N 3 18W
Earn, L., U.K. **13 E4** 56 23N 4 13W
Earnslaw, Mt., N.Z. .. **91 L2** 44 32S 168 27 E
Earth, *U.S.A.* **113 H3** 34 14N 102 24W
Easley, *U.S.A.* **115 H4** 34 50N 82 36W
East Anglia, U.K. .... **14 E9** 52 30N 1 0 E
East Angus, *Canada* . **105 C5** 45 30N 71 40W
East Antarctica,
Antarctica .... **5 D7** 80 0S 90 0 E
East Aurora, *U.S.A.* . **116 D6** 42 46N 78 37W
East Ayrshire □, U.K. **13 F4** 55 26N 4 11W
East Bengal, Bangla. . **67 H17** 24 0N 90 0 E
East Brady, *U.S.A.* .. **116 F5** 40 59N 79 36W
East C., N.Z. .... **91 G7** 37 42S 178 35 E
East Chicago, U.S.A. . **114 E2** 41 38N 87 27W
East China Sea, Asia . **60 C7** 30 5N 126 0 E
East Coulee, *Canada* **102 C6** 51 23N 112 27W
East Dereham =
Dereham, U.K. .... **15 E8** 52 41N 0 57 E
East Dunbartonshire □,
U.K. **13 F4** 55 57N 4 13W
East Falkland, Falk. Is. **128 G5** 51 30S 58 30W
East Grand Forks,
U.S.A. **112 B6** 47 56N 97 1W
East Greenwich, U.S.A. **117 E13** 41 40N 71 27W
East Grinstead, U.K. . **15 F8** 51 7N 0 0 E
East Hartford, U.S.A. **117 E12** 41 46N 72 39W
East Helena, U.S.A. .. **108 C8** 46 35N 111 56W
East Indies, Asia ..... **50 K15** 0 0 120 0 E
East Kilbride, U.K. ... **13 F4** 55 47N 4 11W
East Lansing, U.S.A. . **114 D3** 42 44N 84 29W
East Liverpool, U.S.A. **116 F4** 40 37N 80 35W
East London, S. Africa **89 E4** 33 0S 27 55 E
East Lothian □, U.K. **13 F6** 55 58N 2 44W
East Main = Eastmain,
Canada **104 B4** 52 10N 78 30W
East Northport, U.S.A. **117 F11** 40 53N 73 20W
East Orange, U.S.A. .. **117 F10** 40 46N 74 13W
East Pacific Ridge,
Pac. Oc. **97 J17** 15 0S 110 0W
East Palestine, U.S.A. **116 F4** 40 50N 80 32W
East Pine, *Canada* ... **102 B4** 55 48N 120 12W
East Point, U.S.A. ... **115 J3** 33 41N 84 27W
East Providence, U.S.A. **117 E13** 41 49N 71 23W
East Pt., Br. Virgin Is. **121 e** 18 40N 64 18W
East Pt., *Canada* **105 C7** 46 27N 61 58W
East Renfrewshire □,
U.K. **13 F4** 55 46N 4 21W
East Retford = Retford,
U.K. **14 D7** 53 19N 0 56W
East Riding of
Yorkshire □, U.K. . **14 D7** 53 55N 0 30W
East Rochester, U.S.A. **116 C7** 43 7N 77 29W
East St. Louis, U.S.A. **112 F9** 38 37N 90 9W
East Schelde =
Oosterschelde →,
Neths. .... **17 C4** 51 33N 4 0 E
East Sea = Japan, Sea of,
Asia .... **54 E7** 40 0N 135 0 E
East Siberian Sea,
Russia .... **53 B17** 73 0N 160 0 E
East Stroudsburg, U.S.A. **117 E9** 41 1N 75 11W
East Sussex □, U.K. . **15 G8** 50 56N 0 19 E
East Tawas, *U.S.A.* .. **114 C4** 44 17N 83 29W
East Timor ■, Asia ... **63 F7** 8 50S 126 0 E
East Toorale, *Australia* **95 E4** 30 27S 145 28 E
East Walker →, U.S.A. **110 G7** 38 52N 119 10W
East Windsor, U.S.A. **117 F10** 40 17N 74 34W
Eastbourne, N.Z. .... **91 J5** 41 19S 174 55 E
Eastbourne, U.K. .... **15 G8** 50 46N 0 18 E
Eastend, *Canada* **103 D7** 49 32N 108 50W
Easter I. = Pascua, I. de,
Chile **97 K17** 27 7S 109 23W
Eastern □, Ghana **83 D4** 6 30N 0 30W
Eastern □, Kenya .... **86 C4** 0 0 38 30 E
Eastern □, S. Leone .. **82 D2** 8 15N 11 0W
Eastern Cape □,
S. Africa .... **88 E4** 32 0S 26 0 E
Eastern Cr. →, Australia **94 C3** 20 40S 141 35 E
Eastern Ghats, India . **66 N11** 14 0N 78 50 E
Eastern Group = Lau
Group, Fiji **91 C9** 17 0S 178 30W
Eastern Group,
Australia .... **93 F3** 33 30S 124 30 E
Eastern Transvaal =
Mpumalanga □,
S. Africa .... **89 D5** 26 0S 30 0 E
Easterville, *Canada* .. **103 C9** 53 8N 99 49W
Easthampton, *U.S.A.* **117 D12** 42 16N 72 40W
Eastlake, *U.S.A.* **116 E3** 41 40N 81 26W
Eastland, *U.S.A.* **113 J5** 32 24N 98 49W
Eastleigh, U.K. **15 G6** 50 58N 1 21W
Eastmain, *Canada* ... **104 B4** 52 10N 78 30W
Eastmain →, *Canada* **104 B4** 52 27N 78 26W
Eastman, *Canada* **117 A12** 45 18N 72 19W
Eastman, *U.S.A.* **115 J4** 32 12N 83 11W
Easton, Md., U.S.A. . **114 F7** 38 47N 76 5W
Easton, Pa., U.S.A. .. **117 F9** 40 41N 75 13W
Easton, Wash., U.S.A. **110 C5** 47 14N 121 11W

Eastpointe, *U.S.A.* **116 D2** 42 27N 82 56W
Eastport, *U.S.A.* **115 C12** 44 56N 67 0W
Eastsound, *U.S.A.* **110 B4** 48 42N 122 55W
Eaton, *Canada* **112 E2** 40 32N 104 42W
Eatonia, *Canada* **103 C7** 51 13N 109 25W
Eatonton, *U.S.A.* **115 J4** 33 20N 83 23W
Eatontown, *U.S.A.* **117 F10** 40 19N 74 4W
Eatonville, *U.S.A.* **110 D4** 46 52N 122 16W
Eau Claire, *U.S.A.* **112 C9** 44 49N 91 30W
Eau Claire, L. à l', *Canada* **104 A5** 56 10N 74 25W
Eauze, *France* ..... **20 E4** 43 53N 0 7 E
Eban, *Nigeria* ..... **83 D5** 9 40N 4 50 E
Ebbegebirge △, *Germany* ..... **24 D3** 51 10N 7 55 E
Ebbw Vale, *U.K.* **15 F4** 51 46N 3 12W
Ebeltoft, *Denmark* ..... **11 H4** 56 12N 10 41 E
Ebeltoft Vig, *Denmark* ..... **11 H4** 56 10N 10 35 E
Ebensburg, *U.S.A.* **116 F6** 40 29N 78 44W
Ebensee, *Austria* ..... **26 D6** 47 48N 13 46 E
Eber Gölü, *Turkey* ..... **72 C4** 38 38N 31 11 E
Eberbach, *Germany* ..... **25 F4** 49 28N 8 59 E
Eberswalde-Finow, *Germany* ..... **24 C9** 52 50N 13 49 E
Ebetsu, *Japan* ..... **54 C10** 43 7N 141 34 E
Ebey's Landing △, *U.S.A.* **110 B4** 48 13N 122 41W
Ebian, *China* ..... **58 C4** 29 11N 103 13 E
Ebingen, *Germany* ..... **25 G5** 48 13N 9 1 E
Éboli, *Italy* ..... **43 B8** 40 39N 15 2 E
Ebolowa, *Cameroon* ..... **83 E7** 2 55N 11 10 E
Ebonyi □, *Nigeria* ..... **83 D6** 6 20N 8 0 E
Ebrach, *Germany* ..... **25 F6** 49 51N 10 29 E
Ébrié, Lagune, *Ivory C.* **82 D4** 5 12N 4 26W
Ebro ➤, *Spain* ..... **38 E5** 40 43N 0 54 E
Ebro, Embalse del, *Spain* **36 C7** 43 0N 3 58W
Ebstorf, *Germany* ..... **24 B6** 53 2N 10 24 E
Eceabat, *Turkey* ..... **45 F10** 40 11N 26 21 E
Ech Chéliff, *Algeria* ..... **78 A6** 36 10N 1 20 E
Echigo-Sammyaku, *Japan* ..... **55 F9** 36 50N 139 50 E
Échirolles, *France* ..... **21 C9** 45 8N 5 44 E
Echizen-Misaki, *Japan* ..... **55 G7** 35 59N 135 57 E
Echmiadzin = Yejmiadzin, *Armenia* ..... **35 K7** 40 12N 44 19 E
Echo Bay, *N.W.T.*, *Canada* **100 B8** 66 5N 117 55W
Echo Bay, *Ont., Canada* **104 C3** 46 29N 84 4W
Echoing ➤, *Canada* **104 B1** 55 51N 92 5W
Echterdingen, Stuttgart ✈ (STR), *Germany* ..... **25 G5** 48 42N 9 11 E
Echternach, *Lux.* ..... **17 E6** 49 49N 6 25 E
Echuca, *Australia* ..... **95 F3** 36 10 S 144 45 E
Ecija, *Spain* **37 H5** 37 30N 5 10W
Eckental, *Germany* ..... **25 F7** 49 39N 11 12 E
Eckernförde, *Germany* ..... **24 A5** 54 28N 9 50 E
Eclipse I., *Australia* ..... **93 G2** 35 5 S 117 58 E
Eclipse Is., *Australia* ..... **92 B4** 13 54 S 126 19 E
Eclipse Sd., *Canada* **101 A11** 72 38N 79 0W
Écommoy, *France* ..... **18 E7** 47 50N 0 17 E
Écouché, *France* **18 D6** 48 42N 0 10W
Ecrins △, *France* ..... **21 D10** 44 54N 6 18 E
Ecuador ■, *S. Amer.* ..... **124 D3** 2 0 S 78 0W
Écueillé, *France* ..... **18 E8** 47 5N 1 21 E
Ed, *Sweden* ..... **11 F5** 58 55N 11 55 E
Ed Dabbura, *Sudan* ..... **80 D3** 17 40N 34 15 E
Ed Da'ein, *Sudan* ..... **81 E2** 11 26N 26 9 E
Ed Damazin, *Sudan* ..... **79 F12** 11 46N 34 21 E
Ed Dâmer, *Sudan* ..... **80 D3** 17 27N 34 0 E
Ed Dar el Beida = Casablanca, *Morocco* **78 B4** 33 36N 7 36W
Ed Debba, *Sudan* ..... **80 D3** 18 0N 30 51 E
Ed-Déffa, *Egypt* ..... **80 A2** 30 40N 26 30 E
Ed Deim, *Sudan* ..... **81 E2** 10 10N 28 20 E
Ed Dueim, *Sudan* ..... **81 E3** 14 0N 32 10 E
Edam, *Canada* **103 C7** 53 11N 108 46W
Edam, *Neths.* ..... **17 B5** 52 31N 5 3 E
Edane, *Sweden* ..... **10 E6** 59 38N 12 49 E
Eday, *U.K.* **13 B6** 59 11N 2 47W
Edd, *Eritrea* ..... **81 E5** 14 0N 41 38 E
Eddrachillis B., *U.K.* **13 C3** 58 17N 5 14W
Eddystone, *U.K.* **15 G3** 50 11N 4 16W
Eddystone Pt., *Australia* ..... **95 G4** 40 59 S 148 20 E
Ede, *Neths.* ..... **17 B5** 52 4N 5 40 E
Ede, *Nigeria* ..... **83 D5** 7 45N 4 29 E
Édéa, *Cameroon* ..... **83 E7** 3 51N 10 9 E
Edebäck, *Sweden* ..... **10 D7** 60 4N 13 32 E
Edehon L., *Canada* **103 A9** 60 25N 97 15W
Edekel, *Algeria* ..... **78 D7** 23 56N 6 59 E
Eden, *Australia* ..... **95 F4** 37 3 S 149 55 E
Eden, *N.C., U.S.A.* **115 G6** 36 29N 79 53W
Eden, *N.Y., U.S.A.* **116 D6** 42 39N 78 55W
Eden, *Tex., U.S.A.* **113 K5** 31 13N 99 51W
Eden ➤, *U.K.* **14 C4** 54 57N 3 1W
Edenburg, *S. Africa* ..... **88 D4** 29 43 S 25 58 E
Edendale, *S. Africa* ..... **89 D5** 29 39 S 30 18 E
Edenderry, *Ireland* **12 C4** 53 21N 7 4W
Edenton, *U.S.A.* **115 G7** 36 4N 76 39W
Edenville, *S. Africa* ..... **89 D4** 27 37 S 27 34 E
Eder ➤, *Germany* ..... **24 D5** 51 12N 9 28 E
Eder-Stausee, *Germany* ..... **24 D4** 51 10N 8 57 E
Edewecht, *Germany* ..... **24 B3** 53 8N 7 58 E
Edgar, *U.S.A.* **112 E6** 40 22N 97 58W
Edgartown, *U.S.A.* **117 E14** 41 23N 70 31W
Edge Hill, *U.K.* **15 E6** 52 8N 1 26W
Edgefield, *U.S.A.* **115 J5** 33 47N 81 56W
Edgeley, *U.S.A.* **112 B5** 46 22N 98 43W
Edgemont, *U.S.A.* **112 D3** 43 18N 103 50W
Edgeøya, *Svalbard* ..... **4 B9** 77 45N 22 30 E
Édhessa, *Greece* ..... **46 F5** 40 48N 22 5 E
Ediévale, *N.Z.* ..... **91 L2** 45 49 S 169 22 E
Edina, *Liberia* **82 D2** 6 0N 10 10W
Edina, *U.S.A.* **112 E8** 40 10N 92 11W
Edinboro, *U.S.A.* **116 E4** 41 52N 80 8W
Edinburg, *U.S.A.* **113 M5** 26 18N 98 10W
Edinburgh, *U.K.* **13 F5** 55 57N 3 13W
Edinburgh ✈ (EDI), *U.K.* **13 F5** 55 54N 3 22W
Edinburgh, City of □, *U.K.* **13 F5** 55 57N 3 17W
Edineţ, *Moldova* ..... **29 B12** 48 9N 27 18 E
Edirne, *Turkey* ..... **45 E10** 41 40N 26 34 E
Edirne □, *Turkey* ..... **45 E10** 41 12N 26 30 E
Edison, *U.S.A.* **110 B4** 48 33N 122 27W
Edithburgh, *Australia* ..... **95 F2** 35 5 S 137 43 E
Edmond, *U.S.A.* **113 H6** 35 39N 97 29W
Edmonds, *U.S.A.* **110 C4** 47 49N 122 23W
Edmonton, *Australia* ..... **94 B4** 17 2 S 145 46 E
Edmonton, *Canada* **102 C6** 53 30N 113 30W
Edmund L., *Canada* **104 B1** 54 45N 93 17W
Edmundston, *Canada* **105 C6** 47 23N 68 20W
Edna, *U.S.A.* **113 L6** 28 59N 96 39W
Edo □, *Nigeria* ..... **83 D6** 6 30N 6 0 E
Edolo, *Italy* ..... **40 B7** 46 10N 10 21 E

Edremit, *Turkey* ..... **47 B9** 39 34N 27 0 E
Edremit Körfezi, *Turkey* ..... **47 B8** 39 30N 26 45 E
Edsbro, *Sweden* ..... **10 E12** 59 54N 18 29 E
Edsbyn, *Sweden* ..... **10 C9** 61 23N 15 49 E
Edson, *Canada* **102 C5** 53 35N 116 28W
Eduardo Castex, *Argentina* ..... **126 D3** 35 50 S 64 18W
Edward ➤, *Australia* ..... **95 F3** 35 5 S 143 30 E
Edward, L., *Africa* ..... **86 C2** 0 25 S 29 40 E
Edward River, *Australia* ..... **94 A3** 14 59 S 141 26 E
Edward VII Land, *Antarctica* ..... **5 E13** 80 0 S 150 0W
Edwards, *Calif., U.S.A.* **111 L9** 34 55N 117 51W
Edwards, *N.Y., U.S.A.* **117 B9** 44 20N 75 15W
Edwards Air Force Base, *U.S.A.* **111 L9** 34 50N 117 40W
Edwards Plateau, *U.S.A.* **113 K4** 30 45N 101 20W
Edwardsville, *U.S.A.* **117 E9** 41 15N 75 56W
Edxná, *Mexico* **119 D6** 19 35N 90 15W
Edzo, *Canada* **102 A5** 62 49N 116 4W
Eeklo, *Belgium* ..... **17 C3** 51 11N 3 33 E
Eferding, *Austria* ..... **26 C7** 48 18N 14 1 E
Effigy Mounds △, *U.S.A.* **112 D9** 43 5N 91 11W
Effingham, *U.S.A.* **114 F1** 39 7N 88 33W
Eforie, *Romania* ..... **29 F13** 44 1N 28 37 E
Ega ➤, *Spain* **38 C3** 42 19N 1 55W
Égadi, Ísole, *Italy* ..... **42 E5** 37 55N 12 16 E
Egan Range, *U.S.A.* **108 G6** 39 35N 114 55W
Eganville, *Canada* **116 A7** 45 32N 77 5W
Eger = Cheb, *Czech Rep.* ..... **26 A5** 50 9N 12 28 E
Eger, *Hungary* ..... **28 C5** 47 53N 20 27 E
Eger ➤, *Hungary* ..... **28 C5** 47 38N 20 50 E
Egersund, *Norway* ..... **9 G12** 58 26N 6 1 E
Egg L., *Canada* **103 B7** 55 5N 105 30W
Eggegebirge Südlicher Teutoburger Wald △, *Germany* ..... **24 D4** 51 40N 8 59 E
Eggenburg, *Austria* ..... **26 C8** 48 38N 15 50 E
Eggenfelden, *Germany* ..... **25 G8** 48 23N 12 46 E
Éghezée, *Belgium* ..... **17 D4** 50 35N 4 55 E
Égletons, *France* ..... **20 C6** 45 24N 2 3 E
Egmont, *Canada* **102 D4** 49 45N 123 56W
Egmont △, *N.Z.* ..... **91 H5** 39 17 S 174 4 E
Egmont, C., *N.Z.* ..... **91 H4** 39 16 S 173 45 E
Egmont, Mt. = Taranaki, Mt., *N.Z.* ..... **91 H5** 39 17 S 174 5 E
Egra, *India* ..... **69 J12** 21 54N 87 32 E
Eğridir, *Turkey* ..... **72 D4** 37 52N 30 51 E
Eğridir Gölü, *Turkey* ..... **70 B1** 37 53N 30 50 E
Egtved, *Denmark* ..... **11 J3** 55 38N 9 18 E
Egume, *Nigeria* ..... **83 D6** 7 30N 7 14 E
Eguzon-Chantôme, *France* ..... **19 F8** 46 27N 1 33 E
Egvekinot, *Russia* **53 C19** 66 19N 179 50W
Egyek, *Hungary* ..... **28 C5** 47 39N 20 52 E
Egypt ■, *Africa* ..... **80 B3** 28 0N 31 0 E
Eha Amufu, *Nigeria* ..... **83 D6** 6 30N 7 46 E
Ehime □, *Japan* ..... **55 H6** 33 30N 132 40 E
Ehingen, *Germany* ..... **25 G5** 48 16N 9 43 E
Ehrenberg, *U.S.A.* **111 M12** 33 36N 114 31W
Ehrwald, *Austria* ..... **26 D3** 47 24N 10 56 E
Eibar, *Spain* **38 B2** 43 11N 2 28W
Eichstätt, *Germany* ..... **25 G7** 48 54N 11 11 E
Eider ➤, *Germany* ..... **24 A4** 54 19N 8 57 E
Eidsvold, *Australia* ..... **95 D5** 25 25 S 151 12 E
Eidsvoll, *Norway* ..... **9 F14** 60 19N 11 14 E
Eifel, *Germany* ..... **25 E2** 50 15N 6 50 E
Eiffel Flats, *Zimbabwe* ..... **87 F3** 18 20 S 30 0 E
Eiger, *Switz.* ..... **40 B5** 46 34N 8 1 E
Eigg, *U.K.* **13 E2** 56 54N 6 10W
Eighty Mile Beach, *Australia* ..... **92 C3** 19 30 S 120 40 E
Eil, *Somali Rep.* ..... **75 F4** 8 0N 49 50 E
Eil, L., *U.K.* **13 E3** 56 51N 5 16W
Eildon, L., *Australia* ..... **95 F4** 37 10 S 146 0 E
Eilenburg, *Germany* ..... **24 D8** 51 27N 12 38 E
Ein el Luweiqa, *Sudan* ..... **81 E3** 14 5N 33 50 E
Einasleigh, *Australia* ..... **94 B3** 18 32 S 144 5 E
Einasleigh ➤, *Australia* ..... **94 B3** 17 30 S 142 17 E
Einbeck, *Germany* ..... **24 D5** 51 49N 9 53 E
Eindhoven, *Neths.* ..... **17 C5** 51 26N 5 28 E
Einsiedeln, *Switz.* ..... **25 H4** 47 7N 8 46 E
Eire = Ireland ■, *Europe* **12 C4** 53 50N 7 52W
Eiríksjökull, *Iceland* **8 D3** 64 46N 20 24W
Eirunepé, *Brazil* ..... **124 E5** 6 35 S 69 53W
Eiseb ➤, *Namibia* ..... **88 C2** 20 33 S 20 59 E
Eisenach, *Germany* ..... **24 E6** 50 58N 10 19 E
Eisenberg, *Germany* ..... **24 E7** 50 58N 11 54 E
Eisenerz, *Austria* ..... **26 D7** 47 32N 14 54 E
Eisenhüttenstadt, *Germany* ..... **24 C10** 52 9N 14 38 E
Eisenkappel, *Austria* ..... **26 E7** 46 29N 14 36 E
Eisenstadt, *Austria* ..... **27 D9** 47 51N 16 31 E
Eisfeld, *Germany* ..... **25 E6** 50 25N 10 54 E
Eisleben, *Germany* ..... **24 D7** 51 32N 11 32 E
Eislingen, *Germany* ..... **25 G5** 48 41N 9 42 E
Eivissa, *Spain* ..... **48 C7** 38 54N 1 26 E
Eixe, Serra do, *Spain* **36 C4** 42 24N 6 54W
Ejea de los Caballeros, *Spain* **38 C3** 42 7N 1 9W
Ejeda, *Madag.* ..... **89 C7** 24 20 S 44 31 E
Ejura, *Ghana* **83 D4** 7 23N 1 23W
Ejutla, *Mexico* **119 D5** 16 34N 96 44W
Ekalaka, *U.S.A.* **112 C2** 45 53N 104 33W
Ekenäs = Tammisaari, *Finland* ..... **9 F20** 60 0N 23 26 E
Ekenässjön, *Sweden* ..... **11 G9** 57 28N 15 1 E
Ekerö, *Sweden* ..... **10 E11** 59 16N 17 45 E
Eket, *Nigeria* ..... **83 E6** 4 38N 7 56 E
Eketahuna, *N.Z.* ..... **91 J5** 40 38 S 175 43 E
Ekhínos, *Greece* ..... **45 E9** 41 16N 25 1 E
Ekibastuz, *Kazakhstan* ..... **52 D8** 51 50N 75 10 E
Ekiti □, *Nigeria* ..... **83 D6** 7 25N 5 20 E
Ekoli, *Dem. Rep. of the Congo* ..... **86 C1** 0 23 S 24 13 E
Ekoln, *Sweden* ..... **10 E11** 59 45N 17 37 E
Ekshärad, *Sweden* ..... **10 D7** 60 10N 13 32 E
Eksjö, *Sweden* ..... **11 G8** 57 40N 14 58 E
Ekuma ➤, *Namibia* ..... **88 B2** 18 40 S 16 2 E
Ekwan ➤, *Canada* **104 B3** 53 12N 82 15W
Ekwan Pt., *Canada* **104 B3** 53 16N 82 7W
El Abanico, *Chile* ..... **126 D1** 37 20 S 71 31W
El Abbasiya, *Sudan* ..... **81 E3** 12 10N 31 18 E
El 'Agrûd, *Egypt* ..... **74 E3** 30 14N 34 24 E
El Aïun, W. Sahara **78 C3** 27 9N 13 12W
El Ait, *Egypt* ..... **81 E2** 12 22N 27 27 E
El 'Aiyat, *Egypt* ..... **80 J7** 29 36N 31 15 E
El 'Alamein, *Egypt* ..... **80 A2** 30 48N 28 58 E
El 'Aqaba, W. ➤, *Egypt* ..... **74 E2** 30 7N 33 54 E
El 'Arag, *Egypt* ..... **80 B2** 28 40N 26 20 E
El Arahal, *Spain* **37 H5** 37 15N 5 33W
El Ariñã, *West Bank* ..... **74 D4** 31 52N 35 27 E
El 'Arîsh, *Egypt* ..... **74 D2** 31 8N 33 50 E
El 'Arîsh, W. ➤, *Egypt* ..... **74 D2** 31 8N 33 47 E

El Asnam = Ech Chéliff, *Algeria* ..... **78 A6** 36 10N 1 20 E
El Astillero, *Spain* **36 B7** 43 24N 3 49W
El Badâri, *Egypt* ..... **80 B3** 27 4N 31 25 E
El Bahrein, *Egypt* ..... **80 B2** 28 30N 26 25 E
El Ballás, *Egypt* ..... **80 B3** 26 2N 32 43 E
El Balyana, *Egypt* ..... **80 B3** 26 10N 32 3 E
El Baqeir, *Sudan* ..... **80 D3** 18 40N 33 40 E
El Barco de Ávila, *Spain* **36 E5** 40 21N 5 31W
El Barco de Valdeorras = O Barco, *Spain* **36 C4** 42 23N 6 58W
El Bauga, *Sudan* ..... **80 D3** 18 18N 33 52 E
El Bawiti, *Egypt* ..... **80 B2** 28 25N 28 45 E
El Bayadh, *Algeria* ..... **78 B6** 33 40N 1 1 E
El Bierzo, *Spain* **36 C4** 42 45N 6 30W
El Bluff, *Nic.* **120 D3** 11 59N 83 40W
El Bonillo, *Spain* **39 G2** 38 57N 2 35W
El Brûk, W. ➤, *Egypt* ..... **74 E2** 30 15N 33 50 E
El Buheirat □, *Sudan* ..... **81 F3** 7 0N 30 0 E
El Burgo de Osma, *Spain* **38 D1** 41 35N 3 4W
El Cajon, *U.S.A.* **111 N10** 32 48N 116 58W
El Campo, *U.S.A.* **113 L6** 29 12N 96 16W
El Centro, *U.S.A.* **111 N11** 32 48N 115 34W
El Cerro, *Bolivia* ..... **124 G6** 17 30 S 61 40W
El Cerro de Andévalo, *Spain* **37 H4** 37 45N 6 57W
El Compadre, *Mexico* **111 N10** 32 20N 116 14W
El Coronil, *Spain* **37 H5** 37 5N 5 38W
El Cuy, *Argentina* ..... **128 D3** 39 55 S 68 25W
El Cuyo, *Mexico* **119 C7** 21 30N 87 40W
El Dab'a, *Egypt* ..... **80 H6** 31 0N 28 27 E
El Daheir, *Egypt* ..... **74 D3** 31 13N 34 10 E
El Dátil, *Mexico* **118 B2** 30 7N 112 15W
El Deir, *Egypt* ..... **80 B3** 25 25N 32 20 E
El Dere, *Somali Rep.* ..... **75 G4** 3 50N 47 8 E
El Descanso, *Mexico* **111 N10** 32 12N 116 58W
El Desemboque, *Mexico* **118 A2** 30 30N 112 57W
El Dilingat, *Egypt* ..... **80 H7** 30 50N 30 31 E
El Diviso, *Colombia* **124 C3** 1 22N 78 14W
El Djouf, *Mauritania* **78 D4** 20 0N 9 0W
El Dorado, Ark., *U.S.A.* **113 J8** 33 12N 92 40W
El Dorado, Kans., *U.S.A.* **113 G6** 37 49N 96 52W
El Dorado, *Venezuela* **124 B6** 6 55N 61 37W
El 'Ein, *Sudan* ..... **81 D2** 16 35N 29 22 E
El Ejido, *Spain* **37 J8** 36 47N 2 49W
El Escorial, *Spain* **36 E6** 40 35N 4 7W
El Espinar, *Spain* **36 D6** 41 43N 4 15W
El Faiyûm, *Egypt* ..... **80 J7** 29 19N 30 50 E
El Fâsher, *Sudan* ..... **81 E2** 13 33N 25 26 E
El Fashn, *Egypt* ..... **80 J7** 28 50N 30 54 E
El Ferrol = Ferrol, *Spain* **36 B2** 43 29N 8 15W
El Fifi, *Sudan* ..... **81 E2** 10 3N 25 0 E
El Fuerte, *Mexico* **118 B3** 26 30N 108 40W
El Ga'a, *Sudan* ..... **81 E2** 14 16N 29 59 E
El Gal, *Somali Rep.* ..... **75 E5** 10 58N 50 20 E
El Garef, *Sudan* ..... **81 E3** 14 6N 34 19 E
El Gebir, *Sudan* ..... **81 E2** 13 40N 29 40 E
El Gedida, *Egypt* ..... **80 B2** 25 40N 28 30 E
El Geneina = Al Junaynah, *Sudan* ..... **79 F10** 13 27N 22 45 E
El Geteina, *Sudan* ..... **81 E3** 14 50N 32 27 E
El Gezira □, *Sudan* ..... **81 E3** 15 0N 33 0 E
El Gîr, *Sudan* ..... **80 D2** 19 50N 28 18 E
El Gîza, *Egypt* ..... **80 J7** 30 0N 31 10 E
El Gogorron △, *Mexico* **118 C4** 21 50N 100 50W
El Goléa, *Algeria* ..... **78 B6** 30 30N 2 50 E
El Grau, *Spain* **39 G4** 39 0N 0 7W
El Guácharo △, *Venezuela* **121 D7** 10 8N 63 21W
El Guache △, *Venezuela* **121 E6** 9 45N 69 30W
El Hagiz, *Sudan* ..... **81 D4** 15 15N 35 50 E
El Hâi, *Egypt* ..... **80 J7** 29 39N 31 18 E
El Hammam, *Egypt* ..... **80 A2** 30 52N 29 25 E
El Hawata, *Sudan* ..... **81 E3** 13 25N 34 42 E
El Heiz, *Egypt* ..... **80 B2** 27 50N 28 40 E
El Hideib, *Sudan* ..... **81 E3** 13 0N 33 50 E
El Hilla, *Sudan* ..... **81 E2** 13 24N 27 2 E
El 'Idisât, *Egypt* ..... **80 B3** 25 30N 32 35 E
El Iskandarîya, *Egypt* ..... **80 H7** 31 13N 29 58 E
El Istiwa'iya, *Sudan* ..... **79 G11** 5 0N 28 0 E
El Jadida, *Morocco* **78 B4** 33 11N 8 17W
El Jardal, *Honduras* **120 D2** 14 54N 88 50W
El Jebelein, *Sudan* ..... **81 E3** 12 40N 32 55 E
El Kab, *Sudan* ..... **80 D3** 19 27N 32 46 E
El Kabrît, G., *Egypt* ..... **74 F2** 29 42N 32 58 E
El Kafr el Sharqi, *Egypt* ..... **80 H7** 31 16N 31 10 E
El Kamlin, *Sudan* ..... **81 D3** 15 3N 33 11 E
El Karaba, *Sudan* ..... **80 D3** 18 32N 33 41 E
El Kere, *Ethiopia* ..... **81 F5** 5 50N 42 5 E
El Khandaq, *Sudan* ..... **80 D3** 18 30N 30 30 E
El Khârga, *Egypt* ..... **80 B3** 25 30N 30 33 E
El Khartûm, *Sudan* ..... **81 D3** 15 31N 32 35 E
El Khartûm □, *Sudan* ..... **81 D3** 16 0N 33 0 E
El Khartûm Bahrî, *Sudan* ..... **81 D3** 15 40N 32 31 E
El Kuntilla, *Egypt* ..... **74 E3** 30 1N 34 45 E
El Laqâwa, *Sudan* ..... **81 E2** 11 25N 29 1 E
El Leh, *Ethiopia* ..... **81 G4** 3 46N 39 13 E
El Leiya, *Sudan* ..... **81 D4** 16 15N 35 28 E
El Maestrazgo, *Spain* **38 E4** 40 30N 0 25W
El Mafâza, *Sudan* ..... **81 E3** 13 38N 34 30 E
El Maghra, *Egypt* ..... **80 A2** 30 15N 28 55 E
El Mahalla el Kubra, *Egypt* ..... **80 H7** 31 0N 31 0 E
El Mahârîq, *Egypt* ..... **80 B3** 25 35N 30 35 E
El Maîmûn, *Egypt* ..... **80 J7** 29 14N 31 12 E
El Maks el Bahari, *Egypt* ..... **80 C3** 24 30N 30 40 E
El Malpais △, *U.S.A.* **109 J10** 34 53N 108 0W
El Manshâh, *Egypt* ..... **80 B3** 26 26N 31 50 E
El Mansûra, *Egypt* ..... **80 H7** 31 0N 31 19 E
El Manzala, *Egypt* ..... **80 H7** 31 10N 31 50 E
El Marâgha, *Egypt* ..... **80 B3** 26 35N 31 10 E
El Masid, *Sudan* ..... **81 D3** 15 15N 33 0 E
El Masnou, *Spain* ..... **38 D7** 41 28N 2 20 E
El Matariya, *Egypt* ..... **80 H8** 31 15N 32 0 E
El Meda, *Ethiopia* ..... **81 F5** 5 39N 41 47 E
El Medano, *Canary Is.* **48 F3** 28 3N 16 32W
El Metemma, *Sudan* ..... **81 D3** 16 50N 33 10 E
El Milagro, *Argentina* ..... **126 C2** 30 59 S 65 59W
El Minyâ, *Egypt* ..... **80 B3** 28 7N 30 33 E
El Monte, *U.S.A.* **111 L8** 34 4N 118 1W
El Montseny, *Spain* ..... **38 D7** 41 55N 2 25 E
El Mreyyé, *Mauritania* **82 B3** 18 0N 6 0W
El Niybo, *Ethiopia* ..... **81 G4** 4 40N 39 55 E
El Obeid, *Sudan* ..... **81 E3** 13 8N 30 10 E
El Odaiya, *Sudan* ..... **81 E2** 12 8N 28 12 E
El Oro, *Mexico* **119 D4** 19 48N 100 8W
El Oued, *Algeria* ..... **78 B7** 33 20N 6 58 E
El Palmar △, *Argentina* ..... **126 C4** 32 10 S 58 31W
El Palmito, Presa, *Mexico* **118 B3** 25 40N 105 30W
El Paso, *U.S.A.* **109 L10** 31 45N 106 29W
El Paso Robles, *U.S.A.* **110 K6** 35 38N 120 41W

El Pedernoso, *Spain* **39 F2** 39 29N 2 45W
El Pedroso, *Spain* **37 H5** 37 51N 5 45W
El Pinacate y Gran Desierto de Altar = Gran Desierto del Pinacate △, *Mexico* **118 A2** 31 51N 113 32W
El Pobo de Dueñas, *Spain* **38 E3** 40 46N 1 39W
El Portal, *U.S.A.* **110 H7** 37 41N 119 47W
El Porvenir, *Mexico* **118 A3** 31 15N 105 51W
El Prat de Llobregat, *Spain* ..... **38 D7** 41 18N 2 3 E
El Progreso, *Honduras* **120 C2** 15 26N 87 51W
El Pueblito, *Mexico* **118 B3** 29 3N 105 4W
El Pueblo, *Canary Is.* **48 F2** 28 36N 17 47W
El Puente del Arzobispo, *Spain* **36 F5** 39 48N 5 10W
El Puerto de Santa María, *Spain* **37 J4** 36 36N 6 13W
El Qâhira, *Egypt* ..... **80 H7** 30 1N 31 14 E
El Qantara, *Egypt* ..... **74 E1** 30 51N 32 20 E
El Qasr, *Egypt* ..... **80 B2** 25 44N 28 42 E
El Qubâbât, *Egypt* ..... **80 J7** 29 28N 31 16 E
El Quseima, *Egypt* ..... **74 E3** 30 40N 34 15 E
El Qusîya, *Egypt* ..... **80 B3** 27 29N 30 44 E
El Râshda, *Egypt* ..... **80 B2** 25 36N 28 57 E
El Real, *Panama* **124 B3** 8 0N 77 40W
El Reno, *U.S.A.* **113 H6** 35 32N 97 57W
El Rey △, *Argentina* ..... **126 A3** 24 40 S 64 34W
El Rîdisiya, *Egypt* ..... **80 C3** 24 56N 32 51 E
El Rio, *U.S.A.* **111 L7** 34 14N 119 10W
El Ronquillo, *Spain* **37 H4** 37 44N 6 10W
El Roque, Pta., *Canary Is.* **48 F4** 28 10N 15 25W
El Rosarito, *Mexico* **118 B2** 28 38N 114 4W
El Rubio, *Spain* **37 H5** 37 22N 5 0W
El Saff, *Egypt* ..... **80 J7** 29 34N 31 16 E
El Saheira, W. ➤, *Egypt* ..... **74 E2** 30 5N 33 25 E
El Salto, *Mexico* **118 C3** 23 47N 105 22W
El Salvador ■, *Cent. Amer.* **120 D2** 13 50N 89 0W
El Sauce, *Nic.* **120 D2** 13 0N 86 40W
El Saucejo, *Spain* **37 H5** 37 4N 5 6W
El Shallal, *Egypt* ..... **80 C3** 24 0N 32 53 E
El Simbillawein, *Egypt* ..... **80 H7** 30 48N 31 13 E
El Sueco, *Mexico* **118 B3** 29 54N 106 24W
El Suweis, *Egypt* ..... **80 J8** 29 58N 32 31 E
El Tabbîn, *Egypt* ..... **80 J7** 29 47N 31 18 E
El Tamarâni, W. ➤, *Egypt* ..... **74 E3** 30 7N 34 43 E
El Thamad, *Egypt* ..... **74 F3** 29 40N 34 28 E
El Tigre, *Venezuela* **124 B6** 8 44N 64 15W
El Tîh, Gebal, *Egypt* ..... **74 F3** 29 40N 33 50 E
El Tîna, *Egypt* ..... **80 H8** 31 3N 32 22 E
El Tîna, Khalîg, *Egypt* ..... **74 D1** 31 10N 32 40 E
El Tofo, *Chile* ..... **126 B1** 29 22 S 71 18W
El Tránsito, *Chile* ..... **126 B1** 28 52 S 70 17W
El Tûr, *Egypt* ..... **74 J8** 28 14N 33 36 E
El Turbio, *Argentina* ..... **128 G2** 51 45 S 72 5W
El Uqsur, *Egypt* ..... **80 B3** 25 41N 32 38 E
El Valle △, *Spain* **39 H3** 37 56N 1 6W
El Venado, *Mexico* **118 C4** 22 56N 101 10W
El Vendrell, *Spain* ..... **38 D6** 41 10N 1 30 E
El Vergel, *Mexico* **118 B3** 26 28N 106 22W
El Vigía, *Venezuela* **124 B4** 8 38N 71 39W
El Viso del Alcor, *Spain* **37 H5** 37 23N 5 43W
El Wabeira, *Egypt* ..... **74 F2** 29 34N 33 6 E
El Wak, *Kenya* ..... **86 B5** 2 49N 40 56 E
El Waqf, *Egypt* ..... **80 B3** 25 45N 32 15 E
El Weguet, *Ethiopia* ..... **81 F5** 5 28N 42 17 E
El Wuz, *Sudan* ..... **81 E3** 15 5N 30 7 E
Eláfonisos, *Greece* ..... **46 E4** 36 29N 22 56 E
Élancourt, *France* ..... **19 D8** 48 47N 1 58 E
Élassa, *Greece* ..... **47 F8** 35 18N 26 21 E
Elassón, *Greece* ..... **46 B4** 39 53N 22 12 E
Elat, *Israel* ..... **74 F3** 29 30N 34 56 E
Eláthia, *Greece* ..... **46 C4** 38 37N 22 46 E
Elâzığ, *Turkey* ..... **70 B3** 38 37N 39 14 E
Elba, *Italy* ..... **40 F7** 42 46N 10 17 E
Elba, *U.S.A.* **115 K2** 31 25N 86 4W
Elbasan, *Albania* ..... **44 E4** 41 9N 20 9 E
Elbe ➤, *Europe* ..... **24 B4** 53 50N 9 0 E
Elbe-Seitenkanal, *Germany* ..... **24 C6** 52 45N 10 32 E
Elbert, Mt., *U.S.A.* **109 G10** 39 7N 106 27W
Elberton, *U.S.A.* **115 H4** 34 7N 82 52W
Elbeuf, *France* ..... **18 C8** 49 17N 1 2 E
Elbidtan, *Turkey* ..... **71 B3** 38 13N 37 12 E
Elbing = Elbląg, *Poland* ..... **30 D6** 54 10N 19 25 E
Elbistan, *Turkey* ..... **72 C7** 38 13N 37 15 E
Elbląg, *Poland* ..... **30 D6** 54 10N 19 25 E
Elbow, *Canada* **103 C7** 51 7N 106 35W
Elbrus, *Asia* ..... **35 J6** 43 21N 42 30 E
Elbufer-Drawehn △, *Germany* ..... **24 B6** 53 8N 10 58 E
Elburz Mts. = Alborz, Reshteh-ye Kūhhā-ye, *Iran* ..... **71 C7** 36 0N 52 0 E
Elche, *Spain* **39 G4** 38 15N 0 42W
Elche de la Sierra, *Spain* **39 G2** 38 27N 2 3W
Elcho I., *Australia* ..... **94 A2** 11 55 S 135 45 E
Elda, *Spain* **39 G4** 38 29N 0 47W
Elde ➤, *Germany* ..... **24 B7** 53 7N 11 15 E
Eldon, Mo., *U.S.A.* **112 F8** 38 21N 92 35W
Eldon, Wash., *U.S.A.* **110 C3** 47 33N 123 3W
Eldora, *U.S.A.* **112 D8** 42 22N 93 5W
Eldorado, *Argentina* ..... **127 B5** 26 28 S 54 43W
Eldorado, *Canada* **103 B7** 59 35N 108 30W
Eldorado, *Mexico* **118 C3** 24 20N 107 22W
Eldorado, Ill., *U.S.A.* **114 G1** 37 49N 88 26W
Eldorado, Tex., *U.S.A.* **113 K4** 30 52N 100 36W
Eldorado Springs, *U.S.A.* **113 G8** 37 52N 94 1W
Eldoret, *Kenya* ..... **86 B4** 0 30N 35 17 E
Eldred, *U.S.A.* **116 E6** 41 58N 78 23W
Elea, C., *Cyprus* ..... **49 D13** 35 19N 34 4 E
Eleanora, Pk., *Australia* ..... **93 F3** 32 57 S 121 9 E
Elefantes ➤, *Africa* ..... **89 C5** 24 10 S 32 40 E
Elektrogorsk, *Russia* ..... **32 E10** 55 56N 38 50 E
Elektrostal, *Russia* ..... **32 E10** 55 41N 38 32 E
Elele, *Nigeria* ..... **83 D6** 5 5N 6 50 E
Elena, *Bulgaria* ..... **45 D9** 42 55N 25 53 E
Elephant Butte Reservoir, *U.S.A.* **109 K10** 33 9N 107 11W
Elephant I., *Antarctica* ..... **5 C18** 61 0 S 55 0W
Eleshnitsa, *Bulgaria* ..... **44 E7** 41 52N 23 36 E
Eleskirt, *Turkey* ..... **73 C10** 39 50N 42 50 E
Eleuthera, *Bahamas* **120 B4** 25 0N 76 20W
Elevsís, *Greece* ..... **46 C5** 38 4N 23 26 E
Elevtheroúpolis, *Greece* ..... **45 F8** 40 52N 24 20 E
Elgin, *Canada* **117 B8** 44 36N 76 13W
Elgin, *U.K.* **13 D5** 57 39N 3 19W
Elgin, Ill., *U.S.A.* **114 D1** 42 2N 88 17W
Elgin, N. Dak., *U.S.A.* **112 B4** 46 24N 101 51W
Elgin, Oreg., *U.S.A.* **108 D5** 45 34N 117 55W
Elgin, Tex., *U.S.A.* **113 K6** 30 21N 97 22W

Elgoibar, *Spain* **38 B2** 43 13N 2 24W
Elgon, Mt., *Africa* ..... **86 B3** 1 10N 34 24 E
Eliase, *Indonesia* ..... **63 F8** 8 21 S 130 48 E
Elikón △, *Greece* ..... **46 C4** 38 18N 22 45 E
Elim, *Namibia* ..... **88 B2** 17 48 S 15 31 E
Elim, *S. Africa* ..... **88 E2** 34 35 S 19 45 E
Elin Pelin, *Bulgaria* ..... **44 D7** 42 40N 23 36 E
Elista, *Russia* ..... **35 G7** 46 16N 44 14 E
Elizabeth, *Australia* ..... **95 E2** 34 42 S 138 41 E
Elizabeth, *U.S.A.* **117 F10** 40 40N 74 13W
Elizabeth City, *U.S.A.* **115 G7** 36 18N 76 14W
Elizabethton, *U.S.A.* **115 G4** 36 21N 82 13W
Elizabethtown, Ky., *U.S.A.* **114 G3** 37 42N 85 52W
Elizabethtown, N.Y., *U.S.A.* **117 B11** 44 13N 73 36W
Elizabethtown, Pa., *U.S.A.* **117 F8** 40 9N 76 36W
Elizondo, *Spain* **38 B3** 43 12N 1 30W
Elk, *Poland* ..... **30 E9** 53 50N 22 21 E
Elk ➤, *Canada* **102 C5** 49 11N 115 14W
Elk ➤, *Poland* ..... **30 E9** 53 41N 22 28 E
Elk ➤, *U.S.A.* **115 H2** 34 46N 87 16W
Elk City, *U.S.A.* **113 H5** 35 25N 99 25W
Elk Creek, *U.S.A.* **110 F4** 39 36N 122 32W
Elk Grove, *U.S.A.* **110 G5** 38 25N 121 22W
Elk Island △, *Canada* **102 C6** 53 35N 112 59W
Elk Lake, *Canada* **104 C3** 47 40N 80 25W
Elk Point, *Canada* **103 C6** 53 54N 110 55W
Elk River, Idaho, *U.S.A.* **108 C5** 46 47N 116 11W
Elk River, Minn., *U.S.A.* **112 C8** 45 18N 93 35W
Elkedra ➤, *Australia* ..... **94 C2** 21 8 S 136 22 E
Elkhart, Ind., *U.S.A.* **114 E3** 41 41N 85 58W
Elkhart, Kans., *U.S.A.* **113 G4** 37 0N 101 54W
Elkhorn, *Canada* **103 D8** 49 59N 101 14W
Elkhorn ➤, *U.S.A.* **112 E6** 41 8N 96 19W
Elkhovo, *Bulgaria* ..... **45 D10** 42 10N 26 35 E
Elkin, *U.S.A.* **115 G5** 36 15N 80 51W
Elkins, *U.S.A.* **114 F6** 38 55N 79 51W
Elkland, *U.S.A.* **116 E7** 41 59N 77 19W
Elko, *Canada* **102 D5** 49 20N 115 10W
Elko, *U.S.A.* **108 F6** 40 50N 115 46W
Elkton, *U.S.A.* **116 C1** 43 49N 83 11W
Ell, L., *Australia* ..... **93 E4** 29 13 S 127 46 E
Ellef Ringnes I., *Canada* **4 B2** 78 30N 102 2W
Ellen, Mt., *U.S.A.* **117 B12** 44 9N 72 56W
Ellenburg, *U.S.A.* **117 B11** 44 54N 73 48W
Ellendale, *U.S.A.* **112 B5** 46 0N 98 32W
Ellensburg, *U.S.A.* **108 C3** 46 59N 120 34W
Ellenville, *U.S.A.* **117 E10** 41 43N 74 24W
Ellerton, *Barbados* ..... **121 g** 13 7N 59 33W
Ellery, Mt., *Australia* ..... **95 F4** 37 28 S 148 47 E
Ellesmere, L., *N.Z.* ..... **91 M4** 43 47 S 172 28 E
Ellesmere I., *Canada* **98 B11** 79 30N 80 0W
Ellesmere Port, *U.K.* **14 D5** 53 17N 2 54W
Ellice Is. = Tuvalu ■, *Pac. Oc.* ..... **96 H9** 8 0 S 178 0 E
Ellicottville, *U.S.A.* **116 D6** 42 17N 78 40W
Ellinikón, Athínai, ✈ (ATH), *Greece* ..... **46 D5** 37 52 S 23 55 E
Elliot, *Australia* ..... **94 B1** 17 33 S 133 32 E
Elliot, *S. Africa* ..... **89 E4** 31 22 S 27 48 E
Elliot Lake, *Canada* **104 C3** 46 25N 82 35W
Elliotdale = Xhora, *S. Africa* ..... **89 E4** 31 55 S 28 38 E
Ellis, *U.S.A.* **112 F5** 38 56N 99 34W
Elliston, *Australia* ..... **95 E1** 33 39 S 134 53 E
Ellisville, *U.S.A.* **113 K10** 31 36N 89 12W
Ellon, *U.K.* **13 D6** 57 22N 2 4W
Ellore = Eluru, *India* ..... **67 L12** 16 48N 81 8 E
Ellsworth, Kans., *U.S.A.* **112 F5** 38 44N 98 14W
Ellsworth, Maine, *U.S.A.* **115 C11** 44 33N 68 25W
Ellsworth Land, *Antarctica* ..... **5 D16** 76 0 S 89 0W
Ellsworth Mts., *Antarctica* ..... **5 D16** 78 30 S 85 0W
Ellwangen, *Germany* ..... **25 G6** 48 57N 10 8 E
Ellwood City, *U.S.A.* **116 F4** 40 52N 80 17W
Elm, *Switz.* ..... **25 J5** 46 54N 9 10 E
Elm-Lappwald △, *Germany* ..... **24 C6** 52 15N 10 50 E
Elma, *Canada* **103 D9** 49 52N 95 55W
Elma, *U.S.A.* **110 D3** 47 0N 123 25W
Elmadağ, *Turkey* ..... **72 C5** 39 55N 33 14 E
Elmalı, *Turkey* ..... **47 E11** 36 44N 29 56 E
Elmhurst, *U.S.A.* **114 E2** 41 53N 87 56W
Elmina, *Ghana* **83 D4** 5 5N 1 21W
Elmira, *Canada* **116 C4** 43 36N 80 33W
Elmira, *U.S.A.* **116 D8** 42 6N 76 48W
Elmira Heights, *U.S.A.* **116 D8** 42 8N 76 50W
Elmore, *Australia* ..... **95 F3** 36 30 S 144 37 E
Elmore, *U.S.A.* **111 M11** 33 7N 115 49W
Elmshorn, *Germany* ..... **24 B5** 53 43N 9 40 E
Elmvale, *Canada* **116 B5** 44 35N 79 52W
Elne, *France* ..... **20 F6** 42 36N 2 58 E
Elora, *Canada* **116 C4** 43 41N 80 26W
Elos, *Greece* ..... **46 E4** 36 46N 22 43 E
Eloúnda, *Greece* ..... **49 D7** 35 16N 25 42 E
Éloyes, *France* ..... **19 D13** 48 6N 6 36 E
Elrose, *Canada* **103 C7** 51 12N 108 0W
Elsdorf, *Germany* ..... **24 E2** 50 55N 6 34 E
Elsie, *U.S.A.* **116 D3** 43 5N 84 23W
Elsinore = Helsingør, *Denmark* ..... **11 H6** 56 2N 12 35 E
Elster ➤, *Germany* ..... **24 D7** 51 25N 11 57 E
Elsterwerda, *Germany* ..... **24 D9** 51 27N 13 31 E
Eltham, *N.Z.* ..... **91 H5** 39 26 S 174 19 E
Elton, *Russia* ..... **35 F8** 49 5N 46 52 E
Elton, Ozero, *Russia* ..... **35 F8** 49 5N 46 42 E
Eltville, *Germany* ..... **25 E4** 50 2N 8 7 E
Eluru, *India* ..... **67 L12** 16 48N 81 8 E
Elvas, *Portugal* **37 G3** 38 50N 7 10W
Elven, *France* **18 E4** 47 44N 2 36W
Elverum, *Norway* ..... **9 F14** 60 53N 11 34 E
Elvire ➤, *Australia* ..... **92 C4** 17 51 S 128 11 E
Elvire, Mt., *Australia* ..... **93 E2** 29 22 S 119 36 E
Elvo ➤, *Italy* ..... **40 C5** 45 23N 8 21 E
Elwell, L., *U.S.A.* **108 B8** 48 22N 111 17W
Elwood, Ind., *U.S.A.* **114 E3** 40 17N 85 50W
Elwood, Nebr., *U.S.A.* **112 E5** 40 36N 99 52W
Elx = Elche, *Spain* **39 G4** 38 15N 0 42W
Ely, *U.K.* ..... **15 E8** 52 24N 0 16 E
Ely, Minn., *U.S.A.* **112 B9** 47 55N 91 51W
Ely, Nev., *U.S.A.* **108 G6** 39 15N 114 54W
Elyria, *U.S.A.* **116 E2** 41 22N 82 7W
Elyrus, *Greece* ..... **46 F5** 35 15N 23 45 E
Elz ➤, *Germany* ..... **25 G3** 48 21N 7 45 E
Emådalen, *Sweden* ..... **10 C8** 61 20N 14 44 E
Emāmrūd, *Iran* ..... **71 B7** 36 30N 55 0 E
Emån ➤, *Sweden* ..... **11 G10** 57 3N 16 30 E
Emba, *Kazakhstan* ..... **52 E6** 48 50N 58 8 E
Emba ➤, *Kazakhstan* ..... **52 E6** 46 55N 53 28 E
Embarcación, *Argentina* ..... **126 A3** 23 10 S 64 0W
Embarras Portage, *Canada* **103 B6** 58 27N 111 28W
Embetsu, *Japan* ..... **54 B10** 44 44N 141 47 E

Embi = Emba, *Kazakhstan* .... 52 E6 48 50N 58 8 E
Embi = Emba →, *Kazakhstan* .... 52 E6 46 55N 53 28 E
Embóna, *Greece* ...... 49 C9 36 13S 27 51 E
Embrun, *France* ...... 21 D10 44 34N 6 30 E
Embu, *Kenya* .... 86 C4 0 32 S 37 38 E
Emden, *Germany* .... 24 B3 53 21N 7 12 E
Emecik, *Turkey* ...... 47 E9 36 46N 27 49 E
Emerald, *Australia* .... 94 C4 23 32 S 148 10 E
Emerson, *Canada* 103 D9 49 0N 97 10W
Emet, *Turkey* .... 47 B11 39 20N 29 15 E
Emi Koussi, *Chad* .... 79 E9 19 45N 18 55 E
Emilia-Romagna □, *Italy* .... 40 D8 44 45N 11 0 E
Emilius, Mte., *Italy* .... 40 C4 45 45N 7 20 E
Emine, Nos, *Bulgaria* .. 45 D11 42 40N 27 56 E
Eminska, *Sweden* .... 11 H9 56 37N 15 32 E
Emirdağ, *Turkey* ...... 72 C4 39 2N 31 8 E
Emlenton, *U.S.A.* 116 E5 41 11N 79 43W
Emmaboda, *Sweden* .. 11 H9 56 37N 15 32 E
Emmaus, *S. Africa* .... 88 D4 29 2 S 25 15 E
Emmaus, *U.S.A.* 117 F9 40 32N 75 30W
Emme →, *Switz.* ...... 25 H3 47 14N 7 32 E
Emmeloord, *Neths.* .... 17 B5 52 44N 5 46 E
Emmen, *Neths.* ...... 17 B6 52 48N 6 57 E
Emmen, *Switz.* ...... 25 H4 47 5N 8 18 E
Emmendingen, *Germany* .... 25 G3 48 6N 7 51 E
Emmental, *Switz.* .... 25 J3 46 55N 7 40 E
Emmerich, *Germany* .. 24 D2 51 50N 6 14 E
Emmet, *Australia* .... 94 C3 24 45 S 144 30 E
Emmetsburg, *U.S.A.* .. 112 D7 43 7N 94 41W
Emmett, *Idaho, U.S.A.* 108 E5 43 52N 116 30W
Emmett, *Mich., U.S.A.* 116 D2 42 59N 82 46W
Emmonak, *U.S.A.* 100 B3 62 46N 164 30W
Emo, *Canada* 103 D10 48 38N 93 50W
Emőd, *Hungary* ...... 28 C5 47 57N 20 47 E
Empalme, *Mexico* 118 B2 28 1N 110 49W
Empangeni, *S. Africa* .. 89 D5 28 50 S 31 52 E
Empedrado, *Argentina* 126 B4 28 0 S 58 46W
Emperor Seamount Chain, *Pac. Oc.* .... 96 D9 40 0N 170 0 E
Empoli, *Italy* .... 40 E7 43 43N 10 57 E
Emporia, *Kans., U.S.A.* 112 F6 38 25N 96 11W
Emporia, *Va., U.S.A.* 115 G7 36 42N 77 32W
Emporium, *U.S.A.* 116 E6 41 31N 78 14W
Empress, *Canada* 103 C7 50 57N 110 0W
Empty Quarter = Rub' al Khālī, *Si. Arabia* .. 75 D4 19 0N 48 0 E
Ems →, *Germany* .... 24 B3 53 20N 7 12 E
Emsdale, *Canada* 116 A5 45 32N 79 19W
Emsdetten, *Germany* .. 24 C3 52 10N 7 32 E
Emu, *China* .... 57 C15 43 40N 128 6 E
Emu Park, *Australia* .. 94 C5 23 13 S 150 50 E
'En 'Avrona, *Israel* .... 74 F4 29 43N 35 0 E
En Nahud, *Sudan* .... 81 E2 12 45N 28 25 E
En Nofalab, *Sudan* .... 81 D3 15 52N 32 32 E
Ena, *Japan* .... 55 G8 35 25N 137 25 E
Enana, *Namibia* ...... 88 B2 17 30 S 16 23 E
Enånger, *Sweden* .... 10 C11 61 30N 17 9 E
Enard B., *U.K.* 13 C3 58 5N 5 20W
Enare = Inarijärvi, *Finland* .... 8 B22 69 0N 28 0 E
Enarotali, *Indonesia* .. 63 E9 3 55 S 136 21 E
Encampment, *U.S.A.* .. 108 F10 41 12N 106 47W
Encantadas, Serra, *Brazil* .... 127 C5 30 40 S 53 0W
Encarnación, *Paraguay* 127 B4 27 15 S 55 50W
Encarnación de Díaz, *Mexico* 118 C4 21 30N 102 13W
Enchi, *Ghana* 82 D4 5 53N 2 48W
Encinitas, *U.S.A.* 111 M9 33 3N 117 17W
Encino, *U.S.A.* 109 J11 34 39N 105 28W
Encounter B., *Australia* 95 F2 35 45 S 138 45 E
Encs, *Hungary* ...... 28 B6 48 20N 21 8 E
Endako, *Canada* 102 C3 54 6N 125 2W
Ende, *Indonesia* ...... 63 F6 8 45 S 121 40 E
Endeavour Str., *Australia* .... 94 A3 10 45 S 142 0 E
Endelave, *Denmark* .. 11 J4 55 46N 10 18 E
Enderbury I., *Kiribati* .. 96 H10 3 8 S 171 5W
Enderby, *Canada* 102 C5 50 35N 119 10W
Enderby I., *Australia* .. 92 D2 20 35 S 116 30 E
Enderby Land, *Antarctica* .... 5 C5 66 0 S 53 0 E
Enderlin, *U.S.A.* 112 B6 46 38N 97 36W
Endicott, *U.S.A.* 117 D8 42 6N 76 4W
Endwell, *U.S.A.* 117 D8 42 6N 76 2W
Endyalgout I., *Australia* 92 B5 11 40 S 132 35 E
Eneabba, *Australia* .. 93 E2 29 49 S 115 16 E
Enewetak Atoll, *Marshall Is.* .... 96 F8 11 30N 162 15 E
Enez, *Turkey* .... 45 F10 40 45N 26 5 E
Enfer, Pte. d', *Martinique* .... 120 c 14 22N 60 54W
Enfield, *Canada* 105 D7 44 56N 63 32W
Enfield, *Conn., U.S.A.* 117 E12 41 58N 72 36W
Enfield, *N.H., U.S.A.* 117 C12 43 39N 72 9W
Engadin, *Switz.* ...... 25 J6 46 45N 10 10 E
Engaño, C., *Dom. Rep.* 121 C6 18 30N 68 20W
Engaño, C., *Phil.* .... 63 A6 18 35N 122 23 E
Engaru, *Japan* ...... 54 B11 44 3N 143 31 E
Engcobo, *S. Africa* .. 89 E4 31 37 S 28 0 E
Engelberg, *Switz.* .... 25 J4 46 48N 8 26 E
Engels, *Russia* ...... 34 E8 51 28N 46 6 E
Engemann L., *Canada* 103 B7 58 0N 106 55W
Engershatu, *Eritrea* .. 80 D4 16 7N 36 0 E
Enggano, *Indonesia* .. 62 F2 5 20 S 102 40 E
England, *U.S.A.* 113 H9 34 33N 91 58W
England □, *U.K.* 15 E5 53 0N 2 0W
Englee, *Canada* 105 B8 50 45N 56 5W
Englehart, *Canada* .. 104 C4 47 49N 79 52W
Englewood, *U.S.A.* .. 112 F2 39 39N 104 59W
English □, *Canada* .. 103 C10 49 12N 91 5W
English Bazar = Ingraj Bazar, *India* ...... 69 G13 24 58N 88 10 E
English Channel, *Europe* 15 G6 50 0N 2 0W
English Company's Is., The, *Australia* .... 94 A2 11 50 S 136 32 E
English River, *Canada* 104 C1 49 14N 91 0W
Engures ezers, *Latvia* .. 30 A10 57 16N 23 6 E
Enguri →, *Georgia* .. 35 J5 42 30N 41 38 E
Enid, *U.S.A.* 113 G6 36 24N 97 53W
Enipévs →, *Greece* .. 46 B4 39 22N 22 17 E
Enkhuizen, *Neths.* .... 17 B5 52 42N 5 17 E
Enköping, *Sweden* .. 10 E11 59 37N 17 4 E
Enle, *China* .... 58 F3 24 0N 101 9 E
Enna, *Italy* .... 43 E7 37 34N 14 16 E
Ennadai, *Canada* 103 A8 61 8N 100 53W
Ennadai L., *Canada* .. 103 A8 60 58N 101 20W
Ennedi, *Chad* .... 79 E10 17 15N 22 0 E
Enngonia, *Australia* .. 95 D4 29 21 S 145 50 E

Ennigerloh, *Germany* .. 24 D4 51 50N 8 2 E
Ennis, *Ireland* 12 D3 52 51N 8 59W
Ennis, *Mont., U.S.A.* 108 D8 45 21N 111 44W
Ennis, *Tex., U.S.A.* .. 113 J6 32 20N 96 38W
Enniscorthy, *Ireland* .. 12 D5 52 30N 6 34W
Enniskillen, *Ireland* .. 12 B4 54 21N 7 39W
Ennistimon, *Ireland* .. 12 D2 52 57N 9 17W
Enns, *Austria* .... 26 C7 48 12N 14 28 E
Enns →, *Austria* .... 26 C7 48 14N 14 32 E
Enontekiö, *Finland* .. 8 B20 68 23N 23 37 E
Enosburg Falls, *U.S.A.* 117 B12 44 55N 72 48W
Enping, *China* ...... 59 F9 22 16N 112 21 E
Enriquillo, L., *Dom. Rep.* 121 C5 18 20N 72 5W
Enschede, *Neths.* .... 17 B6 52 13N 6 53 E
Ensenada, *Argentina* .. 126 C4 34 55 S 57 55W
Ensenada, *Mexico* 118 A1 31 50N 116 50W
Ensenada de los Muertos, *Mexico* .. 118 C2 23 59N 109 50W
Enshi, *China* .... 58 B7 30 18N 109 29 E
Ensiola, Pta. de n', *Spain* 48 B9 39 7N 2 55 E
Ensisheim, *France* .. 19 E14 47 50N 7 20 E
Entebbe, *Uganda* .... 86 B3 0 4N 32 28 E
Enterprise, *Canada* .. 102 A5 60 47N 115 45W
Enterprise, *Ala., U.S.A.* 115 K3 31 19N 85 51W
Enterprise, *Oreg., U.S.A.* 108 D5 45 25N 117 17W
Entorno de Doñana △, *Spain* 37 J4 37 0N 6 26W
Entraygues-sur-Truyère, *France* .... 20 D6 44 38N 2 35 E
Entre Ríos, *Bolivia* .. 126 A3 21 30 S 64 25W
Entre Ríos □, *Argentina* 126 C4 30 30 S 58 30W
Entrepeñas, Embalse de, *Spain* 38 E2 40 34N 2 42W
Entroncamento, *Portugal* 37 F2 39 28N 8 28W
Enugu, *Nigeria* ...... 83 D6 6 30N 7 30 E
Enugu □, *Nigeria* .... 83 D6 6 30N 7 45 E
Enugu Ezike, *Nigeria* .. 83 D6 7 0N 7 29 E
Enumclaw, *U.S.A.* .. 110 C5 47 12N 121 59W
Envalira, Port d', *Europe* .... 38 C6 42 33N 1 43 E
Envermeu, *France* .... 18 C8 49 53N 1 15 E
Enviken, *Sweden* .... 10 D9 60 49N 15 46 E
Enying, *Hungary* .... 28 D3 46 56N 18 15 E
Enza →, *Italy* ...... 40 D7 44 54N 10 31 E
Eólie, Ís., *Italy* ...... 43 D7 38 30N 14 57 E
Epanomí, *Greece* .... 44 F6 40 25N 22 59 E
Epe, *Neths.* .... 17 B5 52 21N 5 59 E
Epe, *Nigeria* .... 83 D5 6 36N 3 59 E
Épernay, *France* ...... 19 C10 49 3N 3 56 E
Épernon, *France* .... 19 D8 48 35N 1 40 E
Ephesus, *Turkey* .... 47 D9 37 55N 27 22 E
Ephraim, *U.S.A.* 108 G8 39 22N 111 35W
Ephrata, *Pa., U.S.A.* .. 117 F8 40 11N 76 11W
Ephrata, *Wash., U.S.A.* 108 C4 47 19N 119 33W
Epidaurus Limera, *Greece* .... 46 E5 36 46N 23 0 E
Épila, *Spain* 38 D3 41 36N 1 17W
Épinac, *France* ...... 19 F11 46 59N 4 31 E
Épinal, *France* ...... 19 D13 48 10N 6 27 E
Episkopí, *Cyprus* .... 49 E11 34 40N 32 54 E
Episkopí, *Greece* .... 49 D6 35 20N 24 20 E
Episkopí Bay, *Cyprus* 49 E11 34 35N 32 50 E
Epitálion, *Greece* .... 46 D3 37 37N 21 30 E
Eppan = Appiano, *Italy* 41 B8 46 28N 11 15 E
Eppingen, *Germany* .. 25 F4 49 8N 8 53 E
Epsom, *U.K.* 15 F7 51 19N 0 16W
Epukiro, *Namibia* .... 88 C2 21 40 S 19 9 E
Equatorial Guinea ■, *Africa* .... 84 D1 2 0N 8 0 E
Er Hai, *China* ...... 58 E3 25 48N 100 11 E
Er Rachidia, *Morocco* .. 78 B5 31 58N 4 20W
Er Rahad, *Sudan* .... 81 E3 12 45N 30 32 E
Er Rif, *Morocco* 78 A5 35 1N 4 1W
Er Rogel, *Sudan* .... 80 D4 16 10N 35 25 E
Er Roseires, *Sudan* .. 81 E3 11 55N 34 30 E
Er Rua'at, *Sudan* .... 81 E3 12 21N 32 17 E
Eraclea, *Italy* .... 41 C9 45 35N 12 40 E
Erāwadī Myit = Irrawaddy →, *Burma* 67 M19 15 50N 95 6 E
Erāwadī Myitwanya = Irrawaddy, Mouths of the, *Burma* ...... 67 M19 15 30N 95 0 E
Erba, *Italy* .... 40 C6 45 48N 9 15 E
Erba, *Sudan* .... 80 D4 19 5N 36 51 E
Erba, J., *Sudan* ...... 80 C4 20 48N 36 47 E
Erbaa, *Turkey* ...... 72 B7 40 42N 36 36 E
Erbeskopf, *Germany* .. 25 F3 49 44N 7 2 E
Erbil = Arbīl, *Iraq* .. 70 B5 36 15N 44 5 E
Erbu, *Ethiopia* ...... 81 E3 6 44N 34 53 E
Erçek, *Turkey* ...... 70 B4 38 39N 43 36 E
Erçiş, *Turkey* .... 73 C10 39 2N 43 21 E
Erciyaş Dağı, *Turkey* 70 B2 38 30N 35 30 E
Érd, *Hungary* .... 28 C3 47 22N 18 56 E
Erdao Jiang →, *China* 57 C14 43 0N 127 0 E
Erdek, *Turkey* ...... 45 F11 40 23N 27 47 E
Erdemli, *Turkey* .... 72 D6 36 36N 34 19 E
Erdene = Ulaan-Uul, *Mongolia* .... 56 B6 44 13N 111 10 E
Erdenetsogt, *Mongolia* 56 C4 42 55N 106 5 E
Erding, *Germany* .... 25 G7 48 18N 11 54 E
Erdre →, *France* 18 E5 47 13N 1 32W
Erebus, Mt., *Antarctica* 5 D11 77 35 S 167 0 E
Erechim, *Brazil* ...... 127 B5 27 35 S 52 15W
Ereğli, *Konya, Turkey* 70 B2 37 31N 34 4 E
Ereğli, *Zonguldak, Turkey* .... 72 B4 41 15N 31 24 E
Erei, Monti, *Italy* .... 43 E7 37 20N 14 20 E
Erenhot, *China* ...... 56 C7 43 48N 112 2 E
Eresma →, *Spain* 36 D6 41 26N 4 45W
Eressós, *Greece* ...... 47 B7 39 11N 25 57 E
Erfenisdam, *S. Africa* .. 88 D4 28 30 S 26 50 E
Erfstadt, *Germany* .. 24 E2 50 50N 6 50 E
Erft →, *Germany* .... 24 D2 51 11N 6 44 E
Erfurt, *Germany* .... 24 E7 50 58N 11 2 E
Ergani, *Turkey* ...... 70 B3 38 17N 39 49 E
Ergene →, *Turkey* .. 56 C5 43 8N 109 5 E
Ergel, *Mongolia* ...... 45 E10 41 1N 26 22 E
Ergeni Vozvyshennost, *Russia* .... 35 G7 47 0N 44 0 E
Érgli, *Latvia* .... 9 H21 56 54N 25 38 E
Erhlin, *Taiwan* ...... 59 F13 23 54N 120 22 E
Eria →, *Spain* 36 C5 42 3N 5 44W
Eriboll, L., *U.K.* 13 C4 58 30N 4 42W
Érice, *Italy* .... 42 E5 38 2N 12 35 E
Erie, *U.S.A.* 116 D4 42 8N 80 5W
Erie, L., *N. Amer.* .. 116 D4 42 15N 81 0W
Erie Canal, *U.S.A.* .. 116 C7 43 5N 78 43W
Erieau, *Canada* 116 D3 42 16N 81 57W
Erigavo, *Somali Rep.* .. 75 E4 10 35N 47 20 E
Eriksdale, *Canada* .. 103 C9 50 52N 98 7W
Érimánthos, *Greece* .. 46 D3 37 57N 21 50 E
Erimo-misaki, *Japan* .. 54 D11 41 50N 143 15 E
Erin Pt., *Trin. & Tob.* 125 K15 10 13N 61 40W

Erinpura, *India* ...... 68 G5 25 9N 73 3 E
Eriskay, *U.K.* 13 D1 57 4N 7 18W
Erithraí, *Greece* ...... 46 C5 38 13N 23 20 E
Eritrea ■, *Africa* .... 81 E4 14 0N 38 30 E
Erjas →, *Portugal* .. 36 F3 39 40N 7 1W
Erkelenz, *Germany* .. 24 D2 51 4N 6 19 E
Erkner, *Germany* .... 24 C9 52 25N 13 44 E
Erlangen, *Germany* .. 25 F6 49 36N 11 0 E
Erldunda, *Australia* .. 94 D1 25 14 S 133 12 E
Ermelo, *Neths.* ...... 17 B5 52 18N 5 35 E
Ermelo, *S. Africa* .... 89 D4 26 31 S 29 59 E
Ermenek, *Turkey* .... 70 B2 36 38N 33 0 E
Ermil, *Sudan* .... 81 E2 13 35N 27 40 E
Ermióni, *Greece* ...... 46 D5 37 23N 23 15 E
Ermones, *Greece* .... 49 A3 39 37N 19 46 E
Ernakulam, *India* .... 66 Q10 9 59N 76 22 E
Erne →, *Ireland* 12 B3 54 30N 8 16W
Erne, Lower L., *U.K.* 12 B4 54 28N 7 47W
Erne, Upper L., *U.K.* 12 B4 54 14N 7 32W
Ernée, *France* 18 D6 48 18N 0 56W
Ernest Giles Ra., *Australia* .... 93 E3 27 0 S 123 45 E
Ernstberg, *Germany* .. 25 E2 50 13N 6 47 E
Erode, *India* .... 66 P10 11 24N 77 45 E
Eromanga, *Australia* .. 95 D3 26 40 S 143 11 E
Erongo, *Namibia* .... 88 C2 21 39 S 15 58 E
Erquy, *France* 18 D4 48 38N 2 29W
Erramala Hills, *India* .. 66 M11 15 30N 78 15 E
Errer →, *Ethiopia* .. 81 F5 7 32N 42 35 E
Errigal, *Ireland* 12 A3 55 2N 8 6W
Erris Hd., *Ireland* 12 B1 54 19N 10 0W
Erseke, *Albania* ...... 44 F4 40 22N 20 40 E
Erskine, *U.S.A.* 112 B7 47 40N 96 0W
Erstein, *France* ...... 19 D14 48 25N 7 38 E
Ertholmene, *Denmark* 11 J9 55 19N 15 11 E
Ertil, *Russia* .... 34 E5 51 55N 40 50 E
Ertis = Irtysh →, *Russia* 52 C7 61 4N 68 52 E
Eruh, *Turkey* .... 73 D10 37 46N 42 13 E
Eruwa, *Nigeria* ...... 83 D5 7 33N 3 26 E
Ervy-le-Châtel, *France* 19 D10 48 2N 3 55 E
Erwin, *U.S.A.* 115 G4 36 9N 82 25W
Eryuan, *China* ...... 58 D2 26 7N 99 57 E
Erzgebirge, *Germany* .. 24 E8 50 27N 12 55 E
Erzin, *Russia* .... 53 D10 50 15N 95 10 E
Erzincan, *Turkey* .... 70 B3 39 46N 39 30 E
Erzurum, *Turkey* .... 70 B4 39 57N 41 15 E
Es Caló, *Spain* ...... 48 C8 38 40N 1 30 E
Es Canar, *Spain* .... 48 B8 39 3N 1 36 E
Es Mercadal, *Spain* .. 48 B11 39 59N 4 5 E
Es Migjorn Gran, *Spain* 48 B11 39 57N 4 3 E
Es Safiya, *Sudan* .... 81 D3 15 31N 30 7 E
Es Sahrâ' Esh Sharqîya, *Egypt* .... 80 B3 27 30N 32 30 E
Es Sînâ', *Egypt* ...... 74 F3 29 0N 34 0 E
Es Sûkî, *Sudan* ...... 81 E3 13 20N 33 58 E
Es Vedrà, *Spain* .... 48 C7 38 52N 1 12 E
Esambo, Dem. Rep. of the Congo .... 86 C1 3 48 S 23 30 E
Esan-Misaki, *Japan* .. 54 D10 41 40N 141 10 E
Esashi, *Hokkaidō, Japan* 54 B11 44 56N 142 35 E
Esashi, *Hokkaidō, Japan* 54 D10 41 52N 140 7 E
Esbjerg, *Denmark* .... 11 J2 55 29N 8 29 E
Esbo = Espoo, *Finland* 9 F21 60 12N 24 40 E
Escalante, *U.S.A.* 109 H8 37 47N 111 36W
Escalante →, *U.S.A.* 109 H8 37 24N 110 57W
Escalón, *Mexico* 118 B4 26 46N 104 20W
Escambia →, *U.S.A.* 115 K2 30 32N 87 11W
Escanaba, *U.S.A.* 114 C2 45 45N 87 4W
Esch-sur-Alzette, *Lux.* 17 E6 49 32N 6 0 E
Eschede, *Germany* .. 24 C6 52 44N 10 14 E
Eschwege, *Germany* .. 24 D6 51 11N 10 2 E
Eschweiler, *Germany* .. 24 E2 50 49N 6 15 E
Escondido, *U.S.A.* .. 111 M9 33 7N 117 5W
Escravos →, *Nigeria* 83 D6 5 35N 5 10 E
Escuinapa, *Mexico* .. 118 C3 22 50N 105 50W
Escuintla, *Guatemala* 120 D1 14 20N 90 48W
Eséka, *Cameroon* .... 83 E7 3 41N 10 44 E
Eşen →, *Turkey* .... 47 E11 36 27N 29 16 E
Esenguly, *Turkmenistan* 52 F6 37 37N 53 59 E
Esens, *Germany* ...... 24 B3 53 38N 7 36 E
Esenyurt, *Turkey* .... 45 E12 41 3N 28 48 E
Esera →, *Spain* ...... 38 C5 42 6N 0 15 E
Eşfahān, *Iran* .... 71 C6 32 39N 51 43 E
Eşfahān □, *Iran* ...... 71 C6 32 50N 51 50 E
Esfarāyen, *Iran* ...... 71 B8 37 4N 57 30 E
Esfideh, *Iran* .... 71 C8 33 39N 59 46 E
Esgueva →, *Spain* .. 36 D6 41 40N 4 43W
Esh Sham = Dimashq, *Syria* .... 74 B5 33 30N 36 18 E
Esh Shamâlîya □, *Sudan* 80 D2 19 50N 30 30 E
Esha Ness, *U.K.* 13 A7 60 29N 1 38W
Eshan, *China* .... 58 E4 24 11N 102 24 E
Esher, *U.K.* 15 F7 51 21N 0 20W
Eshkol △, *Israel* .... 74 D3 31 20N 34 30 E
Eshowe, *S. Africa* .... 89 D5 28 50 S 31 30 E
Esiama, *Ghana* 82 E4 4 56N 2 25W
Esigodini, *Zimbabwe* 89 C4 20 18 S 28 56 E
Esil = Ishim →, *Russia* 52 D8 57 45N 71 10 E
Esino →, *Italy* ...... 41 E10 43 39N 13 22 E
Esira, *Madag.* .... 89 C8 24 20 S 46 42 E
Esk →, *Cumb., U.K.* 13 G5 54 58N 3 2W
Esk →, *N. Yorks., U.K.* 14 C7 54 30N 0 37W
Eskān, *Iran* .... 71 E9 26 48N 63 9 E
Esker, *Canada* 105 B6 53 53N 66 25W
Eskifjörður, *Iceland* .. 8 D7 65 3N 13 55W
Eskilsäter, *Sweden* .. 11 F7 58 57N 13 10 E
Eskilstuna, *Sweden* .. 10 E10 59 22N 16 32 E
Eskimalatya, *Turkey* .. 73 C8 38 24N 38 22 E
Eskimo Point = Arviat, *Canada* 103 A10 61 6N 93 59W
Eskişehir, *Turkey* .... 47 B12 39 50N 30 30 E
Eskişehir □, *Turkey* .. 47 B12 39 40N 31 0 E
Esla →, *Spain* 36 D4 41 29N 6 3W
Eslāmābād-e Gharb, *Iran* .... 70 C5 34 10N 46 30 E
Eslāmshahr, *Iran* .... 71 C6 35 40N 51 10 E
Eslöv, *Sweden* ...... 11 J7 55 50N 13 20 E
Eşme, *Turkey* .... 47 C10 38 23N 28 58 E
Esmeraldas, *Ecuador* .. 124 C3 1 0N 79 40W
Esnagi L., *Canada* .. 104 C3 48 36N 84 33W
Espalion, *France* .... 20 D6 44 32N 2 47 E
Espanola, *Canada* 104 C3 46 15N 81 46W
Espanola, *U.S.A.* 109 H10 35 59N 106 5W
Esparreguera, *Spain* .. 38 D6 41 33N 1 52 E
Esparta, *Costa Rica* .. 120 E3 9 59N 84 40W
Espelkamp, *Germany* 24 C4 52 24N 8 36 E
Esperance, *Australia* .. 93 F3 33 45 S 121 55 E
Esperance B., *Australia* 93 F3 33 48 S 121 55 E
Esperance L., *St. Lucia* 121 f 14 4N 60 55W
Esperance, *Antarctica* 5 C18 65 0 S 55 0W
Esperanza, *Argentina* 126 C3 31 29 S 61 3W
Esperanza, *Phil.* ...... 61 G6 8 43N 125 36 E
Esperanza, *Puerto Rico* 121 d 18 6N 65 28W
Esperanza, *La* .... 20 F6 42 56N 2 14 E
Espichel, C., *Portugal* 37 G1 38 22N 9 16W
Espiel, *Spain* 37 G5 38 11N 5 1W
Espigão, Serra do, *Brazil* 127 B5 26 35 S 50 30W

Espinazo, Sierra del = Espinhaço, Serra do, *Brazil* .... 125 G10 17 30 S 43 30W
Espinhaço, Serra do, *Brazil* .... 125 G10 17 30 S 43 30W
Espinho, *Portugal* 36 D2 41 1N 8 38W
Espinilho, Serra do, *Brazil* .... 127 B5 28 30 S 55 0W
Espinosa de los Monteros, *Spain* .. 36 B7 43 5N 3 34W
Espírito Santo □, *Brazil* 125 H10 20 0 S 40 45W
Espíritu Santo, *Vanuatu* 96 J8 15 15 S 166 50 E
Espíritu Santo, B. del, *Mexico* 119 D7 19 15N 87 0W
Espíritu Santo, I., *Mexico* 118 C2 24 30N 110 23W
Espita, *Mexico* 119 C7 21 1N 88 19W
Espiye, *Turkey* ...... 73 B8 40 56N 38 43 E
Espluga de Francolí, *Spain* .... 38 D6 41 24N 1 7 E
Espoo, *Finland* ...... 9 F21 60 12N 24 40 E
España, Sierra de, *Spain* 39 H3 37 51N 1 35W
Espungabera, *Mozam.* 89 C5 20 29 S 32 45 E
Esquel, *Argentina* .... 128 E2 42 55 S 71 20W
Esquimalt, *Canada* .. 102 D4 48 26N 123 25W
Esquina, *Argentina* .. 126 C4 30 0 S 59 30W
Essaouira, *Morocco* .. 78 B4 31 32N 9 42W
Essebie, Dem. Rep. of the Congo .... 86 B3 2 58N 30 40 E
Essen, *Belgium* ...... 17 C4 51 28N 4 28 E
Essen, *Germany* ...... 24 D3 51 28N 7 2 E
Essendon, Mt., *Australia* 93 E3 25 0 S 120 29 E
Essequibo →, *Guyana* 124 B7 6 50N 58 30 E
Essex, *Canada* 116 D2 42 10N 82 49W
Essex, *Calif., U.S.A.* 111 L11 34 44N 115 15W
Essex, *N.Y., U.S.A.* 117 B11 44 19N 73 21W
Essex □, *U.K.* ...... 15 F8 51 54N 0 27 E
Essex Junction, *U.S.A.* 117 B11 44 29N 73 7W
Esslingen, *Germany* .. 25 G5 48 44N 9 18 E
Essonne □, *France* .. 19 D9 48 30N 2 20 E
Estaca de Bares, C. de, *Spain* 36 B3 43 46N 7 42W
Estadilla, *Spain* ...... 38 C5 42 4N 0 16 E
Estados, I. de Los, *Argentina* .... 128 G4 54 40 S 64 30W
Estagel, *France* ...... 20 F6 42 47N 2 40 E
Eşţahbānāt, *Iran* .... 71 D7 29 8N 54 4 E
Estância, *Brazil* ...... 125 F11 11 16 S 37 26W
Estância, *U.S.A.* 109 J10 34 46N 106 4W
Estārm, *Iran* .... 71 D8 28 21N 58 21 E
Estcourt, *S. Africa* .. 89 D4 29 0 S 29 53 E
Este, *Italy* .... 41 C8 45 14N 11 39 E
Este, □ *Dom. Rep.* .. 121 C6 18 45N 68 35 E
Estelí, *Nic.* 120 D2 13 9N 86 22W
Estella, *Spain* 38 C2 42 40N 2 0W
Estellencs, *Spain* .... 48 B9 39 39N 2 29 E
Estena →, *Spain* 37 F6 39 23N 4 44W
Estepa, *Spain* 37 H6 37 17N 4 52W
Estepona, *Spain* 37 J5 36 24N 5 7W
Esterhazy, *Canada* .. 103 C8 50 37N 102 5W
Esternay, *France* .... 19 D10 48 44N 3 33 E
Esterri d'Aneu, *Spain* 38 C6 42 38N 1 5 E
Estevan, *Canada* 103 D8 49 10N 102 59W
Estevan Group, *Canada* 102 C3 53 3N 129 38W
Estherville, *U.S.A.* .. 112 D7 43 24N 94 50W
Estissac, *France* ...... 19 D10 48 16N 3 48 E
Eston, *Canada* 103 C7 51 8N 108 40W
Estonia ■, *Europe* .. 9 G21 58 30N 25 30 E
Estoril, *Portugal* 37 G1 38 42N 9 23W
Estouk, *Mali* .... 83 B5 18 14N 1 2 E
Estreito, *Brazil* ...... 125 E9 6 32 S 47 25W
Estrela, Serra da, *Portugal* 36 E3 40 10N 7 45W
Estrella, *Spain* 37 G7 38 25N 3 35W
Estremoz, *Portugal* .. 37 G3 38 51N 7 39W
Estrondo, Serra do, *Brazil* .... 125 E9 7 20 S 48 0W
Esztergom, *Hungary* .. 28 C3 47 47N 18 44 E
Et Tidra, *Mauritania* .. 82 B1 19 45N 16 20W
Etah, *India* .... 69 F8 27 35N 78 40 E
Étain, *France* .... 19 C12 49 13N 5 38 E
Étampes, *France* .... 19 D9 48 26N 2 10 E
Etanga, *Namibia* .... 88 B1 17 55 S 13 0 E
Étaples, *France* ...... 19 B8 50 30N 1 39 E
Etawah, *India* .... 69 F8 26 48N 79 6 E
Etawney L., *Canada* .. 103 B9 57 50N 96 50W
Ete, *Nigeria* .... 83 D6 7 2N 7 28 E
Ethel, *U.S.A.* 110 D4 46 32N 122 46W
Ethelbert, *Canada* .. 103 C8 51 32N 100 25W
Ethiopia ■, *Africa* .. 75 F3 8 0N 40 0 E
Ethiopian Highlands, *Ethiopia* .... 50 J7 10 0N 37 0 E
Etili, *Turkey* .... 45 G10 39 59N 26 54 E
Etive, L., *U.K.* 13 E3 56 29N 5 10W
Etna, *Italy* .... 43 E7 37 50N 14 55 E
Etoile, Dem. Rep. of the Congo .... 87 E2 11 33 S 27 30 E
Etosha △, *Namibia* .. 88 B2 18 40 S 16 30 E
Etosha Pan, *Namibia* 88 B2 18 40 S 16 30 E
Etowah, *U.S.A.* 115 H3 35 20N 84 32W
Étréchy, *France* ...... 19 D9 48 30N 2 12 E
Étrépagny, *France* .. 19 C8 49 18N 1 36 E
Étretat, *France* ...... 18 C7 49 42N 0 12 E
Étropole, *Bulgaria* .. 45 C8 42 50N 24 0 E
Ettelbruck, *Lux.* ...... 17 E6 49 50N 6 5 E
Ettlingen, *Germany* .. 25 G4 48 56N 8 23 E
Ettrick Water →, *U.K.* 13 F6 55 31N 2 55W
Etuku, Dem. Rep. of the Congo .... 86 C2 3 42 S 25 45 E
Etulia, *Moldova* ...... 29 E13 45 32N 28 35 E
Etzatlán, *Mexico* 118 C4 20 48N 104 5W
Etzná, *Mexico* 119 D6 19 35N 90 15W
Etzná-Tixmucuy = Edxná, *Mexico* .. 119 D6 19 35N 90 15W
Eu, *France* .... 18 B8 50 3N 1 26 E
Eubenangee Swamp △, *Australia* .... 94 B4 16 25 S 146 1 E
Euboea = Évvoia, *Greece* .... 46 C6 38 30N 24 0 E
Eucla, *Australia* ...... 93 F4 31 41 S 128 52 E
Euclid, *U.S.A.* 116 E3 41 34N 81 32W
Eucumbene, L., *Australia* .... 95 F4 36 2 S 148 40 E
Eudora, *U.S.A.* 113 J9 33 7N 91 16W
Eufaula, *Ala., U.S.A.* 115 K3 31 54N 85 9W
Eufaula, *Okla., U.S.A.* 113 H7 35 17N 95 35W
Eufaula L., *U.S.A.* .. 113 H7 35 18N 95 21W
Eugene, *U.S.A.* 108 E2 44 5N 123 4W
Eugowra, *Australia* .. 95 E4 33 22 S 148 24 E
Eulo, *Australia* ...... 95 D4 28 10 S 145 3 E
Eungella △, *Australia* 94 C4 20 57 S 148 40 E
Eunice, *La., U.S.A.* .. 113 K8 30 30N 92 25W
Eunice, *N. Mex., U.S.A.* 113 J3 32 26N 103 10W
Eupen, *Belgium* ...... 17 D6 50 37N 6 3 E
Euphrates = Furāt, Nahr al →, *Asia* .... 70 D5 31 0N 47 25 E

Eure □, *France* ...... 18 C8 49 10N 1 0 E
Eure →, *France* ...... 18 C8 49 18N 1 12 E
Eure-et-Loir □, *France* 18 D8 48 22N 1 30 E
Eureka, *Canada* 4 B3 80 0N 85 56W
Eureka, *Calif., U.S.A.* 108 F1 40 47N 124 9W
Eureka, *Kans., U.S.A.* 113 G6 37 49N 96 17W
Eureka, *Mont., U.S.A.* 108 B6 48 53N 115 3W
Eureka, *Nev., U.S.A.* 108 G5 39 31N 115 58W
Eureka, *S. Dak., U.S.A.* 112 C5 45 46N 99 38W
Eureka, *Mt., Australia* 93 E3 26 35 S 121 35 E
Euroa, *Australia* .... 95 F4 36 44 S 145 35 E
Europa, Île, *Ind. Oc.* 85 J8 22 20 S 40 22 E
Europa, Picos de, *Spain* 36 B6 43 10N 4 49W
Europa, Pta. de, *Gib.* 37 J5 36 3N 5 21W
Europe .... 6 E10 50 0N 20 0 E
Europoort, *Neths.* .. 17 C4 51 57N 4 10 E
Euskirchen, *Germany* 24 E2 50 39N 6 45 E
Eustis, *U.S.A.* 115 L5 28 51N 81 41W
Eutin, *Germany* ...... 24 A6 54 8N 10 36 E
Eutsuk L., *Canada* .. 102 C3 53 20N 126 45W
Evale, *Angola* ...... 88 B2 16 33 S 15 44 E
Evans, *U.S.A.* 112 E2 40 23N 104 41W
Evans, L., *Canada* .. 104 B4 50 50N 77 0W
Evans City, *U.S.A.* .. 116 F4 40 46N 80 4W
Evans Head, *Australia* 95 D5 29 7 S 153 27 E
Evans Mills, *U.S.A.* 117 B9 44 6N 75 48W
Evansburg, *Canada* .. 102 C5 53 36N 114 59W
Evanston, *Ill., U.S.A.* 114 E2 42 3N 87 41W
Evanston, *Wyo., U.S.A.* 108 F8 41 16N 110 58W
Evansville, *U.S.A.* .. 114 G2 37 58N 87 35W
Évaux-les-Bains, *France* 19 F9 46 12N 2 29 E
Evaz, *Iran* .... 71 E7 27 46N 53 59 E
Eveleth, *U.S.A.* 112 B8 47 28N 92 32W
Evensk, *Russia* ...... 53 C16 62 12N 159 30 E
Everard, L., *Australia* 95 E2 31 30 S 135 0 E
Everard Ranges, *Australia* .... 93 E5 27 5 S 132 28 E
Everest, Mt., *Nepal* .. 69 E12 28 5N 86 58 E
Everett, *Pa., U.S.A.* 116 F6 40 1N 78 23W
Everett, *Wash., U.S.A.* 110 C4 47 59N 122 12W
Everglades △, *U.S.A.* 115 N5 25 30N 81 0W
Everglades, The, *U.S.A.* 115 N5 25 50N 81 0W
Everglades City, *U.S.A.* 115 N5 25 52N 81 23W
Evergreen, *Ala., U.S.A.* 115 K2 31 26N 86 57W
Evergreen, *Mont., U.S.A.* 108 B6 48 9N 114 13W
Everöd, *Sweden* ...... 11 J8 55 53N 14 5 E
Evertsberg, *Sweden* .. 10 C7 61 8N 13 58 E
Evesham, *U.K.* 15 E6 52 6N 1 56W
Évian-les-Bains, *France* 19 F13 46 24N 6 35 E
Évinos →, *Greece* .. 46 C3 38 27N 21 40 E
Évisa, *France* ...... 21 F12 42 15N 8 48 E
Evje, *Norway* ...... 9 G12 58 36N 7 51 E
Évora, *Portugal* 37 G3 38 33N 7 57W
Évora □, *Portugal* .. 37 G3 38 33N 7 50W
Evowghlī, *Iran* ...... 70 B5 38 43N 45 13 E
Évreux, *France* ...... 18 C8 49 3N 1 8 E
Évritanía □, *Greece* 46 B3 39 5N 21 30 E
Évron, *France* 18 D6 48 10N 0 24W
Évros □, *Greece* .... 45 E10 41 10N 26 0 E
Évros →, *Greece* .... 72 B2 41 40N 26 34 E
Evrótas →, *Greece* .. 46 E4 36 50N 22 40 E
Évry, *France* .... 19 D9 48 38N 2 27 E
Évvoia, *Greece* ...... 46 C6 38 30N 24 0 E
Évvoia □, *Greece* .... 46 C5 38 40N 23 40 E
Exinoúpolis, *Greece* .. 46 B4 39 12N 22 42 E
Ewe, L., *U.K.* 13 D3 57 49N 5 38W
Ewing, *U.S.A.* 112 D5 42 16N 98 21W
Ewo, *Congo* .... 84 E2 0 48 S 14 45 E
Exaltación, *Bolivia* .. 124 F5 13 10 S 65 20W
Excelsior Springs, *U.S.A.* 112 F7 39 20N 94 13W
Excideuil, *France* .... 20 C5 45 20N 1 4 E
Exe →, *U.K.* 15 G4 50 41N 3 29W
Exeter, *Canada* 116 C3 43 21N 81 29W
Exeter, *U.K.* 15 G4 50 43N 3 31W
Exeter, *Calif., U.S.A.* 110 J7 36 18N 119 9W
Exeter, *N.H., U.S.A.* 117 D14 42 59N 70 57W
Exmoor, *U.K.* 15 F4 51 12N 3 45W
Exmoor △, *U.K.* 15 F4 51 8N 3 42W
Exmouth, *Australia* .. 92 D1 21 54 S 114 10 E
Exmouth, *U.K.* 15 G4 50 37N 3 25W
Exmouth G., *Australia* 92 D1 22 15 S 114 15 E
Expedition △, *Australia* 95 D4 25 41 S 149 7 E
Expedition Ra., *Australia* .... 94 C4 24 30 S 149 12 E
Extremadura □, *Spain* 37 F4 39 30N 6 5W
Exuma Sound, *Bahamas* 120 B4 24 30N 76 20W
Eyasi, L., *Tanzania* .. 86 C4 3 30 S 35 0 E
Eye, L., *U.K.* 13 C2 58 13N 6 10W
Eyemouth, *U.K.* 13 F6 55 52N 2 5W
Eygues = Aigues →, *France* .... 21 D8 44 7N 4 43 E
Eygurande, *France* .. 19 G9 45 40N 2 26 E
Eyjafjörður, *Iceland* .. 8 C4 66 15N 18 30W
Eymet, *France* ...... 20 D4 44 40N 0 25 E
Eymoutiers, *France* .. 20 C5 45 40N 1 45 E
Eynesil, *Turkey* ...... 73 B8 41 4N 39 9 E
Eyre (North), L., *Australia* .... 95 D2 28 30 S 137 20 E
Eyre (South), L., *Australia* .... 95 D2 29 18 S 137 25 E
Eyre Mts., *N.Z.* ...... 91 L2 45 25 S 168 25 E
Eyre Pen., *Australia* .. 95 E2 33 30 S 136 17 E
Eysturoy, *Færoe Is.* .. 8 E9 62 13N 6 54W
Eyvānkī, *Iran* .... 71 C6 35 24N 51 56 E
Ez Zeidab, *Sudan* .... 80 D3 17 25N 33 55 E
Ezcaray, *Spain* 38 C1 42 19N 3 0W
Ēžerėlis, *Lithuania* .. 30 D10 54 53N 23 37 E
Ezhou, *China* ...... 59 B10 30 23N 114 50 E
Ezine, *Turkey* ...... 47 B8 39 48N 26 20 E
Ezouza →, *Cyprus* .. 49 E11 34 44N 32 27 E

F

F.Y.R.O.M. = Macedonia ■, *Europe* 44 E5 41 53N 21 40 E
Fabala, *Guinea* 82 D3 9 44N 9 5W
Fabens, *U.S.A.* 109 L10 31 30N 106 10W
Fabriano, *Italy* ...... 41 E9 43 20N 12 54 E
Făcăeni, *Romania* .. 29 F12 44 32N 27 53 E
Fachi, *Niger* .... 79 E8 18 6N 11 34 E
Fada, *Chad* .... 79 E10 17 13N 21 34 E
Fada-n-Gourma, *Burkina Faso* .... 83 C5 12 10N 0 30 E
Fadd, *Hungary* ...... 28 D3 46 28N 18 49 E
Faddeyevskiy, Ostrov, *Russia* .... 53 B15 76 0N 144 0 E
Faddor, *Sudan* ...... 81 F3 9 7N 32 17 E
Fadghāmī, *Syria* .... 70 C4 35 53N 40 52 E
Fadlab, *Sudan* ...... 80 D3 17 42N 34 2 E

Faenza, Italy ...... **41 D8** 44 17N 11 53 E
Færoe Is. = Føroyar, Atl. Oc. **8 F9** 62 0N 7 0W
Fafa, Mali ...... **83 B5** 15 22N 0 48 E
Fafe, Portugal **36 D2** 41 27N 8 11W
Fagam, Nigeria ...... **83 C7** 11 11N 10 1 E
Făgăraș, Romania ...... **29 E9** 45 48N 24 58 E
Făgăraș, Munții, Romania ...... **29 E9** 45 40N 24 40 E
Fågelmara, Sweden ...... **11 H9** 56 16N 15 58 E
Fagerhult, Sweden ...... **11 G9** 57 8N 15 40 E
Fagersta, Sweden ...... **10 D9** 60 1N 15 46 E
Făget, Romania ...... **28 E7** 45 52N 22 10 E
Făget, Munții, Romania ...... **29 C8** 47 40N 23 10 E
Fagnano, L., Argentina ...... **128 G3** 54 30 S 68 0W
Fagnières, France ...... **19 D11** 48 58N 4 20 E
Faguibine, L., Mali **82 B4** 16 45N 0 15W
Fahliān, Iran ...... **71 D6** 30 11N 51 28 E
Fahraj, Kermān, Iran ...... **71 D8** 29 0N 59 0 E
Fahraj, Yazd, Iran ...... **71 D7** 31 46N 54 36 E
Fai Tsi Long, Vietnam ...... **58 G6** 21 0N 107 30 E
Faial, Madeira **48 D3** 32 47N 16 53W
Fair Haven, U.S.A. **114 D9** 43 36N 73 16W
Fair Oaks, U.S.A. **110 G5** 38 39N 121 16W
Fairbanks, U.S.A. **100 B5** 64 51N 147 43W
Fairbury, U.S.A. **112 E6** 40 8N 97 11W
Fairfax, U.S.A. **117 B11** 44 40N 73 1W
Fairfield, Ala., U.S.A. **115 J2** 33 29N 86 55W
Fairfield, Calif., U.S.A. **110 G4** 38 15N 122 3W
Fairfield, Conn., U.S.A. **117 E11** 41 9N 73 16W
Fairfield, Idaho, U.S.A. **108 E6** 43 21N 114 44W
Fairfield, Ill., U.S.A. **114 F1** 38 23N 88 22W
Fairfield, Iowa, U.S.A. **112 E9** 40 56N 91 57W
Fairfield, Tex., U.S.A. **113 K7** 31 44N 96 10W
Fairford, Canada **103 C9** 51 37N 98 38W
Fairhope, U.S.A. **115 K2** 30 31N 87 54W
Fairlie, N.Z. ...... **91 L3** 44 5 S 170 49 E
Fairmead, U.S.A. **110 H6** 37 5N 120 10W
Fairmont, Minn., U.S.A. **112 D7** 43 39N 94 28W
Fairmont, W. Va., U.S.A. **114 F5** 39 29N 80 9W
Fairmount, Calif., U.S.A. **111 L8** 34 45N 118 26W
Fairmount, N.Y., U.S.A. **117 C8** 43 5N 76 12W
Fairplay, U.S.A. **109 G11** 39 15N 106 2W
Fairport, U.S.A. **116 C7** 43 6N 77 27W
Fairport Harbor, U.S.A. **116 E3** 41 45N 81 17W
Fairview, Canada **102 B5** 56 5N 118 25W
Fairview, Mont., U.S.A. **112 B2** 47 51N 104 3W
Fairview, Okla., U.S.A. **113 G5** 36 16N 98 29W
Fairweather, Mt., U.S.A. **102 B1** 58 55N 137 32W
Faisalabad, Pakistan ...... **68 D5** 31 30N 73 5 E
Faith, U.S.A. **112 C3** 45 2N 102 2W
Faizabad, India ...... **69 F10** 26 45N 82 10 E
Fajardo, Puerto Rico ...... **121 d** 18 20N 65 39W
Fajr, W. →, Si. Arabia ...... **70 D3** 29 10N 38 10 E
Fakenham, U.K. ...... **14 E8** 52 51N 0 51 E
Fåker, Sweden ...... **10 A8** 63 0N 14 34 E
Fakfak, Indonesia ...... **63 E8** 2 55 S 132 18 E
Fakiya, Bulgaria ...... **45 D11** 42 10N 27 6 E
Fakobli, Ivory C. **82 D3** 7 23N 7 23W
Fakse, Denmark ...... **11 J6** 55 15N 12 8 E
Fakse Bugt, Denmark ...... **11 J6** 55 11N 12 15 E
Fakse Ladeplads, Denmark ...... **11 J6** 55 11N 12 11 E
Faku, China ...... **57 C12** 42 32N 123 21 E
Falaba, S. Leone **82 D2** 9 54N 11 22W
Falaise, France **18 D6** 48 54N 0 12W
Falaise, Mui, Vietnam ...... **64 C5** 19 6N 105 45 E
Falakrón Óros, Greece ...... **44 E7** 41 15N 23 58 E
Falam, Burma ...... **67 H18** 23 0N 93 45 E
Falces, Spain **38 C3** 42 24N 1 48W
Fălciu, Romania ...... **29 D13** 46 17N 28 7 E
Falcó, C. des, Spain ...... **48 C7** 38 50N 1 23 E
Falcón, Presa, Mexico **119 B5** 26 35N 99 10W
Falcon Lake, Canada **103 D9** 49 42N 95 15W
Falcon Reservoir, U.S.A. **113 M5** 26 34N 99 10W
Falconara Maríttima, Italy ...... **41 E10** 43 37N 13 24 E
Falcone, C. del, Italy ...... **42 B1** 40 58N 8 12 E
Falconer, U.S.A. **116 D5** 42 7N 79 13W
Faléa, Mali **82 C2** 12 16N 11 17W
Falémé →, Senegal **82 C2** 14 46N 12 14W
Falerum, Sweden ...... **11 F10** 58 8N 16 13 E
Faleshty = Fălești, Moldova ...... **29 C12** 47 32N 27 44 E
Fălești, Moldova ...... **29 C12** 47 32N 27 44 E
Falfurrias, U.S.A. **113 M5** 27 14N 98 9W
Falher, Canada **102 B5** 55 44N 117 15W
Falirakí, Greece ...... **49 C10** 36 22N 28 12 E
Falkenberg, Germany ...... **24 D9** 51 35N 13 14 E
Falkenberg, Sweden ...... **11 H6** 56 54N 12 30 E
Falkensee, Germany ...... **24 C9** 52 34N 13 4 E
Falkirk, U.K. **13 F5** 56 0N 3 47W
Falkirk □, U.K. **13 F5** 55 58N 3 49W
Falkland, U.K. **13 E5** 56 16N 3 12W
Falkland Is. □, Atl. Oc. ...... **128 G5** 51 30 S 59 0W
Falkland Sd., Falk. Is. ...... **128 G5** 52 0 S 60 0W
Falkonéra, Greece ...... **46 E5** 36 50N 23 52 E
Falköping, Sweden ...... **11 F7** 58 12N 13 33 E
Fall River, U.S.A. **117 E13** 41 43N 71 10W
Fallbrook, U.S.A. **111 M9** 33 23N 117 15W
Fallon, U.S.A. **108 G4** 39 28N 118 47W
Falls City, U.S.A. **112 E7** 40 3N 95 36W
Falls Creek, U.S.A. **116 E6** 41 9N 78 48W
Falmouth, Jamaica ...... **120 a** 18 30N 77 40W
Falmouth, U.K. **15 G2** 50 9N 5 5W
Falmouth, U.S.A. **117 E14** 41 33N 70 37W
Falsa, Pta., Mexico **118 B1** 27 51N 115 3W
False B., S. Africa ...... **88 E2** 34 15 S 18 40 E
Falso, C., Honduras **120 C3** 15 12N 83 21W
Falster, Denmark ...... **11 K5** 54 45N 11 55 E
Falsterbo, Sweden ...... **9 J15** 55 23N 12 50 E
Fălticeni, Romania ...... **29 C11** 47 21N 26 20 E
Falun, Sweden ...... **10 D9** 60 37N 15 37 E
Famagusta, Cyprus ...... **49 D12** 35 8N 33 55 E
Famagusta Bay, Cyprus ...... **49 D12** 35 15N 34 0 E
Famalé, Niger ...... **78 F6** 14 33N 1 5 E
Famatina, Sierra de, Argentina ...... **126 B2** 27 30 S 68 0W
Family L., Canada **103 C9** 51 54N 95 27W
Famoso, U.S.A. **111 K7** 35 37N 119 12W
Fan Xian, China ...... **56 G8** 35 55N 115 50 E
Fana, Mali **82 C3** 13 0N 6 56W
Fanad Hd., Ireland **12 A4** 55 17N 7 38W
Fanárion, Greece ...... **38 B4** 39 24N 21 47 E
Fandriana, Madag. ...... **89 C8** 20 14 S 47 21 E
Fánes-Sénnes e Braies □, Italy ...... **41 B9** 46 38N 12 4 E
Fang, Thailand ...... **58 H2** 19 55N 99 13 E
Fang Xian, China ...... **59 A8** 32 3N 110 40 E
Fangaga, Sudan ...... **80 D4** 17 40N 37 50 E
Fangchang, China ...... **59 B12** 31 5N 118 4 E
Fangcheng, China ...... **56 H7** 33 18N 112 59 E
Fangchenggang, China ...... **58 G7** 21 42N 108 21 E
Fangliao, Taiwan ...... **59 F13** 22 22N 120 38 E
Fangshan, China ...... **56 E6** 38 3N 111 25 E

Fangzi, China ...... **57 F10** 36 33N 119 10 E
Fani i Madh →, Albania ...... **44 E4** 41 56N 20 16 E
Fanjakana, Madag. ...... **89 C8** 21 10 S 46 53 E
Fanjiatun, China ...... **57 C13** 43 40N 125 15 E
Fannich, L., U.K. **13 D4** 57 38N 4 59W
Fannūj, Iran ...... **71 E8** 26 35N 59 38 E
Fanø, Denmark ...... **11 J2** 55 25N 8 25 E
Fano, Italy ...... **41 E10** 43 50N 13 1 E
Fanshi, China ...... **56 E7** 39 12N 113 20 E
Fao = Al Fāw, Iraq ...... **71 D6** 30 0N 48 30 E
Faqirwali, Pakistan ...... **68 E5** 29 27N 73 0 E
Fāqūs, Egypt ...... **80 H7** 30 44N 31 47 E
Far East = Dalnevostochnyy □, Russia ...... **53 C14** 67 0N 140 0 E
Far East, Asia ...... **50 E16** 40 0N 130 0 E
Fara in Sabina, Italy ...... **41 F9** 42 12N 12 43 E
Faradje, Dem. Rep. of the Congo ...... **86 B2** 3 50N 29 45 E
Farafangana, Madag. ...... **89 C8** 22 49 S 47 50 E
Farāfra, El Wâhât el-, Egypt ...... **80 B2** 27 15N 28 20 E
Farāh, Afghan. ...... **66 C3** 32 20N 62 7 E
Farāh □, Afghan. ...... **66 C3** 32 25N 62 10 E
Farahalana, Madag. ...... **89 A9** 14 26 S 50 10 E
Faraid, Gebel, Egypt ...... **80 C4** 23 33N 35 19 E
Farako, Ivory C. **82 D4** 10 45N 6 50W
Faramana, Burkina Faso **82 C4** 11 56N 4 45W
Faranah, Guinea **82 C2** 10 3N 10 45W
Farasān, Jazā'ir, Si. Arabia ...... **75 D3** 16 45N 41 55 E
Farasan Is. = Farasān, Jazā'ir, Si. Arabia ...... **75 D3** 16 45N 41 55 E
Faratsiho, Madag. ...... **89 B8** 19 24 S 46 57 E
Fardes →, Spain **37 H7** 37 35N 3 0W
Fareham, U.K. **15 G6** 50 51N 1 11W
Farewell C., N.Z. ...... **91 J4** 40 29 S 172 43 E
Farewell C. = Nunap Isua, Greenland **101 C15** 59 48N 43 55W
Färgelanda, Sweden ...... **11 F5** 58 34N 12 0 E
Farghona, Uzbekistan ...... **52 E8** 40 23N 71 19 E
Fargo, U.S.A. **112 B6** 46 53N 96 48W
Fār'iah, W. al →, West Bank ...... **74 C4** 32 12N 35 27 E
Faribault, U.S.A. **112 C8** 44 18N 93 16W
Faridabad, India ...... **68 E6** 28 26N 77 19 E
Faridkot, India ...... **68 D6** 30 44N 74 45 E
Faridpur, Bangla. ...... **69 H13** 23 15N 89 55 E
Faridpur, India ...... **69 E8** 28 13N 79 33 E
Färila, Sweden ...... **10 C9** 61 48N 15 50 E
Farim, Guinea-Biss. **82 C1** 12 27N 15 9W
Farīmān, Iran ...... **71 C8** 35 40N 59 49 E
Farina, Australia ...... **95 E2** 30 3 S 138 15 E
Fariones, Pta., Canary Is. **48 E6** 29 13N 13 28W
Färiskûr, Egypt ...... **80 H7** 31 20N 31 43 E
Farkadhón, Greece ...... **46 B4** 39 36N 22 4 E
Farleigh, Australia ...... **94 K7** 21 4 S 149 8 E
Farmakonísi, Greece ...... **47 D9** 37 17N 27 5 E
Farmerville, U.S.A. **113 J8** 32 47N 92 24W
Farmingdale, U.S.A. **117 F10** 40 12N 74 10W
Farmington, Canada **102 B4** 55 54N 120 30W
Farmington, Calif., U.S.A. **110 H6** 37 55N 120 59W
Farmington, Maine, U.S.A. **115 C10** 44 40N 70 9W
Farmington, Mo., U.S.A. **113 G9** 37 47N 90 25W
Farmington, N.H., U.S.A. **117 C13** 43 24N 71 4W
Farmington, N. Mex., U.S.A. **109 H9** 36 44N 108 12W
Farmington, Utah, U.S.A. **108 F8** 41 0N 111 12W
Farmington →, U.S.A. **117 E12** 41 51N 72 38W
Farmville, U.S.A. **114 G6** 37 18N 78 24W
Färnäs, Sweden ...... **10 D8** 61 0N 14 39 E
Farne Is., U.K. **14 B6** 55 38N 1 37W
Färnebofjärden □, Sweden ...... **10 D10** 60 10N 16 48 E
Farnham, Canada **117 A12** 45 17N 72 59W
Farnham, Mt., Canada **102 C5** 50 29N 116 30W
Faro, Brazil ...... **125 D7** 2 10 S 56 39W
Faro, Canada **100 B6** 62 11N 133 22W
Faro, Portugal **37 H3** 37 2N 7 55W
Fårö, Sweden ...... **9 H18** 57 55N 19 5 E
Faro □, Portugal **37 H2** 37 12N 8 10W
Faro ✈ (FAO), Portugal **37 H3** 37 7N 7 57W
Fårösund, Sweden ...... **11 G13** 57 52N 19 2 E
Farquhar, C., Australia ...... **93 D1** 23 51 S 113 36 E
Farrars Cr. →, Australia ...... **94 D3** 25 35 S 140 43 E
Farrāshband, Iran ...... **71 D7** 28 57N 52 5 E
Farrell, U.S.A. **116 E4** 41 13N 80 30W
Farrokhī, Iran ...... **71 C8** 33 50N 59 31 E
Farruch, C. = Ferrutx, C., Spain ...... **48 B10** 39 47N 3 21 E
Fārs □, Iran ...... **71 D7** 29 30N 55 0 E
Fársala, Greece ...... **46 B4** 39 17N 22 23 E
Farsø, Denmark ...... **11 H3** 56 46N 9 19 E
Farson, U.S.A. **108 E9** 42 6N 109 27W
Farsund, Norway ...... **9 G12** 58 5N 6 55 E
Fartak, Râs, Si. Arabia ...... **70 D2** 28 5N 34 34 E
Fartak, Ra's, Yemen ...... **75 D5** 15 38N 52 15 E
Fărțănești, Romania ...... **29 E12** 45 49N 27 59 E
Fartura, Serra da, Brazil ...... **127 B5** 26 21 S 52 52W
Faru, Nigeria ...... **83 C6** 12 48N 6 12 E
Fārūj, Iran ...... **71 B8** 37 14N 58 14 E
Fårup, Denmark ...... **11 H3** 56 33N 9 51 E
Farvel, Kap = Nunap Isua, Greenland **101 C15** 59 48N 43 55W
Farwell, U.S.A. **113 H3** 34 23N 103 2W
Fāryāb □, Afghan. ...... **66 B4** 36 0N 65 0 E
Fasā, Iran ...... **71 D7** 29 0N 53 39 E
Fasano, Italy ...... **43 B10** 40 50N 17 22 E
Fashoda, Sudan ...... **81 F3** 9 50N 32 2 E
Fassa, Mali ...... **82 C3** 13 26N 8 15 E
Fastiv, Ukraine ...... **33 G5** 50 7N 29 57 E
Fastnet Rock, Ireland **12 E2** 51 22N 9 37W
Fastov = Fastiv, Ukraine ...... **33 G5** 50 7N 29 57 E
Fatagar, Tanjung, Indonesia ...... **63 E8** 2 46 S 131 57 E
Fatehabad, Haryana, India ...... **68 E6** 29 31N 75 27 E
Fatehabad, Ut. P., India ...... **68 F8** 27 1N 78 19 E
Fatehgarh, India ...... **69 F8** 27 25N 79 35 E
Fatehpur, Bihar, India ...... **69 G11** 24 38N 85 14 E
Fatehpur, Raj., India ...... **68 F6** 28 0N 74 40 E
Fatehpur, Ut. P., India ...... **69 G9** 25 56N 81 13 E
Fatehpur, Ut. P., India ...... **69 F9** 27 10N 81 13 E
Fatehpur Sikri, India ...... **68 F6** 27 6N 77 40 E
Fatesh, Russia ...... **33 F8** 52 8N 35 57 E
Fathai, Sudan ...... **81 F3** 8 5N 31 48 E
Fathom Five △, Canada **116 A3** 45 19N 81 40W
Fatick, Senegal **82 C1** 14 19N 16 27W
Fatima, Canada **105 C7** 47 24N 61 53W
Fátima, Portugal **37 F2** 39 37N 8 39W
Fatoya, Guinea **82 C3** 11 37N 9 10W

Fatsa, Turkey ...... **72 B7** 41 2N 37 31 E
Faucille, Col de la, France ...... **19 F13** 46 22N 6 2 E
Faulkton, U.S.A. **112 C5** 45 2N 99 8W
Faulquemont, France ...... **19 C13** 49 3N 6 36 E
Faure I., Australia ...... **93 E1** 25 52 S 113 50 E
Fauresmith, S. Africa ...... **88 D4** 29 44 S 25 17 E
Fauske, Norway ...... **8 C16** 67 17N 15 25 E
Favara, Italy ...... **42 E6** 37 19N 13 39 E
Favārīx, C. de, Spain ...... **48 B11** 40 0N 4 15 E
Faverges, France ...... **21 C10** 45 45N 6 17 E
Favignana, Italy ...... **42 E5** 37 56N 12 20 E
Favignana, I., Italy ...... **42 E5** 37 56N 12 19 E
Fawcett, Pt., Australia ...... **92 B5** 11 46 S 130 2 E
Fawn →, Canada **104 A2** 55 20N 87 35W
Fawnskin, U.S.A. **111 L10** 34 16N 116 56W
Faxaflói, Iceland **8 D2** 64 29N 23 0W
Faxälven →, Sweden ...... **10 A10** 63 13N 17 13 E
Faya-Largeau, Chad ...... **79 E9** 17 58N 19 6 E
Fayd, Si. Arabia ...... **70 E4** 27 1N 42 52 E
Fayence, France ...... **21 E10** 43 38N 6 42 E
Fayette, Ala., U.S.A. **115 J2** 33 41N 87 50W
Fayette, Mo., U.S.A. **112 F8** 39 9N 92 41W
Fayetteville, Ark., U.S.A. **113 G7** 36 4N 94 10W
Fayetteville, N.C., U.S.A. **115 H6** 35 3N 78 53W
Fayetteville, Tenn., U.S.A. **115 H2** 35 9N 86 34W
Fayied, Egypt ...... **80 H8** 30 18N 32 16 E
Fayón, Spain ...... **38 D5** 41 15N 0 20 E
Fazao-Malfakassa △, Togo ...... **83 D5** 8 45N 0 50 E
Fazilka, India ...... **68 D6** 30 27N 74 2 E
Fazilpur, Pakistan ...... **68 E4** 29 18N 70 29 E
Fdérik, Mauritania **78 D3** 22 40N 12 45W
Feale →, Ireland **12 D2** 52 27N 9 37W
Fear, C., U.S.A. **115 J7** 33 50N 77 58W
Feather →, U.S.A. **108 G3** 38 47N 121 36W
Feather Falls, U.S.A. **110 F5** 39 36N 121 16W
Featherston, N.Z. ...... **91 J5** 41 6 S 175 20 E
Featherstone, Zimbabwe ...... **87 F3** 18 42 S 30 55 E
Fécamp, France ...... **18 C7** 49 45N 0 22 E
Fedala = Mohammedia, Morocco **78 B4** 33 44N 7 21W
Federación, Argentina ...... **126 C4** 31 0 S 57 55W
Féderal, Argentina ...... **128 C5** 30 57 S 58 48W
Federal Capital Terr. □, Nigeria ...... **83 D6** 9 0N 7 10 E
Federal Way, U.S.A. **110 C4** 47 18N 122 19W
Fedeshkūh, Iran ...... **71 D7** 28 49N 53 50 E
Fehérgyarmat, Hungary ...... **28 C7** 47 58N 22 30 E
Fehmarn, Germany ...... **24 A7** 54 27N 11 7 E
Fehmarn Bælt, Europe ...... **11 K5** 54 35N 11 20 E
Fehmarn Belt = Fehmarn Bælt, Europe ...... **11 K5** 54 35N 11 20 E
Fei Xian, China ...... **57 G9** 35 18N 117 59 E
Feijó, Brazil ...... **124 E4** 8 9 S 70 21W
Feilding, N.Z. ...... **91 J5** 40 13 S 175 35 E
Feira de Santana, Brazil ...... **125 F11** 12 15 S 38 57W
Feixi, China ...... **59 B11** 31 43N 117 19 E
Feixiang, China ...... **56 F8** 36 30N 114 45 E
Fejér □, Hungary ...... **28 C3** 47 9N 18 30 E
Fejø, Denmark ...... **11 K5** 54 55N 11 30 E
Feke, Turkey ...... **72 D6** 37 48N 35 56 E
Fekete →, Hungary ...... **28 E3** 45 47N 18 15 E
Felanitx, Spain ...... **48 B10** 39 28N 3 9 E
Feldbach, Austria ...... **26 E8** 46 57N 15 52 E
Feldberg, Baden-W., Germany ...... **25 H3** 47 52N 8 0 E
Feldberg, Mecklenburg-Vorpommern, Germany ...... **24 B9** 53 20N 13 25 E
Feldkirch, Austria ...... **26 D2** 47 15N 9 37 E
Feldkirchen, Austria ...... **26 E7** 46 44N 14 6 E
Felipe Carrillo Puerto, Mexico **119 D7** 19 38N 88 3W
Felixburg, Zimbabwe ...... **89 B5** 19 29 S 30 51 E
Felixstowe, U.K. ...... **15 F9** 51 58N 1 23 E
Felletin, France ...... **20 C6** 45 53N 2 11 E
Fellingsbro, Sweden ...... **10 E9** 59 26N 15 37 E
Felton, U.S.A. **110 H4** 37 3N 122 4W
Feltre, Italy ...... **41 B8** 46 1N 11 54 E
Femer Bælt = Fehmarn Bælt, Europe ...... **11 K5** 54 35N 11 20 E
Femø, Denmark ...... **11 K5** 54 58N 11 37 E
Femunden, Norway ...... **9 E14** 62 10N 11 53 E
Fen He →, China ...... **56 G6** 35 36N 110 42 E
Fene, Spain **36 B2** 43 27N 8 9W
Fenelon Falls, Canada **116 B6** 44 32N 78 45W
Fener Burnu, Turkey ...... **47 E9** 36 58N 27 18 E
Feneroa, Ethiopia ...... **81 E4** 13 5N 39 3 E
Feng Xian, Jiangsu, China ...... **56 G9** 34 43N 116 35 E
Feng Xian, Shaanxi, China ...... **56 H4** 33 54N 106 40 E
Fengári, Greece ...... **45 F9** 40 25N 25 32 E
Fengcheng, Jiangxi, China ...... **59 C10** 28 12N 115 48 E
Fengcheng, Liaoning, China ...... **57 D13** 40 28N 124 5 E
Fengfeng, China ...... **56 F8** 36 28N 114 8 E
Fenggang, China ...... **58 D6** 27 57N 107 47 E
Fenghua, China ...... **59 C13** 29 40N 121 25 E
Fenghuang, China ...... **58 D7** 27 57N 109 29 E
Fengkai, China ...... **59 F8** 23 24N 111 30 E
Fengkang, Taiwan ...... **59 F13** 22 12N 120 41 E
Fengle, China ...... **59 B9** 31 29N 112 29 E
Fenglin, Taiwan ...... **59 F13** 23 45N 121 26 E
Fengning, China ...... **56 D9** 41 10N 116 33 E
Fengqing, China ...... **58 E2** 24 38N 99 55 E
Fengqiu, China ...... **56 G8** 35 2N 114 25 E
Fengrun, China ...... **57 E10** 39 48N 118 8 E
Fengshan, Guangxi Zhuangzu, China ...... **58 E7** 24 31N 107 3 E
Fengshan, Taiwan ...... **59 F13** 22 38N 120 21 E
Fengshan, Guangxi Zhuangzu, China ...... **58 E6** 24 31N 107 3 E
Fengshun, China ...... **59 F11** 23 46N 116 10 E
Fengtai, Anhui, China ...... **59 A11** 32 50N 116 44 E
Fengtai, Beijing, China ...... **56 E9** 39 50N 116 18 E
Fengxian, China ...... **59 B13** 30 55N 121 26 E
Fengxiang, China ...... **56 G4** 34 29N 107 25 E
Fengxin, China ...... **59 C10** 28 41N 115 18 E
Fengyang, China ...... **57 H9** 32 51N 117 29 E
Fengyi, China ...... **58 E3** 25 37N 100 20 E
Fengyuan, Taiwan ...... **59 E13** 24 15N 120 41 E
Fengzhen, China ...... **56 D7** 40 25N 113 2 E
Feno, C. de, France ...... **21 G12** 41 58N 8 33 E
Fenoarivo, Fianarantsoa, Madag. ...... **89 C8** 21 43 S 46 24 E
Fenoarivo, Fianarantsoa, Madag. ...... **89 C8** 20 52 S 46 53 E

Fenoarivo Afovoany, Madag. ...... **89 B8** 18 26 S 46 34 E
Fenoarivo Atsinanana, Madag. ...... **89 B8** 17 22 S 49 25 E
Fens, The, U.K. **14 E7** 52 38N 0 2W
Fensmark, Denmark ...... **11 J5** 55 17N 11 48 E
Fenton, U.S.A. **114 D4** 42 48N 83 42W
Fenxi, China ...... **56 F6** 36 40N 111 31 E
Fenyang, China ...... **56 F6** 37 18N 111 48 E
Fenyi, China ...... **59 D10** 27 45N 114 47 E
Feodosiya, Ukraine ...... **33 K8** 45 2N 35 16 E
Ferdows, Iran ...... **71 C8** 33 58N 58 2 E
Fère-Champenoise, France ...... **19 D10** 48 45N 3 59 E
Fère-en-Tardenois, France ...... **19 C10** 49 10N 3 30 E
Ferfer, Somali Rep. ...... **75 F4** 5 4N 45 9 E
Fergana = Farghona, Uzbekistan ...... **52 E8** 40 23N 71 19 E
Fergus, Canada **116 C4** 43 43N 80 24W
Fergus Falls, U.S.A. **112 B6** 46 17N 96 4W
Feričanci, Croatia ...... **28 E2** 45 32N 18 0 E
Ferihegy, Budapest ✈ (BUD), Hungary ...... **28 C4** 47 25N 19 12 E
Ferkéssédougou, Ivory C. **82 D3** 9 35N 5 6W
Ferlach, Austria ...... **26 E7** 46 32N 14 18 E
Ferland, Canada **104 B2** 50 19N 88 27W
Ferlo, Vallée du, Senegal **82 B2** 15 15N 14 15W
Ferlo-Nord △, Senegal **82 B2** 15 43N 14 0W
Ferlo-Sud △, Senegal **82 B2** 15 43N 14 0W
Fermanagh □, U.K. **12 B4** 54 21N 7 40W
Fermo, Italy ...... **41 E10** 43 9N 13 43 E
Fermont, Canada **105 B6** 52 47N 67 5W
Fermoselle, Spain **36 D4** 41 19N 6 27W
Fermoy, Ireland **12 D3** 52 9N 8 16W
Fernán Nuñez, Spain **37 H6** 37 40N 4 44W
Fernández, Argentina ...... **126 B3** 27 55 S 63 50W
Fernandina Beach, U.S.A. **115 K5** 30 40N 81 27W
Fernando de Noronha, Brazil ...... **125 D12** 4 0 S 33 10W
Fernando Póo = Bioko, Eq. Guin. ...... **83 E6** 3 30N 8 40 E
Ferndale, U.S.A. **110 B4** 48 51N 122 36W
Fernie, Canada **102 D5** 49 30N 115 5W
Fernlees, Australia ...... **94 C4** 23 51 S 148 7 E
Fernley, U.S.A. **108 G4** 39 36N 119 15W
Ferozepore = Firozpur, India ...... **68 D6** 30 55N 74 40 E
Férrai, Greece ...... **45 F10** 40 53N 26 10 E
Ferrandina, Italy ...... **43 B9** 40 29N 16 27 E
Ferrara, Italy ...... **41 D8** 44 50N 11 35 E
Ferrato, C., Italy ...... **42 C2** 39 18N 9 38 E
Ferreira do Alentejo, Portugal **37 G2** 38 4N 8 6W
Ferreñafe, Peru ...... **124 E3** 6 42 S 79 50W
Ferrerías, Spain ...... **48 B11** 39 59N 4 1 E
Ferret, C., France **20 D2** 44 38N 1 15W
Ferrette, France ...... **19 E14** 47 30N 7 20 E
Ferriday, U.S.A. **113 K9** 31 38N 91 33W
Ferriere, Italy ...... **40 D6** 44 40N 9 30 E
Ferrières, France ...... **19 D9** 48 5N 2 48 E
Ferro, Capo, Italy ...... **42 A2** 41 9N 9 31 E
Ferrol, Spain **36 B2** 43 29N 8 15W
Ferron, U.S.A. **109 G8** 39 5N 111 8W
Ferrutx, C., Spain ...... **48 B10** 39 47N 3 21 E
Ferryland, Canada **105 C9** 47 2N 52 53W
Fertile, U.S.A. **112 B6** 47 32N 96 17W
Fertőszentmiklós, Hungary ...... **28 C1** 47 35N 16 53 E
Fertőtavi △, Hungary ...... **28 C1** 47 25N 16 50 E
Fès, Morocco **78 B5** 34 0N 5 0W
Fessenden, U.S.A. **112 B5** 47 39N 99 38W
Festus, U.S.A. **112 F9** 38 13N 90 24W
Feté Bowé, Senegal **82 C2** 14 56N 13 58W
Fethard, Ireland **12 D4** 52 28N 7 50W

Filipstad, Sweden ...... **10 E8** 59 43N 14 9 E
Filisur, Switz. ...... **25 J5** 46 41N 9 40 E
Fillmore, Calif., U.S.A. **111 L8** 34 24N 118 55W
Fillmore, Utah, U.S.A. **109 G7** 38 58N 112 20W
Filótion, Greece ...... **47 D7** 37 3N 25 30 E
Filottrano, Italy ...... **41 E10** 43 26N 13 21 E
Filtu, Ethiopia ...... **81 F5** 5 8N 40 35 E
Fina, Mali **82 C3** 13 5N 8 46W
Finale Emília, Italy ...... **41 D8** 44 50N 11 18 E
Finale Lígure, Italy ...... **40 D5** 44 10N 8 20 E
Fiñana, Spain **37 H8** 37 10N 2 50W
Finch, Canada **117 A9** 45 11N 75 7W
Finch Hatton, Australia ...... **94 K6** 20 25 S 148 39 E
Findhorn →, U.K. **13 D5** 57 38N 3 38W
Findlay, U.S.A. **114 E4** 41 2N 83 39W
Finger, L., Canada **104 B1** 53 33N 93 30W
Finger Lakes, U.S.A. **117 D8** 42 40N 76 30W
Fingoè, Mozam. ...... **87 E3** 14 55 S 31 50 E
Finike, Turkey ...... **47 E12** 36 21N 30 10 E
Finike Körfezi, Turkey ...... **47 E12** 36 17N 30 16 E
Finiq, Albania ...... **44 G4** 39 54N 20 3 E
Finistère □, France **18 D3** 48 20N 4 0W
Finisterre = Fisterra, Spain **36 C1** 42 54N 9 16W
Finisterre, C. = Fisterra, C., Spain **36 C1** 42 50N 9 19W
Finke, Australia ...... **94 D1** 25 34 S 134 35 E
Finke Gorge △, Australia ...... **92 D5** 24 8 S 132 49 E
Finland ■, Europe ...... **8 E22** 63 0N 27 0 E
Finland, G. of, Europe ...... **9 G21** 60 0N 26 0 E
Finlay →, Canada **102 B3** 57 0N 125 10W
Finley, Australia ...... **95 F4** 35 38 S 145 35 E
Finley, U.S.A. **112 B6** 47 31N 97 50W
Finn →, Ireland **12 B4** 54 51N 7 28W
Finnerödja, Sweden ...... **11 F8** 58 57N 14 24 E
Finnigan, Mt., Australia ...... **94 B4** 15 49 S 145 17 E
Finniss, C., Australia ...... **95 E1** 33 8 S 134 51 E
Finnmark, Norway ...... **8 B20** 69 37N 23 57 E
Finnsnes, Norway ...... **8 B18** 69 14N 18 0 E
Finspång, Sweden ...... **11 F9** 58 43N 15 47 E
Finsteraarhorn, Switz. ...... **25 J4** 46 31N 8 10 E
Finsterwalde, Germany ...... **24 D9** 51 37N 13 42 E
Fiora →, Italy ...... **41 F8** 42 20N 11 34 E
Fiordland △, N.Z. ...... **91 L1** 45 46 S 167 0 E
Fiorenzuola d'Arda, Italy ...... **40 D6** 44 56N 9 55 E
Fiq, Syria ...... **74 C4** 32 46N 35 41 E
Firat = Furât, Nahr al →, Asia ...... **70 D5** 31 0N 47 25 E
Fire Island △, U.S.A. **117 F11** 40 38N 73 8W
Firebag →, Canada **103 B6** 57 45N 111 21W
Firebaugh, U.S.A. **110 J6** 36 52N 120 27W
Firedrake L., Canada **103 A8** 61 25N 104 30W
Firenze, Italy ...... **41 E8** 43 46N 11 15 E
Firenze Amerigo Vespucci ✈ (FLR), Italy ...... **40 E8** 43 49N 11 13 E
Firenze Pisa ✈ (PSA), Italy ...... **40 E7** 43 40N 10 22 E
Firenzuola, Italy ...... **41 D8** 44 7N 11 23 E
Firk, Sha'ib →, Iraq ...... **70 D5** 30 59N 44 34 E
Firmi, France ...... **20 D6** 44 33N 2 19 E
Firminy, France ...... **21 C8** 45 23N 4 18 E
Firozabad, India ...... **69 F8** 27 10N 78 25 E
Firozpur, India ...... **68 D6** 30 55N 74 40 E
Firozpur-Jhirka, India ...... **68 F7** 27 48N 76 57 E
Firûzābād, Iran ...... **71 D7** 28 52N 52 35 E
Firûzkûh, Iran ...... **71 C7** 35 50N 52 50 E
Firvale, Canada **102 C3** 52 27N 126 13W
Fish →, Namibia ...... **88 D2** 28 7 S 17 10 E
Fish →, S. Africa ...... **88 E3** 31 30 S 20 16 E
Fish River Canyon, Namibia ...... **88 D2** 27 40 S 17 35 E
Fisher, Australia ...... **93 F5** 30 30 S 131 0 E
Fisher B., Canada **103 C9** 51 35N 97 13W
Fishers I., U.S.A. **117 E13** 41 15N 72 0W
Fishguard, U.K. **15 E3** 52 0N 4 58W
Fishing L., Canada **103 C9** 52 10N 95 24W
Fishkill, U.S.A. **117 E11** 41 32N 73 53W
Fismes, France ...... **19 C10** 49 20N 3 40 E
Fisterra, Spain **36 C1** 42 54N 9 16W
Fisterra, C., Spain **36 C1** 42 50N 9 19W
Fitchburg, U.S.A. **117 D13** 42 35N 71 48W
Fitz Roy, Argentina ...... **128 F3** 47 0 S 67 0W
Fitzgerald, Canada **102 B6** 59 51N 111 36W
Fitzgerald, U.S.A. **115 K4** 31 43N 83 15W
Fitzgerald River △, Australia ...... **93 F3** 33 53 S 120 3 E
Fitzmaurice →, Australia ...... **92 B5** 14 45 S 130 5 E
Fitzroy →, Queens., Australia ...... **94 C5** 23 32 S 150 52 E
Fitzroy →, W. Austral., Australia ...... **92 C3** 17 31 S 123 35 E
Fitzroy, Mte., Argentina ...... **128 F2** 49 17 S 73 5W
Fitzroy Crossing, Australia ...... **92 C4** 18 9 S 125 38 E
Fitzwilliam I., Canada **116 A3** 45 30N 81 45W
Fiuggi, Italy ...... **41 G10** 41 48N 13 13 E
Fiume = Rijeka, Croatia ...... **41 C11** 45 20N 14 21 E
Fiumicino, Roma ✈ (FCO), Italy ...... **41 G9** 41 48N 12 15 E
Five Points, U.S.A. **110 J6** 36 26N 120 6W
Fivizzano, Italy ...... **40 D7** 44 14N 10 8 E
Fizi, Dem. Rep. of the Congo ...... **86 C2** 4 17 S 28 55 E
Fjällbacka, Sweden ...... **11 F5** 58 36N 11 17 E
Fjärdhundra, Sweden ...... **10 E10** 59 47N 16 56 E
Fjellerup, Denmark ...... **11 H4** 56 29N 10 34 E
Fjerritslev, Denmark ...... **11 G3** 57 5N 9 15 E
Fjugesta, Sweden ...... **10 E8** 59 11N 14 52 E
Flagstaff, U.S.A. **109 J8** 35 12N 111 39W
Flagstaff L., U.S.A. **115 C10** 45 12N 70 18W
Flaherty I., Canada **104 A4** 56 15N 79 15W
Flåm, Norway ...... **9 F12** 60 50N 7 7 E
Flambeau →, U.S.A. **112 C9** 45 18N 91 14W
Flamborough Hd., U.K. **14 C7** 54 7N 0 5W
Fläming, Germany ...... **24 C8** 52 0N 12 23 E
Flaming Gorge △, U.S.A. **108 F9** 41 10N 109 25W
Flaming Gorge Reservoir, U.S.A. **108 F9** 41 10N 109 25W
Flamingo, Teluk, Indonesia ...... **63 F9** 5 30 S 138 0 E
Flanders = Flandre, Europe ...... **19 B9** 50 50N 2 30 E
Flandre, Europe ...... **19 B9** 50 50N 2 30 E
Flandre-Occidentale = West-Vlaanderen □, Belgium ...... **17 D2** 51 0N 3 0 E
Flandre-Orientale = Oost-Vlaanderen □, Belgium ...... **17 C3** 51 5N 3 50 E
Flandreau, U.S.A. **112 C6** 44 3N 96 36W
Flanigan, U.S.A. **110 E7** 40 10N 119 53W
Flannan Is., U.K. **13 C1** 58 9N 7 52W

Flåsjön, Sweden ...... 8 D16 64 5N 15 40 E
Flat →, Canada 102 A3 61 33N 125 18W
Flathead L., U.S.A. 108 C7 47 51N 114 8W
Flattery, C., Australia .. 94 A4 14 58S 145 21 E
Flattery, C., U.S.A. 110 B2 48 23N 124 29W
Flatwoods, U.S.A. 114 F4 38 31N 82 43W
Fleetwood, U.K. 14 D4 53 55N 3 1W
Fleetwood, U.S.A. 117 F9 40 27N 75 49W
Flekkefjord, Norway .... 9 G12 58 18N 6 39 E
Flemington, U.S.A. 116 E7 41 7N 77 28W
Flen, Sweden ...... 10 E10 59 4N 16 35 E
Flensburg, Germany .... 24 A5 54 47N 9 27 E
Flers, France 18 D6 48 47N 0 33W
Flesherton, Canada 116 B4 44 16N 80 33W
Flesko, Tanjung,
  Indonesia ...... 63 D6 0 29N 124 30 E
Fleurance, France ...... 20 E4 43 52N 0 40 E
Fleurier, Switz. ...... 25 J2 46 54N 6 35 E
Fleurieu Pen., Australia .. 95 F2 35 40S 138 5 E
Flevoland □, Neths. .... 17 B5 52 30N 5 30 E
Flin Flon, Canada 103 C8 54 46N 101 53W
Flinders →, Australia .. 94 B3 17 36S 140 36 E
Flinders B., Australia .. 93 F2 34 19S 115 19 E
Flinders Group,
  Australia ...... 94 A3 14 11S 144 15 E
Flinders I., S. Austral.,
  Australia ...... 95 E1 33 44S 134 41 E
Flinders I., Tas.,
  Australia ...... 95 G4 40 0S 148 0 E
Flinders Ranges,
  Australia ...... 95 E2 31 30S 138 30 E
Flinders Reefs, Australia 94 B4 17 37S 148 31 E
Flint, U.K. 14 D4 53 15N 3 8W
Flint, U.S.A. 114 D4 43 1N 83 41W
Flint →, U.S.A. 115 K3 30 57N 84 34W
Flint I., Kiribati 97 J12 11 26S 151 48W
Flintshire □, U.K. 14 D4 53 17N 3 17W
Fliseryd, Sweden .... 11 G10 57 6N 16 15 E
Flix, Spain ...... 38 D5 41 14N 0 32 E
Flixecourt, France .... 19 B9 50 1N 2 5 E
Floby, Sweden ...... 11 F7 58 8N 13 20 E
Floda, Sweden ...... 11 G6 57 49N 12 22 E
Flodden, U.K. 14 B5 55 37N 2 8W
Flogny-la-Chapelle,
  France ...... 19 E10 47 57N 3 57 E
Floodwood, U.S.A. 112 B8 46 55N 92 55W
Flora, U.S.A. 114 F1 38 40N 88 29W
Florala, U.S.A. 115 K2 31 0N 86 20W
Florence = Firenze, Italy 41 E8 43 46N 11 15 E
Florence, Ala., U.S.A. .. 115 H2 34 48N 87 41W
Florence, Ariz., U.S.A. .. 109 K8 33 2N 111 23W
Florence, Colo., U.S.A. .. 108 G2 38 23N 105 8W
Florence, Oreg., U.S.A. .. 108 E1 43 58N 124 7W
Florence, S.C., U.S.A. .. 115 H6 34 12N 79 46W
Florence, L., Australia .. 95 D2 28 53S 138 9 E
Florencia, Colombia .. 124 C3 1 36N 75 36W
Florennes, Belgium .... 17 D4 50 15N 4 35 E
Florensac, France ...... 20 E7 43 23N 3 28 E
Florenville, Belgium .... 17 E5 49 40N 5 19 E
Flores, Guatemala 120 C2 16 59N 89 50W
Flores, Indonesia ...... 63 F6 8 35S 121 0 E
Flores I., Canada 102 D3 49 20N 126 10W
Flores Sea, Indonesia .. 63 F6 6 30S 120 0 E
Floresti, Moldova .... 29 C13 47 53N 28 17 E
Floresville, U.S.A. 113 L5 29 8N 98 10W
Floriano, Brazil 125 E10 6 50S 43 0W
Florianópolis, Brazil .. 127 B6 27 30S 48 30W
Florida, Cuba 120 B4 21 32N 78 14W
Florida, Uruguay 127 C4 34 7S 56 10W
Florida □, U.S.A. 115 L5 28 0N 82 0W
Florida, Straits of,
  U.S.A. 120 B4 25 0N 80 0W
Florida B., U.S.A. 120 B3 25 0N 80 45W
Florida Keys, U.S.A. .. 115 N5 24 40N 81 0W
Floridia, Italy ...... 43 E8 37 5N 15 9 E
Flórina, Greece ...... 44 F5 40 48N 21 26 E
Flórina □, Greece .... 44 F5 40 45N 21 20 E
Florø, Norway ...... 9 F11 61 35N 5 1 E
Flower Station, Canada 117 A8 45 10N 76 41W
Flowerpot I., Canada .. 116 A3 45 18N 81 38W
Floydada, U.S.A. 113 J4 33 59N 101 20W
Fluk, Indonesia ...... 63 E7 1 42S 127 44 E
Flúmen →, Spain 38 D4 41 43N 0 9W
Flumendosa →, Italy .. 42 C2 39 26N 9 37 E
Fluminimaggiore, Italy . 42 C1 39 26N 8 30 E
Flushing = Vlissingen,
  Neths. ...... 17 C3 51 26N 3 34 E
Fluviá →, Spain ...... 38 C8 42 12N 3 7 E
Flying Fish, C.,
  Antarctica 5 D15 72 6S 102 29W
Foam Lake, Canada .. 103 C8 51 40N 103 32W
Foča, Bos.-H. ...... 44 C2 43 31N 18 47 E
Foça, Turkey ...... 47 C8 38 39N 26 46 E
Fochabers, U.K. 13 D5 57 37N 3 6W
Focșani, Romania .... 29 E12 45 41N 27 15 E
Fodécontéa, Guinea .. 82 C2 10 50N 14 22W
Fogang, China ...... 59 F9 23 52N 113 30 E
Fóggia, Italy ...... 43 A8 41 27N 15 34 E
Foggo, Nigeria ...... 83 C6 11 21N 9 57 E
Foglia →, Italy ...... 41 E9 43 55N 12 54 E
Fogo, Canada 105 C9 49 43N 54 17W
Fogo I., Canada 105 C9 49 40N 54 5W
Fohnsdorf, Austria .... 26 D7 47 12N 14 40 E
Föhr, Germany ...... 24 A4 54 43N 8 30 E
Foia, Portugal 37 H2 37 19N 8 37W
Foix, France ...... 20 E5 42 58N 1 38 E
Fojnica, Bos.-H. ...... 28 G2 43 59N 17 51 E
Fokino, Russia ...... 32 F8 53 30N 34 22 E
Fokís □, Greece ...... 46 C4 38 30N 22 15 E
Fokku, Nigeria ...... 83 C5 11 36N 4 32 E
Folda, Nord-Trøndelag,
  Norway ...... 8 D14 64 32N 10 30 E
Folda, Nordland,
  Norway ...... 8 C16 67 38N 14 50 E
Földeák, Hungary .... 28 D5 46 19N 20 30 E
Folégandros, Greece .. 46 E6 36 40N 24 55 E
Foley, Botswana ...... 88 C4 21 34S 27 21 E
Foley, U.S.A. 115 K2 30 24N 87 41W
Foleyet, Canada 104 C3 48 15N 82 25W
Folgefonni, Norway .. 9 F12 60 3N 6 23 E
Foligno, Italy ...... 41 F9 42 57N 12 42 E
Folkestone, U.K. ...... 15 F9 51 5N 1 12 E
Folkston, U.S.A. 115 K5 30 50N 82 0W
Follansbee, U.S.A. 116 F4 40 19N 80 35W
Follónica, Italy ...... 40 F7 42 55N 10 45 E
Follónica, G. di, Italy .. 40 F7 42 54N 10 43 E
Folsom L., U.S.A. 110 G5 38 42N 121 9W
Folteşti, Romania .... 29 E13 45 45N 28 3 E
Fond-du-Lac, Canada .. 103 B7 59 19N 107 12W
Fond du Lac, U.S.A. .. 112 D10 43 47N 88 27W
Fond-du-Lac →,
  Canada 103 B7 59 17N 106 0W
Fonda, U.S.A. 117 D10 42 57N 74 22W
Fondi, Italy ...... 42 A6 41 21N 13 25 E
Fonfría, Spain 36 D4 41 37N 6 9W
Fongafale, Tuvalu .... 96 H9 8 31S 179 13 E

Fonni, Italy ...... 42 B2 40 7N 9 15 E
Fonsagrada = A
  Fonsagrada, Spain .. 36 B3 43 8N 7 4W
Fonseca, G. de,
  Cent. Amer. 120 D2 13 10N 87 40W
Font-Romeu-Odeillo-
  Via, France ...... 20 F5 42 31N 2 3 E
Fontaine-Française,
  France ...... 19 E12 47 32N 5 21 E
Fontainebleau, France .. 19 D9 48 24N 2 40 E
Fontana, U.S.A. 111 L9 34 6N 117 26W
Fontas →, Canada 102 B4 58 14N 121 48W
Fonte Boa, Brazil 124 D5 2 33S 66 0W
Fontem, Cameroon .. 83 D6 5 32N 9 52 E
Fontenay-le-Comte,
  France 20 B3 46 28N 0 48W
Fontenelle Reservoir,
  U.S.A. 108 E8 42 1N 110 3W
Fontur, Iceland 8 C6 66 23N 14 32W
Fonyód, Hungary .... 28 D2 46 44N 17 33 E
Foochow = Fuzhou,
  China ...... 59 D12 26 5N 119 16 E
Foping, China ...... 56 H5 33 41N 108 0 E
Forbach, France ...... 19 C13 49 10N 6 52 E
Forbes, Australia ...... 95 E4 33 22S 148 5 E
Forbesganj, India .... 69 F12 26 17N 87 18 E
Forcados, Nigeria .... 83 D6 5 26N 5 26 E
Forcados →, Nigeria .. 83 D6 5 25N 5 19 E
Forcalquier, France .... 21 E9 43 58N 5 47 E
Forchheim, Germany .. 25 F7 49 43N 11 2 E
ForClArE, Guinea 82 D2 9 28N 13 10W
Ford City, Calif., U.S.A. 111 K7 35 9N 119 27W
Ford City, Pa., U.S.A. .. 116 F5 40 46N 79 32W
Førde, Norway ...... 9 F11 61 27N 5 53 E
Ford's Bridge, Australia 95 D4 29 41S 145 29 E
Fordyce, U.S.A. 113 J8 33 49N 92 25W
Forécariah, Guinea 82 D2 9 28N 13 10W
Forel, Mt., Greenland .. 98 C16 66 52N 36 55W
Foremost, Canada 102 D6 49 26N 111 34W
Forest, Canada 116 C3 43 6N 82 0W
Forest, U.S.A. 113 J10 32 22N 89 29W
Forest City, Iowa, U.S.A. 112 D8 43 16N 93 39W
Forest City, N.C., U.S.A. 115 H5 35 20N 81 52W
Forest City, Pa., U.S.A. 117 E9 41 39N 75 28W
Forest Grove, U.S.A. .. 110 E3 45 31N 123 7W
Forestburg, Canada .. 102 C6 52 35N 112 1W
Foreste Casentinesi-
  Monte Falterona-
  Campigna △, Italy .. 41 E8 43 50N 11 48 E
Foresthill, U.S.A. 110 F6 39 1N 120 49W
Forestier Pen., Australia 95 G4 43 0S 148 0 E
Forestville, Canada .. 105 C6 48 48N 69 2W
Forestville, Calif., U.S.A. 110 G4 38 28N 122 54W
Forestville, N.Y., U.S.A. 116 D5 42 28N 79 10W
Forêt d'Orient △, France 19 D11 48 16N 4 25 E
Forez, Mts. du, France . 20 C7 45 40N 3 50 E
Forfar, U.K. 13 E6 56 39N 2 53W
Forillon △, Canada .. 105 C7 48 46N 64 12W
Forks, U.S.A. 110 C2 47 57N 124 23W
Forksville, U.S.A. 117 E8 41 29N 76 35W
Forlì, Italy ...... 41 D9 44 13N 12 3 E
Forman, U.S.A. 112 B6 46 7N 97 38W
Formazza, Italy ...... 40 B5 46 22N 8 26 E
Formby Pt., U.K. 14 D4 53 33N 3 6W
Formentera, Spain .... 48 C7 38 43N 1 27 E
Formentor, C. de, Spain 48 B10 39 58N 3 13 E
Former Yugoslav
  Republic of
  Macedonia =
  Macedonia ■, Europe 44 E5 41 53N 21 40 E
Fórmia, Italy ...... 42 A6 41 15N 13 37 E
Formigine, Italy ...... 40 D7 44 37N 10 51 E
Formosa = Taiwan ■,
  Asia ...... 59 F13 23 30N 121 0 E
Formosa, Argentina .. 126 B4 26 15S 58 10W
Formosa, Brazil 125 G9 15 32S 47 20W
Formosa □, Argentina . 126 B4 25 0S 60 0W
Formosa, Serra, Brazil . 125 F8 12 0S 55 0W
Formosa B. = Ungwana
  B., Kenya ...... 86 C5 2 40S 40 20 E
Fornells, Spain ...... 48 A11 40 3N 4 7 E
Fornos de Algodres,
  Portugal 36 E3 40 38N 7 32W
Fornovo di Taro, Italy .. 40 D7 44 42N 10 6 E
Føroyar, Atl. Oc. 8 F9 62 0N 7 0W
Forres, U.K. 13 D5 57 37N 3 37W
Forrest, Australia ...... 93 F4 30 51S 128 6 E
Forrest, Mt., Australia .. 93 D4 24 48S 127 45 E
Forrest City, U.S.A. .. 113 H9 35 1N 90 47W
Fors, Sweden ...... 10 D10 60 14N 16 20 E
Forsayth, Australia .... 94 B3 18 33S 143 34 E
Forshaga, Sweden .... 10 E7 59 33N 13 29 E
Förslöv, Sweden ...... 11 H6 56 21N 12 48 E
Forsmo, Sweden ...... 10 A11 63 16N 17 11 E
Forssa, Finland ...... 9 F20 60 49N 23 38 E
Forst, Germany ...... 24 D10 51 45N 14 37 E
Forsvik, Sweden ...... 11 F8 58 35N 14 26 E
Forsyth, U.S.A. 108 C10 46 16N 106 41W
Fort Abbas, Pakistan .. 68 E5 29 12N 72 52 E
Fort Albany, Canada .. 104 B3 52 15N 81 35W
Fort Ann, U.S.A. 117 C11 43 25N 73 30W
Fort Assiniboine,
  Canada 102 C6 54 20N 114 45W
Fort Augustus, U.K. .. 13 D4 57 9N 4 42W
Fort Beaufort, S. Africa 88 E4 32 46S 26 40 E
Fort Benton, U.S.A. .. 108 C8 47 49N 110 40W
Fort Bragg, U.S.A. 108 G2 39 26N 123 48W
Fort Bridger, U.S.A. .. 108 F8 41 19N 110 23W
Fort Chipewyan, Canada 103 B6 58 42N 111 8W
Fort Clatsop △, U.S.A. 110 D3 46 8N 123 53W
Fort Collins, U.S.A. .. 112 E2 40 35N 105 5W
Fort-Coulonge, Canada 104 C4 45 50N 76 45W
Fort Covington, U.S.A. 117 B10 44 59N 74 29W
Fort Davis, U.S.A. 113 K3 30 35N 103 54W
Fort-de-France,
  Martinique ...... 120 c 14 36N 61 2W
Fort Defiance, U.S.A. .. 109 J9 35 45N 109 5W
Fort Dodge, U.S.A. .. 112 D7 42 30N 94 11W
Fort Edward, U.S.A. .. 117 C11 43 16N 73 35W
Fort Erie, Canada 116 D6 42 54N 78 56W
Fort Fairfield, U.S.A. .. 115 B12 46 46N 67 50W
Fort Frances, Canada .. 103 D10 48 36N 93 24W
Fort Franklin = Déline,
  Canada 100 B7 65 11N 123 25W
Fort Garland, U.S.A. .. 109 H11 37 26N 105 26W
Fort George = Chisasibi,
  Canada 104 B4 53 50N 79 0W
Fort Good Hope,
  Canada 100 B7 66 14N 128 40W
Fort Hancock, U.S.A. .. 109 L11 31 18N 105 51W
Fort Hope, Canada .. 104 B2 51 30N 88 0W
Fort Irwin, U.S.A. 111 K10 35 16N 116 34W
Fort Kent, U.S.A. 115 B11 47 15N 68 36W
Fort Klamath, U.S.A. .. 108 E3 42 42N 122 0W
Fort Laramie, U.S.A. .. 112 D2 42 13N 104 31W
Fort Lauderdale, U.S.A. 115 M5 26 7N 80 8W
Fort Liard, Canada 102 A4 60 14N 123 28W
Fort Liberté, Haiti 121 C5 19 42N 71 51W

Fort Lupton, U.S.A. ... 112 E2 40 5N 104 49W
Fort MacKay, Canada .. 102 B6 57 12N 111 41W
Fort Macleod, Canada . 102 D6 49 45N 113 30W
Fort McMurray, Canada 102 B6 56 44N 111 7W
Fort McPherson,
  Canada 100 B6 67 30N 134 55W
Fort Madison, U.S.A. .. 112 E9 40 38N 91 27W
Fort Meade, U.S.A. 115 M5 27 45N 81 48W
Fort Morgan, U.S.A. .. 112 E3 40 15N 103 48W
Fort Myers, U.S.A. 115 M5 26 39N 81 52W
Fort Nelson, Canada .. 102 B4 58 50N 122 44W
Fort Nelson →, Canada 102 B4 59 32N 124 0W
Fort Norman = Tulita,
  Canada 100 B7 64 57N 125 30W
Fort Payne, U.S.A. 115 H3 34 26N 85 43W
Fort Peck, U.S.A. 108 B10 48 1N 106 27W
Fort Peck Dam, U.S.A. 108 C10 48 0N 106 26W
Fort Peck L., U.S.A. .. 108 C10 48 0N 106 26W
Fort Pierce, U.S.A. 115 M5 27 27N 80 20W
Fort Pierre, U.S.A. 112 C4 44 21N 100 22W
Fort Plain, U.S.A. 117 D10 42 56N 74 37W
Fort Portal, Uganda .. 86 B3 0 40N 30 20 E
Fort Providence, Canada 102 A5 61 3N 117 40W
Fort Qu'Appelle,
  Canada 103 C8 50 45N 103 50W
Fort Resolution, Canada 102 A6 61 10N 113 40W
Fort Rixon, Zimbabwe . 87 G2 20 2S 29 17 E
Fort Ross, U.S.A. 110 G3 38 32N 123 13W
Fort Rupert =
  Waskaganish, Canada 104 B4 51 30N 78 40W
Fort St. James, Canada 102 C4 54 30N 124 10W
Fort St. John, Canada .. 102 B4 56 15N 120 50W
Fort Saskatchewan,
  Canada 102 C6 53 40N 113 15W
Fort Scott, U.S.A. 113 G7 37 50N 94 42W
Fort Severn, Canada .. 104 A2 56 0N 87 40W
Fort Shevchenko,
  Kazakhstan ...... 35 H10 43 35N 50 23 E
Fort Simpson, Canada 102 A4 61 45N 121 15W
Fort Smith, Canada .. 102 B6 60 0N 111 51W
Fort Smith, U.S.A. 113 H7 35 23N 94 25W
Fort Stockton, U.S.A. .. 113 K3 30 53N 102 53W
Fort Sumner, U.S.A. .. 113 H2 34 28N 104 15W
Fort Thompson, U.S.A. 112 C5 44 3N 99 26W
Fort Union △, U.S.A. .. 113 H2 35 54N 105 1W
Fort Valley, U.S.A. 115 J4 32 33N 83 53W
Fort Vermilion, Canada 102 B5 58 24N 116 0W
Fort Walton Beach,
  U.S.A. 115 K2 30 25N 86 36W
Fort Wayne, U.S.A. .. 114 E3 41 4N 85 9W
Fort William, U.K. 13 E3 56 49N 5 7W
Fort Worth, U.S.A. 113 J6 32 45N 97 18W
Fort Yates, U.S.A. 112 B4 46 5N 100 38W
Fort Yukon, U.S.A. .. 100 B5 66 34N 145 16W
Fortaleza, Brazil 125 D11 3 45S 38 35W
Forteau, Canada 105 B8 51 28N 56 58W
Forth →, U.K. 13 E5 56 9N 3 50W
Forth, Firth of, U.K. .. 13 E6 56 5N 2 55W
Fortore →, Italy ...... 41 G12 41 55N 15 17 E
Fortrose, U.K. 13 D4 57 35N 4 9W
Fortuna, Spain 39 G3 38 11N 1 7W
Fortuna, Calif., U.S.A. 108 F1 40 36N 124 9W
Fortuna, N. Dak., U.S.A. 112 A3 48 55N 103 47W
Fortune, Canada 105 C8 47 4N 55 50W
Fortune B., Canada .. 105 C8 47 30N 55 22W
Forûr, Iran ...... 71 E7 26 17N 54 32 E
Fos-sur-Mer, France .. 21 E8 43 26N 4 56 E
Foshan, China ...... 59 F9 23 4N 113 5 E
Fosna, Norway ...... 8 E14 63 50N 10 20 E
Fosnavåg, Norway .... 9 E11 62 22N 5 38 E
Foso, Ghana 83 D4 5 43N 1 15W
Fossano, Italy ...... 40 D4 44 33N 7 43 E
Fossil, U.S.A. 108 D3 45 0N 120 9W
Fossil Butte △, U.S.A. .. 108 F8 41 50N 110 27W
Fossombrone, Italy .... 41 E9 43 41N 12 48 E
Foster →, Canada 117 A12 45 17N 72 30W
Foster →, Canada 103 B7 55 47N 105 49W
Fosters Ra., Australia .. 94 C1 21 35S 133 48 E
Fostoria, U.S.A. 114 E4 41 10N 83 25W
Fotadrevo, Madag. .... 89 C8 24 3S 45 1 E
Fouesnant, France 18 E2 47 53N 4 1W
Fougamou, Gabon .... 84 E2 1 38S 10 35 E
Fougères, France 18 D5 48 21N 1 14W
Foul Pt., Sri Lanka .... 66 Q12 8 35N 81 18 E
Foula, U.K. 13 A6 60 10N 2 5W
Foulalaba, Mali 82 C3 10 40N 7 20W
Foulness I., U.K. ...... 15 F8 51 36N 0 55 E
Foulpointe, Madag. .... 89 B8 17 41S 49 31 E
Foulweather, C., U.S.A. 106 B2 44 50N 124 5W
Foumban, Cameroon .. 83 D7 5 45N 10 50 E
Foumbot, Cameroon .. 83 D7 5 31N 10 28 E
Foundiougne, Senegal . 82 C1 14 5N 16 4W
Fountain, U.S.A. 112 F2 38 41N 104 42W
Fountain Springs, U.S.A. 111 K8 35 54N 118 51W
Fourchambault, France 19 E10 47 1N 3 3 E
Fouriesburg, S. Africa .. 88 D4 28 38S 28 14 E
Fourmies, France ...... 19 B11 50 1N 4 2 E
Fournás, Greece ...... 46 B3 39 3N 21 52 E
Foúrnoi, Greece ...... 47 D8 37 36N 26 32 E
Fours, France ...... 19 F10 46 50N 3 42 E
Fourth Cataract, Sudan 80 D3 18 47N 32 3 E
Fouta Djallon, Guinea . 82 C2 11 20N 12 10W
Foux, Cap-à-, Haiti 121 C5 19 43N 73 27W
Foveaux Str., N.Z. .... 91 M2 46 42S 168 10 E
Fowey, U.K. 15 G3 50 20N 4 39W
Fowler, Calif., U.S.A. .. 110 J7 36 38N 119 41W
Fowler, Colo., U.S.A. .. 112 F3 38 8N 104 2W
Fowlers B., Australia .. 93 F5 31 59S 132 34 E
Fowman, Iran ...... 71 B6 37 13N 49 19 E
Fox →, Canada 103 B10 56 3N 93 18W
Fox Creek, Canada .. 102 C5 54 24N 116 48W
Fox Lake, Canada 102 B6 58 28N 114 31W
Fox Valley, Canada .. 103 C7 50 30N 109 25W
Foxboro, U.S.A. 117 D13 42 4N 71 16W
Foxdale, Australia .... 94 J6 20 22S 148 35 E
Foxe Basin, Canada .. 101 B12 66 0N 77 0W
Foxe Chan., Canada .. 101 B11 65 0N 80 0W
Foxe Pen., Canada 101 B12 65 0N 76 0W
Foxen, Sweden ...... 10 E5 59 25N 11 55 E
Foxton, N.Z. ...... 91 J5 40 29S 175 18 E
Foyle, Lough, U.K. .. 12 A4 55 7N 7 4W
Foynes, Ireland 12 D2 52 37N 9 7W
Foz, Spain 36 B3 43 33N 7 20W
Foz do Cunene, Angola 88 B1 17 15S 11 48 E
Foz do Iguaçu, Brazil . 127 B5 25 30S 54 30W
Frackville, U.S.A. 117 F8 40 47N 76 14W
Fraga, Spain ...... 38 D5 41 32N 0 21 E
Fraile Muerto, Uruguay 127 C5 32 31S 54 32W
Fram Basin, Arctic .... 4 A 87 30N 80 0 E
Framingham, U.S.A. .. 117 D13 42 17N 71 25W
Frampol, Poland ...... 31 H9 50 41N 22 40 E
Franca, Brazil 125 H9 20 33S 47 30W
Francavilla al Mare, Italy 41 F11 42 25N 14 17 E
Francavilla Fontana,
  Italy ...... 43 B10 40 32N 17 35 E
France ■, Europe .... 7 F6 47 0N 3 0 E
Frances, Australia .... 95 F3 36 41S 140 55 E

Frances →, Canada .. 102 A3 60 16N 129 10W
Frances L., Canada .. 102 A3 61 23N 129 30W
Franceville, Gabon .. 84 E2 1 40S 13 32 E
Franche-Comté □,
  France ...... 19 F12 46 50N 5 55 E
Francis Case, L., U.S.A. 112 D5 43 4N 98 34W
Francisco Beltrão, Brazil 127 B5 26 5S 53 4W
Francisco I. Madero,
  Coahuila, Mexico .. 118 B4 25 48N 103 18W
Francisco I. Madero,
  Durango, Mexico .. 118 C4 24 32N 104 22W
Francistown, Botswana 89 C4 21 7S 27 33 E
Francofonte, Italy .... 43 E7 37 14N 14 53 E
François, Canada 105 C8 47 35N 56 45W
François L., Canada .. 102 C3 54 0N 125 30W
François Peron △,
  Australia ...... 93 E1 25 42S 113 33 E
Franeker, Neths. .... 17 A5 53 12N 5 33 E
Frank Hann △, Australia 93 F3 32 52S 120 19 E
Frankado, Djibouti .... 81 E5 12 30N 43 12 E
Frankenberg, Germany 24 D4 51 3N 8 48 E
Frankenhöhe △,
  Germany ...... 25 F6 49 20N 10 25 E
Frankenwald, Germany 25 E7 50 20N 11 30 E
Frankenwald △,
  Germany ...... 25 E7 50 15N 11 30 E
Frankford, Canada .. 116 B7 44 12N 77 36W
Frankfort, S. Africa .. 89 D4 27 17S 28 30 E
Frankfort, Ind., U.S.A. 114 E2 40 17N 86 31W
Frankfort, Kans., U.S.A. 112 F6 39 42N 96 25W
Frankfort, Ky., U.S.A. 114 F3 38 12N 84 52W
Frankfort, N.Y., U.S.A. 117 C9 43 2N 75 4W
Frankfurt, Brandenburg,
  Germany ...... 24 C10 52 20N 14 32 E
Frankfurt, Hessen,
  Germany ...... 25 E4 50 7N 8 41 E
Frankfurt ✈ (FRA),
  Germany ...... 25 E4 50 7N 8 34 E
Fränkische Alb,
  Germany ...... 25 F7 49 10N 11 23 E
Fränkische Rezat →,
  Germany ...... 25 F7 49 11N 11 1 E
Fränkische Saale →,
  Germany ...... 25 E5 50 3N 9 42 E
Fränkische Schweiz,
  Germany ...... 25 F7 49 50N 11 16 E
Fränkische Schweiz-
  Veldensteiner
  Forst △, Germany .. 25 F7 49 45N 11 22 E
Frankland →, Australia 93 G2 35 0S 116 48 E
Franklin, Ky., U.S.A. .. 115 G2 36 43N 86 35W
Franklin, La., U.S.A. .. 113 L9 29 48N 91 30W
Franklin, Mass., U.S.A. 117 D13 42 5N 71 24W
Franklin, N.H., U.S.A. 117 C13 43 27N 71 39W
Franklin, Nebr., U.S.A. 112 E5 40 6N 98 57W
Franklin, Pa., U.S.A. .. 116 E5 41 24N 79 50W
Franklin, Va., U.S.A. .. 115 G7 36 41N 76 56W
Franklin, W. Va., U.S.A. 114 F6 38 39N 79 20W
Franklin B., Canada .. 100 B7 69 45N 126 0W
Franklin D. Roosevelt
  L., U.S.A. 108 B4 48 18N 118 9W
Franklin-Gordon Wild
  Rivers △, Australia . 95 G4 42 19S 145 51 E
Franklin I., Antarctica . 5 D11 76 10S 168 30 E
Franklin L., U.S.A. 108 F6 40 25N 115 22W
Franklin Mts., Canada . 100 B7 65 0N 125 0W
Franklin Str., Canada .. 100 A10 72 0N 96 0W
Franklinton, U.S.A. .. 113 K9 30 51N 90 9W
Franklinville, U.S.A. .. 116 D6 42 20N 78 27W
Frankston, Australia .. 95 F4 38 8S 145 8 E
Fränö, Sweden ...... 10 B11 62 55N 17 50 E
Fransfontein, Namibia . 88 C2 20 12S 15 1 E
Fränsta, Sweden ...... 10 B10 62 30N 16 11 E
Frantsa Iosifa, Zemlya,
  Russia ...... 52 A6 82 0N 55 0 E
Franz, Canada 104 C3 48 25N 84 30W
Franz Josef Land =
  Frantsa Iosifa,
  Zemlya, Russia .... 52 A6 82 0N 55 0 E
Franz Josef Strauss,
  München ✈ (MUC),
  Germany ...... 25 G7 48 20N 11 50 E
Franzburg, Germany .. 24 A8 54 11N 12 51 E
Frascati, Italy ...... 41 G9 41 48N 12 41 E
Fraser →, B.C., Canada 102 D4 49 7N 123 11W
Fraser →, Nfld. & L.,
  Canada 105 A7 56 39N 62 10W
Fraser, Mt., Australia .. 93 E2 25 35S 118 20 E
Fraser I., Australia .... 95 D5 25 15S 153 10 E
Fraser Lake, Canada .. 102 C4 54 0N 124 50W
Fraserburg, S. Africa .. 88 E3 31 55S 21 30 E
Fraserburgh, U.K. 13 D6 57 42N 2 1W
Fraserdale, Canada .. 104 C3 49 55N 81 37W
Frashër, Albania ...... 44 F4 40 23N 20 26 E
Frasne, France ...... 19 F13 46 50N 6 10 E
Frăteşti, Romania .... 29 G10 43 58N 25 50 E
Frauenfeld, Switz. .... 25 H4 47 34N 8 54 E
Fray Bentos, Uruguay . 126 C4 33 10S 58 15W
Fray Jorge △, Chile .. 126 C1 30 42S 71 40W
Frechilla, Spain 36 C6 42 8N 4 50W
Fredericia, Denmark .. 11 J3 55 34N 9 45 E
Frederick, Md., U.S.A. 114 F7 39 25N 77 25W
Frederick, Okla., U.S.A. 113 H5 34 23N 99 1W
Frederick, S. Dak.,
  U.S.A. 112 C5 45 50N 98 31W
Fredericksburg, Pa.,
  U.S.A. 117 F8 40 27N 76 26W
Fredericksburg, Tex.,
  U.S.A. 113 K5 30 16N 98 52W
Fredericksburg, Va.,
  U.S.A. 114 F7 38 18N 77 28W
Fredericktown, Mo.,
  U.S.A. 113 G9 37 34N 90 18W
Fredericktown, Ohio,
  U.S.A. 116 F2 40 29N 82 33W
Frederico I. Madero,
  Presa, Mexico 118 B3 28 7N 105 40W
Frederico Westphalen,
  Brazil 127 B5 27 22S 53 24W
Fredericton, Canada .. 105 C6 45 57N 66 40W
Fredericton Junction,
  Canada 105 C6 45 41N 66 40W
Frederikshåb = Paamiut,
  Greenland 101 B15 62 0N 49 43W
Frederikshamn =
  Hamina, Finland .. 9 F22 60 34N 27 12 E
Frederikshavn, Denmark 11 G4 57 28N 10 31 E
Frederikssund, Denmark 11 J6 55 50N 12 3 E
Frederiksted,
  U.S. Virgin Is. 121 C7 17 43N 64 53W
Frederiksværk, Denmark 11 J6 55 58N 12 4 E
Fredonia, Ariz., U.S.A. 109 H7 36 57N 112 32W

Fredonia, Kans., U.S.A. 113 G7 37 32N 95 49W
Fredonia, N.Y., U.S.A. 116 D5 42 26N 79 20W
Fredriksberg, Sweden . 10 D8 60 8N 14 23 E
Fredrikstad, Norway .. 9 G14 59 13N 10 57 E
Free State □, S. Africa . 88 D4 28 30S 27 0 E
Freehold, U.S.A. 117 F10 40 16N 74 17W
Freel Peak, U.S.A. 110 G7 38 52N 119 54W
Freeland, U.S.A. 117 E9 41 1N 75 54W
Freels, C., Canada 105 C9 49 15N 53 30W
Freeman, Calif., U.S.A. 111 K9 35 35N 117 53W
Freeman, S. Dak.,
  U.S.A. 112 D6 43 21N 97 26W
Freeport, Bahamas .. 120 A4 26 30N 78 47W
Freeport, Ill., U.S.A. .. 112 D10 42 17N 89 36W
Freeport, N.Y., U.S.A. 117 F11 40 39N 73 35W
Freeport, Ohio, U.S.A. 116 F3 40 12N 81 15W
Freeport, Pa., U.S.A. .. 116 F5 40 41N 79 41W
Freeport, Tex., U.S.A. 113 L7 28 57N 95 21W
Freetown, S. Leone .. 82 D2 8 30N 13 17W
Frégate, L. de la,
  Canada 104 B5 53 15N 74 45W
Fregenal de la Sierra,
  Spain 37 G4 38 10N 6 39W
Fregene, Italy ...... 41 G9 41 51N 12 12 E
Fréhel, C., France 18 D4 48 40N 2 20W
Freiberg, Germany .. 24 E9 50 55N 13 20 E
Freibourg = Fribourg,
  Switz. ...... 25 J3 46 49N 7 9 E
Freiburg, Baden-W.,
  Germany ...... 25 H3 47 59N 7 51 E
Freiburg, Niedersachsen,
  Germany ...... 24 B5 53 49N 9 16 E
Freilassing, Germany .. 25 H8 47 50N 12 58 E
Freire, Chile 128 D2 38 54S 72 38W
Freirina, Chile 126 B1 28 30S 71 10W
Freising, Germany .... 25 G7 48 24N 11 45 E
Freistadt, Austria .... 26 C7 48 30N 14 30 E
Freital, Germany .... 24 D9 51 1N 13 39 E
Fréjus, France ...... 21 E10 43 25N 6 44 E
Fremantle, Australia .. 93 F2 32 7S 115 47 E
Fremont, Calif., U.S.A. 110 H4 37 32N 121 57W
Fremont, Mich., U.S.A. 114 D3 43 28N 85 57W
Fremont, Nebr., U.S.A. 112 E6 41 26N 96 30W
Fremont, Ohio, U.S.A. 114 E4 41 21N 83 7W
Fremont →, U.S.A. .. 109 G8 38 24N 110 42W
French Camp, U.S.A. .. 110 H5 37 53N 121 16W
French Creek →, U.S.A. 116 E5 41 24N 79 50W
French Guiana ☑,
  S. Amer. 125 C8 4 0N 53 0W
French Polynesia ☑,
  Pac. Oc. 97 K13 20 0S 145 0W
Frenchman Cr. →,
  N. Amer. 108 B10 48 31N 107 10W
Frenchman Cr. →,
  U.S.A. 112 E4 40 14N 100 50W
Frenštát pod
  Radhoštěm,
  Czech Rep. ...... 27 B11 49 33N 18 13 E
Fresco, Ivory C. 82 D3 5 3N 5 31W
Fresco →, Brazil 125 E8 7 15S 51 30W
Freshfield, C., Antarctica 5 C10 68 25S 151 10 E
Fresnay-sur-Sarthe,
  France ...... 18 D7 48 17N 0 1 E
Fresnillo, Mexico 118 C4 23 10N 103 0W
Fresno, U.S.A. 110 J7 36 44N 119 47W
Fresno Alhandiga, Spain 36 E5 40 42N 5 37W
Fresno Reservoir, U.S.A. 108 B9 48 36N 109 57W
Freudenstadt, Germany 25 G4 48 27N 8 24 E
Frévent, France ...... 19 B9 50 15N 2 17 E
Frew →, Australia .... 94 C2 20 0S 135 38 E
Frewsburg, U.S.A. 116 D5 42 3N 79 10W
Freycinet △, Australia . 95 G4 42 11S 148 19 E
Freycinet Pen., Australia 95 G4 42 10S 148 25 E
Freyming-Merlebach,
  France ...... 19 C13 49 8N 6 48 E
Freyung, Germany .... 25 G9 48 48N 13 31 E
Fria, Guinea 82 C2 10 27N 13 38W
Fria, C., Namibia .... 88 B1 18 0S 12 0 E
Friant, U.S.A. 110 J7 36 59N 119 43W
Fribourg, Switz. ...... 25 J3 46 49N 7 9 E
Fribourg □, Switz. .... 25 J3 46 40N 7 0 E
Fridafors, Sweden .... 11 H8 56 25N 14 39 E
Friday Harbor, U.S.A. 110 B3 48 32N 123 1W
Friedberg, Bayern,
  Germany ...... 25 G6 48 21N 10 59 E
Friedberg, Hessen,
  Germany ...... 25 E4 50 19N 8 45 E
Friedens, U.S.A. 116 F6 40 3N 78 59W
Friedland, Germany .. 24 B9 53 40N 13 33 E
Friedrichshafen,
  Germany ...... 25 H5 47 39N 9 30 E
Friedrichskoog,
  Germany ...... 24 A4 54 1N 8 53 E
Friedrichstadt, Germany 24 A5 54 23N 9 6 E
Friendly Is. = Tonga ■,
  Pac. Oc. 91 D11 19 50S 174 30W
Friendship, U.S.A. .. 116 D6 42 12N 78 8W
Friesach, Austria .... 26 E7 46 57N 14 24 E
Friesack, Germany .... 24 C8 52 44N 12 34 E
Friesland □, Neths. .. 17 A5 53 5N 5 50 E
Friesoythe, Germany .. 24 B3 53 1N 7 51 E
Friggesund, Sweden .. 10 C10 61 54N 16 33 E
Frillesås, Sweden .... 11 G6 57 20N 12 12 E
Frinnaryd, Sweden .... 11 G8 57 55N 14 50 E
Frio →, U.S.A. 113 L5 28 26N 98 11W
Frio, C., Brazil 122 F6 22 50S 41 50W
Friol, Spain 36 B3 43 2N 7 47W
Friona, U.S.A. 113 H3 34 38N 102 43W
Fristad, Sweden ...... 11 G7 57 50N 13 0 E
Fritch, U.S.A. 113 H4 35 38N 101 36W
Fritsla, Sweden ...... 11 G6 57 33N 12 47 E
Fritzlar, Germany .... 24 D5 51 7N 9 16 E
Friuli-Venézia Giulia □,
  Italy ...... 41 B9 46 0N 13 0 E
Frobisher B., Canada .. 101 B13 63 44N 68 31W
Frobisher Bay = Iqaluit,
  Canada 101 B13 63 44N 68 31W
Frobisher L., Canada .. 103 B7 56 20N 108 15W
Frohavet, Norway .... 8 E13 64 0N 9 30 E
Frohnleiten, Austria .. 26 D8 47 16N 15 19 E
Frolovo, Russia ...... 34 F7 49 45N 43 40 E
Frombork, Poland .... 30 D6 54 21N 19 41 E
Frome, U.K. 15 F5 51 14N 2 19W
Frome →, U.K. 15 G5 50 41N 2 6W
Frome, L., Australia .. 95 E2 30 45S 139 45 E
Frome, The □,
  Australia ...... 95 D2 29 8S 137 54 E
Frómista, Spain 36 C6 42 16N 4 25W
Front Range, U.S.A. .. 106 C5 40 25N 105 45W
Front Royal, U.S.A. .. 114 F6 38 55N 78 12W
Fronteira, Portugal .. 37 F3 39 3N 7 39W
Frontera, Canary Is. .. 48 G2 27 47N 17 59W
Frontera, Mexico 119 D6 18 30N 92 40W
Fronteras, Mexico 118 A3 30 56N 109 31W
Frontignan, France .. 20 E7 43 27N 3 45 E
Frosinone, Italy ...... 42 A6 41 38N 13 19 E

Frostburg, U.S.A. **114 F6** 39 39N 78 56W
Frostisen, Norway ...... **8 B17** 68 14N 17 10 E
Frouard, France ...... **19 D13** 48 47N 6 8 E
Frövi, Sweden ...... **10 E9** 59 28N 15 24 E
Frøya, Norway ...... **8 E13** 63 43N 8 40 E
Frumoasa, Romania .... **29 D10** 46 28N 25 48 E
Frunze = Bishkek,
   Kyrgyzstan ...... **52 E8** 42 54N 74 46 E
Frunzivka, Ukraine .... **29 C14** 47 20N 29 45 E
Fruška Gora,
   Serbia & M. ...... **28 E4** 45 7N 19 30 E
Fruška Gora △,
   Serbia & M. ...... **44 A3** 45 8N 19 40 E
Frutal, Brazil **125 H9** 20 0S 49 0W
Frutigen, Switz. ...... **25 J3** 46 35N 7 38 E
Frýdek-Místek,
   Czech Rep. ...... **27 B11** 49 40N 18 20 E
Frýdlant, Czech Rep. .. **26 A8** 50 56N 15 9 E
Fryeburg, U.S.A. **117 B14** 44 1N 70 59W
Fryvaldov = Jeseník,
   Czech Rep. ...... **27 A10** 50 14N 17 8 E
Fthiótis □, Greece ...... **46 C4** 38 50N 22 25 E
Fu Jiang →, China .... **58 C6** 30 0N 106 10 E
Fu Xian = Wafangdian,
   China ...... **57 E11** 39 38N 121 58 E
Fu Xian, China ...... **56 G5** 36 0N 109 20 E
Fu'an, China ...... **59 D12** 27 11N 119 36 E
Fubian, China ...... **58 B4** 31 17N 102 22 E
Fucécchio, Italy ...... **40 E7** 43 44N 10 48 E
Fucheng, China ...... **56 F9** 37 50N 116 10 E
Fuchou = Fuzhou, China **59 D12** 26 5N 119 16 E
Fuchū, Japan ...... **55 G6** 34 34N 133 14 E
Fuchuan, China ...... **59 E8** 24 50N 111 5 E
Fuchun Jiang →, China **59 B13** 30 5N 120 5 E
Fúcino, Piana del, Italy **41 F10** 42 1N 13 31 E
Fuding, China ...... **59 D13** 27 20N 120 12 E
Fuencaliente, Canary Is. **48 F2** 28 28N 17 50W
Fuencaliente, Spain **37 G6** 38 25N 4 18W
Fuencaliente, Pta.,
   Canary Is. **48 F2** 28 27N 17 51W
Fuengirola, Spain **37 J6** 36 32N 4 41W
Fuenlabrada, Spain **36 E7** 40 17N 3 48W
Fuensalida, Spain **36 E6** 40 5N 4 12W
Fuente-Álamo, Spain .. **39 G3** 38 44N 1 24W
Fuente-Álamo de
   Murcia, Spain **39 H3** 37 42N 1 6W
Fuente de Cantos, Spain **37 G4** 38 15N 6 18W
Fuente del Maestre,
   Spain **37 G4** 38 31N 6 28W
Fuente el Fresno, Spain **37 F7** 39 14N 3 46W
Fuente Obejuna, Spain **37 G5** 38 15N 5 25W
Fuente Palmera, Spain **37 H5** 37 42N 5 6W
Fuentes de Andalucía,
   Spain **37 H5** 37 28N 5 20W
Fuentes de Ebro, Spain **38 D4** 41 31N 0 38W
Fuentes de León, Spain **37 G4** 38 5N 6 32W
Fuentes de Oñoro, Spain **36 E4** 40 33N 6 52W
Fuentesaúco, Spain **36 D5** 41 15N 5 30W
Fuerte →, Mexico **118 B3** 25 50N 109 25W
Fuerte Olimpo,
   Paraguay **126 A4** 21 0S 57 51W
Fuerteventura,
   Canary Is. **48 F6** 28 30N 14 0W
Fuerteventura ✈ (FUE),
   Canary Is. **48 F6** 28 24N 13 52W
Fufeng, China ...... **56 G5** 34 22N 108 0 E
Fuga I., Phil. ...... **61 B4** 18 52N 121 20 E
Fugong, China ...... **58 D2** 27 5N 98 47 E
Fugou, China ...... **56 G8** 34 3N 114 25 E
Fugu, China ...... **56 E6** 39 2N 111 3 E
Fuhai, China ...... **60 B3** 47 2N 87 25 E
Fuḥaymī, Iraq ...... **70 C4** 34 16N 42 10 E
Fuhlsbüttel, Hamburg ✈
   (HAM), Germany .... **24 B5** 53 35N 9 59 E
Fuji, Japan ...... **55 G9** 35 9N 138 39 E
Fuji-Hakone-Izu △,
   Japan ...... **55 G9** 35 15N 138 45 E
Fuji-San, Japan ...... **55 G9** 35 22N 138 44 E
Fuji-Yoshida, Japan .... **55 G9** 35 30N 138 46 E
Fujian □, China ...... **59 E12** 26 0N 118 0 E
Fujinomiya, Japan .... **55 G9** 35 10N 138 40 E
Fujisawa, Japan ...... **55 G9** 35 22N 139 29 E
Fujiyama, Mt. = Fuji-
   San, Japan ...... **55 G9** 35 22N 138 44 E
Fukagawa, Japan ...... **54 C11** 43 43N 142 2 E
Fukien = Fujian □,
   China ...... **59 E12** 26 0N 118 0 E
Fukuchiyama, Japan .. **55 G7** 35 19N 135 9 E
Fukue-Shima, Japan .. **55 H4** 32 40N 128 45 E
Fukui, Japan ...... **55 F8** 36 5N 136 10 E
Fukui □, Japan ...... **55 G8** 36 0N 136 12 E
Fukuoka, Japan ...... **55 H5** 33 39N 130 21 E
Fukuoka □, Japan .... **55 H5** 33 30N 131 0 E
Fukushima, Japan .... **54 F10** 37 44N 140 28 E
Fukushima □, Japan .. **54 F10** 37 30N 140 15 E
Fukuyama, Japan ...... **55 G6** 34 35N 133 20 E
Fulacunda, Guinea-Biss. **82 C1** 11 44N 15 3W
Fulda, Germany ...... **24 E5** 50 32N 9 40 E
Fulda →, Germany .... **24 D5** 51 25N 9 39 E
Fulford Harbour,
   Canada **110 B3** 48 47N 123 27W
Fuliang, China ...... **59 C11** 29 23N 117 14 E
Fullerton, Calif., U.S.A. **111 M9** 33 53N 117 56W
Fullerton, Nebr., U.S.A. **112 E6** 41 22N 97 58W
Fulongquan, China .... **57 B13** 44 20N 124 42 E
Fülöpszállás, Hungary . **28 D4** 46 49N 19 15 E
Fulton, Mo., U.S.A. .. **112 F9** 38 52N 91 57W
Fulton, N.Y., U.S.A. .. **117 C8** 43 19N 76 25W
Fulufjället, Sweden .... **10 C7** 61 18N 13 4 E
Fulufjället, Sweden .... **10 C7** 61 32N 12 41 E
Fumay, France ...... **19 C11** 49 58N 4 40 E
Fumel, France ...... **20 D4** 44 30N 0 58 E
Fumin, China ...... **58 E4** 25 10N 102 20 E
Funabashi, Japan ...... **55 G10** 35 45N 140 0 E
Funafuti = Fongafale,
   Tuvalu ...... **96 H9** 8 31S 179 13 E
Funäsdalen, Sweden .. **10 B6** 62 33N 12 32 E
Funchal, Madeira **48 D3** 32 38N 16 54W
Funchal ✈ (FNC),
   Madeira **48 D3** 32 42N 16 45W
Fundación, Colombia .. **124 A4** 10 31N 74 11W
Fundão, Portugal **36 E3** 40 8N 7 30W
Fundu Moldovei,
   Romania ...... **29 C10** 47 32N 25 12 E
Fundulea, Romania .... **29 F11** 44 28N 26 31 E
Fundy △, Canada **105 C6** 45 35N 65 10W
Fundy, B. of, Canada .. **105 C6** 45 0N 66 0W
Fünen = Fyn, Denmark **11 J4** 55 20N 10 30 E
Funhalouro, Mozam. .. **89 C5** 23 3S 34 25 E
Funing, Hebei, China .. **57 E10** 39 53N 119 12 E
Funing, Jiangsu, China **57 H10** 33 45N 119 50 E
Funing, Yunnan, China **58 F5** 23 35N 105 45 E
Funiu Shan, China .... **56 H7** 33 30N 112 20 E
Funsi, Ghana **82 C4** 10 21N 1 54W
Funtua, Nigeria ...... **83 C6** 11 30N 7 18 E
Fuping, Hebei, China .. **56 E8** 38 48N 114 12 E
Fuping, Shaanxi, China **56 G5** 34 42N 109 10 E
Fuqing, China ...... **59 E12** 25 41N 119 21 E

Fuquan, China ...... **58 D6** 26 40N 107 27 E
Furano, Japan ...... **54 C11** 43 21N 142 23 E
Furāt, Nahr al →, Asia **70 D5** 31 0N 47 25 E
Fürg, Iran ...... **71 D7** 28 18N 55 13 E
Furmanov, Russia ...... **34 B5** 57 10N 41 9 E
Furmanovo, Kazakhstan **34 F9** 49 42N 49 25 E
Furnás, Spain ...... **48 B8** 39 3N 1 32 E
Furnas, Reprêsa de,
   Brazil **127 A6** 20 50S 45 30W
Furneaux Group,
   Australia ...... **95 G4** 40 10S 147 50 E
Furqlus, Syria ...... **74 A6** 34 36N 37 8 E
Fürstenau, Germany .. **24 C3** 52 31N 7 40 E
Fürstenberg, Germany **24 B9** 53 10N 13 8 E
Fürstenfeld, Austria .. **26 D9** 47 3N 16 3 E
Fürstenfeldbruck,
   Germany ...... **25 G7** 48 11N 11 15 E
Fürstenwalde, Germany **24 C10** 52 22N 14 3 E
Fürth, Germany ...... **25 F6** 49 28N 10 59 E
Furth im Wald,
   Germany ...... **25 F8** 49 18N 12 50 E
Furtwangen, Germany . **25 G4** 48 2N 8 12 E
Furudal, Sweden ...... **10 C9** 61 10N 15 11 E
Furukawa, Japan ...... **54 E10** 38 34N 140 58 E
Furulund, Sweden ...... **11 J7** 55 46N 13 6 E
Fury and Hecla Str.,
   Canada **101 B11** 69 56N 84 0W
Fusagasuga, Colombia **124 C4** 4 21N 74 22W
Fuscaldo, Italy ...... **43 C9** 39 25N 16 2 E
Fushan, Shandong,
   China ...... **57 F11** 37 30N 121 15 E
Fushan, Shanxi, China **56 G6** 35 58N 111 51 E
Fushë Arrëz, Albania .. **44 D4** 42 4N 20 2 E
Fushë Krujë, Albania .. **44 E3** 41 29N 19 43 E
Fushun, Liaoning, China **57 D12** 41 50N 123 56 E
Fushun, Sichuan, China **58 C5** 29 13N 104 52 E
Fusong, China ...... **57 C14** 42 20N 127 15 E
Füssen, Germany ...... **25 H6** 47 34N 10 42 E
Fustic, Barbados ...... **121 g** 13 16N 59 38W
Fusui, China ...... **58 F6** 22 40N 107 56 E
Futog, Serbia & M. .... **28 E4** 45 15N 19 42 E
Futuna, Wall. & F. Is. .. **91 B8** 14 25S 178 20W
Fuwa, Egypt ...... **80 H7** 31 12N 30 33 E
Fuxian Hu, China ...... **58 E4** 24 30N 102 53 E
Fuxin, China ...... **57 C11** 42 5N 121 48 E
Fuyang, Anhui, China **56 H8** 33 0N 115 48 E
Fuyang, Zhejiang, China **59 B12** 30 5N 119 57 E
Fuyang He →, China .. **56 E9** 38 12N 117 0 E
Fuying Dao, China .... **59 D13** 26 34N 120 9 E
Fuyu, China ...... **57 B13** 45 12N 124 43 E
Fuyun, China ...... **60 B3** 47 0N 89 28 E
Füzesgyarmat, Hungary **28 C6** 47 6N 21 14 E
Fuzhou, China ...... **59 D12** 26 5N 119 16 E
Fylde, U.K. **14 D5** 53 50N 2 58W
Fyn, Denmark ...... **11 J4** 55 20N 10 30 E
Fyne, L., U.K. **13 F3** 55 59N 5 23W
Fyns Amtskommune □,
   Denmark ...... **11 J4** 55 15N 10 30 E
Fynshav, Denmark .... **11 K3** 54 59N 9 59 E

G

Ga, Ghana **82 D4** 9 47N 2 30W
Gaanda, Nigeria ...... **83 C7** 10 10N 12 27 E
Gabarin, Nigeria ...... **83 C7** 11 8N 10 27 E
Gabas →, France **20 E3** 43 46N 0 42W
Gabela, Angola ...... **84 G2** 11 0S 14 24 E
Gabès, Tunisia ...... **79 B8** 33 53N 10 2 E
Gabès, G. de, Tunisia .. **79 B8** 34 0N 10 30 E
Gabgaba, W. →, Egypt **80 C3** 22 10N 33 5 E
Gabin, Poland ...... **31 F6** 52 23N 19 41 E
Gabon ■, Africa ...... **84 E2** 0 10S 10 0 E
Gaborone, Botswana .. **88 C4** 24 45S 25 57 E
Gabriels, U.S.A. **117 B10** 44 26N 74 12W
Gābrīk, Iran ...... **71 E8** 25 44N 58 28 E
Gabrovo, Bulgaria ...... **45 D9** 42 52N 25 19 E
Gacé, France ...... **18 D7** 48 49N 0 20 E
Gāch Sār, Iran ...... **71 B6** 36 7N 51 19 E
Gachsārān, Iran ...... **71 D6** 30 15N 50 45 E
Gacko, Bos.-H. ...... **44 C2** 43 10N 18 33 E
Gadag, India ...... **66 M9** 15 30N 75 45 E
Gadamai, Sudan ...... **81 D4** 17 11N 36 10 E
Gadap, Pakistan ...... **68 G2** 25 5N 67 28 E
Gadarwara, India ...... **69 H8** 22 50N 78 50 E
Gadebusch, Germany .. **24 B7** 53 42N 11 7 E
Gadein, Sudan ...... **81 F2** 8 10N 28 45 E
Gadhada, India ...... **68 J4** 22 0N 71 35 E
Gádor, Sierra de, Spain **37 J8** 36 57N 2 45W
Gadra, Pakistan ...... **68 G4** 25 40N 70 38 E
Gadsden, U.S.A. **115 H3** 34 1N 86 1W
Gadwal, India ...... **66 L10** 16 10N 77 50 E
Gadyach = Hadyach,
   Ukraine ...... **33 G8** 50 21N 34 0 E
Găeşti, Romania ...... **29 F10** 44 48N 25 19 E
Gaeta, Italy ...... **42 A6** 41 12N 13 35 E
Gaeta, G. di, Italy ...... **42 A6** 41 6N 13 30 E
Gaffney, U.S.A. **115 H5** 35 5N 81 39W
Gafsa, Tunisia ...... **78 B7** 34 24N 8 43 E
Gagarawa, Nigeria .... **83 C6** 12 25N 9 32 E
Gagaria, India ...... **68 G4** 25 43N 70 46 E
Gagarin, Russia ...... **32 E8** 55 38N 35 0 E
Găgăuzia □, Moldova . **29 D13** 46 10N 28 40 E
Gaggenau, Germany .. **25 G4** 48 48N 8 18 E
Gaghamni, Sudan ...... **81 E2** 11 41N 28 19 E
Gagino, Russia ...... **34 C7** 55 15N 45 1 E
Gagliano del Capo, Italy **43 C11** 39 50N 18 22 E
Gagnef, Sweden ...... **10 D9** 60 36N 15 5 E
Gagnoa, Ivory C. **82 D3** 6 56N 5 16W
Gagnon, Canada **105 B6** 51 50N 68 5W
Gagnon, L., Canada .. **103 A6** 62 3N 110 27W
Gagra, Georgia ...... **35 J5** 43 20N 40 10 E
Gahini, Rwanda ...... **86 C3** 1 50S 30 30 E
Gahmar, India ...... **69 G10** 25 27N 83 49 E
Gai Xian = Gaizhou,
   China ...... **57 D12** 40 22N 122 20 E
Gaïdhouronísi, Greece **49 E7** 34 53N 25 41 E
Gail →, Austria ...... **26 E6** 46 36N 13 53 E
Gaillac, France ...... **20 E5** 43 54N 1 54 E
Gaillimh = Galway,
   Ireland **12 C2** 53 17N 9 3W
Gaillon, France ...... **18 C8** 49 10N 1 20 E
Gaines, U.S.A. **116 E7** 41 46N 77 35W
Gainesville, Fla., U.S.A. **115 L4** 29 40N 82 20W
Gainesville, Ga., U.S.A. **115 H4** 34 18N 83 50W
Gainesville, Mo., U.S.A. **113 G8** 36 36N 92 26W
Gainesville, Tex., U.S.A. **113 J6** 33 38N 97 8W
Gainsborough, U.K. .. **14 D7** 53 24N 0 46W

Galala, Gebel el, Egypt **80 J8** 29 21N 32 22 E
Galán, Cerro, Argentina **126 B2** 25 55S 66 52W
Galana →, Kenya ...... **86 C5** 3 9S 40 8 E
Galanta, Slovak Rep. .. **27 C10** 48 11N 17 45 E
Galapagar, Spain **36 E7** 40 36N 3 58W
Galápagos = Colón,
   Arch. de, Ecuador .. **97 H18** 0 0 91 0W
Galashiels, U.K. **13 F6** 55 37N 2 49W
Galatás, Greece ...... **46 D5** 37 30N 23 26 E
Galați, Romania ...... **29 E13** 45 27N 28 2 E
Galați □, Romania .... **29 E12** 45 45N 27 30 E
Galatia, Turkey ...... **72 C5** 39 30N 33 0 E
Galatina, Italy ...... **43 B11** 40 10N 18 10 E
Galátone, Italy ...... **43 B11** 40 9N 18 4 E
Galax, U.S.A. **115 G5** 36 40N 80 56W
Galaxídhion, Greece .. **46 C4** 38 22N 22 23 E
Galcaio, Somali Rep. .. **75 F4** 6 30N 47 30 E
Galdhøpiggen, Norway **9 F12** 61 38N 8 18 E
Galeana, Chihuahua,
   Mexico **118 A3** 30 7N 107 38W
Galeana, Nuevo León,
   Mexico **118 A3** 24 50N 100 4W
Galegu, Sudan ...... **81 E4** 12 36N 35 2 E
Galela, Indonesia ...... **63 D7** 1 50N 127 49 E
Galena, U.S.A. **100 B4** 64 44N 156 56W
Galeota Pt.,
   Trin. & Tob. **125 K16** 10 8N 60 59W
Galera, Spain **39 H2** 37 45N 2 33W
Galera Pt., Trin. & Tob. **121 D7** 10 49N 60 54W
Galesburg, U.S.A. **112 E9** 40 57N 90 22W
Galeton, U.S.A. **116 E7** 41 44N 77 39W
Galga, Ethiopia ...... **81 F4** 6 39N 37 47 E
Galicea Mare, Romania **29 F8** 44 4N 23 19 E
Galich, Russia ...... **34 A6** 58 22N 42 24 E
Galiche, Bulgaria ...... **44 C7** 43 34N 23 53 E
Galicia □, Spain **36 C3** 42 43N 7 45W
Galičica △, Macedonia **44 E4** 41 2N 20 55 E
Galilee = Hagalil, Israel **74 C4** 32 53N 35 18 E
Galilee, L., Australia .. **94 C4** 22 20S 145 50 E
Galilee, Sea of = Yam
   Kinneret, Israel ...... **74 C4** 32 45N 35 35 E
Galim, Cameroon ...... **83 D7** 7 6N 12 25 E
Galina Pt., Jamaica .... **120 a** 18 24N 76 58W
Galinoporni, Cyprus .. **49 D13** 35 31N 34 18 E
Galion, U.S.A. **116 F2** 40 44N 82 47W
Galiuro Mts., U.S.A. .. **109 K8** 32 30N 110 20W
Galiwinku, Australia .. **94 A2** 12 25S 135 34 E
Gallabat, Sudan ...... **81 E4** 12 58N 36 11 E
Gallan Hd., U.K. **13 C1** 58 15N 7 2W
Gallarate, Italy ...... **40 C5** 45 40N 8 48 E
Gallatin, U.S.A. **115 G2** 36 24N 86 27W
Galle, Sri Lanka ...... **66 R12** 6 5N 80 10 E
Gállego →, Spain **38 D4** 41 39N 0 51W
Gallegos →, Argentina **128 G3** 51 35S 69 0W
Galletti →, Ethiopia .. **81 F5** 8 46N 41 10 E
Galley Hd., Ireland **12 E3** 51 32N 8 55W
Galliate, Italy ...... **40 C5** 45 29N 8 42 E
Gallinas, Pta., Colombia **124 A4** 12 28N 71 40W
Gallipoli = Gelibolu,
   Turkey ...... **45 F10** 40 28N 26 43 E
Gallípoli, Italy ...... **43 B10** 40 3N 17 58 E
Gallipolis, U.S.A. **114 F4** 38 49N 82 12W
Gällivare, Sweden ...... **8 C19** 67 9N 20 40 E
Gallneukirchen, Austria **26 C7** 48 25N 14 25 E
Gällö, Sweden ...... **10 B9** 62 55N 15 13 E
Gallo, C., Italy ...... **42 D6** 38 13N 13 19 E
Galloo I., U.S.A. **117 C8** 43 55N 76 25W
Galloway, U.K. **13 F4** 55 1N 4 29W
Galloway, ∴, U.K. **13 F4** 55 6N 4 9W
Galloway, Mull of, U.K. **13 G4** 54 39N 4 52W
Gallup, U.S.A. **109 J9** 35 32N 108 45W
Gallur, Spain **38 D3** 41 52N 1 19W
Galoya, Sri Lanka ...... **66 Q12** 8 10N 80 55 E
Galt, U.S.A. **110 G5** 38 15N 121 18W
Galten, Denmark ...... **11 H3** 56 9N 9 54 E
Galtür, Austria ...... **26 E3** 46 58N 10 11 E
Galty Mts., Ireland **12 D3** 52 22N 8 10W
Galtymore, Ireland **12 D3** 52 21N 8 11W
Galva, U.S.A. **112 E9** 41 10N 90 3W
Galve de Sorbe, Spain **38 D1** 41 13N 3 10W
Galveston, U.S.A. **113 L7** 29 18N 94 48W
Galveston B., U.S.A. .. **113 L7** 29 36N 94 50W
Gálvez, Argentina **126 C3** 32 0S 61 14W
Galway, Ireland **12 C2** 53 17N 9 3W
Galway □, Ireland **12 C2** 53 22N 9 1W
Galway B., Ireland **12 C2** 53 13N 9 10W
Gam →, Vietnam ...... **64 B5** 21 55N 105 12 E
Gamagōri, Japan ...... **55 G8** 34 50N 137 14 E
Gamari, L., Ethiopia .. **81 E5** 11 32N 41 40 E
Gamawa, Nigeria ...... **83 C7** 12 10N 10 31 E
Gamay, Phil. ...... **61 E6** 12 23N 125 18 E
Gambaga, Ghana **83 C4** 10 30N 0 28W
Gambat, Pakistan ...... **68 F3** 27 17N 68 26 E
Gambela, Ethiopia .... **81 F3** 8 14N 34 38 E
Gambela △, Ethiopia .. **81 F3** 8 0N 34 0 E
Gambela-Hizboch □,
   Ethiopia ...... **81 F3** 8 0N 34 0 E
Gambhir →, India ...... **68 F6** 26 58N 77 27 E
Gambia ■, W. Afr. **82 C1** 13 25N 16 0W
Gambia →, W. Afr. **82 C1** 13 28N 16 34W
Gambier, U.S.A. **116 F2** 40 22N 82 23W
Gambier, C., Australia **92 B5** 11 56S 130 57 E
Gambier Is., Australia **95 F2** 35 3S 136 30 E
Gambo, Canada **105 C9** 48 47N 54 13W
Gamboli, Pakistan ...... **68 E3** 29 53N 68 24 E
Gamboma, Congo ...... **84 E3** 1 55S 15 52 E
Gamka →, S. Africa .. **88 E3** 33 18S 21 39 E
Gamkab →, Namibia .. **88 D2** 28 4S 17 54 E
Gamla Uppsala, Sweden **10 E11** 59 54N 17 40 E
Gamlakarleby =
   Kokkola, Finland .... **8 E20** 63 50N 23 8 E
Gamleby, Sweden ...... **11 G10** 57 54N 16 24 E
Gammon →, Canada .. **103 C9** 51 24N 95 44W
Gammon Ranges △,
   Australia ...... **95 E2** 30 38S 139 8 E
Gamo-Gofa, Ethiopia .. **81 F4** 5 40N 36 40 E
Gamou, Niger ...... **83 C6** 14 20N 9 55 E
Gamtoos →, S. Africa **88 E4** 33 58S 25 1 E
Gan, France **20 E3** 43 12N 0 27W
Gan Goriama, Mts.,
   Cameroon ...... **83 D7** 7 44N 12 45 E
Gan Jiang →, China .. **59 C11** 29 15N 116 0 E
Ganado, U.S.A. **109 J9** 35 43N 109 33W
Gananita, Sudan ...... **80 D3** 19 20N 33 30 E
Gananoque, Canada .. **117 B8** 44 20N 76 10W
Ganāveh, Iran ...... **71 D6** 29 35N 50 35 E
Gäncä, Azerbaijan .... **35 K8** 40 45N 46 20 E
Gancheng, China ...... **64 C7** 18 51N 108 37 E
Gand = Gent, Belgium **17 C3** 51 2N 3 42 E
Ganda, Angola ...... **85 G2** 13 3S 14 35 E
Gandajika, Dem. Rep. of
   the Congo ...... **84 F4** 6 45S 23 57 E
Gandak →, India ...... **69 G11** 25 39N 85 13 E
Gandava, Pakistan .... **68 E2** 28 32N 67 32 E
Gandhi Sagar, India .. **68 G6** 24 40N 75 40 E
Gander, Canada **105 C9** 48 58N 54 35W

Gander L., Canada **105 C9** 48 58N 54 35W
Ganderkesee, Germany **24 B4** 53 2N 8 32 E
Ganderowe Falls,
   Zimbabwe ...... **87 F2** 17 20S 29 10 E
Gandesa, Spain ...... **38 D5** 41 3N 0 26 E
Gandhi Sagar, India .. **68 G6** 24 40N 75 40 E
Gandhinagar, India .. **68 H5** 23 15N 72 45 E
Gandi, Nigeria ...... **83 C6** 12 55N 5 49 E
Gandía, Spain **39 G4** 38 58N 0 9W
Gandino, Italy ...... **40 C6** 45 49N 9 54 E
Gando, Pta., Canary Is. **48 G4** 27 55N 15 22W
Gandole, Nigeria ...... **83 D7** 8 28N 11 35 E
Gâneb, Mauritania **82 B2** 18 29N 10 8W
Ganedidalem = Gani,
   Indonesia ...... **63 E7** 0 48S 128 14 E
Ganetti, Sudan ...... **80 D3** 18 0N 31 10 E
Ganga →, India ...... **69 H14** 23 20N 90 30 E
Ganga Sagar, India .... **69 J13** 21 38N 88 5 E
Gangafani, Mali **82 C4** 14 20N 2 20W
Gangan →, India ...... **69 E8** 28 38N 78 58 E
Ganganagar, India .... **68 E5** 29 56N 73 56 E
Gangapur, India ...... **68 F7** 26 32N 76 49 E
Gangara, Niger ...... **83 C6** 14 35N 8 29 E
Gangaw, Burma ...... **67 H19** 22 5N 94 5 E
Gangdisê Shan, China **67 D12** 31 20N 81 0 E
Ganges = Ganga →,
   India ...... **69 H14** 23 20N 90 30 E
Ganges, Canada **102 D4** 48 51N 123 31W
Ganges, France ...... **20 E7** 43 56N 3 42 E
Ganges, Mouths of the,
   India ...... **69 J14** 21 30N 90 0 E
Gânghester, Sweden .. **11 G7** 57 42N 13 1 E
Gangi, Italy ...... **43 E7** 37 48N 14 12 E
Gângiova, Romania .. **29 G8** 43 54N 23 50 E
Gangoh, India ...... **68 E7** 29 46N 77 18 E
Gangotri, India ...... **69 D8** 30 50N 79 10 E
Gangtok, India ...... **67 F16** 27 20N 88 37 E
Gangu, China ...... **56 G3** 34 40N 105 15 E
Gangyao, China ...... **57 B14** 44 12N 126 37 E
Gani, Indonesia ...... **63 E7** 0 48S 128 14 E
Ganj, India ...... **69 F8** 27 45N 78 57 E
Ganluc, China ...... **58 C4** 28 58N 102 59 E
Gannat, France ...... **19 F10** 46 7N 3 11 E
Gannett Peak, U.S.A. .. **108 E9** 43 11N 109 39W
Ganquan, China ...... **56 F5** 36 20N 109 20 E
Ganshui, China ...... **58 C6** 28 40N 106 40 E
Gansu □, China ...... **56 G3** 36 0N 104 0 E
Ganta, Liberia **82 D3** 7 15N 8 59W
Gantheaume, C.,
   Australia ...... **95 F2** 36 4S 137 32 E
Gantheaume B.,
   Australia ...... **93 E1** 27 40S 114 10 E
Gantsevichi =
   Hantsavichy, Belarus **33 F4** 52 49N 26 30 E
Ganye, Nigeria ...... **83 D7** 8 25N 12 2 E
Ganyem = Genyem,
   Indonesia ...... **63 E10** 2 46S 140 12 E
Ganyu, China ...... **57 G10** 34 50N 119 8 E
Ganyushkino,
   Kazakhstan ...... **35 G9** 46 35N 49 20 E
Ganzhou, China ...... **59 E10** 25 51N 114 56 E
Gao, Mali **83 B4** 16 15N 0 5W
Gao Xian, China ...... **58 C5** 28 21N 104 32 E
Gao'an, China ...... **59 C10** 28 15N 115 17 E
Gaochun, China ...... **59 B12** 31 20N 118 49 E
Gaohe, China ...... **59 B11** 30 43N 116 49 E
Gaokeng, China ...... **59 D9** 27 40N 113 58 E
Gaolan Dao, China .... **59 G9** 21 55N 113 10 E
Gaoligong Shan, China **58 E2** 24 45N 98 45 E
Gaoming, China ...... **59 F9** 22 55N 112 50 E
Gaoping, China ...... **56 G7** 35 45N 112 55 E
Gaotang, China ...... **56 F9** 36 50N 116 15 E
Gaoua, Burkina Faso .. **82 C4** 10 20N 3 8W
Gaoual, Guinea **82 C2** 11 45N 13 25W
Gaoxiong = Kaohsiung,
   Taiwan ...... **59 F13** 22 35N 120 16 E
Gaoyang, China ...... **56 E8** 38 40N 115 45 E
Gaoyao, China ...... **59 F9** 23 3N 112 27 E
Gaoyou, China ...... **59 A12** 32 47N 119 26 E
Gaoyou Hu, China .... **57 H10** 32 45N 119 20 E
Gaoyuan, China ...... **57 F9** 37 8N 117 58 E
Gaozhou, China ...... **59 G8** 21 58N 110 50 E
Gap, France ...... **21 D10** 44 33N 6 5 E
Gapan, Phil. ...... **61 D4** 15 19N 120 57 E
Gapat →, India ...... **69 G10** 24 30N 83 28 E
Gapuwiyak, Australia . **94 A2** 12 25S 135 43 E
Gar, China ...... **60 C2** 32 10N 79 58 E
Garabogazköl Aylagy,
   Turkmenistan ...... **52 E6** 41 0N 53 30 E
Garachico, Canary Is. .. **48 F3** 28 22N 16 46W
Garachiné, Panama .. **120 E4** 8 0N 78 12W
Garafia, Canary Is. **48 F2** 28 48N 17 57W
Garah, Australia ...... **95 D4** 29 5S 149 38 E
Garajonay, Canary Is. **48 F2** 28 7N 17 14W
Garamba △, Dem. Rep.
   of the Congo ...... **86 B2** 4 10N 29 40 E
Garango, Burkina Faso **83 C4** 11 48N 0 4W
Garanhuns, Brazil **125 E11** 8 50S 36 30W
Garautha, India ...... **69 G8** 25 34N 79 18 E
Garawe, Liberia **82 E3** 4 35N 8 0W
Garba Tula, Kenya .... **86 B4** 0 30N 38 32 E
Garberville, U.S.A. **108 F2** 40 6N 123 48W
Garbiyang, India ...... **69 D9** 30 8N 80 54 E
Garbsen, Germany .... **24 C5** 52 24N 9 31 E
Garca, Brazil **127 A6** 22 14S 49 47W
Gard □, France ...... **21 D8** 44 2N 4 10 E
Garda, L. di, Italy ...... **40 C7** 45 40N 10 41 E
Gardanne, France ...... **21 E9** 43 27N 5 27 E
Gårdby, Sweden ...... **11 H10** 56 36N 16 38 E
Garde L., Canada **103 A7** 62 50N 106 13W
Gardelegen, Germany **24 C7** 52 32N 11 24 E
Garden City, Ga., U.S.A. **115 J5** 32 6N 81 9W
Garden City, Kans.,
   U.S.A. **113 G4** 37 58N 100 53W
Garden City, Tex.,
   U.S.A. **113 K4** 31 52N 101 29W
Garden Grove, U.S.A. **111 M9** 33 47N 117 55W
Gardez, Afghan. ...... **68 C3** 33 37N 69 9 E
Gardhíki, Greece ...... **46 C3** 38 50N 21 55 E
Gardiner, Maine, U.S.A. **115 C11** 44 14N 69 47W
Gardiner, Mont., U.S.A. **108 D8** 45 2N 110 22W
Gardiners I., U.S.A. .. **117 E12** 41 6N 72 6W
Gardner, U.S.A. **117 D13** 42 34N 71 59W
Gardner Canal, Canada **102 C3** 53 27N 128 8W
Gardnerville, U.S.A. .. **110 G7** 38 56N 119 45W
Gardo, Somali Rep. .. **75 F4** 9 30N 49 6 E
Gardone Val Trómpia,
   Italy ...... **40 C7** 45 41N 10 11 E
Gárdony, Hungary .... **28 C3** 47 12N 18 39 E
Garešnica, Croatia .... **41 C13** 45 36N 16 56 E
Garéssio, Italy ...... **40 D5** 44 12N 8 2 E
Garey, U.S.A. **111 L6** 34 53N 120 19W
Garfagnana, Italy ...... **40 D7** 44 8N 10 23 E

Garforth, U.K. **14 D6** 53 47N 1 24W
Gargaliánoi, Greece .. **46 D3** 37 4N 21 38 E
Gargan, Mt., France .. **20 C5** 45 37N 1 39 E
Gargano △, Italy ...... **41 G12** 41 43N 15 53 E
Gargett, Australia .... **94 K6** 21 9S 148 46 E
Gargouna, Mali ...... **83 B5** 15 56N 0 13 E
Gargždai, Lithuania .. **30 C8** 55 43N 21 24 E
Garibaldi △, Canada .. **102 D4** 49 50N 122 40W
Gariep, L., S. Africa .. **88 E4** 30 40S 25 40 E
Garies, S. Africa ...... **88 E2** 30 32S 17 59 E
Garigliano →, Italy .. **42 A6** 41 13N 13 45 E
Garissa, Kenya ...... **86 C4** 0 25S 39 40 E
Garkida, Nigeria ...... **83 C7** 10 27N 12 36 E
Garko, Nigeria ...... **83 C6** 11 45N 8 53 E
Garland, Tex., U.S.A. **113 J6** 32 55N 96 38W
Garland, Utah, U.S.A. **108 F7** 41 47N 112 10W
Garlasco, Italy ...... **40 C5** 45 12N 8 55 E
Garliava, Lithuania .. **30 D10** 54 49N 23 52 E
Garlin, France **20 E3** 43 33N 0 16W
Garm, Tajikistan ...... **52 F8** 39 0N 70 20 E
Garmāb, Iran ...... **71 C8** 35 25N 56 45 E
Garmisch-
   Partenkirchen,
   Germany ...... **25 H7** 47 30N 11 6 E
Garmo, Qullai =
   Kommunizma, Pik,
   Tajikistan ...... **52 F8** 39 0N 72 2 E
Garmsär, Iran ...... **71 C7** 35 20N 52 25 E
Garner, U.S.A. **112 D8** 43 6N 93 36W
Garnett, U.S.A. **112 F7** 38 17N 95 14W
Garo Hills, India ...... **69 G14** 25 30N 90 30 E
Garoe, Somali Rep. .. **75 F4** 8 25N 48 33 E
Garonne →, France .. **20 C3** 45 2N 0 36W
Garonne, Canal Latéral
   à la, France ...... **20 D4** 44 15N 0 18 E
Garoowe = Garoe,
   Somali Rep. ...... **75 F4** 8 25N 48 33 E
Garot, India ...... **68 G6** 24 19N 75 41 E
Garoua, Cameroon .. **83 D7** 9 19N 13 21 E
Garpenberg, Sweden .. **10 D10** 60 19N 16 12 E
Garphyttan, Sweden .. **10 E8** 59 18N 14 56 E
Garrauli, India ...... **69 G8** 25 5N 79 22 E
Garrel, Germany ...... **24 C4** 52 57N 8 1 E
Garrigues, France ...... **20 E7** 43 40N 3 55 E
Garrison, Mont., U.S.A. **108 C7** 46 31N 112 49W
Garrison, N. Dak.,
   U.S.A. **112 B4** 47 40N 101 25W
Garrison Res. =
   Sakakawea, L., U.S.A. **112 B4** 47 30N 101 25W
Garron Pt., U.K. **12 A6** 55 3N 5 59W
Garrovillas, Spain **37 F4** 39 40N 6 33W
Garrucha, Spain **39 H3** 37 11N 1 49W
Garry →, U.K. **13 E5** 56 44N 3 47W
Garry, L., Canada **100 B9** 65 58N 100 18W
Gärsnäs, Sweden ...... **11 J8** 55 32N 14 18 E
Garson L., Canada **103 B6** 56 19N 110 2W
Garstang, U.K. **14 D5** 53 55N 2 46W
Gartempe →, France .. **20 B4** 46 47N 0 49 E
Gartz, Germany ...... **24 B10** 53 13N 14 22 E
Garu, Ghana **83 C4** 10 55N 0 11W
Garu, India ...... **69 H11** 23 40N 84 14 E
Garub, Namibia ...... **88 D2** 26 37S 16 0 E
Garut, Indonesia ...... **63 G12** 7 14S 107 53 E
Garvão, Portugal **37 H2** 37 42N 8 21W
Garvie Mts., N.Z. ...... **91 L2** 45 30S 168 50 E
Garwa = Garoua,
   Cameroon ...... **83 D7** 9 19N 13 21 E
Garwa, India ...... **69 G10** 24 11N 83 47 E
Garwolin, Poland ...... **31 G8** 51 55N 21 38 E
Gary, U.S.A. **114 E2** 41 36N 87 20W
Garz, Germany ...... **24 A9** 54 19N 13 20 E
Garzê, China ...... **58 B3** 31 38N 100 1 E
Garzón, Colombia **124 C3** 2 10N 75 40W
Gas-San, Japan ...... **54 E10** 38 32N 140 1 E
Gasan Kuli = Esenguly,
   Turkmenistan ...... **52 F6** 37 37N 53 59 E
Gascogne, France ...... **20 E4** 43 45N 0 20 E
Gascogne, G. de, Europe **20 E2** 44 0N 2 0W
Gascony = Gascogne,
   France ...... **20 E4** 43 45N 0 20 E
Gascoyne →, Australia **93 D1** 24 52S 113 37 E
Gascoyne Junction,
   Australia ...... **93 E2** 25 2S 115 17 E
Gascueña, Spain **38 E2** 40 18N 2 31W
Gash, Wad →, Ethiopia **81 D4** 16 48N 35 51 E
Gashagar, Nigeria .... **83 C7** 13 20N 12 47 E
Gashaka, Nigeria ...... **83 D7** 7 20N 11 29 E
Gashaka-Gumti △,
   Nigeria ...... **83 D7** 7 23N 11 34 E
Gasherbrum, Pakistan **69 B7** 35 40N 76 40 E
Gashua, Nigeria ...... **83 C7** 12 54N 11 0 E
Gaspar, Trin. & Tob. .. **125 K15** 10 18N 61 26W
Gaspé, Canada **105 C7** 48 52N 64 30W
Gaspé, C. de, Canada **105 C7** 48 48N 64 7W
Gaspé Pen. = Gaspésie,
   Pén. de la, Canada .. **105 C6** 48 45N 65 40W
Gaspésie △, Canada .. **105 C6** 48 55N 66 10W
Gaspésie, Pén. de la,
   Canada **105 C6** 48 45N 65 40W
Gassan, Burkina Faso . **82 C4** 12 49N 3 12W
Gassol, Nigeria ...... **83 D7** 8 34N 10 25 E
Gasteiz = Vitoria-
   Gasteiz, Spain **38 C2** 42 50N 2 41W
Gastonia, U.S.A. **115 H5** 35 16N 81 11W
Gastoúni, Greece ...... **46 D3** 37 51N 21 15 E
Gastre, Argentina **128 E3** 42 20S 69 15W
Gästrikland, Sweden .. **10 D10** 60 45N 16 40 E
Gata, C., Cyprus ...... **49 E12** 34 34N 33 2 E
Gata, C. de, Spain **39 J2** 36 41N 2 13W
Gata, Sierra de, Spain **36 E4** 40 20N 6 45W
Gataga →, Canada **102 B3** 58 35N 126 59W
Gătaia, Romania ...... **28 E6** 45 26N 21 30 E
Gatchina, Russia ...... **32 C5** 59 35N 30 9 E
Gatehouse of Fleet, U.K. **13 G4** 54 53N 4 12W
Gates, U.S.A. **116 C7** 43 9N 77 42W
Gateshead, U.K. **14 C6** 54 57N 1 35W
Gatesville, U.S.A. **113 K6** 31 26N 97 45W
Gateway △, U.S.A. **117 F11** 40 26N 73 59W
Gaths, Zimbabwe ...... **87 G3** 20 2S 30 32 E
Gatico, Chile **126 A1** 22 29S 70 20W
Gâtinais, France ...... **19 D9** 48 5N 2 40 E
Gâtine, Hauteurs de,
   France **20 B3** 46 35N 0 45W
Gatineau, Canada **117 A9** 45 29N 75 38W
Gatineau →, Canada .. **104 C4** 45 40N 76 0W
Gatineau △, Canada .. **104 C4** 45 40N 76 0W
Gattaran, Phil. ...... **61 B4** 18 4N 121 38 E
Gattinara, Italy ...... **40 C5** 45 37N 8 22 E
Gatton, Australia ...... **95 D5** 27 32S 152 17 E
Gatun, L., Panama **120 E4** 9 7N 79 56W
Gatwick, London ✈
   (LGW), U.K. **15 F7** 51 10N 0 11W
Gatyana, S. Africa .... **89 E4** 32 16S 28 31 E
Gau, Fiji ...... **91 D8** 18 2S 179 18 E

Gaucín, Spain 37 J5 36 31N 5 19W
Gauer L., Canada ... 103 B9 57 0N 97 50W
Gauhati = Guwahati, India .... 67 F17 26 10N 91 45 E
Gauja →, Latvia .... 9 H21 57 10N 24 16 E
Gaula →, Norway ... 8 E14 63 21N 10 14 E
Gauri Phanta, India . 69 E9 28 41N 80 36 E
Gausta, Norway ..... 9 G13 59 48N 8 40 E
Gauteng □, S. Africa . 89 D4 26 0S 28 0 E
Gāv Koshī, Iran ..... 71 D8 28 38N 57 12 E
Gāvakān, Iran ...... 71 D7 29 37N 53 10 E
Gavà, Spain 82 D3 5 8N 1 0W
Gavarnie, France ... 20 F3 42 44N 0 1W
Gavāter, Iran ...... 71 E9 25 10N 61 31 E
Gāvbandī, Iran ..... 71 E7 27 12N 53 4 E
Gavdhopoúla, Greece . 49 E6 34 56N 24 0 E
Gávdhos, Greece .... 49 E6 34 50N 24 5 E
Gavi, Italy .... 40 D5 44 41N 8 49 E
Gavião, Portugal ... 37 F3 39 28N 7 56W
Gaviota, U.S.A. 111 L6 34 29N 120 13W
Gāvkhūnī, Bāţlāq-e, Iran 71 C7 32 6N 52 52 E
Gävle, Sweden ...... 10 D11 60 40N 17 9 E
Gävleborgs län □, Sweden .... 10 C10 61 30N 16 15 E
Gävlebukten, Sweden . 10 D11 60 40N 17 20 E
Gavorrano, Italy ... 40 F7 42 55N 10 54 E
Gavray, France 18 D5 48 55N 1 20W
Gavrilov Yam, Russia . 32 D10 57 18N 39 49 E
Gávrion, Greece .... 46 D6 37 54N 24 44 E
Gawachab, Namibia .. 88 D2 27 4S 17 55 E
Gawilgarh Hills, India 66 J10 21 15N 76 45 E
Gawler, Australia ... 95 E2 34 30S 138 42 E
Gawu, Nigeria ...... 83 D6 9 14N 6 52 E
Gaxun Nur, China ... 60 B5 42 22N 100 30 E
Gaya, India .... 69 G11 24 47N 85 4 E
Gaya, Niger .... 83 C5 11 52N 3 28 E
Gaya, Nigeria ...... 83 C6 11 57N 9 0 E
Gayéri, Burkina Faso . 83 C5 12 39N 0 29 E
Gaylord, U.S.A. 114 C3 45 2N 84 41W
Gayndah, Australia . 95 D5 25 35S 151 32 E
Gaysin = Haysyn, Ukraine .... 33 H5 48 57N 29 25 E
Gayvoron = Hayvoron, Ukraine .... 29 B14 48 22N 29 52 E
Gaza, Gaza Strip ... 74 D3 31 30N 34 28 E
Gaza □, Mozam. .... 89 C5 23 10S 32 45 E
Gaza Strip ⊠, Asia .. 74 D3 31 29N 34 25 E
Gazanjyk, Turkmenistan 71 B7 39 16N 55 32 E
Gazaoua, Niger ..... 83 C6 13 32N 7 55 E
Gāzbor, Iran .... 71 D8 28 5N 58 51 E
Gazi, Dem. Rep. of the Congo .... 86 B1 1 3N 24 30 E
Gaziantep, Turkey .. 70 B3 37 6N 37 23 E
Gazimağusa = Famagusta, Cyprus . 49 D12 35 8N 33 55 E
Gazipaşa, Turkey ... 72 D5 36 16N 32 18 E
Gbarnga, Liberia ... 82 D3 7 19N 9 13W
Gbekebo, Nigeria ... 83 D5 6 20N 4 56 E
Gboko, Nigeria ..... 83 D6 7 17N 9 4 E
Gbongan, Nigeria ... 83 D5 7 28N 4 20 E
Gcoverega, Botswana . 88 B3 19 8S 24 18 E
Gcuwa, S. Africa ... 89 E4 32 20S 28 11 E
Gdańsk, Poland ..... 30 D5 54 22N 18 40 E
Gdansk ✈ (GDN), Poland .... 30 D5 54 22N 18 30 E
Gdańska, Zatoka, Poland .... 30 D6 54 30N 19 20 E
Gdov, Russia .... 9 G22 58 48N 27 55 E
Gdynia, Poland ..... 30 D5 54 35N 18 33 E
Geba →, Guinea-Biss. . 82 C1 11 46N 15 36W
Gebe, Indonesia .... 63 D7 0 5N 129 25 E
Gebeciler, Turkey ... 47 C12 38 46N 30 46 E
Gebeit Mine, Sudan . 80 C4 21 3N 36 29 E
Gebel Abyad, Sudan . 80 D2 19 0N 28 0 E
Gebel Iweibid, Egypt . 80 H8 30 8N 32 13 E
Gebze, Turkey ...... 45 F13 40 47N 29 25 E
Gecha, Ethiopia .... 81 F4 7 30N 35 18 E
Gedaref, Sudan ..... 81 E4 14 2N 35 28 E
Gedaref □, Sudan ... 81 E4 14 0N 35 0 E
Gediz, Turkey ...... 47 B11 39 1N 29 24 E
Gediz →, Turkey .... 47 C8 38 35N 26 48 E
Gedo, Ethiopia ..... 81 F4 9 2N 37 25 E
Gèdre, France ...... 20 F4 42 47N 0 2 E
Gedser, Denmark ... 11 K5 54 35N 11 55 E
Gedung, Pulau, Malaysia 65 c 5 17N 100 23 E
Geegully Cr. →, Australia .... 92 C3 18 32S 123 41 E
Geel, Belgium ...... 17 C4 51 10N 4 59 E
Geelong, Australia .. 95 F3 38 10S 144 22 E
Geelvink B. = Cenderwasih, Teluk, Indonesia .... 63 E9 3 0S 135 20 E
Geelvink Chan., Australia .... 93 E1 28 30S 114 0 E
Geesthacht, Germany . 24 B6 53 26N 10 22 E
Geidam, Nigeria .... 83 C7 12 57N 11 57 E
Geike →, Canada ... 103 B8 57 45N 103 52W
Geikie Gorge △, Australia .... 92 C4 18 3S 125 41 E
Geilenkirchen, Germany 24 E2 50 57N 6 8 E
Geili, Sudan .... 81 D3 16 1N 32 37 E
Geisingen, Germany . 25 H4 47 54N 8 38 E
Geislingen, Germany . 25 G5 48 37N 9 50 E
Geistown, U.S.A. ... 116 F6 40 18N 78 52W
Geita, Tanzania .... 86 C3 2 48S 32 12 E
Geju, China .... 58 F4 23 20N 103 10 E
Gel →, Meydān-e, Iran 71 D7 29 4N 54 50 E
Gel River, Sudan ... 81 F2 7 5N 29 10 E
Gela, Italy .... 43 E7 37 4N 14 15 E
Gela, G. di, Italy ... 43 E7 37 0N 14 20 E
Gelahun, Liberia ... 82 D2 7 55N 10 28W
Gelang Patah, Malaysia 65 d 1 27N 103 35 E
Gelderland □, Neths. . 17 B6 52 5N 6 10 E
Geldern, Germany .. 24 D2 51 31N 6 20 E
Geldrop, Neths. .... 17 C5 51 25N 5 32 E
Geleen, Neths. ..... 17 D5 50 57N 5 49 E
Gelehun, S. Leone .. 82 D2 8 20N 11 40W
Gelembe, Turkey ... 47 B9 39 10N 27 50 E
Gelemso, Ethiopia .. 81 F5 8 49N 40 31 E
Gelendost, Turkey .. 72 C4 38 7N 31 1 E
Gelendzhik, Russia .. 33 K10 44 33N 38 10 E
Gelibolu, Turkey ... 45 F10 40 28N 26 43 E
Gelibolu Yarımadası, Turkey .... 45 F10 40 20N 26 30 E
Gelidonya Burnu, Turkey .... 72 D4 36 12N 30 24 E
Gelnhausen, Germany . 25 E5 50 11N 9 11 E
Gelnica, Slovak Rep. . 27 C13 48 51N 20 55 E
Gelsenkirchen, Germany 24 D3 51 32N 7 1 E
Gelting, Germany ... 24 A5 54 45N 9 53 E
Gelugur, Malaysia .. 65 c 5 22N 100 18 E
Gemas, Malaysia ... 65 L4 2 37N 102 36 E
Gembloux, Belgium . 17 D4 50 34N 4 43 E
Gemena, Dem. Rep. of the Congo .... 84 D3 3 13N 19 48 E

Gemerek, Turkey .... 70 B3 39 15N 36 10 E
Gemla, Sweden ..... 11 H8 56 52N 14 39 E
Gemlik, Turkey ..... 45 F13 40 26N 29 9 E
Gemlik Körfezi, Turkey 45 F12 40 25N 28 55 E
Gemona del Friuli, Italy 41 B10 46 16N 13 9 E
Gemsa, Egypt ...... 80 B3 27 39N 33 35 E
Gemsbok △, Botswana 88 D3 25 5S 21 1 E
Gemünden, Germany . 25 E5 50 3N 9 42 E
Genale →, Ethiopia . 81 F4 6 2N 39 1 E
Genç, Turkey ...... 73 C9 38 44N 40 34 E
Gençay, France ..... 20 B4 46 23N 0 23 E
Geneina, Gebel, Egypt 80 B3 29 2N 33 55 E
General Acha, Argentina 126 D3 37 20S 64 38W
General Alvear, Buenos Aires, Argentina 126 D4 36 0S 60 0W
General Alvear, Mendoza, Argentina . 126 D2 35 0S 67 40W
General Artigas, Paraguay 126 B4 26 52S 56 16W
General Belgrano, Argentina 126 D4 36 35S 58 47W
General Bernardo O'Higgins, Antarctica 5 C18 63 0S 58 3W
General Cabrera, Argentina 126 C3 32 53S 63 52W
General Cepeda, Mexico 118 B4 25 23N 101 27W
General Guido, Argentina 126 D4 36 40S 57 50W
General Juan Madariaga, Argentina 126 D4 37 0S 57 0W
General La Madrid, Argentina 126 D3 37 17S 61 20W
General MacArthur, Phil. .... 61 F6 11 18N 125 28 E
General Martin Miguel de Güemes, Argentina 126 A3 24 50S 65 0W
General Paz, Argentina 126 B4 27 45S 57 36W
General Pico, Argentina 126 D3 35 45S 63 50W
General Pinedo, Argentina 126 B3 27 15S 61 20W
General Pinto, Argentina 126 C3 34 45S 61 50W
General Roca, Argentina 128 D3 39 2S 67 35W
General Santos, Phil. . 61 H6 6 5N 125 14 E
General Toshevo, Bulgaria .... 45 C12 43 42N 28 6 E
General Trevino, Mexico 119 B5 26 14N 99 29W
General Trías, Mexico . 118 B3 28 21N 106 22W
General Viamonte, Argentina 126 D3 35 1S 61 3W
General Villegas, Argentina 126 D3 35 5S 63 0W
Genesee, Idaho, U.S.A. 108 C5 46 33N 116 56W
Genesee, Pa., U.S.A. . 116 E7 41 59N 77 54W
Genesee →, U.S.A. .. 116 C7 43 16N 77 36W
Geneseo, Ill., U.S.A. . 112 E9 41 27N 90 9W
Geneseo, N.Y., U.S.A. 116 D7 42 48N 77 49W
Geneva = Genève, Switz. .... 25 J2 46 12N 6 9 E
Geneva, Ala., U.S.A. . 115 K3 31 2N 85 52W
Geneva, N.Y., U.S.A. . 116 D8 42 52N 76 59W
Geneva, Nebr., U.S.A. 112 E6 40 32N 97 36W
Geneva, Ohio, U.S.A. 116 E4 41 48N 80 57W
Geneva, L. = Léman, L., Europe .... 19 F13 46 26N 6 30 E
Geneva, L., U.S.A. .. 114 D1 42 38N 88 30W
Genève, Switz. ..... 25 J2 46 12N 6 9 E
Gengenbach, Germany 25 G4 48 24N 8 1 E
Gengma, China ..... 58 F2 23 32N 99 20 E
Genichesk = Henichesk, Ukraine .... 33 J8 46 12N 34 50 E
Genil →, Spain 37 H5 37 42N 5 19W
Genk, Belgium ..... 17 D5 50 58N 5 32 E
Genlis, France ..... 19 E12 47 11N 5 12 E
Gennargentu, Mti. del, Italy .... 42 B2 40 1N 9 19 E
Gennes, France 18 E6 47 20N 0 17W
Genoa = Génova, Italy 40 D5 44 25N 8 57 E
Genoa, Australia ... 95 F4 37 29S 149 35 E
Genoa, N.Y., U.S.A. . 117 D8 42 40N 76 32W
Genoa, Nebr., U.S.A. 112 E6 41 27N 97 44W
Genoa, Nev., U.S.A. . 110 F7 39 2N 119 50W
Génova, Italy ...... 40 D5 44 25N 8 57 E
Génova ✈ (GOA), Italy 40 D5 44 25N 8 56 E
Génova, G. di, Italy . 40 E6 44 0N 9 0 E
Genriyetty, Ostrov, Russia .... 53 B16 77 6N 156 30 E
Gent, Belgium ..... 17 C3 51 2N 3 42 E
Genteng, Bali, Indonesia 63 J17 8 22S 114 9 E
Genteng, Jawa, Indonesia .... 63 G12 7 22S 106 24 E
Genthin, Germany .. 24 C8 52 25N 12 9 E
Genyem, Indonesia .. 63 E10 2 46S 140 12 E
Genzano di Lucánia, Italy .... 43 B9 40 51N 16 2 E
Genzano di Roma, Italy 41 G9 41 42N 12 41 E
Geoagiu, Romania .. 29 E8 45 55N 23 12 E
Geographe B., Australia 93 F2 33 30S 115 15 E
Geographe Chan., Australia .... 93 D1 24 30S 113 0 E
Geokchay = Göyçay, Azerbaijan .... 35 K8 40 42N 47 43 E
Georg Forster, Antarctica .... 5 D3 71 0S 12 0 E
Georg von Neumayer, Antarctica 5 D17 71 0S 68 30W
Georga, Zemlya, Russia 52 A5 80 30N 49 0 E
George, S. Africa ... 88 E3 33 58S 22 29 E
George →, Canada .. 105 A6 58 49N 66 10W
George, L., N.S.W., Australia .... 95 F4 35 10S 149 25 E
George, L., S. Austral., Australia .... 95 F3 37 25S 140 0 E
George, L., W. Austral., Australia .... 92 D3 22 45S 123 40 E
George, L., Uganda .. 86 B3 0 5N 30 10 E
George, L., Fla., U.S.A. 115 L5 29 17N 81 36W
George, L., N.Y., U.S.A. 117 C11 43 37N 73 33W
George Gill Ra., Australia .... 92 D5 24 22S 131 45 E
George Pt., Australia . 94 J6 20 6S 148 36 E
George River = Kangiqsualujjuaq, Canada 101 C13 58 30N 65 59W
George Sound, N.Z. . 91 L1 44 52S 167 25 E
George Town, Bahamas 120 B4 23 33N 75 47W
George Town, Cayman Is. 120 C3 19 20N 81 24W
George Town, Malaysia 65 c 5 25N 100 20 E
George V Land, Antarctica .... 5 C10 69 0S 148 0 E
George VI Sound, Antarctica 5 D17 71 0S 68 0W

George West, U.S.A. .. 113 L5 28 20N 98 7W
Georgetown = Janjanbureh, Gambia 82 C2 13 30N 14 47W
Georgetown, Australia 94 B3 18 17S 143 33 E
Georgetown, Ont., Canada 116 C5 43 40N 79 56W
Georgetown, P.E.I., Canada 105 C7 46 13N 62 24W
Georgetown, Guyana . 124 B7 6 50N 58 12W
Georgetown, Calif., U.S.A. 110 G6 38 54N 120 50W
Georgetown, Colo., U.S.A. 108 G11 39 42N 105 42W
Georgetown, Ky., U.S.A. 114 F3 38 13N 84 33W
Georgetown, N.Y., U.S.A. 117 D9 42 46N 75 44W
Georgetown, Ohio, U.S.A. 114 F4 38 52N 83 54W
Georgetown, S.C., U.S.A. 115 J6 33 23N 79 17W
Georgetown, Tex., U.S.A. 113 K6 30 38N 97 41W
Georgia □, U.S.A. .. 115 K5 32 50N 83 15W
Georgia ■, Asia .... 35 J6 42 0N 43 0 E
Georgia, Str. of, Canada 102 D4 49 25N 124 0W
Georgian B., Canada . 116 A4 45 15N 81 0W
Georgian Bay Islands △, Canada 116 B5 44 53N 79 52W
Georgina →, Australia 94 C2 23 30S 139 47 E
Georgina I., Canada . 116 B5 44 22N 79 17W
Georgiyevsk, Russia . 35 H6 44 12N 43 28 E
Georgsmarienhütte, Germany .... 24 C4 52 13N 8 3 E
Gera, Germany ..... 24 E8 50 53N 12 4 E
Geraardsbergen, Belgium .... 17 D3 50 45N 3 53 E
Geral, Serra, Brazil .. 127 B6 26 25S 50 0W
Geral de Goiás, Serra, Brazil 125 F9 12 0S 46 0W
Geraldine, U.S.A. ... 108 C8 47 36N 110 16W
Geraldton, Australia . 93 E1 28 48S 114 32 E
Geraldton, Canada .. 104 C2 49 44N 86 59W
Gérardmer, France .. 19 D13 48 3N 6 50 E
Gercüş, Turkey ..... 73 D9 37 34N 41 23 E
Gerede, Turkey ..... 72 B5 40 45N 32 10 E
Gerês, Sierra do, Portugal 36 D3 41 48N 8 0W
Gereshk, Afghan. ... 66 D4 31 47N 64 35 E
Geretsried, Germany . 25 H7 47 51N 11 28 E
Gérgal, Spain 39 H2 37 7N 2 31W
Gerik, Malaysia .... 65 K3 5 50N 101 10 E
Gering, U.S.A. 112 E3 41 50N 103 40W
Gerlach, U.S.A. 108 F4 40 39N 119 21W
Gerlachovský štit, Slovak Rep. ...... 27 B13 49 11N 20 7 E
German Planina, Macedonia .... 44 D6 42 20N 22 0 E
Germansen Landing, Canada 102 B4 55 43N 124 40W
Germantown, U.S.A. . 113 M10 35 5N 89 49W
Germany ■, Europe . 24 E6 51 0N 10 0 E
Germencik, Turkey .. 47 D9 37 52N 27 37 E
Germering, Germany . 25 G7 48 8N 11 22 E
Germersheim, Germany 25 F4 49 12N 8 22 E
Germ ī, Iran .... 71 B6 39 1N 48 3 E
Germiston, S. Africa . 89 D4 26 15S 28 10 E
Gernsheim, Germany . 25 F4 49 45N 8 30 E
Gero, Japan .... 55 G8 35 48N 137 14 E
Gerokgak, Indonesia . 63 J17 8 15S 114 27 E
Gerolzhofen, Germany 25 F6 49 54N 10 21 E
Gerona = Girona, Spain 38 D7 41 58N 2 46 E
Gerrard, Canada ... 102 C5 50 30N 117 17W
Gers □, France ..... 20 E4 43 35N 0 30 E
Gers →, France .... 20 D4 44 9N 0 39 E
Gersfeld, Germany .. 24 E5 50 27N 9 56 E
Gersthofen, Germany 25 G6 48 25N 10 53 E
Gertak Sanggul, Malaysia .... 65 c 5 17N 100 12 E
Gertak Sanggul, Tanjung, Malaysia . 65 c 5 16N 100 11 E
Gerung, Indonesia .. 63 K19 8 43S 116 7 E
Gerzat, France ..... 20 C7 45 48N 3 8 E
Gerze, Turkey ...... 72 B6 41 48N 35 12 E
Geseke, Germany ... 24 D4 51 38N 8 31 E
Geser, Indonesia .... 63 E8 3 50S 130 54 E
Gesso →, Italy ..... 40 D4 44 24N 7 33 E
Gestro, Wabi →, Ethiopia .... 81 G5 4 12N 42 2 E
Getafe, Spain 36 E7 40 18N 3 44W
Getinge, Sweden ... 11 H6 56 49N 12 44 E
Gettysburg, Pa., U.S.A. 114 F7 39 50N 77 14W
Gettysburg, S. Dak., U.S.A. 112 C5 45 1N 99 57W
Getxo, Spain 38 B2 43 21N 2 59W
Getz Ice Shelf, Antarctica 5 D14 75 0S 130 0W
Gevaş, Turkey ..... 73 C10 38 15N 43 6 E
Gévaudan, France .. 20 D7 44 40N 3 40 E
Gevgelija, Macedonia . 44 E6 41 9N 22 30 E
Gévora →, Spain ... 37 G4 38 53N 6 57W
Gewani, Ethiopia ... 81 E5 10 12N 40 40 E
Gex, France .... 19 F13 46 21N 6 3 E
Geyikli, Turkey ..... 47 B8 39 48N 26 12 E
Geyser, U.S.A. 108 C8 47 16N 110 30W
Geyserville, U.S.A. .. 110 G4 38 42N 122 54W
Geyve, Turkey ..... 72 B4 40 30N 30 18 E
Ghâbat el Arab = Wang Kai, Sudan .... 81 F2 9 3N 29 23 E
Ghabeish, Sudan ... 81 E2 12 9N 27 21 E
Ghaggar →, India .. 68 E6 29 30N 74 53 E
Ghaghara →, India . 69 G11 25 45N 84 40 E
Ghaghat →, Bangla. 69 G13 25 19N 89 38 E
Ghagra, India ...... 69 H11 23 17N 84 33 E
Ghagra →, India ... 69 F9 27 29N 81 9 E
Ghalla, Wadi el →, Sudan .... 81 E2 10 25N 27 32 E
Ghana ■, W. Afr. .. 83 D4 8 0N 1 0W
Ghansor, India ..... 69 H9 22 39N 80 1 E
Ghanzi, Botswana .. 88 C3 21 50S 21 34 E
Gharb el Istiwa'iya □, Sudan .... 81 G3 5 0N 30 0 E
Gharb Kordofân □, Sudan .... 81 E2 13 0N 27 0 E
Gharbîya, Es Sahrâ el, Egypt .... 80 B2 27 40N 26 30 E
Ghardaïa, Algeria ... 78 B6 32 20N 3 37 E
Ghârib, G., Egypt ... 80 B3 28 6N 32 54 E
Gharig, Sudan ..... 81 E2 10 47N 27 23 E
Gharyān, Libya .... 79 B8 32 10N 13 0 E
Ghat, Libya .... 79 D8 24 59N 10 11 E
Ghatal, India ...... 69 H12 22 40N 87 46 E
Ghatampur, India .. 69 F9 26 8N 80 13 E
Ghats, Eastern, India . 66 N11 14 0N 78 50 E
Ghats, Western, India 66 N9 14 0N 75 0 E
Ghatsila, India ..... 69 H12 22 36N 86 29 E
Ghattī, Si. Arabia ... 70 D3 31 16N 37 31 E

Ghawdex = Gozo, Malta 49 C1 36 3N 14 15 E
Ghazal, Bahr el →, Chad .... 79 F9 13 0N 15 47 E
Ghazâl, Bahr el →, Sudan .... 81 F3 9 31N 30 25 E
Ghaziabad, India ... 68 E7 28 42N 77 26 E
Ghazipur, India .... 69 G10 25 38N 83 35 E
Ghazni, Afghan. .... 68 C3 33 30N 68 28 E
Ghaznī □, Afghan. .. 66 C6 32 10N 68 20 E
Ghedi, Italy .... 40 C7 45 24N 10 16 E
Ghelari, Romania ... 28 E7 45 38N 22 45 E
Ghent = Gent, Belgium 17 C3 51 2N 3 42 E
Gheorghe Gheorghiu-Dej = Oneşti, Romania .... 29 D11 46 17N 26 47 E
Gheorgheni, Romania 29 D10 46 43N 25 41 E
Gherla, Romania ... 28 C8 47 2N 23 57 E
Ghidigeni, Romania . 29 D12 46 17N 27 30 E
Ghilarza, Italy ..... 42 B1 40 7N 8 50 E
Ghimes-Făget, Romania 29 D11 46 35N 26 2 E
Ghīnah, Wādī al →, Si. Arabia .... 70 D3 30 27N 38 14 E
Ghisonaccia, France . 21 F13 42 1N 9 26 E
Ghisoni, France .... 21 F13 42 7N 9 12 E
Ghizao, Afghan. .... 68 C1 33 20N 65 44 E
Ghizar →, Pakistan . 69 A5 36 15N 73 43 E
Ghot Ogrein, Egypt . 80 A2 31 10N 25 20 E
Ghotaru, India ..... 68 F4 27 20N 70 1 E
Ghotki, Pakistan ... 68 E3 28 5N 69 21 E
Ghowr □, Afghan. .. 66 C4 34 0N 64 20 E
Ghudāf, W. al →, Iraq 70 C4 32 56N 43 30 E
Ghudāmis, Libya ... 77 C4 30 11N 9 29 E
Ghudāmis □, Libya . 79 B8 30 25N 10 25 E
Ghughri, India ..... 69 H9 22 39N 80 41 E
Ghugus, India ...... 66 K11 19 58N 79 12 E
Ghulam Mohammad Barrage, Pakistan . 68 G3 25 30N 68 20 E
Ghūrīān, Afghan. ... 66 B2 34 17N 61 25 E
Ghusri, India ...... 69 H13 22 39N 88 21 E
Gia Dinh, Vietnam .. 65 G6 10 49N 106 42 E
Gia Lai = Plei Ku, Vietnam .... 64 F7 13 57N 108 0 E
Gia Nghia, Vietnam . 65 G6 11 58N 107 42 E
Gia Ngoc, Vietnam .. 64 E7 14 50N 108 58 E
Gia Vuc, Vietnam ... 64 E7 14 42N 108 34 E
Giannutri, Italy .... 40 F8 42 15N 11 6 E
Giant Forest, U.S.A. . 110 J8 36 36N 118 43W
Giant Mts. = Krkonoše, Czech Rep. .... 26 A8 50 50N 15 35 E
Giant Sequoia △, U.S.A. 110 K8 36 0N 118 32W
Giants Causeway, U.K. 12 A5 55 16N 6 29W
Gianyar, Indonesia .. 63 K18 8 32S 115 20 E
Giarabub = Al Jaghbūb, Libya .... 79 C10 29 42N 24 38 E
Giarre, Italy .... 43 E8 37 43N 15 11 E
Giaveno, Italy ..... 40 C4 45 2N 7 21 E
Gibara, Cuba 120 B4 21 9N 76 11W
Gibb River, Australia 92 C4 16 26S 126 26 E
Gibbon, U.S.A. 112 E5 40 45N 98 51W
Gibe →, Ethiopia ... 81 F4 7 20N 37 36 E
Gibellina Nuova, Italy 42 E5 37 48N 12 52 E
Gibeon, Namibia ... 88 D2 25 9S 17 43 E
Gibraléon, Spain ... 37 H4 37 23N 6 58W
Gibraltar ⊠, Europe . 37 J5 36 7N 5 22W
Gibraltar, Str. of, Medit. S. 37 K5 35 55N 5 40W
Gibraltar Range △, Australia .... 95 D5 29 31S 152 19 E
Gibson Desert, Australia 92 D4 24 0S 126 0 E
Gibsons, Canada ... 102 D4 49 24N 123 32W
Gibsonville, U.S.A. .. 110 F6 39 46N 120 54W
Giddings, U.S.A. ... 113 K6 30 11N 96 56W
Gidole, Ethiopia ... 81 F4 5 40N 37 25 E
Giebnegáisi = Kebnekaise, Sweden 8 C18 67 53N 18 33 E
Gien, France ...... 19 E9 47 40N 2 36 E
Giengen, Germany .. 25 G6 48 37N 10 14 E
Giessen, Germany ... 24 E4 50 34N 8 41 E
Gīfan, Iran .... 71 B8 37 54N 57 28 E
Gifatin, Geziret, Egypt 80 B3 27 10N 33 50 E
Gifhorn, Germany .. 24 C6 52 30N 10 33 E
Gift Lake, Canada .. 102 B5 55 53N 115 49W
Gifu, Japan .... 55 G8 35 30N 136 45 E
Gifu □, Japan ..... 55 G8 35 40N 137 0 E
Gigant, Russia ..... 35 G5 46 28N 41 20 E
Giganta, Sa. de la, Mexico 118 B2 25 30N 111 30W
Gigen, Bulgaria .... 45 C8 43 40N 24 28 E
Gigha, U.K. 13 F3 55 42N 5 44W
Gíglio, Italy .... 40 F7 42 20N 10 52 E
Gignac, France ..... 20 E7 43 39N 3 32 E
Giguela →, Spain .. 37 F7 39 8N 3 44W
Gijón, Spain 36 B5 43 32N 5 42W
Gil I., Canada 102 C3 53 12N 129 15W
Gila →, U.S.A. 109 K6 32 43N 114 33W
Gila Bend, U.S.A. .. 109 K7 32 57N 112 43W
Gila Bend Mts., U.S.A. 109 K7 33 10N 113 0W
Gila Cliff Dwellings △, U.S.A. 109 K9 33 2N 108 16W
Gilān □, Iran ...... 71 B6 37 0N 50 0 E
Gilău, Romania .... 29 D8 46 45N 23 23 E
Gilbert →, Australia 94 B3 16 35S 141 15 E
Gilbert Is., Kiribati .. 96 G9 1 0N 172 0 E
Gilbert River, Australia 94 B3 18 9S 142 52 E
Gilead, U.S.A. 117 B14 44 24N 70 59W
Gilf el Kebîr, Hadabat el, Egypt .... 80 C2 23 50N 25 50 E
Gilford I., Canada .. 102 C3 50 40N 126 30W
Gilgandra, Australia . 95 E4 31 43S 148 39 E
Gilgil, Kenya ...... 86 C4 0 30S 36 20 E
Gilgit, India .... 69 B6 35 50N 74 15 E
Gilgit →, Pakistan .. 69 B6 35 44N 74 37 E
Gili →, Mozam. .... 87 F4 16 39S 38 27 E
Gilimanuk, Indonesia 63 J17 8 10S 114 26 E
Giljeva Planina, Serbia & M. ...... 44 C3 43 9N 20 0 E
Gillam, Canada 103 B10 56 20N 94 40W
Gilleleje, Denmark .. 11 H6 56 8N 12 19 E
Gillen, L., Australia . 93 E3 26 11S 124 38 E
Gilles, L., Australia . 95 E2 32 50S 136 45 E
Gillette, U.S.A. 112 C2 44 18N 105 30W
Gilliat, Australia ... 94 C3 20 40S 141 28 E
Gillingham, U.K. ... 15 F8 51 23N 0 33 E
Gilmer, U.S.A. 113 J7 32 44N 94 57W
Gilmore, L., Australia 93 F3 32 29S 121 37 E
Gilo →, Ethiopia ... 81 F3 8 10N 33 15 E
Gilort →, Romania . 29 F8 44 38N 23 32 E
Gilroy, U.S.A. 110 H5 37 1N 121 34W
Gimbi, Ethiopia .... 81 F4 9 3N 35 42 E
Gimie, Mt., St. Lucia . 121 f 13 54N 61 0W
Gimli, Canada 103 C9 50 40N 97 0W
Gimo, Sweden ..... 10 D12 60 11N 18 12 E
Gimone →, France . 20 E5 44 0N 1 6 E
Gimont, France .... 20 E4 43 38N 0 52 E
Gin Gin, Australia .. 95 D5 25 0S 151 58 E
Gingin, Australia ... 93 F2 31 22S 115 54 E

Gingindlovu, S. Africa 89 D5 29 2S 31 30 E
Ginir, Ethiopia ..... 81 F5 7 6N 40 40 E
Ginosa, Italy ...... 43 B9 40 35N 16 45 E
Ginzo de Limia = Xinzo de Limia, Spain ... 36 C3 42 3N 7 47W
Gióia, G. di, Italy ... 43 D8 38 30N 15 45 E
Gióia del Colle, Italy . 43 B9 40 48N 16 55 E
Gióia Táuro, Italy ... 43 D8 38 25N 15 54 E
Gioiosa Iónica, Italy . 43 D9 38 20N 16 18 E
Gioiosa Marea, Italy . 43 D7 38 10N 14 54 E
Gióna, Óros, Greece . 46 C4 38 38N 22 14 E
Giovi, Passo dei, Italy 40 D5 44 33N 8 57 E
Giovinazzo, Italy ... 43 A9 41 11N 16 40 E
Gir Hills, India .... 68 J4 21 0N 71 0 E
Girab, India .... 68 F4 26 2N 70 38 E
Girâfi, W. →, Egypt . 74 F3 29 58N 34 39 E
Giraltovce, Slovak Rep. 27 B14 49 7N 21 32 E
Girard, Kans., U.S.A. 113 G7 37 31N 94 51W
Girard, Ohio, U.S.A. 116 E4 41 9N 80 42W
Girard, Pa., U.S.A. . 116 E4 42 0N 80 19W
Girdle Ness, U.K. ... 13 D6 57 9N 2 3W
Giresun, Turkey .... 73 B8 40 55N 38 30 E
Girga, Egypt ...... 80 B3 26 17N 31 55 E
Giri →, India ...... 68 D7 30 28N 77 41 E
Giridih, India ...... 69 G12 24 10N 86 21 E
Girifalco, Italy ..... 43 D9 38 49N 16 25 E
Girne = Kyrenia, Cyprus 49 D12 35 20N 33 20 E
Giro, Nigeria ...... 83 C5 11 7N 4 42 E
Giromagny, France . 19 E13 47 45N 6 50 E
Giron = Kiruna, Sweden 8 C19 67 52N 20 15 E
Girona, Spain ...... 38 D7 41 58N 2 46 E
Girona □, Spain .... 38 C7 42 11N 2 30 E
Gironde □, France .. 20 D3 44 45N 0 30W
Gironde →, France . 20 C2 45 32N 1 7W
Gironella, Spain .... 38 C6 42 2N 1 53 E
Girraween △, Australia 95 D5 28 51S 151 54 E
Giru, Australia ..... 94 B4 19 30S 147 5 E
Girvan, U.K. 13 F4 55 14N 4 51W
Gisborne, N.Z. ..... 91 H7 38 39S 178 5 E
Gisenyi, Rwanda ... 86 C2 1 41S 29 15 E
Gisors, France ..... 19 C8 49 15N 1 47 E
Gitega, Burundi .... 86 C2 3 26S 29 56 E
Giuba →, Somali Rep. 75 G3 1 30N 42 35 E
Giugliano in Campania, Italy .... 43 B7 40 56N 14 12 E
Giulianova, Italy ... 41 F10 42 45N 13 57 E
Giurgeni, Romania .. 29 F12 44 45N 27 48 E
Giurgiu, Romania ... 29 G10 43 52N 25 57 E
Giurgiu □, Romania . 29 F10 44 20N 26 0 E
Giurgiuleşti, Moldova 29 E13 45 29N 28 12 E
Give, Denmark ..... 11 J3 55 51N 9 13 E
Givet, France ...... 19 B11 50 8N 4 49 E
Givors, France ..... 21 C8 45 35N 4 45 E
Givry, France ...... 19 F11 46 41N 4 46 E
Giyon, Ethiopia .... 81 F4 8 33N 38 1 E
Giza = El Gîza, Egypt 80 J7 30 0N 31 10 E
Gizhiga, Russia .... 53 C16 62 3N 160 30 E
Gizhiginskaya Guba, Russia .... 53 C16 61 0N 158 0 E
Gizycko, Poland .... 30 D8 54 2N 21 48 E
Gizzeria, Italy ..... 43 D9 38 59N 16 12 E
Gjalicë e Lumës, Mal., Albania .... 44 D4 42 2N 20 25 E
Gjegjan, Albania ... 44 E4 41 58N 20 3 E
Gjirokastër, Albania . 44 F4 40 7N 20 10 E
Gjoa Haven, Canada 100 B10 68 38N 95 53W
Gjøvik, Norway .... 9 F14 60 47N 10 43 E
Gjuhës, Kep i, Albania 44 G2 40 28N 19 15 E
Glace Bay, Canada .. 105 C8 46 11N 59 58W
Glacier △, Canada .. 102 C5 51 15N 117 30W
Glacier △, U.S.A. ... 108 B7 48 30N 113 18W
Glacier Bay △, U.S.A. 102 B1 58 45N 136 30W
Glacier Peak, U.S.A. . 108 B3 48 7N 121 7W
Gladewater, U.S.A. . 113 J7 32 33N 94 56W
Gladstone, Queens., Australia .... 94 C5 23 52S 151 16 E
Gladstone, S. Austral., Australia .... 95 E2 33 15S 138 22 E
Gladstone, Canada .. 103 C9 50 13N 98 57W
Gladstone, U.S.A. .. 114 C2 45 51N 87 1W
Gladwin, U.S.A. ... 114 D3 43 59N 84 29W
Glafsfjorden, Sweden 10 E6 59 30N 12 37 E
Glagah, Indonesia .. 63 J17 8 13S 114 18 E
Głogów Małopolski, Poland .... 31 H8 50 10N 21 56 E
Glåma = Glomma →, Norway .... 9 G14 59 12N 10 57 E
Gláma, Iceland 8 D2 65 48N 23 0W
Glamis, U.S.A. 111 N11 32 55N 115 5W
Glamoč, Bos.-H. .... 41 D13 44 3N 16 51 E
Glamorgan, Vale of □, U.K. 15 F4 51 28N 3 25W
Glamsbjerg, Denmark 11 J4 55 17N 10 6 E
Glarus, Switz. ..... 25 H5 47 3N 9 4 E
Glarus □, Switz. .... 25 J5 47 0N 9 5 E
Glasco, Kans., U.S.A. 112 F6 39 22N 97 50W
Glasco, N.Y., U.S.A. 117 D11 42 3N 73 57W
Glasgow, U.K. 13 F4 55 51N 4 15W
Glasgow, Ky., U.S.A. 114 G3 37 0N 85 55W
Glasgow, Mont., U.S.A. 108 B10 48 12N 106 38W
Glasgow, City of □, U.K. 13 F4 55 51N 4 12W
Glasgow International ✈ (GLA), U.K. 13 F4 55 51N 4 21W
Glaslyn, Canada 103 C7 53 22N 108 21W
Glastonbury, U.K. .. 15 F5 51 9N 2 43W
Glastonbury, U.S.A. . 117 E12 41 43N 72 37W
Glauchau, Germany . 24 E8 50 49N 12 33 E
Glava, Sweden ..... 10 E6 59 33N 12 35 E
Glavice, Croatia .... 41 E13 43 43N 16 41 E
Glazov, Russia ..... 34 A11 58 9N 52 40 E
Gleichen, Canada ... 102 C6 50 52N 113 3W
Gleisdorf, Austria ... 26 D8 47 6N 15 44 E
Gleiwitz = Gliwice, Poland .... 31 H5 50 22N 18 41 E
Glen, U.S.A. 117 B13 44 7N 71 11W
Glen Affric, U.K. ... 13 D3 57 17N 5 1W
Glen Canyon, U.S.A. 109 H8 37 15N 111 0W
Glen Canyon △, U.S.A. 109 H8 37 15N 111 0W
Glen Canyon Dam, U.S.A. 109 H8 36 57N 111 29W
Glen Coe, U.K. 13 E3 56 40N 5 0W
Glen Cove, U.S.A. .. 117 F11 40 52N 73 38W
Glen Garry, U.K. ... 13 D3 57 3N 5 7W
Glen Innes, Australia 95 D5 29 44S 151 44 E
Glen Lyon, U.S.A. .. 117 E8 41 10N 76 5W
Glen Mor, U.K. 13 D4 57 9N 4 37W
Glen More △, U.K. . 13 D5 57 8N 3 40W
Glen Moriston, U.K. 13 D4 57 11N 4 52W
Glen Robertson, Canada 117 A10 45 22N 74 30W
Glen Spean, U.K. ... 13 E4 56 53N 4 40W
Glénan, Is. de, France 18 E3 47 43N 4 0W
Glenariff △, Ireland . 12 A5 55 2N 6 10W
Glencoe, Canada ... 116 D3 42 45N 81 43W
Glencoe, S. Africa .. 89 D5 28 11S 30 11 E
Glencoe, U.S.A. 112 C7 44 46N 94 9W

Glendale, *Ariz., U.S.A.* **109 K7** 33 32N 112 11W
Glendale, *Calif., U.S.A.* **111 L8** 34 9N 118 15W
Glendale, *Zimbabwe* . **87 F3** 17 22 S 31 5 E
Glendive, *U.S.A.* **112 B2** 47 7N 104 43W
Glendo, *U.S.A.* **112 D2** 42 30N 105 2W
Gleneig →, *Australia* .. **95 F2** 38 4 S 140 59 E
Glenfield, *U.S.A.* **117 C9** 43 43N 75 24W
Glengarriff, *Ireland* ... **12 E2** 51 45N 9 34W
Glenmont, *U.S.A.* **116 F2** 40 31N 82 6W
Glenmorgan, *Australia* . **95 D4** 27 14 S 149 42 E
Glenn, *U.S.A.* **110 F4** 39 31N 122 1W
Glennallen, *U.S.A.* ... **100 B5** 62 7N 145 33W
Glennamaddy, *Ireland* . **12 C3** 53 37N 8 33W
Glenns Ferry, *U.S.A.* . **108 E6** 42 57N 115 18W
Glenore, *Australia* ... **94 B3** 17 50 S 141 12 E
Glenreagh, *Australia* .. **95 E5** 30 2 S 153 1 E
Glenrock, *U.S.A.* **108 E11** 42 52N 105 52W
Glenrothes, *U.K.* **13 E5** 56 12N 3 10W
Glens Falls, *U.S.A.* ... **117 C11** 43 19N 73 39W
Glenside, *U.S.A.* **117 F9** 40 6N 75 9W
Glenties, *Ireland* **12 B3** 54 49N 8 16W
Glenveagh △, *Ireland* . **12 A3** 55 3N 8 1W
Glenville, *U.S.A.* **114 F5** 38 56N 80 50W
Glenwood, *Canada* ... **105 C9** 49 0N 54 58W
Glenwood, *Ark., U.S.A.* **113 H8** 34 20N 93 33W
Glenwood, *Iowa, U.S.A.* **112 E7** 41 3N 95 45W
Glenwood, *Minn., U.S.A.* **112 C7** 45 39N 95 23W
Glenwood, *Wash., U.S.A.* **110 D5** 46 1N 121 17W
Glenwood Springs, *U.S.A.* **108 G10** 39 33N 107 19W
Glettinganes, *Iceland* . **8 D7** 65 30N 13 37W
Glifádha, *Greece* .... **46 D5** 37 52N 23 45 E
Glimåkra, *Sweden* ... **11 H8** 56 17N 14 7 E
Glina, *Croatia* ..... **41 C13** 45 20N 16 6 E
Glinojeck, *Poland* ... **31 F7** 52 49N 20 21 E
Gliwice, *Poland* .... **31 H5** 50 22N 18 41 E
Globe, *U.S.A.* **109 K8** 33 24N 110 47W
Glodeanu Siliştea, *Romania* **29 F11** 44 50N 26 48 E
Glodeni, *Moldova* ... **29 C12** 47 45N 27 31 E
Glödnitz, *Austria* ... **26 E7** 46 53N 14 7 E
Gloggnitz, *Austria* .. **26 D8** 47 41N 15 56 E
Głogów, *Poland* .... **31 G3** 51 37N 16 5 E
Głogówek, *Poland* ... **31 H4** 50 21N 17 53 E
Glomma →, *Norway* .. **9 G14** 59 12N 10 57 E
Glorieuses, Is., *Ind. Oc.* **89 A8** 11 30 S 47 20 E
Glóssa, *Greece* ..... **46 B5** 39 10N 23 45 E
Glossop, *U.K.* **14 D6** 53 27N 1 56W
Gloucester, *Australia* . **95 E5** 32 0 S 151 59 E
Gloucester, *U.K.* ... **15 F5** 51 53N 2 15W
Gloucester, *U.S.A.* .. **117 D14** 42 37N 70 40W
Gloucester I., *Australia* **94 J6** 20 2 S 148 30 E
Gloucester Island △, *Australia* **94 J6** 20 2 S 148 30 E
Gloucester Point, *U.S.A.* **114 G7** 37 15N 76 29W
Gloucestershire □, *U.K.* **15 F5** 51 46N 2 15W
Gloversville, *U.S.A.* .. **117 C10** 43 3N 74 21W
Glovertown, *Canada* .. **105 C9** 48 40N 54 3W
Głowno, *Poland* .... **31 G6** 51 59N 19 42 E
Głubczyce, *Poland* ... **31 H4** 50 13N 17 52 E
Glubokiy, *Russia* ... **35 F5** 48 35N 40 25 E
Glubokoye = Hlybokaye, *Belarus* **32 E4** 55 10N 27 45 E
Głuchołazy, *Poland* .. **31 H4** 50 19N 17 24 E
Glücksburg, *Germany* . **24 A5** 54 50N 9 33 E
Glückstadt, *Germany* . **24 B5** 53 45N 9 25 E
Glukhov = Hlukhiv, *Ukraine* **33 G7** 51 40N 33 58 E
Glusk, *Belarus* ..... **32 F5** 52 53N 28 41 E
Głuszyca, *Poland* ... **31 H3** 50 41N 16 23 E
Glyngøre, *Denmark* .. **11 H2** 56 46N 8 52 E
Gmünd, *Kärnten, Austria* **26 E6** 46 54N 13 31 E
Gmünd, *Niederösterreich, Austria* **26 C8** 48 45N 15 0 E
Gmunden, *Austria* ... **26 D6** 47 55N 13 48 E
Gnarp, *Sweden* ..... **10 B11** 62 3N 17 16 E
Gnesta, *Sweden* .... **10 E11** 59 3N 17 17 E
Gniew, *Poland* ..... **30 E5** 53 50N 18 50 E
Gniewkowo, *Poland* .. **31 F5** 52 54N 18 25 E
Gniezno, *Poland* .... **31 F4** 52 30N 17 35 E
Gnjilane, *Serbia & M.* . **44 D5** 42 28N 21 29 E
Gnoien, *Germany* ... **24 B8** 53 58N 12 41 E
Gnosjö, *Sweden* .... **11 G7** 57 22N 13 43 E
Gnowangerup, *Australia* **93 F2** 33 58 S 117 59 E
Go Cong, *Vietnam* ... **65 G6** 10 22N 106 40 E
Gô-no-ura, *Japan* ... **55 H4** 33 44N 129 40 E
Goa, *India* .... **66 M8** 15 33N 73 59 E
Goa □, *India* ..... **66 M8** 15 33N 73 59 E
Goalen Hd., *Australia* . **95 F5** 36 33 S 150 4 E
Goalpara, *India* .... **67 F17** 26 10N 90 40 E
Goaltor, *India* ..... **69 H12** 22 43N 87 10 E
Goalundo Ghat, *Bangla.* **69 H13** 23 50N 89 47 E
Goaso, *Ghana* **82 D4** 6 48N 2 30W
Goat Fell, *U.K.* **13 F3** 55 38N 5 11W
Goba, *Ethiopia* ..... **81 F4** 7 1N 39 59 E
Goba, *Mozam.* ..... **89 D5** 26 15 S 32 13 E
Gobabis, *Namibia* ... **88 C2** 22 30 S 19 0 E
Göbel, *Turkey* ..... **45 F12** 40 10N 28 9 E
Gobi, *Asia* .... **56 C6** 44 0N 111 0 E
Gobō, *Japan* ...... **55 H7** 33 53N 135 10 E
Gobo, *Sudan* ...... **81 F3** 5 40N 31 10 E
Göçbeyli, *Turkey* ... **47 B9** 39 13N 27 25 E
Goch, *Germany* ..... **24 D2** 51 41N 6 9 E
Gochas, *Namibia* ... **88 C2** 24 59 S 18 55 E
Godalming, *U.K.* ... **15 F7** 51 11N 0 36W
Godavari →, *India* .. **67 L13** 16 25N 82 18 E
Godavari Pt., *India* .. **67 L13** 17 0N 82 20 E
Godbout, *Canada* ... **105 C6** 49 20N 67 38W
Godda, *India* ...... **69 G12** 24 50N 87 13 E
Godech, *Bulgaria* ... **44 C7** 43 1N 23 4 E
Goderich, *Canada* ... **116 C3** 43 45N 81 41W
Goderville, *France* ... **18 C7** 49 38N 0 22 E
Godfrey Ra., *Australia* **93 D2** 24 0 S 117 0 E
Godhavn = Qeqertarsuaq, *Greenland* **101 B14** 69 15N 53 38W
Godhra, *India* ..... **68 H5** 22 49N 73 40 E
Gödöllő, *Hungary* ... **28 C4** 47 38N 19 25 E
Godoy Cruz, *Argentina* **126 C2** 32 56 S 68 52W
Gods →, *Canada* ... **104 A1** 56 22N 92 51W
Gods L., *Canada* **104 B1** 54 40N 94 15W
Gods River, *Canada* .. **103 C10** 54 50N 94 5W
Godthåb = Nuuk, *Greenland* **101 B14** 64 10N 51 35W
Goeie Hoop, Kaap die = Good Hope, C. of, *S. Africa* **88 E2** 34 24 S 18 30 E
Goéland, L. au, *Canada* **104 C4** 49 50N 76 48W
Goélands, L. aux, *Canada* **105 A7** 55 27N 64 17W
Goeree, *Neths.* ..... **17 C3** 51 50N 4 0 E
Goes, *Neths.* ...... **17 C3** 51 30N 3 55 E
Goffstown, *U.S.A.* ... **117 C13** 43 1N 71 36W

Gogama, *Canada* **104 C3** 47 35N 81 43W
Gogebic, L., *U.S.A.* .. **112 B10** 46 30N 89 35W
Goggetti, *Ethiopia* ... **81 F4** 8 11N 38 35 E
Gogolin, *Poland* .... **31 H5** 50 30N 18 0 E
Gogonou, *Benin* .... **83 C5** 10 50N 2 50 E
Gogra = Ghaghara →, *India* **69 G11** 25 45N 84 40 E
Gogriâl, *Sudan* ..... **81 F2** 8 30N 28 8 E
Gogti, *Ethiopia* .... **81 E5** 10 7N 42 51 E
Gohana, *India* ..... **68 E7** 29 8N 76 42 E
Gohargaq, *India* .... **68 H7** 23 1N 77 41 E
Goi →, *India* ..... **68 H6** 22 4N 74 46 E
Goiânia, *Brazil* .... **125 G9** 16 43 S 49 20W
Goiás, *Brazil* ...... **125 G8** 15 55 S 50 10W
Goiás □, *Brazil* .... **125 F9** 12 10 S 48 0W
Goio-Erê, *Brazil* .... **127 A5** 24 12 S 53 1W
Góis, *Portugal* **36 E2** 40 10N 8 6W
Gojam, *Ethiopia* .... **81 E4** 10 55N 36 30 E
Gojeb, Wabi →, *Ethiopia* **81 F4** 7 12N 36 40 E
Gojō, *Japan* ...... **55 G7** 34 21N 135 42 E
Gojra, *Pakistan* .... **68 D5** 31 10N 72 40 E
Gökçeada, *Turkey* ... **45 F9** 40 10N 25 50 E
Gökçedağ, *Turkey* ... **47 B10** 39 33N 28 56 E
Gökçen, *Turkey* .... **47 C9** 38 7N 27 53 E
Gökçeören, *Turkey* .. **47 C10** 38 37N 28 35 E
Gökçeyazı, *Turkey* .. **47 B9** 39 40N 27 40 E
Gökırmak →, *Turkey* . **72 B6** 41 25N 35 8 E
Gökova, *Turkey* .... **47 D10** 37 1N 28 17 E
Gökova Körfezi, *Turkey* **47 E9** 36 55N 27 50 E
Göksu →, *Turkey* ... **72 D6** 36 19N 34 5 E
Göksun, *Turkey* .... **72 C7** 38 2N 36 30 E
Gokteik, *Burma* .... **67 H20** 22 26N 97 0 E
Göktepe, *Turkey* ... **47 D10** 37 25N 28 34 E
Gokurt, *Pakistan* ... **68 E2** 29 40N 67 26 E
Gokwe, *Zimbabwe* ... **89 B4** 18 7 S 28 58 E
Gola, *India* ...... **69 E9** 28 3N 80 32 E
Golakganj, *India* ... **69 F13** 26 8N 89 52 E
Golan Heights = Hagolan, *Syria* **74 C4** 33 0N 35 45 E
Gołańcz, *Poland* .... **31 F4** 52 57N 17 18 E
Goläshkerd, *Iran* ... **71 E8** 27 59N 57 16 E
Golaya Pristen = Hola Pristan, *Ukraine* **33 J7** 46 29N 32 32 E
Gölbaşı, *Adiyaman, Turkey* **72 D7** 37 43N 37 25 E
Gölbaşı, *Ankara, Turkey* **72 C5** 39 47N 32 49 E
Golchikha, *Russia* ... **4 B12** 71 45N 83 30 E
Golconda, *U.S.A.* ... **108 F5** 40 58N 117 30W
Gölcük, *Kocaeli, Turkey* **45 F13** 40 42N 29 48 E
Gölcük, *Niğde, Turkey* **72 C6** 38 14N 34 47 E
Gold, *U.S.A.* **116 E7** 41 52N 77 50W
Gold Beach, *U.S.A.* . **108 E1** 42 25N 124 25W
Gold Coast, *W. Afr.* . **83 E4** 4 0N 1 40W
Gold Hill, *U.S.A.* ... **108 E2** 42 26N 123 3W
Gold River, *Canada* .. **102 D3** 49 46N 126 3W
Gołdap, *Poland* .... **30 D9** 54 19N 22 18 E
Goldberg, *Germany* .. **24 B8** 53 35N 12 4 E
Golden, *Canada* **102 C5** 51 20N 116 59W
Golden B., *N.Z.* .... **91 J4** 40 40 S 172 50 E
Golden Gate, *U.S.A.* . **108 H2** 37 54N 122 30W
Golden Gate Highlands △, *S. Africa* **89 D4** 28 40 S 28 40 E
Golden Hinde, *Canada* **102 D3** 49 40N 125 44W
Golden Lake, *Canada* . **116 A7** 45 34N 77 21W
Golden Spike △, *U.S.A.* **108 F7** 41 37N 112 33W
Golden Vale, *Ireland* . **12 D3** 52 33N 8 17W
Goldendale, *U.S.A.* . **108 D3** 45 49N 120 50W
Goldfield, *U.S.A.* ... **109 H5** 37 42N 117 14W
Goldsand L., *Canada* . **103 B8** 57 2N 101 8W
Goldsboro, *U.S.A.* .. **115 H7** 35 23N 77 59W
Goldsmith, *U.S.A.* .. **113 K3** 31 59N 102 37W
Goldsworthy, *Australia* **92 D2** 20 21 S 119 30 E
Goldthwaite, *U.S.A.* . **113 K5** 31 27N 98 34W
Golegã, *Portugal* ... **37 F2** 39 24N 8 29W
Goleniów, *Poland* ... **30 E1** 53 35N 14 50 E
Golestān □, *Iran* ... **71 B7** 37 20N 55 25 E
Golestānak, *Iran* ... **71 D7** 30 36N 54 14 E
Goleta, *U.S.A.* **111 L7** 34 27N 119 50W
Golfito, *Costa Rica* .. **120 E3** 8 41N 83 5W
Golfo Aranci, *Italy* ... **42 B2** 40 59N 9 38 E
Golfo di Orosei e del Gennargentu △, *Italy* **42 B2** 40 5N 9 15 E
Gölgeli Dağları, *Turkey* **47 D10** 37 10N 28 55 E
Gölhisar, *Turkey* ... **47 D11** 37 9N 29 31 E
Goliad, *U.S.A.* **113 L6** 28 40N 97 23W
Golija, *Serbia & M.* .. **44 C2** 43 5N 18 45 E
Golija, *Serbia & M.* .. **44 C4** 43 22N 20 15 E
Golina, *Poland* ..... **31 F5** 52 15N 18 4 E
Gölköy, *Turkey* .... **72 B7** 40 41N 37 37 E
Göllersdorf, *Austria* . **26 C9** 48 29N 16 7 E
Gölmarmara, *Turkey* . **47 C9** 38 42N 27 55 E
Golo →, *France* .... **21 F13** 42 31N 9 32 E
Gölova, *Turkey* .... **47 E12** 36 48N 30 5 E
Golpāyegān, *Iran* ... **71 C6** 33 27N 50 18 E
Gölpazarı, *Turkey* .. **72 B4** 40 16N 30 18 E
Golra, *Pakistan* .... **68 C5** 33 37N 72 56 E
Golspie, *U.K.* **13 D5** 57 58N 3 59W
Golub-Dobrzyń, *Poland* **31 E6** 53 7N 19 2 E
Golubac, *Serbia & M.* . **44 B5** 44 38N 21 38 E
Golyam Perelik, *Bulgaria* **45 E8** 41 36N 24 33 E
Golyama Kamchiya →, *Bulgaria* **45 C11** 43 10N 27 55 E
Goma, *Dem. Rep. of the Congo* **86 C2** 1 37 S 29 10 E
Gomal Pass, *Pakistan* . **68 D3** 31 56N 69 20 E
Gomati →, *India* ... **69 G10** 25 32N 83 11 E
Gombari, *Dem. Rep. of the Congo* **86 B2** 2 45N 29 3 E
Gombe, *Nigeria* .... **83 C7** 10 19N 11 2 E
Gombe →, *Tanzania* . **86 C3** 4 38 S 31 40 E
Gombe □, *Nigeria* .. **83 C7** 10 10N 11 10 E
Gombi, *Nigeria* .... **83 C7** 10 12N 12 30 E
Gomel = Homyel, *Belarus* **33 F6** 52 28N 31 0 E
Gomera, *Canary Is.* . **48 F2** 28 7N 17 14W
Gómez Palacio, *Mexico* **118 B4** 25 40N 104 0W
Gomīshān, *Iran* .... **71 B7** 37 4N 54 6 E
Gommern, *Germany* . **24 C7** 52 4N 11 50 E
Gomogomo, *Indonesia* **63 F8** 6 39 S 134 43 E
Gomoh, *India* ..... **67 H15** 23 52N 86 10 E
Gomotartsi, *Bulgaria* . **44 B6** 44 6N 22 57 E
Gompa = Ganta, *Liberia* **82 D3** 7 15N 8 59W
Gomphi, *Greece* .... **46 B3** 39 26N 21 36 E
Gonābād, *Iran* ..... **71 C8** 34 15N 58 45 E
Gonaïves, *Haiti* **121 C5** 19 20N 72 42W
Gonarezhou △, *Zimbabwe* **87 G3** 21 32 S 31 55 E
Gonâve, G. de la, *Haiti* **121 C5** 19 29N 72 42W
Gonâve, I. de la, *Haiti* **121 C5** 18 45N 73 0W
Gonbad-e Kāvūs, *Iran* **71 B7** 37 20N 55 25 E
Gönc, *Hungary* .... **28 B5** 48 28N 21 14 E
Gonda, *India* ...... **69 F9** 27 9N 81 58 E
Gondal, *India* ..... **68 J4** 21 58N 70 52 E
Gonder, *Ethiopia* ... **81 E4** 12 39N 37 30 E

Gondia, *India* ...... **66 J12** 21 23N 80 10 E
Gondola, *Mozam.* ... **87 F3** 19 10 S 33 37 E
Gondomar, *Portugal* . **36 D2** 41 10N 8 35W
Gondrecourt-le-Château, *France* **19 D12** 48 31N 5 30 E
Gönen, *Balıkesir, Turkey* **45 F11** 40 6N 27 39 E
Gönen, *Isparta, Turkey* **47 D12** 37 57N 30 31 E
Gönen →, *Turkey* ... **45 F11** 40 6N 27 39 E
Gong Xian, *China* ... **58 C5** 28 23N 104 47 E
Gong'an, *China* .... **59 B9** 30 7N 112 12 E
Gongcheng, *China* ... **59 E8** 24 50N 110 49 E
Gongga Shan, *China* . **58 C3** 29 40N 101 55 E
Gonghe, *China* ..... **60 C5** 36 18N 100 32 E
Gongola →, *Nigeria* . **83 D7** 9 30N 12 4 E
Gongolgon, *Australia* . **95 E4** 30 21 S 146 54 E
Gongshan, *China* ... **58 D2** 27 43N 98 29 E
Gongtan, *China* .... **58 C7** 28 55N 108 20 E
Gongzhuling, *China* .. **57 C13** 43 30N 124 40 E
Goniadz, *Poland* .... **30 E9** 53 30N 22 44 E
Goniri, *Nigeria* .... **83 C7** 11 30N 12 15 E
Gonjo, *China* ...... **58 B2** 30 52N 98 17 E
Gonnesa, *Italy* ..... **42 C1** 39 16N 8 28 E
Gónnos, *Greece* .... **46 B4** 39 52N 22 29 E
Gonnosfanádiga, *Italy* **42 C1** 39 29N 8 39 E
Gonzaga, *Phil.* ..... **61 B5** 18 16N 122 0 E
Gonzales, *Calif., U.S.A.* **110 J5** 36 30N 121 26W
Gonzales, *Tex., U.S.A.* **113 L6** 29 30N 97 27W
González Chaves, *Argentina* **126 D3** 38 2 S 60 5W
Good Hope, C. of, *S. Africa* **88 E2** 34 24 S 18 30 E
Gooderham, *Canada* . **116 B6** 44 54N 78 21W
Goodhouse, *S. Africa* . **88 D2** 28 57 S 18 13 E
Gooding, *U.S.A.* **108 E6** 42 56N 114 43W
Goodland, *U.S.A.* ... **112 F4** 39 21N 101 43W
Goodlow, *Canada* ... **102 B4** 56 20N 120 8W
Goodooga, *Australia* . **95 D4** 29 3 S 147 28 E
Goodsprings, *U.S.A.* . **111 K11** 35 49N 115 27W
Goole, *U.K.* **14 D7** 53 42N 0 53W
Goolgowi, *Australia* .. **95 E4** 33 58 S 145 41 E
Goomalling, *Australia* . **93 F2** 31 15 S 116 49 E
Goomeri, *Australia* .. **95 D5** 26 12 S 152 6 E
Goonda, *Mozam.* ... **87 F3** 19 48 S 33 57 E
Goondiwindi, *Australia* **95 D5** 28 30 S 150 21 E
Goongarrie, *Australia* . **93 F3** 30 7 S 121 30 E
Goongarrie, L., *Australia* **93 F3** 30 3 S 121 9 E
Goonyella, *Australia* . **94 C4** 21 47 S 147 58 E
Goose →, *Canada* ... **105 B7** 53 20N 60 35W
Goose Creek, *U.S.A.* . **115 J5** 32 59N 80 2W
Goose L., *U.S.A.* ... **108 F3** 41 56N 120 26W
Gop, *India* .... **66 H6** 22 5N 69 50 E
Gopalganj, *India* ... **69 F11** 26 28N 84 30 E
Göppingen, *Germany* . **25 G5** 48 42N 9 39 E
Goteşti, *Moldova* ... **29 D13** 46 9N 28 10 E
Gotha, *Germany* .... **24 E6** 50 56N 10 42 E
Gothenburg = Göteborg, *Sweden* **11 G5** 57 43N 11 59 E
Gothenburg, *U.S.A.* . **112 E4** 40 56N 100 10W
Gothèye, *Niger* .... **83 C5** 13 52N 1 34 E
Gotland, *Sweden* ... **11 G12** 57 30N 18 33 E
Gotlands län □, *Sweden* **11 G12** 57 15N 18 30 E
Gotō-Rettō, *Japan* .. **55 H4** 32 55N 129 5 E
Gotse Delchev, *Bulgaria* **44 E7** 41 36N 23 46 E
Gotska Sandön, *Sweden* **9 G18** 58 24N 19 15 E
Gōtsu, *Japan* ...... **55 G6** 35 0N 132 14 E
Gott Pk., *Canada* ... **102 C4** 50 18N 122 16W
Göttero, Monte, *Italy* . **40 D6** 44 22N 9 42 E
Göttingen, *Germany* . **24 D5** 51 31N 9 55 E
Gottwald = Zmiyev, *Ukraine* **33 H9** 49 39N 36 27 E
Gottwaldov = Zlín, *Czech Rep.* **27 B10** 49 14N 17 40 E
Goubangzi, *China* ... **57 D11** 41 20N 121 52 E
Gouda, *Neths.* ..... **17 B4** 52 1N 4 42 E
Goúdhoura, Ákra, *Greece* **49 E8** 34 59N 26 6 E
Goudiry, *Senegal* ... **82 C2** 14 15N 12 45W
Goudoumaria, *Niger* . **83 C7** 13 40N 11 10 E
Gouéké, *Guinea* **82 D3** 8 2N 8 43W
Gough I., *Atl. Oc.* ... **2 G9** 40 10 S 9 45 E
Gouin, Rés., *Canada* . **104 C5** 48 35N 74 40W
Goulburn, *Australia* . **95 E4** 34 44 S 149 44 E
Goulburn Is., *Australia* **94 A1** 11 40 S 133 20 E
Goulia, *Ivory C.* **82 D3** 10 1N 7 11W
Goulimine, *Morocco* . **78 C3** 28 56N 10 0W
Goulmima, *Morocco* . **78 B5** 31 41N 4 57W
Goundam, *Mali* **82 B4** 16 27N 3 40W
Goúra, *Greece* ..... **46 D4** 37 56N 22 20 E
Gourbassi, *Mali* **82 C2** 13 24N 11 38W
Gourdon, *France* ... **20 D5** 44 44N 1 23 E
Gouré, *Niger* ...... **83 C7** 14 0N 10 10 E
Gourin, *France* **18 D3** 48 8N 3 37W
Gourits →, *S. Africa* . **88 E3** 34 21 S 21 52 E
Gournay-en-Bray, *France* **19 C8** 49 29N 1 44 E
Gourock, *U.K.* **13 F4** 55 57N 4 49W
Goursi, *Burkina Faso* . **82 C4** 12 42N 2 37W
Gouverneur, *U.S.A.* . **117 B9** 44 20N 75 28W
Gouviá, *Greece* .... **49 A3** 39 39N 19 50 E
Gouzon, *France* .... **19 F9** 46 12N 2 14 E
Governador Valadares, *Brazil* **125 G10** 18 15 S 41 57W
Governor's Harbour, *Bahamas* **120 A4** 25 10N 76 14W
Govindgarh, *India* .. **69 G9** 24 23N 81 18 E
Gowan Ra., *Australia* . **94 D4** 25 0 S 145 0 E
Gowanda, *U.S.A.* ... **116 D6** 42 28N 78 56W
Gower, *U.K.* **15 F3** 51 35N 4 10W
Gowna, L., *Ireland* .. **12 C4** 53 51N 7 34W
Gowrie, *Argentina* .. **126 B4** 29 10N 59 10W
Göyçay, *Azerbaijan* .. **35 K8** 40 42N 47 43 E
Goyder Lagoon, *Australia* **95 D2** 27 3 S 138 58 E
Goyllarisquisga, *Peru* . **124 F3** 10 31 S 76 24W
Göynük, *Antalya, Turkey* **47 E12** 36 41N 30 32 E
Göynük, *Bolu, Turkey* **72 B4** 40 24N 30 48 E
Goz Beïda, *Chad* ... **79 F10** 12 10N 21 20 E
Goz Regeb, *Sudan* .. **81 D4** 16 3N 35 33 E
Gozdnica, *Poland* ... **31 G2** 51 28N 15 4 E
Gozo, *Malta* ...... **49 C1** 36 3N 14 15 E
Graaff-Reinet, *S. Africa* **88 E3** 32 13 S 24 32 E
Grabo, *Ivory C.* **82 D3** 4 57N 7 40W
Grabow, *Germany* .. **24 B7** 53 17N 11 34 E
Grabów nad Prosną, *Poland* **31 G5** 51 31N 18 7 E
Gračac, *Croatia* .... **41 D12** 44 18N 15 57 E
Gračanica, *Bos.-H.* .. **28 F3** 44 43N 18 18 E
Graçay, *France* ..... **19 E8** 47 10N 1 50 E
Gracias a Dios, C., *Honduras* **120 D3** 15 0N 83 10W

Graciosa, I., *Canary Is.* **48 E6** 29 15N 13 32W
Grad Sofiya □, *Bulgaria* **44 D7** 42 35N 23 20 E
Gradac, *Serbia & M.* . **44 D3** 42 23N 19 9 E
Gradačac, *Bos.-H.* ... **28 F3** 44 52N 18 26 E
Gradeška Planina, *Macedonia* **44 E6** 41 30N 22 15 E
Gradets, *Bulgaria* ... **45 D10** 42 46N 26 30 E
Gradišče, *Slovenia* .. **41 B12** 46 37N 15 50 E
Grădiştea de Munte, *Romania* **29 E8** 45 37N 23 18 E
Grado, *Italy* ...... **41 C10** 45 40N 13 23 E
Grado, *Spain* **36 B4** 43 23N 6 4W
Grady, *U.S.A.* **113 H3** 34 49N 103 19W
Graeca, Lacul, *Romania* **29 F11** 44 5N 26 10 E
Grafenau, *Germany* . **25 G9** 48 51N 13 24 E
Gräfenberg, *Germany* **25 F7** 49 39N 11 14 E
Grafham Water, *U.K.* **15 E7** 52 19N 0 18W
Grafton, *Australia* .. **95 D5** 29 38 S 152 58 E
Grafton, *N. Dak., U.S.A.* **112 A6** 48 25N 97 25W
Grafton, *W. Va., U.S.A.* **114 F5** 39 21N 80 2W
Graham, *Canada* ... **104 C1** 49 20N 90 30W
Graham, *U.S.A.* **113 J5** 33 6N 98 35W
Graham Bell, Ostrov = Greem-Bell, Ostrov, *Russia* **52 A7** 81 0N 62 0 E
Graham I., *Canada* .. **102 C2** 53 40N 132 30W
Graham Land, *Antarctica* **5 C17** 65 0 S 64 0W
Grahamstown, *S. Africa* **88 E4** 33 19 S 26 31 E
Grahamsville, *U.S.A.* **117 E10** 41 51N 74 33W
Grahovo, *Serbia & M.* **44 D2** 42 40N 18 40 E
Graie, Alpi, *Europe* .. **21 C4** 45 30N 7 10 E
Grain Coast, *W. Afr.* . **82 E3** 4 20N 10 0W
Grajagan, *Indonesia* . **63 K17** 8 35 S 114 13 E
Grajagan, Teluk, *Indonesia* **63 K17** 8 40 S 114 18 E
Grajaú, *Brazil* ..... **125 E9** 5 50 S 46 4W
Grajaú →, *Brazil* ... **125 D10** 3 41 S 44 48W
Grajewo, *Poland* ... **30 E9** 53 39N 22 30 E
Gramada, *Bulgaria* .. **44 C6** 43 49N 22 39 E
Gramat, *France* .... **20 D5** 44 48N 1 43 E
Grammichele, *Italy* .. **43 E7** 37 13N 14 38 E
Grámmos, Óros, *Greece* **44 F4** 40 18N 20 47 E
Grampian □, *U.K.* .. **116 F6** 40 58N 78 37W
Grampian Highlands = Grampian Mts., *U.K.* **13 E5** 56 50N 4 0W
Grampian Mts., *U.K.* . **13 E5** 56 50N 4 0W
Grampians, The, *Australia* **95 F3** 37 0 S 142 20 E
Gramsh, *Albania* ... **44 F4** 40 52N 20 12 E
Gran Canaria, *Canary Is.* **48 G4** 27 55N 15 35W
Gran Chaco, *S. Amer.* **126 B3** 25 0 S 61 0W
Gran Desierto del Pinacate △, *Mexico* **118 A2** 31 51N 113 32W
Gran Paradiso, *Italy* . **40 C4** 45 33N 7 17 E
Gran Sasso d'Itália, *Italy* **41 F10** 42 27N 13 42 E
Gran Sasso e Monti Della Laga △, *Italy* **41 F10** 42 32N 13 22 E
Granada, *Nic.* **120 D2** 11 58N 86 0W
Granada, *Spain* **37 H7** 37 10N 3 35W
Granada, *U.S.A.* ... **113 F3** 38 4N 102 19W
Granada □, *Spain* .. **37 H7** 37 18N 3 0W
Granadilla de Abona, *Canary Is.* **48 F3** 28 7N 16 33W
Granard, *Ireland* ... **12 C4** 53 47N 7 30W
Granbury, *U.S.A.* ... **113 J6** 32 27N 97 47W
Granby, *Canada* **117 A12** 45 25N 72 45W
Granby, *U.S.A.* **108 F11** 40 5N 105 56W
Grand →, *Canada* .. **116 D5** 42 51N 79 34W
Grand →, *Mo., U.S.A.* **112 F8** 39 23N 93 7W
Grand →, *S. Dak., U.S.A.* **112 C4** 45 40N 100 45W
Grand Bahama, *Bahamas* **120 A4** 26 40N 78 30W
Grand Bank, *Canada* . **105 C8** 47 6N 55 48W
Grand Bassam, *Ivory C.* **82 D4** 5 10N 3 49W
Grand Béréby, *Ivory C.* **82 E3** 4 38N 6 55W
Grand-Bourg, *Guadeloupe* **120 b** 15 53N 61 19W
Grand Canal = Yun Ho →, *China* **57 E9** 39 10N 117 10 E
Grand Canyon, *U.S.A.* **109 H7** 36 3N 112 9W
Grand Canyon △, *U.S.A.* **109 H7** 36 15N 112 30W
Grand Canyon-Parashant △, *U.S.A.* **109 H7** 36 30N 113 20W
Grand Cayman, *Cayman Is.* **120 C3** 19 20N 81 20W
Grand Centre, *Canada* **103 C6** 54 25N 110 13W
Grand Cess, *Liberia* . **82 E3** 4 40N 8 12W
Grand Coulee, *U.S.A.* **108 C4** 47 57N 119 0W
Grand Coulee Dam, *U.S.A.* **108 C4** 47 57N 119 0W
Grand Falls, *Canada* . **105 C6** 47 3N 67 44W
Grand Falls-Windsor, *Canada* **105 C8** 48 56N 55 40W
Grand Forks, *Canada* . **102 D5** 49 0N 118 30W
Grand Forks, *U.S.A.* . **112 B6** 47 55N 97 3W
Grand Gorge, *U.S.A.* **117 D10** 42 21N 74 29W
Grand Haven, *U.S.A.* **114 D2** 43 4N 86 13W
Grand I., *Mich., U.S.A.* **114 B2** 46 31N 86 40W
Grand I., *N.Y., U.S.A.* **116 D6** 43 0N 78 58W
Grand Island, *U.S.A.* **112 E5** 40 55N 98 21W
Grand Isle, *La., U.S.A.* **113 L9** 29 14N 90 0W
Grand Isle, *Vt., U.S.A.* **117 B11** 44 43N 73 18W
Grand Junction, *U.S.A.* **108 G9** 39 4N 108 33W
Grand L., *N.B., Canada* **105 C6** 45 57N 66 7W
Grand L., *Nfld. & L., Canada* **105 C8** 49 0N 57 30W
Grand L., *Nfld. & L., Canada* **105 B7** 53 40N 60 30W
Grand L., *U.S.A.* ... **113 L8** 29 55N 92 47W
Grand Lahou, *Ivory C.* **82 D3** 5 10N 5 5W
Grand Lake, *U.S.A.* . **108 F11** 40 15N 105 49W
Grand-Lieu, L. de, *France* **18 E5** 47 6N 1 40W
Grand Manan I., *Canada* **105 D6** 44 45N 66 52W
Grand Marais, *Canada* **112 B9** 47 45N 90 25W
Grand Marais, *U.S.A.* **114 B3** 46 40N 85 59W
Grand-Mère, *Canada* **104 C5** 46 36N 72 40W
Grand Popo, *Benin* .. **83 D5** 6 15N 1 57 E
Grand Portage, *U.S.A.* **112 B10** 47 58N 89 41W
Grand Prairie, *U.S.A.* **113 J6** 32 47N 97 0W
Grand Rapids, *Canada* **103 C9** 53 12N 99 19W
Grand Rapids, *Mich., U.S.A.* **114 D2** 42 58N 85 40W
Grand Rapids, *Minn., U.S.A.* **112 B8** 47 14N 93 31W
Grand St-Bernard, Col du, *Europe* **25 K3** 45 50N 7 10 E
Grand Staircase-Escalante △, *U.S.A.* **109 H8** 37 30N 111 25W
Grand Teton, *U.S.A.* **108 E8** 43 54N 111 50W
Grand Union Canal, *U.K.* **15 E7** 52 7N 0 53W

Grand-Vigie, Pte. de la, Guadeloupe ...... 120 b 16 32N 61 27W
Grandas de Salime, Spain 36 B4 43 13N 6 53W
Grande →, Jujuy, Argentina ...... 126 A2 24 20 S 65 2W
Grande →, Mendoza, Argentina ...... 126 D2 36 52 S 69 45W
Grande →, Bolivia .... 124 G6 15 51 S 64 39W
Grande →, Bahia, Brazil .... 125 F10 11 30 S 44 30W
Grande →, Minas Gerais, Brazil 125 H8 20 6 S 51 4W
Grande, B., Argentina . 128 G3 50 30 S 68 20W
Grande, Rio →, U.S.A. 113 N6 25 58N 97 9W
Grande Baleine, R. de la →, Canada 104 A4 55 16N 77 47W
Grande Cache, Canada 102 C5 53 53N 119 8W
Grande Casse, Pte. de la, France .... 21 C10 45 24N 6 49 E
Grande-Entrée, Canada 105 C7 47 30N 61 40W
Grande Prairie, Canada 102 B5 55 10N 118 50W
Grande-Rivière, Canada 105 C7 48 26N 64 30W
Grande-Terre, Guadeloupe ...... 120 b 16 20N 61 25W
Grande-Vallée, Canada 105 C6 49 14N 65 8W
Grandfalls, U.S.A. 113 K3 31 20N 102 51W
Grândola, Portugal ... 37 G2 38 12N 8 35W
Grandpré, France .... 19 C11 49 20N 4 50 E
Grands Causses △, France .... 20 D6 44 5N 2 58 E
Grands-Jardins △, Canada 105 C5 47 41N 70 51W
Grandview, Canada ... 103 C8 51 10N 100 42W
Grandview, U.S.A. ... 108 C4 46 15N 119 54W
Grandvilliers, France .. 19 C8 49 40N 1 57 E
Graneros, Chile ...... 126 C1 34 5 S 70 45W
Grangemouth, U.K. ... 13 E5 56 1N 3 42W
Granger, U.S.A. 108 F9 41 35N 109 58W
Grängesberg, Sweden .. 10 D9 60 6N 15 1 E
Grangeville, U.S.A. ... 108 D5 45 56N 116 7W
Granisle, Canada 102 C3 54 53N 126 13W
Granite City, U.S.A. .. 112 F9 38 42N 90 9W
Granite Falls, U.S.A. .. 112 C7 44 49N 95 33W
Granite L., Canada ... 105 C8 48 8N 57 5W
Granite Mt., U.S.A. .. 111 M10 33 5N 116 28W
Granite Pk., U.S.A. ... 108 D9 45 10N 109 48W
Graniteville, U.S.A. ... 117 B12 44 8N 72 29W
Granitola, C., Italy ... 42 E5 37 34N 12 39 E
Granity, N.Z. .... 91 J3 41 39 S 171 51 E
Granja, Brazil .... 125 D10 3 7 S 40 50W
Granja de Moreruela, Spain 36 D5 41 48N 5 44W
Granja de Torrehermosa, Spain 37 G5 38 19N 5 35W
Gränna, Sweden ..... 11 F8 58 1N 14 28 E
Granollers, Spain .... 38 D7 41 39N 2 18 E
Gransee, Germany ... 24 B9 53 1N 13 8 E
Grant, U.S.A. 112 E4 40 53N 101 42W
Grant, U.S.A. 108 G4 38 34N 118 48W
Grant City, U.S.A. ... 112 E7 40 29N 94 25W
Grant I., Australia ... 92 B5 11 10 S 132 52 E
Grant Range, U.S.A. .. 109 G6 38 30N 115 25W
Grantham, U.K. 14 E7 52 55N 0 38W
Grantown-on-Spey, U.K. 13 D5 57 20N 3 36W
Grants, U.S.A. 109 J10 35 9N 107 52W
Grants Pass, U.S.A. .. 108 E2 42 26N 123 19W
Grantsville, U.S.A. ... 108 F7 40 36N 112 28W
Granville, France 18 D5 48 50N 1 35W
Granville, N. Dak., U.S.A. 112 A4 48 16N 100 47W
Granville, N.Y., U.S.A. 117 C11 43 24N 73 16W
Granville, Ohio, U.S.A. 116 F2 40 4N 82 31W
Granville L., Canada .. 103 B8 56 18N 100 30W
Graskop, S. Africa ... 89 C5 24 56 S 30 49 E
Grass →, Canada 103 B9 56 3N 96 33W
Grass Range, U.S.A. .. 108 C9 47 0N 109 0W
Grass River △, Canada 103 C8 54 40N 100 50W
Grass Valley, Calif., U.S.A. 110 F6 39 13N 121 4W
Grass Valley, Oreg., U.S.A. 108 D3 45 22N 120 47W
Grassano, Italy ...... 43 B9 40 38N 16 17 E
Grasse, France ...... 21 E10 43 38N 6 56 E
Grassflat, U.S.A. 116 F6 41 0N 78 6W
Grasslands △, Canada . 103 D7 49 11N 107 38W
Grassy, Australia .... 95 G3 40 3 S 144 5 E
Gråsten, Denmark ... 11 K3 54 55N 9 35 E
Grästorp, Sweden ... 11 F6 58 20N 12 40 E
Gratkorn, Austria .... 26 D8 47 8N 15 21 E
Graubünden □, Switz. . 25 J5 46 45N 9 30 E
Graulhet, France .... 20 E5 43 45N 1 59 E
Graus, Spain .... 38 C5 42 11N 0 20 E
Grave, Pte. de, France 20 C2 45 34N 1 4W
Gravelbourg, Canada . 103 D7 49 50N 106 35W
Gravelines, France ... 19 A9 51 1N 2 10 E
's-Gravenhage, Neths. . 17 B4 52 7N 4 17 E
Gravenhurst, Canada . 116 B5 44 52N 79 20W
Gravesend, Australia .. 95 D5 29 35 S 150 20 E
Gravesend, U.K. ..... 15 F8 51 26N 0 22 E
Gravina in Púglia, Italy 43 B9 40 49N 16 25 E
Gravois, Pointe-à-, Haiti 121 C5 18 15N 73 56W
Gravone →, France ... 21 G12 41 58N 8 45 E
Gray, France .... 19 E12 47 27N 5 35 E
Grayling, U.S.A. 114 C3 44 40N 84 43W
Grays, U.K. .... 15 F8 51 28N 0 21 E
Grays Harbor, U.S.A. . 108 C1 46 59N 124 1W
Grays L., U.S.A. 108 E8 43 4N 111 26W
Grays River, U.S.A. .. 110 D3 46 21N 123 37W
Grayvoron, Russia ... 33 G8 50 29N 35 41 E
Graz, Austria .... 26 D8 47 4N 15 27 E
Grdelica, Serbia & M. . 44 D6 42 55N 22 22 E
Greasy L., Canada ... 102 A4 62 55N 122 12W
Great Abaco I., Bahamas 120 A4 26 25N 77 10W
Great Artesian Basin, Australia .... 94 C3 23 0 S 144 0 E
Great Australian Bight, Australia .... 93 F5 33 30 S 130 0 E
Great Bahama Bank, Bahamas 120 B4 23 15N 78 0W
Great Barrier I., N.Z. . 91 G5 36 11 S 175 25 E
Great Barrier Reef, Australia .... 94 B4 18 0 S 146 50 E
Great Barrier Reef △, Australia .... 94 B4 20 0 S 150 0 E
Great Barrington, U.S.A. 117 D11 42 12N 73 22W
Great Basalt Wall △, Australia .... 94 B4 19 52 S 145 43 E
Great Basin, U.S.A. .. 108 G5 40 0N 117 0W
Great Basin △, U.S.A. 108 G6 38 55N 114 14W
Great Bear →, Canada 100 B7 65 0N 124 0W
Great Bear L., Canada 100 B7 65 30N 120 0W
Great Belt = Store Bælt, Denmark .... 11 J4 55 20N 11 0 E

Great Bend, Kans., U.S.A. 112 F5 38 22N 98 46W
Great Bend, Pa., U.S.A. 117 E9 41 58N 75 45W
Great Blasket I., Ireland 12 D1 52 6N 10 32W
Great Camanoe, Br. Virgin Is. .... 121 e 18 30N 64 35W
Great Codroy, Canada 105 C8 47 51N 59 16W
Great Dividing Ra., Australia .... 94 C4 23 0 S 146 0 E
Great Driffield = Driffield, U.K. 14 C7 54 0N 0 26W
Great Exuma I., Bahamas 120 B4 23 30N 75 50W
Great Falls, U.S.A. ... 108 C8 47 30N 111 17W
Great Fish = Groot Vis →, S. Africa .. 88 E4 33 28 S 27 5 E
Great Guana Cay, Bahamas 120 B4 24 0N 76 20W
Great Inagua I., Bahamas 121 B5 21 0N 73 20W
Great Indian Desert = Thar Desert, India . 68 F5 28 0N 72 0 E
Great Karoo, S. Africa . 88 E3 31 55 S 21 0 E
Great Khingan Mts. = Da Hinggan Ling, China .... 60 B7 48 0N 121 0 E
Great Lake, Australia . 95 G4 41 50 S 146 40 E
Great Lakes, N. Amer. . 98 E11 46 0N 84 0W
Great Malvern, U.K. .. 15 E5 52 7N 2 18W
Great Miami →, U.S.A. 114 F3 39 20N 84 40W
Great Ormes Head, U.K. 14 D4 53 20N 3 52W
Great Ouse →, U.K. .. 14 E8 52 48N 0 21 E
Great Palm I., Australia 94 B4 18 45 S 146 40 E
Great Pedro Bluff, Jamaica .... 120 a 17 51N 77 44W
Great Plains, N. Amer. . 98 E9 47 0N 105 0W
Great Ruaha →, Tanzania .... 86 D4 7 56 S 37 52 E
Great Sacandaga Res., U.S.A. 117 C10 43 6N 74 16W
Great Saint Bernard Pass = Grand St-Bernard, Col du, Europe .... 25 K3 45 50N 7 10 E
Great Salt L., U.S.A. .. 108 F7 41 15N 112 40W
Great Salt Lake Desert, U.S.A. 108 F7 40 50N 113 30W
Great Salt Plains L., U.S.A. 113 G5 36 45N 98 8W
Great Sand Dunes △, U.S.A. 109 H11 37 48N 105 45W
Great Sandy △, Australia .... 95 D5 26 13 S 153 2 E
Great Sandy Desert, Australia .... 92 D3 21 0 S 124 0 E
Great Sangi = Sangihe, Pulau, Indonesia .. 63 D7 3 35N 125 30 E
Great Scarcies →, S. Leone 82 D2 9 0N 13 0W
Great Skellig, Ireland . 12 E1 51 47N 10 33W
Great Slave L., Canada 102 A5 61 23N 115 38W
Great Smoky Mts. △, U.S.A. 115 H4 35 40N 83 40W
Great Snow Mt., Canada 102 B4 57 26N 124 0W
Great Stour = Stour →, U.K. .... 15 F9 51 18N 1 22 E
Great Victoria Desert, Australia .... 93 E4 29 30 S 126 30 E
Great Wall, Antarctica . 5 C18 62 30 S 58 0W
Great Wall, China .... 56 E5 38 30N 109 30 E
Great Whernside, U.K. 14 C6 54 10N 1 58W
Great Yarmouth, U.K. . 15 E9 52 37N 1 44 E
Great Zab = Zāb al Kabīr →, Iraq .... 70 C4 36 1N 43 24 E
Great Zimbabwe, Zimbabwe .... 87 G3 20 16 S 30 54 E
Greater Antilles, W. Indies 121 C5 17 40N 74 0W
Greater Manchester □, U.K. 14 D5 53 30N 2 15W
Greater St. Lucia Wetlands △, S. Africa 89 D5 28 6 S 32 27 E
Greater Sudbury = Sudbury, Canada .. 104 C3 46 30N 81 0W
Greater Sunda Is., Indonesia .... 62 F4 7 0 S 112 0 E
Grebbestad, Sweden .. 11 F5 58 42N 11 15 E
Grebenka = Hrebinka, Ukraine .... 33 G7 50 9N 32 22 E
Greco, C., Cyprus .... 49 E13 34 57N 34 5 E
Greco, Mte., Italy .... 41 G10 41 48N 13 58 E
Gredos, Sierra de, Spain 36 E6 40 20N 5 0W
Greece, U.S.A. 116 C7 43 13N 77 41W
Greece ■, Europe .... 46 B3 40 0N 23 0 E
Greeley, Colo., U.S.A. . 112 E2 40 25N 104 42W
Greeley, Nebr., U.S.A. 112 E5 41 33N 98 32W
Greem-Bell, Ostrov, Russia .... 52 A7 81 0N 62 0 E
Green, U.S.A. 108 E2 43 9N 123 22W
Green →, Ky., U.S.A. . 114 G2 37 54N 87 30W
Green →, Utah, U.S.A. 109 G9 38 11N 109 53W
Green B., U.S.A. 114 C2 45 0N 87 30W
Green Bay, U.S.A. ... 114 C2 44 31N 88 0W
Green C., Australia ... 95 F5 37 13 S 150 1 E
Green Cove Springs, U.S.A. 115 L5 29 59N 81 42W
Green Lake, Canada .. 103 C7 54 17N 107 47W
Green Mts., U.S.A. ... 117 C12 43 45N 72 45W
Green River, Utah, U.S.A. 109 G8 38 59N 110 10W
Green River, Wyo., U.S.A. 108 F9 41 32N 109 28W
Green Valley, U.S.A. .. 109 L8 31 52N 110 56W
Greenbank, U.S.A. ... 110 B4 48 6N 122 34W
Greenbush, Mich., U.S.A. 116 B1 44 35N 83 19W
Greenbush, Minn., U.S.A. 112 A6 48 42N 96 11W
Greencastle, U.S.A. .. 114 F2 39 38N 86 52W
Greene, U.S.A. 117 D9 42 20N 75 46W
Greenfield, Calif., U.S.A. 110 J5 36 19N 121 15W
Greenfield, Calif., U.S.A. 111 K8 35 15N 119 0W
Greenfield, Ind., U.S.A. 114 F3 39 47N 85 46W
Greenfield, Iowa, U.S.A. 112 E7 41 18N 94 28W
Greenfield, Mass., U.S.A. 117 D12 42 35N 72 36W
Greenfield, Mo., U.S.A. 113 G8 37 25N 93 51W
Greenfield Park, Canada 117 A11 45 29N 73 29W
Greenland ☒, N. Amer. 4 C5 66 0N 45 0W
Greenland Sea, Arctic . 4 B7 73 0N 10 0W
Greenock, U.K. 13 F4 55 57N 4 46W
Greenore, Ireland 12 B5 54 2N 6 8W

Greenore Pt., Ireland .. 12 D5 52 14N 6 19W
Greenough, Australia .. 93 E1 28 58 S 114 43 E
Greenough →, Australia 93 E1 28 51 S 114 38 E
Greenough Pt., Canada 116 B3 44 58N 81 26W
Greenport, U.S.A. 117 E12 41 6N 72 22W
Greensboro, Ga., U.S.A. 115 J4 33 35N 83 11W
Greensboro, N.C., U.S.A. 115 G6 36 4N 79 48W
Greensboro, Vt., U.S.A. 117 B12 44 36N 72 18W
Greensburg, Ind., U.S.A. 114 F3 39 20N 85 29W
Greensburg, Kans., U.S.A. 113 G5 37 36N 99 18W
Greensburg, Pa., U.S.A. 116 F5 40 18N 79 33W
Greenstone Pt., U.K. .. 13 D3 57 55N 5 37W
Greenvale, Australia .. 94 B4 18 59 S 145 7 E
Greenville, Liberia ... 82 D3 5 1N 9 6W
Greenville, Ala., U.S.A. 115 K2 31 50N 86 38W
Greenville, Calif., U.S.A. 110 E6 40 8N 120 57W
Greenville, Maine, U.S.A. 115 C11 45 28N 69 35W
Greenville, Mich., U.S.A. 114 D3 43 11N 85 15W
Greenville, Miss., U.S.A. 113 J9 33 24N 91 4W
Greenville, Mo., U.S.A. 113 G9 37 8N 90 27W
Greenville, N.C., U.S.A. 115 H7 35 37N 77 23W
Greenville, N.H., U.S.A. 117 D13 42 46N 71 49W
Greenville, N.Y., U.S.A. 117 D10 42 25N 74 1W
Greenville, Ohio, U.S.A. 114 E3 40 6N 84 38W
Greenville, Pa., U.S.A. 116 E4 41 24N 80 23W
Greenville, S.C., U.S.A. 115 H4 34 51N 82 24W
Greenville, Tenn., U.S.A. 115 G4 36 13N 82 51W
Greenville, Tex., U.S.A. 113 J6 33 8N 96 7W
Greenwater Lake △, Canada 103 C8 52 32N 103 30W
Greenwich, Conn., U.S.A. 117 E11 41 2N 73 38W
Greenwich, N.Y., U.S.A. 117 C11 43 5N 73 30W
Greenwich, Ohio, U.S.A. 116 E2 41 2N 82 31W
Greenwich □, U.K. ... 15 F8 51 29N 0 1 E
Greenwood, Canada .. 102 D5 49 10N 118 40W
Greenwood, Ark., U.S.A. 113 H7 35 13N 94 16W
Greenwood, Ind., U.S.A. 114 F2 39 37N 86 7W
Greenwood, Miss., U.S.A. 113 J9 33 31N 90 11W
Greenwood, S.C., U.S.A. 115 H4 34 12N 82 10W
Greenwood, Mt., Australia .... 92 B5 13 48 S 130 4 E
Gregbe, Ivory C. 82 D3 6 48N 6 43W
Gregory △, Australia .. 92 C5 15 38 S 131 15 E
Gregory →, Australia .. 94 B2 17 53 S 139 17 E
Gregory, L., S. Austral., Australia .... 95 D2 28 55 S 139 0 E
Gregory, L., W. Austral., Australia .... 93 E2 25 38 S 119 58 E
Gregory Downs, Australia .... 94 B2 18 35 S 138 45 E
Gregory Ra., Queens., Australia .... 94 B3 19 30 S 143 40 E
Gregory Ra., W. Austral., Australia 92 D3 21 20 S 121 12 E
Greiffenberg, Germany 24 B9 53 5N 13 57 E
Greifswald, Germany .. 24 A9 54 5N 13 23 E
Greifswalder Bodden, Germany .... 24 A9 54 12N 13 35 E
Grein, Austria .... 26 C7 48 14N 14 51 E
Greiz, Germany ..... 24 E8 50 39N 12 12 E
Gremikha, Russia .... 52 C4 67 59N 39 47 E
Grenå, Denmark .... 11 H4 56 25N 10 53 E
Grenada, U.S.A. 113 J10 33 47N 89 49W
Grenada ■, W. Indies . 121 D7 12 10N 61 40W
Grenade, France .... 20 E5 43 47N 1 7 E
Grenadier I., U.S.A. .. 117 B8 44 3N 76 22W
Grenadines, St. Vincent 121 D7 12 40N 61 20W
Grenchen, Switz. .... 25 H3 47 12N 7 24 E
Grenen, Denmark ... 11 G4 57 44N 10 40 E
Grenfell, Australia ... 95 E4 33 52 S 148 8 E
Grenfell, Canada 103 C8 50 30N 102 56W
Grenoble, France .... 21 C9 45 12N 5 42 E
Grenville, C., Australia 94 A3 12 0 S 143 13 E
Grenville Chan., Canada 102 C3 53 40N 129 46W
Gréoux-les-Bains, France .... 21 E9 43 45N 5 52 E
Gresham, U.S.A. 110 E4 45 30N 122 26W
Gresik, Indonesia .... 63 G15 7 13 S 112 38 E
Gretna, U.K. 13 F5 55 0N 3 3W
Greven, Germany ... 24 C3 52 6N 7 37 E
Grevená, Greece .... 44 F5 40 4N 21 25 E
Grevená □, Greece ... 44 F5 40 2N 21 25 E
Grevenbroich, Germany 24 D2 51 5N 6 35 E
Grevenmacher, Lux. .. 17 E6 49 41N 6 26 E
Grevesmühlen, Germany .... 24 B7 53 51N 11 12 E
Grevestrand, Denmark 11 J6 55 36N 12 19 E
Grey →, Canada 105 C8 47 34N 57 6W
Grey →, N.Z. .... 91 K3 42 27 S 171 12 E
Grey, C., Australia ... 94 A2 13 0 S 136 35 E
Grey Ra., Australia ... 95 D3 27 0 S 143 30 E
Greybull, U.S.A. 108 D9 44 30N 108 3W
Greymouth, N.Z. .... 91 K3 42 29 S 171 13 E
Greystones, Ireland .. 12 C5 53 9N 6 5W
Greytown, N.Z. ..... 91 J5 41 5 S 175 29 E
Greytown, S. Africa .. 89 D5 29 1 S 30 36 E
Gribanovskiy, Russia . 34 E5 51 28N 41 50 E
Gribbell I., Canada ... 102 C3 53 23N 129 0W
Gribës, Mal i, Albania . 44 F3 40 17N 19 45 E
Gridley, U.S.A. 110 F5 39 22N 121 42W
Griekwastad, S. Africa 88 D3 28 49 S 23 15 E
Griesheim, Germany . 25 F4 49 51N 8 33 E
Grieskirchen, Austria . 26 C6 48 16N 13 48 E
Griffin, U.S.A. 115 J3 33 15N 84 16W
Griffith, Australia ... 95 E4 34 18 S 146 2 E
Griffith, Canada 116 A7 45 15N 77 10W
Griffith I., Canada ... 116 B4 44 50N 80 55W
Grignols, France .... 20 D3 44 23N 0 12 E
Grigoriopol, Moldova . 29 C14 47 9N 29 18 E
Grimaylov = Hrymayliv, Ukraine .... 33 H4 49 20N 26 5 E
Grimes, U.S.A. 110 F5 39 4N 121 54W
Grimma, Germany ... 24 D8 51 14N 12 43 E
Grimmen, Germany .. 24 A9 54 7N 13 3 E
Grimsay, U.K. 13 D1 57 29N 7 14W
Grimsby, Canada 116 C5 43 12N 79 34W
Grimsby, U.K. 14 D7 53 34N 0 5W
Grímsey, Iceland 8 C5 66 33N 18 0W
Grimshaw, Canada .. 102 B5 56 10N 117 40W
Grimslöv, Sweden ... 11 H8 56 44N 14 34 E
Grimstad, Norway ... 9 G13 58 20N 8 35 E
Grindelwald, Switz. .. 25 J4 46 38N 8 2 E
Grindsted, Denmark . 11 J3 55 57N 8 55 E
Grindstone I., Canada . 117 B8 44 43N 76 14W
Grindu, Romania .... 29 F11 44 44N 26 50 E
Grinnell, U.S.A. 112 E8 41 45N 92 43W
Grintavec, Slovenia .. 41 B11 46 22N 14 32 E

Gris-Nez, C., France .. 19 B8 50 52N 1 35 E
Grisolles, France .... 20 E5 43 49N 1 19 E
Grisons = Graubünden □, Switz. 25 J5 46 45N 9 30 E
Grisslehamn, Sweden . 10 D12 60 5N 18 49 E
Grmeč Planina, Bos.-H. 41 D13 44 43N 16 16 E
Groais I., Canada 105 B8 50 55N 55 35W
Grobiņa, Latvia ..... 30 B8 56 33N 21 10 E
Groblersdal, S. Africa . 89 D4 25 15 S 29 25 E
Grobming, Austria ... 26 D6 47 27N 13 54 E
Grocka, Serbia & M. .. 44 B4 44 40N 20 42 E
Gródek, Poland ..... 31 E10 53 6N 23 40 E
Grodków, Poland .... 31 H4 50 43N 17 21 E
Grodno = Hrodna, Belarus .... 30 E10 53 42N 23 52 E
Grodzisk Mazowiecki, Poland .... 31 F7 52 7N 20 37 E
Grodzisk Wielkopolski, Poland .... 31 F3 52 15N 16 22 E
Grodzyanka = Hrodzyanka, Belarus 32 F5 53 31N 28 42 E
Groesbeck, U.S.A. ... 113 K6 30 48N 96 31W
Groix, France 18 E3 47 38N 3 28W
Groix, Î. de, France .. 18 E3 47 38N 3 28W
Grójec, Poland ...... 31 G7 51 50N 20 58 E
Gronau, Niedersachsen, Germany .... 24 C5 52 5N 9 47 E
Gronau, Nordrhein-Westfalen, Germany .... 24 C3 52 12N 7 2 E
Grong, Norway ..... 8 D15 64 25N 12 8 E
Grönhögen, Sweden .. 11 H10 56 16N 16 24 E
Groningen, Neths. ... 17 A6 53 15N 6 35 E
Groningen □, Neths. .. 17 A6 53 16N 6 40 E
Groom, U.S.A. 113 H4 35 12N 101 6W
Groot →, S. Africa ... 88 E3 33 45 S 24 36 E
Groot Berg →, S. Africa 88 E2 32 47 S 18 8 E
Groot-Brakrivier, S. Africa .... 88 E3 34 2 S 22 18 E
Groot Karasberge, Namibia .... 88 D2 27 20 S 18 40 E
Groot-Kei →, S. Africa 89 E4 32 41 S 28 22 E
Groot Vis →, S. Africa 88 E4 33 28 S 27 5 E
Grootdrink, S. Africa . 88 D3 28 33 S 21 42 E
Groote Eylandt, Australia .... 94 A2 14 0 S 136 40 E
Grootfontein, Namibia 88 B2 19 31 S 18 6 E
Grootlaagte →, Africa 88 C3 20 55 S 21 27 E
Grootvloer →, S. Africa 88 E3 30 0 S 20 40 E
Gros C., Canada 102 A6 61 59N 113 32W
Gros Islet, St. Lucia .. 121 f 14 5N 60 58W
Gros Morne, Canada . 105 C8 49 40N 57 50W
Gros Piton, St. Lucia . 121 f 13 49N 61 5W
Gros Piton Pt., St. Lucia 121 f 13 49N 61 5W
Grósio, Italy .... 40 B7 46 18N 10 16 E
Grosne →, France ... 19 F11 46 42N 4 56 E
Grossa, Pta., Spain ... 48 B8 39 6N 1 36 E
Grossenbrode, Germany 24 A7 54 21N 11 4 E
Grossenhain, Germany 24 D9 51 17N 13 32 E
Grosser Arber, Germany .... 25 F9 49 6N 13 8 E
Grosser Plöner See, Germany .... 24 A6 54 10N 10 22 E
Grosseto, Italy ...... 41 F8 42 46N 11 8 E
Grossgerungs, Austria . 26 C7 48 34N 14 57 E
Grossglockner, Austria 26 D5 47 5N 12 40 E
Groswater B., Canada . 105 B8 54 20N 57 40W
Groton, Conn., U.S.A. 117 E12 41 21N 72 5W
Groton, N.Y., U.S.A. . 117 D8 42 36N 76 22W
Groton, S. Dak., U.S.A. 112 C5 45 27N 98 6W
Grottáglie, Italy ..... 43 B10 40 32N 17 26 E
Grottaminarda, Italy . 43 A8 41 4N 15 2 E
Grottammare, Italy ... 41 F10 42 59N 13 52 E
Grouard Mission, Canada 102 B5 55 33N 116 9W
Grouin, Pte. du, France 18 D5 48 43N 1 51W
Groundhog →, Canada 104 C3 48 45N 82 58W
Grouw, Neths. ..... 17 A5 53 5N 5 51 E
Grove City, U.S.A. ... 116 E4 41 10N 80 5W
Grove Hill, U.S.A. ... 115 K2 31 42N 87 47W
Groveland, U.S.A. ... 110 H6 37 50N 120 14W
Grover City, U.S.A. .. 111 K6 35 7N 120 37W
Groves, U.S.A. 113 L8 29 57N 93 54W
Groveton, U.S.A. 117 B13 44 36N 71 31W
Grožnjan, Croatia ... 41 C10 45 23N 13 43 E
Groznyy, Russia .... 35 J7 43 20N 45 45 E
Grubišno Polje, Croatia 28 E2 45 44N 17 12 E
Grudovo, Bulgaria ... 45 D11 42 21N 27 10 E
Grudusk, Poland .... 31 E7 53 3N 20 38 E
Grudziądz, Poland ... 30 E5 53 30N 18 47 E
Gruinard B., U.K. ... 13 D3 57 56N 5 35W
Gruissan, France .... 20 E7 43 8N 3 7 E
Grumo Áppula, Italy . 43 A9 41 1N 16 42 E
Grums, Sweden ..... 10 E7 59 22N 13 5 E
Grünberg, Germany .. 24 E4 50 35N 8 58 E
Gründau, Germany .. 25 E5 50 10N 9 6 E
Grundy Center, U.S.A. 112 D8 42 22N 92 47W
Grünstadt, Germany . 25 F4 49 34N 8 10 E
Gruppo di Tessa △, Italy 40 B8 46 47N 11 0 E
Gruvberget, Sweden .. 10 C10 61 6N 16 9 E
Gruver, U.S.A. 113 G4 36 16N 101 24W
Gruyères, Switz. .... 25 J3 46 35N 7 4 E
Gruža, Serbia & M. .. 44 C4 43 54N 20 46 E
Gryazi, Russia ...... 33 F10 52 30N 39 58 E
Gryazovets, Russia ... 32 C11 58 50N 40 10 E
Grybów, Poland ..... 31 J7 49 36N 20 55 E
Grycksbo, Sweden ... 10 D9 60 40N 15 29 E
Gryfice, Poland ..... 30 E2 53 55N 15 13 E
Gryfino, Poland ..... 31 E1 53 16N 14 29 E
Gryfów Śląski, Poland 31 G2 51 2N 15 24 E
Grythyttan, Sweden .. 10 E8 59 41N 14 32 E
Gstaad, Switz. ...... 25 J3 46 28N 7 18 E
Gua, India .... 67 H14 22 18N 85 20 E
Gua Musang, Malaysia 65 K3 4 53N 101 58 E
Guacanayabo, G. de, Cuba 120 B4 20 40N 77 20W
Guachipas →, Argentina 126 B2 25 40 S 65 30W
Guadajoz →, Spain ... 37 H6 37 50N 4 51W
Guadalajara, Mexico . 118 C4 20 40N 103 20W
Guadalajara, Spain ... 38 E1 40 37N 3 12W
Guadalajara □, Spain . 38 E2 40 47N 2 30W
Guadalcanal, Solomon Is. ..... 96 H8 9 32 S 160 12 E
Guadalcanal, Spain .. 37 G5 38 5N 5 52W
Guadalén →, Spain ... 37 G7 38 5N 3 32W
Guadales, Argentina .. 126 C2 34 30 S 67 55W
Guadalete →, Spain .. 37 J4 36 35N 6 13W
Guadalimar →, Spain . 37 G7 38 19N 3 28W
Guadalmena →, Spain 37 G8 38 19N 2 56W
Guadalmez →, Spain . 37 G5 38 46N 5 4W
Guadalope →, Spain .. 38 D4 41 0N 0 11W
Guadalquivir →, Spain 37 J4 36 47N 6 22W
Guadalupe = Guadeloupe ☒, W. Indies .... 120 b 16 20N 61 40W
Guadalupe, Mexico .. 111 N10 32 4N 116 32W
Guadalupe, Spain ... 37 F5 39 27N 5 17W

Guadalupe, U.S.A. ... 111 L6 34 59N 120 33W
Guadalupe →, Mexico 111 N10 32 6N 116 51W
Guadalupe →, U.S.A. . 113 L6 28 27N 96 47W
Guadalupe, Sierra de, Spain 37 F5 39 28N 5 30W
Guadalupe Bravos, Mexico 118 A3 31 20N 106 10W
Guadalupe I., Pac. Oc. . 98 G8 29 0N 118 50W
Guadalupe Mts. △, U.S.A. 113 K2 31 40N 104 30W
Guadalupe Peak, U.S.A. 113 K2 31 50N 104 52W
Guadalupe y Calvo, Mexico 118 B3 26 6N 106 58W
Guadarrama, Sierra de, Spain 36 E7 41 0N 4 0W
Guadauta, Georgia ... 35 J5 43 7N 40 32 E
Guadeloupe ☒, Guadeloupe ...... 120 b 16 10N 61 40W
Guadeloupe ☒, W. Indies .... 120 b 16 20N 61 40W
Guadeloupe Passage, W. Indies 121 C7 16 50N 62 15W
Guadiamar →, Spain . 37 J4 36 55N 6 24W
Guadiana →, Portugal 37 H3 37 14N 7 22W
Guadiana Menor →, Spain 37 H7 37 56N 3 15W
Guadiaro →, Spain ... 37 J5 36 17N 5 17W
Guadiato →, Spain ... 37 H5 37 48N 5 5W
Guadiela →, Spain ... 38 E2 40 22N 2 49W
Guadix, Spain 37 H7 37 18N 3 11W
Guafo, Boca del, Chile . 128 E2 43 35 S 74 0W
Guaico, Trin. & Tob. .. 125 K15 10 35N 61 9W
Guainía →, Colombia . 124 C5 2 1N 67 7W
Guaíra, Brazil ...... 127 A5 24 5 S 54 10W
Guaíra □, Paraguay .. 126 B4 25 45 S 56 30W
Guaitecas, Is., Chile .. 128 E2 44 0 S 74 30W
Guajará-Mirim, Brazil 124 F5 10 50 S 65 20W
Guajira, Pen. de la, Colombia 124 A4 12 0N 72 0W
Gualán, Guatemala ... 120 C2 15 8N 89 22W
Gualdo Tadino, Italy . 41 E9 43 14N 12 47 E
Gualeguay, Argentina . 126 C4 33 10 S 59 14W
Gualeguaychú, Argentina .... 126 C4 33 3 S 59 31W
Gualeguay →, Argentina .... 126 C4 33 19 S 59 39W
Guam ☒, Pac. Oc. ... 96 F6 13 27N 144 45 E
Guaminí, Argentina .. 126 D3 37 1 S 62 28W
Guamúchil, Mexico .. 118 B3 25 25N 108 3W
Guana I., Br. Virgin Is. 121 e 18 30N 64 30W
Guanabacoa, Cuba ... 120 B3 23 8N 82 18W
Guanacaste □, Costa Rica 120 D2 10 57N 85 30W
Guanacaste, Cordillera del, Costa Rica ... 120 D2 10 40N 85 4W
Guanaceví, Mexico ... 118 B3 25 40N 106 0W
Guanahani = San Salvador I., Bahamas 121 B5 24 0N 74 40W
Guanajay, Cuba 120 B3 22 56N 82 42W
Guanajuato, Mexico .. 118 C4 21 0N 101 20W
Guanajuato □, Mexico 118 C4 20 40N 101 20W
Guandacol, Argentina . 126 B2 29 30 S 68 40W
Guane, Cuba 120 B3 22 10N 84 7W
Guang'an, China .... 58 B6 30 28N 106 35 E
Guangchang, China .. 59 D11 26 50N 116 21 E
Guangde, China ..... 59 B12 30 54N 119 25 E
Guangdong □, China . 59 F9 23 0N 113 0 E
Guangfeng, China ... 59 C12 28 20N 118 15 E
Guanghan, China .... 58 B5 30 58N 104 17 E
Guanghua = Laohekou, China .... 59 A8 32 22N 111 38 E
Guangling, China .... 56 E8 39 47N 114 22 E
Guangnan, China .... 58 E5 24 5N 105 4 E
Guangning, China ... 59 F9 23 40N 112 22 E
Guangrao, China .... 57 F10 37 5N 118 25 E
Guangshui, China ... 59 B9 31 37N 114 0 E
Guangshun, China ... 58 D6 26 8N 106 21 E
Guangwu, China .... 56 F3 37 48N 105 57 E
Guangxi Zhuangzu Zizhiqu □, China .. 58 F7 24 0N 109 0 E
Guangyuan, China ... 58 A5 32 26N 105 51 E
Guangze, China ..... 59 D11 27 30N 117 12 E
Guangzhou, China ... 59 F9 23 5N 113 10 E
Guanica, Puerto Rico . 121 d 17 59N 66 55W
Guanipa →, Venezuela 124 B6 9 56N 62 26W
Guanling, China .... 58 E5 25 56N 105 35 E
Guannan, China ..... 57 G10 34 8N 119 21 E
Guantánamo, Cuba ... 121 B4 20 10N 75 14W
Guantánamo B., Cuba 121 C4 19 59N 75 10W
Guantao, China ..... 56 F8 36 42N 115 25 E
Guanyang, China .... 59 E8 25 30N 111 5 E
Guanyun, China ..... 57 G10 34 20N 119 18 E
Guápiles, Costa Rica . 120 D3 10 10N 83 46W
Guapo B., Trin. & Tob. 125 K15 10 12N 61 41W
Guaporé, Brazil ..... 127 B5 28 51 S 51 54W
Guaporé →, Brazil ... 124 F5 11 55 S 65 4W
Guaqui, Bolivia ..... 124 G5 16 41 S 68 54W
Guara, Sierra de, Spain 38 C4 42 19N 0 15W
Guaramacal △, Venezuela 121 E5 9 13N 70 12W
Guarapari, Brazil .... 127 A7 20 40 S 40 30W
Guarapuava, Brazil .. 127 B5 25 20 S 51 30W
Guaratinguetá, Brazil 127 A6 22 49 S 45 9W
Guaratuba, Brazil ... 127 B6 25 53 S 48 38W
Guarda, Portugal 36 E3 40 32N 7 20W
Guarda □, Portugal .. 36 E3 40 40N 7 20W
Guardafui, C. = Asir, Ras, Somali Rep. .. 75 E5 11 55N 51 10 E
Guardamar del Segura, Spain 39 G4 38 5N 0 39W
Guardavalle, Italy ... 43 D9 38 30N 16 30 E
Guárdia Sanframondi, Italy .... 43 A7 41 15N 14 36 E
Guardiagrele, Italy ... 41 F11 42 11N 14 13 E
Guardo, Spain 36 C6 42 47N 4 50W
Guareña, Spain 37 G4 38 51N 6 6W
Guareña →, Spain ... 36 D5 41 29N 5 23W
Guárico □, Venezuela . 124 B5 8 40N 66 35W
Guarujá, Brazil ..... 127 A6 24 2 S 46 25W
Guarulhos, Brazil ... 127 A6 23 29 S 46 33W
Guarus, Brazil ...... 127 A7 21 44 S 41 20W
Guasave, Mexico 118 B3 25 34N 108 27W
Guasdualito, Venezuela 124 B4 7 15N 70 44W
Guastalla, Italy ..... 40 D7 44 55N 10 39 E
Guatemala, Guatemala 120 D1 14 40N 90 22W
Guatemala ■, Cent. Amer. 120 C1 15 40N 90 30W
Guatemala Trench, Pac. Oc. 98 H10 15 0N 95 0W
Guatuaro Pt., Trin. & Tob. 125 K16 10 19N 60 59W
Guaviare □, Colombia 124 C4 2 0N 72 30W
Guaviare →, Colombia 124 C5 4 3N 67 44W
Guaxupé, Brazil ..... 127 A6 21 10 S 46 54W
Guayaguayare, Trin. & Tob. 125 K15 10 12N 61 4W
Guayama, Puerto Rico 121 d 17 59N 66 7W
Guayaquil, Ecuador .. 124 D3 2 15 S 79 52W
Guayaquil, G. de, Ecuador .... 124 D2 3 10 S 81 0W

Guaymas, Mexico 118 B2 27 59N 110 54W
Guba, Dem. Rep. of
  the Congo .... 87 E2 10 38 S 26 27 E
Guba, Ethiopia ...... 81 E4 11 17N 35 20 E
Gûbâl, Madîq, Egypt . 80 B3 27 30N 34 0 E
Gubat, Phil. .... 61 E6 12 55N 124 7 E
Gúbbio, Italy .... 41 E9 43 21N 12 35 E
Guben, Germany ..... 24 D10 51 57N 14 43 E
Gubin, Poland ...... 31 G1 51 57N 14 43 E
Gubio, Nigeria ...... 83 C7 12 30N 12 42 E
Gubkin, Russia ...... 33 G9 51 17N 37 32 E
Guča, Serbia & M. ... 44 C4 43 46N 20 15 E
Gucheng, China ..... 59 A8 32 20N 111 30 E
Gudata = Guadauta,
  Georgia .... 35 J5 43 7N 40 32 E
Gudbrandsdalen,
  Norway .... 9 F14 61 33N 10 10 E
Guddu Barrage,
  Pakistan .... 66 E6 28 30N 69 50 E
Gudenå →, Denmark . 11 H4 56 29N 10 13 E
Gudermes, Russia ... 35 J8 43 24N 46 5 E
Gudhjem, Denmark .. 11 J8 55 12N 14 58 E
Gudur, India .... 66 M11 14 12N 79 55 E
Guebwiller, France .. 19 E14 47 55N 7 12 E
Guecho = Getxo, Spain 38 B2 43 21N 2 59W
Guékédou, Guinea ... 82 D2 8 40N 10 5W
Guéle Mendouka,
  Cameroon .... 83 E7 4 23N 12 55 E
Guelph, Canada 116 C4 43 35N 80 20W
Guémené-Penfao,
  France 18 E5 47 38N 1 50W
Guémené-sur-Scorff,
  France 18 D3 48 4N 3 13W
Guéné, Benin .... 83 C5 11 44N 3 16 E
Guérande, France ... 18 E4 47 54N 2 8W
Guéret, France ...... 19 F8 46 11N 1 51 E
Guérigny, France .... 19 E10 47 5N 3 10 E
Guerneville, U.S.A. . 110 G4 38 30N 123 0W
Guernica = Gernika-
  Lumo, Spain 38 B2 43 19N 2 40W
Guernsey, U.K. 15 H5 49 26N 2 35W
Guernsey, U.S.A. ... 112 D2 42 19N 104 45W
Guerrero □, Mexico . 119 D5 17 30N 100 0W
Guessou-Sud, Benin . 83 C5 12 15N 2 38 E
Gueugnon, France .. 19 F11 46 36N 4 4 E
Guéyo, Ivory C. 82 D3 5 25N 6 5W
Gughe, Ethiopia .... 81 F4 6 12N 37 30 E
Güğher, Iran .... 71 D8 29 28N 56 27 E
Guglionesi, Italy .... 41 G11 41 55N 14 55 E
Guhakolak, Tanjung,
  Indonesia .... 63 G11 6 50 S 105 14 E
Gui Jiang →, China . 59 F8 23 30N 111 15 E
Guia, Canary Is. 48 F4 28 8N 15 38W
Guia de Isora, Canary Is. 48 F3 28 12N 16 46W
Guia Lopes da Laguna,
  Brazil .... 127 A4 21 26 S 56 7W
Guiana Highlands,
  S. Amer. 122 C4 5 10N 60 40W
Guibéroua, Ivory C. . 82 D3 6 14N 6 10W
Guichi, China ...... 59 B11 30 39N 117 27 E
Guider, Cameroon ... 83 D7 9 56N 13 57 E
Guidiguir, Niger .... 83 C6 13 40N 9 50 E
Guidimouni, Niger .. 83 C6 13 42N 9 31 E
Guiding, China ..... 58 D6 26 34N 107 11 E
Guidong, China ..... 59 D9 26 7N 113 57 E
Guidónia-Montecélio,
  Italy .... 41 F9 42 1N 12 45 E
Guiers, L. de, Senegal 82 B1 16 10N 15 50W
Guigang, China ..... 59 F8 23 8N 109 35 E
Guiglo, Ivory C. 82 D3 6 45N 7 30W
Guihulñgan, Phil. ... 61 F5 10 7N 123 16 E
Guijá, Mozam. ...... 89 C5 24 27 S 33 0 E
Guijuelo, Spain 36 E5 40 33N 5 40W
Guildford, U.K. 15 F7 51 14N 0 34W
Guilford, U.S.A. 117 E12 41 17N 72 41W
Guilin, China ...... 59 E8 25 18N 110 15 E
Guillaume-Delisle, L.,
  Canada 104 A4 56 15N 76 17W
Guillaumes, France . 21 D10 44 5N 6 52 E
Guillestre, France .. 21 D10 44 39N 6 40 E
Guilvinec, France .. 18 E2 47 48N 4 17W
Güimar, Canary Is. .. 48 F3 28 18N 16 24W
Guimarães, Portugal . 36 D2 41 28N 8 24W
Guimaras □, Phil. ... 61 F5 10 35N 122 37 E
Guinda, U.S.A. 110 G4 38 50N 122 12W
Guinea, Africa ..... 76 F4 8 0N 8 0 E
Guinea ■, W. Afr. .. 82 C2 10 20N 11 30W
Guinea, Gulf of, Atl. Oc. 83 E5 3 0N 2 30 E
Guinea-Bissau ■, Africa 82 C2 12 0N 15 0W
Güines, Cuba 120 B3 22 50N 82 0W
Guingamp, France .. 18 D3 48 34N 3 10W
Guinguinéo, Senegal 82 C1 14 20N 15 57W
Guipavas, France ... 18 D2 48 26N 4 29W
Guiping, China ..... 59 F8 23 21N 110 2 E
Guipúzcoa □, Spain . 38 B2 43 12N 2 15W
Guir, Mali 82 B4 18 52N 2 52W
Guirel, Mauritania .. 82 B3 15 30N 7 3W
Güiria, Venezuela ... 124 A6 10 32N 62 18W
Guiscard, France ... 19 C10 49 40N 3 1 E
Guise, France ...... 19 C10 49 52N 3 35 E
Guitiriz, Spain 36 B3 43 11N 7 50W
Guitri, Ivory C. 82 D3 5 30N 5 14W
Guiuan, Phil. ...... 61 F6 11 5N 125 55 E
Guixi, China .... 59 C11 28 16N 117 15 E
Guiyang, Guizhou,
  China .... 58 D6 26 32N 106 40 E
Guiyang, Hunan, China 59 E9 25 46N 112 42 E
Guizhou □, China ... 58 D6 27 0N 107 0 E
Gujan-Mestras, France 20 D2 44 38N 1 4W
Gujar Khan, Pakistan 68 C5 33 16N 73 19 E
Gujarat □, India ... 68 H4 23 20N 71 0 E
Gujiang, China ..... 59 D10 27 11N 114 47 E
Gujranwala, Pakistan 68 C6 32 10N 74 12 E
Gujrat, Pakistan ... 68 C6 32 40N 74 2 E
Gukovo, Russia ..... 35 F5 48 1N 39 58 E
Gulbarga, India .... 66 L10 17 20N 76 50 E
Gulbene, Latvia .... 9 H22 57 8N 26 52 E
Gulf, The, Asia ..... 71 E6 27 0N 50 0 E
Gulf Islands □, U.S.A. 115 E2 30 10N 87 10W
Gulfport, U.S.A. 113 K10 30 22N 89 6W
Gulgong, Australia .. 95 E4 32 20 S 149 49 E
Gulin, China .... 58 C5 28 10N 105 50 E
Gulistan, Pakistan .. 68 D2 30 30N 66 35 E
Gull Lake, Canada .. 103 C7 50 10N 108 29W
Gullbrandstorp, Sweden 11 H6 56 42N 12 43 E
Gullspång, Sweden .. 11 F8 58 59N 14 6 E
Güllük, Turkey ..... 47 D9 37 14N 27 35 E
Güllük Dağı △, Turkey 47 E12 37 1N 30 30 E
Güllük Körfezi, Turkey 47 D9 37 12N 27 30 E
Gulma, Nigeria ..... 83 C5 12 40N 4 23 E
Gulmarg, India ..... 69 B6 34 3N 74 25 E
Gulnar, Turkey ..... 72 D5 36 19N 33 24 E
Gülpınar, Turkey ... 47 B8 39 32N 26 7 E
Gülşehir, Turkey ... 72 C6 38 44N 34 37 E

Gulshad, Kazakhstan . 52 E8 46 45N 74 25 E
Gulu, Uganda ...... 86 B3 2 48N 32 17 E
Gülübovo, Bulgaria .. 45 D9 42 8N 25 55 E
Gulud, J., Sudan .... 81 E2 11 41N 29 31 E
Gulwe, Tanzania .... 86 D4 6 30 S 36 25 E
Gulyaypole =
  Hulyaypole, Ukraine 33 J9 47 45N 36 21 E
Gumal →, Pakistan .. 68 D4 31 40N 71 50 E
Gumbaz, Pakistan ... 68 D3 30 2N 69 0 E
Gumel, Nigeria ..... 83 C6 12 39N 9 22 E
Gumiel de Hizán, Spain 36 D7 41 46N 3 41W
Gumla, India .... 69 H11 23 3N 84 33 E
Gumlu, Australia ... 94 B4 19 53 S 147 41 E
Gumma □, Japan .... 55 F9 36 30N 138 20 E
Gummersbach,
  Germany .... 24 D3 51 1N 7 34 E
Gümüldür, Turkey ... 47 C9 38 6N 27 0 E
Gümüşçay, Turkey ... 45 F11 40 16N 27 17 E
Gümüşhacıköy, Turkey 72 B6 40 50N 35 18 E
Gümüşhane, Turkey . 73 B8 40 30N 39 30 E
Gümüşsu, Turkey ... 47 C11 38 14N 29 1 E
Gumzai, Indonesia .. 63 F8 5 28 S 134 42 E
Guna, Ethiopia ..... 81 F4 8 18N 39 52 E
Guna, India .... 68 G7 24 40N 77 19 E
Gundelfingen, Germany 25 G6 48 34N 10 22 E
Güney, Burdur, Turkey 47 D11 37 29N 29 34 E
Güney, Denizli, Turkey 47 C11 38 10N 29 4 E
Güneydoğu Toroslar,
  Turkey .... 73 C9 38 20N 40 30 E
Gunisao →, Canada . 103 C9 53 56N 97 53W
Gunisao L., Canada . 103 C9 53 33N 96 15W
Gunjyal, Pakistan ... 68 C4 32 20N 71 55 E
Günlüce, Turkey .... 47 E10 36 50N 28 20 E
Gunnarskog, Sweden . 10 E6 59 49N 12 34 E
Gunnbjørn Fjeld,
  Greenland 4 C6 68 55N 29 47W
Gunnebo, Sweden ... 11 G10 57 44N 16 32 E
Gunnedah, Australia . 95 E5 30 59 S 150 15 E
Gunnewin, Australia . 95 D4 25 59 S 148 33 E
Gunningbar Cr. →,
  Australia .... 95 E4 31 14 S 147 6 E
Gunnison, Colo., U.S.A. 109 G10 38 33N 106 56W
Gunnison, Utah, U.S.A. 108 G8 39 9N 111 49W
Gunnison →, U.S.A. . 109 G9 39 4N 108 35W
Gunpowder, Australia 94 B2 19 42 S 139 22 E
Guntakal, India ..... 66 M10 15 11N 77 27 E
Guntersville, U.S.A. . 115 H2 34 21N 86 18W
Guntong, Malaysia .. 65 K3 4 36N 101 3 E
Guntur, India ...... 67 L12 16 23N 80 30 E
Gunungapi, Indonesia 63 F7 6 45 S 126 30 E
Gunungsitoli, Indonesia 62 D1 1 15N 97 30 E
Günz →, Germany .. 25 G6 48 27N 10 16 E
Gunza, Angola ..... 84 G2 10 50 S 13 50 E
Günzburg, Germany . 25 G6 48 26N 10 17 E
Gunzenhausen,
  Germany .... 25 F6 49 7N 10 44 E
Guo He →, China .. 57 H9 32 59N 117 10 E
Guoyang, China .... 56 H9 33 32N 116 12 E
Gupis, Pakistan ..... 69 A5 36 15N 73 20 E
Gura Humorului,
  Romania .... 29 C10 47 35N 25 53 E
Gura-Teghii, Romania . 29 E11 45 30N 26 25 E
Gurag, Ethiopia .... 81 F4 8 20N 38 20 E
Gurahonţ, Romania . 28 D7 46 16N 22 21 E
Gurdaspur, India ... 68 C6 32 5N 75 31 E
Gurdon, U.S.A. 113 J8 33 55N 93 9W
Güre, Balıkesir, Turkey 47 B8 39 36N 26 54 E
Güre, Uşak, Turkey . 47 C11 38 39N 29 10 E
Gurgaon, India ..... 68 E7 28 27N 77 1 E
Gürgentepe, Turkey . 72 B7 40 51N 37 50 E
Gurghiu, Munţii,
  Romania .... 29 D10 46 41N 25 15 E
Gurgueia →, Brazil . 125 E10 6 50 S 43 24W
Gurha, India .... 68 G4 25 12N 71 39 E
Guri, Embalse de,
  Venezuela 124 B6 7 50N 62 52W
Gurig △, Australia .. 92 B5 11 36 S 132 7 E
Gurin, Nigeria ..... 83 D7 9 5N 12 54 E
Gurjaani, Georgia .. 35 K7 41 43N 45 52 E
Gurk →, Austria ... 26 E7 46 35N 14 31 E
Gurkha, Nepal ..... 69 E11 28 5N 84 40 E
Gurley, Australia ... 95 D4 29 45 S 149 48 E
Gurnet Point, U.S.A. 117 D14 42 1N 70 34W
Guro, Mozam. ...... 87 F3 17 26 S 32 30 E
Gürpınar, Ist., Turkey 45 F12 40 59N 28 37 E
Gürpınar, Van, Turkey 73 C10 38 18N 43 25 E
Gürsu, Turkey ..... 45 F13 40 13N 29 11 E
Gurué, Mozam. ..... 87 F4 15 25 S 36 58 E
Gurun, Malaysia .... 65 K3 5 49N 100 27 E
Gürün, Turkey ..... 72 C7 38 43N 37 15 E
Gurupá, Brazil ..... 125 D8 1 25 S 51 35W
Gurupá, I. Grande de,
  Brazil .... 125 D8 1 25 S 51 45W
Gurupi, Brazil ...... 125 F9 11 43 S 49 4W
Gurupi →, Brazil ... 125 D9 1 13 S 46 6W
Guruwe, Zimbabwe .. 89 B5 16 40 S 30 42 E
Guryev = Atyraū,
  Kazakhstan .... 52 E6 47 5N 52 0 E
Guryevsk, Russia .... 30 D7 54 47N 20 38 E
Gus-Khrustalnyy, Russia 34 C5 55 42N 40 44 E
Gusau, Nigeria ..... 83 C6 12 12N 6 40 E
Gusev, Russia ...... 9 J20 54 35N 22 10 E
Gushan, China ..... 57 E12 39 50N 123 35 E
Gushgy, Turkmenistan 52 F7 35 20N 62 18 E
Gushi, China .... 59 A10 32 11N 115 41 E
Gushiago, Ghana ... 83 D4 9 55N 0 15W
Gusinje, Serbia & M. . 44 D3 42 35N 19 50 E
Gusinoozersk, Russia . 53 D11 51 16N 106 27 E
Gúspini, Italy ...... 42 C1 39 32N 8 37 E
Güssing, Austria .... 27 D9 47 3N 16 20 E
Gustavsberg, Sweden . 10 E12 59 19N 18 23 E
Gustavus, U.S.A. ... 102 B1 58 25N 135 44W
Gustine, U.S.A. 110 H6 37 16N 121 0W
Güstrow, Germany .. 24 B8 53 47N 12 10 E
Gusum, Sweden .... 11 F10 58 16N 16 30 E
Guta = Kolárovo,
  Slovak Rep. .... 27 D10 47 54N 18 0 E
Gütersloh, Germany . 24 D4 51 54N 8 24 E
Gutha, Australia .... 93 E2 28 58 S 115 55 E
Guthalungra, Australia 94 B4 19 52 S 147 50 E
Guthrie, Okla., U.S.A. 113 H6 35 53N 97 25W
Guthrie, Tex., U.S.A. 113 J4 33 37N 100 19W
Gutian, China ...... 59 D12 26 32N 118 53 E
Guttenberg, U.S.A. . 112 D9 42 47N 91 6W
Gutu, Zimbabwe .... 89 B5 19 41 S 31 9 E
Guwahati, India .... 67 F17 26 10N 91 45 E
Guy Fawkes River △,
  Australia .... 95 D5 30 0 S 152 20 E
Guyana ■, S. Amer. . 124 C7 5 0N 59 0W
Guyane française =
  French Guiana ☑,
  S. Amer. 125 C8 4 0N 53 0W
Guyang, China ..... 56 D6 41 0N 110 5 E
Guyenne, France ... 20 D4 44 30N 0 40 E
Guymon, U.S.A. 113 G4 36 41N 101 29W
Guyra, Australia .... 95 E5 30 15 S 151 40 E

Guyuan, Hebei, China 56 D8 41 37N 115 40 E
Guyuan, Ningxia Huizu,
  China .... 56 G4 36 0N 106 20 E
Güzelbahçe, Turkey . 47 C8 38 21N 26 54 E
Güzelyurt = Morphou,
  Cyprus .... 49 D11 35 12N 32 59 E
Guzhang, China .... 58 C7 28 42N 109 58 E
Guzhen, China ..... 57 H9 33 22N 117 18 E
Guzmán, L. de, Mexico 118 A3 31 25N 107 25W
Gvardeysk, Russia .. 9 J19 54 39N 21 5 E
Gvardeyskoye, Ukraine 33 K8 45 7N 34 1 E
Gwa, Burma .... 67 L19 17 36N 94 34 E
Gwaai, Zimbabwe ... 87 F2 19 15 S 27 45 E
Gwaai →, Zimbabwe 87 F2 17 59 S 26 52 E
Gwabegar, Australia . 95 E4 30 31 S 149 0 E
Gwadabawa, Nigeria . 83 C6 13 28N 5 15 E
Gwādar, Pakistan ... 66 G3 25 10N 62 18 E
Gwagwada, Nigeria . 83 C6 10 15N 7 15 E
Gwaii Haanas △,
  Canada 102 C2 52 21N 131 26W
Gwalior, India ..... 68 F8 26 12N 78 10 E
Gwanara, Nigeria ... 83 D5 8 55N 3 9 E
Gwanda, Zimbabwe . 87 G2 20 55 S 29 0 E
Gwandu, Nigeria ... 83 C5 12 30N 4 41 E
Gwane, Dem. Rep. of
  the Congo .... 86 B2 4 45N 25 48 E
Gwaram, Nigeria ... 83 C7 10 15N 10 25 E
Gwarzo, Nigeria .... 83 C6 12 20N 8 55 E
Gwasero, Nigeria ... 83 D5 9 29N 3 30 E
Gwda →, Poland ... 31 E3 53 3N 16 44 E
Gweebarra B., Ireland 12 B3 54 51N 8 23W
Gweedore, Ireland .. 12 A3 55 3N 8 13W
Gweru, Zimbabwe .. 87 F2 19 28 S 29 45 E
Gwi, Nigeria .... 83 D6 9 0N 7 10 E
Gwinn, U.S.A. 114 B2 46 19N 87 27W
Gwio Kura, Nigeria . 83 C7 12 40N 11 2 E
Gwoza, Nigeria .... 83 C7 11 5N 13 40 E
Gwydir →, Australia 95 D4 29 27 S 149 48 E
Gwynedd □, U.K. .. 14 E3 52 52N 4 10W
Gyandzha = Gäncä,
  Azerbaijan .... 35 K8 40 45N 46 20 E
Gyaring Hu, China .. 60 C4 34 50N 97 40 E
Gydanskiy Poluostrov,
  Russia .... 52 C8 70 0N 78 0 E
Gympie, Australia ... 95 D5 26 11 S 152 38 E
Gyomaendrőd, Hungary 28 D5 46 56N 20 50 E
Gyöngyös, Hungary . 28 C4 47 48N 19 56 E
Győr, Hungary ..... 28 C2 47 41N 17 40 E
Győr-Moson-Sopron □,
  Hungary .... 28 C2 47 40N 17 20 E
Gypsum Pt., Canada . 102 A6 61 53N 114 35W
Gypsumville, Canada . 103 C9 51 45N 98 40W
Gyueshevo, Bulgaria . 44 D6 42 14N 22 28 E
Gyula, Hungary .... 28 D6 46 38N 21 17 E
Gyumri, Armenia ... 35 K6 40 47N 43 50 E
Gyzylarbat,
  Turkmenistan ...... 52 F6 39 4N 56 23 E
Gyzyletrek,
  Turkmenistan ...... 71 B7 37 36N 54 46 E
Gzhatsk = Gagarin,
  Russia .... 32 E8 55 38N 35 0 E

H

Ha 'Arava →, Israel . 74 E4 30 50N 35 20 E
Ha Coi, Vietnam .... 58 G6 21 26N 107 46 E
Ha Dong, Vietnam .. 58 G5 20 58N 105 46 E
Ha Giang, Vietnam .. 58 G5 22 50N 104 59 E
Ha Karmel △, Israel . 74 C4 32 45N 35 3 E
Ha Tien, Vietnam ... 65 G5 10 23N 104 29 E
Ha Tinh, Vietnam ... 64 C5 18 20N 105 54 E
Ha Trung, Vietnam .. 64 C5 19 58N 105 50 E
Ha Yaek Chalong,
  Thailand .... 65 a 7 50N 98 22 E
Haaksbergen, Neths. . 17 B6 52 9N 6 45 E
Haapsalu, Estonia .. 9 G20 58 56N 23 30 E
Haarlem, Neths. .... 17 B4 52 23N 4 39 E
Haast →, N.Z. ..... 91 K2 43 50 S 169 2 E
Haast Bluff, Australia 92 D5 23 22 S 132 0 E
Hab →, Pakistan ... 68 G3 24 53N 66 41 E
Hab Nab Chauki,
  Pakistan .... 68 G2 25 0N 66 50 E
Habahe, China ..... 60 B3 48 0N 86 30 E
Habaswein, Kenya .. 86 B4 1 2N 39 30 E
Habay, Canada 102 B5 58 50N 118 44W
Habbānīyah, Iraq ... 70 C4 33 17N 43 29 E
Habbānīyah, Hawr al,
  Iraq .... 73 F10 33 17N 43 29 E
Habichtswald △,
  Germany .... 24 D5 51 15N 9 15 E
Habo, Sweden ...... 11 G8 57 55N 14 6 E
Haboro, Japan ..... 54 B10 44 22N 141 42 E
Habshān, U.A.E. .... 71 F7 23 50N 53 37 E
Hachenburg, Germany 24 E3 50 40N 7 49 E
Hachijō-Jima, Japan . 55 H9 33 5N 139 45 E
Hachinohe, Japan ... 54 D10 40 30N 141 29 E
Hachiōji, Japan ..... 55 G9 35 40N 139 20 E
Hachōn, N. Korea ... 57 D15 41 29N 129 2 E
Hacıbektaş, Turkey . 72 C6 38 56N 34 33 E
Hacılar, Turkey ..... 72 C6 38 50N 35 26 E
Hackås, Sweden .... 10 B8 62 56N 14 30 E
Hackensack, U.S.A. . 117 F10 40 53N 74 3W
Hackettstown, U.S.A. 117 F10 40 51N 74 50W
Hadali, Pakistan .... 68 C5 32 16N 72 11 E
Hadarba, Ras, Sudan 80 C4 22 4N 36 51 E
Hadarom □, Israel .. 74 E4 31 0N 35 0 E
Hadd, Ra's al, Oman 75 C6 22 35N 59 50 E
Haddington, U.K. ... 13 F6 55 57N 2 47W
Hadejia, Nigeria .... 83 C7 12 30N 10 51 E
Hadejia →, Nigeria . 83 C7 12 50N 10 51 E
Hadera, Israel ...... 74 C3 32 27N 34 55 E
Hadera, N. →, Israel 74 C3 32 28N 34 52 E
Haderslev, Denmark . 11 J3 55 15N 9 30 E
Hadhramaut =
  Hadramawt, Yemen 75 D4 15 30N 49 30 E
Hadiboh, Yemen ... 75 E5 12 35N 54 2 E
Hadím, Turkey ..... 72 D5 36 58N 32 26 E
Hadong, S. Korea ... 57 G14 35 5N 127 44 E
Hadramawt, Yemen . 75 D4 15 30N 49 30 E
Hadrānīyah, Iraq ... 70 C4 35 38N 43 14 E
Hadrian's Wall, U.K. 14 B5 55 0N 2 30W
Hadsten, Denmark .. 11 H4 56 19N 10 3 E
Hadsund, Denmark . 11 H4 56 44N 10 8 E
Hadyach, Ukraine ... 33 G7 50 21N 34 2 E
Haeju, N. Korea .... 57 E13 38 3N 125 45 E
Haenam, S. Korea ... 57 G14 34 34N 126 35 E
Haenertsburg, S. Africa 89 C4 24 0 S 29 50 E
Haerhpin = Harbin,
  China .... 57 B14 45 48N 126 40 E
Hafar al 'Aţk,
  Si. Arabia .... 70 D5 28 32N 45 52 E
Hafik, Turkey ...... 72 C7 39 59N 37 23 E
Hafîrat al 'Aydā,
  Si. Arabia .... 70 E3 26 26N 39 12 E
Hafît, Oman .... 71 F7 23 59N 55 49 E

Hafizabad, Pakistan . 68 C5 32 5N 73 40 E
Haflong, India ..... 67 G18 25 10N 93 5 E
Hafnarfjörður, Iceland 8 D3 64 4N 21 57W
Haft Gel, Iran ..... 71 D6 31 30N 49 32 E
Hafun, Ras, Somali Rep. 75 E5 10 29N 51 30 E
Hagalil, Israel ...... 74 C4 32 53N 35 18 E
Hagby, Sweden ..... 11 H10 56 34N 16 11 E
Hagen, Germany ... 24 D3 51 21N 7 27 E
Hagenow, Germany . 24 B7 53 26N 11 12 E
Hagerman, U.S.A. .. 113 J2 33 7N 104 20W
Hagerman Fossil
  Beds △, U.S.A. 108 E6 42 48N 114 57W
Hagerstown, U.S.A. . 114 F7 39 39N 77 43W
Hagersville, Canada . 116 D4 42 58N 80 3W
Hagetmau, France .. 20 E3 43 39N 0 37W
Hagfors, Sweden ... 10 D7 60 3N 13 45 E
Hagi, Japan .... 55 G5 34 30N 131 22 E
Hagolan, Syria ..... 74 C4 33 0N 35 45 E
Hagondange, France 19 C13 49 16N 6 11 E
Hags Hd., Ireland .. 12 D2 52 57N 9 28W
Hague, C. de la, France 18 C5 49 44N 1 56W
Hague, The = 's-
  Gravenhage, Neths. 17 B4 52 7N 4 17 E
Haguenau, France .. 19 D14 48 49N 7 47 E
Hai Duong, Vietnam 58 G6 20 56N 106 19 E
Hai'an, Guangdong,
  China .... 59 G8 20 18N 110 11 E
Hai'an, Jiangsu, China 59 A13 32 37N 120 27 E
Haicheng, Fujian, China 59 E11 24 23N 117 48 E
Haicheng, Liaoning,
  China .... 57 D12 40 50N 122 45 E
Haidar Khel, Afghan. 68 C3 33 58N 68 38 E
Haidarâbâd =
  Hyderabad =, India 66 L11 17 22N 78 29 E
Haidargarh, India .. 69 F9 26 37N 81 22 E
Haifa = Ḥefa, Israel 74 C4 32 46N 35 0 E
Haifeng, China ..... 59 F10 22 58N 115 10 E
Haiger, Germany ... 24 E4 50 43N 8 12 E
Haikou, China ..... 60 D6 20 1N 110 16 E
Hā'il, Si. Arabia .... 70 E4 27 28N 41 45 E
Hailar, China ...... 60 B6 49 10N 119 38 E
Hailey, U.S.A. 108 E6 43 31N 114 19W
Haileybury, Canada . 104 C4 47 30N 79 38W
Hailin, China ...... 57 B15 44 37N 129 30 E
Hailing Dao, China . 59 G8 21 35N 111 47 E
Hailong, China ..... 57 C13 42 32N 125 40 E
Hailuoto, Finland .. 8 D21 65 3N 24 45 E
Haimen, Guangdong,
  China .... 59 F11 23 15N 116 31 E
Haimen, Jiangsu, China 59 B13 31 52N 121 10 E
Hainan □, China ... 60 E5 19 0N 109 30 E
Hainaut □, Belgium . 17 D4 50 30N 4 0 E
Hainburg, Austria ... 27 C9 48 9N 16 56 E
Haines, Alaska, U.S.A. 102 B1 59 14N 135 26W
Haines, Oreg., U.S.A. 108 D5 44 55N 117 56W
Haines City, U.S.A. . 115 L5 28 7N 81 38W
Haines Junction, Canada 102 A1 60 45N 137 30W
Hainfeld, Austria ... 26 C8 48 3N 15 48 E
Haining, China ..... 59 B13 30 28N 120 40 E
Haiphong, Vietnam . 58 G6 20 47N 106 41 E
Haitan Dao, China .. 59 E12 25 30N 119 45 E
Haiti ■, W. Indies .. 121 C5 19 0N 72 30W
Haiya, Sudan ...... 80 D4 18 20N 36 21 E
Haiyan, China ..... 59 B13 30 28N 120 58 E
Haiyang, China .... 57 F11 36 47N 121 9 E
Haiyuan,
  Guangxi Zhuangzu,
  China .... 58 F6 22 8N 107 35 E
Haiyuan, Ningxia Huizu,
  China .... 56 F3 36 35N 105 52 E
Haizhou, China ..... 57 G10 34 37N 119 7 E
Haizhou Wan, China 57 G10 34 50N 119 20 E
Hajdú-Bihar □,
  Hungary .... 28 C6 47 30N 21 30 E
Hajdúböszörmény,
  Hungary .... 28 C6 47 40N 21 30 E
Hajdúdorog, Hungary 28 C6 47 48N 21 30 E
Hajdúhadház, Hungary 28 C6 47 40N 21 40 E
Hajdúnánás, Hungary 28 C6 47 50N 21 26 E
Hajdúsámson, Hungary 28 C6 47 37N 21 42 E
Hajdúszoboszló,
  Hungary .... 28 C6 47 27N 21 22 E
Hajipur, India ...... 69 G11 25 45N 85 13 E
Ḥājjī Muḥsin, Iraq .. 70 C5 32 35N 45 29 E
Ḥājjīābād, Iran ..... 71 D7 28 19N 55 55 E
Ḥājjīābād-e Zarrīn, Iran 71 C7 33 9N 54 51 E
Hajnówka, Poland .. 31 F10 52 47N 23 35 E
Hakansson, Mts.,
  Dem. Rep. of
  the Congo .... 87 D2 8 40 S 25 45 E
Hakkâri, Turkey .... 70 B4 37 34N 43 44 E
Hakkâri Dağları, Turkey 73 C10 38 21N 42 58 E
Hakken-Zan, Japan . 55 G7 34 10N 135 54 E
Hakodate, Japan ... 54 D10 41 45N 140 44 E
Hakos, Namibia .... 88 C2 23 13 S 16 21 E
Håksberg, Sweden .. 10 D9 60 11N 15 12 E
Haku-San, Japan ... 55 F8 36 9N 136 46 E
Haku-San △, Japan . 55 F8 36 15N 136 47 E
Hakui, Japan .... 55 F8 36 53N 136 47 E
Hala, Pakistan ..... 66 G6 25 43N 68 20 E
Ḥalab, Syria .... 70 B3 36 10N 37 15 E
Ḥalabjah, Iraq ..... 70 C5 35 10N 45 58 E
Halaib, Sudan ...... 80 C4 22 12N 36 30 E
Halasa, Sudan ..... 81 E3 14 26N 30 38 E
Hālat 'Ammār,
  Si. Arabia .... 70 D3 29 10N 36 4 E
Halbā, Lebanon .... 74 A5 34 34N 36 6 E
Halberstadt, Germany 24 D7 51 54N 11 3 E
Halcombe, N.Z. .... 91 J5 40 8N 175 30 E
Halcon, Phil. ...... 63 B6 13 0N 121 30 E
Halden, Norway .... 9 G14 59 9N 11 23 E
Haldensleben, Germany 24 C7 52 17N 11 25 E
Haldia, India ...... 67 H16 22 5N 88 3 E
Haldimand, Canada . 116 D5 42 59N 79 52W
Haldwani, India .... 69 E8 29 31N 79 30 E
Hale →, Australia .. 94 C2 24 56 S 135 53 E
Halesowen, U.K. ... 15 E5 52 27N 2 3W
Halesworth, U.K. ... 15 E9 52 20N 1 31 E
Haleyville, U.S.A. ... 115 H2 34 14N 87 37W
Half Assini, Ghana . 82 D4 5 1N 2 50W
Halfmoon Bay, N.Z. 91 M2 46 50 S 168 5 E
Halfway →, Canada 102 B4 56 12N 121 32W
Halia, India .... 69 G10 24 50N 82 19 E
Haliburton, Canada . 116 A6 45 3N 78 30W
Halifax, Australia .. 94 B4 18 32 S 146 22 E
Halifax, Canada 105 D7 44 38N 63 35W
Halifax, U.K. 14 D6 53 43N 1 52W
Halifax, U.S.A. 116 F8 40 25N 76 55W
Halifax B., Australia 94 B4 18 50 S 147 0 E
Halifax I., Namibia . 88 D2 26 38 S 15 4 E
Ḥalīl →, Iran ...... 71 E8 27 40N 58 30 E
Halkirk, U.K. 13 C5 58 30N 3 29W
Hall Beach = Sanirajak,
  Canada 101 B11 68 46N 81 12W
Hall in Tirol, Austria 26 D4 47 17N 11 30 E

Hall Pen., Canada .. 101 B13 63 30N 66 0W
Hall Pt., Australia .. 92 C3 15 40 S 124 23 E
Hallabro, Sweden ... 11 H9 56 22N 15 5 E
Halland, Sweden ... 9 H15 57 8N 12 47 E
Hallands län □, Sweden 11 H6 57 0N 12 40 E
Hallands Väderö,
  Sweden .... 11 H6 56 27N 12 34 E
Hallandsås, Sweden . 11 H7 56 22N 13 0 E
Hällbybrunn, Sweden 10 E10 59 24N 16 25 E
Halle, Belgium ..... 17 D4 50 44N 4 13 E
Halle,
  Nordrhein-Westfalen,
  Germany .... 24 C4 52 3N 8 22 E
Halle, Sachsen-Anhalt,
  Germany .... 24 D7 51 30N 11 56 E
Hälleforsnäs, Sweden 10 E10 59 10N 14 30 E
Hällekis, Sweden ... 11 F7 58 38N 13 27 E
Hallein, Austria .... 26 D6 47 40N 13 5 E
Hällevadsholm, Sweden 10 E10 59 10N 16 30 E
Hallen, Sweden ..... 10 A8 63 11N 14 4 E
Hallett, Australia ... 95 E2 33 25 S 138 55 E
Hallettsville, U.S.A. . 113 L6 29 27N 96 57W
Hällim, S. Korea .... 57 H14 33 24N 126 15 E
Hallingdalselvi →,
  Norway .... 9 F13 60 23N 9 35 E
Hallock, U.S.A. 112 A6 48 47N 96 57W
Halls Creek, Australia 92 C4 18 16 S 127 38 E
Hallsberg, Sweden .. 10 E9 59 5N 15 7 E
Hallstahammar, Sweden 10 E10 59 38N 16 15 E
Hallstatt, Austria ... 26 D6 47 33N 13 38 E
Hallstavik, Sweden . 10 D12 60 5N 18 37 E
Hallstead, U.S.A. ... 117 E9 41 58N 75 45W
Halmahera, Indonesia 63 D7 0 40N 128 0 E
Halmeu, Romania .. 28 C8 47 57N 23 2 E
Halmstad, Sweden . 11 H6 56 41N 12 52 E
Hals, Denmark ..... 11 H4 57 0N 10 18 E
Hälsingborg =
  Helsingborg, Sweden 11 H6 56 3N 12 42 E
Hälsingland, Sweden 10 C10 61 40N 16 5 E
Halstead, U.K. ...... 15 F8 51 57N 0 40 E
Haltern, Germany .. 24 D3 51 44N 7 11 E
Haltiatunturi, Finland 8 B19 69 17N 21 18 E
Halton □, U.K. 14 D5 53 22N 2 45W
Haltwhistle, U.K. ... 14 C5 54 58N 2 26W
Ḥalūl, Qatar .... 71 E7 25 40N 52 40 E
Halvad, India ...... 68 H4 23 1N 71 11 E
Ḥalvān, Iran .... 71 C8 33 57N 56 15 E
Ham, France .... 19 C10 49 45N 3 4 E
Ham Tan, Vietnam . 65 G6 10 40N 107 45 E
Ham Yen, Vietnam . 64 A5 22 4N 105 3 E
Hamab, Namibia ... 88 D2 28 7 S 19 16 E
Hamad, Sudan .... 81 D3 15 20N 33 32 E
Hamada, Japan ..... 55 G6 34 56N 132 4 E
Hamadān, Iran ..... 71 C6 34 52N 48 32 E
Hamadān □, Iran ... 71 C6 35 0N 49 0 E
Hamāh, Syria ...... 70 C3 35 5N 36 40 E
Hamamatsu, Japan . 55 G8 34 45N 137 45 E
Hamar, Norway .... 9 F14 60 48N 11 7 E
Hambantota, Sri Lanka 66 R12 6 10N 81 10 E
Hamber △, Canada . 102 C5 52 20N 118 0W
Hamburg, Germany . 24 B5 53 33N 9 59 E
Hamburg, Ark., U.S.A. 113 J9 33 14N 91 48W
Hamburg, N.Y., U.S.A. 116 D6 42 43N 78 50W
Hamburg, Pa., U.S.A. 117 F9 40 33N 75 59W
Hamburg, S.C., U.S.A. 24 B5 53 30N 10 0 E
Hamburg Fuhlsbüttel ✈
  (HAM), Germany .. 24 B5 53 35N 9 59 E
Ḥamḍ, W. al →,
  Si. Arabia .... 70 E3 24 55N 36 20 E
Hamden, U.S.A. 117 E12 41 23N 72 54W
Hamdibey, Turkey .. 47 B9 39 50N 27 5 E
Häme, Finland ..... 9 F20 61 38N 25 10 E
Hämeenlinna, Finland 9 F21 61 0N 24 28 E
Hamélé, Ghana 82 C4 10 56N 2 45W
Hamelin Pool, Australia 93 E1 26 22 S 114 20 E
Hameln, Germany .. 24 C5 52 6N 9 21 E
Hamerkaz □, Israel . 74 C3 32 15N 34 55 E
Hamersley Ra.,
  Australia .... 92 D2 22 0 S 117 45 E
Hamhung, N. Korea . 57 E14 39 54N 127 30 E
Hami, China .... 60 B4 42 55N 93 25 E
Hamilton, Australia . 95 F3 37 45 S 142 2 E
Hamilton, Canada .. 116 C5 43 15N 79 50W
Hamilton, N.Z. ..... 91 G5 37 47 S 175 19 E
Hamilton, U.K. 13 F4 55 46N 4 2W
Hamilton, Ala., U.S.A. 115 H1 34 9N 87 59W
Hamilton, Mont., U.S.A. 108 C6 46 15N 114 10W
Hamilton, N.Y., U.S.A. 117 D9 42 50N 75 33W
Hamilton, Ohio, U.S.A. 114 F3 39 24N 84 34W
Hamilton, Tex., U.S.A. 113 K5 31 42N 98 7W
Hamilton →, Australia 94 C2 23 30 S 139 47 E
Hamilton, The →,
  Australia .... 95 D2 26 40 S 135 19 E
Hamilton City, U.S.A. 110 F4 39 45N 122 1W
Hamilton I., Australia 94 J6 20 21 S 148 56 E
Hamilton Inlet, Canada 105 B8 54 0N 57 30W
Hamilton Mt., U.S.A. 117 C10 43 25N 74 22W
Hamina, Finland .... 9 F22 60 34N 27 12 E
Hamīrpur, H.P., India 68 D7 31 41N 76 31 E
Hamirpur, Ut. P., India 69 G9 25 57N 80 9 E
Hamitabat, Turkey .. 45 E11 41 30N 27 17 E
Hamlet, U.S.A. 115 H6 34 53N 79 42W
Hamley Bridge,
  Australia .... 95 E2 34 17 S 138 35 E
Hamlin = Hameln,
  Germany .... 24 C5 52 6N 9 21 E
Hamlin, N.Y., U.S.A. 116 C7 43 17N 77 55W
Hamlin, Tex., U.S.A. 113 J4 32 53N 100 8W
Hamm, Germany ... 24 D3 51 40N 7 50 E
Ḥammār, Hawr al, Iraq 70 D5 30 50N 47 10 E
Hammarstrand, Sweden 10 A10 63 7N 16 20 E
Hammelburg, Germany 25 E5 50 7N 9 54 E
Hammerdal, Sweden 10 A9 63 35N 15 20 E
Hammerfest, Norway 8 A20 70 39N 23 41 E
Hammond, Denmark 11 J8 55 18N 14 47 E
Hamminkeln, Germany 24 D2 51 44N 6 36 E
Hammond, Ind., U.S.A. 114 E2 41 38N 87 30W
Hammond, La., U.S.A. 113 K9 30 30N 90 28W
Hammond, N.Y., U.S.A. 117 B9 44 27N 75 42W
Hammondsport, U.S.A. 116 D7 42 25N 77 13W
Hammonton, U.S.A. . 114 F8 39 39N 74 48W
Hamneda, Sweden . 11 H7 56 41N 13 51 E
Hamoyet, Jebel, Sudan 80 D4 17 33N 38 2 E
Hampden, N.Z. ..... 91 L3 45 18 S 170 50 E
Hampshire □, U.K. . 15 F6 51 7N 1 23W
Hampshire Downs, U.K. 15 F6 51 15N 1 10W
Hampton, N.B., Canada 105 C6 45 30N 65 40W
Hampton, Ont., Canada 116 C6 43 58N 78 45W
Hampton, Ark., U.S.A. 113 J8 33 32N 92 28W
Hampton, Iowa, U.S.A. 112 D8 42 45N 93 13W
Hampton, N.H., U.S.A. 117 D14 42 57N 70 50W
Hampton, S.C., U.S.A. 115 J5 32 52N 81 7W
Hampton, Va., U.S.A. 113 G7 37 2N 76 21W
Hampton Bays, U.S.A. 117 F12 40 53N 72 30W
Hampton Tableland,
  Australia .... 93 F4 32 0 S 127 0 E

Hamra, Sweden ...... 10 C8 61 39N 14 59 E
Hamrat esh Sheykh,
  Sudan .... 81 E2 14 38N 27 55 E
Hamur, Turkey ...... 73 C10 39 37N 43 3 E
Hamyang, S. Korea ... 57 G14 35 32N 127 42 E
Han Jiang →, China . 59 F11 23 25N 116 40 E
Han Shui, China .... 58 A7 30 34N 114 17 E
Han Shui →, China .. 59 B10 30 35N 114 18 E
Hanak, Si. Arabia ... 70 E3 25 32N 37 0 E
Hanamaki, Japan .... 54 E10 39 23N 141 7 E
Hanang, Tanzania ... 86 C4 4 30 S 35 25 E
Hanau, Germany .... 25 E4 50 7N 8 56 E
Hanbogd = Ihbulag,
  Mongolia .... 56 C4 43 11N 107 10 E
Hançalar, Turkey .... 47 C11 38 8N 29 24 E
Hâncești, Moldova ... 29 D13 46 50N 28 36 E
Hancheng, China .... 56 G6 35 31N 110 25 E
Hanchuan, China .... 59 B9 30 40N 113 50 E
Hancock, Mich., U.S.A. 112 B10 47 8N 88 35W
Hancock, N.Y., U.S.A. 117 E9 41 57N 75 17W
Handa, Japan .... 55 G8 34 53N 136 55 E
Handan, China ...... 56 F8 36 35N 114 28 E
Handeni, Tanzania ... 86 D4 5 25 S 38 2 E
Handlová, Slovak Rep. . 27 C11 48 45N 18 35 E
Handub, Sudan ..... 80 D4 19 15N 37 16 E
Handwara, India .... 69 B6 34 21N 74 20 E
Hanegev, Israel ..... 74 E4 30 50N 35 0 E
Hanford, U.S.A. 110 J7 36 20N 119 39W
Hanford Reach △,
  U.S.A. 108 C4 46 40N 119 28W
Hang Chat, Thailand . 64 C2 18 20N 99 21 E
Hang Dong, Thailand . 64 C2 18 41N 98 55 E
Hangang →, S. Korea . 57 F14 37 50N 126 30 E
Hangayn Nuruu,
  Mongolia .... 60 B4 47 30N 99 0 E
Hangchou = Hangzhou,
  China .... 59 B13 30 18N 120 11 E
Hanggin Houqi, China . 56 D4 40 58N 107 4 E
Hanggin Qi, China ... 56 E5 39 52N 108 50 E
Hangu, China ...... 57 E9 39 18N 117 53 E
Hangzhou, China .... 59 B13 30 18N 120 11 E
Hangzhou Wan, China . 59 B13 30 15N 120 45 E
Hanhongor, Mongolia . 56 C3 43 55N 104 28 E
Ḥanīdh, Si. Arabia .. 71 E6 26 35N 48 38 E
Ḥanīsh, Yemen ..... 75 E3 13 45N 42 46 E
Hanjiang, China .... 59 E12 25 26N 119 6 E
Hankinson, U.S.A. ... 112 B6 46 4N 96 54W
Hankö, Finland ..... 9 G20 59 50N 22 57 E
Hankou, China ...... 59 B10 30 35N 114 30 E
Hanksville, U.S.A. ... 109 G8 38 22N 110 43W
Hanle, India .... 69 C8 32 42N 79 4 E
Hanmer Springs, N.Z. . 91 K4 42 32 S 172 50 E
Hann →, Australia ... 92 C4 17 26 S 126 17 E
Hann, Mt., Australia .. 92 C4 15 45 S 126 0 E
Hanna, Canada 102 C6 51 40N 111 54W
Hanna, U.S.A. 108 F10 41 52N 106 34W
Hannah B., Canada .. 104 B4 51 40N 80 0W
Hannibal, Mo., U.S.A. . 112 F9 39 42N 91 22W
Hannibal, N.Y., U.S.A. . 117 C8 43 19N 76 35W
Hannik, Sudan ..... 80 D3 18 12N 32 20 E
Hannover, Germany .. 24 C5 52 22N 9 46 E
Hanö, Sweden ...... 11 H8 56 1N 14 50 E
Hanöbukten, Sweden . 11 H8 55 35N 14 30 E
Hanoi, Vietnam .... 58 G5 21 5N 105 55 E
Hanover = Hannover,
  Germany .... 24 C5 52 22N 9 46 E
Hanover, Canada 116 B3 44 9N 81 2W
Hanover, S. Africa ... 88 E3 31 4 S 24 29 E
Hanover, N.H., U.S.A. . 117 C12 43 42N 72 17W
Hanover, Ohio, U.S.A. . 116 F2 40 4N 82 16W
Hanover, Pa., U.S.A. .. 114 F7 39 48N 76 59W
Hanover, I., Chile ... 128 G2 51 0 S 74 50W
Hans Lollik I.,
  U.S. Virgin Is. ... 121 e 18 24N 64 53W
Hansdiha, India .... 69 G12 24 36N 87 5 E
Hanshou, China .... 59 C8 28 56N 111 50 E
Hansi, India .... 68 E6 29 10N 75 57 E
Hanson, L., Australia . 95 E2 31 0 S 136 15 E
Hanstholm, Denmark . 11 G2 57 7N 8 36 E
Hantsavichy, Belarus . 33 F4 52 49N 26 30 E
Hanumangarh, India . 68 E6 29 35N 74 19 E
Hanyin, China ...... 58 A7 32 54N 108 28 E
Hanyuan, China ..... 58 C4 29 21N 102 40 E
Hanzhong, China .... 56 H4 33 10N 107 1 E
Hanzhuang, China ... 57 G9 34 33N 117 23 E
Haora, India .... 69 H13 22 37N 88 20 E
Haoxue, China ...... 59 B9 30 3N 112 24 E
Haparanda, Sweden .. 8 D21 65 52N 24 8 E
Happy, U.S.A. 113 H4 34 45N 101 52W
Happy Camp, U.S.A. .. 108 F2 41 48N 123 23W
Happy Valley-Goose
  Bay, Canada 105 B7 53 15N 60 20W
Hapsu, N. Korea .... 57 D15 41 13N 128 51 E
Hapur, India ...... 68 E7 28 45N 77 45 E
Ḥaql, Si. Arabia .... 74 F3 29 10N 34 58 E
Har, Indonesia ..... 63 F8 5 16 S 133 14 E
Har-Ayrag, Mongolia . 56 B5 45 47N 109 16 E
Har Hu, China ..... 60 C4 38 20N 97 38 E
Har Us Nuur, Mongolia 60 B4 48 0N 92 0 E
Har Yehuda, Israel .. 74 D3 31 35N 34 57 E
Ḥaraḍ, Si. Arabia ... 75 C4 24 22N 49 0 E
Haradok, Belarus .... 32 E5 55 30N 30 0 E
Härädsbäck, Sweden . 11 H8 56 32N 14 26 E
Haranomachi, Japan . 54 F10 37 38N 140 58 E
Harare, Zimbabwe ... 87 F3 17 43 S 31 2 E
Harat, Eritrea ...... 81 D4 16 5N 39 26 E
Harbin, China ...... 57 B14 45 48N 126 40 E
Harbiye, Turkey .... 72 D7 36 10N 36 8 E
Harbo, Sweden ..... 10 D11 60 7N 17 12 E
Harboør, Denmark ... 11 H2 56 38N 8 10 E
Harbor Beach, U.S.A. . 116 C2 43 51N 82 39W
Harbour Breton,
  Canada 105 C8 47 29N 55 50W
Harbour Deep, Canada 105 B8 50 25N 56 32W
Harburger Berge △,
  Germany .... 24 B5 53 27N 9 58 E
Hårby, Denmark .... 11 J4 55 13N 10 7 E
Harda, India .... 68 H7 22 27N 77 5 E
Hardangerfjorden,
  Norway .... 9 F12 60 5N 6 0 E
Hardangervidda,
  Norway .... 9 F12 60 7N 7 20 E
Hardap △, Namibia .. 88 C2 24 29 S 17 45 E
Hardap Dam, Namibia 88 C2 24 32 S 17 50 E
Hardenberg, Neths. .. 17 B6 52 34N 6 37 E
Harderwijk, Neths. ... 17 B5 52 21N 5 38 E
Hardey →, Australia . 92 D2 22 45 S 116 8 E
Hardin, U.S.A. 108 D10 45 44N 107 37W
Harding, S. Africa ... 89 E4 30 35 S 29 55 E
Harding Ra., Australia . 92 C3 16 17 S 124 55 E
Hardisty, Canada ... 102 C6 52 40N 111 18W
Hardoi, India ...... 69 F9 27 26N 80 6 E
Hardwar = Haridwar,
  India .... 68 E8 29 58N 78 9 E
Hardwick, U.S.A. ... 117 B12 44 30N 72 22W

Hardy, Pen., Chile ... 128 H3 55 30 S 68 20W
Hardy, Pte., St. Lucia . 121 f 14 6N 60 56W
Hare B., Canada 105 B8 51 15N 55 45W
Hareid, Norway ..... 9 E12 62 22N 6 1 E
Haren, Germany .... 24 C3 52 47N 7 13 E
Harer, Ethiopia ..... 81 F5 9 20N 42 8 E
Harerge □, Ethiopia .. 81 F5 7 12N 42 0 E
Hareto, Ethiopia .... 81 F4 9 23N 37 6 E
Harfleur, France .... 18 C7 49 30N 0 10 E
Hargeisa, Somali Rep. . 75 F3 9 30N 44 2 E
Harghita □, Romania . 29 D10 46 30N 25 30 E
Harghita, Munții,
  Romania .... 29 D10 46 25N 25 35 E
Hargshamn, Sweden .. 10 D12 60 12N 18 30 E
Hari →, Indonesia ... 62 E2 1 16 S 104 5 E
Haria, Canary Is. 48 E6 29 8N 13 32W
Haridwar, India .... 68 E8 29 58N 78 9 E
Harim, Jabal al, Oman 71 E8 25 58N 56 14 E
Haringhata →, Bangla. 67 J16 22 0N 89 58 E
Harīrūd →, Asia .... 66 A2 37 24N 60 38 E
Härjedalen, Sweden .. 10 B7 62 22N 13 5 E
Harlan, Iowa, U.S.A. . 112 E7 41 39N 95 19W
Harlan, Ky., U.S.A. .. 115 G4 36 51N 83 19W
Harlech, U.K. 14 E3 52 52N 4 6W
Harlem, U.S.A. 108 B9 48 32N 108 47W
Harlingen, Neths. ... 17 A5 53 11N 5 25 E
Harlingen, U.S.A. ... 113 M6 26 12N 97 42W
Harlow, U.K. ...... 15 F8 51 46N 0 8 E
Harlowton, U.S.A. ... 108 C9 46 26N 109 50W
Harmancık, Turkey .. 47 B11 39 41N 29 9 E
Harmånger, Sweden .. 10 C11 61 55N 17 20 E
Harmil, Eritrea ..... 81 D5 16 30N 40 10 E
Harnai, Pakistan .... 68 D2 30 6N 67 56 E
Harney Basin, U.S.A. . 108 E4 43 30N 119 0W
Harney L., U.S.A. ... 108 E4 43 14N 119 8W
Harney Peak, U.S.A. . 112 D3 43 52N 103 32W
Härnön, Sweden .... 10 B12 62 36N 18 0 E
Härnösand, Sweden .. 10 B11 62 38N 17 55 E
Haro, Spain 38 C2 42 35N 2 55W
Haroldswick, U.K. ... 13 A8 60 48N 0 50W
Harp L., Canada 105 A7 55 5N 61 50W
Harper, Liberia 82 E3 4 25N 7 43W
Harplinge, Sweden ... 11 H6 56 45N 12 45 E
Harrai, India ...... 69 H8 22 37N 79 13 E
Harrand, Pakistan ... 68 E4 29 28N 70 3 E
Harrat Khaybar,
  Si. Arabia ...... 80 B5 25 30N 39 45 E
Harrat Nawāṣīf,
  Si. Arabia ...... 80 C5 21 20N 42 10 E
Harricana →, Canada . 104 B4 50 56N 79 32W
Harriman, U.S.A. ... 115 H3 35 56N 84 33W
Harrington Harbour,
  Canada 105 B8 50 31N 59 30W
Harris, U.K. 13 D2 57 50N 6 55W
Harris, L., Australia .. 95 E2 31 10 S 135 10 E
Harris, Sd. of, U.K. .. 13 D1 57 44N 7 6W
Harris Pt., Canada ... 116 C2 43 6N 82 9W
Harrisburg, Ill., U.S.A. 113 G10 37 44N 88 32W
Harrisburg, Nebr.,
  U.S.A. 112 E3 41 33N 103 44W
Harrisburg, Pa., U.S.A. 116 F8 40 16N 76 53W
Harrismith, S. Africa . 89 D4 28 15 S 29 8 E
Harrison, Ark., U.S.A. . 113 G8 36 14N 93 7W
Harrison, Maine, U.S.A. 117 B14 44 7N 70 39W
Harrison, Nebr., U.S.A. 112 D3 42 41N 103 53W
Harrison, C., Canada . 105 B8 54 55N 57 55W
Harrison L., Canada .. 102 D4 49 33N 121 50W
Harrisonburg, U.S.A. . 114 F6 38 27N 78 52W
Harrisonville, U.S.A. . 112 F7 38 39N 94 21W
Harriston, Canada ... 116 C4 43 57N 80 53W
Harrisville, Mich.,
  U.S.A. 116 B1 44 39N 83 17W
Harrisville, N.Y., U.S.A. 117 B9 44 9N 75 19W
Harrisville, Pa., U.S.A. 116 E5 41 8N 80 0W
Harrodsburg, U.S.A. . 114 G3 37 46N 84 51W
Harrogate, U.K. 14 C6 54 0N 1 33W
Harrow □, U.K. 15 F7 51 35N 0 21W
Harrowsmith, Canada 117 B8 44 24N 76 40W
Harry S. Truman
  Reservoir, U.S.A. .. 112 F7 38 16N 93 24W
Harsefeld, Germany .. 24 B5 53 27N 9 30 E
Harsewinkel, Germany 24 D4 51 56N 8 14 E
Harsın, Iran .... 70 C5 34 18N 47 33 E
Hârșova, Romania ... 29 F12 44 40N 27 59 E
Harstad, Norway .... 8 B17 68 48N 16 30 E
Harsud, India ...... 68 H7 22 6N 76 44 E
Hart, U.S.A. 114 D2 43 42N 86 22W
Hart, L., Australia ... 95 E2 31 10 S 136 25 E
Hartbees →, S. Africa . 88 D3 28 45 S 20 32 E
Hartberg, Austria ... 26 D8 47 17 S 15 58 E
Hartford, Conn., U.S.A. 117 E12 41 46N 72 41W
Hartford, Ky., U.S.A. . 114 G2 37 27N 86 55W
Hartford, S. Dak.,
  U.S.A. 112 D6 43 38N 96 57W
Hartford, Wis., U.S.A. . 112 D10 43 19N 88 22W
Hartford City, U.S.A. . 114 E3 40 27N 85 22W
Hartland, Canada ... 105 C6 46 20N 67 32W
Hartland Pt., U.K. ... 15 F3 51 1N 4 32W
Hartlepool, U.K. 14 C6 54 42N 1 13W
Hartlepool □, U.K. .. 14 C6 54 42N 1 17W
Hartley Bay, Canada . 102 C3 53 25N 129 15W
Hartmannberge,
  Namibia .... 88 B1 17 0 S 13 0 E
Hartney, Canada 103 D8 49 30N 100 35W
Hârtop, Moldova .... 29 D13 46 39N 28 40 E
Harts →, S. Africa ... 88 D3 28 24 S 24 17 E
Hartselle, U.S.A. ... 115 H2 34 27N 86 56W
Hartshorne, U.S.A. .. 113 H7 34 51N 95 34W
Hartstown, U.S.A. ... 116 E4 41 33N 80 23W
Hartsville, U.S.A. ... 115 H5 34 23N 80 4W
Hartswater, S. Africa . 88 D3 27 34 S 24 43 E
Hartwell, U.S.A. 115 H4 34 21N 82 56W
Harunabad, Pakistan . 68 E5 29 35N 73 8 E
Harvand, Iran ...... 71 D7 28 25N 55 43 E
Harvey, Australia ... 93 F2 33 5 S 115 54 E
Harvey, Ill., U.S.A. .. 114 E2 41 36N 87 50W
Harvey, N. Dak., U.S.A. 112 B5 47 47N 99 56W
Harwich, U.K. ..... 15 F9 51 56N 1 17 E
Haryana □, India ... 68 E7 29 0N 76 10 E
Haryn →, Belarus ... 33 F4 52 7N 27 17 E
Harz, Germany ..... 24 D6 51 38N 10 44 E
Harz △, Germany .... 24 D6 51 40N 10 18 E
Harzgerode, Germany 24 D7 51 38N 11 9 E
Hasa □, Si. Arabia ... 71 E6 25 50N 49 0 E
Hasaheisa, Sudan ... 81 E3 14 44N 33 20 E
Ḥasanābād, Iran .... 71 C7 32 8N 52 44 E
Hasdo →, India .... 69 J10 21 44N 82 44 E
Haselünne, Germany . 24 C3 52 40N 7 29 E
Hashimoto, Japan ... 55 G7 34 19N 135 37 E
Hashtjerd, Iran ..... 71 C6 35 52N 50 40 E
Haskell, U.S.A. 113 J5 33 10N 99 44W
Hasköy, Turkey ..... 45 E10 41 38N 26 31 E
Haslach, Germany ... 25 G4 48 16N 8 5 E

Hasle, Denmark .... 11 J8 55 11N 14 44 E
Haslemere, U.K. 15 F7 51 5N 0 43W
Haslev, Denmark ... 11 J5 55 18N 11 57 E
Hasparren, France ... 20 E2 43 24N 1 18 E
Hassa, Turkey ..... 72 D7 36 48N 36 29 E
Hassberge □, Germany 25 E6 50 8N 10 45 E
Hassela, Sweden .... 10 B10 62 7N 16 42 E
Hasselt, Belgium .... 17 D5 50 56N 5 21 E
Hassfurt, Germany .. 25 E6 50 2N 10 32 E
Hassi Messaoud, Algeria 78 B7 31 51N 6 1 E
Hässleholm, Sweden . 11 H7 56 10N 13 46 E
Hassloch, Germany .. 25 F4 49 22N 8 16 E
Hästholmen, Sweden . 11 F8 58 17N 14 38 E
Hastings, N.Z. ..... 91 H6 39 39 S 176 52 E
Hastings, U.K. ..... 15 G8 50 51N 0 35 E
Hastings, Mich., U.S.A. 114 D3 42 39N 85 17W
Hastings, Minn., U.S.A. 112 C8 44 44N 92 51W
Hastings, Nebr., U.S.A. 112 E5 40 35N 98 23W
Hastings Ra., Australia 95 E5 31 15 S 152 14 E
Hästveda, Sweden ... 11 H7 56 17N 13 55 E
Hat, Ukraine ...... 28 B7 48 19N 22 45 E
Hat Yai, Thailand ... 65 J3 7 1N 100 27 E
Hatanbulag = Ergel,
  Mongolia .... 56 C5 43 8N 109 5 E
Hatay = Antalya, Turkey 72 D4 36 52N 30 45 E
Hatch, U.S.A. 109 K10 32 40N 107 9W
Hatchet L., Canada .. 103 B8 58 36N 103 40W
Hațeg, Romania .... 28 E7 45 36N 22 55 E
Hateruma-Shima, Japan 55 M1 24 3N 123 47 E
Hatfield P.O., Australia 95 E3 33 54 S 143 49 E
Hatgal, Mongolia ... 60 A5 50 26N 100 9 E
Hathras, India ..... 68 F8 27 36N 78 6 E
Hatia, Bangla. ..... 67 H17 22 30N 91 5 E
Ḥātibah, Ra's, Si. Arabia 80 C4 22 6N 39 52 E
Hato Mayor, Dom. Rep. 121 C6 18 46N 69 15W
Hatta, India ...... 69 G8 24 7N 79 36 E
Hattah, Australia ... 95 E3 34 48 S 142 17 E
Hatteras, C., U.S.A. .. 115 H8 35 14N 75 32W
Hattiesburg, U.S.A. .. 113 K10 31 20N 89 17W
Hatvan, Hungary ... 28 C4 47 40N 19 45 E
Hau Bon = Cheo Reo,
  Vietnam .... 62 B3 13 25N 108 28 E
Hau Duc, Vietnam ... 64 E7 15 20N 108 13 E
Haugesund, Norway .. 9 G11 59 23N 5 13 E
Haukipudas, Finland . 8 D21 65 12N 25 20 E
Haultain →, Canada . 103 B7 55 51N 106 46W
Hauraki G., N.Z. .... 91 G5 36 35 S 175 5 E
Hausruck, Austria ... 26 C6 48 6N 13 30 E
Haut Atlas, Morocco . 78 B4 32 30N 5 0W
Haut-Jura △, France . 19 F9 46 23N 2 23 E
Haut-Languedoc △,
  France .... 20 E6 43 30N 2 43 E
Haut Niger △, Guinea 82 C2 10 20N 10 20W
Haut-Rhin □, France . 19 E14 48 0N 7 15 E
Haute-Corse □, France 21 F13 42 30N 9 30 E
Haute-Garonne □,
  France .... 20 E5 43 30N 1 30 E
Haute-Loire □, France 20 C7 45 5N 3 50 E
Haute-Marne □, France 19 D12 48 10N 5 20 E
Haute-Normandie □,
  France .... 18 C7 49 20N 1 0 E
Haute-Saône □, France 19 E13 47 45N 6 10 E
Haute-Savoie □, France 21 C10 46 0N 6 20 E
Haute-Vienne □, France 20 C5 45 50N 1 10 E
Hautes-Alpes □, France 21 D10 44 42N 6 20 E
Hautes Fagnes = Hohe
  Venn, Belgium .... 17 D6 50 30N 6 5 E
Hautes Fagnes = Hohes
  Venn-Eifel △, Europe 24 E2 50 30N 6 10 E
Hautes-Pyrénées □,
  France .... 20 F4 43 0N 0 10 E
Hauteville-Lompnès,
  France .... 21 C9 45 58N 5 36 E
Hautmont, France ... 19 B10 50 15N 3 55 E
Hauts-de-Seine □,
  France .... 19 D9 48 52N 2 15 E
Hauts Plateaux, Algeria 76 C4 35 0N 1 0 E
Hauzenberg, Germany 25 G9 48 40N 13 37 E
Havana = La Habana,
  Cuba 120 B3 23 8N 82 22W
Havana, U.S.A. 112 E9 40 18N 90 4W
Havant, U.K. 15 G7 50 51N 0 58W
Havârna, Romania .. 29 B11 48 4N 26 43 E
Havasu, L., U.S.A. ... 111 L12 34 18N 114 28W
Havdhem, Sweden ... 11 G12 57 10N 18 20 E
Havel →, Germany .. 24 C8 52 50N 12 3 E
Havelian, Pakistan ... 68 B5 34 2N 73 10 E
Havelock, Canada ... 116 B7 44 26N 77 53W
Havelock, N.Z. ..... 91 J4 41 17 S 173 48 E
Havelock, U.S.A. 115 H7 34 53N 76 54W
Haverfordwest, U.K. . 15 F3 51 48N 4 58W
Haverhill, U.K. ..... 15 E8 52 5N 0 28 E
Haverhill, U.S.A. ... 117 D13 42 47N 71 5W
Haverstraw, U.S.A. .. 117 E11 41 12N 73 58W
Håverud, Sweden ... 11 F6 58 50N 12 28 E
Havirga, Mongolia .. 56 B7 45 41N 113 5 E
Havířov, Czech Rep. . 27 B11 49 46N 18 20 E
Havlíčkův Brod,
  Czech Rep. ...... 26 B8 49 36N 15 33 E
Havneby, Denmark .. 11 J2 55 5N 8 34 E
Havran, Turkey .... 47 B9 39 33N 27 6 E
Havre, France ...... 18 C7 49 30N 0 5 E
Havre, U.S.A. 108 B9 48 33N 109 41W
Havre-Aubert, Canada 105 C7 47 12N 61 56W
Havre-St.-Pierre,
  Canada 105 B7 50 18N 63 33W
Havsa, Turkey ..... 45 E10 41 33N 26 48 E
Havza, Turkey ..... 72 B6 41 0N 35 35 E
Haw →, U.S.A. 115 H6 35 36N 79 3W
Hawaii □, U.S.A. ... 106 H16 19 30N 156 30W
Hawaii I., Pac. Oc. .. 106 J17 20 0N 155 0W
Hawaiian Is., Pac. Oc. 106 H17 20 30N 156 0W
Hawaiian Ridge,
  Pac. Oc. 97 E11 24 0N 165 0W
Hawarden, U.S.A. ... 112 D6 43 0N 96 29W
Hawea, L., N.Z. .... 91 L2 44 28 S 169 19 E
Hawera, N.Z. ...... 91 H5 39 35 S 174 19 E
Hawick, U.K. 13 F6 55 26N 2 47W
Hawk Junction, Canada 104 C3 48 5N 84 38W
Hawke B., N.Z. .... 91 H6 39 25 S 177 20 E
Hawker, Australia ... 95 E2 31 59 S 138 22 E
Hawkesbury, Canada . 104 C5 45 37N 74 37W
Hawkesbury I., Canada 102 C3 53 37N 129 3W
Hawkesbury Pt.,
  Australia .... 94 A1 11 55 S 134 5 E
Hawkinsville, U.S.A. . 115 J4 32 17N 83 28W
Hawley, Minn., U.S.A. 112 B6 46 53N 96 19W
Hawley, Pa., U.S.A. .. 117 E9 41 28N 75 11W
Hawrān, W. →, Iraq . 70 C4 33 58N 42 34 E
Hawsh Mūssá, Lebanon 74 B4 33 45N 35 55 E
Hawthorne, U.S.A. .. 108 G4 38 32N 118 38W
Hay, Australia ...... 95 E4 34 30 S 144 51 E
Hay →, Australia ... 94 C2 24 50 S 138 0 E
Hay →, Canada 102 A5 60 50N 116 26W
Hay, C., Australia ... 92 B4 14 5 S 129 29 E
Hay I., Canada 116 B4 44 53N 80 58W
Hay L., Canada 102 B5 58 50N 118 50W

Hay-on-Wye, U.K. .. 15 E4 52 5N 3 8W
Hay River, Canada .. 102 A5 60 51N 115 44W
Hay Springs, U.S.A. . 112 D3 42 41N 102 41W
Haya = Tehoru,
  Indonesia .... 63 E7 3 23 S 129 30 E
Hayachine-San, Japan 54 E10 39 34N 141 29 E
Hayange, France .... 19 C13 49 20N 6 2 E
Haydarlı, Turkey ... 47 C12 38 16N 30 23 E
Hayden, U.S.A. 108 F10 40 30N 107 16W
Haydon, Australia ... 94 B3 18 0 S 141 30 E
Hayes, U.S.A. 112 C4 44 23N 101 1W
Hayes →, Canada ... 104 A1 57 3N 92 12W
Hayes Creek, Australia 92 B5 13 43 S 131 22 E
Hayle, U.K. 15 G2 50 11N 5 26W
Hayling I., U.K. 15 G7 50 48N 0 59W
Haymana, Turkey ... 72 C5 39 26N 32 31 E
Hayman I., Australia . 94 b 20 3 S 148 52 E
Hayrabolu, Turkey .. 45 E11 41 12N 27 5 E
Hays, Canada 102 C6 50 6N 111 48W
Hays, U.S.A. 112 F5 38 53N 99 20W
Haysyn, Ukraine .... 33 H5 48 57N 29 25 E
Hayvoron, Ukraine .. 29 B14 48 22N 29 52 E
Hayward, Calif., U.S.A. 110 H4 37 40N 122 5W
Hayward, Wis., U.S.A. 112 B9 46 1N 91 29W
Haywards Heath, U.K. 15 G7 51 0N 0 5W
Hazafon □, Israel ... 74 C4 32 40N 35 20 E
Hazārān, Kūh-e, Iran 71 D8 29 35N 57 20 E
Hazard, U.S.A. 114 G4 37 15N 83 12W
Hazaribag, India ... 69 H11 23 58N 85 26 E
Hazaribag Road, India 69 G11 24 12N 85 57 E
Hazebrouck, France . 19 B9 50 42N 2 31 E
Hazelton, Canada ... 102 B3 55 20N 127 42W
Hazelton, U.S.A. ... 112 B4 46 29N 100 17W
Hazen, U.S.A. 112 B4 47 18N 101 38W
Hazlehurst, Ga., U.S.A. 115 K4 31 52N 82 36W
Hazlehurst, Miss., U.S.A. 113 K9 31 52N 90 24W
Hazlet, U.S.A. 117 F10 40 25N 74 12W
Hazlett, L., Australia . 92 D4 21 30 S 128 48 E
Hazleton, U.S.A. ... 117 F9 40 57N 75 59W
Hazro, Turkey ..... 70 B4 38 15N 40 47 E
He Xian, Anhui, China 59 B12 31 45N 118 20 E
He Xian,
  Guangxi Zhuangzu,
  China .... 59 E8 24 27N 111 30 E
Head of Bight, Australia 93 F5 31 30 S 131 25 E
Headlands, Zimbabwe 87 F3 18 15 S 32 2 E
Healdsburg, U.S.A. .. 110 G4 38 37N 122 52W
Healdton, U.S.A. ... 113 H6 34 14N 97 29W
Healesville, Australia . 95 F4 37 35 S 145 30 E
Heany Junction,
  Zimbabwe .... 89 C4 20 6 S 28 54 E
Heard I., Ind. Oc. ... 3 G13 53 0 S 74 0 E
Hearne, U.S.A. 113 K6 30 53N 96 36W
Hearst, Canada 104 C3 49 40N 83 41W
Heart →, U.S.A. ... 112 B4 46 46N 100 50W
Heart's Content, Canada 105 C9 47 54N 53 27W
Heath, Pte., Canada . 105 C7 49 8N 61 40W
Heathrow, London ✈
  (LHR), U.K. 15 F7 51 28N 0 27W
Heavener, U.S.A. ... 113 H7 34 53N 94 36W
Hebbronville, U.S.A. . 113 M5 27 18N 98 41W
Hebei □, China ..... 56 E9 39 0N 116 0 E
Hebel, Australia .... 95 D4 28 58 S 147 47 E
Heber, U.S.A. 111 N11 32 44N 115 32W
Heber City, U.S.A. ... 108 F8 40 31N 111 25W
Heber Springs, U.S.A. 113 H9 35 30N 92 2W
Hebert, Canada 103 C7 50 30N 107 10W
Hebgen L., U.S.A. ... 108 D8 44 52N 111 20W
Hebi, China .... 56 G8 35 57N 114 7 E
Hebrides, U.K. 6 D4 57 30N 7 0W
Hebrides, Sea of the,
  U.K. 13 D2 57 5N 7 0W
Hebron = Al Khalīl,
  West Bank .... 74 D4 31 32N 35 6 E
Hebron, Canada 101 C13 58 5N 62 30W
Hebron, N. Dak., U.S.A. 112 B3 46 54N 102 3W
Hebron, Nebr., U.S.A. 112 E6 40 10N 97 35W
Heby, Sweden ...... 10 E10 59 56N 16 53 E
Hecate Str., Canada .. 102 C2 53 10N 130 30W
Hechi, China ...... 58 E7 24 40N 108 2 E
Hechingen, Germany . 25 G4 48 21N 8 57 E
Hechuan, China .... 58 B6 30 2N 106 12 E
Hecla, U.S.A. 112 C5 45 53N 98 9W
Hecla I., Canada 103 C9 51 10N 96 43W
Hédé, France 18 D5 48 18N 1 49W
Hede, Sweden ...... 10 B7 62 23N 13 30 E
Hedemora, Sweden .. 10 D9 60 18N 15 58 E
Hedensted, Denmark . 11 J3 55 46N 9 42 E
Hedesunda, Sweden .. 10 D10 60 24N 17 0 E
Heerde, Neths. ..... 17 B6 52 24N 6 2 E
Heerenveen, Neths. .. 17 B5 52 57N 5 55 E
Heerhugowaard, Neths. 17 B4 52 40N 4 51 E
Heerlen, Neths. .... 17 D5 50 55N 5 58 E
Hefa, Israel .... 74 C4 32 46N 35 0 E
Hefa □, Israel ..... 74 C4 32 40N 35 0 E
Hefei, China ...... 59 B11 31 52N 117 18 E
Hefeng, China ..... 59 C8 29 58N 109 52 E
Hegalig, Sudan ..... 81 E3 14 36N 31 54 E
Hegang, China ..... 60 B8 47 20N 130 19 E
Heiban, Sudan ..... 81 E3 11 13N 30 48 E
Heichengzhen, China . 56 F4 36 24N 106 3 E
Heide, Germany .... 24 A5 54 11N 9 6 E
Heidelberg, Germany . 25 F4 49 24N 8 42 E
Heidelberg, S. Africa . 88 E3 34 6 S 20 59 E
Heidenau, Germany .. 24 E9 50 57N 13 52 E
Heidenheim, Germany 25 G6 48 41N 10 9 E
Heijing, China ..... 58 E3 25 22N 101 44 E
Heilbad Heiligenstadt,
  Germany .... 24 D6 51 22N 10 8 E
Heilbron, S. Africa .. 89 D4 27 16 S 27 59 E
Heilbronn, Germany . 25 F5 49 9N 9 13 E
Heiligenblut, Austria . 26 D5 47 2N 12 51 E
Heiligenhafen, Germany 24 A6 54 22N 10 59 E
Heilongjiang □, China 60 B7 48 0N 126 0 E
Heilunkiang =
  Heilongjiang □, China 60 B7 48 0N 126 0 E
Heimaey, Iceland ... 8 E3 63 26N 20 17W
Heinola, Finland .... 9 F22 61 13N 26 2 E
Heinsberg, Germany . 24 D2 51 3N 6 6 E
Heinze Kyun, Burma . 64 E1 14 25N 97 45 E
Heishan, China ..... 57 C12 42 28N 122 30 E
Heishui, Liaoning,
  China .... 57 C10 42 8N 119 30 E
Heishui, Sichuan, China 58 A4 32 4N 103 2 E
Hejaz = Ḥijāz □,
  Si. Arabia ...... 70 E3 24 0N 40 0 E
Hejian, China ...... 56 E9 38 25N 116 5 E
Hejiang, China ..... 58 C5 28 43N 105 46 E
Hejin, China ...... 56 G6 35 35N 110 42 E
Hekimhan, Turkey .. 70 B3 38 50N 37 57 E
Hekla, Iceland 8 E4 63 56N 19 35W
Hekou, Guangdong,
  China .... 59 F9 23 13N 112 45 E
Hekou, Yunnan, China 58 F5 22 30N 103 59 E
Hel, Poland .... 30 D5 54 37N 18 47 E
Helagsfjället, Sweden . 10 B6 62 54N 12 25 E

Helan Shan, China .. 56 E3 38 30N 105 55 E
Helechosa, Spain ... 37 F6 39 22N 4 53W
Helen Atoll, Pac. Oc. . 63 D8 2 40N 132 0 E
Helena, Ark., U.S.A. . 113 H9 34 32N 90 36W
Helena, Mont., U.S.A. 108 C7 46 36N 112 2W
Helendale, U.S.A. ... 111 L9 34 44N 117 19W
Helensburgh, U.K. .. 13 E4 56 1N 4 43W
Helensville, N.Z. ... 91 G5 36 41 S 174 29 E
Helenvale, Australia . 94 B4 15 43 S 145 14 E
Helgasjön, Sweden .. 11 H8 56 55N 14 50 E
Helgeland, Norway .. 8 C15 66 7N 13 29 E
Helgoland, Germany . 24 A3 54 10N 7 53 E
Heligoland = Helgoland,
  Germany .... 24 A3 54 10N 7 53 E
Heligoland B. =
  Deutsche Bucht,
  Germany .... 24 A4 54 15N 8 0 E
Heliopolis, Egypt ... 80 H7 30 6N 31 17 E
Hella, Iceland 8 E3 63 50N 20 24W
Hellertown, U.S.A. .. 117 F9 40 35N 75 21W
Hellespont = Çanakkale
  Boğazı, Turkey ... 45 F10 40 17N 26 32 E
Hellevoetsluis, Neths. 17 C4 51 50N 4 8 E
Hellhole Gorge △,
  Australia .... 94 D3 25 31 S 144 12 E
Hellín, Spain 39 G3 38 31N 1 40W
Hells Canyon △, U.S.A. 108 D5 45 30N 117 45W
Hell's Gate △, Kenya . 86 C4 0 54 S 36 19 E
Helmand □, Afghan. . 66 D4 31 20N 64 0 E
Helmand →, Afghan. 66 D2 31 12N 61 34 E
Helme →, Germany . 24 D7 51 20N 11 21 E
Helmeringhausen,
  Namibia .... 88 D2 25 54 S 16 57 E
Helmond, Neths. ... 17 C5 51 29N 5 41 E
Helmsdale, U.K. 13 C5 58 7N 3 39W
Helmsdale →, U.K. . 13 C5 58 7N 3 40W
Helmstedt, Germany . 24 C7 52 12N 11 0 E
Helong, China ..... 57 C15 42 40N 129 0 E
Helper, U.S.A. 108 G8 39 41N 110 51W
Helsingborg, Sweden . 11 H6 56 3N 12 42 E
Helsinge, Denmark .. 11 H6 56 2N 12 12 E
Helsingfors = Helsinki,
  Finland .... 9 F21 60 15N 25 3 E
Helsingør, Denmark .. 11 H6 56 2N 12 35 E
Helsinki, Finland ... 9 F21 60 15N 25 3 E
Helska, Mierzeja,
  Poland .... 30 D5 54 45N 18 40 E
Helston, U.K. 15 G2 50 6N 5 17W
Helvellyn, U.K. 14 C4 54 32N 3 1W
Helwân, Egypt ..... 80 J7 29 50N 31 20 E
Hemel Hempstead, U.K. 15 F7 51 44N 0 28W
Hemet, U.S.A. 111 M10 33 45N 116 58W
Hemingford, U.S.A. . 112 D3 42 19N 103 4W
Hemmingford, Canada 117 A11 45 3N 73 35W
Hempstead, U.S.A. .. 113 K6 30 6N 96 5W
Hemse, Sweden ..... 11 G12 57 15N 18 22 E
Hemsön, Sweden .... 10 B12 62 42N 18 5 E
Henån, Sweden ..... 11 F5 58 14N 11 40 E
Henan □, China .... 56 H8 34 0N 114 0 E
Henares →, Spain ... 36 E7 40 24N 3 30W
Henashi-Misaki, Japan 54 D9 40 37N 139 51 E
Hendaye, France 20 E2 43 23N 1 47W
Hendek, Turkey .... 72 B4 40 48N 30 44 E
Henderson, Argentina 126 D3 36 18 S 61 43W
Henderson, Ky., U.S.A. 114 G2 37 50N 87 35W
Henderson, N.C., U.S.A. 115 G6 36 20N 78 25W
Henderson, Nev., U.S.A. 111 J12 36 2N 114 59W
Henderson, Tenn.,
  U.S.A. 115 H1 35 26N 88 38W
Henderson, Tex., U.S.A. 113 J7 32 9N 94 48W
Hendersonville, N.C.,
  U.S.A. 115 H4 35 19N 82 28W
Hendersonville, Tenn.,
  U.S.A. 115 G2 36 18N 86 37W
Hendījān, Iran ..... 71 D6 30 14N 49 43 E
Hendorābī, Iran .... 71 E7 26 40N 53 37 E
Heng Jiang, China .. 58 C5 28 40N 104 25 E
Heng Xian, China ... 58 F7 22 40N 109 17 E
Hengcheng, China ... 56 E4 38 18N 106 28 E
Hengchun, Taiwan .. 59 F13 22 0N 120 44 E
Hengdaohezi, China . 57 B15 44 52N 129 0 E
Hengelo, Neths. .... 17 B6 52 16N 6 48 E
Hengfeng, China .... 59 C10 28 12N 117 57 E
Hengshan, Hunan,
  China .... 59 D9 27 16N 112 45 E
Hengshan, Shaanxi,
  China .... 56 F5 37 58N 109 5 E
Hengshui, China .... 56 F8 37 41N 115 40 E
Hengyang, China .... 59 D9 26 59N 112 22 E
Henichesk, Ukraine .. 33 J8 46 12N 34 50 E
Hénin-Beaumont,
  France .... 19 B9 50 25N 2 58 E
Henley-on-Thames,
  U.K. 15 F7 51 32N 0 54W
Henlopen, C., U.S.A. . 114 F8 38 48N 75 6W
Hennan, Sweden .... 10 B9 62 2N 15 54 E
Hennebont, France .. 18 E3 47 49N 3 19W
Hennenman, S. Africa 88 D4 27 59 S 27 1 E
Hennessey, U.S.A. ... 113 G6 36 6N 97 54W
Hennigsdorf, Germany 24 C9 52 38N 13 12 E
Henri Pittier △,
  Venezuela 121 D6 10 26N 67 37W
Henrietta, U.S.A. ... 113 J5 33 49N 98 12W
Henrietta, Ostrov =
  Genriyetty, Ostrov,
  Russia .... 53 B16 77 6N 156 30 E
Henrietta Maria, C.,
  Canada 104 A3 55 9N 82 20W
Henry, U.S.A. 112 E10 41 7N 89 22W
Henryetta, U.S.A. ... 113 H7 35 27N 95 59W
Henryville, Canada .. 117 A11 45 8N 73 11W
Hensall, Canada 116 C3 43 26N 81 30W
Henstedt-Ulzburg,
  Germany .... 24 B6 53 47N 10 0 E
Hentiesbaai, Namibia 88 C1 22 8 S 14 18 E
Hentiyn Nuruu,
  Mongolia .... 60 B5 48 30N 108 30 E
Henty, Australia .... 95 F4 35 30 S 147 0 E
Henzada, Burma .... 67 L19 17 38N 95 26 E
Hephaestia, Greece .. 47 B7 39 55N 25 14 E
Heping, China ..... 59 E10 24 29N 115 0 E
Heppner, U.S.A. 108 D4 45 21N 119 33W
Hepu, China ...... 58 G7 21 40N 109 12 E
Hepworth, Canada .. 116 B3 44 37N 81 9W
Heqing, China ..... 58 D3 26 32N 100 11 E
Héradsflói, Iceland .. 8 D6 65 42N 14 12W
Héradsvötn →, Iceland 8 D4 65 45N 19 25W
Heraklion = Iráklion,
  Greece .... 49 D7 35 20N 25 12 E
Herald Cays, Australia 94 B4 16 58 S 149 9 E
Herāt, Afghan. .... 66 B3 34 20N 62 7 E
Herāt □, Afghan. ... 66 B3 35 0N 62 0 E
Hérault □, France ... 20 E7 43 34N 3 15 E
Hérault →, France .. 20 E7 43 17N 3 26 E
Herbault, France ... 18 E8 47 36N 1 8 E
Herbert →, Australia 94 B4 18 31 S 146 17 E

164 Herbert River Falls INDEX TO WORLD MAPS

Herbert River Falls △, Australia 94 B4 18 15 S 145 32 E
Herberton, Australia 94 B4 17 20 S 145 25 E
Herbertsdale, S. Africa 88 E3 34 1 S 21 46 E
Herbignac, France 18 E4 47 27N 2 18W
Herborn, Germany 24 E4 50 40N 8 18 E
Herby, Poland 31 H5 50 45N 18 50 E
Herceg-Novi, Serbia & M. 44 D2 42 30N 18 33 E
Herchmer, Canada 103 B10 57 22N 94 10W
Herðubreið, Iceland 8 D5 65 11N 16 21W
Hereford, U.K. 15 E5 52 4N 2 43W
Hereford, U.S.A. 113 H3 34 49N 102 24W
Herefordshire □, U.K. 15 E5 52 8N 2 40W
Hereke, Turkey 45 F13 40 47N 29 38 E
Herencia, Spain 37 F7 39 21N 3 22W
Herentals, Belgium 17 C4 51 12N 4 51 E
Herford, Germany 24 C4 52 7N 8 39 E
Héricourt, France 19 E13 47 32N 6 45 E
Herington, U.S.A. 112 F6 38 40N 96 57W
Herisau, Switz. 25 H5 47 22N 9 17 E
Hérisson, France 19 F9 46 32N 2 42 E
Herkimer, U.S.A. 117 D10 43 0N 74 59W
Herlong, U.S.A. 110 E6 40 8N 120 8W
Herm, U.K. 15 H5 49 30N 2 28W
Hermakivka, Ukraine 29 B11 48 42N 26 11 E
Hermann, U.S.A. 112 F9 38 42N 91 27W
Hermannsburg, Australia 92 D5 23 57 S 132 45 E
Hermannsburg, Germany 24 C6 52 50N 10 5 E
Hermanus, S. Africa 88 E2 34 27 S 19 12 E
Herment, France 20 C6 45 45N 2 24 E
Hermidale, Australia 95 E4 31 30 S 146 42 E
Hermiston, U.S.A. 108 D4 45 51N 119 17W
Hermite, I., Chile 128 H3 55 50 S 68 0W
Hermon, U.S.A. 117 B9 44 28N 75 14W
Hermon, Mt. = Shaykh, J. ash, Lebanon 74 B4 33 25N 35 50 E
Hermosillo, Mexico 118 B2 29 10N 111 0W
Hernád →, Hungary 28 C6 47 56N 21 8 E
Hernandarias, Paraguay 127 B5 25 20 S 54 40W
Hernandez, U.S.A. 110 J6 36 24N 120 46W
Hernando, Argentina 126 C3 32 28 S 63 40W
Hernando, U.S.A. 113 H10 34 50N 90 0W
Hernani, Spain 38 B3 43 16N 1 58W
Herndon, U.S.A. 116 F8 40 43N 76 51W
Herne, Germany 17 C7 51 32N 7 14 E
Herne Bay, U.K. 15 F9 51 21N 1 8 E
Herning, Denmark 11 H2 56 8N 8 58 E
Heroica = Caborca, Mexico 118 A2 30 40N 112 10W
Heroica Nogales = Nogales, Mexico 118 A2 31 20N 110 56W
Heron Bay, Canada 104 C2 48 40N 86 25W
Herradura, Pta. de la, Canary Is. 48 F5 28 26N 14 8W
Herreid, U.S.A. 112 C4 45 50N 100 4W
Herrenberg, Germany 25 G4 48 35N 8 52 E
Herrera, Spain 37 H6 37 26N 4 55W
Herrera de Alcántara, Spain 37 F3 39 39N 7 25W
Herrera de Pisuerga, Spain 36 C6 42 35N 4 20W
Herrera del Duque, Spain 37 F5 39 10N 5 3W
Herrestad, Sweden 11 F5 58 21N 11 50 E
Herrin, U.S.A. 113 G10 37 48N 89 2W
Herriot, Canada 103 B8 56 22N 101 16W
Herrljunga, Sweden 11 F7 58 5N 13 1 E
Hersbruck, Germany 25 F7 49 30N 11 26 E
Herschel I., Canada 4 C1 69 35N 139 5W
Hershey, U.S.A. 117 F8 40 17N 76 39W
Hersonissos, Greece 49 D7 35 18N 25 22 E
Herstal, Belgium 17 D5 50 40N 5 38 E
Hertford, U.K. 15 F7 51 48N 0 4W
Hertfordshire □, U.K. 15 F7 51 51N 0 5W
's-Hertogenbosch, Neths. 17 C5 51 42N 5 17 E
Hertsa, Ukraine 29 B11 48 9N 26 15 E
Hertzogville, S. Africa 88 D4 28 9 S 25 30 E
Hervás, Spain 36 E5 40 16N 5 52W
Hervey B., Australia 94 C5 25 0 S 152 52 E
Herzberg, Brandenburg, Germany 24 D9 51 41N 13 14 E
Herzberg, Niedersachsen, Germany 24 D6 51 38N 10 20 E
Herzliyya, Israel 74 C3 32 10N 34 50 E
Herzogenburg, Austria 26 C8 48 17N 15 41 E
Ḥeṣār, Fārs, Iran 71 D6 29 52N 50 16 E
Ḥeṣār, Markazī, Iran 71 C6 35 50N 49 12 E
Hesdin, France 19 B9 50 21N 2 2 E
Heshan, China 58 F7 23 50N 108 53 E
Heshui, China 56 G5 35 48N 108 0 E
Heshun, China 56 F7 37 22N 113 32 E
Hesperia, U.S.A. 111 L9 34 25N 117 18W
Hesse = Hessen □, Germany 24 E4 50 30N 9 0 E
Hessen □, Germany 24 E4 50 30N 9 0 E
Hessenreuther und Manteler Wald △, Germany 25 F8 49 45N 12 1 E
Hestra, Sweden 11 G7 57 26N 13 35 E
Hetch Hetchy Aqueduct, U.S.A. 110 H5 37 29N 122 19W
Hettinger, U.S.A. 112 C3 46 0N 102 42W
Hettstedt, Germany 24 D7 51 39N 11 31 E
Heuvelton, U.S.A. 117 B9 44 37N 75 25W
Heves, Hungary 28 C5 47 36N 20 17 E
Heves □, Hungary 28 C5 47 50N 20 0 E
Hewitt, U.S.A. 113 K6 31 27N 97 11W
Hexham, U.K. 14 C5 54 58N 2 4W
Hexi, Yunnan, China 58 E4 24 9N 102 38 E
Hexi, Zhejiang, China 59 D12 27 58N 119 38 E
Hexigten Qi, China 57 C9 43 18N 117 30 E
Ḥeydarābād, Iran 71 D7 30 33N 55 38 E
Heysham, U.K. 14 C5 54 3N 2 53W
Heyuan, China 59 F10 23 39N 114 40 E
Heywood, Australia 95 F3 38 8 S 141 37 E
Heze, China 56 G8 35 14N 115 20 E
Hezhang, China 58 D5 27 8N 104 41 E
Hi, Ko, Thailand 65 a 7 44N 98 22 E
Hi Vista, U.S.A. 111 L9 34 45N 117 46W
Hialeah, U.S.A. 115 N5 25 50N 80 17W
Hiawatha, U.S.A. 112 F7 39 51N 95 32W
Hibbing, U.S.A. 112 B8 47 25N 92 56W
Hibbs B., Australia 95 G4 42 35 S 145 15 E
Hibernia Reef, Australia 92 B3 12 0 S 123 23 E
Hickman, U.S.A. 113 G10 36 34N 89 11W
Hickory, U.S.A. 115 H5 35 44N 81 21W
Hicks, Pt., Australia 95 F4 37 49 S 149 17 E
Hicks L., Canada 103 A9 61 25N 100 0W
Hicksville, U.S.A. 117 F11 40 46N 73 32W
Hida, Romania 29 C8 47 10N 23 19 E
Hida-Gawa →, Japan 55 G8 35 26N 137 3 E
Hida-Sammyaku, Japan 55 F8 36 30N 137 40 E
Hidaka-Sammyaku, Japan 54 C11 42 35N 142 45 E
Hidalgo, Mexico 119 C5 24 15N 99 26W
Hidalgo □, Mexico 119 C5 20 30N 99 10W
Hidalgo, Presa M., Mexico 118 B3 26 30N 108 35W
Hidalgo del Parral, Mexico 118 B3 26 58N 105 40W
Hiddensee, Germany 24 A9 54 32N 13 6 E
Hieflau, Austria 26 D7 47 36N 14 46 E
Hiendelaencina, Spain 38 D2 41 5N 3 0W
Hierro, Canary Is. 48 G1 27 44N 18 0W
Higashiajima-San, Japan 54 F10 37 40N 140 10 E
Higashiōsaka, Japan 55 G7 34 40N 135 37 E
Higgins, U.S.A. 113 G4 36 7N 100 2W
Higgins Corner, U.S.A. 110 F5 39 2N 121 5W
High Bridge, U.S.A. 117 F10 40 40N 74 54W
High Level, Canada 102 B5 58 31N 117 8W
High Point, U.S.A. 115 H6 35 57N 80 0W
High Prairie, Canada 102 B5 55 30N 116 30W
High River, Canada 102 C6 50 30N 113 50W
High Tatra = Tatry, Slovak Rep. 27 B13 49 20N 20 0 E
High Veld, Africa 76 J6 27 0 S 27 0 E
High Wycombe, U.K. 15 F7 51 37N 0 45W
Highland □, U.K. 13 D4 57 17N 4 21W
Highland Park, U.S.A. 114 D2 42 11N 87 48W
Highmore, U.S.A. 112 C5 44 31N 99 27W
Highrock L., Man., Canada 103 B8 55 45N 100 30W
Highrock L., Sask., Canada 103 B7 57 5N 105 32W
Higüey, Dom. Rep. 121 C6 18 37N 68 42W
Hihya, Egypt 80 H7 30 40N 31 36 E
Hiiumaa, Estonia 9 G20 58 50N 22 45 E
Híjar, Spain 38 D4 41 10N 0 27W
Ḥijāz □, Si. Arabia 70 E3 24 0N 40 0 E
Hijo = Tagum, Phil. 61 H6 7 33N 125 53 E
Hikari, Japan 55 H5 33 58N 131 58 E
Hikmak, Ras el, Egypt 80 A2 31 15N 27 51 E
Hiko, U.S.A. 110 H11 37 32N 115 14W
Hikone, Japan 55 G8 35 15N 136 10 E
Hikurangi, Gisborne, N.Z. 91 H6 37 55 S 178 4 E
Hikurangi, Northland, N.Z. 91 F5 35 36 S 174 17 E
Hildburghausen, Germany 24 E6 50 25N 10 42 E
Hildesheim, Germany 24 C5 52 9N 9 56 E
Hill →, Australia 93 F2 30 23 S 115 3 E
Hill City, Idaho, U.S.A. 108 E6 43 18N 115 3W
Hill City, Kans., U.S.A. 112 F5 39 22N 99 51W
Hill City, S. Dak., U.S.A. 112 D3 43 56N 103 35W
Hill Island L., Canada 103 A7 60 30N 109 50W
Hillaby, Mt., Barbados 121 g 13 12N 59 35W
Hillared, Sweden 11 G7 57 37N 13 10 E
Hillcrest, Barbados 121 g 13 13N 59 32W
Hillcrest Center, U.S.A. 111 K8 35 23N 118 57W
Hillegom, Neths. 17 B4 52 18N 4 35 E
Hillerød, Denmark 11 J6 55 56N 12 19 E
Hillerstorp, Sweden 11 G7 57 20N 13 52 E
Hillsboro, Kans., U.S.A. 112 F6 38 21N 97 12W
Hillsboro, N. Dak., U.S.A. 112 B6 47 26N 97 3W
Hillsboro, N.H., U.S.A. 117 C13 43 7N 71 54W
Hillsboro, Ohio, U.S.A. 114 F4 39 12N 83 37W
Hillsboro, Oreg., U.S.A. 110 E4 45 31N 122 59W
Hillsboro, Tex., U.S.A. 113 J6 32 1N 97 8W
Hillsborough, Grenada 121 D7 12 28N 61 28W
Hillsborough Channel, Australia 94 J7 20 56 S 149 15 E
Hillsdale, Mich., U.S.A. 114 E3 41 56N 84 38W
Hillsdale, N.Y., U.S.A. 117 D11 42 11N 73 30W
Hillsport, Canada 104 C2 49 27N 85 34W
Hillston, Australia 95 E4 33 30 S 145 31 E
Hilo, U.S.A. 106 J17 19 44N 155 5W
Hilton, U.S.A. 116 C7 43 17N 77 48W
Hilton Head Island, U.S.A. 115 J5 32 13N 80 45W
Hilvan, Turkey 73 D8 37 34N 38 58 E
Hilversum, Neths. 17 B5 52 14N 5 10 E
Himachal Pradesh □, India 68 D7 31 30N 77 0 E
Himalaya, Asia 69 E11 29 0N 84 0 E
Himamaylan, Phil. 61 F5 10 6N 122 52 E
Himarë, Albania 44 F3 40 8N 19 43 E
Himatnagar, India 66 H8 23 37N 72 57 E
Himeji, Japan 55 G7 34 50N 134 40 E
Himi, Japan 55 F8 36 50N 136 55 E
Himmerland, Denmark 11 H3 56 45N 9 30 E
Ḥimṣ, Syria 74 A5 34 40N 36 45 E
Ḥimṣ □, Syria 74 A6 34 30N 37 0 E
Hinche, Haiti 121 C5 19 9N 72 1W
Hinchinbrook I., Australia 94 B4 18 20 S 146 15 E
Hinchinbrook Island △, Australia 94 B4 18 14 S 146 6 E
Hinckley, U.K. 15 E6 52 33N 1 22W
Hinckley, U.S.A. 112 B8 46 1N 92 56W
Hindaun, India 68 F7 26 44N 77 5 E
Hindmarsh, L., Australia 95 F3 36 5 S 141 55 E
Hindsholm, Denmark 11 J4 55 30N 10 40 E
Hindu Bagh, Pakistan 68 D2 30 56N 67 50 E
Hindu Kush, Asia 66 B7 36 0N 71 0 E
Hindupur, India 66 N10 13 49N 77 32 E
Hines Creek, Canada 102 B5 56 20N 118 40W
Hinesville, U.S.A. 115 K5 31 51N 81 36W
Hinganghat, India 66 J11 20 30N 78 52 E
Hingham, U.S.A. 108 B8 48 33N 110 25W
Hingir, India 69 J10 21 57N 83 41 E
Hingoli, India 66 K10 19 41N 77 15 E
Hinigaran, Phil. 61 F5 10 16N 122 50 E
Hinis, Turkey 73 C9 39 22N 41 43 E
Hinna = Imi, Ethiopia 81 F5 6 28N 42 10 E
Hinna, Nigeria 83 C7 10 25N 11 35 E
Hinnerup, Denmark 11 H4 56 16N 10 4 E
Hinnøya, Norway 8 B16 68 35N 15 50 E
Hinojosa del Duque, Spain 37 G5 38 30N 5 9W
Hinsdale, U.S.A. 117 D12 42 47N 72 29W
Hinterrhein →, Switz. 25 J5 46 40N 9 25 E
Hinton, Canada 102 C5 53 26N 117 34W
Hinton, U.S.A. 114 G5 37 40N 80 54W
Hınzır Burnu, Turkey 72 D6 36 19N 35 46 E
Hirado, Japan 55 H4 33 22N 129 33 E
Hirakud Dam, India 67 J13 21 32N 83 45 E
Hiran →, India 69 H8 23 6N 79 21 E
Hirapur, India 69 G8 24 22N 79 13 E
Hiratsuka, Japan 55 G9 35 19N 139 21 E
Hirfanlı Barajı, Turkey 72 C5 39 18N 33 31 E
Hiroo, Japan 54 C11 42 17N 143 19 E
Hirosaki, Japan 54 D10 40 34N 140 28 E
Hiroshima, Japan 55 G6 34 24N 132 30 E
Hiroshima □, Japan 55 G6 34 50N 133 0 E
Hirson, France 19 C11 49 55N 4 4 E
Hirtshals, Denmark 11 G3 57 36N 9 57 E
Hisar, India 68 E6 29 12N 75 45 E
Hisarcık, Turkey 47 B11 39 15N 29 14 E
Hisaria, Bulgaria 45 D8 42 30N 24 44 E
Hisb, Sha'ib = Ḥasb, W. →, Iraq 70 D5 31 45N 44 17 E
Ḥismá, Si. Arabia 70 D3 28 30N 36 0 E
Hispaniola, W. Indies 121 C5 19 0N 71 0W
Hīt, Iraq 70 C4 33 38N 42 49 E
Hita, Japan 55 H5 33 20N 130 58 E
Hitachi, Japan 55 F10 36 36N 140 39 E
Hitchin, U.K. 15 F7 51 58N 0 16W
Hitoyoshi, Japan 55 H5 32 13N 130 45 E
Hitra, Norway 8 E13 63 30N 8 45 E
Hitzacker, Germany 24 B7 53 9N 11 2 E
Hixon, Canada 102 C4 53 25N 122 35W
Ḥiyyon, N. →, Israel 74 E4 30 25N 35 10 E
Hjalmar L., Canada 103 A7 61 33N 109 25W
Hjälmaren, Sweden 10 E9 59 18N 15 40 E
Hjältevad, Sweden 11 G9 57 38N 15 20 E
Hjo, Sweden 11 F8 58 22N 14 17 E
Hjørring, Denmark 11 G3 57 29N 9 59 E
Hjortkvarn, Sweden 11 F9 58 54N 15 26 E
Hkakabo Razi, Burma 67 E20 28 25N 97 23 E
Hlinsko, Czech Rep. 26 B8 49 45N 15 54 E
Hlobane, S. Africa 89 D5 27 42 S 31 0 E
Hlohovec, Slovak Rep. 27 C10 48 26N 17 49 E
Hlučín, Czech Rep. 27 B11 49 54N 18 11 E
Hluhluwe, S. Africa 89 D5 28 1 S 32 15 E
Hluhluwe △, S. Africa 89 C5 22 10 S 32 5 E
Hlukhiv, Ukraine 33 G7 51 40N 33 58 E
Hlyboka, Ukraine 29 B10 48 5N 25 56 E
Hlybokaye, Belarus 32 E4 55 10N 27 45 E
Hnúšťa, Slovak Rep. 27 C12 48 35N 19 58 E
Ho, Ghana 83 D5 6 37N 0 27 E
Ho Chi Minh City = Thanh Pho Ho Chi Minh, Vietnam 65 G6 10 58N 106 40 E
Ho Thuong, Vietnam 64 C5 19 32N 105 48 E
Hoa Binh, Vietnam 58 G5 20 50N 105 20 E
Hoa Da, Vietnam 65 G7 11 16N 108 40 E
Hoa Hiep, Vietnam 65 G5 11 34N 105 51 E
Hoai Nhon, Vietnam 64 E7 14 28N 109 1 E
Hoang Lien Son, Vietnam 58 F4 22 0N 104 0 E
Hoanib →, Namibia 88 B2 19 27 S 12 46 E
Hoare B., Canada 101 B13 65 17N 62 30W
Hoarusib →, Namibia 88 B2 19 3 S 12 36 E
Hobart, Australia 95 G4 42 50 S 147 21 E
Hobart, U.S.A. 113 H5 35 1N 99 6W
Hobbs, U.S.A. 113 J3 32 42N 103 8W
Hobbs Coast, Antarctica 5 D14 74 50 S 131 0W
Hobe Sound, U.S.A. 115 M5 27 4N 80 8W
Hoboken, U.S.A. 117 F10 40 45N 74 4W
Hobro, Denmark 11 H3 56 39N 9 46 E
Hoburgen, Sweden 11 H12 56 55N 18 7 E
Hocalar, Turkey 47 C11 38 36N 30 0 E
Hochfeld, Namibia 88 C2 21 28 S 17 58 E
Hochharz △, Germany 24 D6 51 48N 10 38 E
Hochschwab, Austria 26 D8 47 35N 15 0 E
Höchstadt, Germany 25 F6 49 42N 10 47 E
Hochtaunus △, Germany 25 E4 50 20N 8 30 E
Hockenheim, Germany 25 F4 49 19N 8 32 E
Hodaka-Dake, Japan 55 F8 36 17N 137 39 E
Hodeida = Al Ḥudaydah, Yemen 75 E3 14 50N 43 0 E
Hodgeville, Canada 103 C7 50 7N 106 58W
Hodgson, Canada 103 C9 51 13N 97 36W
Hódmezővásárhely, Hungary 28 D5 46 28N 20 22 E
Hodna, Chott el, Algeria 78 A6 35 26N 4 43 E
Hodonín, Czech Rep. 27 C10 48 50N 17 10 E
Hoeamdong, N. Korea 57 C16 42 30N 130 16 E
Hœdic, Î. de, France 18 E4 47 20N 2 53W
Hoek van Holland, Neths. 17 C4 52 0N 4 7 E
Hoengsŏng, S. Korea 57 F14 37 29N 127 59 E
Hoeryong, N. Korea 57 C15 42 30N 129 45 E
Hoeyang, N. Korea 57 E14 38 43N 127 36 E
Hof, Germany 25 E7 50 19N 11 55 E
Hofgeismar, Germany 24 D5 51 29N 9 23 E
Hofheim, Germany 25 E4 50 5N 8 26 E
Hofmeyr, S. Africa 88 E4 31 39 S 25 50 E
Höfn, Iceland 8 D6 64 15N 15 13W
Hofors, Sweden 10 D10 60 31N 16 15 E
Hofsjökull, Iceland 8 D4 64 49N 18 48W
Hōfu, Japan 55 G5 34 3N 131 34 E
Hogan Group, Australia 95 F4 39 13 S 147 1 E
Höganäs, Sweden 11 H6 56 12N 12 33 E
Hogarth, Mt., Australia 94 C2 21 48 S 136 58 E
Hoggar = Ahaggar, Algeria 78 D7 23 0N 6 30 E
Högsäter, Sweden 11 F6 58 38N 12 5 E
Högsby, Sweden 11 G10 57 10N 16 1 E
Högsjö, Sweden 10 E9 59 4N 15 44 E
Hogsty Reef, Bahamas 121 B5 21 41N 73 48W
Hoh →, U.S.A. 110 C2 47 45N 124 29W
Hohe Acht, Germany 25 E3 50 22N 7 0 E
Hohe Tauern, Austria 26 D5 47 11N 12 40 E
Hohe Tauern △, Austria 26 D5 47 5N 12 20 E
Hohe Venn, Belgium 17 D6 50 30N 6 5 E
Hohenau, Austria 27 C9 48 36N 16 55 E
Hohenems, Austria 26 D2 47 22N 9 42 E
Hohenloher Ebene, Germany 25 F5 49 14N 9 36 E
Hohenwald, U.S.A. 115 H2 35 33N 87 33W
Hohenwestedt, Germany 24 A5 54 5N 9 40 E
Hoher Rhön = Rhön, Germany 24 E5 50 24N 9 58 E
Hoher Vogelsberg △, Germany 24 D5 51 45N 9 35 E
Hohes Venn-Eifel △, Europe 24 E2 50 30N 6 10 E
Hohhot, China 56 D6 40 52N 111 40 E
Hóhlakas, Greece 49 D9 35 57N 27 53 E
Hohoe, Ghana 83 D5 7 8N 0 32 E
Hoi An, Vietnam 64 E7 15 30N 108 19 E
Hoi Xuan, Vietnam 58 G5 20 25N 105 9 E
Hoisington, U.S.A. 112 F5 38 31N 98 47W
Højer, Denmark 11 K2 54 58N 8 42 E
Hōjō, Japan 55 H6 33 58N 132 46 E
Hok, Sweden 11 G8 57 31N 14 16 E
Hökensås, Sweden 11 G8 58 0N 14 5 E
Hökerum, Sweden 11 G7 57 51N 13 16 E
Hokianga Harbour, N.Z. 91 F4 35 31 S 173 22 E
Hokitika, N.Z. 91 K3 42 42 S 171 0 E
Hokkaidō □, Japan 54 C11 43 30N 143 0 E
Hol-Hol, Djibouti 81 E5 11 20N 42 50 E
Hola Pristan, Ukraine 33 J7 46 29N 32 32 E
Holbæk, Denmark 11 J5 55 43N 11 43 E
Holbrook, Australia 95 F4 35 42 S 147 18 E
Holbrook, U.S.A. 109 J8 34 54N 110 10W
Holden, U.S.A. 108 G7 39 6N 112 16W
Holdenville, U.S.A. 113 H6 35 5N 96 24W
Holdrege, U.S.A. 112 E5 40 26N 99 23W
Holešov, Czech Rep. 27 B10 49 20N 17 35 E
Holetown, Barbados 121 g 13 11N 59 38W
Holguín, Cuba 120 B4 20 50N 76 20W
Holíč, Slovak Rep. 27 C10 48 49N 17 10 E
Holice, Czech Rep. 26 A8 50 5N 16 0 E
Höljes, Sweden 10 D6 60 50N 12 35 E
Hollabrunn, Austria 26 C9 48 34N 16 5 E
Hollams Bird I., Namibia 88 C1 24 40 S 14 30 E
Holland, Mich., U.S.A. 114 D2 42 47N 86 7W
Holland, N.Y., U.S.A. 116 D6 42 38N 78 32W
Hollandale, U.S.A. 113 J9 33 10N 90 51W
Holley, U.S.A. 116 C6 43 14N 78 2W
Hollfeld, Germany 25 F7 49 56N 11 18 E
Hollidaysburg, U.S.A. 116 F6 40 26N 78 24W
Hollis, U.S.A. 113 H5 34 41N 99 55W
Hollister, Calif., U.S.A. 110 J5 36 51N 121 24W
Hollister, Idaho, U.S.A. 108 E6 42 21N 114 35W
Höllviken = Höllviksnäs, Sweden 11 J6 55 26N 12 58 E
Höllviksnäs, Sweden 11 J6 55 26N 12 58 E
Holly Hill, U.S.A. 115 L5 29 16N 81 3W
Holly Springs, U.S.A. 113 H10 34 46N 89 27W
Hollywood, U.S.A. 115 N5 26 1N 80 9W
Holman, Canada 100 A8 70 44N 117 44W
Hólmavík, Iceland 8 D3 65 42N 21 40W
Holmen, U.S.A. 112 D9 43 58N 91 15W
Holmes Reefs, Australia 94 B4 16 27 S 148 0 E
Holmsjö, Sweden 11 H9 56 25N 15 32 E
Holmsjön, Västernorrland, Sweden 10 B10 62 41N 16 33 E
Holmsjön, Västernorrland, Sweden 10 B9 62 26N 15 20 E
Holmsland Klit, Denmark 11 J2 56 0N 8 5 E
Holmsund, Sweden 8 E19 63 41N 20 20 E
Holod, Romania 28 D7 46 49N 22 8 E
Holovne, Ukraine 31 G11 51 20N 24 5 E
Holozubyntsi, Ukraine 29 B11 48 50N 26 55 E
Holroyd →, Australia 94 A3 14 10 S 141 36 E
Holstebro, Denmark 11 H2 56 22N 8 37 E
Holsteinische Schweiz △, Germany 24 A6 54 8N 10 30 E
Holsworthy, U.K. 15 G3 50 48N 4 22W
Holton, Canada 105 B8 54 31N 57 12W
Holton, U.S.A. 112 F7 39 28N 95 44W
Holtville, U.S.A. 111 N11 32 49N 115 23W
Holwerd, Neths. 17 A5 53 22N 5 54 E
Holy I., Angl., U.K. 14 D3 53 17N 4 37W
Holy I., Northumberland, U.K. 14 B6 55 40N 1 47W
Holyhead, U.K. 14 D3 53 18N 4 38W
Holyoke, Colo., U.S.A. 112 E3 40 35N 102 18W
Holyoke, Mass., U.S.A. 117 D12 42 12N 72 37W
Holyrood, Canada 105 C9 47 27N 53 8W
Holzkirchen, Germany 25 H7 47 52N 11 42 E
Holzminden, Germany 24 D5 51 50N 9 28 E
Homa Bay, Kenya 86 C3 0 36 S 34 30 E
Homalin, Burma 67 G19 24 55N 95 0 E
Homand, Iran 71 C8 32 28N 59 37 E
Homathko →, Canada 102 C4 51 0N 124 56W
Homberg, Germany 24 D5 51 2N 9 25 E
Hombori, Mali 83 B4 15 20N 1 38W
Homburg, Germany 25 F3 49 28N 7 18 E
Home B., Canada 101 B13 68 40N 67 10W
Home Hill, Australia 94 B4 19 43 S 147 25 E
Homedale, U.S.A. 108 E5 43 37N 116 56W
Homer, Alaska, U.S.A. 100 C4 59 39N 151 33W
Homer, La., U.S.A. 113 J8 32 48N 93 4W
Homer City, U.S.A. 116 F5 40 32N 79 10W
Homert △, Germany 24 D4 51 15N 8 0 E
Homestead, Australia 94 C4 20 20 S 145 40 E
Homestead, U.S.A. 115 N5 25 28N 80 29W
Homestead △, U.S.A. 112 E6 40 17N 96 50W
Homewood, U.S.A. 110 F6 39 4N 120 8W
Homoine, Mozam. 89 C6 23 55 S 35 8 E
Homoljske Planina, Serbia & M. 44 B5 44 10N 21 45 E
Homorod, Romania 29 D10 46 5N 25 15 E
Homs = Ḥimṣ, Syria 74 A5 34 40N 36 45 E
Homyel, Belarus 33 F6 52 28N 31 0 E
Hon Chong, Vietnam 65 G5 10 25N 104 30 E
Hon Me, Vietnam 64 C5 19 23N 105 56 E
Honan = Henan □, China 56 H8 34 0N 114 0 E
Honaz, Turkey 47 D11 37 46N 29 18 E
Honbetsu, Japan 54 C11 43 7N 143 37 E
Honcut, U.S.A. 110 F5 39 20N 121 32W
Honda Bay, Phil. 61 G3 9 53N 118 49 E
Hondarribia, Spain 38 B3 43 22N 1 47W
Hondeklipbaai, S. Africa 88 E2 30 19 S 17 17 E
Hondo, Japan 55 H5 32 27N 130 12 E
Hondo, U.S.A. 113 L5 29 21N 99 9W
Hondo →, Belize 119 D7 18 25N 88 21W
Honduras ■, Cent. Amer. 120 D2 14 40N 86 30W
Honduras, G. de, Caribbean 120 C2 16 50N 87 0W
Hønefoss, Norway 9 F14 60 10N 10 18 E
Honesdale, U.S.A. 117 E9 41 34N 75 16W
Honey L., U.S.A. 110 E6 40 15N 120 19W
Honfleur, France 18 C7 49 25N 0 13 E
Høng, Denmark 11 J5 55 31N 11 18 E
Hong →, Vietnam 58 F5 22 0N 104 0 E
Hong Gai, Vietnam 58 G6 20 57N 107 5 E
Hong He →, China 56 H8 32 25N 115 35 E
Hong Hu, China 59 C9 29 54N 113 24 E
Hong Kong □, China 59 F10 22 11N 114 14 E
Hong'an, China 59 B10 31 20N 114 40 E
Hongch'ŏn, S. Korea 57 F14 37 44N 127 53 E
Honghai Wan, China 59 F10 22 40N 115 0 E
Honghe, China 58 F4 23 25N 102 25 E
Honghu, China 59 C9 29 50N 113 30 E
Hongjiang, China 58 D7 27 7N 109 59 E
Hongliu He →, China 56 F5 38 0N 109 50 E
Hongor, Mongolia 56 B7 45 45N 112 50 E
Hongsa, Laos 64 C3 19 43N 101 20 E
Hongshui He →, China 58 F7 23 48N 109 30 E
Hongsŏng, S. Korea 57 F14 36 37N 126 38 E
Hongtong, China 56 F6 36 16N 111 40 E
Honguedo, Détroit d', Canada 105 C7 49 15N 64 0W
Hongwon, N. Korea 57 E14 40 0N 127 56 E
Hongya, China 58 C4 29 57N 103 22 E
Hongyuan, China 58 A4 32 51N 102 40 E
Hongze Hu, China 57 H10 33 15N 118 35 E
Honiara, Solomon Is. 96 H7 9 27 S 159 57 E
Honiton, U.K. 15 G4 50 47N 3 11W
Honjō, Japan 54 E10 39 23N 140 3 E
Honkorāb, Ras, Egypt 80 C4 24 35N 35 10 E
Honningsvåg, Norway 8 A21 70 59N 25 59 E
Hönö, Sweden 11 G5 57 41N 11 39 E
Honolulu, U.S.A. 106 H16 21 19N 157 52W
Hontoria del Pinar, Spain 38 D1 41 50N 3 10W
Hood, Mt., U.S.A. 108 D3 45 23N 121 42W
Hood, Pt., Australia 93 F2 34 23 S 119 34 E
Hood River, U.S.A. 108 D3 45 43N 121 31W
Hoodsport, U.S.A. 110 C3 47 24N 123 9W
Hooge, Germany 24 A4 54 34N 8 33 E
Hoogeveen, Neths. 17 B6 52 44N 6 28 E
Hoogezand-Sappemeer, Neths. 17 A6 53 9N 6 45 E
Hooghly = Hugli →, India 69 J13 21 56N 88 4 E
Hooghly-Chinsura = Chunchura, India 69 H13 22 53N 88 27 E
Hook Hd., Ireland 12 D5 52 7N 6 56W
Hook I., Australia 94 J6 20 4 S 149 0 E
Hook of Holland = Hoek van Holland, Neths. 17 C4 52 0N 4 7 E
Hooker, U.S.A. 113 G4 36 52N 101 13W
Hooker Creek, Australia 92 C5 18 23 S 130 38 E
Hoonah, U.S.A. 102 B1 58 7N 135 27W
Hooper Bay, U.S.A. 100 B3 61 32N 166 6W
Hoopeston, U.S.A. 114 E2 40 28N 87 40W
Hoopstad, S. Africa 88 D4 27 50 S 25 55 E
Höör, Sweden 11 J7 55 56N 13 33 E
Hoorn, Neths. 17 B5 52 38N 5 4 E
Hoover, U.S.A. 115 J2 33 20N 86 11W
Hoover Dam, U.S.A. 111 K12 36 1N 114 44W
Hooversville, U.S.A. 116 F6 40 9N 78 55W
Hop Bottom, U.S.A. 117 E9 41 42N 75 46W
Hopa, Turkey 73 B9 41 28N 41 30 E
Hope, Canada 102 D4 49 25N 121 25W
Hope, Ariz., U.S.A. 111 M13 33 43N 113 42W
Hope, Ark., U.S.A. 113 J8 33 40N 93 36W
Hope, L., S. Austral., Australia 95 D2 28 24 S 139 18 E
Hope, L., W. Austral., Australia 93 F3 32 35 S 120 15 E
Hope, Pt., U.S.A. 4 C17 68 20N 166 50W
Hope I., Canada 116 B4 44 55N 80 11W
Hope Town, Bahamas 120 A4 26 35N 76 57W
Hopedale, Canada 105 A7 55 28N 60 13W
Hopedale, U.S.A. 117 D13 42 8N 71 33W
Hopefield, S. Africa 88 E2 33 3 S 18 22 E
Hopei = Hebei □, China 56 E9 39 0N 116 0 E
Hopelchén, Mexico 119 D7 19 46N 89 50W
Hopetoun, Vic., Australia 95 F3 35 42 S 142 22 E
Hopetoun, W. Austral., Australia 93 F3 33 57 S 120 7 E
Hopetown, S. Africa 88 D3 29 34 S 24 3 E
Hopevale, Australia 94 B4 15 16 S 145 20 E
Hopewell, U.S.A. 114 G7 37 18N 77 17W
Hopfgarten, Austria 26 D5 47 27N 12 10 E
Hopkins, L., Australia 92 D4 24 15 S 128 35 E
Hopkinsville, U.S.A. 115 G2 36 52N 87 29W
Hopland, U.S.A. 110 G3 38 58N 123 7W
Hoquiam, U.S.A. 110 D3 46 59N 123 53W
Hora Hoverla, Ukraine 29 B9 48 7N 24 41 E
Horasan, Turkey 73 B10 40 3N 42 11 E
Horažďovice, Czech Rep. 26 B6 49 19N 13 42 E
Horb, Germany 25 G4 48 26N 8 47 E
Hörby, Sweden 11 J7 55 51N 13 40 E
Horcajo de Santiago, Spain 38 F1 39 50N 3 1W
Horden Hills, Australia 92 D5 20 15 S 130 0 E
Horezu, Romania 29 E8 45 6N 24 0 E
Horgen, Switz. 25 H4 47 15N 8 35 E
Horgoš, Serbia & M. 28 D4 46 10N 20 0 E
Hořice, Czech Rep. 26 A8 50 21N 15 39 E
Horinchove, Ukraine 29 B8 48 16N 23 26 E
Horinger, China 56 D6 40 28N 111 48 E
Horki, Belarus 32 E6 54 17N 30 59 E
Horlick Mts., Antarctica 5 E15 84 0 S 102 0W
Horlivka, Ukraine 33 H10 48 19N 38 5 E
Hormak, Iran 71 D9 29 58N 60 51 E
Hormoz, Iran 71 E7 27 35N 55 0 E
Hormoz, Jaz.-ye, Iran 71 E8 27 8N 56 28 E
Hormozgān □, Iran 71 E8 27 30N 56 0 E
Hormuz, Kūh-e, Iran 71 E7 27 27N 55 10 E
Hormuz, Str. of, The Gulf 71 E8 26 30N 56 30 E
Horn, Austria 26 C8 48 39N 15 40 E
Horn, Iceland 8 C2 66 28N 22 28W
Horn, Sweden 11 G9 57 54N 15 51 E
Horn →, Canada 102 A5 61 30N 118 1W
Horn, Cape = Hornos, C. de, Chile 128 H3 55 50 S 67 30W
Horn Head, Ireland 12 A3 55 14N 8 0W
Horn I., Australia 94 A3 10 37 S 142 17 E
Horn Plateau, Canada 102 A5 62 15N 119 15W
Hornachuelos, Spain 37 H5 37 50N 5 14W
Hornavan, Sweden 8 C17 66 15N 17 30 E
Hornbeck, U.S.A. 113 K8 31 20N 93 24W
Hornbrook, U.S.A. 108 F2 41 55N 122 33W
Hornburg, Germany 24 C6 52 2N 10 37 E
Horncastle, U.K. 14 D7 53 13N 0 7W
Horndal, Sweden 10 D10 60 18N 16 23 E
Hornell, U.S.A. 116 D7 42 20N 77 40W
Hornell L., Canada 102 A5 62 20N 119 25W
Hornepayne, Canada 104 C3 49 14N 84 48W
Horní Planá, Czech Rep. 26 C7 48 46N 14 2 E
Hornings Mills, Canada 116 B4 44 9N 80 12W
Hornitos, U.S.A. 110 H6 37 30N 120 14W
Hornos, C. de, Chile 128 H3 55 50 S 67 30W
Hornoy-le-Bourg, France 19 C8 49 50N 1 54 E
Hornsea, U.K. 14 D7 53 55N 0 11W
Hornslandet, Sweden 10 C11 61 35N 17 37 E
Hörnum, Germany 24 A4 54 45N 8 17 E
Horobetsu = Noboribetsu, Japan 54 C10 42 24N 141 6 E
Horodenka, Ukraine 29 B10 48 41N 25 29 E
Horodnya, Ukraine 33 G6 51 55N 31 33 E
Horodok, Khmelnytskyy, Ukraine 33 H4 49 10N 26 34 E
Horodok, Lviv, Ukraine 33 H2 49 46N 23 32 E
Horodyshche, Ukraine 33 H6 49 17N 31 27 E
Horokhiv, Ukraine 33 G3 50 30N 24 45 E
Horovice, Czech Rep. 26 B6 49 48N 13 53 E
Horqin Youyi Qianqi, China 57 A12 46 5N 122 3 E
Horqueta, Paraguay 126 A4 23 15 S 56 55W
Horred, Sweden 11 G6 57 22N 12 28 E
Horse Creek, U.S.A. 112 E3 41 57N 105 10W
Horse I., Canada 103 C9 53 20N 99 6W
Horse Is., Canada 105 B8 50 15N 55 50W
Horsefly L., Canada 102 C4 52 25N 121 0W
Horseheads, U.S.A. 116 D8 42 10N 76 49W
Horsens, Denmark 11 J3 55 52N 9 51 E
Horsham, Australia 95 F3 36 44 S 142 13 E
Horsham, U.K. 15 F7 51 4N 0 20W
Horšovský Týn, Czech Rep. 26 B5 49 31N 12 58 E
Horten, Norway 9 G14 59 25N 10 32 E
Hortobágy →, Hungary 28 C6 47 30N 21 6 E
Hortobágyi △, Hungary 28 C6 47 36N 21 10 E
Horton, U.S.A. 112 F7 39 40N 95 32W
Horton →, Canada 100 B7 69 56N 126 52W
Horwood L., Canada 104 C3 48 5N 82 20W
Hosaina, Ethiopia 81 F4 7 30N 37 47 E

Hose, Gunung-Gunung,
 Malaysia .... 62 D4 2 5N 114 6 E
Ḥoseynābād, Khūzestān,
 Iran .... 71 C6 32 45N 48 20 E
Ḥoseynābād, Kordestān,
 Iran .... 70 C5 35 33N 47 8 E
Hoshangabad, India .. 68 H7 22 45N 77 45 E
Hoshiarpur, India ... 68 D6 31 30N 75 58 E
Hospet, India .... 66 M10 15 15N 76 20 E
Hoste, I., Chile 128 H3 55 0S 69 0W
Hostens, France 20 D3 44 30N 0 40W
Hot, Thailand .... 64 C2 18 8N 98 29 E
Hot Creek Range,
 U.S.A. 108 G6 38 40N 116 20W
Hot Springs, Ark.,
 U.S.A. 113 H8 34 31N 93 3W
Hot Springs, S. Dak.,
 U.S.A. 112 D3 43 26N 103 29W
Hot Springs △, U.S.A. 113 H8 34 32N 93 4W
Hotagen, Sweden .... 8 E16 63 59N 14 12 E
Hotan, China .... 60 C2 37 25N 79 55 E
Hotazel, S. Africa ... 88 D3 27 17S 22 58 E
Hotchkiss, U.S.A. 109 G10 38 48N 107 43W
Hotham, C., Australia 92 B5 12 2S 131 18 E
Hoting, Sweden ..... 8 D17 64 8N 16 15 E
Hotolisht, Albania ... 44 E4 41 10N 20 25 E
Hotte, Massif de la, Haiti 121 C5 18 30N 73 45W
Hottentotsbaai, Namibia 88 D1 26 8S 14 59 E
Houat, Î. de, France . 18 E4 47 24N 2 58W
Houdan, France ..... 19 D8 48 48N 1 35 E
Houei Sai, Laos ..... 58 G3 20 18N 100 26 E
Houeillès, France .... 20 D4 44 12N 0 2 E
Houffalize, Belgium .. 17 D5 50 8N 5 48 E
Houghton, Mich., U.S.A. 112 B10 47 7N 88 34W
Houghton, N.Y., U.S.A. 116 D6 42 25N 78 10W
Houghton L., U.S.A. . 114 C3 44 21N 84 44W
Houghton-le-Spring,
 U.K. 14 C6 54 51N 1 28W
Houhora Heads, N.Z. . 91 F4 34 49S 173 9 E
Houlton, U.S.A. ..... 115 B12 46 8N .67 51W
Houma, U.S.A. 113 L9 29 36N 90 43W
Houndé, Burkina Faso 82 C4 11 34N 3 31W
Hourtin, France 20 C2 45 11N 1 4W
Hourtin-Carcans, Étang
 d', France 20 C2 45 10N 1 6W
Housatonic →, U.S.A. 117 E11 41 10N 73 7W
Houston, Canada 102 C3 54 25N 126 39W
Houston, Mo., U.S.A. 113 G9 37 22N 91 58W
Houston, Tex., U.S.A. 113 L7 29 46N 95 22W
Hout →, S. Africa ... 89 C4 23 4S 29 36 E
Houtkraal, S. Africa . 88 E3 30 23S 24 5 E
Houtman Abrolhos,
 Australia .... 93 E1 28 43S 113 48 E
Hovd, Mongolia ..... 60 B4 48 2N 91 37 E
Hove, U.K. 15 G7 50 50N 0 10W
Hovenweep △, U.S.A. 109 H9 37 20N 109 0W
Hoveyzeh, Iran ..... 71 D6 31 27N 48 4 E
Hovmantorp, Sweden . 11 H9 56 47N 15 7 E
Hövsgöl, Mongolia ... 56 C5 43 37N 109 39 E
Hövsgöl Nuur, Mongolia 60 A5 51 0N 100 30 E
Hovsta, Sweden ..... 10 E9 59 22N 15 15 E
Howakil, Eritrea .... 81 D5 15 10N 40 16 E
Howar, Wadi →, Sudan 81 D2 17 30N 27 8 E
Howard, Australia ... 95 D5 25 16S 152 32 E
Howard, Pa., U.S.A. . 116 F7 41 1N 77 40W
Howard, S. Dak., U.S.A. 112 C6 44 1N 97 32W
Howe, U.S.A. 108 E7 43 48N 113 0W
Howe, C., Australia .. 95 F5 37 30S 150 0 E
Howe I., Canada 117 B8 44 16N 76 17W
Howell, U.S.A. 114 D4 42 36N 83 56W
Howick, Canada 117 A11 45 11N 73 51W
Howick, S. Africa ... 89 D5 29 28S 30 14 E
Howick Group,
 Australia .... 94 A4 14 20S 145 30 E
Howitt, L., Australia . 95 D2 27 40S 138 40 E
Howland I., Pac. Oc. . 96 G10 0 48N 176 38W
Howrah = Haora, India 69 H13 22 37N 88 20 E
Howth Hd., Ireland .. 12 C5 53 22N 6 3W
Höxter, Germany .... 24 D5 51 46N 9 22 E
Hoy, U.K. 13 C5 58 50N 3 15W
Hoya, Germany ...... 24 C5 52 49N 9 8 E
Høyanger, Norway ... 9 F12 61 13N 6 4 E
Hoyerswerda, Germany 24 D10 51 26N 14 14 E
Hoylake, U.K. 14 D4 53 24N 3 10W
Hoyos, Spain 36 E4 40 9N 6 45W
Hpa-an = Pa-an, Burma 67 L20 16 51N 97 40 E
Hpungan Pass, Burma 67 F20 27 30N 96 55 E
Hradec Králové,
 Czech Rep. .... 26 A8 50 15N 15 50 E
Hrádek, Czech Rep. .. 27 C9 48 46N 16 16 E
Hranice, Czech Rep. . 27 B9 49 34N 17 45 E
Hrazdan, Armenia ... 35 K7 40 30N 44 46 E
Hrebenka, Ukraine ... 33 G4 50 9N 32 22 E
Hrodna, Belarus ..... 30 E10 53 42N 23 52 E
Hrodzyanka, Belarus . 32 F5 53 31N 28 42 E
Hron →, Slovak Rep. . 27 D11 47 49N 18 45 E
Hrubieszów, Poland .. 31 H10 50 49N 23 51 E
Hrubý Jeseník,
 Czech Rep. .... 27 A10 50 5N 17 10 E
Hrvatska = Croatia ■,
 Europe .... 41 C13 45 20N 16 0 E
Hrymayliv, Ukraine .. 33 H4 49 20N 26 5 E
Hrynyava, Ukraine ... 29 C9 47 59N 24 53 E
Hsenwi, Burma ...... 67 H20 23 22N 97 55 E
Hsiamen = Xiamen,
 China .... 59 E12 24 25N 118 4 E
Hsian = Xi'an, China . 56 G5 34 15N 109 0 E
Hsinchu, Taiwan .... 59 E13 24 48N 120 58 E
Hsinhailien =
 Lianyungang, China . 57 G10 34 40N 119 11 E
Hsinying, Taiwan .... 59 F13 23 10N 120 18 E
Hsopket, Burma ..... 58 F2 23 11N 98 26 E
Hsüchou = Xuzhou,
 China .... 57 G9 34 18N 117 10 E
Hu Xian, China ..... 56 G5 34 8N 108 42 E
Hua Hin, Thailand ... 64 F2 12 34N 99 58 E
Hua Xian, Henan, China 56 G8 35 30N 114 30 E
Hua Xian, Shaanxi,
 China .... 56 G5 34 30N 109 48 E
Hua'an, China .... 59 E11 25 1N 117 32 E
Huab →, Namibia ... 88 B2 20 52S 13 25 E
Huacheng, China .... 59 E10 24 4N 115 37 E
Huachinera, Mexico .. 118 A3 30 9N 108 55W
Huacho, Peru 124 F3 11 10S 77 35W
Huade, China .... 56 D7 41 55N 113 59 E
Huadian, China ..... 57 C14 43 0N 126 40 E
Huadu, China .... 59 F9 23 22N 113 12 E
Huai Had △, Thailand 64 D8 16 52N 104 17 E
Huai He →, China ... 59 A12 33 0N 118 30 E
Huai Nam Dang △,
 Thailand .... 64 C2 19 30N 98 30 E
Huai Yot, Thailand .. 65 J2 7 45N 99 37 E
Huai'an, Hebei, China 56 D8 40 30N 114 20 E
Huai'an, Jiangsu, China 57 H10 33 30N 119 10 E
Huaibei, China ...... 56 G9 34 0N 116 48 E
Huaide = Gongzhuling,
 China .... 57 C13 43 30N 124 40 E

Huaidezhen, China ... 57 C13 43 48N 124 50 E
Huaihua, China ..... 58 D7 27 32N 109 57 E
Huaiji, China .... 59 F9 23 55N 112 12 E
Huainan, China ..... 59 A11 32 38N 116 58 E
Huaining, China ..... 59 B11 30 24N 116 40 E
Huairen, China ...... 56 E7 39 48N 113 20 E
Huairou, China ...... 56 D9 40 20N 116 35 E
Huaiyang, China .... 56 H8 33 40N 114 52 E
Huaiyin, China ...... 57 H10 33 30N 119 2 E
Huaiyuan, Anhui, China 57 H9 32 55N 117 10 E
Huaiyuan,
 Guangxi Zhuangzu,
 China .... 58 E7 24 31N 108 22 E
Huajianzi, China .... 57 D13 41 23N 125 20 E
Huajuapan de Leon,
 Mexico 119 D5 17 50N 97 48W
Hualapai Peak, U.S.A. 109 J7 35 5N 113 54W
Hualien, Taiwan .... 59 E13 24 0N 121 30 E
Huallaga →, Peru ... 124 E3 5 15S 75 30W
Huambo, Angola .... 85 G3 12 42S 15 54 E
Huan Jiang →, China 56 G5 34 28N 109 0 E
Huan Xian, China ... 56 F4 36 33N 107 7 E
Huancabamba, Peru . 124 E3 5 10S 79 15W
Huancane, Peru 124 G5 15 10S 69 44W
Huancavelica, Peru .. 124 F3 12 50S 75 5W
Huancayo, Peru 124 F3 12 5S 75 12W
Huanchaca, Bolivia .. 124 H5 20 15S 66 40W
Huang Hai = Yellow
 Sea, China .... 57 G12 35 0N 123 0 E
Huang He →, China . 57 F10 37 55N 118 50 E
Huang Xian, China .. 57 F11 37 38N 120 30 E
Huangchuan, China .. 59 A10 32 15N 115 10 E
Huanggang, China ... 59 B10 30 29N 114 52 E
Huangguoshu, China . 58 E5 26 0N 105 40 E
Huangling, China .... 56 G5 35 34N 109 15 E
Huanglong, China ... 56 G5 35 30N 109 59 E
Huanglongtan, China . 59 A8 32 40N 110 33 E
Huangmei, China .... 59 B10 30 5N 115 56 E
Huangping, China ... 58 D6 26 52N 107 54 E
Huangshan, China ... 59 C12 29 42N 118 25 E
Huangshi, China .... 59 B10 30 10N 115 3 E
Huangsongdian, China 57 C14 43 45N 127 25 E
Huangyan, China .... 59 C13 28 38N 121 19 E
Huangyangsi, China . 59 D8 26 33N 111 39 E
Huaning, China ..... 58 E4 24 17N 102 56 E
Huanjiang, China .... 58 E7 24 50N 108 18 E
Huantai, China ...... 57 F9 36 58N 117 56 E
Huánuco, Peru 124 E3 9 55S 76 15W
Huaping, China ..... 58 D3 26 46N 101 25 E
Huaraz, Peru 124 E3 9 30S 77 32W
Huarmey, Peru 124 F3 10 5S 78 5W
Huarong, China ..... 59 C9 29 29N 112 30 E
Huascarán, Peru 124 E3 9 8S 77 36W
Huasco, Chile 126 B1 28 30S 71 15W
Huasco →, Chile 126 B1 28 27S 71 13W
Huasna, U.S.A. 111 K6 35 6N 120 24W
Huatabampo, Mexico 118 B3 26 50N 109 38W
Huauchinango, Mexico 119 C5 20 11N 98 3W
Huautla de Jiménez,
 Mexico 119 D5 18 8N 96 51W
Huaxi, China .... 58 D6 26 25N 106 40 E
Huay Namota, Mexico 118 C4 21 56N 104 30W
Huayin, China .... 56 G6 34 35N 110 5 E
Huayuan, China ..... 58 C7 28 37N 109 29 E
Huayun, China ...... 58 B6 30 14N 106 40 E
Huazhou, China ..... 59 G8 21 33N 110 33 E
Hubbard, Ohio, U.S.A. 116 E4 41 9N 80 34W
Hubbard, Tex., U.S.A. 113 K6 31 51N 96 48W
Hubbart Pt., Canada . 103 B10 59 21N 94 41W
Hubei □, China ..... 59 B9 31 0N 112 0 E
Hubli, India .... 66 M9 15 22N 75 15 E
Huch'ang, N. Korea . 57 D14 41 25N 127 2 E
Hucknall, U.K. 14 D6 53 3N 1 13W
Huddersfield, U.K. .. 14 D6 53 39N 1 47W
Hude, Germany ..... 24 B4 53 7N 8 26 E
Hudi, Sudan .... 80 D3 17 43N 34 18 E
Hudiksvall, Sweden .. 10 C11 61 43N 17 10 E
Hudson, Canada 104 B1 50 6N 92 9W
Hudson, Mass., U.S.A. 117 D13 42 23N 71 34W
Hudson, N.Y., U.S.A. 117 D11 42 15N 73 46W
Hudson, Wis., U.S.A. 112 C8 44 58N 92 45W
Hudson, Wyo., U.S.A. 108 E9 42 54N 108 35W
Hudson →, U.S.A. .. 117 F10 40 42N 74 2W
Hudson Bay, Nunavut,
 Canada 101 C11 60 0N 86 0W
Hudson Bay, Sask.,
 Canada 103 C8 52 51N 102 23W
Hudson Falls, U.S.A. . 117 C11 43 18N 73 35W
Hudson Mts., Antarctica 5 D16 74 32S 99 20W
Hudson Str., Canada . 101 B13 62 0N 70 0W
Hudson's Hope, Canada 102 B4 56 0N 121 54W
Hue, Vietnam .... 64 D6 16 30N 107 35 E
Huebra →, Spain ... 36 D4 41 2N 6 48W
Huedin, Romania ... 28 D8 46 52N 23 2 E
Huehuetenango,
 Guatemala 120 C1 15 20N 91 28W
Huejúcar, Mexico ... 118 C4 22 21N 103 13W
Huélamo, Spain 38 E3 40 17N 1 48W
Huelgoat, France ... 18 D3 48 22N 3 46W
Huelma, Spain 37 H7 37 39N 3 28W
Huelva, Spain 37 H4 37 18N 6 57W
Huelva □, Spain 37 H4 37 40N 7 0W
Huelva →, Spain ... 37 H5 37 27N 6 0W
Huentelauquén, Chile 126 C1 31 38S 71 33W
Huerta, Sa. de la,
 Argentina 126 C2 31 10S 67 30W
Huertas, C. de las, Spain 39 G4 38 21N 0 24W
Huerva →, Spain ... 38 D4 41 39N 0 52W
Huesca, Spain 38 C4 42 8N 0 25W
Huesca □, Spain .... 38 C5 42 20N 0 1 E
Huéscar, Spain 39 H2 37 44N 2 35W
Huetamo, Mexico ... 118 D4 18 36N 100 54W
Huete, Spain 38 E2 40 10N 2 43W
Hugh →, Australia .. 94 D1 25 1S 134 1 E
Hughenden, Australia 94 C3 20 52S 144 10 E
Hughes, Australia ... 93 F4 30 42S 129 31 E
Hughesville, U.S.A. .. 117 E8 41 14N 76 44W
Hugli →, India ...... 69 J13 21 56N 88 4 E
Hugo, Colo., U.S.A. . 112 F3 39 8N 103 28W
Hugo, Okla., U.S.A. .. 113 H7 34 1N 95 31W
Hugoton, U.S.A. 113 G4 37 11N 101 21W
Hui Xian = Huixian,
 China .... 56 G7 35 27N 113 12 E
Hui Xian, China ..... 56 H4 33 50N 106 4 E
Hui'an, China .... 59 E12 25 1N 118 43 E
Hui'anbu, China ..... 56 F4 37 28N 106 38 E
Huichang, China .... 59 E10 25 32N 115 45 E
Huichapán, Mexico .. 119 C5 20 24N 99 40W
Huidong, Guangdong,
 China .... 59 F10 22 58N 114 43 E
Huidong, Sichuan, China 58 D4 26 34N 102 35 E
Huifa He →, China .. 57 C14 43 0N 127 50 E
Huila, Nevado del,
 Colombia 124 C3 3 0N 76 0W
Huilai, China .... 59 F11 23 0N 116 18 E

Huili, China .... 58 D4 26 35N 102 17 E
Huimin, China ...... 57 F9 37 27N 117 28 E
Huinan, China ...... 57 C14 42 40N 126 2 E
Huinca Renancó,
 Argentina 126 C3 34 51S 64 22W
Huining, China ..... 56 G3 35 38N 105 0 E
Huinong, China ..... 56 E4 39 5N 106 35 E
Huisache, Mexico ... 118 C4 22 55N 100 25W
Huishui, China ..... 58 D6 26 7N 106 38 E
Huiting, China ...... 56 G9 34 5N 116 5 E
Huitong, China ..... 58 D7 26 51N 109 45 E
Huixian, China ..... 56 G7 35 27N 113 12 E
Huixtla, Mexico 119 D6 15 9N 92 28W
Huize, China .... 58 D4 26 24N 103 15 E
Huizhou, China ..... 59 F10 23 0N 114 23 E
Hukawng Valley, Burma 67 C20 26 30N 96 30 E
Hukou, China .... 59 C11 29 45N 116 21 E
Hūksan-chedo, S. Korea 57 G13 34 40N 125 30 E
Hukuntsi, Botswana . 88 C3 23 58S 21 45 E
Ḥulayfā', Si. Arabia . 70 E4 25 58N 40 45 E
Hulin He →, China .. 57 B12 45 0N 122 10 E
Hull = Kingston upon
 Hull, U.K. 14 D7 53 45N 0 21W
Hull, Canada 117 A9 45 25N 75 44W
Hull →, U.K. 14 D7 53 44N 0 20W
Hulst, Neths. .... 17 C4 51 17N 4 2 E
Hultsfred, Sweden ... 11 G9 57 30N 15 52 E
Hulun Nur, China ... 60 B6 49 0N 117 30 E
Hulyaypole, Ukraine . 33 J9 47 45N 36 21 E
Huma, Tanjung,
 Malaysia .... 65 c 5 29N 100 16 E
Humacao, Puerto Rico 121 d 18 9N 65 50W
Humahuaca, Argentina 126 A2 23 10S 65 25W
Humaitá, Brazil 124 E6 7 35S 63 1W
Humaitá, Paraguay .. 126 B4 27 2S 58 31W
Humansdorp, S. Africa 88 E3 34 2S 24 46 E
Humara, J., Sudan .. 81 D3 16 16N 30 9 E
Humbe, Angola ..... 88 B1 16 40S 14 55 E
Humber →, U.K. 14 D7 53 42N 0 27W
Humboldt, Canada ... 103 C7 52 15N 105 9W
Humboldt, Iowa, U.S.A. 112 D7 42 44N 94 13W
Humboldt, Tenn., U.S.A. 113 H10 35 50N 88 55W
Humboldt →, U.S.A. 108 F4 39 59N 118 36W
Humboldt Gletscher =
 Sermersuaq,
 Greenland 4 B4 79 30N 62 0W
Hume, U.S.A. 110 J8 36 48N 118 54W
Hume, L., Australia .. 95 F4 36 0S 147 5 E
Humenné, Slovak Rep. 27 C14 48 55N 21 50 E
Hummelsta, Sweden . 10 E10 59 34N 16 58 E
Humphreys, Mt., U.S.A. 110 H8 37 17N 118 40W
Humphreys Peak, U.S.A. 109 J8 35 21N 111 41W
Humpolec, Czech Rep. 26 B8 49 31N 15 20 E
Humptulips, U.S.A. .. 110 C3 47 14N 123 57W
Hūn, Libya .... 79 C9 29 2N 16 0 E
Hun Jiang →, China 57 D13 40 50N 125 38 E
Húnaflói, Iceland 8 D3 65 50N 20 50W
Hunan □, China .... 59 D9 27 30N 112 0 E
Hunchun, China ..... 57 C16 42 52N 130 28 E
Hundested, Denmark . 11 J5 55 58N 11 52 E
Hundewali, Pakistan . 68 D5 31 55N 72 38 E
Hundred Mile House,
 Canada 102 C4 51 38N 121 18W
Hunedoara, Romania . 28 E7 45 40N 22 50 E
Hunedoara □, Romania 28 E7 45 50N 22 54 E
Hünfeld, Germany ... 24 E5 50 39N 9 46 E
Hung Yen, Vietnam . 58 G6 20 39N 106 4 E
Hungary ■, Europe . 27 D12 47 20N 19 20 E
Hungary, Plain of,
 Europe .... 6 F10 47 0N 20 0 E
Hungerford, Australia 95 D3 28 58S 144 24 E
Hūngnam, N. Korea . 57 E14 39 49N 127 45 E
Hungt'ou Hsü, Taiwan 59 G13 22 1N 121 30 E
Huni Valley, Ghana .. 82 D4 5 33N 1 56W
Hunneberg, Sweden . 11 F6 58 18N 12 30 E
Hunnebostrand, Sweden 11 F5 58 27N 11 18 E
Hunsberge, Namibia . 88 D2 27 45S 17 12 E
Hunsrück, Germany . 25 F3 49 56N 7 27 E
Hunstanton, U.K. ... 14 E8 52 56N 0 29 E
Hunte →, Germany . 24 B4 53 14N 8 28 E
Hunter, U.S.A. 117 D10 42 13N 74 13W
Hunter I., Australia .. 95 G3 40 30S 144 45 E
Hunter I., Canada ... 102 C3 51 55N 128 0W
Hunter Ra., Australia 95 E5 32 45S 150 15 E
Hunters Road,
 Zimbabwe .... 87 F2 19 9S 29 49 E
Hunterville, N.Z. .... 91 H5 39 56S 175 35 E
Huntingburg, U.S.A. . 114 F2 38 18N 86 57W
Huntingdon, Canada . 104 C5 45 6N 74 10W
Huntingdon, U.K. ... 15 E7 52 20N 0 11W
Huntingdon, U.S.A. . 116 F6 40 30N 78 1W
Huntington, Ind., U.S.A. 114 E3 40 53N 85 30W
Huntington, Oreg.,
 U.S.A. 108 D5 44 21N 117 16W
Huntington, Utah,
 U.S.A. 108 G8 39 20N 110 58W
Huntington, W. Va.,
 U.S.A. 114 F4 38 25N 82 27W
Huntington Beach,
 U.S.A. 111 M9 33 40N 118 5W
Huntington Station,
 U.S.A. 117 F11 40 52N 73 26W
Huntly, N.Z. .... 91 G5 37 34S 175 11 E
Huntly, U.K. 13 D6 57 27N 2 47W
Huntsville, Canada .. 116 A5 45 20N 79 14W
Huntsville, Ala., U.S.A. 115 H2 34 44N 86 35W
Huntsville, Tex., U.S.A. 113 K7 30 43N 95 33W
Hunyani →, Zimbabwe 87 F3 15 57S 30 39 E
Hunyuan, China .... 56 E7 39 42N 113 42 E
Hunza →, India .... 69 B6 35 54N 74 20 E
Huo Xian = Huozhou,
 China .... 56 F6 36 36N 111 42 E
Huong Khe, Vietnam 64 C5 18 13N 105 41 E
Huonville, Australia . 95 G4 43 0S 147 5 E
Huoqiu, China ...... 59 A11 32 20N 116 12 E
Huoshan, Anhui, China 59 A12 32 28N 116 30 E
Huoshao Dao = Lü-Tao,
 Taiwan .... 59 F13 22 40N 121 30 E
Huozhou, China ..... 56 F6 36 36N 111 42 E
Hupeh = Hubei □,
 China .... 59 B9 31 0N 112 0 E
Ḥūr, Iran .... 71 D8 30 50N 57 7 E
Hurbanovo, Slovak Rep. 27 D11 47 51N 18 11 E
Hurd, C., Canada ... 116 A3 45 13N 81 44W
Hure Qi, China ..... 57 C11 42 45N 121 45 E
Hurezani, Romania .. 29 F8 44 49N 23 40 E
Hurghada, Egypt ... 80 B3 27 15N 33 50 E
Hurley, N. Mex., U.S.A. 109 K9 32 42N 108 8W
Hurley, Wis., U.S.A. . 112 B9 46 27N 90 11W
Huron, Calif., U.S.A. . 110 J6 36 12N 120 6W
Huron, Ohio, U.S.A. . 116 E2 41 24N 82 33W
Huron, S. Dak., U.S.A. 112 C5 44 22N 98 13W
Huron, L., U.S.A. ... 116 B2 44 30N 82 40W
Huron East, Canada . 116 C3 43 37N 81 18W
Hurricane, U.S.A. ... 109 H7 37 11N 113 17W

Hurso, Ethiopia ..... 81 F5 9 35N 41 33 E
Hurungwe △, Zimbabwe 87 F2 16 7S 29 5 E
Hurunui →, N.Z. .... 91 K4 42 54S 173 18 E
Hurup, Denmark .... 11 H2 56 46N 8 25 E
Húsavík, Iceland 8 C5 66 3N 17 21W
Huşi, Romania ...... 29 D13 46 41N 28 7 E
Huskvarna, Sweden . 11 G8 57 47N 14 15 E
Hustadvika, Norway . 8 E12 63 0N 7 0 E
Hustontown, U.S.A. . 116 F6 40 3N 78 2W
Hustopeče, Czech Rep. 27 C9 48 57N 16 43 E
Husum, Germany ... 24 A5 54 28N 9 4 E
Husum, Sweden ..... 10 A13 63 21N 19 12 E
Hutchinson, Kans.,
 U.S.A. 113 F6 38 5N 97 56W
Hutchinson, Minn.,
 U.S.A. 112 C7 44 54N 94 22W
Hutte Sauvage, L. de la,
 Canada 105 A7 56 15N 64 45W
Hüttenberg, Austria . 26 E7 46 56N 14 33 E
Hüttener Berge △,
 Germany .... 24 A5 54 24N 9 40 E
Hutton, Mt., Australia 95 D4 25 51S 148 20 E
Huwun, Ethiopia .... 81 G5 4 23N 40 6 E
Huy, Belgium .... 17 D5 50 31N 5 15 E
Huzhou, China ...... 59 B13 30 51N 120 8 E
Hvalpsund, Denmark . 11 H3 56 42N 9 11 E
Hvammstangi, Iceland 8 D3 65 24N 20 57W
Hvar, Croatia .... 41 E13 43 11N 16 28 E
Hvarski Kanal, Croatia 41 E13 43 15N 16 35 E
Hvítá →, Iceland 8 D3 64 30N 21 58W
Hvizdets, Ukraine ... 29 B10 48 35N 25 17 E
Hwachŏn-chŏsuji,
 S. Korea .... 57 E14 38 5N 127 50 E
Hwang Ho = Huang
 He →, China ...... 57 F10 37 55N 118 50 E
Hwange, Zimbabwe . 87 F2 18 18S 26 30 E
Hwange △, Zimbabwe 88 B4 19 0S 26 30 E
Hyannis, Mass., U.S.A. 114 E10 41 39N 70 17W
Hyannis, Nebr., U.S.A. 112 E4 42 0N 101 46W
Hyargas Nuur, Mongolia 60 B4 49 0N 93 0 E
Hybo, Sweden ...... 10 C10 61 49N 16 15 E
Hydaburg, U.S.A. 102 B2 55 15N 132 50W
Hyde Park, U.S.A. ... 117 E11 41 47N 73 56W
Hyden, Australia .... 93 F2 32 24S 118 53 E
Hyder, U.S.A. 102 B2 55 55N 130 5W
Hyderabad, India ... 66 L11 17 22N 78 29 E
Hyderabad, Pakistan . 68 G3 25 23N 68 24 E
Hyères, France ...... 21 E10 43 8N 6 9 E
Hyères, Îs. d', France 21 F10 43 0N 6 20 E
Hyesan, N. Korea ... 57 D15 41 20N 128 10 E
Hyland →, Canada . 102 B3 59 52N 128 12W
Hyltebruk, Sweden .. 11 H7 56 59N 13 15 E
Hymia, India .... 69 C8 33 40N 78 2 E
Hyndman Peak, U.S.A. 108 E6 43 45N 114 8W
Hyōgo □, Japan .... 55 G7 35 15N 134 50 E
Hyrum, U.S.A. 108 F8 41 38N 111 51W
Hysham, U.S.A. 108 C10 46 18N 107 14W
Hythe, U.K. .... 15 F9 51 4N 1 5 E
Hyūga, Japan .... 55 H5 32 25N 131 35 E
Hyvinge = Hyvinkää,
 Finland .... 9 F21 60 38N 24 50 E
Hyvinkää, Finland ... 9 F21 60 38N 24 50 E

I-n-Gall, Niger ...... 83 B6 16 51N 7 1 E
I-n-Ouadd, Algeria .. 83 A5 20 17N 4 38 E
I-n-Ouzzal, Algeria .. 83 A5 20 40N 2 35 E
I-n-Tadreft, Niger ... 83 A6 20 58N 3 54 E
Iablaniţa, Romania .. 28 F7 44 57N 22 19 E
Iaco →, Brazil 124 E5 9 3S 68 34W
Iacobeni, Romania .. 29 C10 47 25N 25 20 E
Iakora, Madag. ..... 89 C8 23 6S 46 40 E
Ialomiţa □, Romania 29 F12 44 30N 27 30 E
Ialomiţa →, Romania 29 F12 44 42N 27 51 E
Ialoveni, Moldova ... 29 D13 46 56N 28 47 E
Ialpug →, Moldova . 29 E13 45 41N 28 35 E
Ianca, Romania ..... 29 E12 45 6N 27 29 E
Iara, Romania ...... 29 D8 46 31N 23 35 E
Iarda, Ethiopia ..... 81 E4 11 9N 35 53 E
Iargara, Moldova ... 29 D13 46 24N 28 23 E
Iaşi, Romania ...... 29 C12 47 10N 27 40 E
Iaşi □, Romania .... 29 C12 47 20N 27 0 E
Iasmos, Greece ..... 45 E9 41 8N 25 11 E
Ib →, India .... 69 J10 21 34N 83 48 E
Iba, Phil. .... 61 D3 15 22N 120 0 E
Ibadan, Nigeria ..... 83 D5 7 22N 3 58 E
Ibagué, Colombia ... 124 C3 4 20N 75 20W
Iballë, Albania ...... 44 D4 42 12N 20 0 E
Ibănești, Botoşani,
 Romania .... 29 B11 48 4N 26 22 E
Ibănești, Mureş,
 Romania .... 29 D9 46 45N 24 57 E
Ibar →, Serbia & M. . 44 C4 43 43N 20 45 E
Ibaraki □, Japan ... 55 F10 36 10N 140 10 E
Ibarra, Ecuador 124 C3 0 21N 78 7W
Ibba, Sudan .... 81 G2 4 49N 29 2 E
Ibba, Bahr el →, Sudan 81 F2 5 30N 28 55 E
Ibbenbüren, Germany 24 C3 52 16N 7 43 E
Ibembo, Dem. Rep. of
 the Congo .... 86 B1 2 35N 23 35 E
Ibera, L., Argentina . 126 B4 28 30S 57 9W
Iberian Peninsula,
 Europe 6 H5 40 0N 5 0W
Iberville, Canada 117 A11 45 19N 73 17W
Iberville, Lac d', Canada 104 A5 55 55N 73 15W
Ibi, Nigeria .... 83 D6 8 15N 9 44 E
Ibi, Spain 39 G4 38 38N 0 34W
Ibiá, Brazil 125 G9 19 30S 46 30W
Ibiapaba, Sa. da, Brazil 125 D10 4 0S 41 30W
Ibicuí →, Brazil 127 B4 29 25S 56 47W
Ibicuy, Argentina ... 126 C4 33 55S 59 10W
Ibiza = Eivissa, Spain 48 C7 38 54N 1 26 E
Ibiza ✈ (IBZ), Spain . 48 C7 38 52N 1 24 E
Ibonma, Indonesia .. 63 E8 3 29S 133 31 E
Ibotirama, Brazil ... 125 F10 12 13S 43 12W
Ibrāhīm →, Lebanon 74 A4 34 4N 35 38 E
'Ibrī, Oman .... 71 F8 23 14N 56 30 E
Ibriktepe, Turkey ... 45 E10 41 0N 26 30 E
Ibshawâi, Egypt .... 80 J7 29 21N 30 40 E
Ibu, Indonesia ...... 63 D7 1 35N 127 33 E
Ibusuki, Japan ..... 55 J5 31 12N 130 40 E
Içà →, Brazil 124 D5 2 55S 67 58W
Icacos Pt., Trin. & Tob. 125 K15 10 3N 61 57W
Içana, Brazil 124 C5 0 21N 67 19W
Içana →, Brazil 124 C5 0 26N 67 19W
Içel = Mersin, Turkey 70 B2 36 51N 34 36 E
Iceland ■, Europe .. 8 D4 64 45N 19 0W
Iceland Plateau, Arctic 4 C7 64 0N 10 0W
Ich'ang = Yichang,
 China .... 59 B8 30 40N 111 20 E
Ichchapuram, India .. 67 K14 19 10N 84 40 E

Ichhawar, India ..... 68 H7 23 1N 77 1 E
Ichihara, Japan ..... 55 G10 35 28N 140 5 E
Ichikawa, Japan .... 55 G9 35 44N 139 55 E
Ichilo →, Bolivia ... 124 G6 15 57S 64 50W
Ichinohe, Japan .... 54 D10 40 13N 141 17 E
Ichinomiya, Japan .. 55 G8 35 18N 136 48 E
Ichinoseki, Japan ... 54 E10 38 55N 141 8 E
Ichnya, Ukraine .... 33 G7 50 52N 32 24 E
Icod, Canary Is. 48 F3 28 22N 16 43W
Ida Grove, U.S.A. ... 112 D7 42 21N 95 28W
Idabel, U.S.A. 113 J7 33 54N 94 50W
Idaga Hamus, Ethiopia 81 E4 14 13N 39 48 E
Idah, Nigeria .... 83 D6 7 5N 6 40 E
Idaho □, U.S.A. 108 D7 45 0N 115 0W
Idaho City, U.S.A. .. 108 E6 43 50N 115 50W
Idaho Falls, U.S.A. . 108 E7 43 30N 112 2W
Idalia △, Australia .. 94 C3 24 49S 144 36 E
Idanha-a-Nova, Portugal 36 F3 39 50N 7 15W
Idar-Oberstein,
 Germany .... 25 F3 49 43N 7 16 E
Idensalmi = Iisalmi,
 Finland .... 8 E22 63 32N 27 10 E
Idfû, Egypt .... 80 C3 24 55N 32 49 E
Ídhi Óros, Greece ... 49 D6 35 15N 24 45 E
Ídhra, Greece ...... 46 D5 37 20N 23 28 E
Idi, Indonesia ...... 62 C1 5 2N 97 37 E
Idiofa, Dem. Rep. of
 the Congo .... 84 E3 4 55S 19 42 E
Idkerberget, Sweden . 10 D9 60 22N 15 15 E
Idku, Bahra el, Egypt 80 H7 31 18N 30 18 E
Idlib, Syria .... 70 C3 35 55N 36 36 E
Idre, Sweden .... 10 C6 61 52N 12 42 E
Idria, U.S.A. 110 J6 36 25N 120 41W
Idrija, Slovenia ..... 41 C11 46 0N 14 5 E
Idritsa, Russia ...... 32 C5 56 17N 28 53 E
Idutywa, S. Africa ... 89 E4 32 8S 28 18 E
Ieper, Belgium ...... 17 D2 50 51N 2 53 E
Ierápetra, Greece ... 49 E7 35 1N 25 44 E
Ierissós, Greece .... 44 F7 40 27N 23 52 E
Ierissoú Kólpos, Greece 44 F7 40 27N 23 57 E
Iernut, Romania .... 29 D9 46 27N 24 15 E
Iesi, Italy .... 41 E10 43 31N 13 14 E
Iésolo, Italy .... 41 C9 45 32N 12 38 E
Ifach, Peñón de, Spain 39 G5 38 38N 0 5 E
Ifakara, Tanzania ... 84 F7 8 8S 36 41 E
'Ifâl, W. al →, Si. Arabia 70 D2 28 7N 35 3 E
Ifanadiana, Madag. .. 89 C8 21 19S 47 39 E
Ife, Nigeria .... 83 D5 7 30N 4 31 E
Iférouâne, Niger .... 83 B6 19 5N 8 24 E
Iffley, Australia ..... 94 B3 18 53S 141 12 E
Ifon, Nigeria .... 83 D6 6 58N 5 40 E
Iforas, Adrar des, Africa 83 B5 19 40N 1 40 E
Ifould, L., Australia . 93 F5 30 52S 132 6 E
Iganga, Uganda ..... 86 B3 0 37N 33 28 E
Igarapava, Brazil ... 125 H9 20 3S 47 47W
Igarka, Russia ...... 52 C9 67 30N 86 33 E
Igatimi, Paraguay ... 127 A4 24 5S 55 40W
Igbetti, Nigeria ..... 83 D5 8 44N 4 8 E
Igbo-Ora, Nigeria ... 83 D5 7 29N 3 15 E
Igbohu, Nigeria ..... 83 D5 8 53N 3 50 E
Igbor, Nigeria ...... 83 D6 7 27N 8 34 E
Iğdır, Turkey .... 73 C11 39 55N 44 2 E
Igelfors, Sweden .... 11 F9 58 52N 15 41 E
Iggesund, Sweden ... 10 C11 61 39N 17 10 E
Iglésias, Italy .... 42 C1 39 19N 8 32 E
Igloolik, Canada 101 B11 69 20N 81 49W
Igloulgaarjuk =
 Chesterfield Inlet,
 Canada 100 B10 63 30N 90 45W
Iglulik = Igloolik,
 Canada 101 B11 69 20N 81 49W
'Igma, Gebel el, Egypt 80 B3 28 55N 34 0 E
Ignace, Canada 104 C1 49 30N 91 40W
Iğneada, Turkey .... 45 E11 41 52N 27 59 E
Iğneada Burnu, Turkey 45 E12 41 53N 28 2 E
Igoumenítsa, Greece 46 B2 39 32N 20 18 E
Igra, Russia .... 34 B11 57 33N 53 7 E
Iguaçu →, Brazil ... 127 B5 25 36S 54 36W
Iguaçu △, Brazil 127 B5 25 36S 54 26W
Iguaçu, Cat. del, Brazil 127 B5 25 41S 54 26W
Iguaçu Falls = Iguaçu,
 Cat. del, Brazil 127 B5 25 41S 54 26W
Iguala, Mexico 119 D5 18 20N 99 40W
Igualada, Spain ..... 38 D6 41 37N 1 37 E
Iguassu = Iguaçu →,
 Brazil 127 B5 25 36S 54 36W
Iguatu, Brazil 125 E11 6 20S 39 18W
Iguazú △, Argentina . 127 B5 25 42S 54 22W
Iguidi, Erg, Africa ... 78 C4 27 0N 7 0 E
Iharana, Madag. .... 89 A9 13 25S 50 0 E
Ihbulag, Mongolia .. 56 C4 43 11N 107 10 E
Iheya-Shima, Japan . 55 L3 27 4N 127 58 E
Ihiala, Nigeria ...... 83 D6 5 51N 6 55 E
Ihosy, Madag. ...... 89 C8 22 24S 46 8 E
Ihotry, Farihy, Madag. 89 C7 21 56S 43 41 E
Ihugh, Nigeria ...... 83 D6 7 2N 9 0 E
Ii, Finland .... 8 D21 65 19N 25 22 E
Ii-Shima, Japan .... 55 L3 26 43N 127 47 E
Iida, Japan .... 55 G8 35 35N 137 50 E
Iijoki →, Finland ... 8 D21 65 20N 25 20 E
Iisalmi, Finland ..... 8 E22 63 32N 27 10 E
Iiyama, Japan ...... 55 F9 36 51N 138 22 E
Iizuka, Japan .... 55 H5 33 38N 130 42 E
Ijebu-Igbo, Nigeria . 83 D5 6 56N 4 1 E
Ijebu-Ode, Nigeria .. 83 D5 6 47N 3 58 E
IJmuiden, Neths. ... 17 B4 52 28N 4 35 E
Ijo → = Iijoki →,
 Finland .... 8 D21 65 20N 25 20 E
IJssel →, Neths. .... 17 B5 52 35N 5 50 E
IJsselmeer, Neths. .. 17 B5 52 45N 5 20 E
Ijuí, Brazil 127 B5 28 23S 53 55W
Ijuí →, Brazil 127 B4 27 58S 55 20W
Ikalamavony, Madag. 89 C8 21 9S 46 35 E
Ikale, Nigeria ...... 83 D6 7 40N 5 37 E
Ikalukutiak, Canada . 100 B9 69 10N 105 0W
Ikang, Nigeria ...... 83 E6 4 48N 8 0 E
Ikara, Nigeria ...... 83 C6 11 12N 8 15 E
Ikaría, Greece ...... 47 D8 37 35N 26 10 E
Ikast, Denmark ..... 11 H3 56 8N 9 10 E
Ikeda, Japan .... 55 G6 34 1N 133 48 E
Ikeja, Nigeria ...... 83 D5 6 36N 3 23 E
Ikela, Dem. Rep. of
 the Congo .... 84 E4 1 6S 23 6 E
Ikerre-Ekiti, Nigeria . 83 D6 7 25N 5 19 E
Ikhtiman, Bulgaria .. 44 D7 42 27N 23 48 E
Iki, Japan .... 55 H4 33 45N 129 42 E
Ikimba L., Tanzania . 86 C3 1 30S 31 20 E
Ikire, Nigeria .... 83 D5 7 23N 4 15 E
Ikizdere, Turkey .... 73 B9 40 46N 40 32 E
Ikom, Nigeria ...... 83 D6 5 58N 8 42 E
Ikongo, Madag. ..... 89 C8 21 52S 47 27 E
Ikopa →, Madag. ... 89 B8 16 45S 46 40 E
Ikorongo △, Tanzania 86 C3 1 50S 34 53 E
Ikot Ekpene, Nigeria 83 D6 5 12N 7 40 E
Ikparjuk = Arctic Bay,
 Canada 101 A11 73 1N 85 7W

Ikungu, Tanzania ..... 86 C3 1 33 S 33 42 E
Ikurun, Nigeria ..... 83 D5 7 54N 4 40 E
Ila, Nigeria ..... 83 D5 8 0N 4 39 E
Ilagan, Phil. ..... 61 C4 17 7N 121 53 E
Ilaka, Madag. ..... 89 B8 19 33 S 48 52 E
Ilâm, Iran ..... 70 C5 33 36N 46 36 E
Ilam, Nepal ..... 69 F12 26 58N 87 58 E
Ilam □, Iran ..... 70 C5 33 0N 47 0 E
Ilan, Taiwan ..... 59 E13 24 45N 121 44 E
Ilanskiy, Russia ..... 53 D10 56 14N 96 3 E
Ilaro, Nigeria ..... 83 D5 6 53N 3 3 E
Ilatane, Niger ..... 83 B5 16 30N 4 45 E
Iława, Poland ..... 30 E6 53 36N 19 34 E
Ile →, Kazakhstan ..... 52 E8 45 53N 77 10 E
Île-à-la-Crosse, Canada ..... 103 B7 55 27N 107 53 E
Île-à-la-Crosse, Lac, Canada ..... 103 B7 55 40N 107 45 W
Île-de-France □, France ..... 19 D9 49 0N 2 20 E
Ileanda, Romania ..... 29 C8 47 20N 23 38 E
Ilebo, Dem. Rep. of the Congo ..... 84 E4 4 17 S 20 55 E
Ilek, Russia ..... 52 D6 51 32N 53 21 E
Ilero, Nigeria ..... 83 D5 8 0N 3 20 E
Ilesha, Kwara, Nigeria ..... 83 D5 8 57N 3 28 E
Ilesha, Oyo, Nigeria ..... 83 D5 7 37N 4 40 E
Ilford, Canada ..... 103 B9 56 4N 95 35 W
Ilfracombe, Australia ..... 94 C3 23 30 S 144 30 E
Ilfracombe, U.K. ..... 15 F3 51 12N 4 8 W
Ilgaz, Turkey ..... 72 B5 40 55N 33 37 E
Ilgaz Dağları, Turkey ..... 72 B5 41 10N 33 50 E
Ilgın, Turkey ..... 72 C4 38 16N 31 55 E
Ilha de Moçambique, Mozam. ..... 87 F5 15 4 S 40 52 E
Ilhavo, Portugal ..... 36 E2 40 33N 8 43 W
Ilhéus, Brazil ..... 125 F11 14 49 S 39 2 W
Ili = Ile →, Kazakhstan ..... 52 E8 45 53N 77 10 E
Ilia, Romania ..... 28 E7 45 57N 22 40 E
Ilia □, Greece ..... 46 D3 37 45N 21 35 E
Iliamna L., U.S.A. ..... 100 C4 59 30N 155 0 W
Iliç, Turkey ..... 73 C8 39 27N 38 33 E
Ilıca, Turkey ..... 47 B9 39 52N 27 46 E
Ilichevsk, Azerbaijan ..... 73 C11 39 22N 45 5 E
Iligan, Phil. ..... 61 G6 8 12N 124 13 E
Iligan Bay, Phil. ..... 61 G6 8 25N 124 5 E
Ilíki, L., Greece ..... 46 C5 38 24N 23 15 E
Ilin I., Phil. ..... 61 E4 12 14N 121 5 E
Iliodhrómia, Greece ..... 46 B5 39 12N 23 50 E
Ilion, U.S.A. ..... 117 D9 43 1N 75 2 W
Ilirska-Bistrica, Slovenia ..... 41 C11 45 34N 14 14 E
Ilkeston, U.K. ..... 14 E6 52 58N 1 19 W
Ilkley, U.K. ..... 14 D6 53 56N 1 48 W
Illampu = Ancohuma, Nevado, Bolivia ..... 124 G5 16 0 S 68 50 W
Illana B., Phil. ..... 61 H5 7 35N 123 45 E
Illapel, Chile ..... 126 C1 32 0 S 71 10 W
Ille-et-Vilaine □, France ..... 18 D5 48 10N 1 30 W
Ille-sur-Têt, France ..... 20 F6 42 40N 2 38 E
Illéla, Niger ..... 83 C6 14 32N 5 20 E
Iller →, Germany ..... 25 G5 48 23N 9 58 E
Illertissen, Germany ..... 25 G6 48 12N 10 7 E
Illescas, Spain ..... 36 E7 40 8N 3 51 W
Illetas, Spain ..... 48 B9 39 32N 2 35 E
Illichivsk, Ukraine ..... 33 J6 46 20N 30 35 E
Illiers-Combray, France ..... 18 D8 48 18N 1 15 E
Illimani, Nevado, Bolivia ..... 124 G5 16 30 S 67 50 W
Illinois □, U.S.A. ..... 112 E10 40 15N 89 30 W
Illinois →, U.S.A. ..... 112 F9 38 58N 90 28 W
Illizi, Algeria ..... 78 C7 26 31N 8 32 E
Illkirch-Graffenstaden, France ..... 19 D14 48 34N 7 42 E
Íllora, Spain ..... 37 H7 37 17N 3 53 W
Ilm →, Germany ..... 24 D7 51 6N 11 40 E
Ilmajoki, Finland ..... 9 E20 62 44N 22 34 E
Ilmen, Ozero, Russia ..... 32 C6 58 15N 31 10 E
Ilmenau, Germany ..... 24 E6 50 41N 10 54 E
Ilnytsya, Ukraine ..... 28 B8 48 23N 23 3 E
Ilo, Peru ..... 124 G4 17 40 S 71 20 W
Ilobu, Nigeria ..... 83 D5 7 45N 4 25 E
Iloilo, Phil. ..... 61 F5 10 45N 122 33 E
Ilora, Nigeria ..... 83 D5 7 45N 3 50 E
Ilorin, Nigeria ..... 83 D5 8 30N 4 35 E
Ilovatka, Russia ..... 34 E7 50 30N 45 50 E
Ilovlya, Russia ..... 35 F7 49 15N 44 2 E
Ilovlya →, Russia ..... 35 F7 49 14N 44 0 E
Iłowa, Poland ..... 31 G2 51 30N 15 10 E
Ilubabor □, Ethiopia ..... 81 F4 7 25N 35 0 E
Ilva Mică, Romania ..... 29 C9 47 17N 24 40 E
Ilwaco, U.S.A. ..... 110 D2 46 19N 124 3 W
Ilwaki, Indonesia ..... 63 F7 7 55 S 126 30 E
Ilyichevsk = Illichivsk, Ukraine ..... 33 J6 46 20N 30 35 E
Iłża, Poland ..... 31 G8 51 10N 21 15 E
Ilzanka →, Poland ..... 31 G8 51 14N 21 48 E
Imabari, Japan ..... 55 G6 34 4N 133 0 E
Imaloto →, Madag. ..... 89 C8 23 27 S 45 13 E
Imamoğlu, Turkey ..... 72 D6 37 15N 35 38 E
Imandra, Ozero, Russia ..... 52 C4 67 30N 33 0 E
Imanombo, Madag. ..... 89 C8 24 26 S 45 49 E
Imari, Japan ..... 55 H4 33 15N 129 52 E
Imasa, Sudan ..... 80 D4 18 0N 36 12 E
Imathía □, Greece ..... 44 F6 40 30N 22 15 E
Imatra, Finland ..... 32 B5 61 12N 28 48 E
Imbil, Australia ..... 95 D5 26 22 S 152 32 E
Iménas, Mali ..... 83 B5 16 20N 0 40 E
imeni 26 Bakinskikh Komissarov = Neftçala, Azerbaijan ..... 71 B6 39 19N 49 12 E
imeni 26 Bakinskikh Komissarov, Turkmenistan ..... 71 B7 39 22N 54 10 E
Imeri, Serra, Brazil ..... 124 C5 0 50N 65 25 W
Imerimandroso, Madag. ..... 89 B8 17 26 S 48 35 E
Imi, Ethiopia ..... 81 F5 6 28N 42 10 E
Imishly = Imişli, Azerbaijan ..... 35 L9 39 55N 48 4 E
Imişli, Azerbaijan ..... 35 L9 39 55N 48 4 E
Imlay, U.S.A. ..... 108 F4 40 40N 118 9 W
Imlay City, U.S.A. ..... 116 D1 43 2N 83 5 W
Immaseri, Sudan ..... 81 D2 15 40N 25 31 E
Immenstadt, Germany ..... 25 H6 47 33N 10 13 E
Immingham, U.K. ..... 14 D7 53 37N 0 13 W
Immokalee, U.S.A. ..... 115 M5 26 25N 81 25 W
Imo □, Nigeria ..... 83 D6 5 30N 7 10 E
Imo →, Nigeria ..... 83 E6 4 36N 7 35 E
Ímola, Italy ..... 41 D8 44 20N 11 42 E
Imotski, Croatia ..... 41 E14 43 27N 17 12 E
Imperatriz, Brazil ..... 125 E9 5 30 S 47 29 W
Impéria, Italy ..... 40 E5 43 53N 8 3 E
Imperial, Canada ..... 103 C7 51 21N 105 28 W
Imperial, Calif., U.S.A. ..... 111 N11 32 51N 115 34 W
Imperial, Nebr., U.S.A. ..... 112 E4 40 31N 101 39 W
Imperial Beach, U.S.A. ..... 111 N9 32 35N 117 8 W
Imperial Dam, U.S.A. ..... 111 N12 32 55N 114 25 W
Imperial Reservoir, U.S.A. ..... 111 N12 32 53N 114 28 W
Imperial Valley, U.S.A. ..... 111 N11 33 0N 115 30 W
Imperieuse Reef, Australia ..... 92 C2 17 36 S 118 50 E

Impfondo, Congo ..... 84 D3 1 40N 18 0 E
Imphal, India ..... 67 G18 24 48N 93 56 E
Imphy, France ..... 19 F10 46 55N 3 16 E
Imranlı, Turkey ..... 73 C8 39 54N 38 7 E
Imroz = Gökçeada, Turkey ..... 45 F9 40 10N 25 50 E
Imroz, Turkey ..... 45 F9 40 10N 25 55 E
Imst, Austria ..... 26 D3 47 15N 10 44 E
Imuris, Mexico ..... 118 A2 30 47N 110 52 W
Imuruan B., Phil. ..... 63 B5 10 40N 119 10 E
In Akhmed, Mali ..... 83 B4 19 49N 0 56 W
In Aleï, Mali ..... 82 B4 17 42N 2 30 W
In Delimane, Mali ..... 83 B5 15 52N 1 31 E
In Guezzam, Algeria ..... 83 B6 19 37N 5 52 E
In Koufi, Mali ..... 83 B5 19 11N 1 25 E
In Salah, Algeria ..... 78 C6 27 10N 2 32 E
In Tallak, Mali ..... 83 B5 16 19N 3 15 E
In Tebezas, Mali ..... 83 B5 17 49N 1 53 E
Ina, Japan ..... 55 G8 35 50N 137 55 E
Inagua △, Bahamas ..... 121 B5 21 5N 73 24 W
Inangahua, N.Z. ..... 91 J3 41 52 S 171 59 E
Inanwatan, Indonesia ..... 63 E8 2 8 S 132 10 E
Iñapari, Peru ..... 124 F5 11 0 S 69 40 W
Inari, Finland ..... 8 B22 68 54N 27 1 E
Inarijärvi, Finland ..... 8 B22 69 0N 28 0 E
Inawashiro-Ko, Japan ..... 54 F10 37 29N 140 6 E
Inca, Spain ..... 48 B9 39 43N 2 54 E
Inca de Oro, Chile ..... 126 B2 26 45 S 69 54 W
Incaguasi, Chile ..... 126 B1 29 12 S 71 5 W
Ince Burun, Turkey ..... 72 A6 42 7N 34 56 E
Incekum Burnu, Turkey ..... 72 D5 36 13N 33 57 E
Incesu, Turkey ..... 70 B2 38 38N 35 11 E
Inch'ŏn, S. Korea ..... 57 F14 37 27N 126 40 E
Incio = Cruz de Incio, Spain ..... 36 C3 42 39N 7 21 W
Incirliova, Turkey ..... 47 D9 37 50N 27 41 E
Incline Village, U.S.A. ..... 108 G4 39 10N 119 58 W
Incomáti →, Mozam. ..... 89 D5 25 46 S 32 43 E
Incudine, Mte., France ..... 21 G13 41 50N 9 12 E
Inda Silase, Ethiopia ..... 81 E4 14 10N 38 15 E
Indal, Sweden ..... 10 B11 62 35N 17 5 E
Indalsälven →, Sweden ..... 10 B11 62 36N 17 30 E
Indaw, Burma ..... 67 G20 24 15N 96 5 E
Indbir, Ethiopia ..... 81 F4 8 7N 37 52 E
Independence, Calif., U.S.A. ..... 110 J8 36 48N 118 12 W
Independence, Iowa, U.S.A. ..... 112 D9 42 28N 91 54 W
Independence, Kans., U.S.A. ..... 113 G7 37 14N 95 42 W
Independence, Ky., U.S.A. ..... 114 F3 38 57N 84 33 W
Independence, Mo., U.S.A. ..... 112 F7 39 6N 94 25 W
Independence Fjord, Greenland ..... 4 A6 82 10N 29 0 W
Independence Mts., U.S.A. ..... 108 F5 41 20N 116 0 W
Independența, Romania ..... 29 E12 45 25N 27 42 E
Independence, U.S.A. ..... 110 C5 47 50N 121 33 W
India ■, Asia ..... 66 K11 20 0N 78 0 E
Indian →, U.S.A. ..... 115 M5 27 59N 80 34 W
Indian Cabins, Canada ..... 102 B5 59 52N 117 40 W
Indian Harbour, Canada ..... 105 B8 54 27N 57 13 W
Indian Head, Canada ..... 103 C8 50 30N 103 41 W
Indian Lake, U.S.A. ..... 117 C10 43 47N 74 16 W
Indian Ocean ..... 50 K11 5 0 S 75 0 E
Indian Springs, U.S.A. ..... 111 J11 36 35N 115 40 W
Indiana, U.S.A. ..... 116 F5 40 37N 79 9 W
Indiana □, U.S.A. ..... 114 F3 40 0N 86 0 W
Indianapolis, U.S.A. ..... 114 F2 39 46N 86 9 W
Indianola, Iowa, U.S.A. ..... 112 E8 41 22N 93 34 W
Indianola, Miss., U.S.A. ..... 113 J9 33 27N 90 39 W
Indigirka →, Russia ..... 53 B15 70 48N 148 54 E
Indija, Serbia & M. ..... 28 E5 45 6N 20 7 E
Indio, U.S.A. ..... 111 M10 33 43N 116 13 W
Indira Gandhi Canal, India ..... 68 F5 28 0N 72 0 E
Indo-China, Asia ..... 50 H14 15 0N 102 0 E
Indonesia ■, Asia ..... 62 F5 5 0 S 115 0 E
Indore, India ..... 68 H6 22 42N 75 53 E
Indramayu, Indonesia ..... 63 G13 6 20 S 108 19 E
Indravati →, India ..... 67 K12 19 20N 80 20 E
Indre □, France ..... 19 F8 46 50N 1 39 E
Indre →, France ..... 18 E7 47 16N 0 11 E
Indre-et-Loire □, France ..... 18 E7 47 20N 0 40 E
Indulkana, Australia ..... 95 D1 26 58 S 133 5 E
Indura, Belarus ..... 30 E10 53 26N 23 53 E
Indus →, Pakistan ..... 68 G2 24 20N 67 47 E
Indus, Mouths of the, Pakistan ..... 68 H3 24 0N 68 0 E
Inebolu, Turkey ..... 72 B5 41 55N 33 40 E
Inecik, Turkey ..... 45 F11 40 56N 27 16 E
İnegöl, Turkey ..... 45 F13 40 5N 29 31 E
Ineu, Romania ..... 28 D6 46 26N 21 51 E
Infantes = Villanueva de los Infantes, Spain ..... 37 G7 38 43N 3 1 W
Infiernillo, Presa del, Mexico ..... 118 D4 18 9N 102 0 W
Infiesto, Spain ..... 36 B5 43 21N 5 21 W
Ingelstad, Sweden ..... 11 H8 56 45N 14 56 E
Ingenio, Canary Is. ..... 48 G4 27 55N 15 26 W
Ingenio Santa Ana, Argentina ..... 126 B2 27 25 S 65 40 W
Ingersoll, Canada ..... 116 C4 43 4N 80 55 W
Ingham, Australia ..... 94 B4 18 43 S 146 10 E
Ingleborough, U.K. ..... 14 C5 54 10N 2 22 W
Inglewood, Queens., Australia ..... 95 D5 28 25 S 151 2 E
Inglewood, Vic., Australia ..... 95 F3 36 29 S 143 53 E
Inglewood, N.Z. ..... 91 H5 39 9 S 174 14 E
Inglewood, U.S.A. ..... 111 M8 33 58N 118 21 W
Ingólfshöfði, Iceland ..... 8 E5 63 48N 16 39 W
Ingolstadt, Germany ..... 25 G7 48 46N 11 26 E
Ingomar, U.S.A. ..... 108 C10 46 35N 107 23 W
Ingonish, Canada ..... 105 C7 46 42N 60 18 W
Ingore, Guinea-Biss. ..... 82 C1 12 24N 15 48 W
Ingraj Bazar, India ..... 69 G13 24 58N 88 10 E
Ingrid Christensen Coast, Antarctica ..... 5 C6 69 30 S 76 0 E
Ingul = Inhul →, Ukraine ..... 33 J7 46 50N 32 0 E
Ingulec = Inhulec, Ukraine ..... 33 J7 47 42N 33 14 E
Ingulets = Inhulets →, Ukraine ..... 33 J7 46 46N 32 47 E
Inguri = Enguri →, Georgia ..... 35 J5 42 27N 41 38 E
Ingushetia □, Russia ..... 35 J7 43 20N 44 50 E
Ingwavuma, S. Africa ..... 89 D5 27 9 S 31 59 E
Inhaca, Mozam. ..... 89 D5 26 1 S 32 57 E
Inhafenga, Mozam. ..... 89 C5 20 36 S 33 53 E
Inhambane, Mozam. ..... 89 C6 23 54 S 35 30 E
Inhambane □, Mozam. ..... 89 C5 22 30 S 34 20 E
Inhaminga, Mozam. ..... 87 F4 18 26 S 35 0 E
Inharrime, Mozam. ..... 89 C6 24 30 S 35 0 E

Inharrime →, Mozam. ..... 89 C6 24 30 S 35 0 E
Inhisar, Turkey ..... 47 A12 40 3N 30 23 E
Inhul →, Ukraine ..... 33 J7 46 50N 32 0 E
Inhulec, Ukraine ..... 33 J7 47 42N 33 14 E
Inhulets →, Ukraine ..... 33 J7 46 46N 32 47 E
Iniesta, Spain ..... 39 F3 39 27N 1 45 W
Ining = Yining, China ..... 52 E9 43 58N 81 10 E
Inírida →, Colombia ..... 124 C5 3 55N 67 52 W
Inishbofin, Ireland ..... 12 C1 53 37N 10 13 W
Inisheer, Ireland ..... 12 C2 53 3N 9 32 W
Inishfree B., Ireland ..... 12 A3 55 4N 8 23 W
Inishkea North, Ireland ..... 12 B1 54 9N 10 11 W
Inishkea South, Ireland ..... 12 B1 54 7N 10 12 W
Inishmaan, Ireland ..... 12 C2 53 5N 9 35 W
Inishmore, Ireland ..... 12 C2 53 8N 9 45 W
Inishowen Pen., Ireland ..... 12 A4 55 14N 7 15 W
Inishshark, Ireland ..... 12 C1 53 37N 10 16 W
Inishturk, Ireland ..... 12 C1 53 42N 10 7 W
Inishvickillane, Ireland ..... 12 D1 52 3N 10 37 W
Injibara, Ethiopia ..... 81 E4 10 59N 37 0 E
Injune, Australia ..... 95 D4 25 53 S 148 32 E
Inklin →, Canada ..... 102 B2 58 50N 133 10 W
Inland Kaikoura Ra., N.Z. ..... 91 J4 41 59 S 173 41 E
Inle L., Burma ..... 67 J20 20 30N 96 58 E
Inlet, U.S.A. ..... 117 C10 43 45N 74 48 W
Inn →, Austria ..... 26 C6 48 35N 13 28 E
Innamincka, Australia ..... 95 D3 27 44 S 140 46 E
Inner Hebrides, U.K. ..... 13 E2 57 0N 6 30 W
Inner Mongolia = Nei Monggol Zizhiqu □, China ..... 56 D7 42 0N 112 0 E
Inner Sound, U.K. ..... 13 D3 57 30N 5 55 W
Innerkip, Canada ..... 116 C4 43 13N 80 42 W
Innetalling I., Canada ..... 104 A4 56 0N 79 0 W
Innisfail, Australia ..... 94 B4 17 33 S 146 5 E
Innisfail, Canada ..... 102 C6 52 0N 113 57 W
In'noshima, Japan ..... 55 G6 34 19N 133 10 E
Innsbruck, Austria ..... 26 D4 47 16N 11 23 E
Innviertel, Austria ..... 26 C6 48 10N 13 30 E
Inny →, Ireland ..... 12 C4 53 30N 7 50 W
Inongo, Dem. Rep. of the Congo ..... 84 E3 1 55 S 18 30 E
Inönü, Turkey ..... 47 B12 39 48N 30 9 E
Inoucdjouac = Inukjuak, Canada ..... 101 C12 58 25N 78 15 W
Inowrocław, Poland ..... 31 F5 52 50N 18 12 E
Inpundong, N. Korea ..... 57 D14 41 25N 126 34 E
Inscription, C., Australia ..... 93 E1 25 29 S 112 59 E
Insein, Burma ..... 67 L20 16 50N 96 5 E
Insjön, Sweden ..... 10 D9 60 41N 15 6 E
Ińsko, Poland ..... 30 E2 53 25N 15 32 E
Însurăței, Romania ..... 29 F12 44 50N 27 40 E
Inta, Russia ..... 52 C6 66 5N 60 8 E
Intendente Alvear, Argentina ..... 126 D3 35 12 S 63 32 W
Intepe, Turkey ..... 47 A8 40 1N 26 20 E
Interlaken, Switz. ..... 25 J3 46 41N 7 50 E
Interlaken, U.S.A. ..... 117 D8 42 37N 76 44 W
International Falls, U.S.A. ..... 112 A8 48 36N 93 25 W
Intiyaco, Argentina ..... 126 B3 28 43 S 60 5 W
Íntorsura Buzăului, Romania ..... 29 E11 45 41N 26 2 E
Inukjuak, Canada ..... 101 C12 58 25N 78 15 W
Inútil, B., Chile ..... 128 G2 53 30 S 70 15 W
Inuvik, Canada ..... 100 B6 68 16N 133 40 W
Inveraray, U.K. ..... 13 E3 56 14N 5 5 W
Inverbervie, U.K. ..... 13 E6 56 51N 2 17 W
Invercargill, N.Z. ..... 91 M2 46 24 S 168 24 E
Inverclyde □, U.K. ..... 13 F4 55 55N 4 49 W
Inverell, Australia ..... 95 D5 29 45 S 151 8 E
Invergordon, U.K. ..... 13 D4 57 41N 4 10 W
Inverloch, Australia ..... 95 F4 38 38 S 145 45 E
Invermere, Canada ..... 102 C5 50 30N 116 2 W
Inverness, Canada ..... 105 C7 46 15N 61 19 W
Inverness, U.K. ..... 13 D4 57 29N 4 13 W
Inverness, U.S.A. ..... 115 L4 28 50N 82 20 W
Inverurie, U.K. ..... 13 D6 57 17N 2 23 W
Investigator Group, Australia ..... 95 E1 34 45 S 134 20 E
Investigator Str., Australia ..... 95 F2 35 30 S 137 0 E
Inya, Russia ..... 52 D9 50 28N 86 37 E
Inyanga, Zimbabwe ..... 87 F3 18 12 S 32 40 E
Inyangani, Zimbabwe ..... 87 F3 18 5 S 32 50 E
Inyantue, Zimbabwe ..... 88 B4 18 33 S 26 39 E
Inyo Mts., U.S.A. ..... 110 J9 36 40N 118 0 W
Inyokern, U.S.A. ..... 111 K9 35 39N 117 49 W
Inza, Russia ..... 34 D8 53 55N 46 25 E
Inzhavino, Russia ..... 34 D6 52 22N 42 30 E
Iō-Jima, Japan ..... 55 J5 30 48N 130 18 E
Ioánnina, Greece ..... 46 B3 39 42N 20 47 E
Ioánnina □, Greece ..... 46 B3 39 39N 20 57 E
Iola, U.S.A. ..... 113 G7 37 55N 95 24 W
Ion Corvin, Romania ..... 29 F12 44 7N 27 50 E
Iona, U.K. ..... 13 E2 56 20N 6 25 W
Ione, U.S.A. ..... 110 G6 38 21N 120 56 W
Ionia, U.S.A. ..... 114 D3 42 59N 85 4 W
Ionian Is. = Iónioi Nísoi, Greece ..... 46 C2 38 40N 20 0 E
Ionian Sea, Medit. S. ..... 6 H9 37 30N 17 30 E
Iónioi Nísoi, Greece ..... 46 C2 38 40N 20 0 E
Iónioi Nísoi □, Greece ..... 46 C2 38 40N 20 0 E
Íos, Greece ..... 47 E7 36 41N 25 20 E
Iowa □, U.S.A. ..... 112 D8 42 18N 93 30 W
Iowa →, U.S.A. ..... 112 E9 41 10N 91 1 W
Iowa City, U.S.A. ..... 112 E9 41 40N 91 32 W
Iowa Falls, U.S.A. ..... 112 D8 42 31N 93 16 W
Iowa Park, U.S.A. ..... 113 J5 33 57N 98 40 W
Ipala, Tanzania ..... 86 C3 4 30 S 32 52 E
Ipameri, Brazil ..... 125 G9 17 44 S 48 9 W
Ipáti, Greece ..... 46 C4 38 52N 22 14 E
Ipatinga, Brazil ..... 125 G10 19 32 S 42 30 W
Ipatovo, Russia ..... 35 H6 45 45N 42 50 E
Ipel` →, Europe ..... 27 D11 47 48N 18 53 E
Ipiales, Colombia ..... 124 C3 0 50N 77 37 W
Ipin = Yibin, China ..... 58 C5 28 45N 104 32 E
Ípiros □, Greece ..... 46 B2 39 30N 20 30 E
Ipixuna, Brazil ..... 124 E4 7 0 S 71 40 W
Ipoh, Malaysia ..... 65 K3 4 35N 101 5 E
Ippy, C.A.R. ..... 84 C4 6 5N 21 7 E
Ipsala, Turkey ..... 45 F10 40 55N 26 23 E
Ipsárion, Óros, Greece ..... 45 F8 40 40N 24 40 E
Ipswich, Australia ..... 95 D5 27 35 S 152 40 E
Ipswich, U.K. ..... 15 E9 52 4N 1 10 E
Ipswich, Mass., U.S.A. ..... 117 D14 42 41N 70 50 W
Ipswich, S. Dak., U.S.A. ..... 112 C5 45 27N 99 2 W
Ipu, Brazil ..... 125 D10 4 23 S 40 44 W
Iqaluit, Canada ..... 101 B13 63 44N 68 31 W
Iquique, Chile ..... 124 H4 20 19 S 70 5 W
Iquitos, Peru ..... 124 D4 3 45 S 73 10 W
Irabu-Jima, Japan ..... 55 M2 24 50N 125 10 E
Iracoubo, Fr. Guiana ..... 125 B8 5 30N 53 10 W
Irafshān, Iran ..... 71 E9 26 42N 61 56 E

Irahuan, Phil. ..... 61 G3 9 48N 118 41 E
Iráklia, Kikládhes, Greece ..... 47 E7 36 50N 25 28 E
Iráklia, Sérrai, Greece ..... 44 E7 41 10N 23 16 E
Iráklion, Greece ..... 49 D7 35 20N 25 12 E
Iráklion □, Greece ..... 49 D7 35 10N 25 10 E
Irala, Paraguay ..... 127 B5 25 55 S 54 35 W
Iran ■, Asia ..... 71 C7 33 0N 53 0 E
Iran, Gunung-Gunung, Malaysia ..... 62 D4 2 20N 114 50 E
Iran, Plateau of, Asia ..... 50 F9 32 0N 55 0 E
Iran Ra. = Iran, Gunung-Gunung, Malaysia ..... 62 D4 2 20N 114 50 E
Īrānshahr, Iran ..... 71 E9 27 15N 60 40 E
Irapuato, Mexico ..... 118 C4 20 40N 101 30 W
Iraq ■, Asia ..... 70 C5 33 0N 44 0 E
Irati, Brazil ..... 127 B5 25 25 S 50 38 W
Irbes saurums, Latvia ..... 30 A9 57 45N 22 5 E
Irbid, Jordan ..... 74 C4 32 35N 35 48 E
Irbid □, Jordan ..... 74 C5 32 15N 36 35 E
Iregua →, Spain ..... 38 C7 42 27N 2 24 E
Ireland ■, Europe ..... 12 C4 53 50N 7 52 W
Irele, Nigeria ..... 83 D6 7 40N 5 40 E
Irgiz, Bolshaya →, Russia ..... 34 D9 52 10N 49 10 E
Irhyangdong, N. Korea ..... 57 D15 41 15N 129 30 E
Iri, S. Korea ..... 57 G14 35 59N 127 0 E
Irian Jaya = Papua □, Indonesia ..... 63 E9 4 0 S 137 0 E
Irié, Guinea ..... 82 D3 8 15N 9 10 W
Iriga, Phil. ..... 61 E5 13 25N 123 25 E
Iringa, Tanzania ..... 86 D4 7 48 S 35 43 E
Iringa □, Tanzania ..... 86 D4 7 48 S 35 43 E
Iriomote △, Japan ..... 55 M1 24 29N 123 53 E
Iriomote-Jima, Japan ..... 55 M1 24 19N 123 48 E
Iriona, Honduras ..... 120 C2 15 57N 85 11 W
Iriri →, Brazil ..... 125 D8 3 52 S 52 37 W
Irish Republic ■ = Ireland ■, Europe ..... 12 C4 53 50N 7 52 W
Irish Sea, Europe ..... 14 D3 53 38N 4 48 W
Irkutsk, Russia ..... 53 D11 52 18N 104 20 E
Irlhanlı, Turkey ..... 47 D11 37 53N 29 12 E
Irma, Canada ..... 103 C6 52 55N 111 14 W
Irō-Zaki, Japan ..... 55 G9 34 36N 138 51 E
Iroise, Mer d', France ..... 18 D2 48 15N 4 45 W
Iron Baron, Australia ..... 95 E2 33 0 S 137 11 E
Iron Gate = Portile de Fier, Europe ..... 28 F7 44 44N 22 30 E
Iron Knob, Australia ..... 95 E2 32 46 S 137 8 E
Iron Mountain, U.S.A. ..... 114 C1 45 49N 88 4 W
Iron Range △, Australia ..... 94 A3 12 34 S 143 18 E
Iron River, U.S.A. ..... 112 B10 46 6N 88 39 W
Irondequoit, U.S.A. ..... 116 C7 43 13N 77 35 W
Ironton, Mo., U.S.A. ..... 113 G9 37 36N 90 38 W
Ironton, Ohio, U.S.A. ..... 114 F4 38 32N 82 41 W
Ironwood, U.S.A. ..... 112 B9 46 27N 90 9 W
Ironwood Forest △, U.S.A. ..... 109 K8 32 28N 111 36 W
Iroquois, Canada ..... 117 B9 44 51N 75 19 W
Iroquois Falls, Canada ..... 104 C3 48 46N 80 41 W
Irosin, Phil. ..... 61 E6 12 42N 124 2 E
Irpin, Ukraine ..... 33 G6 50 30N 30 15 E
Irrara Cr. →, Australia ..... 95 D4 29 35 S 145 31 E
Irrawaddy □, Burma ..... 67 L19 17 0N 95 0 E
Irrawaddy →, Burma ..... 67 M19 15 50N 95 6 E
Irrawaddy, Mouths of the, Burma ..... 67 M19 15 30N 95 0 E
Irricana, Canada ..... 102 C6 51 19N 113 37 W
Irshava, Ukraine ..... 28 B8 48 19N 23 3 E
Irsina, Italy ..... 43 B9 40 45N 16 14 E
Irtysh →, Russia ..... 52 C7 61 4N 68 52 E
Irumu, Dem. Rep. of the Congo ..... 86 B2 1 32N 29 53 E
Irún, Spain ..... 38 B3 43 20N 1 52 W
Irunea = Pamplona, Spain ..... 38 C3 42 48N 1 38 W
Irurzun, Spain ..... 38 C3 42 55N 1 50 W
Irvine, U.K. ..... 13 F4 55 37N 4 41 W
Irvine, Calif., U.S.A. ..... 111 M9 33 41N 117 46 W
Irvine, Ky., U.S.A. ..... 114 G4 37 42N 83 58 W
Irving, U.S.A. ..... 113 J6 32 49N 96 56 W
Irvona, U.S.A. ..... 116 F6 40 46N 78 33 W
Irwin →, Australia ..... 93 E1 29 15 S 114 54 E
Irymple, Australia ..... 95 E3 34 14 S 142 8 E
Is, Jebel, Sudan ..... 80 C4 22 3N 35 28 E
Is-sur-Tille, France ..... 19 E12 47 30N 5 10 E
Isa, Nigeria ..... 83 C6 13 14N 6 24 E
Isa Khel, Pakistan ..... 68 C4 32 41N 71 17 E
Isaac →, Australia ..... 94 C4 22 55 S 149 20 E
Isabel, U.S.A. ..... 112 C4 45 24N 101 26 W
Isabela, Phil. ..... 61 H5 6 40N 121 59 E
Isabela, Puerto Rico ..... 121 d 18 30N 67 2 W
Isabela, I., Mexico ..... 118 C3 21 51N 105 55 W
Isabela, Cord., Nic. ..... 120 D2 13 30N 85 25 W
Isabella Ra., Australia ..... 92 D3 21 0 S 121 4 E
Isaccea, Romania ..... 29 E13 45 16N 28 28 E
Ísafjarðardjúp, Iceland ..... 8 C2 66 10N 23 0 W
Ísafjörður, Iceland ..... 8 C2 66 5N 23 9 W
Isagarh, India ..... 68 G7 24 48N 77 51 E
Isahaya, Japan ..... 55 H5 32 52N 130 2 E
Isaka, Tanzania ..... 86 C3 3 56 S 32 59 E
Isakly, Russia ..... 34 C10 54 8N 51 32 E
Işalnița, Romania ..... 29 F8 44 24N 23 44 E
Isalo △, Madag. ..... 89 C8 22 25 S 45 16 E
Isan →, India ..... 69 F9 26 51N 80 7 E
Isana = Içana →, Brazil ..... 124 C5 0 26N 67 19 W
Isangano △, Zambia ..... 87 E3 11 8 S 30 35 E
Isanlu Makutu, Nigeria ..... 83 D6 8 15N 5 50 E
Isar →, Germany ..... 25 G8 48 48N 12 57 E
Ísarco →, Italy ..... 41 B8 46 57N 11 18 E
Ísari, Greece ..... 46 D3 37 22N 22 0 E
Íscar, Spain ..... 36 D6 41 22N 4 32 W
Iscehisar, Turkey ..... 47 C12 38 51N 30 45 E
Íschia, Italy ..... 42 B6 40 44N 13 57 E
Isdell →, Australia ..... 92 C3 16 27 S 124 51 E
Ise, Japan ..... 55 G8 34 25N 136 45 E
Ise-Shima △, Japan ..... 55 G8 34 25N 136 48 E
Ise-Wan, Japan ..... 55 G8 34 43N 136 43 E
Isefjord, Denmark ..... 11 J5 55 53N 11 50 E
Isel →, Austria ..... 26 E5 46 56N 12 47 E
Iseo, Italy ..... 40 C7 45 40N 10 3 E
Iseo, L. d', Italy ..... 40 C7 45 43N 10 4 E
Iseramagazi, Tanzania ..... 86 C3 4 37 S 32 10 E
Isère □, France ..... 21 C9 45 15N 5 40 E
Isère →, France ..... 21 D8 44 59N 4 51 E
Iserlohn, Germany ..... 24 D3 51 22N 7 52 E
Isérnia, Italy ..... 43 A7 41 36N 14 14 E
Iseyin, Nigeria ..... 83 D5 7 59N 3 36 E
Isfahan = Eşfahān, Iran ..... 71 C6 32 39N 51 43 E
Ishëm, Albania ..... 44 E3 41 33N 19 34 E
Ishigaki-Shima, Japan ..... 55 M2 24 20N 124 10 E
Ishikari-Gawa →, Japan ..... 54 C10 43 15N 141 23 E
Ishikari-Sammyaku, Japan ..... 54 C11 43 30N 143 0 E
Ishikari-Wan, Japan ..... 54 C10 43 25N 141 1 E

Ishikawa □, Japan ..... 55 F8 36 30N 136 30 E
Ishim, Russia ..... 52 D7 56 10N 69 30 E
Ishim →, Russia ..... 52 D8 57 45N 71 10 E
Ishinomaki, Japan ..... 54 E10 38 32N 141 20 E
Ishioka, Japan ..... 55 F10 36 11N 140 16 E
Ishkuman, Pakistan ..... 69 A5 36 30N 73 50 E
Ishpeming, U.S.A. ..... 114 B2 46 29N 87 40 W
Isigny-sur-Mer, France ..... 18 C5 49 19N 1 6 W
Işıklar Dağı, Turkey ..... 45 F11 40 45N 27 15 E
Işıklı, Turkey ..... 47 C11 38 19N 29 51 E
Isil Kul, Russia ..... 52 D8 54 55N 71 16 E
Isili, Italy ..... 42 C2 39 44N 9 6 E
Isiolo, Kenya ..... 86 B4 0 24N 37 33 E
Isiro, Dem. Rep. of the Congo ..... 86 B2 2 53N 27 40 E
Isisford, Australia ..... 94 C3 24 15 S 144 21 E
Iskenderun, Turkey ..... 70 B3 36 32N 36 10 E
İskenderun Körfezi, Turkey ..... 72 D6 36 40N 35 50 E
İskilip, Turkey ..... 72 B6 40 45N 34 29 E
Iskůr →, Bulgaria ..... 45 C8 43 45N 24 25 E
Iskŭr, Yazovir, Bulgaria ..... 44 D7 42 23N 23 30 E
Iskut →, Canada ..... 102 B2 56 45N 131 49 W
Isla →, U.K. ..... 13 E5 56 32N 3 20 W
Isla Coiba △, Panama ..... 120 E3 7 33N 81 36 W
Isla Cristina, Spain ..... 37 H3 37 13N 7 17 W
Isla de Salamanca △, Colombia ..... 121 D5 10 59N 74 40 W
Isla Gorge △, Australia ..... 94 D4 25 10 S 149 57 E
Isla Tiburón y San Esteban △, Mexico ..... 118 B2 29 0N 112 27 W
Isla Vista, U.S.A. ..... 111 L7 34 25N 119 53 W
Isláhiye, Turkey ..... 72 D7 37 0N 36 35 E
Islam Headworks, Pakistan ..... 68 E5 29 49N 72 33 E
Islamabad, Pakistan ..... 68 C5 33 40N 73 10 E
Islamgarh, Pakistan ..... 68 F4 27 51N 70 48 E
Islamkot, Pakistan ..... 68 G4 24 42N 70 13 E
Islampur, India ..... 69 G11 25 9N 85 12 E
Island L., Canada ..... 103 C10 53 47N 94 25 W
Island Lagoon, Australia ..... 95 E2 31 30 S 136 40 E
Island Pond, U.S.A. ..... 117 B13 44 49N 71 53 W
Islands, B. of, Canada ..... 105 C8 49 11N 58 15 W
Islands, B. of, N.Z. ..... 91 F5 35 15 S 174 6 E
Islay, U.K. ..... 13 F2 55 46N 6 10 W
Isle →, France ..... 20 D3 44 55N 0 15 W
Isle aux Morts, Canada ..... 105 C8 47 35N 59 0 W
Isle of Wight □, U.K. ..... 15 G6 50 41N 1 17 W
Isle Royale △, U.S.A. ..... 114 B1 48 0N 88 55 W
Isleton, U.S.A. ..... 110 G5 38 10N 121 37 W
Ismail = Izmayil, Ukraine ..... 29 E13 45 22N 28 46 E
Ismâ'ilîya, Egypt ..... 80 H8 30 37N 32 18 E
Ismaning, Germany ..... 25 G7 48 13N 11 40 E
Isna, Egypt ..... 80 B3 25 17N 32 30 E
Isoanala, Madag. ..... 89 C8 23 50 S 45 44 E
Isogstalo, India ..... 69 B8 34 15N 78 46 E
Ísola del Liri, Italy ..... 41 G10 41 41N 13 34 E
Ísola della Scala, Italy ..... 40 C7 45 16N 11 0 E
Ísola di Capo Rizzuto, Italy ..... 43 D10 38 58N 17 6 E
Isparta, Turkey ..... 47 D12 37 47N 30 30 E
Isperikh, Bulgaria ..... 45 C10 43 43N 26 50 E
Íspica, Italy ..... 43 F7 36 47N 14 55 E
Israel ■, Asia ..... 74 D3 32 0N 34 50 E
Isratu, Eritrea ..... 81 D4 16 20N 39 53 E
Issia, Ivory C. ..... 82 D3 6 33N 6 33 W
Issoire, France ..... 20 C7 45 32N 3 15 E
Issoudun, France ..... 19 F8 46 57N 1 59 E
Issyk-Kul, Ozero = Ysyk-Köl, Kyrgyzstan ..... 52 E8 42 25N 77 15 E
Ist, Croatia ..... 41 D11 44 17N 14 47 E
Istállós-kő, Hungary ..... 28 B5 48 4N 20 26 E
Istanbul, Turkey ..... 45 E12 41 0N 29 0 E
Istanbul □, Turkey ..... 45 E12 41 10N 29 0 E
Istanbul ✈ (IST), Turkey ..... 45 F12 40 59N 28 49 E
Istanbul Boğazı, Turkey ..... 45 E13 41 10N 29 10 E
Istiaía, Greece ..... 46 C5 38 57N 23 9 E
Istok, Serbia & M. ..... 44 D4 42 45N 20 24 E
Istokpoga, L., U.S.A. ..... 115 M5 27 23N 81 17 W
Istra, Croatia ..... 41 C10 45 10N 14 0 E
Istres, France ..... 21 E8 43 31N 4 59 E
Istria = Istra, Croatia ..... 41 C10 45 10N 14 0 E
Itá, Paraguay ..... 126 B4 25 29 S 57 21 W
Itaberaba, Brazil ..... 125 F10 12 32 S 40 18 W
Itabira, Brazil ..... 125 G10 19 37 S 43 13 W
Itabirito, Brazil ..... 127 A7 20 15 S 43 48 W
Itabuna, Brazil ..... 125 F11 14 48 S 39 16 W
Itacaúnas →, Brazil ..... 125 E9 5 21 S 49 8 W
Itacoatiara, Brazil ..... 124 D7 3 8 S 58 25 W
Itaipú, Reprêsa de, Brazil ..... 127 B5 25 30 S 54 30 W
Itaituba, Brazil ..... 125 D7 4 10 S 55 50 W
Itajaí, Brazil ..... 127 B6 27 50 S 48 39 W
Itajubá, Brazil ..... 127 A6 22 24 S 45 30 W
Itaka, Tanzania ..... 87 D3 8 50 S 32 49 E
Itala △, S. Africa ..... 89 D5 27 30 S 31 7 E
Italy ■, Europe ..... 7 G8 42 0N 13 0 E
Itamaraju, Brazil ..... 125 G11 17 5 S 39 31 W
Itampolo, Madag. ..... 89 C7 24 41 S 43 57 E
Itandrano, Madag. ..... 89 C8 21 47 S 45 17 E
Itapecuru-Mirim, Brazil ..... 125 D10 3 24 S 44 20 W
Itaperuna, Brazil ..... 127 A7 21 10 S 41 54 W
Itapetininga, Brazil ..... 127 A6 23 36 S 48 7 W
Itapeva, Brazil ..... 127 A6 23 59 S 48 59 W
Itapicuru →, Bahia, Brazil ..... 125 F11 11 47 S 37 32 W
Itapicuru →, Maranhão, Brazil ..... 125 D10 2 52 S 44 12 W
Itapipoca, Brazil ..... 125 D11 3 30 S 39 35 W
Itapuá □, Paraguay ..... 127 B4 26 40 S 55 40 W
Itaquari, Brazil ..... 126 B4 29 8 S 56 30 W
Itaquí, Brazil ..... 126 B4 29 8 S 56 30 W
Itararé, Brazil ..... 127 A6 24 6 S 49 23 W
Itarsi, India ..... 68 H7 22 36N 77 51 E
Itatí, Argentina ..... 126 B4 27 16 S 58 15 W
Itatiaia △, Brazil ..... 127 A7 22 29 S 44 35 W
Itbayat, Phil. ..... 61 A4 20 47N 121 51 E
Itchen →, U.K. ..... 15 G6 50 55N 1 22 W
Itéa, Greece ..... 46 C4 38 25N 22 25 E
Itezhi Tezhi, L., Zambia ..... 87 F2 15 30 S 25 30 E
Ithaca = Itháki, Greece ..... 46 C2 38 25N 20 40 E
Ithaca, U.S.A. ..... 117 D8 42 27N 76 30 W
Itháki, Greece ..... 46 C2 38 25N 20 40 E
Iti △, Greece ..... 46 C4 38 50N 22 15 E
Itiquira →, Brazil ..... 125 G7 17 18 S 56 44 W
Itō, Japan ..... 55 G9 34 58N 139 5 E
Itoigawa, Japan ..... 55 F8 37 5N 137 51 E
Iton →, France ..... 18 C8 49 9N 1 12 E
Itonamas →, Bolivia ..... 124 F6 12 28 S 64 24 W
Íttiri, Italy ..... 42 B1 40 36N 8 34 E
Itu, Brazil ..... 127 A6 23 17 S 47 15 W
Itu, Nigeria ..... 83 D6 5 10N 7 58 E

Itu Aba I., S. China Sea 62 B4 10 23N 114 21 E
Ituiutaba, Brazil 125 G9 19 0 S 49 25W
Itumbiara, Brazil 125 G9 18 20 S 49 10W
Ituna, Canada 103 C8 51 10N 103 24W
Itunge Port, Tanzania 87 D3 9 40 S 33 55 E
Iturbe, Argentina 126 A2 23 0 S 65 25W
Ituri →, Dem. Rep. of the Congo 86 B2 1 40N 27 1 E
Iturup, Ostrov, Russia 53 E15 45 0N 148 0 E
Ituxi →, Brazil 124 E6 7 18 S 64 51W
Ituyuro →, Argentina 126 A3 22 40 S 63 50W
Itzehoe, Germany 24 B5 53 55N 9 31 E
Ivahona, Madag. 89 C8 23 27 S 46 10 E
Ivaí →, Brazil 127 A5 23 18 S 53 42W
Ivalo, Finland 8 B22 68 38N 27 35 E
Ivalojoki →, Finland 8 B22 68 40N 27 40 E
Ivanava, Belarus 33 F3 52 7N 25 29 E
Ivančice, Czech Rep. 27 B9 49 6N 16 23 E
Ivane-Puste, Ukraine 29 B11 48 39N 26 10 E
Ivănești, Romania 29 D12 46 39N 27 27 E
Ivangorod, Russia 32 C5 59 27N 28 13 E
Ivanhoe, Australia 95 E3 32 56 S 144 20 E
Ivanhoe, Calif., U.S.A. 110 J7 36 23N 119 13W
Ivanhoe, Minn., U.S.A. 112 C6 44 28N 96 15W
Ivanhorod, Ukraine 29 B14 48 48N 29 50 E
Ivanić Grad, Croatia 41 C13 45 41N 16 25 E
Ivanjica, Serbia & M. 44 C4 43 35N 20 12 E
Ivanjska, Bos.-H. 28 F2 44 55N 17 4 E
Ivankoyskoye Vdkhr., Russia 32 D9 56 37N 36 32 E
Ivano-Frankivsk, Ukraine 29 B9 48 40N 24 40 E
Ivano-Frankivska □, Ukraine 29 B9 48 45N 24 30 E
Ivanovo = Ivanava, Belarus 33 F3 52 7N 25 29 E
Ivanovo, Russia 32 D11 57 5N 41 0 E
Ivanšćica, Croatia 41 B13 46 12N 16 13 E
Ivato, Madag. 89 C8 20 37 S 47 10 E
Ivatsevichy, Belarus 33 F3 52 43N 25 21 E
Ivaylovgrad, Bulgaria 45 E10 41 32N 26 8 E
Ivinheima →, Brazil 127 A5 23 14 S 53 42W
Ivinhema, Brazil 127 A5 22 10 S 53 37W
Ivohibe, Madag. 89 C8 22 31 S 46 57 E
Ivory Coast, W. Afr. 82 E4 4 20N 5 0W
Ivory Coast ■, Africa 82 D4 7 30N 5 0W
Ivösjön, Sweden 11 H8 56 8N 14 25 E
Ivrea, Italy 40 C4 45 28N 7 52 E
Ivrindi, Turkey 47 B9 39 34N 27 30 E
Ivujivik, Canada 101 B12 62 24N 77 55W
Ivybridge, U.K. 15 G4 50 23N 3 56W
Iwaizumi, Japan 54 E10 39 50N 141 45 E
Iwaki, Japan 55 F10 37 3N 140 55 E
Iwakuni, Japan 55 G6 34 15N 132 8 E
Iwamizawa, Japan 54 C10 43 12N 141 46 E
Iwanai, Japan 54 C10 42 58N 140 30 E
Iwata, Japan 55 G8 34 42N 137 51 E
Iwate □, Japan 54 E10 39 30N 141 30 E
Iwate-San, Japan 54 E10 39 51N 141 0 E
Iwo, Nigeria 83 D5 7 39N 4 9 E
Iwonicz-Zdrój, Poland 31 J8 49 37N 21 47 E
Ixiamas, Bolivia 124 F5 13 50 S 68 5W
Ixopo, S. Africa 89 E5 30 11 S 30 5 E
Ixtepec, Mexico 119 D5 16 32N 95 10W
Ixtlán del Río, Mexico 118 C4 21 5N 104 21W
Iyal Bakhit, Sudan 81 E2 13 20N 28 39 E
Iyo, Japan 55 H6 33 45N 132 45 E
Izabal, L. de, Guatemala 120 C2 15 30N 89 10W
Izamal, Mexico 119 C7 20 56N 89 1W
Izberbash, Russia 35 J8 42 35N 47 52 E
Izbica, Poland 31 H10 50 53N 23 10 E
Izbica Kujawska, Poland 31 F5 52 25N 18 40 E
Izbiceni, Romania 29 G9 43 45N 24 40 E
Izena-Shima, Japan 55 L3 26 56N 127 56 E
Izgrev, Bulgaria 45 C10 43 36N 26 58 E
Izhevsk, Russia 52 D6 56 51N 53 14 E
Izmayil, Ukraine 29 E13 45 22N 28 46 E
İzmir, Turkey 47 C9 38 25N 27 8 E
İzmir □, Turkey 47 C9 38 15N 27 40 E
İzmir Adnan Menderes ✕ (ADB), Turkey 47 C9 38 23N 27 6 E
İzmir Körfezi, Turkey 47 C8 38 30N 26 50 E
İzmit = Kocaeli, Turkey 45 F13 40 45N 29 50 E
İznájar, Spain 37 H6 37 15N 4 19W
Iznalloz, Spain 37 H7 37 24N 3 30W
İznik, Turkey 72 B3 40 23N 29 46 E
İznik Gölü, Turkey 45 F13 40 27N 29 30 E
Izobil'nyy, Russia 35 H5 45 25N 41 44 E
Izola, Slovenia 41 C10 45 32N 13 39 E
Izra, Syria 74 C5 32 51N 36 15 E
Iztochni Rodopi, Bulgaria 45 E9 41 45N 25 30 E
Izu-Shotō, Japan 55 G10 34 30N 140 0 E
Izúcar de Matamoros, Mexico 119 D5 18 36N 98 28W
Izumi-Sano, Japan 55 G7 34 23N 135 18 E
Izumo, Japan 55 G6 35 20N 132 46 E
Izyaslav, Ukraine 33 G4 50 5N 26 50 E
Izyum, Ukraine 33 H9 49 12N 37 19 E

J

Jaba, Ethiopia 81 F4 6 20N 35 7 E
Jabal at Tā'ir, Red Sea 81 D5 15 35N 41 52 E
Jabalón →, Spain 37 G6 38 53N 4 5W
Jabalpur, India 69 H8 23 9N 79 58 E
Jabbūl, Syria 70 B3 36 4N 37 30 E
Jabiru, Australia 92 B5 12 40 S 132 53 E
Jablah, Syria 70 C3 35 20N 36 0 E
Jablanac, Croatia 41 D11 44 42N 14 56 E
Jablanica, Bos.-H. 28 G2 43 40N 17 45 E
Jablonec nad Nisou, Czech Rep. 26 A8 50 43N 15 10 E
Jablonica, Slovak Rep. 27 C10 48 37N 17 26 E
Jabłonowo Pomorskie, Poland 30 E6 53 23N 19 10 E
Jablunkov, Czech Rep. 27 B11 49 35N 18 46 E
Jaboatão, Brazil 125 E11 8 7 S 35 1W
Jaboticabal, Brazil 127 A6 21 15 S 48 17W
Jabukovac, Serbia & M. 44 B6 44 22N 22 21 E
Jaca, Spain 38 C4 42 35N 0 33W
Jacareí, Brazil 127 A6 23 20 S 46 0W
Jacarèzinho, Brazil 127 A6 23 5 S 49 58W
Jackman, U.S.A. 115 C10 45 35N 70 17W
Jacksboro, U.S.A. 113 J5 33 14N 98 15W
Jackson, Barbados 121 g 13 7N 59 36W
Jackson, Ala., U.S.A. 115 K2 31 31N 87 53W
Jackson, Calif., U.S.A. 110 G6 38 21N 120 46W
Jackson, Ky., U.S.A. 114 G4 37 33N 83 23W
Jackson, Mich., U.S.A. 114 D3 42 15N 84 24W
Jackson, Minn., U.S.A. 112 D7 43 37N 95 1W
Jackson, Miss., U.S.A. 113 J9 32 18N 90 12W
Jackson, Mo., U.S.A. 113 G10 37 23N 89 40W
Jackson, N.H., U.S.A. 117 B13 44 10N 71 11W
Jackson, Ohio, U.S.A. 114 F4 39 3N 82 39W
Jackson, Tenn., U.S.A. 115 H1 35 37N 88 49W
Jackson, Wyo., U.S.A. 108 E8 43 29N 110 46W
Jackson B., N.Z. 91 K2 43 58 S 168 42 E
Jackson L., U.S.A. 108 E8 43 52N 110 36W
Jacksons, N.Z. 91 K3 42 46 S 171 32 E
Jackson's Arm, Canada 105 C8 49 52N 56 47W
Jacksonville, Ala., U.S.A. 115 J3 33 49N 85 46W
Jacksonville, Ark., U.S.A. 113 H8 34 52N 92 7W
Jacksonville, Calif., U.S.A. 110 H6 37 52N 120 24W
Jacksonville, Fla., U.S.A. 115 K5 30 20N 81 39W
Jacksonville, Ill., U.S.A. 112 F9 39 44N 90 14W
Jacksonville, N.C., U.S.A. 115 H7 34 45N 77 26W
Jacksonville, Tex., U.S.A. 113 K7 31 58N 95 17W
Jacksonville Beach, U.S.A. 115 K5 30 17N 81 24W
Jacmel, Haiti 121 C5 18 14N 72 32W
Jacob Lake, U.S.A. 109 H7 36 43N 112 13W
Jacobabad, Pakistan 68 E3 28 20N 68 29 E
Jacobina, Brazil 125 F10 11 11 S 40 30W
Jacques-Cartier ⌂, Canada 105 C5 47 15N 71 33W
Jacques-Cartier, Dét. de, Canada 105 C7 50 0N 63 30W
Jacques-Cartier, Mt., Canada 105 C6 48 57N 66 0W
Jacqueville, Ivory C. 82 D4 5 12N 4 25W
Jacuí →, Brazil 127 C5 30 2 S 51 15W
Jacumba, U.S.A. 111 N10 32 37N 116 11W
Jacundá →, Brazil 125 D8 1 57 S 50 26W
Jade, Germany 24 B4 53 20N 8 14 E
Jadebusen, Germany 24 B4 53 29N 8 12 E
Jadovnik, Serbia & M. 44 C3 43 20N 19 45 E
Jadraque, Spain 38 E2 40 55N 2 55W
Jaén, Peru 124 E3 5 25 S 78 40W
Jaén, Spain 37 H7 37 44N 3 43W
Jaén □, Spain 37 H7 37 50N 3 30W
Jafarabad, India 68 J4 20 52N 71 22 E
Jaffa = Tel Aviv-Yafo, Israel 74 C3 32 4N 34 48 E
Jaffa, C., Australia 95 F2 36 58 S 139 40 E
Jaffna, Sri Lanka 66 Q12 9 45N 80 2 E
Jaffray, Canada 103 D10 49 47N 94 26W
Jaffrey, U.S.A. 117 D12 42 49N 72 2W
Jagadhri, India 68 D7 30 10N 77 20 E
Jagadishpur, India 69 G11 25 30N 84 21 E
Jagdalpur, India 67 K13 19 3N 82 0 E
Jagersfontein, S. Africa 88 D4 29 44 S 25 27 E
Jaghīn →, Iran 71 E8 27 17N 57 13 E
Jagodina, Serbia & M. 44 B5 44 5N 21 15 E
Jagraon, India 66 D9 30 50N 75 25 E
Jagst →, Germany 25 F5 49 14N 9 10 E
Jagtial, India 66 K11 18 50N 79 0 E
Jaguariaíva, Brazil 127 A6 24 10 S 49 50W
Jaguaribe →, Brazil 125 D11 4 25 S 37 45W
Jagüey Grande, Cuba 120 B3 22 35N 81 7W
Jahanabad, India 69 G11 25 13N 84 59 E
Jahazpur, India 68 G6 25 37N 75 17 E
Jahrom, Iran 71 D7 28 30N 53 31 E
Jaijon, India 68 D7 31 21N 76 9 E
Jailolo, Indonesia 63 D7 1 5N 127 30 E
Jailolo, Selat, Indonesia 63 D7 0 5N 129 5 E
Jaipur, India 68 F6 27 0N 75 50 E
Jais, India 69 F9 26 15N 81 32 E
Jaisalmer, India 68 F4 26 55N 70 54 E
Jaisinghnagar, India 69 H8 23 38N 78 34 E
Jaitaran, India 68 F5 26 12N 73 56 E
Jaithari, India 69 H8 23 14N 78 37 E
Jājarm, Iran 71 B8 36 58N 56 27 E
Jajce, Bos.-H. 28 F2 44 19N 17 17 E
Jakam →, India 68 H6 23 54N 74 13 E
Jakarta, Indonesia 63 G12 6 9 S 106 49 E
Jakhal, India 68 E6 29 48N 75 50 E
Jakhau, India 68 H3 23 13N 68 43 E
Jakobstad = Pietarsaari, Finland 8 E20 63 40N 22 43 E
Jakupica, Macedonia 44 E5 41 45N 21 22 E
Jal, U.S.A. 113 J3 32 7N 103 12W
Jalālābād, Afghan. 68 B4 34 30N 70 29 E
Jalalabad, India 69 F8 27 41N 79 42 E
Jalalpur Jattan, Pakistan 68 C6 32 38N 74 11 E
Jalama, U.S.A. 111 L6 34 29N 120 29W
Jalapa, Guatemala 120 D2 14 39N 89 59W
Jalapa Enríquez = Xalapa, Mexico 119 D5 19 32N 96 55W
Jalasjärvi, Finland 9 E20 62 29N 22 47 E
Jalaun, India 69 F8 26 8N 79 25 E
Jaldhaka →, Bangla. 69 F13 26 16N 89 16 E
Jalesar, India 68 F8 27 29N 78 19 E
Jaleswar, Nepal 69 F11 26 38N 85 48 E
Jalgaon, India 66 J9 21 0N 75 42 E
Jalībah, Iraq 70 D5 30 35N 46 32 E
Jalingo, Nigeria 83 D7 8 55N 11 25 E
Jalisco □, Mexico 118 D4 20 0N 104 0W
Jalkot, Pakistan 69 B5 35 14N 73 24 E
Jallas →, Spain 36 C1 42 54N 9 8W
Jalna, India 66 K9 19 48N 75 38 E
Jalón →, Spain 38 D3 41 47N 1 4W
Jalor, India 68 G5 25 21N 72 37 E
Jalpa, Mexico 118 C4 21 38N 102 58W
Jalpaiguri, India 67 F16 26 32N 88 46 E
Jaluit I., Marshall Is. 96 G8 6 0N 169 30 E
Jalūlā, Iraq 70 C5 34 16N 45 10 E
Jamaari, Nigeria 83 C6 11 44N 9 53 E
Jamaica ■, W. Indies 120 a 18 10N 77 30W
Jamalpur, Bangla. 67 G16 24 52N 89 56 E
Jamalpur, India 69 G12 25 18N 86 28 E
Jamalpurganj, India 69 H13 23 2N 87 59 E
Jamanxim →, Brazil 125 D7 4 43 S 56 18W
Jambewangi, Indonesia 63 J17 8 17 S 114 7 E
Jambi, Indonesia 62 E2 1 38 S 103 30 E
Jambi □, Indonesia 62 E2 1 30 S 102 30 E
Jambusar, India 68 H5 22 3N 72 51 E
James →, S. Dak., U.S.A. 112 D6 42 52N 97 18W
James →, Va., U.S.A. 114 G7 36 56N 76 27W
James B., Canada 104 B3 54 0N 80 0W
James Ranges, Australia 92 D5 24 10 S 132 30 E
James Ross I., Antarctica 5 C18 63 58 S 57 50W
Jamesabad, Pakistan 68 G3 25 17N 69 15 E
Jamestown, Australia 95 E2 33 10 S 138 32 E
Jamestown, S. Africa 88 E4 31 6 S 26 45 E
Jamestown, N. Dak., U.S.A. 112 B5 46 54N 98 42W
Jamestown, N.Y., U.S.A. 116 D5 42 6N 79 14W
Jamestown, Pa., U.S.A. 116 E4 41 29N 80 27W
Jamīlābād, Iran 71 C6 34 24N 48 28 E
Jamiltepec, Mexico 119 D5 16 17N 97 49W
Jamira →, India 69 J13 21 35N 88 28 E
Jämjö, Sweden 11 H9 56 12N 15 49 E
Jamkhandi, India 66 L9 16 30N 75 15 E
Jammerbugt, Denmark 11 G3 57 15N 9 20 E
Jammu, India 68 C6 32 43N 74 54 E
Jammu & Kashmir □, India 69 B7 34 25N 77 0 E
Jamnagar, India 68 H4 22 30N 70 6 E
Jamni →, India 69 G8 25 13N 78 35 E
Jampur, Pakistan 68 E4 29 39N 70 40 E
Jamrud, Pakistan 68 C4 33 59N 71 24 E
Jämsä, Finland 9 F21 61 53N 25 10 E
Jamshedpur, India 69 H12 22 44N 86 12 E
Jamtara, India 69 H12 23 59N 86 49 E
Jämtland, Sweden 8 E15 63 31N 14 0 E
Jämtlands län □, Sweden 10 B7 63 0N 14 40 E
Jan L., Canada 103 C8 54 56N 102 55W
Jan Mayen, Arctic 4 B7 71 0N 9 0W
Janakkala, Finland 9 F21 60 54N 24 36 E
Janaúba, Brazil 125 G10 15 48 S 43 19W
Jand, Pakistan 68 C5 33 30N 72 6 E
Jandaq, Iran 71 C7 34 3N 54 22 E
Jandía, Canary Is. 48 F5 28 6N 14 21W
Jandía △, Canary Is. 48 F5 28 4N 14 19W
Jandía, Pta. de, Canary Is. 48 F5 28 3N 14 31W
Jandola, Pakistan 68 C4 32 20N 70 9 E
Jandowae, Australia 95 D5 26 45 S 151 7 E
Jándula →, Spain 37 G6 38 3N 4 6W
Janesville, U.S.A. 112 D10 42 41N 89 1W
Janga, Ghana 83 C4 10 5N 1 0W
Jangamo, Mozam. 89 C6 24 6 S 35 21 E
Janghai, India 69 G10 25 33N 82 19 E
Janikowo, Poland 31 F5 52 45N 18 7 E
Janinà = Ioánnina □, Greece 46 B2 39 39N 20 57 E
Janja, Bos.-H. 28 F4 44 40N 19 14 E
Janjanbureh, Gambia 82 C2 13 30N 14 47W
Janjevo, Serbia & M. 44 D5 42 35N 21 19 E
Janjgir, India 69 J10 22 1N 82 34 E
Janjina, Croatia 41 F14 42 58N 17 25 E
Janjina, Madag. 89 C8 20 30 S 45 50 E
Janos, Mexico 118 A3 30 45N 108 10W
Jánoshalma, Hungary 28 D4 46 18N 19 21 E
Jánosháza, Hungary 28 C2 47 8N 17 12 E
Jánossomorja, Hungary 28 C2 47 47N 17 11 E
Janów, Poland 31 H6 50 44N 19 27 E
Janów Lubelski, Poland 31 H9 50 48N 22 23 E
Janów Podlaski, Poland 31 F10 52 11N 23 11 E
Janowiec Wielkopolski, Poland 31 F4 52 45N 17 30 E
Januária, Brazil 125 G10 15 25 S 44 25W
Janub △, Sudan 81 F2 6 50N 28 45 E
Janub Dârfûr □, Sudan 81 E2 11 0N 25 0 E
Janub Kordofân □, Sudan 81 E3 12 0N 30 0 E
Janūb Sīnī □, Egypt 74 F2 29 30N 33 50 E
Janubio, Canary Is. 48 F6 28 56N 13 50W
Janville, France 19 D8 48 10N 1 50 E
Janzé, France 18 E5 47 55N 1 28W
Jaora, India 68 H6 23 40N 75 10 E
Japan ■, Asia 55 G8 36 0N 136 0 E
Japan, Sea of, Asia 54 E7 40 0N 135 0 E
Japan Trench, Pac. Oc. 96 D6 32 0N 142 0 E
Japen = Yapen, Indonesia 63 E9 1 50 S 136 0 E
Japla, India 69 G11 24 33N 84 1 E
Japurá →, Brazil 124 D5 3 8 S 65 46W
Jaquarão, Brazil 127 C5 32 34 S 53 23W
Jaqué, Panama 120 E4 7 27N 78 8W
Jarābulus, Syria 70 B3 36 49N 38 1 E
Jaraicejo, Spain 37 F5 39 40N 5 49W
Jaraíz de la Vera, Spain 36 E5 40 4N 5 45W
Jarama →, Spain 36 E7 40 24N 3 32W
Jaramānah, Syria 72 F7 33 29N 36 21 E
Jarandilla, Spain 36 E5 40 8N 5 39W
Jaranwala, Pakistan 68 D5 31 15N 73 26 E
Jarash, Jordan 74 C4 32 17N 35 54 E
Jarash □, Jordan 74 C4 32 17N 35 54 E
Järbo, Sweden 10 D10 60 43N 16 36 E
Jardim, Brazil 126 A4 21 28 S 56 2W
Jardín →, Spain 39 G2 38 50N 2 10W
Jardine River △, Australia 94 A3 11 9 S 142 21 E
Jardines de la Reina, Arch. de los, Cuba 120 B4 20 50N 78 50W
Jargalang, China 57 C12 43 5N 122 55 E
Jari →, Brazil 125 D8 1 9 S 51 54W
Jarīr, W. al →, Si. Arabia 70 E4 25 38N 42 30 E
Järlåsa, Sweden 10 E11 59 53N 17 12 E
Jarmen, Germany 24 B9 53 54N 13 20 E
Järna, Dalarna, Sweden 10 D8 60 33N 14 26 E
Järna, Stockholm, Sweden 10 E11 59 6N 17 34 E
Jarnac, France 20 C3 45 40N 0 11W
Jarny, France 19 C12 49 9N 5 53 E
Jarocin, Poland 31 G4 51 59N 17 29 E
Jaroměř, Czech Rep. 26 A8 50 22N 15 52 E
Jarosław, Poland 31 H9 50 2N 22 42 E
Järpås, Sweden 11 F6 58 23N 12 57 E
Järpen, Sweden 10 A7 63 21N 13 26 E
Jarrahdale, Australia 93 F2 32 24 S 116 5 E
Jarrahi →, Iran 71 D6 30 49N 48 48 E
Jarres, Plaine des, Laos 64 C4 19 27N 103 10 E
Jarso, Ethiopia 81 F4 5 15N 37 30 E
Jartai, China 56 E3 39 45N 105 48 E
Jarud Qi, China 57 B11 44 28N 120 50 E
Järvenpää, Finland 9 F21 60 29N 25 5 E
Jarvis, Canada 116 D4 42 53N 80 6W
Jarvis I., Pac. Oc. 97 H12 0 15 S 160 5W
Jarvorník, Czech Rep. 27 A10 50 23N 17 2 E
Järvsö, Sweden 10 C10 61 43N 16 10 E
Jarwa, India 69 F10 27 38N 82 30 E
Jaša Tomić, Serbia & M. 28 E5 45 26N 20 50 E
Jasdan, India 68 H4 22 2N 71 12 E
Jashpurnagar, India 69 H11 22 54N 84 9 E
Jasidih, India 69 G12 24 31N 86 39 E
Jasień, Poland 31 G2 51 46N 15 0 E
Jāsimīyah, Iraq 70 C5 33 45N 44 41 E
Jasin, Malaysia 65 L4 2 20N 102 26 E
Jāsk, Iran 71 E8 25 38N 57 45 E
Jasło, Poland 31 J8 49 45N 21 30 E
Jasmund, Germany 24 A9 54 32N 13 35 E
Jasmund △, Germany 24 A9 54 31N 13 38 E
Jaso, India 69 G9 24 30N 80 29 E
Jasper, Alta., Canada 102 C5 52 55N 118 5W
Jasper, Ont., Canada 117 B9 44 52N 75 57W
Jasper, Ala., U.S.A. 115 J2 33 50N 87 17W
Jasper, Fla., U.S.A. 115 K4 30 31N 82 57W
Jasper, Ind., U.S.A. 114 F2 38 24N 86 56W
Jasper, Tex., U.S.A. 113 K8 30 56N 94 1W
Jasper △, Canada 102 C5 52 50N 118 8W
Jasrasar, India 68 F5 27 43N 73 49 E
Jastarnia, Poland 30 D5 54 42N 18 40 E
Jastrebarsko, Croatia 41 C12 45 41N 15 39 E
Jastrowie, Poland 30 E3 53 26N 16 49 E
Jastrzębie Zdrój, Poland 31 J5 49 57N 18 35 E
Jász-Nagykun-Szolnok □, Hungary 28 C5 47 15N 20 30 E
Jászapáti, Hungary 28 C5 47 32N 20 10 E
Jászárokszállás, Hungary 28 C4 47 39N 19 58 E
Jászberény, Hungary 28 C4 47 30N 19 55 E
Jászkisér, Hungary 28 C5 47 27N 20 20 E
Jászladány, Hungary 28 C5 47 23N 20 10 E
Jataí, Brazil 125 G8 17 58 S 51 48W
Jati, Pakistan 68 G3 24 20N 68 19 E
Jatibarang, Indonesia 63 G13 6 28 S 108 18 E
Jatiluwih, Indonesia 63 J18 8 23 S 115 8 E
Jatinegara, Indonesia 63 G12 6 13 S 106 52 E
Játiva = Xàtiva, Spain 39 G4 38 59N 0 32W
Jättendal, Sweden 10 C11 61 58N 17 15 E
Jaú, Brazil 127 A6 22 10 S 48 30W
Jauja, Peru 124 F3 11 45 S 75 15W
Jaunpur, India 69 G10 25 46N 82 44 E
Java = Jawa, Indonesia 62 F3 7 0 S 110 0 E
Java Barat □, Indonesia 63 G12 7 0 S 107 0 E
Java Sea, Indonesia 62 E3 4 35 S 107 15 E
Java Tengah □, Indonesia 63 G14 7 0 S 110 0 E
Java Timur □, Indonesia 63 G15 8 0 S 113 0 E
Java Trench, Ind. Oc. 62 F3 9 0 S 105 0 E
Javalambre, Sa. de, Spain 38 E4 40 6N 1 0W
Jávea, Spain 39 G5 38 48N 0 10 E
Jawa, Indonesia 62 F3 7 0 S 110 0 E
Jawad, India 68 G6 24 36N 74 51 E
Jawor, Poland 31 G3 51 4N 16 11 E
Jaworzno, Poland 31 H6 50 13N 19 11 E
Jaworzyna Śląska, Poland 31 H3 50 55N 16 28 E
Jay Peak, U.S.A. 117 B12 44 55N 72 32W
Jaya, Puncak, Indonesia 63 E9 3 57 S 137 17 E
Jayanti, India 67 F16 26 45N 89 40 E
Jayapura, Indonesia 63 E10 2 28 S 140 38 E
Jayawijaya, Pegunungan, Indonesia 63 E9 5 0 S 139 0 E
Jaynagar, India 67 F15 26 43N 86 9 E
Jayrūd, Syria 70 C3 33 49N 36 44 E
Jayton, U.S.A. 113 J4 33 15N 100 34W
Jāz Mūrīān, Hāmūn-e, Iran 71 E8 27 20N 58 55 E
Jazīreh-ye Shīf, Iran 71 D6 29 4N 50 54 E
Jazminal, Mexico 118 C4 24 56N 101 25W
Jazzīn, Lebanon 74 B4 33 31N 35 35 E
Jean, U.S.A. 111 K11 35 47N 115 20W
Jean Marie River, Canada 102 A4 61 32N 120 38W
Jean Rabel, Haiti 121 C5 19 50N 73 5W
Jeanerette, U.S.A. 113 L9 29 55N 91 40W
Jeanette, Ostrov = Zhannetty, Ostrov, Russia 53 B16 76 43N 158 0 E
Jeannette, U.S.A. 116 F5 40 20N 79 36W
Jebāl Bārez, Kūh-e, Iran 71 D8 28 30N 58 20 E
Jebba, Nigeria 83 D5 9 9N 4 48 E
Jebel, Bahr el →, Sudan 81 F3 9 30N 30 25 E
Jebel Dud, Sudan 81 E3 13 25N 33 9 E
Jebel Qerri, Sudan 81 D3 16 16N 32 50 E
Jedburgh, U.K. 13 F6 55 29N 2 33W
Jedda = Jiddah, Si. Arabia 75 C2 21 29N 39 10 E
Jeddore L., Canada 105 C8 48 3N 55 55W
Jedlicze, Poland 31 J8 49 43N 21 40 E
Jędrzejów, Poland 31 H7 50 35N 20 15 E
Jedwabne, Poland 31 E9 53 17N 22 18 E
Jeetzel →, Germany 24 B7 53 9N 11 3 E
Jefferson, Iowa, U.S.A. 112 D7 42 1N 94 23W
Jefferson, Ohio, U.S.A. 116 E4 41 44N 80 46W
Jefferson, Tex., U.S.A. 113 J7 32 46N 94 21W
Jefferson, Mt., Nev., U.S.A. 108 G5 38 51N 117 0W
Jefferson, Mt., Oreg., U.S.A. 108 D3 44 41N 121 48W
Jefferson City, Mo., U.S.A. 112 F8 38 34N 92 10W
Jefferson City, Tenn., U.S.A. 115 G4 36 7N 83 30W
Jeffersontown, U.S.A. 114 F3 38 12N 85 35W
Jeffersonville, U.S.A. 114 F3 38 17N 85 44W
Jeffrey City, U.S.A. 108 E10 42 30N 107 49W
Jega, Nigeria 83 C5 12 15N 4 23 E
Jeju = Cheju do, S. Korea 57 H14 33 29N 126 34 E
Jēkabpils, Latvia 9 H21 56 29N 25 57 E
Jekyll I., U.S.A. 115 K5 31 4N 81 25W
Jelcz-Laskowice, Poland 31 G4 51 2N 17 19 E
Jelenia Góra, Poland 31 H2 50 50N 15 45 E
Jelgava, Latvia 9 H20 56 41N 23 49 E
Jelgava □, Latvia 30 B10 56 35N 23 45 E
Jelica, Serbia & M. 44 C4 43 50N 20 17 E
Jelli, Sudan 81 F3 5 25N 31 45 E
Jelšava, Slovak Rep. 27 C13 48 37N 20 15 E
Jemaja, Indonesia 65 L5 3 5N 105 45 E
Jemaluang, Malaysia 65 L4 2 16N 103 52 E
Jember, Indonesia 63 H15 8 11 S 113 41 E
Jembongan, Malaysia 62 C5 6 45N 117 20 E
Jena, Germany 24 E7 50 54N 11 35 E
Jena, U.S.A. 113 K8 31 41N 92 8W
Jenbach, Austria 26 D4 47 24N 11 47 E
Jenīn, West Bank 74 C4 32 28N 35 18 E
Jenkins, U.S.A. 114 G4 37 10N 82 38W
Jenner, U.S.A. 110 G3 38 27N 123 7W
Jennings, U.S.A. 113 K8 30 13N 92 40W
Jepara, Indonesia 63 G14 7 40 S 109 14 E
Jeparit, Australia 95 F3 36 8 S 142 1 E
Jequié, Brazil 125 F10 13 51 S 40 5W
Jequitinhonha, Brazil 125 G10 16 30 S 41 0W
Jequitinhonha →, Brazil 125 G11 15 51 S 38 53W
Jerantut, Malaysia 65 L4 3 56N 102 22 E
Jerejak, Pulau, Malaysia 65 c 5 19N 100 19 E
Jérémie, Haiti 121 C5 18 40N 74 10W
Jerez, Punta, Mexico 119 C5 22 58N 97 40W
Jerez de García Salinas, Mexico 118 C4 22 39N 103 0W
Jerez de la Frontera, Spain 37 J4 36 41N 6 7W
Jerez de los Caballeros, Spain 37 G4 38 20N 6 45W
Jericho = El Arīḥā, West Bank 74 D4 31 52N 35 27 E
Jericho, Australia 94 C4 23 38 S 146 6 E
Jerichow, Germany 24 C8 52 30N 12 2 E
Jerid, Chott el = Djerid, Chott, Tunisia 78 B7 33 42N 8 30 E
Jerilderie, Australia 95 F4 35 20 S 145 41 E
Jermyn, U.S.A. 117 E9 41 31N 75 31W
Jerome, U.S.A. 108 E6 42 44N 114 31W
Jerramungup, Australia 93 F2 33 55 S 118 55 E
Jersey, U.K. 15 H5 49 11N 2 7W
Jersey City, U.S.A. 117 F10 40 44N 74 4W
Jersey Shore, U.S.A. 116 E7 41 12N 77 15W
Jerseyville, U.S.A. 112 F9 39 7N 90 20W
Jerusalem, Israel 74 D4 31 47N 35 10 E
Jervis B., Australia 95 F5 35 8 S 150 46 E
Jervis Inlet, Canada 102 C4 50 0N 123 57W
Jerzu, Italy 42 C2 39 47N 9 31 E
Jesenice, Slovenia 41 B11 46 28N 13 3 E
Jeseník, Czech Rep. 27 A10 50 14N 17 8 E
Jesenké, Slovak Rep. 27 C13 48 20N 20 10 E
Jesi = Iesi, Italy 41 E10 43 31N 13 14 E
Jessnitz, Germany 24 D8 51 40N 12 18 E
Jessore, Bangla. 67 H16 23 10N 89 10 E
Jesup, U.S.A. 115 K5 31 36N 81 53W
Jesús Carranza, Mexico 119 D5 17 28N 95 1W
Jesús María, Argentina 126 C3 30 59 S 64 5W
Jetmore, U.S.A. 113 F5 38 4N 99 54W
Jetpur, India 68 J4 21 45N 70 10 E
Jeumont, France 19 B11 50 18N 4 6 E
Jevnaker, Norway 9 F14 60 15N 10 26 E
Jewett, U.S.A. 116 F3 40 22N 81 2W
Jewett City, U.S.A. 117 E13 41 36N 72 0W
Jeyḥūnābād, Iran 71 C6 34 58N 48 59 E
Jeypore, India 67 K13 18 50N 82 38 E
Jeziorak, Jezioro, Poland 30 E6 53 40N 19 35 E
Jeziorany, Poland 30 E7 53 58N 20 46 E
Jeziorka →, Poland 31 F8 52 8N 21 9 E
Jha Jha, India 69 G12 24 46N 86 22 E
Jhaarkand = Jharkhand □, India 69 H11 24 0N 85 50 E
Jhabua, India 68 H6 22 46N 74 36 E
Jhajjar, India 68 E7 28 37N 76 42 E
Jhal, Pakistan 68 E2 28 17N 67 27 E
Jhal Jhao, Pakistan 66 F4 26 20N 65 35 E
Jhalawar, India 68 G7 24 40N 76 10 E
Jhalida, India 69 H11 23 22N 85 58 E
Jhalrapatan, India 68 G7 24 33N 76 10 E
Jhang Maghiana, Pakistan 68 D5 31 15N 72 22 E
Jhansi, India 69 G8 25 30N 78 36 E
Jhargram, India 69 H12 22 27N 86 59 E
Jharia, India 69 H12 23 45N 86 26 E
Jharkhand □, India 69 H11 24 0N 85 50 E
Jharsuguda, India 67 J14 21 56N 84 5 E
Jhelum, Pakistan 68 C5 33 0N 73 45 E
Jhelum →, Pakistan 68 D5 31 20N 72 10 E
Jhilmilli, India 69 H10 23 24N 82 51 E
Jhudo, Pakistan 68 G3 24 58N 69 18 E
Jhunjhunu, India 68 E6 28 10N 75 30 E
Ji-Paraná, Brazil 124 F6 10 52 S 62 57W
Ji Xian, Hebei, China 56 F8 37 35N 115 30 E
Ji Xian, Henan, China 56 G8 35 22N 114 5 E
Ji Xian, Shanxi, China 56 F6 36 7N 110 40 E
Jia Xian, Henan, China 56 H7 33 59N 113 12 E
Jia Xian, Shaanxi, China 56 E6 38 12N 110 28 E
Jiading, China 59 B13 31 22N 121 15 E
Jiahe, China 59 E9 25 38N 112 19 E
Jialing Jiang →, China 58 C6 29 30N 106 20 E
Jiamusi, China 60 B8 46 40N 130 26 E
Ji'an, Jiangxi, China 59 D10 27 6N 114 59 E
Ji'an, Jilin, China 57 D14 41 5N 126 10 E
Jianchang, China 57 D11 40 55N 120 35 E
Jianchangying, China 57 D10 40 10N 118 50 E
Jianchuan, China 58 D2 26 38N 99 55 E
Jiande, China 59 C12 29 23N 119 15 E
Jiang'an, China 58 C5 28 40N 105 3 E
Jiangbei, China 58 C6 29 40N 106 34 E
Jiangcheng, China 58 F3 22 36N 101 52 E
Jiangchuan, China 58 E4 24 8N 102 39 E
Jiangdi, China 58 D4 26 57N 103 37 E
Jiangdu, China 59 A12 32 27N 119 36 E
Jiange, China 58 A5 32 4N 105 32 E
Jianghua, China 59 E8 25 0N 111 47 E
Jiangjin, China 58 C6 29 14N 106 14 E
Jiangkou, China 58 D7 27 40N 108 49 E
Jiangle, China 59 D11 26 42N 117 23 E
Jiangling, China 59 B9 30 25N 112 12 E
Jiangmen, China 59 F9 22 32N 113 0 E
Jiangning, China 59 B12 31 55N 118 50 E
Jiangshan, China 59 C12 28 40N 118 37 E
Jiangsu □, China 57 H11 33 0N 120 0 E
Jiangxi □, China 59 D11 27 30N 116 0 E
Jiangyan, China 59 A13 32 30N 120 7 E
Jiangyin, China 59 B13 31 54N 120 17 E
Jiangyong, China 59 E8 25 20N 111 22 E
Jiangyou, China 58 B5 31 44N 104 43 E
Jianhe, China 58 D7 26 37N 108 31 E
Jianli, China 59 C9 29 46N 112 56 E
Jianning, China 59 D11 26 50N 116 50 E
Jian'ou, China 59 D12 27 3N 118 17 E
Jianshi, China 58 B7 30 37N 109 38 E
Jianshui, China 58 F4 23 36N 102 43 E
Jianyang, Fujian, China 59 D12 27 20N 118 5 E
Jianyang, Sichuan, China 58 B5 30 24N 104 33 E
Jiao Xian = Jiaozhou, China 57 F11 36 18N 120 1 E
Jiaohe, Hebei, China 56 E9 38 2N 116 20 E
Jiaohe, Jilin, China 57 C14 43 40N 127 22 E
Jiaojiang, China 59 C13 28 40N 121 24 E
Jiaoling, China 59 E11 24 41N 116 12 E
Jiaozhou, China 57 F11 36 18N 120 1 E
Jiaozhou Wan, China 57 F11 36 5N 120 10 E
Jiaozuo, China 56 G7 35 16N 113 12 E
Jiashan, China 59 B13 30 55N 120 55 E
Jiawang, China 57 G9 34 28N 117 26 E
Jiaxiang, China 56 G9 35 25N 116 20 E
Jiaxing, China 59 B13 30 49N 120 45 E
Jiayi = Chiai, Taiwan 59 F13 23 29N 120 25 E
Jiayu, China 59 C9 29 55N 113 55 E
Jibiya, Nigeria 83 C6 13 5N 7 12 E
Jibou, Romania 29 C8 47 15N 23 17 E
Jibuti = Djibouti ■, Africa 81 E5 12 0N 43 0 E
Jicarón, I., Panama 120 E3 7 10N 81 50W
Jičín, Czech Rep. 26 A8 50 25N 15 28 E
Jiddah, Si. Arabia 75 C2 21 29N 39 10 E
Jido, India 67 E19 29 2N 94 58 E
Jieshou, China 56 H8 33 18N 115 22 E
Jiexiu, China 56 F6 37 2N 111 55 E
Jieyang, China 59 F11 23 35N 116 21 E
Jigawa □, Nigeria 83 C6 12 0N 9 45 E
Jiggalong, Australia 92 D3 23 21 S 120 47 E
Jigni, India 69 G8 25 45N 79 25 E
Jihlava, Czech Rep. 26 B8 49 28N 15 35 E
Jihlava →, Czech Rep. 27 C9 48 55N 16 36 E
Jihlavský □, Czech Rep. 26 B8 49 30N 15 30 E
Jihočeský □, Czech Rep. 26 B7 49 8N 14 35 E
Jihomoravský □, Czech Rep. 27 B9 49 5N 16 30 E
Jijiga, Ethiopia 75 F3 9 20N 42 50 E
Jikamshi, Nigeria 83 C6 12 12N 7 45 E
Jikau, Sudan 81 F3 8 28N 33 47 E
Jilin, China 57 C14 43 44N 126 30 E
Jilin □, China 57 C14 44 0N 127 0 E
Jiloca →, Spain 38 D3 41 21N 1 39W
Jilong = Chilung, Taiwan 59 E13 25 3N 121 45 E
Jim Thorpe, U.S.A. 117 F9 40 52N 75 44W
Jima, Ethiopia 81 F4 7 40N 36 47 E
Jimbaran, Teluk, Indonesia 63 K18 8 46 S 115 9 E
Jimbolia, Romania 28 E5 45 47N 20 43 E
Jimena de la Frontera, Spain 37 J5 36 27N 5 24W
Jiménez, Mexico 118 B4 27 10N 104 54W

Jimo, China .... **57 F11** 36 23N 120 30 E
Jin Jiang ➤, China ... **59 C10** 28 24N 115 48 E
Jin Xian = Jinzhou,
China .... **56 E8** 38 2N 115 2 E
Jin Xian, China ...... **57 E11** 38 55N 121 42 E
Jinan, China .... **56 F9** 36 38N 117 1 E
Jinchang, China ...... **60 C5** 38 30N 102 10 E
Jincheng, China ...... **56 G7** 35 29N 112 50 E
Jinchuan, China ...... **58 B4** 31 30N 102 3 E
Jind, India .... **68 E7** 29 19N 76 22 E
Jindabyne, Australia .. **95 F4** 36 25 S 148 35 E
Jindřichův Hradec,
Czech Rep. .... **26 B8** 49 10N 15 2 E
Jing He ➤, China .... **56 G5** 34 27N 109 4 E
Jing Shan, China ..... **59 B8** 31 20N 111 35 E
Jing Xian, China ..... **59 B12** 30 38N 118 25 E
Jing'an, China .... **59 C10** 28 50N 115 17 E
Jingbian, China ...... **56 F5** 37 20N 108 30 E
Jingchuan, China ..... **56 G4** 35 20N 107 20 E
Jingde, China .... **59 B12** 30 15N 118 27 E
Jingdezhen, China .... **59 C11** 29 20N 117 11 E
Jingdong, China ...... **58 E3** 24 23N 100 47 E
Jinggangshan, China .. **59 D10** 26 58N 114 15 E
Jinggu, China .... **58 F3** 23 35N 100 41 E
Jinghai, China .... **56 E9** 38 55N 116 55 E
Jinghong, China ...... **58 G3** 22 0N 100 45 E
Jingjiang, China ..... **59 A13** 32 2N 120 16 E
Jingle, China .... **56 E6** 38 20N 111 55 E
Jingmen, China .... **59 B9** 31 0N 112 10 E
Jingning, China ...... **56 G3** 35 30N 105 10 E
Jingpo Hu, China ..... **57 C15** 43 55N 128 55 E
Jingshan, China ...... **59 B9** 31 1N 113 7 E
Jingtai, China .... **56 F3** 37 10N 104 6 E
Jingxi, China .... **58 F6** 23 8N 106 27 E
Jingxing, China ...... **56 E8** 38 2N 114 8 E
Jingyang, China ...... **56 G5** 34 30N 108 50 E
Jingyu, China .... **57 C14** 42 25N 126 45 E
Jingyuan, China ...... **56 F3** 36 30N 104 40 E
Jingzhou, China ...... **58 D7** 26 33N 109 40 E
Jinhua, China .... **59 C12** 29 8N 119 38 E
Jining,
Nei Monggol Zizhiqu,
China .... **56 D7** 41 5N 113 0 E
Jining, Shandong, China **56 G9** 35 22N 116 34 E
Jinja, Uganda .... **86 B3** 0 25N 33 12 E
Jinjang, Malaysia .... **65 L3** 3 13N 101 39 E
Jinji, China .... **56 F4** 37 58N 106 8 E
Jinjiang, Fujian, China **59 E12** 24 43N 118 33 E
Jinjiang, Yunnan, China **58 D3** 26 14N 100 34 E
Jinjini, Ghana **82 D4** 7 26N 2 42W
Jinkou, China .... **59 B10** 30 20N 114 8 E
Jinkouhe, China ...... **58 C4** 29 18N 103 4 E
Jinmen Dao, China .... **59 E12** 24 25N 118 25 E
Jinnah Barrage, Pakistan **66 C7** 32 58N 71 33 E
Jinning, China .... **58 E4** 24 38N 102 38 E
Jinotega, Nic. **120 D2** 13 6N 85 59W
Jinotepe, Nic. **120 D2** 11 50N 86 10W
Jinping, Guizhou, China **58 D7** 26 41N 109 10 E
Jinping, Yunnan, China **58 F5** 22 45N 103 18 E
Jinsha, China .... **58 D6** 27 29N 106 12 E
Jinsha Jiang ➤, China **58 C5** 28 50N 104 36 E
Jinshan, China .... **59 B13** 30 54N 121 10 E
Jinshi, China .... **59 C9** 29 40N 111 50 E
Jintan, China .... **59 B12** 31 42N 119 34 E
Jinxi, Jiangxi, China . **59 D11** 27 56N 116 45 E
Jinxi, Liaoning, China **57 D11** 40 52N 120 50 E
Jinxian, China .... **59 C11** 28 26N 116 17 E
Jinxiang, China ...... **56 G9** 35 5N 116 22 E
Jinyang, China .... **58 D4** 27 28N 103 5 E
Jinyun, China .... **59 C13** 28 35N 120 5 E
Jinzhai, China .... **59 B10** 31 40N 115 53 E
Jinzhou, Hebei, China **56 E8** 38 2N 115 2 E
Jinzhou, Liaoning,
China .... **57 D11** 41 5N 121 3 E
Jiparaná ➤, Brazil ... **124 E6** 8 3 S 62 52W
Jipijapa, Ecuador .... **124 D2** 1 0 S 80 40W
Jiquilpan, Mexico **118 D4** 19 57N 102 42W
Jishan, China .... **56 G6** 35 34N 110 58 E
Jishou, China .... **58 C7** 28 21N 109 43 E
Jishui, China .... **59 D10** 27 12N 115 8 E
Jisr ash Shughūr, Syria **70 C3** 35 49N 36 18 E
Jitarning, Australia . **93 F2** 32 48 S 117 57 E
Jitra, Malaysia ...... **65 J3** 6 16N 100 25 E
Jiu ➤, Romania ...... **29 G8** 43 47N 23 48 E
Jiudengkou, China .... **56 E4** 39 56N 106 40 E
Jiujiang, Guangdong,
China .... **59 F9** 22 50N 113 0 E
Jiujiang, Jiangxi, China **59 C10** 29 42N 115 58 E
Jiuling Shan, China .. **59 C10** 28 40N 114 40 E
Jiulong = Kowloon,
China .... **59 F10** 22 19N 114 11 E
Jiulong, China .... **58 C3** 28 57N 101 31 E
Jiutai, China .... **57 B13** 44 10N 125 50 E
Jiuxincheng, China ... **56 E8** 39 17N 115 59 E
Jiuyuhang, China ..... **59 B12** 30 25N 119 56 E
Jixi, Anhui, China ... **59 B12** 30 5N 118 34 E
Jixi, Heilongjiang, China **57 B16** 45 20N 130 50 E
Jiyang, China .... **56 F9** 37 0N 117 12 E
Jiyuan, China .... **56 G7** 35 7N 112 57 E
Jīzān, Si. Arabia .... **75 D3** 17 0N 42 20 E
Jize, China .... **56 F8** 36 54N 114 56 E
Jizera ➤, Czech Rep. . **26 A7** 50 10N 14 43 E
Jizl, Wādī al ➤,
Si. Arabia .... **70 E3** 25 39N 38 25 E
Jizō-Zaki, Japan ..... **55 G6** 35 34N 133 20 E
Jizzakh, Uzbekistan .. **52 E7** 40 6N 67 50 E
Joaçaba, Brazil ...... **127 B5** 27 5 S 51 31 E
Joal Fadiout, Senegal **82 C1** 14 9N 16 50W
João Pessoa, Brazil .. **125 E12** 7 10 S 34 52W
Joaquín V. González,
Argentina .... **126 B3** 25 10 S 64 0W
Jobat, India .... **68 H6** 22 25N 74 34 E
Jobourg, Nez de, France **18 C5** 49 41N 1 57W
Jódar, Spain **37 H7** 37 50N 3 21W
Jodhpur, India .... **68 F5** 26 23N 73 8 E
Jodiya, India .... **68 H4** 22 42N 70 18 E
Jōetsu, Japan .... **55 F9** 37 12N 138 10 E
Jœuf, France .... **19 C12** 49 12N 5 59 E
Jofane, Mozam. .... **89 C5** 21 15 S 34 18 E
Jogbani, India .... **69 F12** 26 25N 87 15 E
Jõgeva, Estonia ...... **9 G22** 58 45N 26 24 E
Jogjakarta =
Yogyakarta, Indonesia **63 G14** 7 49 S 110 22 E
Johannesburg, S. Africa **89 D4** 26 10 S 28 2 E
Johannesburg, U.S.A. . **111 K9** 35 22N 117 38W
Johansfors, Sweden ... **11 H9** 56 42N 15 32 E
Johilla ➤, India ..... **69 H9** 23 37N 81 14 E
John Crow Mts.,
Jamaica .... **120 a** 18 5N 76 25W
John Day, U.S.A. **108 D4** 44 25N 118 57W
John Day ➤, U.S.A. ... **108 D3** 45 44N 120 39W
John Day Fossil Beds △,
U.S.A. **108 D4** 44 33N 119 38W
John D'Or Prairie,
Canada **102 B5** 58 30N 115 8W

John F. Kennedy
International, New
York ✈ (JFK), U.S.A. **117 F11** 40 38N 73 47W
John H. Kerr Reservoir,
U.S.A. **115 G6** 36 36N 78 18W
John o' Groats, U.K. . **13 C5** 58 38N 3 4W
Johnnie, U.S.A. **111 J10** 36 25N 116 5W
John's Ra., Australia **94 C1** 21 55 S 133 23 E
Johnson, Kans., U.S.A. **113 G4** 37 34N 101 45W
Johnson, Vt., U.S.A. . **117 B12** 44 38N 72 41W
Johnson City, N.Y.,
U.S.A. **117 D9** 42 7N 75 58W
Johnson City, Tenn.,
U.S.A. **115 G4** 36 19N 82 21W
Johnson City, Tex.,
U.S.A. **113 K5** 30 17N 98 25W
Johnsonburg, U.S.A. .. **116 E6** 41 29N 78 41W
Johnsondale, U.S.A. .. **111 K8** 35 58N 118 32W
Johnsons Crossing,
Canada **102 A2** 60 29N 133 18W
Johnston, L., Australia **93 F3** 32 25 S 120 30 E
Johnston Falls =
Mambilima Falls,
Zambia .... **87 E2** 10 31 S 28 45 E
Johnston I., Pac. Oc. . **97 F11** 17 10N 169 8W
Johnstone Str., Canada **102 C3** 50 28N 126 0W
Johnstown, N.Y., U.S.A. **117 C10** 43 0N 74 22W
Johnstown, Ohio, U.S.A. **116 F2** 40 9N 82 41W
Johnstown, Pa., U.S.A. **116 F6** 40 20N 78 55W
Johor, Selat, Asia ... **65 d** 1 28N 103 47 E
Johor Baharu, Malaysia **65 d** 1 28N 103 46 E
Jõhvi, Estonia .... **9 G22** 59 22N 27 27 E
Joigny, France .... **19 E10** 47 58N 3 20 E
Joinville, Brazil .... **127 B6** 26 15 S 48 55W
Joinville, France .... **19 D12** 48 27N 5 10 E
Joinville I., Antarctica **5 C18** 65 0 S 55 30W
Jojutla, Mexico **119 D5** 18 37N 99 11W
Jokkmokk, Sweden .... **8 C18** 66 35N 19 50 E
Jökulsá á Bru ➤,
Iceland **8 D6** 65 40N 14 16W
Jökulsá á Fjöllum ➤,
Iceland **8 C5** 66 10N 16 30W
Jolfà,
Āzarbāyjān-e Sharqī,
Iran .... **70 B5** 38 57N 45 38 E
Jolfà, Eşfahan, Iran . **71 C6** 32 58N 51 37 E
Joliet, U.S.A. **114 E1** 41 32N 88 5W
Joliette, Canada **104 C5** 46 3N 73 24W
Jolo, Phil. .... **61 J4** 6 0N 121 0 E
Jolon, U.S.A. **110 K5** 35 58N 121 9W
Jomalig I., Phil. .... **61 D5** 14 42N 122 22 E
Jombang, Indonesia ... **63 G15** 7 33 S 112 14 E
Jomda, China .... **58 B2** 31 28N 98 12 E
Jonava, Lithuania .... **9 J21** 55 8N 24 12 E
Jones Sound, Canada .. **4 B3** 76 0N 85 0W
Jonesboro, Ark., U.S.A. **113 H9** 35 50N 90 42W
Jonesboro, La., U.S.A. **113 J8** 32 15N 92 43W
Jong ➤, S. Leone **82 D2** 7 32N 12 23W
Jonglei, Sudan .... **81 F3** 6 25N 30 50 E
Jonglei □, Sudan ..... **81 F3** 7 30N 32 30 E
Joniškis, Lithuania .. **9 H20** 56 13N 23 35 E
Jönköping, Sweden .... **11 G8** 57 45N 14 8 E
Jönköpings län □,
Sweden .... **11 G8** 57 30N 14 30 E
Jonquière, Canada **105 C5** 48 27N 71 14W
Jonsered, Sweden ..... **11 G6** 57 45N 12 10 E
Jonzac, France **20 C3** 45 27N 0 28W
Joplin, U.S.A. **113 G7** 37 6N 94 31W
Jora, India .... **68 F6** 26 20N 77 49 E
Jordan, Mont., U.S.A. **108 C10** 47 19N 106 55W
Jordan, N.Y., U.S.A. . **117 C8** 43 4N 76 29W
Jordan ■, Asia .... **74 E5** 31 0N 36 0 E
Jordan ➤, Asia .... **74 D4** 31 48N 35 32 E
Jordan Valley, U.S.A. **108 E5** 42 59N 117 3W
Jordanów, Poland ..... **31 J6** 49 41N 19 49 E
Jorhat, India .... **67 F19** 26 45N 94 12 E
Jörn, Sweden .... **8 D19** 65 4N 20 1 E
Jorong, Indonesia .... **62 E4** 3 58 S 114 56 E
Jørpeland, Norway .... **9 G11** 59 3N 6 1 E
Jorquera ➤, Chile .... **126 B2** 28 3 S 69 58W
Jos, Nigeria .... **83 D6** 9 53N 8 51 E
Jos Plateau, Nigeria . **83 D6** 9 55N 9 0 E
Jošanička Banja,
Serbia & M. ...... **44 C4** 43 24N 20 47 E
José Batlle y Ordóñez,
Uruguay .... **127 C4** 33 20 S 55 10W
Joseni, Romania ...... **29 D10** 46 42N 25 29 E
Joseph, L., Nfld. & L.,
Canada **105 B6** 52 45N 65 18W
Joseph, L., Ont., Canada **116 A5** 45 10N 79 44W
Joseph Bonaparte G.,
Australia .... **92 B4** 14 35 S 128 50 E
Joshinath, India ..... **69 D8** 30 34N 79 34 E
Joshinetsu-Kōgen △,
Japan .... **55 F9** 36 42N 138 32 E
Joshua Tree, U.S.A. .. **111 L10** 34 8N 116 19W
Joshua Tree △, U.S.A. **111 M10** 33 55N 116 0W
Josselin, France **18 E4** 47 57N 2 33W
Jost Van Dyke,
Br. Virgin Is. .... **121 e** 18 29N 64 47W
Jostedalsbreen, Norway **9 F12** 61 40N 6 59 E
Jotunheimen, Norway . **9 F13** 61 35N 8 25 E
Joubertberg, Namibia **88 B1** 18 30 S 14 0 E
Joué-lès-Tours, France **18 E7** 47 21N 0 40 E
Jourdanton, U.S.A. ... **113 L5** 28 55N 98 33W
Joutseno, Finland .... **32 B5** 61 7N 28 31 E
Jovellanos, Cuba **120 B3** 22 40N 81 10W
Joyeuse, France ...... **21 D8** 44 29N 4 16 E
Józefów, Lubelskie,
Poland .... **31 H10** 50 28N 23 2 E
Józefów, Mazowieckie,
Poland .... **31 F8** 52 10N 21 11 E
Ju Xian, China .... **57 F10** 36 35N 118 20 E
Juan Aldama, Mexico . **118 C4** 24 20N 103 23W
Juan Bautista Alberdi,
Argentina .... **126 C3** 34 26 S 61 48W
Juan de Fuca Str.,
Canada **110 B3** 48 15N 124 0W
Juan de Nova, Ind. Oc. **89 B7** 17 3 S 43 45 E
Juan Fernández, Arch.
de, Pac. Oc. ..... **97 L20** 33 50 S 80 0W
Juan José Castelli,
Argentina .... **126 B3** 25 27 S 60 57W
Juan L. Lacaze, Uruguay **126 C4** 34 26 S 57 25W
Juankoski, Finland ... **8 E23** 63 3N 28 19 E
Juárez, Argentina .... **126 D4** 37 40 S 59 43W
Juárez, Mexico **113 N11** 32 20N 115 57W
Juárez, Sierra de,
Mexico **118 A1** 32 0N 116 0W
Juàzeiro, Brazil ..... **125 E10** 9 30 S 40 30W
Juàzeiro do Norte,
Brazil .... **125 E11** 7 10 S 39 18W
Juba = Giuba ➤,
Somali Rep. ...... **75 G3** 1 30N 42 35 E
Juba, Sudan .... **81 G3** 4 50N 31 35 E
Jubany, Antarctica ... **5 C18** 62 15 S 58 37 E
Jubayl, Lebanon ...... **74 A4** 34 5N 35 39 E

Jubbah, Si. Arabia ... **70 D4** 28 2N 40 56 E
Jubbal, India .... **68 D7** 31 5N 77 40 E
Jubbulpore = Jabalpur,
India .... **69 H8** 23 9N 79 58 E
Jübek, Germany .... **24 A5** 54 33N 9 22 E
Jubga, Russia .... **35 H4** 44 19N 38 48 E
Jubilee L., Australia **93 E4** 29 0 S 126 50 E
Juby, C., Morocco **78 C3** 28 0N 12 59W
Júcar = Xúquer ➤,
Spain **39 F4** 39 5N 0 10W
Júcaro, Cuba **120 B4** 21 37N 78 51W
Juchitán, Mexico **119 D5** 16 27N 95 5W
Judaea = Har Yehuda,
Israel .... **74 D3** 31 35N 34 57 E
Judenburg, Austria ... **26 D7** 47 12N 14 38 E
Judith ➤, U.S.A. **108 C9** 47 44N 109 39W
Judith, Pt., U.S.A. .. **117 E13** 41 22N 71 29W
Judith Gap, U.S.A. ... **108 C9** 46 41N 109 45W
Juelsminde, Denmark . **11 J4** 55 43N 10 1 E
Jugoslavia = Serbia &
Montenegro ■,
Europe .... **44 C4** 43 20N 20 0 E
Juigalpa, Nic. **120 D2** 12 6N 85 26W
Juillac, France ...... **20 C5** 45 20N 1 19 E
Juist, Germany .... **24 B2** 53 40N 6 59 E
Juiz de Fora, Brazil **127 A7** 21 43 S 43 19W
Jujuy □, Argentina ... **126 A2** 23 20 S 65 40W
Julesburg, U.S.A. **112 E3** 40 59N 102 16W
Juli, Peru .... **124 G5** 16 10 S 69 25W
Julia Cr. ➤, Australia **94 C3** 20 0 S 141 11 E
Julia Creek, Australia **94 C3** 20 39 S 141 44 E
Juliaca, Peru .... **124 G4** 15 25 S 70 10W
Julian, U.S.A. **111 M10** 33 4N 116 38W
Julian, L., Canada ... **104 B4** 54 25N 77 57W
Julian Alps = Julijske
Alpe, Slovenia ... **41 B11** 46 15N 14 1 E
Julianatop, Suriname **125 C7** 3 40N 56 30W
Julianehåb = Qaqortoq,
Greenland **101 B6** 60 43N 46 0W
Jülich, Germany ...... **24 E2** 50 55N 6 22 E
Julijske Alpe, Slovenia **41 B11** 46 15N 14 1 E
Julimes, Mexico **118 B3** 28 25N 105 27W
Jullundur, India ..... **68 D6** 31 20N 75 40 E
Julu, China .... **56 F8** 37 15N 115 2 E
Jumbo, Zimbabwe ...... **87 F3** 17 30 S 30 58 E
Jumbo Pk., U.S.A. **111 J12** 36 12N 114 11W
Jumentos Cays,
Bahamas **120 B4** 23 0N 75 40W
Jumilla, Spain **39 G3** 38 28N 1 19W
Jumla, Nepal .... **69 E10** 29 15N 82 13 E
Jumna = Yamuna ➤,
India .... **69 G9** 25 30N 81 53 E
Junagadh, India ...... **68 J4** 21 30N 70 30 E
Junction, Tex., U.S.A. **113 K5** 30 29N 99 46W
Junction, Utah, U.S.A. **109 G7** 38 14N 112 13W
Junction B., Australia **94 A1** 11 52 S 133 55 E
Junction City, Kans.,
U.S.A. **112 F6** 39 2N 96 50W
Junction City, Oreg.,
U.S.A. **108 D2** 44 13N 123 12W
Junction Pt., Australia **94 A1** 11 45 S 133 50 E
Jundah, Australia .... **94 C3** 24 46 S 143 2 E
Jundiaí, Brazil ...... **127 A6** 24 30 S 47 0W
Juneau, U.S.A. **102 B2** 58 18N 134 25W
Junee, Australia ..... **95 E4** 34 53 S 147 35 E
Jungfrau, Switz. ..... **25 J3** 46 32N 7 58 E
Junggar Pendi, China **60 B3** 44 30N 86 0 E
Jungshahi, Pakistan . **68 G2** 24 52N 67 44 E
Juniata ➤, U.S.A. **116 F7** 40 30N 77 40W
Junín, Argentina ..... **126 C3** 34 33 S 60 57W
Junín de los Andes,
Argentina .... **128 D2** 39 45 S 71 0W
Jūniyah, Lebanon ..... **74 B4** 33 59N 35 38 E
Junlian, China .... **58 C5** 28 8N 104 29 E
Juntas, Chile .... **126 B2** 28 24 S 69 58W
Juntura, U.S.A. **108 E4** 43 45N 118 5W
Jur, Nahr el ➤, Sudan **81 F2** 8 45N 29 15 E
Jura = Jura, Mts. du,
Europe .... **19 F13** 46 40N 6 5 E
Jura = Schwäbische Alb,
Germany .... **25 G5** 48 20N 9 30 E
Jura, U.K. **13 F3** 56 0N 5 50W
Jura □, France .... **19 F12** 46 47N 5 45 E
Jura □, Switz. .... **25 H3** 47 20N 7 20 E
Jüra ➤, Lithuania .... **30 C9** 55 3N 22 9 E
Jura, Mts. du, Europe **19 F13** 46 40N 6 5 E
Jura, Sd. of, U.K. ... **13 F3** 55 57N 5 45W
Jurbarkas, Lithuania **9 J20** 55 4N 22 46 E
Jurien, Australia .... **93 F2** 30 18 S 115 2 E
Jurilovca, Romania ... **29 F13** 44 46N 28 52 E
Jūrmala, Latvia ...... **9 H20** 56 58N 23 34 E
Jurong, China .... **59 B12** 31 57N 119 12 E
Jurong, Singapore .... **65 d** 1 19N 103 42 E
Juruá ➤, Brazil ...... **124 D5** 2 37 S 65 44W
Juruena, Brazil ...... **124 F7** 13 0 S 58 10W
Juruena ➤, Brazil .... **124 E7** 7 20 S 58 3W
Juruti, Brazil .... **125 D7** 2 9 S 56 4W
Jussey, France .... **19 E12** 47 50N 5 55 E
Justo Daract, Argentina **126 C2** 33 52 S 65 12W
Jutaí ➤, Brazil ...... **124 D5** 2 43 S 66 57W
Jüterbog, Germany .... **24 D9** 51 59N 13 5 E
Juticalpa, Honduras . **120 D2** 14 40N 86 12W
Jutland = Jylland,
Denmark .... **11 H3** 56 25N 9 30 E
Juventud, I. de la, Cuba **120 B3** 21 40N 82 40W
Juvigny-sous-Andaine,
France **18 D6** 48 32N 0 30W
Jüy Zar, Iran .... **70 C5** 33 50N 46 18 E
Juye, China .... **56 G9** 35 22N 116 5 E
Juzennecourt, France **19 D11** 48 10N 4 58 E
Jvari, Georgia .... **35 J6** 42 42N 42 4 E
Jwaneng, Botswana ... **85 C4** 24 45 S 24 50 E
Jyderup, Denmark ..... **11 J5** 55 40N 11 26 E
Jylland, Denmark ..... **11 H3** 56 25N 9 30 E
Jyväskylä, Finland ... **9 E21** 62 14N 25 50 E

K

K2, Pakistan .... **69 B7** 35 58N 76 32 E
Ka ➤, Nigeria .... **83 C5** 11 40N 4 10 E
Kaap Plateau, S. Africa **88 D3** 28 30 S 24 0 E
Kaapkruis, Namibia .. **88 C1** 21 55 S 13 57 E
Kaapstad = Cape Town,
S. Africa .... **88 E2** 33 55 S 18 22 E
Kaba, Guinea **82 C2** 10 9N 11 40W
Kabaena, Indonesia ... **63 F6** 5 15 S 122 0 E
Kabala, S. Leone **82 D2** 9 38N 11 37W
Kabale, Uganda .... **86 C3** 1 15 S 30 0 E
Kabalo, Dem. Rep. of
the Congo .... **86 D2** 6 0 S 27 0 E
Kabambare, Dem. Rep.
of the Congo ..... **86 C2** 4 41 S 27 39 E
Kabango, Dem. Rep. of
the Congo .... **87 D2** 8 35 S 28 30 E
Kabanjahe, Indonesia **62 D1** 3 6N 98 30 E

Kabankalan, Phil. .... **61 G5** 9 59N 122 49 E
Kabara, Mali **82 B4** 16 40N 2 50W
Kabardinka, Russia ... **33 K10** 44 40N 37 57 E
Kabardino-Balkar
Republic =
Kabardino-
Balkaria □, Russia **35 J6** 43 30N 43 30 E
Kabardino-Balkaria □,
Russia .... **35 J6** 43 30N 43 30 E
Kabarega Falls =
Murchison Falls,
Uganda .... **86 B3** 2 15N 31 30 E
Kabasalan, Phil. ..... **61 H5** 7 47N 122 44 E
Kabat, Indonesia ..... **63 J17** 8 16 S 114 19 E
Kabba, Nigeria .... **83 D6** 7 50N 6 3 E
Kabetogama, U.S.A. .. **112 A8** 48 28N 92 59W
Kabi, Niger .... **83 C7** 13 30N 12 35 E
Kabin Buri, Thailand **64 F3** 13 57N 101 43 E
Kabinakagami L.,
Canada **104 C3** 48 54N 84 25W
Kabinda, Dem. Rep. of
the Congo .... **84 F4** 6 19 S 24 20 E
Kabna, Sudan .... **80 D3** 19 6N 32 40 E
Kabompo, Zambia ..... **87 E1** 13 36 S 24 14 E
Kabompo ➤, Zambia ... **85 G4** 14 10 S 23 11 E
Kabondo, Dem. Rep. of
the Congo .... **87 D2** 8 58 S 25 40 E
Kabongo, Dem. Rep. of
the Congo .... **86 D2** 7 22 S 25 33 E
Kabou, Togo .... **83 D5** 9 28N 0 55 E
Kabr, Sudan .... **81 E2** 10 54N 26 50 E
Kabrousse, Senegal ... **82 C1** 12 25N 16 45W
Kabūd Gonbad, Iran .. **71 B8** 37 5N 59 45 E
Kabugao, Phil. .... **61 B4** 18 2N 121 11 E
Kābul, Afghan. .... **66 B6** 34 28N 69 11 E
Kābul □, Afghan. ..... **66 B6** 34 30N 69 0 E
Kābul ➤, Pakistan .... **68 C5** 33 55N 72 14 E
Kabunga, Dem. Rep. of
the Congo .... **86 C2** 1 38 S 28 3 E
Kaburuang, Indonesia **63 D7** 3 50N 126 30 E
Kabushiya, Sudan ..... **81 D3** 16 54N 33 41 E
Kabwe, Zambia .... **87 E2** 14 30 S 28 29 E
Kačanik, Serbia & M. **44 D5** 42 13N 21 12 E
Kačerginė, Lithuania **30 D10** 54 54N 23 42 E
Kachchh, Gulf of, India **68 H3** 22 50N 69 15 E
Kachchh, Rann of, India **68 H4** 24 0N 70 0 E
Kachchhidhana, India **69 J8** 21 44N 78 46 E
Kachebera, Zambia ... **87 E3** 13 50 S 32 50 E
Kachia, Nigeria ...... **83 D6** 9 50N 7 55 E
Kachikau, Botswana .. **88 B3** 18 8 S 24 26 E
Kachin □, Burma ...... **58 D1** 26 0N 97 30 E
Kachira, L., Uganda . **86 C3** 0 40 S 31 7 E
Kachiry, Kazakhstan . **52 D8** 53 10N 75 50 E
Kachisi, Ethiopia .... **81 F4** 9 40N 37 50 E
Kachnara, India ...... **68 H6** 23 50N 75 6 E
Kachot, Cambodia ..... **65 G4** 11 30N 103 3 E
Kaçkar, Turkey .... **73 B9** 40 45N 41 10 E
Kadan, Czech Rep. .... **26 A6** 50 23N 13 16 E
Kadan Kyun, Burma ... **64 F2** 12 30N 98 20 E
Kadanai ➤, Afghan. ... **68 D1** 31 22N 65 45 E
Kadarkút, Hungary ... **28 D2** 46 13N 17 39 E
Kadavu, Fiji .... **91 a** 19 0 S 178 15 E
Kade, Ghana **83 D4** 6 7N 0 56W
Kadhimain = Al
Kāẓimīyah, Iraq ... **70 C5** 33 22N 44 18 E
Kadi, India .... **68 H5** 23 18N 72 23 E
Kadina, Australia .... **95 E2** 33 55 S 137 43 E
Kadınhanı, Turkey ... **72 C5** 38 14N 32 13 E
Kadiolo, Mali **82 C3** 10 35N 7 41W
Kadipur, India .... **69 F10** 26 10N 82 23 E
Kadirli, Turkey ...... **70 B3** 37 23N 36 5 E
Kadiyevka = Stakhanov,
Ukraine .... **33 H10** 48 35N 38 40 E
Kadodo, Sudan .... **81 E2** 11 4N 29 31 E
Kadoka, U.S.A. **112 D4** 43 50N 101 31W
Kadom, Russia .... **34 C6** 54 37N 42 30 E
Kadoma, Zimbabwe .... **87 F2** 18 20 S 29 52 E
Kādugli, Sudan .... **81 E2** 11 0N 29 45 E
Kaduna, Nigeria ...... **83 C6** 10 30N 7 21 E
Kaduna □, Nigeria .... **83 C6** 11 0N 7 30 E
Kaduy, Russia .... **32 C9** 59 12N 37 9 E
Kaédi, Mauritania **82 B2** 16 9N 13 28W
Kaélé, Cameroon ...... **83 C7** 10 5N 14 27 E
Kaeng Khoï, Thailand **64 E3** 14 35N 101 0 E
Kaeng Kra Chan △,
Thailand .... **64 F2** 12 58N 99 34 E
Kaeng Tana △, Thailand **64 E5** 15 25N 105 32 E
Kaesŏng, N. Korea ... **57 F14** 37 58N 126 35 E
Kāf, Si. Arabia ...... **70 D3** 31 25N 37 29 E
Kafan = Kapan,
Armenia .... **70 B5** 39 18N 46 27 E
Kafanchan, Nigeria .. **83 D6** 9 40N 8 20 E
Kafareti, Nigeria .... **83 C7** 11 11N 11 12 E
Kaffrine, Senegal **82 C1** 14 8N 15 36W
Kafin, Nigeria .... **83 D6** 9 30N 7 4 E
Kafin Madaki, Nigeria **83 C6** 10 41N 9 46 E
Kafinda, Zambia ...... **87 E3** 12 32 S 30 20 E
Kafirévs, Ákra, Greece **46 C6** 38 9N 24 38 E
Kafue, Zambia .... **87 F2** 15 46 S 28 9 E
Kafue ➤, Zambia ...... **85 H5** 15 30 S 29 0 E
Kafue Flats, Zambia . **87 F2** 15 40 S 27 25 E
Kafulwe, Zambia ...... **87 D2** 9 0 S 29 1 E
Kaga, Afghan. .... **68 B4** 34 14N 70 10 E
Kaga Bandoro, C.A.R. **84 C3** 7 0N 19 10 E
Kagan, Uzbekistan .... **52 F7** 39 43N 64 33 E
Kagawa □, Japan ...... **55 G7** 34 15N 134 0 E
Kagera □, Tanzania ... **86 C3** 2 0 S 31 30 E
Kagera ➤, Uganda ..... **86 C3** 0 57 S 31 47 E
Kağızman, Turkey .... **73 B10** 40 5N 43 10 E
Kagmar, Sudan .... **81 E3** 14 24N 30 25 E
Kagoshima, Japan ..... **55 J5** 31 30N 130 30 E
Kagoshima □, Japan ... **55 J5** 31 30N 130 30 E
Kagul = Cahul, Moldova **29 E13** 45 50N 28 15 E
Kahak, Iran .... **71 B6** 36 6N 49 46 E
Kahama, Tanzania ..... **86 C3** 4 8 S 32 30 E
Kahan, Pakistan ...... **68 E3** 29 18N 68 54 E
Kahang, Malaysia ..... **65 L4** 2 12N 103 32 E
Kahayan ➤, Indonesia **62 E4** 3 40 S 114 0 E
Kahnūj, Iran .... **71 E8** 27 55N 57 40 E
Kahoka, U.S.A. **112 E9** 40 25N 91 44W
Kahoolawe, U.S.A. **106 H16** 20 33N 156 37W
Kahramanmaraş, Turkey **70 B3** 37 37N 36 53 E
Kâhta, Turkey .... **73 D8** 37 48N 38 36 E
Kahul, Ozero, Ukraine **29 E13** 45 24N 28 24 E
Kahurangi △, N.Z. .... **91 J4** 41 10 S 172 32 E
Kahuta, Pakistan ..... **68 C5** 33 35N 73 24 E

Kai Besar, Indonesia **63 F8** 5 35 S 133 0 E
Kai Is. = Kai,
Kepulauan, Indonesia **63 F8** 5 55 S 132 45 E
Kai Kecil, Indonesia **63 F8** 5 45 S 132 40 E
Kai Xian, China ...... **58 B7** 31 11N 108 21 E
Kaiama, Nigeria ...... **83 D5** 9 36N 4 1 E
Kaiapoi, N.Z. .... **91 K4** 43 24 S 172 40 E
Kaieteur Falls, Guyana **124 B7** 5 1N 59 10W
Kaifeng, China .... **56 G8** 34 48N 114 21 E
Kaihua, China .... **59 C12** 29 12N 118 20 E
Kaijiang, China ...... **58 B6** 31 7N 107 55 E
Kaikohe, N.Z. .... **91 F4** 35 25 S 173 49 E
Kaikoura, N.Z. .... **91 K4** 42 25 S 173 43 E
Kailahun, S. Leone ... **82 D2** 8 18N 10 39W
Kailash = Kangrinboqê
Feng, China ...... **69 D9** 31 0N 81 25 E
Kaili, China .... **58 D6** 26 33N 107 59 E
Kailu, China .... **57 C11** 43 38N 121 18 E
Kailua Kona, U.S.A. .. **106 J17** 19 39N 155 59W
Kaimana, Indonesia ... **63 E8** 3 39 S 133 45 E
Kaimanawa Mts., N.Z. **91 H5** 39 15 S 175 56 E
Kaimganj, India ...... **69 F8** 27 33N 79 24 E
Kaimur Hills, India . **69 G10** 24 30N 82 0 E
Kainab ➤, Namibia .... **88 D2** 28 32 S 19 34 E
Kainji Dam, Nigeria . **83 D5** 9 55N 4 35 E
Kainji Lake △, Nigeria **83 C5** 10 1N 4 6 E
Kainji Res., Nigeria . **83 C5** 10 1N 4 40 E
Kainuu, Finland ...... **8 D23** 64 30N 29 7 E
Kaipara Harbour, N.Z. **91 G5** 36 25 S 174 14 E
Kaiping, China .... **59 F9** 22 33N 112 42 E
Kaipokok B., Canada . **105 B8** 54 54N 59 47W
Kaira, India .... **68 H5** 22 45N 72 50 E
Kairana, India .... **68 E7** 29 24N 77 15 E
Kaironi, Indonesia ... **63 E8** 0 47 S 133 40 E
Kairouan, Tunisia .... **79 A8** 35 45N 10 5 E
Kaiserslautern, Germany **25 F3** 49 26N 7 45 E
Kaiserstuhl, Germany **25 G3** 48 4N 7 40 E
Kaitaia, N.Z. .... **91 F4** 35 8 S 173 17 E
Kaitangata, N.Z. ..... **91 M2** 46 17 S 169 51 E
Kaithal, India .... **68 E7** 29 48N 76 26 E
Kaitu ➤, Pakistan .... **68 C4** 33 10N 70 30 E
Kaiyang, China .... **58 D6** 27 4N 106 59 E
Kaiyuan, Liaoning,
China .... **57 C13** 42 28N 124 1 E
Kaiyuan, Yunnan, China **58 F4** 23 40N 103 12 E
Kaiyuh Mts., U.S.A. . **106 C8** 64 30N 158 0W
Kajaani, Finland ..... **8 D22** 64 17N 27 46 E
Kajabbi, Australia ... **94 C3** 20 0 S 140 1 E
Kajana = Kajaani,
Finland .... **8 D22** 64 17N 27 46 E
Kajang, Malaysia ..... **65 L3** 2 59N 101 48 E
Kajaran, Armenia ..... **73 C12** 39 10N 46 7 E
Kajiado, Kenya .... **86 C4** 1 53 S 36 48 E
Kajo Kaji, Sudan ..... **81 G3** 3 58N 31 40 E
Kajuru, Nigeria ...... **83 C6** 10 15N 7 34 E
Kaka, Sudan .... **81 E3** 10 38N 32 10 E
Kakabeka Falls, Canada **104 C2** 48 24N 89 37W
Kakadu △, Australia . **92 B5** 12 0 S 132 3 E
Kakamas, S. Africa ... **88 D3** 28 45 S 20 33 E
Kakamega, Kenya ..... **86 B3** 0 20N 34 46 E
Kakanj, Bos.-H. ...... **28 F3** 44 4N 18 4 E
Kakanui Mts., N.Z. ... **91 L3** 45 10 S 170 30 E
Kakata, Liberia **82 D2** 6 35N 10 20W
Kakdwip, India .... **69 J13** 21 53N 88 11 E
Kake, Japan .... **55 G6** 34 36N 132 19 E
Kake, U.S.A. **102 B2** 56 59N 133 57W
Kakegawa, Japan ...... **55 G9** 34 45N 138 1 E
Kakeroma-Jima, Japan **55 K4** 28 8N 129 14 E
Kakhib, Russia .... **35 J8** 42 28N 46 34 E
Kakhovka, Ukraine .... **33 J7** 46 45N 33 30 E
Kakhovske Vdskh.,
Ukraine .... **33 J7** 47 5N 34 0 E
Kakinada, India ...... **67 L13** 16 57N 82 11 E
Kakisa ➤, Canada **102 A5** 61 3N 118 10W
Kakisa L., Canada **102 A5** 60 56N 117 43W
Kakogawa, Japan ...... **55 G7** 34 46N 134 51 E
Kakwa ➤, Canada **102 C5** 54 37N 118 28W
Kāl Gūsheh, Iran ..... **71 D8** 30 59N 58 12 E
Kāl Safīd, Iran ...... **70 C5** 34 52N 47 23 E
Kala, Nigeria .... **83 C7** 12 2N 14 40 E
Kalaallit Nunaat =
Greenland =
N. Amer. **4 C5** 66 0N 45 0W
Kalabagh, Pakistan ... **68 C4** 33 0N 71 28 E
Kalabahi, Indonesia . **63 F6** 8 13 S 124 31 E
Kalabáka, Greece ..... **46 B3** 39 42N 21 39 E
Kalabana, Mali **82 C3** 14 10N 8 35W
Kalach, Russia .... **34 E5** 50 22N 41 0 E
Kalach na Donu, Russia **35 F6** 48 43N 43 32 E
Kaladan ➤, Burma ..... **67 J18** 20 20N 93 5 E
Kaladar, Canada **116 B7** 44 37N 77 5W
Kalahari, Africa ..... **88 C3** 24 0 S 21 30 E
Kalahari Gemsbok △,
S. Africa .... **88 D3** 25 30 S 20 30 E
Kalajoki, Finland .... **8 D20** 64 12N 24 10 E
Kalakamati, Botswana **89 C4** 20 40 S 27 25 E
Kalakan, Russia ...... **53 D12** 55 15N 116 45 E
K'alak'unlun Shank'ou =
Karakoram Pass, Asia **69 B7** 35 33N 77 50 E
Kalam, Pakistan ...... **69 B5** 35 34N 72 30 E
Kalama, Dem. Rep. of
the Congo .... **86 C2** 2 52 S 28 35 E
Kalama, U.S.A. **110 E4** 46 1N 122 51W
Kalámai, Greece ...... **46 D4** 37 3N 22 10 E
Kalamandzi, Greece ... **44 F6** 40 33N 22 55 E
Kalamazoo, U.S.A. **114 D3** 42 17N 85 35W
Kalamazoo ➤, U.S.A. . **114 D2** 42 40N 86 10W
Kalambo Falls, Tanzania **87 D3** 8 37 S 31 35 E
Kálamos, Greece ...... **46 C5** 38 17N 20 52 E
Kálamos, Greece ...... **46 C2** 38 37N 20 55 E
Kalan, Turkey .... **70 B3** 39 7N 39 32 E
Kalankalan, Guinea .. **82 C3** 10 7N 8 54W
Kalannie, Australia . **93 F2** 30 22 S 117 5 E
Kalāntarī, Iran ...... **71 C7** 32 10N 54 8 E
Kalao, Indonesia ..... **63 F6** 7 21 S 121 0 E
Kalaotoa, Indonesia . **63 F6** 7 20 S 121 50 E
Kälarne, Sweden ...... **10 B10** 62 59N 16 5 E
Kalasin, Thailand .... **64 D4** 16 26N 103 30 E
Kalāt, Iran .... **71 E8** 25 29N 59 22 E
Kalat, Pakistan ...... **66 E5** 29 8N 66 31 E
Kalāt, Iran .... **71 B7** 36 33N 55 41 E
Kalāteh, Iran .... **71 B7** 36 33N 55 41 E
Kalāteh-ye Ganj, Iran **71 E8** 27 31N 57 55 E
Kálathos, Greece ..... **47 E10** 36 9N 28 8 E
Kalávrita, Greece .... **46 C4** 38 3N 22 8 E
Kalbarri, Australia . **93 E1** 27 51 S 114 30 E
Kale, Antalya, Turkey **47 E12** 36 14N 30 0 E
Kale, Denizli, Turkey **47 D10** 37 27N 29 8 E
Kalecik, Turkey ...... **72 B5** 40 4N 33 26 E
Kalegauk Kyun, Burma **67 M20** 15 33N 97 35 E
Kalehe, Dem. Rep. of
the Congo .... **86 C2** 2 6 S 28 50 E
Kalema, Tanzania ..... **86 C3** 1 12 S 31 55 E
Kalemie, Dem. Rep. of
the Congo .... **86 D2** 5 55 S 29 9 E
Kalety, Poland .... **31 H5** 50 35N 18 52 E

Kalewa, Burma .... **67 H19** 23 10N 94 15 E
Kaleybar, Iran ...... **70 B5** 38 47N 47 2 E
Kalgoorlie-Boulder,
  Australia .... **93 F3** 30 40 S 121 22 E
Kali →, India ...... **69 F8** 27 6N 79 55 E
Kali Sindh →, India .. **68 G6** 25 32 S 76 17 E
Kaliakra, Nos, Bulgaria **45 C12** 43 21N 28 30 E
Kalianda, Indonesia .. **62 F3** 5 50 S 105 45 E
Kalibo, Phil. .... **61 F5** 11 43N 122 22 E
Kalima, Dem. Rep. of
  the Congo .... **86 C2** 2 33 S 26 32 E
Kalimantan, Indonesia . **62 E4** 0 0 114 0 E
Kalimantan Barat □,
  Indonesia .... **62 E4** 0 0 110 30 E
Kalimantan Selatan □,
  Indonesia .... **62 E5** 2 30 S 115 30 E
Kalimantan Tengah □,
  Indonesia .... **62 E4** 2 0 S 113 30 E
Kalimantan Timur □,
  Indonesia .... **62 D5** 1 30N 116 30 E
Kálimnos, Greece .... **47 D8** 37 0N 27 0 E
Kalimpong, India .... **69 F13** 27 4N 88 35 E
Kaliningrad, Russia ... **9 J19** 54 42N 20 32 E
Kaliningrad ✈ (KGD),
  Russia .... **30 D7** 54 50N 20 33 E
Kalininsk, Russia .... **34 E7** 51 30N 44 40 E
Kalinkavichy, Belarus . **33 F5** 52 12N 29 20 E
Kalinkovichi =
  Kalinkavichy, Belarus **33 F5** 52 12N 29 20 E
Kalinovik, Bos.-H. .... **44 C2** 43 31N 18 25 E
Kalipetrovo, Bulgaria . **45 B11** 44 5N 27 14 E
Kaliro, Uganda ..... **86 B3** 0 56N 33 30 E
Kalírrákhi, Greece ... **45 F8** 40 40N 24 35 E
Kalispell, U.S.A. **108 B6** 48 12N 114 19W
Kalisz, Poland ...... **31 G5** 51 45N 18 8 E
Kalisz Pomorski, Poland **31 E2** 53 17N 15 55 E
Kaliua, Tanzania .... **86 D3** 5 5 S 31 48 E
Kalívia Thorikoú,
  Greece .... **46 D5** 37 50N 23 55 E
Kalix = Kalixälven →,
  Sweden .... **8 D20** 65 50N 23 11 E
Kalix, Sweden ...... **8 D20** 65 53N 23 12 E
Kalixälven →, Sweden . **8 D20** 65 50N 23 11 E
Kalka, India .... **68 D7** 30 46N 76 57 E
Kalkan, Turkey ..... **47 E11** 36 15N 29 23 E
Kalkarindji, Australia . **92 C5** 17 30 S 130 47 E
Kalkaska, U.S.A. **114 C3** 44 44N 85 11W
Kalkfeld, Namibia ... **88 C2** 20 57 S 16 14 E
Kalkfontein, Botswana . **88 C3** 22 4 S 20 57 E
Kalkım, Turkey ..... **47 B9** 39 48N 27 13 E
Kalkrand, Namibia ... **88 C2** 24 1 S 17 35 E
Kållandsö, Sweden ... **11 F7** 58 40N 13 5 E
Kallavesi, Finland ... **8 E22** 62 58N 27 30 E
Källby, Sweden ..... **11 F7** 58 30N 13 8 E
Kållered, Sweden .... **11 G6** 57 32N 12 4 E
Kallinge, Sweden .... **11 H9** 56 15N 15 18 E
Kallithéa, Greece .... **46 D5** 37 55N 23 41 E
Kallmet, Albania .... **44 E3** 41 51N 19 41 E
Kalloní, Greece ..... **47 B8** 39 14N 26 12 E
Kallonís, Kólpos, Greece **47 B8** 39 10N 26 10 E
Kallsjön, Sweden .... **8 E15** 63 38N 13 0 E
Kalmalo, Nigeria .... **83 C6** 13 40N 5 20 E
Kalmar, Sweden .... **11 H10** 56 40N 16 20 E
Kalmar län □, Sweden . **11 G10** 57 25N 16 0 E
Kalmar sund, Sweden .. **11 H10** 56 40N 16 25 E
Kalmyk Republic =
  Kalmykia □, Russia . **35 G8** 46 5N 46 1 E
Kalmykia □, Russia .. **35 G8** 46 5N 46 1 E
Kalmykovo, Kazakhstan **35 F9** 49 0N 51 47 E
Kalna, India .... **69 H13** 23 13N 88 25 E
Kalnai, India ...... **69 J8** 22 46N 83 30 E
Kalocsa, Hungary ... **28 D4** 46 32N 19 0 E
Kalofer, Bulgaria ... **45 D8** 42 37N 24 59 E
Kalokhorio, Cyprus .. **49 E12** 34 51N 33 2 E
Kaloko, Dem. Rep. of
  the Congo .... **86 D2** 6 47 S 25 48 E
Kalol, Gujarat, India . **68 H5** 22 37N 73 31 E
Kalol, Gujarat, India . **68 H5** 23 15N 72 33 E
Kalolímnos, Greece ... **47 D9** 37 4N 27 5 E
Kalomo, Zambia .... **87 F2** 17 0 S 26 30 E
Kalonerón, Greece ... **46 D3** 37 20N 21 38 E
Kalpi, India .... **69 F8** 26 8N 79 47 E
Kaltern = Caldaro, Italy **41 B8** 46 25N 11 14 E
Kaltungo, Nigeria ... **83 D7** 9 48N 11 19 E
Kalu, Pakistan ..... **68 G2** 25 5N 67 39 E
Kaluga, Russia ..... **32 E9** 54 35N 36 10 E
Kalulushi, Zambia ... **87 E2** 12 50 S 28 3 E
Kalundborg, Denmark . **11 J5** 55 41N 11 5 E
Kalush, Ukraine .... **33 H3** 49 3N 24 23 E
Kałuszyn, Poland ... **31 F8** 52 13N 21 52 E
Kalutara, Sri Lanka .. **66 R12** 6 35N 80 0 E
Kalvarija, Lithuania .. **30 D10** 54 24N 23 14 E
Kalyan, India ...... **66 K8** 19 15N 73 9 E
Kalyazin, Russia .... **32 D9** 57 15N 37 55 E
Kam, Albania ...... **44 D4** 42 17N 20 18 E
Kam →, Nigeria .... **83 D7** 8 15N 1 10 E
Kama, Dem. Rep. of
  the Congo .... **86 C2** 3 30 S 27 5 E
Kama →, Russia .... **6 D16** 55 45N 52 0 E
Kamachumu, Tanzania **86 C3** 1 37 S 31 37 E
Kamaishi, Japan .... **54 E10** 39 16N 141 53 E
Kamalia, Pakistan ... **68 D5** 30 44N 72 42 E
Kaman, India ...... **68 F6** 27 39N 77 16 E
Kaman, Turkey ..... **72 C5** 39 22N 33 44 E
Kamanjab, Namibia .. **88 B2** 19 35 S 14 51 E
Kamarān, Yemen ... **75 D3** 15 21N 42 35 E
Kamativi, Zimbabwe . **88 B4** 18 20 S 27 6 E
Kamba, Nigeria ..... **83 C5** 11 50N 3 45 E
Kambalda, Australia .. **93 F3** 31 10 S 121 37 E
Kambar, Pakistan ... **68 F3** 27 37N 68 1 E
Kambia, S. Leone **82 D2** 9 3N 12 53W
Kambolé, Togo ..... **83 D5** 8 43N 1 39 E
Kambos, Cyprus .... **49 D11** 35 2N 32 44 E
Kambove, Dem. Rep. of
  the Congo .... **87 E2** 10 51 S 26 33 E
Kamchatka, Poluostrov,
  Russia .... **53 D16** 57 0N 160 0 E
Kamchatka Pen. =
  Kamchatka,
  Poluostrov, Russia .. **53 D16** 57 0N 160 0 E
Kamchiya →, Bulgaria **45 C11** 43 4N 27 44 E
Kame Ruins, Zimbabwe **87 G2** 20 7 S 28 25 E
Kamen, Russia ...... **52 D9** 53 50N 81 30 E
Kamen-Rybolov, Russia **54 B6** 44 46N 132 2 E
Kamenica, Serbia & M. **44 C5** 43 27N 22 27 E
Kamenica, Serbia & M. **44 B3** 44 25N 19 45 E
Kamenice nad Lipou,
  Czech Rep. .... **26 B8** 49 18N 15 2 E
Kamenjak, Rt, Croatia . **41 D10** 44 47N 13 55 E
Kamenka =
  Kamianka,
  Ukraine .... **33 H7** 49 3N 32 6 E
Kamenka, Kazakhstan . **34 E10** 51 7N 50 19 E
Kamenka, Penza, Russia **34 D6** 53 10N 44 5 E
Kamenka, Voronezh,
  Russia .... **33 G10** 50 47N 39 20 E

Kamenka Bugskaya =
  Kamyanka-Buzka,
  Ukraine .... **33 G3** 50 8N 24 16 E
Kamenka
  Dneprovskaya =
  Kamyanka-
  Dniprovska, Ukraine **33 J8** 47 29N 34 28 E
Kamennomostskiy,
  Russia .... **35 H5** 44 18N 40 13 E
Kameno, Bulgaria .... **45 D11** 42 34N 27 18 E
Kamenolomni, Russia . **35 G5** 47 40N 40 14 E
Kamensk-Shakhtinskiy,
  Russia .... **35 F5** 48 23N 40 20 E
Kamensk Uralskiy,
  Russia .... **52 D7** 56 25N 62 2 E
Kamenskiy, Russia .... **34 E7** 50 48N 45 25 E
Kamenskoye, Russia .. **53 C17** 62 45N 165 30 E
Kamenyak, Bulgaria .. **45 C10** 43 24N 26 57 E
Kamenz, Germany ... **24 D10** 51 15N 14 5 E
Kameoka, Japan .... **55 G7** 35 0N 135 35 E
Kamiah, U.S.A. **108 C5** 46 14N 116 2W
Kamień Krajeński,
  Poland .... **30 E4** 53 32N 17 32 E
Kamień Pomorski,
  Poland .... **30 E1** 53 57N 14 43 E
Kamienna →, Poland . **31 G8** 51 6N 21 47 E
Kamienna Góra, Poland **31 H3** 50 47N 16 2 E
Kamieńsk, Poland ... **31 G6** 51 12N 19 29 E
Kamieskroon, S. Africa **88 E2** 30 9 S 17 56 E
Kamilukuak L., Canada **103 A8** 62 22N 101 40W
Kamin-Kashyrskyy,
  Ukraine .... **33 G3** 51 39N 24 56 E
Kamina, Dem. Rep. of
  the Congo .... **87 D2** 8 45 S 25 0 E
Kaminak L., Canada .. **103 A10** 62 10N 95 0W
Kaministiquia, Canada **104 C1** 48 32N 89 35W
Kaminka, Ukraine ... **33 H7** 49 3N 32 6 E
Kaminoyama, Japan .. **54 E10** 38 9N 140 17 E
Kamiros, Greece .... **49 C9** 36 20N 27 56 E
Kamituga, Dem. Rep. of
  the Congo .... **86 C2** 3 2 S 28 10 E
Kamla →, India ..... **69 G12** 25 35N 86 36 E
Kamloops, Canada ... **102 C4** 50 40N 120 20W
Kamnik, Slovenia .... **41 B11** 46 14N 14 37 E
Kamo, Armenia ..... **35 K7** 40 21N 45 7 E
Kamo, Japan .... **54 F9** 37 39N 139 3 E
Kamoke, Pakistan ... **68 C6** 32 4N 74 4 E
Kamp →, Austria .... **26 C8** 48 23N 15 42 E
Kampala, Uganda ... **86 B3** 0 20N 32 30 E
Kampar, Malaysia ... **65 K3** 4 18N 101 9 E
Kampar →, Indonesia . **62 D2** 0 30N 103 8 E
Kampen, Neths. ..... **17 B5** 52 33N 5 53 E
Kampene, Dem. Rep. of
  the Congo .... **84 E5** 3 36 S 26 40 E
Kamphaeng Phet,
  Thailand .... **64 D2** 16 28N 99 30 E
Kampinoski △, Poland **31 F7** 52 21N 20 40 E
Kampolombo, L.,
  Zambia .... **87 E2** 11 37 S 29 42 E
Kampong Chhnang,
  Cambodia .... **65 F5** 12 20N 104 35 E
Kampong Pengerang,
  Malaysia .... **65 d** 1 22N 104 7 E
Kampong Punggai,
  Malaysia .... **65 d** 1 27N 104 18 E
Kampong Saom,
  Cambodia .... **65 G4** 10 38N 103 30 E
Kampong Saom, Chaak,
  Cambodia .... **65 G4** 10 50N 103 32 E
Kampong Tanjong
  Langsat, Malaysia .. **65 d** 1 28N 104 1 E
Kampong Telok
  Ramunia, Malaysia . **65 d** 1 22N 104 15 E
Kampong To, Thailand **65 J3** 6 3N 101 13 E
Kampot, Cambodia .. **65 G5** 10 36N 104 10 E
Kampti, Burkina Faso **82 C4** 10 7N 3 25W
Kampuchea =
  Cambodia ■, Asia . **64 F5** 12 15N 105 0 E
Kampung Air Putih,
  Malaysia .... **65 K4** 4 15N 103 10 E
Kampung Jerangau,
  Malaysia .... **65 K4** 4 50N 103 10 E
Kampung Raja,
  Malaysia .... **65 K4** 5 45N 102 35 E
Kampungbaru = Tolitoli,
  Indonesia .... **63 D6** 1 5N 120 50 E
Kamrau, Teluk,
  Indonesia .... **63 E8** 3 30 S 133 36 E
Kamsack, Canada ... **103 C8** 51 34N 101 54W
Kamsai, Ghana **82 C2** 10 40N 14 36W
Kamskoye Ustye, Russia **34 C9** 55 10N 49 20 E
Kamuchawie L., Canada **103 B8** 56 18N 101 59W
Kamui-Misaki, Japan .. **54 C10** 43 20N 140 21 E
Kamyanets-Podilskyy,
  Ukraine .... **29 B11** 48 45N 26 40 E
Kamyanka-Buzka,
  Ukraine .... **33 G3** 50 8N 24 16 E
Kamyanka-Dniprovska,
  Ukraine .... **33 J8** 47 29N 34 28 E
Kamyanets, Belarus .. **31 F10** 52 23N 23 49 E
Kamyanyuki, Belarus . **31 F10** 52 32N 23 49 E
Kämyärän, Iran ..... **70 C5** 34 47N 46 56 E
Kamyshin, Russia ... **34 E7** 50 10N 45 24 E
Kamyzyak, Russia ... **35 G9** 46 4N 48 10 E
Kan, Sudan .... **81 F3** 9 1N 31 47 E
Kanaaupscow, Canada **101 C12** 53 39N 77 9W
Kanaaupscow →,
  Canada **104 B4** 54 2N 76 30W
Kanab, U.S.A. **109 H7** 37 3N 112 32W
Kanab →, U.S.A. **109 H7** 36 24N 112 38W
Kanagi, Japan ...... **54 D10** 40 54N 140 27 E
Kanairiktok →, Canada **105 A7** 55 2N 60 18W
Kanália, Greece ..... **46 B4** 39 30N 22 53 E
Kananga, Dem. Rep. of
  the Congo .... **84 F4** 5 55 S 22 18 E
Kanash, Russia ..... **34 C8** 55 30N 47 32 E
Kanaskat, U.S.A. **110 C5** 47 19N 121 54W
Kanastraíon, Ákra =
  Palioúrion, Ákra,
  Greece .... **44 G7** 39 57N 23 45 E
Kanawha →, U.S.A. .. **114 F4** 38 50N 82 9W
Kanazawa, Japan ... **55 F8** 36 30N 136 38 E
Kanchanaburi, Thailand **64 E2** 14 2N 99 31 E
Kanchenjunga, Nepal . **69 F13** 27 50N 88 10 E
Kanchipuram, India .. **66 N11** 12 52N 79 45 E
Kańczuga, Poland ... **31 J9** 49 59N 22 25 E
Kandaghat, India ... **68 D7** 30 59N 77 7 E
Kandahar = Qandahār,
  Afghan. .... **66 D4** 31 32N 65 43 E
Kandalaksha, Russia .. **52 C4** 67 9N 32 30 E
Kandangan, Indonesia **62 E5** 2 50 S 115 20 E
Kandanghaur, Indonesia **63 G13** 6 21 S 108 6 E
Kandanos, Greece ... **49 D5** 35 19N 23 44 E
Kandava, Latvia .... **30 A9** 57 2N 22 46 E
Kandavu = Kadavu, Fiji **91 D8** 19 0 S 178 15 E
Kandhila, Greece .... **46 D4** 37 46N 22 22 E
Kandhkot, Pakistan .. **68 E3** 28 16N 69 8 E

Kandhla, India ...... **68 E7** 29 18N 77 19 E
Kandi, Benin .... **83 C5** 11 7N 2 55 E
Kandi, India .... **69 H13** 23 58N 88 5 E
Kandiaro, Pakistan .. **68 F3** 27 4N 68 13 E
Kandıra, Turkey .... **72 B4** 41 4N 30 9 E
Kandla, India ...... **68 H4** 23 0N 70 10 E
Kandos, Australia ... **95 E4** 32 45 S 149 58 E
Kandreho, Madag. ... **89 B8** 17 29 S 46 6 E
Kandy, Sri Lanka .... **66 R12** 7 18N 80 43 E
Kane, U.S.A. **116 E6** 41 40N 78 49W
Kangri Mposhi, Zambia **87 E2** 13 59 S 28 43 E
Kanel, Senegal **82 B2** 15 30N 13 8W
Kaneohe, U.S.A. **106 H16** 21 25N 157 48W
Kanevskaya, Russia .. **35 G4** 46 3N 38 57 E
Kanfanar, Croatia ... **41 C10** 45 7N 13 50 E
Kang, Botswana .... **88 C3** 23 41 S 22 50 E
Kang Krung △, Thailand **65 H2** 9 30N 98 50 E
Kangaba, Mali **82 C3** 11 56N 8 25W
Kangal, Turkey ..... **72 C7** 39 14N 37 23 E
Kangān, Fārs, Iran .. **71 E7** 27 50N 52 3 E
Kangān, Hormozgān,
  Iran .... **71 E8** 25 48N 57 28 E
Kangar, Malaysia ... **65 J3** 6 27N 100 12 E
Kangaré, Mali **82 C3** 11 36N 8 4W
Kangaroo I., Australia . **95 F2** 35 45 S 137 0 E
Kangaroo Mts.,
  Australia .... **94 C3** 23 29 S 141 51 E
Kangasala, Finland ... **9 F21** 61 28N 24 4 E
Kangāvar, Iran ..... **71 C6** 34 40N 48 0 E
Kangding, China .... **58 B3** 30 0N 101 57 E
Kangdong, N. Korea .. **57 E14** 39 9N 126 5 E
Kangean, Kepulauan,
  Indonesia .... **62 F5** 6 55 S 115 23 E
Kangean Is. = Kangean,
  Kepulauan, Indonesia **62 F5** 6 55 S 115 23 E
Kangen →, Sudan ... **81 F3** 6 47N 33 9 E
Kanggye, N. Korea ... **57 D14** 41 0N 126 35 E
Kanggyŏng, S. Korea . **57 F14** 36 10N 127 0 E
Kanghwa, S. Korea .. **57 F14** 37 45N 126 30 E
Kangikajik, Greenland . **4 B6** 70 7N 22 0W
Kangiqliniq = Rankin
  Inlet, Canada **100 B10** 62 30N 93 0W
Kangiqsualujjuaq,
  Canada **101 C13** 58 30N 65 59W
Kangiqsujuaq, Canada **101 B12** 61 30N 72 0W
Kangiqtugaapik = Clyde
  River, Canada **101 A13** 70 30N 68 30W
Kangirsuk, Canada ... **101 B13** 60 0N 70 0W
Kangkar Chemaran,
  Malaysia .... **65 d** 1 34N 104 12 E
Kangkar Sungai Tiram,
  Malaysia .... **65 d** 1 35N 103 55 E
Kangkar Teberau,
  Malaysia .... **65 d** 1 32N 103 51 E
Kangnŭng, S. Korea .. **57 F15** 37 45N 128 54 E
Kangping, China .... **57 C12** 42 43N 123 18 E
Kangra, India ...... **68 C7** 32 6N 76 16 E
Kangrinboqê Feng,
  China .... **69 D9** 31 0N 81 25 E
Kangto, India ...... **67 F18** 27 50N 92 35 E
Kanhar →, India .... **69 G10** 24 28N 83 8 E
Kani, Ivory C. **82 D3** 8 29N 6 36W
Kaniama, Dem. Rep. of
  the Congo .... **86 D1** 7 30 S 24 12 E
Kaniapiskau =
  Caniapiscau →,
  Canada **105 A6** 56 40N 69 30W
Kaniapiskau, L. =
  Caniapiscau, L. de,
  Canada **105 B6** 54 10N 69 55W
Kanin, Poluostrov,
  Russia .... **52 C5** 68 0N 45 0 E
Kanin Nos, Mys, Russia **52 C5** 68 39N 43 32 E
Kanin Pen. = Kanin,
  Poluostrov, Russia .. **52 C5** 68 0N 45 0 E
Kaninë, Albania .... **44 F3** 40 23N 19 30 E
Kaniva, Australia ... **95 F3** 36 22 S 141 18 E
Kanjiža, Serbia & M. .. **28 D5** 46 3N 20 4 E
Kanjut Sar, Pakistan .. **69 A6** 36 7N 75 25 E
Kankaanpää, Finland . **9 F20** 61 44N 22 50 E
Kankakee, U.S.A. **114 E2** 41 7N 87 52W
Kankakee →, U.S.A. . **114 E1** 41 23N 88 15W
Kankan, Guinea **82 C3** 10 23N 9 15W
Kankendy = Xankändi,
  Azerbaijan .... **70 B5** 39 52N 46 49 E
Kanker, India ...... **67 J12** 20 10N 81 40 E
Kankossa, Mauritania **82 B2** 15 54N 11 31W
Kankroli, India ..... **68 G5** 25 4N 73 53 E
Kannapolis, U.S.A. .. **115 H5** 35 30N 80 37W
Kannauj, India ..... **69 F8** 27 3N 79 56 E
Kannod, India ...... **66 H10** 22 45N 76 40 E
Kano, Japan .... **83 C6** 12 2N 8 30 E
Kano □, Nigeria .... **83 C6** 11 30N 8 30 E
Kan'onji, Japan .... **55 G6** 34 7N 133 39 E
Kanoroba, Ivory C. .. **82 D3** 9 7N 6 8W
Kanowit, Malaysia .. **62 D4** 2 14N 112 20 E
Kanoya, Japan ..... **55 J5** 31 25N 130 50 E
Kanpetlet, Burma ... **67 J18** 21 10N 93 59 E
Kanpur, India ...... **69 F9** 26 28N 80 20 E
Kansas □, U.S.A. **112 F6** 38 30N 99 0W
Kansas →, U.S.A. ... **112 F7** 39 7N 94 37W
Kansas City, Kans.,
  U.S.A. **112 F7** 39 7N 94 38W
Kansas City, Mo., U.S.A. **112 F7** 39 6N 94 35W
Kansenia, Dem. Rep. of
  the Congo .... **87 E2** 10 20 S 26 0 E
Kansk, Russia ...... **53 D10** 56 20N 95 37 E
Kansŏng, S. Korea ... **57 E15** 38 24N 128 30 E
Kansu = Gansu □,
  China .... **56 G3** 36 0N 104 0 E
Kantaphor, India ... **68 H7** 22 35N 76 34 E
Kantchari, Burkina Faso **83 C5** 12 37N 1 37 E
Kanthé, Niger ...... **83 C6** 13 31N 8 30 E
Kanté, Togo .... **83 D5** 9 57N 1 3 E
Kantemirovka, Russia **33 H10** 49 43N 39 55 E
Kantharalak, Thailand **64 E5** 14 39N 104 39 E
Kantli →, India ..... **68 E6** 28 20N 75 30 E
Kantō □, Japan ..... **55 F9** 36 15N 139 30 E
Kantō-Sanchi, Japan .. **55 G9** 35 59N 138 50 E
Kanturk, Ireland ... **12 D3** 52 11N 8 54W
Kanuma, Japan ..... **55 F9** 36 34N 139 42 E
Kanus, Namibia .... **88 D2** 27 50 S 18 39 E
Kanye, Botswana .... **88 C4** 24 55 S 25 28 E
Kanzenze, Dem. Rep. of
  the Congo .... **87 E2** 10 30 S 25 12 E
Kanzi, Ras, Tanzania . **86 D4** 7 1 S 39 5 E
Kao Phara, Thailand .. **65 a** 8 3N 98 22 E
Kaohsiung, Taiwan .. **59 F13** 22 35N 120 16 E
Kaokoveld, Namibia . **88 B1** 19 15 S 14 30 E
Kaolack, Senegal ... **82 C1** 14 5N 16 8W
Kaoshan, U.S.A. **106 G15** 22 5N 159 19W
Kapadvanj, India ... **68 H5** 23 5N 73 0 E
Kapaklı, Turkey .... **45 E11** 41 19N 27 59 E
Kapan, Armenia .... **70 B5** 39 18N 46 27 E
Kapanga, Dem. Rep. of
  the Congo .... **84 F4** 8 30 S 22 40 E

Kapchagai =
  Qapshaghay,
  Kazakhstan ...... **52 E8** 43 51N 77 14 E
Kapela = Velika Kapela,
  Croatia .... **41 C12** 45 10N 15 5 E
Kapéllo, Ákra, Greece . **46 E5** 36 9N 23 3 E
Kapema, Dem. Rep. of
  the Congo .... **87 E2** 10 45 S 28 22 E
Kapfenberg, Austria .. **26 D8** 47 26N 15 18 E
Kapı Dağı, Turkey .. **45 F11** 40 28N 27 50 E
Kapıl Mposhi, Zambia **87 E2** 13 59 S 28 43 E
Kāpīsā □, Afghan. ... **66 B6** 35 0N 69 20 E
Kapiskau →, Canada . **104 B3** 52 47N 81 55W
Kapit, Malaysia .... **62 D4** 2 0N 112 55 E
Kapiti I., N.Z. ...... **91 J5** 40 50 S 174 56 E
Kaplan, U.S.A. **113 K8** 30 0N 92 17W
Kaplice, Czech Rep. .. **26 C7** 48 42N 14 30 E
Kapoe, Thailand .... **65 H2** 9 34N 98 32 E
Kapoeta, Sudan .... **81 G3** 4 50N 33 35 E
Kápolnásnyék, Hungary **28 C3** 47 16N 18 41 E
Kapos →, Hungary .. **28 D3** 46 44N 18 30 E
Kaposvár, Hungary .. **28 D2** 46 25N 17 47 E
Kapowsin, U.S.A. ... **110 D4** 46 59N 122 13W
Kappeln, Germany .. **24 A5** 54 40N 9 55 E
Kappelshamn, Sweden **11 G12** 57 52N 18 47 E
Kapps, Namibia .... **88 C2** 22 32 S 17 18 E
Kaprije, Croatia .... **41 E12** 43 42N 15 43 E
Kapsan, N. Korea ... **57 D15** 41 4N 128 19 E
Kapsukas =
  Marijampolė,
  Lithuania .... **9 J20** 54 33N 23 19 E
Kaptai L., Bangla. ... **67 H18** 22 40N 92 20 E
Kapuas →, Indonesia . **62 E3** 0 25 S 109 20 E
Kapuas Hulu,
  Pegunungan, Malaysia **62 D4** 1 30N 113 30 E
Kapuas Hulu Ra. =
  Kapuas Hulu,
  Pegunungan, Malaysia **62 D4** 1 30N 113 30 E
Kapulo, Dem. Rep. of
  the Congo .... **87 D2** 8 18 S 29 15 E
Kapunda, Australia .. **95 E2** 34 20 S 138 56 E
Kapuni, N.Z. .... **91 H5** 39 29 S 174 8 E
Kapurthala, India ... **68 D6** 31 23N 75 25 E
Kapuskasing, Canada **104 C3** 49 25N 82 30W
Kapuskasing →, Canada **104 C3** 49 49N 82 0W
Kapustin Yar, Russia . **35 F7** 48 37N 45 40 E
Kaputar, Australia ... **95 E5** 30 15 S 150 10 E
Kaputir, Kenya ..... **86 B4** 2 5N 35 28 E
Kapuvár, Hungary .. **28 C2** 47 36N 17 1 E
Kara, Russia .... **52 C7** 69 10N 65 0 E
Kará, W. →, Si. Arabia **80 C5** 20 45N 41 42 E
Kara Ada, Turkey ... **47 E9** 36 58N 27 28 E
Kara Bogaz Gol, Zaliv =
  Garabogazköl Aylagy,
  Turkmenistan ..... **52 E6** 41 0N 53 30 E
Kara Burun, Turkey .. **47 E9** 36 33N 27 58 E
Kara Kalpak Republic =
  Qoraqalpoghiston □,
  Uzbekistan .... **52 E6** 43 0N 58 0 E
Kara Kum,
  Turkmenistan ..... **52 F6** 39 30N 60 0 E
Kara Sea, Russia .... **52 B7** 75 0N 70 0 E
Karaadilli, Turkey ... **47 C12** 38 18N 30 37 E
Karabiğa, Turkey ... **45 F11** 40 23N 27 17 E
Karabük, Turkey .... **72 B5** 41 12N 32 37 E
Karaburun, Albania .. **44 F3** 40 25N 19 20 E
Karaburun, Turkey .. **47 C8** 38 41N 26 28 E
Karabutak = Qarabutaq,
  Kazakhstan ...... **52 E7** 49 59N 60 14 E
Karacabey, Turkey .. **45 F12** 40 12N 28 21 E
Karacakılavuz, Turkey **45 E11** 41 8N 27 21 E
Karacaköy, Turkey .. **45 E12** 41 24N 28 22 E
Karacasu, Turkey ... **47 D10** 37 43N 28 35 E
Karachala = Qaraçala,
  Azerbaijan .... **35 L9** 39 45N 48 53 E
Karachayevsk, Russia **35 J5** 43 50N 41 55 E
Karachev, Russia .... **33 F8** 53 10N 35 5 E
Karachey-Cherkessia □,
  Russia .... **35 J5** 43 40N 41 30 E
Karachi, Pakistan ... **68 G2** 24 53N 67 0 E
Karad, India .... **66 L9** 17 15N 74 10 E
Karadirek, Turkey ... **47 C12** 38 34N 30 11 E
Karaga, Ghana **83 D4** 9 58N 0 28W
Karaganda =
  Qaraghandy,
  Kazakhstan ...... **52 E8** 49 50N 73 10 E
Karagayly = Qaraghayly,
  Kazakhstan ...... **52 E8** 49 26N 76 0 E
Karaginskiy, Ostrov,
  Russia .... **53 D17** 58 45N 164 0 E
Karagola Road, India **69 G12** 25 29N 87 23 E
Karagüney Dağları,
  Turkey .... **72 B6** 40 30N 34 40 E
Karahallı, Turkey ... **47 C11** 38 21N 29 33 E
Karaikal, India ..... **66 P11** 10 59N 79 50 E
Karaikkudi, India ... **66 P11** 10 5N 78 45 E
Karaisalı, Turkey ... **72 D6** 37 16N 35 2 E
Karaj, Iran .... **71 C6** 35 48N 51 0 E
Karak, Malaysia .... **65 L4** 3 25N 102 2 E
Karakalpakstan =
  Qoraqalpoghiston □,
  Uzbekistan .... **52 E6** 43 0N 58 0 E
Karakelong, Indonesia **63 D7** 4 35N 126 50 E
Karakitang, Indonesia **63 D7** 3 14N 125 28 E
Karakoçan, Turkey .. **73 C9** 38 57N 40 2 E
Karakol, Kyrgyzstan .. **52 E8** 42 30N 78 20 E
Karakoram Pass, Asia **69 B7** 35 33N 77 50 E
Karakoram Ra.,
  Pakistan .... **69 B7** 35 30N 77 0 E
Karakurt, Turkey ... **73 B10** 40 10N 42 37 E
Karakuwisa, Namibia **88 B2** 18 56 S 19 40 E
Karalon, Russia ..... **53 D12** 57 5N 115 50 E
Karaman, Jordan ... **74 D4** 31 57N 35 35 E
Karaman, Balıkesir,
  Turkey .... **47 B9** 39 39N 28 0 E
Karaman, Konya,
  Turkey .... **70 B2** 37 14N 33 13 E
Karamanlı, Turkey .. **47 D11** 37 25N 29 36 E
Karamay, China .... **60 B3** 45 30N 84 58 E
Karamea Bight, N.Z. .. **91 J3** 41 22 S 171 40 E
Karamnasa →, India . **69 G10** 25 31N 83 52 E
Karamürsel, Turkey .. **45 F13** 40 41N 29 36 E
Karand, Iran .... **70 C5** 34 16N 46 15 E
Karanganyar, Indonesia **63 G13** 7 38 S 109 37 E
Karangasem, Indonesia **63 J18** 8 27 S 115 37 E
Karanjia, India ..... **69 J11** 21 47N 85 58 E
Karankasso,
  Burkina Faso **82 C4** 10 50N 3 53W
Karapınar, Turkey .. **72 D5** 37 43N 33 6 E
Karasburg, Namibia . **88 D2** 28 0 S 18 44 E
Karasino, Russia .... **52 C9** 66 50N 86 50 E
Karasjok, Norway ... **8 B21** 69 27N 25 30 E
Karasu →, Turkey ... **72 B4** 41 30N 30 46 E
Karasu →, Turkey ... **47 E12** 36 18N 30 10 E

Karasuk, Russia ..... **52 D8** 53 44N 78 2 E
Karasuyama, Japan .. **55 F10** 36 39N 140 9 E
Karataş, Adana, Turkey **72 D6** 36 36N 35 21 E
Karataş, Manisa, Turkey **47 C10** 38 35N 28 16 E
Karataş Burnu, Turkey **72 D6** 36 31N 35 24 E
Karatau, Khrebet =
  Qarataū, Kazakhstan **52 E7** 43 30N 69 30 E
Karatoprak, Turkey .. **47 D9** 37 2N 27 15 E
Karatsu, Japan ..... **55 H5** 33 26N 129 58 E
Karaul, Russia ..... **52 B9** 70 6N 82 15 E
Karauli, India ...... **68 F7** 26 30N 77 4 E
Karavastasë, L. e,
  Albania .... **44 F3** 40 55N 19 30 E
Karávi, Greece ..... **46 E5** 36 49N 23 37 E
Karavostasi, Cyprus . **49 D11** 35 8N 32 50 E
Karawang, Indonesia . **63 G12** 6 30 S 107 15 E
Karawanken, Europe .. **26 E7** 46 30N 14 40 E
Karayazı, Turkey .... **73 C10** 39 41N 42 9 E
Karazhal, Kazakhstan . **52 E8** 48 2N 70 49 E
Karbalā', Iraq ...... **70 C5** 32 36N 44 3 E
Kårböle, Sweden .... **10 C9** 61 59N 15 22 E
Karcag, Hungary .... **28 C5** 47 19N 20 57 E
Karchana, India .... **69 G9** 25 17N 81 56 E
Karczew, Poland .... **31 F8** 52 5N 21 15 E
Kardam, Bulgaria ... **45 C12** 43 45N 28 6 E
Kardeljevo = Ploče,
  Croatia .... **41 E14** 43 4N 17 26 E
Kardhámila, Greece .. **47 C8** 38 35N 26 5 E
Kardhamíli, Greece .. **46 E4** 36 53N 22 13 E
Kardhítsa, Greece ... **46 B3** 39 23N 21 54 E
Kardhítsa □, Greece .. **46 B3** 39 15N 21 50 E
Kärdla, Estonia ..... **9 G20** 59 0N 22 45 E
Kareeberge, S. Africa . **88 E3** 30 59 S 21 50 E
Kareha →, India .... **69 G12** 25 44N 86 21 E
Kareima, Sudan .... **80 D3** 18 30N 31 49 E
Karelia □, Russia ... **52 C4** 65 30N 32 30 E
Karelian Republic =
  Karelia □, Russia .. **52 C4** 65 30N 32 30 E
Karera, India ...... **68 G8** 25 32N 78 9 E
Kārevāndar, Iran ... **71 E9** 27 53N 60 44 E
Kargasok, Russia .... **52 D9** 59 3N 80 53 E
Kargat, Russia ..... **52 D9** 55 10N 80 15 E
Kargı, Turkey ...... **72 B6** 41 11N 34 30 E
Kargil, India .... **69 B7** 34 32N 76 12 E
Kargopol, Russia .... **32 B10** 61 30N 38 58 E
Kargowa, Poland .... **31 F2** 52 5N 15 51 E
Karguéri, Niger ..... **83 C7** 13 27N 10 30 E
Karhal, India ...... **69 F8** 27 1N 78 57 E
Kariá, Greece ...... **46 C2** 38 45N 20 39 E
Kariaí, Greece ..... **45 F8** 40 14N 24 19 E
Karīān, Iran .... **71 E8** 26 57N 57 14 E
Karianga, Madag. ... **89 C8** 22 25 S 47 22 E
Kariba, Zimbabwe ... **87 F2** 16 28 S 28 50 E
Kariba, L., Zimbabwe . **87 F2** 16 40 S 28 25 E
Kariba Dam, Zimbabwe **87 F2** 16 30 S 28 35 E
Kariba Gorge, Zambia **87 F2** 16 30 S 28 50 E
Karibib, Namibia .... **88 C2** 22 0 S 15 56 E
Karijini △, Australia .. **92 D2** 23 8 S 118 15 E
Karimata, Kepulauan,
  Indonesia .... **62 E3** 1 25 S 109 0 E
Karimata, Selat,
  Indonesia .... **62 E3** 2 0 S 108 40 E
Karimata Is. = Karimata,
  Kepulauan, Indonesia **62 E3** 1 25 S 109 0 E
Karimnagar, India ... **66 K11** 18 26N 79 10 E
Karimun Kecil, Pulau,
  Indonesia .... **65 d** 1 8N 103 22 E
Karimunjawa,
  Kepulauan, Indonesia **62 F4** 5 50 S 110 30 E
Karin, Somali Rep. ... **75 E4** 10 50N 45 52 E
Káristos, Greece .... **46 C6** 38 1N 24 29 E
Karīt, Iran .... **71 C8** 33 29N 56 55 E
Kariya, Japan ...... **55 G8** 34 58N 137 1 E
Kariyangwe, Zimbabwe **89 B4** 18 0 S 27 38 E
Karjala, Finland .... **32 A5** 62 0N 30 25 E
Karkaralinsk =
  Qarqaraly,
  Kazakhstan ...... **52 E8** 49 26N 75 30 E
Karkheh →, Iran .... **70 D5** 31 2N 47 29 E
Karkinitska Zatoka,
  Ukraine .... **33 K7** 45 56N 33 0 E
Karkinitskiy Zaliv =
  Karkinitska Zatoka,
  Ukraine .... **33 K7** 45 56N 33 0 E
Karkur Tohl, Egypt ... **80 C2** 22 5N 29 5 E
Karleby = Kokkola,
  Finland .... **8 E20** 63 50N 23 8 E
Karlholmsbruk, Sweden **10 D11** 60 31N 17 37 E
Karlino, Poland .... **30 D2** 54 3N 15 53 E
Karlivka, Ukraine ... **33 H8** 49 29N 35 8 E
Karlobag, Croatia ... **41 D12** 44 32N 15 5 E
Karlovac, Croatia ... **41 C12** 45 31N 15 36 E
Karlovarský □,
  Czech Rep. .... **26 A5** 50 10N 12 50 E
Karlovka = Karlivka,
  Ukraine .... **33 H8** 49 29N 35 8 E
Karlovo, Bulgaria ... **45 D8** 42 38N 24 47 E
Karlovy Vary,
  Czech Rep. .... **26 A5** 50 13N 12 51 E
Karlsbad = Karlovy
  Vary, Czech Rep. .. **26 A5** 50 13N 12 51 E
Karlsborg, Sweden .. **11 F8** 58 33N 14 33 E
Karlshamn, Sweden .. **11 H8** 56 10N 14 51 E
Karlskoga, Sweden .. **10 E8** 59 28N 14 33 E
Karlskrona, Sweden . **11 H9** 56 10N 15 35 E
Karlsruhe, Germany . **25 F4** 49 0N 8 23 E
Karlstad, Sweden ... **10 E7** 59 23N 13 30 E
Karlstad, U.S.A. **112 A6** 48 35N 96 31W
Karlstadt, Germany .. **25 F5** 49 57N 9 47 E
Karma, Niger ...... **83 C5** 13 38N 1 52 E
Karmëlava, Lithuania **30 D11** 54 58N 24 4 E
Karmi'el, Israel .... **74 C4** 32 55N 35 18 E
Karnak, Egypt ..... **80 B3** 25 43N 32 39 E
Karnal, India ...... **68 E7** 29 42N 77 2 E
Karnali →, Nepal ... **69 E9** 28 45N 81 16 E
Karnaphuli Res. =
  Kaptai L., Bangla. .. **67 H18** 22 40N 92 20 E
Karnaprayag, India .. **69 D8** 30 16N 79 15 E
Karnataka □, India .. **66 N10** 13 15N 77 0 E
Karnes City, U.S.A. .. **113 L6** 28 53N 97 54W
Karnische Alpen,
  Europe .... **26 E6** 46 36N 13 0 E
Kärnten □, Austria .. **26 E6** 46 52N 13 30 E
Karo, Mali **82 C4** 12 16N 3 18W
Karoi, Zimbabwe ... **87 F2** 16 48 S 29 45 E
Karonga, Malawi ... **87 D3** 9 57 S 33 55 E
Karoo □, S. Africa .. **88 E3** 32 18 S 23 28 E
Karoonda, Australia . **95 F2** 35 1 S 139 59 E
Karor, Pakistan .... **68 D4** 31 15N 70 59 E
Karora, Sudan ..... **80 D4** 17 44N 38 15 E
Káros, Greece ..... **47 E7** 36 54N 25 40 E
Karounga, Mali **82 B3** 15 20N 7 35W
Karousádhes, Greece . **46 B1** 39 47N 19 45 E

Karpacz, Poland ...... 31 H2 50 46N 15 46 E
Karpasia, Cyprus .... 49 D13 35 32N 34 15 E
Kárpathos, Greece ... 47 F9 35 37N 27 10 E
Kárpathos, Stenón,
  Greece .... 47 F9 36 0N 27 30 E
Karpatsky △, Ukraine . 29 B9 48 20N 24 35 E
Karpenísion, Greece .. 46 C3 38 55N 21 40 E
Karpuz Burnu =
  Apostolos Andreas,
  C., Cyprus .... 49 D13 35 42N 34 35 E
Karpuzlu, Turkey .... 47 D9 37 33N 27 51 E
Karratha, Australia .. 92 D2 20 53 S 116 40 E
Kars, Turkey .... 73 B10 40 40N 43 5 E
Karsakpay, Kazakhstan 52 E7 47 55N 66 40 E
Karsha, Kazakhstan .. 34 F10 49 45N 51 35 E
Karshi = Qarshi,
  Uzbekistan .... 52 F7 38 53N 65 48 E
Karsiyang, India .... 69 F13 26 56N 88 18 E
Karsog, India .... 68 D7 31 23N 77 12 E
Karst = Kras, Croatia . 41 C10 45 35N 14 0 E
Kartal, Turkey ...... 45 F13 40 53N 29 11 E
Kartál Óros, Greece .. 45 E9 41 15N 25 13 E
Kartaly, Russia ..... 52 D7 53 3N 60 40 E
Kartapur, India ..... 68 D6 31 27N 75 32 E
Karthaus, U.S.A. 116 E6 41 8N 78 9W
Kartuzy, Poland ..... 30 D5 54 22N 18 0 E
Karufa, Indonesia ... 63 E8 3 50 S 133 20 E
Karuma △, Uganda ... 86 B3 2 5N 32 15 E
Karumba, Australia .. 94 B3 17 31 S 140 50 E
Karumo, Tanzania ... 86 C3 2 25 S 32 50 E
Karumwa, Tanzania .. 86 C3 3 12 S 32 38 E
Kärun →, Iran ...... 71 D6 30 26N 48 10 E
Karungu, Kenya ..... 86 C3 0 50 S 34 10 E
Karup, Denmark ..... 11 H3 56 19N 9 10 E
Karviná, Czech Rep. .. 27 B11 49 53N 18 31 E
Karwan →, India .... 68 F8 27 26N 78 4 E
Karwar, India .... 66 M9 14 55N 74 13 E
Karwendel △, Austria . 26 E4 47 25N 11 30 E
Karwi, India .... 69 G9 25 12N 80 57 E
Kaş, Turkey .... 47 E11 36 11N 29 37 E
Kasaba, Turkey ..... 47 E11 36 18N 29 44 E
Kasache, Malawi .... 87 E3 13 25 S 34 20 E
Kasai →, Dem. Rep. of
  the Congo .... 84 E3 3 30 S 16 10 E
Kasai-Oriental □,
  Dem. Rep. of
  the Congo .... 86 D1 5 0 S 24 30 E
Kasaji, Dem. Rep. of
  the Congo .... 87 E1 10 25 S 23 27 E
Kasama, Zambia ..... 87 E3 10 16 S 31 9 E
Kasan-dong, N. Korea . 57 D14 41 18N 126 55 E
Kasane, Namibia .... 88 B3 17 34 S 24 50 E
Kasanga, Tanzania ... 87 D3 8 30 S 31 10 E
Kasanka △, Zambia .. 87 E3 11 34 S 30 15 E
Kasar, Ras, Sudan ... 80 D4 18 2N 38 36 E
Kasaragod, India .... 66 N9 12 30N 74 58 E
Kasba L., Canada 103 A8 60 20N 102 10W
Käseh Garān, Iran ... 70 C5 34 5N 46 2 E
Kasempa, Zambia .... 87 E2 13 30 S 25 44 E
Kasenga, Dem. Rep. of
  the Congo .... 87 E2 10 20 S 28 45 E
Kasese, Uganda ..... 86 B3 0 13N 30 3 E
Kasewa, Zambia ..... 87 E2 14 28 S 28 53 E
Kasganj, India ...... 69 F8 27 48N 78 42 E
Kashabowie, Canada . 104 C1 48 40N 90 26W
Kashaf →, Iran ..... 71 C9 35 58N 61 7 E
Kāshān, Iran .... 71 C6 34 5N 51 30 E
Kashechewan, Canada . 104 B3 52 18N 81 37W
Kashgar = Kashi, China 60 C2 39 30N 76 2 E
Kashi, China .... 60 C2 39 30N 76 2 E
Kashimbo, Dem. Rep. of
  the Congo .... 87 E2 11 12 S 26 19 E
Kashin, Russia ...... 32 D9 57 20N 37 36 E
Kashipur, India ..... 69 E8 29 15N 79 0 E
Kashira, Russia ..... 32 E10 54 45N 38 10 E
Kashiwazaki, Japan .. 55 F9 37 22N 138 33 E
Kashk-e Kohneh,
  Afghan. .... 66 B3 34 55N 62 30 E
Kashkū'īyeh, Iran ... 71 D7 30 31N 55 40 E
Kāshmar, Iran ...... 71 C8 35 16N 58 26 E
Kashmir, Asia ...... 69 C7 34 0N 76 0 E
Kashmor, Pakistan .. 68 E3 28 28N 69 32 E
Kashpirovka, Russia .. 34 D9 53 0N 48 30 E
Kashun Noerh = Gaxun
  Nur, China .... 60 B5 42 22N 100 30 E
Kasiari, India ...... 69 H12 22 8N 87 14 E
Kasimov, Russia .... 34 C5 54 55N 41 20 E
Kasinge, Dem. Rep. of
  the Congo .... 86 D2 6 15 S 26 58 E
Kasiruta, Indonesia .. 63 E7 0 25 S 127 12 E
Kaskaskia →, U.S.A. . 112 G10 37 58N 89 57W
Kaskattama →, Canada 103 B10 57 3N 90 4W
Kaskinen, Finland ... 9 E19 62 22N 21 15 E
Kaskö = Kaskinen,
  Finland .... 9 E19 62 22N 21 15 E
Kaslo, Canada 102 D5 49 55N 116 55W
Kasmere L., Canada . 103 B8 59 34N 101 10W
Kasongo, Dem. Rep. of
  the Congo .... 86 C2 4 30 S 26 33 E
Kasongo Lunda,
  Dem. Rep. of
  the Congo .... 84 F3 6 35 S 16 49 E
Kásos, Greece ...... 47 F8 35 20N 26 55 E
Kásos, Stenón, Greece 47 F8 35 30N 26 30 E
Kaspi, Georgia ..... 35 K7 41 59N 44 26 E
Kaspichan, Bulgaria .. 45 C11 43 18N 27 11 E
Kaspiysk, Russia .... 35 J8 42 52N 47 40 E
Kaspiyskiy, Russia ... 35 H8 45 22N 47 23 E
Kassab ed Doleib, Sudan 81 E3 13 30N 33 35 E
Kassaba, Egypt ..... 80 C2 22 40N 29 55 E
Kassalâ, Sudan ..... 81 D4 15 30N 36 0 E
Kassalâ □, Sudan ... 81 D4 15 20N 36 26 E
Kassándra, Greece ... 44 F7 40 0N 23 30 E
Kassándrinon, Greece 44 F7 40 1N 23 27 E
Kassel, Germany .... 24 D5 51 18N 9 26 E
Kassinger, Sudan .... 80 D3 18 46N 31 51 E
Kassiópi, Greece .... 49 A3 39 48N 19 53 E
Kasson, U.S.A. 112 C8 44 2N 92 45W
Kastav, Croatia ..... 41 C11 45 22N 14 20 E
Kastélli, Greece ..... 49 D5 35 29N 23 38 E
Kastéllion, Greece ... 49 D7 35 12N 25 20 E
Kastellórizon = Megiste,
  Greece .... 47 E11 36 8N 29 34 E
Kástellos, Greece .... 47 F9 36 16N 27 49 E
Kastellou, Ákra, Greece 47 F8 35 30N 27 15 E
Kasterlee, Belgium ... 17 C4 51 15N 4 59 E
Kastlösa, Sweden ... 11 H10 56 26N 16 25 E
Kastóri, Greece ..... 46 D4 37 10N 22 17 E
Kastoría, Greece .... 44 F5 40 30N 21 19 E
Kastoría □, Greece .. 44 F5 40 30N 21 22 E
Kastorías, Límni, Greece 44 F5 40 30N 21 20 E
Kastornoye, Russia .. 33 G10 51 55N 38 2 E
Kastós Nísís, Greece . 46 C2 38 34N 20 55 E
Kastrosikiá, Greece .. 46 B2 39 6N 20 38 E
Kastrup, København ✈
  (CPH), Denmark .. 11 J6 55 37N 12 39 E

Kastsyukovichy, Belarus 32 F7 53 20N 32 4 E
Kasulu, Tanzania .... 86 C3 4 37 S 30 5 E
Kasumi, Japan ...... 55 G7 35 38N 134 38 E
Kasumkent, Russia .. 35 K9 41 47N 48 15 E
Kasungu, Malawi ... 87 E3 13 0 S 33 29 E
Kasungu △, Malawi .. 87 E3 12 53 S 33 9 E
Kasur, Pakistan .... 68 D6 31 5N 74 25 E
Kataba, Zambia ..... 87 F2 16 5 S 25 10 E
Katagum, Nigeria ... 83 C7 12 18N 10 21 E
Katahdin, Mt., U.S.A. 115 C11 45 54N 68 56W
Katako Kombe,
  Dem. Rep. of
  the Congo .... 86 C1 3 25 S 24 20 E
Katákolon, Greece ... 46 D3 37 38N 21 19 E
Katale, Tanzania .... 86 C3 4 52 S 31 7 E
Katanda, Katanga,
  Dem. Rep. of
  the Congo .... 86 D1 7 52 S 24 13 E
Katanda, Nord-Kivu,
  Dem. Rep. of
  the Congo .... 86 C2 0 55 S 29 21 E
Katanga □, Dem. Rep.
  of the Congo ...... 86 D2 8 0 S 25 0 E
Katangi, India ...... 66 J11 21 56N 79 50 E
Katanning, Australia . 93 F2 33 40 S 117 33 E
Katástari, Greece .... 46 D3 37 50N 20 45 E
Katavi △, Tanzania .. 86 D3 6 51 S 31 3 E
Katavi Swamp, Tanzania 86 D3 6 51 S 31 10 E
Katerini, Greece .... 44 F6 40 18N 22 37 E
Katghora, India ..... 69 H10 22 30N 82 33 E
Katha, Burma ...... 67 G20 24 10N 96 30 E
Katherîna, Gebel, Egypt 70 D2 28 30N 33 57 E
Katherine, Australia . 92 B5 14 27 S 132 20 E
Katherine Gorge,
  Australia .... 92 B5 14 18 S 132 28 E
Kathi, India .... 68 J6 21 47N 74 3 E
Kathiawar, India .... 68 H4 22 20N 71 0 E
Kathikas, Cyprus .... 49 E11 34 55N 32 25 E
Kathmandu =
  Katmandu, Nepal .. 69 F11 27 45N 85 20 E
Kathua, India .... 68 C6 32 23N 75 34 E
Kati, Mali 82 C3 12 41N 8 4W
Katihar, India ...... 69 G12 25 34N 87 36 E
Katima Mulilo, Zambia 88 B3 17 28 S 24 13 E
Katimbira, Malawi .. 87 E3 12 40 S 34 0 E
Katingan =
  Mendawai →,
  Indonesia .... 62 E4 3 30 S 113 0 E
Katiola, Ivory C. 82 D3 8 10N 5 10W
Katlabukh, Ozero,
  Ukraine .... 29 E14 45 30N 28 30 E
Katlanovo, Macedonia 44 E5 41 52N 21 40 E
Katmandu, Nepal ... 69 F11 27 45N 85 20 E
Katni, India .... 69 H9 23 51N 80 24 E
Káto Akhaḯa, Greece . 46 C3 38 8N 21 33 E
Káto Arkhánai, Greece 49 D7 35 15N 25 10 E
Káto Khorió, Greece . 49 D7 35 3N 25 47 E
Káto Pyrgos, Cyprus . 49 D11 35 11N 32 41 E
Káto Stavros, Greece . 44 F7 40 39N 23 43 E
Katokhí, Greece ..... 46 C3 38 8N 21 15 E
Katompe, Dem. Rep. of
  the Congo .... 86 D2 6 2 S 26 23 E
Katong, Singapore ... 65 d 1 18N 103 53 E
Katonga →, Uganda . 86 B3 0 34N 31 50 E
Katoomba, Australia . 95 E5 33 41 S 150 19 E
Katoúna, Greece .... 46 C3 38 47N 21 7 E
Katowice, Poland ... 31 H6 50 17N 19 5 E
Katranci Dağı, Turkey 47 D12 37 27N 30 25 E
Katrine, L., U.K. 13 E4 56 15N 4 30W
Katrineholm, Sweden . 10 E10 59 9N 16 12 E
Katsepe, Madag. .... 89 B8 15 45 S 46 15 E
Katsina, Nigeria .... 83 C6 13 0N 7 32 E
Katsina □, Nigeria .. 83 C6 12 30N 7 30 E
Katsina Ala, Nigeria . 83 D6 7 10N 9 30 E
Katsina Ala →, Nigeria 83 D6 7 10N 9 20 E
Katsumoto, Japan ... 55 H4 33 51N 129 42 E
Katsuura, Japan .... 55 G10 35 10N 140 20 E
Katsuyama, Japan ... 55 F8 36 3N 136 30 E
Kattaviá, Greece .... 49 D9 35 57N 27 46 E
Kattegat, Denmark .. 11 H5 56 40N 11 20 E
Katthammarsvik,
  Sweden .... 11 G12 57 26N 18 51 E
Katul, J., Sudan .... 81 E2 14 12N 29 25 E
Katumba, Dem. Rep. of
  the Congo .... 86 D2 7 40 S 25 17 E
Katwa, India .... 69 H13 23 30N 88 5 E
Katwijk, Neths. ..... 17 B4 52 12N 4 24 E
Kąty Wrocławskie,
  Poland .... 31 G3 51 2N 16 45 E
Kauai, U.S.A. 106 H15 22 3N 159 30W
Kauai Channel, U.S.A. 106 H15 21 45N 158 50W
Kaub, Germany ..... 25 E3 50 5N 7 46 E
Kaudom △, Namibia . 88 B3 18 45 S 20 51 E
Kaufbeuren, Germany 25 H6 47 53N 10 37 E
Kaufman, U.S.A. 113 J6 32 35N 96 19W
Kauhajoki, Finland .. 9 E20 62 25N 22 10 E
Kaukauna, U.S.A. ... 114 C1 44 17N 88 17W
Kaukauveld, Namibia 88 C3 20 0 S 20 15 E
Kaunakakai, U.S.A. . 106 H16 21 6N 157 1W
Kaunas, Lithuania .. 9 J20 54 54N 23 54 E
Kaunas ✈ (KUN),
  Lithuania .... 30 D11 54 57N 24 3 E
Kaunia, Bangla. .... 69 G13 25 46N 89 26 E
Kaura Namoda, Nigeria 83 C6 12 37N 6 33 E
Kauru, Nigeria ..... 83 C6 10 33N 8 12 E
Kautokeino, Norway . 8 B20 69 0N 23 4 E
Kauwapur, India .... 69 F10 27 31N 82 18 E
Kavacha, Russia .... 53 C17 60 16N 169 51 E
Kavadarci, Macedonia 44 E6 41 26N 22 3 E
Kavajë, Albania .... 44 E3 41 11N 19 33 E
Kavak, Turkey ...... 72 B7 41 4N 36 3 E
Kavak Dağı, Turkey . 47 D10 37 10N 28 10 E
Kavaklı, Turkey ..... 45 E11 41 39N 27 10 E
Kavaklıdere, Turkey . 47 D10 37 27N 28 21 E
Kavalerovo, Russia .. 54 B7 44 15N 135 4 E
Kavali, India .... 66 M12 14 55N 80 1 E
Kaválla, Greece ..... 45 F8 40 57N 24 28 E
Kaválla □, Greece ... 45 E8 41 5N 24 30 E
Kaválla Kólpos, Greece 45 F8 40 50N 24 25 E
Kavār, Iran .... 71 D7 29 11N 52 44 E
Kavarna, Bulgaria ... 45 C12 43 26N 28 22 E
Kavi, India .... 68 H5 22 12N 72 38 E
Kavīr, Dasht-e, Iran . 71 C7 34 30N 55 0 E
Kavkaz, Russia ..... 33 K9 45 20N 36 40 E
Kavos, Greece ...... 49 B4 39 23N 20 3 E
Kavoúsi, Greece .... 47 F7 35 7N 25 51 E
Kaw, Fr. Guiana 125 C8 4 30N 52 15W
Kawagama L., Canada 116 A6 45 18N 78 45W
Kawagoe, Japan .... 55 G9 35 55N 139 29 E
Kawaguchi, Japan ... 55 G9 35 52N 139 45 E
Kawaihae, U.S.A. ... 106 H17 20 3N 155 50W
Kawambwa, Zambia . 87 D2 9 48 S 29 3 E
Kawanoe, Japan .... 55 G6 34 1N 133 34 E
Kawardha, India .... 69 J9 22 0N 81 17 E

Kawasaki, Japan .... 55 G9 35 31N 139 43 E
Kawasi, Indonesia ... 63 E7 1 38 S 127 28 E
Kawerau, N.Z. ..... 91 H6 38 7 S 176 42 E
Kawhia Harbour, N.Z. 91 H5 38 5 S 174 51 E
Kawio, Kepulauan,
  Indonesia .... 63 D7 4 30N 125 30 E
Kawnro, Burma ..... 67 H21 22 48N 99 8 E
Kawthaung, Burma .. 65 H2 10 5N 98 36 E
Kawthoolei = Kayin □,
  Burma .... 67 L20 18 0N 97 30 E
Kawthule = Kayin □,
  Burma .... 67 L20 18 0N 97 30 E
Kaxholmen, Sweden . 11 G8 57 51N 14 19 E
Kaya, Burkina Faso .. 83 C4 13 4N 1 10W
Kayah □, Burma .... 67 K20 19 15N 97 15 E
Kayalıköy Barajı,
  Turkey .... 45 E11 41 50N 27 5 E
Kayan →, Indonesia . 62 D5 2 55N 117 35 E
Kaycee, U.S.A. 108 E10 43 43N 106 38W
Kayeli, Indonesia ... 63 E7 3 20 S 127 10 E
Kayenta, U.S.A. 109 H8 36 44N 110 15W
Kayes, Mali 82 C2 14 25N 11 30W
Kayı, Turkey .... 47 B12 39 12N 30 46 E
Kayima, S. Leone ... 82 D2 8 54N 11 15W
Kayin □, Burma .... 67 L20 18 0N 97 30 E
Kaymakçı, Turkey .. 47 C10 38 10N 28 4 E
Kaynarca, Turkey ... 45 F13 41 2N 30 18 E
Kayoa, Indonesia ... 63 D7 0 1N 127 28 E
Kayomba, Zambia .. 87 E1 13 11 S 24 2 E
Kaysatskoye, Russia . 34 F8 49 47N 46 49 E
Kayseri, Turkey .... 70 B2 38 45N 35 30 E
Kaysville, U.S.A. ... 108 F8 41 2N 111 56W
Kaz Dağı, Turkey ... 47 B8 39 42N 26 50 E
Kazachye, Russia ... 53 B14 70 52N 135 58 E
Kazakhstan ■, Asia . 52 E7 50 0N 70 0 E
Kazan, Russia ...... 34 C9 55 50N 49 10 E
Kazan →, Canada ... 103 A9 64 2N 95 29W
Kazan-Rettō, Pac. Oc. 96 E6 25 0N 141 0 E
Kazanlŭk, Bulgaria .. 45 D9 42 38N 25 20 E
Kazanskaya, Russia . 34 F5 49 50N 41 10 E
Kazatin = Kozyatyn,
  Ukraine .... 33 H5 49 45N 28 50 E
Kazaure, Nigeria ... 83 C6 12 42N 8 28 E
Kazbek, Russia ..... 35 J7 42 42N 44 30 E
Kāzerūn, Iran ...... 71 D6 29 38N 51 40 E
Kazi Magomed =
  Qazimämmäd,
  Azerbaijan .... 35 K9 40 3N 49 0 E
Kazimierz Dolny,
  Poland .... 31 G8 51 19N 21 57 E
Kazimierza Wielka,
  Poland .... 31 H7 50 15N 20 30 E
Kazincbarcika, Hungary 28 B5 48 17N 20 36 E
Kazlų Rūda, Lithuania 30 D10 54 46N 23 30 E
Kaztalovka, Kazakhstan 34 F9 49 47N 48 43 E
Kazuma Pan △,
  Zimbabwe .... 87 F2 18 20 S 25 48 E
Kazuno, Japan ...... 54 D10 40 10N 140 45 E
Kazym →, Russia ... 52 C7 63 54N 65 50 E
Kcynia, Poland ..... 31 F4 53 0N 17 30 E
Ké-Macina, Mali 82 C3 13 58N 5 22W
Kéa, Greece .... 46 D6 37 35N 24 22 E
Keady, U.K. 12 B5 54 15N 6 42W
Kearney, U.S.A. 112 E5 40 42N 99 5W
Kearny, U.S.A. 109 K8 33 3N 110 55W
Kearsarge, Mt., U.S.A. 117 C13 43 22N 71 50W
Keban, Turkey ..... 73 C8 38 50N 38 50 E
Keban Baraji, Turkey 70 B3 38 41N 38 33 E
Kebbi, Nigeria ..... 83 C5 11 35N 4 0 E
Kebbi □, Nigeria ... 83 C5 11 30N 4 0 E
Kebnekaise, Sweden . 8 C18 67 53N 18 33 E
Kebri Dehar, Ethiopia 75 F3 6 45N 44 17 E
Kebumen, Indonesia 63 G13 7 42 S 109 40 E
Kecel, Hungary ..... 28 D4 46 31N 19 16 E
Kechika →, Canada . 102 B3 59 41N 127 12W
Keçiborlu, Turkey ... 47 D12 37 57N 30 18 E
Kecskemét, Hungary 28 D4 46 57N 19 42 E
Kedada, Ethiopia ... 81 F4 5 25N 35 58 E
Kédainiai, Lithuania 9 J21 55 15N 24 2 E
Kedarnath, India ... 69 D8 30 44N 79 4 E
Kedgwick, Canada .. 105 C6 47 40N 67 20W
Kédhros Óros, Greece 49 D6 35 11N 24 37 E
Kediri, Indonesia ... 63 G15 7 51 S 112 1 E
Kedjebi, Ghana ..... 83 D5 8 12N 0 25 E
Kédougou, Senegal .. 82 C2 12 35N 12 10W
Kędzierzyn-Koźle,
  Poland .... 31 H5 50 20N 18 12 E
Keeler, U.S.A. 110 J9 36 29N 117 52W
Keeley L., Canada ... 103 C7 54 54N 108 8W
Keeling Is. = Cocos Is.,
  Ind. Oc. .... 96 J1 12 10 S 96 55 E
Keelung = Chilung,
  Taiwan .... 59 E13 25 3N 121 45 E
Keene, Canada 116 B6 44 15N 78 10W
Keene, Calif., U.S.A. . 111 K8 35 13N 118 33W
Keene, N.H., U.S.A. . 117 D12 42 56N 72 17W
Keene, N.Y., U.S.A. . 117 B11 44 16N 73 46W
Keep River △, Australia 92 C4 15 49 S 129 8 E
Keeper Hill, Ireland . 12 D3 52 45N 8 16W
Keer-Weer, C., Australia 94 A3 14 0 S 141 32 E
Keeseville, U.S.A. ... 117 B11 44 29N 73 30W
Keetmanshoop, Namibia 88 D2 26 35 S 18 8 E
Keewatin, Canada .. 103 D10 49 46N 94 34W
Keewatin →, Canada 103 B8 56 29N 100 46W
Kefa, Ethiopia ..... 81 F4 6 55N 36 30 E
Kefallinía, Greece .. 46 C2 38 20N 20 30 E
Kefallinía □, Greece . 46 C2 38 15N 20 30 E
Kéfalos, Greece .... 47 E9 36 45N 26 57 E
Kefamenanu, Indonesia 63 F6 9 28 S 124 29 E
Kefar Sava, Israel ... 74 C3 32 11N 34 54 E
Keffi, Nigeria ...... 83 D6 8 55N 7 43 E
Keffin Hausa, Nigeria 83 C6 11 46N 9 14 E
Keflavík, Iceland ... 8 D2 64 2N 22 35W
Kegaska, Canada ... 105 B7 50 9N 61 18W
Keheili, Sudan ..... 80 D3 19 25N 32 50 E
Kehl, Germany ..... 25 G3 48 34N 7 50 E
Keighley, U.K. 14 D6 53 52N 1 54W
Keila, Estonia ...... 9 G21 59 18N 24 25 E
Keimoes, S. Africa .. 88 D3 28 41 S 20 59 E
Keita, Niger .... 83 C6 14 46N 5 56 E
Keitele, Finland .... 8 E22 63 10N 26 20 E
Keith, Australia .... 95 F3 36 6 S 140 20 E
Keith, U.K. 13 D6 57 32N 2 57W
Keizer, U.S.A. 108 D2 44 57N 123 1W
Kejimkujik △, Canada 105 D6 44 25N 65 25W
Kekri, India .... 68 G6 26 0N 75 10 E
Kelam, Ethiopia .... 81 G4 4 48N 35 58 E
Kelamet, Eritrea .... 81 D4 16 0N 38 30 E
Kelan, China .... 56 E6 38 43N 111 31 E
Kelang, Malaysia ... 65 L3 3 2N 101 26 E
Kelantan →, Malaysia 65 J4 6 13N 102 14 E

Keleti-főcsatorna,
  Hungary .... 28 C6 47 45N 21 20 E
Kelheim, Germany .. 25 G7 48 54N 11 52 E
Kelkit, Turkey ...... 73 B8 40 7N 39 16 E
Kelkit →, Turkey ... 72 B7 40 45N 36 32 E
Kellerberrin, Australia 93 F2 31 36 S 117 38 E
Kellett, C., Canada .. 4 B1 72 0N 126 0W
Kelleys I., U.S.A. ... 116 E2 41 36N 82 42W
Kellogg, U.S.A. 108 C5 47 32N 116 7W
Kells = Ceanannus Mor,
  Ireland 12 C5 53 44N 6 53W
Kelmė, Lithuania ... 30 C9 55 38N 22 56 E
Kelmentsi, Ukraine .. 29 B11 48 28N 26 50 E
Kelokedhara, Cyprus 49 E11 34 48N 32 39 E
Kelowna, Canada ... 102 D5 49 50N 119 25W
Kelsey Creek, Australia 94 J6 20 26 S 148 31 E
Kelseyville, U.S.A. .. 110 G4 38 59N 122 50W
Kelso, N.Z. .... 91 L2 45 54 S 169 15 E
Kelso, U.K. 13 F6 55 36N 2 26W
Kelso, U.S.A. 110 D4 46 9N 122 54W
Keluang, Malaysia .. 65 L4 2 3N 103 18 E
Kelvington, Canada . 103 C8 52 10N 103 30W
Kem, Russia .... 52 C4 65 0N 34 38 E
Kema, Indonesia ... 63 D7 1 22N 125 8 E
Kemah, Turkey ..... 70 B3 39 32N 39 5 E
Kemaliye, Erzincan,
  Turkey .... 73 C8 39 16N 38 29 E
Kemaliye, Manisa,
  Turkey .... 47 C10 38 27N 28 25 E
Kemalpaşa, Turkey .. 47 C9 38 25N 27 27 E
Kemaman, Malaysia . 62 D2 4 12N 103 18 E
Kemano, Canada ... 102 C3 53 35N 128 0W
Kemasik, Malaysia .. 65 K4 4 25N 103 27 E
Kembolcha, Ethiopia 81 E4 11 2N 39 42 E
Kemer, Antalya, Turkey 47 E12 36 36N 30 34 E
Kemer, Burdur, Turkey 47 D12 37 21N 30 4 E
Kemer, Muğla, Turkey 47 E11 36 40N 29 22 E
Kemer Baraji, Turkey 47 D10 37 30N 28 37 E
Kemerovo, Russia ... 52 D9 55 20N 86 5 E
Kemeru □, Latvia ... 30 B10 56 58N 23 32 E
Kemi, Finland ...... 8 D21 65 44N 24 34 E
Kemi älv = Kemijoki →,
  Finland .... 8 D21 65 47N 24 32 E
Kemi träsk = Kemijärvi,
  Finland .... 8 C22 66 43N 27 22 E
Kemijärvi, Finland .. 8 C22 66 43N 27 22 E
Kemijoki →, Finland 8 D21 65 47N 24 32 E
Kemmerer, U.S.A. .. 108 F8 41 48N 110 32W
Kemmuna = Comino,
  Malta .... 49 C1 36 1N 14 20 E
Kemp, L., U.S.A. ... 113 J5 33 46N 99 9W
Kemp Land, Antarctica 5 C5 69 0 S 55 0 E
Kempas, Malaysia ... 65 d 1 33N 103 42 E
Kempsey, Australia . 95 E5 31 1 S 152 50 E
Kempt, L., Canada .. 104 C5 47 25N 74 22W
Kempten, Germany . 25 H6 47 45N 10 17 E
Kempton, Australia . 95 G4 42 31 S 147 12 E
Kemptville, Canada . 117 B9 45 0N 75 38W
Ken →, India ...... 69 G9 25 13N 80 27 E
Kenai, U.S.A. 100 B4 60 33N 151 16W
Kendai, India ...... 69 H10 22 45N 82 37 E
Kendal, Indonesia .. 63 G14 6 56 S 110 14 E
Kendal, U.K. 14 C5 54 20N 2 44W
Kendall, Australia .. 95 E5 31 35 S 152 44 E
Kendall →, Australia 94 A3 14 4 S 141 35 E
Kendall, U.S.A. 115 N5 25 41N 80 19W
Kendallville, U.S.A. . 114 E3 41 27N 85 16W
Kendari, Indonesia .. 63 E6 3 50 S 122 30 E
Kendawangan,
  Indonesia .... 62 E4 2 32 S 110 17 E
Kende, Nigeria ..... 83 C5 11 30N 4 12 E
Kendi, Pulau, Malaysia 65 c 5 13N 100 11 E
Kendrapara, India .. 67 J15 20 35N 86 30 E
Kendrew, S. Africa .. 88 E3 32 32 S 24 30 E
Kene Thao, Laos .... 64 D3 17 44N 101 10 E
Kenedy, U.S.A. 113 L6 28 49N 97 51W
Kenema, S. Leone .. 82 D2 7 50N 11 14W
Keng Kok, Laos .... 64 D5 16 26N 105 12 E
Keng Tawng, Burma . 64 D5 20 45N 98 18 E
Keng Tung, Burma .. 58 G2 21 0N 99 30 E
Kengeja, Tanzania .. 86 D4 5 26 S 39 45 E
Kenhardt, S. Africa . 88 D3 29 19 S 21 12 E
Kéniéba, Mali 82 C2 12 54N 11 17W
Kenitra, Morocco ... 78 B4 34 15N 6 40W
Kenli, China .... 57 F10 37 30N 118 20 E
Kenmare, Ireland ... 12 E2 51 53N 9 36W
Kenmare, U.S.A. ... 112 A3 48 41N 102 5W
Kenmare River, Ireland 12 E2 51 48N 9 51W
Kennebago Lake, U.S.A. 117 A14 45 4N 70 40W
Kennebec →, U.S.A. 115 D11 43 45N 69 46W
Kennebunk, U.S.A. . 117 C14 43 23N 70 33W
Kennedy, Zimbabwe . 88 B4 18 52 S 27 10 E
Kennedy →, Australia 93 D2 24 45 S 115 10 E
Kennedy Range △,
  Australia .... 93 D2 24 58 S 115 2 E
Kenner, U.S.A. 113 L9 29 59N 90 15W
Kennet →, U.K. ... 15 F7 51 27N 0 57W
Kenneth Ra., Australia 93 D2 23 50 S 117 8 E
Kennett, U.S.A. .... 113 G9 36 14N 90 3 E
Kennewick, U.S.A. . 108 C4 46 12N 119 7W
Kenogami →, Canada 104 B3 51 6N 84 28W
Kenora, Canada 103 D10 49 47N 94 29W
Kenosha, U.S.A. 114 D2 42 35N 87 49W
Kent, Ohio, U.S.A. .. 116 E3 41 9N 81 22W
Kent, Tex., U.S.A. .. 113 K2 31 4N 104 13W
Kent, Wash., U.S.A. . 110 C4 47 23N 122 14W
Kent □, U.K. .... 15 F8 51 12N 0 40 E
Kent Group, Australia 95 F4 39 30 S 147 20 E
Kent Pen., Canada .. 100 B9 68 30N 107 0W
Kentau, Kazakhstan . 52 E7 43 32N 68 36 E
Kentland, U.S.A. ... 114 E2 40 46N 87 27W
Kenton, U.S.A. 114 E4 40 39N 83 37W
Kentucky □, U.S.A. . 114 G3 37 0N 84 0W
Kentucky →, U.S.A. 114 F3 38 41N 85 11W
Kentucky L., U.S.A. . 115 G2 37 1N 88 16W
Kentville, Canada ... 105 C7 45 6N 64 29W
Kentwood, U.S.A. .. 113 K9 30 56N 90 31W
Kenya ■, Africa .... 86 B4 1 0N 38 0 E
Kenya, Mt., Kenya .. 86 C4 0 10 S 37 18 E
Keo Neua, Deo,
  Vietnam .... 64 C5 18 23N 105 10 E
Keokuk, U.S.A. 112 E9 40 24N 91 24W
Keonjhargarh, India . 69 J11 21 28N 85 35 E
Kep, Cambodia ..... 65 G5 10 29N 104 29 E
Kep, Vietnam ...... 64 B6 21 24N 106 16 E
Kepala Batas, Malaysia 65 c 5 31N 100 26 E
Kepez, S. Africa .... 89 D4 28 18 S 24 30 E
Kepi, Indonesia ..... 63 F9 6 32 S 139 19 E
Képice, Poland ..... 30 D3 54 16N 16 51 E
Kępno, Poland ..... 31 G4 51 18N 17 58 E
Kepsut, Turkey ..... 47 B10 39 40N 28 9 E
Kerala □, India .... 66 P10 11 0N 76 15 E
Kerama-Rettō, Japan 55 L3 26 5N 127 15 E

Keran, Pakistan ..... 69 B5 34 35N 73 59 E
Keran △, Togo ...... 83 C5 10 9N 0 41 E
Kerang, Australia ... 95 F3 35 40 S 143 55 E
Keranyo, Ethiopia .. 81 F4 5 3N 38 18 E
Kerao →, Sudan .... 81 E3 11 0N 32 41 E
Keratéa, Greece .... 46 D5 37 48N 23 58 E
Keraudren, C., Australia 92 C2 19 58 S 119 45 E
Kerava, Finland .... 9 F21 60 25N 25 5 E
Kerch, Ukraine ..... 33 K9 45 20N 36 20 E
Kerchenskiy Proliv,
  Black Sea .... 33 K9 45 10N 36 30 E
Kerchoual, Mali .... 83 B5 17 12N 0 20 E
Kerempe Burnu, Turkey 72 A5 42 2N 33 20 E
Keren, Eritrea ...... 81 D4 15 45N 38 28 E
Kerewan, Gambia .. 82 C1 13 29N 16 10W
Kerguelen, Ind. Oc. . 3 G13 49 15 S 69 10 E
Keri, Greece .... 46 D2 37 40N 20 49 E
Keri Kera, Sudan ... 81 E3 12 21N 32 42 E
Kericho, Kenya ..... 86 C4 0 22 S 35 15 E
Kerinci, Indonesia .. 62 E2 1 40 S 101 15 E
Kerki, Turkmenistan 52 F7 37 50N 65 12 E
Kerkínitis, Límni,
  Greece .... 44 E7 41 12N 23 10 E
Kérkira, Greece .... 49 A3 39 38N 19 50 E
Kérkira □, Greece .. 46 B1 39 37N 19 50 E
Kérkira ✈ (CFU),
  Greece .... 46 B1 39 35N 19 54 E
Kerkouane, Tunisia . 42 F4 36 58N 11 2 E
Kerkrade, Neths. ... 17 D6 50 53N 6 4 E
Kerma, Sudan ...... 80 D3 19 33N 30 32 E
Kermadec Is., Pac. Oc. 96 L10 30 0 S 178 15W
Kermadec Trench,
  Pac. Oc. .... 96 L10 30 30 S 176 0W
Kermān, Iran .... 71 D8 30 15N 57 1 E
Kerman, U.S.A. 110 J6 36 43N 120 4W
Kermān □, Iran .... 71 D8 30 0N 57 0 E
Kermān, Bīābān-e, Iran 71 D8 28 45N 59 45 E
Kermānshāh =
  Bākhtarān, Iran ... 70 C5 34 23N 47 0 E
Kermen, Bulgaria ... 45 D10 42 30N 26 16 E
Kermit, U.S.A. 113 K3 31 52N 103 6W
Kern →, U.S.A. 111 K7 35 16N 119 18W
Kernhof, Austria .... 26 D8 47 49N 15 32 E
Kernow = Cornwall □,
  U.K. 15 G3 50 26N 4 40W
Kernville, U.S.A. ... 111 K8 35 45N 118 26W
Keroh, Malaysia .... 65 K3 5 43N 101 1 E
Kérou, Benin ...... 83 C5 10 50N 2 5 E
Kérouane, Guinea .. 82 D3 9 15N 9 0W
Kerpen, Germany ... 24 E2 50 51N 6 41 E
Kerrera, U.K. 13 E3 56 24N 5 33W
Kerrobert, Canada .. 103 C7 51 56N 109 8W
Kerrville, U.S.A. ... 113 K5 30 3N 99 8W
Kerry □, Ireland ... 12 D2 52 7N 9 35W
Kerry Hd., Ireland .. 12 D2 52 25N 9 56W
Kersa, Ethiopia .... 81 F5 9 28N 41 48 E
Kerulen →, Asia ... 60 B6 48 48N 117 0 E
Kervo = Kerava, Finland 9 F21 60 25N 25 5 E
Kerzaz, Algeria 78 C5 29 29N 1 37W
Kesagami →, Canada 104 B4 51 40N 79 45W
Kesagami L., Canada 104 B3 50 23N 80 15W
Keşan, Turkey ...... 45 F10 40 49N 26 38 E
Kesennuma, Japan .. 54 E10 38 54N 141 35 E
Keshit, Iran .... 71 D8 29 43N 58 17 E
Keşiş Dağ, Turkey .. 73 C8 39 47N 39 46 E
Keskin, Turkey ..... 72 C5 39 40N 33 36 E
Kestell, S. Africa ... 89 D4 28 17 S 28 42 E
Kestenga, Russia ... 52 C4 65 50N 31 45 E
Keswick, U.K. 14 C4 54 36N 3 8W
Keszthely, Hungary . 28 D2 46 50N 17 15 E
Ket →, Russia ..... 52 D9 58 55N 81 32 E
Keta, Ghana .... 83 D5 5 49N 1 0 E
Keta Lagoon, Ghana 83 D5 5 50N 0 55 E
Ketapang, Bali,
  Indonesia .... 63 J17 8 9 S 114 23 E
Ketapang, Kalimantan,
  Indonesia .... 62 E4 1 55 S 110 0 E
Ketchenery, Russia . 35 G7 47 18N 44 32 E
Ketchikan, U.S.A. .. 102 B2 55 21N 131 39W
Ketchum, U.S.A. ... 108 E6 43 41N 114 22W
Kete Krachi, Ghana . 83 D4 7 46N 0 1W
Ketef, Khalig Umm el,
  Egypt .... 70 F2 23 40N 35 35 E
Keti Bandar, Pakistan 68 G2 24 8N 67 27 E
Kétou, Benin ...... 83 D5 7 25N 2 45 E
Ketri, India .... 68 E6 28 1N 75 50 E
Kętrzyn, Poland .... 30 D8 54 7N 21 22 E
Kettering, U.K. 15 E7 52 24N 0 43W
Kettering, U.S.A. ... 114 F3 39 41N 84 10W
Kettle →, Canada .. 103 B11 56 40N 89 34W
Kettle Falls, U.S.A. . 108 B4 48 37N 118 3W
Kettle Pt., Canada .. 116 C2 43 13N 82 1W
Kettleman City, U.S.A. 110 J7 36 1N 119 58W
Kęty, Poland .... 31 J6 49 51N 19 16 E
Keuka L., U.S.A. ... 116 D7 42 30N 77 9W
Keuruu, Finland .... 9 E21 62 16N 24 41 E
Kevelaer, Germany . 24 D2 51 36N 6 15 E
Kewanee, U.S.A. ... 112 E10 41 14N 89 56W
Kewaunee, U.S.A. .. 114 C2 44 27N 87 31W
Keweenaw B., U.S.A. 114 B1 47 0N 88 15W
Keweenaw Pen., U.S.A. 114 B2 47 30N 88 0W
Keweenaw Pt., U.S.A. 114 B2 47 25N 87 43W
Key Largo, U.S.A. .. 115 N5 25 5N 80 27W
Key West, U.S.A. ... 107 F10 24 33N 81 48W
Keyala, Sudan ..... 81 G3 4 27N 32 52 E
Keynsham, U.K. 15 F5 51 24N 2 29W
Keyser, U.S.A. 114 F6 39 26N 78 59W
Kezhma, Russia .... 53 D11 58 59N 101 9 E
Kežmarok, Slovak Rep. 27 B13 49 10N 20 28 E
Kgalagadi
  Transfrontier △,
  Africa .... 88 D3 25 10 S 21 0 E
Khabarovsk, Russia . 53 E14 48 30N 135 5 E
Khabr, Iran .... 71 D8 28 51N 56 22 E
Khābūr →, Syria ... 70 C4 35 17N 40 35 E
Khachmas = Xaçmaz,
  Azerbaijan .... 35 K9 41 31N 48 42 E
Khachrod, India .... 68 H6 23 25N 75 20 E
Khadari, W. el →,
  Sudan .... 81 E2 10 29N 27 15 E
Khadro, Pakistan ... 68 F3 26 11N 68 50 E
Khadyzhensk, Russia 35 H4 44 26N 39 32 E
Khadzhilyangar, China 69 B8 35 45N 79 20 E
Khaga, India .... 69 G9 25 47N 81 7 E
Khagaria, India .... 69 G12 25 30N 86 32 E
Khaipur, Pakistan .. 68 E5 29 34N 72 17 E
Khair, India .... 68 F7 27 57N 77 46 E
Khairabad, India ... 69 F9 27 33N 80 47 E
Khairagarh, India .. 69 J9 21 27N 81 2 E
Khairpur, Pakistan .. 68 F3 27 32N 68 49 E
Khairpur Nathan Shah,
  Pakistan .... 68 F2 27 6N 67 44 E
Khairwara, India ... 68 H5 23 58N 73 38 E
Khaisor →, Pakistan 68 D3 31 17N 68 59 E
Khajuri Kach, Pakistan 68 C3 32 4N 69 51 E
Khakassia □, Russia 52 D9 53 0N 90 0 E

Khakhea, Botswana .... 88 C3 24 48 S 23 22 E
Khalafābād, Iran ...... 71 D6 30 54N 49 24 E
Khalilabad, India ...... 69 F10 26 48N 83 5 E
Khalīl, Iran .... 71 E10 27 38N 53 17 E
Khalkhāl, Iran .... 71 B6 37 37N 48 32 E
Khálki, Dhodhekánisos,
  Greece .... 47 E9 36 17N 27 35 E
Khálki, Thessalía,
  Greece .... 46 B4 39 36N 22 30 E
Khalkidhikí □, Greece .. 44 F7 40 25N 23 20 E
Khalkís, Greece .... 46 C5 38 27N 23 42 E
Khalmer Yu, Russia .... 52 C7 67 58N 65 1 E
Khalūf, Oman .... 75 C6 20 30N 58 13 E
Kham Keut, Laos ...... 64 C5 18 15N 104 43 E
Khamaria, India .... 69 H9 23 5N 80 48 E
Khambhaliya, India .... 68 H3 22 14N 69 41 E
Khambhat, India .... 68 H5 22 23N 72 33 E
Khambhat, G. of, India 66 J8 20 45N 72 30 E
Khamilonísion, Greece .. 47 F8 35 50N 26 15 E
Khamir, Iran .... 71 E7 26 57N 55 36 E
Khamir, Yemen .... 75 D3 16 2N 44 0 E
Khamsa, Egypt .... 74 E1 30 27N 32 23 E
Khan —, Namibia ..... 88 C2 22 37S 14 56 E
Khān Abū Shāmat, Syria 74 B5 33 39N 36 53 E
Khān Azād, Iraq ...... 70 C5 33 7N 44 22 E
Khān Mujiddah, Iraq ... 70 C4 32 21N 43 48 E
Khān Shaykhūn, Syria .. 70 C3 35 26N 36 38 E
Khān Yūnis, Gaza Strip 74 D3 31 21N 34 18 E
Khanai, Pakistan ...... 68 D2 30 30N 67 8 E
Khānaqīn, Iraq .... 70 C5 34 23N 45 25 E
Khānbāghī, Iran .... 71 B7 36 10N 55 25 E
Khandrá, Greece .... 47 F8 35 3N 26 10 E
Khandwa, India .... 66 J10 21 49N 76 22 E
Khandyga, Russia ...... 53 C14 62 42N 135 35 E
Khāneh, Iran .... 70 B5 36 41N 45 8 E
Khanewal, Pakistan .... 68 D4 30 20N 71 55 E

Khangah Dogran,
  Pakistan .... 68 D5 31 50N 73 37 E
Khanh Duong, Vietnam 64 F7 12 44N 108 44 E
Khaniá, Greece .... 49 D6 35 30N 24 4 E
Khaniá □, Greece ..... 49 D6 35 30N 24 0 E
Khaniadhana, India .... 68 G8 25 1N 78 8 E
Khaníon, Kólpos, Greece 49 D5 35 33N 23 55 E
Khanka, L., Asia ..... 53 E14 45 0N 132 24 E
Khankendy = Xankändi,
  Azerbaijan .... 70 B5 39 52N 46 49 E
Khanna, India .... 68 D7 30 42N 76 16 E
Khanozai, Pakistan .... 68 D2 30 37N 67 19 E
Khanpur, Pakistan ..... 68 E4 28 42N 70 35 E
Khanty-Mansiysk,
  Russia .... 52 C7 61 0N 69 0 E
Khao Laem △, Thailand 64 E2 14 56N 98 31 E
Khao Laem Res.,
  Thailand .... 64 E2 14 50N 98 30 E
Khao Luang △, Thailand 65 H2 8 34N 99 42 E
Khao Phlu, Thailand .. 65 b 9 29N 99 59 E
Khao Pu-Khao Ya △,
  Thailand .... 65 J2 7 26N 99 57 E
Khao Sam Roi Yot △,
  Thailand .... 65 F2 12 13N 99 57 E
Khao Sok △, Thailand . 65 H2 8 55N 98 38 E
Khao Yai △, Thailand . 64 E3 14 21N 101 29 E
Khaoen Si Nakarin △,
  Thailand .... 64 E2 14 47N 99 0 E
Khapalu, Pakistan ..... 69 B7 35 10N 76 20 E
Khapcheranga, Russia .. 53 E12 49 42N 112 24 E
Kharabali, Russia ..... 35 G8 47 25N 47 15 E
Kharaghoda, India ..... 68 H4 23 11N 71 46 E
Kharagpur, India ...... 69 H12 22 20N 87 25 E
Kharax, Greece .... 49 D7 35 1N 25 7 E
Kharan Kalat, Pakistan 66 E4 28 34N 65 21 E
Kharānaq, Iran .... 71 C7 32 20N 54 45 E
Kharda, India .... 66 K9 18 40N 75 34 E
Khardung La, India .... 69 B7 34 20N 77 43 E
Kharg = Khārk, Jazīreh-
  ye, Iran .... 71 D6 29 15N 50 28 E
Khárga, El Wâhât-el,
  Egypt .... 80 B3 25 10N 30 35 E
Khargon, India .... 66 J9 21 45N 75 40 E
Khari —, India .... 68 G6 25 54N 74 31 E
Kharian, Pakistan ..... 68 C5 32 49N 73 52 E
Kharit, Wadi el —,
  Egypt .... 80 C3 24 26N 33 3 E
Khārk, Jazīreh-ye, Iran 71 D6 29 15N 50 28 E
Kharkiv, Ukraine ...... 33 H9 49 58N 36 20 E
Kharkov = Kharkiv,
  Ukraine .... 33 H9 49 58N 36 20 E
Kharmanli, Bulgaria ... 45 E9 41 55N 25 55 E
Kharovsk, Russia ...... 32 C11 59 56N 40 13 E
Kharsawan, India ..... 69 H11 22 48N 85 50 E
Kharta, Turkey .... 72 B3 40 55N 29 7 E
Khartoum = El
  Khartûm, Sudan .... 81 D3 15 31N 32 35 E
Khasan, Russia .... 54 C5 42 25N 130 40 E
Khasavyurt, Russia .... 35 J8 43 16N 46 40 E
Khāsh, Iran .... 66 E2 28 15N 61 15 E
Khashm el Girba, Sudan 81 E4 14 59N 35 58 E
Khashum, Sudan ...... 81 E2 12 27N 28 2 E
Khashuri, Georgia ..... 35 J6 42 1N 43 35 E
Khaskovo, Bulgaria .... 45 E9 41 56N 25 30 E
Khaskovo □, Bulgaria .. 45 E9 41 50N 25 40 E
Khatanga, Russia ..... 53 B11 72 0N 102 20 E
Khatanga —, Russia .. 53 B11 72 55N 106 0 E
Khatauli, India .... 68 E7 29 17N 77 43 E
Khatra, India .... 69 H12 22 59N 86 51 E
Khātūnābād, Iran ..... 71 D7 30 1N 55 25 E
Khatyrka, Russia ..... 53 C18 62 3N 175 15 E
Khavda, India .... 68 H3 23 51N 69 43 E
Khaybar, Ḥarrat,
  Si. Arabia .... 70 E4 25 45N 40 0 E
Khayelitsha, S. Africa .. 85 L3 34 5S 18 42 E
Khāzimiyah, Iraq ..... 70 C4 34 46N 43 37 E
Khazzan Jabal al
  Awliyâ, Sudan ..... 81 D3 15 24N 32 20 E
Khe Bo, Vietnam ..... 64 C5 19 8N 104 41 E
Khe Long, Vietnam ... 64 D6 16 37N 106 45 E
Khed Brahma, India ... 68 G5 24 7N 73 5 E
Khekra, India .... 68 E7 28 52N 77 20 E
Khemarak Phouminville,
  Cambodia .... 65 G4 11 37N 102 59 E
Khemisset, Morocco ... 78 B4 33 50N 6 1W
Khemmarat, Thailand .. 64 D5 16 10N 105 15 E
Khenāmān, Iran ...... 71 D8 30 27N 56 29 E
Khenchela, Algeria .... 78 A7 35 28N 7 11 E
Khersān —, Iran ..... 71 D6 31 33N 50 2 E
Khérson, Greece ...... 44 E6 41 5N 22 47 E
Kherson, Ukraine ..... 33 J7 46 35N 32 35 E
Khersónisos Akrotíri,
  Greece .... 49 D6 35 30N 24 10 E
Khérson —, Russia ... 53 B11 71 54N 102 6 E
Khewari, Pakistan ..... 68 F3 26 36N 68 52 E
Khilchipur, India ..... 68 G7 24 2N 76 34 E
Khiliomódhion, Greece .. 46 D4 37 48N 22 51 E
Khimki, Russia .... 32 E9 55 50N 37 20 E
Khíos, Greece .... 47 C8 38 27N 26 9 E

Khíos □, Greece ...... 47 C8 38 27N 26 9 E
Khirsadoh, India ...... 69 H8 22 11N 78 47 E
Khiuma = Hiiumaa,
  Estonia .... 9 G20 58 50N 22 45 E
Khiva, Uzbekistan .... 52 E7 41 30N 60 18 E
Khīyāv, Iran .... 70 B5 38 30N 47 45 E
Khlebarovo, Bulgaria .. 45 C10 43 37N 26 15 E
Khlong Khlung,
  Thailand .... 64 D2 16 12N 99 43 E
Khmelnik, Ukraine .... 33 H4 49 33N 27 58 E
Khmelnitskiy =
  Khmelnytskyy,
  Ukraine .... 33 H4 49 23N 27 0 E
Khmelnytskyy, Ukraine 33 H4 49 23N 27 0 E
Khmer Rep. =
  Cambodia ■, Asia .. 64 F5 12 15N 105 0 E
Khoai, Hon, Vietnam .. 65 H5 8 26N 104 50 E
Khodoriv, Ukraine .... 33 H3 49 24N 24 19 E
Khodzent = Khŭjand,
  Tajikistan .... 52 E7 40 17N 69 37 E
Khojak Pass, Afghan. .. 68 D2 30 51N 66 34 E
Khok Kloi, Thailand .. 65 a 8 17N 98 19 E
Khok Pho, Thailand .. 65 J3 6 43N 101 6 E
Kholm, Russia .... 32 D6 57 10N 31 15 E
Kholmsk, Russia ...... 53 E15 47 40N 142 5 E
Khomas Hochland,
  Namibia .... 88 C2 22 40S 16 0 E
Khombole, Senegal 82 C1 14 43N 16 42W
Khomeyn, Iran .... 71 C6 33 40N 50 7 E
Khomeynī Shahr, Iran . 71 C6 32 41N 51 31 E
Khomodino, Botswana . 88 C3 22 46S 23 52 E
Khon Kaen, Thailand .. 64 D4 16 30N 102 47 E
Khong —, Cambodia .. 64 F5 13 32N 105 58 E
Khong Sedone, Laos ... 64 E5 15 34N 105 49 E
Khonuu, Russia .... 53 C15 66 30N 143 12 E
Khoper —, Russia .... 34 F6 49 30N 42 20 E
Khor el 'Atash, Sudan . 81 E3 13 20N 34 15 E
Khóra, Greece .... 46 D3 37 3N 21 42 E
Khóra Sfakíon, Greece . 49 D6 35 15N 24 9 E
Khorāsān □, Iran ..... 71 C8 34 0N 58 0 E
Khorat = Nakhon
  Ratchasima, Thailand 64 E4 14 59N 102 12 E
Khorat, Cao Nguyen,
  Thailand .... 64 E4 15 30N 102 50 E
Khorixas, Namibia .... 88 C1 20 16S 14 59 E
Khorol, Ukraine ...... 33 H7 49 48N 33 15 E
Khorramābād,
  Khorāsān, Iran ..... 71 C8 35 6N 57 57 E
Khorramābād, Lorestān,
  Iran .... 71 C6 33 30N 48 25 E
Khorrāmshahr, Iran ... 71 D6 30 29N 48 15 E
Khorugh, Tajikistan ... 52 F8 37 30N 71 36 E
Khosravī, Iran .... 71 D6 30 48N 51 28 E
Khosrowābād,
  Khuzestān, Iran .... 71 D6 30 10N 48 25 E
Khosrowābād,
  Kordestān, Iran .... 70 C5 35 31N 47 38 E
Khost, Pakistan ...... 68 D2 30 13N 67 35 E
Khosūyeh, Iran .... 71 D7 28 32N 54 26 E
Khotyn, Ukraine ...... 29 B11 48 31N 26 27 E
Khouribga, Morocco ... 78 B4 32 58N 6 57W
Khowst, Afghan. ..... 68 C3 33 22N 69 58 E
Khowst □, Afghan. ... 66 C6 33 20N 70 0 E
Khoyniki, Belarus ..... 33 G5 51 54N 29 55 E
Khrami —, Georgia ... 35 K7 41 25N 45 0 E
Khrenovoye, Russia ... 34 E5 51 4N 40 16 E
Khrisoúpolis, Greece .. 45 F8 40 58N 24 42 E
Khristianá, Greece .... 47 E7 36 14N 25 13 E
Khrysokhou B., Cyprus 49 D11 35 6N 32 25 E
Khtapodhiá, Greece ... 47 D7 37 24N 25 34 E
Khu Khan, Thailand .. 64 E5 14 42N 104 12 E
Khuan Wa, Thailand .. 65 a 7 53N 98 17 E
Khudzhand = Khŭjand,
  Tajikistan .... 52 E7 40 17N 69 37 E
Khuff, Si. Arabia ..... 70 E5 24 55N 44 53 E
Khūgīānī, Afghan. .... 68 D2 31 34N 66 32 E
Khuis, Botswana ...... 88 D3 26 40S 21 49 E
Khuiyala, India ...... 68 F4 27 9N 70 25 E
Khŭjand, Tajikistan ... 52 E7 40 17N 69 37 E
Khujner, India .... 68 H7 23 47N 76 36 E
Khulna, Bangla. ...... 67 H16 22 45N 89 34 E
Khulna □, Bangla. .... 67 H16 22 25N 89 35 E
Khulo, Georgia .... 35 K6 41 33N 42 19 E
Khumago, Botswana ... 88 C3 20 26S 24 32 E
Khūnsorkh, Iran ...... 71 E8 27 9N 56 7 E
Khunti, India .... 69 H11 23 5N 85 17 E
Khūr, Iran .... 71 C8 32 55N 58 18 E
Khurai, India .... 68 G8 24 3N 78 23 E
Khurayṣ, Si. Arabia ... 71 E6 25 6N 48 2 E
Khureit, Sudan .... 81 E2 13 5N 26 3 E
Khurīya Murīya, Jazā'ir,
  Oman .... 75 D6 17 30N 55 58 E
Khurja, India .... 68 E7 28 15N 77 58 E
Khūrmāl, Iraq .... 70 C5 35 18N 46 2 E
Khurr, Wādi al, Iraq .. 70 C4 32 3N 43 52 E
Khūsf, Iran .... 71 C8 32 46N 58 53 E
Khush, Afghan. ...... 66 C3 32 55N 62 10 E
Khushab, Pakistan .... 68 C5 32 20N 72 20 E
Khust, Ukraine .... 29 B8 48 10N 23 18 E
Khutse △, Botswana .. 88 C3 23 31 S 24 12 E
Khuzdar, Pakistan .... 68 F2 27 52N 66 30 E
Khūzestān □, Iran .... 71 D6 31 0N 49 0 E
Khvāf, Iran .... 71 C9 34 33N 60 8 E
Khvājeh, Iran .... 70 B5 38 9N 46 35 E
Khvalynsk, Russia .... 34 D9 52 30N 48 2 E
Khvānsār, Iran .... 71 D7 29 56N 54 8 E
Khvatovka, Russia .... 34 D8 52 24N 46 32 E
Khvor, Iran .... 71 C7 33 45N 55 0 E
Khvorgū, Iran .... 71 E8 27 34N 56 27 E
Khvormūj, Iran .... 71 D6 28 40N 51 30 E
Khvoy, Iran .... 70 B5 38 35N 45 0 E
Khvoynaya, Russia .... 32 C8 58 58N 34 28 E
Khyber Pass, Afghan. .. 68 B4 34 10N 71 8 E
Khyriv, Ukraine ...... 28 49 32N 22 50 E
Kiabukwa, Dem. Rep. of
  the Congo .... 87 D1 8 40S 24 48 E
Kiama, Australia ..... 95 E5 34 40S 150 50 E
Kiamba, Phil. .... 61 H6 6 2N 124 46 E
Kiambi, Dem. Rep. of
  the Congo .... 86 D2 7 15S 28 0 E
Kiambu, Kenya .... 86 C4 1 8S 36 50 E
Kiang West △, Gambia 82 C1 13 15N 15 50W
Kiangara, Madag. ..... 89 B8 17 58 S 47 2 E
Kiangsi = Jiangxi □,
  China .... 59 D11 27 30N 116 0 E
Kiangsu = Jiangsu □,
  China .... 57 H11 33 0N 120 0 E
Kiáton, Greece .... 46 C4 38 1N 22 45 E
Kibæk, Denmark ...... 11 H2 56 2N 8 51 E
Kibale △, Uganda .... 86 B3 0 16N 30 18 E
Kibanga Port, Uganda . 86 B3 0 10N 32 58 E
Kibara, Tanzania ..... 86 C3 2 8S 33 30 E
Kibare, Mts., Dem. Rep.
  of the Congo ...... 86 D2 8 25 S 27 10 E
Kibira △, Burundi .... 86 C2 3 6S 30 24 E
Kibombo, Dem. Rep. of
  the Congo .... 86 C2 3 57S 25 53 E

Kibondo, Tanzania .... 86 C3 3 35 S 30 45 E
Kibre Mengist, Ethiopia 81 F4 5 54N 38 59 E
Kibumbu, Burundi .... 86 C2 3 32 S 29 45 E
Kibungo, Rwanda ..... 86 C3 2 10S 30 32 E
Kibuye, Burundi ...... 86 C2 3 39 S 29 59 E
Kibuye, Rwanda ...... 86 C2 2 3S 29 21 E
Kibwesa, Tanzania .... 86 D2 6 30S 29 58 E
Kibwezi, Kenya ...... 86 C4 2 27 S 37 57 E
Kicasalih, Turkey ..... 45 E10 41 23N 26 48 E
Kičevo, Macedonia .... 44 E4 41 34N 20 59 E
Kichha, India .... 69 E8 28 53N 79 30 E
Kichha —, India ..... 69 E8 28 41N 79 18 E
Kicking Horse Pass,
  Canada 102 C5 51 28N 116 16W
Kidal, Mali .... 83 B5 18 26N 1 22 E
Kidderminster, U.K. .. 15 E5 52 24N 2 15W
Kidepo Valley △,
  Uganda .... 86 B3 3 52N 33 50 E
Kidete, Tanzania ..... 86 D4 6 25 S 37 17 E
Kidira, Senegal 82 C2 14 28N 12 13W
Kidnappers, C., N.Z. .. 91 H6 39 38 S 177 5 E
Kidsgrove, U.K. 14 D5 53 5N 2 14W
Kidston, Australia .... 94 B3 18 52 S 144 8 E
Kidugallo, Tanzania ... 86 D4 6 49 S 38 15 E
Kiel, Germany .... 24 A6 54 19N 10 8 E
Kiel Canal = Nord-
  Ostsee-Kanal,
  Germany .... 24 A5 54 12N 9 32 E
Kielce, Poland .... 31 H7 50 52N 20 42 E
Kielder Water, U.K. ... 14 B5 55 11N 2 31W
Kieler Bucht, Germany 24 A6 54 35N 10 25 E
Kiembara, Burkina Faso 82 C4 13 15N 2 44W
Kien Binh, Vietnam ... 65 H5 9 55N 105 19 E
Kien Tan, Vietnam ... 65 G5 10 7N 105 17 E
Kienge, Dem. Rep. of
  the Congo .... 87 E2 10 30S 27 30 E
Kiessé, Niger .... 83 C5 13 29N 4 1 E
Kiev = Kyyiv, Ukraine . 33 G6 50 30N 30 28 E
Kifaya, Guinea 82 C2 12 10N 13 4W
Kiffa, Mauritania 82 B2 16 37N 11 24W
Kifisiá, Greece .... 46 C5 38 4N 23 49 E
Kifissós —, Greece ... 46 C5 38 35N 23 20 E
Kifrī, Iraq .... 70 C5 34 45N 45 0 E
Kigali, Rwanda .... 86 C3 1 59 S 30 4 E
Kigarama, Tanzania ... 86 C3 1 1S 31 50 E
Kigelle, Sudan .... 81 F3 8 40N 34 2 E
Kigezi □, Uganda ..... 86 C2 0 34 S 29 55 E
Kigoma □, Tanzania .. 86 D3 5 0S 30 0 E
Kigoma-Ujiji, Tanzania 86 C2 4 55 S 29 36 E
Kigomasha, Ras,
  Tanzania .... 86 C4 4 58 S 38 58 E
Kığzı, Turkey .... 70 B4 38 18N 43 25 E
Kihei, U.S.A. 106 H16 20 47N 156 28W
Kihnu, Estonia .... 9 G21 58 9N 24 1 E
Kii-Sanchi, Japan ..... 55 G8 34 20N 136 0 E
Kii-Suidō, Japan ..... 55 H7 33 40N 134 45 E
Kikaiga-Shima, Japan . 55 K4 28 19N 129 59 E
Kikinda, Serbia & M. .. 28 E5 45 50N 20 30 E
Kikládhes, Greece .... 46 E6 37 0N 24 30 E
Kikládhes □, Greece .. 46 E6 37 0N 25 0 E
Kikwit, Dem. Rep. of
  the Congo .... 84 E3 5 0S 18 45 E
Kil, Sweden .... 10 E7 59 30N 13 20 E
Kilafors, Sweden ..... 10 C10 61 14N 16 36 E
Kilar, India .... 68 C7 33 6N 76 25 E
Kilauea Crater, U.S.A. . 106 J17 19 25N 155 17W
Kilbrannan Sd., U.K. .. 13 F3 55 37N 5 26W
Kilchu, N. Korea ..... 57 D15 40 57N 129 25 E
Kilcoy, Australia ..... 95 D5 26 59 S 152 30 E
Kildare, Ireland 12 C5 53 10N 6 55W
Kildare □, Ireland 12 C5 53 10N 6 50W
Kilfinnane, Ireland ... 12 D3 52 21N 8 28W
Kilgore, U.S.A. 113 J7 32 23N 94 53W
Kilibo, Benin .... 83 D5 8 32N 2 38 E
Kilifi, Kenya .... 86 C4 3 40S 39 48 E
Kilimanjaro, Tanzania . 86 C4 3 7S 37 20 E
Kilimanjaro □, Tanzania 86 C4 4 0S 38 0 E
Kilimli, Turkey ...... 72 B4 41 28N 31 50 E
Kilindini, Kenya ..... 86 C4 4 4S 39 40 E
Kilis, Turkey .... 70 B3 36 42N 37 6 E
Kiliya, Ukraine ...... 29 E14 45 28N 29 16 E
Kilkee, Ireland 12 D2 52 41N 9 39W
Kilkeel, U.K. 12 B5 54 4N 6 0W
Kilkenny, Ireland 12 D4 52 39N 7 15W
Kilkenny □, Ireland ... 12 D4 52 35N 7 15W
Kilkieran B., Ireland .. 12 C2 53 20N 9 41W
Kilkís, Greece .... 44 E6 40 58N 22 57 E
Kilkís □, Greece ..... 44 E6 41 5N 22 50 E
Killala, Ireland 12 B2 54 13N 9 12W
Killala B., Ireland 12 B2 54 16N 9 8W
Killaloe, Canada 116 A7 45 33N 77 25W
Killaloe, Ireland 12 D3 52 48N 8 28W
Killarney, Australia ... 95 D5 28 20 S 152 18 E
Killarney, Canada 103 D9 49 10N 99 40W
Killarney, Ireland 12 D2 52 4N 9 30W
Killarney △, Ireland .. 12 D2 52 0N 9 33W
Killary Harbour, Ireland 12 C2 53 38N 9 52W
Killdeer, U.S.A. 112 B3 47 26N 102 48W
Killeberg, Sweden .... 11 H8 56 14N 14 1 E
Killeen, U.S.A. 113 K6 31 7N 97 44W
Killin, U.K. 13 E4 56 28N 4 19W
Killíni, Ilía, Greece ... 46 D3 37 55N 21 8 E
Killíni, Korinthía, Greece 46 D4 37 54N 22 25 E
Killorglin, Ireland 12 D2 52 6N 9 47W
Killybegs, Ireland 12 B3 54 38N 8 26W
Kilmarnock, U.K. 13 F4 55 37N 4 29W
Kilmez, Russia .... 34 B10 56 58N 50 55 E
Kilmez —, Russia .... 34 B10 56 58N 50 28 E
Kilmore, Australia .... 95 F3 37 25 S 144 53 E
Kilondo, Tanzania .... 87 D4 9 45 S 34 20 E
Kilosa, Tanzania ..... 86 D4 6 48 S 37 0 E
Kilrush, Ireland 12 D2 52 38N 9 29W
Kilwa Kisiwani,
  Tanzania .... 87 D4 8 58 S 39 32 E
Kilwa Kivinje, Tanzania 87 D4 8 45 S 39 25 E
Kilwa Masoko, Tanzania 87 D4 8 55 S 39 30 E
Kilwinning, U.K. 13 F4 55 39N 4 43W
Kim, U.S.A. 113 G3 37 15N 103 21W
Kim —, Cameroon ... 83 D7 5 28N 11 7 E
Kimaam, Indonesia ... 63 F9 7 58 S 138 53 E
Kimamba, Tanzania ... 86 D4 6 45 S 37 10 E
Kimba, Australia ..... 95 E2 33 8S 136 23 E
Kimball, Nebr., U.S.A. 112 E3 41 14N 103 40W
Kimball, S. Dak., U.S.A. 112 D5 43 45N 98 57W
Kimberley, Australia .. 92 C4 16 20 S 127 0 E
Kimberley, Canada 102 D5 49 40N 115 59W
Kimberley, S. Africa .. 88 D3 28 43 S 24 46 E
Kimberly, U.S.A. 108 E6 42 32N 114 22W
Kimch'aek, N. Korea . 57 D15 40 40N 129 10 E
Kimch'ŏn, S. Korea .. 57 F15 36 11N 128 4 E
Kími, Greece .... 46 C6 38 38N 24 6 E
Kimje, S. Korea ...... 57 G14 35 48N 126 45 E
Kimmirut, Canada 101 B13 62 50N 69 50W
Kímolos, Greece ..... 46 E6 36 48N 24 37 E
Kimovsk, Moskva,
  Russia .... 32 E9 55 21N 37 28 E

Kimovsk, Tula, Russia . 32 E10 54 0N 38 29 E
Kimparana, Mali 82 C4 12 48N 5 0W
Kimpese, Dem. Rep. of
  the Congo .... 84 F2 5 35 S 14 26 E
Kimry, Russia .... 32 D9 56 55N 37 15 E
Kimstad, Sweden ..... 11 F9 58 35N 15 58 E
Kinabalu, Gunong,
  Malaysia .... 62 C5 6 3N 116 14 E
Kínaros, Greece ...... 47 E8 36 59N 26 15 E
Kinaskan L., Canada .. 102 B2 57 38N 130 8W
Kinbasket L., Canada . 102 C5 52 0N 118 10W
Kincardine, Canada ... 116 B3 44 10N 81 40W
Kincolith, Canada 102 C3 55 0N 129 57W
Kinda, Dem. Rep. of
  the Congo .... 87 D2 9 18 S 25 4 E
Kindberg, Austria .... 26 D8 47 30N 15 27 E
Kinde, U.S.A. 116 C2 43 56N 83 0W
Kinder Scout, U.K. ... 14 D6 53 24N 1 52W
Kindersley, Canada ... 103 C7 51 30N 109 10W
Kindia, Guinea 82 D2 10 0N 12 52W
Kindu, Dem. Rep. of
  the Congo .... 86 C2 2 55 S 25 50 E
Kinel, Russia .... 34 D10 53 15N 50 40 E
Kineshma, Russia .... 34 B6 57 30N 42 5 E
Kinesi, Tanzania ..... 86 C3 1 25 S 33 50 E
King, L., Australia .... 93 F2 33 10 S 119 35 E
King, Mt., Australia ... 94 D4 25 10 S 147 30 E
King City, U.S.A. 110 J5 36 13N 121 8W
King Cr. —, Australia 94 C2 24 35 S 139 30 E
King Edward —,
  Australia .... 92 B4 14 14 S 126 35 E
King Frederick VI
  Land = Kong Frederik
  VI Kyst, Greenland . 101 B15 63 0N 43 0W
King George B., Falk. Is. 128 G4 51 30 S 60 30W
King George I.,
  Antarctica 5 C18 60 0S 60 0W
King George Is., Canada 101 C11 57 20N 80 30W
King I. = Kadan Kyun,
  Burma .... 64 F2 12 30N 98 20 E
King I., Australia ..... 95 F3 39 50 S 144 0 E
King I., Canada 102 C3 52 10N 127 40W
King Leopold Ranges,
  Australia .... 92 C4 17 30 S 125 45 E
King of Prussia, U.S.A. 117 F9 40 5N 75 23W
King Sd., Australia ... 92 C3 16 50 S 123 20 E
King Sejong, Antarctica 5 C18 62 30 S 58 0W
King William I., Canada 100 B10 69 10N 97 25W
King William's Town,
  S. Africa .... 88 E4 32 51 S 27 22 E
Kingait = Cape Dorset,
  Canada 101 B12 64 14N 76 32W
Kingaok = Bathurst
  Inlet, Canada 100 B9 66 50N 108 1W
Kingaroy, Australia ... 95 D5 26 32 S 151 51 E
Kingfisher, U.S.A. ... 113 H6 35 52N 97 56W
Kingirbān, Iraq ...... 70 C5 34 40N 44 54 E
Kingisepp = Kuressaare,
  Estonia .... 9 G20 58 15N 22 30 E
Kingisepp, Russia .... 32 C5 59 25N 28 40 E
Kingman, Ariz., U.S.A. 111 K12 35 12N 114 4W
Kingman, Kans., U.S.A. 113 G5 37 39N 98 7W
Kingoonya, Australia .. 95 E2 30 55 S 135 19 E
Kingri, Pakistan ..... 68 D3 30 27N 69 49 E
Kings —, U.S.A. 110 J7 36 3N 119 50W
Kings Canyon △, U.S.A. 110 J8 36 50N 118 40W
Kings Mountain, U.S.A. 115 H5 35 15N 81 20W
King's Lynn, U.K. .... 14 E8 52 45N 0 24 E
Kings Park, U.S.A. ... 117 F11 40 53N 73 16W
King's Peak, U.S.A. .. 108 F8 40 46N 110 27W
Kingsbridge, U.K. 15 G4 50 17N 3 47W
Kingsburg, U.S.A. 110 J7 36 31N 119 33W
Kingscote, Australia .. 95 F2 35 40 S 137 38 E
Kingscourt, Ireland ... 12 C5 53 55N 6 48W
Kingsford, U.S.A. 114 C1 45 48N 88 4W
Kingsland, U.S.A. 115 K5 30 48N 81 41W
Kingsley, U.S.A. 112 D7 42 35N 95 58W
Kingsport, U.S.A. 115 G4 36 33N 82 33W
Kingston, Canada 116 B8 44 14N 76 30W
Kingston, Jamaica .... 120 a 18 0N 76 50W
Kingston, N.Z. .... 91 L2 45 20 S 168 43 E
Kingston, N.H., U.S.A. 117 D13 42 56N 71 3W
Kingston, N.Y., U.S.A. 117 E11 41 56N 73 59W
Kingston, Pa., U.S.A. . 117 E9 41 16N 75 54W
Kingston, R.I., U.S.A. . 117 E13 41 29N 71 30W
Kingston Pk., U.S.A. .. 111 K11 35 45N 115 54W
Kingston South East,
  Australia .... 95 F2 36 51 S 139 55 E
Kingston upon Hull,
  U.K. 14 D7 53 45N 0 21W
Kingston upon Hull □,
  U.K. 14 D7 53 45N 0 21W
Kingston-upon-
  Thames □, U.K. 15 F7 51 24N 0 17W
Kingstown, St. Vincent . 121 D7 13 10N 61 10W
Kingstree, U.S.A. 115 J6 33 40N 79 50W
Kingsville, Canada 116 D2 42 2N 82 45W
Kingsville, U.S.A. 113 M6 27 31N 97 52W
Kingussie, U.K. 13 D4 57 6N 4 2W
Kingwood, U.S.A. 113 K7 29 54N 95 18W
Kınık, Antalya, Turkey 47 E11 36 20N 29 20 E
Kınık, İzmir, Turkey .. 47 B9 39 6N 27 24 E
Kinistino, Canada 103 C7 52 57N 105 2W
Kinkala, Congo ...... 84 E2 4 18 S 14 49 E
Kinki □, Japan ...... 55 H8 33 45N 136 0 E
Kinleith, N.Z. .... 91 H5 38 20 S 175 56 E
Kinlochleven, U.K. ... 13 E4 56 43N 5 0W
Kinmount, Canada ... 116 B6 44 48N 78 45W
Kinna, Sweden ...... 11 G6 57 32N 12 42 E
Kinnairds Hd., U.K. .. 13 D6 57 43N 2 1W
Kinnarp, Sweden ..... 11 F7 58 2N 13 35 E
Kinneviken, Sweden .. 11 F7 58 35N 13 15 E
Kino, Mexico 118 B2 28 45N 111 59W
Kinoje —, Canada ... 104 B3 52 8N 81 25W
Kinomoto, Japan ..... 55 G8 35 30N 136 13 E
Kinoni, Uganda ...... 86 C3 0 41 S 30 28 E
Kinoosao, Canada 103 B8 57 5N 102 1W
Kinross, U.K. 13 E5 56 13N 3 25W
Kinsale, Ireland 12 E3 51 42N 8 31W
Kinsale, Old Hd. of,
  Ireland 12 E3 51 37N 8 33W
Kinsha = Chang
  Jiang —, China .... 59 B13 31 48N 121 10 E
Kinshasa, Dem. Rep. of
  the Congo .... 84 E3 4 20 S 15 15 E
Kinsley, U.S.A. 113 G5 37 55N 99 25W
Kinsman, U.S.A. 116 E4 41 26N 80 35W
Kintamani, Indonesia . 63 J18 8 14 S 115 19 E
Kintore, U.K. 13 D6 57 14N 2 20W
Kintore Ra., Australia . 92 D4 23 15 S 128 47 E
Kintyre, U.K. 13 F3 55 30N 5 35W
Kintyre, Mull of, U.K. . 13 F3 55 17N 5 47W
Kinushseo —, Canada 104 A3 55 15N 83 45W
Kinuso, Canada 102 B5 55 20N 115 25W

Kinyangiri, Tanzania .. 86 C3 4 25 S 34 37 E
Kinyeti, Sudan .... 81 G3 3 57N 32 54 E
Kinzig —, Germany .. 25 G3 48 36N 7 49 E
Kinzua, U.S.A. 116 E6 41 52N 78 58W
Kinzua Dam, U.S.A. . 116 E6 41 53N 79 0W
Kióni, Greece .... 46 C2 38 27N 20 41 E
Kiosk, Canada 104 C4 46 6N 78 53W
Kiowa, Kans., U.S.A. . 113 G5 37 1N 98 29W
Kiowa, Okla., U.S.A. . 113 H7 34 43N 95 54W
Kipahigan L., Canada . 103 B8 55 20N 101 55W
Kipanga, Tanzania ... 86 D4 6 15 S 35 20 E
Kiparissía, Greece .... 46 D3 37 15N 21 40 E
Kiparissiakós Kólpos,
  Greece .... 46 D3 37 25N 21 25 E
Kipawa, L., Canada ... 104 C4 46 50N 79 0W
Kipembawe, Tanzania . 86 D3 7 38 S 35 25 E
Kipengere Ra., Tanzania 87 D3 9 12 S 34 15 E
Kipili, Tanzania ...... 86 D3 7 28 S 30 32 E
Kipini, Kenya .... 86 C5 2 30 S 40 32 E
Kipling, Canada 103 C8 50 6N 102 38W
Kippure, Ireland 12 C5 53 11N 6 21W
Kipushi, Dem. Rep. of
  the Congo .... 87 E2 11 48 S 27 12 E
Kirane, Mali 82 B2 15 20N 10 20W
Kiranomena, Madag. . 89 B8 18 17 S 46 2 E
Kiraz, Turkey .... 47 C10 38 14N 28 13 E
Kirazlı, Turkey ...... 45 F10 40 2N 26 41 E
Kirchhain, Germany .. 24 E4 50 47N 8 54 E
Kirchheim, Germany .. 25 G5 48 39N 9 27 E
Kirchheimbolanden,
  Germany .... 25 F3 49 40N 8 0 E
Kirchschlag, Austria .. 27 D9 47 30N 16 19 E
Kireç, Turkey .... 47 B10 39 33N 28 22 E
Kirensk, Russia ...... 53 D11 57 50N 107 55 E
Kirghizia =
  Kyrgyzstan ■, Asia . 52 E8 42 0N 75 0 E
Kirghizstan =
  Kyrgyzstan ■, Asia . 52 E8 42 0N 75 0 E
Kiribati ■, Pac. Oc. .. 96 H10 5 0S 180 0 E
Kırıkhan, Turkey ..... 72 D7 36 31N 36 21 E
Kırıkkale, Turkey ..... 72 C5 39 51N 33 32 E
Kirillov, Russia ...... 32 C10 59 49N 38 24 E
Kirin = Jilin, China ... 57 C14 43 44N 126 30 E
Kirinyaga = Kenya, Mt.,
  Kenya .... 86 C4 0 10 S 37 18 E
Kirishi, Russia .... 32 C7 59 28N 31 59 E
Kirishima Yaku △,
  Japan .... 55 J5 31 24N 130 50 E
Kiritimati, Kiribati 97 G12 1 58N 157 27W
Kırka, Turkey .... 47 B12 39 17N 30 33 E
Kirkağaç, Turkey ..... 47 B9 39 39N 27 40 E
Kirkby, U.K. 14 D5 53 30N 2 54W
Kirkby-in-Ashfield, U.K. 14 D6 53 6N 1 14W
Kirkby Lonsdale, U.K. . 14 C5 54 12N 2 36W
Kirkby Stephen, U.K. . 14 C5 54 29N 2 21W
Kirkcaldy, U.K. 13 E5 56 7N 3 9W
Kirkcudbright, U.K. .. 13 G4 54 50N 4 2W
Kirkee, India .... 66 K8 18 34N 73 56 E
Kirkenes, Norway .... 8 B23 69 40N 30 5 E
Kirkfield, Canada 116 B6 44 34N 78 59W
Kirkintilloch, U.K. 13 F4 55 56N 4 8W
Kirkjubæjarklaustur,
  Iceland 8 E4 63 47N 18 4W
Kirkkonummi, Finland 9 F21 60 8N 24 26 E
Kirkland Lake, Canada 104 C3 48 9N 80 2W
Kırklareli, Turkey .... 45 E11 41 44N 27 15 E
Kirklareli □, Turkey .. 45 E11 41 45N 27 15 E
Kirksville, U.S.A. 112 E8 40 12N 92 35W
Kirkūk, Iraq .... 70 C5 35 30N 44 21 E
Kirkwall, U.K. 13 C6 58 59N 2 58W
Kirkwood, S. Africa .. 88 E4 33 22 S 25 15 E
Kirn, Germany .... 25 F3 49 47N 7 26 E
Kirov, Kaluga, Russia . 32 E8 54 3N 34 20 E
Kirov, Kirov, Russia .. 52 D5 58 35N 49 40 E
Kirovabad = Gäncä,
  Azerbaijan .... 35 K8 40 45N 46 20 E
Kirovograd =
  Kirovohrad, Ukraine 33 H7 48 35N 32 20 E
Kirovohrad, Ukraine .. 33 H7 48 35N 32 20 E
Kirovskiy, Astrakhan,
  Russia .... 35 H9 45 51N 48 11 E
Kirovskiy, Kamchatka,
  Russia .... 53 D16 54 27N 155 42 E
Kirovskiy, Primorsk,
  Russia .... 54 B6 45 7N 133 30 E
Kirriemuir, U.K. 13 E5 56 41N 3 1W
Kirsanov, Russia ..... 34 D6 52 35N 42 40 E
Kırşehir, Turkey ..... 70 B2 39 14N 34 5 E
Kirtachi, Niger .... 83 C5 12 52N 2 30 E
Kirthar Range, Pakistan 68 F2 27 0N 67 0 E
Kirtland, U.S.A. 109 H9 36 44N 108 21W
Kiruna, Sweden ...... 8 C19 67 52N 20 15 E
Kirundu, Dem. Rep. of
  the Congo .... 86 C2 0 50 S 25 35 E
Kirya, Russia .... 34 C8 55 5N 46 55 E
Kiryū, Japan .... 55 F9 36 24N 139 20 E
Kisa, Sweden .... 11 G9 58 0N 15 39 E
Kisaga, Tanzania ..... 86 C3 4 30 S 34 23 E
Kisalaya, Nic. 120 D3 14 40N 84 3W
Kisalföld, Hungary ... 28 C2 47 30N 17 0 E
Kisámou, Kólpos,
  Greece .... 49 D5 35 30N 23 38 E
Kisanga, Dem. Rep. of
  the Congo .... 86 B2 2 30N 26 35 E
Kisangani, Dem. Rep. of
  the Congo .... 86 B2 0 35N 25 15 E
Kisar, Indonesia ..... 63 F7 8 5S 127 10 E
Kisarawe, Tanzania ... 86 D4 6 53 S 39 0 E
Kisarazu, Japan ...... 55 G9 35 23N 139 55 E
Kisbér, Hungary ..... 28 C3 47 30N 18 2 E
Kishanganga —,
  Pakistan .... 69 B5 34 18N 73 28 E
Kishanganj, India .... 69 F13 26 3N 88 14 E
Kishangarh, Raj., India 68 F6 26 34N 74 52 E
Kishangarh, Raj., India 68 F4 27 50N 70 30 E
Kishi, Nigeria .... 83 D5 9 1N 3 52 E
Kishinev = Chişinău,
  Moldova .... 29 C13 47 2N 28 50 E
Kishiwada, Japan ..... 55 G7 34 28N 135 22 E
Kishtwar, India ...... 69 C6 33 20N 75 48 E
Kisielice, Poland ..... 30 E6 53 36N 19 16 E
Kisigo —, Tanzania .. 86 D3 6 35 S 34 17 E
Kisii, Kenya .... 86 C3 0 40 S 34 45 E
Kisiju, Tanzania ..... 86 D4 7 23 S 39 19 E
Kisir, Turkey .... 73 B10 41 0N 43 5 E
Kisizi, Uganda .... 86 C2 1 0S 29 58 E
Kiskomárom =
  Zalakomár, Hungary 28 D2 46 33N 17 10 E
Kiskőrei-víztároló,
  Hungary .... 28 C5 47 31N 20 36 E
Kiskőrös, Hungary ... 28 D4 46 37N 19 20 E
Kiskundorozsma,
  Hungary .... 28 D5 46 16N 20 5 E
Kiskunfélegyháza,
  Hungary .... 28 D4 46 42N 19 53 E
Kiskunhalas, Hungary 28 D4 46 28N 19 37 E
Kiskunmajsa, Hungary 28 D4 46 30N 19 48 E

Kiskunsági △, *Hungary* **28 D4** 46 39N 19 30 E
Kislovodsk, *Russia* **35 J6** 43 50N 42 45 E
Kismayu = Chisimaio,
  Somali Rep. **77 G8** 0 22 S 42 32 E
Kiso-Gawa →, *Japan* **55 G8** 35 20N 136 45 E
Kiso-Sammyaku, *Japan* **55 G8** 35 45N 137 45 E
Kisofukushima, *Japan* **55 G8** 35 52N 137 43 E
Kisoro, *Uganda* **86 C2** 1 17 S 29 48 E
Kissidougou, *Guinea* **82 D2** 9 5N 10 5W
Kissimmee, *U.S.A.* **115 L5** 28 18N 81 24W
Kissimmee →, *U.S.A.* **115 M5** 27 9N 80 52W
Kississing L., *Canada* **103 B8** 55 10N 101 20W
Kissónerga, *Cyprus* **49 E11** 34 49N 32 24 E
Kissu, J., *Sudan* **80 C2** 21 37N 25 10 E
Kistanje, *Croatia* **41 E12** 43 58N 15 55 E
Kisújszállás, *Hungary* **28 C5** 47 12N 20 50 E
Kisumu, *Kenya* **86 C3** 0 3 S 34 45 E
Kisvárda, *Hungary* **28 B7** 48 14N 22 4 E
Kiswani, *Tanzania* **86 C4** 4 5 S 37 57 E
Kiswere, *Tanzania* **87 D4** 9 27 S 39 30 E
Kit Carson, *U.S.A.* **112 F3** 38 46N 102 48W
Kita, *Mali* **82 C3** 13 5N 9 25W
Kitaibaraki, *Japan* **55 F10** 36 50N 140 45 E
Kitakami, *Japan* **54 E10** 39 20N 141 10 E
Kitakami-Gawa →,
  Japan **54 E10** 38 25N 141 19 E
Kitakami-Sammyaku,
  Japan **54 E10** 39 30N 141 30 E
Kitakata, *Japan* **54 F9** 37 39N 139 52 E
Kitakyūshū, *Japan* **55 H5** 33 50N 130 50 E
Kitale, *Kenya* **86 B4** 1 0N 35 0 E
Kitami, *Japan* **54 C11** 43 48N 143 54 E
Kitami-Sammyaku,
  Japan **54 B11** 44 22N 142 43 E
Kitangiri, L., *Tanzania* **86 C3** 4 5 S 34 20 E
Kitaya, *Tanzania* **87 E5** 10 38 S 40 8 E
Kitchener, *Canada* **116 C4** 43 27N 80 29W
Kitee, *Finland* **32 A6** 62 5N 30 8 E
Kitega = Gitega,
  Burundi **86 C2** 3 26 S 29 56 E
Kitengo, *Dem. Rep. of
  the Congo* **86 D1** 7 26 S 24 8 E
Kitgum, *Uganda* **86 B3** 3 17N 32 52 E
Kíthira, *Greece* **46 E5** 36 8N 23 0 E
Kíthnos, *Greece* **46 D6** 37 26N 24 27 E
Kiti, *Cyprus* **49 E12** 34 50N 33 34 E
Kiti, C., *Cyprus* **49 E12** 34 48N 33 36 E
Kitimat, *Canada* **102 C3** 54 3N 128 38W
Kitinen →, *Finland* **8 C22** 67 14N 27 27 E
Kitiyab, *Sudan* **81 D3** 17 13N 33 35 E
Kítros, *Greece* **44 F6** 40 22N 22 34 E
Kitsman, *Ukraine* **29 B10** 48 26N 25 46 E
Kitsuki, *Japan* **55 H5** 33 25N 131 37 E
Kittakittaooloo, L.,
  Australia **95 D2** 28 3 S 138 14 E
Kittanning, *U.S.A.* **116 F5** 40 49N 79 31W
Kittatinny Mts., *U.S.A.* **117 F10** 41 0N 75 0W
Kittery, *U.S.A.* **115 D10** 43 5N 70 45W
Kittilä, *Finland* **8 C21** 67 40N 24 51 E
Kitui, *Kenya* **86 C4** 1 17 S 38 0 E
Kitwanga, *Canada* **102 B3** 55 6N 128 4W
Kitwe, *Zambia* **87 E2** 12 54 S 28 13 E
Kitzbühel, *Austria* **26 D5** 47 27N 12 24 E
Kitzbüheler Alpen,
  Austria **26 D5** 47 20N 12 20 E
Kitzingen, *Germany* **25 F6** 49 44N 10 9 E
Kivarli, *India* **68 G5** 24 33N 72 46 E
Kivertsi, *Ukraine* **33 G3** 50 50N 25 28 E
Kividhes, *Cyprus* **49 E11** 34 46N 32 53 E
Kivik, *Sweden* **11 J8** 55 41N 14 13 E
Kivotós, *Greece* **44 F5** 40 13N 21 26 E
Kivu, L., *Dem. Rep. of
  the Congo* **86 C2** 1 48 S 29 0 E
Kiyev = Kyyiv, *Ukraine* **33 G6** 50 30N 30 28 E
Kiyevskoye Vdkhr. =
  Kyyivske Vdskh.,
  Ukraine **33 G6** 51 0N 30 25 E
Kıyıköy, *Turkey* **45 E12** 41 38N 28 5 E
Kiziguru, *Rwanda* **86 C3** 1 46 S 30 23 E
Kızıl Adalar, *Turkey* **45 F13** 40 52N 29 5 E
Kızıl Irmak →, *Turkey* **72 B6** 41 44N 35 58 E
Kizil Jilga, *China* **69 B8** 35 26N 78 50 E
Kizil Yurt, *Russia* **35 J8** 43 13N 46 54 E
Kızılcabölük, *Turkey* **47 D11** 37 37N 29 1 E
Kızılcadağ, *Turkey* **47 D11** 37 1N 29 58 E
Kızılcahamam, *Turkey* **72 B5** 40 30N 32 30 E
Kızılırmak, *Turkey* **72 D3** 37 35N 29 17 E
Kızılırmak, *Turkey* **72 B5** 40 21N 33 59 E
Kızılkaya, *Turkey* **47 D12** 37 18N 30 27 E
Kızılören, *Turkey* **47 D12** 38 15N 30 10 E
Kızıltepe, *Turkey* **70 B4** 37 12N 40 35 E
Kizimkazi, *Tanzania* **86 D4** 6 28 S 39 30 E
Kizlyar, *Russia* **35 J8** 43 51N 46 40 E
Kizyl-Arvat =
  Gyzylarbat,
  Turkmenistan **52 F6** 39 4N 56 23 E
Kjellerup, *Denmark* **11 H3** 56 17N 9 25 E
Kjölur, *Iceland* **8 D4** 64 50N 19 25W
Kladanj, *Bos.-H.* **28 F3** 44 14N 18 42 E
Kladno, *Czech Rep.* **26 A7** 50 10N 14 7 E
Kladovo, *Serbia & M.* **44 B6** 44 36N 22 33 E
Klaeng, *Thailand* **64 F3** 12 47N 101 39 E
Klagenfurt, *Austria* **26 E7** 46 38N 14 20 E
Klaipėda, *Lithuania* **9 J19** 55 43N 21 10 E
Klaipėda □, *Lithuania* **30 C8** 55 43N 21 7 E
Klaksvík, *Færøe Is.* **8 E9** 62 14N 6 35W
Klamath →, *U.S.A.* **108 F1** 41 33N 124 5W
Klamath Falls, *U.S.A.* **108 E3** 42 13N 121 46W
Klamath Mts., *U.S.A.* **108 F2** 41 20N 123 0W
Klamono, *Indonesia* **63 E8** 1 8 S 131 30 E
Klanjec, *Croatia* **41 B12** 46 3N 15 45 E
Klappan →, *Canada* **102 B3** 58 0N 129 43W
Klarälven →, *Sweden* **10 E7** 59 23N 13 32 E
Klässbol, *Sweden* **10 E6** 59 33N 12 45 E
Klatovy, *Czech Rep.* **26 B6** 49 23N 13 18 E
Klawer, *S. Africa* **88 E2** 31 44 S 18 36 E
Klazienaveen, *Neths.* **17 B6** 52 44N 7 0 E
Klé, *Mali* **82 C3** 12 0N 6 28W
Kłecko, *Poland* **31 F4** 52 38N 17 25 E
Kleczew, *Poland* **31 F5** 52 22N 18 9 E
Kleena Kleene, *Canada* **102 C4** 52 0N 124 59W
Klein-Karas, *Namibia* **88 D2** 27 33 S 18 7 E
Klekovača, *Bos.-H.* **41 D13** 44 25N 16 32 E
Klembivka, *Ukraine* **29 B13** 48 28N 28 25 E
Klenoec, *Macedonia* **44 E4** 41 32N 20 49 E
Klenovec, *Slovak Rep.* **27 C12** 48 36N 19 54 E
Klerksdorp, *S. Africa* **88 D4** 26 53 S 26 38 E
Kleszczele, *Poland* **31 F10** 52 35N 23 19 E
Kletnya, *Russia* **32 F7** 53 23N 33 12 E
Kletsk = Klyetsk,
  Belarus **33 F4** 53 5N 26 45 E
Kletskiy, *Russia* **35 F6** 49 16N 43 11 E
Kleve, *Germany* **24 D2** 51 47N 6 11 E
Klickitat, *U.S.A.* **108 D3** 45 49N 121 9W
Klickitat →, *U.S.A.* **110 E5** 45 42N 121 17W
Klidhes, *Cyprus* **49 D13** 35 42N 34 36 E

Klimovichi, *Belarus* **32 F6** 53 36N 32 0 E
Klin, *Russia* **32 D9** 56 20N 36 48 E
Klina, *Serbia & M.* **44 D4** 42 37N 20 35 E
Klinaklini →, *Canada* **102 C3** 51 21N 125 40W
Klintehamn, *Sweden* **11 G12** 57 24N 18 12 E
Klintsy, *Russia* **33 F7** 52 50N 32 10 E
Klip →, *S. Africa* **89 D4** 27 3 S 29 3 E
Klipdale, *S. Africa* **88 E2** 34 19 S 19 57 E
Klippan, *Sweden* **11 H7** 56 8N 13 10 E
Klipplaat, *S. Africa* **88 E3** 33 1 S 24 22 E
Klishkivtsi, *Ukraine* **29 B11** 48 26N 26 16 E
Kljajićevo, *Serbia & M.* **28 E4** 45 45N 19 17 E
Ključ, *Bos.-H.* **41 D13** 44 32N 16 48 E
Kłobuck, *Poland* **31 H5** 50 55N 18 55 E
Klockestrand, *Sweden* **10 B11** 62 53N 17 45 E
Kłodawa, *Poland* **31 F5** 52 15N 18 55 E
Kłodzko, *Poland* **31 H3** 50 28N 16 38 E
Klong Wang Chao △,
  Thailand **64 D2** 16 20N 99 9 E
Klos, *Albania* **44 E4** 41 28N 20 10 E
Klosterneuburg, *Austria* **27 C9** 48 18N 16 19 E
Klosters, *Switz.* **25 J5** 46 52N 9 52 E
Klötze, *Germany* **24 C7** 52 37N 11 10 E
Klouto, *Togo* **83 D5** 6 57N 0 44 E
Kluane →, *Canada* **102 A1** 60 45N 139 30W
Kluane L., *Canada* **100 B6** 61 15N 138 40W
Kluczbork, *Poland* **31 H5** 50 58N 18 12 E
Klukwan, *U.S.A.* **102 B1** 59 24N 135 54W
Klungkung, *Indonesia* **63 K18** 8 32 S 115 24 E
Klyetsk, *Belarus* **33 F4** 53 5N 26 45 E
Klyuchevskaya, Gora,
  Russia **53 D17** 55 50N 160 30 E
Knäred, *Sweden* **11 H7** 56 31N 13 19 E
Knaresborough, *U.K.* **14 C6** 54 1N 1 28W
Knee L., *Man., Canada* **104 A1** 55 3N 94 45W
Knee L., *Sask., Canada* **103 B7** 55 51N 107 0W
Knezha, *Bulgaria* **45 C8** 43 30N 24 5 E
Knight Inlet, *Canada* **102 C3** 50 45N 125 40W
Knighton, *U.K.* **15 E4** 52 21N 3 3W
Knights Ferry, *U.S.A.* **110 H6** 37 50N 120 40W
Knights Landing, *U.S.A.* **110 G5** 38 48N 121 43W
Knin, *Croatia* **41 D13** 44 1N 16 17 E
Knislinge, *Sweden* **11 H8** 56 12N 14 5 E
Knittelfeld, *Austria* **26 D7** 47 13N 14 51 E
Knivsta, *Sweden* **10 E11** 59 43N 17 48 E
Knjaževac, *Serbia & M.* **44 C6** 43 35N 22 18 E
Knob, C., *Australia* **93 F2** 34 32 S 119 16 E
Knock, *Ireland* **12 C3** 53 48N 8 55W
Knockmealdown Mts.,
  Ireland **12 D4** 52 14N 7 56W
Knokke-Heist, *Belgium* **17 C3** 51 21N 3 17 E
Knossós, *Greece* **49 D7** 35 16N 25 10 E
Knowlton, *Canada* **117 A12** 45 13N 72 31W
Knox, *U.S.A.* **114 E2** 41 18N 86 37W
Knox Coast, *Antarctica* **5 C8** 66 30 S 108 0 E
Knoxville, *Iowa, U.S.A.* **112 E8** 41 19N 93 6W
Knoxville, *Pa., U.S.A.* **116 E7** 41 57N 77 27W
Knoxville, *Tenn., U.S.A.* **115 H4** 35 58N 83 55W
Knud Rasmussen Land,
  Greenland **4 A5** 79 0N 60 0W
Knysna, *S. Africa* **88 E3** 34 2 S 23 2 E
Knyszyn, *Poland* **30 E9** 53 20N 22 56 E
Ko Kha, *Thailand* **64 C2** 18 11N 99 24 E
Ko Tarutao △, *Thailand* **65 J2** 6 31N 99 26 E
Ko Yao, *Thailand* **65 a** 8 7N 98 35 E
Koartac = Quaqtaq,
  Canada **101 B13** 60 55N 69 40W
Koba, *Indonesia* **63 F8** 6 37 S 134 37 E
Kobarid, *Slovenia* **41 B10** 46 15N 13 30 E
Kobayashi, *Japan* **55 J5** 31 56N 130 59 E
Kōbe, *Japan* **55 G7** 34 45N 135 10 E
Kobelyaky, *Ukraine* **33 H8** 49 11N 34 9 E
København, *Denmark* **11 J6** 55 41N 12 34 E
København ✈ (CPH),
  Denmark **11 J6** 55 37N 12 39 E
Københavns
  Amtskommune □,
  Denmark **11 J6** 55 42N 12 21 E
Kobenni, *Mauritania* **82 B3** 15 58N 9 24W
Kōbi-Sho, *Japan* **55 M1** 25 56N 123 41 E
Koblenz, *Germany* **25 E3** 50 21N 7 36 E
Kobo, *Ethiopia* **81 E4** 12 2N 39 56 E
Kobryn, *Belarus* **33 F3** 52 15N 24 22 E
Kobuleti, *Georgia* **35 K5** 41 55N 41 45 E
Kobyletska Polyana,
  Ukraine **29 B9** 48 3N 24 4 E
Kobylin, *Poland* **31 G4** 51 43N 17 12 E
Kobyłka, *Poland* **31 F8** 52 21N 21 10 E
Kobylkino, *Russia* **34 C6** 54 8N 43 56 E
Koca →, *Turkey* **45 F11** 40 8N 27 57 E
Kocabaş, *Turkey* **47 D11** 37 49N 29 20 E
Kocaeli, *Turkey* **45 F13** 40 45N 29 50 E
Kocaeli □, *Turkey* **45 F13** 40 45N 29 55 E
Kočane, *Serbia & M.* **44 C5** 43 12N 21 52 E
Kočani, *Macedonia* **44 E6** 41 55N 22 25 E
Koçarlı, *Turkey* **47 D9** 37 45N 27 43 E
Koceljevo, *Serbia & M.* **44 B3** 44 28N 19 50 E
Kočevje, *Slovenia* **41 C11** 45 39N 14 50 E
Koch Bihar, *India* **67 F16** 26 22N 89 29 E
Kochang, *S. Korea* **57 G14** 35 41N 127 55 E
Kochas, *India* **69 G10** 25 15N 83 56 E
Kocher →, *Germany* **25 F5** 49 13N 9 12 E
Kochi = Cochin, *India* **66 Q10** 9 58N 76 20 E
Kōchi, *Japan* **55 H6** 33 30N 133 35 E
Kōchi □, *Japan* **55 H6** 33 40N 133 30 E
Kochiu = Gejiu, *China* **58 F4** 23 20N 103 10 E
Kock, *Poland* **31 G9** 51 38N 22 27 E
Kodarma, *India* **69 G11** 24 28N 85 36 E
Kode, *Sweden* **11 G5** 57 57N 11 51 E
Kodiak, *U.S.A.* **100 C4** 57 47N 152 24W
Kodiak I., *U.S.A.* **100 C4** 57 30N 152 45W
Kodinar, *India* **68 J4** 20 46N 70 46 E
Kodok, *Sudan* **81 F3** 9 53N 32 7 E
Kodori →, *Georgia* **35 J5** 42 47N 41 10 E
Koedoesberge, *S. Africa* **88 E3** 32 40 S 20 11 E
Koes, *Namibia* **88 D2** 26 0 S 19 15 E
Kofçaz, *Turkey* **45 E11** 41 58N 27 12 E
Koffiefontein, *S. Africa* **88 D4** 29 30 S 25 0 E
Kofiau, *Indonesia* **63 E7** 1 11 S 129 50 E
Köflach, *Austria* **26 D8** 47 4N 15 5 E
Koforidua, *Ghana* **83 D4** 6 3N 0 17W
Kōfu, *Japan* **55 G9** 35 40N 138 30 E
Koga, *Japan* **55 F9** 36 11N 139 43 E
Kogaluc →, *Canada* **105 A7** 56 12N 61 44W
Køge, *Denmark* **11 J6** 55 27N 12 11 E
Køge Bugt, *Denmark* **11 J6** 55 30N 12 20 E
Kogi, *Nigeria* **83 D6** 7 45N 6 45 E
Kogin Baba, *Nigeria* **83 D7** 7 55N 11 35 E
Koh-i-Khurd, *Afghan.* **68 C1** 33 30N 65 59 E
Koh-i-Maran, *Pakistan* **68 E2** 29 18N 66 50 E
Kohat, *Pakistan* **68 C4** 33 40N 71 29 E
Kohima, *India* **67 G19** 25 35N 94 10 E
Kohkīlūyeh va Būyer
  Ahmadi □, *Iran* **71 D6** 31 30N 50 30 E
Kohler Ra., *Antarctica* **5 D15** 77 0 S 110 0W

Kohlu, *Pakistan* **68 E3** 29 54N 69 15 E
Kohtla-Järve, *Estonia* **9 G22** 59 20N 27 20 E
Kohylnyk →, *Ukraine* **29 E14** 45 49N 29 40 E
Koi Sanjaq, *Iraq* **70 B5** 36 5N 44 38 E
Koillismaa, *Finland* **8 D23** 65 44N 28 36 E
Koin-dong, *N. Korea* **57 D14** 40 28N 126 18 E
Koinare, *Bulgaria* **45 C8** 43 21N 24 8 E
Koindu, *S. Leone* **82 D2** 8 26N 10 19W
Kojetín, *Czech Rep.* **27 B10** 49 21N 17 20 E
Kojŏ, *N. Korea* **57 E14** 38 58N 127 58 E
Kojonup, *Australia* **93 F2** 33 48 S 117 10 E
Kojūr, *Iran* **71 B6** 36 23N 51 43 E
Koka, *Sudan* **80 C3** 20 5N 30 35 E
Kokand = Qŭqon,
  Uzbekistan **52 E8** 40 30N 70 57 E
Kokas, *Indonesia* **63 E8** 2 42 S 132 26 E
Kokava, *Slovak Rep.* **27 C12** 48 35N 19 50 E
Kokchetav = Kökshetaü,
  Kazakhstan **52 D7** 53 20N 69 25 E
Kokemäenjoki →,
  Finland **9 F19** 61 32N 21 44 E
Kokhma, *Russia* **34 B5** 56 57N 41 8 E
Koki, *Senegal* **82 B1** 15 30N 15 59W
Kokkola, *Finland* **8 E20** 63 50N 23 8 E
Koko, *Nigeria* **83 C5** 11 28N 4 29 E
Koko Kyunzu, *Burma* **67 M18** 14 10N 93 25 E
Kokolopozo, *Ivory C.* **82 D3** 5 8N 6 5W
Kokomo, *U.S.A.* **114 E2** 40 29N 86 8W
Kokoro, *Niger* **83 C5** 14 12N 0 55 E
Koksan, *N. Korea* **57 E14** 38 46N 126 40 E
Koksoak →, *Canada* **101 C13** 58 30N 68 10W
Kokstad, *S. Africa* **89 E4** 30 32 S 29 29 E
Kokubu, *Japan* **55 J5** 31 44N 130 46 E
Kola, *Indonesia* **63 F8** 5 35 S 134 30 E
Kola Pen. = Kolskiy
  Poluostrov, *Russia* **52 C4** 67 30N 38 0 E
Kolachi →, *Pakistan* **68 F2** 27 8N 67 2 E
Kolahoi, *India* **69 B6** 34 12N 75 22 E
Kolahun, *Liberia* **82 D2** 8 15N 10 4W
Kolaka, *Indonesia* **63 E6** 4 3 S 121 46 E
Kolar, *India* **66 N11** 13 12N 78 15 E
Kolar Gold Fields, *India* **66 N11** 12 58N 78 16 E
Kolaras, *India* **68 G7** 25 14N 77 36 E
Kolari, *Finland* **8 C20** 67 20N 23 48 E
Kolárovo, *Slovak Rep.* **27 D10** 47 54N 18 0 E
Kolašin, *Serbia & M.* **44 D3** 42 50N 19 31 E
Kolayat, *India* **66 F8** 27 50N 72 50 E
Kolbäck, *Sweden* **10 E10** 59 34N 16 15 E
Kolbäcksån →, *Sweden* **10 E10** 59 36N 16 16 E
Kolbermoor, *Germany* **25 H8** 47 51N 12 4 E
Kolbuszowa, *Poland* **31 H8** 50 15N 21 46 E
Kolchugino, *Russia* **32 D10** 56 17N 39 22 E
Kolda, *Senegal* **82 C2** 12 55N 14 57W
Koldegi, *Sudan* **81 E3** 12 3N 30 16 E
Kolding, *Denmark* **11 J3** 55 30N 9 29 E
Kolepom = Dolak,
  Pulau, *Indonesia* **63 F9** 8 0 S 138 30 E
Kolguyev, Ostrov,
  Russia **52 C5** 69 20N 48 30 E
Kolhapur, *India* **66 L9** 16 43N 74 15 E
Kolia, *Ivory C.* **82 D3** 9 46N 6 28W
Kolín, *Czech Rep.* **26 A8** 50 2N 15 9 E
Kolind, *Denmark* **11 H4** 56 21N 10 34 E
Kolkas rags, *Latvia* **9 H20** 57 46N 22 37 E
Kolkata, *India* **69 H13** 22 36N 88 24 E
Kollam = Quilon, *India* **66 Q10** 8 50N 76 38 E
Kolleda, *Germany* **24 D7** 51 11N 11 15 E
Kollum, *Neths.* **17 A6** 53 17N 6 10 E
Kolmanskop, *Namibia* **88 D2** 26 45 S 15 14 E
Köln, *Germany* **24 E2** 50 56N 6 57 E
Kolno, *Poland* **30 E8** 53 25N 21 56 E
Koło, *Poland* **31 F5** 52 14N 18 40 E
Kołobrzeg, *Poland* **30 D2** 54 10N 15 35 E
Kolochava, *Ukraine* **29 B8** 48 26N 23 41 E
Kolokani, *Mali* **82 C3** 13 35N 7 45W
Koloko, *Burkina Faso* **82 C3** 11 5N 5 19W
Kololo, *Ethiopia* **81 F5** 7 29N 41 58 E
Kolomna, *Russia* **32 E10** 55 8N 38 45 E
Kolomyya, *Ukraine* **29 B10** 48 31N 25 2 E
Kolondiéba, *Mali* **82 C3** 11 5N 6 54W
Kolonodale, *Indonesia* **63 E6** 2 0 S 121 19 E
Kolonowskie, *Poland* **31 H5** 50 39N 18 22 E
Kolosib, *India* **67 G18** 24 15N 92 45 E
Kolpashevo, *Russia* **52 D9** 58 20N 83 5 E
Kolpino, *Russia* **32 C6** 59 44N 30 39 E
Kolpny, *Russia* **33 F9** 52 17N 37 1 E
Kolskiy Poluostrov,
  Russia **52 C4** 67 30N 38 0 E
Kolsva, *Sweden* **10 E9** 59 36N 15 51 E
Kolubara →,
  Serbia & M. **44 B4** 44 35N 20 15 E
Koluszki, *Poland* **31 G6** 51 45N 19 46 E
Kolwezi, *Dem. Rep. of
  the Congo* **87 E2** 10 40 S 25 25 E
Kolyma →, *Russia* **53 C17** 69 30N 161 0 E
Kolymskoye Nagorye,
  Russia **53 C16** 63 0N 157 0 E
Kôm Hamâda, *Egypt* **80 H7** 30 46N 30 41 E
Kôm Ombo, *Egypt* **80 C3** 24 25N 32 52 E
Komadugu Gana →,
  Nigeria **83 C7** 13 5N 12 24 E
Komandorskie Is. =
  Komandorskiye
  Ostrova, *Russia* **53 D17** 55 0N 167 0 E
Komandorskiye
  Ostrova, *Russia* **53 D17** 55 0N 167 0 E
Komárno, *Slovak Rep.* **27 D11** 47 49N 18 5 E
Komarnyky, *Ukraine* **29 B8** 48 59N 23 3 E
Komárom, *Hungary* **28 C3** 47 43N 18 7 E
Komárom-Esztergom □,
  Hungary **28 C3** 47 35N 18 20 E
Komatipoort, *S. Africa* **89 D5** 25 25 S 31 55 E
Komatou Yialou,
  Cyprus **49 D13** 35 25 S 34 8 E
Komatsu, *Japan* **55 F8** 36 25N 136 30 E
Komatsushima, *Japan* **55 H7** 34 0N 134 35 E
Kombissiri,
  Burkina Faso **83 C4** 12 4N 1 20W
Kombori, *Burkina Faso* **82 C4** 13 26N 3 56W
Kombóti, *Greece* **46 B3** 39 6N 21 5 E
Komen, *Slovenia* **41 C10** 45 49N 13 45 E
Komenda, *Ghana* **83 D4** 5 4N 1 28W
Komi □, *Russia* **52 C6** 64 0N 55 0 E
Komiža, *Croatia* **41 E13** 43 3N 16 11 E
Komló, *Hungary* **28 D3** 46 15N 18 16 E
Kommunarsk =
  Alchevsk, *Ukraine* **33 H10** 48 30N 38 45 E
Kommunizma, Pik,
  Tajikistan **52 F8** 39 0N 72 2 E
Komodo, *Indonesia* **63 F5** 8 37 S 119 20 E
Komoé →, *Ivory C.* **82 D4** 5 12N 3 44W
Komoran, Pulau,
  Indonesia **63 F9** 8 18 S 138 45 E
Komoro, *Japan* **55 F9** 36 19N 138 26 E
Komotini, *Greece* **45 E8** 41 9N 25 26 E
Komovi, *Serbia & M.* **44 D3** 42 41N 19 39 E
Kompasberg, *S. Africa* **88 E3** 31 45 S 24 32 E

Kompong Bang,
  Cambodia **65 F5** 12 24N 104 40 E
Kompong Cham,
  Cambodia **65 F5** 12 0N 105 30 E
Kompong Chhnang =
  Kampong Chhnang,
  Cambodia **65 F5** 12 20N 104 35 E
Kompong Chikreng,
  Cambodia **64 F5** 13 5N 104 18 E
Kompong Kleang,
  Cambodia **64 F5** 13 6N 104 8 E
Kompong Luong,
  Cambodia **65 G5** 11 49N 104 48 E
Kompong Pranak,
  Cambodia **64 F5** 13 35N 104 55 E
Kompong Som =
  Kampong Saom,
  Cambodia **65 G4** 10 38N 103 30 E
Kompong Som,
  Chhung = Kampong
  Saom, Chaak,
  Cambodia **65 G4** 10 50N 103 32 E
Kompong Speu,
  Cambodia **65 G5** 11 26N 104 32 E
Kompong Sralau,
  Cambodia **64 E5** 14 5N 105 46 E
Kompong Thom,
  Cambodia **64 F5** 12 35N 104 51 E
Kompong Trabeck,
  Cambodia **64 F5** 13 6N 105 14 E
Kompong Trabeck,
  Cambodia **65 G5** 11 9N 105 28 E
Kompong Trach,
  Cambodia **65 G5** 11 25N 105 48 E
Kompong Tralach,
  Cambodia **65 G5** 11 54N 104 47 E
Komrat = Comrat,
  Moldova **29 D13** 46 18N 28 40 E
Komsberg, *S. Africa* **88 E3** 32 40 S 20 45 E
Komsomolets, Ostrov,
  Russia **53 A10** 80 30N 95 0 E
Komsomolsk, *Amur,
  Russia* **53 D14** 50 30N 137 0 E
Komsomolsk, *Ivanovo,
  Russia* **32 D11** 57 2N 40 20 E
Komsomolskiy, *Russia* **34 C7** 54 27N 45 33 E
Kömür Burnu, *Turkey* **47 C8** 38 39N 26 12 E
Kon Tum, *Vietnam* **64 E7** 14 24N 108 0 E
Kon Tum, Plateau du,
  Vietnam **64 E7** 14 30N 108 30 E
Kona, *Mali* **82 C4** 14 57N 3 53W
Konakovo, *Russia* **32 D9** 56 40N 36 51 E
Konarhā □, *Afghan.* **66 B7** 34 30N 71 3 E
Konārī, *Iran* **71 D6** 28 13N 51 36 E
Konch, *India* **69 G8** 26 0N 79 10 E
Konde, *Tanzania* **86 C4** 4 57 S 39 45 E
Kondiá, *Greece* **47 B8** 39 49N 25 10 E
Kondoa, *Tanzania* **86 C4** 4 55 S 35 50 E
Kondókali, *Greece* **49 A3** 39 38N 19 51 E
Kondopaga, *Russia* **32 A8** 62 12N 34 17 E
Kondratyevo, *Russia* **53 D10** 57 22N 98 15 E
Kondrovo, *Russia* **32 E8** 54 48N 35 56 E
Konduga, *Nigeria* **83 C7** 11 35N 13 26 E
Köneürgench,
  Turkmenistan **52 E6** 42 19N 59 10 E
Konevo, *Russia* **32 A10** 62 8N 39 20 E
Kong = Khong →,
  Cambodia **64 F5** 13 32N 105 58 E
Kong, *Ivory C.* **82 D4** 8 54N 4 36W
Kong, Koh, *Cambodia* **65 G4** 11 20N 103 0 E
Kong Christian IX Land,
  Greenland **4 C6** 68 0N 36 0W
Kong Christian X Land,
  Greenland **4 B6** 74 0N 29 0W
Kong Frederik IX Land,
  Greenland **4 C5** 67 0N 52 0W
Kong Frederik VI Kyst,
  Greenland **101 B15** 63 0N 43 0W
Kong Frederik VIII
  Land, *Greenland* **4 B6** 78 30N 26 0W
Kong Oscar Fjord,
  Greenland **4 B6** 72 20N 24 0W
Kongeå →, *Denmark* **11 J2** 55 23N 8 39 E
Kongerslev, *Denmark* **11 H4** 56 57N 10 6 E
Kongju, *S. Korea* **57 F14** 36 30N 127 0 E
Konglu, *Burma* **67 F20** 27 13N 97 57 E
Kongola, *Namibia* **88 B3** 17 45 S 23 20 E
Kongolo, Kasai-Or.,
  *Dem. Rep. of
  the Congo* **86 D1** 5 26 S 24 49 E
Kongolo, Katanga,
  *Dem. Rep. of
  the Congo* **86 D2** 5 22 S 27 0 E
Kongor, *Sudan* **81 F3** 7 1N 31 27 E
Kongoussi,
  Burkina Faso **83 C4** 13 19N 1 32W
Kongsberg, *Norway* **9 G13** 59 39N 9 39 E
Kongsvinger, *Norway* **9 F15** 60 12N 12 2 E
Kongwa, *Tanzania* **86 D4** 6 11 S 36 26 E
Koni, *Dem. Rep. of
  the Congo* **87 E2** 10 40 S 27 11 E
Koni, Mts., *Dem. Rep. of
  the Congo* **87 E2** 10 36 S 27 10 E
Koniakari, *Mali* **82 C2** 14 35N 10 50W
Koniecpol, *Poland* **31 H6** 50 46N 19 40 E
Königs Wusterhausen,
  Germany **24 C9** 52 19N 13 38 E
Königsbrunn, *Germany* **25 G6** 48 16N 10 54 E
Königslutter, *Germany* **24 C6** 52 15N 10 49 E
Konin, *Poland* **31 F5** 52 12N 18 15 E
Konispol, *Albania* **44 G4** 39 42N 20 10 E
Kónitsa, *Greece* **46 A2** 40 5N 20 48 E
Konjic, *Bos.-H.* **28 G2** 43 42N 17 58 E
Konkiep, *Namibia* **88 D2** 26 49 S 17 15 E
Konkouré →, *Guinea* **82 D2** 9 50N 13 42W
Konnongorr, *Ghana* **24 D7** 51 41N 11 45 E
Kono, *S. Leone* **82 D2** 8 30N 11 5W
Konongo, *Ghana* **83 D4** 6 40N 1 31W
Konosha, *Russia* **32 B11** 61 0N 40 5 E
Kōnosu, *Japan* **55 F9** 36 3N 139 31 E
Konotop, *Ukraine* **33 G7** 51 12N 33 7 E
Konqi He →, *China* **60 B4** 41 0N 86 0 E
Końskie, *Poland* **31 G7** 51 15N 20 23 E
Konstancin-Jeziorna,
  Poland **31 F8** 52 5N 21 17 E
Konstantinovka =
  Kostyantynivka,
  Ukraine **33 H9** 48 32N 37 39 E
Konstantynów Łódzki,
  Poland **31 G6** 51 45N 19 20 E
Konstanz, *Germany* **25 H5** 47 40N 9 10 E
Kont, *Iran* **71 E9** 26 55N 61 50 E
Kontagora, *Nigeria* **83 C6** 10 23N 5 27 E
Kontcha, *Cameroon* **83 D7** 7 59N 12 15 E
Konya, *Turkey* **70 B2** 37 52N 32 35 E
Konya Ovası, *Turkey* **72 C5** 38 30N 33 5 E

Konz, *Germany* **25 F2** 49 42N 6 34 E
Konza, *Kenya* **86 C4** 1 45 S 37 7 E
Koocanusa, L., *Canada* **108 B6** 49 20N 115 15W
Kookynie, *Australia* **93 E3** 29 17 S 121 22 E
Koolyanobbing,
  Australia **93 F2** 30 48 S 119 36 E
Koonibba, *Australia* **95 E1** 31 54 S 133 25 E
Koorawatha, *Australia* **95 E4** 34 2 S 148 33 E
Koorda, *Australia* **93 F2** 30 48 S 117 35 E
Kooskia, *U.S.A.* **108 C6** 46 9N 115 59W
Kootenay →, *U.S.A.* **102 C5** 5 0N 116 0W
Kootenay →, *U.S.A.* **102 D5** 49 19N 117 39W
Kootenay L., *Canada* **102 D5** 49 45N 116 50W
Kootjieskolk, *S. Africa* **88 E3** 31 15 S 20 21 E
Kopanovka, *Russia* **35 G8** 47 28N 46 50 E
Kopaonik, *Serbia & M.* **44 C4** 43 10N 20 50 E
Kopaonik △,
  Serbia & M. **44 C4** 43 20N 20 50 E
Kópavogur, *Iceland* **8 D3** 64 6N 21 55W
Kopayhorod, *Ukraine* **29 B12** 48 52N 27 47 E
Koper, *Slovenia* **41 C10** 45 31N 13 44 E
Kopet Dagh, *Asia* **71 B8** 38 0N 58 0 E
Kopi, *Australia* **95 E2** 33 24 S 135 40 E
Köping, *Sweden* **10 E10** 59 31N 16 3 E
Köpingsvik, *Sweden* **11 H10** 56 53N 16 43 E
Kopište, *Croatia* **41 F13** 42 48N 16 42 E
Koplik, *Albania* **44 D3** 42 15N 19 22 E
Köpmanholmen, *Sweden* **10 A12** 63 10N 18 35 E
Kopparberg, *Sweden* **10 E9** 59 52N 15 0 E
Koppeh Dāgh = Kopet
  Dagh, *Asia* **71 B8** 38 0N 58 0 E
Koppies, *S. Africa* **89 D4** 27 20 S 27 30 E
Koppom, *Sweden* **10 E6** 59 43N 12 10 E
Koprivlen, *Bulgaria* **44 E7** 41 31N 23 53 E
Koprivnica, *Croatia* **41 B13** 46 12N 16 45 E
Koprivnitsa, *Bulgaria* **45 D8** 42 40N 24 19 E
Köprübaşı, *Turkey* **47 C10** 38 43N 28 23 E
Kopychyntsi, *Ukraine* **33 H3** 49 7N 25 58 E
Kora △, *Kenya* **86 C4** 0 14 S 38 44 E
Korab, *Macedonia* **44 E4** 41 44N 20 40 E
Korakiána, *Greece* **49 A3** 39 42N 19 45 E
Koral, *India* **68 J5** 21 50N 73 12 E
Korarou, L., *Mali* **82 B4** 15 15N 3 15W
Korba, *India* **69 H10** 22 20N 82 45 E
Korbach, *Germany* **24 D4** 51 16N 8 52 E
Korbu, G., *Malaysia* **65 K3** 4 41N 101 18 E
Korçë, *Albania* **44 F4** 40 37N 20 50 E
Korčula, *Croatia* **41 F13** 42 56N 16 57 E
Korčulanski Kanal,
  Croatia **41 E13** 43 3N 16 40 E
Kord Kūy, *Iran* **71 B7** 36 48N 54 7 E
Kord Sheykh, *Iran* **71 D7** 28 31N 52 53 E
Kordestan = Kurdistan,
  Asia **73 D10** 37 20N 43 30 E
Kordestān □, *Iran* **70 C5** 36 0N 47 0 E
Kordofân, *Sudan* **79 F11** 13 0N 29 0 E
Koré Mayroua, *Niger* **83 C5** 13 18N 3 55 E
Korea, North ■, *Asia* **57 E14** 40 0N 127 0 E
Korea, South ■, *Asia* **57 G15** 36 0N 128 0 E
Korea Bay, *Korea* **57 E13** 39 0N 124 0 E
Korea Strait, *Asia* **57 H15** 34 0N 129 30 E
Korem, *Ethiopia* **81 E4** 12 30N 39 32 E
Korenevo, *Russia* **33 G8** 51 27N 34 55 E
Korenovsk, *Russia* **35 H4** 45 30N 39 22 E
Korets, *Ukraine* **33 G4** 50 40N 27 5 E
Korfantów, *Poland* **31 H4** 50 29N 17 36 E
Korgan, *Turkey* **72 B7** 40 44N 37 13 E
Korgus, *Sudan* **80 D3** 19 16N 33 29 E
Korhogo, *Ivory C.* **82 D3** 9 29N 5 28W
Koribundu, *S. Leone* **82 D2** 7 41N 11 46W
Korienzé, *Mali* **82 B4** 15 22N 3 50W
Korinthía □, *Greece* **46 D4** 37 50N 22 35 E
Kórinthos, *Greece* **46 D4** 37 56N 22 55 E
Korioumé, *Mali* **82 B4** 16 35N 3 0W
Korissa, Límni, *Greece* **49 B3** 39 27N 19 53 E
Kōriyama, *Japan* **54 F10** 37 24N 140 23 E
Korkuteli, *Turkey* **47 D12** 37 4N 30 13 E
Korla, *China* **60 B4** 41 45N 86 4 E
Kormakiti, C., *Cyprus* **49 D11** 35 23N 32 56 E
Körmend, *Hungary* **28 C1** 47 5N 16 35 E
Kornat, *Croatia* **41 E12** 43 50N 15 20 E
Kornat, *Croatia* **41 E12** 43 50N 15 12 E
Korneshty = Cornești,
  Moldova **29 C13** 47 21N 28 1 E
Korneuburg, *Austria* **27 C9** 48 20N 16 20 E
Kórnik, *Poland* **31 F4** 52 15N 17 6 E
Koro, *Fiji* **91 C8** 17 19 S 179 23 E
Koro, *Ivory C.* **82 D3** 8 32N 7 30W
Koro, *Mali* **82 C4** 14 1N 2 58W
Koro Sea, *Fiji* **91 C9** 17 30 S 179 45W
Korocha, *Russia* **33 G9** 50 55N 37 30 E
Köroğlu Dağları, *Turkey* **72 B5** 40 38N 33 0 E
Korogwe, *Tanzania* **86 D4** 5 5 S 38 25 E
Koroit, *Australia* **95 F3** 38 18 S 142 24 E
Koronadal, *Phil.* **61 H6** 6 12N 125 1 E
Koronowo, *Poland* **31 E4** 53 12N 17 51 E
Koróni, *Greece* **46 E3** 36 48N 21 57 E
Korónia, Limni, *Greece* **44 F7** 40 47N 23 37 E
Koronís, *Greece* **47 D7** 37 12N 25 35 E
Koronowo, *Poland* **29 B10** 48 56N 25 10 E
Koror, *Palau* **96 G5** 7 20N 134 28 E
Körös →, *Hungary* **28 D5** 46 43N 20 12 E
Körös Maros △,
  Hungary **28 C5** 47 8N 20 52 E
Köröstarcsa, *Hungary* **28 D6** 46 53N 21 3 E
Korosten, *Ukraine* **33 G5** 50 54N 28 36 E
Korostyshev, *Ukraine* **33 G5** 50 19N 29 4 E
Korotoyak, *Russia* **33 G10** 51 1N 39 2 E
Korraraika, Helodranon'
  i, *Madag.* **89 B7** 17 45 S 43 57 E
Korsakov, *Russia* **53 E15** 46 36N 142 42 E
Korsberga, *Sweden* **11 G9** 57 19N 15 1 E
Korshiv, *Ukraine* **29 B10** 48 39N 25 1 E
Korshunovo, *Russia* **53 D12** 58 37N 110 10 E
Korsør, *Denmark* **11 J5** 55 20N 11 9 E
Korsun
  Shevchenkovskiy,
  Ukraine **33 H6** 49 26N 31 16 E
Korsze, *Poland* **30 D8** 54 11N 21 9 E
Korti, *Sudan* **80 D3** 18 6N 31 33 E
Kortrijk, *Belgium* **17 D3** 50 50N 3 17 E
Korucu, *Turkey* **47 B9** 39 28N 27 3 E
Korwai, *India* **68 G8** 24 7N 78 5 E
Koryakskoye Nagorye,
  Russia **53 C18** 61 0N 171 0 E
Koryŏng, *S. Korea* **57 G15** 35 44N 128 15 E
Kos, *Greece* **47 E9** 36 50N 27 15 E
Kosa, *Ethiopia* **81 F4** 7 50N 36 50 E
Kosaya Gora, *Russia* **32 E9** 54 10N 37 30 E
Kościan, *Poland* **31 F3** 52 5N 16 40 E
Kościerzyna, *Poland* **30 D4** 54 8N 17 59 E
Kosciusko, *U.S.A.* **113 J10** 33 4N 89 35W
Kosciuszko, Mt.,
  Australia **95 F4** 36 27 S 148 16 E

Kösély ➤, Hungary .... 28 C6 47 25N 21 5 E
Kosha, Sudan .... 80 C3 20 50N 30 30 E
Koshava, Bulgaria .... 44 B7 44 4N 23 2 E
K'oshih = Kashi, China 60 C2 39 30N 76 2 E
Koshiki-Rettō, Japan .. 55 J4 31 45N 129 49 E
Kosi, India .... 68 F7 27 48N 77 29 E
Kosi ➤, India .... 69 E8 28 41N 78 57 E
Košice, Slovak Rep. ... 27 C14 48 42N 21 15 E
Košický □, Slovak Rep. 27 C14 48 45N 21 0 E
Kosiv, Ukraine .... 29 B10 48 19N 25 6 E
Kosjerić, Serbia & M. .. 44 B3 44 0N 19 55 E
Köşk, Turkey .... 47 D10 37 50N 28 3 E
Koskinoú, Greece ..... 49 C10 36 23N 28 13 E
Koslan, Russia .... 52 C5 63 34N 49 14 E
Kosmach, Ukraine .... 29 B9 48 20N 24 50 E
Kosŏng, N. Korea .... 57 E15 38 40N 128 22 E
Kosovo □, Serbia & M. 44 D4 42 30N 21 0 E
Kosovo Polje,
  Serbia & M. .... 44 D5 42 40N 21 5 E
Kosovska Kamenica,
  Serbia & M. .... 44 D5 42 35N 21 35 E
Kosovska Mitrovica,
  Serbia & M. .... 44 D4 42 54N 20 52 E
Kossou, L. de, Ivory C. . 82 D3 6 59N 5 31W
Kosta, Sweden .... 11 H9 56 50N 15 24 E
Kostajnica, Croatia ... 41 C13 45 17N 16 30 E
Kostanjevica, Slovenia . 41 C12 45 51N 15 27 E
Kostelec, Bulgaria .... 44 D7 42 15N 23 52 E
Koster, S. Africa ..... 88 D4 25 52 S 26 54 E
Kôstî, Sudan .... 81 E3 13 8N 32 43 E
Kostinbrod, Bulgaria .. 44 D7 42 49N 23 13 E
Kostolac, Serbia & M. . 44 B5 44 37N 21 15 E
Kostopil, Ukraine .... 33 G4 50 51N 26 22 E
Kostroma, Russia ..... 32 D11 57 50N 40 58 E
Kostromskoye Vdkhr.,
  Russia .... 32 D11 57 52N 40 49 E
Kostryzhivka, Ukraine . 29 B10 48 39N 25 43 E
Kostrzyn, Lubuskie,
  Poland .... 31 F1 52 35N 14 39 E
Kostrzyn, Wielkopolskie,
  Poland .... 31 F4 52 24N 17 14 E
Kostyantynivka, Ukraine 33 H9 48 32N 37 39 E
Kostyukovichi =
  Kastsyukovichy,
  Belarus .... 32 F7 53 20N 32 4 E
Koszalin, Poland ..... 30 D3 54 11N 16 8 E
Kőszeg, Hungary ..... 28 C1 47 23N 16 33 E
Kot Addu, Pakistan ... 68 D4 30 30N 71 0 E
Kot Kapura, India .... 68 D6 30 35N 74 50 E
Kot Moman, Pakistan . 68 C5 32 13N 73 0 E
Kot Sultan, Pakistan .. 68 D4 30 46N 70 56 E
Kota, India .... 68 G6 25 14N 75 49 E
Kota Baharu, Malaysia 65 J4 6 7N 102 14 E
Kota Barrage, India .. 68 G6 24 55N 76 10 E
Kota Belud, Malaysia . 62 C5 6 21N 116 26 E
Kota Kinabalu, Malaysia 62 C5 6 0N 116 4 E
Kota Kubu Baharu,
  Malaysia .... 65 L3 3 34N 101 39 E
Kota Tinggi, Malaysia . 65 M4 1 44N 103 53 E
Kotaagung, Indonesia . 62 F2 5 38 S 104 29 E
Kotabaru, Indonesia .. 62 E5 3 20 S 116 20 E
Kotabumi, Indonesia .. 62 E2 4 49 S 104 54 E
Kotamobagu, Indonesia 63 D6 0 57N 124 31 E
Kotcho L., Canada 102 B4 59 7N 121 12W
Kotdwara, India ...... 69 E8 29 45N 78 32 E
Kotel, Bulgaria ...... 45 D10 42 52N 26 26 E
Kotelnich, Russia .... 34 A9 58 22N 48 24 E
Kotelnikovo, Russia .. 35 G6 47 38N 43 8 E
Kotelnyy, Ostrov, Russia 53 B14 75 10N 139 0 E
Kothari ➤, India ..... 68 G5 25 20N 75 4 E
Köthen, Germany .... 24 D7 51 45N 11 59 E
Kothi, Chhattisgarh,
  India .... 69 H10 23 21N 82 3 E
Kothi, Mad. P., India . 69 G9 24 45N 80 40 E
Kotiro, Pakistan ..... 68 F2 26 17N 67 13 E
Kotka, Finland .... 9 F22 60 28N 26 58 E
Kotli, Pakistan ...... 68 G3 25 22N 68 22 E
Kótorus, Russia ...... 52 C5 61 17N 46 43 E
Kotlenska Planina,
  Bulgaria .... 45 D10 42 56N 26 30 E
Kotli, Pakistan ...... 68 C5 33 30N 73 55 E
Kotma, India .... 69 H9 23 12N 81 58 E
Kotmul, Pakistan .... 69 B6 35 32N 75 10 E
Koton-Karifi, Nigeria . 83 D6 8 0N 6 48 E
Kotonkoro, Nigeria ... 83 C6 11 3N 5 58 E
Kotor, Serbia & M. ... 44 D2 42 25N 18 47 E
Kotor Varoš, Bos.-H. . 28 F2 44 38N 17 22 E
Kotoriba, Croatia .... 41 B13 46 23N 16 48 E
Kotovo, Russia ...... 34 E7 50 22N 44 45 E
Kotovsk, Russia ..... 34 D5 52 36N 41 32 E
Kotovsk, Ukraine .... 33 J5 47 45N 29 35 E
Kotputli, India ...... 68 F7 27 43N 76 12 E
Kotri, Pakistan ...... 68 G3 25 22N 68 22 E
Kótronas, Greece ..... 46 E4 36 38N 22 29 E
Kötschach-Mauthen,
  Austria .... 26 E6 46 41N 13 1 E
Kotturu, India .... 66 M10 14 45N 76 10 E
Kotuy ➤, Russia ..... 53 B11 71 54N 102 6 E
Kotyuzhany, Ukraine . 29 B12 48 48N 27 42 E
Kotzebue, U.S.A. 100 B3 66 53N 162 39W
Kouchibouguac △,
  Canada 105 C6 46 50N 65 0W
Koudougou,
  Burkina Faso 82 C4 12 10N 2 20W
Koufonísi, Greece .... 49 E8 34 56N 26 8 E
Koufonísia, Greece ... 47 E7 36 57N 25 35 E
Kougaberge, S. Africa . 88 E3 33 48 S 23 50 E
Kouibli, Ivory C. 82 D3 7 15N 7 14W
Kouilou ➤, Congo .... 84 E2 4 10 S 12 5 E
Koula Moutou, Gabon . 84 E2 1 15 S 12 25 E
Koulen = Kulen,
  Cambodia .... 64 F5 13 50N 104 40 E
Koulikoro, Mali 82 C3 12 40N 7 50W
Kouloúra, Greece .... 49 A3 39 42N 19 54 E
Koûm-bournoú, Ákra,
  Greece .... 49 C10 36 15N 28 11 E
Koumala, Australia ... 94 C4 21 38 S 149 15 E
Koumankou, Mali 82 C3 11 58N 6 6W
Koumbia, Burkina Faso 82 C4 11 10N 3 50W
Koumbia, Guinea 82 C2 11 48N 13 29W
Koumboum, Guinea .. 82 C2 10 25N 13 0W
Koumpenntoum,
  Senegal 82 C2 13 59N 14 34W
Koun-Fao, Ivory C. ... 82 D4 7 30N 3 15W
Koundara, Guinea 82 C2 12 29N 13 18W
Koundheul, Senegal .. 82 C2 14 0N 14 50W
Kounradskiy,
  Kazakhstan .... 52 E8 46 59N 75 0 E
Koupéla, Burkina Faso 83 C4 12 11N 0 21W
Kouroussa, Guinea ... 82 C3 10 45N 9 45W
Kourémalé, Mali 82 C3 11 59N 8 42W
Kouris ➤, Cyprus .... 49 E11 34 38N 32 54 E
Kouroussa, Guinea ... 82 C3 10 45N 9 45W
Kourou, Fr. Guiana ... 125 B8 5 9N 52 39W
Kourouma,
  Burkina Faso 82 C4 11 35N 4 50W

Kourouninkoto, Mali .. 82 C3 13 52N 9 35W
Kouroussa, Guinea ... 82 C3 10 45N 9 45W
Koussanar, Senegal ... 82 C2 13 52N 14 5W
Koussané, Mali 82 C2 14 53N 11 14W
Koussane, Senegal ... 82 C2 14 10N 12 22W
Kousséri, Cameroon .. 79 F8 12 0N 14 55 E
Koutiala, Mali 82 C3 12 25N 5 23W
Kouto, Ivory C. 82 D3 9 53N 6 25W
Kouvé, Togo .... 83 D5 6 25N 1 25 E
Kouvola, Finland ..... 9 F22 60 52N 26 43 E
Kovačica, Serbia & M. . 28 E5 45 5N 20 38 E
Kovel, Ukraine .... 33 G3 51 11N 24 38 E
Kovin, Serbia & M. ... 28 F5 44 44N 20 59 E
Kovrov, Russia .... 34 B5 56 25N 41 25 E
Kowal, Poland .... 31 F6 52 32N 19 7 E
Kowalewo Pomorskie,
  Poland .... 31 E5 53 10N 18 52 E
Kowanyama, Australia . 94 B3 15 29 S 141 44 E
Kowloon, China ..... 59 F10 22 19N 114 11 E
Kowŏn, N. Korea .... 57 E14 39 26N 127 14 E
Koyampattur =
  Coimbatore, India .. 66 P10 11 2N 76 59 E
Köyceğiz, Turkey .... 47 E10 36 57N 28 40 E
Köyceğiz Gölü, Turkey 47 E10 36 56N 28 42 E
Koyulhisar, Turkey ... 72 B7 40 20N 37 52 E
Koyunyeri, Turkey ... 45 F10 40 50N 26 26 E
Koza, Japan .... 55 L3 26 19N 127 46 E
Kozak, Turkey .... 47 B9 39 15N 27 6 E
Kozan, Turkey .... 70 B2 37 26N 35 50 E
Kozáni, Greece ...... 44 F5 40 19N 21 47 E
Kozáni □, Greece .... 44 F5 40 18N 21 45 E
Kozara, Bos.-H. ..... 41 D14 45 0N 17 0 E
Kozara △, Bos.-H. ... 28 F2 45 0N 17 0 E
Kozarac, Bos.-H. ..... 41 D13 44 58N 16 48 E
Kozelets, Ukraine .... 33 G6 50 55N 31 7 E
Kozelsk, Russia ...... 32 E8 54 2N 35 48 E
Kozhikode = Calicut,
  India .... 66 P9 11 15N 75 43 E
Koziegłowy, Poland .. 31 H6 50 37N 19 8 E
Kozienice, Poland .... 31 G8 51 35N 21 34 E
Kozje, Slovenia ...... 41 B12 46 5N 15 35 E
Kozlodży, Bulgaria ... 44 C7 43 45N 23 42 E
Kozlovets, Bulgaria .. 45 C9 43 30N 25 20 E
Kozlovka, Russia ..... 34 C9 55 32N 48 14 E
Kozlu, Turkey .... 72 B4 41 26N 31 45 E
Kozluk, Turkey ...... 73 C9 38 11N 41 31 E
Koźmin, Poland ...... 31 G4 51 48N 17 27 E
Kozmodemyansk, Russia 34 B8 56 20N 46 36 E
Kozhukhovo, Poland .. 31 G2 51 45N 15 31 E
Kozyatyn, Ukraine .... 33 H5 49 45N 28 50 E
Kpabia, Ghana 83 D4 9 10N 0 20W
Kpalimé, Togo .... 83 D5 6 57N 0 44 E
Kpandae, Ghana 83 D4 8 30N 0 2W
Kpessi, Togo .... 83 D5 8 4N 1 16 E
Kra, Isthmus of = Kra,
  Kho Khot, Thailand . 65 G2 10 15N 99 30 E
Kra, Kho Khot,
  Thailand .... 65 G2 10 15N 99 30 E
Kra Buri, Thailand ... 65 G2 10 22N 98 46 E
Kraai ➤, S. Africa .... 88 E4 30 40 S 26 45 E
Krabi, Thailand ...... 65 H2 8 4N 98 55 E
Kracheh, Cambodia .. 64 F6 12 32N 106 10 E
Kragan, Indonesia .... 63 G14 6 43 S 111 38 E
Kragerø, Norway ..... 9 G13 58 52N 9 25 E
Kragujevac, Serbia & M. 44 B4 44 2N 20 56 E
Krajenka, Poland ..... 31 E3 53 18N 16 59 E
Krakatau = Rakata,
  Pulau, Indonesia ... 62 F3 6 10 S 105 20 E
Krakatoa = Rakata,
  Pulau, Indonesia ... 62 F3 6 10 S 105 20 E
Krakor, Cambodia ... 64 F5 12 32N 104 12 E
Kraków, Poland ...... 31 H6 50 4N 19 57 E
Kraków ✈ (KRK),
  Poland .... 31 H6 50 5N 19 52 E
Kralanh, Cambodia .. 64 F4 13 35N 103 25 E
Králíky, Czech Rep. .. 27 A9 50 6N 16 45 E
Kraljevo, Serbia & M. . 44 C4 43 44N 20 41 E
Kralovéhradecký □,
  Czech Rep. .... 26 A8 50 25N 15 50 E
Královský Chlmec,
  Slovak Rep. .... 27 C14 48 27N 22 0 E
Kralupy nad Vltavou,
  Czech Rep. .... 26 A7 50 13N 14 20 E
Kramatorsk, Ukraine . 33 H9 48 50N 37 30 E
Kramfors, Sweden .... 10 B11 62 55N 17 48 E
Kraniá, Greece ...... 44 G5 39 53N 21 18 E
Kranía Elassónas,
  Greece .... 46 B4 39 57N 22 2 E
Kraníthion, Greece ... 46 D5 37 20N 23 10 E
Kranj, Slovenia ...... 41 B11 46 16N 14 22 E
Kranjska Gora, Slovenia 41 B11 46 29N 13 48 E
Krankskop, S. Africa . 89 D5 28 0 S 30 47 E
Krapina, Croatia ..... 41 B12 46 10N 15 52 E
Krapina ➤, Croatia ... 41 C12 45 50N 15 50 E
Krapkowice, Poland .. 31 H4 50 29N 17 56 E
Kras, Croatia .... 41 C10 45 35N 14 0 E
Kraskino, Russia ..... 53 E14 42 44N 130 48 E
Kräslava, Latvia ..... 32 E4 55 54N 27 10 E
Kraslice, Czech Rep. .. 26 A5 50 19N 12 31 E
Krasnaya Gorbatka,
  Russia .... 34 C5 55 52N 41 45 E
Krasnaya Polyana,
  Russia .... 35 J5 43 40N 40 13 E
Krasne, Ukraine ...... 29 D14 46 7N 29 15 E
Krasni Okny, Ukraine . 29 C14 47 32N 29 27 E
Kraśnik, Poland ...... 31 H9 50 55N 22 15 E
Krasnoarmeisk, Ukraine 33 H9 48 18N 37 11 E
Krasnoarmeysk, Russia 34 E7 51 0N 45 42 E
Krasnoarmeyskiy,
  Russia .... 35 G6 47 0N 42 12 E
Krasnobrod, Poland .. 31 H10 50 33N 23 12 E
Krasnodar, Russia .... 35 H4 45 5N 39 0 E
Krasnodon, Ukraine .. 33 H10 48 17N 39 44 E
Krasnogorskiy, Russia . 34 B9 56 10N 48 28 E
Krasnograd =
  Krasnohrad, Ukraine 33 H8 49 27N 35 27 E
Krasnogvardeysk,
  Ukraine .... 33 K8 45 32N 34 16 E
Krasnogvardeyskoye,
  Russia .... 35 H5 45 52N 41 33 E
Krasnohrad, Ukraine . 33 H8 49 27N 35 27 E
Krasnokutsk, Ukraine . 33 G8 50 10N 34 50 E
Krasnolesnyy, Russia . 33 G10 51 53N 39 35 E
Krasnoperekopsk,
  Ukraine .... 33 J7 46 0N 33 54 E
Krasnorechenskiy,
  Russia .... 54 B7 44 41N 135 14 E
Krasnoselkup, Russia . 52 C9 65 20N 82 10 E
Krasnoslobodsk,
  Mordvinia, Russia . 34 C6 54 25N 43 45 E
Krasnoslobodsk,
  Volgograd, Russia . 35 F7 48 42N 44 33 E
Krasnoturinsk, Russia . 52 D7 59 46N 60 12 E
Krasnoufimsk, Russia . 52 D6 56 36N 57 38 E
Krasnoyarsk, Russia .. 53 D10 56 8N 93 0 E
Krasnoyarskoye, Russia 30 D8 54 31N 21 56 E
Krasnoye = Krasnyy,
  Russia .... 32 E6 54 25N 31 30 E
Krasnoyilsk, Ukraine . 29 C10 47 59N 25 28 E

Krasnozavodsk, Russia 32 D10 56 27N 38 25 E
Krasnoznamensk, Russia 30 D9 54 57N 22 30 E
Krasny Sulin, Russia .. 33 J11 47 52N 40 8 E
Krasnystaw, Poland .. 31 H10 50 57N 23 5 E
Krasny, Russia .... 32 E6 54 25N 31 30 E
Krasnyy Kholm, Russia 32 C9 58 10N 37 10 E
Krasnyy Kut, Russia .. 34 E8 50 50N 47 0 E
Krasnyy Liman, Ukraine 33 H9 48 58N 37 50 E
Krasnyy Luch, Ukraine 33 H10 48 13N 39 0 E
Krasnyy Profintern,
  Russia .... 32 D11 57 45N 40 27 E
Krasnyy Yar, Astrakhan,
  Russia .... 35 G9 46 43N 48 23 E
Krasnyy Yar, Samara,
  Russia .... 34 D10 53 30N 50 22 E
Krasnyy Yar, Volgograd,
  Russia .... 34 E7 50 42N 44 45 E
Krasnyye Baki, Russia . 34 B7 57 8N 45 10 E
Krasnyyoskolske
  Vdskh., Ukraine ... 33 H9 49 27N 37 40 E
Kraszna ➤, Hungary . 28 B7 48 4N 22 20 E
Kratie = Kracheh,
  Cambodia .... 64 F6 12 32N 106 10 E
Kratovo, Macedonia .. 44 D6 42 6N 22 10 E
Krau, Indonesia ...... 63 E10 3 19 S 140 5 E
Kravanh, Chuor Phnum,
  Cambodia .... 65 G4 12 0N 103 32 E
Krefeld, Germany .... 24 D2 51 20N 6 33 E
Krémaston, Límni,
  Greece .... 46 C3 38 52N 21 30 E
Kremen, Croatia ..... 41 D12 44 28N 15 53 E
Kremenchuk, Ukraine . 33 H7 49 5N 33 25 E
Kremenchuksk Vdskh.,
  Ukraine .... 33 H7 49 20N 32 30 E
Kremenets, Ukraine .. 33 G3 50 8N 25 43 E
Kremennaya, Ukraine . 33 H10 49 1N 38 10 E
Kremges = Svitlovodsk,
  Ukraine .... 33 H7 49 20N 33 13 E
Kremmen, Germany .. 24 C9 52 45N 13 1 E
Kremmling, U.S.A. ... 108 F10 40 4N 106 24W
Krems, Austria .... 26 C8 48 25N 15 36 E
Kremsmünster, Austria 26 C7 48 3N 14 8 E
Kretinga, Lithuania ... 9 J19 55 53N 21 15 E
Krettsy, Russia ...... 32 C7 58 15N 32 30 E
Kreuzberg, Germany .. 25 E5 50 27N 9 58 E
Kreuztal, Germany ... 24 E4 50 57N 8 0 E
Kría Vrísi, Greece .... 44 F6 40 41N 22 18 E
Kribi, Cameroon ..... 83 E6 2 57N 9 56 E
Krichem, Bulgaria .... 45 D8 42 8N 24 28 E
Krichev = Krychaw,
  Belarus .... 32 F6 53 40N 31 41 E
Krim, Slovenia .... 41 C11 45 53N 14 30 E
Kriós, Ákra, Greece ... 49 D5 35 13N 23 34 E
Krishna ➤, India ..... 67 M12 15 57N 80 59 E
Krishnanagar, India .. 69 H13 23 24N 88 33 E
Kristdala, Sweden .... 11 G10 57 24N 16 13 E
Kristiansand, Norway . 9 G13 58 8N 8 1 E
Kristianstad, Sweden . 11 H8 56 2N 14 9 E
Kristiansund, Norway . 8 E12 63 7N 7 45 E
Kristiinankaupunki,
  Finland .... 9 E19 62 16N 21 21 E
Kristinehamn, Sweden . 10 E8 59 18N 14 7 E
Kristinestad =
  Kristiinankaupunki,
  Finland .... 9 E19 62 16N 21 21 E
Kríti, Greece .... 49 D7 35 15N 25 0 E
Kritsá, Greece .... 49 D7 35 10N 25 41 E
Kriva ➤, Macedonia .. 44 D5 42 5N 21 47 E
Kriva Palanka,
  Macedonia .... 44 D6 42 11N 22 19 E
Krivaja ➤, Bos.-H. ... 28 F3 44 27N 18 9 E
Krivelj, Serbia & M. .. 44 B6 44 10N 22 5 E
Křivoklátsko △,
  Czech Rep. .... 26 A6 50 1N 13 51 E
Krivoy Rog = Kryvyy
  Rih, Ukraine ...... 33 J7 47 51N 33 20 E
Križevci, Croatia ..... 41 B13 46 3N 16 32 E
Krk, Croatia .... 41 C11 45 8N 14 40 E
Krka ➤, Slovenia ..... 41 C12 45 50N 15 30 E
Krka △, Slovenia ..... 41 C12 45 50N 15 56 E
Krkonoše, Czech Rep. . 26 A8 50 50N 15 35 E
Krkonoše △, Czech Rep. 26 A8 50 43N 15 39 E
Krnov, Czech Rep. ... 27 A10 50 5N 17 40 E
Krobia, Poland ...... 31 G3 51 47N 16 59 E
Krokeaí, Greece ..... 46 E4 36 53N 22 32 E
Krokek, Sweden ..... 11 F10 58 40N 16 24 E
Krokodil ➤, Mozam. . 89 D5 25 14 S 32 18 E
Krokom, Sweden ..... 10 A8 63 20N 14 30 E
Krokowa, Poland .... 30 D5 54 47N 18 9 E
Krolevets, Ukraine ... 33 G7 51 35N 33 20 E
Kroměříž, Czech Rep. . 27 B10 49 18N 17 21 E
Krompachy, Slovak Rep. 27 C13 48 54N 20 52 E
Kromy, Russia .... 33 F8 52 48N 35 48 E
Kronach, Germany ... 25 E7 50 14N 11 19 E
Krong Kaoh Kong,
  Cambodia .... 62 B2 11 35N 103 0 E
Kronobergs län □,
  Sweden .... 11 H8 56 45N 14 30 E
Kronprins Olav Kyst,
  Antarctica .... 5 C5 69 0 S 42 0 E
Kronprinsesse Märtha
  Kyst, Antarctica ... 5 D2 73 30 S 10 0W
Kronshtadt, Russia ... 32 C5 59 57N 29 51 E
Kroonstad, S. Africa .. 88 D4 27 43 S 27 19 E
Kröpelin, Germany ... 24 A7 54 4N 11 47 E
Kropotkin, Russia .... 35 H5 45 28N 40 28 E
Kropp, Germany ..... 24 A5 54 24N 9 31 E
Krosna, Lithuania .... 30 D10 54 23N 23 33 E
Krośniewice, Poland .. 31 F6 52 15N 19 11 E
Krosno, Poland ...... 31 J8 49 42N 21 46 E
Krosno Odrzańskie,
  Poland .... 31 F2 52 3N 15 7 E
Krotoszyn, Poland ... 31 G4 51 42N 17 23 E
Krotovka, Russia ..... 34 D10 53 18N 51 10 E
Kroussón, Greece .... 49 D6 35 13N 24 59 E
Krrabë, Albania ..... 44 E4 41 27N 19 48 E
Krško, Slovenia ...... 41 C12 45 57N 15 30 E
Krstača, Serbia & M. . 44 D4 42 57N 20 8 E
Kruger △, S. Africa ... 89 C5 24 50 S 26 10 E
Krugersdorp, S. Africa 89 D4 26 5 S 27 46 E
Kruisfontein, S. Africa 88 E3 33 59 S 24 43 E
Krujë, Albania .... 44 E3 41 31N 19 46 E
Krulevshchina =
  Krulyewshchyna,
  Belarus .... 32 E4 55 5N 27 45 E
Krulyewshchyna,
  Belarus .... 32 E4 55 5N 27 45 E
Krumbach, Germany . 25 G6 48 15N 10 22 E
Krumë, Albania ..... 44 D4 42 11N 20 25 E
Krumovgrad, Bulgaria 45 E9 41 29N 25 38 E
Krung Thep = Bangkok,
  Thailand .... 64 F3 13 45N 100 35 E
Krupanj, Serbia & M. . 44 B3 44 25N 19 22 E
Krupina, Slovak Rep. . 27 C12 48 21N 19 5 E
Krupinica ➤,
  Slovak Rep. .... 27 C11 48 4N 18 55 E
Krupki, Belarus ...... 32 E5 54 19N 29 8 E

Kruševac, Serbia & M. . 44 C5 43 35N 21 28 E
Kruševo, Macedonia .. 44 E5 41 23N 21 19 E
Krushelnyksya, Ukraine 31 J10 49 7N 23 29 E
Kruszwica, Poland ... 31 F5 52 40N 18 20 E
Krychaw, Belarus .... 32 F6 53 40N 31 41 E
Krymsk, Russia ...... 33 K10 44 50N 38 0 E
Krymskiy Poluostrov =
  Krymskyy Pivostriv,
  Ukraine .... 33 K8 45 0N 34 0 E
Krymskyy Pivostriv,
  Ukraine .... 33 K8 45 0N 34 0 E
Krynica, Poland ...... 31 J7 49 25N 20 57 E
Krynica Morska, Poland 30 D6 54 23N 19 28 E
Krynki, Poland ...... 31 E10 53 17N 23 43 E
Krynychne, Ukraine .. 29 E13 45 32N 28 40 E
Kryvyy Rih, Ukraine . 33 J7 47 51N 33 20 E
Kryzhopil, Ukraine ... 29 B13 48 23N 28 53 E
Krzepice, Poland ..... 31 H5 50 58N 18 50 E
Krzeszów, Poland .... 31 H9 50 24N 22 21 E
Krzna ➤, Poland ..... 31 F10 52 3N 23 32 E
Krzywiń, Poland ..... 31 G3 51 58N 16 50 E
Krzyż Wielkopolski,
  Poland .... 31 F2 52 53N 16 0 E
Ksar el Kebir, Morocco 78 B4 35 0N 6 0W
Ksar es Souk = Er
  Rachidia, Morocco . 78 B5 31 58N 4 20W
Ksiąz Wielkopolski,
  Poland .... 31 F4 52 4N 17 14 E
Kstovo, Russia ...... 34 B7 56 12N 44 13 E
Ku, W. el ➤, Sudan .. 81 E2 13 37N 25 15 E
Kuah, Malaysia ...... 65 J2 6 19N 99 51 E
Kuala Belait, Malaysia . 62 D4 4 35N 114 11 E
Kuala Berang, Malaysia 65 K4 5 5N 103 1 E
Kuala Dungun =
  Dungun, Malaysia .. 65 K4 4 45N 103 25 E
Kuala Kangsar, Malaysia 65 K3 4 46N 100 56 E
Kuala Kelawang,
  Malaysia .... 65 L4 2 56N 102 5 E
Kuala Kerai, Malaysia . 65 K4 5 30N 102 12 E
Kuala Kerian, Malaysia 65 c 5 10N 100 25 E
Kuala Lipis, Malaysia . 65 K4 4 10N 102 3 E
Kuala Lumpur, Malaysia 65 L3 3 9N 101 41 E
Kuala Nerang, Malaysia 65 J3 6 16N 100 37 E
Kuala Pilah, Malaysia . 65 L4 2 45N 102 15 E
Kuala Rompin, Malaysia 65 L4 2 49N 103 29 E
Kuala Selangor,
  Malaysia .... 65 L3 3 20N 101 15 E
Kuala Sepetang,
  Malaysia .... 65 K3 4 49N 100 28 E
Kuala Terengganu,
  Malaysia .... 65 K4 5 20N 103 8 E
Kualajelai, Indonesia . 62 E4 2 58 S 110 46 E
Kualakapuas, Indonesia 62 E4 2 55 S 114 20 E
Kualakurun, Indonesia 62 E4 1 10 S 113 50 E
Kualapembuang,
  Indonesia .... 62 E4 3 14 S 112 38 E
Kualasimpang,
  Indonesia .... 62 D1 4 17N 98 3 E
Kuancheng, China ... 57 D10 40 37N 118 30 E
Kuandang, Indonesia . 63 D6 0 56N 123 1 E
Kuandian, China ..... 57 D13 40 45N 124 45 E
Kuangchou =
  Guangzhou, China . 59 F9 23 5N 113 10 E
Kuanshan, Taiwan ... 59 F13 23 11N 121 9 E
Kuantan, Malaysia ... 65 L4 3 49N 103 20 E
Kuba = Quba,
  Azerbaijan .... 35 K9 41 21N 48 32 E
Kuban ➤, Russia ..... 33 K9 45 20N 37 30 E
Kuban Depression =
  Prikubanskaya
  Nizmennost, Russia . 35 H4 45 39N 38 33 E
Kubenskoye, Ozero,
  Russia .... 32 C10 59 40N 39 25 E
Kubokawa, Japan .... 55 H6 33 12N 133 8 E
Kubrat, Bulgaria ..... 45 C10 43 49N 26 31 E
Kubu, Indonesia ..... 63 J18 8 16 S 115 35 E
Kubutambahan,
  Indonesia .... 63 J18 8 5 S 115 10 E
Kucar, Tanjung,
  Indonesia .... 63 F5 8 39 S 114 34 E
Kučevo, Serbia & M. .. 44 B5 44 30N 21 40 E
Kuchaman, India .... 68 F6 27 13N 74 47 E
Kuchenspitze, Austria . 26 D3 47 7N 10 12 E
Kuchinda, India ..... 69 J11 21 44N 84 21 E
Kuching, Malaysia ... 62 D4 1 33N 110 25 E
Kuchino-eruba-Jima,
  Japan .... 55 J5 30 28N 130 12 E
Kuchino-Shima, Japan 55 K4 29 57N 129 55 E
Kuchinotsu, Japan ... 55 H5 32 36N 130 11 E
Kuchl, Austria .... 26 D6 47 37N 13 9 E
Kuchurhan ➤, Ukraine 29 D14 46 50N 29 57 E
Kucing = Kuching,
  Malaysia .... 62 D4 1 33N 110 25 E
Kuçovë, Albania ..... 44 F3 40 47N 19 57 E
Küçükbahçe, Turkey . 47 C8 38 33N 26 24 E
Küçükköy, Turkey ... 47 B8 39 16N 26 42 E
Küçükkuyu, Turkey .. 47 B8 39 34N 26 36 E
Küçükmenderes ➤,
  Turkey .... 47 D9 37 57N 27 16 E
Kud ➤, Pakistan ..... 68 F2 26 5N 66 20 E
Kuda, India .... 66 H7 23 10N 71 15 E
Kudat, Malaysia ..... 62 C5 6 55N 116 55 E
Kudirkos Naumiestis,
  Lithuania .... 30 D9 54 46N 22 53 E
Kudowa-Zdrój, Poland 31 H3 50 27N 16 15 E
Kudus, Indonesia .... 63 G14 6 48 S 110 51 E
Kudymkar, Russia ... 52 D6 59 1N 54 39 E
Kueiyang = Guiyang,
  China .... 58 D6 26 32N 106 40 E
Kufra Oasis = Al
  Kufrah, Libya ..... 79 D10 24 17N 23 15 E
Kufstein, Austria ..... 26 D5 47 35N 12 11 E
Kugaaruk = Pelly Bay,
  Canada 101 B11 68 38N 89 50W
Kugluktuk, Canada .. 100 B8 67 50N 115 5W
Kugong I., Canada ... 104 A4 56 18N 79 50W
Kūhak, Iran .... 66 F3 27 12N 63 10 E
Kuhan, Pakistan ..... 68 E2 28 19N 67 14 E
Kühbonān, Iran ..... 71 D8 31 23N 56 19 E
Kühestak, Iran ...... 71 E8 26 47N 57 2 E
Kühīn, Iran .... 71 B6 36 22N 49 40 E
Kühīrī, Iran .... 71 E9 26 55N 61 2 E
Kuhn Ø, Greenland .. 4 B6 75 12N 18 50W
Kühpāyeh, Esfahan, Iran 71 C7 32 44N 52 20 E
Kühpāyeh, Kermān, Iran 71 D8 30 35N 57 15 E
Kührān, Kūh-e, Iran .. 71 E8 26 46N 58 12 E
Kui Buri, Thailand ... 65 F2 12 3N 99 52 E
Kuiseb ➤, Namibia ... 88 C1 22 59N 14 58 E
Kuito, Angola .... 85 G3 12 22 S 16 55 E
Kuiu I., U.S.A. 102 B2 57 45N 134 10W
Kujang, N. Korea .... 57 E14 39 57N 126 1 E
Kujawsko-Pomorskie □,
  Poland .... 31 E5 53 16N 18 30 E
Kuji, Japan .... 54 D10 40 11N 141 46 E
Kujū-San, Japan ..... 55 H5 33 5N 131 15 E
Kukava, Ukraine ..... 29 B12 48 27N 27 43 E
Kukawa, Nigeria ..... 83 C7 12 58N 13 27 E
Kukës, Albania ...... 44 D4 42 5N 20 27 E
Kukmor, Russia ..... 34 B10 56 11N 50 54 E
Kukup, Malaysia .... 65 d 1 20N 103 27 E
Kukup, Pulau, Malaysia 65 d 1 18N 103 25 E
Kukvidze, Russia .... 34 E6 50 40N 43 0 E
Kula, Bulgaria ...... 44 C6 43 52N 22 36 E
Kula, Serbia & M. .... 28 E4 45 37N 19 32 E
Kula, Turkey .... 47 C10 38 32N 28 40 E
Kulachi, Pakistan .... 68 D4 31 56N 70 27 E
Kuladia, Russia ...... 65 M4 1 44N 103 35 E
Kulaly, Ostrov,
  Kazakhstan .... 35 H10 45 0N 50 0 E
Kulasekarappattinam,
  India .... 66 Q11 8 20N 78 5 E
Kulautuva, Lithuania . 30 D10 54 56N 23 36 E
Kuldīga, Latvia ...... 9 H19 56 58N 21 59 E
Kuldīga □, Latvia .... 30 B8 56 55N 22 0 E
Kuldu, Sudan .... 81 E2 12 50N 28 58 E
Kulebaki, Russia ..... 34 C6 55 22N 42 25 E
Kulen, Cambodia .... 64 F5 13 50N 104 40 E
Kulen Vakuf, Bos.-H. . 41 D13 44 35N 16 2 E
Kulgam, India .... 69 C6 33 36N 75 2 E
Kulgera, Australia ... 94 D1 25 50 S 133 18 E
Kulim, Malaysia ..... 65 K3 5 22N 100 34 E
Kulin, Australia ..... 93 F2 32 40 S 118 2 E
Kulkayu = Hartley Bay,
  Canada 102 C3 53 25N 129 15W
Kullen, Sweden ...... 11 H6 56 18N 12 26 E
Kulmbach, Germany . 25 E7 50 6N 11 26 E
Kŭlob, Tajikistan .... 52 F7 37 55N 69 50 E
Kulp, Turkey .... 73 C9 38 29N 41 2 E
Kulpawn ➤, Ghana .. 83 D4 10 20N 1 5W
Kulsary, Kazakhstan . 52 E6 46 59N 54 1 E
Kulti, India .... 69 H12 23 43N 86 50 E
Kulu, India .... 68 D7 31 58N 77 6 E
Kulu, Turkey .... 72 C5 39 5N 33 4 E
Kulumbura, Australia . 92 B4 13 55 S 126 35 E
Kulunda, Russia ..... 52 D8 52 35N 78 57 E
Kulungar, Afghan. ... 68 C3 34 0N 69 2 E
Kulvand, Iran .... 71 D7 31 21N 54 35 E
Kulwin, Australia .... 95 F3 35 0 S 142 42 E
Kulyab = Kŭlob,
  Tajikistan .... 52 F7 37 55N 69 50 E
Kuma ➤, Russia ..... 35 H8 44 55N 47 0 E
Kumafşarı, Turkey .. 47 D11 37 19N 29 32 E
Kumagaya, Japan .... 55 F9 36 9N 139 22 E
Kumai, Indonesia .... 62 E4 2 44 S 111 43 E
Kumalar Dağı, Turkey 47 C12 38 15N 30 20 E
Kumamba, Kepulauan,
  Indonesia .... 63 E9 1 36 S 138 45 E
Kumamoto, Japan ... 55 H5 32 45N 130 45 E
Kumamoto □, Japan . 55 H5 32 55N 130 55 E
Kumanovo, Macedonia 44 D5 42 9N 21 42 E
Kumara, N.Z. .... 91 K3 42 37 S 171 12 E
Kumarina, Australia .. 93 D2 24 41 S 119 32 E
Kumasi, Ghana 82 D4 6 41N 1 38W
Kumba, Cameroon ... 83 E6 4 36N 9 24 E
Kumbağ, Turkey .... 45 F11 40 51N 27 27 E
Kumbakonam, India . 66 P11 10 58N 79 25 E
Kumbarilla, Australia . 95 D5 27 15 S 150 55 E
Kumbhraj, India ..... 68 G7 24 22N 77 3 E
Kumbia, Australia ... 95 D5 26 41 S 151 39 E
Kumbo, Cameroon ... 83 D7 6 15N 10 36 E
Kŭmch'ŏn, N. Korea . 57 E14 38 10N 126 29 E
Kumdok, India ...... 69 C8 33 32N 78 10 E
Kume-Shima, Japan .. 55 L3 26 20N 126 47 E
Kumeny, Russia ..... 34 A9 58 10N 49 47 E
Kumharsain, India ... 68 D7 31 19N 77 27 E
Kumhwa, S. Korea ... 57 E14 38 17N 127 28 E
Kumi, Uganda .... 86 B3 1 30N 33 58 E
Kumkale, Turkey .... 45 G10 39 59N 26 11 E
Kumla, Sweden ...... 10 E9 59 8N 15 10 E
Kumluca, Turkey .... 47 E12 36 22N 30 20 E
Kummerower See,
  Germany .... 24 B8 53 49N 12 51 E
Kumo, Nigeria .... 83 C7 10 1N 11 12 E
Kumo älv ➤ =
  Kokemäenjoki ➤,
  Finland .... 9 F19 61 32N 21 44 E
Kumon Bum, Burma . 67 F20 26 30N 97 15 E
Kumylzhenskaya, Russia 34 F6 49 51N 42 38 E
Kunágota, Hungary .. 28 D6 46 26N 21 3 E
Kunashir, Ostrov, Russia 53 E15 44 0N 146 0 E
Kunda, Estonia ...... 9 G22 59 30N 26 34 E
Kunda, India .... 69 G9 25 43N 81 31 E
Kundar ➤, Pakistan .. 68 D3 31 56N 69 19 E
Kundelungu △,
  Dem. Rep. of
  the Congo .... 87 E2 10 30 S 27 40 E
Kundelungu Ouest △,
  Dem. Rep. of
  the Congo .... 87 D2 9 55 S 27 17 E
Kundian, Pakistan ... 68 C4 32 27N 71 28 E
Kundla, India .... 68 J4 21 21N 71 25 E
Kung, Ao, Thailand .. 65 a 8 5N 98 24 E
Kunga ➤, Bangla. ... 69 J13 21 46N 89 30 E
Kungälv, Sweden .... 11 G5 57 53N 11 59 E
Kunghit I., Canada ... 102 C2 52 6N 131 3W
Kungrad = Qŭnghirot,
  Uzbekistan .... 52 E6 43 6N 58 54 E
Kungsängen, Sweden . 10 E11 59 29N 17 45 E
Kungsbacka, Sweden . 11 G6 57 30N 12 5 E
Kungsgården, Sweden 10 D10 60 37N 16 53 E
Kungshamn, Sweden . 11 F5 58 22N 11 21 E
Kungsör, Sweden .... 10 E10 59 25N 16 5 E
Kungur, Russia ...... 52 D6 57 25N 56 57 E
Kungurri, Australia .. 94 K6 21 4 S 148 45 E
Kunhar ➤, Pakistan . 69 B5 34 20N 73 30 E
Kunhegyes, Hungary . 28 C5 47 22N 20 36 E
Kuningan, Indonesia . 63 G13 6 59 S 108 29 E
Kunlong, Burma ..... 58 F2 23 20N 98 50 E
Kunlun Shan, Asia ... 60 C3 36 0N 86 30 E
Kunmadaras, Hungary 28 C5 47 28N 20 45 E
Kunming, China ..... 58 E4 25 1N 102 41 E
Kunsan, S. Korea .... 57 G14 35 59N 126 45 E
Kunshan, China ..... 59 B13 31 22N 120 58 E
Kunszentmárton,
  Hungary .... 28 D5 46 50N 20 11 E
Kunszentmiklós,
  Hungary .... 28 C4 47 1N 19 8 E
Kuntaur, Senegal 82 C2 13 40N 14 48W
Kununurra, Australia . 92 C4 15 40 S 128 50 E
Kunwari ➤, India .... 69 F8 26 26N 79 11 E
Kunya-Urgench =
  Köneürgench,
  Turkmenistan ..... 52 E6 42 19N 59 10 E
Künzelsau, Germany . 25 F5 49 17N 9 42 E
Kuopio, Finland ..... 8 E22 62 53N 27 35 E
Kupa ➤, Croatia ..... 41 C13 45 28N 16 24 E
Kupang, Indonesia ... 63 F6 10 19 S 123 39 E
Kupreanof I., U.S.A. . 102 B2 56 50N 133 30W
Kupres, Bos.-H. ..... 28 G2 43 59N 17 15 E
Kupyansk-Uzlovoi,
  Ukraine .... 33 H9 49 40N 37 43 E

Kuqa, China .... 60 B3 41 35N 82 30 E
Kür →, Azerbaijan .. 73 C13 39 29N 49 15 E
Kür Dili, Azerbaijan .. 71 B6 39 3N 49 13 E
Kura = Kür →,
　Azerbaijan ..... 73 C13 39 29N 49 15 E
Kuranda, Australia .... 94 B4 16 48 S 145 35 E
Kuranga, India ..... 68 H3 22 4N 69 10 E
Kurashiki, Japan .... 55 G6 34 40N 133 50 E
Kurayoshi, Japan .... 55 G6 35 26N 133 50 E
Kürdämir, Azerbaijan .. 35 K9 40 25N 48 3 E
Kurdistan, Asia ..... 73 D10 37 20N 43 30 E
Kürdzhali, Bulgaria .. 45 E9 41 38N 25 21 E
Kure, Japan .... 55 G6 34 14N 132 32 E
Küre, Turkey ...... 72 B5 41 48N 33 43 E
Küre Dağları, Turkey .. 72 B5 41 50N 34 10 E
Kuressaare, Estonia .. 9 G20 58 15N 22 30 E
Kurgan, Russia ..... 52 D7 55 26N 65 18 E
Kurganinsk, Russia .. 35 H5 44 54N 40 34 E
Kurgannaya =
　Kurganinsk, Russia .. 35 H5 44 54N 40 34 E
Kuri, India .... 68 F4 26 37N 70 43 E
Kuria Maria Is. =
　Khurīyā Murīyā,
　Jazā'ir, Oman ..... 75 D6 17 30N 55 58 E
Kuridala, Australia .... 94 C3 21 16 S 140 29 E
Kurigram, Bangla. .... 67 G16 25 49N 89 39 E
Kurikka, Finland ..... 9 E20 62 36N 22 24 E
Kuril Is. = Kurilskiye
　Ostrova, Russia .... 53 E15 45 0N 150 0 E
Kuril Trench, Pac. Oc. .. 96 C7 44 0N 153 0 E
Kurilsk, Russia ..... 53 E15 45 14N 147 53 E
Kurilskiye Ostrova,
　Russia .... 53 E15 45 0N 150 0 E
Kurino, Japan ...... 55 J5 31 57N 130 43 E
Kurinskaya Kosa = Kür
　Dili, Azerbaijan .... 71 B6 39 3N 49 13 E
Kurkur, Egypt ...... 80 C3 23 50N 32 0 E
Kurlovskiy, Russia .... 34 C5 55 25N 40 40 E
Kurmuk, Sudan ..... 81 E3 10 33N 34 21 E
Kurnool, India ..... 66 M11 15 45N 78 0 E
Kuro-Shima,
　Kagoshima, Japan .. 55 J4 30 50N 129 57 E
Kuro-Shima, Okinawa,
　Japan .... 55 M2 24 14N 124 1 E
Kuror, J., Sudan .... 80 C3 20 27N 31 30 E
Kurow, N.Z. .... 91 L3 44 44 S 170 29 E
Kurów, Poland ..... 31 G9 51 23N 22 12 E
Kurram →, Pakistan .. 68 C4 32 36N 71 20 E
Kurri Kurri, Australia .. 95 E5 32 50 S 151 28 E
Kurrimine, Australia .. 94 B4 17 47 S 146 6 E
Kursavka, Russia .... 35 H6 44 29N 42 32 E
Kurshskaya Kosa △,
　Russia .... 30 C7 55 7N 20 45 E
Kurshskiy Zaliv, Russia .. 9 J19 55 9N 21 6 E
Kuršių Nerijos =
　Lithuania .... 30 C8 55 30N 21 6 E
Kursk, Russia ...... 33 G9 51 42N 36 11 E
Kuršumlija, Serbia & M. .. 44 C5 43 9N 21 19 E
Kuršumlijska Banja,
　Serbia & M. ..... 44 C5 43 3N 21 11 E
Kurşunlu, Bursa, Turkey .. 45 F13 40 3N 29 40 E
Kurşunlu, Çankırı,
　Turkey .... 72 B5 40 51N 33 15 E
Kurtalan, Turkey .... 73 D7 37 56N 41 4 E
Kurtbey, Turkey .... 45 E10 41 9N 26 35 E
Kuru, Sudan .... 81 F2 7 43N 26 31 E
Kuru, Bahr el →, Sudan .. 81 F2 8 10N 26 50 E
Kurucaşile, Turkey .. 72 B5 41 49N 32 42 E
Kuruçay, Turkey .... 70 B3 39 39N 38 29 E
Kuruktag, China .... 60 B3 41 0N 89 0 E
Kuruman, S. Africa .. 88 D3 27 28 S 23 28 E
Kuruman →, S. Africa .. 88 D3 26 56 S 20 39 E
Kurume, Japan ..... 55 H5 33 15N 130 30 E
Kurun →, Sudan .... 81 F3 5 30N 34 17 E
Kurunegala, Sri Lanka .. 66 R12 7 30N 80 23 E
Kurya, Russia ...... 52 C6 61 42N 57 9 E
Kus Gölü, Turkey .... 45 F11 40 10N 27 55 E
Kuşadası, Turkey .... 72 D2 37 52N 27 15 E
Kuşadası Körfezi,
　Turkey .... 47 D8 37 56N 27 0 E
Kusamba, Indonesia .. 63 K18 8 34 S 115 27 E
Kusatsu, Japan ..... 55 F9 36 37N 138 36 E
Kusawa L., Canada .. 102 A1 60 20N 136 13 W
Kusel, Germany ..... 25 F3 49 32N 7 24 E
Kushaka, Nigeria .... 83 C6 10 32N 6 48 E
Kushalgarh, India .... 68 H6 23 10N 74 27 E
Kushchevskaya, Russia .. 35 G4 46 33N 39 35 E
Kusheriki, Nigeria .... 83 C6 10 30N 6 26 E
Kushikino, Japan .... 55 J5 31 44N 130 16 E
Kushima, Japan ..... 55 J5 31 29N 131 14 E
Kushimoto, Japan .... 55 H7 33 28N 135 47 E
Kushiro, Japan ..... 54 C12 43 0N 144 30 E
Kushiro-Gawa →, Japan .. 54 C12 42 59N 144 23 E
Kushiro Shitsugen △,
　Japan .... 54 C12 43 9N 144 26 E
Kūshk, Iran .... 71 D8 28 46N 56 51 E
Kushka = Gushgy,
　Turkmenistan .... 52 F7 35 20N 62 18 E
Kūshkī, Iran .... 70 C5 33 31N 47 13 E
Kushnytsya, Ukraine .. 29 B8 48 27N 23 15 E
Kushol, India ...... 69 C7 33 40N 76 36 E
Kushtia, Bangla. .... 67 H16 23 55N 89 5 E
Kushum →, Kazakhstan .. 34 F10 49 0N 50 20 E
Kuskokwim B., U.S.A. .. 100 C3 59 45N 162 25 W
Kusmi, India ...... 69 H10 23 17N 83 55 E
Kussharo-Ko, Japan .. 54 C12 43 38N 144 21 E
Kustanay = Qostanay,
　Kazakhstan ..... 52 D7 53 10N 63 35 E
Kut, Ko, Thailand .... 65 G4 11 40N 102 35 E
Kuta, Indonesia .... 63 K18 8 43 S 115 11 E
Kütahya, Turkey .... 47 B11 39 30N 30 2 E
Kütahya □, Turkey .. 47 B11 39 10N 29 30 E
Kutaisi, Georgia .... 35 J6 42 19N 42 40 E
Kutaraja = Banda Aceh,
　Indonesia ...... 62 C1 5 35N 95 20 E
Kutch, Gulf of =
　Kachchh, Gulf of,
　India .... 68 H3 22 50N 69 15 E
Kutch, Rann of =
　Kachchh, Rann of,
　India .... 68 H4 24 0N 70 0 E
Kutina, Croatia ..... 41 C13 45 29N 16 48 E
Kutiyana, India ..... 68 J4 21 36N 70 2 E
Kutjevo, Croatia .... 42 E2 45 23N 17 53 E
Kutkashen, Azerbaijan .. 35 K8 40 58N 47 47 E
Kutná Hora, Czech Rep. .. 26 B8 49 57N 15 16 E
Kutno, Poland ..... 31 F6 52 15N 19 23 E
Kutse, Botswana .... 88 C3 21 7 S 24 36 E
Kuttabul, Australia .. 94 K6 21 1 S 148 54 E
Kutu, Dem. Rep. of
　the Congo ...... 84 E3 2 40 S 18 11 E
Kutum, Sudan ..... 81 E1 14 10N 24 40 E
Kúty, Slovak Rep. .... 27 C10 48 40N 17 3 E
Kuty, Ukraine ...... 29 B10 48 16N 25 1 E
Kuujjuaq, Canada .... 101 C13 58 6N 68 15 W
Kuujjuarapik, Canada .. 104 A4 55 20N 77 35 W

Kuusamo, Finland .... 8 D23 65 57N 29 8 E
Kuusankoski, Finland .. 9 F22 60 55N 26 38 E
Kuvshinovo, Russia .. 32 D8 57 2N 34 11 E
Kuwait = Al Kuwayt,
　Kuwait .... 70 D5 29 30N 48 0 E
Kuwait ■, Asia ..... 70 D5 29 30N 47 30 E
Kuwana, Japan ..... 55 G8 35 5N 136 43 E
Kuwana →, India .... 69 F10 26 25N 83 15 E
Kuybyshev = Samara,
　Russia .... 34 D10 53 8N 50 6 E
Kuybyshev, Russia .. 52 D8 55 27N 78 19 E
Kuybyshevo, Ukraine .. 33 J9 47 25N 36 40 E
Kuybyshevskoye
　Vdkhr., Russia .... 34 C9 55 2N 49 30 E
Kuye He →, China .. 56 E6 38 23N 110 46 E
Küyeh, Iran .... 70 B5 38 45N 47 57 E
Kuyucak, Turkey .... 47 D10 37 55N 28 28 E
Kuyumba, Russia .... 53 C10 60 58N 96 59 E
Kuzey Anadolu Dağları,
　Turkey .... 72 B7 41 30N 35 0 E
Kuzmin, Serbia & M. .. 28 E4 45 2N 19 25 E
Kuznetsk, Russia .... 34 D8 53 12N 46 40 E
Kuzomen, Russia .... 52 C4 66 22N 36 50 E
Kvænangen, Norway .. 8 A19 70 5N 21 15 E
Kværndrup, Denmark .. 11 J4 55 10N 10 31 E
Kvaløy, Norway .... 8 B18 69 40N 18 30 E
Kvänum, Sweden .... 11 F7 58 18N 13 11 E
Kvareli = Qvareli,
　Georgia .... 35 K7 41 57N 45 47 E
Kvarner, Croatia .... 41 D11 44 50N 14 10 E
Kvarnerič, Croatia .. 41 D11 44 43N 14 37 E
Kvicksund, Sweden .. 10 E10 59 27N 16 19 E
Kvillsfors, Sweden .. 11 G9 57 24N 15 29 E
Kvismare kanal, Sweden .. 10 E9 59 11N 15 35 E
Kvissleby, Sweden .. 10 B11 62 18N 17 22 E
Kwa-Nobuhle, S. Africa .. 85 L5 33 50 S 25 22 E
Kwabhaca, S. Africa .. 89 E4 30 51 S 29 0 E
Kwakhanai, Botswana .. 88 C3 21 39 S 21 16 E
Kwakoegron, Suriname .. 125 B7 5 12N 55 25 W
Kwale, Kenya ...... 86 C4 4 15 S 39 31 E
Kwale, Nigeria ..... 83 D6 5 46N 6 26 E
Kwando →, Africa .. 88 B3 18 27 S 23 32 E
Kwangchow =
　Guangzhou, China .. 59 F9 23 5N 113 10 E
Kwangdaeri, N. Korea .. 57 D14 40 31N 127 32 E
Kwangju, S. Korea .. 57 G14 35 9N 126 54 E
Kwango →, Dem. Rep.
　of the Congo ..... 84 E3 3 14 S 17 22 E
Kwangsi-Chuang =
　Guangxi Zhuangzu
　Zizhiqu □, China .. 58 F7 24 0N 109 0 E
Kwangtung =
　Guangdong □, China .. 59 F9 23 0N 113 0 E
Kwara □, Nigeria .. 83 D6 8 45N 4 30 E
Kwataboahegan →,
　Canada .... 104 B3 51 9N 80 50 W
Kwatisore, Indonesia .. 63 E8 3 18 S 134 50 E
KwaZulu Natal □,
　S. Africa .... 89 D5 29 0 S 30 0 E
Kweichow = Guizhou □,
　China .... 58 D6 27 0N 107 0 E
Kwekwe, Zimbabwe .. 87 F2 18 58 S 29 48 E
Kwidzyn, Poland .... 30 E5 53 44N 18 55 E
Kwiha, Ethiopia .... 81 E4 13 29N 39 32 E
Kwinana New Town,
　Australia .... 93 F2 32 15 S 115 47 E
Kwisa →, Poland .... 31 G2 51 34N 15 24 E
Kwoka, Indonesia .... 63 E8 0 31 S 132 27 E
Kwolla, Nigeria ..... 83 D6 9 0N 9 15 E
Kyabra Cr. →, Australia .. 95 D3 25 36 S 142 55 E
Kyabram, Australia .. 95 F4 36 19 S 145 4 E
Kyaikto, Burma ..... 64 D1 17 20N 97 3 E
Kyakhta, Russia .... 53 D11 50 30N 106 25 E
Kyambura →, Uganda .. 86 C3 0 7 S 30 9 E
Kyancutta, Australia .. 95 E2 33 8 S 135 33 E
Kyaukpadaung, Burma .. 67 J19 20 52N 95 8 E
Kyaukpyu, Burma .... 67 K18 19 28N 93 30 E
Kyaukse, Burma .... 67 J20 21 36N 96 10 E
Kybartai, Lithuania .. 30 D9 54 39N 22 45 E
Kyburz, U.S.A. ..... 110 G6 38 47N 120 18 W
Kyelang, India ..... 68 C7 32 35N 77 2 E
Kyenjojo, Uganda .... 86 B3 0 40N 30 37 E
Kyjov, Czech Rep. .. 27 B10 49 1N 17 7 E
Kyle, Canada ...... 103 C7 50 50N 108 2 W
Kyle Dam, Zimbabwe .. 87 G3 20 15 S 31 0 E
Kyle of Lochalsh, U.K. .. 13 D3 57 17N 5 44 W
Kyll →, Germany .... 25 F2 49 48N 6 41 E
Kyllburg, Germany .. 25 E2 50 2N 6 34 E
Kymijoki →, Finland .. 9 F22 60 30N 26 55 E
Kyneton, Australia .. 95 F3 37 10 S 144 29 E
Kynuna, Australia .. 94 C3 21 37 S 141 55 E
Kyō-ga-Saki, Japan .. 55 G7 35 45N 135 15 E
Kyoga, L., Uganda .. 86 B3 1 35N 33 0 E
Kyogle, Australia .. 95 D5 28 40 S 153 0 E
Kyom →, Sudan .... 81 F2 6 58N 28 13 E
Kyongju, S. Korea .. 57 G15 35 51N 129 14 E
Kyongpyaw, Burma .. 67 L19 17 12N 95 10 E
Kyŏngsŏng, N. Korea .. 57 D15 41 35N 129 36 E
Kyōto, Japan ...... 55 G7 35 0N 135 45 E
Kyōto □, Japan .... 55 G7 35 15N 135 45 E
Kyparissovouno, Cyprus .. 49 D12 35 19N 33 10 E
Kyperounda, Cyprus .. 49 E11 34 56N 32 58 E
Kyrenia, Cyprus .... 49 D12 35 20N 33 20 E
Kyrgyzstan ■, Asia .. 52 E8 42 0N 75 0 E
Kyritz, Germany .... 24 C8 52 56N 12 24 E
Kyrkhult, Sweden .. 11 H8 56 22N 14 34 E
Kyrnasivka, Ukraine .. 29 B13 48 35N 28 58 E
Kyrnychky, Ukraine .. 29 E14 45 42N 29 4 E
Kyrö älv =
　Kyrönjoki →, Finland .. 8 E19 63 14N 21 45 E
Kyrönjoki →, Finland .. 8 E19 63 14N 21 45 E
Kystatyam, Russia .. 53 C13 67 20N 123 10 E
Kysucké Nové Mesto,
　Slovak Rep. ..... 27 B11 49 18N 18 47 E
Kytay, Ozero, Ukraine .. 29 E14 45 40N 29 13 E
Kythréa, Cyprus .... 49 D12 35 15N 33 29 E
Kyunhla, Burma .... 67 H19 23 25N 95 15 E
Kyuquot Sound, Canada .. 102 D3 50 2N 127 22 W
Kyurdamir = Kürdämir,
　Azerbaijan ...... 35 K9 40 25N 48 3 E
Kyūshū, Japan ..... 55 H5 33 0N 131 0 E
Kyūshū □, Japan .... 55 H5 33 0N 131 0 E
Kyūshū-Sanchi, Japan .. 55 H5 32 35N 131 17 E
Kyustendil, Bulgaria .. 44 D6 42 16N 22 41 E
Kyusyur, Russia .... 53 B13 70 19N 127 30 E
Kyyiv, Ukraine ..... 33 G6 50 30N 30 28 E
Kyyivske Vdskh.,
　Ukraine .... 33 G6 51 0N 30 25 E
Kyzyl, Russia ...... 53 D10 51 50N 94 30 E
Kyzyl Kum, Uzbekistan .. 52 E7 42 30N 65 0 E
Kyzyl-Kyya, Kyrgyzstan .. 52 E8 40 16N 72 8 E
Kyzyl-Orda =
　Qyzylorda,
　Kazakhstan ..... 52 E7 44 48N 65 28 E

L

La Albuera, Spain 37 G4 38 45N 6 49W
La Alcarria, Spain .. 38 E2 40 31N 2 45W
La Almarcha, Spain .. 38 F2 39 41N 2 24W
La Almunia de Doña
　Godina, Spain 38 D3 41 29N 1 23W
La Asunción, Venezuela .. 124 A6 11 2N 63 53W
La Baie, Canada 105 C5 48 19N 70 53W
La Banda, Argentina .. 126 B3 27 45 S 64 10W
La Bañeza, Spain 36 C5 42 17N 5 54W
La Barca, Mexico 118 C4 20 20N 102 40W
La Barge, U.S.A. 108 E8 42 16N 110 12W
La Bastide-Puylaurent,
　France .... 20 D7 44 35N 3 55 E
La Baule, France 18 E4 47 17N 2 24W
La Belle, U.S.A. 115 M5 26 46N 81 26W
La Biche →, Canada .. 102 B4 59 57N 123 50W
La Biche, L., Canada .. 102 C6 54 50N 112 5W
La Bisbal d'Empordà,
　Spain .... 38 D8 41 58N 3 2 E
La Blanquilla, Venezuela 121 D7 11 51N 64 37W
La Bomba, Mexico .. 118 A1 31 53N 115 2W
La Brea, Trin. & Tob. .. 125 K15 10 15N 61 37W
La Brède, France 20 D3 44 41N 0 32W
La Bresse, France .. 19 D13 48 2N 6 53 E
La Bureba, Spain 36 C2 42 36N 3 24W
La Calera, Chile .... 126 C1 32 50 S 71 10W
La Campana △, Chile .. 126 C1 32 58 S 71 14W
La Campiña, Spain .. 37 H6 37 45N 4 45W
La Canal = Sa Canal,
　Spain .... 48 C7 38 51N 1 23 E
La Cañiza = A Cañiza,
　Spain 36 C2 42 13N 8 16W
La Canourgue, France .. 20 D7 44 26N 3 13 E
La Capelle, France .. 19 C10 49 59N 3 50 E
La Carlota, Argentina .. 126 C3 33 30 S 63 20W
La Carlota, Phil. ... 61 F5 10 25N 122 55 E
La Carlota, Spain .. 37 H6 37 40N 4 56W
La Carolina, Spain .. 37 G7 38 17N 3 38W
La Cavalerie, France .. 20 D7 44 1N 3 10 E
La Ceiba, Honduras .. 120 C2 15 40N 86 50W
La Chaise-Dieu, France .. 20 C7 45 18N 3 42 E
La Chapelle d'Angillon,
　France .... 19 E9 47 21N 2 25 E
La Chapelle-St-Luc,
　France .... 19 D11 48 20N 4 3 E
La Chapelle-sur-Erdre,
　France 18 E5 47 18N 1 34W
La Charité-sur-Loire,
　France .... 19 E10 47 10N 3 1 E
La Chartre-sur-le-Loir,
　France .... 18 E7 47 44N 0 34 E
La Châtaigneraie,
　France 20 B3 46 39N 0 44W
La Châtre, France .. 19 F9 46 35N 2 0 E
La Chaux-de-Fonds,
　Switz. .... 25 H2 47 7N 6 50 E
La Chorrera, Panama .. 120 E4 8 53N 79 47W
La Ciotat, France .. 21 E9 43 10N 5 37 E
La Clayette, France .. 19 F11 46 17N 4 19 E
La Cocha, Argentina .. 126 B2 27 50 S 65 40W
La Concepción, Panama .. 120 E3 8 31N 82 37W
La Concordia, Mexico .. 119 D6 16 8N 92 38W
La Coruña = A Coruña,
　Spain 36 B2 43 20N 8 25W
La Coruña □, Spain .. 36 B2 43 10N 8 30W
La Côte-St-André,
　France .... 21 C9 45 24N 5 15 E
La Courtine, France .. 20 C6 45 41N 2 15 E
La Crau,
　Bouches-du-Rhône,
　France .... 21 E8 43 32N 4 40 E
La Crau, Var, France .. 21 E10 43 9N 6 4 E
La Crescent, U.S.A. .. 112 D9 43 50N 91 18W
La Crete, Canada .. 102 B5 58 11N 116 24W
La Crosse, Kans., U.S.A. .. 112 F5 38 32N 99 18W
La Crosse, Wis., U.S.A. .. 112 D9 43 48N 91 15W
La Cruz, Costa Rica .. 120 D2 11 4N 85 39W
La Cruz, Mexico 118 C3 23 55N 106 54W
La Désirade,
　Guadeloupe ..... 120 b 16 18N 61 3W
La Escondida, Mexico .. 118 C5 24 6N 99 55W
La Esmeralda, Paraguay .. 126 A3 22 16 S 62 33W
La Esperanza, Cuba .. 120 B3 22 46N 83 44W
La Esperanza, Honduras 120 D2 14 15N 88 10W
La Estrada = A Estrada,
　Spain 36 C2 42 43N 8 27W
La Faouët, France .. 18 D3 48 2N 3 30W
La Fayette, U.S.A. .. 115 H3 34 42N 85 17W
La Fé, Cuba 120 B3 22 2N 84 15W
La Fère, France .... 19 C10 49 39N 3 21 E
La Ferté-Bernard,
　France .... 18 D7 48 10N 0 40 E
La Ferté-Gaucher,
　France .... 19 D10 48 47N 3 19 E
La Ferté-Macé, France .. 18 D6 48 35N 0 22W
La Ferté-St-Aubin,
　France .... 19 E8 47 42N 1 57 E
La Ferté-sous-Jouarre,
　France .... 19 D10 48 56N 3 8 E
La Ferté-Vidame,
　France .... 18 D7 48 37N 0 53 E
La Flèche, France .. 18 E6 47 42N 0 4W
La Follette, U.S.A. .. 115 G3 36 23N 84 7W
La Fregeneda, Spain .. 36 E4 40 58N 6 54W
La Fuente de San
　Esteban, Spain 36 E4 40 49N 6 15W
La Gacilly, France .. 18 E4 47 46N 2 8W
La Gineta, Spain 39 F2 39 8N 2 1W
La Grand'Combe,
　France .... 21 D8 44 13N 4 2 E
La Grande, U.S.A. .. 108 D4 45 20N 118 5W
La Grande →, Canada .. 104 B5 53 50N 79 0W
La Grande-Motte,
　France .... 21 E8 43 23N 4 5 E
La Grande Quatre, Rés.,
　Canada 104 B5 54 0N 76 55W
La Grande Trois, Rés.,
　Canada 104 B4 53 40N 75 10W
La Grange, Calif.,
　U.S.A. 110 H6 37 42N 120 27W
La Grange, Ga., U.S.A. .. 115 J3 33 2N 85 2W
La Grange, Ky., U.S.A. .. 113 F3 38 25N 85 23W
La Grange, Tex., U.S.A. .. 113 L6 29 54N 96 52W
La Grave, France .. 21 C10 45 3N 6 18 E
La Guaira, Venezuela .. 124 A5 10 36N 66 56W
La Guardia = A Guarda,
　Spain 36 D2 41 56N 8 52W
La Gudiña = A Gudiña,
　Spain 36 C3 42 4N 7 8W
La Guerche-de-
　Bretagne, France .. 18 E5 47 57N 1 16W

La Guerche-sur-
　l'Aubois, France .. 19 F9 46 58N 2 56 E
La Habana, Cuba 120 B3 23 8N 82 22W
La Haute Vallée de
　Chevreuse △, France .. 19 D8 48 35N 1 58 E
La Haye-du-Puits,
　France 18 C5 49 17N 1 33W
La Horra, Spain 36 D7 41 44N 3 53W
La Independencia,
　Mexico 119 D6 16 31N 91 47W
La Isabela, Dom. Rep. .. 121 C5 19 58N 71 2W
La Jonquera, Spain .. 38 C7 42 25N 2 53 E
La Junta, U.S.A. 113 F3 37 59N 103 33W
La Laguna, Canary Is. .. 48 F3 28 28N 16 18W
La Libertad, Guatemala 120 C1 16 47N 90 7W
La Libertad, Mexico .. 118 B2 29 55N 112 41W
La Ligua, Chile .... 126 C1 32 30 S 71 16W
La Línea de la
　Concepción, Spain .. 37 J5 36 15N 5 23W
La Loche, Canada .. 103 B7 56 29N 109 26W
La Londe-les-Maures,
　France .... 21 E10 43 8N 6 14 E
La Lora, Spain 36 C7 42 45N 4 0W
La Loupe, France .. 18 D8 48 28N 1 1 E
La Louvière, Belgium .. 17 D4 50 27N 4 10 E
La Lune, Trin. & Tob. .. 125 K15 10 3N 61 22W
La Machine, France .. 19 F10 46 54N 3 27 E
La Maddalena, Italy .. 42 A2 41 13N 9 24 E
La Malbaie, Canada .. 105 C5 47 40N 70 10W
La Malinche △, Mexico 119 D5 19 14N 98 3W
La Mancha, Spain .. 39 F2 39 10N 2 54W
La Mariña, Spain 36 B3 43 30N 7 40W
La Martre, L., Canada .. 102 A5 63 15N 117 55W
La Mesa, U.S.A. 111 N9 32 46N 117 3W
La Misión, Mexico .. 118 A1 32 5N 116 50W
La Mothe-Achard,
　France 18 F5 46 37N 1 40W
La Motte-Chalançon,
　France .... 21 D9 44 30N 5 21 E
La Motte-du-Caire,
　France .... 21 D10 44 20N 6 3 E
La Motte-Servolex,
　France .... 21 C9 45 35N 5 53 E
La Moure, U.S.A. 112 B5 46 21N 98 18W
La Muela, Spain 38 D3 41 36N 1 7W
La Mure, France .... 21 D9 44 55N 5 48 E
La Negra, Chile .... 126 A1 23 46 S 70 18W
La Oliva, Canary Is. .. 48 F6 28 36N 13 57W
La Orotava, Canary Is. .. 48 F3 28 22N 16 31W
La Oroya, Peru .... 124 F3 11 32 S 75 54W
La Pacaudière, France .. 19 F10 46 11N 3 52 E
La Palma, Canary Is. .. 48 F2 28 40N 17 50W
La Palma, Panama .. 120 E4 8 15N 78 0W
La Palma del Condado,
　Spain 37 H4 37 21N 6 38W
La Paloma, Chile .... 126 C1 30 35 S 71 0W
La Pampa □, Argentina .. 126 D2 36 50 S 66 0W
La Paragua, Venezuela .. 124 B6 6 50N 63 20W
La Paz, Entre Ríos,
　Argentina ...... 126 C4 30 50 S 59 45W
La Paz, San Luis,
　Argentina ...... 126 C2 33 30 S 67 20W
La Paz, Bolivia .... 124 G5 16 20 S 68 10W
La Paz, Honduras .. 120 D2 14 20N 87 47W
La Paz, Mexico 118 C2 24 10N 110 20W
La Paz Centro, Nic. .. 120 D2 12 20N 86 41W
La Pedrera, Colombia .. 124 D5 1 18 S 69 43W
La Pérade, Canada .. 105 C5 46 35N 72 12W
La Perouse Str., Asia .. 54 B11 45 40N 142 0 E
La Pesca, Mexico .. 119 C5 23 46N 97 45W
La Piedad, Mexico .. 118 C4 20 20N 102 1W
La Pine, U.S.A. 108 E3 43 40N 121 30W
La Plata, Argentina .. 126 D4 35 0 S 57 55W
La Pobla de Lillet, Spain 38 C6 42 16N 1 59 E
La Pocatière, Canada .. 105 C5 47 22N 70 2W
La Pola de Gordón,
　Spain 36 C5 42 51N 5 41W
La Porta, France .... 21 F13 42 25N 9 20 E
La Porte, Ind., U.S.A. .. 114 E2 41 36N 86 43W
La Porte, Tex., U.S.A. .. 113 L7 29 39N 95 1W
La Presanella, Italy .. 40 B7 46 13N 10 40 E
La Puebla = Sa Pobla,
　Spain .... 38 F8 39 46N 3 1 E
La Puebla de Cazalla,
　Spain 37 H5 37 10N 5 20W
La Puebla de los
　Infantes, Spain 37 H5 37 47N 5 24W
La Puebla de
　Montalbán, Spain .. 36 F6 39 52N 4 22W
La Puebla del Río, Spain .. 37 H4 37 16N 6 3W
La Puerta de Segura,
　Spain 37 G8 38 22N 2 45W
La Purísima, Mexico .. 118 B2 26 10N 112 4W
La Push, U.S.A. 110 C2 47 55N 124 38W
La Quiaca, Argentina .. 126 A2 22 5 S 65 35W
La Réole, France .. 20 D3 44 35N 0 1W
La Restinga, Canary Is. .. 48 G2 27 38N 17 59W
La Rioja, Argentina .. 126 B2 29 20 S 67 0W
La Rioja □, Argentina .. 126 B2 29 30 S 67 0W
La Rioja □, Spain .. 38 C2 42 20N 2 20W
La Robla, Spain 36 C5 42 50N 5 41W
La Roche-Bernard,
　France 18 E4 47 31N 2 19W
La Roche-Canillac,
　France .... 20 C5 45 12N 1 57 E
La Roche-en-Ardenne,
　Belgium .... 17 D5 50 11N 5 35 E
La Roche-sur-Foron,
　France .... 19 F13 46 4N 6 19 E
La Roche-sur-Yon,
　France 18 F5 46 40N 1 25W
La Rochefoucauld,
　France .... 20 C4 45 44N 0 24 E
La Rochelle, France .. 20 B2 46 10N 1 9W
La Roda, Spain 39 F2 39 13N 2 15W
La Roda de Andalucía,
　Spain 37 H6 37 12N 4 46W
La Romana, Dom. Rep. 121 C6 18 27N 68 57W
La Ronge, Canada .. 103 B7 55 5N 105 20W
La Rumorosa, Mexico .. 111 N10 32 33N 116 4W
La Sabina = Sa Savina,
　Spain .... 38 C7 38 44N 1 25 E
La Sagra, Spain 39 H2 37 57N 2 35W
La Salle, U.S.A. 112 E10 41 20N 89 6W
La Sanabria, Spain .. 36 C4 42 0N 6 30W
La Santa, Canary Is. .. 48 E6 29 5N 13 40W
La Sarre, Canada .. 104 C4 48 45N 79 15W
La Scie, Canada 105 C8 49 57N 55 36W
La Selva, Spain .... 38 D7 41 55N 2 30 E
La Selva Beach, U.S.A. .. 110 J5 36 56N 121 51W
La Selva del Camp,
　Spain .... 38 D6 41 13N 1 8 E
La Serena, Chile .... 126 B1 29 55 S 71 10W
La Serena, Spain 37 G5 38 45N 5 40W
La Seu d'Urgell, Spain .. 38 C6 42 22N 1 23 E
La Seyne-sur-Mer,
　France .... 21 E9 43 7N 5 52 E

La Sila, Italy .... 43 C9 39 15N 16 35 E
La Solana, Spain 37 G7 38 59N 3 14W
La Soufrière, St. Vincent 121 D7 13 20N 61 11W
La Souterraine, France .. 19 F8 46 15N 1 30 E
La Spézia, Italy ..... 40 D6 44 7N 9 50 E
La Suze-sur-Sarthe,
　France .... 18 E7 47 53N 0 2 E
La Tagua, Colombia .. 124 C4 0 3N 74 40W
La Teste-de-Buch,
　France 20 D2 44 37N 1 8W
La Tortuga, Venezuela .. 121 D6 11 0N 65 22W
La Tour-du-Pin, France .. 21 C9 45 33N 5 27 E
La Tranche-sur-Mer,
　France 18 F5 46 20N 1 27W
La Tremblade, France .. 20 C2 45 46N 1 8W
La Trinité, Martinique .. 120 c 14 43N 60 58W
La Tuque, Canada .. 104 C5 47 30N 72 50W
La Unión, Chile .... 128 E2 40 10 S 73 0W
La Unión, El Salv. .. 120 D2 13 20N 87 50W
La Unión, Mexico .. 118 D4 17 58N 101 49W
La Unión, Spain 39 H4 37 38N 0 53W
La Urbana, Venezuela .. 124 B5 7 8N 66 56W
La Vache Pt.,
　Trin. & Tob. 125 K15 10 47N 61 37W
La Vall d'Uixó, Spain .. 38 F4 39 49N 0 15W
La Vecilla de Curveño,
　Spain 36 C5 42 51N 5 27W
La Vega, Dom. Rep. .. 121 C5 19 20N 70 30W
La Vela de Coro,
　Venezuela 124 A5 11 27N 69 34W
La Veleta, Spain 37 H7 37 1N 3 22W
La Venta, Mexico .. 119 D6 18 8N 94 3W
La Ventura, Mexico .. 118 C4 24 38N 100 54W
La Voulte-sur-Rhône,
　France .... 21 D8 44 48N 4 46 E
Laa an der Thaya,
　Austria .... 27 C9 48 43N 16 23 E
Laaber, Grosse →,
　Germany .... 25 G8 48 55N 12 30 E
Laage, Germany .... 24 B8 53 55N 12 21 E
Laas Caanood = Las
　Anod, Somali Rep. .. 75 F4 8 26N 47 19 E
Laatzen, Germany .. 24 C5 52 19N 9 48 E
Laba →, Russia .... 35 H4 45 11N 39 42 E
Labasa, Fiji .... 91 C8 16 30 S 179 27 E
Labason, Phil. ..... 61 G5 8 4N 122 14 E
Labastide-Murat, France 20 D5 44 39N 1 33 E
Labastide-Rouairoux,
　France .... 20 E6 43 28N 2 39 E
Labbézenga, Mali .. 83 B5 15 2N 0 48 E
Labe →, Europe .... 24 B4 53 50N 9 0 E
Laberge, L., Canada .. 102 A1 61 11N 135 12W
Labin, Croatia ..... 41 C11 45 5N 14 8 E
Labinsk, Russia .... 35 H5 44 40N 40 48 E
Labis, Malaysia .... 65 L4 2 22N 103 2 E
Łabiszyn, Poland .. 31 F4 52 57N 17 54 E
Labo, Phil. .... 61 D5 14 9N 122 51 E
Laboe, Germany .... 24 A6 54 24N 10 13 E
Laborec →, Slovak Rep. .. 27 C14 48 37N 21 58 E
Laborie, St. Lucia .. 121 f 13 45N 61 2W
Labouheyre, France .. 20 D3 44 13N 0 55W
Laboulaye, Argentina .. 126 C3 34 10 S 63 30W
Labrador, Canada .. 105 B7 53 20N 61 0W
Labrador City, Canada 105 B6 52 57N 66 55W
Labrador Sea, Atl. Oc. .. 101 C14 57 0N 54 0W
Lábrea, Brazil ..... 124 E6 7 15 S 64 51W
Labruguière, France .. 20 E6 43 31N 2 16 E
Labuan, Malaysia .. 62 C5 5 20N 115 14 E
Labuan, Pulau, Malaysia 62 C5 5 21N 115 13 E
Labuha, Indonesia .. 63 E7 0 30 S 127 30 E
Labuhan, Indonesia .. 63 G11 6 22 S 105 50 E
Labuhanbajo, Indonesia 63 F6 8 28 S 119 54 E
Labuk, Telok, Malaysia 62 C5 6 10N 117 50 E
Labyrinth, L., Australia 95 E2 30 40 S 135 11 E
Labytnangi, Russia .. 52 C7 66 39N 66 21 E
Laç, Albania ...... 44 E3 41 38N 19 43 E
Lac-Bouchette, Canada 105 C5 48 16N 72 11W
Lac Édouard, Canada .. 104 C5 47 40N 72 16W
Lac La Biche, Canada .. 102 C6 54 45N 111 58W
Lac la Martre = Wha Ti,
　Canada 100 B8 63 8N 117 16W
Lac La Ronge △,
　Canada 103 B7 55 9N 104 41W
Lac-Mégantic, Canada 105 C5 45 35N 70 53W
Lac Thien, Vietnam .. 64 F7 12 25N 108 11 E
Lacanau, Canada .. 20 D2 44 58N 1 5W
Lacanau, Étang de,
　France 20 D2 44 58N 1 7W
Lacantún →, Mexico 119 D6 16 36N 90 40W
Lacara →, Spain 37 G4 38 55N 6 25W
Lacaune, France .... 20 E6 43 43N 2 40 E
Lacaune, Mts. de, France 20 E6 43 43N 2 50 E
Laccadive Is. =
　Lakshadweep Is.,
　India .... 50 H11 10 0N 72 30 E
Lacepede B., Australia 95 F2 36 40 S 139 40 E
Lacepede Is., Australia 92 C3 16 55 S 122 0 E
Lacerdónia, Mozam. .. 87 F4 18 3 S 35 35 E
Lacey, U.S.A. 110 C4 47 7N 122 49W
Lachhmangarh, India .. 68 F6 27 50N 75 4 E
Lachi, Pakistan .... 68 C4 33 25N 71 20 E
Lachine, Canada 104 C5 45 30N 73 40W
Lachlan →, Australia .. 95 E3 34 22 S 143 55 E
Lachute, Canada 104 C5 45 39N 74 21W
Lackawanna, U.S.A. .. 116 D6 42 50N 78 50W
Lackawaxen, U.S.A. .. 117 E10 41 29N 74 59W
Lacolle, Canada 117 A11 45 5N 73 22W
Lacombe, Canada .. 102 C6 52 30N 113 44W
Lacona, U.S.A. 117 C8 43 39N 76 10W
Láconi, Italy ...... 42 C2 39 54N 9 4 E
Laconia, U.S.A. 117 C13 43 32N 71 28W
Lacq, France 20 E3 43 25N 0 35W
Ladakh Ra., India .. 69 C8 34 0N 78 0 E
Ładek-Zdrój, Poland .. 31 H3 50 21N 16 53 E
Ladik, Turkey ..... 72 B6 40 57N 35 58 E
Ladismith, S. Africa .. 88 E3 33 28 S 21 15 E
Ladíspoli, Italy ..... 41 G9 41 56N 12 5 E
Ladnun, India ..... 68 F6 27 38N 74 25 E
Ladoga, L. =
　Ladozhskoye Ozero,
　Russia .... 32 B6 61 15N 30 30 E
Ladozhskoye Ozero,
　Russia .... 32 B6 61 15N 30 30 E
Ladushkin, Russia .. 30 D7 54 34N 20 10 E
Lady Elliott I., Australia 94 C5 24 7 S 152 42 E
Lady Grey, S. Africa .. 88 E4 30 43 S 27 13 E
Ladybrand, S. Africa .. 88 D4 29 9 S 27 29 E
Ladysmith, Canada .. 102 D4 49 0N 123 49W
Ladysmith, S. Africa .. 89 D4 28 32 S 29 46 E
Ladysmith, U.S.A. .. 112 C9 45 28N 91 12W
Ladyzhyn, Ukraine .. 29 B14 48 40N 29 13 E
Lae, Papua N.G. .... 96 H6 6 40 S 147 2 E
Laem Hin Khom,
　Thailand .... 65 b 9 25N 99 56 E

Laem Khat, Thailand .. 65 a 8 6N 98 26 E
Laem Nga, Thailand ... 65 a 7 55N 98 27 E
Laem Ngop, Thailand .. 65 F4 12 10N 102 26 E
Laem Phan Wa, Thailand .. 65 a 7 47N 98 25 E
Laem Pho, Thailand ... 65 J3 6 55N 101 19 E
Laem Phrom Thep, Thailand .. 65 a 7 45N 98 19 E
Laem Riang, Thailand . 65 a 8 7N 98 27 E
Laem Sam Rong, Thailand .. 65 b 9 35N 100 4 E
Laem Son, Thailand ... 65 a 7 59N 98 16 E
Laem Yamu, Thailand . 65 a 7 59N 98 26 E
Læsø, Denmark ...... 11 G5 57 15N 11 5 E
Læsø Rende, Denmark . 11 G4 57 20N 10 45 E
Lafayette, Colo., U.S.A. 112 F2 39 58N 105 12W
Lafayette, Ind., U.S.A. 114 E2 40 25N 86 54W
Lafayette, La., U.S.A. . 113 K9 30 14N 92 1W
Lafayette, Tenn., U.S.A. 115 G2 36 31N 86 2W
Laferte →, Canada ... 102 A5 61 53N 117 44W
Lafia, Nigeria .... 83 D6 8 30N 8 34 E
Lafiagi, Nigeria ...... 83 D6 8 52N 5 20 E
Lafleche, Canada 103 D7 49 45N 106 40W
Lafon, Sudan .... 81 F3 5 5N 32 29 E
Lagan →, Sweden .... 11 H7 56 56N 13 58 E
Lagan →, U.K. 13 B6 54 36N 5 55W
Lagarfljót →, Iceland . 8 D6 65 40N 14 18W
Lage, Germany .... 24 D4 51 59N 8 48 E
Lågen →, Oppland, Norway .. 9 F14 61 8N 10 25 E
Lågen →, Vestfold, Norway .. 9 G14 59 3N 10 3 E
Lägerdorf, Germany ... 24 B5 53 53N 9 34 E
Laghouat, Algeria .... 78 B6 33 50N 2 59 E
Lagnieu, France ...... 21 C9 45 55N 5 20 E
Lagny-sur-Marne, France .. 19 D9 48 52N 2 44 E
Lago, Italy .... 43 C9 39 10N 16 9 E
Lago de Sanabria y Entorno △, Spain .. 36 C4 42 9N 6 45W
Lagôa, Portugal 37 H2 37 8N 8 27W
Lagoa do Peixe △, Brazil .. 127 C5 31 12 S 50 55W
Lagoa Vermelha, Brazil 127 B5 28 13 S 51 32W
Lagoaça, Portugal 36 D4 41 11N 6 44W
Lagodekhi, Georgia ... 35 K8 41 50N 46 22 E
Lagónegro, Italy ..... 43 B8 40 8N 15 45 E
Lagonoy G., Phil. ..... 61 E5 13 35N 123 50 E
Lagos, Nigeria .... 83 D5 6 25N 3 27 E
Lagos, Portugal 37 H2 37 5N 8 41W
Lagos □, Nigeria ..... 83 D5 6 28N 3 25 E
Lagos de Moreno, Mexico .. 118 C4 21 21N 101 55W
Lagrange, Australia ... 92 C3 18 45 S 121 43 E
Lagrange B., Australia . 92 C3 18 38 S 121 42 E
Laguardia, Spain 38 C2 42 33N 2 35W
Laguépie, France ..... 20 D5 44 8N 1 57 E
Laguna, Brazil .... 127 B6 28 30 S 48 50W
Laguna, U.S.A. 109 J10 35 2N 107 25W
Laguna Beach, U.S.A. . 111 M9 33 33N 117 47W
Laguna de Duera, Spain 36 D6 41 35N 4 43W
Laguna de la Restinga △, Venezuela 121 D6 10 58N 64 0W
Laguna del Laja △, Chile .. 126 D1 37 27 S 71 20W
Laguna del Tigre △, Guatemala .. 120 C1 17 32N 90 56W
Laguna Limpia, Argentina .. 126 B4 26 32 S 59 45W
Lagunas, Chile .... 126 A2 21 0 S 69 45W
Lagunas, Peru .... 124 E3 5 10 S 75 35W
Lagunas de Chacahua △, Mexico .. 119 D5 16 0N 97 43W
Lagunas de Montebello △, Mexico 119 D6 16 6N 91 41W
Lagunas de Ruidera △, Spain .. 39 G2 38 57N 2 52W
Lahad Datu, Malaysia . 63 C5 5 0N 118 20 E
Lahad Datu, Teluk, Malaysia .. 63 D5 4 50N 118 20 E
Lahan Sai, Thailand .. 64 E4 14 25N 102 52 E
Lahanam, Laos ...... 64 D5 16 16N 105 16 E
Lahar, India .... 69 F8 26 12N 78 57 E
Laharpur, India ...... 69 F9 27 43N 80 56 E
Lahat, Indonesia ..... 62 E2 3 45 S 103 30 E
Lahewa, Indonesia .... 62 D1 1 22N 97 12 E
Lähijän, Iran .... 71 B6 37 10N 50 6 E
Lahn →, Germany .... 25 E3 50 19N 7 37 E
Lahnstein, Germany .. 25 E3 50 19N 7 37 E
Laholm, Sweden ..... 11 H7 56 30N 13 2 E
Laholmsbukten, Sweden 11 H6 56 30N 12 45 E
Lahore, Pakistan ..... 68 D6 31 32N 74 22 E
Lahr, Germany .... 25 G3 48 20N 7 53 E
Lahri, Pakistan ...... 68 E3 29 11N 68 13 E
Lahti, Finland .... 9 F21 60 58N 25 40 E
Lahtis = Lahti, Finland 9 F21 60 58N 25 40 E
Laï, Chad .... 79 G9 9 25N 16 18 E
Lai Chau, Vietnam ... 58 F4 22 5N 103 3 E
Lai'an, China .... 59 A12 32 28N 118 30 E
Laibin, China .... 58 F7 23 42N 109 14 E
Laifeng, China .... 58 C7 29 27N 109 20 E
L'Aigle, France ...... 18 D7 48 46N 0 38 E
Laignes, France ...... 19 E11 47 50N 4 20 E
L'Aiguillon-sur-Mer, France .. 20 B2 46 20N 1 18W
Laila = Layla, Si. Arabia 75 C4 22 10N 46 40 E
Laingsburg, S. Africa . 88 E3 33 9 S 20 52 E
Lainioälven →, Sweden 8 C20 67 35N 22 40 E
Lairg, U.K. 13 C4 58 2N 4 24W
Laishui, China .... 56 E8 39 23N 115 45 E
Laissac, France ...... 20 D6 44 23N 2 50 E
Láives, Italy .... 41 B8 46 26N 11 20 E
Laiwu, China .... 57 F9 36 15N 117 40 E
Laixi, China .... 57 F11 36 50N 120 31 E
Laiyang, China .... 57 F11 36 59N 120 45 E
Laiyuan, China .... 56 E8 39 20N 114 40 E
Laizhou, China .... 57 F10 37 8N 119 57 E
Laizhou Wan, China .. 57 F10 37 30N 119 30 E
Laja →, Mexico 118 C4 20 55N 100 46W
Lajere, Nigeria .... 83 C7 12 10N 11 25 E
Lajes, Brazil .... 127 B5 27 48 S 50 20W
Lajkovac, Serbia & M. . 44 B4 44 27N 20 14 E
Lajosmizse, Hungary .. 42 C4 47 5N 19 16 E
Lak Sao, Laos .... 64 C5 18 11N 104 59 E
Lakaband, Pakistan .. 68 D3 31 2N 69 15 E
Lakamané, Mali 82 C3 14 35N 9 44W
Lake Alpine, U.S.A. .. 110 G7 38 29N 120 0W
Lake Andes, U.S.A. .. 112 D5 43 9N 98 32W
Lake Arthur, U.S.A. .. 113 K8 30 5N 92 41W
Lake Bindegolly △, Australia 95 D3 28 0 S 144 12 E
Lake Cargelligo, Australia 95 E4 33 15 S 146 22 E
Lake Charles, U.S.A. .. 113 K8 30 14N 93 13W
Lake City, Colo., U.S.A. 109 G10 38 2N 107 19W
Lake City, Fla., U.S.A. . 115 K4 30 11N 82 38W

Lake City, Mich., U.S.A. 114 C3 44 20N 85 13W
Lake City, Minn., U.S.A. 112 C8 44 27N 92 16W
Lake City, Pa., U.S.A. . 116 D4 42 1N 80 21W
Lake City, S.C., U.S.A. 115 J6 33 52N 79 45W
Lake Cowichan, Canada 102 D4 48 49N 124 3W
Lake District □, U.K. . 14 C4 54 30N 3 21W
Lake Elsinore, U.S.A. . 111 M9 33 38N 117 20W
Lake Eyre △, Australia 95 D2 28 40 S 137 31 E
Lake Gairdner △, Australia 95 E2 31 41 S 135 51 E
Lake George, U.S.A. .. 117 C11 43 26N 73 43W
Lake Grace, Australia . 93 F2 33 7 S 118 28 E
Lake Harbour = Kimmirut, Canada .. 101 B13 62 50N 69 50W
Lake Havasu City, U.S.A. .. 111 L12 34 27N 114 22W
Lake Hughes, U.S.A. .. 111 L8 34 41N 118 26W
Lake Isabella, U.S.A. . 111 K8 35 38N 118 28W
Lake Jackson, U.S.A. . 113 L7 29 3N 95 27W
Lake Junction, U.S.A. . 108 D8 44 35N 110 28W
Lake King, Australia .. 93 F2 33 5 S 119 45 E
Lake Lenore, Canada . 103 C8 52 24N 104 59W
Lake Louise, Canada . 102 C5 51 30N 116 10W
Lake Malawi △, Malawi 87 E3 12 0 S 34 0 E
Lake Mburo △, Uganda 86 C3 0 35 S 30 56 E
Lake Mead △, U.S.A. . 111 K12 36 15N 114 30W
Lake Meredith △, U.S.A. .. 113 H4 35 50N 101 50W
Lake Mills, U.S.A. 112 D8 43 25N 93 32W
Lake Nakuru △, Kenya 86 C4 0 21 S 36 8 E
Lake Placid, U.S.A. ... 117 B11 44 17N 73 59W
Lake Pleasant, U.S.A. . 117 C10 43 28N 74 25W
Lake Providence, U.S.A. 113 J9 32 48N 91 10W
Lake Roosevelt △, U.S.A. .. 108 C4 47 57N 118 59W
Lake St. Peter, Canada 116 A6 45 18N 78 2W
Lake Superior △, Canada .. 104 C3 47 45N 84 45W
Lake Torrens △, Australia 95 E2 30 55 S 137 40 E
Lake Village, U.S.A. .. 113 J9 33 20N 91 17W
Lake Wales, U.S.A. ... 115 M5 27 54N 81 35W
Lake Worth, U.S.A. ... 115 M5 26 37N 80 3W
Lakeba, Fiji .... 91 D9 18 13 S 178 47W
Lakefield, Canada 116 B6 44 25N 78 16W
Lakefield △, Australia . 94 B3 15 24 S 144 26 E
Lakehurst, U.S.A. 117 F10 40 1N 74 19W
Lakeland, Australia ... 94 B3 15 49 S 144 57 E
Lakeland, U.S.A. 115 M5 28 3N 81 57W
Lakemba = Lakeba, Fiji 91 D9 18 13 S 178 47W
Lakeport, Calif., U.S.A. 110 F4 39 3N 122 55W
Lakeport, Mich., U.S.A. 116 C2 43 7N 82 30W
Lakes Entrance, Australia 95 F4 37 50 S 148 0 E
Lakeside, Ariz., U.S.A. 109 J9 34 9N 109 58W
Lakeside, Calif., U.S.A. 111 N10 32 52N 116 55W
Lakeside, Nebr., U.S.A. 112 D3 42 3N 102 26W
Lakeside, Ohio, U.S.A. 116 E2 41 32N 82 46W
Lakeview, U.S.A. 108 E3 42 11N 120 21W
Lakeville, U.S.A. 112 C8 44 39N 93 14W
Lakewood, Colo., U.S.A. 112 F2 39 44N 105 5W
Lakewood, N.J., U.S.A. 117 F10 40 6N 74 13W
Lakewood, N.Y., U.S.A. 116 D5 42 6N 79 19W
Lakewood, Ohio, U.S.A. 116 E3 41 28N 81 48W
Lakewood, Wash., U.S.A. .. 110 C4 47 11N 122 32W
Lakha, India .... 68 F4 26 9N 70 54 E
Lakhaniá, Greece .... 49 D9 35 58N 27 54 E
Lakhimpur, India ..... 69 F9 27 57N 80 46 E
Lakhnadon, India .... 69 H8 22 36N 79 36 E
Lakhnau = Lucknow, India .. 69 F9 26 50N 81 0 E
Lakhonpheng, Laos .. 64 E5 15 54N 105 34 E
Lakhpat, India .... 68 H3 23 48N 68 47 E
Läki, Azerbaijan ..... 35 K8 40 34N 47 22 E
Lakin, U.S.A. 113 G4 37 57N 101 15W
Lakitusaki →, Canada . 104 B3 54 21N 82 25W
Lakki, Pakistan ...... 68 C4 32 36N 70 55 E
Lákkoi, Greece ...... 49 D5 35 24N 23 57 E
Lakonía □, Greece ... 46 E4 36 55N 22 30 E
Lakonikós Kólpos, Greece .. 46 E4 36 40N 22 40 E
Lakor, Indonesia ..... 63 F7 8 15 S 128 17 E
Lakota, Ivory C. 82 D3 5 50N 5 30W
Lakota, U.S.A. 112 A5 48 2N 98 21W
Laksar, India .... 68 E8 29 46N 78 3 E
Laksefjorden, Norway . 8 A22 70 45N 26 50 E
Lakselv, Norway ..... 8 A21 70 2N 25 0 E
Lakshadweep Is., India 50 H11 10 0N 72 30 E
Lakshmanpur, India .. 69 H10 22 58N 83 3 E
Lakshmikantapur, India 69 H13 22 5N 88 20 E
Lala Musa, Pakistan .. 68 C5 32 40N 73 57 E
Lalaghat, India ...... 67 G18 24 30N 92 40 E
Lalago, Tanzania ..... 86 C3 3 28 S 33 58 E
Lalapanzi, Zimbabwe . 87 F3 19 20 S 30 15 E
Lalapaşa, Turkey ..... 45 E10 41 49N 26 44 E
Lalbenque, France .... 20 D5 44 19N 1 34 E
L'Albufera, Spain 39 F4 39 20N 0 21W
Lalganj, India .... 69 G11 25 52N 85 13 E
Lalgola, India .... 69 G13 24 25N 88 15 E
Lālī, Iran .... 71 C6 32 21N 49 6 E
Lalibela, Ethiopia .... 81 E4 12 3N 39 0 E
Lalin, China .... 57 B14 45 12N 127 0 E
Lalín, Spain 36 C2 42 40N 8 5W
Lalin He →, China ... 57 B13 45 32N 125 40 E
Lalinde, France ...... 20 D4 44 50N 0 44 E
Lalitapur, Nepal ..... 69 F11 27 40N 85 20 E
Lalitpur, India .... 69 G8 24 42N 78 28 E
Lalkua, India .... 69 E8 29 5N 79 31 E
Lalsot, India .... 68 F7 26 34N 76 20 E
Lam, Vietnam .... 64 B6 21 21N 106 31 E
Lam Pao Res., Thailand 64 D4 16 50N 103 15 E
Lama Kara, Togo .... 83 D5 9 30N 1 15 E
Lamaing, Burma ..... 67 M20 15 25N 97 53 E
Lamar, Colo., U.S.A. . 112 F3 38 5N 102 37W
Lamar, Mo., U.S.A. .. 113 G7 37 30N 94 16W
Lamas, Peru .... 124 E3 6 28 S 76 31W
Lamastre, France .... 21 D8 44 59N 4 35 E
Lambach, Austria .... 26 C7 48 6N 13 51 E
Lamballe, France 18 D4 48 29N 2 31W
Lambaréné, Gabon ... 84 E2 0 41 S 10 12 E
Lambasa = Labasa, Fiji 91 C8 16 30 S 179 27 E
Lambay I., Ireland 12 C5 53 29N 6 1W
Lambert Glacier, Antarctica .. 5 D6 71 0 S 70 0 E
Lambert's Bay, S. Africa 88 E2 32 5 S 18 17 E
Lambesc, France ..... 21 E9 43 39N 5 16 E
Lambeth, Canada 116 D3 42 54N 81 18W
Lámbia, Greece ...... 46 D3 37 52N 21 53 E
Lambomakondro, Madag. .. 89 C7 22 41 S 44 44 E
Lambro →, Italy ..... 40 C6 45 8N 9 32 E
Lambton Shores, Canada .. 116 C3 43 10N 81 56W
Lame, Nigeria .... 83 C6 10 30N 9 20 E
Lame Deer, U.S.A. ... 108 D10 45 37N 106 40W
Lamego, Portugal 36 D3 41 5N 7 52W

Lamèque, Canada 105 C7 47 45N 64 38W
Lameroo, Australia ... 95 F3 35 19 S 140 33 E
Lamesa, U.S.A. 113 J4 32 44N 101 58W
Lamía, Greece .... 46 C4 38 55N 22 26 E
Lamington △, Australia 95 D5 28 13 S 153 12 E
Lamitan, Phil. .... 63 C6 6 39N 122 8 E
Lammermuir Hills, U.K. 13 F6 55 50N 2 40W
Lammhult, Sweden ... 11 G8 57 10N 14 35 E
Lamoille →, U.S.A. .. 117 B11 44 38N 73 13W
Lamon B., Phil. ...... 61 D5 14 30N 122 20 E
Lamont, Canada 102 C6 53 46N 112 50W
Lamont, Calif., U.S.A. 111 K8 35 15N 118 55W
Lamont, Wyo., U.S.A. 108 E10 42 13N 107 29W
Lamotte-Beuvron, France .. 19 E9 47 36N 2 2 E
Lampa, Peru .... 124 G4 15 22 S 70 22W
Lampang, Thailand ... 64 C2 18 16N 99 32 E
Lampasas, U.S.A. 113 K5 31 4N 98 11W
Lampazos de Naranjo, Mexico .. 118 B4 27 2N 100 32W
Lampertheim, Germany 25 F4 49 35N 8 27 E
Lampeter, U.K. 15 E3 52 7N 4 4W
Lampman, Canada ... 103 D8 49 25N 102 50W
Lamprechtshausen, Austria .. 26 D5 48 0N 12 58 E
Lampung □, Indonesia 62 F2 5 30 S 104 30 E
Lamta, India .... 69 H9 22 8N 80 7 E
Lamu, Kenya .... 86 C5 2 16 S 40 55 E
Lamy, U.S.A. 109 J11 35 29N 105 53W
Lan Xian, China ..... 56 E6 38 15N 111 35 E
Lan Yu = Hungt'ou Hsü, Taiwan .. 59 G13 22 0N 121 30 E
Lanak La, China ..... 69 B8 34 27N 79 32 E
Lanak'o Shank'ou = Lanak La, China .... 69 B8 34 27N 79 32 E
Lanao, L., Phil. ...... 61 H6 7 52N 124 15 E
Lanark, Canada 117 A8 45 1N 76 22W
Lanark, U.K. 13 F5 55 40N 3 47W
Lanbi Kyun, Burma .. 65 G2 10 50N 98 20 E
Lancang, China ...... 58 G3 22 36N 99 58 E
Lancang Jiang →, China 58 G3 21 40N 101 10 E
Lancashire □, U.K. ... 14 D5 53 50N 2 48W
Lancaster, U.K. 14 C5 54 3N 2 48W
Lancaster, Calif., U.S.A. 111 L8 34 42N 118 8W
Lancaster, Ky., U.S.A. 114 G3 37 37N 84 35W
Lancaster, N.H., U.S.A. 117 B13 44 29N 71 34W
Lancaster, N.Y., U.S.A. 116 D6 42 54N 78 40W
Lancaster, Pa., U.S.A. 117 F8 40 2N 76 19W
Lancaster, S.C., U.S.A. 115 H5 34 43N 80 46W
Lancaster, Wis., U.S.A. 112 D9 42 51N 90 43W
Lancaster Sd., Canada 101 A11 74 13N 84 0W
Lancelin, Australia ... 93 F2 31 0 S 115 18 E
Lanchow = Lanzhou, China .. 56 F2 36 1N 103 52 E
Lanchyn, Ukraine .... 29 B9 48 33N 24 45 E
Lanciano, Italy ...... 41 F11 42 14N 14 23 E
Lancun, China .... 57 F11 36 25N 120 10 E
Łańcut, Poland ...... 31 H9 50 10N 22 13 E
Land Between the Lakes △, U.S.A. 115 G1 36 55N 88 7W
Landau, Bayern, Germany .. 25 G8 48 40N 12 41 E
Landau, Rhld.-Pfz., Germany .. 25 F4 49 12N 8 6 E
Landeck, Austria ..... 26 D3 47 9N 10 34 E
Lander, U.S.A. 108 E9 42 50N 108 44W
Lander →, Australia .. 92 D5 22 0 S 132 0 E
Landerneau, France .. 18 D2 48 28N 4 17W
Landeryd, Sweden ... 11 G7 57 7N 13 15 E
Landes, France 20 D4 44 0N 1 0W
Landes □, France 20 E3 43 57N 0 48W
Landes de Gascogne △, France .. 20 D3 44 23N 0 50W
Landete, Spain 38 F3 39 56N 1 25W
Landi Kotal, Pakistan . 68 B4 34 7N 71 6 E
Landisburg, U.S.A. ... 116 F7 40 21N 77 19W
Landívisiau, France .. 18 D2 48 31N 4 6W
Landquart, Switz. .... 25 J5 46 58N 9 32 E
Landrecies, France ... 19 B10 50 7N 3 40 E
Land's End, U.K. 15 G2 50 4N 5 44W
Landsberg, Germany . 25 G6 48 3N 10 53 E
Landsborough Cr. →, Australia 94 C3 22 28 S 144 35 E
Landsbro, Sweden ... 11 G8 57 24N 14 56 E
Landshut, Germany .. 25 G8 48 34N 12 8 E
Landskrona, Sweden . 11 J6 55 53N 12 50 E
Landstuhl, Germany .. 25 F3 49 24N 7 34 E
Landvetter, Sweden .. 11 G6 57 41N 12 17 E
Lanesboro, U.S.A. ... 117 E9 41 57N 75 34W
Lanester, France 18 E3 47 46N 3 22W
Lanett, U.S.A. 115 J3 32 52N 85 12W
Lang Qua, Vietnam .. 64 A5 22 16N 104 27 E
Lang Shan, China .... 56 D4 41 0N 106 30 E
Lang Son, Vietnam ... 58 G6 21 52N 106 42 E
Lang Suan, Thailand . 65 H2 9 57N 99 4 E
Langå, Denmark ..... 11 H3 56 23N 9 54 E
La'nga Co, China .... 67 D12 30 45N 81 15 E
Lángádhás, Greece ... 44 F7 40 46N 23 6 E
Langádhia, Greece ... 46 D4 37 43N 22 1 E
Långan →, Sweden .. 10 A8 63 19N 14 44 E
Langano, L., Ethiopia . 81 F4 7 36N 38 43 E
Langar, Iran .... 71 C9 35 23N 60 25 E
Langara I., Canada ... 102 C2 54 14N 133 1W
Långås, Sweden ..... 11 H6 56 58N 12 26 E
Langdai, China ...... 58 D5 26 6N 105 21 E
Langdon, U.S.A. 112 A5 48 45N 98 22W
Lange Jan = Ölands södra udde, Sweden . 11 H10 56 12N 16 23 E
Langeac, France ..... 20 C7 45 7N 3 29 E
Langeais, France .... 18 E7 47 20N 0 24 E
Langeb Baraka →, Sudan .. 80 D4 17 28N 36 50 E
Langeberg, S. Africa .. 88 E3 33 55 S 21 0 E
Langeberge, S. Africa . 88 D3 28 15 S 22 33 E
Langeland, Denmark . 11 K4 54 56N 10 48 E
Langelands Bælt, Denmark .. 11 K4 54 50N 10 55 E
Langen, Hessen, Germany .. 25 F4 49 59N 8 40 E
Langen, Niedersachsen, Germany .. 24 B4 53 36N 8 36 E
Langenburg, Canada . 103 C8 50 51N 101 43W
Langeneß, Germany .. 24 A4 54 38N 8 36 E
Langenlois, Austria ... 26 C8 48 29N 15 40 E
Langeoog, Germany .. 24 B3 53 45N 7 32 E
Langeskov, Denmark . 11 J4 55 22N 10 35 E
Länghem, Sweden ... 11 G7 57 36N 13 14 E
Langhirano, Italy ..... 41 D7 44 37N 10 16 E
Langholm, U.K. 13 F5 55 9N 3 0W
Langjökull, Iceland ... 8 D3 64 39N 20 12W
Langkawi, Pulau, Malaysia .. 65 J2 6 25N 99 45 E
Langkon, Malaysia ... 62 C5 6 30N 116 40 E
Langkop, S. Africa ... 88 D3 28 12 S 20 20 E
Langlade, St-P. & M. . 105 C8 46 50N 56 20W

Larose, U.S.A. 113 L9 29 34N 90 23W
Larrimah, Australia .. 92 C5 15 35 S 133 12 E
Larsen Ice Shelf, Antarctica .. 5 C17 67 0 S 62 0W
Laruns, France 20 F3 43 0N 0 26W
Larvik, Norway ...... 9 G14 59 4N 10 2 E
Larzac, Causse du, France .. 20 E7 43 55N 3 17 E
Las Alpujarras, Spain . 39 J1 36 55N 3 20W
Las Animas, U.S.A. .. 113 F3 38 4N 103 13W
Las Anod, Somali Rep. 75 F4 8 26N 47 19 E
Las Arenas, Spain ... 36 B6 43 18N 4 50W
Las Aves, Is., W. Indies 121 C7 15 45N 63 55W
Las Batuecas △, Spain 36 E4 40 26N 6 5W
Las Breñas, Argentina . 126 B3 27 5 S 61 7W
Las Cabezas de San Juan, Spain .. 37 J5 36 57N 5 58W
Las Cañadas del Teide △, Canary Is. . 48 F3 28 15N 16 37W
Las Cejas, Argentina . 128 B4 26 53 S 64 44W
Las Chimeneas, Mexico 111 N10 32 38N 116 5W
Las Cruces, U.S.A. ... 109 K10 32 19N 106 47W
Las Flores, Argentina . 126 D4 36 10 S 59 7W
Las Heras, Argentina . 126 C2 32 51 S 68 49W
Las Lajas, Argentina . 128 D2 38 30 S 70 25W
Las Lomitas, Argentina 126 A3 24 43 S 60 35W
Las Marismas, Spain . 37 H4 37 5N 6 20W
Las Minas, Spain 39 G3 38 20N 1 41W
Las Navas de la Concepción, Spain .. 37 H5 37 56N 5 30W
Las Navas del Marqués, Spain .. 36 E6 40 36N 4 20W
Las Palmas, Argentina . 126 B4 27 8 S 58 45W
Las Palmas, Canary Is. . 48 F4 28 7N 15 26W
Las Palmas →, Mexico 111 N10 32 26N 116 54W
Las Palmas ✈ (LPA), Canary Is. .. 48 G4 27 55N 15 25W
Las Palmas de Cocalán △, Chile ... 126 C1 34 18 S 71 4W
Las Pedroñas, Spain . 39 F2 39 26N 2 40W
Las Piedras, Uruguay . 127 C4 34 44 S 56 14W
Las Pipinas, Argentina . 126 D4 35 30 S 57 19W
Las Plumas, Argentina 128 E3 43 40 S 67 15W
Las Rosas, Argentina . 126 C3 32 30 S 61 35W
Las Rozas, Spain 36 E7 40 29N 3 52W
Las Tablas, Panama .. 120 E3 7 49N 80 14W
Las Termas, Argentina . 126 B3 27 29 S 64 52W
Las Toscas, Argentina . 126 B4 28 21 S 59 18W
Las Truchas, Mexico . 118 D4 17 57N 102 13W
Las Varillas, Argentina 126 C3 31 50 S 62 50W
Las Vegas, N. Mex., U.S.A. .. 109 J11 35 36N 105 13W
Las Vegas, Nev., U.S.A. 111 J11 36 10N 115 9W
Las Vegas McCarran International ✈ (LAS), U.S.A. .. 111 J11 36 5N 115 9W
Lasarte, Spain 38 B2 43 16N 2 1W
Lascano, Uruguay ... 127 C5 33 35 S 54 12W
Lash-e Joveyn, Afghan. 66 D2 31 45N 61 30 E
Lashburn, Canada ... 103 C7 53 10N 109 40W
Lashio, Burma .... 67 H20 22 56N 97 45 E
Lashkar, India .... 68 F8 26 10N 78 10 E
Łasin, Poland .... 30 E6 53 30N 19 2 E
Lasíthi □, Greece .... 49 D7 35 11N 25 31 E
Lasíthi, Greece ...... 49 D7 35 5N 25 50 E
Läsjerd, Iran .... 71 C7 35 24N 53 4 E
Lask, Poland .... 31 G6 51 34N 19 8 E
Łaskarzew, Poland .. 31 G8 51 48N 21 36 E
Laško, Slovenia ..... 41 B12 46 10N 15 16 E
Lassay-les-Châteaux, France .. 18 D6 48 27N 0 30W
Lassen Pk., U.S.A. ... 108 F3 40 29N 121 31W
Lassen Volcanic △, U.S.A. .. 108 F3 40 30N 121 20W
Last Mountain L., Canada .. 103 C7 51 5N 105 14W
Lastchance Cr. →, U.S.A. .. 110 E5 40 2N 121 15W
Lastoursville, Gabon . 84 E2 0 55 S 12 38 E
Lastovo, Croatia ..... 41 F13 42 46N 16 55 E
Lastovski Kanal, Croatia 41 F14 42 50N 17 0 E
Lat Yao, Thailand .... 64 E2 15 45N 99 48 E
Latacunga, Ecuador .. 124 D3 0 50 S 78 35W
Latakia = Al Lādhiqīyah, Syria ... 70 C2 35 30N 35 45 E
Latchford, Canada ... 104 C4 47 20N 79 50W
Latehar, India .... 69 H11 23 45N 84 30 E
Laterza, Italy .... 43 B9 40 37N 16 48 E
Latham, Australia .... 93 E2 29 44 S 116 20 E
Lathen, Germany .... 24 C3 52 52N 7 19 E
Lathi, India .... 68 F4 27 43N 71 23 E
Lathrop Wells, U.S.A. 111 J10 36 39N 116 24W
Latiano, Italy .... 43 B10 40 33N 17 43 E
Latina, Italy .... 42 A5 41 28N 12 52 E
Latium = Lazio □, Italy 42 A5 42 0N 12 30 E
Laton, U.S.A. 110 J7 36 26N 119 41W
Latorytsya →, Slovak Rep. .. 27 C14 48 28N 21 50 E
Latouche Treville, C., Australia .. 92 C3 18 27 S 121 49 E
Latrobe, Australia .... 95 G4 41 14 S 146 30 E
Latrobe, U.S.A. 116 F5 40 19N 79 23W
Latrónico, Italy ...... 43 B9 40 5N 16 1 E
Latvia ■, Europe .... 9 H20 56 50N 24 0 E
Lau, Nigeria .... 83 D7 9 11N 11 19 E
Lau Group, Fiji ...... 91 C9 17 0 S 178 30W
Lauchhammer, Germany 24 D9 51 29N 13 47 E
Lauda-Königshofen, Germany .. 25 F5 49 33N 9 42 E
Lauenburg, Germany . 24 B6 53 22N 10 32 E
Lauenburgische Seen △, Germany .. 24 B6 53 38N 10 45 E
Lauf, Germany .... 25 F7 49 30N 11 16 E
Laughlin, U.S.A. 109 J6 35 8N 114 35W
Laujar de Andarax, Spain .. 39 H2 37 0N 2 54W
Laukaa, Finland ..... 9 E21 62 24N 25 56 E
Launceston, Australia . 95 G4 41 24 S 147 8 E
Launceston, U.K. 15 G3 50 38N 4 22W
Laune →, Ireland 12 D2 52 7N 9 47W
Launglon Bok, Burma 64 F1 13 50N 97 54 E
Laupheim, Germany . 25 G5 48 14N 9 52 E
Laura, Australia ...... 94 B3 15 32 S 144 32 E
Laureana di Borrello, Italy .. 43 D9 38 30N 16 5 E
Laurel, Miss., U.S.A. . 113 K10 31 41N 89 8W
Laurel, Mont., U.S.A. 108 D9 45 40N 108 46W
Laurencekirk, U.K. ... 13 E6 56 50N 2 28W
Laurens, U.S.A. 115 H4 34 30N 82 1W
Laurentian Plateau, Canada .. 105 B6 52 0N 70 0W
Lauria, Italy .... 43 B8 40 2N 15 50 E
Laurie L., Canada 103 B8 56 35N 101 57W
Laurinburg, U.S.A. ... 115 H6 34 47N 79 28W
Laurium, U.S.A. 114 B1 47 14N 88 27W
Lausanne, Switz. ..... 25 J2 46 32N 6 38 E

Laut, Indonesia .... 62 D3 4 45N 108 0 E
Laut, Pulau, Indonesia .. 62 E5 3 40 S 116 10 E
Laut Kecil, Kepulauan, Indonesia .... 62 E5 4 45 S 115 40 E
Lauterbach, Germany .. 24 E5 50 37N 9 24 E
Lauterecken, Germany .. 25 F3 49 38N 7 35 E
Lautoka, Fiji .... 91 C7 17 37 S 177 27 E
Lauzès, France ...... 20 D5 44 34N 1 35 E
Lava →, Russia ...... 30 D8 54 37N 21 14 E
Lava Beds △, ... 108 F3 41 40N 121 30W
Lavagh More, Ireland .. 12 B3 54 46N 8 6W
Lavagna, Italy ...... 40 D6 44 18N 9 2 E
Laval, France 18 D6 48 4N 0 48W
Lavalle, Argentina .... 126 B2 28 15 S 65 15W
Lavant Station, Canada . 117 A8 45 3N 76 42W
Lāvar Meydān, Iran ... 71 D7 30 20N 54 30 E
Lávara, Greece ...... 45 E10 41 19N 26 22 E
Lavardac, France .... 20 D4 44 12N 0 20 E
Lavaur, France ...... 20 E5 43 40N 1 49 E
Lavelanet, France .... 20 F5 42 57N 1 51 E
Lavello, Italy .... 43 A8 41 3N 15 48 E
Laverton, Australia ... 93 E3 28 44 S 122 29 E
Lavis, Italy .... 40 B4 46 9N 11 5 E
Lávkos, Greece ...... 46 B5 39 9N 23 14 E
Lavos, Portugal 36 E2 40 6N 8 49W
Lavradio, Portugal ... 37 G1 38 40N 9 3W
Lavras, Brazil ...... 127 A7 21 20 S 45 0W
Lavre, Portugal 37 G2 38 46N 8 22W
Lávrion, Greece ..... 46 D6 37 40N 24 4 E
Lávris, Greece ...... 49 D6 35 25N 24 40 E
Lavumisa, Swaziland .. 89 D5 27 20 S 31 55 E
Lavushi Manda △, Zambia .... 87 E3 12 46 S 31 0 E
Lawas, Malaysia ..... 62 D5 4 55N 115 25 E
Lawele, Indonesia .... 63 F6 5 13 S 122 57 E
Lawn Hill △, Australia . 94 B2 18 15 S 138 6 E
Lawng Pit, Burma .... 67 G20 25 30N 97 25 E
Lawqah, Si. Arabia ... 70 D4 29 49N 42 45 E
Lawra, Ghana 82 C4 10 39N 2 51W
Lawrence, N.Z. ...... 91 L2 45 55 S 169 41 E
Lawrence, Kans., U.S.A. 112 F7 38 58N 95 14W
Lawrence, Mass., U.S.A. 117 D13 42 43N 71 10W
Lawrenceburg, Ind., U.S.A. 114 F3 39 6N 84 52W
Lawrenceburg, Tenn., U.S.A. 115 H2 35 14N 87 20W
Lawrenceville, Ga., U.S.A. 115 J4 33 57N 83 59W
Lawrenceville, Pa., U.S.A. 116 E7 41 59N 77 8W
Laws, U.S.A. 110 H8 37 24N 118 20W
Lawton, U.S.A. 113 H5 34 37N 98 25W
Lawu, Indonesia ..... 63 G14 7 40 S 111 13 E
Lawz, J. al, Si. Arabia .. 80 B4 28 39N 35 18 E
Laxá, Sweden .... 11 F8 58 59N 14 37 E
Laxford, L., U.K. 13 C3 58 24N 5 6W
Laxou, France ...... 19 D13 48 41N 6 8 E
Lay →, France 20 B2 46 18N 1 17W
Layla, Si. Arabia .... 75 C4 22 10N 46 40 E
Laylān, Iraq .... 70 C5 35 18N 44 31 E
Layon →, France 18 E6 47 20N 0 45W
Layton, U.S.A. 108 F7 41 4N 111 58W
Laytonville, U.S.A. ... 108 G2 39 41N 123 29W
Lazarevac, Serbia & M. . 44 B4 44 23N 20 17 E
Lazarevskoye, Russia .. 35 J4 43 55N 39 21 E
Lazarivo, Madag. .... 89 C8 23 54 S 44 59 E
Lazdijai, Lithuania ... 30 D10 54 14N 23 31 E
Lazio □, Italy ...... 41 F9 42 10N 12 30 E
Lazo, Moldova ...... 29 C13 47 33N 28 2 E
Lazo, Russia .... 54 C6 43 25N 133 55 E
Le Beausset, France .. 21 E9 43 12N 5 48 E
Le Bic, Canada 105 C6 48 20N 68 41W
Le Blanc, France .... 20 B5 46 37N 1 3 E
Le Bleymard, France .. 20 D7 44 30N 3 42 E
Le Bourgneuf-la-Fôret, France 18 D6 48 10N 0 59W
Le Bugue, France .... 20 D4 44 55N 0 56 E
Le Cateau Cambrésis, France .... 19 B10 50 7N 3 32 E
Le Caylar, France .... 20 E7 43 51N 3 19 E
Le Chambon-Feugerolles, France . 21 C8 45 24N 4 19 E
Le Châtelet, France .. 19 F9 46 38N 2 16 E
Le Chesne, France ... 19 C11 49 30N 4 45 E
Le Cheylard, France .. 21 D8 44 55N 4 25 E
Le Conquet, France .. 18 D2 48 21N 4 46W
Le Creusot, France ... 19 F11 46 48N 4 24 E
Le Croisic, France ... 18 E4 47 18N 2 30W
Le Donjon, France ... 19 F10 46 20N 3 48 E
Le Dorat, France .... 20 B5 46 14N 1 5 E
Le François, Martinique 120 c 14 38N 60 57W
Le Grand-Lucé, France 18 E7 47 52N 0 28 E
Le Grand-Pressigny, France .... 18 F7 46 55N 0 48 E
Le Grand-Quevilly, France .... 18 C8 49 24N 1 3 E
Le Havre, France .... 18 C7 49 30N 0 5 E
Le Lamentin, Martinique .... 120 c 14 35N 61 2W
Le Lavandou, France . 21 E10 43 8N 6 22 E
Le Lion-d'Angers, France 18 E6 47 37N 0 43W
Le Louroux-Béconnais, France 18 E6 47 30N 0 55W
Le Luc, France ..... 21 E10 43 23N 6 21 E
Le Lude, France .... 18 E7 47 39N 0 9 E
Le Mans, France .... 18 E7 48 0N 0 10 E
Le Marin, Martinique . 120 c 14 27N 60 55W
Le Mars, U.S.A. 112 D6 42 47N 96 10W
Le Mayet-de-Montagne, France .... 19 F10 46 4N 3 40 E
Le Mêle-sur-Sarthe, France .... 18 D7 48 31N 0 22 E
Le Monastier-sur-Gazeille, France ... 20 D7 44 57N 3 59 E
Le Monêtier-les-Bains, France .... 21 D10 44 58N 6 30 E
Le Mont-Dore, France . 20 C6 45 35N 2 49 E
Le Mont-St-Michel, France 18 D5 48 40N 1 30W
Le Muy, France ..... 21 E10 43 28N 6 34 E
Le Palais, France 18 E3 47 20N 3 10W
Le Perthus, France ... 20 F6 42 30N 2 53 E
Le Prêcheur, Martinique 120 c 14 50N 61 12W
Le Puy-en-Velay, France 20 C7 45 3N 3 52 E
Le Robert, Martinique . 120 c 14 40N 60 56W
Le Sueur, U.S.A. 112 C8 44 28N 93 55W
Le Teil, France ..... 21 D8 44 33N 4 40 E
Le Teilleul, France ... 18 D6 48 32N 0 53W
Le Theil, France .... 18 D7 48 16N 0 42 E
Le Thillot, France ... 19 E13 47 53N 6 46 E
Le Thuy, Vietnam ... 64 D6 17 14N 106 49 E
Le Touquet-Paris-Plage, France .... 19 B8 50 30N 1 36 E
Le Tréport, France ... 18 B8 50 3N 1 20 E
Le Val-d'Ajol, France . 19 E13 47 55N 6 30 E

Le Verdon-sur-Mer, France 20 C2 45 33N 1 4W
Le Vigan, France .... 20 E7 43 59N 3 36 E
Lea →, U.K. .... 15 F8 51 31N 0 1 E
Leach, Cambodia .... 65 F4 12 21N 103 46 E
Lead, U.S.A. 112 C3 44 21N 103 46W
Leader, Canada 103 C7 50 50N 109 30W
Leadville, U.S.A. 109 G10 39 15N 106 18W
Leaf →, U.S.A. 113 K10 30 59N 88 44W
Leaf Rapids, Canada .. 103 B9 56 30N 99 59W
Leamington, Canada .. 116 D2 42 3N 82 36W
Leamington, U.S.A. .. 108 G7 39 32N 112 17W
Leamington Spa = Royal Leamington Spa, U.K. 15 E6 52 18N 1 31W
Le'an, China .... 59 D10 27 22N 115 48 E
Leandro Norte Alem, Argentina .... 127 B4 27 34 S 55 15W
Leane, L., Ireland ... 12 D2 52 2N 9 32W
Learmonth, Australia . 92 D1 22 13 S 114 10 E
Leask, Canada 103 C7 53 5N 106 45W
Leatherhead, U.K. ... 15 F7 51 18N 0 20W
Leavenworth, Kans., U.S.A. 112 F7 39 19N 94 55W
Leavenworth, Wash., U.S.A. 108 C3 47 36N 120 40W
Łeba, Poland .... 30 D4 54 45N 17 32 E
Łeba →, Poland .... 30 D4 54 46N 17 33 E
Lebach, Germany ... 25 F2 49 25N 6 54 E
Lebak, Phil. .... 61 H6 6 32N 124 5 E
Lebam, U.S.A. 110 D3 46 34N 123 33W
Lebane, Serbia & M. .. 44 D5 42 56N 21 44 E
Lebanon, Ind., U.S.A. . 114 E2 40 3N 86 28W
Lebanon, Kans., U.S.A. 112 F5 39 49N 98 33W
Lebanon, Ky., U.S.A. . 114 G3 37 34N 85 15W
Lebanon, Mo., U.S.A. . 113 G8 37 41N 92 40W
Lebanon, N.H., U.S.A. . 117 C12 43 39N 72 15W
Lebanon, Oreg., U.S.A. 108 D2 44 32N 122 55W
Lebanon, Pa., U.S.A. . 117 F8 40 20N 76 26W
Lebanon, Tenn., U.S.A. 115 G2 36 12N 86 18W
Lebanon ■, Asia .... 74 B5 34 0N 36 0 E
Lebec, U.S.A. 111 L8 34 50N 118 52W
Lebedyan, Russia ... 33 F10 53 0N 39 10 E
Lebedyn, Ukraine ... 33 G8 50 35N 34 30 E
Lebel-sur-Quévillon, Canada 104 C4 49 3N 76 59W
Lebomboberge, S. Africa .... 89 C5 24 30 S 32 0 E
Lębork, Poland ..... 30 D4 54 33N 17 46 E
Lebrija, Spain 37 J4 36 53N 6 5W
Łebsko, Jezioro, Poland 30 D4 54 40N 17 25 E
Leca da Palmeira, Portugal 36 D2 41 12N 8 42W
Lecce, Italy .... 43 B11 40 23N 18 11 E
Lecco, Italy .... 40 C6 45 51N 9 23 E
Lecco, L. di, Italy ... 40 C6 45 51N 9 22 E
Lécera, Spain 38 D4 41 13N 0 43W
Lech, Austria ...... 26 D3 47 13N 10 9 E
Lech →, Germany ... 25 G6 48 43N 10 56 E
Lechang, China ..... 59 E9 25 10N 113 20 E
Lechtaler Alpen, Austria 26 D3 47 15N 10 30 E
Lecontes Mills, U.S.A. . 116 E6 41 5N 78 17W
Lectoure, France ... 20 E4 43 56N 0 38 E
Łęczna, Poland ..... 31 G9 51 18N 22 53 E
Łęczyca, Poland .... 31 F6 52 5N 19 15 E
Ledesma, Spain 36 D5 41 6N 5 59W
Ledong, China ..... 64 C7 18 41N 109 5 E
Leduc, Canada 102 C6 53 15N 113 30W
Lee, U.S.A. 117 D11 42 19N 73 15W
Lee →, Ireland 12 E3 51 53N 8 56W
Lee Vining, U.S.A. .. 110 H7 37 58N 119 7W
Leech L., U.S.A. 112 B7 47 10N 94 24W
Leechburg, U.S.A. ... 116 F5 40 37N 79 36W
Leeds, U.K. 14 D6 53 48N 1 33W
Leeds, U.S.A. 115 J2 33 33N 86 33W
Leek, Neths. .... 17 A6 53 10N 6 24 E
Leek, U.K. 14 D5 53 7N 2 1W
Leeman, Australia ... 93 E1 29 57 S 114 58 E
Leeper, U.S.A. 116 E5 41 22N 79 18W
Leer, Germany ..... 24 B3 53 13N 7 26 E
Leesburg, U.S.A. ... 115 L5 28 49N 81 53W
Leesville, U.S.A. 113 K8 31 9N 93 16W
Leeton, Australia ... 95 E4 34 33 S 146 23 E
Leetonia, U.S.A. 116 F4 40 53N 80 45W
Leeu Gamka, S. Africa 88 E3 32 47 S 21 59 E
Leeuwarden, Neths. . 17 A5 53 15N 5 48 E
Leeuwin, C., Australia 93 F2 34 20 S 115 9 E
Leeuwin Naturaliste △, Australia .... 93 F2 34 6 S 115 3 E
Leeward Is., Atl. Oc. .. 121 C7 16 30N 63 30W
Lefka, Cyprus ...... 49 D11 35 6N 32 51 E
Lefkoníko, Cyprus ... 49 D12 35 18N 33 44 E
Lefroy, Canada 116 B5 44 16N 79 34W
Lefroy, L., Australia .. 93 F3 31 21 S 121 40 E
Łeg →, Poland ..... 31 H8 50 42N 21 50 E
Leganés, Spain 36 E7 40 19N 3 45W
Legazpi, Phil. ...... 61 E5 13 10N 123 45 E
Lège-Cap-Ferret, France 20 D2 44 48N 1 9W
Lege Hida, Ethiopia .. 81 F5 7 56N 41 4 E
Legendre I., Australia . 92 D2 20 22 S 116 55 E
Leghorn = Livorno, Italy 40 E7 43 33N 10 19 E
Legionowo, Poland .. 31 F7 52 25N 20 50 E
Legnago, Italy ..... 41 C8 45 11N 11 18 E
Legnano, Italy ..... 40 C5 45 36N 8 54 E
Legnica, Poland .... 31 G3 51 12N 16 10 E
Legrad, Croatia .... 41 B13 46 17N 16 51 E
Leh, India .... 69 B7 34 9N 77 35 E
Lehigh Acres, U.S.A. . 115 M5 26 36N 81 39W
Lehighton, U.S.A. ... 117 F9 40 50N 75 43W
Leho, Sudan .... 81 F3 7 7N 33 52 E
Lehrte, Germany ... 24 C5 52 22N 9 58 E
Lehututu, Botswana . 88 C3 23 54 S 21 55 E
Lei Shui →, China .. 59 D9 26 55N 112 35 E
Leiah, Pakistan .... 68 D4 30 58N 70 58 E
Leibnitz, Austria ... 26 E8 46 47N 15 34 E
Leibo, China ...... 58 C4 28 11N 103 34 E
Leicester, U.K. 15 E6 52 38N 1 8W
Leicester City □, U.K. . 15 E6 52 38N 1 9W
Leicestershire □, U.K. . 15 E6 52 41N 1 17W
Leichhardt →, Australia 94 B2 17 35 S 139 48 E
Leichhardt Ra., Australia .... 94 C4 20 46 S 147 40 E
Leiden, Neths. ..... 17 B4 52 9N 4 30 E
Leie →, Belgium .... 17 C3 51 2N 3 45 E
Leifers = Láives, Italy . 41 B8 46 26N 11 20 E
Leigh →, U.K. 15 F4 51 5N 2 38W
Leine →, Germany .. 24 C5 52 43N 9 36 E
Leinefelde, Germany . 24 D6 51 23N 10 19 E
Leinster, Australia .. 93 E3 27 51 S 120 36 E
Leinster □, Ireland .. 12 C4 53 3N 7 8W
Leinster, Mt., Ireland . 12 D5 52 37N 6 46W
Leipalingis, Lithuania . 30 D10 54 5N 23 51 E
Leipzig, Germany ... 24 D8 51 18N 12 22 E
Leiria, Portugal 36 F2 39 46N 8 53W
Leiria □, Portugal ... 36 F2 39 46N 8 53W
Leirvik, Norway .... 9 G11 59 47N 5 28 E

Leishan, China ..... 58 D7 26 15N 108 20 E
Leisler, Mt., Australia . 92 D4 23 23 S 129 20 E
Leith, U.K. 13 F5 55 59N 3 11W
Leith Hill, U.K. 15 F7 51 11N 0 22W
Leitha →, Europe ... 27 D10 47 50N 17 15 E
Leitrim, Ireland 12 B3 54 0N 8 5W
Leitrim □, Ireland ... 12 B4 54 8N 8 0W
Leitza, Spain 38 B3 43 5N 1 55W
Leiyang, China ..... 59 D9 26 27N 112 45 E
Leizhou, China ..... 58 G7 20 52N 110 8 E
Leizhou Bandao, China 58 G7 21 0N 110 0 E
Leizhou Wan, China . 59 G8 20 50N 110 20 E
Lek →, Neths. ..... 17 C4 51 54N 4 35 E
Leka, Norway ..... 8 D14 65 5N 11 35 E
Lekáni, Greece ..... 45 E8 41 10N 24 35 E
Lekbibaj, Albania ... 44 D3 42 17N 19 56 E
Lekeitio, Spain 38 B2 43 20N 2 32W
Lekhainá, Greece ... 46 D3 37 57N 21 16 E
Lekoui, Burkina Faso . 82 C4 12 37N 3 40W
Leksand, Sweden ... 10 D9 60 44N 15 1 E
Lékva Óros, Greece .. 49 D6 35 18N 24 3 E
Leland, Mich., U.S.A. . 114 C3 45 1N 85 45W
Leland, Miss., U.S.A. . 113 J9 33 24N 90 54W
Lelâng, Sweden .... 10 E6 59 10N 12 5 E
Leleque, Argentina .. 128 E2 42 28 S 71 0W
Lelystad, Neths. .... 17 B5 52 30N 5 25 E
Lem, Denmark ..... 11 H2 56 1N 8 24 E
Lema, Nigeria ..... 83 C5 12 58N 4 13 E
Lema Shilindi, Ethiopia 81 G5 4 50N 42 6 E
Léman, L., Europe .. 19 F13 46 26N 6 30 E
Lembar, Indonesia .. 63 K19 8 45 S 116 4 E
Lembuak, Indonesia . 63 K18 8 36 S 116 11 E
Lemera, Dem. Rep. of the Congo .... 86 C2 3 0 S 28 55 E
Lemery, Phil. ...... 61 E4 13 51N 120 56 E
Lemhi Ra., U.S.A. ... 108 D7 44 30N 113 30W
Lemmer, Neths. .... 17 B5 52 51N 5 43 E
Lemmon, U.S.A. 112 C3 45 57N 102 10W
Lemon Grove, U.S.A. 111 N9 32 45N 117 2W
Lemoore, U.S.A. 110 J7 36 18N 119 46W
Lempdes, France ... 20 C7 45 22N 3 17 E
Lemvig, Denmark ... 11 H2 56 33N 8 20 E
Lena →, Russia .... 53 B13 72 52N 126 40 E
Lenart, Slovenia .... 41 B12 46 36N 15 48 E
Lenartovce, Slovak Rep. 27 C13 48 18N 20 19 E
Lencloître, France .. 18 F7 46 50N 0 20 E
Léndas, Greece ..... 49 E6 34 56N 24 56 E
Lendava, Slovenia ... 41 B13 46 35N 16 25 E
Lendeh, Iran ...... 71 D6 30 58N 50 25 E
Lendinara, Italy .... 41 C8 45 5N 11 36 E
Lengerich, Germany . 24 C3 52 11N 7 52 E
Lenggong, Malaysia . 65 K3 5 6N 100 58 E
Lenggries, Germany . 25 H7 47 41N 11 34 E
Lengshuijiang, China . 59 D8 27 40N 111 26 E
Lengshuitan, China .. 59 D8 26 27N 111 35 E
Lengua de Vaca, Pta., Chile .... 126 C1 30 14 S 71 38W
Lengwe △, Malawi .. 87 F3 16 14 S 34 45 E
Lengyeltóti, Hungary . 28 D7 46 40N 17 40 E
Lenhovda, Sweden .. 11 G9 57 0N 15 16 E
Lenina, Kanal →, Russia .... 35 J7 43 44N 45 17 E
Leningrad = Sankt-Peterburg, Russia .. 32 C6 59 55N 30 20 E
Lenino, Ukraine .... 33 K8 45 17N 35 46 E
Leninogorsk, Kazakhstan ...... 52 D9 50 20N 83 30 E
Leninsk, Russia .... 35 F7 48 40N 45 15 E
Leninsk-Kuznetskiy, Russia .... 52 D9 54 44N 86 10 E
Leninskoye, Russia .. 34 A8 58 23N 47 3 E
Lenk, Switz. .... 25 J3 46 27N 7 28 E
Lenkoran = Länkäran, Azerbaijan .... 71 B6 38 48N 48 52 E
Lenmalu, Indonesia . 63 E8 1 45 S 130 15 E
Lenne →, Germany . 24 D3 51 25N 7 29 E
Lennestadt, Germany 24 D4 51 8N 8 2 E
Lennox, U.S.A. 112 D6 43 21N 96 53W
Lennoxville, Canada . 117 A13 45 22N 71 51W
Leno, Italy .... 40 C7 45 22N 10 13 E
Lenoir, U.S.A. 115 H5 35 55N 81 32W
Lenoir City, U.S.A. .. 115 H3 35 48N 84 16W
Lenore L., Canada ... 103 C8 52 30N 104 59W
Lenox, U.S.A. 117 D11 42 22N 73 17W
Lens, France .... 19 B9 50 26N 2 50 E
Lensahn, Germany .. 24 A6 54 13N 10 53 E
Lensk, Russia ...... 53 C12 60 48N 114 55 E
Lentekhi, Georgia ... 35 J6 42 47N 42 45 E
Lenti, Hungary ..... 28 D1 46 37N 16 33 E
Lentini, Italy ...... 43 E8 37 17N 15 0 E
Lenwood, U.S.A. ... 111 L9 34 53N 117 7W
Lenya, Burma ...... 62 B1 11 33N 98 57 E
Lenzen, Germany ... 24 B7 53 5N 11 29 E
Léo, Burkina Faso ... 82 C4 11 3N 2 2W
Leoben, Austria .... 26 D8 47 22N 15 5 E
Leodhas = Lewis, U.K. 13 C2 58 9N 6 40W
Leola, U.S.A. 112 C5 45 43N 98 56W
Leominster, U.K. 15 E5 52 14N 2 43W
Leominster, U.S.A. .. 117 D13 42 32N 71 46W
Léon, France 20 E2 43 53N 1 18W
León, Mexico 118 C4 21 7N 101 40W
León, Nic. 120 D2 12 20N 86 51W
León, Spain 36 C5 42 38N 5 34W
León □, Spain 36 C5 42 40N 5 55W
León, Montes de, Spain 36 C4 42 30N 6 18W
Leonardo da Vinci, Roma ✈ (FCO), Italy 41 G9 41 48N 12 15 E
Leonardtown, U.S.A. 114 F7 38 17N 76 38W
Leonardville, Namibia 88 C2 23 29 S 18 49 E
Leonberg, Germany . 25 G5 48 48N 9 1 E
Leonding, Austria ... 26 C7 48 16N 14 15 E
Leonessa, Italy ..... 41 F9 42 34N 12 58 E
Leonforte, Italy ..... 43 E7 37 38N 14 23 E
Leongatha, Australia . 95 F4 38 30 S 145 58 E
Leonídhion, Greece .. 46 D4 37 9N 22 52 E
Leonora, Australia .. 93 E3 28 49 S 121 19 E
Leopoldina, Brazil ... 127 A7 21 28 S 42 40W
Leopoldsburg, Belgium 17 C5 51 7N 5 13 E
Leoti, U.S.A. 112 F4 38 29N 101 21W
Leova, Moldova .... 29 D13 46 28N 28 15 E
Leoville, Canada 103 C7 53 39N 107 33W
Lepe, Spain 37 H3 37 15N 7 12W
Lepel = Lyepyel, Belarus 32 E5 54 50N 28 40 E
Lepenoú, Greece ... 46 C3 38 42N 21 7 E
Leping, China ...... 59 C11 28 47N 117 7 E
Lépo, L. do, Angola .. 88 B2 17 0 S 19 0 E
Lepontine, Alpi, Italy . 40 B5 46 22N 8 27 E
Leppävirta, Finland .. 9 E22 62 29N 27 46 E
Lepsény, Hungary .. 28 D3 47 0N 18 15 E
Lequeitio = Lekeitio, Spain 38 B2 43 20N 2 32W
Lercara Friddi, Italy .. 42 E6 37 45N 13 36 E
Lerdo, Mexico 118 B4 25 32N 103 32W
Léré, Chad .... 83 D7 9 39N 14 13 E
Léré, Mali 82 B4 15 45N 4 55W

Lere, Bauchi, Nigeria . 83 D6 9 43N 9 18 E
Lere, Kaduna, Nigeria 83 C6 10 23N 8 35 E
Leribe, Lesotho ..... 89 D4 28 51 S 28 3 E
Lérici, Italy .... 40 D6 44 4N 9 58 E
Lérida = Lleida, Spain 38 D5 41 37N 0 39 E
Lérins, Îs. de, France . 21 E11 43 31N 7 3 E
Lerma, Spain 36 C7 42 0N 3 47W
Léros, Greece ...... 47 D8 37 10N 26 50 E
Lérouville, France .. 19 D12 48 51N 5 30 E
Lerum, Sweden ..... 11 G6 57 46N 12 16 E
Lerwick, U.K. 13 A7 60 9N 1 9W
Leş, Romania ...... 28 D6 46 58N 21 50 E
Les Abrets, France .. 21 C9 45 32N 5 35 E
Les Andelys, France . 18 C8 49 15N 1 25 E
Les Borges Blanques, Spain .... 38 D5 41 31N 0 52 E
Les Cayes, Haiti 121 C5 18 15N 73 46W
Les Coteaux, Canada . 117 A10 45 15N 74 13W
Les Essarts, France .. 18 F5 46 47N 1 12W
Les Herbiers, France . 18 F5 46 52N 1 1W
Les Minquiers, Plateau des, Chan. Is. 18 D4 48 58N 2 8W
Les Pieux, France ... 18 C4 49 31N 1 48W
Les Ponts-de-Cé, France 18 E6 47 25N 0 30W
Les Riceys, France .. 19 E11 47 59N 4 22 E
Les Sables-d'Olonne, France 20 B2 46 30N 1 45W
Les Vans, France ... 21 D8 44 25N 4 7 E
Lesbos = Lésvos, Greece 47 B8 39 10N 26 20 E
L'Escala, Spain .... 38 C8 42 7N 3 8 E
Leshan, China ..... 58 C4 29 33N 103 41 E
Leshwe △, Dem. Rep. of the Congo .... 87 E2 12 45 S 29 30 E
Lésina, Italy .... 41 G12 41 52N 15 21 E
Lésina, L. di, Italy ... 41 G12 41 53N 15 26 E
Lesjöfors, Sweden ... 10 E8 59 58N 14 11 E
Lesko, Poland ..... 31 J9 49 30N 22 23 E
Leskov I., Antarctica . 5 B1 56 0 S 28 0W
Leskovac, Serbia & M. 44 C5 43 0N 21 58 E
Leskovik, Albania ... 44 F4 40 10N 20 34 E
Leśna, Poland ..... 31 G2 51 1N 15 15 E
Lesnaya →, Russia .. 30 E10 52 21N 26 32 E
Lesneven, France ... 18 D2 48 35N 4 20W
Leśnica, Poland .... 31 H5 50 26N 18 11 E
Leśnica, Serbia & M. . 44 B3 44 39N 19 20 E
Lesnoye, Russia .... 32 C8 58 15N 35 18 E
Lesopilnoye, Russia . 54 A7 46 44N 134 20 E
Lesotho ■, Africa ... 89 D4 29 40 S 28 0 E
Lesozavodsk, Russia . 53 E14 45 30N 133 29 E
Lesparre-Médoc, France 20 C3 45 18N 0 57W
Lessay, France 18 C5 49 14N 1 30W
Lesse →, Belgium .. 17 D5 50 15N 4 54 E
Lesse et Lomme △, Belgium .... 17 D5 50 8N 5 9 E
Lessebo, Sweden ... 11 H9 56 45N 15 16 E
Lesser Antilles, W. Indies 121 D7 15 0N 61 0W
Lesser Slave L., Canada 102 B5 55 30N 115 25W
Lesser Sunda Is., Indonesia .... 63 F6 8 0 S 120 0 E
Lessines, Belgium ... 17 D3 50 42N 3 50 E
Lester, U.S.A. 110 C5 47 12N 121 29W
Lester B. Pearson International, Toronto ✈ (YYZ), Canada 116 C5 43 40N 79 34W
Lestock, Canada 103 C8 51 19N 103 59W
Lesuer I., Australia .. 92 B4 13 50 S 127 17 E
Lesueur △, Australia . 93 F2 30 11 S 115 10 E
Lésvos, Greece ..... 47 B8 39 10N 26 20 E
Leszno, Poland .... 31 G3 51 50N 16 30 E
Letaba, S. Africa .... 89 C5 23 59 S 31 50 E
Letälven, Sweden ... 10 E8 59 5N 14 5 E
Létavértes, Hungary . 28 C6 47 23N 21 55 E
Letchworth, U.K. ... 15 F7 51 59N 0 13W
Letea, Ostrov, Romania 29 E14 45 18N 29 20 E
Lethbridge, Canada . 102 D6 49 45N 112 45W
Lethem, Guyana 124 C7 3 20N 59 50W
Leti, Kepulauan, Indonesia .... 63 F7 8 10 S 128 0 E
Leti Is. = Leti, Kepulauan, Indonesia 63 F7 8 10 S 128 0 E
Letiahau →, Botswana 88 C3 21 16 S 24 0 E
Leticia, Colombia ... 124 D5 4 9 S 70 0W
Leting, China ...... 57 E10 39 23N 118 55 E
Letjiesbos, S. Africa . 88 E3 32 34 S 22 16 E
Letlhakane, Botswana 88 C4 21 27 S 25 30 E
Letlhakeng, Botswana 88 C3 24 0 S 24 59 E
Letong, Indonesia ... 62 D3 2 58N 105 42 E
Letpadan, Burma ... 67 L19 17 45N 95 45 E
Letpan, Burma ..... 67 K19 19 28N 94 10 E
Letsôk-aw Kyun, Burma 65 G2 11 30N 98 25 E
Letterkenny, Ireland . 12 B4 54 57N 7 45W
Leu, Romania ...... 29 F9 44 10N 24 0 E
Leucadia, U.S.A. 111 M9 33 4N 117 18W
Leucate, France .... 20 F7 42 56N 3 3 E
Leucate, Étang de, France .... 20 F7 42 50N 3 0 E
Leuchars, U.K. 13 E6 56 24N 2 53W
Leuk, Switz. .... 25 J3 46 19N 7 37 E
Leuşeni, Moldova ... 29 D13 46 58N 28 11 E
Leuser, G., Indonesia . 62 D1 3 46N 97 12 E
Leutkirch, Germany . 25 H6 47 50N 10 1 E
Leuven, Belgium ... 17 D4 50 52N 4 42 E
Leuze-en-Hainaut, Belgium .... 17 D3 50 36N 3 37 E
Lev Tolstoy, Russia .. 32 F10 53 13N 39 29 E
Levádhia, Greece ... 46 C4 38 27N 22 54 E
Levanger, Norway .. 8 E14 63 45N 11 19 E
Levant, Î. du, France . 21 E10 43 3N 6 28 E
Lévanto, Italy ...... 40 D6 44 10N 9 37 E
Lévanzo, Italy ..... 42 D5 38 0N 12 20 E
Levelland, U.S.A. ... 113 J3 33 35N 102 23W
Leven, U.K. 13 E6 56 12N 3 0W
Leven, L., U.K. 13 E5 56 12N 3 22W
Leven, Toraka, Madag. 89 A8 12 30 S 47 45 E
Leveque C., Australia 92 C3 16 20 S 123 0 E
Leverano, Italy ..... 43 B10 40 17N 18 0 E
Leverkusen, Germany 24 D2 51 1N 7 1 E
Levice, Slovak Rep. .. 27 C11 48 13N 18 35 E
Lévico Terme, Italy .. 41 C8 46 0N 11 18 E
Levie, France ...... 21 G13 41 40N 9 7 E
Levier, France ..... 19 F13 46 58N 6 8 E
Levin, N.Z. .... 91 J5 40 37 S 175 18 E
Lévis, Canada 105 C5 46 48N 71 9W
Levis, L., Canada ... 102 A5 62 37N 117 58W
Levítha, Greece .... 47 D8 37 0N 26 28 E
Levittown, N.Y., U.S.A. 117 F11 40 44N 73 31W
Levittown, Pa., U.S.A. 117 F10 40 9N 74 51W
Levka, Bulgaria .... 45 E10 41 52N 26 15 E
Levkás □, Greece ... 46 C2 38 40N 20 43 E
Levkími, Greece .... 49 B4 39 25N 20 4 E
Levkímmi, Ákra, Greece 49 B4 39 29N 20 3 E
Levkôsia = Nicosia, Cyprus .... 49 D12 35 10N 33 25 E
Levoča, Slovak Rep. . 27 B13 49 2N 20 35 E

Levroux, France .... 19 F8 46 59N 1 38 E
Levski, Bulgaria .... 45 C9 43 21N 25 10 E
Levskigrad = Karlovo, Bulgaria .... 45 D8 42 38N 24 47 E
Lewes, U.K. .... 15 G8 50 52N 0 1 E
Lewes, U.S.A. 114 F8 38 46N 75 9W
Lewin Brzeski, Poland 31 H4 50 45N 17 37 E
Lewis, U.K. 13 C2 58 9N 6 40W
Lewis →, U.S.A. 110 E4 45 51N 122 48W
Lewis, Butt of, U.K. . 13 C2 58 31N 6 16W
Lewis Ra., Australia . 92 D4 20 3 S 128 50 E
Lewis Range, U.S.A. . 108 C7 48 5N 113 5W
Lewis Run, U.S.A. .. 116 E6 41 52N 78 40W
Lewisburg, Pa., U.S.A. 116 F8 40 58N 76 54W
Lewisburg, Tenn., U.S.A. 115 H2 35 27N 86 48W
Lewisburg, W. Va., U.S.A. 114 G5 37 48N 80 27W
Lewisporte, Canada . 105 C8 49 15N 55 3W
Lewiston, Idaho, U.S.A. 108 C5 46 25N 117 1W
Lewiston, Maine, U.S.A. 115 C11 44 6N 70 13W
Lewiston, N.Y., U.S.A. 116 C5 43 11N 79 3W
Lewistown, Mont., U.S.A. 108 C9 47 4N 109 26W
Lewistown, Pa., U.S.A. 116 F7 40 36N 77 34W
Lexington, Ill., U.S.A. 112 E10 40 39N 88 47W
Lexington, Ky., U.S.A. 114 F3 38 3N 84 30W
Lexington, Mich., U.S.A. 116 C2 43 16N 82 32W
Lexington, Mo., U.S.A. 112 F8 39 11N 93 52W
Lexington, N.C., U.S.A. 115 H5 35 49N 80 15W
Lexington, N.Y., U.S.A. 117 D10 42 15N 74 22W
Lexington, Nebr., U.S.A. 112 E5 40 47N 99 45W
Lexington, Ohio, U.S.A. 116 F2 40 41N 82 35W
Lexington, Tenn., U.S.A. 115 H1 35 39N 88 24W
Lexington, Va., U.S.A. 114 G6 37 47N 79 27W
Lexington Park, U.S.A. 114 F7 38 16N 76 27W
Leyburn, U.K. 14 C6 54 19N 1 48W
Leye, China .... 58 E6 24 48N 106 29 E
Leyland, U.K. 14 D5 53 42N 2 43W
Leyre →, France ... 20 D2 44 39N 1 1W
Leyte □, Phil. ...... 61 F6 11 0N 125 0 E
Leyte Gulf, Phil. .... 61 F6 10 50N 125 25 E
Leżajsk, Poland .... 31 H9 50 16N 22 25 E
Lezay, France 20 B3 46 15N 0 1W
Lezhë, Albania ..... 44 E3 41 47N 19 39 E
Lezhi, China .... 58 B5 30 19N 104 58 E
Lézignan-Corbières, France .... 20 E6 43 13N 2 43 E
Lezoux, France ..... 20 C7 45 49N 3 21 E
Lgov, Russia .... 33 G8 51 42N 35 16 E
Lhasa, China ...... 60 D4 29 25N 90 58 E
Lhazê, China ...... 60 D3 29 5N 87 38 E
Lhokkruet, Indonesia 62 D1 4 55N 95 24 E
Lhokseumawe, Indonesia .... 62 C1 5 10N 97 10 E
L'Hospitalet de Llobregat, Spain .. 38 D7 41 21N 2 6 E
Li, Thailand .... 64 D2 17 48N 98 57 E
Li Shui →, China ... 59 C9 29 24N 112 1 E
Li Xian, Gansu, China 56 G3 34 10N 105 5 E
Li Xian, Hebei, China 56 E8 38 30N 115 35 E
Li Xian, Hunan, China 59 C8 29 36N 111 42 E
Liádhoi, Greece .... 47 E8 36 50N 26 11 E
Liancheng, China ... 59 E11 25 42N 116 40 E
Liancourt Rocks = Tok-do, Asia .... 55 F5 37 15N 131 52 E
Lianga, Phil. ...... 61 G7 8 38N 126 6 E
Liangcheng, Nei Monggol Zizhiqu, China .... 56 D7 40 28N 112 25 E
Liangcheng, Shandong, China .... 57 G10 35 32N 119 37 E
Liangdang, China ... 56 H4 33 56N 106 18 E
Lianghekou, China .. 58 C7 29 11N 108 44 E
Liangping, China ... 58 B6 30 38N 107 47 E
Lianhua, China ..... 59 D9 27 3N 113 54 E
Lianjiang, Fujian, China 59 D12 26 12N 119 27 E
Lianjiang, Guangdong, China .... 59 G8 21 40N 110 20 E
Lianping, China .... 59 E10 24 26N 114 30 E
Lianshan, China .... 59 E9 24 38N 112 8 E
Lianshanguan, China 57 D12 40 53N 123 43 E
Lianshui, China .... 57 H10 33 42N 119 20 E
Lianyuan, China .... 59 D8 27 40N 111 38 E
Lianyungang, China . 57 G10 34 40N 119 11 E
Lianzhou, China .... 59 E9 24 51N 112 2 E
Liao He →, China .. 57 D11 41 0N 121 50 E
Liaocheng, China ... 56 F8 36 28N 115 58 E
Liaodong Bandao, China .... 57 E12 40 0N 122 30 E
Liaodong Wan, China 57 D11 40 20N 121 10 E
Liaoning □, China .. 57 D12 41 40N 122 30 E
Liaotung, G. of = Liaodong Wan, China 57 D11 40 20N 121 10 E
Liaoyang, China .... 57 D12 41 15N 122 58 E
Liaoyuan, China .... 57 C13 42 58N 125 2 E
Liaozhong, China ... 57 D12 41 23N 122 50 E
Liapádhes, Greece .. 46 B1 39 42N 19 40 E
Liard →, Canada ... 102 A4 61 51N 121 18W
Liard River, Canada . 102 B3 59 25N 126 5W
Liari, Pakistan ..... 68 G2 25 37N 66 30 E
Libau = Liepāja, Latvia 9 H19 56 30N 21 0 E
Libby, U.S.A. 108 B6 48 23N 115 33W
Libenge, Dem. Rep. of the Congo .... 84 D3 3 40N 18 55 E
Liberal, U.S.A. 113 G4 37 3N 100 55W
Liberec, Czech Rep. . 26 A8 50 47N 15 7 E
Liberec □, Czech Rep. 26 A8 50 45N 15 2 E
Liberia, Costa Rica .. 120 D2 10 40N 85 30W
Liberia ■, W. Afr. ... 82 D3 6 30N 9 30W
Liberty, Mo., U.S.A. . 112 F7 39 15N 94 25W
Liberty, N.Y., U.S.A. . 117 E10 41 48N 74 45W
Liberty, Pa., U.S.A. .. 116 E7 41 34N 77 6W
Liberty, Tex., U.S.A. . 113 K7 30 3N 94 48W
Libiąż, Poland ..... 31 H6 50 7N 19 21 E
Libîya, Sahrâ', Africa 79 C10 25 0N 25 0 E
Libo, China .... 58 E6 25 22N 107 53 E
Libobo, Tanjung, Indonesia .... 63 E7 0 54 S 128 28 E
Libode, S. Africa .... 89 E4 31 33 S 29 2 E
Libohovë, Albania .. 44 F4 40 3N 20 10 E
Libourne, France ... 20 D3 44 55N 0 14W
Libramont, Belgium . 17 E5 49 55N 5 23 E
Libreville, Gabon ... 84 D1 0 25N 9 26 E
Libya ■, N. Afr. .... 79 C9 27 0N 17 0 E
Libyan Desert = Libîya, Sahrâ', Africa ..... 79 C10 25 0N 25 0 E
Libyan Plateau = Ed-Défa, Egypt ...... 80 A2 30 40N 26 30 E
Licantén, Chile ..... 126 D1 35 55 S 72 0W
Licata, Italy .... 42 E6 37 6N 13 56 E
Lice, Turkey .... 73 C9 38 27N 40 39 E
Licheng, China ..... 56 F7 36 28N 113 20 E
Lichfield, U.K. 15 E6 52 41N 1 49W
Lichinga, Mozam. ... 87 E4 13 13 S 35 11 E

Lichtenburg, S. Africa . **88 D4** 26 8 S 26 8 E
Lichtenfels, Germany .. **25 E7** 50 8N 11 4 E
Lichuan, Hubei, China . **58 B7** 30 18N 108 57 E
Lichuan, Jiangxi, China **59 D11** 27 18N 116 55 E
Licking →, U.S.A. **114 F3** 39 6N 84 30W
Licosa, Punta, Italy .... **43 B7** 40 15N 14 55 E
Licungo →, Mozam. ... **87 F4** 17 40 S 37 15 E
Lida, Belarus .... **9 K21** 53 53N 16 48 E
Liden, Sweden .... **10 B10** 62 42N 16 48 E
Lidhorikíon, Greece ... **46 C4** 38 32N 22 14 E
Lidhult, Sweden ...... **11 H7** 56 50N 13 27 E
Lidköping, Sweden .... **11 F7** 58 31N 13 7 E
Lido, Italy .... **41 C9** 45 25N 12 22 E
Lido, Niger .... **83 C5** 12 54N 3 44 E
Lido di Roma = Óstia,
  Lido di, Italy ...... **41 G9** 41 43N 12 17 E
Lidzbark, Poland ..... **31 E6** 53 15N 19 49 E
Lidzbark Warmiński,
  Poland .... **30 D7** 54 7N 20 34 E
Liebenwalde, Germany . **24 C9** 52 52N 13 24 E
Lieberose, Germany ... **24 D10** 51 59N 14 17 E
Liebig, Mt., Australia .. **92 D5** 23 18 S 131 22 E
Liebling, Romania .... **28 E6** 45 36N 21 20 E
Liechtenstein ■, Europe **25 H5** 47 8N 9 35 E
Liège, Belgium .... **17 D5** 50 38N 5 35 E
Liège □, Belgium ..... **17 D5** 50 32N 5 35 E
Liegnitz = Legnica,
  Poland .... **31 G3** 51 12N 16 10 E
Lienart, Dem. Rep. of
  the Congo .... **86 B2** 3 3N 25 31 E
Lienyünchiangshih =
  Lianyungang, China . **57 G10** 34 40N 119 11 E
Lienz, Austria .... **26 E5** 46 50N 12 46 E
Liepāja, Latvia ...... **9 H19** 56 30N 21 0 E
Liepāja □, Latvia .... **30 B8** 56 30N 21 30 E
Liepājas ezers, Latvia . **30 B8** 56 27N 21 3 E
Lier, Belgium .... **17 C4** 51 7N 4 34 E
Liernais, France ..... **19 E11** 47 13N 4 16 E
Liești, Romania ...... **29 E12** 45 38N 27 34 E
Liévin, France .... **19 B9** 50 24N 2 47 E
Lièvre →, Canada **104 C4** 45 31N 75 26W
Liezen, Austria ...... **26 E7** 47 34N 14 15 E
Liffey →, Ireland **12 C5** 53 21N 6 13W
Lifford, Ireland **12 B4** 54 51N 7 29W
Liffré, France **18 D5** 48 12N 1 30W
Lifudzin, Russia ..... **54 B7** 44 21N 134 58 E
Ligao, Phil. .... **61 E5** 13 14N 123 32 E
Lightning Ridge,
  Australia .... **95 D4** 29 22 S 148 0 E
Lignano Sabbiadoro,
  Italy .... **41 C10** 45 42N 13 9 E
Ligny-en-Barrois, France **19 D12** 48 36N 5 20 E
Ligonha →, Mozam. .. **87 F4** 16 54 S 39 9 E
Ligonier, U.S.A. **116 F5** 40 15N 79 14W
Ligourion, Greece .... **46 D5** 37 37N 23 4 E
Ligueil, France ...... **18 E7** 47 2N 0 49 E
Liguria □, Italy ...... **40 D5** 44 30N 8 50 E
Ligurian Sea, Medit. S. . **6 G7** 43 20N 9 0 E
Lihou Reefs and Cays,
  Australia .... **94 B5** 17 25 S 151 40 E
Lihue, U.S.A. **106 H15** 21 59N 159 23W
Lihué Calel △,
  Argentina .... **126 D2** 38 0 S 65 10W
Lijiang, China .... **58 D3** 26 55N 100 20 E
Likasi, Dem. Rep. of
  the Congo .... **87 E2** 10 55 S 26 48 E
Likenäs, Sweden ..... **10 D7** 60 37N 13 3 E
Likhoslavl, Russia .... **32 D8** 57 12N 35 30 E
Likoma I., Malawi .... **87 E3** 12 3 S 34 45 E
Likumburu, Tanzania .. **87 D4** 9 43 S 35 8 E
L'Île-Bouchard, France **18 E7** 47 7N 0 26 E
L'Île-Rousse, France .. **21 F12** 42 38N 8 57 E
Liling, China .... **59 D9** 27 42N 113 29 E
Lilla Edet, Sweden .... **11 F6** 58 9N 12 8 E
Lille, France .... **19 B10** 50 38N 3 3 E
Lille Bælt, Denmark ... **11 J3** 55 20N 9 45 E
Lillebonne, France ... **18 C7** 49 30N 0 32 E
Lillehammer, Norway .. **9 F14** 61 8N 10 30 E
Lillesand, Norway .... **9 G13** 58 15N 8 23 E
Lillhärdal, Sweden ... **10 C8** 61 51N 14 5 E
Lillian Pt., Australia .. **93 E4** 27 40 S 126 6 E
Lillo, Spain **36 F7** 39 45N 3 20W
Lillooet, Canada **102 C4** 50 44N 121 57W
Lillooet →, Canada ... **102 D4** 49 15N 121 57W
Lilongwe, Malawi .... **87 E3** 14 0 S 33 48 E
Liloy, Phil. .... **63 C6** 8 4N 122 39 E
Lim →, Bos.-H. ..... **44 C3** 43 45N 19 15 E
Lim Chu Kang,
  Singapore .... **65 d** 1 26N 103 43 E
Lima, Indonesia ..... **63 E7** 3 39 S 127 58 E
Lima, Mont., U.S.A. .. **108 D7** 44 38N 112 36W
Lima, Ohio, U.S.A. ... **114 E3** 40 44N 84 6W
Lima →, Portugal ... **36 D2** 41 41N 8 50W
Liman, Indonesia .... **63 G14** 7 48 S 111 45 E
Liman, Russia .... **35 H8** 45 45N 47 12 E
Limanowa, Poland ... **31 J7** 49 42N 20 22 E
Limassol, Cyprus .... **49 E12** 34 42N 33 1 E
Limavady, U.K. **12 A5** 55 3N 6 56W
Limay →, Argentina . **128 D3** 39 0 S 68 0W
Limay Mahuida,
  Argentina .... **126 D2** 37 10 S 66 45W
Limbach-Oberfrohna,
  Germany .... **24 E8** 50 52N 12 43 E
Limbang, Brunei ..... **62 D5** 4 42N 115 6 E
Limbara, Mte., Italy ... **42 B2** 40 51N 9 10 E
Limbaži, Latvia ...... **9 H21** 57 31N 24 42 E
Limbdi, India .... **68 H4** 22 34N 71 51 E
Limbe, Cameroon .... **83 E6** 4 1N 9 10 E
Limburg, Germany ... **25 E4** 50 22N 8 4 E
Limburg □, Belgium .. **17 C5** 51 2N 5 25 E
Limburg □, Neths. ... **17 C5** 51 20N 5 55 E
Limedsforsen, Sweden . **10 D7** 60 52N 13 25 E
Limeira, Brazil ...... **127 A6** 22 35 S 47 28W
Limenária, Greece ... **45 F8** 40 38N 24 32 E
Limerick, Ireland **12 D3** 52 40N 8 37W
Limerick, U.S.A. **117 C14** 43 41N 70 48W
Limerick □, Ireland .. **12 D3** 52 30N 8 50W
Limestone, U.S.A. **116 D6** 42 2N 78 38W
Limestone →, Canada **103 B10** 56 31N 94 7W
Limfjorden, Denmark . **11 H3** 56 55N 9 0 E
Limia = Lima →,
  Portugal **36 D2** 41 41N 8 50W
Limín Khersónisou,
  Greece .... **47 F7** 35 18N 25 21 E
Limingen, Norway .... **8 D15** 64 48N 13 35 E
Limmared, Sweden ... **11 G7** 57 31N 13 21 E
Limmen Bight, Australia **94 A2** 14 40 S 135 35 E
Limmen Bight →,
  Australia .... **94 B2** 15 7 S 135 44 E
Límni, Greece .... **46 C5** 38 43N 23 18 E
Límnos, Greece ...... **47 B7** 39 50N 25 5 E
Limoges, Canada **117 A9** 45 20N 75 16W
Limoges, France ..... **20 C5** 45 50N 1 15 E
Limón, Costa Rica ... **120 E3** 10 0N 83 2W
Limon, U.S.A. **112 F3** 39 16N 103 41W

Limone Piemonte, Italy **40 D4** 44 12N 7 34 E
Limousin □, France .. **20 C5** 45 30N 1 30 E
Limousin, Plateau du,
  France .... **20 C5** 45 45N 1 15 E
Limoux, France ...... **20 E6** 43 4N 2 12 E
Limpopo □, S. Africa .. **89 C4** 24 5 S 29 0 E
Limpopo →, Africa ... **89 D5** 25 5 S 33 30 E
Limuru, Kenya ...... **86 C4** 1 2 S 36 35 E
Lin Xian, China ..... **56 F6** 37 57N 110 58 E
Lin'an, China .... **59 B12** 30 15N 119 42 E
Linapacan I., Phil. ... **61 F3** 11 27N 119 49 E
Linapacan Str., Phil. .. **61 F3** 11 37N 119 52 E
Linares, Chile .... **126 D1** 35 50 S 71 40W
Linares, Mexico **119 C5** 24 50N 99 40W
Linares, Spain **37 G7** 38 10N 3 40W
Linaro, Capo, Italy ... **41 F8** 42 2N 11 50 E
Línas Mte., Italy ..... **42 C1** 39 25N 8 38 E
Linate, Milano ✈ (LIN),
  Italy .... **40 C6** 45 27N 9 16 E
Lincang, China ...... **58 F3** 23 58N 100 1 E
Lincheng, China ..... **56 F8** 37 25N 114 30 E
Linchuan, China ..... **59 D11** 27 57N 116 15 E
Lincoln = Beamsville,
  Canada **116 C5** 43 12N 79 28W
Lincoln, Argentina ... **126 C3** 34 55 S 61 30W
Lincoln, N.Z. .... **91 K4** 43 38 S 172 30 E
Lincoln, U.K. **14 D7** 53 14N 0 32W
Lincoln, Calif., U.S.A. . **110 G5** 38 54N 121 17W
Lincoln, Ill., U.S.A. ... **112 E10** 40 9N 89 22W
Lincoln, Kans., U.S.A. . **112 F5** 39 3N 98 9W
Lincoln, Maine, U.S.A. . **115 C11** 45 22N 68 30W
Lincoln, N.H., U.S.A. .. **117 B13** 44 3N 71 40W
Lincoln, N. Mex., U.S.A. **109 K11** 33 30N 105 23W
Lincoln, Nebr., U.S.A. . **112 E6** 40 49N 96 41W
Lincoln City, U.S.A. .. **108 D1** 44 57N 124 1W
Lincoln Sea, Arctic ... **4 A5** 84 0N 55 0W
Lincoln Sea, Arctic ... **4 A5** 84 0N 55 0W
Lincolnshire □, U.K. .. **14 D7** 53 14N 0 32W
Lincolnshire Wolds,
  U.K. **14 D7** 53 26N 0 13W
Lincolnton, U.S.A. ... **115 H5** 35 29N 81 16W
Lind, U.S.A. **108 C4** 46 58N 118 37W
Linda, U.S.A. **110 F5** 39 8N 121 34W
Lindau, Germany .... **25 H5** 47 33N 9 41 E
Linden, Guyana **124 B7** 6 0N 58 10W
Linden, Ala., U.S.A. .. **115 J2** 32 18N 87 48W
Linden, Calif., U.S.A. . **110 G5** 38 1N 121 5W
Linden, Tex., U.S.A. .. **113 J7** 33 1N 94 22W
Lindenhurst, U.S.A. .. **117 F11** 40 41N 73 23W
Lindesberg, Sweden .. **10 E9** 59 36N 15 15 E
Lindesnes, Norway ... **9 H12** 57 58N 7 3 E
Líndhos, Greece ..... **49 C10** 36 6N 28 4 E
Líndhos, Ákra, Greece . **49 C10** 36 4N 28 10 E
Lindi, Tanzania ...... **87 D4** 9 58 S 39 38 E
Lindi □, Tanzania .... **87 D4** 9 40 S 38 30 E
Lindi →, Dem. Rep. of
  the Congo .... **86 B2** 0 33N 25 5 E
Lindö, Sweden .... **11 F10** 58 37N 16 15 E
Lindome, Sweden .... **11 G6** 57 35N 12 5 E
Lindoso, Portugal **36 D2** 41 52N 8 11W
Lindow, Germany .... **24 C8** 52 58N 12 59 E
Lindsay, Canada **116 B6** 44 22N 78 43W
Lindsay, Calif., U.S.A. . **110 J7** 36 12N 119 5W
Lindsay, Okla., U.S.A. . **113 H6** 34 50N 97 38W
Lindsborg, U.S.A. **112 F6** 38 35N 97 40W
Lindsdal, Sweden .... **11 H10** 56 44N 16 18 E
Line Islands, Pac. Oc. . **97 H12** 7 0N 160 0W
Linesville, U.S.A. **116 E4** 41 39N 80 26W
Linfen, China .... **56 F6** 36 3N 111 30 E
Ling Xian, Hunan,
  China .... **59 D9** 26 29N 113 48 E
Ling Xian, Shandong,
  China .... **56 F9** 37 22N 116 30 E
Lingao, China .... **64 C7** 19 56N 109 42 E
Lingayen, Phil. ...... **63 A6** 16 1N 120 14 E
Lingayen G., Phil. .... **61 C4** 16 10N 120 15 E
Lingbi, China .... **57 H9** 33 33N 117 33 E
Lingbo, Sweden ..... **10 C10** 61 3N 16 41 E
Linchuan,
  Guangxi Zhuangzu,
  China .... **59 E8** 25 26N 110 21 E
Lingchuan, Shanxi,
  China .... **56 G7** 35 45N 113 12 E
Lingen, Germany .... **24 C3** 52 31N 7 19 E
Lingga, Indonesia .... **62 E2** 0 12 S 104 37 E
Lingga, Kepulauan,
  Indonesia .... **62 E2** 0 10 S 104 30 E
Lingga Arch. = Lingga,
  Kepulauan, Indonesia **62 E2** 0 10 S 104 30 E
Linghem, Sweden .... **11 F9** 58 26N 15 47 E
Lingle, U.S.A. **112 D2** 42 8N 104 21W
Lingqiu, China ...... **56 E8** 39 28N 114 22 E
Lingshan, China ..... **58 F7** 22 25N 109 18 E
Lingshi, China ...... **56 F6** 36 48N 111 48 E
Lingshou, China ..... **56 E8** 38 20N 114 20 E
Lingshui, China ..... **64 C8** 18 27N 110 0 E
Lingtai, China ...... **56 G4** 35 0N 107 40 E
Linguère, Senegal **82 B1** 15 25N 15 5W
Lingui, China .... **58 E8** 25 12N 110 2 E
Lingwu, China ...... **56 E4** 38 6N 106 20 E
Lingyuan, China ..... **57 D10** 41 10N 119 15 E
Lingyun, China ...... **58 E6** 25 2N 106 35 E
Linhai, China .... **59 C13** 28 50N 121 8 E
Linhares, Brazil ..... **125 G10** 19 25 S 40 4W
Linhe, China .... **56 D4** 40 48N 107 20 E
Linjiang, China ...... **57 D14** 41 50N 127 0 E
Linköping, Sweden ... **11 F9** 58 28N 15 36 E
Linkou, China .... **57 B16** 45 15N 130 18 E
Linli, China .... **59 C8** 29 27N 111 30 E
Linqi, China .... **56 G7** 35 45N 113 52 E
Linqing, China ...... **56 F8** 36 50N 115 42 E
Linqu, China .... **57 F10** 36 25N 118 30 E
Linru, China .... **56 G7** 34 11N 112 52 E
Lins, Brazil .... **127 A6** 21 40 S 49 44W
Linshui, China ...... **58 B6** 30 2N 106 57 E
Linstead, Jamaica .... **120 a** 18 8N 77 2W
Linth →, Switz. ..... **25 H5** 47 7N 9 7 E
Linthal, Switz. ...... **25 J5** 46 54N 9 0 E
Linton, Ind., U.S.A. .. **114 F2** 39 2N 87 10W
Linton, N. Dak., U.S.A. **112 B4** 46 16N 100 14W
Lintong, China ...... **56 G5** 34 20N 109 10 E
Linwood, Canada **116 C4** 43 35N 80 43W
Linwu, China .... **59 E9** 25 19N 112 31 E
Linxi, China .... **57 C10** 43 36N 118 2 E
Linxia, China .... **60 C5** 35 36N 103 10 E
Linxiang, China ..... **59 C9** 29 28N 113 23 E
Linyanti →, Africa ... **88 B4** 17 50 S 25 5 E
Linyi, China .... **57 G10** 35 5N 118 21 E
Linz, Austria .... **26 C7** 48 18N 14 18 E
Linz, Germany ...... **24 E3** 50 34N 7 17 E
Linzhenzhen, China .. **56 F5** 36 30N 108 58 E
Linzi, China .... **57 F10** 36 50N 118 20 E
Lion, G. du, France .. **20 E7** 43 10N 4 0 E

Lionárisso, Cyprus .... **49 D13** 35 28N 34 8 E
Lioni, Italy .... **43 B8** 40 52N 15 11 E
Lions, G. of = Lion, G.
  du, France .... **20 E7** 43 10N 4 0 E
Lion's Den, Zimbabwe **87 F3** 17 15 S 30 5 E
Lion's Head, Canada .. **116 B3** 44 58N 81 15W
Liozno = Lyozna,
  Belarus .... **32 E6** 55 0N 30 50 E
Lipa, Phil. .... **61 E4** 13 57N 121 10 E
Lipali, Mozam. ...... **87 F4** 15 50 S 35 50 E
Lipany, Slovak Rep. ... **27 B13** 49 9N 20 58 E
Lípari, Italy .... **43 D7** 38 26N 14 58 E
Lípari, I., Italy ...... **43 D7** 38 29N 14 56 E
Lípari, Is. = Eólie, Ís.,
  Italy .... **43 D7** 38 30N 14 57 E
Lipcani, Moldova .... **29 B11** 48 14N 26 48 E
Lipetsk, Russia ...... **33 F10** 52 37N 39 35 E
Lipiany, Poland ..... **31 E1** 53 2N 14 58 E
Lipkany = Lipcani,
  Moldova .... **29 B11** 48 14N 26 48 E
Lipník nad Bečvou,
  Czech Rep. .... **27 B10** 49 32N 17 36 E
Lipno, Poland .... **31 F6** 52 49N 19 15 E
Lipova, Romania ..... **28 D6** 46 8N 21 42 E
Lipovcy Manzovka,
  Russia .... **54 B5** 44 12N 132 26 E
Lipovets, Ukraine .... **33 H5** 49 12N 29 1 E
Lippe →, Germany .. **24 D2** 51 39N 6 36 E
Lippstadt, Germany .. **24 D4** 51 41N 8 22 E
Lipscomb, U.S.A. **113 G4** 36 14N 100 16W
Lipsk, Poland .... **30 E10** 53 44N 23 24 E
Lipsko, Poland ...... **31 G8** 51 9N 21 40 E
Lipsoí, Greece ...... **47 D8** 37 19N 26 50 E
Liptovský Hrádok,
  Slovak Rep. .... **27 B12** 49 2N 19 44 E
Liptovský Milkuláš,
  Slovak Rep. .... **27 B12** 49 6N 19 35 E
Liptrap, C., Australia .. **95 F4** 38 50 S 145 55 E
Lipu, China .... **59 E8** 24 30N 110 22 E
Liquillo, Sierra de,
  Puerto Rico .... **121 d** 18 20N 65 47W
Lira, Uganda .... **86 B3** 2 17N 32 57 E
Liri →, Italy .... **42 A6** 41 25N 13 52 E
Liria = Llíria, Spain .. **39 F4** 39 37N 0 35W
Lisala, Dem. Rep. of
  the Congo .... **84 D4** 2 12N 21 38 E
Lisboa, Portugal **37 G1** 38 42N 9 10W
Lisboa □, Portugal ... **37 F1** 39 0N 9 12W
Lisboa ✈ (LIS), Portugal **37 G1** 38 46N 9 8W
Lisbon = Lisboa,
  Portugal **37 G1** 38 42N 9 10W
Lisbon, N. Dak., U.S.A. **112 B6** 46 27N 97 41W
Lisbon, N.H., U.S.A. .. **117 B13** 44 13N 71 55W
Lisbon, Ohio, U.S.A. .. **116 F4** 40 46N 80 46W
Lisbon Falls, U.S.A. .. **115 D10** 44 0N 70 4W
Lisburn, U.K. **12 B5** 54 31N 6 3W
Lisburne, C., U.S.A. .. **4 C17** 68 53N 166 13W
Liscannor B., Ireland . **12 D2** 52 55N 9 24W
Liscia →, Italy ...... **42 A2** 41 11N 9 9 E
Lishe Jiang →, China . **58 E3** 24 15N 101 35 E
Lishi, China .... **56 F6** 37 31N 111 8 E
Lishu, China .... **57 C13** 43 20N 124 18 E
Lishui, Jiangsu, China . **59 B12** 31 38N 119 2 E
Lishui, Zhejiang, China **59 C12** 28 28N 119 54 E
Lisianski I., Pac. Oc. .. **96 E10** 26 2N 173 58W
Lisichansk =
  Lysychansk, Ukraine **33 H10** 48 55N 38 30 E
Lisieux, France ...... **18 C7** 49 10N 0 12 E
Liski, Russia .... **33 G10** 51 3N 39 30 E
L'Isle-Jourdain, Gers,
  France .... **20 E5** 43 36N 1 5 E
L'Isle-Jourdain, Vienne,
  France .... **20 B4** 46 13N 0 31 E
L'Isle-sur-la-Sorgue,
  France .... **21 E9** 43 54N 5 2 E
Lisle-sur-Tarn, France . **20 E5** 43 52N 1 49 E
Lismore, Australia ... **95 D5** 28 44 S 153 21 E
Lismore, Ireland **12 D4** 52 8N 7 55W
Lista, Norway .... **9 G12** 58 7N 6 39 E
Lister, Mt., Antarctica . **5 D11** 78 0 S 162 0 E
Liston, Australia ..... **95 D5** 28 39 S 152 6 E
Listowel, Canada **116 C4** 43 44N 80 58W
Listowel, Ireland **12 D2** 52 27N 9 29W
Lit, Sweden .... **10 A8** 63 19N 14 51 E
Lit-et-Mixe, France ... **20 D2** 44 2N 1 15W
Litang,
  Guangxi Zhuangzu,
  China .... **58 F7** 23 12N 109 8 E
Litang, Sichuan, China **58 B3** 30 1N 100 17 E
Litang Qu →, China .. **58 C3** 28 6N 101 32 E
Litani →, Lebanon ... **74 B4** 33 20N 35 15 E
Litchfield, Calif., U.S.A. **110 E6** 40 24N 120 23W
Litchfield, Conn., U.S.A. **117 E11** 41 45N 73 11W
Litchfield, Ill., U.S.A. . **112 F10** 39 11N 89 39W
Litchfield, Minn., U.S.A. **112 C7** 45 8N 94 32W
Litchfield △, Australia . **92 B5** 13 14 S 131 1 E
Liteni, Romania ..... **29 C11** 47 32N 26 32 E
Lithgow, Australia ... **95 E5** 33 25 S 150 8 E
Líthinon, Ákra, Greece **49 E6** 34 55N 24 44 E
Lithuania ■, Europe .. **9 J20** 55 30N 24 0 E
Litija, Slovenia ...... **41 B11** 46 3N 14 50 E
Lititz, U.S.A. **117 F8** 40 9N 76 18W
Litókhoron, Greece ... **44 F6** 40 8N 22 34 E
Litoměřice, Czech Rep. **26 A7** 50 33N 14 10 E
Litomyšl, Czech Rep. . **27 B9** 49 52N 16 20 E
Litschau, Austria .... **26 C8** 48 58N 15 4 E
Little Abaco I.,
  Bahamas **120 A4** 26 50N 77 30W
Little Barrier I., N.Z. .. **91 G5** 36 12 S 175 8 E
Little Belt Mts., U.S.A. **108 C8** 46 40N 110 45W
Little Bighorn
  Battlefield △, U.S.A. **108 D10** 45 34N 107 26W
Little Blue →, U.S.A. . **112 F6** 39 42N 96 41W
Little Buffalo →,
  Canada **102 A6** 61 0N 113 46W
Little Cayman,
  Cayman Is. **120 C3** 19 41N 80 3W
Little Churchill →,
  Canada **103 B9** 57 30N 95 22W
Little Colorado →,
  U.S.A. **109 H8** 36 12N 111 48W
Little Current, Canada **104 C3** 45 55N 82 0W
Little Current →,
  Canada **104 B3** 50 57N 84 36W
Little Falls, Minn.,
  U.S.A. **112 C7** 45 59N 94 22W
Little Falls, N.Y., U.S.A. **117 C10** 43 3N 74 51W
Little Fork →, U.S.A. . **112 A8** 48 31N 93 35W
Little Grand Rapids,
  Canada **103 C9** 52 0N 95 29W
Little Humboldt →,
  U.S.A. **108 F5** 41 1N 117 43W
Little Inagua I.,
  Bahamas **121 B5** 21 40N 73 50W
Little Karoo, S. Africa . **88 E3** 33 45 S 21 0 E

Little Khingan Mts. =
  Xiao Hinggan Ling,
  China .... **60 B7** 49 0N 127 0 E
Little Lake, U.S.A. ... **111 K9** 35 56N 117 55W
Little Laut Is. = Laut
  Kecil, Kepulauan,
  Indonesia .... **62 E5** 4 45 S 115 40 E
Little Mecatina = Petit-
  Mécatina →, Canada **105 B8** 50 40N 59 30W
Little Minch, U.K. **13 D2** 57 35N 6 45W
Little Missouri →,
  U.S.A. **112 B3** 47 36N 102 25W
Little Ouse →, U.K. .. **15 E9** 52 22N 1 12 E
Little Rann, India .... **68 H4** 23 25N 71 25 E
Little Red →, U.S.A. . **113 H9** 35 11N 91 27W
Little River, N.Z. .... **91 K4** 43 45 S 172 49 E
Little Rock, U.S.A. ... **113 H8** 34 45N 92 17W
Little Ruaha →,
  Tanzania .... **86 D4** 7 57 S 37 53 E
Little Sable Pt., U.S.A. **114 D2** 43 38N 86 33W
Little Scarcies →,
  S. Leone **82 D2** 8 50N 13 10W
Little Sioux →, U.S.A. **112 E6** 41 48N 96 4W
Little Smoky →,
  Canada **102 C5** 54 44N 117 11W
Little Snake →, U.S.A. **108 F9** 40 27N 108 26W
Little Valley, U.S.A. .. **116 D6** 42 15N 78 48W
Little Wabash →,
  U.S.A. **114 G1** 37 55N 88 5W
Little White →, U.S.A. **112 D4** 43 40N 100 40W
Little Zab = Zāb aş
  Şaghir →, Iraq .... **70 C4** 35 17N 43 29 E
Littlefield, U.S.A. **113 J3** 33 55N 102 20W
Littlehampton, U.K. .. **15 G7** 50 49N 0 32W
Littleton, U.S.A. **117 B13** 44 18N 71 46W
Litvinov, Czech Rep. .. **26 A6** 50 36N 13 37 E
Liu He →, China .... **57 D11** 40 55N 121 35 E
Liu Jiang →, China .. **58 F7** 23 55N 109 30 E
Liuba, China .... **56 H4** 33 38N 106 55 E
Liucheng, China ..... **58 E7** 24 38N 109 14 E
Liugou, China .... **57 D10** 40 57N 118 15 E
Liuhe, China .... **57 C13** 42 17N 125 43 E
Liuheng Dao, China .. **59 C14** 29 40N 122 5 E
Liujiang, China ...... **58 E7** 24 26N 109 11 E
Liukang Tenggaja =
  Sabalana, Kepulauan,
  Indonesia .... **63 F5** 6 45 S 118 50 E
Liuli, Tanzania ...... **87 E3** 11 3 S 34 38 E
Liuwa Plain, Zambia . **85 G4** 14 20 S 22 30 E
Liuyang, China ...... **59 C9** 28 10N 113 37 E
Liuzhou, China ...... **58 E7** 24 22N 109 22 E
Liuzhuang, China .... **57 H11** 33 12N 120 18 E
Livada, Romania .... **28 C8** 47 52N 23 5 E
Livadherón, Greece .. **44 F5** 40 2N 21 57 E
Livadhia, Cyprus .... **49 E12** 34 57N 33 38 E
Livádhion, Greece ... **46 A4** 40 8N 22 9 E
Livarot, France ...... **18 D7** 48 58N 0 9 E
Live Oak, Calif., U.S.A. **110 F5** 39 17N 121 40W
Live Oak, Fla., U.S.A. . **115 K4** 30 18N 82 59W
Liveras, Cyprus ...... **49 D11** 35 23N 32 57 E
Livermore, U.S.A. **110 H5** 37 41N 121 47W
Livermore, Mt., U.S.A. **113 K2** 30 38N 104 11W
Livermore Falls, U.S.A. **115 C11** 44 29N 70 11W
Liverpool, Canada ... **105 D7** 44 5N 64 41W
Liverpool, U.K. **14 D4** 53 25N 3 0W
Liverpool, U.S.A. **117 C8** 43 6N 76 13W
Liverpool Bay, U.K. .. **14 D4** 53 30N 3 20W
Liverpool Ra., Australia **95 E5** 31 50 S 150 30 E
Livigno, Italy .... **40 B7** 46 32N 10 4 E
Livingston, Guatemala **120 C2** 15 50N 88 50W
Livingston, U.K. **13 F5** 55 54N 3 30W
Livingston, Ala., U.S.A. **115 J1** 32 35N 88 11W
Livingston, Calif., U.S.A. **110 H6** 37 23N 120 43W
Livingston, Mont.,
  U.S.A. **108 D8** 45 40N 110 34W
Livingston, S.C., U.S.A. **115 J5** 33 32N 80 53W
Livingston, Tenn.,
  U.S.A. **115 G3** 36 23N 85 19W
Livingston, Tex., U.S.A. **113 K7** 30 43N 94 56W
Livingston, L., U.S.A. . **113 K7** 30 50N 95 10W
Livingston Manor,
  U.S.A. **117 E10** 41 54N 74 50W
Livingstone, Zambia .. **87 F2** 17 46 S 25 52 E
Livingstone Mts.,
  Tanzania .... **87 D3** 9 40 S 34 20 E
Livingstonia, Malawi . **87 E3** 10 38 S 34 5 E
Livno, Bos.-H. .... **28 G2** 43 50N 17 0 E
Livny, Russia .... **33 F9** 52 30N 37 30 E
Livonia, Mich., U.S.A. **114 D4** 42 23N 83 23W
Livonia, N.Y., U.S.A. . **116 D7** 42 49N 77 40W
Livorno, Italy .... **40 E7** 43 33N 10 19 E
Livradois-Forez □,
  France .... **20 E7** 44 0N 3 0 E
Livramento, Brazil ... **127 C4** 30 55 S 55 30W
Livron-sur-Drôme,
  France .... **21 D8** 44 46N 4 51 E
Livvntsi, Ukraine .... **29 B11** 48 25N 26 37 E
Liwale, Tanzania .... **87 D4** 9 48 S 37 58 E
Liwiec →, Poland ... **31 F8** 52 36N 21 34 E
Liwonde △, Malawi .. **87 E4** 14 48 S 35 20 E
Lixi, China .... **58 D3** 26 23N 101 59 E
Lixian, China .... **56 G3** 34 27N 105 2 E
Lixoúrion, Greece ... **46 C2** 38 12N 20 26 E
Liyang, China .... **59 B12** 31 26N 119 28 E
Lizard I., Australia ... **94 A4** 14 42 S 145 30 E
Lizard Pt., U.K. **15 H2** 49 57N 5 13W
Lizzano, Italy .... **43 B10** 40 23N 17 27 E
Ljig, Serbia & M. .... **44 B4** 44 13N 20 18 E
Ljubija, Bos.-H. ..... **41 D13** 44 55N 16 35 E
Ljubinje, Bos.-H. .... **44 D2** 42 58N 18 5 E
Ljubljana, Slovenia .. **41 B11** 46 4N 14 33 E
Ljubljana ✈ (LJU),
  Slovenia .... **41 B11** 46 14N 14 28 E
Ljubno, Slovenia ..... **41 B11** 46 25N 14 46 E
Ljubovija, Serbia & M. **44 B3** 44 11N 19 22 E
Ljugarn, Sweden ..... **11 G12** 57 20N 18 43 E
Ljung, Sweden ...... **11 G7** 57 59N 13 3 E
Ljungan →, Sweden . **10 B11** 62 18N 17 23 E
Ljungaverk, Sweden .. **10 B10** 62 30N 16 5 E
Ljungby, Sweden .... **11 H7** 56 49N 13 55 E
Ljungbyhed, Sweden . **11 H10** 56 39N 16 3 E
Ljungdalen, Sweden .. **10 B6** 62 52N 12 46 E
Ljungsbro, Sweden ... **11 F9** 58 31N 15 30 E
Ljungskile, Sweden .. **11 G6** 58 14N 11 55 E
Ljusdal, Sweden ..... **10 C10** 61 46N 16 3 E
Ljusfallshammar,
  Sweden .... **11 F9** 58 48N 15 30 E
Ljusnan →, Sweden . **10 C11** 61 13N 17 7 E
Ljusne, Sweden ..... **10 C11** 61 13N 17 7 E
Ljutomer, Slovenia .. **41 B13** 46 31N 16 11 E
Llagostera, Spain .... **38 D7** 41 50N 2 54 E
Llancanelo, Salina,
  Argentina .... **126 D2** 35 40 S 69 8W

Llandrindod Wells, U.K. **15 E4** 52 14N 3 22W
Llandudno, U.K. **14 D4** 53 19N 3 50W
Llanelli, U.K. **15 F3** 51 41N 4 10W
Llanes, Spain **36 B6** 43 25N 4 50W
Llangollen, U.K. **14 E4** 52 58N 3 11W
Llanidloes, U.K. **15 E4** 52 27N 3 31W
Llano, U.S.A. **113 K5** 30 45N 98 41W
Llano →, U.S.A. **113 K5** 30 39N 98 26W
Llano Estacado, U.S.A. **113 J3** 33 30N 103 0W
Llanos, S. Amer. **124 C4** 5 0N 71 35W
Llanos de Challe △,
  Chile .... **126 B1** 28 8 S 71 1W
Llanquihue, L., Chile .. **128 E1** 41 10 S 72 50W
Llanwrtyd Wells, U.K. **15 E4** 52 7N 3 38W
Llebeig, C., des Spain . **48 B9** 39 33N 2 18 E
Lleida, Spain .... **38 D5** 41 37N 0 39 E
Lleida □, Spain ...... **38 C6** 42 6N 1 0 E
Llentrisca, C., Spain .. **48 C7** 38 52N 1 15 E
Llera, Mexico **119 C5** 23 19N 99 1W
Llerena, Spain **37 G5** 38 17N 6 0W
Lleyn Peninsula, U.K. . **14 E3** 52 51N 4 36W
Llico, Chile .... **126 C1** 34 46 S 72 5W
Lliria, Spain **39 F4** 39 37N 0 35W
Llobregat →, Spain .. **38 D7** 41 19N 2 9 E
Llodio, Spain **38 B2** 43 9N 2 58W
Lloret de Mar, Spain . **38 D7** 41 41N 2 53 E
Lloyd B., Australia ... **94 A3** 12 45 S 143 27 E
Lloyd L., Canada **103 B7** 57 22N 108 57W
Lloydminster, Canada **103 C7** 53 17N 110 0W
Llucena del Cid, Spain **38 E4** 40 9N 0 17W
Llucmajor, Spain .... **48 B9** 39 29N 2 53 E
Llullaillaco △, Chile .. **126 A2** 24 50 S 68 51W
Llullaillaco, Volcán,
  S. Amer. .... **126 A2** 24 43 S 68 30W
Lo →, Vietnam ..... **64 B5** 21 18N 105 25 E
Loa, U.S.A. **109 G8** 38 24N 111 39W
Loa →, Chile .... **126 A1** 21 26 S 70 41W
Loaita I., S. China Sea **62 B4** 10 41N 114 25 E
Loange →, Dem. Rep.
  of the Congo ...... **84 E4** 4 17 S 20 2 E
Loano, Italy .... **40 D5** 44 8N 8 15 E
Lobatse, Botswana ... **88 D4** 25 12 S 25 40 E
Löbau, Germany .... **24 D10** 51 5N 14 40 E
Lobenstein, Germany . **24 E7** 50 25N 11 39 E
Lobería, Argentina ... **126 D4** 38 10 S 58 40W
Łobez, Poland .... **30 E2** 53 38N 15 39 E
Lobito, Angola ...... **85 G2** 12 18 S 13 35 E
Lobo →, Ivory C. ... **82 D3** 6 2N 6 45W
Lobos, Argentina .... **126 D4** 35 10 S 59 0W
Lobos, I. de, Canary Is. **48 F6** 28 45N 13 50W
Łobżenica, Poland ... **31 E4** 53 18N 17 15 E
Loc Binh, Vietnam ... **64 B6** 21 46N 106 54 E
Loc Ninh, Vietnam ... **65 G6** 11 50N 106 34 E
Locarno, Switz. ...... **25 J4** 46 10N 8 47 E
Loch Baghasdail =
  Lochboisdale, U.K. .. **13 D1** 57 9N 7 20W
Loch Garman =
  Wexford, Ireland .. **12 D5** 52 20N 6 28W
Loch Lomond and the
  Trossachs △, U.K. .. **13 E4** 56 10N 4 40W
Loch Nam Madadh =
  Lochmaddy, U.K. ... **13 D1** 57 36N 7 10W
Lochaber, U.K. **13 E3** 56 59N 5 1W
Locharbriggs, U.K. ... **13 F5** 55 7N 3 35W
Lochboisdale, U.K. ... **13 D1** 57 9N 7 20W
Loche, L. La, Canada .. **103 B7** 56 30N 109 30W
Lochem, Neths. ...... **17 B6** 52 9N 6 26 E
Loches, France ...... **18 E7** 47 7N 1 0 E
Lochgilphead, U.K. ... **13 E3** 56 2N 5 26W
Lochinvar △, Zambia . **87 F2** 15 55 S 27 15 E
Lochinver, U.K. **13 C3** 58 9N 5 14W
Lochmaddy, U.K. **13 D1** 57 36N 7 10W
Lochnagar, Australia . **94 C4** 23 33 S 145 38 E
Lochnagar, U.K. **13 E5** 56 57N 3 15W
Łochów, Poland ..... **31 F8** 52 33N 21 42 E
Lochy, L., U.K. **13 E4** 57 0N 4 53W
Lock, Australia ...... **95 E2** 33 34 S 135 46 E
Lock Haven, U.S.A. .. **116 E7** 41 8N 77 28W
Lockeford, U.S.A. **110 G5** 38 10N 121 9W
Lockeport, Canada ... **105 D6** 43 47N 65 4W
Lockerbie, U.K. **13 F5** 55 7N 3 21W
Lockhart, U.S.A. **113 L6** 29 53N 97 40W
Lockhart, L., Australia **93 F2** 33 15 S 119 3 E
Lockhart River,
  Australia .... **94 A3** 12 58 S 143 30 E
Lockney, U.S.A. **113 H4** 34 7N 101 27W
Lockport, U.S.A. **116 C6** 43 10N 78 42W
Locminé, France **18 E4** 47 54N 2 51W
Locri, Italy .... **43 D9** 38 14N 16 16 E
Locronan, France **18 D2** 48 7N 4 15W
Lod, Israel .... **74 D3** 31 57N 34 54 E
Lodeinoye Pole, Russia **32 B7** 60 44N 33 33 E
Lodève, France ...... **20 E7** 43 44N 3 19 E
Lodge Bay, Canada ... **105 B8** 52 14N 55 51W
Lodge Grass, U.S.A. .. **108 D10** 45 19N 107 22W
Lodgepole Cr. →,
  U.S.A. **112 E2** 41 20N 104 30W
Lodhran, Pakistan ... **68 E4** 29 32N 71 30 E
Lodi, Italy .... **40 C6** 45 19N 9 30 E
Lodi, Calif., U.S.A. ... **110 G5** 38 8N 121 16W
Lodi, Ohio, U.S.A. ... **116 E3** 41 2N 82 0W
Lodja, Dem. Rep. of
  the Congo .... **86 C1** 3 30 S 23 23 E
Lodosa, Spain **38 C2** 42 25N 2 4W
Lodwar, Kenya ...... **86 B4** 3 10N 35 40 E
Łódź, Poland .... **31 G6** 51 45N 19 27 E
Łódzkie □, Poland ... **31 G6** 51 30N 19 30 E
Loei, Thailand ...... **64 D3** 17 29N 101 35 E
Loengo, Dem. Rep. of
  the Congo .... **86 C2** 4 48 S 26 30 E
Loeriesfontein, S. Africa **88 E2** 31 0 S 19 26 E
Lofa □, Liberia **82 D2** 8 35N 11 8W
Lofa Mano △, Liberia **82 D2** 7 55N 10 25W
Lofer, Austria .... **26 D5** 47 35N 12 41 E
Lofoten, Norway .... **8 B15** 68 30N 14 0 E
Lofsdalen, Sweden ... **10 B7** 62 10N 13 30 E
Lofsen →, Sweden .. **10 B7** 62 7N 13 57 E
Loftahammar, Sweden **11 G10** 57 54N 16 41 E
Logan, Iowa, U.S.A. .. **112 E7** 41 39N 95 47W
Logan, Ohio, U.S.A. .. **114 F4** 39 32N 82 25W
Logan, Utah, U.S.A. .. **108 F8** 41 44N 111 50W
Logan, W. Va., U.S.A. **114 G5** 37 51N 81 59W
Logan, Mt., Canada .. **100 B5** 60 34N 140 23W
Logandale, U.S.A. ... **111 J12** 36 36N 114 29W
Logansport, Ind., U.S.A. **114 E2** 40 45N 86 22W
Logansport, La., U.S.A. **113 K8** 31 58N 94 0W
Logirim, Sudan ..... **81 G3** 4 43N 33 14 E
Logo, Sudan .... **81 F3** 5 20N 30 18 E
Logone →, Chad .... **79 F9** 12 6N 15 2 E
Logroño, Spain **38 C2** 42 28N 2 27W
Logrosán, Spain **37 F5** 39 20N 5 32W
Løgstør, Denmark ... **11 H3** 56 58N 9 14 E
Løgumkloster, Denmark **11 J2** 55 4N 8 57 E

Lohals, *Denmark* ...... **11 J4** 55 8N 10 55 E
Lohardaga, *India* ...... **69 H11** 23 27N 84 45 E
Loharia, *India* ...... **68 H6** 23 45N 74 14 E
Loharu, *India* ...... **68 E7** 28 27N 75 49 E
Lohja, *Finland* ...... **9 F21** 60 12N 24 5 E
Löhne, *Germany* ...... **24 C4** 52 11N 8 40 E
Lohr, *Germany* ...... **25 F5** 49 59N 9 35 E
Lohri Wah →, *Pakistan* **68 F2** 27 27N 67 37 E
Loi-kaw, *Burma* ...... **67 K20** 19 40N 97 17 E
Loimaa, *Finland* ...... **9 F20** 60 50N 23 5 E
Loir →, *France* **18 E6** 47 33N 0 32W
Loir-et-Cher □, *France* **18 E8** 47 40N 1 20 E
Loire □, *France* ...... **21 C8** 45 40N 4 5 E
Loire →, *France* **18 E4** 47 16N 2 10W
Loire Anjou
  Touraine △, *France* **18 E6** 47 14N 0 5W
Loire-Atlantique □,
  France **18 E5** 47 25N 1 40W
Loiret □, *France* ...... **19 E9** 47 55N 2 30 E
Loitz, *Germany* ...... **24 B9** 53 58N 13 8 E
Loja, *Ecuador* ...... **124 D3** 3 59 S 79 16W
Loja, *Spain* **37 H6** 37 10N 4 10W
Loji = Kawasi, *Indonesia* **63 E7** 1 38 S 127 28 E
Lojo = Lohja, *Finland* **9 F21** 60 12N 24 5 E
Løjt Kirkeby, *Denmark* **11 J3** 55 7N 9 26 E
Lojung, *China* ...... **58 E7** 24 27N 109 36 E
Loka, *Sudan* ...... **81 G3** 4 13N 31 0 E
Lokandu, *Dem. Rep. of
  the Congo* ...... **86 C2** 2 30 S 25 45 E
Lokeren, *Belgium* ...... **17 C3** 51 6N 3 59 E
Lokgwabe, *Botswana* .. **88 C3** 24 10 S 21 50 E
Lokhvitsa, *Ukraine* ... **33 G7** 50 25N 33 18 E
Lokichokio, *Kenya* .... **86 B3** 4 19N 34 13 E
Lokitaung, *Kenya* .... **86 B4** 4 12N 35 48 E
Lokkan tekojärvi,
  Finland ...... **8 C22** 67 55N 27 35 E
Løkken, *Denmark* ..... **11 G3** 57 22N 9 41 E
Loknya, *Russia* ...... **32 D6** 56 49N 30 4 E
Loko, *Nigeria* ...... **83 D6** 8 1N 7 53 E
Lokoja, *Nigeria* ...... **83 D6** 7 47N 6 45 E
Lokot, *Russia* ...... **33 F8** 52 34N 34 36 E
Lol →, *Sudan* ...... **81 F2** 9 13N 26 30 E
Lola, *Guinea* **82 D3** 7 52N 8 29W
Lola, Mt., *U.S.A.* **110 F6** 39 26N 120 22W
Lolibai, Gebel, *Sudan* . **81 G3** 3 50N 33 0 E
Lolimi, *Sudan* ...... **81 G3** 4 35N 34 0 E
Loliondo, *Tanzania* .... **86 C4** 2 2 S 35 39 E
Lolland, *Denmark* ..... **11 K5** 54 45N 11 30 E
Lollar, *Germany* ...... **24 E4** 50 39N 8 43 E
Lolo, *U.S.A.* **108 C6** 46 45N 114 5W
Lolodorf, *Cameroon* ... **83 E7** 3 16N 10 49 E
Lom, *Bulgaria* ...... **44 C7** 43 48N 23 12 E
Lom →, *Bulgaria* ..... **44 C7** 43 45N 23 15 E
Lom Kao, *Thailand* ... **64 D3** 16 53N 101 14 E
Lom Sak, *Thailand* ... **64 D3** 16 47N 101 15 E
Loma, *U.S.A.* **108 C8** 47 56N 110 30W
Loma Linda, *U.S.A.* .. **111 L9** 34 3N 117 16W
Lomami →, *Dem. Rep.
  of the Congo* ...... **86 B1** 0 46N 24 16 E
Lomas de Zamóra,
  Argentina ...... **126 C4** 34 45 S 58 25W
Lombadina, *Australia* .. **92 C3** 16 31 S 122 54 E
Lombárdia □, *Italy* .... **40 C6** 45 40N 9 30 E
Lombardy =
  Lombárdia □, *Italy* .. **40 C6** 45 40N 9 30 E
Lombez, *France* ...... **20 E4** 43 29N 0 55 E
Lomblen, *Indonesia* ... **63 F6** 8 30 S 123 32 E
Lombok, *Indonesia* ... **62 F5** 8 45 S 116 30 E
Lombok, Selat,
  Indonesia ...... **63 K18** 8 30 S 115 50 E
Lomé, *Togo* ...... **83 D5** 6 9N 1 20 E
Lomela, *Dem. Rep. of
  the Congo* ...... **84 E4** 2 19 S 23 15 E
Lomela →, *Dem. Rep.
  of the Congo* ...... **84 E4** 0 15 S 20 40 E
Lomianki, *Poland* ..... **31 F7** 52 21N 20 54 E
Lomma, *Sweden* ...... **11 J7** 55 43N 13 6 E
Lommel, *Belgium* ..... **17 C5** 51 14N 5 19 E
Lomond, *Canada* **102 C6** 50 24N 112 36W
Lomond, L., *U.K.* **13 E4** 56 8N 4 38W
Lomonosov Ridge,
  Arctic ...... **4 A** 88 0N 140 0 E
Lomphat, *Cambodia* .. **64 F6** 13 30N 106 59 E
Lompobatang, *Indonesia* **63 F5** 5 24 S 119 56 E
Lompoc, *U.S.A.* **111 L6** 34 38N 120 28W
Łomża, *Poland* ...... **31 E9** 53 10N 22 2 E
Lon, Ko, *Thailand* .... **65 a** 7 47N 98 23 E
Loncoche, *Chile* ...... **128 D2** 39 20 S 72 50W
Londa, *India* ...... **66 M9** 15 30N 74 30 E
Londiani, *Kenya* ...... **86 C4** 0 10 S 35 33 E
Londinières, *France* ... **18 C8** 49 50N 1 25 E
London, *Canada* **116 D3** 42 59N 81 15W
London, *U.K.* **15 F7** 51 30N 0 3W
London, Ky., *U.S.A.* .. **114 G3** 37 8N 84 5W
London, Ohio, *U.S.A.* **114 F4** 39 53N 83 27W
London, Greater □,
  U.K. **15 F7** 51 36N 0 5W
London Gatwick ✈
  (LGW), *U.K.* **15 F7** 51 10N 0 11W
London Heathrow ✈
  (LHR), *U.K.* **15 F7** 51 28N 0 27W
London Stansted ✈
  (STN), *U.K.* ...... **15 F8** 51 54N 0 14 E
Londonderry, *U.K.* **12 B4** 55 0N 7 20W
Londonderry □, *U.K.* . **12 B4** 55 0N 7 20W
Londonderry, C.,
  Australia ...... **92 B4** 13 45 S 126 55 E
Londonderry, I., *Chile* **128 H2** 55 0 S 71 0W
Londres, *Argentina* .... **128 B3** 27 43 S 67 7W
Londrina, *Brazil* ...... **127 A5** 23 18 S 51 10W
Lone Pine, *U.S.A.* **110 J8** 36 36N 118 4W
Lonely Mine, *Zimbabwe* **89 B4** 19 30 S 28 49 E
Long B., *U.S.A.* **115 J6** 33 35N 78 45W
Long Beach, Calif.,
  U.S.A. **111 M8** 33 47N 118 11W
Long Beach, N.Y.,
  U.S.A. **117 F11** 40 35N 73 39W
Long Beach, Wash.,
  U.S.A. **110 D2** 46 21N 124 3W
Long Branch, *U.S.A.* . **117 F11** 40 18N 74 0W
Long Creek, *U.S.A.* ... **108 D4** 44 43N 119 6W
Long Eaton, *U.K.* **14 E6** 52 53N 1 15W
Long I., *Australia* ..... **94 J6** 20 22 S 148 51 E
Long I., *Bahamas* **121 B4** 23 20N 75 10W
Long I., *Canada* **104 B4** 54 50N 79 20W
Long I., *Ireland* **12 E2** 51 30N 9 34W
Long I., *U.S.A.* **117 F11** 40 45N 73 30W
Long Island Sd., *U.S.A.* **117 E12** 41 10N 73 0W
Long Lake, *Canada* ... **117 C10** 43 58N 74 25W
Long L., *Canada* **104 C2** 49 30N 86 50W
Long Point B., *Canada* **116 D4** 42 40N 80 10W
Long Prairie →, *U.S.A.* **112 C7** 46 20N 94 36W
Long Pt., *Canada* **116 D4** 42 35N 80 2W
Long Range Mts.,
  Canada **105 C8** 49 30N 57 30W
Long Reef, *Australia* .. **92 B4** 14 1 S 125 48 E
Long Spruce, *Canada* . **103 B10** 56 24N 94 21W

Long Str. = Longa,
  Proliv, *Russia* ...... **4 C16** 70 0N 175 0 E
Long Thanh, *Vietnam* . **65 G6** 10 47N 106 57 E
Long Xian, *China* ..... **56 G4** 34 55N 106 55 E
Long Xuyen, *Vietnam* . **65 G5** 10 19N 105 28 E
Longá, *Greece* ...... **46 E3** 36 53N 21 55 E
Longa, Proliv, *Russia* . **4 C16** 70 0N 175 0 E
Long'an, *China* ...... **58 F6** 23 10N 107 40 E
Longarone, *Italy* ...... **41 B9** 46 16N 12 18 E
Longboat Key, *U.S.A.* **115 M4** 27 23N 82 39W
Longchang, *China* ..... **58 C5** 29 18N 105 20 E
Longchi, *China* ...... **58 C4** 29 25N 103 24 E
Longchuan, Guangdong,
  China ...... **59 E10** 24 5N 115 17 E
Longchuan, Yunnan,
  China ...... **58 E1** 24 23N 97 58 E
Longde, *China* ...... **56 G4** 35 30N 106 20 E
Longeau, *France* ...... **19 E12** 47 47N 5 20 E
Longford, *Australia* ... **95 G4** 41 32 S 147 3 E
Longford, *Ireland* **12 C4** 53 43N 7 49W
Longford □, *Ireland* .. **12 C4** 53 42N 7 45W
Longhai, *China* ...... **59 E11** 24 25N 117 46 E
Longhua, *China* ...... **57 D9** 41 18N 117 45 E
Longhui, *China* ...... **59 D8** 27 7N 111 2 E
Longido, *Tanzania* .... **86 C4** 2 43 S 36 42 E
Longiram, *Indonesia* .. **62 E5** 0 5 S 115 45 E
Longkou, Jiangxi, *China* **59 D10** 28 8N 115 10 E
Longkou, Shandong,
  China ...... **57 F11** 37 40N 120 18 E
Longlac, *Canada* **104 C2** 49 45N 86 25W
Longli, *China* ...... **58 D6** 26 25N 106 58 E
Longlin, *China* ...... **58 E5** 24 47N 105 20 E
Longling, *China* ...... **58 E2** 24 37N 98 39 E
Longmeadow, *U.S.A.* . **117 D12** 42 3N 72 34W
Longmen, *China* ...... **59 F10** 23 40N 114 18 E
Longming, *China* ...... **58 F6** 22 59N 107 7 E
Longmont, *U.S.A.* **112 E2** 40 10N 105 6W
Longnan, *China* ...... **59 E10** 24 55N 114 47 E
Longnawan, *Indonesia* **62 D4** 1 51N 114 55 E
Longobucco, *Italy* ..... **43 C9** 39 27N 16 37 E
Longquan, *China* ...... **59 C12** 28 7N 119 10 E
Longreach, *Australia* .. **94 C3** 23 28 S 144 14 E
Longshan, *China* ...... **58 C7** 29 29N 109 25 E
Longsheng, *China* ..... **59 E8** 25 48N 110 0 E
Longué-Jumelles, *France* **18 E6** 47 22N 0 8W
Longueau, *France* ..... **19 C9** 49 52N 2 21 E
Longueuil, *Canada* **117 A11** 45 32N 73 28W
Longuyon, *France* ..... **19 C12** 49 27N 5 35 E
Longvic, *France* ...... **19 E12** 47 17N 5 4 E
Longview, Tex., *U.S.A.* **113 J7** 32 30N 94 44W
Longview, Wash., *U.S.A.* **110 D4** 46 8N 122 57W
Longwy, *France* ...... **19 C12** 49 30N 5 46 E
Longxi, *China* ...... **56 G3** 34 53N 104 40 E
Longyan, *China* ...... **59 E11** 25 10N 117 0 E
Longyearbyen, *Svalbard* **4 B8** 78 13N 15 40 E
Longyou, *China* ...... **59 C12** 29 1N 119 8 E
Longzhou, *China* ...... **58 F6** 22 22N 106 50 E
Longo, *Italy* ...... **41 C8** 45 23N 11 23 E
Löningen, *Germany* ... **24 C3** 52 44N 7 46 E
Lonja →, *Croatia* ..... **41 C13** 45 22N 16 40 E
Lonoke, *U.S.A.* **113 H9** 34 47N 91 54W
Lons-le-Saunier, *France* **19 F12** 46 40N 5 31 E
Lönsboda, *Sweden* .... **11 H8** 56 24N 14 20 E
Looe, *U.K.* **15 G3** 50 22N 4 28W
Lookout, C., *Canada* .. **104 A3** 55 18N 83 56W
Lookout, C., *U.S.A.* .. **115 H7** 34 35N 76 32W
Loolmalasin, *Tanzania* **86 C4** 3 0 S 35 53 E
Loon →, Alta., *Canada* **102 B5** 57 8N 115 3W
Loon →, Man., *Canada* **103 B8** 55 53N 101 59W
Loon Lake, *Canada* ... **103 C7** 54 2N 109 10W
Loongana, *Australia* ... **93 F4** 30 52 S 127 5 E
Loop Hd., *Ireland* **12 D2** 52 34N 9 56W
Lop Buri, *Thailand* .... **64 E3** 14 48N 100 37 E
Lop Nor = Lop Nur,
  China ...... **60 B4** 40 20N 90 10 E
Lop Nur, *China* ...... **60 B4** 40 20N 90 10 E
Lopare, Bos.-H. ...... **28 F3** 44 39N 18 46 E
Lopatin, *Russia* ...... **35 J8** 43 50N 47 35 E
Lopatina, Gora, *Russia* **53 D15** 50 47N 143 10 E
Lopaye, *Sudan* ...... **81 F3** 6 37N 33 40 E
Lopez, *Phil.* ...... **61 E5** 13 53N 122 15 E
Lopez, *U.S.A.* **117 E8** 41 27N 76 20W
Lopez, C., *Gabon* ..... **84 E1** 0 47 S 8 40 E
Lopphavet, *Norway* ... **8 A19** 70 27N 21 15 E
Lora →, *Afghan.* ...... **66 D4** 31 35N 66 32 E
Lora Cr. →, *Australia* . **95 D2** 28 10 S 135 22 E
Lora del Río, *Spain* ... **37 H5** 37 39N 5 33W
Lorain, *U.S.A.* **116 E2** 41 28N 82 11W
Loralai, *Pakistan* ...... **68 D3** 30 20N 68 41 E
Lorca, *Spain* **39 H3** 37 41N 1 42W
Lord Howe I., Pac. Oc. **96 L7** 31 33 S 159 6 E
Lord Howe Ridge,
  Pac. Oc. ...... **96 L8** 30 0 S 162 30 E
Lordsburg, *U.S.A.* **109 K9** 32 21N 108 43W
Lorestan □, *Iran* ...... **71 C6** 33 30N 48 40 E
Loreto, *Brazil* ...... **125 E9** 7 5 S 45 10W
Loreto, *Italy* ...... **41 E10** 43 26N 13 36 E
Loreto, *Mexico* **118 B2** 26 1N 111 21W
Lorgues, *France* ...... **21 E10** 43 28N 6 22 E
Lorhosso, *Burkina Faso* **82 C4** 10 17N 3 38W
Lorient, *France* **18 E3** 47 45N 3 23W
Lőrinci, *Hungary* ..... **28 C4** 47 44N 19 41 E
Lormi, *India* ...... **69 H9** 22 17N 81 41 E
Lorn, *U.K.* **13 E3** 56 26N 5 10W
Lorn, Firth of, *U.K.* .. **13 E3** 56 20N 5 40W
Lórne, *Italy* ...... **40 C7** 45 49N 10 4 E
Lorne, *Australia* ...... **95 F3** 38 33 S 143 59 E
Loronyo, *Sudan* ...... **81 G3** 4 38N 32 38 E
Lorraine □, *France* .... **19 D12** 48 53N 6 0 E
Lorraine △, *France* .... **19 D13** 48 53N 5 50 E
Lorraine □, *France* .... **19 D13** 48 53N 6 0 E
Los, *Sweden* ...... **10 C9** 61 45N 15 10 E
Los, Îles de, *Guinea* ... **82 D2** 9 30N 13 50W
Los Alamos, Calif.,
  U.S.A. **111 L6** 34 44N 120 17W
Los Alamos, N. Mex.,
  U.S.A. **109 J10** 35 53N 106 19W
Los Alcornocales △,
  Spain **37 J5** 36 21N 5 32W
Los Altos, *U.S.A.* **110 H4** 37 23N 122 7W
Los Andes, *Chile* ...... **126 C1** 32 50 S 70 40W
Los Ángeles, *Chile* .... **126 D1** 37 28 S 72 23W
Los Ángeles, *U.S.A.* .. **111 M8** 34 4N 118 15W
Los Ángeles, Bahía de,
  Mexico **118 B2** 28 56N 113 34W
Los Ángeles Aqueduct,
  U.S.A. **111 K9** 35 22N 118 5W
Los Ángeles
  International ✈
  (LAX), *U.S.A.* **111 M8** 33 57N 118 25W
Los Banos, *U.S.A.* **110 H6** 37 4N 120 51W
Los Barrios, *Spain* **37 J5** 36 11N 5 30W
Los Blancos, *Argentina* **126 A3** 23 40 S 62 30W

Los Cardones △,
  Argentina ...... **126 B2** 25 8 S 65 55W
Los Chiles, *Costa Rica* **120 D3** 11 2N 84 43W
Los Corrales de Buelna,
  Spain **36 B6** 43 16N 4 4W
Los Cristianos,
  Canary Is. **48 F3** 28 3N 16 42W
Los Gallardos, *Spain* .. **39 H3** 37 10N 1 57W
Los Gatos, *U.S.A.* **110 H5** 37 14N 121 59W
Los Haïtises △,
  Dom. Rep. **121 C6** 19 4N 69 36W
Los Hermanos Is.,
  Venezuela **121 D7** 11 45N 64 25W
Los Islotes, *Canary Is.* **48 E6** 29 4N 13 44W
Los Llanos de Aridane,
  Canary Is. **48 F2** 28 38N 17 54W
Los Loros, *Chile* ...... **126 B1** 27 50 S 70 6W
Los Lunas, *U.S.A.* **109 J10** 34 48N 106 44W
Los Mochis, *Mexico* .. **118 B3** 25 45N 108 57W
Los Monegros, *Spain* . **38 D4** 41 29N 0 13W
Los Nietos, *Spain* **39 H4** 37 39N 0 47W
Los Olivos, *U.S.A.* **111 L6** 34 40N 120 7W
Los Palacios, *Cuba* ... **120 B3** 22 35N 83 15W
Los Palacios y
  Villafranca, *Spain* ... **37 H5** 37 10N 5 55W
Los Reyes, *Mexico* **118 D4** 19 34N 102 30W
Los Roques Is.,
  Venezuela **121 D6** 11 50N 66 45W
Los Santos de Maimona,
  Spain **37 G4** 38 27N 6 22W
Los Teques, *Venezuela* **124 A5** 10 21N 67 2W
Los Testigos, Is.,
  Venezuela **124 A6** 11 23N 63 6W
Los Vilos, *Chile* ...... **126 C1** 32 10 S 71 30W
Los Yébenes, *Spain* ... **37 F7** 39 36N 3 55W
Łosice, *Poland* ...... **31 F9** 52 13N 22 43 E
Loskop Dam, *S. Africa* **89 D4** 25 23 S 29 20 E
Løsning, *Denmark* ..... **11 J3** 55 48N 9 42 E
Lossiemouth, *U.K.* **13 D5** 57 42N 3 17W
Lossen →, *Sweden* ..... **10 B6** 62 26N 12 45 E
Lostwithiel, *U.K.* **15 G3** 50 24N 4 41W
Lot □, *France* ...... **20 D5** 44 39N 1 40 E
Lot →, *France* ...... **20 D4** 44 18N 0 20 E
Lot-et-Garonne □,
  France ...... **20 D4** 44 22N 0 30 E
Lota, *Chile* ...... **126 D1** 37 5 S 73 10W
Lotagipi Swamp, *Sudan* **86 B3** 4 35N 35 53 E
Lotfābād, *Iran* ...... **71 B8** 37 32N 59 20 E
Lothair, *S. Africa* ...... **89 D5** 26 22 S 30 27 E
Lotorp, *Sweden* ...... **11 F9** 58 44N 15 50 E
Lötschbergtunnel, *Switz.* **25 J3** 46 26N 7 43 E
Lotung, *Taiwan* ...... **59 E13** 24 41N 121 46 E
Loubomo, *Congo* ...... **84 E2** 4 9 S 12 47 E
Loudéac, *France* **18 D4** 48 11N 2 47W
Loudi, *China* ...... **59 D8** 27 42N 111 59 E
Loudonville, *U.S.A.* ... **116 F2** 40 38N 82 14W
Loudun, *France* ...... **18 E7** 47 0N 0 5 E
Loue →, *France* ...... **19 E12** 47 1N 5 28 E
Louga, *Senegal* **82 B1** 15 45N 16 5W
Loughborough, *U.K.* .. **14 E6** 52 47N 1 11W
Loughrea, *Ireland* **12 C3** 53 12N 8 33W
Loughros More B.,
  Ireland **12 B3** 54 48N 8 32W
Louhans, *France* ...... **19 F12** 46 38N 5 12 E
Louis Trichardt,
  S. Africa ...... **89 C4** 23 1 S 29 43 E
Louis XIV, Pte., *Canada* **104 B4** 54 37N 79 45W
Louisa, *U.S.A.* **114 F4** 38 7N 82 36W
Louisbourg, *Canada* ... **105 C8** 45 55N 60 0W
Louise I., *Canada* **102 C2** 52 55N 131 50W
Louiseville, *Canada* ... **104 C5** 46 20N 72 56W
Louisiade Arch.,
  Papua N. G. ...... **96 J7** 11 10 S 153 0 E
Louisiana, *U.S.A.* **112 F9** 39 27N 91 3W
Louisiana □, *U.S.A.* .. **113 K9** 30 50N 92 0W
Louisville, Ky., *U.S.A.* **114 F3** 38 15N 85 46W
Louisville, Miss., *U.S.A.* **113 J10** 33 7N 89 3W
Louisville, Ohio, *U.S.A.* **116 F3** 40 50N 81 16W
Loulay, *France* **20 B3** 46 3N 0 30W
Loulé, *Portugal* **37 H3** 37 9N 8 0W
Louny, *Czech Rep.* .... **26 A6** 50 20N 13 48 E
Loup City, *U.S.A.* **112 E5** 41 17N 98 58W
Loups Marins, Lacs des,
  Canada **104 A5** 56 30N 73 45W
Lourdes, *France* **20 E3** 43 6N 0 3W
Lourinhã, *Portugal* **37 F1** 39 14N 9 17W
Lousã, *Portugal* **36 E2** 40 7N 8 14W
Louta, Burkina Faso **82 C4** 13 30N 1 25W
Louth, *Australia* ...... **95 E4** 30 30 S 145 8 E
Louth, *Ireland* **12 C5** 53 58N 6 32W
Louth □, *Ireland* **12 C5** 53 56N 6 34W
Louth, *U.K.* **14 D7** 53 22N 0 1W
Loutrá Aidhipsoú,
  Greece ...... **46 C5** 38 54N 23 2 E
Loutráki, *Greece* ...... **46 D4** 37 58N 22 57 E
Louvain = Leuven,
  Belgium ...... **17 D4** 50 52N 4 42 E
Louviers, *France* ...... **18 C8** 49 12N 1 10 E
Louwsburg, *S. Africa* .. **89 D5** 27 37 S 31 7 E
Lovat →, *Russia* ...... **32 C6** 58 14N 31 28 E
Lovćen, Serbia & M. ... **44 D2** 42 23N 18 51 E
Lovćen △, Serbia & M. **44 D2** 42 20N 18 50 E
Lovech, *Bulgaria* ...... **45 C8** 43 8N 24 42 E
Lovech □, *Bulgaria* ... **45 C8** 43 15N 24 45 E
Loveland, *U.S.A.* **112 E2** 40 24N 105 5W
Lovell, *U.S.A.* **108 D9** 44 50N 108 24W
Lovelock, *U.S.A.* **108 F4** 40 11N 118 28W
Lóvere, *Italy* ...... **40 C7** 45 49N 10 4 E
Lövestad, *Sweden* ..... **11 J7** 55 40N 13 54 E
Loviisa, *Finland* ...... **9 F22** 60 28N 26 12 E
Loving, *U.S.A.* **113 J2** 32 17N 104 6W
Lovington, *U.S.A.* **113 J3** 32 57N 103 21W
Lovisa = Loviisa,
  Finland ...... **9 F22** 60 28N 26 12 E
Lovosice, *Czech Rep.* . **26 A7** 50 30N 14 2 E
Lovran, *Croatia* ...... **41 C11** 45 18N 14 15 E
Lovrin, *Romania* ...... **28 E5** 45 58N 20 48 E
Lövstabruk, *Sweden* ... **10 D11** 60 35N 17 53 E
Lövstabukten, *Sweden* . **10 D11** 60 35N 17 45 E
Low, L., *Canada* **104 B4** 52 29N 76 17W
Low Pt., *Australia* ..... **93 F4** 32 25 S 127 25 E
Low Tatra = Nízke
  Tatry, Slovak Rep. ... **27 C12** 48 55N 19 30 E
Lowa, Dem. Rep. of
  the Congo ...... **86 C2** 1 25 S 25 47 E
Lowa →, Dem. Rep. of
  the Congo ...... **86 C2** 1 24 S 25 51 E
Lowell, *U.S.A.* **117 D13** 42 38N 71 19W
Lowellville, *U.S.A.* **116 E4** 41 2N 80 32W
Löwen →, *Namibia* .... **88 D2** 26 51 S 18 17 E
Lower Alkali L., *U.S.A.* **108 F3** 41 16N 120 2W
Lower Arrow L.,
  Canada **102 D5** 49 40N 118 5W
Lower Austria =
  Niederösterreich □,
  Austria ...... **26 C8** 48 25N 15 40 E

Lower California = Baja
  California, *Mexico* ... **118 A1** 31 10N 115 12W
Lower Hutt, *N.Z.* ..... **91 J5** 41 10 S 174 55 E
Lower Lake, *U.S.A.* ... **110 G4** 38 55N 122 37W
Lower Manitou L.,
  Canada **103 D10** 49 15N 93 0W
Lower Post, *Canada* ... **102 B3** 59 58N 128 30W
Lower Red L., *U.S.A.* . **112 B7** 47 58N 95 0W
Lower Saxony =
  Niedersachsen □,
  Germany ...... **24 C4** 52 50N 9 0 E
Lower Tunguska =
  Tunguska,
  Nizhnyaya →, *Russia* **53 C9** 65 48N 88 4 E
Lower Zambezi △,
  Zambia ...... **87 F2** 15 25 S 29 40 E
Lowestoft, *U.K.* ...... **15 E9** 52 29N 1 45 E
Lowgar □, *Afghan.* .... **66 B6** 34 0N 69 0 E
Łowicz, *Poland* ...... **31 F6** 52 6N 19 55 E
Lowville, *U.S.A.* **117 C9** 43 47N 75 29W
Loxton, *Australia* ...... **95 E3** 34 28 S 140 31 E
Loxton, S. Africa ...... **88 E3** 31 30 S 22 22 E
Loyalton, *U.S.A.* **110 F6** 39 41N 120 14W
Loyalty Is. = Loyauté,
  Îs., N. Cal. ...... **96 K8** 20 50 S 166 30 E
Loyang = Luoyang,
  China ...... **56 G7** 34 40N 112 26 E
Loyauté, Îs., N. Cal. ... **96 K8** 20 50 S 166 30 E
Loyev = Loyew, Belarus **33 G6** 51 56N 30 46 E
Loyew, Belarus ...... **33 G6** 51 56N 30 46 E
Loyoro, Uganda ...... **86 B3** 3 22N 34 14 E
Lož, Slovenia ...... **41 C11** 45 43N 14 30 E
Lozère □, *France* ...... **20 D7** 44 35N 3 30 E
Loznica, Serbia & M. .. **44 B3** 44 32N 19 12 E
Lozova, Ukraine ...... **33 H9** 49 0N 36 20 E
Lü Shan, *China* ...... **59 C11** 29 30N 115 55 E
Lü-Tao, Taiwan ...... **59 F13** 22 40N 121 30 E
Luachimo, Angola ..... **84 F4** 7 23 S 20 48 E
Luajan →, *India* ...... **69 G11** 24 44N 85 1 E
Lualaba →, Dem. Rep.
  of the Congo ...... **86 B2** 0 26N 25 20 E
Luampa, Zambia ...... **87 F1** 15 4 S 24 20 E
Lu'an, China ...... **59 B11** 31 45N 116 29 E
Luan Chau, Vietnam ... **58 G4** 21 38N 103 24 E
Luan He →, *China* .... **57 E10** 39 20N 119 5 E
Luan Xian, *China* ..... **57 E10** 39 40N 118 40 E
Luancheng,
  Guangxi Zhuangzu,
  China ...... **58 F7** 22 48N 108 55 E
Luancheng, Hebei,
  China ...... **56 F8** 37 53N 114 40 E
Luanco, Spain **36 B5** 43 37N 5 48W
Luanda, Angola ...... **84 F2** 8 50 S 13 15 E
Luang, Thale, Thailand **65 J3** 7 30N 100 15 E
Luang Prabang, Laos .. **58 H4** 19 52N 102 10 E
Luangwa, Zambia ...... **87 F3** 15 35 S 30 16 E
Luangwa →, Zambia ... **87 E3** 14 25 S 30 25 E
Luangwa Valley,
  Zambia ...... **87 E3** 13 30 S 31 30 E
Luanne, China ...... **57 D9** 40 55N 117 40 E
Luanping, China ...... **57 D9** 40 53N 117 23 E
Luanshya, Zambia ..... **87 E2** 13 3 S 28 28 E
Luapula □, Zambia .... **87 E2** 11 0 S 29 0 E
Luapula →, Africa ..... **87 D2** 9 26 S 28 33 E
Luarca, Spain **36 B4** 43 32N 6 32W
Luashi, Dem. Rep. of
  the Congo ...... **87 E1** 10 50 S 23 36 E
Luau, Angola ...... **84 G4** 10 40 S 22 10 E
Lubaczów, Poland ..... **31 H10** 50 10N 23 8 E
Lubań, Poland ...... **31 G2** 51 5N 15 15 E
Lubana, Ozero =
  Lubānas Ezers, Latvia **9 H22** 56 45N 27 0 E
Lubānas Ezers, Latvia . **9 H22** 56 45N 27 0 E
Lubang, Phil. ...... **61 E4** 13 52N 120 7 E
Lubang Is., Phil. ...... **63 B6** 13 50N 120 12 E
Lubango, Angola ...... **85 G2** 14 55 S 13 30 E
Lubao, Dem. Rep. of
  the Congo ...... **86 D2** 5 17 S 25 42 E
Lubartów, Poland ...... **31 G9** 51 28N 22 42 E
Lubawa, Poland ...... **30 E6** 53 30N 19 48 E
Lübbecke, Germany .... **24 C4** 52 18N 8 37 E
Lübben, Germany ...... **24 D9** 51 56N 13 54 E
Lübbenau, Germany ... **24 D9** 51 53N 13 58 E
Lubbock, *U.S.A.* **113 J4** 33 35N 101 51W
Lübeck, Germany ...... **24 B6** 53 52N 10 40 E
Lübecker Bucht,
  Germany ...... **24 A6** 54 3N 10 54 E
Lubefu, Dem. Rep. of
  the Congo ...... **86 C1** 4 47 S 24 27 E
Lubefu →, Dem. Rep. of
  the Congo ...... **86 C1** 4 10 S 23 0 E
Lubelskie □, Poland ... **31 G9** 51 20N 22 50 E
Lubero = Luofu,
  Dem. Rep. of
  the Congo ...... **86 C2** 0 10 S 29 15 E
Luberon △, *France* .... **21 E9** 43 52N 5 25 E
Lubersac, *France* ...... **20 C5** 45 26N 1 23 E
Lubicon L., Canada **102 B5** 56 23N 115 56W
Lubień Kujawski,
  Poland ...... **31 F6** 52 23N 19 9 E
Lubilash →, Dem. Rep.
  of the Congo ...... **84 F4** 6 2 S 23 45 E
Lubin, Poland ...... **31 G3** 51 24N 16 11 E
Lublin, Poland ...... **31 G9** 51 12N 22 38 E
Lubliniec, Poland ...... **31 H5** 50 43N 18 45 E
Lubnān, Jabal, Lebanon **74 B4** 33 45N 35 40 E
Lubnewice, Poland ..... **31 F2** 52 31N 15 15 E
Lubny, Ukraine ...... **33 G7** 50 3N 32 58 E
Lubomierz, Poland ..... **31 G2** 51 1N 15 31 E
Luboń, Poland ...... **31 F3** 52 21N 16 51 E
Lubongola, Dem. Rep.
  of the Congo ...... **86 C2** 2 35 S 27 50 E
L'ubotín, Slovak Rep. .. **27 B13** 49 17N 20 53 E
Lubraniec, Poland ..... **31 F5** 52 33N 18 50 E
Lubsko, Poland ...... **31 G1** 51 45N 14 57 E
Lübtheen, Germany .... **24 B7** 53 18N 11 5 E
Lubuagan, Phil. ...... **61 C4** 17 21N 121 10 E
Lubudi, Dem. Rep. of
  the Congo ...... **84 F5** 9 57 S 25 58 E
Lubudi →, Dem. Rep. of
  the Congo ...... **83 D2** 9 0 S 25 35 E
Lubuklinggau, Indonesia **62 E2** 3 15 S 102 55 E
Lubuksikaping,
  Indonesia ...... **62 D2** 0 10N 100 15 E
Lubumbashi, Dem. Rep.
  of the Congo ...... **87 E2** 11 40 S 27 28 E
Lubunda, Dem. Rep. of
  the Congo ...... **86 D2** 5 12 S 26 41 E
Lubungu, Zambia ...... **87 E2** 14 35 S 26 24 E
Lubuskie □, Poland .... **31 F2** 52 10N 15 20 E
Lubutu, Dem. Rep. of
  the Congo ...... **86 C2** 0 45 S 26 30 E

Lucban, Phil. ...... **61 D4** 14 6N 121 33 E
Lucca, Italy ...... **40 E7** 43 50N 10 29 E
Lucé, France ...... **18 D8** 48 26N 1 27 E
Luce Bay, *U.K.* **13 G4** 54 45N 4 48W
Lucea, Jamaica ...... **120 a** 18 25N 78 10W
Lucedale, *U.S.A.* **115 K1** 30 56N 88 35W
Lucena, Phil. ...... **61 D4** 13 56N 121 37 E
Lucena, Spain **37 H6** 37 27N 4 31W
Lučenec, Slovak Rep. .. **27 C12** 48 18N 19 42 E
Lucera, Italy ...... **43 A8** 41 30N 15 20 E
Lucerne = Luzern,
  Switz. ...... **25 H4** 47 3N 8 18 E
Lucerne, *U.S.A.* **110 F4** 39 6N 122 48W
Lucerne Valley, *U.S.A.* **111 L10** 34 27N 116 57W
Lucero, Mexico **118 A3** 30 49N 106 30W
Luchena →, Spain **39 H3** 37 44N 1 50W
Lucheng, China ...... **56 F7** 36 20N 113 11 E
Lucheringo →, Mozam. **87 E4** 11 43 S 36 17 E
Lüchow, Germany ..... **24 C7** 52 58N 11 8 E
Luchuan, China ...... **59 F8** 22 21N 110 12 E
Lucia, *U.S.A.* **110 J5** 36 2N 121 33W
Lucinda, Australia ..... **94 B4** 18 32 S 146 20 E
Luckau, Germany ...... **24 D9** 51 50N 13 42 E
Luckenwalde, Germany **24 C9** 52 5N 13 10 E
Luckhoff, S. Africa ..... **88 D3** 29 44 S 24 43 E
Lucknow, Canada **116 C3** 43 57N 81 31W
Lucknow, India ...... **69 F9** 26 50N 81 0 E
Luçon, France **20 B2** 46 28N 1 10W
Lüda = Dalian, China .. **57 E11** 38 50N 121 40 E
Luda Kamchiya →,
  Bulgaria ...... **45 C11** 43 3N 27 29 E
Ludbreg, Croatia ...... **41 B13** 46 15N 16 38 E
Lüdenscheid, Germany **24 D3** 51 13N 7 37 E
Lüderitz, Namibia ..... **88 D2** 26 41 S 15 8 E
Lüderitzbaai, Namibia . **88 D2** 26 36 S 15 8 E
Ludhiana, India ...... **68 D6** 30 57N 75 56 E
Ludian, China ...... **58 D4** 27 10N 103 33 E
Luding Qiao, China .... **58 C4** 29 53N 102 12 E
Lüdinghausen, Germany **24 D3** 51 46N 7 27 E
Ludington, *U.S.A.* **114 D2** 43 57N 86 27W
Ludlow, *U.K.* **15 E5** 52 22N 2 42W
Ludlow, Calif., *U.S.A.* **111 L10** 34 43N 116 10W
Ludlow, Pa., *U.S.A.* .. **116 E6** 41 43N 78 56W
Ludlow, Vt., *U.S.A.* .. **117 C12** 43 24N 72 42W
Ludus, Romania ...... **29 D9** 46 29N 24 5 E
Ludvika, Sweden ...... **10 D9** 60 8N 15 14 E
Ludwigsburg, Germany **25 G5** 48 53N 9 11 E
Ludwigsfelde, Germany **24 C9** 52 17N 13 17 E
Ludwigshafen, Germany **25 F4** 49 29N 8 26 E
Ludwigslust, Germany . **24 B7** 53 19N 11 30 E
Ludza, Latvia ...... **32 D4** 56 32N 27 43 E
Lueki, Dem. Rep. of
  the Congo ...... **86 C2** 3 20 S 25 48 E
Luena, Dem. Rep. of
  the Congo ...... **87 D2** 9 28 S 25 43 E
Luena, Zambia ...... **87 E3** 10 40 S 30 25 E
Luenha = Ruenya →,
  Africa ...... **87 F3** 16 24 S 33 48 E
Lüeyang, China ...... **56 H4** 33 22N 106 10 E
Lufeng, Guangdong,
  China ...... **59 F10** 22 57N 115 38 E
Lufeng, Yunnan, China **58 E4** 25 0N 102 5 E
Lufira →, Dem. Rep. of
  the Congo ...... **87 D2** 9 30 S 27 0 E
Lufkin, *U.S.A.* **113 K7** 31 21N 94 44W
Lufupa, Dem. Rep. of
  the Congo ...... **87 E1** 10 37 S 24 56 E
Luga, Russia ...... **32 C5** 58 40N 29 55 E
Luga →, Russia ...... **32 C5** 59 40N 28 18 E
Lugano, Switz. ...... **25 J4** 46 1N 8 57 E
Lugano, L. di, Switz. .. **40 C6** 46 0N 9 0 E
Lugansk = Luhansk,
  Ukraine ...... **33 H10** 48 38N 39 15 E
Lugard's Falls, Kenya .. **86 C4** 3 6 S 38 41 E
Lugela, Mozam. ...... **87 F4** 16 25 S 36 43 E
Lugenda →, Mozam. .. **87 E4** 11 25 S 38 33 E
Lugh Ganana =
  Somali Rep. ...... **75 G3** 3 48N 42 34 E
Lugnaquillia, Ireland ... **12 D5** 52 58N 6 28W
Lugo, Italy ...... **41 D8** 44 25N 11 54 E
Lugo, Spain **36 B3** 43 2N 7 35W
Lugo □, Spain **36 C3** 43 0N 7 30W
Lugoj, Romania ...... **28 E6** 45 42N 21 57 E
Lugovoy = Qulan,
  Kazakhstan ...... **52 E8** 42 55N 72 43 E
Luhansk, Ukraine ...... **33 H10** 48 38N 39 15 E
Luhe, China ...... **59 A12** 32 19N 118 50 E
Luhe →, Germany ..... **24 B6** 53 23N 10 13 E
Luhuo, China ...... **58 B3** 31 21N 100 48 E
Luiana, Angola ...... **88 B3** 17 25 S 22 59 E
Luichow Pen. = Leizhou
  Bandao, China ...... **58 G7** 21 0N 110 0 E
Luimneach = Limerick,
  Ireland **12 D3** 52 40N 8 37W
Luing, *U.K.* **13 E3** 56 14N 5 39W
Luino, Italy ...... **40 C5** 45 59N 8 44 E
Luís Correia, Brazil .... **125 D10** 3 0 S 41 35W
Luitpold Coast,
  Antarctica ...... **5 D1** 78 30 S 32 0W
Luiza, Dem. Rep. of
  the Congo ...... **84 F4** 7 40 S 22 30 E
Luizi, Dem. Rep. of
  the Congo ...... **86 D2** 6 0 S 27 25 E
Luján, Argentina ...... **126 C4** 34 45 S 59 5W
Lujiang, China ...... **59 B11** 31 20N 117 15 E
Lukang, Taiwan ...... **59 E13** 24 1N 120 22 E
Lukanga Swamp,
  Zambia ...... **87 E2** 14 30 S 27 40 E
Lukavac, Bos.-H. ...... **28 F3** 44 33N 18 32 E
Lukenie →, Dem. Rep.
  of the Congo ...... **84 E3** 3 0 S 18 50 E
Lukhisaral, India ...... **69 G12** 25 11N 86 5 E
Lüki, Bulgaria ...... **45 E8** 41 50N 24 43 E
Lukolela, Dem. Rep. of
  the Congo ...... **86 D1** 5 23 S 24 32 E
Lukosi, Zimbabwe ..... **87 F2** 18 30 S 26 30 E
Lukovit, Bulgaria ...... **45 C8** 43 13N 24 11 E
Lukovo Šugorje, *Croatia* **31 G9** 51 55N 22 23 E
Lukoyanov, Russia ..... **34 C7** 55 2N 44 29 E
Łukusuzi □, Zambia ... **87 E3** 12 53 S 32 50 E
Luleå, Sweden ...... **8 D20** 65 35N 22 10 E
Luleälven →, Sweden .. **8 D19** 65 35N 22 10 E
Lüleburgaz, Turkey .... **45 E11** 41 23N 27 22 E
Luling, *U.S.A.* **113 L6** 29 41N 97 39W
Lulong, China ...... **57 E10** 39 53N 118 51 E
Lulonga →, Dem. Rep.
  of the Congo ...... **84 D3** 1 0N 18 10 E
Lulua →, Dem. Rep. of
  the Congo ...... **84 E4** 4 30 S 20 30 E
Lumajang, Indonesia ... **63 H15** 8 8 S 113 13 E
Lumbala N'guimbo,
  Angola ...... **85 G4** 14 18 S 21 18 E
Lumberton, *U.S.A.* **115 H6** 34 37N 79 0W
Lumsden, Canada **103 C8** 50 39N 104 52W
Lumsden, N.Z. ...... **91 L2** 45 44 S 168 27 E

Lumut, *Malaysia* ...... **65 K3** 4 13N 100 37 E
Lumut, Tanjung,
 Indonesia ...... **62 E3** 3 50 S 105 58 E
Luna, *India* ...... **68 HJ3** 23 43N 69 16 E
Lunan, *China* ...... **58 E4** 24 40N 103 18 E
Lunavada, *India* ...... **68 H5** 23 8N 73 37 E
Lunca, *Romania* ...... **29 C10** 47 22N 25 1 E
Lunca Corbului,
 Romania ...... **29 F9** 44 42N 24 45 E
Lund, *Sweden* ...... **11 J7** 55 44N 13 12 E
Lundazi, *Zambia* ...... **87 E3** 12 20 S 33 7 E
Lunderskov, *Denmark* ...... **11 J3** 55 29N 9 19 E
Lundi →, *Zimbabwe* ...... **87 G3** 21 43 S 32 34 E
Lundu, *Malaysia* ...... **62 D3** 1 40N 109 50 E
Lundy, *U.K.* **15 F3** 51 10N 4 41W
Lune →, *U.K.* **14 C5** 54 0N 2 51W
Lüneburg, *Germany* ...... **24 B6** 53 15N 10 24 E
Lüneburg Heath =
 Lüneburger Heide,
 Germany ...... **24 B6** 53 10N 10 12 E
Lüneburger Heide,
 Germany ...... **24 B6** 53 10N 10 12 E
Lunel, *France* ...... **21 E8** 43 32N 4 9 E
Lünen, *Germany* ...... **24 D3** 51 37N 7 32 E
Lunenburg, *Canada* **105 D7** 44 22N 64 18W
Lunéville, *France* ...... **19 D13** 48 36N 6 30 E
Lunga →, *Zambia* ...... **87 E2** 14 34 S 26 25 E
Lungi Airport, *S. Leone* **82 D2** 8 40N 13 17W
Lunglei, *India* ...... **67 H18** 22 55N 92 45 E
Luni, *India* ...... **68 G5** 26 0N 73 6 E
Luni →, *India* ...... **68 G4** 24 41N 71 14 E
Luninets = Luninyets,
 Belarus ...... **33 F4** 52 15N 26 50 E
Luning, *U.S.A.* **108 G4** 38 30N 118 11W
Lunino, *Russia* ...... **34 D7** 53 38N 45 18 E
Luninyets, *Belarus* ...... **33 F4** 52 15N 26 50 E
Lunkaransar, *India* ...... **68 E5** 28 29N 73 44 E
Lunsemfwa →, *Zambia* ...... **87 E3** 14 54 S 30 12 E
Lunsemfwa Falls,
 Zambia ...... **87 E2** 14 30 S 29 6 E
Luo He →, *China* ...... **56 G6** 34 35N 110 20 E
Luochuan, *China* ...... **56 G5** 35 45N 109 26 E
Luoci, *China* ...... **58 E4** 25 19N 102 18 E
Luodian, *China* ...... **58 E6** 25 24N 106 43 E
Luoding, *China* ...... **59 F8** 22 45N 111 40 E
Luofu, *Dem. Rep. of*
 the Congo ...... **86 C2** 0 10 S 29 15 E
Luohe, *China* ...... **56 H8** 33 32N 114 2 E
Luojiang, *China* ...... **58 B5** 31 18N 104 33 E
Luonan, *China* ...... **56 G6** 34 5N 110 10 E
Luoning, *China* ...... **56 G6** 34 35N 111 40 E
Luoshan, *China* ...... **59 A10** 32 13N 114 30 E
Luotian, *China* ...... **59 B10** 30 46N 115 22 E
Luoxiao Shan, *China* ...... **59 D10** 26 30N 114 1 E
Luoyang, *China* ...... **56 G7** 34 40N 112 26 E
Luoyuan, *China* ...... **59 D12** 26 28N 119 30 E
Luozigou, *China* ...... **57 C16** 43 42N 130 18 E
Lupanshui, *China* ...... **58 D5** 26 38N 104 48 E
Lupeni, *Romania* ...... **29 E8** 45 21N 23 13 E
Lupilichi, *Mozam.* ...... **87 E4** 11 47 S 35 13 E
Łupków, *Poland* ...... **31 J9** 49 15N 22 4 E
Luping, *China* ...... **58 E5** 24 53N 104 21 E
Luquan, *China* ...... **58 E4** 25 35N 102 25 E
Luque, *Paraguay* ...... **126 B4** 25 19 S 57 25W
Lúras, *Italy* ...... **42 B2** 40 56N 9 10 E
Luray, *U.S.A.* **114 F6** 38 40N 78 28W
Lure, *France* ...... **19 E13** 47 40N 6 30 E
Lurgan, *U.K.* **12 B5** 54 28N 6 19W
Lusaka, *Zambia* ...... **87 F2** 15 28 S 28 16 E
Lusaka □, *Zambia* ...... **87 F2** 15 30 S 29 0 E
Lusambo, *Dem. Rep. of*
 the Congo ...... **86 C1** 4 58 S 23 28 E
Lusangaye, *Dem. Rep. of*
 the Congo ...... **86 C2** 4 54 S 26 0 E
Luseland, *Canada* **103 C7** 52 5N 109 24W
Lusenga Plain △,
 Zambia ...... **87 D2** 9 22 S 29 14 E
Lushan, *Henan, China* ...... **56 H7** 33 45N 112 55 E
Lushan, *Sichuan, China* ...... **58 B4** 30 12N 102 52 E
Lushi, *China* ...... **56 G6** 34 3N 111 3 E
Lushnjë, *Albania* ...... **44 F3** 40 55N 19 41 E
Lushoto, *Tanzania* ...... **86 C4** 4 47 S 38 20 E
Lushui, *China* ...... **58 E2** 25 58N 98 44 E
Lushun, *China* ...... **57 E11** 38 45N 121 15 E
Lusignan, *France* ...... **20 B4** 46 26N 0 8 E
Lusigny-sur-Barse,
 France ...... **19 D11** 48 16N 4 15 E
Lusk, *U.S.A.* **112 D2** 42 46N 104 27W
Lussac-les-Châteaux,
 France ...... **20 B4** 46 24N 0 43 E
Lustenau, *Austria* ...... **26 D7** 47 26N 9 39 E
Lūt, Dasht-e, *Iran* ...... **71 D8** 31 30N 58 0 E
Luta = Dalian, *China* ...... **57 E11** 38 50N 121 40 E
Lutherstadt Wittenberg,
 Germany ...... **24 D8** 51 53N 12 39 E
Luton, *U.K.* **15 F7** 51 53N 0 24W
Luton □, *U.K.* **15 F7** 51 53N 0 24W
Łutselk'e, *Canada* **103 A6** 62 24N 110 44W
Lutsk, *Ukraine* ...... **33 G3** 50 50N 25 15 E
Lützow Holmbukta,
 Antarctica ...... **5 C4** 69 10 S 37 30 E
Lutzputs, *S. Africa* ...... **88 D3** 28 3 S 20 40 E
Luuq = Lugh Ganana,
 Somali Rep. ...... **75 G3** 3 48N 42 34 E
Luverne, *Ala., U.S.A.* **115 K2** 31 43N 86 16W
Luverne, *Minn., U.S.A.* **112 D6** 43 39N 96 13W
Luvua, *Dem. Rep. of*
 the Congo ...... **87 D2** 8 48 S 25 17 E
Luvua →, *Dem. Rep. of*
 the Congo ...... **86 D2** 6 50 S 27 30 E
Luvuvhu →, *S. Africa* ...... **89 C5** 22 25 S 31 18 E
Luwegu →, *Tanzania* ...... **87 D4** 8 31 S 37 23 E
Luwuk, *Indonesia* ...... **63 E6** 0 56 S 122 47 E
Luxembourg, *Lux.* ...... **17 E6** 49 37N 6 9 E
Luxembourg □, *Belgium* ...... **17 E5** 49 58N 5 30 E
Luxembourg ■, *Europe* ...... **17 E7** 49 45N 6 0 E
Luxembourg ✈ (LUX),
 Lux. ...... **17 E6** 49 37N 6 10 E
Luxeuil-les-Bains,
 France ...... **19 E13** 47 49N 6 24 E
Luxi, *Hunan, China* ...... **59 C8** 28 20N 110 7 E
Luxi, *Yunnan, China* ...... **58 E4** 24 40N 103 55 E
Luxi, *Yunnan, China* ...... **58 E2** 24 27N 98 36 E
Luxor = El Uqsur, *Egypt* ...... **80 B3** 25 41N 32 38 E
Luy-de-Béarn →,
 France **20 E3** 43 39N 0 48W
Luy-de-France →,
 France **20 E3** 43 39N 0 48W
Luyi, *China* ...... **56 H8** 33 50N 115 35 E
Luz-St-Sauveur, *France* ...... **20 F4** 42 53N 0 0 W
Luzern, *Switz.* ...... **25 H4** 47 3N 8 18 E
Luzern □, *Switz.* ...... **25 H4** 47 2N 7 55 E
Luzhai, *China* ...... **58 E7** 24 29N 109 42 E
Luzhany, *Ukraine* ...... **29 B11** 48 22N 25 45 E
Luzhi, *China* ...... **58 D5** 26 21N 105 16 E
Luzhou, *China* ...... **58 C5** 28 52N 105 20 E

Luziânia, *Brazil* ...... **125 G9** 16 20 S 48 0W
Lužnice →, *Czech Rep.* ...... **26 B7** 49 18N 14 23 E
Luzon, *Phil.* ...... **61 D4** 16 0N 121 0 E
Luzon Strait, *Asia* ...... **59 G13** 21 0N 120 40 E
Luzy, *France* ...... **19 F10** 46 47N 3 58 E
Luzzi, *Italy* ...... **43 C9** 39 27N 16 17 E
Lviv, *Ukraine* ...... **33 H3** 49 50N 24 0 E
Lvov = Lviv, *Ukraine* ...... **33 H3** 49 50N 24 0 E
Lwówek, *Poland* ...... **31 F3** 52 28N 16 10 E
Lwówek Śląski, *Poland* ...... **31 G2** 51 7N 15 38 E
Lyakhavichy, *Belarus* ...... **33 F4** 53 2N 26 32 E
Lyakhovskiye, Ostrova,
 Russia ...... **53 B15** 73 40N 141 0 E
Lyaki = Läki, *Azerbaijan* ...... **35 K8** 40 34N 47 22 E
Lyal I., *Canada* **116 B3** 44 57N 81 24W
Lyaskovets, *Bulgaria* ...... **45 C9** 43 6N 25 44 E
Lyasnaya, *Belarus* ...... **31 F10** 52 9N 23 31 E
Lybster, *U.K.* **13 C5** 58 18N 3 15W
Lycaonia, *Turkey* ...... **72 D5** 38 0N 33 0 E
Lychen, *Germany* ...... **24 B9** 53 12N 13 18 E
Lychkova, *Russia* ...... **32 D7** 57 55N 32 24 E
Lycia, *Turkey* ...... **47 E11** 36 30N 29 30 E
Lyckebyån →, *Sweden* ...... **11 H9** 56 12N 15 39 E
Lycksele, *Sweden* ...... **8 D18** 64 38N 18 40 E
Lycosura, *Greece* ...... **46 D4** 37 20N 22 3 E
Lydda = Lod, *Israel* ...... **74 D3** 31 57N 34 54 E
Lydenburg, *S. Africa* ...... **89 D5** 25 10 S 30 29 E
Lydia, *Turkey* ...... **47 C10** 38 48N 28 19 E
Łydynia →, *Poland* ...... **31 F7** 52 43N 20 26 E
Lyell, *N.Z.* ...... **91 J4** 41 48 S 172 4 E
Lyell I., *Canada* **102 C2** 52 40N 131 35W
Lyepyel, *Belarus* ...... **32 E5** 54 50N 28 40 E
Lygnern, *Sweden* ...... **11 G6** 57 30N 12 15 E
Lykens, *U.S.A.* **117 F8** 40 34N 76 42W
Lyman, *Ukraine* ...... **29 E14** 45 41N 29 45 E
Lyman, *U.S.A.* **108 F8** 41 20N 110 18W
Lymanske, *Ukraine* ...... **29 D14** 46 40N 29 58 E
Lyme B., *U.K.* **15 G4** 50 42N 2 53W
Lyme Regis, *U.K.* **15 G5** 50 43N 2 57W
Lymington, *U.K.* **15 G6** 50 45N 1 32W
Łyna →, *Poland* ...... **9 J19** 54 37N 21 14 E
Lynchburg, *U.S.A.* **114 G6** 37 25N 79 9W
Lynd →, *Australia* ...... **94 B3** 16 28 S 143 18 E
Lynd Ra., *Australia* ...... **95 D4** 25 30 S 149 20 E
Lynden, *Canada* **116 C4** 43 14N 80 9W
Lynden, *U.S.A.* **110 B4** 48 57N 122 27W
Lyndhurst, *Australia* ...... **95 E2** 30 15 S 138 18 E
Lyndon →, *Australia* ...... **93 D1** 23 29 S 114 6 E
Lyndonville, *N.Y.,*
 U.S.A. **116 C6** 43 20N 78 23W
Lyndonville, *Vt., U.S.A.* **117 B12** 44 31N 72 1W
Lyngen, *Norway* ...... **8 B19** 69 45N 20 30 E
Lynher Reef, *Australia* ...... **92 C3** 15 27 S 121 55 E
Lynn, *U.S.A.* **117 D14** 42 28N 70 57W
Lynn Lake, *Canada* **103 B8** 56 51N 101 3W
Lynnwood, *U.S.A.* **110 C4** 47 49N 122 19W
Lynton, *U.K.* **15 F4** 51 13N 3 50W
Lyntupy, *Belarus* ...... **9 J22** 55 4N 26 23 E
Lynx L., *Canada* **103 A7** 62 25N 106 15W
Lyon, *France* ...... **21 C8** 45 46N 4 50 E
Lyon St-Exupery ✈
 (LYS), *France* ...... **21 C9** 45 44N 5 2 E
Lyonnais, *France* ...... **21 C8** 45 45N 4 15 E
Lyons = Lyon, *France* ...... **21 C8** 45 46N 4 50 E
Lyons, *Ga., U.S.A.* **115 J4** 32 12N 82 19W
Lyons, *Kans., U.S.A.* **112 F5** 38 21N 98 12W
Lyons, *N.Y., U.S.A.* **116 C8** 43 5N 77 0W
Lyons →, *Australia* ...... **93 E2** 25 2 S 115 9 E
Lyons Falls, *U.S.A.* **117 C9** 43 37N 75 22W
Lyozna, *Belarus* ...... **32 E6** 55 0N 30 50 E
Lys = Leie →, *Belgium* ...... **17 C3** 51 2N 3 45 E
Lysá nad Labem,
 Czech Rep. ...... **26 A7** 50 11N 14 51 E
Lysekil, *Sweden* ...... **11 F5** 58 17N 11 26 E
Lysets, *Ukraine* ...... **29 B9** 48 52N 24 36 E
Lyskovo, *Russia* ...... **34 B7** 56 0N 45 3 E
Lystrup, *Denmark* ...... **11 H4** 56 14N 10 14 E
Lysva, *Sweden* ...... **10 D7** 60 1N 13 9 E
Lysychansk, *Ukraine* ...... **33 H10** 48 55N 38 30 E
Lytham St. Anne's, *U.K.* **14 D4** 53 45N 3 0W
Lyttelton, *N.Z.* ...... **91 K4** 43 35 S 172 44 E
Lytton, *Canada* **102 C4** 50 13N 121 31W
Lyuban, *Russia* ...... **32 C6** 59 16N 31 18 E
Lyubertsy, *Russia* ...... **32 E9** 55 39N 37 50 E
Lyubim, *Russia* ...... **32 C11** 58 20N 40 39 E
Lyubimets, *Bulgaria* ...... **45 E10** 41 50N 26 5 E
Lyuboml, *Ukraine* ...... **31 G11** 51 11N 24 4 E
Lyubotyn, *Ukraine* ...... **33 H8** 50 0N 36 0 E
Lyubytino, *Russia* ...... **32 C7** 58 50N 33 16 E
Lyudinovo, *Russia* ...... **32 F8** 53 52N 34 28 E

M

M.R. Gomez, Presa,
 Mexico **119 B5** 26 10N 99 0W
M.R. Štefánik,
 Bratislava ✈ (BTS),
 Slovak Rep. ...... **27 C10** 48 11N 17 9 E
Ma →, *Vietnam* ...... **58 H5** 19 47N 105 56 E
Ma'adaba, *Jordan* ...... **74 E4** 30 43N 35 47 E
Maamba, *Zambia* ...... **88 B4** 17 17 S 26 28 E
Ma'ān, *Jordan* ...... **74 E4** 30 12N 35 44 E
Ma'ān □, *Jordan* ...... **74 F5** 30 0N 36 0 E
Maanselkä, *Finland* ...... **8 C23** 63 52N 28 32 E
Ma'anshan, *China* ...... **59 B12** 31 44N 118 29 E
Maarianhamina, *Finland* ...... **9 F18** 60 5N 19 55 E
Ma'arrat an Nu'mān,
 Syria ...... **70 C3** 35 43N 36 43 E
Maas →, *Neths.* ...... **17 C4** 51 45N 4 32 E
Maaseik, *Belgium* ...... **17 C5** 51 6N 5 45 E
Maasin, *Phil.* ...... **63 B6** 10 8N 124 50 E
Maastricht, *Neths.* ...... **17 D5** 50 50N 5 40 E
Maave, *Mozam.* ...... **89 C5** 21 4 S 34 47 E
Mababe Depression,
 Botswana ...... **88 B3** 18 50 S 24 15 E
Mabalane, *Mozam.* ...... **89 C5** 23 37 S 32 31 E
Mabel L., *Canada* **102 C5** 50 35N 118 43W
Mabenge, *Dem. Rep. of*
 the Congo ...... **86 B1** 4 15N 24 12 E
Maberly, *Canada* **117 B8** 44 50N 76 32W
Mabian, *China* ...... **58 C4** 28 47N 103 37 E
Mabil, *Ethiopia* ...... **81 E4** 10 26N 36 52 E
Mablethorpe, *U.K.* ...... **14 D8** 53 20N 0 15 E
Mably, *France* ...... **19 F11** 46 5N 4 4 E
Maboma, *Dem. Rep. of*
 the Congo ...... **86 B2** 2 30N 28 10 E
Mabonto, *S. Leone* **82 D2** 8 53N 11 50W
Mabrouk, *Mali* **83 B4** 19 29N 1 15W
Mabuasehube △,
 Botswana ...... **88 D3** 25 5 S 21 10 E
Mac Bac, *Vietnam* ...... **65 H6** 9 46N 106 7 E
Macachín, *Argentina* ...... **126 D3** 37 10 S 63 43W
Macaé, *Brazil* ...... **127 A7** 22 20 S 41 43W
Macael, *Spain* **39 H2** 37 20N 2 18W
McAlester, *U.S.A.* **113 H7** 34 56N 95 46W

McAllen, *U.S.A.* **113 M5** 26 12N 98 14W
MacAlpine L., *Canada* **100 B9** 66 32N 102 45W
Macamic, *Canada* **104 C4** 48 45N 79 0W
Macao = Macau, *China* ...... **59 F9** 22 12N 113 33 E
Macão, *Portugal* **37 F3** 39 35N 7 59W
Macapá, *Brazil* **125 C8** 0 5N 51 4W
Macarao △, *Venezuela* **121 D6** 10 22N 67 7W
Macau, *Brazil* ...... **125 E11** 5 15 S 36 40W
Macau, *China* ...... **59 F9** 22 12N 113 33 E
McBride, *Canada* **102 C4** 53 20N 120 19W
McCall, *U.S.A.* **108 D5** 44 55N 116 6W
McCamey, *U.S.A.* **113 K3** 31 8N 102 14W
McCammon, *U.S.A.* **108 E7** 42 39N 112 12W
McCauley I., *Canada* **102 C2** 53 40N 130 15W
McCleary, *U.S.A.* **110 C3** 47 3N 123 16W
Macclenny, *U.S.A.* **115 K4** 30 17N 82 7W
Macclesfield, *U.K.* **14 D5** 53 15N 2 8W
M'Clintock Chan.,
 Canada **100 A9** 72 0N 102 0W
McClintock Ra.,
 Australia ...... **92 C4** 18 44 S 127 38 E
McCloud, *U.S.A.* **108 F2** 41 15N 122 8W
McCluer I., *Australia* ...... **92 A5** 11 5 S 133 0 E
McClure, *U.S.A.* **116 F7** 40 42N 77 19W
McClure, L., *U.S.A.* **110 H6** 37 35N 120 16W
M'Clure Str., *Canada* **98 B8** 75 0N 119 0W
McClusky, *U.S.A.* **112 B4** 47 29N 100 27W
McComb, *U.S.A.* **113 K9** 31 15N 90 27W
McConaughy, L., *U.S.A.* **112 E4** 41 14N 101 40W
McCook, *U.S.A.* **112 E4** 40 12N 100 38W
McCreary, *Canada* **103 C9** 50 47N 99 29W
McCullough Mt., *U.S.A.* **111 K11** 35 35N 115 13W
McCusker →, *Canada* **103 B7** 55 32N 108 39W
McDame, *Canada* **102 B3** 59 44N 128 59W
McDermitt, *U.S.A.* **108 F5** 41 59N 117 43W
McDonald, *U.S.A.* **116 F4** 40 22N 80 14W
Macdonald, L., *Australia* ...... **92 D4** 23 30 S 129 0 E
McDonald Is., *Ind. Oc.* ...... **3 G13** 53 0 S 73 0 E
MacDonnell Ranges,
 Australia ...... **92 D5** 23 40 S 133 0 E
MacDowell L., *Canada* **104 B1** 52 15N 92 45W
Macduff, *U.K.* **13 D6** 57 40N 2 31W
Maceda, *Spain* **36 C3** 42 16N 7 39W
Macedonia, *U.S.A.* **116 E3** 41 19N 81 31W
Macedonia, *Europe* ...... **44 E5** 41 53N 21 40 E
Maceió, *Brazil* ...... **125 E11** 9 40 S 35 41W
Maceira, *Portugal* **36 F2** 39 41N 8 55W
Macenta, *Guinea* **82 D3** 8 35N 9 32W
Macerata, *Italy* ...... **41 E10** 43 18N 13 27 E
McFarland, *U.S.A.* **111 K7** 35 41N 119 14W
McFarlane →, *Canada* **103 B7** 59 12N 107 58W
Macfarlane, L., *Australia* ...... **95 E2** 32 0 S 136 40 E
McGehee, *U.S.A.* **113 J9** 33 38N 91 24W
McGill, *U.S.A.* **108 G6** 39 23N 114 47W
Macgillycuddy's Reeks,
 Ireland **12 E2** 51 58N 9 45W
McGraw, *U.S.A.* **117 D8** 42 36N 76 8W
McGregor, *U.S.A.* **112 D9** 43 1N 91 11W
McGregor Ra., *Australia* ...... **95 D3** 27 0 S 142 45 E
McGuire, Mt, *Australia* ...... **94 J6** 20 18 S 148 23 E
Mach, *Pakistan* ...... **66 E5** 29 50N 67 20 E
Māch Kowr, *Iran* ...... **71 E9** 25 48N 61 28 E
Machado = Jiparaná →,
 Brazil ...... **124 E6** 8 3 S 62 52W
Machagai, *Argentina* ...... **126 B3** 26 56 S 60 2W
Machakos, *Kenya* ...... **86 C4** 1 30 S 37 15 E
Machala, *Ecuador* ...... **124 D3** 3 20 S 79 57W
Machanga, *Mozam.* ...... **89 C6** 20 59 S 35 0 E
Machattie, L., *Australia* ...... **94 C2** 24 50 S 139 48 E
Machault, *France* ...... **19 C11** 49 21N 4 29 E
Machava, *Mozam.* ...... **89 D5** 25 54 S 32 28 E
Machece, *Mozam.* ...... **87 F4** 19 15 S 35 32 E
Macheke, *Zimbabwe* ...... **89 B5** 18 5 S 31 51 E
Macheng, *China* ...... **59 B10** 31 12N 115 2 E
Machero, *Spain* **37 F6** 39 21N 4 20W
Machhu →, *India* ...... **68 H4** 23 6N 70 46 E
Machias, *Maine, U.S.A.* **115 C12** 44 43N 67 28W
Machias, *N.Y., U.S.A.* **116 D6** 42 25N 78 30W
Machichi →, *Canada* **103 B10** 57 3N 92 6W
Machico, *Madeira* **48 D3** 32 43N 16 44W
Machilipatnam, *India* ...... **67 L12** 16 12N 81 8 E
Machiques, *Venezuela* **124 A4** 10 4N 72 34W
Machupicchu, *Peru* ...... **124 F4** 13 8 S 72 30W
Machynlleth, *U.K.* **15 E4** 52 35N 3 50W
Macia, *Mozam.* ...... **89 D5** 25 2 S 33 8 E
Maciejowice, *Poland* ...... **31 G8** 51 36N 21 26 E
McIlwraith Ra.,
 Australia ...... **94 A3** 13 50 S 143 20 E
Măcin, *Romania* ...... **29 E13** 45 16N 28 8 E
Macina, *Mali* **82 C4** 14 50N 5 0W
McInnes L., *Canada* **103 C10** 52 13N 93 45W
McIntosh, *U.S.A.* **112 C4** 45 55N 101 21W
McIntosh L., *Canada* **103 B8** 55 45N 105 0W
Macintosh Ra., *Australia* ...... **93 E4** 27 39 S 125 32 E
Macintyre →, *Australia* ...... **95 D5** 28 37 S 150 47 E
Macizo Galaico, *Spain* **36 C3** 42 30N 7 30W
Mackay, *Australia* ...... **94 K7** 21 8 S 149 11 E
Mackay, *U.S.A.* **108 E7** 43 55N 113 37W
MacKay →, *Canada* **102 B6** 57 10N 111 38W
Mackay, L., *Australia* ...... **92 D4** 22 30 S 129 0 E
McKay Ra., *Australia* ...... **92 D3** 23 0 S 122 30 E
McKeesport, *U.S.A.* **116 F5** 40 21N 79 52W
McKellar, *Canada* **116 A5** 45 30N 79 55W
McKenna, *U.S.A.* **110 D4** 46 56N 122 33W
Mackenzie, *Canada* **102 B4** 55 20N 123 5W
Mackenzie →, *Australia* ...... **94 C4** 23 38 S 149 46 E
Mackenzie →, *Canada* **100 B6** 69 10N 134 20W
McKenzie →, *U.S.A.* **108 D2** 44 7N 123 6W
Mackenzie Bay, *Canada* **4 B1** 69 0N 137 30W
Mackenzie City =
 Linden, *Guyana* **124 B7** 6 0N 58 10W
Mackenzie Mts., *Canada* **100 B6** 64 0N 130 0W
Mackinaw City, *U.S.A.* **114 C3** 45 47N 84 44W
McKinlay, *Australia* ...... **94 C3** 21 16 S 141 18 E
McKinlay →, *Australia* ...... **94 C3** 20 50 S 141 28 E
McKinley, Mt., *U.S.A.* **100 B4** 63 4N 151 0W
McKinley Sea, *Arctic* ...... **4 A7** 82 0N 0 0 E
McKinney, *U.S.A.* **113 J6** 33 12N 96 37W
Mackinnon Road, *Kenya* ...... **86 C4** 3 40 S 39 1 E
McKittrick, *U.S.A.* **111 K7** 35 18N 119 37W
Macklin, *Canada* **103 C7** 52 20N 109 56W
Macksville, *Australia* ...... **95 E5** 30 40 S 152 56 E
McLaughlin, *U.S.A.* **112 C4** 45 49N 100 49W
Maclean, *Australia* ...... **95 D5** 29 26 S 153 16 E
McLean, *U.S.A.* **113 H4** 35 14N 100 36W
McLeansboro, *U.S.A.* **112 F10** 38 6N 88 32W
Maclear, *S. Africa* ...... **89 E4** 31 2 S 28 23 E
Maclear, C., *Malawi* ...... **87 E3** 13 54 S 34 49 E
Macleay →, *Australia* ...... **95 E5** 30 56 S 153 0 E
McLennan, *Canada* **102 B5** 55 42N 116 50W
McLeod →, *Canada* **102 C5** 54 9N 115 44W
McLeod, B., *Canada* **103 A7** 62 53N 110 0W

McLeod, L., *Australia* ...... **93 D1** 24 9 S 113 47 E
MacLeod Lake, *Canada* **102 C4** 54 58N 123 0W
McLoughlin, Mt., *U.S.A.* **108 E2** 42 27N 122 19W
McMechen, *U.S.A.* **116 G4** 39 57N 80 44W
McMinnville, *Oreg.,*
 U.S.A. **108 D2** 45 13N 123 12W
McMinnville, *Tenn.,*
 U.S.A. **115 H3** 35 41N 85 46W
McMurdo Sd.,
 Antarctica ...... **5 D11** 77 0 S 170 0 E
McMurray = Fort
 McMurray, *Canada* **102 B6** 56 44N 111 7W
McMurray, *U.S.A.* **110 B4** 48 19N 122 14W
Macodoene, *Mozam.* ...... **89 C6** 23 32 S 35 5 E
Macomb, *U.S.A.* **112 E9** 40 27N 90 40W
Macomer, *Italy* ...... **42 B1** 40 16N 8 47 E
Mâcon, *France* ...... **19 F11** 46 19N 4 50 E
Macon, *Ga., U.S.A.* **115 J4** 32 51N 83 38W
Macon, *Miss., U.S.A.* **115 J1** 33 7N 88 34W
Macon, *Mo., U.S.A.* **112 F8** 39 44N 92 28W
Macossa, *Mozam.* ...... **87 F3** 17 55 S 33 56 E
Macoun L., *Canada* **103 B8** 56 32N 103 40W
Macovane, *Mozam.* ...... **89 C6** 21 30 S 35 2 E
McPherson, *U.S.A.* **112 F6** 38 22N 97 40W
McPherson Pk., *U.S.A.* **111 L7** 34 53N 119 53W
McPherson Ra.,
 Australia ...... **95 D5** 28 15 S 153 15 E
Macquarie →, *Australia* ...... **95 E4** 30 7 S 147 24 E
Macquarie Harbour,
 Australia ...... **95 G3** 42 15 S 145 23 E
Macquarie Is., *Pac. Oc.* ...... **96 N7** 54 36 S 158 55 E
MacRobertson Land,
 Antarctica ...... **5 D6** 71 0 S 64 0 E
Macroom, *Ireland* **12 E3** 51 54N 8 57W
MacTier, *Canada* **116 A5** 45 9N 79 46W
Macubela, *Mozam.* ...... **87 F4** 16 53 S 37 49 E
Macugnaga, *Italy* ...... **40 C4** 45 58N 7 58 E
Macuira △, *Colombia* **121 D5** 12 9N 71 21W
Macuiza, *Mozam.* ...... **87 F3** 18 7 S 34 29 E
Macumba, The →,
 Australia ...... **95 D2** 27 52 S 137 12 E
Macuro, *Venezuela* **125 K15** 10 42N 61 55W
Macusani, *Peru* ...... **124 F4** 14 4 S 70 29W
Macuse, *Mozam.* ...... **87 F4** 17 45 S 37 10 E
Macuspana, *Mexico* **119 D6** 17 46N 92 36W
Macusse, *Angola* ...... **88 B3** 17 48 S 20 23 E
Mada →, *Nigeria* ...... **83 D6** 7 59N 7 55 E
Ma'dabā □, *Jordan* ...... **74 D4** 31 43N 35 47 E
Madadeni, *S. Africa* ...... **89 D5** 27 43 S 30 3 E
Mada'in Sālih, *Si. Arabia* ...... **70 E3** 26 46N 37 57 E
Madama, *Niger* ...... **79 D8** 22 0N 13 40 E
Madame, I., *Canada* **105 C7** 45 30N 60 58W
Madan, *Bulgaria* ...... **45 E8** 41 30N 24 57 E
Madaoua, *Niger* ...... **83 C6** 14 5N 6 27 E
Madara, *Nigeria* ...... **83 C7** 11 45N 10 35 E
Madaripur, *Bangla.* ...... **67 H17** 23 19N 90 15 E
Madauk, *Burma* ...... **67 L20** 17 56N 96 52 E
Madawaska, *Canada* **116 A7** 45 30N 78 0W
Madawaska →, *Canada* **116 A8** 45 27N 76 21W
Madaya, *Burma* ...... **67 H20** 22 12N 96 10 E
Madbar, *Sudan* ...... **81 F3** 6 17N 30 45 E
Maddalena, *Italy* ...... **42 A2** 41 16N 9 23 E
Maddaloni, *Italy* ...... **43 A7** 41 2N 14 23 E
Madeira →, *Brazil* ...... **124 D7** 3 22 S 58 45W
Madeira, Atl. Oc. **48 D3** 32 50N 17 0W
Madeleine, Îs. de la,
 Canada **105 C7** 47 30N 61 40W
Magdalen Is. =
 Madeleine, Îs. de la,
 Canada **105 C7** 47 30N 61 40W
Madera, *Mexico* **118 B3** 29 12N 108 7W
Madera, *Calif., U.S.A.* **110 J6** 36 57N 120 3W
Madera, *Pa., U.S.A.* **116 F6** 40 49N 78 26W
Madha, *India* ...... **66 L9** 18 0N 75 30 E
Madhavpur, *India* ...... **68 J3** 21 15N 69 58 E
Madhepura, *India* ...... **69 F12** 25 16N 86 23 E
Madhubani, *India* ...... **69 F12** 26 21N 86 7 E
Madhupur, *India* ...... **69 G12** 24 16N 86 39 E
Madhya Pradesh □,
 India ...... **68 J8** 22 50N 78 0 E
Madidi →, *Bolivia* ...... **124 F5** 12 32 S 66 52W
Madikeri, *India* ...... **66 N9** 12 30N 75 45 E
Madikwe □, *S. Africa* ...... **89 D4** 24 42 S 26 45 E
Madill, *U.S.A.* **113 H6** 34 6N 96 46W
Madimba, *Dem. Rep. of*
 the Congo ...... **84 E3** 4 58 S 15 5 E
Ma'din, *Syria* ...... **70 C3** 35 45N 39 36 E
Madina, *Mali* **82 C3** 11 16N 10 37W
Madinani, *Ivory C.* **82 D3** 9 37N 6 57W
Madingou, *Congo* ...... **84 E2** 4 10 S 13 33 E
Madirovalo, *Madag.* ...... **89 B8** 16 26 S 46 32 E
Madison, *Calif., U.S.A.* **110 G5** 38 41N 121 59W
Madison, *Fla., U.S.A.* **115 K4** 30 28N 83 25W
Madison, *Ind., U.S.A.* **114 F3** 38 44N 85 23W
Madison, *Nebr., U.S.A.* **112 E6** 41 50N 97 27W
Madison, *Ohio, U.S.A.* **116 E3** 41 46N 81 3W
Madison, *S. Dak., U.S.A.* **112 D6** 44 0N 97 7W
Madison, *Wis., U.S.A.* **112 D10** 43 4N 89 24W
Madison →, *U.S.A.* **108 D8** 45 56N 111 31W
Madison Heights, *U.S.A.* **114 G6** 37 25N 79 8W
Madisonville, *Ky.,*
 U.S.A. **114 G2** 37 20N 87 30W
Madisonville, *Tex.,*
 U.S.A. **113 K7** 30 57N 95 55W
Madista, *Botswana* ...... **88 C4** 21 15 S 25 6 E
Madiun, *Indonesia* ...... **63 G14** 7 38 S 111 32 E
Madoc, *Canada* **116 B7** 44 30N 77 28W
Madol, *Sudan* ...... **81 F2** 9 3N 27 45 E
Madon →, *France* ...... **19 D13** 48 36N 6 6 E
Madona, *Latvia* ...... **9 H22** 56 53N 26 5 E
Madonie, *Italy* ...... **42 E6** 37 50N 13 50 E
Madonna di Campíglio,
 Italy ...... **40 B7** 46 14N 10 48 E
Madra Dağı, *Turkey* ...... **47 B9** 39 23N 27 12 E
Madrakah, Ra's al,
 Oman ...... **75 D6** 19 0N 57 50 E
Madras = Chennai, *India* ...... **66 N12** 13 8N 80 19 E
Madras = Tamil
 Nadu □, *India* ...... **66 P10** 11 0N 77 0 E
Madras, *U.S.A.* **108 D3** 44 38N 121 8W
Madre, Laguna, *U.S.A.* **113 M6** 27 0N 97 30W
Madre, Sierra, *Phil.* ...... **61 C5** 17 0N 122 0 E
Madre de Dios →,
 Bolivia ...... **124 F5** 10 59 S 66 8W
Madre de Dios, I., *Chile* ...... **128 G1** 50 20 S 75 10W
Madre del Sur, Sierra,
 Mexico **119 D5** 17 30N 100 0W
Madre Occidental,
 Sierra, *Mexico* **118 B3** 27 0N 107 0W
Madre Oriental, Sierra,
 Mexico **118 C5** 25 0N 100 0W
Madri, *India* ...... **68 G5** 24 16N 73 32 E
Madrid, *Spain* **36 E7** 40 24N 3 42W
Madrid, *U.S.A.* **117 B9** 44 45N 75 8W
Madrid □, *Spain* **36 E7** 40 30N 3 45W
Madrid Barajas ✈
 (MAD), *Spain* **36 E7** 40 26N 3 34W

Madridejos, *Spain* **37 F7** 39 28N 3 33W
Madrigal de las Altas
 Torres, *Spain* **36 D6** 41 5N 5 0W
Madrona, Sierra, *Spain* **37 G6** 38 27N 4 16W
Madroñera, *Spain* **37 F5** 39 26N 5 42W
Madu, *Sudan* ...... **81 E2** 14 37N 26 4 E
Madura, *Australia* ...... **93 F4** 31 55 S 127 0 E
Madura, *Indonesia* ...... **63 G15** 7 30 S 114 0 E
Madura, Selat, *Indonesia* ...... **63 G15** 7 30 S 113 20 E
Madurai, *India* ...... **66 Q11** 9 55N 78 10 E
Madurantakam, *India* ...... **66 N11** 12 30N 79 50 E
Madzhalis, *Russia* ...... **35 J8** 42 9N 47 47 E
Mae Chan, *Thailand* ...... **64 B2** 20 9N 99 52 E
Mae Hong Son,
 Thailand ...... **64 C2** 19 16N 97 56 E
Mae Khlong →,
 Thailand ...... **64 F3** 13 24N 100 0 E
Mae Phrik, *Thailand* ...... **64 D2** 17 27N 99 7 E
Mae Ping △, *Thailand* ...... **64 D2** 17 37N 98 51 E
Mae Ramat, *Thailand* ...... **64 D2** 16 58N 98 31 E
Mae Rim, *Thailand* ...... **64 C2** 18 54N 98 57 E
Mae Sot, *Thailand* ...... **64 D2** 16 43N 98 34 E
Mae Suai, *Thailand* ...... **58 H2** 19 39N 99 33 E
Mae Tha, *Thailand* ...... **64 C2** 18 28N 99 8 E
Mae Wong △, *Thailand* ...... **64 E2** 15 54N 99 12 E
Mae Yom △, *Thailand* ...... **64 C3** 18 43N 100 15 E
Maebashi, *Japan* ...... **55 F9** 36 24N 139 4 E
Maella, *Spain* ...... **38 D5** 41 8N 0 7 E
Maesteg, *U.K.* **15 F4** 51 36N 3 40W
Maestra, Sierra, *Cuba* **120 B4** 20 15N 77 0W
Maevatanana, *Madag.* ...... **89 B8** 16 56 S 46 49 E
Mafeking = Mafikeng,
 S. Africa ...... **88 D4** 25 50 S 25 38 E
Mafeking, *Canada* **103 C8** 52 40N 101 10W
Maféré, *Ivory C.* **82 D4** 5 30N 3 2W
Mafeteng, *Lesotho* ...... **88 D4** 29 51 S 27 15 E
Maffra, *Australia* ...... **95 F4** 37 53 S 146 58 E
Mafia I., *Tanzania* ...... **86 D4** 7 45 S 39 50 E
Mafikeng, *S. Africa* ...... **88 D4** 25 50 S 25 38 E
Mafra, *Brazil* ...... **127 B6** 26 10 S 49 55W
Mafra, *Portugal* **37 G1** 38 55N 9 20W
Mafungbusi Plateau,
 Zimbabwe ...... **87 F2** 18 30 S 29 8 E
Magadan, *Russia* ...... **53 D16** 59 38N 150 50 E
Magadi, *Kenya* ...... **86 C4** 1 54 S 36 19 E
Magadi, L., *Kenya* ...... **86 C4** 1 54 S 36 19 E
Magaliesburg, *S. Africa* ...... **89 D4** 26 0 S 27 32 E
Magallanes, Estrecho de,
 Chile ...... **128 G2** 52 30 S 75 0W
Magaluf, *Spain* ...... **38 B9** 39 29N 2 32 E
Magangué, *Colombia* **124 B4** 9 14N 74 45W
Magaria, *Niger* ...... **83 C6** 13 4N 9 5 E
Magburaka, *S. Leone* **82 D2** 8 47N 12 0W
Magdalen Is. =
 Madeleine, Îs. de la,
 Canada **105 C7** 47 30N 61 40W
Magdalena, *Argentina* ...... **126 D4** 35 5 S 57 30W
Magdalena, *Bolivia* ...... **124 F6** 13 13 S 63 57W
Magdalena, *Mexico* **118 A2** 30 50N 112 0W
Magdalena →,
 Colombia **124 A4** 11 6N 74 51W
Magdalena →, *Mexico* **118 A2** 30 40N 112 25W
Magdalena, B., *Mexico* **118 C2** 24 30N 112 10W
Magdalena, Llano de la,
 Mexico **118 C2** 25 0N 111 30W
Magdeburg, *Germany* ...... **24 C7** 52 7N 11 38 E
Magdelaine Cays,
 Australia ...... **94 B5** 16 33 S 150 18 E
Magdub, *Sudan* ...... **81 E2** 13 42N 25 5 E
Magee, *U.S.A.* **113 K10** 31 52N 89 44W
Magelang, *Indonesia* ...... **63 G14** 7 29 S 110 13 E
Magellan's Str. =
 Magallanes, Estrecho
 de, *Chile* ...... **128 G2** 52 30 S 75 0W
Magenta, *Italy* ...... **40 C5** 45 28N 8 53 E
Magenta, L., *Australia* ...... **93 F2** 33 30 S 119 2 E
Magerøya, *Norway* ...... **8 A21** 71 3N 25 40 E
Maggia →, *Switz.* ...... **25 J4** 46 18N 8 36 E
Maggiorasca, Mte., *Italy* ...... **40 D6** 44 33N 9 29 E
Maggiore, Lago, *Italy* ...... **40 C5** 45 57N 8 39 E
Maggotty, *Jamaica* ...... **120 a** 18 9N 77 46W
Maghâgha, *Egypt* ...... **80 B3** 28 38N 30 50 E
Maghama, *Mauritania* **82 B2** 15 32N 12 57W
Magherafelt, *U.K.* **12 B5** 54 45N 6 37W
Maghreb, *N. Afr.* **78 B5** 32 0N 4 0W
Magione, *Italy* ...... **41 E9** 43 8N 12 12 E
Magistralnyy, *Russia* ...... **53 D11** 56 16N 107 36 E
Maglaj, *Bos.-H.* ...... **28 F3** 44 33N 18 7 E
Magliano in Toscana,
 Italy ...... **41 F8** 42 36N 11 17 E
Máglie, *Italy* ...... **43 B11** 40 7N 18 18 E
Magnac-Laval, *France* ...... **20 B5** 46 13N 1 11 E
Magnetic Pole (North),
 Canada **4 A2** 88 30N 107 0W
Magnetic Pole (South),
 Antarctica ...... **5 C9** 64 8 S 138 8 E
Magnésia □, *Greece* ...... **46 B5** 39 15N 23 0 E
Magnitogorsk, *Russia* ...... **52 D6** 53 27N 59 4 E
Magnolia, *Ark., U.S.A.* **113 J8** 33 16N 93 14W
Magnolia, *Miss., U.S.A.* **113 K9** 31 9N 90 28W
Magny-en-Vexin, *France* ...... **19 C8** 49 9N 1 47 E
Mago △, *Ethiopia* ...... **81 F4** 5 40N 36 18 E
Magog, *Canada* **117 A12** 45 18N 72 9W
Magoro, *Uganda* ...... **86 B3** 1 45N 34 12 E
Magosa = Famagusta,
 Cyprus ...... **49 D12** 35 8N 33 55 E
Magouládhes, *Greece* ...... **49 A3** 39 45N 19 42 E
Magoye, *Zambia* ...... **87 F2** 16 1 S 27 30 E
Magozal, *Mexico* **119 C5** 21 34N 97 59W
Magpie, L., *Canada* **105 B7** 51 0N 64 41W
Magrath, *Canada* **102 D6** 49 25N 112 50W
Magre →, *Spain* **39 F4** 39 11N 0 25W
Magrur, *Sudan* ...... **81 E3** 14 1N 30 27 E
Magrur, Wadi →, *Sudan* ...... **81 D2** 16 5N 26 30 E
Magta Lahjar,
 Mauritania **82 B2** 17 28N 13 17W
Maguan, *China* ...... **58 F5** 23 0N 104 21 E
Maguarinho, C., *Brazil* ...... **125 D9** 0 15 S 48 30W
Maguarichi △, *Poland* ...... **31 J8** 49 30N 21 30 E
Magusa = Famagusta,
 Cyprus ...... **49 D12** 35 8N 33 55 E
Magwe L., *Canada* **103 A9** 61 37N 95 10W
Magwe Pt., *Canada* **103 A10** 61 20N 93 50W
Magvana, *India* ...... **68 H3** 23 13N 69 22 E
Magwe, *Burma* ...... **67 J19** 20 10N 95 0 E
Magwe, *Sudan* ...... **81 G3** 4 8N 32 17 E
Maha Sarakham,
 Thailand ...... **64 D4** 16 12N 103 16 E
Mahābād, *Iran* ...... **70 B5** 36 50N 45 45 E
Mahabharat Lekh,
 Nepal ...... **69 E10** 28 30N 82 0 E
Mahabo, *Madag.* ...... **89 C7** 20 23 S 44 40 E
Mahadeo Hills, *India* ...... **69 H8** 22 20N 78 30 E
Mahadeopur, *India* **116 F6** 40 53N 78 44W
Mahagi, *Dem. Rep. of*
 the Congo ...... **86 B3** 2 20N 31 0 E

Mahajamba →, Madag. 89 B8 15 33 S 47 8 E
Mahajamba,
  Helodranon' i, Madag. 89 B8 15 24 S 47 5 E
Mahajan, India 68 E5 28 48N 73 56 E
Mahajanga, Madag. 89 B8 15 40 S 46 25 E
Mahajanga □, Madag. 89 B8 17 0 S 47 0 E
Mahajilo →, Madag. 89 B8 19 42 S 45 22 E
Mahakam →, Indonesia 62 E5 0 35 S 117 17 E
Mahalapye, Botswana 88 C4 23 1 S 26 51 E
Mahale Mts., Tanzania 86 D3 6 20 S 30 0 E
Mahale Mts. △,
  Tanzania 86 D2 6 10 S 29 50 E
Maḩallāt, Iran 71 C6 33 55N 50 30 E
Māhān, Iran 71 D8 30 5N 57 18 E
Mahan →, India 67 H13 22 30N 82 50 E
Mahanadi →, India 67 J15 20 20N 86 25 E
Mahananda →, India 69 G12 25 12N 87 52 E
Mahanoro, Madag. 89 B8 19 54 S 48 48 E
Mahanoy City, U.S.A. 117 F8 40 49N 76 9W
Maharashtra □, India 66 J9 20 30N 75 30 E
Mahasham, W. →,
  Egypt 74 E3 30 15N 34 10 E
Mahasoa, Madag. 89 C8 22 12 S 46 6 E
Mahasolo, Madag. 89 B8 19 7 S 46 22 E
Mahattat ash Shīdīyah,
  Jordan 74 F4 29 55N 35 55 E
Mahattat 'Unayzah,
  Jordan 74 E4 30 30N 35 47 E
Mahavavy →, Madag. 89 B8 15 57 S 45 54 E
Mahaxay, Laos 64 D5 17 22N 105 12 E
Mahbubnagar, India 66 L10 16 45N 77 59 E
Maḩḑah, Oman 71 E7 24 24N 55 59 E
Mahdia, Tunisia 79 A8 35 28N 11 0 E
Mahe, India 69 C8 33 10N 78 32 E
Mahendragarh, India 68 E7 28 17N 76 14 E
Mahenge, Tanzania 87 D4 8 45 S 36 41 E
Maheno, N.Z. 91 L3 45 10 S 170 50 E
Mahesana, India 68 H5 23 39N 72 26 E
Maheshwar, India 68 H6 22 11N 75 35 E
Mahgawan, India 69 F8 26 29N 78 37 E
Mahi →, India 68 H5 22 15N 72 55 E
Mahia Pen., N.Z. 91 H6 39 9 S 177 55 E
Mahilyow, Belarus 32 F6 53 55N 30 18 E
Mahmud Kot, Pakistan 68 D4 30 16N 71 0 E
Mahmudia, Romania 29 E14 45 5N 29 5 E
Mahmudiye, Turkey 47 B12 39 48N 30 15 E
Mahmutbey, Turkey 45 E12 41 3N 28 49 E
Mahnomen, U.S.A. 112 B7 47 19N 95 58W
Mahoba, India 69 G8 25 15N 79 55 E
Mahón = Maó, Spain 48 B11 39 53N 4 16 E
Mahon, Menorca ✕
  (MAH), Spain 38 F9 39 50N 4 16 E
Mahone Bay, Canada 105 D7 44 30N 64 20W
Mahopac, U.S.A. 117 E11 41 22N 73 45W
Mahuta, Nigeria 83 C5 11 32N 4 58 E
Mahuva, India 68 J4 21 5N 71 48 E
Mahya Daği, Turkey 45 E11 41 47N 27 36 E
Mai-Ndombe, L.,
  Dem. Rep. of
  the Congo 84 E3 2 0 S 18 20 E
Mai-Sai, Thailand 58 G2 20 20N 99 55 E
Mai Thon, Ko, Thailand 65 a 7 40N 98 28 E
Maia, Portugal 36 D2 41 14N 8 37W
Maia, Spain 38 B3 43 12N 1 29W
Maials, Spain 38 D5 41 22N 0 30 E
Maîche, France 19 E13 47 16N 6 48 E
Maicurú →, Brazil 125 D8 2 14 S 54 17W
Máida, Italy 43 D9 38 51N 16 22 E
Maidan Khula, Afghan. 68 C3 33 36N 69 50 E
Maidenhead, U.K. 15 F7 51 31N 0 42W
Maidstone, Canada 103 C7 53 5N 109 20W
Maidstone, U.K. 15 F8 51 16N 0 32 E
Maiduguri, Nigeria 83 C7 12 0N 13 20 E
Maiella △, Italy 41 F11 42 5N 14 5 E
Măierus, Romania 29 E10 45 53N 25 31 E
Maigatari, Nigeria 83 C6 12 46N 9 27 E
Maignelay Montigny,
  France 19 C9 49 32N 2 30 E
Maigo, Phil. 61 G5 8 10N 123 57 E
Maigudo, Ethiopia 81 F4 7 30N 37 8 E
Maihar, India 69 G9 24 16N 80 45 E
Maijdi, Bangla. 67 H17 22 48N 91 10 E
Maikala Ra., India 67 J12 22 0N 81 0 E
Maiko △, Dem. Rep. of
  the Congo 86 C2 0 30 S 27 50 E
Mailani, India 69 E9 28 17N 80 21 E
Maillezais, France 20 B3 46 22N 0 45W
Mailsi, Pakistan 68 E5 29 48N 72 15 E
Main →, Germany 25 F4 50 0N 8 18 E
Main →, U.K. 12 B5 54 48N 6 18W
Main Range △, Australia 95 D5 28 11 S 152 27 E
Main Ridge,
  Trin. & Tob. 125 J16 11 16N 60 40W
Mainburg, Germany 25 G7 48 38N 11 47 E
Maine, France 18 D6 48 20N 0 15W
Maine □, U.S.A. 115 C11 45 20N 69 0W
Maine →, Ireland 12 D2 52 9N 9 45W
Maine-et-Loire □,
  France 18 E6 47 31N 0 30W
Maïne-Soroa, Niger 83 C7 13 13N 12 2 E
Maingkwan, Burma 67 F20 26 15N 96 37 E
Mainit, L., Phil. 61 G6 9 31N 125 30 E
Mainland, Orkney, U.K. 13 C5 58 59N 3 8W
Mainland, Shet., U.K. 13 A7 60 15N 1 22W
Mainoru, Australia 94 A1 14 0 S 134 6 E
Mainpuri, India 69 F8 27 18N 79 4 E
Maintal, Germany 25 E4 50 7N 8 52 E
Maintenon, France 19 D8 48 35N 1 35 E
Maintirano, Madag. 89 B7 18 3 S 44 1 E
Mainz, Germany 25 E4 50 0N 8 14 E
Maipú, Argentina 126 D4 36 52 S 57 50W
Maiquetía, Venezuela 124 A5 10 36N 66 57W
Máira →, Italy 40 D4 44 49N 7 38 E
Mairabari, India 67 F18 26 30N 92 22 E
Maisí, Cuba 121 B5 20 17N 74 9W
Maisí, Pta. de, Cuba 121 B5 20 10N 74 10W
Maitland, N.S.W.,
  Australia 95 E5 32 33 S 151 36 E
Maitland, S. Austral.,
  Australia 95 E2 34 23 S 137 40 E
Maitland →, Canada 116 C3 43 45N 81 43W
Maitri, Antarctica 5 D3 70 0 S 0 E
Maiyema, Nigeria 83 C5 12 5N 4 25 E
Maiyuan, China 59 E11 25 34N 117 28 E
Maiz, Is. del, Nic. 120 D3 12 15N 83 4W
Maizuru, Japan 55 G7 35 25N 135 22 E
Majalengka, Indonesia 63 G13 6 50 S 108 13 E
Majene, Indonesia 63 E5 3 38 S 118 57 E
Majete △, Malawi 87 F3 15 54 S 34 34 E
Majevica, Bos.-H. 28 F3 44 45N 18 50 E
Maji, Ethiopia 81 F4 6 12N 35 30 E
Majiang, China 58 D6 26 28N 107 32 E
Majorca = Mallorca,
  Spain 48 B10 39 30N 3 0 E
Maka, Senegal 82 C2 13 40N 14 10W
Makaha, Zimbabwe 89 B5 17 20 S 32 39 E

Makak, Cameroon 83 E7 3 36N 11 0 E
Makalamabedi,
  Botswana 88 C3 20 19 S 23 51 E
Makale, Indonesia 63 E5 3 6 S 119 51 E
Makamba, Burundi 86 C2 4 8 S 29 49 E
Makari, Cameroon 83 C7 12 35N 10 27 E
Makarikari =
  Makgadikgadi Salt
  Pans, Botswana 88 C4 20 40 S 25 45 E
Makarov Basin, Arctic 4 A 87 0N 150 0W
Makarovo, Russia 53 D11 57 40N 107 45 E
Makarska, Croatia 41 E14 43 20N 17 2 E
Makaryev, Russia 34 B6 57 52N 43 50 E
Makasar = Ujung
  Pandang, Indonesia 63 F5 5 10 S 119 20 E
Makasar, Selat,
  Indonesia 63 E5 1 0 S 118 20 E
Makasar, Str. of =
  Makasar, Selat,
  Indonesia 63 E5 1 0 S 118 20 E
Makat, Kazakhstan 52 E6 47 39N 53 19 E
Makedhonía =
  Macedonia ■, Europe 44 E5 41 53N 21 40 E
Makeni, S. Leone 82 D2 8 55N 12 5W
Makeyevka =
  Makiyivka, Ukraine 33 H9 48 0N 38 0 E
Makgadikgadi △,
  Botswana 88 C3 20 27 S 24 47 E
Makgadikgadi Salt Pans,
  Botswana 88 C4 20 40 S 25 45 E
Makhachkala, Russia 35 J8 43 0N 47 30 E
Makhado = Louis
  Trichardt, S. Africa 89 C4 23 1 S 29 43 E
Makharadze = Ozurgeti,
  Georgia 35 K5 41 55N 42 2 E
Makhfar al Buşayyah,
  Iraq 70 D5 30 0N 46 10 E
Makhmūr, Iraq 70 C4 35 46N 43 35 E
Makian, Indonesia 63 D7 0 20N 127 20 E
Makindu, Kenya 86 C4 2 18 S 37 50 E
Makinsk, Kazakhstan 52 D8 52 37N 70 26 E
Makiv, Ukraine 29 B11 48 48N 26 43 E
Makiyivka, Ukraine 33 H9 48 0N 38 0 E
Makkah, Si. Arabia 75 C2 21 30N 39 54 E
Makkovik, Canada 105 A8 55 10N 59 10W
Makó, Hungary 28 D5 46 14N 20 33 E
Mako, Senegal 82 C2 12 52N 12 20W
Makokou, Gabon 84 D2 0 40N 12 50 E
Makongo, Dem. Rep. of
  the Congo 86 B2 3 25N 26 17 E
Makoro, Dem. Rep. of
  the Congo 86 B2 3 10N 29 59 E
Maków Mazowiecki,
  Poland 31 F8 52 52N 21 6 E
Maków Podhalański,
  Poland 31 J6 49 43N 19 45 E
Makrá, Greece 47 E7 36 15N 25 54 E
Makrai, India 66 H10 22 2N 77 0 E
Makran Coast Range,
  Pakistan 66 G4 25 40N 64 0 E
Makrana, India 68 F6 27 2N 74 46 E
Makrany, Belarus 31 G11 51 48N 24 17 E
Mákri, Greece 45 F9 40 52N 25 40 E
Makriyialos, Greece 49 D7 35 2N 25 59 E
Makū, Iran 70 B5 39 15N 44 31 E
Makunda, Botswana 88 C3 22 30 S 20 7 E
Makung, Taiwan 59 F12 23 34N 119 34 E
Makurazaki, Japan 55 J5 31 15N 130 20 E
Makurdi, Nigeria 83 D6 7 43N 8 35 E
Makūyeh, Iran 71 D7 28 7N 53 9 E
Makwassie, S. Africa 88 D4 27 17 S 26 0 E
Makwiro, Zimbabwe 89 B5 17 58 S 30 25 E
Mâl, Mauritania 82 B2 16 58N 13 23W
Mal B., Ireland 12 D2 52 50N 9 30W
Mala, Pta., Panama 120 E3 7 28N 80 2W
Mala Belozërka,
  Ukraine 33 J8 47 12N 34 56 E
Malá Fatra △,
  Slovak Rep. 27 B12 49 10N 19 0 E
Mala Kapela, Croatia 41 D12 44 45N 15 30 E
Mała Panew →, Poland 31 H4 50 43N 17 54 E
Mala Vyska, Ukraine 33 H6 48 39N 31 36 E
Malabang, Phil. 61 H6 7 36N 124 3 E
Malabar Coast, India 66 P9 11 0N 75 0 E
Malabon, Phil. 61 D4 14 21N 121 0 E
Malabu, Nigeria 83 D7 9 32N 12 48 E
Malacca, Str. of,
  Indonesia 65 L3 3 0N 101 0 E
Malacky, Slovak Rep. 27 C10 48 27N 17 0 E
Malad City, U.S.A. 108 E7 42 12N 112 15W
Maladeta, Spain 38 C5 42 39N 0 39 E
Maladzyechna, Belarus 32 E4 54 20N 26 50 E
Málaga, Spain 37 J6 36 43N 4 23W
Málaga □, Spain 37 J6 36 38N 4 58W
Malagarasi, Tanzania 86 D3 5 5 S 30 50 E
Malagarasi →, Tanzania 86 D2 5 12 S 29 47 E
Malagasy Rep. =
  Madagascar ■, Africa 89 C8 20 0 S 47 0 E
Malagón, Spain 37 F7 39 11N 3 52W
Malagón →, Spain 37 H3 37 35N 7 29W
Malahide, Ireland 12 C5 53 26N 6 9W
Malaimbandy, Madag. 89 C8 20 20 S 45 36 E
Malakāl, Sudan 81 F3 9 33N 31 40 E
Malakand, Pakistan 68 B4 34 40N 71 55 E
Malakwal, Pakistan 68 C5 32 34N 73 13 E
Malamala, Indonesia 63 E6 3 21 S 120 55 E
Malanda, Australia 94 B4 17 22 S 145 35 E
Malang, Indonesia 63 G15 7 59 S 112 45 E
Malangen, Norway 8 B18 69 24N 18 37 E
Malanje, Angola 84 F3 9 36 S 16 17 E
Mälaren, Sweden 10 E11 59 30N 17 10 E
Malargüe, Argentina 126 D2 35 32 S 69 30W
Malartic, Canada 104 C4 48 9N 78 9W
Malaryta, Belarus 31 G11 51 50N 24 3 E
Malatya, Turkey 70 B3 38 25N 38 20 E
Malawi ■, Africa 87 E3 11 55 S 34 0 E
Malawi, L. = Nyasa, L.,
  Africa 87 E3 12 30 S 34 30 E
Malay Pen., Asia 65 J3 7 25N 100 0 E
Malaya Belozërka =
  Mala Belozërka,
  Ukraine 33 J8 47 12N 34 56 E
Malaya Vishera, Russia 32 C7 58 55N 32 25 E
Malaya Viska = Mala
  Vyska, Ukraine 33 H6 48 39N 31 36 E
Malaybalay, Phil. 61 G6 8 5N 125 7 E
Malāyer, Iran 71 C6 34 19N 48 51 E
Malaysia ■, Asia 65 K4 5 0N 110 0 E
Malazgirt, Turkey 70 B4 39 10N 42 33 E
Malbaza, Niger 83 C6 13 59N 5 38 E
Malbon, Australia 94 C3 21 5 S 140 17 E
Malbooma, Australia 95 E1 30 41 S 134 11 E
Malbork, Poland 31 F6 54 3N 19 1 E
Malcésine, Italy 40 C7 45 46N 10 48 E
Malchin, Germany 24 B8 53 44N 12 44 E
Malchow, Germany 24 B8 53 28N 12 25 E
Malcolm, Australia 93 E3 28 51 S 121 25 E

Malcolm, Pt., Australia 93 F3 33 48 S 123 45 E
Malczyce, Poland 31 G3 51 14N 16 29 E
Maldah, India 69 G13 25 2N 88 9 E
Maldegem, Belgium 17 C3 51 14N 3 26 E
Malden, Mass., U.S.A. 117 D13 42 26N 71 4W
Malden, Mo., U.S.A. 113 G10 36 34N 89 57W
Malden I., Kiribati 97 H12 4 3 S 155 1 W
Maldives ■, Ind. Oc. 50 J11 5 0N 73 0 E
Maldon, U.K. 15 F8 51 44N 0 42 E
Maldonado, Uruguay 127 C5 34 59 S 55 0W
Maldonado, Punta,
  Mexico 119 D5 16 19N 98 35W
Malè, Italy 40 B7 46 21N 10 55 E
Male, Maldives 51 J11 4 0N 73 28 E
Malé Karpaty,
  Slovak Rep. 27 C10 48 30N 17 20 E
Maléa, Ákra, Greece 46 E5 36 28N 23 7 E
Malegaon, India 66 J9 20 30N 74 38 E
Malei, Mozam. 87 F4 17 12 S 36 58 E
Malek, Sudan 81 F3 6 4N 31 36 E
Malek Kandī, Iran 70 B5 37 9N 46 6 E
Malela, Dem. Rep. of
  the Congo 86 C2 4 22 S 26 8 E
Malema, Mozam. 87 E4 14 57 S 37 20 E
Máleme, Greece 49 D5 35 31N 23 49 E
Malerkotla, India 68 D6 30 32N 75 58 E
Máles, Greece 49 D7 35 6N 25 35 E
Malesherbes, France 19 D9 48 15N 2 24 E
Maleshevska Planina,
  Europe 44 E7 41 38N 23 7 E
Malesína, Greece 46 C5 38 37N 23 14 E
Malestroit, France 18 E4 47 49N 2 25W
Malfa, Italy 43 D7 38 35N 14 50 E
Malgobek, Russia 35 J7 43 30N 44 34 E
Malgrat de Mar, Spain 38 D7 41 39N 2 46 E
Malha, Sudan 81 D2 15 8N 25 10 E
Malhargarh, India 68 G6 24 17N 74 59 E
Malheur →, U.S.A. 108 D5 44 4N 116 59W
Malheur L., U.S.A. 108 E4 43 20N 118 48W
Mali, Guinea 82 C2 12 10N 12 20W
Mali ■, Africa 82 B4 17 0N 3 0 E
Mali →, Burma 67 G20 25 40N 97 40 E
Mali Kanal, Serbia & M. 28 E4 45 36N 19 24 E
Mali Kyun, Burma 64 F2 13 0N 98 20 E
Malibu, U.S.A. 111 L8 34 2N 118 41W
Maliku, Indonesia 63 E6 0 39 S 123 16 E
Malili, Indonesia 63 E6 2 42 S 121 6 E
Målilla, Sweden 11 G9 57 23N 15 48 E
Malimba, Mts.,
  Dem. Rep. of
  the Congo 86 D2 7 30 S 29 30 E
Malin Hd., Ireland 12 A4 55 23N 7 24W
Malin Pen., Ireland 12 A4 55 20N 7 17W
Malindi, Kenya 86 C5 3 12 S 40 5 E
Malines = Mechelen,
  Belgium 17 C4 51 2N 4 29 E
Malino, Indonesia 63 D6 1 0N 121 0 E
Malinyi, Tanzania 87 D4 8 56 S 36 0 E
Malipo, China 58 F5 23 7N 104 42 E
Maliq, Albania 44 F4 40 45N 20 48 E
Malita, Phil. 63 C7 6 19N 125 39 E
Maliwun, Burma 62 B1 10 17N 98 40 E
Maliya, India 68 H4 23 5N 70 46 E
Maljenik, Serbia & M. 44 C5 43 54N 21 43 E
Malka Mari, Kenya 86 B5 4 11N 40 46 E
Malkara, Turkey 45 F10 40 53N 26 53 E
Malkinia Górna, Poland 31 F9 52 42N 22 5 E
Malko Tŭrnovo,
  Bulgaria 45 E11 41 59N 27 31 E
Mallacoota Inlet,
  Australia 95 F4 37 34 S 149 40 E
Mallaig, U.K. 13 D3 57 0N 5 50W
Mallaoua, Niger 83 C6 13 2N 9 36 E
Mallawan, India 69 F9 27 4N 80 12 E
Mallawi, Egypt 80 B3 27 44N 30 44 E
Mallemort, France 21 E9 43 43N 5 11 E
Málles Venosta, Italy 40 B7 46 41N 10 32 E
Mállia, Greece 49 D7 35 17N 25 32 E
Mallion, Kólpos, Greece 49 D7 35 19N 25 27 E
Mallorca, Spain 48 B10 39 30N 3 0 E
Mallorytown, Canada 117 B9 44 29N 75 53W
Mallow, Ireland 12 D3 52 8N 8 39W
Malmbäck, Sweden 11 G8 57 34N 14 28 E
Malmberget, Sweden 8 C19 67 11N 20 40 E
Malmédy, Belgium 17 D6 50 25N 6 2 E
Malmesbury, S. Africa 88 E2 33 28 S 18 41 E
Malmivaara =
  Malmberget, Sweden 8 C19 67 11N 20 40 E
Malmköping, Sweden 10 E10 59 8N 16 44 E
Malmö, Sweden 11 J7 55 36N 12 59 E
Malmslätt, Sweden 11 F9 58 27N 15 33 E
Malmyzh, Russia 34 B10 56 31N 50 41 E
Malnaş, Romania 29 D10 46 2N 25 49 E
Malo Konare, Bulgaria 45 D8 42 12N 24 24 E
Maloarkhangelsk, Russia 33 F9 52 28N 36 30 E
Malolos, Phil. 63 B6 14 50N 120 49 E
Malolotja →, Swaziland 89 D5 26 4N 31 6 E
Malombe L., Malawi 87 E4 14 40 S 35 15 E
Małomice, Poland 31 G2 51 34N 15 2 E
Malomir, Bulgaria 45 D10 42 16N 26 32 E
Malone, U.S.A. 117 B10 44 51N 74 18W
Malong, China 58 E4 25 24N 103 34 E
Małopolskie □, Poland 31 H7 49 50N 20 0 E
Malorad, Bulgaria 44 C7 43 28N 23 41 E
Måløy, Norway 9 F11 61 57N 5 6 E
Maloyaroslovets, Russia 32 E9 55 2N 36 20 E
Malpartida, Spain 37 F4 39 26N 6 30W
Malpaso, Canary Is. 48 G1 27 43N 18 3W
Malpelo, I. de, Colombia 124 C2 4 3N 81 35W
Malpica de Bergantiños,
  Spain 36 B2 43 19N 8 48W
Malpur, India 68 H5 23 21N 73 27 E
Malpura, India 68 F6 26 17N 75 23 E
Mals = Málles Venosta,
  Italy 40 B7 46 41N 10 32 E
Malta, Idaho, U.S.A. 108 E7 42 18N 113 22W
Malta, Mont., U.S.A. 108 B10 48 21N 107 52W
Malta ■, Europe 49 D1 35 50N 14 26 E
Maltahöhe, Namibia 88 C2 24 55 S 17 0 E
Maltepe, Turkey 45 F13 40 55N 29 8 E
Malton, Canada 116 C5 43 42N 79 38W
Malton, U.K. 14 C7 54 8N 0 49W
Maluku, Indonesia 63 E7 1 0 S 127 0 E
Maluku □, Indonesia 63 E7 3 0 S 128 0 E
Maluku Sea = Molucca
  Sea, Indonesia 63 E6 0 0 125 0 E
Malumfashi, Nigeria 83 C6 11 48N 7 39 E
Malung, Sweden 10 D7 60 42N 13 44 E
Malungsfors, Sweden 10 D7 60 44N 13 33 E
Maluwe, Ghana 82 D4 8 40N 2 17W
Malvan, India 66 L8 16 2N 73 30 E
Malvern, U.S.A. 113 H8 34 22N 92 49W
Malvern Hills, U.K. 15 E5 52 0N 2 19W
Malvinas, Is. = Falkland
  Is. ☑, Atl. Oc. 128 G5 51 30 S 59 0W

Malý Dunaj →,
  Slovak Rep. 27 D11 47 45N 18 9 E
Malya, Tanzania 86 C3 3 5 S 33 38 E
Malye Derbety, Russia 35 G7 47 57N 44 42 E
Malyn, Ukraine 33 G5 50 46N 29 3 E
Malyy Lyakhovskiy,
  Ostrov, Russia 53 B15 74 7N 140 36 E
Mama, Russia 53 D12 58 18N 112 54 E
Mamadysh, Russia 34 C10 55 44N 51 23 E
Mamanguape, Brazil 125 E11 6 50 S 35 4W
Mamarr Mitla, Egypt 74 E1 30 2N 32 54 E
Mamasa, Indonesia 63 E5 2 55 S 119 20 E
Mambasa, Dem. Rep. of
  the Congo 86 B2 1 22N 29 3 E
Mamberamo →,
  Indonesia 63 E9 2 0 S 137 50 E
Mambilima Falls,
  Zambia 87 E2 10 31 S 28 45 E
Mambirima, Dem. Rep.
  of the Congo 87 E2 11 25 S 27 33 E
Mambo, Tanzania 86 C4 4 52 S 38 22 E
Mambrui, Kenya 86 C5 3 5 S 40 5 E
Mamburao, Phil. 61 E4 13 13N 120 39 E
Mameigwess L., Canada 104 B2 52 35N 87 50W
Mamers, France 18 D7 48 21N 0 22 E
Mamfé, Cameroon 83 D6 5 50N 9 15 E
Mammoth, U.S.A. 109 K8 32 43N 110 39W
Mammoth Cave △,
  U.S.A. 114 G3 37 8N 86 13W
Mamonovo, Russia 30 D6 54 28N 19 55 E
Mamoré →, Bolivia 124 F5 10 23 S 65 53W
Mamou, Guinea 82 C2 10 15N 12 0W
Mamoudzou, Mayotte 77 H8 12 48 S 45 14 E
Mampatá, Guinea-Biss. 82 C2 11 54N 14 53W
Mampikony, Madag. 89 B8 16 6 S 47 38 E
Mampong, Ghana 83 D4 7 6N 1 26W
Mamry, Jezioro, Poland 30 D8 54 5N 21 50 E
Mamuju, Indonesia 63 E5 2 41 S 118 50 E
Mamuno, Botswana 88 C3 22 16 S 20 1 E
Mamuras, Albania 44 E3 41 34N 19 41 E
Man, Ivory C. 82 D3 7 30N 7 40W
Man, I. of, U.K. 14 C3 54 15N 4 30W
Man-Bazar, India 69 H12 23 4N 86 39 E
Man Na, Burma 67 H20 23 27N 97 19 E
Mana →, Fr. Guiana 125 B8 5 45N 53 55W
Mana Pools △,
  Zimbabwe 87 F2 15 56 S 29 25 E
Manaar, G. of =
  Mannar, G. of, Asia 66 Q11 8 30N 79 0 E
Manacapuru, Brazil 124 D6 3 16 S 60 37W
Manacor, Spain 48 B10 39 34N 3 13 E
Manado, Indonesia 63 D6 1 29N 124 51 E
Managua, Nic. 120 D2 12 6N 86 20W
Managua, L. de, Nic. 120 D2 12 20N 86 30W
Manakara, Madag. 89 C8 22 8 S 48 1 E
Manali, India 68 C7 32 16N 77 10 E
Manama = Al
  Manāmah, Bahrain 71 E6 26 10N 50 30 E
Manambao →, Madag. 89 B7 17 35 S 44 0 E
Manambato, Madag. 89 A8 13 43 S 49 7 E
Manambolo →, Madag. 89 B7 19 18 S 44 22 E
Manambolosy, Madag. 89 B8 16 2 S 49 40 E
Mananara →, Madag. 89 C8 23 21 S 47 42 E
Mananara Avaratra,
  Madag. 89 B8 16 10 S 49 46 E
Mananara △, Madag. 89 B8 16 14 S 49 45 E
Mananjary, Madag. 89 C8 21 13 S 48 20 E
Manankoro, Mali 82 C3 10 28N 7 25W
Manantenina, Madag. 89 C8 24 17 S 47 19 E
Manaos = Manaus,
  Brazil 124 D7 3 0 S 60 0W
Manapire →, Venezuela 124 B5 7 42N 66 7W
Manapouri, N.Z. 91 L1 45 34 S 167 39 E
Manapouri, L., N.Z. 91 L1 45 32 S 167 32 E
Manaqil, Sudan 81 E3 14 15N 32 59 E
Manār, Jabal, Yemen 75 E3 14 2N 44 17 E
Manaravolo, Madag. 89 C8 23 55 S 45 39 E
Manas, China 60 B3 44 17N 85 56 E
Manas →, India 67 F17 26 12N 90 40 E
Manaslu, Nepal 69 E11 28 33N 84 33 E
Manasquan, U.S.A. 117 F10 40 8N 74 3W
Manassa, U.S.A. 109 H11 37 11N 105 56W
Manatí, Puerto Rico 121 d 18 26N 66 29W
Manaung, Burma 67 K18 18 45N 93 40 E
Manaus, Brazil 124 D7 3 0 S 60 0W
Manavgat, Turkey 72 D4 36 47N 31 26 E
Manawan L., Canada 103 B8 55 24N 103 14W
Manay, Phil. 61 H7 7 17N 126 33 E
Manbij, Syria 70 B3 36 31N 37 57 E
Mancha Real, Spain 37 H7 37 48N 3 39W
Manche □, France 18 C5 49 10N 1 20W
Manchegorsk, Russia 52 C4 67 54N 32 58 E
Manchester, U.K. 14 D5 53 29N 2 12W
Manchester, Calif.,
  U.S.A. 110 G3 38 58N 123 41W
Manchester, Conn.,
  U.S.A. 117 E12 41 47N 72 31W
Manchester, Ga., U.S.A. 115 J3 32 51N 84 37W
Manchester, Iowa,
  U.S.A. 112 D9 42 29N 91 27W
Manchester, Ky., U.S.A. 114 G4 37 9N 83 46W
Manchester, N.H.,
  U.S.A. 117 D13 42 59N 71 28W
Manchester, N.Y.,
  U.S.A. 116 D7 42 56N 77 16W
Manchester, Pa., U.S.A. 117 F8 40 4N 76 43W
Manchester, Tenn.,
  U.S.A. 115 H2 35 29N 86 5W
Manchester, Vt., U.S.A. 117 C11 43 10N 73 5W
Manchester
  International ✕
  (MAN), U.K. 14 D5 53 21N 2 17W
Manchester L., Canada 103 A7 61 28N 107 29W
Manchhar L., Pakistan 68 F2 26 25N 67 39 E
Manchuria = Dongbei,
  China 57 D13 45 0N 125 0 E
Manchurian Plain, China 50 E16 47 0N 124 0 E
Manciano, Italy 41 F8 42 35N 11 31 E
Mancifa, Ethiopia 81 F5 6 53N 41 50 E
Mand →, India 69 J10 21 42N 83 15 E
Mand →, Iran 71 D7 28 20N 52 30 E
Manda, Ludewe,
  Tanzania 87 E3 10 30 S 34 40 E
Manda, Mbeya,
  Tanzania 86 D3 7 58 S 29 2 E
Manda, Mbeya,
  Tanzania 86 D3 8 30 S 32 49 E
Mandabé, Madag. 89 C7 21 0 S 44 55 E
Mandaguari, Brazil 127 A5 23 32 S 51 42W
Mandah = Töhöm,
  Mongolia 56 B5 44 27N 108 2 E
Mandal, Norway 9 G12 58 2N 7 25 E
Mandala, Puncak,
  Indonesia 63 E10 4 44 S 140 20 E
Mandalay, Burma 67 J20 22 0N 96 4 E
Mandale = Mandalay,
  Burma 67 J20 22 0N 96 4 E
Mandalgarh, India 68 G6 25 12N 75 6 E

Mandalgovi, Mongolia 56 B4 45 45N 106 10 E
Mandalī, Iraq 70 C5 33 43N 45 28 E
Mandan, U.S.A. 112 B4 46 50N 100 54W
Mandaon, Phil. 61 E5 12 13N 123 17 E
Mandar, Teluk,
  Indonesia 63 E5 3 35 S 119 15 E
Mándas, Italy 42 C2 39 40N 9 8 E
Mandaue, Phil. 61 F5 10 20N 123 56 E
Mandelieu-la-Napoule,
  France 21 E10 43 34N 6 57 E
Mandera, Kenya 86 B5 3 55N 41 53 E
Mandeville, Jamaica 120 a 18 2N 77 31W
Mandi, India 68 D7 31 39N 76 58 E
Mandi Dabwali, India 68 E6 29 58N 74 42 E
Mandiana, Guinea 82 C3 10 37N 8 39W
Mandimba, Mozam. 87 E4 14 20 S 35 40 E
Mandioli, Indonesia 63 E7 0 40 S 127 20 E
Mandla, India 69 H9 22 39N 80 30 E
Mandø, Denmark 11 J2 55 18N 8 33 E
Mandorah, Australia 92 B5 12 32 S 130 42 E
Mandoto, Madag. 89 B8 19 34 S 46 17 E
Mandoúdhion, Greece 46 C5 38 48N 23 29 E
Mándra, Greece 46 C5 38 4N 23 30 E
Mandrákı, Greece 47 E9 36 36N 27 11 E
Mandrare →, Madag. 89 D8 25 10 S 46 30 E
Mandritsara, Madag. 89 B8 15 50 S 48 49 E
Mandronarivo, Madag. 89 C8 21 7 S 45 38 E
Mandsaur, India 68 G6 24 3N 75 8 E
Mandurah, Australia 93 F2 32 36 S 115 48 E
Mandúria, Italy 43 B10 40 24N 17 38 E
Mandvi, India 68 H3 22 51N 69 22 E
Mandya, India 66 N10 12 30N 77 0 E
Mandzai, Pakistan 68 D2 30 55N 67 6 E
Mané, Burkina Faso 83 C4 12 59N 1 21W
Maneh, Iran 71 B8 37 39N 57 7 E
Manengouba, Mts.,
  Cameroon 83 E6 5 0N 9 50 E
Manera, Madag. 89 C7 22 55 S 44 20 E
Manérbio, Italy 40 C7 45 21N 10 8 E
Maneroo Cr. →,
  Australia 94 C3 23 21 S 143 53 E
Manfalût, Egypt 80 B3 27 20N 30 52 E
Manfredónia, Italy 41 G12 41 38N 15 55 E
Manfredónia, G. di, Italy 41 G13 41 35N 16 5 E
Manga, Burkina Faso 83 C4 11 40N 1 4W
Manga, Niger 83 C7 15 0N 14 0 E
Mangabeiras, Chapada
  das, Brazil 125 F9 10 0 S 46 30W
Mangalia, Romania 29 G13 43 50N 28 35 E
Mangalore, India 66 N9 12 55N 74 47 E
Mangan, India 69 F13 27 31N 88 32 E
Mangaung, S. Africa 85 K5 29 10 S 26 25 E
Mangawan, India 69 G9 24 41N 81 33 E
Mangaweka, N.Z. 91 H5 39 48 S 175 47 E
Manggar, Indonesia 62 E3 2 50 S 108 10 E
Manggawitu, Indonesia 63 E8 4 8 S 133 32 E
Manggis, Indonesia 63 J18 8 29 S 115 31 E
Mangindrano, Madag. 89 A8 14 17 S 48 58 E
Mangkalihat, Tanjung,
  Indonesia 63 D5 1 2N 118 59 E
Mangla, Pakistan 68 C5 33 7N 73 39 E
Mangla Dam, Pakistan 69 C5 33 9N 73 44 E
Manglaur, India 68 E7 29 44N 77 49 E
Mangnai, China 60 C4 37 52N 91 43 E
Mango, Togo 83 C5 10 20N 0 30 E
Mangoche, Malawi 87 E4 14 25 S 35 16 E
Mangoky →, Madag. 89 C7 21 29 S 43 41 E
Mangole, Indonesia 63 E6 1 50 S 125 55 E
Mangombe, Dem. Rep.
  of the Congo 86 C2 1 20 S 26 48 E
Mangonui, N.Z. 91 F4 35 1 S 173 32 E
Mangoro →, Madag. 89 B8 20 0 S 48 45 E
Mangrol, Mad. P., India 68 J4 21 7N 70 7 E
Mangrol, Raj., India 68 G6 25 20N 76 31 E
Mangualde, Portugal 36 E3 40 38N 7 48W
Mangueira, L. da, Brazil 127 C5 33 0 S 52 50W
Mangum, U.S.A. 113 H5 34 53N 99 30W
Mangyshlak, Poluostrov,
  Kazakhstan 52 E6 44 30N 52 30 E
Manhattan, U.S.A. 112 F6 39 11N 96 35W
Manhiça, Mozam. 89 D5 25 23 S 32 49 E
Mania →, Madag. 89 B8 19 42 S 45 22 E
Maniago, Italy 41 B9 46 10N 12 43 E
Manica, Mozam. 89 B5 18 58 S 32 59 E
Manica □, Mozam. 89 B5 19 10 S 33 45 E
Manicaland □,
  Zimbabwe 87 F3 19 0 S 32 30 E
Manicoré, Brazil 124 E6 5 48 S 61 16W
Manicouagan →,
  Canada 105 C6 49 30N 68 30W
Manicouagan, Rés.,
  Canada 105 B6 51 5N 68 40W
Maniema □, Dem. Rep.
  of the Congo 86 C2 3 0 S 26 0 E
Manīfah, Si. Arabia 71 E6 27 44N 49 0 E
Manifold, C., Australia 94 C5 22 41 S 150 50 E
Manigango, China 58 B2 31 56N 99 10 E
Manigotagan, Canada 103 C9 51 6N 96 18W
Manigotagan →,
  Canada 103 C9 51 7N 96 20W
Manihari, India 69 G12 25 21N 87 38 E
Manihiki, Cook Is. 97 J11 10 24 S 161 1W
Manika, Plateau de la,
  Dem. Rep. of
  the Congo 87 E2 10 0 S 25 5 E
Manikpur, India 69 G9 25 4N 81 7 E
Manila, Phil. 61 D4 14 40N 121 3 E
Manila, U.S.A. 108 F9 40 59N 109 43W
Manila B., Phil. 61 D4 14 40N 120 35 E
Manilla, Australia 95 E5 30 45 S 150 43 E
Maningrida, Australia 94 A1 12 3 S 134 13 E
Maninian, Ivory C. 82 C3 10 3N 7 52W
Manipur □, India 67 G19 25 0N 94 0 E
Manipur →, Burma 67 H19 23 45N 94 20 E
Manisa, Turkey 47 C9 38 38N 27 30 E
Manistee, U.S.A. 114 C2 44 15N 86 19W
Manistee →, U.S.A. 114 C2 44 15N 86 21W
Manistique, U.S.A. 114 C2 45 57N 86 15W
Manitoba □, Canada 103 B9 55 30N 97 0W
Manitoba, L., Canada 103 C9 51 0N 98 45W
Manitou, Canada 103 D9 49 15N 98 32W
Manitou, L., Canada 105 B6 50 55N 65 17W
Manitou Is., U.S.A. 114 C3 45 8N 86 0W
Manitou L., Canada 103 C7 52 43N 109 43W
Manitou Springs, U.S.A. 112 F2 38 52N 104 55W
Manitoulin I., Canada 104 C3 45 40N 82 30W
Manitouwadge, Canada 104 C2 49 8N 85 48W
Manitowoc, U.S.A. 114 C2 44 5N 87 40W
Manizales, Colombia 124 B3 5 5N 75 32W
Manja, Madag. 89 C7 21 26 S 44 20 E
Manjacaze, Mozam. 89 C5 24 45 S 34 0 E
Manjakandriana,
  Madag. 89 B8 18 55 S 47 47 E
Manjhand, Pakistan 68 G3 25 50N 68 10 E

Manjil, *Iran* .... 71 B6 36 46N 49 30 E
Manjimup, *Australia* ... 93 F2 34 15 S 116 6 E
Manjra →, *India* ...... 66 K10 18 49N 77 52 E
Mankato, *Kans., U.S.A.* 112 F5 39 47N 98 13W
Mankato, *Minn., U.S.A.* 112 C8 44 10N 94 0W
Mankayane, *Swaziland* 89 D5 26 40 S 31 4 E
Mankera, *Pakistan* .... 68 D4 31 23N 71 26 E
Mankim, *Cameroon* .... 83 D7   5 6N 12 3 E
Mankono, *Ivory C.* 82 D3   8 1N   6 10W
Mankota, *Canada* 103 D7 49 25N 107 5W
Manlay = Üydzin,
  Mongolia .... 56 B4 44 9N 107 0 E
Manlleu, *Spain* .... 38 C7 42 2N   2 17 E
Manmad, *India* ...... 66 J9 20 18N 74 28 E
Mann Ranges, *Australia* 93 E5 26 6 S 130 5 E
Manna, *Indonesia* .... 62 E2   4 25 S 102 55 E
Mannahill, *Australia* . 95 E3 32 25 S 140 0 E
Mannar, *Sri Lanka* ... 66 Q11 9 1N 79 54 E
Mannar, G. of, *Asia* .. 66 Q11 8 30N 79 0 E
Mannar I., *Sri Lanka* . 66 Q11 9 5N 79 45 E
Mannheim, *Germany* ... 25 F4 49 29N   8 29 E
Manning, *Canada* 102 B5 56 53N 117 39W
Manning, *Oreg., U.S.A.* 110 E3 45 45N 123 13W
Manning, *S.C., U.S.A.* 115 J5 33 42N 80 13W
Mannu →, *Italy* ...... 42 C2 39 16N   9 0 E
Mannu, C., *Italy* ..... 42 B1 40 3N   8 21 E
Mannum, *Australia* ... 95 E2 34 50 S 139 20 E
Mano, *S. Leone* ...... 82 D2   8 3N 12 2 E
Mano, *Liberia* 82 D2   6 56N 11 30W
Mano River, *Liberia* .. 82 D2   7 20N 11 6W
Manohparpur, *India* .. 69 H11 22 23N 85 12 E
Manokwari, *Indonesia* . 63 E8   0 54 S 134 0 E
Manolás, *Greece* ..... 46 C3 38 4N 21 21 E
Manombo, *Madag.* .... 89 C7 22 57 S 43 28 E
Manono, *Dem. Rep. of
  the Congo* .... 86 D2   7 15 S 27 25 E
Manoppello, *Italy* .... 41 F11 42 15N 14 3 E
Manosque, *France* .... 21 E9 43 49N   5 47 E
Manotick, *Canada* 117 A9 45 13N 75 41W
Manouane →, *Canada* . 105 C5 49 30N 71 10W
Manouane, L., *Canada* 105 B5 50 45N 70 45W
Manp'o, *N. Korea* ... 57 D14 41 6N 126 24 E
Manpojin = Manp'o,
  N. Korea .... 57 D14 41 6N 126 24 E
Manpur, *Chhattisgarh,
  India* .... 69 H10 23 17N 83 35 E
Manpur, *Mad. P., India* 68 H6 22 26N 75 37 E
Manresa, *Spain* ...... 38 D6 41 48N   1 50 E
Mansa, *Gujarat, India* . 68 H5 23 27N 72 45 E
Mansa, *Punjab, India* . 68 E6 30 0N 75 27 E
Mansa, *Zambia* ...... 87 E2 11 13 S 28 55 E
Månsåsen, *Sweden* ... 10 A8 63 5N 14 18 E
Mansehra, *Pakistan* .. 68 B5 34 20N 73 15 E
Mansel I., *Canada* ... 101 B11 62 0N 80 0W
Mansfield, *Australia* .. 95 F4 37 4 S 146 6 E
Mansfield, *U.K.* 14 D6 53 9N   1 11W
Mansfield, *La., U.S.A.* 113 J8 32 2N 93 43W
Mansfield, *Mass., U.S.A.* 117 D13 42 2N 71 13W
Mansfield, *Ohio, U.S.A.* 116 F2 40 45N 82 31W
Mansfield, *Pa., U.S.A.* 116 E7 41 48N 77 5W
Mansfield, Mt., *U.S.A.* 117 B12 44 33N 72 49W
Mansilla de las Mulas,
  Spain 36 C5 42 30N   5 25W
Mansle, *France* ...... 20 C4 45 52N   0 12 E
Mansoa, *Guinea-Biss.* . 82 C1 12 0N 15 20W
Manson Creek, *Canada* 102 B4 55 37N 124 32W
Manta, *Ecuador* ...... 124 D2   1 0 S 80 40W
Mantadia △, *Madag.* . 89 B8 18 54 S 48 21 E
Mantalingajan, Mt., *Phil.* 61 G3 8 55N 117 45 E
Mantare, *Tanzania* ... 86 C3   2 42 S 33 13 E
Manteca, *U.S.A.* 110 H5 37 48N 121 13W
Manteo, *U.S.A.* 115 H8 35 55N 75 40W
Mantes-la-Jolie, *France* 19 D8 48 58N   1 41 E
Manthani, *India* ..... 66 K11 18 40N 79 35 E
Manti, *U.S.A.* 108 G8 39 16N 111 38W
Mantiqueira, Serra da,
  Brazil .... 127 A7 22 0 S 44 0W
Manton, *U.S.A.* 114 C3 44 25N 85 24W
Mantorp, *Sweden* .... 11 F8 58 21N 15 20 E
Mántova, *Italy* ...... 40 C7 45 9N 10 48 E
Mänttä, *Finland* ..... 9 E21 62 3N 24 40 E
Mantua = Mántova, *Italy* 40 C7 45 9N 10 48 E
Manturovo, *Russia* ... 34 A7 58 23N 44 45 E
Manu, *Peru* .... 124 F4 12 10 S 70 51W
Manu →, *Peru* .... 124 F4 12 16 S 70 55W
Manu'a Is. =
  Amer. Samoa ..... 91 B14 14 13 S 169 35W
Manuel Alves →, *Brazil* 125 F9 11 19 S 48 28W
Manui, *Indonesia* .... 63 E6   3 35 S 123 5 E
Manukau, *N.Z.* ...... 91 G5 37 0 S 174 52 E
Manuripi →, *Bolivia* . 124 F5 11 6 S 67 36W
Many, *U.S.A.* 113 K8 31 34N 93 29W
Manyara, L., *Tanzania* . 86 C4   3 40 S 35 50 E
Manyas, *Turkey* ..... 45 F11 40 2N 27 59 E
Manyava, *Ukraine* ... 29 B9 48 39N 24 21 E
Manych →, *Russia* ... 35 G5 47 13N 40 40 E
Manych-Gudilo, Ozero,
  Russia .... 35 G6 46 24N 42 38 E
Manyonga →, *Tanzania* 86 C3   4 10 S 34 15 E
Manyoni, *Tanzania* ... 86 D3   5 45 S 34 55 E
Manzai, *Pakistan* .... 68 C4 32 12N 70 15 E
Manzala, Bahra el,
  Egypt .... 80 H7 31 10N 31 56 E
Manzanar △, *U.S.A.* . 110 J7 36 44N 119 5W
Manzanares, *Spain* ... 37 F7 39 2N   3 22W
Manzaneda, *Spain* ... 36 C3 42 12N   7 15W
Manzanillo, *Cuba* 120 B4 20 20N 77 31W
Manzanillo, *Mexico* .. 118 D4 19 0N 104 20W
Manzanillo, Pta.,
  Panama 120 E4   9 30N 79 40W
Manzano Mts., *U.S.A.* 109 J10 34 40N 106 20W
Manzarīyeh, *Iran* .... 71 C6 34 53N 50 50 E
Manzhouli, *China* .... 60 B6 49 35N 117 25 E
Manzini, *Swaziland* .. 89 D5 26 30 S 31 25 E
Mao, *Chad* .... 79 F9 14 4N 15 19 E
Maó, *Spain* .... 48 B11 39 53N 4 16 E
Maoke, Pegunungan,
  Indonesia .... 63 E9   3 40 S 137 30 E
Maolin, *China* ...... 57 C12 43 58N 123 30 E
Maoming, *China* ..... 59 G8 21 50N 110 54 E
Maopi T'ou, *China* ... 59 G13 21 56N 120 43 E
Maouri, Dallol →, *Niger* 83 C5 12 5N   3 32 E
Maoxian, *China* ..... 58 B4 31 41N 103 49 E
Mapam Yumco, *China* . 60 C3 30 45N 81 28 E
Mapastepec, *Mexico* .. 119 D6 15 26N 92 54W
Maphrao, Ko, *Thailand* 65 a   7 56N 98 26 E
Mapia, Kepulauan,
  Indonesia .... 63 D8   0 50N 134 20 E
Mapimí, *Mexico* 118 B4 25 50N 103 50W
Mapimí, Bolsón de,
  Mexico 118 B4 27 30N 104 15W
Maping, *China* ...... 59 B9 31 34N 113 32 E
Mapinga, *Tanzania* ... 86 D4   6 40 S 39 12 E
Mapinhane, *Mozam.* . 89 C6 22 20 S 35 0 E
Maple Creek, *Canada* . 103 D7 49 55N 109 29W
Maple Valley, *U.S.A.* . 110 C4 47 25N 122 3W

Mapleton, *U.S.A.* 108 D2 44 2N 123 52W
Mapuera →, *Brazil* .. 124 D7   1 5 S 57 2W
Mapulanguene, *Mozam.* 89 C5 24 59 S 32 6 E
Maputo, *Mozam.* ..... 89 D5 25 58 S 32 32 E
Maputo →, *Mozam.* .. 89 D5 25 58 S 32 32 E
Maputo □, *Mozam.* ... 89 D5 26 0 S 32 25 E
Maputo, B. de, *Mozam.* 89 D5 25 50 S 32 45 E
Maqiaohe, *China* .... 57 B16 44 40N 130 30 E
Maqnā, *Si. Arabia* ... 70 D2 28 25N 34 50 E
Maquan He =
  Brahmaputra →, *Asia* 69 H13 23 40N 90 35 E
Maqueda, *Spain* 36 E6 40 4N   4 22W
Maquela do Zombo,
  Angola .... 84 F3   6 0 S 15 15 E
Maquinchao, *Argentina* 128 E3 41 15 S 68 50W
Maquoketa, *U.S.A.* .. 112 D9 42 4N 90 40W
Mar, Serra do, *Brazil* . 127 B6 25 30 S 49 0W
Mar Chiquita, L.,
  Argentina .... 126 C3 30 40 S 62 50W
Mar del Plata, *Argentina* 126 D4 38 0 S 57 30W
Mar Menor, *Spain* ... 39 H4 37 40N   0 45W
Mara, *Tanzania* ...... 86 C3   1 30 S 34 32 E
Mara □, *Tanzania* .... 86 C3   1 45 S 34 20 E
Maraã, *Brazil* .... 124 D5   1 52 S 65 25W
Marabá, *Brazil* ...... 125 E9   5 20 S 49 5W
Maracá, I. de, *Brazil* . 125 C8   2 10N 50 30W
Maracaibo, *Venezuela* 124 A4 10 40N 71 37W
Maracaibo, L. de,
  Venezuela 124 B4   9 40N 71 30W
Maracaju, *Brazil* .... 127 A4 21 38 S 55 9W
Maracas Bay Village,
  Trin. & Tob. 125 K15 10 46N 61 28W
Maracay, *Venezuela* .. 124 A5 10 15N 67 28W
Maracena, *Spain* 37 H7 37 12N   3 38W
Maradi, *Niger* .... 83 C6 13 29N   7 20 E
Marāgheh, *Iran* ..... 70 B5 37 30N 46 12 E
Marāh, *Si. Arabia* ... 70 E5 25 0N 45 35 E
Marahoue →, *Ivory C.* 82 D3   8 0N   7 8W
Marais du Cotentin et du
  Bessin △, *France* .. 18 C5 49 10N   1 30W
Marais Poitevin, Val de
  Sèvre et Vendée △,
  France 20 B3 46 18N   0 35W
Marajó, I. de, *Brazil* .. 125 D9   1 0 S 49 30W
Marākand, *Iran* ..... 70 B5 38 51N 45 16 E
Marakele △, *S. Africa* 89 E4 32 14 S 27 27 E
Maralal, *Kenya* ...... 86 B4   1 0N 36 38 E
Maralinga, *Australia* .. 93 F5 30 13 S 131 32 E
Maramaraereğlisi,
  Turkey .... 45 F11 40 57N 27 57 E
Marambio, *Antarctica* . 5 C18 64 0 S 56 0W
Marampa, *S. Leone* .. 82 D2   8 45N 12 28W
Maramureş □, *Romania* 29 C9 47 45N 24 0 E
Maran, *Malaysia* ..... 65 L4   3 35N 102 45 E
Marana, *U.S.A.* 109 K8 32 27N 111 13W
Maranboy, *Australia* .. 92 B5 14 40 S 132 39 E
Maranchón, *Spain* ... 38 D2 41 6N   2 15W
Marand, *Iran* .... 70 B5 38 30N 45 45 E
Marang, *Malaysia* .... 65 K4   5 12N 103 13 E
Maranguape, *Brazil* .. 125 D11 3 55 S 38 50W
Maranhão = São Luís,
  Brazil .... 125 D10 2 39 S 44 15W
Maranhão □, *Brazil* .. 125 E9   5 0 S 46 0W
Marano, L. di, *Italy* .. 41 C10 45 44N 13 10 E
Maranoa →, *Australia* 95 D4 27 50 S 148 37 E
Marañón →, *Peru* .... 124 D4   4 30 S 73 35W
Marão, *Mozam.* ...... 89 C5 24 18 S 34 2 E
Maras =
  Kahramanmaraş,
  Turkey .... 70 B3 37 37N 36 53 E
Mărăşeşti, *Romania* .. 29 E12 45 52N 27 14 E
Maratea, *Italy* ...... 43 C8 39 59N 15 43 E
Marateca, *Portugal* .. 37 G2 38 34N   8 40W
Marathasa, *Cyprus* .. 49 E11 34 59N 32 51 E
Marathókambos, *Greece* 47 D8 37 43N 26 42 E
Marathon, *Australia* .. 94 C3 20 51 S 143 32 E
Marathon, *Canada* ... 104 C2 48 44N 86 23W
Marathón, *Greece* .... 46 C5 38 11N 23 58 E
Marathon, *N.Y., U.S.A.* 117 D8 42 27N 76 2W
Marathon, *Tex., U.S.A.* 113 K3 30 12N 103 15W
Marathóvouno, *Cyprus* 49 D12 35 13N 33 37 E
Maratua, *Indonesia* .. 63 D5   2 10N 118 35 E
Maraval, *Trin. & Tob.* 125 K15 10 43N 61 32W
Maravatío, *Mexico* ... 118 D4 19 51N 100 25W
Marawi City, *Phil.* .... 61 G6   8 0N 124 21 E
Marāwih, *U.A.E.* ..... 71 E7 24 18N 53 18 E
Marazliyivka, *Ukraine* 29 D15 46 38N 30 3 E
Marbella, *Spain* 37 J6 36 30N   4 57W
Marble Bar, *Australia* 92 D2 21 9 S 119 44 E
Marble Falls, *U.S.A.* . 113 K5 30 35N 98 16W
Marblehead, *U.S.A.* .. 117 D14 42 30N 70 51W
Marburg, *Germany* ... 24 E4 50 47N   8 46 E
Marcal →, *Hungary* .. 28 C2 47 41N 17 40 E
Marcali, *Hungary* .... 28 D2 46 35N 17 25 E
Marcaria, *Italy* ..... 40 C7 45 7N 10 32 E
Mărcăuţi, *Moldova* .. 29 B12 48 20N 27 14 E
March, *U.K.* .... 15 E8 52 33N   0 5 E
Marche, *France* ...... 20 B5 46 5N   1 20 E
Marche □, *Italy* ...... 41 E10 43 30N 13 15 E
Marche-en-Famenne,
  Belgium .... 17 D5 50 14N   5 19 E
Marchena, *Spain* 37 H5 37 18N   5 23W
Marches = Marche □,
  Italy .... 41 E10 43 30N 13 15 E
Marchesale □, *Italy* .. 43 D9 38 32N 16 13 E
Marciana Marina, *Italy* 40 F7 42 48N 10 12 E
Marcianise, *Italy* ..... 43 A7 41 2N 14 17 E
Marcigny, *France* .... 19 F11 46 17N   4 2 E
Marcillat-en-Combraille,
  France .... 19 F9 46 12N   2 38 E
Marck, *France* ...... 19 B8 50 57N   1 57 E
Marckolsheim, *France* 19 D14 48 10N   7 30 E
Marco, *U.S.A.* 115 N5 25 58N 81 44W
Marcos Juárez,
  Argentina .... 126 C3 32 42 S 62 5W
Mărculeşti, *Moldova* . 29 C12 47 52N 28 14 E
Marcus I. = Minami-
  Tori-Shima, *Pac. Oc.* 96 E7 24 20N 153 58 E
Marcus Necker Ridge,
  Pac. Oc. .... 96 F9 20 0N 175 0 E
Marcy, Mt., *U.S.A.* .. 117 B11 44 7N 73 56W
Mardan, *Pakistan* .... 68 B5 34 20N 72 0 E
Mardarivka, *Ukraine* . 29 C14 47 32N 29 44 E
Mardin, *Turkey* ...... 70 B4 37 20N 40 43 E
Maree, L., *U.K.* 13 D3 57 40N   5 26W
Mareeba, *Australia* ... 94 B4 16 59 S 145 28 E
Mareetsane, *S. Africa* 88 D4 26 9 S 25 25 E
Maremma, *Italy* ..... 41 F8 42 35N 11 10 E
Maremma □, *Italy* .... 41 F8 42 35N 11 8 E
Maréna, Kayes, *Mali* . 82 C2 14 36N 10 45W
Maréna, Koulikouro,
  Mali 82 C3 13 55N   7 20W
Marengo, *U.S.A.* 112 E8 41 48N 92 4W
Marennes, *France* 20 C2 45 49N   1 7W
Marerano, *Madag.* ... 89 C7 21 23 S 44 52 E

Maréttimo, *Italy* ..... 42 E5 37 58N 12 4 E
Mareuil, *France* ...... 20 C4 45 26N   0 29 E
Marfa, *U.S.A.* 113 K2 30 19N 104 1W
Marfa Pt., *Malta* ..... 49 D1 35 59N 14 19 E
Marganets = Marhanets,
  Ukraine .... 33 J8 47 40N 34 40 E
Margaret →, *Australia* 92 C4 18 9 S 125 41 E
Margaret Bay, *Canada* 102 C3 51 20N 127 35W
Margaret L., *Canada* . 102 B5 58 56N 115 25W
Margaret River,
  Australia .... 93 F2 33 57 S 115 4 E
Margarita, I. de,
  Venezuela 124 A6 11 0N 64 0W
Margarition, *Greece* .. 46 B2 39 22N 20 26 E
Margaritovo, *Russia* . 54 C7 43 25N 134 45 E
Margate, *S. Africa* ... 89 E5 30 50 S 30 20 E
Margate, *U.K.* .... 15 F9 51 23N   1 23 E
Margeride, Mts. de la,
  France .... 20 D7 44 43N   3 38 E
Margherita di Savóia,
  Italy .... 43 A9 41 22N 16 9 E
Margherita Pk., *Uganda* 86 B3   0 22N 29 51 E
Marghita, *Romania* ... 28 C7 47 22N 22 22 E
Margonin, *Poland* .... 31 F4 52 58N 17 5 E
Margosatubig, *Phil.* .. 61 H5   7 34N 123 10 E
Mārgow, Dasht-e,
  Afghan. .... 66 D3 30 40N 62 30 E
Marguerite, *Canada* .. 102 C4 52 30N 122 25W
Marhanets, *Ukraine* .. 33 J8 47 40N 34 40 E
Mari El □, *Russia* .... 34 B8 56 30N 48 0 E
Mari Indus, *Pakistan* . 68 C4 32 57N 71 34 E
Mari Republic = Mari
  El □, *Russia* ...... 34 B8 56 30N 48 0 E
María, Sa. de, *Spain* . 39 H2 37 39N   2 14W
María Elena, *Chile* ... 126 A2 22 18 S 69 40W
María Grande,
  Argentina .... 126 C4 31 45 S 59 55W
Maria I., *N. Terr.,
  Australia* .... 94 A2 14 52 S 135 45 E
Maria I., *Tas., Australia* 95 G4 42 35 S 148 0 E
Maria Island △,
  Australia .... 95 G4 42 38 S 148 5 E
Maria van Diemen, C.,
  N.Z. .... 91 F4 34 29 S 172 40 E
Mariager, *Denmark* .. 11 H3 56 40N   9 59 E
Mariager Fjord,
  Denmark .... 11 H4 56 42N 10 19 E
Mariakani, *Kenya* .... 86 C4   3 50 S 39 27 E
Mariala △, *Australia* . 95 D4 25 57 S 145 2 E
Marian, *Australia* .... 94 K6 21 9 S 148 57 E
Marian L., *Canada* ... 102 A5 63 0N 116 15W
Mariana Trench,
  Pac. Oc. .... 96 F6 13 0N 145 0 E
Marianao, *Cuba* 120 B3 23 8N 82 24W
Marianna, *Ark., U.S.A.* 113 H9 34 46N 90 46W
Marianna, *Fla., U.S.A.* 115 K3 30 46N 85 14W
Mariannelund, *Sweden* 11 G9 57 37N 15 35 E
Mariánské Lázně,
  Czech Rep. .... 26 B5 49 58N 12 41 E
Marias →, *U.S.A.* 108 C8 47 56N 110 30W
Mariato, Punta, *Panama* 120 E3   7 12N 80 52W
Mariazell, *Austria* ... 26 D8 47 47N 15 19 E
Maribo, *Denmark* .... 11 K5 54 48N 11 30 E
Maribor, *Slovenia* .... 41 B12 46 36N 15 40 E
Marico →, *Africa* .... 88 C4 23 35 S 26 57 E
Maricopa, *Ariz., U.S.A.* 109 K7 33 4N 112 3W
Maricopa, *Calif., U.S.A.* 111 K7 35 4N 119 24W
Marīdī, *Sudan* .... 81 G2 4 55N 29 25 E
Marīdī, Wadi →, *Sudan* 81 F2 6 15N 29 21 E
Marié →, *Brazil* ..... 124 D5   0 27 S 66 26W
Marie Byrd Land,
  Antarctica .... 5 D14 79 30 S 125 0W
Marie-Galante,
  Guadeloupe ...... 120 b 15 56N 61 16W
Mariecourt =
  Kangiqsujuaq, *Canada* 101 B12 61 30N 72 0W
Mariefred, *Sweden* ... 10 E11 59 15N 17 12 E
Mariehamn =
  Maarianhamina,
  Finland .... 9 F18 60 5N 19 55 E
Marieholm, *Sweden* .. 11 J7 55 53N 13 10 E
Mariembourg, *Belgium* 17 D4 50 6N   4 31 E
Marienbad = Mariánské
  Lázně, *Czech Rep.* . 26 B5 49 58N 12 41 E
Marienberg, *Germany* 24 E9 50 39N 13 9 E
Mariental, *Namibia* .. 88 C2 24 36 S 18 0 E
Marienville, *U.S.A.* .. 116 E5 41 28N 79 8W
Mariestad, *Sweden* ... 11 F7 58 43N 13 50 E
Marietta, *Ga., U.S.A.* 115 J3 33 57N 84 33W
Marietta, *Ohio, U.S.A.* 114 F5 39 25N 81 27W
Marieville, *Canada* ... 117 A11 45 26N 73 10W
Mariga →, *Nigeria* ... 83 C6   9 40N   5 55 E
Marihatag, *Phil.* ..... 61 G7   8 48N 126 18 E
Marijampolė, *Lithuania* 9 J20 54 33N 23 19 E
Marijampolės □,
  Lithuania .... 30 D10 54 34N 23 21 E
Marília, *Brazil* ...... 127 A6 22 13 S 50 0W
Marín, *Spain* 36 C2 42 23N   8 42W
Marina, *U.S.A.* 110 J5 36 41N 121 48W
Marinduque, *Phil.* ... 63 B6 13 25N 122 0 E
Marine City, *U.S.A.* .. 116 D2 42 43N 82 30W
Marineo, *Italy* ...... 42 E6 37 57N 13 25 E
Marinette, *U.S.A.* 114 C2 45 6N 87 38W
Maringá, *Brazil* ..... 127 A5 23 26 S 52 2W
Marinha Grande,
  Portugal 36 F2 39 45N   8 56W
Marino, *Italy* .... 41 G9 41 46N 12 39 E
Marion, *Ala., U.S.A.* . 115 J2 32 38N 87 19W
Marion, *Ill., U.S.A.* .. 113 G10 37 44N 88 56W
Marion, *Ind., U.S.A.* . 114 E3 40 32N 85 40W
Marion, *Iowa, U.S.A.* 112 D9 42 2N 91 36W
Marion, *Kans., U.S.A.* 112 F6 38 21N 97 1W
Marion, *N.C., U.S.A.* . 115 H5 35 41N 82 1W
Marion, *Ohio, U.S.A.* 114 E4 40 35N 83 8W
Marion, *S.C., U.S.A.* . 115 H6 34 11N 79 24W
Marion, *Va., U.S.A.* .. 115 G5 36 50N 81 31W
Marion, L., *U.S.A.* ... 115 J5 33 28N 80 10W
Mariposa, *U.S.A.* 110 H7 37 29N 119 58W
Mariscal Estigarribia,
  Paraguay .... 126 A3 22 3 S 60 40W
Maritime Alps =
  Maritimes, Alpes,
  Europe .... 21 D11 44 10N   7 10 E
Maritimes, Alpes,
  Europe .... 21 D11 44 10N   7 10 E
Maritsa = Évros →,
  Greece .... 73 B2 41 40N 26 34 E
Maritsá, *Greece* ..... 49 C10 36 22N 28 8 E
Mariupol, *Ukraine* ... 33 J9 47 5N 37 31 E
Marīvān, *Iran* .... 70 C5 35 30N 46 25 E
Marj 'Uyūn, *Lebanon* 74 B4 33 20N 35 35 E
Marka = Merca,
  Somali Rep. ...... 75 G3   1 48N 44 50 E

Marka, *Si. Arabia* .... 80 D5 18 14N 41 19 E
Markam, *China* ...... 58 C2 29 42N 98 38 E
Markazī □, *Iran* ..... 71 C6 35 0N 49 30 E
Markdale, *Canada* ... 116 B4 44 19N 80 39W
Marked Tree, *U.S.A.* . 113 H9 35 32N 90 25W
Markelsdorfer Huk,
  Germany .... 24 A7 54 33N 11 4 E
Market Drayton, *U.K.* 14 E5 52 54N   2 29W
Market Harborough,
  U.K. 15 E7 52 29N   0 55W
Market Rasen, *U.K.* .. 14 D7 53 24N   0 20W
Markham, *Canada* ... 116 C5 43 52N 79 16W
Markham, Mt.,
  Antarctica .... 5 E11 83 0 S 164 0 E
Marki, *Poland* ...... 31 F8 52 20N 21 2 E
Märkische Schweiz △,
  Germany .... 24 C9 52 32N 14 3 E
Markkleeberg, *Germany* 24 D8 51 16N 12 23 E
Markleeville, *U.S.A.* . 110 G7 38 42N 119 47W
Markoupoulon, *Greece* 46 D5 37 53N 23 57 E
Markovac, *Serbia & M.* 44 B5 44 14N 21 7 E
Markovo, *Russia* .... 53 C17 64 40N 170 24 E
Markoye, *Burkina Faso* 83 C5 14 39N   0 2 E
Marks, *Russia* ...... 34 E8 51 45N 46 50 E
Marksville, *U.S.A.* ... 113 K8 31 8N 92 4W
Markt Schwaben,
  Germany .... 25 G7 48 11N 11 52 E
Marktoberdorf,
  Germany .... 25 H6 47 45N 10 37 E
Marktredwitz, *Germany* 25 E8 50 1N 12 5 E
Marl, *Germany* ...... 24 D3 51 39N   7 4 E
Marla, *Australia* ..... 95 D1 27 19 S 133 33 E
Marlbank, *Canada* ... 116 B7 44 26N 77 6W
Marlboro, *Mass., U.S.A.* 117 D13 42 19N 71 33W
Marlboro, *N.Y., U.S.A.* 117 E11 41 36N 73 59W
Marlborough, *Australia* 94 C4 22 46 S 149 52 E
Marlborough, *U.K.* ... 15 F6 51 25N   1 43W
Marlborough Downs,
  U.K. 15 F6 51 27N   1 53W
Marle, *France* ...... 19 C10 49 43N   3 47 E
Marlin, *U.S.A.* 113 K6 31 18N 96 54W
Marlow, *Germany* .... 24 A8 54 9N 12 33 E
Marlow, *U.K.* 15 F7 51 34N   0 46W
Marlow, *U.S.A.* 113 H6 34 39N 97 58W
Marmagao, *India* .... 66 M8 15 25N 73 56 E
Marmande, *France* ... 20 D4 44 30N   0 10 E
Marmara, *Turkey* .... 45 F11 40 35N 27 34 E
Marmara, Sea of =
  Marmara Denizi,
  Turkey .... 45 F12 40 45N 28 15 E
Marmara Denizi, *Turkey* 45 F12 40 45N 28 15 E
Marmara Gölü, *Turkey* 47 C10 38 37N 28 2 E
Marmaris, *Turkey* ... 47 E10 36 50N 28 14 E
Marmara Limanı,
  Turkey .... 47 E10 36 50N 28 19 E
Marmion, Mt., *Australia* 93 E2 29 16 S 119 50 E
Marmion L., *Canada* . 104 C1 48 55N 91 20W
Marmolada, Mte., *Italy* 41 B8 46 26N 11 51 E
Marmolejo, *Spain* ... 37 G6 38 3N   4 13W
Marmora, *Canada* ... 116 B7 44 28N 77 41W
Mármora, La, *Italy* .. 42 C2 39 59N   9 20 E
Marnay, *France* ..... 19 E12 47 16N   5 48 E
Marne □, *France* .... 19 D11 48 50N   4 10 E
Marne →, *France* .... 19 D9 48 48N   2 24 E
Marneuli, *Georgia* ... 35 K7 41 30N 44 48 E
Maroala, *Madag.* .... 89 B8 15 23 S 47 59 E
Maroantsetra, *Madag.* 89 B8 15 26 S 49 44 E
Maroelaboom, *Namibia* 88 B2 19 15 S 18 53 E
Marofandilia, *Madag.* 89 C7 20 7 S 44 34 E
Marojejy △, *Madag.* . 89 A8 14 26 S 49 21 E
Marolambo, *Madag.* . 89 C8 20 2 S 48 7 E
Maromandia, *Madag.* 89 A8 14 13 S 48 5 E
Maromokotro, *Madag.* 89 A8 14 0 S 49 12 E
Marondera, *Zimbabwe* 87 F3 18 5 S 31 42 E
Maroni →, *Fr. Guiana* 125 B8   5 30N 54 0W
Marónia, *Greece* ..... 45 F9 40 53N 25 30 E
Maronne →, *France* .. 20 C5 45 5N   1 56 E
Maroochydore, *Australia* 95 D5 26 29 S 153 5 E
Maroona, *Australia* .. 95 F3 37 27 S 142 54 E
Maros →, *Hungary* .. 28 D5 46 15N 20 13 E
Marosakoa, *Madag.* . 89 B8 15 26 S 46 38 E
Maroseranana, *Madag.* 89 B8 18 32 S 48 51 E
Maróstica, *Italy* ..... 41 C8 45 44N 11 40 E
Marotandrano, *Madag.* 89 B8 16 10 S 48 50 E
Marotaolano, *Madag.* 89 A8 12 47 S 49 15 E
Maroua, *Cameroon* .. 83 C7 10 40N 14 20 E
Marovato, *Madag.* ... 89 B8 15 48 S 48 5 E
Marovoay, *Madag.* .. 89 B8 16 6 S 46 39 E
Marquard, S. *Africa* . 88 D4 28 40 S 27 28 E
Marquesas Is. =
  Marquises, Îs.,
  French Polynesia .. 97 H14 9 30 S 140 0W
Marquette, *U.S.A.* ... 114 B2 46 33N 87 24W
Marquis, *St. Lucia* ... 121 f 14 2N 60 54W
Marquise, *France* .... 19 B8 50 50N   1 40 E
Marquises, Îs.,
  French Polynesia .. 97 H14 9 30 S 140 0W
Marra, Djebel, *Sudan* 79 F10 13 10N 24 22 E
Marra, Gebel, *Sudan* 81 F2 7 20N 27 35 E
Marracuene, *Mozam.* 89 D5 25 45 S 32 35 E
Marradi, *Italy* ...... 41 D8 44 4N 11 37 E
Marrakech, *Morocco* . 78 B4 31 9N   8 0W
Marratxi, *Spain* ..... 38 F7 39 39N   2 48 E
Marrawah, *Australia* . 95 G3 40 55 S 144 42 E
Marree, *Australia* .... 95 D2 29 39 S 138 1 E
Marrero, *U.S.A.* 113 L9 29 54N 90 6W
Marrimane, *Mozam.* . 89 C5 22 58 S 33 34 E
Marromeu, *Mozam.* .. 89 B6 18 15 S 36 25 E
Marromeu △, *Mozam.* 89 B6 19 0 S 36 0 E
Marroquí, Punta, *Spain* 37 K5 36 0N   5 37W
Marrowie Cr. →,
  Australia .... 95 E4 33 23 S 145 40 E
Marrubane, *Mozam.* . 89 F4 18 0 S 37 0 E
Marrúbiu, *Italy* ..... 42 C1 39 46N   8 35 E
Marrupa, *Mozam.* ... 87 E4 13 8 S 37 30 E
Mars Hill, *U.S.A.* ... 115 B12 46 31N 67 52W
Marsá 'Alam, *Egypt* . 80 B3 25 5N 34 54 E
Marsá Matrûḥ, *Egypt* 80 A2 31 19N 27 9 E
Marsá Sha'b, *Sudan* . 80 C4 21 5N 36 36 E
Marsabit, *Kenya* ..... 86 B4   2 18N 38 0 E
Marsabit △, *Kenya* ... 86 B4   2 15N 38 10 E
Marsala, *Italy* .... 42 E5 37 48N 12 26 E
Marsalforn, *Malta* ... 49 C1 36 4N 14 16 E
Mârşani, *Romania* ... 29 F9 44 1N 24 1 E
Marsberg, *Germany* .. 24 D4 51 28N   8 52 E
Marsciano, *Italy* ..... 41 F9 42 54N 12 20 E
Marsden, *Australia* .. 95 E4 33 47 S 147 32 E
Marseillan, *France* ... 20 E7 43 21N   3 32 E
Marseille, *France* .... 21 E9 43 18N   5 23 E
Marseille ✈ (MRS),
  France .... 21 E9 43 26N   5 14 E
Marseilles = Marseille,
  France .... 21 E9 43 18N   5 23 E

Marshall, *Mich., U.S.A.* 114 D3 42 16N 84 58W
Marshall, *Minn., U.S.A.* 112 C7 44 25N 95 45W
Marshall, *Mo., U.S.A.* 112 F8 39 7N 93 12W
Marshall, *Tex., U.S.A.* 113 J7 32 33N 94 23W
Marshall →, *Australia* 94 C2 22 59 S 136 59 E
Marshall Is. ■, *Pac. Oc.* 96 G9   9 0N 171 0 E
Marshalltown, *U.S.A.* 112 D8 42 3N 92 55W
Marshbrook, *Zimbabwe* 89 B5 18 33 S 31 9 E
Marshfield, *Mo., U.S.A.* 113 G8 37 15N 92 54W
Marshfield, *Vt., U.S.A.* 117 B12 44 20N 72 24W
Marshfield, *Wis., U.S.A.* 112 C9 44 40N 90 10W
Marshūn, *Iran* .... 71 B6 36 19N 49 23 E
Mársico Nuovo, *Italy* 43 B8 40 25N 15 44 E
Märsta, *Sweden* ..... 10 E11 59 37N 17 52 E
Marstal, *Denmark* ... 11 K4 54 51N 10 30 E
Marstrand, *Sweden* .. 11 G5 57 53N 11 35 E
Mart, *U.S.A.* 113 K6 31 33N 96 50W
Marta →, *Italy* ...... 41 F8 42 14N 11 42 E
Martaban, *Burma* .... 67 L20 16 30N 97 35 E
Martaban, G. of, *Burma* 67 L20 16 5N 96 30 E
Martano, *Italy* ...... 43 B11 40 12N 18 18 E
Martapura, *Kalimantan,
  Indonesia* .... 62 E4 3 22 S 114 47 E
Martapura, *Sumatera,
  Indonesia* .... 62 E2 4 19 S 104 22 E
Marte, *Italy* .... 83 C7 12 23N 13 46 E
Martel, *France* ...... 20 D5 44 57N   1 37 E
Martelange, *Belgium* . 17 E5 49 49N   5 43 E
Martellago, *Italy* .... 41 C9 45 33N 12 9 E
Martés, Sierra, *Spain* 39 F4 39 20N   1 0W
Martfű, *Hungary* .... 28 C5 47 1N 20 17 E
Martha's Vineyard,
  U.S.A. 117 E14 41 25N 70 38W
Martigné-Ferchaud,
  France 18 E5 47 50N   1 20W
Martigny, *Switz.* .... 25 J3 46 6N   7 3 E
Martigues, *France* ... 21 E9 43 24N   5 4 E
Martin, *Slovak Rep.* . 27 B11 49 6N 18 58 E
Martin, *S. Dak., U.S.A.* 112 D4 43 11N 101 44W
Martin, *Tenn., U.S.A.* 113 G10 36 21N 88 51W
Martín →, *Spain* 38 D4 41 18N   0 19W
Martin, L., *U.S.A.* ... 115 J3 32 41N 85 55W
Martina Franca, *Italy* 43 B10 40 42N 17 20 E
Martinborough, *N.Z.* 91 J5 41 14 S 175 29 E
Martinez, *Calif., U.S.A.* 110 G4 38 1N 122 8W
Martinez, *Ga., U.S.A.* 115 J4 33 31N 82 4W
Martinique ☑, *W. Indies* 120 c 14 40N 61 0W
Martinique Passage,
  W. Indies 121 C7 15 15N 61 0W
Martínon, *Greece* .... 46 C5 38 35N 23 12 E
Martinópolis, *Brazil* . 127 A5 22 11 S 51 12W
Martins Ferry, *U.S.A.* 116 F4 40 6N 80 44W
Martins Bay, *Barbados* 121 g 13 12N .59 29W
Martinsberg, *Austria* 26 C8 48 22N 15 9 E
Martinsburg, *Pa., U.S.A.* 116 F6 40 19N 78 20W
Martinsburg, *W. Va.,
  U.S.A.* 114 F7 39 27N 77 58W
Martinsicuro, *Italy* .. 41 F10 42 54N 13 54 E
Martinsville, *Ind., U.S.A.* 114 F2 39 26N 86 25W
Martinsville, *Va., U.S.A.* 115 G6 36 41N 79 52W
Marton, *N.Z.* .... 91 J5 40 4 S 175 23 E
Martorell, *Spain* .... 38 D6 41 28N   1 56 E
Martos, *Spain* 37 H7 37 44N   3 58W
Martuni, *Armenia* ... 35 K7 40 8N 45 20 E
Maru, *Nigeria* ...... 83 C6 12 22N   6 22 E
Marudi, *Malaysia* ... 62 D4 4 11N 114 19 E
Maruf, *Afghan.* ...... 66 D5 31 30N 67 6 E
Marugame, *Japan* ... 55 G6 34 15N 133 40 E
Marunga, *Angola* ... 88 B3 17 28 S 20 2 E
Marungu, Mts.,
  *Dem. Rep. of
  the Congo* .... 86 D3   7 30 S 30 0 E
Marv Dasht, *Iran* .... 71 D7 29 50N 52 40 E
Marvast, *Iran* .... 71 D7 30 30N 54 15 E
Marvejols, *France* ... 20 D7 44 33N   3 19 E
Marvel Loch, *Australia* 93 F2 31 28 S 119 29 E
Marwar, *India* ...... 68 G5 25 43N 73 45 E
Mary, *Turkmenistan* .. 52 F7 37 40N 61 50 E
Maryborough = Port
  Laoise, *Ireland* 12 C4 53 2N   7 18W
Maryborough, *Queens.,
  Australia* .... 95 D5 25 31 S 152 37 E
Maryborough, *Vic.,
  Australia* .... 95 F3 37 0 S 143 44 E
Maryfield, *Canada* ... 103 D8 49 50N 101 35W
Maryland □, *U.S.A.* . 114 F7 39 0N 76 30W
Maryland Junction,
  Zimbabwe .... 87 F3 17 45 S 30 31 E
Maryport, *U.K.* 14 C4 54 44N   3 28W
Mary's Harbour, *Canada* 105 B8 52 18N 55 51W
Marystown, *Canada* . 105 C8 47 10N 55 10W
Marysville, *Canada* .. 102 D5 49 35N 116 0W
Marysville, *Calif., U.S.A.* 110 F5 39 9N 121 35W
Marysville, *Kans., U.S.A.* 112 F6 39 51N 96 39W
Marysville, *Mich., U.S.A.* 116 D2 42 54N 82 29W
Marysville, *Ohio, U.S.A.* 114 E4 40 14N 83 22W
Marysville, *Wash.,
  U.S.A.* 110 B4 48 3N 122 11W
Maryville, *Mo., U.S.A.* 112 E7 40 21N 94 52W
Maryville, *Tenn., U.S.A.* 115 H4 35 46N 83 58W
Marzūq, *Libya* ...... 79 C8 25 53N 13 57 E
Masahunga, *Tanzania* 86 C3   2 6 S 33 8 E
Masai, *Malaysia* ..... 65 d   1 29N 103 53 E
Masai Mara △, *Kenya* 86 C4   1 25 S   35 5 E
Masai Steppe, *Tanzania* 86 C4   4 30 S 36 30 E
Masaka, *Uganda* .... 86 C3   0 21 S 31 45 E
Masalembo, Kepulauan,
  Indonesia .... 62 F4 5 35 S 114 30 E
Masalima, Kepulauan,
  Indonesia .... 62 F5   5 4 S 117 5 E
Masallı, *Azerbaijan* .. 73 C13 39 3N 48 40 E
Masamba, *Indonesia* 63 E6 2 30 S 120 15 E
Masan, *S. Korea* .... 57 G15 35 11N 128 32 E
Masandam, Ra's, *Oman* 71 E8 26 30N 56 30 E
Masasi, *Tanzania* ... 87 E4 10 45 S 38 52 E
Masaya, *Nic.* 120 D2 12 0N 86 7W
Masba, *Nigeria* ..... 83 C7 11 35N 13 1 E
Masbate, *Phil.* ...... 61 E5 12 21N 123 36 E
Máscali, *Italy* .... 43 E8 37 45N 15 12 E
Mascara, *Algeria* .... 78 A6 35 26N   0 6 E
Mascota, *Mexico* 118 C4 20 30N 104 50W
Masela, *Indonesia* ... 63 F7 8 9 S 129 51 E
Maseru, *Lesotho* .... 88 D4 29 18 S 27 30 E
Mashaba, *Zimbabwe* 87 G3 20 2 S 30 6 E
Mashábih, *Si. Arabia* 70 E3 25 35N 36 30 E
Mashan, *China* ...... 58 F7 23 40N 108 11 E
Mashhad, *Iran* ...... 71 B8 36 20N 59 35 E
Mashi, *Nigeria* ...... 83 C6 13 0N   7 54 E
Mashīz, *Iran* .... 71 D8 29 56N 56 37 E
Mashki Chāh, *Pakistan* 66 E3 29 5N 62 30 E
Mashonaland,
  Zimbabwe .... 85 H6 16 30 S 31 0 E

Mashonaland Central □,
  Zimbabwe ...... **89 B5** 17 30 S 31 0 E
Mashonaland East □,
  Zimbabwe ...... **89 B5** 18 0 S 32 0 E
Mashonaland West □,
  Zimbabwe ...... **89 B4** 17 30 S 29 30 E
Mashrakh, India ..... **69 F11** 26 7N 84 48 E
Mashtaga = Maştağa,
  Azerbaijan ...... **35 K10** 40 35N 49 57 E
Masindi, Uganda ...... **86 B3** 1 40N 31 43 E
Masindi Port, Uganda . **86 B3** 1 43N 32 2 E
Maşīrah, Oman ...... **75 C6** 21 0N 58 50 E
Maşīrah, Khalīj, Oman **75 C6** 20 10N 58 10 E
Masisi, Dem. Rep. of
  the Congo ...... **86 C2** 1 23 S 28 49 E
Masjed Soleyman, Iran **71 D6** 31 55N 49 18 E
Mask, L., Ireland **12 C2** 53 36N 9 22W
Maskin, Oman ...... **71 F8** 23 30N 56 50 E
Maslen Nos, Bulgaria . **45 D11** 42 18N 27 48 E
Maslinica, Croatia ..... **41 E13** 43 24N 16 13 E
Masnou = El Masnou,
  Spain ...... **38 D7** 41 28N 2 20 E
Masoala, Madag. ...... **89 B9** 15 30 S 50 12 E
Masoala, Tanjon'i,
  Madag. ...... **89 B9** 15 59 S 50 13 E
Masoarivo, Madag. ..... **89 B7** 19 3 S 44 19 E
Masohi = Amahai,
  Indonesia ...... **63 E7** 3 20 S 128 55 E
Masomeloka, Madag. .. **89 C8** 20 17 S 48 37 E
Mason, Nev., U.S.A. ... **110 G7** 38 56N 119 8W
Mason, Tex., U.S.A. ... **113 K5** 30 45N 99 14W
Mason City, U.S.A. ... **112 D8** 43 9N 93 12W
Maspalomas, Canary Is. **48 G4** 27 46N 15 35W
Maspalomas, Pta.,
  Canary Is. **48 G4** 27 43N 15 36W
Masqaţ, Oman ...... **75 C6** 23 37N 58 36 E
Massa, Italy ...... **40 D7** 44 1N 10 9 E
Massa Marittima, Italy . **40 E7** 43 3N 10 52 E
Massachusetts □, U.S.A. **117 D13** 42 30N 72 0W
Massachusetts B., U.S.A. **117 D14** 42 20N 70 50W
Massafra, Italy ...... **43 B10** 40 35N 17 7 E
Massakory, Chad ..... **79 F9** 13 0N 15 49 E
Massanella, Spain ..... **48 B9** 39 48N 2 51 E
Massangena, Mozam. .. **89 C5** 21 34 S 33 0 E
Massango, Angola ..... **84 F3** 8 2 S 16 21 E
Massat, France ...... **20 F5** 42 53N 1 21 E
Massawa = Mitsiwa,
  Eritrea ...... **81 D4** 15 35N 39 25 E
Massena, U.S.A. **117 B10** 44 56N 74 54W
Masséna, Chad ...... **79 F9** 11 21N 16 9 E
Masset, Canada **102 C2** 54 2N 132 10W
Masseube, France ..... **20 E4** 43 25N 0 34 E
Massiac, France ...... **20 C7** 45 15N 3 11 E
Massiah Street,
  Barbados ...... **121 g** 13 9N 59 29W
Massif Central, France . **20 D7** 44 55N 3 0 E
Massif des Bauges △,
  France ...... **19 G13** 45 40N 6 10 E
Massigui, Mali **82 C3** 11 48N 6 50W
Massillon, U.S.A. **116 F3** 40 48N 81 32W
Massinga, Mozam. ..... **89 C6** 23 15 S 35 22 E
Massingir, Mozam. ..... **89 C5** 23 51 S 32 4 E
Masson-Angers, Canada **117 A9** 45 32N 75 25W
Masson I., Antarctica . **5 C7** 66 10 S 93 20 E
Maştağa, Azerbaijan .. **35 K10** 40 35N 49 57 E
Mastanli =
  Momchilgrad,
  Bulgaria ...... **45 E9** 41 33N 25 23 E
Masterton, N.Z. ...... **91 J5** 40 56 S 175 39 E
Mastic, U.S.A. **117 F12** 40 47N 72 54W
Mastuj, Pakistan ..... **69 A5** 36 20N 72 36 E
Mastung, Pakistan .... **66 E5** 29 50N 66 56 E
Mastūrah, Si. Arabia .. **80 C4** 23 7N 38 52 E
Masty, Belarus ...... **32 F3** 53 27N 24 38 E
Masuda, Japan ...... **55 G5** 34 40N 131 51 E
Masvingo, Zimbabwe .. **87 G3** 20 8 S 30 49 E
Masvingo □, Zimbabwe **87 G3** 21 0 S 31 30 E
Maswa □, Tanzania ... **86 C3** 2 58 S 34 19 E
Maşyāf, Syria ...... **70 C3** 35 4N 36 20 E
Maszewo, Poland ..... **30 E2** 53 29N 15 3 E
Mat →, Albania ...... **44 E3** 41 40N 19 35 E
Matabeleland,
  Zimbabwe ...... **85 H5** 18 0 S 27 0 E
Matabeleland North □,
  Zimbabwe ...... **87 F2** 19 0 S 28 0 E
Matabeleland South □,
  Zimbabwe ...... **87 G2** 21 0 S 29 0 E
Matachel →, Spain ... **37 G4** 38 50N 6 17W
Matachewan, Canada .. **104 C3** 47 56N 80 39W
Matadi, Dem. Rep. of
  the Congo ...... **84 F2** 5 52 S 13 31 E
Matagalpa, Nic. **120 D2** 13 0N 85 58W
Matagami, Canada ... **104 C4** 49 45N 77 34W
Matagami, L., Canada . **104 C4** 49 50N 77 40W
Matagorda B., U.S.A. . **113 L6** 28 40N 96 0W
Matagorda I., U.S.A. .. **113 L6** 28 15N 96 30W
Matak, Indonesia ..... **62 D3** 3 18N 106 16 E
Mátala, Greece ...... **49 E6** 34 59N 24 45 E
Matam, Senegal **82 B2** 15 34N 13 17W
Matameye, Niger ..... **83 C6** 13 26N 8 28 E
Matamoros, Campeche,
  Mexico **119 D6** 18 50N 90 50W
Matamoros, Coahuila,
  Mexico **118 B4** 25 33N 103 15W
Matamoros, Tamaulipas,
  Mexico **119 B5** 25 50N 97 30W
Ma'tan as Sarra, Libya **79 D10** 21 45N 22 0 E
Matandu →, Tanzania **87 D3** 8 45 S 34 19 E
Matane, Canada **105 C6** 48 50N 67 33W
Matang, China ...... **58 F5** 23 30N 104 7 E
Matankari, Niger ..... **83 C5** 13 46N 4 1 E
Matanomadh, India ... **68 H3** 23 33N 68 57 E
Matanzas, Cuba **120 B3** 23 0N 81 40W
Matapa, Botswana .... **88 C3** 23 11 S 24 39 E
Matapan, C. = Taínaron,
  Ákra, Greece ...... **46 E4** 36 22N 22 27 E
Matapédia, Canada ... **105 C6** 48 0N 66 59W
Matapo = Matapo △,
  Zimbabwe ...... **87 G2** 20 36 S 28 20 E
Matara, Sri Lanka .... **66 S12** 5 58N 80 30 E
Mataram, Indonesia ... **63 K19** 8 35 S 116 7 E
Matarani, Peru ...... **124 D3** 14 55 S 72 10W
Mataranka, Australia . **92 B5** 14 55 S 133 4 E
Matarma, Râs, Egypt . **74 E1** 30 27N 32 44 E
Mataró, Spain ...... **38 D7** 41 32N 2 29 E
Matarraña →, Spain . **38 D5** 41 14N 0 22 E
Mataruška Banja,
  Serbia & M. ...... **44 C4** 43 40N 20 40 E
Matatiele, S. Africa ... **89 E4** 30 20 S 28 49 E
Mataura, N.Z. ...... **91 M2** 46 11 S 168 51 E
Matehuala, Mexico **118 C4** 23 40N 100 40W
Mateke Hills, Zimbabwe **87 G3** 21 48 S 31 0 E
Matelot, Trin. & Tob. . **125 K15** 10 50N 61 7W
Matera, Italy ...... **43 B9** 40 40N 16 36 E
Matese △, Italy ...... **43 A7** 41 25N 14 23 E
Matese, Monti del, Italy **43 A7** 41 30N 14 22 E
Mátészalka, Hungary . **28 C7** 47 58N 22 20 E

Matetsi, Zimbabwe .... **87 F2** 18 12 S 26 0 E
Matfors, Sweden ...... **10 B11** 62 21N 17 2 E
Matha, France **20 C3** 45 52N 0 20W
Matheniko △, Uganda . **86 B3** 2 49N 34 27 E
Mathis, U.S.A. **113 L6** 28 6N 97 50W
Mathráki, Greece ..... **49 A3** 39 48N 19 31 E
Mathura, India ...... **68 F7** 27 30N 77 40 E
Mati, Phil. ...... **61 H7** 6 55N 126 15 E
Matiakoali,
  Burkina Faso ...... **83 C5** 12 28N 1 2 E
Matiali, India ...... **69 F13** 26 56N 88 49 E
Matías Romero, Mexico **119 D5** 16 53N 95 2W
Matibane, Mozam. .... **87 E5** 14 49 S 40 45 E
Matiri Ra., N.Z. ..... **91 J4** 41 38 S 172 20 E
Matjiesfontein, S. Africa **88 E3** 33 14 S 20 35 E
Matla →, India ...... **69 J13** 21 40N 88 40 E
Matlamanyane,
  Botswana ...... **88 B4** 19 33 S 25 57 E
Matli, Pakistan ...... **68 G3** 25 2N 68 39 E
Matlock, U.K. **14 D6** 53 9N 1 33W
Matna, Sudan ...... **81 E4** 13 49N 35 10 E
Mato Grosso □, Brazil **125 F8** 14 0 S 55 0W
Mato Grosso, Planalto
  do, Brazil ...... **125 G8** 15 0 S 55 0W
Mato Grosso do Sul □,
  Brazil ...... **125 G8** 18 0 S 55 0W
Matobo = Matapo △,
  Zimbabwe ...... **87 G2** 20 36 S 28 20 E
Matochkin Shar, Russia **52 B6** 73 10N 56 40 E
Matopo Hills, Zimbabwe **87 G2** 20 36 S 28 20 E
Matopos, Zimbabwe ... **87 G2** 20 20 S 28 29 E
Matosinhos, Portugal . **36 D2** 41 11N 8 42W
Matour, France ...... **19 F11** 46 19N 4 29 E
Matroosberg, S. Africa . **88 E2** 33 23 S 19 40 E
Matsena, Nigeria ..... **83 C7** 13 5N 10 5 E
Matsesta, Russia ..... **35 J4** 43 34N 39 51 E
Matsu Tao, Taiwan ... **59 E13** 26 19N 119 56 E
Matsue, Japan ...... **55 G6** 35 25N 133 10 E
Matsum, Ko, Thailand . **65 b** 9 22N 99 59 E
Matsumae, Japan ..... **54 D10** 41 26N 140 7 E
Matsumoto, Japan .... **55 F9** 36 15N 138 0 E
Matsusaka, Japan .... **55 G8** 34 34N 136 32 E
Matsuura, Japan ..... **55 H4** 33 20N 129 49 E
Matsuyama, Japan .... **55 H6** 33 45N 132 45 E
Mattagami →, Canada **104 B3** 50 43N 81 29W
Mattancheri, India ... **66 Q10** 9 50N 76 15 E
Mattawa, Canada **104 C4** 46 20N 78 45W
Matterhorn, Switz. ... **25 K3** 45 58N 7 39 E
Mattersburg, Austria . **27 D9** 47 44N 16 24 E
Matthew Town,
  Bahamas **121 B5** 20 57N 73 40W
Matthew's Ridge,
  Guyana **124 B6** 7 37N 60 10W
Mattice, Canada **104 C3** 49 40N 83 20W
Mattituck, U.S.A. **117 F12** 40 59N 72 32W
Mattō, Japan ...... **55 F8** 36 31N 136 34 E
Mattoon, U.S.A. **114 F1** 39 29N 88 23W
Matuba, Mozam. ..... **89 C5** 24 28 S 32 49 E
Matucana, Peru ...... **124 F3** 11 55 S 76 25W
Matūn = Khowst,
  Afghan. ...... **68 C3** 33 22N 69 58 E
Matveyev Kurgan,
  Russia ...... **33 J10** 47 35N 38 57 E
Matxitxako, C., Spain . **38 B2** 43 28N 2 47W
Mau, Mad. P., India .. **69 F8** 26 17N 78 41 E
Mau, Ut. P., India ... **69 G10** 25 56N 83 33 E
Mau, Ut. P., India ... **69 G9** 25 17N 81 23 E
Mau Escarpment, Kenya **86 C4** 0 40 S 36 0 E
Mau Ranipur, India ... **69 G8** 25 16N 79 8 E
Maubeuge, France ... **19 B10** 50 17N 3 57 E
Maubourguet, France . **20 E4** 43 29N 0 1 E
Maud, Pt., Australia .. **92 D1** 23 6 S 113 45 E
Maude, Australia ..... **95 E3** 34 29 S 144 18 E
Maudin Sun, Burma .. **67 M19** 16 0N 94 30 E
Maués, Brazil ...... **124 D7** 3 20 S 57 45W
Mauganj, India ...... **69 G12** 24 50N 81 55 E
Maughold Hd., U.K. .. **14 C3** 54 18N 4 18W
Mauguio, France ..... **20 E7** 43 37N 4 1 E
Maui, U.S.A. **106 H16** 20 48N 156 20W
Maulamyaing =
  Moulmein, Burma .. **67 L20** 16 30N 97 40 E
Maule □, Chile ...... **126 D1** 36 5 S 72 30W
Mauléon-Licharre,
  France **20 E3** 43 14N 0 54W
Maumee, U.S.A. **114 E4** 41 34N 83 39W
Maumee →, U.S.A. ... **114 E4** 41 42N 83 28W
Maumere, Indonesia .. **63 F6** 8 38 S 122 13 E
Maun, Botswana ...... **88 C3** 20 0 S 23 26 E
Mauna Kea, U.S.A. ... **106 J17** 19 50N 155 28W
Mauna Loa, U.S.A. ... **106 J17** 19 30N 155 35W
Maungmagan Kyunzu,
  Burma ...... **64 E1** 14 0N 97 48 E
Maupin, U.S.A. **108 D3** 45 11N 121 5W
Maure-de-Bretagne,
  France **18 E5** 47 53N 1 58W
Maurepas, L., U.S.A. . **113 K9** 30 15N 90 30W
Maures, France ...... **21 E10** 43 15N 6 15 E
Mauriac, France ..... **20 C6** 45 13N 2 19 E
Maurice, L., Australia . **93 E5** 29 30 S 131 0 E
Mauricie △, Canada .. **104 C5** 46 45N 73 0W
Maurienne, France ... **21 C10** 45 13N 6 30 E
Mauritania ■, Africa . **78 E3** 20 50N 10 0W
Mauritius ■, Ind. Oc. **77 J9** 20 0 S 57 0 E
Mauron, France **18 D4** 48 9N 2 18W
Maurs, France ...... **20 D6** 44 43N 2 12 E
Mauston, U.S.A. **112 D9** 43 48N 90 5W
Mauterndorf, Austria . **26 D6** 47 9N 13 40 E
Mauthen, Austria ..... **26 E6** 46 40N 13 0 E
Mauvezin, France .... **20 E4** 43 44N 0 53 E
Mauzé-sur-le-Mignon,
  France **20 B3** 46 12N 0 41W
Mavli, India ...... **68 G5** 24 45N 73 55 E
Mavrovë, Albania .... **44 F3** 40 26N 19 32 E
Mavrovo △, Macedonia **44 E4** 41 40N 20 45 E
Mavuradonha Mts.,
  Zimbabwe ...... **87 F3** 16 30 S 31 30 E
Mawa, Dem. Rep. of
  the Congo ...... **86 B2** 2 45N 26 40 E
Mawai, India ...... **69 H9** 22 30N 81 4 E
Mawana, India ...... **68 E7** 29 6N 77 58 E
Mawand, Pakistan .... **68 E3** 29 33N 68 38 E
Mawk Mai, Burma ... **67 J20** 20 14N 97 37 E
Mawlaik, Burma ..... **67 H19** 23 40N 94 26 E
Mawlamyine =
  Moulmein, Burma .. **67 L20** 16 30N 97 40 E
Mawqaq, Si. Arabia .. **70 E4** 27 25N 41 8 E
Mawson Base,
  Antarctica ...... **5 C6** 67 30 S 62 53 E
Mawson Coast,
  Antarctica ...... **5 C6** 68 30 S 63 0 E

Max, U.S.A. **112 B4** 47 49N 101 18W
Maxcanú, Mexico **119 C6** 20 40N 92 0W
Maxesibeni, S. Africa . **89 E4** 30 49 S 29 23 E
Maxhamish L., Canada **102 B4** 59 50N 123 17W
Maxixe, Mozam. ...... **89 C6** 23 54 S 35 17 E
Maxville, Canada **117 A10** 45 17N 74 51W
Maxwell, U.S.A. **110 F4** 39 17N 122 11W
Maxwelton, Australia . **94 C3** 20 43 S 142 41 E
May, C., U.S.A. **114 F8** 38 56N 74 58W
May Pen, Jamaica .... **120 a** 17 58N 77 15W
Maya →, Russia ..... **53 D14** 60 28N 134 28 E
Maya Mts., Belize **119 D7** 16 30N 89 0W
Mayaguana, Bahamas . **121 B5** 22 30N 72 44W
Mayagüez, Puerto Rico **121 d** 18 12N 67 9W
Mayahi, Niger ...... **83 C6** 13 58N 7 40 E
Mayaky, Ukraine ..... **29 C14** 47 26N 29 33 E
Mayals = Maials, Spain **38 D5** 41 22N 0 30 E
Mayāmey, Iran ...... **71 B7** 36 24N 55 42 E
Mayang, China ...... **58 D7** 27 53N 109 49 E
Mayanup, Australia ... **93 F2** 33 57 S 116 27 E
Mayapán, Mexico **119 C7** 20 28N 89 11W
Mayapán, Yucatán,
  Mexico **119 C7** 20 30N 89 25W
Mayarí, Cuba **121 B4** 20 40N 75 41W
Mayaro B., Trin. & Tob. **125 K16** 10 13N 61 0W
Maybell, U.S.A. **108 F9** 40 31N 108 5W
Maybole, U.K. **13 F4** 55 21N 4 42W
Maychew, Ethiopia ... **81 E4** 12 50N 39 31 E
Maydān, Iraq ...... **70 C5** 34 55N 45 37 E
Maydan, Ukraine ..... **29 B8** 48 36N 23 29 E
Maydena, Australia ... **95 G4** 42 45 S 146 30 E
Mayen, Germany ..... **25 E3** 50 19N 7 13 E
Mayenne, France **18 D6** 48 20N 0 38W
Mayenne □, France ... **18 D6** 48 10N 0 40W
Mayenne →, France .. **18 E6** 47 30N 0 32W
Mayer, U.S.A. **109 J7** 34 24N 112 14W
Mayerthorpe, Canada . **102 C5** 53 57N 115 8W
Mayfield, Ky., U.S.A. . **114 G1** 36 44N 88 38W
Mayfield, N.Y., U.S.A. **117 C10** 43 6N 74 16W
Mayhill, U.S.A. **109 K11** 32 53N 105 29W
Maykop, Russia ...... **35 H5** 44 35N 40 10 E
Maymyo, Burma ..... **64 A1** 22 2N 96 28 E
Maynard, Mass., U.S.A. **117 D13** 42 26N 71 27W
Maynard, Wash., U.S.A. **110 C4** 47 59N 122 55W
Maynard Hills, Australia **93 E2** 28 28 S 119 49 E
Mayne →, Australia .. **94 C3** 23 40 S 141 55 E
Maynooth, Ireland ... **12 C5** 53 23N 6 34W
Mayo, Canada **100 B6** 63 38N 135 57W
Mayo □, Ireland **12 C2** 53 53N 9 3W
Mayo Daga, Nigeria .. **83 D7** 6 59N 11 25 E
Mayo Faran, Nigeria . **83 D7** 8 59N 12 4 E
Mayon Volcano, Phil. . **61 E5** 13 15N 123 41 E
Mayor I., N.Z. ...... **91 G6** 37 16 S 176 17 E
Mayorga, Spain **36 C5** 42 10N 5 16W
Mayotte □, Ind. Oc. .. **85 G9** 12 50 S 45 10 E
Mayraira Pt., Phil. ... **61 B4** 18 39N 120 51 E
Maysān □, Iraq ...... **70 D5** 31 55N 47 15 E
Mayskiy, Russia ...... **35 J7** 43 47N 44 2 E
Maysville, U.S.A. **114 F4** 38 39N 83 46W
Mayu, Indonesia ..... **63 D7** 1 30N 126 30 E
Mayville, N. Dak.,
  U.S.A. **112 B6** 47 30N 97 20W
Mayville, N.Y., U.S.A. . **116 D5** 42 15N 79 30W
Mayya, Russia ...... **53 C14** 61 44N 130 18 E
Mazabuka, Zambia ... **87 F2** 15 52 S 27 44 E
Mazagán = El Jadida,
  Morocco **78 B4** 33 11N 8 17W
Mazagão, Brazil ..... **125 D8** 0 7 S 51 16W
Mazamet, France ..... **20 E6** 43 30N 2 20 E
Mazán, Peru ...... **124 D4** 3 30 S 73 0W
Mãzandarān □, Iran .. **71 B7** 36 30N 52 0 E
Mazapil, Mexico **118 C4** 24 38N 101 34W
Mazara del Vallo, Italy **42 E5** 37 39N 12 35 E
Mazarrón, Spain **39 H3** 37 38N 1 19W
Mazarrón, G. de, Spain **39 H3** 37 27N 1 19W
Mazaruni →, Guyana **124 B7** 6 25N 58 35W
Mazatán, Mexico **118 B2** 29 0N 110 8W
Mazatenango,
  Guatemala **120 D1** 14 35N 91 30W
Mazatlán, Mexico **118 C3** 23 13N 106 25W
Mažeikiai, Lithuania . **9 H20** 56 20N 22 20 E
Mãzhān, Iran ...... **71 C8** 32 30N 59 0 E
Mazīnān, Iran ...... **71 B8** 36 19N 56 56 E
Mazoe, Mozam. ...... **87 F3** 16 42 S 33 7 E
Mazoe →, Mozam. ... **87 F3** 16 20 S 33 30 E
Mazowe, Zimbabwe .. **87 F3** 17 28 S 30 58 E
Mazowieckie □, Poland **31 F8** 52 40N 21 0 E
Mazrūb, Sudan ...... **81 E2** 14 0N 29 20 E
Mazu Dao, China .... **59 D12** 26 10N 119 55 E
Mazurian Lakes =
  Mazurski, Pojezierze,
  Poland ...... **30 E7** 53 50N 21 0 E
Mazurski, Pojezierze,
  Poland ...... **30 E7** 53 50N 21 0 E
Mazyr, Belarus ...... **33 F5** 51 59N 29 15 E
Mba, Senegal **82 C1** 14 59N 16 44W
Mbaba, Senegal **82 C1** 14 59N 16 44W
Mbabane, Swaziland .. **89 D5** 26 18 S 31 6 E
Mbagne, Mauritania .. **82 B2** 16 6N 14 47W
M'bahiakro, Ivory C. . **82 D4** 7 33N 4 19W
Mbaïki, C.A.R. ...... **84 D3** 3 53N 18 1 E
Mbala, Zambia ...... **87 D3** 8 46 S 31 24 E
Mbalabala, Zimbabwe **89 C4** 20 27 S 29 3 E
Mbale, Uganda ...... **86 B3** 1 8N 34 12 E
Mbalmayo, Cameroon **83 E7** 3 33N 11 33 E
Mbam →, Cameroon . **83 E7** 4 24N 11 17 E
Mbamba Bay, Tanzania **87 E3** 11 13 S 34 49 E
Mbandaka, Dem. Rep. of
  the Congo ...... **84 D3** 0 1N 18 18 E
Mbanga, Cameroon .. **83 E6** 4 30N 9 33 E
Mbanza Congo, Angola **84 F2** 6 18 S 14 16 E
Mbanza Ngungu,
  Dem. Rep. of
  the Congo ...... **84 F2** 5 12 S 14 53 E
Mbarangandu, Tanzania **87 D4** 10 11 S 36 48 E
Mbarara, Uganda .... **86 C3** 0 35 S 30 40 E
Mbashe →, S. Africa . **89 E4** 32 15 S 28 54 E
Mbatto, Ivory C. **82 D4** 6 28N 4 22W
Mbenkuru →, Tanzania **87 D4** 9 25 S 39 50 E
Mberengwa, Zimbabwe **87 G2** 20 29 S 29 57 E
Mberengwa, Mt.,
  Zimbabwe ...... **87 G2** 20 37 S 29 55 E
Mberubu, Nigeria .... **83 D6** 6 10N 7 38 E
Mbesuma, Zambia ... **87 E3** 10 0 S 32 2 E
Mbeya, Tanzania ..... **87 D3** 8 54 S 33 29 E
Mbeya □, Tanzania .. **86 D3** 8 15 S 33 30 E
Mbini = Río Muni □,
  Eq. Guin. ...... **84 D2** 1 30N 10 0 E
Mboki, C.A.R. ...... **86 A2** 5 19N 25 58 E
M'bonge, Cameroon .. **83 E6** 4 33N 9 5 E
Mboro, Senegal **82 C1** 15 9N 16 54W
M'boukou, Rés. de,
  Cameroon ...... **83 D7** 6 28N 12 22 E
Mboune, Senegal **82 C2** 14 42N 13 34W
Mbour, Senegal **82 C1** 14 22N 16 54W
Mbout, Mauritania ... **82 B2** 16 1N 12 38W

Mbuji-Mayi, Dem. Rep.
  of the Congo ...... **86 D1** 6 9 S 23 40 E
Mbulu, Tanzania ..... **86 C4** 3 45 S 35 30 E
Mburucuyá, Argentina **126 B4** 28 1 S 58 14W
McCarran International,
  Las Vegas ✈ (LAS),
  U.S.A. **111 J11** 36 5N 115 9W
Mchinja, Tanzania .... **87 D4** 9 44 S 39 45 E
Mchinji, Malawi ..... **87 E3** 13 47 S 32 58 E
McMurdo, Antarctica . **5 D11** 77 0 S 140 0 E
Mdantsane, S. Africa . **85 L5** 32 56 S 27 46 E
Mead, L., U.S.A. **111 J12** 36 1N 114 44W
Meade, U.S.A. **113 G4** 37 17N 100 20W
Meadow Lake, Canada **103 C7** 54 10N 108 26W
Meadow Lake △,
  Canada **103 C7** 54 27N 109 0W
Meadow Valley
  Wash →, U.S.A. ... **111 J12** 36 40N 114 34W
Meadville, U.S.A. **116 E4** 41 39N 80 9W
Meaford, Canada **116 B4** 44 36N 80 35W
Mealhada, Portugal .. **36 E2** 40 22N 8 27W
Mealy Mts., Canada .. **105 B8** 53 10N 58 0W
Meander River, Canada **102 B5** 59 2N 117 42W
Meares, C., U.S.A. ... **108 D2** 45 37N 124 0W
Mearim →, Brazil .... **125 D10** 3 4 S 44 35W
Meath □, Ireland **12 C5** 53 40N 6 57W
Meath Park, Canada .. **103 C7** 53 27N 105 22W
Meaulne, France ..... **19 F9** 46 36N 2 36 E
Meaux, France ...... **19 D9** 48 58N 2 50 E
Mebechi-Gawa →,
  Japan ...... **54 D10** 40 31N 141 31 E
Mebulu, Tanjung,
  Indonesia ...... **63 K18** 8 50 S 115 5 E
Mecanhelas, Mozam. . **87 F4** 15 12 S 35 54 E
Mecca = Makkah,
  Si. Arabia ...... **70 E3** 21 30N 39 54 E
Mecca, U.S.A. **111 M10** 33 34N 116 5W
Mechanicsburg, U.S.A. **116 F8** 40 13N 77 1W
Mechanicville, U.S.A. . **117 D11** 42 54N 73 41W
Mechara, Ethiopia .... **81 F5** 8 36N 40 20 E
Mechelen, Belgium ... **17 C4** 51 2N 4 29 E
Mecheria, Algeria **78 B5** 33 35N 0 18W
Mechernich, Germany . **24 E2** 50 35N 6 39 E
Mechetinskaya, Russia **35 G5** 46 45N 40 32 E
Mecidiye, Turkey ..... **45 F10** 40 38N 26 32 E
Mecitözü, Turkey ..... **72 B6** 40 32N 35 17 E
Mecklenburg-
  Vorpommern □,
  Germany ...... **24 B8** 53 45N 12 15 E
Mecklenburger Bucht,
  Germany ...... **24 A7** 54 20N 11 40 E
Meconta, Mozam. .... **87 E4** 14 59 S 39 50 E
Mecsek, Hungary .... **28 D3** 46 10N 18 18 E
Meda, Portugal **36 E3** 40 57N 7 18W
Medan, Indonesia .... **62 D1** 3 40N 98 38 E
Médanos de Coro △,
  Venezuela **121 D6** 11 35N 69 44W
Medanosa, Pta.,
  Argentina ...... **128 F3** 48 8 S 66 0W
Médéa, Algeria ...... **78 A6** 36 12N 2 50 E
Medebach, Bos.-H. ... **28 G4** 43 44N 19 10 E
Medellín, Colombia ... **124 B3** 6 15N 75 35W
Medelpad, Sweden ... **10 B10** 62 33N 16 30 E
Medemblik, Neths. ... **17 B5** 52 46N 5 8 E
Menderawa, Mauritania **82 B1** 17 0N 15 38W
Medford, Mass., U.S.A. **117 D13** 42 25N 71 7W
Medford, Oreg., U.S.A. **108 E2** 42 19N 122 52W
Medford, Wis., U.S.A. . **112 C9** 45 9N 90 20W
Medgidia, Romania ... **29 F13** 44 15N 28 19 E
Medi, Sudan ...... **81 F3** 5 4N 30 42 E
Media Agua, Argentina **126 C2** 31 58 S 68 25W
Media Luna, Argentina **126 C2** 34 45 S 66 44W
Medianeira, Brazil ... **127 B5** 25 17 S 54 5W
Mediaş, Romania .... **29 D9** 46 9N 24 22 E
Medicina, Italy ...... **41 D8** 44 28N 11 38 E
Medicine Bow, U.S.A. . **108 F10** 41 54N 106 12W
Medicine Bow Pk.,
  U.S.A. **108 F10** 41 10N 106 19W
Medicine Bow Ra.,
  U.S.A. **108 F10** 41 10N 106 25W
Medicine Hat, Canada **103 D6** 50 0N 110 45W
Medicine Lake, U.S.A. **112 A2** 48 30N 104 30W
Medicine Lodge, U.S.A. **113 G5** 37 17N 98 35W
Medina = Al Madīnah,
  Si. Arabia ...... **70 E3** 24 35N 39 52 E
Medina, N. Dak., U.S.A. **112 B5** 46 54N 99 18W
Medina, N.Y., U.S.A. . **116 C6** 43 13N 78 23W
Medina, Ohio, U.S.A. . **116 E3** 41 8N 81 52W
Medina →, U.S.A. ... **113 L5** 29 16N 98 29W
Medina de Pomar, Spain **36 C7** 42 56N 3 29W
Medina de Ríoseco,
  Spain **36 D5** 41 53N 5 3W
Medina del Campo,
  Spain **36 D6** 41 18N 4 55W
Medina L., U.S.A. **113 L5** 29 32N 98 56W
Medina Sidonia, Spain . **37 J5** 36 28N 5 57W
Medinaceli, Spain **38 D2** 41 12N 2 30W
Medinipur, India ..... **69 H12** 22 25N 87 21 E
Mediterranean Sea,
  Europe ...... **6 H7** 35 0N 15 0 E
Médoc, France **20 C3** 45 10N 0 50W
Medulin, Croatia ..... **41 D10** 44 49N 13 55 E
Medveda, Serbia & M. **44 D5** 42 50N 21 32 E
Medvedevo, Russia ... **34 B8** 56 37N 47 47 E
Medveditsa →, Tver,
  Russia ...... **32 D9** 57 5N 37 30 E
Medveditsa →,
  Volgograd, Russia .. **34 F6** 49 35N 42 41 E
Medvedok, Russia .... **34 B10** 57 20N 50 1 E
Medvezhi, Ostrava,
  Russia ...... **53 B17** 71 0N 161 0 E
Medvezhyegorsk, Russia **52 C4** 63 0N 34 25 E
Medway →, U.K. ..... **15 F8** 51 25N 0 32 E
Medway □, U.K. ..... **15 F8** 51 27N 0 46 E
Medzev, Slovak Rep. . **27 C13** 48 43N 20 55 E
Medzilaborce,
  Slovak Rep. ...... **27 B14** 49 17N 21 52 E
Međimurje □, Macedonia **44 F6** 40 56N 21 26 E
Meekatharra, Australia **93 E2** 26 32 S 118 29 E
Meeker, U.S.A. **108 F10** 40 2N 107 55W
Meelpaeg Res., Canada **105 C8** 48 15N 56 50W
Meersburg, Germany . **25 H5** 47 41N 9 16 E
Meerut, India ...... **68 E7** 29 1N 77 42 E
Meeteetse, U.S.A. **108 D9** 44 9N 108 52W
Mega, Ethiopia ...... **81 G4** 3 57N 38 19 E
Megála Khorío, Greece **47 E9** 36 27N 27 24 E
Megálo Petalí, Greece **46 D6** 38 0N 24 15 E
Megálópolis, Greece .. **46 D4** 37 25N 22 7 E
Meganisí, Greece ..... **46 C2** 38 38N 20 45 E
Mégara, Greece ...... **46 D5** 37 58N 23 22 E
Megasini, India ...... **69 J12** 21 38N 86 21 E
Megdhova →, Greece . **46 C3** 39 10N 21 45 E
Mégève, France ...... **21 C10** 45 51N 6 37 E
Meghalaya □, India .. **67 G17** 25 50N 91 0 E
Meghezez, Ethiopia .. **81 F4** 9 18N 39 26 E
Meghna →, Bangla. .. **67 H17** 22 50N 90 50 E

Mégiscane, L., Canada **104 C4** 48 35N 75 55W
Megiste, Greece ...... **47 E11** 36 8N 29 34 E
Megra, Russia ...... **32 B9** 60 11N 37 14 E
Mehadia, Romania ... **28 F7** 44 56N 22 23 E
Meharry, Mt., Australia **92 D2** 22 59 S 118 35 E
Mehedeby, Sweden ... **10 D11** 60 27N 17 25 E
Mehedinţi □, Romania **28 F7** 44 40N 22 45 E
Meheisa, Sudan ...... **80 D3** 19 38N 32 57 E
Mehlville, U.S.A. **112 F9** 38 30N 90 19W
Mehndawal, India ... **69 F10** 26 58N 83 5 E
Mehr Jān, Iran ...... **71 C7** 33 50N 55 6 E
Mehrābād, Iran ..... **70 B5** 36 53N 47 55 E
Mehrān, Iran ...... **70 C5** 33 7N 46 10 E
Mehrīz, Iran ...... **71 D7** 31 35N 54 28 E
Mehun-sur-Yèvre,
  France ...... **19 E9** 47 10N 2 13 E
Mei Jiang →, China .. **59 E11** 24 25N 116 35 E
Mei Xian, China ..... **56 G4** 34 18N 107 55 E
Meicheng, China ..... **59 C12** 29 29N 119 16 E
Meichengzhen, China . **59 C8** 28 9N 111 40 E
Meichuan, China ..... **59 B10** 30 11N 115 31 E
Meigu, China ...... **58 C4** 28 16N 103 20 E
Meiktila, Burma ..... **67 J19** 20 53N 95 54 E
Meinerzhagen, Germany **24 D3** 51 6N 7 38 E
Meiningen, Germany . **24 E6** 50 34N 10 25 E
Meira, Serra de, Spain **36 B3** 43 15N 7 15W
Meiringen, Switz. .... **25 J4** 46 43N 8 12 E
Meishan, China ...... **58 B4** 30 3N 103 23 E
Meissen, Germany ... **24 D9** 51 9N 13 29 E
Meissner-Kaufunger
  Wald △, Germany .. **24 D5** 51 16N 9 45 E
Meitan, China ...... **58 D6** 27 45N 107 29 E
Meizhou, China ...... **59 E11** 24 16N 116 6 E
Meja, India ...... **69 G10** 25 9N 82 7 E
Mejillones, Chile ..... **126 A1** 23 10 S 70 30W
Mekdela, Ethiopia .... **81 E4** 11 24N 39 10 E
Mekele, Ethiopia ..... **81 E4** 13 33N 39 30 E
Mekhtar, Pakistan ... **66 D6** 30 30N 69 15 E
Meknès, Morocco **78 B4** 33 57N 5 33W
Meko, Nigeria ...... **83 D5** 7 27N 2 52 E
Mekong →, Asia ..... **65 H6** 9 30N 106 15 E
Mekongga, Indonesia . **63 E6** 3 39 S 121 15 E
Mekrou →, Benin .... **83 C5** 12 25N 2 50 E
Mekvari = Kür →,
  Azerbaijan ...... **73 C13** 39 29N 49 15 E
Mel, Italy ...... **41 B9** 46 4N 12 5 E
Melagiri Hills, India .. **66 N10** 12 20N 77 30 E
Melaka, Malaysia .... **65 L4** 2 15N 102 15 E
Melalap, Malaysia .... **62 C5** 5 10N 116 5 E
Mélambes, Greece .... **49 D6** 35 8N 24 40 E
Melanesia, Pac. Oc. .. **96 H7** 4 0 S 155 0 E
Melaya, Indonesia .... **63 J17** 8 15 S 114 30 E
Melbourne, Australia . **95 F4** 37 50 S 145 0 E
Melbourne, U.S.A. ... **115 L5** 28 5N 80 37W
Melchor Múzquiz,
  Mexico **118 B4** 27 50N 101 30W
Melchor Ocampo,
  Mexico **118 C4** 24 52N 101 40W
Méldola, Italy ...... **41 D9** 44 7N 12 5 E
Meldorf, Germany ... **24 A5** 54 5N 9 5 E
Melegnano, Italy ..... **40 C6** 45 21N 9 19 E
Melenci, Serbia & M. . **28 E5** 45 32N 20 20 E
Melenki, Russia ...... **34 C5** 55 20N 41 37 E
Mélèzes →, Canada .. **104 A5** 57 40N 69 29W
Melfi, Italy ...... **43 B8** 41 0N 15 39 E
Melfort, Canada **103 C8** 52 50N 104 37W
Melfort, Zimbabwe ... **87 F3** 18 0 S 31 25 E
Melgaço, Portugal **36 C2** 42 7N 8 15W
Melgar de Fernamental,
  Spain **36 C6** 42 27N 4 17W
Melhus, Norway ..... **8 E14** 63 17N 10 18 E
Melide, Spain **36 C2** 42 55N 8 1W
Melilla, N. Afr. **78 A5** 35 21N 2 57W
Melilli, Italy ...... **43 E8** 37 11N 15 7 E
Melipilla, Chile ...... **126 C1** 33 42 S 71 15W
Mélissa, Ákra, Greece **49 D6** 35 6N 24 33 E
Mélissa Óros, Greece . **47 D8** 37 32N 26 4 E
Melita, Canada **103 D8** 49 15N 101 0W
Mélito di Porto Salvo,
  Italy ...... **43 E8** 37 55N 15 47 E
Melitopol, Ukraine ... **33 J8** 46 50N 35 22 E
Melk, Austria ...... **26 D8** 48 13N 15 20 E
Mellan Fryken, Sweden **10 E7** 59 45N 13 10 E
Mellansel, Sweden ... **8 E18** 63 26N 18 19 E
Mellbystrand, Sweden **11 H6** 56 30N 12 56 E
Melle, France **20 B3** 46 14N 0 10W
Melle, Germany ...... **24 C4** 52 12N 8 20 E
Mellen, U.S.A. **112 B9** 46 20N 90 40W
Mellerud, Sweden .... **11 F6** 58 41N 12 28 E
Mellette, U.S.A. **112 C5** 45 9N 98 30W
Mellid = Melide, Spain **36 C2** 42 55N 8 1W
Mellieha, Malta ...... **49 D1** 35 57N 14 22 E
Mellit, Sudan ...... **81 E2** 14 7N 25 34 E
Mellrichstadt, Germany **24 E6** 50 25N 10 17 E
Melnik, Bulgaria ..... **44 E7** 41 30N 23 25 E
Mělník, Czech Rep. .. **26 A7** 50 22N 14 23 E
Melnytsya Podilska,
  Ukraine ...... **29 B11** 48 37N 26 10 E
Melo, Uruguay ...... **127 C5** 32 20 S 54 10W
Melolo, Indonesia .... **63 F6** 9 53 S 120 40 E
Melouprey, Cambodia **64 F5** 13 48N 105 16 E
Melrose, Australia .... **95 E4** 32 42 S 146 57 E
Melrose, U.K. **13 F6** 55 36N 2 43W
Melrose, Minn., U.S.A. **112 C7** 45 40N 94 49W
Melrose, N. Mex., U.S.A. **113 H3** 34 26N 103 38W
Melstone, U.S.A. **108 C10** 46 36N 107 52W
Melsungen, Germany . **24 D5** 51 7N 9 32 E
Melton Mowbray, U.K. **14 E7** 52 47N 0 54W
Melun, France ...... **19 D9** 48 32N 2 39 E
Melut, Sudan ...... **81 E3** 10 30N 32 13 E
Melville, Canada **103 C8** 50 55N 102 50W
Melville, C., Australia . **94 A3** 14 11 S 144 30 E
Melville, L., Canada .. **105 B8** 53 30N 60 0W
Melville B., Australia . **94 A2** 12 0 S 136 45 E
Melville I., Australia .. **92 B5** 11 30 S 131 0 E
Melville I., Canada ... **98 B8** 75 30N 112 0W
Melville Pen., Canada **101 B11** 68 0N 84 0W
Melvin →, U.S.A. .... **28 D4** 46 11N 9 25 E
Mélykút, Hungary ... **28 D4** 46 11N 19 25 E
Memaliaj, Albania ... **44 F3** 40 25N 19 58 E
Memba, Mozam. ..... **87 E5** 14 11 S 40 30 E
Memboro, Indonesia . **63 F5** 9 30 S 119 30 E
Membrilla, Spain **37 G7** 38 59N 3 21W
Memel = Klaipeda,
  Lithuania ...... **9 J19** 55 43N 21 10 E
Memel, S. Africa ..... **89 D4** 27 38 S 29 36 E
Memmingen, Germany **25 H6** 47 58N 10 10 E
Mempawah, Indonesia **62 D3** 0 30N 109 5 E
Memphis, Egypt ..... **80 J7** 29 52N 31 12 E
Memphis, Mich., U.S.A. **116 D2** 42 54N 82 46W
Memphis, Tenn., U.S.A. **113 H10** 35 8N 90 3W
Memphis, Tex., U.S.A. **113 H4** 34 44N 100 33W
Memphrémagog, L.,
  U.S.A. **117 B12** 45 0N 72 12W
Mena, Ukraine ...... **33 G7** 51 31N 32 13 E
Mena, U.S.A. **113 H7** 34 35N 94 15W

Mena →, Ethiopia .. 81 F5 5 40N 40 50 E
Menai Strait, U.K. .. 14 D3 53 11N 4 13W
Ménaka, Mali ...... 83 B5 15 59N 2 18 E
Menan = Chao
  Phraya →, Thailand . 64 F3 13 32N 100 36 E
Menarandra →, Madag. 89 D7 25 17 S 44 30 E
Menard, U.S.A. 113 K5 30 55N 99 47W
Menawashei, Sudan .. 81 E1 12 41N 24 59 E
Mendawai →, Indonesia 62 E4 3 30 S 113 0 E
Mende, France ...... 20 D7 44 31N 3 30 E
Mendebo Mts., Ethiopia 81 F4 7 0N 39 22 E
Mendeleyev Ridge,
  Arctic 4 B17 80 0N 178 0W
Menden, Germany .... 24 D3 51 26N 7 47 E
Menderes, Turkey .... 47 C9 38 14N 27 8 E
Mendez, Mexico 119 B5 25 7N 98 34W
Mendhar, India ..... 69 C6 33 35N 74 10 E
Mendi, Ethiopia ..... 81 F4 9 47N 35 4 E
Mendip Hills, U.K. .. 15 F5 51 17N 2 40W
Mendocino, U.S.A. ... 108 G2 39 19N 123 48W
Mendocino, C., U.S.A. 108 G1 40 26N 124 25W
Mendota, Calif., U.S.A. 110 J6 36 45N 120 23W
Mendota, Ill., U.S.A. 112 E10 41 33N 89 7W
Mendoyo, Indonesia .. 63 J17 8 23 S 114 42 E
Mendoza, Argentina .. 126 C2 32 50 S 68 52W
Mendoza □, Argentina 126 C2 33 0 S 69 0W
Mene Grande,
  Venezuela 124 B4 9 49N 70 56W
Menemen, Turkey .... 47 C9 38 34N 27 3 E
Menen, Belgium ..... 17 D3 50 47N 3 7 E
Menfi, Italy .... 42 E5 37 36N 12 58 E
Mengdingjie, China .. 58 F2 23 31N 98 58 E
Mengeš, Slovenia .... 41 B11 46 10N 14 35 E
Menggala, Indonesia .. 62 E3 4 30 S 105 15 E
Menghai, China ..... 58 G3 21 49N 100 55 E
Mengíbar, Spain 37 H7 37 58N 3 48W
Mengla, China ...... 56 G7 34 55N 112 45 E
Mengla, China ...... 58 G3 21 20N 101 25 E
Menglian, China .... 58 F2 22 20N 99 58 E
Mengshan, China .... 59 E8 24 14N 110 55 E
Mengyin, China ..... 57 G9 35 40N 117 58 E
Mengzhe, China ..... 58 F2 22 20N 100 15 E
Mengzi, China ...... 58 F4 23 20N 103 22 E
Menihek, Canada 105 B6 54 28N 56 36W
Menihek L., Canada .. 105 B6 54 0N 67 0W
Menin = Menen,
  Belgium .... 17 D3 50 47N 3 7 E
Menindee, Australia .. 95 E3 32 20 S 142 25 E
Menindee L., Australia 95 E3 32 20 S 142 25 E
Meningie, Australia .. 95 F2 35 50 S 139 18 E
Menjangan, Pulau,
  Indonesia .... 63 J17 8 7 S 114 31 E
Menlo Park, U.S.A. .. 110 H4 37 27N 122 12W
Menominee, U.S.A. .. 114 C2 45 6N 87 37W
Menominee →, U.S.A. 114 C2 45 6N 87 36W
Menomonie, U.S.A. .. 112 C9 44 53N 91 55W
Menongue, Angola ... 85 G3 14 48 S 17 52 E
Menorca, Spain ..... 48 B11 40 0N 4 0 E
Menorca ✈ (MAH),
  Spain .... 38 F9 39 50N 4 16 E
Mentakab, Malaysia .. 65 L4 3 29N 102 21 E
Mentawai, Kepulauan,
  Indonesia .... 62 E1 2 0 S 99 0 E
Menton, France ..... 21 E11 43 50N 7 29 E
Mentor, U.S.A. 116 E3 41 40N 81 21W
Menzies, Australia .. 93 E3 29 40 S 121 2 E
Meob B., Namibia .... 88 C1 24 25 S 14 34 E
Me'ona, Israel ..... 74 B4 33 1N 35 15 E
Meoqui, Mexico 118 B3 28 17N 105 29W
Mepaco, Mozam. .... 87 F3 15 57 S 30 48 E
Meppel, Neths. ..... 17 B6 52 42N 6 12 E
Meppen, Germany .... 24 C3 52 42N 7 17 E
Mequinenza, Spain ... 38 D5 41 22N 0 17 E
Mequinenza, Embalse
  de, Spain .... 38 D5 41 25N 0 15 E
Mer, France .... 18 E8 47 42N 1 30 E
Merabéllou, Kólpos,
  Greece .... 49 D7 35 10N 25 50 E
Merak, Indonesia .... 63 F12 6 10N 106 26 E
Meramangye, L.,
  Australia .... 93 E5 28 25 S 132 13 E
Meran = Merano, Italy 40 B4 46 40N 11 9 E
Merano, Italy ...... 40 B4 46 40N 11 9 E
Merate, Italy .... 40 C6 45 42N 9 25 E
Merauke, Indonesia .. 63 F10 8 29 S 140 24 E
Merbein, Australia .. 95 E3 34 10 S 142 2 E
Merbuk, Gunung,
  Indonesia .... 63 J17 8 13 S 114 39 E
Merca, Somali Rep. .. 75 G3 1 48N 44 50 E
Mercantour □, France 21 D10 44 16N 6 43 E
Mercato Saraceno, Italy 41 E9 43 57N 12 12 E
Merced, U.S.A. 110 H6 37 18N 120 29W
Merced →, U.S.A. .. 110 H6 37 21N 120 59W
Merced Pk., U.S.A. .. 110 H7 37 36N 119 24W
Mercedes, Buenos Aires,
  Argentina .... 126 C4 34 40 S 59 30W
Mercedes, Corrientes,
  Argentina .... 126 B4 29 10 S 58 5W
Mercedes, San Luis,
  Argentina .... 126 C2 33 40 S 65 21W
Mercedes, Uruguay .. 126 C4 33 12 S 58 0W
Merceditas, Chile .... 126 B1 28 20 S 70 35W
Mercer, N.Z. .... 91 G5 37 16 S 175 5 E
Mercer, U.S.A. 116 C4 41 14N 80 15W
Mercer Island, U.S.A. 110 C4 47 35N 122 15W
Mercury, U.S.A. 111 J11 36 40N 115 58W
Mercy, C., Canada ... 101 B13 65 0N 63 30W
Merdrignac, France .. 18 D4 48 11N 2 27W
Mere, U.K. 15 F5 51 6N 2 16W
Meredith, C., Falk. Is. 128 G4 52 15 S 60 40W
Meredith, L., U.S.A. . 113 H4 35 43N 101 33W
Merefa, Ukraine ..... 33 H9 49 48N 36 3 E
Merei, Romania ..... 29 E11 45 7N 26 43 E
Merga = Nukheila,
  Sudan .... 80 D2 19 1N 26 21 E
Mergui, Burma ...... 64 F2 12 26N 98 34 E
Mergui Arch. = Myeik
  Kyunzu, Burma ... 65 G1 11 30N 97 30 E
Méribel-les-Allues,
  France .... 21 C10 45 25N 6 34 E
Meriç, Turkey ...... 45 F10 40 52N 26 12 E
Meriç →, Turkey .... 45 F10 40 52N 26 12 E
Mérida, Mexico 119 C7 20 58N 89 37W
Mérida, Spain 37 G4 38 55N 6 25W
Mérida, Venezuela ... 124 B4 8 24N 71 8W
Mérida, Cord. de,
  Venezuela 124 B4 9 0N 71 0W
Meriden, U.K. 15 E6 52 26N 1 38W
Meriden, U.S.A. 117 E12 41 32N 72 48W
Meridian, Calif., U.S.A. 110 F5 39 9N 121 55W
Meridian, Idaho, U.S.A. 108 E5 43 37N 116 24W
Meridian, Miss., U.S.A. 115 J1 32 22N 88 42W
Mérignac, France 20 D3 44 51N 0 39W
Merijärvi, Finland ... 8 D21 64 17N 24 29 E
Merinda, Australia .. 94 C4 20 2 S 148 11 E
Mering, Germany .... 25 G6 48 16N 10 59 E

Meringa, Nigeria .... 83 C7 10 44N 12 9 E
Merir, Pac. Oc. ..... 63 D8 4 10N 132 30 E
Merirumã, Brazil 125 C8 1 15N 54 50W
Merkel, U.S.A. 113 J5 32 28N 100 1W
Mermaid Reef, Australia 92 C2 17 6 S 119 36 E
Merowe, Sudan ..... 80 D3 18 29N 31 46 E
Merredin, Australia .. 93 F2 31 28 S 118 18 E
Merrick, U.K. 13 F4 55 8N 4 28W
Merrickville, Canada . 117 B9 44 55N 75 50W
Merrill, Oreg., U.S.A. 108 E3 42 1N 121 36W
Merrill, Wis., U.S.A. 112 C10 45 11N 89 41W
Merrimack →, U.S.A. 117 D14 42 49N 70 49W
Merriman, U.S.A. ... 112 D4 42 55N 101 42W
Merritt, Canada 102 C4 50 10N 120 45W
Merritt Island, U.S.A. 115 L5 28 21N 80 42W
Merriwa, Australia .. 95 E5 32 6 S 150 22 E
Merry I., Canada 104 A4 55 29N 77 31W
Merryville, U.S.A. .. 113 K8 30 45N 93 33W
Mersa Fatma, Eritrea . 81 E5 14 57N 40 17 E
Mersch, Lux. .... 17 E6 49 44N 6 7 E
Merse →, Italy ..... 41 E8 43 5N 11 22 E
Mersea I., U.K. ..... 15 F8 51 47N 0 58 E
Merseburg, Germany . 24 D7 51 22N 11 59 E
Mersey →, U.K. 14 D4 53 25N 3 1W
Merseyside □, U.K. .. 14 D4 53 31N 3 2W
Mersin, Turkey ..... 70 B2 36 51N 34 36 E
Mersing, Malaysia ... 65 L4 2 25N 103 50 E
Merta, India .... 68 F6 26 39N 74 4 E
Merta Road, India ... 68 F5 26 43N 73 55 E
Merthyr Tydfil, U.K. 15 F4 51 45N 3 22W
Merthyr Tydfil □, U.K. 15 F4 51 46N 3 21W
Mértola, Portugal 37 H3 37 40N 7 40W
Mertzon, U.S.A. 113 K4 31 16N 100 49W
Méru, France .... 19 C9 49 13N 2 8 E
Meru, Kenya .... 86 B4 0 3N 37 40 E
Meru, Tanzania ..... 86 C4 3 15 S 36 46 E
Meru △, Kenya ..... 86 B4 0 5N 38 10 E
Merville, France .... 19 B9 50 38N 2 38 E
Méry-sur-Seine, France 19 D10 48 31N 3 54 E
Merzifon, Turkey .... 72 B6 40 53N 35 32 E
Merzig, Germany .... 25 F2 49 26N 6 38 E
Mesa, U.S.A. 109 K8 33 25N 111 50W
Mesa Verde △, U.S.A. 109 H9 37 11N 108 29W
Mesagne, Italy ...... 43 B10 40 34N 17 48 E
Mesanagrós, Greece .. 49 C9 36 1N 27 49 E
Mesaoría, Cyprus .... 49 D12 35 12N 33 14 E
Mesarás, Kólpos, Greece 49 D6 35 6N 24 47 E
Meschede, Germany .. 24 D4 51 20N 8 18 E
Mescit, Turkey ..... 73 B9 40 21N 41 11 E
Mesfinto, Ethiopia ... 81 E4 13 20N 37 22 E
Mesgouez, L., Canada 104 B5 51 20N 75 0W
Meshed = Mashhad, Iran 71 B8 36 20N 59 35 E
Meshoppen, U.S.A. .. 117 E8 41 36N 76 3W
Meshra er Req, Sudan 81 F2 8 25N 29 18 E
Mesilinka →, Canada 102 B4 56 6N 124 30W
Mesilla, U.S.A. 109 K10 32 16N 106 48W
Meslay-du-Maine,
  France 18 E6 47 58N 0 33W
Mesocco, Switz. .... 25 J5 46 23N 9 12 E
Mesolóngion, Greece . 46 C3 38 21N 21 28 E
Mesopotamia = Al
  Jazirah, Iraq ..... 70 C5 33 30N 44 0 E
Mesopotamia, U.S.A. 116 E4 41 27N 80 57W
Mesopótamon, Greece 46 B2 39 14N 20 32 E
Mesoraca, Italy ..... 43 C9 39 5N 16 48 E
Mésou Volímais =
  Volímai, Greece ... 46 D2 37 52N 20 39 E
Mesquite, U.S.A. ... 109 H6 36 47N 114 6W
Messaad, Algeria .... 78 B6 34 8N 3 30 E
Messac, France 18 E5 47 49N 1 50W
Messalo →, Mozam. . 87 E4 12 25 S 39 15 E
Méssaména, Cameroon 83 E7 3 48N 12 49 E
Messeue, Greece .... 46 D3 37 12N 21 58 E
Messina =
  S. Africa .... 89 C5 22 20 S 30 5 E
Messina, Italy ...... 43 D8 38 11N 15 34 E
Messina, Str. di, Italy 43 D8 38 15N 15 35 E
Messíni, Greece ..... 46 D4 37 4N 22 1 E
Messínia □, Greece .. 46 D3 37 10N 22 0 E
Messiniakós Kólpos,
  Greece .... 46 E4 36 45N 22 5 E
Messkirch, Germany . 25 H5 47 59N 9 7 E
Messlingen, Sweden .. 10 B6 62 40N 12 50 E
Messonghi, Greece ... 49 B3 39 29N 19 56 E
Mesta →, Bulgaria .. 44 E7 40 54N 24 49 E
Mestá, Ákra, Greece . 47 C7 38 16N 25 53 E
Mestanza, Spain 37 G6 38 35N 4 4W
Mestre, Italy .... 41 C9 45 29N 12 15 E
Mesudiye, Turkey ... 72 B7 40 28N 37 46 E
Meta →, S. Amer. ... 124 B5 6 12N 67 28W
Meta Incognita Pen.,
  Canada 101 B13 62 45N 68 30W
Metabetchouan, Canada 105 C5 48 26N 71 52W
Metairie, U.S.A. 113 L9 29 58N 90 10W
Metalici, Munţii,
  Romania .... 28 D7 46 15N 22 50 E
Metaline Falls, U.S.A. 108 B5 48 52N 117 22W
Metallifere, Colline,
  Italy .... 40 E8 43 10N 11 0 E
Metán, Argentina .... 126 B3 25 30 S 65 0W
Metangula, Mozam. . 87 E3 12 40 S 34 50 E
Metauro →, Italy ... 41 E10 43 50N 13 8 E
Metema, Ethiopia ... 81 E4 12 56N 36 13 E
Metengobalame,
  Mozam. .... 87 E3 14 49 S 34 30 E
Méthana, Greece .... 46 D5 37 35N 23 23 E
Methóni, Greece .... 46 E3 36 49N 21 42 E
Methven, N.Z. ...... 91 K3 43 38 S 171 40 E
Metil, Mozam. ...... 87 F4 16 24 S 39 0 E
Metkovets, Bulgaria . 44 C7 43 37N 23 10 E
Metković, Croatia ... 41 E14 43 6N 17 39 E
Metlakatla, U.S.A. .. 100 C6 55 8N 131 35W
Metlika, Slovenia ... 41 C12 45 40N 15 20 E
Metropolis, U.S.A. .. 113 G10 37 9N 88 44W
Métsovon, Greece ... 46 B3 39 48N 21 12 E
Metu, Ethiopia ..... 81 F4 8 18N 35 35 E
Metz, France .... 19 C13 49 8N 6 10 E
Metzingen, Germany . 25 G5 48 31N 9 17 E
Meulaboh, Indonesia . 62 D1 4 11N 96 3 E
Meung-sur-Loire, France 19 E8 47 50N 1 40 E
Meureudu, Indonesia . 62 C1 5 19N 96 10 E
Meurthe →, France . 19 D13 48 47N 6 9 E
Meurthe-et-Moselle □,
  France .... 19 D13 48 52N 6 0 E
Meuse □, France .... 19 C12 49 8N 5 25 E
Meuse →, Europe ... 17 D5 50 45N 5 41 E
Meuselwitz, Germany 24 D8 51 2N 12 17 E
Mexia, U.S.A. 113 K6 31 41N 96 29W
Mexiana, I., Brazil .. 125 D9 0 0 49 30W
Mexicali, Mexico 111 N11 32 40N 115 30W
Mexican Plateau,
  Mexico 98 G9 25 0N 104 0W
Mexican Water, U.S.A. 109 H9 36 57N 109 32W
México, Mexico 119 D5 19 20N 99 10W
Mexico, Maine, U.S.A. 117 B14 44 34N 70 33W
Mexico, Mo., U.S.A. 112 F9 39 10N 91 53W

Mexico, N.Y., U.S.A. 117 C8 43 28N 76 18W
Méxic □, Mexico 119 D5 19 20N 99 10W
Mexico ■, Cent. Amer. 118 C4 25 0N 105 0W
Mexico, G. of,
  Cent. Amer. 119 C7 25 0N 90 0W
Mexico B., U.S.A. ... 117 C8 43 35N 76 20W
Meydān-e Naftūn, Iran 71 D6 31 56N 49 18 E
Meydani, Ra's-e, Iran 71 E8 25 24N 59 6 E
Meyenburg, Germany 24 B8 53 18N 12 14 E
Meymac, France .... 20 C6 45 32N 2 10 E
Meymaneh, Afghan. . 66 B4 35 53N 64 38 E
Meyrueis, France .... 20 D7 44 12N 3 27 E
Meyssac, France .... 20 D5 45 3N 1 40 E
Meyzieu, France .... 21 C8 45 46N 4 59 E
Mezdra, Bulgaria .... 44 C7 43 12N 23 42 E
Mèze, France .... 20 E7 43 25N 3 36 E
Mezen, Russia ...... 52 C5 65 50N 44 20 E
Mezen →, Russia ... 52 C5 65 44N 44 22 E
Mézenc, Mt., France . 21 D8 44 54N 4 11 E
Mezeş, Munţii, Romania 28 C8 47 5N 23 5 E
Mezha →, Russia ... 32 E6 55 44N 31 33 E
Mezhdurechenskiy,
  Russia .... 52 D7 59 36N 65 56 E
Mézidon-Canon, France 18 C6 49 5N 0 1W
Mézières-en-Brenne,
  France .... 20 B5 46 49N 1 13 E
Mézilhac, France .... 21 D8 44 49N 4 21 E
Mézin, France ...... 20 D4 44 4N 0 16 E
Mezőberény, Hungary 28 D6 46 49N 21 3 E
Mezőfalva, Hungary . 28 D3 46 55N 18 49 E
Mezőhegyes, Hungary 28 D5 46 19N 20 49 E
Mezőkövácsháza,
  Hungary .... 28 D5 46 25N 20 57 E
Mezőkövesd, Hungary 28 C5 47 49N 20 35 E
Mézos, France 20 D2 44 5N 1 10W
Mezőtúr, Hungary .. 28 C5 47 1N 20 41 E
Mezquital, Mexico ... 118 C4 23 29N 104 23W
Mezzolombardo, Italy 40 B8 46 13N 11 5 E
Mgeta, Tanzania .... 87 D4 8 22 S 36 6 E
Mglin, Russia ...... 33 F7 53 2N 32 50 E
Mhlaba Hills, Zimbabwe 87 F3 18 30 S 30 30 E
Mhow, India .... 68 H6 22 33N 75 50 E
Miahuatlán, Mexico . 119 D5 16 21N 96 36W
Miajadas, Spain 37 F5 39 9N 5 54W
Miami, Fla., U.S.A. .. 115 N5 25 47N 80 11W
Miami, Okla., U.S.A. 113 G7 36 53N 94 53W
Miami, Tex., U.S.A. . 113 H4 35 42N 100 38W
Miami Beach, U.S.A. 115 N5 25 47N 80 8W
Mian Xian, China ... 56 H4 33 10N 106 32 E
Mianchi, China ..... 56 G6 34 48N 111 48 E
Miāndarreh, Iran .... 71 C7 35 37N 53 39 E
Miāndowāb, Iran .... 70 B5 37 0N 46 5 E
Miandrivazo, Madag. 89 B8 19 31 S 45 29 E
Miāneh, Iran .... 70 B5 37 30N 47 40 E
Mianning, China .... 58 C4 28 32N 102 9 E
Mianwali, Pakistan .. 68 C4 32 38N 71 28 E
Mianyang, China .... 58 B5 31 22N 104 47 E
Mianzhu, China ..... 58 B5 31 22N 104 7 E
Miaoli, Taiwan ..... 59 E13 24 37N 120 49 E
Miarinarivo,
  Antananarivo, Madag. 89 B8 18 57 S 46 55 E
Miarinarivo, Toamasina,
  Madag. .... 89 B8 16 38 S 48 15 E
Miarivaratra, Madag. 89 C8 20 13 S 47 31 E
Miass, Russia ...... 52 D7 54 59N 60 6 E
Miastko, Poland .... 30 E3 54 0N 16 58 E
Miastko, Poland .... 30 E3 54 0N 16 58 E
Mica, S. Africa ..... 89 C5 24 10 S 30 48 E
Micăsasa, Romania .. 29 D9 46 7N 24 7 E
Michalovce, Slovak Rep. 27 C14 48 47N 21 58 E
Michigan □, U.S.A. .. 114 C3 44 0N 85 0W
Michigan, L., U.S.A. 114 D2 44 0N 87 0W
Michigan City, U.S.A. 114 E2 41 43N 86 54W
Michika, Nigeria .... 83 C7 10 36N 13 23 E
Michipicoten I., Canada 104 C2 47 40N 85 40W
Michoacan □, Mexico 118 D4 19 0N 102 0W
Michurin, Bulgaria .. 45 D11 42 9N 27 51 E
Michurinsk, Russia .. 34 D5 52 58N 40 27 E
Mico, Pta., Nic. 120 D3 12 0N 83 30W
Micoud, St. Lucia ... 121 f 13 49N 60 54W
Micronesia, Pac. Oc. . 96 G7 11 0N 160 0 E
Micronesia, Federated
  States of ■, Pac. Oc. 96 G7 9 0N 150 0 E
Mid-Oceanic Ridge,
  Ind. Oc. .... 96 M1 42 0 S 90 0 E
Midai, Indonesia .... 62 D3 3 0N 107 47 E
Midale, Canada 103 D8 49 25N 103 20W
Middelburg, Neths. .. 17 C3 51 30N 3 36 E
Middelburg,
  Eastern Cape,
  S. Africa .... 88 E4 31 30 S 25 0 E
Middelburg,
  Mpumalanga,
  S. Africa .... 89 D4 25 49 S 29 28 E
Middelfart, Denmark . 11 J3 55 30N 9 43 E
Middelpos, S. Africa . 88 E3 31 55 S 20 13 E
Middelwit, S. Africa . 88 C4 24 51 S 27 3 E
Middle Alkali L., U.S.A. 108 F3 41 27N 120 5W
Middle Bass I., U.S.A. 116 E2 41 41N 82 49W
Middle East, Asia ... 50 F7 38 0N 40 0 E
Middle Fork Feather →,
  U.S.A. 110 F5 38 33N 121 30W
Middle I., Australia .. 93 F3 34 6 S 123 11 E
Middle Loup →, U.S.A. 112 E5 41 17N 98 24W
Middle Sackville,
  Canada 105 D7 44 47N 63 42W
Middleboro, U.S.A. .. 117 E14 41 54N 70 55W
Middleburg, Fla., U.S.A. 115 K5 30 4N 81 52W
Middleburg, N.Y.,
  U.S.A. 117 D10 42 36N 74 20W
Middleburg, Pa., U.S.A. 116 F7 40 47N 77 3W
Middlebury, U.S.A. .. 117 B11 44 1N 73 10W
Middlemount, Australia 94 C4 22 50 S 148 40 E
Middleport, N.Y., U.S.A. 116 C6 43 13N 78 29W
Middleport, Ohio,
  U.S.A. 114 F4 39 0N 82 3W
Middlesboro, U.S.A. . 115 G4 36 36N 83 43W
Middlesbrough, U.K. 14 C6 54 35N 1 13W
Middlesbrough □, U.K. 14 C6 54 28N 1 13W
Middlesex, Belize 120 C2 17 2N 88 31W
Middlesex, N.J., U.S.A. 117 F10 40 36N 74 30W
Middlesex, N.Y., U.S.A. 116 D7 42 42N 77 16W
Middleton, Australia . 94 C3 22 22 S 141 32 E
Middleton, Canada .. 105 D6 44 57N 65 4W
Middleton Cr. →,
  Australia .... 94 C3 22 35 S 141 51 E
Middletown, U.K. ... 12 B5 54 17N 6 51W
Middletown, Calif.,
  U.S.A. 110 G4 38 45N 122 37W
Middletown, Conn.,
  U.S.A. 117 E12 41 34N 72 39W
Middletown, N.Y.,
  U.S.A. 117 E10 41 27N 74 25W
Middletown, Ohio,
  U.S.A. 114 F3 39 31N 84 24W

Middletown, Pa., U.S.A. 117 F8 40 12N 76 44W
Midge Point, Australia 94 J6 20 39 S 148 43 E
Midhurst, U.K. 15 G7 50 59N 0 44W
Mīdī, Yemen .... 81 D5 16 20N 42 45 E
Midi, Canal du →,
  France .... 20 E5 43 45N 1 21 E
Midi d'Ossau, Pic du,
  France 20 F3 42 50N 0 26W
Midi-Pyrénées □, France 20 E5 43 55N 1 45 E
Midland, Canada 116 B5 44 45N 79 50W
Midland, Calif., U.S.A. 111 M12 33 52N 114 48W
Midland, Mich., U.S.A. 114 D3 43 37N 84 14W
Midland, Pa., U.S.A. 116 F4 40 39N 80 27W
Midland, Tex., U.S.A. 113 K3 32 0N 102 3W
Midlands □, Zimbabwe 87 F2 19 40 S 29 0 E
Midleton, Ireland ... 12 E3 51 55N 8 10W
Midlothian, U.S.A. .. 113 J6 32 30N 97 0W
Midlothian □, U.K. .. 13 F5 55 51N 3 5W
Midongy,
  Tangorombohitr' i,
  Madag. .... 89 C8 23 30 S 47 0 E
Midongy Atsimo,
  Madag. .... 89 C8 23 35 S 47 1 E
Midou →, France ... 20 E3 43 54N 0 30W
Midouze →, France . 20 E3 43 48N 0 51W
Midsayap, Phil. .... 61 H6 7 12N 124 32 E
Midu, China .... 58 E3 25 18N 100 30 E
Midway Is., Pac. Oc. 96 E10 28 13N 177 22W
Midway Wells, U.S.A. 111 N11 32 41N 115 7W
Midwest, U.S.A. 107 B9 42 0N 90 0W
Midwest, Wyo., U.S.A. 108 E10 43 25N 106 16W
Midwest City, U.S.A. 113 H6 35 27N 97 24W
Midyat, Turkey ..... 70 B4 37 25N 41 23 E
Midzŏr, Bulgaria .... 44 C6 43 24N 22 40 E
Mie □, Japan .... 55 G8 34 30N 136 10 E
Miechów, Poland .... 31 H7 50 21N 20 5 E
Miedwie, Jezioro,
  Poland .... 31 E1 53 17N 14 54 E
Międzybórz, Poland . 31 G3 51 25N 17 34 E
Międzychód, Poland . 31 F2 52 35N 15 53 E
Międzylesie, Poland . 31 H3 50 8N 16 40 E
Międzyrzec Podlaski,
  Poland .... 31 G9 51 58N 22 45 E
Międzyrzecz, Poland . 31 F2 52 26N 15 35 E
Międzyzdroje, Poland 30 E1 53 56N 14 26 E
Miélan, France ..... 20 E4 43 27N 0 19 E
Mielec, Poland ..... 31 H8 50 15N 21 25 E
Mienga, Angola ..... 88 B2 17 12 S 19 48 E
Miercurea-Ciuc,
  Romania .... 29 D10 46 21N 25 48 E
Miercurea Sibiului,
  Romania .... 29 E8 45 53N 23 48 E
Mieres, Spain 36 B5 43 18N 5 48W
Mieroszów, Poland .. 31 H3 50 40N 16 11 E
Mieso, Ethiopia ..... 81 F5 9 15N 40 43 E
Mieszkowice, Poland 31 F1 52 47N 14 30 E
Mifflintown, U.S.A. . 116 F7 40 34N 77 24W
Mifraz Hefa, Israel .. 74 C4 32 52N 35 0 E
Migennes, France ... 19 E10 47 58N 3 31 E
Migliarino, Italy .... 41 D8 44 46N 11 56 E
Migliarino-San Rossore-
  Massaciuccoli □, Italy 40 E7 43 44N 10 20 E
Miguel Alemán, Presa,
  Mexico 119 D5 18 15N 96 40W
Miguelturra, Spain .. 37 G7 38 58N 3 53W
Mihăileni, Romania . 29 C11 47 58N 26 9 E
Mihăileşti, Romania . 29 F10 44 20N 25 54 E
Mihailovca, Moldova 29 D13 46 33N 28 56 E
Mihalgazi, Turkey .. 47 A12 40 2N 30 34 E
Mihaliçcik, Turkey .. 72 C4 39 53N 31 30 E
Mihara, Japan ...... 55 G6 34 24N 133 5 E
Miheşu de Cîmpie,
  Romania .... 29 D9 46 41N 24 9 E
Mijas, Spain 37 J6 36 36N 4 40W
Mikese, Tanzania ... 86 D4 6 48 S 37 55 E
Mikha-Tskhakaya =
  Senaki, Georgia ... 35 J6 42 15N 42 7 E
Mikhailovka =
  Mykhaylivka, Ukraine 33 J8 47 12N 35 15 E
Mikhaylov, Russia ... 32 E10 54 14N 39 0 E
Mikhaylovgrad =
  Montana, Bulgaria . 44 C7 43 27N 23 16 E
Mikhaylovka, Russia 34 E6 50 3N 43 5 E
Mikhnevo, Russia ... 32 E9 55 4N 37 59 E
Mikínai, Greece .... 46 D4 37 43N 22 46 E
Mikkeli, Finland .... 9 F22 61 43N 27 15 E
Mikkwa →, Canada . 102 B6 58 25N 114 46W
Mikniya, Sudan .... 81 D3 17 0N 33 45 E
Mikołajki, Poland ... 30 E8 53 49N 21 37 E
Míkonos, Greece .... 47 D7 37 30N 25 25 E
Mikrí Préspa, Límni,
  Greece .... 44 F5 40 47N 21 3 E
Mikrón Dhérion, Greece 45 E10 41 19N 26 6 E
Mikstat, Poland .... 31 G4 51 32N 17 59 E
Mikumi, Tanzania .. 86 D4 7 26 S 37 0 E
Mikumi △, Tanzania 86 D4 7 35 S 37 15 E
Milaca, U.S.A. 112 C8 45 45N 93 39W
Milagro, Ecuador ... 124 D3 2 11 S 79 36W
Milagros, Phil. ..... 61 E5 12 13N 123 30 E
Milan = Milano, Italy 40 C6 45 28N 9 10 E
Milan, Mo., U.S.A. .. 112 E8 40 12N 93 7W
Milan, Tenn., U.S.A. 115 H1 35 55N 88 46W
Milange, Mozam. ... 87 F4 16 3 S 35 45 E
Milano, Italy .... 40 C6 45 28N 9 12 E
Milano Linate ✈ (LIN),
  Italy .... 40 C6 45 27N 9 16 E
Milanoa, Madag. .... 89 A8 13 35 S 49 47 E
Milâs, Turkey ...... 47 D9 37 20N 27 50 E
Milatos, Greece ..... 49 D7 35 18N 25 34 E
Milazzo, Italy ...... 43 D8 38 13N 15 15 E
Milbank, U.S.A. 112 C6 45 13N 96 38W
Milbank Sd., Canada 102 C3 52 15N 128 35W
Milden, Canada 103 C7 51 29N 107 32W
Mildenhall, U.K. .... 15 E8 52 21N 0 32 E
Mildmay, Canada ... 116 B3 44 3N 81 7W
Mildura, Australia .. 95 E3 34 13 S 142 9 E
Mile, China .... 58 E4 24 28N 103 20 E
Miléai, Greece ..... 46 B5 39 20N 23 9 E
Miles, Australia ..... 95 D5 26 40 S 150 9 E
Miles City, U.S.A. .. 112 B2 46 25N 105 51W
Mileşti, Moldova ... 29 C13 47 16N 28 15 E
Milestone, Canada .. 103 D8 49 59N 104 31W
Miletto, Mte., Italy .. 43 A7 41 27N 14 22 E
Mīletus, Turkey .... 47 D9 37 30N 27 18 E
Milevsko, Czech Rep. 26 B7 49 27N 14 21 E
Milford, Calif., U.S.A. 110 E6 40 10N 120 22W
Milford, Conn.,
  U.S.A. 117 E12 41 14N 73 3W
Milford, Del., U.S.A. 114 F8 38 55N 75 26W
Milford, Mass., U.S.A. 117 D13 42 8N 71 31W
Milford, N.H., U.S.A. 117 D13 42 50N 71 39W
Milford, Pa., U.S.A. 117 E10 41 19N 74 48W
Milford, Utah, U.S.A. 109 G7 38 24N 113 1W
Milford Haven, U.K. 15 F2 51 42N 5 7W
Milford Sd., N.Z. ... 91 L1 44 41 S 167 47 E
Milford Sound, N.Z. 91 L1 44 41 S 167 55 E

Milh, Baḥr al = Razāzah,
  Buḥayrat ar, Iraq .. 70 C4 32 40N 43 35 E
Milicz, Poland ...... 31 G4 51 31N 17 19 E
Milikapiti, Australia . 92 B5 11 26 S 130 40 E
Miling, Australia .... 93 F2 30 30 S 116 17 E
Militello in Val di
  Catánia, Italy ..... 43 E7 37 16N 14 48 E
Milk →, U.S.A. 108 B10 48 4N 106 19W
Milk, Wadi el →, Sudan 80 D3 17 55N 30 20 E
Milk River, Canada . 102 D6 49 10N 112 5W
Mill I., Antarctica ... 5 C8 66 0 S 101 30 E
Mill Valley, U.S.A. .. 110 H4 37 54N 122 32W
Millárs →, Spain ... 38 F4 39 55N 0 1W
Millau, France ...... 20 D7 44 8N 3 4 E
Millbridge, Canada . 116 B7 44 41N 77 36W
Millbrook, Canada .. 116 B6 44 10N 78 29W
Millbrook, U.S.A. .. 117 E11 41 47N 73 42W
Mille Lacs, L. des,
  Canada 104 C1 48 45N 90 35W
Mille Lacs L., U.S.A. 112 B8 46 15N 93 39W
Milledgeville, U.S.A. 115 J4 33 5N 83 14W
Millen, U.S.A. 115 J5 32 48N 81 57W
Millennium I. = Caroline
  I., Kiribati .... 97 H12 9 58 S 150 13W
Miller, U.S.A. 112 C5 44 31N 98 59W
Millerovo, Russia ... 35 F5 48 57N 40 28 E
Millersburg, Ohio,
  U.S.A. 116 F3 40 33N 81 55W
Millersburg, Pa., U.S.A. 116 F8 40 32N 76 58W
Millerton, U.S.A. ... 117 E11 41 57N 73 31W
Millerton L., U.S.A. 110 J7 37 1N 119 41W
Millet, St. Lucia .... 121 f 13 55N 60 59W
Millevaches, Plateau de,
  France .... 20 C6 45 45N 2 0 E
Millheim, U.S.A. ... 116 F7 40 54N 77 29W
Millicent, Australia .. 95 F3 37 34 S 140 21 E
Millington, Australia 95 D5 27 53 S 151 16 E
Millinocket, U.S.A. .. 115 C11 45 39N 68 43W
Millmerran, Australia 95 D5 27 53 S 151 16 E
Millom, U.K. 14 C4 54 13N 3 16W
Mills L., Canada 102 A5 61 30N 118 20W
Millsboro, U.S.A. ... 116 G5 40 0N 80 0W
Millstream-
  Chichester △,
  Australia .... 92 D2 21 35 S 117 6 E
Milltown Malbay,
  Ireland 12 D2 52 52N 9 24W
Millville, N.J., U.S.A. 114 F8 39 24N 75 2W
Millville, Pa., U.S.A. 117 E8 41 7N 76 32W
Millwood L., U.S.A. 113 J8 33 42N 93 58W
Milna, Croatia ..... 41 E13 43 20N 16 28 E
Milne →, Australia . 94 C2 21 10 S 137 33 E
Milo, U.S.A. 115 C11 45 15N 68 59W
Mílos, Greece ...... 46 E6 36 44N 24 25 E
Miłosław, Poland ... 31 F4 52 12N 17 32 E
Milot, Albania ..... 44 E3 41 41N 19 43 E
Milparinka, Australia 95 D3 29 46 S 141 57 E
Miltenberg, Germany 25 F5 49 41N 9 16 E
Milton, N.S., Canada 105 D7 44 4N 64 45W
Milton, Ont., Canada 116 C5 43 31N 79 53W
Milton, N.Z. .... 91 M2 46 7 S 169 59 E
Milton, Calif., U.S.A. 110 G6 38 3N 120 51W
Milton, Fla., U.S.A. 115 K2 30 38N 87 3W
Milton, Pa., U.S.A. 116 F8 41 1N 76 51W
Milton, Vt., U.S.A. . 117 B11 44 38N 73 7W
Milton-Freewater,
  U.S.A. 108 D4 45 56N 118 23W
Milton Keynes, U.K. 15 E7 52 1N 0 44W
Milton Keynes □, U.K. 15 E7 52 1N 0 44W
Miluo, China .... 59 C9 29 0N 112 59 E
Milverton, Canada .. 116 C4 43 34N 80 55W
Milwaukee, U.S.A. .. 114 D2 43 2N 87 55W
Milwaukee Deep,
  Atl. Oc. 121 C6 19 50N 68 0W
Milwaukie, U.S.A. .. 110 E4 45 27N 122 38W
Mim, Ghana 82 D4 6 57N 2 33W
Mimizan, France 20 D2 44 12N 1 13W
Mimoň, Czech Rep. . 26 A7 50 38N 14 43 E
Min Jiang →, Fujian,
  China .... 59 E12 26 0N 119 35 E
Min Jiang →, Sichuan,
  China .... 58 C5 28 45N 104 40 E
Min Xian, China ... 56 G3 34 25N 104 5 E
Mina Pirquitas,
  Argentina .... 126 A2 22 40 S 66 30W
Mīnā Su'ud, Si. Arabia 71 D6 28 45N 48 28 E
Mīnā' al Aḥmadī, Kuwait 71 D6 29 5N 48 10 E
Minago →, Canada . 103 C9 54 33N 98 59W
Minaki, Canada 103 D10 49 59N 94 40W
Minamata, Japan ... 55 H5 32 10N 130 30 E
Minami-Arapusa △,
  Japan .... 55 G9 35 30N 138 9 E
Minami-Tori-Shima,
  Pac. Oc. .... 96 E7 24 20N 153 58 E
Minas, Uruguay .... 127 C4 34 20 S 55 10W
Minas, Sierra de las,
  Guatemala 120 C2 15 9N 89 31W
Minas Basin, Canada 105 C7 45 20N 64 12W
Minas de Ríotinto, Spain 37 H4 37 42N 6 35W
Minas Gerais □, Brazil 125 G9 18 50 S 46 0W
Minatitlán, Mexico .. 119 D6 17 59N 94 31W
Minbu, Burma ..... 67 J19 20 10N 94 52 E
Minchinabad, Pakistan 68 D5 30 10N 73 34 E
Mincio →, Italy .... 40 C7 45 4N 10 59 E
Minčol, Slovak Rep. . 27 B13 49 15N 20 58 E
Mindanao, Phil. .... 61 H6 8 0N 125 0 E
Mindanao Sea = Bohol
  Sea, Phil. .... 63 C6 9 0N 124 0 E
Mindanao Trench,
  Pac. Oc. .... 61 F7 12 0N 126 6 E
Mindel →, Germany 25 G6 48 31N 10 23 E
Mindelheim, Germany 25 G6 48 3N 10 29 E
Minden, Canada 116 B6 44 55N 78 43W
Minden, Germany ... 24 C4 52 17N 8 55 E
Minden, La., U.S.A. 113 J8 32 37N 93 17W
Minden, Nev., U.S.A. 110 G7 38 57N 119 46W
Mindiptana, Indonesia 63 F10 5 55 S 140 22 E
Mindoro, Phil. ..... 61 E4 13 0N 121 0 E
Mindoro Str., Phil. .. 61 E4 12 30N 120 30 E
Mine, Japan .... 55 G5 34 12N 131 7 E
Minehead, U.K. 15 F4 51 12N 3 29W
Mineola, N.Y., U.S.A. 117 F11 40 45N 73 39W
Mineola, Tex., U.S.A. 113 J7 32 40N 95 29W
Mineral King, U.S.A. 110 J8 36 27N 118 36W
Mineral Wells, U.S.A. 113 J5 32 48N 98 7W
Mineralnyye Vody,
  Russia .... 35 H6 44 15N 43 8 E
Minersville, U.S.A. .. 117 F8 40 41N 76 16W
Minerva, U.S.A. 116 F3 40 44N 81 6W
Minervino Murge, Italy 43 A9 41 5N 16 5 E
Minetto, U.S.A. 117 C8 43 24N 76 28W
Mingäçevir, Azerbaijan 35 K8 40 45N 47 0 E
Mingäçevir Su Anbarı,
  Azerbaijan .... 35 K8 40 57N 46 50 E
Mingan, Canada 105 B7 50 20N 64 0W
Mingechaur =
  Mingäçevir,
  Azerbaijan .... 35 K8 40 45N 47 0 E

Mingechaurskoye
Vdkhr. = Mingeçaçevir
Su Anbarı, Azerbaijan ... 35 K8 40 57N 46 50 E
Mingela, Australia ...... 94 C2 19 52 S 146 38 E
Mingenew, Australia .... 93 E2 29 12 S 115 21 E
Mingera Cr. →,
Australia .... 94 C2 20 38 S 137 45 E
Minggang, China .... 59 A10 32 24N 114 3 E
Mingguang, China ...... 59 A11 32 46N 117 59 E
Mingin, Burma .... 67 H19 22 50N 94 30 E
Mingir, Moldova .... 29 D13 46 40N 28 20 E
Minglanilla, Spain 39 F3 39 34N 1 38W
Minglun, China .... 58 E7 25 10N 108 21 E
Mingo Junction, U.S.A. 116 F4 40 19N 80 37W
Mingorria, Spain 36 E6 40 45N 4 40W
Mingshan, China .... 58 B4 30 6N 103 10 E
Mingteke Daban =
Mintaka Pass,
Pakistan .... 69 A6 37 0N 74 58 E
Mingxi, China .... 59 D11 26 18N 117 12 E
Mingyuegue, China .... 57 C15 43 2N 128 50 E
Minhe, China .... 58 D5 26 0N 119 15 E
Minho = Miño →, Spain 36 D2 41 52N 8 40W
Minhou, China .... 59 E12 26 0N 119 15 E
Minićevo, Serbia & M. .. 28 G7 43 42N 22 18 E
Minidoka, U.S.A. 108 E7 42 45N 113 29W
Minigwal, L., Australia . 93 E3 29 31 S 123 14 E
Minilya →, Australia ... 93 D1 23 45 S 114 0 E
Minilya Roadhouse,
Australia .... 93 D1 23 55 S 114 0 E
Minipi L., Canada 105 B7 52 25N 60 45W
Mink L., Canada 102 A5 61 54N 117 40W
Minkammen, Sudan .... 81 F3 6 3N 31 32 E
Minna, Nigeria .... 83 D6 9 37N 6 30 E
Minneapolis, Kans.,
U.S.A. 112 F6 39 8N 97 42W
Minneapolis, Minn.,
U.S.A. 112 C8 44 59N 93 16W
Minnedosa, Canada 103 C9 50 14N 99 50W
Minnesota □, U.S.A. ... 112 B8 46 0N 94 15W
Minnesota →, U.S.A. .. 112 C8 44 54N 93 9W
Minnewaukan, U.S.A. .. 112 A5 48 4N 99 15W
Minnipa, Australia .... 95 E2 32 51 S 135 9 E
Minnitaki L., Canada .. 104 C1 49 57N 92 10W
Mino, Japan .... 55 G8 35 32N 136 55 E
Miño, Spain 36 B2 43 12N 8 15W
Miño →, Spain 36 D2 41 52N 8 40W
Minoa, U.S.A. .... 47 F7 35 6N 25 45 E
Minorca = Menorca,
Spain .... 48 B11 40 0N 4 0 E
Minot, U.S.A. 112 A4 48 14N 101 18W
Minqin, China .... 56 E2 38 38N 103 20 E
Minqing, China .... 59 D12 26 15N 118 50 E
Minsen, Germany ...... 24 B3 53 41N 7 58 E
Minsk, Belarus .... 32 F4 53 52N 27 30 E
Mińsk Mazowiecki,
Poland .... 31 F8 52 10N 21 33 E
Mintabie, Australia ... 95 D1 27 15 S 133 7 E
Mintaka Pass, Pakistan . 69 A6 37 0N 74 58 E
Minto, Canada 105 C6 46 5N 66 5W
Minto, L., Canada 104 A5 57 13N 75 0W
Minton, Canada 103 D8 49 10N 104 35W
Minturn, U.S.A. 108 G10 39 35N 106 26W
Minturno, Italy .... 42 A6 41 15N 13 45 E
Minúf, Egypt .... 80 H7 30 26N 30 52 E
Minusinsk, Russia ..... 53 D10 53 43N 91 20 E
Minutang, India ...... 67 E20 28 15N 96 30 E
Minya el Qamh, Egypt .. 80 H7 30 31N 31 21 E
Minya Konka = Gongga
Shan, China .... 58 C3 29 40N 101 55 E
Mionica, Bos.-H. ...... 44 B4 44 51N 18 29 E
Mionica, Serbia & M. .. 44 B4 44 14N 20 6 E
Miquelon, Canada 104 C4 49 25N 76 27W
Miquelon, St-P. & M. .. 105 C8 47 8N 56 22W
Mir, Niger .... 83 C7 14 5N 11 59 E
Mīr Kūh, Iran .... 71 E8 26 22N 58 55 E
Mīr Shahdād, Iran ..... 71 E8 26 15N 58 29 E
Mira, Italy .... 41 C9 45 26N 12 8 E
Mira, Portugal 36 E2 40 26N 8 44W
Mira →, Portugal 37 H2 37 43N 8 47W
Mira por vos Cay,
Bahamas 121 B5 22 9N 74 30W
Mirabella Eclano, Italy . 43 A7 41 2N 14 59 E
Mirador-Río Azul △,
Guatemala 120 C2 17 45N 89 50W
Miraj, India .... 66 L9 16 50N 74 45 E
Miram Shah, Pakistan .. 68 C4 33 0N 70 2 E
Miramar, Argentina ... 126 D4 38 15 S 57 50W
Miramar, Mozam. ..... 89 C6 23 50 S 35 35 E
Miramas, France ...... 21 E8 43 33N 4 59 E
Mirambeau, France 20 C3 45 23N 0 35W
Miramichi, Canada 105 C6 47 2N 65 28W
Miramichi B., Canada .. 105 C7 47 15N 65 0W
Miramont-de-Guyenne,
France .... 20 D4 44 37N 0 21 E
Miranda, Brazil ...... 125 H7 20 10 S 56 15W
Miranda →, Brazil .... 124 G7 19 25 S 57 20W
Miranda de Ebro, Spain 38 C2 42 41N 2 57W
Miranda do Corvo,
Portugal 36 E2 40 6N 8 20W
Miranda do Douro,
Portugal 36 D4 41 30N 6 16W
Mirande, France ...... 20 E4 43 31N 0 25 E
Mirandela, Portugal ... 36 D3 41 32N 7 10W
Mirándola, Italy ...... 41 D8 44 53N 11 4 E
Mirandópolis, Brazil .. 127 A5 21 9 S 51 6W
Mirango, Malawi ..... 87 E3 13 32 S 34 58 E
Mirani, Australia ..... 94 K6 21 8 S 148 53 E
Mirano, Italy .... 41 C9 45 30N 12 7 E
Miras, Albania .... 44 F4 40 40N 20 56 E
Mirassol, Brazil ...... 127 A6 20 46 S 49 28W
Mirbāṭ, Oman .... 75 D5 17 0N 54 45 E
Mirear, Egypt .... 80 C4 23 15N 35 41 E
Mirebeau, France ..... 18 F7 46 49N 0 10 E
Mirebeau-sur-Bèze,
France .... 19 E12 47 25N 5 20 E
Mirecourt, France .... 19 D13 48 20N 6 10 E
Mirgorod = Myrhorod,
Ukraine .... 33 H7 49 58N 33 37 E
Miri, Malaysia .... 62 D4 4 23N 113 59 E
Miriam Vale, Australia . 94 C5 24 20 S 151 33 E
Miribel, France ...... 19 G11 45 50N 4 57 E
Mirim, L., S. Amer. ... 127 C5 32 45 S 52 50W
Mirnyy, Russia .... 53 C12 62 33N 113 53 E
Miroc, Serbia & M. .... 44 B6 44 32N 22 16 E
Mirokhan, Pakistan ... 68 F3 27 46N 68 6 E
Mirond L., Canada 103 B8 55 6N 102 47W
Mirosławiec, Poland ... 30 E3 53 20N 16 5 E
Mirpur, Pakistan ..... 69 C5 33 32N 73 56 E
Mirpur Batoro, Pakistan 68 G3 24 44N 68 13 E
Mirpur Bibiwari,
Pakistan .... 68 E2 28 33N 67 44 E
Mirpur Khas, Pakistan . 68 G3 25 30N 69 0 E
Mirpur Sakro, Pakistan 68 G2 24 33N 67 41 E
Mirria, Niger .... 83 C6 13 43N 9 7 E
Mirsk, Poland .... 31 H2 50 58N 15 23 E
Mirtağ, Turkey .... 70 B4 38 23N 41 56 E
Miryang, S. Korea .... 57 G15 35 31N 128 44 E

Mirzaani, Georgia ..... 35 K8 41 24N 46 5 E
Mirzapur, India ...... 69 G10 25 10N 82 34 E
Mirzapur-cum-
Vindhyachal =
Mirzapur, India .... 69 G10 25 10N 82 34 E
Misantla, Mexico 119 D5 19 56N 96 50W
Misawa, Japan .... 54 D10 40 41N 141 24 E
Miscou I., Canada 105 C7 47 57N 64 31W
Mish'āb, Ra's al,
Si. Arabia .... 71 D6 28 15N 48 43 E
Mishan, China .... 60 B8 45 37N 131 48 E
Mishawaka, U.S.A. 114 E2 41 40N 86 11W
Mishbih, Gebel, Egypt . 80 C3 22 38N 34 44 E
Mishima, Japan ...... 55 G9 35 10N 138 52 E
Misión, Mexico 111 N10 32 6N 116 53W
Misiones □, Argentina . 127 B5 27 0 S 55 0W
Misiones □, Paraguay .. 126 B4 27 0 S 56 0W
Miskah, Si. Arabia .... 70 E4 24 49N 42 56 E
Miskitos, Cayos, Nic. .. 120 D3 14 26N 82 50W
Miskolc, Hungary ..... 28 B5 48 7N 20 50 E
Misoke, Dem. Rep. of
the Congo .... 86 C2 0 42 S 28 2 E
Misool, Indonesia ..... 63 E8 1 52 S 130 10 E
Miṣrātah, Libya ...... 79 B9 32 24N 15 3 E
Missanabie, Canada ... 104 C3 48 20N 84 6W
Missinaibi →, Canada . 104 B3 50 43N 81 29W
Missinaibi L., Canada .. 104 C3 48 23N 83 40W
Mission, Canada 102 D4 49 10N 122 15W
Mission, S. Dak., U.S.A. 112 D4 43 18N 100 39W
Mission, Tex., U.S.A. .. 113 M5 26 13N 98 20W
Mission Beach, Australia 94 B4 17 53 S 146 6 E
Mission Viejo, U.S.A. .. 111 M9 33 36N 117 40W
Missirah, Senegal 82 C1 13 40N 16 30W
Missisa L., Canada 104 B2 52 20N 85 7W
Missisicabi →, Canada . 104 B4 51 14N 79 31W
Mississagi →, Canada .. 104 C3 46 15N 83 9W
Mississauga, Canada ... 116 C5 43 32N 79 35W
Mississippi □, U.S.A. .. 113 J10 33 0N 90 0W
Mississippi →, U.S.A. . 113 L10 29 9N 89 15W
Mississippi L., Canada .. 117 A8 45 5N 76 10W
Mississippi River Delta,
U.S.A. 113 L9 29 10N 89 15W
Mississippi Sd., U.S.A. . 113 K10 30 20N 89 0W
Missoula, U.S.A. 108 C7 46 52N 114 1W
Missouri □, U.S.A. 112 F8 38 25N 92 30W
Missouri →, U.S.A. ... 112 F9 38 49N 90 7W
Missouri City, U.S.A. .. 113 L7 29 37N 95 32W
Missouri Valley, U.S.A. 112 E7 41 34N 95 53W
Mist, U.S.A. 110 E3 45 59N 123 15W
Mistassibi →, Canada . 105 B5 48 53N 72 13W
Mistassini →, Canada . 105 C5 48 42N 72 20W
Mistassini L., Canada .. 104 B5 51 0N 73 30W
Mistastin L., Canada ... 105 A7 55 57N 63 20W
Mistelbach, Austria ... 27 C9 48 34N 16 34 E
Misterbianco, Italy .... 43 E8 37 31N 15 1 E
Mistinibi, L., Canada .. 105 A7 55 56N 64 17W
Mistissini, Canada 105 C5 48 53N 72 13W
Mistretta, Italy ...... 43 E7 37 56N 14 22 E
Misty L., Canada 103 B8 58 53N 101 40W
Misurata = Miṣrātah,
Libya .... 79 B9 32 24N 15 3 E
Mit Ghamr, Egypt .... 80 H7 30 42N 31 12 E
Mitatib, Sudan .... 81 D4 15 59N 36 12 E
Mitchell, Australia .... 95 D4 26 29 S 147 58 E
Mitchell, Canada 116 C3 43 28N 81 12W
Mitchell, Nebr., U.S.A. . 112 E3 41 57N 103 49W
Mitchell, Oreg., U.S.A. . 108 D3 44 34N 120 9W
Mitchell, S. Dak., U.S.A. 112 D6 43 43N 98 2W
Mitchell →, Australia .. 94 B3 15 12 S 141 35 E
Mitchell, Mt., U.S.A. .. 115 H4 35 46N 82 16W
Mitchell and Alice
Rivers △, Australia . 94 B3 15 28 S 142 5 E
Mitchell Ranges,
Australia .... 94 A2 12 49 S 135 36 E
Mitchelstown, Ireland .. 12 D3 52 15N 8 16W
Mitha Tiwana, Pakistan 68 C5 32 13N 72 6 E
Mithi, Pakistan ...... 68 G3 24 44N 69 48 E
Mithimna, Greece .... 47 B8 39 20N 26 12 E
Mithrao, Pakistan .... 68 F3 27 28N 69 40 E
Mitilíni, Greece ...... 47 B8 39 6N 26 35 E
Mitilinoí, Greece ..... 47 D8 37 42N 26 56 E
Mito, Japan .... 55 F10 36 20N 140 30 E
Mitrofanovka, Russia .. 33 H10 49 58N 39 42 E
Mitrovica = Kosovska
Mitrovica,
Serbia & M. .... 44 D4 42 54N 20 52 E
Mitsinjo, Madag. ..... 89 B8 16 1 S 45 52 E
Mitsiwa, Eritrea ..... 81 D4 15 35N 39 25 E
Mitsiwa Channel, Eritrea 81 D5 15 30N 40 0 E
Mitsukaidō, Japan .... 55 F9 36 1N 139 59 E
Mittagong, Australia .. 95 E5 34 28 S 150 29 E
Mittelberg, Austria ... 26 D3 47 20N 10 10 E
Mittelfranken □,
Germany .... 25 F6 49 25N 10 40 E
Mittellandkanal →,
Germany .... 24 C4 52 20N 8 28 E
Mittenwalde, Germany 24 C9 52 15N 13 31 E
Mittersill, Austria .... 26 D5 47 16N 12 29 E
Mitterteich, Germany .. 25 F8 49 57N 12 14 E
Mittimatalik = Pond
Inlet, Canada 101 A12 72 40N 77 0W
Mittweida, Germany ... 24 E8 50 59N 12 59 E
Mitú, Colombia 124 C4 1 15N 70 13W
Mitumba, Tanzania ... 86 D3 7 8 S 31 2 E
Mitumba, Mts.,
Dem. Rep. of
the Congo .... 86 D2 7 0 S 27 30 E
Mitwaba, Dem. Rep. of
the Congo .... 87 D2 8 2 S 27 17 E
Mityana, Uganda ..... 86 B3 0 23N 32 2 E
Mixteco →, Mexico ... 119 D5 18 11N 98 30W
Miyagi □, Japan ...... 54 E10 38 15N 140 45 E
Miyah, W. el →, Egypt . 80 C3 25 0N 33 23 E
Miyāh, W. el →, Syria . 70 C3 34 44N 39 57 E
Miyake-Jima, Japan ... 55 G9 34 5N 139 30 E
Miyako, Japan .... 54 E10 39 40N 141 59 E
Miyako-Jima, Japan ... 55 M2 24 45N 125 20 E
Miyako-Rettō, Japan .. 55 M2 24 24N 125 0 E
Miyakonojō, Japan .... 55 J5 31 40N 131 5 E
Miyani, India .... 68 J3 21 50N 69 26 E
Miyanoura-Dake, Japan 55 J5 30 20N 130 31 E
Miyazaki, Japan ...... 55 J5 31 56N 131 30 E
Miyazaki □, Japan .... 55 H5 32 30N 131 30 E
Miyazu, Japan .... 55 G7 35 35N 135 10 E
Miyet, Bahr el = Dead
Sea, Asia .... 74 D4 31 30N 35 30 E
Miyi, China .... 58 D4 26 47N 102 9 E
Miyoshi, Japan ...... 55 G6 34 48N 132 51 E
Miyun, China .... 56 D9 40 28N 116 50 E
Miyun Shuiku, China .. 57 D9 40 30N 117 0 E
Mizan Teferi, Ethiopia . 81 F4 6 57N 35 3 E
Mizdah, Libya .... 79 B8 31 30N 13 0 E
Mizen Hd., Cork,
Ireland 12 E2 51 27N 9 50W
Mizen Hd., Wicklow,
Ireland 12 D5 52 51N 6 4W
Mizhhirya, Ukraine ... 29 B8 48 32N 23 30 E

Mizhi, China .... 56 F6 37 47N 110 12 E
Mizil, Romania .... 29 F11 44 59N 26 29 E
Mizoram □, India ..... 67 H18 23 30N 92 40 E
Mizpe Ramon, Israel .. 74 E3 30 34N 34 49 E
Mizuho, Antarctica ... 5 D5 70 30 S 41 0 E
Mizusawa, Japan ..... 54 E10 39 8N 141 8 E
Mjällby, Sweden ..... 11 H8 56 3N 14 40 E
Mjöbäck, Sweden ..... 11 G6 57 28N 12 53 E
Mjölby, Sweden ...... 11 F9 58 20N 15 10 E
Mjörn, Sweden .... 11 G6 57 55N 12 25 E
Mjøsa, Norway .... 9 F14 60 40N 11 0 E
Mkata, Tanzania ..... 86 D4 5 45 S 38 20 E
Mkhaya △, Swaziland . 89 D5 26 34 S 31 45 E
Mkokotoni, Tanzania .. 86 D4 5 55 S 39 15 E
Mkomazi, Tanzania ... 86 C4 4 40 S 38 7 E
Mkomazi △, Tanzania . 86 C4 4 4 S 30 2 E
Mkomazi →, S. Africa . 89 E5 30 12 S 30 50 E
Mkulwe, Tanzania .... 87 D3 8 37 S 32 20 E
Mkumbi, Ras, Tanzania 86 D4 7 38 S 39 55 E
Mkushi, Zambia ...... 87 E2 14 25 S 29 15 E
Mkushi River, Zambia . 87 E2 13 32 S 29 45 E
Mkuze, S. Africa ..... 89 D5 27 10 S 32 0 E
Mkuze △, S. Africa ... 89 D4 29 27 S 29 30 E
Mladá Boleslav,
Czech Rep. .... 26 A7 50 27N 14 53 E
Mladenovac,
Serbia & M. .... 44 B4 44 28N 20 44 E
Mlala Hills, Tanzania .. 86 D3 6 50 S 31 40 E
Mlange = Mulanje,
Malawi .... 87 F4 16 2 S 35 33 E
Mlanje, Pic, Malawi ... 85 H7 15 57 S 35 38 E
Mlava →, Serbia & M. . 44 B5 44 45N 21 13 E
Mława, Poland .... 31 E7 53 9N 20 25 E
Mlawula △, Swaziland . 89 D5 26 23 S 32 2 E
Mlinište, Bos.-H. ..... 41 D13 44 15N 16 50 E
Mljet, Croatia .... 41 F14 42 43N 17 30 E
Mljetski Kanal, Croatia 41 F14 42 48N 17 35 E
Mlynary, Poland ..... 30 D6 54 12N 19 46 E
Mmabatho, S. Africa .. 88 D4 25 49 S 25 30 E
Mme, Cameroon ...... 83 D7 6 18N 10 14 E
Mnichovo Hradiště,
Czech Rep. .... 26 A7 50 32N 14 59 E
Mo i Rana, Norway ... 8 C16 66 20N 14 7 E
Moa, Cuba 121 B4 20 40N 74 56W
Moa, Indonesia ...... 63 F7 8 0 S 128 0 E
Moa →, S. Leone 82 D2 6 59N 11 36W
Moab, U.S.A. 109 G9 38 35N 109 33W
Moala, Fiji .... 91 D8 18 36 S 179 53 E
Moama, Australia .... 95 F3 36 7 S 144 46 E
Moamba, Mozam. ..... 89 D5 25 36 S 32 15 E
Moapa, U.S.A. 111 J12 36 40N 114 37W
Moate, Ireland 12 C4 53 24N 7 44W
Moba, Dem. Rep. of
the Congo .... 86 D2 7 0 S 29 48 E
Mobārakābād, Iran ... 71 D7 28 24N 53 20 E
Mobaye, C.A.R. ...... 84 D4 4 25N 21 5 E
Mobayi, Dem. Rep. of
the Congo .... 84 D4 4 15N 21 8 E
Moberley Lake, Canada 102 B4 55 50N 121 44W
Moberly, U.S.A. 112 F8 39 25N 92 26W
Mobile, U.S.A. 115 K1 30 41N 88 3W
Mobile B., U.S.A. 115 K2 30 30N 88 0W
Mobridge, U.S.A. 112 C4 45 32N 100 26W
Moc Chau, Vietnam ... 64 B5 20 50N 104 38 E
Moc Hoa, Vietnam .... 65 G5 10 46N 105 56 E
Mocabe Kasari,
Dem. Rep. of
the Congo .... 87 D2 9 58 S 26 12 E
Moçambique, Mozam. . 87 F5 15 3 S 40 42 E
Mocanaqua, U.S.A. ... 117 E8 41 9N 76 8W
Mochima △, Venezuela 124 A5 10 30N 64 5W
Mochudi, Botswana ... 88 C4 24 27 S 26 7 E
Mocimboa da Praia,
Mozam. .... 87 E5 11 25 S 40 20 E
Mociu, Romania ...... 29 D9 46 46N 24 3 E
Möckeln, Sweden ..... 11 H8 56 40N 14 15 E
Mockfjärd, Sweden ... 10 D8 60 30N 14 57 E
Moclips, U.S.A. 110 C2 47 14N 124 13W
Mocoa, Colombia 124 C3 1 7N 76 35W
Mococa, Brazil ...... 127 A6 21 28 S 47 0W
Mocorito, Mexico 118 B3 25 30N 107 53W
Moctezuma, Mexico ... 118 B3 29 50N 109 0W
Moctezuma →, Mexico 119 C5 21 59N 98 34W
Mocuba, Mozam. ..... 87 F4 16 54 S 36 57 E
Mocúzari, Presa, Mexico 118 B3 27 10N 109 10W
Modane, France ...... 21 C10 45 12N 6 40 E
Modasa, India .... 68 H5 23 30N 73 21 E
Modder →, S. Africa .. 88 D3 29 2 S 24 37 E
Modderrivier, S. Africa 88 D3 29 2 S 24 38 E
Módena, Italy .... 40 D7 44 40N 10 55 E
Modena, U.S.A. 109 H7 37 48N 113 56W
Modesto, U.S.A. 110 H6 37 39N 121 0W
Módica, Italy .... 43 F7 36 52N 14 46 E
Modimolle, S. Africa .. 89 C4 24 42 S 28 22 E
Mödling, Austria ..... 27 C9 48 5N 16 17 E
Modo, Sudan .... 81 F3 5 31N 30 33 E
Modra, Slovak Rep. ... 27 C10 48 19N 17 20 E
Modriča, Bos.-H. ..... 28 F3 44 57N 18 17 E
Moe, Australia .... 95 F4 38 12 S 146 19 E
Moebase, Mozam. .... 87 F4 17 3 S 38 41 E
Moëlan-sur-Mer, France 18 E3 47 49N 3 38W
Moengo, Suriname 125 B8 5 45N 54 20W
Moffat, U.K. 13 F5 55 21N 3 27W
Moga, India .... 68 D6 30 48N 75 8 E
Mogadishu = Muqdisho,
Somali Rep. .... 75 G4 2 2N 45 25 E
Mogador = Essaouira,
Morocco 78 B4 31 32N 9 42W
Mogadouro, Portugal .. 36 D4 41 22N 6 47W
Mogalakwena →,
S. Africa .... 89 C4 22 38 S 28 40 E
Mogami-Gawa →,
Japan .... 54 E10 38 45N 140 0 E
Mogán, Canary Is. 48 G4 27 53N 15 43W
Mogaung, Burma ..... 67 G20 25 20N 97 0 E
Mogente = Moixent,
Spain 39 G4 38 52N 0 45W
Mogho, Ethiopia ..... 81 G5 4 54N 40 16 E
Mogi das Cruzes, Brazil 127 A6 23 31 S 46 11W
Mogi-Guaçu →, Brazil . 127 A6 20 53 S 48 10W
Mogi-Mirim, Brazil ... 127 A6 22 29 S 47 0W
Mogielnica, Poland ... 31 G7 51 42N 20 41 E
Mogige, Ethiopia ..... 81 F4 5 24N 36 14 E
Mogilev = Mahilyow,
Belarus .... 32 F6 53 55N 30 18 E
Mogilev-Podolskiy =
Mohyliv-Podilskyy,
Ukraine .... 29 B12 48 26N 27 48 E
Mogincual, Mozam. ... 87 F5 15 35 S 40 25 E
Mogliano Véneto, Italy 41 C9 45 33N 12 14 E
Mogocha, Russia ..... 53 D12 53 40N 119 50 E
Mogok, Burma .... 67 H20 23 0N 96 40 E
Mogollon Rim, U.S.A. . 109 J8 34 10N 110 50W
Mógoro, Italy .... 42 C1 39 41N 8 47 E
Mograt, Sudan .... 80 D3 19 28N 33 16 E

Moguer, Spain 37 H4 37 15N 6 52W
Mogumber, Australia . 93 F2 31 2 S 116 3 E
Mohács, Hungary ..... 28 E3 45 58N 18 41 E
Mohales Hoek, Lesotho 88 E4 30 7 S 27 26 E
Mohall, U.S.A. 112 A4 48 46N 101 31W
Moḥammadābād, Iran . 71 B8 37 52N 59 5 E
Mohammedia, Morocco 78 B4 33 44N 7 21W
Mohana →, India ..... 69 G11 24 43N 85 0 E
Mohanlalganj, India .. 69 F9 26 41N 80 58 E
Mohave, L., U.S.A. ... 111 K12 35 12N 114 34W
Mohawk →, U.S.A. ... 117 D11 42 47N 73 41W
Moheda, Sweden ...... 11 G8 57 1N 14 35 E
Mohenjodaro, Pakistan 68 F3 27 19N 68 7 E
Moher, Cliffs of, Ireland 12 D2 52 58N 9 27W
Mohicanville Reservoir,
U.S.A. 116 F3 40 45N 82 0W
Möhne →, Germany ... 24 D3 51 29N 7 57 E
Mohoro, Tanzania .... 86 D4 8 6 S 39 8 E
Mohyliv-Podilskyy,
Ukraine .... 29 B12 48 26N 27 48 E
Moia, Sudan .... 81 F2 5 3N 28 2 E
Moidart, L., U.K. 13 E3 56 47N 5 52W
Moineşti, Romania .... 29 D11 46 28N 26 31 E
Moira →, Canada 116 B7 44 21N 77 24W
Moirans, France ...... 21 C9 45 20N 5 33 E
Moirans-en-Montagne,
France .... 19 F12 46 26N 5 43 E
Moíres, Greece .... 49 D6 35 4N 24 56 E
Moisaküla, Estonia ... 9 G21 58 3N 25 12 E
Moisie, Canada 105 B6 50 12N 66 1W
Moisie →, Canada 105 B6 50 14N 66 5W
Moissac, France ...... 20 D5 44 7N 1 5 E
Moita, Portugal 37 G2 38 38N 8 58W
Moixent, Spain 39 G4 38 52N 0 45W
Möja, Sweden .... 10 E12 59 26N 18 55 E
Mojácar, Spain 39 H3 37 6N 1 55W
Mojados, Spain 36 D6 41 26N 4 40W
Mojave, U.S.A. 111 K8 35 3N 118 10W
Mojave △, U.S.A. 111 K11 35 7N 115 30W
Mojave Desert, U.S.A. . 111 L10 35 0N 116 30W
Mojiang, China ...... 58 F3 23 37N 101 35 E
Mojo, Bolivia .... 126 A2 21 48 S 65 33W
Mojo, Ethiopia ...... 81 F4 8 35N 39 5 E
Mojokerto, Indonesia . 63 G15 7 28 S 112 26 E
Mokai, N.Z. .... 91 H5 38 32 S 175 56 E
Mokambo, Dem. Rep. of
the Congo .... 87 E2 12 25 S 28 20 E
Mokameh, India ...... 69 G11 25 24N 85 55 E
Mokau, N.Z. .... 91 H5 38 42 S 174 39 E
Mokelumne →, U.S.A. 110 G5 38 13N 121 28W
Mokelumne Hill, U.S.A. 110 G6 38 18N 120 43W
Mokhós, Greece ...... 49 D7 35 16N 25 27 E
Mokhotlong, Lesotho .. 89 D4 29 22 S 29 2 E
Möklinta, Sweden .... 10 D10 60 4N 16 33 E
Mokokchung, India ... 67 F19 26 15N 94 30 E
Mokolo, Cameroon .... 83 C7 10 50N 13 55 E
Mokolo →, S. Africa .. 89 C4 23 14 S 27 43 E
Mokopane, S. Africa .. 89 C4 24 10 S 28 55 E
Mokp'o, S. Korea ..... 57 G14 34 50N 126 25 E
Mokra Gora,
Serbia & M. .... 44 D4 42 50N 20 30 E
Mokronog, Slovenia ... 41 C12 45 57N 15 9 E
Moksha →, Russia .... 34 C6 54 45N 41 53 E
Mokshan, Russia ..... 34 D7 53 25N 44 35 E
Mokwa, Nigeria ...... 83 D6 9 19N 5 0 E
Mol, Belgium .... 17 C5 51 11N 5 5 E
Mola di Bari, Italy .... 43 A10 41 4N 17 5 E
Molale, Ethiopia ..... 81 F4 10 10N 39 41 E
Moláoi, Greece ...... 46 E4 36 49N 22 56 E
Molara, Italy .... 42 A5 40 52N 9 43 E
Molat, Croatia .... 41 D11 44 15N 14 50 E
Molchanovo, Russia ... 52 D9 57 40N 83 50 E
Mold, U.K. 14 D4 53 9N 3 8W
Moldava nad Bodvou,
Slovak Rep. .... 27 C14 48 38N 21 0 E
Moldavia = Moldova ■,
Europe .... 29 C13 47 0N 28 0 E
Moldavia, Romania ... 29 C10 47 0N 27 0 E
Molde, Norway .... 8 E12 62 45N 7 9 E
Moldova ■, Europe ... 29 C13 47 0N 28 0 E
Moldova Nouă,
Romania .... 28 F6 44 45N 21 41 E
Moldoveanu, Vf.,
Romania .... 29 E9 45 36N 24 45 E
Moldoviţa, Romania .. 29 C10 47 41N 25 32 E
Mole →, Ghana 83 D4 9 43N 1 44W
Mole →, U.K. 15 F7 51 24N 0 21W
Mole Creek, Australia . 95 G4 41 34 S 146 24 E
Molepolole, Botswana . 88 C4 24 28 S 25 28 E
Molfetta, Italy .... 43 A9 41 12N 16 36 E
Molina de Aragón,
Spain 38 E3 40 46N 1 52W
Molina de Segura, Spain 39 G3 38 3N 1 12W
Moline, U.S.A. 112 E9 41 30N 90 31W
Molinella, Italy ...... 41 D8 44 37N 11 40 E
Molinos, Argentina ... 126 B2 25 28 S 66 15W
Moliro, Dem. Rep. of
the Congo .... 86 D3 8 12 S 30 30 E
Moliterno, Italy ...... 43 B8 40 14N 15 52 E
Molkom, Sweden ..... 10 E7 59 37N 13 44 E
Mölle, Sweden .... 11 H6 56 17N 12 31 E
Molledo, Spain 36 B6 43 8N 4 6W
Mollendo, Peru ...... 124 G4 17 0 S 72 0W
Mollerin, L., Australia . 93 F2 30 30 S 117 35 E
Mollerussa, Spain .... 38 D5 41 37N 0 54 E
Mollina, Spain 37 H6 37 8N 4 38W
Mölln, Germany ...... 24 B6 53 37N 10 41 E
Mölltorp, Sweden ..... 11 F8 58 30N 14 26 E
Mölnlycke, Sweden ... 11 G6 57 40N 12 8 E
Molochansk, Ukraine .. 33 J8 47 15N 35 35 E
Molochnoye, Ozero,
Ukraine .... 33 J8 46 30N 35 20 E
Molodechno =
Maladzyechna,
Belarus .... 32 E4 54 20N 26 50 E
Molokai, U.S.A. 106 H16 21 8N 157 0W
Molong, Australia .... 95 E4 33 5 S 148 54 E
Molopo →, Africa ..... 88 D3 28 30 S 20 12 E
Mólos, Greece .... 46 C4 38 47N 22 37 E
Molson L., Canada 103 C9 54 22N 96 40W
Molteno, S. Africa .... 88 E4 31 22 S 26 22 E
Molu, Indonesia ...... 63 F8 6 45 S 131 40 E
Molucca Sea, Indonesia 63 E6 0 0 125 0 E
Moluccas = Maluku,
Indonesia .... 63 E7 1 0 S 127 0 E
Moma, Dem. Rep. of
the Congo .... 86 C1 1 35 S 23 52 E
Moma, Mozam. .... 87 F4 16 47 S 39 4 E
Mombasa, Kenya ..... 86 C4 4 2 S 39 43 E
Mombetsu, Japan ..... 54 B11 44 21N 143 22 E
Momchilgrad, Bulgaria 45 E9 41 33N 25 23 E
Momi, Dem. Rep. of
the Congo .... 86 C2 1 42 S 27 0 E

Mompós, Colombia 124 B4 9 14N 74 26W
Møn, Denmark .... 11 K6 54 57N 12 20 E
Mon □, Burma .... 67 L20 16 0N 97 30 E
Mona, Canal de la =
Mona Passage,
W. Indies 121 C6 18 30N 67 45W
Mona, Isla, Puerto Rico 121 C6 18 5N 67 54W
Mona, Pta., Costa Rica 120 E3 9 37N 82 36W
Mona Passage, W. Indies 121 C6 18 30N 67 45W
Monaca, U.S.A. 116 F4 40 41N 80 17W
Monaco ■, Europe .... 21 E11 43 46N 7 23 E
Monadhliath Mts., U.K. 13 D4 57 10N 4 4W
Monadnock, Mt., U.S.A. 117 D12 42 52N 72 7W
Monaghan, Ireland ... 12 B5 54 15N 6 57W
Monaghan □, Ireland .. 12 B5 54 11N 6 56W
Monahans, U.S.A. 113 K3 31 36N 102 54W
Monapo, Mozam. ..... 87 E5 14 56 S 40 19 E
Monar, L., U.K. 13 D3 57 26N 5 8W
Monarch Mt., Canada . 102 C3 51 55N 125 57W
Monashee Mts., Canada 102 C5 51 0N 118 43W
Monasterevin, Ireland . 12 C4 53 8N 7 4W
Monastir = Bitola,
Macedonia .... 44 E5 41 1N 21 20 E
Moncada, Phil. .... 61 D4 15 44N 120 34 E
Moncalieri, Italy ..... 40 C4 45 0N 7 41 E
Moncalvo, Italy ...... 40 C5 45 3N 8 16 E
Moncão, Portugal 36 C2 42 4N 8 27W
Monção, Portugal 36 E2 40 9N 8 52W
Moncontour, France ... 18 D4 48 22N 2 38W
Moncton, Canada 105 C7 46 7N 64 51W
Mondariz, Spain 36 C2 42 14N 8 27W
Mondego →, Portugal . 36 E2 40 9N 8 52W
Mondego, C., Portugal . 36 E2 40 11N 8 54W
Mondeodo, Indonesia . 63 E6 3 34 S 122 9 E
Mondeville, France ... 18 C6 49 10N 0 18W
Mondo, Chad .... 79 F9 13 47N 15 34 E
Mondolfo, Italy ...... 41 E10 43 45N 13 6 E
Mondoñedo, Spain 36 B3 43 25N 7 23W
Mondoví, Italy .... 40 D4 44 23N 7 49 E
Mondovi, U.S.A. 112 C9 44 34N 91 40W
Mondragon, Phil. ..... 61 E6 12 31N 124 45 E
Mondragone, Italy .... 42 A6 41 7N 13 53 E
Mondrain I., Australia . 93 F3 34 9 S 122 14 E
Moneague, Jamaica ... 120 a 18 16N 77 7W
Monemvasía, Greece .. 46 E5 36 41N 23 3 E
Monessen, U.S.A. 116 F5 40 9N 79 54W
Monesterio, Spain 37 G4 38 6N 6 15W
Monestier-de-Clermont,
France .... 21 D9 44 55N 5 38 E
Monett, U.S.A. 113 G8 36 55N 93 55W
Moneymore, U.K. 12 B5 54 41N 6 40W
Monfalcone, Italy ..... 41 C10 45 49N 13 32 E
Monflanquin, France .. 20 D4 44 32N 0 47 E
Monforte, Portugal ... 37 F3 39 6N 7 25W
Monforte de Lemos,
Spain 36 C3 42 31N 7 33W
Mong Cai, Vietnam ... 64 B6 21 27N 107 54 E
Mong Hsu, Burma .... 58 G2 21 54N 98 30 E
Mong Kung, Burma ... 67 J20 21 35N 97 35 E
Mong Nai, Burma ..... 67 J20 20 32N 97 46 E
Mong Pawk, Burma ... 67 H21 22 4N 99 16 E
Mong Ping, Burma .... 58 G2 21 22N 99 2 E
Mong Ton, Burma .... 67 J21 20 17N 98 45 E
Mong Wa, Burma ..... 67 J22 21 26N 100 27 E
Mong Yai, Burma ..... 67 H21 22 21N 98 3 E
Mongalla, Sudan ..... 81 F3 5 8N 31 42 E
Mongers, L., Australia . 93 E2 29 25 S 117 5 E
Monghyr = Munger,
India .... 69 G12 25 23N 86 30 E
Mongibello = Etna, Italy 43 E7 37 50N 14 55 E
Mongo, Chad .... 79 F9 12 14N 18 43 E
Mongolia ■, Asia ..... 53 E10 47 0N 103 0 E
Mongolia, Plateau of,
Asia .... 50 E14 45 0N 105 0 E
Mongonu, Nigeria .... 83 C7 12 40N 13 32 E
Mongu, Zambia ...... 85 H4 15 16 S 23 12 E
Môngua, Angola ..... 88 B2 16 43 S 15 20 E
Monifieth, U.K. 13 E6 56 30N 2 48W
Monistrol-sur-Loire,
France .... 21 C8 45 17N 4 11 E
Monkey Bay, Malawi .. 87 E4 14 7 S 35 1 E
Monkey Mia, Australia 93 E1 25 48 S 113 43 E
Monkey River, Belize .. 119 D7 16 22N 88 29W
Mońki, Poland .... 30 E9 53 23N 22 48 E
Monkoto, Dem. Rep. of
the Congo .... 84 E4 1 38 S 20 35 E
Monkton, Canada 116 C3 43 35N 81 5W
Monmouth, U.K. 15 F5 51 48N 2 42W
Monmouth, Ill., U.S.A. 112 E9 40 55N 90 39W
Monmouth, Oreg.,
U.S.A. 108 D2 44 51N 123 14W
Monmouthshire □, U.K. 15 F5 51 48N 2 54W
Mono L., U.S.A. 110 H7 38 1N 119 1W
Monólithos, Greece ... 49 C9 36 7N 27 45 E
Monongahela, U.S.A. . 116 F5 40 12N 79 56W
Monópoli, Italy ...... 43 B10 40 57N 17 18 E
Monor, Hungary ..... 28 C4 47 21N 19 27 E
Monos I., Trin. & Tob. . 125 K15 10 42N 61 44W
Monóvar, Spain 39 G4 38 28N 0 53W
Monreal del Campo,
Spain 38 E3 40 47N 1 20W
Monreale, Italy ...... 42 E6 38 5N 13 17 E
Monroe, Ga., U.S.A. .. 115 J4 33 47N 83 43W
Monroe, La., U.S.A. .. 113 J8 32 30N 92 7W
Monroe, Mich., U.S.A. . 114 E4 41 55N 83 24W
Monroe, N.C., U.S.A. . 115 H5 34 59N 80 33W
Monroe, N.Y., U.S.A. . 117 E10 41 20N 74 11W
Monroe, Utah, U.S.A. . 109 G7 38 38N 112 7W
Monroe, Wash., U.S.A. 110 C5 47 51N 121 58W
Monroe, Wis., U.S.A. . 112 D10 42 36N 89 38W
Monroe City, U.S.A. .. 112 F9 39 39N 91 44W
Monroeton, U.S.A. 117 E8 41 43N 76 29W
Monroeville, Ala.,
U.S.A. 115 K2 31 31N 87 20W
Monroeville, Pa., U.S.A. 116 F5 40 26N 79 45W
Monrovia, Liberia 82 D2 6 18N 10 47W
Mons, Belgium .... 17 D3 50 27N 3 58 E
Møns Klint, Denmark . 11 K6 54 57N 12 8 E
Monsaraz, Portugal ... 37 G3 38 28N 7 22W
Monse, Indonesia ..... 63 E6 4 7 S 123 15 E
Monségur, France .... 20 D4 44 38N 0 4 E
Monsélice, Italy ...... 41 C8 45 14N 11 45 E
Mönsterås, Sweden ... 11 G10 57 3N 16 26 E
Mont Cenis, Col du,
France .... 21 C10 45 15N 6 55 E
Mont-de-Marsan, France 20 E3 43 54N 0 31W
Mont-Joli, Canada 105 C6 48 37N 68 10W
Mont-Laurier, Canada . 104 C4 46 35N 75 30W
Mont-Louis, Canada .. 105 C6 49 15N 65 44W
Mont Peko △, Ivory C. 82 D3 7 30N 7 15W

Mont-roig del Camp, Spain 38 D5 41 5N 0 58 E
Mont-St-Michel, Le, France 18 D5 48 40N 1 30W
Mont Sangbe △, Ivory C. 82 D3 8 0N 7 10W
Mont-Tremblant △, Canada 104 C5 46 30N 74 30W
Montabaur, Germany 24 E3 50 25N 7 50 E
Montagnac, France 20 E7 43 29N 3 28 E
Montagnana, Italy 41 C8 45 14N 11 28 E
Montagne d'Ambre △, Madag. 89 A8 12 37 S 49 8 E
Montagne de Reims △, France 19 C11 49 8N 4 0 E
Montagu, S. Africa 88 E3 33 45 S 20 8 E
Montagu I., Antarctica 5 B1 58 25 S 26 20W
Montague, Canada 105 C7 46 10N 62 39W
Montague, I., Mexico 118 A2 31 40N 114 56W
Montague Ra., Australia 93 E2 27 15 S 119 30 E
Montague Sd., Australia 92 B4 14 28 S 125 20 E
Montaigu, France 18 F5 46 59N 1 18W
Montalbán, Spain 38 E4 40 50N 0 45W
Montalbano Iónico, Italy 43 B9 40 17N 16 34 E
Montalbo, Spain 38 F2 39 53N 2 42W
Montalcino, Italy 41 E8 43 3N 11 29 E
Montalegre, Portugal 36 D3 41 49N 7 47W
Montalto, Italy 43 D8 38 10N 15 55 E
Montalto di Castro, Italy 41 F8 42 21N 11 37 E
Montalto Uffugo, Italy 43 C9 39 24N 16 9 E
Montalvo, U.S.A. 111 L7 34 15N 119 12W
Montamarta, Spain 36 D5 41 39N 5 49W
Montana, Bulgaria 44 C7 43 27N 23 16 E
Montana, Peru 124 E4 6 0 S 73 0W
Montana □, Bulgaria 44 C7 43 30N 23 20 E
Montana □, U.S.A. 108 C9 47 0N 110 0W
Montaña Clara, I., Canary Is. 48 E6 29 17N 13 33W
Montañas de Malaga △, Spain 37 J6 36 48N 4 32W
Montánchez, Spain 37 F4 39 15N 6 8W
Montargil, Portugal 37 F2 39 5N 8 10W
Montargis, France 19 E9 47 59N 2 43 E
Montauban, France 20 D5 44 2N 1 21 E
Montauk, U.S.A. 117 E13 41 3N 71 57W
Montauk Pt., U.S.A. 117 E13 41 4N 71 52W
Montbard, France 19 E11 47 38N 4 20 E
Montbarrey, France 19 E12 47 1N 5 39 E
Montbéliard, France 19 E13 47 31N 6 48 E
Montblanc, Spain 38 D6 41 23N 1 4 E
Montbrison, France 21 C8 45 36N 4 3 E
Montcalm, Pic de, France 20 F5 42 40N 1 25 E
Montceau-les-Mines, France 19 F11 46 40N 4 23 E
Montcenis, France 21 B8 46 47N 4 23 E
Montclair, U.S.A. 117 F10 40 49N 74 13W
Montcornet, France 19 C11 49 40N 4 1 E
Montcuq, France 20 D5 44 21N 1 13 E
Montdidier, France 19 C9 49 38N 2 35 E
Monte Albán, Mexico 119 D5 17 2N 96 45W
Monte Alegre, Brazil 125 D8 2 0 S 54 0W
Monte Azul, Brazil 125 G10 15 9 S 42 53W
Monte Bello Is., Australia 92 D2 20 30 S 115 45 E
Monte-Carlo, Monaco 21 E11 43 44N 7 25 E
Monte Caseros, Argentina 126 C4 30 10 S 57 50W
Monte Comán, Argentina 126 C2 34 40 S 67 53W
Monte Cristi, Dom. Rep. 121 C5 19 52N 71 39W
Monte Cucco △, Italy 41 E9 43 22N 12 43 E
Monte Lindo →, Paraguay 126 A4 23 56 S 57 12W
Monte Patria, Chile 126 C1 30 42 S 70 58W
Monte Quemado, Argentina 126 B3 25 53 S 62 41W
Monte Redondo, Portugal 36 F2 39 53N 8 50W
Monte Rio, U.S.A. 110 G4 38 28N 123 0W
Monte San Giovanni Campano, Italy 42 A6 41 38N 13 31 E
Monte Sant' Savino, Italy 41 E8 43 20N 11 43 E
Monte Sant' Ángelo, Italy 41 G12 41 42N 15 59 E
Monte Santu, C. di, Italy 42 B2 40 5N 9 44 E
Monte Sibillini △, Italy 41 F10 42 55N 13 15 E
Monte Subasio △, Italy 41 E9 43 5N 12 40 E
Monte Vista, U.S.A. 109 H10 37 35N 106 9W
Monteagudo, Argentina 127 B5 27 14 S 54 8W
Montealegre del Castillo, Spain 39 G3 38 48N 1 17W
Montebello, Canada 104 C5 45 40N 74 55W
Montebello Iónico, Italy 43 E8 37 59N 15 45 E
Montebelluna, Italy 41 C9 45 47N 12 3 E
Montebourg, France 18 C5 49 30N 1 20W
Montecastrilli, Italy 41 F9 42 39N 12 29 E
Montecatini Terme, Italy 40 E7 43 53N 10 46 E
Montecito, U.S.A. 111 L7 34 26N 119 40W
Montecristo, Italy 40 F7 42 20N 10 19 E
Montefalco, Italy 41 F9 42 54N 12 39 E
Montefiascone, Italy 41 F9 42 32N 12 2 E
Montefrío, Spain 37 H7 37 20N 4 0W
Montegiórgio, Italy 41 E10 43 6N 13 33 E
Montego Bay, Jamaica 120 a 18 30N 78 0W
Montehermoso, Spain 36 E4 40 5N 6 21W
Montejicar, Spain 37 H7 37 33N 3 30W
Montélimar, France 21 D8 44 33N 4 45 E
Montella, Italy 43 B8 40 51N 15 1 E
Montellano, Spain 37 J5 36 59N 5 29W
Montello, U.S.A. 112 D10 43 48N 89 20W
Montemor-o-Novo, Portugal 37 G2 38 40N 8 12W
Montemor-o-Velho, Portugal 36 E2 40 11N 8 40W
Montendre, France 20 C3 45 16N 0 26W
Montenegro, Brazil 127 B5 29 39 S 51 29W
Montenegro □, Serbia & M. 44 D3 42 40N 19 20 E
Montenero di Bisáccia, Italy 41 G11 41 57N 14 47 E
Montepuez, Mozam. 87 E4 13 8 S 38 59 E
Montepuez →, Mozam. 87 E5 12 32 S 40 27 E
Montepulciano, Italy 41 E8 43 5N 11 46 E
Montereale, Italy 41 F10 42 31N 13 15 E
Montereau-Faut-Yonne, France 19 D9 48 22N 2 57 E
Monterey, U.S.A. 110 J5 36 37N 121 55W
Monterey B., U.S.A. 110 J5 36 45N 122 0W
Montería, Colombia 124 B3 8 46N 75 53W
Monteros, Argentina 126 B2 27 11 S 65 30W
Monterotondo, Italy 41 F9 42 3N 12 37 E
Monterrey, Mexico 118 B4 25 40N 100 30W
Montes Azules △, Mexico 119 D6 16 21N 91 3W
Montes Claros, Brazil 125 G10 16 30 S 43 50W

Montesano, U.S.A. 110 D3 46 59N 123 36W
Montesano sulla Marcellana, Italy 43 B8 40 16N 15 42 E
Montescághioso, Italy 43 B9 40 33N 16 40 E
Montesilvano, Italy 41 F11 42 29N 14 8 E
Montevarchi, Italy 41 E8 43 31N 11 34 E
Montevideo, Uruguay 127 C4 34 50 S 56 11W
Montevideo, U.S.A. 112 C7 44 57N 95 43W
Montezuma, U.S.A. 112 E8 41 35N 92 32W
Montezuma Castle △, U.S.A. 109 J8 34 34N 111 45W
Montfaucon, France 18 E5 47 6N 1 7W
Montfaucon-d'Argonne, France 19 C12 49 16N 5 8 E
Montfaucon-en-Velay, France 21 C8 45 11N 4 20 E
Montfort-le-Gesnois, France 18 D7 48 3N 0 25 E
Montfort-sur-Meu, France 18 D5 48 9N 1 58W
Montfragüe △, Spain 36 F5 39 48N 5 52W
Montgenèvre, France 21 D10 44 56N 6 43 E
Montgomery, U.K. 15 E4 52 34N 3 8W
Montgomery, Ala., U.S.A. 115 J2 32 23N 86 19W
Montgomery, Pa., U.S.A. 116 E8 41 10N 76 53W
Montgomery, W. Va., U.S.A. 114 F5 38 11N 81 19W
Montgomery City, U.S.A. 112 F9 38 59N 91 30W
Montguyon, France 20 C3 45 12N 0 12W
Monthermé, France 19 C11 49 52N 4 42 E
Monthey, Switz. 25 J2 46 15N 6 56 E
Monthois, France 19 C11 49 19N 4 43 E
Monti, France 42 B2 40 49N 9 19 E
Monti Lucrétili △, Italy 41 F9 42 5N 12 50 E
Monti Picentini △, Italy 43 B8 40 45N 15 2 E
Monti Simbruini △, Italy 41 G10 41 55N 13 13 E
Monticelli d'Ongina, Italy 40 C6 45 5N 9 56 E
Monticello, Ark., U.S.A. 113 J9 33 38N 91 47W
Monticello, Fla., U.S.A. 115 K4 30 33N 83 52W
Monticello, Ind., U.S.A. 114 E2 40 45N 86 46W
Monticello, Iowa, U.S.A. 112 E9 42 15N 91 12W
Monticello, Ky., U.S.A. 115 G3 36 50N 84 51W
Monticello, Minn., U.S.A. 112 C8 45 18N 93 48W
Monticello, Miss., U.S.A. 113 K9 31 33N 90 7W
Monticello, N.Y., U.S.A. 117 E10 41 39N 74 42W
Monticello, Utah, U.S.A. 109 H9 37 52N 109 21W
Montichiari, Italy 40 C7 45 25N 10 23 E
Montier-en-Der, France 19 D11 48 30N 4 45 E
Montignac, France 20 C5 45 4N 1 10 E
Montigny-les-Metz, France 19 C13 49 7N 6 10 E
Montigny-sur-Aube, France 19 E11 47 57N 4 45 E
Montijo, Portugal 37 G2 38 41N 8 54W
Montijo, Spain 37 G4 38 52N 6 39W
Montilla, Spain 37 H6 37 36N 4 40W
Montivilliers, France 18 C7 49 33N 0 12 E
Montluçon, France 19 F9 46 22N 2 36 E
Montmagny, Canada 105 C5 46 58N 70 34W
Montmarault, France 19 F9 46 19N 2 57 E
Montmartre, Canada 103 C8 50 14N 103 27W
Montmédy, France 19 C12 49 30N 5 20 E
Montmélian, France 21 C10 45 30N 6 4 E
Montmirail, France 19 D10 48 51N 3 30 E
Montmoreau-St-Cybard, France 20 C4 45 23N 0 8 E
Montmorillon, France 20 B4 46 26N 0 50 E
Montmort-Lucy, France 19 D10 48 55N 3 49 E
Monto, Australia 94 C5 24 52 S 151 6 E
Montoire-sur-le-Loir, France 18 E7 47 45N 0 52 E
Montório al Vomano, Italy 41 F10 42 35N 13 38 E
Montoro, Spain 37 G6 38 1N 4 27W
Montour Falls, U.S.A. 116 D8 42 21N 76 51W
Montoursville, U.S.A. 116 E8 41 15N 76 55W
Montpelier, Idaho, U.S.A. 108 E8 42 19N 111 18W
Montpelier, Vt., U.S.A. 117 B12 44 16N 72 35W
Montpellier, France 20 E7 43 37N 3 52 E
Montpezat-de-Quercy, France 20 D5 44 15N 1 30 E
Montpon-Ménestérol, France 20 D4 45 0N 0 11 E
Montréal, Canada 117 A11 45 31N 73 34W
Montréal, Aude, France 20 E6 43 13N 2 8 E
Montréal, Gers, France 20 E4 43 56N 0 11 E
Montreal →, Canada 104 C3 47 14N 84 39W
Montreal L., Canada 103 C7 54 20N 105 45W
Montreal Lake, Canada 103 C7 54 3N 105 46W
Montredon-Labessonnié, France 20 E6 43 45N 2 18 E
Montrésor, France 18 E8 47 10N 1 10 E
Montret, France 19 F12 46 40N 5 7 E
Montreuil, Pas-de-Calais, France 19 B8 50 27N 1 45 E
Montreuil, Seine-St-Denis, France 19 D9 48 51N 2 27 E
Montreuil-Bellay, France 18 E6 47 8N 0 9W
Montreux, Switz. 25 J2 46 26N 6 55 E
Montrevel-en-Bresse, France 19 F12 46 21N 5 8 E
Montrichard, France 18 E8 47 20N 1 10 E
Montrose, U.K. 13 E6 56 44N 2 27W
Montrose, Colo., U.S.A. 109 G10 38 29N 107 53W
Montrose, Pa., U.S.A. 117 E9 41 50N 75 53W
Monts, Pte. des, Canada 105 C6 49 20N 67 12W
Montsalvy, France 20 D6 44 41N 2 30 E
Montsant, Serra de, Spain 38 D6 41 17N 1 0 E
Montsauche-les-Settons, France 19 E11 47 13N 4 2 E
Montsec, Serra del, Spain 38 C5 42 5N 0 45 E
Montseny △, Spain 38 D2 41 43N 2 22W
Montserrat, Spain 38 D6 41 36N 1 49 E
Montserrat ☑, W. Indies 121 C7 16 40N 62 10W
Montuenga, Spain 36 D6 41 3N 4 38W
Montuiri, Spain 48 B9 39 34N 2 59 E
Monywa, Burma 67 H19 22 7N 95 11 E
Monza, Italy 40 C6 45 35N 9 16 E
Monze, Zambia 87 F2 16 17 S 27 29 E
Monze, C., Pakistan 68 G2 24 47N 66 37 E
Monzón, Spain 38 D5 41 52N 0 10 E
Mooers, U.S.A. 117 B11 44 58N 73 35W
Mooi →, S. Africa 89 D5 28 45 S 30 34 E
Mooi River, S. Africa 89 D4 29 13 S 29 50 E

Moonah →, Australia 94 C2 22 3 S 138 33 E
Moonda, L., Australia 94 D3 25 52 S 140 25 E
Moonie, Australia 95 D5 27 46 S 150 20 E
Moonie →, Australia 95 D4 29 19 S 148 43 E
Moonta, Australia 95 E2 34 6 S 137 32 E
Moora, Australia 93 F2 30 37 S 115 58 E
Moorcroft, U.S.A. 112 C2 44 16N 104 57W
Moore →, Australia 93 F2 31 22 S 115 30 E
Moore, L., Australia 93 E2 29 50 S 117 35 E
Moore Park, Australia 94 C5 24 43 S 152 17 E
Moore River △, Australia 93 F2 31 7 S 115 39 E
Moorefield, U.S.A. 114 F6 39 5N 78 59W
Moores Res., U.S.A. 117 B13 44 45N 71 50W
Moorfoot Hills, U.K. 13 F5 55 44N 3 8W
Moorhead, U.S.A. 112 B6 46 53N 96 45W
Moormerland, Germany 24 B3 53 19N 7 24 E
Moorpark, U.S.A. 111 L8 34 17N 118 53W
Moorreesburg, S. Africa 88 E2 33 6 S 18 38 E
Moorrinya △, Australia 94 C3 21 42 S 144 58 E
Moosburg, Germany 25 G7 48 27N 11 56 E
Moose →, Canada 104 B3 51 20N 80 25W
Moose →, U.S.A. 117 C9 43 38N 75 24W
Moose Creek, Canada 117 A10 45 15N 74 58W
Moose Factory, Canada 104 B3 51 16N 80 32W
Moose Jaw, Canada 103 C7 50 24N 105 30W
Moose Jaw →, Canada 103 C7 50 34N 105 18W
Moose Lake, Canada 112 B8 46 27N 92 46W
Moose Mountain △, Canada 103 D8 49 48N 102 25W
Moosehead L., U.S.A. 115 C11 45 38N 69 40W
Mooselookmeguntic L., U.S.A. 115 C10 44 55N 70 49W
Moosilauke, Mt., U.S.A. 117 B13 44 3N 71 40W
Moosomin, Canada 103 C8 50 9N 101 40W
Moosonee, Canada 104 B3 51 17N 80 39W
Moosup, U.S.A. 117 E13 41 43N 71 53W
Mopane, S. Africa 89 C4 22 37 S 29 52 E
Mopeia Velha, Mozam. 87 F4 17 30 S 35 40 E
Mopipi, Botswana 88 C3 21 6 S 24 55 E
Mopoi, C.A.R. 86 A2 5 6N 26 54 E
Mopti, Mali 82 C4 14 30N 4 0W
Moqatta, Sudan 81 E4 14 38N 35 50 E
Moqor, Afghan. 68 C2 32 50N 67 42 E
Moquegua, Peru 124 G4 17 15 S 70 46W
Mór, Hungary 28 C3 47 25N 18 12 E
Mora, Cameroon 83 C7 11 2N 14 7 E
Mora, Portugal 37 G2 38 55N 8 10W
Mora, Spain 37 F7 39 41N 3 46W
Mora, Sweden 10 C8 61 2N 14 38 E
Mora, Minn., U.S.A. 112 C8 45 53N 93 18W
Mora, N. Mex., U.S.A. 109 J11 35 58N 105 20W
Mora de Rubielos, Spain 38 E4 40 15N 0 45W
Mòra d'Ebre, Spain 38 D5 41 6N 0 38 E
Mòra la Nova, Spain 38 D5 41 7N 0 39 E
Moraća →, Serbia & M. 44 D3 42 20N 19 9 E
Moradabad, India 69 E8 28 50N 78 50 E
Morafenobe, Madag. 89 B7 17 50 S 44 53 E
Morag, Poland 30 E6 53 55N 19 56 E
Moral de Calatrava, Spain 37 G7 38 51N 3 33W
Moraleja, Spain 36 E4 40 6N 6 43W
Moramanga, Madag. 89 B8 18 56 S 48 12 E
Moran, Kans., U.S.A. 113 G7 37 55N 95 10W
Moran, Wyo., U.S.A. 108 E8 43 53N 110 37W
Moranbah, Australia 94 C4 22 1 S 148 6 E
Morano Cálabro, Italy 43 C9 39 50N 16 8 E
Morant Bay, Jamaica 120 a 17 22N 76 0W
Morant Cays, Jamaica 120 a 17 22N 76 0W
Morant Pt., Jamaica 120 a 17 55N 76 12W
Morar, India 68 F8 26 14N 78 14 E
Morar, L., U.K. 13 E3 56 57N 5 40W
Moratalla, Spain 39 G3 38 14N 1 49W
Moratuwa, Sri Lanka 66 R11 6 45N 79 55 E
Morava →, Slovak Rep. 27 C9 48 10N 16 59 E
Moravia, U.S.A. 117 D8 42 43N 76 25W
Moravian Hts. = Českomoravská Vrchovina, Czech Rep. 26 B8 49 30N 15 40 E
Moravica →, Serbia & M. 44 C4 43 52N 20 8 E
Moravița, Romania 28 E6 45 17N 21 14 E
Moravská Třebová, Czech Rep. 27 B9 49 45N 16 40 E
Moravské Budějovice, Czech Rep. 26 B8 49 4N 15 49 E
Morawa, Australia 93 E2 29 13 S 116 0 E
Morawhanna, Guyana 124 B7 8 30N 59 40W
Moray □, U.K. 13 D5 57 31N 3 18W
Moray Firth, U.K. 13 D5 57 40N 3 52W
Morbach, Germany 25 F3 49 48N 7 6 E
Morbegno, Italy 40 B6 46 8N 9 34 E
Morbi, India 68 H4 22 50N 70 42 E
Morbihan □, France 18 E4 47 55N 2 50W
Mörbylånga, Sweden 11 H10 56 32N 16 22 E
Morcenx, France 20 D3 44 3N 0 55W
Morcone, Italy 43 A7 41 20N 14 40 E
Mordelles, France 18 E5 48 5N 1 52W
Morden, Canada 103 D9 49 15N 98 10W
Mordovian Republic = Mordvinia □, Russia 34 C7 54 20N 44 30 E
Mordovo, Russia 34 D5 52 6N 40 50 E
Mordvinia □, Russia 34 C7 54 20N 44 30 E
Mordy, Poland 31 F9 52 13N 22 31 E
Morea, Greece 6 H10 37 45N 22 10 E
Moreau →, U.S.A. 112 C4 45 18N 100 43W
Morecambe, U.K. 14 C5 54 5N 2 52W
Morecambe B., U.K. 14 C5 54 7N 3 0W
Moree, Australia 95 D4 29 28 S 149 54 E
Morehead, U.S.A. 114 F4 38 11N 83 26W
Morehead City, U.S.A. 115 H7 34 43N 76 43W
Morel →, India 68 F7 26 13N 76 36 E
Morelia, Mexico 118 D4 19 42N 101 7W
Morella, Australia 94 C3 23 0 S 143 52 E
Morella, Spain 38 E4 40 35N 0 5W
Morelos, Mexico 118 B3 26 42N 107 40W
Morelos □, Mexico 119 D5 18 40N 99 10W
Moremi △, Botswana 88 B3 19 18 S 23 10 E
Morena, India 68 F8 26 30N 78 4 E
Morena, Sierra, Spain 37 G7 38 20N 4 0W
Moreni, Romania 29 F10 44 59N 25 36 E
Moreno Valley, U.S.A. 111 M10 33 56N 117 15W
Moresby I., Canada 102 C2 52 30N 131 40W
Morestel, France 21 C9 45 40N 5 28 E
Moreton I., Australia 95 D5 27 10 S 153 25 E
Moreton Island △, Australia 95 D5 27 2 S 153 24 E
Moreuil, France 19 C9 49 46N 2 30 E
Morey, Spain 48 B10 39 44N 3 20 E
Morez, France 19 F13 46 31N 6 2 E
Morgan, U.S.A. 108 F8 41 2N 111 41W
Morgan City, U.S.A. 113 L9 29 42N 91 12W
Morgan Hill, U.S.A. 110 H5 37 8N 121 39W
Morganfield, U.S.A. 114 G2 37 41N 87 55W

Morganton, U.S.A. 115 H5 35 45N 81 41W
Morgantown, U.S.A. 114 F6 39 38N 79 57W
Morgenzon, S. Africa 89 D4 26 45 S 29 36 E
Morges, Switz. 25 J2 46 31N 6 29 E
Morghak, Iran 71 D8 29 7N 57 54 E
Morgongåva, Sweden 10 E10 59 57N 16 58 E
Morhange, France 19 D13 48 55N 6 38 E
Morhar →, India 69 G11 25 29N 85 11 E
Mori, Italy 40 C7 45 51N 10 59 E
Mori, Japan 54 C10 42 6N 140 35 E
Moriarty, U.S.A. 109 J10 34 59N 106 3W
Moribaya, Guinea 82 D3 9 53N 9 32W
Morice L., Canada 102 C3 53 50N 127 40W
Moriki, Nigeria 83 C6 12 52N 6 30 E
Morinville, Canada 102 C6 53 49N 113 41W
Morioka, Japan 54 E10 39 45N 141 8 E
Moris, Mexico 118 B3 28 8N 108 32W
Morlaàs, France 20 E3 43 21N 0 18W
Morlaix, France 18 D3 48 36N 3 52W
Mörlunda, Sweden 11 G9 57 19N 15 52 E
Mormanno, Italy 43 C8 39 53N 15 59 E
Mormant, France 19 D9 48 37N 2 52 E
Mornington, Australia 95 F4 38 15 S 145 5 E
Mornington, I., Chile 128 F1 49 50 S 75 30W
Mornington I., Australia 94 B2 16 30 S 139 30 E
Mórnos →, Greece 46 C3 38 25N 21 50 E
Moro, Pakistan 68 F2 26 40N 68 0 E
Moro, Sudan 81 E3 10 50N 30 9 E
Moro →, Pakistan 68 E2 29 42N 67 22 E
Moro G., Phil. 61 H5 6 30N 123 0 E
Morocco ■, N. Afr. 78 B4 32 0N 5 50W
Morogoro, Tanzania 86 D4 6 50 S 37 40 E
Morogoro □, Tanzania 86 D4 8 0 S 37 0 E
Moroleón, Mexico 118 C4 20 8N 101 32W
Morombe, Madag. 89 C7 21 45 S 43 22 E
Moron, Argentina 126 C4 34 39 S 58 37W
Morón, Cuba 120 B4 22 8N 78 39W
Morón de Almazán, Spain 38 D2 41 29N 2 27W
Morón de la Frontera, Spain 37 H5 37 6N 5 28W
Morona →, Peru 124 D3 4 40 S 77 10W
Morondava, Madag. 89 C7 20 17 S 44 17 E
Morondo, Ivory C. 82 D3 8 57N 6 47W
Morongo Valley, U.S.A. 111 L10 34 3N 116 37W
Moroni, Comoros Is. 77 H8 11 40 S 43 16 E
Moroni, U.S.A. 108 G8 39 32N 111 35W
Moronou, Ivory C. 82 D4 6 16N 4 59W
Morotai, Indonesia 63 D7 2 10N 128 30 E
Moroto, Uganda 86 B3 2 28N 34 42 E
Moroto, Mt., Uganda 86 B3 2 30N 34 43 E
Morozov, Bulgaria 45 D9 42 30N 25 10 E
Morozovsk, Russia 35 F5 48 25N 41 50 E
Morpeth, U.K. 14 B6 55 10N 1 41W
Morphou, Cyprus 49 D11 35 12N 32 59 E
Morphou Bay, Cyprus 49 D11 35 15N 32 50 E
Morrilton, U.S.A. 113 H8 35 9N 92 44W
Morrinhos, Brazil 125 G9 17 45 S 49 10W
Morrinsville, N.Z. 91 G5 37 40 S 175 32 E
Morris, Canada 103 D9 49 25N 97 22W
Morris, Ill., U.S.A. 112 E10 41 22N 88 26W
Morris, Minn., U.S.A. 112 C7 45 35N 95 55W
Morris, N.Y., U.S.A. 117 D9 42 33N 75 15W
Morris, Pa., U.S.A. 116 E7 41 35N 77 17W
Morris, Mt., Australia 93 E5 26 9 S 131 4 E
Morris Jesup, Kap, Greenland 4 A5 83 40N 34 0W
Morrisburg, Canada 117 B9 44 55N 75 7W
Morristown, Ariz., U.S.A. 109 K7 33 51N 112 37W
Morristown, N.J., U.S.A. 117 F10 40 48N 74 29W
Morristown, N.Y., U.S.A. 117 B9 44 35N 75 39W
Morristown, Tenn., U.S.A. 115 G4 36 13N 83 18W
Morrisville, N.Y., U.S.A. 117 D9 42 53N 75 35W
Morrisville, Pa., U.S.A. 117 F10 40 13N 74 47W
Morrisville, Vt., U.S.A. 117 B12 44 34N 72 36W
Morro, Pta., Chile 126 B1 27 6 S 71 0W
Morro Bay, U.S.A. 110 K6 35 22N 120 51W
Morro del Jable, Canary Is. 48 F5 28 3N 14 23W
Morro Jable, Pta. de, Canary Is. 48 F5 28 2N 14 20W
Morrocoy △, Venezuela 121 D6 10 48N 68 13W
Morrosquillo, G. de, Colombia 120 E4 9 35N 75 40W
Mörrum, Sweden 11 H8 56 12N 14 45 E
Morrumbene, Mozam. 89 C6 23 31 S 35 16 E
Mörrumsån →, Sweden 11 H8 56 10N 14 45 E
Mors, Denmark 11 H2 56 50N 8 45 E
Morshansk, Russia 34 D5 53 28N 41 50 E
Mörsil, Sweden 10 A7 63 19N 13 40 E
Mortagne →, France 19 D13 48 33N 6 27 E
Mortagne-au-Perche, France 18 D7 48 31N 0 33 E
Mortagne-sur-Gironde, France 20 C3 45 28N 0 47W
Mortagne-sur-Sèvre, France 18 F6 47 0N 0 59W
Mortain, France 18 D6 48 40N 0 57W
Mortara, Italy 40 C5 45 15N 8 44 E
Morteau, France 19 E13 47 3N 6 35 E
Morteros, Argentina 126 C3 30 50 S 62 0W
Mortlach, Canada 103 C7 50 27N 106 4W
Mortlake, Australia 95 F3 38 5 S 142 50 E
Morton, Tex., U.S.A. 113 J3 33 44N 102 46W
Morton, Wash., U.S.A. 110 D4 46 34N 122 17W
Moruga, Trin. & Tob. 125 K15 10 4N 61 16W
Morundah, Australia 95 E4 34 57 S 146 19 E
Moruya, Australia 95 F5 35 58 S 150 3 E
Morvan, France 19 E11 47 5N 4 0 E
Morven, Australia 95 D4 26 22 S 147 5 E
Morven, U.K. 13 E5 56 38N 5 44W
Morwell, Australia 95 F4 38 10 S 146 22 E
Moryń, Poland 31 F1 52 51N 14 22 E
Morzine, France 21 B10 46 11N 6 42 E
Mosalsk, Russia 32 E8 54 30N 34 55 E
Mosbach, Germany 25 F5 49 21N 9 9 E
Mošćenice, Croatia 41 C11 45 17N 14 16 E
Mosciano Sant' Ángelo, Italy 41 F10 42 42N 13 52 E
Moscos Is., Burma 64 E1 14 0N 97 30 E
Moscow = Moskva, Russia 32 E9 55 45N 37 35 E
Moscow, Idaho, U.S.A. 108 C5 46 44N 117 0W
Moscow, Pa., U.S.A. 117 E9 41 20N 75 31W
Mosel →, Europe 19 B14 50 22N 7 36 E
Moselle = Mosel →, Europe 19 B14 50 22N 7 36 E
Moselle □, France 19 D13 48 59N 6 33 E
Moses Lake, U.S.A. 108 C4 47 8N 119 17W
Mosgiel, N.Z. 91 L3 45 53 S 170 21 E
Moshaweng →, S. Africa 88 D3 26 35 S 22 50 E
Moshi, Tanzania 86 C4 3 22 S 37 18 E

Moshupa, Botswana 88 C4 24 46 S 25 29 E
Mosina, Poland 31 F3 52 15N 16 50 E
Mosjøen, Norway 8 D15 65 51N 13 12 E
Moskenesøya, Norway 8 C15 67 58N 13 0 E
Moskenstraumen, Norway 8 C15 67 47N 12 45 E
Moskva, Russia 32 E9 55 45N 37 35 E
Moskva →, Russia 32 E10 55 5N 38 51 E
Moslavačka Gora, Croatia 41 C13 45 40N 16 37 E
Mosomane, Botswana 88 C4 24 2 S 26 19 E
Mosonmagyaróvár, Hungary 28 C2 47 52N 17 18 E
Mošorin, Serbia & M. 28 E5 45 19N 20 4 E
Mospino, Ukraine 33 J9 47 52N 38 0 E
Mosquera, Colombia 124 C3 2 35N 78 24W
Mosquero, U.S.A. 113 H3 35 47N 103 58W
Mosqueruela, Spain 38 E4 40 21N 0 27W
Mosquitia, Honduras 120 C3 15 20N 84 10W
Mosquito Coast = Mosquitia, Honduras 120 C3 15 20N 84 10W
Mosquito Creek L., U.S.A. 116 E4 41 18N 80 46W
Mosquito L., Canada 103 A8 62 35N 103 20W
Mosquitos, G. de los, Panama 120 E3 9 15N 81 10W
Moss, Norway 9 G14 59 27N 10 40 E
Moss Vale, Australia 95 E5 34 32 S 150 25 E
Mossbank, Canada 103 D7 49 56N 105 56W
Mossburn, N.Z. 91 L2 45 41 S 168 15 E
Mosselbaai, S. Africa 88 E3 34 11 S 22 8 E
Mossendjo, Congo 84 E2 2 55 S 12 42 E
Mossgiel, Australia 95 E3 33 15 S 144 5 E
Mossingen, Germany 25 G5 48 24N 9 4 E
Mossman, Australia 94 B4 16 21 S 145 15 E
Mossoró, Brazil 125 E11 5 10 S 37 15W
Mossuril, Mozam. 87 E5 14 58 S 40 42 E
Most, Czech Rep. 26 A6 50 31N 13 38 E
Mosta, Malta 49 D1 35 55N 14 26 E
Mostaganem, Algeria 78 A6 35 54N 0 5 E
Mostar, Bos.-H. 28 G2 43 22N 17 50 E
Mostardas, Brazil 127 C5 31 2 S 50 51W
Mostiska = Mostyska, Ukraine 31 J10 49 48N 23 4 E
Móstoles, Spain 36 E7 40 19N 3 53W
Mosty = Masty, Belarus 31 F3 53 27N 24 38 E
Mostyska, Ukraine 31 J10 49 48N 23 4 E
Mosul = Al Mawşil, Iraq 70 B4 36 15N 43 5 E
Mosûlpo, S. Korea 57 H14 33 20N 126 17 E
Mota, Ethiopia 81 E4 11 5N 37 52 E
Mota del Cuervo, Spain 39 F2 39 30N 2 52W
Mota del Marqués, Spain 36 D5 41 38N 5 11W
Motagua →, Guatemala 120 C2 15 44N 88 14W
Motala, Sweden 11 F9 58 32N 15 1 E
Motaze, Mozam. 89 C5 24 48 S 32 52 E
Moţca, Romania 29 C11 47 15N 26 37 E
Moth, India 69 G8 25 43N 78 57 E
Motherwell, U.K. 13 F5 55 47N 3 58W
Motihari, India 69 F11 26 30N 84 55 E
Motilla del Palancar, Spain 39 F3 39 34N 1 55W
Motnik, Slovenia 41 B11 46 14N 14 54 E
Motovun, Croatia 41 C10 45 20N 13 50 E
Motozintla de Mendoza, Mexico 119 D6 15 21N 92 14W
Motril, Spain 37 J7 36 31N 3 37W
Motru, Romania 28 F7 44 48N 22 59 E
Motru →, Romania 29 F8 44 44N 22 31 E
Mott, U.S.A. 112 B3 46 23N 102 20W
Móttola, Italy 43 B10 40 38N 17 2 E
Motueka, N.Z. 91 J4 41 7 S 173 1 E
Motueka →, N.Z. 91 J4 41 5 S 173 1 E
Motul, Mexico 119 C7 21 0N 89 20W
Mouchalagane →, Canada 105 B6 50 56N 68 41W
Moúdhros, Greece 47 B7 39 50N 25 18 E
Mouding, China 58 E3 25 20N 101 28 E
Moudjeria, Mauritania 82 B2 17 50N 12 28W
Moudon, Switz. 25 J2 46 40N 6 49 E
Mouila, Gabon 84 E2 1 50 S 11 0 E
Moulamein, Australia 95 F3 35 3 S 144 1 E
Moule, Guadeloupe 120 b 16 20N 61 21W
Moule à Chique, C., St. Lucia 121 f 13 43N 60 57W
Mouliana, Greece 49 D7 35 10N 25 59 E
Moulins, France 19 F10 46 35N 3 19 E
Moulmein, Burma 67 L20 16 30N 97 40 E
Moulouya, O. →, Morocco 78 B5 35 5N 2 25W
Moultrie, U.S.A. 115 K4 31 11N 83 47W
Moultrie, L., U.S.A. 115 J5 33 20N 80 5W
Mound City, Mo., U.S.A. 112 E7 40 7N 95 14W
Mound City, S. Dak., U.S.A. 112 C4 45 44N 100 4W
Moúnda, Ákra, Greece 46 C2 38 3N 20 47 E
Moundou, Chad 79 G9 8 40N 16 10 E
Moundsville, U.S.A. 116 G4 39 55N 80 44W
Moung, Cambodia 64 F4 12 46N 103 27 E
Mount Airy, U.S.A. 115 G5 36 31N 80 37W
Mount Albert, Canada 116 B5 44 8N 79 19W
Mount Aspiring △, N.Z. 91 L2 44 19 S 168 47 E
Mount Barker, S. Austral., Australia 95 F2 35 5 S 138 52 E
Mount Barker, W. Austral., Australia 93 F2 34 38 S 117 40 E
Mount Brydges, Canada 116 D3 42 54N 81 29W
Mount Burr, Australia 95 F3 37 34 S 140 26 E
Mount Carmel = Ha Karmel △, Israel 74 C4 32 45N 35 5 E
Mount Carmel, Ill., U.S.A. 114 F2 38 25N 87 46W
Mount Carmel, Pa., U.S.A. 117 F8 40 47N 76 24W
Mount Charleston, U.S.A. 111 J11 36 16N 115 37W
Mount Coolon, Australia 94 C4 21 25 S 147 25 E
Mount Darwin, Zimbabwe 87 F3 16 47 S 31 38 E
Mount Desert I., U.S.A. 115 C11 44 21N 68 20W
Mount Dora, U.S.A. 115 L5 28 48N 81 38W
Mount Edziza △, Canada 102 B2 57 30N 130 45W
Mount Elgon △, E. Afr. 86 B3 1 4N 34 42 E
Mount Field △, Australia 95 G4 42 39 S 146 35 E
Mount Fletcher, S. Africa 89 E4 30 40 S 28 30 E
Mount Forest, Canada 116 C4 43 59N 80 43W
Mount Gambier, Australia 95 F3 37 50 S 140 46 E
Mount Garnet, Australia 94 B4 17 37 S 145 6 E
Mount Holly, U.S.A. 117 G10 39 59N 74 47W
Mount Holly Springs, U.S.A. 116 F7 40 7N 77 12W
Mount Hope, N.S.W., Australia 95 E4 32 51 S 145 51 E

Mount Hope, S. Austral.,
Australia .... **95 E2** 34 7 S 135 23 E
Mount Isa, Australia .. **94 C2** 20 42 S 139 26 E
Mount Jewett, U.S.A. . **116 E6** 41 44N 78 39W
Mount Kaputar △,
Australia .... **95 E5** 30 16 S 150 10 E
Mount Kenya △, Kenya **86 C4** 0 7 S 37 21 E
Mount Kilimanjaro △,
Tanzania .... **86 C4** 3. 2 S 37 19 E
Mount Kisco, U.S.A. .. **117 E11** 41 12N 73 44W
Mount Laguna, U.S.A. **111 N10** 32 52N 116 25W
Mount Larcom,
Australia .... **94 C5** 23 48 S 150 59 E
Mount Lofty Ra.,
Australia .... **95 E2** 34 35 S 139 5 E
Mount Magnet,
Australia .... **93 E2** 28 2 S 117 47 E
Mount Maunganui, N.Z. **91 G6** 37 40 S 176 14 E
Mount Molloy, Australia **94 B4** 16 42 S 145 20 E
Mount Morgan,
Australia .... **94 C5** 23 40 S 150 25 E
Mount Morris, U.S.A. . **116 D7** 42 44N 77 52W
Mount Pearl, Canada .. **105 C9** 47 31N 52 47W
Mount Penn, U.S.A. ... **117 F9** 40 20N 75 54W
Mount Perry, Australia **95 D5** 25 13 S 151 42 E
Mount Pleasant, Iowa,
U.S.A. **112 E9** 40 58N 91 33W
Mount Pleasant, Mich.,
U.S.A. **114 D3** 43 36N 84 46W
Mount Pleasant, Pa.,
U.S.A. **116 F5** 40 9N 79 33W
Mount Pleasant, S.C.,
U.S.A. **115 J6** 32 47N 79 52W
Mount Pleasant, Tenn.,
U.S.A. **115 H2** 35 32N 87 12W
Mount Pleasant, Tex.,
U.S.A. **113 J7** 33 9N 94 58W
Mount Pleasant, Utah,
U.S.A. **108 G8** 39 33N 111 27W
Mount Pocono, U.S.A. **117 E9** 41 7N 75 22W
Mount Rainier △,
U.S.A. **110 D5** 46 55N 121 50W
Mount Revelstoke △,
Canada **102 C5** 51 5N 118 30W
Mount Robson △,
Canada **102 C5** 53 0N 119 0W
Mount St. Helens △,
U.S.A. **110 D4** 46 14N 122 11W
Mount Selinda,
Zimbabwe .... **89 C5** 20 24 S 32 43 E
Mount Shasta, U.S.A. **108 F2** 41 19N 122 19W
Mount Signal, U.S.A. . **111 N11** 32 39N 115 37W
Mount Sterling, Ill.,
U.S.A. **112 F9** 39 59N 90 45W
Mount Sterling, Ky.,
U.S.A. **114 F4** 38 4N 83 56W
Mount Surprise,
Australia .... **94 B3** 18 10 S 144 17 E
Mount Union, U.S.A. . **116 F7** 40 23N 77 53W
Mount Upton, U.S.A. . **117 D9** 42 26N 75 23W
Mount Vernon, Ill.,
U.S.A. **114 F1** 38 19N 88 55W
Mount Vernon, Ind.,
U.S.A. **112 F10** 38 17N 88 57W
Mount Vernon, N.Y.,
U.S.A. **117 F11** 40 55N 73 50W
Mount Vernon, Ohio,
U.S.A. **116 F2** 40 23N 82 29W
Mount Vernon, Wash.,
U.S.A. **110 B4** 48 25N 122 20W
Mount William △,
Australia .... **95 G4** 40 56 S 148 14 E
Mountain Ash, U.K. ... **13 F4** 51 40N 3 23W
Mountain Center, U.S.A. **111 M10** 33 42N 116 44W
Mountain City, Nev.,
U.S.A. **108 F6** 41 50N 115 58W
Mountain City, Tenn.,
U.S.A. **115 G5** 36 29N 81 48W
Mountain Dale, U.S.A. **117 E10** 41 41N 74 32W
Mountain Grove, U.S.A. **113 G8** 37 8N 92 16W
Mountain Home, Ark.,
U.S.A. **113 G8** 36 20N 92 23W
Mountain Home, Idaho,
U.S.A. **108 E6** 43 8N 115 41W
Mountain Iron, U.S.A. **112 B8** 47 32N 92 37W
Mountain Pass, U.S.A. **111 K11** 35 29N 115 35W
Mountain View, Ark.,
U.S.A. **113 H8** 35 52N 92 7W
Mountain View, Calif.,
U.S.A. **110 H4** 37 23N 122 5W
Mountain View, Hawaii,
U.S.A. **106 J17** 19 33N 155 7W
Mountain Zebra △,
S. Africa .... **88 E4** 32 14 S 25 27 E
Mountainair, U.S.A. .. **109 J10** 34 31N 106 15W
Mountlake Terrace,
U.S.A. **110 C4** 47 47N 122 19W
Mountmellick, Ireland . **12 C4** 53 7N 7 20W
Mountrath, Ireland **12 D4** 53 0N 7 28W
Moura, Australia ..... **94 C4** 24 35 S 149 58 E
Moura, Brazil .... **124 D6** 1 32 S 61 38W
Moura, Portugal **37 G3** 38 7N 7 30W
Mourão, Portugal **37 G3** 38 22N 7 22W
Mourdi, Dépression du,
Chad .... **79 E10** 18 10N 23 0 E
Mourdiah, Mali **82 C3** 14 35N 7 25W
Mourenx, France **20 E3** 43 22N 0 38W
Mouri, Ghana **83 D4** 5 6N 1 14W
Mourilyan, Australia .. **94 B4** 17 35 S 146 3 E
Mourmelon-le-Grand,
France .... **19 C11** 49 8N 4 22 E
Mourne →, U.K. **12 B4** 54 52N 7 26W
Mourne Mts., U.K. ... **12 B5** 54 10N 6 0W
Mournies, Greece ..... **49 D6** 35 29N 24 1 E
Mournies = Mourniaí,
Greece .... **49 D6** 35 29N 24 1 E
Mouscron, Belgium .. **17 D3** 50 45N 3 12 E
Moussoro, Chad ...... **79 F9** 13 41N 16 35 E
Mouthe, France ...... **19 F13** 46 44N 6 12 E
Moutier, Switz. ...... **25 H3** 47 16N 7 21 E
Moûtiers, France ..... **21 C10** 45 29N 6 32 E
Moutong, Indonesia .. **63 D6** 0 28N 121 13 E
Mouy, France .... **19 C9** 49 18N 2 20 E
Mouzáki, Greece ..... **46 B3** 39 25N 21 37 E
Mouzon, France ..... **19 C12** 49 36N 5 3 E
Movas, Mexico **118 B3** 28 10N 109 25W
Moville, Ireland **12 A4** 55 11N 7 3W
Mowandjum, Australia **92 C3** 17 22 S 123 40 E
Moy →, Ireland **12 B2** 54 8N 9 8W
Moyale, Kenya ...... **81 G4** 3 30N 39 0 E
Moyamba, S. Leone .. **82 D2** 8 4N 12 30W
Moyen Atlas, Morocco **78 B4** 33 0N 5 0W
Moyne, L. le, Canada .. **105 A6** 56 45N 68 47W
Moyo, Indonesia ..... **62 F5** 8 10 S 117 40 E
Moyobamba, Peru .... **124 E3** 6 0 S 77 0W
Moyyero →, Russia .. **53 C11** 68 44N 103 42 E
Moyynty, Kazakhstan . **52 E8** 47 10N 73 18 E

Mozambique =
Moçambique, Mozam. **87 F5** 15 3 S 40 42 E
Mozambique ■, Africa **87 F4** 19 0 S 35 0 E
Mozambique Chan.,
Africa .... **89 B7** 17 30 S 42 30 E
Mozdok, Russia ..... **35 J7** 43 45N 44 48 E
Mozdūrān, Iran ..... **71 B9** 36 9N 60 35 E
Mozhaysk, Russia .... **32 E9** 55 30N 36 2 E
Mozhga, Russia ..... **34 B11** 56 26N 52 15 E
Mozhnābād, Iran .... **71 C9** 34 7N 60 6 E
Mozirje, Slovenia .... **41 B11** 46 22N 14 58 E
Mozyr = Mazyr, Belarus **33 F5** 51 59N 29 15 E
Mpanda, Tanzania .... **86 D3** 6 23 S 31 1 E
Mpésoba, Mali **82 C3** 12 31N 5 39W
Mphoengs, Zimbabwe **89 C4** 21 10 S 27 51 E
Mpika, Zambia ...... **87 E3** 11 51 S 31 25 E
Mpulungu, Zambia .. **87 D3** 8 51 S 31 5 E
Mpumalanga, S. Africa **89 D5** 29 50 S 30 33 E
Mpumalanga □,
S. Africa .... **89 D5** 26 0 S 30 0 E
Mpwapwa, Tanzania .. **86 D4** 6 23 S 36 30 E
Mqanduli, S. Africa ... **89 E4** 31 49 S 28 45 E
Mqinvartsveri = Kazbek,
Russia .... **35 J7** 42 42N 44 30 E
Mragowo, Poland .... **30 E8** 53 52N 21 18 E
Mramor, Serbia & M. .. **44 C5** 43 20N 21 45 E
Mrkonjić Grad, Bos.-H. **28 F2** 44 26N 17 4 E
Mrkopalj, Croatia .... **41 C11** 45 21N 14 52 E
Mrocza, Poland ..... **31 E4** 53 16N 17 35 E
Msambansovu,
Zimbabwe .... **87 F3** 15 50 S 30 3 E
M'sila →, Algeria ... **78 A6** 35 30N 4 29 E
Msoro, Zambia ...... **87 E3** 13 35 S 31 50 E
Msta →, Russia ..... **32 C6** 58 25N 31 20 E
Mstislavl = Mstsislaw,
Belarus .... **32 E6** 54 0N 31 50 E
Mstsislaw, Belarus ... **32 E6** 54 0N 31 50 E
Mszana Dolna, Poland **31 J7** 49 41N 20 5 E
Mszczonów, Poland .. **31 G7** 51 58N 20 33 E
Mtama, Tanzania .... **87 E4** 10 17 S 39 21 E
Mtamvuna →, S. Africa **89 E5** 31 6 S 30 12 E
Mtilikwe →, Zimbabwe **87 G3** 21 9 S 31 30 E
Mtsensk, Russia ..... **32 F9** 53 17N 36 36 E
Mtskheta, Georgia ... **35 K7** 41 52N 44 45 E
Mtubatuba, S. Africa . **89 D5** 28 30 S 32 8 E
Mtwalume, S. Africa . **89 E5** 30 30 S 30 38 E
Mtwara-Mikindani,
Tanzania .... **87 E5** 10 20 S 40 20 E
Mu Gia, Deo, Vietnam **64 D5** 17 40N 105 47 E
Mu Ko Chang △,
Thailand .... **65 G4** 11 59N 102 22 E
Mu Us Shamo, China . **56 E5** 39 0N 109 0 E
Muang Chiang Rai =
Chiang Rai, Thailand **58 H2** 19 52N 99 50 E
Muang Khong, Laos .. **64 E5** 14 7N 105 51 E
Muang Lamphun,
Thailand .... **64 C2** 18 40N 99 2 E
Muang Mai, Thailand **65 a** 8 5N 98 21 E
Muang Pak Beng, Laos **58 H3** 19 54N 101 8 E
Muar, Malaysia ..... **65 L4** 2 3N 102 34 E
Muarabungo, Indonesia **62 E2** 1 28 S 102 52 E
Muaraenim, Indonesia **62 E2** 3 40 S 103 50 E
Muarajuloi, Indonesia **62 E4** 0 12 S 114 3 E
Muarakaman, Indonesia **62 E5** 0 2 S 116 45 E
Muaratebo, Indonesia **62 E2** 1 30 S 102 26 E
Muaratembesi,
Indonesia .... **62 E2** 1 42 S 103 8 E
Muaratewe, Indonesia **62 E4** 0 58 S 114 52 E
Mubarakpur, India ... **69 F10** 26 6N 83 18 E
Mubarraz = Al
Mubarraz, Si. Arabia **71 E6** 25 30N 49 40 E
Mubende, Uganda ... **86 B3** 0 33N 31 22 E
Mubi, Nigeria .... **83 C7** 10 18N 13 16 E
Mucajaí →, Brazil .. **124 C6** 2 25N 60 52W
Muchachos, Roque de
los, Canary Is. **48 F2** 28 44N 17 52W
Mücheln, Germany ... **24 D7** 51 17N 11 47 E
Muchinga Mts., Zambia **87 E3** 11 30 S 31 30 E
Muchkapskiy, Russia .. **34 E6** 51 52N 42 28 E
Muchuan, China ..... **58 C5** 28 57N 103 55 E
Muck, U.K. **13 E2** 56 50N 6 15W
Muckadilla, Australia . **95 D4** 26 35 S 148 23 E
Muckle Flugga, U.K. .. **13 A8** 60 51N 0 54W
Mucojo, Mozam. .... **87 E5** 12 S 40 27 E
Mucomeze →, Mozam. **87 F3** 16 S 35 35 E
Mucuri, Brazil ...... **125 G11** 18 0 S 39 36W
Mucusso, Angola .... **88 B3** 18 1 S 21 25 E
Muda, Canary Is. **48 F6** 28 34N 13 57W
Mudanjiang, China .. **57 B15** 44 38N 129 30 E
Mudanya, Turkey .... **45 F12** 40 25N 28 50 E
Muddy Cr. →, U.S.A. **109 H8** 38 24N 110 42W
Mudgee, Australia ... **95 E4** 32 32 S 149 31 E
Mudjatik →, Canada **103 B7** 56 1N 107 36W
Mudurnu, Turkey .... **72 B4** 40 27N 31 12 E
Muecate, Mozam. .... **87 E4** 14 55 S 39 40 E
Mueda, Mozam. ..... **87 E4** 11 36 S 39 28 E
Mueller Ra., Australia **92 C4** 18 18 S 126 46 E
Muende, Mozam. .... **87 E3** 14 28 S 33 0 E
Muerto, Mar, Mexico . **119 D6** 16 10N 94 10W
Mufulira, Zambia .... **87 E2** 12 32 S 28 15 E
Mufumbiro Range,
Africa .... **86 C2** 1 25 S 29 30 E
Mugardos, Spain **36 B2** 43 27N 8 15W
Muge →, Portugal .. **37 F2** 39 8N 8 44W
Múggia, Italy .... **41 C10** 45 36N 13 46 E
Mughal Sarai, India .. **69 G10** 25 18N 83 7 E
Mughayrā', Si. Arabia **70 D3** 29 17N 37 41 E
Mugi, Japan .... **55 H7** 33 40N 134 25 E
Mugia = Muxía, Spain **36 B1** 43 3N 9 10W
Mugila, Mts., Dem. Rep.
of the Congo .... **86 D2** 7 0 S 28 50 E
Muğla, Turkey ...... **47 D10** 37 15N 28 22 E
Muğla □, Turkey .... **47 D10** 37 15N 28 0 E
Muglad, Sudan ...... **81 E2** 11 11N 27 50 E
Müglizh, Bulgaria ... **45 D9** 42 37N 25 32 E
Mugu, Nepal .... **69 E10** 29 45N 82 30 E
Muhammad, Râs, Egypt **70 E2** 27 44N 34 16 E
Muhammad Qol, Sudan **80 C4** 20 53N 37 9 E
Muhammadabad, India **69 F10** 26 4N 83 25 E
Muhesi →, Tanzania . **86 D4** 7 0 S 35 20 E
Mühlacker, Germany . **25 G4** 48 57N 8 51 E
Mühldorf, Germany .. **25 G8** 48 14N 12 32 E
Mühlhausen, Germany **24 D6** 51 12N 10 27 E
Mühlig Hofmann fjell,
Antarctica ...... **5 D3** 72 30 S 5 0 E
Mühlviertel, Austria .. **26 C7** 48 30N 14 10 E
Muhos, Finland ..... **8 D22** 64 47N 25 59 E
Muhu, Estonia ...... **9 G20** 58 36N 23 11 E
Muhutwe, Tanzania .. **86 C3** 1 35 S 31 45 E
Muine Bheag, Ireland **12 D5** 52 42N 6 58W
Muir, L., Australia ... **93 F2** 34 30 S 116 40 E
Muir of Ord, U.K. ... **13 D4** 57 32N 4 28W
Mujnak = Muynak,
Uzbekistan ...... **52 E6** 43 44N 59 10 E
Muka, Tanjung,
Malaysia .... **65 c** 5 28N 100 11 E
Mukacheve, Ukraine . **28 B7** 48 27N 22 45 E

Mukachevo =
Mukacheve, Ukraine **28 B7** 48 27N 22 45 E
Mukah, Malaysia .... **62 D4** 2 55N 112 5 E
Mukandwara, India .. **68 G6** 24 49N 75 59 E
Mukawwa, Geziret,
Egypt .... **80 C4** 23 55N 35 53 E
Mukawwar, Sudan ... **80 C4** 20 50N 37 17 E
Mukdahan, Thailand . **64 D5** 16 32N 104 43 E
Mukden = Shenyang,
China .... **57 D12** 41 48N 123 27 E
Mukerian, India ..... **68 D6** 31 57N 75 37 E
Mukhavyets, Belarus . **31 F10** 52 5N 23 39 E
Mukhtolovo, Russia .. **34 C6** 55 29N 43 15 E
Mukishi, Dem. Rep. of
the Congo ...... **87 D1** 8 30 S 24 44 E
Mukomuko, Indonesia **62 E2** 2 30 S 101 10 E
Mukomwenze,
Dem. Rep. of
the Congo ...... **86 D2** 6 49 S 27 15 E
Muktsar, India ..... **68 D6** 30 30N 74 30 E
Mukur = Moqor,
Afghan. .... **68 C2** 32 50N 67 42 E
Mukutawa →, Canada **103 C9** 53 10N 97 24W
Mukwela, Zambia ... **87 F2** 17 0 S 26 40 E
Mula, Spain **39 G3** 38 3N 1 33W
Mula →, Pakistan ... **68 F2** 27 57N 67 36 E
Mulange, Dem. Rep. of
the Congo ...... **86 C2** 3 40 S 27 10 E
Mulanje, Malawi .... **87 F4** 16 5 S 35 33 E
Mulanje, Mt., Malawi **87 F4** 16 0 S 35 30 E
Mulchén, Chile ..... **126 D1** 37 45 S 72 20W
Mulde →, Germany . **24 D8** 51 53N 12 15 E
Mule Creek Junction,
U.S.A. **112 D2** 43 19N 104 8W
Muleba, Tanzania ... **86 C3** 1 50 S 31 37 E
Mulejé, Mexico **118 B2** 26 53N 112 1W
Muleshoe, U.S.A. **113 H3** 34 13N 102 43W
Muletta, Gara, Ethiopia **81 F5** 9 15N 41 44 E
Mulgrave, Canada ... **105 C7** 45 38N 61 31W
Mulhacén, Spain **37 H7** 37 4N 3 20W
Mülheim, Germany .. **24 D2** 51 25N 6 54 E
Mulhouse, France ... **19 E14** 47 40N 7 20 E
Muli, China .... **58 D3** 27 52N 101 8 E
Muling, China ...... **57 B16** 44 35N 130 10 E
Mull, U.K. **13 E3** 56 25N 5 56W
Mull, Sound of, U.K. . **13 E3** 56 30N 5 50W
Mullaittivu, Sri Lanka **66 Q12** 9 15N 80 49 E
Mullen, U.S.A. **112 D4** 42 3N 101 1W
Mullens, U.S.A. **114 G5** 37 35N 81 23W
Muller, Pegunungan,
Indonesia ...... **62 D4** 0 30N 113 30 E
Mullet Pen., Ireland . **12 B1** 54 13N 10 2W
Mullewa, Australia ... **93 E2** 28 29 S 115 30 E
Müllheim, Germany .. **25 H3** 47 47N 7 36 E
Mulligan →, Australia **94 D2** 25 0 S 139 0 E
Mullingar, Ireland ... **12 C4** 53 31N 7 21W
Mullins, U.S.A. **115 H6** 34 12N 79 15W
Mullsjö, Sweden .... **11 G7** 57 56N 13 55 E
Mullumbimby, Australia **95 D5** 28 30 S 153 30 E
Mulobezi, Zambia ... **87 F2** 16 45 S 25 7 E
Mulroy B., Ireland .. **12 A4** 55 15N 7 46W
Multan, Pakistan .... **68 D4** 30 15N 71 36 E
Mulumbe, Mts.,
Dem. Rep. of
the Congo ...... **87 D2** 8 40 S 27 30 E
Mulungushi Dam,
Zambia .... **87 E2** 14 48 S 28 48 E
Mulvane, U.S.A. **113 G6** 37 29N 97 15W
Mulwad, Sudan ..... **80 D3** 18 45N 30 39 E
Mumbai, India ...... **66 K8** 18 55N 72 50 E
Mumbwa, Zambia ... **87 F2** 15 0 S 27 0 E
Mumra, Russia ...... **35 H8** 45 45N 47 41 E
Mun →, Thailand ... **64 E5** 15 19N 105 30 E
Muna, Indonesia .... **63 F6** 5 0 S 122 30 E
Munabao, India ..... **68 G4** 25 45N 70 17 E
Munamağı, Estonia .. **9 H22** 57 43N 27 4 E
Muncan, Indonesia .. **63 K18** 8 34 S 115 11 E
Muncar, Indonesia .. **63 J17** 8 26 S 114 20 E
Münchberg, Germany **25 E7** 50 11N 11 47 E
Müncheberg, Germany **24 C10** 52 30N 14 9 E
München, Germany .. **25 G7** 48 8N 11 34 E
Munchen-Gladbach =
Mönchengladbach,
Germany .... **24 D2** 51 11N 6 27 E
München
International ✈
(MUC), Germany .. **25 G7** 48 20N 11 50 E
Muncho Lake, Canada **102 B3** 59 0N 125 50W
Munch'ŏn, N. Korea . **57 E14** 39 14N 127 19 E
Muncie, U.S.A. **114 E3** 40 12N 85 23W
Muncoonie, L., Australia **94 D2** 25 12 S 138 40 E
Mundabbera, Australia **95 D5** 25 36 S 151 18 E
Munday, U.S.A. **113 J5** 33 27N 99 38W
Münden, Germany ... **24 D5** 51 25N 9 38 E
Münden →, Germany **24 D5** 51 28N 9 42 E
Mundiwindi, Australia **92 D3** 23 47 S 120 9 E
Mundo →, Spain ... **39 G2** 38 30N 2 15W
Mundo Novo, Brazil . **125 F10** 11 50 S 40 29W
Mundra, India ...... **68 H3** 22 54N 69 48 E
Mundrabilla, Australia **93 F4** 31 52 S 127 51 E
Munera, Spain **39 F2** 39 2N 2 29W
Mungallala, Australia **95 D4** 26 28 S 147 34 E
Mungallala Cr. →,
Australia .... **95 D4** 28 53 S 147 5 E
Mungana, Australia .. **94 B3** 17 8 S 144 27 E
Mungaoli, India ..... **68 G8** 24 24N 78 7 E
Mungari, Mozam. .... **87 F3** 17 12 S 33 30 E
Mungbere, Dem. Rep.
of the Congo .... **86 B2** 2 36N 28 28 E
Mungeli, India ...... **69 H9** 22 4N 81 41 E
Munger, India ...... **69 G12** 25 23N 86 30 E
Mungkan Kandju △,
Australia .... **94 A3** 13 35 S 142 52 E
Munich = München,
Germany .... **25 G7** 48 8N 11 34 E
Munising, U.S.A. **114 B2** 46 25N 86 40W
Munka-Ljungby, Sweden **11 H6** 56 16N 12 58 E
Munkedal, Sweden .. **11 F5** 58 28N 11 40 E
Munkfors, Sweden ... **10 E7** 59 47N 13 30 E
Munku-Sardyk, Russia **53 D11** 51 45N 100 20 E
Münnerstadt, Germany **25 E6** 50 14N 10 12 E
Muñoz Gamero, Pen.,
Chile .... **128 G2** 52 30 S 73 5W
Munroe L., Canada .. **103 B9** 59 13N 98 35W
Munsan, S. Korea ... **57 F14** 37 51N 126 48 E
Münster, France .... **19 D14** 48 2N 7 8 E
Münster, Niedersachsen,
Germany .... **24 C6** 52 59N 10 5 E
Münster,
Nordrhein-Westfalen,
Germany .... **24 D3** 51 58N 7 37 E
Munster □, Ireland .. **12 D3** 52 18N 8 44W
Muntadgin, Australia **93 F2** 31 45 S 118 33 E
Muntele Mare, Vf.,
Romania .... **29 D8** 46 30N 23 12 E

Muntok, Indonesia .. **62 E3** 2 5 S 105 10 E
Munyama, Zambia ... **87 F2** 16 5 S 28 31 E
Munzur Dağları, Turkey **73 C8** 39 30N 39 10 E
Muong Beng, Laos .. **58 G3** 20 23N 101 46 E
Muong Boum, Vietnam **58 F4** 22 24N 102 49 E
Muong Et, Laos ..... **64 B5** 20 49N 104 1 E
Muong Hai, Laos .... **58 G3** 21 3N 101 49 E
Muong Hiem, Laos .. **64 B4** 20 5N 103 22 E
Muong Houn, Laos .. **58 G3** 20 8N 101 23 E
Muong Hung, Vietnam **58 G4** 20 56N 103 53 E
Muong Kau, Laos ... **64 E5** 15 6N 105 47 E
Muong Khao, Laos .. **64 C4** 19 38N 103 32 E
Muong Khoua, Laos . **58 G4** 21 5N 102 31 E
Muong Liep, Laos ... **64 C3** 18 29N 101 40 E
Muong May, Laos ... **64 E6** 14 49N 106 56 E
Muong Ngeun, Laos . **58 G3** 20 36N 101 3 E
Muong Ngoi, Laos .. **58 G4** 20 43N 102 41 E
Muong Nhie, Vietnam **58 F4** 22 12N 102 28 E
Muong Nong, Laos .. **64 D6** 16 22N 106 30 E
Muong Ou Tay, Laos . **58 F3** 22 7N 101 48 E
Muong Oua, Laos ... **64 C3** 18 18N 101 20 E
Muong Peun, Laos .. **58 G4** 20 13N 103 52 E
Muong Phalane, Laos **64 D5** 16 39N 105 34 E
Muong Phieng, Laos . **64 C3** 19 6N 101 32 E
Muong Phine, Laos .. **64 D6** 16 32N 106 2 E
Muong Sai, Laos .... **58 G3** 20 42N 101 59 E
Muong Saiapoun, Laos **64 C3** 18 24N 101 31 E
Muong Sen, Vietnam **64 C5** 19 24N 104 8 E
Muong Sing, Laos ... **58 G3** 21 11N 101 9 E
Muong Son, Laos ... **58 G4** 20 27N 103 19 E
Muong Soui, Laos ... **64 C4** 19 33N 102 52 E
Muong Va, Laos .... **58 G4** 21 53N 102 19 E
Muong Xia, Vietnam **64 B5** 20 19N 104 50 E
Muonio, Finland .... **8 C20** 67 57N 23 40 E
Muonio älv →,
Muonionjoki →,
Finland .... **8 C20** 67 11N 23 34 E
Muonioälven =
Muonionjoki →,
Finland .... **8 C20** 67 11N 23 34 E
Muonionjoki →,
Finland .... **8 C20** 67 11N 23 34 E
Muping, China ...... **57 F11** 37 22N 121 36 E
Mupoi, Sudan ...... **81 F2** 5 28N 27 40 E
Muqaddam, Wadi →,
Sudan .... **80 D3** 18 4N 31 30 E
Muqdisho, Somali Rep. **75 G4** 2 2N 45 25 E
Musay'īd, Qatar .... **71 E6** 25 0N 51 33 E
Muscat = Masqat, Oman **75 C6** 23 37N 58 36 E
Muscatine, U.S.A. ... **112 E9** 41 25N 91 3W
Musengezi =
Unsengedsi →,
Zimbabwe ...... **87 F3** 15 43 S 31 14 E
Musgrave Harbour,
Canada **105 C9** 49 27N 53 58W
Musgrave Ranges,
Australia .... **93 E5** 26 0 S 132 0 E
Mushie, Dem. Rep. of
the Congo ...... **84 E3** 2 56 S 16 55 E
Mushin, Nigeria .... **83 D5** 6 32N 3 21 E
Musi →, Indonesia .. **62 E2** 2 20 S 104 56 E
Musina, S. Africa ... **89 C5** 22 20 S 30 5 E
Muskeg →, Canada . **102 A4** 60 20N 123 20W
Muskegon, U.S.A. ... **114 D2** 43 14N 86 16W
Muskegon →, U.S.A. **114 D2** 43 14N 86 21W
Muskegon Heights,
U.S.A. **114 D2** 43 12N 86 16W
Muskogee, U.S.A. ... **113 H7** 35 45N 95 22W
Muskoka, L., Canada **116 B5** 45 0N 79 25W
Muskwa →, Canada . **102 B4** 58 47N 122 48W
Muslimiyah, Syria ... **70 B3** 36 19N 37 12 E
Musmar, Sudan ..... **80 D4** 18 13N 35 40 E
Musofu, Zambia .... **87 E2** 13 30 S 29 0 E
Musoma, Tanzania .. **86 C3** 1 30 S 33 48 E
Musquaro, L., Canada **105 B7** 50 38N 61 5W
Musquodoboit Harbour,
Canada **105 D7** 44 50N 63 9W
Musselburgh, U.K. .. **13 F5** 55 57N 3 2W
Musselshell →, U.S.A. **108 C10** 47 21N 107 57W
Mussidan, France ... **20 C4** 45 2N 0 22 E
Mussomeli, Italy .... **42 E6** 37 35N 13 45 E
Mussoorie, India .... **68 D8** 30 27N 78 6 E
Mussuco, Angola ... **88 B2** 17 2 S 19 3 E
Mustafakemalpaşa,
Turkey .... **45 F12** 40 2N 28 24 E
Mustang, Nepal .... **69 E10** 29 10N 83 55 E
Musters, L., Argentina **128 F3** 45 20 S 69 25W
Musudan, N. Korea .. **57 D15** 40 50N 129 43 E
Muswellbrook, Australia **95 E5** 32 16 S 150 56 E
Muszyna, Poland .... **31 J7** 49 22N 20 55 E
Mût, Egypt .... **80 B2** 25 28N 28 58 E
Mut, Turkey .... **70 B2** 36 40N 33 28 E
Mutanda, Mozam. .. **89 C5** 21 0 S 33 34 E
Mutanda, Zambia ... **87 E2** 12 24 S 26 13 E
Mutare, Zimbabwe .. **87 F3** 18 58 S 32 38 E
Muting, Indonesia ... **63 F10** 7 23 S 140 20 E
Mutoko, Zimbabwe . **89 B5** 17 24 S 32 13 E
Mutoray, Russia .... **53 C11** 60 56N 101 0 E
Mutshatsha, Dem. Rep.
of the Congo .... **87 E1** 10 35 S 24 20 E
Mutsu, Japan ...... **54 D10** 41 5N 140 55 E
Mutsu-Wan, Japan .. **54 D10** 41 5N 140 55 E
Muttaburra, Australia **94 C3** 22 38 S 144 29 E
Muttalip, Turkey .... **47 B12** 39 50N 30 32 E
Mutton I., Ireland ... **12 D2** 52 49N 9 32W
Mutuáli, Mozam. .... **87 E4** 14 55 S 37 0 E
Mutum Biyu, Nigeria **83 D7** 8 40N 10 50 E
Muweilih, Egypt .... **74 E3** 30 42N 34 19 E
Muxía, Spain **36 B1** 43 3N 9 10W
Muy Muy, Nic. **120 D2** 12 39N 85 36W
Muyinga, Burundi .. **86 C3** 3 14 S 30 33 E
Muynak, Uzbekistan . **52 E6** 43 44N 59 10 E
Muzaffarabad, Pakistan **69 B5** 34 25N 73 30 E
Muzaffargarh, Pakistan **68 D4** 30 5N 71 14 E
Muzaffarnagar, India **68 E7** 29 26N 77 40 E
Muzaffarpur, India .. **69 F11** 26 7N 85 23 E
Muzafirpur, Pakistan **68 D4** 30 58N 69 9 E
Muzhi, Russia ...... **52 C7** 65 25N 64 40 E
Muzillac, France **18 E4** 47 35N 2 30W
Muzόn, C., U.S.A. ... **102 C2** 54 40N 132 42W
Muztagh, Egypt .... **80 J7** 28 53N 30 48 E
Mvϋlΰ, Angola ..... **81 F2** 6 2N 29 53 E
Mvurwi, Zimbabwe .. **87 F3** 19 16 S 30 30 E
Mvuma, Zimbabwe .. **87 F3** 19 16 S 30 30 E
Mvurwi, Zimbabwe .. **87 F3** 17 0 S 30 57 E
Mwabvi △, Malawi .. **87 F3** 16 42 S 35 0 E
Mwadui, Tanzania .. **86 C3** 3 26 S 33 32 E
Mwali = Mohéli, Comoros **85 a** 12 20 S 43 40 E
Mwandi, Zambia .... **87 F1** 17 30 S 24 51 E
Mwanza, Dem. Rep. of
the Congo ...... **86 D2** 7 55 S 26 43 E
Mwanza, Tanzania .. **86 C3** 2 30 S 32 58 E
Mwanza, Zambia ... **87 F1** 16 58 S 24 28 E
Mwanza □, Tanzania **86 C3** 2 0 S 33 0 E
Mwaya, Tanzania ... **87 D3** 9 32 S 33 55 E
Mweelrea, Ireland ... **12 C2** 53 39N 9 49W
Mweka, Dem. Rep. of
the Congo ...... **84 E4** 4 50 S 21 34 E
Mwenezi, Zimbabwe **87 G3** 21 15 S 30 48 E
Mwenezi →, Mozam. **87 G3** 22 40 S 31 50 E
Mwenga, Dem. Rep. of
the Congo ...... **86 C2** 3 1 S 28 28 E
Mweru, L., Zambia .. **87 D2** 9 0 S 28 40 E
Mweru Wantipa △,
Zambia .... **87 D2** 8 39 S 29 25 E
Mweza Range,
Zimbabwe ...... **87 G3** 21 0 S 30 0 E

Mwilambwe, Dem. Rep. of the Congo 86 D2 8 7S 25 5E
Mwimbi, Tanzania 87 D3 8 38S 31 39E
Mwinilunga, Zambia 87 E1 11 43S 24 25E
My Tho, Vietnam 65 G6 10 29N 106 23E
Myajlar, India 68 F4 26 15N 70 20E
Myanaung, Burma 67 K19 18 18N 95 22E
Myanmar = Burma ■, Asia 67 J20 21 0N 96 30E
Myaungmya, Burma 67 L19 16 30N 94 40E
Myedna, Belarus 31 G10 51 52N 23 42E
Myeik Kyunzu, Burma 65 G1 11 30N 97 30E
Myers Chuck, U.S.A. 102 B2 55 44N 132 11W
Myerstown, U.S.A. 117 F8 40 22N 76 19W
Myingyan, Burma 67 J19 21 30N 95 20E
Myitkyina, Burma 67 G20 25 24N 97 26E
Myjava, Slovak Rep. 27 C10 48 41N 17 37E
Mykhaylivka, Ukraine 33 J8 47 12N 35 15E
Mykines, Færoe Is. 8 E9 62 7N 7 35W
Mykolayiv, Ukraine 33 J7 46 58N 32 0E
Mymensingh, Bangla. 67 G17 24 45N 90 24E
Mynydd Du, U.K. 15 F4 51 52N 3 50W
Mýrdalsjökull, Iceland 8 E4 63 40N 19 6W
Myrhorod, Ukraine 33 H7 49 58N 33 37E
Myrtle Beach, U.S.A. 115 J6 33 42N 78 53W
Myrtle Creek, U.S.A. 108 E2 43 1N 123 17W
Myrtle Point, U.S.A. 108 E1 43 4N 124 8W
Myrtou, Cyprus 49 D12 35 18N 33 4E
Mysia, Turkey 45 G11 39 50N 27 0E
Myślenice, Poland 31 J6 49 51N 19 57E
Myślibórz, Poland 31 F1 52 55N 14 50E
Mysłowice, Poland 31 H6 50 15N 19 12E
Mysore = Karnataka □, India 66 N10 13 15N 77 0E
Mysore, India 66 N10 12 17N 76 41E
Mystic, U.S.A. 117 E13 41 21N 71 58W
Myszków, Poland 31 H6 50 45N 19 22E
Myszyniec, Poland 30 E8 53 23N 21 21E
Mytishchi, Russia 32 E9 55 50N 37 50E
Mývatn, Iceland 8 D5 65 36N 17 0W
Mže →, Czech Rep. 26 B6 49 46N 13 24E
Mzimba, Malawi 87 E3 11 55S 33 39E
Mzimkulu →, S. Africa 89 E5 30 44S 30 28E
Mzimvubu →, S. Africa 89 E4 31 38S 29 33E
Mzuzu, Malawi 87 E3 11 30S 33 55E

N

Na Hearadh = Harris, U.K. 13 D2 57 50N 6 55W
Na Noi, Thailand 64 C3 18 19N 100 43E
Na Phao, Laos 64 D5 17 35N 105 44E
Na Sam, Vietnam 58 F6 22 3N 106 37E
Na San, Vietnam 64 B5 21 12N 104 2E
Na Thon, Thailand 65 b 9 32N 99 56E
Naab →, Germany 25 F8 49 1N 12 2E
Na'am, Sudan 81 F2 9 42N 28 27E
Na'am →, Sudan 81 F2 6 48N 29 57E
Naantali, Finland 9 F19 60 29N 22 2E
Naas, Ireland 12 C5 53 12N 6 40W
Nababeep, S. Africa 88 D2 29 36S 17 46E
Nabadwip = Navadwip, India 69 H13 23 34N 88 20E
Nabawa, Australia 93 E1 28 30S 114 48E
Nabberu, L., Australia 93 E3 25 50S 120 30E
Nabburg, Germany 25 F8 49 27N 12 11E
Naberezhnyye Chelny, Russia 34 C11 55 42N 52 19E
Nabeul, Tunisia 79 A8 36 30N 10 44E
Nabha, India 68 D7 30 26N 76 14E
Nabīd, Iran 71 D8 29 40N 57 38E
Nabire, Indonesia 63 E9 3 15S 135 26E
Nabisar, Pakistan 68 G3 25 8N 69 40E
Nabisipi →, Canada 105 B7 50 14N 62 13W
Nabiswera, Uganda 86 B3 1 27N 32 15E
Nāblus = Nābulus, West Bank 74 C4 32 14N 35 15E
Naboomspruit, S. Africa 89 C4 24 32S 28 40E
Nabou, Burkina Faso 82 C4 11 25N 2 50W
Nabua, Phil. 61 E5 13 24N 123 22E
Nābulus, West Bank 74 C4 32 14N 35 15E
Nacala, Mozam. 87 E5 14 31S 40 34E
Nacala-Velha, Mozam. 87 E5 14 32S 40 34E
Nacaome, Honduras 120 D2 13 31N 87 30W
Nacaroa, Mozam. 87 E4 14 22S 39 56E
Naches, U.S.A. 108 C3 46 44N 120 42W
Naches →, U.S.A. 110 D6 46 38N 120 31W
Nachicapau, L., Canada 105 A6 56 40N 68 5W
Nachingwea, Tanzania 87 E4 10 23S 38 49E
Nachna, India 68 F4 27 34N 71 41E
Náchod, Czech Rep. 26 A9 50 25N 16 8E
Nacimiento L., U.S.A. 110 K6 35 46N 120 53W
Naco, Mexico 118 A3 31 20N 109 56W
Nacogdoches, U.S.A. 113 K7 31 36N 94 39W
Nácori Chico, Mexico 118 B3 29 39N 109 1W
Nacozari, Mexico 118 A3 30 24N 109 39W
Nådendal = Naantali, Finland 9 F19 60 29N 22 2E
Nadi, Fiji 91 C7 17 42S 177 20E
Nadi, Sudan 80 D3 18 40N 33 41E
Nadiad, India 68 H5 22 41N 72 56E
Nădlac, Romania 28 D5 46 10N 20 50E
Nador, Morocco 78 B5 35 14N 2 58W
Nadur, Malta 49 C1 36 2N 14 18E
Nadūshan, Iran 71 C7 32 2N 53 35E
Nadvirna, Ukraine 29 B9 48 37N 24 30E
Nadvornaya = Nadvirna, Ukraine 29 B9 48 37N 24 30E
Nadym, Russia 52 C8 65 35N 72 42E
Nadym →, Russia 52 C8 66 12N 72 0E
Nærbø, Norway 9 G11 58 40N 5 39E
Næstved, Denmark 11 J5 55 13N 11 44E
Nafada, Nigeria 83 C7 11 8N 11 20E
Naft-e Safīd, Iran 71 D6 31 40N 49 17E
Naftshahr, Iran 70 C5 34 0N 45 30E
Nafud Desert = An Nafūd, Si. Arabia 70 D4 28 15N 41 0E
Nag Hammâdi, Egypt 80 B3 26 2N 32 18E
Naga, Phil. 61 E5 13 38N 123 15E
Nagahama, Japan 55 G8 35 23N 136 16E
Nagai, Japan 54 E10 38 6N 140 2E
Nagaland □, India 67 G19 26 0N 94 30E
Nagano, Japan 55 F9 36 40N 138 10E
Nagano □, Japan 55 F9 36 15N 138 0E
Nagaoka, Japan 55 F9 37 27N 138 51E
Nagappattinam, India 66 P11 10 46N 79 51E
Nagar →, Bangla. 69 G13 24 27N 89 12E
Nagar Parkar, Pakistan 68 G4 24 28N 70 46E
Nagasaki, Japan 55 H4 32 47N 129 50E
Nagasaki □, Japan 55 H4 32 50N 129 40E
Nagato, Japan 55 G5 34 19N 131 5E
Nagaur, India 68 F5 27 15N 73 45E
Nagda, India 68 H6 23 27N 75 25E
Nagercoil, India 66 Q10 8 12N 77 26E
Nagina, India 69 E8 29 30N 78 30E
Nagīneh, Iran 71 C8 34 20N 57 15E
Nagir, Pakistan 69 A6 36 12N 74 42E
Naglarby, Sweden 10 D9 60 25N 15 34E
Nagod, India 69 G9 24 34N 80 36E
Nagold, Germany 25 G4 48 32N 8 43E
Nagold →, Germany 25 G4 48 52N 8 42E
Nagoorin, Australia 94 C5 24 17S 151 15E
Nagorno-Karabakh □, Azerbaijan 70 B5 39 55N 46 45E
Nagornyy, Russia 53 D13 55 58N 124 57E
Nagoya, Japan 55 G8 35 10N 136 50E
Nagpur, India 66 J11 21 8N 79 10E
Nagua, Dom. Rep. 121 C6 19 23N 69 50W
Naguabo, Puerto Rico 121 d 18 13N 65 44W
Nagyatád, Hungary 28 D2 46 14N 17 22E
Nagyecsed, Hungary 28 C7 47 53N 22 24E
Nagykálló, Hungary 28 C6 47 53N 21 51E
Nagykanizsa, Hungary 28 D2 46 28N 17 0E
Nagykáta, Hungary 28 C4 47 25N 19 45E
Nagykőrös, Hungary 28 C4 47 5N 19 48E
Naha, Japan 55 L3 26 13N 127 42E
Nahan, India 68 D7 30 33N 77 18E
Nahanni △, Canada 102 A4 61 36N 125 41W
Nahanni Butte, Canada 102 A4 61 2N 123 31W
Nahargarh, Mad. P., India 68 G6 24 10N 75 14E
Nahargarh, Raj., India 68 G7 24 55N 76 50E
Nahariyya, Israel 70 C2 33 1N 35 5E
Nahāvand, Iran 71 C6 34 10N 48 22E
Nahe →, Germany 25 F3 49 58N 7 54E
Nahirne, Ukraine 29 E13 45 26N 28 27E
Nahîya, W. →, Egypt 80 B3 28 55N 31 0E
Nahuelbuta △, Chile 126 D1 37 44S 72 57W
Nai Yong, Thailand 65 a 8 14N 98 22E
Naicá, Mexico 118 B3 27 53N 105 31W
Naicam, Canada 103 C8 52 30N 104 30W
Naikoon ⌓, Canada 102 C2 53 55N 131 55W
Naila, Germany 25 E7 50 19N 11 42E
Naimisharanya, India 69 F9 27 21N 80 30E
Nain, Canada 105 A7 56 34N 61 40W
Nā'īn, Iran 71 C7 32 54N 53 0E
Naini Tal, India 69 E8 29 30N 79 30E
Nainpur, India 66 H12 22 30N 80 10E
Naintré, France 18 F7 46 46N 0 29E
Nainwa, India 68 G6 25 46N 75 51E
Naipu, Romania 29 F10 44 12N 25 47E
Nairn, U.K. 13 D5 57 35N 3 53W
Nairobi, Kenya 86 C4 1 17S 36 48E
Nairobi △, Kenya 86 C4 1 22S 36 50E
Naissaar, Estonia 9 G21 59 34N 24 29E
Naita, Mt., Ethiopia 81 F4 5 30N 35 18E
Naivasha, Kenya 86 C4 0 40S 36 30E
Naivasha, L., Kenya 86 C4 0 48S 36 20E
Najac, France 20 D5 44 14N 1 58E
Najaf = An Najaf, Iraq 70 C5 32 3N 44 15E
Najafābād, Iran 71 C6 32 40N 51 15E
Najd, Si. Arabia 75 B3 26 30N 42 0E
Nájera, Spain 38 C2 42 26N 2 48W
Najerilla →, Spain 38 C2 42 32N 2 48W
Najibabad, India 68 E8 29 40N 78 20E
Najin, N. Korea 57 C16 42 12N 130 15E
Najmah, Si. Arabia 71 E6 26 42N 50 6E
Najrān, Si. Arabia 75 D3 17 34N 44 18E
Naju, S. Korea 57 G14 35 3N 126 43E
Nakadōri-Shima, Japan 55 H4 32 57N 129 4E
Nakalagba, Dem. Rep. of the Congo 86 B2 2 50N 27 58E
Nakaminato, Japan 55 F10 36 21N 140 36E
Nakamura, Japan 55 H6 32 59N 132 56E
Nakano, Japan 55 F9 36 45N 138 22E
Nakano-Shima, Japan 55 K4 29 51N 129 52E
Nakashibetsu, Japan 54 C12 43 33N 144 59E
Nakfa, Eritrea 81 D4 16 40N 38 32E
Nakfa ⌓, Eritrea 81 D4 17 28N 38 55E
Nakha Yai, Ko, Thailand 65 a 8 3N 98 28E
Nakhichevan = Naxçıvan, Azerbaijan 70 B5 39 12N 45 15E
Nakhichevan Rep. = Naxçıvan □, Azerbaijan 52 F5 39 25N 45 26E
Nakhl, Egypt 74 F2 29 55N 33 43E
Nakhl-e Taqī, Iran 71 E7 27 28N 52 36E
Nakhodka, Russia 53 E14 42 53N 132 54E
Nakhon Nayok, Thailand 64 E3 14 12N 101 13E
Nakhon Pathom, Thailand 64 F3 13 49N 100 3E
Nakhon Phanom, Thailand 64 D5 17 23N 104 43E
Nakhon Ratchasima, Thailand 64 E4 14 59N 102 12E
Nakhon Sawan, Thailand 64 E3 15 35N 100 10E
Nakhon Si Thammarat, Thailand 65 H3 8 29N 100 0E
Nakhon Thai, Thailand 64 D3 17 5N 100 44E
Nakhtarana, India 68 H3 23 20N 69 15E
Nakina, Canada 104 B2 50 10N 86 40W
Nakło nad Notecią, Poland 31 E4 53 9N 17 38E
Nako, Burkina Faso 82 C4 10 40N 3 4W
Nakodar, India 68 D6 31 8N 75 31E
Nakskov, Denmark 11 K5 54 50N 11 8E
Naktong →, S. Korea 57 G15 35 7N 128 57E
Nakuru, Kenya 86 C4 0 15S 36 4E
Nakuru, L., Kenya 86 C4 0 23S 36 5E
Nakusp, Canada 102 C5 50 20N 117 45W
Nal, Pakistan 68 F2 27 40N 66 12E
Nal →, Pakistan 68 G1 25 20N 65 30E
Nalázi, Mozam. 89 C5 24 3S 33 20E
Nalchik, Russia 35 J6 43 30N 43 33E
Nałęczów, Poland 31 G9 51 17N 22 9E
Nalerigu, Ghana 83 C4 10 35N 0 25W
Nalgonda, India 66 L11 17 6N 79 15E
Nalhati, India 69 G12 24 17N 87 52E
Naliya, India 68 H3 23 16N 68 50E
Nallamalai Hills, India 66 M11 15 30N 78 50E
Nallıhan, Turkey 72 B4 40 11N 31 20E
Nalón →, Spain 36 B4 43 32N 6 4W
Nālūt, Libya 79 B8 31 54N 11 0E
Nam Can, Vietnam 65 H5 8 46N 104 59E
Nam-ch'on, N. Korea 57 E14 38 15N 126 26E
Nam Co, China 60 C4 30 30N 90 45E
Nam Dinh, Vietnam 58 G6 20 25N 106 5E
Nam Du, Hon, Vietnam 65 H5 9 41N 104 21E
Nam Nao △, Thailand 64 D3 16 44N 101 32E
Nam Ngum Dam, Laos 64 C4 18 35N 102 34E
Nam-Phan, Vietnam 65 G6 10 30N 106 0E
Nam Phong, Thailand 64 D4 16 42N 102 52E
Nam Tha, Laos 58 G3 20 58N 101 30E
Nam Tok, Thailand 64 E2 14 21N 99 4E
Namacunde, Angola 88 B2 17 18S 15 50E
Namacurra, Mozam. 89 B6 17 30S 36 50E
Namak, Daryācheh-ye, Iran 71 C7 34 30N 52 0E
Namak, Kavir-e, Iran 71 C8 34 30N 57 30E
Namakzār, Daryācheh-ye, Iran 71 C9 34 0N 60 30E
Namaland, Namibia 88 C2 26 0S 17 0E
Namangan, Uzbekistan 52 E8 41 0N 71 40E
Namapa, Mozam. 87 E4 13 43S 39 50E
Namaqualand, S. Africa 88 E2 30 0S 17 25E
Namasagali, Uganda 86 B3 1 2N 33 0E
Namber, Indonesia 63 E8 1 2S 134 49E
Nambour, Australia 95 D5 26 32S 152 58E
Nambucca Heads, Australia 95 E5 30 37S 153 0E
Nambung △, Australia 93 F2 30 30S 115 5E
Namche Bazar, Nepal 69 F12 27 51N 86 47E
Namchonjŏm = Nam-ch'on, N. Korea 57 E14 38 15N 126 26E
Namecunda, Mozam. 87 E4 14 54S 37 37E
Nameponda, Mozam. 87 F4 15 50S 39 50E
Náměšť nad Oslavou, Czech Rep. 27 B9 49 12N 16 10E
Námestovo, Slovak Rep. 27 B12 49 24N 19 25E
Nametil, Mozam. 87 F4 15 40S 39 21E
Namew L., Canada 103 C8 54 14N 101 56W
Namgia, India 69 D8 31 48N 78 40E
Namhkam, Burma 58 E1 23 50N 97 41E
Namib Desert, Namibia 88 C2 22 30S 15 0E
Namib-Naukluft ⌓, Namibia 88 C2 24 40S 15 16E
Namibe, Angola 85 H2 15 7S 12 11E
Namibe □, Angola 88 B1 16 35S 12 30E
Namibia ■, Africa 88 C2 22 0S 18 9E
Namibwoestyn = Namib Desert, Namibia 88 C2 22 30S 15 0E
Namīn, Iran 73 C13 38 25N 48 30E
Namlea, Indonesia 63 E7 3 18S 127 5E
Namoi →, Australia 95 E4 30 12S 149 30E
Nampa, U.S.A. 108 E5 43 34N 116 34W
Nampala, Mali 82 B3 15 20N 5 30W
Namp'o, N. Korea 57 E13 38 52N 125 10E
Nampō-Shotō, Japan 55 J10 32 0N 140 0E
Nampula, Mozam. 87 F4 15 6S 39 15E
Namrole, Indonesia 63 E7 3 46S 126 46E
Namse Shankou, China 67 E13 30 0N 82 25E
Namsen →, Norway 8 D14 64 28N 11 37E
Namsos, Norway 8 D14 64 29N 11 30E
Namtok Chat Trakan △, Thailand 64 D3 17 17N 100 40E
Namtok Mae Surin △, Thailand 64 C2 18 55N 98 2E
Namtsy, Russia 53 C13 62 43N 129 37E
Namtu, Burma 67 H20 23 5N 97 28E
Namtumbo, Tanzania 87 E4 10 30S 36 4E
Namu, Canada 102 C3 51 52N 127 50W
Namur, Belgium 17 D4 50 27N 4 52E
Namur □, Belgium 17 D4 50 17N 5 0E
Namutoni, Namibia 88 B2 18 49S 16 55E
Namwala, Zambia 87 F2 15 44S 26 30E
Namwŏn, S. Korea 57 G14 35 23N 127 23E
Namysłów, Poland 31 G4 51 6N 17 42E
Nan, Thailand 64 C3 18 48N 100 46E
Nan →, Thailand 64 E3 15 42N 100 9E
Nan-ch'ang = Nanchang, China 59 C10 28 42N 115 55E
Nan Ling, China 59 E8 25 0N 112 30E
Nan Xian, China 59 C9 29 20N 112 22E
Nana, Romania 29 F11 44 17N 26 34E
Nana Kru, Liberia 82 E3 4 55N 8 45W
Nanaimo, Canada 102 D4 49 10N 124 0W
Nanam, N. Korea 57 D15 41 44N 129 40E
Nanan, China 59 E12 24 59N 118 21E
Nanango, Australia 95 D5 26 40S 152 0E
Nan'ao, China 59 F11 23 28N 117 5E
Nanao, Japan 55 F8 37 0N 137 0E
Nanbu, China 58 B6 31 18N 106 3E
Nanchang, Jiangxi, China 59 C10 28 42N 115 55E
Nanchang, Kiangsi, China 59 C10 28 34N 115 48E
Nancheng, China 59 D11 27 33N 116 35E
Nanching = Nanjing, China 59 A12 32 2N 118 47E
Nanchong, China 58 B6 30 43N 106 2E
Nanchuan, China 58 C6 29 9N 107 6E
Nancy, France 19 D13 48 42N 6 12E
Nanda Devi, India 69 D8 30 23N 79 59E
Nanda Kot, India 69 D9 30 17N 80 5E
Nandan, China 58 E6 24 58N 107 29E
Nandan, Japan 55 G7 34 10N 134 42E
Nanded, India 66 K10 19 10N 77 20E
Nandewar Ra., Australia 95 E5 30 15S 150 35E
Nandi = Nadi, Fiji 91 C7 17 42S 177 20E
Nandigram, India 69 H12 22 1N 87 58E
Nandurbar, India 66 J9 21 20N 74 15E
Nandyal, India 66 M11 15 30N 78 30E
Nanfeng, Guangdong, China 59 F8 23 45N 111 47E
Nanfeng, Jiangxi, China 59 D11 27 12N 116 28E
Nanga-Eboko, Cameroon 83 E7 4 41N 12 22E
Nanga Parbat, Pakistan 69 B6 35 10N 74 35E
Nangade, Mozam. 87 E4 11 5S 39 36E
Nangapinoh, Indonesia 62 E4 0 20S 111 44E
Nangarhār □, Afghan. 66 B7 34 20N 70 0E
Nangatayap, Indonesia 62 E4 1 32S 110 34E
Nangeya Mts., Uganda 86 B3 3 30N 33 30E
Nangis, France 19 D10 48 33N 3 1E
Nangong, China 56 F8 37 23N 115 22E
Nanhua, China 58 E3 25 13N 101 21E
Nanhuang, China 57 F11 36 58N 121 48E
Nanhui, China 59 B13 31 5N 121 44E
Nanjeko, Zambia 87 F1 15 31S 23 30E
Nanji Shan, China 59 D13 27 27N 121 4E
Nanjian, China 58 E3 25 2N 100 25E
Nanjiang, China 58 A6 32 28N 106 51E
Nanjing, Fujian, China 59 E11 24 25N 117 20E
Nanjing, Jiangsu, China 59 A12 32 2N 118 47E
Nanjirinji, Tanzania 87 D4 9 41S 39 5E
Nankana Sahib, Pakistan 68 D5 31 27N 73 38E
Nankang, China 59 E10 25 40N 114 45E
Nanking = Nanjing, China 59 A12 32 2N 118 47E
Nankoku, Japan 55 H6 33 39N 133 44E
Nanling, China 59 B12 30 55N 118 20E
Nanning, China 58 F7 22 48N 108 20E
Nannup, Australia 93 F2 33 59S 115 48E
Nanpan Jiang →, China 58 E6 25 10N 106 5E
Nanpara, India 69 F9 27 52N 81 33E
Nanpi, China 56 E9 38 2N 116 45E
Nanping, Fujian, China 59 D12 26 38N 118 10E
Nanping, Henan, China 59 C9 29 55N 112 3E
Nanri Dao, China 59 E12 25 15N 119 25E
Nanripe, Mozam. 87 E4 13 52S 38 52E
Nansei-Shotō = Ryūkyū-rettō, Japan 55 M3 26 0N 126 0E
Nansen Basin, Arctic 4 A10 84 0N 50 0E
Nansen Cordillera, Arctic 4 A 87 0N 90 0E
Nansen Sd., Canada 4 A3 81 0N 91 0W
Nanshan I., S. China Sea 62 B5 10 45N 115 49E
Nansio, Tanzania 86 C3 2 3S 33 4E
Nant, France 20 D7 44 1N 3 18E
Nanterre, France 19 D9 48 53N 2 13E
Nantes, France 18 E5 47 12N 1 33W
Nantiat, France 20 B5 46 1N 1 11E
Nanticoke, U.S.A. 117 E8 41 12N 76 0W
Nanton, Canada 102 C6 50 21N 113 46W
Nantong, China 59 A13 32 1N 120 52E
Nantou, Taiwan 59 F13 23 57N 120 35E
Nantua, France 19 F12 46 10N 5 35E
Nantucket I., U.S.A. 114 E10 41 16N 70 5W
Nantwich, U.K. 14 D5 53 4N 2 31W
Nanty Glo, U.S.A. 116 F6 40 28N 78 50W
Nanuque, Brazil 125 G10 17 50S 40 21W
Nanusa, Kepulauan, Indonesia 63 D7 4 45N 127 1E
Nanutarra Roadhouse, Australia 92 D2 22 32S 115 30E
Nanxi, China 58 C5 28 54N 104 59E
Nanxiong, China 59 E10 25 6N 114 15E
Nanyang, China 56 H7 33 11N 112 30E
Nanyi Hu, China 59 B12 31 5N 119 0E
Nanyuki, Kenya 86 B4 0 2N 37 4E
Nanzhang, China 59 B8 31 45N 111 50E
Nao, C. de la, Spain 39 G5 38 44N 0 14E
Naococane, L., Canada 105 B5 52 50N 70 45W
Náousa, Imathía, Greece 44 F6 40 42N 22 9E
Náousa, Kikládhes, Greece 47 D7 37 7N 25 14E
Naozhou Dao, China 59 G8 20 55N 110 20E
Napa, U.S.A. 110 G4 38 18N 122 17W
Napa →, U.S.A. 110 G4 38 10N 122 19W
Napanee, Canada 116 B8 44 15N 77 0W
Napanoch, U.S.A. 117 E10 41 44N 74 22W
Nape, Laos 64 C5 18 18N 105 6E
Nape Pass = Keo Neua, Deo, Vietnam 64 C5 18 23N 105 10E
Napier, N.Z. 91 H6 39 30S 176 56E
Napier Broome B., Australia 92 B4 14 2S 126 37E
Napier Pen., Australia 94 A2 12 4S 135 43E
Napierville, Canada 117 A11 45 11N 73 25W
Naples = Nápoli, Italy 43 B7 40 50N 14 15E
Naples, U.S.A. 115 M5 26 8N 81 48W
Napo, China 58 F5 23 22N 105 50E
Napo →, Peru 124 D4 3 20S 72 40W
Napoleon, N. Dak., U.S.A. 112 B5 46 30N 99 46W
Napoleon, Ohio, U.S.A. 114 E3 41 23N 84 8W
Nápoli, Italy 43 B7 40 50N 14 15E
Nápoli, G. di, Italy 43 B7 40 43N 14 10E
Nápoli Capodichino ✈ (NAP), Italy 43 B7 40 53N 14 16E
Napopo, Dem. Rep. of the Congo 86 B2 4 15N 28 0E
Naqâda, Egypt 80 B3 25 53N 32 42E
Naqadeh, Iran 73 D11 36 57N 45 23E
Naqb, Ra's an, Jordan 74 F4 30 0N 35 29E
Naqqāsh, Iran 71 C6 35 40N 49 6E
Nara, Japan 55 G7 34 40N 135 49E
Nara, Mali 82 B3 15 10N 7 20W
Nara □, Japan 55 G8 34 30N 136 0E
Nara Canal, Pakistan 68 G3 24 30N 69 20E
Nara Visa, U.S.A. 113 H3 35 37N 103 6W
Naracoorte, Australia 95 F3 36 58S 140 45E
Naradhan, Australia 95 E4 33 34S 146 17E
Naraini, India 69 G9 25 11N 80 29E
Narasapur, India 67 L12 16 26N 81 40E
Narathiwat, Thailand 65 J3 6 30N 101 48E
Narayanganj, Bangla. 67 H17 23 40N 90 33E
Narayanpet, India 66 L10 16 45N 77 30E
Narberth, U.K. 15 F3 51 47N 4 44W
Narbonne, France 20 E7 43 11N 3 0E
Narcea →, Spain 36 B4 43 33N 6 44W
Nardīn, Iran 71 B7 37 3N 55 59E
Nardò, Italy 43 B11 40 11N 18 2E
Narembeen, Australia 93 F2 32 7S 118 24E
Narendranagar, India 68 D8 30 10N 78 18E
Nares Str., Arctic 98 A13 80 0N 70 0W
Naretha, Australia 93 F3 31 0S 124 45E
Narew →, Poland 31 F7 52 26N 20 41E
Nari →, Pakistan 68 F2 28 0N 67 40E
Narin, Afghan. 66 A6 36 5N 69 0E
Narindra, Helodranon' i, Madag. 89 A8 14 55S 47 30E
Narita, Japan 55 G10 35 47N 140 19E
Nariva Swamp, Trin. & Tob. 125 K15 10 26N 61 4W
Närke, Sweden 10 E8 59 10N 15 0E
Narmada →, India 68 J5 21 38N 72 36E
Narman, Turkey 73 B9 40 26N 41 57E
Narmland, Sweden 9 F15 60 0N 13 30E
Narnaul, India 68 E7 28 5N 76 11E
Narni, Italy 41 F9 42 30N 12 30E
Naro, Ghana 82 C4 10 22N 2 27W
Naro Fominsk, Russia 32 E9 55 23N 36 43E
Narodnaya, Russia 6 B17 65 5N 59 58E
Narok, Kenya 86 C4 1 55S 35 52E
Narón, Spain 36 B2 43 32N 8 9W
Narooma, Australia 95 F5 36 14S 150 4E
Narowal, Pakistan 68 C6 32 6N 74 52E
Narrabri, Australia 95 E4 30 19S 149 46E
Narran →, Australia 95 D4 28 37S 148 12E
Narrandera, Australia 95 E4 34 42S 146 31E
Narrogin, Australia 93 F2 32 58S 117 14E
Narromine, Australia 95 E4 32 12S 148 12E
Narrow Hills ⌓, Canada 103 C8 54 0N 104 37W
Narsimhapur, India 69 H8 22 54N 79 14E
Narsinghgarh, India 68 H7 23 45N 76 40E
Nartes, L. e, Albania 44 F3 40 32N 19 25E
Nartkala, Russia 35 J6 43 33N 43 51E
Naruto, Japan 55 G7 34 11N 134 37E
Narva, Estonia 32 C5 59 23N 28 12E
Narva →, Russia 9 G22 59 27N 28 2E
Narva Bay = Narva Laht, Estonia 9 G19 59 35N 27 35E
Narva Laht, Estonia 9 G19 59 35N 27 35E
Narvik, Norway 8 B17 68 28N 17 26E
Narvskoye Vdkhr., Russia 32 C5 59 18N 28 14E
Narwana, India 68 E7 29 39N 76 6E
Narwiański △, Poland 31 F9 52 5N 22 53E
Naryan-Mar, Russia 52 C6 67 42N 53 12E
Narym, Russia 52 D9 59 0N 81 30E
Naryn, Kyrgyzstan 52 E8 41 26N 75 58E
Nasa, Norway 8 C16 66 29N 15 23E
Năsăud, Romania 29 C9 47 19N 24 29E
Naseby, N.Z. 91 L3 45 1S 170 10E
Naselle, U.S.A. 110 D3 46 22N 123 49W
Naser, Buheirat en, Egypt 80 C3 23 0N 32 30E
Nashua, Mont., U.S.A. 108 B10 48 8N 106 22W
Nashua, N.H., U.S.A. 117 D13 42 45N 71 28W
Nashville, Ark., U.S.A. 113 J8 33 57N 93 51W
Nashville, Ga., U.S.A. 115 K4 31 12N 83 15W
Nashville, Tenn., U.S.A. 115 G2 36 10N 86 47W
Našice, Croatia 28 E3 45 32N 18 4E
Nasielsk, Poland 31 F7 52 35N 20 50E
Nasik, India 66 K8 19 58N 73 50E
Nasipit, Phil. 61 G6 8 57N 125 19E
Nasir, Sudan 81 F3 8 36N 33 4E
Nasirabad, India 68 F6 26 15N 74 45E
Nasirabad, Pakistan 68 E3 28 23N 68 24E
Nasiriyah = An Nāşirīyah, Iraq 70 D5 31 0N 46 15E
Naskaupi →, Canada 105 B7 53 47N 60 51W
Naso, Italy 43 D7 38 7N 14 47E
Naşrābād, Iran 71 C6 34 8N 51 26E
Naşriān-e Pā'īn, Iran 70 C5 32 52N 46 52E
Nass →, Canada 102 C3 55 0N 129 40W
Nassarawa, Nigeria 83 D6 8 32N 7 41E
Nassarawa □, Nigeria 83 D6 8 30N 8 20E
Nassau, Bahamas 120 A4 25 5N 77 20W
Nassau, U.S.A. 117 D11 42 31N 73 37W
Nassau, B., Chile 128 H3 55 20S 68 0W
Nasser, L. = Naser, Buheirat en, Egypt 80 C3 23 0N 32 30E
Nassian, Ivory C. 82 D4 8 28N 3 28W
Nässjö, Sweden 11 G8 57 39N 14 42E
Nastapoka →, Canada 104 A4 56 55N 76 33W
Nastapoka, Is., Canada 104 A4 56 55N 76 50W
Nasugbu, Phil. 61 D4 14 5N 120 38E
Näsum, Sweden 11 H8 56 10N 14 29E
Näsviken, Sweden 10 C10 61 46N 16 52E
Nata, Botswana 88 C4 20 12S 26 12E
Nata →, Botswana 88 C4 20 14S 26 10E
Natal, Brazil 125 E11 5 47S 35 13W
Natal, Indonesia 62 D1 0 35N 99 7E
Natal, S. Africa 85 K6 28 30S 30 30E
Natal Drakensberg ⌓, S. Africa 89 D4 29 27S 29 30E
Natalinci, Serbia & M. 28 F5 44 15N 20 49E
Naţanz, Iran 71 C6 33 30N 51 55E
Natashquan, Canada 105 B7 50 14N 61 46W
Natashquan →, Canada 105 B7 50 7N 61 50W
Natchez, U.S.A. 113 K9 31 34N 91 24W
Natchitoches, U.S.A. 113 K8 31 46N 93 5W
Nathalia, Australia 95 F4 36 1S 145 13E
Nathdwara, India 68 G5 24 55N 73 50E
Nati, Pta., Spain 48 A10 40 3N 3 50E
Natimuk, Australia 95 F3 36 42S 142 0E
Nation →, Canada 102 B4 55 30N 123 32W
National City, U.S.A. 111 N9 32 41N 117 6W
Natitingou, Benin 83 C5 10 20N 1 26E
Natividad, I., Mexico 118 B1 27 50N 115 10W
Natkyizin, Burma 64 E1 14 57N 97 59E
Natron, L., Tanzania 86 C4 2 20S 36 0E
Natrona Heights, U.S.A. 116 F5 40 37N 79 44W
Natrûn, W. el →, Egypt 80 H7 30 25N 30 13E
Nättraby, Sweden 11 H9 56 13N 15 31E
Natukanaoka Pan, Namibia 88 B2 18 40S 15 45E
Natuna Besar, Kepulauan, Indonesia 62 D3 4 0N 108 15E
Natuna Is. = Natuna Besar, Kepulauan, Indonesia 62 D3 4 0N 108 15E
Natuna Selatan, Kepulauan, Indonesia 62 D3 2 45N 109 0E
Natural Bridge, U.S.A. 117 B9 44 5N 75 30W
Natural Bridges ⌓, U.S.A. 109 H8 37 36N 110 1W
Naturaliste, C., Australia 95 G4 40 50S 148 15E
Nau Qala, Afghan. 68 B3 34 5N 68 5E
Naucelle, France 20 D6 44 13N 2 20E
Nauders, Austria 26 E3 46 54N 10 30E
Nauen, Germany 24 C8 52 36N 12 52E
Naugatuck, U.S.A. 117 E11 41 30N 73 3W
Naujaat = Repulse Bay, Canada 101 B11 66 30N 86 30W
Naujoji Akmenė, Lithuania 30 B9 56 19N 22 54E
Naumburg, Germany 24 D7 51 9N 11 47E
Nā'ūr at Tunayb, Jordan 74 D4 31 48N 35 57E
Nauru ■, Pac. Oc. 96 H8 1 0S 166 0E
Naushahra = Nowshera, Pakistan 66 C8 34 0N 72 0E
Naushahro, Pakistan 68 F3 26 50N 68 7E
Naushon I., U.S.A. 117 E14 41 29N 70 45W
Nauta, Peru 124 D4 4 31S 73 35W
Nautanwa, India 67 F13 27 20N 83 25E
Naute ⌓, Namibia 88 D2 26 55S 17 57E
Nautla, Mexico 119 C5 20 20N 96 50W
Nava, Mexico 118 B4 28 25N 100 46W
Nava, Spain 36 B5 43 21N 5 31W
Nava del Rey, Spain 36 D5 41 22N 5 6W
Navadwip, India 69 H13 23 34N 88 20E
Navahermosa, Spain 37 F6 39 41N 4 28W
Navahrudak, Belarus 32 F3 53 40N 25 50E
Navajo Reservoir, U.S.A. 109 H10 36 48N 107 36W
Navalcarnero, Spain 36 E6 40 17N 4 5W
Navalmoral de la Mata, Spain 36 F5 39 52N 5 33W
Navalvillar de Pela, Spain 37 F5 39 9N 5 24W
Navan = An Uaimh, Ireland 12 C5 53 39N 6 41W
Navapolatsk, Belarus 32 E5 55 32N 28 37E
Navarin, Mys, Russia 4 C16 62 15N 179 5E
Navarino, I., Chile 128 H3 55 0S 67 40W
Navarra □, Spain 38 C3 42 40N 1 40W
Navarre, U.S.A. 116 F3 40 43N 81 31W
Navarro →, U.S.A. 110 F3 39 11N 123 45W
Navas de San Juan, Spain 37 G7 38 30N 3 19W
Navasota, U.S.A. 113 K6 30 23N 96 5W
Navassa I., W. Indies 121 C5 18 30N 75 0W
Nävekvarn, Sweden 11 F10 58 38N 16 49E
Naver →, U.K. 13 C4 58 32N 4 14W
Navia, Spain 36 B4 43 35N 6 42W
Navia →, Spain 36 B4 43 15N 6 50W
Navia de Suarna, Spain 36 C3 42 58N 7 3W
Navibandar, India 68 J3 21 26N 69 48E
Navidad, Chile 126 C1 33 57S 71 50W
Naviraí, Brazil 127 A5 23 8S 54 13W
Navlakhi, India 68 H4 22 58N 70 28E
Navlya, Russia 33 F8 52 53N 34 30E
Năvodari, Romania 29 F13 44 19N 28 36E
Navoi = Nawoiy, Uzbekistan 52 E7 40 9N 65 22E
Navojoa, Mexico 118 B3 27 0N 109 30W
Navolato, Mexico 118 C3 24 47N 107 42W
Návpaktos, Greece 46 C3 38 24N 21 50E
Návplion, Greece 46 D4 37 33N 22 50E
Navrongo, Ghana 83 C4 10 51N 1 3W
Navsari, India 66 J8 20 57N 72 59E
Nawa Kot, Pakistan 68 E4 28 21N 71 24E
Nawab Khan, Pakistan 68 D3 30 17N 69 12E
Nawabganj, Ut. P., India 69 F9 26 56N 81 14E
Nawabganj, Ut. P., India 69 E8 28 32N 79 40E
Nawabshah, Pakistan 68 F3 26 15N 68 25E
Nawada, India 69 G11 24 50N 85 33E
Nawakot, Nepal 69 F11 27 55N 85 10E
Nawalgarh, India 68 F6 27 50N 75 15E

Nawanshahr, India .... 69 C6 32 33N 74 48 E
Nawar, Dasht-i-,
 Afghan. .... 68 C3 33 52N 68 0 E
Nawi, Sudan ...... 80 D3 18 32N 30 50 E
Nawoiy, Uzbekistan .. 52 E7 40 9N 65 22 E
Naxçivan, Azerbaijan . 70 B5 39 12N 45 15 E
Naxçivan □, Azerbaijan 70 B5 39 25N 45 26 E
Náxos, Greece ...... 47 D7 37 8N 25 25 E
Nay, France 20 E3 43 10N 0 18W
Nay, Mui, Vietnam .. 62 B3 12 55N 109 23 E
Nãy Band, Büshehr, Iran 71 E7 27 20N 52 40 E
Nãy Band, Khorãsãn,
 Iran .... 71 C8 32 20N 57 34 E
Nayakhan, Russia ... 53 C16 61 56N 159 0 E
Nayarit □, Mexico ... 118 C4 22 0N 105 0W
Nayé, Senegal 82 C2 14 28N 12 12W
Nayong, China ...... 58 D5 26 50N 105 20 E
Nayoro, Japan ...... 54 B11 44 21N 142 28 E
Nayyãl, W. →,
 Si. Arabia .... 70 D3 28 35N 39 4 E
Nazaré, Brazil 125 F11 13 2S 39 0W
Nazaré, Portugal ... 37 F1 39 36N 9 4W
Nazareth = Nazerat,
 Israel .... 74 C4 32 42N 35 17 E
Nazareth, U.S.A. ... 117 F9 40 44N 75 19W
Nazas, Mexico 118 B4 25 10N 104 6W
Nazas →, Mexico ... 118 B4 25 35N 103 25W
Nazca, Peru 124 F4 14 50S 74 57W
Naze, The, U.K. ... 15 F9 51 53N 1 18 E
Nazerat, Israel .... 74 C4 32 42N 35 17 E
Nãzik, Iran .... 70 B5 39 1N 45 4 E
Nazilli, Turkey .... 47 D10 37 55N 28 15 E
Nazko, Canada 102 C4 53 1N 123 37W
Nazko →, Canada ... 102 C4 53 7N 123 34W
Nazret, Ethiopia ... 81 F4 8 32N 39 22 E
Nazwa, Oman ...... 75 C6 22 56N 57 32 E
Nchanga, Zambia ... 87 E2 12 30S 27 49 E
Ncheu, Malawi ..... 87 E3 14 50S 34 47 E
Ndala, Tanzania .... 86 C3 4 45S 33 15 E
Ndalatando, Angola .. 84 F2 9 12S 14 48 E
Ndali, Benin ...... 83 D5 9 50N 2 46 E
Ndareda, Tanzania ... 86 C4 4 12S 35 30 E
Ndélé, C.A.R. ..... 84 C4 8 25N 20 36 E
Ndiael △, Senegal .. 82 B1 16 15N 16 0W
Ndikinimeki, Cameroon 83 E7 4 46N 10 50 E
N'Dioum, Senegal ... 82 B2 16 31N 14 39W
Ndjamena, Chad ... 79 F8 12 10N 14 59 E
Ndola, Zambia ..... 87 E2 13 0S 28 34 E
Ndoto Mts., Kenya .. 86 B4 2 0N 37 0 E
Nduguti, Tanzania ... 86 C3 4 18S 34 41 E
Ndumu △, S. Africa .. 89 D5 26 52S 32 15 E
Néa Alikarnassós,
 Greece .... 47 F7 35 18N 25 13 E
Néa Ankhíalos, Greece 46 B4 39 16N 22 45 E
Néa Epídhavros, Greece 46 D5 37 40N 23 7 E
Néa Flippiás, Greece .. 46 B2 39 12N 20 53 E
Néa Ionía, Greece ... 46 B4 39 21N 22 56 E
Néa Kallikrátia, Greece 46 C4 40 21N 23 3 E
Néa Mákri, Greece ... 46 C5 38 8N 23 59 E
Néa Moudhaniá, Greece 44 F7 40 15N 23 17 E
Néa Péramos, Attikí,
 Greece .... 46 C5 38 0N 23 26 E
Néa Péramos, Kaválla,
 Greece .... 45 F8 40 50N 24 18 E
Néa Víssi, Greece ... 45 E10 41 34N 26 33 E
Néa Zíkhna, Greece .. 44 E7 41 2N 23 49 E
Neagh, Lough, U.K. .. 12 B5 54 37N 6 25W
Neah Bay, U.S.A. .. 110 B2 48 22N 124 37W
Neale, L., Australia .. 92 D5 24 15S 130 0 E
Neales, The →,
 Australia .... 95 D2 28 8S 136 47 E
Neamţ □, Romania .. 29 C11 47 0N 26 20 E
Neápolis, Kozáni,
 Greece .... 44 F5 40 20N 21 24 E
Neápolis, Kríti, Greece . 49 D7 35 15N 25 37 E
Neápolis, Lakonía,
 Greece .... 46 E5 36 27N 23 8 E
Near Is., U.S.A. ... 100 C1 52 30N 174 0 E
Neath, U.K. 15 F4 51 39N 3 48W
Neath Port Talbot □,
 U.K. 15 F4 51 42N 3 45W
Nebbou, Burkina Faso . 83 C4 11 9N 1 51W
Nebelat el Hagana,
 Sudan .... 81 E2 13 13N 29 2 E
Nebine Cr. →, Australia 95 D4 29 27S 146 56 E
Nebitdag, Turkmenistan 52 F6 39 30N 54 22 E
Nebo, Australia ..... 94 C4 21 42S 148 42 E
Nebolchy, Russia ... 32 C7 59 8N 33 18 E
Nebraska □, U.S.A. .. 112 E5 41 30N 99 30W
Nebraska City, U.S.A. 112 E7 40 41N 95 52W
Nébrodi, Monti, Italy . 43 E7 37 54N 14 35 E
Necedah, U.S.A. ... 112 C9 44 2N 90 4W
Nechako →, Canada .. 102 C4 53 55N 122 42W
Neches →, U.S.A. ... 113 L8 29 58N 93 51W
Nechisar △, Ethiopia . 81 F4 5 50N 37 55 E
Neckar →, Germany .. 25 F4 49 27N 8 29 E
Neckartal-Odenwald △,
 Germany .... 25 F5 49 30N 9 5 E
Necochea, Argentina . 126 D4 38 30S 58 50W
Neda, Spain 36 B2 43 30N 8 9W
Nedelino, Bulgaria ... 45 E9 41 27N 25 3 E
Nedelišće, Croatia ... 41 B13 46 23N 16 22 E
Nédha →, Greece ... 46 D3 37 25N 21 6 E
Nedoboyivtsi, Ukraine . 29 B11 48 26N 26 21 E
Needles, Canada ... 102 D5 49 53N 118 7W
Needles, U.S.A. ... 111 L12 34 51N 114 37W
Needles, The, U.K. .. 15 G6 50 39N 1 35W
Neembucú □, Paraguay 126 B4 27 0S 58 0W
Neemuch = Nimach,
 India .... 68 G6 24 30N 74 56 E
Neenah, U.S.A. ... 114 C1 44 11N 88 28W
Neepawa, Canada ... 103 C9 50 15N 99 30W
Neftçala, Azerbaijan . 71 B6 39 19N 49 12 E
Neftegorsk, Russia .. 35 H4 44 25N 39 45 E
Neftekumsk, Russia .. 35 H7 44 46N 44 50 E
Nefyn, U.K. 14 E3 52 56N 4 31W
Négala, Mali 82 C3 12 52N 8 30W
Negapatam =
 Nagappattinam, India 66 P11 10 46N 79 51 E
Negara, Indonesia ... 63 J17 8 22S 114 37 E
Negaunee, U.S.A. .. 114 B2 46 30N 87 36W
Negele =
 Hanegev, Israel ... 74 E4 30 50N 35 0 E
Negombo, Sri Lanka . 66 R11 7 12N 79 50 E
Negotin, Serbia & M. . 44 B6 44 16N 22 37 E
Negotino, Macedonia . 44 E6 41 29N 22 7 E
Negra, Peña, Spain .. 36 C4 42 11N 6 30W
Negra, Pta., Peru .. 124 E2 6 6S 81 10W
Negrais = C. = Maudin
 Sun, Burma ...... 67 M19 16 0N 94 30 E
Negreşti, Romania ... 29 D12 46 50N 27 30 E
Negreşti-Oaş, Romania 29 C8 47 52N 23 27 E
Negril, Jamaica .... 120 a 18 22N 78 20W
Negra →, Argentina . 128 E4 41 2S 62 47W
Negro →, Brazil 124 D7 3 0S 60 0W

Negro →, Uruguay .. 127 C4 33 24S 58 22W
Negros, Phil. ...... 61 G5 9 30N 122 40 E
Negru Vodă, Romania . 29 G13 43 47N 28 21 E
Neguac, Canada 105 C6 47 15N 65 5W
Nehalem →, U.S.A. .. 110 E3 45 40N 123 56W
Nehãvand, Iran .... 71 C6 35 56N 49 31 E
Nehbandãn, Iran ... 71 D9 31 35N 60 5 E
Nehoiu, Romania ... 29 E11 45 24N 26 20 E
Nei Monggol Zizhiqu □,
 China .... 56 D7 42 0N 112 0 E
Neijiang, China .... 58 C5 29 35N 104 55 E
Neillsville, U.S.A. ... 112 C9 44 34N 90 36W
Neilton, U.S.A. 110 C2 47 25N 123 53W
Neiqiu, China ...... 56 F8 37 15N 114 30 E
Neiva, Colombia ... 124 C3 2 56N 75 18W
Neixiang, China .... 56 H6 33 10N 111 52 E
Nejanilini L., Canada . 103 B9 59 33N 97 48W
Nejd = Najd, Si. Arabia 75 B3 26 30N 42 0 E
Nejo, Ethiopia ..... 81 F4 9 30N 35 28 E
Nekã, Iran .... 71 B7 36 39N 53 19 E
Nekemte, Ethiopia ... 81 F4 9 4N 36 30 E
Nekheb, Egypt .... 80 B3 25 10N 32 48 E
Neksø, Denmark ... 11 J9 55 4N 15 8 E
Nelas, Portugal 36 E3 40 32N 7 52W
Nelia, Australia .... 94 C3 20 39S 142 12 E
Nelidovo, Russia ... 32 D7 56 13N 32 49 E
Neligh, U.S.A. 112 D5 42 8N 98 2W
Nelkan, Russia .... 53 D14 57 40N 136 4 E
Nellore, India .... 66 M11 14 27N 79 59 E
Nelson, Canada 102 D5 49 30N 117 20W
Nelson, N.Z. ...... 91 J4 41 18S 173 16 E
Nelson, U.K. 14 D5 53 50N 2 13W
Nelson, Ariz., U.S.A. . 109 J7 35 31N 113 19W
Nelson, Nev., U.S.A. . 111 K12 35 42N 114 50W
Nelson →, Canada .. 103 C9 54 33N 98 2W
Nelson, C., Australia . 95 F3 38 26S 141 32 E
Nelson, Estrecho, Chile 128 G2 51 30S 75 0W
Nelson Forks, Canada . 102 B4 59 30N 124 0W
Nelson House, Canada . 103 B9 55 47N 98 51W
Nelson L., Canada .. 103 B8 55 48N 100 7W
Nelson Lakes △, N.Z. . 91 J4 41 55S 172 44 E
Nelspoort, S. Africa .. 88 E3 32 7S 23 0 E
Nelspruit, S. Africa .. 89 D5 25 29S 30 59 E
Néma, Mauritania ... 82 B3 16 40N 7 15W
Neman = Nemunas →,
 Lithuania .... 9 J19 55 25N 21 10 E
Neman, Russia .... 9 J20 55 2N 22 2 E
Neméa, Greece .... 46 D4 37 49N 22 40 E
Nemeiben L., Canada . 103 B7 55 20N 105 20W
Nemercke, Mal, Albania 44 F4 40 15N 20 15 E
Nemira, Vf., Romania . 29 D11 46 17N 26 19 E
Nemiscau, Canada .. 104 B4 51 18N 76 54W
Nemiscau, L., Canada . 104 B4 51 25N 76 40W
Nemours, France ... 19 D9 48 16N 2 40 E
Nemšová, Slovak Rep. . 27 C11 48 58N 18 7 E
Nemunas →, Lithuania . 9 J19 55 25N 21 10 E
Nemuro, Japan .... 54 C12 43 20N 145 35 E
Nemuro-Kaikyō, Japan 54 C12 43 30N 145 30 E
Nen Jiang →, China .. 57 B13 45 28N 124 30 E
Nenagh, Ireland ... 12 D3 52 52N 8 11W
Nenasi, Malaysia ... 65 L4 3 9N 103 23 E
Nene →, U.K. ..... 15 E8 52 49N 0 11 E
Nénita, Greece .... 47 C8 38 14N 26 6 E
Nenjiang, China ... 60 B7 49 10N 125 10 E
Neno, Malawi ..... 87 F3 15 25S 34 40 E
Neodesha, U.S.A. .. 113 G7 37 25N 95 41W
Neokhórion,
 Aitolía kai Akarnanía,
 Greece .... 46 C3 38 25N 21 17 E
Neokhórion, Árta,
 Greece .... 46 B2 39 4N 21 0 E
Néon Karlovásion,
 Greece .... 47 D8 37 45N 26 42 E
Néon Petrítsi, Greece .. 44 E7 41 16N 23 15 E
Neosho, U.S.A. 113 G7 36 52N 94 22W
Neosho →, U.S.A. .. 113 H7 36 48N 95 18W
Nepal ■, Asia ..... 69 F11 28 0N 84 30 E
Nepalganj, Nepal ... 69 E9 28 5N 81 40 E
Nepalganj Road, India 69 E9 28 1N 81 41 E
Nephi, U.S.A. 108 G8 39 43N 111 50W
Nephin, Ireland ... 12 B2 54 1N 9 22W
Nepi, Italy .... 41 F9 42 14N 12 21 E
Nepomuk, Czech Rep. . 26 B6 49 29N 13 35 E
Neptune, U.S.A. ... 117 F10 40 13N 74 2W
Nera →, Italy ..... 41 F9 42 26N 12 24 E
Nera →, Romania ... 28 F6 44 48N 21 25 E
Nérac, France .... 20 D4 44 8N 0 21 E
Nerang, Australia ... 95 D5 27 58S 153 20 E
Neratovice, Czech Rep. 26 A7 50 16N 14 31 E
Nereju, Romania ... 29 E11 45 43N 26 43 E
Nerekhta, Russia ... 32 D11 57 26N 40 38 E
Neresnytsya, Ukraine . 29 B8 48 7N 23 46 E
Néret, L., Canada .. 105 B5 54 45N 70 44W
Neretvanski Kanal,
 Croatia .... 41 E14 43 7N 17 10 E
Neringa, Lithuania .. 9 J19 55 20N 21 5 E
Neris →, Lithuania .. 9 J21 55 8N 24 16 E
Nerja, Spain 37 J7 36 43N 3 55W
Nerl →, Russia .... 32 D11 56 11N 40 34 E
Nerpio, Spain 39 G2 38 11N 2 16W
Nerva, Spain 37 H4 37 42N 6 30W
Nervi, Italy ...... 40 D6 44 23N 9 2 E
Neryungri, Russia ... 53 D13 57 38N 124 28 E
Nescopeck, U.S.A. .. 117 E8 41 3N 76 12W
Nesebŭr, Bulgaria ... 45 D11 42 41N 27 46 E
Ness, L., U.K. 13 D4 57 15N 4 32W
Ness City, U.S.A. .. 112 F5 38 27N 99 54W
Nesterov, Russia ... 30 D9 54 38N 22 41 E
Nesterov, Ukraine .. 33 G2 50 4N 23 58 E
Nestórion, Greece ... 44 F5 40 24N 21 5 E
Néstos →, Greece ... 45 E8 41 20N 24 35 E
Nesvady, Slovak Rep. . 27 D11 47 56N 18 7 E
Nesvizh = Nyasvizh,
 Belarus .... 33 F4 53 14N 26 38 E
Netanya, Israel .... 74 C3 32 20N 34 51 E
Netarhat, India .... 69 H11 23 29N 84 16 E
Nete →, Belgium ... 17 C4 51 7N 4 14 E
Netherdale, Australia . 94 K6 21 10S 148 33 E
Netherlands ■, Europe 17 C5 52 0N 5 30 E
Netherlands Antilles ☑,
 W. Indies 124 A5 12 15N 69 0W
Neto →, Italy ..... 43 C10 39 12N 17 9 E
Netrang, India .... 68 J5 21 39N 73 21 E
Nettancourt, France .. 19 D11 48 51N 4 57 E
Nettetal, Germany .. 24 D2 51 19N 6 12 E
Nettilling L., Canada . 101 B12 66 30N 71 0W
Nettuno, Italy ..... 42 A5 41 27N 12 39 E
Netzahualcoyotl, Presa,
 Mexico 119 D6 17 10N 93 30W
Neu-Isenburg, Germany 25 E4 50 3N 8 42 E
Neu-Ulm, Germany .. 25 G6 48 23N 10 1 E
Neubrandenburg,
 Germany .... 24 B9 53 33N 13 15 E
Neubukow, Germany . 24 A7 54 1N 11 40 E
Neuburg, Germany .. 25 G7 48 44N 11 11 E

Neuchâtel, Switz. ... 25 J2 47 0N 6 55 E
Neuchâtel □, Switz. .. 25 J2 47 0N 6 55 E
Neuchâtel, Lac de,
 Switz. .... 25 J2 46 53N 6 50 E
Neudau, Austria .... 26 D9 47 11N 16 6 E
Neuenhagen, Germany 24 C9 52 32N 13 38 E
Neuenhaus, Germany . 24 C2 52 30N 6 58 E
Neuf-Brisach, France . 19 D14 48 1N 7 30 E
Neufahrn, Bayern,
 Germany .... 25 G8 48 41N 12 11 E
Neufahrn, Bayern,
 Germany .... 25 G7 48 18N 11 40 E
Neufchâteau, Belgium . 17 E5 49 50N 5 25 E
Neufchâteau, France .. 19 D12 48 21N 5 40 E
Neufchâtel-en-Bray,
 France .... 18 C8 49 44N 1 26 E
Neufchâtel-sur-Aisne,
 France .... 19 C11 49 26N 4 1 E
Neuhaus, Germany .. 24 B6 53 17N 10 56 E
Neuillé-Pont-Pierre,
 France .... 18 E7 47 33N 0 33 E
Neuilly-St-Front, France 19 C10 49 10N 3 15 E
Neukalen, Germany .. 24 B8 53 49N 12 46 E
Neumarkt, Germany . 25 F7 49 16N 11 27 E
Neumünster, Germany 24 A5 54 4N 9 58 E
Neung-sur-Beuvron,
 France .... 19 E8 47 30N 1 50 E
Neunkirchen, Austria . 26 D9 47 43N 16 4 E
Neunkirchen, Germany 25 F3 49 20N 7 9 E
Neuquén, Argentina . 128 D3 38 55S 68 0W
Neuquén □, Argentina 126 D2 38 0S 69 50W
Neuruppin, Germany . 24 C8 52 55N 12 48 E
Neusäss, Germany .. 25 G6 48 24N 10 50 E
Neuse →, U.S.A. ... 115 H7 35 6N 76 29W
Neusiedl, Austria ... 27 D9 47 57N 16 50 E
Neusiedler See, Austria 27 D9 47 50N 16 47 E
Neusiedler See-
 Seewinkel △, Austria 27 D9 47 50N 16 45 E
Neuss, Germany .... 24 D2 51 11N 6 42 E
Neussargues-Moissac,
 France .... 20 C7 45 9N 3 0 E
Neustadt, Bayern,
 Germany .... 25 F8 49 44N 12 10 E
Neustadt, Bayern,
 Germany .... 25 G7 48 48N 11 46 E
Neustadt, Bayern,
 Germany .... 25 F6 49 34N 10 37 E
Neustadt, Bayern,
 Germany .... 25 E7 50 19N 11 7 E
Neustadt, Brandenburg,
 Germany .... 24 C8 52 50N 12 27 E
Neustadt, Hessen,
 Germany .... 24 E5 50 51N 9 9 E
Neustadt, Niedersachsen,
 Germany .... 24 C5 52 30N 9 30 E
Neustadt, Rhld.-Pfz.,
 Germany .... 25 F4 49 21N 8 10 E
Neustadt, Sachsen,
 Germany .... 24 D10 51 2N 14 12 E
Neustadt,
 Schleswig-Holstein,
 Germany .... 24 A6 54 6N 10 49 E
Neustadt, Thüringen,
 Germany .... 24 E7 50 45N 11 43 E
Neustrelitz, Germany . 24 B9 53 21N 13 4 E
Neuvic, France .... 20 C6 45 23N 2 16 E
Neuville-sur-Saône,
 France .... 21 C8 45 52N 4 51 E
Neuvy-le-Roi, France . 18 E7 47 36N 0 36 E
Neuvy-St-Sépulchre,
 France .... 19 F8 46 35N 1 48 E
Neuvy-sur-Barangeon,
 France .... 19 E9 47 20N 2 15 E
Neuwerk, Germany .. 24 B4 53 55N 8 30 E
Neuwied, Germany .. 24 E3 50 26N 7 29 E
Neva →, Russia .... 32 C6 59 50N 30 30 E
Nevada, Iowa, U.S.A. . 112 D8 42 1N 93 27W
Nevada, Mo., U.S.A. . 113 G7 37 51N 94 22W
Nevada □, U.S.A. .. 108 G5 39 0N 117 0W
Nevada City, U.S.A. . 110 F6 39 16N 121 1W
Nevado, Cerro,
 Argentina 126 D2 35 30S 68 32W
Nevado de Colima =
 Volcán de Colima △,
 Mexico 118 D4 19 30N 103 40W
Nevado de Tres
 Cruces △, Chile ... 126 B2 27 13S 69 5W
Nevel, Russia ..... 32 D5 56 0N 29 55 E
Nevers, France .... 19 F10 47 0N 3 9 E
Nevertire, Australia .. 95 E4 31 50S 147 44 E
Nevesinje, Bos.-H. .. 44 C2 43 14N 18 6 E
Neville, Canada 103 D7 49 58N 107 39W
Nevinnomyssk, Russia . 35 H6 44 40N 42 0 E
Nevis, St. Kitts & Nevis 121 C7 17 0N 62 30W
Nevrokop = Gotse
 Delchev, Bulgaria .. 44 E7 41 36N 23 46 E
Nevşehir, Turkey ... 70 B2 38 33N 34 40 E
Nevskoye, Russia ... 30 D9 54 32N 22 39 E
New →, U.S.A. 114 F5 38 10N 81 12W
New Aiyansh, Canada . 102 B3 55 12N 129 4W
New Albany, Ind.,
 U.S.A. 114 F3 38 18N 85 49W
New Albany, Miss.,
 U.S.A. 113 H10 34 29N 89 0W
New Albany, Pa., U.S.A. 117 E8 41 36N 76 27W
New Amsterdam,
 Guyana 124 B7 6 15N 57 36W
New Angledool,
 Australia .... 95 D4 29 5S 147 55 E
New Baltimore, U.S.A. 116 D2 42 41N 82 44W
New Bedford, U.S.A. . 117 E14 41 38N 70 56W
New Berlin, N.Y., U.S.A. 117 D9 42 37N 75 20W
New Berlin, Pa., U.S.A. 116 F8 40 50N 76 57W
New Bern, U.S.A. .. 115 H7 35 7N 77 3W
New Bethlehem, U.S.A. 116 F5 41 0N 79 20W
New Bloomfield, U.S.A. 116 F7 40 25N 77 11W
New Boston, U.S.A. . 113 J7 33 28N 94 25W
New Braunfels, U.S.A. 113 L5 29 42N 98 8W
New Brighton, N.Z. .. 91 K4 43 29S 172 43 E
New Brighton, U.S.A. . 116 F4 40 42N 80 19W
New Britain,
 Papua N. G. ...... 96 H7 5 50S 150 20 E
New Britain, U.S.A. . 117 E12 41 40N 72 47W
New Brunswick, U.S.A. 117 F10 40 30N 74 27W
New Brunswick □,
 Canada 105 C6 46 50N 66 30W
New Bussa, Nigeria .. 83 D5 9 53N 4 31 E
New Caledonia ☑,
 Pac. Oc. .... 96 K8 21 0S 165 0 E
New Castile = Castilla-
 La Mancha □, Spain . 6 H5 39 30N 3 30W
New Castle, Ind., U.S.A. 114 F3 39 55N 85 22W
New Castle, Pa., U.S.A. 116 F4 41 0N 80 21W
New City, U.S.A. .. 117 E11 41 9N 73 59W
New Concord, U.S.A. . 116 G3 39 59N 81 54W
New Cumberland,
 U.S.A. 116 F4 40 30N 80 36W

New Cuyama, U.S.A. . 111 L7 34 57N 119 38W
New Delhi, India ... 68 E7 28 37N 77 13 E
New Denver, Canada . 102 D5 50 0N 117 25W
New Don Pedro
 Reservoir, U.S.A. .. 110 H6 37 43N 120 24W
New England, U.S.A. . 107 B12 43 0N 71 0W
New England, N. Dak.,
 U.S.A. 112 B3 46 32N 102 52W
New England Ra.,
 Australia .... 95 E5 30 20S 151 45 E
New Forest △, U.K. .. 15 G6 50 53N 1 34W
New Galloway, U.K. . 13 F4 55 5N 4 9W
New Glasgow, Canada 105 C7 45 35N 62 36W
New Guinea, Oceania . 96 H5 4 0S 136 0 E
New Hamburg, Canada 116 C4 43 23N 80 42W
New Hampshire □,
 U.S.A. 117 C13 44 0N 71 30W
New Hampton, U.S.A. 112 D8 43 3N 92 19W
New Hanover, S. Africa 89 D5 29 22S 30 31 E
New Hartford, U.S.A. . 117 C9 43 4N 75 18W
New Haven, Conn.,
 U.S.A. 117 E12 41 18N 72 55W
New Haven, Mich.,
 U.S.A. 116 D2 42 44N 82 48W
New Hazelton, Canada 102 B3 55 20N 127 30W
New Hebrides =
 Vanuatu ■, Pac. Oc. . 96 J8 15 0S 168 0 E
New Holland, U.S.A. . 116 F8 40 6N 76 5W
New Iberia, U.S.A. .. 113 K9 30 1N 91 49W
New Ireland,
 Papua N. G. ...... 96 H7 3 20S 151 50 E
New Jersey □, U.S.A. . 114 E8 40 0N 74 30W
New Kensington, U.S.A. 116 F5 40 34N 79 46W
New Lexington, U.S.A. 114 F4 39 43N 82 13W
New Liskeard, Canada 104 C4 47 31N 79 41W
New London, Conn.,
 U.S.A. 117 E12 41 22N 72 6W
New London, Ohio,
 U.S.A. 116 E2 41 5N 82 24W
New London, Wis.,
 U.S.A. 112 C10 44 23N 88 45W
New Madrid, U.S.A. . 113 G10 36 36N 89 32W
New Martinsville, U.S.A. 114 F5 39 39N 80 52W
New Meadows, U.S.A. 108 D5 44 58N 116 18W
New Melones L., U.S.A. 110 H6 37 57N 120 31W
New Mexico □, U.S.A. 109 J10 34 30N 106 0W
New Milford, Conn.,
 U.S.A. 117 E11 41 35N 73 25W
New Milford, Pa., U.S.A. 117 E9 41 52N 75 44W
New Norcia, Australia . 93 F2 30 57S 116 13 E
New Norfolk, Australia 95 G4 42 46S 147 2 E
New Orleans, U.S.A. . 113 L9 29 58N 90 4W
New Philadelphia,
 U.S.A. 116 F3 40 30N 81 27W
New Plymouth, N.Z. . 91 H5 39 4S 174 5 E
New Plymouth, U.S.A. 108 E5 43 58N 116 49W
New Port Richey, U.S.A. 115 L4 28 16N 82 43W
New Providence I.,
 Bahamas 120 A4 25 25N 78 35W
New Quay, U.K. 15 E3 52 13N 4 21W
New Radnor, U.K. .. 15 E4 52 15N 3 9W
New Richmond, Canada 105 C6 48 7N 65 45W
New Richmond, U.S.A. 112 C8 45 7N 92 32W
New River Gorge △,
 U.S.A. 114 G5 37 53N 81 5W
New Roads, U.S.A. .. 113 K9 30 42N 91 26W
New Rochelle, U.S.A. . 117 F11 40 55N 73 47W
New Rockford, U.S.A. 112 B5 47 41N 99 8W
New Romney, U.K. .. 15 G8 50 59N 0 57 E
New Ross, Ireland .. 12 D5 52 23N 6 57W
New Salem, U.S.A. .. 112 B4 46 51N 101 25W
New Scone = Scone,
 U.K. 13 E5 56 25N 3 24W
New Siberian I. =
 Novaya Sibir, Ostrov,
 Russia .... 53 B16 75 10N 150 0 E
New Siberian Is. =
 Novosibirskiye
 Ostrova, Russia ... 53 B15 75 0N 142 0 E
New Smyrna Beach,
 U.S.A. 115 L5 29 1N 80 56W
New South Wales □,
 Australia .... 95 E4 33 0S 146 0 E
New Tecumseth, Canada 116 B5 44 9N 79 52W
New Town, U.S.A. .. 112 B3 47 59N 102 30W
New Tredegar, U.K. . 15 F4 51 44N 3 16W
New Ulm, U.S.A. ... 112 C7 44 19N 94 28W
New Waterford, Canada 105 C7 46 13N 60 4W
New-Wes-Valley,
 Canada 105 C9 49 8N 53 36W
New Westminster,
 Canada 110 A4 49 13N 122 55W
New York, U.S.A. .. 117 F11 40 45N 74 0W
New York □, U.S.A. . 117 D9 43 0N 75 0W
New York J.F. Kennedy
 International ✈ (JFK) . 117 F11 40 38N 73 47W
New York Mts., U.S.A. 109 J6 35 0N 115 20W
New Zealand ■,
 Oceania .... 91 J6 40 0S 176 0 E
Newaj →, India .... 68 G7 24 24N 76 49 E
Newala, Tanzania ... 87 E4 10 58S 39 18 E
Newark, Del., U.S.A. . 114 F8 39 41N 75 46W
Newark, N.J., U.S.A. . 117 F10 40 44N 74 10W
Newark, N.Y., U.S.A. . 116 C7 43 3N 77 6W
Newark, Ohio, U.S.A. . 116 F2 40 3N 82 24W
Newark International ✈
 (EWR), U.S.A. 117 F10 40 42N 74 10W
Newark-on-Trent, U.K. 14 D7 53 5N 0 48W
Newark Valley, U.S.A. 117 D8 42 14N 76 11W
Newberg, U.S.A. ... 108 D2 45 18N 122 58W
Newberry, Mich., U.S.A. 114 B3 46 21N 85 30W
Newberry, S.C., U.S.A. 115 H5 34 17N 81 37W
Newberry □, U.S.A. . 108 E2 43 42N 122 43W
Newberry Springs,
 U.S.A. 111 L10 34 50N 116 41W
Newboro L., Canada . 117 B8 44 38N 76 20W
Newbridge = Droichead
 Nua, Ireland 12 C5 53 11N 6 48W
Newburgh, Canada .. 116 B8 44 19N 76 52W
Newburgh, U.S.A. .. 117 E11 41 30N 74 1W
Newbury, U.K. 15 F6 51 24N 1 20W
Newbury, N.H., U.S.A. 117 B12 43 19N 72 3W
Newbury, Vt., U.S.A. . 117 B12 44 5N 72 4W
Newburyport, U.S.A. . 115 D10 42 49N 70 53W
Newcastle, Australia . 95 E5 33 0S 151 46 E
Newcastle, N.B., Canada 105 C6 47 1N 65 38W
Newcastle, Ont., Canada 116 C6 43 55N 78 35W
Newcastle, S. Africa .. 89 D4 27 45S 29 58 E
Newcastle, U.K. 12 B6 54 13N 5 54W
Newcastle, Calif., U.S.A. 110 G5 38 53N 121 8W
Newcastle, Wyo., U.S.A. 112 D2 43 50N 104 11W
Newcastle Emlyn, U.K. 15 E3 52 2N 4 28W
Newcastle Ra., Australia 92 C5 15 45S 130 15 E
Newcastle-under-Lyme,
 U.K. 14 D5 53 1N 2 14W
Newcastle-upon-Tyne,
 U.K. 14 C6 54 58N 1 36W

Newcastle Waters,
 Australia .... 94 B1 17 30S 133 28 E
Newcastle West, Ireland 12 D2 52 27N 9 3W
Newcomb, U.S.A. .. 117 C10 43 58N 74 10W
Newcomerstown, U.S.A. 116 F3 40 16N 81 36W
Newdegate, Australia . 93 F2 33 6S 119 0 E
Newell, Australia ... 94 B4 16 20S 145 16 E
Newell, U.S.A. 112 C3 44 43N 103 25W
Newfane, U.S.A. ... 116 C6 43 17N 78 43W
Newfield, U.S.A. ... 117 D8 42 18N 76 33W
Newfound L., U.S.A. . 117 C13 43 40N 71 47W
Newfoundland, Canada 105 C8 49 0N 55 0W
Newfoundland, U.S.A. 117 E9 41 18N 75 19W
Newfoundland &
 Labrador □, Canada . 105 B8 53 0N 58 0W
Newhall, U.S.A. 111 L8 34 23N 118 32W
Newhaven, U.K. .... 15 G8 50 47N 0 3 E
Newkirk, U.S.A. ... 113 G6 36 53N 97 3W
Newlyn, U.K. 15 G2 50 6N 5 34W
Newman, Australia .. 92 D2 23 18S 119 45 E
Newman, U.S.A. ... 110 H5 37 19N 121 1W
Newmarket, Canada . 116 B5 44 3N 79 28W
Newmarket, Ireland . 12 D2 52 13N 9 0W
Newmarket, U.K. ... 15 E8 52 15N 0 25 E
Newmarket, U.S.A. . 117 C14 43 4N 70 56W
Newnan, U.S.A. ... 115 J3 33 23N 84 48W
Newport, Ireland ... 12 C2 53 53N 9 33W
Newport, I. of W., U.K. 15 G6 50 42N 1 17W
Newport, Newp., U.K. 15 F5 51 35N 3 0W
Newport, Ark., U.S.A. 113 H9 35 37N 91 16W
Newport, Ky., U.S.A. . 114 F3 39 5N 84 30W
Newport, N.H., U.S.A. 117 C12 43 22N 72 10W
Newport, N.Y., U.S.A. 117 C9 43 11N 75 1W
Newport, Oreg., U.S.A. 108 D1 44 39N 124 3W
Newport, Pa., U.S.A. . 116 F7 40 29N 77 8W
Newport, R.I., U.S.A. . 117 E13 41 29N 71 19W
Newport, Tenn., U.S.A. 115 H4 35 58N 83 11W
Newport, Vt., U.S.A. . 117 B12 44 56N 72 13W
Newport, Wash., U.S.A. 108 B5 48 11N 117 3W
Newport □, U.K. ... 15 F4 51 33N 3 1W
Newport Beach, U.S.A. 111 M9 33 37N 117 56W
Newport News, U.S.A. 114 G7 36 59N 76 25W
Newport Pagnell, U.K. 15 E7 52 5N 0 43W
Newquay, U.K. 15 G2 50 25N 5 6W
Newry, U.K. 12 B5 54 11N 6 21W
Newton, Ill., U.S.A. . 112 F10 38 59N 88 10W
Newton, Iowa, U.S.A. 112 E8 41 42N 93 3W
Newton, Kans., U.S.A. 113 F6 38 3N 97 21W
Newton, Mass., U.S.A. 117 D13 42 21N 71 12W
Newton, Miss., U.S.A. 113 J10 32 19N 89 10W
Newton, N.C., U.S.A. 115 H5 35 40N 81 13W
Newton, N.J., U.S.A. . 117 E10 41 3N 74 45W
Newton, Tex., U.S.A. 113 K8 30 51N 93 46W
Newton Abbot, U.K. . 15 G4 50 32N 3 37W
Newton Aycliffe, U.K. 14 C6 54 37N 1 34W
Newton Falls, U.S.A. . 116 E4 41 11N 80 59W
Newton Stewart, U.K. 13 G4 54 57N 4 30W
Newtonmore, U.K. .. 13 D4 57 4N 4 8W
Newtown, U.K. 15 E4 52 31N 3 19W
Newtownabbey, U.K. . 12 B6 54 40N 5 56W
Newtownards, U.K. .. 12 B6 54 36N 5 42W
Newtownbarry =
 Bunclody, Ireland . 12 D5 52 39N 6 40W
Newtownstewart, U.K. 12 B4 54 43N 7 23W
Neville, U.S.A. 116 F7 40 10N 77 24W
Nexon, France .... 20 C5 45 41N 1 11 E
Neya, Russia ..... 34 A6 58 21N 43 49 E
Neyrīz, Iran ...... 71 D7 29 15N 54 19 E
Neyshābūr, Iran ... 71 B8 36 10N 58 50 E
Nezhin = Nizhyn,
 Ukraine .... 33 G6 51 5N 31 55 E
Nezperce, U.S.A. ... 108 C5 46 14N 116 14W
Nezvysko, Ukraine .. 29 B10 48 45N 25 5 E
Ngabang, Indonesia . 62 D3 0 23N 109 55 E
Ngabordamlu, Tanjung,
 Indonesia .... 63 F8 6 56S 134 11 E
N'Gage, Angola .... 84 F3 7 46S 15 16 E
Ngala, Nigeria .... 83 C7 12 20N 14 11 E
Ngambé, Centre,
 Cameroon .... 83 D7 5 48N 11 29 E
Ngambé, Littoral,
 Cameroon .... 83 E7 4 21N 10 40 E
Ngami Depression,
 Botswana .... 88 C3 20 30S 22 46 E
Ngamo, Zimbabwe .. 87 F2 19 3S 27 32 E
Ngangala, Sudan ... 81 G3 4 42N 31 55 E
Nganglong Kangri,
 China .... 67 C12 33 0N 81 0 E
Ngao, Thailand .... 64 C2 18 46N 99 59 E
Ngaoundéré, Cameroon 84 C2 7 15N 13 35 E
Ngapara, N.Z. ..... 91 L3 44 57S 170 46 E
Ngara, Tanzania ... 86 C3 2 29S 30 40 E
Ngawi, Indonesia ... 63 G14 7 24S 111 26 E
Nghia Lo, Vietnam .. 58 G5 21 33N 104 28 E
Ngoboli, Sudan .... 81 G3 4 57N 32 37 E
Ngoma, Malawi .... 87 E3 13 8S 33 45 E
Ngomahura, Zimbabwe 87 G3 20 26S 30 43 E
Ngomba, Tanzania .. 87 D3 8 20S 32 53 E
Ngop, Sudan ...... 81 F3 6 17N 30 9 E
Ngoring Hu, China .. 60 C4 34 55N 97 5 E
Ngorkou, Mali 82 B4 15 40N 3 41W
Ngorongoro, Tanzania 86 C4 3 11S 35 32 E
Ngorongoro △,
 Tanzania .... 86 C4 2 40S 35 30 E
Ngozi, Burundi .... 86 C2 2 54S 29 50 E
Ngudu, Tanzania ... 86 C3 2 58S 33 25 E
Nguigmi, Niger .... 79 F8 14 20N 13 20 E
Nguila, Cameroon .. 83 E7 4 41N 11 43 E
Nguiu, Australia ... 92 B5 11 46S 130 38 E
Ngukurr, Australia .. 94 A1 14 44S 134 44 E
Ngunga, Tanzania .. 86 C3 3 37S 33 37 E
Nguru, Nigeria .... 83 C7 12 56N 10 29 E
Nguru Mts., Tanzania 86 D4 6 0S 37 30 E
Ngusi, Malawi ..... 87 E3 9 4S 33 53 E
Nguyen Binh, Vietnam 58 F5 22 39N 105 56 E
Nha Trang, Vietnam . 65 F7 12 16N 109 10 E
Nhacoongo, Mozam. . 89 C6 24 18S 35 14 E
Nhamundá →, Brazil . 125 D7 2 12S 56 41W
Nhangulaze, L., Mozam. 89 C5 24 0S 34 30 E
Nhill, Australia .... 95 F3 36 18S 141 40 E
Nho Quan, Vietnam . 58 G5 20 18N 105 45 E
Nhulunbuy, Australia . 94 A2 12 10S 137 20 E
Nia-nia, Dem. Rep. of
 the Congo .... 86 B2 1 30N 27 40 E
Niafounké, Mali ... 82 B4 16 0N 4 5W
Niagara Falls, Canada 116 C5 43 7N 79 5W
Niagara Falls, U.S.A. . 116 C5 43 5N 79 4W
Niagara-on-the-Lake,
 Canada 116 C5 43 15N 79 4W
Niah, Malaysia .... 62 D4 3 58N 113 46 E
Niamey, Niger .... 83 C5 13 27N 2 6 E
Niandan-Koro, Guinea 82 D3 11 5N 9 52W
Nianforando, Guinea . 82 D2 9 37N 10 36W
Niangara, Dem. Rep. of
 the Congo .... 86 B2 3 42N 27 50 E
Niangbo, Ivory C. .. 82 D3 8 49N 5 10W

Niangoloko,
  Burkina Faso **82 C4** 10 15N 4 55W
Niantic, U.S.A. **117 E12** 41 20N 72 11W
Niaro, Sudan .... **81 E3** 10 38N 33 31 E
Nias, Indonesia .... **62 D1** 1 0N 97 30 E
Niassa □, Mozam. .... **87 E4** 13 30 S 36 0 E
Niassa □, Mozam. .... **87 E4** 13 30 S 36 0 E
Nibāk, Si. Arabia .... **71 E7** 24 25N 50 50 E
Nibe, Denmark .... **11 H3** 56 59N 9 38 E
Nicaragua ■,
  Cent. Amer. **120 D2** 11 40N 85 30W
Nicaragua, L. de, Nic. **120 D2** 12 0N 85 30W
Nicastro, Italy .... **43 D9** 38 59N 16 19 E
Nice, France .... **21 E11** 43 42N 7 14 E
Nice ✈ (NCE), France .... **21 E11** 43 42N 7 14 E
Niceville, U.S.A. **115 K2** 30 31N 86 30W
Nichicun, L., Canada **105 B5** 53 5N 71 0W
Nichinan, Japan .... **55 J5** 31 38N 131 23 E
Nicholás, Canal,
  W. Indies **120 B3** 23 30N 80 5W
Nicholasville, U.S.A. **114 G3** 37 53N 84 34W
Nichols, U.S.A. **117 D8** 42 1N 76 22W
Nicholson, Australia .... **93 C5** 18 2 S 128 54 E
Nicholson ➜, Australia **93 C5** 17 31N 75 47W
Nicholson, U.S.A. **117 E9** 41 37N 75 47W
Nicholson ➜, Australia .... **94 B2** 17 31 S 139 36 E
Nicholson L., Canada **103 A8** 62 40N 102 40W
Nicholson Ra., Australia .... **93 E2** 27 15 S 116 45 E
Nicholville, U.S.A. **117 B10** 44 41N 74 39W
Nicobar Is., Ind. Oc. .... **50 J13** 8 0N 93 30 E
Nicola, Canada **102 C4** 50 12N 120 40W
Nicolls Town, Bahamas **120 A4** 25 8N 78 0W
Nicopolis, Greece .... **46 B2** 39 5N 20 43 E
Nicosia, Cyprus .... **49 D12** 35 10N 33 25 E
Nicosia, Italy .... **43 E7** 37 45N 14 24 E
Nicótera, Italy .... **43 D8** 38 33N 15 56 E
Nicoya, Costa Rica **120 D2** 10 9N 85 27W
Nicoya, G. de,
  Costa Rica **120 E3** 10 0N 85 0W
Nicoya, Pen. de,
  Costa Rica **120 E2** 9 45N 85 40W
Nida, Lithuania .... **30 C8** 55 20N 21 4 E
Nidd ➜, U.K. **14 D6** 53 59N 1 23W
Nidda, Germany .... **25 E5** 50 23N 9 1 E
Nidda ➜, Germany .... **25 E4** 50 17N 8 48 E
Nidwalden □, Switz. .... **25 J4** 46 50N 8 25 E
Nidzica, Poland .... **31 E7** 53 25N 20 28 E
Niebüll, Germany .... **24 A4** 54 46N 8 48 E
Nied ➜, Germany .... **19 C13** 49 23N 6 40 E
Niederaula, Germany .... **24 E5** 50 47N 9 36 E
Niederbayern □,
  Germany .... **25 G8** 48 40N 12 50 E
Niederbronn-les-Bains,
  France .... **19 D14** 48 57N 7 39 E
Niedere Tauern, Austria .... **26 D7** 47 20N 14 0 E
Niederlausitz, Germany .... **24 D9** 51 42N 13 59 E
Niederösterreich □,
  Austria .... **26 C8** 48 25N 15 40 E
Niedersachsen □,
  Germany .... **24 C4** 52 50N 9 0 E
Niedersächsisches
  Wattenmeer △,
  Germany .... **24 B3** 53 45N 7 30 E
Niekerkshoop, S. Africa .... **88 D3** 29 19 S 22 51 E
Niellé, Ivory C. **82 C3** 10 5N 5 38W
Niemba, Dem. Rep. of
  the Congo .... **86 D2** 5 58 S 28 24 E
Niemen = Nemunas ➜,
  Lithuania .... **9 J19** 55 25N 21 10 E
Niemodlin, Poland .... **31 H4** 50 38N 17 38 E
Nienburg, Germany .... **24 C5** 52 39N 9 13 E
Niepołomice, Poland .... **31 H7** 50 3N 20 13 E
Niers ➜, Germany .... **24 D1** 51 43N 5 57 E
Niesky, Germany .... **24 D10** 51 17N 14 49 E
Nieszawa, Poland .... **31 F5** 52 52N 18 50 E
Nieu Bethesda, S. Africa .... **88 E3** 31 51 S 24 34 E
Nieuw Amsterdam,
  Suriname **125 B7** 5 53N 55 5W
Nieuw Nickerie,
  Suriname **125 B7** 6 0N 56 59W
Nieuwoudtville,
  S. Africa .... **88 E2** 31 23 S 19 7 E
Nieuwpoort, Belgium .... **17 C2** 51 8N 2 45 E
Nieves, Pico de las,
  Canary Is. **48 G4** 27 57N 15 35W
Nièvre □, France .... **19 E10** 47 10N 3 40 E
Niğa, Mali **82 C3** 13 38N 5 27W
Niğde, Turkey .... **70 B2** 37 58N 34 40 E
Nigel, S. Africa .... **89 D4** 26 27 S 28 25 E
Niger □, Nigeria .... **83 D6** 10 0N 5 30 E
Niger ■, W. Afr. .... **83 B7** 17 30N 10 0 E
Niger ➜, W. Afr. .... **83 D6** 5 33N 6 33 E
Niger Delta, Africa .... **83 E6** 5 0N 6 0 E
Nigeria ■, W. Afr. .... **83 D6** 8 30N 8 0 E
Nighasin, India .... **69 E9** 28 14N 80 52 E
Nightcaps, N.Z. .... **91 L2** 45 57 S 168 2 E
Nigríta, Greece .... **44 D5** 40 56N 23 29 E
Nii-Jima, Japan .... **55 G9** 34 20N 139 15 E
Niigata, Japan .... **54 F9** 37 58N 139 0 E
Niigata □, Japan .... **55 F9** 37 15N 138 45 E
Niihama, Japan .... **55 H6** 33 55N 133 16 E
Niihau, U.S.A. **106 H14** 21 54N 160 9W
Niimi, Japan .... **55 G6** 34 59N 133 28 E
Niitsu, Japan .... **54 F9** 37 48N 139 7 E
Níjar, Spain **39 J2** 36 53N 2 15W
Nijil, Jordan .... **74 E4** 30 32N 35 33 E
Nijkerk, Neths. .... **17 B5** 52 13N 5 30 E
Nijmegen, Neths. .... **17 C5** 51 50N 5 52 E
Nijverdal, Neths. .... **17 B6** 52 22N 6 28 E
Nīk Pey, Iran .... **71 B6** 36 50N 48 10 E
Nike, Nigeria .... **83 D6** 6 26N 7 29 E
Nikiniki, Indonesia .... **63 F6** 9 49 S 124 30 E
Nikkí, Benin .... **45 F8** 40 57N 24 9 E
Nikítas, Greece .... **44 F7** 40 13N 23 43 E
Nikki, Benin .... **83 D5** 9 58N 3 12 E
Nikkō, Japan .... **55 F9** 36 45N 139 35 E
Nikkō △, Japan .... **55 F9** 36 56N 139 37 E
Nikolayev = Mykolayiv,
  Ukraine .... **33 J7** 46 58N 32 0 E
Nikolayevsk, Russia .... **34 E7** 50 0N 45 35 E
Nikolayevsk-na-Amur,
  Russia .... **53 D15** 53 8N 140 44 E
Nikolsk, Russia .... **34 D8** 53 49N 46 4 E
Nikolskoye, Russia .... **53 D17** 55 12N 166 0 E
Nikopol, Bulgaria .... **45 C8** 43 43N 24 54 E
Nikopol, Ukraine .... **33 J8** 47 35N 34 25 E
Niksar, Turkey .... **72 B7** 40 31N 37 2 E
Nīkshahr, Iran .... **71 E9** 26 15N 60 10 E
Nikšić, Serbia & M. .... **44 D2** 42 50N 18 57 E
Nīl, Nahr en ➜, Africa .... **80 H7** 30 10N 31 6 E
Nīl el Abyad ➜, Sudan .... **81 D3** 15 38N 32 31 E
Nīl el Azraq ➜, Sudan .... **81 D3** 15 38N 32 31 E
Nila, Indonesia .... **63 F7** 6 44 S 129 31 E
Nile = Nīl, Nahr en ➜,
  Africa **111 M11** 33 14N 115 31W
Nile = Nīl, Nahr en ➜,
  Africa .... **80 H7** 30 10N 31 6 E
Nile Delta, Egypt .... **80 H7** 31 40N 31 0 E
Niles, Mich., U.S.A. **114 E2** 41 50N 86 15W

Niles, Ohio, U.S.A. **116 E4** 41 11N 80 46W
Nilüfer ➜, Turkey .... **45 F12** 40 18N 28 27 E
Nim Ka Thana, India .... **68 F6** 27 44N 75 48 E
Nimach, India .... **68 G6** 24 30N 74 56 E
Nimbahera, India .... **68 G6** 24 37N 74 45 E
Nîmes, France .... **21 E8** 43 50N 4 23 E
Nimfaíon, Ákra =
  Pínnes, Ákra, Greece .... **45 F8** 40 5N 24 20 E
Nimmitabel, Australia .... **95 F4** 36 29 S 149 15 E
Nimule, Sudan .... **81 G3** 3 32N 32 3 E
Nimule △, Sudan .... **81 G3** 3 38N 32 2 E
Nin, Croatia .... **41 D12** 44 16N 15 12 E
Ninawá, Iraq .... **70 B4** 36 25N 43 10 E
Ninawá □, Iraq .... **70 B4** 36 15N 43 0 E
Nindigully, Australia .... **95 D4** 28 21 S 148 50 E
Nineveh = Nīnawā, Iraq .... **70 B4** 36 25N 43 10 E
Ning Xian, China .... **56 G4** 35 30N 107 58 E
Ning'an, China .... **57 B15** 44 22N 129 20 E
Ningbo, China .... **59 C13** 29 51N 121 28 E
Ningcheng, China .... **57 D10** 41 32N 119 53 E
Ningde, China .... **59 D12** 26 38N 119 23 E
Ningdu, China .... **59 D10** 26 25N 115 59 E
Ninggang, China .... **59 D9** 26 42N 113 55 E
Ningguo, China .... **59 B12** 30 35N 119 0 E
Ninghai, China .... **59 C13** 29 15N 121 27 E
Ninghua, China .... **59 D11** 26 14N 116 45 E
Ningi, Nigeria .... **83 C6** 10 55N 9 30 E
Ningjin, China .... **56 F8** 37 35N 114 57 E
Ningjing Shan, China .... **58 C2** 30 0N 98 20 E
Ninglang, China .... **58 D3** 27 20N 100 55 E
Ningling, China .... **56 G8** 34 25N 115 22 E
Ningming, China .... **58 F6** 22 8N 107 4 E
Ningnan, China .... **58 D4** 27 5N 102 36 E
Ningpo = Ningbo, China .... **59 C13** 29 51N 121 28 E
Ningqiang, China .... **56 H4** 32 47N 106 15 E
Ningshan, China .... **56 H5** 33 21N 108 21 E
Ningsia Hui A.R. =
  Ningxia Huizu
  Zizhiqu □, China .... **56 F4** 38 0N 106 0 E
Ningwu, China .... **56 E7** 39 0N 112 18 E
Ningxia Huizu
  Zizhiqu □, China .... **56 F4** 38 0N 106 0 E
Ningxiang, China .... **59 C9** 28 15N 112 30 E
Ningyang, China .... **56 G9** 35 47N 116 45 E
Ningyuan, China .... **59 E8** 25 37N 111 57 E
Ninh Binh, Vietnam .... **58 G5** 20 15N 105 55 E
Ninh Giang, Vietnam .... **64 B6** 20 44N 106 24 E
Ninh Hoa, Vietnam .... **64 F7** 12 30N 109 7 E
Ninh Ma, Vietnam .... **64 F7** 12 48N 109 21 E
Nini-Suhien △, Ghana **82 D4** 5 20N 2 34W
Ninove, Belgium .... **17 D4** 50 51N 4 2 E
Nioaque, Brazil .... **127 A4** 21 5 S 55 50W
Niobrara, U.S.A. **112 D6** 42 45N 98 2W
Niobrara ➜, U.S.A. **112 D6** 42 46N 98 3W
Niokolo-Koba △,
  Senegal **82 C2** 13 3N 13 2W
Niono, Mali **82 C3** 14 15N 6 0W
Nionsamoridougou,
  Guinea **82 D3** 8 45N 8 50W
Nioro du Rip, Senegal **82 C1** 13 40N 15 50W
Nioro du Sahel, Mali **82 B3** 15 15N 9 30W
Niort, France **20 B3** 46 19N 0 29W
Nipawin, Canada **103 C8** 53 20N 104 0W
Nipigon, Canada **104 C2** 49 0N 88 17W
Nipigon, L., Canada **104 C2** 49 50N 88 30W
Nipishish L., Canada **105 B7** 54 12N 60 45W
Nipissing L., Canada **104 C4** 46 20N 80 0W
Nipomo, U.S.A. **111 K6** 35 3N 120 29W
Nipton, U.S.A. **111 K11** 35 28N 115 16W
Niquelândia, Brazil .... **125 F9** 14 33 S 48 23W
Nīr, Iran .... **70 B5** 38 2N 47 59 E
Nirasaki, Japan .... **55 G9** 35 42N 138 27 E
Nirmal, India .... **66 K11** 19 3N 78 20 E
Nirmali, India .... **69 F12** 26 20N 86 35 E
Niš, Serbia & M. .... **44 C5** 43 19N 21 58 E
Niša, Portugal **37 F3** 39 30N 7 41W
Nişāb, Si. Arabia .... **70 D5** 29 11N 44 43 E
Nişāb, Yemen .... **75 E4** 14 25N 46 29 E
Nišava ➜, Serbia & M. .... **44 C5** 43 20N 21 46 E
Niscemi, Italy .... **43 E7** 37 9N 14 23 E
Nishinomiya, Japan .... **55 G7** 34 45N 135 20 E
Nishino'omote, Japan .... **55 J5** 30 43N 130 59 E
Nishiwaki, Japan .... **55 G7** 34 59N 134 58 E
Nísiros, Greece .... **47 E9** 36 35N 27 12 E
Niška Banja,
  Serbia & M. .... **44 C6** 43 18N 22 1 E
Niskibi ➜, Canada **104 A2** 56 29N 88 9W
Nisko, Poland .... **31 H9** 50 35N 22 7 E
Nisporeni, Moldova .... **29 C13** 47 4N 28 10 E
Nisqually ➜, U.S.A. **110 C4** 47 6N 122 42W
Nissáki, Greece .... **49 A3** 39 43N 19 52 E
Nissan ➜, Sweden .... **11 H6** 56 40N 12 51 E
Nissum Bredning,
  Denmark .... **11 H2** 56 40N 8 20 E
Nissum Fjord, Denmark .... **11 H2** 56 20N 8 11 E
Nistru = Dnister ➜,
  Europe .... **33 J6** 46 18N 30 17 E
Nisutlin ➜, Canada **102 A2** 60 14N 132 34W
Nitchequon, Canada **105 B5** 53 10N 70 58W
Niterói, Brazil .... **127 A7** 22 52 S 43 0W
Nith ➜, Canada **116 C4** 43 12N 80 23W
Nith ➜, U.K. **13 F5** 55 14N 3 33W
Nitmiluk △, Australia .... **92 B5** 14 6 S 132 15 E
Nitra, Slovak Rep. .... **27 C11** 48 19N 18 4 E
Nitra ➜, Slovak Rep. .... **27 D11** 47 46N 18 10 E
Nitriansky □,
  Slovak Rep. .... **27 C11** 48 30N 18 30 E
Nittenau, Germany .... **25 F8** 49 12N 12 16 E
Niuafo'ou, Tonga .... **91 B11** 15 30 S 175 58W
Niulan Jiang ➜, China .... **58 D4** 27 30N 103 5 E
Niut, Indonesia .... **62 D4** 0 55N 110 6 E
Niutou Shan, China .... **59 C13** 29 51N 121 59 E
Niuzhuang, China .... **57 D12** 40 58N 122 28 E
Nivala, Finland .... **8 E21** 63 56N 24 57 E
Nivelles, Belgium .... **17 D4** 50 35N 4 20 E
Nivernais, France .... **19 E10** 47 15N 3 30 E
Niwas, India .... **69 H9** 23 3N 80 26 E
Nixon, U.S.A. **113 L6** 29 16N 97 46W
Nizamabad, India .... **66 K11** 18 45N 78 7 E
Nizamghat, India .... **67 E19** 28 20N 95 45 E
Nizhne Kolymsk, Russia .... **53 C17** 68 34N 160 55 E
Nizhnegansk, Russia .... **53 C13** 55 47N 109 30 E
Nizhnegorskiy =
  Nyzhnohirskyy,
  Ukraine .... **33 K8** 45 27N 34 38 E
Nizhnekamsk, Russia .... **34 C10** 55 38N 51 49 E
Nizhneudinsk, Russia .... **53 D10** 54 54N 99 3 E
Nizhnevartovsk, Russia .... **52 C8** 60 56N 76 38 E
Nizhniy Chir, Russia .... **35 F6** 48 22N 43 5 E
Nizhniy Lomov, Russia .... **34 D6** 53 54N 43 38 E
Nizhniy Novgorod,
  Russia .... **34 B7** 56 20N 44 0 E
Nizhniy Tagil, Russia .... **52 D6** 57 55N 59 57 E
Nizhyn, Ukraine .... **33 G6** 51 5N 31 55 E

Nizina Mazowiecka,
  Poland .... **31 F8** 52 30N 21 0 E
Nizip, Turkey .... **70 B3** 37 5N 37 50 E
Nízké Tatry, Slovak Rep. .... **27 C12** 48 55N 19 30 E
Nízké Tatry △,
  Slovak Rep. .... **27 C12** 48 55N 19 37 E
Nízký Jeseník,
  Czech Rep. .... **27 B10** 49 50N 17 45 E
Nizza Monferrato, Italy .... **40 D5** 44 46N 8 21 E
Njakwa, Malawi .... **87 E3** 11 1 S 33 56 E
Njanji, Zambia .... **87 E3** 14 25 S 31 46 E
Njinjo, Tanzania .... **87 D4** 8 48 S 38 54 E
Njombe, Tanzania .... **87 D3** 9 20 S 34 50 E
Njombe ➜, Tanzania .... **86 D4** 6 56 S 35 6 E
Njurundabommen,
  Sweden .... **10 B11** 62 15N 17 25 E
Nkambe, Cameroon .... **83 D7** 6 35N 10 40 E
Nkana, Zambia .... **87 E2** 12 50 S 28 8 E
Nkandla, S. Africa .... **89 D5** 28 37 S 31 5 E
Nkawkaw, Ghana **83 D4** 6 36N 0 49W
Nkayi, Zimbabwe .... **87 F2** 19 41 S 29 20 E
Nkhotakota, Malawi .... **87 E3** 12 56 S 34 15 E
Nkhotakota △, Malawi .... **87 E3** 12 50 S 34 0 E
Nkongsamba, Cameroon .... **83 E6** 4 55N 9 55 E
Nkurenkuru, Namibia .... **88 B2** 17 42 S 18 32 E
Nkwanta, Ghana **82 D4** 6 10N 2 10W
Nmai ➜, Burma .... **67 G20** 25 30N 97 25 E
Noakhali = Maijdi,
  Bangla. .... **67 H17** 22 48N 91 10 E
Nobel, Canada **116 A4** 45 25N 80 6W
Nobeoka, Japan .... **55 H5** 32 36N 131 41 E
Noblejas, Spain **36 F7** 39 58N 3 26W
Noblesville, U.S.A. **114 E3** 40 3N 86 1W
Noboribetsu, Japan .... **54 C10** 42 24N 141 6 E
Noce ➜, Italy .... **40 B8** 46 9N 11 4 E
Nocera Inferiore, Italy .... **43 B7** 40 44N 14 38 E
Nocera Umbra, Italy .... **41 F9** 43 7N 12 47 E
Noci, Italy .... **43 B10** 40 48N 17 7 E
Nocona, U.S.A. **113 J6** 33 47N 97 44W
Nocrich, Romania .... **29 E9** 45 55N 24 26 E
Noda, Japan .... **55 G9** 35 56N 139 52 E
Nogales, Mexico **118 A2** 31 20N 110 56W
Nogales, U.S.A. **109 L8** 31 20N 110 56W
Nogaro, France **20 E3** 43 45N 0 2W
Nogat ➜, Poland .... **30 D6** 54 17N 19 17 E
Nogent, France .... **19 D12** 48 1N 5 20 E
Nogent-le-Rotrou,
  France .... **18 D7** 48 20N 0 50 E
Nogent-sur-Seine,
  France .... **19 D10** 48 30N 3 30 E
Noggerup, Australia .... **93 F2** 33 32 S 116 5 E
Noginsk, Moskva, Russia .... **32 E10** 55 50N 38 25 E
Noginsk, Tunguska,
  Russia .... **53 C10** 64 30N 90 50 E
Nogoa ➜, Australia .... **94 C4** 23 40 S 147 55 E
Nogoyá, Argentina .... **126 C4** 32 24 S 59 48W
Nógrád □, Hungary .... **28 C4** 48 0N 19 30 E
Noguera Pallaresa ➜,
  Spain .... **38 D5** 41 55N 0 55 E
Noguera
  Ribagorzana ➜,
  Spain .... **38 D5** 41 40N 0 43 E
Nohar, India .... **68 E6** 29 11N 74 49 E
Nohfelden, Germany .... **25 F3** 49 35N 7 7 E
Nohta, India .... **69 H8** 23 40N 79 34 E
Noia, Spain **36 C2** 42 48N 8 53W
Noire, Montagne, France .... **20 E6** 43 28N 2 18 E
Noires, Mts., France **18 D3** 48 11N 3 40W
Noirétable, France .... **20 C7** 45 48N 3 46 E
Noirmoutier, Î. de,
  France **18 F4** 46 58N 2 10W
Noirmoutier-en-l'Île,
  France **18 F4** 47 0N 2 14W
Nojane, Botswana .... **88 C3** 23 15 S 20 14 E
Nojima-Zaki, Japan .... **55 G9** 34 54N 139 53 E
Nok Kundi, Pakistan .... **66 E3** 28 50N 62 45 E
Nok Ta Phao, Ko,
  Thailand .... **65 b** 9 23N 99 40 E
Nokaneng, Botswana .... **88 B3** 19 40 S 22 17 E
Nokia, Finland .... **9 F20** 61 30N 23 30 E
Nokomis, Canada **103 C8** 51 35N 105 0W
Nokomis L., Canada **103 B8** 57 0N 103 0W
Nola, C.A.R. .... **84 D3** 3 35N 16 4 E
Nola, Italy .... **43 B7** 40 55N 14 33 E
Nolay, France .... **19 F11** 46 58N 4 35 E
Noli, C. di, Italy .... **40 D5** 44 12N 8 25 E
Nolinsk, Russia .... **34 B9** 57 28N 49 57 E
Noma Omuramba ➜,
  Namibia .... **88 B3** 18 52 S 20 53 E
Nombre de Dios,
  Panama **120 E4** 9 34N 79 28W
Nome, U.S.A. **100 B3** 64 30N 165 25W
Nomo-Zaki, Japan .... **55 H4** 32 35N 129 44 E
Nonacho L., Canada **103 A7** 61 42N 109 40W
Nonancourt, France .... **18 D8** 48 47N 1 11 E
Nonda, Australia .... **94 C3** 20 40 S 142 28 E
None, Italy .... **40 D4** 44 56N 7 32 E
Nong Chang, Thailand .... **64 E2** 15 23N 99 51 E
Nong Het, Laos .... **64 C4** 19 29N 103 59 E
Nong Khai, Thailand .... **64 D4** 17 50N 102 46 E
Nong'an, China .... **57 B13** 44 25N 125 5 E
Nongoma, S. Africa .... **89 D5** 27 58 S 31 35 E
Nongsa, Indonesia .... **65 d** 1 11N 104 8 E
Nonoava, Mexico **118 B3** 27 28N 106 44W
Nonoava →, Mexico **118 B3** 27 29N 106 45W
Nonthaburi, Thailand .... **64 F3** 13 51N 100 34 E
Nontron, France .... **20 C4** 45 31N 0 40 E
Nonza, France .... **21 F13** 42 47N 9 21 E
Noonamah, Australia .... **92 B5** 12 40 S 131 4 E
Noord Brabant □,
  Neths. .... **17 C5** 51 40N 5 0 E
Noord Holland □,
  Neths. .... **17 B4** 52 30N 4 45 E
Noordbeveland, Neths. .... **17 C3** 51 35N 3 50 E
Noordoostpolder, Neths. .... **17 B5** 52 45N 5 45 E
Noordwijk, Neths. .... **17 B4** 52 14N 4 26 E
Nootka I., Canada **102 D3** 49 32N 126 42W
Nopiming △, Canada **103 C9** 50 30N 95 37W
Nora, Eritrea .... **81 D5** 16 6N 40 4 E
Nora, Sweden .... **10 E9** 60 6N 15 56 E
Noralee, Canada **102 C3** 53 59N 126 26W
Noranda = Rouyn-
  Noranda, Canada **104 C4** 48 20N 79 0W
Norberg, Sweden .... **10 D9** 60 4N 15 56 E
Nórcia, Italy .... **41 F10** 42 48N 13 5 E
Norco, U.S.A. **111 M9** 33 56N 117 33W
Nord □, France .... **19 B10** 50 15N 3 30 E
Nord-Kivu □, Dem. Rep.
  of the Congo .... **86 C2** 1 0 S 29 0 E
Nord-Ostsee-Kanal,
  Germany .... **24 A5** 54 12N 9 32 E
Nord-Pas-de-Calais □,
  France .... **19 B9** 50 30N 2 50 E
Nordaustlandet,
  Svalbard .... **4 B9** 79 14N 23 0 E

Nordborg, Denmark .... **11 J3** 55 5N 9 50 E
Norddeich, Germany .... **24 B3** 55 27N 8 24 E
Norddeich, Germany .... **24 B3** 53 36N 7 9 E
Nordegg, Canada **102 C5** 52 29N 116 5W
Norden, Germany .... **24 B3** 53 35N 7 12 E
Nordenham, Germany .... **24 B4** 53 30N 8 30 E
Norderney, Germany .... **24 B3** 53 42N 7 9 E
Norderstedt, Germany .... **24 B6** 53 42N 10 1 E
Nordfjord, Norway .... **9 F11** 61 55N 5 30 E
Nordfriesische Inseln,
  Germany .... **24 A4** 54 40N 8 20 E
Nordhausen, Germany .... **24 D6** 51 30N 10 47 E
Nordhorn, Germany .... **24 C3** 52 26N 7 4 E
Nordingrå, Sweden .... **10 B12** 62 56N 18 17 E
Nordjyllands
  Amtskommune □,
  Denmark .... **11 G4** 57 20N 10 0 E
Nordkapp, Norway .... **8 A21** 71 10N 25 50 E
Nordkapp, Svalbard .... **4 A9** 80 31N 20 0 E
Nordkinnhalvøya,
  Norway .... **8 A22** 70 55N 27 40 E
Nördlicher Teutoburger
  Wald-
  Wiehengebirge △,
  Germany .... **24 C4** 52 18N 8 10 E
Nördlingen, Germany .... **25 G6** 48 48N 10 30 E
Nordrhein-Westfalen □,
  Germany .... **24 D3** 51 45N 7 30 E
Nordstrand, Germany .... **24 A4** 54 30N 8 52 E
Nordvik, Russia .... **53 B12** 74 2N 111 32 E
Nore ➜, Ireland **12 D4** 52 25N 6 58W
Norfolk, Canada **116 D4** 42 50N 80 23W
Norfolk, Nebr., U.S.A. **112 D6** 42 2N 97 25W
Norfolk, Va., U.S.A. **114 G7** 36 51N 76 17W
Norfolk □, U.K. .... **15 E8** 52 39N 0 54 E
Norfolk I., Pac. Oc. .... **96 K8** 28 58 S 168 3 E
Norfolk ➜, U.S.A. **113 G8** 36 15N 92 14W
Norilsk, Russia .... **53 C9** 69 20N 88 6 E
Norma, Mt., Australia .... **94 C3** 20 55 S 140 42 E
Normal, U.S.A. **112 E10** 40 31N 88 59W
Norman, U.S.A. **113 H6** 35 13N 97 26W
Norman ➜, Australia .... **94 B3** 19 18 S 141 51 E
Norman Wells, Canada **100 B7** 65 17N 126 51W
Normanby ➜, Australia .... **94 A3** 14 23 S 144 10 E
Normandie-Maine △,
  France **18 D6** 48 30N 0 20W
Normandin, Canada **104 C5** 48 49N 72 31W
Normanhurst, Mt.,
  Australia .... **93 E3** 25 4 S 122 30 E
Normanton, Australia .... **94 B3** 17 40 S 141 10 E
Normétal, Canada **104 C4** 49 0N 79 22W
Norquay, Canada **103 C8** 51 53N 102 5W
Norquinco, Argentina .... **128 E2** 41 51 S 70 55W
Norra Dellen, Sweden .... **10 C10** 61 53N 16 43 E
Norra Kvill △, Sweden .... **11 G9** 57 46N 15 35 E
Norra Ulvön, Sweden .... **10 A12** 63 1N 18 40 E
Norrahammar, Sweden .... **11 G8** 57 43N 14 7 E
Norrbottens län □,
  Sweden .... **8 C19** 66 50N 20 0 E
Nørre Åby, Denmark .... **11 J3** 55 27N 9 52 E
Nørre Alslev, Denmark .... **11 K5** 54 54N 11 52 E
Nørresundby, Denmark .... **11 G3** 57 5N 9 52 E
Norrhult-Klavreström,
  Sweden .... **11 G9** 57 1N 15 10 E
Norris Point, Canada **105 C8** 49 31N 57 53W
Norristown, U.S.A. **117 F9** 40 7N 75 21W
Norrköping, Sweden .... **11 F10** 58 37N 16 11 E
Norrland, Sweden .... **9 E16** 62 15N 15 45 E
Norrsundet, Sweden .... **10 D11** 60 56N 17 8 E
Norrtälje, Sweden .... **10 E12** 59 46N 18 42 E
Norseman, Australia .... **93 F3** 32 8 S 121 43 E
Norsk, Russia .... **53 D14** 52 30N 130 5 E
Norte, Pta. del,
  Canary Is. **48 G2** 27 51N 17 57W
Norte, Serra do, Brazil .... **124 F7** 11 20 S 59 0W
North, C., Canada **105 C7** 47 2N 60 20W
North Adams, U.S.A. **117 D11** 42 42N 73 7W
North America **98 F10** 40 0N 100 0W
North Arm, Canada **102 A5** 62 0N 114 30W
North Atlantic Ocean,
  Atl. Oc. **2 C7** 30 0N 50 0W
North Augusta, U.S.A. **115 J5** 33 30N 81 59W
North Ayrshire □, U.K. **13 F4** 55 45N 4 44W
North Bass I., U.S.A. **116 E2** 41 44N 82 53W
North Battleford,
  Canada **103 C7** 52 50N 108 17W
North Bay, Canada **104 C4** 46 20N 79 30W
North Belcher Is.,
  Canada **104 A4** 56 50N 79 50W
North Bend, Oreg.,
  U.S.A. **108 E1** 43 24N 124 14W
North Bend, Pa., U.S.A. **116 E7** 41 20N 77 42W
North Bend, Wash.,
  U.S.A. **110 C5** 47 30N 121 47W
North Bennington,
  U.S.A. **117 D11** 42 56N 73 15W
North Berwick, U.K. **13 E6** 56 4N 2 42W
North Berwick, U.S.A. **117 C14** 43 18N 70 44W
North C., Canada **105 C7** 47 5N 64 0W
North C., N.Z. .... **91 F4** 34 23 S 173 4 E
North Canadian ➜,
  U.S.A. **113 H7** 35 16N 95 31W
North Canton, U.S.A. **116 F3** 40 53N 81 24W
North Cape =
  Nordkapp, Norway .... **8 A21** 71 10N 25 50 E
North Cape =
  Nordkapp, Svalbard .... **4 A9** 80 31N 20 0 E
North Caribou L.,
  Canada **104 B1** 52 50N 90 40W
North Carolina □,
  U.S.A. **115 H6** 35 30N 80 0W
North Cascades △,
  U.S.A. **110 B3** 48 45N 121 10W
North Channel, Canada **104 C3** 46 0N 83 0W
North Channel, U.K. **13 F3** 55 13N 5 52W
North Charleston,
  U.S.A. **115 J6** 32 53N 79 58W
North Chicago, U.S.A. **114 D2** 42 19N 87 51W
North Creek, U.S.A. **117 C11** 43 41N 73 59W
North Dakota □, U.S.A. **112 B5** 47 30N 100 15W
North Downs, U.K. .... **15 F8** 51 19N 0 21 E
North East, U.S.A. **116 D5** 42 13N 79 50W
North East Frontier
  Agency = Arunachal
  Pradesh □, India .... **67 F19** 28 0N 95 0 E
North East
  Lincolnshire □, U.K. .... **14 D7** 53 34N 0 2 E
North Eastern □, Kenya .... **86 B5** 1 30N 40 0 E
North Esk ➜, U.K. **13 E6** 56 46N 2 24W
North European Plain,
  Europe .... **6 E10** 55 0N 25 0 E
North Foreland, U.K. .... **15 F9** 51 22N 1 28 E
North Fork, U.S.A. **110 H7** 37 14N 119 21W
North Fork
  American ➜, U.S.A. **110 G5** 38 57N 120 59W

North Fork Feather ➜,
  U.S.A. **110 F5** 38 33N 121 30W
North Fork Grand ➜,
  U.S.A. **112 C3** 45 47N 102 16W
North Fork Red ➜,
  U.S.A. **113 H5** 34 24N 99 14W
North Frisian Is. =
  Nordfriesische Inseln,
  Germany .... **24 A4** 54 40N 8 20 E
North Gower, Canada **117 A9** 45 8N 75 43W
North Hd., Australia .... **93 F1** 30 14 S 114 59 E
North Henik L., Canada **103 A9** 61 45N 97 40W
North Highlands,
  U.S.A. **110 G5** 38 40N 121 23W
North Horr, Kenya .... **86 B4** 3 20N 37 8 E
North I., Kenya .... **86 B4** 4 5N 36 5 E
North I., N.Z. .... **91 H5** 38 0 S 175 0 E
North Kingsville, U.S.A. **116 E4** 41 54N 80 42W
North Kitui △, Kenya .... **86 C4** 0 15 S 38 29 E
North Knife ➜, Canada **103 B10** 58 53N 94 45W
North Koel ➜, India .... **69 G10** 24 45N 83 50 E
North Korea ■, Asia .... **57 E14** 40 0N 127 0 E
North Lakhimpur, India .... **67 F19** 27 14N 94 7 E
North Lanarkshire □,
  U.K. **13 F5** 55 52N 3 56W
North Las Vegas, U.S.A. **111 J11** 36 12N 115 7W
North Lincolnshire □,
  U.K. **14 D7** 53 36N 0 30W
North Little Rock,
  U.S.A. **113 H8** 34 45N 92 16W
North Loup ➜, U.S.A. **112 E5** 41 17N 98 24W
North Luangwa △,
  Zambia .... **87 E3** 11 49 S 32 9 E
North Magnetic Pole,
  Canada **4 A2** 88 30N 107 0W
North Minch, U.K. **13 C3** 58 5N 5 55W
North Moose L., Canada **103 C8** 54 11N 100 6W
North Moose L., Man.,
  Canada **103 C8** 54 4N 100 12W
North Myrtle Beach,
  U.S.A. **115 J6** 33 48N 78 42W
North Nahanni ➜,
  Canada **102 A4** 62 15N 123 20W
North Olmsted, U.S.A. **116 E3** 41 25N 81 56W
North Ossetia □, Russia .... **35 J7** 43 30N 44 30 E
North Pagai, I. = Pagai
  Utara, Pulau,
  Indonesia .... **62 E2** 2 35 S 100 0 E
North Palisade, U.S.A. **110 H8** 37 6N 118 31W
North Platte, U.S.A. **112 E4** 41 8N 100 46W
North Platte ➜, U.S.A. **112 E4** 41 7N 100 42W
North Pole, Arctic .... **4 A** 90 0N 0 0W
North Portal, Canada **103 D8** 49 0N 102 33W
North Powder, U.S.A. **108 D5** 45 2N 117 55W
North Pt., Barbados .... **121 g** 13 20N 59 37W
North Pt., Trin. & Tob. **125 J16** 11 21N 60 31W
North Pt., U.S.A. **116 A1** 45 2N 83 16W
North Rhine
  Westphalia =
  Nordrhein-
  Westfalen □,
  Germany .... **24 D3** 51 45N 7 30 E
North River, Canada **105 B8** 53 49N 57 6W
North Ronaldsay, U.K. **13 B6** 59 22N 2 26W
North Saskatchewan ➜,
  Canada **103 C7** 53 15N 105 5W
North Sea, Europe .... **16** 56 0N 4 0 E
North Seal ➜, Canada **103 B9** 58 50N 98 7W
North Somerset □, U.K. **15 F5** 51 24N 2 45W
North Sporades = Vóriai
  Sporádhes, Greece .... **46 B5** 39 15N 23 30 E
North Sydney, Canada **105 C7** 46 12N 60 15W
North Syracuse, U.S.A. **117 C8** 43 8N 76 7W
North Taranaki Bight,
  N.Z. .... **91 H5** 38 50 S 174 15 E
North Thompson ➜,
  Canada **102 C4** 50 40N 120 20W
North Tonawanda,
  U.S.A. **116 C6** 43 2N 78 53W
North Troy, U.S.A. **117 B12** 45 0N 72 24W
North Truchas Pk.,
  U.S.A. **109 J11** 36 0N 105 30W
North Twin I., Canada **104 B4** 53 20N 80 0W
North Tyne ➜, U.K. **14 B5** 55 0N 2 8W
North Uist, U.K. **13 D1** 57 40N 7 15W
North Vancouver,
  Canada **102 D4** 49 19N 123 4W
North Vernon, U.S.A. **114 F3** 39 0N 85 38W
North Wabasca L.,
  Canada **102 B6** 56 0N 113 55W
North Walsham, U.K. .... **14 E9** 52 50N 1 22 E
North West = Severo-
  Zapadnyy □, Russia .... **52 C4** 65 0N 40 0 E
North-West □, S. Africa .... **88 D4** 27 0 S 25 0 E
North-West C., Australia .... **92 D1** 21 45 S 114 9 E
North West Christmas I.
  Ridge, Pac. Oc. **97 G11** 6 30N 165 0W
North West Frontier □,
  Pakistan .... **68 C4** 34 0N 72 0 E
North West Highlands,
  U.K. **13 D4** 57 33N 4 58W
North West River,
  Canada **105 B7** 53 30N 60 10W
North Western □,
  Zambia .... **87 E2** 13 30 S 25 30 E
North Wildwood, U.S.A. **114 F8** 39 0N 74 48W
North York Moors, U.K. **14 C7** 54 23N 0 53W
North York Moors △,
  U.K. **14 C7** 54 27N 0 51W
North Yorkshire □, U.K. **14 C6** 54 15N 1 25W
Northallerton, U.K. **14 C6** 54 20N 1 26W
Northam, Australia .... **93 F2** 31 35 S 116 42 E
Northam, S. Africa .... **88 C4** 24 56 S 27 18 E
Northampton, Australia .... **93 E1** 28 27 S 114 33 E
Northampton, Mass.,
  U.S.A. **117 D12** 42 19N 72 38W
Northampton, Pa.,
  U.S.A. **117 F9** 40 41N 75 30W
Northamptonshire □,
  U.K. **15 E7** 52 16N 0 55W
Northbridge, Australia **117 D13** 42 9N 71 39W
Northcliffe, Australia .... **93 F2** 34 39 S 116 7 E
Northeast Providence
  Chan., W. Indies **120 A4** 26 0N 76 0W
Northeim, Germany .... **24 D6** 51 42N 10 0 E
Northern = Limpopo □,
  S. Africa .... **89 C4** 24 5 S 29 0 E
Northern □, Ghana **83 D4** 9 30N 1 0W
Northern □, Malawi .... **87 E3** 11 0 S 34 0 E
Northern □, S. Leone **82 D2** 9 15N 11 30W
Northern □, Zambia .... **87 E3** 10 30 S 31 0 E
Northern Areas □,
  Pakistan .... **69 A5** 36 30N 73 0 E
Northern Cape □,
  S. Africa .... **88 D3** 30 0 S 20 0 E
Northern Circars, India .... **67 L13** 17 30N 82 30 E
Northern Indian L.,
  Canada **103 B9** 57 20N 97 20W

Northern Ireland □,
  U.K. **12 B5** 54 45N   7 0W
Northern Light L.,
  Canada **104 C1** 48 15N 90 39W
Northern Marianas ☑,
  Pac. Oc. ...... **96 F6** 17 0N 145 0 E
Northern Mid-Atlantic
  Ridge, *Atl. Oc.* ... **4 D6** 35 0N 35 0W
Northern Province □,
  S. Africa ...... **89 C4** 24 0 S 29 0 E
Northern Range,
  Trin. & Tob. **125 K15** 10 46N 61 15W
Northern Territory □,
  Australia ...... **92 D5** 20 0 S 133 0 E
Northfield, *Minn.,*
  U.S.A. **112 C8** 44 27N 93 9W
Northfield, *Vt., U.S.A.* **117 B12** 44 9N 72 40W
Northland □, *N.Z.* .... **91 F4** 35 30 S 173 30 E
Northome, *U.S.A.* **112 B7** 47 52N 94 17W
Northport, *Ala., U.S.A.* **115 J2** 33 14N 87 35W
Northport, *Wash.,*
  U.S.A. **108 B5** 48 55N 117 48W
Northumberland □,
  U.K. **14 B6** 55 12N   2 0W
Northumberland, C.,
  Australia ...... **95 F3** 38 5 S 140 40 E
Northumberland Is.,
  Australia ...... **94 C4** 21 30 S 149 50 E
Northumberland Str.,
  Canada **105 C7** 46 20N 64 0W
Northville, *U.S.A.* ... **117 C10** 43 13N 74 11W
Northwest Providence
  Channel, *W. Indies* **120 A4** 26 0N 78 0W
Northwest Territories □,
  Canada **100 B9** 63 0N 118 0W
Northwich, *U.K.* **14 D5** 53 15N   2 31W
Northwood, *Iowa,*
  U.S.A. **112 D8** 43 27N 93 13W
Northwood, *N. Dak.,*
  U.S.A. **112 B6** 47 44N 97 34W
Norton, *U.S.A.* **112 F5** 39 50N 99 53W
Norton, *Zimbabwe* ... **87 F3** 17 52 S 30 40 E
Norton Sd., *U.S.A.* ... **100 B3** 63 50N 164 0W
Nortorf, *Germany* ... **24 A5** 54 10N   9 50 E
Norwalk, *Calif., U.S.A.* **117 M8** 33 54N 118 5W
Norwalk, *Conn., U.S.A.* **117 E11** 41 7N 73 22W
Norwalk, *Iowa, U.S.A.* **112 C8** 41 29N 93 41W
Norwalk, *Ohio, U.S.A.* **116 E2** 41 15N 82 37W
Norway, *Maine, U.S.A.* **115 C10** 44 13N 70 32W
Norway, *Mich., U.S.A.* **114 C2** 45 47N 87 55W
Norway ■, *Europe* ... **8 E14** 63 0N 11 0 E
Norway House, *Canada* **103 C9** 53 59N 97 50W
Norwegian Sea, *Atl. Oc.* **7 B6** 66 0N   1 0 E
Norwich, *Canada* **116 D4** 42 59N 80 36W
Norwich, *U.K.* ...... **15 E9** 52 38N   1 18 E
Norwich, *Conn., U.S.A.* **117 E12** 41 31N 72 5W
Norwich, *N.Y., U.S.A.* **117 D9** 42 32N 75 32W
Norwood, *Canada* ... **116 B7** 44 23N 77 59W
Norwood, *U.S.A.* **117 B10** 44 45N 75 0W
Noshiro, *Japan* ...... **54 D10** 40 12N 140 0 E
Nosivka, *Ukraine* .... **33 G6** 50 50N 31 37 E
Nosovka = Nosivka,
  Ukraine .... **33 G6** 50 50N 31 37 E
Noṣratābād, *Iran* .... **71 D8** 29 55N 60 0 E
Noss Hd., *U.K.* **13 C5** 58 28N   3 3W
Nossebro, *Sweden* ... **11 F6** 58 12N 12 43 E
Nossob →, *S. Africa* .. **88 D3** 26 55 S 20 45 E
Nossombougou, *Mali* . **82 C3** 13 5N   7 55W
Nosy Barren, *Madag.* . **85 H8** 18 25 S 43 40 E
Nosy Be, *Madag.* .... **85 G9** 13 25 S 48 15 E
Nosy Boraha, *Madag.* . **89 B8** 16 50 S 49 55 E
Nosy Lava, *Madag.* ... **89 A8** 14 33 S 47 36 E
Nosy Varika, *Madag.* . **89 C8** 20 35 S 48 32 E
Noteć →, *Poland* .... **31 F2** 52 44N 15 26 E
Notikewin →, *Canada* . **102 B5** 57 2N 117 38W
Notio Aigaio = Notios
  Aiyaíon □, *Greece* .. **47 E7** 36 52N 25 34 E
Notios Aiyaíon □,
  Greece .... **47 E7** 36 52N 25 34 E
Notios Evvoïkos Kólpos,
  Greece .... **46 C5** 38 20N 24 0 E
Noto, *Italy* .... **43 F8** 36 53N 15 4 E
Noto, G. di, *Italy* .... **43 F8** 36 50N 15 12 E
Notodden, *Norway* ... **9 G13** 59 35N   9 17 E
Notre Dame B., *Canada* **105 C8** 49 45N 55 30W
Notre-Dame-de-
  Koartac = Quaqtaq,
  Canada **101 B13** 60 55N 69 40W
Notre-Dame-des-Bois,
  Canada **117 A13** 45 24N 71 4W
Notre-Dame-
  d'Ivugivic = Ivujivik,
  Canada **101 B12** 62 24N 77 55W
Notre-Dame-du-Nord,
  Canada **104 C4** 47 36N 79 30W
Notsé, *Togo* .... **83 D5** 7 0N   1 17 E
Nottawasaga B., *Canada* **116 B4** 44 35N 80 15W
Nottaway →, *Canada* . **104 B4** 51 22N 78 55W
Nottingham, *U.K.* ... **14 E6** 52 58N   1 10W
Nottingham, City of □,
  U.K. **14 E6** 52 58N   1 10W
Nottingham I., *Canada* **101 B12** 63 20N 77 55W
Nottinghamshire □,
  U.K. **14 D6** 53 10N   1 3W
Nottoway →, *U.S.A.* .. **114 G7** 36 33N 76 55W
Notwane →, *Botswana* . **88 C4** 23 35 S 26 58 E
Nouâdhibou, *Mauritania* **78 D2** 20 54N 17 0W
Nouâdhibou, Ras,
  Mauritania **78 D2** 20 50N 17 0W
Nouakchott, *Mauritania* **82 B1** 18 9N 15 58W
Nouâmghâr, *Mauritania* **82 B1** 19 20N 16 20W
Nouméa, *N. Cal.* .... **96 K8** 22 17 S 166 30 E
Nouna, *Burkina Faso* . **82 C4** 12 45N   3 52W
Noupoort, *S. Africa* ... **88 E3** 31 10 S 24 57 E
Nouveau Comptoir =
  Wemindji, *Canada* . **104 B4** 53 0N 78 49W
Nouveau-Amsterdam, Î.,
  Ind. Oc. .... **3 F13** 38 30 S 77 30 E
Nouvelle-Calédonie =
  New Caledonia ☑,
  Pac. Oc. .... **96 K8** 21 0 S 165 0 E
Nouzonville, *France* ... **19 C11** 49 48N   4 44 E
Nová Baňa, *Slovak Rep.* **27 C11** 48 28N 18 39 E
Nová Bystřice,
  Czech Rep. ...... **26 B8** 49 2N 15 8 E
Nova Casa Nova, *Brazil* **125 E10** 9 25 S 41 5W
Nova Esperança, *Brazil* **127 A5** 23 8 S 52 24W
Nova Friburgo, *Brazil* . **127 A7** 22 16 S 42 30W
Nova Gradiška, *Croatia* **28 E2** 45 17N 17 28 E
Nova Gorica, *Slovenia* . **41 C10** 45 31N 13 39 E
Nova Iguaçu, *Brazil* .. **127 A7** 22 45 S 43 28W
Nova Iorque, *Brazil* ... **125 E10** 7 0 S 44 5W
Nova Kakhovka,
  Ukraine .... **33 J7** 46 42N 33 27 E
Nova Lamego,
  Guinea-Biss. **82 C2** 12 19N 14 11W
Nova Lima, *Brazil* .... **127 A7** 19 59 S 43 51W

Nova Lusitânia, *Mozam.* **87 F3** 19 50 S 34 34 E
Nova Mambone,
  Mozam. .... **89 C6** 21 0 S 35 3 E
Nova Odesa, *Ukraine* .. **33 J6** 47 19N 31 47 E
Nova Sarzyna, *Poland* . **31 H9** 50 21N 22 21 E
Nová Paka, *Czech Rep.* **26 A8** 50 29N 15 30 E
Nova Pavova,
  Serbia & M. ..... **28 F5** 44 56N 20 14 E
Nova Scotia □, *Canada* **105 C7** 45 10N 63 0W
Nova Siri, *Italy* ...... **43 B9** 40 10N 16 35 E
Nova Sofala, *Mozam.* .. **89 C5** 20 7 S 34 42 E
Nova Ushytsya, *Ukraine* **29 B12** 48 50N 27 17 E
Nova Varoš,
  Serbia & M. ..... **44 C3** 43 29N 19 48 E
Nova Venécia, *Brazil* .. **125 G10** 18 45 S 40 24W
Nova Zagora, *Bulgaria* . **45 D10** 42 32N 26 1 E
Novaci, *Macedonia* ... **44 E5** 41 5N 21 29 E
Novaci, *Romania* .... **29 E8** 45 10N 23 42 E
Novaféltria, *Italy* .... **41 E9** 43 53N 12 17 E
Novannenskiy =
  Novoannenskiy,
  Russia .... **34 E6** 50 32N 42 39 E
Novar, *Canada* **116 A5** 45 27N 79 15W
Novara, *Italy* .... **40 C5** 45 28N   8 38 E
Novato, *U.S.A.* **110 G4** 38 6N 122 35W
Novaya Kakhovka =
  Nova Kakhovka,
  Ukraine .... **33 J7** 46 42N 33 27 E
Novaya Kazanka,
  Kazakhstan ...... **35 F9** 48 56N 49 36 E
Novaya Ladoga, *Russia* **32 B7** 60 7N 32 16 E
Novaya Lyalya, *Russia* . **52 D7** 59 4N 60 45 E
Novaya Sibir, Ostrov,
  Russia .... **53 B16** 75 10N 150 0 E
Novaya Zemlya, *Russia* **52 B6** 75 0N 56 0 E
Nové Město,
  Slovak Rep. ..... **27 C10** 48 45N 17 50 E
Nové Město na Moravě,
  Czech Rep. ...... **26 B9** 49 34N 16 5 E
Nové Město nad Metují,
  Czech Rep. ...... **27 A9** 50 20N 16 10 E
Nové Zámky,
  Slovak Rep. ..... **27 C11** 48 2N 18 8 E
Novelda, *Spain* **39 G4** 38 24N   0 45W
Novellara, *Italy* ..... **40 D7** 44 51N 10 44 E
Noventa Vicentina, *Italy* **41 C8** 45 17N 11 32 E
Novgorod, *Russia* .... **32 C6** 58 30N 31 25 E
Novgorod-Severskiy =
  Novhorod-Siverskyy,
  Ukraine .... **33 G7** 52 2N 33 10 E
Novhorod-Siverskyy,
  Ukraine .... **33 G7** 52 2N 33 10 E
Novi Bečej, *Serbia & M.* **28 E5** 45 36N 20 10 E
Novi Iskar, *Bulgaria* .. **44 D7** 42 48N 23 21 E
Novi Kneževac,
  Serbia & M. ..... **28 D5** 46 4N 20 8 E
Novi Lígure, *Italy* .... **40 D5** 44 46N   8 47 E
Novi Pazar, *Bulgaria* .. **45 C11** 43 25N 27 15 E
Novi Pazar, *Serbia & M.* **44 C4** 43 12N 20 28 E
Novi Sad, *Serbia & M.* . **28 E4** 45 18N 19 52 E
Novi Slankamen,
  Serbia & M. ..... **28 E5** 45 8N 20 15 E
Novi Travnik, *Bos.-H.* . **42 F2** 44 10N 17 40 E
Novi Vinodolski, *Croatia* **41 C11** 45 10N 14 48 E
Novigrad, *Istra, Croatia* **41 C10** 45 19N 13 33 E
Novigrad, *Zadar,*
  Croatia .... **41 D12** 44 10N 15 32 E
Novigradsko More,
  Croatia .... **41 D12** 44 10N 15 32 E
Novo Hamburgo, *Brazil* **127 B5** 29 37 S 51 7W
Novo Ivanivka, *Ukraine* **29 E14** 45 55N 29 5 E
Novo Mesto, *Slovenia* . **41 C12** 45 47N 15 12 E
Novo Miloševo,
  Serbia & M. ..... **28 E5** 45 42N 20 20 E
Novo Remanso, *Brazil* . **125 E10** 9 41 S 42 4W
Novoaleksandrovsk,
  Russia .... **35 H5** 45 29N 41 17 E
Novoaleksandrovskaya =
  Novoaleksandrovsk,
  Russia .... **35 H5** 45 29N 41 17 E
Novoaltaysk, *Russia* .. **52 D9** 53 30N 84 0 E
Novoannenskiy, *Russia* **34 E6** 50 32N 42 39 E
Novoazovsk, *Ukraine* . **33 J10** 47 15N 38 4 E
Novocheboksarsk,
  Russia .... **34 B8** 56 5N 47 27 E
Novocherkassk, *Russia* **35 G5** 47 27N 40 15 E
Novodevichye, *Russia* . **34 D9** 53 37N 48 50 E
Novogrudok =
  Navahrudak, *Belarus* **32 F3** 53 40N 25 50 E
Novohrad-Volynskyy,
  Ukraine .... **33 G4** 50 34N 27 35 E
Novokachalinsk, *Russia* **54 B6** 45 5N 132 0 E
Novokhopersk, *Russia* . **34 E5** 51 5N 41 39 E
Novokuybyshevsk,
  Russia .... **34 D9** 53 7N 49 58 E
Novokuznetsk, *Russia* . **52 D9** 53 45N 87 10 E
Novomirgorod, *Ukraine* **33 H6** 48 45N 31 33 E
Novomoskovsk, *Russia* **32 E10** 54 5N 38 15 E
Novomoskovsk, *Ukraine* **33 H8** 48 33N 35 17 E
Novopolotsk =
  Navapolatsk, *Belarus* **32 E5** 55 32N 28 44 E
Novorossiysk, *Russia* .. **33 K9** 44 43N 37 46 E
Novorybnoye, *Russia* . **53 B11** 72 50N 105 50 E
Novorzhev, *Russia* ... **32 D5** 57 3N 29 25 E
Novosej, *Albania* .... **44 E4** 41 56N 20 35 E
Novoselytsya, *Ukraine* . **29 B11** 48 14N 26 15 E
Novoshakhtinsk, *Russia* **33 J10** 47 46N 39 58 E
Novosibirsk, *Russia* .. **52 D9** 55 0N 83 5 E
Novosibirskiye Ostrova,
  Russia .... **53 B15** 75 0N 142 0 E
Novosil, *Russia* ...... **33 F9** 52 59N 37 2 E
Novosokolniki, *Russia* . **32 D6** 56 20N 30 2 E
Novotitarovskaya,
  Russia .... **35 H4** 45 17N 38 43 E
Novotroitsk, *Russia* .. **52 D6** 51 10N 58 15 E
Novoukrayinka, *Ukraine* **33 H6** 48 25N 31 30 E
Novouljanovsk, *Russia* **34 C9** 54 10N 48 25 E
Novouzensk, *Russia* .. **34 E9** 50 32N 48 17 E
Novovoronezhskiy,
  Russia .... **33 G10** 51 19N 39 13 E
Novoyavoriske, *Ukraine* **31 J10** 49 53N 23 33 E
Novozybkov, *Russia* .. **33 F6** 52 30N 31 58 E
Novska, *Croatia* ..... **41 C14** 45 19N 17 0 E
Novvy Urengoy, *Russia* **52 C8** 65 48N 76 52 E
Novyy Bor, *Czech Rep.* **26 A7** 50 46N 14 35 E
Novyy Bug = Novyy Buh,
  Ukraine .... **33 J7** 47 34N 32 29 E
Nový Bydžov,
  Czech Rep. ...... **26 A8** 50 14N 15 29 E
Novyy Dvor, *Belarus* .. **31 F11** 52 50N 24 21 E
Novyy Dwór Mazowiecki,
  Poland .... **31 F7** 52 26N 20 44 E
Nový Jičín, *Czech Rep.* **27 B11** 49 30N 18 0 E
Novyy Port, *Russia* ... **52 C8** 67 40N 72 30 E

Now Shahr, *Iran* ..... **71 B6** 36 40N 51 30 E
Nowa Deba, *Poland* .. **31 H8** 50 26N 21 41 E
Nowa Ruda, *Poland* .. **31 H3** 50 35N 16 30 E
Nowa Sarzyna, *Poland* **31 H9** 50 21N 22 21 E
Nowa Sól, *Poland* ... **31 G2** 51 48N 15 44 E
Nowata, *U.S.A.* **113 G7** 36 42N 95 38W
Nowbaran, *Iran* ..... **71 C6** 35 8N 49 42 E
Nowe, *Poland* ...... **30 E5** 53 41N 18 44 E
Nowe Miasteczko,
  Poland .... **31 G2** 51 42N 15 42 E
Nowe Miasto, *Poland* . **31 G7** 51 38N 20 34 E
Nowe Miasto
  Lubawskie, *Poland* .. **30 E6** 53 27N 19 33 E
Nowe Skalmierzyce,
  Poland .... **31 G4** 51 43N 18 0 E
Nowe Warpno, *Poland* **30 E1** 53 42N 14 18 E
Nowghāb, *Iran* ..... **71 C8** 33 53N 59 4 E
Nowgong, *Assam, India* **67 F18** 26 20N 92 50 E
Nowgong, *Mad. P., India* **69 G8** 25 4N 79 27 E
Nowogard, *Poland* ... **30 E2** 53 41N 15 10 E
Nowogród, *Poland* ... **31 E8** 53 14N 21 53 E
Nowogród Bobrzanski,
  Poland .... **31 G2** 51 48N 15 15 E
Nowogrodziec, *Poland* **31 G2** 51 12N 15 24 E
Nowra, *Australia* .... **95 E5** 34 53 S 150 35 E
Nowshera, *Pakistan* .. **66 C8** 34 0N 72 0 E
Nowy Dwór Gdański,
  Poland .... **30 D6** 54 13N 19 7 E
Nowy Sącz, *Poland* .. **31 J7** 49 40N 20 41 E
Nowy Staw, *Poland* .. **30 D6** 54 13N 19 2 E
Nowy Targ, *Poland* .. **31 J7** 49 29N 20 2 E
Nowy Tomyśl, *Poland* **31 F3** 52 19N 16 10 E
Nowy Wiśnicz, *Poland* **31 J7** 49 55N 20 28 E
Noxen, *U.S.A.* **117 E8** 41 25N 76 4W
Noxon, *U.S.A.* **108 C6** 48 0N 115 43W
Noyabr'sk, *Russia* ... **52 C8** 64 34N 76 21 E
Noyant, *France* ..... **18 E7** 47 30N   0 6 E
Noyers, *France* ..... **19 E10** 47 40N   4 0 E
Noyon, *France* ...... **19 C9** 49 34N   2 59 E
Noyon, *Mongolia* ... **56 C2** 43 2N 102 4 E
Nozay, *France* **18 E5** 47 34N   1 38W
Nqutu, *S. Africa* .... **89 D5** 28 13 S 30 32 E
Nsanje, *Malawi* ..... **87 F4** 16 55 S 35 12 E
Nsawam, *Ghana* **83 D4** 5 50N   0 24W
Nsomba, *Zambia* .... **87 E2** 10 45 S 29 51 E
Nsukka, *Nigeria* ..... **83 D6** 6 51N   7 29 E
Ntui, *Cameroon* ..... **83 E7** 4 27N 11 38 E
Nu Jiang →, *China* ... **58 E2** 29 58N 97 25 E
Nu Shan, *China* ..... **58 E2** 26 0N 99 20 E
Nuba Mts. = Nubah,
  Jibalan, *Sudan* .... **81 E3** 12 0N 31 0 E
Nubah, Jibalan, *Sudan* **81 E3** 12 0N 31 0 E
Nubia, *Africa* ...... **76 D7** 21 0N 32 0 E
Nubian Desert =
  Nûbîya, Es Sahrâ en,
  Sudan .... **80 C3** 21 30N 33 30 E
Nûbîya, Es Sahrâ en,
  Sudan .... **80 C3** 21 30N 33 30 E
Nubledo, *Spain* **36 B5** 43 31N   5 52W
Nuboai, *Indonesia* ... **63 E9** 2 10 S 136 30 E
Nubra →, *India* ..... **69 B7** 34 35N 77 35 E
Nucet, *Romania* ..... **28 D7** 46 28N 22 35 E
Nueces →, *U.S.A.* ... **113 M6** 27 51N 97 30W
Nueltin L., *Canada* ... **103 A9** 60 30N 99 30W
Nueva Carteya, *Spain* . **37 H6** 37 35N   4 28W
Nueva Gerona, *Cuba* . **120 B3** 21 53N 82 49W
Nueva Palmira, *Uruguay* **126 C4** 33 52 S 58 20W
Nueva Rosita, *Mexico* . **118 B4** 28 0N 101 11W
Nueva San Salvador,
  El Salv. **120 D2** 13 40N 89 18W
Nueva Tabarca, *Spain* . **39 G4** 38 17N   0 30 E
Nuéve de Julio,
  Argentina ...... **126 D3** 35 30 S 61 0W
Nuevitas, *Cuba* **120 B4** 21 30N 77 20W
Nuevo, G., *Argentina* . **128 E4** 43 0 S 64 30W
Nuevo Casas Grandes,
  Mexico **118 A3** 30 22N 108 0W
Nuevo Guerrero,
  Mexico **119 B5** 26 34N 99 15W
Nuevo Laredo, *Mexico* **119 B5** 27 30N 99 30W
Nuevo León □, *Mexico* **118 C5** 25 0N 100 0W
Nuevo Rocafuerte,
  Ecuador .... **124 D3** 0 55 S 75 27W
Nugget Pt., *N.Z.* .... **91 M2** 46 27 S 169 50 E
Nugrus, Gebel, *Egypt* . **80 C3** 24 47N 34 35 E
Nuhaka, *N.Z.* .... **91 H6** 39 3 S 177 45 E
Nuits-St-Georges,
  France .... **19 E11** 47 10N   4 56 E
Nukey Bluff, *Australia* . **95 E2** 32 26 S 135 29 E
Nukhayb, *Iraq* ...... **70 C4** 32 4N 42 3 E
Nukheila, *Sudan* .... **80 D2** 19 1N 26 21 E
Nuku'alofa, *Tonga* ... **91 E12** 21 10 S 174 0W
Nukus, *Uzbekistan* ... **52 E6** 42 27N 59 41 E
Nules, *Spain* **38 F4** 39 51N   0 9W
Nullagine, *Australia* .. **92 D3** 21 53 S 120 7 E
Nullagine →, *Australia* **92 D3** 21 20 S 120 20 E
Nullarbor, *Australia* .. **93 F5** 31 28 S 130 55 E
Nullarbor →, *Australia* **93 F2** 32 39 S 115 37 E
Nullarbor Plain,
  Australia ...... **93 F4** 31 10 S 129 0 E
Numalla, L., *Australia* . **95 D3** 28 43 S 144 20 E
Numan, *Nigeria* ..... **83 D7** 9 29N 12 3 E
Numata, *Japan* ...... **55 F9** 36 45N 139 4 E
Numatinna →, *Sudan* . **81 F2** 7 38N 27 20 E
Numazu, *Japan* ..... **55 G9** 35 7N 138 51 E
Numbulwar, *Australia* . **94 A2** 14 15 S 135 45 E
Numfoor, *Indonesia* .. **63 E8** 1 0 S 134 50 E
Numurkah, *Australia* . **95 F4** 36 5 S 145 26 E
Nunaksaluk I., *Canada* **105 A7** 55 49N 60 20W
Nunap Isua, *Greenland* **101 C15** 59 48N 43 55W
Nunavut □, *Canada* .. **101 D8** 66 0N 85 0W
Nunda, *U.S.A.* **116 D7** 42 35N 77 56W
Nuneaton, *U.K.* **15 E6** 52 32N   1 27W
Nungarin, *Australia* .. **93 F2** 31 12 S 118 6 E
Nungo, *Mozam.* ..... **87 E4** 13 23 S 37 43 E
Nungwe, *Tanzania* ... **86 C3** 2 48 S 32 2 E
Nunivak I., *U.S.A.* ... **100 B3** 60 10N 166 30W
Nunkun, *India* ...... **69 C7** 33 57N 76 2 E
Núoro, *Italy* .... **42 B2** 40 20N   9 20 E
Nūrābād, *Iran* ...... **71 E8** 27 47N 57 12 E
Nure →, *Italy* ...... **40 C6** 45 3N   9 49 E
Nuremberg = Nürnberg,
  Germany .... **25 F7** 49 27N 11 3 E
Nuri, *Mexico* **118 B3** 28 2N 109 22W
Nuri, Sudan .... **80 D3** 18 29N 31 59 E
Nuriootpa, *Australia* .. **95 E2** 34 27 S 139 0 E
Nurlat, *Russia* ...... **34 C9** 54 26N 50 45 E
Nurmes, *Finland* .... **8 E23** 63 33N 29 10 E
Nurpur, *Pakistan* .... **68 D4** 31 53N 71 54 E
Nurra, Là, *Italy* ..... **42 B1** 40 45N   8 15 E
Nurran = Terewah,
  L., *Australia* .... **95 D4** 29 52 S 147 35 E
Nurrari Lakes, *Australia* **93 E5** 29 1 S 130 5 E

Nurri, *Italy* .... **42 C2** 39 43N   9 14 E
Nürtingen, *Germany* .. **25 G5** 48 37N   9 19 E
Nurzec →, *Poland* ... **31 F9** 52 37N 22 25 E
Nus, *Italy* .... **40 C4** 45 45N   7 28 E
Nusa Barung, *Indonesia* **63 H15** 8 30 S 113 30 E
Nusa Dua, *Indonesia* . **63 K18** 8 48 S 115 14 E
Nusa Kambangan,
  Indonesia ...... **63 G13** 7 40 S 108 10 E
Nusa Tenggara Barat □,
  Indonesia ...... **62 F5** 8 50 S 117 30 E
Nusa Tenggara Timur □,
  Indonesia ...... **63 F6** 9 30 S 122 0 E
Nusaybin, *Turkey* .... **73 D9** 37 3N 41 10 E
Nushki, *Pakistan* .... **68 E2** 29 35N 66 0 E
Nuuk, *Greenland* **101 B14** 64 10N 51 35W
Nuwakot, *Nepal* ..... **69 E10** 28 10N 83 55 E
Nuweiba', *Egypt* .... **70 D2** 28 59N 34 39 E
Nuwerus, *S. Africa* ... **88 E2** 31 8 S 18 24 E
Nuweveldberge,
  S. Africa .... **88 E3** 32 10 S 21 45 E
Nuyts, C., *Australia* .. **93 F5** 32 2 S 132 21 E
Nuyts, Pt., *Australia* . **93 G2** 35 4 S 116 38 E
Nuyts Arch., *Australia* **95 E1** 32 35 S 133 20 E
Nxai Pan △, *Botswana* **88 B3** 19 50 S 24 46 E
Nxau-Nxau, *Botswana* **88 B3** 18 57 S 21 4 E
Nyaake, *Liberia* **82 E3** 4 52N   7 37W
Nyabing, *Australia* ... **93 F2** 33 33 S 118 9 E
Nyack, *U.S.A.* **117 E11** 41 5N 73 55W
Nyagan, *Russia* ..... **52 C7** 62 30N 65 38 E
Nyahanga, *Tanzania* .. **86 C3** 2 20 S 33 37 E
Nyahua, *Tanzania* ... **86 D3** 5 25 S 33 23 E
Nyahururu, *Kenya* ... **86 B4** 0 2N 36 27 E
Nyainqentanglha Shan,
  China .... **60 C4** 30 0N 90 0 E
Nyakanazi, *Tanzania* . **86 C3** 3 2 S 31 10 E
Nyakrom, *Ghana* **83 D4** 5 40N   0 50W
Nyâlâ, *Sudan* ...... **81 E1** 12 2N 24 58 E
Nyamandhlovu,
  Zimbabwe ...... **87 F2** 19 55 S 28 16 E
Nyambiti, *Tanzania* .. **86 C3** 2 48 S 33 27 E
Nyamlell, *Sudan* .... **81 F2** 9 7N 26 59 E
Nyamwaga, *Tanzania* . **86 C3** 1 27 S 34 33 E
Nyandekwa, *Tanzania* **86 C3** 3 57 S 32 32 E
Nyanding →, *Sudan* .. **81 F3** 8 40N 32 41 E
Nyandoma, *Russia* ... **32 B11** 61 40N 40 12 E
Nyanga →, *Zimbabwe* **87 F3** 18 37 S 32 46 E
Nyangana, *Namibia* .. **88 B3** 18 0 S 20 40 E
Nyanguge, *Tanzania* . **86 C3** 2 30 S 33 12 E
Nyankpala, *Ghana* ... **83 D4** 9 21N   0 58W
Nyanza, *Rwanda* .... **86 C2** 2 20 S 29 42 E
Nyanza □, *Kenya* .... **86 C3** 0 10 S 34 15 E
Nyanza-Lac, *Burundi* . **86 C2** 4 21 S 29 36 E
Nyaponges, *Sudan* ... **81 F3** 5 5N 33 45 E
Nyasa, L., *Africa* .... **87 E3** 12 30 S 34 30 E
Nyasvizh, *Belarus* ... **33 F4** 53 14N 26 38 E
Nyazura, *Zimbabwe* .. **87 F3** 18 40 S 32 16 E
Nyazwidzi →,
  Zimbabwe ...... **87 G3** 20 0 S 31 17 E
Nyborg, *Denmark* ... **11 J4** 55 18N 10 47 E
Nybro, *Sweden* ..... **11 H9** 56 44N 15 55 E
Nyda, *Russia* .... **52 C8** 66 40N 72 58 E
Nyeri, *Kenya* .... **86 C4** 0 23 S 36 56 E
Nyerol, *Sudan* ...... **81 F3** 8 41N 32 1 E
Nyhammar, *Sweden* . **10 D8** 60 17N 14 58 E
Nyika △, *Malawi* .... **87 E3** 10 30 S 33 53 E
Nyíinahin, *Ghana* ... **82 D4** 6 43N   2 3W
Nyíradony, *Hungary* .. **28 C6** 47 41N 21 55 E
Nyírbátor, *Hungary* .. **28 C7** 47 49N 22 9 E
Nyíregyháza, *Hungary* **28 C6** 47 58N 21 47 E
Nykarleby =
  Uusikaarlepyy,
  Finland .... **8 E20** 63 32N 22 31 E
Nykøbing, Storstrøm,
  Denmark .... **11 K5** 54 56N 11 52 E
Nykøbing, Vestsjælland,
  Denmark .... **11 J5** 55 55N 11 40 E
Nykøbing, Viborg,
  Denmark .... **11 H2** 56 48N   8 51 E
Nyköping, *Sweden* ... **11 F11** 58 45N 17 1 E
Nykroppa, *Sweden* .. **10 E8** 59 37N 14 18 E
Nykvarn, *Sweden* ... **10 E11** 59 11N 17 25 E
Nyland, *Sweden* ..... **10 A11** 63 1N 17 45 E
Nylstroom = Modimolle,
  S. Africa .... **89 C4** 24 42 S 28 22 E
Nymagee, *Australia* .. **95 E4** 32 7 S 146 20 E
Nymboida →, *Australia* **95 D5** 29 38 S 152 26 E
Nymburk, *Czech Rep.* **26 A8** 50 10N 15 1 E
Nynäshamn, *Sweden* . **11 F11** 58 54N 17 57 E
Nyngan, *Australia* ... **95 E4** 31 30 S 147 8 E
Nyoma Rap, *India* ... **69 C8** 33 10N 78 40 E
Nyoman = Nemunas →,
  Lithuania ...... **9 J19** 55 25N 21 10 E
Nyon, *Switz.* .... **25 J2** 46 23N   6 14 E
Nyong →, *Cameroon* . **83 E6** 3 17N   9 54 E
Nyons, *France* ...... **21 D9** 44 22N   5 10 E
Nyou, *Burkina Faso* ... **82 C4** 12 46N   1 58W
Nýrsko, *Czech Rep.* .. **26 B6** 49 18N 13 9 E
Nysa, *Poland* .... **31 H4** 50 30N 17 2 E
Nysa →, *Europe* .... **24 C10** 52 4N 14 46 E
Nysa Kłodzka →,
  Poland .... **31 H4** 50 49N 17 40 E
Nysäter, *Sweden* .... **10 E6** 59 17N 12 47 E
Nyslott = Savonlinna,
  Finland .... **32 B5** 61 52N 28 53 E
Nyssa, *U.S.A.* **108 E5** 43 53N 117 0W
Nystad = Uusikaupunki,
  Finland .... **9 F19** 60 47N 21 25 E
Nysted, *Denmark* .... **11 K5** 54 40N 11 44 E
Nyunzu, Dem. Rep. of
  the Congo .... **86 D2** 5 57 S 27 58 E
Nyurba, *Russia* ..... **53 C12** 63 17N 118 28 E
Nyzhankovychi, *Ukraine* **31 J9** 49 40N 22 49 E
Nyzhnohirskyy, *Ukraine* **33 K8** 45 27N 34 38 E
Nyzhnyy Vorota, *Ukraine* **29 B8** 48 46N 23 6 E
Nzébéla, *Guinea* **82 D3** 8 9N   9 7W
Nzega, *Tanzania* .... **86 C3** 4 10 S 33 12 E
Nzérékoré, *Guinea* ... **82 D3** 7 49N   8 48W
Nzeto, *Angola* ...... **84 F2** 7 10 S 12 52 E
Nzilo, Chutes de,
  *Dem. Rep. of
  the Congo* ...... **87 E2** 10 18 S 25 27 E
N'zo →, *Ivory C.* **82 D3** 6 15N   7 15W
N'zo →, *Ivory C.* **82 D3** 6 15N   7 3W
Nzubuka, *Tanzania* .. **86 C3** 4 45 S 32 50 E

O

Oahe, L., *U.S.A.* **112 C4** 44 27N 100 24W
Oahe Dam, *U.S.A.* ... **112 C4** 44 27N 100 24W
Oahu, *U.S.A.* **106 H16** 21 28N 157 58W
Oak Harbor, *U.S.A.* .. **110 B4** 48 18N 122 39W
Oak Hill, *U.S.A.* **114 G5** 37 59N 81 9W
Oak Ridge, *U.S.A.* ... **115 G3** 36 1N 84 16W
Oak View, *U.S.A.* ... **111 L7** 34 24N 119 18W
Oakan-Dake, *Japan* .. **54 C12** 43 27N 144 10 E
Oakdale, *Calif., U.S.A.* **110 H6** 37 46N 120 51W
Oakdale, *La., U.S.A.* . **113 K8** 30 49N 92 40W
Oakes, *U.S.A.* **112 B5** 46 8N 98 6W
Oakesdale, *U.S.A.* ... **108 C5** 47 8N 117 15W
Oakey, *Australia* .... **95 D5** 27 25 S 151 43 E
Oakfield, *U.S.A.* **116 C6** 43 4N 78 16W
Oakham, *U.K.* **15 E7** 52 40N   0 43W
Oakhurst, *U.S.A.* ... **110 H7** 37 19N 119 40W
Oakland, *U.S.A.* **110 H4** 37 49N 122 16W
Oakley, *Idaho, U.S.A.* **108 E7** 42 15N 113 53W
Oakley, *Kans., U.S.A.* **112 F4** 39 8N 100 51W
Oakover →, *Australia* **92 D3** 21 0 S 120 40 E
Oakridge, *U.S.A.* ... **108 E2** 43 45N 122 28W
Oakville, *Canada* **116 C5** 43 27N 79 41W
Oakville, *U.S.A.* **110 D3** 46 51N 123 14W
Oamaru, *N.Z.* ...... **91 L3** 45 5 S 170 59 E
Oancea, *Romania* ... **29 E12** 45 21N 27 42 E
Oasi Faunistica di
  Vendicari △, *Italy* .. **43 F8** 36 49N 15 6 E
Oasis, *Calif., U.S.A.* . **111 M10** 33 28N 116 6W
Oasis, *Nev., U.S.A.* .. **110 H9** 37 29N 117 55W
Oates Land, *Antarctica* **5 C11** 69 0 S 160 0 E
Oatlands, *Australia* .. **95 G4** 42 17 S 147 21 E
Oatman, *U.S.A.* **111 K12** 35 1N 114 19W
Oaxaca, *Mexico* **119 D5** 17 2N 96 40W
Oaxaca □, *Mexico* ... **119 D5** 17 0N 97 0W
Ob →, *Russia* ...... **52 C7** 66 45N 69 30 E
Oba, *Canada* **104 C3** 49 4N 84 7W
Obala, *Cameroon* ... **83 E7** 4 9N 11 32 E
Obama, *Japan* ...... **55 G7** 35 30N 135 45 E
Oban, *Nigeria* ...... **83 D6** 5 17N   8 33 E
Oban, *U.K.* **13 E3** 56 25N   5 29W
Obbia, *Somali Rep.* .. **75 F4** 5 25N 48 30 E
Obera, *Argentina* .... **127 B4** 27 21 S 55 2W
Oberammergau,
  Germany .... **25 H7** 47 36N 11 4 E
Oberasbach, *Germany* **25 F6** 49 25N 10 57 E
Oberbayern □,
  Germany .... **25 G7** 48 5N 11 50 E
Oberdrauburg, *Austria* **26 E5** 46 44N 12 58 E
Obere Donau △,
  Germany .... **25 G5** 48 5N   9 0 E
Oberer Bayerischer
  Wald △, *Germany* . **25 F8** 49 15N 12 40 E
Oberfranken □,
  Germany .... **25 E7** 50 10N 11 20 E
Oberhausen, *Germany* **24 D2** 51 28N   6 51 E
Oberkirch, *Germany* .. **25 G4** 48 31N   8 4 E
Oberlausitz, *Germany* **24 D10** 51 16N 14 18 E
Oberlin, *Kans., U.S.A.* **112 F4** 39 49N 100 32W
Oberlin, *La., U.S.A.* .. **113 K8** 30 37N 92 46W
Oberlin, *Ohio, U.S.A.* **116 E2** 41 18N 82 13W
Obernai, *France* .... **19 D14** 48 28N   7 30 E
Oberndorf, *Germany* . **25 G4** 48 17N   8 34 E
Oberon, *Australia* ... **95 E4** 33 45 S 149 52 E
Oberösterreich □,
  Austria .... **26 C7** 48 10N 14 0 E
Oberpfalz □, *Germany* **25 F8** 49 20N 12 10 E
Oberpfälzer Wald □,
  Germany .... **25 F8** 49 30N 12 30 E
Oberpfälzer Wald △,
  Germany .... **25 F8** 49 40N 12 20 E
Oberstdorf, *Germany* . **25 H6** 47 24N 10 15 E
Obertyn, *Ukraine* ... **29 B10** 48 42N 25 10 E
Oberursel, *Germany* .. **25 E4** 50 11N   8 34 E
Oberwart, *Austria* ... **27 D9** 47 17N 16 12 E
Obi, *Indonesia* ...... **63 E7** 1 23 S 127 45 E
Obiaruku, *Nigeria* ... **83 D6** 5 51N   6 9 E
Óbidos, *Brazil* ...... **125 D7** 1 50 S 55 30W
Óbidos, *Portugal* **37 F1** 39 19N   9 10W
Obihiro, *Japan* ...... **54 C11** 42 56N 143 12 E
Obilatu, *Indonesia* ... **63 E7** 1 25 S 127 20 E
Obilnoye, *Russia* .... **35 G7** 47 32N 44 30 E
Obing, *Germany* ..... **25 G8** 48 0N 12 24 E
Objat, *France* ...... **20 C5** 45 16N   1 24 E
Obluchye, *Russia* .... **53 E14** 49 1N 131 4 E
Obninsk, *Russia* .... **32 E9** 55 8N 36 37 E
Obo, *C.A.R.* .... **86 A2** 5 20N 26 32 E
Oboa, Mt., *Uganda* .. **86 B3** 1 45N 34 45 E
Obodivka, *Ukraine* ... **29 B14** 48 24N 29 15 E
Oborniki, *Poland* .... **31 F3** 52 39N 16 50 E
Oborniki Śląskie,
  Poland .... **31 G3** 51 17N 16 53 E
Oboyan, *Russia* ..... **33 G9** 51 15N 36 21 E
Obozerskaya =
  Obozerskiy, *Russia* . **52 C5** 63 34N 40 21 E
Obozerskiy, *Russia* .. **52 C5** 63 34N 40 21 E
Obrenovac, *Serbia & M.* **44 B4** 44 40N 20 11 E
Obrovac, *Croatia* .... **41 D12** 44 11N 15 41 E
Obruk, *Turkey* ...... **72 C5** 38 7N 33 12 E
Obrzycko, *Poland* ... **31 F3** 52 42N 16 32 E
Observatory Inlet,
  Canada **102 B3** 55 10N 129 54W
Obshchi Syrt, *Russia* . **6 E16** 52 0N 53 0 E
Obskaya Guba, *Russia* **52 C8** 69 0N 73 0 E
Obuasi, *Ghana* **83 D4** 6 17N   1 40W
Obubra, *Nigeria* ..... **83 D6** 6 8N   8 20 E
Obudu, *Nigeria* ..... **83 D6** 6 38N   9 5 E
Obwalden □, *Switz.* .. **25 J4** 46 55N   8 15 E
Obzor, *Bulgaria* ..... **45 D11** 42 50N 27 52 E
Ocala, *U.S.A.* **115 L4** 29 11N 82 8W
Ocampo, *Chihuahua,*
  Mexico **118 B3** 28 9N 108 24W
Ocampo, *Tamaulipas,*
  Mexico **119 C5** 22 50N 99 20W
Ocaña, *Spain* **36 F7** 39 55N   3 30W
Ocanomowoc, *U.S.A.* **112 D10** 43 7N 88 30W
Ocaña, *Spain* **36 F7** 39 55N   3 30W
Occidental, Cordillera,
  Colombia **124 C3** 5 0N 76 0W
Occidental, Grand Erg,
  Algeria .... **78 B6** 30 20N   1 0 E
Ocean City, *Md., U.S.A.* **114 F8** 38 20N 75 5W
Ocean City, *N.J., U.S.A.* **114 F8** 39 17N 74 35W
Ocean City, *Wash.,*
  U.S.A. **110 C2** 47 4N 124 10W
Ocean Falls, *Canada* . **102 C3** 52 18N 127 48W
Ocean I. = Banaba,
  Kiribati .... **96 H8** 0 45 S 169 50 E
Ocean Park, *U.S.A.* .. **110 D2** 46 30N 124 3W
Oceano, *U.S.A.* **111 K6** 35 6N 120 37W
Oceanport, *U.S.A.* .. **117 F10** 40 19N 74 3W
Oceanside, *U.S.A.* .. **111 M9** 33 12N 117 23W
Ochagavía, *Spain* ... **38 C3** 42 55N   1 5W
Ochakiv, *Ukraine* .... **33 J6** 46 37N 31 33 E
Ochamchira, *Georgia* **35 J5** 42 46N 41 32 E
Ochil Hills, *U.K.* **13 E5** 56 14N   3 40W
Ocho Rios, *Jamaica* .. **120 a** 18 24N 77 6W
Ochsenfurt, *Germany* **25 F6** 49 40N 10 4 E

Ochsenhausen, Germany 25 G5 48 4N 9 57 E
Ocilla, U.S.A. 115 K4 31 36N 83 15W
Ockelbo, Sweden . . . . . 10 D10 60 54N 16 45 E
Ocmulgee →, U.S.A. . . 115 K4 31 58N 82 33W
Ocna Mureş, Romania . . 29 D8 46 23N 23 55 E
Ocna Sibiului, Romania . 29 E9 45 52N 24 2 E
Ocnele Mari, Romania . . 29 E8 45 8N 24 18 E
Ocniţa, Moldova . . . . . 29 B12 48 25N 27 30 E
Oconee →, U.S.A. 115 K4 31 58N 82 33W
Oconto, U.S.A. 114 C2 44 53N 87 52W
Oconto Falls, U.S.A. . . . 114 C1 44 52N 88 9W
Ocosingo, Mexico 119 D6 17 10N 92 15W
Ocotal, Nic. 120 D2 13 41N 86 31W
Ocotlán, Mexico 118 C4 20 21N 102 42W
Ocotlán de Morelos,
Mexico 119 D5 16 48N 96 40W
Ocreza →, Portugal . . . 37 F3 39 32N 7 50W
Ócsa, Hungary . . . . . . 28 C4 47 17N 19 15 E
Octeville, France 18 C5 49 38N 1 40W
Oda, Ghana 83 D4 5 50N 0 51W
Öda, Japan . . . . 55 G6 35 11N 132 30 E
Öda, J., Sudan . . . . . . 80 C4 21 36N 36 39 E
Óðáðahraun, Iceland . . . 8 D5 65 5N 17 0W
Odate, Japan . . . . 54 D10 40 16N 140 34 E
Odawara, Japan . . . . . 55 G9 35 20N 139 6 E
Odda, Norway . . . . . . 9 F12 60 3N 6 35 E
Odder, Denmark . . . . . 11 J4 55 58N 10 10 E
Odei →, Canada 103 B9 56 6N 96 54W
Odemira, Portugal 37 H2 37 35N 8 40W
Ödemiş, Turkey . . . . . 47 C9 38 15N 28 0 E
Odendaalsrus, S. Africa . 88 D4 27 48 S 26 45 E
Odensbacken, Sweden . . 10 E9 59 10N 15 32 E
Odense, Denmark . . . . 11 J4 55 22N 10 23 E
Odenwald = Neckartal-
Odenwald △,
Germany . . . . 25 F5 49 30N 9 5 E
Odenwald, Germany . . . 25 F5 49 35N 9 0 E
Oder →, Europe . . . . . 24 B10 53 33N 14 38 E
Oder-Havel Kanal,
Germany . . . . 24 C10 52 52N 14 2 E
Oderzo, Italy . . . . 41 C9 45 47N 12 29 E
Odesa, Ukraine . . . . . . 33 J6 46 30N 30 45 E
Ödeshög, Sweden . . . . . 11 F8 58 14N 14 39 E
Odessa = Odesa,
Ukraine . . . . 33 J6 46 30N 30 45 E
Odessa, Canada 117 B8 44 17N 76 43W
Odessa, Tex., U.S.A. . . . 113 K3 31 52N 102 23W
Odessa, Wash., U.S.A. . . 108 C4 47 20N 118 41W
Odiakwe, Botswana . . . 88 C4 20 12 S 25 17 E
Odiel →, Spain 37 H4 37 10N 6 55W
Odienné, Ivory C. 82 D3 9 30N 7 34W
Odintsovo, Russia . . . . 32 E9 55 39N 37 15 E
Odiongan, Phil. . . . . . 61 E4 12 24N 121 59 E
Odobeşti, Romania . . . . 29 E12 45 43N 27 4 E
Odolanów, Poland . . . . 31 G4 51 34N 17 40 E
O'Donnell, U.S.A. 113 J4 32 58N 101 50W
Odorheiu Secuiesc,
Romania . . . . 29 D10 46 21N 25 21 E
Odoyevo, Russia . . . . . 32 F9 53 56N 36 42 E
Odra = Oder →, Europe 24 B10 53 33N 14 38 E
Odra →, Spain 36 C6 42 14N 4 17W
Odžaci, Serbia & M. . . . 28 E4 45 30N 19 17 E
Odžak, Bos.-H. . . . . . . 28 E3 45 3N 18 18 E
Odzi, Zimbabwe . . . . . 89 B5 19 0 S 32 20 E
Odzi →, Zimbabwe . . . 89 B5 19 45 S 32 23 E
Oebisfelde, Germany . . . 24 C6 52 27N 10 57 E
Oeiras, Brazil . . . . 125 E10 7 0 S 42 8W
Oeiras, Portugal 37 G1 38 41N 9 18W
Oelrichs, U.S.A. 112 D3 43 11N 103 14W
Oelsnitz, Germany . . . . 25 E8 50 24N 12 10 E
Oelwein, U.S.A. 112 D9 42 41N 91 55W
Oenpelli, Australia . . . 92 B5 12 20 S 133 4 E
Oetz, Austria . . . . 26 D3 47 13N 10 53 E
Of, Turkey . . . . 73 B9 40 59N 40 23 E
Ofanto →, Italy . . . . . 43 A9 41 22N 16 13 E
Offa, Nigeria . . . . 83 D5 8 13N 4 42 E
Offaly □, Ireland 12 C4 53 15N 7 30W
Offenbach, Germany . . . 25 E4 50 6N 8 44 E
Offenburg, Germany . . . 25 G3 48 28N 7 56 E
Officer, The →,
Australia . . . . 93 E5 27 46 S 132 30 E
Offida, Italy . . . . 41 F10 42 56N 13 41 E
Ofidhousa, Greece . . . . 47 E8 36 33N 26 8 E
Ofotfjorden, Norway . . . 8 B17 68 27N 17 0 E
Ōfunato, Japan . . . . . . 54 E10 39 4N 141 43 E
Oga, Japan . . . . 54 E9 39 55N 139 50 E
Oga-Hantō, Japan . . . . 54 E9 39 58N 139 47 E
Ogaden, Ethiopia . . . . 75 F3 7 30N 45 30 E
Ōgaki, Japan . . . . 55 G8 35 21N 136 37 E
Ogallala, U.S.A. 112 E4 41 8N 101 43W
Ogasawara Gunto,
Pac. Oc. . . . . 96 E6 27 0N 142 0 E
Ogbomosho, Nigeria . . . 83 D5 8 1N 4 11 E
Ogden, U.S.A. 108 F7 41 13N 111 58W
Ogdensburg, U.S.A. . . . 117 B9 44 42N 75 30W
Ogeechee →, U.S.A. . . . 115 K5 31 50N 81 3W
Ogilby, U.S.A. 111 N12 32 49N 114 50W
Óglio →, Italy . . . . . . 40 C7 45 2N 10 39 E
Óglio Nord △, Italy . . . 40 C6 45 22N 9 54 E
Óglio Sud △, Italy . . . . 40 C7 45 7N 10 24 E
Ogmore, Australia . . . . 94 C4 22 37 S 149 35 E
Ognon →, France . . . . 19 E12 47 16N 5 28 E
Ogoja, Nigeria . . . . . . 83 D6 6 38N 8 39 E
Ogoki, Canada 104 B2 51 38N 85 58W
Ogoki →, Canada 104 B2 51 38N 85 57W
Ogoki L., Canada 104 B2 50 50N 87 10W
Ogoki Res., Canada . . . 104 B2 50 45N 88 15W
Ogooué →, Gabon . . . . 84 E1 1 0 S 9 0 E
Ogosta →, Bulgaria . . . 44 C7 43 48N 23 55 E
Ogowe = Ogooué →,
Gabon . . . . 84 E1 1 0 S 9 0 E
Ogr = Sharafa, Sudan . . 81 E1 11 59N 27 7 E
Ograzden, Macedonia . . 44 E6 41 30N 22 50 E
Ogre, Latvia . . . . 9 H21 56 49N 24 36 E
Ogrein, Sudan . . . . . . 80 D3 17 55N 34 50 E
Ogulin, Croatia . . . . . . 41 C12 45 16N 15 16 E
Ogun □, Nigeria . . . . . 83 D5 7 0N 3 0 E
Ogurchinsky, Ostrov,
Turkmenistan . . . . . 71 B7 38 55N 53 2 E
Oguta, Nigeria . . . . . . 83 D6 5 44N 6 44 E
Ogwashi-Uku, Nigeria . 83 D6 6 15N 6 30 E
Ogwe, Nigeria . . . . . . 83 E6 5 0N 7 14 E
Ohai, N.Z. . . . . 91 L2 45 55N 167 52 E
Ohakune, N.Z. . . . . . . 91 H5 39 24 S 175 24 E
Ohata, Japan . . . . 54 D10 41 24N 141 10 E
Ohau, L., N.Z. . . . . . . 91 L2 44 15 S 169 53 E
Ohio □, U.S.A. 114 G1 36 59N 89 8W
Ohio →, U.S.A. 114 G1 36 59N 89 8W
Ohre →, Czech Rep. . . . 26 A7 50 30N 14 10 E
Ohre →, Germany . . . . 24 C7 52 18N 11 46 E
Ohrid, Macedonia . . . . 44 E4 41 8N 20 52 E
Ohridsko Jezero,
Macedonia . . . . . . 44 E4 41 8N 20 52 E
Ohrigstad, S. Africa . . . 89 C5 24 39 S 30 36 E
Ohringen, Germany . . . 25 F5 49 12N 9 31 E
Oi Qu, China . . . . 58 C2 28 17N 98 16 E

Oiapoque, Brazil 125 3 50N 51 50W
Oikou, China . . . . 57 E9 38 35N 117 42 E
Oil City, U.S.A. 116 E5 41 26N 79 42W
Oil Springs, Canada . . . 116 D2 42 47N 82 7W
Oildale, U.S.A. 111 K7 35 25N 119 1W
Oinousa, Greece . . . . . 47 C8 38 33N 26 14 E
Oise □, France . . . . . . 19 C9 49 28N 2 30 E
Oise →, France . . . . . . 19 C9 49 0N 2 4 E
Oiseaux du Djoudj △,
Senegal 82 B1 16 24N 16 14W
Oistins, Barbados . . . . 121 g 13 4N 59 33W
Oistins B., Barbados . . . 121 g 13 4N 59 33W
Oita, Japan . . . . 55 H5 33 14N 131 36 E
Oita □, Japan . . . . 55 H5 33 15N 131 30 E
Oiticica, Brazil . . . . . . 125 E10 5 3 S 41 5W
Ojacaliente, Mexico . . . 118 C4 22 34N 102 15W
Ojai, U.S.A. 111 L7 34 27N 119 15W
Ojcowski △, Poland . . . 31 H6 50 15N 19 50 E
Ojinaga, Mexico 118 B4 29 34N 104 25W
Ojiya, Japan . . . . 55 F9 37 18N 138 48 E
Ojo de Liebre △, Mexico 118 B2 27 50N 114 0W
Ojos del Salado, Cerro,
Argentina . . . . 126 B2 27 0 S 68 40W
Oka →, Russia . . . . . . 34 B7 56 20N 43 59 E
Okaba, Indonesia . . . . 63 F9 8 6 S 139 42 E
Okahandja, Namibia . . . 88 C2 22 0 S 16 59 E
Okanagan L., Canada . . 102 D5 50 0N 119 30W
Okanogan, U.S.A. 108 B4 48 22N 119 35W
Okanogan →, U.S.A. . . . 108 B4 48 6N 119 44W
Okány, Hungary . . . . . 28 D6 46 52N 21 21 E
Okapi △, Dem. Rep. of
the Congo . . . . 86 B2 2 30N 27 20 E
Okaputa, Namibia . . . . 88 C2 20 5 S 17 0 E
Okara, Pakistan . . . . . 68 D5 30 50N 73 31 E
Okaukuejo, Namibia . . . 88 B2 19 10 S 16 0 E
Okavango Delta,
Botswana . . . . 88 B3 18 45 S 22 45 E
Okavango Swamp =
Okavango Delta,
Botswana . . . . 88 B3 18 45 S 22 45 E
Okaya, Japan . . . . 55 F9 36 5N 138 10 E
Okayama, Japan . . . . . 55 G6 34 40N 133 54 E
Okayama □, Japan . . . . 55 G6 35 0N 133 50 E
Okazaki, Japan . . . . . . 55 G8 34 57N 137 10 E
Oke-Iho, Nigeria . . . . . 83 D5 8 1N 3 18 E
Okęcie, Warszawa ✈
(WAW), Poland . . . . 31 F7 52 9N 20 59 E
Okeechobee, U.S.A. . . . 115 M5 27 15N 80 50W
Okeechobee, L., U.S.A. . 115 M5 27 0N 80 50W
Okefenokee △, U.S.A. . . 115 K4 30 44N 82 7W
Okefenokee Swamp,
U.S.A. 115 K4 30 40N 82 20W
Okehampton, U.K. 15 G4 50 44N 4 0W
Okene, Nigeria . . . . . . 83 D6 7 32N 6 11 E
Oker →, Germany . . . . 24 C6 52 32N 10 22 E
Okha, India . . . . 68 H3 22 27N 69 4 E
Okha, Russia . . . . 53 D15 53 40N 143 0 E
Ókhi Óros, Greece . . . . 46 C6 38 5N 24 25 E
Okhotsk, Russia . . . . . 53 D15 59 20N 143 10 E
Okhotsk, Sea of, Asia . . 53 D15 55 0N 145 0 E
Okhotskiy Perevoz,
Russia . . . . 53 C14 61 52N 135 35 E
Okhtyrka, Ukraine . . . . 33 G8 50 25N 35 0 E
Oki-Shotō, Japan . . . . . 55 F6 36 5N 133 15 E
Okiep, S. Africa . . . . . 88 D2 29 39 S 17 53 E
Okigwi, Nigeria . . . . . 83 D6 5 52N 7 20 E
Okija, Nigeria . . . . . . 83 D6 5 54N 6 55 E
Okinawa □, Japan . . . . 55 L4 26 40N 128 0 E
Okinawa-Guntō, Japan . 55 L4 26 40N 128 0 E
Okinawa-Jima, Japan . . 55 L4 26 32N 128 0 E
Okino-erabu-Shima,
Japan . . . . 55 L4 27 21N 128 33 E
Okitipupa, Nigeria . . . . 83 D5 6 31N 4 50 E
Oklahoma □, U.S.A. . . . 113 H6 35 20N 97 30W
Oklahoma City, U.S.A. . 113 H6 35 30N 97 30W
Okmulgee, U.S.A. 113 H7 35 37N 95 58W
Oknitsa = Ocniţa,
Moldova . . . . 29 B12 48 25N 27 30 E
Oko, W. → , Sudan . . . . 80 C4 21 15N 35 56 E
Okolo, Uganda . . . . . . 86 B3 2 37N 31 8 E
Okolona, U.S.A. 113 J10 34 0N 88 45W
Okombahe, Namibia . . . 88 C2 21 23 S 15 22 E
Okonek, Poland . . . . . 30 E3 53 32N 16 51 E
Okotoks, Canada 102 C6 50 43N 113 58W
Okrika, Nigeria . . . . . 83 E6 4 40N 7 10 E
Oksibil, Indonesia . . . . 63 E10 4 59 S 140 35 E
Oktabrsk = Oktyabrsk,
Kazakhstan . . . . . . 52 E6 49 28N 57 25 E
Oktyabrsk, Kazakhstan . 52 E6 49 28N 57 25 E
Oktyabrsk, Russia . . . . 34 D9 53 11N 48 40 E
Oktyabrskiy =
Aktsyabrski, Belarus . 33 F5 52 38N 28 53 E
Oktyabrskiy, Russia . . . 35 G5 47 30N 40 4 E
Oktyabrskoy
Revolyutsii, Ostrov,
Russia . . . . 53 B10 79 30N 97 0 E
Oktyabrskoye =
Zhovtneve, Ukraine . 33 J7 46 54N 32 3 E
Okulovka, Russia . . . . 32 C7 58 25N 33 19 E
Okuru, N.Z. . . . . 91 K2 43 55 S 168 55 E
Okushiri-Tō, Japan . . . 54 C9 42 15N 139 30 E
Okuta, Nigeria . . . . . . 83 D5 9 14N 3 12 E
Okwa →, Botswana . . . 88 C3 22 30 S 23 0 E
Ola, U.S.A. 113 H8 35 2N 93 13W
Olancha, U.S.A. 111 J8 36 17N 118 1W
Olancha Pk., U.S.A. . . . 111 J8 36 15N 118 7W
Olanchito, Honduras . . 120 C2 15 30N 86 30W
Öland, Sweden . . . . . . 11 H10 56 45N 16 38 E
Ölands norra udde,
Sweden . . . . 11 G11 57 22N 17 5 E
Ölands södra udde,
Sweden . . . . 11 H10 56 12N 16 23 E
Olargues, France . . . . . 20 E6 43 34N 2 53 E
Olary, Australia . . . . . 95 E3 32 18 S 140 19 E
Olascoaga, Argentina . . 126 D3 35 15 S 60 39W
Olathe, U.S.A. 112 F7 38 53N 94 49W
Olavarría, Argentina . . . 126 D3 36 55 S 60 20W
Oława, Poland . . . . . . 31 H4 50 57N 17 20 E
Olbernhau, Germany . . 24 E9 50 40N 13 19 E
Ólbia, Italy . . . . 42 B2 40 55N 9 31 E
Ólbia, G. di, Italy . . . . 42 B2 40 55N 9 39 E
Olching, Germany . . . . 25 G7 48 12N 11 21 E
Olcott, U.S.A. 116 C6 43 20N 78 42W
Old Bahama Chan. =
Bahama, Canal Viejo
de, W. Indies 120 B4 22 10N 77 30W
Old Baldy Mt. = San
Antonio, Mt., U.S.A. . 111 L9 34 17N 117 38W
Old Castile = Castilla y
Leon □, Spain 36 D6 42 0N 5 0W
Old Crow, Canada 100 B6 67 30N 139 55W
Old Dale, U.S.A. 111 L11 34 8N 115 47W
Old Forge, N.Y., U.S.A. . 117 C10 43 43N 74 58W
Old Forge, Pa., U.S.A. . . 117 E9 41 22N 75 45W

Old Perlican, Canada . . 105 C9 48 5N 53 1W
Old Shinyanga,
Tanzania . . . . 86 C3 3 33 S 33 27 E
Old Speck Mt., U.S.A. . . 117 B14 44 34N 70 57W
Old Town, U.S.A. 115 C11 44 56N 68 39W
Old Washington, U.S.A. . 116 F3 40 2N 81 27W
Old Wives L., Canada . . 103 C7 50 5N 106 0W
Oldbury, U.K. 15 F5 51 38N 2 33W
Oldcastle, Ireland 12 C4 53 46N 7 10W
Oldeani, Tanzania . . . . 86 C4 3 22 S 35 35 E
Oldenburg,
Niedersachsen,
Germany . . . . 24 B4 53 9N 8 13 E
Oldenburg,
Schleswig-Holstein,
Germany . . . . 24 A6 54 17N 10 52 E
Oldenzaal, Neths. . . . . 17 B6 52 19N 6 53 E
Oldham, U.K. 14 D5 53 33N 2 7W
Oldman →, Canada . . . 102 D6 49 57N 111 42W
Oldmeldrum, U.K. 13 D6 57 20N 2 19W
Olds, Canada 102 C6 51 50N 114 10W
Olduvai Gorge,
Tanzania . . . . 86 C4 2 57 S 35 23 E
Oldziyt, Mongolia . . . . 56 B5 44 40N 109 1 E
Olean, U.S.A. 116 D6 42 5N 78 26W
Olecko, Poland . . . . . . 30 D9 54 2N 22 31 E
Oléggio, Italy . . . . 40 C5 45 36N 8 38 E
Oleiros, Portugal 36 F3 39 56N 7 56W
Oleiros, Spain 36 B2 43 20N 8 19W
Olekma →, Russia . . . . 53 C13 60 22N 120 42 E
Olekminsk, Russia . . . . 53 C13 60 25N 120 30 E
Oleksandriya,
Kirovohrad, Ukraine . 33 H7 48 42N 33 3 E
Oleksandriya, Rivne,
Ukraine . . . . 33 G4 50 37N 26 19 E
Oleksandrovka, Ukraine 33 H7 48 38N 30 56 E
Olema, U.S.A. 110 G4 38 3N 122 47W
Olenek, Russia . . . . . . 53 C12 68 28N 112 18 E
Olenek →, Russia . . . . 53 B13 73 0N 120 10 E
Olenino, Russia . . . . . 32 D7 56 15N 33 30 E
Oléron, Î. d', France . . . 20 C2 45 55N 1 15W
Olesk, Ukraine . . . . . . 31 G11 51 6N 24 11 E
Olešnica, Poland . . . . . 31 G4 51 13N 17 22 E
Olesno, Poland . . . . . . 31 H5 50 51N 18 26 E
Olevsk, Ukraine . . . . . 33 G4 51 12N 27 39 E
Olga, Russia . . . . 53 E14 43 50N 135 14 E
Olga, L., Canada 104 C4 49 47N 77 15W
Olga, Mt., Australia . . . 93 E5 25 20 S 130 50 E
Ølgod, Denmark . . . . . 11 J2 55 49N 8 36 E
Olhão, Portugal 37 H3 37 3N 7 48W
Olhopil, Ukraine . . . . . 29 B14 48 12N 29 30 E
Olhovatka, Russia . . . . 30 30 54 30N 22 18 E
Olib, Croatia . . . . 41 D11 44 23N 14 44 E
Oliena, Italy . . . . 42 B2 40 16N 9 24 E
Oliete, Spain 38 D4 41 1N 0 41W
Olifants = Elefantes →,
Africa . . . . 89 C5 24 10 S 32 40 E
Olifants →, Namibia . . . 88 C2 25 30 S 19 30 E
Olifantshoek, S. Africa . 88 D3 27 57 S 22 42 E
Ólimbos, Greece . . . . . 47 F9 35 44N 27 11 E
Ólimbos, Óros, Greece . 44 F6 40 6N 22 23 E
Olímpia, Brazil . . . . . . 127 A6 20 44 S 48 54W
Olinda, Brazil . . . . 125 E12 8 1 S 34 51W
Olite, Spain 38 C3 42 29N 1 40W
Oliva, Argentina . . . . . 126 C3 32 0 S 63 38W
Oliva, Spain 39 G4 38 58N 0 9W
Oliva, Punta del, Spain . 36 B5 43 37N 5 28W
Oliva de la Frontera,
Spain 37 G4 38 17N 6 54W
Olivares, Spain 38 F2 39 46N 2 20W
Olivehurst, U.S.A. 110 F5 39 6N 121 34W
Oliveira de Azeméis,
Portugal 36 E2 40 49N 8 29W
Oliveira do Douro,
Portugal 36 D2 41 5N 8 2W
Olivenza, Spain 37 G3 38 41N 7 9W
Oliver, Canada 102 D5 49 13N 119 37W
Oliver L., Canada 103 B8 56 56N 103 22W
Olivet, France . . . . . . 19 E8 47 51N 1 55 E
Olkhovka, Russia . . . . 34 F7 49 48N 44 32 E
Olkusz, Poland . . . . . . 31 H6 50 18N 19 33 E
Ollagüe, Chile . . . . . . 126 A2 21 15 S 68 10W
Olmedo, Spain 36 D6 41 20N 4 43W
Olmeto, France . . . . . . 21 G12 41 43N 8 55 E
Olney, Ill., U.S.A. 114 F1 38 44N 88 5W
Olney, Tex., U.S.A. 113 J5 33 22N 98 45W
Olofström, Sweden . . . 11 H8 56 17N 14 32 E
Oloma, Cameroon . . . . 83 E7 3 29N 11 19 E
Olomane →, Canada . . . 105 B7 50 14N 60 37W
Olomouc, Czech Rep. . . 27 B9 49 38N 17 12 E
Olomoucký □,
Czech Rep. . . . . . . 27 B10 49 45N 17 5 E
Olonets, Russia . . . . . 32 B7 61 0N 32 54 E
Olongapo, Phil. . . . . . 61 D4 14 50N 120 18 E
Olonne-sur-Mer, France 20 B2 46 32N 1 47W
Oloron, Gave d' →,
France 20 E2 43 33N 1 5W
Oloron-Ste-Marie,
France 20 E3 43 11N 0 38W
Olot, Spain . . . . 38 C7 42 11N 2 30 E
Olovo, Bos.-H. . . . . . . 28 E3 44 8N 18 35 E
Olovyannaya, Russia . . 53 D12 50 58N 115 35 E
Oloy →, Russia . . . . . 53 C16 66 29N 159 29 E
Olsberg, Germany . . . . 24 D4 51 21N 8 31 E
Olshammar, Sweden . . . 11 F8 58 45N 14 48 E
Olshanka, Ukraine . . . . 33 H6 48 16N 30 58 E
Olshany, Ukraine . . . . 33 G8 50 3N 35 53 E
Olsztyn, Poland . . . . . 30 E7 53 48N 20 29 E
Olsztynek, Poland . . . . 30 E7 53 34N 20 19 E
Olt □, Romania . . . . . . 29 F9 44 20N 24 30 E
Olt →, Romania . . . . . 29 G9 43 43N 24 51 E
Oltenia, Romania . . . . 29 F11 44 7N 26 42 E
Olton, U.S.A. 113 H3 34 11N 102 8W
Oltu, Turkey . . . . 73 B9 40 35N 41 58 E
Oluanpi, Taiwan . . . . . 59 G13 21 54N 120 51 E
Olula del Río, Spain . . . 39 H2 37 21N 2 18W
Olur, Turkey . . . . 73 B10 40 49N 42 14 E
Olutanga, Phil. . . . . . . 61 H5 7 26N 122 54 E
Olvega, Spain 38 D2 41 47N 1 59W
Olvera, Spain 37 J5 36 55N 5 18W
Olymbos, Cyprus . . . . 49 D12 35 11N 33 45 E
Olympia, Greece . . . . . 46 D3 37 39N 21 39 E
Olympia, U.S.A. 110 D4 47 3N 122 53W
Olympic △, Australia . . 95 E2 30 30 S 136 55 E
Olympic Dam, Australia 95 E2 30 30 S 136 55 E
Olympic Mts., U.S.A. . . 110 C3 47 55N 123 45W
Olympus, Cyprus . . . . 49 E11 34 56N 32 52 E
Olympus, Mt. =
Ólimbos, Óros, Greece 44 F6 40 6N 22 23 E
Olympus, Mt. = Uludağ,
Turkey . . . . 47 F13 40 4N 29 13 E
Olympus, Mt., U.S.A. . . 110 C3 47 48N 123 43W
Olyphant, U.S.A. 117 E9 41 27N 75 36W
Om →, Russia . . . . . . 52 D8 54 59N 73 22 E

Om Hajer, Eritrea . . . . 81 E4 14 20N 36 41 E
Om Koi, Thailand . . . . 64 D2 17 48N 98 22 E
Ōmachi, Japan . . . . . . 54 D10 41 45N 141 5 E
Ōmachi, Japan . . . . . . 55 F8 36 30N 137 50 E
Omae-Zaki, Japan . . . . 55 G9 34 36N 138 14 E
Ōmagari, Japan . . . . . 54 E10 39 27N 140 29 E
Omagh, U.K. 12 B4 54 36N 7 19W
Omagh □, U.K. 12 B4 54 35N 7 15W
Omaha, U.S.A. 112 E7 41 17N 95 58W
Omak, U.S.A. 108 B4 48 25N 119 31W
Omalos, Greece . . . . . 49 D5 35 19N 23 55 E
Oman ■, Asia . . . . . . 75 C6 23 0N 58 0 E
Oman, G. of, Asia . . . . 71 E8 24 30N 58 30 E
Omaruru, Namibia . . . . 88 C2 21 26 S 16 0 E
Omaruru →, Namibia . . 88 C1 22 7 S 14 15 E
Omate, Peru . . . . 124 G4 16 45 S 71 0W
Ombai, Selat, Indonesia 63 F6 8 30 S 124 50 E
Omboué, Gabon . . . . . 84 E1 1 35 S 9 15 E
Ombrone →, Italy . . . . 40 F8 42 42N 11 5 E
Omdurmân, Sudan . . . 81 D3 15 40N 32 28 E
Omegna, Italy . . . . . . 40 C5 45 53N 8 24 E
Omemee, Canada 116 B6 44 18N 78 33W
Omeonga, Dem. Rep. of
the Congo . . . . 86 C1 3 40 S 24 22 E
Ometepe, I. de, Nic. . . . 120 D2 11 32N 85 35W
Ometepec, Mexico 119 D5 16 39N 98 23W
Ominato, Japan . . . . . 54 D10 41 17N 141 10 E
Omineca →, Canada . . . 102 B4 56 3N 124 16W
Omiš, Croatia . . . . 41 E13 43 28N 16 40 E
Omišalj, Croatia . . . . . 41 C11 45 13N 14 32 E
Omitara, Namibia . . . . 88 C2 22 16 S 18 2 E
Ōmiya, Japan . . . . 55 G9 35 54N 139 38 E
Ommen, Neths. . . . . . . 17 B6 52 31N 6 26 E
Ömnögovi □, Mongolia . 56 C3 43 15N 104 0 E
Omo →, Ethiopia . . . . 81 F4 5 54N 35 55 E
Omo Valley, Ethiopia . . 81 F4 6 25N 36 10 E
Omodeo, L., Italy . . . . 42 B1 40 8N 8 56 E
Omodhos, Cyprus . . . . 49 E11 34 51N 32 48 E
Omoko, Nigeria . . . . . 83 D6 5 19N 6 40 E
Omolon →, Russia . . . . 53 C16 68 42N 158 36 E
Omono-Gawa →, Japan . 54 E10 39 46N 140 3 E
Omsk, Russia . . . . 52 D8 55 0N 73 12 E
Omsukchan, Russia . . . 53 C16 62 32N 155 48 E
Ōmu, Japan . . . . 54 B11 44 34N 142 58 E
Omul, Vf., Romania . . . 29 E10 45 27N 25 29 E
Omulew →, Poland . . . 31 E8 53 5N 21 33 E
Ōmura, Japan . . . . 55 H4 32 56N 129 57 E
Omuramba
Omatako →, Namibia . 88 B2 17 45 S 20 25 E
Omuramba Ovambo →,
Namibia . . . . 88 B3 18 45 S 16 59 E
Omurtag, Bulgaria . . . . 45 C10 43 8N 26 26 E
Ōmuta, Japan . . . . 55 H5 33 5N 130 26 E
Oña, Spain 36 C7 42 43N 3 25W
Onaga, U.S.A. 112 F6 39 29N 96 10W
Onalaska, U.S.A. 112 D9 43 53N 91 14W
Onancock, U.S.A. 114 G8 37 43N 75 45W
Onang, Indonesia . . . . 63 E5 3 2 S 118 49 E
Onaping L., Canada . . . 104 C3 47 3N 81 30W
Oñati, Spain 38 B2 43 3N 2 25W
Onavas, Mexico 118 B3 28 28N 109 30W
Onawa, U.S.A. 112 D6 42 2N 96 6W
Oncócua, Angola . . . . . 88 B1 16 30 S 13 25 E
Onda, Spain 38 F4 39 55N 0 17W
Ondaejin, N. Korea . . . 57 D15 41 34N 129 40 E
Ondangwa, Namibia . . . 88 B2 17 57 S 16 4 E
Ondarroa, Spain 38 B2 43 19N 2 25W
Ondava →, Slovak Rep. . 27 C14 48 27N 21 48 E
Ondjiva, Angola . . . . . 88 B2 16 48 S 15 50 E
Ondo, Nigeria . . . . . . 83 D5 7 4N 4 47 E
Ondo □, Nigeria . . . . . 83 D6 6 45N 5 0 E
Öndörshil, Mongolia . . 56 B5 45 13N 108 5 E
Öndverðarnes, Iceland . 8 D1 64 52N 24 0W
One Tree, Australia . . . 95 E3 34 11 S 144 43 E
Onega, Russia . . . . . . 52 C4 64 0N 38 10 E
Onega →, Russia . . . . . 6 C13 63 58N 38 2 E
Onega, L. =
Onezhskoye Ozero,
Russia . . . . 32 B8 61 44N 35 22 E
Oneida, U.S.A. 117 C9 43 6N 75 39W
Oneida L., U.S.A. 117 C9 43 12N 75 54W
O'Neill, U.S.A. 112 D5 42 27N 98 39W
Onekotan, Ostrov,
Russia . . . . 53 E16 49 25N 154 45 E
Onema, Dem. Rep. of
the Congo . . . . 86 C1 4 35 S 24 30 E
Oneonta, U.S.A. 117 D9 42 27N 75 4W
Oneşti, Romania . . . . . 29 D11 46 17N 26 47 E
Onezhskoye Ozero,
Russia . . . . 32 B8 61 44N 35 22 E
Ongarue, N.Z. . . . . . . 91 H5 38 42 S 175 19 E
Ongers →, S. Africa . . . 88 E3 31 4 S 23 13 E
Ongerup, Australia . . . 93 F2 33 58 S 118 28 E
Ongjin, N. Korea . . . . . 57 F13 37 56N 125 21 E
Ongkharak, Thailand . . 64 E3 14 8N 101 1 E
Ongniud Qi, China . . . 57 C10 43 0N 118 38 E
Ongoka, Dem. Rep. of
the Congo . . . . 86 C2 1 20 S 26 0 E
Ongole, India . . . . 66 M12 15 33N 80 2 E
Ongon = Havirga,
Mongolia . . . . 56 B7 45 41N 113 5 E
Oni, Georgia . . . . 35 J6 42 33N 43 26 E
Onida, U.S.A. 112 C4 44 42N 100 4W
Onilahy →, Madag. . . . 89 C7 23 34 S 43 45 E
Onitsha, Nigeria . . . . . 83 D6 6 6N 6 42 E
Onoda, Japan . . . . . . 55 G5 33 59N 131 11 E
Onpyŏng-ni, S. Korea . . 57 H14 33 25N 126 55 E
Onsala, Sweden . . . . . 11 G6 57 26N 12 0 E
Onslow, Australia . . . . 92 D2 21 40 S 115 12 E
Onslow B., U.S.A. 115 H7 34 20N 77 15W
Ontake-San, Japan . . . 55 G8 35 53N 137 29 E
Ontario, Calif., U.S.A. . . 111 L9 34 4N 117 39W
Ontario, Oreg., U.S.A. . . 108 D5 44 2N 116 58W
Ontario □, Canada 104 B2 48 0N 83 0W
Ontario, L., N. Amer. . . 116 C8 43 20N 78 0W
Ontinyent, Spain 39 G4 38 50N 0 35W
Ontonagon, U.S.A. . . . 112 B10 46 52N 89 19W
Ontur, Spain 39 G3 38 38N 1 29W
Onyx, U.S.A. 111 K8 35 41N 118 14W
Oodnadatta, Australia . . 95 D2 27 33 S 135 30 E
Ooldea, Australia . . . . 93 F5 30 27 S 131 50 E
Oombulgurri, Australia . 92 C4 15 15 S 127 45 E
Oorindi, Australia . . . . 94 C3 20 40 S 141 1 E
Oost-Vlaanderen □,
Belgium . . . . 17 C3 51 5N 3 50 E
Oostende, Belgium . . . 17 C2 51 15N 2 54 E
Oosterhout, Neths. . . . 17 C4 51 39N 4 47 E
Oosterschelde →, Neths. 17 C4 51 33N 4 0 E
Oosterwolde, Neths. . . 17 B6 53 0N 6 17 E

Opala, Dem. Rep. of
the Congo . . . . 86 C1 0 40 S 24 20 E
Opalenica, Poland . . . . 31 F3 52 18N 16 24 E
Opan, Bulgaria . . . . . . 45 D9 42 13N 25 41 E
Opanake, Sri Lanka . . . 66 R12 6 35N 80 40 E
Opasatika, Canada 104 C3 49 30N 82 50W
Opasquia △, Canada . . . 104 B1 53 33N 93 5W
Opatija, Croatia . . . . . 41 C11 45 21N 14 17 E
Opatów, Poland . . . . . 31 H8 50 50N 21 27 E
Opava, Czech Rep. . . . . 27 B10 49 57N 17 58 E
Opelika, U.S.A. 115 J3 32 39N 85 23W
Opelousas, U.S.A. 113 K8 30 32N 92 5W
Opémisca, L., Canada . . 104 C5 50 0N 75 0W
Opheim, U.S.A. 108 B10 48 51N 106 24W
Ophthalmia Ra.,
Australia . . . . 92 D2 23 15 S 119 30 E
Opi, Nigeria . . . . 83 D6 6 36N 7 28 E
Opinaca →, Canada . . . 104 B4 52 15N 78 2W
Opinaca, Rés., Canada . 104 B4 52 39N 76 20W
Opinnagau →, Canada . 104 B3 54 12N 82 25W
Opiscotéo, L., Canada . . 105 B6 53 10N 68 10W
Opobo, Nigeria . . . . . . 83 E6 4 35N 7 34 E
Opochka, Russia . . . . . 32 D5 56 42N 28 45 E
Opoczno, Poland . . . . . 31 G7 51 22N 20 18 E
Opol, Phil. . . . . 61 G6 8 31N 124 34 E
Opole, Poland . . . . . . 31 H4 50 42N 17 58 E
Opole Lubelskie, Poland 31 G8 51 9N 21 58 E
Opolskie □, Poland . . . 31 H5 50 30N 17 45 E
Oponono L., Namibia . . 88 B2 18 8 S 15 45 E
Oporto = Porto,
Portugal 36 D2 41 8N 8 40W
Opotiki, N.Z. . . . . 91 H6 38 1 S 177 19 E
Opp, U.S.A. 115 K2 31 17N 86 16W
Oppdal, Norway . . . . . 9 E13 62 35N 9 41 E
Óppido Mamertina, Italy 43 D8 38 16N 15 59 E
Opportunity, U.S.A. . . . 108 C5 47 39N 117 15W
Oprişor, Romania . . . . 29 F8 44 17N 23 5 E
Oprtalj, Croatia . . . . . 41 C10 45 23N 13 50 E
Opua, N.Z. . . . . 91 F5 35 19 S 174 9 E
Opunake, N.Z. . . . . . . 91 H4 39 26 S 173 52 E
Opuwo, Namibia . . . . . 88 B1 18 3 S 13 45 E
Opuzen, Croatia . . . . . 41 E14 43 1N 17 34 E
Ora, Cyprus . . . . 49 E12 34 51N 33 12 E
Oracle, U.S.A. 109 K8 32 37N 110 46W
Oradea, Romania . . . . 28 C6 47 2N 21 58 E
Öræfajökull, Iceland . . . 8 D5 64 2N 16 39W
Orahovac, Serbia & M. . 44 D4 42 24N 20 40 E
Orahovica, Croatia . . . 28 E2 45 35N 17 52 E
Orai, India . . . . 69 G8 25 58N 79 30 E
Oraison, France . . . . . 21 E9 43 55N 5 55 E
Oral = Zhayyq →,
Kazakhstan . . . . . . 52 E6 47 0N 51 48 E
Oral, Kazakhstan . . . . 34 E10 51 20N 51 20 E
Oran, Algeria 78 A5 35 45N 0 39W
Orange, Australia . . . . 95 E4 33 15 S 149 7 E
Orange, France . . . . . . 21 D8 44 8N 4 47 E
Orange, Calif., U.S.A. . . 111 M9 33 47N 117 51W
Orange, Mass., U.S.A. . . 117 D12 42 35N 72 19W
Orange, Tex., U.S.A. . . . 113 K8 30 6N 93 44W
Orange, Va., U.S.A. . . . 114 F6 38 15N 78 7W
Orange →, S. Africa . . . 88 D2 28 41 S 16 28 E
Orange, C., Brazil 125 C8 4 20N 51 30W
Orange Cove, U.S.A. . . . 110 J7 36 38N 119 19W
Orange Free State =
Free State □, S. Africa 88 D4 28 30 S 27 0 E
Orange Grove, U.S.A. . . 113 M6 27 58N 97 56W
Orange Walk, Belize . . . 119 D7 18 6N 88 33W
Orangeburg, U.S.A. . . . 115 J5 33 30N 80 52W
Orangeville, Canada . . . 104 D3 43 55N 80 5W
Orango, Guinea-Biss. . . 82 C1 11 5N 16 0W
Orani, Phil. . . . . 61 D4 14 49N 120 32 E
Oranienburg, Germany . 24 C9 52 45N 13 14 E
Oranje = Orange →,
S. Africa . . . . 88 D2 28 41 S 16 28 E
Oranjemund, Namibia . 88 D2 28 38 S 16 29 E
Oranjerivier, S. Africa . . 88 D3 29 40 S 24 12 E
Oranjestad, Aruba 121 D5 12 32N 70 2W
Orapa, Botswana . . . . . 85 J5 21 15 S 25 30 E
Orarak, Sudan . . . . . . 81 F3 6 15N 32 23 E
Oras, Phil. . . . . 61 E6 12 9N 125 28 E
Orašje, Bos.-H. . . . . . . 28 E3 45 1N 18 42 E
Orăştie, Romania . . . . 29 E8 45 50N 23 10 E
Orava →, Slovak Rep. . . 27 B12 49 9N 19 8 E
Orava, Vodná nádrž,
Slovak Rep. . . . . . . 27 B12 49 25N 19 35 E
Oraviţa, Romania . . . . 28 E6 45 6N 21 43 E
Orb →, France . . . . . . 20 E7 43 15N 3 18 E
Orba →, Italy . . . . 40 D5 44 53N 8 37 E
Ørbæk, Denmark . . . . . 11 J4 55 17N 10 39 E
Orbe, Switz. . . . . 25 J2 46 43N 6 32 E
Orbec, France . . . . . . 18 C7 49 1N 0 23 E
Orbetello, Italy . . . . . . 41 F8 42 27N 11 13 E
Órbigo →, Spain 36 C5 42 5N 5 42W
Orbisonia, U.S.A. 116 F7 40 15N 77 54W
Orbost, Australia . . . . . 95 F4 37 40 S 148 29 E
Ørbyhus, Sweden . . . . 10 D11 60 15N 17 43 E
Orcadas, Antarctica . . . 5 C18 60 44 S 44 37W
Orcas I., U.S.A. 110 B4 48 42N 122 56W
Orce, Spain 39 H2 37 44N 2 28W
Orce →, Spain 39 H2 37 44N 2 28W
Orchard City, U.S.A. . . . 109 G10 38 50N 107 58W
Orchies, France . . . . . 19 B10 50 28N 3 14 E
Orchila, I., Venezuela . . 121 D6 11 48N 66 10W
Orchilla, Pta., Canary Is. 48 G1 27 42N 18 10W
Órcia →, Italy . . . . . . 41 F8 42 58N 11 21 E
Orco →, Italy . . . . 40 C4 45 10N 7 52 E
Orcutt, U.S.A. 111 L6 34 52N 120 27W
Ord →, Australia . . . . . 92 C4 15 33 S 128 15 E
Ord, Mt., Australia . . . . 92 C4 17 20 S 125 34 E
Ordenes = Ordes, Spain 36 B2 43 5N 8 29W
Orderville, U.S.A. 109 H7 37 17N 112 38W
Ordes, Spain 36 B2 43 5N 8 29W
Ordesa y Monte
Perdido △, Spain . . . 38 C4 42 40N 0 10W
Ording = St-Peter-
Ording, Germany . . . 24 A4 54 20N 8 36 E
Ordos = Mu Us Shamo,
China . . . . 56 E5 39 0N 109 0 E
Ordu, Turkey . . . . 72 B7 40 55N 37 53 E
Ordubad, Azerbaijan . . 73 C12 38 54N 46 1 E
Orduña, Álava, Spain . . 38 C2 42 58N 2 58W
Orduña, Granada, Spain 37 H7 37 20N 3 30W
Ore →, Italy . . . . 40 C4 45 10N 7 52 E
Ore, Dem. Rep. of
the Congo . . . . 86 B2 3 17N 29 30 E
Ore Mts. = Erzgebirge,
Germany . . . . 24 E8 50 27N 12 55 E
Orebić, Croatia . . . . . . 41 F14 43 0N 17 11 E
Örebro, Sweden . . . . . 10 E9 59 20N 15 18 E
Örebro län □, Sweden . 10 E9 59 20N 15 0 E
Orecchiella △, Italy . . . 40 D7 44 16N 10 22 E
Oregon, U.S.A. 112 D10 42 1N 89 20W
Oregon □, U.S.A. 108 E3 44 0N 121 0W
Oregon City, U.S.A. . . . 110 E4 45 21N 122 36W
Oregon Dunes △, U.S.A. 108 E1 43 3N 123 26W

Öregrund, Sweden .... 10 D12 60 21N 18 30 E
Öregrundsgrepen,
 Sweden .... 10 D12 60 25N 18 15 E
Orekhov = Orikhiv,
 Ukraine .... 33 J8 47 30N 35 48 E
Orekhovo-Zuyevo,
 Russia .... 32 E10 55 50N 38 55 E
Orel, Russia ...... 33 F9 52 57N 36 3 E
Orel →, Ukraine .... 33 H8 48 40N 34 39 E
Orellana, Spain 37 F5 39 1N 5 32W
Orellana, Canal de,
 Spain 37 F5 39 2N 6 0W
Orellana, Embalse de,
 Spain 37 F5 39 5N 5 10W
Orem, U.S.A. 108 F8 40 19N 111 42W
Ören, Turkey ...... 47 D9 37 3N 27 57 E
Orenburg, Russia ... 52 D6 51 45N 55 6 E
Örencik, Turkey .... 47 B11 39 16N 29 33 E
Orense = Ourense,
 Spain 36 C3 42 19N 7 55W
Orense □, Spain 36 C3 42 15N 7 51W
Orepuki, N.Z. ..... 91 M1 46 19 S 167 46 E
Orestiás, Greece ... 45 E10 41 30N 26 33 E
Orestos Pereyra, Mexico 118 B3 26 31N 105 40W
Öresund, Europe ... 11 J6 55 45N 12 45 E
Orford Ness, U.K. .. 15 E9 52 5N 1 35 E
Organ Pipe Cactus △,
 U.S.A. 109 K7 32 0N 113 10W
Organos, Pta. de los,
 Canary Is. 48 F2 28 12N 17 17W
Organyà, Spain .... 38 C6 42 13N 1 20 E
Orgaz, Spain 37 F7 39 39N 3 53W
Orgeyev = Orhei,
 Moldova .... 29 C13 47 24N 28 50 E
Orhaneli, Turkey ... 45 G12 39 54N 28 59 E
Orhaneli →, Turkey . 45 G12 39 50N 28 55 E
Orhangazi, Turkey .. 45 F13 40 29N 29 18 E
Orhei, Moldova .... 29 C13 47 24N 28 50 E
Orhon Gol →,
 Mongolia .... 60 A5 50 21N 106 0 E
Ória, Italy .... 43 B10 40 30N 17 38 E
Oriental, Cordillera,
 Colombia 124 B4 6 0N 73 0W
Oriental, Grand Erg,
 Algeria .... 78 B7 30 0N 6 30 E
Orientale □, Dem. Rep.
 of the Congo .... 86 B2 2 20N 26 0 E
Oriente, Argentina .. 126 D3 38 44 S 60 37W
Orihuela, Spain 39 G4 38 7N 0 55W
Orihuela del Tremedal,
 Spain 38 E3 40 33N 1 39W
Orikhiv, Ukraine ... 33 J8 47 30N 35 48 E
Orikum, Albania .... 44 F3 40 20N 19 30 E
Orillia, Canada 116 B5 44 40N 79 24W
Orinoco →, Venezuela 124 B6 9 15N 61 30W
Orion, Canada 103 D6 49 27N 110 49W
Oriskany, U.S.A. ... 117 C9 43 10N 75 20W
Orissa □, India .... 67 K14 20 0N 84 0 E
Orissaare, Estonia .. 9 G20 58 34N 23 5 E
Oristano, Italy .... 42 C1 39 54N 8 36 E
Oristano, G. di, Italy 42 C1 39 50N 8 29 E
Orizaba, Mexico ... 119 D5 18 51N 97 6W
Orizaba, Pico de, Mexico 119 D5 19 0N 97 20W
Orizare, Bulgaria ... 45 D11 42 44N 27 39 E
Orjen, Bos.-H. ..... 44 D2 42 35N 18 34 E
Orjiva, Spain 37 J7 36 53N 3 24W
Orkanger, Norway .. 8 E13 63 18N 9 52 E
Örkelljunga, Sweden 11 H7 56 17N 13 17 E
Örken, Sweden .... 11 G9 56 9N 15 1 E
Örkény, Hungary ... 28 C4 47 9N 19 26 E
Orkla →, Norway ... 8 E13 63 18N 9 51 E
Orkney, S. Africa ... 88 D4 26 58 S 26 40 E
Orkney □, U.K. 13 B5 59 2N 3 13W
Orkney Is., U.K. ... 13 B5 59 0N 3 0W
Orland, U.S.A. 110 F4 39 45N 122 12W
Orlando, U.S.A. 115 L5 28 33N 81 23W
Orlando, C. d', Italy . 43 D7 38 10N 14 43 E
Orléanais, France .. 19 C8 48 0N 2 0 E
Orléans, France .... 19 E8 47 54N 1 52 E
Orleans, U.S.A. 117 B12 44 49N 72 12W
Orléans, Î. d', Canada 105 C5 46 54N 70 58W
Orlice →, Czech Rep. 26 A8 50 13N 15 50 E
Orlivka, Ukraine ... 29 E13 45 19N 28 27 E
Orlov, Slovak Rep. .. 27 B13 49 17N 20 51 E
Orlov Gay, Russia .. 34 E9 50 56N 48 19 E
Orlová, Czech Rep. . 27 B11 49 51N 18 26 E
Orlovat, Serbia & M. 28 E5 45 14N 20 33 E
Orly, Paris ✈ (ORY),
 France .... 19 D9 48 44N 2 23 E
Ormara, Pakistan ... 66 G4 25 16N 64 33 E
Ormea, Italy ...... 40 D4 44 9N 7 54 E
Ormília, Greece .... 44 F7 40 16N 23 39 E
Ormoc, Phil. ...... 61 F6 11 0N 124 37 E
Ormond, N.Z. ..... 91 H6 38 33 S 177 56 E
Ormond Beach, U.S.A. 115 L5 29 17N 81 3W
Ormož, Slovenia ... 41 B13 46 25N 16 10 E
Ormskirk, U.K. 14 D5 53 35N 2 54W
Ormstown, Canada .. 117 A11 45 8N 74 0W
Ornans, France .... 19 E13 47 7N 6 10 E
Orne □, France .... 18 D7 48 40N 0 5 E
Orne →, France 18 C6 49 18N 0 15W
Orneta, Poland .... 30 D7 54 8N 20 9 E
Örnö, Sweden ..... 10 E12 59 4N 18 24 E
Örnsköldsvik, Sweden 10 A12 63 17N 18 40 E
Oro, N. Korea ..... 57 D14 40 1N 127 27 E
Oro →, Mexico 118 B3 25 35N 105 2W
Oro Grande, U.S.A. . 111 L9 34 36N 117 20W
Oro Valley, U.S.A. .. 109 K8 32 26N 110 58W
Orobie, Alpi, Italy .. 40 B6 46 7N 10 0 E
Orobie Bergamasche △,
 Italy .... 40 C6 46 0N 9 45 E
Orobie Valtellinesi △,
 Italy .... 40 C6 46 5N 9 45 E
Orocué, Colombia .. 124 C4 4 48N 71 20W
Orodara, Burkina Faso 82 C4 11 0N 4 55W
Orodo, Nigeria .... 83 D6 5 34N 7 4 E
Orofino, U.S.A. 108 C5 46 29N 116 15W
Orol Dengizi = Aral Sea,
 Asia .... 52 E7 44 30N 60 0 E
Oromíya □, Ethiopia 81 F5 7 0N 40 0 E
Oromocto, Canada .. 105 C6 45 54N 66 29W
Oron, Nigeria ..... 83 E6 4 48N 8 14 E
Orono, Canada 116 C6 43 59N 78 37W
Orono, U.S.A. 115 C11 44 53N 68 40W
Oronsay, U.K. 13 E2 56 1N 6 15W
Oropesa, Spain 36 F5 39 57N 5 10W
Oroquieta, Phil. ... 61 G5 8 32N 123 44 E
Orosei, Italy ...... 42 B2 40 23N 9 42 E
Orosei, G. di, Italy .. 42 B2 40 15N 9 44 E
Orosháza, Hungary . 28 D5 46 32N 20 42 E
Orotukan, Russia ... 53 C16 62 16N 151 42 E
Oroville, Calif., U.S.A. 110 F5 39 31N 121 33W
Oroville, Wash., U.S.A. 108 B4 48 56N 119 26W
Oroville, L., U.S.A. . 110 F5 39 33N 121 29W
Orrefors, Sweden ... 11 H9 56 50N 15 45 E
Orroroo, Australia .. 95 E2 32 43 S 138 38 E

Orrviken, Sweden ... 10 A8 63 6N 14 26 E
Orrville, U.S.A. 116 F3 40 50N 81 46W
Orsa, Sweden ...... 10 C8 61 7N 14 37 E
Orsara di Púglia, Italy 43 A8 41 17N 15 16 E
Orsasjön, Sweden .. 10 C8 61 7N 14 37 E
Orsha, Belarus .... 32 E6 54 30N 30 25 E
Orsk, Russia ...... 52 D6 51 12N 58 34 E
Orşova, Romania ... 28 F7 44 41N 22 25 E
Ørsted, Denmark ... 11 H4 56 30N 10 20 E
Orsundsbro, Sweden 10 E11 59 44N 17 18 E
Orta, L. d', Italy .... 40 C5 45 49N 8 24 E
Orta Nova, Italy .... 43 A8 41 19N 15 42 E
Ortaca, Turkey .... 47 E10 36 49N 28 45 E
Ortakent, Turkey ... 47 D9 37 5N 27 21 E
Ortaklar, Turkey ... 47 D9 37 53N 27 30 E
Ortaköy, Çorum, Turkey 72 B6 40 16N 35 15 E
Ortaköy, Niğde, Turkey 72 C6 38 44N 34 3 E
Orte, Italy .... 41 F9 42 27N 12 23 E
Ortegal, C., Spain .. 36 B3 43 43N 7 52W
Orthez, France 20 E3 43 29N 0 48W
Ortigueira, Spain ... 36 B3 43 40N 7 50W
Orting, U.S.A. 110 C4 47 6N 122 12W
Ortisei, Italy ...... 41 B8 46 34N 11 40 E
Ortles, Italy ...... 40 B7 46 31N 10 33 E
Ortón →, Bolivia ... 124 F5 10 50 S 67 0W
Ortona, Italy ...... 41 F11 42 21N 14 24 E
Ortonville, U.S.A. .. 112 C6 45 19N 96 27W
Orümíyeh, Iran .... 70 B5 37 40N 45 0 E
Orümíyeh, Daryächeh-
 ye, Iran .... 70 B5 37 50N 45 30 E
Orune, Italy ...... 42 B2 40 24N 9 22 E
Oruro, Bolivia ..... 124 G5 18 0 S 67 9W
Orust, Sweden ..... 11 F5 58 10N 11 40 E
Oruzgān □, Afghan. . 66 C5 33 30N 66 0 E
Orvault, France 18 E5 47 17N 1 38W
Orvieto, Italy ...... 41 F9 42 43N 12 7 E
Orwell, N.Y., U.S.A. 117 C9 43 35N 75 50W
Orwell, Ohio, U.S.A. 116 E4 41 32N 80 52W
Orwell →, U.K. .... 15 F9 51 59N 1 18 E
Orwigsburg, U.S.A. . 117 F8 40 38N 76 6W
Oryakhovo, Bulgaria 44 C7 43 40N 23 57 E
Orynyn, Ukraine ... 29 B11 48 46N 26 24 E
Orzinuovi, Italy .... 40 C6 45 24N 9 55 E
Oryc →, Poland .... 31 F8 52 46N 21 14 E
Orzysz, Poland .... 30 E8 53 50N 21 58 E
Osa →, Poland .... 30 E5 53 33N 18 46 E
Osa, Pen. de, Costa Rica 120 E3 8 0N 84 0W
Osage, U.S.A. 112 D8 43 17N 92 49W
Osage →, U.S.A. .. 112 F9 38 35N 91 57W
Osage City, U.S.A. . 112 F7 38 38N 95 50W
Ōsaka, Japan ..... 55 G7 34 40N 135 30 E
Osan, S. Korea .... 57 F14 37 11N 127 4 E
Osawatomie, U.S.A. 112 F7 38 31N 94 57W
Osborne, U.S.A. ... 112 F5 39 26N 98 42W
Osby, Sweden ..... 11 H7 56 23N 13 59 E
Osceola, Ark., U.S.A. 113 H10 35 42N 89 58W
Osceola, Iowa, U.S.A. 112 E8 41 2N 93 46W
Oschatz, Germany .. 24 D9 51 17N 13 6 E
Oschersleben, Germany 24 C7 52 2N 11 14 E
Óschiri, Italy ...... 42 B2 40 43N 9 7 E
Oscoda, U.S.A. 116 B1 44 26N 83 20W
Osečina, Serbia & M. 44 B3 44 23N 19 34 E
Ösel = Saaremaa,
 Estonia .... 9 G20 58 30N 22 30 E
Osery, Russia ..... 32 E10 54 52N 38 28 E
Osgoode, Canada .. 117 A9 45 8N 75 36W
Osh, Kyrgyzstan ... 52 E8 40 37N 72 49 E
Oshakati, Namibia .. 85 H3 17 45 S 15 40 E
Oshawa, Canada ... 116 C6 43 50N 78 50W
Oshigambo, Namibia 88 B2 17 45 S 16 5 E
Oshkosh, Nebr., U.S.A. 112 E3 41 24N 102 21W
Oshkosh, Wis., U.S.A. 112 C10 44 1N 88 33W
Oshmyany = Ashmyany,
 Belarus .... 9 J21 54 26N 25 52 E
Oshnovíyeh, Iran ... 70 B5 37 2N 45 6 E
Oshogbo, Nigeria .. 83 D5 7 48N 4 37 E
Oshtorinãn, Iran ... 71 C6 34 1N 48 38 E
Oshwe, Dem. Rep. of
 the Congo ...... 84 E3 3 25 S 19 28 E
Osi, Nigeria .... 83 D6 8 0N 5 14 E
Osiecznica, Poland . 31 G3 51 55N 16 40 E
Osijek, Croatia .... 28 E3 45 34N 18 41 E
Ósilo, Italy .... 42 B1 40 45N 8 40 E
Ósimo, Italy ...... 41 E10 43 28N 13 30 E
Osintorf, Belarus ... 32 E6 54 40N 30 39 E
Osipovichi =
 Asipovichy, Belarus 32 F5 53 19N 28 33 E
Osiyan, India ..... 68 F5 26 43N 72 55 E
Osizweni, S. Africa . 89 D5 27 49 S 30 7 E
Oskaloosa, U.S.A. .. 112 E8 41 18N 92 39W
Oskarshamn, Sweden 11 G10 57 15N 16 27 E
Oskarström, Sweden 11 H6 56 48N 12 58 E
Oskélanéo, Canada . 104 C4 48 5N 75 15W
Öskemen, Kazakhstan 52 E9 50 0N 82 36 E
Oskol →, Ukraine .. 33 H9 49 6N 37 25 E
Oslo, Norway ..... 9 G14 59 55N 10 45 E
Oslob, Phil. .... 61 G5 9 31N 123 26 E
Oslofjorden, Norway 9 G14 59 20N 10 35 E
Osmanabad, India .. 66 K10 18 5N 76 10 E
Osmancık, Turkey .. 72 B6 40 58N 34 47 E
Osmaniye, Turkey .. 70 B3 37 5N 36 10 E
Osmanlı, Turkey ... 45 E10 41 35N 26 51 E
Ösmo, Sweden .... 10 F11 58 58N 17 55 E
Osnabrück, Germany 24 C4 52 17N 8 3 E
Ośno Lubuskie, Poland 31 F1 52 28N 14 51 E
Osoblaha, Czech Rep. 27 A10 50 17N 17 44 E
Osogovska Planina,
 Macedonia ...... 44 D6 42 10N 22 30 E
Osor, Italy .... 41 D11 44 42N 14 24 E
Osorio, Brazil ..... 127 B5 29 53 S 50 17W
Osorno, Chile ..... 128 E2 40 25 S 73 0W
Osorno, Spain 36 C6 42 24N 4 22W
Osoyoos, Canada .. 102 D5 49 0N 119 30W
Osøyro, Norway ... 9 F11 60 9N 5 30 E
Ospika →, Canada . 102 B4 56 20N 124 0W
Osprey Reef, Australia 94 A4 13 52 S 146 36 E
Oss, Neths. .... 17 C5 51 46N 5 32 E
Ossa, Mt., Australia . 95 G4 41 52 S 146 3 E
Óssa, Óros, Greece . 44 E4 39 47N 22 42 E
Ossa de Montiel, Spain 39 G2 38 58N 2 45W
Ossabaw I., U.S.A. . 115 K5 31 50N 81 5W
Osse →, France .... 20 D4 44 7N 0 17 E
Osse →, Nigeria ... 83 D6 6 10N 5 20 E
Ossi, Italy .... 42 B1 40 40N 8 34 E
Ossining, U.S.A. ... 117 E11 41 10N 73 55W
Ossipee, U.S.A. 117 C13 43 41N 71 7W
Ossokmanuan L.,
 Canada 105 B7 53 25N 65 0W
Ossora, Russia .... 53 D17 59 20N 163 13 E
Ostashkov, Russia .. 32 D7 57 4N 33 2 E
Ostavall, Sweden ... 10 B9 62 26N 15 29 E
Oste →, Germany .. 24 B5 53 30N 9 12 E
Ostend = Oostende,
 Belgium .... 17 C2 51 15N 2 54 E
Oster, Ukraine ..... 33 G6 50 57N 30 53 E
Österbotten =
 Pohjanmaa, Finland 8 E20 62 58N 22 50 E

Osterburg, Germany 24 C7 52 47N 11 45 E
Osterburg, U.S.A. .. 116 F6 40 16N 78 31W
Osterburken, Germany 25 F5 49 25N 9 26 E
Österbybruk, Sweden 10 D11 60 13N 17 55 E
Österbymo, Sweden 11 G9 57 49N 15 15 E
Österdalälven, Sweden 10 D8 61 30N 13 45 E
Österfärnebo, Sweden 10 D10 60 13N 16 48 E
Osterforse, Sweden . 10 A11 63 9N 17 3 E
Östergötlands län □,
 Sweden .... 11 F9 58 35N 15 45 E
Osterholz-Scharmbeck,
 Germany .... 24 B4 53 13N 8 47 E
Østerild, Denmark .. 11 G2 57 2N 8 51 E
Östermyra = Seinäjoki,
 Finland .... 9 E20 62 40N 22 51 E
Osterode, Germany . 24 D6 51 43N 10 15 E
Östersund, Sweden . 10 A8 63 10N 14 38 E
Östervåla, Sweden . 10 D11 60 11N 17 11 E
Ostfriesische Inseln,
 Germany .... 24 B3 53 42N 7 0 E
Ostfriesland, Germany 24 B3 53 20N 7 30 E
Osthammar, Sweden 10 D12 60 16N 18 22 E
Óstia, Lido di, Italy . 41 G9 41 43N 12 17 E
Ostíglia, Italy ..... 41 C8 45 4N 11 8 E
Ostmark, Sweden .. 10 D6 60 17N 12 45 E
Ostra Husby, Sweden 11 F10 58 35N 16 33 E
Ostrava, Czech Rep. 27 B11 49 51N 18 18 E
Ostróda, Poland ... 30 E6 53 42N 19 58 E
Ostrogozhsk, Russia 33 G10 50 55N 39 7 E
Ostroh, Ukraine ... 33 G4 50 20N 26 30 E
Ostrołęka, Poland .. 31 E8 53 4N 21 32 E
Ostrov, Bulgaria ... 45 C8 43 40N 24 9 E
Ostrov, Czech Rep. . 26 A5 50 18N 12 57 E
Ostrov, Romania ... 29 F12 44 6N 27 24 E
Ostrov, Russia ..... 32 D5 57 25N 28 20 E
Ostrów Lubelski, Poland 31 G9 51 29N 22 51 E
Ostrów Mazowiecka,
 Poland .... 31 E8 52 50N 21 51 E
Ostrów Wielkopolski,
 Poland .... 31 G4 51 36N 17 44 E
Ostrowiec-
 Świętokrzyski, Poland 31 H8 50 55N 21 22 E
Ostrožac, Bos.-H. .. 28 G2 43 43N 17 49 E
Ostrzeszów, Poland 31 G4 51 25N 17 52 E
Ostseebad
 Kühlungsborn,
 Germany .... 24 A7 54 8N 11 44 E
Osttirol □, Austria .. 26 E5 46 50N 12 30 E
Ostuni, Italy ...... 43 B10 40 44N 17 35 E
Osum →, Albania .. 44 F4 40 40N 20 10 E
Osüm →, Bulgaria . 45 C8 43 40N 24 9 E
Ōsumi-Kaikyō, Japan 55 J5 30 55N 131 0 E
Ōsumi-Shotō, Japan 55 J5 30 30N 130 0 E
Osun □, Nigeria ... 83 D5 7 30N 4 30 E
Osuna, Spain 37 H5 37 14N 5 8W
Oswegatchie →, U.S.A. 117 B9 44 42N 75 30W
Oswego, U.S.A. 117 C8 43 27N 76 31W
Oswego →, U.S.A. . 117 C8 43 27N 76 30W
Oswestry, U.K. 14 E4 52 52N 3 3W
Oświęcim, Poland .. 31 H6 50 2N 19 11 E
Otaci, Moldova .... 29 B12 48 27N 27 47 E
Otago □, N.Z. ..... 91 L2 45 15 S 170 0 E
Otago Harbour, N.Z. 91 L3 45 47 S 170 42 E
Otaheite B.,
 Trin. & Tob. 125 K15 10 20N 61 30W
Otake, Japan ...... 55 G6 34 12N 132 13 E
Otaki, N.Z. .... 91 J5 40 45 S 175 10 E
Otaru, Japan ...... 54 C10 43 10N 141 0 E
Otaru-Wan = Ishikari-
 Wan, Japan ..... 54 C10 43 25N 141 1 E
Otava →, Czech Rep. 26 B7 49 26N 14 12 E
Otavalo, Ecuador .. 124 C3 0 13N 78 20W
Otavi, Namibia .... 88 B2 19 40 S 17 24 E
Otchinjau, Angola .. 88 B1 16 30 S 13 56 E
Otelec, Romania ... 28 E5 45 36N 20 50 E
Otelnuk, L., Canada 105 A6 56 9N 68 12W
Oţelu Roşu, Romania 28 E7 45 30N 22 22 E
Otero de Rey = Outeiro
 de Rei, Spain 36 B3 43 7N 7 36W
Othello, U.S.A. 108 C4 46 50N 119 10W
Othonoí, Greece ... 46 B4 39 52N 19 22 E
Óthris, Óros, Greece 46 B4 39 4N 22 42 E
Oti →, Togo ...... 83 C5 10 40N 0 35 E
Otjiwarongo, Namibia 88 C2 20 30 S 16 33 E
Otmuchów, Poland . 31 H4 50 28N 17 10 E
Otočac, Croatia .... 41 D12 44 53N 15 12 E
Otoineppu, Japan .. 54 B11 44 44N 142 16 E
Otok, Croatia ..... 41 E13 43 42N 16 44 E
Otopeni, Bucureşti ✈
 (OTP), Romania .. 45 B10 44 30N 26 11 E
Otorohanga, N.Z. .. 91 H5 38 12 S 175 14 E
Otoskwin →, Canada 104 B2 52 13N 88 6W
Otra →, Norway ... 9 G13 58 9N 8 1 E
Otradnyy, Russia ... 34 D10 53 20N 51 21 E
Otranto, Italy ..... 43 B11 40 9N 18 28 E
Otranto, C. d', Italy . 43 B11 40 7N 18 30 E
Otranto, Str. of, Italy 43 B11 40 15N 18 40 E
Otrokovice, Czech Rep. 27 B9 49 12N 17 32 E
Otse, S. Africa ..... 88 D4 25 2 S 25 45 E
Ōtsu, Japan ...... 55 G7 35 0N 135 50 E
Ōtsuki, Japan ..... 55 G9 35 36N 138 57 E
Ottawa = Outaouais →,
 Canada 104 C5 45 27N 74 8W
Ottawa, Canada ... 117 A9 45 27N 75 42W
Ottawa, Ill., U.S.A. . 112 E10 41 21N 88 51W
Ottawa, Kans., U.S.A. 112 F7 38 37N 95 16W
Ottawa Is., Canada . 101 C11 59 35N 80 10W
Ottélé, Cameroon .. 83 E7 3 38N 11 19 E
Ottensheim, Austria 26 C7 48 21N 14 12 E
Otter Cr. →, U.S.A. 117 B11 44 13N 73 17W
Otter L., Canada ... 103 B8 55 35N 104 39W
Otterndorf, Germany 24 B4 53 48N 8 53 E
Otterup, Denmark .. 11 J4 55 30N 10 22 E
Otterville, Canada .. 116 D4 42 55N 80 36W
Ottery St. Mary, U.K. 15 G4 50 44N 3 17W
Otto Beit Bridge,
 Zimbabwe ...... 87 F2 15 59 S 28 56 E
Ottosdal, S. Africa .. 88 D4 26 46 S 25 59 E
Ottumwa, U.S.A. .. 112 E8 41 1N 92 25W
Otu, Nigeria ...... 83 D5 8 14N 3 22 E
Otukpa, Nigeria ... 83 D6 7 9N 7 41 E
Oturkpo, Nigeria .. 83 D6 7 16N 8 8 E
Otway, B., Chile ... 128 G2 53 30 S 74 0W
Otway, C., Australia 95 F3 38 52 S 143 30 E
Otwock, Poland .... 31 F8 52 5N 21 20 E
Otyniya, Ukraine ... 29 B10 48 44N 24 51 E
Ou →, Laos .... 58 B3 20 4N 102 13 E
Ou Neua, Laos .... 58 A3 22 18N 101 48 E
Ou-Sammyaku, Japan 54 E10 39 20N 140 35 E
Ouachita →, U.S.A. 113 K9 31 38N 91 49W
Ouachita, L., U.S.A. 113 H8 34 34N 93 12W
Ouachita Mts., U.S.A. 113 H7 34 40N 94 25W

Ouagadougou,
 Burkina Faso 83 C4 12 25N 1 30W
Ouahigouya,
 Burkina Faso 82 C4 13 31N 2 25W
Ouahran = Oran,
 Algeria 78 A5 35 45N 0 39W
Oualâta, Mauritania 82 B3 17 20N 6 55W
Ouallam, Niger .... 83 C5 14 23N 2 10 E
Ouallene, Algeria .. 78 D6 24 41N 1 11 E
Ouargaye, Burkina Faso 83 C5 11 34N 0 19 E
Ouargla, Algeria ... 78 B7 31 59N 5 16 E
Ouarkoye, Burkina Faso 82 C4 12 5N 3 40W
Ouarzazate, Morocco 78 B4 30 55N 6 50W
Ouassouas, Mali ... 83 B5 16 10N 1 23 E
Ouatagouna, Mali .. 83 B5 15 11N 0 43 E
Oubangi →, Dem. Rep.
 of the Congo .... 84 E3 0 30 S 17 50 E
Ouche →, France .. 19 E12 47 6N 5 16 E
Ouddorp, Neths. ... 17 C3 51 50N 3 57 E
Oude Rijn →, Neths. 17 B4 52 12N 4 24 E
Oudeïka, Mali 83 B4 17 30N 1 40W
Oudenaarde, Belgium 17 D3 50 50N 3 37 E
Oudon →, France .. 18 E6 47 41N 0 53W
Oudtshoorn, S. Africa 88 E3 33 35 S 22 14 E
Ouellé, Ivory C. ... 82 D4 7 26N 4 1W
Ouémé →, Benin .. 83 D5 6 30N 2 30 E
Ouessa, Burkina Faso 82 C4 11 4N 2 47W
Ouessant, Î. d', France 18 D1 48 28N 5 6W
Ouesso, Congo .... 84 D3 1 37N 16 5 E
Ouest, Pte. de l', Canada 105 C7 49 52N 64 40W
Ouezzane, Morocco 78 B4 34 51N 5 35W
Ougarou, Burkina Faso 83 C5 12 10N 0 58 E
Oughterard, Ireland 12 C2 53 26N 9 18W
Ouidah, Benin ..... 83 D5 6 25N 2 0 E
Ouidi, Niger ...... 83 C7 14 10N 13 0 E
Ouistreham, France 18 C6 49 17N 0 18W
Oujda, Morocco ... 78 B5 34 41N 1 55W
Oujeft, Mauritania .. 82 A2 20 2N 13 0W
Oulainen, Finland .. 8 D21 64 17N 24 47 E
Ould Yenjé, Mauritania 82 B2 15 38N 12 16W
Oulins, France ..... 21 C8 45 43N 4 49 E
Oulu, Finland ..... 8 D21 65 1N 25 29 E
Oulujärvi, Finland .. 8 D22 64 25N 27 15 E
Oulujoki →, Finland 8 D21 65 1N 25 30 E
Oulx, Italy .... 40 C3 45 2N 6 50 E
Oum Chalouba, Chad 79 E10 15 48N 20 46 E
Oum Hadjer, Chad . 79 F9 13 18N 19 41 E
Oumé, Ivory C. 82 D3 6 21N 5 27W
Ounasjoki →, Finland 8 C21 66 31N 25 40 E
Ounguati, Namibia . 88 C2 22 0 S 15 46 E
Ounianga Sérir, Chad 79 E10 18 54N 20 51 E
Our →, Lux. ...... 17 E6 49 55N 6 5 E
Ouranópolis, Greece 44 F7 40 20N 23 59 E
Ourârene, Niger ... 83 B6 19 30N 7 10 E
Ouray, U.S.A. 109 G10 38 1N 107 40W
Ourcq →, France .. 19 C10 49 1N 3 1 E
Ouricuri, Brazil .... 125 E10 7 53 S 40 5W
Ourinhos, Brazil ... 127 A6 22 16 S 46 25W
Ourique, Portugal .. 37 H2 37 38N 8 16W
Ouro Fino, Brazil .. 127 A6 22 16 S 46 25W
Ouro-Ndia, Mali ... 82 B4 15 8N 4 35W
Ouro Prêto, Brazil .. 127 A7 20 20 S 43 30W
Ouro Sogui, Senegal 82 B2 15 36N 13 19W
Oursi, Burkina Faso 83 C4 14 41N 0 27W
Ouse →, E. Susx., U.K. 15 G8 50 47N 0 4 E
Ouse →, N. Yorks.,
 U.K. 14 D7 53 44N 0 55W
Oust, France ...... 20 F5 42 52N 1 13 E
Oust →, France ... 18 E4 47 35N 2 6W
Outamba-Kilimi △,
 S. Leone 82 D2 9 50N 12 40W
Outaouais →, Canada 104 C5 45 27N 74 8W
Outardes →, Canada 105 C6 49 24N 69 30W
Outeiro de Rei, Spain 36 B3 43 7N 7 36W
Outer Hebrides, U.K. 13 D1 57 30N 7 40W
Outes = Serra de Outes,
 Spain 36 C2 42 52N 8 55W
Outjo, Namibia .... 88 C2 20 5 S 16 7 E
Outlook, Canada ... 103 C7 51 30N 107 0W
Outokumpu, Finland 8 E23 62 43N 29 1 E
Outreau, France ... 19 B8 50 40N 1 36 E
Ouvèze →, France . 21 E8 43 59N 4 51 E
Ouyen, Australia ... 95 F3 35 1 S 142 22 E
Ouzouer-le-Marché,
 France .... 18 E8 47 54N 1 32 E
Ovada, Italy ...... 40 D5 44 38N 8 38 E
Ovalau, Fiji .... 91 C8 17 40 S 178 48 E
Ovalle, Chile ...... 126 C1 30 33 S 71 18W
Ovamboland, Namibia 88 B2 18 30 S 16 0 E
Ovar, Portugal 36 E2 40 51N 8 40W
Overath, Germany .. 24 E3 50 56N 7 17 E
Overflakkee, Neths. 17 C4 51 44N 4 10 E
Overijssel □, Neths. 17 B6 52 25N 6 35 E
Overland Park, U.S.A. 112 F7 38 55N 94 50W
Overton, U.S.A. ... 111 J12 36 33N 114 27W
Övertorneå, Sweden 8 C20 66 23N 23 38 E
Överum, Sweden ... 11 F10 58 0N 16 20 E
Ovid, U.S.A. 117 D8 42 41N 76 49W
Ovidiopol, Ukraine . 33 J6 46 15N 30 30 E
Ovidiu, Romania ... 29 F13 44 16N 28 34 E
Oviedo, Spain 36 B5 43 25N 5 50W
Oviksfjällen, Sweden 10 A7 63 0N 13 49 E
Oviši, Latvia ...... 9 H19 57 33N 21 44 E
Ovoot, Mongolia ... 56 B7 45 21N 113 45 E
Övör Hangay □,
 Mongolia .... 56 B2 45 0N 102 30 E
Ovoro, Nigeria .... 83 D6 5 26N 7 16 E
Øvre Årdal, Norway 9 F12 61 19N 7 48 E
Øvre Fryken, Sweden 10 E7 59 47N 13 14 E
Ovruch, Ukraine ... 33 G5 51 25N 28 45 E
Owaka, N.Z. ...... 91 M2 46 27 S 169 40 E
Owambo =
 Ovamboland, Namibia 88 B2 18 30 S 16 0 E
Owasco, L., U.S.A. . 117 D8 42 50N 76 31W
Owase, Japan ..... 55 G8 34 7N 136 12 E
Owatonna, U.S.A. .. 112 C8 44 5N 93 14W
Owbeh, Afghan. ... 66 B3 34 28N 63 10 E
Owego, U.S.A. 117 D8 42 6N 76 16W
Owen Falls Dam,
 Uganda .... 86 B3 0 30N 33 5 E
Owen Sound, Canada 116 B4 44 35N 80 55W
Owens →, U.S.A. . 111 J9 36 32N 117 59W
Owens L., U.S.A. .. 111 J9 36 26N 117 57W
Owensboro, U.S.A. . 114 G2 37 46N 87 7W
Owerri, Nigeria ... 83 D6 5 29N 7 0 E
Owl →, Canada 103 B10 57 51N 92 44W
Owo, Nigeria ...... 83 D6 7 10N 5 39 E
Owosso, U.S.A. ... 114 D3 43 0N 84 10W
Owyhee, U.S.A. ... 108 F5 41 57N 116 6W
Owyhee →, U.S.A. 108 E5 43 49N 117 2W
Owyhee, L., U.S.A. 108 E5 43 38N 117 14W
Ox Mts. = Slieve
 Gamph, Ireland .. 12 B3 54 6N 9 0W
Oxarfjörður, Iceland 8 C5 66 15N 16 45W
Oxbow, Canada 103 D8 49 14N 102 10W

Oxelösund, Sweden . 11 F11 58 43N 17 5 E
Oxford, N.Z. ...... 91 K4 43 18 S 172 11 E
Oxford, U.K. 15 F6 51 46N 1 15W
Oxford, Mass., U.S.A. 117 D13 42 7N 71 52W
Oxford, Miss., U.S.A. 113 H10 34 22N 89 31W
Oxford, N.C., U.S.A. 115 G6 36 19N 78 35W
Oxford, N.Y., U.S.A. 117 D9 42 27N 75 36W
Oxford, Ohio, U.S.A. 114 F3 39 31N 84 45W
Oxford L., Canada .. 103 C9 54 51N 95 37W
Oxfordshire □, U.K. 15 F6 51 48N 1 16W
Oxía Nísís, Greece .. 46 C3 38 18N 21 6 E
Oxie, Sweden ..... 11 J7 55 33N 13 6 E
Oxílithos, Greece .. 46 C6 38 35N 24 7 E
Oxnard, U.S.A. 111 L7 34 12N 119 11W
Oxsjövålen, Sweden 10 B7 62 34N 13 57 E
Oxus = Amudarya →,
 Uzbekistan ..... 52 E6 43 58N 59 34 E
Oya, Malaysia ..... 62 D4 2 55N 111 55 E
Oyama, Japan ..... 55 F9 36 18N 139 48 E
Oyambre △, Spain . 36 B6 43 22N 4 21W
Oyem, Gabon ..... 84 D2 1 34N 11 31 E
Oyen, Canada 103 C6 51 22N 110 28W
Oykel →, U.K. 13 D4 57 56N 4 26W
Oymyakon, Russia . 53 C15 63 25N 142 44 E
Oyo, Nigeria ...... 83 D5 7 46N 3 56 E
Oyo □, Nigeria .... 83 D5 8 15N 3 30 E
Oyonnax, France ... 19 F12 46 16N 5 40 E
Oyster Bay, U.S.A. . 117 F11 40 52N 73 32W
Oyūbari, Japan .... 54 C11 43 1N 142 5 E
Özalp, Turkey ..... 73 C10 38 39N 43 59 E
Ozamiz, Phil. ...... 61 G5 8 15N 123 50 E
Ozark, Ala., U.S.A. . 115 K3 31 28N 85 39W
Ozark, Ark., U.S.A. . 113 H8 35 29N 93 50W
Ozark, Mo., U.S.A. . 113 G8 37 1N 93 12W
Ozark Plateau, U.S.A. 113 G9 37 20N 91 40W
Ozarks, L. of the, U.S.A. 112 F8 38 12N 92 38W
Ozarów, Poland .... 31 H8 50 53N 21 40 E
Ózd, Hungary ..... 28 B5 48 14N 20 15 E
Ozernoye, Russia .. 34 E10 51 46N 61 24 E
Ozersk, Russia .... 30 D8 54 25N 22 0 E
Ozette L., U.S.A. ... 110 B2 48 6N 124 38W
Ozieri, Italy .... 42 B2 40 35N 9 0 E
Ozimek, Poland .... 31 H5 50 41N 18 11 E
Ozinki, Russia ..... 34 E9 51 10N 49 40 E
Ozona, U.S.A. 113 K4 30 43N 101 12W
Ozorków, Poland ... 31 G6 51 57N 19 16 E
Ozren, Bos.-H. .... 28 G3 43 55N 18 29 E
Ozuluama, Mexico . 119 C5 21 40N 97 50W
Ozun, Romania .... 29 E10 45 47N 25 50 E
Özurgeti, Georgia .. 35 K5 41 55N 42 2 E

P

Pa, Burkina Faso 82 C4 11 33N 3 19W
Pa-an, Burma ..... 67 L20 16 51N 97 40 E
Pa Mong Dam, Thailand 64 D4 18 0N 102 22 E
Pa Sak →, Thailand 62 B2 15 30N 101 0 E
Paamiut, Greenland 101 B15 62 0N 49 43W
Paar →, Germany .. 25 G7 48 46N 11 36 E
Paarl, S. Africa .... 88 E2 33 45 S 18 56 E
Pab Hills, Pakistan . 68 F2 26 30N 66 45 E
Pabbay, U.K. 13 D1 57 46N 7 14W
Pabianice, Poland .. 31 G6 51 40N 19 20 E
Pabna, Bangla. .... 67 G16 24 1N 89 18 E
Pabo, Uganda ..... 86 B3 3 1N 32 10 E
Pacaja →, Brazil ... 125 D8 1 56 S 50 50W
Pacaraima, Sa., S. Amer. 124 C6 4 0N 62 30W
Pacasmayo, Peru ... 124 E3 7 20 S 79 35W
Paceco, Italy ...... 42 E5 37 59N 12 33 E
Pachhar, India .... 68 G7 24 40N 77 42 E
Pachino, Italy ..... 43 F8 36 43N 15 5 E
Pachitea →, Peru .. 124 E4 8 46 S 74 33W
Pachmarhi, India ... 69 H8 22 28N 78 26 E
Pachpadra, India ... 66 G8 25 58N 72 10 E
Pachuca, Mexico ... 119 C5 20 10N 98 40W
Pacific, Canada 102 C3 54 48N 128 28W
Pacific-Antarctic Ridge,
 Pac. Oc. .... 97 M16 43 0 S 115 0W
Pacific Grove, U.S.A. 110 J5 36 38N 121 56W
Pacific Ocean 97 G14 10 0N 140 0W
Pacific Rim △, Canada 102 D4 48 40N 124 45W
Pacifica, U.S.A. 110 H4 37 36N 122 30W
Pacitan, Indonesia . 63 H14 8 12 S 111 7 E
Packwood, U.S.A. .. 110 D5 46 36N 121 40W
Pacov, Czech Rep. . 26 B8 49 27N 15 0 E
Pacy-sur-Eure, France 18 C8 49 1N 1 23 E
Padaido, Kepulauan,
 Indonesia ...... 63 E9 1 15 S 136 30 E
Padang, Indonesia . 62 E2 1 0 S 100 20 E
Padang Endau, Malaysia 65 L4 2 40N 103 38 E
Padangpanjang,
 Indonesia ...... 62 E2 0 40 S 100 20 E
Padangsidempuan,
 Indonesia ...... 62 D1 1 30N 99 15 E
Padborg, Denmark . 11 K3 54 49N 9 21 E
Paddle Prairie, Canada 102 B5 57 57N 117 29W
Paddockwood, Canada 103 C7 53 30N 105 30W
Paderborn, Germany 24 D4 51 42N 8 45 E
Padeş, Vf., Romania 28 E7 45 40N 22 22 E
Padina, Romania ... 29 F12 44 50N 27 8 E
Padma, India ...... 69 G11 24 12N 85 22 E
Pádova, Italy ...... 41 C8 45 25N 11 53 E
Padra, India .... 68 H5 22 15N 73 7 E
Padrauna, India .... 69 F10 26 54N 83 59 E
Padre I. △, U.S.A. . 113 M6 26 36N 97 17W
Padrón, Spain 36 C2 42 41N 8 39W
Padstow, U.K. 15 G3 50 33N 4 58W
Padua = Pádova, Italy 41 C8 45 25N 11 53 E
Paducah, Ky., U.S.A. 114 G1 37 5N 88 37W
Paducah, Tex., U.S.A. 113 H4 34 1N 100 18W
Padul, Spain 37 H7 37 1N 3 38W
Paengnyŏng-do,
 S. Korea .... 57 F13 37 57N 124 40 E
Paeroa, N.Z. ...... 91 G5 37 23 S 175 41 E
Paesana, Italy ..... 40 D4 44 41N 7 16 E
Pag, Croatia ...... 41 D12 44 25N 15 3 E
Paga, Ghana 83 C4 11 1N 1 8W
Pagadian, Phil. .... 61 H5 7 55N 123 30 E
Pagai Selatan, Pulau,
 Indonesia ...... 62 E2 3 0 S 100 15 E
Pagai Utara, Pulau,
 Indonesia ...... 62 E2 2 35 S 100 0 E
Pagalu = Annobón,
 Atl. Oc. .... 77 G4 1 25 S 5 36 E
Pagara, India ...... 69 G9 24 22N 80 1 E
Pagastikós Kólpos,
 Greece .... 46 B5 39 15N 23 0 E
Pagatan, Indonesia . 62 E5 3 33 S 115 59 E
Page, U.S.A. 109 H8 36 57N 111 27W
Pagėgiai, Lithuania . 30 C8 55 9N 21 54 E
Pago Pago,
 Amer. Samoa ... 91 B13 14 16 S 170 43W
Pagosa Springs, U.S.A. 109 H10 37 16N 107 1W

Pagwa River, Canada .. 104 B2 50 2N 85 14W
Pahala, U.S.A. 106 J17 19 12N 155 29W
Pahang →, Malaysia .. 65 L4 3 30N 103 9 E
Pahiatua, N.Z. .... 91 J5 40 27 S 175 50 E
Pahokee, U.S.A. 115 M5 26 50N 80 40W
Pahrump, U.S.A. 111 J11 36 12N 115 59W
Pahute Mesa, U.S.A. .. 110 H10 37 20N 116 45W
Pai, Thailand .... 64 C2 19 19N 98 27 E
Paicines, U.S.A. 110 J5 36 44N 121 17W
Paide, Estonia .... 9 G21 58 53N 25 33 E
Paignton, U.K. 15 G4 50 26N 3 35W
Paiho, Taiwan .... 59 F13 23 21N 120 25 E
Päijänne, Finland ..... 9 F21 61 30N 25 30 E
Pailani, India .... 69 G9 25 45N 80 26 E
Pailin, Cambodia ...... 64 F4 12 46N 102 36 E
Paimpol, France 18 D3 48 48N 3 4W
Painan, Indonesia ..... 62 E2 1 21 S 100 34 E
Painesville, U.S.A. 116 E3 41 43N 81 15W
Paint Hills = Wemindji,
Canada 104 B4 53 0N 78 49W
Paint L., Canada 103 B9 55 28N 97 57W
Painted Desert, U.S.A. . 109 J8 36 0N 111 0W
Paintsville, U.S.A. 114 G4 37 49N 82 48W
País Vasco □, Spain ... 38 C2 42 50N 2 45W
Paisley, Canada 116 B3 44 18N 81 16W
Paisley, U.K. 13 F4 55 50N 4 25W
Paisley, U.S.A. 108 E3 42 42N 120 32W
Paita, Peru .... 124 E2 5 11 S 81 9W
Paiva →, Portugal 36 D2 41 4N 8 16W
Paizhou, China .... 59 B9 30 12N 113 55 E
Pajares, Spain 36 B5 43 1N 5 46W
Pajares, Puerto de, Spain 36 C5 42 58N 5 46W
Pajęczno, Poland ...... 31 G5 51 10N 19 0 E
Pak Lay, Laos .... 64 C3 18 15N 101 27 E
Pak Phanang, Thailand 65 H3 8 21N 100 12 E
Pak Sane, Laos .... 64 C4 18 22N 103 39 E
Pak Song, Laos .... 64 E6 15 11N 106 14 E
Pak Suong, Laos ...... 58 H4 19 58N 102 15 E
Pakaur, India .... 69 G12 24 38N 87 51 E
Pakenham, Canada 117 A8 45 18N 76 18W
Pákhnes, Greece ...... 49 D6 35 16N 24 4 E
Pakhuis, S. Africa .... 88 E2 32 9 S 19 5 E
Pakistan ■, Asia ...... 68 E4 30 0N 70 0 E
Pakkading, Laos ...... 64 C4 18 19N 103 59 E
Paklenica △, Croatia .. 41 D12 44 20N 15 39 E
Pakokku, Burma ...... 67 J19 21 20N 95 0 E
Pakość, Poland .... 31 F5 52 48N 18 6 E
Pakowki L., Canada ... 103 D6 49 20N 111 0W
Pakpattan, Pakistan ... 68 D5 30 25N 73 27 E
Pakrac, Croatia .... 28 E2 45 27N 17 12 E
Pakruojis, Lithuania ... 30 C10 55 58N 23 52 E
Paks, Hungary .... 28 D3 46 38N 18 55 E
Paktīā □, Afghan. ..... 66 C6 33 30N 69 15 E
Paktīkā □, Afghan. .... 66 C6 32 30N 69 0 E
Pakwach, Uganda ..... 86 B3 2 28N 31 27 E
Pakxe, Laos .... 64 E5 15 5N 105 52 E
Pal Lahara, India ...... 69 J11 21 27N 85 11 E
Pala, Chad .... 79 G9 9 25N 15 5 E
Pala, Dem. Rep. of
the Congo .... 86 D2 6 45 S 29 30 E
Pala, U.S.A. 111 M9 33 22N 117 5W
Palabek, Uganda ...... 86 B3 3 22N 32 33 E
Palacios, U.S.A. 113 L6 28 42N 96 13W
Palafrugell, Spain ..... 38 D8 41 55N 3 10 E
Palagiano, Italy ...... 43 B10 40 35N 17 2 E
Palagonía, Italy ...... 43 E7 37 19N 14 45 E
Palagruža, Croatia .... 41 F13 42 24N 16 15 E
Palaiókastron, Greece . 49 D8 35 12N 26 15 E
Palaiokhóra, Greece ... 49 D5 35 16N 23 39 E
Pálairos, Greece ...... 46 C2 38 47N 20 53 E
Palaiseau, France ..... 19 D9 48 43N 2 15 E
Palam, India .... 66 K10 19 0N 77 0 E
Palamás, Greece ...... 46 B4 39 26N 22 4 E
Palamòs, Spain .... 38 D8 41 50N 3 10 E
Palampur, India ...... 68 C7 32 10N 76 30 E
Palamut, Turkey ...... 47 C9 38 59N 27 41 E
Palana, Australia ..... 95 F4 39 45 S 147 55 E
Palana, Russia .... 53 D16 59 10N 159 59 E
Palanan, Phil. .... 61 C5 17 8N 122 29 E
Palanan Pt., Phil. ..... 61 C5 17 17N 122 30 E
Palandri, Pakistan .... 69 C5 33 42N 73 40 E
Palanga, Lithuania .... 9 J19 55 58N 21 3 E
Palangkaraya, Indonesia 62 E4 2 16 S 113 56 E
Palani Hills, India .... 66 P10 10 14N 77 33 E
Palanpur, India ...... 68 G5 24 10N 72 25 E
Palapye, Botswana .... 88 C4 22 30 S 27 7 E
Palas, Pakistan .... 69 B5 35 4N 73 14 E
Palas de Rei, Spain ... 36 C3 42 52N 7 52W
Palashi, India .... 69 H13 23 47N 88 15 E
Palasponga, India ..... 69 J11 21 47N 85 34 E
Palatka, Russia .... 53 C16 60 6N 150 54 E
Palatka, U.S.A. 115 L5 29 39N 81 38W
Palau, Italy .... 42 A2 41 11N 9 23 E
Palau ■, Pac. Oc. ..... 96 G5 7 30N 134 30 E
Palauk, Burma .... 64 F2 13 10N 98 40 E
Palawan, Phil. .... 61 G3 9 30N 118 30 E
Palayankottai, India ... 66 Q10 8 45N 77 45 E
Palazzo, Pte., France .. 21 F12 42 28N 8 30 E
Palazzo San Gervásio,
Italy .... 43 B8 40 56N 15 59 E
Palazzolo Acréide, Italy 43 E7 37 4N 14 54 E
Paldiski, Estonia ...... 9 G21 59 23N 24 9 E
Pale, Bos.-H. .... 28 G3 43 50N 18 38 E
Paleleh, Indonesia .... 63 D6 1 10N 121 50 E
Palembang, Indonesia .. 62 E2 3 0 S 104 50 E
Palencia, Spain 36 C6 42 1N 4 34W
Palencia □, Spain 36 C6 42 31N 4 33W
Palenque, Mexico 119 D6 17 31N 91 58W
Paleokastrítsa, Greece . 49 A3 39 40N 19 41 E
Paleometokho, Cyprus . 49 D12 35 7N 33 11 E
Palermo, Italy .... 42 D6 38 7N 13 22 E
Palermo, U.S.A. 108 G3 39 26N 121 33W
Palermo ✕ (PMO), Italy 42 D6 38 11N 13 5 E
Palestina, Chile ...... 128 A3 23 50 S 69 47W
Palestine, Asia .... 74 D4 32 0N 35 0 E
Palestine, U.S.A. 113 K7 31 46N 95 38W
Palestrina, Italy ...... 41 G9 41 50N 12 53 E
Paletwa, Burma .... 67 J18 21 10N 92 50 E
Palghat, India .... 66 P10 10 46N 76 42 E
Palgrave, Mt., Australia 92 D2 23 22 S 115 58 E
Pali, India .... 68 G5 25 50N 73 20 E
Palikir, Micronesia .... 96 G7 6 55N 158 9 E
Palinuro, Italy .... 43 B8 40 2N 15 17 E
Palinuro, C., Italy ..... 43 B8 40 2N 15 16 E
Paliouríon, Ákra, Greece 44 G7 39 57N 23 45 E
Palisades Reservoir,
U.S.A. 108 E8 43 20N 111 12W
Paliseul, Belgium ..... 17 E5 49 54N 5 8 E
Palitana, India .... 68 J4 21 32N 71 49 E
Palizada, Mexico 119 D6 18 18N 92 8W
Palk Bay, Asia .... 66 Q11 9 30N 79 15 E
Palk Strait, Asia ...... 66 Q11 10 0N 79 45 E
Palkānah, Iraq .... 70 C5 35 49N 44 26 E
Palkot, India .... 69 H11 22 53N 84 39 E
Pallanza = Verbánia,
Italy .... 40 C5 45 56N 8 33 E
Pallarenda, Australia .. 94 B4 19 12 S 146 46 E
Pallasovka, Russia .... 34 E8 50 4N 47 0 E
Pallës, Bishti i, Albania 44 E3 41 24N 19 24 E
Pallinup →, Australia .. 93 F2 34 27 S 118 50 E
Pallisa, Uganda ...... 86 B3 1 12N 33 43 E
Pallu, India .... 68 E6 28 59N 74 14 E
Palm Bay, U.S.A. 115 L5 28 2N 80 35W
Palm Beach, U.S.A. ... 115 M6 26 43N 80 2W
Palm Coast, U.S.A. ... 115 L5 29 32N 81 10W
Palm Desert, U.S.A. ... 111 M10 33 43N 116 22W
Palm Is., Australia ... 94 B4 18 40 S 146 35 E
Palm Springs, U.S.A. .. 111 M10 33 50N 116 33W
Palma, Mozam. .... 87 E5 10 46 S 40 29 E
Palma, B. de, Spain ... 48 B9 39 30N 2 39 E
Palma de Mallorca,
Spain .... 48 B9 39 35N 2 39 E
Palma de Mallorca ✕
(PMI), Spain .... 39 F7 39 34N 2 43 E
Palma del Río, Spain .. 37 H5 37 43N 5 17W
Palma di Montechiaro,
Italy .... 42 E6 37 11N 13 46 E
Palma Soriano, Cuba .. 120 B4 20 15N 76 0W
Palmares, Brazil ..... 125 E11 8 41 S 35 28W
Palmarola, Italy ...... 42 B5 40 56N 12 51 E
Palmas, Brazil .... 127 B5 26 29 S 52 0W
Palmas, C., Liberia ... 82 E3 4 27N 7 46W
Pálmas, G. di, Italy ... 42 D1 39 0N 8 30 E
Palmdale, U.S.A. 111 L8 34 35N 118 7W
Palmeira das Missões,
Brazil .... 127 B5 27 55 S 53 17W
Palmeira dos Índios,
Brazil .... 125 E11 9 25 S 36 37W
Palmela, Portugal 37 G2 38 32N 8 57W
Palmer, Antarctica .... 5 C17 64 35 S 65 0W
Palmer, U.S.A. 100 B5 61 36N 149 7W
Palmer →, Australia ... 94 B3 16 0 S 142 26 E
Palmer Arch., Antarctica 5 C17 64 15 S 65 0W
Palmer Lake, U.S.A. ... 112 F2 39 7N 104 55W
Palmer Land, Antarctica 5 D18 73 0 S 63 0W
Palmerston, Canada ... 116 C4 43 50N 80 51W
Palmerston, N.Z. ..... 91 L3 45 29 S 170 43 E
Palmerston North, N.Z. 91 J5 40 21 S 175 39 E
Palmerton, U.S.A. 117 F9 40 48N 75 37W
Palmetto, U.S.A. 115 M4 27 31N 82 34W
Palmi, Italy .... 43 D8 38 21N 15 51 E
Palmira, Argentina .... 126 C2 32 59 S 68 34W
Palmira, Colombia 124 C3 3 32N 76 16W
Palmyra = Tudmur,
Syria .... 70 C3 34 36N 38 15 E
Palmyra, Mo., U.S.A. .. 112 F9 39 48N 91 32W
Palmyra, N.J., U.S.A. .. 117 F9 40 1N 75 1W
Palmyra, N.Y., U.S.A. . 116 C7 43 5N 77 18W
Palmyra, Pa., U.S.A. .. 117 F8 40 18N 76 36W
Palmyra Is., Pac. Oc. . 97 G11 5 52N 162 5W
Palo Alto, U.S.A. 110 H4 37 27N 122 10W
Palo Seco, Trin. & Tob. 125 K15 10 4N 61 36W
Palo Verde, U.S.A. 111 M12 33 26N 114 44W
Palo Verde △,
Costa Rica 120 D2 10 21N 85 21W
Paloich, Sudan .... 81 E3 10 28N 32 32 E
Palomar Mt., U.S.A. ... 111 M10 33 22N 116 50W
Palompon, Phil. ...... 61 F6 11 3N 124 23 E
Palopo, Indonesia ..... 63 E6 3 0 S 120 16 E
Palos, C. de, Spain 39 H4 37 38N 0 40W
Palos de la Frontera,
Spain 37 H4 37 14N 6 53W
Palos Verdes, U.S.A. .. 111 M8 33 48N 118 23W
Palos Verdes, Pt., U.S.A. 111 M8 33 43N 118 26W
Pålsboda, Sweden ..... 10 E9 59 3N 15 22 E
Palu, Indonesia .... 63 E5 1 0 S 119 52 E
Palu, Turkey .... 70 B3 38 45N 40 0 E
Paluke, Liberia 82 D3 5 2N 8 5W
Paluzza, Italy .... 41 B10 46 32N 13 1 E
Palwal, India .... 68 E7 28 8N 77 19 E
Pama, Burkina Faso ... 83 C5 11 19N 0 44 E
Pama △, Burkina Faso . 83 C5 11 27N 0 40 E
Pamanukan, Indonesia . 63 G12 6 16 S 107 49 E
Pamekasan, Indonesia . 63 G15 7 10 S 113 28 E
Pamenang, Indonesia .. 63 J19 8 24 S 116 6 E
Pamiers, France ...... 20 E5 43 7N 1 39 E
Pamir, Tajikistan ..... 52 F8 37 40N 73 0 E
Pamlico →, U.S.A. 115 H7 35 20N 76 28W
Pamlico Sd., U.S.A. ... 115 H8 35 20N 76 0W
Pampa, U.S.A. 113 H4 35 32N 100 58W
Pampa de las Salinas,
Argentina .... 126 C2 32 1 S 66 58W
Pampanua, Indonesia .. 63 E6 4 16 S 120 8 E
Pampas, Argentina .... 126 D3 35 0 S 63 0W
Pampas, Peru .... 124 F4 12 20 S 74 50W
Pamphylia, Turkey .... 72 D4 37 0N 31 20 E
Pamplona, Colombia ... 124 B4 7 23N 72 39W
Pamplona, Spain 38 C3 42 48N 1 38W
Pampoenpoort, S. Africa 88 E3 31 3 S 22 40 E
Pamukçu, Turkey ..... 47 B9 39 30N 27 54 E
Pamukkale, Turkey .... 47 D11 37 55N 29 8 E
Pan de Azúcar △, Chile 126 B1 26 0 S 70 40W
Pan Xian, China ...... 58 E5 25 46N 104 38 E
Pana, U.S.A. 112 F10 39 23N 89 5W
Panabo, Phil. .... 61 H6 7 19N 125 42 E
Panaca, U.S.A. 109 H6 37 47N 114 23W
Panagyurishte, Bulgaria 45 D8 42 30N 24 15 E
Panaitan, Indonesia ... 63 G11 6 36 S 105 12 E
Panaji, India .... 66 M8 15 25N 73 50 E
Panamá, Panama 120 E4 9 0N 79 25W
Panama ■, Cent. Amer. 120 E4 8 48N 79 55W
Panamá, G. de, Panama 120 E4 8 4N 79 20W
Panama Canal, Panama 120 E4 9 10N 79 37W
Panama City, U.S.A. ... 115 K3 30 10N 85 40W
Panamint Range, U.S.A. 111 J9 36 20N 117 20W
Panamint Springs,
U.S.A. 111 J9 36 20N 117 28W
Panão, Peru .... 124 E3 9 55 S 75 55W
Panaon I., Phil. .... 61 F6 10 3N 125 13 E
Panare, Thailand ..... 65 J3 6 51N 101 30 E
Panarea, Italy .... 43 D8 38 38N 15 4 E
Panaro →, Italy ...... 41 D8 44 55N 11 25 E
Panay, Phil. .... 61 F5 11 10N 122 30 E
Panay, G., Phil. ...... 63 B6 11 0N 122 30 E
Pančevo, Serbia & M. .. 28 F5 44 52N 20 41 E
Panch'iao, Taiwan .... 59 E13 25 1N 121 27 E
Panciu, Romania ..... 29 E12 45 54N 27 8 E
Pancorbo, Desfiladero,
Spain 36 C7 42 32N 3 5W
Pâncota, Romania .... 28 D6 46 20N 21 45 E
Panda, Mozam. .... 89 C5 24 2 S 34 45 E
Pandan, Malaysia ..... 65 d 1 32N 103 46 E
Pandan, Antique, Phil. . 61 F5 11 45N 122 10 E
Pandan, Catanduanes,
Phil. .... 61 D6 14 3N 124 10 E
Pandan, Selat, Singapore 65 d 1 15N 103 44 E
Pandan Tampoi =
Tampoi, Malaysia ... 65 d 1 30N 103 39 E
Pandegelang, Indonesia 63 G12 6 25 S 106 5 E
Pandhana, India ...... 68 J7 21 42N 76 13 E
Pandharpur, India .... 66 L9 17 41N 75 20 E
Pando, Uruguay ...... 127 C4 34 44 S 56 0W
Pando, L. = Hope, L.,
Australia .... 95 D2 28 24 S 139 18 E
Pandokrátor, Greece .. 49 A3 39 45N 19 50 E
Pandora, Costa Rica .. 120 E3 9 43N 83 3W
Pandrup, Denmark .... 11 G3 57 14N 9 40 E
Panevéggio-Pale di San
Martino △, Italy .... 41 B8 46 14N 11 46 E
Panevėžys, Lithuania .. 9 J21 55 42N 24 25 E
Panfilov, Kazakhstan .. 52 E8 44 10N 80 0 E
Panfilovo, Russia ..... 34 E6 50 25N 42 46 E
Pang-Long, Burma .... 67 H21 23 11N 98 45 E
Pang Sida △, Thailand . 64 E4 14 5N 102 17 E
Pang-Yang, Burma .... 67 H21 22 7N 98 48 E
Panga, Dem. Rep. of
the Congo .... 86 B2 1 52N 26 18 E
Pangaíon Óros, Greece 45 F8 40 50N 24 0 E
Pangalanes, Canal des =
Ampangalana,
Lakandranon',
Madag. .... 89 C8 22 48 S 47 50 E
Pangani, Tanzania .... 86 D4 5 25 S 38 58 E
Pangani →, Tanzania .. 86 D4 5 26 S 38 58 E
Pangfou = Bengbu,
China .... 57 H9 32 58N 117 20 E
Pangil, Dem. Rep. of
the Congo .... 86 C2 3 10 S 26 35 E
Pangkah, Tanjung,
Indonesia .... 63 G15 6 51 S 112 33 E
Pangkajene, Indonesia . 63 E5 4 46 S 119 34 E
Pangkalanbrandan,
Indonesia .... 62 D1 4 1N 98 20 E
Pangkalanbuun,
Indonesia .... 62 E4 2 41 S 111 37 E
Pangkalpinang,
Indonesia .... 62 E3 2 0 S 106 0 E
Pangnirtung, Canada .. 101 B13 66 8N 65 43W
Pangong Tso, India ... 68 B8 34 40N 78 40 E
Panguitch, U.S.A. 109 H7 37 50N 112 26W
Pangutaran Group, Phil. 61 H4 6 18N 120 34 E
Panhandle, U.S.A. 113 H4 35 21N 101 23W
Pani Mines, India ..... 68 H5 22 29N 73 50 E
Pania-Mutombo,
Dem. Rep. of
the Congo .... 86 D1 5 11 S 23 51 E
Panikota I., India ..... 68 J4 20 46N 71 21 E
Panipat, India .... 68 E7 29 25N 77 2 E
Panjal Range = Pir
Panjal Range, India . 68 C7 32 30N 76 50 E
Panjang, Hon, Vietnam 65 H4 9 20N 103 28 E
Panjgur, Pakistan .... 66 F4 27 0N 64 5 E
Panjim = Panaji, India . 66 M8 15 25N 73 50 E
Panjin, China .... 57 D12 41 3N 122 2 E
Panjinad Barrage,
Pakistan .... 66 E7 29 22N 71 15 E
Panjnad →, Pakistan .. 68 E4 28 57N 70 30 E
Panjwai, Afghan. ..... 68 D1 31 26N 65 27 E
Pankshin, Nigeria .... 83 D6 9 16N 9 25 E
Panmunjŏm, N. Korea . 57 F14 37 59N 126 38 E
Panna, India .... 69 G9 24 40N 80 15 E
Panna Hills, India .... 69 G9 24 40N 81 15 E
Pannawonica, Australia 92 D2 21 39 S 116 19 E
Pannirtuuq =
Pangnirtung, Canada 101 B13 66 8N 65 43W
Pano Akil, Pakistan ... 68 F3 27 51N 69 7 E
Pano Lefkara, Cyprus . 49 E12 34 53N 33 20 E
Pano Panayia, Cyprus . 49 E11 34 55N 32 38 E
Panorama, Brazil ..... 127 A5 21 21 S 51 51W
Pánormon, Greece .... 49 D6 35 25N 24 41 E
Pansemal, India ...... 68 J6 21 39N 74 42 E
Panshan = Panjin, China 57 D12 41 3N 122 2 E
Panshi, China .... 57 C14 42 58N 126 5 E
Pantanal, Brazil ..... 124 H7 17 30 S 57 40W
Pantanos de Centla △,
Mexico 119 D6 18 25N 92 25W
Pantar, Indonesia .... 63 F6 8 28 S 124 10 E
Pante Macassar,
E. Timor .... 63 F6 9 30 S 123 58 E
Pante Makasar = Pante
Macassar, E. Timor . 63 F6 9 30 S 123 58 E
Pantelleria, Italy ..... 42 F4 36 50N 11 57 E
Pantón, Spain 36 C3 42 31N 7 37W
Pánuco, Mexico 119 C5 22 0N 98 15W
Panyam, Nigeria ..... 83 D6 9 27N 9 8 E
Panyu, China .... 59 F9 22 51N 113 20 E
Panzhihua, China .... 58 D3 26 33N 101 44 E
Páola, Italy .... 43 C9 39 21N 16 2 E
Paola, Malta .... 49 D2 35 52N 14 30 E
Paola, U.S.A. 112 F7 38 35N 94 53W
Paonia, U.S.A. 109 G10 38 52N 107 36W
Paoting = Baoding,
China .... 56 E8 38 50N 115 28 E
Paot'ou = Baotou, China 56 D6 40 32N 110 2 E
Paoua, C.A.R. .... 84 C3 7 9N 16 20 E
Pápa, Hungary ...... 28 C2 47 22N 17 30 E
Papa Stour, U.K. 13 A7 60 20N 1 42W
Papa Westray, U.K. ... 13 B6 59 20N 2 55W
Papagayo →, Mexico .. 119 D5 16 36N 99 43W
Papagayo, G. de,
Costa Rica 120 D2 10 30N 85 50W
Papakura, N.Z. ...... 91 G5 37 4 S 174 59 E
Papantla, Mexico 119 C5 20 30N 97 30W
Papar, Malaysia ..... 62 C5 5 45N 116 0 E
Paparoa △, N.Z. ..... 91 K3 42 7 S 171 26 E
Pápas, Ákra, Greece .. 46 C3 38 13N 21 20 E
Papeete, Tahiti ...... 97 J13 17 32 S 149 34W
Papenburg, Germany .. 24 B3 53 5N 7 23 E
Paphlagonia, Turkey .. 72 B5 41 30N 33 0 E
Paphos, Cyprus ...... 49 E11 34 46N 32 25 E
Papigochic →, Mexico . 118 B3 29 9N 109 40W
Paposo, Chile .... 126 B1 25 0 S 70 30W
Papoutsa, Cyprus .... 49 E12 34 54N 33 4 E
Papua □, Indonesia ... 63 E9 4 0 S 137 0 E
Papua New Guinea ■,
Oceania .... 96 H6 8 0 S 145 0 E
Papudo, Chile .... 126 C1 32 29 S 71 27W
Papuk, Croatia ...... 28 E2 45 30N 17 30 E
Papun, Burma .... 67 K20 18 2N 97 30 E
Papunya, Australia ... 92 D5 23 15 S 131 54 E
Pará = Belém, Brazil . 125 D9 1 20 S 48 30W
Pará □, Brazil ...... 125 D8 3 20 S 52 0W
Paraburdoo, Australia . 92 D2 23 14 S 117 32 E
Paracale, Phil. ...... 61 D5 14 17N 122 48 E
Paracatu, Brazil ..... 125 G9 17 10 S 46 50W
Paracel Is., S. China Sea 62 A4 15 50N 112 0 E
Parachilna, Australia . 95 E2 31 10 S 138 21 E
Parachinar, Pakistan . 68 C4 33 55N 70 5 E
Paraćin, Serbia & M. .. 44 C5 43 54N 21 27 E
Paradas, Spain 37 H5 37 18N 5 29W
Paradela, Spain 36 C3 42 44N 7 37W
Paradhísi, Greece ... 49 C10 36 18N 28 7 E
Paradip, India ...... 67 J15 20 15N 86 35 E
Paradise, Calif., U.S.A. 110 F5 39 46N 121 37W
Paradise, Nev., U.S.A. 111 J11 36 9N 115 10W
Paradise →, Canada .. 105 B8 53 27N 57 19W
Paradise Hill, Canada 103 C7 53 32N 109 28W
Paradise River, Canada 105 B8 53 27N 57 17W
Paradise Valley, U.S.A. 108 F5 41 30N 117 32W
Parado, Indonesia .... 63 F5 8 42 S 118 30 E
Paragould, U.S.A. 113 G9 36 3N 90 29W
Paragua →, Venezuela 124 B6 6 55N 62 55W
Paraguaçu →, Brazil .. 125 F11 12 45 S 38 54W
Paraguaçu Paulista,
Brazil .... 127 A5 22 22 S 50 35W
Paraguaná, Pen. de,
Venezuela 124 A5 12 0N 70 0W
Paraguarí, Paraguay .. 126 B4 25 36 S 57 0W
Paraguarí □, Paraguay 126 B4 26 0 S 57 10W
Paraguay ■, S. Amer. .. 126 A4 23 0 S 57 0W
Paraguay →, Paraguay 126 B4 27 18 S 58 38W
Paraíba = João Pessoa,
Brazil .... 125 E12 7 10 S 34 52W
Paraíba □, Brazil .... 125 E11 7 0 S 36 0W
Paraíba do Sul →,
Brazil .... 127 A7 21 37 S 41 3W
Parainen, Finland .... 9 F20 60 18N 22 18 E
Paraiso, Mexico 119 D6 18 24N 93 14W
Parak, Iran .... 71 E7 27 38N 52 25 E
Parakhino Paddubye,
Russia .... 32 C7 58 26N 33 10 E
Parakou, Benin ...... 83 D5 9 25N 2 40 E
Paralimni, Cyprus .... 49 D12 35 2N 33 58 E
Parálion-Astrous,
Greece .... 46 D4 37 25N 22 45 E
Paramaribo, Suriname . 125 B7 5 50N 55 10W
Paramithiá, Greece ... 46 B2 39 30N 20 35 E
Páramos del Batallón y
La Negra △,
Venezuela 121 E5 8 2N 71 55W
Paramushir, Ostrov,
Russia .... 53 D16 50 24N 156 0 E
Paran →, Israel ..... 74 E4 30 20N 35 10 E
Paraná, Argentina ... 126 C3 31 45 S 60 30W
Paranã, Brazil ...... 125 F9 12 30 S 47 48W
Paraná □, Brazil .... 127 A5 24 30 S 51 0W
Paraná →, Argentina .. 126 C4 33 43 S 59 15W
Paranaguá, Brazil ... 127 B6 25 30 S 48 30W
Paranaíba, Brazil ... 125 G8 19 40 S 51 11W
Paranaíba →, Brazil .. 125 H8 20 6 S 51 4W
Paranapanema →,
Brazil .... 127 A5 22 40 S 53 9W
Paranapiacaba, Serra do,
Brazil .... 127 A6 24 31 S 48 35W
Paranas, Phil. ...... 61 F6 11 42N 125 2 E
Paranavaí, Brazil .... 127 A5 23 4 S 52 56W
Parang, Maguindanao,
Phil. .... 63 C6 7 23N 124 16 E
Parang, Sulu, Phil. ... 61 J4 5 55N 120 54 E
Parângul Mare, Vf.,
Romania .... 29 E8 45 20N 23 37 E
Paraparaumu, N.Z. ... 91 J5 40 57 S 175 3 E
Parapóla, Greece .... 46 E5 36 55N 23 27 E
Paraspóri, Ákra, Greece 47 F9 35 55N 27 15 E
Paray-le-Monial, France 19 F11 46 27N 4 7 E
Parbati →, Mad. P.,
India .... 68 G7 25 50N 76 30 E
Parbati →, Raj., India . 68 F7 26 54N 77 53 E
Parbhani, India ..... 66 K10 19 8N 76 52 E
Parchim, Germany ... 24 B7 53 26N 11 52 E
Parczew, Poland .... 31 G9 51 40N 22 52 E
Pardes Hanna-Karkur,
Israel .... 74 C3 32 28N 34 57 E
Pardilla, Spain 36 D7 41 33N 3 43W
Pardo →, Bahia, Brazil 125 G11 15 40 S 39 0W
Pardo →, Mato Grosso,
Brazil .... 127 A5 21 46 S 52 9W
Pardubice, Czech Rep. . 26 A8 50 3N 15 45 E
Pardubický □,
Czech Rep. .... 26 B8 49 50N 16 0 E
Pare, Indonesia ..... 63 G15 7 43 S 112 12 E
Pare Mts., Tanzania .. 86 C4 4 0 S 37 45 E
Parecis, Serra dos, Brazil 124 F7 13 0 S 60 0W
Paredes de Nava, Spain 36 C6 42 9N 4 42W
Paren, Russia .... 53 C17 62 30N 163 15 E
Parent, Canada 104 C5 47 55N 74 35W
Parent, L., Canada ... 104 C4 48 31N 77 1W
Parentis-en-Born,
France 20 D2 44 21N 1 4W
Parepare, Indonesia .. 63 E5 4 0 S 119 40 E
Parfino, Russia ..... 32 D6 57 59N 31 34 E
Párga, Greece ...... 46 B2 39 15N 20 29 E
Pargas = Parainen,
Finland .... 9 F20 60 18N 22 18 E
Pargo, Pta. do, Madeira 48 D2 32 49N 17 17W
Paria, G. de, Venezuela 125 K14 10 20N 62 0W
Pariaguán, Venezuela . 124 B6 8 51N 64 34W
Paricutín, Cerro, Mexico 118 D4 19 28N 102 15W
Parigi, Indonesia .... 63 E6 0 50 S 120 5 E
Parika, Guyana 124 B7 6 50N 58 20W
Parikkala, Finland ... 32 B5 61 33N 29 31 E
Parima, Serra, Brazil . 124 C6 2 30N 64 0W
Parinari, Peru ...... 124 D4 4 35 S 74 25W
Pariñas, Pta., S. Amer. 122 D2 4 30 S 82 0W
Parincea, Romania ... 29 D12 46 27N 27 9 E
Parintins, Brazil .... 125 D7 2 40 S 56 50W
Paripatit Kyun, Burma 67 M18 14 55N 93 45 E
Paris, Canada 116 C4 43 12N 80 25W
Paris, France .... 19 D9 48 50N 2 20 E
Paris, Idaho, U.S.A. .. 108 E8 42 14N 111 24W
Paris, Ky., U.S.A. ... 114 F3 38 13N 84 15W
Paris, Tenn., U.S.A. .. 115 G1 36 18N 88 19W
Paris, Tex., U.S.A. ... 113 J7 33 40N 95 33W
Paris, Ville de □, France 19 D9 48 50N 2 20 E
Paris Charles de
Gaulle ✕ (CDG),
France .... 19 D9 49 0N 2 32 E
Paris Orly ✕ (ORY),
France .... 19 D9 48 44N 2 23 E
Parish, U.S.A. 117 C8 43 25N 76 8W
Parishville, U.S.A. ... 117 B10 44 38N 74 49W
Park, U.S.A. 110 B4 48 45N 122 18W
Park City, U.S.A. 113 G6 37 48N 97 20W
Park Falls, U.S.A. ... 112 C9 45 56N 90 27W
Park Head, Canada ... 116 B3 44 36N 81 9W
Park Hills, U.S.A. ... 113 G9 37 53N 90 28W
Park Range, U.S.A. .. 108 G10 40 0N 106 30W
Park Rapids, U.S.A. .. 112 B7 46 55N 95 4W
Park River, U.S.A. ... 112 A6 48 24N 97 45W
Park Rynie, S. Africa . 89 E5 30 25 S 30 45 E
Parkā Bandar, Iran .. 71 E8 25 55N 59 35 E
Parkano, Finland .... 9 E20 62 1N 23 0 E
Parker, Ariz., U.S.A. . 111 L12 34 9N 114 17W
Parker, Pa., U.S.A. .. 116 E5 41 5N 79 41W
Parker Dam, U.S.A. .. 111 L12 34 18N 114 8W
Parkersburg, U.S.A. .. 114 F5 39 16N 81 34W
Parkes, Australia .... 95 E4 33 9 S 148 11 E
Parkfield, U.S.A. 110 K6 35 54N 120 26W
Parkhill, Canada 116 C3 43 15N 81 38W
Parkland, U.S.A. 110 C4 47 9N 122 26W
Parkston, U.S.A. 112 D6 43 24N 97 59W
Parksville, Canada ... 102 D4 49 20N 124 21W
Parla, Spain 36 E7 40 14N 3 46W
Pârlita, Moldova .... 29 C12 47 19N 27 52 E
Parma, Italy .... 40 D7 44 48N 10 20 E
Parma, Idaho, U.S.A. . 108 E5 43 47N 116 57W
Parma, Ohio, U.S.A. .. 116 E3 41 23N 81 43W
Parma →, Italy ...... 40 D7 44 56N 10 26 E
Parnaguá, Brazil .... 125 F10 10 10 S 44 38W
Parnaíba, Brazil .... 125 D10 2 54 S 41 47W
Parnaíba →, Brazil .. 125 D10 3 0 S 41 50W
Parnassós, Greece ... 46 C4 38 35N 22 30 E
Párnis, Greece ...... 46 C5 38 14N 23 45 E
Párnitha △, Greece .. 46 C5 38 12N 23 44 E
Párnon Óros, Greece . 46 D4 37 15N 22 45 E
Pärnu, Estonia ..... 9 G21 58 28N 24 33 E
Paroo →, Australia .. 95 E3 31 28 S 143 32 E
Páros, Greece ...... 47 D7 37 5N 25 12 E
Parowan, U.S.A. 109 H7 37 51N 112 50W
Parpaillon, France ... 21 D10 44 30N 6 40 E
Parral, Chile .... 126 D1 36 10 S 71 52W
Parras, Mexico 118 B4 25 30N 102 20W
Parrett →, U.K. 15 F4 51 12N 3 1W
Parris I., U.S.A. 115 J5 32 20N 80 41W
Parrsboro, Canada ... 105 C7 45 30N 64 25W
Parry I., Canada 116 A4 45 18N 80 10W
Parry Is., Canada ... 98 B8 77 0N 110 0W
Parry Sound, Canada . 116 A5 45 20N 80 0W
Parsberg, Germany .. 25 F7 49 10N 11 43 E
Parsęta →, Poland ... 30 D2 54 11N 15 34 E
Parsnip →, Canada .. 102 B4 55 10N 123 2W
Parsons, U.S.A. 113 G7 37 20N 95 16W
Parsons Ra., Australia 94 A2 13 30 S 135 15 E
Partanna, Italy ..... 42 E5 37 43N 12 53 E
Partenio △, Italy ... 43 B7 40 56N 14 38 E
Parthenay, France ... 18 F6 46 38N 0 16W
Partinico, Italy ..... 42 D6 38 3N 13 7 E
Partizánske, Slovak Rep. 27 C11 48 38N 18 23 E
Partridge I., Canada .. 104 A2 55 59N 87 37W
Paru →, Brazil ..... 125 D8 1 33 S 52 38W
Parvān □, Afghan. ... 66 B6 35 0N 69 0 E
Parvatipuram, India .. 67 K13 18 50N 83 25 E
Parvatsar, India .... 68 F6 26 52N 74 49 E
Påryd, Sweden ..... 11 H9 56 34N 15 55 E
Parys, S. Africa .... 88 D4 26 52 S 27 29 E
Pas, Pta. des, Spain .. 48 C7 38 46N 1 26 E
Pas-de-Calais □, France 19 B9 50 30N 2 10 E
Pasada, Spain 36 B5 43 23N 5 40W
Pasadena, Canada ... 105 C8 49 1N 57 36W
Pasadena, Calif., U.S.A. 111 L8 34 9N 118 9W
Pasadena, Tex., U.S.A. 113 L7 29 43N 95 13W
Pasaje →, Argentina .. 126 B3 25 39 S 63 56W
Paşalimanı, Turkey .. 45 F11 40 29N 27 36 E
Pasar, Indonesia ... 63 J17 8 27 S 114 54 E
Pasay, Phil. .... 61 D4 14 33N 121 0 E
Pascagoula, U.S.A. .. 113 K10 30 21N 88 33W
Pascagoula →, U.S.A. 113 K10 30 23N 88 37W
Paşcani, Romania ... 29 C11 47 14N 26 45 E
Pasco, U.S.A. 108 C4 46 14N 119 6W
Pasco, Cerro de, Peru 124 F3 10 45 S 76 10W
Pasco I., Australia .. 92 D2 20 57 S 115 20 E
Pascoag, U.S.A. 117 E13 41 57N 71 42W
Pascua, I. de, Chile .. 97 K17 27 7 S 109 23W
Pasewalk, Germany .. 24 B9 53 30N 13 58 E
Pasfield L., Canada .. 103 B7 58 24N 105 20W
Pasha →, Russia .... 32 B7 60 29N 32 55 E
Pasinler, Turkey .... 73 C9 39 59N 41 41 E
Pasir Mas, Malaysia .. 65 J4 6 2N 102 8 E
Pasir Panjang, Singapore 65 d 1 18N 103 46 E
Pasir Putih, Malaysia . 65 K4 5 50N 102 24 E
Pasirian, Indonesia .. 63 H15 8 13 S 113 8 E
Pasirkuning, Indonesia 62 E2 0 30 S 104 33 E
Påskallavik, Sweden .. 11 G10 57 10N 16 26 E
Paskūh, Iran ...... 71 E9 27 34N 61 39 E
Pasłęk, Poland ..... 30 D6 54 3N 19 41 E
Pasłęka →, Poland .. 30 D6 54 26N 19 46 E
Pasley, C., Australia . 93 F3 33 52 S 123 35 E
Pašman, Croatia .... 41 E12 43 58N 15 20 E
Pasni, Pakistan .... 66 G3 25 15N 63 27 E
Paso Cantinela, Mexico 111 N11 32 33N 115 47W
Paso de Indios,
Argentina .... 128 E3 43 55 S 69 0W
Paso de los Libres,
Argentina .... 126 B4 29 44 S 57 10W
Paso de los Toros,
Uruguay .... 126 C4 32 45 S 56 30W
Paso Robles, U.S.A. .. 109 J3 35 38N 120 41W
Paspébiac, Canada .. 105 C6 48 3N 65 17W
Pasrur, Pakistan ... 68 C6 32 16N 74 43 E
Passage West, Ireland 12 E3 51 52N 8 21W
Passaic, U.S.A. 117 F10 40 51N 74 7W
Passau, Germany ... 25 G9 48 34N 13 28 E
Passero, C., Italy ... 43 F8 36 41N 15 10 E
Passo Fundo, Brazil . 127 B5 28 10 S 52 20W
Passos, Brazil ..... 125 H9 20 45 S 46 37W
Passow, Germany ... 24 B10 53 8N 14 6 E
Passy, France ..... 21 C10 45 55N 6 41 E
Pastavy, Belarus ... 9 J22 55 4N 26 50 E
Pastaza →, Peru ... 124 D3 4 50 S 76 52W
Pasto, Colombia ... 124 C3 1 13N 77 17W
Pastrana, Spain ... 38 E2 40 27N 2 53W
Pasuruan, Indonesia . 63 G15 7 40 S 112 44 E
Pasym, Poland .... 30 E7 53 48N 20 49 E
Pásztó, Hungary ... 28 C4 47 52N 19 43 E
Patagonia, Argentina . 128 F3 45 0 S 69 0W
Patagonia, U.S.A. .. 109 L8 31 33N 110 45W
Patambar, Iran .... 71 D9 29 45N 60 17 E
Patan = Lalitapur, Nepal 69 F11 27 40N 85 20 E
Patan, Gujarat, India .. 66 H8 23 54N 72 14 E
Patan, Maharashtra,
India .... 68 H5 23 54N 72 14 E
Patani, Indonesia ... 63 D7 0 20N 128 50 E
Pătârlagele, Romania . 29 E11 45 19N 26 21 E
Pataudi, India ..... 68 E7 28 18N 76 48 E
Patchewollock, Australia 95 F3 35 22 S 142 12 E
Patchogue, U.S.A. .. 117 F11 40 46N 73 1W
Pate, Kenya ...... 86 C5 2 10 S 41 0 E
Patea, N.Z. .... 91 H5 39 45 S 174 30 E
Pategi, Nigeria .... 83 D6 8 50N 5 45 E
Patensie, S. Africa .. 88 E3 33 46 S 24 49 E
Paterna, Spain 39 F4 39 30N 0 26W
Paternion, Austria .. 26 E6 46 43N 13 38 E
Paternò, Italy ..... 43 E7 37 34N 14 54 E
Pateros, U.S.A. 108 B4 48 3N 119 54W
Paterson, U.S.A. ... 117 F10 40 55N 74 11W
Paterson Ra., Australia 92 D3 21 45 S 122 10 E
Pathankot, India ... 68 C6 32 18N 75 45 E
Pathein = Bassein,
Burma .... 67 L19 16 45N 94 30 E
Pathfinder Reservoir,
U.S.A. 108 E10 42 28N 106 51W
Pathiu, Thailand ... 65 G2 10 42N 99 19 E
Pathum Thani, Thailand 64 E3 14 1N 100 32 E
Pati, Indonesia .... 63 G14 6 45 S 111 1 E
Patía →, Colombia .. 124 C3 2 13N 78 40W
Patiala, Punjab, India . 68 D7 30 23N 76 26 E
Patiala, Ut. P., India .. 69 F8 27 43N 79 1 E
Patine Kouka, Senegal 82 C2 12 45N 13 45W
Patitíron, Greece ... 46 B5 39 8N 23 50 E
Patkai Bum, India .. 67 F19 27 0N 95 30 E
Pátmos, Greece .... 47 D8 37 21N 26 36 E
Patna, India ...... 69 G11 25 35N 85 12 E
Patnos, Turkey .... 73 C10 39 13N 42 51 E

Pato Branco, Brazil 127 B5 26 13 S 52 40W
Patong, Ao, Thailand 65 a 7 54N 98 17 E
Patonga, Uganda 86 B3 2 45N 33 15 E
Patos, Albania 44 F3 40 42N 19 38 E
Patos, Brazil 125 E11 6 55 S 37 16W
Patos, L. dos, Brazil 127 C5 31 20 S 51 0W
Patos, Río de los →, Argentina 126 C2 31 18 S 69 25W
Patos de Minas, Brazil 125 G9 18 35 S 46 32W
Patquía, Argentina 126 C2 30 2 S 66 55W
Pátrai, Greece 46 C3 38 14N 21 47 E
Patraikós Kólpos, Greece 46 C3 38 17N 21 30 E
Patras = Pátrai, Greece 46 C3 38 14N 21 47 E
Patrocínio, Brazil 125 G9 18 57 S 47 0W
Pattada, Italy 42 B2 40 35N 9 6 E
Pattani, Thailand 65 J3 6 48N 101 15 E
Pattaya, Thailand 62 B2 12 52N 100 55 E
Patten, U.S.A. 115 C11 46 0N 68 38W
Patterson, Calif., U.S.A. 110 H5 37 28N 121 8W
Patterson, La., U.S.A. 113 L9 29 42N 91 18W
Patterson, Mt., U.S.A. 110 G7 38 29N 119 20W
Patti, Punjab, India 68 D6 31 17N 74 54 E
Patti, Ut. P., India 69 G10 25 55N 82 12 E
Patti, Italy 43 D7 38 8N 14 58 E
Pattoki, Pakistan 68 D5 31 5N 73 52 E
Patton, U.S.A. 116 F6 40 38N 78 39W
Patuakhali, Bangla. 67 H17 22 20N 90 25 E
Patuanak, Canada 103 B7 55 55N 107 43W
Patuca →, Honduras 120 C3 15 50N 84 18W
Patuca, Punta, Honduras 120 C3 15 49N 84 14W
Pătulele, Romania 28 F7 44 21N 22 47 E
Pátzcuaro, Mexico 118 D4 19 30N 101 40W
Pau, France 20 E3 43 19N 0 25W
Pau, Gave de →, France 20 E2 43 33N 1 12W
Pauillac, France 20 C3 45 11N 0 46W
Pauk, Burma 67 J19 21 27N 94 30 E
Paul I., Canada 105 A7 56 30N 61 20W
Paul Smiths, U.S.A. 117 B10 44 26N 74 15W
Paulatuk, Canada 100 B7 69 25N 124 0W
Paulhan, France 20 E7 43 33N 3 28 E
Paulistana, Brazil 125 E10 8 9 S 41 9W
Paulo Afonso, Brazil 125 E11 9 21 S 38 15W
Paulpietersburg, S. Africa 89 D5 27 23 S 30 50 E
Pauls Valley, U.S.A. 113 H6 34 44N 97 13W
Pauma Valley, U.S.A. 111 M10 33 16N 116 58W
Pauri, India 69 D8 30 9N 78 47 E
Pāveh, Iran 70 C5 35 3N 46 2 E
Pavelets, Russia 32 F10 53 49N 39 14 E
Pavia, Italy 40 C6 45 7N 9 8 E
Pavilion, U.S.A. 116 D6 42 52N 78 1W
Pavilly, France 18 C7 49 34N 0 57 E
Pāvilosta, Latvia 9 H19 56 53N 21 14 E
Pavlikeni, Bulgaria 45 C9 43 14N 25 20 E
Pavlodar, Kazakhstan 52 D8 52 33N 77 0 E
Pavlograd = Pavlohrad, Ukraine 33 H8 48 30N 35 52 E
Pavlohrad, Ukraine 33 H8 48 30N 35 52 E
Pavlovo, Russia 34 C6 55 58N 43 5 E
Pavlovsk, Russia 34 E5 50 26N 40 5 E
Pavlovskaya, Russia 35 G4 46 17N 39 47 E
Pavlovskiy-Posad, Russia 32 E10 55 47N 38 42 E
Pavullo nel Frignano, Italy 40 D7 44 20N 10 50 E
Pawai, Pulau, Singapore 65 d 1 11N 103 44 E
Pawayan, India 69 E9 28 4N 80 6 E
Pawhuska, U.S.A. 113 G6 36 40N 96 20W
Pawling, U.S.A. 117 E11 41 34N 73 36W
Pawnee, U.S.A. 113 G6 36 20N 96 48W
Pawnee City, U.S.A. 112 E6 40 7N 96 9W
Pawtucket, U.S.A. 117 E13 41 53N 71 23W
Paximádhia, Greece 49 E6 35 0N 24 35 E
Paxton, Ill., U.S.A. 114 E1 40 27N 88 6W
Paxton, Nebr., U.S.A. 112 E4 41 7N 101 21W
Payakumbuh, Indonesia 62 E2 0 20 S 100 35 E
Payerne, Switz. 25 J2 46 49N 6 56 E
Payette, U.S.A. 108 D5 44 5N 116 56W
Paymogo, Spain 37 H3 37 44N 7 21W
Payne Bay = Kangirsuk, Canada 101 B13 60 0N 70 0W
Payne L., Canada 101 C12 59 30N 74 30W
Paynes Find, Australia 93 E2 29 15 S 117 42 E
Paynesville, Liberia 82 D2 6 20N 10 45W
Paynesville, U.S.A. 112 C7 45 23N 94 43W
Pays de la Loire □, France 18 E6 47 45N 0 25W
Paysandú, Uruguay 126 C4 32 19 S 58 8W
Payson, U.S.A. 109 J8 34 14N 111 20W
Paz →, Guatemala 120 D1 13 44N 90 10W
Paz, B. de la, Mexico 118 C2 24 15N 110 25W
Pāzanān, Iran 71 D6 30 35N 49 59 E
Pazar, Turkey 73 B9 41 10N 40 50 E
Pazarcık, Turkey 72 D7 37 30N 37 17 E
Pazardzhik, Bulgaria 45 D8 42 12N 24 20 E
Pazarköy, Turkey 47 B9 39 51N 27 24 E
Pazarlar, Turkey 47 C11 39 0N 29 7 E
Pazaryeri, Turkey 47 B11 40 0N 29 56 E
Pazaryolu, Turkey 73 B9 40 21N 40 47 E
Pazin, Croatia 41 C10 45 14N 13 56 E
Pčinja →, Macedonia 44 E5 41 50N 21 45 E
Pe Ell, U.S.A. 110 D3 46 34N 123 18W
Peabody, U.S.A. 117 D14 42 31N 70 56W
Peace →, Canada 102 B6 59 0N 111 25W
Peace Point, Canada 102 B6 59 7N 112 27W
Peace River, Canada 102 B5 56 15N 117 18W
Peach Springs, U.S.A. 109 J7 35 32N 113 25W
Peachland, Canada 102 D5 49 47N 119 45W
Peachtree City, U.S.A. 115 J3 33 25N 84 35W
Peak, The = Kinder Scout, U.K. 14 D6 53 24N 1 52W
Peak Charles △, Australia 93 F3 32 42 S 121 10 E
Peak District △, U.K. 14 D6 53 24 S 1 46W
Peak Hill, N.S.W., Australia 95 E4 32 47 S 148 11 E
Peak Hill, W. Austral., Australia 93 E2 25 35 S 118 43 E
Peak Ra., Australia 94 C4 22 50 S 148 20 E
Peake Cr. →, Australia 95 D2 28 2 S 136 7 E
Peal de Becerro, Spain 37 H7 37 55N 3 7W
Peale, Mt., U.S.A. 109 G9 38 26N 109 14W
Pearblossom, U.S.A. 111 L9 34 30N 117 55W
Pearl →, U.S.A. 113 K10 30 11N 89 32W
Pearl City, U.S.A. 106 H16 21 24N 157 59W
Pearl Harbor, U.S.A. 106 H16 21 21N 157 57W
Pearl River = Zhu Jiang →, China 59 F9 22 45N 113 37 E
Pearl River, U.S.A. 117 E10 41 4N 74 2W
Pearsall, U.S.A. 113 L5 28 54N 99 6W
Peary Land, Greenland 4 A6 82 40N 33 0W
Pease →, U.S.A. 113 H5 34 2N 99 2W
Peawanuck, Canada 101 C11 55 15N 85 12W
Pebane, Mozam. 87 F4 17 10 S 38 8 E

Pebas, Peru 124 D4 3 10 S 71 46W
Pebble Beach, U.S.A. 110 J5 36 34N 121 57W
Peć, Serbia & M. 44 D4 42 40N 20 17 E
Péccioli, Italy 40 E7 43 33N 10 43 E
Pechea, Romania 29 E12 45 36N 27 49 E
Pechenga, Russia 52 C4 69 29N 31 4 E
Pechenizhyn, Ukraine 29 B9 48 30N 24 48 E
Pechiguera, Pta., Canary Is. 48 F6 28 51N 13 53W
Pechnezhskoye Vdkhr., Ukraine 33 G9 50 5N 36 54 E
Pechora, Russia 52 C6 65 10N 57 11 E
Pechora →, Russia 52 C6 68 13N 54 15 E
Pechorskaya Guba, Russia 52 C6 68 40N 54 0 E
Pechory, Russia 9 H22 57 48N 27 40 E
Pecica, Romania 28 D6 46 10N 21 3 E
Pecka, Serbia & M. 44 B3 44 18N 19 33 E
Pécora, C., Italy 42 C1 39 27N 8 23 E
Pecos, U.S.A. 113 K3 31 26N 103 30W
Pecos →, U.S.A. 113 L3 29 42N 101 22W
Pécs, Hungary 28 D3 46 5N 18 15 E
Pedder, L., Australia 95 G4 42 55 S 146 10 E
Peddie, S. Africa 89 E4 33 14 S 27 7 E
Pedernales, Dom. Rep. 121 C5 18 2N 71 44W
Pedirka, Australia 95 D2 26 40 S 135 14 E
Pedra Azul, Brazil 125 G10 16 2 S 41 17W
Pedreguer, Spain 39 G5 38 48N 0 3 E
Pedreiras, Brazil 125 D10 4 32 S 44 40W
Pedro Afonso, Brazil 125 E9 9 0 S 48 10W
Pedro Cays, Jamaica 120 C4 17 5N 77 48W
Pedro de Valdivia, Chile 126 A2 22 55 S 69 38W
Pedro Juan Caballero, Paraguay 127 A4 22 30 S 55 40W
Pedro Muñoz, Spain 37 F8 39 25N 2 56W
Pedrógão Grande, Portugal 36 F2 39 55N 8 9W
Pee Dee →, U.S.A. 115 J6 33 22N 79 16W
Peebinga, Australia 95 E3 34 52 S 140 57 E
Peebles, U.K. 13 F5 55 40N 3 11W
Peekskill, U.S.A. 117 E11 41 17N 73 55W
Peel, U.K. 14 C3 54 13N 4 40W
Peel →, Australia 95 E5 30 50 S 150 29 E
Peel →, Canada 100 B6 67 0N 135 0W
Peel Sd., Canada 100 A10 73 0N 96 0W
Peene →, Germany 24 A9 54 9N 13 46 E
Peera Peera Poolanna L., Australia 95 D2 26 30 S 138 0 E
Peerless Lake, Canada 102 B6 56 37N 114 40W
Peers, Canada 102 C5 53 40N 116 0W
Pegasus Bay, N.Z. 91 K4 43 20 S 173 10 E
Peggau, Austria 26 D8 47 12N 15 21 E
Pegnitz, Germany 25 F7 49 44N 11 31 E
Pegnitz →, Germany 25 F6 49 30N 10 59 E
Pego, Spain 39 G4 38 51N 0 8W
Pegu, Burma 67 L20 17 20N 96 29 E
Pegu Yoma, Burma 67 K20 19 0N 96 0 E
Pehčevo, Macedonia 44 E6 41 41N 22 55 E
Pehlivanköy, Turkey 45 E10 41 20N 26 55 E
Pehuajó, Argentina 126 D3 35 45 S 62 0W
Pei Xian = Pizhou, China 56 G9 34 44N 116 55 E
Peine, Chile 126 A2 23 45 S 68 8W
Peine, Germany 24 C6 52 19N 10 14 E
Peip'ing = Beijing, China 56 E9 39 55N 116 20 E
Peipus, L. = Chudskoye, Ozero, Russia 9 G22 58 13N 27 30 E
Peissenberg, Germany 25 H7 47 48N 11 4 E
Peitz, Germany 24 D10 51 51N 14 24 E
Peixe, Brazil 125 F9 12 0 S 48 40W
Peixe →, Brazil 125 H8 21 31 S 51 58W
Pek →, Serbia & M. 44 B5 44 45N 21 29 E
Pekalongan, Indonesia 63 G13 6 53 S 109 40 E
Pekan, Malaysia 65 L4 3 30N 103 25 E
Pekan Nenas, Malaysia 65 d 1 31N 103 31 E
Pekanbaru, Indonesia 62 D2 0 30N 101 15 E
Pekang, Taiwan 59 F13 23 34N 120 18 E
Pekin, U.S.A. 112 E10 40 35N 89 40W
Peking = Beijing, China 56 E9 39 55N 116 20 E
Pekutatan, Indonesia 63 J17 8 25 S 114 49 E
Péla, Guinea 82 D3 7 37N 9 7W
Pelabuhan Kelang, Malaysia 65 L3 3 0N 101 23 E
Pelabuhan Ratu, Teluk, Indonesia 63 G12 7 5 S 106 30 E
Pelabuhanratu, Indonesia 63 G12 7 0 S 106 32 E
Pélagos, Greece 46 B6 39 17N 24 4 E
Pelaihari, Indonesia 62 E4 3 55 S 114 45 E
Pelat, Mt., France 21 D10 44 16N 6 42 E
Pełczyce, Poland 31 E2 53 3N 15 16 E
Peleaga, Vf., Romania 28 E7 45 22N 22 55 E
Pelée, Mt., Martinique 120 c 14 48N 61 10W
Pelee, Pt., Canada 104 D3 41 54N 82 31W
Pelee I., Canada 116 E2 41 47N 82 40W
Pelekech, Kenya 86 B4 3 52N 35 8 E
Peleng, Indonesia 63 E6 1 20 S 123 30 E
Pelentong, Malaysia 65 d 1 32N 103 49 E
Pélézi, Ivory C. 82 D3 7 17N 6 54W
Pelhřimov, Czech Rep. 26 B8 49 24N 15 12 E
Pelican, U.S.A. 102 B1 57 58N 136 14W
Pelican L., Canada 103 C8 52 28N 100 20W
Pelican Narrows, Canada 103 B8 55 10N 102 56W
Pelister △, Macedonia 44 F5 41 0N 21 10 E
Pelješac, Croatia 41 F14 42 55N 17 25 E
Pelkosenniemi, Finland 8 C22 67 6N 27 28 E
Pella, Greece 44 F6 40 46N 22 28 E
Pella, S. Africa 88 D2 29 1 S 19 6 E
Pella □, Greece 44 F6 40 52N 22 0 E
Pello, Finland 8 C21 66 47N 23 59 E
Pellworm, Germany 24 A4 54 31N 8 39 E
Pelly →, Canada 100 B6 62 47N 137 19W
Pelly Bay, Canada 101 B11 68 38N 89 50W
Peloponnese = Pelopónnisos □, Greece 46 D4 37 10N 22 0 E
Pelopónnisos □, Greece 46 D4 37 10N 22 0 E
Peloritani, Monti, Italy 43 D8 38 3N 15 0 E
Pelorus Sd., N.Z. 91 J4 40 59 S 173 59 E
Pelotas, Brazil 127 C5 31 42 S 52 23W
Pelotas →, Brazil 127 B5 27 28 S 51 55W
Pelovo, Bulgaria 45 C8 43 26N 24 17 E
Pelplin, Poland 30 E5 53 55N 18 42 E
Pelvoux, Massif du, France 21 D10 44 52N 6 20 E
Pemalang, Indonesia 63 G13 6 53 S 109 23 E
Pemanggil, Pulau, Malaysia 65 L5 2 37N 104 21 E
Pematangsiantar, Indonesia 62 D1 2 57N 99 5 E
Pemba, Mozam. 87 E5 12 58 S 40 30 E
Pemba, Zambia 87 F2 16 30 S 27 28 E
Pemba Channel, Tanzania 86 D4 5 0 S 39 37 E

Pemba I., Tanzania 86 D4 5 0 S 39 45 E
Pemberton, Australia 93 F2 34 30 S 116 0 E
Pemberton, Canada 102 C4 50 25N 122 50W
Pembina, U.S.A. 112 A6 48 58N 97 15W
Pembroke, Canada 104 C4 45 50N 77 7W
Pembroke, U.K. 15 F3 51 41N 4 55W
Pembrokeshire □, U.K. 15 F3 51 52N 4 56W
Pembrokeshire Coast △, U.K. 15 F2 51 50N 5 2W
Pen-y-Ghent, U.K. 14 C5 54 10N 2 14W
Peña, Sierra de la, Spain 38 C4 42 32N 0 45W
Peña de Francia, Sierra de la, Spain 36 E4 40 32N 6 0W
Penafiel, Portugal 36 D2 41 12N 8 17W
Peñafiel, Spain 36 D7 41 35N 4 7W
Peñaflor, Spain 37 H5 37 43N 5 21W
Penal, Trin. & Tob. 125 K15 10 9N 61 29W
Peñalara, Spain 36 E7 40 51N 3 57W
Penamacôr, Portugal 36 E3 40 10N 7 10W
Penang = Pinang, Malaysia 65 c 5 25N 100 15 E
Penápolis, Brazil 127 A6 21 30 S 50 0W
Peñaranda de Bracamonte, Spain 36 E5 40 53N 5 13W
Peñarroya, Spain 38 E4 40 25N 0 40W
Peñarroya-Pueblonuevo, Spain 37 G5 38 19N 5 16W
Penarth, U.K. 15 F4 51 26N 3 11W
Peñas, C. de, Spain 36 B5 43 42N 5 52W
Penas, G. de, Chile 128 F2 47 0 S 75 0W
Peñas de San Pedro, Spain 39 G3 38 44N 2 0W
Peñas del Chache, Canary Is. 48 E6 29 6N 13 33W
Peñausende, Spain 36 D5 41 17N 5 52W
Pench'i = Benxi, China 57 D12 41 20N 123 48 E
Pend Oreille →, U.S.A. 108 B5 49 4N 117 37W
Pend Oreille, L., U.S.A. 108 C5 48 10N 116 21W
Pendálofon, Greece 44 F5 40 14N 21 12 E
Pendembu, Eastern, S. Leone 82 D2 8 30N 10 42W
Pendembu, Northern, S. Leone 82 D2 9 7N 11 14W
Pender B., Australia 92 C3 16 45 S 122 42 E
Pendik, Turkey 45 F13 40 53N 29 13 E
Pendjari →, Benin 83 C5 11 15N 1 32 E
Pendjari □, Benin 83 C5 10 55N 0 50 E
Pendleton, U.S.A. 108 D4 45 40N 118 47W
Pendra, India 69 H9 22 46N 81 57 E
Peneda-Gerês △, Portugal 36 D2 41 57N 8 15W
Penedo, Brazil 125 F11 10 15 S 36 36W
Penelokan, Indonesia 63 J18 8 17 S 115 22 E
Penetanguishene, Canada 116 B5 44 50N 79 55W
Penfield, U.S.A. 116 E6 41 13N 78 35W
Pengalengan, Indonesia 63 G12 7 9 S 107 30 E
Penge, Kasai-Or., Dem. Rep. of the Congo 86 D1 5 30 S 24 33 E
Penge, Sud-Kivu, Dem. Rep. of the Congo 86 C2 4 27 S 28 25 E
P'enghu Ch'üntou, Taiwan 59 F12 23 34N 119 30 E
Penglai, China 57 F11 37 48N 120 42 E
Pengshan, China 58 B4 30 14N 103 58 E
Pengshui, China 58 C7 29 17N 108 12 E
Penguin, Australia 95 G4 41 8 S 146 6 E
Pengxi, China 58 B5 30 44N 105 45 E
Pengze, China 59 C11 29 52N 116 32 E
Penhalonga, Zimbabwe 87 F3 18 52 S 32 40 E
Peniche, Portugal 37 F1 39 19N 9 22W
Penicuik, U.K. 13 F5 55 50N 3 13W
Penida, Nusa, Indonesia 63 K18 8 45 S 115 30 E
Peninnes, Alpes = Pennine, Alpi, Alps 25 J3 46 4N 7 30 E
Peninsular Malaysia □, Malaysia 65 L4 4 0N 102 0 E
Peñíscola, Spain 38 E5 40 22N 0 24 E
Penitente, Serra do, Brazil 125 E9 8 45 S 46 20W
Penkridge, U.K. 14 E5 52 44N 2 6W
Penmarch, France 18 E2 47 49N 4 21W
Penmarch, Pte. de, France 18 E2 47 48N 4 22W
Penn Hills, U.S.A. 116 F5 40 28N 79 52W
Penn Yan, U.S.A. 116 D7 42 40N 77 3W
Penna, Punta della, Italy 41 F11 42 10N 14 43 E
Pennant, Canada 103 C7 50 32N 108 14W
Penne, Italy 41 F10 42 27N 13 55 E
Penner →, India 66 M12 14 35N 80 10 E
Pennine, Alpi, Alps 25 J3 46 4N 7 30 E
Pennines, U.K. 14 C5 54 45N 2 27W
Pennington, U.S.A. 110 F3 39 15N 121 47W
Pennington →, Nigeria 83 E6 4 45N 5 35 E
Pennino, Mte., Italy 41 E9 43 6N 12 53 E
Pennsburg, U.S.A. 117 F9 40 23N 75 29W
Pennsylvania □, U.S.A. 114 E7 40 45N 77 30W
Penny, Canada 102 C4 53 51N 121 20W
Peno, Russia 32 D7 57 2N 32 49 E
Penobscot →, U.S.A. 115 C11 44 30N 68 48W
Penobscot B., U.S.A. 115 C11 44 35N 68 50W
Penola, Australia 95 F3 37 25 S 140 48 E
Penong, Australia 93 F5 31 56 S 133 1 E
Penonomé, Panama 120 E3 8 31N 80 21W
Penrith, Australia 95 E5 33 43 S 150 38 E
Penrith, U.K. 14 C5 54 40N 2 45W
Penryn, U.K. 15 G2 50 9N 5 7W
Pensacola, U.S.A. 115 K2 30 25N 87 13W
Pensacola Mts., Antarctica 5 E1 84 0 S 40 0W
Pense, Canada 103 C8 50 25N 104 59W
Penshurst, Australia 95 F3 37 49 S 142 20 E
Penticton, Canada 102 D5 49 30N 119 38W
Pentland, Australia 94 C4 20 32 S 145 25 E
Pentland Firth, U.K. 13 C5 58 43N 3 10W
Pentland Hills, U.K. 13 F5 55 48N 3 25W
Pentland Hills △, U.K. 13 F5 55 50N 3 20W
Penza, Russia 34 D7 53 15N 45 5 E
Penzance, U.K. 15 G2 50 7N 5 33W
Penzberg, Germany 25 H7 47 45N 11 23 E
Penzhino, Russia 53 C17 63 30N 167 55 E
Penzhinskaya Guba, Russia 53 C17 61 30N 163 0 E
Penzhou, China 58 B4 31 4N 103 32 E
Penzlin, Germany 24 B9 53 30N 13 5 E
Peoria, Ariz., U.S.A. 109 K7 33 35N 112 14W
Peoria, Ill., U.S.A. 112 E10 40 42N 89 36W
Pepacton Reservoir, U.S.A. 117 D10 42 5N 74 58W
Pepani →, S. Africa 88 D3 25 49 S 22 47 E
Pepel, S. Leone 82 D2 8 40N 13 5W
Peqin, Albania 44 E3 41 4N 19 44 E
Pera Hd., Australia 94 A3 12 55 S 141 37 E
Perabumulih, Indonesia 62 E2 3 27 S 104 15 E
Perak →, Malaysia 65 K3 4 0N 100 50 E

Perakhóra, Greece 46 C4 38 2N 22 56 E
Perales de Alfambra, Spain 38 E4 40 38N 1 0W
Perales del Puerto, Spain 36 E4 40 10N 6 40W
Pérama, Kérkira, Greece 49 A3 39 34N 19 54 E
Pérama, Kríti, Greece 49 D6 35 20N 24 40 E
Perancak, Indonesia 63 J17 8 23 S 114 37 E
Peräpohjola, Finland 8 C22 66 16N 26 10 E
Perast, Serbia & M. 44 D2 42 31N 18 47 E
Percé, Canada 105 C7 48 31N 64 13W
Perche, France 18 D8 48 31N 1 1 E
Perche □, France 18 D7 48 24N 0 46 E
Perchtoldsdorf, Austria 27 C9 48 7N 16 16 E
Percival Lakes, Australia 92 D4 21 25 S 125 0 E
Percy, France 18 D5 48 55N 1 11W
Percy Is., Australia 94 C5 21 39 S 150 16 E
Perdido, Mte., Spain 38 C5 42 40N 0 5 E
Perdu, Mt. = Perdido, Mte., Spain 38 C5 42 40N 0 5 E
Perechyn, Ukraine 28 B7 48 44N 22 28 E
Perehinske, Ukraine 29 B9 48 49N 24 11 E
Pereira, Colombia 124 C3 4 49N 75 43W
Perelazovskiy, Russia 35 F6 49 8N 42 35 E
Perenjori, Australia 93 E2 29 26 S 116 16 E
Peresecina, Moldova 29 C13 47 16N 28 46 E
Pereslavl-Zalesskiy, Russia 32 D10 56 45N 38 50 E
Peretu, Romania 29 F10 44 3N 25 5 E
Pereyaslav-Khmelnytskyy, Ukraine 33 G6 50 3N 31 28 E
Pereyma, Ukraine 29 B14 48 4N 29 30 E
Pérez, I., Mexico 119 C7 22 24N 89 42W
Perg, Austria 26 C7 48 15N 14 38 E
Pergamino, Argentina 126 C3 33 52 S 60 30W
Pergau →, Malaysia 65 K3 5 23N 102 2 E
Pérgine Valsugana, Italy 41 B8 46 4N 11 14 E
Pérgola, Italy 41 E9 43 34N 12 50 E
Perham, U.S.A. 112 B7 46 36N 95 34W
Perhentian, Kepulauan, Malaysia 65 K4 5 54N 102 42 E
Periam, Romania 28 D5 46 2N 20 52 E
Péribonka →, Canada 105 C5 48 45N 72 5W
Péribonka, L., Canada 105 B5 50 1N 71 10W
Perico, Argentina 126 A2 24 20 S 65 5W
Pericos, Mexico 118 B3 25 3N 107 42W
Périers, France 18 C5 49 11N 1 25W
Périgord, France 20 D4 45 0N 0 40 E
Périgord-Limousin △, France 20 C4 45 40N 0 50 E
Périgueux, France 20 C4 45 10N 0 42 E
Perijá, ∠Venezuela 121 E5 9 30N 72 55W
Perijá, Sierra de, Colombia 124 B4 9 30N 73 3W
Peristéra, Greece 46 B5 39 15N 23 58 E
Peristerona →, Cyprus 49 D12 35 8N 33 5 E
Perito Moreno, Argentina 128 F2 46 36 S 70 56W
Perivol = Dragovishtitsa, Bulgaria 44 D6 42 22N 22 39 E
Perkasie, U.S.A. 117 F9 40 22N 75 18W
Perković, Croatia 41 E13 43 41N 16 10 E
Perlas, Arch. de las, Panama 120 E4 8 41N 79 7W
Perlas, Punta de, Nic. 120 D3 12 30N 83 30W
Perleberg, Germany 24 B7 53 5N 11 52 E
Perlez, Serbia & M. 42 E5 45 11N 20 22 E
Perm, Russia 52 D6 58 0N 56 10 E
Përmet, Albania 44 F4 40 15N 20 21 E
Pernambuco = Recife, Brazil 125 E12 8 0 S 35 0W
Pernambuco □, Brazil 125 E11 8 0 S 37 0W
Pernatty Lagoon, Australia 95 E2 31 30 S 137 12 E
Pernik, Bulgaria 44 D7 42 35N 23 2 E
Peron Is., Australia 92 B5 13 9 S 130 4 E
Peron Pen., Australia 93 E1 26 0 S 113 10 E
Péronne, France 19 C9 49 55N 2 57 E
Perosa Argentina, Italy 40 D4 44 58N 7 10 E
Perow, Canada 102 C3 54 35N 126 10W
Perpignan, France 20 F6 42 42N 2 53 E
Perris, U.S.A. 111 M9 33 47N 117 14W
Perros-Guirec, France 18 D3 48 49N 3 28W
Perry, Fla., U.S.A. 115 K4 30 7N 83 35W
Perry, Ga., U.S.A. 115 J4 32 28N 83 44W
Perry, Iowa, U.S.A. 112 E7 41 51N 94 6W
Perry, Okla., U.S.A. 113 G6 36 17N 97 14W
Perryton, U.S.A. 113 G4 36 24N 100 48W
Perryville, U.S.A. 113 G10 37 43N 89 52W
Persan, France 19 C9 49 9N 2 18 E
Persberg, Sweden 10 E8 59 47N 14 15 E
Perşembe, Turkey 72 B7 41 5N 37 46 E
Persepolis, Iran 71 D7 29 55N 52 50 E
Pershotravensk, Ukraine 33 G4 50 13N 27 40 E
Persia = Iran ■, Asia 71 C7 33 0N 53 0 E
Persian Gulf = Gulf, The, Asia 71 E6 27 0N 50 0 E
Perstorp, Sweden 11 H7 56 10N 13 25 E
Pertek, Turkey 73 C8 38 51N 39 19 E
Perth, Australia 93 F2 31 57 S 115 52 E
Perth, Canada 117 B8 44 55N 76 15W
Perth, U.K. 13 E5 56 24N 3 26W
Perth & Kinross □, U.K. 13 E5 56 45N 3 55W
Perth Amboy, U.S.A. 117 F10 40 31N 74 16W
Perth-Andover, Canada 105 C6 46 44N 67 42W
Pertuis, France 21 E9 43 42N 5 30 E
Pertusato, C., France 21 G13 41 21N 9 11 E
Peru, Ind., U.S.A. 114 E2 40 45N 86 4W
Peru, N.Y., U.S.A. 117 B11 44 35N 73 32W
Peru ■, S. Amer. 124 D4 4 0 S 75 0W
Peru Basin, Pac. Oc. 97 J18 20 0 S 95 0W
Peru-Chile Trench, Pac. Oc. 124 G3 20 0 S 72 0W
Perúgia, Italy 41 E9 43 7N 12 23 E
Perušić, Croatia 41 D12 44 40N 15 22 E
Pervomaysk, Russia 34 C6 54 56N 43 58 E
Pervomaysk, Ukraine 33 H6 48 10N 30 46 E
Pervouralsk, Russia 52 D6 56 59N 59 59 E
Pésaro, Italy 41 E9 43 54N 12 55 E
Pescadores = P'enghu Ch'üntou, Taiwan 59 F12 23 34N 119 30 E
Pescara, Italy 41 F11 42 28N 14 13 E
Pescara →, Italy 41 F11 42 28N 14 13 E
Peschanokopskoye, Russia 35 G5 46 14N 41 4 E
Péscia, Italy 40 E7 43 54N 10 41 E
Pescina, Italy 41 F10 42 2N 13 39 E
Peshawar, Pakistan 68 B4 34 2N 71 37 E
Peshkopi, Albania 44 E4 41 41N 20 25 E
Peshtera, Bulgaria 45 D8 42 2N 24 18 E
Peshtigo, U.S.A. 114 C2 45 4N 87 46W
Peski, Russia 34 E6 51 14N 42 29 E
Peso da Régua, Portugal 36 D3 41 10N 7 47W
Pesqueira, Brazil 125 E11 8 20 S 36 42W
Pessac, France 20 D3 44 48N 0 37W
Pest □, Hungary 28 C4 47 29N 19 5 E
Pestovo, Russia 32 C8 58 33N 35 42 E

Pestravka, Russia 34 D9 52 28N 49 57 E
Péta, Greece 46 B3 39 10N 21 2 E
Petah Tiqwa, Israel 74 C3 32 6N 34 53 E
Petalídhion, Greece 46 E3 36 57N 21 55 E
Petaling Jaya, Malaysia 65 L3 3 4N 101 42 E
Petaloudhes, Greece 49 C10 36 20N 24 40 E
Petaluma, U.S.A. 110 G4 38 14N 122 39W
Pétange, Lux. 17 E5 49 33N 5 55 E
Petaro, Pakistan 68 G3 25 31N 68 18 E
Petatlán, Mexico 118 D4 17 31N 101 16W
Petauke, Zambia 87 E3 14 14 S 31 20 E
Petawawa, Canada 104 C4 45 54N 77 17W
Petén Itzá, L., Guatemala 120 C2 16 58N 89 50W
Peter I., Br. Virgin Is. 121 e 18 22N 64 35W
Peter I.s Øy, Antarctica 5 C16 69 0 S 91 0W
Peter Pond L., Canada 103 B7 55 55N 108 44W
Peterbell, Canada 104 C3 48 36N 83 21W
Peterborough, Australia 95 E2 32 58 S 138 51 E
Peterborough, Canada 116 B6 44 20N 78 20W
Peterborough, U.K. 15 E7 52 35N 0 15W
Peterborough, U.S.A. 117 D13 42 53N 71 57W
Peterborough □, U.K. 15 E7 52 35N 0 15W
Peterculter, U.K. 13 D6 57 6N 2 16W
Peterhead, U.K. 13 D7 57 31N 1 48W
Peterlee, U.K. 14 C6 54 47N 1 20W
Petermann Ranges, Australia 92 E5 26 0 S 130 30 E
Petersburg, Alaska, U.S.A. 100 C6 56 48N 132 58W
Petersburg, Pa., U.S.A. 116 F6 40 34N 78 3W
Petersburg, Va., U.S.A. 114 G7 37 14N 77 24W
Petersburg, W. Va., U.S.A. 114 F6 39 1N 79 5W
Petersfield, U.K. 15 F7 51 1N 0 56W
Petershagen, Germany 24 C4 52 23N 8 58 E
Petília Policastro, Italy 43 C9 39 7N 16 48 E
Petit-Canal, Guadeloupe 120 b 16 25N 61 31W
Petit Goâve, Haiti 121 C5 18 27N 72 51W
Petit Jardin, Canada 105 C8 48 28N 59 14W
Petit Lac Manicouagan, Canada 105 B6 51 25N 67 40W
Petit-Mécatina →, Canada 105 B8 50 40N 59 30W
Petit-Mécatina, Î. du, Canada 105 B8 50 30N 59 25W
Petit Piton, St. Lucia 121 f 13 51N 61 5W
Petit-Saguenay, Canada 105 C5 48 15N 70 4W
Petit Saint Bernard, Col du, Italy 21 C10 45 40N 6 52 E
Petitcodiac, Canada 105 C6 45 57N 65 11W
Petite Terre, Iles de la, Guadeloupe 120 b 16 13N 61 9W
Petitot →, Canada 102 A4 60 14N 123 29W
Petitsikapau L., Canada 105 B6 54 37N 66 25W
Petlad, India 68 H5 22 30N 72 45 E
Peto, Mexico 119 C7 20 10N 88 53W
Petone, N.Z. 91 J5 41 13 S 174 53 E
Petorca, Chile 126 C1 32 15 S 70 56W
Petoskey, U.S.A. 114 C3 45 22N 84 57W
Petra, Jordan 74 E4 30 20N 35 22 E
Petra, Spain 48 B10 39 37N 3 6 E
Petra, Ostrova, Russia 4 B13 76 15N 118 30 E
Petra Velikogo, Zaliv, Russia 54 C6 42 40N 132 0 E
Petrel = Petrer, Spain 39 G4 38 30N 0 46W
Petrella, Monte, Italy 42 A6 41 18N 13 40 E
Petrer, Spain 39 G4 38 30N 0 46W
Petreto-Bicchisano, France 21 G12 41 47N 8 58 E
Petrich, Bulgaria 44 E7 41 24N 23 13 E
Petrijanec, Croatia 41 B13 46 23N 16 17 E
Petrikov = Pyetrikaw, Belarus 33 F5 52 11N 28 29 E
Petrila, Romania 29 E8 45 29N 23 29 E
Petrinja, Croatia 41 C13 45 28N 16 18 E
Petrodvorets, Russia 32 C5 59 52N 29 54 E
Petrolândia, Brazil 125 E11 9 5 S 38 20W
Petrolia, Canada 116 D2 42 54N 82 9W
Petrolina, Brazil 125 E10 9 24 S 40 30W
Petropavl, Kazakhstan 52 D7 54 53N 69 13 E
Petropavlovsk = Petropavl, Kazakhstan 52 D7 54 53N 69 13 E
Petropavlovsk-Kamchatskiy, Russia 53 D16 53 3N 158 43 E
Petropavlovskoye = Akhtubinsk, Russia 35 F8 48 13N 46 7 E
Petrópolis, Brazil 127 A7 22 33 S 43 9W
Petroşani, Romania 29 E8 45 28N 23 20 E
Petrova Gora, Croatia 41 C12 45 15N 15 45 E
Petrovac, Serbia & M. 44 B5 44 22N 21 26 E
Petrovac, Serbia & M. 44 D2 42 13N 18 57 E
Petrovaradin, Serbia & M. 28 E4 45 16N 19 55 E
Petrovsk, Russia 34 D7 52 22N 45 19 E
Petrovsk-Zabaykalskiy, Russia 53 D11 51 20N 108 55 E
Petrovskaya, Russia 33 K9 45 25N 37 58 E
Petrozavodsk, Russia 32 B8 61 41N 34 20 E
Petrus Steyn, S. Africa 89 D4 27 38 S 28 8 E
Petrusburg, S. Africa 88 D4 29 4 S 25 26 E
Petzeck, Austria 26 E5 46 57N 12 48 E
Peumo, Chile 126 C1 34 21 S 71 12W
Peureulak, Indonesia 62 D1 4 48N 97 45 E
Pevek, Russia 53 C18 69 41N 171 19 E
Peveragno, Italy 40 D4 44 20N 7 37 E
Peyrehorade, France 20 E2 43 34N 1 7W
Peyruis, France 21 D9 44 1N 5 56 E
Pézenas, France 20 E7 43 28N 3 24 E
Pezinok, Slovak Rep. 27 C10 48 17N 17 17 E
Pfaffenhofen, Germany 25 G7 48 31N 11 31 E
Pfälzerwald △, Germany 25 F5 49 18N 9 55 E
Pfarrkirchen, Germany 25 G8 48 25N 12 56 E
Pfeffenhausen, Germany 25 G7 48 39N 11 58 E
Pforzheim, Germany 25 G4 48 52N 8 41 E
Pfullendorf, Germany 25 H5 47 55N 9 15 E
Pfungstadt, Germany 25 F4 49 48N 8 35 E
Pha Taem △, Thailand 64 E5 15 32N 105 30 E
Phagwara, India 68 D6 31 10N 75 40 E
Phaistós, Greece 49 D6 35 2N 24 50 E
Phala, Botswana 88 C4 23 45 S 26 50 E
Phalera = Phulera, India 68 F6 26 52N 75 16 E
Phalodi, India 68 F5 27 12N 72 24 E
Phalsbourg, France 19 D14 48 46N 7 15 E
Phaluai, Ko, Thailand 65 b 9 32N 99 52 E
Phan, Thailand 64 C2 19 28N 99 43 E
Phan Rang, Vietnam 65 G7 11 34N 109 0 E
Phan Ri = Hoa Da, Vietnam 65 G7 11 16N 108 40 E
Phan Thiet, Vietnam 65 G7 11 1N 108 9 E
Phanae, Greece 47 C7 38 15N 25 59 E
Phanat Nikhom, Thailand 64 F3 13 27N 101 11 E
Phangan, Ko, Thailand 65 H3 9 45N 100 0 E
Phangnga, Thailand 65 H2 8 28N 98 30 E

Phangnga, Ao, *Thailand* **65 a** 8 16N 98 33 E
Phanom Sarakham,
  Thailand .... **64 F3** 13 45N 101 21 E
Phaphund, *India* ...... **69 F8** 26 36N 79 28 E
Pharenda, *India* ...... **69 F10** 27 5N 83 17 E
Pharr, *U.S.A.* **113 M5** 26 12N 98 11W
Phatthalung, *Thailand* **65 J3** 7 39N 100 6 E
Phayao, *Thailand* ..... **64 C2** 19 11N 99 55 E
Phelps, *U.S.A.* **116 D7** 42 58N 77 3W
Phelps L., *Canada* **103 B8** 59 15N 103 15W
Phenix City, *U.S.A.* .. **115 J3** 32 28N 85 0W
Phet Buri, *Thailand* .. **64 F2** 13 1N 99 55 E
Phetchabun, *Thailand* . **64 D3** 16 25N 101 8 E
Phetchabun, Thiu Khao,
  Thailand .... **64 E3** 16 0N 101 20 E
Phetchaburi = Phet Buri,
  Thailand .... **64 F2** 13 1N 99 55 E
Phi Phi, Ko, *Thailand* . **65 J2** 7 45N 98 46 E
Phiafay, *Laos* .... **64 E6** 14 48N 106 0 E
Phibun Mangsahan,
  Thailand .... **64 E5** 15 14N 105 14 E
Phichai, *Thailand* ..... **64 D3** 17 22N 100 10 E
Phichit, *Thailand* ..... **64 D3** 16 26N 100 22 E
Philadelphia, *Miss.*,
  U.S.A. **113 J10** 32 46N 89 7W
Philadelphia, *N.Y.*,
  U.S.A. **117 B9** 44 9N 75 43W
Philadelphia, *Pa.*, *U.S.A.* **117 G9** 39 57N 75 10W
Philip, *U.S.A.* **112 C4** 44 2N 101 40W
Philippeville, *Belgium* . **17 D4** 50 12N 4 33 E
Philippi, *Greece* ...... **45 E8** 41 1N 24 16 E
Philippi, *U.S.A.* **114 F5** 39 9N 80 3W
Philippine Sea, *Pac. Oc.* **50 H16** 18 0N 125 0 E
Philippines ■, *Asia* ... **61 F5** 12 0N 123 0 E
Philippolis, *S. Africa* .. **88 E4** 30 15 S 25 16 E
Philippopolis = Plovdiv,
  Bulgaria .... **45 D8** 42 8N 24 44 E
Philipsburg, *Canada* .. **117 A11** 45 2N 73 5W
Philipsburg, *Mont.*,
  U.S.A. **108 C7** 46 20N 113 18W
Philipsburg, *Pa.*, *U.S.A.* **116 F6** 40 54N 78 13W
Philipstown = Daingean,
  Ireland **12 C4** 53 18N 7 17W
Philipstown, *S. Africa* . **88 E3** 30 28 S 24 30 E
Phillip I., *Australia* ... **95 F4** 38 30 S 145 12 E
Phillips, *U.S.A.* **112 C9** 45 42N 90 24W
Phillipsburg, *Kans.*,
  U.S.A. **112 F5** 39 45N 99 19W
Phillipsburg, *N.J.*, *U.S.A.* **117 F9** 40 42N 75 12W
Philmont, *U.S.A.* **117 D11** 42 15N 73 39W
Philomath, *U.S.A.* **108 D2** 44 32N 123 22W
Phimai, *Thailand* ..... **64 E4** 15 13N 102 30 E
Phitsanulok, *Thailand* . **64 D3** 16 50N 100 12 E
Phnom Dangrek,
  Thailand .... **62 B2** 14 20N 104 0 E
Phnom Penh, *Cambodia* **65 G5** 11 33N 104 55 E
Phnom Penh = Phnom
  Penh, *Cambodia* .... **65 G5** 11 33N 104 55 E
Phoenicia, *U.S.A.* **117 D10** 42 5N 74 14W
Phoenix, *Ariz.*, *U.S.A.* **109 K7** 33 27N 112 4W
Phoenix, *N.Y.*, *U.S.A.* **117 C8** 43 14N 76 18W
Phoenix Is., *Kiribati* .. **96 H10** 3 30 S 172 0W
Phoenixville, *U.S.A.* .. **117 F9** 40 8N 75 31W
Phon, *Thailand* .... **64 E4** 15 49N 102 36 E
Phon Tiou, *Laos* ..... **64 D5** 17 53N 104 37 E
Phong ➤, *Thailand* ... **64 D4** 17 53N 102 56 E
Phong Saly, *Laos* ..... **58 G4** 21 42N 102 9 E
Phong Tho, *Vietnam* .. **64 A4** 22 32N 103 21 E
Phonhong, *Laos* ...... **64 C4** 18 30N 102 25 E
Phonum, *Thailand* .... **65 H2** 8 49N 98 48 E
Phosphate Hill,
  Australia .... **94 C2** 21 53 S 139 58 E
Photharam, *Thailand* .. **64 F2** 13 41N 99 51 E
Phra Nakhon Si
  Ayutthaya, *Thailand* **64 E3** 14 25N 100 30 E
Phra Thong, Ko,
  Thailand .... **65 H2** 9 5N 98 17 E
Phrae, *Thailand* ...... **64 C3** 18 7N 100 9 E
Phrom Phiram, *Thailand* **64 D3** 17 2N 100 12 E
Phrygia, *Turkey* ...... **72 C4** 38 40N 30 0 E
Phu Chong-Na Yoi △,
  Thailand .... **64 E5** 14 25N 105 30 E
Phu Dien, *Vietnam* ... **64 C5** 18 58N 105 31 E
Phu Hin Rang Kla △,
  Thailand .... **64 D3** 17 0N 100 59 E
Phu Kradung △,
  Thailand .... **64 D3** 17 2N 101 44 E
Phu Loi, *Laos* .... **64 B4** 20 14N 103 14 E
Phu Luang △, *Thailand* **64 D3** 17 15N 101 29 E
Phu Ly, *Vietnam* ..... **58 G5** 20 35N 105 50 E
Phu Phan △, *Thailand* **64 D4** 17 0N 103 56 E
Phu Quoc, Dao, *Vietnam* **65 G4** 10 20N 104 0 E
Phu Tho, *Vietnam* .... **58 G5** 21 24N 105 13 E
Phuc Yen, *Vietnam* ... **58 G5** 21 16N 105 45 E
Phuket, *Thailand* ..... **65 a** 7 53N 98 24 E
Phuket, Ko, *Thailand* . **65 a** 8 0N 98 22 E
Phul, *India* .... **68 D6** 30 19N 75 14 E
Phulad, *India* .... **68 G5** 25 38N 73 49 E
Phulchari, *Bangla.* .... **69 G13** 25 11N 89 37 E
Phulera, *India* .... **68 F6** 26 52N 75 16 E
Phulpur, *India* .... **69 G10** 25 31N 82 49 E
Phun Phin, *Thailand* .. **65 H2** 9 7N 99 12 E
Piacenza, *Italy* .... **40 C6** 45 1N 9 40 E
Piai, Tanjung, *Malaysia* **65 d** 1 17N 103 30 E
Pian Cr. ➤, *Australia* . **95 E4** 30 2 S 148 12 E
Pian-Upe ➤, *Uganda* . **86 B3** 1 44N 34 20 E
Piana, *France* .... **21 F12** 42 15N 8 34 E
Pianella, *Italy* .... **41 F11** 42 24N 14 2 E
Pianosa, *Puglia*, *Italy* . **41 F12** 42 12N 15 44 E
Pianosa, *Toscana*, *Italy* **40 F7** 42 35N 10 5 E
Piapot, *Canada* **103 D7** 49 59N 109 8W
Pias, *Portugal* **37 G3** 38 1N 7 29W
Piaseczno, *Poland* .... **31 F8** 52 5N 21 2 E
Piaski, *Poland* .... **31 G9** 51 8N 22 52 E
Piastów, *Poland* ...... **31 F7** 52 10N 20 48 E
Piatra, *Romania* ...... **29 G10** 43 51N 25 9 E
Piatra Craiului △,
  Romania .... **29 E10** 45 30N 25 12 E
Piatra Neamț, *Romania* **29 D11** 46 56N 26 21 E
Piatra Olt, *Romania* .. **29 F9** 44 22N 24 16 E
Piauí □, *Brazil* .... **125 E10** 7 0 S 43 0W
Piauí ➤, *Brazil* .... **125 E10** 6 38 S 42 42W
Piave ➤, *Italy* .... **41 C9** 45 32N 12 44 E
Piazza Armerina, *Italy* . **43 E7** 37 21N 14 20 E
Pibor ➤, *Sudan* ...... **81 F3** 7 35N 33 0 E
Pibor Post, *Sudan* .... **81 F3** 6 47N 33 3 E
Pica, *Chile* .... **124 H5** 20 35 S 69 25W
Picardie □, *France* .... **19 C10** 49 50N 3 0 E
Picardie, Plaine de,
  France .... **19 C9** 50 0N 2 0 E
Picardy = Picardie □,
  France .... **19 C10** 49 50N 3 0 E
Picayune, *U.S.A.* **113 K10** 30 32N 89 41W
Picerno, *Italy* .... **43 B8** 40 38N 15 38 E
Pichhor, *India* .... **69 G8** 25 58N 78 20 E
Pichilemu, *Chile* ...... **126 C1** 34 22 S 72 0W
Pichor, *India* .... **68 G8** 25 11N 78 11 E

Pickerel L., *Canada* ... **104 C1** 48 40N 91 25W
Pickering, *U.K.* **14 C7** 54 15N 0 46W
Pickering, Vale of, *U.K.* **14 C7** 54 14N 0 45W
Pickle Lake, *Canada* .. **104 B1** 51 30N 90 12W
Pickwick L., *U.S.A.* ... **115 H1** 35 4N 88 15W
Pico Bonito △,
  Honduras **120 C2** 15 34N 86 48W
Pico Truncado,
  Argentina .... **128 F3** 46 40 S 68 0W
Picos, *Brazil* .... **125 E10** 7 5 S 41 28W
Picos de Europa △,
  Spain **36 B6** 43 12N 4 58W
Picton, *Australia* ..... **95 E5** 34 12 S 150 34 E
Picton, *Canada* **116 B7** 44 1N 77 9W
Picton, *N.Z.* .... **91 J5** 41 18 S 174 3 E
Pictou, *Canada* **105 C7** 45 41N 62 42W
Picture Butte, *Canada* . **102 D6** 49 55N 112 45W
Pictured Rocks △,
  U.S.A. **114 B2** 46 30N 86 30W
Picún Leufú, *Argentina* **128 D3** 39 30 S 69 5W
Pidbuzh, *Ukraine* ..... **31 J10** 49 19N 23 14 E
Piduruталagala,
  Sri Lanka .... **66 R12** 7 10N 80 50 E
Piechowice, *Poland* ... **31 H2** 50 51N 15 36 E
Piedimonte Matese, *Italy* **43 A7** 41 22N 14 22 E
Piedmont = Piemonte □,
  Italy .... **40 D5** 45 0N 8 0 E
Piedmont, *Ala.*, *U.S.A.* **115 J3** 33 55N 85 37W
Piedmont, *S.C.*, *U.S.A.* **107 D10** 34 0N 81 30W
Piedra ➤, *Spain* **38 D3** 41 18N 1 47W
Piedrabuena, *Spain* ... **37 G6** 39 0N 4 10W
Piedrahita, *Spain* **36 E5** 40 28N 5 23W
Piedralaves, *Spain* **36 E6** 40 19N 4 42W
Piedras Blancas, *Spain* **36 B5** 43 43 S 5 58W
Piedras Negras, *Mexico* **118 B4** 28 42N 100 31W
Piekary Śląskie, *Poland* **31 H5** 50 24N 18 57 E
Pieksämäki, *Finland* ... **9 E22** 62 18N 27 10 E
Piemonte □, *Italy* .... **40 D5** 45 0N 8 0 E
Pienaarsrivier, *S. Africa* **89 D4** 25 15 S 28 18 E
Pieniężno, *Poland* .... **30 D7** 54 14N 20 8 E
Pieniński △, *Europe* ... **27 B13** 49 25N 20 28 E
Pieńsk, *Poland* .... **31 G2** 51 16N 15 2 E
Piercefield, *U.S.A.* ... **117 B10** 44 13N 74 35W
Pierceland, *Canada* ... **103 C7** 54 20N 109 46W
Piería □, *Greece* ...... **44 F6** 40 13N 22 25 E
Pierpont, *U.S.A.* **116 E4** 41 45N 80 34W
Pierre, *U.S.A.* **112 C4** 44 22N 100 21W
Pierre-Buffière, *France* **20 C5** 45 41N 1 22 E
Pierre-de-Bresse, *France* **19 F12** 46 54N 5 13 E
Pierrefontaine-les-
  Varans, *France* ..... **19 E13** 47 14N 6 32 E
Pierrefort, *France* .... **20 D6** 44 55N 2 50 E
Pierrelatte, *France* .... **21 D8** 44 23N 4 43 E
Pierreville, *Trin. & Tob.* **125 K16** 10 16N 61 0W
Piešťany, *Slovak Rep.* . **27 C10** 48 38N 17 55 E
Piesting ➤, *Austria* ... **27 C9** 48 6N 16 40 E
Pieszyce, *Poland* ..... **31 H3** 50 43N 16 33 E
Piet Retief, *S. Africa* .. **89 D5** 27 1 S 30 50 E
Pietarsaari, *Finland* ... **8 E20** 63 40N 22 43 E
Pietermaritzburg,
  S. Africa .... **89 D5** 29 35 S 30 25 E
Pietersburg =
  Polokwane, *S. Africa* **89 C4** 23 54 S 29 25 E
Pietragalla, *Italy* ...... **43 B8** 40 45N 15 53 E
Pietrasanta, *Italy* ..... **40 E7** 43 57N 10 14 E
Pietroşiţa, *Romania* ... **29 E10** 45 11N 25 26 E
Pietrosul, Vf.,
  Maramureş, *Romania* **29 C9** 47 35N 24 43 E
Pietrosul, Vf., *Suceava*,
  Romania .... **29 C10** 47 12N 25 18 E
Pieve di Cadore, *Italy* . **41 B9** 46 26N 12 22 E
Pieve di Teco, *Italy* ... **40 D4** 44 3N 7 56 E
Pievepélago, *Italy* .... **40 D7** 44 12N 10 37 E
Pigadhítsa, *Greece* .... **44 G5** 39 59N 21 23 E
Pigeon L., *Canada* **116 B6** 44 27N 78 30W
Piggott, *U.S.A.* **113 G9** 36 23N 90 11W
Pigna, *Italy* .... **40 E4** 43 56N 7 40 E
Pigüe, *Argentina* ..... **126 D3** 37 36 S 62 25W
Pihani, *India* .... **69 F9** 27 36N 80 15 E
Pihlajavesi, *Finland* ... **9 F23** 61 45N 28 45 E
Pijijiapan, *Mexico* **119 D6** 15 42N 93 14W
Pikalevo, *Russia* ..... **32 C8** 59 37N 34 9 E
Pikangikum Berens,
  Canada **103 C10** 51 49N 94 0W
Pikes Peak, *U.S.A.* ... **112 F2** 38 50N 105 3W
Piketberg, *S. Africa* ... **88 E2** 32 55 S 18 40 E
Pikeville, *U.S.A.* **114 G4** 37 29N 82 31W
Pikou, *China* .... **57 E12** 39 18N 122 22 E
Pikwitonei, *Canada* ... **103 B9** 55 35N 97 9W
Piła, *Poland* .... **31 E3** 53 10N 16 48 E
Pila, *Italy* **39 G3** 38 16N 1 11W
Pilaía, *Greece* .... **44 F6** 40 32N 22 59 E
Pilanesberg △, *S. Africa* **88 D4** 25 15 S 27 4 E
Pilani, *India* .... **68 E6** 28 22N 75 33 E
Pilar, *Paraguay* ...... **126 B4** 26 50 S 58 20W
Pilar de la Horadada,
  Spain **39 H4** 37 52N 0 47W
Pilat, *France* .... **21 C8** 45 20N 4 30 E
Pilawa, *Poland* .... **31 G8** 51 57N 21 32 E
Pilaya ➤, *Bolivia* ..... **124 H6** 20 55 S 64 4W
Pilbara, *Australia* ..... **92 D2** 23 35 S 117 25 E
Pilcomayo ➤, *Paraguay* **126 B4** 25 21 S 57 42W
Pilgrim's Rest, *S. Africa* **89 C5** 24 55 S 30 44 E
Pilgrimstad, *Sweden* .. **10 B9** 62 57N 15 2 E
Pili, *Greece* .... **47 E9** 36 50N 27 15 E
Pilibhit, *India* .... **69 E8** 28 40N 79 50 E
Pilica ➤, *Poland* ...... **31 G8** 51 52N 21 17 E
Pilion, *Greece* .... **46 B5** 39 27N 23 3 E
Pilis, *Hungary* .... **28 C4** 47 17N 19 35 E
Pilisvörösvár, *Hungary* **28 C3** 47 38N 18 56 E
Pilkhawa, *India* .... **68 E7** 28 43N 77 42 E
Pilliga, *Australia* ...... **95 E4** 30 21 S 148 54 E
Pílos, *Greece* .... **46 E3** 36 55N 21 42 E
Pilot Mound, *Canada* . **103 D9** 49 15N 98 54W
Pilot Point, *U.S.A.* ... **113 J6** 33 24N 96 58W
Pilot Rock, *U.S.A.* ... **108 D4** 45 29N 118 50W
Pilštanj, *Slovenia* ..... **41 B12** 46 8N 15 39 E
Piltene, *Latvia* .... **30 A8** 57 13N 21 40 E
Pilzno, *Poland* .... **31 J8** 49 58N 21 16 E
Pima, *U.S.A.* **109 K9** 32 54N 109 50W
Pimba, *Australia* ...... **95 E2** 31 18 S 136 46 E
Pimenta Bueno, *Brazil* **124 F6** 11 35 S 61 10W
Pimentel, *Peru* .... **124 E3** 6 45 S 79 55W
Pina de Ebro, *Spain* .. **38 D4** 41 29N 0 33W
Pinamalayan, *Phil.* .... **61 E4** 13 2N 121 29 E
Pinang, *Malaysia* ..... **65 c** 5 25N 100 15 E
Pinar, C. des, *Spain* .. **38 B10** 39 53N 3 12 E
Pinar del Río, *Cuba* ... **120 B3** 22 26N 83 40W
Pınarbaşı, *Çanakkale*,
  Turkey .... **47 B8** 39 53N 26 15 E
Pınarbaşı, *Kayseri*,
  Turkey .... **72 C7** 38 43N 36 23 E
Pinarhisar, *Turkey* .... **45 E11** 41 37N 27 30 E
Pinatubo, Mt., *Phil.* ... **61 D3** 15 8N 120 21 E
Pincehely, *Hungary* ... **28 D3** 46 41N 18 27 E
Pinchang, *China* ...... **58 B6** 31 36N 107 3 E
Pincher Creek, *Canada* **102 D6** 49 30N 113 57W

Pinchi L., *Canada* **102 C4** 54 38N 124 30W
Pinckneyville, *U.S.A.* .. **112 F10** 38 5N 89 23W
Pindar, *Australia* ..... **93 E2** 28 30 S 115 47 E
Pindi Gheb, *Pakistan* .. **68 C5** 33 14N 72 21 E
Pindiga, *Nigeria* ...... **83 D7** 9 58N 10 53 E
Pindos △, *Greece* ..... **46 B3** 39 52N 21 11 E
Pindos Óros, *Greece* .. **46 B3** 40 0N 21 0 E
Pindus Mts. = Pindos
  Óros, *Greece* ...... **46 B3** 40 0N 21 0 E
Pine ➤, *B.C.*, *Canada* . **102 B4** 56 8N 120 43W
Pine ➤, *Sask.*, *Canada* **103 B7** 58 50N 105 38W
Pine, C., *Canada* **105 C9** 46 37N 53 32W
Pine Bluff, *U.S.A.* **113 H9** 34 13N 92 1W
Pine Bluffs, *U.S.A.* ... **112 E2** 41 11N 104 4W
Pine City, *U.S.A.* **112 C8** 45 50N 92 59W
Pine Cr. ➤, *U.S.A.* ... **116 E7** 41 10N 77 16W
Pine Creek, *Australia* . **92 B5** 13 50 S 131 50 E
Pine Falls, *Canada* **103 C9** 50 34N 96 11W
Pine Flat Res., *U.S.A.* . **110 J7** 36 50N 119 20W
Pine Grove, *U.S.A.* ... **117 F8** 40 33N 76 23W
Pine Pass, *Canada* **102 B4** 55 25N 122 42W
Pine Point, *Canada* ... **102 A6** 60 50N 114 28W
Pine Ridge, *U.S.A.* ... **112 D3** 43 2N 102 33W
Pine River, *Canada* ... **103 C8** 51 45N 100 30W
Pine River, *U.S.A.* **112 B7** 46 43N 94 24W
Pine Valley, *U.S.A.* ... **111 N10** 32 50N 116 32W
Pinecrest, *U.S.A.* **110 G6** 38 12N 120 1W
Pineda de Mar, *Spain* . **38 D7** 41 37N 2 42 E
Pinedale, *Calif.*, *U.S.A.* **110 J7** 36 50N 119 48W
Pinedale, *Wyo.*, *U.S.A.* **108 E9** 42 52N 109 52W
Pinega ➤, *Russia* ..... **52 C5** 64 30N 44 19 E
Pinehill, *Australia* ..... **94 C4** 23 38 S 146 57 E
Pinehouse L., *Canada* . **103 B7** 55 32N 106 35W
Pineimuta ➤, *Canada* . **104 B1** 52 8N 88 33W
Pinerolo, *Italy* .... **40 D4** 44 53N 7 21 E
Pineto, *Italy* .... **41 F11** 42 36N 14 4 E
Pinetop, *U.S.A.* **109 J9** 34 8N 109 56W
Pinetown, *S. Africa* ... **89 D5** 29 48 S 30 54 E
Pineville, *U.S.A.* **113 K8** 31 19N 92 26W
Piney, *France* .... **19 D11** 48 22N 4 21 E
Ping ➤, *Thailand* ..... **64 E3** 15 42N 100 9 E
Pingaring, *Australia* ... **93 F2** 32 40 S 118 32 E
Pingba, *China* .... **58 D6** 26 23N 106 12 E
Pingbian, *China* ...... **58 F4** 22 55N 103 42 E
Pingchuan, *China* ..... **58 D3** 27 35N 101 55 E
Pingding, *China* ...... **56 F7** 37 47N 113 38 E
Pingdingshan, *China* .. **56 H7** 33 43N 113 27 E
Pingdong, *Taiwan* .... **59 F13** 22 39N 120 30 E
Pingdu, *China* .... **57 F10** 36 42N 119 59 E
Pingelly, *Australia* ..... **93 F2** 32 32 S 117 5 E
Pingguo, *China* .... **58 F6** 23 19N 107 36 E
Pinghe, *China* .... **59 E11** 24 17N 117 21 E
Pinghu, *China* .... **59 B13** 30 40N 121 2 E
Pingjiang, *China* ...... **59 C9** 28 45N 113 36 E
Pingle, *China* .... **59 E8** 24 40N 110 40 E
Pingli, *China* .... **58 A7** 32 27N 109 22 E
Pingliang, *China* ...... **56 G4** 35 35N 106 31 E
Pinglu, *China* .... **56 E7** 39 31N 112 30 E
Pingluo, *China* .... **56 E4** 38 52N 106 30 E
Pingnan,
  Guangxi Zhuangzu,
  China .... **59 F8** 23 33N 110 22 E
Pingquan, *China* ...... **57 D10** 41 1N 118 37 E
Pingrup, *Australia* ..... **93 F2** 33 32 S 118 29 E
Pingshan, *China* ...... **58 C5** 28 39N 104 3 E
Pingtan, *China* .... **59 E12** 25 31N 119 47 E
Pingtang, *China* ...... **58 E6** 25 49N 107 17 E
P'ingtung, *Taiwan* .... **59 F13** 22 38N 120 30 E
Pingwu, *China* .... **56 H3** 32 25N 104 30 E
Pingxiang,
  Guangxi Zhuangzu,
  China .... **58 F6** 22 6N 106 46 E
Pingxiang, *Jiangxi*,
  China .... **59 D9** 27 43N 113 48 E
Pingyao, *China* .... **56 F7** 37 12N 112 10 E
Pingyi, *China* .... **57 G9** 35 30N 117 35 E
Pingyin, *China* .... **56 F9** 36 20N 116 25 E
Pingyuan, *Guangdong*,
  China .... **59 E10** 24 37N 115 57 E
Pingyuan, *Shandong*,
  China .... **56 F9** 37 10N 116 22 E
Pingyuanjie, *China* .... **58 F4** 23 45N 103 48 E
Pinhal, *Brazil* .... **127 A6** 22 10 S 46 46W
Pinhal Novo, *Portugal* . **37 G2** 38 38N 8 55W
Pinheiro, *Brazil* ...... **125 D9** 2 31 S 45 5W
Pinheiro Machado,
  Brazil .... **127 C5** 31 34 S 53 23W
Pinhel, *Portugal* **36 E3** 40 50N 7 1W
Pini, *Indonesia* .... **62 D1** 0 10N 98 40 E
Piniós ➤, *Ília*, *Greece* . **46 D3** 37 48N 21 20 E
Piniós ➤, *Tríkkala*,
  Greece .... **46 B4** 39 55N 22 41 E
Pinjarra, *Australia* ..... **93 F2** 32 37 S 115 52 E
Pink Mountain, *Canada* **102 B4** 57 3N 122 52W
Pinkafeld, *Austria* .... **27 D9** 47 22N 16 9 E
Pinnacles, *U.S.A.* **110 J5** 36 33N 121 19W
Pinnacles △, *U.S.A.* .. **110 J5** 36 25N 121 12W
Pinnaroo, *Australia* ... **95 F3** 35 17 S 140 53 E
Pinneberg, *Germany* .. **24 B5** 53 40N 9 48 E
Pínnes, Ákra, *Greece* . **45 F8** 40 5N 24 20 E
Pinon Hills, *U.S.A.* ... **111 L9** 34 26N 117 39W
Pinos, *Mexico* **118 C4** 22 20N 101 40W
Pinos, Mt., *U.S.A.* **111 L7** 34 49N 119 8W
Pinos Pt., *U.S.A.* **109 H3** 36 38N 121 57W
Pinos Puente, *Spain* .. **37 H7** 37 15N 3 45W
Pinotepa Nacional,
  Mexico **119 D5** 16 19N 98 3W
Pinrang, *Indonesia* .... **63 E5** 3 46 S 119 41 E
Pins, Pte. aux, *Canada* **116 D3** 42 15N 81 51W
Pinsk, *Belarus* .... **33 F4** 52 10N 26 1 E
Pintados, *Chile* .... **124 H5** 20 35 S 69 40W
Pinyang, *China* .... **59 D13** 27 42N 120 31 E
Pinyug, *Russia* .... **52 C5** 60 5N 48 4 E
Pioche, *U.S.A.* **109 H6** 37 56N 114 27W
Piombino, *Italy* .... **40 F7** 42 55N 10 32 E
Piombino, Canale di,
  Italy .... **40 F7** 42 53N 10 30 E
Pioner, Ostrov, *Russia* **53 B10** 79 50N 92 0 E
Pionerskiy, *Russia* .... **30 D7** 54 56N 20 14 E
Pionki, *Poland* .... **31 G8** 51 29N 21 28 E
Piorini, L., *Brazil* ..... **124 D6** 3 15 S 62 35W
Piotrków Trybunalski,
  Poland .... **31 G6** 51 23N 19 43 E
Piove di Sacco, *Italy* .. **41 C9** 45 18N 12 2 E
Píp, *Iran* .... **71 E9** 26 45N 60 10 E
Pipar, *India* .... **68 F5** 26 25N 73 31 E
Pipar Road, *India* ..... **68 F5** 26 27N 73 27 E
Piparia, *Mad. P.*, *India* **68 H8** 22 45N 78 23 E
Piparia, *Mad. P.*, *India* **68 J7** 21 49N 77 37 E
Pipéri, *Greece* .... **46 B6** 39 20N 24 19 E
Pipestone, *U.S.A.* **112 D6** 44 0N 96 19W
Pipestone ➤, *Canada* . **104 B2** 52 53N 89 23W
Pipestone Cr. ➤,
  Canada **103 D8** 49 38N 100 15W
Piplan, *Pakistan* ...... **68 C4** 32 17N 71 21 E

Piploda, *India* .... **68 H6** 23 37N 74 56 E
Pipmuacan, Rés.,
  Canada **105 C5** 49 45N 70 30W
Pippingarra, *Australia* . **92 D2** 20 27 S 118 42 E
Pipriac, *France* **18 E5** 47 59N 1 58W
Piqua, *U.S.A.* **114 E3** 40 9N 84 15W
Piquiri ➤, *Brazil* ...... **127 A5** 24 3 S 54 14W
Pir Panjal Range, *India* **68 C7** 32 30N 76 50 E
Pira, *Benin* .... **83 D5** 8 28N 1 48 E
Piracicaba, *Brazil* ..... **127 A6** 22 45 S 47 40W
Piracuruca, *Brazil* .... **125 D10** 3 50 S 41 50W
Piraeus = Piraiévs,
  Greece .... **46 D5** 37 57N 23 42 E
Piraiévs, *Greece* ...... **46 D5** 37 57N 23 42 E
Pirajuí, *Brazil* .... **127 A6** 21 59 S 49 29W
Piram I., *India* .... **68 J5** 21 36N 72 21 E
Piran, *Slovenia* .... **41 C10** 45 31N 13 33 E
Pirané, *Argentina* ..... **126 B4** 25 42 S 59 6W
Pirano = Piran, *Slovenia* **41 C10** 45 31N 13 33 E
Pirapora, *Brazil* ...... **125 G10** 17 20 S 44 56W
Pirawa, *India* .... **68 G7** 24 10N 76 2 E
Pirdop, *Bulgaria* ...... **45 C8** 42 40N 24 10 E
Pírgos, *Ília*, *Greece* ... **46 D3** 37 40N 21 27 E
Pírgos, *Kríti*, *Greece* .. **47 F7** 35 0N 25 9 E
Pirgovo, *Bulgaria* ..... **45 C9** 43 44N 25 43 E
Piribebuy, *Paraguay* ... **126 B4** 25 26 S 57 2W
Pirimapun, *Indonesia* . **63 F9** 6 20 S 138 24 E
Pirin △, *Bulgaria* ..... **44 E7** 41 40N 23 22 E
Pirin Planina, *Bulgaria* **44 E7** 41 40N 23 30 E
Pireneos = Pyrénées,
  Europe .... **20 F4** 42 45N 0 18 E
Piripiri, *Brazil* .... **125 D10** 4 15 S 41 46W
Pirmasens, *Germany* .. **25 F3** 49 12N 7 36 E
Pirna, *Germany* .... **24 E9** 50 57N 13 56 E
Pirot, *Serbia & M.* .... **44 C6** 43 9N 22 33 E
Piru, *Indonesia* .... **63 E7** 3 4 S 128 12 E
Piru, *U.S.A.* **111 L8** 34 25N 118 48W
Piryatin = Pyryatyn,
  Ukraine .... **33 G7** 50 15N 32 25 E
Piryí, *Greece* .... **47 C7** 38 13N 25 59 E
Pisa, *Italy* .... **40 E7** 43 43N 10 23 E
Pisa ➤, *Poland* .... **31 E8** 53 14N 21 52 E
Pisagne, *Italy* .... **40 C7** 45 48N 10 10 E
Pisagua, *Chile* .... **124 G4** 19 40 S 70 15W
Pisarovina, *Croatia* .... **41 C12** 45 35N 15 50 E
Pisco, *Peru* .... **124 F3** 13 50 S 76 12W
Piscu, *Romania* .... **29 E12** 45 30N 27 43 E
Písek, *Czech Rep.* ..... **26 B7** 49 19N 14 10 E
Pishan, *China* .... **60 C2** 37 30N 78 33 E
Pishcha, *Ukraine* ...... **31 G10** 51 35N 23 50 E
Pishchanka, *Ukraine* .. **29 B13** 48 28N 28 54 E
Pīshīn, *Iran* .... **71 E9** 26 6N 61 47 E
Pishin, *Pakistan* ...... **68 D2** 30 35N 67 0 E
Pishin Lora ➤, *Pakistan* **68 E1** 29 9N 64 5 E
Pisidia, *Turkey* .... **72 D4** 37 30N 31 40 E
Pising, *Indonesia* ..... **63 F6** 5 8 S 121 53 E
Pismo Beach, *U.S.A.* .. **111 K6** 35 9N 120 38W
Piso, L., *Liberia* **82 D2** 6 50N 11 15W
Pissila, *Burkina Faso* .. **83 C4** 13 5N 0 50W
Pissis, Cerro, *Argentina* **126 B2** 27 45 S 68 48W
Pissos, *France* **20 D3** 44 19N 0 49W
Pissouri, *Cyprus* ...... **49 E11** 34 40N 32 42 E
Pisticci, *Italy* .... **43 B9** 40 23N 16 33 E
Pistóia, *Italy* .... **40 E7** 43 55N 10 54 E
Pistol B., *Canada* **103 A10** 62 25N 92 37W
Pisuerga ➤, *Spain* **36 D6** 41 33N 4 52W
Pisz, *Poland* .... **30 E8** 53 38N 21 49 E
Pit ➤, *U.S.A.* **108 F2** 40 47N 122 6W
Pita, *Guinea* **82 C2** 11 5N 12 15W
Pitarpunga, L., *Australia* **95 E3** 34 24 S 143 30 E
Pitcairn I., *Pac. Oc.* ... **97 K14** 25 5 S 130 5W
Pitch L., *Trin. & Tob.* . **125 K15** 10 12N 61 39W
Piteå, *Sweden* .... **8 D19** 65 20N 21 25 E
Piteälven ➤, *Sweden* .. **8 D19** 65 20N 21 25 E
Piterka, *Russia* .... **34 E8** 50 41N 47 29 E
Piteşti, *Romania* ...... **29 F9** 44 52N 24 54 E
Pithapuram, *India* .... **67 L13** 17 10N 82 15 E
Pithara, *Australia* ..... **93 F2** 30 20 S 116 35 E
Píthion, *Greece* .... **45 E10** 41 24N 26 40 E
Pithiviers, *France* ..... **19 D9** 48 10N 2 13 E
Pithoragarh, *India* .... **69 E9** 29 35N 80 13 E
Pithoro, *Pakistan* ..... **68 G3** 25 31N 69 23 E
Pitigliano, *Italy* .... **41 F8** 42 38N 11 40 E
Pitkyaranta, *Russia* ... **32 B6** 61 31N 31 13 E
Pitlochry, *U.K.* **13 E5** 56 42N 3 44W
Pitsilia, *Cyprus* .... **49 E12** 34 55N 33 0 E
Pitt I., *Canada* **102 C3** 53 30N 129 50W
Pittsburg, *Calif.*, *U.S.A.* **110 G5** 38 2N 121 53W
Pittsburg, *Kans.*, *U.S.A.* **113 G7** 37 25N 94 42W
Pittsburg, *Tex.*, *U.S.A.* **113 J7** 33 0N 94 59W
Pittsburgh, *U.S.A.* **116 F5** 40 26N 80 1W
Pittsfield, *Ill.*, *U.S.A.* . **112 F9** 39 36N 90 49W
Pittsfield, *Maine*, *U.S.A.* **115 C11** 44 47N 69 23W
Pittsfield, *Mass.*, *U.S.A.* **117 D11** 42 27N 73 15W
Pittsfield, *N.H.*, *U.S.A.* **117 C13** 43 18N 71 20W
Pittston, *U.S.A.* **117 E9** 41 19N 75 47W
Pittsworth, *Australia* .. **95 D5** 27 41 S 151 37 E
Pituri ➤, *Australia* ... **94 C2** 22 35 S 138 30 E
Piura, *Peru* .... **124 E2** 5 15 S 80 38W
Piva ➤, *Serbia & M.* .. **44 C2** 43 20N 18 51 E
Piwniczna, *Poland* .... **31 J7** 49 27N 20 42 E
Pixley, *U.S.A.* **110 K7** 35 58N 119 18W
Piyai, *Greece* .... **46 B3** 39 17N 21 25 E
Pizarra, *Spain* **37 J6** 36 46N 4 42W
Pizhou, *China* .... **56 G9** 34 44N 116 55 E
Pizzo, *Italy* .... **43 D9** 38 44N 16 10 E
Placentia, *Canada* **105 C9** 47 20N 54 0W
Placentia B., *Canada* .. **105 C9** 47 0N 54 40W
Placer, *Masbate*, *Phil.* . **61 F5** 11 52N 123 55 E
Placer, *Surigao N.*, *Phil.* **61 G6** 9 36N 125 38 E
Placerville, *U.S.A.* **110 G6** 38 44N 120 48W
Placetas, *Cuba* **120 B4** 22 15N 79 44W
Plačkovica, *Macedonia* **44 E6** 41 45N 22 30 E
Plainfield, *N.J.*, *U.S.A.* **117 F10** 40 37N 74 25W
Plainfield, *Ohio*, *U.S.A.* **116 F3** 40 13N 81 43W
Plainfield, *Vt.*, *U.S.A.* . **117 B12** 44 17N 72 26W
Plains, *Mont.*, *U.S.A.* . **108 C6** 47 28N 114 53W
Plains, *Tex.*, *U.S.A.* ... **113 J3** 33 11N 102 50W
Plainview, *Nebr.*, *U.S.A.* **112 D6** 42 21N 97 47W
Plainview, *Tex.*, *U.S.A.* **113 H4** 34 11N 101 43W
Plainwell, *U.S.A.* **114 D3** 42 27N 85 38W
Plaisance, *France* ..... **20 E4** 43 36N 0 3 E
Plaistow, *U.S.A.* **117 D13** 42 50N 71 6W
Pláka, *Greece* .... **47 B7** 40 0N 25 24 E
Pláka, Ákra, *Greece* ... **49 D8** 35 11N 26 19 E
Plakenska Planina,
  Macedonia .... **44 E4** 41 14N 21 2 E
Planá, *Czech Rep.* ..... **26 B5** 49 50N 12 44 E
Planada, *U.S.A.* **110 H6** 37 16N 120 19W
Plandište, *Serbia & M.* **28 E6** 45 16N 21 10 E
Plano, *U.S.A.* **113 J6** 33 1N 96 42W
Plant City, *U.S.A.* **115 M4** 28 1N 82 7W

Plaquemine, *U.S.A.* ... **113 K9** 30 17N 91 14W
Plasencia, *Spain* **36 E4** 40 3N 6 8W
Plaški, *Croatia* .... **41 C12** 45 4N 15 22 E
Plaster City, *U.S.A.* ... **111 N11** 32 47N 115 51W
Plaster Rock, *Canada* . **105 C6** 46 53N 67 22W
Plastun, *Russia* .... **54 B8** 44 45N 136 19 E
Plasy, *Czech Rep.* ..... **26 B6** 49 56N 13 24 E
Plata, Río de la,
  S. Amer. .... **126 C4** 34 45 S 57 30W
Plátani ➤, *Italy* ...... **42 E6** 37 23N 13 16 E
Plátanos, *Greece* ..... **49 D5** 35 28N 23 33 E
Plateau □, *Nigeria* .... **83 D6** 8 30N 9 0 E
Platí, Ákra, *Greece* .... **45 F8** 40 27N 24 0 E
Platte, *U.S.A.* **112 D5** 43 23N 98 51W
Platte ➤, *Mo.*, *U.S.A.* **112 F7** 39 16N 94 50W
Platte ➤, *Nebr.*, *U.S.A.* **112 E7** 41 4N 95 53W
Platteville, *U.S.A.* **112 D9** 42 44N 90 29W
Plattling, *Germany* .... **25 G8** 48 46N 12 53 E
Plattsburgh, *U.S.A.* ... **117 B11** 44 42N 73 28W
Plattsmouth, *U.S.A.* .. **112 E7** 41 1N 95 53W
Plau, *Germany* .... **24 B8** 53 27N 12 15 E
Plauen, *Germany* ..... **24 E8** 50 30N 12 8 E
Plauer See, *Germany* .. **24 B8** 53 28N 12 17 E
Plav, *Serbia & M.* ..... **44 D3** 42 38N 19 57 E
Plavinas, *Latvia* ...... **9 H21** 56 35N 25 46 E
Plavnica, *Serbia & M.* . **44 D3** 42 20N 19 13 E
Plavno, *Croatia* .... **41 D13** 44 9N 16 10 E
Plavsk, *Russia* .... **32 F9** 53 40N 37 18 E
Playa Blanca, *Canary Is.* **48 F6** 28 55N 13 37W
Playa Blanca Sur,
  Canary Is. **48 F6** 28 51N 13 50W
Playa de las Americas,
  Canary Is. **48 F3** 28 5N 16 43W
Playa de Mogán,
  Canary Is. **48 G4** 27 48N 15 47W
Playa del Inglés,
  Canary Is. **48 G4** 27 45N 15 33W
Playa Esmeralda,
  Canary Is. **48 F5** 28 8N 14 16W
Playgreen L., *Canada* . **103 C9** 54 0N 98 15W
Pleasant Bay, *Canada* . **105 C7** 46 51N 60 48W
Pleasant Hill, *U.S.A.* .. **110 H4** 37 57N 122 4W
Pleasant Mount, *U.S.A.* **117 E9** 41 44N 75 26W
Pleasanton, *Calif.*,
  U.S.A. **110 H5** 37 39N 121 52W
Pleasanton, *Tex.*, *U.S.A.* **113 L5** 28 58N 98 29W
Pleasantville, *N.J.*,
  U.S.A. **114 F8** 39 24N 74 32W
Pleasantville, *Pa.*, *U.S.A.* **116 E5** 41 35N 79 34W
Pléaux, *France* .... **20 C6** 45 8N 2 13 E
Plei Ku, *Vietnam* ..... **64 F7** 13 57N 108 0 E
Plélan-le-Grand, *France* **18 D4** 48 0N 2 7W
Pléneuf-Val-André,
  France **18 D4** 48 35N 2 32W
Plenița, *Romania* ..... **29 F8** 44 14N 23 10 E
Plenty ➤, *Australia* ... **94 C2** 23 25 S 136 31 E
Plenty, B. of, *N.Z.* .... **91 G6** 37 45 S 177 0 E
Plentywood, *U.S.A.* ... **112 A2** 48 47N 104 34W
Plérin, *France* **18 D4** 48 32N 2 46W
Plessisville, *Canada* **105 C5** 46 14N 71 47W
Plestin-les-Grèves,
  France **18 D3** 48 40N 3 39W
Pleszew, *Poland* ...... **31 G4** 51 53N 17 47 E
Pleternica, *Croatia* .... **28 E2** 45 17N 17 48 E
Plétipi, L., *Canada* **105 B5** 51 44N 70 6W
Pleven, *Bulgaria* ...... **45 C8** 43 26N 24 37 E
Plevlja, *Serbia & M.* ... **44 C3** 43 21N 19 21 E
Plevna, *Canada* **116 B8** 44 58N 76 59W
Plitvička Jezera △,
  Croatia .... **41 D12** 44 54N 15 35 E
Plješevica, *Croatia* ..... **41 D12** 44 45N 15 45 E
Ploaghe, *Italy* .... **42 B1** 40 40N 8 45 E
Ploče, *Croatia* .... **41 E14** 43 4N 17 26 E
Płock, *Poland* .... **31 F6** 52 32N 19 40 E
Plöckenpass, *Italy* ..... **41 B9** 46 37N 12 57 E
Plöckenstein, *Germany* **25 G9** 48 46N 13 51 E
Ploemeur, *France* **18 E3** 47 44N 3 26W
Ploërmel, *France* **18 E4** 47 55N 2 26W
Ploiești, *Romania* ..... **29 F11** 44 57N 26 5 E
Plomárion, *Greece* .... **47 C8** 38 59N 26 22 E
Plombières-les-Bains,
  France .... **19 E13** 47 58N 6 27 E
Plomin, *Croatia* .... **41 C11** 45 8N 14 10 E
Plön, *Germany* .... **24 A6** 54 9N 10 24 E
Plonge, Lac la, *Canada* **103 B7** 55 8N 107 20W
Płońsk, *Poland* .... **31 F7** 52 37N 20 21 E
Plopiș, *Romania* ...... **29 E10** 45 4N 25 59 E
Plopişului, Munții,
  Romania .... **28 C7** 47 0N 22 20 E
Płoty, *Poland* .... **30 E2** 53 48N 15 18 E
Plouaret, *France* **18 D3** 48 37N 3 28W
Plouay, *France* **18 E3** 47 55N 3 21W
Ploučnice ➤,
  Czech Rep. .... **26 A7** 50 46N 14 13 E
Ploudalmézeau, *France* **18 D2** 48 34N 4 41W
Plouescat, *France* **18 D2** 48 39N 4 10W
Plougasnou, *France* ... **18 D3** 48 42N 3 49W
Plougastel-Daoulas,
  France **18 D2** 48 22N 4 17W
Plouguerneau, *France* . **18 D2** 48 36N 4 30W
Plouha, *France* **18 D4** 48 41N 2 57W
Plouhinec, *France* **18 E2** 48 1N 4 29W
Plovdiv, *Bulgaria* ..... **45 D8** 42 8N 24 44 E
Plovdiv □, *Bulgaria* ... **45 D8** 42 8N 24 44 E
Plum, *U.S.A.* **116 F5** 40 29N 79 47W
Plum I., *U.S.A.* **117 E12** 41 11N 72 12W
Plumas, *U.S.A.* **110 F7** 39 45N 120 4W
Plummer, *U.S.A.* **108 C5** 47 20N 116 53W
Plumtree, *Zimbabwe* . **87 G2** 20 27 S 27 55 E
Plunge, *Lithuania* ..... **9 J19** 55 53N 21 59 E
Pluvigner, *France* **18 E3** 47 46N 3 1W
Plymouth, *Trin. & Tob.* **125 J16** 11 14N 60 48W
Plymouth, *U.K.* **15 G3** 50 22N 4 10W
Plymouth, *Calif.*, *U.S.A.* **110 G6** 38 29N 120 51W
Plymouth, *Ind.*, *U.S.A.* **114 E2** 41 21N 86 19W
Plymouth, *Mass.*, *U.S.A.* **117 E14** 41 57N 70 40W
Plymouth, *N.C.*, *U.S.A.* **117 H7** 35 52N 76 43W
Plymouth, *N.H.*, *U.S.A.* **117 C13** 43 46N 71 41W
Plymouth, *Wis.*, *U.S.A.* **114 D2** 43 45N 87 59W
Plympton-Wyoming,
  Canada **116 D2** 42 57N 82 7W
Plynlimon = Pumlumon
  Fawr, *U.K.* **15 E4** 52 28N 3 46W
Plyusa, *Russia* .... **32 C5** 58 28N 29 27 E
Plyussa ➤, *Russia* ..... **32 C5** 59 0N 28 5 E
Plzeň, *Czech Rep.* ..... **26 B6** 49 45N 13 22 E
Plzeňský □, *Czech Rep.* **26 B6** 49 35N 13 12 E
Pniewy, *Poland* .... **31 F3** 52 31N 16 16 E
Pô, *Burkina Faso* **83 C4** 11 14N 1 5W
Po ➤, *Italy* .... **41 D9** 44 57N 12 4 E
Pô △, *Burkina Faso* ... **83 C4** 11 25N 1 5W
Po, Foci del, *Italy* ..... **41 D9** 44 55N 12 30 E
Po Hai = Bo Hai, *China* **57 E10** 39 0N 119 0 E
Pobé, *Benin* .... **83 D5** 7 0N 2 56 E
Pobé-Mengao,
  Burkina Faso **83 C4** 13 53N 1 42W
Pobeda, *Russia* .... **53 C15** 65 12N 146 12 E

Pobedy, Pik, Kyrgyzstan 52 E8 42 0N 79 58 E
Pobiedziska, Poland 31 F4 52 29N 17 11 E
Pobla de Segur, Spain 38 C5 42 15N 0 58 E
Pobladura del Valle, Spain 36 C5 42 6N 5 44W
Pobra de Trives, Spain 36 C3 42 20N 7 10W
Pocahontas, Ark., U.S.A. 113 G9 36 16N 90 58W
Pocahontas, Iowa, U.S.A. 112 D7 42 44N 94 40W
Pocatello, U.S.A. 108 E7 42 52N 112 27W
Počátky, Czech Rep. 26 B8 49 15N 15 14 E
Pochep, Russia 33 F7 52 58N 33 29 E
Pochinki, Russia 34 C7 54 41N 44 59 E
Pochinok, Russia 32 E7 54 28N 32 29 E
Pöchlarn, Austria 26 C8 48 12N 15 12 E
Pochutla, Mexico 119 D5 15 50N 96 31W
Pocito Casas, Mexico 118 B2 28 32N 111 6W
Pocking, Germany 25 G9 48 23N 13 19 E
Pocomoke City, U.S.A. 114 F8 38 5N 75 34W
Poços de Caldas, Brazil 127 A6 21 50 S 46 33W
Podbořany, Czech Rep. 26 A6 50 14N 13 25 E
Poddębice, Poland 31 G5 51 54N 18 58 E
Poděbrady, Czech Rep. 26 A8 50 9N 15 8 E
Podensac, France 20 D3 44 40N 0 22W
Podenzano, Italy 40 D6 44 57N 9 41 E
Podgorač, Croatia 28 E3 45 27N 18 13 E
Podgorica, Serbia & M. 44 D3 42 30N 19 19 E
Podgorie, Albania 44 F4 40 49N 20 48 E
Podilska Vysochyna, Ukraine 29 B13 49 0N 28 0 E
Podkarpackie □, Poland 31 H9 50 0N 22 10 E
Podkova, Bulgaria 45 E9 41 24N 25 24 E
Podlapača, Croatia 41 D12 44 37N 15 47 E
Podlaskie □, Poland 31 E10 53 10N 23 0 E
Podoleni, Romania 29 D11 46 46N 26 39 E
Podolínec, Slovak Rep. 27 B13 49 16N 20 31 E
Podolsk, Russia 32 E9 55 25N 37 30 E
Podor, Senegal 82 B1 16 40N 15 2W
Podporozhye, Russia 32 B8 60 55N 34 2 E
Podu Iloaiei, Romania 29 C12 47 13N 27 16 E
Podu Turcului, Romania 29 D12 46 11N 27 25 E
Podujevo, Serbia & M. 44 D5 42 54N 21 10 E
Podyjí △, Czech Rep. 26 C8 48 51N 15 57 E
Poel, Germany 24 B6 54 0N 11 25 E
Pofadder, S. Africa 88 D2 29 10 S 19 22 E
Poggiardo, Italy 43 B11 40 3N 18 23 E
Poggibonsi, Italy 40 E8 43 28N 11 9 E
Póggio Mirteto, Italy 41 F9 42 16N 12 41 E
Pogoanele, Romania 29 F12 44 55N 27 0 E
Pogorzela, Poland 31 G4 51 50N 17 12 E
Pogradec, Albania 44 F4 40 54N 20 37 E
Pogranichnyy, Russia 54 B5 44 25N 131 24 E
Poh, Indonesia 63 E6 0 46 S 122 51 E
P'ohang, S. Korea 57 F15 36 1N 129 23 E
Pohjanmaa, Finland 8 E20 62 58N 22 50 E
Pohnpei, Micronesia 96 G7 6 55N 158 10 E
Pohorelá, Slovak Rep. 27 C13 48 50N 20 2 E
Pohořelice, Czech Rep. 27 C9 48 59N 16 31 E
Pohorje, Slovenia 41 B12 46 30N 15 20 E
Pohri, India 68 G6 25 32N 77 22 E
Poiana Mare, Romania 28 G8 43 57N 23 5 E
Poiana Ruscăi, Munţii, Romania 28 E7 45 45N 22 25 E
Poiana Stampei, Romania 29 C10 47 19N 25 8 E
Poinsett, C., Antarctica 5 C8 65 42 S 113 18 E
Point Arena, U.S.A. 110 G3 38 55N 123 41W
Point Baker, U.S.A. 102 B2 56 21N 133 37W
Point Edward, Canada 104 D3 43 0N 82 30W
Point Fortin, Trin. & Tob. 125 K15 10 10N 61 42W
Point Hope, U.S.A. 100 B3 68 21N 166 47W
Point L., Canada 100 B8 65 15N 113 4W
Point Lisas, Trin. & Tob. 125 K15 10 24N 61 30W
Point Pedro, Sri Lanka 66 Q12 9 50N 80 15 E
Point Pelee △, Canada 116 E2 41 57N 82 31W
Point Pleasant, N.J., U.S.A. 117 F10 40 5N 74 4W
Point Pleasant, W. Va., U.S.A. 114 F4 38 51N 82 8W
Point Reyes △, U.S.A. 110 G2 38 10N 122 55W
Pointe-à-Pitre, Guadeloupe 120 b 16 10N 61 32W
Pointe-au-Pic = La Malbaie, Canada 105 C5 47 40N 70 10W
Pointe-Claire, Canada 117 A11 45 26N 73 50W
Pointe-Gatineau, Canada 117 A9 45 28N 75 42W
Pointe-Noire, Congo 84 E2 4 48 S 11 53 E
Pointe Noire, Guadeloupe 120 b 16 14N 61 47W
Poio, Spain 36 C2 42 28N 8 41W
Poirino, Italy 40 D4 44 56N 7 48 E
Poisonbush Ra., Australia 92 D3 22 30 S 121 30 E
Poissonnier Pt., Australia 92 C2 19 57 S 119 10 E
Poitiers, France 18 F7 46 35N 0 20 E
Poitou, France 20 B3 46 40N 0 10W
Poitou-Charentes □, France 20 B4 46 10N 0 15 E
Poix-de-Picardie, France 19 C8 49 47N 1 58 E
Poix-Terron, France 19 C11 49 38N 4 38 E
Pojoaque, U.S.A. 109 J11 35 54N 106 1W
Pokaran, India 66 F7 27 0N 71 50 E
Pokataroo, Australia 95 D4 29 30 S 148 36 E
Pokhara, Nepal 69 E10 28 14N 83 58 E
Pokhvistnevo, Russia 34 D11 53 36N 52 0 E
Poko, Dem. Rep. of the Congo 86 B2 3 7N 26 52 E
Poko, Sudan 81 F3 5 41N 31 55 E
Pokrov, Russia 32 E10 55 55N 39 7 E
Pokrovsk, Russia 53 C13 61 29N 129 0 E
Pokrovskoye, Russia 33 J10 47 25N 38 54 E
Pola = Pula, Croatia 41 D10 44 54N 13 57 E
Pola, Russia 32 D7 57 55N 32 0 E
Pola de Allande, Spain 36 B4 43 16N 6 37W
Pola de Lena, Spain 36 B5 43 10N 5 49W
Pola de Siero, Spain 36 B5 43 24N 5 39W
Pola de Somiedo, Spain 36 B4 43 5N 6 15W
Polacca, U.S.A. 109 J8 35 50N 110 23W
Polan, Iran 71 E9 25 30N 61 10 E
Pol'ana, Slovak Rep. 27 C12 48 38N 19 29 E
Poland ■, Europe 31 G3 52 0N 20 0 E
Polanica-Zdrój, Poland 31 H3 50 24N 16 32 E
Połaniec, Poland 31 H8 50 26N 21 17 E
Polanów, Poland 30 D3 54 7N 16 41 E
Polar Bear △, Canada 104 A2 55 0N 83 45W
Polatlı, Turkey 72 C5 39 36N 32 9 E
Polatsk, Belarus 32 E5 55 30N 28 50 E
Polcura, Chile 126 D1 37 17 S 71 43W
Połczyn-Zdrój, Poland 30 E3 53 47N 16 5 E
Poleski △, Poland 31 G10 51 29N 23 5 E
Polessk, Russia 9 J19 54 50N 21 8 E
Polesye = Pripet Marshes, Europe 33 F5 52 10N 28 10 E
Polgar, Hungary 28 C6 47 54N 21 6 E
Pŏlgyo-ri, S. Korea 57 G14 34 51N 127 21 E
Poli, Cameroon 83 C7 8 34N 13 15 E
Políaigos, Greece 46 E6 36 45N 24 38 E
Policastro, G. di, Italy 43 C8 40 0N 15 35 E
Police, Poland 30 E1 53 33N 14 33 E
Polička, Czech Rep. 27 B9 49 43N 16 15 E
Policoro, Italy 43 B9 40 13N 16 41 E
Polignano a Mare, Italy 43 A9 41 0N 17 13 E
Poligny, France 19 F12 46 50N 5 42 E
Políkhnitas, Greece 47 B8 39 6N 26 10 E
Polillo Is., Phil. 61 D4 14 56N 122 0 E
Polillo Strait, Phil. 61 D4 14 44N 121 51 E
Polis, Cyprus 49 D11 35 2N 32 26 E
Polístena, Italy 43 D9 38 24N 16 4 E
Políyiros, Greece 44 F7 40 23N 23 25 E
Polk, U.S.A. 116 E5 41 22N 79 56W
Polkowice, Poland 31 G3 51 29N 16 3 E
Polla, Italy 43 B8 40 31N 15 29 E
Pollachi, India 66 P10 10 35N 77 0 E
Pollença, Spain 48 B10 39 54N 3 1 E
Pollença, B. de, Spain 48 B10 39 53N 3 8 E
Póllica, Italy 43 B8 40 11N 15 3 E
Pollino △, Italy 43 C9 40 0N 16 12 E
Pollino, Mte., Italy 43 C9 39 55N 16 11 E
Polna, Russia 32 C5 58 31N 28 5 E
Polnovat, Russia 52 C7 63 50N 65 54 E
Pology, Ukraine 33 J9 47 29N 36 15 E
Polokwane, S. Africa 89 C4 23 54 S 29 25 E
Polonne, Ukraine 33 G4 50 6N 27 30 E
Polonnoye = Polonne, Ukraine 33 G4 50 6N 27 30 E
Polski Trŭmbesh, Bulgaria 45 C9 43 20N 25 38 E
Polsko Kosovo, Bulgaria 45 C9 43 23N 25 38 E
Polson, U.S.A. 108 C6 47 41N 114 9W
Poltár, Slovak Rep. 27 C12 48 26N 19 48 E
Poltava, Ukraine 33 H8 49 35N 34 35 E
Põltsamaa, Estonia 9 G21 58 39N 25 58 E
Polunochnoye, Russia 52 C7 60 52N 60 25 E
Põlva, Estonia 9 G22 58 3N 27 3 E
Polyana, Ukraine 28 B7 48 38N 22 58 E
Polynesia, Pac. Oc. 97 F11 10 0 S 162 0W
Polynésie française = French Polynesia ☑, Pac. Oc. 97 K13 20 0 S 145 0W
Pomarance, Italy 40 E7 43 18N 10 52 E
Pomaro, Mexico 118 D4 18 20N 103 18W
Pombal, Portugal 36 F2 39 55N 8 40W
Pómbia, Greece 49 E6 35 0N 24 51 E
Pomene, Mozam. 89 C6 22 53 S 35 33 E
Pomeroy, Ohio, U.S.A. 114 F4 39 2N 82 2W
Pomeroy, Wash., U.S.A. 108 C5 46 28N 117 36W
Pomézia, Italy 42 A5 41 40N 12 30 E
Pomichna, Ukraine 33 H6 48 13N 31 36 E
Pomona, Australia 95 D5 26 22 S 152 52 E
Pomona, U.S.A. 111 L9 34 4N 117 45W
Pomorie, Bulgaria 45 D11 42 32N 27 41 E
Pomorskie □, Poland 30 D5 54 30N 18 0 E
Pomorskie, Pojezierze, Poland 30 E3 53 40N 16 37 E
Pomos, Cyprus 49 D11 35 9N 32 33 E
Pomos, C., Cyprus 49 D11 35 10N 32 33 E
Pompano Beach, U.S.A. 115 M5 26 14N 80 8W
Pompei, Italy 43 B7 40 45N 14 30 E
Pompey, France 19 D13 48 46N 6 6 E
Pompeys Pillar, U.S.A. 108 D10 45 59N 107 57W
Pompeys Pillar △, U.S.A. 108 D10 46 0N 108 0W
Pompton Lakes, U.S.A. 117 F10 41 0N 74 17W
Ponape = Pohnpei, Micronesia 96 G7 6 55N 158 10 E
Ponask L., Canada 104 B1 54 0N 92 41W
Ponca, U.S.A. 112 D6 42 34N 96 43W
Ponca City, U.S.A. 113 G6 36 42N 97 5W
Ponce, Puerto Rico 121 d 18 1N 66 37W
Ponchatoula, U.S.A. 113 K9 30 26N 90 26W
Poncheville, L., Canada 104 B4 50 10N 76 55W
Pond, U.S.A. 111 K7 35 43N 119 20W
Pond Inlet, Canada 101 A12 72 40N 77 0W
Pondicherry, India 66 P11 11 59N 79 50 E
Ponds, I. of, Canada 105 B8 53 27N 55 52W
Ponferrada, Spain 36 C4 42 32N 6 35W
Pongo, Wadi →, Sudan 81 F2 8 42N 27 40 E
Poniatowa, Poland 31 G9 51 11N 22 3 E
Poniec, Poland 31 G3 51 48N 16 50 E
Ponikva, Slovenia 41 B12 46 16N 15 26 E
Ponnani, India 66 P9 10 45N 75 59 E
Ponoka, Canada 102 C6 52 42N 113 40W
Ponorogo, Indonesia 63 G14 7 52 S 111 27 E
Pons = Ponts, Spain 38 D6 41 55N 1 12 E
Pons, France 20 C3 45 35N 0 34W
Ponsul →, Portugal 36 F3 39 40N 7 31W
Pont-à-Mousson, France 19 D13 48 54N 6 1 E
Pont-Audemer, France 18 C7 49 21N 0 30 E
Pont-Aven, France 18 E3 47 51N 3 47W
Pont Canavese, Italy 40 C4 45 25N 7 36 E
Pont-d'Ain, France 19 F12 46 3N 5 21 E
Pont-de-Roide, France 19 E13 47 23N 6 45 E
Pont-de-Salars, France 20 D6 44 18N 2 44 E
Pont-de-Vaux, France 19 F11 46 26N 4 56 E
Pont-de-Veyle, France 19 F11 46 17N 4 53 E
Pont-du-Château, France 19 G10 45 47N 3 15 E
Pont-l'Abbé, France 18 E2 47 52N 4 15W
Pont-l'Évêque, France 18 C7 49 18N 0 11 E
Pont-St-Esprit, France 21 D8 44 16N 4 40 E
Pont-St-Martin, Italy 40 C4 45 36N 7 48 E
Pont-Ste-Maxence, France 19 C9 49 18N 2 35 E
Pont-sur-Yonne, France 19 D10 48 18N 3 10 E
Ponta do Sol, Madeira 48 D2 32 42N 17 7W
Ponta Grossa, Brazil 127 B5 25 7 S 50 10W
Ponta Pora, Brazil 127 A4 22 20 S 55 35W
Pontacq, France 20 E3 43 11N 0 8W
Pontailler-sur-Saône, France 19 E12 47 13N 5 25 E
Pontarlier, France 19 F13 46 54N 6 20 E
Pontassieve, Italy 41 E8 43 46N 11 26 E
Pontaumur, France 20 C6 45 52N 2 40 E
Pontcharra, France 21 C10 45 26N 6 1 E
Pontchartrain L., U.S.A. 113 K10 30 5N 90 5W
Pontchâteau, France 18 E4 47 25N 2 5W
Ponte da Barca, Portugal 36 D2 41 48N 8 25W
Ponte de Sor, Portugal 37 F2 39 17N 8 1W
Ponte dell'Ólio, Italy 40 D6 44 52N 9 39 E
Ponte di Legno, Italy 40 B7 46 16N 10 31 E
Ponte do Lima, Portugal 36 D2 41 46N 8 35W
Ponte do Pungué, Mozam. 87 F3 19 30 S 34 33 E
Ponte-Leccia, France 21 F13 42 28N 9 13 E
Ponte nelle Alpi, Italy 41 B9 46 11N 12 16 E
Ponte Nova, Brazil 127 A7 20 25 S 42 54W
Ponteareas, Spain 36 C2 42 10N 8 28W
Pontebba, Italy 41 B10 46 30N 13 18 E
Ponteceso, Spain 36 B2 43 15N 8 54W
Pontecorvo, Italy 42 A6 41 27N 13 40 E
Pontedeume, Spain 36 B2 43 24N 8 10W
Ponteix, Canada 103 D7 49 46N 107 29W
Pontevedra, Spain 36 C2 42 26N 8 40W
Pontevedra □, Spain 36 C2 42 25N 8 39W
Pontevedra, R. de →, Spain 36 C2 42 22N 8 45W
Pontevico, Italy 40 C7 45 16N 10 5 E
Pontiac, Ill., U.S.A. 112 E10 40 53N 88 38W
Pontiac, Mich., U.S.A. 114 D4 42 38N 83 18W
Pontian Kechil, Malaysia 65 d 1 29N 103 23 E
Pontianak, Indonesia 62 E3 0 3 S 109 15 E
Pontine Is. = Ponziane, Ísole, Italy 42 B5 40 55N 12 57 E
Pontine Mts. = Kuzey Anadolu Dağları, Turkey 72 B7 41 30N 35 0 E
Pontínia, Italy 42 A6 41 25N 13 2 E
Pontivy, France 18 D4 48 5N 2 58W
Pontoise, France 19 C9 49 3N 2 5 E
Ponton →, Canada 102 B5 58 27N 116 11W
Pontorson, France 18 D5 48 34N 1 30W
Pontrémoli, Italy 40 D6 44 22N 9 53 E
Pontrieux, France 18 D3 48 42N 3 10W
Ponts, Spain 38 D6 41 55N 1 12 E
Pontypool, Canada 116 B6 44 6N 78 38W
Pontypool, U.K. 15 F4 51 42N 3 2W
Ponza, Italy 42 B5 40 54N 12 58 E
Ponziane, Ísole, Italy 42 B5 40 55N 12 57 E
Poochera, Australia 95 E1 32 43 S 134 51 E
Poole, U.K. 15 G6 50 43N 1 59W
Poole □, U.K. 15 G6 50 43N 1 59W
Poona = Pune, India 66 K8 18 29N 73 57 E
Pooncarie, Australia 95 E3 33 22 S 142 31 E
Poopelloe L., Australia 95 E3 31 40 S 144 0 E
Poopó, L. de, Bolivia 124 G5 18 30 S 67 35W
Popayán, Colombia 124 C3 2 27N 76 36W
Poperinge, Belgium 17 D2 50 51N 2 42 E
Popilta L., Australia 95 E3 33 10 S 141 42 E
Popina, Bulgaria 45 B10 44 7N 26 57 E
Popio L., Australia 95 E3 33 10 S 141 52 E
Poplar, U.S.A. 112 A2 48 7N 105 12W
Poplar →, Canada 103 C9 53 0N 97 19W
Poplar Bluff, U.S.A. 113 G9 36 46N 90 24W
Poplarville, U.S.A. 113 K10 30 51N 89 32W
Popocatépetl, Volcán, Mexico 119 D5 19 2N 98 38W
Popokabaka, Dem. Rep. of the Congo 84 F3 5 41 S 16 40 E
Pópoli, Italy 41 F10 42 10N 13 50 E
Popovača, Croatia 41 C13 45 30N 16 41 E
Popovo, Bulgaria 45 C10 43 21N 26 18 E
Poppberg, Germany 25 F7 49 26N 11 37 E
Poppi, Italy 41 E8 43 43N 11 46 E
Poprad, Slovak Rep. 27 B13 49 3N 20 18 E
Poprad →, Slovak Rep. 27 B13 49 38N 20 42 E
Porali →, Pakistan 68 G2 25 58N 66 26 E
Porbandar, India 68 J3 21 44N 69 43 E
Porcher I., Canada 102 C2 53 50N 130 30W
Porcuna, Spain 37 H6 37 52N 4 11W
Porcupine →, Canada 103 B8 59 11N 104 46W
Porcupine →, U.S.A. 100 B5 66 34N 145 19W
Porcupine Gorge △, Australia 94 C3 20 22 S 144 26 E
Pordenone, Italy 41 C9 45 57N 12 39 E
Pordim, Bulgaria 45 C8 43 23N 24 51 E
Poreč, Croatia 41 C10 45 14N 13 36 E
Poretskoye, Russia 34 C8 55 9N 46 21 E
Pori, Finland 9 F19 61 29N 21 48 E
Porí, Greece 46 F5 35 58N 23 13 E
Porkhov, Russia 32 D5 57 45N 29 38 E
Porlamar, Venezuela 124 A6 10 57N 63 51W
Porlezza, Italy 40 B6 46 2N 9 7 E
Porma →, Spain 36 C5 42 49N 5 28W
Pornic, France 18 E4 47 7N 2 5W
Poronaysk, Russia 53 E15 49 13N 143 0 E
Póros, Greece 46 D5 37 30N 23 30 E
Poroshiri-Dake, Japan 54 C11 42 41N 142 52 E
Poroszló, Hungary 28 C5 47 39N 20 40 E
Poroto Mts., Tanzania 87 D3 9 0 S 33 30 E
Porpoise B., Antarctica 5 C9 66 0 S 127 0 E
Porquerolles, Î. de, France 21 F10 43 0N 6 13 E
Porrentruy, Switz. 25 H3 47 25N 7 6 E
Porreres, Spain 48 B10 39 31N 3 2 E
Porsangen, Norway 8 A21 70 40N 25 40 E
Porsgrunn, Norway 9 G13 59 10N 9 40 E
Port Alberni, Canada 102 D4 49 14N 124 50W
Port Alfred, S. Africa 88 E4 33 36 S 26 55 E
Port Alice, Canada 102 C3 50 20N 127 25W
Port Allegany, U.S.A. 116 E6 41 48N 78 17W
Port Allen, U.S.A. 113 K9 30 27N 91 12W
Port Alma, Australia 94 C5 23 38 S 150 53 E
Port Angeles, U.S.A. 110 B3 48 7N 123 27W
Port Antonio, Jamaica 120 a 18 10N 76 30W
Port Aransas, U.S.A. 113 M6 27 50N 97 4W
Port Arthur, Australia 95 G4 43 7 S 147 50 E
Port Arthur, U.S.A. 113 L8 29 54N 93 56W
Port au Choix, Canada 105 B8 50 43N 57 22W
Port au Port B., Canada 105 C8 48 40N 58 50W
Port-au-Prince, Haiti 121 C5 18 40N 72 20W
Port Augusta, Australia 95 E2 32 30 S 137 50 E
Port Austin, U.S.A. 116 B2 44 3N 83 1W
Port Bell, Uganda 86 B3 0 18N 32 35 E
Port Bergé Vaovao, Madag. 89 B8 15 33 S 47 40 E
Port Blandford, Canada 105 C9 48 20N 54 10W
Port-Bouët, Ivory C. 82 D4 5 16N 3 57W
Port Bradshaw, Australia 94 A2 12 30 S 137 20 E
Port Broughton, Australia 95 E2 33 37 S 137 56 E
Port Burwell, Canada 116 D4 42 40N 80 48W
Port Canning, India 69 H13 22 23N 88 40 E
Port-Cartier, Canada 105 B6 50 2N 66 50W
Port Chalmers, N.Z. 91 L3 45 49 S 170 30 E
Port Charlotte, U.S.A. 115 M4 26 59N 82 6W
Port Chester, U.S.A. 117 F11 41 0N 73 40W
Port Clements, Canada 102 C2 53 40N 132 10W
Port Clinton, U.S.A. 114 E4 41 31N 82 56W
Port Colborne, Canada 116 D5 42 50N 79 10W
Port Coquitlam, Canada 102 D4 49 15N 122 45W
Port Credit, Canada 116 C5 43 33N 79 35W
Port-Cros △, France 21 F10 43 0N 6 24 E
Port Curtis, Australia 94 C5 23 57 S 151 20 E
Port d'Alcúdia, Spain 48 B10 39 50N 3 7 E
Port Dalhousie, Canada 116 C5 43 13N 79 16W
Port d'Andratx, Spain 48 B9 39 32N 2 23 E
Port Darwin, Australia 92 B5 12 24 S 130 45 E
Port Darwin, Falk. Is. 128 G5 51 50 S 59 0W
Port Davey, Australia 95 G4 43 16 S 145 55 E
Port-de-Bouc, France 21 E8 43 24N 4 59 E
Port-de-Paix, Haiti 121 C5 19 50N 72 50W
Port de Pollença, Spain 48 B10 39 54N 3 4 E
Port de Sóller, Spain 48 B9 39 48N 2 42 E
Port Dickson, Malaysia 65 L3 2 30N 101 49 E
Port Douglas, Australia 94 B4 16 30 S 145 30 E
Port Dover, Canada 116 D4 42 47N 80 12W
Port Edward, Canada 102 C2 54 12N 130 10W
Port Elgin, Canada 116 B3 44 25N 81 25W
Port Elizabeth, S. Africa 88 E4 33 58 S 25 40 E
Port Ellen, U.K. 13 F2 55 38N 6 11W
Port-en-Bessin-Huppain, France 18 C6 49 21N 0 45W
Port Erin, U.K. 14 C3 54 5N 4 45W
Port Essington, Australia 92 B5 11 15 S 132 10 E
Port Ewen, U.S.A. 117 E11 41 54N 73 59W
Port Fairy, Australia 95 F3 38 22 S 142 12 E
Port Fouâd = Bûr Fuad, Egypt 80 H8 31 15N 32 20 E
Port Gamble, U.S.A. 110 C4 47 51N 122 35W
Port-Gentil, Gabon 84 E1 0 40 S 8 50 E
Port Germein, Australia 95 E2 33 1 S 138 1 E
Port Gibson, U.S.A. 113 K9 31 58N 90 59W
Port Glasgow, U.K. 13 F4 55 56N 4 41W
Port Harcourt, Nigeria 83 E6 4 40N 7 10 E
Port Hardy, Canada 102 C3 50 41N 127 30W
Port Harrison = Inukjuak, Canada 101 C12 58 25N 78 15W
Port Hawkesbury, Canada 105 C7 45 36N 61 22W
Port Hedland, Australia 92 D2 20 25 S 118 35 E
Port Henry, U.S.A. 117 B11 44 3N 73 28W
Port Hood, Canada 105 C7 46 0N 61 32W
Port Hope, Canada 116 C6 43 56N 78 20W
Port Hope, U.S.A. 116 C2 43 57N 82 43W
Port Hope Simpson, Canada 105 B8 52 33N 56 18W
Port Hueneme, U.S.A. 111 L7 34 7N 119 12W
Port Huron, U.S.A. 116 D2 42 58N 82 26W
Port Iliç, Azerbaijan 73 C13 38 53N 48 47 E
Port Jefferson, U.S.A. 117 F11 40 57N 73 3W
Port Jervis, U.S.A. 117 E10 41 22N 74 41W
Port-Joinville, France 18 F4 46 45N 2 23W
Port Katon, Russia 33 J10 46 52N 38 46 E
Port Kelang = Pelabuhan Kelang, Malaysia 65 L3 3 0N 101 23 E
Port Kenny, Australia 95 E1 33 10 S 134 41 E
Port-la-Nouvelle, France 20 E7 43 1N 3 3 E
Port Lairge = Waterford, Ireland 12 D4 52 15N 7 8W
Port Laoise, Ireland 12 C4 53 2N 7 18W
Port Lavaca, U.S.A. 113 L6 28 37N 96 38W
Port Leyden, U.S.A. 117 C9 43 35N 75 21W
Port Lincoln, Australia 95 E2 34 42 S 135 52 E
Port Loko, S. Leone 82 D2 8 48N 12 46W
Port Louis, France 18 E3 47 42N 3 22W
Port-Louis, Guadeloupe 120 b 16 28N 61 32W
Port Louis, Mauritius 77 H9 20 10 S 57 30 E
Port MacDonnell, Australia 95 F3 38 5 S 140 48 E
Port McNeill, Canada 102 C3 50 35N 127 6W
Port Macquarie, Australia 95 E5 31 25 S 152 25 E
Port Maria, Jamaica 120 a 18 25N 76 55W
Port Matilda, U.S.A. 116 F6 40 48N 78 3W
Port Mellon, Canada 102 D4 49 32N 123 31W
Port-Menier, Canada 105 C7 49 51N 64 15W
Port Moody, Canada 110 A4 49 17N 122 51W
Port Morant, Jamaica 120 a 17 54N 76 19W
Port Moresby, Papua N. G. 96 H6 9 24 S 147 8 E
Port Musgrave, Australia 94 A3 11 55 S 141 50 E
Port-Navalo, France 18 E4 47 34N 2 54W
Port Neches, U.S.A. 113 L8 30 0N 93 59W
Port Nolloth, S. Africa 88 D2 29 17 S 16 52 E
Port Nouveau-Québec = Kangiqsualujjuaq, Canada 101 C13 58 30N 65 59W
Port of Spain, Trin. & Tob. 121 D7 10 40N 61 31W
Port Orange, U.S.A. 115 L5 29 9N 80 59W
Port Orchard, U.S.A. 110 C4 47 32N 122 38W
Port Orford, U.S.A. 108 E1 42 45N 124 30W
Port Pegasus, N.Z. 91 M1 47 12 S 167 41 E
Port Perry, Canada 116 B6 44 6N 78 56W
Port Phillip B., Australia 95 F3 38 10 S 144 50 E
Port Pirie, Australia 95 E2 33 10 S 138 1 E
Port Renfrew, Canada 102 D4 48 30N 124 20W
Port Roper, Australia 94 A2 14 45 S 135 25 E
Port Rowan, Canada 116 D4 42 40N 80 30W
Port Safaga = Bûr Safâga, Egypt 70 E2 26 43N 33 57 E
Port Said = Bûr Sa'îd, Egypt 80 H8 31 16N 32 18 E
Port St. Joe, U.S.A. 115 L3 29 49N 85 18W
Port St. Johns = Umzimvubu, S. Africa 89 E4 31 38 S 29 33 E
Port-St-Louis-du-Rhône, France 21 E8 43 23N 4 49 E
Port St. Lucie, U.S.A. 115 M5 27 20N 80 20W
Port-Ste-Marie, France 20 D4 44 15N 0 25 E
Port Sanilac, U.S.A. 116 C2 43 26N 82 33W
Port Severn, Canada 116 B5 44 48N 79 43W
Port Shepstone, S. Africa 89 E5 30 44 S 30 28 E
Port Simpson, Canada 102 C2 54 30N 130 20W
Port Stanley = Stanley, Falk. Is. 128 G5 51 40 S 59 51W
Port Stanley, Canada 116 D3 42 40N 81 10W
Port Sudan = Bûr Sûdân, Sudan 80 D4 19 32N 37 9 E
Port Sulphur, U.S.A. 113 L10 29 29N 89 42W
Port-sur-Saône, France 19 E13 47 42N 6 2 E
Port Talbot, U.K. 15 F4 51 35N 3 47W
Port Taufiq = Bûr Taufiq, Egypt 80 J8 29 54N 32 32 E
Port Townsend, U.S.A. 110 B4 48 7N 122 45W
Port-Vendres, France 20 F7 42 32N 3 8 E
Port Vila, Vanuatu 96 J8 17 45 S 168 18 E
Port Wakefield, Australia 95 E2 34 12 S 138 10 E
Port Washington, U.S.A. 114 D2 43 23N 87 53W
Portadown, U.K. 12 B5 54 25N 6 27W
Portaferry, U.K. 12 B6 54 23N 5 33W
Portage, Pa., U.S.A. 116 F6 40 23N 78 41W
Portage, Wis., U.S.A. 112 D10 43 33N 89 28W
Portage la Prairie, Canada 103 D9 49 58N 98 18W
Portageville, U.S.A. 113 G10 36 26N 89 42W
Portalegre, Portugal 37 F3 39 19N 7 25W
Portalegre □, Portugal 37 F3 39 20N 7 40W
Portales, U.S.A. 113 H3 34 11N 103 20W
Portarlington, Ireland 12 C4 53 9N 7 14W
Portbou, Spain 38 C8 42 25N 3 9 E
Portel, Portugal 37 G3 38 19N 7 41W
Portela, Lisboa ✕ (LIS), Portugal 37 G1 38 46N 9 8W
Porter L., N.W.T., Canada 103 A7 61 41N 108 5W
Porter L., Sask., Canada 103 B7 56 20N 107 20W
Porterville, S. Africa 88 E2 33 0 S 19 0 E
Porterville, U.S.A. 110 J8 36 4N 119 1W
Portes-lès-Valence, France 21 D8 44 52N 4 54 E
Porthcawl, U.K. 15 F4 51 29N 3 42W
Porthill, U.S.A. 108 B5 48 59N 116 30W
Porthmadog, U.K. 14 E3 52 55N 4 8W
Portile de Fier, Europe 28 F7 44 44N 22 30 E
Portimão, Portugal 37 H2 37 8N 8 32W
Portishead, U.K. 15 F5 51 29N 2 46W
Portiţei, Gura, Romania 29 F14 44 41N 29 0 E
Portknockie, U.K. 13 D6 57 42N 2 51W
Portland, N.S.W., Australia 95 E5 33 20 S 150 0 E
Portland, Vic., Australia 95 F3 38 20 S 141 35 E
Portland, Canada 117 B8 44 42N 76 12W
Portland, Conn., U.S.A. 117 E12 41 34N 72 38W
Portland, Maine, U.S.A. 101 D12 43 39N 70 16W
Portland, Mich., U.S.A. 114 D3 42 52N 84 54W
Portland, Oreg., U.S.A. 110 E4 45 32N 122 37W
Portland, Pa., U.S.A. 117 F9 40 55N 75 6W
Portland, Tex., U.S.A. 113 M6 27 53N 97 20W
Portland ✕ (PDX), U.S.A. 110 E4 45 35N 122 36W
Portland, I. of, U.K. 15 G5 50 33N 2 26W
Portland B., Australia 95 F3 38 15 S 141 45 E
Portland Bight, Jamaica 120 a 17 52N 77 5W
Portland Bill, U.K. 15 G5 50 31N 2 28W
Portland Canal, U.S.A. 102 B2 55 56N 130 0W
Portland Pt., Jamaica 120 a 17 42N 77 11W
Portmadoc = Porthmadog, U.K. 14 E3 52 55N 4 8W
Portmore, Jamaica 120 a 17 53N 77 53W
Porto, France 21 F12 42 16N 8 42 E
Porto, Portugal 36 D2 41 8N 8 40W
Porto □, Portugal 36 D2 41 8N 8 20W
Porto, G. de, France 21 F12 42 17N 8 34 E
Pôrto Alegre, Brazil 127 C5 30 5 S 51 10W
Porto Azzurro, Italy 40 F7 42 46N 10 24 E
Porto Cristo, Spain 48 B10 39 33N 3 20 E
Pôrto de Móz, Brazil 125 D8 1 41 S 52 13W
Porto Empédocle, Italy 42 E6 37 17N 13 32 E
Pôrto Esperança, Brazil 124 G7 19 37 S 57 29W
Pôrto Franco, Brazil 125 E9 6 20 S 47 24W
Pôrto Lágos, Greece 45 E9 41 1N 25 6 E
Pôrto Mendes, Brazil 127 A5 24 30 S 54 15W
Porto Moniz, Madeira 48 D2 32 52N 17 11W
Pôrto Murtinho, Brazil 124 H7 21 45 S 57 55W
Pôrto Nacional, Brazil 125 F9 10 40 S 48 30W
Porto-Novo, Benin 83 D5 6 23N 2 42 E
Porto Petro, Spain 48 B10 39 22N 3 13 E
Porto San Giórgio, Italy 41 E10 43 11N 13 48 E
Porto Sant' Elpídio, Italy 41 E10 43 15N 13 43 E
Porto Santo, I. de, Madeira 78 B2 33 45N 16 25W
Porto Santo Stéfano, Italy 40 F8 42 26N 11 7 E
Pôrto São José, Brazil 127 A5 22 43 S 53 10W
Pôrto Seguro, Brazil 125 G11 16 26 S 39 5W
Porto Tolle, Italy 41 D9 44 56N 12 22 E
Porto Tórres, Italy 42 B1 40 50N 8 24 E
Pôrto União, Brazil 127 B5 26 10 S 51 10W
Pôrto Válter, Brazil 124 E4 8 15 S 72 40W
Porto-Vecchio, France 21 G13 41 35N 9 16 E
Pôrto Velho, Brazil 124 E6 8 46 S 63 54W
Portobelo, Panama 120 E4 9 35N 79 42W
Portoferráio, Italy 40 F7 42 48N 10 20 E
Portogruaro, Italy 41 C9 45 47N 12 50 E
Portola, U.S.A. 110 F6 39 49N 120 28W
Portomaggiore, Italy 41 D8 44 42N 11 48 E
Portoscuso, Italy 42 C1 39 12N 8 24 E
Portovénere, Italy 40 D6 44 3N 9 51 E
Portoviejo, Ecuador 124 D2 1 7 S 80 28W
Portpatrick, U.K. 13 G3 54 51N 5 7W
Portree, U.K. 13 D2 57 25N 6 12W
Portrush, U.K. 12 A5 55 12N 6 40W
Portsmouth, Domin. 121 C7 15 34N 61 27W
Portsmouth, U.K. 15 G6 50 48N 1 6W
Portsmouth, N.H., U.S.A. 115 D10 43 5N 70 45W
Portsmouth, Ohio, U.S.A. 114 F4 38 44N 82 57W
Portsmouth, R.I., U.S.A. 117 E13 41 36N 71 15W
Portsmouth, Va., U.S.A. 114 G7 36 50N 76 18W
Portsmouth □, U.K. 15 G6 50 48N 1 6W
Portsoy, U.K. 13 D6 57 41N 2 41W
Portstewart, U.K. 12 A5 55 11N 6 43W
Porttipahdan tekojärvi, Finland 8 B22 68 5N 26 40 E
Portugal ■, Europe 36 F3 40 0N 8 0W
Portugalete, Spain 38 B1 43 19N 3 4W
Portumna, Ireland 12 C3 53 6N 8 14W
Portville, U.S.A. 116 D6 42 3N 78 20W
Porvenir, Chile 128 G2 53 10 S 70 16W
Porvoo, Finland 9 F21 60 24N 25 40 E
Porzuna, Spain 37 F6 39 9N 4 9W
Posada, Italy 42 B2 40 38N 9 43 E
Posada →, Italy 42 B2 40 39N 9 45 E
Posadas, Argentina 127 B4 27 30 S 55 50W
Posadas, Spain 37 H5 37 47N 5 11W
Poschiavo, Switz. 25 J6 46 19N 10 4 E
Posets, Spain 38 C5 42 39N 0 25 E
Posht-e Badam, Iran 71 C7 33 2N 55 23 E
Posidhion, Ákra, Greece 44 G7 39 57N 23 30 E
Posidium, Greece 47 F9 35 30N 27 10 E
Poso, Indonesia 63 E6 1 20 S 120 55 E
Posong, S. Korea 57 G14 34 46N 127 5 E
Posse, Brazil 125 F9 14 4 S 46 18W
Possession I., Antarctica 5 D11 72 4 S 172 0 E
Pössneck, Germany 24 E7 50 42N 11 35 E
Possum Kingdom L., U.S.A. 113 J5 32 52N 98 26W
Post, U.S.A. 113 J4 33 12N 101 23W
Post Falls, U.S.A. 108 C5 47 43N 116 57W
Postavy = Pastavy, Belarus 9 J22 55 4N 26 50 E
Poste-de-la-Baleine = Kuujjuarapik, Canada 104 A4 55 20N 77 35W
Postmasburg, S. Africa 88 D3 28 18 S 23 5 E
Postojna, Slovenia 41 C11 45 46N 14 12 E
Poston, U.S.A. 111 M12 34 0N 114 24W
Postville, Canada 105 B8 54 54N 59 47W
Potamós, Andikíthira, Greece 46 F5 35 52N 23 15 E
Potamós, Kíthira, Greece 46 E4 36 15N 22 58 E
Potchefstroom, S. Africa 88 D4 26 41 S 27 7 E
Potcoava, Romania 29 F9 44 30N 24 39 E
Poteau, U.S.A. 113 H7 35 3N 94 37W
Poteet, U.S.A. 113 L5 29 2N 98 35W
Potenza, Italy 43 B8 40 38N 15 48 E
Potenza →, Italy 41 E10 43 25N 13 40 E
Potenza Picena, Italy 41 E10 43 22N 13 37 E
Poteriteri, L., N.Z. 91 M1 46 5 S 167 10 E
Potgietersrus = Mokopane, S. Africa 89 C4 24 10 S 28 55 E
Poti, Georgia 35 J5 42 10N 41 38 E
Potiskum, Nigeria 83 C7 11 39N 11 2 E
Potlogi, Romania 29 F10 44 34N 25 34 E
Potomac →, U.S.A. 114 G7 38 0N 76 23W
Potosí, Bolivia 124 G5 19 38 S 65 50W
Potosi Mt., U.S.A. 111 K11 35 57N 115 29W

Pototan, *Phil.* . . . . **61 F5** 10 54N 122 38 E
Potrerillos, *Chile* . . . . **126 B2** 26 30 S 69 30W
Potsdam, *Germany* . . . . **24 C9** 52 25N 13 4 E
Potsdam, *U.S.A.* **117 B10** 44 40N 74 59W
Pottersville, *U.S.A.* **117 C11** 43 43N 73 50W
Pottstown, *U.S.A.* **117 F9** 40 15N 75 39W
Pottsville, *U.S.A.* **117 F8** 40 41N 76 12W
Pottuvil, *Sri Lanka* . . . . **66 R12** 6 55N 81 50 E
P'otzu, *Taiwan* . . . . . . **59 F13** 23 30N 120 25 E
Pouancé, *France* **18 E5** 47 44N 1 10W
Pouce Coupé, *Canada* . . **102 B4** 55 40N 120 10W
Poughkeepsie, *U.S.A.* . . **117 E11** 41 42N 73 56W
Pouilly-sur-Loire, *France* **19 E9** 47 17N 2 57 E
Poulaphouca Res.,
    Ireland **12 C5** 53 8N 6 30W
Poulsbo, *U.S.A.* **110 C4** 47 44N 122 39W
Poultney, *U.S.A.* **117 C11** 43 31N 73 14W
Poulton-le-Fylde, *U.K.* . . **14 D5** 53 51N 2 58W
Pouso Alegre, *Brazil* . . **127 A6** 22 14 S 45 57W
Pout, *Senegal* **82 C1** 14 45N 17 0W
Pouthisat, *Cambodia* . . **64 F4** 12 34N 103 50 E
Pouzauges, *France* **18 F6** 46 47N 0 50W
Pova de Santa Iria,
    Portugal **37 G1** 38 51N 9 4W
Považská Bystrica,
    Slovak Rep. . . . . **27 B11** 49 8N 18 27 E
Poverty B., *N.Z.* . . . . . . **91 H7** 38 43 S 178 2 E
Povlen, *Serbia & M.* . . **44 B3** 44 9N 19 44 E
Póvoa de Lanhoso,
    Portugal **36 D2** 41 33N 8 15W
Póvoa de Varzim,
    Portugal **36 D2** 41 25N 8 46W
Povorino, *Russia* . . . . **34 E6** 51 12N 42 5 E
Povungnituk = Puvirnituq, *Canada* . . **101 B12** 60 2N 77 10W
Powassan, *Canada* **104 C4** 46 5N 79 25W
Poway, *U.S.A.* **111 N9** 32 58N 117 2W
Powder →, *U.S.A.* **112 B2** 46 45N 105 26W
Powder River, *U.S.A.* . . **108 E10** 43 2N 106 59W
Powell, *U.S.A.* **108 D9** 44 45N 108 46W
Powell, L., *U.S.A.* **109 H8** 36 57N 111 29W
Powell River, *Canada* . . **102 D4** 49 50N 124 35W
Powers, *U.S.A.* **114 C2** 45 41N 87 32W
Powys □, *U.K.* **15 E4** 52 20N 3 20W
Poyang Hu, *China* . . . . **59 C11** 29 5N 116 20 E
Poyarkovo, *Russia* . . . . **53 E13** 49 36N 128 41 E
Poysdorf, *Austria* . . . . **27 C9** 48 40N 16 37 E
Poza de la Sal, *Spain* . . **36 C7** 42 35N 3 31W
Poza Rica, *Mexico* **119 C5** 20 33N 97 27W
Pozanti, *Turkey* . . . . . . **72 D6** 37 25N 34 50 E
Požarevac, *Serbia & M.* . . **44 B5** 44 35N 21 18 E
Pozazal, *Puerto, Spain* . . **36 C7** 42 56N 4 10W
Požega, *Croatia* . . . . . . **28 E2** 45 20N 17 40 E
Požega, *Serbia & M.* . . **44 C4** 43 53N 20 2 E
Poznań, *Poland* . . . . . . **31 F3** 52 25N 16 55 E
Poznań ✈ (POZ),
    Poland . . . . . . **31 F3** 52 26N 16 45 E
Pozo, *U.S.A.* **111 K6** 35 20N 120 24W
Pozo Alcón, *Spain* **37 H8** 37 42N 2 56W
Pozo Almonte, *Chile* . . **124 H5** 20 10 S 69 50W
Pozo Colorado,
    Paraguay . . . . . . **126 A4** 23 30 S 58 45W
Pozoblanco, *Spain* **37 G6** 38 23N 4 51W
Pozzallo, *Italy* . . . . . . **43 F7** 36 43N 14 51 E
Pozzomaggiore, *Italy* . . **42 B1** 40 24N 8 39 E
Pozzuoli, *Italy* . . . . . . **43 B7** 40 49N 14 7 E
Pra →, *Ghana* **83 D4** 5 1N 1 37W
Prabuty, *Poland* . . . . . . **30 E6** 53 47N 19 15 E
Prača, *Bos.-H.* . . . . . . **28 G3** 43 47N 18 43 E
Prachatice, *Czech Rep.* . . **26 B6** 49 1N 14 0 E
Prachin Buri, *Thailand* . . **64 E3** 14 0N 101 25 E
Prachuap Khiri Khan,
    Thailand . . . . . . **65 G2** 11 49N 99 48 E
Pradelles, *France* . . . . **20 D7** 44 46N 3 52 E
Prades, *France* . . . . . . **20 F6** 42 38N 2 23 E
Prado, *Brazil* . . . . . . **125 G11** 17 20 S 39 13W
Prado del Rey, *Spain* . . **37 J5** 36 48N 5 33W
Præstø, *Denmark* . . . . **11 J6** 55 8N 12 2 E
Pragersko, *Slovenia* . . **41 B12** 46 27N 15 42 E
Prague = Praha,
    Czech Rep. . . . . **26 A7** 50 5N 14 22 E
Praha, *Czech Rep.* . . . . **26 A7** 50 5N 14 22 E
Praha ✈ (PRG),
    Czech Rep. . . . . **26 A7** 50 7N 14 15 E
Prahecq, *France* **20 B3** 46 19N 0 26W
Prahova □, *Romania* . . **29 E10** 45 10N 26 0 E
Prahova →, *Romania* . . **29 F10** 44 50N 25 50 E
Prahovo, *Serbia & M.* . . **44 B6** 44 18N 22 39 E
Praia, *C. Verde Is.* **77 E1** 15 2N 23 34W
Práia a Mare, *Italy* . . . . **43 C8** 39 50N 15 45 E
Praid, *Romania* . . . . . . **29 D10** 46 32N 25 10 E
Prainha, *Amazonas,
    Brazil* . . . . . . **124 E6** 7 10 S 60 30W
Prainha, *Pará, Brazil* . . **125 D8** 1 45 S 53 30W
Prairie, *Australia* . . . . **94 C3** 20 50 S 144 35 E
Prairie City, *U.S.A.* . . **108 D4** 44 28N 118 43W
Prairie Dog Town
    Fork →, *U.S.A.* . . **113 H5** 34 30N 99 23W
Prairie du Chien, *U.S.A.* **112 D9** 43 3N 91 9W
Prairies, L. of the,
    Canada **103 C8** 51 16N 101 32W
Pramánda, *Greece* . . . . **46 B3** 39 32N 21 8 E
Prampram, *Ghana* . . . . **83 D5** 5 43N 0 8 E
Pran Buri, *Thailand* . . **64 F2** 12 23N 99 55 E
Prang, *Ghana* **83 D4** 8 1N 0 56W
Prapat, *Indonesia* . . . . **62 D1** 2 41N 98 58 E
Prasonísi, Ákra, *Greece* **49 D9** 35 42N 27 46 E
Prästmon, *Sweden* . . . . **10 A11** 63 5N 17 45 E
Praszka, *Poland* . . . . . . **31 G5** 51 5N 18 31 E
Prata, *Brazil* . . . . . . **125 G9** 19 25 S 48 54W
Pratabpur, *India* . . . . **69 H10** 23 28N 83 15 E
Pratapgarh, *Raj., India* . . **68 G6** 24 2N 74 40 E
Pratapgarh, *Ut. P., India* . . **69 G9** 25 56N 81 59 E
Pratas Is. = Dongsha
    Dao, *China* . . . . **59 G11** 20 45N 116 43 E
Prato, *Italy* . . . . . . **40 E8** 43 53N 11 6 E
Prátola Peligna, *Italy* . . **41 F10** 42 7N 13 52 E
Prats-de-Mollo-la-
    Preste, *France* . . . . **20 F6** 42 25N 2 27 E
Pratt, *U.S.A.* **113 G5** 37 39N 98 44W
Prattville, *U.S.A.* **115 J2** 32 28N 86 29W
Pravdinsk, *Russia* . . . . **30 D8** 54 27N 21 1 E
Pravia, *Spain* **36 B4** 43 30N 6 12W
Pravets, *Bulgaria* . . . . **44 D7** 42 53N 23 55 E
Praya, *Indonesia* . . . . **62 F5** 8 39 S 116 17 E
Pré-en-Pail, *France* . . **18 D6** 48 28N 0 12W
Precipice △, *Australia* . . **95 D5** 25 18 S 150 5 E
Precordillera, *Argentina* **126 C2** 30 0 S 69 1W
Predazzo, *Italy* . . . . . . **41 B8** 46 19N 11 37 E
Predeal, *Romania* . . . . **29 E10** 45 30N 25 28 E
Predejane, *Serbia & M.* **44 D6** 42 51N 22 9 E
Preeceville, *Canada* . . **103 C8** 51 57N 102 40W
Preetz, *Germany* . . . . **24 A6** 54 14N 10 18 E
Pregolya →, *Russia* . . **30 D7** 54 41N 20 22 E

Pregrada, *Croatia* . . . . **41 B12** 46 11N 15 45 E
Preiļi, *Latvia* . . . . . . **9 H22** 56 18N 26 43 E
Preko, *Croatia* . . . . . . **41 D12** 44 7N 15 10 E
Prelog, *Croatia* . . . . . . **41 B13** 46 18N 16 32 E
Prémery, *France* . . . . **19 E10** 47 10N 3 18 E
Premià de Mar, *Spain* . . **38 D7** 41 29N 2 22 E
Premont, *U.S.A.* **113 M5** 27 22N 98 7W
Premuda, *Croatia* . . . . **41 D11** 44 20N 14 36 E
Prentice, *U.S.A.* **112 C9** 45 33N 90 17W
Prenzlau, *Germany* . . **24 B9** 53 19N 13 50 E
Preobrazheniye, *Russia* **54 C6** 42 54N 133 54 E
Preparis North Channel,
    Ind. Oc. . . . . . . **67 M18** 15 12N 93 40 E
Preparis South Channel,
    Ind. Oc. . . . . . . **67 M18** 14 36N 93 40 E
Přerov, *Czech Rep.* . . **27 B10** 49 28N 17 27 E
Prescott, *Canada* **117 B9** 44 45N 75 30W
Prescott, *Ariz., U.S.A.* . . **109 J7** 34 33N 112 28W
Prescott, *Ark., U.S.A.* . . **113 J8** 33 48N 93 23W
Prescott Valley, *U.S.A.* **109 J7** 34 40N 112 18W
Preservation Inlet, *N.Z.* **91 M1** 46 8 S 166 35 E
Preševo, *Serbia & M.* . . **44 D5** 42 19N 21 39 E
Presho, *U.S.A.* **112 D4** 43 54N 100 3W
Presicce, *Italy* . . . . . . **43 C11** 39 54N 18 16 E
Presidencia de la Plaza,
    Argentina . . . . **126 B4** 27 0 S 59 50W
Presidencia Roque
    Saenz Peña, *Argentina* **126 B3** 26 45 S 60 30W
Presidente Epitácio,
    Brazil . . . . . . **125 H8** 21 56 S 52 6W
Presidente Hayes □,
    Paraguay . . . . **126 A4** 24 0 S 59 0W
Presidente Prudente,
    Brazil . . . . . . **127 A5** 22 5 S 51 25W
Presidio, *Mexico* **118 B4** 29 29N 104 23W
Presidio, *U.S.A.* **113 L2** 29 34N 104 22W
Preslav, *Bulgaria* . . . . **45 C10** 43 10N 26 52 E
Preslavska Planina,
    Bulgaria . . . . . . **45 C10** 43 10N 26 45 E
Prešov, *Slovak Rep.* . . **27 B14** 49 0N 21 15 E
Prešovský □,
    Slovak Rep. . . . . **27 B13** 49 10N 21 0 E
Prespa, *Bulgaria* . . . . **45 E8** 41 44N 24 55 E
Préspa, L. = Prespansko
    Jezero, *Macedonia* **44 F5** 40 55N 21 0 E
Prespansko Jezero,
    Macedonia . . . . **44 F5** 40 55N 21 0 E
Presque, *U.S.A.* **116 D4** 42 9N 80 6W
Presque Isle, *U.S.A.* . . **115 B12** 46 41N 68 1W
Prestatyn, *U.K.* **14 D4** 53 20N 3 24W
Prestea, *Ghana* **82 D4** 5 22N 2 7W
Presteigne, *U.K.* **15 E5** 52 17N 3 0W
Přeštice, *Czech Rep.* . . **26 B6** 49 34N 13 20 E
Preston, *Canada* **116 C4** 43 23N 80 21W
Preston, *U.K.* **14 D5** 53 46N 2 42W
Preston, *Idaho, U.S.A.* . . **108 E8** 42 6N 111 53W
Preston, *Minn., U.S.A.* . . **112 D8** 43 40N 92 5W
Preston, C., *Australia* . . **92 D2** 20 51 S 116 12 E
Prestonburg, *U.S.A.* . . **114 G4** 37 39N 82 46W
Prestwick, *U.K.* **13 F4** 55 29N 4 37W
Pretoria, *S. Africa* . . . . **89 D4** 25 44 S 28 12 E
Preuilly-sur-Claise,
    France . . . . . . **18 F7** 46 51N 0 56 E
Préveza, *Greece* . . . . **46 C2** 38 57N 20 45 E
Préveza □, *Greece* . . . . **46 B2** 39 10N 20 40 E
Prey Veng, *Cambodia* . . **65 G5** 11 35N 105 29 E
Priazovskoye, *Ukraine* . . **33 J8** 46 44N 35 40 E
Pribilof Is., *U.S.A.* **100 C2** 57 0N 170 0W
Priboj, *Serbia & M.* . . **44 C3** 43 35N 19 32 E
Příbram, *Czech Rep.* . . **26 B7** 49 41N 14 2 E
Price, *U.S.A.* **108 G8** 39 36N 110 49W
Price I., *Canada* **102 C3** 52 23N 128 41W
Prichard, *U.S.A.* **115 K1** 30 44N 88 5W
Priego, *Spain* **38 E2** 40 26N 2 21W
Priego de Córdoba,
    Spain **37 H6** 37 27N 4 12W
Priekule, *Latvia* . . . . **9 H19** 56 26N 21 35 E
Prien, *Germany* . . . . . . **25 H8** 47 51N 12 20 E
Prienai, *Lithuania* . . . . **9 J20** 54 38N 23 57 E
Prieska, *S. Africa* . . . . **88 D3** 29 40 S 22 42 E
Priest L., *U.S.A.* **108 B5** 48 35N 116 52W
Priest River, *U.S.A.* . . **108 B5** 48 10N 116 54W
Priest Valley, *U.S.A.* . . **110 J6** 36 10N 120 39W
Prievidza, *Slovak Rep.* . . **27 C11** 48 46N 18 36 E
Prignitz, *Germany* . . . . **24 B7** 53 6N 11 45 E
Prijedor, *Bos.-H.* . . . . **41 D13** 44 58N 16 41 E
Prijepolje, *Serbia & M.* **44 C3** 43 27N 19 40 E
Prikaspiyskaya
    Nizmennost = Caspian
    Depression, *Eurasia* **35 G9** 47 0N 48 0 E
Prikro, *Ivory C.* **82 D4** 7 40N 3 59W
Prikubanskaya
    Nizmennost, *Russia* **35 H4** 45 39N 38 33 E
Prilep, *Macedonia* . . . . **44 E5** 41 21N 21 32 E
Priluki = Pryluky,
    Ukraine . . . . . . **33 G7** 50 30N 32 24 E
Prime Seal I., *Australia* **95 G4** 40 3 S 147 43 E
Primorsk, *Russia* . . . . **30 D6** 54 44N 20 0 E
Primorsk, *Russia* . . . . **32 B5** 60 22N 28 37 E
Primorsko, *Bulgaria* . . **45 D11** 42 15N 27 44 E
Primorsko-Akhtarsk,
    Russia . . . . . . **33 J10** 46 2N 38 10 E
Primorskoye, *Ukraine* . . **33 J9** 46 48N 36 5 E
Primrose L., *Canada* . . **103 C7** 54 55N 109 45W
Prince Albert, *Canada* . . **103 C7** 53 15N 105 50W
Prince Albert, *S. Africa* **88 E3** 33 12 S 22 2 E
Prince Albert △, *Canada* **103 C7** 54 0N 106 25W
Prince Albert Mts.,
    Antarctica . . . . **5 D11** 76 0 S 161 30 E
Prince Albert Pen.,
    Canada **100 A8** 72 30N 116 0W
Prince Albert Sd.,
    Canada **100 A8** 70 25N 115 0W
Prince Alfred, C.,
    Canada **4 B1** 74 20N 124 40W
Prince Charles I.,
    Canada **101 B12** 67 47N 76 12W
Prince Charles Mts.,
    Antarctica . . . . **5 D6** 72 0 S 67 0 E
Prince Edward I. □,
    Canada **105 C7** 46 20N 63 20W
Prince Edward Is.,
    Ind. Oc. . . . . . . **3 G11** 46 35 S 38 0 E
Prince Edward Pt.,
    Canada **116 C8** 43 56N 76 52W
Prince George, *Canada* **102 C4** 53 55N 122 50W
Prince of Wales, C.,
    U.S.A. **98 C3** 65 36N 168 5W
Prince of Wales I.,
    Australia . . . . **94 A3** 10 40 S 142 10 E
Prince of Wales I.,
    Canada **100 A10** 73 0N 99 0W
Prince of Wales I.,
    U.S.A. **100 C6** 55 47N 132 50W
Prince Patrick I., *Canada* **4 B2** 77 0N 120 0W
Prince Regent Inlet,
    Canada **4 B3** 73 0N 90 0W

Prince Rupert, *Canada* **102 C2** 54 20N 130 20W
Princes Town,
    Trin. & Tob. **125 K15** 10 16N 61 23W
Princess Charlotte B.,
    Australia . . . . **94 A3** 14 25 S 144 0 E
Princess May Ranges,
    Australia . . . . **92 C4** 15 30 S 125 30 E
Princess Royal I.,
    Canada **102 C3** 53 0N 128 40W
Princeton, *Canada* . . **102 D4** 49 27N 120 30W
Princeton, *Calif., U.S.A.* **110 F4** 39 24N 122 1W
Princeton, *Ill., U.S.A.* . . **112 E10** 41 23N 89 28W
Princeton, *Ind., U.S.A.* . . **114 F2** 38 21N 87 34W
Princeton, *Ky., U.S.A.* . . **114 G2** 37 7N 87 53W
Princeton, *Mo., U.S.A.* . . **112 E8** 40 24N 93 35W
Princeton, *N.J., U.S.A.* . . **117 F10** 40 21N 74 39W
Princeton, *W. Va.,
    U.S.A.* **114 G5** 37 22N 81 6W
Principe, I. de, *Atl. Oc.* **76 F4** 1 37N 7 27 E
Principe da Beira, *Brazil* **124 F6** 12 20 S 64 30W
Prineville, *U.S.A.* **108 D3** 44 18N 120 51W
Prins Harald Kyst,
    Antarctica . . . . **5 D4** 70 0 S 35 1 E
Prinsesse Astrid Kyst,
    Antarctica . . . . **5 D3** 70 45 S 12 30 E
Prinsesse Ragnhild Kyst,
    Antarctica . . . . **5 D4** 70 15 S 27 30 E
Prinzapolca, *Nic.* **120 D3** 13 20N 83 35W
Prior, C., *Spain* **36 B2** 43 34N 8 17W
Priozersk, *Russia* . . . . **32 B6** 61 2N 30 7 E
Pripet = Prypyat →,
    Europe . . . . . . **33 G6** 51 20N 30 15 E
Pripet Marshes = Pripyat
    Marshes, *Europe* . . **33 F5** 52 10N 28 10 E
Pripyat Marshes = Pripet
    Marshes, *Europe* . . **33 F5** 52 10N 28 10 E
Pripyats = Prypyat →,
    Europe . . . . . . **33 G6** 51 20N 30 15 E
Prislop, Pasul, *Romania* **29 C9** 47 37N 24 48 E
Pristen, *Russia* . . . . . . **33 G9** 51 15N 36 44 E
Priština, *Serbia & M.* . . **44 D5** 42 40N 21 13 E
Pritzwalk, *Germany* . . **24 B8** 53 9N 12 10 E
Privas, *France* . . . . . . **21 D8** 44 45N 4 37 E
Priverno, *Italy* . . . . . . **42 A6** 41 29N 13 11 E
Privolzhsk, *Russia* . . . . **34 B5** 57 23N 41 16 E
Privolzhskaya
    Vozvyshennost,
    Russia . . . . . . **34 E7** 51 0N 46 0 E
Privolzhskiy, *Russia* . . **34 E8** 51 25N 46 3 E
Privolzhskiy □, *Russia* **34 B10** 56 0N 50 0 E
Privolzhye, *Russia* . . . . **34 D9** 52 52N 48 33 E
Priyutnoye, *Russia* . . . . **35 G6** 46 12N 44 19 E
Prizren, *Serbia & M.* . . **44 D4** 42 13N 20 45 E
Prizzi, *Italy* . . . . . . **42 E6** 37 43N 13 26 E
Prnjavor, *Bos.-H.* . . . . **28 F2** 44 52N 17 43 E
Probolinggo, *Indonesia* **63 G15** 7 46 S 113 13 E
Prochowice, *Poland* . . **31 G3** 51 17N 16 20 E
Proctor, *U.S.A.* **117 C11** 43 40N 73 2W
Proddatur, *India* . . . . **66 M11** 14 45N 78 30 E
Prodhromos, *Cyprus* . . **49 E11** 34 57N 32 50 E
Proença-a-Nova,
    Portugal **36 F3** 39 45N 7 54W
Profítis Ilías, *Greece* . . **49 C9** 36 17N 27 56 E
Profondeville, *Belgium* **17 D4** 50 23N 4 52 E
Progreso, *Coahuila,
    Mexico* **118 B4** 27 28N 101 4W
Progreso, *Yucatán,
    Mexico* **119 C7** 21 20N 89 40W
Prokhladnyy, *Russia* . . **35 J7** 43 50N 44 2 E
Prokletije, *Albania* . . **44 D3** 42 30N 19 45 E
Prokopyevsk, *Russia* . . **52 D9** 54 0N 86 45 E
Prokuplje, *Serbia & M.* **44 C5** 43 16N 21 36 E
Proletarsk, *Russia* . . . . **35 G5** 46 42N 41 50 E
Proletarskaya =
    Proletarsk, *Russia* . . **35 G5** 46 42N 41 50 E
Prome, *Burma* . . . . . . **67 K19** 18 49N 95 13 E
Prophet →, *Canada* . . **102 B4** 58 48N 122 40W
Prophet River, *Canada* **102 B4** 58 6N 122 43W
Propriá, *Brazil* . . . . **125 F11** 10 13 S 36 51W
Propriano, *France* . . . . **21 G12** 41 41N 8 52 E
Proserpine, *Australia* . . **94 J6** 20 21 S 148 36 E
Prosna →, *Poland* . . . . **31 F4** 52 6N 17 44 E
Prospect, *U.S.A.* **117 C9** 43 18N 75 9W
Prosser, *U.S.A.* **108 C4** 46 12N 119 46W
Prostějov, *Czech Rep.* . . **27 B10** 49 30N 17 9 E
Prostki, *Poland* . . . . **30 E9** 53 42N 22 25 E
Proston, *Australia* . . . . **95 D5** 26 8 S 151 32 E
Proszowice, *Poland* . . **31 H7** 50 13N 20 16 E
Próti, *Greece* . . . . . . **46 D3** 37 5N 21 32 E
Provadiya, *Bulgaria* . . **45 C11** 43 12N 27 30 E
Provence, *France* . . . . **21 E9** 43 40N 5 46 E
Provence-Alpes-Côte
    d'Azur □, *France* . . **21 D10** 44 0N 6 15 E
Providence, *Ky., U.S.A.* **114 G2** 37 24N 87 46W
Providence, *R.I., U.S.A.* **117 E13** 41 49N 71 24W
Providence Bay, *Canada* **104 C3** 45 41N 82 15W
Providence Mts., *U.S.A.* **111 K11** 35 10N 115 15W
Providencia, I. de,
    Colombia **120 D3** 13 25N 81 26W
Provideniya, *Russia* . . **53 C19** 64 23N 173 18W
Provins, *France* . . . . **19 D10** 48 33N 3 15 E
Provo, *U.S.A.* **108 F8** 40 14N 111 39W
Provost, *Canada* **103 C6** 52 25N 110 20W
Prozor, *Bos.-H.* . . . . . . **28 G2** 43 50N 17 34 E
Prrenjas, *Albania* . . . . **44 E4** 41 4N 20 25 E
Prudhoe Bay, *U.S.A.* . . **100 A5** 70 18N 148 22W
Prudhoe I., *Australia* . . **94 C4** 21 19 S 149 41 E
Prud'homme, *Canada* . . **103 C7** 52 20N 105 54W
Prudnik, *Poland* . . . . **31 H4** 50 20N 17 38 E
Prüm, *Germany* . . . . . . **25 E2** 50 12N 6 25 E
Prundu, *Romania* . . . . **29 F11** 44 6N 26 14 E
Pruszcz Gdański, *Poland* **30 D5** 54 17N 18 40 E
Pruszków, *Poland* . . . . **31 F7** 52 9N 20 49 E
Prut →, *Romania* . . . . **29 E13** 45 28N 28 10 E
Pruzhany, *Belarus* . . . . **33 F3** 52 33N 24 28 E
Prvič, *Croatia* . . . . . . **41 D11** 44 55N 14 47 E
Prydz B., *Antarctica* . . **5 C6** 69 0 S 74 0 E
Pryluky, *Ukraine* . . . . **33 G7** 50 30N 32 24 E
Pryor, *U.S.A.* **113 G7** 36 19N 95 19W
Prypyat →, *Europe* . . **33 G6** 51 20N 30 15 E
Przasnysz, *Poland* . . . . **31 E7** 53 2N 20 54 E
Przedbórz, *Poland* . . . . **31 G6** 51 6N 19 53 E
Przedecz, *Poland* . . . . **31 F5** 52 20N 18 53 E
Przemków, *Poland* . . . . **31 G2** 51 31N 15 48 E
Przemyśl, *Poland* . . . . **31 J9** 49 50N 22 45 E
Przeworsk, *Poland* . . . . **31 H9** 50 6N 22 32 E
Przewóz, *Poland* . . . . **31 G1** 51 28N 14 57 E
Przhevalsk = Karakol,
    Kyrgyzstan . . . . **52 E8** 42 30N 78 20 E
Przysucha, *Poland* . . . . **31 G7** 51 22N 20 38 E
Psakhná, *Greece* . . . . **46 C5** 38 34N 23 35 E
Psará, *Greece* . . . . . . **47 C7** 38 37N 25 38 E
Psathoúra, *Greece* . . . . **46 B5** 39 30N 24 12 E
Psel →, *Ukraine* . . . . **33 H7** 49 10N 33 37 E
Pserimos, *Greece* . . . . **47 E9** 36 56N 27 5 E
Psíra, *Greece* . . . . . . **49 D7** 35 12N 25 52 E
Pskov, *Russia* . . . . . . **32 C5** 57 50N 28 25 E
Pskovskoye, Ozero,
    Russia . . . . . . **32 D5** 58 0N 27 58 E

Psunj, *Croatia* . . . . . . **28 E2** 45 25N 17 19 E
Pteleón, *Greece* . . . . **46 B4** 39 3N 22 57 E
Ptich = Ptsich →,
    Belarus . . . . . . **33 F5** 52 9N 28 52 E
Ptolemaís, *Greece* . . . . **44 F5** 40 30N 21 43 E
Ptsich →, *Belarus* . . . . **33 F5** 52 9N 28 52 E
Ptuj, *Slovenia* . . . . . . **41 B12** 46 28N 15 50 E
Ptujska Gora, *Slovenia* **41 B12** 46 23N 15 47 E
Pu Xian, *China* . . . . **56 F6** 36 24N 111 6 E
Pua, *Thailand* . . . . . . **64 C3** 19 11N 100 55 E
Puán, *Argentina* . . . . **126 D3** 37 30 S 62 45W
Pu'an, *China* . . . . . . **58 E5** 25 46N 104 57 E
Puan, S. Korea . . . . . . **57 G14** 35 44N 126 44 E
Pubei, *China* . . . . . . **58 F7** 22 16N 109 31 E
Pucallpa, *Peru* . . . . . . **124 E4** 8 25 S 74 30W
Pucheng, *China* . . . . **59 D12** 27 59N 118 31 E
Pucheni, *Romania* . . . . **29 E10** 45 25N 25 17 E
Puchheim, *Germany* . . **25 G7** 48 9N 11 21 E
Púchov, *Slovak Rep.* . . **27 B11** 49 8N 18 20 E
Pucioasa, *Romania* . . . . **29 E10** 45 5N 25 25 E
Pučišća, *Croatia* . . . . **41 E13** 43 22N 16 43 E
Puck, *Poland* . . . . . . **30 D5** 54 45N 18 23 E
Pucka, Zatoka, *Poland* **30 D5** 54 30N 18 40 E
Pudasjärvi, *Finland* . . . . **8 D22** 65 23N 26 53 E
Pudeto →, *Angola* ... (no entry)
Pudozh, *Russia* . . . . **32 B9** 61 48N 36 32 E
Puducherry, India =
    Pondicherry, *India* . . **66 P11** 11 59N 79 50 E
Pudukkottai, *India* . . . . **66 P11** 10 28N 78 47 E
Puebla, *Mexico* **119 D5** 19 3N 98 12W
Puebla □, *Mexico* **119 D5** 18 30N 98 0W
Puebla de Alcocer,
    Spain **37 G5** 38 59N 5 14W
Puebla de Don
    Fadrique, *Spain* . . **39 H2** 37 58N 2 25W
Puebla de Don Rodrigo,
    Spain **37 F6** 39 5N 4 37W
Puebla de Guzmán,
    Spain **37 H3** 37 37N 7 15W
Puebla de la Calzada,
    Spain **37 G4** 38 54N 6 37W
Puebla de Sanabria,
    Spain **36 C4** 42 4N 6 38W
Puebla de Trives =
    Pobra de Trives, *Spain* **36 C3** 42 20N 7 10W
Pueblo, *U.S.A.* **108 G12** 38 16N 104 37W
Pueblo Hundido, *Chile* **126 B1** 26 20 S 70 5W
Puelches, *Argentina* . . **126 D2** 38 5 S 65 51W
Puelén, *Argentina* . . . . **126 D2** 37 32 S 67 38W
Puente Alto, *Chile* . . **126 C1** 33 32 S 70 35W
Puente-Genil, *Spain* . . **37 H6** 37 22N 4 47W
Puente la Reina, *Spain* **38 C3** 42 40N 1 49W
Puentearas =
    Ponteareas, *Spain* . . **36 C2** 42 10N 8 28W
Puentedeume =
    Pontedeume, *Spain* **36 B2** 43 24N 8 10W
Puentes de García
    Rodríguez = As
    Pontes de García
    Rodríguez, *Spain* . . **36 B3** 43 27N 7 50W
Puerca, Pta., *Puerto Rico* **121 d** 18 13N 65 36W
Puerco →, *U.S.A.* . . **109 J10** 34 22N 107 50W
Puerto Aisén, *Chile* . . **128 F2** 45 27 S 73 0W
Puerto Ángel, *Mexico* . . **119 D5** 15 40N 96 29W
Puerto Arista, *Mexico* . . **119 D6** 15 56N 93 48W
Puerto Armuelles,
    Panama **120 E3** 8 20N 82 51W
Puerto Ayacucho,
    Venezuela **124 B5** 5 40N 67 35W
Puerto Barrios,
    Guatemala **120 C2** 15 40N 88 32W
Puerto Bermejo,
    Argentina . . . . **126 B4** 26 55 S 58 34W
Puerto Bermúdez, *Peru* **124 F4** 10 20 S 74 58W
Puerto Bolívar, *Ecuador* **124 D3** 3 19 S 79 55W
Puerto Cabello,
    Venezuela **124 A5** 10 28N 68 1W
Puerto Cabezas, *Nic.* . . **120 D3** 14 0N 83 30W
Puerto Cabo Gracias á
    Dios, *Nic.* **120 D3** 15 0N 83 10W
Puerto Carreño,
    Colombia **124 B5** 6 12N 67 22W
Puerto Castilla,
    Honduras **120 C2** 16 0N 86 0W
Puerto Chicama, *Peru* . . **124 E3** 7 45 S 79 20W
Puerto Coig, *Argentina* **128 G3** 50 54 S 69 15W
Puerto Cortés,
    Costa Rica **120 E3** 8 55N 84 0W
Puerto Cortés,
    Honduras **120 C2** 15 51N 88 0W
Puerto Cumarebo,
    Venezuela **124 A5** 11 29N 69 30W
Puerto de Alcudia =
    Port d'Alcúdia, *Spain* **48 B10** 39 50N 3 7 E
Puerto de Cabrera,
    Spain . . . . . . **48 B9** 39 8N 2 56 E
Puerto de Gran Tarajal,
    Canary Is. **48 F5** 28 13N 14 1W
Puerto de la Cruz,
    Canary Is. **48 F3** 28 24N 16 32W
Puerto de los Ángeles △,
    Mexico **118 C3** 23 39N 105 45W
Puerto de Mazarrón,
    Spain **39 H3** 37 34N 1 15W
Puerto de Pozo Negro,
    Canary Is. **48 F6** 28 19N 13 55W
Puerto de Sóller = Port
    de Sóller, *Spain* . . **48 B9** 39 48N 2 42 E
Puerto de Somosierra,
    Spain **36 D7** 41 9N 3 35W
Puerto del Carmen,
    Canary Is. **48 F6** 28 55N 13 38W
Puerto del Rosario,
    Canary Is. **48 F6** 28 30N 13 52W
Puerto Deseado,
    Argentina . . . . **128 F3** 47 55 S 66 0W
Puerto Escondido,
    Mexico **119 D5** 15 50N 97 3W
Puerto Heath, *Bolivia* . . **124 F5** 12 34 S 68 39W
Puerto Inírida,
    Colombia **124 C5** 3 53N 67 52W
Puerto Juárez, *Mexico* . . **119 C7** 21 11N 86 49W
Puerto La Cruz,
    Venezuela **124 A6** 10 13N 64 38W
Puerto Leguízamo,
    Colombia . . . . **124 D4** 0 12 S 74 46W
Puerto Limón, *Colombia* **124 C4** 3 23N 73 30W
Puerto Lobos, *Argentina* **128 E3** 42 0 S 65 3W
Puerto Lumbreras,
    Spain **39 H3** 37 34N 1 48W
Puerto Madryn,
    Argentina . . . . **128 E3** 42 48 S 65 4W
Puerto Maldonado, *Peru* **124 F5** 12 30 S 69 10W
Puerto Manotí, *Cuba* . . **120 B4** 21 22N 76 50W
Puerto Montt, *Chile* . . **128 E2** 41 28 S 73 0W

Puerto Morazán, *Nic.* . . **120 D2** 12 51N 87 11W
Puerto Morelos, *Mexico* **119 C7** 20 49N 86 52W
Puerto Natales, *Chile* . . **128 G2** 51 45 S 72 15W
Puerto Padre, *Cuba* . . **120 B4** 21 13N 76 35W
Puerto Páez, *Venezuela* **124 B5** 6 13N 67 28W
Puerto Peñasco, *Mexico* **118 A2** 31 20N 113 33W
Puerto Pinasco,
    Paraguay . . . . **126 A4** 22 36 S 57 50W
Puerto Plata, *Dom. Rep.* **121 C5** 19 48N 70 45W
Puerto Pollensa = Port
    de Pollença, *Spain* . . **48 B10** 39 54N 3 4 E
Puerto Princesa, *Phil.* . . **61 G3** 9 46N 118 45 E
Puerto Quepos,
    Costa Rica **120 E3** 9 29N 84 6W
Puerto Real, *Spain* . . **37 J4** 36 33N 6 12W
Puerto Rico, *Canary Is.* **48 G4** 27 47N 15 42W
Puerto Rico ☑, *W. Indies* **121 d** 18 15N 66 45W
Puerto Rico Trench,
    Atl. Oc. **121 C6** 19 50N 66 0W
Puerto San Julián,
    Argentina . . . . **128 F3** 49 18 S 67 43W
Puerto Sastre, *Paraguay* **126 A4** 22 2 S 57 55W
Puerto Serrano, *Spain* . . **37 J5** 36 56N 5 33W
Puerto Suárez, *Bolivia* . . **124 G7** 18 58 S 57 52W
Puerto Vallarta, *Mexico* **118 C3** 20 36N 105 15W
Puerto Wilches,
    Colombia **124 B4** 7 21N 73 54W
Puertollano, *Spain* . . **37 G6** 38 43N 4 7W
Pueyrredón, L.,
    Argentina . . . . **128 F2** 47 20 S 72 0W
Púez Odle △, *Italy* . . **41 B8** 46 37N 11 48 E
Puffin I., *Ireland* **12 E1** 51 50N 10 24W
Pugachev, *Russia* . . . . **34 D9** 52 0N 48 49 E
Pugal, *India* . . . . . . **68 E5** 28 30N 72 48 E
Puge, *China* . . . . . . **58 D4** 27 20N 102 31 E
Puge, *Tanzania* . . . . **86 C3** 4 45 S 33 11 E
Puget Sound, *U.S.A.* . . **108 C2** 47 50N 122 30W
Puget-Théniers, *France* **21 E10** 43 58N 6 53 E
Púglia □, *Italy* . . . . **43 A9** 41 15N 16 15 E
Pugŏdong, N. Korea . . **57 C16** 42 5N 130 0 E
Pugu, *Tanzania* . . . . **86 D4** 6 55 S 39 4 E
Pūgūnzī, *Iran* . . . . . . **71 E8** 25 49N 59 10 E
Pui, *Romania* . . . . . . **28 E8** 45 30N 23 4 E
Puiești, *Romania* . . . . **29 D12** 46 25N 27 33 E
Puig Major, *Spain* . . **48 B9** 39 48N 2 47 E
Puigcerdà, *Spain* . . . . **38 C6** 42 24N 1 50 E
Puigmal, *Spain* . . . . **38 C7** 42 23N 2 7 E
Puigpunyent, *Spain* . . **48 B9** 39 38N 2 32 E
Puijiang, *China* . . . . **58 B4** 30 14N 103 30 E
Puisaye, Collines de la,
    France . . . . . . **19 E10** 47 37N 3 20 E
Puiseaux, *France* . . . . **19 D9** 48 11N 2 30 E
Pujehun, S. Leone **82 D2** 7 23N 11 45W
Pujiang, *China* . . . . **59 C12** 29 29N 119 54 E
Pujols, *France* **20 D3** 44 48N 0 2W
Pujon-chōsuji, N. Korea **57 D14** 40 35N 127 35 E
Pukaki, L., *N.Z.* . . . . **91 L3** 44 4 S 170 1 E
Pukapuka, Cook Is. . . . . **97 J11** 10 53 S 165 49W
Pukaskwa △, *Canada* . . **104 C2** 48 20N 86 0W
Pukatawagan, *Canada* . . **103 B8** 55 45N 101 20W
Pukchin, N. Korea . . . . **57 D13** 40 12N 125 45 E
Pukch'ŏng, N. Korea . . **57 D15** 40 14N 128 10 E
Pukë, *Albania* . . . . . . **44 D3** 42 2N 19 53 E
Pukekohe, *N.Z.* . . . . **91 G5** 37 12 S 174 55 E
Pukhrayan, *India* . . . . **69 F8** 26 14N 79 51 E
Pukou, *China* . . . . . . **59 A12** 32 7N 118 38 E
Pula, *Croatia* . . . . . . **41 D10** 44 54N 13 57 E
Pula, *Italy* . . . . . . **42 C1** 39 1N 9 0 E
Pulacayo, *Bolivia* . . . . **124 H5** 20 25 S 66 41W
Pulai, *Malaysia* . . . . **65 d** 1 20N 103 31 E
Pulandian, *China* . . . . **57 E11** 39 25N 121 58 E
Pularumpi, *Australia* . . **92 B5** 11 24 S 130 26 E
Pulaski, N.Y., *U.S.A.* . . **117 C8** 43 34N 76 8W
Pulaski, *Tenn., U.S.A.* . . **115 H2** 35 12N 87 2W
Pulaski, *Va., U.S.A.* . . **114 G5** 37 3N 80 47W
Pulau →, *Indonesia* . . **63 F9** 5 50 S 138 15 E
Puławy, *Poland* . . . . **31 G8** 51 23N 21 59 E
Pulga, *U.S.A.* **110 F5** 39 48N 121 29W
Pulicat L., *India* . . . . **66 N12** 13 40N 80 15 E
Pullman, *U.S.A.* **108 C5** 46 44N 117 10W
Pulog, Mt., *Phil.* . . . . **61 C4** 16 40N 120 50 E
Pułtusk, *Poland* . . . . **31 F8** 52 43N 21 6 E
Pülümür, *Turkey* . . . . **73 C8** 39 30N 39 51 E
Pumlumon Fawr, *U.K.* . . **15 E4** 52 28N 3 46W
Puná, I., *Ecuador* . . . . **124 D2** 2 55 S 80 5W
Punakha, *Bhutan* . . . . **67 F16** 27 42N 89 52 E
Punasar, *India* . . . . **68 F5** 27 6N 73 6 E
Punata, *Bolivia* . . . . **124 G5** 17 32 S 65 50W
Punch, *India* . . . . . . **69 C6** 33 48N 74 4 E
Punda Maria, *S. Africa* **89 C5** 22 40 S 31 5 E
Pune, *India* . . . . . . **66 K8** 18 29N 73 57 E
P'ungsan, N. Korea . . **57 D15** 40 50N 128 9 E
Pungue, Ponte de,
    Mozam. . . . . . . **87 F3** 19 0 S 34 0 E
Puning, *China* . . . . . . **59 F11** 23 20N 116 12 E
Punjab □, *India* . . . . **68 D7** 31 0N 76 0 E
Punjab □, *Pakistan* . . **68 E6** 32 0N 72 30 E
Puno, *Peru* . . . . . . **124 G4** 15 55 S 70 3W
Punpun →, *India* . . . . **69 G11** 25 31N 85 18 E
Punta, Cerro de,
    Puerto Rico . . . . **121 d** 18 10N 66 37W
Punta Alta, *Argentina* . . **128 D4** 38 53 S 62 4W
Punta Arenas, *Chile* . . **128 G2** 53 10 S 71 0W
Punta de Díaz, *Chile* . . **126 B1** 28 0 S 70 45W
Punta del Hidalgo,
    Canary Is. **48 F3** 28 33N 16 19W
Punta Gorda, *Belize* . . **119 D7** 16 10N 88 45W
Punta Gorda, *U.S.A.* . . **115 M5** 26 56N 82 3W
Punta Prieta, *Mexico* . . **118 B2** 28 58N 114 17W
Punta Prima, *Spain* . . **48 B11** 39 48N 4 16 E
Punta Umbría, *Spain* . . **37 H4** 37 10N 6 56W
Puntarenas, *Costa Rica* **120 E3** 10 0N 84 50W
Punto Fijo, *Venezuela* . . **124 A4** 11 50N 70 13W
Punxsatawney, *U.S.A.* . . **116 F6** 40 57N 78 59W
Puqi, *China* . . . . . . **59 C9** 29 40N 113 50 E
Puquio, *Indonesia* . . . . **63 J18** 8 19 S 114 9 E
Puqi, *China* . . . . . . **59 C9** 29 40N 113 50 E
Pur →, *Russia* . . . . **52 C8** 67 31N 77 55 E
Puracé, Vol., *Colombia* **124 C3** 2 21N 76 23W
Puralia = Puruliya, *India* **69 H12** 23 17N 86 24 E
Puranpur, *India* . . . . **69 E9** 28 31N 80 9 E
Purbeck, Isle of, *U.K.* . . **15 G5** 50 39N 1 59W
Purcell, *U.S.A.* **113 H6** 35 1N 97 22W
Purcell Mts., *Canada* . . **102 D5** 49 55N 116 15W
Puri, *India* . . . . . . **67 K14** 19 50N 85 58 E
Purmerend, *Neths.* . . **17 B4** 52 32N 4 58 E
Purnia, *India* . . . . . . **69 G12** 25 45N 87 31 E
Pursat = Pouthisat,
    Cambodia . . . . **64 F4** 12 34N 103 50 E
Purukcahu, *Indonesia* . . **62 E4** 0 35 S 114 35 E
Puruliya, *India* . . . . **69 H12** 23 17N 86 24 E
Purus →, *Brazil* . . . . **124 D6** 3 42 S 61 28W
Puruvesi, *Finland* . . . . **32 B5** 61 50N 29 30 E
Purvis, *U.S.A.* **113 K10** 31 9N 89 25W
Pŭrvomay, *Bulgaria* . . **45 D9** 42 8N 25 17 E

Purwa, *India* .... **69 F9** 26 28N 80 47 E
Purwakarta, *Indonesia* . **63 G12** 6 35 S 107 29 E
Purwo, Tanjung,
  Indonesia .... **63 K18** 8 44 S 114 21 E
Purwodadi, *Indonesia* .. **63 G14** 7 7 S 110 55 E
Purwokerto, *Indonesia* . **63 G13** 7 25 S 109 14 E
Puryŏng, *N. Korea* .... **57 C15** 42 5N 129 43 E
Pusa, *India* .... **69 G11** 25 59N 85 41 E
Pusan, *S. Korea* ...... **57 G15** 35 5N 129 0 E
Pushkino, *Moskva,*
  Russia .... **32 C6** 59 45N 30 25 E
Pushkino, *Saratov,*
  Russia .... **34 E8** 51 16N 47 0 E
Püspökladány, *Hungary* . **28 C6** 47 19N 21 6 E
Pustoshka, *Russia* .... **32 D5** 56 20N 29 30 E
Puszczykowo, *Poland* .. **31 F3** 52 18N 16 49 E
Putahow L., *Canada* ... **103 B8** 59 54N 100 40W
Putao, *Burma* .... **67 F20** 27 28N 97 30 E
Putaruru, *N.Z.* .... **91 H5** 38 2 S 175 50 E
Putbus, *Germany* ..... **24 A9** 54 22N 13 28 E
Putian, *China* .... **59 E12** 25 23N 119 0 E
Putignano, *Italy* ...... **43 B10** 40 51N 17 7 E
Puting, Tanjung,
  Indonesia .... **62 E4** 3 31 S 111 46 E
Putlitz, *Germany* ..... **24 B8** 53 15N 12 3 E
Putna, *Romania* ...... **29 C10** 47 50N 25 33 E
Putna →, *Romania* .... **29 E12** 45 42N 27 26 E
Putnam, *U.S.A.* **117 E13** 41 55N 71 55W
Putnok, *Hungary* ..... **28 B5** 48 18N 20 26 E
Putorana, Gory, *Russia* . **53 C10** 69 0N 95 0 E
Putrajaya, *Malaysia* ... **65 L3** 2 55N 101 40 E
Puttalam, *Sri Lanka* ... **66 Q11** 8 1N 79 55 E
Puttgarden, *Germany* .. **24 A7** 54 30N 11 10 E
Püttlingen, *Germany* ... **25 F2** 49 17N 6 53 E
Putumayo →, *S. Amer.* . **124 D5** 3 7 S 67 58W
Putuo, *China* .... **59 C14** 29 56N 122 20 E
Putussibau, *Indonesia* .. **62 D4** 0 50N 112 56 E
Putyla, *Ukraine* ...... **29 B10** 48 0N 25 5 E
Puvirnituq, *Canada* ... **101 B12** 60 2N 77 10W
Puy-de-Dôme, *France* .. **20 C6** 45 46N 2 57 E
Puy-de-Dôme □, *France* . **20 C7** 45 40N 3 5 E
Puy-l'Évêque, *France* ... **20 D5** 44 31N 1 9 E
Puyallup, *U.S.A.* **110 C4** 47 12N 122 18W
Puyang, *China* .... **56 G8** 35 40N 115 1 E
Puylaurens, *France* .... **20 E6** 43 35N 2 0 E
Püzeh Rīg, *Iran* ...... **71 E8** 27 20N 58 40 E
Puzhaykove, *Ukraine* .. **29 B14** 48 7N 29 50 E
Pwani □, *Tanzania* .... **86 D4** 7 0 S 39 0 E
Pweto, Dem. Rep. of
  the Congo .... **87 D2** 8 25 S 28 51 E
Pwllheli, *U.K.* **14 E3** 52 53N 4 25W
Pyana →, *Russia* ..... **34 C8** 55 43N 46 1 E
Pyapon, *Burma* ...... **67 L19** 16 20N 95 40 E
Pyasina →, *Russia* .... **53 B9** 73 30N 87 0 E
Pyatigorsk, *Russia* .... **35 H6** 44 2N 43 6 E
Pyatykhatky, *Ukraine* .. **33 H7** 48 28N 33 38 E
Pydna, *Greece* .... **46 F6** 40 20N 22 34 E
Pyè = Prome, *Burma* .. **67 K19** 18 49N 95 13 E
Pyetrikaw, *Belarus* .... **33 F5** 52 11N 28 29 E
Pyhäjoki, *Finland* ..... **8 D21** 64 28N 24 14 E
Pyinmana, *Burma* .... **67 K20** 19 45N 96 12 E
Pyla, C., *Cyprus* ..... **49 E12** 34 56N 33 51 E
Pymatuning Reservoir,
  U.S.A. **116 E4** 41 30N 80 28W
Pyŏktong, *N. Korea* ... **57 D13** 40 50N 125 50 E
Pyŏnggang, *N. Korea* .. **57 E14** 38 24N 127 17 E
P'yŏngt'aek, *S. Korea* .. **57 F14** 37 1N 127 4 E
P'yŏngyang, *N. Korea* .. **57 E13** 39 0N 125 30 E
Pyote, *U.S.A.* **113 K3** 31 32N 103 8W
Pyramid L., *U.S.A.* ... **108 G4** 40 1N 119 35W
Pyramid Pk., *U.S.A.* .. **111 J10** 36 25N 116 37W
Pyramids, *Egypt* ..... **80 J7** 29 58N 31 9 E
Pyrénées, *Europe* ..... **20 F4** 42 45N 0 18 E
Pyrénées □, *France* **20 F3** 42 52N 0 10W
Pyrénées-Atlantiques □,
  France **20 E3** 43 10N 0 50W
Pyrénées-Orientales □,
  France .... **20 F6** 42 35N 2 26 E
Pyryatyn, *Ukraine* .... **33 G7** 50 15N 32 25 E
Pyrzyce, *Poland* ...... **31 E1** 53 10N 14 55 E
Pyskowice, *Poland* .... **31 H5** 50 24N 18 38 E
Pytalovo, *Russia* ..... **32 D4** 57 5N 27 55 E
Pyu, *Burma* .... **67 K20** 18 30N 96 28 E
Pyzdry, *Poland* ...... **31 F4** 52 11N 17 42 E

Q

Qaanaaq, *Greenland* ... **4 B4** 77 40N 69 0W
Qabirri →, *Azerbaijan* .. **35 K8** 41 3N 46 17 E
Qachasnek, *S. Africa* ... **89 E4** 30 6 S 28 42 E
Qa'el Jafr, *Jordan* ..... **74 E5** 30 20N 36 25 E
Qa'emābād, *Iran* ..... **71 D9** 31 44N 60 2 E
Qā'emshahr, *Iran* ..... **71 B7** 36 30N 52 53 E
Qagan Nur, *China* .... **56 C8** 43 30N 114 55 E
Qahar Youyi Zhongqi,
  China .... **56 D7** 41 12N 112 40 E
Qahremānshahr =
  Bākhtarān, *Iran* .... **70 C5** 34 23N 47 0 E
Qaidam Pendi, *China* .. **60 C4** 37 0N 95 0 E
Qajarīyeh, *Iran* ...... **71 D6** 31 1N 48 22 E
Qala, Ras il, *Malta* .... **49 C1** 36 2N 14 20 E
Qala-i-Jadid = Spīn
  Būldak, *Afghan.* .... **68 D2** 31 1N 66 25 E
Qala Point = Qala, Ras
  il, *Malta* .... **49 C1** 36 2N 14 20 E
Qala Viala, *Pakistan* ... **68 D2** 30 49N 67 17 E
Qala Yangi, *Afghan.* ... **68 B2** 34 20N 66 30 E
Qal'at al Akhḍar,
  Si. Arabia .... **70 E3** 28 0N 37 10 E
Qal'at Dīzah, *Iraq* .... **70 B5** 36 11N 45 7 E
Qal'at Ṣāliḥ, *Iraq* ..... **70 D5** 31 31N 47 16 E
Qal'at Sukkar, *Iraq* .... **70 D5** 31 51N 46 5 E
Qalyûb, *Egypt* .... **80 H7** 30 12N 31 11 E
Qamani'tuaq = Baker
  Lake, *Canada* **100 B10** 64 20N 96 3W
Qamdo, *China* .... **58 B1** 31 15N 97 6 E
Qamruddin Karez,
  Pakistan .... **68 D3** 31 45N 68 20 E
Qandahār, *Afghan.* .... **66 D4** 31 32N 65 43 E
Qandahār □, *Afghan.* .. **66 D4** 31 0N 65 0 E
Qapān, *Iran* .... **71 B7** 37 40N 55 47 E
Qapshagay,
  Kazakhstan .... **52 E8** 43 51N 77 14 E
Qâra, *Egypt* .... **80 B2** 29 38N 26 30 E
Qara Qash →, *China* .. **69 B8** 35 0N 78 30 E
Qarabutaq, *Kazakhstan* . **52 E7** 49 59N 60 14 E
Qaraçala, *Azerbaijan* ... **35 L9** 39 45N 48 53 E
Qaraghandy,
  Kazakhstan .... **52 E8** 49 50N 73 10 E
Qaraghayly, *Kazakhstan* . **52 E8** 49 26N 76 0 E
Qārah, *Si. Arabia* ..... **70 D4** 29 55N 40 3 E
Qaratau, *Kazakhstan* ... **52 E8** 43 10N 70 28 E
Qaratau, *Kazakhstan* ... **52 E7** 43 30N 69 30 E

Qardho = Gardo,
  Somali Rep. .... **75 F4** 9 30N 49 6 E
Qarqud, *Sudan* .... **81 E2** 10 20N 29 56 E
Qareh →, *Iran* .... **70 B5** 39 25N 47 22 E
Qareh Tekān, *Iran* .... **71 B6** 36 38N 49 29 E
Qarqan He →, *China* .. **60 C3** 39 30N 88 30 E
Qarqaraly, *Kazakhstan* . **52 E8** 49 26N 75 30 E
Qarrasa, *Sudan* ...... **81 E3** 14 38N 32 5 E
Qarshi, *Uzbekistan* .... **52 F7** 38 53N 65 48 E
Qartabā, *Lebanon* .... **74 A4** 34 4N 35 50 E
Qaryat al Gharab, *Iraq* . **70 D5** 31 27N 44 48 E
Qaryat al 'Ulyā,
  Si. Arabia .... **70 E5** 27 33N 47 42 E
Qasr 'Amra, *Jordan* ... **70 D3** 31 48N 36 35 E
Qasr-e Qand, *Iran* .... **71 E9** 26 15N 60 45 E
Qasr Farâfra, *Egypt* ... **80 B2** 27 0N 28 1 E
Qaṭanā, *Syria* .... **74 B5** 33 26N 36 4 E
Qatar ■, *Asia* .... **71 E6** 25 30N 51 15 E
Qatlīsh, *Iran* .... **71 B8** 37 50N 57 19 E
Qattâra, *Egypt* ...... **80 A2** 30 12N 27 3 E
Qattâra, Munkhafed el,
  Egypt .... **80 B2** 29 30N 27 30 E
Qattâra Depression =
  Qattâra, Munkhafed
  el, *Egypt* .... **80 B2** 29 30N 27 30 E
Qawām al Ḥamzah = Al
  Ḩamzah, *Iraq* ...... **70 D5** 31 43N 44 58 E
Qāyen, *Iran* .... **71 C8** 33 40N 59 10 E
Qazaqstan =
  Kazakhstan ■, *Asia* . **52 E7** 50 0N 70 0 E
Qazimämmäd,
  Azerbaijan .... **35 K9** 40 3N 49 0 E
Qazvin, *Iran* .... **71 B6** 36 15N 50 0 E
Qazvin □, *Iran* ...... **71 B6** 36 20N 50 0 E
Qena, *Egypt* .... **81 E3** 1 4N 34 40 E
Qena, *Egypt* .... **80 B3** 26 10N 32 43 E
Qena, W. →, *Egypt* ... **80 B3** 26 12N 32 44 E
Qeqertarsuaq,
  Greenland **101 B5** 69 45N 53 30W
Qeqertarsuaq,
  Greenland **101 B14** 69 15N 53 38W
Qeshlāq, *Iran* .... **70 C5** 34 55N 46 28 E
Qeshm, *Iran* .... **71 E8** 26 55N 56 10 E
Qeys, *Iran* .... **71 E7** 26 32N 53 58 E
Qezel Owzen →, *Iran* . **71 B6** 36 45N 49 22 E
Qezi'ot, *Israel* .... **74 E3** 30 52N 34 26 E
Qi Xian, *China* ...... **56 G8** 34 40N 114 48 E
Qian Gorlos, *China* ... **57 B13** 45 5N 124 42 E
Qian Xian, *China* ..... **56 G5** 34 31N 108 15 E
Qiancheng, *China* .... **58 D7** 27 12N 109 50 E
Qianjiang,
  Guangxi Zhuangzu,
  China .... **58 F7** 23 38N 108 58 E
Qianjiang, *Hubei, China* **59 B9** 30 24N 112 55 E
Qianjiang, *Sichuan,*
  China .... **58 C7** 29 30N 108 47 E
Qianshan, *China* ..... **59 B11** 30 37N 116 35 E
Qianwei, *China* ...... **58 C4** 29 13N 103 56 E
Qianxi, *China* .... **58 D6** 27 3N 106 3 E
Qianyang, *Hunan, China* **59 D8** 27 18N 110 10 E
Qianyang, *Shaanxi,*
  China .... **56 G4** 34 40N 107 8 E
Qianyang, *Zhejiang,*
  China .... **59 B12** 30 1N 119 25 E
Qiaojia, *China* .... **58 D4** 26 56N 102 58 E
Qichun, *China* .... **59 B10** 30 18N 115 25 E
Qidong, *Hunan, China* . **59 D9** 26 49N 112 7 E
Qidong, *Jiangsu, China* . **59 B13** 31 48N 121 38 E
Qijiang, *China* .... **58 C6** 28 57N 106 35 E
Qikiqtarjuaq, *Canada* .. **101 B13** 67 33N 63 0W
Qila Safed, *Pakistan* ... **66 E2** 29 0N 61 30 E
Qila Saifullāh, *Pakistan* . **68 D3** 30 45N 68 17 E
Qilian Shan, *China* .... **60 C4** 38 30N 96 0 E
Qimen, *China* .... **59 C11** 29 50N 117 42 E
Qin He →, *China* ..... **56 G7** 35 1N 113 22 E
Qin Jiang →,
  Guangxi Zhuangzu,
  China .... **58 F7** 21 53N 108 35 E
Qin Jiang →, *Jiangxi,*
  China .... **59 D10** 26 15N 115 55 E
Qin Ling = Qinling
  Shandi, *China* ...... **56 H5** 33 50N 108 10 E
Qin'an, *China* .... **56 G3** 34 48N 105 40 E
Qing Xian, *China* ..... **56 E9** 38 35N 116 45 E
Qingcheng, *China* .... **57 F9** 37 15N 117 40 E
Qingdao, *China* ...... **57 F11** 36 5N 120 20 E
Qingfeng, *China* ..... **56 G8** 35 52N 115 8 E
Qinghai □, *China* ..... **60 C4** 36 0N 98 0 E
Qinghai Hu, *China* .... **60 C5** 36 40N 100 10 E
Qinghecheng, *China* ... **57 D13** 41 28N 124 15 E
Qinghemen, *China* .... **57 D11** 41 48N 121 25 E
Qingjian, *China* ...... **56 F6** 37 8N 110 8 E
Qingjiang = Huaiyin,
  China .... **57 H10** 33 30N 119 2 E
Qingliu, *China* .... **59 D11** 26 11N 116 48 E
Qinglong, *China* ..... **58 E5** 25 49N 105 12 E
Qingping, *China* ...... **58 D6** 26 39N 107 47 E
Qingpu, *China* .... **59 B13** 31 10N 121 6 E
Qingshui, *China* ...... **56 G4** 34 48N 106 8 E
Qingshuihe, *China* .... **56 E6** 39 55N 111 35 E
Qingtian, *China* ...... **59 C13** 28 12N 120 15 E
Qingtongxia Shuiku,
  China .... **56 F3** 37 50N 105 58 E
Qingxi, *China* .... **58 D7** 26 38N 108 43 E
Qingxu, *China* .... **56 F7** 37 34N 112 22 E
Qingyang, *Anhui, China* **59 B11** 30 38N 117 50 E
Qingyang, *Gansu, China* **56 F4** 36 2N 107 55 E
Qingyi Jiang →, *China* . **58 C4** 29 32N 103 44 E
Qingyuan, *Guangdong,*
  China .... **59 F9** 23 40N 112 59 E
Qingyuan, *Liaoning,*
  China .... **57 C13** 42 10N 124 55 E
Qingyuan, *Zhejiang,*
  China .... **59 D12** 27 36N 119 3 E
Qingyun, *China* ...... **57 F9** 37 45N 117 20 E
Qingzhen, *China* ..... **58 D6** 26 31N 106 25 E
Qinhuangdao, *China* .. **57 E10** 39 56N 119 30 E
Qinling Shandi, *China* . **56 H5** 33 50N 108 10 E
Qinshui, *China* ...... **56 G7** 35 40N 112 8 E
Qinyang = Jiyuan, *China* **56 G7** 35 7N 112 57 E
Qinyuan, *China* ...... **56 F7** 36 29N 112 20 E
Qinzhou, *China* ...... **58 G7** 21 58N 108 38 E
Qionghai, *China* ..... **64 C8** 19 15N 110 26 E
Qionglai, *China* ...... **58 B4** 30 25N 103 31 E
Qionglai Shan, *China* .. **58 B4** 30 1N 102 30 E
Qiongzhou Haixia,
  China .... **64 B8** 20 10N 110 15 E
Qiqihar, *China* ...... **53 E13** 47 26N 124 0 E
Qiraîya, W. →, *Egypt* . **74 E3** 30 27N 34 0 E
Qiryat Ata, *Israel* ..... **74 C4** 32 47N 35 6 E
Qiryat Gat, *Israel* ..... **74 D3** 31 32N 34 46 E
Qiryat Mal'akhi, *Israel* . **74 D3** 31 44N 34 44 E
Qiryat Shemona, *Israel* . **74 B4** 33 13N 35 35 E
Qiryat Yam, *Israel* .... **74 C4** 32 51N 35 4 E
Qishan, *China* .... **56 G4** 34 25N 107 38 E
Qitai, *China* .... **60 B3** 44 2N 89 35 E
Qiubei, *China* .... **58 E5** 24 4N 104 12 E

Qixia, *China* .... **57 F11** 37 17N 120 52 E
Qiyang, *China* .... **59 D8** 26 35N 111 50 E
Qızılağac Körfäzi,
  Azerbaijan .... **71 B6** 39 9N 49 0 E
Qojūr, *Iran* .... **70 B5** 36 12N 47 55 E
Qom, *Iran* .... **71 C6** 34 40N 51 0 E
Qom □, *Iran* .... **71 C6** 34 40N 51 0 E
Qomolangma Feng =
  Everest, Mt., *Nepal* . **69 E12** 28 5N 86 58 E
Qomsheh, *Iran* ...... **71 D6** 32 0N 51 55 E
Qoraqalpoghistan □,
  Uzbekistan .... **52 E6** 43 0N 58 0 E
Qorveh, *Iran* .... **73 E12** 35 10N 47 48 E
Qostanay, *Kazakhstan* . **52 D7** 53 10N 63 35 E
Qoṭūr, *Iran* .... **73 C11** 38 28N 44 58 E
Qu Jiang →, *China* ... **58 B6** 30 1N 106 24 E
Qu Xian, *China* ...... **58 B6** 30 48N 106 58 E
Quabbin Reservoir,
  U.S.A. **117 D12** 42 20N 72 20W
Quairading, *Australia* .. **93 F2** 32 0 S 117 21 E
Quakenbrück, *Germany* **24 C3** 52 41N 7 57 E
Quakertown, *U.S.A.* ... **117 F9** 40 26N 75 21W
Qualicum Beach,
  Canada **102 D4** 49 22N 124 26W
Quambatook, *Australia* **95 F3** 35 49 S 143 34 E
Quambone, *Australia* .. **95 E4** 30 57 S 147 53 E
Quamby, *Australia* .... **94 C3** 20 22 S 140 17 E
Quan Long = Ca Mau,
  Vietnam .... **65 H5** 9 7N 105 8 E
Quanah, *U.S.A.* **113 H5** 34 18N 99 44W
Quang Ngai, *Vietnam* . **64 E7** 15 13N 108 58 E
Quang Tri, *Vietnam* ... **64 D6** 16 45N 107 13 E
Quang Yen, *Vietnam* .. **58 G6** 20 56N 106 52 E
Quannan, *China* ...... **59 E10** 24 45N 114 33 E
Quantock Hills, *U.K.* .. **15 F4** 51 8N 3 10W
Quanzhou, *Fujian,*
  China .... **59 E12** 24 55N 118 34 E
Quanzhou,
  Guangxi Zhuangzu,
  China .... **59 E8** 25 57N 111 5 E
Qu'Appelle, *Canada* ... **103 C8** 50 33N 103 53W
Quaqtaq, *Canada* **101 B13** 60 55N 69 40W
Quaraí, *Brazil* .... **126 C4** 30 15 S 56 20W
Quarré-les-Tombes,
  France .... **19 E11** 47 21N 4 0 E
Quarteira, *Portugal* ... **37 H2** 37 4N 8 6W
Quartu Sant'Élena, *Italy* **42 C2** 39 15N 9 10 E
Quartzsite, *U.S.A.* **111 M12** 33 40N 114 13W
Quatsino Sd., *Canada* . **102 C3** 50 25N 127 58W
Quba, *Azerbaijan* ..... **35 K9** 41 21N 48 32 E
Qūchān, *Iran* .... **71 B8** 37 10N 58 27 E
Queanbeyan, *Australia* . **95 F4** 35 17 S 149 14 E
Québec, *Canada* **105 C5** 46 52N 71 13W
Québec □, *Canada* **105 C6** 48 0N 74 0W
Quebrada del
  Condorito △,
  Argentina .... **126 C3** 31 49 S 64 40W
Quedlinburg, *Germany* . **24 D7** 51 47N 11 8 E
Queen Alexandra Ra.,
  Antarctica .... **5 E11** 85 0 S 170 0 E
Queen Charlotte City,
  Canada **102 C2** 53 15N 132 2W
Queen Charlotte Is.,
  Canada **102 C2** 53 20N 132 10W
Queen Charlotte Sd.,
  Canada **102 C3** 51 0N 128 0W
Queen Charlotte Strait,
  Canada **102 C3** 50 45N 127 10W
Queen Elizabeth △,
  U.K. **13 E4** 56 7N 4 30W
Queen Elizabeth △,
  Uganda .... **86 C3** 0 0 30 0 E
Queen Elizabeth Is.,
  Canada **98 B10** 76 0N 95 0W
Queen Mary Land,
  Antarctica .... **5 D7** 70 0 S 95 0 E
Queen Maud G.,
  Canada **100 B9** 68 15N 102 30W
Queen Maud Land =
  Dronning Maud Land,
  Antarctica .... **5 D3** 72 30 S 12 0 E
Queen Maud Mts.,
  Antarctica .... **5 E13** 86 0 S 160 0W
Queens Chan., *Australia* **94 C4** 15 0 S 129 30 E
Queenscliff, *Australia* .. **95 F3** 38 16 S 144 39 E
Queensland □, *Australia* **94 C3** 22 0 S 142 0 E
Queenstown, *Australia* . **95 G4** 42 4 S 145 35 E
Queenstown, *N.Z.* .... **91 L2** 45 1 S 168 40 E
Queenstown, *Singapore* **65 d** 1 18N 103 48 E
Queenstown, *S. Africa* . **88 E4** 31 52 S 26 52 E
Queets, *U.S.A.* **110 C2** 47 32N 124 20W
Queguay Grande →,
  Uruguay .... **126 C4** 32 9 S 58 9W
Queimadas, *Brazil* .... **125 F11** 11 0 S 39 38W
Quelimane, *Mozam.* ... **87 F4** 17 53 S 36 58 E
Quellón, *Chile* .... **128 E2** 43 7 S 73 37W
Quelpart = Cheju do,
  S. Korea .... **57 H14** 33 29N 126 34 E
Queluz, *Portugal* **37 G1** 38 45N 9 15W
Quemado, *N. Mex.,*
  U.S.A. **109 J9** 34 20N 108 30W
Quemado, *Tex., U.S.A.* **113 L4** 28 58N 100 35W
Quemoy = Chinmen,
  Taiwan .... **59 E13** 24 26N 118 19 E
Quemú-Quemú,
  Argentina .... **126 D3** 36 3 S 63 36W
Quequén, *Argentina* ... **126 D4** 38 30 S 58 30W
Querétaro, *Mexico* **118 C4** 20 36N 100 23W
Querétaro □, *Mexico* .. **118 C5** 20 30N 100 0W
Querfurt, *Germany* .... **24 D7** 51 23N 11 35 E
Quérigut, *France* ..... **20 F6** 42 42N 2 6 E
Querqueville, *France* ... **18 C5** 49 40N 1 42W
Quesada, *Spain* **37 H7** 37 51N 3 4W
Queshan, *China* ...... **56 H8** 32 55N 114 2 E
Quesnel, *Canada* **102 C4** 53 0N 122 30W
Quesnel →, *Canada* ... **102 C4** 52 58N 122 29W
Quesnel L., *Canada* ... **102 C4** 52 30N 121 20W
Questa, *U.S.A.* **109 H11** 36 42N 105 36W
Questembert, *France* ... **18 E4** 47 40N 2 28W
Quetico △, *Canada* **104 C1** 48 30N 91 45W
Quetta, *Pakistan* ..... **68 D2** 30 15N 66 55 E
Queyras △, *France* .... **21 D10** 44 45N 6 50 E
Quezaltenango,
  Guatemala **120 D1** 14 50N 91 30W
Quezon City, *Phil.* .... **61 D4** 14 38N 121 0 E
Qufār, *Si. Arabia* ..... **70 E4** 27 26N 41 37 E
Qui Nhon, *Vietnam* ... **64 F7** 13 40N 109 13 E
Quiaca, La, *Argentina* .. **126 A2** 22 5 S 65 35W
Quibaxe, *Angola* ..... **84 F2** 8 24 S 14 27 E
Quibdo, *Colombia* **124 B3** 5 42N 76 40W
Quiberon, *France* **18 E3** 47 29N 3 9W
Quiberon, Presqu'île de,
  France **18 E3** 47 30N 3 8W
Quickborn, *Germany* .. **24 B5** 53 44N 9 52 E
Quiet L., *Canada* ..... **102 A2** 61 5N 133 5 E
Quiindy, *Paraguay* .... **126 B4** 25 58 S 57 14W
Quila, *Mexico* **118 C3** 24 23N 107 13W
Quilán, C., *Chile* ..... **128 E2** 43 15 S 74 30W

Quilcene, *U.S.A.* **110 C4** 47 49N 122 53W
Quilimarí, *Chile* ...... **126 C1** 32 5 S 71 30W
Quilino, *Argentina* .... **126 C3** 30 14 S 64 29W
Quill Lakes, *Canada* ... **103 C8** 51 55N 104 13W
Quillabamba, *Peru* .... **124 F4** 12 50 S 72 50W
Quillagua, *Chile* ...... **126 A2** 21 40 S 69 40W
Quillaicillo, *Chile* ..... **126 C1** 31 17 S 71 40W
Quillan, *France* ...... **20 F6** 42 53N 2 10 E
Quillota, *Chile* .... **126 C1** 32 54 S 71 16W
Quilmes, *Argentina* ... **126 C4** 34 43 S 58 15W
Quilon, *India* .... **66 Q10** 8 50N 76 38 E
Quilpie, *Australia* ..... **95 D3** 26 35 S 144 11 E
Quilpué, *Chile* .... **126 C1** 33 5 S 71 33W
Quilua, *Mozam.* ...... **87 F4** 16 17 S 39 54 E
Quimili, *Argentina* .... **126 B3** 27 40 S 62 30W
Quimper, *France* **18 E2** 48 0N 4 9W
Quimperlé, *France* **18 E3** 47 53N 3 33W
Quinault →, *U.S.A.* ... **110 C2** 47 21N 124 18W
Quincy, *Calif., U.S.A.* . **110 F3** 39 56N 120 57W
Quincy, *Fla., U.S.A.* .. **115 K3** 30 35N 84 34W
Quincy, *Ill., U.S.A.* ... **112 F9** 39 56N 91 23W
Quincy, *Mass., U.S.A.* . **117 D14** 42 15N 71 0W
Quincy, *Wash., U.S.A.* **108 C4** 47 22N 119 56W
Quines, *Argentina* .... **126 C2** 32 13 S 65 48W
Quinga, *Mozam.* ..... **87 F5** 15 49 S 40 15 E
Quingey, *France* ...... **19 E6** 47 7N 5 52 E
Quinns Rocks, *Australia* **93 F2** 31 40 S 115 42 E
Quintana de la Serena,
  Spain **37 G5** 38 45N 5 40W
Quintana Roo □,
  Mexico **119 D7** 19 0N 88 0W
Quintanar de la Orden,
  Spain **37 F7** 39 36N 3 5W
Quintanar de la Sierra,
  Spain **38 D2** 41 57N 2 55W
Quintanar del Rey,
  Spain **39 F3** 39 21N 1 56W
Quinte West, *Canada* .. **116 B7** 44 10N 77 34W
Quintero, *Chile* ...... **126 C1** 32 45 S 71 30W
Quintin, *France* **18 D4** 48 26N 2 56W
Quinto, *Spain* **38 D4** 41 25N 0 32W
Quípar →, *Spain* **39 G3** 38 15N 1 40W
Quirihue, *Chile* ...... **126 D1** 36 15 S 72 35W
Quirindi, *Australia* .... **95 E5** 31 28 S 150 40 E
Quirinópolis, *Brazil* ... **125 G8** 18 32 S 50 30W
Quiroga, *Spain* **36 C3** 42 28N 7 18W
Quissac, *France* ...... **21 E8** 43 55N 4 0 E
Quissanga, *Mozam.* ... **87 E5** 12 24 S 40 28 E
Quissico, *Mozam.* .... **89 C5** 24 42 S 34 44 E
Quitilipi, *Argentina* ... **126 B3** 26 50 S 60 13W
Quitman, *U.S.A.* **115 K4** 30 47N 83 34W
Quito, *Ecuador* ...... **124 D3** 0 15 S 78 35W
Quixadá, *Brazil* ...... **125 D11** 4 55 S 39 0W
Quixaxe, *Mozam.* ..... **87 F5** 15 17 S 40 4 E
Qujing, *China* .... **58 E4** 25 32N 103 41 E
Qul'an, Jazā'ir, *Egypt* . **70 E2** 24 22N 35 31 E
Qumbu, *S. Africa* ..... **89 E4** 31 10 S 28 48 E
Quneitra, *Syria* ...... **74 B4** 33 7N 35 48 E
Qŭnghirot, *Uzbekistan* . **52 E6** 43 6N 58 54 E
Qu'nyido, *China* ...... **58 B2** 31 15N 98 6 E
Quoin I., *Australia* .... **94 B4** 14 54 S 129 32 E
Quoin Pt., *S. Africa* ... **88 E2** 34 46 S 19 37 E
Quorn, *Australia* ..... **95 E2** 32 25 S 138 5 E
Qŭqon, *Uzbekistan* ... **52 E8** 40 30N 70 57 E
Qurein, *Sudan* .... **81 E3** 13 30N 34 50 E
Qurnat as Sawdā',
  Lebanon .... **74 A5** 34 18N 36 6 E
Qûs, *Egypt* .... **80 B3** 25 55N 32 50 E
Qusar, *Azerbaijan* .... **35 K9** 41 25N 48 26 E
Quṣaybā', *Si. Arabia* ... **70 E4** 26 53N 43 35 E
Qusaybah, *Iraq* ...... **70 C4** 34 24N 40 59 E
Quseir, *Egypt* .... **70 E2** 26 7N 34 16 E
Qūshchī, *Iran* .... **70 B5** 37 59N 45 3 E
Quthing, *Lesotho* ..... **89 E4** 30 25 S 27 36 E
Qūṭīābād, *Iran* ...... **71 C6** 35 47N 48 30 E
Quwo, *China* .... **56 G6** 35 38N 111 25 E
Quyang, *China* .... **56 E8** 38 35N 114 40 E
Quynh Nhai, *Vietnam* . **64 B4** 21 49N 103 33 E
Quyon, *Canada* **117 A8** 45 31N 76 14W
Quzhou, *China* .... **59 C12** 28 57N 118 54 E
Quzi, *China* .... **56 F4** 36 20N 107 20 E
Qvareli, *Georgia* ..... **35 K7** 41 57N 45 47 E
Qyzylorda, *Kazakhstan* . **52 E7** 44 48N 65 28 E

R

Ra, Ko, *Thailand* ..... **65 H2** 9 13N 98 16 E
Raab, *Austria* .... **26 C6** 48 21N 13 39 E
Raahe, *Finland* ...... **8 D21** 64 40N 24 28 E
Raalte, *Neths.* .... **17 B6** 52 23N 6 16 E
Raasay, *U.K.* **13 D2** 57 25N 6 4W
Raasay, Sd. of, *U.K.* .. **13 D2** 57 30N 6 8W
Rab, *Croatia* .... **41 D11** 44 45N 14 45 E
Raba, *Indonesia* ...... **63 F5** 8 36 S 118 55 E
Rába →, *Hungary* ..... **28 C3** 47 38N 17 38 E
Raba →, *Poland* ...... **31 H7** 50 8N 20 30 E
Rabaçal →, *Portugal* .. **36 D3** 41 30N 7 12W
Rabah, *Nigeria* ...... **83 C6** 13 5N 5 30 E
Rabai, *Kenya* .... **86 C4** 3 50 S 39 31 E
Rabak, *Sudan* .... **81 E3** 13 43N 32 44 E
Rabastens, *France* .... **20 E5** 43 50N 1 43 E
Rabastens-de-Bigorre,
  France .... **20 E4** 43 23N 0 9 E
Rabat = Victoria, *Malta* **49 C1** 36 3N 14 14 E
Rabat, *Malta* .... **49 D1** 35 53N 14 24 E
Rabat, *Morocco* **78 B4** 34 2N 6 48W
Rabaul, *Papua N. G.* .. **96 H7** 4 24 S 152 18 E
Rābigh, *Si. Arabia* .... **80 C4** 22 50N 39 5 E
Rabka, *Poland* .... **31 J6** 49 37N 19 59 E
Râbniţa, *Moldova* .... **29 C14** 47 45N 29 0 E
Râbor, *Iran* .... **71 D8** 29 17N 56 55 E
Rača, *Serbia & M.* .... **44 B4** 44 14N 21 0 E
Răcăciuni, *Romania* ... **29 E11** 46 20N 26 43 E
Răcăşdia, *Romania* ... **28 F6** 44 59N 21 36 E
Racconigi, *Italy* ...... **40 D7** 44 46N 7 46 E
Race, C., *Canada* **105 C9** 46 40N 53 5W
Rach Gia, *Vietnam* .... **65 G5** 10 5N 105 5 E
Rachid, *Mauritania* ... **82 B2** 18 45N 11 35W
Racibórz, *Poland* ..... **31 H5** 50 7N 18 18 E
Racichy, *Belarus* ..... **30 E10** 53 44N 27 10 E
Racine, *U.S.A.* **114 D2** 42 41N 87 51W
Rackerby, *U.S.A.* **110 F5** 39 26N 121 22W
Radama, Nosy, *Madag.* **89 A8** 14 0 S 47 47 E
Radama, Saikanosy,
  Madag. .... **89 A8** 14 16 S 47 53 E
Radan, *Serbia & M.* ... **44 D5** 42 59N 21 29 E
Rădăuți, *Romania* .... **29 C10** 47 50N 25 59 E
Rădăuți-Prut, *Romania* **29 B11** 48 14N 26 48 E
Radbuza →, *Czech Rep.* **26 B6** 49 35N 13 5 E
Radcliff, *U.S.A.* **114 G3** 37 51N 85 57W
Radeberg, *Germany* ... **24 D9** 51 6N 13 55 E
Radebeul, *Germany* ... **24 D9** 51 6N 13 39 E
Radeče, *Slovenia* ..... **41 B12** 46 5N 15 14 E

Radekhiv, *Ukraine* .... **33 G3** 50 25N 24 32 E
Radekhov = Radekhiv,
  Ukraine .... **33 G3** 50 25N 24 32 E
Radenthein, *Austria* ... **26 E6** 46 48N 13 43 E
Radew →, *Poland* ..... **30 D2** 54 2N 15 52 E
Radford, *U.S.A.* **114 G5** 37 8N 80 34W
Radhanpur, *India* ..... **68 H4** 23 50N 71 38 E
Radhwa, Jabal,
  Si. Arabia .... **70 E3** 24 34N 38 18 E
Radika →, *Macedonia* . **44 E4** 41 38N 20 37 E
Radisson, *Qué., Canada* **104 B4** 53 47N 77 37W
Radisson, *Sask., Canada* **103 C7** 52 30N 107 20W
Radium Hot Springs,
  Canada **102 C5** 50 35N 116 2W
Radlje ob Dravi,
  Slovenia .... **41 B12** 46 38N 15 13 E
Radnevo, *Bulgaria* .... **45 D9** 42 17N 25 58 E
Radnice, *Czech Rep.* .. **26 B6** 49 51N 13 35 E
Radnor Forest, *U.K.* ... **15 E4** 52 17N 3 10W
Radolfzell, *Germany* ... **25 H4** 47 39N 8 59 E
Radom, *Poland* ...... **31 G8** 51 23N 21 12 E
Radomir, *Bulgaria* .... **44 D6** 42 37N 22 59 E
Radomka →, *Poland* .. **31 G8** 51 43N 21 28 E
Radomsko, *Poland* .... **31 G6** 51 5N 19 28 E
Radomyshl, *Ukraine* .. **33 G5** 50 30N 29 12 E
Radomyśl Wielki,
  Poland .... **31 H8** 50 14N 21 15 E
Radoszyce, *Poland* .... **31 G7** 51 4N 20 15 E
Radoviš, *Macedonia* ... **44 E6** 41 38N 22 28 E
Radovljica, *Slovenia* ... **41 B11** 46 22N 14 12 E
Radstadt, *Austria* ..... **26 D6** 47 24N 13 28 E
Radstock, C., *Australia* . **95 E1** 33 12 S 134 20 E
Răducăneni, *Romania* . **29 D12** 46 58N 27 54 E
Raduša, *Macedonia* ... **44 D5** 42 7N 21 15 E
Radvanichy, *Belarus* ... **31 F11** 52 1N 24 0 E
Radviliškis, *Lithuania* .. **9 J20** 55 49N 23 33 E
Radville, *Canada* **103 D8** 49 30N 104 15W
Radwá, J., Si. Arabia ... **80 C4** 24 34N 38 18 E
Radymno, *Poland* .... **31 J9** 49 59N 22 52 E
Radziejów, *Poland* .... **31 F5** 52 40N 18 30 E
Radzyń Chelmiński,
  Poland .... **30 E5** 53 23N 18 55 E
Radzyń Podlaski,
  Poland .... **31 G9** 51 47N 22 37 E
Rae, *Canada* **102 A5** 62 50N 116 3W
Rae Bareli, *India* ..... **69 F9** 26 18N 81 20 E
Rae Isthmus, *Canada* .. **101 B11** 66 40N 87 30W
Raeren, *Belgium* ...... **17 D6** 50 41N 6 7 E
Raeside, L., *Australia* .. **93 E3** 29 20 S 122 0 E
Raetihi, *N.Z.* .... **91 H5** 39 25 S 175 17 E
Rafaela, *Argentina* .... **126 C3** 31 10 S 61 30W
Rafah, *Gaza Strip* .... **74 D3** 31 18N 34 14 E
Rafai, *C.A.R.* .... **86 B1** 4 59N 23 58 E
Raffadali, *Italy* ...... **42 E6** 37 24N 13 32 E
Raffili, *Sudan* .... **81 F2** 6 50N 28 0 E
Rafḥā, *Si. Arabia* ..... **70 D4** 29 35N 43 35 E
Rafsanjān, *Iran* ...... **71 D8** 30 30N 56 5 E
Raft Pt., *Australia* .... **92 C3** 16 4 S 124 26 E
Râga, *Sudan* .... **81 F2** 8 28N 25 41 E
Raga →, *Sudan* ...... **81 F2** 8 41N 25 52 E
Ragachow, *Belarus* .... **33 F6** 53 8N 30 5 E
Ragag, *Sudan* .... **81 E1** 10 59N 24 40 E
Ragama, *Sri Lanka* .... **66 R11** 7 0N 79 50 E
Ragged, Mt., *Australia* . **93 F3** 33 27 S 123 25 E
Ragged Pt., *Barbados* .. **121 g** 13 10N 59 10W
Raghunathpalli, *India* .. **69 H11** 22 14N 84 48 E
Raghunathpur, *India* .. **69 H12** 23 33N 86 40 E
Raglan, *N.Z.* .... **91 G5** 37 55 S 174 55 E
Ragusa, *Italy* .... **43 F7** 36 55N 14 44 E
Raha, *Indonesia* ..... **63 E6** 4 55 S 123 0 E
Rahad, Nahr ed →,
  Sudan .... **81 E3** 14 28N 33 31 E
Rahaeng = Tak,
  Thailand .... **64 D2** 16 52N 99 8 E
Rahatgarh, *India* ..... **69 H8** 23 47N 78 22 E
Rahden, *Germany* .... **24 C4** 52 26N 8 36 E
Raheita, *Eritrea* ...... **81 E5** 12 46N 43 4 E
Rahimyar Khan,
  Pakistan .... **68 E4** 28 30N 70 25 E
Rāhjerd, *Iran* .... **71 C6** 34 22N 50 22 E
Rahole △, *Kenya* ..... **86 B4** 3 30N 38 57 E
Rahon, *India* .... **68 D7** 31 3N 76 7 E
Raiajganj, *India* ...... **66 L10** 16 10N 77 20 E
Raiganj, *India* .... **69 G13** 25 37N 88 10 E
Raigarh, *India* .... **67 J13** 21 56N 83 25 E
Raijua, *Indonesia* ..... **63 F6** 10 37 S 121 36 E
Raikot, *India* .... **68 D6** 30 41N 75 42 E
Railton, *Australia* .... **95 G4** 41 25 S 146 28 E
Rainbow Bridge △,
  U.S.A. **109 H8** 37 5N 110 58W
Rainbow Lake, *Canada* **102 B5** 58 30N 119 23W
Rainier, *U.S.A.* **110 D4** 46 53N 122 41W
Rainier, Mt., *U.S.A.* ... **110 D5** 46 52N 121 46W
Rainy L., *Canada* **103 D10** 48 42N 93 10W
Rainy River, *Canada* .. **103 D10** 48 43N 94 29W
Raippaluoto, *Finland* .. **8 E19** 63 13N 21 14 E
Raipur, *India* .... **67 J12** 21 17N 81 45 E
Ra'is, *Si. Arabia* ..... **80 C4** 23 33N 38 43 E
Raisen, *India* .... **68 H8** 23 20N 77 48 E
Raisio, *Finland* ...... **9 F20** 60 28N 22 11 E
Raj Nandgaon, *India* .. **67 J12** 21 5N 81 5 E
Raj Nilgiri, *India* ..... **69 J12** 21 28N 86 46 E
Raja, Ujung, *Indonesia* . **62 D1** 3 40N 96 25 E
Raja Ampat, Kepulauan,
  Indonesia .... **63 E7** 0 30 S 130 0 E
Rajahmundry, *India* ... **67 L12** 17 1N 81 48 E
Rajang →, *Malaysia* ... **62 D4** 2 30N 112 0 E
Rajanpur, *Pakistan* .... **68 E4** 29 6N 70 19 E
Rajapalaiyam, *India* ... **66 Q10** 9 25N 77 35 E
Rajasthan □, *India* .... **68 F5** 26 45N 73 30 E
Rajasthan Canal =
  Indira Gandhi Canal,
  India .... **68 F5** 28 0N 72 0 E
Rajauri, *India* .... **69 C6** 33 25N 74 21 E
Rajgarh, Mad. P., India . **68 G7** 24 2N 76 45 E
Rajgarh, *Raj., India* ... **68 E6** 28 40N 75 25 E
Rajgarh, *Raj., India* ... **68 F7** 27 14N 76 38 E
Rajgir, *India* .... **69 G11** 25 2N 85 25 E
Rajgród, *Poland* ..... **30 E9** 53 42N 22 42 E
Rajkot, *India* .... **68 H4** 22 15N 70 56 E
Rajmahal Hills, *India* .. **69 G12** 24 30N 87 30 E
Rajpipla, *India* ...... **66 J8** 21 50N 73 30 E
Rajpur, *India* .... **68 H6** 22 18N 74 21 E
Rajpura, *India* .... **68 D7** 30 25N 76 32 E
Rajshahi, *Bangla.* .... **67 G16** 24 22N 88 39 E
Rajshahi □, *Bangla.* ... **69 G13** 25 0N 89 0 E
Rajula, *India* .... **68 J4** 21 3N 71 26 E
Rakaia, *N.Z.* .... **91 K4** 43 45 S 172 1 E
Rakaia →, *N.Z.* ...... **91 K4** 43 36 S 172 15 E
Rakan, Ra's, *Qatar* ... **71 E6** 26 10N 51 20 E
Rakaposhi, *Pakistan* ... **69 A6** 36 10N 74 25 E
Rakata, Pulau, *Indonesia* **62 F3** 6 10 S 105 20 E
Rakhiv, *Ukraine* ..... **29 B9** 48 3N 24 12 E
Rakhni, *Pakistan* ..... **68 D3** 30 4N 69 56 E
Rakhni →, *Pakistan* ... **68 E3** 29 31N 69 36 E
Rakhny-Lisovi, *Ukraine* **29 B13** 48 47N 28 50 E

Rakitnoye, Russia ..... **54 B7** 45 36N 134 17 E
Rakitovo, Bulgaria ... **45 E8** 41 59N 24 5 E
Rakops, Botswana .... **88 C3** 21 1 S 24 28 E
Rakovica, Croatia .... **41 D12** 44 59N 15 38 E
Rakovník, Czech Rep. .. **26 A6** 50 6N 13 42 E
Rakovski, Bulgaria ... **45 D8** 42 21N 24 57 E
Rakvere, Estonia ..... **9 G22** 59 20N 26 25 E
Raleigh, U.S.A. **115 H6** 35 47N 78 39W
Ralja, Serbia & M. .... **44 B4** 44 33N 20 34 E
Ralls, U.S.A. **113 J4** 33 41N 101 24W
Ralston, U.S.A. **116 E8** 41 30N 76 57W
Ram →, Canada **102 A4** 62 1N 123 41W
Rām Allāh, West Bank .. **74 D4** 31 55N 35 10 E
Rama, Nic. **120 D3** 12 9N 84 15W
Ramacca, Italy .... **43 E7** 37 23N 14 42 E
Ramakona, India ..... **69 J8** 21 43N 78 50 E
Ramales de la Victoria,
Spain **36 B7** 43 15N 3 28W
Rāmallāh = Rām Allāh,
West Bank .... **74 D4** 31 55N 35 10 E
Raman, Thailand ..... **65 J3** 6 29N 101 18 E
Ramanathapuram, India **66 Q11** 9 25N 78 55 E
Ramanetaka, B. de,
Madag. .... **89 A8** 14 13 S 47 52 E
Ramanujganj, India ... **69 H10** 23 48N 83 42 E
Ramat Gan, Israel .... **74 C3** 32 4N 34 48 E
Ramatlhabama,
S. Africa .... **88 D4** 25 37 S 25 33 E
Ramban, India .... **69 C6** 33 14N 75 12 E
Rambervillers, France .. **19 D13** 48 20N 6 38 E
Rambipuji, Indonesia .. **63 H15** 8 12 S 113 37 E
Rambouillet, France ... **19 D8** 48 39N 1 50 E
Rame Hd., Australia ... **95 F4** 37 47 S 149 30 E
Ramechhap, Nepal .... **69 F12** 27 25N 86 10 E
Ramenskoye, Russia ... **32 E10** 55 32N 38 15 E
Ramganga →, India .. **69 F8** 27 5N 79 58 E
Ramgarh, Jharkhand,
India .... **69 H11** 23 40N 85 35 E
Ramgarh, Raj., India .. **68 F6** 27 16N 75 14 E
Ramgarh, Raj., India .. **68 F4** 27 30N 70 36 E
Rāmhormoz, Iran ..... **71 D6** 31 15N 49 35 E
Ramīān, Iran .... **71 B7** 37 3N 55 16 E
Ramingining, Australia . **94 A2** 12 19 S 135 3 E
Ramla, Israel .... **74 D3** 31 55N 34 52 E
Ramlu, Eritrea .... **81 E5** 13 32N 41 40 E
Ramm = Rum, Jordan . **74 F4** 29 39N 35 26 E
Ramm, Jabal, Jordan .. **74 F4** 29 35N 35 24 E
Râmna →, Romania .. **29 E12** 45 36N 27 3 E
Ramnad =
Ramanathapuram,
India .... **66 Q11** 9 25N 78 55 E
Ramnagar,
Jammu & Kashmir,
India .... **69 C6** 32 47N 75 18 E
Ramnagar, Uttaranchal,
India .... **69 E8** 29 24N 79 7 E
Ramnäs, Sweden ..... **10 E10** 59 46N 16 12 E
Râmnicu Sărat,
Romania .... **29 E12** 45 26N 27 3 E
Râmnicu Vâlcea,
Romania .... **29 E9** 45 9N 24 21 E
Ramon, Russia .... **33 G10** 51 55N 39 21 E
Ramona, U.S.A. **111 M10** 33 2N 116 52W
Ramonville-St-Agne,
France .... **20 E5** 43 33N 1 28 E
Ramore, Canada **104 C3** 48 30N 80 25W
Ramos →, Nigeria ... **83 D6** 5 8N 5 22 E
Ramotswa, Botswana .. **88 C4** 24 50 S 25 52 E
Rampur, H.P., India ... **68 D7** 31 26N 77 43 E
Rampur, Mad. P., India **68 H5** 23 25N 73 53 E
Rampur, Ut. P., India .. **69 E8** 28 50N 79 5 E
Rampur Hat, India .... **69 G12** 24 10N 87 50 E
Rampura, India ...... **68 G6** 24 30N 75 27 E
Ramrama Tola, India .. **69 J8** 21 52N 79 55 E
Ramree I., Burma .... **67 K19** 19 0N 93 40 E
Rämsar, Iran .... **71 B6** 36 53N 50 41 E
Ramsey, U.K. **14 C3** 54 20N 4 22W
Ramsey, U.S.A. **117 E10** 41 4N 74 9W
Ramsey L., Canada ... **104 C3** 47 13N 82 15W
Ramsgate, U.K. ..... **15 F9** 51 20N 1 25 E
Ramsjö, Sweden ..... **10 B9** 62 11N 15 37 E
Ramstein, Germany ... **25 F3** 49 27N 7 32 E
Ramtek, India .... **66 J11** 21 20N 79 15 E
Ramvik, Sweden ..... **10 B11** 62 49N 17 51 E
Rana Pratap Sagar Dam,
India .... **68 G6** 24 58N 75 38 E
Ranaghat, India ...... **69 H13** 23 15N 88 35 E
Ranahu, Pakistan .... **68 G3** 25 55N 69 45 E
Ranau, Malaysia ..... **62 C5** 6 2N 116 40 E
Rancagua, Chile ..... **126 C1** 34 10 S 70 50W
Rance →, France **18 D5** 48 34N 1 59W
Rancheria →, Canada **102 A3** 60 13N 129 7W
Ranchester, U.S.A. ... **114 D10** 44 54N 107 10W
Ranchi, India .... **69 H11** 23 19N 85 27 E
Rancho Cucamonga,
U.S.A. **111 L9** 34 10N 117 30W
Randalstown, U.K. ... **12 B5** 54 45N 6 19W
Randan, France ...... **19 F10** 46 2N 3 21 E
Randazzo, Italy ...... **43 E7** 37 53N 14 57 E
Randers, Denmark .... **11 H4** 56 29N 10 1 E
Randers Fjord,
Denmark .... **11 H4** 56 37N 10 20 E
Randfontein, S. Africa . **89 D4** 26 8 S 27 45 E
Randle, U.S.A. **110 D5** 46 32N 121 57W
Randolph, Mass., U.S.A. **117 D13** 42 10N 71 2W
Randolph, N.Y., U.S.A. **116 D6** 42 10N 78 59W
Randolph, Utah, U.S.A. **108 F8** 41 40N 111 11W
Randolph, Vt., U.S.A. . **117 C12** 43 55N 72 40W
Randsburg, U.S.A. ... **111 K9** 35 22N 117 39W
Råneälven →, Sweden . **8 D20** 65 50N 22 20 E
Rangae, Thailand .... **65 J3** 6 19N 101 44 E
Rangaunu B., N.Z. ... **91 F4** 34 51 S 173 15 E
Rangeley, U.S.A. **117 B14** 44 58N 70 39W
Rangeley L., U.S.A. .. **117 B14** 44 55N 70 43W
Rangely, U.S.A. **108 F9** 40 5N 108 48W
Ranger, U.S.A. **113 J5** 32 28N 98 41W
Rangia, India .... **67 F17** 26 28N 91 38 E
Rangiora, N.Z. ...... **91 K4** 43 19 S 172 36 E
Rangitaiki →, N.Z. .. **91 G6** 37 54 S 176 49 E
Rangitata →, N.Z. .. **91 K3** 43 45 S 171 15 E
Rangkasbitung,
Indonesia .... **63 G12** 6 21 S 106 15 E
Rangon →, Burma ... **67 L20** 16 28N 96 40 E
Rangoon, Burma .... **67 L20** 16 45N 96 20 E
Rangpur, Bangla. .... **67 G16** 25 42N 89 22 E
Rangsit, Thailand .... **64 F3** 13 59N 100 37 E
Ranibennur, India .... **66 M9** 14 35N 75 30 E
Raniganj, Ut. P., India **69 F9** 27 3N 82 13 E
Raniganj, W. Bengal,
India .... **67 H15** 23 40N 87 5 E
Ranikhet, India ..... **69 E8** 29 39N 79 25 E
Raniwara, India ..... **68 G8** 24 50N 72 10 E
Rānīya, Iraq .... **70 B5** 36 15N 44 53 E
Ranka, India .... **69 H10** 23 59N 83 47 E
Ranken →, Australia . **94 C2** 20 31 S 137 36 E
Rankin, U.S.A. **113 K4** 31 13N 101 56W

Rankin Inlet, Canada . **100 B10** 62 30N 93 0W
Rankins Springs,
Australia .... **95 E4** 33 49 S 146 14 E
Rankweil, Austria .... **26 D2** 47 17N 9 39 E
Rannoch, L., U.K. **13 E4** 56 41N 4 20W
Rannoch Moor, U.K. .. **13 E4** 56 38N 4 48W
Ranobe, Helodranon' i,
Madag. .... **89 C7** 23 3 S 43 33 E
Ranohira, Madag. .... **89 C8** 22 29 S 45 24 E
Ranomafana,
Toamasina, Madag. . **89 B8** 18 57 S 48 50 E
Ranomafana, Toliara,
Madag. .... **89 C8** 24 34 S 47 0 E
Ranomafana △, Madag. **89 C8** 21 16 S 47 25 E
Ranomena △, Madag. . **89 C8** 23 25 S 47 17 E
Ranong, Thailand .... **65 H2** 9 56N 98 40 E
Ranotsara Nord, Madag. **89 C8** 22 48 S 46 36 E
Rânsa, Iran .... **71 C6** 33 39N 48 18 E
Ransiki, Indonesia ... **63 E8** 1 30 S 134 10 E
Rantabe, Madag. ..... **89 B8** 15 42 S 49 39 E
Rantauprapat, Indonesia **62 D1** 2 15N 99 50 E
Rantemario, Indonesia . **63 E5** 3 15 S 119 57 E
Rantoul, U.S.A. **114 E1** 40 19N 88 9W
Ranum, Denmark .... **11 H3** 56 54N 9 14 E
Ranyah, W. →,
Si. Arabia .... **80 C5** 21 18N 43 20 E
Raon l'Étape, France .. **19 D13** 48 24N 6 50 E
Raoping, China ...... **59 F11** 23 42N 117 1 E
Raoyang, China ...... **56 E8** 38 15N 115 45 E
Rap, Ko, Thailand .... **65 b** 9 19N 99 58 E
Rapa, French Polynesia **97 K13** 27 35 S 144 20W
Rapa Nui = Pascua, I.
de, Chile .... **97 K17** 27 7 S 109 23W
Rapallo, Italy .... **40 D6** 44 21N 9 14 E
Rapar, India .... **68 H4** 23 34N 70 38 E
Rāpch, Iran .... **71 E8** 25 40N 59 15 E
Raper, C., Canada **101 B13** 69 44N 67 6W
Rapid City, U.S.A. ... **112 D3** 44 5N 103 14W
Rapid River, U.S.A. .. **114 C2** 45 55N 86 58W
Rapla, Estonia ...... **9 G21** 59 1N 24 52 E
Rapti →, India ..... **69 F10** 26 18N 83 41 E
Rapu Rapu I., Phil. ... **61 E6** 13 12N 124 9 E
Raqaba ez Zarqa →,
Sudan .... **81 F2** 9 14N 29 44 E
Raquette →, U.S.A. . **117 B10** 45 0N 74 42W
Raquette Lake, U.S.A. **117 C10** 43 49N 74 40W
Rarotonga, Cook Is. .. **97 K12** 21 30 S 160 0W
Ra's al 'Ayn, Syria ... **70 B4** 36 45N 40 12 E
Ra's al Khaymah,
U.A.E. .... **71 E7** 25 50N 55 59 E
Râs el Mâ, Mali **82 B4** 16 35N 4 30W
Râs Ghârib, Egypt ... **80 B3** 28 6N 33 18 E
Râs Mallap, Egypt ... **80 B3** 29 18N 32 50 E
Râs Muhammad △,
Egypt .... **80 B3** 27 45N 34 16 E
Rasca, Pta. de la,
Canary Is. **48 G3** 27 59N 16 41W
Râşcani, Moldova .... **29 C12** 47 59N 27 33 E
Raseiniai, Lithuania .. **9 J20** 55 25N 23 5 E
Rashad, Sudan ...... **81 E3** 11 55N 31 0 E
Rashîd, Egypt .... **80 H7** 31 21N 30 22 E
Rashîd, Masabb, Egypt **80 H7** 31 22N 30 17 E
Rashmi, India .... **68 G6** 25 4N 74 22 E
Rasht, Iran .... **71 B6** 37 20N 49 40 E
Rasi Salai, Thailand .. **64 E5** 15 20N 104 9 E
Raška, Serbia & M. ... **44 C4** 43 19N 20 39 E
Râsnov, Romania .... **29 E10** 45 35N 25 27 E
Rason L., Australia ... **93 E3** 28 45 S 124 25 E
Raşova, Romania .... **29 F12** 44 15N 27 55 E
Rasovo, Bulgaria .... **44 C7** 43 42N 23 17 E
Rasra, India .... **69 G10** 25 50N 83 50 E
Rasskazovo, Russia .. **34 D5** 52 35N 41 50 E
Rast, Romania ...... **29 G8** 43 53N 23 16 E
Rastatt, Germany .... **25 G4** 48 50N 8 11 E
Rastede, Germany ... **24 B4** 53 15N 8 12 E
Răstoliţa, Romania .. **29 D9** 46 59N 24 58 E
Rasul, Pakistan ..... **68 C5** 32 42N 73 34 E
Raszków, Poland .... **31 G4** 51 43N 17 40 E
Rat Buri, Thailand ... **64 F2** 13 30N 99 54 E
Rat Islands, U.S.A. .. **100 C1** 52 0N 178 0 E
Rat L., Canada **103 B9** 56 10N 99 40W
Ratangarh, India .... **68 E6** 28 5N 74 35 E
Raţāwī, Iraq .... **70 D5** 30 38N 47 13 E
Rath, India .... **69 G8** 25 36N 79 37 E
Rath Luirc, Ireland ... **12 D3** 52 21N 8 40W
Rathdrum, Ireland ... **12 D5** 52 56N 6 14W
Rathenow, Germany .. **24 C8** 52 37N 12 19 E
Rathkeale, Ireland ... **12 D3** 52 32N 8 56W
Rathlin I., U.K. **12 A5** 55 18N 6 14W
Rathmelton, Ireland .. **12 A4** 55 2N 7 38W
Ratibor = Racibórz,
Poland .... **31 H5** 50 7N 18 18 E
Rätikon, Austria ..... **26 D2** 47 0N 9 55 E
Ratingen, Germany ... **24 D2** 51 18N 6 52 E
Ratlam, India .... **68 H6** 23 20N 75 0 E
Ratnagiri, India ..... **66 L8** 16 57N 73 18 E
Ratodero, Pakistan ... **68 F3** 27 48N 68 18 E
Raton, U.S.A. **113 G2** 36 54N 104 24W
Rattaphum, Thailand . **65 J3** 7 8N 100 16 E
Ratten, Austria ...... **26 D8** 47 28N 15 44 E
Rattray Hd., U.K. **13 D7** 57 38N 1 50W
Rättvik, Sweden ..... **10 D9** 60 52N 15 7 E
Ratz, Mt., Canada ... **102 B2** 57 23N 132 12W
Ratzeburg, Germany . **24 B6** 53 40N 10 46 E
Raub, Malaysia ..... **65 L3** 3 47N 101 52 E
Rauch, Argentina .... **126 D4** 36 45 S 59 5W
Raudales de Malpaso,
Mexico **119 D6** 17 30N 23 30W
Raufarhöfn, Iceland .. **8 C6** 66 27N 15 57W
Raufoss, Norway .... **9 F14** 60 44N 10 37 E
Raukumara Ra., N.Z. . **91 H6** 38 5 S 177 55 E
Rauma, Finland ..... **9 F19** 61 10N 21 30 E
Raumo = Rauma,
Finland .... **9 F19** 61 10N 21 30 E
Raung, Gunung,
Indonesia .... **63 J17** 8 8 S 114 3 E
Raurkela, India ..... **69 H11** 22 14N 84 50 E
Rausu-Dake, Japan .. **54 B12** 44 4N 145 7 E
Răut →, Moldova ... **29 C14** 47 15N 28 7 E
Rava-Ruska, Ukraine . **31 H10** 50 15N 23 42 E
Rava Russkaya = Rava-
Ruska, Ukraine .... **31 H10** 50 15N 23 42 E
Ravalli, U.S.A. **108 C6** 47 17N 114 11W
Ravānsar, Iran ...... **70 C5** 34 43N 46 40 E
Ravanusa, Italy ..... **42 E6** 37 16N 13 58 E
Rāvar, Iran .... **71 D8** 31 20N 56 51 E
Ravena, U.S.A. **117 D11** 42 28N 73 49W
Ravenna, Italy ...... **41 D9** 44 25N 12 12 E
Ravenna, Nebr., U.S.A. **112 E5** 41 1N 98 55W
Ravenna, Ohio, U.S.A. **116 E3** 41 9N 81 15W
Ravensburg, Germany **25 H5** 47 46N 9 36 E
Ravenshoe, Australia . **94 B4** 17 37 S 145 29 E
Ravensthorpe, Australia **93 F3** 33 35 S 120 2 E
Ravenswood, Australia **94 C4** 20 6 S 146 54 E
Ravenswood, U.S.A. . **114 F5** 38 57N 81 46W
Ravi →, Pakistan .... **68 D4** 30 35N 71 49 E

Ravna Gora, Croatia .. **41 C11** 45 24N 14 50 E
Ravna Reka,
Serbia & M. .... **44 B5** 44 1N 21 35 E
Ravne na Koroškem,
Slovenia .... **41 B11** 46 36N 14 59 E
Rawa Mazowiecka,
Poland .... **31 G7** 51 46N 20 12 E
Rawalpindi, Pakistan . **68 C5** 33 38N 73 8 E
Rawāndūz, Iraq ..... **70 B5** 36 40N 44 30 E
Rawang, Malaysia ... **65 L3** 3 20N 101 35 E
Rawene, N.Z. .... **91 F4** 35 25 S 173 32 E
Rawicz, Poland ...... **31 G3** 51 36N 16 52 E
Rawlinna, Australia .. **93 F4** 30 58 S 125 28 E
Rawlins, U.S.A. **108 F10** 41 47N 107 14W
Rawson, Argentina ... **128 E3** 43 15 S 65 5W
Raxaul, India .... **69 F11** 26 59N 84 51 E
Ray, U.S.A. **112 A3** 48 21N 103 10W
Ray, C., Canada **105 C8** 47 33N 59 15W
Raya Ring, Ko, Thailand **65 b** 8 18N 98 29 E
Rayadurg, India ..... **66 M10** 14 40N 76 50 E
Rayagada, India ..... **67 K13** 19 15N 83 20 E
Raychikhinsk, Russia . **53 E13** 49 46N 129 25 E
Rāyen, Iran .... **71 D8** 29 34N 57 26 E
Rayleigh, U.K. ...... **15 F8** 51 36N 0 37 E
Raymond, Canada ... **102 D6** 49 30N 112 35W
Raymond, Calif., U.S.A. **110 H7** 37 13N 119 54W
Raymond, N.H., U.S.A. **117 C13** 43 2N 71 11W
Raymond, Wash., U.S.A. **110 D3** 46 41N 123 44W
Raymondville, U.S.A. **113 M6** 26 29N 97 47W
Raymore, Canada **103 C8** 51 25N 104 31W
Rayón, Mexico **118 B2** 29 43N 110 35W
Rayong, Thailand .... **64 F3** 12 40N 101 20 E
Rayville, U.S.A. **113 J9** 32 29N 91 46W
Raz, Pte. du, France . **18 D2** 48 2N 4 47W
Razan, Iran .... **71 C6** 35 23N 49 2 E
Ražana, Serbia & M. . **44 B4** 44 6N 19 55 E
Ražanj, Serbia & M. .. **44 C5** 43 40N 21 31 E
Razāzah, Buḩayrat ar,
Iraq .... **70 C4** 32 40N 43 35 E
Razāzah, L. = Razāzah,
Buḩayrat ar, Iraq .. **70 C4** 32 40N 43 35 E
Razdelna, Bulgaria ... **45 C11** 43 13N 27 41 E
Razdel'naya = Rozdilna,
Ukraine .... **29 D15** 46 50N 30 2 E
Razdolnoye, Russia .. **54 C5** 43 30N 131 52 E
Razdolnoye, Ukraine . **33 K7** 45 46N 33 29 E
Razeh, Iran .... **71 C6** 32 47N 48 9 E
Razgrad, Bulgaria ... **45 C10** 43 33N 26 34 E
Razim, Lacul, Romania **29 F14** 44 50N 29 0 E
Razlog, Bulgaria .... **44 E7** 41 53N 23 28 E
Razmak, Pakistan ... **68 C3** 32 45N 69 50 E
Ré, Î. de, France **20 B2** 46 12N 1 30W
Reading, U.K. **15 F7** 51 27N 0 58W
Reading, U.S.A. **117 F9** 40 20N 75 56W
Reading □, U.K. **15 F7** 51 27N 0 58W
Realicó, Argentina ... **126 D3** 35 0 S 64 15W
Réalmont, France .... **20 E6** 43 48N 2 10 E
Ream, Cambodia .... **65 G4** 10 34N 103 39 E
Reata, Mexico **118 B4** 26 8N 101 5W
Reay Forest, U.K. **13 C4** 58 22N 4 55W
Rebais, France ...... **19 D10** 48 50N 3 10 E
Rebi, Indonesia ..... **63 F8** 6 23 S 134 7 E
Rebiana, Libya ...... **79 D10** 24 12N 22 10 E
Rebiana, Sahrâ', Libya **79 D10** 24 30N 21 0 E
Rebun-Tō, Japan .... **54 B10** 45 23N 141 2 E
Recanati, Italy ...... **41 E10** 43 24N 13 32 E
Recaş, Romania ..... **28 E6** 45 46N 21 30 E
Recco, Italy .... **40 D6** 44 22N 9 9 E
Recherche, Arch. of the,
Australia .... **95 E2** 32 48 S 138 10 E
Rechna Doab, Pakistan **68 D5** 31 35N 73 30 E
Rechytsa, Belarus ... **33 F6** 52 21N 30 24 E
Recife, Brazil .... **125 E12** 8 0 S 35 0W
Recklinghausen,
Germany .... **17 C7** 51 37N 7 12 E
Reconquista, Argentina **126 B4** 29 10 S 59 45W
Recreo, Argentina ... **126 B2** 29 25 S 65 10W
Recz, Poland .... **31 E2** 53 16N 15 31 E
Red →, La., U.S.A. . **113 K9** 31 1N 91 45W
Red →, N. Dak., U.S.A. **100 C10** 49 0N 97 15W
Red Bank, U.S.A. ... **117 F10** 40 21N 74 5W
Red Bay, Canada **105 B8** 51 44N 56 25W
Red Bluff, U.S.A. **108 F2** 40 11N 122 15W
Red Bluff L., U.S.A. .. **113 K3** 31 54N 103 55W
Red Cliffs, Australia .. **95 E3** 34 19 S 142 11 E
Red Cloud, U.S.A. ... **112 E5** 40 5N 98 32W
Red Creek, U.S.A. ... **117 C8** 43 14N 76 45W
Red Deer, Canada ... **102 C6** 52 20N 113 50W
Red Deer →, Alta.,
Canada **103 C7** 50 58N 110 0W
Red Deer →, Man.,
Canada **103 C8** 52 53N 101 1W
Red Deer L., Canada . **103 C8** 52 55N 101 20W
Red Hook, U.S.A. ... **117 E11** 41 55N 73 53W
Red Indian L., Canada **105 C8** 48 35N 57 0W
Red L., Canada **103 C10** 51 3N 93 49W
Red Lake, Canada ... **103 C10** 51 3N 93 49W
Red Lake Falls, U.S.A. **112 B6** 47 53N 96 16W
Red Lake Road, Canada **103 C10** 49 59N 93 25W
Red Lodge, U.S.A. .. **108 D9** 45 11N 109 15W
Red Mountain, U.S.A. **111 K9** 35 37N 117 38W
Red Oak, U.S.A. **112 E7** 41 1N 95 14W
Red Rock, Canada ... **104 C2** 48 55N 88 15W
Red Rock, L., U.S.A. . **112 E8** 41 22N 92 59W
Red Rocks Pt., Australia **93 F4** 32 13 S 127 32 E
Red Sea, Asia ...... **75 C2** 25 0N 36 0 E
Red Slate Mt., U.S.A. **110 H8** 37 31N 118 52W
Red Sucker L., Canada **104 B1** 54 9N 93 40W
Red Tower Pass = Turnu
Roşu, P., Romania . **29 E9** 45 33N 24 17 E
Red Wing, U.S.A. ... **112 C8** 44 34N 92 31W
Reda, Poland .... **30 D5** 54 40N 18 19 E
Redang, Malaysia ... **65 K4** 5 49N 103 2 E
Redange, Lux. ...... **17 E5** 49 46N 5 52 E
Redcar, U.K. **14 C6** 54 37N 1 4W
Redcar & Cleveland □,
U.K. **14 C7** 54 29N 1 0W
Redcliff, Canada **103 C6** 50 10N 110 50W
Redcliffe, Australia .. **95 D5** 27 12 S 153 0 E
Redcliffe, Mt., Australia **93 E3** 28 30 S 121 30 E
Redding, U.S.A. **108 F2** 40 35N 122 24W
Redditch, U.K. **15 E6** 52 18N 1 55W
Redfield, U.S.A. **112 C5** 44 53N 98 31W
Redford, U.S.A. **117 B11** 44 38N 73 48W
Redhead, Trin. & Tob. **125 K16** 10 48N 60 3W
Redkino, Russia ..... **32 D9** 56 36N 36 16 E
Redlands, U.S.A. **111 M9** 34 4N 117 11W
Redmond, Oreg., U.S.A. **108 D3** 44 17N 121 11W
Redmond, Wash., U.S.A. **110 C4** 47 41N 122 7W
Redon, France **18 E4** 47 40N 2 6W
Redonda, Antigua & B. **121 C7** 16 58N 62 19W
Redondela, Spain ... **36 C2** 42 15N 8 38W
Redondo, Portugal ... **37 G3** 38 39N 7 37W
Redondo Beach, U.S.A. **111 M8** 33 50N 118 23W

Redruth, U.K. **15 G2** 50 14N 5 14W
Redvers, Canada **103 D8** 49 35N 101 40W
Redwater, Canada ... **102 C6** 53 55N 113 6W
Redwood, U.S.A. **117 B9** 44 18N 75 48W
Redwood City, U.S.A. **110 H4** 37 30N 122 15W
Redwood Falls, U.S.A. **112 C7** 44 32N 95 7W
Ree, L., Ireland **12 C3** 53 35N 8 0W
Reed, L., Canada **103 C8** 54 38N 100 30W
Reed City, U.S.A. **114 D3** 43 53N 85 31W
Reedley, U.S.A. **110 J7** 36 36N 119 27W
Reedsburg, U.S.A. .. **112 D9** 43 32N 90 0W
Reedsport, U.S.A. ... **108 E1** 43 42N 124 6W
Reedsville, U.S.A. ... **116 F7** 40 39N 77 35W
Reefton, N.Z. .... **91 K3** 42 6 S 171 51 E
Rees, Germany ...... **24 D2** 51 46N 6 24 E
Reese →, U.S.A. ... **108 F5** 40 48N 117 4W
Refahiye, Turkey .... **73 C8** 39 54N 38 47 E
Reftele, Sweden ..... **11 G7** 57 11N 13 35 E
Refugio, U.S.A. **113 L6** 28 18N 97 17W
Rega →, Poland .... **30 D2** 54 10N 15 18 E
Regen, Germany .... **25 G9** 48 58N 13 9 E
Regen →, Germany . **25 F8** 49 1N 12 6 E
Regensburg, Germany **25 F8** 49 1N 12 6 E
Regenstauf, Germany **25 F8** 49 7N 12 8 E
Reggâne = Zaouiet
Reggâne, Algeria ... **78 C6** 26 32N 0 3 E
Reggello, Italy ...... **41 E8** 43 41N 11 32 E
Réggio di Calábria, Italy **43 D8** 38 6N 15 39 E
Réggio nell'Emília, Italy **40 D7** 44 43N 10 36 E
Reghin, Romania .... **29 D9** 46 46N 24 42 E
Regina, Canada **103 C8** 50 27N 104 35W
Regina Beach, Canada **103 C8** 50 47N 105 0W
Registro, Brazil ..... **127 A6** 24 29 S 47 49W
Reguengos de
Monsaraz, Portugal **37 G3** 38 25N 7 32W
Rehar →, India ..... **69 H10** 23 55N 82 40 E
Rehli, India .... **69 H8** 23 38N 79 5 E
Rehoboth, Namibia .. **88 C2** 23 15 S 17 4 E
Rehovot, Israel ..... **74 D3** 31 54N 34 48 E
Reichenbach, Germany **24 E8** 50 37N 12 17 E
Reid, Australia ...... **93 F4** 30 49 S 128 26 E
Reidsville, U.S.A. **115 G6** 36 21N 79 40W
Reigate, U.K. **15 F7** 51 14N 0 12W
Reillo, Spain **38 F3** 39 54N 1 53W
Reims, France ...... **19 C11** 49 15N 4 1 E
Reina Adelaida, Arch.,
Chile .... **128 G2** 52 20 S 74 0W
Reina Sofía, Tenerife ✈
(TFS), Canary Is. .. **48 F3** 28 3N 16 33W
Reinbek, Germany ... **24 B6** 53 30N 10 16 E
Reindeer →, Canada **103 B8** 55 36N 103 11W
Reindeer I., Canada .. **103 C9** 52 30N 98 0W
Reindeer L., Canada . **103 B8** 57 15N 102 15W
Reinga, C., N.Z. ..... **91 F4** 34 35 S 172 43 E
Reinosa, Spain **36 B6** 43 2N 4 15W
Reitz, S. Africa ...... **89 D4** 27 48 S 28 29 E
Reivilo, S. Africa .... **88 D3** 27 36 S 24 8 E
Rejaf, Sudan .... **81 G3** 4 48N 31 35 E
Rejmyre, Sweden ... **11 F9** 58 50N 15 55 E
Rejowiec Fabryczny,
Poland .... **31 G10** 51 5N 23 17 E
Reka →, Slovenia ... **41 C11** 45 40N 14 0 E
Rekovac, Serbia & M. **44 C5** 43 51N 21 3 E
Reliance, Canada **103 A7** 63 0N 109 20W
Rémalard, France .... **18 D7** 48 26N 0 47 E
Remarkable, Mt.,
Australia .... **95 E2** 32 48 S 138 10 E
Rembang, Indonesia . **63 G14** 6 42 S 111 21 E
Remedios, Panama .. **120 E3** 8 15N 81 50W
Remeshk, Iran ...... **71 E8** 26 55N 58 50 E
Remetea, Romania .. **29 D10** 46 45N 25 29 E
Remich, Lux. .... **17 E6** 49 32N 6 22 E
Remiremont, France . **19 D13** 48 2N 6 36 E
Remo, Ethiopia ..... **81 F5** 6 48N 41 20 E
Remontnoye, Russia . **35 G6** 46 34N 43 37 E
Remoulins, France .. **21 E8** 43 55N 4 35 E
Remscheid, Germany **17 C7** 51 11N 7 12 E
Ren Xian, China ..... **56 F8** 37 8N 114 40 E
Rendang, Indonesia . **63 J18** 8 26 S 115 25 E
Rende, Italy .... **43 C9** 39 20N 16 11 E
Rendína, Greece .... **46 B3** 39 4N 21 58 E
Rendsburg, Germany **24 A5** 54 17N 9 39 E
Renfrew, Canada **117 A8** 45 30N 76 40W
Renfrewshire □, U.K. **13 F4** 55 49N 4 38W
Rengat, Indonesia ... **62 E2** 0 30 S 102 45 E
Rengo, Chile .... **126 C1** 34 24 S 70 50W
Renhua, China ...... **59 E9** 25 5N 113 40 E
Renhuai, China ..... **58 D6** 27 48N 106 24 E
Renk, Sudan .... **81 E3** 11 50N 32 50 E
Renmark, Australia .. **95 E3** 34 11 S 140 43 E
Rennell Sd., Canada . **102 C2** 53 23N 132 35W
Renner Springs,
Australia .... **94 B1** 18 20 S 133 47 E
Rennes, France **18 D5** 48 7N 1 41W
Rennie L., Canada ... **103 A7** 61 32N 105 35W
Reno, U.S.A. **110 F7** 39 31N 119 48W
Reno →, Italy ...... **41 D9** 44 38N 12 16 E
Renovo, U.S.A. **116 E7** 41 20N 77 45W
Renqiu, China ...... **56 E9** 38 43N 116 5 E
Rens, Denmark ..... **11 K3** 54 54N 9 5 E
Renshou, China ..... **58 C5** 30 3N 104 9 E
Rensselaer, Ind., U.S.A. **114 E2** 40 57N 87 9W
Rensselaer, N.Y., U.S.A. **117 D11** 42 38N 73 45W
Rentería, Spain **38 B3** 43 19N 1 54W
Renton, U.S.A. **110 C4** 47 29N 122 12W
Réo, Burkina Faso ... **82 C4** 12 28N 2 35W
Reocín, Spain **36 B6** 43 21N 4 5W
Reotipur, India ..... **69 G10** 25 33N 83 45 E
Repalle, India ...... **67 L12** 16 2N 80 45 E
Repcelak, Hungary .. **28 C2** 47 24N 17 1 E
Republic, Wash., U.S.A. **108 B4** 48 39N 118 44W
Republican →, U.S.A. **112 F6** 39 4N 96 48W
Repulse B., Australia . **94 J6** 20 35 S 148 46 E
Repulse Bay, Canada **101 B11** 66 30N 86 30W
Requena, Peru ...... **124 E4** 5 5 S 73 52W
Requena, Spain **39 F3** 39 30N 1 4W
Réquista, France .... **20 D6** 44 2N 2 33 E
Reşadiye = Datça,
Turkey .... **47 E9** 36 46N 27 40 E
Reşadiye, Turkey .... **72 B7** 40 23N 37 20 E
Reşadiye Yarımadası,
Turkey .... **47 E9** 36 40N 27 45 E
Resavica, Serbia & M. **44 B5** 44 5N 21 59 E
Resen, Macedonia ... **44 E5** 41 5N 21 0 E
Reserve, U.S.A. **109 K9** 33 43N 108 45W
Resht = Rasht, Iran .. **71 B6** 37 20N 49 40 E
Resistencia, Argentina **126 B4** 27 30 S 59 0W
Reşiţa, Romania .... **28 E6** 45 18N 21 53 E
Resko, Poland ...... **30 E2** 53 47N 15 25 E
Resolution I., Canada **101 B13** 61 30N 65 0W
Resolution I., N.Z. ... **91 L1** 45 40 S 166 40 E
Ressano Garcia,
Mozam. .... **89 D5** 25 25 S 32 0 E

Reston, Canada **103 D8** 49 33N 101 6W
Reszel, Poland ...... **30 D8** 54 4N 21 10 E
Retalhuleu, Guatemala **120 D1** 14 33N 91 46W
Retenue, L. de,
Dem. Rep. of
the Congo .... **87 E2** 11 0 S 27 0 E
Retezat ○, Romania . **28 E7** 45 23N 22 56 E
Retezat, Munţii,
Romania .... **28 E8** 45 25N 23 0 E
Retford, U.K. **14 D7** 53 19N 0 56W
Rethem, Germany ... **24 C5** 52 47N 9 22 E
Réthimnon, Greece .. **49 D6** 35 18N 24 30 E
Réthímnon □, Greece **49 D6** 35 23N 24 28 E
Reti, Pakistan .... **68 E3** 28 5N 69 48 E
Retiche, Alpi, Switz. .. **25 J6** 46 30N 10 0 E
Retiers, France **18 E5** 47 55N 1 23W
Retortillo, Spain **36 E4** 40 48N 6 21W
Retournac, France ... **21 C8** 45 12N 4 2 E
Rétság, Hungary .... **28 C4** 47 58N 19 10 E
Réunion ☒, Ind. Oc. . **77 J9** 21 0 S 56 0 E
Reus, Spain .... **38 D6** 41 10N 1 5 E
Reuterstadt
Stavenhagen,
Germany .... **24 B8** 53 42N 12 54 E
Reutlingen, Germany **25 G5** 48 29N 9 12 E
Reutte, Austria ..... **26 D3** 47 29N 10 42 E
Reval = Tallinn, Estonia **9 G21** 59 22N 24 48 E
Revel, France .... **20 E6** 43 28N 2 1 E
Revelganj, India .... **69 G11** 25 50N 84 40 E
Revelstoke, Canada . **102 C5** 51 0N 118 10W
Reventazón, Peru ... **124 E2** 6 10 S 80 58W
Revigny-sur-Ornain,
France .... **19 D11** 48 50N 4 59 E
Revillagigedo, Is. de,
Pac. Oc. **118 D2** 18 40N 112 0W
Revin, France .... **19 C11** 49 55N 4 39 E
Revúca, Slovak Rep. . **27 C13** 48 41N 20 7 E
Revuè →, Mozam. .. **87 F3** 19 50 S 34 0 E
Rewa, India .... **69 G9** 24 33N 81 25 E
Rewari, India .... **68 E7** 28 15N 76 40 E
Rexburg, U.S.A. **108 E8** 43 49N 111 47W
Rey, Iran .... **71 C6** 35 35N 51 25 E
Rey, I. del, Panama .. **120 E4** 8 20N 78 30W
Rey Malabo, Eq. Guin. **83 E6** 3 45N 8 50 E
Reyðarfjörður, Iceland **8 D6** 65 2N 14 13W
Reyes, Pt., U.S.A. .. **110 H3** 38 0N 123 0W
Reyhanlı, Turkey .... **72 D7** 36 16N 36 35 E
Reykjahlíð, Iceland .. **8 D5** 65 40N 16 55W
Reykjanes, Iceland .. **8 E2** 63 48N 22 40W
Reykjavík, Iceland ... **8 D3** 64 10N 21 57W
Reynolds Ra., Australia **92 D5** 22 30 S 133 0 E
Reynoldsville, U.S.A. **116 E6** 41 5N 78 58W
Reynosa, Mexico ... **119 B5** 26 5N 98 18W
Rēzekne, Latvia ..... **9 H22** 56 30N 27 17 E
Rezina, Moldova .... **29 C13** 47 45N 28 58 E
Rezovo, Bulgaria ... **45 D12** 42 0N 28 0 E
Rezvān, Iran .... **71 E8** 27 34N 56 6 E
Rgotina, Serbia & M. **44 B6** 44 1N 22 17 E
Rhamnus, Greece ... **46 C6** 38 12N 24 3 E
Rhayader, U.K. **15 E4** 52 18N 3 29W
Rheda-Wiedenbrück,
Germany .... **24 D4** 51 50N 8 20 E
Rhede, Germany .... **24 D2** 51 50N 6 42 E
Rhein →, Europe ... **17 C6** 51 52N 6 2 E
Rhein-Main-Donau-
Kanal, Germany ... **25 F7** 49 1N 11 27 E
Rhein-Ruhr,
Düsseldorf ✈ (DUS),
Germany .... **24 D2** 51 17N 6 46 E
Rhein-Taunus ○,
Germany .... **25 E4** 50 10N 8 10 E
Rhein-Westerwald ○,
Germany .... **24 E3** 50 32N 7 20 E
Rheinbach, Germany **24 E2** 50 38N 6 57 E
Rheine, Germany ... **24 C3** 52 17N 7 26 E
Rheinfelden, Germany **25 H3** 47 33N 7 47 E
Rheinhessen-Pfalz □,
Germany .... **25 F3** 49 20N 8 0 E
Rheinland-Pfalz □,
Germany .... **25 E2** 50 0N 7 0 E
Rheinsberg, Germany **24 B8** 53 6N 12 54 E
Rhin = Rhein →,
Europe .... **17 C6** 51 52N 6 2 E
Rhine = Rhein →,
Europe .... **17 C6** 51 52N 6 2 E
Rhinebeck, U.S.A. .. **117 E11** 41 56N 73 55W
Rhineland-Palatinate =
Rheinland-Pfalz □,
Germany .... **25 E2** 50 0N 7 0 E
Rhinelander, U.S.A. . **112 C10** 45 38N 89 25W
Rhinns Pt., U.K. **13 F2** 55 40N 6 29W
Rhino Camp, Uganda **86 B3** 3 0N 31 22 E
Rhir, Cap, Morocco .. **78 B4** 30 38N 9 54W
Rho, Italy .... **40 C6** 45 32N 9 2 E
Rhode Island □, U.S.A. **117 E13** 41 40N 71 30W
Rhodes = Ródhos,
Greece .... **49 C10** 36 15N 28 10 E
Rhodope Mts. =
Rhodopi Planina,
Bulgaria .... **45 E8** 41 40N 24 20 E
Rhodopi Planina,
Bulgaria .... **45 E8** 41 40N 24 20 E
Rhön, Germany ..... **24 E5** 50 24N 9 58 E
Rhondda, U.K. **15 F4** 51 39N 3 31W
Rhondda Cynon Taff □,
U.K. **15 F4** 51 42N 3 27W
Rhône □, France .... **21 C8** 45 54N 4 35 E
Rhône →, France ... **21 E8** 43 28N 4 42 E
Rhône-Alpes □, France **21 C9** 45 40N 6 0 E
Rhum, U.K. **13 E2** 57 0N 6 20W
Rhyl, U.K. **14 D4** 53 20N 3 29W
Ri-Aba, Eq. Guin. ... **83 E6** 3 28N 8 40 E
Ria Formosa ○,
Portugal **37 H3** 37 1N 7 48W
Riachão, Brazil ..... **125 E9** 7 20 S 46 37W
Riangnom, Sudan ... **81 F3** 9 55N 30 1 E
Riaño, Spain **36 C6** 42 59N 4 59W
Riansáres →, Spain . **39 F1** 39 32N 3 18W
Riasi, India .... **69 C6** 33 10N 74 50 E
Riau □, Indonesia ... **62 D2** 0 0 102 35 E
Riau, Kepulauan,
Indonesia .... **62 D2** 0 30N 104 20 E
Riau Arch. = Riau,
Kepulauan, Indonesia **62 D2** 0 30N 104 20 E
Riaza, Spain **30 D7** 41 18N 3 29W
Riaza →, Spain **36 D7** 41 42N 3 55W
Riba de Saelices, Spain **38 E2** 40 55N 2 17W
Riba-Roja de Turia,
Spain **39 F4** 39 33N 0 34W
Ribadavia, Spain **36 C2** 42 17N 8 8W
Ribadeo, Spain **36 B3** 43 35N 7 5W
Ribadesella, Spain .. **36 B5** 43 30N 5 7W
Ribado, Cameroon .. **83 D7** 9 16N 12 47 E
Ribao, Cameroon ... **83 D7** 8 28N 11 30 E
Ribas = Ribes de Freser,
Spain .... **38 C7** 42 19N 2 15 E

Ribas do Rio Pardo, Brazil **125 H8** 20 27 S 53 46W
Ribauè, Mozam. **87 E4** 14 57 S 38 17 E
Ribble →, U.K. **14 D5** 53 52N 2 25W
Ribe, Denmark **11 J2** 55 19N 8 44 E
Ribe Amtskommune □, Denmark **11 J2** 55 35N 8 45 E
Ribeauvillé, France **19 D14** 48 10N 7 20 E
Ribécourt-Dreslincourt, France **19 C9** 49 30N 2 55 E
Ribeira = Santa Uxía, Spain **36 C2** 42 36N 8 58W
Ribeira Brava, Madeira **48 D2** 32 41N 17 4W
Ribeirão Prêto, Brazil **127 A6** 21 10 S 47 50W
Ribemont, France **19 C10** 49 47N 3 27 E
Ribera, Italy **42 E6** 37 30N 13 16 E
Ribérac, France **20 C4** 45 15N 0 20 E
Riberalta, Bolivia **124 F5** 11 0 S 66 0W
Ribes de Freser, Spain **38 C7** 42 19N 2 15 E
Ribnica, Slovenia **41 C11** 45 45N 14 45 E
Ribnitz-Damgarten, Germany **24 A8** 54 15N 12 27 E
Ričany, Czech Rep. **26 B7** 50 0N 14 40 E
Riccarton, N.Z. **91 K4** 43 32 S 172 37 E
Ríccia, Italy **43 A7** 41 30N 14 50 E
Riccione, Italy **41 E9** 43 59N 12 39 E
Rice, U.S.A. **111 L12** 34 5N 114 51W
Rice L., Canada **116 B6** 44 12N 78 10W
Rice Lake, U.S.A. **112 C9** 45 30N 91 44W
Rich, C., Canada **116 B4** 44 43N 80 38W
Richard Toll, Senegal **82 B1** 16 25N 15 42W
Richards Bay, S. Africa **89 D5** 28 48 S 32 6 E
Richardson →, Canada **103 B6** 58 25N 111 14W
Richardson Lakes, U.S.A. **114 C10** 44 46N 70 58W
Richardson Springs, U.S.A. **110 F5** 39 51N 121 46W
Riche, C., Australia **93 F2** 34 36 S 118 47 E
Richelieu, France **18 E7** 47 1N 0 20 E
Richey, U.S.A. **112 B2** 47 39N 105 4W
Richfield, U.S.A. **109 G8** 38 46N 112 5W
Richfield Springs, U.S.A. **117 D10** 42 51N 74 59W
Richford, U.S.A. **117 B12** 45 0N 72 40W
Richibucto, Canada **105 C7** 46 42N 64 54W
Richland, Ga., U.S.A. **115 J3** 32 5N 84 40W
Richland, Wash., U.S.A. **108 C4** 46 17N 119 18W
Richland Center, U.S.A. **112 D9** 43 21N 90 23W
Richlands, U.S.A. **114 G5** 37 6N 81 48W
Richmond, Australia **94 C3** 20 43 S 143 8 E
Richmond, N.Z. **91 J4** 41 20 S 173 12 E
Richmond, U.K. **14 C6** 54 25N 1 43W
Richmond, Calif., U.S.A. **110 H4** 37 56N 122 21W
Richmond, Ind., U.S.A. **114 F3** 39 50N 84 53W
Richmond, Ky., U.S.A. **114 G3** 37 45N 84 18W
Richmond, Mich., U.S.A. **116 D2** 42 49N 82 45W
Richmond, Mo., U.S.A. **112 F8** 39 17N 93 58W
Richmond, Tex., U.S.A. **113 L7** 29 35N 95 46W
Richmond, Utah, U.S.A. **108 F8** 41 56N 111 48W
Richmond, Va., U.S.A. **114 G7** 37 33N 77 27W
Richmond, Vt., U.S.A. **117 B12** 44 24N 72 59W
Richmond Hill, Canada **116 C5** 43 52N 79 27W
Richmond Ra., Australia **95 D5** 29 0 S 152 45 E
Richtersveld △, S. Africa **88 D2** 28 15 S 17 10 E
Richwood, U.S.A. **114 F5** 38 14N 80 32W
Ricla, Spain **38 D3** 41 31N 1 24W
Ridder = Leninogorsk, Kazakhstan **52 D9** 50 20N 83 30 E
Riddlesburg, U.S.A. **116 F6** 40 9N 78 15W
Ridgecrest, U.S.A. **111 K9** 35 38N 117 40W
Ridgefield, Conn., U.S.A. **117 E11** 41 17N 73 30W
Ridgefield, Wash., U.S.A. **110 E4** 45 49N 122 45W
Ridgeland, U.S.A. **115 J5** 32 29N 80 59W
Ridgetown, Canada **116 D3** 42 26N 81 52W
Ridgewood, U.S.A. **117 F10** 40 59N 74 7W
Ridgway, U.S.A. **116 E6** 41 25N 78 44W
Riding Mountain △, Canada **103 C9** 50 50N 100 0W
Ridley, Mt., Australia **93 F3** 33 12 S 122 7 E
Riebeek-Oos, S. Africa **88 E4** 33 10 S 26 10 E
Ried, Austria **26 C6** 48 14N 13 30 E
Riedlingen, Germany **25 G5** 48 9N 9 28 E
Riedstadt, Germany **25 F4** 49 45N 8 30 E
Rienza →, Italy **41 B8** 46 49N 11 47 E
Riesa, Germany **24 D9** 51 17N 13 17 E
Riesi, Italy **43 E7** 37 17N 14 5 E
Riet →, S. Africa **88 D3** 29 0 S 23 54 E
Rietavas, Lithuania **30 C8** 55 44N 21 56 E
Rietbron, S. Africa **88 E3** 32 54 S 23 10 E
Rietfontein, Namibia **88 C3** 21 58 S 20 58 E
Rieti, Italy **41 F9** 42 24N 12 51 E
Rieupeyroux, France **20 D6** 44 19N 2 12 E
Riez, France **21 E10** 43 49N 6 6 E
Rif = Er Rif, Morocco **78 A5** 35 1N 4 1W
Riffe L., U.S.A. **110 D4** 46 32N 122 26W
Rifle, U.S.A. **108 G10** 39 32N 107 47W
Rift Valley, Africa **76 G7** 7 0N 30 0 E
Rift Valley □, Kenya **86 B4** 0 20N 36 0 E
Rīga, Latvia **9 H21** 56 53N 24 8 E
Rīga ✈ (RIX), Latvia **30 B10** 56 54N 23 59 E
Riga, G. of, Latvia **9 H20** 57 40N 23 45 E
Rigacikun, Nigeria **83 C6** 10 40N 7 28 E
Rīgān, Iran **71 D8** 28 37N 58 58 E
Rīgas Jūras Līcis = Riga, G. of, Latvia **9 H20** 57 40N 23 45 E
Rigaud, Canada **117 A10** 45 29N 74 18W
Rigby, U.S.A. **108 E8** 43 40N 111 55W
Rīgestān, Afghan. **66 D4** 30 15N 65 0 E
Riggins, U.S.A. **108 D5** 45 25N 116 19W
Rignac, France **20 D6** 44 25N 2 16 E
Rigolet, Canada **105 B8** 54 10N 58 23W
Rihand Dam, India **69 G10** 24 9N 83 2 E
Riihimäki, Finland **9 F21** 60 45N 24 48 E
Riiser-Larsen-halvøya, Antarctica **5 C4** 68 0 S 35 0 E
Rijau, Nigeria **83 C6** 11 8N 5 17 E
Rijeka, Croatia **41 C11** 45 20N 14 21 E
Rijeka Crnojevića, Serbia & M. **44 D3** 42 24N 19 1 E
Rijssen, Neths. **17 B6** 52 19N 6 31 E
Rika →, Ukraine **29 B8** 48 11N 23 16 E
Rike, Ethiopia **81 E4** 10 50N 39 53 E
Rikuchū-Kaigan △, Japan **54 E11** 39 20N 142 0 E
Rikuzentakada, Japan **54 E10** 39 0N 141 40 E
Rila, Bulgaria **44 D7** 42 7N 23 7 E
Rila Planina, Bulgaria **44 D7** 42 10N 23 20 E
Riley, U.S.A. **108 E4** 43 32N 119 28W
Rima →, Nigeria **83 C6** 13 4N 5 10 E
Rimah, Wadi ar →, Si. Arabia **70 E4** 26 5N 41 30 E
Rimau, Pulau, Malaysia **65 c** 5 15N 100 16 E
Rimavská Sobota, Slovak Rep. **27 C13** 48 22N 20 2 E
Rimbey, Canada **102 C6** 52 35N 114 15W
Rimbo, Sweden **10 E12** 59 44N 18 21 E
Rimersburg, U.S.A. **116 E5** 41 3N 79 30W
Rimforsa, Sweden **11 F9** 58 6N 15 43 E
Rimi, Nigeria **83 C6** 12 58N 7 43 E
Rímini, Italy **41 D9** 44 3N 12 33 E
Rimouski, Canada **105 C6** 48 27N 68 30W
Rimrock, U.S.A. **110 D5** 46 38N 121 10W
Rinca, Indonesia **63 F5** 8 45 S 119 35 E
Rincón de la Victoria, Spain **37 J6** 36 43N 4 18W
Rincón de Romos, Mexico **118 C4** 22 14N 102 18W
Rinconada, Argentina **126 A2** 22 26 S 66 10W
Rind →, India **69 G9** 25 53N 80 33 E
Ringarum, Sweden **11 F10** 58 21N 16 26 E
Ringas, India **68 F6** 27 21N 75 34 E
Ringe, Denmark **11 J4** 55 13N 10 28 E
Ringim, Nigeria **83 C6** 12 13N 9 10 E
Ringkøbing, Denmark **11 H2** 56 5N 8 15 E
Ringkøbing Amtskommune □, Denmark **11 H2** 56 10N 8 45 E
Ringkøbing Fjord, Denmark **11 H2** 56 0N 8 15 E
Ringsjön, Sweden **11 J7** 55 55N 13 30 E
Ringsted, Denmark **11 J5** 55 25N 11 46 E
Ringvassøy, Norway **8 B18** 69 56N 19 15 E
Ringwood, U.S.A. **117 E10** 41 7N 74 15W
Rinía, Greece **47 D7** 37 23N 25 13 E
Rinjani, Indonesia **62 F5** 8 24 S 116 28 E
Rinteln, Germany **24 C5** 52 10N 9 8 E
Río, Punta del, Spain **39 J2** 36 49N 2 24W
Rio Branco, Brazil **124 E5** 9 58 S 67 49W
Río Branco, Uruguay **127 C5** 32 40 S 53 40W
Río Bravo ⌓, N. Amer. **118 B4** 29 2N 102 45W
Río Bravo del Norte →, Mexico **119 B5** 25 57N 97 9W
Rio Brilhante, Brazil **127 A5** 21 48 S 54 33W
Rio Claro, Brazil **127 A6** 22 19 S 47 35W
Rio Claro, Trin. & Tob. **121 D7** 10 20N 61 25W
Río Colorado, Argentina **128 D4** 39 0 S 64 0W
Río Cuarto, Argentina **126 C3** 33 10 S 64 25W
Rio das Pedras, Mozam. **89 C6** 23 8 S 35 28 E
Rio de Janeiro, Brazil **127 A7** 23 0 S 43 12W
Rio de Janeiro □, Brazil **127 A7** 22 50 S 43 0W
Rio do Sul, Brazil **127 B6** 27 13 S 49 37W
Río Dulce △, Guatemala **120 C2** 15 43N 88 50W
Río Gallegos, Argentina **128 G3** 51 35 S 69 15W
Río Grande, Argentina **128 G3** 53 50 S 67 45W
Rio Grande, Brazil **127 C5** 32 0 S 52 20W
Río Grande, Mexico **118 C4** 23 50N 103 2W
Río Grande, Nic. **120 D3** 12 54N 83 33W
Rio Grande, Puerto Rico **121 d** 18 23N 65 50W
Rio Grande, U.S.A. **113 N6** 25 58N 97 9W
Rio Grande City, U.S.A. **113 M5** 26 23N 98 49W
Río Grande de Santiago →, Mexico **118 C3** 21 36N 105 26W
Rio Grande do Norte □, Brazil **125 E11** 5 40 S 36 0W
Rio Grande do Sul □, Brazil **127 C5** 30 0 S 53 0W
Río Hato, Panama **120 E3** 8 22N 80 10W
Río Lagartos, Mexico **119 C7** 21 36N 88 10W
Rio Largo, Brazil **125 E11** 9 28 S 35 50W
Rio Maior, Portugal **37 F2** 39 19N 8 57W
Rio Marina, Italy **40 F7** 42 49N 10 25 E
Río Mulatos, Bolivia **124 G5** 19 40 S 66 50W
Río Muni □, Eq. Guin. **84 D2** 1 30N 10 0 E
Rio Negro, Brazil **127 B6** 26 0 S 49 55W
Rio Pardo, Brazil **127 C5** 30 0 S 52 30W
Río Pilcomayo △, Argentina **126 B4** 25 5 S 58 5W
Río Platano ⌓, Honduras **120 C3** 15 45N 85 0W
Rio Rancho, U.S.A. **109 J10** 35 14N 106 38W
Río Segundo, Argentina **126 C3** 31 40 S 63 59W
Río Tercero, Argentina **126 C3** 32 15 S 64 8W
Rio Tinto, Portugal **36 D2** 41 11N 8 34W
Rio Verde, Brazil **125 G8** 17 50 S 51 0W
Río Verde, Mexico **119 C5** 21 56N 99 59W
Rio Vista, U.S.A. **110 G5** 38 10N 121 42W
Ríobamba, Ecuador **124 D3** 1 50 S 78 45W
Ríohacha, Colombia **124 A4** 11 33N 72 55W
Riom, France **20 C7** 45 54N 3 7 E
Riom-ès-Montagnes, France **20 C6** 45 17N 2 39 E
Rion-des-Landes, France **20 E3** 43 55N 0 56W
Rionero in Vúlture, Italy **43 B8** 40 55N 15 40 E
Rioni →, Georgia **35 J5** 42 14N 41 44 E
Riós, Spain **36 D3** 41 58N 7 16W
Ríosucio, Colombia **124 B3** 7 27N 77 7W
Riou L., Canada **103 B7** 59 7N 106 25W
Rioz, France **19 E13** 47 26N 6 5 E
Ripatransone, Italy **41 F10** 42 59N 13 46 E
Ripley, Canada **116 B3** 44 4N 81 35W
Ripley, Calif., U.S.A. **111 M12** 33 32N 114 39W
Ripley, N.Y., U.S.A. **116 D5** 42 16N 79 43W
Ripley, Tenn., U.S.A. **113 H10** 35 45N 89 32W
Ripley, W. Va., U.S.A. **114 F5** 38 49N 81 43W
Ripoll, Spain **38 C7** 42 15N 2 13 E
Ripon, U.K. **14 C6** 54 9N 1 31W
Ripon, Calif., U.S.A. **110 H5** 37 44N 121 7W
Ripon, Wis., U.S.A. **114 D1** 43 51N 88 50W
Riposto, Italy **43 E8** 37 44N 15 12 E
Risan, Serbia & M. **44 D2** 42 32N 18 42 E
Riscle, France **20 E3** 43 39N 0 5W
Rishā', W. ar →, Si. Arabia **70 E5** 25 33N 44 5 E
Rishiri-Rebun-Sarobetsu △, Japan **54 B10** 45 26N 141 30 E
Rishiri-Tō, Japan **54 B10** 45 11N 141 15 E
Rishon le Ẕiyyon, Israel **74 D3** 31 58N 34 48 E
Risle →, France **18 C7** 49 26N 0 23 E
Risnjak △, Croatia **41 C11** 45 25N 14 36 E
Rison, U.S.A. **113 J8** 33 58N 92 11W
Risør, Norway **9 G13** 58 43N 9 13 E
Rita Blanca Cr. →, U.S.A. **113 H3** 35 40N 102 29W
Riti, Nigeria **83 D6** 7 57N 9 41 E
Ritter, Mt., U.S.A. **110 H7** 37 41N 119 12W
Rittman, U.S.A. **116 F3** 40 58N 81 47W
Ritzville, U.S.A. **108 C4** 47 8N 118 23W
Riva del Garda, Italy **40 C7** 45 53N 10 50 E
Riva Lígure, Italy **40 E4** 43 50N 7 50 E
Rivadavia, Buenos Aires, Argentina **126 D3** 35 29 S 62 59W
Rivadavia, Mendoza, Argentina **126 C2** 33 13 S 68 30W
Rivadavia, Salta, Argentina **126 A3** 24 5 S 62 54W
Rivadavia, Chile **126 B1** 29 57 S 70 35W
Rivarolo Canavese, Italy **40 C4** 45 19N 7 43 E
Rivas, Nic. **120 D2** 11 30N 85 50W
Rive-de-Gier, France **21 C8** 45 32N 4 37 E
River Cess, Liberia **82 D3** 5 30N 9 32W
River Jordan, Canada **110 B2** 48 26N 124 3W
Rivera, Argentina **126 D3** 37 12 S 63 14W
Rivera, Uruguay **127 C4** 31 0 S 55 50W
Riverbank, U.S.A. **110 H6** 37 44N 120 56W
Riverdale, U.S.A. **110 J7** 36 26N 119 52W
Riverhead, U.S.A. **117 F12** 40 55N 72 40W
Riverhurst, Canada **103 C7** 50 55N 106 50W
Rivers, Canada **103 C8** 50 2N 100 14W
Rivers □, Nigeria **83 E6** 4 30N 7 10 E
Rivers Inlet, Canada **102 C3** 51 42N 127 15W
Riversdale, S. Africa **88 E3** 34 7 S 21 15 E
Riverside, U.S.A. **111 M9** 33 59N 117 22W
Riverton, Australia **95 E2** 34 10 S 138 46 E
Riverton, Canada **103 C9** 51 1N 97 0W
Riverton, N.Z. **91 M2** 46 21 S 168 0 E
Riverton, U.S.A. **108 E9** 43 2N 108 23W
Riverton Heights, U.S.A. **110 C4** 47 28N 122 17W
Rives, France **21 C9** 45 21N 5 31 E
Rivesaltes, France **20 F6** 42 47N 2 50 E
Riviera, U.S.A. **111 K12** 35 4N 114 35W
Riviera di Levante, Italy **40 D6** 44 15N 9 30 E
Riviera di Ponente, Italy **40 D5** 44 10N 8 20 E
Rivière-au-Renard, Canada **105 C7** 48 59N 64 23W
Rivière-du-Loup, Canada **105 C6** 47 50N 69 30W
Rivière-Pentecôte, Canada **105 C6** 49 57N 67 1W
Rivière-Pilote, Martinique **120 c** 14 26N 60 53W
Rivière St-Paul, Canada **105 B8** 51 28N 57 45W
Rivière-Salée, Martinique **120 c** 14 31N 61 0W
Rivne, Ukraine **29 D14** 46 1N 29 10 E
Rivne, Ukraine **33 G4** 50 40N 26 10 E
Rívoli, Italy **40 C4** 45 3N 7 31 E
Rivoli B., Australia **95 F3** 37 32 S 140 3 E
Rixheim, France **19 E14** 47 40N 7 24 E
Riyadh = Ar Riyāḍ, Si. Arabia **70 E5** 24 41N 46 42 E
Rize, Turkey **73 B9** 41 0N 40 30 E
Rizhao, China **57 G10** 35 25N 119 30 E
Rizokarpaso, Cyprus **49 D13** 35 36N 34 23 E
Rizzuto, C., Italy **43 D10** 38 53N 17 5 E
Rjukan, Norway **9 G13** 59 54N 8 33 E
Ro, Greece **47 E11** 36 9N 29 33 E
Roa, Spain **36 D7** 41 41N 3 56W
Road Town, Br. Virgin Is. **121 e** 18 27N 64 37W
Roan Plateau, U.S.A. **108 G9** 39 20N 109 20W
Roanne, France **19 F11** 46 3N 4 4 E
Roanoke, Ala., U.S.A. **115 J3** 33 9N 85 22W
Roanoke, Va., U.S.A. **114 G6** 37 16N 79 56W
Roanoke →, U.S.A. **115 H7** 35 57N 76 42W
Roanoke I., U.S.A. **115 H8** 35 55N 75 40W
Roanoke Rapids, U.S.A. **115 G7** 36 28N 77 40W
Roatán, Honduras **120 C2** 16 18N 86 35W
Robāt Sang, Iran **71 C8** 35 35N 59 10 E
Robāṭkarīm, Iran **71 C6** 35 25N 50 59 E
Robāṭkarīm □, Iran **71 B6** 35 26N 50 59 E
Robbins I., Australia **95 G4** 40 42 S 145 0 E
Róbbio, Italy **40 C5** 45 17N 8 35 E
Robe →, Australia **92 D2** 21 42 S 116 15 E
Röbel, Germany **24 B8** 53 22N 12 35 E
Robert Lee, U.S.A. **113 K4** 31 54N 100 29W
Robertsdale, U.S.A. **116 F6** 40 11N 78 6W
Robertsganj, India **69 G10** 24 44N 83 4 E
Robertson, S. Africa **88 E2** 33 46 S 19 50 E
Robertson I., Antarctica **5 C18** 65 15 S 59 30W
Robertson Ra., Australia **92 D3** 23 15 S 121 0 E
Robertsport, Liberia **82 D2** 6 45N 11 26W
Robertstown, Australia **95 E2** 33 58 S 139 5 E
Roberval, Canada **105 C5** 48 32N 72 15W
Robeson Chan., N. Amer. **4 A4** 82 0N 61 30W
Robesonia, U.S.A. **117 F8** 40 21N 76 8W
Robi, Ethiopia **81 F4** 7 52N 39 38 E
Robinson, U.S.A. **114 F2** 39 0N 87 44W
Robinson →, Australia **94 B2** 16 3 S 137 16 E
Robinson Ra., Australia **93 E2** 25 40 S 119 0 E
Robinvale, Australia **95 E3** 34 40 S 142 45 E
Robledo, Spain **39 G2** 38 46N 2 26W
Roblin, Canada **103 C8** 51 14N 101 21W
Roboré, Bolivia **124 G7** 18 10 S 59 45W
Robson, Canada **102 D5** 49 20N 117 41W
Robson, Mt., Canada **102 C5** 53 10N 119 10W
Robstown, U.S.A. **113 M6** 27 47N 97 40W
Roca, C. da, Portugal **37 G1** 38 40N 9 31W
Roca Partida, I., Mexico **118 D2** 19 1N 112 2W
Rocamadour, France **20 D5** 44 48N 1 37 E
Rocas, I., Brazil **125 D12** 4 0 S 34 1W
Rocca San Casciano, Italy **41 D8** 44 3N 11 50 E
Roccadáspide, Italy **43 B8** 40 27N 15 10 E
Roccastrada, Italy **41 F8** 43 0N 11 10 E
Roccella Iónica, Italy **43 D9** 38 19N 16 24 E
Rocha, Uruguay **127 C5** 34 30 S 54 25W
Rochdale, U.K. **14 D5** 53 38N 2 9W
Rochechouart, France **20 C4** 45 50N 0 49 E
Rochefort, Belgium **17 D5** 50 9N 5 12 E
Rochefort, France **20 C3** 45 56N 0 57W
Rochefort-en-Terre, France **18 E4** 47 42N 2 22W
Rochelle, U.S.A. **112 E10** 41 56N 89 4W
Rocher River, Canada **102 A6** 61 23N 112 44W
Rocheservière, France **18 F5** 46 57N 1 30W
Rochester, U.K. **15 F8** 51 23N 0 31 E
Rochester, Ind., U.S.A. **114 E2** 41 4N 86 13W
Rochester, Minn., U.S.A. **112 C8** 44 1N 92 28W
Rochester, N.H., U.S.A. **117 C14** 43 18N 70 59W
Rochester, N.Y., U.S.A. **116 C7** 43 10N 77 37W
Rociu, Romania **29 F10** 44 43N 25 2 E
Rock →, Canada **102 A3** 60 7N 127 7W
Rock Creek, U.S.A. **116 E4** 41 40N 80 52W
Rock Falls, U.S.A. **112 E10** 41 47N 89 41W
Rock Hill, U.S.A. **115 H5** 34 56N 81 1W
Rock Island, U.S.A. **112 E9** 41 30N 90 34W
Rock Rapids, U.S.A. **112 D6** 43 26N 96 10W
Rock Sound, Bahamas **120 B4** 24 54N 76 12W
Rock Springs, Mont., U.S.A. **108 C10** 46 49N 106 15W
Rock Springs, Wyo., U.S.A. **108 F9** 41 35N 109 14W
Rock Valley, U.S.A. **112 D6** 43 12N 96 18W
Rockall, Atl. Oc. **6 D3** 57 37N 13 42W
Rockdale, Tex., U.S.A. **113 K6** 30 39N 97 0W
Rockdale, Wash., U.S.A. **110 C5** 47 22N 121 28W
Rockeby = Mungkan Kandju △, Australia **94 A3** 13 35 S 142 52 E
Rockefeller Plateau, Antarctica **5 E14** 80 0 S 140 0W
Rockford, U.S.A. **112 D10** 42 16N 89 6W
Rockglen, Canada **103 D7** 49 11N 105 57W
Rockhampton, Australia **94 C5** 23 22 S 150 32 E
Rockingham, Australia **93 F2** 32 15 S 115 38 E
Rockingham, U.S.A. **115 H6** 34 57N 79 46W
Rockingham B., Australia **94 B4** 18 5 S 146 10 E
Rocklake, U.S.A. **112 A5** 48 47N 99 15W
Rockland, Canada **117 A9** 45 33N 75 17W
Rockland, Idaho, U.S.A. **108 E7** 42 34N 112 53W
Rockland, Maine, U.S.A. **115 C11** 44 6N 69 7W
Rockland, Mich., U.S.A. **112 B10** 46 44N 89 11W
Rocklin, U.S.A. **110 G5** 38 48N 121 14W
Rockly B., Trin. & Tob. **125 J16** 11 9N 60 46W
Rockmart, U.S.A. **115 H3** 34 0N 85 3W
Rockport, Mass., U.S.A. **117 D14** 42 39N 70 37W
Rockport, Mo., U.S.A. **112 E7** 40 25N 95 31W
Rockport, Tex., U.S.A. **113 L6** 28 2N 97 3W
Rocksprings, U.S.A. **113 K4** 30 1N 100 13W
Rockville, Conn., U.S.A. **117 E12** 41 52N 72 28W
Rockville, Md., U.S.A. **114 F7** 39 5N 77 9W
Rockwall, U.S.A. **113 J6** 32 56N 96 28W
Rockwell City, U.S.A. **112 D7** 42 24N 94 38W
Rockwood, Canada **116 C4** 43 37N 80 8W
Rockwood, Maine, U.S.A. **115 C11** 45 41N 69 45W
Rockwood, Tenn., U.S.A. **115 H3** 35 52N 84 41W
Rocky Ford, U.S.A. **112 F3** 38 3N 103 43W
Rocky Gully, Australia **93 F2** 34 30 S 116 57 E
Rocky Harbour, Canada **105 C8** 49 36N 57 55W
Rocky Island L., Canada **104 C3** 46 55N 83 0W
Rocky Lane, Canada **102 B5** 58 31N 116 22W
Rocky Mount, U.S.A. **115 H7** 35 57N 77 48W
Rocky Mountain △, U.S.A. **108 F11** 40 25N 105 45W
Rocky Mountain House, Canada **102 C6** 52 22N 114 55W
Rocky Mts., N. Amer. **108 G10** 49 0N 115 0W
Rocky Point, Namibia **88 B2** 19 3 S 12 30 E
Rocroi, France **19 C11** 49 55N 4 30 E
Rod, Pakistan **66 E3** 28 10N 63 5 E
Rødby, Denmark **11 K5** 54 41N 11 23 E
Rødbyhavn, Denmark **11 K5** 54 39N 11 22 E
Roddickton, Canada **105 B8** 50 51N 56 8W
Rødding, Denmark **11 J3** 55 23N 9 3 E
Rödeby, Sweden **11 H9** 56 15N 15 37 E
Rødekro, Denmark **11 J3** 55 4N 9 20 E
Rodenkirchen, Germany **24 B4** 53 23N 8 26 E
Rodez, France **20 D6** 44 21N 2 33 E
Rodholívas, Greece **44 F7** 40 55N 24 0 E
Rodhópi □, Greece **45 E9** 41 5N 25 30 E
Rodhopoú, Greece **49 D5** 35 34N 23 45 E
Ródhos, Greece **49 C10** 36 15N 28 10 E
Ródhos ✈ (RHO), Greece **47 E10** 36 23N 28 12 E
Rodi Gargánico, Italy **41 G12** 41 55N 15 53 E
Rodna, Romania **29 C9** 47 25N 24 50 E
Rodnei, Munţii, Romania **29 C9** 47 35N 24 35 E
Rodney, Canada **116 D3** 42 34N 81 41W
Rodney, C., N.Z. **91 G5** 36 17 S 174 50 E
Rodniki, Russia **34 B5** 57 7N 41 47 E
Rodonit, Kepi i, Albania **44 E3** 41 35N 19 27 E
Rodriguez, Ind. Oc. **3 E13** 19 45 S 63 20 E
Roe →, U.K. **12 A5** 55 6N 6 59W
Roebling, U.S.A. **117 F10** 40 7N 74 47W
Roebourne, Australia **92 D2** 20 44 S 117 9 E
Roebuck B., Australia **92 C3** 18 5 S 122 20 E
Roermond, Neths. **17 C6** 51 12N 6 0 E
Roes Welcome Sd., Canada **101 B11** 65 0N 87 0W
Roeselare, Belgium **17 D3** 50 57N 3 7 E
Rogachev = Ragachow, Belarus **33 F6** 53 8N 30 5 E
Rogačica, Serbia & M. **44 B3** 44 4N 19 40 E
Rogagua, L., Bolivia **124 F5** 13 43 S 66 50W
Rogaška Slatina, Slovenia **41 B12** 46 15N 15 42 E
Rogatec, Slovenia **41 B12** 46 15N 15 46 E
Rogatica, Bos.-H. **28 G4** 43 47N 19 0 E
Rogatyn, Ukraine **33 H3** 49 24N 24 36 E
Rogdhia, Greece **49 D7** 35 22N 25 1 E
Rogers, U.S.A. **113 G7** 36 20N 94 7W
Rogers City, U.S.A. **114 C4** 45 25N 83 49W
Rogersville, Canada **105 C6** 46 44N 65 26W
Roggan →, Canada **104 B4** 54 24N 79 25W
Roggan L., Canada **104 B4** 54 8N 77 50W
Roggeveldberge, S. Africa **88 E3** 32 10 S 20 10 E
Roggiano Gravina, Italy **43 C9** 39 37N 16 9 E
Rogliano, France **21 F13** 42 57N 9 30 E
Rogliano, Italy **43 C9** 39 10N 16 19 E
Rogoaguado, L., Bolivia **124 F5** 13 0 S 65 30W
Rogojampi, Indonesia **63 J17** 8 19 S 114 17 E
Rogoźno, Poland **31 F3** 52 45N 16 59 E
Rogue →, U.S.A. **108 E1** 42 26N 124 26W
Rohan, France **18 D4** 48 4N 2 45W
Róhda, Greece **49 A3** 39 48N 19 46 E
Rohnert Park, U.S.A. **110 G4** 38 16N 122 40W
Rohri, Pakistan **68 F3** 27 45N 68 51 E
Rohri Canal, Pakistan **68 F3** 26 15N 68 27 E
Rohtak, India **68 E7** 28 55N 76 43 E
Roi Et, Thailand **64 D4** 16 4N 103 40 E
Roja, Latvia **9 H20** 57 29N 22 43 E
Rojas, Argentina **126 C3** 34 10 S 60 45W
Rojişte, Romania **29 F8** 44 4N 23 56 E
Rojo, C., Mexico **119 C5** 21 33N 97 20W
Rokan →, Indonesia **62 D2** 2 0N 100 50 E
Rokel →, S. Leone **82 D2** 8 30N 12 48W
Rokiškis, Lithuania **9 J21** 55 55N 25 35 E
Rokitno, Russia **33 G8** 50 57N 35 56 E
Rokycany, Czech Rep. **26 B6** 49 43N 13 35 E
Rolândia, Brazil **127 A5** 23 18 S 51 23W
Rolla, U.S.A. **113 G9** 37 57N 91 46W
Rolleston, Australia **94 C4** 24 28 S 148 35 E
Rollingstone, Australia **94 B4** 19 2 S 146 24 E
Rom, Sudan **81 F3** 9 54N 32 16 E
Roma, Australia **95 D4** 26 32 S 148 49 E
Roma, Italy **41 G9** 41 54N 12 29 E
Roma, Sweden **11 G12** 57 32N 18 26 E
Roma, U.S.A. **113 M5** 26 25N 99 1W
Roma Fiumicino ✈ (FCO), Italy **41 G9** 41 48N 12 15 E
Romain C., U.S.A. **115 J6** 33 0N 79 22W
Romaine, Canada **105 B7** 50 13N 60 40W
Romaine →, Canada **105 B7** 50 18N 63 47W
Roman, Bulgaria **44 C7** 43 8N 23 57 E
Roman, Romania **29 D11** 46 57N 26 55 E
Roman-Kosh, Gora, Ukraine **33 K8** 44 37N 34 15 E
Romanche →, France **21 C9** 45 5N 5 43 E
Romang, Indonesia **63 F7** 7 30 S 127 20 E
Romāni, Egypt **74 E1** 30 59N 32 38 E
Romania ■, Europe **29 D10** 46 0N 25 0 E
Romanija, Bos.-H. **28 G3** 43 50N 18 45 E
Romano, Cayo, Cuba **120 B4** 22 0N 77 30W
Romans-sur-Isère, France **21 C9** 45 3N 5 3 E
Romanshorn, Switz. **25 H5** 47 33N 9 22 E
Rombari, Sudan **81 G3** 4 33N 31 2 E
Romblon, Phil. **61 E5** 12 33N 122 17 E
Rome = Roma, Italy **41 G9** 41 54N 12 29 E
Rome, Ga., U.S.A. **115 H3** 34 15N 85 10W
Rome, N.Y., U.S.A. **117 C9** 43 13N 75 27W
Rome, Pa., U.S.A. **117 E8** 41 51N 76 21W
Rometta, Italy **43 D8** 38 10N 15 25 E
Romilly-sur-Seine, France **19 D10** 48 31N 3 44 E
Romney, U.S.A. **114 F6** 39 21N 78 45W
Romney Marsh, U.K. **15 F8** 51 2N 0 54 E
Romny, Ukraine **33 G7** 50 48N 33 28 E
Rømø, Denmark **11 J2** 55 10N 8 30 E
Romodan, Ukraine **33 G7** 49 55N 33 15 E
Romodanovo, Russia **34 C7** 54 26N 45 23 E
Romont, Switz. **25 J2** 46 42N 6 54 E
Romorantin-Lanthenay, France **19 E8** 47 21N 1 45 E
Romsdalen, Norway **9 E12** 62 25N 7 52 E
Romsey, U.K. **15 G6** 51 0N 1 29W
Ron, Vietnam **64 D6** 17 53N 106 27 E
Rona, U.K. **13 D3** 57 34N 5 59W
Ronan, U.S.A. **108 C6** 47 32N 114 6W
Roncador, Cayos, Colombia **120 D3** 13 32N 80 4W
Roncador, Serra do, Brazil **125 F8** 12 30 S 52 30W
Ronciglione, Italy **41 F9** 42 17N 12 13 E
Ronco →, Italy **41 D9** 44 24N 12 12 E
Ronda, Spain **37 J5** 36 46N 5 12W
Ronda, Serranía de, Spain **37 J5** 36 44N 5 3W
Rondane, Norway **9 F13** 61 57N 9 50 E
Rondônia □, Brazil **124 F6** 11 0 S 63 0W
Rondonópolis, Brazil **125 G8** 16 28 S 54 38W
Rong, Koh, Cambodia **65 G4** 10 45N 103 15 E
Rong Jiang →, China **58 E7** 24 35N 109 20 E
Rong Xian, Guangxi Zhuangzu, China **59 F8** 22 50N 110 31 E
Rong Xian, Sichuan, China **58 C5** 29 23N 104 22 E
Rong'an, China **58 E7** 25 14N 109 22 E
Rongchang, China **58 C5** 29 20N 105 32 E
Ronge, L. la, Canada **103 B7** 55 6N 105 17W
Rongjiang, China **58 E7** 25 57N 108 28 E
Rongshui, China **58 E7** 25 5N 109 12 E
Rønne, Denmark **11 J8** 55 6N 14 43 E
Ronne Ice Shelf, Antarctica **5 D18** 78 0 S 60 0W
Ronneby, Sweden **11 H9** 56 12N 15 17 E
Ronnebyån →, Sweden **11 H9** 56 11N 15 18 E
Rönneshytta, Sweden **11 F9** 58 56N 15 2 E
Ronsard, C., Australia **93 D1** 24 46 S 113 10 E
Ronse, Belgium **17 D3** 50 45N 3 35 E
Roodepoort, S. Africa **89 D4** 26 11 S 27 54 E
Roof Butte, U.S.A. **109 H9** 36 28N 109 5W
Rooiboklaagte →, Namibia **88 C3** 20 50 S 21 0 E
Roorkee, India **68 E7** 29 52N 77 59 E
Roosendaal, Neths. **17 C4** 51 32N 4 29 E
Roosevelt, U.S.A. **108 F8** 40 18N 109 59W
Roosevelt →, Brazil **124 E6** 7 35 S 60 20W
Roosevelt, Mt., Canada **102 B3** 58 26N 125 20W
Roosevelt I., Antarctica **5 D12** 79 30 S 162 0W
Ropczyce, Poland **31 H8** 50 4N 21 38 E
Roper →, Australia **94 A2** 14 43 S 135 27 E
Roper Bar, Australia **94 A1** 14 44 S 134 44 E
Roque Pérez, Argentina **126 D4** 35 25 S 59 24W
Roquefort, France **20 D3** 44 2N 0 20W
Roquemaure, France **21 D8** 44 3N 4 48 E
Roquetas de Mar, Spain **39 J2** 36 46N 2 36W
Roquetes, Spain **38 E5** 40 50N 0 30 E
Roquevaire, France **21 E9** 43 20N 5 36 E
Roraima □, Brazil **124 C6** 2 0N 61 30W
Roraima, Mt., Venezuela **124 B6** 5 10N 60 40W
Røros, Norway **9 E14** 62 35N 11 23 E
Rorschach, Switz. **25 H5** 47 28N 9 28 E
Rosa, Zambia **87 D3** 9 33 S 31 15 E
Rosa, L., Bahamas **121 B5** 21 0N 73 30W
Rosa, Monte, Europe **40 C4** 45 57N 7 53 E
Rosal de la Frontera, Spain **37 H3** 37 59N 7 13W
Rosalia, U.S.A. **108 C5** 47 14N 117 22W
Rosamond, U.S.A. **111 L8** 34 52N 118 10W
Rosans, France **21 D9** 44 24N 5 29 E
Rosario, Argentina **126 C3** 33 0 S 60 40W
Rosário, Brazil **125 D10** 3 0 S 44 15W
Rosario, Baja Calif., Mexico **118 B1** 30 0N 115 50W
Rosario, Sinaloa, Mexico **118 C3** 23 0N 105 52W
Rosario, Paraguay **126 A4** 24 30 S 57 35W
Rosario de la Frontera, Argentina **126 B3** 25 50 S 65 0W
Rosario de Lerma, Argentina **126 A2** 24 59 S 65 35W
Rosario del Tala, Argentina **126 C4** 32 20 S 59 10W
Rosário do Sul, Brazil **127 C5** 30 15 S 54 55W
Rosarito, Mexico **111 N9** 32 18N 117 4W
Rosarno, Italy **43 D8** 38 29N 15 58 E
Rosas = Roses, Spain **38 C8** 42 19N 3 10 E
Roscoe, U.S.A. **117 E10** 41 56N 74 55W
Roscoff, France **18 D3** 48 44N 3 58W
Roscommon, Ireland **12 C3** 53 38N 8 11W
Roscommon □, Ireland **12 C3** 53 49N 8 23W
Roscrea, Ireland **12 D4** 52 57N 7 49W
Rose →, Australia **94 A2** 14 16 S 135 45 E
Rose Blanche-Harbour Le Cou, Canada **105 C8** 47 38N 58 45W
Rose Pt., Canada **102 C2** 54 11N 131 39W
Rose Valley, Canada **103 C8** 52 19N 103 49W
Roseau, Domin. **121 C7** 15 20N 61 24W
Roseau, U.S.A. **112 A7** 48 51N 95 46W
Rosebery, Australia **95 G4** 41 46 S 145 33 E
Rosebud, S. Dak., U.S.A. **112 D4** 43 14N 100 51W
Rosebud, Tex., U.S.A. **113 K6** 31 4N 96 59W
Roseburg, U.S.A. **108 E2** 43 13N 123 20W
Rosedale, U.S.A. **113 J9** 33 51N 91 2W
Rosehearty, U.K. **13 D6** 57 42N 2 7W
Roseland, U.S.A. **110 G4** 38 25N 122 43W
Rosemary, Canada **102 C6** 50 46N 112 5W
Rosenberg, U.S.A. **113 L7** 29 34N 95 49W
Rosendaël, France **19 A9** 51 3N 2 24 E
Rosenheim, Germany **25 H8** 47 51N 12 7 E
Roses, Spain **38 C8** 42 19N 3 10 E
Roses, G. de, Spain **38 C8** 42 10N 3 15 E
Roseto degli Abruzzi, Italy **41 F11** 42 41N 14 1 E
Rosetown, Canada **103 C7** 51 35N 107 59W
Rosetta = Rashîd, Egypt **80 H7** 31 21N 30 22 E
Roseville, Calif., U.S.A. **110 G5** 38 45N 121 17W
Roseville, Mich., U.S.A. **116 D2** 42 30N 82 56W
Rosewood, Australia **95 D5** 27 38 S 152 36 E
Roshkhvār, Iran **71 C8** 34 58N 59 37 E
Rosières-en-Santerre, France **19 C9** 49 49N 2 42 E
Rosignano Maríttimo, Italy **40 E7** 43 24N 10 28 E
Rosignol, Guyana **124 B7** 6 15N 57 30W
Roşiori de Vede, Romania **29 F10** 44 9N 25 0 E

Rositsa, *Bulgaria* 45 C11 43 57N 27 57 E
Rositsa →, *Bulgaria* 45 C9 43 10N 25 30 E
Roskilde, *Denmark* 11 J6 55 38N 12 3 E
Roskilde Amtskommune □, *Denmark* 11 J6 55 35N 12 5 E
Roskovec, *Albania* 44 F3 40 44N 19 43 E
Roslavl, *Russia* 32 F7 53 57N 32 55 E
Rosmaninhal, *Portugal* 36 F3 39 44N 7 5W
Rosmead, *S. Africa* 88 E4 31 29 S 25 8 E
Røsnæs, *Denmark* 11 J4 55 44N 10 55 E
Rosolini, *Italy* 43 F7 36 49N 14 57 E
Rosporden, *France* 18 E3 47 57N 3 50W
Ross, *Australia* 95 G4 42 2 S 147 30 E
Ross, *N.Z.* 91 K3 42 53 S 170 49 E
Ross Béthio, *Mauritania* 82 B1 16 15N 16 8W
Ross Dependency, *Antarctica* 5 D12 76 0 S 170 0W
Ross I., *Antarctica* 5 D11 77 30 S 168 0 E
Ross Ice Shelf, *Antarctica* 5 E12 80 0 S 180 0 E
Ross L., *U.S.A.* 108 B3 48 44N 121 4W
Ross-on-Wye, *U.K.* 15 F5 51 54N 2 34W
Ross River, *Australia* 94 C1 23 44 S 134 30 E
Ross River, *Canada* 102 A2 62 30N 131 30W
Ross Sea, *Antarctica* 5 D11 74 0 S 178 0 E
Rossall Pt., *U.K.* 14 D4 53 55N 3 3W
Rossan Pt., *Ireland* 12 B3 54 42N 8 47W
Rossano, *Italy* 43 C9 39 36N 16 39 E
Rossburn, *Canada* 103 C8 50 40N 100 49W
Rosseau, *Canada* 116 A5 45 16N 79 39W
Rosseau, L., *Canada* 116 A5 45 10N 79 35W
Rosses, The, *Ireland* 12 A3 55 2N 8 20W
Rossignol, L., *Canada* 104 B5 52 43N 73 40W
Rossignol L., *Canada* 105 D6 44 12N 65 10W
Rossland, *Canada* 102 D5 49 6N 117 50W
Rosslare, *Ireland* 12 D5 52 17N 6 24W
Rosslare Harbour, *Ireland* 12 D5 52 15N 6 20W
Rosslau, *Germany* 24 D8 51 52N 12 15 E
Rosso, *Mauritania* 82 B1 16 40N 15 45W
Rosso, C., *France* 21 F12 42 13N 8 32 E
Rossosh, *Russia* 33 G10 50 15N 39 28 E
Røssvatnet, *Norway* 8 D16 65 45N 14 5 E
Røst, *Norway* 8 C15 67 32N 12 0 E
Rosthern, *Canada* 103 C7 52 40N 106 20W
Rostock, *Germany* 24 A8 54 5N 12 8 E
Rostov, *Don, Russia* 33 J10 47 15N 39 45 E
Rostov, *Yaroslavl, Russia* 32 D10 57 14N 39 25 E
Rostrenen, *France* 18 D3 48 14N 3 21W
Roswell, *Ga., U.S.A.* 115 H3 34 2N 84 22W
Roswell, *N. Mex., U.S.A.* 113 J2 33 24N 104 32W
Rota, *Spain* 37 J4 36 37N 6 20W
Rotan, *U.S.A.* 113 J4 32 51N 100 28W
Rotenburg, *Hessen, Germany* 24 E5 50 59N 9 44 E
Rotenburg, *Niedersachsen, Germany* 24 B5 53 6N 9 25 E
Roth, *Germany* 25 F7 49 15N 11 5 E
Rothaargebirge, *Germany* 24 D4 51 2N 8 13 E
Rothaargebirge ⌓, *Germany* 24 E4 51 0N 8 15 E
Rothenburg ob der Tauber, *Germany* 25 F6 49 23N 10 11 E
Rother →, *U.K.* 15 G8 50 59N 0 45 E
Rothera, *Antarctica* 5 C17 67 20 S 63 0W
Rotherham, *U.K.* 14 D6 53 26N 1 20W
Rothes, *U.K.* 13 D5 57 32N 3 13W
Rothesay, *Canada* 105 C6 45 23N 66 0W
Rothesay, *U.K.* 13 F3 55 50N 5 3W
Roti, *Indonesia* 63 F6 10 50 S 123 0 E
Rotja, Pta., *Spain* 39 G6 38 38N 1 35 E
Roto, *Australia* 95 E4 33 0 S 145 30 E
Rotondo, Mte., *France* 21 F13 42 14N 9 8 E
Rotoroa, L., *N.Z.* 91 J4 41 55 S 172 39 E
Rotorua, *N.Z.* 91 H6 38 9 S 176 16 E
Rotorua, L., *N.Z.* 91 H6 38 5 S 176 18 E
Rott →, *Germany* 25 G9 48 27N 13 25 E
Rottenburg, *Germany* 25 G4 48 28N 8 55 E
Rottenmann, *Austria* 26 D7 47 31N 14 22 E
Rotterdam, *Neths.* 17 C4 51 55N 4 30 E
Rotterdam, *U.S.A.* 117 D10 42 48N 74 1W
Rottne, *Sweden* 11 G8 57 1N 14 54 E
Rottnest I., *Australia* 93 F2 32 0 S 115 27 E
Rottumeroog, *Neths.* 17 A6 53 33N 6 34 E
Rottweil, *Germany* 25 G4 48 9N 8 37 E
Rotuma, *Fiji* 96 J9 12 25 S 177 5 E
Roubaix, *France* 19 B10 50 40N 3 10 E
Roudnice nad Labem, *Czech Rep.* 26 A7 50 25N 14 15 E
Rouen, *France* 18 C8 49 27N 1 4 E
Rouergue, *France* 20 D5 44 15N 2 0 E
Rouillac, *France* 20 C3 45 47N 0 4W
Rouleau, *Canada* 103 C8 50 10N 104 56W
Round Mountain, *U.S.A.* 108 G5 38 43N 117 4W
Round Mt., *Australia* 95 E5 30 26 S 152 16 E
Round Rock, *U.S.A.* 113 K6 30 31N 97 41W
Roundup, *U.S.A.* 108 C9 46 27N 108 33W
Rousay, *U.K.* 13 B5 59 10N 3 2W
Rouses Point, *U.S.A.* 117 B11 44 59N 73 22W
Rouseville, *U.S.A.* 116 E5 41 28N 79 42W
Roussillon, *Isère, France* 21 C8 45 24N 4 49 E
Roussillon, *Pyrénées-Or., France* 20 F6 42 30N 2 35 E
Rouxville, *S. Africa* 88 E4 30 25 S 26 50 E
Rouyn-Noranda, *Canada* 104 C4 48 20N 79 0W
Rovaniemi, *Finland* 8 C21 66 29N 25 41 E
Rovato, *Italy* 40 C7 45 34N 10 0 E
Rovenki, *Ukraine* 33 H10 48 5N 39 21 E
Rovereto, *Italy* 40 C8 45 53N 11 3 E
Rovigo, *Italy* 41 C8 45 4N 11 47 E
Rovinj, *Croatia* 41 C10 45 5N 13 40 E
Rovno = Rivne, *Ukraine* 33 G4 50 40N 26 10 E
Rovnoye, *Russia* 34 E8 50 52N 46 3 E
Rovuma = Ruvuma →, *Tanzania* 87 E5 10 29 S 40 28 E
Row'ān, *Iran* 71 C6 35 8N 48 51 E
Rowena, *Australia* 95 D4 29 48 S 148 55 E
Rowley Shoals, *Australia* 92 C2 17 30 S 119 0 E
Roxa, *Guinea-Biss.* 82 C1 11 15N 15 45W
Roxas, *Capiz, Phil.* 61 F5 11 36N 122 49 E
Roxas, *Isabela, Phil.* 61 C4 17 8N 121 36 E
Roxas, *Mind. Or., Phil.* 61 E4 12 35N 121 31 E
Roxboro, *U.S.A.* 115 G6 36 24N 78 59W
Roxborough, *Trin. & Tob.* 125 J16 11 15N 60 35W
Roxburgh, *N.Z.* 91 L2 45 33 S 169 19 E
Roxbury, *U.S.A.* 116 F7 40 6N 77 39W
Roxen, *Sweden* 11 F9 58 30N 15 40 E
Roy, *Mont., U.S.A.* 108 C9 47 20N 108 58W
Roy, *N. Mex., U.S.A.* 113 H2 35 57N 104 12W
Roy, *Utah, U.S.A.* 108 F7 41 10N 112 2W
Royal Canal, *Ireland* 12 C4 53 30N 7 13W
Royal Leamington Spa, *U.K.* 15 E6 52 18N 1 31W
Royal Natal △, *S. Africa* 89 D4 28 43 S 28 51 E
Royal Tunbridge Wells, *U.K.* 15 F8 51 7N 0 16 E
Royale, Isle, *U.S.A.* 112 B10 48 0N 88 54W
Royan, *France* 20 C2 45 37N 1 2W
Roye, *France* 19 C9 49 42N 2 48 E
Royston, *U.K.* 15 E7 52 3N 0 0W
Rožaj, *Serbia & M.* 44 D4 42 50N 20 11 E
Różan, *Poland* 31 F8 52 52N 21 25 E
Rozay-en-Brie, *France* 19 D9 48 41N 2 58 E
Rozdilna, *Ukraine* 29 D15 46 50N 30 2 E
Rozhnyativ, *Ukraine* 29 B9 48 56N 24 9 E
Rozhyshche, *Ukraine* 33 G3 50 54N 25 15 E
Rožmitál pod Třemšínem, *Czech Rep.* 26 B6 49 36N 13 53 E
Rožňava, *Slovak Rep.* 27 C13 48 37N 20 35 E
Rozogi, *Poland* 30 E8 53 28N 21 19 E
Rozoy-sur-Serre, *France* 19 C11 49 40N 4 8 E
Roztoczański △, *Poland* 31 H10 50 37N 23 0 E
Rozzano, *Italy* 40 C6 45 22N 9 10 E
Rrëshen, *Albania* 44 E3 41 47N 19 49 E
Rrogozhine, *Albania* 44 E3 41 4N 19 50 E
Rtanj, *Serbia & M.* 44 C5 43 45N 21 50 E
Rtishchevo, *Russia* 34 D6 52 18N 43 46 E
Rúa = A Rúa, *Spain* 36 C3 42 24N 7 6W
Ruacaná, *Namibia* 88 B1 17 27 S 14 21 E
Ruaha △, *Tanzania* 86 D3 7 41 S 34 30 E
Ruahine Ra., *N.Z.* 91 H6 39 55 S 176 2 E
Ruapehu, *N.Z.* 91 H5 39 17 S 175 35 E
Ruapuke I., *N.Z.* 91 M2 46 46 S 168 31 E
Ruâq, W. →, *Egypt* 74 F2 30 0N 33 49 E
Rub' al Khālī, *Si. Arabia* 75 D4 19 0N 48 0 E
Rubeho Mts., *Tanzania* 86 D4 6 50 S 36 25 E
Rubezhnoye = Rubizhne, *Ukraine* 33 H10 49 6N 38 25 E
Rubh a' Mhail, *U.K.* 13 F2 55 56N 6 8W
Rubha Hunish, *U.K.* 13 D2 57 42N 6 20W
Rubha Robhanais = Lewis, Butt of, *U.K.* 13 C2 58 31N 6 16W
Rubi, *Spain* 38 D7 41 29N 2 2 E
Rubicon →, *U.S.A.* 110 G5 38 53N 121 4W
Rubicone →, *Italy* 41 D9 44 8N 12 28 E
Rubik, *Albania* 44 E3 41 46N 19 47 E
Rubino, *Ivory C.* 82 D4 6 4N 4 18W
Rubio, *Venezuela* 124 B4 7 43N 72 22W
Rubizhne, *Ukraine* 33 H10 49 6N 38 25 E
Rubondo △, *Tanzania* 86 C3 2 18 S 31 58 E
Rubtsovsk, *Russia* 52 D9 51 30N 81 10 E
Ruby L., *U.S.A.* 108 F6 40 10N 115 28W
Ruby Mts., *U.S.A.* 108 F6 40 30N 115 20W
Rubyvale, *Australia* 94 C4 23 25 S 147 42 E
Rucheng, *China* 59 E9 25 33N 113 38 E
Ruciane-Nida, *Poland* 30 E8 53 40N 21 32 E
Rūd Sar, *Iran* 71 B6 37 8N 50 18 E
Ruda, *Sweden* 11 G10 57 6N 16 7 E
Ruda Śląska, *Poland* 31 H5 50 16N 18 50 E
Rudall, *Australia* 95 E2 33 43 S 136 17 E
Rudall →, *Australia* 92 D3 22 34 S 122 13 E
Rudall River △, *Australia* 92 D3 22 38 S 122 30 E
Rüdersdorf, *Germany* 24 C9 52 27N 13 47 E
Rudewa, *Tanzania* 87 E3 10 7 S 34 40 E
Rudkøbing, *Denmark* 11 K4 54 56N 10 41 E
Rudky, *Ukraine* 31 J10 49 38N 23 29 E
Rudna, *Poland* 31 G3 51 30N 16 17 E
Rudnik, *Bulgaria* 45 D11 42 36N 27 30 E
Rudnik, *Poland* 31 H9 50 26N 22 15 E
Rudnik, *Serbia & M.* 44 B4 44 7N 20 35 E
Rudnya, *Russia* 32 E6 54 55N 31 7 E
Rudnytsa, *Ukraine* 29 B13 48 16N 28 54 E
Rudnyy, *Kazakhstan* 52 D7 52 57N 63 7 E
Rudo, *Bos.-H.* 28 G4 43 41N 19 23 E
Rudolfa, Ostrov, *Russia* 52 A6 81 45N 58 30 E
Rudolstadt, *Germany* 24 E7 50 44N 11 19 E
Rudong, *China* 59 A13 32 20N 121 12 E
Rudozem, *Bulgaria* 45 E8 41 29N 24 51 E
Rudyard, *U.S.A.* 114 B3 46 14N 84 36W
Rue, *France* 19 B8 50 15N 1 40 E
Ruenya →, *Africa* 87 F3 16 24 S 33 48 E
Rufa'a, *Sudan* 81 E3 14 44N 33 22 E
Rufiji →, *Tanzania* 86 D4 7 50 S 39 15 E
Rufino, *Argentina* 126 C3 34 20 S 62 50W
Rufisque, *Senegal* 82 C1 14 40N 17 15W
Rufling Pt., *Br. Virgin Is.* 121 e 18 44N 64 27W
Rufunsa, *Zambia* 87 F2 15 4 S 29 34 E
Rugao, *China* 59 A13 32 23N 120 31 E
Rugby, *U.K.* 15 E6 52 23N 1 16W
Rugby, *U.S.A.* 112 A5 48 22N 100 0W
Rügen, *Germany* 24 A9 54 22N 13 24 E
Rügen ⌓, *Germany* 24 A9 54 25N 13 25 E
Rugles, *France* 18 D7 48 50N 0 40 E
Ruhengeri, *Rwanda* 86 C2 1 30 S 29 36 E
Ruhla, *Germany* 24 E6 50 54N 10 23 E
Ruhland, *Germany* 24 D9 51 27N 13 51 E
Ruhnu, *Estonia* 9 H20 57 48N 23 15 E
Ruhr →, *Germany* 24 D2 51 27N 6 43 E
Ruhuhu →, *Tanzania* 87 E3 10 31 S 34 34 E
Rui'an, *China* 59 D13 27 47N 120 40 E
Ruichang, *China* 59 C10 29 40N 115 39 E
Ruidoso, *U.S.A.* 109 K11 33 20N 105 41W
Ruijin, *China* 59 E10 25 48N 116 0 E
Ruili, *China* 58 E1 24 1N 97 43 E
Ruivo, Pico, *Madeira* 48 D3 32 45N 16 56W
Ruj, *Bulgaria* 44 D6 42 52N 22 34 E
Rujen, *Macedonia* 44 D6 42 9N 22 30 E
Rujm Tal'at al Jamā'ah, *Jordan* 74 E4 30 24N 35 30 E
Ruk, *Pakistan* 68 F3 27 50N 68 42 E
Rukhla, *Pakistan* 68 C4 32 27N 71 57 E
Ruki →, *Dem. Rep. of the Congo* 84 E3 0 5N 18 17 E
Rukwa □, *Tanzania* 86 D3 7 0 S 31 30 E
Rukwa, L., *Tanzania* 86 D3 8 0 S 32 20 E
Rulhieres, C., *Australia* 92 B4 13 56 S 127 22 E
Rum = Rhum, *U.K.* 13 E2 57 0N 6 20W
Rum, *Jordan* 74 F4 29 39N 35 26 E
Rum Cay, *Bahamas* 121 B5 23 40N 74 58W
Rum Jungle, *Australia* 92 B5 13 0 S 130 59 E
Ruma, *Serbia & M.* 28 E4 45 0N 19 50 E
Ruma △, *Kenya* 86 C3 0 39 S 34 18 E
Rumāḩ, *Si. Arabia* 70 E5 25 29N 47 10 E
Rumania = Romania ■, *Europe* 29 D10 46 0N 25 0 E
Rumaylah, *Iraq* 70 D5 30 47N 47 37 E
Rumbêk, *Sudan* 81 F2 6 54N 29 37 E
Rumburk, *Czech Rep.* 26 A7 50 57N 14 32 E
Rumford, *U.S.A.* 115 C10 44 33N 70 33W
Rumia, *Poland* 30 D5 54 37N 18 25 E
Rumilly, *France* 21 C9 45 53N 5 56 E
Rumoi, *Japan* 54 C10 43 56N 141 39 E
Rumonge, *Burundi* 86 C2 3 59 S 29 26 E
Rumson, *U.S.A.* 117 F11 40 23N 74 0W
Rumuruti, *Kenya* 86 B4 0 17N 36 32 E
Runan, *China* 56 H8 33 0N 114 30 E
Runanga, *N.Z.* 91 K3 42 25 S 171 15 E
Runaway, C., *N.Z.* 91 G6 37 32 S 177 59 E
Runaway Bay, *Jamaica* 120 a 18 27N 77 20W
Runcorn, *U.K.* 14 D5 53 21N 2 44W
Rundu, *Namibia* 88 B2 17 52 S 19 43 E
Rungwa, *Tanzania* 86 D3 6 55 S 33 32 E
Rungwa ⌓, *Tanzania* 86 D3 6 53 S 34 2 E
Rungwa →, *Tanzania* 86 D3 7 36 S 31 50 E
Rungwe, *Tanzania* 87 D3 9 11 S 33 32 E
Rungwe, Mt., *Tanzania* 84 F6 9 8 S 33 40 E
Runka, *Nigeria* 83 C6 12 28N 7 20 E
Runn, *Sweden* 10 D9 60 30N 15 40 E
Runton Ra., *Australia* 92 D3 23 31 S 123 6 E
Ruokolahti, *Finland* 32 B5 61 17N 28 50 E
Ruoqiang, *China* 60 C3 38 55N 88 10 E
Rupa, *India* 67 F18 27 15N 92 21 E
Rupar, *India* 68 D7 31 2N 76 38 E
Rupat, *Indonesia* 62 D2 1 45N 101 40 E
Rupea, *Romania* 29 D10 46 2N 25 13 E
Rupen →, *India* 68 H4 23 28N 71 31 E
Rupert, *U.S.A.* 108 E7 42 37N 113 41W
Rupert →, *Canada* 104 B4 51 29N 78 45W
Rupert B., *Canada* 104 B4 51 35N 79 0W
Rupert House = Waskaganish, *Canada* 104 B4 51 30N 78 40W
Rupsa, *India* 69 J12 21 37N 87 1 E
Rur →, *Germany* 24 D1 51 11N 5 59 E
Rurrenabaque, *Bolivia* 124 F5 14 30 S 67 32W
Rus →, *Spain* 39 F2 39 30N 2 30W
Rusambo, *Zimbabwe* 87 F3 16 30 S 32 4 E
Rusape, *Zimbabwe* 87 F3 18 35 S 32 8 E
Ruschuk = Ruse, *Bulgaria* 45 C9 43 48N 25 59 E
Ruse, *Bulgaria* 45 C9 43 48N 25 59 E
Ruse □, *Bulgaria* 45 C10 43 35N 26 20 E
Rusenski Lom △, *Bulgaria* 44 C7 43 40N 26 10 E
Rușețu, *Romania* 29 F12 44 57N 27 14 E
Rush, *Ireland* 12 C5 53 31N 6 6W
Rushan, *China* 57 F11 36 56N 121 30 E
Rushden, *U.K.* 15 E7 52 18N 0 35W
Rushmore, Mt., *U.S.A.* 112 D3 43 53N 103 28W
Rushville, *Ill., U.S.A.* 112 E9 40 7N 90 34W
Rushville, *Ind., U.S.A.* 114 F3 39 37N 85 27W
Rushville, *Nebr., U.S.A.* 112 D3 42 43N 102 28W
Russas, *Brazil* 125 D11 4 55 S 37 50W
Russell, *Canada* 103 C8 50 50N 101 20W
Russell, *Kans., U.S.A.* 112 F5 38 54N 98 52W
Russell, *N.Y., U.S.A.* 117 B9 44 27N 75 9W
Russell, *Pa., U.S.A.* 116 E5 41 56N 79 8W
Russell Cave ⌓, *U.S.A.* 115 H3 34 59N 85 49W
Russell L., *Man., Canada* 103 B8 56 15N 101 30W
Russell L., *N.W.T., Canada* 102 A5 63 5N 115 44W
Russellkonda, *India* 67 K14 19 57N 84 42 E
Russellville, *Ala., U.S.A.* 115 H2 34 30N 87 44W
Russellville, *Ark., U.S.A.* 113 H8 35 17N 93 8W
Russellville, *Ky., U.S.A.* 115 G2 36 51N 86 53W
Rüsselsheim, *Germany* 25 F4 49 59N 8 23 E
Russi, *Italy* 41 D9 44 22N 12 2 E
Russia ■, *Eurasia* 53 C11 62 0N 105 0 E
Russian →, *U.S.A.* 110 G3 38 27N 123 8W
Russkoye Ustie, *Russia* 4 B15 71 0N 149 0 E
Rust, *Austria* 27 D9 47 49N 16 42 E
Rustam, *Pakistan* 68 B5 34 25N 72 13 E
Rustam Shahr, *Pakistan* 68 F2 26 58N 66 6 E
Rustavi, *Georgia* 35 K7 41 30N 45 0 E
Rustenburg, *S. Africa* 88 D4 25 41 S 27 14 E
Ruston, *U.S.A.* 113 J8 32 32N 92 38W
Rutana, *Burundi* 86 C3 3 55 S 30 0 E
Rute, *Spain* 37 H6 37 19N 4 23W
Ruteng, *Indonesia* 63 F6 8 35 S 120 30 E
Ruth, *U.S.A.* 116 C2 43 42N 82 45W
Rutherford, *U.S.A.* 110 G4 38 26N 122 24W
Rutland, *U.S.A.* 117 C12 43 37N 72 58W
Rutland □, *U.K.* 15 E7 52 38N 0 40W
Rutland Water, *U.K.* 15 E7 52 39N 0 38W
Rutledge →, *Canada* 103 A6 61 4N 112 0W
Rutledge L., *Canada* 103 A6 61 33N 110 47W
Rutqa, W. →, *Syria* 73 E9 34 30N 41 3 E
Rutshuru, *Dem. Rep. of the Congo* 86 C2 1 13 S 29 25 E
Ruvo di Púglia, *Italy* 43 A9 41 7N 16 29 E
Ruvu, *Tanzania* 86 D4 6 49 S 38 43 E
Ruvu →, *Tanzania* 86 D4 6 23 S 38 52 E
Ruvuba △, *Burundi* 86 C2 3 3 S 29 33 E
Ruvuma □, *Tanzania* 87 E4 10 20 S 36 0 E
Ruvuma →, *Tanzania* 87 E5 10 29 S 40 28 E
Ruwais, *U.A.E.* 71 E7 24 5N 52 50 E
Ruwenzori, *Africa* 86 B2 0 30N 29 55 E
Ruwenzori △, *Uganda* 86 B2 0 20 S 30 0 E
Ruya →, *Zimbabwe* 89 B5 16 27 S 32 5 E
Ruyigi, *Burundi* 86 C3 3 29 S 30 15 E
Ruyuan, *China* 59 E9 24 46N 113 16 E
Ruzayevka, *Russia* 34 C7 54 4N 45 0 E
Růzhevo Konare, *Bulgaria* 45 D8 42 23N 24 46 E
Ružomberok, *Slovak Rep.* 27 B12 49 3N 19 17 E
Ruzyne, Praha ✕ (PRG), *Czech Rep.* 26 A7 50 7N 14 15 E
Rwanda ■, *Africa* 86 C3 2 0 S 30 0 E
Ryakhovo, *Bulgaria* 45 C10 43 58N 26 18 E
Ryan, L., *U.K.* 13 G3 55 0N 5 2W
Ryazan, *Russia* 32 E10 54 40N 39 40 E
Ryazhsk, *Russia* 32 F11 53 45N 40 3 E
Rybache = Rybachye, *Kazakhstan* 52 E9 46 40N 81 20 E
Rybachiy, *Russia* 30 C7 55 10N 20 50 E
Rybachye, *Kazakhstan* 52 E9 46 40N 81 20 E
Rybinsk, *Russia* 32 C10 58 5N 38 50 E
Rybinskoye Vdkhr., *Russia* 32 C10 58 30N 38 25 E
Rybnik, *Poland* 31 H5 50 6N 18 32 E
Rybnitsa = Râbniţa, *Moldova* 29 C14 47 45N 29 0 E
Rybnoye, *Russia* 32 E10 54 45N 39 30 E
Rychnov nad Kněžnou, *Czech Rep.* 27 A9 50 10N 16 17 E
Rychwał, *Poland* 31 F5 52 4N 18 10 E
Rycroft, *Canada* 102 B5 55 45N 118 40W
Ryd, *Sweden* 11 H8 56 27N 14 42 E
Rydaholm, *Sweden* 11 H8 56 59N 14 18 E
Ryde, *U.K.* 15 G6 50 43N 1 9W
Ryderwood, *U.S.A.* 110 D3 46 23N 123 3W
Rydzyna, *Poland* 31 G3 51 47N 16 39 E
Rye, *U.K.* 15 G8 50 57N 0 45 E
Rye →, *U.K.* 14 C7 54 11N 0 44W
Rye Bay, *U.K.* 15 G8 50 52N 0 49 E
Rye Patch Reservoir, *U.S.A.* 108 F4 40 28N 118 19W
Ryegate, *U.S.A.* 108 C9 46 18N 109 15W
Ryki, *Poland* 31 G8 51 38N 21 56 E
Ryley, *Canada* 102 C6 53 17N 112 26W
Rylsk, *Russia* 33 G8 51 36N 34 43 E
Rylstone, *Australia* 95 E4 32 46 S 149 58 E
Rymanów, *Poland* 31 J8 49 35N 21 51 E
Ryn, *Poland* 30 E8 53 57N 21 34 E
Ryn Peski, *Kazakhstan* 35 G9 47 30N 49 0 E
Ryōtsu, *Japan* 54 E9 38 5N 138 26 E
Rypin, *Poland* 31 E6 53 3N 19 25 E
Ryssby, *Sweden* 11 H8 56 52N 14 10 E
Rysy, *Europe* 27 B13 49 10N 20 4 E
Ryūgasaki, *Japan* 55 G10 35 54N 140 11 E
Ryūkyū Is. = Ryūkyū-rettō, *Japan* 55 M3 26 0N 126 0 E
Ryūkyū-rettō, *Japan* 55 M3 26 0N 126 0 E
Rzepin, *Poland* 31 F1 52 20N 14 49 E
Rzeszów, *Poland* 31 H8 50 5N 21 58 E
Rzhev, *Russia* 32 D8 56 20N 34 20 E

S

Sa, *Thailand* 64 C3 18 34N 100 45 E
Sa Canal, *Spain* 48 C7 38 51N 1 23 E
Sa Conillera, *Spain* 48 C7 38 59N 1 13 E
Sa Dec, *Vietnam* 65 G5 10 20N 105 46 E
Sa Dragonera, *Spain* 48 B9 39 35N 2 19 E
Sa Mesquida, *Spain* 48 B11 39 55N 4 16 E
Sa Pobla, *Spain* 38 F8 39 46N 3 1 E
Sa Savina, *Spain* 48 C7 38 44N 1 25 E
Sa'ādatābād, *Fārs, Iran* 71 D7 30 10N 53 5 E
Sa'ādatābād, *Hormozgān, Iran* 71 D7 28 3N 55 53 E
Sa'ādatābād, *Kermān, Iran* 71 D7 29 40N 55 51 E
Saale →, *Germany* 24 D7 51 56N 11 54 E
Saaler Bodden, *Germany* 24 A8 54 20N 12 27 E
Saalfeld, *Germany* 24 E7 50 38N 11 21 E
Saalfelden, *Austria* 26 D5 47 25N 12 51 E
Saane →, *Switz.* 25 H3 47 8N 7 10 E
Saanich, *Canada* 110 B3 48 29N 123 26W
Saar →, *Europe* 17 E6 49 41N 6 32 E
Saar-Hunsrück ⌓, *Germany* 25 F2 49 30N 6 50 E
Saarbrücken, *Germany* 25 F2 49 14N 6 59 E
Saarburg, *Germany* 25 F2 49 36N 6 32 E
Saaremaa, *Estonia* 9 G20 58 30N 22 30 E
Saarijärvi, *Finland* 9 E21 62 43N 25 16 E
Saariselkä, *Finland* 8 B23 68 16N 28 15 E
Saarland □, *Germany* 25 F2 49 20N 7 0 E
Saarlouis, *Germany* 25 F2 49 18N 6 45 E
Sab 'Ābar, *Syria* 70 C3 33 46N 37 41 E
Saba, *W. Indies* 121 C7 17 42N 63 26W
Šabac, *Serbia & M.* 44 B3 44 48N 19 42 E
Sabadell, *Spain* 38 D7 41 28N 2 7 E
Sabah □, *Malaysia* 62 C5 6 0N 117 0 E
Sabak Bernam, *Malaysia* 65 L3 3 46N 100 58 E
Sabalān, Kūhhā-ye, *Iran* 70 B5 38 15N 47 45 E
Sabalana, Kepulauan, *Indonesia* 63 F5 6 45 S 118 50 E
Sábana de la Mar, *Dom. Rep.* 121 C6 19 7N 69 24W
Sábanalarga, *Colombia* 124 A4 10 38N 74 55W
Sabang, *Indonesia* 62 C1 5 50N 95 15 E
Săbăoani, *Romania* 29 C11 47 1N 26 51 E
Sabará, *Brazil* 125 G10 19 55 S 43 46W
Sabarmati →, *India* 68 H5 22 18N 72 22 E
Sabattis, *U.S.A.* 117 B10 44 6N 74 40W
Sabáudia, *Italy* 42 A6 41 18N 13 1 E
Saberania, *Indonesia* 63 E9 2 5 S 138 18 E
Sabhah, *Libya* 79 C8 27 9N 14 29 E
Sabi →, *India* 68 E7 28 29N 76 44 E
Sabidana, J., *Sudan* 80 D4 18 4N 36 50 E
Sabie, *S. Africa* 89 D5 25 10 S 30 48 E
Sabinal, *Mexico* 118 A3 30 58N 107 25W
Sabinal, *U.S.A.* 113 L5 29 19N 99 28W
Sabiñánigo, *Spain* 38 C4 42 31N 0 22W
Sabinar, Punta del, *Spain* 39 J2 36 43N 2 44W
Sabinas, *Mexico* 118 B4 27 50N 101 10W
Sabinas →, *Mexico* 118 B4 27 37N 100 42W
Sabinas Hidalgo, *Mexico* 118 B4 26 33N 100 10W
Sabine →, *U.S.A.* 113 L8 29 59N 93 47W
Sabine L., *U.S.A.* 113 L8 29 53N 93 51W
Sabine Pass, *U.S.A.* 113 L8 29 44N 93 54W
Sabinov, *Slovak Rep.* 27 B14 49 6N 21 5 E
Sabinsville, *U.S.A.* 116 E7 41 52N 77 31W
Sabirabad, *Azerbaijan* 35 K9 40 5N 48 30 E
Sablayan, *Phil.* 61 E4 12 50N 120 50 E
Sable, *Canada* 105 A6 55 30N 68 21W
Sable, C., *Canada* 105 D6 43 29N 65 38W
Sable, C., *U.S.A.* 107 E10 25 9N 81 8W
Sable I., *Canada* 105 D8 44 0N 60 0W
Sablé-sur-Sarthe, *France* 18 E6 47 50N 0 20W
Sabonkafi, *Niger* 83 C6 14 40N 8 45 E
Sabor →, *Portugal* 36 D3 41 10N 7 7W
Sabou, *Burkina Faso* 82 C4 12 1N 2 15W
Sabres, *France* 20 D3 44 9N 0 43W
Sabrina Coast, *Antarctica* 5 C9 68 0 S 120 0 E
Sabugal, *Portugal* 36 E3 40 20N 7 5W
Sabulubbek, *Indonesia* 62 E1 1 36 S 98 40 E
Sabuncu, *Turkey* 47 B12 39 33N 30 12 E
Sabzevār, *Iran* 71 B8 36 15N 57 40 E
Sabzvārān, *Iran* 71 D8 28 45N 57 50 E
Sac City, *U.S.A.* 112 D7 42 25N 95 0W
Sacedón, *Spain* 38 E2 40 29N 2 41W
Săcele, *Romania* 29 E10 45 37N 25 41 E
Sachigo →, *Canada* 104 A2 55 6N 88 58W
Sachigo, L., *Canada* 104 B1 53 50N 92 12W
Sachkhere, *Georgia* 35 J6 42 25N 43 28 E
Sachsen □, *Germany* 24 E9 50 55N 13 10 E
Sachsen-Anhalt □, *Germany* 24 D7 52 0N 12 0 E
Sächsische Schweiz △, *Germany* 24 E10 50 55N 14 10 E
Sacile, *Italy* 41 C9 45 57N 12 30 E
Sackets Harbor, *U.S.A.* 117 C8 43 57N 76 7W
Sackville, *Canada* 105 C7 45 54N 64 22W
Saco, *Maine, U.S.A.* 115 D10 43 30N 70 27W
Saco, *Mont., U.S.A.* 108 B10 48 28N 107 21W
Sacramento, *U.S.A.* 110 G5 38 35N 121 29W
Sacramento →, *U.S.A.* 110 G5 38 3N 121 56W
Sacramento Mts., *U.S.A.* 109 K11 32 30N 105 30W
Sacramento Valley, *U.S.A.* 110 G5 39 30N 122 0W
Sacratif, C., *Spain* 37 J7 36 42N 3 28W
Săcueni, *Romania* 28 C7 47 20N 22 5 E
Sada, *Spain* 36 B2 43 22N 8 15W
Sada-Misaki, *Japan* 55 H6 33 20N 132 1 E
Sádaba, *Spain* 38 C3 42 19N 1 12W
Sadabad, *India* 68 F8 27 27N 78 3 E
Sadani, *Tanzania* 86 D4 5 58 S 38 35 E
Sadao, *Thailand* 65 J3 6 38N 100 26 E
Sadd el Aali, *Egypt* 80 C3 23 54N 32 54 E
Saddle Mt., *U.S.A.* 110 E3 45 58N 123 41W
Sade, *Nigeria* 83 C7 11 22N 10 45 E
Sadimi, *Dem. Rep. of the Congo* 87 D1 9 25 S 23 32 E
Sadiola, *Mali* 82 C2 13 50N 11 40W
Sa'dīyah, Hawr as, *Iraq* 73 F12 32 15N 46 30 E
Sado, *Japan* 54 F9 38 0N 138 25 E
Sado →, *Portugal* 37 G2 38 29N 8 55W
Sadon, *Burma* 67 G20 25 28N 97 55 E
Sadon, *Russia* 35 J6 42 52N 43 58 E
Sadovoye, *Russia* 35 G7 47 47N 44 31 E
Sadra, *India* 68 H5 23 21N 72 43 E
Sadri, *India* 68 G5 25 11N 73 26 E
Sæby, *Denmark* 11 G4 57 21N 10 30 E
Saegertown, *U.S.A.* 116 E4 41 43N 80 9W
Saelices, *Spain* 38 F2 39 55N 2 49W
Safaalan, *Turkey* 45 E12 41 26N 28 6 E
Safaga, *Egypt* 80 B3 26 42N 34 0 E
Şafājah, *Si. Arabia* 70 E3 26 25N 39 0 E
Šafárikovo = Tornal'a, *Slovak Rep.* 27 C13 48 25N 20 20 E
Säffle, *Sweden* 10 E6 59 8N 12 55 E
Safford, *U.S.A.* 109 K9 32 50N 109 43W
Saffron Walden, *U.K.* 15 E8 52 1N 0 16 E
Safi, *Morocco* 78 B4 32 18N 9 20W
Şafīābād, *Iran* 71 B8 36 45N 57 58 E
Safīd Dasht, *Iran* 71 C6 33 27N 48 11 E
Safīd Kūh, *Afghan.* 66 B3 34 45N 63 0 E
Safīd Rūd →, *Iran* 71 B6 37 23N 50 11 E
Safipur, *India* 69 F9 26 44N 80 21 E
Safonovo, *Russia* 32 E7 55 4N 33 16 E
Safranbolu, *Turkey* 72 B5 41 15N 32 41 E
Saft Rashīn, *Egypt* 80 J7 28 58N 30 55 E
Şafwān, *Iraq* 70 D5 30 7N 47 43 E
Sag Harbor, *U.S.A.* 117 F12 41 0N 72 18W
Saga, *Japan* 55 H5 33 15N 130 16 E
Saga □, *Japan* 55 H5 33 15N 130 20 E
Sagae, *Japan* 54 E10 38 22N 140 17 E
Sagala, *Mali* 82 C3 14 9N 6 38W
Sagamartha = Everest, Mt., *Nepal* 69 E12 28 5N 86 58 E
Sagamore, *U.S.A.* 116 F5 40 46N 79 14W
Sagar, *Karnataka, India* 66 M9 14 14N 75 6 E
Sagar, *Mad. P., India* 69 H8 23 50N 78 44 E
Sagara, L., *Tanzania* 86 D3 5 20 S 31 0 E
Sagay, *Phil.* 61 F5 10 57N 123 25 E
Saginaw, *U.S.A.* 114 D4 43 26N 83 56W
Saginaw →, *U.S.A.* 114 D4 43 39N 83 51W
Saginaw B., *U.S.A.* 114 D4 43 50N 83 40W
Sagleipie, *Liberia* 82 D3 7 0N 8 52W
Saglouc = Salluit, *Canada* 101 B12 62 14N 75 38W
Sagŏ-ri, *S. Korea* 57 G14 35 25N 126 49 E
Sagone, *France* 21 F12 42 7N 8 42 E
Sagone, G. de, *France* 21 F12 42 4N 8 40 E
Sagres, *Portugal* 37 J2 37 0N 8 58W
Sagua la Grande, *Cuba* 120 B3 22 50N 80 10W
Saguache, *U.S.A.* 109 G10 38 5N 106 8W
Saguaro △, *U.S.A.* 109 K8 32 12N 110 38W
Saguenay →, *Canada* 105 C5 48 22N 71 0W
Sagunt, *Spain* 38 F4 39 42N 0 18W
Sagunto = Sagunt, *Spain* 38 F4 39 42N 0 18W
Sagwara, *India* 68 H6 23 41N 74 1 E
Sahaba, *Sudan* 80 D3 18 57N 30 25 E
Sahagún, *Spain* 36 C5 42 18N 5 2W
Saḩam al Jawlān, *Syria* 74 C4 32 45N 35 55 E
Sahamandrevo, *Madag.* 89 C8 23 15 S 45 35 E
Sahand, Kūh-e, *Iran* 70 B5 37 44N 46 27 E
Sahara, *Africa* 78 D6 23 0N 5 0 E
Saharan Atlas = Saharien, Atlas, *Algeria* 78 B6 33 30N 1 0 E
Saharanpur, *India* 68 E7 29 58N 77 33 E
Saharien, Atlas, *Algeria* 78 B6 33 30N 1 0 E
Saharsa, *India* 69 G12 25 53N 86 36 E
Sahasinaka, *Madag.* 89 C8 21 49 S 47 49 E
Sahaswan, *India* 69 E8 28 5N 78 45 E
Sahel, *Africa* 78 E5 16 0N 5 0 E
Sahel, Canal du, *Mali* 82 C3 14 20N 6 0W
Sahibganj, *India* 69 G12 25 12N 87 40 E
Sāḩilīyah, *Iraq* 70 C4 33 43N 42 42 E
Sahiwal, *Pakistan* 68 D5 30 45N 73 8 E
Şaḩneh, *Iran* 70 C5 34 29N 47 41 E
Sahrawi = Western Sahara ■, *Africa* 78 D3 25 0N 13 0W
Sahuaripa, *Mexico* 118 B3 29 0N 109 13W
Sahuarita, *U.S.A.* 109 L8 31 57N 110 58W
Sahuayo, *Mexico* 118 C4 20 4N 102 43W
Šahy, *Slovak Rep.* 27 C11 48 4N 18 55 E
Sai →, *India* 69 G10 25 39N 82 47 E
Sai Buri, *Thailand* 65 J3 6 43N 101 45 E
Sa'id Bundas, *Sudan* 79 G10 8 24N 24 48 E
Sa'īdābād = Sīrjān, *Iran* 71 D7 29 30N 55 45 E
Sa'īdābād, *Iran* 71 B7 36 8N 54 11 E
Sa'īdīyeh, *Iran* 71 B6 36 20N 48 55 E
Saidpur, *Bangla.* 67 G16 25 48N 89 0 E
Saidpur, *India* 69 G10 25 33N 83 11 E
Saidu, *Pakistan* 69 B5 34 43N 72 24 E
Saignes, *France* 20 C6 45 20N 2 31 E
Saigon = Thanh Pho Ho Chi Minh, *Vietnam* 65 G6 10 58N 106 40 E
Saijō, *Japan* 55 H6 33 55N 133 11 E
Saikai △, *Japan* 55 H4 33 12N 129 36 E
Saikanosy Masoala, *Madag.* 89 B9 15 45 S 50 10 E
Saikhoa Ghat, *India* 67 F19 27 50N 95 40 E
Saiki, *Japan* 55 H5 32 58N 131 51 E
Sailana, *India* 68 H6 23 28N 74 55 E
Saillans, *France* 21 D9 44 42N 5 12 E
Sailolof, *Indonesia* 63 E8 1 15 S 130 46 E
Saimaa, *Finland* 9 F23 61 15N 28 15 E
Saimbeyli, *Turkey* 72 D7 37 59N 36 6 E
Saimen = Saimaa, *Finland* 9 F23 61 15N 28 15 E
Şa'īn Dezh, *Iran* 70 B5 36 40N 46 25 E
St. Abb's Head, *U.K.* 13 F6 55 55N 2 8W
St-Affrique, *France* 20 E6 43 57N 2 53 E
St-Agrève, *France* 21 C8 45 0N 4 23 E
St-Aignan, *France* 18 E8 47 16N 1 22 E
St. Alban's, *Canada* 105 C8 47 51N 55 50W
St. Albans, *U.K.* 15 F7 51 45N 0 19W
St. Albans, *Vt., U.S.A.* 117 B11 44 49N 73 5W
St. Albans, *W. Va., U.S.A.* 114 F5 38 23N 81 50W
St. Alban's Head, *U.K.* 15 G5 50 34N 2 4W
St. Albert, *Canada* 102 C6 53 37N 113 32W
St-Amand-en-Puisaye, *France* 19 E10 47 32N 3 5 E
St-Amand-les-Eaux, *France* 19 B10 50 27N 3 25 E
St-Amand-Montrond, *France* 19 F9 46 43N 2 30 E
St-Amarin, *France* 19 E14 47 54N 7 2 E
St-Amour, *France* 19 F12 46 26N 5 21 E
St-André-de-Cubzac, *France* 20 D3 44 59N 0 26W
St-André-les-Alpes, *France* 21 E10 43 58N 6 30 E
St. Andrew's, *Canada* 105 C8 47 45N 59 15W
St. Andrews, *U.K.* 13 E6 56 20N 2 47W
St-Anicet, *Canada* 117 A10 45 8N 74 22W

St. Anns B., Canada 105 C7 46 22N 60 25W
St. Ann's Bay, Jamaica 120 a 18 26N 77 15W
St. Anthony, Canada 105 B8 51 22N 55 35W
St. Anthony, U.S.A. 108 E8 43 58N 111 41W
St-Antoine, Canada 105 C7 46 22N 64 45W
St-Antonin-Noble-Val, France 20 D5 44 10N 1 45 E
St. Arnaud, Australia 95 F3 36 40 S 143 16 E
St-Astier, France 20 C4 45 8N 0 31 E
St-Aubin-du-Cormier, France 18 D5 48 15N 1 26W
St-Augustin, Canada 105 B8 51 13N 58 38W
St-Augustin →, Canada 105 B8 51 16N 58 40W
St. Augustine, U.S.A. 115 L5 29 54N 81 19W
St-Aulaye, France 20 C4 45 12N 0 9 E
St. Austell, U.K. 15 G3 50 20N 4 47W
St-Avold, France 19 C13 49 6N 6 43 E
St. Barbe, Canada 105 B8 51 12N 56 46W
St-Barthélemy, W. Indies 121 C7 17 50N 62 50W
St-Béat, France 20 F4 42 55N 0 41 E
St. Bees Hd., U.K. 14 C4 54 31N 3 38W
St. Bees I., Australia 94 J7 20 56 S 149 26 E
St-Benoît-du-Sault, France 20 B5 46 26N 1 24 E
St-Bonnet-en-Champsaur, France 21 D10 44 40N 6 5 E
St-Brevin-les-Pins, France 18 E4 47 14N 2 10W
St-Brice-en-Coglès, France 18 D5 48 25N 1 22W
St. Bride's, Canada 105 C9 46 56N 54 10W
St. Brides B., U.K. 15 F2 51 49N 5 9W
St-Brieuc, France 18 D4 48 30N 2 46W
St-Calais, France 18 E7 47 55N 0 45 E
St-Cast-le-Guildo, France 18 D4 48 37N 2 18W
St. Catharines, Canada 116 C5 43 10N 79 15W
St. Catherines I., U.S.A. 115 K5 31 40N 81 10W
St. Catherine's Pt., U.K. 15 G6 50 34N 1 18W
St-Céré, France 20 D5 44 51N 1 54 E
St-Cergue, Switz. 25 J2 46 27N 6 10 E
St-Cernin, France 20 C6 45 5N 2 25 E
St-Chamond, France 21 C8 45 28N 4 31 E
St. Charles, Ill., U.S.A. 114 E1 41 54N 88 19W
St. Charles, Mo., U.S.A. 112 F9 38 47N 90 29W
St. Charles, Va., U.S.A. 114 F7 36 48N 83 4W
St-Chély-d'Apcher, France 20 D7 44 48N 3 17 E
St-Chinian, France 20 E6 43 25N 2 56 E
St. Christopher-Nevis = St. Kitts & Nevis ■, W. Indies 121 C7 17 20N 62 40W
St-Ciers-sur-Gironde, France 20 C3 45 17N 0 37W
St. Clair, Mich., U.S.A. 116 D2 42 50N 82 30W
St. Clair, Pa., U.S.A. 117 F8 40 43N 76 12W
St. Clair →, U.S.A. 116 D2 42 38N 82 31W
St. Clair, L., Canada 104 D3 42 30N 82 45W
St. Clair, L., U.S.A. 116 D2 42 27N 82 39W
St. Clairsville, U.S.A. 116 F4 40 5N 80 54W
St-Claud, France 20 C4 45 54N 0 28 E
St. Claude, Canada 103 D9 49 40N 98 20W
St-Claude, France 19 F12 46 22N 5 52 E
St. Clears, U.K. 15 F3 51 49N 4 31W
St-Clet, Canada 117 A10 45 21N 74 13W
St. Cloud, Fla., U.S.A. 115 L5 28 15N 81 17W
St. Cloud, Minn., U.S.A. 112 C7 45 34N 94 10W
St. Cricq, C., Australia 93 E1 25 17 S 113 6 E
St. Croix, U.S. Virgin Is. 121 C7 17 45N 64 45W
St. Croix →, U.S.A. 112 C8 44 45N 92 48W
St. Croix Falls, U.S.A. 112 C8 45 24N 92 38W
St-Cyprien, France 20 F7 42 37N 3 2 E
St-Cyr-sur-Mer, France 21 E9 43 11N 5 43 E
St. David's, Canada 105 C8 48 12N 58 52W
St. David's, U.K. 15 F2 51 53N 5 16W
St. David's Head, U.K. 15 F2 51 54N 5 19W
St-Denis, France 19 D9 48 56N 2 22 E
St-Dié, France 19 D13 48 17N 6 56 E
St-Dizier, France 19 D11 48 38N 4 56 E
St-Égrève, France 21 C9 45 14N 5 41 E
St. Elias, Mt., U.S.A. 100 B5 60 18N 140 56W
St. Elias Mts., N. Amer. 102 A1 60 33N 139 28W
St-Eloy-les-Mines, France 19 F9 46 10N 2 51 E
St-Émilion, France 20 D3 44 53N 0 9W
St-Étienne, France 21 C8 45 27N 4 22 E
St-Étienne-de-Tinée, France 21 D10 44 16N 6 56 E
St-Étienne-du-Rouvray, France 18 C8 49 23N 1 6 E
St. Eugène, Canada 117 A10 45 30N 74 28W
St. Eustatius, W. Indies 121 C7 17 20N 63 0W
St-Exupery, Lyon ✕ (LYS), France 21 C9 45 44N 5 2 E
St-Fargeau, France 19 E10 47 39N 3 4 E
St-Félicien, Canada 104 C5 48 40N 72 25W
St-Florent, France 21 F13 42 41N 9 18 E
St-Florent, G. de, France 21 F13 42 47N 9 12 E
St-Florent-sur-Cher, France 19 F9 46 59N 2 15 E
St-Florentin, France 19 E10 48 0N 3 45 E
St-Flour, France 20 C7 45 2N 3 6 E
St. Francis, U.S.A. 112 F4 39 47N 101 48W
St. Francis →, U.S.A. 113 H9 34 38N 90 36W
St. Francis, C., S. Africa 88 E3 34 14 S 24 49 E
St. Francisville, U.S.A. 113 K9 30 47N 91 23W
St-François, L., Canada 117 A10 45 10N 74 22W
St-Fulgent, France 18 F5 46 50N 1 10W
St-Gabriel, Canada 104 C5 46 17N 73 24W
St. Gallen = Sankt Gallen, Switz. 25 H5 47 26N 9 22 E
St-Galmier, France 19 G11 45 35N 4 19 E
St-Gaudens, France 20 E4 43 6N 0 44 E
St-Gaultier, France 18 F8 46 39N 1 26 E
St-Gengoux-le-National, France 19 F11 46 37N 4 40 E
St-Geniez-d'Olt, France 20 D6 44 27N 2 58 E
St. George, Australia 95 D4 28 1 S 148 30 E
St. George, Canada 105 C6 45 11N 66 50W
St. George, S.C., U.S.A. 115 J5 33 11N 80 35W
St. George, Utah, U.S.A. 109 H7 37 6N 113 35W
St. George, C., Canada 105 C8 48 30N 59 16W
St. George, C., U.S.A. 115 L3 29 40N 85 5W
St. George Ra., Australia 92 C4 18 40 S 125 0 E
St. George's, Canada 105 C8 48 26N 58 31W
St-Georges, Canada 105 C5 46 8N 70 40W
St. George's, Grenada 121 D7 12 5N 61 43W
St. George's B., Canada 105 C8 48 24N 58 53W
St. Georges Basin, N.S.W., Australia 95 F5 35 7 S 150 36 E
St. Georges Basin, W. Austral., Australia 92 C4 15 23 S 125 2 E
St. George's Channel, Europe 12 E6 52 0N 6 0W
St. Georges Hd., Australia 95 F5 35 12 S 150 42 E
St-Georges-lès-Baillargeaux, France 20 B4 46 41N 0 22 E
St-Germain-de-Calberte, France 20 D7 44 13N 3 48 E
St-Germain-en-Laye, France 19 D9 48 54N 2 6 E
St-Germain-Lembron, France 20 C7 45 27N 3 14 E
St-Gervais-d'Auvergne, France 19 F9 46 4N 2 50 E
St-Gervais-les-Bains, France 21 C10 45 53N 6 42 E
St-Gildas, Pte. de, France 18 E4 47 8N 2 14W
St-Gilles, France 21 E8 43 40N 4 26 E
St-Girons, Ariège, France 20 F5 42 59N 1 8 E
St-Girons, Landes, France 20 E2 43 56N 1 18W
St. Gotthard P. = San Gottardo, P. del, Switz. 25 J4 46 33N 8 33 E
St. Helena, Atl. Oc. 76 H3 15 58 S 5 42W
St. Helena, U.S.A. 108 G2 38 30N 122 28W
St. Helena, Mt., U.S.A. 110 G4 38 40N 122 36W
St. Helena B., S. Africa 88 E2 32 40 S 18 10 E
St. Helens, Australia 95 G4 41 20 S 148 15 E
St. Helens, U.K. 14 D5 53 27N 2 44W
St. Helens, U.S.A. 110 E4 45 52N 122 48W
St. Helens, Mt., U.S.A. 110 D4 46 12N 122 12W
St. Helier, U.K. 15 H5 49 10N 2 7W
St-Herblain, France 18 E5 47 13N 1 40W
St-Hilaire-du-Harcouët, France 18 D5 48 35N 1 5W
St-Hippolyte, France 19 E13 47 19N 6 50 E
St-Hippolyte-du-Fort, France 20 E7 43 58N 3 52 E
St-Honoré-les-Bains, France 19 F10 46 54N 3 50 E
St-Hubert, Belgium 17 D5 50 2N 5 23 E
St-Hyacinthe, Canada 104 C5 45 40N 72 58W
St. Ignace, U.S.A. 114 C3 45 52N 84 44W
St. Ignace I., Canada 104 C2 48 45N 88 0W
St. Ignatius, U.S.A. 108 C6 47 19N 114 6W
St-Imier, Switz. 25 H2 47 9N 6 58 E
St. Ives, Cambs., U.K. 15 E7 52 20N 0 4W
St. Ives, Corn., U.K. 15 G2 50 12N 5 30W
St-James, France 18 D5 48 31N 1 20W
St. James, U.S.A. 112 D7 43 59N 94 38W
St-Jean →, Canada 105 B7 50 17N 64 20W
St-Jean, L., Canada 105 C5 48 40N 72 0W
St-Jean-d'Angély, France 20 C3 45 57N 0 31W
St-Jean-de-Braye, France 19 E8 47 53N 1 58 E
St-Jean-de-Luz, France 20 E2 43 23N 1 39W
St-Jean-de-Maurienne, France 21 C10 45 16N 6 21 E
St-Jean-de-Monts, France 18 F4 46 47N 2 4W
St-Jean-du-Gard, France 20 D7 44 7N 3 52 E
St-Jean-en-Royans, France 21 C9 45 1N 5 18 E
St-Jean-Pied-de-Port, France 20 E2 43 10N 1 14W
St-Jean-Port-Joli, Canada 105 C5 47 15N 70 13W
St-Jean-sur-Richelieu, Canada 117 A11 45 20N 73 20W
St-Jérôme, Canada 104 C5 45 47N 74 0W
St. John, Canada 105 C6 45 20N 66 8W
St. John, U.S.A. 113 G5 38 0N 98 46W
St. John →, Liberia 82 D2 6 40N 9 10W
St. John →, U.S.A. 115 C12 45 12N 66 5W
St. John, C., Canada 105 C8 50 0N 55 32W
St. John I., U.S. Virgin Is. 121 e 18 20N 64 42W
St. John's, Antigua & B. 121 C7 17 6N 61 51W
St. John's, Canada 105 C9 47 35N 52 40W
St. Johns, Ariz., U.S.A. 109 J9 34 30N 109 22W
St. Johns, Mich., U.S.A. 114 D3 43 0N 84 33W
St. Johns →, U.S.A. 115 K5 30 24N 81 24W
St. John's Pt., Ireland 12 B3 54 34N 8 27W
St. Johnsbury, U.S.A. 117 B12 44 25N 72 1W
St. Johnsville, U.S.A. 117 D10 43 0N 74 43W
St-Joseph, Martinique 120 c 14 39N 61 4W
St. Joseph, La., U.S.A. 113 K9 31 55N 91 14W
St. Joseph, Mo., U.S.A. 112 F7 39 46N 94 50W
St. Joseph →, U.S.A. 114 D2 42 7N 86 29W
St. Joseph, I., Canada 104 C3 46 12N 83 58W
St. Joseph, L., Canada 104 B1 51 10N 90 35W
St-Jovite, Canada 104 C5 46 8N 74 38W
St-Juéry, France 20 E6 43 57N 2 12 E
St-Julien-Chapteuil, France 21 C8 45 2N 4 4 E
St-Julien-de-Vouvantes, France 18 E5 47 38N 1 13W
St-Julien-en-Genevois, France 19 F13 46 9N 6 5 E
St-Junien, France 20 C4 45 53N 0 55 E
St-Just-en-Chaussée, France 19 C9 49 30N 2 25 E
St-Just-en-Chevalet, France 20 C7 45 55N 3 50 E
St. Kitts & Nevis ■, W. Indies 121 C7 17 20N 62 40W
St. Laurent, Canada 103 C9 50 25N 97 58W
St-Laurent-de-la-Salanque, France 20 F6 42 46N 2 59 E
St-Laurent-du-Pont, France 21 C9 45 23N 5 45 E
St-Laurent-en-Grandvaux, France 19 F12 46 35N 5 58 E
St-Laurent-Médoc, France 20 C3 45 8N 0 49W
St. Lawrence, Australia 94 C4 22 16 S 149 31 E
St. Lawrence, Canada 105 C8 46 54N 55 23W
St. Lawrence →, Canada 105 C6 49 30N 66 0W
St. Lawrence, Gulf of, Canada 105 C7 48 25N 62 0W
St. Lawrence I., U.S.A. 100 B3 63 30N 170 30W
St. Lawrence Islands △, Canada 117 B9 44 27N 75 52W
St. Leonard, Canada 105 C6 47 12N 67 58W
St-Léonard-de-Noblat, France 20 C5 45 49N 1 29 E
St. Lewis →, Canada 105 B8 52 26N 56 11W
St-Lô, France 18 C5 49 7N 1 5W
St-Louis, France 19 E14 47 30N 7 34 E
St-Louis, Guadeloupe 120 b 15 56N 61 19W
St. Louis, Senegal 82 B1 16 8N 16 27W
St. Louis, U.S.A. 112 F9 38 37N 90 12W
St. Louis →, U.S.A. 112 B8 47 15N 92 45W
St-Loup-sur-Semouse, France 19 E13 47 53N 6 16 E
St. Lucia ■, W. Indies 121 f 14 0N 60 50W
St. Lucia, L., S. Africa 89 D5 28 5 S 32 30 E
St. Lucia Channel, W. Indies 121 D7 14 15N 61 0W
St. Maarten ☒, W. Indies 121 C7 18 0N 63 5W
St. Magnus B., U.K. 13 A7 60 25N 1 35W
St-Maixent-l'École, France 20 B3 46 24N 0 12W
St-Malo, France 18 D4 48 39N 2 1W
St-Malo, G. de, France 18 D4 48 50N 2 30W
St-Mandrier-sur-Mer, France 21 E9 43 4N 5 57 E
St-Marc, Haiti 121 C5 19 10N 72 41W
St-Marcellin, France 21 C9 45 9N 5 20 E
St-Marcouf, Îs., France 18 C5 49 30N 1 10W
St. Maries, U.S.A. 108 C5 47 19N 116 35W
St-Martin ☒, W. Indies 121 C7 18 0N 63 0W
St-Martin, C., Martinique 120 c 14 52N 61 14W
St. Martin, L., Canada 103 C9 51 40N 98 30W
St-Martin-de-Crau, France 21 E8 43 38N 4 48 E
St-Martin-de-Ré, France 20 B2 46 12N 1 21W
St-Martin-d'Hères, France 21 C9 45 9N 5 45 E
St-Martin-Vésubie, France 21 D11 44 4N 7 15 E
St. Martins, Barbados 121 g 13 5N 59 28W
St-Martory, France 20 E4 43 9N 0 56 E
St. Mary Pk., Australia 95 E2 31 32 S 138 34 E
St. Marys, Australia 95 G4 41 35 S 148 11 E
St. Marys, Canada 116 C3 43 20N 81 10W
St. Mary's, Corn., U.K. 15 H1 49 55N 6 18W
St. Mary's, Orkney, U.K. 13 C6 58 54N 2 54W
St. Marys, Ga., U.S.A. 115 K5 30 44N 81 33W
St. Marys, Pa., U.S.A. 116 E6 41 26N 78 34W
St. Mary's, C., Canada 105 C9 46 50N 54 12W
St. Mary's B., Canada 105 C9 46 50N 53 50W
St. Marys Bay, Canada 105 D6 44 25N 66 10W
St-Mathieu, Pte., France 18 D2 48 20N 4 45W
St. Matthew I., U.S.A. 100 B2 60 24N 172 42W
St-Maurice →, Canada 104 C5 46 21N 72 31W
St. Mawes, U.K. 15 G2 50 10N 5 2W
St-Maximin-la-Ste-Baume, France 21 E9 43 27N 5 52 E
St-Médard-en-Jalles, France 20 D3 44 53N 0 43W
St-Méen-le-Grand, France 18 D4 48 11N 2 12W
St-Mihiel, France 19 D12 48 54N 5 32 E
St. Moritz, Switz. 25 J5 46 30N 9 51 E
St-Nazaire, France 18 E4 47 17N 2 12W
St. Neots, U.K. 15 E7 52 14N 0 15W
St-Nicolas-de-Port, France 19 D13 48 38N 6 18 E
St-Niklaas, Belgium 17 C4 51 10N 4 8 E
St-Omer, France 19 B9 50 45N 2 15 E
St-Palais-sur-Mer, France 20 C2 45 38N 1 5W
St-Pamphile, Canada 105 C6 46 58N 69 48W
St-Pardoux-la-Rivière, France 20 C4 45 29N 0 45 E
St-Pascal, Canada 105 C6 47 32N 69 48W
St. Paul, Canada 102 C6 54 0N 111 17W
St-Paul, France 21 D10 44 31N 6 45 E
St. Paul, Minn., U.S.A. 112 C8 44 57N 93 6W
St. Paul, Nebr., U.S.A. 112 E5 41 13N 98 27W
St-Paul →, Canada 105 B8 51 27N 57 42W
St. Paul →, Liberia 82 D2 6 25N 10 48W
St. Paul, I., Ind. Oc. 3 F13 38 55 S 77 34 E
St-Paul-de-Fenouillet, France 20 F6 42 48N 2 30 E
St. Paul I., Canada 105 C7 47 12N 60 9W
St-Paul-lès-Dax, France 20 E2 43 44N 1 3W
St-Péray, France 21 D8 44 57N 4 50 E
St. Peter, U.S.A. 112 C8 44 20N 93 57W
St-Peter-Ording, Germany 24 A4 54 20N 8 36 E
St. Peter Port, U.K. 15 H5 49 26N 2 33W
St. Peters, N.S., Canada 105 C7 45 40N 60 53W
St. Peters, P.E.I., Canada 105 C7 46 25N 62 35W
St. Petersburg = Sankt-Peterburg, Russia 32 C6 59 55N 30 20 E
St. Petersburg, U.S.A. 115 M4 27 46N 82 39W
St-Philbert-de-Grand-Lieu, France 18 E5 47 2N 1 39W
St-Pie, Canada 117 A12 45 30N 72 54W
St-Pierre, Martinique 120 c 14 45N 61 10W
St-Pierre, St-P. & M. 105 C8 46 46N 56 12W
St-Pierre, L., Canada 104 C5 46 12N 72 52W
St-Pierre-d'Oléron, France 20 C2 45 57N 1 19W
St-Pierre-en-Port, France 18 C7 49 48N 0 30 E
St-Pierre-et-Miquelon ☒, N. Amer. 105 C8 46 55N 56 10W
St-Pierre-le-Moûtier, France 19 F10 46 47N 3 7 E
St-Pierre-sur-Dives, France 18 C6 49 2N 0 1W
St-Pol-de-Léon, France 18 D3 48 41N 4 0W
St-Pol-sur-Mer, France 19 A9 51 1N 2 20 E
St-Pol-sur-Ternoise, France 19 B9 50 23N 2 20 E
St-Pons, France 20 E6 43 30N 2 45 E
St-Pourçain-sur-Sioule, France 19 F10 46 18N 3 18 E
St-Priest, France 21 C8 45 42N 4 57 E
St-Quay-Portrieux, France 18 D4 48 39N 2 51W
St-Quentin, Canada 105 C6 47 30N 67 23W
St-Quentin, France 19 C10 49 50N 3 16 E
St-Rambert-d'Albon, France 21 C8 45 17N 4 49 E
St-Raphaël, France 21 E10 43 25N 6 46 E
St. Regis, U.S.A. 108 C6 47 18N 115 6W
St-Renan, France 18 D2 48 26N 4 37W
St-Saëns, France 18 C8 49 41N 1 16 E
St-Savin, France 20 B4 46 34N 0 53 E
St-Savinien, France 20 C3 45 53N 0 42W
St. Sebastien, Tanjon' i, Madag. 89 A8 12 26 S 48 44 E
St-Seine-l'Abbaye, France 19 E11 47 26N 4 47 E
St-Sernin-sur-Rance, France 20 E6 43 54N 2 35 E
St-Sever, France 20 E3 43 45N 0 35W
St-Siméon, Canada 105 C6 47 51N 69 54W
St. Simons I., U.S.A. 115 K5 31 12N 81 15W
St. Simons Island, U.S.A. 115 K5 31 9N 81 22W
St. Stephen, Canada 105 C6 45 16N 67 17W
St-Sulpice, France 20 E5 43 46N 1 41 E
St-Sulpice-Laurière, France 20 B5 46 3N 1 29 E
St-Sulpice-les-Feuilles, France 20 B5 46 19N 1 21 E
St-Syprien = St-Cyprien, France 20 F7 42 37N 3 2 E
St-Thégonnec, France 18 D3 48 31N 3 57W
St. Thomas, Canada 116 D3 42 45N 81 10W
St. Thomas I., U.S. Virgin Is. 121 e 18 20N 64 55W
St-Tite, Canada 104 C5 46 45N 72 34W
St-Tropez, France 21 E10 43 17N 6 38 E
St-Troud = St. Truiden, Belgium 17 D5 50 48N 5 10 E
St. Truiden, Belgium 17 D5 50 48N 5 10 E
St-Vaast-la-Hougue, France 18 C5 49 35N 1 17W
St-Valery-en-Caux, France 18 C7 49 52N 0 43 E
St-Valéry-sur-Somme, France 19 B8 50 11N 1 38 E
St-Vallier, France 19 F11 46 38N 4 22 E
St-Vallier-de-Thiey, France 21 E10 43 42N 6 51 E
St-Varent, France 18 F6 46 53N 0 13W
St-Vaury, France 20 B5 46 12N 1 46 E
St. Vincent, Italy 40 C4 45 45N 7 39 E
St. Vincent, G., Australia 95 F2 35 0 S 138 0 E
St. Vincent & the Grenadines ■, W. Indies 121 D7 13 0N 61 10W
St-Vincent-de-Tyrosse, France 20 E2 43 39N 1 19W
St. Vincent Passage, W. Indies 121 D7 13 30N 61 0W
St-Vith, Belgium 17 D6 50 17N 6 9 E
St-Vivien-de-Médoc, France 20 C2 45 25N 1 2W
St. Walburg, Canada 103 C7 53 39N 109 12W
St-Yrieix-la-Perche, France 20 C5 45 31N 1 12 E
Ste-Adresse, France 18 C7 49 31N 0 5 E
Ste-Agathe-des-Monts, Canada 104 C5 46 3N 74 17W
Ste-Anne, Guadeloupe 120 b 16 13N 61 24W
Ste-Anne, L., Canada 105 B6 50 0N 67 42W
Ste-Anne-des-Monts-Tourelle, Canada 105 C6 49 8N 66 30W
Ste-Croix, Switz. 25 J2 46 49N 6 34 E
Ste-Enimie, France 20 D7 44 22N 3 26 E
Ste-Foy-la-Grande, France 20 D4 44 50N 0 13 E
Ste. Genevieve, U.S.A. 112 G9 37 59N 90 2W
Ste-Hermine, France 20 B2 46 32N 1 4W
Ste-Livrade-sur-Lot, France 20 D4 44 24N 0 36 E
Ste-Marguerite →, Canada 105 B6 50 9N 66 36W
Ste-Marie, Canada 105 C5 46 26N 71 0W
Ste-Marie, Martinique 120 c 14 48N 61 1W
Ste-Marie-aux-Mines, France 19 D14 48 15N 7 12 E
Ste-Maure-de-Touraine, France 18 E7 47 7N 0 37 E
Ste-Maxime, France 21 E10 43 19N 6 39 E
Ste-Menehould, France 19 C11 49 5N 4 54 E
Ste-Mère-Église, France 18 C5 49 24N 1 19W
Ste-Rose, Guadeloupe 120 b 16 20N 61 45W
Ste. Rose du Lac, Canada 103 C9 51 4N 99 30W
Ste-Savine, France 19 D11 48 18N 4 3 E
Ste-Sigolène, France 21 C8 45 15N 4 14 E
Saintes, France 20 C3 45 45N 0 37W
Saintes, Îs. des, Guadeloupe 120 b 15 50N 61 35W
Stes-Maries-de-la-Mer, France 21 E8 43 26N 4 26 E
Saintfield, U.K. 12 B6 54 28N 5 49W
Saintonge, France 20 C3 45 40N 0 50W
Saipan, Pac. Oc. 96 F6 15 12N 145 45 E
Sairang, India 67 H18 23 50N 92 45 E
Sairecábur, Cerro, Bolivia 126 A2 22 43 S 67 54W
Saitama □, Japan 55 F9 36 25N 139 30 E
Saiteli = Kadınhanı, Turkey 72 C5 38 14N 32 13 E
Saiţi, Moldova 29 D14 46 30N 29 24 E
Saiyid, Pakistan 68 C5 33 7N 73 2 E
Saja-Besaya △, Spain 36 B6 43 10N 4 9W
Sajama, Bolivia 124 G5 18 7 S 69 0W
Sajan, Serbia & M. 28 E5 45 50N 20 20 E
Sajó →, Hungary 28 C6 47 56N 21 7 E
Sajószentpéter, Hungary 28 B5 48 12N 20 44 E
Sajum, India 69 C8 33 20N 79 0 E
Sak →, S. Africa 88 E3 30 52 S 20 25 E
Sakaba, Nigeria 83 C6 11 4N 5 35 E
Sakai, Japan 55 G7 34 30N 135 30 E
Sakaide, Japan 55 G6 34 19N 133 50 E
Sakaiminato, Japan 55 G6 35 38N 133 11 E
Sakākah, Si. Arabia 70 D4 30 0N 40 8 E
Sakakawea, L., U.S.A. 112 B4 47 30N 101 25W
Sakami →, Canada 104 B4 53 40N 76 40W
Sakami, L., Canada 104 B4 53 15N 77 0W
Sâkâne, 'Erg i-n, Mali 83 A4 20 30N 1 30W
Sakania, Dem. Rep. of the Congo 87 E2 12 43 S 28 30 E
Sakaraha, Madag. 89 C7 22 55 S 44 32 E
Sakarya, Turkey 72 B4 40 48N 30 25 E
Sakarya →, Turkey 72 B4 41 7N 30 39 E
Sakashima-Guntō, Japan 55 M2 24 46N 124 0 E
Sakassou, Ivory C. 82 D3 7 29N 5 19W
Sakata, Japan 54 E9 38 55N 139 50 E
Sakchu, N. Korea 57 D13 40 23N 125 2 E
Sakeny →, Madag. 89 C8 20 0 S 45 25 E
Sakété, Benin 83 D5 6 40N 2 45 E
Sakha □, Russia 53 C13 66 0N 130 0 E
Sakhalin, Russia 53 D15 51 0N 143 0 E
Sakhalinskiy Zaliv, Russia 53 D15 54 0N 141 0 E
Şaki, Azerbaijan 35 K8 41 10N 47 5 E
Šakiai, Lithuania 9 J20 54 59N 23 2 E
Sakon Nakhon, Thailand 64 D5 17 10N 104 9 E
Sakrand, Pakistan 68 F3 26 10N 68 15 E
Sakri, India 69 F12 26 13N 86 5 E
Sakrivier, S. Africa 88 E3 30 54 S 20 28 E
Sakskøbing, Denmark 11 K5 54 49N 11 39 E
Sakti, India 69 H10 22 2N 82 58 E
Sakuma, Japan 55 G8 35 3N 137 49 E
Sakurai, Japan 55 G7 34 30N 135 51 E
Saky, Ukraine 33 K7 45 9N 33 34 E
Sal →, Russia 35 G5 47 31N 40 45 E
Sala, Eritrea 81 D4 16 53N 37 36 E
Sal'a, Slovak Rep. 27 C10 48 10N 17 50 E
Sala, Sweden 10 E10 59 58N 16 35 E
Sala →, Eritrea 81 D4 16 53N 37 36 E
Sala Consilina, Italy 43 B8 40 23N 15 36 E
Sala-y-Gómez, Pac. Oc. 97 K17 26 28 S 105 28W
Salaberry-de-Valleyfield, Canada 117 A10 45 15N 74 8W
Salacgrīva, Latvia 30 A11 57 45N 24 21 E
Salada, L., Mexico 109 K6 32 20N 115 40W
Saladas, Argentina 126 B4 28 15 S 58 40W
Saladillo, Argentina 126 D4 35 40 S 59 55W
Salado →, Buenos Aires, Argentina 126 D4 35 44 S 57 22W
Salado →, La Pampa, Argentina 128 D3 37 30 S 67 0W
Salado →, Santa Fe, Argentina 126 C3 31 40 S 60 41W
Salado →, Mexico 113 M5 26 52N 99 19W
Salaga, Ghana 83 D4 8 31N 0 31W
Şalāh, Syria 74 C5 32 40N 36 45 E
Şalāḥ ad Dīn □, Iraq 70 C4 34 35N 43 35 E
Sălaj □, Romania 28 C8 47 15N 23 0 E
Sálakhos, Greece 49 C9 36 17N 27 57 E
Salala, Liberia 82 D2 6 42N 10 7W
Salala, Sudan 80 C4 21 17N 36 16 E
Salālah, Oman 75 D5 16 56N 53 59 E
Salamanca, Chile 126 C1 31 46 S 70 59W
Salamanca, Spain 36 E5 40 58N 5 39W
Salamanca, U.S.A. 116 D6 42 10N 78 43W
Salamanca □, Spain 36 E5 40 57N 5 40W
Salāmatābād, Iran 70 C5 35 39N 47 50 E
Salamis, Cyprus 49 D12 35 11N 33 54 E
Salamís, Greece 46 D5 37 56N 23 30 E
Salar de Atacama, Chile 126 A2 23 30 S 68 25W
Salar de Uyuni, Bolivia 124 H5 20 30 S 67 45W
Sălard, Romania 28 C7 47 12N 22 3 E
Salas, Spain 36 B4 43 25N 6 15W
Salas de los Infantes, Spain 36 C7 42 2N 3 17W
Salatiga, Indonesia 63 G14 7 19 S 110 30 E
Salaverry, Peru 124 E3 8 15 S 79 0W
Salawati, Indonesia 63 E8 1 7 S 130 52 E
Salaya, India 68 H3 22 19N 69 35 E
Salayar, Indonesia 63 F6 6 7 S 120 30 E
Salazar →, Spain 38 C3 42 40N 1 20W
Salbris, France 19 E9 47 25N 2 3 E
Sălcia, Romania 29 G9 43 56N 24 55 E
Sălciua, Romania 29 D8 46 24N 23 26 E
Salcombe, U.K. 15 G4 50 14N 3 47W
Saldaña, Spain 36 C6 42 32N 4 48W
Saldanha, S. Africa 88 E2 33 0 S 17 58 E
Saldanha B., S. Africa 88 E2 33 6 S 18 0 E
Saldus, Latvia 9 H20 56 38N 22 30 E
Saldus □, Latvia 30 B9 56 35N 22 30 E
Sale, Australia 95 F4 38 6 S 147 6 E
Sale, Italy 40 D5 44 59N 8 48 E
Salé, Morocco 78 B4 34 3N 6 48W
Sale, U.K. 14 D5 53 26N 2 19W
Salekhard, Russia 52 C7 66 30N 66 35 E
Salem, India 66 P11 11 40N 78 11 E
Salem, Ill., U.S.A. 114 F1 38 38N 88 57W
Salem, Ind., U.S.A. 114 F2 38 36N 86 6W
Salem, Mass., U.S.A. 117 D14 42 31N 70 53W
Salem, Mo., U.S.A. 113 G9 37 39N 91 32W
Salem, N.H., U.S.A. 117 D13 42 45N 71 12W
Salem, N.J., U.S.A. 114 F8 39 34N 75 28W
Salem, N.Y., U.S.A. 117 C11 43 10N 73 20W
Salem, Ohio, U.S.A. 116 F4 40 54N 80 52W
Salem, Oreg., U.S.A. 108 D2 44 56N 123 2W
Salem, S. Dak., U.S.A. 112 D6 43 44N 97 23W
Salem, Va., U.S.A. 114 G5 37 18N 80 3W
Salemi, Italy 42 E5 37 49N 12 48 E
Sälen, Sweden 10 C7 61 15N 13 22 E
Salernes, France 21 E10 43 34N 6 15 E
Salerno, Italy 43 B7 40 41N 14 47 E
Salerno, G. di, Italy 43 B7 40 32N 14 42 E
Salford, U.K. 14 D5 53 30N 2 18W
Salgir →, Ukraine 33 K8 45 38N 35 1 E
Salgótarján, Hungary 28 B4 48 5N 19 47 E
Salgueiro, Brazil 125 E11 8 4 S 39 6W
Salibabu, Indonesia 63 D7 3 51N 126 40 E
Salibea, Trin. & Tob. 125 K15 10 43N 61 2W
Salida, U.S.A. 106 C5 38 32N 106 0W
Salies-de-Béarn, France 20 E3 43 28N 0 56W
Salihli, Turkey 72 C3 38 28N 28 8 E
Salihorsk, Belarus 33 F4 52 51N 27 27 E
Salima, Malawi 85 G6 13 47 S 34 28 E
Salina, Italy 43 D7 38 34N 14 50 E
Salina, Kans., U.S.A. 112 F6 38 50N 97 37W
Salina, Utah, U.S.A. 109 G8 38 58N 111 51W
Salina Cruz, Mexico 119 D5 16 10N 95 10W
Salina di Margherita di Savoia ⌂, Italy 43 A9 41 23N 16 4 E
Salinas, Brazil 125 G10 16 10 S 42 10W
Salinas, Chile 126 A2 23 31 S 69 29W
Salinas, Ecuador 124 D2 2 10 S 80 58W
Salinas, U.S.A. 110 J5 36 40N 121 39W
Salinas →, Guatemala 119 D6 16 28N 90 31W
Salinas →, U.S.A. 110 J5 36 45N 121 48W
Salinas, B. de, Nic. 120 D2 11 4N 85 45W
Salinas, Pampa de las, Argentina 126 C2 31 58 S 66 42W
Salinas Ambargasta, Argentina 126 B3 29 0 S 65 0W
Salinas de Hidalgo, Mexico 118 C4 22 30N 101 40W
Salinas Grandes, Argentina 126 C3 30 0 S 65 0W
Salinas Pueblo Missions ⌂, U.S.A. 109 J10 34 16N 106 5W
Saline →, Ark., U.S.A. 113 J8 33 10N 92 8W
Saline →, Kans., U.S.A. 112 F6 38 52N 97 30W
Saline di Trapani e Paceco ⌂, Italy 42 E5 37 59N 12 28 E
Salines, C. de ses, Spain 48 B10 39 16N 3 4 E
Salinópolis, Brazil 125 D9 0 40 S 47 20W
Salins-les-Bains, France 19 F12 46 58N 5 52 E
Salir, Portugal 37 H2 37 14N 8 2W
Salisbury, U.K. 15 F6 51 4N 1 47W
Salisbury, Md., U.S.A. 114 F8 38 22N 75 36W
Salisbury, N.C., U.S.A. 115 H5 35 40N 80 29W
Salisbury I., Canada 101 B12 63 30N 77 0W
Salisbury Plain, U.K. 15 F6 51 14N 1 55W
Sălişte, Romania 29 E8 45 45N 23 56 E
Salka, Nigeria 83 C5 10 20N 4 58 E
Şalkhad, Syria 74 C5 32 29N 36 43 E
Salkove, Ukraine 29 B14 48 15N 29 59 E
Salla, Finland 8 C23 66 50N 28 49 E
Sallanches, France 21 C10 45 55N 6 38 E
Sallent, Spain 38 D6 41 49N 1 54 E
Salles, France 20 D3 44 33N 0 52W
Salles-Curan, France 20 D6 44 11N 2 48 E
Salling, Denmark 11 H2 56 40N 8 55 E
Salliq = Coral Harbour, Canada 101 B11 64 8N 83 10W
Sallisaw, U.S.A. 113 H7 35 28N 94 47W
Sallom Junction, Sudan 80 D4 19 17N 37 6 E
Salluit, Canada 101 B12 62 14N 75 38W
Salmās, Iran 70 B5 38 11N 44 47 E
Salmerón, Spain 38 E2 40 33N 2 29W
Salmo, Canada 102 D5 49 10N 117 20W
Salmon, U.S.A. 108 D7 45 11N 113 54W
Salmon →, Canada 102 C4 54 3N 122 40W
Salmon →, U.S.A. 108 D5 45 51N 116 47W
Salmon Arm, Canada 102 C5 50 40N 119 15W
Salmon Gums, Australia 93 F3 32 59 S 121 38 E
Salmon River Mts., U.S.A. 108 D6 45 0N 114 30W
Salo, Finland 9 F20 60 22N 23 10 E
Salò, Italy 40 C7 45 36N 10 31 E

Salobreña, *Spain* **37 J7** 36 44N 3 35W
Salome, *U.S.A.* **111 M13** 33 47N 113 37W
Salon, *India* ...... **69 F9** 26 2N 81 27 E
Salon-de-Provence,
  France ...... **21 E9** 43 39N 5 6 E
Salonica = Thessaloníki,
  Greece ...... **44 F6** 40 38N 22 58 E
Salonta, *Romania* ...... **28 D6** 46 49N 21 42 E
Salor →, *Spain* ...... **37 F3** 39 39N 7 3 W
Salou, *Spain* ...... **38 D6** 41 4N 1 8 E
Salou, C. de, *Spain* ...... **38 D6** 41 3N 1 10 E
Saloum →, *Senegal* **82 C1** 13 50N 16 45W
Salpausselkä, *Finland* ...... **9 F22** 61 3N 26 15 E
Salsacate, *Argentina* ...... **126 C2** 31 20 S 65 5W
Salses, *France* ...... **20 F6** 42 50N 2 55 E
Salsk, *Russia* ...... **35 G5** 46 28N 41 30 E
Salso →, *Italy* ...... **42 E6** 37 6N 13 57 E
Salsomaggiore Terme,
  Italy ...... **40 D6** 44 49N 9 59 E
Salt, *Spain* ...... **38 D7** 41 59N 2 47 E
Salt →, *Canada* **102 B6** 60 0N 112 25W
Salt →, *U.S.A.* **109 K7** 33 23N 112 19W
Salt L., *The, Australia* ...... **95 E3** 30 6 S 142 8 E
Salt Lake City, *U.S.A.* **108 F8** 40 45N 111 53W
Salt Range, *Pakistan* ...... **68 C5** 32 30N 72 25 E
Salta, *Argentina* ...... **126 A2** 24 57 S 65 25W
Salta □, *Argentina* ...... **126 A2** 24 48 S 65 30W
Saltara, *Italy* ...... **41 E9** 43 45N 12 50 E
Saltash, *U.K.* **15 G3** 50 24N 4 14W
Saltburn by the Sea,
  U.K. **14 C7** 54 35N 0 58W
Saltcoats, *U.K.* **13 F4** 55 38N 4 47W
Saltee Is., *Ireland* **12 D5** 52 7N 6 37W
Saltfjellet, *Norway* ...... **8 C16** 66 40N 15 15 E
Saltfjorden, *Norway* ...... **8 C16** 67 15N 14 10 E
Saltholm, *Denmark* ...... **11 J6** 55 38N 12 43 E
Saltillo, *Mexico* **118 B4** 25 25N 101 0W
Salto, *Argentina* ...... **126 C3** 34 20 S 60 15W
Salto, *Uruguay* ...... **126 C4** 31 27 S 57 50W
Salto del Guairá,
  Paraguay ...... **127 A5** 24 3 S 54 17W
Salton City, *U.S.A.* **111 M11** 33 29N 115 51W
Salton Sea, *U.S.A.* **111 M11** 33 15N 115 45W
Saltpond, *Ghana* **83 D4** 5 15N 1 3W
Saltsburg, *U.S.A.* **116 F5** 40 29N 79 27W
Saltsjöbaden, *Sweden* ...... **10 E12** 59 15N 18 20 E
Saluda →, *U.S.A.* **115 J5** 34 1N 81 4W
Salûm, *Egypt* ...... **80 A2** 31 31N 25 7 E
Salûm, Khâlig el, *Egypt* ...... **80 A2** 31 35N 25 24 E
Salur, *India* ...... **67 K13** 18 27N 83 18 E
Saluzzo, *Italy* ...... **40 D4** 44 39N 7 29 E
Salvador, *Brazil* ...... **125 F11** 13 0 S 38 30W
Salvador, *Canada* **103 C7** 52 10N 109 32W
Salvador, El ■,
  Cent. Amer. **120 D2** 13 50N 89 0W
Salvador, L., *U.S.A.* **113 L9** 29 43N 90 15W
Salvaterra de Magos,
  Portugal **37 F2** 39 1N 8 47W
Sálvora, I. de, *Spain* **36 C2** 42 30N 8 58W
Salween →, *Burma* ...... **67 L20** 16 31N 97 37 E
Salyan, *Azerbaijan* ...... **52 F5** 39 33N 48 59 E
Salza →, *Austria* ...... **26 D7** 47 40N 14 43 E
Salzach →, *Austria* ...... **26 C5** 48 12N 12 56 E
Salzburg, *Austria* ...... **26 D6** 47 48N 13 2 E
Salzburg □, *Austria* ...... **26 D6** 47 15N 13 0 E
Salzgitter, *Germany* ...... **24 C6** 52 9N 10 19 E
Salzkotten, *Germany* ...... **24 D4** 51 40N 8 37 E
Salzwedel, *Germany* ...... **24 C7** 52 52N 11 10 E
Sam, *India* ...... **68 F4** 26 50N 70 31 E
Sam Neua, *Laos* ...... **58 G5** 20 29N 104 5 E
Sam Ngao, *Thailand* ...... **64 D2** 17 18N 99 0 E
Sam Rayburn Reservoir,
  U.S.A. **113 K7** 31 4N 94 5W
Sam Son, *Vietnam* ...... **64 C5** 19 44N 105 54 E
Sam Teu, *Laos* ...... **64 C5** 19 59N 104 38 E
Sama de Langreo =
  Langreo, *Spain* **36 B5** 43 18N 5 40W
Samagaltay, *Russia* ...... **53 D10** 50 36N 95 3 E
Samâlût, *Egypt* ...... **80 B3** 28 20N 30 42 E
Samana, *India* ...... **68 D7** 30 10N 76 13 E
Samana Cay, *Bahamas* **121 B5** 23 3N 73 45W
Samandağı, *Turkey* ...... **72 D6** 36 5N 35 59 E
Samandra, *Turkey* ...... **45 F13** 40 59N 29 13 E
Samanga, *Tanzania* ...... **87 D4** 8 20 S 39 13 E
Samangân □, *Afghan.* ...... **66 B5** 36 15N 68 3 E
Samangwa, Dem. Rep. of
  the Congo ...... **86 C1** 4 23 S 24 10 E
Samani, *Japan* ...... **54 C11** 42 7N 142 56 E
Samanli Dağları, *Turkey* ...... **45 F13** 40 32N 29 10 E
Samar, *Phil.* ...... **61 F6** 12 0N 125 0 E
Samara, *Russia* ...... **34 D10** 53 8N 50 6 E
Samara →, *Russia* ...... **34 D10** 53 10N 50 4 E
Samara →, *Ukraine* ...... **33 H8** 48 28N 35 7 E
Samaria = Shōmron,
  West Bank ...... **74 C4** 32 15N 35 13 E
Samariá, *Greece* ...... **49 D5** 35 17N 23 58 E
Samaria △, *Greece* ...... **46 F5** 35 18N 23 57 E
Samarinda, *Indonesia* ...... **62 E5** 0 30 S 117 9 E
Samarkand =
  Samarqand,
  Uzbekistan ...... **52 F7** 39 40N 66 55 E
Samarqand, *Uzbekistan* ...... **52 F7** 39 40N 66 55 E
Sāmarrā', *Iraq* ...... **70 C4** 34 12N 43 52 E
Samastipur, *India* ...... **69 G11** 25 50N 85 50 E
Samaxi, *Azerbaijan* ...... **35 K9** 40 38N 48 32 E
Samba, Dem. Rep. of
  the Congo ...... **86 C2** 4 38 S 26 22 E
Samba, *India* ...... **69 C6** 32 32N 75 10 E
Sambalpur, *India* ...... **67 J14** 21 28N 84 4 E
Sambar, Tanjung,
  Indonesia ...... **62 E4** 2 59 S 110 19 E
Sambas, *Indonesia* ...... **62 D3** 1 20N 109 20 E
Sambava, *Madag.* ...... **89 A9** 14 16 S 50 10 E
Sambawizi, *Zimbabwe* ...... **87 F2** 18 24 S 26 13 E
Sambhal, *India* ...... **69 E8** 28 35N 78 37 E
Sambhar, *India* ...... **68 F6** 26 52N 75 6 E
Sambhar L., *India* ...... **68 F6** 26 55N 75 12 E
Sambiase, *Italy* ...... **43 D9** 38 58N 16 17 E
Sambir, *Ukraine* ...... **31 J10** 49 30N 23 10 E
Sambor, *Cambodia* ...... **64 F6** 12 46N 106 0 E
Samborombón, B.,
  Argentina ...... **126 D4** 36 5 S 57 20W
Sambuca di Sicília, *Italy* ...... **42 E6** 37 39N 13 7 E
Samburu, *Kenya* ...... **86 B4** 3 37 S 37 31 E
Samch'ŏk, *S. Korea* ...... **57 F15** 37 30N 129 10 E
Samch'onp'o, *S. Korea* ...... **57 G15** 35 0N 128 6 E
Same, *Tanzania* ...... **86 C4** 4 2 S 37 38 E
Samfya, *Zambia* ...... **87 E2** 11 22 S 29 31 E
Sámi, *Greece* ...... **46 C2** 38 15N 20 39 E
Şämkir, *Azerbaijan* ...... **35 K8** 40 50N 46 0 E
Samli, *Turkey* ...... **47 B9** 39 48N 27 51 E
Sammañ, Si. Arabia ...... **70 E3** 25 10N 37 15 E
Samo Alto, *Chile* ...... **126 C1** 30 22 S 71 0W
Samoa ■, *Pac. Oc.* ...... **91 B13** 14 0 S 172 0W
Samoan Is., *Pac. Oc.* ...... **91 A13** 14 0 S 171 0W
Samobor, *Croatia* ...... **41 C12** 45 47N 15 44 E

Samoëns, *France* ...... **19 F13** 46 5N 6 45 E
Samokov, *Bulgaria* ...... **44 D7** 42 18N 23 35 E
Šamorín, Slovak Rep. ...... **27 C10** 48 2N 17 19 E
Samorogouan,
  Burkina Faso **82 C4** 11 21N 4 57W
Sámos, *Greece* ...... **47 D8** 37 45N 26 50 E
Samoš, *Serbia & M.* ...... **28 E5** 45 13N 20 46 E
Samos, *Spain* **36 C3** 42 44N 7 20W
Sámos □, *Greece* ...... **47 D8** 37 45N 26 50 E
Samothráki = Mathráki,
  Greece ...... **49 A3** 39 48N 19 31 E
Samothráki, *Greece* ...... **45 F9** 40 28N 25 28 E
Samoylovka, *Russia* ...... **34 E6** 51 12N 43 43 E
Sampa, *Ghana* **82 D4** 8 0N 2 36W
Sampacho, *Argentina* ...... **126 C3** 33 20 S 64 50W
Sampalan, *Indonesia* ...... **63 K18** 8 41 S 115 34 E
Sampang, *Indonesia* ...... **63 G15** 7 11 S 113 13 E
Samper de Calanda,
  Spain **38 D4** 41 11N 0 28W
Sampéyre, *Italy* ...... **40 D4** 44 34N 7 11 E
Sampit, *Indonesia* ...... **62 E4** 2 34 S 113 0 E
Sampit, Teluk, *Indonesia* ...... **62 E4** 3 5 S 113 3 E
Samrong, *Cambodia* ...... **64 E4** 14 15N 103 30 E
Samrong, *Thailand* ...... **64 E3** 15 10N 100 40 E
Samsø, *Denmark* ...... **11 J4** 55 50N 10 35 E
Samsø Bælt, *Denmark* ...... **11 J4** 55 45N 10 45 E
Samsun, *Turkey* ...... **72 B7** 41 15N 36 22 E
Samtredia, *Georgia* ...... **35 J6** 42 7N 42 24 E
Samui, Ko, *Thailand* ...... **65 b** 9 30N 100 0 E
Samur →, *Russia* ...... **35 K9** 41 53N 48 32 E
Samurskiy Khrebet,
  Russia ...... **35 K8** 41 55N 47 11 E
Samusole, Dem. Rep. of
  the Congo ...... **87 E1** 10 2 S 24 0 E
Samut Prakan, *Thailand* ...... **64 F3** 13 32N 100 40 E
Samut Songkhram □,
  Thailand ...... **62 B1** 13 24N 100 1 E
Samwari, *Pakistan* ...... **68 E2** 28 30N 66 46 E
San, *Mali* **82 C4** 13 15N 4 57W
San →, *Cambodia* ...... **64 F5** 13 32N 105 57 E
San →, *Poland* ...... **31 H8** 50 45N 21 51 E
San Adrián, *Spain* **38 C3** 42 20N 1 56W
San Adrián, C. de, *Spain* **36 B2** 43 21N 8 50W
San Agustín, C., *Phil.* ...... **61 H7** 6 20N 126 13 E
San Agustín de Valle
  Fértil, *Argentina* ...... **126 C2** 30 35 S 67 30W
San Ambrosio, Pac. Oc. ...... **97 K20** 26 28 S 79 53W
San Andreas, *U.S.A.* **110 G6** 38 12N 120 41W
San Andrés, *Phil.* ...... **61 E6** 13 36N 124 6 E
San Andrés, I. de,
  Caribbean **120 D3** 12 42N 81 46W
San Andrés del
  Rabanedo, *Spain* **36 C5** 42 37N 5 36W
San Andres Mts., *U.S.A.* **109 K10** 33 0N 106 30W
San Andrés Tuxtla,
  Mexico **119 D5** 18 30N 95 20W
San Angelo, *U.S.A.* **113 K4** 31 28N 100 26W
San Anselmo, *U.S.A.* **110 H4** 37 59N 122 34W
San Antonio, *Belize* **119 D7** 16 15N 89 2W
San Antonio, *Chile* ...... **126 C1** 33 40 S 71 40W
San Antonio, *Phil.* ...... **61 D4** 14 57N 120 5 E
San Antonio, N. Mex.,
  U.S.A. **109 K10** 33 55N 106 52W
San Antonio, Tex.,
  U.S.A. **113 L5** 29 25N 98 30W
San Antonio →, *U.S.A.* **113 L6** 28 30N 96 54W
San Antonio, C.,
  Argentina ...... **126 D4** 36 15 S 56 40W
San Antonio, C., Cuba **120 B3** 21 50N 84 57W
San Antonio, C. de,
  Spain ...... **39 G5** 38 48N 0 12 E
San Antonio, Mt.,
  U.S.A. **111 L9** 34 17N 117 38W
San Antonio de los
  Baños, Cuba **120 B3** 22 54N 82 31W
San Antonio de los
  Cobres, *Argentina* ...... **126 A2** 24 10 S 66 17W
San Antonio Oeste,
  Argentina ...... **128 E4** 40 40 S 65 0W
San Arcángelo, *Italy* ...... **43 B9** 40 14N 16 14 E
San Ardo, *U.S.A.* **110 J6** 36 1N 120 54W
San Augustine, *U.S.A.* **113 K7** 31 30N 94 7W
San Bartolomé,
  Canary Is. **48 F6** 28 59N 13 37W
San Bartolomé de
  Tirajana, Canary Is. **48 G4** 27 54N 15 34W
San Bartolomeo in
  Galdo, *Italy* ...... **43 A8** 41 24N 15 1 E
San Benedetto del
  Tronto, *Italy* ...... **41 F10** 42 57N 13 53 E
San Benedetto Po, *Italy* ...... **40 C7** 45 2N 10 55 E
San Benedicto, I.,
  Mexico **118 D2** 19 18N 110 49W
San Benito, *U.S.A.* **113 N6** 26 8N 97 38W
San Benito →, *U.S.A.* **110 J5** 36 53N 121 34W
San Benito Mt., *U.S.A.* **110 J6** 36 22N 120 37W
San Bernardino, *U.S.A.* **111 L9** 34 7N 117 19W
San Bernardino Mts.,
  U.S.A. **111 L10** 34 10N 116 45W
San Bernardino Str.,
  Phil. ...... **61 E6** 13 0N 125 0 E
San Bernardo, *Chile* ...... **126 C1** 33 40 S 70 50W
San Bernardo, I. de,
  Colombia **124 B3** 9 45N 75 50W
San Blas, *Mexico* **118 B3** 26 4N 108 46W
San Blas, Arch. de,
  Panama **120 E4** 9 50N 78 31W
San Blas, C., *U.S.A.* **115 L3** 29 40N 85 21W
San Bonifacio, *Italy* ...... **41 C8** 45 24N 11 16 E
San Borja, *Bolivia* ...... **124 F5** 14 50 S 66 52W
San Buenaventura =
  Ventura, *U.S.A.* **111 L7** 34 17N 119 18W
San Buenaventura,
  Mexico **118 B4** 27 5N 101 32W
San Carlos = Sant
  Carles, *Spain* ...... **48 B8** 39 3N 1 34 E
San Carlos, *Argentina* ...... **126 C2** 33 50 S 69 0W
San Carlos, *Chile* ...... **126 D1** 36 10 S 72 0W
San Carlos,
  Baja Calif. S., Mexico **118 C2** 24 47N 112 6W
San Carlos, Coahuila,
  Mexico **118 B4** 29 0N 100 54W
San Carlos, Nic. **120 D3** 11 12N 84 50W
San Carlos, Neg. Occ.,
  Phil. ...... **61 F5** 10 29N 123 25 E
San Carlos, Pangasinan,
  Phil. ...... **61 D4** 15 55N 120 20 E
San Carlos, Uruguay ...... **127 C5** 34 46 S 54 58W
San Carlos, U.S.A. **109 K8** 33 21N 110 27W
San Carlos, Venezuela **124 B5** 9 40N 68 36W
San Carlos de Bariloche,
  Argentina ...... **128 E2** 41 10 S 71 25W
San Carlos de Bolívar,
  Argentina ...... **128 D4** 36 15 S 61 6W
San Carlos de la
  Rápita = Sant Carles
  de la Ràpita, *Spain* ...... **38 E5** 40 37N 0 35 E

San Carlos del Zulia,
  Venezuela **124 B4** 9 1N 71 55W
San Carlos L., *U.S.A.* **109 K8** 33 11N 110 32W
San Cataldo, *Italy* ...... **42 E6** 37 29N 13 59 E
San Celoni = Sant
  Celoni, *Spain* ...... **38 D7** 41 42N 2 30 E
San Clemente, *Chile* ...... **126 D1** 35 30 S 71 29W
San Clemente, *Spain* **39 F2** 39 24N 2 25W
San Clemente, *U.S.A.* **111 M9** 33 26N 117 37W
San Clemente I., *U.S.A.* **111 N8** 32 53N 118 29W
San Cristóbal = Es
  Migjorn Gran, *Spain* ...... **48 B11** 39 57N 4 3 E
San Cristóbal, *Argentina* ...... **126 C3** 30 20 S 61 10W
San Cristóbal,
  Dom. Rep. **121 C5** 18 25N 70 6W
San Cristóbal, Venezuela **124 B4** 7 46N 72 14W
San Cristóbal de la
  Casas, *Mexico* **119 D6** 16 50N 92 33W
San Damiano d'Asti,
  Italy ...... **40 D5** 44 50N 8 4 E
San Daniele del Friuli,
  Italy ...... **41 B10** 46 9N 13 1 E
San Diego, Calif., U.S.A. **111 N9** 32 43N 117 9W
San Diego, Tex., U.S.A. **113 M5** 27 46N 98 14W
San Diego, C., Argentina ...... **128 G3** 54 40 S 65 10W
San Diego de la Unión,
  Mexico **118 C4** 21 28N 100 52W
San Diego
  International ✈
  (SAN), U.S.A. **111 N9** 32 44N 117 11W
San Dimitri, Ras, Malta ...... **49 C1** 36 4N 14 11 E
San Dimitri Point = San
  Dimitri, Ras, Malta ...... **49 C1** 36 4N 14 11 E
San Donà di Piave, Italy ...... **41 C9** 45 38N 12 34 E
San Estanislao,
  Paraguay ...... **126 A4** 24 39 S 56 26W
San Esteban de Gormaz,
  Spain **38 D1** 41 34N 3 13W
San Felice Circeo, Italy ...... **42 A6** 41 14N 13 5 E
San Felice sul Panaro,
  Italy ...... **41 D8** 44 50N 11 8 E
San Felipe, *Chile* ...... **126 C1** 32 43 S 70 42W
San Felipe, *Mexico* **118 A2** 31 0N 114 52W
San Felipe, Venezuela **124 A5** 10 20N 68 44W
San Felipe →, U.S.A. **111 M11** 33 12N 115 49W
San Félix, Chile ...... **126 B1** 28 56 S 70 28W
San Félix, Pac. Oc. ...... **97 K20** 26 23 S 80 0W
San Fernando = Sant
  Ferran, *Spain* ...... **48 C7** 38 42N 1 28 E
San Fernando, Chile ...... **126 C1** 34 30 S 71 0W
San Fernando,
  Baja Calif., Mexico **118 B1** 29 55N 115 10W
San Fernando,
  Tamaulipas, Mexico **119 C5** 24 51N 98 10W
San Fernando,
  La Union, Phil. ...... **61 C4** 16 40N 120 23 E
San Fernando,
  Pampanga, Phil. ...... **61 D4** 15 5N 120 37 E
San Fernando, Spain **37 J4** 36 28N 6 17W
San Fernando,
  Trin. & Tob. **121 D7** 10 20N 61 30W
San Fernando, U.S.A. **111 L8** 34 17N 118 26W
San Fernando de Apure,
  Venezuela **124 B5** 7 54N 67 15W
San Fernando de
  Atabapo, Venezuela **124 C5** 4 3N 67 42W
San Fernando di Púglia,
  Italy ...... **43 A9** 41 18N 16 5 E
San Francisco, Argentina ...... **126 C3** 31 30 S 62 5W
San Francisco, U.S.A. **110 H4** 37 47N 122 25W
San Francisco →, U.S.A. **109 K9** 32 59N 109 22W
San Francisco, C. de,
  Colombia **122 C3** 6 18N 77 29W
San Francisco, Paso de,
  S. Amer. ...... **126 B2** 27 0 S 68 0W
San Francisco de
  Macorís, Dom. Rep. **121 C5** 19 19N 70 15W
San Francisco del Monte
  de Oro, Argentina ...... **126 C2** 32 36 S 66 8W
San Francisco del Oro,
  Mexico **118 B3** 26 52N 105 50W
San Francisco
  International ✈
  (SFO), U.S.A. **110 H4** 37 37N 122 22W
San Francisco Javier =
  Sant Francesc de
  Formentera, *Spain* ...... **48 C7** 38 42N 1 26 E
San Fratello, *Italy* ...... **43 D7** 38 1N 14 36 E
San Gabriel, *Chile* ...... **126 C1** 33 47 S 70 15W
San Gabriel Mts., *U.S.A.* **111 L9** 34 20N 118 0W
San Gavino Monreale,
  Italy ...... **42 C1** 39 33N 8 47 E
San German,
  Puerto Rico ...... **121 d** 18 4N 67 4W
San Gimignano, *Italy* ...... **40 E8** 43 28N 11 2 E
San Giórgio di Nogaro,
  Italy ...... **41 C10** 45 50N 13 13 E
San Giórgio Iónico, Italy ...... **43 B10** 40 27N 17 23 E
San Giovanni Bianco,
  Italy ...... **40 C6** 45 52N 9 39 E
San Giovanni in Fiore,
  Italy ...... **43 C9** 39 15N 16 42 E
San Giovanni in
  Persiceto, *Italy* ...... **41 D8** 44 38N 11 11 E
San Giovanni Rotondo,
  Italy ...... **41 G12** 41 42N 15 44 E
San Giovanni Valdarno,
  Italy ...... **41 E8** 43 34N 11 32 E
San Giuliano Terme,
  Italy ...... **40 E7** 43 46N 10 26 E
San Gorgonio Mt.,
  U.S.A. **111 L10** 34 7N 116 51W
San Gottardo, P. del,
  Switz. ...... **25 J4** 46 33N 8 33 E
San Gregorio, *Uruguay* ...... **127 C4** 32 37 S 55 40W
San Gregorio, *U.S.A.* **110 H4** 37 20N 122 23W
San Guiseppe Jato, Italy ...... **42 E6** 37 57N 13 11 E
San Ignacio, *Belize* **119 D7** 17 10N 89 0W
San Ignacio, *Bolivia* ...... **124 G6** 16 20 S 60 55W
San Ignacio, *Mexico* **118 B2** 27 27N 113 0W
San Ignacio, *Paraguay* ...... **120 C2** 26 52 S 57 3W
San Ignacio △, *Mexico* **118 B2** 26 50N 113 11W
San Ildefonso, C., *Phil.* ...... **61 C5** 16 0N 122 1 E
San Isidro, *Argentina* ...... **126 C4** 34 29 S 58 31W
San Isidro, *Phil.* ...... **61 H7** 6 50N 126 5 E
San Jacinto, *U.S.A.* **111 M10** 33 47N 116 57W
San Jaime = Sant Jaume,
  Spain ...... **48 B11** 39 54N 4 4 E
San Javier, *Misiones,*
  Argentina ...... **127 B4** 27 55 S 55 5W
San Javier, *Santa Fe,*
  Argentina ...... **126 C4** 30 40 S 59 55W
San Javier, *Bolivia* ...... **124 G6** 16 18 S 62 30W
San Javier, *Chile* ...... **126 D1** 35 40 S 71 45W
San Javier, *Spain* **39 H4** 37 49N 0 50W
San Jeronimo Taviche,
  Mexico **119 D5** 16 38N 96 32W

San Joaquin, *U.S.A.* **110 J6** 36 36N 120 11W
San Joaquin →, *U.S.A.* **110 G5** 38 4N 121 51W
San Joaquin Valley,
  U.S.A. **110 J6** 37 20N 121 0W
San Jon, *U.S.A.* **113 H3** 35 6N 103 20W
San Jordi = Sant Jordi,
  Spain ...... **48 B9** 39 33N 2 46 E
San Jorge, *Argentina* ...... **126 C3** 31 54 S 61 50W
San Jorge, B. de, Mexico **118 A2** 31 20N 113 20W
San Jorge, G., *Argentina* ...... **128 F3** 46 0 S 66 0W
San José = San Josep,
  Spain ...... **48 C7** 38 55N 1 18 E
San José, Costa Rica **120 E3** 9 55N 84 2W
San José, Guatemala **120 D1** 14 0N 90 50W
San José, Mexico **118 C2** 25 0N 110 50W
San Jose, Mind. Occ.,
  Phil. ...... **61 E4** 12 27N 121 4 E
San Jose, Nueva Écija,
  Phil. ...... **61 D4** 15 45N 120 55 E
San Jose, U.S.A. **110 H5** 37 20N 121 53W
San Jose →, U.S.A. **109 J10** 34 25N 106 45W
San Jose de Buenavista,
  Phil. ...... **63 B6** 10 45N 121 56 E
San José de Chiquitos,
  Bolivia ...... **124 G6** 17 53 S 60 50W
San José de Feliciano,
  Argentina ...... **126 C4** 30 26 S 58 46W
San José de Jáchal,
  Argentina ...... **126 C2** 30 15 S 68 46W
San José de Mayo,
  Uruguay ...... **126 C4** 34 27 S 56 40W
San José del Cabo,
  Mexico **118 C3** 23 0N 109 40W
San José del Guaviare,
  Colombia **124 C4** 2 35N 72 38W
San Josep, *Spain* ...... **48 C7** 38 55N 1 18 E
San Juan, *Argentina* ...... **126 C2** 31 30 S 68 30W
San Juan, *Mexico* **118 C4** 21 20N 102 50W
San Juan, *Phil.* ...... **61 F6** 10 16N 125 10 E
San Juan, Puerto Rico ...... **121 d** 18 28N 66 7W
San Juan, Trin. & Tob. **125 K15** 10 39N 61 29W
San Juan □, *Argentina* ...... **126 C2** 31 9 S 69 0W
San Juan →, *Argentina* ...... **126 C2** 32 20 S 67 25W
San Juan →, *Nic.* **120 D3** 10 56N 83 42W
San Juan →, *U.S.A.* **109 H8** 37 16N 110 26W
San Juan Bautista = Sant
  Joan Baptista, *Spain* ...... **48 B8** 39 5N 1 31 E
San Juan Bautista,
  Paraguay ...... **126 B4** 26 37 S 57 6W
San Juan Bautista,
  U.S.A. **110 J5** 36 51N 121 32W
San Juan Bautista Valle
  Nacional, *Mexico* **119 D5** 17 47N 96 19W
San Juan Capistrano,
  U.S.A. **111 M9** 33 30N 117 40W
San Juan Cr. →, *U.S.A.* **110 J5** 35 40N 120 22W
San Juan de Alicante,
  Spain **39 G4** 38 24N 0 26W
San Juan de Guadalupe,
  Mexico **118 C4** 24 38N 102 44W
San Juan de la Costa,
  Mexico **118 C2** 24 23N 110 45W
San Juan de los Morros,
  Venezuela **124 B5** 9 55N 67 21W
San Juan del Norte, Nic. **120 D3** 10 58N 83 40W
San Juan del Norte, B.
  de, Nic. **120 D3** 11 0N 83 40W
San Juan del Río,
  Mexico **119 C5** 20 25N 100 0W
San Juan del Sur, Nic. **120 D2** 11 20N 85 51W
San Juan I., *U.S.A.* **110 B3** 48 32N 123 5W
San Juan Island △,
  U.S.A. **110 B4** 48 27N 123 0W
San Juan Mts., *U.S.A.* **109 H10** 37 30N 107 0W
San Just, Sierra de,
  Spain **38 E4** 40 45N 0 49W
San Justo, *Argentina* ...... **126 C3** 30 47 S 60 30W
San Kamphaeng,
  Thailand ...... **64 C2** 18 45N 99 8 E
San Lázaro, C., *Mexico* **118 C2** 24 50N 112 18W
San Lázaro, Sa., Mexico **118 C3** 23 25N 110 0W
San Leandro, *U.S.A.* **110 H4** 37 44N 122 9W
San Leonardo de Yagüe,
  Spain **38 D1** 41 51N 3 5W
San Lorenzo = Sant
  Llorenç des
  Cardassar, *Spain* ...... **48 B10** 39 37N 3 17 E
San Lorenzo, *Argentina* ...... **126 C3** 32 45 S 60 45W
San Lorenzo, *Ecuador* **124 C3** 1 15N 78 50W
San Lorenzo, *Paraguay* ...... **126 B4** 25 20 S 57 32W
San Lorenzo, *U.S.A.* **118 C3** 24 15N 107 24W
San Lorenzo, I., Mexico **118 B2** 28 35N 112 50W
San Lorenzo, Mte.,
  Argentina ...... **128 F2** 47 40 S 72 20W
San Lorenzo de la
  Parrilla, *Spain* **38 F2** 39 51N 2 22W
San Lorenzo de
  Morunys = Sant
  Llorenç de Morunys,
  Spain ...... **38 C6** 42 8N 1 35 E
San Lucas, *Bolivia* ...... **124 H5** 20 5 S 65 7W
San Lucas, Baja Calif. S.,
  Mexico **118 C3** 22 53N 109 54W
San Lucas, Baja Calif. S.,
  Mexico **118 B2** 27 10N 112 14W
San Lucas, U.S.A. **110 J5** 36 8N 121 1W
San Lucas, C., Mexico **118 C3** 22 50N 110 0W
San Lúcido, *Italy* ...... **43 C9** 39 18N 16 3 E
San Luis, *Argentina* ...... **126 C2** 33 20 S 66 20W
San Luis, Cuba **120 B3** 22 17N 83 46W
San Luis, Guatemala **120 C2** 16 14N 89 27W
San Luis, Ariz., U.S.A. **109 K6** 32 29N 114 47W
San Luis, Colo., U.S.A. **109 H11** 37 12N 105 25W
San Luis □, *Argentina* ...... **126 C2** 34 0 S 66 0W
San Luis, Sierra de,
  Argentina ...... **126 C2** 32 30 S 66 10W
San Luis de la Paz,
  Mexico **118 C4** 21 19N 100 32W
San Luis Obispo, *U.S.A.* **111 K6** 35 17N 120 40W
San Luis Potosí, *Mexico* **118 C4** 22 9N 100 59W
San Luis Potosí □,
  Mexico **118 C4** 22 10N 101 0W
San Luis Reservoir,
  U.S.A. **110 H5** 37 4N 121 5W
San Luis Río Colorado,
  Mexico **118 A2** 32 29N 114 58W
San Manuel, *U.S.A.* **109 K8** 32 36N 110 38W
San Marco, C., *Italy* ...... **42 C1** 39 51N 8 26 E
San Marco Argentano,
  Italy ...... **43 C9** 39 33N 16 7 E
San Marco in Lámis,
  Italy ...... **41 G12** 41 43N 15 38 E
San Marcos, Guatemala **120 D1** 14 59N 91 52W
San Marcos, Mexico **118 B2** 27 13N 112 6W
San Marcos, Calif.,
  U.S.A. **111 M9** 33 9N 117 10W

San Marcos, Tex., U.S.A. **113 L6** 29 53N 97 56W
San Marino, San Marino ...... **41 E9** 43 55N 12 30 E
San Marino ■, Europe ...... **41 E9** 43 56N 12 25 E
San Martín, Antarctica ...... **5 C17** 68 11 S 67 0W
San Martín, Argentina ...... **126 C2** 33 5 S 68 28W
San Martín →, Bolivia ...... **124 F6** 13 8 S 63 43W
San Martín, L.,
  Argentina ...... **128 F2** 48 50 S 72 50W
San Martín de la Vega,
  Spain **36 E7** 40 13N 3 34W
San Martín de los
  Andes, *Argentina* ...... **128 E2** 40 10 S 71 20W
San Martín de
  Valdeiglesias, *Spain* **36 E6** 40 21N 4 24W
San Mateo = Sant
  Mateu, Baleares,
  Spain ...... **48 B7** 39 3N 1 23 E
San Mateo = Sant
  Mateu, Valencia,
  Spain ...... **38 E5** 40 28N 0 10 E
San Mateo, Phil. ...... **61 C4** 16 54N 121 33 E
San Mateo, U.S.A. **110 H4** 37 34N 122 19W
San Matías, Bolivia ...... **124 G7** 16 25 S 58 20W
San Matías, G.,
  Argentina ...... **128 E4** 41 30 S 64 0W
San Miguel = Sant
  Miguel, *Spain* ...... **48 B7** 39 3N 1 26 E
San Miguel, El Salv. **120 D2** 13 30N 88 12W
San Miguel, Panama **120 E4** 8 27N 78 55W
San Miguel, U.S.A. **110 K6** 35 45N 120 42W
San Miguel →, Bolivia ...... **124 F6** 13 52 S 63 56W
San Miguel de Tucumán,
  Argentina ...... **126 B2** 26 50 S 65 20W
San Miguel del Monte,
  Argentina ...... **126 D4** 35 23 S 58 50W
San Miguel I., *U.S.A.* **111 L6** 34 2N 120 23W
San Miniato, *Italy* ...... **40 E7** 43 41N 10 51 E
San Nicolás, Canary Is. **48 G4** 27 58N 15 47W
San Nicolas, Phil. ...... **61 B4** 18 10N 120 36 E
San Nicolás de los
  Arroyas, *Argentina* ...... **126 C3** 33 25 S 60 10W
San Nicolas I., *U.S.A.* **111 M7** 33 15N 119 30W
San Onofre, *U.S.A.* **111 M9** 33 22N 117 34W
San Pablo, *Bolivia* ...... **126 A2** 21 43 S 66 38W
San Pablo, Phil. ...... **61 D4** 14 11N 121 31 E
San Pablo, *U.S.A.* **110 H4** 37 58N 122 21W
San Páolo di Civitate,
  Italy ...... **41 G12** 41 44N 15 15 E
San Pedro,
  Buenos Aires,
  Argentina ...... **126 C4** 33 40 S 59 40W
San Pedro, Misiones,
  Argentina ...... **127 B5** 26 30 S 54 10W
San Pédro, Chile ...... **126 C1** 33 54 S 71 28W
San Pédro, Ivory C. **82 E3** 4 50N 6 33W
San Pedro, Mexico **118 C2** 23 55N 110 17W
San Pedro □, Paraguay ...... **126 A4** 24 0 S 57 0W
San Pedro →,
  Chihuahua, Mexico **118 B3** 28 20N 106 10W
San Pedro →, Nayarit,
  Mexico **118 C3** 21 45N 105 30W
San Pedro, Pta., Chile ...... **126 B1** 25 30 S 70 38W
San Pedro, Sierra de,
  Spain **37 F4** 39 18N 6 40W
San Pedro Channel,
  U.S.A. **111 M8** 33 30N 118 25W
San Pedro de Atacama,
  Chile ...... **126 A2** 22 55 S 68 15W
San Pedro de Jujuy,
  Argentina ...... **126 A3** 24 12 S 64 55W
San Pedro de las
  Colonias, Mexico **118 B4** 25 50N 102 59W
San Pedro de Macorís,
  Dom. Rep. **121 C6** 18 30N 69 18W
San Pedro del Norte,
  Nic. **120 D3** 13 4N 84 33W
San Pedro del Paraná,
  Paraguay ...... **126 B4** 26 43 S 56 13W
San Pedro del Pinatar,
  Spain **39 H4** 37 50N 0 50W
San Pedro Mártir △,
  Mexico **118 A1** 31 0N 115 21W
San Pedro Mártir,
  Sierra, *Mexico* **118 A1** 31 0N 115 30W
San Pedro Mixtepec,
  Mexico **119 D5** 16 2N 97 7W
San Pedro Ocampo =
  Melchor Ocampo,
  Mexico **118 C4** 24 52N 101 40W
San Pedro Sula,
  Honduras **120 C2** 15 30N 88 0W
San Pietro, *Italy* ...... **42 C1** 39 8N 8 17 E
San Pietro Vernótico,
  Italy ...... **43 B11** 40 29N 18 0 E
San Quintín, Mexico **118 A1** 30 29N 115 57W
San Rafael, *Argentina* ...... **126 C2** 34 40 S 68 21W
San Rafael, Calif.,
  U.S.A. **110 H4** 37 58N 122 32W
San Rafael, N. Mex.,
  U.S.A. **109 J10** 35 7N 107 53W
San Rafael Mt., U.S.A. **111 L7** 34 41N 119 52W
San Rafael Mtn., U.S.A. **111 L7** 34 40N 119 50W
San Ramón de la Nueva
  Orán, *Argentina* ...... **126 A3** 23 10 S 64 20W
San Remo, *Italy* ...... **40 E4** 43 49N 7 46 E
San Roque, *Argentina* ...... **126 B4** 28 25 S 58 45W
San Roque, *Spain* **37 J5** 36 17N 5 21W
San Rosendo, *Chile* ...... **126 D1** 37 16 S 72 43W
San Saba, *U.S.A.* **113 K5** 31 12N 98 43W
San Salvador, El Salv. **120 D2** 13 40N 89 10W
San Salvador de Jujuy,
  Argentina ...... **126 A3** 24 10 S 64 48W
San Salvador I.,
  Bahamas **121 B5** 24 0N 74 40W
San Salvo, *Italy* ...... **41 F11** 42 3N 14 44 E
San Sebastián =
  Donostia-San
  Sebastián, *Spain* **38 B3** 43 17N 1 58W
San Sebastián, Argentina ...... **128 G3** 53 10 S 68 30W
San Sebastián,
  Puerto Rico ...... **121 d** 18 20N 66 59W
San Sebastián de la
  Gomera, Canary Is. **48 F2** 28 5N 17 7W
San Serra = Son Serra,
  Spain ...... **48 B10** 39 43N 3 13 E
San Severino Marche,
  Italy ...... **41 E10** 43 13N 13 10 E
San Severo, *Italy* ...... **41 G12** 41 41N 15 23 E
San Simeon, *U.S.A.* **110 K5** 35 39N 121 11W
San Simon, *U.S.A.* **109 K9** 32 16N 109 14W
San Stéfano di Cadore,
  Italy ...... **41 B9** 46 34N 12 33 E
San Stino di Livenza,
  Italy ...... **41 C9** 45 44N 12 41 E
San Telmo = Sant Telm,
  Spain ...... **48 B9** 39 35N 2 21 E

San Telmo, *Mexico* **118 A1** 30 58N 116 6W
San Tiburcio, *Mexico* ... **118 C4** 24 8N 101 32W
San Valentin, Mte.,
  Chile .... **128 F2** 46 30 S 73 30W
San Vicente de
  Alcántara, *Spain* ... **37 F3** 39 22N 7 8W
San Vicente de la
  Barquera, *Spain* **36 B6** 43 23N 4 29W
San Vincente del
  Raspeig, *Spain* **39 G4** 38 24N 0 31W
San Vincenzo, *Italy* ... **40 E7** 43 6N 10 32 E
San Vito, *Costa Rica* .. **120 E3** 8 50N 82 58W
San Vito, *Italy* .... **42 C2** 39 26N 9 32 E
San Vito, C., *Italy* .... **42 D5** 38 11N 12 41 E
San Vito al Tagliamento,
  Italy .... **41 C9** 45 54N 12 52 E
San Vito Chietino, *Italy* **41 F11** 42 18N 14 27 E
San Vito dei Normanni,
  Italy .... **43 B10** 40 39N 17 42 E
Sana', *Yemen* .... **75 D3** 15 27N 44 12 E
Sana →, *Bos.-H.* ...... **41 C13** 45 3N 16 23 E
Sanaba, *Burkina Faso* .. **82 C4** 12 25N 3 47W
Sanāfir, *Si. Arabia* .... **80 B3** 27 56N 34 42 E
Sanaga →, *Cameroon* .. **83 E6** 3 35N 9 38 E
Sanaloa, Presa, *Mexico* **118 C3** 24 50N 107 20W
Sanana, *Indonesia* .... **63 E7** 2 4 S 125 58 E
Sanand, *India* .... **68 H5** 22 59N 72 25 E
Sanandaj, *Iran* .... **70 C5** 35 18N 47 1 E
Sanandita, *Bolivia* ... **126 A3** 21 40 S 63 45W
Sanary-sur-Mer, *France* **21 E9** 43 7N 5 48 E
Sanawad, *India* ...... **68 H7** 22 11N 76 5 E
Sancellas = Sencelles,
  Spain .... **48 B9** 39 39N 2 54 E
Sancergues, *France* ... **19 E9** 47 10N 2 54 E
Sancerre, *France* ..... **19 E9** 47 20N 2 50 E
Sancerrois, Collines du,
  France .... **19 E9** 47 20N 2 40 E
Sancha He →, *China* .. **58 D6** 26 48N 106 7 E
Sanchahe, *China* ..... **57 B14** 44 50N 126 2 E
Sánchez, *Dom. Rep.* .. **121 C6** 19 15N 69 36W
Sanchor, *India* .... **68 G4** 24 45N 71 55 E
Sancoins, *France* ..... **19 F9** 46 47N 2 55 E
Sancti Spíritus, *Cuba* . **120 B4** 21 52N 79 33W
Sancy, Puy de, *France* . **20 C6** 45 32N 2 50 E
Sand →, *S. Africa* ..... **89 C5** 22 25 S 30 5 E
Sand Hills, *U.S.A.* **112 D4** 42 10N 101 30W
Sand Lakes △, *Canada* **103 B7** 57 51N 98 32W
Sand Springs, *U.S.A.* .. **113 G6** 36 9N 96 7W
Sanda, *Japan* .... **55 G7** 34 53N 135 14 E
Sandakan, *Malaysia* .. **62 C5** 5 53N 118 4 E
Sandan = Sambor,
  Cambodia .... **64 F6** 12 46N 106 0 E
Sandanski, *Bulgaria* .. **44 E7** 41 35N 23 16 E
Sandaré, *Mali* **82 C2** 14 40N 10 15W
Sandared, *Sweden* .... **11 G6** 57 43N 12 47 E
Sandarne, *Sweden* .... **10 C11** 61 16N 17 9 E
Sanday, *U.K.* **13 B6** 59 16N 2 31W
Sandefjord, *Norway* .. **9 G14** 59 10N 10 15 E
Sanders, *U.S.A.* **109 J9** 35 13N 109 20W
Sanderson, *U.S.A.* **113 K3** 30 9N 102 24W
Sandersville, *U.S.A.* .. **115 J4** 32 59N 82 48W
Sandfire Roadhouse,
  Australia .... **92 C3** 19 45 S 121 15 E
Sandfly L., *Canada* ... **103 B7** 55 43N 106 6W
Sandfontein, *Namibia* . **88 C2** 23 48 S 29 1 E
Sandhammaren, C.,
  Sweden .... **11 J8** 55 23N 14 14 E
Sandheads, The, *India* . **69 J13** 21 10N 88 20 E
Sandía, *Peru* .... **124 F5** 14 10 S 69 30W
Sandıklı, *Turkey* ..... **47 C12** 38 28N 30 17 E
Sandila, *India* .... **69 F9** 27 5N 80 31 E
Sandnes, *Norway* .... **9 G11** 58 50N 5 45 E
Sandnessjøen, *Norway* . **8 C15** 66 2N 12 38 E
Sandoa, *Dem. Rep. of
  the Congo* .... **84 F4** 9 41 S 23 0 E
Sandomierz, *Poland* ... **31 H8** 50 40N 21 43 E
Sândominic, *Romania* . **29 D10** 46 35N 25 47 E
Sandover →, *Australia* **94 C2** 21 43 S 136 32 E
Sandoway, *Burma* .... **67 K19** 18 20N 94 30 E
Sandoy, *Færoe Is.* **8 F9** 61 52N 6 46W
Sandpoint, *U.S.A.* **108 B5** 48 17N 116 33W
Sandray, *U.K.* **13 E1** 56 53N 7 31W
Sandringham, *U.K.* ... **14 E8** 52 51N 0 31 E
Sandstone, *Australia* .. **93 E2** 27 59 S 119 16 E
Sandu, *China* .... **58 E6** 26 0N 107 52 E
Sandusky, *Mich., U.S.A.* **116 C2** 43 25N 82 50W
Sandusky, *Ohio, U.S.A.* **116 E2** 41 27N 82 42W
Sandvig, *Sweden* ..... **11 J8** 55 18N 14 47 E
Sandviken, *Sweden* ... **10 D10** 60 38N 16 46 E
Sandwich, C., *Australia* **94 B4** 18 14 S 146 18 E
Sandwich B., *Canada* .. **105 B8** 53 40N 57 15W
Sandwich B., *Namibia* . **88 C1** 23 25 S 14 20 E
Sandy, *Oreg., U.S.A.* .. **110 E4** 45 24N 122 16W
Sandy, *Pa., U.S.A.* **116 E6** 41 6N 78 46W
Sandy, *Utah, U.S.A.* ... **108 F8** 40 35N 111 50W
Sandy Bay, *Canada* ... **103 B8** 55 31N 102 19W
Sandy Bight, *Australia* . **93 F3** 33 50 S 123 20 E
Sandy C., *Queens.,
  Australia* .... **94 C5** 24 42 S 153 15 E
Sandy C., *Tas., Australia* **95 G3** 41 25 S 144 45 E
Sandy Cay, *Bahamas* .. **121 B4** 23 13N 75 18W
Sandy Cr. →, *U.S.A.* .. **108 F9** 41 51N 109 47W
Sandy L., *Canada* **104 B1** 53 2N 93 0W
Sandy Lake, *Canada* .. **104 B1** 53 0N 93 0W
Sandy Valley, *U.S.A.* .. **111 K11** 35 49N 115 36W
Sånfjällets △, *Sweden* . **10 B7** 62 17N 13 35 E
Sanford, *Fla., U.S.A.* .. **115 L5** 28 48N 81 16W
Sanford, *N.C., U.S.A.* .. **115 H6** 35 29N 79 10W
Sanford →, *Australia* .. **93 E2** 27 22 S 115 53 E
Sanford, Mt., *U.S.A.* ... **100 B5** 62 13N 144 8W
Sang-i-Masha, *Afghan.* **68 C2** 33 8N 67 27 E
Sanga, *Mozam.* ...... **87 E4** 12 22 S 35 21 E
Sanga →, *Congo* ..... **84 E3** 1 5 S 17 0 E
Sangamner, *India* .... **66 K9** 19 37N 74 15 E
Sanganeb Atoll △,
  Sudan .... **80 D4** 19 33N 37 11 E
Sangar, *Afghan.* ..... **68 C1** 32 56N 65 30 E
Sangar, *Russia* ...... **53 C13** 64 2N 127 31 E
Sangar Sarai, *Afghan.* . **68 B4** 34 27N 70 35 E
Sangarh →, *Pakistan* . **68 D4** 30 43N 70 44 E
Sangasso, *Mali* **82 C3** 12 5N 5 35W
Sangatte, *France* ..... **19 B8** 50 56N 1 46 E
Sangay, *Ecuador* ..... **124 D3** 2 0 S 78 20W
Sange, *Dem. Rep. of
  the Congo* .... **86 D2** 6 58 S 28 21 E
Sangeang, *Indonesia* .. **63 F5** 8 12 S 119 6 E
Sangeorz-Băi, *Romania* **29 C9** 47 22N 24 41 E
Sanger, *U.S.A.* **110 J7** 36 42N 119 33W
Sângera, *Moldova* .... **29 D13** 46 55N 28 58 E
Sangerhausen, *Germany* **24 D7** 51 28N 11 18 E
Sanggan He →, *China* **56 E9** 38 12N 117 15 E
Sanggau, *Indonesia* ... **62 D4** 0 5N 110 30 E
Sanghar, *Pakistan* .... **68 F3** 26 2N 68 57 E
Sangihe, Kepulauan,
  Indonesia .... **63 D7** 3 0N 125 30 E

Sangihe, Pulau,
  Indonesia .... **63 D7** 3 35N 125 30 E
Sangju, *S. Korea* ..... **57 F15** 36 25N 128 10 E
Sangkapura, *Indonesia* **62 F4** 5 52 S 112 40 E
Sangkhla, *Thailand* ... **64 E2** 14 57N 98 28 E
Sangkulirang, *Indonesia* **62 D5** 0 59N 117 58 E
Sangla, *Pakistan* ..... **68 D5** 31 43N 73 23 E
Sangli, *India* .... **66 L9** 16 55N 74 33 E
Sangmélima, *Cameroon* **83 E7** 2 57N 12 1 E
Sangod, *India* .... **68 G7** 24 55N 76 17 E
Sangre de Cristo Mts.,
  U.S.A. **113 G2** 37 30N 105 20W
Sangre Grande,
  Trin. & Tob. **125 K15** 10 35N 61 8W
Sangro →, *Italy* ...... **41 F11** 42 14N 14 32 E
Sangrur, *India* .... **68 D6** 30 14N 75 50 E
Sangudo, *Canada* **102 C6** 53 50N 114 54W
Sangue →, *Brazil* .... **124 F7** 11 1 S 58 39W
Sangüesa, *Spain* **38 C3** 42 37N 1 17W
Sanguinaires, Ís., *France* **21 G12** 41 51N 8 36 E
Sangzhi, *China* ...... **59 C8** 29 25N 110 12 E
Sanhala, *Ivory C.* **82 C3** 10 3N 6 51W
Sanibel, *U.S.A.* **115 M4** 26 26N 82 1W
Sanin-Kaigan △, *Japan* **55 G7** 35 39N 134 37 E
Sanirajak, *Canada* **101 B11** 68 46N 81 12W
Sanjawi, *Pakistan* .... **68 D3** 30 17N 68 21 E
Sanje, *Uganda* .... **86 C3** 0 49 S 31 30 E
Sanjiang, *China* ...... **58 E7** 25 48N 109 37 E
Sanjo, *Japan* .... **54 F9** 37 37N 138 57 E
Sankh →, *India* ...... **69 H11** 22 15N 84 48 E
Sankt Andrä, *Austria* .. **26 E7** 46 46N 14 50 E
Sankt Augustin,
  Germany .... **24 E3** 50 45N 7 10 E
Sankt Blasien, *Germany* **25 H4** 47 47N 8 7 E
Sankt Gallen, *Switz.* .. **25 H5** 47 26N 9 22 E
Sankt Gallen □, *Switz.* **25 H5** 47 25N 9 22 E
Sankt Goar, *Germany* . **25 E3** 50 12N 7 43 E
Sankt Ingbert, *Germany* **25 F3** 49 16N 7 6 E
Sankt Johann im
  Pongau, *Austria* .... **26 D6** 47 22N 13 12 E
Sankt Johann in Tirol,
  Austria .... **26 D5** 47 30N 12 25 E
Sankt Michel = Mikkeli,
  Finland .... **9 F22** 61 43N 27 15 E
Sankt-Peterburg, *Russia* **32 C6** 59 55N 30 20 E
Sankt Pölten, *Austria* .. **26 C8** 48 12N 15 38 E
Sankt Ulrich = Ortisei,
  Italy .... **41 B8** 46 34N 11 40 E
Sankt Valentin, *Austria* **26 C7** 48 11N 14 33 E
Sankt Veit an der Glan,
  Austria .... **26 E7** 46 47N 14 22 E
Sankt Wendel, *Germany* **25 F3** 49 27N 7 9 E
Sankt Wolfgang, *Austria* **26 D6** 47 43N 13 27 E
Sankuru →, *Dem. Rep.
  of the Congo* .... **84 E4** 4 17 S 20 25 E
Sanliurfa, *Turkey* .... **70 B3** 37 12N 38 50 E
Sanlúcar de Barrameda,
  Spain **37 J4** 36 46N 6 21W
Sanluri, *Italy* .... **42 C1** 39 34N 8 54 E
Sânmartin, *Romania* .. **29 D10** 46 19N 25 58 E
Sanmen, *China* ...... **59 C13** 29 5N 121 34 E
Sanmenxia, *China* .... **56 G6** 34 47N 111 12 E
Sanming, *China* ...... **59 D11** 26 15N 117 40 E
Sannaspos, *S. Africa* .. **88 D4** 29 6 S 26 34 E
Sannicandro Gargánico,
  Italy .... **41 G12** 41 50N 15 34 E
Sânnicolau Mare,
  Romania .... **28 D5** 46 5N 20 39 E
Sannieshof, *S. Africa* .. **88 D4** 26 30 S 25 47 E
Sannin, J., *Lebanon* ... **74 B4** 33 57N 35 52 E
Sanniquellie, *Liberia* .. **82 D3** 7 19N 8 38W
Sannûr, W. →, *Egypt* . **80 B3** 28 59N 31 3 E
Sanoe, *Antarctica* .... **5 D2** 70 20 S 9 0W
Sanok, *Poland* .... **31 J9** 49 35N 22 10 E
Sanquhar, *U.K.* **13 F5** 55 22N 3 54W
Sans Souci, *Trin. & Tob.* **125 K16** 10 50N 61 0W
Sansanding, *Mali* **82 C3** 13 48N 6 0W
Sansepolcro, *Italy* .... **41 E9** 43 34N 12 8 E
Sansha, *China* .... **59 D13** 26 58N 120 12 E
Sanshui, *China* ...... **59 F9** 23 10N 112 56 E
Sanski Most, *Bos.-H.* . **41 D13** 44 46N 16 40 E
Sansui, *China* .... **58 D7** 26 58N 108 39 E
Sant Antoni Abat, *Spain* **48 C7** 38 59N 1 19 E
Sant Boi de Llobregat,
  Spain .... **38 D7** 41 21N 2 2 E
Sant Carles, *Spain* ... **48 B8** 39 3N 1 34 E
Sant Carles de la Ràpita,
  Spain .... **38 E5** 40 37N 0 35 E
Sant Celoni, *Spain* ... **38 D7** 41 42N 2 30 E
Sant Feliu de Guíxols,
  Spain .... **38 D8** 41 45N 3 1 E
Sant Feliu de Llobregat,
  Spain .... **38 D7** 41 23N 2 2 E
Sant Ferran, *Spain* ... **48 C7** 38 42N 1 28 E
Sant Francesc de
  Formentera, *Spain* .. **48 C7** 38 42N 1 26 E
Sant Jaume, *Spain* ... **48 B11** 39 54N 4 4 E
Sant Joan Baptista,
  Spain .... **48 B8** 39 5N 1 31 E
Sant Jordi, *Ibiza, Spain* **48 C7** 38 53N 1 24 E
Sant Jordi, *Mallorca,
  Spain* .... **48 B9** 39 33N 2 46 E
Sant Jordi, G. de, *Spain* **38 E6** 40 53N 1 2 E
Sant Llorenç de
  Morunys, *Spain* ..... **38 C6** 42 8N 1 35 E
Sant Llorenç del Munt y
  l'Obac △, *Spain* **38 D3** 41 39N 1 55W
Sant Llorenç des
  Cardassar, *Spain* .... **48 B10** 39 37N 3 17 E
Sant Mateu, *Baleares,
  Spain* .... **48 B7** 39 3N 1 23 E
Sant Mateu, *Valencia,
  Spain* .... **38 E5** 40 28N 0 10 E
Sant Miguel, *Spain* ... **48 B7** 39 3N 1 26 E
Sant Telm, *Spain* .... **48 B9** 39 35N 2 21 E
Sant' Ágata Militello,
  Italy .... **43 D7** 38 2N 14 8 E
Santa Agnès, *Spain* ... **48 B7** 39 3N 1 21 E
Santa Ana, *Bolivia* ... **124 F5** 13 50 S 65 40W
Santa Ana, *El Salv.* ... **120 D2** 14 0N 89 31W
Santa Ana, *Mexico* ... **118 A2** 30 31N 111 8W
Santa Ana, *U.S.A.* **111 M9** 33 46N 117 52W

Santa Catalina, Gulf of,
  U.S.A. **111 N9** 33 10N 117 50W
Santa Catalina, I.,
  Mexico **118 B2** 25 40N 110 50W
Santa Catalina I., *U.S.A.* **111 M8** 33 23N 118 25W
Santa Catarina □, *Brazil* **127 B6** 27 25 S 48 30W
Santa Catarina, I. de,
  Brazil .... **127 B6** 27 30 S 48 40W
Santa Caterina di
  Pittinuri, *Italy* ..... **42 B1** 40 6N 8 27 E
Santa Cecília,
  Villarmosa, *Italy* ... **43 E7** 37 35N 14 2 E
Santa Cecília, *Brazil* .. **127 B5** 26 56 S 50 18W
Santa Clara, *Cuba* **120 B4** 22 20N 80 0W
Santa Clara, *Calif.,
  U.S.A.* **110 H5** 37 21N 121 57W
Santa Clara, *Utah,
  U.S.A.* **109 H7** 37 8N 113 39W
Santa Clara, El Golfo
  de, *Mexico* **118 A2** 31 42N 114 30W
Santa Clara de Olimar,
  Uruguay .... **127 C5** 32 50 S 54 54W
Santa Clarita, *U.S.A.* .. **111 L8** 34 24N 118 30W
Santa Clotilde, *Peru* .. **124 D4** 2 33 S 73 45W
Santa Coloma de
  Farners, *Spain* ..... **38 D7** 41 50N 2 39 E
Santa Coloma de
  Gramenet, *Spain* ... **38 D7** 41 27N 2 13 E
Santa Comba, *Spain* .. **36 B2** 43 2N 8 49W
Santa Croce Camerina,
  Italy .... **43 F7** 36 50N 14 31 E
Santa Croce di
  Magliano, *Italy* .... **41 G11** 41 42N 14 59 E
Santa Cruz, *Argentina* **128 G3** 50 0 S 68 32W
Santa Cruz, *Bolivia* ... **124 G6** 17 43 S 63 10W
Santa Cruz, *Chile* .... **126 C1** 34 38 S 71 27W
Santa Cruz, *Costa Rica* **120 D2** 10 15N 85 35W
Santa Cruz, *Madeira* .. **48 D3** 32 42N 16 46W
Santa Cruz, *Phil.* ..... **61 D4** 14 20N 121 24 E
Santa Cruz, *U.S.A.* ... **110 J4** 36 58N 122 1W
Santa Cruz →,
  Argentina .... **128 G3** 50 10 S 68 20W
Santa Cruz de la Palma,
  Canary Is. **48 F2** 28 41N 17 46W
Santa Cruz de la
  Palma ✈ (SPC),
  Canary Is. **48 F2** 28 40N 17 45W
Santa Cruz de Mudela,
  Spain **37 G7** 38 39N 3 28W
Santa Cruz de Tenerife,
  Canary Is. **48 F3** 28 28N 16 15W
Santa Cruz del Norte,
  Cuba **120 B3** 23 9N 81 55W
Santa Cruz del Retamar,
  Spain **36 E6** 40 8N 4 14W
Santa Cruz del Sur,
  Cuba **120 B4** 20 44N 78 0W
Santa Cruz do Rio
  Pardo, *Brazil* ...... **127 A6** 22 54 S 49 37W
Santa Cruz do Sul,
  Brazil .... **127 B5** 29 42 S 52 25W
Santa Cruz I., *U.S.A.* .. **111 M7** 34 1N 119 43W
Santa Cruz Is.,
  Solomon Is. .... **96 J8** 10 30 S 166 0 E
Santa Cruz Mts.,
  Jamaica .... **120 a** 17 58N 77 43W
Santa Domingo, Cay,
  Bahamas **120 B4** 21 25N 75 15W
Sant' Egídio alla
  Vibrata, *Italy* ...... **41 F10** 42 49N 13 42 E
Santa Elena, *Argentina* **126 C4** 30 58 S 59 47W
Santa Elena, C.,
  Costa Rica **120 D2** 10 54N 85 56W
Sant' Eufémia, G. di,
  Italy .... **43 D9** 38 51N 16 4 E
Santa Eulàlia des Riu,
  Spain .... **48 C8** 38 59N 1 32 E
Santa Fe, *Argentina* .. **126 C3** 31 35 S 60 41W
Santa Fe, *Spain* **37 H7** 37 11N 3 43W
Santa Fe, *U.S.A.* **109 J11** 35 41N 105 57W
Santa Fé □, *Argentina* **126 C3** 31 50 S 60 55W
Santa Fé do Sul, *Brazil* **125 H8** 20 13 S 50 56W
Santa Filomena, *Brazil* **125 E9** 9 6 S 45 50W
Santa Fiora, *Italy* .... **41 F8** 42 50N 11 35 E
Santa Gertrudis, *Spain* **48 C7** 39 0N 1 26 E
Santa Giustina, *Italy* .. **41 B9** 46 10N 12 5 E
Santa Inês, *Brazil* .... **125 F11** 3 17 S 39 48W
Santa Inés, *Spain* **37 G5** 38 32N 5 37W
Santa Inés, I., *Chile* ... **128 G2** 54 0 S 73 0W
Santa Isabel, *Argentina* **126 D2** 36 10 S 66 54W
Santa Isabel, Pico,
  Eq. Guin. .... **83 E6** 3 36N 8 49 E
Santa Isabel do Morro,
  Brazil .... **125 F8** 11 34 S 50 40W
Santa Lucía, *Corrientes,
  Argentina* .... **126 B4** 28 58 S 59 5W
Santa Lucía, *San Juan,
  Argentina* .... **126 C2** 31 30 S 68 30W
Santa Lucía, *Spain* ... **39 H4** 37 35N 0 58W
Santa Lucia, *Uruguay* . **126 C4** 34 27 S 56 24W
Santa Lucia Range,
  U.S.A. **110 K5** 36 0N 121 20W
Santa Magdalena, I.,
  Mexico **118 C2** 24 40N 112 15W
Santa Margarita,
  Argentina .... **126 D3** 38 28 S 61 35W
Santa Margarita, *Spain* **48 B10** 39 42N 3 6 E
Santa Margarita, *U.S.A.* **110 K6** 35 23N 120 37W
Santa Margarita →,
  U.S.A. **111 M9** 33 13N 117 23W
Santa Margarita, I.,
  Mexico **118 C2** 24 30N 111 50W
Santa Margherita, *Italy* **42 D1** 38 58N 8 58 E
Santa Margherita
  Ligure, *Italy* .... **40 D6** 44 20N 9 11 E
Santa María, *Argentina* **126 B2** 26 40 S 66 0W
Santa Maria, *Brazil* ... **127 B5** 29 40 S 53 48W
Santa Maria, *Phil.* .... **61 C4** 17 22N 120 29 E
Santa Maria, *U.S.A.* .. **111 L6** 34 57N 120 26W
Santa María →, *Mexico* **118 A3** 31 0N 107 14W
Santa Maria, B. de,
  Mexico **118 B3** 25 10N 108 40W
Santa Maria, C. de,
  Portugal **37 J3** 36 58N 7 53W
Santa María Cápua
  Vétere, *Italy* .... **43 A7** 41 5N 14 15 E
Santa Maria da Feira,
  Portugal **36 E2** 40 55N 8 35W
Santa Maria da Vitória,
  Brazil .... **125 F10** 13 24 S 44 12W
Santa Maria del Camí,
  Spain .... **48 B9** 39 38N 2 47 E
Santa Maria di Léuca,
  C., *Italy* .... **43 C11** 39 47N 18 22 E
Santa María la Real de
  Nieva, *Spain* **36 D6** 41 4N 4 24W
Santa Marinella, *Italy* . **41 F8** 42 2N 11 52 E

Santa Marta, *Colombia* **124 A4** 11 15N 74 13W
Santa Marta, Sierra
  Nevada de, *Colombia* **124 A4** 10 55N 73 50W
Santa Marta de Tormes,
  Spain **36 E5** 40 57N 5 38W
Santa Marta Grande, C.,
  Brazil .... **127 B6** 28 43 S 48 50W
Santa Marta Ortigueira,
  Ría de, *Spain* **36 B3** 43 44N 7 45W
Santa Maura = Levkás,
  Greece .... **46 C2** 38 40N 20 43 E
Santa Monica, *U.S.A.* . **111 M8** 34 1N 118 29W
Santa Monica Mts. △,
  U.S.A. **111 L8** 34 4N 118 44W
Santa Olalla, *Huelva,
  Spain* **37 H4** 37 54N 6 14W
Santa Olalla, *Toledo,
  Spain* **36 E6** 40 2N 4 25W
Santa Paula, *U.S.A.* ... **111 L7** 34 21N 119 4W
Santa Pola, *Spain* **39 G4** 38 13N 0 35W
Santa Ponça, *Spain* ... **48 B9** 39 30N 2 28 E
Santa Rita, *U.S.A.* **109 K10** 32 48N 108 4W
Santa Rosa, *La Pampa,
  Argentina* .... **126 D3** 36 40 S 64 17W
Santa Rosa, *San Luis,
  Argentina* .... **126 C2** 32 21 S 65 10W
Santa Rosa, *Brazil* .... **127 B5** 27 52 S 54 29W
Santa Rosa, *Calif.,
  U.S.A.* **110 G4** 38 26N 122 43W
Santa Rosa, *N. Mex.,
  U.S.A.* **113 H2** 34 57N 104 41W
Santa Rosa I., *Calif.,
  U.S.A.* **111 M6** 33 58N 120 6W
Santa Rosa I., *Fla.,
  U.S.A.* **115 K2** 30 20N 86 50W
Santa Rosa Range,
  U.S.A. **108 F5** 41 45N 117 40W
Santa Rosalía, *Mexico* **118 B2** 27 20N 112 20W
Santa Sylvina, *Argentina* **126 B3** 27 50 S 61 10W
Santa Tecla = Nueva San
  Salvador, *El Salv.* .. **120 D2** 13 40N 89 18W
Santa Teresa, *Argentina* **126 C3** 33 25 S 60 47W
Santa Teresa, *Australia* **94 C1** 24 8 S 134 22 E
Santa Teresa, *Mexico* . **119 B5** 25 17N 97 51W
Santa Teresa △,
  Uruguay .... **127 C5** 33 57 S 53 31W
Santa Teresa di Riva,
  Italy .... **43 E8** 37 57N 15 22 E
Santa Teresa Gallura,
  Italy .... **42 A2** 41 14N 9 11 E
Santa Uxía, *Spain* **36 C2** 42 36N 8 58W
Santa Vitória do Palmar,
  Brazil .... **127 C5** 33 32 S 53 25W
Santa Ynez →, *U.S.A.* **111 L6** 35 41N 120 36W
Santa Ynez Mts., *U.S.A.* **111 L6** 34 30N 120 0W
Santa Ysabel, *U.S.A.* .. **111 M10** 33 7N 116 40W
Santadi, *Italy* .... **42 C1** 39 5N 8 43 E
Santaella, *Spain* **37 H6** 37 34N 4 51W
Santai, *China* .... **58 B5** 31 5N 104 58 E
Santana, *Madeira* **48 D3** 32 48N 16 52W
Sântana, *Romania* ... **28 D6** 46 20N 21 30 E
Santana, Coxilha de,
  Brazil .... **127 C4** 30 50 S 55 35W
Santana do Livramento,
  Brazil .... **127 C4** 30 55 S 55 30W
Santander, *Spain* **36 B7** 43 27N 3 51W
Santander Jiménez,
  Mexico **119 C5** 24 11N 98 29W
Santanilla, Is., *Honduras* **120 C3** 17 22N 83 57W
Santanyí, *Spain* ...... **48 B10** 39 20N 3 5 E
Santaquin, *U.S.A.* **108 G8** 39 59N 111 47W
Santarcángelo di
  Romagna, *Italy* .... **41 D9** 44 4N 12 26 E
Santarém, *Brazil* ..... **125 D8** 2 25 S 54 42W
Santarém, *Portugal* .. **37 F2** 39 12N 8 42W
Santarém □, *Portugal* **37 F2** 39 10N 8 40W
Santaren Channel,
  W. Indies **120 B4** 24 0N 79 30W
Santee, *U.S.A.* **111 N10** 32 50N 116 58W
Santee →, *U.S.A.* **115 J6** 33 7N 79 17W
Santérem in Colle, *Italy* **43 B9** 40 49N 16 45 E
Santerno →, *Italy* .... **41 D8** 44 34N 11 58 E
Santhià, *Italy* .... **40 C5** 45 22N 8 10 E
Santi-Quaranta =
  Sarandë, *Albania* ... **44 G3** 39 52N 19 55 E
Santiago, *Brazil* ..... **127 B5** 29 11 S 54 52W
Santiago, *Canary Is.* .. **48 F2** 28 2N 17 12W
Santiago, *Chile* ...... **126 C1** 33 24 S 70 40W
Santiago, *Panama* **120 E3** 8 0N 81 0W
Santiago, *Phil.* .... **61 C4** 16 41N 121 33 E
Santiago □, *Chile* .... **126 C1** 33 30 S 70 50W
Santiago →, *Mexico* .. **98 G9** 25 11N 105 26W
Santiago →, *Peru* .... **124 D3** 4 27 S 77 38W
Santiago, Punta de,
  Eq. Guin. .... **83 E6** 3 12N 8 40 E
Santiago de Compostela,
  Spain **36 C2** 42 52N 8 37W
Santiago de Cuba, *Cuba* **120 C4** 20 0N 75 49W
Santiago de los
  Cabelleros, *Dom. Rep.* **121 C5** 19 30N 70 40W
Santiago del Estero,
  Argentina .... **126 B3** 27 50 S 64 15W
Santiago del Estero □,
  Argentina .... **126 B3** 27 40 S 63 15W
Santiago del Teide,
  Canary Is. **48 F3** 28 17N 16 48W
Santiago do Cacém,
  Portugal **37 G2** 38 1N 8 42W
Santiago Ixcuintla,
  Mexico **118 C3** 21 50N 105 11W
Santiago Papasquiaro,
  Mexico **118 C3** 25 0N 105 20W
Santiaguillo, L. de,
  Mexico **118 C4** 24 50N 104 50W
Santigi, *Mali* **82 C3** 12 42N 7 25W
Santillana, *Spain* **36 B6** 43 24N 4 6W
Santisteban del Puerto,
  Spain **37 G7** 38 17N 3 15W
Santo Amaro, *Brazil* .. **125 F11** 12 30 S 38 43W
Santo Anastácio, *Brazil* **125 A5** 21 58 S 51 39W
Santo André, *Brazil* .. **127 A6** 23 39 S 46 29W
Santo Ângelo, *Brazil* .. **127 B5** 28 15 S 54 15W
Santo Antônio do Içá,
  Brazil .... **124 D5** 3 5 S 67 57W
Santo Antônio do
  Leverger, *Brazil* .... **125 G7** 15 52 S 56 5W
Santo Domingo,
  Dom. Rep. **121 C6** 18 30N 69 59W
Santo Domingo,
  Baja Calif., Mexico . **118 A1** 30 43N 116 2W

Santo Domingo,
  Baja Calif. S., Mexico **118 B2** 25 32N 112 2W
Santo Domingo, *Nic.* . **120 D3** 12 14N 84 59W
Santo Domingo de la
  Calzada, *Spain* **38 C2** 42 26N 2 57W
Santo Domingo de los
  Colorados, *Ecuador* . **124 D3** 0 15 S 79 9W
Santo Domingo Pueblo,
  U.S.A. **109 J10** 35 31N 106 22W
Santo Stéfano di
  Camastro, *Italy* .... **43 D7** 38 1N 14 22 E
Santo Tirso, *Portugal* . **36 D2** 41 21N 8 28W
Santo Tomás, *Mexico* . **118 A1** 31 33N 116 24W
Santo Tomás, *Peru* ... **124 F4** 14 26 S 72 8W
Santo Tomé, *Argentina* **127 B4** 28 40 S 56 5W
Santo Tomé de
  Guayana = Ciudad
  Guayana, *Venezuela* **124 B6** 8 0N 62 30W
Santomera, *Spain* **39 G3** 38 4N 1 3W
Santoña, *Spain* **36 B7** 43 29N 3 27W
Santoríni = Thíra,
  Greece .... **47 E7** 36 23N 25 27 E
Santos, *Brazil* .... **127 A6** 24 0 S 46 20W
Santos, Sierra de los,
  Spain **37 G5** 38 7N 5 12W
Santos Dumont, *Brazil* **127 A7** 22 55 S 43 10W
Sanur, *Indonesia* ..... **63 K18** 8 41 S 115 15 E
Sanwer, *India* .... **68 H6** 22 59N 75 50 E
Sanxenxo, *Spain* **36 C2** 42 24N 8 49W
Sanyuan, *China* ...... **56 G5** 34 35N 108 58 E
São Bartolomeu de
  Messines, *Portugal* . **37 H2** 37 15N 8 17W
São Bernardo do
  Campo, *Brazil* ..... **127 A6** 23 45 S 46 34W
São Borja, *Brazil* ..... **127 B4** 28 39 S 56 0W
São Brás de Alportel,
  Portugal **37 H3** 37 8N 7 37W
São Carlos, *Brazil* .... **127 A6** 22 0 S 47 50W
São Cristóvão, *Brazil* . **125 F11** 11 1 S 37 15W
São Domingos, *Brazil* . **125 F9** 13 25 S 46 19W
São Domingos,
  Guinea-Biss. .... **82 C1** 12 19N 16 13 E
São Francisco, *Brazil* . **125 G10** 16 0 S 44 50W
São Francisco →, *Brazil* **125 F11** 10 30 S 36 24W
São Francisco do Sul,
  Brazil .... **127 B6** 26 15 S 48 36W
São Gabriel, *Brazil* ... **127 C5** 30 20 S 54 20W
São Gonçalo, *Brazil* .. **127 A7** 22 48 S 43 5W
São Hill, *Tanzania* .... **87 D4** 8 20 S 35 12 E
São João, *Guinea-Biss.* **82 C1** 11 32N 15 25W
São João da Boa Vista,
  Brazil .... **127 A6** 22 0 S 46 52W
São João da Madeira,
  Portugal **36 E2** 40 54N 8 30W
São João da Pesqueira,
  Portugal **36 D3** 41 8N 7 24W
São João del Rei, *Brazil* **127 A7** 21 8 S 44 15W
São João do Araguaia,
  Brazil .... **125 E9** 5 23 S 48 46W
São João do Piauí,
  Brazil .... **125 E10** 8 21 S 42 15W
São Joaquim, *Brazil* .. **127 B6** 28 18 S 49 56W
São Joaquim △, *Brazil* **127 B6** 28 12 S 49 37W
São Jorge, Pta. de,
  Madeira **48 D3** 32 50N 16 53W
São José do Norte,
  Brazil .... **127 C5** 32 1 S 52 3W
São José do Rio Prêto,
  Brazil .... **127 A6** 20 50 S 49 20W
São José dos Campos,
  Brazil .... **127 A6** 23 7 S 45 52W
São Leopoldo, *Brazil* . **127 B5** 29 50 S 51 10W
São Lourenço, *Brazil* . **127 A6** 22 7 S 45 3W
São Lourenço →, *Brazil* **125 G7** 17 53 S 57 27W
São Lourenço, Pta. de,
  Madeira **48 D3** 32 44N 16 39W
São Lourenço do Sul,
  Brazil .... **127 C5** 31 22 S 51 58W
São Luís, *Brazil* ...... **125 D10** 2 39 S 44 15W
São Luís Gonzaga,
  Brazil .... **127 B5** 28 25 S 55 0W
São Marcos →, *Brazil* **125 G9** 18 15 S 47 37W
São Marcos, B. de,
  Brazil .... **125 D10** 2 0 S 44 0W
São Martinho da
  Cortiça, *Portugal* ... **36 E2** 40 18N 8 8W
São Mateus, *Brazil* ... **125 G11** 18 44 S 39 50W
São Mateus do Sul,
  Brazil .... **127 B5** 25 52 S 50 23W
São Miguel do Oeste,
  Brazil .... **127 B5** 26 45 S 53 34W
São Paulo, *Brazil* ..... **127 A6** 23 32 S 46 37W
São Paulo □, *Brazil* .. **127 A6** 22 0 S 49 0W
São Paulo, I., *Atl. Oc.* . **2 D8** 0 50N 31 40W
São Paulo de Olivença,
  Brazil .... **124 D5** 3 27 S 68 48W
São Pedro do Sul,
  Portugal **36 E2** 40 46N 8 4W
São Roque, *Madeira* .. **48 D3** 32 46N 16 48W
São Roque, C. de, *Brazil* **125 E11** 5 30 S 35 16W
São Sebastião, I. de,
  Brazil .... **127 A6** 23 50 S 45 18W
São Sebastião do
  Paraíso, *Brazil* ..... **127 A6** 20 54 S 46 59W
São Teotónio, *Portugal* **37 H2** 37 30N 8 42W
São Tomé,
  São Tomé & Príncipe **76 F4** 0 10N 6 39 E
São Tomé, C. de, *Brazil* **127 A7** 22 0 S 40 59W
São Tomé & Príncipe ■,
  Africa .... **77 F4** 0 12N 6 39 E
São Vicente, *Brazil* ... **127 A6** 23 57 S 46 23W
São Vicente, *Madeira* . **48 D2** 32 48N 17 3W
São Vicente, C. de,
  Portugal **37 H1** 37 0N 9 0W
São Vicente, *Dem. Rep.* **121 C6** 18 10N 68 40W
Saône →, *France* ..... **19 G11** 45 44N 4 50 E
Saône-et-Loire □,
  France .... **19 F11** 46 30N 4 50 E
Saonek, *Indonesia* .... **63 E8** 0 30 S 130 55 E
Sápai, *Greece* .... **45 E9** 41 2N 25 43 E
Sapam, Ao, *Thailand* . **65 a** 8 0N 98 20 E
Sapanca, *Turkey* ..... **72 B4** 40 41N 30 16 E
Saparua, *Indonesia* ... **63 E7** 3 33 S 128 40 E
Sapele, *Nigeria* ...... **83 D6** 5 50N 5 40 E
Sapelo I., *U.S.A.* **115 K5** 31 25N 81 12W
Saphane, *Turkey* ..... **47 B11** 39 1N 29 13 E
Sapi △, *Zimbabwe* .... **87 F2** 15 48 S 29 42 E
Sapiéntza, *Greece* .... **46 E3** 36 45N 21 43 E
Sapo △, *Liberia* **82 D3** 5 15N 8 30W
Sapone, *Burkina Faso* . **83 C4** 12 3N 1 35W
Saposoa, *Peru* .... **124 E3** 6 55 S 76 45W
Sapotskina, *Belarus* .. **30 E10** 53 49N 23 41 E
Sapouy, *Burkina Faso* . **83 C4** 11 34N 1 44W
Sapozhok, *Russia* .... **34 D5** 53 59N 40 41 E
Sapphire, *Australia* ... **94 C4** 23 28 S 147 43 E
Sappho, *U.S.A.* **110 B2** 48 4N 124 16W

Sapporo, Japan .... 54 C10 43 0N 141 21 E
Sapri, Italy .... 43 B8 40 4N 15 38 E
Sapulpa, U.S.A. 113 H6 35 59N 96 5W
Saqqez, Iran ...... 70 B5 36 15N 46 20 E
Sar Dasht,
   Āzarbāyjān-e Gharbī,
   Iran .... 73 D11 36 9N 45 28 E
Sar Dasht, Khuzestān,
   Iran .... 71 C6 32 32N 48 52 E
Sar-e Pol □, Afghan. .. 66 B4 36 20N 65 50 E
Sar Gachīneh = Yāsūj,
   Iran .... 71 D6 30 31N 51 31 E
Sar Planina, Macedonia 44 E4 42 0N 21 0 E
Sara, Burkina Faso ... 82 C4 11 40N 3 53W
Sara, Phil. .... 61 F5 11 16N 123 1 E
Šara □, Serbia & M. .. 44 D5 42 12N 21 0 E
Sara Buri = Saraburi,
   Thailand .... 64 E3 14 30N 100 55 E
Sarāb, Iran .... 70 B5 37 55N 47 40 E
Sarabadi, Iraq ...... 70 C5 33 1N 44 48 E
Saraburi, Thailand ... 64 E3 14 30N 100 55 E
Saradiya, India .... 68 J4 21 34N 70 2 E
Saraféré, Mali 82 B4 15 50N 3 40W
Saragossa = Zaragoza,
   Spain 38 D4 41 39N 0 53W
Saraguro, Ecuador ... 124 D3 3 35 S 79 16W
Sarai Naurang, Pakistan 68 C4 32 50N 70 47 E
Saraikela, India .... 69 H11 22 42N 85 56 E
Saraiu, Romania ..... 29 F13 44 43N 28 10 E
Sarajevo, Bos.-H. .... 28 G3 43 52N 18 26 E
Sarakhs, Turkmenistan 71 B9 36 32N 61 13 E
Saran, Gunung,
   Indonesia .... 62 E4 0 30 S 111 25 E
Saranac L., U.S.A. .. 117 B10 44 20N 74 10W
Saranac Lake, U.S.A. 117 B10 44 20N 74 8W
Saranda, Tanzania ... 86 D3 5 45 S 34 59 E
Sarandë, Albania .... 44 G3 39 52N 19 55 E
Sarandí del Yi, Uruguay 127 C4 33 18 S 55 38W
Sarandí Grande,
   Uruguay .... 126 C4 33 44 S 56 20W
Sarangani B., Phil. .. 61 J6 6 0N 125 13 E
Sarangani Is., Phil. .. 61 J6 5 25N 125 25 E
Sarangarh, India .... 67 J13 21 30N 83 5 E
Saransk, Russia .... 34 C7 54 10N 45 10 E
Sarapul, Russia .... 52 D6 56 28N 53 48 E
Sarasota, U.S.A. ... 115 M4 27 20N 82 32W
Sarata, Ukraine .... 29 D14 46 1N 29 40 E
Sarata →, Ukraine ... 29 E14 45 51N 29 40 E
Saratoga, Calif., U.S.A. 110 H4 37 16N 122 2W
Saratoga, Wyo., U.S.A. 108 F10 41 27N 106 49W
Saratoga □, U.S.A. .. 117 D14 43 0N 73 37W
Saratoga Springs, U.S.A. 117 C11 43 5N 73 47W
Saratok, Malaysia ... 62 D4 1 55N 111 17 E
Saratov, Russia .... 34 E7 51 30N 46 2 E
Sarävän, Iran ..... 71 E9 27 25N 62 15 E
Saravane, Laos ..... 64 E6 15 43N 106 25 E
Sarawak □, Malaysia .. 62 D4 2 0N 113 0 E
Saray, Tekirdağ, Turkey 45 E11 41 26N 27 55 E
Saray, Van, Turkey ... 73 C11 38 38N 44 9 E
Saraya, Guinea 82 C2 12 50N 11 45W
Saraya, Senegal 82 C2 12 50N 11 45W
Saraycık, Turkey .... 47 B11 39 1N 29 49 E
Sarayköy, Turkey .... 47 D10 37 55N 28 54 E
Saraylar, Turkey .... 45 F11 40 39N 27 42 E
Sarayönü, Turkey .... 72 C5 38 16N 32 24 E
Sarbāz, Iran ...... 71 E9 26 38N 61 19 E
Sarbīsheh, Iran .... 71 C8 32 30N 59 40 E
Sárbogárd, Hungary .. 28 D3 46 50N 18 40 E
Sarca →, Italy ..... 40 C7 45 52N 10 52 E
Sarcelles, France ... 19 D9 49 1N 2 23 E
Sarda →, India ..... 67 F12 27 21N 81 23 E
Sardarshahr, India .. 68 E6 28 30N 74 29 E
Sardegna □, Italy ... 42 B1 40 0N 9 0 E
Sardhana, India .... 68 E7 29 9N 77 39 E
Sardina, Pta., Canary Is. 48 F4 28 9N 15 44W
Sardinia = Sardegna □,
   Italy .... 42 B1 40 0N 9 0 E
Sardis, Turkey ..... 47 C10 38 28N 28 2 E
Sārdūīyeh = Dar Mazār,
   Iran .... 71 D8 29 14N 57 20 E
Saren, Indonesia .... 63 J18 8 26 S 115 34 E
S'Arenal, Spain .... 48 B9 39 30N 2 45 E
Sarentino, Italy .... 40 B4 46 38N 11 21 E
Saréyamou, Mali 82 B4 16 7N 3 10W
Sargasso Sea, Atl. Oc. 97 D20 27 0N 72 0W
Sargodha, Pakistan .. 68 C5 32 10N 72 40 E
Sarh, Chad .... 79 G9 9 5N 18 23 E
Sarhala, Ivory C. .. 82 D3 8 22N 6 8W
Sārī, Iran .... 71 B7 36 30N 53 4 E
Sari d'Orcino, France 21 F12 42 3N 8 49 E
Sária, Greece ..... 47 F9 35 54N 27 17 E
Saria, India ...... 69 J10 21 38N 83 22 E
Sariab, Pakistan .... 68 D2 30 6N 66 59 E
Saribeyler, Turkey .. 47 B9 39 24N 27 35 E
Sarıgöl, Turkey .... 72 C3 38 14N 28 41 E
Sarikamiş, Turkey ... 73 B10 40 22N 42 35 E
Sarıkaya, Turkey ... 72 C6 39 29N 35 22 E
Sarikei, Malaysia ... 62 D4 2 8N 111 30 E
Sarila, India ..... 69 G8 25 46N 79 41 E
Sarina, Australia ... 94 C4 21 22 S 149 13 E
Sariñena, Spain 38 D4 41 47N 0 10W
Sarita, U.S.A. 113 M6 27 13N 97 47W
Sariwŏn, N. Korea ... 57 E13 38 31N 125 46 E
Sariyar Baraji, Turkey 72 B4 40 2N 31 33 E
Sariyer, Turkey .... 45 E13 41 10N 29 3 E
Sarju →, India ..... 69 F9 27 21N 81 23 E
Sark, U.K. 15 H5 49 25N 2 22W
Sarkad, Hungary .... 28 D6 46 47N 21 23 E
Sarkari Tala, India .. 68 F4 27 39N 70 52 E
Şarkışla, Turkey ... 72 C7 39 21N 36 25 E
Şarköy, Turkey .... 45 F11 40 36N 27 6 E
Sarlat-la-Canéda, France 20 D5 44 54N 1 13 E
Sărmaşag, Romania .. 28 C7 47 21N 22 50 E
Sărmaşu, Romania ... 29 D9 46 45N 24 13 E
Sarmi, Indonesia ... 63 E9 1 49 S 138 44 E
Sarmiento, Argentina 128 C2 45 35 S 69 5W
Sarmizegetusa, Romania 28 E7 45 31N 22 47 E
Särna, Sweden ..... 10 C7 61 41N 13 8 E
Sarnano, Italy ..... 41 E10 43 2N 13 18 E
Sarnen, Switz. .... 25 J4 46 53N 8 13 E
Sarnia, Canada 116 D2 42 58N 82 23W
Sarno, Italy ...... 43 B7 40 49N 14 37 E
Sarnthein = Sarentino,
   Italy .... 41 B8 46 38N 11 21 E
Särö, Sweden ..... 11 G5 57 31N 11 57 E
Sarolangun, Indonesia 62 E2 2 19 S 102 42 E
Saronikós Kólpos,
   Greece .... 46 D5 37 45N 23 45 E
Saronno, Italy ..... 40 C6 45 38N 9 2 E
Saros Körfezi, Turkey 45 F10 40 30N 26 15 E
Sárospatak, Hungary . 28 B6 48 18N 21 33 E
Sarpsborg, Norway .. 9 G14 59 16N 11 7 E
Sarracín, Spain 36 C7 42 15N 3 45W
Sarralbe, France ... 19 D14 49 0N 7 1 E
Sarre = Saar →, Europe 17 E6 49 41N 6 32 E
Sarre, Italy .... 40 C4 45 40N 7 15 E

Sarre-Union, France ... 19 D14 48 57N 7 4 E
Sarrebourg, France .. 19 D14 48 43N 7 3 E
Sarreguemines, France 19 C14 49 5N 7 4 E
Sarria, Spain 36 C3 42 49N 7 29W
Sarrión, Spain 38 E4 40 9N 0 49W
Sarro, Mali 82 C3 13 40N 5 15W
Sarstedt, Germany ... 24 C5 52 14N 9 52 E
Sartène, France .... 21 G12 41 38N 8 58 E
Sarthe □, France ... 18 D7 48 10N 0 10 E
Sarthe →, France 18 E6 47 33N 0 31W
Sartilly, France 18 D5 48 45N 1 28W
Saruhanlı, Turkey ... 47 C9 38 44N 27 36 E
Sărulești, Romania .. 29 F11 44 25N 26 39 E
Saruna →, Pakistan .. 68 F2 26 31N 67 7 E
Sárvár, Hungary ... 28 C1 47 15N 16 56 E
Sarvar, India ...... 68 F6 26 4N 75 0 E
Sarvestān, Iran .... 71 D7 29 20N 53 10 E
Sárvíz →, Hungary ... 28 D3 46 24N 18 41 E
Sary-Tash, Kyrgyzstan 52 F8 39 44N 73 15 E
Sarych, Mys, Ukraine . 33 K7 44 25N 33 45 E
Saryshagan, Kazakhstan 52 E8 46 12N 73 38 E
Sarzana, Italy ..... 40 D6 44 7N 9 58 E
Sarzeau, France 18 E4 47 31N 2 48W
Sasan Gir, India .... 68 J4 21 10N 70 36 E
Sasaram, India ..... 69 G11 24 57N 84 5 E
Sasebo, Japan ..... 55 H4 33 10N 129 43 E
Saser, India ...... 69 B7 34 50N 77 50 E
Saskatchewan □,
   Canada 103 C7 54 40N 106 0W
Saskatchewan →,
   Canada 103 C8 53 37N 100 40W
Saskatoon, Canada .. 103 C7 52 10N 106 38W
Saskylakh, Russia ... 53 B12 71 55N 114 1 E
Saslaya △, Nic. 120 D2 13 45N 85 4W
Sasolburg, S. Africa . 89 D4 26 46 S 27 49 E
Sasovo, Russia .... 34 C5 54 25N 41 55 E
Sassandra, Ivory C. . 82 E3 4 58N 6 8W
Sassandra →, Ivory C. 82 E3 4 58N 6 5W
Sássari, Italy ..... 42 B1 40 43N 8 34 E
Sassnitz, Germany ... 24 A9 54 29N 13 39 E
Sasso Marconi, Italy . 41 D8 44 24N 11 15 E
Sassocorvaro, Italy .. 41 E9 43 47N 12 30 E
Sassoferrato, Italy .. 41 E9 43 26N 12 51 E
Sasstown, Liberia ... 82 E3 4 45N 8 27W
Sássuolo, Italy .... 40 D7 44 33N 10 47 E
Sástago, Spain 38 D4 41 19N 0 21W
Sasyk, Ozero, Ukraine 29 E14 45 45N 29 20 E
Sata-Misaki, Japan .. 55 J5 31 0N 130 40 E
Satadougou, Mali ... 82 C2 12 25N 11 25W
Satakunta = Satakunta,
   Finland .... 9 F20 61 45N 23 0 E
Satakunta, Finland .. 9 F20 61 45N 23 0 E
Satama-Soukoura,
   Ivory C. 82 D4 7 55N 4 27W
Satara, India ...... 66 L8 17 44N 73 58 E
Satara, S. Africa .... 89 C5 24 29 S 31 47 E
Satbarwa, India .... 69 H11 23 55N 84 16 E
Sätenäs, Sweden .... 11 F6 58 27N 12 41 E
Säter, Sweden ..... 10 D9 60 21N 15 45 E
Satevó, Mexico 118 B3 27 57N 106 7W
Satilla →, U.S.A. ... 115 K5 30 59N 81 29W
Satmala Hills, India . 66 J9 20 15N 74 40 E
Satna, India ...... 69 G9 24 35N 80 50 E
Šator, Bos.-H. ..... 41 D13 44 11N 16 37 E
Sátoraljaújhely, Hungary 28 B6 48 25N 21 41 E
Satpura Ra., India .. 66 J10 21 25N 76 10 E
Satrup, Germany ... 24 A5 54 41N 9 36 E
Satsuna-Shotō, Japan . 55 K5 30 0N 130 0 E
Sattahip, Thailand .. 64 F3 12 41N 100 54 E
Satu Mare, Romania . 28 C7 47 46N 22 55 E
Satu Mare □, Romania 28 C8 47 45N 23 0 E
Satui, Indonesia .... 62 E5 3 50 S 115 27 E
Satun, Thailand .... 65 J3 6 43N 100 2 E
Saturnina →, Brazil . 124 F7 12 15 S 58 10W
Sauce, Argentina ... 126 C4 30 5 S 58 46W
Sauceda, Mexico ... 118 B4 25 55N 101 18W
Saucillo, Mexico ... 118 B3 28 1N 105 17W
Sauda, Norway .... 9 G12 59 40N 6 20 E
Sauðarkrókur, Iceland 8 D4 65 45N 19 40W
Saudi Arabia ■, Asia 70 B3 26 0N 44 0 E
Saugeen →, Canada .. 116 B3 44 30N 81 22W
Saugerties, U.S.A. .. 117 D11 42 5N 73 57W
Saugues, France .... 20 D7 44 58N 3 32 E
Saugus, U.S.A. 111 L8 34 25N 118 32W
Saujon, France 20 D3 45 41N 0 55W
Sauk Centre, U.S.A. . 112 C7 45 44N 94 57W
Sauk Rapids, U.S.A. . 112 C7 45 35N 94 10W
Saulgau, Germany ... 25 G5 48 1N 9 29 E
Saulieu, France .... 19 E11 47 17N 4 14 E
Sault, France ...... 21 D9 44 6N 5 24 E
Sault Ste. Marie, Canada 104 C3 46 30N 84 20W
Sault Ste. Marie, U.S.A. 101 D11 46 30N 84 21W
Saumlaki, Indonesia . 63 F8 7 55 S 131 20 E
Saumur, France 18 E6 47 15N 0 5W
Saunders, C., N.Z. .. 91 L3 45 53 S 170 45 E
Saunders I., Antarctica 5 B1 57 48 S 26 28W
Saunders Point,
   Australia .... 93 E4 27 52 S 125 38 E
Sauri, Nigeria ..... 83 C6 11 42N 6 44 E
Saurimo, Angola ... 84 F4 9 40 S 20 12 E
Sausalito, U.S.A. ... 110 H4 37 51N 122 29W
Sauveterre-de-Béarn,
   France 20 E3 43 24N 0 57W
Sauzé-Vaussais, France 20 B4 46 8N 0 8 E
Savá, Honduras 120 C2 15 32N 86 15W
Sava, Italy .... 43 B10 40 24N 17 33 E
Sava →, Serbia & M. . 28 F5 44 50N 20 26 E
Savage, U.S.A. 112 B2 47 27N 104 21W
Savage I. = Niue,
   Cook Is. .... 97 J11 19 2 S 169 54W
Savage River, Australia 95 G4 41 31 S 145 14 E
Savai'i, Samoa .... 91 A12 13 28 S 172 24W
Savalou, Benin .... 83 D5 7 57N 1 58 E
Savane, Mozam. .... 87 F4 19 37 S 35 8 E
Savanna, U.S.A. ... 112 D9 42 5N 90 8W
Savanna-la-Mar,
   Jamaica .... 120 a 18 10N 78 10W
Savannah, Ga., U.S.A. 115 J5 32 5N 81 6W
Savannah, Mo., U.S.A. 112 F7 39 56N 94 50W
Savannah, Tenn., U.S.A. 115 H1 35 14N 88 15W
Savannah →, U.S.A. . 115 J5 32 2N 80 53W
Savannakhet, Laos .. 64 D5 16 30N 104 49 E
Savant L., Canada ... 104 B1 50 16N 90 44W
Savant Lake, Canada . 104 B1 50 14N 90 40W
Săvârşin, Romania .. 28 D7 46 1N 22 14 E
Savaştepe, Turkey ... 47 B9 39 22N 27 42 E
Savé, Benin .... 83 D5 8 2N 2 29 E
Save →, France ..... 20 E5 43 47N 1 17 E
Save →, Mozam. .... 89 C5 21 16 S 34 0 E
Säveh, Iran .... 71 C6 35 2N 50 20 E
Savelugu, Ghana ... 83 D4 9 38N 0 54W
Savenay, France 18 E5 47 20N 1 55W
Săveni, Romania ... 29 C11 47 57N 26 52 E
Saverdun, France ... 20 E5 43 14N 1 34 E
Saverne, France .... 19 D14 48 43N 7 20 E
Savigliano, Italy .... 40 D4 44 38N 7 40 E

Savigny-sur-Braye,
   France .... 18 E7 47 53N 0 49 E
Sávio →, Italy ..... 41 D9 44 19N 12 20 E
Savnik, Serbia & M. . 44 D3 42 59N 19 10 E
Savo, Finland ..... 8 E22 62 45N 27 30 E
Savoie □, France .... 21 C10 45 26N 6 35 E
Savolax = Savo, Finland 8 E22 62 45N 27 30 E
Savona, Italy ...... 40 D5 44 17N 8 30 E
Savona, U.S.A. 116 D7 42 17N 77 13W
Savonlinna, Finland . 32 B5 61 52N 28 53 E
Savoy = Savoie □,
   France .... 21 C10 45 26N 6 25 E
Şavşat, Turkey ..... 73 B10 41 15N 42 20 E
Sävsjö, Sweden .... 11 G8 57 20N 14 40 E
Savur, Turkey ..... 70 B4 37 34N 40 53 E
Sawahlunto, Indonesia 62 E2 0 40 S 100 52 E
Sawai, Indonesia ... 63 E7 3 0 S 129 5 E
Sawai Madhopur, India 68 G7 26 0N 76 25 E
Sawang Daen Din,
   Thailand .... 64 D4 17 28N 103 28 E
Sawankhalok, Thailand 64 D2 17 19N 99 50 E
Sawara, Japan ..... 55 G10 35 55N 140 30 E
Sawatch Range, U.S.A. 109 G10 38 30N 106 30W
Sawel Mt., U.K. 12 B4 54 50N 7 2W
Sawi, Thailand .... 65 G2 10 14N 99 5 E
Sawla, Ghana 82 D4 9 17N 2 25W
Sawmills, Zimbabwe . 87 F2 19 30 S 28 2 E
Sawtooth △, U.S.A. . 108 D6 44 0N 114 50W
Sawtooth Range, U.S.A. 108 E6 44 3N 114 58W
Sawu, Indonesia .... 63 F6 10 35 S 121 50 E
Sawu Sea, Indonesia . 63 F6 9 30 S 121 50 E
Saxby →, Australia .. 94 B3 18 25 S 140 53 E
Saxmundham, U.K. .. 15 E9 52 13N 1 30 E
Saxony = Sachsen □,
   Germany .... 24 E9 50 55N 13 10 E
Saxony, Lower =
   Niedersachsen □,
   Germany .... 24 C4 52 50N 9 0 E
Saxton, U.S.A. 116 F6 40 13N 78 15W
Say, Mali 82 C4 13 50N 4 57W
Say, Niger .... 83 C5 13 8N 2 22 E
Saya, Nigeria ..... 83 D5 9 30N 3 18 E
Sayabec, Canada ... 105 C6 48 35N 67 41W
Sayaboury, Laos ... 64 C3 19 15N 101 45 E
Sayán, Peru ...... 124 F3 11 8 S 77 12W
Sayan, Vostochnyy,
   Russia .... 53 D10 54 0N 96 0 E
Sayan, Zapadnyy, Russia 53 D10 52 30N 94 0 E
Saydā, Lebanon .... 74 B4 33 35N 35 25 E
Sayhandulaan = Oldziyt,
   Mongolia .... 56 B5 44 40N 109 1 E
Sayhût, Yemen .... 75 D5 15 12N 51 10 E
Saykhin, Kazakhstan . 35 F8 48 50N 46 47 E
Saylac = Zeila,
   Somali Rep. ...... 75 E3 11 21N 43 30 E
Saynshand, Mongolia . 60 B6 44 55N 110 11 E
Sayre, Okla., U.S.A. . 113 H5 35 18N 99 38W
Sayre, Pa., U.S.A. .. 117 E8 41 59N 76 32W
Sayreville, U.S.A. ... 117 F10 40 28N 74 22W
Sayula, Mexico 118 D4 19 50N 103 40W
Sayward, Canada ... 102 C3 50 21N 125 55W
Sazanit, Albania ... 44 F3 40 30N 19 20 E
Sázava →, Czech Rep. 26 B7 49 53N 14 24 E
Sazin, Pakistan .... 69 B5 35 35N 73 30 E
Sazlika →, Bulgaria . 45 E9 41 59N 25 50 E
Scaër, France 18 D3 48 2N 3 42W
Scafell Pike, U.K. ... 14 C4 54 27N 3 14W
Scalea, Italy ...... 43 C8 39 49N 15 47 E
Scalloway, U.K. 13 A7 60 9N 1 17W
Scalpay, U.K. 13 D3 57 18N 6 0W
Scandia, Canada ... 102 C6 50 20N 112 2W
Scandiano, Italy ... 40 D7 44 36N 10 43 E
Scandicci, Italy .... 41 E8 43 45N 11 11 E
Scandinavia, Europe . 8 E16 64 0N 12 0 E
Scansano, Italy .... 41 F8 42 41N 11 20 E
Scapa Flow, U.K. ... 13 C5 58 53N 3 3W
Scappoose, U.S.A. .. 110 E4 45 45N 122 53W
Scarámia, Capo, Italy 43 F7 36 47N 14 29 E
Scarba, U.K. 13 E3 56 11N 5 43W
Scarborough,
   Trin. & Tob. 121 D7 11 11N 60 42W
Scarborough, U.K. .. 14 C7 54 17N 0 24W
Scariff I., Ireland ... 12 E1 51 44N 10 15W
Scarp, U.K. 13 C1 58 1N 7 8W
Scarpe-Escaut →, France 19 B10 50 26N 3 23 E
Scebeli, Wabi →,
   Somali Rep. ...... 75 G3 2 0N 44 0 E
Šćedro, Croatia .... 41 E13 43 6N 16 43 E
Schaal See, Germany . 24 B6 53 36N 10 55 E
Schaalsee △, Germany 24 B6 53 40N 10 59 E
Schaffhausen, Switz. . 25 H4 47 42N 8 39 E
Schagen, Neths. .... 17 B4 52 49N 4 48 E
Schaghticoke, U.S.A. 117 D11 42 54N 73 35W
Schärding, Austria .. 26 C6 48 27N 13 27 E
Scharhörn, Germany . 24 B4 53 57N 8 24 E
Scheessel, Germany . 24 B5 53 10N 9 33 E
Schefferville, Canada 105 B6 54 48N 66 50W
Scheibbs, Austria ... 26 D8 48 1N 15 9 E
Schelde →, Belgium . 17 C4 51 15N 4 16 E
Schell Creek Ra., U.S.A. 108 G6 39 15N 114 30W
Schellsburg, U.S.A. . 116 F6 40 3N 78 39W
Schenectady, U.S.A. . 117 D11 42 49N 73 57W
Schenevus, U.S.A. .. 117 D10 42 33N 74 50W
Scherfede, Germany . 24 D5 51 32N 9 2 E
Schesslitz, Germany . 25 F7 49 58N 11 1 E
Schiedam, Neths. ... 17 C4 51 55N 4 25 E
Schiermonnikoog, Neths. 17 A6 53 30N 6 15 E
Schilthigheim, France 19 D14 48 35N 7 45 E
Schio, Italy ...... 41 C8 45 43N 11 21 E
Schiphol, Amsterdam ✈
   (AMS), Neths. .... 17 B4 52 18N 4 45 E
Schladming, Austria . 26 D6 47 23N 13 41 E
Schlanders = Silandro,
   Italy .... 40 B7 46 38N 10 46 E
Schlei →, Germany .. 24 A5 54 40N 10 0 E
Schleiden, Germany . 24 E2 50 31N 6 28 E
Schleiz, Germany ... 24 E7 50 35N 11 49 E
Schleswig, Germany . 24 A5 54 31N 9 34 E
Schleswig-Holstein □,
   Germany .... 24 A5 54 30N 9 30 E
Schlüchtern, Germany 25 E5 50 20N 9 32 E
Schmalkalden, Germany 24 E6 50 43N 10 27 E
Schmölln, Germany . 24 E8 50 54N 12 22 E
Schneeberg, Austria . 26 D8 47 47N 15 48 E
Schneeberg, Germany 24 E8 50 35N 12 38 E
Schneverdingen,
   Germany .... 24 B5 53 7N 9 48 E
Schœlcher, Martinique 120 c 14 36N 61 7W
Schoharie, U.S.A. .. 117 D10 42 40N 74 19W
Schoharie →, U.S.A. 117 D10 42 57N 74 18W
Scholls, U.S.A. 110 E4 45 24N 122 56W
Schönberg,
   Mecklenburg-Vorpommern,
   Germany .... 24 B6 53 52N 10 56 E
Schönberg,
   Schleswig-Holstein,
   Germany .... 24 A6 54 23N 10 21 E

Schönbuch △, Germany 25 G5 48 35N 9 2 E
Schönebeck, Germany 24 C7 52 2N 11 44 E
Schongau, Germany . 25 H6 47 47N 10 53 E
Schöningen, Germany 24 C6 52 8N 10 56 E
Schopfheim, Germany 25 H3 47 38N 7 50 E
Schorndorf, Germany 25 G5 48 47N 9 32 E
Schortens, Germany . 24 B3 53 31N 7 56 E
Schouten, I., Australia 95 G4 42 20 S 148 20 E
Schouten Is. = Supiori,
   Indonesia .... 63 E9 1 0 S 136 0 E
Schouwen, Neths. ... 17 C3 51 43N 3 45 E
Schramberg, Germany 25 G4 48 13N 8 22 E
Schrankogel, Austria . 26 D4 47 3N 11 7 E
Schreiber, Canada .. 104 C2 48 45N 87 20W
Schrems, Austria ... 26 C8 48 47N 15 4 E
Schrobenhausen,
   Germany .... 25 G7 48 34N 11 16 E
Schroon Lake, U.S.A. 117 C11 43 50N 73 46W
Schruns, Austria ... 26 D2 47 5N 9 56 E
Schuler, Canada ... 103 C6 50 20N 110 6W
Schumacher, Canada 104 C3 48 30N 81 16W
Schurz, U.S.A. 108 G4 38 57N 118 49W
Schuyler, U.S.A. ... 112 E6 41 27N 97 4W
Schuylerville, U.S.A. 117 C11 43 6N 73 35W
Schuylkill →, U.S.A. 117 G9 39 53N 75 12W
Schuylkill Haven, U.S.A. 117 F8 40 37N 76 11W
Schwabach, Germany 25 F7 49 19N 11 2 E
Schwaben □, Germany 25 G6 48 15N 10 30 E
Schwäbisch-Fränkischer
   Wald △, Germany . 25 G5 49 0N 9 30 E
Schwäbisch Gmünd,
   Germany .... 25 G5 48 48N 9 47 E
Schwäbisch Hall,
   Germany .... 25 F5 49 6N 9 44 E
Schwäbische Alb,
   Germany .... 25 G5 48 20N 9 30 E
Schwabmünchen,
   Germany .... 25 G6 48 10N 10 46 E
Schwalmstadt, Germany 24 E5 50 55N 9 10 E
Schwandorf, Germany 25 F8 49 19N 12 7 E
Schwaner, Pegunungan,
   Indonesia .... 62 E4 1 0 S 112 30 E
Schwanewede, Germany 24 B4 53 14N 8 35 E
Schwarmstedt, Germany 24 C5 52 39N 9 38 E
Schwarze Elster →,
   Germany .... 24 D8 51 48N 12 50 E
Schwarzenberg,
   Germany .... 24 E8 50 32N 12 47 E
Schwarzrand, Namibia 88 D2 25 37 S 16 50 E
Schwarzwald, Germany 25 G4 48 30N 8 20 E
Schwaz, Austria .... 26 D4 47 20N 11 44 E
Schwechat, Austria .. 27 C9 48 8N 16 28 E
Schwechat, Wien ✈
   (VIA), Austria .... 27 C9 48 7N 16 35 E
Schwedt, Germany .. 24 B10 53 3N 14 16 E
Schweinfurt, Germany 25 E6 50 3N 10 14 E
Schweizer-Reneke,
   S. Africa .... 88 D4 27 11 S 25 18 E
Schwenningen =
   Villingen-
   Schwenningen,
   Germany .... 25 G4 48 3N 8 26 E
Schwerin, Germany . 24 B7 53 36N 11 22 E
Schweriner See,
   Germany .... 24 B7 53 43N 11 28 E
Schwetzingen, Germany 25 F4 49 23N 8 35 E
Schwyz, Switz. .... 25 H4 47 2N 8 39 E
Schwyz □, Switz. ... 25 H4 47 2N 8 39 E
Sciacca, Italy ..... 42 E6 37 31N 13 3 E
Scicli, Italy ...... 43 F7 36 47N 14 42 E
Sciliar △, Italy .... 41 B8 46 31N 11 35 E
Scilla, Italy ...... 43 D8 38 15N 15 43 E
Scilly, Isles of, U.K. . 15 H1 49 56N 6 22W
Ścinawa, Poland ... 31 G3 51 25N 16 26 E
Scione, Greece ..... 44 G7 39 57N 23 36 E
Scioto →, U.S.A. ... 114 F4 38 44N 83 1W
Scituate, U.S.A. ... 117 D14 42 12N 70 44W
Scobey, U.S.A. 112 A2 48 47N 105 25W
Scone, Australia ... 95 E5 32 5 S 150 52 E
Scone, U.K. 13 E5 56 25N 3 24W
Scordia, Italy ..... 43 E7 37 18N 14 51 E
Scoresbysund =
   Ittoqqortoormiit,
   Greenland 4 B6 70 20N 23 0W
Scornicești, Romania 29 F9 44 34N 24 33 E
Scotia, Calif., U.S.A. 108 F1 40 29N 124 6W
Scotia, N.Y., U.S.A. 117 D11 42 50N 73 58W
Scotia Sea, Antarctica 5 D11 56 5 S 56 0W
Scotland, Canada ... 116 C4 43 1N 80 22W
Scotland □, U.K. ... 13 E5 57 0N 4 0W
Scott, Antarctica ... 5 D11 77 0 S 165 0 E
Scott, C., U.S.A. .. 92 B4 13 30 S 129 49 E
Scott City, U.S.A. .. 112 F4 38 29N 100 54W
Scott Glacier, Antarctica 5 C8 66 15 S 100 5 E
Scott I., Antarctica .. 5 C11 67 0 S 179 0 E
Scott Is., Canada ... 102 C3 50 48N 128 40W
Scott L., Canada ... 103 B7 59 55N 106 18W
Scott Reef, Australia . 92 B3 14 0 S 121 50 E
Scottburgh, S. Africa 89 E5 30 15 S 30 47 E
Scottdale, U.S.A. ... 116 F5 40 6N 79 35W
Scottish Borders □, U.K. 13 F6 55 35N 2 50W
Scottsbluff, U.S.A. .. 112 E3 41 52N 103 40W
Scottsboro, U.S.A. .. 115 H3 34 40N 86 2W
Scottsburg, U.S.A. .. 114 F3 38 41N 85 47W
Scottsdale, Australia 95 G4 41 9 S 147 31 E
Scottsdale, U.S.A. .. 109 K7 33 29N 111 56W
Scottsville, Ky., U.S.A. 115 G2 36 45N 86 11W
Scottsville, N.Y., U.S.A. 116 C7 43 2N 77 47W
Scottville, U.S.A. ... 114 D2 43 58N 86 17W
Scranton, U.S.A. ... 117 E9 41 25N 75 40W
Scugog, L., Canada . 116 B6 44 10N 78 55W
Sculeni, Moldova ... 29 C12 47 20N 27 37 E
Scunthorpe, U.K. ... 14 D7 53 36N 0 39W
Scuol Schuls, Switz. . 25 J6 46 48N 10 17 E
Scutari = Shkodër,
   Albania .... 44 D3 42 4N 19 32 E
Scutari = Üsküdar,
   Turkey .... 45 F13 41 0N 29 5 E
Seabrook, L., Australia 93 F2 30 55 S 119 40 E
Seaford, U.K. ..... 15 G8 50 47N 0 7 E
Seaford, U.S.A. 114 F8 38 39N 75 37W
Seaforth, Australia . 94 J6 20 55 S 148 57 E
Seaforth, Canada ... 116 C3 43 35N 81 25W
Seaforth, L., U.K. .. 13 D2 57 52N 6 36W
Seagraves, U.S.A. .. 113 J3 32 57N 102 34W
Seaham, U.K. 14 C6 54 50N 1 20W
Seal →, Canada 103 B10 59 4N 94 48W
Seal L., Canada 105 B7 54 20N 61 30W
Sealy, U.S.A. 113 L6 29 47N 96 9W
Searchlight, U.S.A. . 111 K12 35 28N 114 55W
Searcy, U.S.A. 113 H9 35 15N 91 44W
Searles L., U.S.A. .. 111 K9 35 44N 117 21W
Seascale, U.K. 14 C4 54 24N 3 29W
Seaside, Calif., U.S.A. 110 J5 36 37N 121 50W
Seaside, Oreg., U.S.A. 110 E3 46 0N 123 56W
Seaspray, Australia . 95 F4 38 25 S 147 15 E

Seattle, U.S.A. 110 C4 47 36N 122 20W
Seattle-Tacoma
   International ✈
   (SEA), U.S.A. 110 C4 47 27N 122 18W
Seaview Ra., Australia 94 B4 18 40 S 145 45 E
Sebago L., U.S.A. .. 117 C14 43 52N 70 34W
Sebago Lake, U.S.A. 117 C14 43 51N 70 34W
Sebastián Vizcaíno, B.,
   Mexico 118 B2 28 0N 114 30W
Sebastopol = Sevastopol,
   Ukraine .... 33 K7 44 35N 33 30 E
Sebastopol, U.S.A. . 110 G4 38 24N 122 49W
Sebba, Burkina Faso 83 C5 13 35N 0 32 E
Sebderat, Eritrea ... 81 D4 15 26N 36 42 E
Sébékoro, Mali 82 C3 12 58N 9 0W
Seben, Turkey ..... 72 B4 40 24N 31 34 E
Sebeş, Romania .... 29 E8 45 58N 23 34 E
Sebeşului, Munţii,
   Romania .... 29 E8 45 36N 23 40 E
Sebewaing, U.S.A. .. 114 D4 43 44N 83 27W
Sebezh, Russia .... 32 D5 56 14N 28 22 E
Sebha = Sabhah, Libya 79 C8 27 9N 14 29 E
Sébi, Mali 82 B4 15 50N 4 12W
Şebinkarahisar, Turkey 73 B8 40 22N 38 28 E
Sebiş, Romania .... 28 D7 46 23N 22 13 E
Sebnitz, Germany ... 24 E10 50 58N 14 15 E
Sebring, Fla., U.S.A. 115 M5 27 30N 81 27W
Sebring, Ohio, U.S.A. 116 F3 40 55N 81 2W
Sebringville, Canada 116 C3 43 24N 81 4W
Sebta = Ceuta, N. Afr. 78 A4 35 52N 5 18W
Sebuku, Indonesia .. 62 E5 3 30 S 116 25 E
Sebuku, Teluk, Malaysia 62 D5 4 0N 118 10 E
Sečanj, Serbia & M. . 28 E5 45 25N 20 47 E
Secchia →, Italy ... 40 C8 44 43N 11 7 E
Sechelt, Canada ... 102 D4 49 25N 123 42W
Sechura, Desierto de,
   Peru .... 124 E2 6 0 S 80 30W
Seclin, France ..... 19 B10 50 33N 3 2 E
Secondigny, France . 18 F6 46 37N 0 26W
Sečovce, Slovak Rep. 27 C14 48 42N 21 40 E
Secretary I., N.Z. ... 91 L1 45 15 S 166 56 E
Secunda, S. Africa .. 66 L11 17 28N 78 30 E
Secunderabad, India 66 L11 17 28N 78 30 E
Security-Widefield,
   U.S.A. 112 F2 38 45N 104 45W
Sedalia, U.S.A. 112 F8 38 42N 93 14W
Sedan, France ..... 19 C11 49 43N 4 57 E
Sedan, U.S.A. 113 G6 37 8N 96 11W
Sedano, Spain 36 C7 42 43N 3 49W
Sedbergh, U.K. 14 C5 54 20N 2 31W
Seddon, N.Z. ..... 91 J5 41 40 S 174 7 E
Seddonville, N.Z. ... 91 J4 41 33 S 172 1 E
Sedé Boqér, Israel .. 74 E3 30 52N 34 47 E
Sedeh, Fārs, Iran ... 71 D7 30 45N 52 11 E
Sedeh, Khorāsān, Iran 71 C8 33 20N 59 14 E
Séderon, France .... 21 D9 44 12N 5 32 E
Sederot, Israel .... 74 D3 31 32N 34 37 E
Sédhiou, Senegal ... 82 C1 12 44N 15 30W
Sedico, Italy ...... 41 B9 46 8N 12 6 E
Sedlčany, Czech Rep. 26 B7 49 40N 14 25 E
Sedley, Canada 103 C8 50 10N 104 0W
Sedona, U.S.A. 109 J8 34 52N 111 46W
Sedova, Pik, Russia . 52 B6 73 29N 54 58 E
Sedro Woolley, U.S.A. 110 B4 48 30N 122 14W
Šeduva, Lithuania .. 30 C10 55 45N 23 45 E
Sędziszów, Poland .. 31 H7 50 35N 20 4 E
Sędziszów Małopolski,
   Poland .... 31 H8 50 5N 21 45 E
Seebad Ahlbeck,
   Germany .... 24 B10 53 56N 14 10 E
Seefeld in Tirol, Austria 26 D4 47 19N 11 13 E
Seehausen, Germany 24 C7 52 54N 11 45 E
Seeheim, Namibia .. 88 D2 26 50 S 17 45 E
Seeheim-Jugenheim,
   Germany .... 25 F4 49 46N 8 40 E
Seeis, Namibia .... 88 C2 22 29 S 17 39 E
Seekoei →, S. Africa 88 E4 30 18 S 25 1 E
Seeley's Bay, Canada 117 B8 44 29N 76 14W
Seelow, Germany ... 24 C10 52 32N 14 23 E
Sées, France ...... 18 D7 48 38N 0 10 E
Seesen, Germany ... 24 D6 51 54N 10 10 E
Seevetal, Germany . 24 B6 53 26N 10 1 E
Seewinkel = Neusiedler
   See-Seewinkel △,
   Austria .... 27 D9 47 50N 16 45 E
Sefadu, S. Leone ... 82 D2 8 35N 10 58W
Seferihisar, Turkey .. 47 C8 38 10N 26 50 E
Séfeto, Mali 82 C3 14 16N 9 48W
Sefwi Bekwai, Ghana 82 D4 6 10N 2 25W
Segamat, Malaysia .. 65 L4 2 30N 102 50 E
Segarcea, Romania .. 29 F8 44 6N 23 43 E
Ségbana, Benin .... 83 C5 10 56N 3 42 E
Segbwema, S. Leone . 82 D2 8 0N 11 0W
Seget, Indonesia ... 63 E8 1 24 S 130 58 E
Segezha, Russia 52 C3 45 36N 0 14W
Gegonzac, France .. 20 C3 45 36N 0 14W
Segorbe, Spain 38 F4 39 50N 0 30W
Ségou, Mali 82 C3 13 30N 6 16W
Segovia = Coco →,
   Cent. Amer. 120 D3 15 0N 83 8W
Segovia, Spain 36 E6 40 57N 4 10W
Segovia □, Spain ... 36 E6 40 55N 4 10W
Segré, France 18 E6 47 40N 0 52W
Segre →, Spain .... 38 D5 41 40N 0 43 E
Séguéla, Ivory C. .. 82 D3 7 55N 6 40W
Séguénéga,
   Burkina Faso 83 C4 13 25N 1 58W
Seguin, U.S.A. 113 L6 29 34N 97 58W
Segundo →, Argentina 126 C3 30 53 S 62 44W
Segura →, Spain ... 39 G4 38 3N 0 44W
Segura, Sierra de, Spain 39 G2 38 5N 2 45W
Seh Konj, Kūh-e, Iran 71 D8 30 6N 57 30 E
Seh Qal'eh, Iran ... 71 C8 33 40N 58 24 E
Sehitwa, Botswana .. 88 C3 20 30 S 22 30 E
Sehlabathebe △,
   Lesotho .... 89 D4 29 53 S 29 7 E
Sehore, India ..... 68 H7 23 10N 77 5 E
Sehwan, Pakistan .. 68 F2 26 28N 67 53 E
Şeica Mare, Romania 29 D9 46 1N 24 10 E
Seil, U.K. 13 E3 56 18N 5 38W
Seiland, Norway ... 8 A20 70 25N 23 15 E
Seilhac, France .... 20 C5 45 22N 1 43 E
Seiling, U.S.A. 113 G5 36 9N 98 56W
Seille →, Moselle,
   France .... 19 C13 49 7N 6 11 E
Seille →,
   Saône-et-Loire, France 19 F11 46 31N 4 57 E
Sein, Î. de, France . 18 D2 48 2N 4 52W
Seinäjoki, Finland .. 9 E20 62 40N 22 51 E
Seine →, France ... 18 C7 49 26N 0 26 E
Seine, B. de la, France 18 C6 49 40N 0 40W
Seine-et-Marne □,
   France .... 19 D10 48 45N 3 0 E
Seine-Maritime □,
   France .... 18 C7 49 40N 1 0 E
Seine-St-Denis □,
   France .... 19 D9 48 58N 2 24 E
Seini, Romania .... 29 C8 47 44N 23 21 E
Seirijai, Lithuania .. 30 D10 54 14N 23 54 E

Seistan = Sīstān, *Asia* **71 D9** 30 50N 61 0 E
Seistan, Daryācheh-ye =
Sīstān, Daryācheh-ye,
Iran **71 D9** 31 0N 61 0 E
Sejerø, *Denmark* **11 J5** 55 54N 11 9 E
Sejerø Bugt, *Denmark* **11 J5** 55 53N 11 15 E
Sejny, *Poland* **30 D10** 54 6N 23 21 E
Seka, *Ethiopia* **81 F4** 8 10N 36 52 E
Sekayu, *Indonesia* **62 E2** 2 51 S 103 51 E
Seke, *Tanzania* **86 C3** 3 20 S 33 31 E
Sekenke, *Tanzania* **86 C3** 4 18 S 34 11 E
Seki, *Turkey* **47 E11** 36 48N 29 33 E
Sekondi-Takoradi,
Ghana **82 E4** 4 58N 1 45W
Sekota, *Ethiopia* **81 E4** 12 40N 39 2 E
Seksna, *Russia* **32 C10** 59 13N 38 30 E
Sekudai, *Malaysia* **65 d** 1 32N 103 39 E
Sekuma, *Botswana* **88 C3** 24 36 S 23 50 E
Selah, *U.S.A.* **108 C3** 46 39N 120 32W
Selama, *Malaysia* **65 K3** 5 12N 100 42 E
Selárgius, *Italy* **42 C2** 39 16N 9 10 E
Selaru, *Indonesia* **63 F8** 8 9 S 131 0 E
Selatan, Selat, *Malaysia* **65 c** 5 15N 100 20 E
Selb, *Germany* **25 E8** 50 10N 12 7 E
Selby, *U.K.* **14 D6** 53 47N 1 5W
Selby, *U.S.A.* **112 C4** 45 31N 100 2W
Selca, *Croatia* **41 E13** 43 20N 16 50 E
Selçuk, *Turkey* **47 D9** 37 56N 27 22 E
Selden, *U.S.A.* **112 F4** 39 33N 100 34W
Sele →, *Italy* **43 B7** 40 29N 14 56 E
Selebi-Pikwe, *Botswana* **89 C4** 21 58 S 27 48 E
Selemdzha →, *Russia* **53 D13** 51 42N 128 53 E
Selendi, *Manisa, Turkey* **47 C10** 38 43N 28 50 E
Selendi, *Manisa, Turkey* **47 C9** 38 46N 27 53 E
Selenga = Selenge
Mörön →, *Asia* **60 A5** 52 16N 106 16 E
Selenge Mörön →, *Asia* **60 A5** 52 16N 106 16 E
Selenicë, *Albania* **44 F3** 40 33N 19 39 E
Selenter See, *Germany* **24 A6** 54 18N 10 26 E
Sélestat, *France* **19 D14** 48 16N 7 26 E
Seletan, Tanjung,
Indonesia **62 E4** 4 10 S 114 40 E
Selevac, *Serbia & M.* **44 B4** 44 28N 20 52 E
Sélibabi, *Mauritania* **82 B2** 15 10N 12 15W
Seliger, Ozero, *Russia* **32 D7** 57 15N 33 0 E
Seligman, *U.S.A.* **109 J7** 35 20N 112 53W
Şelim, *Turkey* **73 B10** 40 30N 42 46 E
Selima, El Wâhât el,
Sudan **80 C2** 21 22N 29 19 E
Selimiye, *Turkey* **47 D9** 37 24N 27 40 E
Selinda Spillway →,
Botswana **88 B3** 18 35 S 23 10 E
Selinoûs, *Greece* **46 D3** 37 35N 21 37 E
Selinsgrove, *U.S.A.* **116 F8** 40 48N 76 52W
Selizharovo, *Russia* **32 D7** 56 51N 33 27 E
Selkirk, *Canada* **103 C9** 50 10N 96 55W
Selkirk, *U.K.* **13 F6** 55 33N 2 50W
Selkirk I. = Horse I.,
Canada **103 C9** 53 20N 99 6W
Selkirk Mts., *Canada* **100 C8** 51 15N 117 40W
Sellafield, *U.K.* **14 C4** 54 25N 3 29W
Sellama, *Sudan* **81 E2** 12 51N 29 46 E
Selliá, *Greece* **49 D6** 35 12N 24 23 E
Sellières, *France* **19 F12** 46 50N 5 32 E
Sells, *U.S.A.* **109 L8** 31 55N 111 53W
Sellye, *Hungary* **28 E2** 45 52N 17 51 E
Selma, *Ala., U.S.A.* **115 J2** 32 25N 87 1W
Selma, *Calif., U.S.A.* **110 J7** 36 34N 119 37W
Selma, *N.C., U.S.A.* **115 H6** 35 32N 78 17W
Selmer, *U.S.A.* **115 H1** 35 10N 88 36W
Selongey, *France* **19 E12** 47 36N 5 11 E
Selous →, *Tanzania* **87 D4** 8 37 S 37 42 E
Selowandoma Falls,
Zimbabwe **87 G3** 21 15 S 31 50 E
Selpele, *Indonesia* **63 E8** 0 1 S 130 5 E
Selsey Bill, *U.K.* **15 G7** 50 43N 0 47W
Seltso, *Russia* **32 F8** 53 22N 34 4 E
Seltz, *France* **19 D15** 48 54N 8 4 E
Selu, *Indonesia* **63 F8** 7 32 S 130 55 E
Sélune →, *France* **18 D5** 48 38N 1 22W
Selva = La Selva del
Camp, *Spain* **38 D6** 41 13N 1 8 E
Selva, *Argentina* **126 B3** 29 50 S 62 0W
Selva Lancandona =
Montes Azules △,
Mexico **119 D6** 16 21N 91 3W
Selvas, *Brazil* **124 E5** 6 30 S 67 0W
Selwyn L., *Canada* **103 B8** 60 0N 104 30W
Selwyn Mts., *Canada* **100 B6** 63 0N 130 0W
Selwyn Ra., *Australia* **94 C3** 21 10 S 140 0 E
Selyatyn, *Ukraine* **29 C10** 47 50N 25 12 E
Seman →, *Albania* **44 F3** 40 47N 19 30 E
Semarang, *Indonesia* **63 G14** 7 0 S 110 26 E
Sembabule, *Uganda* **86 C3** 0 4 S 31 25 E
Sembawang, *Singapore* **65 d** 1 27N 103 50 E
Sembung, *Indonesia* **63 J18** 8 28 S 115 11 E
Şemdinli, *Turkey* **73 D11** 37 18N 44 35 E
Sémé, *Senegal* **82 B2** 15 4N 13 41W
Semeih, *Sudan* **81 E3** 12 43N 30 53 E
Semenanjung
Blambangan,
Indonesia **63 K17** 8 42 S 114 29 E
Semenov, *Russia* **34 B7** 56 43N 44 30 E
Semenovka, Chernihiv,
Ukraine **33 F7** 52 8N 32 36 E
Semenovka,
Kremenchuk, *Ukraine* **33 H7** 49 37N 33 10 E
Semeru, *Indonesia* **63 H15** 8 4 S 112 55 E
Semey, *Kazakhstan* **52 D9** 50 30N 80 10 E
Semikarakorskiy, *Russia* **35 G5** 47 31N 40 48 E
Semiluki, *Russia* **33 G10** 51 41N 39 2 E
Seminoe Reservoir,
U.S.A. **108 F10** 42 9N 106 55W
Seminole, *Okla., U.S.A.* **113 H6** 35 14N 96 41W
Seminole, *Tex., U.S.A.* **113 J3** 32 43N 102 39W
Seminole Draw →,
U.S.A. **113 J3** 32 27N 102 20W
Semipalatinsk = Semey,
Kazakhstan **52 D9** 50 30N 80 10 E
Semirara Is., *Phil.* **61 F4** 12 0N 121 20 E
Semitau, *Indonesia* **62 D4** 0 29N 111 57 E
Semiyarka, *Kazakhstan* **52 D8** 50 55N 78 23 E
Semiyarskoye =
Semiyarka,
Kazakhstan **52 D8** 50 55N 78 23 E
Semmering P., *Austria* **26 D8** 47 41N 15 45 E
Semnān, *Iran* **71 C7** 35 40N 53 23 E
Semnān □, *Iran* **71 C7** 36 0N 54 0 E
Semporna, *Malaysia* **63 D5** 4 30N 118 33 E
Semuda, *Indonesia* **62 E4** 2 51 S 112 58 E
Semur-en-Auxois,
France **19 E11** 47 30N 4 20 E
Sen →, *Cambodia* **62 B3** 13 45N 105 12 E
Sena, *Iran* **71 D6** 28 27N 51 36 E
Sena, *Mozam.* **87 F4** 17 25 S 35 0 E
Sena Madureira, *Brazil* **124 E5** 9 5 S 68 45W
Senador Pompeu, *Brazil* **125 E11** 5 40 S 39 20W
Senaki, *Georgia* **35 J6** 42 15N 42 7 E
Senang, Pulau,
Singapore **65 d** 1 10N 103 44 E
Senanga, *Zambia* **85 H4** 16 7 S 23 16 E
Senatobia, *U.S.A.* **113 H10** 34 37N 89 58W
Sencelles, *Spain* **48 B9** 39 39N 2 54 E
Sendafa, *Ethiopia* **81 F4** 9 11N 39 3 E
Sendai, Kagoshima,
Japan **55 J5** 31 50N 130 20 E
Sendai, Miyagi, *Japan* **54 E10** 38 15N 140 53 E
Sendai-Wan, *Japan* **54 E10** 38 15N 141 0 E
Senden, Bayern,
Germany **25 G6** 48 19N 10 4 E
Senden,
Nordrhein-Westfalen,
Germany **24 D3** 51 52N 7 22 E
Sendhwa, *India* **68 J6** 21 41N 75 6 E
Sene →, *Ghana* **83 D4** 7 30N 0 33W
Senec, *Slovak Rep.* **27 C10** 48 12N 17 23 E
Seneca, *U.S.A.* **115 H4** 34 41N 82 57W
Seneca Falls, *U.S.A.* **117 D8** 42 55N 76 48W
Seneca L., *U.S.A.* **116 D8** 42 40N 76 54W
Senecaville L., *U.S.A.* **116 G3** 39 55N 81 25W
Senegal ■, *W. Afr.* **82 C2** 14 30N 14 30W
Sénégal →, *W. Afr.* **82 B1** 15 48N 16 32W
Senegambia, *Africa* **76 E2** 12 45N 12 0W
Senekal, *S. Africa* **89 D4** 28 20 S 27 36 E
Senftenberg, *Germany* **24 D10** 51 32N 14 0 E
Senga Hill, *Zambia* **87 D3** 9 19 S 31 11 E
Senge Khambab =
Indus →, *Pakistan* **68 G2** 24 20N 67 47 E
Sengiley, *Russia* **34 D9** 53 58N 48 46 E
Sengua →, *Zimbabwe* **87 F2** 17 7 S 28 5 E
Senhor-do-Bonfim,
Brazil **125 F10** 10 30 S 40 10W
Senica, *Slovak Rep.* **27 C10** 48 41N 17 25 E
Senigállia, *Italy* **41 E10** 43 43N 13 13 E
Senio →, *Italy* **41 D9** 44 35N 12 15 E
Senirkent, *Turkey* **47 C12** 38 6N 30 33 E
Senj, *Croatia* **41 D11** 45 0N 14 58 E
Senja, *Norway* **8 B17** 69 25N 17 30 E
Senkaku-Shotō, *Japan* **55 L1** 25 45N 124 0 E
Senkuang, *Indonesia* **65 d** 1 11N 104 2 E
Senlis, *France* **19 C9** 49 13N 2 35 E
Senmonorom, *Cambodia* **64 F6** 12 27N 107 12 E
Sennâr, *Sudan* **81 E3** 13 30N 33 35 E
Sennar □, *Sudan* **81 E3** 13 0N 34 0 E
Senneterre, *Canada* **104 C4** 48 25N 77 15W
Senno, *Belarus* **32 E5** 54 45N 29 43 E
Sénnori, *Italy* **42 B1** 40 47N 8 35 E
Seno, *Laos* **64 D5** 16 35N 104 50 E
Senonches, *France* **18 D8** 48 34N 1 2 E
Senorbi, *Italy* **42 C2** 39 32N 9 8 E
Senožeče, *Slovenia* **41 C11** 45 43N 14 3 E
Sens, *France* **19 D10** 48 11N 3 15 E
Senta, *Serbia & M.* **28 E5** 45 55N 20 3 E
Sentani, *Indonesia* **63 E10** 2 36 S 140 37 E
Sentery = Lubao,
Dem. Rep. of
the Congo **86 D2** 5 17 S 25 42 E
Sentinel, *U.S.A.* **109 K7** 32 52N 113 13W
Sentjur, *Slovenia* **41 B12** 46 14N 15 24 E
Sentosa, *Singapore* **65 d** 1 15N 103 50 E
Senya Beraku, *Ghana* **83 D4** 5 28N 0 31W
Seo de Urgel = La Seu
d'Urgell, *Spain* **38 C6** 42 22N 1 23 E
Seohara, *India* **69 E8** 29 15N 78 33 E
Seonath →, *India* **69 J10** 21 44N 82 28 E
Seondha, *India* **69 F8** 26 9N 78 48 E
Seoni, *India* **69 H8** 22 5N 79 30 E
Seoni Malwa, *India* **68 H8** 22 27N 77 28 E
Seoul = Sŏul, *S. Korea* **57 F14** 37 31N 126 58 E
Sepīdān, *Iran* **71 D7** 30 20N 52 5 E
Sepo-ri, *N. Korea* **57 E14** 38 57N 127 25 E
Sępólno Krajeńskie,
Poland **30 E4** 53 26N 17 30 E
Sepone, *Laos* **64 D6** 16 45N 106 13 E
Sepopol, *Poland* **30 D8** 54 16N 21 2 E
Sept-Îles, *Canada* **105 B6** 50 13N 66 22W
Septemvri, *Bulgaria* **45 D8** 42 13N 24 6 E
Sepúlveda, *Spain* **36 D7** 41 18N 3 45W
Sequeros, *Spain* **36 E4** 40 31N 6 2W
Sequim, *U.S.A.* **110 B3** 48 5N 123 6W
Sequoia △, *U.S.A.* **110 J8** 36 30N 118 30W
Serafimovich, *Russia* **34 F6** 49 36N 42 43 E
Seraing, *Belgium* **17 D5** 50 35N 5 32 E
Serakhis →, *Cyprus* **49 D11** 35 13N 32 55 E
Seram, *Indonesia* **63 E7** 3 10 S 129 0 E
Seram Sea, *Indonesia* **63 E7** 2 30 S 128 30 E
Seranantsara, *Madag.* **89 B8** 18 30 S 49 5 E
Serang, *Indonesia* **63 G12** 6 8 S 106 10 E
Serangoon, *Singapore* **65 d** 1 23N 103 54 E
Serasan, *Indonesia* **62 D3** 2 29N 109 4 E
Seravezza, *Italy* **40 E7** 43 59N 10 13 E
Şerbettar, *Turkey* **45 E10** 41 27N 26 46 E
Serbia □, *Serbia & M.* **44 C5** 43 30N 21 0 E
Serbia & Montenegro ■
Europe **44 C4** 43 20N 20 0 E
Sercaia, *Romania* **29 E10** 45 49N 25 9 E
Serdo, *Ethiopia* **81 E5** 11 56N 41 14 E
Serdobsk, *Russia* **34 D7** 52 28N 44 10 E
Seredka, *Russia* **32 C5** 58 12N 28 10 E
Serednye, *Ukraine* **29** 48 32N 22 30 E
Şereflikoçhisar, *Turkey* **72 C5** 38 56N 33 32 E
Seregno, *Italy* **40 C6** 45 39N 9 12 E
Seremban, *Malaysia* **65 L3** 2 43N 101 53 E
Serengeti △, *Tanzania* **86 C3** 2 11 S 35 0 E
Serengeti Plain,
Tanzania **86 C4** 2 40 S 35 0 E
Serenje, *Zambia* **87 E3** 13 14 S 30 15 E
Sereth = Siret →,
Romania **29 E12** 45 24N 28 1 E
Sergach, *Russia* **34 C7** 55 30N 45 30 E
Sergen, *Turkey* **45 E11** 41 41N 27 42 E
Sergino, *Russia* **52 C7** 62 25N 65 12 E
Sergipe □, *Brazil* **125 F11** 10 30 S 37 30W
Sergiyev Posad, *Russia* **32 D10** 56 20N 38 10 E
Seria, *Brunei* **62 D4** 4 37N 114 23 E
Serian, *Malaysia* **62 D4** 1 10N 110 31 E
Seriate, *Italy* **40 C6** 45 41N 9 43 E
Seribu, Kepulauan,
Indonesia **62 F3** 5 36 S 106 33 E
Sérifontaine, *France* **19 C8** 49 20N 1 45 E
Sérifos, *Greece* **46 D6** 37 9N 24 30 E
Sérignan, *France* **20 E7** 43 17N 3 17 E
Sérigny →, *Canada* **105 A6** 56 47N 66 0W
Serik, *Turkey* **72 D4** 36 55N 31 7 E
Seringapatam Reef,
Australia **92 B3** 13 38 S 122 5 E
Serinhisar, *Turkey* **47 D11** 37 36N 29 18 E
Seririt, *Indonesia* **63 J17** 8 12 S 114 56 E
Sermaize-les-Bains,
France **19 D11** 48 47N 4 54 E
Sermata, *Indonesia* **63 F7** 8 15 S 128 50 E
Sermersuaq, *Greenland* **4 B4** 79 30N 62 0W
Sérmide, *Italy* **41 D8** 45 0N 11 18 E
Sernovodsk, *Russia* **34 D10** 53 54N 51 16 E
Sernur, *Russia* **34 B9** 56 52N 49 2 E
Serock, *Poland* **31 F8** 52 31N 21 4 E
Serón, *Spain* **39 H2** 37 20N 2 29W
Seròs, *Spain* **38 D5** 41 27N 0 24 E
Serov, *Russia* **52 D7** 59 29N 60 35 E
Serowe, *Botswana* **88 C4** 22 25 S 26 43 E
Serpa, *Portugal* **37 H3** 37 57N 7 38W
Serpeddì, Punta, *Italy* **42 C2** 39 19N 9 18 E
Serpentara, *Italy* **42 C2** 39 8N 9 36 E
Serpentine Lakes,
Australia **93 E4** 28 30 S 129 10 E
Serpent's Mouth =
Sierpe, Bocas de la,
Venezuela **125 L15** 10 0N 61 30W
Serpis →, *Spain* **39 G4** 38 59N 0 9W
Serpneve, *Ukraine* **29 D14** 46 18N 29 1 E
Serpukhov, *Russia* **32 E9** 54 55N 37 28 E
Serra da Estrela △,
Portugal **36 E3** 40 27N 7 33W
Serra de Outes, *Spain* **36 C2** 42 52N 8 55W
Serra do Navio, *Brazil* **125 C8** 0 59N 52 3W
Serra San Bruno, *Italy* **43 D9** 38 35N 16 20 E
Serradilla, *Spain* **36 F4** 39 50N 6 9W
Sérrai, *Greece* **44 E7** 41 5N 23 31 E
Sérrai □, *Greece* **44 E7** 41 5N 23 37 E
Serramanna, *Italy* **42 C1** 39 25N 8 55 E
Serranía San Luís △,
Paraguay **126 A4** 22 35 S 57 22W
Serras d'Aire e
Candeeiros △,
Portugal **37 F2** 39 31N 8 48W
Serravalle Scrívia, *Italy* **40 D5** 44 43N 8 51 E
Serre-Ponçon, L. de,
France **21 D10** 44 22N 6 20 E
Serres, *France* **21 D10** 44 26N 5 43 E
Serrezuela, *Argentina* **126 C2** 30 40 S 65 20W
Serrinha, *Brazil* **125 F11** 11 39 S 39 0W
Sersale, *Italy* **43 C9** 39 1N 16 43 E
Sertã, *Portugal* **36 F2** 39 48N 8 6W
Sertanópolis, *Brazil* **127 A5** 23 4 S 51 2W
Sêrtar, *China* **58 A3** 32 20N 100 41 E
Serua, *Indonesia* **63 F8** 6 18 S 130 1 E
Serui, *Indonesia* **63 E9** 1 53 S 136 10 E
Serule, *Botswana* **88 C4** 21 57 S 27 20 E
Sérvia, *Greece* **44 F6** 40 11N 22 0 E
Serzedelo, *Portugal* **36 D2** 41 24N 8 14W
Ses Salines, *Spain* **48 B10** 39 21N 3 3 E
Sese Is., *Uganda* **86 C3** 0 20 S 32 20 E
Sesepe, *Indonesia* **63 E7** 1 30 S 127 59 E
Sesfontein, *Namibia* **88 B1** 19 7 S 13 39 E
Sesheke, *Zambia* **88 B3** 17 29 S 24 13 E
Sésia →, *Italy* **40 C5** 45 5N 8 37 E
Sesimbra, *Portugal* **37 G1** 38 28N 9 6W
S'Espalmador, *Spain* **48 C7** 38 47N 1 26 E
S'Espardell, *Spain* **48 C7** 38 48N 1 29 E
Sessa Aurunca, *Italy* **42 A6** 41 14N 13 56 E
S'Estanyol, *Spain* **48 B9** 39 22N 2 54 E
Sestao, *Spain* **38 B2** 43 18N 3 0W
Sesto Calende, *Italy* **40 C5** 45 43N 8 37 E
Sesto San Giovanni,
Italy **40 C6** 45 32N 9 14 E
Sestri Levante, *Italy* **40 D6** 44 16N 9 24 E
Sestriere, *Italy* **40 D3** 44 58N 6 56 E
Sestroretsk, *Russia* **32 B6** 60 5N 29 58 E
Sestrunj, *Croatia* **41 D11** 44 10N 15 0 E
Sestu, *Italy* **42 C2** 39 18N 9 5 E
Setana, *Japan* **54 C9** 42 26N 139 51 E
Sète, *France* **20 E7** 43 25N 3 42 E
Sete Lagôas, *Brazil* **125 G10** 19 27 S 44 16W
Sétif, *Algeria* **78 A7** 36 9N 5 26 E
Seto, *Japan* **55 G8** 35 14N 137 6 E
Setonaikai, *Japan* **55 G6** 34 20N 133 30 E
Setonaikai △, *Japan* **55 G6** 34 15N 133 15 E
Settat, *Morocco* **78 B4** 33 0N 7 40W
Setting L., *Canada* **103 C9** 55 0N 98 38W
Settle, *U.K.* **14 C5** 54 5N 2 16W
Settlement Pt., *Bahamas* **115 M6** 26 40N 79 0W
Settlers, *S. Africa* **89 C4** 25 2 S 28 30 E
Setúbal, *Portugal* **37 G2** 38 30N 8 58W
Setúbal □, *Portugal* **37 G2** 38 30N 8 35W
Setúbal, B. de, *Portugal* **37 G2** 38 40N 8 56W
Seugne →, *France* **20 C3** 45 42N 0 32W
Seul, Lac, *Canada* **104 B1** 50 20N 92 30W
Seurre, *France* **19 F12** 47 0N 5 8 E
Sevan, *Armenia* **35 K7** 40 33N 44 56 E
Sevan, Ozero = Sevana
Lich, *Armenia* **35 K7** 40 30N 45 20 E
Sevana Lich, *Armenia* **35 K7** 40 30N 45 20 E
Sevastopol, *Ukraine* **33 K7** 44 35N 33 30 E
Seven Sisters, *Canada* **102 C3** 54 56N 128 10W
Sever →, *Spain* **37 F3** 39 40N 7 32W
Sévérac-le-Château,
France **20 D7** 44 20N 3 5 E
Severn →, *Canada* **104 A2** 56 2N 87 36W
Severn →, *U.K.* **15 F5** 51 35N 2 40W
Severn L., *Canada* **104 B1** 53 54N 90 48W
Severnaya Zemlya,
Russia **53 B10** 79 0N 100 0 E
Severo-Kurilsk, *Russia* **53 D16** 50 40N 156 8 E
Severo-Yeniseyskiy,
Russia **53 C10** 60 22N 93 1 E
Severo-Zapadnyy □,
Russia **52 C4** 65 0N 40 0 E
Severočeský □,
Czech Rep. **26 A7** 50 30N 14 0 E
Severodonetsk =
Syeverodonetsk,
Ukraine **33 H10** 48 58N 38 35 E
Severodvinsk, *Russia* **52 C4** 64 27N 39 58 E
Severomoravský □,
Czech Rep. **27 B10** 49 38N 17 40 E
Sevier, *U.S.A.* **109 G7** 38 39N 112 11W
Sevier →, *U.S.A.* **109 G7** 39 4N 113 6W
Sevier Desert, *U.S.A.* **108 G7** 39 40N 112 45W
Sevier L., *U.S.A.* **108 G7** 38 54N 113 9W
Sevilla, *Spain* **37 H5** 37 23N 5 58W
Sevilla □, *Spain* **37 H5** 37 25N 5 30W
Seville = Sevilla, *Spain* **37 H5** 37 23N 5 58W
Sevlievo, *Bulgaria* **45 C9** 43 2N 25 6 E
Sevnica, *Slovenia* **41 B12** 46 2N 15 19 E
Sèvre-Nantaise →,
France **18 E5** 47 12N 1 33W
Sèvre-Niortaise →,
France **20 B3** 46 28N 0 56W
Sevsk, *Russia* **33 F8** 52 10N 34 30 E
Sewa →, *S. Leone* **82 D2** 7 20N 12 10W
Sewani, *India* **68 E6** 28 58N 75 39 E
Seward, *Alaska, U.S.A.* **100 B5** 60 7N 149 27W
Seward, *Nebr., U.S.A.* **112 E6** 40 55N 97 6W
Seward, *Pa., U.S.A.* **116 F5** 40 25N 79 1W
Seward Peninsula,
U.S.A. **100 B3** 65 30N 166 0W
Sewell, *Chile* **126 C1** 34 10 S 70 23W
Sewer, *Indonesia* **63 F8** 5 53 S 134 40 E
Sewickley, *U.S.A.* **116 F4** 40 32N 80 12W
Sexsmith, *Canada* **102 B5** 55 21N 118 47W
Seychelles ■, *Ind. Oc.* **50 K9** 5 0 S 56 0 E
Seyðisfjörður, *Iceland* **8 D6** 65 16N 13 57W
Seydişehir, *Turkey* **72 D4** 37 25N 31 51 E
Seydvān, *Iran* **70 B5** 38 34N 45 2 E
Seyhan →, *Turkey* **70 B2** 36 43N 34 53 E
Seyhan Barajı, *Turkey* **72 D6** 37 2N 35 18 E
Seyitgazi, *Turkey* **47 B12** 39 26N 30 43 E
Seyitömer, *Turkey* **47 B11** 39 34N 29 52 E
Seym →, *Ukraine* **33 G7** 51 27N 32 34 E
Seymen, *Turkey* **45 E11** 41 6N 27 57 E
Seymour, *Australia* **95 F4** 37 0 S 145 10 E
Seymour, *S. Africa* **89 E4** 32 33 S 26 46 E
Seymour, *Conn., U.S.A.* **117 E11** 41 24N 73 4W
Seymour, *Ind., U.S.A.* **114 F3** 38 58N 85 53W
Seymour, *Tex., U.S.A.* **113 J5** 33 35N 99 16W
Seyne, *France* **21 D10** 44 21N 6 22 E
Seyssel, *France* **21 C9** 45 57N 5 50 E
Sežana, *Slovenia* **41 C10** 45 43N 13 41 E
Sézanne, *France* **19 D10** 48 40N 3 40 E
Sezze, *Italy* **42 A6** 41 30N 13 3 E
Sfântu Gheorghe,
Covasna, *Romania* **29 E10** 45 52N 25 48 E
Sfântu Gheorghe,
Tulcea, *Romania* **29 F14** 44 53N 29 36 E
Sfântu Gheorghe,
Brațul →, *Romania* **29 F14** 44 51N 29 36 E
Sfax, *Tunisia* **79 B8** 34 49N 10 48 E
Sha Xi →, *China* **59 D12** 26 35N 118 0 E
Sha Xian, *China* **59 D11** 26 23N 117 45 E
Shaanxi □, *China* **56 G5** 35 0N 109 0 E
Shaba = Katanga □,
Dem. Rep. of
the Congo **86 D2** 8 0 S 25 0 E
Shaba △, *Kenya* **86 B4** 0 38N 37 48 E
Shaballe = Scebeli,
Wabi →, *Somali Rep.* **75 G3** 2 0N 44 0 E
Shabla, *Bulgaria* **45 C12** 43 31N 28 32 E
Shabogamo L., *Canada* **105 B6** 53 15N 66 30W
Shabunda, *Dem. Rep. of*
the Congo **86 C2** 2 40 S 27 16 E
Shache, *China* **60 C2** 38 20N 77 10 E
Shackleton Ice Shelf,
Antarctica **5 C8** 66 0 S 100 0 E
Shackleton Inlet,
Antarctica **5 E11** 83 0 S 160 0 E
Shādegān, *Iran* **71 D6** 30 40N 48 38 E
Shadi, *China* **59 D10** 26 7N 114 47 E
Shadi, *India* **69 C7** 33 24N 77 14 E
Shadrinsk, *Russia* **52 D7** 56 5N 63 32 E
Shadyside, *U.S.A.* **116 G4** 39 58N 80 45W
Shaffa, *Nigeria* **83 C7** 10 30N 12 6 E
Shafter, *U.S.A.* **111 K7** 35 30N 119 16W
Shaftesbury, *U.K.* **15 F5** 51 0N 2 11W
Shagamu, *Nigeria* **83 D5** 6 51N 3 39 E
Shagram, *Pakistan* **69 A5** 36 24N 72 20 E
Shah Alizai, *Pakistan* **68 E2** 29 25N 66 33 E
Shah Bunder, *Pakistan* **68 G2** 24 13N 67 56 E
Shahabad, *Punjab, India* **68 D7** 30 10N 76 55 E
Shahabad, *Raj., India* **69 G7** 25 15N 77 11 E
Shahabad, *Ut. P., India* **69 F8** 27 36N 79 56 E
Shahadpur, *Pakistan* **68 G3** 25 55N 68 35 E
Shahba, *Syria* **74 C5** 32 52N 36 38 E
Shahdād, *Iran* **71 D8** 30 30N 57 40 E
Shahdād, Namakzār-e,
Iran **71 D8** 30 20N 58 20 E
Shahdadkot, *Pakistan* **68 F2** 27 50N 67 55 E
Shahdol, *India* **69 H9** 23 19N 81 26 E
Shahe, *China* **56 F8** 37 0N 114 32 E
Shahganj, *India* **69 F10** 26 3N 82 44 E
Shahgarh, *India* **66 F6** 27 15N 69 50 E
Shahjahanpur, *India* **69 F8** 27 54N 79 57 E
Shahpur, *India* **68 H7** 22 12N 77 58 E
Shahpur, Baluchistan,
Pakistan **68 E3** 28 46N 68 27 E
Shahpur, Punjab,
Pakistan **68 C5** 32 17N 72 26 E
Shahpur Chakar,
Pakistan **68 F3** 26 9N 68 39 E
Shahpura, Mad. P., India* **69 H9** 23 10N 80 45 E
Shahpura, Raj., India* **68 G6** 25 38N 74 56 E
Shahr-e Babak, *Iran* **71 D7** 30 7N 55 9 E
Shahr-e Kord, *Iran* **71 C6** 32 15N 50 55 E
Shāhrakht, *Iran* **71 C9** 33 38N 60 16 E
Shahrig, *Pakistan* **68 D2** 30 15N 67 40 E
Shahukou, *China* **56 D7** 40 20N 112 18 E
Shaikhabad, *Afghan.* **68 B3** 34 2N 68 45 E
Shajapur, *India* **68 H7** 23 27N 76 21 E
Shakargarh, *Pakistan* **68 C6** 32 17N 75 10 E
Shakawe, *Botswana* **88 B3** 18 28 S 21 49 E
Shaker Heights, *U.S.A.* **116 E3** 41 29N 81 32W
Shakhty, *Russia* **35 G5** 47 40N 40 16 E
Shakhunya, *Russia* **34 B8** 57 40N 46 46 E
Shaki, *Nigeria* **83 D5** 8 41N 3 21 E
Shākir, *Egypt* **80 B3** 27 30N 33 59 E
Shaksam Valley, *Asia* **69 A7** 36 0N 76 20 E
Shala, L., *Ethiopia* **81 F4** 7 30N 38 30 E
Shali, *Russia* **35 J7** 43 9N 45 55 E
Shallow Lake, *Canada* **116 B3** 44 36N 81 5W
Shalqar, *Kazakhstan* **52 E6** 47 48N 59 39 E
Shalskiy, *Russia* **32 B8** 61 48N 35 58 E
Shaluli Shan, *China* **58 B2** 30 40N 99 55 E
Shām, *Iran* **71 E8** 26 39N 57 21 E
Shām, Bādiyat ash, *Asia* **70 C3** 32 0N 40 0 E
Shamâl Bahr el
Ghazal □, *Sudan* **81 F2** 8 0N 27 30 E
Shamâl Dârfûr □, *Sudan* **81 E2** 15 0N 25 0 E
Shamâl Kordofân □,
Sudan **81 E3** 15 0N 30 0 E
Shamâl Sînî □, *Egypt* **74 D3** 30 30N 33 30 E
Shamattawa, *Canada* **104 A1** 55 51N 92 5W
Shamattawa →, *Canada* **104 A2** 55 1N 85 23W
Shambe, *Sudan* **81 F3** 7 8N 30 46 E
Shambu, *Ethiopia* **81 F4** 9 32N 37 3 E
Shamīl, *Iran* **71 E8** 27 30N 56 55 E
Shamkhor =
Şämkir,
Azerbaijan **35 K8** 40 50N 46 0 E
Shāmkūh, *Iran* **71 C8** 35 47N 57 50 E
Shamli, *India* **68 E7** 29 32N 77 18 E
Shammar, Jabal,
Si. Arabia **70 E4** 27 40N 41 0 E
Shamo = Gobi, *Asia* **56 C6** 44 0N 111 0 E
Shamo, L., *Ethiopia* **81 F4** 5 45N 37 30 E
Shamokin, *U.S.A.* **117 F8** 40 47N 76 34W
Shamrock, *U.S.A.* **113 H4** 35 13N 100 15W
Shamva, *Zimbabwe* **87 F3** 17 20 S 31 32 E
Shan □, *Burma* **67 J21** 21 30N 98 30 E
Shan Xian, *China* **56 G9** 34 50N 116 4 E
Shanan →, *Ethiopia* **81 F5** 8 0N 40 20 E
Shanchengzhen, *China* **57 C13** 42 20N 125 20 E
Shāndak, *Iran* **71 D9** 28 28N 60 27 E
Shandon, *U.S.A.* **110 K6** 35 39N 120 23W
Shandong □, *China* **57 G10** 36 0N 118 0 E
Shandong Bandao,
China **57 F11** 37 0N 121 0 E
Shang Xian =
Shangzhou, *China* **56 H5** 33 50N 109 58 E
Shanga, *Nigeria* **78 F6** 11 12N 4 33 E
Shangalowe, Dem. Rep.
of the Congo **87 E2** 10 50 S 26 30 E
Shangani, *Zimbabwe* **89 B4** 19 41 S 29 20 E
Shangani →, *Zimbabwe* **87 F2** 18 41 S 27 10 E
Shangbancheng, *China* **57 D10** 40 50N 118 1 E
Shangcheng, *China* **59 B10** 31 47N 115 26 E
Shangchuan Dao, *China* **59 G9** 21 40N 112 50 E
Shangdu, *China* **56 D7** 41 30N 113 30 E
Shanggao, *China* **59 C10** 28 17N 114 55 E
Shanghai, *China* **59 B13** 31 15N 121 26 E
Shanghai Shi □, *China* **59 B13** 31 10N 121 30 E
Shanghe, *China* **57 F9** 37 20N 117 10 E
Shanglin, *China* **58 F7** 23 27N 108 57 E
Shangnan, *China* **56 H6** 33 32N 110 50 E
Shangqiu, *China* **56 G8** 34 26N 115 36 E
Shangrao, *China* **59 C11** 28 25N 117 59 E
Shangshui, *China* **60 C6** 33 42N 114 35 E
Shangsi, *China* **58 F6** 22 8N 107 58 E
Shangyou, *China* **59 E10** 25 48N 114 32 E
Shangzhi, *China* **57 B14** 45 22N 127 56 E
Shangzhou, *China* **56 H5** 33 50N 109 58 E
Shanhetun, *China* **57 B14** 44 33N 127 15 E
Shani, *Nigeria* **83 C7** 10 14N 12 2 E
Shanklin, *U.K.* **15 G6** 50 38N 1 11W
Shannon, *N.Z.* **91 J5** 40 33 S 175 25 E
Shannon △, *Australia* **93 F2** 31 55 S 117 51 E
Shannon →, *Ireland* **12 D2** 52 35N 9 30W
Shannon, Mouth of the,
Ireland **12 D2** 52 30N 9 55W
Shannon Airport,
Ireland **12 D3** 52 42N 8 57W
Shansi = Shanxi □,
China **56 F7** 37 0N 112 0 E
Shantar, Ostrov
Bolshoy, *Russia* **53 D14** 55 9N 137 40 E
Shantipur, *India* **69 H13** 23 17N 88 25 E
Shantou, *China* **59 F11** 23 18N 116 40 E
Shantung = Shandong □,
China **57 G10** 36 0N 118 0 E
Shanwei, *China* **59 F10** 22 48N 115 22 E
Shanxi □, *China* **56 F7** 37 0N 112 0 E
Shanyang, *China* **56 H5** 33 31N 109 55 E
Shanyin, *China* **56 E7** 39 25N 112 56 E
Shaodong, *China* **59 D8** 27 15N 111 43 E
Shaoguan, *China* **59 E9** 24 48N 113 35 E
Shaoshan, *China* **59 D9** 27 55N 112 33 E
Shaowu, *China* **59 D11** 27 22N 117 28 E
Shaoxing, *China* **59 C13** 30 0N 120 35 E
Shaoyang, Hunan, China* **59 D8** 26 59N 111 20 E
Shaoyang, Hunan, China* **59 D8** 27 14N 111 25 E
Shap, *U.K.* **14 C5** 54 32N 2 40W
Shapinsay, *U.K.* **13 B6** 59 3N 2 51W
Shaqq el Gi'eifer →,
Sudan **81 D2** 15 16N 26 0 E
Shaqra', *Si. Arabia* **70 E5** 25 15N 45 16 E
Shaqrā', *Yemen* **75 E4** 13 22N 45 44 E
Sharafa, *Sudan* **81 E2** 11 59N 27 7 E
Sharafkhāneh, *Iran* **70 B5** 38 11N 45 29 E
Sharashova, *Belarus* **31 F11** 52 34N 24 12 E
Sharbot Lake, *Canada* **117 B8** 44 46N 76 41W
Sharhorod, *Ukraine* **29 B13** 48 45N 28 3 E
Shari, *Japan* **54 C12** 43 55N 144 40 E
Sharjah = Ash Shāriqah,
U.A.E. **71 E7** 25 23N 55 26 E
Shark B., *Australia* **93 E1** 25 30 S 113 32 E
Shark Bay △, *Australia* **93 F2** 32 49 S 118 49 E
Sharm el Sheikh, *Egypt* **80 B3** 27 53N 34 15 E
Sharon, *Mass., U.S.A.* **117 D13** 42 7N 71 11W
Sharon, *Pa., U.S.A.* **116 E4** 41 14N 80 31W
Sharon Springs, Kans.,
U.S.A. **112 F4** 38 54N 101 45W
Sharon Springs, N.Y.,
U.S.A. **117 D10** 42 48N 74 37W
Sharp Pt., *Australia* **94 A3** 10 58 S 142 43 E
Sharpe L., *Canada* **104 B1** 54 24N 93 40W
Sharpsville, *U.S.A.* **116 E4** 41 15N 80 29W
Sharq el Istiwa'iya □,
Sudan **81 G3** 5 0N 33 0 E
Sharya, *Russia* **34 A7** 58 22N 45 20 E
Shasha, *Ethiopia* **81 F4** 6 29N 35 59 E
Shashemene, *Ethiopia* **81 F4** 7 13N 38 33 E
Shashi, *Botswana* **89 C4** 21 15 S 27 27 E
Shashi →, *Africa* **87 G2** 21 14 S 29 20 E
Shashi, *China* **59 B9** 30 25N 112 14 E
Shasta, Mt., *U.S.A.* **108 F2** 41 25N 122 12W
Shasta L., *U.S.A.* **108 F2** 40 43N 122 25W
Shatawi, *Sudan* **81 E3** 14 39N 32 6 E
Shatsk, *Russia* **34 C5** 54 5N 41 45 E
Shatsk, *Ukraine* **31 G10** 51 29N 23 55 E
Shatskyi △, *Ukraine* **31 G10** 51 30N 23 52 E
Shatt al'Arab →, *Iran* **71 D6** 30 0N 48 31 E
Shatura, *Russia* **32 E10** 55 33N 39 21 E
Shaumyani = Shulaveri,
Georgia **35 K7** 41 22N 44 45 E
Shaunavon, *Canada* **103 D7** 49 35N 108 25W
Shaver L., *U.S.A.* **110 H7** 37 9N 119 18W
Shaw →, *Australia* **92 D2** 20 21 S 119 17 E
Shaw I., *Australia* **94 J7** 20 30 S 149 2 E
Shawanaga, *Canada* **116 A4** 45 31N 80 17W
Shawangunk Mts.,
U.S.A. **117 E10** 41 35N 74 30W
Shawano, *U.S.A.* **114 C1** 44 47N 88 36W
Shawinigan, *Canada* **104 C5** 46 35N 72 50W
Shawnee, *U.S.A.* **113 H6** 35 20N 96 55W
Shay Gap, *Australia* **92 D3** 20 30 S 120 10 E
Shayang, *China* **59 B9** 30 42N 112 29 E
Shaybārā, *Si. Arabia* **70 E3** 25 26N 36 47 E
Shayib el Banat, Gebel,
Egypt **80 B3** 26 59N 33 29 E
Shaykh, J. ash, *Lebanon* **74 B4** 33 25N 35 50 E
Shaykh Miskīn, *Syria* **74 C4** 32 49N 36 9 E
Shaykh Sa'id, *Iraq* **70 C5** 32 34N 46 17 E
Shchekino, *Russia* **32 E9** 54 11N 37 34 E
Shchigry, *Russia* **33 G9** 51 55N 36 58 E
Shchors, *Ukraine* **33 G6** 51 48N 31 56 E
Shchuchinsk,
Kazakhstan **52 D8** 52 56N 70 12 E
She Xian, Anhui, China* **59 C12** 29 50N 118 25 E
She Xian, Hebei, China* **56 F8** 36 30N 113 40 E
Shebekino, *Russia* **33 G9** 50 28N 36 54 E
Shebele = Scebeli,
Wabi →, *Somali Rep.* **75 G3** 2 0N 44 0 E
Sheboygan, *U.S.A.* **114 D2** 43 46N 87 45W
Shebshi Mts., *Nigeria* **83 D7** 8 30N 12 0 E
Shediac, *Canada* **105 C7** 46 14N 64 32W
Sheelin, L., *Ireland* **12 C4** 53 48N 7 20W
Sheep Haven, *Ireland* **12 A4** 55 11N 7 52W
Sheerness, *U.K.* **15 F8** 51 26N 0 47 E
Sheet Harbour, *Canada* **105 D7** 44 56N 62 31W
Sheffield, *U.K.* **14 D6** 53 23N 1 28W
Sheffield, *Ala., U.S.A.* **115 H2** 34 46N 87 41W
Sheffield, *Mass., U.S.A.* **117 D11** 42 5N 73 21W

Sheffield, Pa., U.S.A. . . **116 E5** 41 42N 79 3W
Shehojele, Ethiopia . . . . **81 E4** 10 40N 35 9 E
Shehong, China . . . . . . **58 B5** 30 54N 105 18 E
Sheikh Idris, Sudan . . . . **81 E3** 11 43N 33 30 E
Sheikhpura, India . . . . . **69 G11** 25 9N 85 53 E
Shek Hasan, Ethiopia . . . **81 E4** 12 5N 35 58 E
Shekhupura, Pakistan . . . **68 D5** 31 42N 73 58 E
Sheki = Şaki, Azerbaijan . **35 K8** 41 10N 47 5 E
Shelburne, N.S., Canada . **105 D6** 43 47N 65 20W
Shelburne, Ont., Canada . **116 B4** 44 4N 80 15W
Shelburne, U.S.A. **117 B11** 44 23N 73 14W
Shelburne B., Australia . . **94 A3** 11 50 S 142 50 E
Shelburne Falls, U.S.A. . . **117 D12** 42 36N 72 45W
Shelby, Mich., U.S.A. . . . **114 D2** 43 37N 86 22W
Shelby, Miss., U.S.A. . . . **113 J9** 33 57N 90 46W
Shelby, Mont., U.S.A. . . . **108 B8** 48 30N 111 51W
Shelby, N.C., U.S.A. **115 H5** 35 17N 81 32W
Shelby, Ohio, U.S.A. **116 F2** 40 53N 82 40W
Shelbyville, Ill., U.S.A. . . **112 F10** 39 24N 88 48W
Shelbyville, Ind., U.S.A. . . **114 F3** 39 31N 85 47W
Shelbyville, Ky., U.S.A. . . **114 F3** 38 13N 85 14W
Shelbyville, Tenn.,
U.S.A. **115 H2** 35 29N 86 28W
Sheldon, U.S.A. **112 D7** 43 11N 95 51W
Sheldrake, Canada **105 B7** 50 20N 64 51W
Shelengo, Khawr →,
Sudan . . . . **81 E2** 10 33N 28 40 E
Shelikhova, Zaliv,
Russia . . . . **53 D16** 59 30N 157 0 E
Shell Lakes, Australia . . . **93 E4** 29 20 S 127 30 E
Shellbrook, Canada **103 C7** 53 13N 106 24W
Shellharbour, Australia . . **95 E5** 34 31 S 150 51 E
Shelon →, Russia . . . . . **32 C6** 58 10N 30 47 E
Shelter I., U.S.A. **117 E12** 41 5N 72 21W
Shelton, Conn., U.S.A. . . **117 E11** 41 19N 73 5W
Shelton, Wash., U.S.A. . . **110 C3** 47 13N 123 6W
Shemakha = Şamaxi,
Azerbaijan . . . . **35 K9** 40 38N 48 37 E
Shëmri, Albania . . . . . . **44 D4** 42 7N 20 13 E
Shemsi, Sudan . . . . **80 D2** 19 2N 29 57 E
Shen Xian, China . . . . . **56 F8** 36 15N 115 40 E
Shenandoah, Iowa,
U.S.A. **112 E7** 40 46N 95 22W
Shenandoah, Pa., U.S.A. . **117 F8** 40 49N 76 12W
Shenandoah, Va., U.S.A. . **114 F6** 38 29N 78 37W
Shenandoah △, U.S.A. . . **114 F6** 38 35N 78 22W
Shenandoah →, U.S.A. . . **114 F7** 39 19N 77 44W
Shenchi, China . . . . **56 E7** 39 8N 112 10 E
Shendam, Nigeria . . . . . **83 D6** 8 49N 9 30 E
Shendī, Sudan . . . . **81 D3** 16 46N 33 22 E
Shenge, S. Leone **82 D2** 7 54N 12 55W
Shengfang, China . . . . . **56 E9** 39 3N 116 42 E
Shëngjergj, Albania . . . . **44 E4** 41 17N 20 10 E
Shëngjin, Albania . . . . . **44 E3** 41 50N 19 35 E
Shengzhou, China . . . . . **59 C13** 29 35N 120 50 E
Shenjingzi, China . . . . . **57 B13** 44 40N 124 30 E
Shenmu, China . . . . **56 E6** 38 50N 110 29 E
Shennongjia, China . . . . **59 B8** 31 43N 110 44 E
Shenqiu, China . . . . **56 H8** 33 25N 115 5 E
Shensi = Shaanxi □,
China . . . . **56 G5** 35 0N 109 0 E
Shenyang, China . . . . . . **57 D12** 41 48N 123 27 E
Shenzhen, China . . . . . . **59 F10** 22 32N 114 5 E
Sheo, India . . . . **68 F4** 26 11N 71 15 E
Sheopur Kalan, India . . . **66 G10** 25 40N 76 40 E
Shepetivka, Ukraine . . . . **33 G4** 50 10N 27 10 E
Shepetovka =
Shepetivka, Ukraine . . **33 G4** 50 10N 27 10 E
Shepparton, Australia . . . **95 F4** 36 23 S 145 26 E
Sheppey, I. of, U.K. . . . . **15 F8** 51 25N 0 48 E
Shepton Mallet, U.K. . . . **15 F5** 51 11N 2 33W
Sheqi, China . . . . **56 H7** 33 12N 112 57 E
Sher Qila, Pakistan . . . . **69 A6** 36 7N 74 2 E
Sherab, Sudan . . . . **81 E1** 10 44N 24 41 E
Sherborne, U.K. **15 G5** 50 57N 2 31W
Sherbro I., S. Leone **82 D2** 7 30N 12 40W
Sherbro I., S. Leone **82 D2** 7 30N 12 40W
Sherbrooke, N.S.,
Canada **105 C7** 45 8N 61 59W
Sherbrooke, Qué.,
Canada **117 A13** 45 28N 71 57W
Sherburne, U.S.A. **117 D9** 42 41N 75 30W
Shereik, Sudan . . . . **80 D3** 18 44N 33 47 E
Shergarh, India . . . . . . **68 F5** 26 20N 72 18 E
Sherghati, India . . . . . . **69 G11** 24 34N 84 47 E
Sheridan, Ark., U.S.A. . . **113 H8** 34 19N 92 24W
Sheridan, Wyo., U.S.A. . . **108 D10** 44 48N 106 58W
Sheringham, U.K. . . . . . **14 E9** 52 56N 1 13 E
Sherkin I., Ireland **12 E2** 51 28N 9 26W
Sherkot, India . . . . **69 E8** 29 22N 78 35 E
Sherpur, India . . . . **69 G14** 25 34N 87 47 E
Sherridon, Canada **103 B8** 55 8N 101 5W
Sherwood Forest, U.K. . . **14 D6** 53 6N 1 7W
Sherwood Park, Canada . . **102 C6** 53 31N 113 19W
Sheslay →, Canada **102 B2** 58 48N 132 5W
Shethanei L., Canada . . . **103 B9** 58 48N 97 50W
Shetland □, U.K. **13 A7** 60 30N 1 30W
Shetland Is., U.K. **13 A7** 60 30N 1 30W
Shetrunji →, India . . . . **68 J5** 21 19N 72 7 E
Shevchenkovo, Ukraine . . **29 E14** 45 33N 29 20 E
Shewa, Ethiopia . . . . . . **81 F4** 9 33N 38 10 E
Shewa Gimira, Ethiopia . . **81 F4** 7 4N 35 51 E
Sheyenne →, U.S.A. . . . **112 B6** 47 2N 96 50W
Shibām, Yemen . . . . **75 D4** 15 59N 48 36 E
Shibata, Japan . . . . **54 F9** 37 57N 139 20 E
Shibecha, Japan . . . . . . **54 C12** 43 17N 144 36 E
Shibetsu, Japan . . . . . . **54 B11** 44 10N 142 23 E
Shibīn el Kôm, Egypt . . . **80 H7** 30 31N 30 55 E
Shibīn el Qanâtir, Egypt . **80 H7** 30 19N 31 19 E
Shibing, China . . . . **58 D7** 27 20N 108 7 E
Shibogama L., Canada . . **104 B2** 53 35N 88 15W
Shibushi, Japan . . . . . . **55 J5** 31 25N 131 8 E
Shicheng, China . . . . . . **59 D11** 26 22N 116 20 E
Shickshinny, U.S.A. **117 E8** 41 9N 76 9W
Shickshock Mts. = Chic-
Chocs, Mts., Canada . . **105 C6** 48 55N 66 0W
Shidao, China . . . . **57 F12** 36 50N 122 25 E
Shidian, China . . . . **58 E2** 24 40N 99 5 E
Shido, Japan . . . . **55 G7** 34 19N 134 10 E
Shiel, L., U.K. **13 E3** 56 48N 5 34W
Shield, C., Australia . . . . **94 A2** 13 20 S 136 20 E
Shīeli, Kazakhstan . . . . . **52 E7** 44 20N 66 15 E
Shifang, China . . . . **58 B5** 31 8N 104 10 E
Shiga □, Japan . . . . **55 G8** 35 20N 136 0 E
Shigu, China . . . . **58 D2** 26 51N 99 56 E
Shiguaigou, China . . . . . **56 D6** 40 52N 110 15 E
Shihchiachuangi =
Shijiazhuang, China . . **56 E8** 38 2N 114 28 E
Shihezi, China . . . . **60 B3** 44 15N 86 2 E
Shijak, Albania . . . . **44 E3** 41 21N 19 33 E
Shijiazhuang, China . . . . **56 E8** 38 2N 114 28 E
Shijiu Hu, China . . . . . . **59 B12** 31 25N 118 52 E
Shikarpur, India . . . . . . **68 E8** 28 17N 78 7 E
Shikarpur, Pakistan . . . . **68 F3** 27 57N 68 39 E
Shikohabad, India . . . . . **69 F8** 27 6N 78 36 E
Shikoku □, Japan . . . . . **55 H6** 33 30N 133 30 E

Shikoku-Sanchi, Japan . . **55 H6** 33 30N 133 30 E
Shikotsu-Ko, Japan . . . . **54 C10** 42 45N 141 25 E
Shikotsu-Tōya △, Japan . **54 C10** 44 4N 145 8 E
Shiliguri, India . . . . **67 F16** 26 45N 88 25 E
Shilka, Russia . . . . **53 D12** 53 20N 121 26 E
Shilka →, Russia . . . . . **53 D13** 53 20N 121 26 E
Shillelagh, Ireland **12 D5** 52 45N 6 32W
Shillington, U.S.A. **117 F9** 40 18N 75 58W
Shillong, India . . . . **67 G17** 25 35N 91 53 E
Shilo, West Bank . . . . . . **74 C4** 32 4N 35 18 E
Shilong, China . . . . **59 F9** 23 5N 113 52 E
Shilou, China . . . . **56 F6** 37 0N 110 48 E
Shilovo, Russia . . . . **34 C5** 54 25N 40 57 E
Shimabara, Japan . . . . . **55 H5** 32 48N 130 20 E
Shimada, Japan . . . . . . **55 G9** 34 49N 138 10 E
Shimane □, Japan . . . . . **55 G6** 35 0N 132 30 E
Shimanovsk, Russia . . . . **53 D13** 52 15N 127 30 E
Shimba Hills △, Kenya . . **86 C4** 4 14 S 39 25 E
Shimen, China . . . . **59 C8** 29 35N 111 0 E
Shimenjie, China . . . . . . **59 C11** 29 29N 116 48 E
Shimian, China . . . . **58 C4** 29 17N 102 23 E
Shimizu, Japan . . . . **55 G9** 35 0N 138 30 E
Shimodate, Japan . . . . . **55 F9** 36 20N 139 55 E
Shimoga, India . . . . **66 N9** 13 57N 75 32 E
Shimoni, Kenya . . . . **86 C4** 4 38 S 39 20 E
Shimonoseki, Japan . . . . **55 H5** 33 58N 130 55 E
Shimpuru Rapids,
Namibia . . . . **88 B2** 17 45 S 19 55 E
Shimsk, Russia . . . . **32 C6** 58 15N 30 50 E
Shin, L., U.K. **13 C4** 58 5N 4 30W
Shinan, China . . . . **58 F7** 22 44N 109 53 E
Shinano-Gawa →,
Japan . . . . **55 F9** 36 50N 138 30 E
Shināṣ, Oman . . . . **71 E8** 24 46N 56 28 E
Shīndand, Afghan. . . . . . **66 C3** 33 12N 62 8 E
Shinglehouse, U.S.A. . . . **116 E6** 41 58N 78 12W
Shingū, Japan . . . . **55 H7** 33 40N 135 55 E
Shingwidzi, S. Africa . . . **89 C5** 23 5 S 31 25 E
Shinjō, Japan . . . . **54 E10** 38 46N 140 18 E
Shinkafe, Nigeria . . . . . **83 C6** 13 8N 6 29 E
Shinshār, Syria . . . . **74 A5** 34 36N 36 43 E
Shinyanga, Tanzania . . . **86 C3** 3 45 S 33 27 E
Shinyanga □, Tanzania . . **86 C3** 3 50 S 34 0 E
Shio-no-Misaki, Japan . . **55 H7** 33 25N 135 45 E
Shiogama, Japan . . . . . . **54 E10** 38 19N 141 1 E
Shiojiri, Japan . . . . **55 F8** 36 6N 137 58 E
Shipchenski Prokhod,
Bulgaria . . . . **45 D9** 42 45N 25 15 E
Shiping, China . . . . **58 F4** 23 45N 102 23 E
Shippagan, Canada **105 C7** 47 45N 64 45W
Shippensburg, U.S.A. . . . **116 F7** 40 3N 77 31W
Shippenville, U.S.A. **116 E5** 41 15N 79 28W
Shiprock, U.S.A. **109 H9** 36 47N 108 41W
Shiqian, China . . . . **58 D7** 27 32N 108 13 E
Shiqma, N. →, Israel . . . **74 D3** 31 37N 34 30 E
Shiquan, China . . . . **56 H5** 33 5N 108 15 E
Shiquan He = Indus →,
Pakistan . . . . **68 G2** 24 20N 67 47 E
Shīr Kūh, Iran . . . . **71 D7** 31 39N 54 3 E
Shiragami-Misaki, Japan . **54 D10** 41 24N 140 12 E
Shirakawa, Fukushima,
Japan . . . . **55 F10** 37 7N 140 13 E
Shirakawa, Gifu, Japan . . **55 F8** 36 17N 136 56 E
Shirane-San, Gumma,
Japan . . . . **55 F9** 36 48N 139 22 E
Shirane-San, Yamanashi,
Japan . . . . **55 G9** 35 42N 138 9 E
Shiraoi, Japan . . . . **54 C10** 42 33N 141 21 E
Shīrāz, Iran . . . . **71 D7** 29 42N 52 30 E
Shirbīn, Egypt . . . . **80 H7** 31 11N 31 32 E
Shire →, Africa . . . . **87 F4** 17 42 S 35 19 E
Shiretoko-Misaki, Japan . **54 B12** 44 21N 145 20 E
Shirinab →, Pakistan . . . **68 D2** 30 5N 66 28 E
Shiriya-Zaki, Japan . . . . **54 D10** 41 25N 141 30 E
Shiroishi, Japan . . . . . . **54 F10** 38 0N 140 37 E
Shīrvān, Iran . . . . **71 B8** 37 30N 57 50 E
Shirwa, L. = Chilwa, L.,
Malawi . . . . **87 F4** 15 15 S 35 40 E
Shishi, China . . . . **59 E12** 24 44N 118 37 E
Shishou, China . . . . **59 C9** 29 38N 112 22 E
Shitai, China . . . . **59 B11** 30 12N 117 25 E
Shivpuri, India . . . . **68 G7** 25 26N 77 42 E
Shixian, China . . . . **57 C15** 43 5N 129 50 E
Shixing, China . . . . **59 E10** 24 46N 114 5 E
Shiyan, China . . . . **59 A8** 32 35N 110 45 E
Shiyata, Egypt . . . . **80 B2** 29 25N 25 7 E
Shizhu, China . . . . **58 C7** 29 58N 108 7 E
Shizong, China . . . . **58 E5** 24 50N 104 0 E
Shizuishan, China . . . . . **56 E4** 39 15N 106 50 E
Shizuoka, Japan . . . . . . **55 G9** 34 57N 138 24 E
Shizuoka □, Japan . . . . . **55 G9** 35 15N 138 40 E
Shklov = Shklow,
Belarus . . . . **32 E6** 54 16N 30 15 E
Shklow, Belarus . . . . . . **32 E6** 54 16N 30 15 E
Shkodër, Albania . . . . . . **44 D3** 42 4N 19 32 E
Shkumbini →, Albania . . **44 E3** 41 2N 19 31 E
Shmidta, Ostrov, Russia . **53 A10** 81 0N 91 0 E
Shō-Gawa →, Japan . . . **55 F8** 36 47N 137 4 E
Shoal L., Canada **103 D9** 49 33N 95 1W
Shoal Lake, Canada **103 C8** 50 30N 100 35W
Shōdo-Shima, Japan . . . . **55 G7** 34 30N 134 15 E
Sholapur = Solapur,
India . . . . **66 L9** 17 43N 75 56 E
Shōmrōn, West Bank . . . **74 C4** 32 15N 35 13 E
Shoreham by Sea, U.K. . . **15 G7** 50 50N 0 16W
Shori →, Pakistan . . . . . **68 E3** 28 29N 69 44 E
Shorkot Road, Pakistan . . **68 D5** 30 47N 72 15 E
Shoshone, Calif., U.S.A. . **111 K10** 35 58N 116 16W
Shoshone, Idaho, U.S.A. . **108 E6** 42 56N 114 25W
Shoshone L., U.S.A. **108 D8** 44 22N 110 43W
Shoshone Mts., U.S.A. . . **108 G5** 39 20N 117 25W
Shoshong, Botswana . . . **88 C4** 22 56 S 26 31 E
Shoshoni, U.S.A. **108 E9** 43 14N 108 7W
Shostka, Ukraine . . . . . . **33 G7** 51 57N 33 32 E
Shou Xian, China . . . . . **59 A11** 32 37N 116 42 E
Shouchang, China . . . . . **59 C12** 29 19N 119 18 E
Shouguang, China . . . . . **57 F10** 37 52N 118 45 E
Shouning, China . . . . . . **59 D12** 27 19N 119 31 E
Shouyang, China . . . . . . **56 F7** 37 54N 113 8 E
Show Low, U.S.A. **109 J9** 34 15N 110 2W
Shpola, Ukraine . . . . . . **33 H6** 49 1N 31 30 E
Shpykiv, Ukraine . . . . . . **29 B13** 48 47N 28 58 E
Shreveport, U.S.A. **113 J8** 32 31N 93 45W
Shrewsbury, U.K. **15 E5** 52 43N 2 45W
Shri Mohangarh, India . . **68 F4** 27 17N 71 18 E
Shrirampur, India . . . . . **69 H13** 22 44N 88 21 E
Shropshire □, U.K. **15 E5** 52 36N 2 45W
Shū, Kazakhstan . . . . . . **52 E8** 43 36N 73 42 E
Shū →, Kazakhstan . . . . **50 E10** 45 0N 67 44 E
Shuangcheng, China . . . . **58 E3** 24 42N 101 38 E
Shuangcheng, China . . . . **57 B14** 45 20N 126 15 E
Shuangfeng, China . . . . . **59 D9** 27 29N 112 11 E
Shuanggou, China . . . . . **57 H9** 34 2N 117 30 E
Shuangjiang, China . . . . **58 F2** 23 26N 99 58 E
Shuangliao, China . . . . . **57 C12** 43 29N 123 30 E
Shuangshanzi, China . . . **57 D10** 40 20N 119 8 E
Shuangyang, China . . . . **57 C13** 43 28N 125 40 E

Shuangyashan, China . . . **60 B8** 46 28N 131 5 E
Shubra el Kheima, Egypt . **80 H7** 30 6N 31 15 E
Shubra Khīt, Egypt . . . . **80 H7** 31 2N 30 42 E
Shucheng, China . . . . . . **59 B11** 31 28N 116 57 E
Shugozero, Russia . . . . . **32 C5** 59 54N 34 10 E
Shuguri Falls, Tanzania . . **87 D4** 8 33 S 37 22 E
Shuiji, China . . . . **59 D12** 27 13N 118 20 E
Shuiye, China . . . . **56 F8** 36 7N 114 8 E
Shujalpur, India . . . . . . **68 H7** 23 18N 76 46 E
Shukpa Kunzang, India . . **69 B8** 34 22N 78 22 E
Shulan, China . . . . **57 B14** 44 28N 127 0 E
Shulaveri, Georgia . . . . . **35 K7** 41 22N 44 45 E
Shule, China . . . . **60 C2** 39 25N 76 3 E
Shumagin Is., U.S.A. . . . **100 C4** 55 7N 160 30W
Shumen, Bulgaria . . . . . **45 C10** 43 18N 26 55 E
Shumerlya, Russia . . . . . **34 C8** 55 30N 46 25 E
Shumikha, Russia . . . . . **52 D7** 55 10N 63 15 E
Shunchang, China . . . . . **59 D11** 26 54N 117 48 E
Shunde, China . . . . **59 F9** 22 42N 113 14 E
Shungay, Kazakhstan . . . **35 F8** 48 30N 46 45 E
Shuo Xian = Shuozhou,
China . . . . **56 E7** 39 20N 112 33 E
Shuozhou, China . . . . . . **56 E7** 39 20N 112 33 E
Shūr →, Fārs, Iran . . . . **71 D7** 28 30N 55 0 E
Shūr →, Kermān, Iran . . **71 D8** 30 52N 57 37 E
Shūr →, Yazd, Iran . . . . **71 D7** 31 45N 55 15 E
Shūr Āb, Iran . . . . **71 C6** 34 23N 51 11 E
Shūr Gaz, Iran . . . . **71 D8** 29 10N 59 20 E
Shūrāb, Iran . . . . **71 C8** 33 43N 56 29 E
Shūrjestān, Iran . . . . . . **71 D7** 31 24N 52 25 E
Shurugwi, Zimbabwe . . . **87 F3** 19 40 S 30 0 E
Shūsf, Iran . . . . **71 D9** 31 50N 60 5 E
Shūsh, Iran . . . . **73 F13** 32 11N 48 15 E
Shūshtar, Iran . . . . **71 D6** 32 0N 48 50 E
Shuswap L., Canada **102 C5** 50 55N 119 3W
Shuya, Russia . . . . **34 B5** 56 50N 41 28 E
Shuyang, China . . . . **57 G10** 34 10N 118 42 E
Shūzū, Iran . . . . **71 D7** 29 52N 54 30 E
Shwebo, Burma . . . . **67 H19** 22 30N 95 45 E
Shwegu, Burma . . . . **67 G20** 24 15N 96 26 E
Shweli →, Burma . . . . . **67 H20** 23 45N 96 45 E
Shymkent, Kazakhstan . . **52 E7** 42 18N 69 36 E
Shyok, India . . . . **69 B8** 34 13N 78 12 E
Shyok →, Pakistan . . . . **69 B6** 35 13N 75 53 E
Shyroke, Ukraine . . . . . . **28 B8** 48 13N 34 9 E
Shyroke, Ukraine . . . . . . **29 E15** 45 59N 30 5 E
Si Chon, Thailand . . . . . **65 H2** 9 0N 99 54 E
Si Kiang = Xi Jiang →,
China . . . . **59 F9** 22 5N 113 20 E
Si Lanna △, Thailand . . . **64 C2** 19 17N 99 12 E
Si-ngan = Xi'an, China . . **56 G5** 34 15N 109 0 E
Si Prachan, Thailand . . . **64 E3** 14 37N 100 9 E
Si Racha, Thailand . . . . **64 F3** 13 10N 100 48 E
Si Xian, China . . . . **57 H9** 33 43N 117 50 E
Siachen Glacier, Asia . . . **69 B7** 35 20N 77 30 E
Siahaf →, Pakistan . . . . **68 E3** 29 3N 68 57 E
Siahan Range, Pakistan . . **66 F4** 27 30N 64 40 E
Siaksriindrapura,
Indonesia . . . . **62 D2** 0 51N 102 0 E
Sialkot, Pakistan . . . . . . **68 C6** 32 32N 74 30 E
Siam = Thailand ■, Asia . **64 E4** 16 0N 102 0 E
Sian = Xi'an, China . . . . **56 G5** 34 15N 109 0 E
Sian Ka'an, Mexico **119 D7** 19 35N 87 40W
Sianów, Poland . . . . **30 D3** 54 13N 16 18 E
Siantan, Indonesia . . . . . **62 D3** 3 10N 106 15 E
Siãreh, Iran . . . . **71 D9** 28 5N 60 14 E
Siargao I., Phil. . . . . **61 G7** 9 52N 126 3 E
Siari, Pakistan . . . . **69 B7** 34 55N 76 40 E
Siasi, Phil. . . . . **63 C6** 5 34N 120 50 E
Siasi I., Phil. . . . . **61 J4** 5 33N 120 51 E
Siátista, Greece . . . . . . **44 F5** 40 15N 21 33 E
Siau, Indonesia . . . . **63 D7** 2 50N 125 25 E
Šiauliai, Lithuania . . . . . **9 J20** 55 56N 23 15 E
Šiauliai □, Lithuania . . . **30 C10** 55 56N 23 19 E
Siazan = Siyäzän,
Azerbaijan . . . . **35 K9** 41 3N 49 10 E
Sibã̈, Gebel el, Egypt . . . **70 E2** 25 45N 34 10 E
Sibang, Indonesia . . . . . **63 K18** 8 34 S 115 13 E
Sibayi, L., S. Africa . . . . **89 D5** 27 20 S 32 45 E
Sibdu, Sudan . . . . **81 E2** 10 57N 26 17 E
Šibenik, Croatia . . . . . . **41 E12** 43 48N 15 54 E
Siberia = Sibirskiy □,
Russia . . . . **53 D10** 58 0N 90 0 E
Siberia, Russia . . . . **50 C13** 60 0N 100 0 E
Siberut, Indonesia . . . . . **62 E1** 1 30 S 99 0 E
Sibi, Pakistan . . . . **68 E2** 29 30N 67 54 E
Sibil = Oksibil,
Indonesia . . . . **63 E10** 4 59 S 140 35 E
Sibiloi △, Kenya . . . . . . **86 B4** 4 0N 36 20 E
Sibirskiy □, Russia . . . . **53 D10** 58 0N 90 0 E
Sibiti, Congo . . . . **84 E2** 3 38 S 13 19 E
Sibiu, Romania . . . . **29 E9** 45 45N 24 9 E
Sibiu □, Romania . . . . . **29 E9** 45 50N 24 15 E
Sibley, U.S.A. **112 D7** 43 24N 95 45W
Sibolga, Indonesia . . . . . **62 D1** 1 42N 98 45 E
Sibsagar, India . . . . **67 F19** 27 0N 94 36 E
Sibu, Malaysia . . . . **62 D4** 2 18N 111 49 E
Sibuco, Phil. . . . . **61 H5** 7 20N 122 10 E
Sibuguey B., Phil. . . . . . **61 H5** 7 50N 122 45 E
Sibut, C.A.R. . . . . **84 C3** 5 46N 19 10 E
Sibutu, Phil. . . . . **63 D5** 4 45N 119 30 E
Sibutu Group, Phil. . . . . **61 J3** 4 45N 119 20 E
Sibutu Passage, E. Indies **63 D5** 4 50N 120 0 E
Sibuyan I., Phil. . . . . . . **61 E5** 12 25N 122 40 E
Sibuyan Sea, Phil. . . . . . **61 E5** 12 30N 122 20 E
Sic, Romania . . . . **29 D8** 46 56N 23 53 E
Sicamous, Canada **102 C5** 50 49N 119 0W
Siccus →, Australia . . . . **95 E2** 31 55 S 139 17 E
Sichuan □, China . . . . . **58 B5** 30 30N 103 0 E
Sichuan Pendi, China . . . **58 B5** 31 0N 105 0 E
Sicilia, Italy . . . . **43 E7** 37 30N 14 30 E
Sicily = Sicilia, Italy . . . **43 E7** 37 30N 14 30 E
Sicily, Str. of . . . . **42 E5** 37 35N 11 56 E
Sicuani, Peru . . . . **124 F4** 14 21 S 71 10W
Šid, Serbia & M. . . . . . . **28 E4** 45 8N 19 14 E
Sidamo, Ethiopia . . . . . . **81 G4** 5 0N 37 50 E
Sidaouet, Niger . . . . **83 B6** 18 34N 8 3 E
Sidári, Greece . . . . **49 A3** 39 47N 19 41 E
Siddhapur, India . . . . . . **68 H5** 23 56N 72 25 E
Siddipet, India . . . . **66 K11** 18 5N 78 51 E
Sidensjö, Sweden . . . . . **10 A12** 63 18N 18 17 E
Sidéradougou,
Burkina Faso **82 C4** 10 42N 4 12W
Siderno, Italy . . . . **43 E9** 38 16N 16 18 E
Sidhauli, India . . . . **69 F9** 27 17N 80 50 E
Sidheros, Ákra, Greece . . **49 D8** 35 19N 26 19 E
Sidhi, India . . . . **69 G9** 24 25N 81 53 E
Sidhirókastron, Greece . . **44 E7** 41 13N 23 24 E
Sîdi Abd el Rahmân,
Egypt . . . . **80 A2** 30 55N 28 41 E
Sîdi Barrâni, Egypt . . . . **80 A2** 31 38N 25 58 E
Sidi-bel-Abbès, Algeria . . **78 A5** 35 13N 0 39W
Sidi Haneish, Egypt . . . . **80 A2** 31 10N 27 35 E
Sidi Ifni, Morocco **78 C3** 29 29N 10 12W
Sîdi Omar, Egypt . . . . . . **80 A1** 31 24N 24 57 E
Sidlaw Hills, U.K. **13 E5** 56 32N 3 2W
Sidley, Mt., Antarctica . . **5 D14** 77 2 S 126 2W

Sidmouth, U.K. **15 G4** 50 40N 3 15W
Sidmouth, C., Australia . . **94 A3** 13 25 S 143 36 E
Sidney, Canada **102 D4** 48 39N 123 24W
Sidney, Mont., U.S.A. . . . **112 B2** 47 43N 104 9W
Sidney, N.Y., U.S.A. **117 D9** 42 19N 75 24W
Sidney, Nebr., U.S.A. . . . **112 E3** 41 8N 102 59W
Sidney, Ohio, U.S.A. . . . **114 E3** 40 17N 84 9W
Sidney Lanier, L., U.S.A. . **115 H4** 34 10N 84 4W
Sido, Mali **82 C3** 11 37N 7 29W
Sidoarjo, Indonesia . . . . **63 G15** 7 27 S 112 43 E
Sidon = Saydā, Lebanon . **74 B4** 33 35N 35 25 E
Sidra, G. of = Surt,
Khalīj, Libya . . . . **79 B9** 31 40N 18 30 E
Siedlce, Poland . . . . **31 F9** 52 10N 22 20 E
Sieg →, Germany . . . . . **24 E3** 50 46N 7 6 E
Siegburg, Germany . . . . **24 E3** 50 47N 7 12 E
Siegen, Germany . . . . . . **24 E4** 50 51N 8 0 E
Siem Pang, Cambodia . . . **64 E6** 14 7N 106 23 E
Siem Reap = Siemreab,
Cambodia . . . . **64 F4** 13 20N 103 52 E
Siemiatycze, Poland . . . . **31 F9** 52 27N 22 53 E
Siemreab, Cambodia . . . **64 F4** 13 20N 103 52 E
Siena, Italy . . . . **41 E8** 43 19N 11 21 E
Sieniawa, Poland . . . . . . **31 H9** 50 11N 22 38 E
Sieradz, Poland . . . . **31 G5** 51 37N 18 41 E
Sieraków, Poland . . . . . . **31 F3** 52 39N 16 2 E
Sierck-les-Bains, France . **19 C13** 49 26N 6 20 E
Sierning, Austria . . . . . . **26 C7** 48 2N 14 18 E
Sierpc, Poland . . . . **31 F6** 52 55N 19 43 E
Sierpe, Bocas de la,
Venezuela **125 L15** 10 0N 61 30W
Sierra Blanca, U.S.A. . . . **109 L11** 31 11N 105 22W
Sierra Blanca Peak,
U.S.A. **109 K11** 33 23N 105 49W
Sierra City, U.S.A. **110 F6** 39 34N 120 38W
Sierra Colorada,
Argentina . . . . **128 E3** 40 35 S 67 50W
Sierra de Aracena y
Picas de Aroche △,
Spain **37 H4** 37 53N 6 41W
Sierra de Bahoruco △,
Dom. Rep. **121 C5** 18 10N 71 25W
Sierra de Baza △, Spain . **39 H2** 37 20N 2 48W
Sierra de Castril △,
Spain **39 H2** 37 54N 2 50W
Sierra de España △,
Spain **39 H3** 37 50N 1 31W
Sierra de Gata, Spain . . . **36 E3** 40 20N 6 45W
Sierra de Gorbea, Spain . **38 B2** 43 0N 2 50W
Sierra de Grazalema △,
Spain **37 J5** 36 45N 5 28W
Sierra de Gredos △,
Spain **36 E5** 40 17N 5 17W
Sierra de
Hornachuelos △,
Spain **37 H5** 37 56N 5 14W
Sierra de Huétor △,
Spain **37 H7** 37 14N 3 30W
Sierra de La Culata △,
Venezuela **121 E5** 8 45N 71 10W
Sierra de Lancandón △,
Guatemala **120 C1** 16 59N 90 23W
Sierra de las Nieves △,
Spain **37 J6** 36 42N 5 0W
Sierra de las Quijadas △,
Argentina . . . . **126 C2** 32 29 S 67 5W
Sierra de María-Los
Vélez △, Spain **39 H2** 37 41N 2 10W
Sierra de San Luis △,
Venezuela **121 D6** 11 20N 69 43W
Sierra de Yeguas, Spain . **37 H6** 37 7N 4 52W
Sierra del São
Mamede △, Portugal . **37 F3** 39 17N 7 18W
Sierra Gorda, Chile . . . . **126 A2** 22 50 S 69 15W
Sierra Leone ■, W. Afr. . . **82 D2** 9 0N 12 0W
Sierra Madre, Mexico . . . **119 D6** 16 0N 93 0W
Sierra Mágina △, Spain . **39 H7** 37 44N 3 28W
Sierra Mojada, Mexico . . **118 B4** 27 19N 103 42W
Sierra Nevada, Spain . . . **37 H7** 37 3N 3 15W
Sierra Nevada, U.S.A. . . . **110 H8** 39 0N 120 30W
Sierra Nevada △, Spain . **37 H7** 37 4N 3 5W
Sierra Nevada △,
Venezuela **121 E5** 8 35N 70 45W
Sierra Nevada de Santa
Marta △, Colombia . . **121 D5** 10 56N 73 36W
Sierra Norte de
Seville △, Spain **37 H5** 37 55N 5 46W
Sierra Subbéticas △,
Spain **37 H6** 37 26N 4 18W
Sierra Vista, U.S.A. **109 L8** 31 33N 110 18W
Sierras de Cardeña y
Montoro △, Spain . . . **37 G6** 38 13N 4 15W
Sierras de Cazorla,
Segura y las Villas △,
Spain **39 J2** 37 0N 2 45W
Sierraville, U.S.A. **110 F6** 39 36N 120 22W
Sierre, Switz. . . . . **25 J3** 46 17N 7 31 E
Sifani, Ethiopia . . . . **81 E5** 12 18N 40 19 E
Sifié, Ivory C. **82 D3** 6 6N 7 15W
Sifnos, Greece . . . . **46 E6** 37 0N 24 45 E
Sifton, Canada **103 C8** 51 21N 100 8W
Sifton Pass, Canada **102 B3** 57 52N 126 15W
Sigean, France . . . . **20 E6** 43 2N 2 58 E
Sighetu-Marmaţiei,
Romania . . . . **29 C8** 47 57N 23 52 E
Sighişoara, Romania . . . . **29 D9** 46 12N 24 50 E
Sigli, Indonesia . . . . **62 C1** 5 25N 96 0 E
Siglufjörður, Iceland . . . **8 C4** 66 12N 18 55W
Sigmaringen, Germany . . **25 G5** 48 5N 9 12 E
Signa, Italy . . . . **40 E8** 43 45N 11 6 E
Signakhi = Tsnori,
Georgia . . . . **35 K7** 41 40N 45 57 E
Signal, U.S.A. **111 L13** 34 30N 113 38W
Signal de Botrang,
Belgium . . . . **17 D6** 50 29N 6 4 E
Signal Pk., U.S.A. **111 M12** 33 20N 114 2W
Signy I., Antarctica . . . . **5 C18** 60 45 S 45 56W
Signy-l'Abbaye, France . . **19 C11** 49 40N 4 25 E
Sigsig, Ecuador . . . . **124 D3** 3 0 S 78 50W
Sigüenza, Spain **38 D2** 41 3N 2 40W
Siguiri, Guinea **82 C3** 11 31N 9 10W
Sigulda, Latvia . . . . **9 H21** 57 10N 24 55 E
Sihora, India . . . . **69 H9** 23 29N 80 6 E
Sihui, China . . . . **59 F9** 23 20N 112 40 E
Siikajoki →, Finland . . . **8 D21** 64 50N 24 43 E
Siilinjärvi, Finland . . . . . **8 E22** 63 4N 27 39 E
Siirt, Turkey . . . . **73 D9** 37 57N 41 55 E
Sijarira Ra. = Chizarira,
Zimbabwe . . . . **87 F2** 17 36 S 27 45 E
Sika, India . . . . **68 H3** 22 26N 69 47 E
Sikani Chief →, Canada . **102 B4** 57 47N 122 15W
Sikao, Thailand . . . . **65 J2** 7 34N 99 21 E
Sikar, India . . . . **68 F6** 27 33N 75 10 E
Sikasso, Mali **82 C3** 11 18N 5 35W
Sikeston, U.S.A. **113 G10** 36 53N 89 35W
Sikhote Alin, Khrebet,
Russia . . . . **53 E14** 45 0N 136 0 E
Sikhote Alin Ra. =
Sikhote Alin, Khrebet,
Russia . . . . **53 E14** 45 0N 136 0 E

Sikiá, Greece . . . . **44 F7** 40 2N 23 56 E
Síkinos, Greece . . . . **47 E7** 36 40N 25 8 E
Sikkim □, India . . . . **67 F16** 27 50N 88 30 E
Siklós, Hungary . . . . **28 E3** 45 50N 18 19 E
Sil →, Spain **36 C3** 42 27N 7 43W
Silacayoapan, Mexico . . . **119 D5** 17 30N 98 9W
Silale, Lithuania . . . . . . **30 C9** 55 28N 22 12 E
Silandro, Italy . . . . **40 B7** 46 38N 10 46 E
Silawad, India . . . . **68 J6** 21 54N 74 54 E
Silay, Phil. . . . . **61 F5** 10 47N 122 58 E
Silba, Croatia . . . . **41 D11** 44 24N 14 41 E
Silchar, India . . . . **67 G18** 24 49N 92 48 E
Şile, Turkey . . . . **45 E13** 41 10N 29 37 E
Siler City, U.S.A. **115 H6** 35 44N 79 28W
Silgarhi Doti, Nepal . . . . **69 E9** 29 15N 81 0 E
Silghat, India . . . . **67 F18** 26 35N 93 0 E
Sili, Burkina Faso **82 C4** 11 37N 2 30W
Silifke, Turkey . . . . **70 B2** 36 22N 33 58 E
Siliguri = Shiliguri, India **67 F16** 26 45N 88 25 E
Siling Co, China . . . . . . **60 C3** 31 50N 89 20 E
Silistea Nouă, Romania . . **29 F10** 44 23N 25 1 E
Silistra, Bulgaria . . . . . . **45 B11** 44 6N 27 19 E
Silivri, Turkey . . . . **45 E12** 41 4N 28 14 E
Siljan, Sweden . . . . **10 D8** 60 55N 14 45 E
Siljansnäs, Sweden . . . . **10 D8** 60 47N 14 52 E
Silkeborg, Denmark . . . . **11 H3** 56 10N 9 32 E
Silkwood, Australia . . . . **94 B4** 17 45 S 146 2 E
Silla, Spain **39 F4** 39 22N 0 25W
Sillajhuay, Cordillera,
Chile . . . . **124 G5** 19 46 S 68 40W
Sillamäe, Estonia . . . . . **9 G22** 59 24N 27 45 E
Sillé-le-Guillaume,
France **18 D6** 48 10N 0 8W
Silleda, Spain **36 C2** 42 42N 8 14W
Silloth, U.K. **14 C4** 54 52N 3 23W
Síño, Greece . . . . **45 E9** 41 10N 25 53 E
Siloam Springs, U.S.A. . . **113 G7** 36 11N 94 32W
Silopi, Turkey . . . . **73 D10** 37 15N 42 27 E
Silsbee, U.S.A. **113 K7** 30 21N 94 11W
Siluko, Nigeria . . . . **83 D6** 6 35N 5 10 E
Silutė, Lithuania . . . . . . **9 J19** 55 21N 21 33 E
Silvan, Turkey . . . . **73 C9** 38 7N 41 2 E
Silvani, India . . . . **69 H8** 23 18N 78 25 E
Silver City, U.S.A. **109 K9** 32 46N 108 17W
Silver Cr. →, U.S.A. **108 E4** 43 16N 119 13W
Silver Creek, U.S.A. **116 D5** 42 33N 79 10W
Silver L., U.S.A. **110 G6** 38 39N 120 6W
Silver Lake, Calif.,
U.S.A. **111 K10** 35 21N 116 7W
Silver Lake, Oreg.,
U.S.A. **108 E3** 43 8N 121 3W
Silverdalen, Sweden . . . . **11 G9** 57 32N 15 45 E
Silverton, Colo., U.S.A. . . **109 H10** 37 49N 107 40W
Silverton, Tex., U.S.A. . . . **113 H4** 34 28N 101 19W
Silves, Portugal **37 H2** 37 11N 8 26W
Silvi Marina, Italy . . . . . **41 F11** 42 34N 14 5 E
Silvies →, U.S.A. **108 E4** 43 34N 119 2W
Silvretta群, Switz. . . . . . **40 B7** 46 50N 10 6 E
Silwa Bahari, Egypt . . . . **80 C3** 24 45N 32 55 E
Silz, Austria . . . . **26 D3** 47 16N 10 56 E
Simaltala, India . . . . **69 G12** 24 43N 86 33 E
Simanggang = Bandar
Sri Aman, Malaysia . . . **62 D4** 1 15N 111 32 E
Simao, China . . . . **58 F3** 22 47N 101 5 E
Simard, L., Canada **104 C4** 47 40N 78 40W
Şīmareh →, Iran . . . . . . **73 F12** 33 9N 47 41 E
Simav, Turkey . . . . **47 B10** 39 4N 28 58 E
Simav →, Turkey . . . . . **45 F12** 40 23N 28 31 E
Simav Dağları, Turkey . . **47 B10** 39 10N 28 50 E
Simba, Tanzania . . . . . . **86 C4** 2 10 S 37 36 E
Simbach, Germany . . . . . **25 G9** 48 16N 13 2 E
Simbirsk, Russia . . . . . . **34 C9** 54 20N 48 25 E
Simbo, Tanzania . . . . . . **86 C2** 4 51 S 29 41 E
Simcoe, Canada **116 D4** 42 50N 80 20W
Simcoe, L., Canada **116 B5** 44 25N 79 20W
Simdega, India . . . . **69 H11** 22 37N 84 31 E
Simeonovgrad, Bulgaria . **45 D9** 42 1N 25 50 E
Simeria, Romania . . . . . **28 E8** 45 51N 23 1 E
Simeto →, Italy . . . . **43 E8** 37 24N 15 6 E
Simeulue, Indonesia . . . . **62 D1** 2 45N 95 45 E
Simferopol, Ukraine . . . . **33 K8** 44 55N 34 3 E
Sími, Greece . . . . **47 E9** 36 35N 27 50 E
Simi Valley, U.S.A. **111 L8** 34 16N 118 47W
Simien Mts. △, Ethiopia . **81 E4** 13 19N 38 0 E
Simikot, Nepal . . . . **69 E9** 30 0N 81 50 E
Simitli, Bulgaria . . . . . . **44 E7** 41 52N 23 7 E
Simla, India . . . . **68 D7** 31 2N 77 9 E
Simlångsdalen, Sweden . . **11 H7** 56 43N 13 6 E
Şimleu-Silvaniei,
Romania . . . . **28 C7** 47 17N 22 50 E
Simmern, Germany . . . . **25 F3** 49 58N 7 30 E
Simmie, Canada **103 D7** 49 56N 108 6W
Simmler, U.S.A. **111 K7** 35 21N 119 59W
Simnas, Lithuania . . . . . **30 D10** 54 24N 23 39 E
Simo älv = Simojoki →,
Finland . . . . **8 D21** 65 35N 25 1 E
Simojoki →, Finland . . . **8 D21** 65 35N 25 1 E
Simojovel, Mexico **119 D6** 17 12N 92 38W
Simonette →, Canada . . **102 B5** 55 9N 118 15W
Simonstown, S. Africa . . **88 E2** 34 14 S 18 26 E
Simontornya, Hungary . . **28 D3** 46 45N 18 33 E
Simpang Empat,
Malaysia . . . . **65 c** 5 27N 100 29 E
Simplonpass, Switz. . . . . **25 J4** 46 15N 8 3 E
Simplontunnel, Switz. . . . **25 J4** 46 15N 8 7 E
Simpson Desert,
Australia . . . . **94 D2** 25 0 S 137 0 E
Simpson Desert △,
Australia . . . . **94 C2** 25 S 138 21 E
Simpson Pen., Canada . . **101 B11** 68 34N 88 45W
Simpungdong, N. Korea . **57 D15** 40 56N 129 29 E
Simrishamn, Sweden . . . **11 J8** 55 33N 14 22 E
Simsbury, U.S.A. **117 E12** 41 53N 72 48W
Simushir, Ostrov, Russia . **53 E16** 46 50N 152 30 E
Sin Cowe I.,
S. China Sea . . . . **62 C4** 9 53N 114 19 E
Sinabang, Indonesia . . . . **62 D1** 2 30N 96 24 E
Sinadogo, Somali Rep. . . **75 F4** 5 50N 46 0 E
Sinai = Es Sînâ', Egypt . **74 F3** 29 0N 34 0 E
Sinai, Mt. =
Gebel, Egypt . . . . **70 D2** 28 33N 33 59 E
Sinai Peninsula, Egypt . . **50 G7** 29 30N 34 0 E
Sinaia, Romania . . . . . . **29 E10** 45 21N 25 24 E
Sinaloa □, Mexico **118 C3** 25 0N 107 30W
Sinaloa de Leyva,
Mexico **118 B3** 25 50N 108 20W
Sinalunga, Italy . . . . **41 E8** 43 12N 11 44 E
Sinan, China . . . . **58 D7** 27 56N 108 13 E
Sinandrei, Romania . . . . **28 E6** 45 52N 21 13 E
Sinarádhes, Greece . . . . **49 A3** 39 34N 19 51 E
Sincan, Turkey . . . . **72 B5** 39 58N 32 36 E
Sincanlı, Turkey . . . . . . **47 C12** 38 45N 30 15 E
Sincelejo, Colombia **124 B3** 9 18N 75 24W
Sinch'ang, N. Korea . . . . **57 D15** 40 7N 128 28 E
Sinch'ang-ni, N. Korea . . **57 E14** 39 24N 126 8 E
Sinclair, U.S.A. **108 F10** 41 47N 107 7W
Sinclair Mills, Canada . . **102 C4** 54 5N 121 40W

Sinclair's B., U.K. **13 C5** 58 31N 3 5W
Sinclairville, U.S.A. **116 D5** 42 16N 79 16W
Sincorá, Serra do, Brazil **125 F10** 13 30 S 41 0W
Sind, Pakistan .... **68 G3** 26 0N 68 30 E
Sind □, Pakistan .... **68 G3** 26 0N 69 0 E
Sind →,
   Jammu & Kashmir,
   India .... **69 B6** 34 18N 74 45 E
Sind →, Mad. P., India **69 F8** 26 26N 79 13 E
Sind Sagar Doab,
   Pakistan .... **68 D4** 32 0N 71 30 E
Sindal, Denmark .... **11 G4** 57 28N 10 10 E
Sindangan, Phil. .... **61 G5** 8 10N 123 5 E
Sindangbarang,
   Indonesia .... **63 G12** 7 27 S 107 1 E
Sinde, Zambia .... **87 F2** 17 28 S 25 51 E
Sindelfingen, Germany .. **25 G4** 48 42N 9 0 E
Sindh = Sind □, Pakistan **68 G3** 26 0N 69 0 E
Sındırgı, Turkey .... **47 B10** 39 13N 28 10 E
Sindou, Burkina Faso ... **82 C3** 10 35N 5 4W
Sindri, India .... **69 H12** 23 45N 86 42 E
Sine →, Senegal **82 C1** 14 10N 16 28W
Sinelki, Turkey .... **45 E12** 41 14N 26 23 E
Sinelnikove =
   Synelnykove, Ukraine **33 H8** 48 25N 35 30 E
Sinendé, Benin .... **83 C5** 10 20N 2 22 E
Sines, Portugal **37 H2** 37 56N 8 51W
Sines, C. de, Portugal .. **37 H2** 37 58N 8 53W
Sineu, Spain .... **48 B10** 39 38N 3 1 E
Sinfra, Ivory C. **82 D3** 6 35N 5 56W
Sing Buri, Thailand .... **64 E3** 14 53N 100 25 E
Singa, Sudan .... **81 E3** 13 10N 33 57 E
Singapore ■, Asia .... **65 d** 1 17N 103 51 E
Singapore, Straits of,
   Asia .... **65 d** 1 15N 104 0 E
Singapore Changi ✈
   (SIN), Singapore .... **65 M4** 1 23N 103 59 E
Singaraja, Indonesia ... **63 J18** 8 7 S 115 6 E
Singen, Germany .... **25 H4** 47 45N 8 50 E
Singida, Tanzania ...... **86 C3** 4 49 S 34 48 E
Singida □, Tanzania ... **86 D3** 6 0 S 34 30 E
Singitikós Kólpos,
   Greece .... **44 F7** 40 6N 24 0 E
Singkaling Hkamti,
   Burma .... **67 G19** 26 0N 95 39 E
Singkang, Indonesia .... **63 E6** 4 8 S 120 1 E
Singkawang, Indonesia .. **62 D3** 1 0N 108 57 E
Singkep, Indonesia ..... **62 E2** 0 30 S 104 25 E
Singleton, Australia .... **95 E5** 32 33 S 151 0 E
Singleton, Mt., N. Terr.,
   Australia .... **92 D5** 22 0 S 130 46 E
Singleton, Mt.,
   W. Austral., Australia **93 E2** 29 27 S 117 15 E
Singö, Sweden .... **10 D12** 60 12N 18 45 E
Singoli, India .... **68 G6** 25 0N 75 22 E
Singora = Songkhla,
   Thailand .... **65 J3** 7 13N 100 37 E
Singosan, N. Korea ..... **57 E14** 38 52N 127 25 E
Sinhung, N. Korea ..... **57 D14** 40 11N 127 34 E
Siniátsikon, Óros,
   Greece .... **44 F5** 40 6N 21 35 E
Siniscóla, Italy .... **42 B2** 40 34N 9 41 E
Sinj, Croatia .... **41 E13** 43 42N 16 39 E
Sinjai, Indonesia ...... **63 F6** 5 7 S 120 20 E
Sinjar, Iraq .... **70 B4** 36 19N 41 52 E
Sinjār, Iraq .... **80 D4** 18 55N 36 49 E
Sinkat, Sudan .... **80 D4** 18 55N 36 49 E
Sinkiang Uighur =
   Xinjiang Uygur
   Zizhiqu □, China .... **60 B3** 42 0N 86 0 E
Sinmak, N. Korea ...... **57 E14** 38 25N 126 14 E
Sinnai, Italy .... **42 C2** 39 18N 9 13 E
Sinnamary, Fr. Guiana . **125 B8** 5 25N 53 0W
Sinni →, Italy .... **43 B9** 40 8N 16 41 E
Sínnuris, Egypt .... **80 J7** 29 26N 30 31 E
Sinoie, Lacul, Romania . **29 F13** 44 35N 28 50 E
Sinop, Turkey .... **72 A6** 42 1N 35 11 E
Sinor, India .... **68 J5** 21 55N 73 20 E
Sinp'o, N. Korea ...... **57 E15** 40 0N 128 13 E
Sinsheim, Germany ..... **25 F4** 49 15N 8 52 E
Sinsk, Russia .... **53 C13** 61 8N 126 48 E
Sintang, Indonesia ..... **62 D4** 0 5N 111 35 E
Sinton, U.S.A. **113 L6** 28 2N 97 31W
Sintra, Portugal **37 G1** 38 47N 9 25W
Sintra-Cascais △,
   Portugal **37 G1** 38 50N 9 25W
Sinŭiju, N. Korea ...... **57 D13** 40 5N 124 24 E
Sinyukha →, Ukraine .. **33 H6** 48 3N 30 51 E
Sinzig, Germany .... **24 E3** 50 32N 7 14 E
Siocon, Phil. .... **61 H5** 7 40N 122 10 E
Siófok, Hungary .... **28 D3** 46 54N 18 3 E
Sion, Switz. .... **25 J3** 46 14N 7 20 E
Sion Mills, U.K. **12 B4** 54 48N 7 29W
Sioux City, U.S.A. **112 D6** 42 30N 96 24W
Sioux Falls, U.S.A. **112 D6** 43 33N 96 44W
Sioux Lookout, Canada . **104 B1** 50 10N 91 50W
Sioux Narrows, Canada . **103 D10** 49 25N 94 10W
Sipalay, Phil. .... **61 G5** 9 45N 122 24 E
Şipan, Croatia .... **44 D1** 42 45N 17 52 E
Siparia, Trin. & Tob. ... **125 K15** 10 8N 61 31W
Sipil Dağı △, Turkey .. **47 C9** 38 35N 27 30 E
Siping, China .... **57 C13** 43 8N 124 21 E
Sipiwesk L., Canada ... **103 B9** 55 5N 97 35W
Siple, Antarctica ...... **5 D7** 75 0 S 74 0 E
Sípovo, Bos.-H. .... **28 F2** 44 16N 17 6 E
Sipra →, India .... **68 H6** 23 55N 75 28 E
Sipura, Indonesia ...... **62 E1** 2 18 S 99 40 E
Siquia →, Nic. **120 D3** 12 10N 84 20W
Siquijor, Phil. .... **61 G5** 9 12N 123 35 E
Siquirres, Costa Rica .. **120 D3** 10 6N 83 30W
Şır Abu Nu'ayr, U.A.E. **71 E7** 25 20N 54 20 E
Şır Banı Yās, U.A.E. .. **71 E7** 24 19N 52 37 E
Sir Edward Pellew
   Group, Australia .... **94 B2** 15 40 S 137 10 E
Sir Graham Moore Is.,
   Australia .... **92 B4** 13 53 S 126 34 E
Sir James MacBrien,
   Mt., Canada **100 B7** 62 7N 127 41W
Sira →, Norway ...... **9 G12** 58 23N 6 34 E
Siracusa, Italy .... **43 E8** 37 4N 15 17 E
Sirajganj, Bangla. ..... **69 G13** 24 25N 89 47 E
Sirakoro, Mali **82 C3** 12 41N 9 14W
Şiran, Turkey .... **73 B8** 40 11N 39 7 E
Sirasso, Ivory C. **82 D3** 9 16N 6 6W
Sirathu, India .... **69 G9** 25 39N 81 19 E
Şirdān, Iran .... **71 B6** 36 39N 49 12 E
Sirdaryo = Syrdarya →,
   Kazakhstan .... **52 E7** 46 3N 61 0 E
Sire, Ethiopia .... **81 F4** 6 55N 38 10 E
Siren, U.S.A. **112 C8** 45 47N 92 24W
Sirente-Velino △, Italy **40 C7** 42 10N 13 30 E
Sirer, Spain .... **48 C7** 38 56N 1 22 E
Siret, Romania .... **29 C11** 47 55N 26 5 E
Siret →, Romania ..... **29 E12** 45 24N 28 1 E
Sirghāyā, Syria .... **74 B5** 33 51N 36 8 E

Şiria, Romania .... **28 D6** 46 16N 21 38 E
Sirinath □, Thailand ... **65 a** 8 16N 98 17 E
Sirino, Mte., Italy ..... **43 B8** 40 7N 15 50 E
Şırjan, Iran .... **71 D7** 29 30N 55 45 E
Sirmaur, India .... **69 G9** 24 51N 81 23 E
Şırnak, Turkey .... **73 D10** 37 32N 42 28 E
Sírna, Greece .... **47 E8** 36 22N 26 42 E
Sirohi, India .... **68 G5** 24 52N 72 53 E
Sironj, India .... **68 G7** 24 5N 77 39 E
Síros, Greece .... **46 D6** 37 28N 24 57 E
Sirretta Pk., U.S.A. ... **111 K8** 35 56N 118 19W
Sırrı, Iran .... **71 E7** 25 55N 54 32 E
Sirsa, India .... **68 E6** 29 33N 75 4 E
Sirsa →, India .... **69 F8** 26 51N 79 4 E
Siruela, Spain **37 G5** 38 58N 5 3W
Sisak, Croatia .... **41 C13** 45 30N 16 21 E
Sisaket, Thailand ...... **64 E5** 15 8N 104 23 E
Sisante, Spain **39 F2** 39 25N 2 12W
Sisargas, Is., Spain **36 B2** 43 21N 8 50W
Sishen, S. Africa ...... **88 D3** 27 47 S 22 59 E
Sishui, Henan, China .. **56 G7** 34 48N 113 15 E
Sishui, Shandong, China **57 G9** 35 42N 117 18 E
Sisipuk L., Canada **103 B8** 55 45N 101 50W
Sisophon, Cambodia ... **64 F4** 13 38N 102 59 E
Sisseton, U.S.A. **112 C6** 45 40N 97 3W
Sissonne, France ...... **19 C10** 49 34N 3 51 E
Sīstān, Asia .... **71 D9** 30 50N 61 0 E
Sīstān, Daryācheh-ye,
   Iran .... **71 D9** 31 0N 61 0 E
Sīstān va Balūchestān □,
   Iran .... **71 E9** 27 0N 62 0 E
Sisteron, France ...... **21 D9** 44 12N 5 57 E
Sisters, U.S.A. **108 D3** 44 18N 121 33W
Siswa Bazar, India .... **69 F10** 27 9N 83 46 E
Sitakili, Mali **82 C2** 13 7N 11 14W
Sitamarhi, India ...... **69 F11** 26 37N 85 30 E
Sitampiky, Madag. ..... **89 B8** 16 41 S 46 6 E
Sitapur, India .... **69 F9** 27 38N 80 45 E
Siteki, Swaziland ...... **89 D5** 26 32 S 31 58 E
Sitges, Spain .... **38 D6** 41 17N 1 47 E
Sithonía, Greece ...... **44 F7** 40 0N 23 45 E
Sitía, Greece .... **49 D8** 35 13N 26 6 E
Sitka, U.S.A. **102 B1** 57 3N 135 20W
Sitoti, Botswana ...... **88 C3** 23 15 S 23 40 E
Sitra, Egypt .... **80 B2** 28 40N 26 53 E
Sittang Myit →, Burma **67 L20** 17 20N 96 45 E
Sittard, Neths. .... **17 C5** 51 0N 5 52 E
Sittensen, Germany .... **24 B5** 53 17N 9 32 E
Sittingbourne, U.K. .... **15 F8** 51 21N 0 45 E
Sittona, Eritrea .... **81 E4** 14 25N 37 23 E
Sittoung = Sittang
   Myit →, Burma .... **67 L20** 17 20N 96 45 E
Sittwe, Burma .... **67 J18** 20 18N 92 45 E
Situbondo, Indonesia .. **63 G16** 7 42 S 114 0 E
Siuna, Nic. **120 D3** 13 37N 84 45W
Siuri, India .... **69 H12** 23 50N 87 34 E
Sivand, Iran .... **71 D7** 30 5N 52 55 E
Sivas, Turkey .... **70 B3** 39 43N 36 58 E
Sivaslı, Turkey .... **47 C11** 38 31N 29 42 E
Siverek, Turkey .... **70 B3** 37 50N 39 19 E
Sivrihisar, Turkey ..... **72 C4** 39 30N 31 35 E
Sîwa, El Wâhât es, Egypt **80 B2** 29 10N 25 31 E
Sîwa Oasis = Sîwa, El
   Wâhât es, Egypt ... **80 B2** 29 10N 25 30 E
Siwalik Range, Nepal .. **69 F10** 28 0N 83 0 E
Siwan, India .... **69 F11** 26 13N 84 21 E
Siwana, India .... **68 G5** 25 38N 72 25 E
Six Cross Roads,
   Barbados .... **121 g** 13 10N 59 28W
Sixmilebridge, Ireland . **12 D3** 52 44N 8 46W
Sixth Cataract, Sudan . **81 D3** 16 20N 32 42 E
Siyâl, Jazâ'ir, Egypt ... **80 C4** 22 49N 36 12 E
Siyäzän, Azerbaijan ... **35 K9** 41 3N 49 10 E
Siziwang Qi, China .... **56 D6** 41 25N 111 40 E
Sjælland, Denmark .... **11 J5** 55 30N 11 30 E
Sjælland Odde,
   Denmark .... **11 J5** 55 58N 11 24 E
Sjenica, Serbia & M. .. **44 C3** 43 16N 20 0 E
Sjöbo, Sweden .... **11 J7** 55 37N 13 45 E
Sjötofta, Sweden ..... **11 G7** 57 22N 13 17 E
Sjötorp, Sweden ...... **11 F8** 58 50N 14 0 E
Sjumen = Shumen,
   Bulgaria .... **45 C10** 43 18N 26 55 E
Sjuntorp, Sweden ..... **11 F6** 58 12N 12 13 E
Skadarsko Jezero,
   Serbia & M. .... **44 D3** 42 10N 19 20 E
Skadovsk, Ukraine .... **33 J7** 46 17N 32 52 E
Skælskør, Denmark ... **11 J5** 55 15N 11 18 E
Skærbæk, Denmark ... **11 J2** 55 9N 8 45 E
Skaftafell, Iceland **8 D5** 64 1N 17 0W
Skagafjörður, Iceland .. **8 D4** 65 54N 19 35W
Skagastølstindane,
   Norway .... **9 F12** 61 28N 7 52 E
Skagaströnd, Iceland .. **8 D3** 65 50N 20 19W
Skagen, Denmark ..... **11 G4** 57 43N 10 35 E
Skagern, Sweden ..... **10 E8** 59 0N 14 20 E
Skagerrak, Denmark ... **11 G2** 57 30N 9 0 E
Skagit →, U.S.A. **110 B4** 48 23N 122 22W
Skagway, U.S.A. **100 C6** 59 28N 135 19W
Skala-Podilska, Ukraine **29 B11** 48 50N 26 15 E
Skala Podolskaya =
   Skala-Podilska,
   Ukraine .... **29 B11** 48 50N 26 15 E
Skalat, Ukraine .... **33 H3** 49 23N 25 55 E
Skalbmierz, Poland ... **31 H7** 50 20N 20 25 E
Skälderviken, Sweden . **11 H6** 56 22N 12 30 E
Skalica, Slovak Rep. ... **27 C10** 48 50N 17 15 E
Skallingen, Denmark ... **11 J2** 55 32N 8 13 E
Skalni Dol = Kamenyak,
   Bulgaria .... **45 C10** 43 24N 26 57 E
Skanderborg, Denmark **11 H3** 56 2N 9 55 E
Skåne, Sweden ...... **11 J7** 55 59N 13 30 E
Skåne län □, Sweden .. **11 H7** 56 15N 13 30 E
Skaneateles, U.S.A. .. **117 D8** 42 57N 76 26W
Skaneateles L., U.S.A. . **117 D8** 42 51N 76 22W
Skänninge, Sweden ... **11 F9** 58 24N 15 5 E
Skanör med Falsterbo,
   Sweden .... **11 J6** 55 24N 12 50 E
Skantzoúra, Greece ... **46 B6** 39 5N 24 6 E
Skara, Sweden .... **11 F7** 58 25N 13 30 E
Skärblacka, Sweden ... **11 F9** 58 35N 15 54 E
Skardu, Pakistan ..... **69 B6** 35 20N 75 44 E
Skåre, Sweden .... **10 E7** 59 26N 13 30 E
Skärhamn, Sweden ... **11 G5** 57 59N 11 34 E
Skarszewy, Poland ... **30 D5** 54 4N 18 25 E
Skärvången, Sweden .. **10 A8** 63 34N 14 20 E
Skaryszew, Poland .... **31 G8** 51 19N 21 15 E
Skarżysko-Kamienna,
   Poland .... **31 G7** 51 7N 20 52 E
Skattkärr, Sweden .... **10 E7** 59 25N 13 34 E
Skattungbyn, Sweden . **10 C8** 61 10N 14 56 E
Skawina, Poland ...... **31 J6** 49 59N 19 50 E
Skebokvarn, Sweden . **10 E10** 59 7N 16 45 E
Skeena →, Canada ... **102 C2** 54 9N 130 5W
Skeena Mts., Canada .. **102 B3** 56 40N 128 30W

Skegness, U.K. .... **14 D8** 53 9N 0 20 E
Skeldon, Guyana **124 B7** 5 55N 57 20W
Skeleton Coast, Namibia **85 H2** 20 0 S 13 0 E
Skeleton Coast △,
   Namibia .... **88 C1** 20 0 S 13 20 E
Skellefteå, Sweden .... **8 D19** 64 45N 20 50 E
Skelleftealven →,
   Sweden .... **8 D19** 64 45N 21 10 E
Skelleftehamn, Sweden **8 D19** 64 40N 21 9 E
Skender Vakuf, Bos.-H. **28 F2** 44 29N 17 22 E
Skerries, The, U.K. **14 D3** 53 25N 4 36W
Skhidnytsya, Ukraine . **31 J10** 49 13N 23 20 E
Skhíza, Greece .... **46 E3** 36 41N 21 40 E
Skhoinoúsa, Greece .. **47 E7** 36 53N 25 31 E
Ski, Norway .... **9 G14** 59 43N 10 52 E
Skíathos, Greece ..... **46 B5** 39 12N 23 30 E
Skibbereen, Ireland ... **12 E2** 51 33N 9 16W
Skiddaw, U.K. **14 C4** 54 39N 3 9W
Skidegate, Canada **102 C2** 53 15N 132 1W
Skídhra, Greece ...... **44 F6** 40 46N 22 10 E
Skien, Norway .... **9 G13** 59 12N 9 35 E
Skierniewice, Poland .. **31 G7** 51 58N 20 10 E
Skikda, Algeria ...... **78 A7** 36 50N 6 58 E
Skillingaryd, Sweden .. **11 G8** 57 27N 14 5 E
Skillinge, Sweden .... **11 J8** 55 30N 14 16 E
Skilloura, Cyprus ..... **49 D12** 35 14N 33 10 E
Skinári, Ákra, Greece . **46 D2** 37 56N 20 42 E
Skinnskatteberg, Sweden **10 E9** 59 50N 15 42 E
Skipton, U.K. **14 D5** 53 58N 2 3W
Skirmish Pt., Australia **94 A1** 11 59 S 134 17 E
Skiropoúla, Greece ... **46 C6** 38 50N 24 21 E
Skíros, Greece .... **46 C6** 38 55N 24 34 E
Skivarp, Sweden ..... **11 J7** 55 26N 13 34 E
Skive, Denmark ...... **11 H3** 56 33N 9 2 E
Skjálfandafljót →,
   Iceland **8 D5** 65 59N 17 25W
Skjálfandi, Iceland ... **8 C5** 66 5N 17 30W
Skjern, Denmark ..... **11 J2** 55 57N 8 30 E
Skoczów, Poland ..... **31 J5** 49 49N 18 45 E
Škofja Loka, Slovenia . **41 B11** 46 9N 14 19 E
Skoghall, Sweden .... **10 E7** 59 20N 13 30 E
Skogstorp, Sweden ... **10 E10** 59 12N 16 29 E
Skoki, Poland .... **31 F4** 52 40N 17 11 E
Skole, Ukraine .... **33 H2** 49 3N 23 30 E
Skópelos, Greece ..... **46 B5** 39 9N 23 47 E
Skopí, Greece .... **49 D8** 35 11N 26 2 E
Skopin, Russia .... **32 F10** 53 55N 39 32 E
Skopje, Macedonia ... **44 D5** 42 1N 21 26 E
Skopje ✈ (SKP),
   Macedonia .... **44 E5** 41 59N 21 29 E
Skórcz, Poland .... **30 E5** 53 47N 18 30 E
Skørping, Denmark ... **11 H3** 56 50N 9 53 E
Skövde, Sweden ...... **11 F7** 58 24N 13 50 E
Skovorodino, Russia .. **53 D13** 54 0N 124 0 E
Skowhegan, U.S.A. ... **115 C11** 44 46N 69 43W
Skradin, Croatia ...... **41 E12** 43 52N 15 53 E
Skrea, Sweden .... **11 H6** 56 53N 12 34 E
Skrunda, Latvia ...... **30 B9** 56 41N 22 1 E
Skrwa →, Poland .... **31 F6** 52 35N 19 32 E
Skuleskogen △, Sweden **10 A12** 63 6N 18 30 E
Skull, Ireland **12 E2** 51 32N 9 34W
Skultorp, Sweden .... **11 F7** 58 24N 13 51 E
Skultuna, Sweden .... **10 E10** 59 43N 16 25 E
Skunk →, U.S.A. **112 E9** 40 42N 91 7W
Skuodas, Lithuania ... **9 H19** 56 16N 21 33 E
Skurup, Sweden ...... **11 J7** 55 28N 13 30 E
Skutskär, Sweden .... **10 D11** 60 37N 17 25 E
Skvyra, Ukraine ...... **33 H5** 49 44N 29 40 E
Skwierzyna, Poland .. **31 F2** 52 33N 15 30 E
Skye, U.K. **13 D2** 57 15N 6 10W
Skykomish, U.S.A. ... **108 C3** 47 42N 121 22W
Skyros = Skíros, Greece **46 C6** 38 55N 24 34 E
Skyttorp, Sweden .... **10 D11** 60 5N 17 44 E
Slade Pt., Australia ... **94 K7** 21 5 S 149 13 E
Slættaratindur, Faroe Is. **8 E9** 62 18N 7 1W
Slagelse, Denmark .... **11 J5** 55 23N 11 19 E
Slamet, Indonesia .... **63 G13** 7 16 S 109 8 E
Slaney →, Ireland ... **12 D5** 52 26N 6 33W
Slangberge, S. Africa .. **88 E3** 31 32 S 20 48 E
Slánic, Romania ...... **29 E10** 45 14N 25 58 E
Slano, Croatia .... **44 D1** 42 48N 17 53 E
Slantsy, Russia ...... **32 C5** 59 7N 28 5 E
Slaný, Czech Rep. .... **26 A7** 50 13N 14 6 E
Śląskie □, Poland .... **31 H6** 50 30N 19 0 E
Slátbaken, Sweden ... **11 F10** 58 25N 16 45 E
Slate Is., Canada **104 C2** 48 40N 87 0W
Slatina, Croatia ...... **28 E2** 45 42N 17 45 E
Slatina, Romania ..... **29 F9** 44 28N 24 22 E
Slatina Timiş, Romania **28 E7** 45 15N 22 17 E
Slatington, U.S.A. **117 F9** 40 45N 75 37W
Slaton, U.S.A. **113 J4** 33 26N 101 39W
Slave →, Canada **102 A6** 61 18N 113 39W
Slave Coast, W. Afr. .. **82 D5** 6 0N 2 30 E
Slave Lake, Canada ... **102 B6** 55 17N 114 43W
Slave Pt., Canada **102 A5** 61 11N 115 56W
Slavgorod, Russia .... **52 D8** 53 1N 78 37 E
Slavinja, Serbia & M. . **44 C6** 43 9N 22 50 E
Slavkov u Brna,
   Czech Rep. .... **27 B9** 49 10N 16 52 E
Slavkovský Les △,
   Czech Rep. .... **26 A5** 50 5N 12 44 E
Slavonija, Europe ..... **28 E2** 45 20N 17 40 E
Slavonski Brod, Croatia **28 E3** 45 11N 18 1 E
Slavsk, Russia .... **30 C8** 55 3N 21 41 E
Slavuta, Ukraine ..... **33 G4** 50 15N 27 2 E
Slavyanka, Russia .... **54 C5** 42 53N 131 21 E
Slavyanovo, Bulgaria . **45 C8** 43 28N 24 52 E
Slavyansk = Slovyansk,
   Ukraine .... **33 H9** 48 55N 37 36 E
Slavyansk-na-Kubani,
   Russia .... **33 K10** 45 15N 38 11 E
Sława, Poland .... **31 G3** 51 52N 16 2 E
Slawharad, Belarus ... **32 F6** 53 27N 31 0 E
Sławno, Poland ...... **30 D3** 54 20N 16 41 E
Sławoborze, Poland .. **30 E2** 53 55N 15 42 E
Sleaford, U.K. **14 D7** 53 0N 0 24W
Sleaford B., Australia . **95 E2** 34 55 S 135 45 E
Sleat, Sd. of, U.K. **13 D3** 57 5N 5 47W
Sleeper Is., Canada ... **101 C11** 58 30N 81 0W
Sleeping Bear Dunes △,
   U.S.A. **114 C2** 44 50N 86 5W
Sleepy Eye, U.S.A. ... **112 C7** 44 18N 94 43W
Slemon L., Canada ... **102 A5** 63 13N 116 4W
Ślesin, Poland .... **31 F5** 52 22N 18 14 E
Slide Mt., U.S.A. **117 E10** 42 0N 74 25W
Slidell, U.S.A. **113 K10** 30 17N 89 47W
Sliema, Malta .... **49 D2** 35 55N 14 30 E
Slieve Aughty, Ireland **12 C3** 53 4N 8 30W
Slieve Bloom, Ireland . **12 C4** 53 4N 7 40W
Slieve Donard, U.K. .. **12 B6** 54 11N 5 55W
Slieve Gamph, Ireland **12 B3** 54 6N 9 0W
Slieve Gullion, U.K. .. **12 B5** 54 7N 6 26W
Slieve League, Ireland **12 B3** 54 40N 8 42W
Slieve Mish, Ireland .. **12 D2** 52 12N 9 50W

Slievenamon, Ireland . **12 D4** 52 25N 7 34W
Sligeach = Sligo, Ireland **12 B3** 54 16N 8 28W
Sligo, Ireland **12 B3** 54 16N 8 28W
Sligo, U.S.A. **116 E5** 41 6N 79 29W
Sligo □, Ireland **12 B3** 54 8N 8 42W
Sligo B., Ireland **12 B3** 54 18N 8 40W
Slippery Rock, U.S.A. **116 E4** 41 3N 80 3W
Slite, Sweden .... **11 G12** 57 42N 18 48 E
Šliteres, Latvia ...... **30 A9** 57 41N 22 21 E
Sliven, Bulgaria ...... **45 D10** 42 42N 26 19 E
Slivnitsa, Bulgaria .... **44 D7** 42 50N 23 2 E
Sljeme, Croatia ...... **41 C12** 45 57N 15 58 E
Sloan, U.S.A. **111 K11** 35 57N 115 13W
Sloansville, U.S.A. ... **117 D10** 42 45N 74 22W
Slobidka, Ukraine .... **29 D14** 47 54N 29 15 E
Slobozia, Argeş,
   Romania .... **29 F10** 44 30N 25 14 E
Slobozia, Ialomiţa,
   Romania .... **29 F12** 44 34N 27 23 E
Slocan, Canada **102 D5** 49 48N 117 28W
Słomniki, Poland ..... **31 H7** 50 16N 20 4 E
Slonim, Belarus ...... **33 F3** 53 4N 25 19 E
Slough, U.K. **15 F7** 51 30N 0 36W
Slough □, U.K. **15 F7** 51 30N 0 36W
Sloughhouse, U.S.A. . **110 G5** 38 26N 121 12W
Slovak Rep. ■, Europe **27 C13** 48 30N 20 0 E
Slovakia = Slovak
   Rep. ■, Europe .... **27 C13** 48 30N 20 0 E
Slovakian Ore Mts. =
   Slovenské Rudohorie,
   Slovak Rep. .... **27 C12** 48 45N 20 0 E
Slovenia ■, Europe ... **41 C11** 45 58N 14 30 E
Slovenia = Slovenia ■,
   Europe .... **41 C11** 45 58N 14 30 E
Slovenj Gradec, Slovenia **41 B12** 46 31N 15 5 E
Slovenska Bistrica,
   Slovenia .... **41 B12** 46 24N 15 35 E
Slovenské Konjice,
   Slovenia .... **41 B12** 46 20N 15 28 E
Slovenské Rudohorie,
   Slovak Rep. .... **27 C12** 48 45N 20 0 E
Slovenský Raj △,
   Slovak Rep. .... **27 C13** 48 55N 20 25 E
Slovyansk, Ukraine ... **33 H9** 48 55N 37 36 E
Słowiński □, Poland .. **30 D4** 54 43N 17 26 E
Słubice, Poland ...... **31 F1** 52 22N 14 35 E
Sluch →, Ukraine .... **33 G4** 51 37N 26 38 E
Sluis, Neths. .... **17 C3** 51 18N 3 23 E
Slŭnchev Bryag,
   Bulgaria .... **45 D11** 42 40N 27 41 E
Slunj, Croatia .... **41 C12** 45 6N 15 33 E
Słupca, Poland .... **31 F4** 52 15N 17 52 E
Słupia →, Poland .... **30 D4** 54 30N 16 51 E
Słupsk, Poland .... **30 D4** 54 30N 17 3 E
Slurry, S. Africa ...... **88 D4** 25 49 S 25 42 E
Slutsk, Belarus ...... **33 F4** 53 2N 27 31 E
Slyne Hd., Ireland ... **12 C1** 53 25N 10 10W
Slyudyanka, Russia ... **53 D11** 51 40N 103 40 E
Słmåland, Sweden .... **11 G9** 57 15N 15 25 E
Slmålandsfarvandet,
   Denmark .... **11 J5** 55 10N 11 20 E
Słmålandsstenar, Sweden **11 G7** 57 10N 13 25 E
Smalltree L., Canada .. **103 A8** 61 0N 105 0W
Smallwood Res., Canada **105 B7** 54 5N 64 30W
Smarhon, Belarus .... **32 E4** 54 20N 26 24 E
Smarje, Slovenia ..... **41 B12** 46 15N 15 34 E
Smartt Syndicate Dam,
   S. Africa .... **88 E3** 30 45 S 23 10 E
Smartville, U.S.A. **110 F5** 39 13N 121 18W
Smeaton, Canada **103 C8** 53 30N 104 49W
Smederevo, Serbia & M. **44 B4** 44 40N 20 57 E
Smederevska Palanka,
   Serbia & M. .... **44 B4** 44 22N 20 58 E
Smedjebacken, Sweden **10 D9** 60 8N 15 25 E
Smela = Smila, Ukraine **33 H6** 49 30N 31 58 E
Smerwick Harbour,
   Ireland **12 D1** 52 12N 10 23W
Smethport, U.S.A. **116 E6** 41 49N 78 27W
Smidovich, Russia .... **53 E14** 48 36N 133 49 E
Šmigiel, Poland ...... **31 F3** 52 1N 16 32 E
Smiley, Canada **103 C7** 51 38N 109 29W
Smith, Canada **102 B6** 55 10N 114 0W
Smith Center, U.S.A. . **112 F5** 39 47N 98 47W
Smith River △, U.S.A. **108 F2** 41 55N 124 0W
Smith Sd., N. Amer. .. **4 B4** 78 25N 74 0W
Smithburne →,
   Australia .... **94 B3** 17 3 S 140 57 E
Smithers, Canada **102 C3** 54 45N 127 10W
Smithfield, S. Africa .. **89 E4** 30 9 S 26 30 E
Smithfield, N.C., U.S.A. **115 H6** 35 31N 78 21W
Smithfield, Utah, U.S.A. **108 F8** 41 50N 111 50W
Smiths Falls, Canada .. **117 B9** 44 55N 76 0W
Smithton, Australia ... **95 G4** 40 53 S 145 6 E
Smithton, Canada **116 C5** 43 6N 79 33W
Smithville, U.S.A. **113 K6** 30 1N 97 10W
Smoky →, Canada ... **102 B5** 56 10N 117 21W
Smoky Bay, Australia . **95 E1** 32 22 S 134 13 E
Smoky Hill →, U.S.A. **112 F6** 39 4N 96 48W
Smoky Hills, U.S.A. .. **112 F5** 39 15N 99 30W
Smoky Lake, Canada .. **102 C6** 54 10N 112 30W
Smøla, Norway ...... **8 E13** 63 23N 8 3 E
Smolensk, Russia ..... **32 E7** 54 45N 32 5 E
Smolikas, Óros, Greece **44 F4** 40 9N 20 58 E
Smolník, Slovak Rep. . **27 C13** 48 44N 20 44 E
Smolyan, Bulgaria .... **45 E8** 41 36N 24 38 E
Smooth Rock Falls,
   Canada **104 C3** 49 17N 81 37W
Smoothstone L., Canada **103 C7** 54 40N 106 50W
Smorgon = Smarhon,
   Belarus .... **32 E4** 54 20N 26 24 E
Smotrych →, Ukraine **29 B11** 48 34N 26 39 E
Smulţi, Romania ..... **29 E12** 45 57N 27 44 E
Smyadovo, Bulgaria .. **45 C11** 43 2N 27 1 E
Smygehamn, Sweden . **11 J7** 55 21N 13 22 E
Smyrna = İzmir, Turkey **47 C9** 38 25N 27 8 E
Smyrna, U.S.A. **114 F8** 39 18N 75 36W
Snæfell, Iceland **8 D6** 64 48N 15 34W
Snaefell, U.K. **14 C3** 54 16N 4 27W
Snæfellsjökull, Iceland **8 D2** 64 49N 23 46W
Snake →, U.S.A. **108 C4** 46 12N 119 2W
Snake I., Australia ... **95 F4** 38 47 S 146 33 E
Snake Range, U.S.A. . **108 G6** 39 0N 114 20W
Snake River Plain,
   U.S.A. **108 E7** 42 50N 114 0W
Snåsavatnet, Norway . **8 D14** 64 12N 12 0 E
Sneads, U.S.A. **115 K3** 35 17N 85 10W
Sneek, Neths. .... **17 A5** 53 2N 5 40 E
Sneeuberge, S. Africa . **88 E3** 31 46 S 24 20 E
Snejbjerg, Denmark .. **11 H2** 56 8N 8 54 E
Snelling, U.S.A. **110 H6** 37 31N 120 26W
Snezhnoye, Ukraine .. **33 J10** 48 0N 38 58 E
Snežnik, Slovenia .... **41 C11** 45 36N 14 35 E
Śniadowo, Poland ... **31 E8** 53 2N 21 0 E

Śniardwy, Jezioro,
   Poland .... **30 E8** 53 48N 21 50 E
Śnieżka, Europe ..... **26 A8** 50 44N 15 44 E
Snigirevka = Snihurivka,
   Ukraine .... **33 J7** 47 2N 32 49 E
Snihurivka, Ukraine .. **33 J7** 47 2N 32 49 E
Snina, Slovak Rep. .... **27 C15** 48 58N 22 9 E
Snizort, L., U.K. **13 D2** 57 33N 6 28W
Snøhetta, Norway .... **9 E13** 62 19N 9 16 E
Snohomish, U.S.A. ... **110 C4** 47 55N 122 6W
Snoul, Cambodia ..... **65 F6** 12 4N 106 26 E
Snow Hill, U.S.A. **114 F8** 38 11N 75 24W
Snow Lake, Canada .. **103 C8** 54 52N 100 3W
Snow Mt., Calif., U.S.A. **110 F4** 39 23N 122 45W
Snow Mt., Maine, U.S.A. **117 A14** 45 18N 70 48W
Snow Shoe, U.S.A. ... **116 E7** 41 2N 77 57W
Snowbird L., Canada . **103 A8** 60 45N 103 0W
Snowdon, U.K. **14 D3** 53 4N 4 5W
Snowdonia △, U.K. ... **14 D4** 53 7N 3 59W
Snowdrift = Łutselk'e,
   Canada **103 A6** 62 24N 110 44W
Snowdrift →, Canada **103 A6** 62 24N 110 44W
Snowflake, U.S.A. **109 J8** 34 30N 110 5W
Snowshoe Pk., U.S.A. **108 B6** 48 13N 115 41W
Snowtown, Australia . **95 E2** 33 46 S 138 14 E
Snowville, U.S.A. **108 F7** 41 58N 112 43W
Snowy →, Australia .. **95 F4** 37 46 S 148 30 E
Snowy Mt., U.S.A. ... **117 C10** 43 42N 74 23W
Snowy Mts., Australia **95 F4** 36 30 S 148 20 E
Snug Corner, Bahamas **121 B5** 22 33N 73 52W
Snyatyn, Ukraine ..... **29 B10** 48 27N 25 38 E
Snyder, Okla., U.S.A. . **113 H5** 34 40N 98 57W
Snyder, Tex., U.S.A. .. **113 J4** 32 44N 100 55W
Soahanina, Madag. ... **89 B7** 18 42 S 44 13 E
Soalala, Madag. ...... **89 B8** 16 6 S 45 20 E
Soaloka, Madag. ..... **89 B8** 18 32 S 45 15 E
Soamanonga, Madag. . **89 C7** 23 52 S 44 47 E
Soan →, Pakistan .... **68 C4** 33 1N 71 44 E
Soanierana-Ivongo,
   Madag. .... **89 B8** 16 55 S 49 35 E
Soanindraniny, Madag. **89 B8** 19 54 S 47 14 E
Şoarş, Romania ...... **29 E9** 45 56N 24 55 E
Soavina, Madag. ..... **89 C8** 20 23 S 46 56 E
Soavinandriana, Madag. **89 B8** 19 9 S 46 45 E
Sob →, Ukraine ..... **29 B14** 48 40N 29 15 E
Soba, Nigeria .... **83 C6** 10 58N 8 4 E
Sobat, Nahr →, Sudan **81 F3** 9 22N 31 33 E
Soběslav, Czech Rep. . **26 B7** 49 16N 14 45 E
Sobhapur, India ...... **68 H8** 22 47N 78 17 E
Sobinka, Russia ...... **32 E11** 56 0N 40 0 E
Sobótka, Poland ...... **31 H3** 50 54N 16 44 E
Sobra, Croatia .... **41 F14** 42 44N 17 34 E
Sobradinho, Reprêsa de,
   Brazil .... **125 E10** 9 30 S 42 0W
Sobral, Brazil .... **125 D10** 3 50 S 40 20W
Sobrance, Slovak Rep. **27 C15** 48 45N 22 11 E
Sobreira Formosa,
   Portugal **36 F3** 39 46N 7 51W
Soc Giang, Vietnam .. **58 F6** 22 54N 106 1 E
Soc Trang, Vietnam .. **65 H5** 9 37N 105 50 E
Soča →, Europe ..... **26 E6** 46 20N 13 40 E
Socastee, U.S.A. **115 J6** 33 41N 79 1W
Sochaczew, Poland .. **31 F7** 52 15N 20 13 E
Soch'e = Shache, China **60 C2** 38 20N 77 10 E
Sochi, Russia .... **35 J4** 43 35N 39 40 E
Société, Is. de la,
   French Polynesia ... **97 J12** 17 0 S 151 0W
Society Is. = Société, Is.
   de la,
   French Polynesia ... **97 J12** 17 0 S 151 0W
Socompa, Portezuelo de,
   Chile .... **126 A2** 24 27 S 68 18W
Socorro, N. Mex., U.S.A. **109 J10** 34 4N 106 54W
Socorro, Tex., U.S.A. . **109 L10** 31 39N 106 18W
Socorro, I., Mexico ... **118 D2** 18 45N 110 58W
Socotra, Yemen ...... **75 E5** 12 30N 54 0 E
Socovos, Spain **39 G3** 38 20N 1 58W
Socuéllamos, Spain .. **39 F2** 39 16N 2 47W
Soda L., U.S.A. **109 J5** 35 10N 116 4W
Soda Plains, India .... **69 B8** 35 30N 79 0 E
Soda Springs, U.S.A. . **108 E8** 42 39N 111 36W
Sodankylä, Finland ... **8 C22** 67 29N 26 40 E
Soddy-Daisy, U.S.A. . **115 H3** 35 17N 85 10W
Söderåsen, Sweden .. **10 C10** 61 16N 16 55 E
Söderbärke, Sweden . **10 D9** 60 5N 15 33 E
Söderfors, Sweden ... **10 D11** 60 23N 17 25 E
Söderhamn, Sweden . **10 C11** 61 18N 17 10 E
Söderköping, Sweden . **11 F10** 58 31N 16 20 E
Södermanland →,
   Sweden .... **9 G17** 58 56N 16 55 E
Södermanlands län □,
   Sweden .... **10 E10** 59 10N 16 30 E
Södertälje, Sweden ... **10 E11** 59 12N 17 39 E
Sodiri, Sudan .... **81 E2** 14 27N 29 0 E
Sodo, Ethiopia .... **81 F4** 7 0N 37 41 E
Södra Dellen, Sweden **10 C10** 61 48N 16 43 E
Södra Finnskoga,
   Sweden .... **10 D6** 60 42N 12 34 E
Södra Sandby, Sweden **11 J7** 55 43N 13 21 E
Södra Ulvön, Sweden **10 B12** 62 59N 18 38 E
Södra Vi, Sweden .... **11 G9** 57 45N 15 45 E
Sodražica, Slovenia .. **41 C11** 45 45N 14 39 E
Sodus, U.S.A. **116 C7** 43 14N 77 4W
Sodwana Bay △,
   S. Africa .... **89 D5** 27 35 S 32 43 E
Soekmekaar, S. Africa **89 C4** 23 30 S 29 55 E
Soest, Germany ...... **24 D4** 51 34N 8 7 E
Soest, Neths. .... **17 B5** 52 9N 5 19 E
Sofádhes, Greece .... **46 B4** 39 20N 22 4 E
Sofala □, Mozam. .... **89 B5** 19 30 S 34 30 E
Sofia = Sofiya, Bulgaria **44 D7** 42 45N 23 20 E
Sofia →, Madag. ..... **89 B8** 15 27 S 47 23 E
Sofievka, Ukraine .... **33 H7** 48 5N 33 55 E
Sofikón, Greece ...... **46 D5** 37 47N 23 3 E
Sofiya, Bulgaria ...... **44 D7** 42 45N 23 20 E
Sofiya □, Bulgaria .... **44 D7** 42 15N 23 20 E
Sofiya ✈ (SOF),
   Bulgaria .... **44 D7** 42 46N 23 28 E
Sōfu-Gan, Japan ..... **55 K10** 29 49N 140 21 E
Sogakofe, Ghana ..... **83 D5** 6 2N 0 39 E
Sogamoso, Colombia . **124 B4** 5 43N 72 56W
Sogār, Iran .... **71 E8** 25 53N 58 6 E
Sögel, Germany ...... **24 C3** 52 50N 7 31 E
Sogndalsfjøra, Norway **9 F12** 61 14N 7 5 E
Søgne, Norway ...... **9 G12** 58 5N 7 48 E
Sognefjorden, Norway **9 F11** 61 10N 5 50 E
Söğüt, Bilecik, Turkey **47 A12** 40 2N 30 11 E
Söğüt, Burdur, Turkey **47 D11** 37 2N 29 22 E
Söğütlü, Turkey ...... **47 D11** 37 50N 29 55 E
Soh, Iran .... **71 C6** 33 26N 51 27 E
Sohâg, Egypt .... **80 B3** 26 33N 31 43 E
Sohagpur, India ...... **68 H8** 22 42N 78 12 E
Sohori, N. Korea ..... **57 D15** 40 7N 128 23 E
Soignies, Belgium .... **17 D4** 50 35N 4 5 E

Soin, Burkina Faso 82 C4 12 47N 3 50W
Soira, Eritrea .... 81 E4 14 45N 39 30 E
Soissons, France ..... 19 C10 49 25N 3 19 E
Sōja, Japan .... 55 G6 34 40N 133 45 E
Sojat, India .... 68 G5 25 55N 73 45 E
Sok →, Russia ...... 34 D10 53 24N 50 8 E
Sokal, Ukraine ...... 33 G3 50 31N 24 15 E
Söke, Turkey .... 47 D9 37 48N 27 28 E
Sokelo, Dem. Rep. of
   the Congo .... 87 D1 9 55 S 24 36 E
Sokhós, Greece ...... 44 F7 40 48N 23 22 E
Sokhumi, Georgia .... 35 J5 43 0N 41 0 E
Soko Banja, Serbia & M. 44 C5 43 40N 21 51 E
Sokodé, Togo .... 83 D5 9 0N 1 11 E
Sokol, Russia .... 32 C11 59 30N 40 5 E
Sokolac, Bos.-H. ..... 28 G3 43 56N 18 48 E
Sokółka, Poland ..... 30 E10 53 25N 23 30 E
Sokolo, Ségou, Mali .. 82 C3 14 53N 6 8W
Sokolo, Sikasso, Mali . 82 C3 10 55N 6 0 E
Sokoto □, Nigeria .... 83 C5 11 20N 4 10 E
Sokoto →, Nigeria ... 83 C5 11 20N 4 10 E
Sokyrnytsya, Ukraine . 29 B8 48 7N 23 23 E
Sokyryany, Ukraine ... 29 B12 48 27N 27 25 E
Sol Iletsk, Russia .... 52 D6 51 10N 55 0 E
Sola →, Poland ..... 31 H6 50 4N 19 15 E
Solai, Kenya .... 86 B4 0 2N 36 12 E
Solan, India .... 68 D7 30 55N 77 7 E
Solano, Phil. .... 61 C4 16 31N 121 15 E
Solapur, India ...... 66 L9 17 43N 75 56 E
Solca, Romania ...... 29 C10 47 40N 25 50 E
Solda Gölü, Turkey ... 47 D11 37 33N 29 42 E
Soldăneşti, Moldova .. 29 C13 47 49N 28 48 E
Soldeu, Andorra ..... 38 C6 42 35N 1 40 E
Soldotna, U.S.A. 100 B4 60 29N 151 3W
Soléa, Cyprus .... 49 D12 35 5N 33 4 E
Solec Kujawski, Poland 31 E5 53 5N 18 14 E
Soledad, Colombia ... 124 A4 10 55N 74 46W
Soledad, U.S.A. 110 J5 36 26N 121 20W
Soledad, Venezuela ... 124 B6 8 10N 63 34W
Solent, The, U.K. 15 G6 50 45N 1 25W
Solenzara, France .... 21 G13 41 53N 9 23 E
Solesmes, France .... 19 B10 50 10N 3 30 E
Solfonn, Norway ..... 9 F12 60 2N 6 57 E
Solhan, Turkey ...... 70 B4 38 57N 41 3 E
Soligorsk = Salihorsk,
   Belarus .... 33 F4 52 51N 27 27 E
Solihull, U.K. 15 E6 52 26N 1 47W
Solikamsk, Russia .... 52 D6 59 38N 56 50 E
Solila, Madag. ...... 89 C8 21 25 S 46 37 E
Solimões =
   Amazonas →,
   S. Amer. .... 125 D9 0 5 S 50 0W
Solin, Croatia .... 41 E13 43 33N 16 30 E
Solingen, Germany ... 24 D3 51 10N 7 5 E
Sollebrunn, Sweden .. 11 F6 58 8N 12 32 E
Sollefteå, Sweden .... 10 A11 63 12N 17 20 E
Sollentuna, Sweden ... 10 E11 59 26N 17 56 E
Sóller, Spain .... 48 B9 39 46N 2 43 E
Sollerön, Sweden .... 10 D8 60 55N 14 37 E
Solling, Germany .... 24 D5 51 46N 9 38 E
Solling-Vogler △,
   Germany .... 24 D5 51 45N 9 32 E
Solnechnogorsk, Russia 32 D9 56 10N 36 57 E
Solo →, Indonesia ... 63 G15 6 47 S 112 22 E
Solofra, Italy .... 43 B7 40 50N 14 51 E
Sologne, France ..... 19 E8 47 40N 1 45 E
Solok, Indonesia .... 62 E2 0 45 S 100 40 E
Sololá, Guatemala ... 120 D1 14 49N 91 10W
Solomon, N. Fork →,
   U.S.A. 112 F5 39 29N 98 26W
Solomon, S. Fork →,
   U.S.A. 112 F5 39 25N 99 12W
Solomon Is. ■, Pac. Oc. 96 H7 6 0 S 155 0 E
Solon, China .... 60 B7 46 32N 121 10 E
Solon Springs, U.S.A. . 112 B9 46 22N 91 49W
Solor, Indonesia ..... 63 F6 8 27 S 123 0 E
Solotcha, Russia ..... 32 E10 54 48N 39 53 E
Solothurn, Switz. .... 25 H3 47 13N 7 32 E
Solothurn □, Switz. .. 25 H3 47 18N 7 40 E
Solotvyn, Ukraine .... 29 B9 48 42N 24 25 E
Solsona, Spain ...... 38 C6 42 0N 1 31 E
Solt, Hungary .... 28 D4 46 45N 19 1 E
Şolta, Croatia .... 41 E13 43 24N 16 15 E
Solţānābād, Khorāsān,
   Iran .... 71 C8 34 13N 59 58 E
Solţānābād, Khorāsān,
   Iran .... 71 B8 36 29N 58 5 E
Soltau, Germany .... 24 C5 52 59N 9 50 E
Soltsy, Russia .... 32 C6 58 10N 30 30 E
Solunska Glava,
   Macedonia .... 44 E5 41 44N 21 31 E
Solvang, U.S.A. 111 L6 34 36N 120 8W
Solvay, U.S.A. 117 C8 43 3N 76 13W
Sölvesborg, Sweden .. 11 H8 56 5N 14 35 E
Solway Firth, U.K. ... 14 C4 54 49N 3 35W
Solwezi, Zambia ..... 87 E2 12 11 S 26 21 E
Sōma, Japan .... 54 F10 37 40N 140 50 E
Soma, Turkey .... 47 B9 39 10N 27 35 E
Somabhula, Zimbabwe 89 B4 19 42 S 29 40 E
Somali Pen., Africa .. 76 F8 7 0N 46 0 E
Somali Rep. ■, Africa 75 F4 7 0N 47 0 E
Somalia = Somali
   Rep. ■, Africa .... 75 F4 7 0N 47 0 E
Sombernon, France .. 19 E11 47 20N 4 40 E
Sombor, Serbia & M. . 28 E4 45 46N 19 9 E
Sombra, Canada 116 D2 42 43N 82 29W
Sombrerete, Mexico .. 118 C4 23 40N 103 40W
Sombrero, Anguilla .. 121 C7 18 37N 63 30W
Somcuta Mare, Romania 29 C8 47 31N 23 33 E
Somdari, India ...... 68 G5 25 47N 72 38 E
Someiro □, Spain 36 B4 43 5N 5 50W
Somers, U.S.A. 108 B6 48 5N 114 13W
Somerset, Ky., U.S.A. . 114 G3 37 5N 84 36W
Somerset, Mass., U.S.A. 117 E13 41 47N 71 8W
Somerset □, U.K. 15 F5 51 9N 3 0W
Somerset East, S. Africa 88 E4 32 42 S 25 35 E
Somerset I., Canada .. 100 A10 73 30N 93 0W
Somerset West, S. Africa 88 E2 34 8 S 18 50 E
Somersworth, U.S.A. . 117 C14 43 16N 70 52W
Somerton, U.S.A. 109 K6 32 36N 114 43W
Somerville, U.S.A. ... 117 F10 40 35N 74 38W
Someş →, Romania .. 28 C7 47 49N 22 43 E
Someşul Mare →,
   Romania .... 29 C8 47 9N 23 55 E
Somme □, France .... 19 C9 49 57N 2 20 E
Somme →, France ... 19 B8 50 11N 1 38 E
Somme, B. de la, France 18 B8 50 14N 1 33 E
Sommen, Jönköping,
   Sweden .... 11 F8 58 12N 14 58 E

Sommen, Östergötland,
   Sweden .... 11 F9 58 0N 15 15 E
Sommepy-Tahure,
   France .... 19 C11 49 15N 4 31 E
Sömmerda, Germany . 24 D7 51 9N 11 7 E
Sommesous, France .. 19 D11 48 44N 4 12 E
Sommières, France ... 21 E8 43 47N 4 6 E
Somnath, India ..... 68 J4 20 53N 70 22 E
Somogy □, Hungary . 28 D2 46 19N 17 30 E
Somogyszob, Hungary 28 D2 46 18N 17 20 E
Somoto, Nic. 120 D2 13 28N 86 37W
Sompolno, Poland ... 31 F5 52 26N 18 30 E
Somport, Puerto de,
   Spain 38 C4 42 48N 0 31W
Son →, India .... 69 G11 25 42N 84 52 E
Son Ha, Vietnam .... 64 E7 15 3N 108 34 E
Son Hoa, Vietnam ... 64 F7 13 2N 108 58 E
Son La, Vietnam .... 58 G4 21 20N 103 50 E
Son Serra, Spain .... 48 B10 39 43N 3 13 E
Son Servera, Spain ... 38 F8 39 37N 3 21 E
Son Tay, Vietnam ... 58 G5 21 8N 105 30 E
Soná, Panama 120 E3 8 0N 81 20W
Sonamarg, India .... 69 B6 34 18N 75 21 E
Sonamukhi, India ... 69 H12 23 18N 87 27 E
Sonar →, India ..... 69 G8 24 24N 79 56 E
Sŏnch'ŏn, N. Korea .. 57 E13 39 48N 124 55 E
Sondags →, S. Africa 88 E4 33 44 S 25 51 E
Sóndalo, Italy ...... 40 B7 46 20N 10 19 E
Sondar, India .... 69 C6 33 28N 75 56 E
Sønder Felding,
   Denmark .... 11 J2 55 57N 8 47 E
Sønder Omme,
   Denmark .... 11 J2 55 50N 8 54 E
Sønderborg, Denmark 11 K3 54 55N 9 49 E
Sønderjyllands
   Amtskommune □,
   Denmark .... 11 J3 55 10N 9 10 E
Sondershausen,
   Germany .... 24 D6 51 22N 10 51 E
Sóndrio, Italy .... 40 B6 46 10N 9 52 E
Sone, Mozam. ...... 87 F3 17 23 S 34 55 E
Sonepur, India ...... 67 J13 20 55N 83 50 E
Song, Nigeria ...... 83 D7 9 0N 12 0 E
Song Cau, Vietnam .. 64 F7 13 27N 109 18 E
Song Xian, China ... 56 G7 34 12N 112 8 E
Songan, Indonesia ... 63 J18 8 13 S 115 24 E
Songch'ŏn, N. Korea . 57 E14 39 12N 126 15 E
Songea, Tanzania .... 87 E4 10 40 S 35 40 E
Songeons, France .... 19 C8 49 32N 1 50 E
Songhua Hu, China . 57 C14 43 35N 126 50 E
Songhua Jiang →, China 60 B8 47 45N 132 30 E
Songjiang, China .... 59 B13 31 1N 121 12 E
Songjin, N. Korea ... 57 D15 40 40N 129 10 E
Songjŏng-ni, S. Korea 57 G14 35 8N 126 47 E
Songkan, China ..... 58 C6 28 35N 106 52 E
Songkhla, Thailand .. 65 J3 7 13N 100 37 E
Songming, China .... 58 E4 25 12N 103 2 E
Songnim, N. Korea .. 57 E13 38 45N 125 39 E
Songo, Mozam. ..... 85 H6 15 34 S 32 38 E
Songo, Sudan ...... 79 G10 9 47N 24 21 E
Songpan, China ..... 58 A4 32 40N 103 30 E
Songtao, China ..... 58 C7 28 11N 109 0 E
Songwe, Dem. Rep. of
   the Congo .... 86 C2 3 20 S 26 16 E
Songwe →, Africa ... 87 D3 9 44 S 33 58 E
Songxi, China .... 59 D12 27 31N 118 44 E
Songzi, China .... 59 B8 30 12N 111 45 E
Sonhat, India .... 69 H10 23 29N 82 31 E
Sonid Youqi, China .. 56 C7 42 45N 112 48 E
Sonipat, India ...... 68 E7 29 0N 77 5 E
Sonkach, India ...... 68 H7 22 59N 76 21 E
Sonkovo, Russia .... 32 D9 57 50N 37 5 E
Sonmiani, Pakistan .. 68 G2 25 25N 66 40 E
Sonmiani B., Pakistan 68 G2 25 15N 66 30 E
Sonnino, Italy ...... 42 A6 41 25N 13 14 E
Sono →, Brazil ..... 125 E9 9 58 S 48 11W
Sonoma, U.S.A. 110 G4 38 18N 122 28W
Sonora, Calif., U.S.A. . 110 H6 37 59N 120 23W
Sonora, Tex., U.S.A. .. 113 K4 30 34N 100 39W
Sonora □, Mexico ... 118 B2 28 50N 111 33W
Sonora →, Mexico .. 118 B2 28 50N 111 33W
Sonoran Desert, U.S.A. 111 L12 33 40N 114 15W
Sonoyta, Mexico 118 A2 31 51N 112 50W
Sonqor, Iran .... 73 E12 34 47N 47 36 E
Sŏnsan, S. Korea .... 57 F15 36 14N 128 17 E
Sonseca, Spain 37 F7 39 42N 3 38W
Sonsonate, El Salv. .. 120 D2 13 43N 89 44W
Sonstorp, Sweden ... 11 F9 58 44N 15 38 E
Sonthofen, Germany . 25 H6 47 30N 10 16 E
Soochow = Suzhou,
   China .... 59 B13 31 19N 120 38 E
Sooke, Canada 110 B3 48 13N 123 43W
Sop Hao, Laos ...... 58 G5 20 33N 104 27 E
Sop Prap, Thailand .. 64 D2 17 53N 99 20 E
Sopelana, Spain 38 B2 43 23N 2 58W
Sopi, Indonesia ..... 63 D7 2 34N 128 28 E
Sopo, N → , Sudan .. 81 F2 8 40N 26 30 E
Sopot, Bulgaria ..... 45 D8 42 39N 24 45 E
Sopot, Poland ...... 30 D5 54 27N 18 31 E
Sopot, Serbia & M. .. 44 B4 44 29N 20 36 E
Sopotnica, Macedonia 44 E5 41 18N 21 13 E
Sopron, Hungary .... 28 C1 47 45N 16 32 E
Sopur, India .... 69 B6 34 18N 74 27 E
Sør-Rondane, Antarctica 5 D4 72 0 S 25 0 E
Sora, Italy .... 41 G10 41 43N 13 37 E
Sorah, Pakistan ..... 68 F3 27 13N 68 56 E
Söråker, Sweden .... 10 B11 62 30N 17 32 E
Sorano, Italy .... 41 F8 42 41N 11 43 E
Soraon, India ...... 69 G9 25 37N 81 51 E
Sörbygden, Sweden .. 10 B10 62 48N 16 12 E
Sore, France 20 D3 44 18N 0 35W
Sorel-Tracy, Canada . 104 C5 46 0N 73 10W
Soresina, Italy ...... 40 C6 45 17N 9 51 E
Sörforsa, Sweden .... 10 C10 61 43N 16 58 E
Sórgono, Italy ...... 42 B2 40 1N 9 6 E
Sorgues, France ..... 21 D8 44 1N 4 53 E
Sorgun, Turkey ..... 72 C6 39 46N 35 11 E
Soria, Spain 38 D2 41 43N 2 32W
Soria □, Spain 38 D2 41 46N 2 28W
Soriano, Uruguay ... 126 C4 33 24 S 58 19W
Soriano nel Cimino, Italy 41 F9 42 25N 12 14 E
Sorkh, Kuh-e, Iran ... 71 C8 35 40N 58 30 E
Sorø, Denmark ..... 11 J5 55 26N 11 32 E
Soro, Guinea 82 C3 10 9N 9 48W
Soroca, Moldova .... 29 B13 48 8N 28 12 E
Sorocaba, Brazil .... 127 A6 23 31 S 47 27W
Soroki = Soroca,
   Moldova .... 29 B13 48 8N 28 12 E
Sorong, Indonesia ... 63 E8 0 55 S 131 15 E
Soroní, Greece ...... 49 C10 36 21N 28 1 E
Soroti, Uganda ..... 86 B3 1 43N 33 35 E
Sørøya, Norway .... 8 A20 70 40N 22 30 E
Sørøysundet, Norway 8 A20 70 25N 23 0 E
Sorraia →, Portugal . 37 G2 38 55N 8 53W

Sorrell, Australia .... 95 G4 42 47 S 147 34 E
Sorrento, Italy ...... 43 B7 40 37N 14 22 E
Sorsele, Sweden ..... 8 D17 65 31N 17 30 E
Sörsjön, Sweden .... 10 C7 61 24N 13 5 E
Sorso, Italy .... 42 B1 40 48N 8 34 E
Sorsogon, Phil. ..... 61 E6 13 0N 124 0 E
Sortavala, Russia .... 32 B5 61 42N 30 41 E
Sortland, Norway ... 8 B16 68 42N 15 25 E
Sorvizhi, Russia .... 34 B9 57 52N 48 32 E
Sos del Rey Católico,
   Spain 38 C3 42 30N 1 13W
Sŏsan, S. Korea ..... 57 F14 36 47N 126 27 E
Soscumica, L., Canada 104 B4 50 15N 77 27W
Sösdala, Sweden .... 11 H7 56 2N 13 41 E
Sosna →, Russia .... 33 F10 52 42N 38 55 E
Sosnovka, Kirov, Russia 34 B10 56 17N 51 17 E
Sosnovka, Tambov,
   Russia .... 34 D5 53 13N 41 24 E
Sosnovyy Bor, Russia . 32 C5 59 55N 29 6 E
Sosnowiec, Poland ... 31 H6 50 20N 19 10 E
Sospel, France ...... 21 E11 43 52N 7 27 E
Sossus Vlei, Namibia . 88 C2 24 40 S 15 23 E
Šoštanj, Slovenia .... 41 B12 46 23N 15 4 E
Sŏsura, N. Korea .... 57 C16 42 16N 130 36 E
Sot →, India .... 69 F8 27 27N 79 37 E
Sotkamo, Finland ... 8 D23 64 8N 28 23 E
Soto del Barco, Spain 36 B4 43 32N 6 4W
Soto la Marina →,
   Mexico 119 C5 23 40N 97 40W
Soto y Amío, Spain .. 36 C5 42 46N 5 53W
Sotrondio, Spain 36 B5 43 17N 5 36W
Sotuta, Mexico 119 C7 20 29N 89 43W
Souanké, Congo .... 84 D2 2 10N 14 3 E
Soubré, Ivory C. 82 D3 5 50N 6 35W
Souderton, U.S.A. ... 117 F9 40 19N 75 19W
Soúdha, Greece ..... 49 D6 35 29N 24 4 E
Soúdhas, Kólpos, Greece 49 D6 35 25N 24 10 E
Soufflon, France .... 45 E10 41 12N 26 18 E
Soufrière, Guadeloupe 120 b 16 5N 61 40W
Soufrière, St. Lucia .. 121 f 13 51N 61 3W
Soufrière Bay, Domin. 121 f 15 20N 61 6W
Souillac, France ..... 20 D5 44 53N 1 29 E
Souilly, France ...... 19 C12 49 1N 5 17 E
Soukhouma, Laos ... 64 E5 14 38N 105 48 E
Soúl = Seoul, S. Korea 57 F14 37 31N 126 58 E
Soulac-sur-Mer, France 20 C2 45 30N 1 7W
Soulougou,
   Burkina Faso ..... 83 C5 13 1N 0 25 E
Soultz-sous-Forêts,
   France .... 19 D14 48 57N 7 52 E
Sound, The = Øresund,
   Europe .... 11 J6 55 45N 12 45 E
Sound, The, U.K. 15 G3 50 20N 4 10W
Soúnion, Ákra, Greece 46 D6 37 37N 24 1 E
Sources, Mt. aux,
   Lesotho .... 89 D4 28 45 S 28 50 E
Soure, Brazil .... 125 D9 0 35 S 48 30W
Soure, Portugal 36 E2 40 4N 8 38W
Souris, Man., Canada 103 D8 49 40N 100 20W
Souris, P.E.I., Canada 105 C7 46 21N 62 15W
Souris →, Canada ... 112 A5 49 40N 99 34W
Sourou →, Africa ... 82 C4 12 45N 3 25W
Soúrpi, Greece ..... 46 B4 39 6N 22 54 E
Sousa, Brazil .... 125 E11 6 45 S 38 10W
Sousel, Portugal 37 G3 38 57N 7 40W
Sousse, Tunisia ..... 79 A8 35 50N 10 38 E
Soustons, France 20 E2 43 45N 1 19W
Sout →, S. Africa ... 88 E2 31 35 S 18 24 E
South Africa ■, Africa 88 E3 32 0 S 23 0 E
South America ...... 122 E5 10 0 S 60 0W
South Atlantic Ocean 2 F8 20 0 S 10 0W
South Aulatsivik I.,
   Canada 105 A7 56 45N 61 30W
South Australia □,
   Australia .... 95 E2 32 0 S 139 0 E
South Ayrshire □, U.K. 14 F4 55 18N 4 41W
South Baldy, U.S.A. . 109 J10 33 59N 107 11W
South Bass I., U.S.A. . 116 E2 41 38N 82 53W
South Bend, Ind., U.S.A. 114 E2 41 41N 86 15W
South Bend, Wash.,
   U.S.A. 110 D3 46 40N 123 48W
South Boston, U.S.A. . 115 G6 36 42N 78 54W
South Branch, Canada 105 C8 47 55N 59 2W
South Brook, Canada 105 C8 49 26N 56 5W
South Carolina □,
   U.S.A. 115 J5 34 0N 81 0W
South Charleston,
   U.S.A. 114 F5 38 22N 81 44W
South China Sea, Asia 62 C4 10 0N 113 0 E
South Cumberland Is. □,
   Australia .... 94 J7 20 42 S 149 11 E
South Dakota □, U.S.A. 112 C5 44 15N 100 0W
South Deerfield, U.S.A. 117 D12 42 29N 72 37W
South Downs, U.K. .. 15 G7 50 52N 0 25W
South East C., Australia 95 G4 43 40 S 146 50 E
South-East Indian Rise,
   Ind. Oc. .... 5 B10 43 0 S 80 0 E
South East Is., Australia 93 F3 34 17 S 123 30 E
South Esk →, U.K. .. 13 E6 56 43N 2 31W
South Foreland, U.K. . 15 F9 51 8N 1 24 E
South Fork
   American →, U.S.A. 110 G5 38 45N 121 5W
South Fork Feather →,
   U.S.A. 110 F5 39 17N 121 36W
South Fork Grand →,
   U.S.A. 112 C3 45 43N 102 17W
South Fork
   Republican →, U.S.A. 112 E4 40 3N 101 31W
South Georgia,
   Antarctica .... 128 G9 54 30 S 37 0W
South
   Gloucestershire □,
   U.K. 15 F5 51 32N 2 28W
South Hadley, U.S.A. . 117 D12 42 16N 72 35W
South Haven, U.S.A. . 114 D2 42 24N 86 16W
South Henik L., Canada 103 A9 61 30N 97 20W
South Honshu Ridge,
   Pac. Oc. .... 96 E6 23 0N 143 0 E
South Horr, Kenya ... 86 B4 2 12N 36 56 E
South I., Kenya ..... 86 B4 2 35N 36 35 E
South I., N.Z. .... 91 L3 44 0 S 170 0 E
South Indian Lake,
   Canada 103 B9 56 47N 98 56W
South Invercargill, N.Z. 91 M2 46 26 S 168 23 E
South Island △, Kenya 86 B4 2 39N 36 35 E
South Kitui △, Kenya 86 C4 1 48 S 38 46 E
South Knife →, Canada 103 B10 58 55N 94 37W
South Koel →, India . 69 H11 22 32N 85 14 E
South Korea ■, Asia . 57 G15 36 0N 128 0 E
South Lake Tahoe,
   U.S.A. 110 G6 38 57N 119 59W
South Lanarkshire □,
   U.K. 13 F5 55 37N 3 53W
South Loup →, U.S.A. 112 E5 41 4N 98 39W
South Luangwa △,
   Zambia .... 87 E3 13 0 S 31 20 E

South Magnetic Pole,
   Antarctica .... 5 C9 64 8 S 138 8 E
South Milwaukee,
   U.S.A. 114 D2 42 55N 87 52W
South Molton, U.K. .. 15 F4 51 1N 3 51W
South Moose L., Canada 103 C8 53 46N 100 8W
South Nahanni →,
   Canada 102 A4 61 3N 123 21W
South Nation →,
   Canada 117 A9 45 34N 75 6W
South Natuna Is. =
   Natuna Selatan,
   Kepulauan, Indonesia 62 D3 2 45N 109 0 E
South Negril Pt.,
   Jamaica .... 120 a 18 14N 78 30W
South Orkney Is.,
   Antarctica .... 5 C18 63 0 S 45 0W
South Ossetia □,
   Georgia .... 35 J7 42 21N 44 2 E
South Pagai, I. = Pagai
   Selatan, Pulau,
   Indonesia .... 62 E2 3 0 S 100 15 E
South Paris, U.S.A. .. 117 B14 44 14N 70 31W
South Pittsburg, U.S.A. 115 H3 35 1N 85 42W
South Platte →, U.S.A. 112 E4 41 7N 100 42W
South Pole, Antarctica 5 E 90 0 S 0 0 E
South Porcupine,
   Canada 104 C3 48 30N 81 12W
South Portland, U.S.A. 115 D10 43 38N 70 15W
South Pt., Barbados .. 121 g 13 2N 59 32W
South Pt., U.S.A. 116 B1 44 52N 83 19W
South River, Canada . 104 C4 45 52N 79 23W
South River, U.S.A. .. 117 F10 40 27N 74 23W
South Ronaldsay, U.K. 13 C6 58 48N 2 58W
South Sandwich Is.,
   Antarctica .... 5 B1 57 0 S 27 0W
South Saskatchewan →,
   Canada 103 C7 53 15N 105 5W
South Seal →, Canada 103 B9 58 48N 98 8W
South Shetland Is.,
   Antarctica .... 5 C18 62 0 S 59 0W
South Shields, U.K. .. 14 C6 55 0N 1 25W
South Sioux City, U.S.A. 112 D6 42 28N 96 24W
South Taranaki Bight,
   N.Z. .... 91 H5 39 40 S 174 5 E
South Thompson →,
   Canada 102 C4 50 40N 120 20W
South Twin I., Canada 104 B4 53 7N 79 52W
South Tyne →, U.K. . 14 C5 54 59N 2 8W
South Uist, U.K. 13 D1 57 20N 7 15W
South West C., Australia 95 G4 43 34 S 146 3 E
South Williamsport,
   U.S.A. 116 E8 41 13N 77 0W
South Yorkshire □, U.K. 14 D6 53 27N 1 36W
Southampton, Canada 116 B3 44 30N 81 25W
Southampton, U.K. .. 15 G6 50 54N 1 23W
Southampton □, U.K. 15 G6 50 54N 1 23W
Southampton I., Canada 101 B11 64 30N 84 0W
Southaven, U.S.A. ... 113 H9 34 59N 90 2W
Southbank, Canada .. 102 C3 54 2N 125 46W
Southbridge, N.Z. ... 91 K4 43 48 S 172 16 E
Southbridge, U.S.A. . 117 D12 42 5N 72 2W
Southeast Pacific Basin,
   Pac. Oc. .... 5 C15 16 30 S 92 0W
Southend, Canada ... 103 B8 56 19N 103 22W
Southend-on-Sea, U.K. 15 F8 51 32N 0 44 E
Southend-on-Sea □,
   U.K. .... 15 F8 51 32N 0 44 E
Southern = Janub □,
   Sudan .... 81 F2 6 50N 28 45 E
Southern = Yedebub
   Biheroch
   Bihereseboch na
   Hizboch □, Ethiopia 81 F4 10 0N 36 0 E
Southern = Yuzhnyy □,
   Russia .... 35 H5 44 0N 40 0 E
Southern □, Malawi . 87 F4 15 0 S 35 0 E
Southern □, S. Leone 82 D2 8 0N 12 30W
Southern □, Zambia . 87 F2 16 20 S 26 20 E
Southern Alps, N.Z. . 91 K3 43 41 S 170 11 E
Southern Cross,
   Australia .... 93 F2 31 12 S 119 15 E
Southern Indian L.,
   Canada 103 B9 57 10N 98 30W
Southern Ocean,
   Antarctica .... 5 C6 62 0 S 60 0 E
Southern Pines, U.S.A. 115 H6 35 11N 79 24W
Southern Uplands, U.K. 13 F5 55 28N 3 52W
Southington, U.S.A. . 117 E12 41 36N 72 53W
Southland □, N.Z. .. 91 L1 45 30 S 168 0 E
Southold, U.S.A. 117 E12 41 4N 72 26W
Southport, Australia . 95 D5 27 58 S 153 25 E
Southport, U.K. 14 D4 53 39N 3 0W
Southport, Fla., U.S.A. 115 K3 30 17N 85 38W
Southport, N.Y., U.S.A. 116 D8 42 3N 76 49W
Southwest △, Australia 95 G4 43 8 S 146 5 E
Southwest C., N.Z. .. 91 M1 47 17 S 167 28 E
Southwestern Pacific
   Basin, Pac. Oc. .... 5 A12 42 0 S 170 0W
Southwold, U.K. .... 15 E9 52 20N 1 41 E
Southwood △, Australia 95 D5 27 48 S 150 8 E
Soutpansberg, S. Africa 89 C4 23 0 S 29 30 E
Souvigny, France .... 19 F10 46 33N 3 10 E
Sovata, Romania .... 29 D10 46 35N 25 3 E
Soverato, Italy ...... 43 D9 38 41N 16 33 E
Sovetsk, Kaliningrad,
   Russia .... 9 J19 55 6N 21 50 E
Sovetsk, Kirov, Russia 34 B9 57 38N 48 53 E
Sovetskaya Gavan =
   Vanino, Russia .... 53 E15 48 50N 140 5 E
Soviche, Italy ...... 41 E8 43 17N 11 13 E
Soweto, S. Africa .... 89 D4 26 14 S 27 54 E
Sōya-Kaikyō = La
   Perouse Str., Asia . 54 B11 45 40N 142 0 E
Sōya-Misaki, Japan .. 54 B10 45 30N 141 55 E
Soyaux, France ..... 20 C4 45 39N 0 12 E
Sozh →, Belarus .... 33 F6 51 57N 30 48 E
Sozopol, Bulgaria ... 45 D11 42 23N 27 42 E
Spa, Belgium .... 17 D5 50 29N 5 53 E
Spain ■, Europe 7 H5 39 0N 4 0W
Spalding, Australia .. 95 E2 33 30 S 138 37 E
Spalding, U.K. 14 E7 52 48N 0 9W
Spangler, U.S.A. 116 F6 40 39N 78 48W
Spanish, Canada 104 C3 46 12N 82 20W
Spanish Fork, U.S.A. 108 F8 40 7N 111 39W
Spanish Town,
   Br. Virgin Is. ..... 121 e 17 43N 64 26W
Spanish Town, Jamaica 120 a 18 0N 76 57W
Sparks, U.S.A. 110 F7 39 32N 119 45W

Spárti, Greece ...... 46 D4 37 5N 22 25 E
Spartivento, C.,
   Calabria, Italy .... 43 E9 37 55N 16 4 E
Spartivento, C., Sard.,
   Italy .... 42 D1 38 53N 8 50 E
Sparwood, Canada .. 102 D6 49 44N 114 53W
Spas-Demensk, Russia 32 E7 54 20N 34 0 E
Spas-Klepiki, Russia . 32 E11 55 10N 40 10 E
Spassk Dalniy, Russia 53 E14 44 40N 132 48 E
Spassk-Ryazanskiy,
   Russia .... 32 E11 54 24N 40 25 E
Spátha, Ákra, Greece 49 D5 35 42N 23 43 E
Spatsizi →, Canada . 102 B3 57 42N 128 7W
Spatsizi Plateau
   Wilderness △, Canada 102 B3 57 40N 128 0W
Spean →, U.K. 13 E4 56 55N 4 59W
Spearfish, U.S.A. 112 C3 44 30N 103 52W
Spearman, U.S.A. ... 113 G4 36 12N 101 12W
Speculator, U.S.A. .. 117 C10 43 30N 74 25W
Speia, Moldova ..... 29 C14 46 59N 29 19 E
Speightstown, Barbados 121 g 13 15N 59 39W
Speke Gulf, Tanzania 86 C3 2 20 S 32 50 E
Spello, Italy .... 41 F9 42 59N 12 40 E
Spence Bay = Taloyoak,
   Canada 100 B10 69 32N 93 32W
Spencer, Idaho, U.S.A. 108 D7 44 22N 112 11W
Spencer, Iowa, U.S.A. 112 D7 43 9N 95 9W
Spencer, N.Y., U.S.A. 117 D8 42 13N 76 30W
Spencer, Nebr., U.S.A. 112 D5 42 53N 98 42W
Spencer, C., Australia 95 F2 35 20 S 136 53 E
Spencer B., Namibia . 88 D1 25 30 S 14 47 E
Spencer G., Australia 95 E2 34 0 S 137 20 E
Spencerville, Canada 117 B9 44 51N 75 33W
Spences Bridge, Canada 102 C4 50 25N 121 20W
Spennymoor, U.K. ... 14 C6 54 42N 1 36W
Spentrup, Denmark .. 11 H4 56 33N 10 4 E
Sperkhiós →, Greece 46 C4 38 57N 22 3 E
Sperrin Mts., U.K. ... 12 B5 54 50N 7 0W
Spessart, Germany .. 25 F5 49 56N 9 18 E
Spétsai, Greece ..... 46 D5 37 15N 23 10 E
Spey →, U.K. 13 D5 57 40N 3 6W
Speyer, Germany .... 25 F4 49 29N 8 25 E
Spezand, Pakistan ... 68 E2 29 59N 67 0 E
Spezzano Albanese,
   Italy .... 43 C9 39 40N 16 19 E
Spiekeroog, Germany 24 B3 53 46N 7 42 E
Spiez, Switz. .... 25 J3 46 40N 7 40 E
Spíli, Greece .... 49 D6 35 13N 24 31 E
Spilimbergo, Italy ... 41 B9 46 7N 12 54 E
Spinalónga, Greece .. 49 D7 35 18N 25 44 E
Spinazzola, Italy .... 43 B9 40 58N 16 5 E
Spineni, Romania ... 29 F9 44 43N 24 37 E
Spirit Lake, U.S.A. .. 110 D4 46 15N 122 9W
Spirit River, Canada . 102 B5 55 45N 118 50W
Spiritwood, Canada .. 103 C7 53 24N 107 33W
Spišská Nová Ves,
   Slovak Rep. ...... 27 C13 48 58N 20 34 E
Spišské Podhradie,
   Slovak Rep. ...... 27 B13 49 0N 20 48 E
Spital, Austria ...... 26 D7 47 42N 14 18 E
Spithead, U.K. 15 G6 50 45N 1 10W
Spittal an der Drau,
   Austria .... 26 E6 46 48N 13 31 E
Spitzbergen = Svalbard,
   Arctic .... 51 B5 78 0N 17 0 E
Spjelkavik, Norway .. 9 E12 62 28N 6 22 E
Split, Croatia .... 41 E13 43 31N 16 26 E
Split ✈ (SPU), Croatia 41 E13 43 33N 16 15 E
Split L., Canada 103 B9 56 8N 96 15W
Split Lake, Canada .. 103 B9 56 8N 96 15W
Splitski Kanal, Croatia 41 E13 43 31N 16 20 E
Splügenpass, Switz. . 25 J5 46 30N 9 20 E
Spofford, U.S.A. 113 L4 29 10N 100 25W
Spokane, U.S.A. 108 C5 47 40N 117 24W
Spoleto, Italy .... 41 F9 42 44N 12 44 E
Spooner, U.S.A. 112 C9 45 50N 91 53W
Sporry Navolok, Mys,
   Russia .... 52 B7 75 50N 68 40 E
Sprague, U.S.A. 108 C5 47 18N 117 59W
Spratly I., S. China Sea 62 C4 8 38N 111 55 E
Spratly Is., S. China Sea 62 C4 8 20N 112 0 E
Spray, U.S.A. 108 D4 44 50N 119 48W
Spreča →, Bos.-H. .. 28 F3 44 44N 18 6 E
Spree →, Germany .. 24 C9 52 32N 13 13 E
Spreewald, Germany 24 D9 51 58N 13 51 E
Spremberg, Germany 24 D10 51 34N 14 22 E
Sprengisandur, Iceland 8 D5 64 52N 18 7W
Spring City, U.S.A. .. 117 F9 40 11N 75 33W
Spring Creek, U.S.A. 108 F6 40 45N 115 38W
Spring Garden, U.S.A. 110 F6 39 52N 120 47W
Spring Hall, Barbados 121 g 13 18N 59 36W
Spring Hill, U.S.A. .. 115 L4 28 27N 82 41W
Spring Mts., U.S.A. .. 109 H6 36 0N 115 45W
Spring Valley, U.S.A. 111 N10 32 45N 117 5W
Springbok, S. Africa . 88 D2 29 42 S 17 54 E
Springboro, U.S.A. .. 116 E4 41 48N 80 22W
Springdale, Canada .. 105 C8 49 30N 56 6W
Springdale, U.S.A. .. 113 G7 36 11N 94 8W
Springe, Germany ... 24 C5 52 13N 9 33 E
Springerville, U.S.A. 109 J9 34 8N 109 17W
Springfield, Canada . 116 D4 42 50N 80 56W
Springfield, N.Z. .... 91 K3 43 19 S 171 56 E
Springfield, Colo.,
   U.S.A. 113 G3 37 24N 102 37W
Springfield, Ill., U.S.A. 112 F10 39 48N 89 39W
Springfield, Mass.,
   U.S.A. 117 D12 42 6N 72 35W
Springfield, Mo., U.S.A. 113 G8 37 13N 93 17W
Springfield, Ohio, U.S.A. 114 F4 39 55N 83 49W
Springfield, Oreg.,
   U.S.A. 108 D2 44 3N 123 1W
Springfield, Tenn.,
   U.S.A. 115 G2 36 31N 86 53W
Springfield, Vt., U.S.A. 117 C12 43 18N 72 29W
Springfontein, S. Africa 88 E4 30 15 S 25 40 E
Springhill, Canada .. 105 C7 45 40N 64 4W
Springhill, U.S.A. ... 113 J8 33 0N 93 28W
Springhouse, Canada 102 C4 51 56N 122 7W
Springs, S. Africa .... 89 D4 26 13 S 28 25 E
Springsure, Australia 94 C4 24 8 S 148 6 E
Springvale, U.S.A. .. 117 C14 43 28N 70 48W
Springville, Calif., U.S.A. 110 J8 36 8N 118 49W
Springville, N.Y., U.S.A. 116 D6 42 31N 78 40W
Springville, Utah, U.S.A. 108 F8 40 10N 111 37W
Springwater, U.S.A. . 116 D7 42 38N 77 35W
Spruce-Creek, U.S.A. 116 F6 40 36N 78 9W
Spruce Knob-Seneca
   Rocks △, U.S.A. .. 114 F6 38 50N 79 30W
Spruce Mt., U.S.A. .. 117 B12 44 12N 72 19W
Spur, U.S.A. 113 J4 33 28N 100 52W
Spurn Hd., U.K. .... 14 D8 53 35N 0 8 E
Spuž, Serbia & M. ... 44 D3 42 32N 19 10 E
Spuzzum, Canada ... 102 D4 49 37N 121 23W
Squam L., U.S.A. ... 117 C13 43 45N 71 32W

Squamish, *Canada* **102 D4** 49 45N 123 10W
Square Islands, *Canada* **105 B8** 52 47N 55 47W
Squillace, G. di, *Italy* . **43 D9** 38 45N 16 50 E
Squinzano, *Italy* ...... **43 B11** 40 26N 18 2 E
Squires, Mt., *Australia* **93 E4** 26 14 S 127 28 E
Srbac, *Bos.-H.* .... **28 E2** 45 7N 17 30 E
Srbica, *Serbia & M.* ... **44 C5** 43 30N 20 47 E
Srbija = Serbia □,
  Serbia & M. ...... **44 C5** 43 30N 21 0 E
Srbobran, *Serbia & M.* **28 E4** 45 32N 19 48 E
Sre Ambel, *Cambodia* . **65 G4** 11 8N 103 46 E
Sre Khtum, *Cambodia* . **65 F6** 12 10N 106 52 E
Sre Umbell = Sre
  Ambel, *Cambodia* .. **65 G4** 11 8N 103 46 E
Srebrenica, *Bos.-H.* ... **28 F4** 44 6N 19 18 E
Sredinny Ra. =
  Sredinnyy Khrebet,
  Russia .... **53 D16** 57 0N 160 0 E
Sredinnyy Khrebet,
  Russia .... **53 D16** 57 0N 160 0 E
Središče, *Slovenia* ..... **41 B13** 46 24N 16 17 E
Sredna Gora, *Bulgaria* **45 D8** 42 40N 24 20 E
Srednekolymsk, *Russia* **53 C16** 67 27N 153 40 E
Sredni Rodopi, *Bulgaria* **45 E8** 41 40N 24 45 E
Srednogorie, *Bulgaria* . **45 D8** 42 43N 24 10 E
Śrem, *Poland* .... **31 F4** 52 6N 17 2 E
Sremska Mitrovica,
  Serbia & M. ...... **44 A4** 44 59N 19 38 E
Sremski Karlovci,
  Serbia & M. ...... **28 E4** 45 12N 19 56 E
Srepok →, *Cambodia* .. **64 F6** 13 33N 106 16 E
Sretensk, *Russia* ...... **53 D12** 52 10N 117 40 E
Sri Lanka ■, *Asia* .... **66 R12** 7 30N 80 50 E
Srikakulam, *India* ..... **67 K13** 18 14N 83 58 E
Srinagar, *India* .... **69 B6** 34 5N 74 50 E
Srinagarind Res.,
  Thailand .... **64 E2** 14 35N 99 0 E
Środa Śląska, *Poland* . **31 G3** 51 10N 16 36 E
Środa Wielkopolski,
  Poland .... **31 F4** 52 15N 17 19 E
Srono, *Indonesia* ...... **63 J17** 8 24 S 114 16 E
Srpska Crnja,
  Serbia & M. ...... **28 E5** 45 38N 20 44 E
Srpski Itebej,
  Serbia & M. ...... **28 E5** 45 35N 20 44 E
Staaten →, *Australia* . **94 B3** 16 24 S 141 17 E
Staaten River △,
  Australia .... **94 B3** 16 15 S 142 40 E
Staberhuk, *Germany* ... **24 A7** 54 23N 11 18 E
Stade, *Germany* .... **24 B5** 53 35N 9 29 E
Stadskanaal, *Neths.* ... **17 A6** 53 4N 6 55 E
Stadtallendorf, *Germany* **24 C5** 50 48N 9 1 E
Stadthagen, *Germany* .. **24 C5** 52 19N 9 13 E
Stadtlohn, *Germany* ... **24 D2** 51 59N 6 55 E
Stadtroda, *Germany* ... **24 E7** 50 52N 11 44 E
Staffa, *U.K.* **13 E2** 56 27N 6 21W
Staffanstorp, *Sweden* .. **11 J7** 55 39N 13 13 E
Stafford, *U.K.* **14 E5** 52 49N 2 7W
Stafford, *U.S.A.* **113 G5** 37 58N 98 36W
Stafford Springs, *U.S.A.* **117 E12** 41 57N 72 18W
Staffordshire □, *U.K.* . **14 E5** 52 53N 2 10W
Stagnone, *Italy* .... **42 E5** 37 53N 12 26 E
Stagnone di Marsala △,
  Italy .... **42 E5** 37 52N 12 26 E
Staines, *U.K.* **15 F7** 51 26N 0 29W
Stainz, *Austria* .... **26 E8** 46 53N 15 17 E
Stakhanov, *Ukraine* ... **33 H10** 48 35N 38 40 E
Stalać, *Serbia & M.* ... **44 C5** 43 43N 21 28 E
Stalingrad = Volgograd,
  Russia .... **35 F7** 48 40N 44 25 E
Stalis, *Greece* .... **49 D7** 35 17N 25 25 E
Ställdalen, *Sweden* .... **10 E11** 59 22N 17 12 E
Stalowa Wola, *Poland* . **31 H9** 50 34N 22 3 E
Stalybridge, *U.K.* **14 D5** 53 28N 2 3W
Stamford, *Australia* ... **94 C3** 21 15 S 143 46 E
Stamford, *U.K.* **15 E7** 52 39N 0 29W
Stamford, *Conn., U.S.A.* **117 E11** 41 3N 73 32W
Stamford, *N.Y., U.S.A.* **117 D10** 42 25N 74 38W
Stamford, *Tex., U.S.A.* **113 J5** 32 57N 99 48W
Stampriet, *Namibia* .... **88 C2** 24 20 S 18 28 E
Stamps, *U.S.A.* **113 J8** 33 22N 93 30W
Stančevo = Kalipetrovo,
  Bulgaria .... **45 B11** 44 5N 27 14 E
Standerton, *S. Africa* .. **89 D4** 26 55 S 29 7 E
Standish, *U.S.A.* **114 D4** 43 59N 83 57W
Stanford, *S. Africa* .... **88 E2** 34 26 S 19 29 E
Stanford, *U.S.A.* **108 C8** 47 9N 110 13W
Stånga, *Sweden* .... **11 G12** 57 17N 18 29 E
Stanger, *S. Africa* ..... **89 D5** 29 27 S 31 14 E
Stängselåsen =
  Salpausselkä, *Finland* **9 F22** 61 3N 26 15 E
Stanišić, *Serbia & M.* . **28 E4** 45 56N 19 10 E
Stanislaus →, *U.S.A.* . **110 H5** 37 40N 121 14W
Stanislawów, *Poland* .. **31 F8** 52 18N 21 33 E
Stanley, *Australia* ..... **95 G4** 40 46 S 145 19 E
Stanley, *Falk. Is.* ..... **128 G5** 51 40 S 59 51W
Stanley, *U.K.* **14 C6** 54 53N 1 41W
Stanley, *Idaho, U.S.A.* **108 D6** 44 13N 114 56W
Stanley, *N. Dak., U.S.A.* **112 A3** 48 19N 102 23W
Stanley, *N.Y., U.S.A.* .. **116 D7** 42 48N 77 6W
Stanley Mission, *Canada* **103 B8** 55 25N 104 33W
Stanovoy Khrebet,
  Russia .... **53 D13** 55 0N 130 0 E
Stanovoy Ra. =
  Stanovoy Khrebet,
  Russia .... **53 D13** 55 0N 130 0 E
Stansmore Ra., *Australia* **92 D4** 21 23 S 128 33 E
Stansted, London ✈
  (STN), *U.K.* ...... **15 F8** 51 54N 0 14 E
Stanthorpe, *Australia* .. **95 D5** 28 36 S 151 59 E
Stanton, *U.S.A.* **113 J4** 32 8N 101 48W
Stanwood, *U.S.A.* **110 B4** 48 15N 122 23W
Staples, *U.S.A.* **112 B7** 46 21N 94 48W
Stąporków, *Poland* .... **31 G7** 51 9N 20 31 E
Star City, *Canada* **103 C8** 52 50N 104 20W
Star Lake, *U.S.A.* **117 B9** 44 10N 75 2W
Stará L'ubovňa,
  Slovak Rep. .... **27 B13** 49 18N 20 42 E
Stara Moravica,
  Serbia & M. ...... **28 E4** 45 50N 19 30 E
Stara Pazova,
  Serbia & M. ...... **28 F5** 44 58N 20 10 E
Stara Planina, *Bulgaria* **28 F7** 43 15N 23 0 E
Stara Sil, *Ukraine* ..... **31 J9** 49 29N 22 58 E
Stará Turá, *Slovak Rep.* **27 C10** 48 47N 17 42 E
Stara Ushytsya, *Ukraine* **29 B12** 48 35N 27 8 E
Stara Zagora, *Bulgaria* **45 D9** 42 26N 25 39 E
Starachowice, *Poland* .. **31 G8** 51 3N 21 2 E
Staraya Russa, *Russia* . **32 D6** 57 58N 31 23 E
Starbuck I., *Kiribati* ... **97 H12** 5 37 S 155 55W
Starchiojd, *Romania* ... **29 E11** 45 19N 26 11 E
Starcke △, *Australia* .. **94 A4** 14 56 S 145 2 E
Stargard Szczeciński,
  Poland .... **30 E2** 53 20N 15 0 E
Stari Bar, *Serbia & M.* **44 D3** 42 7N 19 10 E
Stari Trg, *Slovenia* .... **41 C12** 45 29N 15 7 E

Staritsa, *Russia* .... **32 D8** 56 33N 34 55 E
Starke, *U.S.A.* **115 L4** 29 57N 82 7W
Starnberg, *Germany* ... **25 H7** 48 0N 11 21 E
Starnberger See,
  Germany .... **25 H7** 47 54N 11 19 E
Starobilsk, *Ukraine* .... **33 H10** 49 16N 39 0 E
Starodub, *Russia* ..... **33 F7** 52 30N 32 50 E
Starogard Gdański,
  Poland .... **30 E5** 53 59N 18 30 E
Starokonstantinov =
  Starokonstyantyniv,
  Ukraine .... **33 H4** 49 48N 27 10 E
Starokonstyantyniv,
  Ukraine .... **33 H4** 49 48N 27 10 E
Starokozache, *Ukraine* **29 D14** 46 20N 29 59 E
Starominskaya, *Russia* **33 J10** 46 33N 39 0 E
Staroshcherbinovskaya,
  Russia .... **33 J10** 46 40N 38 53 E
Start Pt., *U.K.* **15 G4** 50 13N 3 39W
Stary Sącz, *Poland* .... **31 J7** 49 33N 20 35 E
Staryy Biryuzyak, *Russia* **35 H8** 44 46N 46 50 E
Staryy Chartoriysk,
  Ukraine .... **33 G3** 51 15N 25 54 E
Staryy Krym, *Ukraine* . **33 K8** 45 3N 35 8 E
Staryy Oskol, *Russia* .. **33 G9** 51 19N 37 55 E
Staryy Sambir, *Ukraine* **31 J9** 49 27N 22 59 E
Stassfurt, *Germany* .... **24 D7** 51 51N 11 35 E
Staszów, *Poland* ...... **31 H8** 50 33N 21 10 E
State College, *U.S.A.* . **116 F7** 40 48N 77 52W
Stateline, *U.S.A.* **110 G7** 38 57N 119 56W
Staten, I. = Estados, I.
  de Los, *Argentina* .. **128 G4** 54 40 S 64 30W
Staten I., *U.S.A.* **117 F10** 40 35N 74 9W
Statesboro, *U.S.A.* **115 J5** 32 27N 81 47W
Statesville, *U.S.A.* **115 H5** 35 47N 80 53W
Stauffer, *U.S.A.* **111 L7** 34 45N 119 3W
Staunton, *Ill., U.S.A.* . **112 F10** 39 1N 89 47W
Staunton, *Va., U.S.A.* . **114 F6** 38 9N 79 4W
Stavanger, *Norway* .... **9 G11** 58 57N 5 40 E
Staveley, *N.Z.* .... **91 K3** 43 40 S 171 32 E
Stavelot, *Belgium* ..... **17 D5** 50 23N 5 55 E
Stavern, *Norway* ...... **9 G14** 59 0N 10 1 E
Stavoren, *Neths.* ...... **17 B5** 52 53N 5 22 E
Stavropol, *Russia* ..... **35 H6** 45 5N 42 0 E
Stavros, *Cyprus* ...... **49 D11** 35 1N 32 38 E
Stavrós, *Greece* ...... **46 D6** 35 12N 24 45 E
Stavrós, *Greece* ...... **49 D6** 36 25N 24 58 E
Stavroúpolis, *Greece* .. **45 E8** 41 12N 24 45 E
Stawell, *Australia* ..... **95 F3** 37 5 S 142 47 E
Stawell →, *Australia* . **94 C3** 20 20 S 142 55 E
Stawiski, *Poland* ...... **30 E9** 53 22N 22 9 E
Stawiszyn, *Poland* .... **31 G5** 51 56N 18 4 E
Stayner, *Canada* **116 B4** 44 25N 80 5W
Stayton, *U.S.A.* **108 D2** 44 48N 122 48W
Steamboat Springs,
  U.S.A. **108 F10** 40 29N 106 50W
Steblevë, *Albania* ..... **44 E4** 41 21N 20 33 E
Steele, *U.S.A.* **112 B5** 46 51N 99 55W
Steelton, *U.S.A.* **116 F8** 40 14N 76 50W
Steen River, *Canada* ... **102 B5** 59 40N 117 12W
Steenwijk, *Neths.* ..... **17 B6** 52 47N 6 7 E
Steep Pt., *Australia* .... **93 E1** 26 8 S 113 8 E
Steep Rock, *Canada* ... **103 C9** 51 30N 98 48W
Ştefan Vodă, *Moldova* **29 D14** 46 27N 29 42 E
Ştefănesti, *Romania* ... **29 C12** 47 44N 27 15 E
Stefanie △, *Ethiopia* .. **81 G4** 4 55N 36 55 E
Stefanie L. = Chew
  Bahir, *Ethiopia* .... **81 G4** 4 40N 36 50 E
Stefansson Bay,
  Antarctica .... **5 C5** 67 20 S 59 8 E
Stege, *Denmark* ...... **11 K6** 54 59N 12 18 E
Ştei, *Romania* .... **28 D7** 46 32N 22 27 E
Steiermark □, *Austria* **26 D8** 47 26N 15 0 E
Steigerwald, *Germany* . **25 F6** 49 44N 10 26 E
Steigerwald △, *Germany* **25 F6** 49 50N 10 30 E
Steilacoom, *U.S.A.* **110 C4** 47 10N 122 36W
Steilrandberge, *Namibia* **88 B1** 17 45 S 13 20 E
Steinbach, *Canada* **103 D9** 49 32N 96 40W
Steinfurt, *Germany* .... **24 C3** 52 9N 7 21 E
Steinhausen, *Namibia* .. **88 C2** 21 49 S 18 20 E
Steinheim, *Germany* ... **24 D5** 51 51N 9 5 E
Steinhuder Meer,
  Germany .... **24 C5** 52 29N 9 21 E
Steinhuder Meer △,
  Germany .... **24 C5** 52 30N 9 16 E
Steinkjer, *Norway* ..... **8 D14** 64 1N 11 31 E
Steinkopf, *S. Africa* ... **88 D2** 29 18 S 17 43 E
Steinwald △, *Germany* **25 F8** 49 55N 12 8 E
Stellarton, *Canada* **105 C7** 45 32N 62 30W
Stellenbosch, *S. Africa* . **88 E2** 33 58 S 18 50 E
Stelvio, Paso dello, *Italy* **40 B7** 46 32N 10 27 E
Stenay, *France* .... **19 C12** 49 29N 5 12 E
Stendal, *Germany* ..... **24 C7** 52 36N 11 53 E
Stende, *Latvia* .... **30 A9** 57 11N 22 33 E
Stenhamra, *Sweden* ... **10 E11** 59 20N 17 41 E
Stenshuvud △, *Sweden* **11 J8** 55 39N 14 15 E
Stenstorp, *Sweden* .... **11 F7** 58 17N 13 45 E
Stenungsund, *Sweden* . **11 F5** 58 6N 11 50 E
Steornabhaigh =
  Stornoway, *U.K.* ... **13 C2** 58 13N 6 23W
Stepanakert =
  Xankändi, *Azerbaijan* **70 B5** 39 52N 46 49 E
Stepanavan, *Armenia* . **35 K7** 41 1N 44 23 E
Stephens Creek,
  Australia .... **95 E3** 31 50 S 141 30 E
Stephens I., *Canada* ... **102 C2** 54 10N 130 45W
Stephens L., *Canada* ... **103 B9** 56 32N 95 0W
Stephenville, *Canada* .. **105 C8** 48 31N 58 35W
Stephenville, *U.S.A.* .. **113 J5** 32 13N 98 12W
Stepnica, *Poland* ...... **30 E1** 53 38N 14 36 E
Steppe, *Asia* .... **50 D9** 50 0N 50 0 E
Stereá Ellas □, *Greece* **46 C4** 38 50N 23 0 E
Sterkstroom, *S. Africa* . **88 E4** 31 32 S 26 32 E
Sterling, *Colo., U.S.A.* **112 E3** 40 37N 103 13W
Sterling, *Ill., U.S.A.* ... **112 E10** 41 48N 89 42W
Sterling, *Kans., U.S.A.* **112 F5** 38 13N 98 12W
Sterling City, *U.S.A.* .. **113 K4** 31 51N 101 0W
Sterling Heights, *U.S.A.* **114 D4** 42 35N 83 0W
Sterling Run, *U.S.A.* .. **116 E6** 41 25N 78 12W
Sterlitamak, *Russia* ... **52 D6** 53 40N 56 0 E
Sternberg, *Germany* ... **24 B7** 53 42N 11 50 E
Šternberk, *Czech Rep.* **27 B10** 49 45N 17 15 E
Stérnes, *Greece* ...... **49 D6** 35 30N 24 9 E
Sterzing = Vipiteno,
  Italy .... **41 B8** 46 54N 11 26 E
Stettin = Szczecin,
  Poland .... **30 E1** 53 27N 14 27 E
Stettiner Haff, *Germany* **30 E1** 53 47N 14 15 E
Stettler, *Canada* **102 C6** 52 19N 112 40W
Steubenville, *U.S.A.* .. **116 F4** 40 22N 80 37W
Stevenage, *U.K.* **15 F7** 51 55N 0 13W
Stevens Point, *U.S.A.* . **112 C10** 44 31N 89 34W
Stevenson, *U.S.A.* **110 E5** 45 42N 121 53W
Stevenson L., *Canada* . **103 C9** 53 55N 96 0W

Stevensville, *U.S.A.* ... **108 C6** 46 30N 114 5W
Stevns Klint, *Denmark* **11 J6** 55 17N 12 28 E
Stewart, *Canada* **102 B3** 55 56N 129 57W
Stewart, *U.S.A.* **110 F7** 39 5N 119 46W
Stewart →, *Canada* ... **100 B6** 63 19N 139 26W
Stewart, C., *Australia* . **94 A1** 11 57 S 134 56 E
Stewart, I., *Chile* ..... **128 G2** 54 50 S 71 15W
Stewart I., *N.Z.* ...... **91 M1** 46 58 S 167 54 E
Stewarts Point, *U.S.A.* **110 G3** 38 39N 123 24W
Stewartville, *U.S.A.* ... **112 D8** 43 51N 92 29W
Stewiacke, *Canada* **105 C7** 45 9N 63 22W
Steynsburg, *S. Africa* . **88 E4** 31 15 S 25 49 E
Steyr, *Austria* .... **26 C7** 48 3N 14 25 E
Steyr →, *Austria* ..... **26 C7** 48 3N 14 25 E
Steytlerville, *S. Africa* . **88 E3** 33 17 S 24 19 E
Stia, *Italy* .... **41 E8** 43 48N 11 42 E
Stigler, *U.S.A.* **113 H7** 35 15N 95 8W
Stigliano, *Italy* .... **43 B9** 40 24N 16 14 E
Stigtomta, *Sweden* .... **11 F10** 58 47N 16 48 E
Stikine →, *Canada* **102 B2** 56 40N 132 30W
Stilfontein, *S. Africa* ... **88 D4** 26 51 S 26 50 E
Stilís, *Greece* .... **46 C4** 38 55N 22 47 E
Stillwater, *N.Z.* .... **91 K3** 42 27 S 171 20 E
Stillwater, *Minn., U.S.A.* **112 C8** 45 3N 92 49W
Stillwater, *N.Y., U.S.A.* **117 D11** 42 55N 73 41W
Stillwater, *Okla., U.S.A.* **113 G6** 36 7N 97 4W
Stillwater Range, *U.S.A.* **108 G4** 39 50N 118 5 E
Stillwater Reservoir,
  U.S.A. **117 C9** 43 54N 75 3W
Stilo, Pta., *Italy* ...... **43 D9** 38 25N 16 35 E
Stilwell, *U.S.A.* **113 H7** 35 49N 94 38W
Stînga Nistrului □,
  Moldova .... **29 C14** 47 20N 29 15 E
Ştip, *Macedonia* ...... **44 E6** 41 42N 22 10 E
Stíra, *Greece* .... **46 C6** 38 9N 24 14 E
Stirling, *Canada* **116 B7** 44 18N 77 33W
Stirling, *U.K.* **13 E5** 56 8N 3 57W
Stirling □, *U.K.* **13 E4** 56 12N 4 18W
Stirling Ra., *Australia* . **93 F2** 34 23 S 118 0 E
Stirling Range △,
  Australia .... **93 F2** 34 26 S 118 20 E
Stittsville, *Canada* **117 A9** 45 15N 75 55W
Stjernøya, *Norway* .... **8 A20** 70 20N 22 40 E
Stjørdalshalsen, *Norway* **8 E14** 63 29N 10 51 E
Stockach, *Germany* .... **25 H5** 47 50N 9 1 E
Stockaryd, *Sweden* .... **11 G8** 57 19N 14 36 E
Stockerau, *Austria* .... **27 C9** 48 24N 16 12 E
Stockholm, *Sweden* ... **10 E12** 59 20N 18 3 E
Stockholm Arlanda ✈
  (ARN), *Sweden* .... **10 E11** 59 41N 17 56 E
Stockholms län □,
  Sweden .... **10 E12** 59 30N 18 20 E
Stockport, *U.K.* **14 D5** 53 25N 2 9W
Stocksbridge, *U.K.* **14 D6** 53 29N 1 35W
Stockton, *Calif., U.S.A.* **110 H5** 37 58N 121 17W
Stockton, *Kans., U.S.A.* **112 F5** 39 26N 99 16W
Stockton, *Mo., U.S.A.* **113 G8** 37 42N 93 48W
Stockton-on-Tees, *U.K.* **14 C6** 54 35N 1 19W
Stockton-on-Tees □,
  U.K. **14 C6** 54 35N 1 19W
Stockton Plateau, *U.S.A.* **113 K3** 30 30N 102 30W
Stoczek Łukowski,
  Poland .... **31 G8** 51 58N 21 58 E
Stöde, *Sweden* .... **10 B10** 62 28N 16 35 E
Stoeng Treng, *Cambodia* **64 F5** 13 31N 105 58 E
Stoer, Pt. of, *U.K.* **13 C3** 58 16N 5 23W
Stogovo, *Macedonia* ... **44 E4** 41 31N 20 38 E
Stoholm, *Denmark* .... **11 H3** 56 30N 9 4 E
Stoke-on-Trent, *U.K.* .. **14 D5** 53 1N 2 11W
Stoke-on-Trent □, *U.K.* **14 D5** 53 1N 2 11W
Stokes →, *Australia* ... **93 E2** 29 55 S 115 6 E
Stokes Pt., *Australia* ... **95 G3** 40 10 S 143 56 E
Stokes Ra., *Australia* .. **92 C5** 15 50 S 130 50 E
Stokksnes, *Iceland* **8 D6** 64 14N 14 58W
Stokmarknes, *Norway* . **8 B16** 68 34N 14 54 E
Stolac, *Bos.-H.* .... **44 C1** 43 5N 17 59 E
Stolberg, *Germany* .... **24 E2** 50 47N 6 13 E
Stolbovoy, Ostrov,
  Russia .... **53 B14** 74 44N 135 14 E
Stolbtsy = Stowbtsy,
  Belarus .... **32 F4** 53 30N 26 43 E
Stolin, *Belarus* .... **33 G4** 51 53N 26 50 E
Stöllet, *Sweden* ...... **10 D7** 60 26N 13 15 E
Stolnici, *Romania* ..... **29 F9** 44 31N 24 48 E
Stomíon, *Greece* ...... **49 D5** 35 21N 23 32 E
Ston, *Croatia* .... **41 F14** 42 51N 17 43 E
Stone, *U.K.* **14 E5** 52 55N 2 9W
Stoneboro, *U.S.A.* **116 E4** 41 20N 80 7W
Stonehaven, *U.K.* **13 E6** 56 59N 2 12W
Stonehenge, *Australia* . **94 C3** 24 22 S 143 17 E
Stonehenge, *U.K.* **15 F6** 51 9N 1 45W
Stonewall, *Canada* **103 C9** 50 10N 97 19W
Stony L., *Man., Canada* **103 B9** 58 51N 98 40W
Stony L., *Ont., Canada* **116 B6** 44 30N 78 5W
Stony Point, *U.S.A.* ... **117 E11** 41 14N 73 59W
Stony Pt., *U.S.A.* **117 C8** 43 50N 76 18W
Stony Rapids, *Canada* . **103 B7** 59 16N 105 50W
Stony Tunguska =
  Tunguska,
  Podkamennaya →,
  Russia .... **53 C10** 61 50N 90 13 E
Stonyford, *U.S.A.* **110 F4** 39 23N 122 33W
Stopnica, *Poland* ...... **31 H7** 50 27N 20 57 E
Storå, *Sweden* .... **10 E9** 59 42N 15 6 E
Stora →, *Denmark* .... **11 H2** 56 20N 8 19 E
Stora Gla, *Sweden* .... **10 E6** 59 30N 12 30 E
Stora Le, *Sweden* ..... **10 E5** 59 5N 11 55 E
Stora Lulevatten,
  Sweden .... **8 C18** 67 10N 19 30 E
Storavan, *Sweden* ..... **8 D18** 65 45N 18 10 E
Stord, *Norway* .... **9 G11** 59 52N 5 23 E
Store Bælt, *Denmark* .. **11 J4** 55 20N 11 0 E
Store Heddinge,
  Denmark .... **11 J6** 55 18N 12 23 E
Store Mosse △, *Sweden* **11 G7** 57 18N 13 55 E
Storebro, *Sweden* ..... **11 G9** 57 35N 15 52 E
Storfors, *Sweden* ..... **10 E8** 59 32N 14 17 E
Storlien, *Sweden* ...... **10 A6** 63 19N 12 5 E
Storm B., *Australia* .... **95 G4** 43 10 S 147 30 E
Storm Lake, *U.S.A.* ... **112 D7** 42 39N 95 13W
Stormberge, *S. Africa* . **88 E4** 31 16 S 26 17 E
Stormsrivier, *S. Africa* . **88 E3** 33 59 S 23 52 E
Stornoway, *U.K.* **13 C2** 58 13N 6 23W
Storo, *Italy* .... **40 C7** 45 51N 10 35 E
Storozhynets,
  Storozhynets, *Ukraine* **29 B10** 48 14N 25 45 E
Storozhynets, *Ukraine* . **29 B10** 48 14N 25 45 E
Storrs, *U.S.A.* **117 E12** 41 49N 72 15W
Storsjön, *Gävleborg,
  Sweden* .... **10 D10** 60 35N 16 45 E
Storsjön, *Jämtland,
  Sweden* .... **10 B7** 62 48N 13 7 E
Storsjön, *Jämtland,
  Sweden* .... **10 A8** 63 9N 14 30 E
Storstrøms
  Amtskommune □,
  Denmark .... **11 J5** 54 50N 11 45 E

Storuman, *Sweden* .... **8 D17** 65 5N 17 10 E
Storuman, *Sweden* .... **8 D17** 65 13N 16 50 E
Storvätteshågna, *Sweden* **10 B6** 62 6N 12 30 E
Storvik, *Sweden* ...... **10 D10** 60 35N 16 33 E
Storvreta, *Sweden* ..... **10 E11** 59 58N 17 44 E
Stouffville, *Canada* **116 C5** 43 58N 79 15W
Stoughton, *Canada* **103 D8** 49 40N 103 0W
Stour →, *Dorset, U.K.* **15 G6** 50 43N 1 47W
Stour →, *Kent, U.K.* . **15 F9** 51 18N 1 22 E
Stour →, *Suffolk, U.K.* **15 F9** 51 57N 1 4 E
Stourbridge, *U.K.* **15 E5** 52 28N 2 8W
Stout L., *Canada* **103 C10** 52 0N 94 40W
Stove Pipe Wells
  Village, *U.S.A.* **111 J9** 36 35N 117 11W
Støvring, *Denmark* .... **11 H3** 56 54N 9 50 E
Stow, *U.S.A.* **116 E3** 41 10N 81 27W
Stowbtsy, *Belarus* ..... **32 F4** 53 30N 26 43 E
Stowmarket, *U.K.* ..... **15 E9** 52 12N 1 0 E
Strabane, *U.K.* **12 B4** 54 50N 7 27W
Stracin, *Macedonia* .... **44 D6** 42 13N 22 2 E
Stradella, *Italy* .... **40 C6** 45 5N 9 18 E
Strahan, *Australia* ..... **95 G4** 42 9 S 145 20 E
Strajitsa, *Bulgaria* ..... **45 C9** 43 14N 25 58 E
Strakonice, *Czech Rep.* **26 B6** 49 15N 13 53 E
Straldzha, *Bulgaria* .... **45 D10** 42 35N 26 40 E
Stralsund, *Germany* ... **24 A9** 54 18N 13 4 E
Strand, *S. Africa* ..... **88 E2** 34 9 S 18 48 E
Stranda,
  Møre og Romsdal,
  Norway .... **9 E12** 62 19N 6 58 E
Stranda,
  Nord-Trøndelag,
  Norway .... **8 E14** 63 33N 10 14 E
Strandby, *Denmark* .... **11 G4** 57 30N 10 29 E
Strangford L., *U.K.* ... **12 B6** 54 30N 5 37W
Strängnäs, *Sweden* .... **10 E11** 59 23N 17 2 E
Stranraer, *U.K.* **13 G3** 54 54N 5 1W
Strasbourg, *Canada* ... **103 C8** 51 4N 104 55W
Strasbourg, *France* .... **19 D14** 48 35N 7 42 E
Strasburg, *Germany* ... **24 B9** 53 30N 13 43 E
Strasburg, *U.S.A.* **112 B4** 46 8N 100 10W
Straßen □, *Germany* ... **29 C13** 47 8N 28 36 E
Stratford, *Canada* **116 C4** 43 23N 81 0W
Stratford, *N.Z.* .... **91 H5** 39 20 S 174 19 E
Stratford, *Calif., U.S.A.* **110 J7** 36 11N 119 49W
Stratford, *Conn., U.S.A.* **117 E11** 41 12N 73 8W
Stratford, *Tex., U.S.A.* **113 G3** 36 20N 102 4W
Stratford-upon-Avon,
  U.K. **15 E6** 52 12N 1 42W
Strath Spey, *U.K.* **13 D5** 57 9N 3 49W
Strathalbyn, *Australia* . **95 F2** 35 13 S 138 53 E
Strathaven, *U.K.* **13 F4** 55 40N 4 5W
Strathcona △, *Canada* **102 D3** 49 38N 125 40W
Strathmore, *Canada* ... **102 C6** 51 5N 113 18W
Strathmore, *U.K.* **13 E5** 56 37N 3 7W
Strathmore, *U.S.A.* **110 J7** 36 9N 119 4W
Strathnaver, *Canada* ... **102 C4** 53 20N 122 33W
Strathpeffer, *U.K.* **13 D4** 57 35N 4 32W
Strathroy, *Canada* **116 D3** 42 58N 81 38W
Strathy Pt., *U.K.* **13 C4** 58 36N 4 1W
Strattanville, *U.S.A.* ... **116 E5** 41 12N 79 19W
Stratton, *U.S.A.* **117 A14** 45 8N 70 26W
Stratton Mt., *U.S.A.* .. **117 C12** 43 4N 72 55W
Straubing, *Germany* ... **25 G8** 48 52N 12 34 E
Straumnes, *Iceland* **8 C2** 66 26N 23 8W
Strausberg, *Germany* .. **24 C9** 52 35N 13 54 E
Strawberry →, *U.S.A.* **108 F8** 40 10N 110 24W
Strážnice, *Czech Rep.* . **27 C10** 48 54N 17 19 E
Streaky B., *Australia* ... **95 E1** 32 48 S 134 13 E
Streaky Bay, *Australia* . **95 E1** 32 51 S 134 18 E
Streator, *U.S.A.* **112 E10** 41 8N 88 50W
Středočeský □,
  Czech Rep. .... **26 B7** 49 55N 14 30 E
Streetsboro, *U.S.A.* **116 E3** 41 14N 81 21W
Streetsville, *Canada* ... **116 C5** 43 35N 79 42W
Strehaia, *Romania* .... **29 F8** 44 37N 23 10 E
Strelcha, *Bulgaria* ..... **45 D8** 42 25N 24 19 E
Strelka, *Russia* .... **53 D10** 58 5N 93 3 E
Streng →, *Cambodia* .. **64 F4** 13 12N 103 37 E
Stresa, *Italy* .... **40 C5** 45 52N 8 28 E
Streymoy, *Færoe Is.* .. **8 E9** 62 8N 7 5W
Strezhevoy, *Russia* .... **52 C8** 60 42N 77 34 E
Stříbro, *Czech Rep.* .... **26 A6** 49 44N 13 0 E
Strilky, *Ukraine* ...... **31 J9** 49 20N 22 59 E
Strimón →, *Greece* ... **44 F7** 40 46N 23 51 E
Strimonikós Kólpos,
  Greece .... **44 F7** 40 33N 24 0 E
Strofádhes, *Greece* .... **46 D3** 37 15N 21 0 E
Stroma, *U.K.* **13 C5** 58 41N 3 7W
Stromberg-
  Heuchelberg △,
  Germany .... **25 F4** 49 2N 8 50 E
Strómboli, *Italy* ...... **43 D8** 38 47N 15 13 E
Stromeferry, *U.K.* **13 D3** 57 21N 5 33W
Stromness, *U.K.* **13 C5** 58 58N 3 17W
Strömsbruk, *Sweden* .. **10 C11** 61 52N 17 18 E
Stromsburg, *U.S.A.* ... **112 E6** 41 7N 97 36W
Strömsnäsbruk, *Sweden* **11 H7** 56 35N 13 45 E
Strömstad, *Sweden* .... **11 F5** 58 56N 11 10 E
Strömsund, *Sweden* ... **8 E16** 63 51N 15 33 E
Strongilí, *Greece* ..... **47 E11** 36 6N 29 42 E
Stróngoli, *Italy* .... **43 C10** 39 16N 17 3 E
Strongsville, *U.S.A.* **116 E3** 41 19N 81 50W
Stronie Śląskie, *Poland* **31 H3** 50 18N 16 53 E
Stronsay, *U.K.* **13 B6** 59 7N 2 35W
Stropkov, *Slovak Rep.* . **27 B14** 49 13N 21 39 E
Stroud, *U.K.* **15 F5** 51 45N 2 13W
Stroud Road, *Australia* **95 E5** 32 18 S 151 57 E
Stroudsburg, *U.S.A.* ... **117 F9** 40 59N 75 12W
Stroumbi, *Cyprus* ..... **49 E11** 34 53N 32 29 E
Struer, *Denmark* ...... **11 H2** 56 30N 8 35 E
Struga, *Macedonia* .... **44 E4** 41 11N 20 44 E
Strugi Krasnyye, *Russia* **32 C5** 58 21N 29 1 E
Strumica, *Macedonia* .. **44 E6** 41 28N 22 41 E
Strumica →, *Europe* .. **44 E7** 41 20N 23 22 E
Strumok, *Ukraine* ..... **29 E14** 45 43N 29 27 E
Struthers, *Canada* **104 C2** 48 41N 85 51W
Struthers, *U.S.A.* **116 E4** 41 4N 80 39W
Stryama, *Bulgaria* ..... **45 D8** 42 16N 24 54 E
Stryker, *U.S.A.* **108 B6** 48 41N 114 46W
Stryków, *Poland* ...... **31 G6** 51 55N 19 33 E
Stryy, *Ukraine* .... **33 H2** 49 16N 23 48 E
Strzegom, *Poland* ..... **31 H3** 50 58N 16 20 E
Strzelce Krajeńskie,
  Poland .... **31 F2** 52 52N 15 33 E
Strzelce Opolskie,
  Poland .... **31 H5** 50 31N 18 18 E
Strzelecki Cr. →,
  Australia .... **95 D2** 29 37 S 139 59 E
Strzelin, *Poland* .... **31 H4** 50 46N 17 2 E
Strzelno, *Poland* ...... **31 F5** 52 35N 18 9 E
Strzybnica, *Poland* .... **31 H5** 50 27N 18 51 E
Strzyżów, *Poland* ..... **31 J8** 49 52N 21 47 E
Stuart, *Fla., U.S.A.* ... **115 M5** 27 12N 80 15W
Stuart, *Nebr., U.S.A.* .. **112 D5** 42 36N 99 8W
Stuart →, *Canada* **102 C4** 54 0N 123 35W
Stuart Bluff Ra.,
  Australia .... **92 D5** 22 50 S 131 52 E

Stuart L., *Canada* **102 C4** 54 30N 124 30W
Stuart Ra., *Australia* ... **95 D1** 29 10 S 134 56 E
Stubbekøbing, *Denmark* **11 K6** 54 53N 12 9 E
Stuben, *Austria* .... **26 D3** 47 10N 10 8 E
Studen Kladenets,
  Yazovir, *Bulgaria* .. **45 E9** 41 37N 25 30 E
Studenka, *Czech Rep.* . **27 B11** 49 44N 18 1 E
Stugun, *Sweden* ...... **10 A9** 63 10N 15 40 E
Stuhr, *Germany* ...... **24 B4** 53 5N 8 44 E
Stull L., *Canada* **104 B1** 54 24N 92 34W
Stung Treng = Stoeng
  Treng, *Cambodia* ... **64 F5** 13 31N 105 58 E
Stupart →, *Canada* ... **104 A1** 56 0N 93 25W
Stupino, *Russia* ...... **32 D10** 54 57N 38 2 E
Stupava, *Slovak Rep.* . **27 C10** 48 17N 17 2 E
Sturgeon B., *Canada* .. **103 C9** 52 0N 97 50W
Sturgeon Bay, *U.S.A.* . **114 C2** 44 50N 87 23W
Sturgeon Falls, *Canada* **104 C4** 46 25N 79 57W
Sturgeon L., *Alta.,
  Canada* **102 B5** 55 6N 117 32W
Sturgeon L., *Ont.,
  Canada* **104 C1** 50 0N 90 45W
Sturgeon L., *Ont.,
  Canada* **116 B6** 44 28N 78 43W
Sturgis, *Canada* **103 C8** 51 56N 102 36W
Sturgis, *Mich., U.S.A.* **114 E3** 41 48N 85 25W
Sturgis, *S. Dak., U.S.A.* **112 C3** 44 25N 103 31W
Sturkö, *Sweden* ...... **11 H9** 56 5N 15 42 E
Štúrovo, *Slovak Rep.* . **27 D11** 47 48N 18 41 E
Sturt →, *Australia* .... **95 D3** 27 17 S 141 37 E
Sturt Cr. →, *Australia* **92 C4** 19 3 S 127 50 E
Stutterheim, *S. Africa* . **88 E4** 32 33 S 27 28 E
Stuttgart, *Germany* .... **25 G5** 48 48N 9 11 E
Stuttgart, *U.S.A.* **113 H9** 34 30N 91 33W
Stuttgart
  Echterdingen ✈
  (STR), *Germany* ... **25 G5** 48 42N 9 11 E
Stuyvesant, *U.S.A.* **117 D11** 42 23N 73 45W
Stykkishólmur, *Iceland* **8 D2** 65 2N 22 40W
Styria = Steiermark □,
  Austria .... **26 D8** 47 26N 15 0 E
Styrsö, *Sweden* .... **11 G5** 57 37N 11 46 E
Su Xian = Suzhou,
  China .... **56 H9** 33 41N 116 59 E
Suakin, *Sudan* .... **80 D4** 19 8N 37 20 E
Suan, *N. Korea* .... **57 E14** 38 42N 126 22 E
Suaqui, *Mexico* **118 B3** 29 12N 109 41W
Suar, *India* .... **69 E8** 29 2N 79 3 E
Subang, *Indonesia* ..... **63 G12** 6 34 S 107 45 E
Subansiri →, *India* .... **67 F18** 26 48N 93 50 E
Subarnarekha →, *India* **69 H12** 22 34N 87 24 E
Subayhah, *Si. Arabia* . **70 D3** 30 2N 38 50 E
Subcetate, *Romania* ... **28 E8** 45 36N 23 0 E
Subi, *Indonesia* .... **65 L6** 2 58N 108 50 E
Subiaco, *Italy* .... **41 G10** 41 56N 13 5 E
Subotica, *Serbia & M.* **28 D4** 46 6N 19 29 E
Suca, *Ethiopia* .... **81 F4** 6 31N 39 14 E
Suceava, *Romania* .... **29 C11** 47 38N 26 16 E
Suceava □, *Romania* .. **29 C10** 47 37N 25 40 E
Suceava →, *Romania* . **29 C11** 47 32N 26 32 E
Sucha-Beskidzka,
  Poland .... **31 J6** 49 44N 19 35 E
Suchań, *Poland* .... **31 E2** 53 18N 15 18 E
Suchan, *Russia* .... **54 C6** 43 8N 133 9 E
Suchedniów, *Poland* ... **31 G7** 51 3N 20 49 E
Suchitoto, *El Salv.* **120 D2** 13 56N 89 0W
Suchou = Suzhou, *China* **59 B13** 31 19N 120 38 E
Süchow = Xuzhou,
  China .... **57 G9** 34 18N 117 10 E
Suchowola, *Poland* .... **30 E10** 53 33N 23 3 E
Suck →, *Ireland* **12 C3** 53 17N 8 3W
Sucre, *Bolivia* .... **124 G5** 19 0 S 65 15W
Sućuraj, *Croatia* ...... **41 E14** 43 10N 17 8 E
Sucuriú →, *Brazil* ..... **125 H8** 20 47 S 51 38W
Sud, Pte. du, *Canada* . **105 C7** 49 3N 62 14W
Sud-Kivu □, *Dem. Rep.
  of the Congo* .... **86 C2** 3 0 S 28 30 E
Sud-Ouest, Pte., *Canada* **105 C7** 49 23N 63 36W
Suda →, *Russia* ...... **32 C9** 59 0N 37 40 E
Sudak, *Ukraine* .... **33 K8** 44 51N 34 57 E
Sudan, *U.S.A.* **113 H3** 34 4N 102 32W
Sudan ■, *Africa* ...... **81 E3** 15 0N 30 0 E
Sudbury, *Canada* **104 C3** 46 30N 81 0W
Sudbury, *U.K.* .... **15 E8** 52 2N 0 45 E
Südd, *Sudan* .... **81 F3** 8 20N 30 0 E
Sudeifel = Deutsch-
  Luxemburgischer △,
  Germany .... **25 F2** 49 58N 6 12 E
Süderbrarup, *Germany* **24 A5** 54 38N 9 45 E
Süderlügum, *Germany* . **24 A4** 54 52N 8 54 E
Süderoogsand, *Germany* **24 A4** 54 27N 8 28 E
Sudeten Mts. = Sudety,
  Europe .... **27 A9** 50 20N 16 45 E
Sudety, *Europe* .... **27 A9** 50 20N 16 45 E
Südheide △, *Germany* . **24 C6** 52 46N 10 10 E
Suðuroy, *Færoe Is.* **8 F9** 61 32N 6 50W
Sudi, *Tanzania* .... **87 E4** 10 11 S 39 57 E
Sudirman, Pegunungan,
  Indonesia .... **63 E9** 4 30 S 137 0 E
Sudiți, *Romania* ...... **29 F12** 44 35N 27 38 E
Sudogda, *Russia* ...... **34 C5** 55 55N 40 50 E
Sudong, Pulau,
  Singapore .... **65 d** 1 12N 103 43 E
Sudova Vyshnya,
  Ukraine .... **31 J9** 49 46N 23 22 E
Sudr, *Egypt* .... **80 B3** 29 40N 32 42 E
Sudzha, *Russia* .... **33 G8** 51 14N 35 17 E
Sue →, *Sudan* .... **81 F2** 7 41N 28 3 E
Sueca, *Spain* **39 F4** 39 12N 0 21W
Suedinenie, *Bulgaria* .. **45 D8** 42 16N 24 33 E
Suemez I., *U.S.A.* **102 B2** 55 15N 133 20W
Suez = El Suweis, *Egypt* **80 J8** 29 58N 32 31 E
Suez, G. of = Suweis,
  Khalig el, *Egypt* .... **80 J8** 28 40N 33 0 E
Suez Canal = Suweis,
  Qanâ es, *Egypt* ..... **80 H8** 31 0N 32 20 E
Suffield, *Canada* **102 C6** 50 12N 111 10W
Suffolk, *U.S.A.* **114 G7** 36 44N 76 35W
Suffolk □, *U.K.* ...... **15 E9** 52 16N 1 0 E
Şugag, *Romania* ...... **29 E8** 45 46N 23 39 E
Sugarcreek, *U.S.A.* **116 E5** 41 59N 79 21W
Sugargrove, *U.S.A.* ... **116 E5** 41 59N 79 21W
Sugarive →, *India* .... **69 F12** 26 16N 86 24 E
Suğla Gölü, *Turkey* ... **72 D5** 37 20N 32 0 E
Sugluk = Salluit, *Canada* **101 B12** 62 14N 75 38W
Suhaia, Lacul, *Romania* **29 G10** 43 45N 25 15 E
Şuḩār, *Oman* .... **71 E8** 24 20N 56 40 E
Sühbaatar, *Mongolia* .. **56 B8** 45 30N 114 0 E
Sühbaatar □, *Mongolia* **56 B8** 46 30N 108 50 E
Suhl, *Germany* .... **24 E6** 50 36N 10 42 E
Şuhut, *Turkey* .... **47 C12** 38 31N 30 32 E
Sui, *Pakistan* .... **68 E3** 28 37N 69 19 E
Sui Xian, *China* .... **56 H8** 34 25N 115 2 E
Suichang, *China* ...... **59 C12** 28 29N 119 15 E
Suichuan, *China* ...... **59 D10** 26 20N 114 32 E
Suide, *China* .... **56 F6** 37 30N 110 12 E
Suifenhe, *China* ...... **57 B16** 44 25N 131 10 E
Suihua, *China* .... **60 B7** 46 32N 126 55 E

Suijiang, China ...... 58 C4 28 40N 103 59 E
Suining, Hunan, China . 59 D8 26 35N 110 10 E
Suining, Jiangsu, China 57 H9 33 56N 117 58 E
Suining, Sichuan, China 58 B5 30 26N 105 35 E
Suiping, China ...... 56 H7 33 10N 113 59 E
Suippes, France ...... 19 C11 49 8N 4 30 E
Suir →, Ireland 12 D4 52 16N 7 9W
Suisun City, U.S.A. 110 G4 38 15N 122 2W
Suixi, China .... 59 G8 21 19N 110 18 E
Suiyang, Guizhou, China 58 D6 27 58N 107 18 E
Suiyang, Heilongjiang,
  China .... 57 B16 44 30N 130 56 E
Suizhong, China ...... 57 D11 40 21N 120 20 E
Suizhou, China .... 59 B9 31 42N 113 24 E
Sujangarh, India ..... 68 F6 27 42N 74 31 E
Sukabumi, Indonesia . 63 G12 6 56 S 106 50 E
Sukadana, Indonesia .. 62 E3 1 10 S 110 0 E
Sukagawa, Japan .... 55 F10 37 17N 140 23 E
Sukaraja, Indonesia .. 62 E4 2 28 S 110 25 E
Sukawati, Indonesia . 63 K18 8 35 S 115 17 E
Sukch'ŏn, N. Korea ... 57 E13 39 22N 125 35 E
Sukhindol, Bulgaria .. 45 C9 43 11N 25 10 E
Sukhinichi, Russia ... 32 E8 54 8N 35 10 E
Sukhona →, Russia ... 52 D4 61 15N 46 39 E
Sukhothai, Thailand .. 64 D2 17 1N 99 49 E
Sukhumi = Sokhumi,
  Georgia .... 35 J5 43 0N 41 0 E
Sukkur, Pakistan ..... 68 F3 27 42N 68 54 E
Sukkur Barrage,
  Pakistan .... 68 F3 27 40N 68 50 E
Sukovo, Serbia & M. .. 44 C6 43 4N 22 37 E
Sukri →, India .... 68 G4 25 4N 71 43 E
Sukumo, Japan .... 55 H6 32 56N 132 44 E
Sukunka →, Canada .. 102 B4 55 45N 121 15W
Sula →, Ukraine ..... 33 H7 49 40N 32 41 E
Sula, Kepulauan,
  Indonesia .... 63 E7 1 45 S 125 0 E
Sulaco →, Honduras . 120 C2 15 2N 87 44W
Sulaiman Range,
  Pakistan .... 68 D3 30 30N 69 50 E
Sulak →, Russia ..... 35 J8 43 20N 47 34 E
Sūlār, Iran .... 71 D6 31 53N 51 54 E
Sulawesi, Indonesia .. 63 E6 2 0 S 120 0 E
Sulawesi Sea = Celebes
  Sea, Indonesia .... 63 D6 3 0N 123 0 E
Sulawesi Selatan □,
  Indonesia .... 63 E6 2 30 S 120 0 E
Sulawesi Utara □,
  Indonesia .... 63 D6 1 0N 122 30 E
Sulechów, Poland .... 31 F2 52 5N 15 40 E
Sulęcin, Poland ...... 31 F2 52 26N 15 10 E
Sulejów, Poland ...... 31 G6 51 26N 19 53 E
Sulejówek, Poland ... 31 F8 52 13N 21 17 E
Süleymanlı, Turkey ... 47 C9 38 58N 37 47 E
Sulima, S. Leone 82 D2 6 58N 11 32W
Sulina, Romania ..... 29 E14 45 10N 29 40 E
Sulina, Brațul →,
  Romania .... 29 E14 45 10N 29 40 E
Sulingen, Germany ... 24 C4 52 41N 8 48 E
Sulița, Romania ...... 29 C11 47 39N 26 59 E
Sulitjelma, Norway ... 8 C17 67 9N 16 3 E
Sullana, Peru .... 124 D2 4 52 S 80 39W
Süller, Turkey .... 47 C11 38 9N 29 58 E
Sullivan, Ill., U.S.A. .. 112 F10 39 36N 88 37W
Sullivan, Ind., U.S.A. . 114 F2 39 6N 87 24W
Sullivan, Mo., U.S.A. . 112 F9 38 13N 91 10W
Sullivan Bay, Canada . 102 C3 50 55N 126 50W
Sullivan I. = Lanbi
  Kyun, Burma ..... 65 G2 10 50N 98 20 E
Sullom Voe, U.K. 13 A7 60 27N 1 20W
Sully-sur-Loire, France 19 E9 47 45N 2 20 E
Sulmierzyce, Poland .. 31 G4 51 37N 17 32 E
Sulmona, Italy .... 41 F10 42 3N 13 55 E
Sulphur, La., U.S.A. .. 113 K8 30 14N 93 23W
Sulphur, Okla., U.S.A. 113 H6 34 31N 96 58W
Sulphur Pt., Canada .. 102 A6 60 56N 114 48W
Sulphur Springs, U.S.A. 113 J7 33 8N 95 36W
Sultan, Canada 104 C3 47 36N 82 47W
Sultan, U.S.A. 110 C5 47 52N 121 49W
Sultan Dağları, Turkey 72 C4 38 20N 31 20 E
Sultanhisar, Turkey .. 47 D10 37 53N 28 9 E
Sultaniye, Turkey .... 45 F10 40 37N 26 8 E
Sultanpur, Mad. P.,
  India .... 68 H8 23 9N 77 56 E
Sultanpur, Punjab, India 68 D6 31 13N 75 11 E
Sultanpur, Ut. P., India 69 F10 26 18N 82 4 E
Sulu Arch., Phil. ..... 61 J4 6 0N 121 0 E
Sulu Sea, E. Indies ... 61 G4 8 0N 120 0 E
Sülüklü, Turkey ...... 72 C5 38 53N 32 20 E
Sululta, Ethiopia ..... 81 F4 9 10N 38 43 E
Suluova, Turkey ..... 72 B6 40 46N 35 32 E
Suluq, Libya .... 79 B10 31 44N 20 14 E
Sulzbach, Germany .. 25 F3 49 18N 7 3 E
Sulzbach-Rosenberg,
  Germany .... 25 F7 49 30N 11 44 E
Sulzberger Ice Shelf,
  Antarctica .... 5 E13 78 0 S 150 0W
Sumalata, Indonesia . 63 D6 1 0N 122 31 E
Sumampa, Argentina . 126 B3 29 25 S 63 29W
Sumatera □, Indonesia 62 D2 0 40N 100 20 E
Sumatera Barat □,
  Indonesia .... 62 E2 1 0 S 101 0 E
Sumatera Utara □,
  Indonesia .... 62 D1 2 30N 98 0 E
Sumatra = Sumatera □,
  Indonesia .... 62 D2 0 40N 100 20 E
Sumava △, Czech Rep. 26 C6 49 0N 13 49 E
Sumba, Indonesia .... 63 F5 9 45 S 119 35 E
Sumba, Selat, Indonesia 63 F5 9 0 S 118 40 E
Sumbawa, Indonesia . 62 F5 8 26 S 117 30 E
Sumbawa Besar,
  Indonesia .... 62 F5 8 30 S 117 26 E
Sumbawanga □,
  Tanzania .... 84 F6 8 0 S 31 30 E
Sumbe, Angola ...... 84 G2 11 10 S 13 48 E
Sumbu □, Zambia .... 87 D3 8 43 S 30 22 E
Sumburgh Hd., U.K. . 13 B7 59 52N 1 17W
Sumdeo, India .... 69 D8 31 26N 78 44 E
Sumdo, China .... 69 B8 35 6N 78 41 E
Sumedang, Indonesia 63 G12 6 52N 107 55 E
Sümeg, Hungary .... 28 D2 46 59N 17 20 E
Sumeih, Sudan ...... 81 F2 9 50N 27 39 E
Sumen = Shumen,
  Bulgaria .... 45 C10 43 18N 26 55 E
Sumenep, Indonesia . 63 G15 7 1 S 113 52 E
Sumgait = Sumqayıt,
  Azerbaijan .... 35 K9 40 34N 49 38 E
Summer L., U.S.A. ... 108 E3 42 50N 120 45W
Summerland, Canada . 102 D5 49 32N 119 41W
Summerside, Canada . 105 C7 46 24N 63 47W
Summerville, U.S.A. . 114 F5 38 17N 80 51W
Summerville, Ga.,
  U.S.A. 115 H3 34 29N 85 21W
Summerville, S.C.,
  U.S.A. 115 J5 33 1N 80 11W

Summit Lake, Canada . 102 C4 54 20N 122 40W
Summit Peak, U.S.A. . 109 H10 37 21N 106 42W
Sumner, Iowa, U.S.A. . 112 D8 42 51N 92 6W
Sumner, Wash., U.S.A. 110 C4 47 12N 122 14W
Sumoto, Japan .... 55 G7 34 21N 134 54 E
Šumperk, Czech Rep. . 27 B9 49 59N 16 59 E
Sumqayıt, Azerbaijan . 35 K9 40 34N 49 38 E
Sumter, U.S.A. 115 J5 33 55N 80 21W
Sumy, Ukraine .... 33 G8 50 57N 34 50 E
Sun City, S. Africa .... 88 D4 25 17 S 27 3 E
Sun City, Ariz., U.S.A. 109 K7 33 36N 112 17W
Sun City, Calif., U.S.A. 111 M9 33 42N 117 11W
Sun City Center, U.S.A. 115 M4 27 43N 82 18W
Sun Lakes, U.S.A. 109 K8 33 10N 111 52W
Sun Valley, U.S.A. 108 E6 43 42N 114 21W
Sunagawa, Japan .... 54 C10 43 29N 141 55 E
Sunan, N. Korea ..... 57 E13 39 15N 125 40 E
Sunart, L., U.K. 13 E3 56 42N 5 43W
Sunburst, U.S.A. 108 B8 48 53N 111 55W
Sunbury, Australia ... 95 F3 37 35 S 144 44 E
Sunbury, U.S.A. 117 F8 40 52N 76 48W
Sunchales, Argentina . 126 C3 30 58 S 61 35W
Suncho Corral,
  Argentina .... 126 B3 27 55 S 63 27W
Sunch'ŏn, S. Korea .. 57 G14 34 52N 127 31 E
Suncook, U.S.A. 117 C13 43 8N 71 27W
Sunda, Selat, Indonesia 62 F3 6 20 S 105 30 E
Sunda Is., Indonesia . 96 H2 5 0 S 105 0 E
Sunda Str. = Sunda,
  Selat, Indonesia ... 62 F3 6 20 S 105 30 E
Sundance, Canada ... 103 B10 56 32N 94 4W
Sundance, U.S.A. 112 C2 44 24N 104 23W
Sundar Nagar, India . 68 D7 31 32N 76 53 E
Sundarbans, Asia .... 67 J16 22 0N 89 0 E
Sundargarh, India ... 67 H14 22 4N 84 5 E
Sundays = Sondags →,
  S. Africa .... 88 E4 33 44 S 25 51 E
Sunderland, Canada .. 116 B5 44 16N 79 4W
Sunderland, U.K. 14 C6 54 55N 1 23W
Sundown △, Australia 95 D5 28 49 S 151 38 E
Sundre, Canada 102 C6 51 49N 114 38W
Sunds, Denmark ..... 11 H3 56 13N 9 1 E
Sundsvall, Sweden ... 10 B11 62 23N 17 17 E
Sundsvallsbukten,
  Sweden .... 10 B11 62 21N 17 25 E
Sung Hei, Vietnam ... 65 G6 10 20N 106 2 E
Sungai Acheh, Malaysia 65 c 5 7N 100 30 E
Sungai Kolok, Thailand 65 J3 6 2N 101 58 E
Sungai Lembing,
  Malaysia .... 65 L4 3 55N 103 3 E
Sungai Petani, Malaysia 65 K3 5 37N 100 30 E
Sungaigerong, Indonesia 62 E2 2 59 S 104 52 E
Sungailiat, Indonesia . 62 E2 1 51 S 106 8 E
Sungaipenuh, Indonesia 62 E2 2 1 S 101 20 E
Sungari = Songhua
  Jiang →, China ... 60 B8 47 45N 132 30 E
Songhua Chiang =
  Songhua Jiang →,
  China .... 60 B8 47 45N 132 30 E
Sungikai, Sudan ..... 81 E2 12 20N 29 51 E
Sungurlu, Turkey .... 72 B6 40 12N 34 21 E
Sunja, Croatia .... 41 C13 45 21N 16 35 E
Sunland Park, U.S.A. 109 L10 31 50N 106 40W
Sunnansjö, Norway .. 10 D8 60 13N 14 58 E
Sunndalsøra, Norway . 9 E13 62 40N 8 33 E
Sunne, Sweden ...... 10 E7 59 52N 13 5 E
Sunnemo, Sweden ... 10 E7 59 53N 13 44 E
Sunnyside, U.S.A. ... 108 C3 46 20N 120 0W
Sunnyvale, U.S.A. ... 110 H4 37 23N 122 2W
Suntar, Russia .... 53 C12 62 15N 117 30 E
Sunyani, Ghana 82 D4 7 21N 2 22W
Suomenselkä, Finland 8 E21 62 52N 24 0 E
Suomussalmi, Finland 8 D23 64 54N 29 10 E
Suoyarvi, Russia ..... 32 A7 62 3N 32 20 E
Supai, U.S.A. 109 H7 36 15N 112 41W
Supaul, India .... 69 F12 26 10N 86 40 E
Superior, Ariz., U.S.A. 109 K8 33 18N 111 6W
Superior, Mont., U.S.A. 108 C6 47 12N 114 53W
Superior, Nebr., U.S.A. 112 E5 40 1N 98 4W
Superior, Wis., U.S.A. 112 B8 46 44N 92 6W
Superior, L., N. Amer. 104 C2 47 0N 87 0W
Supetar, Croatia ..... 41 E13 43 25N 16 32 E
Suphan Buri, Thailand 64 E3 14 14N 100 10 E
Suphan Dağı, Turkey . 70 B4 38 54N 42 48 E
Supiori, Indonesia ... 63 E9 1 0 S 136 0 E
Supraśl, Poland ...... 31 E10 53 13N 23 19 E
Supraśl →, Poland ... 31 E9 53 11N 22 57 E
Supung Shuiku, China 57 D13 40 35N 124 50 E
Süq Suwayq, Si. Arabia 70 E3 24 23N 38 27 E
Suqian, China .... 57 H10 33 54N 118 8 E
Suquţra = Socotra,
  Yemen .... 75 E5 12 30N 54 0 E
Şūr, Lebanon .... 74 B4 33 19N 35 16 E
Şür, Oman .... 75 C6 22 34N 59 32 E
Sur, Pt., U.S.A. 110 J5 36 18N 121 54W
Sura →, Russia ...... 34 C8 56 6N 46 0 E
Surab, Pakistan ...... 68 E2 28 25N 66 15 E
Surabaja = Surabaya,
  Indonesia .... 63 G15 7 17 S 112 45 E
Surabaya, Indonesia . 63 G15 7 17 S 112 45 E
Surahammar, Sweden 10 E10 59 43N 16 13 E
Suraia, Romania ..... 29 E12 45 40N 27 25 E
Surakarta, Indonesia . 63 G14 7 35 S 110 48 E
Surakhany, Azerbaijan 35 K10 40 25N 50 1 E
Šuřany, Slovak Rep. . 27 C11 48 6N 18 10 E
Surat, Australia ...... 95 D4 27 10 S 149 6 E
Surat, India .... 66 J8 21 12N 72 55 E
Surat Thani, Thailand 65 H2 9 6N 99 20 E
Suratgarh, India ..... 68 E5 29 18N 73 55 E
Suraż, Poland .... 31 F9 52 57N 22 57 E
Surazh, Belarus ..... 32 E6 55 25N 30 44 E
Surazh, Russia ...... 33 F7 53 5N 32 27 E
Surduc, Romania .... 29 C8 47 15N 23 19 E
Surduc Pasul, Romania 29 E8 45 21N 23 23 E
Surdulica, Serbia & M. 44 D6 42 41N 22 11 E
Surendranagar, India 68 H4 22 45N 71 40 E
Surf, U.S.A. 111 L6 34 41N 120 36W
Surgères, France 20 B3 46 7N 0 47W
Surgut, Russia .... 52 C8 61 14N 73 20 E
Sùria, Spain .... 38 D6 41 50N 1 45 E
Suriapet, India ...... 66 L11 17 10N 79 40 E
Surigao, Phil. .... 61 G6 9 45N 125 23 E
Surigao Strait, Phil. . 61 F6 10 15N 125 23 E
Surin, Thailand ...... 64 E4 14 50N 103 34 E
Surin Nua, Ko, Thailand 65 H1 9 30N 97 55 E
Surinam = Suriname ■,
  S. Amer. 125 C7 4 0N 56 0W
Suriname ■, S. Amer. 125 C7 4 0N 56 0W
Suriname →, Suriname 125 B7 5 50N 55 15W
Şürmaq, Iran .... 71 D7 31 3N 52 48 E
Sürmene, Turkey .... 73 B9 41 0N 40 1 E
Surovikino, Russia ... 35 F6 48 32N 42 55 E
Surrey, Canada 110 A4 49 10N 122 54W
Surrey □, U.K. 15 F7 51 15N 0 31W
Sursand, India .... 69 F11 26 39N 85 43 E
Sursar →, India ..... 69 F12 26 14N 87 3 E
Sursee, Switz. .... 25 H4 47 11N 8 6 E

Sursk, Russia .... 34 D7 53 3N 45 40 E
Surskoye, Russia ..... 34 D8 54 30N 46 44 E
Surt, Libya .... 79 B9 31 11N 16 39 E
Surt, Khalīj, Libya ... 79 B9 31 40N 18 30 E
Surte, Sweden .... 11 G6 57 50N 12 1 E
Surtsey, Iceland 8 E3 63 20N 20 30W
Sürüç, Turkey .... 73 D8 36 58N 38 25 E
Suruga-Wan, Japan .. 55 G9 34 45N 138 30 E
Susa, Italy .... 40 C4 45 8N 7 3 E
Suså →, Denmark ... 11 J5 55 12N 11 42 E
Sušac, Croatia .... 41 F13 42 46N 16 30 E
Susak, Croatia .... 41 D11 44 30N 14 18 E
Susaki, Japan .... 55 H6 33 22N 133 17 E
Susangerd, Iran ..... 71 D6 31 35N 48 6 E
Susanville, U.S.A. ... 108 F3 40 25N 120 39W
Susch, Switz. .... 25 J6 46 46N 10 5 E
Suşehri, Turkey ..... 73 B8 40 10N 38 6 E
Sušice, Czech Rep. ... 26 B6 49 17N 13 30 E
Susleni, Moldova .... 29 C13 47 25N 28 59 E
Susner, India .... 68 H7 23 57N 76 5 E
Susong, China .... 59 B11 30 10N 116 5 E
Susquehanna, U.S.A. . 117 E9 41 57N 75 36W
Susquehanna →, U.S.A. 117 G8 39 33N 76 5W
Susques, Argentina .. 126 A2 23 35 S 66 25W
Sussex, Canada 105 C6 45 45N 65 37W
Sussex, U.S.A. 117 E10 41 13N 74 37W
Sussex, E. □, U.K. ... 15 G8 51 0N 0 20 E
Sussex, W. □, U.K. .. 15 G7 51 0N 0 30W
Sustut →, Canada ... 102 B3 56 20N 127 30W
Susuman, Russia .... 53 C15 62 47N 148 10 E
Susunu, Indonesia ... 63 E8 3 7 S 133 39 E
Susurluk, Turkey .... 47 B10 39 54N 28 8 E
Susuz, Turkey .... 73 B10 40 46N 43 9 E
Susz, Poland .... 30 E6 53 44N 19 20 E
Sütçüler, Turkey .... 72 D4 37 29N 30 57 E
Sutherland, S. Africa . 88 E3 32 24 S 20 40 E
Sutherland, U.K. 13 C4 58 12N 4 50W
Sutherland, U.S.A. ... 112 E4 41 10N 101 8W
Sutherland Falls, N.Z. 91 L1 44 48 S 167 46 E
Sutherlin, U.S.A. 108 E2 43 23N 123 19W
Suthri, India .... 68 H3 23 3N 68 55 E
Sutlej →, Pakistan .. 68 E4 29 23N 71 3 E
Sutter, U.S.A. 110 F5 39 10N 121 45W
Sutter Creek, U.S.A. . 110 G6 38 24N 120 48W
Sutton, Canada 117 A12 45 6N 72 37W
Sutton, Nebr., U.S.A. . 112 E6 40 36N 97 52W
Sutton, W. Va., U.S.A. 114 F5 38 40N 80 43W
Sutton →, Canada ... 104 A3 55 15N 83 45W
Sutton Coldfield, U.K. 15 E6 52 35N 1 49W
Sutton in Ashfield, U.K. 14 D6 53 8N 1 16W
Sutton L., Canada 104 B3 54 15N 84 42W
Suttor →, Australia .. 94 C4 21 36 S 147 2 E
Suttsu, Japan .... 54 C10 42 48N 140 14 E
Suva, Fiji .... 91 D8 18 6 S 178 30 E
Suva Gora, Macedonia 44 E5 41 45N 21 3 E
Suva Planina,
  Serbia & M. .... 44 C6 43 10N 22 5 E
Suva Reka, Serbia & M. 44 D4 42 21N 20 50 E
Suvorov, Russia ..... 32 E9 54 7N 36 30 E
Suvorov Is. = Suwarrow
  Is., Cook Is. ...... 97 J11 15 0 S 163 0W
Suvorovo, Ukraine ... 29 E13 45 35N 28 59 E
Suvorovo, Bulgaria .. 45 C11 43 20N 27 35 E
Suwałki, Poland ..... 30 D9 54 8N 22 59 E
Suwana, Indonesia .. 63 K18 8 44 S 115 16 E
Suwannaphum, Thailand 64 E4 15 33N 103 47 E
Suwannee →, U.S.A. . 115 L4 29 17N 83 10W
Suwarrow Is., Cook Is. 97 J11 15 0 S 163 0W
Suwayq aş Şuqban, Iraq 70 D5 31 32N 46 7 E
Suweis, Khalîg el, Egypt 80 J8 28 40N 33 0 E
Suweis, Qanâ es, Egypt 80 H8 31 0N 32 20 E
Suwŏn, S. Korea .... 57 F14 37 17N 127 1 E
Suzdal, Russia .... 34 B5 56 29N 40 26 E
Suzhou, Anhui, China 56 H9 33 41N 116 59 E
Suzhou, Jiangsu, China 59 B13 31 19N 120 38 E
Suzu, Japan .... 55 F8 37 25N 137 17 E
Suzu-Misaki, Japan .. 55 F8 37 31N 137 21 E
Suzuka, Japan .... 55 G8 34 55N 136 36 E
Suzzara, Italy .... 40 D7 44 59N 10 45 E
Svalbard, Arctic ..... 51 B5 78 0N 17 0 E
Svalbard Radio =
  Longyearbyen,
  Svalbard .... 4 B8 78 13N 15 40 E
Svalöv, Sweden ...... 11 J7 55 57N 13 8 E
Svalyava, Ukraine ... 28 B7 48 33N 22 59 E
Svaneke, Denmark .. 11 J9 55 8N 15 8 E
Svängsta, Sweden ... 11 H8 56 16N 14 47 E
Svanskog, Sweden ... 10 E6 59 11N 12 33 E
Svappavaara, Sweden 8 C19 67 40N 21 3 E
Svärdsjö, Sweden ... 10 D9 60 45N 15 54 E
Svartå, Sweden ...... 10 E8 59 8N 14 32 E
Svartisen, Norway ... 8 C16 66 40N 13 50 E
Svartvik, Sweden .... 10 B11 62 19N 17 24 E
Svatove, Ukraine .... 33 H10 49 22N 38 15 E
Svatovo = Svatove,
  Ukraine .... 33 H10 49 22N 38 15 E
Svay Chek, Cambodia 64 F4 13 48N 102 58 E
Svay Rieng, Cambodia 65 G5 11 9N 105 45 E
Svealand □, Sweden . 10 D9 60 20N 15 0 E
Svedala, Sweden .... 11 J7 55 30N 13 15 E
Sveg, Sweden .... 10 B8 62 2N 14 21 E
Svendborg, Denmark . 11 J4 55 4N 10 35 E
Svenljunga, Sweden . 11 G7 57 29N 13 5 E
Svenstavik, Sweden . 10 B8 62 45N 14 26 E
Svenstrup, Denmark . 11 H3 56 58N 9 50 E
Sverdlovsk, Ukraine . 33 H10 48 5N 39 47 E
Sverdrup Is., Canada . 98 B10 79 0N 97 0W
Svetac, Croatia ...... 41 E12 43 3N 15 43 E
Sveti Nikola, Prokhod,
  Europe .... 44 C6 43 27N 22 6 E
Sveti Nikole, Macedonia 44 E5 41 51N 21 56 E
Sveti Rok, Croatia ... 41 D12 44 22N 15 39 E
Svetlaya, Russia ..... 54 A9 46 33N 138 18 E
Svetlogorsk =
  Svyetlahorsk, Belarus 33 F6 52 38N 29 46 E
Svetlogorsk, Russia .. 30 D7 54 56N 20 10 E
Svetlograd, Russia ... 35 H6 45 25N 42 58 E
Svetlovodsk =
  Svitlovodsk, Ukraine 33 H7 49 2N 33 13 E
Svetlyy, Russia ...... 30 D7 54 41N 20 8 E
Svidník, Slovak Rep. . 27 B14 49 15N 21 37 E
Svilaja Planina, Croatia 41 E13 43 49N 16 31 E
Svilajnac, Serbia & M. 44 B5 44 15N 21 11 E
Svilengrad, Bulgaria . 45 E10 41 49N 26 12 E
Svir →, Russia ...... 32 B7 60 30N 32 48 E
Sviritsa, Russia ...... 32 B7 60 30N 32 48 E
Svishtov, Bulgaria ... 45 C9 43 36N 25 23 E
Svislach, Belarus .... 31 E11 53 3N 24 2 E
Svitava →, Czech Rep. 27 B9 49 11N 16 37 E
Svitavy, Czech Rep. . 27 B9 49 47N 16 28 E
Svitlovodsk, Ukraine . 33 H7 49 2N 33 13 E
Svobodnyy, Russia ... 53 D13 51 20N 128 0 E

Svoge, Bulgaria ...... 44 D7 42 59N 23 23 E
Svolvær, Norway .... 8 B16 68 15N 14 34 E
Svratka →, Czech Rep. 27 B9 49 11N 16 38 E
Svrljig, Serbia & M. .. 44 C6 43 25N 22 6 E
Svyetlahorsk, Belarus 33 F5 52 38N 29 46 E
Swabian Alps =
  Schwäbische Alb,
  Germany .... 25 G5 48 20N 9 30 E
Swaffham, U.K. ..... 15 E8 52 39N 0 42 E
Swainsboro, U.S.A. .. 115 J4 32 36N 82 20W
Swakop →, Namibia 88 C2 22 38 S 14 36 E
Swakopmund, Namibia 88 C1 22 37 S 14 30 E
Swale →, U.K. 14 C6 54 5N 1 20W
Swan →, Australia ... 93 F2 32 3 S 115 45 E
Swan →, Canada 103 C8 52 30N 100 45W
Swan Hill, Australia .. 95 F3 35 20 S 143 33 E
Swan Hills, Canada .. 102 C5 54 43N 115 24W
Swan Is. = Santanilla, Is.,
  Honduras 120 C3 17 22N 83 57W
Swan L., Canada 103 C8 52 30N 100 40W
Swan Peak, U.S.A. ... 108 C7 47 43N 113 38W
Swan Ra., U.S.A. 108 C7 48 0N 113 45W
Swan River, Canada . 103 C8 52 10N 101 16W
Swanage, U.K. 15 G6 50 36N 1 58W
Swansea, Australia .. 95 G4 42 8 S 148 4 E
Swansea, Canada 116 C5 43 38N 79 28W
Swansea, U.K. 15 F4 51 37N 3 57W
Swansea, U.S.A. 117 E13 41 45N 71 11W
Swansea □, U.K. 15 F3 51 38N 4 3W
Swar →, Pakistan ... 69 B5 34 40N 72 5 E
Swartberge, S. Africa 88 E3 33 20 S 22 0 E
Swartmodder, S. Africa 88 D3 28 1 S 20 32 E
Swartnossob →,
  Namibia .... 88 C2 23 8 S 18 42 E
Swartruggens, S. Africa 88 D4 25 39 S 26 42 E
Swarzędz, Poland .... 31 F4 52 25N 17 4 E
Swastika, Canada 104 C3 48 7N 80 6W
Swatow = Shantou,
  China .... 59 F11 23 18N 116 40 E
Swaziland ■, Africa . 89 D5 26 30 S 31 30 E
Sweden ■, Europe .. 9 G16 57 0N 15 0 E
Swedru, Ghana 83 D4 5 32N 0 41W
Sweet Home, U.S.A. . 108 D2 44 24N 122 44W
Sweetgrass, U.S.A. .. 108 B8 48 59N 111 58W
Sweetwater, Nev., U.S.A. 110 G7 38 27N 119 9W
Sweetwater, Tenn.,
  U.S.A. 115 H3 35 36N 84 28W
Sweetwater, Tex., U.S.A. 113 J4 32 28N 100 25W
Sweetwater →, U.S.A. 108 E10 42 31N 107 2W
Swellendam, S. Africa 88 E3 34 1 S 20 26 E
Swider →, Poland ... 31 F8 52 6N 21 14 E
Świdnica, Poland .... 31 H3 50 50N 16 30 E
Świdnik, Poland ..... 31 G9 51 13N 22 39 E
Świdwin, Poland ..... 30 E2 53 47N 15 49 E
Świebodzice, Poland . 31 H3 50 51N 16 20 E
Świebodzin, Poland .. 31 F2 52 15N 15 31 E
Świecie, Poland ...... 30 E5 53 25N 18 30 E
Świerzawa, Poland .. 31 G2 51 1N 15 54 E
Świętokrzyskie □,
  Poland .... 31 H7 50 53N 20 59 E
Świętokrzyskie, Góry,
  Poland .... 31 H7 51 0N 20 30 E
Swift Current, Canada 103 C7 50 20N 107 45W
Swift Current →,
  Canada 103 C7 50 38N 107 44W
Swilly, L., Ireland ... 12 A4 55 12N 7 33W
Swindon, U.K. 15 F6 51 34N 1 46W
Swindon □, U.K. 15 F6 51 34N 1 46W
Swinemünde =
  Świnoujście, Poland 30 E1 53 54N 14 16 E
Swinford, Ireland 12 C3 53 57N 8 58W
Świnoujście, Poland . 30 E1 53 54N 14 16 E
Switzerland ■, Europe 25 J4 46 30N 8 0 E
Swords, Ireland 12 C5 53 28N 6 13W
Swoyerville, U.S.A. .. 117 E9 41 18N 75 53W
Syasstroy, Russia .... 32 B7 60 9N 32 33 E
Sychevka, Russia .... 32 E8 55 59N 34 16 E
Syców, Poland ...... 31 G4 51 19N 17 40 E
Sydenham →, Canada 116 D2 42 33N 82 25W
Sydney, Australia .... 95 E5 33 53 S 151 10 E
Sydney, Canada 105 C7 46 7N 60 7W
Sydney L., Canada ... 103 C10 50 41N 94 25W
Sydney Mines, Canada 105 C7 46 18N 60 15W
Sydprøven = Alluitsup
  Paa, Greenland 101 B15 60 30N 45 35W
Sydra, G. of = Surt,
  Khalīj, Libya ...... 79 B9 31 40N 18 30 E
Syeverodonetsk,
  Ukraine .... 33 H10 48 58N 38 35 E
Syke, Germany ...... 24 C4 52 55N 8 50 E
Sykesville, U.S.A. ... 116 E6 41 3N 78 50W
Syktyvkar, Russia ... 52 C6 61 45N 50 40 E
Sylacauga, U.S.A. ... 115 J2 33 10N 86 15W
Sylarna, Sweden .... 8 E15 63 2N 12 13 E
Sylhet, Bangla. ...... 67 G17 24 54N 91 52 E
Sylhet □, Bangla. .... 67 G17 24 50N 91 50 E
Sylt, Germany .... 24 A4 54 54N 8 22 E
Sylvan Beach, U.S.A. 117 C9 43 12N 75 44W
Sylvan Lake, Canada . 102 C6 52 20N 114 3W
Sylvania, U.S.A. 115 J5 32 45N 81 38W
Sylvester, U.S.A. 115 K4 31 32N 83 50W
Sym, Russia .... 52 C9 60 20N 88 18 E
Symón, Mexico 118 C4 24 42N 102 35W
Synelnykove, Ukraine 33 H8 48 25N 35 30 E
Synevyr △, Ukraine . 29 B8 48 30N 23 40 E
Synevyrska Polyana,
  Ukraine .... 29 B8 48 35N 23 41 E
Synnott Ra., Australia 92 C4 16 30 S 125 20 E
Synyak, Ukraine .... 28 B7 48 35N 22 51 E
Syowa, Antarctica ... 5 C5 68 5 S 39 10 E
Syracuse, Kans., U.S.A. 113 G4 37 59N 101 45W
Syracuse, N.Y., U.S.A. 117 C8 43 3N 76 9W
Syracuse, Nebr., U.S.A. 112 E6 40 39N 96 11W
Syrdarya →,
  Kazakhstan .... 52 E7 46 3N 61 0 E
Syria ■, Asia .... 70 C3 35 0N 38 0 E
Syrian Desert = Shām,
  Bādiyat ash, Asia . 70 C3 32 0N 40 0 E
Sysslebäck, Sweden . 10 D6 60 44N 12 52 E
Syzran, Russia ...... 34 D9 53 23N 48 30 E
Szabolcs-Szatmár-
  Bereg □, Hungary . 28 B6 48 2N 21 45 E
Szadek, Poland ...... 31 G5 51 41N 18 59 E
Szamocin, Poland ... 31 E4 53 2N 17 7 E
Szamos →, Hungary . 28 B7 48 7N 22 20 E
Szamotuły, Poland ... 31 F3 52 35N 16 5 E
Száraz →, Hungary . 28 D6 46 10N 21 15 E
Szarvas, Hungary ... 28 D5 46 50N 20 38 E
Százhalombatta,
  Hungary .... 28 C3 47 20N 18 58 E
Szczawnica, Poland . 31 J7 49 26N 20 33 E
Szczebrzeszyn, Poland 31 H9 50 42N 22 59 E
Szczecin, Poland .... 30 E1 53 27N 14 27 E
Szczecinek, Poland .. 30 E3 53 43N 16 41 E
Szczeciński, Zalew =
  Stettiner Haff,
  Germany .... 24 B10 53 47N 14 15 E

Szczekociny, Poland . 31 H6 50 38N 19 48 E
Szczucin, Poland .... 31 H8 50 18N 21 4 E
Szczuczyn, Poland .. 30 E9 53 36N 22 19 E
Szczyrk, Poland ..... 31 J6 49 43N 19 2 E
Szczytna, Poland .... 31 H3 50 25N 16 28 E
Szczytno, Poland .... 30 E7 53 33N 21 0 E
Szechuan = Sichuan □,
  China .... 58 B5 31 0N 105 0 E
Szechwan Basin =
  Sichuan Pendi,
  China .... 58 B5 31 0N 105 0 E
Szechwan = Sichuan □,
  China .... 58 B5 30 30N 103 0 E
Szécsény, Hungary .. 28 B4 48 7N 19 30 E
Szeged, Hungary .... 28 D5 46 16N 20 10 E
Szeghalom, Hungary 28 C6 47 1N 21 10 E
Székesfehérvár,
  Hungary .... 28 C3 47 15N 18 25 E
Szekszárd, Hungary . 28 D3 46 22N 18 42 E
Szendrő, Hungary ... 28 B5 48 24N 20 41 E
Szentendre, Hungary 28 C4 47 39N 19 4 E
Szentes, Hungary ... 28 D5 46 39N 20 21 E
Szentgotthárd, Hungary 28 D1 46 58N 16 19 E
Szentlőrinc, Hungary 28 D3 46 3N 18 1 E
Szerencs, Hungary .. 28 B6 48 10N 21 12 E
Szigetszentmiklós,
  Hungary .... 28 C4 47 21N 19 3 E
Szigetvár, Hungary .. 28 D2 46 3N 17 46 E
Szikszó, Hungary .... 28 B5 48 12N 20 56 E
Szklarska Poreba,
  Poland .... 31 H2 50 50N 15 33 E
Szkwa →, Poland ... 31 E8 53 11N 21 43 E
Szlichtyngowa, Poland 31 G3 51 42N 16 15 E
Szob, Hungary ...... 28 C3 47 48N 18 53 E
Szolnok, Hungary ... 28 C5 47 10N 20 15 E
Szombathely, Hungary 28 C1 47 14N 16 38 E
Szprotawa, Poland ... 31 G2 51 33N 15 35 E
Sztum, Poland ...... 30 E6 53 55N 19 1 E
Sztutowo, Poland ... 30 D6 54 20N 19 15 E
Szubin, Poland ...... 31 E4 53 1N 17 45 E
Szydłowiec, Poland . 31 G7 51 15N 20 51 E
Szypliszki, Poland ... 30 D10 54 17N 23 2 E

T

Ta Khli Khok, Thailand 64 E3 15 18N 100 20 E
Ta Lai, Vietnam ..... 65 G6 11 24N 107 23 E
Tab, Hungary .... 28 D3 46 44N 18 2 E
Tabacal, Argentina .. 126 A3 23 15 S 64 15W
Tabaco, Phil. .... 61 E5 13 22N 123 44 E
Tabagné, Ivory C. ... 82 D4 7 59N 3 4W
Ţabah, Si. Arabia ... 70 E4 26 55N 42 38 E
Tabanan, Indonesia . 63 K18 8 32 S 115 8 E
Tabankort, Niger .... 83 B5 17 44N 0 20 E
Ţabas, Khorāsān, Iran 71 C9 32 48N 60 12 E
Ţabas, Khorāsān, Iran 71 C8 33 35N 56 55 E
Tabasará, Serranía de,
  Panama 120 E3 8 35N 81 40W
Tabasco □, Mexico .. 119 D6 17 45N 93 30W
Tabāsīn, Iran .... 71 D8 31 12N 57 54 E
Tabatinga, Serra da,
  Brazil .... 125 F10 10 30 S 44 0W
Taber, Canada 102 D6 49 47N 112 8W
Taberg, Sweden ..... 11 G8 57 40N 14 6 E
Taberg, U.S.A. 117 C9 43 18N 75 37W
Tabla, Niger .... 83 C5 13 46N 3 1 E
Tablas de Daimiel △,
  Spain 37 F7 39 9N 3 40W
Tablas I., Phil. ...... 61 E5 12 25N 122 2 E
Tablas Strait, Phil. .. 61 E4 12 40N 121 48 E
Table B., Canada 105 B8 50 40N 56 25W
Table B., S. Africa ... 88 E2 33 35 S 18 25 E
Table Mt., S. Africa .. 88 E2 34 0 S 18 22 E
Table Rock L., U.S.A. 113 G8 36 36N 93 19W
Tabletop, Mt., Australia 94 C4 23 24 S 147 11 E
Tábor, Czech Rep. ... 26 B7 49 25N 14 39 E
Tabora, Tanzania .... 86 D3 5 2 S 32 50 E
Tabora □, Tanzania . 86 D3 5 0 S 33 0 E
Tabou, Ivory C. 82 E3 4 30N 7 20W
Tabrīz, Iran .... 70 B5 38 7N 46 20 E
Tabuaeran, Kiribati . 97 G12 3 51N 159 22W
Tabuenca, Spain 38 D3 41 42N 1 33W
Tabūk, Si. Arabia ... 70 D3 28 23N 36 36 E
Taburno-
  Camposauro △, Italy 43 A7 41 8N 14 37 E
Täby, Sweden .... 10 E12 59 28N 18 4 E
Tacámbaro de Codallos,
  Mexico 118 D4 19 14N 101 28W
Tacheng, China ..... 60 B3 46 40N 82 58 E
Tach'i, Taiwan ...... 59 E13 24 46N 121 18 E
Tachia, Taiwan ...... 59 E13 24 25N 120 28 E
Tach'ing Shan = Daqing
  Shan, China ...... 56 D6 40 40N 111 0 E
Tachov, Czech Rep. . 26 B5 49 47N 12 39 E
Tácina →, Italy ..... 43 D9 38 57N 16 55 E
Tacloban, Phil. ...... 61 F6 11 15N 124 58 E
Tacna, Peru .... 124 G4 18 0 S 70 20W
Tacoma, U.S.A. 110 C4 47 14N 122 26W
Tacuarembó, Uruguay 127 C4 31 45 S 56 0W
Tademaït, Plateau du,
  Algeria .... 78 C6 28 30N 2 30 E
Tadio, L., Ivory C. ... 82 D3 5 10N 5 15W
Tadjoura, Djibouti ... 81 E5 11 50N 42 55 E
Tadjoura, Golfe de,
  Djibouti .... 81 E5 11 50N 43 0 E
Tadmor, N.Z. .... 91 J4 41 27 S 172 45 E
Tadoule L., Canada .. 103 B9 58 36N 98 20W
Tadoussac, Canada .. 105 C6 48 11N 69 42W
Tadrés →, Niger .... 83 B6 16 0N 7 10 E
Tadzhikistan =
  Tajikistan ■, Asia . 52 F8 38 30N 70 0 E
Taechŏn-ni, S. Korea 57 F14 36 21N 126 36 E
Taegu, S. Korea ..... 57 G15 35 50N 128 37 E
Taegwan, N. Korea .. 57 D13 40 13N 125 12 E
Taejŏn, S. Korea .... 57 F14 36 20N 127 28 E
Taen, Ko, Thailand .. 65 b 9 22N 99 57 E
Tafalla, Spain 38 C3 42 30N 1 41W
Tafar, Sudan .... 81 F2 6 52N 28 15 E
Tafelbaai = Table B.,
  S. Africa .... 88 E2 33 35 S 18 25 E
Tafermaar, Indonesia 63 F8 6 47 S 134 10 E
Tafí Viejo, Argentina . 126 B2 26 43 S 65 17W
Tafīhān, Iran .... 71 D7 29 25N 52 39 E
Tafiré, Ivory C. 82 D3 9 4N 5 4W
Tafo, Ghana 83 D4 6 15N 0 20W
Tafresh, Iran .... 71 C6 34 45N 49 57 E
Taft, Iran .... 71 D7 31 45N 54 14 E
Taft, Phil. .... 61 F6 11 57N 125 30 E
Taft, U.S.A. 111 K7 35 8N 119 28W
Taftān, Kūh-e, Iran .. 71 D9 28 40N 61 0 E
Taga Dzong, Bhutan . 67 F17 27 5N 89 55 E
Taganrog, Russia .... 33 J10 47 12N 38 50 E
Taganrogskiy Zaliv,
  Russia .... 33 J10 47 0N 38 30 E
Tagânt, Mauritania .. 82 B2 18 20N 11 0W
Tagatay, Phil. .... 61 D4 14 6N 120 56 E
Tagbilaran, Phil. .... 61 G5 9 39N 123 51 E
Tággia, Italy .... 40 E4 43 52N 7 51 E

Tagish, *Canada* **102 A2** 60 19N 134 16W
Tagish L., *Canada* **102 A2** 60 10N 134 20W
Tagliacozzo, *Italy* **41 F10** 42 4N 13 14 E
Tagliamento →, *Italy* **41 C10** 45 38N 13 6 E
Táglio di Po, *Italy* **41 D9** 45 0N 12 12 E
Tago, *Phil.* **61 G7** 9 2N 126 13 E
Tagomago, *Spain* **48 B8** 39 2N 1 39 E
Tagourāret, *Mauritania* **82 B3** 17 45N 7 45W
Taguatinga, *Brazil* **125 F10** 12 16 S 42 26W
Tagudin, *Phil.* **61 C4** 16 56N 120 27 E
Tagum, *Phil.* **61 H6** 7 33N 125 53 E
Tagus = Tejo →, *Europe* **37 F2** 38 40N 9 24W
Tahakopa, *N.Z.* **91 M2** 46 30 S 169 23 E
Tahan, Gunong, *Malaysia* **65 K4** 4 34N 102 17 E
Tahat, *Algeria* **78 D7** 23 18N 5 33 E
Tāherī, *Iran* **71 E7** 27 43N 52 20 E
Tahiti, *French Polynesia* **97 J13** 17 37 S 149 27W
Tahlequah, *U.S.A.* **113 H7** 35 55N 94 58W
Tahoe, L., *U.S.A.* **110 G6** 39 6N 120 2W
Tahoe City, *U.S.A.* **110 F6** 39 10N 120 9W
Tahoka, *U.S.A.* **113 J4** 33 10N 101 48W
Taholah, *U.S.A.* **110 C2** 47 21N 124 17W
Tahoua, *Niger* **83 C6** 14 57N 5 16 E
Tahrūd, *Iran* **71 D8** 29 26N 57 49 E
Tahsis, *Canada* **102 D3** 49 55N 126 40W
Tahta, *Egypt* **80 B3** 26 44N 31 32 E
Tahtaköprü, *Turkey* **45 G13** 39 57N 29 39 E
Tahtalı Dağları, *Turkey* **72 C7** 38 20N 36 0 E
Tahulandang, *Indonesia* **63 D7** 2 27N 125 23 E
Tahuna, *Indonesia* **63 D7** 3 38N 125 30 E
Taï, *Ivory C.* **82 D3** 5 55N 7 30W
Taï △, *Ivory C.* **82 D3** 5 25N 7 5W
Tai Hu, *China* **59 B12** 31 5N 120 10 E
Tai Rom Yen △, *Thailand* **65 H2** 8 45N 99 30 E
Tai Shan, *China* **57 F9** 36 25N 117 20 E
Tai'an, *China* **57 F9** 36 12N 117 8 E
Taibei = T'aipei, *Taiwan* **59 E13** 25 2N 121 30 E
Taibique, *Canary Is.* **48 G2** 27 42N 17 58W
Taibus Qi, *China* **56 D8** 41 54N 115 22 E
Taicang, *China* **59 B13** 31 30N 121 5 E
T'aichung, *Taiwan* **59 E13** 24 9N 120 37 E
Taieri →, *N.Z.* **91 M3** 46 3 S 170 12 E
Taigu, *China* **56 F7** 37 28N 112 30 E
Taihang Shan, *China* **56 G7** 36 0N 113 30 E
Taihape, *N.Z.* **91 H5** 39 41 S 175 48 E
Taihe, *Anhui, China* **56 H8** 33 20N 115 42 E
Taihe, *Jiangxi, China* **59 D10** 26 47N 114 52 E
Taihu, *China* **59 B11** 30 22N 116 20 E
Taijiang, *China* **58 D7** 26 39N 108 21 E
Taikang, *China* **56 G8** 34 5N 114 50 E
Tailem Bend, *Australia* **95 F2** 35 12 S 139 29 E
Tailfingen, *Germany* **25 G5** 48 15N 9 1 E
Tailuko, *Taiwan* **59 E13** 24 9N 121 37 E
Taimyr Peninsula = Taymyr, Poluostrov, *Russia* **53 B11** 75 0N 100 0 E
Tain, *U.K.* **13 D4** 57 49N 4 4W
T'ainan, *Taiwan* **59 F13** 23 0N 120 10 E
Taínaron, Ákra, *Greece* **46 E4** 36 22N 22 27 E
Taining, *China* **59 D11** 26 54N 117 9 E
T'aipei, *Taiwan* **59 E13** 25 2N 121 30 E
Taiping, *China* **59 B12** 30 15N 118 6 E
Taiping, *Malaysia* **65 K3** 4 51N 100 44 E
Taipingzhen, *China* **56 H6** 33 35N 111 42 E
Tairbeart = Tarbert, *U.K.* **13 D2** 57 54N 6 49W
Taishan, *China* **59 F9** 22 14N 112 41 E
Taishun, *China* **59 D12** 27 30N 119 42 E
Taita Hills, *Kenya* **86 C4** 3 25 S 38 15 E
Taitao, Pen. de, *Chile* **128 F2** 46 30 S 75 0W
T'aitung, *Taiwan* **59 F13** 22 43N 121 4 E
Taivalkoski, *Finland* **8 D23** 65 33N 28 12 E
Taiwan ■, *Asia* **59 F13** 23 30N 121 0 E
Taiwan Strait, *Asia* **59 E12** 24 40N 120 0 E
Taixing, *China* **59 A13** 32 11N 120 0 E
Taiyara, *Sudan* **81 E3** 13 12N 30 47 E
Taïyetos Óros, *Greece* **46 D4** 37 0N 22 23 E
Taiyiba, *Israel* **74 C4** 32 36N 35 27 E
Taiyuan, *China* **56 F7** 37 52N 112 33 E
Taizhong = T'aichung, *Taiwan* **59 E13** 24 9N 120 37 E
Taizhou, *China* **59 A12** 32 28N 119 55 E
Taizhou Liedao, *China* **59 C13** 28 30N 121 55 E
Ta'izz, *Yemen* **75 E3** 13 35N 44 2 E
Tājābād, *Iran* **71 D7** 30 2N 54 24 E
Tajikistan ■, *Asia* **52 F8** 38 30N 70 0 E
Tajima, *Japan* **55 F9** 37 12N 139 46 E
Tajo = Tejo →, *Europe* **37 F2** 38 40N 9 24W
Tajrīsh, *Iran* **71 C6** 35 48N 51 25 E
Tak, *Thailand* **64 D2** 16 52N 99 8 E
Takāb, *Iran* **70 B5** 36 24N 47 7 E
Takachiho, *Japan* **55 H5** 32 42N 131 18 E
Takachu, *Botswana* **88 C3** 22 37 S 21 58 E
Takada, *Japan* **55 F9** 37 7N 138 15 E
Takahagi, *Japan* **55 F10** 36 43N 140 45 E
Takaka, *N.Z.* **91 J4** 40 51 S 172 50 E
Takamatsu, *Japan* **55 G7** 34 20N 134 5 E
Takaoka, *Japan* **55 F8** 36 47N 137 0 E
Takapuna, *N.Z.* **91 G5** 36 47 S 174 47 E
Takasaki, *Japan* **55 F9** 36 20N 139 0 E
Takatsuki, *Japan* **55 G7** 34 51N 135 37 E
Takaungu, *Kenya* **86 C4** 3 38 S 39 52 E
Takayama, *Japan* **55 F8** 36 18N 137 11 E
Take-Shima, *Japan* **55 J5** 30 49N 130 26 E
Takefu, *Japan* **55 G8** 35 50N 136 10 E
Takengon, *Indonesia* **62 D1** 4 45N 96 50 E
Takeo, *Japan* **55 H5** 33 12N 130 1 E
Tåkern, *Sweden* **11 F8** 58 22N 14 45 E
Takeshima = Tok-do, *Asia* **55 F5** 37 15N 131 52 E
Tākestān, *Iran* **71 C6** 36 0N 49 40 E
Taketa, *Japan* **55 H5** 32 58N 131 24 E
Takev, *Cambodia* **65 G5** 10 59N 104 47 E
Takh, *India* **69 C7** 33 6N 77 32 E
Takht-Sulaiman, *Pakistan* **68 D3** 31 40N 69 58 E
Takikawa, *Japan* **54 C10** 43 33N 141 54 E
Takla L., *Canada* **102 B3** 55 15N 125 45W
Takla Landing, *Canada* **102 B3** 55 30N 125 50W
Takla Makan = Taklamakan Shamo, *China* **60 C3** 38 0N 83 0 E
Taklamakan Shamo, *China* **60 C3** 38 0N 83 0 E
Taku →, *Canada* **102 B2** 58 30N 133 50W
Takua Thung, *Thailand* **65 a** 8 24N 98 27 E
Takum, *Nigeria* **83 D6** 7 18N 9 36 E
Tal Halāl, *Iran* **71 D7** 28 54N 55 1 E
Tala, *Uruguay* **127 C4** 34 21 S 55 46W
Talachyn, *Belarus* **32 E5** 54 25N 29 42 E
Talacogan, *Phil.* **61 G6** 8 32N 125 39 E
Talagang, *Pakistan* **68 C5** 32 55N 72 25 E
Talagante, *Chile* **126 C1** 33 40 S 70 50W
Talak, *Niger* **83 B6** 18 0N 5 0 E
Talamanca, Cordillera de, *Cent. Amer.* **120 E3** 9 20N 83 20W
Talant, *France* **19 E11** 47 19N 4 58 E
Talara, *Peru* **124 D2** 4 38 S 81 18W
Talas, *Kyrgyzstan* **52 E8** 42 30N 72 13 E
Talas, *Turkey* **72 C6** 38 41N 35 33 E
Talâta, *Egypt* **74 E1** 30 36N 32 20 E
Talata Mafara, *Nigeria* **83 C6** 12 38N 6 4 E
Talaud, Kepulauan, *Indonesia* **63 D7** 4 30N 126 50 E
Talaud Is. = Talaud, Kepulauan, *Indonesia* **63 D7** 4 30N 126 50 E
Talavera de la Reina, *Spain* **36 F6** 39 55N 4 46W
Talavera la Real, *Spain* **37 G4** 38 53N 6 46W
Talayan, *Phil.* **61 H6** 6 52N 124 24 E
Talayuela, *Spain* **36 F5** 39 59N 5 36W
Talbandh, *India* **69 H12** 22 3N 86 20 E
Talbert, Sillon de, *France* **18 D3** 48 53N 3 5W
Talbot, C., *Australia* **92 B4** 13 48 S 126 43 E
Talbragar →, *Australia* **95 E4** 32 12 S 148 37 E
Talca, *Chile* **126 D1** 35 28 S 71 40W
Talcahuano, *Chile* **126 D1** 36 40 S 73 10W
Talcher, *India* **67 J14** 21 0N 85 18 E
Talcho, *Niger* **83 C5** 14 44N 3 28 E
Taldy Kurgan = Taldyqorghan, *Kazakhstan* **52 E8** 45 10N 78 45 E
Taldyqorghan, *Kazakhstan* **52 E8** 45 10N 78 45 E
Tālesh, *Iran* **71 B6** 37 58N 48 58 E
Tālesh, Kūhhā-ye, *Iran* **71 B6** 37 42N 48 55 E
Talguharai, *Sudan* **80 D4** 18 19N 35 56 E
Tali Post, *Sudan* **81 F3** 5 55N 30 44 E
Taliabu, *Indonesia* **63 E6** 1 50 S 125 0 E
Talibon, *Phil.* **63 B6** 10 9N 124 20 E
Talibong, Ko, *Thailand* **65 J2** 7 15N 99 23 E
Talihina, *U.S.A.* **113 H7** 34 45N 95 3W
Talisayan, *Phil.* **61 G6** 9 0N 124 55 E
Taliwang, *Indonesia* **62 F5** 8 50 S 116 55 E
Tall 'Afar, *Iraq* **70 B4** 36 22N 42 27 E
Tall Kalakh, *Syria* **74 A5** 34 41N 36 15 E
Talla, *Egypt* **80 B3** 28 5N 30 43 E
Talladega, *U.S.A.* **115 J2** 33 26N 86 6W
Tallahassee, *U.S.A.* **115 K3** 30 27N 84 17W
Tallangatta, *Australia* **95 F4** 36 15 S 147 19 E
Tallard, *France* **21 D10** 44 28N 6 3 E
Tällberg, *Sweden* **10 D9** 60 51N 15 2 E
Tallering Pk., *Australia* **93 E2** 28 6 S 115 37 E
Talli, *Pakistan* **68 E3** 29 32N 68 8 E
Tallinn, *Estonia* **9 G21** 59 22N 24 48 E
Tallmadge, *U.S.A.* **116 E3** 41 6N 81 27W
Tallulah, *U.S.A.* **113 J9** 32 25N 91 11W
Tălmaciu, *Romania* **29 E9** 45 38N 24 19 E
Talmont-St-Hilaire, *France* **20 B2** 46 27N 1 37W
Talne, *Ukraine* **33 H6** 48 50N 30 44 E
Talnoye = Talne, *Ukraine* **33 H6** 48 50N 30 44 E
Talodi, *Sudan* **81 E3** 10 35N 30 22 E
Talovaya, *Russia* **34 E5** 51 6N 40 45 E
Taloyoak, *Canada* **100 B10** 69 32N 93 32W
Talpa de Allende, *Mexico* **118 C4** 20 23N 104 51W
Talparo, *Trin. & Tob.* **125 K15** 10 30N 61 17W
Talsi, *Latvia* **9 H20** 57 10N 22 30 E
Talsi □, *Latvia* **30 A9** 57 20N 22 40 E
Taltal, *Chile* **126 B1** 25 23 S 70 33W
Taltson →, *Canada* **102 A6** 61 24N 112 46W
Talwood, *Australia* **95 D4** 28 29 S 149 29 E
Talyawalka Cr. →, *Australia* **95 E3** 32 28 S 142 22 E
Tam Ky, *Vietnam* **64 E7** 15 34N 108 29 E
Tam Quan, *Vietnam* **64 E7** 14 35N 109 3 E
Tama, *U.S.A.* **112 E8** 41 58N 92 35W
Tama ⌓, *Ethiopia* **81 F4** 5 55N 36 5 E
Tamale, *Ghana* **83 D4** 9 22N 0 50W
Taman, *Russia* **33 K9** 45 14N 36 41 E
Taman Negara △, *Malaysia* **65 K4** 4 38N 102 26 E
Tamani, *Mali* **82 C3** 13 20N 6 50W
Tamano, *Japan* **55 G6** 34 29N 133 59 E
Tamanrasset, *Algeria* **78 D7** 22 50N 5 30 E
Tamaqua, *U.S.A.* **117 F9** 40 48N 75 58W
Tamar →, *U.K.* **15 G3** 50 27N 4 15W
Tamarinda, *Spain* **48 B10** 39 55N 3 49 E
Tamarite de Litera, *Spain* **38 D5** 41 52N 0 25 E
Tamashima, *Japan* **55 G6** 34 32N 133 40 E
Tamási, *Hungary* **28 D3** 46 40N 18 18 E
Tamaské, *Niger* **83 C6** 14 49N 5 43 E
Tamaulipas □, *Mexico* **119 C5** 24 0N 99 0W
Tamaulipas, Sierra de, *Mexico* **119 C5** 23 30N 98 20W
Tamazula, *Mexico* **118 C3** 24 55N 106 58W
Tamazunchale, *Mexico* **119 C5** 21 16N 98 47W
Tamba-Dabatou, *Guinea* **82 C2** 11 50N 10 40W
Tambacounda, *Senegal* **82 C2** 13 45N 13 40W
Tambelan, Kepulauan, *Indonesia* **62 D3** 1 0N 107 30 E
Tambellup, *Australia* **93 F2** 34 4 S 117 37 E
Tambo, *Australia* **94 C4** 24 54 S 146 14 E
Tambo de Mora, *Peru* **124 F3** 13 30 S 76 8W
Tambohorano, *Madag.* **89 B7** 17 30 S 43 58 E
Tambora, *Indonesia* **62 F5** 8 12 S 118 5 E
Tambov, *Russia* **34 D5** 52 45N 41 28 E
Tambre →, *Spain* **36 C2** 42 49N 8 53W
Tambuku, *Indonesia* **63 G15** 7 8 S 113 40 E
Tamburâ, *Sudan* **81 F2** 5 40N 27 25 E
Tâmchekket, *Mauritania* **82 B2** 17 25N 10 40W
Tâmega →, *Portugal* **36 D2** 41 5N 8 21W
Tamenglong, *India* **67 G18** 25 0N 93 35 E
Tamgué, Massif du, *Guinea* **82 C2** 12 0N 12 18W
Tamiahua, L. de, *Mexico* **119 C5** 21 30N 97 30W
Tamil Nadu □, *India* **66 P10** 11 0N 77 0 E
Tamis →, *Serbia & M.* **28 F5** 44 51N 20 39 E
Tamluk, *India* **69 H12** 22 18N 87 58 E
Tammerfors = Tampere, *Finland* **9 F20** 61 30N 23 50 E
Tammisaari, *Finland* **9 F20** 60 0N 23 26 E
Tämnaren, *Sweden* **10 D11** 60 10N 17 25 E
Tamo Abu, Pegunungan, *Malaysia* **62 D5** 3 10N 115 5 E
Tampa, *U.S.A.* **115 M4** 27 57N 82 27W
Tampa, Tanjung, *Indonesia* **63 K19** 8 55 S 116 12 E
Tampa B., *U.S.A.* **115 M4** 27 50N 82 30W
Tampere, *Finland* **9 F20** 61 30N 23 50 E
Tampico, *Mexico* **119 C5** 22 20N 97 50W
Tampin, *Malaysia* **65 L4** 2 28N 102 13 E
Tampoi, *Malaysia* **65 d** 1 30N 103 39 E
Tamsweg, *Austria* **26 D6** 47 7N 13 49 E
Tamu, *Burma* **67 G19** 24 13N 94 12 E
Tamuja →, *Spain* **37 F4** 39 38N 6 29W
Tamworth, *Australia* **95 E5** 31 7 S 150 58 E
Tamworth, *Canada* **116 B8** 44 29N 77 0W
Tamworth, *U.K.* **15 E6** 52 39N 1 41W
Tamyang, *S. Korea* **57 G14** 35 19N 126 59 E
Tan An, *Vietnam* **65 G6** 10 32N 106 25 E
Tan Chau, *Vietnam* **65 G5** 10 48N 105 12 E
Tan-Tan, *Morocco* **78 C3** 28 29N 11 1W
Tana →, *Kenya* **86 C5** 2 32 S 40 31 E
Tana →, *Norway* **8 A23** 70 30N 28 14 E
Tana, L., *Ethiopia* **81 E4** 13 5N 37 30 E
Tana River Primate ⌓, *Kenya* **86 C5** 1 55 S 40 7 E
Tanabe, *Japan* **55 H7** 33 44N 135 22 E
Tanafjorden, *Norway* **8 A23** 70 45N 28 25 E
Tanahbala, *Indonesia* **62 E1** 0 30 S 98 30 E
Tanahgrogot, *Indonesia* **62 E5** 1 55 S 116 15 E
Tanahjampea, *Indonesia* **63 F6** 7 10 S 120 35 E
Tanahmasa, *Indonesia* **62 E1** 0 12 S 98 39 E
Tanahmerah, *Indonesia* **63 F10** 6 5 S 140 16 E
Tanakpur, *India* **69 E9** 29 5N 80 7 E
Tanakura, *Japan* **55 F10** 37 10N 140 20 E
Tanami, *Australia* **92 C4** 19 59 S 129 43 E
Tanami Desert, *Australia* **92 C5** 18 50 S 132 0 E
Tanana →, *U.S.A.* **100 B4** 65 10N 151 58W
Tananarive = Antananarivo, *Madag.* **89 B8** 18 55 S 47 31 E
Tánaro →, *Italy* **40 D5** 44 55N 8 40 E
Tancheng, *China* **57 G10** 34 25N 118 20 E
Tanch'ŏn, *N. Korea* **57 D15** 40 27N 128 54 E
Tanda, *Ut. P., India* **69 F10** 26 33N 82 35 E
Tanda, *Ut. P., India* **69 E8** 28 57N 78 56 E
Tanda, *Ivory C.* **82 D4** 7 48N 3 10W
Tandag, *Phil.* **61 G7** 9 4N 126 9 E
Tandaia, *Tanzania* **87 D3** 9 25 S 34 15 E
Tăndărei, *Romania* **29 F12** 44 39N 27 40 E
Tandaué, *Angola* **88 B2** 16 58 S 18 5 E
Tandil, *Argentina* **126 D4** 37 15 S 59 6W
Tandil, Sa. del, *Argentina* **126 D4** 37 30 S 59 0W
Tandlianwala, *Pakistan* **68 D5** 31 3N 73 9 E
Tando Adam, *Pakistan* **68 G3** 25 45N 68 40 E
Tando Allahyar, *Pakistan* **68 G3** 25 28N 68 43 E
Tando Bago, *Pakistan* **68 G3** 24 47N 68 58 E
Tando Mohommed Khan, *Pakistan* **68 G3** 25 8N 68 32 E
Tandou L., *Australia* **95 E3** 32 40 S 142 5 E
Tandragee, *U.K.* **12 B5** 54 21N 6 24W
Tandsjöborg, *Sweden* **10 C8** 61 42N 14 43 E
Tane-ga-Shima, *Japan* **55 J5** 30 30N 131 0 E
Taneatua, *N.Z.* **91 H6** 38 4 S 177 1 E
Tanen Tong Dan = Dawna Ra., *Burma* **64 D2** 16 30N 98 30 E
Tanew →, *Poland* **31 H9** 50 29N 22 16 E
Tanezrouft, *Algeria* **78 D6** 23 9N 0 11 E
Tang, Koh, *Cambodia* **65 G4** 10 16N 103 7 E
Tang, Ra's-e, *Iran* **71 E8** 25 21N 59 52 E
Tang Krasang, *Cambodia* **64 F5** 12 34N 105 3 E
Tanga, *Tanzania* **86 D4** 5 5 S 39 2 E
Tanga □, *Tanzania* **86 D4** 5 20 S 38 0 E
Tanganyika, L., *Africa* **86 D3** 6 40 S 30 0 E
Tangaza, *Nigeria* **83 C5** 13 19N 4 55 E
Tanger, *Morocco* **78 A4** 35 50N 5 49W
Tangerang, *Indonesia* **63 G12** 6 11 S 106 37 E
Tangerhütte, *Germany* **24 C7** 52 26N 11 48 E
Tangermünde, *Germany* **24 C7** 52 33N 11 58 E
Tanggu, *China* **57 E9** 39 2N 117 40 E
Tanggula Shan, *China* **60 C4** 32 40N 92 10 E
Tanghe, *China* **56 H7** 32 47N 112 50 E
Tanghla Range = Tanggula Shan, *China* **60 C4** 32 40N 92 10 E
Tangier = Tanger, *Morocco* **78 A4** 35 50N 5 49W
Tangorin, *Australia* **94 C3** 21 47 S 144 12 E
Tangorombohitr'i Makay, *Madag.* **89 C8** 21 0 S 45 15 E
Tangshan, *China* **57 E10** 39 38N 118 10 E
Tangtou, *China* **57 G10** 35 28N 118 30 E
Tanguiéta, *Benin* **83 C5** 10 35N 1 21 E
Tangxi, *China* **59 C12** 29 3N 119 25 E
Tangyan He →, *China* **58 C7** 28 54N 108 19 E
Tanimbar, Kepulauan, *Indonesia* **63 F8** 7 30 S 131 30 E
Tanimbar Is. = Tanimbar, Kepulauan, *Indonesia* **63 F8** 7 30 S 131 30 E
Taninthari = Tenasserim, *Burma* **65 F2** 12 6N 99 3 E
Tanjay, *Phil.* **61 G5** 9 30N 123 5 E
Tanjong Malim, *Malaysia* **65 L3** 3 42N 101 31 E
Tanjong Pelepas, *Malaysia* **65 d** 1 21N 103 33 E
Tanjore = Thanjavur, *India* **66 P11** 10 48N 79 12 E
Tanjung, *Indonesia* **63 J19** 8 21 S 116 9 E
Tanjung, *Phil.* **62 E5** 2 10 S 115 25 E
Tanjung Tokong, *Malaysia* **65 c** 5 28N 100 18 E
Tanjungbalai, *Indonesia* **62 D1** 2 55N 99 44 E
Tanjungbatu, *Indonesia* **62 D5** 2 23N 118 3 E
Tanjungkarang Telukbetung, *Indonesia* **62 F3** 5 20 S 105 10 E
Tanjungpandan, *Indonesia* **62 E3** 2 43 S 107 38 E
Tanjungpinang, *Indonesia* **62 D2** 1 5N 104 30 E
Tanjungredeb, *Indonesia* **62 D5** 2 9N 117 29 E
Tanjungselor, *Indonesia* **62 D5** 2 55N 117 25 E
Tank, *Pakistan* **68 C4** 32 14N 70 25 E
Tankhala, *India* **68 J5** 21 58N 73 47 E
Tankwa-Karoo △, *S. Africa* **88 E2** 32 14 S 19 50 E
Tännäs, *Sweden* **10 B6** 62 26N 12 42 E
Tannersville, *U.S.A.* **117 E9** 41 3N 75 18W
Tannis Bugt, *Denmark* **11 G4** 57 40N 10 15 E
Tannu-Ola, *Russia* **53 D10** 51 0N 94 0 E
Tannum Sands, *Australia* **94 C5** 23 57 S 151 22 E
Tano →, *Ghana* **82 D4** 5 7N 2 56W
Tanon Str., *Phil.* **61 F5** 10 20N 123 30 E
Tanout, *Niger* **83 C6** 14 50N 8 55 E
Tanshui, *Taiwan* **59 E13** 25 10N 121 28 E
Tansilla, *Burkina Faso* **82 C4** 12 25N 4 23W
Tanta, *Egypt* **80 H7** 30 45N 30 57 E
Tantoyuca, *Mexico* **119 C5** 21 21N 98 10W
Tantung = Dandong, *China* **57 D13** 40 10N 124 20 E
Tanumshede, *Sweden* **11 F5** 58 42N 11 20 E
Tanunda, *Australia* **95 E2** 34 30 S 139 0 E
Tanus, *France* **20 D6** 44 8N 2 19 E
Tanzania ■, *Africa* **86 D3** 6 0 S 34 0 E
Tanzilla →, *Canada* **102 B2** 58 8N 130 43W
Tao, Ko, *Thailand* **65 G2** 10 5N 99 52 E
Tao'an = Taonan, *China* **57 B12** 45 22N 122 40 E
Tao'er He →, *China* **57 B13** 45 45N 124 5 E
Taohua Dao, *China* **59 C14** 29 50N 122 20 E
Taolanaro, *Madag.* **89 D8** 25 2 S 47 0 E
Taole, *China* **56 E4** 38 48N 106 40 E
Taonan, *China* **57 B12** 45 22N 122 40 E
Taormina, *Italy* **43 E8** 37 51N 15 17 E
Taos, *U.S.A.* **109 H11** 36 24N 105 35W
Taoudenni, *Mali* **78 D5** 22 40N 3 55W
Taoyuan, *China* **59 C8** 28 55N 111 16 E
T'aoyüan, *Taiwan* **59 E13** 25 0N 121 4 E
Tapa, *Estonia* **9 G21** 59 15N 25 50 E
Tapa Shan = Daba Shan, *China* **58 B7** 32 0N 109 0 E
Tapachula, *Mexico* **119 E6** 14 54N 92 17W
Tapah, *Malaysia* **65 K3** 4 12N 101 15 E
Tapajós →, *Brazil* **125 D8** 2 24 S 54 41W
Tapaktuan, *Indonesia* **62 D1** 3 15N 97 10 E
Tapanahoni →, *Suriname* **125 C8** 4 20N 54 25W
Tapanui, *N.Z.* **91 L2** 45 56 S 169 18 E
Tapauá →, *Brazil* **124 E6** 5 40 S 64 21W
Tapes, *Brazil* **127 C5** 30 40 S 51 23W
Tapeta, *Liberia* **82 D3** 6 29N 8 52W
Taphan Hin, *Thailand* **64 D3** 16 13N 100 26 E
Tapi →, *India* **66 J8** 21 8N 72 41 E
Tapia de Casariego, *Spain* **36 B4** 43 34N 6 56W
Tapirapecó, Serra, *Venezuela* **124 C6** 1 10N 65 0W
Tapo-Capara △, *Venezuela* **121 E5** 7 55N 71 15W
Tapolca, *Hungary* **28 D2** 46 53N 17 29 E
Tapuaenuku, *N.Z.* **91 K4** 42 0 S 173 39 E
Tapul Group, *Phil.* **61 J4** 5 35N 120 50 E
Tapurucuará, *Brazil* **124 D5** 0 24 S 65 2W
Ţaqţaq, *Iraq* **70 C5** 35 53N 44 35 E
Taquara, *Brazil* **127 B5** 29 36 S 50 46W
Taquari →, *Brazil* **124 G7** 19 15 S 57 17W
Tara, *Australia* **95 D5** 27 17 S 150 31 E
Tara, *Canada* **116 B3** 44 28N 81 9W
Tara, *Russia* **52 D8** 56 55N 74 24 E
Tara, *Zambia* **87 F2** 16 58 S 26 45 E
Tara △, *Serbia & M.* **44 C3** 43 55N 19 30 E
Tara →, *Serbia & M.* **44 C2** 43 21N 18 51 E
Taraba □, *Nigeria* **83 D7** 8 0N 10 30 E
Taraba →, *Nigeria* **83 D7** 8 30N 10 15 E
Tarābulus, *Lebanon* **74 A4** 34 31N 35 50 E
Tarābulus, *Libya* **79 B8** 32 49N 13 7 E
Taraclía, *Taraclia, Moldova* **29 E13** 45 54N 28 40 E
Taraclia, *Tighina, Moldova* **29 D14** 46 34N 29 7 E
Taradehi, *India* **69 H8** 23 18N 79 21 E
Tarajalejo, *Canary Is.* **48 F5** 28 12N 14 7W
Tarakan, *Indonesia* **62 D5** 3 20N 117 35 E
Tarakit, Mt., *Kenya* **86 B4** 2 2N 35 10 E
Tarama-Jima, *Japan* **55 M2** 24 39N 124 42 E
Taran, Mys, *Russia* **9 J18** 54 56N 19 59 E
Taranagar, *India* **68 E6** 28 43N 74 50 E
Taranaki □, *N.Z.* **91 H5** 39 25 S 174 30 E
Taranaki, Mt., *N.Z.* **91 H5** 39 17 S 174 5 E
Tarancón, *Spain* **38 E1** 40 1N 3 1W
Tarangire △, *Tanzania* **86 C4** 4 21 S 36 7 E
Taransay, *U.K.* **13 D1** 57 54N 7 0W
Táranto, *Italy* **43 B10** 40 28N 17 14 E
Táranto, G. di, *Italy* **43 B10** 40 8N 17 20 E
Tarapacá, *Colombia* **124 D5** 2 56 S 69 46W
Tarapacá □, *Chile* **126 A2** 20 45 S 69 30W
Tarapoto, *Peru* **124 E3** 6 30 S 76 20W
Tarare, *France* **21 C8** 45 54N 4 26 E
Tararua Ra., *N.Z.* **91 J5** 40 45 S 175 25 E
Tarascon, *France* **21 E8** 43 48N 4 39 E
Tarascon-sur-Ariège, *France* **20 F5** 42 50N 1 36 E
Tarashcha, *Ukraine* **33 H6** 49 30N 30 31 E
Tarauacá, *Brazil* **124 E4** 8 6 S 70 48W
Tarauacá →, *Brazil* **124 E5** 6 42 S 69 48W
Taravo →, *France* **21 G12** 41 42N 8 49 E
Tarawa, *Kiribati* **96 G9** 1 30N 173 0 E
Tarawera, *N.Z.* **91 H6** 39 2 S 176 36 E
Tarawera, L., *N.Z.* **91 H6** 38 13 S 176 27 E
Taraz, *Kazakhstan* **52 E8** 42 54N 71 22 E
Tarazona, *Spain* **38 D3** 41 55N 1 43W
Tarazona de la Mancha, *Spain* **39 F3** 39 16N 1 55W
Tarbagatay, Khrebet, *Kazakhstan* **52 E9** 48 0N 83 0 E
Tarbat Ness, *U.K.* **13 D5** 57 52N 3 47W
Tarbela Dam, *Pakistan* **68 B5** 34 8N 72 52 E
Tarbert, *Arg. & Bute, U.K.* **13 F3** 55 52N 5 25W
Tarbert, *W. Isles, U.K.* **13 D2** 57 54N 6 49W
Tarbes, *France* **20 E4** 43 15N 0 3 E
Tarboro, *U.S.A.* **115 H7** 35 54N 77 32W
Tărcău, Munţii, *Romania* **29 D11** 46 39N 26 7 E
Tarcento, *Italy* **41 B10** 46 13N 13 13 E
Tarcoola, *Australia* **95 E1** 30 44 S 134 36 E
Tarcoon, *Australia* **95 E4** 30 15 S 146 43 E
Tardets-Sorholus, *France* **20 E3** 43 8N 0 52W
Tardoire →, *France* **20 C4** 45 52N 0 14 E
Taree, *Australia* **95 E5** 31 50 S 152 30 E
Tarfa, W. el →, *Egypt* **80 B3** 28 25N 30 50 E
Tarfaya, *Morocco* **78 C3** 27 55N 12 55W
Târgovişte, *Romania* **29 F10** 44 55N 25 27 E
Târgu Bujor, *Romania* **29 E12** 45 52N 27 54 E
Târgu Cărbuneşti, *Romania* **29 F8** 44 57N 23 31 E
Târgu Frumos, *Romania* **29 C12** 47 12N 27 2 E
Târgu-Jiu, *Romania* **29 E8** 45 5N 23 19 E
Târgu Lăpuş, *Romania* **29 C8** 47 27N 23 52 E
Târgu Mureş, *Romania* **29 D9** 46 31N 24 38 E
Târgu Neamţ, *Romania* **29 C11** 47 12N 26 25 E
Târgu Ocna, *Romania* **29 D11** 46 16N 26 39 E
Târgu Secuiesc, *Romania* **29 E11** 46 0N 26 10 E
Târguşor, *Romania* **29 F13** 44 27N 28 25 E
Tărhăus, Vf., *Romania* **29 D11** 46 40N 26 8 E
Ţarif, *U.A.E.* **71 E7** 24 3N 53 46 E
Tarífa, *Spain* **37 J5** 36 1N 5 36W
Tarija, *Bolivia* **126 A3** 21 30 S 64 40W
Tarija □, *Bolivia* **126 A3** 21 30 S 63 30W
Tariku →, *Indonesia* **63 E9** 2 55 S 138 26 E
Tarim Basin = Tarim Pendi, *China* **60 C3** 40 0N 84 0 E
Tarim He →, *China* **60 C3** 39 30N 88 30 E
Tarim Pendi, *China* **60 C3** 40 0N 84 0 E
Taritatu →, *Indonesia* **63 E9** 2 54 S 138 27 E
Tarka →, *S. Africa* **88 E4** 32 10 S 26 0 E
Tarkastad, *S. Africa* **88 E4** 32 0 S 26 16 E
Tarkhankut, Mys, *Ukraine* **33 K7** 45 25N 32 30 E
Tarko Sale, *Russia* **52 C8** 64 55N 77 50 E
Tarkwa, *Ghana* **82 D4** 5 20N 2 0W
Tarlac, *Phil.* **61 D4** 15 29N 120 35 E
Tarm, *Denmark* **11 J2** 55 56N 8 31 E
Tarma, *Peru* **124 F3** 11 25 S 75 45W
Tarn □, *France* **20 E6** 43 49N 2 8 E
Tarn →, *France* **20 D5** 44 5N 1 6 E
Tarn-et-Garonne □, *France* **20 D5** 44 8N 1 20 E
Tarna →, *Hungary* **28 C4** 47 31N 19 59 E
Târnava Mare →, *Romania* **29 D8** 46 10N 23 43 E
Târnava Mică →, *Romania* **29 D8** 46 9N 23 55 E
Târnăveni, *Romania* **29 D9** 46 19N 24 13 E
Tarnica, *Poland* **31 J9** 49 4N 22 44 E
Tarnobrzeg, *Poland* **31 H8** 50 35N 21 41 E
Tarnogród, *Poland* **31 H9** 50 22N 22 45 E
Tarnos, *France* **20 E2** 43 32N 1 28W
Târnova, *Moldova* **29 B12** 48 10N 27 40 E
Târnova, *Romania* **28 E6** 45 23N 21 59 E
Tarnów, *Poland* **31 H8** 50 3N 21 0 E
Tarnowskie Góry, *Poland* **31 H5** 50 27N 18 54 E
Tärnsjö, *Sweden* **10 D10** 60 9N 16 56 E
Táro →, *Italy* **40 C7** 45 2N 10 15 E
Ţārom, *Iran* **71 D7** 28 11N 55 46 E
Taroom, *Australia* **95 D4** 25 36 S 149 48 E
Taroudannt, *Morocco* **78 B4** 30 30N 8 52W
Tarp, *Germany* **24 A5** 54 39N 9 24 E
Tarpon Springs, *U.S.A.* **115 L4** 28 9N 82 45W
Tarquínia, *Italy* **41 F8** 42 15N 11 45 E
Tarragona, *Spain* **38 D6** 41 5N 1 17 E
Tarragona □, *Spain* **38 D6** 41 5N 1 0 E
Tarraleah, *Australia* **95 G4** 42 17 S 146 26 E
Tarrasa = Terrassa, *Spain* **38 D7** 41 34N 2 1 E
Tàrrega, *Spain* **38 D6** 41 39N 1 9 E
Tarrytown, *U.S.A.* **117 E11** 41 4N 73 52W
Tårs, *Denmark* **11 G4** 57 23N 10 7 E
Tarshiha = Me'ona, *Israel* **74 B4** 33 1N 35 15 E
Tarsus, *Turkey* **70 B2** 36 58N 34 55 E
Tartagal, *Argentina* **126 A3** 22 30 S 63 50W
Tärtär, *Azerbaijan* **35 K8** 40 20N 46 58 E
Tärtär →, *Azerbaijan* **35 K8** 40 26N 47 20 E
Tartas, *France* **20 E3** 43 50N 0 49W
Tartu, *Estonia* **9 G22** 58 20N 26 44 E
Ţarţūs, *Syria* **70 C2** 34 55N 35 55 E
Tarumizu, *Japan* **55 J5** 31 29N 130 42 E
Tarussa, *Russia* **32 E9** 54 44N 37 10 E
Tarutao = Ko Tarutao △, *Thailand* **65 J2** 6 31N 99 26 E
Tarutao, Ko, *Thailand* **65 J2** 6 33N 99 40 E
Tarutung, *Indonesia* **62 D1** 2 0N 98 54 E
Tarutyne, *Ukraine* **29 D14** 46 12N 29 9 E
Tarvísio, *Italy* **41 B10** 46 30N 13 35 E
Taseko →, *Canada* **102 C4** 52 8N 123 45W
Tash-Kömür, *Kyrgyzstan* **52 E8** 41 40N 72 10 E
Tash-Kumyr = Tash-Kömür, *Kyrgyzstan* **52 E8** 41 40N 72 10 E
Tashauz = Dashhowuz, *Turkmenistan* **52 E6** 41 49N 59 58 E
Tashi Chho Dzong = Thimphu, *Bhutan* **67 F16** 27 31N 89 45 E
Ţashk, Daryācheh-ye, *Iran* **71 D7** 29 45N 53 35 E
Tashkent = Toshkent, *Uzbekistan* **52 E7** 41 20N 69 10 E
Tashtagol, *Russia* **52 D9** 52 47N 87 53 E
Tasiilaq, *Greenland* **4 C6** 65 40N 37 20W
Tasikmalaya, *Indonesia* **63 G13** 7 18 S 108 12 E
Tåsinge, *Denmark* **11 J4** 55 0N 10 35 E
Tåsjön, *Sweden* **8 D16** 64 15N 15 40 E
Taskan, *Russia* **53 C16** 62 59N 150 20 E
Tasker, *Niger* **83 C7** 15 8N 10 40 E
Taşköprü, *Turkey* **72 B6** 41 30N 34 15 E
Taşlâc, *Moldova* **29 C14** 47 4N 29 24 E
Tasman B., *N.Z.* **91 J4** 40 59 S 173 25 E
Tasman Mts., *N.Z.* **91 J4** 41 3 S 172 25 E
Tasman Pen., *Australia* **95 G4** 43 10 S 148 0 E
Tasman Plateau, *S. Ocean* **5 A10** 48 0 S 146 0 E
Tasman Sea, *Pac. Oc.* **96 L8** 36 0 S 160 0 E
Tasmania □, *Australia* **95 G4** 42 0 S 146 30 E
Tăşnad, *Romania* **28 C7** 47 30N 22 33 E
Tassili n'Ajjer, *Algeria* **78 C7** 25 47N 8 1 E
Tassili Tin-Rerhoh, *Algeria* **83 A5** 20 5N 3 55 E
Tata, *Hungary* **28 C3** 47 37N 18 19 E
Tatabánya, *Hungary* **28 C3** 47 32N 18 25 E
Tatahouine, *Tunisia* **79 B8** 32 56N 10 27 E
Tataouine, *Tunisia* **79 B8** 32 57N 10 29 E
Tatar Republic = Tatarstan □, *Russia* **34 C10** 55 30N 51 30 E
Tatarbunary, *Ukraine* **29 E14** 45 50N 29 39 E
Tatarsk, *Russia* **52 D8** 55 14N 76 0 E
Tatarstan □, *Russia* **34 C10** 55 30N 51 30 E
Tateyama, *Japan* **55 G9** 35 0N 139 50 E
Tathlina L., *Canada* **102 A5** 60 33N 117 39W
Tathra, *Australia* **95 F4** 36 44 S 149 59 E
Tatinnai L., *Canada* **103 A9** 60 55N 97 40W
Tatla L., *Canada* **102 C4** 52 0N 124 20W
Tatlısu, *Turkey* **45 F11** 40 24N 27 55 E
Tatnam, C., *Canada* **103 B10** 57 16N 91 0W
Tatra = Tatry, *Slovak Rep.* **27 B13** 49 20N 20 0 E
Tatranský △, *Slovak Rep.* **27 B13** 49 10N 20 0 E
Tatry, *Slovak Rep.* **27 B13** 49 20N 20 0 E
Tatshenshini →, *Canada* **102 B1** 59 28N 137 45W
Tatsuno, *Japan* **55 G7** 34 52N 134 33 E
Tatta, *Pakistan* **68 G2** 24 42N 67 55 E
Tatuī, *Brazil* **127 A6** 23 25 S 47 53W
Tatum, *U.S.A.* **113 J3** 33 16N 103 19W
Tat'ung = Datong, *China* **56 D7** 40 6N 113 18 E
Tatvan, *Turkey* **70 B4** 38 31N 42 15 E
Taubaté, *Brazil* **127 A6** 23 0 S 45 36W
Tauberbischofsheim, *Germany* **25 F5** 49 37N 9 39 E
Taucha, *Germany* **24 D8** 51 23N 12 29 E
Tauern-tunnel, *Austria* **26 D6** 47 0N 13 12 E
Taufikia, *Sudan* **81 F3** 9 24N 31 37 E
Taulé, *France* **18 D3** 48 37N 3 55W
Taumarunui, *N.Z.* **91 H5** 38 53 S 175 15 E
Taumaturgo, *Brazil* **124 E4** 8 54 S 72 51W
Taung, *S. Africa* **88 D3** 27 33 S 24 47 E
Taungdwingyi, *Burma* **67 J19** 20 1N 95 40 E
Taunggyi, *Burma* **67 J20** 20 50N 97 0 E
Taungup, *Burma* **67 K19** 18 51N 94 14 E
Taungup Taunggya, *Burma* **67 K18** 18 20N 93 40 E
Taunsa, *Pakistan* **68 D4** 30 42N 70 39 E
Taunsa Barrage, *Pakistan* **68 D4** 30 42N 70 50 E
Taunton, *U.K.* **15 F4** 51 1N 3 5W
Taunton, *U.S.A.* **117 E13** 41 54N 71 6W
Taunus, *Germany* **25 E4** 50 13N 8 34 E
Taupo, *N.Z.* **91 H6** 38 41 S 176 7 E
Taupo, L., *N.Z.* **91 H5** 38 46 S 175 55 E
Tauragė, *Lithuania* **9 J20** 55 14N 22 16 E
Tauragė □, *Lithuania* **30 C9** 55 15N 22 17 E

Tauranga, N.Z. **91 G6** 37 42 S 176 11 E
Tauranga Harb., N.Z. **91 G6** 37 30 S 176 5 E
Taureau, Rés., Canada **104 C5** 46 46N 73 50W
Taurianova, Italy **43 D9** 38 21N 16 1 E
Taurus Mts. = Toros
　Dağları, Turkey **70 B2** 37 0N 32 30 E
Tauste, Spain **38 D3** 41 58N 1 18W
Tauz = Tovuz,
　Azerbaijan **35 K7** 41 0N 45 40 E
Tavas, Turkey **47 D11** 37 34N 29 4 E
Tavastehus =
　Hämeenlinna, Finland **9 F21** 61 0N 24 28 E
Tavda, Russia **52 D7** 58 7N 65 8 E
Tavda →, Russia **52 D7** 57 47N 67 18 E
Tavernes de la
　Valldigna, Spain **39 F4** 39 5N 0 13W
Taveta, Tanzania **86 C4** 3 23 S 37 37 E
Taveuni, Fiji **91 C9** 16 51 S 179 58W
Taviano, Italy **43 C11** 39 59N 18 5 E
Tavignano →, France **21 F13** 42 7N 9 33 E
Tavira, Portugal **37 H3** 37 8N 7 40W
Tavistock, Canada **116 C4** 43 19N 80 50W
Tavistock, U.K. **15 G3** 50 33N 4 9W
Tavolara, Italy **42 B2** 40 54N 9 42 E
Távora →, Portugal **36 D3** 41 8N 7 35W
Tavoy, Burma **64 E2** 14 2N 98 12 E
Tavşanlı, Turkey **47 B11** 39 32N 29 30 E
Taw →, U.K. **15 F3** 51 4N 4 4W
Tawa →, India **68 H8** 22 48N 77 48 E
Tawas City, U.S.A. **114 C4** 44 16N 83 31W
Tawau, Malaysia **62 D5** 4 20N 117 55 E
Taweisha, Sudan **81 E2** 12 19N 26 40 E
Tawitawi, Phil. **63 B6** 5 10N 120 0 E
Tawu, Taiwan **59 F13** 22 30N 120 50 E
Taxco de Alarcón,
　Mexico **119 D5** 18 33N 99 36W
Taxila, Pakistan **68 C5** 33 42N 72 52 E
Tay →, U.K. **13 E5** 56 43N 3 59W
Tay →, U.K. **13 E5** 56 37N 3 38W
Tay, Firth of, U.K. **13 E5** 56 25N 3 8W
Tay, L., Australia **93 F3** 32 55 S 120 48 E
Tay, L., U.K. **13 E4** 56 32N 4 8W
Tay Ninh, Vietnam **65 G6** 11 20N 106 5 E
Tayabamba, Peru **124 E3** 8 15 S 77 16W
Tayabas Bay, Phil. **61 E4** 13 45N 121 45 E
Taylakova, Russia **52 D8** 59 13N 74 0 E
Taylakovy = Taylakova,
　Russia **52 D8** 59 13N 74 0 E
Taylor, Canada **102 B4** 56 13N 120 40W
Taylor, Nebr., U.S.A. **112 E5** 41 46N 99 23W
Taylor, Pa., U.S.A. **117 E9** 41 23N 75 43W
Taylor, Tex., U.S.A. **113 K6** 30 34N 97 25W
Taylor, Mt., U.S.A. **109 J10** 35 14N 107 37W
Taylorville, U.S.A. **112 F10** 39 33N 89 18W
Taymā, Si. Arabia **70 E3** 27 35N 38 45 E
Taymyr, Oz., Russia **53 B11** 74 20N 102 0 E
Taymyr, Poluostrov,
　Russia **53 B11** 75 0N 100 0 E
Tayport, U.K. **13 E6** 56 27N 2 52W
Tayrona △, Colombia **121 D15** 11 20N 74 2W
Tayshet, Russia **53 D10** 55 58N 98 1 E
Taytay, Phil. **61 F3** 10 45N 119 30 E
Tāyyebād, Iran **71 C9** 34 45N 60 45 E
Tāyyebād □, Iran **71 C9** 34 44N 60 44 E
Taz →, Russia **52 C8** 67 32N 78 40 E
Taza, Morocco **78 B5** 34 16N 4 6W
Tāza Khurmātū, Iraq **70 C5** 35 18N 44 20 E
Tazawa-Ko, Japan **54 E10** 39 43N 140 40 E
Tazin, Canada **103 B7** 59 48N 109 55W
Tazin, L., Canada **103 B7** 59 44N 108 42W
Tazovskiy, Russia **52 C8** 67 30N 78 44 E
Tbilisi, Georgia **35 K7** 41 43N 44 50 E
Tchad = Chad ■, Africa **79 F8** 15 0N 17 15 E
Tchad, L., Chad **79 F8** 13 30N 14 30 E
Tchaourou, Benin **83 D5** 8 58N 2 40 E
Tch'eng-tou = Chengdu,
　China **58 B5** 30 38N 104 2 E
Tchentlo L., Canada **102 B4** 55 15N 125 0W
Tchetti, Benin **83 D5** 7 50N 1 40 E
Tchibanga, Gabon **84 E2** 2 45 S 11 0 E
Tchien, Liberia **82 D3** 5 59N 8 15W
Tchin Tabaraden, Niger **83 B6** 15 58N 5 56 E
Tch'ong-k'ing =
　Chongqing, China **58 C6** 29 35N 106 25 E
Tczew, Poland **30 D5** 54 8N 18 50 E
Te Anau, N.Z. **91 L1** 45 15 S 167 45 E
Te Aroha, N.Z. **91 G5** 37 32 S 175 44 E
Te Awamutu, N.Z. **91 H5** 38 1 S 175 20 E
Te Kuiti, N.Z. **91 H5** 38 20 S 175 11 E
Te-n-Dghâmcha,
　Sebkhet, Mauritania **82 B1** 18 30N 15 55W
Te Puke, N.Z. **91 G6** 37 46 S 176 22 E
Te Waewae B., N.Z. **91 M1** 46 13 S 167 33 E
Teaca, Romania **29 D9** 46 55N 24 30 E
Teague, U.S.A. **113 K6** 31 38N 96 17W
Teano, Italy **43 A7** 41 15N 14 4 E
Teapa, Mexico **119 D6** 18 35N 92 56W
Teba, Spain **37 J6** 36 59N 4 55W
Tebakang, Malaysia **62 D4** 1 6N 110 30 E
Teberda, Russia **35 J5** 43 30N 41 46 E
Teberu, Malaysia **65 d** 1 30N 103 42 E
Tébessa, Algeria **78 A7** 35 22N 8 8 E
Tebicuary →, Paraguay **126 B4** 26 36 S 58 16W
Tebingtinggi, Riau,
　Indonesia **62 E2** 1 0N 102 45 E
Tebingtinggi,
　Sumatera Utara,
　Indonesia **62 D1** 3 20N 99 9 E
Tebulos, Georgia **35 J7** 42 36N 45 17 E
Tecate, Mexico **111 N10** 32 34N 116 38W
Tecer Dağları, Turkey **72 C7** 39 27N 37 27 E
Tech →, France **20 F7** 42 36N 3 3 E
Techiman, Ghana **82 D4** 7 35N 1 58W
Techirghiol, Romania **29 F13** 44 4N 28 32 E
Tecka, Argentina **128 E2** 43 29 S 70 48W
Tecomán, Mexico **118 D4** 18 55N 103 53W
Tecopa, U.S.A. **111 K10** 35 51N 116 13W
Tecoripa, Mexico **118 B3** 28 37N 109 57W
Tecuala, Mexico **118 C3** 22 23N 105 27W
Tecuci, Romania **29 E12** 45 51N 27 27 E
Tecumseh, Canada **116 D2** 42 19N 82 54W
Tecumseh, Mich., U.S.A. **114 D4** 42 0N 83 57W
Tecumseh, Okla., U.S.A. **113 H6** 35 15N 96 56W
Tedzhen = Tejen,
　Turkmenistan **52 F7** 37 23N 60 31 E
Tees →, U.K. **14 C6** 54 37N 1 10W
Tees B., U.K. **14 C6** 54 40N 1 9W
Teeswater, Canada **116 C3** 43 59N 81 17W
Tefé, Brazil **124 D6** 3 25 S 64 50W
Tefenni, Turkey **47 D11** 37 18N 29 45 E
Tegal, Indonesia **63 G13** 6 52 S 109 8 E
Tegallalang, Indonesia **63 J18** 8 25 S 115 17 E
Tegalsari, Indonesia **63 J17** 8 25 S 114 8 E
Tegel, Berlin ✈ (TXL),
　Germany **24 C9** 52 35N 13 14 E
Tegernsee, Germany **25 H7** 47 43N 11 46 E
Teggiano, Italy **43 B8** 40 23N 15 32 E

Tegid, L. = Bala, L.,
　U.K. **14 E4** 52 53N 3 37W
Tegina, Nigeria **83 C6** 10 5N 6 11 E
Tegucigalpa, Honduras **120 D2** 14 5N 87 14W
Teguidda-i-n-Tessoum,
　Niger **83 B6** 17 25N 6 58 E
Tehachapi, U.S.A. **111 K8** 35 8N 118 27W
Tehachapi Mts., U.S.A. **111 L8** 35 0N 118 30W
Tehamiyam, Sudan **80 D4** 18 20N 36 32 E
Teheran = Tehrān, Iran **71 C6** 35 44N 51 30 E
Tehilla, Sudan **80 D4** 17 42N 36 6 E
Téhini, Ivory C. **82 D4** 9 39N 3 40W
Tehrān, Iran **71 C6** 35 44N 51 30 E
Tehrān □, Iran **71 C6** 35 40N 51 30 E
Tehri, India **69 D8** 30 23N 78 29 E
Tehuacán, Mexico **119 D5** 18 30N 97 30W
Tehuantepec, Mexico **119 D5** 16 21N 95 13W
Tehuantepec, G. de,
　Mexico **119 D5** 15 50N 95 12W
Tehuantepec, Istmo de,
　Mexico **119 D6** 17 0N 94 30W
Teide, Pico de,
　Canary Is. **48 F3** 28 15N 16 38W
Teifi →, U.K. **15 E3** 52 5N 4 41W
Teign →, U.K. **15 G4** 50 32N 3 32W
Teignmouth, U.K. **15 G4** 50 33N 3 31W
Teiuș, Romania **29 D8** 46 12N 23 40 E
Teixeira Pinto,
　Guinea-Biss. **82 C1** 12 3N 16 0W
Tejakula, Indonesia **63 J18** 8 8 S 115 20 E
Tejam, India **69 E9** 29 57N 80 11 E
Tejen, Turkmenistan **52 F7** 37 23N 60 31 E
Tejen →, Turkmenistan **52 F7** 37 24N 60 38 E
Tejo →, Europe **37 F2** 38 40N 9 24W
Tejon Pass, U.S.A. **111 L8** 34 49N 118 53W
Tekamah, U.S.A. **112 E6** 41 47N 96 13W
Tekapo, L., N.Z. **91 K3** 43 53 S 170 33 E
Tekax, Mexico **119 C7** 20 11N 89 18W
Teke, Turkey **45 E13** 41 4N 29 39 E
Tekeli, Kazakhstan **52 E8** 44 50N 79 0 E
Tekeze →, Ethiopia **81 E4** 14 20N 35 50 E
Tekija, Serbia & M. **44 B6** 44 42N 22 26 E
Tekirdağ, Turkey **45 F11** 40 58N 27 30 E
Tekirdağ □, Turkey **45 F11** 41 0N 27 0 E
Tekirova, Turkey **47 E12** 36 30N 30 32 E
Tekkali, India **67 K14** 18 37N 84 15 E
Tekke, Turkey **72 B7** 40 42N 36 12 E
Tekman, Turkey **73 C9** 39 38N 41 30 E
Tekoa, U.S.A. **108 C5** 47 14N 117 4W
Tekong Besar, Pulau,
　Singapore **65 d** 1 25N 104 3 E
Tel Aviv ✈ (TLV), Israel **74 C3** 32 5N 34 49 E
Tel Aviv-Yafo, Israel **74 C3** 32 4N 34 48 E
Tel Lakhish, Israel **74 D3** 31 34N 34 51 E
Tel Megiddo, Israel **74 C4** 32 35N 35 11 E
Tela, Honduras **120 C2** 15 40N 87 28W
Telanaipura = Jambi,
　Indonesia **62 E2** 1 38 S 103 30 E
Telašćica △, Croatia **41 E12** 43 53N 15 10 E
Telavi, Georgia **35 J7** 42 0N 45 30 E
Telč, Czech Rep. **26 B8** 49 11N 15 28 E
Telciu, Romania **29 C9** 47 25N 24 24 E
Telde, Canary Is. **48 G4** 27 59N 15 25W
Telegraph Creek,
　Canada **102 B2** 58 0N 131 10W
Telekhany =
　Tsyelyakhany, Belarus **33 F3** 52 30N 25 46 E
Telemark, Norway **9 G12** 59 15N 7 40 E
Telén, Argentina **126 D2** 36 15 S 65 31W
Teleng, Iran **71 E9** 25 47N 61 3 E
Teleño, Spain **36 C4** 42 23N 6 22W
Teleorman □, Romania **29 G10** 44 0N 25 0 E
Teleorman →, Romania **29 G10** 43 52N 25 26 E
Teles Pires →, Brazil **124 E7** 7 21 S 58 3W
Telescope Pk., U.S.A. **111 J9** 36 10N 117 5W
Teletaye, Mali **83 B5** 16 31N 1 30 E
Telfer Mine, Australia **92 C3** 21 40 S 122 12 E
Telford, U.K. **15 E5** 52 40N 2 27W
Telford and Wrekin □,
　U.K. **14 E5** 52 45N 2 27W
Telfs, Austria **26 D4** 47 19N 11 4 E
Télimélé, Guinea **82 C2** 10 54N 13 2W
Teljo, J., Sudan **81 E2** 14 42N 25 26 E
Telkwa, Canada **102 C3** 54 41N 127 5W
Tell City, U.S.A. **114 G2** 37 57N 86 46W
Tellicherry, India **66 P9** 11 45N 75 30 E
Telluride, U.S.A. **109 H10** 37 56N 107 49W
Teloloapán, Mexico **119 D5** 18 21N 99 51W
Telpos Iz, Russia **6 C17** 63 16N 59 13 E
Telsen, Argentina **128 E3** 42 30 S 66 50W
Telšiai, Lithuania **9 H20** 55 59N 22 14 E
Telšiai □, Lithuania **24 C9** 55 59N 22 15 E
Teltow, Germany **24 C9** 52 24N 13 15 E
Teluk Anson = Teluk
　Intan, Malaysia **65 K3** 4 3N 101 0 E
Teluk Bahang, Malaysia **65 c** 5 28N 100 11 E
Teluk Betung =
　Tanjungkarang
　Telukbetung,
　Indonesia **62 F3** 5 20 S 105 10 E
Teluk Intan, Malaysia **65 K3** 4 3N 101 0 E
Teluk Kumbar, Malaysia **65 c** 5 18N 100 14 E
Telukbutun, Indonesia **62 D3** 4 13N 108 12 E
Telukdalem, Indonesia **62 D1** 0 33N 97 50 E
Tema, Ghana **83 D5** 5 41N 0 0W
Temax, Mexico **119 C7** 21 10N 88 50W
Temba, S. Africa **89 D4** 25 20 S 28 17 E
Tembagapura, Indonesia **63 E9** 4 20 S 137 0 E
Tembe, Dem. Rep. of
　the Congo **86 C2** 0 16 S 28 14 E
Tembe, S. Africa **89 D5** 26 51 S 32 24 E
Tembeling →, Malaysia **65 c** 4 4N 102 20 E
Tembleque, Spain **36 F7** 39 41N 3 30W
Temblor Range, U.S.A. **111 K7** 35 20N 119 50W
Teme →, U.K. **15 E5** 52 11N 2 13W
Temecula, U.S.A. **111 M9** 33 30N 117 9W
Temerloh, Malaysia **62 D2** 3 27N 102 25 E
Teminabuan, Indonesia **63 E8** 1 26 S 132 1 E
Temir, Kazakhstan **52 E6** 49 1N 57 14 E
Temirtau, Kazakhstan **52 D8** 50 5N 72 56 E
Temirtau, Russia **52 D9** 53 10N 87 30 E
Témiscamie →, Canada **105 B5** 50 59N 73 5W
Témiscaming, Canada **104 C4** 46 44N 79 5W
Témiscamingue, L.,
　Canada **104 C4** 47 10N 79 25W
Temnikov, Russia **34 C6** 54 40N 43 11 E
Temo →, Italy **42 B1** 40 20N 8 30 E
Temora, Australia **95 E4** 34 30 S 147 30 E
Temosachic, Mexico **118 B3** 28 58N 107 50W
Tempe, U.S.A. **109 K8** 33 25N 111 56W
Tempio Pausánia, Italy **42 B2** 40 54N 9 6 E
Tempiute, U.S.A. **110 H11** 37 39N 115 38W
Temple, U.S.A. **113 K6** 31 6N 97 21W
Temple B., Australia **94 A3** 12 15 S 143 3 E
Templemore, Ireland **12 D4** 52 47N 7 51W
Templeton, U.S.A. **110 K6** 35 33N 120 42W
Templeton →, Australia **94 C2** 21 0 S 138 40 E

Templin, Germany **24 B9** 53 7N 13 28 E
Tempoal, Mexico **119 C5** 21 31N 98 23W
Temryuk, Russia **33 K9** 45 15N 37 24 E
Temska →, Serbia & M. **44 C6** 43 17N 22 33 E
Temuco, Chile **128 D2** 38 45 S 72 40W
Temuka, N.Z. **91 L3** 44 14 S 171 17 E
Tenabo, Mexico **119 C6** 20 2N 90 12W
Tenaha, U.S.A. **113 K7** 31 57N 94 15W
Tenakee Springs, U.S.A. **102 B1** 57 47N 135 13W
Tenali, India **67 L12** 16 15N 80 35 E
Tenancingo, Mexico **119 D5** 19 0N 99 33W
Tenango, Mexico **119 D5** 19 7N 99 33W
Tenasserim, Burma **65 F2** 12 6N 99 3 E
Tenasserim □, Burma **64 F2** 14 0N 98 30 E
Tenby, U.K. **15 F3** 51 40N 4 42W
Tenda, Colle di, France **21 D11** 44 7N 7 36 E
Tendaho, Ethiopia **81 E5** 11 48N 40 54 E
Tende, France **21 D11** 44 5N 7 35 E
Tendelti, Sudan **81 E3** 13 1N 31 55 E
Tendrovskaya Kosa,
　Ukraine **33 J6** 46 16N 31 35 E
Tendukhera, India **69 H8** 23 24N 79 33 E
Teneguía, Volcanes de,
　Canary Is. **48 F2** 28 28N 17 51W
Teneida, Egypt **80 B2** 25 30N 29 19 E
Tenenkou, Mali **82 C4** 14 28N 4 55W
Ténéré, Niger **83 B7** 19 0N 10 30 E
Tenerife, Canary Is. **48 F3** 28 15N 16 35W
Tenerife, Pico,
　Canary Is. **48 G1** 27 43N 18 1W
Tenerife Norte ✈
　(TFN), Canary Is. **48 F3** 28 28N 16 17W
Tenerife Sur ✈ (TFS),
　Canary Is. **48 F3** 28 3N 16 33W
Teng Xian,
　Guangxi Zhuangzu,
　China **59 F8** 23 21N 110 56 E
Teng Xian, Shandong,
　China **57 G9** 35 5N 117 10 E
Tengah □, Indonesia **63 E6** 1 30 S 121 0 E
Tengah, Kepulauan,
　Indonesia **62 F5** 7 5 S 118 15 E
Tengchong, China **58 E2** 25 0N 98 28 E
Tengchowfu = Penglai,
　China **57 F11** 37 48N 120 42 E
Tenggara □, Indonesia **63 E6** 3 50 S 122 0 E
Tenggarong, Indonesia **62 E5** 0 24 S 116 58 E
Tenggol, Pulau,
　Malaysia **65 K4** 4 48N 103 41 E
Tengiz, Ozero,
　Kazakhstan **52 D7** 50 30N 69 0 E
Tenhult, Sweden **11 G8** 57 41N 14 20 E
Teniente Enciso △,
　Paraguay **126 A3** 21 5 S 61 8W
Teniente Rodolfo
　Marsh, Antarctica **5 C18** 62 30 S 58 0W
Tenino, U.S.A. **110 D4** 46 51N 122 51W
Tenkasi, India **66 Q10** 8 55N 77 20 E
Tenke, Katanga,
　Dem. Rep. of
　the Congo **87 E2** 11 22 S 26 40 E
Tenke, Katanga,
　Dem. Rep. of
　the Congo **87 E2** 10 32 S 26 7 E
Tenkodogo,
　Burkina Faso **83 C4** 11 54N 0 19W
Tenna →, Italy **41 E10** 43 14N 13 47 E
Tennant Creek,
　Australia **94 B1** 19 30 S 134 15 E
Tennessee □, U.S.A. **115 H2** 36 0N 86 30W
Tennessee →, U.S.A. **114 G1** 37 4N 88 34W
Teno, Pta. de, Canary Is. **48 F3** 28 21N 16 55W
Tenom, Malaysia **62 C5** 5 4N 115 57 E
Tenosique, Mexico **119 D6** 17 30N 91 24W
Tenryū-Gawa →, Japan **55 G8** 35 39N 137 48 E
Tenterden, U.K. **15 F8** 51 4N 0 42 E
Tenterfield, Australia **95 D5** 29 0 S 152 0 E
Teo, Spain **36 C2** 42 45N 8 30W
Teófilo Otoni, Brazil **125 G10** 17 50 S 41 30W
Tepa, Indonesia **63 F7** 7 52 S 129 31 E
Tepalcatepec →, Mexico **118 D4** 18 35N 101 59W
Tepecik, Bursa, Turkey **45 F12** 40 7N 28 25 E
Tepecik, Kütahya,
　Turkey **47 B11** 39 32N 29 28 E
Tepehuanes, Mexico **118 B3** 25 21N 105 44W
Tepelenë, Albania **44 F4** 40 17N 20 2 E
Tepetongo, Mexico **118 C4** 22 28N 103 9W
Tepic, Mexico **118 C4** 21 30N 104 54W
Teplá, Czech Rep. **26 B5** 49 59N 12 52 E
Teplice, Czech Rep. **26 A6** 50 40N 13 48 E
Teplyk, Ukraine **29 B14** 48 40N 29 44 E
Tepoca, C., Mexico **118 A2** 30 20N 112 25W
Tequila, Mexico **118 C4** 20 54N 103 47W
Ter →, Spain **38 C8** 42 0N 3 12 E
Ter Apel, Neths. **17 B7** 52 53N 7 5 E
Téra, Niger **83 C5** 14 0N 0 45 E
Tera →, Spain **36 D5** 41 54N 5 44W
Teraina, Kiribati **97 G11** 4 43N 160 25W
Terakeka, Sudan **81 F3** 5 26N 31 45 E
Téramo, Italy **41 F10** 42 39N 13 42 E
Terang, Australia **95 F3** 38 15 S 142 55 E
Terang, Teluk, Indonesia **63 K19** 8 44 S 116 0 E
Terazit, Massif de, Niger **83 A6** 20 2N 8 30 E
Tercan, Turkey **73 C9** 39 47N 40 23 E
Tercero →, Argentina **126 C3** 32 58 S 61 47W
Terebovlya, Ukraine **33 H3** 49 18N 25 44 E
Teregova, Romania **28 E7** 45 10N 22 16 E
Tereida, Sudan **81 E3** 10 35N 31 17 E
Terek →, Russia **35 J8** 44 0N 47 30 E
Terepaima △, Venezuela **121 E6** 9 58N 69 17W
Tereshka →, Russia **34 E8** 51 48N 46 26 E
Teresina, Brazil **125 E10** 5 9 S 42 45W
Terespol, Poland **31 F10** 52 5N 23 37 E
Teresva, Ukraine **29 B8** 48 0N 23 42 E
Terewah, L., Australia **95 D4** 29 52 S 147 35 E
Terges →, Portugal **37 H3** 37 49N 7 41W
Tergnier, France **19 C10** 49 40N 3 17 E
Teridgerie Cr. →,
　Australia **95 E4** 30 25 S 148 50 E
Terlizzi, Italy **43 A9** 41 8N 16 32 E
Termez = Termiz,
　Uzbekistan **52 F7** 37 15N 67 15 E
Términi Imerese, Italy **42 E6** 37 59N 13 42 E
Términos, L. de, Mexico **119 D6** 18 37N 91 33W
Termiz, Uzbekistan **52 F7** 37 15N 67 15 E
Térmoli, Italy **41 F12** 42 0N 15 0 E
Ternate, Indonesia **63 D7** 0 45N 127 25 E
Terneuzen, Neths. **17 C3** 51 20N 3 50 E
Terney, Russia **53 E14** 45 3N 136 37 E
Terni, Italy **41 F9** 42 34N 12 37 E
Ternitz, Austria **26 D8** 47 43N 16 2 E
Ternivka, Ukraine **29 B14** 48 8N 29 58 E
Ternopil, Ukraine **33 H3** 49 30N 25 40 E
Ternopol = Ternopil,
　Ukraine **33 H3** 49 30N 25 40 E
Terowie, Australia **95 E2** 33 8 S 138 55 E

Terpní, Greece **44 F7** 40 55N 23 26 E
Terra Bella, U.S.A. **111 K7** 35 58N 119 3W
Terra Nova △, Canada **105 C9** 48 33N 53 55W
Terrace, Canada **102 C3** 54 30N 128 35W
Terrace Bay, Canada **104 C2** 48 47N 87 5W
Terracina, Italy **42 A6** 41 17N 13 15 E
Terralba, Italy **42 C1** 39 43N 8 39 E
Terrassini, Italy **42 E6** 38 10N 13 4 E
Terrassa, Spain **38 D7** 41 34N 2 1 E
Terrasson-la-Villedieu,
　France **20 C5** 45 8N 1 18 E
Terre Haute, U.S.A. **114 F2** 39 28N 87 25W
Terrebonne B., U.S.A. **113 L9** 29 5N 90 35W
Terrell, U.S.A. **113 J6** 32 44N 96 17W
Terrenceville, Canada **105 C9** 47 40N 54 44W
Terry, U.S.A. **112 B2** 46 47N 105 19W
Terryville, U.S.A. **117 E11** 41 41N 73 3W
Terschelling, Neths. **17 A5** 53 25N 5 20 E
Tersko-Kumskiy Kanal,
　Russia **35 H7** 44 32N 44 38 E
Tertenía, Italy **42 C2** 39 42N 9 34 E
Terter = Tärtär →,
　Azerbaijan **35 K8** 40 26N 47 20 E
Teruel, Spain **38 E4** 40 22N 1 8W
Teruel □, Spain **38 E4** 40 48N 1 0W
Tervel, Bulgaria **45 C11** 43 45N 27 28 E
Tervola, Finland **8 C21** 66 6N 24 49 E
Teryaweyna L.,
　Australia **95 E3** 32 18 S 143 22 E
Tešanj, Bos.-H. **28 F2** 44 38N 18 1 E
Teseney, Eritrea **81 D4** 15 5N 36 42 E
Tesha →, Russia **34 C6** 55 38N 42 9 E
Teshio, Japan **54 B10** 44 53N 141 44 E
Teshio-Gawa →, Japan **54 B10** 44 53N 141 45 E
Tešica, Serbia & M. **44 C5** 43 27N 21 45 E
Tesiyn Gol →,
　Mongolia **60 A4** 50 40N 93 20 E
Teslić, Bos.-H. **28 F2** 44 37N 17 54 E
Teslin, Canada **102 A2** 60 10N 132 43W
Teslin →, Canada **102 A2** 61 34N 134 35W
Teslin L., Canada **102 A2** 60 15N 132 57W
Tessalit, Mali **83 A5** 20 12N 1 0 E
Tessaoua, Niger **83 C6** 13 47N 7 56 E
Tessin, Germany **24 A8** 54 2N 12 26 E
Tessit, Mali **83 B5** 15 13N 0 18 E
Test →, U.K. **15 G6** 50 56N 1 29W
Testa del Gargano, Italy **41 G13** 41 50N 16 10 E
Testigos, Is. Las,
　Venezuela **121 D7** 11 23N 63 7W
Tét, Hungary **28 C2** 47 30N 17 33 E
Têt →, France **20 F7** 42 44N 3 2 E
Tetachuck L., Canada **102 C3** 53 18N 125 55W
Tetas, Pta., Chile **126 A1** 23 31 S 70 38W
Tete, Mozam. **87 F3** 16 13 S 33 33 E
Tete □, Mozam. **87 F3** 15 15 S 32 40 E
Teterev →, Ukraine **33 G6** 51 1N 30 5 E
Teterow, Germany **24 B8** 53 46N 12 34 E
Teteven, Bulgaria **45 D8** 42 58N 24 17 E
Tethul →, Canada **102 A6** 60 35N 112 12W
Tetiyev, Ukraine **33 H5** 49 22N 29 38 E
Teton →, U.S.A. **108 C8** 47 56N 110 31W
Tétouan, Morocco **78 A4** 35 35N 5 21W
Tetovo, Macedonia **44 D4** 42 1N 20 59 E
Tetyushi, Russia **34 C9** 54 55N 48 49 E
Teuco →, Argentina **126 B3** 25 35 S 60 11W
Teulada, Italy **42 D1** 38 58N 8 46 E
Teulon, Canada **103 C9** 50 23N 97 16W
Teun, Indonesia **63 F7** 6 59 S 129 8 E
Teutoburger Wald,
　Germany **24 C4** 52 5N 8 22 E
Tevere →, Italy **41 F9** 41 44N 12 14 E
Teverya, Israel **74 C4** 32 47N 35 32 E
Teviot →, U.K. **13 F6** 55 29N 2 38W
Tewantin, Australia **95 D5** 26 27 S 153 3 E
Tewkesbury, U.K. **15 F5** 51 59N 2 9W
Texada I., Canada **102 D4** 49 40N 124 25W
Texarkana, Ark., U.S.A. **113 J8** 33 26N 94 2W
Texarkana, Tex., U.S.A. **113 J7** 33 26N 94 3W
Texas, Australia **95 D5** 28 49 S 151 9 E
Texas □, U.S.A. **113 K5** 31 40N 98 30W
Texas City, U.S.A. **113 L7** 29 24N 94 54W
Texel, Neths. **17 A4** 53 5N 4 50 E
Texline, U.S.A. **113 G3** 36 23N 103 2W
Texoma, L., U.S.A. **113 J6** 33 50N 96 34W
Teykovo, Russia **32 D11** 56 55N 40 30 E
Teza →, Russia **34 B5** 56 32N 41 53 E
Tezin, Afghan. **68 B3** 34 24N 69 30 E
Teziutlán, Mexico **119 D5** 19 50N 97 22W
Tezpur, India **67 F18** 26 40N 92 45 E
Tezzeron L., Canada **102 C4** 54 43N 124 30W
Tha-anne →, Canada **103 A10** 60 31N 94 37W
Tha Deua, Laos **64 D4** 17 57N 102 53 E
Tha Deua, Laos **64 C3** 19 26N 101 50 E
Tha Pla, Thailand **64 D3** 17 48N 100 32 E
Tha Rua, Thailand **64 E3** 14 34N 100 44 E
Tha Sala, Thailand **65 H2** 8 40N 99 56 E
Tha Song Yang,
　Thailand **64 D1** 17 34N 97 55 E
Thaba Putsoa, Lesotho **89 D4** 29 45 S 28 0 E
Thabana Ntlenyana,
　Lesotho **89 D4** 29 30 S 29 16 E
Thabazimbi, S. Africa **89 C4** 24 40 S 27 21 E
Thādiq, Si. Arabia **70 E5** 25 18N 45 52 E
Thai Binh, Vietnam **58 G6** 20 35N 106 1 E
Thai Muang, Thailand **65 H2** 8 24N 98 16 E
Thai Nguyen, Vietnam **58 G5** 21 35N 105 55 E
Thailand ■, Asia **64 E4** 16 0N 102 0 E
Thailand, G. of, Asia **65 G3** 11 30N 101 0 E
Thakhek, Laos **64 D5** 17 25N 104 45 E
Thal, Pakistan **68 C4** 33 28N 70 33 E
Thal Desert, Pakistan **68 D4** 31 10N 71 30 E
Thala La = Hkakabo
　Razi, Burma **67 E20** 28 25N 97 23 E
Thalabarivat, Cambodia **64 F5** 13 33N 105 57 E
Thallon, Australia **95 D4** 28 39 S 148 49 E
Thalwil, Switz. **25 H4** 47 17N 8 35 E
Thames, N.Z. **91 G5** 37 7 S 175 34 E
Thames →, Canada **114 D2** 42 20N 82 25W
Thames →, U.K. **15 F8** 51 29N 0 34 E
Thames →, U.S.A. **117 E12** 41 18N 72 5W
Thames Estuary, U.K. **15 F8** 51 29N 0 52 E
Thamesford, Canada **116 C4** 43 4N 81 0W
Thamesville, Canada **116 D3** 42 33N 81 59W
Than, India **68 H4** 22 34N 71 11 E
Than Uyen, Vietnam **64 B4** 22 0N 103 54 E
Thana Gazi, India **68 F7** 27 25N 76 19 E
Thandla, India **68 H6** 23 0N 74 34 E
Thane, India **66 K8** 19 12N 72 59 E
Thanesar, India **68 D7** 30 1N 76 52 E
Thanet, I. of, U.K. **15 F9** 51 21N 1 20 E
Thangool, Australia **94 C5** 24 38 S 150 42 E
Thanh Hoa, Vietnam **64 C5** 19 48N 105 46 E
Thanh Hung, Vietnam **65 H5** 9 55N 105 43 E
Thanh Pho Ho Chi
　Minh, Vietnam **65 G6** 10 58N 106 40 E

Thanh Thuy, Vietnam **64 A5** 22 55N 104 51 E
Thanjavur, India **66 P11** 10 48N 79 12 E
Thann, France **19 E14** 47 48N 7 5 E
Thano Bula Khan,
　Pakistan **68 G2** 25 22N 67 50 E
Thaolinta L., Canada **103 A9** 61 30N 96 25W
Thaon-les-Vosges,
　France **19 D13** 48 15N 6 24 E
Thap Lan △, Thailand **64 E4** 14 15N 102 16 E
Thap Sakae, Thailand **65 G2** 11 30N 99 37 E
Thap Than, Thailand **64 E2** 15 27N 99 54 E
Thar Desert, India **68 F5** 28 0N 72 0 E
Tharad, India **68 G4** 24 30N 71 44 E
Thargomindah, Australia **95 D3** 27 58 S 143 46 E
Tharrawaddy, Burma **67 L19** 17 38N 95 48 E
Tharthār, Buhayrat ath,
　Iraq **70 C4** 34 0N 43 15 E
Tharthar, L. = Tharthār,
　Buhayrat ath, Iraq **70 C4** 34 0N 43 15 E
Tharthār, W. ath →,
　Iraq **70 C4** 33 59N 43 12 E
Thasopoúla, Greece **45 F8** 40 49N 24 45 E
Thásos, Greece **45 F8** 40 40N 24 40 E
That Khe, Vietnam **58 F6** 22 16N 106 28 E
Thatcher, Ariz., U.S.A. **109 K9** 32 51N 109 46W
Thatcher, Colo., U.S.A. **113 G2** 37 33N 104 7W
Thaton, Burma **67 L20** 16 55N 97 22 E
Thau, Bassin de, France **20 E7** 43 23N 3 36 E
Thaungdut, Burma **67 G19** 24 30N 94 40 E
Thayer, U.S.A. **113 G9** 36 31N 91 33W
Thayetmyo, Burma **67 K19** 19 20N 95 10 E
Thazi, Burma **67 J20** 21 0N 96 5 E
The Bight, Bahamas **121 B4** 24 19N 75 24W
The Crane, Barbados **121 g** 13 6N 59 27W
The Dalles, U.S.A. **108 D3** 45 36N 121 10W
The Great Divide =
　Great Dividing Ra.,
　Australia **94 C4** 23 0 S 146 0 E
The Hague = 's-
　Gravenhage, Neths. **17 B4** 52 7N 4 17 E
The Pas, Canada **103 C8** 53 45N 101 15W
The Range, Zimbabwe **87 F3** 19 2 S 31 2 E
The Rock, Australia **95 F4** 35 15 S 147 2 E
The Settlement,
　Br. Virgin Is. **121 e** 18 43N 64 22W
The Woodlands, U.S.A. **113 K7** 30 9N 95 27W
Thebes = Thívai, Greece **46 C5** 38 19N 23 19 E
Thebes, Egypt **80 B3** 25 40N 32 35 E
Thedford, U.S.A. **112 E4** 41 59N 100 35W
Theebine, Australia **95 D5** 25 57 S 152 34 E
Thekulthili L., Canada **103 A7** 61 3N 110 0W
Thelon →, Canada **103 A8** 64 16N 96 4W
Thénezay, France **18 F6** 46 44N 0 2W
Thenon, France **20 C5** 45 9N 1 4 E
Theodore, Australia **94 C5** 24 55 S 150 3 E
Theodore, Canada **103 C8** 51 26N 102 55W
Theodore, U.S.A. **115 K1** 30 33N 88 10W
Theodore Roosevelt △,
　U.S.A. **112 B3** 47 0N 103 25W
Theodore Roosevelt L.,
　U.S.A. **109 K8** 33 40N 111 10W
Thepha, Thailand **65 J3** 6 52N 100 58 E
Thérain →, France **19 C9** 49 15N 2 27 E
Theresa, U.S.A. **117 B9** 44 13N 75 48W
Thermaïkós Kólpos,
　Greece **44 F6** 40 15N 22 45 E
Thermi, Greece **47 B8** 39 11N 26 29 E
Thermopolis, U.S.A. **108 E9** 43 39N 108 13W
Thermopylae P., Greece **46 C4** 38 48N 22 35 E
Thesprotía □, Greece **46 B2** 39 27N 20 22 E
Thessalía □, Greece **46 B4** 39 25N 22 0 E
Thessalon, Canada **104 C3** 46 20N 83 30W
Thessaloníki, Greece **44 F6** 40 38N 22 58 E
Thessaloníki □, Greece **44 F7** 40 45N 23 0 E
Thessaloníki ✈ (SKG),
　Greece **44 F7** 40 30N 23 0 E
Thessaloníki, Gulf of =
　Thermaïkós Kólpos,
　Greece **44 F6** 40 15N 22 45 E
Thessaly = Thessalía □,
　Greece **46 B4** 39 25N 22 0 E
Thetford, U.K. **15 E8** 52 25N 0 45 E
Thetford Mines, Canada **105 C5** 46 8N 71 18W
Theun →, Laos **64 C5** 18 19N 104 0 E
Theunissen, S. Africa **88 D4** 28 26 S 26 43 E
Thevenard, Australia **95 E1** 32 9 S 133 38 E
Thiámis →, Greece **46 B2** 39 15N 20 6 E
Thibault, France **18 C7** 49 8N 0 27 E
Thibodaux, U.S.A. **113 L9** 29 48N 90 49W
Thicket Portage, Canada **103 B9** 55 19N 97 42W
Thief River Falls, U.S.A. **112 A6** 48 7N 96 10W
Thiel Mts., Antarctica **5 E16** 85 15 S 91 0W
Thiene, Italy **41 C8** 45 42N 11 29 E
Thiérache, France **19 C10** 49 51N 3 45 E
Thiers, France **20 C7** 45 52N 3 33 E
Thiès, Senegal **82 C1** 14 50N 16 51W
Thiesi, Italy **42 B1** 40 31N 8 43 E
Thiet, Sudan **81 F2** 7 37N 28 49 E
Thika, Kenya **86 C4** 1 1 S 37 5 E
Thikombia, Fiji **91 B9** 15 44 S 179 55W
Thille-Boubacar, Senegal **82 B1** 16 31N 15 5W
Thimphu, Bhutan **67 F16** 27 31N 89 45 E
Pingvallavatn, Iceland **8 D3** 64 11N 21 9W
Thionville, France **19 C13** 49 20N 6 10 E
Thíra, Greece **47 E7** 36 23N 25 27 E
Thirasía, Greece **47 E7** 36 26N 25 21 E
Third Cataract, Sudan **80 D3** 19 42N 30 20 E
Thirsk, U.K. **14 C6** 54 14N 1 19W
Thiruvananthapuram =
　Trivandrum, India **66 Q10** 8 41N 77 0 E
Thisted, Denmark **11 H2** 56 58N 8 40 E
Thistle I., Australia **95 F2** 35 0 S 136 8 E
Thívai, Greece **46 C5** 38 19N 23 19 E
Thiviers, France **20 C4** 45 25N 0 54 E
Thizy, France **19 F11** 46 2N 4 18 E
Þjórsá →, Iceland **8 E3** 63 47N 20 48W
Thlewiaza →, Canada **103 A10** 60 29N 94 40W
Thmar Puok, Cambodia **64 F4** 13 57N 103 4 E
Tho Vinh, Vietnam **64 C5** 19 16N 105 42 E
Thoa →, Canada **103 A7** 60 31N 109 47W
Thoen, Thailand **64 D2** 17 43N 99 12 E
Thoeng, Thailand **64 C3** 19 41N 100 12 E
Thohoyandou, S. Africa **85 J6** 22 58 S 30 29 E
Tholdi, Pakistan **69 B7** 35 5N 76 6 E
Thomas, U.S.A. **113 H5** 35 45N 98 45W
Thomas, L., Australia **95 D2** 26 4 S 137 58 E
Thomaston, U.S.A. **115 J3** 32 53N 84 20W
Thomasville, Ala.,
　U.S.A. **115 K2** 31 55N 87 44W
Thomasville, Ga., U.S.A. **115 K4** 30 50N 83 59W
Thomasville, N.C.,
　U.S.A. **115 H5** 35 53N 80 5W
Thompson, Canada **103 B9** 55 45N 97 52W
Thompson, U.S.A. **117 E9** 41 52N 75 31W
Thompson →, Canada **102 C4** 50 15N 121 24W
Thompson →, U.S.A. **112 F8** 39 46N 93 37W
Thompson Falls, U.S.A. **108 C6** 47 36N 115 21W

Thompson Pk., U.S.A. . 108 F2 41 0N 123 0W
Thompson Springs,
  U.S.A. 109 G9 38 58N 109 43W
Thompsontown, U.S.A. . 116 F7 40 33N 77 14W
Thomson, U.S.A. 115 J4 33 28N 82 30W
Thomson →, Australia . 94 C3 25 11 S 142 53 E
Thônes, France . . . . . . 21 C10 45 54N 6 18 E
Thong Yang, Thailand . 65 b 9 28N 99 56 E
Thonon-les-Bains,
  France . . . . 19 F13 46 22N 6 29 E
Thorez, Ukraine . . . . . 33 H10 48 4N 38 34 E
Þórisvatn, Iceland 8 D4 64 20N 18 55W
Thornaby on Tees, U.K. . 14 C5 54 33N 1 18W
Thornbury, Canada . . . 116 B4 44 34N 80 26W
Thorne, U.K. 14 D7 53 37N 0 57W
Thornhill, Canada 102 C3 54 31N 128 32W
Thorold, Canada 116 C5 43 7N 79 12W
Thouin, C., Australia . . 92 D2 20 20 S 118 10 E
Thousand Oaks, U.S.A. . 111 L8 34 10N 118 50W
Thrace, Turkey . . . . . . 45 F10 41 0N 27 0 E
Thrakikón Pélagos,
  Greece . . . . 45 F8 40 30N 25 0 E
Three Forks, U.S.A. . . . 108 D8 45 54N 111 33W
Three Gorges Dam,
  China . . . . 59 B8 30 45N 111 15 E
Three Hills, Canada . . . 102 C6 51 43N 113 15W
Three Hummock I.,
  Australia . . . . 95 G3 40 25 S 144 55 E
Three Pagodas Pass,
  Asia . . . . 64 E2 15 20N 98 30 E
Three Points, C., Ghana . 82 E4 4 42N 2 6W
Three Rivers, Calif.,
  U.S.A. 110 J8 36 26N 118 54W
Three Rivers, Tex.,
  U.S.A. 113 L5 28 28N 98 11W
Three Sisters, U.S.A. . . 108 D3 44 4N 121 51W
Three Springs, Australia 93 E2 29 32 S 115 45 E
Throssell, L., Australia . 93 E3 27 33 S 124 10 E
Throssell Ra., Australia 92 D3 22 3 S 121 43 E
Thrushton △, Australia 95 D4 27 47 S 147 40 E
Thuan Hoa, Vietnam . . 65 H5 8 58N 105 30 E
Thubun Lakes, Canada . 103 A6 61 30N 112 0W
Thueyts, France . . . . . 21 D8 44 41N 4 9 E
Thuin, Belgium . . . . . 17 D4 50 20N 4 17 E
Thuir, France . . . . . . 20 F6 42 38N 2 45 E
Thule = Qaanaaq,
  Greenland 4 B4 77 40N 69 0W
Thule Air Base =
  Uummannaq,
  Greenland 4 B5 70 58N 52 0W
Thun, Switz. . . . . 25 J3 46 45N 7 38 E
Thunder B., U.S.A. . . . 116 B1 45 0N 83 20W
Thunder Bay, Canada . . 104 C2 48 20N 89 15W
Thunersee, Switz. . . . . 25 J3 46 43N 7 39 E
Thung Salaeng Luang △,
  Thailand . . . . 64 D3 16 43N 100 50 E
Thung Song, Thailand . 65 H2 8 10N 99 40 E
Thunkar, Bhutan . . . . 67 F17 27 55N 91 0 E
Thuong Tra, Vietnam . . 64 D6 16 2N 107 42 E
Thur →, Switz. . . . . . 25 H5 47 32N 9 10 E
Thurgau □, Switz. . . . . 25 H5 47 34N 9 10 E
Thüringen □, Germany . 24 D6 51 0N 11 0 E
Thüringer Wald,
  Germany . . . . 24 E6 50 35N 11 0 E
Thurles, Ireland 12 D4 52 41N 7 49W
Thurn P., Austria . . . . 26 E5 47 20N 12 25 E
Thurrock □, U.K. . . . . 15 F8 51 31N 0 23 E
Thursday I., Australia . 94 A3 10 30 S 142 3 E
Thurso, Canada 104 C4 45 36N 75 15W
Thurso, U.K. 13 C5 58 36N 3 32W
Thurso →, U.K. 13 C5 58 36N 3 32W
Thurston I., Antarctica . 5 D16 72 0 S 100 0W
Thury-Harcourt, France 18 D6 48 59N 0 30W
Thutade L., Canada . . . 102 B3 57 0N 126 55W
Thy, Denmark . . . . . . 11 H2 56 52N 8 25 E
Thyborøn, Denmark . . . 11 H2 56 42N 8 12 E
Thyolo, Malawi . . . . . 87 F4 16 7 S 35 5 E
Ti-n-Amzi →, Niger . . . 83 B5 18 20N 4 32 E
Ti-n-Barraouene, O. →,
  Africa . . . . 83 B5 18 40N 4 5 E
Ti-n-Zaouatene, Algeria 83 B5 19 55N 2 55 E
Ti Tree, Australia . . . . 94 C1 22 5 S 133 22 E
Tiadiaye, Senegal 82 C1 14 25N 16 40W
Tian Shan, Asia . . . . . 60 B3 40 30N 76 0 E
Tianchang, China . . . . 59 A12 32 40N 119 0 E
Tiandeng, China . . . . . 58 F6 23 6N 107 7 E
Tiandong, China . . . . . 58 F6 23 36N 107 8 E
Tian'e, China . . . . 58 E6 25 1N 107 9 E
Tianhe, China . . . . . . 58 E7 24 48N 108 40 E
Tianjin, China . . . . . . 57 E9 39 8N 117 10 E
Tiankoura,
  Burkina Faso 82 C4 10 47N 3 17W
Tianlin, China . . . . . . 58 E6 24 21N 106 12 E
Tianmen, China . . . . . 59 B9 30 39N 113 9 E
Tianquan, China . . . . . 58 B4 30 7N 102 43 E
Tianshui, China . . . . . 56 G3 34 32N 105 40 E
Tianyang, China . . . . . 58 F6 23 42N 106 53 E
Tianyar, Indonesia . . . 63 J18 8 12 S 115 30 E
Tianzhen, China . . . . . 56 D8 40 24N 114 5 E
Tianzhu, China . . . . . 58 D7 26 54N 109 11 E
Tianzhuangtai, China . . 57 D12 40 43N 122 5 E
Tiaret, Algeria . . . . . . 78 A6 35 20N 1 21 E
Tiassalé, Ivory C. 82 D4 5 58N 4 57W
Tibagi, Brazil . . . . . . 127 A5 24 30 S 50 24W
Tibagi →, Brazil . . . . . 127 A5 22 47 S 51 1W
Tibati, Cameroon . . . . 83 D7 6 22N 12 30 E
Tibe, Ethiopia . . . . . . 81 F4 9 24N 37 12 E
Tiber = Tevere →, Italy 41 G9 41 44N 12 14 E
Tiberias = Teverya,
  Israel . . . . 74 C4 32 47N 35 32 E
Tiberias, L. = Yam
  Kinneret, Israel . . . . 74 C4 32 45N 35 35 E
Tibesti, Chad . . . . . . 79 D9 21 0N 17 30 E
Tibet = Xizang
  Zizhiqu □, China . . . 60 C3 32 0N 88 0 E
Tibiao, Phil. . . . . 61 F5 11 17N 122 2 E
Tibiri, Niger . . . . 83 C6 13 34N 7 4 E
Tibleş, Vf., Romania . . 29 C9 47 32N 24 15 E
Tibleşu, Munţii,
  Romania . . . . 29 C9 47 32N 24 15 E
Tibnī, Syria . . . . 70 C3 35 36N 39 50 E
Tibooburra, Australia . 95 D3 29 26 S 142 1 E
Tibro, Sweden . . . . . . 11 F8 58 28N 14 10 E
Tiburón, I., Mexico . . . 118 B2 29 0N 112 30W
Ticao I., Phil. . . . . 61 E5 12 31N 123 42 E
Tîchît, Mauritania 82 B3 18 21N 9 29W
Ticho, Ethiopia . . . . . 81 F4 7 50N 39 32 E
Ticino □, Switz. . . . . . 25 J4 46 20N 8 45 E
Ticino →, Italy . . . . . . 25 K5 45 9N 9 14 E
Ticleni, Romania . . . . 29 F8 44 53N 23 24 E
Ticonderoga, U.S.A. . . 117 C11 43 51N 73 26W

Ticul, Mexico 119 C7 20 20N 89 31W
Tidaholm, Sweden . . . . 11 F7 58 12N 13 58 E
Tidan, Sweden . . . . . . 11 F8 58 34N 14 1 E
Tiddim, Burma . . . . . . 67 H18 23 28N 93 45 E
Tidioute, U.S.A. 116 E5 41 41N 79 24W
Tidjikja, Mauritania . . 82 B2 18 29N 11 35W
Tidore, Indonesia . . . . 63 D7 0 40N 127 25 E
Tiel, Neths. . . . . 17 C5 51 53N 5 26 E
Tiel, Senegal 82 C1 14 55N 15 5W
Tieling, China . . . . . . 57 C12 42 20N 123 55 E
Tielt, Belgium . . . . . . 17 C3 51 0N 3 20 E
Tien Shan = Tian Shan,
  Asia . . . . 60 B3 40 30N 76 0 E
Tien-tsin = Tianjin,
  China . . . . 57 E9 39 8N 117 10 E
Tien Yen, Vietnam . . . . 64 B6 21 20N 107 24 E
T'ienching = Tianjin,
  China . . . . 57 E9 39 8N 117 10 E
Tienen, Belgium . . . . . 17 D4 50 48N 4 57 E
Tiénigbé, Ivory C. 82 D3 8 11N 5 43W
Tientsin = Tianjin, China 57 E9 39 8N 117 10 E
Tieri, Australia . . . . . . 94 C4 23 2 S 148 21 E
Tierp, Sweden . . . . . . 10 D11 60 20N 17 30 E
Tierra Amarilla, Chile . 126 B1 27 28 S 70 18W
Tierra Amarilla, U.S.A. . 109 H10 36 42N 106 33W
Tierra Colorada, Mexico 119 D5 17 10N 99 35W
Tierra de Barros, Spain . 37 G4 38 40N 6 30W
Tierra de Campos, Spain 36 C6 42 10N 4 50W
Tierra del Fuego, I. Gr.
  de, Argentina . . . . . 128 G3 54 0 S 69 0W
Tiétar →, Spain 36 F4 39 50N 6 1W
Tieté →, Brazil . . . . . . 127 A5 20 40 S 51 35W
Tiffin, U.S.A. 114 E2 41 7N 83 11W
Tifton, U.S.A. 115 K4 31 27N 83 31W
Tifu, Indonesia . . . . . . 63 E7 3 39 S 126 24 E
Tighina, Moldova . . . . 29 D14 46 50N 29 30 E
Tigil, Russia . . . . 53 D16 57 49N 158 40 E
Tignish, Canada 105 C7 46 58N 64 2W
Tigray □, Ethiopia . . . . 81 E4 13 35N 39 15 E
Tigre →, Peru . . . . 124 D4 4 30 S 74 10W
Tigre →, Venezuela . . . 124 B6 9 20N 62 30W
Tigris = Dijlah, Nahr →,
  Asia . . . . 70 D5 31 0N 47 25 E
Tigveni, Romania . . . . 29 E9 45 10N 24 31 E
Tigyaing, Burma . . . . . 67 H20 23 45N 96 10 E
Tîh, Gebel el, Egypt . . . 80 B3 29 32N 33 26 E
Tijara, India . . . . 68 F7 27 56N 76 31 E
Tijuana, Mexico 111 N9 32 30N 117 10W
Tikal, Guatemala 120 C2 17 13N 89 24W
Tikal △, Guatemala . . . 120 C2 17 13N 89 34W
Tikamgarh, India . . . . 69 G8 24 44N 78 50 E
Tikaré, Burkina Faso . . 83 C4 13 15N 1 43W
Tikhoretsk, Russia . . . 35 H5 45 56N 40 5 E
Tikhvin, Russia . . . . . 32 C7 59 35N 33 30 E
Tikiraqjuaq = Whale
  Cove, Canada 103 A10 62 10N 92 34W
Tiko, Cameroon . . . . . 83 E6 4 4N 9 20 E
Tikrīt, Iraq . . . . 70 C4 34 35N 43 37 E
Tiksi, Russia . . . . 53 B13 71 40N 128 45 E
Tilamuta, Indonesia . . . 63 D6 0 32N 122 23 E
Tilburg, Neths. . . . . . . 17 C5 51 31N 5 6 E
Tilbury, Canada 116 D2 42 17N 82 23W
Tilbury, U.K. . . . . 15 F8 51 27N 0 22 E
Tilcara, Argentina . . . . 126 A2 23 36 S 65 23W
Tilden, U.S.A. 112 D6 42 3N 97 50W
Tilemses, Niger . . . . . 83 B5 15 37N 4 44 E
Tilemsi, Vallée du, Mali 83 B5 17 42N 0 15 E
Tilichiki, Russia . . . . . 53 C17 60 27N 166 5 E
Tilissos, Greece . . . . . 49 D7 35 20N 25 1 E
Till →, U.K. 14 B5 55 41N 2 13W
Tillabéri, Niger . . . . . 83 C5 14 28N 1 28 E
Tillamook, U.S.A. 108 D2 45 27N 123 51W
Tillberga, Sweden . . . . 10 E10 59 40N 16 39 E
Tillia, Niger . . . . 83 B5 16 8N 4 47 E
Tillsonburg, Canada . . 116 D4 42 53N 80 44W
Tillyeria, Cyprus . . . . . 49 D11 35 6N 32 40 E
Tilogne, Senegal 82 B2 16 1N 13 40W
Tílos, Greece . . . . 47 E9 36 27N 27 27 E
Tilpa, Australia . . . . . 95 E3 30 57 S 144 24 E
Tilt →, U.K. 13 E5 56 46N 3 51W
Tilton, U.S.A. 117 C13 43 27N 71 36W
Tiltonsville, U.S.A. . . . 116 F4 40 10N 80 41W
Tim, Denmark . . . . . . 11 H2 56 12N 8 19 E
Timagami, L., Canada . 104 C3 47 0N 80 10W
Timanfaya △, Canary Is. 48 F6 29 0N 13 46W
Timaru, N.Z. . . . . 91 L3 44 23N 171 14 E
Timashevo, Russia . . . 34 D10 53 22N 51 9 E
Timashevsk, Russia . . . 35 H4 45 35N 39 0 E
Timau, Kenya . . . . . . 86 B4 0 4N 37 15 E
Timbákion, Greece . . . 49 D6 35 4N 24 45 E
Timbedgha, Mauritania 82 B3 16 17N 8 16W
Timber Creek, Australia 92 C5 15 40 S 130 29 E
Timber Lake, U.S.A. . . 112 C4 45 26N 101 5W
Timber Mt., U.S.A. . . . 110 H10 37 6N 116 28W
Timbo, Guinea 82 C2 10 35N 11 50W
Timbo, Liberia 82 D3 5 35N 9 45W
Timbuktu =
  Tombouctou, Mali . . 82 B4 16 50N 3 0W
Timeiaouine, Algeria . . 83 A5 20 27N 1 50 E
Timétrine, Mts., Mali . 83 B4 19 25N 1 0W
Timfi Óros, Greece . . . 46 B2 39 59N 20 45 E
Timfristós, Óros, Greece 46 C3 38 57N 21 50 E
Timi, Cyprus . . . . 49 E11 34 44N 32 31 E
Timia, Niger . . . . 83 B6 18 4N 8 40 E
Timimoun, Algeria . . . 78 C6 29 14N 0 16 E
Timirist, Râs, Mauritania 82 B1 19 21N 16 30W
Timiş →, Serbia & M. . . 28 E5 44 51N 20 39 E
Timiş →,
  Serbia & M. . . . . . . 28 E6 45 40N 21 30 E
Timişoara, Romania . . 28 E6 45 43N 21 15 E
Timmersdala, Sweden . 11 F7 58 32N 13 46 E
Timmins, Canada 104 C3 48 28N 81 25W
Timok →, Serbia & M. . 44 B6 44 10N 22 40 E
Timor, Asia . . . . 63 F7 9 0 S 125 0 E
Timor Leste = East
  Timor ■, Asia . . . . . 63 F7 8 50 S 126 0 E
Timor Sea, Ind. Oc. . . . 92 B4 12 0 S 127 0 E
Timrå, Sweden . . . . . . 10 B11 62 29N 17 18 E
Tin Can Bay, Australia . 95 D5 25 56 S 153 0 E
Tin Ethisane, Mali . . . 83 B4 19 3N 0 52W
Tin Gornai, Mali 83 B4 16 38N 0 38W
Tin Mt., U.S.A. 110 J9 36 50N 117 10W
Tina, Khalîg el, Egypt . 80 A3 31 20N 32 42 E
Tinaca Pt., Phil. . . . . . 61 J6 5 30N 125 25 E
Tinajo, Canary Is. 48 E6 29 4N 13 42W
Tinca, Romania . . . . . 28 D6 46 46N 21 58 E
Tindal, Australia . . . . . 92 B5 14 31 S 132 22 E
Tindouf, Algeria 78 C4 27 42N 8 10W
Tineo, Spain 36 B4 43 21N 6 27W
Tinfunque △, Paraguay . 126 A3 23 55 S 60 17W

Ting Jiang →, China . . . 59 E11 24 45N 116 35 E
Tinggi, Pulau, Malaysia 65 L5 2 18N 104 7 E
Tinglev, Denmark . . . . 11 K3 54 57N 9 13 E
Tingo Maria, Peru . . . . 124 E3 9 10 S 75 54W
Tingrela, Ivory C. 82 C3 10 27N 6 25W
Tingsryd, Sweden . . . . 11 H9 56 31N 15 0 E
Tingstäde, Sweden . . . 11 G12 57 44N 18 37 E
Tinh Bien, Vietnam . . . 65 G5 10 36N 104 57 E
Tinnevelly = Tirunelveli,
  India . . . . 66 Q10 8 45N 77 45 E
Tinogasta, Argentina . . 126 B2 28 5 S 67 32W
Tínos, Greece . . . . 47 D7 37 33N 25 8 E
Tiñoso, C., Spain 39 H3 37 32N 1 6W
Tinpahar, India . . . . . 69 G12 24 59N 87 44 E
Tintina, Argentina . . . . 126 B3 27 2 S 62 45W
Tintinara, Australia . . . 95 F3 35 48 S 140 2 E
Tintioulé, Guinea 82 C3 10 13N 9 12W
Tinto →, Spain 37 H4 37 12N 6 55W
Tioga, N. Dak., U.S.A. . 112 A3 48 23N 102 56W
Tioga, Pa., U.S.A. 116 E7 41 55N 77 8W
Tioman, Pulau, Malaysia 65 L5 2 50N 104 10 E
Tione di Trento, Italy . . 40 B7 46 2N 10 43 E
Tionesta, U.S.A. 116 E5 41 30N 79 28W
Tior, Sudan . . . . 81 F3 6 26N 31 11 E
Tipongpani, India . . . . 67 F19 27 20N 95 55 E
Tipperary, Ireland 12 D3 52 28N 8 10W
Tipperary □, Ireland . . 12 D4 52 37N 7 55W
Tipton, Calif., U.S.A. . . 110 J7 36 4N 119 19W
Tipton, Iowa, U.S.A. . . 112 E9 41 46N 91 8W
Tipton, Mt., U.S.A. . . . 111 K12 35 32N 114 12W
Tiptonville, U.S.A. 113 G10 36 23N 89 29W
Tîrân, Iran . . . . 71 C6 32 45N 51 8 E
Tîrân, Si. Arabia . . . . . 80 B3 27 57N 34 32 E
Tiranë, Albania . . . . . 44 E3 41 18N 19 49 E
Tiranë ✈ (TIA), Albania 43 A12 41 57N 19 42 E
Tirano, Italy . . . . 40 B7 46 13N 10 10 E
Tiraspol, Moldova . . . . 29 D14 46 55N 29 35 E
Tirdout, Mali 83 B4 16 7N 1 5W
Tire, Turkey . . . . 47 C9 38 5N 27 45 E
Tirebolu, Turkey . . . . . 73 B8 40 58N 38 45 E
Tiree, U.K. 13 E2 56 31N 6 55W
Tiree, Passage of, U.K. . 13 E2 56 30N 6 30W
Tîrgoviste = Târgoviste,
  Romania . . . . 29 F10 44 55N 25 27 E
Tîrgu-Jiu = Târgu-Jiu,
  Romania . . . . 29 E8 45 5N 23 19 E
Tîrgu Mures = Târgu
  Mureş, Romania . . . 29 D9 46 31N 24 38 E
Tirich Mir, Pakistan . . . 66 A7 36 15N 71 55 E
Tiriolo, Italy . . . . 43 D9 38 57N 16 32 E
Tiriro, Guinea 82 C3 10 27N 8 40W
Tírodi, India . . . . 66 J11 21 40N 79 44 E
Tirol □, Austria . . . . . 26 E4 47 3N 10 43 E
Tirschenreuth, Germany 25 F8 49 53N 12 19 E
Tirso →, Italy . . . . 42 C1 39 53N 8 32 E
Tirstrup, Denmark . . . . 11 H4 56 18N 10 42 E
Tiruchchirappalli, India 66 P11 10 45N 78 45 E
Tirunelveli, India . . . . 66 Q10 8 45N 77 45 E
Tirupati, India . . . . . . 66 N11 13 39N 79 25 E
Tiruppur, India . . . . . 66 P10 11 5N 77 22 E
Tiruvannamalai, India . 66 N11 12 15N 79 5 E
Tisa, India . . . . 68 C7 32 50N 76 9 E
Tisa →, Serbia & M. . . . 28 E5 45 15N 20 17 E
Tisdale, Canada 103 C8 52 50N 104 0W
Tishomingo, U.S.A. . . . 113 H6 34 14N 96 41W
Tisjön, Sweden . . . . . . 10 D7 60 56N 13 0 E
Tisnaren, Sweden . . . . 11 F9 58 58N 15 56 E
Tišnov, Czech Rep. . . . 27 B9 49 21N 16 25 E
Tisovec, Slovak Rep. . . 27 C12 48 41N 19 56 E
Tisza = Tisa →,
  Serbia & M. . . . . . . 28 E5 45 15N 20 17 E
Tiszaföldvár, Hungary . 28 D5 46 58N 20 14 E
Tiszafüred, Hungary . . 28 C5 47 38N 20 50 E
Tiszalök, Hungary . . . . 28 B6 48 1N 21 20 E
Tiszavasvári, Hungary . 28 C6 47 58N 21 18 E
Tit-Ary, Russia . . . . . . 53 B13 71 55N 127 2 E
Titaguas, Spain 38 F3 39 53N 1 6W
Titao, Burkina Faso . . . 83 C4 13 45N 2 5W
Titel, Serbia & M. . . . . 28 E5 45 10N 20 18 E
Tithwal, Pakistan . . . . 69 B5 34 21N 73 50 E
Titicaca, L., S. Amer. . . 124 G5 15 30 S 69 30W
Titisee, Germany . . . . 25 H4 47 54N 8 10 E
Titiwa, Nigeria . . . . . . 83 C7 12 14N 12 53 E
Tito, Italy . . . . 43 B8 40 35N 15 40 E
Titova Korenica, Croatia 41 D12 44 43N 15 41 E
Titu, Romania . . . . . . 29 F10 44 39N 25 32 E
Titule, Dem. Rep. of
  the Congo . . . . 86 B2 3 15N 25 31 E
Titusville, Fla., U.S.A. . 115 L5 28 37N 80 49W
Titusville, Pa., U.S.A. . 116 E5 41 38N 79 41W
Tivaouane, Senegal . . . 82 C1 14 56N 16 45W
Tivat, Serbia & M. . . . . 44 D2 42 28N 18 43 E
Tivedens △, Sweden . . 11 F8 58 45N 14 35 E
Tiverton, U.K. 15 G4 50 54N 3 29W
Tívoli, Italy . . . . 41 G9 41 58N 12 45 E
Tiyo, Eritrea . . . . 81 E5 14 41N 40 15 E
Tizi-Ouzou, Algeria . . . 78 A6 36 42N 4 3 E
Tizimín, Mexico 119 C7 21 0N 88 1W
Tjæreborg, Denmark . . 11 J2 55 28N 8 36 E
Tjällmo, Sweden . . . . . 11 F9 58 43N 15 21 E
Tjeggelvas, Sweden . . . 8 C17 66 37N 17 45 E
Tjieggelvas = Tjeggelvas,
  Sweden . . . . 8 C17 66 37N 17 45 E
Tjirebon = Cirebon,
  Indonesia . . . . 63 G13 6 45 S 108 32 E
Tjluring, Indonesia . . . 63 J17 8 25 S 114 13 E
Tjörn, Sweden . . . . . . 11 F5 58 0N 11 35 E
Tkibuli = Tqibuli,
  Georgia . . . . 35 J6 42 26N 43 0 E
Tkvarcheli = Tqvarcheli,
  Georgia . . . . 35 J5 42 47N 41 42 E
Tlacotalpan, Mexico . . 119 D5 18 37N 95 40W
Tlahualilo, Mexico . . . 118 B4 26 20N 103 30W
Tlaquepaque, Mexico . . 118 C4 20 39N 103 19W
Tlaxcala, Mexico 119 D5 19 20N 98 14W
Tlaxcala □, Mexico . . . 119 D5 19 30N 98 20W
Tlaxiaco, Mexico 119 D5 17 18N 97 40W
Tlemcen, Algeria 78 B5 34 52N 1 21W
Tłuszcz, Poland . . . . . 31 F8 52 25N 21 25 E
Tlyarata, Russia . . . . . 35 J8 42 9N 46 26 E
To Bong, Vietnam . . . . 64 F7 12 45N 109 16 E
Toa Payoh, Singapore . 65 d 1 20N 103 51 E
Toad →, Canada 102 B4 59 25N 124 57W
Toad River, Canada . . . 102 B3 58 51N 125 14W
Toamasina, Madag. . . . 89 B8 18 10 S 49 25 E
Toamasina □, Madag. . 89 B8 18 0 S 49 0 E
Toay, Argentina . . . . . 126 D3 36 43 S 64 38W
Toba, China . . . . 58 B1 31 19N 97 42 E
Toba, Japan . . . . 55 G8 34 30N 136 51 E
Toba, Danau, Indonesia 62 D1 2 30N 97 30 E
Toba Tek Singh,
  Pakistan . . . . 68 D5 30 55N 72 25 E
Tobago, Trin. & Tob. . . 121 D7 11 10N 60 30W
Tobarra, Spain 39 G3 38 37N 1 44W

Tobelo, Indonesia . . . . 63 D7 1 45N 127 56 E
Tobermory, Canada . . . 116 A3 45 12N 81 40W
Tobermory, U.K. 13 E2 56 38N 6 5W
Tobin, Pac. Oc. . . . . . . 63 D8 2 40N 131 10 E
Tobin, U.S.A. 110 F5 39 55N 121 19W
Tobin, L., Australia . . . 92 D4 21 45 S 125 49 E
Tobin L., Canada 103 C8 53 35N 103 30W
Toblach = Dobbiaco,
  Italy . . . . 41 B9 46 44N 12 14 E
Toboali, Indonesia . . . 62 E3 3 0 S 106 25 E
Tobol →, Russia . . . . . 52 D7 58 10N 68 12 E
Toboli, Indonesia . . . . 63 E6 0 38 S 120 5 E
Tobolsk, Russia . . . . . 52 D7 58 15N 68 10 E
Tobor, Senegal 82 C1 12 40N 16 15W
Tobruk = Tubruq, Libya 79 B10 32 7N 23 55 E
Tobyhanna, U.S.A. . . . 117 E9 41 11N 75 25W
Tobyl = Tobol →,
  Russia . . . . 52 D7 58 10N 68 12 E
Tocantinópolis, Brazil . 125 E9 6 20 S 47 25W
Tocantins □, Brazil . . . 125 F9 10 0 S 48 0W
Tocantins →, Brazil . . . 125 D9 1 45 S 49 10W
Toccoa, U.S.A. 115 H4 34 35N 83 19W
Toce →, Italy . . . . 40 C5 45 56N 8 29 E
Tochi →, Pakistan . . . . 68 C4 32 49N 70 41 E
Tochigi, Japan . . . . . . 55 F9 36 25N 139 45 E
Tochigi □, Japan . . . . . 55 F9 36 45N 139 45 E
Tocina, Spain 37 H5 37 37N 5 44W
Töcksfors, Sweden . . . 10 E5 59 31N 11 50 E
Toco, Trin. & Tob. 125 K16 10 50N 60 4W
Toconao, Chile . . . . . . 126 A2 22 5 S 68 1W
Tocopilla, Chile . . . . . 126 A1 22 5 S 70 10W
Tocumwal, Australia . . 95 F4 35 51 S 145 31 E
Tocuyo →, Venezuela . . 124 A5 11 3N 68 23W
Todd →, Australia . . . . 94 C2 24 52 S 135 48 E
Todeli, Indonesia . . . . 63 E6 1 40 S 124 29 E
Todenyang, Kenya . . . . 86 B4 4 35N 35 56 E
Todgarh, India . . . . . . 68 G5 25 42N 73 58 E
Todi, Italy . . . . 41 F9 42 47N 12 24 E
Todos os Santos, B. de,
  Brazil . . . . 125 F11 12 48 S 38 38W
Todos Santos, Mexico . 118 C2 23 27N 110 13W
Todtmang, Germany . . 25 H3 47 49N 7 56 E
Toe Hd., U.K. 13 D1 57 50N 7 8W
Toecé, Burkina Faso . . 83 C4 11 50N 1 16W
Tofield, Canada 102 C6 53 25N 112 40W
Tofino, Canada 102 D3 49 11N 125 55W
Töfsingdalens △,
  Sweden . . . . 10 B6 62 10N 12 28 E
Tofua, Tonga . . . . 91 D11 19 45 S 175 5W
Tōgane, Japan . . . . . . 55 G10 35 33N 140 22 E
Togba, Mauritania . . . 82 B2 17 26N 10 12W
Togian, Kepulauan,
  Indonesia . . . . 63 E6 0 20 S 121 50 E
Togliatti, Russia . . . . . 34 D9 53 32N 49 24 E
Togo ■, W. Afr. . . . . . 83 D5 8 30N 1 35 E
Togtoh, China . . . . . . 56 D6 40 15N 111 10 E
Tohma →, Turkey . . . . 72 C7 38 29N 38 23 E
Tōhoku □, Japan . . . . . 54 E10 39 50N 141 45 E
Töhöm, Mongolia . . . . 56 B5 44 27N 108 2 E
Toinya, Sudan . . . . . . 81 F2 6 17N 29 46 E
Toiyabe Range, U.S.A. . 108 G5 39 30N 117 0W
Tojikiston =
  Tajikistan ■, Asia . . 52 F8 38 30N 70 0 E
Tojo, Indonesia . . . . . 63 E6 1 20 S 121 15 E
Tōjō, Japan . . . . 55 G6 34 53N 133 16 E
Tok, U.S.A. 100 B5 63 20N 142 59W
Tok-do, Asia . . . . 55 F5 37 15N 131 52 E
Tokachi-Dake, Japan . . 54 C11 43 17N 142 5 E
Tokachi-Gawa →,
  Japan . . . . 54 C11 42 44N 143 42 E
Tokaj, Hungary . . . . . 28 B6 48 8N 21 27 E
Tokala, Indonesia . . . . 63 E6 1 30 S 121 40 E
Tōkamachi, Japan . . . . 55 F9 37 8N 138 43 E
Tokanui, N.Z. . . . . 91 M2 46 34 S 168 56 E
Tokar, Sudan . . . . 80 D4 18 27N 37 56 E
Tokara-Rettō, Japan . . 55 K4 29 37N 129 43 E
Tokarahi, N.Z. . . . . . . 91 L3 44 56 S 170 39 E
Tokashiki-Shima, Japan 55 L3 26 11N 127 21 E
Tokat, Turkey . . . . 72 B7 40 22N 36 35 E
Tŏkch'ŏn, N. Korea . . . 57 E14 39 45N 126 18 E
Tokeland, U.S.A. 110 D3 46 42N 123 59W
Tokelau Is., Pac. Oc. . . 96 H10 9 0 S 171 45W
Tokmak, Kyrgyzstan . . 52 E8 42 49N 75 15 E
Tokmak, Ukraine . . . . 33 J8 47 16N 35 42 E
Toko Ra., Australia . . . 94 C2 23 5 S 138 20 E
Tokoro-Gawa →, Japan 54 B12 44 7N 144 5 E
Tokuno-Shima, Japan . 55 L4 27 56N 128 55 E
Tokushima, Japan . . . . 55 H7 34 4N 134 34 E
Tokushima □, Japan . . 55 H7 33 55N 134 0 E
Tokuyama, Japan . . . . 55 G5 34 3N 131 50 E
Tōkyō, Japan . . . . 55 G9 35 45N 139 45 E
Tolaga Bay, N.Z. . . . . . 91 H7 38 21 S 178 20 E
Tolbukhin = Dobrich,
  Bulgaria . . . . 45 C11 43 37N 27 49 E
Toledo, Brazil . . . . . . 127 A5 24 44 S 53 45W
Toledo, Spain 36 F6 39 50N 4 2W
Toledo, Ohio, U.S.A. . . 114 E4 41 39N 83 33W
Toledo, Oreg., U.S.A. . . 108 D2 44 37N 123 56W
Toledo, Wash., U.S.A. . 108 C2 46 26N 122 51W
Toledo, Montes de,
  Spain 37 F6 39 33N 4 20W
Toledo Bend Reservoir,
  U.S.A. 113 K8 31 11N 93 34W
Tolentino, Italy . . . . . 41 E10 43 12N 13 17 E
Tolfa, Italy . . . . 41 F8 42 9N 11 56 E
Tolga, Australia . . . . . 94 B4 17 15 S 145 29 E
Toliara, Madag. . . . . . 89 C7 23 21 S 43 40 E
Toliara □, Madag. . . . . 89 C8 21 0 S 45 0 E
Tolima, Colombia 124 C3 4 40N 75 19W
Tolitoli, Indonesia . . . . 63 D6 1 5N 120 50 E
Tolkmicko, Poland . . . 30 D6 54 19N 19 31 E
Tollarp, Sweden . . . . . 11 J7 55 55N 13 58 E
Tollensesee, Germany . 24 B9 53 30N 13 20 E
Tollhouse, U.S.A. 110 H7 37 1N 119 24W
Tolmachovo, Russia . . 32 C5 58 56N 29 51 E
Tolmezzo, Italy . . . . . 41 B10 46 24N 13 1 E
Tolmin, Slovenia . . . . . 28 D3 46 25N 13 44 E
Tolna, Hungary . . . . . 28 D3 46 25N 18 48 E
Tolna □, Hungary . . . . 28 D3 46 30N 18 30 E
Tolo, Teluk, Indonesia . 63 E6 2 20 S 122 10 E
Tolochin = Talachyn,
  Belarus . . . . 32 E5 54 25N 29 42 E
Tolosa, Spain 38 B2 43 8N 2 5W
Tolox, Spain 37 J6 36 41N 4 54W
Toluca, Mexico 119 D5 19 17N 99 40W
Tom Burke, S. Africa . . 89 C4 23 5 S 28 0 E
Tom Price, Australia . . 92 D2 22 40 S 117 48 E
Toma, Burkina Faso . . . 82 C4 12 45N 2 53W
Tomah, U.S.A. 112 D9 43 59N 90 30W
Tomahawk, U.S.A. 112 C10 45 28N 89 44W
Tomai, Moldova . . . . . 29 D13 46 34N 28 19 E
Tomakomai, Japan . . . 54 C10 42 38N 141 36 E
Tomales, U.S.A. 110 G4 38 15N 122 53W
Tomales B., U.S.A. . . . 110 G3 38 15N 123 58W
Tomar, Portugal 37 F2 39 36N 8 25W
Tómaros, Óros, Greece . 46 B2 39 29N 20 48 E
Tomarza, Turkey . . . . 72 C6 38 27N 35 48 E

Tomashevka, Belarus . . 31 G10 51 33N 23 36 E
Tomashpil, Ukraine . . . 29 B13 48 32N 28 31 E
Tomaszów Lubelski,
  Poland . . . . 31 H10 50 27N 23 25 E
Tomaszów Mazowiecki,
  Poland . . . . 31 G7 51 30N 20 2 E
Tomatlán, Mexico 118 D3 19 56N 105 15W
Tombador, Serra do,
  Brazil . . . . 124 F7 12 0 S 58 0W
Tombe, Sudan . . . . . . 81 F3 5 53N 31 40 E
Tombigbee →, U.S.A. . . 115 K2 31 8N 87 57W
Tomboco, Angola . . . . 84 F2 6 50 S 13 3 E
Tombouctou, Mali 82 B4 16 50N 3 0W
Tombstone, U.S.A. 109 L8 31 43N 110 4W
Tombua, Angola . . . . . 88 B1 15 55 S 11 55 E
Tomé, Chile . . . . 126 D1 36 36 S 72 57W
Tomelilla, Sweden . . . . 11 J7 55 33N 13 58 E
Tomelloso, Spain 37 F7 39 10N 3 2W
Tomini, Indonesia . . . . 63 D6 0 30N 120 30 E
Tomini, Teluk,
  Indonesia . . . . 63 E6 0 10 S 121 0 E
Tominian, Mali 82 C4 13 17N 4 35W
Tomiño, Spain 36 D2 41 59N 8 46W
Tomintoul, U.K. 13 D5 57 15N 3 23W
Tomislavgrad, Bos.-H. . 28 G2 43 42N 17 13 E
Tommot, Russia . . . . . 53 D13 59 4N 126 20 E
Tomnop Ta Suos,
  Cambodia . . . . 65 G5 11 20N 104 15 E
Tomo →, Colombia . . . 124 B5 5 20N 67 48W
Toms Place, U.S.A. . . . 110 H8 37 34N 118 41W
Toms River, U.S.A. . . . 117 G10 39 58N 74 12W
Tomsk, Russia . . . . . . 52 D9 56 30N 85 5 E
Tomtabacken, Sweden . 11 G8 57 30N 14 30 E
Tona, Spain . . . . 38 D7 41 51N 2 14 E
Tonalá, Mexico 119 D6 16 8N 93 41W
Tonale, Passo del, Italy 40 B7 46 16N 10 35 E
Tonantins, Brazil . . . . 124 D5 2 45 S 67 45W
Tonasket, U.S.A. 108 B4 48 42N 119 26W
Tonawanda, U.S.A. . . . 116 D6 43 1N 78 53W
Tonb, Iran . . . . 71 E7 26 15N 55 15 E
Tonbridge, U.K. . . . . . 15 F8 51 11N 0 17 E
Tondano, Indonesia . . . 63 D6 1 35N 124 54 E
Tondela, Portugal 36 E2 40 31N 8 5W
Tønder, Denmark . . . . 11 K2 54 58N 8 50 E
Tondi Kiwindi, Niger . . 83 C5 14 28N 2 2 E
Tondibi, Mali 83 B4 16 39N 0 14W
Tondoro, Namibia . . . . 88 B2 17 45 S 18 50 E
Tone →, Australia . . . . 93 F2 34 25 S 116 25 E
Tone-Gawa →, Japan . . 55 F9 35 44N 140 51 E
Tonekābon, Iran . . . . . 71 B6 36 45N 51 12 E
Tong Xian, China . . . . 56 E9 39 55N 116 35 E
Tŏnga, Sudan . . . . . . 81 F3 9 28N 31 3 E
Tonga ■, Pac. Oc. . . . . 91 D11 19 50 S 174 30W
Tonga Trench, Pac. Oc. . 96 J10 18 0 S 173 0W
Tongaat, S. Africa . . . . 89 D5 29 33 S 31 9 E
Tong'an, China . . . . . . 59 E12 24 37N 118 8 E
Tongareva, Cook Is. . . . 97 H12 9 0 S 158 0W
Tongariro △, N.Z. . . . . 91 H5 39 13 S 175 31 E
Tongatapu Group,
  Tonga . . . . 91 E12 21 0 S 175 0W
Tongbai, China . . . . . . 59 A9 32 20N 113 23 E
Tongcheng, Anhui,
  China . . . . 59 B11 31 4N 116 56 E
Tongcheng, Hubei,
  China . . . . 59 C9 29 15N 113 50 E
Tongchŏn-ni, N. Korea . 57 E14 39 50N 127 25 E
Tongdao, China . . . . . 58 D7 26 10N 109 42 E
Tongeren, Belgium . . . 17 D5 50 47N 5 28 E
Tonggu, China . . . . . . 59 C10 28 31N 114 20 E
Tongguan, China . . . . 56 G6 34 40N 110 25 E
Tonghae, S. Korea . . . 57 F15 37 29N 129 7 E
Tonghua, China . . . . . 57 D13 41 42N 125 58 E
Tongjiang, China . . . . 58 B6 31 58N 107 11 E
Tongjosŏn Man,
  N. Korea . . . . 57 E15 39 30N 128 0 E
Tongking, G. of =
  Tonkin, G. of, Asia . . 60 E5 20 0N 108 0 E
Tongliang, China . . . . 58 C6 29 50N 106 3 E
Tongliao, China . . . . . 57 C12 43 38N 122 18 E
Tongling, China . . . . . 59 B11 30 55N 117 48 E
Tonglu, China . . . . . . 59 C12 29 45N 119 37 E
Tongnan = Anyue,
  China . . . . 58 B5 30 9N 105 50 E
Tongobory, Madag. . . . 89 C7 23 32 S 44 20 E
Tongoy, Chile . . . . . . 126 C1 30 16 S 71 31W
Tongren, China . . . . . 58 D7 27 43N 109 11 E
Tongres = Tongeren,
  Belgium . . . . 17 D5 50 47N 5 28 E
Tongsa Dzong, Bhutan . 67 F17 27 31N 90 31 E
Tongue →, U.S.A. 112 B2 46 25N 105 52W
Tongwei, China . . . . . 56 G3 35 0N 105 5 E
Tongxiang, China . . . . 59 B13 30 38N 120 23 E
Tongxin, China . . . . . 56 F3 36 59N 105 58 E
Tongyang, N. Korea . . 57 E14 39 9N 126 53 E
Tongyu, China . . . . . . 57 B12 44 45N 123 4 E
Tongzi, China . . . . . . 58 C6 28 9N 106 49 E
Tonj, Sudan . . . . 81 F2 7 20N 28 44 E
Tonj →, Sudan . . . . . . 81 F2 7 31N 28 55 E
Tonk, India . . . . 68 F6 26 6N 75 54 E
Tonkawa, U.S.A. 113 G6 36 41N 97 18W
Tonkin = Bac Phan,
  Vietnam . . . . 64 B5 22 0N 105 0 E
Tonkin, G. of, Asia . . . 60 E5 20 0N 108 0 E
Tonle Sap, Cambodia . . 64 F4 13 0N 104 0 E
Tonnay-Charente,
  France 20 C3 45 56N 0 55W
Tonneins, France . . . . 20 D4 44 23N 0 19 E
Tonnerre, France . . . . 19 E10 47 51N 3 59 E
Tönning, Germany . . . 24 A4 54 19N 8 56 E
Tono, Japan . . . . 54 E10 39 19N 141 32 E
Tonopah, U.S.A. 109 G5 38 4N 117 14W
Tonosí, Panama 120 E3 7 20N 80 20W
Tons →, Haryana, India 68 D7 30 30N 77 39 E
Tons →, Ut. P., India . . 69 F10 31 18N 81 0 E
Tønsberg, Norway . . . 9 G14 59 19N 10 25 E
Tonto △, U.S.A. 109 K8 33 51N 110 55W
Tonya, Turkey . . . . . . 73 B8 40 53N 39 16 E
Toobanna, Australia . . 94 B4 18 42 S 146 9 E
Toodyay, Australia . . . 93 F2 31 34 S 116 28 E
Tooele, U.S.A. 108 F7 40 32N 112 18W
Toompine, Australia . . 95 D3 27 15 S 144 19 E
Toora, Australia . . . . . 95 F4 38 39 S 146 23 E
Toora-Khem, Russia . . 53 D10 52 28N 96 17 E
Toowoomba, Australia . 95 D5 27 32 S 151 56 E
Top Springs, Australia . 92 C5 16 37 S 131 51 E
Topalu, Romania . . . . 29 F13 44 31N 28 3 E
Topaz, U.S.A. 110 G7 38 41N 119 30W
Topeka, U.S.A. 112 F7 39 3N 95 40W
Topl'a →, Slovak Rep. . . 27 C14 48 45N 21 44 E
Topley, Canada 102 C3 54 49N 126 18W
Toplica →, Serbia & M. . 44 C5 43 15N 21 49 E

Toplița, *Romania* **29 D10** 46 55N 25 20 E
Topocalma, Pta., *Chile* **126 C1** 34 10 S 72 2W
Topock, *U.S.A.* **111 L12** 34 46N 114 29W
Topola, *Serbia & M.* **44 B4** 44 17N 20 41 E
Topolčani, *Macedonia* **44 E5** 41 14N 21 25 E
Topol'čany, *Slovak Rep.* **27 C11** 48 35N 18 12 E
Topolnitsa →, *Bulgaria* **45 D8** 42 11N 24 18 E
Topolobampo, *Mexico* **118 B3** 25 40N 109 4W
Topoloveni, *Romania* **29 F10** 44 49N 25 5 E
Topolovgrad, *Bulgaria* **45 D10** 42 5N 26 20 E
Topolvăţu Mare, *Romania* **28 E6** 45 46N 21 41 E
Toppenish, *U.S.A.* **108 C3** 46 23N 120 19W
Topraisar, *Romania* **29 F13** 44 1N 28 27 E
Topusko, *Croatia* **41 C12** 45 18N 15 59 E
Torà, *Spain* **38 D6** 41 49N 1 25 E
Tora Kit, *Sudan* **81 E3** 11 2N 32 36 E
Toraka Vestale, *Madag.* **89 B7** 16 20 S 43 58 E
Torata, *Peru* **124 G4** 17 23 S 70 1W
Torbalı, *Turkey* **47 C9** 38 10N 27 21 E
Torbat-e Heydārīyeh, *Iran* **71 C8** 35 15N 59 12 E
Torbat-e Jām, *Iran* **71 C9** 35 16N 60 35 E
Torbay, *Canada* **105 C9** 47 40N 52 42W
Torbay □, *U.K.* **15 G4** 50 26N 3 31W
Torbjörntorp, *Sweden* **11 F7** 58 12N 13 36 E
Tordesillas, *Spain* **36 D6** 41 30N 5 0W
Töreboda, *Sweden* **11 F8** 58 41N 14 7 E
Torekov, *Sweden* **11 H6** 56 26N 12 37 E
Torellò, *Spain* **38 C7** 42 3N 2 16 E
Toreno, *Spain* **36 C4** 42 42N 6 30W
Torfaen □, *U.K.* **15 F4** 51 43N 3 3W
Torgau, *Germany* **24 D8** 51 34N 13 0 E
Torgelow, *Germany* **24 B10** 53 37N 14 1 E
Torhamn, *Sweden* **11 H9** 56 6N 15 50 E
Torhout, *Belgium* **17 C3** 51 5N 3 7 E
Torhovytsya, *Ukraine* **29 B10** 48 36N 25 26 E
Tori, *Ethiopia* **81 F3** 7 53N 33 35 E
Tori-Shima, *Japan* **55 J10** 30 29N 140 19 E
Torigni-sur-Vire, *France* **18 C6** 49 3N 0 58W
Torija, *Spain* **38 E1** 40 44N 3 2W
Torin, *Mexico* **118 B2** 27 33N 110 15W
Torino, *Italy* **40 C4** 45 3N 7 40 E
Torit, *Sudan* **81 G3** 4 27N 32 31 E
Torkamān, *Iran* **70 B5** 37 35N 47 23 E
Torkovichi, *Russia* **32 C6** 58 51N 30 21 E
Tormac, *Romania* **28 E6** 45 30N 21 30 E
Tormes →, *Spain* **36 D4** 41 18N 6 29W
Tornado Mt., *Canada* **102 D6** 49 55N 114 40W
Tornal'a, *Slovak Rep.* **27 C13** 48 25N 20 20 E
Torneå = Tornio, *Finland* **8 D21** 65 50N 24 12 E
Torneälven →, *Europe* **8 D21** 65 50N 24 12 E
Torneträsk, *Sweden* **8 B18** 68 24N 19 15 E
Tornio, *Finland* **8 D21** 65 50N 24 12 E
Tornionjoki = Torneälven →, *Europe* **8 D21** 65 50N 24 12 E
Tornquist, *Argentina* **126 D3** 38 8 S 62 15W
Toro, *Baleares, Spain* **48 B11** 39 59N 4 8 E
Toro, *Zamora, Spain* **36 D5** 41 35N 5 24W
Torö, *Sweden* **11 F11** 58 48N 17 50 E
Toro △, *Uganda* **86 C3** 0 5 S 30 22 E
Toro, Cerro del, *Chile* **126 B2** 29 10 S 69 50W
Toro Pk., *U.S.A.* **111 M10** 33 34N 116 24W
Törökszentmiklós, *Hungary* **28 C5** 47 11N 20 27 E
Toronaíos Kólpos, *Greece* **44 F7** 40 5N 23 30 E
Toronto, *Canada* **116 C5** 43 39N 79 20W
Toronto, *U.S.A.* **116 F4** 40 28N 80 36W
Toronto Lester B. Pearson International ✈ (YYZ), *Canada* **116 C5** 43 40N 79 34W
Toropets, *Russia* **32 D6** 56 30N 31 40 E
Tororo, *Uganda* **86 B3** 0 45N 34 12 E
Toros Dağları, *Turkey* **70 B2** 37 0N 32 30 E
Torpa, *India* **69 H11** 22 57N 85 6 E
Torquay, *U.K.* **15 G4** 50 27N 3 32W
Torquemada, *Spain* **36 C6** 42 2N 4 19W
Torrance, *U.S.A.* **111 M8** 33 50N 118 19W
Torrão, *Portugal* **37 G2** 38 16N 8 11W
Torre Annunziata, *Italy* **43 B7** 40 45N 14 27 E
Torre de Moncorvo, *Portugal* **36 D3** 41 12N 7 8W
Torre del Campo, *Spain* **37 H7** 37 46N 3 53W
Torre del Greco, *Italy* **43 B7** 40 47N 14 22 E
Torre del Mar, *Spain* **37 J6** 36 44N 4 6W
Torre-Pacheco, *Spain* **39 H4** 37 44N 0 57W
Torre Péllice, *Italy* **40 D4** 44 49N 7 13 E
Torreblanca, *Spain* **38 E5** 40 14N 0 12 E
Torrecampo, *Spain* **37 G6** 38 29N 4 41W
Torrecilla en Cameros, *Spain* **38 C2** 42 15N 2 38W
Torredembarra, *Spain* **38 D6** 41 9N 1 24 E
Torredonjimeno, *Spain* **37 H7** 37 46N 3 57W
Torrejón de Ardoz, *Spain* **36 E7** 40 27N 3 29W
Torrejoncillo, *Spain* **36 F4** 39 54N 6 28W
Torrelaguna, *Spain* **36 E7** 40 50N 3 38W
Torrelavega, *Spain* **36 B6** 43 20N 4 5W
Torremaggiore, *Italy* **41 G12** 41 41N 15 17 E
Torremolinos, *Spain* **37 J6** 36 38N 4 30W
Torrens, L., *Australia* **95 E2** 31 0 S 137 50 E
Torrens Cr. →, *Australia* **94 C4** 22 23 S 145 9 E
Torrens Creek, *Australia* **94 C4** 20 48 S 145 3 E
Torrent, *Spain* **39 F4** 39 27N 0 28W
Torrenueva, *Spain* **37 G7** 38 38N 3 22W
Torreón, *Mexico* **118 B4** 25 33N 103 26W
Torreperogil, *Spain* **37 G7** 38 2N 3 17W
Torres, *Brazil* **127 B5** 29 21 S 49 44W
Torres, *Mexico* **118 B2** 28 46N 110 47W
Torres Novas, *Portugal* **37 F2** 39 27N 8 33W
Torres Strait, *Australia* **96 H6** 9 50 S 142 20 E
Torres Vedras, *Portugal* **37 F1** 39 5N 9 15W
Torrevieja, *Spain* **39 H4** 37 59N 0 42W
Torrey, *U.S.A.* **109 G8** 38 18N 111 25W
Torridge →, *U.K.* **15 G3** 51 0N 4 13W
Torridon, L., *U.K.* **13 D3** 57 35N 5 50W
Torrijos, *Spain* **36 F6** 39 59N 4 18W
Tørring, *Denmark* **11 J3** 55 52N 9 29 E
Torrington, *Conn., U.S.A.* **117 E11** 41 48N 73 7W
Torrington, *Wyo., U.S.A.* **112 D2** 42 4N 104 11W
Torroella de Montgrì, *Spain* **38 C8** 42 2N 3 8 E
Torrox, *Spain* **37 J7** 36 46N 3 57W
Torsås, *Sweden* **11 H9** 56 24N 16 0 E
Torsby, *Sweden* **10 D6** 60 7N 13 0 E
Torshälla, *Sweden* **10 E10** 59 25N 16 28 E
Tórshavn, *Færoe Is.* **8 E9** 62 5N 6 56W
Torslanda, *Sweden* **11 G5** 57 44N 11 45 E
Torsö, *Sweden* **11 F7** 58 48N 13 45 E
Tortola, *Br. Virgin Is.* **121 e** 18 19N 64 45W
Tórtoles de Esgueva, *Spain* **36 D6** 41 49N 4 2W
Tortolì, *Italy* **42 C2** 39 55N 9 39 E
Tortona, *Italy* **40 D5** 44 54N 8 52 E
Tortorici, *Italy* **43 D7** 38 2N 14 49 E
Tortosa, *Spain* **38 E5** 40 49N 0 31 E
Tortosa, C., *Spain* **38 E5** 40 41N 0 52 E
Tortosendo, *Portugal* **36 E3** 40 15N 7 31W
Tortue, I. de la, *Haiti* **121 B5** 20 5N 72 57W
Tortuguero △, *Costa Rica* **120 D3** 10 31N 83 29W
Tortum, *Turkey* **73 B9** 40 19N 41 35 E
Ţorūd, *Iran* **71 C7** 35 25N 55 5 E
Torul, *Turkey* **73 B8** 40 34N 39 18 E
Toruń, *Poland* **31 E5** 53 2N 18 39 E
Torun, *Ukraine* **29 B8** 48 40N 23 34 E
Tory I., *Ireland* **12 A3** 55 16N 8 14W
Torysa →, *Slovak Rep.* **27 C14** 48 39N 21 21 E
Torzhok, *Russia* **32 D8** 57 5N 34 55 E
Torzym, *Poland* **31 F2** 52 19N 15 5 E
Tosa, *Japan* **55 H6** 33 24N 133 23 E
Tosa-Shimizu, *Japan* **55 H6** 32 52N 132 58 E
Tosa-Wan, *Japan* **55 H6** 33 15N 133 30 E
Toscana □, *Italy* **40 E8** 43 25N 11 0 E
Toscano, Arcipelago, *Italy* **40 F7** 42 30N 10 30 E
Toshkent, *Uzbekistan* **52 E7** 41 20N 69 10 E
Tosno, *Russia* **32 C6** 59 38N 30 46 E
Tossa de Mar, *Spain* **38 D7** 41 43N 2 56 E
Tösse, *Sweden* **11 F6** 58 58N 12 39 E
Tostado, *Argentina* **126 B3** 29 15 S 61 50W
Tostedt, *Germany* **24 B5** 53 17N 9 42 E
Tostón, Pta. de, *Canary Is.* **48 F5** 28 42N 14 2W
Tosu, *Japan* **55 H5** 33 22N 130 31 E
Tosya, *Turkey* **72 B6** 41 1N 34 2 E
Toszek, *Poland* **31 H5** 50 27N 18 32 E
Totana, *Spain* **39 H3** 37 45N 1 30W
Totebo, *Sweden* **11 G10** 57 38N 16 12 E
Toteng, *Botswana* **88 C3** 20 22 S 22 58 E
Tôtes, *France* **18 C8** 49 41N 1 2 E
Tótkomlós, *Hungary* **28 D5** 46 24N 20 45 E
Totma, *Russia* **52 C5** 60 0N 42 40 E
Totnes, *U.K.* **15 G4** 50 26N 3 42W
Totness, *Suriname* **125 B7** 5 53N 56 19W
Toto, *Nigeria* **83 D6** 8 26N 7 5 E
Totonicapán, *Guatemala* **120 D1** 14 58N 91 12W
Totten Glacier, *Antarctica* **5 C8** 66 45 S 116 10 E
Tottenham, *Australia* **95 E4** 32 14 S 147 21 E
Tottenham, *Canada* **116 B5** 44 1N 79 49W
Tottori, *Japan* **55 G7** 35 30N 134 15 E
Tottori □, *Japan* **55 G7** 35 30N 134 12 E
Touaret, *Niger* **83 A6** 20 17N 7 8 E
Touba, *Ivory C.* **82 D3** 8 22N 7 40W
Touba, *Senegal* **82 C1** 14 50N 15 55W
Toubkal, Djebel, *Morocco* **78 B4** 31 0N 8 0W
Toucy, *France* **19 E10** 47 44N 3 15 E
Tougan, *Burkina Faso* **82 C4** 13 11N 2 58W
Touggourt, *Algeria* **78 B7** 33 6N 6 4 E
Tougouri, *Burkina Faso* **83 C4** 13 20N 0 30W
Tougué, *Guinea* **82 C2** 11 25N 11 50W
Toukoto, *Mali* **82 C3** 13 27N 9 52W
Toul, *France* **19 D12** 48 40N 5 53 E
Toulepleu, *Ivory C.* **82 D3** 6 32N 8 24W
Toulon, *France* **21 E9** 43 10N 5 55 E
Toulouse, *France* **20 E5** 43 37N 1 27 E
Toulouse Blagnac ✈ (TLS), *France* **20 E5** 43 37N 1 22 E
Toummo, *Niger* **79 D8** 22 45N 14 8 E
Toumodi, *Ivory C.* **82 D3** 6 32N 5 4W
Tounan, *Taiwan* **59 F13** 23 41N 120 28 E
Toungo, *Nigeria* **83 D7** 8 20N 12 3 E
Toungoo, *Burma* **67 K20** 19 0N 96 30 E
Touques →, *France* **18 C7** 49 22N 0 8 E
Touraine, *France* **18 E7** 47 20N 0 30 E
Tourcoing, *France* **19 B10** 50 42N 3 10 E
Touriñán, C., *Spain* **36 B1** 43 3N 9 17W
Tournai, *Belgium* **17 D3** 50 35N 3 25 E
Tournan-en-Brie, *France* **19 D9** 48 44N 2 46 E
Tournay, *France* **20 E4** 43 13N 0 13 E
Tournon-St-Martin, *France* **18 F7** 46 45N 0 58 E
Tournon-sur-Rhône, *France* **21 C8** 45 4N 4 50 E
Tournus, *France* **19 F11** 46 35N 4 54 E
Tours, *France* **18 E7** 47 22N 0 40 E
Toussora, Mt., *C.A.R.* **84 C4** 9 7N 23 14 E
Touws →, *S. Africa* **88 E3** 33 45 S 21 11 E
Touwsrivier, *S. Africa* **88 E3** 33 20 S 20 2 E
Tovarkovskiy, *Russia* **32 F10** 53 40N 38 14 E
Tovste, *Ukraine* **29 B10** 48 50N 25 44 E
Tovuz, *Azerbaijan* **35 K7** 41 0N 45 40 E
Towada, *Japan* **54 D10** 40 37N 141 13 E
Towada-Hachimantai △, *Japan* **54 D10** 40 20N 140 55 E
Towada-Ko, *Japan* **54 D10** 40 28N 140 55 E
Towanda, *U.S.A.* **117 E8** 41 46N 76 27W
Towang, *India* **67 F17** 27 37N 91 50 E
Tower, *U.S.A.* **112 B8** 47 48N 92 17W
Towerhill Cr. →, *Australia* **94 C3** 22 28 S 144 35 E
Towner, *U.S.A.* **112 A4** 48 21N 100 25W
Townsend, *U.S.A.* **108 C8** 46 19N 111 31W
Townshend I., *Australia* **94 C5** 22 10 S 150 31 E
Townsville, *Australia* **94 B4** 19 15 S 146 45 E
Towraghondi, *Afghan.* **66 B3** 35 13N 62 16 E
Towson, *U.S.A.* **114 F7** 39 24N 76 36W
Towuti, Danau, *Indonesia* **63 E6** 2 45 S 121 32 E
Toya-Ko, *Japan* **54 C10** 42 35N 140 51 E
Toyama, *Japan* **55 F8** 36 40N 137 15 E
Toyama □, *Japan* **55 F8** 36 45N 137 30 E
Toyama-Wan, *Japan* **55 F8** 37 0N 137 30 E
Toyapakeh, *Indonesia* **63 K18** 8 41 S 115 29 E
Toyohashi, *Japan* **55 G8** 34 45N 137 25 E
Toyokawa, *Japan* **55 G8** 34 48N 137 27 E
Toyonaka, *Japan* **55 G7** 34 50N 135 28 E
Toyooka, *Japan* **55 G7** 35 35N 134 48 E
Toyota, *Japan* **55 G8** 35 3N 137 7 E
Tozeur, *Tunisia* **78 B7** 33 56N 8 8 E
Tozkhurmato, *Iraq* **70 C5** 34 56N 44 38 E
Tqibuli, *Georgia* **35 J6** 42 26N 43 0 E
Tqvarcheli, *Georgia* **35 J5** 42 47N 41 42 E
Trá Li = Tralee, *Ireland* **12 D2** 52 16N 9 42W
Tra On, *Vietnam* **65 H5** 9 58N 105 55 E
Trabancos →, *Spain* **36 D5** 41 36N 5 15W
Traben-Trarbach, *Germany* **25 F3** 49 57N 7 7 E
Trabzon, *Turkey* **73 B8** 41 0N 39 45 E
Tracadie-Sheila, *Canada* **105 C7** 47 30N 64 55W
Tracy, *Calif., U.S.A.* **110 H5** 37 44N 121 26W
Tracy, *Minn., U.S.A.* **112 C7** 44 14N 95 37W
Tradate, *Italy* **40 C5** 45 43N 8 54 E
Trade Town, *Liberia* **82 D3** 5 40N 9 50W
Trafalgar, C., *Spain* **37 J4** 36 10N 6 2W
Traian, *Brăila, Romania* **29 E12** 45 11N 27 44 E
Traian, *Tulcea, Romania* **29 E13** 45 2N 28 15 E
Trail, *Canada* **102 D5** 49 5N 117 40W
Trainor L., *Canada* **102 A4** 60 24N 120 17W
Trákhonas, *Cyprus* **49 D12** 35 12N 33 21 E
Tralee, *Ireland* **12 D2** 52 16N 9 42W
Tralee B., *Ireland* **12 D2** 52 17N 9 55W
Tramore, *Ireland* **12 D4** 52 10N 7 10W
Tramore B., *Ireland* **12 D4** 52 9N 7 10W
Tran Ninh, Cao Nguyen, *Laos* **64 C4** 19 30N 103 10 E
Tranås, *Sweden* **11 F8** 58 3N 14 59 E
Tranbjerg, *Denmark* **11 H4** 56 6N 10 9 E
Trancas, *Argentina* **126 B2** 26 11 S 65 20W
Trancoso, *Portugal* **36 E3** 40 49N 7 21W
Tranebjerg, *Denmark* **11 J4** 55 51N 10 36 E
Tranemo, *Sweden* **11 G7** 57 30N 13 20 E
Trang, *Thailand* **65 J2** 7 33N 99 38 E
Trangahy, *Madag.* **89 B7** 19 7 S 44 31 E
Trangan, *Indonesia* **63 F8** 6 40 S 134 20 E
Trangie, *Australia* **95 E4** 32 4 S 148 0 E
Trångsviken, *Sweden* **10 A7** 63 19N 13 59 E
Trani, *Italy* **43 A9** 41 17N 16 25 E
Tranoroa, *Madag.* **89 C8** 24 42 S 45 4 E
Tranqueras, *Uruguay* **127 C4** 31 13 S 55 45W
Transantarctic Mts., *Antarctica* **5 E12** 85 0 S 170 0W
Transilvania, *Romania* **29 D9** 46 30N 24 0 E
Transilvanian Alps = Carpaţii Meridionali, *Romania* **29 E9** 45 30N 25 0 E
Transnistria = Stînga Nistrului □, *Moldova* **29 C14** 47 20N 29 15 E
Transtrand, *Sweden* **10 C7** 61 6N 13 20 E
Transtrandsfjällen, *Sweden* **10 C6** 61 8N 13 0 E
Transylvania = Transilvania, *Romania* **29 D9** 46 30N 24 0 E
Trápani, *Italy* **42 D5** 38 1N 12 29 E
Trapper Pk., *U.S.A.* **108 D6** 45 54N 114 18W
Traralgon, *Australia* **95 F4** 38 12 S 146 34 E
Trarza, *Mauritania* **82 B2** 17 30N 15 0W
Trasacco, *Italy* **41 G10** 41 57N 13 32 E
Trăscău, Munţii, *Romania* **29 D8** 46 14N 23 14 E
Trasimeno, L., *Italy* **41 E9** 43 8N 12 6 E
Träslövsläge, *Sweden* **11 G6** 57 4N 12 16 E
Trasvase Tajo-Segura, Canal de, *Spain* **38 E2** 40 15N 2 55W
Trat, *Thailand* **65 F4** 12 14N 102 33 E
Tratani →, *Pakistan* **68 E3** 29 19N 68 20 E
Traun, *Austria* **26 C7** 48 14N 14 15 E
Traunreut, *Germany* **25 H8** 47 57N 12 36 E
Traunsee, *Austria* **26 D6** 47 55N 13 50 E
Traunstein, *Germany* **25 H8** 47 52N 12 37 E
Traveller's L., *Australia* **95 E3** 33 20 S 142 0 E
Travemünde, *Germany* **24 B6** 53 57N 10 52 E
Travers, Mt., *N.Z.* **91 K4** 42 1 S 172 45 E
Traverse City, *U.S.A.* **114 C3** 44 46N 85 38W
Travis, L., *U.S.A.* **113 K5** 30 24N 97 55W
Travnik, *Bos.-H.* **28 F2** 44 17N 17 39 E
Trbovlje, *Slovenia* **41 B12** 46 12N 15 5 E
Trébbia →, *Italy* **40 C6** 45 4N 9 41 E
Trebel →, *Germany* **24 B9** 53 54N 13 2 E
Trébeurden, *France* **18 D3** 48 46N 3 35W
Trebević △, *Bos.-H.* **28 G3** 43 20N 18 45 E
Třebíč, *Czech Rep.* **26 B8** 49 14N 15 55 E
Trebinje, *Bos.-H.* **44 D2** 42 44N 18 22 E
Trebisacce, *Italy* **43 C9** 39 52N 16 32 E
Trebišnjica →, *Bos.-H.* **44 D2** 42 47N 18 8 E
Trebišov, *Slovak Rep.* **27 C14** 48 38N 21 41 E
Trebižat →, *Bos.-H.* **41 E14** 43 15N 17 30 E
Trebnje, *Slovenia* **41 C12** 45 54N 15 1 E
Třeboň, *Czech Rep.* **26 B7** 49 1N 14 48 E
Trebonne, *Australia* **94 B4** 18 37 S 146 5 E
Třeboňsko △, *Czech Rep.* **26 B7** 49 1N 14 49 E
Trebujena, *Spain* **37 J4** 36 52N 6 11W
Trecate, *Italy* **40 C5** 45 26N 8 44 E
Tregaron, *U.K.* **15 E4** 52 14N 3 56W
Tregnago, *Italy* **41 C8** 45 31N 11 10 E
Tregrosse Is., *Australia* **94 B5** 17 41 S 150 43 E
Tréguier, *France* **18 D3** 48 47N 3 16W
Trégunc, *France* **18 E3** 47 51N 3 51W
Treherne, *Canada* **103 D9** 49 38N 98 42W
Tréia, *Italy* **41 E10** 43 19N 13 19 E
Treignac, *France* **20 C5** 45 32N 1 48 E
Treinta y Tres, *Uruguay* **127 C5** 33 16 S 54 17W
Treis-karden, *Germany* **25 E3** 50 10N 7 18 E
Treklyano, *Bulgaria* **44 D6** 42 33N 22 36 E
Trelawney, *Zimbabwe* **89 B5** 17 30 S 30 30 E
Trélazé, *France* **18 E6** 47 26N 0 30W
Trelew, *Argentina* **128 E3** 43 10 S 65 20W
Trélissac, *France* **20 C4** 45 11N 0 47 E
Trelleborg, *Sweden* **11 J7** 55 20N 13 10 E
Tremadog Bay, *U.K.* **14 E3** 52 51N 4 18W
Trémiti, *Italy* **41 F12** 42 8N 15 30 E
Tremonton, *U.S.A.* **108 F7** 41 43N 112 10W
Tremp, *Spain* **38 C5** 42 10N 0 52 E
Trenche →, *Canada* **104 C5** 47 46N 72 53W
Trenčiansky □, *Slovak Rep.* **27 C11** 48 45N 18 20 E
Trenčín, *Slovak Rep.* **27 C11** 48 52N 18 4 E
Trenggalek, *Indonesia* **63 H14** 8 3 S 111 43 E
Trenque Lauquen, *Argentina* **126 D3** 36 5 S 62 45W
Trent →, *Canada* **116 B7** 44 6N 77 34W
Trent →, *U.K.* **14 D7** 53 41N 0 42W
Trentino-Alto Adige □, *Italy* **41 B8** 46 30N 11 20 E
Trento, *Italy* **40 B8** 46 4N 11 8 E
Trenton = Quinte West, *Canada* **116 B7** 44 10N 77 34W
Trenton, *Mo., U.S.A.* **112 E8** 40 5N 93 37W
Trenton, *N.J., U.S.A.* **117 F10** 40 14N 74 46W
Trenton, *Nebr., U.S.A.* **112 E4** 40 11N 101 1W
Trepassey, *Canada* **105 C9** 46 43N 53 25W
Trepuzzi, *Italy* **43 B11** 40 24N 18 4 E
Tres Arroyos, *Argentina* **126 D3** 38 26 S 60 20W
Três Corações, *Brazil* **127 A6** 21 44 S 45 15W
Três Lagoas, *Brazil* **125 H8** 20 50 S 51 43W
Tres Lomas, *Argentina* **126 D3** 36 27 S 62 51W
Tres Marías, Islas, *Mexico* **118 C3** 21 25N 106 28W
Tres Montes, C., *Chile* **128 F1** 46 50 S 75 30W
Tres Pinos, *U.S.A.* **110 J5** 36 48N 121 19W
Três Pontas, *Brazil* **127 A6** 21 23 S 45 29W
Tres Puentes, *Chile* **126 B1** 27 50 S 70 15W
Tres Puntas, C., *Argentina* **128 F3** 47 0 S 66 0W
Três Rios, *Brazil* **127 A7** 22 6 S 43 15W
Tres Valles, *Mexico* **119 D5** 18 15N 96 8W
Tresco, *U.K.* **15 H1** 49 57N 6 20W
Treska →, *Macedonia* **44 E5** 42 0N 21 20 E
Treskavica, *Bos.-H.* **28 G3** 43 40N 18 20 E
Trespaderne, *Spain* **36 C7** 42 47N 3 24W
Trestickland △, *Sweden* **11 F5** 59 0N 11 42 E
Trets, *France* **21 E9** 43 27N 5 41 E
Treuchtlingen, *Germany* **25 G6** 48 58N 10 54 E
Treuenbrietzen, *Germany* **24 C8** 52 5N 12 52 E
Trevi, *Italy* **41 F9** 42 52N 12 45 E
Treviglio, *Italy* **40 C6** 45 31N 9 35 E
Trevinca, Peña, *Spain* **36 C4** 42 15N 6 46W
Treviso, *Italy* **41 C9** 45 40N 12 15 E
Trévoux, *France* **21 C8** 45 57N 4 47 E
Trgovište, *Serbia & M.* **44 D6** 42 20N 22 10 E
Triabunna, *Australia* **95 G4** 42 30 S 147 55 E
Triánda, *Greece* **49 C10** 36 25N 28 10 E
Triangle, *Zimbabwe* **89 C5** 21 2 S 31 28 E
Triaucourt-en-Argonne, *France* **19 D12** 48 59N 5 2 E
Tribal Areas □, *Pakistan* **68 C4** 33 0N 70 0 E
Tribsees, *Germany* **24 A8** 54 5N 12 44 E
Tribulation, C., *Australia* **94 B4** 16 5 S 145 29 E
Tribune, *U.S.A.* **112 F4** 38 28N 101 45W
Tricárico, *Italy* **43 B9** 40 37N 16 9 E
Tricase, *Italy* **43 C11** 39 56N 18 22 E
Trichinopoly = Tiruchchirappalli, *India* **66 P11** 10 45N 78 45 E
Trichur, *India* **66 P10** 10 30N 76 18 E
Trida, *Australia* **95 E4** 33 1 S 145 1 E
Trier, *Germany* **25 F2** 49 45N 6 38 E
Trieste, *Italy* **41 C10** 45 40N 13 46 E
Trieste, G. di, *Italy* **41 C10** 45 40N 13 35 E
Trieux →, *France* **18 D3** 48 43N 3 9W
Triggiano, *Italy* **43 A9** 41 4N 16 55 E
Triglav, *Slovenia* **41 B10** 46 21N 13 50 E
Triglavski △, *Slovenia* **41 B10** 46 20N 13 50 E
Trigno →, *Italy* **41 F11** 42 4N 14 48 E
Trigueros, *Spain* **37 H4** 37 24N 6 50W
Tríkeri, *Greece* **46 B5** 39 6N 23 5 E
Tríkhonis, Límni, *Greece* **46 C3** 38 34N 21 30 E
Tríkkala, *Greece* **46 B3** 39 34N 21 47 E
Tríkkala □, *Greece* **46 B3** 39 41N 21 30 E
Trikomo, *Cyprus* **49 D12** 35 17N 33 52 E
Trikora, Puncak, *Indonesia* **63 E9** 4 15 S 138 45 E
Trilj, *Croatia* **41 E13** 43 38N 16 42 E
Trillo, *Spain* **38 E2** 40 42N 2 35W
Trim, *Ireland* **12 C5** 53 33N 6 48W
Trincomalee, *Sri Lanka* **66 Q12** 8 38N 81 15 E
Trindade, *Brazil* **125 G9** 16 40 S 49 30W
Trindade, I., *Atl. Oc.* **2 F8** 20 20 S 29 50W
Třinec, *Czech Rep.* **27 B11** 49 41N 18 39 E
Trinidad, *Bolivia* **124 F6** 14 46 S 64 50W
Trinidad, *Cuba* **120 B4** 21 48N 80 0W
Trinidad, *Trin. & Tob.* **121 D7** 10 30N 61 15W
Trinidad, *Uruguay* **126 C4** 33 30 S 56 50W
Trinidad, *U.S.A.* **113 G2** 37 10N 104 31W
Trinidad →, *Mexico* **119 D5** 17 49N 95 9W
Trinidad & Tobago ■, *W. Indies* **121 D7** 10 30N 61 20W
Trinitápoli, *Italy* **43 A9** 41 21N 16 5 E
Trinity, *Canada* **105 C9** 48 59N 53 55W
Trinity, *U.S.A.* **113 K7** 30 57N 95 22W
Trinity →, *Calif., U.S.A.* **108 F2** 41 11N 123 42W
Trinity →, *Tex., U.S.A.* **113 L7** 29 45N 94 43W
Trinity B., *Canada* **105 C9** 48 20N 53 10W
Trinity Hills, *Trin. & Tob.* **125 K15** 10 16N 61 6W
Trinity Is., *U.S.A.* **100 C4** 56 33N 154 25W
Trinity Range, *U.S.A.* **108 F4** 40 15N 118 45W
Trinkitat, *Sudan* **80 D4** 18 45N 37 51 E
Trino, *Italy* **40 C5** 45 12N 8 18 E
Trinway, *U.S.A.* **116 F2** 40 9N 82 1W
Trionto, C., *Italy* **43 C9** 39 37N 16 43 E
Triora, *Italy* **40 D4** 44 1N 7 46 E
Tripoli = Tarābulus, *Lebanon* **74 A4** 34 31N 35 50 E
Tripoli = Tarābulus, *Libya* **79 B8** 32 49N 13 7 E
Trípolis, *Greece* **46 D4** 37 31N 22 25 E
Tripolitania, *N. Afr.* **79 B8** 31 0N 13 0 E
Tripura □, *India* **67 H18** 24 0N 92 0 E
Tripylos, *Cyprus* **49 E11** 34 59N 32 41 E
Trischen, *Germany* **24 A4** 54 4N 8 40 E
Tristan da Cunha, *Atl. Oc.* **77 K2** 37 6 S 12 20W
Trisul, *India* **69 D8** 30 19N 79 47 E
Trivandrum, *India* **66 Q10** 8 41N 77 0 E
Trivento, *Italy* **41 G11** 41 47N 14 33 E
Trnava, *Slovak Rep.* **27 C10** 48 23N 17 35 E
Trnavský □, *Slovak Rep.* **27 C10** 48 30N 17 45 E
Troarn, *France* **18 C6** 49 11N 0 11W
Trochu, *Canada* **102 C6** 51 50N 113 13W
Trodely I., *Canada* **104 B4** 52 15N 79 26W
Troezen, *Greece* **46 D5** 37 25N 23 15 E
Trogir, *Croatia* **41 E13** 43 32N 16 15 E
Troglav, *Croatia* **41 E13** 43 56N 16 36 E
Tróia, *Italy* **43 A8** 41 22N 15 18 E
Troilus, L., *Canada* **104 B5** 50 50N 74 35W
Troina, *Italy* **43 E7** 37 47N 14 36 E
Trois-Pistoles, *Canada* **105 C6** 48 5N 69 10W
Trois-Rivières, *Canada* **104 C5** 46 25N 72 34W
Trois-Rivières, *Guadeloupe* **120 b** 15 57N 61 40W
Troisdorf, *Germany* **24 E3** 50 48N 7 11 E
Troitsk, *Russia* **52 D7** 54 10N 61 35 E
Troitsko Pechorsk, *Russia* **52 C6** 62 40N 56 10 E
Troitskoye, *Russia* **35 G7** 46 26N 44 15 E
Trölladyngja, *Iceland* **8 D5** 64 54N 17 16W
Trollhättan, *Sweden* **11 F6** 58 17N 12 20 E
Trollheimen, *Norway* **8 E13** 62 46N 9 1 E
Trombetas →, *Brazil* **125 D7** 1 55 S 55 35W
Tromsø, *Norway* **8 B18** 69 40N 18 56 E
Trona, *U.S.A.* **111 K9** 35 46N 117 23W
Tronador, Mte., *Argentina* **128 E2** 41 10 S 71 50W
Trøndelag, *Norway* **8 D14** 64 17N 11 50 E
Trondheim, *Norway* **8 E14** 63 36N 10 25 E
Trondheimsfjorden, *Norway* **8 E14** 63 35N 10 30 E
Trönninge, *Sweden* **11 H6** 56 37N 12 51 E
Tronto →, *Italy* **41 F10** 42 54N 13 55 E
Troodos, *Cyprus* **49 E11** 34 55N 32 52 E
Troon, *U.K.* **13 F4** 55 33N 4 39W
Tropea, *Italy* **43 D8** 38 41N 15 54 E
Tropic, *U.S.A.* **109 H7** 37 37N 112 5W
Tropojë, *Albania* **44 D4** 42 23N 20 10 E
Trosa, *Sweden* **11 F11** 58 54N 17 33 E
Trostan, *U.K.* **12 A5** 55 3N 6 10W
Trostberg, *Germany* **25 G8** 48 1N 12 33 E
Trostyanets, *Ukraine* **29 B14** 48 31N 29 11 E
Trostyanets, *Ukraine* **33 G8** 50 33N 34 59 E
Trou Gras Pt., *St. Lucia* **121 f** 13 54N 60 53W
Trout →, *Canada* **102 A5** 61 19N 119 51W
Trout L., *N.W.T., Canada* **102 A4** 60 40N 121 14W
Trout L., *Ont., Canada* **103 C10** 51 20N 93 15W
Trout Lake, *Canada* **102 B6** 56 30N 114 32W
Trout Lake, *U.S.A.* **110 E5** 46 0N 121 32W
Trout River, *Canada* **105 C8** 49 29N 58 8W
Trout Run, *U.S.A.* **116 E7** 41 23N 77 3W
Trouville-sur-Mer, *France* **18 C7** 49 21N 0 5 E
Trowbridge, *U.K.* **15 F5** 51 18N 2 12W
Troy, *Turkey* **47 B8** 39 57N 26 12 E
Troy, *Ala., U.S.A.* **115 K3** 31 48N 85 58W
Troy, *Kans., U.S.A.* **112 F7** 39 47N 95 5W
Troy, *Mo., U.S.A.* **112 F9** 38 59N 90 59W
Troy, *Mont., U.S.A.* **108 B6** 48 28N 115 53W
Troy, *N.Y., U.S.A.* **117 D11** 42 44N 73 41W
Troy, *Ohio, U.S.A.* **114 E3** 40 2N 84 12W
Troy, *Pa., U.S.A.* **117 E8** 41 47N 76 47W
Troyan, *Bulgaria* **45 D8** 42 57N 24 43 E
Troyes, *France* **19 D11** 48 19N 4 3 E
Trpanj, *Croatia* **41 E14** 43 1N 17 15 E
Trstenik, *Serbia & M.* **44 C5** 43 36N 21 0 E
Trubchevsk, *Russia* **33 F7** 52 33N 33 47 E
Truchas Peak, *U.S.A.* **113 H2** 35 58N 105 39W
Trucial States = United Arab Emirates ■, *Asia* **71 F7** 23 50N 54 0 E
Truckee, *U.S.A.* **110 F6** 39 20N 120 11W
Trudfront, *Russia* **35 H8** 45 56N 47 40 E
Trudovoye, *Russia* **54 C6** 43 17N 132 5 E
Trujillo, *Honduras* **120 C2** 16 0N 86 0W
Trujillo, *Peru* **124 E3** 8 6 S 79 0W
Trujillo, *Spain* **37 F5** 39 28N 5 55W
Trujillo, *U.S.A.* **113 H2** 35 32N 104 42W
Trujillo, *Venezuela* **124 B4** 9 22N 70 38W
Truk, *Micronesia* **96 G7** 7 25N 151 46 E
Trumann, *U.S.A.* **113 H9** 35 41N 90 31W
Trumansburg, *U.S.A.* **117 D8** 42 33N 76 40W
Trumbull, Mt., *U.S.A.* **109 H7** 36 25N 113 8W
Trŭn, *Bulgaria* **44 D6** 42 51N 22 38 E
Trun, *France* **18 D7** 48 50N 0 2 E
Trundle, *Australia* **95 E4** 32 53 S 147 35 E
Trung-Phan = Annam, *Vietnam* **64 E7** 16 0N 108 0 E
Truro, *Canada* **105 C7** 45 21N 63 14W
Truro, *U.K.* **15 G2** 50 16N 5 4W
Truskavets, *Ukraine* **33 H2** 49 17N 23 30 E
Trŭstenik, *Bulgaria* **45 C8** 43 31N 24 28 E
Trustrup, *Denmark* **11 H4** 56 20N 10 46 E
Trutch, *Canada* **102 B4** 57 44N 122 57W
Truth or Consequences, *U.S.A.* **109 K10** 33 8N 107 15W
Trutnov, *Czech Rep.* **26 A8** 50 37N 15 54 E
Truxton, *U.S.A.* **117 D8** 42 45N 76 2W
Truyère →, *France* **20 D6** 44 38N 2 34 E
Tryavna, *Bulgaria* **45 D9** 42 54N 25 25 E
Tryonville, *U.S.A.* **116 E5** 41 42N 79 48W
Trzcianka, *Poland* **31 E3** 53 3N 16 25 E
Trzciel, *Poland* **31 F2** 52 23N 15 50 E
Trzcińsko Zdrój, *Poland* **31 F1** 52 58N 14 35 E
Trzebiatów, *Poland* **30 D2** 54 3N 15 18 E
Trzebiez, *Poland* **30 E1** 53 38N 14 31 E
Trzebnica, *Poland* **31 G4** 51 20N 17 1 E
Trzemeszno, *Poland* **31 F4** 52 33N 17 48 E
Tržič, *Slovenia* **41 B11** 46 22N 14 18 E
Tsagan Aman, *Russia* **35 G8** 47 34N 46 43 E
Tsamandás, *Greece* **46 B2** 39 46N 20 21 E
Tsandi, *Namibia* **88 B1** 17 42 S 14 50 E
Tsaratanana, *Madag.* **89 B8** 16 47 S 47 39 E
Tsaratanana △, *Madag.* **89 A8** 13 57 S 48 52 E
Tsaratanana, Mt. de = Maromokotro, *Madag.* **89 A8** 14 0 S 49 0 E
Tsarevo, *Bulgaria* **45 D9** 42 28N 25 52 E
Tsaritsáni, *Greece* **46 B4** 39 53N 22 14 E
Tsau, *Botswana* **88 C3** 20 8 S 22 22 E
Tsavo East △, *Kenya* **86 C4** 2 44 S 38 47 E
Tsavo West △, *Kenya* **86 C4** 3 19 S 37 57 E
Tsebrykove, *Ukraine* **33 J6** 47 9N 30 10 E
Tsentralnyy □, *Russia* **34 D4** 52 0N 40 0 E
Tses, *Namibia* **88 D2** 25 58 S 18 8 E
Tsetserleg, *Mongolia* **60 B5** 47 36N 101 32 E
Tsévié, *Togo* **83 D5** 6 25N 1 20 E
Tshabong, *Botswana* **88 D3** 26 2 S 22 29 E
Tshane, *Botswana* **88 C3** 24 5 S 21 54 E
Tshela, *Dem. Rep. of the Congo* **84 E2** 4 57 S 13 4 E
Tshesebe, *Botswana* **89 C4** 21 51 S 27 32 E
Tshibeke, *Dem. Rep. of the Congo* **86 C2** 2 40 S 28 35 E
Tshibinda, *Dem. Rep. of the Congo* **86 C2** 2 23 S 28 43 E
Tshikapa, *Dem. Rep. of the Congo* **84 F4** 6 28 S 20 48 E
Tshilenge, *Dem. Rep. of the Congo* **86 D1** 6 17 S 23 48 E
Tshinsenda, *Dem. Rep. of the Congo* **87 E2** 12 20 S 28 0 E
Tshofa, *Dem. Rep. of the Congo* **86 D2** 5 13 S 25 16 E
Tshwane, *Botswana* **88 C3** 22 24 S 22 1 E
Tsigara, *Botswana* **88 C4** 20 22 S 25 54 E
Tsihombe, *Madag.* **89 D8** 25 10 S 45 41 E
Tsiigehtchic, *Canada* **100 B6** 67 15N 134 0W
Tsimlyansk, *Russia* **35 G6** 47 40N 42 6 E
Tsimlyansk Res. = Tsimlyanskoye Vdkhr., *Russia* **35 F6** 48 0N 43 0 E
Tsimlyanskoye Vdkhr., *Russia* **35 F6** 48 0N 43 0 E
Tsinan = Jinan, *China* **56 F9** 36 38N 117 1 E
Tsineng, *S. Africa* **88 D3** 27 5 S 23 5 E
Tsínga, *Greece* **45 E8** 41 23N 24 44 E
Tsinghai = Qinghai □, *China* **60 C4** 36 0N 98 0 E
Tsingtao = Qingdao, *China* **57 F11** 36 5N 120 20 E
Tsingy de Bemaraha △, *Madag.* **89 B8** 18 35 S 45 25 E
Tsingy de Namoroka △, *Madag.* **89 B8** 16 29 S 45 25 E
Tsinjoarivo, *Madag.* **89 B8** 19 37 S 47 40 E
Tsinjomitondraka, *Madag.* **89 B8** 15 40 S 47 8 E
Tsiroanomandidy, *Madag.* **89 B8** 18 46 S 46 2 E
Tsiteli-Tsqaro, *Georgia* **35 K8** 41 33N 46 0 E
Tsitondroina, *Madag.* **89 C8** 21 19 S 46 0 E
Tsitsikamma △, *S. Africa* **88 E3** 34 3 S 23 40 E
Tsivilsk, *Russia* **34 C8** 55 50N 47 25 E
Tsivory, *Madag.* **89 C8** 24 4 S 46 5 E
Tskhinvali, *Georgia* **35 J7** 42 14N 44 1 E
Tsna →, *Russia* **34 C6** 54 55N 41 58 E
Tsnori, *Georgia* **35 K7** 41 40N 45 57 E
Tso Moriri, L., *India* **69 C8** 32 50N 78 20 E
Tsobis, *Namibia* **88 B2** 19 27 S 17 30 E
Tsodilo Hill, *Botswana* **88 B3** 18 49 S 21 43 E
Tsogttsetsiy = Baruunsuu, *Mongolia* **56 C3** 43 43N 105 35 E
Tsolo, *S. Africa* **89 E4** 31 18 S 28 37 E
Tsomo, *S. Africa* **89 E4** 32 0 S 27 42 E
Tsu, *Japan* **55 G8** 34 45N 136 25 E
Tsu L., *Canada* **102 A6** 60 40N 111 52W

216 Tsuchiura INDEX TO WORLD MAPS

Tsuchiura, *Japan* **55 F10** 36 5N 140 15 E
Tsuen Wan, *China* **59 F10** 22 22N 114 6 E
Tsugaru-Kaikyō, *Japan* **54 D10** 41 35N 141 0 E
Tsumeb, *Namibia* **88 B2** 19 9 S 17 44 E
Tsumis, *Namibia* **88 C2** 23 39 S 17 29 E
Tsuruga, *Japan* **55 G8** 35 45N 136 2 E
Tsurugi-San, *Japan* **55 H7** 33 51N 134 6 E
Tsuruoka, *Japan* **54 E9** 38 44N 139 50 E
Tsushima, *Gifu, Japan* **55 G8** 35 10N 136 43 E
Tsushima, *Nagasaki, Japan* **55 G4** 34 20N 129 20 E
Tsuyama, *Japan* **55 G7** 35 3N 134 0 E
Tsvetkovo, *Ukraine* **33 H6** 49 8N 31 33 E
Tsyelyakhany, *Belarus* **33 F3** 52 30N 25 46 E
Tua →, *Portugal* **36 D3** 41 13N 7 26W
Tual, *Indonesia* **63 F8** 5 38 S 132 44 E
Tuam, *Ireland* **12 C3** 53 31N 8 51W
Tuamotu Arch. = Tuamotu Is., *French Polynesia* **97 J13** 17 0 S 144 0W
Tuamotu Is., *French Polynesia* **97 J13** 17 0 S 144 0W
Tuamotu Ridge, *Pac. Oc.* **97 K14** 20 0 S 138 0W
Tuanfeng, *China* **59 B10** 30 38N 114 52 E
Tuanxi, *China* **58 D6** 27 28N 107 8 E
Tuao, *Phil.* **61 C4** 17 55N 121 22 E
Tuapse, *Russia* **35 H4** 44 5N 39 10 E
Tuas, *Singapore* **65 d** 1 19N 103 39 E
Tuatapere, *N.Z.* **91 M1** 46 8 S 167 41 E
Tuba City, *U.S.A.* **109 H8** 36 8N 111 14W
Tuban, *Indonesia* **63 G15** 6 54 S 112 3 E
Tubani, *Botswana* **88 C3** 24 46 S 24 18 E
Tubarão, *Brazil* **127 B6** 28 30 S 49 0W
Tūbās, *West Bank* **74 C4** 32 20N 35 22 E
Tubas →, *Namibia* **88 C2** 22 54 S 14 35 E
Tübingen, *Germany* **25 G5** 48 31N 9 4 E
Tubruq, *Libya* **79 B10** 32 7N 23 55 E
Tubuai Is., *French Polynesia* **97 K13** 25 0 S 150 0W
Tuc Trung, *Vietnam* **65 G6** 11 1N 107 12 E
Tucacas, *Venezuela* **124 A5** 10 48N 68 19W
T'uch'ang, *Taiwan* **59 E13** 24 42N 121 25 E
Tuchodi →, *Canada* **102 B4** 58 17N 123 42W
Tuchola, *Poland* **30 E4** 53 33N 17 52 E
Tuchów, *Poland* **31 J8** 49 54N 21 1 E
Tuckanarra, *Australia* **93 E2** 27 7 S 118 5 E
Tucson, *U.S.A.* **109 K8** 32 13N 110 58W
Tucumán □, *Argentina* **126 B2** 26 48 S 66 2W
Tucumcari, *U.S.A.* **113 H3** 35 10N 103 44W
Tucupita, *Venezuela* **124 B6** 9 2N 62 3W
Tucuruí, *Brazil* **125 D9** 3 42 S 49 44W
Tucuruí, Reprêsa de, *Brazil* **125 D9** 4 0 S 49 30W
Tuczno, *Poland* **31 E3** 53 13N 16 10 E
Tudela, *Spain* **38 C3** 42 4N 1 39W
Tudmur, *Syria* **70 C3** 34 36N 38 15 E
Tudor, L., *Canada* **105 A6** 55 50N 65 25W
Tudora, *Romania* **29 C11** 47 31N 26 45 E
Tuella →, *Portugal* **36 D3** 41 30N 7 12W
Tugela →, *S. Africa* **89 D5** 29 14 S 31 30 E
Tuguegarao, *Phil.* **61 C4** 17 35N 121 42 E
Tugur, *Russia* **53 D14** 53 44N 136 45 E
Tui, *Spain* **36 C2** 42 3N 8 39W
Tuineje, *Canary Is.* **48 F5** 28 19N 14 3W
Tukangbesi, Kepulauan, *Indonesia* **63 F6** 6 0 S 124 0 E
Tukarak I., *Canada* **104 A4** 56 15N 78 45W
Tukayyid, *Iraq* **70 D5** 29 47N 45 36 E
Tûkh, *Egypt* **80 H7** 30 21N 31 12 E
Tukhlya, *Ukraine* **29 B8** 48 55N 23 28 E
Tukkae, Ao, *Thailand* **65 a** 7 51N 98 25 E
Tukobo, *Ghana* **82 D4** 5 1N 2 47W
Tuktoyaktuk, *Canada* **100 B6** 69 27N 133 2W
Tukums, *Latvia* **9 H20** 56 58N 23 10 E
Tukums □, *Latvia* **30 B10** 56 55N 23 0 E
Tukuyu, *Tanzania* **87 D3** 9 17 S 33 35 E
Tula, *Hidalgo, Mexico* **119 C5** 20 5N 99 20W
Tula, *Tamaulipas, Mexico* **119 C5** 23 0N 99 40W
Tula, *Nigeria* **83 D7** 9 51N 11 27 E
Tula, *Russia* **32 E9** 54 13N 37 38 E
Tulancingo, *Mexico* **119 C5** 20 5N 99 22W
Tulare, *Serbia & M.* **44 D5** 42 48N 21 28 E
Tulare, *U.S.A.* **110 J7** 36 13N 119 21W
Tulare Lake Bed, *U.S.A.* **110 K7** 36 0N 119 48W
Tularosa, *U.S.A.* **109 K10** 33 5N 106 1W
Tulbagh, *S. Africa* **88 E2** 33 16 S 19 6 E
Tulcán, *Ecuador* **124 C3** 0 48N 77 43W
Tulcea, *Romania* **29 E13** 45 13N 28 46 E
Tulcea □, *Romania* **29 E13** 45 0N 28 30 E
Tulchyn, *Ukraine* **29 B13** 48 41N 28 49 E
Tūleh, *Iran* **71 C7** 34 35N 52 33 E
Tulemalu L., *Canada* **103 A9** 62 58N 99 25W
Tulgheş, *Romania* **29 D10** 46 58N 25 45 E
Tuli, *Zimbabwe* **87 G2** 21 58 S 29 13 E
Tulia, *U.S.A.* **113 H4** 34 32N 101 46W
Tuliszków, *Poland* **31 F5** 52 5N 18 18 E
Tulita, *Canada* **100 B7** 64 57N 125 30W
Ţūlkarm, *West Bank* **74 C4** 32 19N 35 2 E
Tulla, *Ireland* **12 D3** 52 53N 8 46W
Tullahoma, *U.S.A.* **115 H2** 35 22N 86 13W
Tullamore, *Australia* **95 E4** 32 39 S 147 36 E
Tullamore, *Ireland* **12 C4** 53 16N 7 31W
Tulle, *France* **20 C5** 45 16N 1 46 E
Tulln, *Austria* **26 C9** 48 20N 16 4 E
Tullow, *Ireland* **12 D5** 52 49N 6 45W
Tullus, *Sudan* **81 E1** 11 7N 24 31 E
Tully, *Australia* **94 B4** 17 56 S 145 55 E
Tully, *U.S.A.* **117 D8** 42 48N 76 7W
Tulnici, *Romania* **29 E11** 45 51N 26 38 E
Tulovo, *Bulgaria* **45 D9** 42 33N 25 32 E
Tulsa, *U.S.A.* **113 G7** 36 10N 95 55W
Tulsequah, *Canada* **102 B2** 58 39N 133 35W
Tulu Milki, *Ethiopia* **81 F4** 9 55N 38 20 E
Tulu Welel, *Ethiopia* **81 F3** 8 56N 34 47 E
Tulua, *Colombia* **124 C3** 4 6N 76 11W
Tuluceşti, *Romania* **29 E13** 45 34N 28 2 E
Tulun, *Russia* **53 D11** 54 32N 100 35 E
Tulungagung, *Indonesia* **63 H14** 8 5 S 111 54 E
Tuma, *Russia* **32 E11** 55 10N 40 30 E
Tuma →, *Nic.* **120 D3** 13 6N 84 35W
Tumacacori △, *U.S.A.* **109 L8** 31 34N 111 3W
Tumaco, *Colombia* **124 C3** 1 50N 78 45W
Tumatumari, *Guyana* **124 B7** 5 20N 58 55W
Tumba, *Sweden* **10 E11** 59 12N 17 48 E
Tumba, L., *Dem. Rep. of the Congo* **84 E3** 0 50 S 18 0 E
Tumbarumba, *Australia* **95 F4** 35 44 S 148 0 E
Tumbaya, *Argentina* **126 A2** 23 50 S 65 26W
Tumbes, *Peru* **124 D2** 3 37 S 80 27W
Tumbur, *Sudan* **81 G3** 4 20N 31 34 E
Tumbwe, *Dem. Rep. of the Congo* **87 E2** 11 25 S 27 15 E
Tumby Bay, *Australia* **95 E2** 34 21 S 136 8 E
Tumd Youqi, *China* **56 D6** 40 30N 110 30 E
Tumen, *China* **57 C15** 43 0N 129 50 E
Tumen Jiang →, *China* **57 C16** 42 20N 130 35 E
Tumeremo, *Venezuela* **124 B6** 7 18N 61 30W
Tumkur, *India* **66 N10** 13 18N 77 6 E
Tump, *Pakistan* **66 F3** 26 7N 62 16 E
Tumpat, *Malaysia* **65 J4** 6 11N 102 10 E
Tumu, *Ghana* **82 C4** 10 56N 1 56W
Tumucumaque, Serra, *Brazil* **125 C8** 2 0N 55 0W
Tumut, *Australia* **95 F4** 35 16 S 148 13 E
Tumwater, *U.S.A.* **110 C4** 47 1N 122 54W
Tuna, *India* **68 H4** 22 59N 70 5 E
Tunadal, *Sweden* **10 B11** 62 26N 17 22 E
Tunapuna, *Trin. & Tob.* **125 K15** 10 38N 61 24W
Tunas de Zaza, *Cuba* **120 B4** 21 39N 79 34W
Tunbridge Wells = Royal Tunbridge Wells, *U.K.* **15 F8** 51 7N 0 16 E
Tunçbilek, *Turkey* **47 B11** 39 37N 29 29 E
Tunceli, *Turkey* **73 C8** 39 6N 39 31 E
Tuncurry, *Australia* **95 E5** 32 17 S 152 29 E
Tundla, *India* **68 F8** 27 12N 78 17 E
Tundubai, *Sudan* **80 D2** 18 36N 28 35 E
Tunduru, *Tanzania* **87 E4** 11 8 S 37 25 E
Tundzha →, *Bulgaria* **45 E10** 41 40N 26 35 E
Tungabhadra →, *India* **66 M11** 15 57N 78 15 E
Tungaru, *Sudan* **81 E3** 10 9N 30 52 E
Tungla, *Nic.* **120 D3** 13 24N 84 21W
Tungsha Tao = Dongsha Dao, *China* **59 G11** 20 45N 116 43 E
Tungshih, *Taiwan* **59 E13** 24 12N 120 43 E
Tungsten, *Canada* **102 A3** 61 57N 128 16W
Tunguska, Nizhnyaya →, *Russia* **53 C9** 65 48N 88 4 E
Tunguska, Podkamennaya →, *Russia* **53 C10** 61 50N 90 13 E
Tunica, *U.S.A.* **113 H9** 34 41N 90 23W
Tunis, *Tunisia* **78 A7** 36 50N 10 11 E
Tunis ✕ (TUN), *Tunisia* **42 F3** 36 52N 10 14 E
Tunisia ■, *Africa* **78 B6** 33 30N 9 10 E
Tunja, *Colombia* **124 B4** 5 33N 73 25W
Tunkhannock, *U.S.A.* **117 E9** 41 32N 75 57W
Tunliu, *China* **56 F7** 36 13N 112 52 E
Tunnel Creek △, *Australia* **92 C4** 17 41 S 125 18 E
Tunnsjøen, *Norway* **8 D15** 64 45N 13 25 E
Tunø, *Denmark* **11 J4** 55 57N 10 27 E
Tunungayualok I., *Canada* **105 A7** 56 0N 61 0W
Tunuyán, *Argentina* **126 C2** 33 35 S 69 0W
Tunuyán →, *Argentina* **126 C2** 33 33 S 67 30W
Tuo Jiang →, *China* **58 C5** 28 50N 105 35 E
Tuolumne, *U.S.A.* **110 H6** 37 58N 120 15W
Tuolumne →, *U.S.A.* **110 H5** 37 36N 121 13W
Tūp Āghāj, *Iran* **70 B5** 36 3N 47 50 E
Tupã, *Brazil* **127 A5** 21 57 S 50 28W
Tupelo, *U.S.A.* **115 H1** 34 16N 88 43W
Tupik, *Russia* **32 E7** 55 42N 33 22 E
Tupinambaranas, *Brazil* **124 D7** 3 0 S 58 0W
Tupiza, *Bolivia* **126 A2** 21 30 S 65 40W
Tupižnica, *Serbia & M.* **44 C6** 43 43N 22 10 E
Tupman, *U.S.A.* **111 K7** 35 18N 119 21W
Tupper, *Canada* **102 B4** 55 32N 120 1W
Tupper Lake, *U.S.A.* **117 B10** 44 14N 74 28W
Tupungato, Cerro, *S. Amer.* **126 C2** 33 15 S 69 50W
Tuquan, *China* **57 B11** 45 18N 121 38 E
Túquerres, *Colombia* **124 C3** 1 5N 77 37W
Tura, *Russia* **53 C11** 64 20N 100 17 E
Turabah, *Ḥā'il, Si. Arabia* **70 D4** 28 20N 43 15 E
Turabah, *Makkah, Si. Arabia* **80 C5** 21 15N 41 34 E
Tūrān, *Iran* **71 C8** 35 39N 56 42 E
Turan, *Russia* **53 D10** 51 55N 95 0 E
Ţurayf, *Si. Arabia* **70 D3** 31 41N 38 39 E
Turbacz, *Poland* **31 J7** 49 30N 20 8 E
Turbe, *Bos.-H.* **28 F2** 44 15N 17 35 E
Turčianske Teplice, *Slovak Rep.* **27 C11** 48 52N 18 52 E
Turcoaia, *Romania* **29 E13** 45 7N 28 11 E
Turda, *Romania* **29 D8** 46 34N 23 47 E
Turek, *Poland* **31 F5** 52 3N 18 30 E
Turen, *Venezuela* **124 B5** 9 17N 69 6W
Turfan = Turpan, *China* **60 B3** 43 58N 89 10 E
Turfan Basin = Turpan Hami, *China* **50 E12** 42 40N 89 25 E
Turfan Depression = Turpan Hami, *China* **50 E12** 42 40N 89 25 E
Turgeon →, *Canada* **104 C4** 50 0N 78 56W
Tŭrgovishte, *Bulgaria* **45 C10** 43 17N 26 38 E
Turgut, *Turkey* **47 D10** 37 22N 28 4 E
Turgutlu, *Turkey* **47 C9** 38 30N 27 43 E
Turgwe →, *Zimbabwe* **89 C5** 21 31 S 32 15 E
Turhal, *Turkey* **72 B7** 40 24N 36 5 E
Turia →, *Spain* **39 F4** 39 27N 0 19W
Turiaçu, *Brazil* **125 D9** 1 40 S 45 19W
Turiaçu →, *Brazil* **125 D9** 1 36 S 45 19W
Turiec →, *Slovak Rep.* **27 B11** 49 7N 18 55 E
Turin = Torino, *Italy* **40 C4** 45 3N 7 40 E
Turka, *Ukraine* **31 J10** 49 10N 23 2 E
Turkana, L., *Africa* **86 B4** 3 30N 36 5 E
Türkeli, *Turkey* **45 F11** 40 30N 27 30 E
Turkestan = Türkistan, *Kazakhstan* **52 E7** 43 17N 68 16 E
Túrkeve, *Hungary* **28 C5** 47 6N 20 44 E
Turkey ■, *Eurasia* **72 C7** 39 0N 36 0 E
Turkey Creek, *Australia* **92 C4** 17 2 S 128 12 E
Turki, *Russia* **34 D6** 52 0N 43 15 E
Türkistan, *Kazakhstan* **52 E7** 43 17N 68 16 E
Türkmenbashi, *Turkmenistan* **52 E6** 40 5N 53 5 E
Turkmenistan ■, *Asia* **52 F6** 39 0N 59 0 E
Türkmenli, *Turkey* **47 B8** 39 45N 26 30 E
Türkoğlu, *Turkey* **72 D7** 37 23N 36 50 E
Turks & Caicos Is. ☑, *W. Indies* **121 B5** 21 20N 71 20W
Turks Island Passage, *W. Indies* **121 B5** 21 30N 71 30W
Turku, *Finland* **9 F20** 60 30N 22 19 E
Turkwel →, *Kenya* **86 B4** 3 6N 36 6 E
Turlock, *U.S.A.* **110 H6** 37 30N 120 51W
Turnagain →, *Canada* **102 B3** 59 12N 127 35W
Turnagain, C., *N.Z.* **91 J6** 40 28 S 176 38 E
Turneffe Is., *Belize* **119 D7** 17 20N 87 50W
Turner, *U.S.A.* **108 B9** 48 51N 108 24W
Turner Pt., *Australia* **94 A1** 11 47 S 133 32 E
Turner Valley, *Canada* **102 C6** 50 40N 114 17W
Turners Falls, *U.S.A.* **117 D12** 42 36N 72 33W
Turnhout, *Belgium* **17 C4** 51 19N 4 57 E
Türnitz, *Austria* **26 D8** 47 55N 15 29 E
Turnor L., *Canada* **103 B7** 56 35N 108 35W
Turnov, *Czech Rep.* **26 A8** 50 34N 15 10 E
Tŭrnovo = Veliko Tŭrnovo, *Bulgaria* **45 C9** 43 5N 25 41 E
Turnu Măgurele, *Romania* **29 G9** 43 46N 24 56 E
Turnu Roşu, P., *Romania* **29 E9** 45 33N 24 17 E
Turobin, *Poland* **31 H9** 50 50N 22 44 E
Turpan, *China* **60 B3** 43 58N 89 10 E
Turpan Hami, *China* **50 E12** 42 40N 89 25 E
Turrës, Kala e, *Albania* **44 E3** 41 10N 19 28 E
Turriff, *U.K.* **13 D6** 57 32N 2 27W
Tursāq, *Iraq* **70 C5** 33 27N 45 47 E
Tursi, *Italy* **43 B9** 40 15N 16 28 E
Turtle Head I., *Australia* **94 A3** 10 56 S 142 37 E
Turtle Is., *S. Leone* **82 D2** 7 40N 13 0 E
Turtle L., *Canada* **103 C7** 53 36N 108 38W
Turtle Lake, *U.S.A.* **112 B4** 47 31N 100 53W
Turtleford, *Canada* **103 C7** 53 23N 108 57W
Turuépano △, *Venezuela* **121 D7** 10 34N 62 43W
Turukhansk, *Russia* **53 C9** 65 21N 88 5 E
Turzovka, *Slovak Rep.* **27 B11** 49 25N 18 35 E
Tuscaloosa, *U.S.A.* **115 J2** 33 12N 87 34W
Tuscánia, *Italy* **41 F8** 42 25N 11 52 E
Tuscany = Toscana □, *Italy* **40 E8** 43 25N 11 0 E
Tuscarawas →, *U.S.A.* **116 F3** 40 24N 81 25W
Tuscarora Mt., *U.S.A.* **116 F7** 40 55N 77 55W
Tuscola, *Ill., U.S.A.* **114 F1** 39 48N 88 17W
Tuscola, *Tex., U.S.A.* **113 J5** 32 12N 99 48W
Tuscumbia, *U.S.A.* **115 H2** 34 44N 87 42W
Tuskegee, *U.S.A.* **115 J3** 32 25N 85 42W
Tustin, *U.S.A.* **111 M9** 33 44N 117 49W
Tuszyn, *Poland* **31 G6** 51 36N 19 33 E
Tutak, *Turkey* **73 C10** 39 31N 42 46 E
Tutayev, *Russia* **32 D10** 57 53N 39 32 E
Tuticorin, *India* **66 Q11** 8 50N 78 12 E
Tutin, *Serbia & M.* **44 D4** 42 58N 20 20 E
Tutóia, *Brazil* **125 D10** 2 45 S 42 20W
Tutong, *Brunei* **62 D4** 4 47N 114 40 E
Tutova →, *Romania* **29 D12** 46 7N 27 30 E
Tutrakan, *Bulgaria* **45 B10** 44 2N 26 40 E
Tuttle Creek L., *U.S.A.* **112 F6** 39 22N 96 40W
Tuttlingen, *Germany* **25 H4** 47 58N 8 48 E
Tutuala, *E. Timor* **63 F7** 8 25 S 127 15 E
Tutuila, *Amer. Samoa* **91 B13** 14 19 S 170 50W
Tutume, *Botswana* **85 J5** 20 30 S 27 5 E
Tutun, *Egypt* **80 J7** 29 9N 30 46 E
Tututepec, *Mexico* **119 D5** 16 9N 97 38W
Tuva □, *Russia* **53 D10** 51 30N 95 0 E
Tuvalu ■, *Pac. Oc.* **96 H9** 8 0 S 178 0 E
Tuxer Alpen, *Austria* **26 D4** 47 10N 11 45 E
Tuxpan, *Mexico* **119 C5** 20 58N 97 23W
Tuxtla Gutiérrez, *Mexico* **119 D6** 16 50N 93 10W
Tuy = Tui, *Spain* **36 C2** 42 3N 8 39W
Tuy An, *Vietnam* **64 F7** 13 17N 109 16 E
Tuy Duc, *Vietnam* **65 F6** 12 15N 107 27 E
Tuy Hoa, *Vietnam* **64 F7** 13 5N 109 10 E
Tuy Phong, *Vietnam* **65 G7** 11 14N 108 43 E
Tuya L., *Canada* **102 B2** 59 7N 130 35W
Tuyen Hoa, *Vietnam* **64 D6** 17 50N 106 10 E
Tuyen Quang, *Vietnam* **58 G5** 21 50N 105 10 E
Tūysarkān, *Iran* **71 C6** 34 33N 48 27 E
Tuz Gölü, *Turkey* **72 C5** 38 42N 33 18 E
Ţūz Khurmātū = Tozkhurmato, *Iraq* **70 C5** 34 56N 44 38 E
Tuzi, *Serbia & M.* **44 D3** 42 22N 19 20 E
Tuzigoot △, *U.S.A.* **109 J7** 34 46N 112 2W
Tuzla, *Bos.-H.* **28 F3** 44 34N 18 41 E
Tuzlov →, *Russia* **33 J10** 47 17N 39 57 E
Tuzluca, *Turkey* **73 B10** 40 3N 43 39 E
Tuzly **29 E15** 45 54N 30 6 E
Tvååker, *Sweden* **11 G6** 57 4N 12 25 E
Tvardiţa, *Moldova* **29 D13** 46 9N 28 58 E
Tver, *Russia* **32 D8** 56 55N 35 55 E
Tvrdošin, *Slovak Rep.* **27 B12** 49 21N 19 35 E
Tvrdošovce, *Slovak Rep.* **27 C11** 48 6N 18 4 E
Tvŭrditsa, *Bulgaria* **45 D9** 42 42N 25 53 E
Twain, *U.S.A.* **110 E5** 40 1N 121 3W
Twain Harte, *U.S.A.* **110 G6** 38 2N 120 14W
Twardogóra, *Poland* **31 G4** 51 23N 17 28 E
Tweed, *Canada* **116 B7** 44 29N 77 19W
Tweed →, *U.K.* **13 F6** 55 45N 2 0W
Tweed Heads, *Australia* **95 D5** 28 10 S 153 31 E
Tweedsmuir △, *Canada* **102 C3** 53 0N 126 20W
Twentynine Palms, *U.S.A.* **111 L10** 34 8N 116 3W
Twillingate, *Canada* **105 C9** 49 42N 54 45W
Twin Bridges, *U.S.A.* **108 D7** 45 33N 112 20W
Twin Falls, *Canada* **105 B7** 53 30N 64 32W
Twin Falls, *U.S.A.* **108 E6** 42 34N 114 28W
Twin Valley, *U.S.A.* **112 B6** 47 16N 96 16W
Twinsburg, *U.S.A.* **116 E3** 41 18N 81 26W
Twistringen, *Germany* **24 C4** 52 48N 8 37 E
Twitchell Reservoir, *U.S.A.* **111 L6** 34 59N 120 19W
Two Harbors, *U.S.A.* **112 B9** 47 2N 91 40W
Two Hills, *Canada* **102 C6** 53 43N 111 52W
Two Rivers, *U.S.A.* **114 C2** 44 9N 87 34W
Two Rocks, *Australia* **93 F2** 31 30 S 115 35 E
Twofold B., *Australia* **95 F4** 37 8 S 149 59 E
Tyachiv, *Ukraine* **33 H2** 48 1N 23 35 E
Tychy, *Poland* **31 H5** 50 9N 18 59 E
Tyczyn, *Poland* **31 J9** 49 58N 22 2 E
Tykocin, *Poland* **31 E9** 53 13N 22 46 E
Tyler, *Minn., U.S.A.* **112 C6** 44 18N 96 8W
Tyler, *Tex., U.S.A.* **113 J7** 32 21N 95 18W
Tyligul →, *Ukraine* **33 J6** 47 4N 30 57 E
Tymanivka, *Ukraine* **29 B13** 48 34N 28 50 E
Týn nad Vltavou, *Czech Rep.* **26 B7** 49 13N 14 26 E
Tynda, *Russia* **53 D13** 55 10N 124 43 E
Tyndall, *U.S.A.* **112 D6** 43 0N 97 50W
Tyne →, *U.K.* **14 C6** 54 59N 1 32W
Tyne & Wear □, *U.K.* **14 B6** 55 6N 1 17W
Týnec nad Sázavou, *Czech Rep.* **26 B7** 49 50N 14 36 E
Tynemouth, *U.K.* **14 B6** 55 1N 1 26W
Tyre = Sūr, *Lebanon* **74 B4** 33 19N 35 16 E
Tyresta △, *Sweden* **10 E12** 59 12N 18 14 E
Tyrifjorden, *Norway* **9 F14** 60 2N 10 8 E
Tyringe, *Sweden* **11 H7** 56 9N 13 35 E
Tyrnyauz, *Russia* **35 J6** 43 21N 42 45 E
Tyrol = Tirol □, *Austria* **26 D3** 47 3N 10 43 E
Tyrone, *U.S.A.* **116 F6** 40 40N 78 14W
Tyrone □, *U.K.* **12 B4** 54 38N 7 11W
Tyrrell →, *Australia* **95 F3** 35 26 S 142 51 E
Tyrrell, L., *Australia* **95 F3** 35 20 S 142 50 E
Tyrrell L., *Canada* **103 A7** 63 7N 105 27W
Tyrrhenian Sea, *Medit. S.* **6 G8** 40 0N 12 30 E
Tysfjorden, *Norway* **8 B17** 68 7N 16 25 E
Tysmenytsya, *Ukraine* **29 B9** 48 54N 24 51 E
Tystberga, *Sweden* **11 F11** 58 51N 17 15 E
Tytuvėnai, *Lithuania* **30 C10** 55 36N 23 12 E
Tyub Karagan, Mys, *Kazakhstan* **35 H10** 44 40N 50 19 E
Tyuleni, Ostrova, *Kazakhstan* **35 H10** 45 2N 50 16 E
Tyuleniy, *Russia* **35 H8** 44 28N 47 30 E
Tyuleniy, Mys, *Azerbaijan* **35 K10** 40 12N 50 22 E
Tyumen, *Russia* **52 D7** 57 11N 65 29 E
Tywi →, *U.K.* **15 F3** 51 48N 4 21W
Tywyn, *U.K.* **15 E3** 52 35N 4 5W
Tzaneen, *S. Africa* **89 C5** 23 47 S 30 9 E
Tzermiádhes, *Greece* **49 D7** 35 12N 25 29 E
Tzoumérka, Óros, *Greece* **46 B3** 39 30N 21 26 E
Tzukong = Zigong, *China* **58 C5** 29 15N 104 48 E

U

U Taphao, *Thailand* **64 F3** 12 35N 101 0 E
U.S.A. = United States of America ■, *N. Amer.* **106 C7** 37 0N 96 0W
U.S. Virgin Is. ☑, *W. Indies* **121 e** 18 20N 65 0W
Uatumã →, *Brazil* **124 D7** 2 26 S 57 37W
Uaupés, *Brazil* **124 D5** 0 8 S 67 5W
Uaupés →, *Brazil* **124 C5** 0 2N 67 16W
Uaxactún, *Guatemala* **120 C2** 17 25N 89 29W
Ub, *Serbia & M.* **44 B4** 44 28N 20 6 E
Ubá, *Brazil* **127 A7** 21 8 S 43 0W
Uba, *Nigeria* **83 C7** 10 29N 13 13 E
Ubaitaba, *Brazil* **125 F11** 14 18 S 39 20W
Ubangi = Oubangi →, *Dem. Rep. of the Congo* **84 E3** 0 30 S 17 50 E
Ubauro, *Pakistan* **68 E3** 28 15N 69 45 E
Ubaye →, *France* **21 D10** 44 28N 6 18 E
Ubayyiḍ, W. al →, *Iraq* **70 C4** 32 34N 43 48 E
Ube, *Japan* **55 H5** 33 56N 131 15 E
Úbeda, *Spain* **37 G7** 38 3N 3 23W
Uberaba, *Brazil* **125 G9** 19 50 S 47 55W
Uberlândia, *Brazil* **125 G9** 19 0 S 48 20W
Überlingen, *Germany* **25 H5** 47 46N 9 10 E
Ubiaja, *Nigeria* **83 D6** 6 41N 6 22 E
Ubin, Pulau, *Singapore* **65 d** 1 25N 103 56 E
Ubolratna Res., *Thailand* **64 D4** 16 45N 102 30 E
Ubombo, *S. Africa* **89 D5** 27 31 S 32 4 E
Ubon Ratchathani, *Thailand* **64 E5** 15 15N 104 50 E
Ubondo, *Dem. Rep. of the Congo* **86 C2** 0 55 S 25 42 E
Ubort →, *Belarus* **33 F5** 52 6N 28 30 E
Ubrique, *Spain* **37 J5** 36 41N 5 27W
Ubud, *Indonesia* **63 J18** 8 30 S 115 16 E
Ubundu, *Dem. Rep. of the Congo* **86 C2** 0 22 S 25 30 E
Ucayali →, *Peru* **124 D4** 4 30 S 73 30W
Uchab, *Namibia* **88 B2** 19 47 S 17 42 E
Uchiura-Wan, *Japan* **54 C10** 42 25N 140 40 E
Uchquduq, *Uzbekistan* **52 E7** 41 50N 62 50 E
Uchte, *Germany* **24 C4** 52 30N 8 54 E
Uchur →, *Russia* **53 D14** 58 48N 130 35 E
Uckermark, *Germany* **24 B9** 53 5N 13 30 E
Ucluelet, *Canada* **102 D3** 48 57N 125 32W
Uda →, *Russia* **53 D14** 54 42N 135 14 E
Udagamandalam, *India* **66 P10** 11 30N 76 44 E
Udainagar, *India* **68 H7** 22 33N 76 13 E
Udaipur, *India* **68 G5** 24 36N 73 44 E
Udaipur Garhi, *Nepal* **69 F12** 27 0N 86 35 E
Udala, *India* **69 J12** 21 35N 86 34 E
Udbina, *Croatia* **41 D12** 44 31N 15 47 E
Uddeholm, *Sweden* **10 D7** 60 1N 13 38 E
Uddevalla, *Sweden* **11 F5** 58 21N 11 55 E
Uddjaure, *Sweden* **8 D17** 65 56N 17 49 E
Uden, *Neths.* **17 C5** 51 40N 5 37 E
Udgir, *India* **66 K10** 18 25N 77 5 E
Udhampur, *India* **69 C6** 33 0N 75 5 E
Udi, *Nigeria* **83 D6** 6 17N 7 21 E
Údine, *Italy* **41 B10** 46 3N 13 14 E
Udmurtia □, *Russia* **52 D6** 57 30N 52 30 E
Udon Thani, *Thailand* **64 D4** 17 29N 102 46 E
Udupi, *India* **66 N9** 13 25N 74 42 E
Udvoy Balkan, *Bulgaria* **45 D10** 42 50N 26 50 E
Udzungwa △, *Tanzania* **86 D4** 7 52 S 36 35 E
Udzungwa Range, *Tanzania* **87 D4** 9 30 S 35 10 E
Ueckermünde, *Germany* **24 B10** 53 44N 14 1 E
Ueda, *Japan* **55 F9** 36 24N 138 16 E
Uedineniya, Os., *Russia* **4 B12** 78 0N 85 0 E
Uele →, *Dem. Rep. of the Congo* **84 D4** 3 45N 24 45 E
Uelen, *Russia* **53 C19** 66 10N 170 0W
Uelzen, *Germany* **24 C6** 52 57N 10 32 E
Uetersen, *Germany* **24 B5** 53 40N 9 40 E
Uetze, *Germany* **24 C6** 52 28N 10 11 E
Ufa, *Russia* **52 D6** 54 45N 55 55 E
Uffenheim, *Germany* **25 F6** 49 33N 10 14 E
Ugab →, *Namibia* **88 C1** 20 55 S 13 30 E
Ugalla →, *Tanzania* **86 D3** 5 8 S 30 42 E
Ugalla River △, *Tanzania* **86 D3** 5 50 S 31 54 E
Uganda ■, *Africa* **86 B3** 2 0N 32 0 E
Ugento, *Italy* **43 C11** 39 56N 18 10 E
Ugep, *Nigeria* **83 D6** 5 53N 8 2 E
Ughelli, *Nigeria* **83 D6** 5 33N 6 0 E
Ugie, *S. Africa* **89 E4** 31 10 S 28 13 E
Ugíjar, *Spain* **37 J7** 36 58N 3 7W
Ugine, *France* **21 C10** 45 45N 6 25 E
Uglegorsk, *Russia* **53 E15** 49 5N 142 2 E
Uglich, *Russia* **32 D10** 57 33N 38 20 E
Ugljan, *Croatia* **41 D12** 44 12N 15 10 E
Ugljane, *Croatia* **41 E13** 43 35N 16 46 E
Ugra →, *Russia* **32 E9** 54 30N 36 7 E
Ugŭrchin, *Bulgaria* **45 C8** 43 6N 24 26 E
Uh →, *Slovak Rep.* **27 C15** 48 37N 22 0 E
Uherské Hradiště, *Czech Rep.* **27 B10** 49 4N 17 30 E
Uherský Brod, *Czech Rep.* **27 B10** 49 1N 17 40 E
Úhlava →, *Czech Rep.* **26 B6** 49 45N 13 24 E
Uhlenhorst, *Namibia* **88 C2** 23 45 S 17 55 E
Uhniv, *Ukraine* **31 H10** 50 22N 23 45 E
Uhrichsville, *U.S.A.* **116 F3** 40 24N 81 21W
Uibhist a Deas = South Uist, *U.K.* **13 D1** 57 20N 7 15W
Uibhist a Tuath = North Uist, *U.K.* **13 D1** 57 40N 7 15W
Uig, *U.K.* **13 D2** 57 35N 6 21W
Uíge, *Angola* **84 F2** 7 30 S 14 40 E
Uijŏngbu, *S. Korea* **57 F14** 37 48N 127 0 E
Ŭiju, *N. Korea* **57 D13** 40 15N 124 35 E
Uinta Mts., *U.S.A.* **108 F8** 40 45N 110 30W
Uis, *Namibia* **88 C1** 21 8 S 14 49 E
Uitenhage, *S. Africa* **88 E4** 33 40 S 25 28 E
Uithuizen, *Neths.* **17 A6** 53 24N 6 41 E
Ujazd, *Poland* **31 H5** 50 23N 18 21 E
Újfehértó, *Hungary* **28 C6** 47 49N 21 41 E
Ujh →, *India* **68 C6** 32 10N 75 18 E
Ujhani, *India* **69 F8** 28 0N 79 6 E
Uji-guntō, *Japan* **55 J4** 31 15N 129 25 E
Ujjain, *India* **68 H6** 23 9N 75 43 E
Ujście, *Poland* **31 E3** 53 3N 16 45 E
Újszász, *Hungary* **28 C5** 47 19N 20 7 E
Ujung Pandang, *Indonesia* **63 F5** 5 10 S 119 20 E
Uka, *Russia* **53 D17** 57 50N 162 0 E
Ukara I., *Tanzania* **86 C3** 1 50 S 33 0 E
Uke-Shima, *Japan* **55 K4** 28 2N 129 14 E
Ukerewe I., *Tanzania* **86 C3** 2 0 S 33 0 E
Ukholovo, *Russia* **34 D5** 53 47N 40 30 E
Ukhrul, *India* **67 G19** 25 10N 94 25 E
Ukhta, *Russia* **52 C6** 63 34N 53 41 E
Ukiah, *U.S.A.* **110 F3** 39 9N 123 13W
Ukmergė, *Lithuania* **9 J21** 55 15N 24 45 E
Ukraine ■, *Europe* **33 H7** 49 0N 32 0 E
Ukwi, *Botswana* **88 C3** 23 29 S 20 30 E
Ulaan-Uul, *Mongolia* **56 B6** 44 13N 111 10 E
Ulaanbaatar, *Mongolia* **53 E11** 47 55N 106 53 E
Ulaangom, *Mongolia* **60 A4** 50 5N 92 10 E
Ulaanjirem, *Mongolia* **56 B3** 45 5N 105 30 E
Ulamba, *Dem. Rep. of the Congo* **87 D1** 9 3 S 23 38 E
Ulan Bator = Ulaanbaatar, *Mongolia* **53 E11** 47 55N 106 53 E
Ulan Erge, *Russia* **35 G7** 46 19N 44 53 E
Ulan Khol, *Russia* **35 H8** 45 18N 47 4 E
Ulan Ude, *Russia* **53 D11** 51 45N 107 40 E
Ulanów, *Poland* **31 H9** 50 30N 22 16 E
Ulaş, *Sivas, Turkey* **72 C7** 39 26N 37 2 E
Ulaş, *Tekirdağ, Turkey* **45 E11** 41 14N 27 42 E
Ulaya, *Morogoro, Tanzania* **86 D4** 7 3 S 36 55 E
Ulaya, *Tabora, Tanzania* **86 C3** 4 25 S 33 30 E
Ulcinj, *Serbia & M.* **44 E3** 41 58N 19 10 E
Ulco, *S. Africa* **88 D3** 28 21 S 24 15 E
Ule älv = Oulujoki →, *Finland* **8 D21** 65 1N 25 30 E
Ule träsk = Oulujärvi, *Finland* **8 D22** 64 25N 27 15 E
Uleåborg = Oulu, *Finland* **8 D21** 65 1N 25 29 E
Ulefoss, *Norway* **9 G13** 59 17N 9 16 E
Ulëz, *Albania* **44 E3** 41 46N 19 54 E
Ulfborg, *Denmark* **11 H2** 56 16N 8 20 E
Ulhasnagar, *India* **66 K8** 19 15N 73 10 E
Uliastay, *Mongolia* **60 B4** 47 56N 97 28 E
Uljma, *Serbia & M.* **28 E6** 45 2N 21 10 E
Ulla →, *Spain* **36 C2** 42 39N 8 44W
Ulladulla, *Australia* **95 F5** 35 21 S 150 29 E
Ullapool, *U.K.* **13 D3** 57 54N 5 9W
Ullared, *Sweden* **11 G6** 57 8N 12 42 E
Ulldecona, *Spain* **38 E5** 40 36N 0 20 E
Ullswater, *U.K.* **14 C5** 54 34N 2 52W
Ullŭng-do, *S. Korea* **55 F5** 37 30N 130 30 E
Ulm, *Germany* **25 G5** 48 23N 9 58 E
Ulmarra, *Australia* **95 D5** 29 37 S 153 4 E
Ulmeni, *Buzău, Romania* **29 E11** 45 4N 26 40 E
Ulmeni, *Maramureş, Romania* **29 C8** 47 28N 23 18 E
Ulonguè, *Mozam.* **87 E3** 14 37 S 34 19 E
Ulricehamn, *Sweden* **11 G7** 57 46N 13 26 E
Ulrika, *Sweden* **11 F9** 58 5N 15 23 E
Ulsan, *S. Korea* **57 G15** 35 20N 129 15 E
Ulsta, *U.K.* **13 A7** 60 30N 1 9W
Ulster □, *U.K.* **12 B5** 54 35N 6 30W
Ulstrem, *Bulgaria* **45 D10** 42 1N 26 27 E
Ulubat Gölü, *Turkey* **45 F12** 40 9N 28 35 E
Ulubey, *Turkey* **47 C11** 38 25N 29 18 E
Uluborlu, *Turkey* **47 C12** 38 4N 30 28 E
Uluçinar, *Turkey* **72 D6** 36 21N 35 57 E
Uludağ, *Turkey* **45 F13** 40 4N 29 13 E
Uludağ △, *Turkey* **45 F13** 40 5N 29 12 E
Uludere, *Turkey* **73 D10** 37 28N 42 42 E
Uluguru Mts., *Tanzania* **86 D4** 7 15 S 37 40 E
Ulukışla, *Turkey* **72 D6** 37 33N 34 28 E
Ulungur He →, *China* **60 B3** 47 1N 87 24 E
Uluru = Ayers Rock, *Australia* **93 E5** 25 23 S 131 5 E
Uluru-Kata Tjuta △, *Australia* **93 E5** 25 19 S 131 1 E
Ulutau, *Kazakhstan* **52 E7** 48 39N 67 1 E
Uluwatu, *Indonesia* **63 K18** 8 50 S 115 5 E
Ulva, *U.K.* **13 E2** 56 29N 6 13W
Ulverston, *U.K.* **14 C4** 54 13N 3 5W
Ulverstone, *Australia* **95 G4** 41 11 S 146 11 E
Ulya, *Russia* **53 D15** 59 10N 142 0 E
Ulyanovo, *Russia* **30 D9** 54 50N 22 6 E
Ulyanovsk = Simbirsk, *Russia* **34 C9** 54 20N 48 25 E
Ulyasutay = Uliastay, *Mongolia* **60 B4** 47 56N 97 28 E
Ulysses, *U.S.A.* **113 G4** 37 35N 101 22W
Umag, *Croatia* **41 C10** 45 26N 13 31 E
Umala, *Bolivia* **124 G5** 17 25 S 68 5W
Uman, *Ukraine* **33 H6** 48 40N 30 12 E
Umaria, *India* **67 H12** 23 35N 80 50 E
Umarkot, *Pakistan* **66 G6** 25 15N 69 40 E
Umarpada, *India* **68 J5** 21 27N 73 30 E
Umatilla, *U.S.A.* **108 D4** 45 55N 119 21W
Umbagog L., *U.S.A.* **117 B13** 44 46N 71 3W
Umbakumba, *Australia* **94 A2** 13 47 S 136 50 E
Umbértide, *Italy* **41 E9** 43 18N 12 20 E
Umbrella Mts., *N.Z.* **91 L2** 45 35 S 169 5 E
Umbria □, *Italy* **41 F9** 42 53N 12 30 E
Umeå, *Sweden* **8 E19** 63 45N 20 20 E
Umeälven →, *Sweden* **8 E19** 63 45N 20 20 E
Umera, *Indonesia* **63 E7** 0 12 S 129 37 E
Umfolozi △, *S. Africa* **89 D5** 28 18 S 31 50 E
Umfuli →, *Zimbabwe* **87 F2** 17 30 S 29 23 E
Umfurudzi △, *Zimbabwe* **87 F3** 17 6 S 31 40 E
Umgusa, *Zimbabwe* **87 F2** 19 29 S 27 52 E
Umim Urūmah, *Si. Arabia* **80 B4** 25 43N 36 35 E
Umka, *Serbia & M.* **44 B4** 44 40N 20 19 E
Umkomaas, *S. Africa* **89 E5** 30 13 S 30 48 E
Umlazi, *S. Africa* **85 L6** 29 59 S 30 54 E
Umm ad Daraj, J., *Jordan* **74 C4** 32 18N 35 48 E
Umm al Qaywayn, *U.A.E.* **71 E7** 25 30N 55 35 E
Umm al Qittayn, *Jordan* **74 C5** 32 18N 36 40 E
Umm Arda, *Sudan* **81 D3** 15 17N 32 31 E
Umm Bāb, *Qatar* **71 E6** 25 12N 50 48 E
Umm Badr, *Sudan* **81 E2** 14 13N 27 58 E
Umm Baiyud, *Sudan* **81 E3** 12 5N 31 40 E
Umm Bel, *Sudan* **81 E2** 13 35N 28 0 E
Umm Birkah, *Si. Arabia* **80 B4** 27 44N 36 31 E
Umm Boim, *Sudan* **81 E2** 11 43N 25 27 E
Umm Dam, *Sudan* **81 E3** 13 45N 30 59 E
Umm Debi, *Sudan* **81 E3** 14 37N 30 23 E
Umm Dubban, *Sudan* **81 D3** 15 23N 32 52 E
Umm Durman = Omdurmân, *Sudan* **81 D3** 15 40N 32 28 E
Umm el Fahm, *Israel* **74 C4** 32 31N 35 9 E

Umm Gafala, *Sudan* .. **81 E2** 13 22N 27 15 E
Umm Gimala, *Sudan* .. **81 E2** 11 27N 28 12 E
Umm Inderaba, *Sudan* **80 D3** 15 58N 30 41 E
Umm Keddada, *Sudan* . **81 E2** 13 33N 26 35 E
Umm Koweika, *Sudan* . **81 E3** 13 10N 32 16 E
Umm Lajj, *Si. Arabia* .. **70 E3** 25 0N 37 23 E
Umm Merwa, *Sudan* .. **80 D3** 18 4N 32 30 E
Umm Qantur, *Sudan* .. **81 E3** 14 17N 31 22 E
Umm Ruwaba, *Sudan* .. **81 F3** 12 50N 31 20 E
Umm Saiyala, *Sudan* .. **81 E3** 14 25N 31 10 E
Umm Shanqa, *Sudan* .. **81 E2** 13 14N 27 14 E
Umm Shutur, *Sudan* .. **81 F3** 7 17N 33 14 E
Umm Sidr, *Sudan* ..... **81 E2** 14 29N 25 10 E
Umnak I., *U.S.A.* **100 C3** 53 15N 168 20W
Umniati →, *Zimbabwe* **87 F2** 16 49 S 28 45 E
Umpqua →, *U.S.A.* **108 E1** 43 40N 124 12W
Umreth, *India* .... **68 H5** 22 41N 73 4 E
Umtata, *S. Africa* .... **89 E4** 31 36 S 28 49 E
Umuahia, *Nigeria* .... **83 D6** 5 31N 7 26 E
Umuarama, *Brazil* .... **127 A5** 23 45 S 53 20W
Umurbey, *Turkey* ..... **45 F10** 40 13N 26 36 E
Umvukwe Ra.,
  Zimbabwe .... **87 F3** 16 45 S 30 45 E
Umzimvubu, *S. Africa* . **89 E4** 31 38 S 29 33 E
Umzingwane →,
  Zimbabwe .... **87 G2** 22 12 S 29 56 E
Umzinto, *S. Africa* .... **89 E5** 30 15 S 30 45 E
Una, *India* .... **68 J4** 20 46N 71 8 E
Una →, *Bos.-H.* ...... **41 D13** 45 0N 16 20 E
Unac →, *Bos.-H.* ..... **41 D13** 44 30N 16 9 E
Unadilla, *U.S.A.* **117 D9** 42 20N 75 19W
Unalakleet, *U.S.A.* **100 B3** 63 52N 160 47W
Unalaska, *U.S.A.* **100 C3** 53 53N 166 32W
Unalaska I., *U.S.A.* ... **100 C3** 53 35N 166 50W
'Unayzah, *Si. Arabia* .. **70 E4** 26 6N 43 58 E
'Unayzah, J., *Asia* .... **70 C3** 32 12N 39 18 E
Uncastillo, *Spain* **38 C3** 42 21N 1 8W
Uncía, *Bolivia* ...... **124 G5** 18 25 S 66 40W
Uncompahgre Peak,
  U.S.A. **109 G10** 38 4N 107 28W
Uncompahgre Plateau,
  U.S.A. **109 G9** 38 20N 108 15W
Undara Volcanic △,
  Australia .... **94 B3** 18 14 S 144 41 E
Unden, *Sweden* ...... **11 F8** 58 45N 14 25 E
Underbool, *Australia* .. **95 F3** 35 10 S 141 51 E
Undersaker, *Sweden* .. **10 A7** 63 19N 13 21 E
Unecha, *Russia* ...... **33 F7** 52 50N 32 37 E
Ungarie, *Australia* .... **95 E4** 33 38 S 146 56 E
Ungarra, *Australia* .... **95 E2** 34 12 S 136 2 E
Ungava, Pén. d', *Canada* **101 C12** 60 0N 74 0W
Ungava B., *Canada* ... **101 C13** 59 30N 67 30W
Ungeny = Ungheni,
  Moldova .... **29 C12** 47 11N 27 51 E
Unggi, *N. Korea* ..... **57 C16** 42 16N 130 28 E
Ungheni, *Moldova* ... **29 C12** 47 11N 27 51 E
Unguala →, *Ethiopia* . **81 F5** 8 6N 41 9 E
Ungwana B., *Kenya* ... **86 C5** 2 40 S 40 20 E
Ungwatiri, *Sudan* .... **81 D4** 16 52N 36 10 E
Uni, *Russia* .... **34 B10** 57 46N 51 31 E
União da Vitória, *Brazil* **127 B5** 26 13 S 51 5W
Uničov, *Czech Rep.* ... **27 B10** 49 46N 17 8 E
Uniejów, *Poland* ..... **31 G5** 51 59N 18 46 E
Unije, *Croatia* ...... **41 D11** 44 40N 14 15 E
Unimak I., *U.S.A.* **100 C3** 54 45N 164 0W
Union, *Miss., U.S.A.* .. **113 J10** 32 34N 89 7W
Union, *Mo., U.S.A.* ... **112 F9** 38 27N 91 0W
Union, *S.C., U.S.A.* ... **115 H5** 34 43N 81 37W
Union City, *Calif.,*
  U.S.A. **110 H4** 37 36N 122 1W
Union City, *N.J., U.S.A.* **117 F10** 40 45N 74 2W
Union City, *Pa., U.S.A.* **116 E5** 41 54N 79 51W
Union City, *Tenn.,*
  U.S.A. **113 G10** 36 26N 89 3W
Union Gap, *U.S.A.* ... **108 C3** 46 33N 120 28W
Union Springs, *U.S.A.* **115 J3** 32 9N 85 43W
Uniondale, *S. Africa* .. **88 E3** 33 39 S 23 7 E
Uniontown, *U.S.A.* ... **114 F6** 39 54N 79 44W
Unionville, *U.S.A.* ... **112 E8** 40 29N 93 1W
Unirea, *Romania* .... **29 F12** 44 15N 27 35 E
United Arab
  Emirates ■, *Asia* ... **71 F7** 23 50N 54 0 E
United Kingdom ■,
  Europe **7 E5** 53 0N 2 0W
United States of
  America ■, *N. Amer.* **106 C7** 37 0N 96 0W
Unity, *Canada* **103 C7** 52 30N 109 5W
Universales, Mtes.,
  Spain **38 E3** 40 18N 1 33W
University Park, *U.S.A.* **109 K10** 32 17N 106 45W
Unjha, *India* .... **68 H5** 23 46N 72 24 E
Unna, *Germany* ..... **24 D3** 51 32N 7 42 E
Unnao, *India* .... **69 F9** 26 35N 80 30 E
Uno, Ilha, *Guinea-Biss.* **82 C1** 11 15N 16 13W
Unsengedsi →,
  Zimbabwe .... **87 F3** 15 43 S 31 14 E
Unst, *U.K.* **13 A8** 60 44N 0 53W
Unstrut →, *Germany* . **24 D7** 51 10N 11 48 E
Unterfranken □,
  Germany .... **25 F5** 50 0N 10 0 E
Unterschleissheim,
  Germany .... **25 G7** 48 17N 11 34 E
Unuk →, *Canada* **102 B2** 56 5N 131 3W
Ünye, *Turkey* .... **72 B7** 41 5N 37 15 E
Unzen-Amakusa △,
  Japan .... **55 H5** 32 15N 130 10 E
Unzha, *Russia* ...... **34 A7** 58 0N 44 0 E
Unzha →, *Russia* .... **34 B6** 57 49N 43 47 E
Uozu, *Japan* .... **55 F8** 36 48N 137 24 E
Upata, *Venezuela* **124 B6** 8 1N 62 24W
Upemba △, *Dem. Rep.*
  of the Congo ..... **87 D2** 9 0 S 26 35 E
Upemba, L., *Dem. Rep.*
  of the Congo ..... **87 D2** 8 30 S 26 20 E
Upernavik, *Greenland* . **4 B5** 72 49N 56 20W
Upington, *S. Africa* ... **88 D3** 28 25 S 21 15 E
Upleta, *India* .... **68 J4** 21 46N 70 16 E
'Upolu, *Samoa* ...... **91 A13** 13 58 S 172 0W
Upper □, *Ghana* **83 C4** 10 30N 1 30W
Upper Alkali L., *U.S.A.* **108 F3** 41 47N 120 8W
Upper Arrow L.,
  Canada **102 C5** 50 30N 117 50W
Upper Foster L., *Canada* **103 B7** 56 47N 105 20W
Upper Hutt, *N.Z.* .... **91 J5** 41 8 S 175 5 E
Upper Klamath L.,
  U.S.A. **108 E3** 42 25N 121 55W
Upper Lake, *U.S.A.* ... **110 F4** 39 10N 122 54W
Upper Manzanilla,
  Trin. & Tob. **125 K15** 10 31N 61 4W
Upper Missouri River
  Breaks △, *U.S.A.* .. **108 C9** 47 50N 108 55W
Upper Musquodoboit,
  Canada **105 C7** 45 10N 62 58W
Upper Red L., *U.S.A.* . **112 A7** 48 8N 94 45W
Upper Sandusky, *U.S.A.* **114 E4** 40 50N 83 17W

Upper Volta = Burkina
  Faso ■, *Africa* **82 C4** 12 0N 1 0W
Upphärad, *Sweden* ... **11 F6** 58 9N 12 19 E
Uppland, *Sweden* .... **10 D12** 59 59N 17 48 E
Upplands-Väsby,
  Sweden .... **10 E11** 59 31N 17 54 E
Uppsala, *Sweden* .... **10 E11** 59 53N 17 38 E
Uppsala län □, *Sweden* **10 D11** 60 0N 17 30 E
Upshi, *India* .... **69 C7** 33 48N 77 52 E
Upstart, C., *Australia* . **94 B4** 19 41 S 147 45 E
Upton, *U.S.A.* **112 C2** 44 6N 104 38W
Uqsuqtuuq = Gjoa
  Haven, *Canada* ... **100 B10** 68 38N 95 53W
Ur, *Iraq* .... **70 D5** 30 55N 46 25 E
Urad Qianqi, *China* .. **56 D5** 40 40N 108 30 E
Urakawa, *Japan* ..... **54 C11** 42 9N 142 47 E
Ural = Uralskiy □,
  Russia .... **52 C7** 64 0N 70 0 E
Ural = Zhayyq →,
  Kazakhstan ...... **52 E6** 47 0N 51 48 E
Ural, *Australia* ...... **95 E4** 33 21 S 146 12 E
Ural Mts. = Uralskie
  Gory, *Eurasia* .... **52 D6** 60 0N 59 0 E
Uralla, *Australia* .... **95 E5** 30 37 S 151 29 E
Uralsk = Oral,
  Kazakhstan ...... **34 E10** 51 20N 51 20 E
Uralskie Gory, *Eurasia* **52 D6** 60 0N 59 0 E
Uralskiy □, *Russia* ... **52 C7** 64 0N 70 0 E
Urambo, *Tanzania* ... **86 D3** 5 4 S 32 0 E
Urandangi, *Australia* . **94 C2** 21 32 S 138 14 E
Uranium City, *Canada* **103 B7** 59 34N 108 37W
Uraricoera →, *Brazil* . **124 C6** 3 2N 60 30W
Urawa, *Japan* .... **55 G9** 35 50N 139 40 E
Uray, *Russia* .... **52 C7** 60 5N 65 15 E
'Uray'irah, *Si. Arabia* . **71 E6** 25 57N 48 53 E
Urbana, *Ill., U.S.A.* .. **114 E1** 40 7N 88 12W
Urbana, *Ohio, U.S.A.* . **114 E4** 40 7N 83 45W
Urbánia, *Italy* ...... **41 E9** 43 40N 12 31 E
Urbel →, *Spain* **36 C7** 42 21N 3 40W
Urbino, *Italy* .... **41 E9** 43 43N 12 38 E
Urbión, Picos de, *Spain* **38 C2** 42 1N 2 52W
Urcos, *Peru* .... **124 F4** 13 40 S 71 38W
Urdinarrain, *Argentina* **126 C4** 32 37 S 58 52W
Urdos, *France* **20 F3** 42 51N 0 35W
Urdzhar, *Kazakhstan* . **52 E9** 47 5N 81 38 E
Ure →, *U.K.* **14 C6** 54 5N 1 20W
Uren, *Russia* .... **34 B7** 57 35N 45 55 E
Ures, *Mexico* **118 B2** 29 30N 110 30W
Urewera △, *N.Z.* .... **91 H6** 38 29 S 177 7 E
Urfa = Şanlıurfa, *Turkey* **70 B3** 37 12N 38 50 E
Urganch, *Uzbekistan* . **52 E7** 41 40N 60 41 E
Urgench = Urganch,
  Uzbekistan ...... **52 E7** 41 40N 60 41 E
Ürgüp, *Turkey* ...... **70 B2** 38 38N 34 56 E
Uri, *India* .... **69 B6** 34 8N 74 2 E
Uri □, *Switz.* .... **25 J4** 46 43N 8 35 E
Uribia, *Colombia* **124 A4** 11 43N 72 16W
Uricani, *Romania* .... **28 E8** 45 20N 23 9 E
Uriondo, *Bolivia* .... **126 A3** 21 41 S 64 41W
Urique, *Mexico* **118 B3** 27 13N 107 55W
Urique →, *Mexico* ... **118 B3** 26 29N 107 58W
Urk, *Neths.* .... **17 B5** 52 39N 5 36 E
Urkiola □, *Spain* **38 B3** 43 6N 1 2W
Urla, *Turkey* .... **47 C8** 38 20N 26 47 E
Urlaţi, *Romania* ..... **29 F11** 44 59N 26 15 E
Urmia = Orūmīyeh, *Iran* **70 B5** 37 40N 45 0 E
Uroševac, *Serbia & M.* . **44 D5** 42 23N 21 10 E
Uroyan, Montañas de,
  Puerto Rico ...... **121 d** 18 12N 67 0W
Urshult, *Sweden* .... **11 H8** 56 31N 14 50 E
Uruaçu, *Brazil* ...... **125 F9** 14 30 S 49 10W
Uruapan, *Mexico* **118 D4** 19 30N 102 0W
Urubamba →, *Peru* .. **124 F4** 10 43 S 73 48W
Uruburuça, *Brazil* .... **124 D7** 2 32 S 57 45W
Uruçuí, *Brazil* ...... **125 E10** 7 20 S 44 28W
Uruguai →, *Brazil* ... **127 B5** 26 0 S 53 30W
Uruguaiana, *Brazil* ... **126 B4** 29 50 S 57 0W
Uruguay ■, *S. Amer.* . **126 C4** 32 30 S 56 30W
Uruguay →, *S. Amer.* . **126 C4** 34 12 S 58 18W
Urumchi = Ürümqi,
  China .... **52 E9** 43 45N 87 45 E
Ürümqi, *China* ..... **52 E9** 43 45N 87 45 E
Urup →, *Russia* ..... **35 H5** 45 0N 41 10 E
Urup, Ostrov, *Russia* . **53 E16** 46 0N 151 0 E
Uryupinsk, *Russia* ... **34 E5** 50 45N 41 58 E
Urzhum, *Russia* ..... **34 B9** 57 10N 49 56 E
Urziceni, *Romania* ... **29 F11** 44 40N 26 42 E
Usa →, *Russia* ...... **52 C6** 66 16N 59 49 E
Uşak, *Turkey* .... **47 C11** 38 43N 29 28 E
Uşak □, *Turkey* ..... **47 C11** 38 30N 29 0 E
Usakos, *Namibia* .... **88 C2** 21 54 S 15 31 E
Ušće, *Serbia & M.* ... **44 C4** 43 30N 20 39 E
Usedom, *Germany* ... **24 B10** 53 55N 14 2 E
Usedom →, *Germany* . **24 B10** 53 55N 14 0 E
Useless Loop, *Australia* **93 E1** 26 8 S 113 23 E
'Usfān, *Si. Arabia* ... **80 C4** 21 58N 39 27 E
Ush-Tobe, *Kazakhstan* **52 E8** 45 16N 78 0 E
Ushakova, Ostrov,
  Russia .... **4 A12** 82 0N 80 0 E
Ushakovo, *Russia* ... **30 D7** 54 37N 20 16 E
Ushant = Ouessant, Î. d',
  France **18 D1** 48 28N 5 6W
Ushashi, *Tanzania* ... **86 C3** 1 59 S 33 57 E
Ushuaia, *Argentina* .. **128 G3** 54 50 S 68 23W
Ushumun, *Russia* .... **53 D13** 52 47N 126 32 E
Ushytsya →, *Ukraine* . **29 B12** 48 35N 27 8 E
Usk, *Canada* **102 C3** 54 38N 128 26W
Usk →, *U.K.* **15 F5** 51 33N 2 58W
Uska, *India* .... **69 F10** 27 12N 83 7 E
Üsküdar, *Turkey* .... **45 F13** 41 0N 29 5 E
Uslar, *Germany* ..... **24 D5** 51 39N 9 38 E
Usman, *Russia* ...... **33 F10** 52 5N 39 48 E
Usoke, *Tanzania* .... **86 D3** 5 8 S 32 24 E
Usolye Sibirskoye,
  Russia .... **53 D11** 52 48N 103 40 E
Usoro, *Nigeria* ..... **83 D6** 5 33N 7 21 E
Uspallata, P. de,
  Argentina .... **126 C2** 32 37 S 69 22W
Uspenskiy, *Kazakhstan* **52 E8** 48 41N 72 43 E
Ussel, *France* ...... **20 C6** 45 32N 2 18 E
Usson-du-Poitou, *France* **20 B4** 46 16N 0 31 E
Ussuri →, *Asia* ..... **54 A7** 48 27N 135 0 E
Ussuriysk, *Russia* ... **53 E14** 43 48N 131 59 E
Ussurka, *Russia* .... **54 B6** 45 12N 133 31 E
Ust-Bolsheretsk, *Russia* **53 D16** 52 50N 156 15 E
Ust-Buzulukskaya,
  Russia .... **34 E6** 50 8N 42 11 E
Ust-Chaun, *Russia* ... **53 C18** 68 47N 170 30 E
Ust-Chorna, *Ukraine* . **29 B8** 48 19N 23 56 E
Ust-Donetskiy, *Russia* **35 G5** 47 35N 40 55 E
Ust-Ilimsk, *Russia* ... **53 D11** 58 3N 102 39 E
Ust-Ishim, *Russia* ... **52 D8** 57 45N 71 10 E
Ust-Kamchatsk, *Russia* **53 D17** 56 10N 162 28 E

Ust-Kamenogorsk =
  Öskemen, *Kazakhstan* **52 E9** 50 0N 82 36 E
Ust-Khayryuzovo,
  Russia .... **53 D16** 57 15N 156 45 E
Ust-Kut, *Russia* ..... **53 D11** 56 50N 105 42 E
Ust-Kuyga, *Russia* ... **53 B14** 70 1N 135 43 E
Ust-Labinsk, *Russia* .. **35 H4** 45 15N 39 41 E
Ust-Luga, *Russia* .... **32 C5** 59 35N 28 20 E
Ust-Maya, *Russia* .... **53 C14** 60 30N 134 28 E
Ust-Nera, *Russia* .... **53 C15** 64 35N 143 15 E
Ust-Nyukzha, *Russia* . **53 D13** 56 34N 121 37 E
Ust-Olenek, *Russia* .. **53 B12** 73 0N 120 5 E
Ust-Omchug, *Russia* . **53 C15** 61 9N 149 38 E
Ust-Port, *Russia* .... **52 C9** 69 40N 84 26 E
Ust-Tsilma, *Russia* ... **52 C6** 65 28N 52 11 E
Ust Urt = Ustyurt
  Plateau, *Asia* ..... **52 E6** 44 0N 55 0 E
Ustaritz, *France* **20 E2** 43 24N 1 27W
Ustecký □, *Czech Rep.* **26 A7** 50 30N 14 0 E
Uster, *Switz.* .... **25 H4** 47 22N 8 43 E
Ústí nad Labem,
  Czech Rep. ...... **26 A7** 50 41N 14 3 E
Ústí nad Orlicí,
  Czech Rep. ...... **27 B9** 49 58N 16 24 E
Ústica, *Italy* .... **42 D6** 38 42N 13 11 E
Ustinov = Izhevsk,
  Russia .... **52 D6** 56 51N 53 14 E
Ustka, *Poland* ...... **30 D3** 54 35N 16 55 E
Ustroń, *Poland* ..... **31 B11** 49 43N 18 48 E
Ustrzyki Dolne, *Poland* **31 J9** 49 27N 22 40 E
Ustyluh, *Ukraine* .... **31 H11** 50 51N 24 10 E
Ustyurt Plateau, *Asia* . **52 E6** 44 0N 55 0 E
Ustyuzhna, *Russia* ... **32 C9** 58 50N 36 32 E
Usu, *China* .... **60 B3** 44 27N 84 40 E
Usuki, *Japan* .... **55 H5** 33 8N 131 49 E
Usulután, *El Salv.* ... **120 D2** 13 25N 88 28W
Usumacinta →, *Mexico* **119 D6** 17 0N 91 0W
Usumbura =
  Bujumbura, *Burundi* **86 C2** 3 16 S 29 18 E
Usure, *Tanzania* .... **86 C3** 4 40 S 34 22 E
Usutuo →, *Mozam.* .. **89 D5** 26 48 S 32 7 E
Uta, *Indonesia* ..... **63 E9** 4 33 S 136 0 E
Utah □, *U.S.A.* **108 G8** 39 20N 111 30W
Utah L., *U.S.A.* **108 F8** 40 10N 111 58W
Utansjö, *Sweden* .... **10 B11** 62 46N 17 55 E
Utara, Selat, *Malaysia* **65 c** 5 28N 100 20 E
Utarni, *India* .... **68 F4** 26 5N 71 58 E
Utattlan, *Guatemala* . **120 C1** 15 2N 91 11W
Ute Creek →, *U.S.A.* . **113 H3** 35 21N 103 50W
Utebo, *Spain* **38 D3** 41 43N 1 0W
Utena, *Lithuania* .... **9 J21** 55 27N 25 40 E
Utete, *Tanzania* ..... **86 D4** 8 0 S 38 45 E
Uthai Thani, *Thailand* **64 E3** 15 22N 100 3 E
Uthal, *Pakistan* ..... **68 G2** 25 44N 66 40 E
Utiariti, *Brazil* ..... **124 F7** 13 0 S 58 10W
Utica, *N.Y., U.S.A.* .. **117 C9** 43 6N 75 14W
Utica, *Ohio, U.S.A.* .. **116 F2** 40 14N 82 27W
Utiel, *Spain* **39 F3** 39 37N 1 11W
Utikuma L., *Canada* .. **102 B5** 55 50N 115 30W
Utö, *Sweden* .... **10 F12** 58 56N 18 16 E
Utopia, *Australia* .... **94 C1** 22 14 S 134 33 E
Utraula, *India* ...... **69 F10** 27 19N 82 25 E
Utrecht, *Neths.* ..... **17 B5** 52 5N 5 8 E
Utrecht, *S. Africa* .... **89 D5** 27 38 S 30 20 E
Utrecht □, *Neths.* .... **17 B5** 52 6N 5 7 E
Utrera, *Spain* **37 H5** 37 12N 5 48W
Utsjoki →, *Finland* .. **8 B22** 69 51N 26 59 E
Utsunomiya, *Japan* .. **55 F9** 36 30N 139 50 E
Uttar Pradesh □, *India* **69 F9** 27 0N 80 0 E
Uttaradit, *Thailand* .. **64 D3** 17 36N 100 5 E
Uttaranchal □, *India* . **69 D8** 30 0N 79 30 E
Uttoxeter, *U.K.* **14 E6** 52 54N 1 52W
Utuado, *Puerto Rico* . **121 d** 18 16N 66 42W
Uummannaq, *Greenland* **4 B4** 70 58N 52 0W
Uummannaq, *Greenland* **4 B5** 70 58N 52 0W
Uummannarsuaq =
  Nunap Isua,
  Greenland **101 C15** 59 48N 43 55W
Uusikaarlepyy, *Finland* **8 E20** 63 32N 22 31 E
Uusikaupunki, *Finland* **9 F19** 60 47N 21 25 E
Uva, *Russia* .... **34 B11** 56 59N 52 13 E
Uvac →, *Serbia & M.* . **44 C3** 43 35N 19 30 E
Uvalde, *U.S.A.* **113 L5** 29 13N 99 47W
Uvarovo, *Russia* .... **34 E6** 51 59N 42 14 E
Uvat, *Russia* .... **52 D7** 59 5N 68 50 E
Uvinza, *Tanzania* ... **86 D3** 5 5 S 30 24 E
Uvira, *Dem. Rep. of*
  the Congo .... **86 C2** 3 22 S 29 3 E
Uvs Nuur, *Mongolia* . **60 A4** 50 20N 92 30 E
'Uwairidh, Ḥarrat al,
  Si. Arabia .... **70 E3** 26 50N 38 0 E
Uwajima, *Japan* .... **55 H6** 33 10N 132 35 E
Uwanda □, *Tanzania* . **86 D3** 7 46 S 32 0 E
Uweinat, Jebel, *Sudan* **80 C1** 21 54N 24 58 E
Uxbridge, *Canada* ... **116 B5** 44 6N 79 7W
Uxin Qi, *China* ..... **56 E5** 38 50N 109 5 E
Uxmal, *Mexico* **119 C7** 20 22N 89 46W
Uydzin, *Mongolia* ... **56 B4** 44 9N 107 0 E
Uyo, *Nigeria* .... **83 D6** 5 1N 7 53 E
Üyüklü Tepe, *Turkey* . **47 D9** 37 5N 27 21 E
Uyûn Mûsa, *Egypt* .. **74 F1** 29 53N 32 40 E
Uyuni, *Bolivia* ..... **124 H5** 20 28 S 66 47W
Uzbekistan ■, *Asia* .. **52 E7** 41 30N 65 0 E
Uzen, Bolshoi →,
  Kazakhstan ...... **35 F9** 49 6N 49 56 E
Uzen, Mal →,
  Kazakhstan ...... **35 F9** 49 4N 49 44 E
Uzerche, *France* .... **20 C5** 45 25N 1 34 E
Uzès, *France* .... **21 D8** 44 4N 4 26 E
Uzh →, *Ukraine* .... **33 G6** 51 15N 30 12 E
Uzhgorod = Uzhhorod,
  Ukraine .... **28 B7** 48 36N 22 18 E
Uzhhorod, *Ukraine* .. **28 B7** 48 36N 22 18 E
Užhok, *Ukraine* ..... **28 B7** 48 59N 22 52 E
Užice, *Serbia & M.* ... **44 C3** 43 55N 19 50 E
Uzlovaya, *Russia* .... **32 F10** 54 0N 38 5 E
Üzümlü, *Turkey* .... **47 E11** 36 44N 29 14 E
Uzunköprü, *Turkey* .. **45 E10** 41 16N 26 43 E
Uzunkuyu, *Turkey* .. **47 C8** 38 17N 26 33 E

V

Vaal →, *S. Africa* .... **88 D3** 29 4 S 23 38 E
Vaal Dam, *S. Africa* .. **89 D4** 27 0 S 28 14 E
Vaalbos △, *S. Africa* . **88 D3** 28 35 S 24 20 E
Vaalwater, *S. Africa* .. **89 C4** 24 15 S 28 8 E
Vaasa, *Finland* ..... **8 E19** 63 6N 21 38 E
Vabre, *France* ...... **20 E6** 43 42N 2 24 E
Vác, *Hungary* ...... **28 C4** 47 49N 19 10 E
Vacaria, *Brazil* ..... **127 B5** 28 31 S 50 52W
Vacaville, *U.S.A.* **110 G5** 38 21N 121 59W
Vaccarès, Étang de,
  France .... **21 E8** 43 32N 4 34 E

Vach = Vakh →, *Russia* **52 C8** 60 45N 76 45 E
Vache, Î. à, *Haiti* **121 C5** 18 2N 73 35W
Väckelsång, *Sweden* .. **11 H8** 56 37N 14 58 E
Väddö, *Sweden* ..... **10 D12** 60 0N 18 50 E
Väderstad, *Sweden* ... **11 F8** 58 19N 14 55 E
Vadnagar, *India* .... **68 H5** 23 47N 72 40 E
Vado Lígure, *Italy* ... **40 D5** 44 17N 8 26 E
Vadodara, *India* .... **68 H5** 22 20N 73 10 E
Vadsø, *Norway* ..... **8 A23** 70 3N 29 50 E
Vadstena, *Sweden* ... **11 F8** 58 28N 14 54 E
Vaduz, *Liech.* ...... **25 H5** 47 8N 9 31 E
Værøy, *Norway* ..... **8 C15** 67 40N 12 40 E
Vágar, *Færoe Is.* **8 E9** 62 5N 7 15W
Vaggeryd, *Sweden* ... **11 G8** 57 30N 14 10 E
Vagney, *France* ..... **19 D13** 48 1N 6 43 E
Vagnhärad, *Sweden* .. **11 F11** 58 57N 17 33 E
Vagos, *Portugal* **36 E2** 40 33N 8 42W
Vågsfjorden, *Norway* . **8 B17** 68 50N 16 50 E
Váh →, *Slovak Rep.* .. **27 D11** 47 43N 18 7 E
Vahsel B., *Antarctica* . **5 D1** 75 0 S 35 0W
Váhtjer = Gällivare,
  Sweden .... **8 C19** 67 9N 20 40 E
Vái, *Greece* .... **49 D8** 35 15N 26 18 E
Vaigach, *Russia* .... **52 B6** 70 10N 59 0 E
Vaiges, *France* **18 D6** 48 2N 0 30W
Vaihingen, *Germany* . **25 G4** 48 54N 8 57 E
Vail, *U.S.A.* **106 C5** 39 40N 106 20W
Vailly-sur-Aisne, *France* **19 C10** 49 24N 3 31 E
Vaisali →, *India* .... **69 F8** 26 28N 78 53 E
Vaison-la-Romaine,
  France .... **21 D9** 44 14N 5 4 E
Vakarel, *Bulgaria* ... **44 D7** 42 35N 23 40 E
Vakfikebir, *Turkey* ... **73 B8** 41 3N 39 17 E
Vakh →, *Russia* ..... **52 C8** 60 45N 76 45 E
Vakhtan, *Russia* .... **34 B8** 57 53N 46 47 E
Vál, *Hungary* ...... **28 C3** 47 22N 18 40 E
Val-de-Marne □, *France* **19 D9** 48 45N 2 28 E
Val-d'Isère □, *France* . **21 C10** 45 27N 6 59 E
Val-d'Oise □, *France* . **19 C9** 49 5N 2 0 E
Val-d'Or, *Canada* ... **104 C4** 48 7N 77 47W
Val Grande △, *Italy* .. **40 B5** 46 5N 8 30 E
Val Marie, *Canada* ... **103 D7** 49 15N 107 45W
Val Thorens, *France* . **21 C10** 45 20N 6 33 E
Valaam, *Russia* ..... **32 B6** 61 22N 30 57 E
Valadares, *Portugal* .. **36 D2** 41 4N 8 38W
Valahia, *Romania* ... **29 F9** 44 35N 25 0 E
Valais □, *Switz.* ..... **25 J3** 46 12N 7 45 E
Valais, Alpes du, *Switz.* **25 J3** 46 5N 7 35 E
Valandovo, *Macedonia* **44 E6** 41 19N 22 34 E
Valašské Meziříčí,
  Czech Rep. ...... **27 B10** 49 29N 17 59 E
Valáxa, *Greece* ..... **46 C6** 38 50N 24 29 E
Vålberg, *Sweden* .... **10 E7** 59 23N 13 11 E
Valbo, *Sweden* ..... **10 D10** 60 38N 17 2 E
Valbondione, *Italy* ... **40 B7** 46 20N 10 1 E
Vălcani, *Romania* ... **28 D5** 46 0N 20 26 E
Vâlcea □, *Romania* .. **29 F8** 45 0N 24 10 E
Valchetka, *Argentina* . **128 E3** 40 40 S 66 8W
Valdagno, *Italy* ..... **41 C8** 45 39N 11 18 E
Valdahon, *France* ... **19 E13** 47 8N 6 21 E
Valdai Hills =
  Valdayskaya
  Vozvyshennost,
  Russia .... **32 D7** 57 0N 33 30 E
Valday, *Russia* ..... **32 D7** 57 58N 33 9 E
Valdayskaya
  Vozvyshennost,
  Russia .... **32 D7** 57 0N 33 30 E
Valdeazogues →, *Spain* **37 G6** 38 45N 4 55W
Valdecañas, Embalse de,
  Spain **37 F5** 39 45N 5 25W
Valdemarsvik, *Sweden* **11 F10** 58 14N 16 40 E
Valdemoro, *Spain* ... **36 E7** 40 12N 3 40W
Valdepeñas, *Spain* ... **37 G7** 38 43N 3 23W
Valderaduey →, *Spain* **36 D5** 41 31N 5 42W
Valdérice, *Italy* ..... **42 E5** 38 3N 12 37 E
Valderrobres, *Spain* .. **38 E5** 40 53N 0 9 E
Valdés, Pen., *Argentina* **128 E4** 42 30 S 63 45W
Valdez, *U.S.A.* **100 B5** 61 7N 146 16W
Valdivia, *Chile* ..... **128 D2** 39 50 S 73 14W
Valdobbiádene, *Italy* . **41 C8** 45 54N 12 0 E
Valdosta, *U.S.A.* **115 K4** 30 50N 83 17W
Valdoviño, *Spain* ... **36 B2** 43 36N 8 8W
Valdres, *Norway* .... **9 F13** 61 5N 9 5 E
Vale, *Georgia* ...... **35 K6** 41 30N 42 58 E
Vale, *U.S.A.* **108 E5** 43 59N 117 15W
Vale of Glamorgan □,
  U.K. **15 F4** 51 28N 3 25W
Valea lui Mihai,
  Romania .... **28 C7** 47 32N 22 11 E
Valea Mărului, *Romania* **29 E12** 45 49N 27 42 E
Valemount, *Canada* .. **102 C5** 52 50N 119 15W
Valença, *Brazil* ..... **125 F11** 13 20 S 39 5W
Valença, *Portugal* ... **36 C2** 42 1N 8 34W
Valença do Piauí, *Brazil* **125 E10** 6 20 S 41 45W
Valençay, *France* .... **19 E8** 47 9N 1 34 E
Valence, *France* .... **21 D8** 44 57N 4 54 E
Valence d'Agen, *France* **20 D4** 44 6N 0 53 E
Valencia, *Spain* **39 F4** 39 27N 0 23W
Valencia, *Trin. & Tob.* **125 K15** 10 39N 61 11W
Valencia, *Venezuela* . **124 A5** 10 11N 68 0W
Valencia □, *Spain* ... **39 F4** 39 20N 0 40W
Valencia ✈ (VLC),
  Spain **39 F4** 39 29N 0 26W
Valencia, G. de, *Spain* **39 F5** 39 30N 0 20 E
Valencia de Alcántara,
  Spain **37 F3** 39 25N 7 14W
Valencia de Don Juan,
  Spain **36 C5** 42 17N 5 31W
Valencia I., *Ireland* .. **12 E1** 51 54N 10 22W
Valenciennes, *France* . **19 B10** 50 20N 3 34 E
Văleni, *Romania* .... **29 F9** 44 15N 24 45 E
Vălenii de Munte,
  Romania .... **29 E11** 45 11N 26 2 E
Valensole, *France* ... **21 E9** 43 50N 5 59 E
Valentigney, *France* . **19 E13** 47 27N 6 51 E
Valentim, Sa. do, *Brazil* **125 E10** 6 0 S 43 30W
Valentine, *U.S.A.* ... **113 K2** 30 35N 104 30W
Valenza, *Italy* ...... **40 C5** 45 1N 8 38 E
Valera, *Venezuela* ... **124 B4** 9 19N 70 37W
Valga, *Estonia* ..... **9 H22** 57 47N 26 2 E
Valguarnera Caropepe,
  Italy .... **43 E7** 37 30N 14 23 E
Valier, *U.S.A.* **108 B7** 48 18N 112 16W
Valinco, G. de, *France* **21 G12** 41 40N 8 52 E
Valjevo, *Serbia & M.* . **44 B3** 44 18N 19 53 E
Valka, *Latvia* ...... **9 H21** 57 42N 25 57 E
Valkeakoski, *Finland* . **9 F20** 61 16N 24 2 E
Valkenswaard, *Neths.* **17 C5** 51 21N 5 29 E
Vall de Uxó = La Vall
  d'Uixó, *Spain* **38 F4** 39 49N 0 15W
Valladolid, *Mexico* .. **119 C7** 20 40N 88 11W
Valladolid, *Spain* ... **36 D6** 41 38N 4 43W

Valladolid □, *Spain* .. **36 D6** 41 38N 4 43W
Vallata, *Italy* ...... **43 A8** 41 2N 15 16 E
Valldemossa, *Spain* .. **48 B9** 39 43N 2 37 E
Valle d'Aosta □, *Italy* **40 C4** 45 45N 7 15 E
Valle de Arán, *Spain* . **38 C5** 42 50N 0 55 E
Valle de la Pascua,
  Venezuela **124 B5** 9 13N 66 0W
Valle de las Palmas,
  Mexico **111 N10** 32 20N 116 43W
Valle de Santiago,
  Mexico **118 C4** 20 25N 101 15W
Valle de Suchil, *Mexico* **118 C4** 23 38N 103 55W
Valle de Zaragoza,
  Mexico **118 B3** 27 28N 105 49W
Valle del Ticino △, *Italy* **40 C6** 45 22N 9 0 E
Valle Fértil, Sierra del,
  Argentina .... **126 C2** 30 20 S 68 0W
Valle Gran Rey,
  Canary Is. **48 F2** 28 5N 17 20W
Valle Hermoso, *Mexico* **119 B5** 25 35N 97 40W
Valledupar, *Colombia* . **124 A4** 10 29N 73 15W
Vallehermoso,
  Canary Is. **48 F2** 28 10N 17 15W
Vallejo, *U.S.A.* **110 G4** 38 7N 122 14W
Vallenar, *Chile* ..... **126 B1** 28 30 S 70 50W
Vallentuna, *Sweden* .. **10 E12** 59 32N 18 5 E
Valleraugue, *France* . **20 D7** 44 6N 3 39 E
Vallet, *France* **18 E5** 47 10N 1 15W
Valletta, *Malta* ..... **49 D2** 35 54N 14 31 E
Valley Center, *U.S.A.* . **111 M9** 33 13N 117 2W
Valley Falls, *Oreg.,*
  U.S.A. **108 E3** 42 29N 120 17W
Valley Falls, *R.I., U.S.A.* **117 E13** 41 54N 71 24W
Valley of the Kings,
  Egypt .... **80 B3** 25 41N 32 34 E
Valley Springs, *U.S.A.* **110 G6** 38 12N 120 50W
Valley View, *U.S.A.* .. **117 F8** 40 39N 76 33W
Valley Wells, *U.S.A.* . **111 K11** 35 27N 115 46W
Valleyview, *Canada* .. **102 B5** 55 5N 117 17W
Valli di Comácchio, *Italy* **41 D9** 44 40N 12 15 E
Vallimanca, Arroyo,
  Argentina .... **126 D4** 35 40 S 59 10W
Vallo della Lucánia,
  Italy .... **43 B8** 40 14N 15 16 E
Vallon-Pont-d'Arc,
  France .... **21 D8** 44 24N 4 24 E
Vallorbe, *Switz.* ..... **25 J2** 46 42N 6 20 E
Valls, *Spain* .... **38 D6** 41 18N 1 15 E
Valmaseda =
  Balmaseda, *Spain* . **38 B1** 43 11N 3 12W
Valmiera, *Latvia* .... **9 H21** 57 37N 25 29 E
Valnera, *Spain* **36 B7** 43 9N 3 40W
Valognes, *France* **18 C5** 49 30N 1 28W
Valona = Vlorë, *Albania* **44 F3** 40 32N 19 28 E
Valongo, *Portugal* ... **36 D2** 41 8N 8 30W
Valozhyn, *Belarus* ... **32 E4** 54 3N 26 30 E
Valpaços, *Portugal* .. **36 D3** 41 36N 7 17W
Valparaíso, *Chile* .... **126 C1** 33 2 S 71 40W
Valparaíso, *Mexico* .. **118 C4** 22 50N 103 32W
Valparaiso, *U.S.A.* ... **114 E2** 41 28N 87 4W
Valparaíso □, *Chile* .. **126 C1** 33 2 S 71 40W
Valpovo, *Croatia* .... **28 E3** 45 39N 18 25 E
Valréas, *France* ..... **21 D9** 44 24N 5 0 E
Vals, *Switz.* .... **25 J5** 46 39N 9 11 E
Vals →, *S. Africa* .... **88 D4** 27 23 S 26 30 E
Vals, Tanjung, *Indonesia* **63 F9** 8 26 S 137 25 E
Vals-les-Bains, *France* **21 D8** 44 42N 4 24 E
Valsad, *India* ...... **66 J8** 20 40N 72 58 E
Valtellina, *Italy* ..... **40 B6** 46 11N 9 55 E
Valuyki, *Russia* ..... **33 G10** 50 10N 38 5 E
Valverde, *Canary Is.* . **48 G2** 27 48N 17 55W
Valverde del Camino,
  Spain **37 H4** 37 35N 6 47W
Valverde del Fresno,
  Spain **36 E4** 40 15N 6 51W
Vama, *Romania* ..... **29 C10** 47 34N 25 42 E
Vamdrup, *Denmark* .. **11 J3** 55 25N 9 17 E
Vámhus, *Sweden* .... **10 C8** 61 7N 14 29 E
Vammala, *Finland* ... **9 F20** 61 20N 22 54 E
Vámos, *Greece* ..... **49 D6** 35 24N 24 13 E
Van, *Turkey* .... **70 B4** 38 30N 43 20 E
Van, L. = Van Gölü,
  Turkey .... **70 B4** 38 30N 43 0 E
Van Alstyne, *U.S.A.* . **113 J6** 33 25N 96 35W
Van Blommestein Meer,
  Suriname **125 C7** 4 45N 55 5W
Van Buren, *Canada* .. **105 C6** 47 10N 67 55W
Van Buren, *Ark., U.S.A.* **113 H7** 35 26N 94 21W
Van Buren, *Maine,*
  U.S.A. **115 B11** 47 10N 67 58W
Van Buren, *Mo., U.S.A.* **113 G9** 37 0N 91 1W
Van Canh, *Vietnam* .. **64 F7** 13 37N 109 0 E
Van Diemen, C.,
  N. Terr., Australia . **92 B5** 11 9 S 130 24 E
Van Diemen, C.,
  Queens., Australia . **94 B2** 16 30 S 139 46 E
Van Diemen G.,
  Australia .... **92 B5** 11 45 S 132 0 E
Van Gölü, *Turkey* ... **70 B4** 38 30N 43 0 E
Van Horn, *U.S.A.* ... **113 K2** 31 3N 104 50W
Van Ninh, *Vietnam* .. **64 F7** 12 42N 109 14 E
Van Rees, Pegunungan,
  Indonesia .... **63 E9** 2 35 S 138 15 E
Van Wert, *U.S.A.* ... **114 E3** 40 52N 84 35W
Van Yen, *Vietnam* ... **58 G5** 21 4N 104 42 E
Vanadzor, *Armenia* .. **35 K7** 40 48N 44 30 E
Vanavara, *Russia* ... **53 C11** 60 22N 102 16 E
Vancouver, *Canada* .. **102 D4** 49 15N 123 10W
Vancouver, *U.S.A.* ... **110 E4** 45 38N 122 40W
Vancouver, C., *Australia* **93 G2** 35 2 S 118 11 E
Vancouver I., *Canada* . **102 D3** 49 50N 126 0W
Vancouver
  International ✈
  (YVR), *U.S.A.* **110 A3** 49 10N 123 10W
Vanda = Vantaa,
  Finland .... **9 F21** 60 18N 24 58 E
Vandalia, *Ill., U.S.A.* . **112 F10** 38 58N 89 6W
Vandalia, *Mo., U.S.A.* **112 F9** 39 19N 91 29W
Vandenburg, *U.S.A.* . **111 L6** 34 35N 120 33W
Vanderbijlpark,
  S. Africa .... **89 D4** 26 42 S 27 54 E
Vandergrift, *U.S.A.* .. **116 F5** 40 36N 79 34W
Vanderhoof, *Canada* . **102 C4** 54 0N 124 0W
Vanderkloof Dam,
  S. Africa .... **88 E3** 30 4 S 24 40 E
Vanderlin I., *Australia* **94 B2** 15 44 S 137 2 E
Vänern, *Sweden* .... **11 F7** 58 47N 13 30 E
Vänersborg, *Sweden* . **11 F6** 58 26N 12 19 E
Vang Vieng, *Laos* ... **64 C4** 18 58N 102 32 E
Vanga, *Kenya* ...... **86 C4** 4 35 S 39 12 E
Vangaindrano, *Madag.* **89 C8** 23 21 S 47 36 E
Vanguard, *Canada* ... **103 D7** 49 55N 107 20W
Vanino, *Russia* ..... **53 E15** 48 50N 140 5 E
Vânju Mare, *Romania* **28 F7** 44 25N 22 52 E
Vanna, *Norway* ..... **8 A18** 70 6N 19 50 E

Vännäs, Sweden ...... 8 E18 63 58N 19 48 E
Vannes, France 18 E4 47 40N 2 47W
Vanoise, Massif de la,
  France .... 21 C10 45 25N 6 40 E
Vanrhynsdorp, S. Africa 88 E2 31 36 S 18 44 E
Vansbro, Sweden ..... 10 D8 60 32N 14 15 E
Vansittart B., Australia 92 B4 14 3 S 126 17 E
Vantaa, Finland ..... 9 F21 60 18N 24 58 E
Vanua Balavu, Fiji .... 91 C9 17 40 S 178 57W
Vanua Levu, Fiji ..... 91 C8 16 33 S 179 15 E
Vanuatu ■, Pac. Oc. ... 96 J8 15 0 S 168 0 E
Vanwyksvlei, S. Africa . 88 E3 30 18 S 21 49 E
Vanzylsrus, S. Africa . 88 D3 26 52 S 22 4 E
Vapnyarka, Ukraine .. 29 B13 48 32N 28 45 E
Var □, France .... 21 E10 43 27N 6 18 E
Var →, France .... 21 E11 43 39N 7 12 E
Vara, Sweden .... 11 F6 58 16N 12 55 E
Varades, France 18 E5 47 25N 1 1W
Varáita →, Italy ...... 40 D4 44 9N 7 53 E
Varallo, Italy .... 40 C5 45 49N 8 15 E
Varāmīn, Iran .... 71 C6 35 20N 51 39 E
Varāmīn □, Iran ..... 71 B6 35 18N 51 35 E
Varanasi, India ...... 69 G10 25 22N 83 0 E
Varangerfjorden,
  Norway .... 8 A23 70 3N 29 25 E
Varangerhalvøya,
  Norway .... 8 A23 70 25N 29 30 E
Varano, Lago di, Italy . 41 G12 41 53N 15 45 E
Varaždin, Croatia .... 41 B13 46 20N 16 20 E
Varazze, Italy .... 40 D5 44 22N 8 34 E
Varberg, Sweden ..... 11 G6 57 6N 12 20 E
Vardak □, Afghan. .... 66 B6 34 0N 68 0 E
Vardar = Axiós →,
  Greece .... 44 F6 40 57N 22 35 E
Varde, Denmark ..... 11 J2 55 38N 8 29 E
Varde Å →, Denmark . 11 J2 55 35N 8 19 E
Vardø, Norway .... 8 A24 70 23N 31 5 E
Varel, Germany ...... 24 B4 53 23N 8 8 E
Varella, Mui, Vietnam . 64 F7 12 54N 109 26 E
Varēna, Lithuania .... 9 J21 54 12N 24 30 E
Varennes-sur-Allier,
  France .... 19 F10 46 19N 3 24 E
Varennes-Vauzelles,
  France .... 19 E10 47 3N 3 9 E
Vareš, Bos.-H. .... 28 F3 44 12N 18 23 E
Varese, Italy .... 40 C5 45 48N 8 50 E
Vârfurile, Romania ... 28 D7 46 19N 22 31 E
Vårgårda, Sweden .... 11 F6 58 2N 12 48 E
Varginha, Brazil ..... 127 A6 21 33 S 45 25W
Vargön, Sweden ...... 11 F6 58 22N 12 20 E
Varillas, Chile .... 126 A1 24 0 S 70 10W
Varkaus, Finland .... 9 E22 62 19N 27 50 E
Värmdölandet, Sweden 10 E12 59 20N 18 33 E
Värmeln, Sweden .... 10 E6 59 35N 12 54 E
Värmlands län □,
  Sweden .... 10 E6 60 0N 13 20 E
Värmlandsbro, Sweden 10 E7 59 11N 13 0 E
Varna, Bulgaria ..... 45 C11 43 13N 27 56 E
Varna □, Bulgaria .... 45 C11 43 20N 27 30 E
Värnamo, Sweden .... 11 G8 57 10N 14 3 E
Varnsdorf, Czech Rep. . 26 A7 50 55N 14 35 E
Várpalota, Hungary .. 28 C3 47 12N 18 8 E
Vars, Canada 117 A9 45 21N 75 21W
Vars, France .... 21 D10 44 37N 6 42 E
Varto, Turkey .... 73 C9 39 10N 41 27 E
Varvarin, Serbia & M. . 44 C5 43 43N 21 20 E
Varysburg, U.S.A. 116 D6 42 46N 78 19W
Varzaneh, Iran ...... 71 C7 32 25N 52 40 E
Varzi, Italy .... 40 D6 44 49N 9 12 E
Varzo, Italy .... 40 B5 46 12N 8 15 E
Varzy, France .... 19 E10 47 22N 3 20 E
Vas □, Hungary ...... 28 C1 47 10N 16 55 E
Vasa = Vaasa, Finland . 8 E19 63 6N 21 38 E
Vasa Barris →, Brazil . 125 F11 11 10 S 37 10W
Vásárosnamény,
  Hungary .... 28 B7 48 9N 22 19 E
Vascão →, Portugal .. 37 H3 37 31N 7 31W
Vaşcău, Romania .... 28 D7 46 28N 22 30 E
Vascongadas = País
  Vasco □, Spain 38 C2 42 50N 2 45W
Vashkivtsi, Ukraine .. 29 B10 48 23N 25 31 E
Vasht = Khāsh, Iran .. 66 E2 28 15N 61 15 E
Vasilevichi, Belarus .. 33 F5 52 15N 29 50 E
Vasilikón, Greece .... 46 C5 38 25N 23 40 E
Vasilkov = Vasylkiv,
  Ukraine .... 33 G6 50 7N 30 15 E
Vaslui, Romania ..... 29 D12 46 38N 27 42 E
Vaslui □, Romania ... 29 D12 46 30N 27 45 E
Väsman, Sweden .... 10 D9 60 9N 15 5 E
Vassar, Canada 103 D9 49 10N 95 55W
Vassar, U.S.A. 114 D4 43 22N 83 35W
Västerbotten, Sweden . 8 D16 64 36N 20 4 E
Västerdalälven →,
  Sweden .... 10 D8 60 30N 14 7 E
Västergötland, Sweden 11 F7 58 0N 13 10 E
Västerhaninge, Sweden 10 E12 59 7N 18 6 E
Västervik, Sweden ... 11 G10 57 43N 16 33 E
Västmanland, Sweden 9 G16 59 45N 16 20 E
Västmanlands län □,
  Sweden .... 11 F6 59 45N 16 20 E
Vasto, Italy .... 41 F11 42 8N 14 40 E
Västra Götalands
  Län □, Sweden .... 11 F6 58 0N 13 0 E
Vasvár, Hungary .... 28 C1 47 3N 16 47 E
Vasylkiv, Ukraine ... 29 E13 45 38N 28 50 E
Vasylkiv, Ukraine ... 33 G6 50 7N 30 15 E
Vatan, France .... 19 E8 47 4N 1 50 E
Vatersay, U.K. 13 E1 56 55N 7 32W
Váthia, Greece ...... 46 E4 36 29N 22 29 E
Vatican City ■, Europe 41 G9 41 54N 12 27 E
Vaticano, C., Italy ... 43 D8 38 37N 15 50 E
Vatili, Cyprus .... 49 D12 35 6N 33 40 E
Vatin, Serbia & M. ... 28 E6 45 12N 21 20 E
Vatnajökull, Iceland . 8 D5 64 30N 16 48W
Vatoa, Fiji .... 91 D9 19 50 S 178 13W
Vatólakkos, Greece ... 49 D5 35 27N 23 53 E
Vatoloha, Madag. .... 89 B8 17 52 S 47 48 E
Vatra-Dornei, Romania 29 C10 47 22N 25 22 E
Vatrak →, India ..... 68 H5 23 9N 73 2 E
Vättern, Sweden ..... 11 F8 58 25N 14 30 E
Vaucluse □, France .. 21 E9 44 3N 5 10 E
Vaucouleurs, France . 19 D12 48 37N 5 40 E
Vaud □, Switz. ...... 25 J2 46 35N 6 30 E
Vaudreuil-Dorion,
  Canada 117 A10 45 23N 74 2W
Vaughn, Mont., U.S.A. 108 C8 47 33N 111 33W
Vaughn, N. Mex., U.S.A. 109 J11 34 36N 105 13W
Vaujours L., Canada . 104 A5 55 27N 74 15W
Vaupés = Uaupés →,
  Brazil 124 C5 0 2N 67 16W
Vaupés □, Colombia .. 124 C4 1 0N 71 0W
Vauvert, France ..... 21 E8 43 42N 4 17 E
Vauxhall, Canada 102 C6 50 5N 112 9W
Vav, India .... 68 G4 24 22N 71 31 E

Vavatenina, Madag. .. 89 B8 17 28 S 49 12 E
Vava'u, Tonga ...... 91 D12 18 36 S 174 0W
Vavoua, Ivory C. 82 D3 7 23N 6 29W
Vawkavysk, Belarus .. 33 F3 53 9N 24 30 E
Vaxholm, Sweden ... 10 E12 59 25N 18 20 E
Växjö, Sweden ...... 11 H8 56 52N 14 50 E
Växtorp, Sweden .... 11 H7 56 25N 13 8 E
Vaygach, Ostrov, Russia 52 C6 70 0N 60 0 E
Váyia, Greece ...... 46 C5 38 19N 23 11 E
Váyia, Ákra, Greece .. 49 C10 36 15N 28 11 E
Veaikevárri =
  Svappavaara, Sweden 8 C19 67 40N 21 3 E
Vechelde, Germany .. 24 C6 52 16N 10 22 E
Vechta, Germany .... 24 C4 52 44N 8 17 E
Vechte →, Neths. .... 17 B6 52 34N 6 6 E
Vecsés, Hungary .... 28 C4 47 26N 19 19 E
Veddige, Sweden .... 11 G6 57 17N 12 20 E
Vedea →, Romania ... 29 G10 43 42N 25 41 E
Vedia, Argentina .... 126 C3 34 30 S 61 31W
Vedrette di Ries-
  Aurina △, Italy .... 41 B9 46 54N 12 5 E
Vedum, Sweden ..... 11 F7 58 11N 13 0 E
Veendam, Neths. .... 17 A6 53 5N 6 52 E
Veenendaal, Neths. .. 17 B5 52 2N 5 34 E
Vefsna →, Norway ... 8 D15 65 48N 13 10 E
Vega, Norway ...... 8 D14 65 40N 11 55 E
Vega, U.S.A. 113 H3 35 15N 102 26W
Vega Baja, Puerto Rico 121 d 18 27N 66 23W
Vegadeo, Spain 36 B3 43 27N 7 4W
Vegorrítis, Límni,
  Greece .... 44 F5 40 45N 21 45 E
Vegreville, Canada .. 102 C6 53 30N 112 5W
Veinge, Sweden ..... 11 H7 56 33N 13 4 E
Veisiejai, Lithuania .. 9 J20 54 6N 23 42 E
Vejbystrand, Sweden . 11 H6 56 19N 12 45 E
Vejen, Denmark ..... 11 J3 55 30N 9 9 E
Vejer de la Frontera,
  Spain 37 J5 36 15N 5 59W
Vejle, Denmark ..... 11 J3 55 43N 9 30 E
Vejle Amtskommune □,
  Denmark .... 11 J3 55 45N 9 20 E
Vejle Fjord, Denmark . 11 J3 55 40N 9 50 E
Vela Luka, Croatia ... 41 F13 42 59N 16 44 E
Velas, C., Costa Rica . 120 D2 10 21N 85 52W
Velasco, Sierra de,
  Argentina .... 126 B2 29 20 S 67 10W
Velay, Mts. du, France 20 D7 45 0N 3 40 E
Velbert, Germany ... 24 D3 51 20N 7 3 E
Velddrif, S. Africa ... 88 E2 32 42 S 18 11 E
Velebit △, Croatia ... 41 D12 44 50N 15 15 E
Velebit Planina, Croatia 41 D12 44 50N 15 20 E
Velebitski Kanal,
  Croatia .... 41 D11 44 45N 14 55 E
Veleka →, Bulgaria .. 45 D11 42 4N 27 58 E
Velenci-tó, Hungary .. 28 C3 47 13N 18 36 E
Velenje, Slovenia .... 41 B12 46 23N 15 8 E
Veles, Macedonia .... 44 E5 41 46N 21 47 E
Velestínon, Greece ... 46 B4 39 23N 22 43 E
Vélez-Málaga, Spain . 37 J6 36 48N 4 5W
Vélez Rubio, Spain ... 39 H2 37 41N 2 5W
Velhas →, Brazil .... 125 G10 17 13 S 44 49W
Velika, Croatia ...... 28 E2 45 27N 17 40 E
Velika Gorica, Croatia 41 C13 45 44N 16 5 E
Velika Kapela, Croatia 41 C12 45 10N 15 5 E
Velika Kladuša, Bos.-H. 41 C12 45 11N 15 48 E
Velika Kruša,
  Serbia & M. ...... 44 D4 42 19N 20 39 E
Velika Morava →,
  Serbia & M. ...... 44 B5 44 43N 21 3 E
Velika Plana,
  Serbia & M. ...... 44 B5 44 20N 21 1 E
Velikaya →, Russia .. 32 D5 57 48N 28 10 E
Velikaya Kema, Russia 54 B8 45 30N 137 12 E
Velikaya Lepetikha,
  Ukraine .... 33 J7 47 2N 33 58 E
Veliké Kapušany,
  Slovak Rep. ...... 27 C15 48 34N 22 5 E
Velike Lašče, Slovenia 41 C11 45 49N 14 45 E
Veliki Jastrebac,
  Serbia & M. ...... 44 C5 43 25N 21 30 E
Veliki Kanal,
  Serbia & M. ...... 28 E4 45 45N 19 15 E
Veliki Popović,
  Serbia & M. ...... 44 B5 44 8N 21 18 E
Velikiye Luki, Russia . 32 D6 56 25N 30 32 E
Veliko Gradište,
  Serbia & M. ...... 44 B5 44 46N 21 29 E
Veliko Tŭrnovo,
  Bulgaria .... 45 C9 43 5N 25 41 E
Velikonda Range, India 66 M11 14 45N 79 10 E
Vélingara, Kolda,
  Senegal 82 C2 13 12N 14 5W
Vélingara, Louga,
  Senegal 82 B2 15 0N 14 40W
Velingrad, Bulgaria .. 44 D7 42 4N 23 58 E
Velino, Mte., Italy ... 41 F10 42 9N 13 23 E
Velizh, Russia ...... 32 E6 55 36N 31 11 E
Velké Karlovice,
  Czech Rep. .... 27 B11 49 20N 18 17 E
Velké Meziříčí,
  Czech Rep. .... 26 B9 49 21N 16 1 E
Vel'ký Javorník,
  Slovak Rep. ...... 27 B11 49 19N 18 22 E
Vel'ký Krtíš,
  Slovak Rep. ...... 27 C12 48 12N 19 21 E
Vel'ký Meder,
  Slovak Rep. ...... 27 D10 47 52N 17 46 E
Vel'ký Tribeč,
  Slovak Rep. ...... 27 C11 48 28N 18 15 E
Velletri, Italy .... 42 A5 41 41N 12 47 E
Vellinge, Sweden .... 11 J6 55 29N 13 0 E
Vellmar, Germany ... 24 D5 51 22N 9 28 E
Vellore, India .... 66 N11 12 57N 79 10 E
Veluwezoom △, Neths. 17 B6 52 5N 6 0 E
Velva, U.S.A. 112 A4 48 4N 100 56W
Velvendós, Greece ... 44 F6 40 15N 22 6 E
Velyka Mykhaylivka,
  Ukraine .... 29 C14 47 4N 29 52 E
Velyki Luchky, Ukraine 28 B7 48 25N 22 34 E
Velykyy Bereznyy,
  Ukraine .... 28 B7 48 54N 22 28 E
Velykyy Bychkiv,
  Ukraine .... 29 C7 47 58N 24 1 E
Vemb, Denmark ..... 11 H2 56 21N 8 21 E
Vemdalen, Sweden .. 10 B7 62 27N 13 51 E
Ven, Sweden .... 11 J6 55 55N 12 45 E
Venado, Italy .... 21 F13 42 14N 9 11 E
Venado Tuerto,
  Argentina .... 126 C3 33 50 S 62 0W
Venango, U.S.A. .... 112 E3 41 23N 103 37 E
Venaria, Italy ...... 40 C4 45 8N 7 38 E
Vençane, Serbia & M. . 44 B4 44 24N 20 28 E

Vence, France ...... 21 E11 43 43N 7 6 E
Vendas Novas, Portugal 37 G2 38 39N 8 27W
Vendée □, France ... 18 F5 46 50N 1 35W
Vendée →, France ... 18 F5 46 20N 1 10W
Vendéen, Bocage,
  France 20 B2 46 40N 1 20W
Vendeuvre-sur-Barse,
  France .... 19 D11 48 14N 4 28 E
Vendôme, France ... 18 E8 47 47N 1 3 E
Vendrell = El Vendrell,
  Spain .... 38 D6 41 10N 1 30 E
Vendsyssel, Denmark 11 G4 57 22N 10 0 E
Vendychany, Ukraine 29 B12 48 38N 27 48 E
Venelles, France .... 21 E9 43 35N 5 28 E
Véneta, L., Italy .... 41 C9 45 23N 12 25 E
Véneto □, Italy ..... 41 C9 45 40N 12 0 E
Venev, Russia ...... 32 E10 54 22N 38 17 E
Venézia, Italy ...... 41 C9 45 27N 12 21 E
Venézia, G. di, Italy .. 41 C10 45 15N 13 0 E
Venezuela ■, S. Amer. 124 B5 8 0N 66 0W
Venezuela, G. de,
  Venezuela 124 A4 11 30N 71 0W
Vengurla, India ..... 66 M8 15 53N 73 45 E
Venice = Venézia, Italy 41 C9 45 27N 12 21 E
Venice, U.S.A. 115 M4 27 6N 82 27W
Vénissieux, France .. 21 C8 45 42N 4 53 E
Venjansjön, Sweden . 10 D8 60 54N 14 0 E
Venkatapuram, India . 67 K12 18 20N 80 30 E
Venlo, Neths. ...... 17 C6 51 22N 6 11 E
Vennesla, Norway ... 9 G12 58 15N 7 59 E
Venosa, Italy .... 43 B8 40 58N 15 49 E
Venray, Neths. ..... 17 C6 51 31N 6 0 E
Venta, Lithuania .... 30 B9 56 12N 22 42 E
Venta →, Latvia .... 30 A8 57 24N 21 33 E
Venta de Baños, Spain 36 D6 41 55N 4 30W
Venta de Cardeña =
  Cardeña, Spain 37 G6 38 16N 4 20W
Ventana, Punta de la,
  Mexico 118 C3 24 4N 109 48W
Ventana, Sa. de la,
  Argentina .... 126 D3 38 0 S 62 30W
Ventersburg, S. Africa 88 D4 28 7 S 27 9 E
Venterstad, S. Africa . 88 E4 30 47 S 25 48 E
Ventimiglia, Italy ... 40 E4 43 47N 7 36 E
Ventnor, U.K. 15 G6 50 36N 1 12W
Ventoténe, Italy .... 42 B6 40 47N 13 25 E
Ventoux, Mt., France 21 D9 44 10N 5 17 E
Ventspils, Latvia .... 9 H19 57 25N 21 32 E
Ventspils □, Latvia .. 30 A8 57 20N 21 50 E
Ventuari →, Venezuela 124 C5 3 58N 67 2W
Ventucopa, U.S.A. ... 111 L7 34 50N 119 29W
Ventura, U.S.A. 111 L7 34 17N 119 18W
Venus B., Australia .. 95 F4 38 40 S 145 42 E
Vera, Argentina ..... 126 B3 29 30 S 60 20W
Vera, Spain 39 H3 37 15N 1 51W
Veracruz, Mexico 119 D5 19 10N 96 10W
Veracruz □, Mexico .. 119 D5 19 10N 96 15W
Veraval, India ...... 68 J4 20 53N 70 27 E
Verbánia, Italy ..... 40 C5 45 56N 8 33 E
Verbicaro, Italy ..... 43 C8 39 45N 15 55 E
Verbier, Switz. ...... 25 J3 46 6N 7 13 E
Vercelli, Italy ...... 40 C5 45 19N 8 25 E
Verchovchevo, Ukraine 33 H8 48 32N 34 10 E
Vercors □, France ... 21 D9 45 0N 5 25 E
Verdalsøra, Norway .. 8 E14 63 48N 11 30 E
Verde →, Argentina .. 128 E3 41 56 S 65 5W
Verde →, Goiás, Brazil 125 G8 18 1 S 50 14W
Verde →,
  Mato Grosso do Sul,
  Brazil .... 125 H8 21 25 S 52 20W
Verde →, Chihuahua,
  Mexico 118 B3 26 29N 107 58W
Verde →, Oaxaca,
  Mexico 119 D5 15 59N 97 50W
Verde →, Veracruz,
  Mexico 118 C4 21 10N 102 50W
Verde →, Paraguay .. 126 A4 23 9 S 57 37W
Verde →, U.S.A. 106 D4 33 33N 111 40W
Verde, Cay, Bahamas . 120 B4 23 0N 75 5W
Verde Island Pass, Phil. 61 E4 13 34N 120 51 E
Verden, Germany ... 24 C5 52 55N 9 14 E
Verdhikoúsa, Greece . 46 B3 39 47N 21 59 E
Verdi, U.S.A. 110 F7 39 31N 119 59W
Verdon →, France .. 21 E10 43 50N 6 5 E
Verdon-sur-Mer, France 20 C2 45 33N 1 4W
Verdun, France ..... 19 C12 49 9N 5 24 E
Verdun-sur-le-Doubs,
  France .... 19 F12 46 54N 5 2 E
Vereeniging, S. Africa 89 D4 26 38 S 27 57 E
Verga, C., Guinea ... 82 C2 10 30N 14 10W
Vergara, Uruguay ... 127 C5 32 56 S 53 57W
Vergato, Italy ...... 40 D8 44 17N 11 7 E
Vergemont Cr. →,
  Australia .... 94 C3 24 16 S 143 16 E
Vergennes, U.S.A. ... 117 B11 44 10N 73 15W
Vergt, France ...... 20 C4 45 2N 0 43 E
Verín, Spain 36 D3 41 57N 7 27W
Verkhnedvinsk =
  Vyerkhnyadzvinsk,
  Belarus .... 32 E4 55 45N 27 58 E
Verkhnevilyuysk, Russia 53 C13 63 27N 120 18 E
Verkhniy Baskunchak,
  Russia .... 35 F8 48 14N 46 44 E
Verkhovyna, Ukraine 29 B9 48 9N 24 47 E
Verkhoyansk, Russia . 53 C14 67 35N 133 25 E
Verkhoyansk Ra. =
  Verkhoyanskiy
  Khrebet, Russia .... 53 C13 66 0N 129 0 E
Verkhoyanskiy Khrebet,
  Russia .... 53 C13 66 0N 129 0 E
Vermenton, France .. 19 E10 47 40N 3 42 E
Vermilion, Canada .. 103 C6 53 20N 110 50W
Vermilion, U.S.A. ... 116 E2 41 25N 82 22W
Vermilion →, Canada 103 C6 53 22N 110 51W
Vermilion Bay, Canada 103 D10 49 51N 93 34W
Vermilion L., U.S.A. . 112 B8 47 53N 92 26W
Vermillion, U.S.A. .. 112 D6 42 47N 96 56W
Vermillion →, Canada 104 C5 47 38N 72 56W
Vermont □, U.S.A. .. 117 C12 44 0N 73 0W
Vermosh, Albania ... 44 D3 42 35N 19 42 E
Vernadsky, Antarctica 5 C17 65 0 S 64 0W
Vernal, U.S.A. 108 F9 40 27N 109 32W
Vernalis, U.S.A. 110 H5 37 36N 121 17W
Vernazza, Italy ..... 40 D6 44 10N 9 45 E
Verner, Canada 104 C3 46 25N 80 8W
Verneuil-sur-Avre,
  France .... 18 D7 48 45N 0 55 E
Verneukpan, S. Africa 88 E3 30 0 S 21 0 E
Vernier, Switz. ..... 25 J2 46 11N 6 6 E
Vérnio, Italy .... 43 A7 41 29N 14 2 E
Vernon, Canada 102 C5 50 20N 119 15W
Vernon, France ..... 18 C8 49 5N 1 30 E
Vernon, U.S.A. 113 H5 34 9N 99 17W
Vernonia, U.S.A. ... 110 E3 45 52N 123 11W

Vernouillet, France .. 18 D8 48 58N 1 58 E
Vero Beach, U.S.A. .. 115 M5 27 38N 80 24W
Véroia, Greece ..... 44 F6 40 34N 22 12 E
Véroli, Italy .... 41 G10 41 41N 13 25 E
Verona, Canada 117 B8 44 29N 76 42W
Verona, Italy .... 40 C7 45 27N 10 59 E
Verona, U.S.A. 112 D10 42 59N 89 32W
Verrès, Italy .... 40 C4 45 40N 7 42 E
Versailles, France ... 19 D9 48 48N 2 8 E
Versmold, Germany . 24 C4 52 2N 8 9 E
Vert, C., Senegal 82 C1 14 45N 17 30W
Vertou, France 18 E5 47 10N 1 28W
Vertus, France ...... 19 D11 48 54N 4 2 E
Verulam, S. Africa .. 89 D5 29 38 S 31 2 E
Verviers, Belgium ... 17 D5 50 37N 5 52 E
Vervins, France ..... 19 C10 49 50N 3 53 E
Veržej, Slovenia ..... 41 B13 46 34N 16 13 E
Verzy, France ...... 19 C11 49 9N 4 10 E
Vescovato, France ... 21 F13 42 30N 9 27 E
Veselí nad Lužnicí,
  Czech Rep. .... 26 B7 49 12N 14 43 E
Veselie, Bulgaria .... 45 D11 42 18N 27 38 E
Veselovskoye Vdkhr.,
  Russia .... 35 G5 46 58N 41 25 E
Veshenskaya, Russia . 34 F5 49 35N 41 44 E
Vesle →, France ..... 19 C10 49 23N 3 28 E
Vesoul, France ..... 19 E13 47 40N 6 11 E
Vessigebro, Sweden . 11 H6 56 58N 12 40 E
Vesterålen, Norway . 8 B16 68 45N 15 0 E
Vestfjorden, Norway . 8 C15 67 55N 14 0 E
Vestmannaeyjar, Iceland 8 E3 63 27N 20 15W
Vestsjællands
  Amtskommune □,
  Denmark .... 11 J5 55 30N 11 20 E
Vestspitsbergen,
  Svalbard .... 4 B8 78 40N 17 0 E
Vestvågøy, Norway .. 8 B15 68 18N 13 50 E
Vesuvio, Italy ...... 43 B7 40 49N 14 26 E
Vesuvius, Mt. = Vesuvio,
  Italy .... 43 B7 40 49N 14 26 E
Vesyegonsk, Russia .. 32 C9 58 40N 37 16 E
Veszprém, Hungary .. 28 C2 47 8N 17 57 E
Veszprém □, Hungary 28 C2 47 5N 17 55 E
Vésztő, Hungary .... 28 D6 46 55N 21 16 E
Vetlanda, Sweden ... 11 G9 57 24N 15 3 E
Vetluga, Russia ..... 34 B7 57 53N 45 45 E
Vetlugu →, Russia ... 34 B8 56 36N 46 4 E
Vetluzhskiy, Kostroma,
  Russia .... 34 B7 57 17N 45 12 E
Vetluzhskiy,
  Nizhniy Novgorod,
  Russia .... 34 B7 57 17N 45 12 E
Vetovo, Bulgaria .... 45 C10 43 42N 26 16 E
Vetralla, Italy ...... 41 F9 42 20N 12 2 E
Vetren, Bulgaria .... 45 D8 42 15N 24 3 E
Vettore, Mte., Italy .. 41 F10 42 49N 13 16 E
Veurne, Belgium .... 17 C2 51 5N 2 40 E
Veveno →, Sudan ... 81 F3 6 40N 32 58 E
Vevey, Switz. .... 25 J2 46 28N 6 51 E
Vévi, Greece .... 44 F5 40 47N 21 38 E
Veynes, France ..... 21 D9 44 32N 5 49 E
Veys, Iran .... 71 D6 31 30N 49 0 E
Vézelay, France ..... 19 E10 47 27N 3 45 E
Vézelise, France .... 19 D13 48 30N 6 5 E
Vézère →, France ... 20 D4 44 53N 0 53 E
Vezhen, Bulgaria .... 45 D8 42 50N 24 20 E
Vezirköprü, Turkey .. 72 B6 41 8N 35 27 E
Vezzani, France ..... 21 F13 42 10N 9 15 E
Vi Thanh, Vietnam .. 65 H5 9 42N 105 26 E
Viacha, Bolivia ..... 124 G5 16 39 S 68 18W
Viadana, Italy ...... 40 D7 44 56N 10 30 E
Viamão, Brazil ..... 127 C5 30 5 S 51 0W
Viana, Brazil .... 125 D10 3 13 S 44 55W
Viana, Spain 38 C2 42 31N 2 22W
Viana do Alentejo,
  Portugal 37 G3 38 17N 7 59W
Viana do Bolo, Spain 36 C3 42 11N 7 6W
Viana do Castelo,
  Portugal 36 D2 41 42N 8 50W
Viana do Castelo □,
  Portugal 36 D2 41 50N 8 30W
Vianden, Lux. ...... 17 E6 49 56N 6 12 E
Viangchan = Vientiane,
  Laos .... 64 D4 17 58N 102 36 E
Vianópolis, Brazil ... 125 G9 16 40 S 48 35W
Viar →, Spain 37 H5 37 36N 5 50W
Viaréggio, Italy ..... 40 E7 43 52N 10 14 E
Viaur →, France .... 20 D5 44 8N 1 58 E
Vibble, Sweden ..... 11 G12 57 37N 18 16 E
Vibo Valéntia, Italy .. 43 D9 38 40N 16 6 E
Viborg, Denmark .... 11 H3 56 27N 9 23 E
Viborg
  Amtskommune □,
  Denmark .... 11 H3 56 30N 9 10 E
Vibraye, France ..... 18 D7 48 3N 0 44 E
Vic, France .... 20 E7 43 29N 3 50 E
Vic-en-Bigorre, France 20 E4 43 24N 0 3 E
Vic-Fezensac, France . 20 E4 43 47N 0 19 E
Vic-le-Comte, France 19 G10 45 39N 3 14 E
Vic-sur-Cère, France . 20 D6 44 59N 2 38 E
Vícar, Spain 39 J2 36 50N 2 38W
Vicenza, Italy ...... 41 C8 45 33N 11 33 E
Vich = Vic, Spain ... 38 D7 41 58N 2 19 E
Vichada →, Colombia 124 C5 4 55N 67 50W
Vichuga, Russia ..... 34 B5 57 12N 41 55 E
Vichy, France ...... 19 F10 46 9N 3 26 E
Vicksburg, Ariz., U.S.A. 111 M13 33 45N 113 45W
Vicksburg, Miss., U.S.A. 113 J9 32 21N 90 53W
Vico, France .... 21 F12 42 10N 8 49 E
Vico, L. di, Italy .... 41 F9 42 20N 12 10 E
Vico del Gargano, Italy 41 G12 41 54N 15 57 E
Vicovu de Sus, Romania 29 C10 47 56N 25 41 E
Victor, India .... 68 J4 21 0N 71 30 E
Victor, U.S.A. 116 D7 42 58N 77 24W
Victor Harbor, Australia 95 F2 35 30 S 138 37 E
Victoria, Argentina .. 126 C3 32 40 S 60 10W
Victoria, Chile ..... 128 D2 38 13 S 72 20W
Victoria, Malta ..... 49 C1 36 3N 14 14 E
Victoria, Phil. ...... 61 D4 15 35N 120 41 E
Victoria, Romania ... 29 E9 45 44N 24 41 E
Victoria, Kans., U.S.A. 112 F5 38 52N 99 9W
Victoria, Tex., U.S.A. . 113 L6 28 48N 97 0W
Victoria □, Australia . 95 F3 37 0 S 144 0 E
Victoria →, Australia 92 C4 15 10 S 129 40 E
Victoria, Grand L.,
  Canada 104 C4 47 31N 77 30W
Victoria, L., Africa .. 86 C3 1 0 S 33 0 E
Victoria, L., Australia 95 E3 33 57 S 141 15 E
Victoria, Mt., Burma . 67 J18 21 15N 93 55 E
Victoria Beach, Canada 103 C9 50 40N 96 35W
Victoria de Durango =
  Durango, Mexico .. 118 C4 24 3N 104 39W
Victoria de las Tunas,
  Cuba 120 B4 20 58N 76 59W

Victoria Falls,
  Zimbabwe .... 87 F2 17 58 S 25 52 E
Victoria Harbour,
  Canada 116 B5 44 45N 79 45W
Victoria I., Canada .. 100 A8 71 0N 111 0W
Victoria L., Canada .. 105 C8 48 20N 57 27W
Victoria Ld., Antarctica 5 D11 75 0 S 160 0 E
Victoria Nile →,
  Uganda .... 86 B3 2 14N 31 26 E
Victoria River, Australia 92 C5 16 25 S 131 0 E
Victoria Str., Canada . 100 B9 69 31N 100 30W
Victoria West, S. Africa 88 E3 31 25 S 23 4 E
Victorias, Phil. ..... 61 F5 10 54N 123 5 E
Victoriaville, Canada 105 C5 46 4N 71 56W
Victorica, Argentina . 126 D2 36 20 S 65 30W
Victorville, U.S.A. ... 111 L9 34 32N 117 18W
Vicuña, Chile ...... 126 C1 30 0 S 70 50W
Vicuña Mackenna,
  Argentina .... 126 C3 33 53 S 64 25W
Vidal, U.S.A. 111 L12 34 7N 114 31W
Vidal Junction, U.S.A. 111 L12 34 11N 114 34W
Vidalia, U.S.A. 115 J4 32 13N 82 25W
Vidamlya, Belarus ... 31 F10 52 19N 23 47 E
Vidauban, France ... 21 E10 43 25N 6 27 E
Videbæk, Denmark .. 11 H2 56 6N 8 38 E
Videle, Romania .... 29 F10 44 17N 25 31 E
Vídho, Greece ...... 49 A3 39 38N 19 55 E
Vidigueira, Portugal . 37 G3 38 12N 7 48W
Vidin, Bulgaria ..... 44 C6 43 59N 22 50 E
Vidio, C., Spain 36 B4 43 35N 6 14W
Vidisha, India ...... 68 H7 23 28N 77 53 E
Vidra, Romania ..... 29 E11 45 56N 26 55 E
Viduša, Bos.-H. ..... 44 D2 42 55N 18 21 E
Vidzy, Belarus ...... 9 J22 55 23N 26 37 E
Viechtach, Germany . 25 F8 49 4N 12 53 E
Viedma, Argentina .. 128 E4 40 50 S 63 0W
Viedma, L., Argentina 128 F2 49 30 S 72 30W
Vieira do Minho,
  Portugal 36 D2 41 38N 8 8W
Vielha, Spain ...... 38 C5 42 43N 0 44 E
Viella = Vielha, Spain 38 C5 42 43N 0 44 E
Vielsalm, Belgium ... 17 D5 50 17N 5 54 E
Vienenburg, Germany 24 D6 51 57N 10 34 E
Vienna = Wien, Austria 27 C9 48 12N 16 22 E
Vienna, Ill., U.S.A. .. 113 G10 37 25N 88 54W
Vienna, Mo., U.S.A. . 112 F9 38 11N 91 57W
Vienne, France ..... 21 C8 45 31N 4 53 E
Vienne □, France ... 20 B4 46 30N 0 42 E
Vienne →, France ... 18 E7 47 13N 0 5 E
Vientiane, Laos ..... 64 D4 17 58N 102 36 E
Vientos, Paso de los,
  Caribbean 121 C5 20 0N 74 0W
Vieques, Isla de,
  Puerto Rico .... 121 d 18 8N 65 25W
Vierge Pt., St. Lucia . 121 f 13 49N 60 53W
Viernheim, Germany 25 F4 49 31N 8 35 E
Viersen, Germany ... 24 D2 51 15N 6 23 E
Vierwaldstättersee,
  Switz. .... 25 J4 47 0N 8 30 E
Vierzon, France ..... 19 E9 47 13N 2 5 E
Vieste, Italy .... 41 G13 41 53N 16 10 E
Vietnam ■, Asia .... 64 C6 19 0N 106 0 E
Vieux-Boucau-les-Bains,
  France 20 E2 43 48N 1 23W
Vieux Fort, St. Lucia . 121 f 13 46N 60 58W
Vif, France .... 21 C9 45 5N 5 41 E
Vigan, Phil. .... 61 C4 17 35N 120 28 E
Vigévano, Italy ..... 40 C5 45 19N 8 51 E
Vigia, Brazil .... 125 D9 0 50 S 48 5W
Vigía Chico, Mexico . 119 D7 19 46N 87 35W
Víglas, Ákra, Greece . 49 D9 35 54N 27 51 E
Vignemale, France .. 20 F3 42 47N 0 10W
Vigneulles-lès-
  Hattonchâtel, France 19 D12 48 59N 5 43 E
Vignola, Italy ...... 40 D8 44 29N 11 1 E
Vigo, Spain 36 C2 42 12N 8 41W
Vigo, Ría de, Spain .. 36 C2 42 15N 8 45W
Vigsø Bugt, Denmark 11 G2 57 8N 8 47 E
Vihiers, France 18 E6 47 10N 0 30W
Vihowa, Pakistan ... 68 D4 31 8N 70 30 E
Vihowa →, Pakistan . 68 D4 31 8N 70 41 E
Vijayawada, India ... 67 L12 16 31N 80 39 E
Vijosë →, Albania ... 44 F3 40 37N 19 24 E
Vík, Iceland 8 E4 63 25N 19 1W
Vika, Sweden ...... 10 D8 60 57N 14 28 E
Vikarbyn, Sweden .. 10 D9 60 55N 15 1 E
Vikeke = Viqueque,
  E. Timor .... 63 F7 8 52 S 126 23 E
Viken, Skåne, Sweden 11 H6 56 9N 12 34 E
Viken, Västra Götaland,
  Sweden .... 11 F8 58 39N 14 20 E
Viking, Canada 102 C6 53 7N 111 50W
Vikmanshyttan, Sweden 10 D9 60 18N 15 50 E
Vikna, Norway ..... 8 D14 64 55N 10 58 E
Vikos-Aoos △, Greece 46 B2 40 0N 20 45 E
Vila da Maganja,
  Mozam. .... 87 F4 17 18 S 37 30 E
Vila de Rei, Portugal . 36 F2 39 41N 8 9W
Vila do Bispo, Portugal 37 H2 37 5N 8 53W
Vila do Conde, Portugal 36 D2 41 21N 8 45W
Vila Franca de Xira,
  Portugal 37 G2 38 57N 8 59W
Vila Gamito, Mozam. 87 E3 14 12 S 33 0 E
Vila Gomes da Costa,
  Mozam. .... 89 C5 24 20 S 33 37 E
Vila Machado, Mozam. 87 F3 19 15 S 34 14 E
Vila Mouzinho, Mozam. 87 E3 14 48 S 34 25 E
Vila Nova de Famalicão,
  Portugal 36 D2 41 25N 8 32W
Vila Nova de Fos Côa,
  Portugal 36 D3 41 5N 7 9W
Vila Nova de Gaia,
  Portugal 36 D2 41 4N 8 40W
Vila Nova de Ourém,
  Portugal 36 F2 39 40N 8 35W
Vila Pouca de Aguiar,
  Portugal 36 D3 41 30N 7 38W
Vila Real, Portugal .. 36 D3 41 17N 7 48W
Vila Real □, Portugal 36 D3 41 36N 7 35W
Vila-real de los Infantes,
  Spain 38 F4 39 55N 0 3W
Vila Real de Santo
  António, Portugal .. 37 H3 37 10N 7 28W
Vila Vasco da Gama,
  Mozam. .... 87 E3 14 54 S 32 14 E
Vila Velha, Brazil ... 127 A7 20 20 S 40 17W
Vila Viçosa, Portugal 37 G3 38 45N 7 27W
Vilafranca del Maestrat,
  Spain 38 E4 40 26N 0 16W
Vilafranca del Penedès,
  Spain .... 38 D6 41 21N 1 40 E
Vilagarcía de Arousa,
  Spain 36 C2 42 34N 8 46W
Vilaine →, France ... 18 E4 47 30N 2 27W
Vilanandro, Tanjona,
  Madag. .... 89 B7 16 11 S 44 27 E

Vilanculos, *Mozam.* ... 89 C6 22 1 S 35 17 E
Vilanova de Castelló, *Spain* ... 39 F4 39 5N 0 31W
Vilanova i la Geltrú, *Spain* ... 38 D6 41 13N 1 40 E
Vilar Formosa, *Portugal* 36 E4 40 38N 6 45W
Vilaseca-Salou = Vilaseca, *Spain* ... 38 D6 41 7N 1 9 E
Vilbjerg, *Denmark* ... 11 H2 56 12N 8 46 E
Vilcheka, Zemlya, *Russia* ... 4 A11 80 30N 60 30 E
Vilches, *Spain* ... 37 G7 38 12N 3 30W
Vileyka, *Belarus* ... 32 E4 54 30N 26 53 E
Vilhelmina, *Sweden* ... 8 D17 64 35N 16 39 E
Vilhena, *Brazil* ... 124 F6 12 40 S 60 5W
Viliya = Neris →, *Lithuania* ... 9 J21 55 8N 24 16 E
Viljandi, *Estonia* ... 9 G21 58 28N 25 30 E
Vilkaviškis, *Lithuania* ... 30 D10 54 39N 23 2 E
Vilkija, *Lithuania* ... 30 C10 55 3N 23 35 E
Vilkitskogo, Proliv, *Russia* ... 53 B11 78 0N 103 0 E
Vilkovo = Vylkove, *Ukraine* ... 29 E14 45 28N 29 32 E
Villa Abecia, *Bolivia* ... 126 A2 21 0 S 68 18W
Villa Ahumada, *Mexico* 118 A3 30 38N 106 30W
Villa Ana, *Argentina* ... 126 B4 28 28 S 59 40W
Villa Ángela, *Argentina* 126 B3 27 34 S 60 45W
Villa Bella, *Bolivia* ... 124 F5 10 25 S 65 22W
Villa Cañás, *Argentina* 126 C3 34 0 S 61 35W
Villa Colón, *Argentina* 126 C2 31 38 S 68 20W
Villa Constitución, *Argentina* ... 126 C3 33 15 S 60 20W
Villa de María, *Argentina* ... 126 B3 29 55 S 63 43W
Villa del Rio, *Spain* ... 37 H6 37 59N 4 17W
Villa Dolores, *Argentina* 126 C2 31 58 S 65 15W
Villa Frontera, *Mexico* ... 118 B4 26 56N 101 27W
Villa Guillermina, *Argentina* ... 126 B4 28 15 S 59 29W
Villa Hayes, *Paraguay* ... 126 B4 25 5 S 57 20W
Villa Iris, *Argentina* ... 126 D3 38 12 S 63 12W
Villa Juárez, *Mexico* ... 118 B4 27 37N 100 44W
Villa María, *Argentina* 126 C3 32 20 S 63 10W
Villa Mazán, *Argentina* 126 B2 28 40 S 66 30W
Villa Minozzo, *Italy* ... 40 D7 44 22N 10 28 E
Villa Montes, *Bolivia* ... 126 A3 21 10 S 63 30W
Villa Ocampo, *Argentina* 126 B4 28 30 S 59 20W
Villa Ocampo, *Mexico* ... 118 B3 26 29N 105 30W
Villa Ojo de Agua, *Argentina* ... 126 B3 29 30 S 63 44W
Villa San Giovanni, *Italy* 43 D8 38 13N 15 38 E
Villa San José, *Argentina* 126 C4 32 12 S 58 15W
Villa San Martín, *Argentina* ... 126 B3 28 15 S 64 9W
Villa Santina, *Italy* ... 41 B9 46 24N 12 55 E
Villa Unión, *Mexico* ... 118 C3 23 12N 106 14W
Villablino, *Spain* ... 36 C4 42 57N 6 19W
Villacarlos, *Spain* ... 48 B11 39 53N 4 17 E
Villacarriedo, *Spain* ... 36 B7 43 14N 3 48W
Villacarrillo, *Spain* ... 37 G7 38 7N 3 3W
Villacastín, *Spain* ... 36 E6 40 46N 4 25W
Villach, *Austria* ... 26 E6 46 37N 13 51 E
Villacidro, *Italy* ... 42 C1 39 27N 8 44 E
Villada, *Spain* ... 36 C6 42 15N 4 59W
Villadiego, *Spain* ... 36 C6 42 31N 4 1W
Villadóssola, *Italy* ... 40 B5 46 4N 8 16 E
Villafeliche, *Spain* ... 38 D3 41 10N 1 30W
Villaffranca, *Spain* ... 38 C3 42 17N 1 46W
Villafranca de los Barros, *Spain* ... 37 G4 38 35N 6 18W
Villafranca de los Caballeros, *Baleares, Spain* ... 48 B10 39 34N 3 25 E
Villafranca de los Caballeros, *Toledo, Spain* ... 37 F7 39 26N 3 21W
Villafranca del Cid = Vilafranca del Maestrat, *Spain* ... 38 E4 40 26N 0 16W
Villafranca del Panadés = Vilafranca del Penedès, *Spain* 38 D6 41 21N 1 40 E
Villafranca di Verona, *Italy* ... 40 C7 45 21N 10 50 E
Villafranca Tirrena, *Italy* 43 D8 38 20N 15 25 E
Villagrán, *Mexico* ... 119 C5 24 29N 99 29W
Villaguay, *Argentina* ... 126 C4 32 0 S 59 0W
Villaharta, *Spain* ... 37 G6 38 9N 4 54W
Villahermosa, *Mexico* ... 119 D6 17 59N 92 55W
Villahermosa, *Spain* ... 39 G2 38 46N 2 52W
Villaines-la-Juhel, *France* ... 18 D6 48 21N 0 20W
Villajoyosa, *Spain* ... 39 G4 38 30N 0 12W
Villalba, *Spain* ... 36 B3 43 26N 7 40W
Villalba de Guardo, *Spain* ... 36 C6 42 42N 4 49W
Villalón de Campos, *Spain* ... 36 C5 42 5N 5 4W
Villalpando, *Spain* ... 36 D5 41 51N 5 25W
Villaluenga, *Spain* ... 36 E7 40 2N 3 54W
Villamanán, *Spain* ... 36 C5 42 19N 5 35W
Villamartín, *Spain* ... 37 J5 36 52N 5 38W
Villamayor de Santiago, *Spain* ... 38 F2 39 50N 2 59W
Villamblard, *France* ... 20 C4 45 2N 0 32 E
Villanova Monteleone, *Italy* ... 42 B1 40 30N 8 28 E
Villanueva, *U.S.A.* ... 113 H2 35 16N 105 22W
Villanueva de Castello = Vilanova de Castelló, *Spain* ... 39 F4 39 5N 0 31W
Villanueva de Córdoba, *Spain* ... 37 G6 38 20N 4 38W
Villanueva de la Fuente, *Spain* ... 39 G2 38 42N 2 42W
Villanueva de la Serena, *Spain* ... 37 G5 38 59N 5 50W
Villanueva de la Sierra, *Spain* ... 36 E4 40 12N 6 24W
Villanueva de los Castillejos, *Spain* ... 37 H3 37 30N 7 15W
Villanueva de los Infantes, *Spain* ... 37 G7 38 43N 3 1W
Villanueva del Arzobispo, *Spain* ... 39 G2 38 10N 3 0W
Villanueva del Fresno, *Spain* ... 37 G3 38 23N 7 10W
Villanueva y Geltrú = Vilanova i la Geltrú, *Spain* ... 38 D6 41 13N 1 40 E
Villaputzu, *Italy* ... 42 C2 39 26N 9 34 E
Villaquilambre, *Spain* ... 36 C5 42 37N 5 33W
Villar del Arzobispo, *Spain* ... 38 F4 39 44N 0 50W

Villar del Rey, *Spain* ... 37 F4 39 7N 6 50W
Villard-de-Lans, *France* 21 C9 45 3N 5 33 E
Villarramiel, *Spain* ... 36 C6 42 2N 4 55W
Villarreal = Vila-real de los Infantes, *Spain* ... 38 F4 39 55N 0 3W
Villarrica, *Chile* ... 128 D2 39 15 S 72 15W
Villarrica, *Paraguay* ... 126 B4 25 40 S 56 30W
Villarrobledo, *Spain* ... 39 F2 39 18N 2 36W
Villarroya de la Sierra, *Spain* ... 38 D3 41 27N 1 46W
Villarrubia de los Ojos, *Spain* ... 37 F7 39 14N 3 36W
Villars-les-Dombes, *France* ... 19 F12 46 0N 5 3 E
Villasayas, *Spain* ... 38 D2 41 24N 2 39W
Villaseca de los Gamitos = Villaseco de los Gamitos, *Spain* 36 D4 41 2N 6 7W
Villaseco de los Gamitos, *Spain* ... 36 D4 41 2N 6 7W
Villasimíus, *Italy* ... 42 C2 39 8N 9 31 E
Villastar, *Spain* ... 38 E3 40 17N 1 9W
Villatobas, *Spain* ... 36 F7 39 54N 3 20W
Villavicencio, *Argentina* 126 C2 32 28 S 69 0W
Villavicencio, *Colombia* 124 C4 4 9N 73 37W
Villaviciosa, *Spain* ... 36 B5 43 32N 5 27W
Villazón, *Bolivia* ... 126 A2 22 0 S 65 35W
Ville Platte, *U.S.A.* ... 113 K8 30 41N 92 17W
Villedieu-les-Poêles, *France* ... 18 D5 48 50N 1 13W
Villefort, *France* ... 20 D7 44 28N 3 56 E
Villefranche-de-Lauragais, *France* ... 20 E5 43 25N 1 44 E
Villefranche-de-Rouergue, *France* ... 20 D6 44 21N 2 2 E
Villefranche-du-Périgord, *France* ... 20 D5 44 38N 1 5 E
Villefranche-sur-Saône, *France* ... 21 C8 45 59N 4 43 E
Villel, *Spain* ... 38 E3 40 14N 1 12W
Villemur-sur-Tarn, *France* ... 20 E5 43 51N 1 31 E
Villena, *Spain* ... 39 G4 38 39N 0 52W
Villenauxe-la-Grande, *France* ... 19 D10 48 35N 3 33 E
Villeneuve-d'Ornon, *France* ... 20 D3 44 46N 0 33W
Villeneuve-d'Ascq, *France* ... 19 B10 50 38N 3 9 E
Villeneuve-l'Archevêque, *France* 19 D10 48 14N 3 32 E
Villeneuve-lès-Avignon, *France* ... 21 E8 43 58N 4 49 E
Villeneuve-sur-Allier, *France* ... 19 F10 46 40N 3 13 E
Villeneuve-sur-Lot, *France* ... 20 D4 44 24N 0 42 E
Villeneuve-sur-Yonne, *France* ... 19 D10 48 5N 3 18 E
Villeréal, *France* ... 20 D4 44 38N 0 45 E
Villers-Bocage, *France* 18 C6 49 3N 0 40W
Villers-Cotterêts, *France* 19 C10 49 15N 3 4 E
Villers-sur-Mer, *France* 18 C6 49 21N 0 2W
Villersexel, *France* ... 19 E13 47 33N 6 26 E
Villerupt, *France* ... 19 C12 49 28N 5 55 E
Villeurbanne, *France* . 21 C8 45 46N 4 55 E
Villiers, *S. Africa* ... 89 D4 27 2 S 28 36 E
Villingen-Schwenningen, *Germany* ... 25 G4 48 3N 8 26 E
Villmanstrand = Lappeenranta, *Finland* ... 9 F23 61 3N 28 12 E
Vilna, *Canada* ... 102 C6 54 7N 111 55W
Vilnius, *Lithuania* ... 9 J21 54 38N 25 19 E
Vils, *Austria* ... 26 D3 47 33N 10 38 E
Vils →, *Bayern, Germany* ... 25 G9 48 37N 13 11 E
Vils →, *Bayern, Germany* ... 25 F7 49 10N 11 57 E
Vilsbiburg, *Germany* . 25 G8 48 26N 12 22 E
Vilshofen, *Germany* ... 25 G9 48 37N 13 11 E
Vilusi, *Serbia & M.* ... 44 D2 42 44N 18 34 E
Vilvoorde, *Belgium* ... 17 D4 50 56N 4 26 E
Vilyuy →, *Russia* ... 53 C13 64 24N 126 26 E
Vilyuysk, *Russia* ... 53 C13 63 40N 121 35 E
Vimianzo, *Spain* ... 36 B1 43 7N 9 2W
Vimioso, *Portugal* ... 36 D4 41 35N 6 31W
Vimmerby, *Sweden* ... 11 G9 57 40N 15 55 E
Vimoutiers, *France* ... 18 D7 48 57N 0 10 E
Vimperk, *Czech Rep.* . 26 B6 49 3N 13 46 E
Viña del Mar, *Chile* ... 126 C1 33 0 S 71 30W
Vinaròs, *Spain* ... 38 E5 40 30N 0 27 E
Vincennes, *U.S.A.* ... 114 F2 38 41N 87 32W
Vincent, *U.S.A.* ... 111 L8 34 33N 118 11W
Vinchina, *Argentina* ... 126 B2 28 45 S 68 15W
Vindelälven →, *Sweden* 8 E18 63 55N 19 50 E
Vindeln, *Sweden* ... 8 D18 64 12N 19 43 E
Vinderup, *Denmark* ... 11 H2 56 29N 8 45 E
Vindhya Ra., *India* ... 68 H7 22 50N 77 0 E
Vineland, *U.S.A.* ... 114 F8 39 29N 75 2W
Vineuil, *France* ... 18 47 35N 1 22 E
Vinga, *Romania* ... 28 D6 46 1N 21 14 E
Vingåker, *Sweden* ... 10 E9 59 2N 15 52 E
Vinh, *Vietnam* ... 64 C5 18 45N 105 38 E
Vinh Linh, *Vietnam* ... 64 D6 17 4N 107 2 E
Vinh Long, *Vietnam* ... 65 G5 10 16N 105 57 E
Vinh Yen, *Vietnam* ... 58 G5 21 21N 105 35 E
Vinhais, *Portugal* ... 36 D3 41 50N 7 5W
Vinica, *Croatia* ... 41 B13 46 20N 16 9 E
Vinica, *Macedonia* ... 44 E6 41 53N 22 30 E
Vinica, *Slovenia* ... 41 C12 45 28N 15 16 E
Vinita, *U.S.A.* ... 113 G7 36 39N 95 9W
Vinkovci, *Croatia* ... 28 E3 45 19N 18 48 E
Vinnitsa = Vinnytsya, *Ukraine* ... 33 H5 49 15N 28 30 E
Vinnytsya, *Ukraine* ... 33 H5 49 15N 28 30 E
Vinslöv, *Sweden* ... 11 H7 56 7N 13 55 E
Vinson Massif, *Antarctica* ... 5 D16 78 35 S 85 25W
Vintjärn, *Sweden* ... 10 D10 60 50N 16 4 E
Vinton, *Calif., U.S.A.* . 110 F6 39 48N 120 10W
Vinton, *Iowa, U.S.A.* . 112 D8 42 10N 92 1W
Vinton, *La., U.S.A.* ... 113 K8 30 11N 93 35W
Vințu de Jos, *Romania* 29 D8 46 0N 23 30 E
Viöl, *Germany* ... 24 A5 54 34N 9 11 E
Vipava, *Slovenia* ... 41 C10 45 51N 13 58 E
Vipiteno, *Italy* ... 41 B8 46 54N 11 26 E
Viqueque, *E. Timor* ... 63 F7 8 52 S 126 23 E
Vir, *Croatia* ... 41 D12 44 17N 15 3 E
Virac, *Phil.* ... 61 E6 13 30N 124 20 E
Virachey, *Cambodia* ... 64 F6 13 59N 106 49 E
Virachey △, *Cambodia* 64 E6 14 1N 106 55 E
Virago Sd., *Canada* ... 102 C2 54 0N 132 30W
Viramgam, *India* ... 68 H5 23 5N 72 0 E
Virananşehir, *Turkey* . 70 B3 37 13N 39 45 E

Virawah, *Pakistan* ... 68 G4 24 31N 70 46 E
Virbalis, *Lithuania* ... 30 D9 54 39N 22 49 E
Virden, *Canada* ... 103 D8 49 50N 100 56W
Vire, *France* ... 18 D6 48 50N 0 53W
Vire →, *France* ... 18 C5 49 20N 1 7W
Vírgenes, C., *Argentina* 128 G3 52 19 S 68 21W
Virgin →, *U.S.A.* ... 109 H6 36 28N 114 21W
Virgin Gorda, *Br. Virgin Is.* ... 121 e 18 30N 64 26W
Virgin Is. (British) ☑, *W. Indies* ... 121 e 18 30N 64 30W
Virgin Is. (U.S.) ☑, *W. Indies* ... 121 e 18 20N 65 0W
Virgin Islands △, *Virgin Is.* ... 121 C7 18 21N 64 43W
Virginia, *S. Africa* ... 88 D4 28 8 S 26 55 E
Virginia, *U.S.A.* ... 112 B8 47 31N 92 32W
Virginia □, *U.S.A.* ... 114 G7 37 30N 78 45W
Virginia Beach, *U.S.A.* 114 G8 36 51N 75 59W
Virginia City, *Mont., U.S.A.* ... 108 D8 45 18N 111 56W
Virginia City, *Nev., U.S.A.* ... 110 F7 39 19N 119 39W
Virginia Falls, *Canada* 102 A3 61 38N 125 42W
Virginiatown, *Canada* 104 C4 48 9N 79 36W
Virje, *Croatia* ... 41 B13 46 4N 16 59 E
Viroqua, *U.S.A.* ... 112 D9 43 34N 90 53W
Virovitica, *Croatia* ... 28 E2 45 51N 17 21 E
Virpazar, *Serbia & M.* 44 D3 42 14N 19 6 E
Virpur, *India* ... 68 J4 21 51N 70 42 E
Virserum, *Sweden* ... 11 G9 57 20N 15 35 E
Virton, *Belgium* ... 17 E5 49 35N 5 32 E
Virudunagar, *India* ... 66 Q10 9 30N 77 58 E
Virunga △, *Dem. Rep. of the Congo* ... 86 B2 0 5N 29 38 E
Vis, *Croatia* ... 41 E13 43 4N 16 10 E
Visalia, *U.S.A.* ... 110 J7 36 20N 119 18W
Visayan Sea, *Phil.* ... 61 F5 11 30N 123 30 E
Visby, *Sweden* ... 11 G12 57 37N 18 18 E
Viscount Melville Sd., *Canada* ... 98 B9 74 10N 108 0W
Visé, *Belgium* ... 17 D5 50 44N 5 41 E
Višegrad, *Bos.-H.* ... 28 G4 43 47N 19 17 E
Viseu, *Brazil* ... 125 D9 1 10 S 46 5W
Viseu, *Portugal* ... 36 E3 40 40N 7 55W
Viseu □, *Portugal* ... 36 E3 40 40N 7 55W
Vişeu de Sus, *Romania* 29 C9 47 45N 24 25 E
Vishakhapatnam, *India* 67 L13 17 45N 83 20 E
Vişina, *Romania* ... 29 G9 43 52N 24 27 E
Vişineşti, *Moldova* ... 29 D13 46 28N 28 27 E
Visingsö, *Sweden* ... 11 F8 58 2N 14 20 E
Viskafors, *Sweden* ... 11 G6 57 37N 12 50 E
Viskan →, *Sweden* ... 11 G6 57 14N 12 12 E
Viški Kanal, *Croatia* .. 41 E13 43 4N 16 5 E
Vislanda, *Sweden* ... 11 H8 56 46N 14 30 E
Visnagar, *India* ... 68 H5 23 45N 72 32 E
Višnja Gora, *Slovenia* 41 C11 45 58N 14 45 E
Viso, Mte., *Italy* ... 40 D4 44 38N 7 5 E
Viso del Marqués, *Spain* 37 G7 38 32N 3 34W
Visoko, *Bos.-H.* ... 28 G3 43 58N 18 10 E
Visokoi I., *Antarctica* 5 B1 56 43 S 27 15W
Visp, *Switz.* ... 25 J3 46 17N 7 52 E
Vissefjärda, *Sweden* .. 11 H9 56 32N 15 35 E
Visselhövede, *Germany* 24 C5 52 59N 9 34 E
Vissenbjerg, *Denmark* 11 J4 55 23N 10 7 E
Vista, *U.S.A.* ... 111 M9 33 12N 117 14W
Vistonikos, Ormos = Vistonís, Límni, *Greece* ... 45 E9 41 0N 25 7 E
Vistonís, Límni, *Greece* 45 E9 41 0N 25 7 E
Vistula = Wisła →, *Poland* ... 30 D5 54 22N 18 55 E
Vit →, *Bulgaria* ... 45 C8 43 30N 24 30 E
Vitanje, *Slovenia* ... 41 B12 46 25N 15 18 E
Vitebsk = Vitsyebsk, *Belarus* ... 32 E6 55 10N 30 15 E
Viterbo, *Italy* ... 41 F9 42 25N 12 6 E
Vitez, *Bos.-H.* ... 28 F2 44 10N 17 48 E
Viti Levu, *Fiji* ... 91 C7 17 30 S 177 30 E
Vitigudino, *Spain* ... 36 D4 41 1N 6 26W
Vitim, *Russia* ... 53 D12 59 28N 112 35 E
Vitim →, *Russia* ... 53 D12 59 26N 112 34 E
Vitina, *Bos.-H.* ... 41 E14 43 17N 17 29 E
Vitina, *Greece* ... 46 D4 37 40N 22 10 E
Vítkov, *Czech Rep.* ... 27 B10 49 46N 17 45 E
Vitória, *Brazil* ... 125 H10 20 20 S 40 22W
Vitória da Conquista, *Brazil* ... 125 F10 14 51 S 40 51W
Vitória de Santo Antão, *Brazil* ... 125 E11 8 10 S 35 20W
Vitoria-Gasteiz, *Spain* 38 C2 42 50N 2 41W
Vitosha △, *Bulgaria* ... 44 D7 42 36N 23 18 E
Vitré, *France* ... 18 D5 48 8N 1 12W
Vitry-le-François, *France* 19 D11 48 43N 4 33 E
Vitry-sur-Seine, *France* 19 D9 48 47N 2 24 E
Vitsand, *Sweden* ... 10 D7 60 20N 13 0 E
Vitsi, Óros, *Greece* ... 44 F5 40 40N 21 25 E
Vitsyebsk, *Belarus* ... 32 E6 55 10N 30 15 E
Vittangi, *Sweden* ... 8 C19 67 58N 21 0 E
Vitteaux, *France* ... 19 E11 47 24N 4 30 E
Vittel, *France* ... 19 D12 48 12N 5 57 E
Vittória, *Italy* ... 43 F7 36 57N 14 32 E
Vittório Véneto, *Italy* . 41 C9 45 59N 12 18 E
Vittsjö, *Sweden* ... 11 H7 56 20N 13 40 E
Viveiro, *Spain* ... 36 B3 43 39N 7 38W
Vivian, *U.S.A.* ... 113 J8 32 53N 93 59W
Viviers, *France* ... 21 D8 44 30N 4 40 E
Vivonne, *France* ... 20 B4 46 25N 0 15 E
Vizcaíno, Desierto de, *Mexico* ... 118 B2 27 40N 113 50W
Vizcaíno, Sierra, *Mexico* 118 B2 27 30N 114 0W
Vizcaya □, *Spain* ... 38 B2 43 15N 2 45W
Vize, *Turkey* ... 45 E11 41 34N 27 45 E
Vizianagaram, *India* .. 67 K13 18 6N 83 30 E
Vizille, *France* ... 21 C9 45 5N 5 46 E
Viziñada, *Croatia* ... 41 C10 45 20N 13 46 E
Viziru, *Romania* ... 29 E12 45 0N 27 43 E
Vizzini, *Italy* ... 43 F7 37 10N 14 45 E
Vlaardingen, *Neths.* ... 17 C4 51 55N 4 21 E
Vlădeasa, Vf., *Romania* 28 D7 46 47N 22 50 E
Vladičin Han, *Serbia & M.* ... 44 D6 42 42N 22 1 E
Vladikavkaz, *Russia* ... 35 J7 43 0N 44 35 E
Vladimir, *Russia* ... 32 D11 56 15N 40 30 E
Vladimir Volynskiy = Volodymyr-Volynskyy, *Ukraine* 33 G3 50 50N 24 18 E
Vladimirci, *Serbia & M.* 44 B3 44 36N 19 50 E
Vladimirovac, *Serbia & M.* ... 28 E5 45 1N 20 53 E
Vladimirovo, *Bulgaria* 44 C7 43 32N 23 22 E
Vladimirovka, *Kazakhstan* ... 34 E10 50 51N 51 8 E
Vladislavovka, *Ukraine* 33 K8 45 12N 35 29 E
Vladivostok, *Russia* ... 53 E14 43 10N 131 53 E

Vlăhiţa, *Romania* ... 29 D10 46 21N 25 31 E
Vlakhiótis, *Greece* ... 46 E4 36 52N 22 42 E
Vlasenica, *Bos.-H.* ... 28 F3 44 11N 18 59 E
Vlašić, *Bos.-H.* ... 28 F2 44 19N 17 37 E
Vlašim, *Czech Rep.* ... 26 B7 49 40N 14 53 E
Vlasinsko Jezero, *Serbia & M.* ... 44 D6 42 44N 22 22 E
Vlasotince, *Serbia & M.* 44 D6 42 59N 22 7 E
Vlieland, *Neths.* ... 17 A4 53 16N 4 55 E
Vlissingen, *Neths.* ... 17 C3 51 26N 3 34 E
Vlorë, *Albania* ... 44 F3 40 32N 19 28 E
Vlorës, Gjiri i, *Albania* 44 F3 40 29N 19 27 E
Vltava →, *Czech Rep.* 26 A7 50 21N 14 30 E
Vo Dat, *Vietnam* ... 65 G6 11 9N 107 31 E
Vobarno, *Italy* ... 40 C7 45 39N 10 30 E
Voćin, *Croatia* ... 28 E2 45 37N 17 33 E
Vöcklabruck, *Austria* . 26 C6 48 1N 13 39 E
Vodice, *Croatia* ... 41 E12 43 47N 15 47 E
Vodňany, *Czech Rep.* . 26 B7 49 9N 14 11 E
Vodnjan, *Croatia* ... 41 D10 44 59N 13 52 E
Voe, *U.K.* ... 13 A7 60 21N 1 16W
Vogel Pk., *Nigeria* ... 83 D7 8 24N 11 47 E
Vogelkop = Doberai, Jazirah, *Indonesia* . 63 E8 1 25 S 133 0 E
Vogelsberg, *Germany* 24 E5 50 31N 9 12 E
Voghera, *Italy* ... 40 D6 44 59N 9 1 E
Vohibinany, *Madag.* . 89 B8 18 49 S 49 4 E
Vohilava, *Madag.* ... 89 C8 21 4 S 48 0 E
Vohimarina = Iharana, *Madag.* ... 89 A9 13 25 S 50 0 E
Vohimena, Tanjon' i, *Madag.* ... 89 D8 25 36 S 45 8 E
Vohipeno, *Madag.* ... 89 C8 22 22 S 47 51 E
Voi, *Kenya* ... 86 C4 3 25 S 38 32 E
Void-Vacon, *France* ... 19 D12 48 40N 5 36 E
Voineşti, *Iaşi, Romania* 29 C12 47 5N 27 27 E
Voineşti, *Prahova, Romania* ... 29 E10 45 5N 25 14 E
Voiron, *France* ... 21 C9 45 22N 5 35 E
Voisey B., *Canada* ... 105 A7 56 15N 61 50W
Voitsberg, *Austria* ... 26 D8 47 3N 15 9 E
Vojens, *Denmark* ... 11 J3 55 16N 9 18 E
Vojmsjön, *Sweden* ... 8 D17 65 0N 16 24 E
Vojnić, *Croatia* ... 41 C12 45 19N 15 43 E
Vojnik, *Italy* ... 41 B12 46 18N 15 19 E
Vojvodina □, *Serbia & M.* ... 28 E5 45 20N 20 0 E
Vokhtoga, *Russia* ... 32 C11 58 46N 41 8 E
Volary, *Czech Rep.* ... 26 C6 48 54N 13 52 E
Volborg, *U.S.A.* ... 112 C2 45 51N 105 41W
Volcán de Colima △, *Mexico* ... 118 D4 19 30N 103 40W
Volcano Is. = Kazan-Rettō, *Pac. Oc.* ... 96 E6 25 0N 141 0 E
Volcans △, *Rwanda* .. 86 C2 1 30 S 29 26 E
Volcans d'Auvergne △, *France* ... 20 C6 45 20N 2 40 E
Volchansk = Vovchansk, *Ukraine* ... 33 G9 50 17N 36 58 E
Volchya →, *Ukraine* . 33 H8 48 32N 36 0 E
Volda, *Norway* ... 9 E12 62 9N 6 5 E
Volga = Privolzhskiy □, *Russia* ... 34 B10 56 0N 50 0 E
Volga, *Russia* ... 32 C10 57 58N 38 16 E
Volga →, *Russia* ... 35 G9 46 0N 48 30 E
Volga Hts. = Privolzhskaya Vozvyshennost, *Russia* ... 34 E7 51 0N 46 0 E
Volgo-Baltiyskiy Kanal, *Russia* ... 32 B9 60 0N 38 0 E
Volgodonsk, *Russia* ... 35 F7 48 40N 43 37 E
Volgograd, *Russia* ... 35 F7 48 40N 44 25 E
Volgogradskoye Vdkhr., *Russia* ... 34 E8 50 0N 45 20 E
Volgorechensk, *Russia* 32 C11 57 28N 41 14 E
Volímai, *Greece* ... 46 D2 37 30N 20 39 E
Volíntiri, *Moldova* ... 29 D14 46 26N 29 37 E
Volissós, *Greece* ... 47 C6 38 29N 25 54 E
Volkach, *Germany* ... 25 F6 49 52N 10 13 E
Völkermarkt, *Austria* . 26 E7 46 39N 14 39 E
Volkhov, *Russia* ... 32 C7 59 55N 32 15 E
Volkhov →, *Russia* .. 32 B7 60 8N 32 20 E
Völklingen, *Germany* 25 F2 49 15N 6 50 E
Volkovysk = Vawkavysk, *Belarus* ... 33 F3 53 9N 24 30 E
Volksrust, *S. Africa* ... 89 D4 27 24 S 29 53 E
Volnansk, *Ukraine* ... 33 H8 48 25N 35 30 E
Volnovakha, *Ukraine* . 33 J9 47 35N 37 30 E
Volochanka, *Russia* ... 53 B10 71 0N 94 28 E
Volodarsk, *Russia* ... 34 B6 56 12N 43 15 E
Volodymyr-Volynskyy, *Ukraine* ... 33 G3 50 50N 24 18 E
Vologda, *Russia* ... 32 C10 59 10N 39 45 E
Volokolamsk, *Russia* . 32 D8 56 5N 35 57 E
Volokonovka, *Russia* . 33 G9 50 33N 37 52 E
Vólos, *Greece* ... 46 B4 39 24N 22 59 E
Volosovo, *Russia* ... 32 C5 59 27N 29 32 E
Volovets, *Ukraine* ... 29 B8 48 43N 23 11 E
Volovo, *Russia* ... 32 F10 53 35N 38 1 E
Volozhin = Valozhyn, *Belarus* ... 32 E4 54 3N 26 30 E
Volsk, *Russia* ... 34 D8 52 5N 47 22 E
Volta □, *Ghana* ... 83 D5 7 30N 0 15 E
Volta →, *Ghana* ... 83 D5 5 46N 0 41 E
Volta, L., *Ghana* ... 83 D5 7 30N 0 0W
Volta Blanche = White Volta →, *Ghana* ... 83 D4 9 10N 1 15W
Volta Redonda, *Brazil* 127 A7 22 31 S 44 5W
Voltaire, C., *Australia* 92 B4 14 16 S 125 35 E
Volterra, *Italy* ... 40 E7 43 24N 10 51 E
Voltri, *Italy* ... 40 D5 44 25N 8 45 E
Volturno →, *Italy* ... 42 A6 41 1N 13 55 E
Vólvi, L., *Greece* ... 44 F7 40 40N 23 34 E
Volyne, *Czech Rep.* ... 26 B6 49 10N 13 53 E
Volzhsk, *Russia* ... 34 C9 55 57N 48 23 E
Volzhskiy, *Russia* ... 35 F7 48 56N 44 46 E
Vondrozo, *Madag.* ... 89 C8 22 49 S 47 20 E
Vónitsa, *Greece* ... 46 C2 38 53N 20 58 E
Vopnafjörður, *Iceland* 8 D6 65 45N 14 50W
Vóras Óros, *Greece* ... 44 F5 40 57N 21 45 E
Vorarlberg □, *Austria* 26 D3 47 20N 10 0 E
Vorchdorf, *Austria* ... 26 C6 48 0N 13 54 E
Vorden, *Switz.* ...
Voríai Sporádhes, *Greece* ... 46 B5 39 15N 23 30 E
Vóriai Aiyaíon □, *Greece* ... 47 C7 38 50N 25 30 E

Vórios Evvoïkós Kólpos, *Greece* ... 46 C5 38 45N 23 15 E
Vorkuta, *Russia* ... 52 C7 67 48N 64 20 E
Vormsi, *Estonia* ... 9 G20 59 1N 23 13 E
Vóroi, *Greece* ... 46 F6 35 4N 24 49 E
Vorona →, *Russia* ... 34 E6 51 22N 42 3 E
Voronezh, *Russia* ... 33 G10 51 40N 39 10 E
Voronezh, *Ukraine* ... 33 G7 51 47N 33 28 E
Voronezh →, *Russia* . 33 G10 51 56N 39 10 E
Vorontsovo-Aleksandrovskoye = Zelenokumsk, *Russia* 35 H6 44 24N 44 0 E
Vorpommersche Boddenlandschaft △, *Germany* ... 24 A8 54 25N 12 32 E
Vorskla →, *Ukraine* .. 33 H8 49 50N 34 10 E
Võrts Järv, *Estonia* ... 9 G22 58 16N 26 3 E
Võru, *Estonia* ... 9 H22 57 48N 26 54 E
Vosges, *France* ... 19 D14 48 20N 7 10 E
Vosges □, *France* ... 19 D13 48 12N 6 20 E
Vosges du Nord △, *France* ... 19 D14 49 0N 7 30 E
Voskopojë, *Albania* .. 44 F4 40 35N 20 37 E
Voskresensk, *Russia* . 32 E10 55 19N 38 43 E
Voskresenskoye, *Russia* 34 B7 56 51N 45 30 E
Voss, *Norway* ... 9 F12 60 38N 6 26 E
Vostok, *Antarctica* ... 5 D8 78 30 S 106 50 E
Vostok I., *Kiribati* ... 97 J12 10 5 S 152 23W
Votice, *Czech Rep.* ... 26 B7 49 39N 14 39 E
Votkinsk, *Russia* ... 34 C10 57 0N 53 55 E
Votsuri-Shima, *Japan* 55 M1 25 45N 123 29 E
Vouga →, *Portugal* .. 36 E2 40 41N 8 40W
Vouillé, *France* ... 18 F7 46 38N 0 10 E
Voúxa, Ákra, *Greece* . 49 D5 35 37N 23 32 E
Vouziers, *France* ... 19 C11 49 22N 4 40 E
Vovchansk, *Ukraine* . 33 G9 50 17N 36 58 E
Vowchyn, *Belarus* ... 31 F10 52 18N 23 18 E
Voyageurs △, *U.S.A.* . 112 A8 48 32N 93 0W
Vozhe, Ozero, *Russia* 32 B10 60 45N 39 0 E
Vozhega, *Russia* ... 32 B11 60 29N 40 12 E
Voznesensk, *Ukraine* 33 J6 47 35N 31 21 E
Voznesenye, *Russia* .. 32 B8 61 0N 35 28 E
Vrå, *Denmark* ... 11 G3 57 21N 9 56 E
Vráble, *Slovak Rep.* .. 27 C11 48 15N 18 16 E
Vračevšnica, *Serbia & M.* ... 44 B4 44 2N 20 34 E
Vrakhnéika, *Greece* .. 46 C3 38 10N 21 40 E
Vrancea □, *Romania* . 29 E11 45 50N 26 45 E
Vrancei, Munţii, *Romania* ... 29 E11 46 0N 26 30 E
Vrangelya, Ostrov, *Russia* ... 53 B19 71 0N 180 0 E
Vranica, *Bos.-H.* ... 28 G2 43 55N 17 50 E
Vranje, *Serbia & M.* . 44 D5 42 34N 21 54 E
Vranjska Banja, *Serbia & M.* ... 44 D6 42 34N 22 1 E
Vranov nad Topľou, *Slovak Rep.* ... 27 C14 48 53N 21 40 E
Vransko, *Slovenia* ... 41 B11 46 17N 14 58 E
Vransko Jezero, *Croatia* 41 E12 43 53N 15 34 E
Vrapčište, *Macedonia* 44 E4 41 50N 20 53 E
Vratsa, *Bulgaria* ... 44 C7 43 15N 23 30 E
Vrbas, *Serbia & M.* .. 28 E4 45 40N 19 40 E
Vrbas →, *Bos.-H.* ... 28 E2 45 8N 17 29 E
Vrbnik, *Croatia* ... 41 C11 45 4N 14 40 E
Vrbovec, *Croatia* ... 41 C13 45 53N 16 28 E
Vrbovsko, *Croatia* ... 41 C12 45 24N 15 5 E
Vrchlabí, *Czech Rep.* . 26 A8 50 38N 15 37 E
Vrede, *S. Africa* ... 89 D4 27 24 S 29 6 E
Vredefort, *S. Africa* .. 88 D4 27 0 S 27 22 E
Vreden, *Germany* ... 24 C2 52 2N 6 50 E
Vredenburg, *S. Africa* 88 E2 32 56 S 18 0 E
Vredendal, *S. Africa* . 88 E2 31 41 S 18 35 E
Vretstorp, *Sweden* ... 10 E8 59 1N 14 53 E
Vrgorac, *Croatia* ... 41 E14 43 12N 17 20 E
Vrhnika, *Slovenia* ... 41 C11 45 58N 14 15 E
Vríði, *Ivory C.* ... 82 D4 5 15N 4 3W
Vrigstad, *Sweden* ... 11 G8 57 21N 14 28 E
Vrindavan, *India* ... 68 F7 27 37N 77 40 E
Vríses, *Greece* ... 49 D6 35 23N 24 13 E
Vrnograč, *Bos.-H.* ... 41 C12 45 10N 15 57 E
Vrondádhes, *Greece* . 47 C8 38 25N 26 7 E
Vrpolje, *Croatia* ... 28 E3 45 13N 18 24 E
Vršac, *Serbia & M.* .. 28 E6 45 8N 21 20 E
Vrsacki Kanal, *Serbia & M.* ... 28 E5 45 15N 21 0 E
Vrútky, *Slovak Rep.* . 27 B11 49 7N 18 55 E
Vryburg, *S. Africa* ... 88 D3 26 55 S 24 45 E
Vryheid, *S. Africa* ... 89 D5 27 45 S 30 47 E
Vsetín, *Czech Rep.* ... 27 B11 49 20N 18 0 E
Vu Liet, *Vietnam* ... 64 C5 18 43N 105 23 E
Vúcha →, *Bulgaria* .. 45 D8 42 10N 24 26 E
Vučitrn, *Serbia & M.* . 44 D4 42 49N 20 59 E
Vukovar, *Croatia* ... 28 E3 45 21N 18 59 E
Vulcan, *Canada* ... 102 C6 50 25N 113 15W
Vulcan, *Romania* ... 29 E8 45 23N 23 17 E
Vulcănești, *Moldova* . 29 E13 45 41N 28 18 E
Vulcano, *Italy* ... 43 D7 38 24N 14 58 E
Vŭlchedrŭma, *Bulgaria* 44 C7 43 42N 23 27 E
Vulkaneshty = Vulcănești, *Moldova* 29 E13 45 41N 28 18 E
Vunduzi →, *Mozam.* . 87 F3 18 56 S 34 1 E
Vung Tau, *Vietnam* ... 65 G6 10 21N 107 4 E
Vŭrbitsa, *Bulgaria* ... 45 D10 42 59N 26 40 E
Vŭrshets, *Bulgaria* ... 44 C7 43 13N 23 23 E
Vutcani, *Romania* ... 29 D12 46 26N 27 59 E
Vuya, *Sudan* ... 81 F2 5 21N 29 60 E
Vuzlove, *Ukraine* ... 28 B8 48 22N 22 24 E
Vwaza △, *Malawi* ... 87 E3 10 58 S 33 25 E
Vyartsilya, *Russia* ... 32 A6 62 8N 30 45 E
Vyatka = Kirov, *Russia* 52 D5 58 35N 49 40 E
Vyatka →, *Russia* ... 34 C10 55 37N 51 28 E
Vyatskiye Polyany, *Russia* ... 34 B10 56 14N 51 5 E
Vyazemskiy, *Russia* .. 53 E14 47 32N 134 45 E
Vyazma, *Russia* ... 32 E8 55 10N 34 15 E
Vyazniki, *Russia* ... 34 B6 56 10N 42 10 E
Vyborg, *Russia* ... 32 B5 60 43N 28 47 E
Vychodné Beskydy, *Europe* ... 27 B15 49 20N 22 0 E
Vyerkhnyadzvinsk, *Belarus* ... 32 E4 55 45N 27 58 E
Vyksa, *Russia* ... 34 C6 55 19N 42 11 E
Vylkove, *Ukraine* ... 29 E14 45 28N 29 32 E
Vylok, *Ukraine* ... 28 B7 48 6N 22 54 E
Vynohradiv, *Ukraine* 28 B8 48 9N 23 13 E
Vyrnwy, L., *U.K.* ... 14 E4 52 48N 3 31W
Vyshkiv, *Ukraine* ... 28 B8 48 23N 23 55 E
Vyshkove, *Ukraine* .. 29 B8 48 3N 23 15 E
Vyshniy Volochek, *Russia* ... 32 D8 57 30N 34 30 E
Vyshzha = imeni 26 Bakinskikh Komissarov, *Turkmenistan* ... 71 B7 39 22N 54 10 E

Vyškov, *Czech Rep.* ... 27 B9 49 17N 17 0 E
Vysokaye, *Belarus* ... 31 F10 52 22N 23 22 E
Vysoké Mýto, *Czech Rep.* ... 26 B8 49 58N 16 10 E
Vysokovsk, *Russia* ... 32 D9 56 22N 36 30 E
Vyšší Brod, *Czech Rep.* ... 26 C7 48 37N 14 19 E
Vytegra, *Russia* ... 8 B9 61 0N 36 27 E
Vyzhnytsya, *Ukraine* ... 29 B10 48 15N 25 11 E
Vyzhnytsya △, *Ukraine* ... 29 B10 48 7N 25 15 E

W

W du Benin △, *Benin* ... 83 C5 11 57N 2 43 E
W du Burkina Faso △, *Burkina Faso* ... 83 C4 11 52N 2 50W
W du Niger △, *Niger* ... 83 C5 11 53N 2 28 E
W.A.C. Bennett Dam, *Canada* ... 102 B4 56 2N 122 6W
Wa, *Ghana* ... 82 C4 10 7N 2 25W
Waal →, *Neths.* ... 17 C5 51 37N 5 0 E
Waalwijk, *Neths.* ... 17 C5 51 42N 5 4 E
Waat, *Sudan* ... 81 F3 8 10N 32 7 E
Wabakimi △, *Canada* ... 104 B2 50 43N 89 29W
Wabana, *Canada* ... 105 C9 47 40N 53 0W
Wabasca →, *Canada* ... 102 B5 58 22N 115 20W
Wabasca-Desmarais, *Canada* ... 102 B6 55 57N 113 56W
Wabash, *U.S.A.* ... 114 E3 40 48N 85 49W
Wabash →, *U.S.A.* ... 114 G1 37 48N 88 2W
Wabi →, *Ethiopia* ... 81 F5 7 45N 40 50 E
Wabigoon L., *Canada* ... 103 D10 49 44N 92 44W
Wabowden, *Canada* ... 103 C9 54 55N 98 38W
Wąbrzeźno, *Poland* ... 31 E5 53 16N 18 57 E
Wabu Hu, *China* ... 59 A11 32 20N 116 50 E
Wabuk Pt., *Canada* ... 104 A2 55 20N 85 5W
Wabush, *Canada* ... 105 B6 52 55N 66 52W
Wąchock, *Poland* ... 31 G8 51 4N 21 1 E
Wächtersbach, *Germany* ... 25 E5 50 14N 9 17 E
Waco, *U.S.A.* ... 113 K6 31 33N 97 9W
Waconichi, L., *Canada* ... 104 B5 50 8N 74 0W
Wad Ban Naqa, *Sudan* ... 81 D3 16 32N 33 9 E
Wad Banda, *Sudan* ... 81 E2 13 10N 27 56 E
Wad el Haddad, *Sudan* ... 81 E3 13 50N 33 30 E
Wad en Nau, *Sudan* ... 81 E3 14 10N 33 34 E
Wad Hamid, *Sudan* ... 81 D3 16 30N 32 45 E
Wad Medanî, *Sudan* ... 81 E3 14 28N 33 30 E
Wad Thana, *Pakistan* ... 68 F2 27 22N 66 23 E
Wadai, *Africa* ... 76 E5 12 0N 19 0 E
Wadayama, *Japan* ... 55 G7 35 19N 134 52 E
Waddeneilanden, *Neths.* ... 17 A5 53 5N 5 10 E
Waddenzee, *Neths.* ... 17 A5 53 6N 5 10 E
Waddi, Chappal, *Nigeria* ... 83 D7 7 2N 11 43W
Waddington, *U.S.A.* ... 117 B9 44 52N 75 12W
Waddington, Mt., *Canada* ... 102 C3 51 23N 125 15W
Waddy Pt., *Australia* ... 95 C5 24 58 S 153 21 E
Wadebridge, *U.K.* ... 15 G3 50 31N 4 51W
Wadena, *Canada* ... 103 C8 51 57N 103 47W
Wadena, *U.S.A.* ... 112 B7 46 26N 95 8W
Wädenswil, *Switz.* ... 25 H4 47 14N 8 40 E
Wadern, *Germany* ... 25 F2 49 32N 6 53 E
Wadeye, *Australia* ... 92 B4 14 28 S 129 52 E
Wadhams, *Canada* ... 102 C3 51 30N 127 30W
Wādī as Sīr, *Jordan* ... 74 D4 31 56N 35 49 E
Wadi Gemâl, *Egypt* ... 80 C4 24 35N 35 10 E
Wadi Halfa, *Sudan* ... 80 C3 21 53N 31 19 E
Wadi Rum △, *Jordan* ... 74 F4 29 30N 35 20 E
Wadian, *China* ... 59 A9 32 42N 112 29 E
Wadlew, *Poland* ... 31 G6 51 31N 19 23 E
Wadowice, *Poland* ... 31 J6 49 52N 19 30 E
Wadsworth, Nev., *U.S.A.* ... 108 G4 39 38N 119 17W
Wadsworth, Ohio, *U.S.A.* ... 116 E3 41 2N 81 44W
Waegwan, *S. Korea* ... 57 G15 35 59N 128 23 E
Wafangdian, *China* ... 57 E11 39 38N 121 58 E
Wafrah, *Si. Arabia* ... 70 D5 28 33N 47 56 E
Wageningen, *Neths.* ... 17 C5 51 58N 5 40 E
Wager B., *Canada* ... 101 B11 65 26N 88 40W
Wagga Wagga, *Australia* ... 95 F4 35 7 S 147 24 E
Waghete, *Indonesia* ... 63 E9 4 10 S 135 50 E
Wagin, *Australia* ... 93 F2 33 17 S 117 25 E
Wagner, *U.S.A.* ... 112 D5 43 5N 98 18W
Wagon Mound, *U.S.A.* ... 113 G2 36 1N 104 42W
Wagoner, *U.S.A.* ... 113 H7 35 58N 95 22W
Wągrowiec, *Poland* ... 31 F4 52 48N 17 11 E
Wah, *Pakistan* ... 68 C5 33 45N 72 40 E
Wahai, *Indonesia* ... 63 E7 2 48 S 129 35 E
Wahiawa, *U.S.A.* ... 106 H15 21 30N 158 2W
Wâḥid, *Egypt* ... 74 E1 30 48N 32 21 E
Wahnai, *Afghan.* ... 68 C1 32 40N 65 50 E
Wahni, *Ethiopia* ... 81 E4 12 40N 36 39 E
Wahoo, *U.S.A.* ... 112 E6 41 13N 96 37W
Wahpeton, *U.S.A.* ... 112 B6 46 16N 96 36W
Waiau →, *N.Z.* ... 91 K4 42 47 S 173 22 E
Waibeem, *Indonesia* ... 63 E8 0 30 S 132 59 E
Waiblingen, *Germany* ... 25 G5 48 49N 9 18 E
Waidhofen an der Thaya, *Austria* ... 26 C8 48 49N 15 17 E
Waidhofen an der Ybbs, *Austria* ... 26 D7 47 57N 14 46 E
Waigeo, *Indonesia* ... 63 E8 0 20 S 130 40 E
Waihi, *N.Z.* ... 91 G5 37 23 S 175 52 E
Waihou →, *N.Z.* ... 91 G5 37 15 S 175 40 E
Waika, *Dem. Rep. of the Congo* ... 86 C2 2 22 S 25 42 E
Waikabubak, *Indonesia* ... 63 F5 9 45 S 119 25 E
Waikaremoana, L., *N.Z.* ... 91 H6 38 49 S 177 9 E
Waikari, *N.Z.* ... 91 K4 42 58 S 172 41 E
Waikato →, *N.Z.* ... 91 G5 37 23 S 174 43 E
Waikerie, *Australia* ... 95 E3 34 9 S 140 0 E
Waikokopu, *N.Z.* ... 91 H6 39 3 S 177 52 E
Waikouaiti, *N.Z.* ... 91 L3 45 36 S 170 41 E
Wailuku, *U.S.A.* ... 106 H16 20 53N 156 30W
Waimakariri →, *N.Z.* ... 91 K4 43 24 S 172 42 E
Waimate, *N.Z.* ... 91 L3 44 45 S 171 3 E
Wainganga →, *India* ... 66 K11 18 50N 79 55 E
Waingapu, *Indonesia* ... 63 F6 9 35 S 120 11 E
Waini →, *Guyana* ... 124 B7 8 20N 59 50W
Wainwright, *Canada* ... 103 C6 52 50N 110 50W
Waiouru, *N.Z.* ... 91 H5 39 28 S 175 41 E
Waipara, *N.Z.* ... 91 K4 43 3 S 172 46 E
Waipawa, *N.Z.* ... 91 H6 39 56 S 176 38 E
Waipiro, *N.Z.* ... 91 H7 38 2 S 178 22 E
Waipu, *N.Z.* ... 91 F5 35 59 S 174 29 E
Waipukurau, *N.Z.* ... 91 J6 40 1 S 176 33 E
Wairakei, *N.Z.* ... 91 H6 38 37 S 176 6 E
Wairarapa, L., *N.Z.* ... 91 J5 41 14 S 175 15 E
Wairoa, *N.Z.* ... 91 H6 39 3 S 177 25 E
Waitaki →, *N.Z.* ... 91 L3 44 56 S 171 7 E
Waitara, *N.Z.* ... 91 H5 38 59 S 174 15 E
Waitsburg, *U.S.A.* ... 108 C5 46 16N 118 9W
Waiuku, *N.Z.* ... 91 G5 37 15 S 174 45 E
Wajima, *Japan* ... 55 F8 37 30N 137 0 E
Wajir, *Kenya* ... 86 B5 1 42N 40 5 E

Waka, *Ethiopia* ... 81 F4 7 2N 37 20 E
Wakasa, *Japan* ... 55 G7 35 20N 134 24 E
Wakasa-Wan, *Japan* ... 55 G7 35 40N 135 30 E
Wakatipu, L., *N.Z.* ... 91 L2 45 5 S 168 33 E
Wakaw, *Canada* ... 103 C7 52 39N 105 44W
Wakayama, *Japan* ... 55 G7 34 15N 135 15 E
Wakayama □, *Japan* ... 55 H7 33 50N 135 30 E
Wake Forest, *U.S.A.* ... 115 H6 35 59N 78 30W
Wake I., *Pac. Oc.* ... 96 F8 19 18N 166 36 E
WaKeeney, *U.S.A.* ... 112 F5 39 1N 99 53W
Wakefield, *Jamaica* ... 120 a 18 26N 77 42W
Wakefield, *N.Z.* ... 91 J4 41 24 S 173 5 E
Wakefield, *U.K.* ... 14 D6 53 41N 1 29W
Wakefield, *Mass., U.S.A.* ... 117 D13 42 30N 71 4W
Wakefield, *Mich., U.S.A.* ... 112 B10 46 29N 89 56W
Wakkanai, *Japan* ... 54 B10 45 28N 141 35 E
Wakkerstroom, *S. Africa* ... 89 D5 27 24 S 30 10 E
Wakool, *Australia* ... 95 F3 35 28 S 144 23 E
Wakool →, *Australia* ... 95 F3 35 5 S 143 33 E
Wakre, *Indonesia* ... 63 E8 0 19 S 131 5 E
Wakuach, L., *Canada* ... 105 A6 55 34N 67 32W
Walamba, *Zambia* ... 87 E2 13 30 S 28 42 E
Wałbrzych, *Poland* ... 31 H3 50 45N 16 18 E
Walbury Hill, *U.K.* ... 15 F6 51 21N 1 28W
Walcha, *Australia* ... 95 E5 30 55 S 151 31 E
Walcheren, *Neths.* ... 17 C3 51 30N 3 35 E
Walcott, *U.S.A.* ... 108 F10 41 46N 106 51W
Wałcz, *Poland* ... 31 E3 53 17N 16 27 E
Waldbröl, *Germany* ... 24 E3 50 52N 7 37 E
Waldburg Ra., *Australia* ... 93 D2 24 40 S 117 35 E
Waldeck, *Germany* ... 24 D5 51 12N 9 4 E
Walden, *Colo., U.S.A.* ... 108 F10 40 44N 106 17W
Walden, *N.Y., U.S.A.* ... 117 E10 41 34N 74 11W
Waldkirch, *Germany* ... 25 G3 48 5N 7 58 E
Waldkirchen, *Germany* ... 25 G9 48 43N 13 36 E
Waldkraiburg, *Germany* ... 25 G8 48 11N 12 24 E
Waldport, *U.S.A.* ... 108 D1 44 26N 124 4W
Waldron, *U.S.A.* ... 113 H7 34 54N 94 5W
Waldviertel, *Austria* ... 26 C8 48 30N 15 30 E
Walebing, *Australia* ... 93 F2 30 41 S 116 13 E
Walembele, *Ghana* ... 82 C4 10 30N 1 58W
Walensee, *Switz.* ... 25 H5 47 7N 9 13 E
Wales □, *U.K.* ... 15 E3 52 19N 4 43W
Walewale, *Ghana* ... 83 C4 10 21N 0 50W
Walgett, *Australia* ... 95 E4 30 0 S 148 5 E
Walgreen Coast, *Antarctica* ... 5 D15 75 15 S 105 0W
Walker, *U.S.A.* ... 112 B7 47 6N 94 35W
Walker, L., *Canada* ... 105 B6 50 20N 67 11W
Walker L., *Canada* ... 103 C9 54 42N 95 57W
Walker L., *U.S.A.* ... 108 G4 38 42N 118 43W
Walkerston, *Australia* ... 94 K7 21 11 S 149 8 E
Walkerton, *Canada* ... 116 B3 44 10N 81 10W
Wall, *U.S.A.* ... 112 D3 44 0N 102 8W
Walla Walla, *U.S.A.* ... 108 C4 46 4N 118 20W
Wallace, *Idaho, U.S.A.* ... 108 C6 47 28N 115 56W
Wallace, *N.C., U.S.A.* ... 115 H7 34 44N 77 59W
Wallaceburg, *Canada* ... 116 D2 42 34N 82 23W
Wallachia = Valahia, *Romania* ... 29 F9 44 35 S 25 0 E
Wallal, *Australia* ... 95 D4 26 32 S 146 7 E
Wallam Cr. →, *Australia* ... 95 D4 28 40 S 147 20 E
Wallambin, L., *Australia* ... 93 F2 30 57 S 117 35 E
Wallangarra, *Australia* ... 95 D5 28 56 S 151 58 E
Wallaroo, *Australia* ... 95 E2 33 56 S 137 39 E
Walldürn, *Germany* ... 25 F5 49 34N 9 22 E
Wallenhorst, *Germany* ... 24 C4 52 21N 8 1 E
Wallenpaupack, L., *U.S.A.* ... 117 E9 41 25N 75 15W
Wallingford, *U.S.A.* ... 117 E12 41 27N 72 50W
Wallis & Futuna, Is., *Pac. Oc.* ... 96 J10 13 18 S 176 10W
Wallowa, *U.S.A.* ... 108 D5 45 34N 117 32W
Wallowa Mts., *U.S.A.* ... 108 D5 45 20N 117 30W
Walls, *U.K.* ... 13 A7 60 14N 1 33W
Walls of Jerusalem △, *Australia* ... 95 G4 41 56 S 146 15 E
Wallula, *U.S.A.* ... 108 C4 46 5N 118 54W
Wallumbilla, *Australia* ... 95 D4 26 33 S 149 9 E
Walmsley, L., *Canada* ... 103 A7 63 25N 108 36W
Walney, I. of, *U.K.* ... 14 C4 54 6N 3 15W
Walnut Canyon △, *U.S.A.* ... 109 J8 35 15N 111 20W
Walnut Creek, *U.S.A.* ... 110 H4 37 54N 122 4W
Walnut Ridge, *U.S.A.* ... 113 G9 36 4N 90 57W
Walpole, *Australia* ... 93 F2 34 58 S 116 44 E
Walpole, *U.S.A.* ... 117 D13 42 9N 71 15W
Wals, *Austria* ... 26 D5 47 47N 12 58 E
Walsall, *U.K.* ... 15 E6 52 35N 1 58W
Walsenburg, *U.S.A.* ... 113 G2 37 38N 104 47W
Walsh, *U.S.A.* ... 113 G3 37 23N 102 17W
Walsh →, *Australia* ... 94 B3 16 31 S 143 42 E
Walsrode, *Germany* ... 24 C5 52 51N 9 35 E
Walterboro, *U.S.A.* ... 115 J5 32 55N 80 40W
Walters, *U.S.A.* ... 113 H5 34 22N 98 19W
Waltershausen, *Germany* ... 24 E6 50 54N 10 33 E
Waltham, *U.S.A.* ... 117 D13 42 23N 71 14W
Waltman, *U.S.A.* ... 108 E10 43 4N 107 12W
Walton, *U.S.A.* ... 117 D9 42 10N 75 8W
Walton-on-the-Naze, *U.K.* ... 15 F9 51 51N 1 17 E
Walvis Bay, *Namibia* ... 88 C1 23 0 S 14 28 E
Walvisbaai = Walvis Bay, *Namibia* ... 88 C1 23 0 S 14 28 E
Wamba, *Dem. Rep. of the Congo* ... 86 B2 2 10N 27 57 E
Wamba, *Kenya* ... 86 B4 0 58N 37 19 E
Wamba, *Nigeria* ... 83 D6 8 57N 8 42 E
Wamego, *U.S.A.* ... 112 F6 39 12N 96 18W
Wamena, *Indonesia* ... 63 E9 4 4 S 138 57 E
Wamsutter, *U.S.A.* ... 108 F9 41 40N 107 58W
Wan Xian, *China* ... 56 E8 38 47N 115 7 E
Wana, *Pakistan* ... 68 C3 32 20N 69 32 E
Wanaaring, *Australia* ... 95 D3 29 38 S 144 9 E
Wanaka, *N.Z.* ... 91 L2 44 42 S 169 9 E
Wanaka, L., *N.Z.* ... 91 L2 44 33 S 169 7 E
Wan'an, *China* ... 59 D10 26 26N 114 49 E
Wanapitei L., *Canada* ... 104 C3 46 45N 80 40W
Wandel Sea = McKinley Sea, *Arctic* ... 4 A7 82 0N 0 0W
Wandérama, *Ivory C.* ... 82 D4 8 37N 4 25W
Wanderer, *Zimbabwe* ... 87 F3 19 36 S 30 1 E
Wandhari, *Pakistan* ... 68 F2 27 42N 66 48 E
Wanding, *China* ... 58 E2 24 5N 98 4 E
Wandoan, *Australia* ... 95 D4 26 5 S 149 55 E
Wanfu, *China* ... 57 D12 40 8N 122 38 E
Wang →, *Thailand* ... 64 D2 17 8N 99 2 E
Wang Kai, *Sudan* ... 81 F2 9 3N 29 23 E
Wang Noi, *Thailand* ... 64 E3 14 13N 100 44 E
Wang Saphung, *Thailand* ... 64 D3 17 18N 101 46 E
Wang Thong, *Thailand* ... 64 D3 16 50N 100 26 E
Wangá, *Dem. Rep. of the Congo* ... 86 B2 2 58N 29 12 E

Wangal, *Indonesia* ... 63 F8 6 8 S 134 9 E
Wanganella, *Australia* ... 95 F3 35 6 S 144 49 E
Wanganui, *N.Z.* ... 91 H5 39 56 S 175 3 E
Wangaratta, *Australia* ... 95 F4 36 21 S 146 19 E
Wangary, *Australia* ... 95 E2 34 35 S 135 29 E
Wangcang, *China* ... 58 A6 32 18N 106 20 E
Wangcheng, *China* ... 59 C9 28 22N 112 49 E
Wangdu, *China* ... 56 E8 38 40N 115 7 E
Wangen, *Germany* ... 25 H5 47 41N 9 50 E
Wangerooge, *Germany* ... 24 B3 53 47N 7 54 E
Wangiwangi, *Indonesia* ... 63 F6 5 22 S 123 37 E
Wangjiang, *China* ... 59 B11 30 10N 116 42 E
Wangmo, *China* ... 58 E6 25 11N 106 5 E
Wangolodougou, *Ivory C.* ... 82 D3 9 55N 5 10W
Wangqing, *China* ... 57 C15 43 12N 129 42 E
Wankaner, *India* ... 68 H4 22 35N 71 0 E
Wanless, *Canada* ... 103 C8 54 11N 101 21W
Wannian, *China* ... 59 C11 28 42N 117 4 E
Wanning, *China* ... 64 C8 18 48N 110 22 E
Wanon Niwat, *Thailand* ... 64 D4 17 38N 103 46 E
Wanquan, *China* ... 56 D8 40 50N 114 40 E
Wanrong, *China* ... 56 G6 35 25N 110 50 E
Wanshan, *China* ... 58 D7 27 30N 109 12 E
Wanshengchang, *China* ... 58 C6 28 57N 106 53 E
Wantage, *U.K.* ... 15 F6 51 35N 1 25W
Wanxian, *China* ... 58 B7 30 42N 108 20 E
Wanyuan, *China* ... 58 A7 32 4N 108 3 E
Wanzai, *China* ... 59 C10 28 7N 114 30 E
Wapakoneta, *U.S.A.* ... 114 E3 40 34N 84 12W
Wapato, *U.S.A.* ... 108 C3 46 27N 120 25W
Wapawekka L., *Canada* ... 103 C8 54 55N 104 40W
Wapikopa L., *Canada* ... 104 B2 52 56N 87 53W
Wapiti →, *Canada* ... 102 B5 55 5N 118 18W
Wappingers Falls, *U.S.A.* ... 117 E11 41 36N 73 55W
Wapsipinicon →, *U.S.A.* ... 112 E9 41 44N 90 19W
Wapusk △, *Canada* ... 103 B10 57 46N 93 22W
Warab □, *Sudan* ... 81 F2 7 30N 28 30 E
Warangal, *India* ... 66 L11 17 58N 79 35 E
Waraseoni, *India* ... 69 J9 21 45N 80 2 E
Waratah, *Australia* ... 95 G4 41 30 S 145 30 E
Waratah B., *Australia* ... 95 F4 38 54 S 146 5 E
Warburg, *Germany* ... 24 D5 51 28N 9 11 E
Warburton, *Vic., Australia* ... 95 F4 37 47 S 145 42 E
Warburton, *W. Austral., Australia* ... 93 E4 26 8 S 126 35 E
Warburton, The →, *Australia* ... 95 D2 28 4 S 137 28 E
Warburton Ra., *Australia* ... 93 E4 25 55 S 126 28 E
Ward, *N.Z.* ... 91 J5 41 49 S 174 11 E
Ward →, *Australia* ... 95 D4 26 28 S 146 6 E
Ward Mt., *U.S.A.* ... 110 H8 37 12N 118 54W
Warden, *S. Africa* ... 89 D4 27 50 S 29 0 E
Wardha, *India* ... 66 J11 20 45N 78 39 E
Wardha →, *India* ... 66 K11 19 57N 79 11 E
Ware, *Canada* ... 102 B3 57 26N 125 41W
Ware, *U.K.* ... 15 F8 51 49N 0 0W
Ware, *U.S.A.* ... 117 D12 42 16N 72 14W
Waregem, *Belgium* ... 17 D3 50 53N 3 27 E
Wareham, *U.S.A.* ... 117 E14 41 46N 70 43W
Waremme, *Belgium* ... 17 D5 50 43N 5 15 E
Waren, *Germany* ... 24 B8 53 31N 12 40 E
Warendorf, *Germany* ... 24 D4 51 57N 8 1 E
Warialda, *Australia* ... 95 D5 29 29 S 150 33 E
Wariap, *Indonesia* ... 63 E8 1 30 S 134 5 E
Warin Chamrap, *Thailand* ... 64 E5 15 12N 104 53 E
Warka, *Poland* ... 31 G8 51 47N 21 12 E
Warkopi, *Indonesia* ... 63 E8 1 12 S 134 9 E
Warm Springs, *U.S.A.* ... 109 G5 38 10N 116 20W
Warman, *Canada* ... 103 C7 52 19N 106 30W
Warmbad = Bela Bela, *S. Africa* ... 89 C4 24 51 S 28 19 E
Warmbad, *Namibia* ... 88 D2 28 25 S 18 42 E
Warmińsko-Mazurskie □, *Poland* ... 30 D8 54 0N 21 0 E
Warminster, *U.K.* ... 15 F5 51 12N 2 10W
Warminster, *U.S.A.* ... 117 F9 40 12N 75 6W
Warnemünde, *Germany* ... 24 A8 54 10N 12 4 E
Warner Mts., *U.S.A.* ... 108 F3 41 40N 120 15W
Warner Robins, *U.S.A.* ... 115 J4 32 37N 83 36W
Warnow →, *Germany* ... 24 A8 54 6N 12 9 E
Waroona, *Australia* ... 93 F2 32 50 S 115 58 E
Warracknabeal, *Australia* ... 95 F3 36 9 S 142 26 E
Warragul, *Australia* ... 95 F4 38 10 S 145 58 E
Warrego →, *Australia* ... 95 E4 30 24 S 145 21 E
Warrego Ra., *Australia* ... 94 C4 24 58 S 146 0 E
Warren, *Australia* ... 95 E4 31 42 S 147 51 E
Warren, *Ark., U.S.A.* ... 113 J8 33 37N 92 4W
Warren, *Mich., U.S.A.* ... 114 D4 42 30N 83 0W
Warren, *Minn., U.S.A.* ... 112 A6 48 12N 96 46W
Warren, *Ohio, U.S.A.* ... 116 E4 41 14N 80 49W
Warren, *Pa., U.S.A.* ... 116 E5 41 51N 79 9W
Warrenpoint, *U.K.* ... 12 B5 54 6N 6 15W
Warrensburg, *Mo., U.S.A.* ... 112 F8 38 46N 93 44W
Warrensburg, *N.Y., U.S.A.* ... 117 C11 43 29N 73 46W
Warrenton, *S. Africa* ... 88 D3 28 9 S 24 47 E
Warrenton, *U.S.A.* ... 110 D3 46 10N 123 56W
Warri, *Nigeria* ... 83 D6 5 30N 5 41 E
Warrina, *Australia* ... 95 D2 28 12 S 135 50 E
Warrington, *U.K.* ... 14 D5 53 24N 2 35W
Warrington □, *U.K.* ... 14 D5 53 24N 2 35W
Warrnambool, *Australia* ... 95 F3 38 25 S 142 30 E
Warroad, *U.S.A.* ... 112 A7 48 54N 95 19W
Warruwi, *Australia* ... 94 A1 11 36 S 133 20 E
Warsa, *Indonesia* ... 63 E9 0 47 S 135 55 E
Warsak Dam, *Pakistan* ... 68 B4 34 11N 71 19 E
Warsaw = Warszawa, *Poland* ... 31 F8 52 13N 21 0 E
Warsaw, *Ind., U.S.A.* ... 114 E3 41 14N 85 51W
Warsaw, *N.Y., U.S.A.* ... 116 D6 42 45N 78 8W
Warsaw, *Ohio, U.S.A.* ... 116 F3 40 20N 82 0W
Warstein, *Germany* ... 24 D4 51 26N 8 22 E
Warszawa, *Poland* ... 31 F8 52 13N 21 0 E
Warszawa ✈ (WAW), *Poland* ... 31 F7 52 9N 20 59 E
Warta, *Poland* ... 31 G5 51 43N 18 38 E
Warta →, *Poland* ... 31 F1 52 35N 14 39 E
Warthe = Warta →, *Poland* ... 31 F1 52 35N 14 39 E
Waru, *Indonesia* ... 63 E8 3 30 S 130 36 E
Warwick, *Australia* ... 95 D5 28 10 S 152 1 E
Warwick, *U.K.* ... 15 E6 52 18N 1 35W
Warwick, *N.Y., U.S.A.* ... 117 E10 41 16N 74 22W
Warwick, *R.I., U.S.A.* ... 117 E13 41 42N 71 28W
Warwickshire □, *U.K.* ... 15 E6 52 14N 1 38W
Wasaga Beach, *Canada* ... 116 B4 44 31N 80 1W
Wasagaming, *Canada* ... 103 C9 50 39N 99 58W
Wasatch Ra., *U.S.A.* ... 108 F8 40 30N 111 15W
Wasbank, *S. Africa* ... 89 D5 28 15 S 30 9 E

Wasco, *Calif., U.S.A.* ... 111 K7 35 36N 119 20W
Wasco, *Oreg., U.S.A.* ... 108 D3 45 36N 120 42W
Wase, *Nigeria* ... 83 D6 9 4N 9 54 E
Waseca, *U.S.A.* ... 112 C8 44 5N 93 30W
Wasekamio L., *Canada* ... 103 B7 56 45N 108 45W
Wash, The, *U.K.* ... 14 E8 52 58N 0 20 E
Washago, *Canada* ... 116 B5 44 45N 79 20W
Washburn, *N. Dak., U.S.A.* ... 112 B4 47 17N 101 2W
Washburn, *Wis., U.S.A.* ... 112 B9 46 40N 90 54W
Washim, *India* ... 66 J10 20 3N 77 0 E
Washington, *U.K.* ... 14 C6 54 55N 1 30W
Washington, *D.C., U.S.A.* ... 114 F7 38 54N 77 2W
Washington, *Ga., U.S.A.* ... 115 J4 33 44N 82 44W
Washington, *Ind., U.S.A.* ... 114 F2 38 40N 87 10W
Washington, *Iowa, U.S.A.* ... 112 E9 41 18N 91 42W
Washington, *Mo., U.S.A.* ... 112 F9 38 33N 91 1W
Washington, *N.C., U.S.A.* ... 115 H7 35 33N 77 3W
Washington, *N.J., U.S.A.* ... 117 F10 40 46N 74 59W
Washington, *Pa., U.S.A.* ... 116 F4 40 10N 80 15W
Washington, *Utah, U.S.A.* ... 109 H7 37 8N 113 31W
Washington □, *U.S.A.* ... 108 C3 47 30N 120 30W
Washington, Mt., *U.S.A.* ... 117 B13 44 16N 71 18W
Washington Court House, *U.S.A.* ... 114 F4 39 32N 83 26W
Washington I., *U.S.A.* ... 114 C2 45 23N 86 54W
Washougal, *U.S.A.* ... 110 E4 45 35N 122 21W
Washpool △, *Australia* ... 95 D5 29 22 S 152 21 E
Wasian, *Indonesia* ... 63 E8 1 47 S 133 19 E
Wasilków, *Poland* ... 31 E10 53 12N 23 13 E
Wasilla, *U.S.A.* ... 100 B5 61 35N 149 26W
Wasior, *Indonesia* ... 63 E8 2 43 S 134 30 E
Wāsiṭ □, *Iraq* ... 70 C5 32 30N 46 0 E
Waskaganish, *Canada* ... 104 B4 51 30N 78 40W
Waskaiowaka, L., *Canada* ... 103 B9 56 33N 96 23W
Waskesiu Lake, *Canada* ... 103 C7 53 55N 106 5W
Wasserburg, *Germany* ... 25 G8 48 3N 12 14 E
Wasserkuppe, *Germany* ... 24 E5 50 29N 9 55 E
Wassy, *France* ... 19 D11 48 30N 4 58 E
Waswanipi, *Canada* ... 104 C4 49 40N 76 29W
Waswanipi, L., *Canada* ... 104 C4 49 35N 76 40W
Watampone, *Indonesia* ... 63 E6 4 29 S 120 25 E
Watamu, *Kenya* ... 86 C5 3 23 S 40 0 E
Waterberg Plateau △, *Namibia* ... 88 C2 20 25 S 17 18 E
Waterberge, *S. Africa* ... 89 C4 24 10 S 28 0 E
Waterbury, *Conn., U.S.A.* ... 117 E11 41 33N 73 3W
Waterbury, *Vt., U.S.A.* ... 117 B12 44 20N 72 46W
Waterbury L., *Canada* ... 103 B8 58 10N 104 22W
Waterdown, *Canada* ... 116 C5 43 20N 79 53W
Waterford, *Canada* ... 116 D4 42 56N 80 17W
Waterford, *Ireland* ... 12 D4 52 15N 7 8W
Waterford, *Calif., U.S.A.* ... 110 H6 37 38N 120 46W
Waterford, *Pa., U.S.A.* ... 116 E5 41 57N 79 59W
Waterford □, *Ireland* ... 12 D4 52 10N 7 40W
Waterford Harbour, *Ireland* ... 12 D5 52 8N 6 58W
Waterloo, *Belgium* ... 17 D4 50 43N 4 25 E
Waterloo, *Ont., Canada* ... 116 C4 43 30N 80 32W
Waterloo, *Qué., Canada* ... 117 A12 45 22N 72 32W
Waterloo, *S. Leone* ... 82 D2 8 26N 13 8W
Waterloo, *Ill., U.S.A.* ... 112 F9 38 20N 90 9W
Waterloo, *Iowa, U.S.A.* ... 112 D8 42 30N 92 21W
Waterloo, *N.Y., U.S.A.* ... 116 D8 42 54N 76 52W
Watermeet, *U.S.A.* ... 112 B10 46 16N 89 11W
Waterton Lakes △, *Canada* ... 102 D6 48 45N 115 0W
Watertown, *Conn., U.S.A.* ... 117 E11 41 36N 73 7W
Watertown, *N.Y., U.S.A.* ... 117 C9 43 59N 75 55W
Watertown, *S. Dak., U.S.A.* ... 112 C6 44 54N 97 7W
Watertown, *Wis., U.S.A.* ... 112 D10 43 12N 88 43W
Waterval-Boven, *S. Africa* ... 89 D5 25 40 S 30 18 E
Waterville, *Canada* ... 117 A13 45 16N 71 54W
Waterville, *Maine, U.S.A.* ... 115 C11 44 33N 69 38W
Waterville, *N.Y., U.S.A.* ... 117 D9 42 56N 75 23W
Waterville, *Pa., U.S.A.* ... 116 E7 41 19N 77 21W
Waterville, *Wash., U.S.A.* ... 108 C3 47 39N 120 4W
Watervliet, *U.S.A.* ... 117 D11 42 44N 73 42W
Wates, *Indonesia* ... 63 G14 7 51 S 110 10 E
Watford, *Canada* ... 116 D3 42 57N 81 53W
Watford, *U.K.* ... 15 F7 51 40N 0 24W
Watford City, *U.S.A.* ... 112 B3 47 48N 103 17W
Wathaman →, *Canada* ... 103 B8 57 16N 102 59W
Wathaman L., *Canada* ... 103 B8 56 58N 103 44W
Watheroo, *Australia* ... 93 F2 30 15 S 116 0 E
Watheroo △, *Australia* ... 93 F2 30 19 S 115 48 E
Wating, *China* ... 56 G4 35 40N 106 38 E
Watkins Glen, *U.S.A.* ... 116 D8 42 23N 76 52W
Watling I. = San Salvador I., *Bahamas* ... 121 B5 24 0N 74 40W
Watonga, *U.S.A.* ... 113 H5 35 51N 98 25W
Watrous, *Canada* ... 103 C7 51 40N 105 25W
Watrous, *U.S.A.* ... 113 H2 35 48N 104 59W
Watsa, *Dem. Rep. of the Congo* ... 86 B2 3 4N 29 30 E
Watseka, *U.S.A.* ... 114 E2 40 47N 87 44W
Watson, *Australia* ... 95 E5 30 29 S 131 31 E
Watson, *Canada* ... 103 C8 52 10N 104 30W
Watson Lake, *Canada* ... 102 A3 60 6N 128 49W
Watsontown, *U.S.A.* ... 116 E8 41 5N 76 52W
Watsonville, *U.S.A.* ... 110 J5 36 55N 121 45W
Wattiwarriganna Cr. →, *Australia* ... 95 D2 28 57 S 136 10 E
Wattwil, *Switz.* ... 25 H5 47 18N 9 6 E
Watuata = Batuata, *Indonesia* ... 63 F6 6 12 S 122 42 E
Watubela, Kepulauan, *Indonesia* ... 63 E8 4 28 S 131 35 E
Watubela Is. = Watubela, Kepulauan, *Indonesia* ... 63 E8 4 28 S 131 35 E
Wau = Wâw, *Sudan* ... 81 F2 7 45N 28 1 E
Waubamik, *Canada* ... 116 A4 45 27N 80 1W
Waubay, *U.S.A.* ... 112 C6 45 20N 97 18W
Wauchope, *N.S.W., Australia* ... 95 E5 31 28 S 152 45 E
Wauchope, *N. Terr., Australia* ... 94 C1 20 36 S 134 15 E
Wauchula, *U.S.A.* ... 115 M5 27 33N 81 49W
Waukarlycarly, L., *Australia* ... 92 D3 21 18 S 121 56 E

Waukegan, *U.S.A.* ... 114 D2 42 22N 87 50W
Waukesha, *U.S.A.* ... 114 D1 43 1N 88 14W
Waukon, *U.S.A.* ... 112 D9 43 16N 91 29W
Waupaca, *U.S.A.* ... 112 C10 44 21N 89 5W
Waupun, *U.S.A.* ... 112 D10 43 38N 88 44W
Waurika, *U.S.A.* ... 113 H6 34 10N 98 0W
Wausau, *U.S.A.* ... 112 C10 44 58N 89 38W
Wautoma, *U.S.A.* ... 112 C10 44 4N 89 18W
Wauwatosa, *U.S.A.* ... 114 D2 43 3N 88 0W
Waveney →, *U.K.* ... 15 E9 52 35N 1 39 E
Waverley, *N.Z.* ... 91 H5 39 46 S 174 37 E
Waverly, *Iowa, U.S.A.* ... 112 D8 42 44N 92 29W
Waverly, *N.Y., U.S.A.* ... 117 E8 42 1N 76 32W
Wavre, *Belgium* ... 17 D4 50 43N 4 38 E
Wâw, *Sudan* ... 81 F2 7 45N 28 1 E
Wawa, *Nigeria* ... 83 D5 9 54N 4 27 E
Wawa, *Sudan* ... 80 C3 20 30N 30 22 E
Wawanesa, *Canada* ... 103 D9 49 36N 99 40W
Wawona, *U.S.A.* ... 110 H7 37 32N 119 39W
Waxahachie, *U.S.A.* ... 113 J6 32 24N 96 51W
Way, L., *Australia* ... 93 E3 26 45 S 120 16 E
Waycross, *U.S.A.* ... 115 K4 31 13N 82 21W
Wayi, *Sudan* ... 81 F3 5 8N 30 10 E
Wayland, *U.S.A.* ... 116 D7 42 34N 77 35W
Wayne, *Nebr., U.S.A.* ... 112 D6 42 14N 97 1W
Wayne, *W. Va., U.S.A.* ... 114 F4 38 13N 82 27W
Waynesboro, *Ga., U.S.A.* ... 115 J4 33 6N 82 1W
Waynesboro, *Miss., U.S.A.* ... 115 K1 31 40N 88 39W
Waynesboro, *Pa., U.S.A.* ... 114 F7 39 45N 77 35W
Waynesboro, *Va., U.S.A.* ... 114 F6 38 4N 78 53W
Waynesburg, *U.S.A.* ... 114 F5 39 54N 80 11W
Waynesville, *U.S.A.* ... 115 H4 35 28N 82 58W
Waynoka, *U.S.A.* ... 113 G5 36 35N 98 53W
Wazirabad, *Pakistan* ... 68 C6 32 30N 74 8 E
Wda →, *Poland* ... 30 E5 53 25N 18 29 E
We, *Indonesia* ... 62 C1 5 51N 95 18 E
Weald, The, *U.K.* ... 15 F8 51 4N 0 20 E
Wear →, *U.K.* ... 14 C6 54 55N 1 23W
Weatherford, *Okla., U.S.A.* ... 113 H5 35 32N 98 43W
Weatherford, *Tex., U.S.A.* ... 113 J6 32 46N 97 48W
Weaverville, *U.S.A.* ... 108 F2 40 44N 122 56W
Webb City, *U.S.A.* ... 113 G7 37 9N 94 28W
Webequie, *Canada* ... 104 B2 52 59N 87 21W
Webo = Nyaake, *Liberia* ... 82 E3 4 52N 7 37W
Webster, *Mass., U.S.A.* ... 117 D13 42 3N 71 53W
Webster, *N.Y., U.S.A.* ... 116 C7 43 13N 77 26W
Webster, *S. Dak., U.S.A.* ... 112 C6 45 20N 97 31W
Webster City, *U.S.A.* ... 112 D8 42 28N 93 49W
Webster Springs, *U.S.A.* ... 114 F5 38 29N 80 25W
Weda, *Indonesia* ... 63 D7 0 21N 127 50 E
Weda, Teluk, *Indonesia* ... 63 D7 0 20N 128 0 E
Weddell I., *Falk. Is.* ... 128 G4 51 50 S 61 0W
Weddell Sea, *Antarctica* ... 5 D1 72 30 S 40 0W
Wedderburn, *Australia* ... 95 F3 36 26 S 143 33 E
Wedel, *Germany* ... 24 B5 53 34N 9 42 E
Wedemark, *Germany* ... 24 C5 52 32N 9 43 E
Wedgeport, *Canada* ... 105 D6 43 44N 65 59W
Wedza, *Zimbabwe* ... 87 F3 18 40 S 31 33 E
Wee Waa, *Australia* ... 95 E4 30 11 S 149 26 E
Weed, *U.S.A.* ... 108 F2 41 25N 122 23W
Weed Heights, *U.S.A.* ... 110 G7 38 59N 119 13W
Weedsport, *U.S.A.* ... 117 C8 43 3N 76 35W
Weedville, *U.S.A.* ... 116 E6 41 17N 78 30W
Weenen, *S. Africa* ... 89 D5 28 48 S 30 7 E
Weener, *Germany* ... 24 B3 53 9N 7 20 E
Weert, *Neths.* ... 17 C5 51 15N 5 43 E
Węgierska-Górka, *Poland* ... 31 J6 49 36N 19 7 E
Węgliniec, *Poland* ... 31 G2 51 18N 15 14 E
Węgorzewo, *Poland* ... 30 D8 54 13N 21 43 E
Węgorzyno, *Poland* ... 30 E2 53 32N 15 33 E
Węgrów, *Poland* ... 31 F9 52 24N 22 0 E
Wehda □, *Sudan* ... 81 F3 8 30N 30 0 E
Wei He →, *Hebei, China* ... 56 F8 36 10N 115 45 E
Wei He →, *Shaanxi, China* ... 56 G6 34 38N 110 15 E
Weichang, *China* ... 57 D9 41 58N 117 49 E
Weichuan, *China* ... 56 G7 34 20N 113 59 E
Weida, *Germany* ... 24 E8 50 46N 12 2 E
Weiden, *Germany* ... 25 F8 49 41N 12 10 E
Weifang, *China* ... 57 F10 36 44N 119 7 E
Weihai, *China* ... 57 F12 37 30N 122 6 E
Weil, *Germany* ... 25 H3 47 35N 7 37 E
Weilburg, *Germany* ... 24 E4 50 28N 8 17 E
Weilheim, *Germany* ... 25 H7 47 50N 11 9 E
Weimar, *Germany* ... 24 E7 50 58N 11 19 E
Weinan, *China* ... 56 G5 34 31N 109 29 E
Weingarten, *Germany* ... 25 F4 49 3N 8 31 E
Weinheim, *Germany* ... 25 F4 49 32N 8 40 E
Weining, *China* ... 58 D5 26 50N 104 17 E
Weipa, *Australia* ... 94 A3 12 40 S 141 50 E
Weir →, *Australia* ... 95 D4 28 20 S 149 50 E
Weir →, *Canada* ... 103 B10 56 49N 94 6W
Weir River, *Canada* ... 103 B10 56 49N 94 6W
Weirton, *U.S.A.* ... 116 F4 40 24N 80 35W
Weiser, *U.S.A.* ... 108 D5 44 10N 117 0W
Weishan, *Shandong, China* ... 57 G9 34 47N 117 5 E
Weishan, *Yunnan, China* ... 58 E3 25 12N 100 20 E
Weissenburg, *Germany* ... 25 F6 49 2N 10 58 E
Weissenfels, *Germany* ... 24 D7 51 11N 12 0 E
Weisswasser, *Germany* ... 24 D10 51 30N 14 36 E
Wéitra, *Austria* ... 26 C7 48 41N 14 54 E
Weixi, *China* ... 58 D2 27 10N 99 10 E
Weixin, *China* ... 58 D5 27 48N 105 3 E
Weiyuan, *China* ... 56 G3 35 7N 104 10 E
Weiz, *Austria* ... 26 D8 47 13N 15 39 E
Weizhou Dao, *China* ... 58 G7 21 0N 109 5 E
Wejherowo, *Poland* ... 30 D5 54 35N 18 12 E
Wekusko L., *Canada* ... 103 C9 54 40N 99 50W
Welch, *U.S.A.* ... 114 G5 37 26N 81 35W
Weldya, *Ethiopia* ... 81 E4 11 50N 39 34 E
Welega □, *Ethiopia* ... 81 F3 9 25N 34 20 E
Welford △, *Australia* ... 94 D3 25 5 S 143 16 E
Welkite, *Ethiopia* ... 81 F4 8 15N 37 42 E
Welkom, *S. Africa* ... 88 D4 28 0 S 26 46 E
Welland, *Canada* ... 116 D5 43 0N 79 15W
Welland →, *U.K.* ... 15 E7 52 51N 0 5W
Wellesley Is., *Australia* ... 94 B2 16 42 S 139 30 E
Wellingborough, *U.K.* ... 15 E7 52 19N 0 41W
Wellington, *Australia* ... 95 E4 32 35 S 148 59 E
Wellington, *Canada* ... 116 C7 43 57N 77 20W
Wellington, *N.Z.* ... 91 J5 41 19 S 174 46 E
Wellington, *S. Africa* ... 88 E2 33 38 S 19 1 E
Wellington, *Somst., U.K.* ... 15 G4 50 58N 3 13W
Wellington, *Telford & Wrekin, U.K.* ... 15 E5 52 42N 2 30W
Wellington, *Colo., U.S.A.* ... 112 E2 40 42N 105 0W

Wellington, *Kans.,*
U.S.A. **113 G6** 37 16N 97 24W
Wellington, *Nev., U.S.A.* **110 G7** 38 45N 119 23W
Wellington, *Ohio,*
U.S.A. **116 E2** 41 10N 82 13W
Wellington, *Tex., U.S.A.* **113 H4** 34 51N 100 13W
Wellington, *I., Chile* .. **128 F2** 49 30 S 75 0W
Wellington, *L., Australia* **95 F4** 38 6 S 147 20 E
Wells, *U.K.* **15 F5** 51 13N 2 39W
Wells, *Maine, U.S.A.* .. **117 C14** 43 20N 70 35W
Wells, *N.Y., U.S.A.* .. **117 C10** 43 24N 74 17W
Wells, *Nev., U.S.A.* .. **108 F6** 41 7N 114 58W
Wells, *L., Australia* .. **93 E3** 26 44 S 123 15 E
Wells, *Mt., Australia* .. **14 E8** 17 25 S 127 8 E
Wells Gray △, *Canada* .. **102 C4** 52 30N 120 15W
Wells-next-the-Sea, *U.K.* **14 E8** 52 57N 0 51 E
Wells River, *U.S.A.* .. **117 B12** 44 9N 72 4W
Wellsboro, *U.S.A.* **116 E7** 41 45N 77 18W
Wellsburg, *U.S.A.* **116 F4** 40 16N 80 37W
Wellsville, *N.Y., U.S.A.* **116 D7** 42 7N 77 57W
Wellsville, *Ohio, U.S.A.* **116 F4** 40 36N 80 39W
Wellsville, *Utah, U.S.A.* **108 F8** 41 38N 111 56W
Wellton, *U.S.A.* **109 K6** 32 40N 114 8W
Welmel, Wabi →,
Ethiopia .... **81 F5** 5 38N 40 47 E
Welo, *Ethiopia* ...... **81 E4** 11 50N 39 48 E
Wels, *Austria* ...... **26 C7** 48 9N 14 1 E
Welshpool, *U.K.* **15 E4** 52 39N 3 8W
Welwyn Garden City,
U.K. **15 F7** 51 48N 0 12W
Wem, *U.K.* **14 E5** 52 52N 2 44W
Wembere →, *Tanzania* .. **86 C3** 4 10 S 34 15 E
Wemindji, *Canada* **104 B4** 53 0N 78 49W
Wen Xian, *China* .... **56 G7** 34 55N 113 5 E
Wenatchee, *U.S.A.* .. **108 C3** 47 25N 120 19W
Wenchang, *China* .... **64 C8** 19 38N 110 42 E
Wencheng, *China* .... **59 D13** 27 46N 120 4 E
Wenchi, *Ghana* **82 D4** 7 46N 2 8W
Wenchow = Wenzhou,
China .... **59 D13** 28 0N 120 38 E
Wenchuan, *China* .... **58 B4** 31 22N 103 35 E
Wenden, *U.S.A.* **111 M13** 33 49N 113 33W
Wendeng, *China* .... **57 F12** 37 15N 122 5 E
Wendesi, *Indonesia* .. **63 E8** 2 30 S 134 17 E
Wendo, *Ethiopia* .... **81 F4** 6 40N 38 27 E
Wendover, *U.S.A.* .. **108 F6** 40 44N 114 2W
Weng'an, *China* ...... **58 D6** 27 5N 107 25 E
Wengcheng, *China* .... **59 E9** 24 22N 113 50 E
Wengyuan, *China* .... **59 E10** 24 20N 114 9 E
Wenjiang, *China* .... **58 B4** 30 44N 103 55 E
Wenling, *China* ...... **59 C13** 28 21N 121 20 E
Wenlock →, *Australia* .. **94 A3** 12 2 S 141 55 E
Wenshan, *China* ...... **58 F5** 23 20N 104 18 E
Wenshang, *China* .... **56 G9** 35 45N 116 30 E
Wenshui, *China* ...... **56 F7** 37 26N 112 1 E
Wensleydale, *U.K.* .. **14 C6** 54 17N 2 0W
Wensu, *China* .... **60 B3** 41 15N 80 10 E
Wensum →, *U.K.* .... **14 E8** 52 40N 1 15 E
Wentworth, *Australia* .. **95 E3** 34 2 S 141 54 E
Wentzel L., *Canada* .. **102 B6** 59 2N 114 28W
Wenut, *Indonesia* .... **63 E8** 3 11 S 133 19 E
Wenxi, *China* .... **56 G6** 35 20N 111 10 E
Wenxian, *China* ...... **56 H3** 32 43N 104 36 E
Wenzhou, *China* ...... **59 D13** 28 0N 120 38 E
Weott, *U.S.A.* **108 F2** 40 20N 123 55W
Wepener, *S. Africa* .. **88 D4** 29 42 S 27 3 E
Werda, *Botswana* .... **88 D3** 25 24 S 23 15 E
Werdau, *Germany* .... **24 E8** 50 44N 12 22 E
Werder, *Germany* .... **24 C8** 52 23N 12 55 E
Werdohl, *Germany* .. **24 D3** 51 15N 7 46 E
Wereilu, *Ethiopia* .... **81 E4** 10 40N 39 28 E
Weri, *Indonesia* ...... **63 E8** 3 10 S 132 38 E
Werneck, *Germany* .. **25 F6** 49 58N 10 5 E
Wernigerode, *Germany* **24 D6** 51 50N 10 47 E
Werra →, *Germany* .. **24 D5** 51 24N 9 39 E
Werrimull, *Australia* .. **95 E3** 34 25 S 141 38 E
Werris Creek, *Australia* **95 E5** 31 18 S 150 38 E
Wertach →, *Germany* .. **25 G6** 48 22N 10 54 E
Wertheim, *Germany* .. **25 F5** 49 45N 9 32 E
Wertingen, *Germany* .. **25 G6** 48 33N 10 41 E
Wesel, *Germany* ...... **24 D2** 51 39N 6 37 E
Weser →, *Germany* .. **24 B4** 53 36N 8 28 E
Weser-Ems □, *Germany* **24 C3** 53 0N 7 30 E
Weserbergland,
Germany .... **24 C5** 52 12N 9 7 E
Weserbergland
Schaumburg
Hameln △, *Germany* **24 C5** 52 8N 9 20 E
Wesiri, *Indonesia* .... **63 F7** 7 30 S 126 30 E
Weslemkoon L., *Canada* **116 A7** 45 2N 77 25W
Wesleyville, *U.S.A.* .. **116 D4** 42 9N 80 0W
Wessel, *C., Australia* .. **94 A2** 10 59 S 136 46 E
Wessel Is., *Australia* .. **94 A2** 11 10 S 136 45 E
Wesselburen, *Germany* **24 A4** 54 13N 8 54 E
Wessington Springs,
U.S.A. **112 C5** 44 5N 98 34W
West, *U.S.A.* **113 K6** 31 48N 97 6W
West →, *U.S.A.* **117 D12** 42 52N 72 33W
West Antarctica,
Antarctica .... **5 D15** 80 0 S 90 0W
West Baines →,
Australia .... **92 C4** 15 38 S 129 59 E
West Bank ⊘, *Asia* .. **74 C4** 32 6N 35 13 E
West Bend, *U.S.A.* .. **114 D1** 43 25N 88 11W
West Bengal □, *India* .. **69 H13** 23 0N 88 0 E
West Berkshire □, *U.K.* **15 F6** 51 25N 1 17W
West Beskids = Západné
Beskydy, *Europe* .. **27 B12** 49 30N 19 0 E
West Branch, *U.S.A.* .. **114 C3** 44 17N 84 14W
West Branch
Susquehanna →,
U.S.A. **117 F8** 40 53N 76 48W
West Bromwich, *U.K.* .. **15 E6** 52 32N 1 59W
West Burra, *U.K.* **13 A7** 60 5N 1 21W
West Canada Cr. →,
U.S.A. **117 C10** 43 1N 74 58W
West Cape Howe,
Australia .... **93 G2** 35 8 S 117 36 E
West Chazy, *U.S.A.* .. **117 B11** 44 49N 73 28W
West Chester, *U.S.A.* .. **117 G9** 39 58N 75 36W
West Coast △, *Namibia* **88 C1** 21 53 S 14 14 E
West Coast △, *S. Africa* **88 E2** 33 13 S 18 0 E
West Columbia, *U.S.A.* **113 L7** 29 9N 95 39W
West Covina, *U.S.A.* .. **111 L9** 34 4N 117 54W
West Des Moines,
U.S.A. **112 E8** 41 35N 93 43W
West Dunbartonshire □,
U.K. **13 F4** 55 59N 4 30W
West End, *Bahamas* .. **120 A4** 26 41N 78 58W
West Falkland, *Falk. Is.* **128 G5** 51 40 S 60 0W
West Fargo, *U.S.A.* .. **112 B6** 46 52N 96 54W
West Farmington,
U.S.A. **116 E4** 41 23N 80 58W
West Fjord = Vest-
fjorden, *Norway* .. **8 C15** 67 55N 14 0 E
West Fork Trinity →,
U.S.A. **113 J6** 32 48N 96 54W

West Frankfort, *U.S.A.* **112 G10** 37 54N 88 55W
West Hartford, *U.S.A.* **117 E12** 41 45N 72 44W
West Haven, *U.S.A.* .. **117 E12** 41 17N 72 57W
West Hazleton, *U.S.A.* **117 F9** 40 58N 76 0W
West Helena, *U.S.A.* .. **113 H9** 34 33N 90 38W
West Hurley, *U.S.A.* .. **117 E10** 41 59N 74 7W
West Ice Shelf,
Antarctica .... **5 C7** 67 0 S 85 0 E
West Indies, *Cent. Amer.* **121 D7** 15 0N 65 0W
West Jordan, *U.S.A.* .. **108 F8** 40 36N 111 56W
West Lorne, *Canada* .. **116 D3** 42 36N 81 36W
West Lothian □, *U.K.* .. **13 F5** 55 54N 3 36W
West Lunga →, *Zambia* **87 E1** 13 6 S 24 39 E
West MacDonnell △,
Australia .... **92 D5** 23 38 S 132 59 E
West Memphis, *U.S.A.* **113 H9** 35 9N 90 11W
West Midlands □, *U.K.* **15 E6** 52 26N 2 0W
West Mifflin, *U.S.A.* .. **116 F5** 40 22N 79 52W
West Milton, *U.S.A.* .. **116 E8** 41 1N 76 50W
West Monroe, *U.S.A.* .. **113 J8** 32 31N 92 9W
West Newton, *U.S.A.* .. **116 F5** 40 14N 79 46W
West Nicholson,
Zimbabwe .... **87 G2** 21 2 S 29 20 E
West Palm Beach,
U.S.A. **115 M5** 26 43N 80 3W
West Plains, *U.S.A.* .. **113 G9** 36 44N 91 51W
West Point, *N.Y., U.S.A.* **117 E11** 41 24N 73 58W
West Point, *Nebr.,*
U.S.A. **112 E6** 41 51N 96 43W
West Pt. = Ouest, Pte. de
l', *Canada* **105 C7** 49 52N 64 40W
West Pt., *Australia* .. **95 F2** 35 1 S 135 56 E
West Road →, *Canada* **102 C4** 53 18N 122 53W
West Rutland, *U.S.A.* .. **117 C11** 43 38N 73 5W
West Schelde =
Westerschelde →,
Neths. .... **17 C3** 51 25N 3 25 E
West Seneca, *U.S.A.* .. **116 D6** 42 51N 78 48W
West Siberian Plain,
Russia .... **50 C11** 62 0N 75 0 E
West Sussex □, *U.K.* .. **15 G7** 50 55N 0 30W
West-Terschelling,
Neths. .... **17 A5** 53 22N 5 13 E
West Valley City, *U.S.A.* **108 F8** 40 42N 111 57W
West Virginia □, *U.S.A.* **114 F5** 38 45N 80 30W
West-Vlaanderen □,
Belgium .... **17 D2** 51 0N 3 0 E
West Walker →, *U.S.A.* **110 G7** 38 54N 119 9W
West Wyalong, *Australia* **95 E4** 33 56 S 147 10 E
West Yellowstone,
U.S.A. **108 D8** 44 40N 111 6W
West Yorkshire □, *U.K.* **14 D6** 53 45N 1 40W
Westall, Pt., *Australia* .. **95 E1** 32 55 S 134 4 E
Westbrook, *U.S.A.* .. **115 D10** 43 41N 70 22W
Westbury, *Australia* .. **95 G4** 41 30 S 146 51 E
Westby, *U.S.A.* **112 A2** 48 52N 104 3W
Westend, *U.S.A.* **111 K9** 35 42N 117 24W
Westerland, *Germany* .. **9 J13** 54 54N 8 17 E
Westerly, *U.S.A.* **117 E13** 41 22N 71 50W
Western □, *Ghana* .. **82 D4** 5 30N 2 30W
Western □, *Kenya* .. **86 B3** 0 30N 34 30 E
Western □, *S. Leone* .. **82 D2** 8 30N 13 0W
Western □, *Zambia* .. **87 F1** 15 0 S 24 4 E
Western Australia □,
Australia .... **93 E2** 25 0 S 118 0 E
Western Cape □,
S. Africa .... **88 E3** 34 0 S 20 0 E
Western Dvina =
Daugava →, *Latvia* **9 H21** 57 4N 24 3 E
Western Ghats, *India* .. **66 N9** 14 0N 75 0 E
Western Isles □, *U.K.* .. **13 D1** 57 30N 7 10W
Western Sahara ■,
Africa **78 D3** 25 0N 13 0W
Western Samoa =
Samoa ■, *Pac. Oc.* .. **91 B13** 14 0 S 172 0W
Westernport, *U.S.A.* .. **114 F6** 39 29N 79 3W
Westerschelde →,
Neths. .... **17 C3** 51 25N 3 25 E
Westerstede, *Germany* **24 B3** 53 15N 7 55 E
Westerwald, *Germany* **24 E3** 50 38N 7 56 E
Westfield, *Mass., U.S.A.* **117 D12** 42 7N 72 45W
Westfield, *N.Y., U.S.A.* **116 D5** 42 20N 79 35W
Westfield, *Pa., U.S.A.* .. **116 E7** 41 55N 77 32W
Westhill, *U.K.* **13 D6** 57 9N 2 19W
Westhope, *U.S.A.* .. **112 A4** 48 55N 101 1W
Westland △, *N.Z.* .. **91 K2** 43 16 S 170 16 E
Westland Bight, *N.Z.* .. **91 K3** 42 55 S 170 5 E
Westlock, *Canada* .. **102 C6** 54 9N 113 55W
Westmar, *Australia* .. **95 D4** 27 55 S 149 44 E
Westmeath □, *Ireland* **12 C4** 53 33N 7 34W
Westminster, *U.S.A.* .. **114 F7** 39 34N 76 59W
Westmont, *U.S.A.* .. **116 F6** 40 19N 78 58W
Westmoreland,
Barbados .... **121 g** 13 13N 59 37W
Westmorland, *U.S.A.* .. **111 M11** 33 2N 115 37W
Weston, *Oreg., U.S.A.* **108 D4** 45 49N 118 26W
Weston, *W. Va., U.S.A.* **114 F5** 39 2N 80 28W
Weston I., *Canada* .. **104 B4** 52 33N 79 36W
Weston-super-Mare,
U.K. **15 F5** 51 21N 2 58W
Westover, *U.S.A.* **116 F6** 40 45N 78 40W
Westport, *Canada* .. **117 B8** 44 40N 76 25W
Westport, *Ireland* .. **12 C2** 53 48N 9 31W
Westport, *N.Z.* ...... **91 J3** 41 46 S 171 37 E
Westport, *N.Y., U.S.A.* **117 B11** 44 11N 73 26W
Westport, *Oreg., U.S.A.* **110 D3** 46 8N 123 23W
Westport, *Wash., U.S.A.* **110 D2** 46 53N 124 6W
Westray, *Canada* **103 C8** 53 36N 101 24W
Westray, *U.K.* **13 B5** 59 18N 3 0W
Westree, *Canada* **104 C3** 47 26N 81 34W
Westville, *U.S.A.* **110 F6** 39 8N 120 42W
Westwood, *U.S.A.* .. **108 F3** 40 18N 121 0W
Wetar, *Indonesia* .... **63 F7** 7 48 S 126 30 E
Wetaskiwin, *Canada* .. **102 C6** 52 55N 113 24W
Wete, *Tanzania* ...... **84 F7** 5 4 S 39 43 E
Wetherby, *U.K.* **14 D6** 53 56N 1 23W
Wethersfield, *U.S.A.* .. **117 E12** 41 42N 72 40W
Wetteren, *Belgium* .. **17 D3** 51 0N 3 53 E
Wetzlar, *Germany* .. **24 E4** 50 32N 8 31 E
Wewoka, *U.S.A.* **113 H6** 35 9N 96 30W
Wexford, *Ireland* .. **12 D5** 52 20N 6 28W
Wexford □, *Ireland* .. **12 D5** 52 20N 6 25W
Wexford Harbour,
Ireland **12 D5** 52 20N 6 25W
Weyburn, *Canada* .. **103 D8** 49 40N 103 50W
Weyer Markt, *Austria* .. **26 D7** 47 51N 14 40 E
Weyhe, *Germany* .... **24 C4** 52 58N 8 49 E
Weyib →, *Ethiopia* .. **81 F5** 7 15N 40 15 E
Weymouth, *Canada* .. **105 D6** 44 30N 66 1W
Weymouth, *U.K.* **15 G5** 50 37N 2 28W
Weymouth, *U.S.A.* .. **117 D14** 42 13N 70 58W
Weymouth, *C., Australia* **94 A3** 12 37 S 143 27 E
Wha Ti, *Canada* **100 B8** 63 8N 117 16W
Whakatane, *N.Z.* .... **91 G6** 37 57 S 177 1 E

Whale Cove, *Canada* .. **103 A10** 62 10N 92 34W
Whales, B. of, *Antarctica* **5 D12** 78 0 S 165 0W
Whalsay, *U.K.* **13 A8** 60 22N 0 59W
Whangamomona, *N.Z.* **91 H5** 39 8 S 174 44 E
Whanganui, *N.Z.* .... **91 H5** 39 17 S 174 53 E
Whangarei, *N.Z.* .... **91 F5** 35 43 S 174 21 E
Whangarei Harb., *N.Z.* **91 F5** 35 45 S 174 28 E
Wharfe →, *U.K.* **14 D6** 53 51N 1 9W
Wharfedale, *U.K.* **14 C5** 54 6N 2 1W
Wharton, *N.J., U.S.A.* **117 F10** 40 54N 74 35W
Wharton, *Pa., U.S.A.* **116 E6** 41 31N 78 1W
Wharton, *Tex., U.S.A.* **113 L6** 29 19N 96 6W
Wheatland, *Calif.,*
U.S.A. **110 F5** 39 1N 121 25W
Wheatland, *Wyo., U.S.A.* **112 D2** 42 3N 104 58W
Wheatley, *Canada* .. **116 D2** 42 6N 82 27W
Wheaton, *Md., U.S.A.* **114 F7** 39 3N 77 3W
Wheaton, *Minn., U.S.A.* **112 C6** 45 48N 96 30W
Wheelbarrow Pk.,
U.S.A. **110 H10** 37 26N 116 5W
Wheeler, *Oreg., U.S.A.* **108 D2** 45 41N 123 53W
Wheeler, *Tex., U.S.A.* **113 H4** 35 27N 100 16W
Wheeler →, *Canada* .. **105 A5** 57 2N 67 13W
Wheeler L., *U.S.A.* .. **115 H2** 34 48N 87 23W
Wheeler Pk., *N. Mex.,*
U.S.A. **109 H11** 36 34N 105 25W
Wheeler Pk., *Nev.,*
U.S.A. **109 G6** 38 57N 114 15W
Wheeler Ridge, *U.S.A.* **111 L8** 35 0N 118 57W
Wheeling, *U.S.A.* **116 F4** 40 4N 80 43W
Whernside, *U.K.* **14 C5** 54 14N 2 24W
Whiskey Jack L.,
Canada **103 B8** 58 23N 101 55W
Whiskeytown-Shasta-
Trinity △, *U.S.A.* .. **108 F2** 40 45N 122 15W
Whistleduck Cr. →,
Australia .... **94 C2** 20 15 S 135 18 E
Whistler, *Canada* **102 C4** 50 7N 122 58W
Whitby, *Canada* **116 C6** 43 52N 78 56W
Whitby, *U.K.* **14 C7** 54 29N 0 37W
White →, *Ark., U.S.A.* **113 J9** 33 57N 91 5W
White →, *Ind., U.S.A.* **114 F2** 38 25N 87 45W
White →, *S. Dak.,*
U.S.A. **112 D5** 43 42N 99 27W
White →, *Tex., U.S.A.* **113 J4** 33 14N 100 56W
White →, *Utah, U.S.A.* **108 F9** 40 4N 109 41W
White →, *Vt., U.S.A.* **117 C12** 43 37N 72 20W
White →, *Wash., U.S.A.* **110 C4** 47 12N 122 15W
White, L., *Australia* .. **92 D4** 21 9 S 128 56 E
White B., *Canada* **105 C8** 50 0N 56 35W
White Bird, *U.S.A.* .. **108 D5** 45 46N 116 18W
White Butte, *U.S.A.* .. **112 B3** 46 23N 103 18W
White City, *U.S.A.* .. **108 E2** 42 26N 122 51W
White Cliffs, *Australia* **95 E3** 30 50 S 143 10 E
White Hall, *U.S.A.* .. **112 F9** 39 26N 90 24W
White Haven, *U.S.A.* .. **117 E9** 41 4N 75 47W
White Horse, Vale of,
U.K. **15 F6** 51 37N 1 30W
White I., *N.Z.* .... **91 G6** 37 30 S 177 13 E
White L., *Canada* **117 A8** 45 18N 76 31W
White L., *U.S.A.* **113 L8** 29 44N 92 30W
White Mountain Peak,
U.S.A. **109 G4** 37 38N 118 15W
White Mts., *Calif.,*
U.S.A. **110 H8** 37 30N 118 15W
White Mts., *N.H., U.S.A.* **117 B13** 44 15N 71 15W
White Mts. △, *Australia* **94 C4** 20 43 S 145 12 E
White Nile = Nîl el
Abyaḍ →, *Sudan* .. **81 D3** 15 38N 32 31 E
White Nile Dam =
Khazzân Jabal al
Awliyâ, *Sudan* .. **81 D3** 15 24N 32 20 E
White Otter L., *Canada* **104 C1** 49 5N 91 55W
White Pass, *Canada* .. **110 D5** 46 38N 121 24W
White Plains, *U.S.A.* .. **117 E11** 41 2N 73 46W
White River, *Canada* .. **104 C2** 48 35N 85 20W
White River, *S. Africa* **89 D5** 25 20 S 31 0 E
White River, *U.S.A.* .. **112 D4** 43 34N 100 45W
White Rock, *Canada* .. **110 A4** 49 2N 122 48W
White Russia =
Belarus ■, *Europe* .. **32 F4** 53 30N 27 0 E
White Sands, *U.S.A.* .. **109 K10** 32 46N 106 20W
White Sea = Beloye
More, *Russia* ...... **52 C4** 66 30N 38 0 E
White Sulphur Springs,
Mont., U.S.A. **108 C8** 46 33N 110 54W
White Sulphur Springs,
W. Va., U.S.A. **114 G5** 37 48N 80 18W
White Swan, *U.S.A.* .. **110 D6** 46 23N 120 44W
White Volta →, *Ghana* **83 D4** 9 10N 1 15W
Whitecliffs, *N.Z.* .... **91 K3** 43 26 S 171 55 E
Whitecourt, *Canada* .. **102 C5** 54 10N 115 45W
Whiteface Mt., *U.S.A.* **117 B11** 44 22N 73 54W
Whitefield, *U.S.A.* .. **117 B13** 44 23N 71 36W
Whitefish, *U.S.A.* .. **108 B6** 48 25N 114 20W
Whitefish L., *Canada* **103 A7** 62 41N 106 48W
Whitefish Point, *U.S.A.* **114 B3** 46 45N 84 59W
Whitegull, L. =
Goélands, L. aux,
Canada **105 A7** 55 27N 64 17W
Whitehall, *Mich., U.S.A.* **114 D2** 43 24N 86 21W
Whitehall, *Mont., U.S.A.* **108 D7** 45 52N 112 6W
Whitehall, *N.Y., U.S.A.* **117 C11** 43 33N 73 24W
Whitehall, *Wis., U.S.A.* **112 C9** 44 22N 91 19W
Whitehaven, *U.K.* **14 C4** 54 33N 3 35W
Whitehorse, *Canada* .. **102 A1** 60 43N 135 3W
Whitemark, *Australia* .. **95 G4** 40 7 S 148 3 E
Whiteplains, *Liberia* .. **82 D2** 6 28N 10 40W
Whiteriver, *U.S.A.* .. **109 K9** 33 50N 109 58W
Whitesand →, *Canada* **102 A5** 60 9N 115 45W
Whitesands, *S. Africa* **88 E3** 34 23 S 20 50 E
Whitesboro, *N.Y.,*
U.S.A. **117 C9** 43 7N 75 18W
Whitesboro, *Tex., U.S.A.* **113 J6** 33 39N 96 54W
Whiteshell △, *Canada* **103 D9** 50 0N 95 40W
Whitesville, *U.S.A.* .. **116 D7** 42 2N 77 46W
Whiteville, *U.S.A.* .. **115 H6** 34 20N 78 42W
Whitewater, *U.S.A.* .. **114 D1** 42 50N 88 44W
Whitewater Baldy,
U.S.A. **109 K9** 33 20N 108 39W
Whitewater L., *Canada* **104 B2** 50 50N 89 10W
Whitewood, *Australia* **94 C3** 21 28 S 143 30 E
Whitewood, *Canada* .. **103 C8** 50 20N 102 20W
Whithorn, *U.K.* **13 G4** 54 44N 4 26W
Whitianga, *N.Z.* ...... **91 G5** 36 47 S 175 41 E
Whitman, *U.S.A.* **116 A6** 45 3N 74 0W
Whitney, *Canada* **116 A6** 45 31N 78 14W
Whitney, Mt., *U.S.A.* .. **110 J8** 36 35N 118 18W
Whitney Point, *U.S.A.* **117 D9** 42 20N 75 58W
Whitstable, *U.K.* .... **15 F9** 51 21N 1 3 E
Whitsunday I., *Australia* **94 J7** 20 15 S 149 4 E
Whitsunday Islands △,
Australia .... **94 J7** 20 15 S 149 0 E
Whitsunday Passage,
Australia .... **94 J6** 20 16 S 148 51 E
Whittier, *U.S.A.* **111 M8** 33 58N 118 3W

Whittlesea, *Australia* .. **95 F4** 37 27 S 145 9 E
Wholdaia L., *Canada* **103 A8** 60 43N 104 20W
Whyalla, *Australia* .. **95 E2** 33 2 S 137 30 E
Wiang Kosai △,
Thailand .... **64 D2** 17 54N 99 29 E
Wiarton, *Canada* **116 B3** 44 40N 81 10W
Wiawso, *Ghana* **82 D4** 6 10N 2 25W
Wiay, *U.K.* **13 D1** 57 24N 7 13W
Wichian Buri, *Thailand* **64 E3** 15 39N 101 7 E
Wichita, *U.S.A.* **113 G6** 37 42N 97 20W
Wichita Falls, *U.S.A.* **113 J5** 33 54N 98 30W
Wick, *U.K.* **13 C5** 58 26N 3 5W
Wicked Pt., *Canada* .. **116 C7** 43 52N 77 15W
Wickenburg, *U.S.A.* .. **109 K7** 33 58N 112 44W
Wickepin, *Australia* .. **93 F2** 32 50 S 117 30 E
Wickham, *Australia* .. **92 D2** 20 42 S 117 11 E
Wickham, *C., Australia* **95 F3** 39 35 S 143 57 E
Wickliffe, *U.S.A.* **116 E3** 41 36N 81 28W
Wicklow, *Ireland* **12 D5** 52 59N 6 3W
Wicklow □, *Ireland* .. **12 D5** 52 57N 6 25W
Wicklow Hd., *Ireland* **12 D6** 52 58N 6 0W
Wicklow Mts., *Ireland* **12 C5** 52 58N 6 26W
Wicklow Mts. △, *Ireland* **12 C5** 53 6N 6 21W
Widawa, *Poland* ...... **31 G5** 51 27N 18 51 E
Widawa →, *Poland* .. **31 G5** 51 27N 18 52 E
Widgeegoara Cr. →,
Australia .... **95 D4** 28 51 S 146 34 E
Widgiemooltha,
Australia .... **93 F3** 31 30 S 121 34 E
Widnes, *U.K.* **14 D5** 53 23N 2 45W
Więcbork, *Poland* .. **31 E4** 53 21N 17 30 E
Wiehengebirge =
Nördlicher
Teutoburger Wald-
Wiehengebirge △,
Germany .... **24 C4** 52 18N 8 10 E
Wiehl, *Germany* .... **24 E3** 50 56N 7 34 E
Wiek, *Germany* ...... **24 A9** 54 37N 13 17 E
Wielbark, *Poland* .. **30 E7** 53 24N 20 55 E
Wieleń, *Poland* ...... **31 F3** 52 53N 16 9 E
Wielichowo, *Poland* .. **31 F3** 52 11N 16 22 E
Wieliczka, *Poland* .. **31 J7** 50 0N 20 5 E
Wielkopolski △, *Poland* **31 F3** 52 18N 16 45 E
Wielkopolskie □,
Poland .... **31 F4** 52 0N 17 30 E
Wieluń, *Poland* ...... **31 G5** 51 15N 18 34 E
Wien, *Austria* .... **27 C9** 48 12N 16 22 E
Wien ✈ (VIA), *Austria* **27 C9** 48 7N 16 35 E
Wiener Neustadt,
Austria .... **27 D9** 47 49N 16 16 E
Wieprz →, *Poland* .. **31 G9** 51 34N 21 49 E
Wieprza →, *Poland* .. **30 D3** 54 26N 16 35 E
Wieruszów, *Poland* .. **31 G5** 51 19N 18 9 E
Wiesbaden, *Germany* **25 E4** 50 4N 8 14 E
Wiesental, *Germany* **25 F4** 49 13N 8 31 E
Wiesloch, *Germany* .. **25 F4** 49 18N 8 41 E
Wiesmoor, *Germany* **24 B3** 53 24N 7 47 E
Wieżyca, *Poland* .... **30 D5** 54 14N 18 8 E
Wigan, *U.K.* **14 D5** 53 33N 2 38W
Wiggins, *Colo., U.S.A.* **112 E2** 40 14N 104 4W
Wiggins, *Miss., U.S.A.* **113 K10** 30 51N 89 8W
Wight, I. of □, *U.K.* .. **15 G6** 50 40N 1 20W
Wigierski △, *Poland* .. **30 D10** 54 5N 23 5 E
Wigry, *Jezioro, Poland* **30 D10** 54 2N 23 8 E
Wigston, *U.K.* **15 E6** 52 35N 1 6W
Wigton, *U.K.* **14 C4** 54 50N 3 10W
Wigtown, *U.K.* **13 G4** 54 53N 4 27W
Wigtown B., *U.K.* .. **13 G4** 54 46N 4 15W
Wil, *Switz.* .... **25 H5** 47 28N 9 3 E
Wilamowice, *Poland* **31 J6** 49 55N 19 9 E
Wilber, *U.S.A.* **112 E6** 40 29N 96 58W
Wilberforce, *Canada* **116 A6** 45 2N 78 13W
Wilberforce, C.,
Australia .... **94 A2** 11 54 S 136 35 E
Wilburton, *U.S.A.* .. **113 H7** 34 55N 95 19W
Wilcannia, *Australia* .. **95 E3** 31 30 S 143 26 E
Wilcox, *U.S.A.* **116 E6** 41 35N 78 41W
Wildbad, *Germany* .. **25 G4** 48 44N 8 33 E
Wildeshausen, *Germany* **24 C4** 52 54N 8 27 E
Wildeshauser Geest △,
Germany .... **24 C4** 52 54N 8 30 E
Wildon, *Austria* ...... **26 E8** 46 52N 15 31 E
Wildrose, *U.S.A.* **111 J9** 36 14N 117 11W
Wildspitze, *Austria* .. **26 E3** 46 53N 10 53 E
Wilga →, *Poland* .... **31 G8** 51 52N 21 18 E
Wilge →, *S. Africa* .. **89 D4** 27 3 S 28 20 E
Wilhelm II Coast,
Antarctica .... **5 C7** 68 0 S 90 0 E
Wilhelmsburg, *Austria* **26 C8** 48 6N 15 36 E
Wilhelmshaven,
Germany .... **24 B4** 53 31N 8 7 E
Wilhelmstal, *Namibia* **88 C2** 21 58 S 16 21 E
Wilkes-Barre, *U.S.A.* **117 E9** 41 15N 75 53W
Wilkes Land, *Antarctica* **5 D9** 69 0 S 120 0 E
Wilkie, *Canada* **103 C7** 52 27N 108 42W
Wilkinsburg, *U.S.A.* .. **116 F5** 40 26N 79 53W
Wilkinson Lakes,
Australia .... **93 E5** 29 40 S 132 39 E
Willandra Creek →,
Australia .... **95 E4** 33 22 S 145 52 E
Willapa B., *U.S.A.* .. **108 C2** 46 40N 124 0W
Willapa Hills, *U.S.A.* **110 D3** 46 35N 123 25W
Willard, *U.S.A.* **110 D8** 42 40N 76 50W
Willard, *Ohio, U.S.A.* **114 E2** 41 3N 82 44W
Willcox, *U.S.A.* **109 K9** 32 15N 109 50W
Willemstad, *Neth. Ant.* **121 D6** 12 5N 69 0W
Willet, *U.S.A.* **117 D9** 42 28N 75 55W
William →, *Canada* .. **103 B7** 59 8N 109 19W
William 'Bill' Dannely
Res., *U.S.A.* **115 J2** 32 10N 87 10W
William Creek, *Australia* **95 D2** 28 58 S 136 22 E
Williams, *Australia* .. **93 F2** 33 2 S 116 52 E
Williams, *Ariz., U.S.A.* **109 J7** 35 15N 112 11W
Williams, *Calif., U.S.A.* **110 F4** 39 9N 122 9W
Williams Harbour,
Canada **105 B8** 52 33N 55 47W
Williams Lake, *Canada* **102 C4** 52 10N 122 10W
Williamsburg, *Ky.,*
U.S.A. **115 G3** 36 44N 84 10W
Williamsburg, *Pa.,*
U.S.A. **116 F6** 40 28N 78 12W
Williamsburg, *Va.,*
U.S.A. **114 G7** 37 17N 76 44W
Williamson, *N.Y., U.S.A.* **116 C7** 43 14N 77 11W
Williamson, *W. Va.,*
U.S.A. **114 G4** 37 41N 82 17W
Williamsport, *U.S.A.* **116 E7** 41 15N 77 0W
Williamston, *U.S.A.* .. **115 H7** 35 51N 77 4W
Williamstown, *Australia* **95 F3** 37 51 S 144 52 E
Williamstown, *Mass.,*
U.S.A. **117 D11** 42 41N 73 12W
Williamstown, *N.Y.,*
U.S.A. **117 C9** 43 26N 75 53W

Willimantic, *U.S.A.* .. **117 E12** 41 43N 72 13W
Willingboro, *U.S.A.* .. **114 E8** 40 3N 74 54W
Williston, *S. Africa* .. **88 E3** 31 20 S 20 53 E
Williston, *Fla., U.S.A.* **115 L4** 29 23N 82 27W
Williston, *N. Dak.,*
U.S.A. **112 A3** 48 9N 103 37W
Williston L., *Canada* **102 B4** 56 0N 124 0W
Willits, *U.S.A.* **108 G2** 39 25N 123 21W
Willmar, *U.S.A.* **112 C7** 45 7N 95 3W
Willmore Wilderness □,
Canada **102 C5** 53 45N 119 30W
Willoughby, *U.S.A.* .. **116 E3** 41 39N 81 24W
Willow Bunch, *Canada* **103 D7** 49 20N 105 35W
Willow L., *Canada* .. **102 A5** 62 10N 119 8W
Willow Wall, The, *China* **57 C12** 42 10N 122 0 E
Willowick, *U.S.A.* .. **116 E3** 41 38N 81 28W
Willowlake →, *Canada* **102 A4** 62 42N 123 8W
Willowmore, *S. Africa* **88 E3** 33 15 S 23 30 E
Willows, *U.S.A.* **110 F4** 39 31N 122 12W
Willowvale = Gatyana,
S. Africa .... **89 E4** 32 16 S 28 31 E
Wills, L., *Australia* .. **92 D4** 21 25 S 128 51 E
Wills Cr. →, *Australia* **94 C3** 22 43 S 140 2 E
Willsboro, *U.S.A.* .. **117 B11** 44 21N 73 24W
Willunga, *Australia* .. **95 F2** 35 15 S 138 30 E
Wilmette, *U.S.A.* **114 D2** 42 5N 87 42W
Wilmington, *Australia* **95 E2** 32 39 S 138 7 E
Wilmington, *Del., U.S.A.* **114 F8** 39 45N 75 33W
Wilmington, *N.C.,*
U.S.A. **115 H7** 34 14N 77 55W
Wilmington, *Ohio,*
U.S.A. **114 F4** 39 27N 83 50W
Wilmington, *Vt., U.S.A.* **117 D12** 42 52N 72 52W
Wilmslow, *U.K.* **14 D5** 53 19N 2 13W
Wilpena Cr. →,
Australia .... **95 E2** 31 25 S 139 29 E
Wilsall, *U.S.A.* **108 D8** 45 59N 110 38W
Wilson, *N.C., U.S.A.* **115 H7** 35 44N 77 55W
Wilson, *N.Y., U.S.A.* **116 C6** 43 19N 78 50W
Wilson, *Pa., U.S.A.* .. **117 F9** 40 41N 75 15W
Wilson →, *Australia* **92 C4** 16 48 S 128 16 E
Wilson Bluff, *Australia* **93 F4** 31 41 S 129 0 E
Wilson Inlet, *Australia* **93 G2** 35 0 S 117 22 E
Wilsons Promontory,
Australia .... **95 F4** 38 55 S 146 25 E
Wilster, *Germany* .. **24 B5** 53 55N 9 23 E
Wilton, *U.S.A.* **112 B4** 47 10N 100 47W
Wilton →, *Australia* .. **94 A1** 14 45 S 134 33 E
Wiltshire □, *U.K.* .. **15 F6** 51 18N 1 53W
Wiltz, *Lux.* .... **17 E5** 49 57N 5 55 E
Wiluna, *Australia* .... **93 E3** 26 36 S 120 14 E
Wimborne Minster, *U.K.* **15 G6** 50 48N 1 59W
Wimereux, *France* .. **19 B8** 50 45N 1 37 E
Wimmera →, *Australia* **95 F3** 36 8 S 141 56 E
Winam G., *Kenya* .... **86 C3** 0 20 S 34 15 E
Winburg, *S. Africa* .. **88 D4** 28 30 S 27 2 E
Winchendon, *U.S.A.* **117 D12** 42 41N 72 3W
Winchester, *U.K.* **15 F6** 51 4N 1 18W
Winchester, *Conn.,*
U.S.A. **117 E11** 41 53N 73 9W
Winchester, *Idaho,*
U.S.A. **108 C5** 46 14N 116 38W
Winchester, *Ind., U.S.A.* **114 E3** 40 10N 84 59W
Winchester, *Ky., U.S.A.* **114 G3** 38 0N 84 11W
Winchester, *N.H.,*
U.S.A. **117 D12** 42 46N 72 23W
Winchester, *Nev., U.S.A.* **111 J11** 36 5N 115 10W
Winchester, *Tenn.,*
U.S.A. **115 H2** 35 11N 86 7W
Winchester, *Va., U.S.A.* **114 F6** 39 11N 78 10W
Wind →, *U.S.A.* **108 E9** 43 12N 108 12W
Wind Cave △, *U.S.A.* **112 D3** 43 32N 103 17W
Wind River Range,
U.S.A. **108 E9** 43 0N 109 30W
Windau = Ventspils,
Latvia .... **9 H19** 57 25N 21 32 E
Windber, *U.S.A.* **116 F6** 40 14N 78 50W
Winder, *U.S.A.* **115 J4** 34 0N 83 45W
Windermere, *U.K.* .. **14 C5** 54 23N 2 55W
Windham, *U.S.A.* **116 E3** 41 14N 81 3W
Windhoek, *Namibia* .. **88 C2** 22 35 S 17 4 E
Windischgarsten, *Austria* **26 D7** 47 42N 14 21 E
Windom, *U.S.A.* **112 D7** 43 52N 95 7W
Windorah, *Australia* .. **94 D3** 25 24 S 142 36 E
Window Rock, *U.S.A.* **109 J9** 35 41N 109 3W
Windrush →, *U.K.* .. **15 F6** 51 43N 1 24W
Windsor, *Australia* .. **95 E5** 33 37 S 150 50 E
Windsor, *N.S., Canada* **105 D7** 44 59N 64 5W
Windsor, *Ont., Canada* **116 D2** 42 18N 83 0W
Windsor, *U.K.* **15 F7** 51 29N 0 36W
Windsor, *Colo., U.S.A.* **112 E2** 40 29N 104 54W
Windsor, *Conn., U.S.A.* **117 E12** 41 50N 72 39W
Windsor, *Mo., U.S.A.* **112 F8** 38 32N 93 31W
Windsor, *N.Y., U.S.A.* **117 D9** 42 5N 75 37W
Windsor, *Vt., U.S.A.* **117 C12** 43 29N 72 24W
Windsor &
Maidenhead □, *U.K.* **15 F7** 51 29N 0 40W
Windsorton, *S. Africa* **88 D3** 28 16 S 24 44 E
Windward Is., *W. Indies* **121 D7** 13 0N 61 0W
Windward Passage =
Vientos, Paso de los,
Caribbean **121 C5** 20 0N 74 0W
Winefred L., *Canada* **103 B6** 55 30N 110 30W
Winejok, *Sudan* ...... **81 F2** 9 1N 27 30 E
Winfield, *U.S.A.* **113 G6** 37 15N 96 59W
Wingate Mts., *Australia* **92 B5** 14 25 S 130 40 E
Wingham, *Australia* .. **95 E5** 31 48 S 152 22 E
Wingham, *Canada* .. **116 C3** 43 55N 81 20W
Winisk, *Canada* **104 A2** 55 20N 85 15W
Winisk →, *Canada* .. **104 A2** 55 17N 85 5W
Winisk L., *Canada* .. **104 B2** 52 55N 87 22W
Wink, *U.S.A.* **113 K3** 31 45N 103 9W
Winkler, *Canada* **103 D9** 49 10N 97 56W
Winklern, *Austria* .. **26 E5** 46 52N 12 52 E
Winlock, *U.S.A.* **110 D4** 46 30N 122 56W
Winneba, *Ghana* **83 D4** 5 25N 0 36W
Winnebago, L., *U.S.A.* **114 D1** 44 0N 88 26W
Winnecke Cr. →,
Australia .... **92 C5** 18 35 S 131 34 E
Winnemucca, *U.S.A.* **108 F5** 40 58N 117 44W
Winnemucca L., *U.S.A.* **108 F4** 40 7N 119 21W
Winnett, *U.S.A.* **108 C9** 47 0N 108 21W
Winnfield, *U.S.A.* **113 K8** 31 56N 92 38W
Winnibigoshish, L.,
U.S.A. **112 B7** 47 27N 94 13W
Winnipeg, *Canada* .. **103 D9** 49 54N 97 9W
Winnipeg →, *Canada* **103 C9** 50 38N 96 19W
Winnipeg, L., *Canada* **103 C9** 52 0N 97 0W
Winnipeg Beach,
Canada **103 C9** 50 30N 96 58W
Winnipegosis, *Canada* **103 C9** 51 39N 99 55W
Winnipegosis L., *Canada* **103 C9** 52 30N 100 0W
Winnipesaukee, L.,
U.S.A. **117 C13** 43 38N 71 21W
Winnisquam L., *U.S.A.* **117 C13** 43 33N 71 31W
Winnsboro, *La., U.S.A.* **113 J9** 32 10N 91 43W
Winnsboro, *S.C., U.S.A.* **115 H5** 34 23N 81 5W

Winnsboro, *Tex., U.S.A.* **113 J7** 32 58N 95 17W
Winokapau, L., *Canada* .. **105 B7** 53 15N 62 50W
Winona, *Minn., U.S.A.* .. **112 C9** 44 3N 91 39W
Winona, *Miss., U.S.A.* .. **113 J10** 33 29N 89 44W
Winooski, *U.S.A.* **117 B11** 44 29N 73 11W
Winooski →, *U.S.A.* **117 B11** 44 32N 73 17W
Winschoten, *Neths.* ..... **17 A7** 53 9N 7 3 E
Winsen, *Germany* ...... **24 B6** 53 22N 10 13 E
Winsford, *U.K.* **14 D5** 53 12N 2 31W
Winslow, *Ariz., U.S.A.* .. **109 J8** 35 2N 110 42W
Winslow, *Wash., U.S.A.* .. **110 C4** 47 38N 122 31W
Winsted, *U.S.A.* **117 E11** 41 55N 73 4W
Winston-Salem, *U.S.A.* .. **115 G5** 36 6N 80 15W
Winter Garden, *U.S.A.* .. **115 L5** 28 34N 81 35W
Winter Haven, *U.S.A.* ... **115 M5** 28 1N 81 44W
Winter Park, *U.S.A.* **115 L5** 28 36N 81 20W
Winterberg, *Germany* ... **24 D4** 51 11N 8 33 E
Winterhaven, *U.S.A.* **111 N12** 32 47N 114 39W
Winters, *U.S.A.* **110 G5** 38 32N 121 58W
Wintersville, *U.S.A.* **116 F4** 40 23N 80 42W
Winterswijk, *Neths.* .... **17 C6** 51 58N 6 43 E
Winterthur, *Switz.* ..... **25 H4** 47 30N 8 44 E
Winthrop, *U.S.A.* **108 B3** 48 28N 120 10W
Winton, *Australia* ...... **94 C3** 22 24 S 143 3 E
Winton, *N.Z.* .... **91 M2** 46 8 S 168 20 E
Wipper →, *Germany* .... **24 D7** 51 16N 11 12 E
Wirrulla, *Australia* ..... **95 E1** 32 24 S 134 31 E
Wisbech, *U.K.* .... **15 E8** 52 41N 0 9 E
Wisconsin □, *U.S.A.* **112 C10** 44 45N 89 30W
Wisconsin →, *U.S.A.* ... **112 D9** 43 0N 91 15W
Wisconsin Rapids,
  U.S.A. **112 C10** 44 23N 89 49W
Wisdom, *U.S.A.* **108 D7** 45 37N 113 27W
Wishaw, *U.K.* **13 F5** 55 46N 3 54W
Wishek, *U.S.A.* **112 B5** 46 16N 99 33W
Wisła, *Poland* .... **31 J5** 49 38N 18 53 E
Wisła →, *Poland* ...... **30 D5** 54 22N 18 55 E
Wisłok →, *Poland* ..... **31 H9** 50 13N 22 32 E
Wisłoka →, *Poland* .... **31 H8** 50 27N 21 23 E
Wismar, *Germany* ..... **24 B7** 53 54N 11 29 E
Wisner, *U.S.A.* **112 E6** 41 59N 96 55W
Wissant, *France* ...... **19 B8** 50 52N 1 40 E
Wissembourg, *France* ... **19 C14** 49 2N 7 57 E
Wisznice, *Poland* ...... **31 G10** 51 48N 23 13 E
Witbank, *S. Africa* ..... **89 D4** 25 51 S 29 14 E
Witdraai, *S. Africa* ..... **88 D3** 26 58 S 20 48 E
Witham, *U.K.* .... **15 F8** 51 48N 0 40 E
Witham →, *U.K.* **14 E7** 52 59N 0 2W
Withernsea, *U.K.* ...... **14 D8** 53 44N 0 1 E
Witjira △, *Australia* .... **95 D2** 26 22 S 135 37 E
Witkowo, *Poland* ...... **31 F4** 52 26N 17 45 E
Witney, *U.K.* **15 F6** 51 48N 1 28W
Witnica, *Poland* .... **31 F1** 52 40N 14 54 E
Witnossob →, *Namibia* . **88 D3** 23 55 S 18 45 E
Witten, *Germany* ...... **24 A4** 54 38N 8 2 E
Witten, *Germany* ...... **24 D3** 51 26N 7 20 E
Wittenberge, *Germany* .. **24 B7** 53 0N 11 45 E
Wittenburg, *Germany* ... **24 B7** 53 31N 11 4 E
Wittenheim, *France* .... **19 E14** 47 44N 7 20 E
Wittenoom, *Australia* ... **92 D2** 22 15 S 118 20 E
Wittingen, *Germany* .... **24 C6** 52 44N 10 44 E
Wittlich, *Germany* ..... **25 F2** 49 59N 6 53 E
Wittmund, *Germany* .... **24 B3** 53 34N 7 46 E
Wittow, *Germany* ...... **24 A9** 54 38N 13 20 E
Wittstock, *Germany* .... **24 B8** 53 10N 12 28 E
Witvlei, *Namibia* ...... **88 C2** 22 23 S 18 32 E
Witzenhausen, *Germany* . **24 D5** 51 20N 9 51 E
Wkra →, *Poland* ...... **31 F7** 52 27N 20 44 E
Władysławowo, *Poland* . **30 D5** 54 48N 18 25 E
Wleń, *Poland* .... **31 G2** 51 2N 15 39 E
Wlingi, *Indonesia* ...... **63 H15** 8 5 S 112 25 E
Włocławek, *Poland* ..... **31 F6** 52 40N 19 3 E
Włodawa, *Poland* ...... **31 G10** 51 33N 23 31 E
Włoszczowa, *Poland* .... **31 H6** 50 50N 19 55 E
Woburn, *U.S.A.* **117 D13** 42 29N 71 9W
Wodian, *China* .... **56 H7** 32 50N 112 35 E
Wodonga = Albury-
  Wodonga, *Australia* . **95 F4** 36 3 S 146 56 E
Wodzisław Śląski,
  Poland .... **31 H5** 50 1N 18 26 E
Wœrth, *France* .... **19 D14** 48 57N 7 45 E
Woinbogoin, *China* ..... **58 A2** 32 51N 98 39 E
Woippy, *France* .... **19 C13** 49 10N 6 4 E
Wojcieszow, *Poland* .... **31 H2** 50 58N 15 55 E
Wokam, *Indonesia* ..... **63 F8** 5 45 S 134 28 E
Woking, *U.K.* **15 F7** 51 19N 0 34W
Wokingham, *U.K.* **15 F7** 51 24N 0 49W
Wokingham □, *U.K.* **15 F7** 51 25N 0 51W
Wolbrom, *Poland* ...... **31 H6** 50 24N 19 45 E
Wołczyn, *Poland* ...... **31 G5** 51 1N 18 3 E
Woldegk, *Germany* ..... **24 B9** 53 27N 13 34 E
Wolf →, *Canada* **102 A2** 60 17N 132 33W
Wolf Creek, *U.S.A.* **108 C7** 47 0N 112 4W
Wolf L., *Canada* **102 A2** 60 24N 131 40W
Wolf Point, *U.S.A.* **112 A2** 48 5N 105 39W
Wolfe I., *Canada* **117 B8** 44 7N 76 20W
Wolfeboro, *U.S.A.* **117 C13** 43 35N 71 13W
Wolfen, *Germany* ...... **24 D8** 51 39N 12 15 E
Wolfenbüttel, *Germany* .. **24 C6** 52 10N 10 33 E
Wolfratshausen,
  Germany .... **25 H7** 47 54N 11 24 E
Wolfsberg, *Austria* ..... **26 E7** 46 50N 14 52 E
Wolfsburg, *Germany* .... **24 C6** 52 25N 10 48 E
Wolgast, *Germany* ..... **24 A9** 54 3N 13 44 E
Wolhusen, *Switz.* ...... **25 H4** 47 4N 8 4 E
Wolin, *Poland* .... **30 E1** 53 50N 14 37 E
Woliński △, *Poland* .... **30 E1** 53 55N 14 26 E
Wollaston, Is., *Chile* .... **128 H3** 55 40 S 67 30W
Wollaston L., *Canada* ... **103 B8** 58 7N 103 10W
Wollaston Lake, *Canada* . **103 B8** 58 3N 103 33W
Wollaston Pen., *Canada* . **100 B8** 69 30N 115 0W
Wollongong, *Australia* ... **95 E5** 34 25 S 150 54 E
Wolmaransstad,
  S. Africa .... **88 D4** 27 12 S 25 59 E
Wolmirstedt, *Germany* .. **24 C7** 52 14N 11 37 E
Wołomin, *Poland* ...... **31 F8** 52 19N 21 15 E
Wołów, *Poland* .... **31 G3** 51 20N 16 38 E
Wolseley, *S. Africa* ..... **88 E2** 33 26 S 19 7 E
Wolsey, *U.S.A.* **112 C5** 44 24N 98 28W
Wolstenholme, C.,
  Canada **98 C12** 62 35N 77 30W
Wolsztyn, *Poland* ...... **31 F3** 52 8N 16 5 E
Wolvega, *Neths.* ...... **17 B6** 52 52N 6 0 E
Wolverhampton, *U.K.* ... **15 E5** 52 35N 2 7W
Wondai, *Australia* ...... **95 D5** 26 20 S 151 49 E
Wongalarroo L.,
  Australia .... **95 E3** 31 32 S 144 0 E
Wongan Hills, *Australia* . **93 F2** 30 51 S 116 37 E
Wŏnju, *S. Korea* ...... **57 F14** 37 22N 127 58 E
Wonosari, *Indonesia* .... **63 G14** 7 58 S 110 36 E
Wonosobo, *Indonesia* ... **63 G13** 7 22 S 109 54 E
Wonowon, *Canada* **102 B4** 56 44N 121 48W
Wŏnsan, *N. Korea* ..... **57 E14** 39 11N 127 27 E
Wonthaggi, *Australia* ... **95 F4** 38 37 S 145 37 E
Wood Buffalo △,
  Canada **102 B6** 59 0N 113 41W

Wood Is., *Australia* ..... **92 C3** 16 24 S 123 19 E
Wood L., *Canada* **103 B8** 55 17N 103 17W
Woodah I., *Australia* .... **94 A2** 13 27 S 136 10 E
Woodbourne, *U.S.A.* ... **117 E10** 41 46N 74 36W
Woodbridge, *Canada* ... **116 C5** 43 47N 79 36W
Woodbridge, *U.K.* ..... **15 E9** 52 6N 1 20 E
Woodburn, *U.S.A.* **108 D2** 45 9N 122 51W
Woodenbong, *Australia* . **95 D5** 28 24 S 152 39 E
Woodend, *Australia* .... **95 F3** 37 20 S 144 33 E
Woodford, *Australia* .... **95 D5** 26 58 S 152 47 E
Woodfords, *U.S.A.* **110 G7** 38 47N 119 50W
Woodlake, *U.S.A.* **110 J7** 36 25N 119 6W
Woodland, *Calif., U.S.A.* . **110 G5** 38 41N 121 46W
Woodland, Maine,
  U.S.A. **115 C12** 45 9N 67 25W
Woodland, *Pa., U.S.A.* .. **116 F6** 40 59N 78 21W
Woodland, Wash.,
  U.S.A. **110 E4** 45 54N 122 45W
Woodland Caribou △,
  Canada **103 C10** 51 0N 94 45W
Woodlands, *Singapore* .. **65 d** 1 27N 103 47 E
Woodridge, *Canada* **103 D9** 49 20N 96 9W
Woodroffe, Mt.,
  Australia .... **93 E5** 26 20 S 131 45 E
Woods, L., *Australia* .... **94 B1** 17 50 S 133 30 E
Woods, L. of the,
  Canada **103 D10** 49 15N 94 45W
Woodstock, *Australia* ... **94 B4** 19 35 S 146 50 E
Woodstock, N.B.,
  Canada **105 C6** 46 11N 67 37W
Woodstock, *Ont.,
  Canada* **116 C4** 43 10N 80 45W
Woodstock, *U.K.* **15 F6** 51 51N 1 20W
Woodstock, *Ill., U.S.A.* .. **112 D10** 42 19N 88 27W
Woodstock, *Vt., U.S.A.* . **117 C12** 43 37N 72 31W
Woodsville, *U.S.A.* **117 B13** 44 9N 72 2W
Woodville, *N.Z.* .... **91 J5** 40 20 S 175 53 E
Woodville, *Miss., U.S.A.* . **113 K9** 31 6N 91 18W
Woodville, *Tex., U.S.A.* . **113 K7** 30 47N 94 25W
Woodward, *U.S.A.* **113 G5** 36 26N 99 24W
Woody, *U.S.A.* **111 K8** 35 42N 118 50W
Woody →, *Canada* **103 C8** 52 31N 100 51W
Woolacombe, *U.K.* **15 F3** 51 10N 4 13W
Woolamai, C., *Australia* . **95 F4** 38 30 S 145 23 E
Wooler, *U.K.* **14 B5** 55 33N 2 1W
Woolgoolga, *Australia* .. **95 E5** 30 6 S 153 11 E
Woomera, *Australia* .... **95 E2** 31 5 S 136 50 E
Woonsocket, R.I.,
  U.S.A. **117 E13** 42 0N 71 31W
Woonsocket, S. Dak.,
  U.S.A. **112 C5** 44 3N 98 17W
Wooramel →, *Australia* . **93 E1** 25 47 S 114 10 E
Wooramel Roadhouse,
  Australia .... **93 E1** 25 45 S 114 17 E
Wooster, *U.S.A.* **116 F3** 40 48N 81 56W
Worcester, *S. Africa* .... **88 E2** 33 39 S 19 27 E
Worcester, *U.K.* **15 E5** 52 11N 2 12W
Worcester, *Mass., U.S.A.* **117 D13** 42 16N 71 48W
Worcester, *N.Y., U.S.A.* . **117 D10** 42 36N 74 45W
Worcestershire □, *U.K.* . **15 E5** 52 13N 2 10W
Worg], *Austria* .... **26 D5** 47 29N 12 3 E
Workington, *U.K.* **14 C4** 54 39N 3 33W
Worksop, *U.K.* **14 D6** 53 18N 1 7W
Workum, *Neths.* ...... **17 B5** 52 59N 5 26 E
Worland, *U.S.A.* **108 D10** 44 1N 107 57W
Wormhout, *France* ..... **19 B9** 50 52N 2 28 E
Worms, *Germany* ...... **25 F4** 49 37N 8 21 E
Worsley, *Canada* **102 B5** 56 31N 119 8W
Wörth, *Germany* ...... **25 F8** 49 1N 12 24 E
Wortham, *U.S.A.* **113 K6** 31 47N 96 28W
Wörther See, *Austria* ... **26 E7** 46 37N 14 10 E
Worthing, *Barbados* .... **121 g** 13 4N 59 35W
Worthing, *U.K.* **15 G7** 50 49N 0 21W
Worthington, Minn.,
  U.S.A. **112 D7** 43 37N 95 36W
Worthington, Pa., U.S.A. . **116 F5** 40 50N 79 38W
Wosi, *Indonesia* .... **63 E7** 0 15 S 128 0 E
Wou-han = Wuhan,
  China .... **59 B10** 30 31N 114 18 E
Wousi = Wuxi, *China* ... **59 B13** 31 33N 120 18 E
Wowoni, *Indonesia* ..... **63 E6** 4 5 S 123 5 E
Wrangel I. = Vrangelya,
  Ostrov, *Russia* ...... **53 B19** 71 0N 180 0 E
Wrangell, *U.S.A.* **102 B2** 56 28N 132 23W
Wrangell Mts., *U.S.A.* .. **100 B5** 61 30N 142 0W
Wrath, C., *U.K.* **13 C3** 58 38N 5 1W
Wray, *U.S.A.* **112 E3** 40 5N 102 13W
Wrekin, The, *U.K.* **15 E5** 52 41N 2 32W
Wrens, *U.S.A.* **115 J4** 33 12N 82 23W
Wrexham, *U.K.* **14 D4** 53 3N 3 0W
Wrexham □, *U.K.* **14 D5** 53 1N 2 58W
Wriezen, *Germany* ..... **24 C10** 52 43N 14 7 E
Wright = Paranas, Phil. .. **61 F6** 11 42N 125 2 E
Wright, *U.S.A.* **112 D2** 43 47N 105 30W
Wrightson, Mt., *U.S.A.* . **109 L8** 31 42N 110 51W
Wrightwood, *U.S.A.* **111 L9** 34 21N 117 38W
Wrigley, *Canada* **100 B7** 63 16N 123 37W
Wrocław, *Poland* ...... **31 G4** 51 5N 17 5 E
Wronki, *Poland* .... **31 F3** 52 41N 16 21 E
Września, *Poland* ...... **31 F4** 52 21N 17 36 E
Wschowa, *Poland* ..... **31 G3** 51 48N 16 20 E
Wu Jiang →, *China* .... **58 C6** 29 40N 107 20 E
Wu'an, *China* .... **56 F8** 36 40N 114 15 E
Wubin, *Australia* ...... **93 F2** 30 6 S 116 37 E
Wubu, *China* .... **56 F6** 37 28N 110 42 E
Wuchang, *China* ...... **57 B14** 44 55N 127 5 E
Wucheng, *China* ...... **56 F9** 37 12N 116 20 E
Wuchuan, Guangdong,
  China .... **59 G8** 21 33N 110 43 E
Wuchuan, Guizhou,
  China .... **58 C7** 28 25N 108 3 E
Wuchuan,
  Nei Monggol Zizhiqu,
  China .... **56 D6** 41 5N 111 28 E
Wudi, *China* .... **57 F9** 37 40N 117 35 E
Wuding He →, *China* ... **56 F6** 37 2N 110 23 E
Wudinna, *Australia* ..... **95 E2** 33 0 S 135 22 E
Wudu, *China* .... **56 H3** 33 22N 104 54 E
Wufeng, *China* .... **59 B8** 30 12N 110 42 E
Wugang, *China* .... **59 D8** 26 44N 110 35 E
Wugong Shan, *China* ... **59 D9** 27 30N 114 0 E
Wuhan, *China* .... **59 B10** 30 31N 114 18 E
Wuhe, *China* .... **57 H9** 33 10N 117 50 E
Wuhsi = Wuxi, *China* ... **59 B13** 31 33N 120 18 E
Wuhu, *China* .... **59 B12** 31 22N 118 21 E
Wujiang, *China* .... **59 B13** 31 10N 120 38 E
Wukari, *Nigeria* .... **83 D6** 7 51N 9 42 E
Wulajie, *China* .... **57 B14** 44 6N 126 33 E
Wulanbulang, *China* .... **56 D6** 41 5N 110 55 E
Wular L., *India* .... **69 B6** 34 20N 74 30 E
Wulehe, *Ghana* .... **83 D5** 8 39N 0 0 W
Wulian, *China* .... **57 G10** 35 40N 119 12 E
Wuliang Shan, *China* ... **58 E3** 24 30N 100 40 E
Wuliaru, *Indonesia* ..... **63 F8** 7 27 S 131 0 E

Wuling Shan, *China* .... **58 C7** 30 0N 110 0 E
Wulong, *China* .... **58 C6** 29 12N 107 43 E
Wulumuchi = Ürümqi,
  China .... **52 E9** 43 45N 87 45 E
Wum, *Cameroon* ...... **83 D7** 6 24N 10 2 E
Wuming, *China* .... **58 F7** 23 12N 108 18 E
Wun Rog, *Sudan* ...... **81 F2** 9 0N 28 20 E
Wundowie, *Australia* ... **93 F2** 31 47 S 116 23 E
Wuning, *China* .... **59 C10** 29 17N 115 5 E
Wunnummin L., *Canada* . **104 B2** 52 55N 89 10W
Wunsiedel, *Germany* .... **25 E8** 50 2N 12 0 E
Wunstorf, *Germany* .... **24 C5** 52 25N 9 26 E
Wuntho, *Burma* .... **67 H19** 23 55N 95 45 E
Wupatki △, *U.S.A.* **109 J8** 35 35N 111 20W
Wuping, *China* .... **59 E11** 25 5N 116 5 E
Wuppertal, *Germany* ... **24 D3** 51 16N 7 12 E
Wuppertal, *S. Africa* .... **88 E2** 32 13 S 19 12 E
Wuqing, *China* .... **57 E9** 39 23N 117 4 E
Wurtsboro, *U.S.A.* **117 E10** 41 35N 74 29W
Würzburg, *Germany* .... **25 F5** 49 46N 9 55 E
Wurzen, *Germany* ..... **24 D8** 51 22N 12 44 E
Wushan, *China* .... **56 G3** 34 43N 104 53 E
Wushishi, *Nigeria* ...... **83 D6** 9 46N 6 7 E
Wusuli Jiang =
  Ussuri →, *Asia* ..... **54 A7** 48 27N 135 0 E
Wutach →, *Germany* ... **25 H4** 47 37N 8 15 E
Wutai, *China* .... **56 E7** 38 40N 113 12 E
Wuting = Huimin, *China* **57 F9** 37 27N 117 28 E
Wutong, *China* .... **58 E8** 25 24N 110 4 E
Wutonghaolai, *China* ... **57 C11** 42 50N 120 5 E
Wutongqiao, *China* ..... **58 C4** 29 22N 103 50 E
Wuwei, *Anhui, China* ... **59 B11** 31 18N 117 54 E
Wuwei, *Gansu, China* ... **60 C5** 37 57N 102 34 E
Wuxi, *Jiangsu, China* ... **59 B13** 31 33N 120 18 E
Wuxi, *Sichuan, China* ... **58 B7** 31 23N 109 35 E
Wuxiang, *China* .... **56 F7** 36 49N 112 50 E
Wuxuan, *China* .... **58 F7** 23 30N 109 35 E
Wuxue, *China* .... **59 C10** 29 52N 115 30 E
Wuyang, *China* .... **56 H7** 33 25N 113 35 E
Wuyi, *Hebei, China* .... **56 F8** 37 46N 115 56 E
Wuyi, *Zhejiang, China* .. **59 C12** 28 52N 119 50 E
Wuyi Shan, *China* ..... **59 D11** 27 0N 117 0 E
Wuyishan, *China* ...... **59 D12** 27 45N 118 0 E
Wuyo, *Nigeria* .... **83 C7** 10 23N 11 50 E
Wuyuan, *Jiangxi, China* . **59 C11** 29 15N 117 50 E
Wuyuan,
  Nei Monggol Zizhiqu,
  China .... **56 D5** 41 2N 108 20 E
Wuzhai, *China* .... **56 E6** 38 54N 111 48 E
Wuzhi Shan, *China* .... **64 C7** 18 45N 109 45 E
Wuzhong, *China* ...... **56 E4** 38 2N 106 12 E
Wuzhou, *China* .... **59 F9** 23 30N 111 18 E
Wyaaba Cr. →,
  Australia .... **94 B3** 16 27 S 141 35 E
Wyalkatchem, *Australia* . **93 F2** 31 8 S 117 22 E
Wyalusing, *U.S.A.* **117 E8** 41 40N 76 16W
Wyandotte, *U.S.A.* **114 D4** 42 12N 83 9W
Wyandra, *Australia* ..... **95 D4** 27 12 S 145 56 E
Wyangala, L., *Australia* . **95 E4** 33 54 S 149 0 E
Wyara, L., *Australia* .... **95 D3** 28 42 S 144 14 E
Wycheproof, *Australia* .. **95 F3** 36 5 S 143 17 E
Wye →, *U.K.* **15 F5** 51 38N 2 40W
Wyemandoo, *Australia* . **93 E2** 28 28 S 118 29 E
Wyk, *Germany* .... **24 A4** 54 41N 8 33 E
Wymondham, *U.K.* .... **15 E9** 52 35N 1 7 E
Wymore, *U.S.A.* **112 E6** 40 7N 96 40W
Wyndham, *Australia* ... **92 C4** 15 33 S 128 3 E
Wyndham, *N.Z.* .... **91 M2** 46 20 S 168 51 E
Wynne, *U.S.A.* **113 H9** 35 14N 90 47W
Wynyard, *Australia* ..... **95 G4** 41 5 S 145 44 E
Wynyard, *Canada* **103 C8** 51 45N 104 10W
Wyola L., *Australia* ..... **93 E5** 29 8 S 130 17 E
Wyoming = Plympton-
  Wyoming, *Canada* ... **116 D2** 42 57N 82 7W
Wyoming □, *U.S.A.* **108 E10** 43 0N 107 30W
Wyomissing, *U.S.A.* **117 F9** 40 20N 75 59W
Wyong, *Australia* ...... **95 E5** 33 14 S 151 24 E
Wyrzysk, *Poland* ...... **31 E4** 53 10N 17 17 E
Wysła Mazowieckie,
  Poland .... **31 E8** 52 55N 22 30 E
Wyszków, *Poland* ...... **31 F8** 52 36N 21 25 E
Wyszogród, *Poland* .... **31 F7** 52 23N 20 9 E
Wytheville, *U.S.A.* **114 G5** 36 57N 81 5W
Wyżyna Małopolska,
  Poland .... **31 H7** 50 45N 20 0 E

X

Xaafuun, *Somali Rep.* ... **75 E5** 10 25N 51 16 E
Xaçmaz, *Azerbaijan* .... **35 K9** 41 31N 48 42 E
Xai-Xai, *Mozam.* ...... **89 D5** 25 6 S 33 31 E
Xainza, *China* .... **60 C3** 30 58N 88 35 E
Xalapa, *Mexico* **119 D5** 19 32N 96 55W
Xangongo, *Angola* ..... **88 B2** 16 45 S 15 5 E
Xankändi, *Azerbaijan* ... **70 B5** 39 52N 46 49 E
Xanlar, *Azerbaijan* ..... **35 K8** 40 37N 46 12 E
Xanten, *Germany* ...... **24 D2** 51 39N 6 26 E
Xánthi, *Greece* .... **45 E8** 41 10N 24 58 E
Xánthi □, *Greece* ...... **45 E8** 41 10N 24 58 E
Xanthos, *Turkey* ...... **47 E11** 36 19N 29 18 E
Xanxerê, *Brazil* .... **127 B5** 26 53 S 52 23W
Xapuri, *Brazil* .... **124 F5** 10 35 S 68 35W
Xar Moron He →,
  China .... **57 C11** 43 25N 120 35 E
Xarrë, *Albania* .... **44 G4** 39 44N 20 3 E
Xátiva, *Spain* **39 G4** 38 59N 0 32W
Xau, L., *Botswana* ..... **88 C3** 21 15 S 24 44 E
Xavantina, *Brazil* ...... **127 A5** 21 15 S 52 48W
Xenia, *U.S.A.* **114 F4** 39 41N 83 56W
Xeropotamos →,
  Cyprus .... **49 E11** 34 42N 32 33 E
Xertigny, *France* ...... **19 D13** 48 3N 6 24 E
Xhora, *S. Africa* .... **89 E4** 31 55 S 28 38 E
Xhumo, *Botswana* ..... **88 C3** 21 7 S 24 35 E
Xi Jiang →, *China* ..... **59 F9** 22 5N 113 20 E
Xi Xian, *Henan, China* .. **59 A10** 32 20N 114 43 E
Xi Xian, *Shanxi, China* . **56 F6** 36 41N 110 58 E
Xia Xian, *China* .... **56 G6** 35 8N 111 12 E
Xiachengzi, *China* ..... **57 B16** 44 40N 130 18 E
Xiachuan Dao, *China* ... **59 G9** 21 40N 112 40 E
Xiaguan, *China* .... **60 D5** 25 32N 100 16 E
Xiajiang, *China* .... **59 D10** 27 30N 115 10 E
Xiajin, *China* .... **56 F9** 36 56N 116 0 E
Xiamen, *China* .... **59 E12** 24 25N 118 4 E
Xi'an, *China* .... **56 G5** 34 15N 109 0 E
Xian Xian, *China* ...... **56 E9** 38 12N 116 6 E
Xianfeng, *China* .... **58 C7** 29 40N 109 8 E
Xiang Jiang →, *China* .. **59 C9** 28 55N 112 50 E
Xiangcheng, Henan,
  China .... **56 H8** 33 29N 114 52 E

Xiangcheng, Henan,
  China .... **56 H7** 33 50N 113 27 E
Xiangcheng, Sichuan,
  China .... **58 C2** 28 53N 99 47 E
Xiangdu, *China* .... **58 F6** 23 13N 106 58 E
Xiangfan, *China* .... **59 A9** 32 2N 112 8 E
Xianggang = Hong
  Kong □, *China* ...... **59 F10** 22 11N 114 14 E
Xianghuang Qi, *China* .. **56 C7** 42 2N 113 50 E
Xiangning, *China* ...... **56 G6** 35 58N 110 50 E
Xiangquan, *China* ..... **56 F7** 36 30N 113 1 E
Xiangquan He =
  Sutlej →, *Pakistan* .. **68 E4** 29 23N 71 3 E
Xiangshan, *China* ..... **59 C13** 29 29N 121 51 E
Xiangshui, *China* ...... **57 G10** 34 12N 119 33 E
Xiangtan, *China* .... **59 D9** 27 51N 112 54 E
Xiangxiang, *China* ..... **59 D9** 27 43N 112 28 E
Xiangyin, *China* .... **59 C9** 28 38N 112 54 E
Xiangzhou, *China* ...... **58 F7** 23 58N 109 40 E
Xianju, *China* .... **59 C13** 28 51N 120 44 E
Xianning, *China* .... **59 C10** 29 51N 114 16 E
Xianshui He →, *China* .. **58 B3** 30 10N 100 59 E
Xiantao, *China* .... **59 B9** 30 25N 113 25 E
Xianyang, *China* ...... **56 G5** 34 20N 108 40 E
Xianyou, *China* .... **59 E12** 25 12N 118 38 E
Xiao Hinggan Ling,
  China .... **60 B7** 49 0N 127 0 E
Xiao Xian, *China* ...... **56 G9** 34 15N 116 55 E
Xiaofeng, *China* ...... **59 B12** 30 35N 119 32 E
Xiaogan, *China* .... **59 B9** 30 52N 113 55 E
Xiaojin, *China* .... **58 B4** 30 59N 102 21 E
Xiaolan, *China* .... **59 F9** 22 38N 113 20 E
Xiaoshan, *China* ...... **59 B13** 30 12N 120 18 E
Xiaoyi, *China* .... **56 F6** 37 8N 111 48 E
Xiapu, *China* .... **57 C11** 26 54N 119 59 E
Xiawa, *China* .... **57 C11** 42 35N 120 38 E
Xiayi, *China* .... **56 G9** 34 15N 116 10 E
Xichang, *China* .... **58 D4** 27 51N 102 19 E
Xichong, *China* .... **58 B5** 30 57N 105 54 E
Xichou, *China* .... **58 E5** 23 25N 104 42 E
Xichuan, *China* .... **56 H6** 33 0N 111 30 E
Xide, *China* .... **58 C4** 28 20N 102 23 E
Xiemahe, *China* .... **59 B8** 31 38N 111 12 E
Xieng Khouang, *Laos* .. **64 C4** 19 17N 103 25 E
Xifei He →, *China* ..... **56 H9** 32 45N 116 40 E
Xifeng, Gansu, *China* ... **56 G4** 35 40N 107 40 E
Xifeng, Guizhou, China .. **58 D6** 27 7N 106 42 E
Xifeng, Liaoning, China .. **57 C13** 42 42N 124 45 E
Xifengzhen = Xifeng,
  China .... **56 G4** 35 40N 107 40 E
Xigazê, *China* .... **60 D3** 29 5N 88 45 E
Xihe, *China* .... **56 G3** 34 2N 105 20 E
Xihua, *China* .... **56 H8** 33 45N 114 30 E
Xilaganí, *Greece* ...... **45 F9** 40 58N 25 28 E
Xiliao He →, *China* .... **57 C12** 43 32N 123 35 E
Xilin, *China* .... **58 E5** 24 30N 105 6 E
Xilókastron, *Greece* .... **46 C4** 38 5N 22 38 E
Ximana, *Mozam.* ...... **87 F3** 19 24 S 33 58 E
Xime, Guinea-Biss. **82 C2** 11 59N 14 57W
Ximeng, *China* .... **58 F2** 22 50N 99 27 E
Xin Jiang →, *China* .... **59 C11** 28 45N 116 35 E
Xin Xian = Xinzhou,
  China .... **56 E7** 38 22N 112 46 E
Xinavane, *Mozam.* ..... **89 D5** 25 2 S 32 47 E
Xinbin, *China* .... **57 D13** 41 40N 125 2 E
Xincai, *China* .... **59 A10** 32 43N 114 58 E
Xinchang, *China* ...... **59 C13** 29 28N 120 52 E
Xincheng,
  Guangxi Zhuangzu,
  China .... **58 E7** 24 5N 108 39 E
Xincheng, Jiangxi, China . **59 D10** 26 48N 114 6 E
Xincheng, *China* ...... **58 B5** 30 50N 104 10 E
Xinfeng, Guangdong,
  China .... **59 E10** 24 5N 114 16 E
Xinfeng, Jiangxi, China .. **59 D11** 27 7N 116 11 E
Xinfeng, Jiangxi, China .. **59 E10** 25 27N 114 58 E
Xinfengjiang Skuiku,
  China .... **59 F10** 23 52N 114 30 E
Xing Xian, *China* ...... **56 E6** 38 27N 111 7 E
Xing'an,
  Guangxi Zhuangzu,
  China .... **59 E8** 25 38N 110 40 E
Xingan, Jiangxi, China ... **59 D10** 27 46N 115 20 E
Xingcheng, *China* ..... **57 D11** 40 40N 120 45 E
Xingguo, *China* .... **59 D10** 26 21N 115 21 E
Xinghe, *China* .... **56 D7** 40 55N 113 55 E
Xinghua, *China* .... **57 H10** 32 58N 119 48 E
Xinghua Wan, *China* ... **59 E12** 25 15N 119 20 E
Xinglong, *China* .... **57 D9** 40 25N 117 30 E
Xingning, *China* .... **59 E10** 24 3N 115 42 E
Xingping, *China* .... **56 G5** 34 20N 108 28 E
Xingren, *China* .... **58 E5** 25 24N 105 11 E
Xingshan, *China* ...... **59 B8** 31 15N 110 45 E
Xingtai, *China* .... **56 F8** 37 3N 114 32 E
Xingu →, *Brazil* ...... **125 D8** 1 30 S 51 53W
Xingwen, *China* .... **58 C5** 28 22N 104 50 E
Xingyang, *China* ...... **56 G7** 34 45N 112 52 E
Xinhe, *China* .... **56 F8** 37 30N 115 15 E
Xinhua, *China* .... **59 D8** 27 42N 111 13 E
Xinhuang, *China* ...... **58 D7** 27 21N 109 12 E
Xinhui, *China* .... **59 F9** 22 25N 113 0 E
Xining, *China* .... **60 C5** 36 34N 101 40 E
Xinjian, *China* .... **59 C10** 28 37N 115 46 E
Xinjiang, *China* .... **56 G6** 35 34N 111 11 E
Xinjiang Uygur
  Zizhiqu □, *China* .... **60 B3** 42 0N 86 0 E
Xinjie, *China* .... **58 D3** 26 48N 101 15 E
Xinjin = Pulandian,
  China .... **57 E11** 39 25N 121 58 E
Xinjin, *China* .... **58 B4** 30 24N 103 47 E
Xinkai He →, *China* .... **57 C12** 43 32N 123 35 E
Xinle, *China* .... **56 E8** 38 25N 114 40 E
Xinlitun, *China* .... **57 D12** 42 0N 122 8 E
Xinlong, *China* .... **58 B3** 30 57N 100 12 E
Xinmin, *China* .... **57 D12** 41 59N 122 50 E
Xinning, *China* .... **59 D8** 26 28N 110 50 E
Xinshao, *China* .... **59 D8** 27 21N 111 26 E
Xintai, *China* .... **57 G9** 35 55N 117 45 E
Xintian, *China* .... **59 E9** 25 55N 112 15 E
Xinxiang, *China* ...... **56 G7** 35 18N 113 50 E
Xinxing, *China* .... **59 F9** 22 5N 112 15 E
Xinye, *China* .... **59 A10** 32 30N 112 21 E
Xinyi, *China* .... **59 F9** 22 30N 110 21 E
Xinyu, *China* .... **59 D10** 27 49N 114 58 E
Xinzheng, *China* ...... **56 G7** 34 20N 113 45 E
Xinzhou, *China* .... **59 B10** 31 0N 114 15 E
Xinzhou, Shanxi, China . **56 E7** 38 22N 112 46 E
Xinzo de Limia, *Spain* .. **36 C3** 42 3N 7 47W
Xiongyuecheng, *China* . **57 D12** 40 12N 122 5 E
Xiping, Henan, *China* ... **56 H8** 33 22N 114 5 E
Xiping, Henan, *China* ... **56 H6** 33 25N 111 8 E

Xiping, Zhejiang, China .. **59 C12** 28 16N 119 29 E
Xique-Xique, *Brazil* .... **125 F10** 10 50 S 42 40W
Xisha Qundao = Paracel
  Is., S. China Sea ..... **62 A4** 15 50N 112 0 E
Xishui, Guizhou, China .. **58 C6** 28 19N 106 9 E
Xishui, Hubei, China .... **59 B10** 30 30N 115 15 E
Xitole, Guinea-Biss. **82 C2** 11 43N 14 50W
Xiu Shui →, *China* ..... **59 C10** 29 13N 116 0 E
Xiuning, *China* .... **59 C12** 29 45N 118 10 E
Xiuren, *China* .... **59 E8** 24 27N 110 42 E
Xiushan, *China* .... **58 C7** 28 25N 108 57 E
Xiushui, *China* .... **59 C10** 29 2N 114 33 E
Xiuwen, *China* .... **58 D6** 26 49N 106 40 E
Xiuyan, *China* .... **57 D12** 40 18N 123 11 E
Xixabangma Feng,
  China .... **67 E14** 28 20N 85 40 E
Xixia, *China* .... **56 H6** 33 25N 111 29 E
Xixiang, *China* .... **56 H4** 33 0N 107 44 E
Xiyang, *China* .... **56 F7** 37 38N 113 38 E
Xizang Zizhiqu □, China . **60 C3** 32 0N 88 0 E
Xlendi, *Malta* .... **49 C1** 36 1N 14 12 E
Xochob, *Mexico* **119 D7** 19 28N 89 45W
Xu Jiang →, *China* .... **59 D11** 28 0N 116 25 E
Xuan Loc, *Vietnam* .... **65 G6** 10 56N 107 14 E
Xuan'en, *China* .... **58 C7** 30 0N 109 30 E
Xuanhan, *China* .... **58 B6** 31 18N 107 38 E
Xuanhua, *China* .... **56 D8** 40 40N 115 2 E
Xuanwei, *China* .... **58 C5** 26 15N 103 59 E
Xuanzhou, *China* ...... **59 B12** 30 56N 118 43 E
Xuchang, *China* .... **56 G7** 34 2N 113 48 E
Xudat, *Azerbaijan* ..... **35 K9** 41 38N 48 41 E
Xuefeng Shan, *China* ... **59 D8** 27 5N 110 35 E
Xuejiaping, *China* ...... **59 B8** 31 39N 110 16 E
Xun Jiang →, *China* .... **59 F8** 23 35N 111 30 E
Xun Xian, *China* ...... **56 G8** 35 42N 114 33 E
Xundian, *China* .... **58 E4** 25 36N 103 15 E
Xunwu, *China* .... **59 E10** 24 54N 115 37 E
Xunyang, *China* .... **56 H5** 32 48N 109 22 E
Xunyi, *China* .... **56 G5** 35 8N 108 20 E
Xupu, *China* .... **59 D8** 27 53N 110 32 E
Xúquer →, *Spain* **39 F4** 39 5N 0 10W
Xushui, *China* .... **56 E8** 39 2N 115 40 E
Xuwen, *China* .... **59 G8** 20 20N 110 10 E
Xuyen Moc, *Vietnam* ... **65 G6** 10 34N 107 25 E
Xuyong, *China* .... **58 C5** 28 10N 105 22 E
Xuzhou, *China* .... **57 G9** 34 18N 117 18 E
Xylophagou, *Cyprus* ... **49 E12** 34 54N 33 51 E

Y

Ya Xian, *China* .... **64 C7** 18 14N 109 29 E
Yaamba, *Australia* ..... **94 C5** 23 8 S 150 22 E
Ya'an, *China* .... **58 C4** 29 58N 103 5 E
Yaapeet, *Australia* ..... **95 F3** 35 45 S 142 3 E
Yabassi, *Cameroon* .... **83 E6** 4 30N 9 57 E
Yabelo, *Ethiopia* ...... **81 G4** 4 50N 38 8 E
Yabelo △, *Ethiopia* .... **81 F4** 6 0N 37 50 E
Yablanitsa, *Bulgaria* .... **45 C8** 43 2N 24 5 E
Yablonovy Ra. =
  Yablonovyy Khrebet,
  Russia .... **53 D12** 53 0N 114 0 E
Yablonovyy Khrebet,
  Russia .... **53 D12** 53 0N 114 0 E
Yabluniv, *Ukraine* ..... **29 B9** 48 24N 24 57 E
Yablunytsya, *Ukraine* .. **29 B9** 48 19N 24 29 E
Yabrai Shan, *China* .... **56 E2** 39 40N 103 0 E
Yabrūd, *Syria* .... **74 B5** 33 58N 36 39 E
Yabucoa, Puerto Rico ... **121 d** 18 3N 65 53W
Yacambú △, *Venezuela* . **121 E6** 9 42N 69 27W
Yacheng, *China* .... **64 C7** 18 22N 109 6 E
Yacuiba, *Bolivia* ...... **126 A3** 22 0 S 63 43W
Yacuma →, *Bolivia* .... **124 F5** 13 38 S 65 23W
Yadgir, *India* .... **66 L10** 16 45N 77 5 E
Yadkin →, *U.S.A.* **115 H5** 35 29N 80 9W
Yadrin, *Russia* .... **34 C8** 55 57N 46 12 E
Yaeyama-Rettō, *Japan* .. **55 M1** 24 30N 123 40 E
Yagaba, *Ghana* **83 C4** 10 14N 1 20W
Yağcılar, *Turkey* ...... **47 B10** 39 25N 28 23 E
Yagodnoye, *Russia* .... **53 C15** 62 33N 149 40 E
Yahila, Dem. Rep. of
  the Congo .... **86 B1** 0 13N 24 28 E
Yahk, *Canada* **102 D5** 49 6N 116 10W
Yahotyn, *Ukraine* ..... **33 G6** 50 17N 31 46 E
Yahuma, Dem. Rep. of
  the Congo .... **84 D4** 1 0N 23 10 E
Yahyalı, *Turkey* .... **72 C6** 38 5N 35 2 E
Yaita, *Japan* .... **55 F9** 36 48N 139 56 E
Yaiza, Canary Is. **48 F6** 28 57N 13 46W
Yajiang, *China* .... **58 B3** 30 2N 100 57 E
Yajua, *Nigeria* .... **83 C7** 11 27N 12 49 E
Yakima, *U.S.A.* **108 C3** 46 36N 120 31W
Yakima →, *U.S.A.* **108 C3** 47 0N 120 30W
Yako, Burkina Faso **82 C4** 12 59N 2 15W
Yakobi I., U.S.A. **102 B1** 58 0N 136 30W
Yakoruda, *Bulgaria* .... **44 D7** 42 1N 23 39 E
Yakovlevka, *Russia* .... **54 B6** 44 26N 133 28 E
Yaku-Shima, *Japan* .... **55 J5** 30 20N 130 30 E
Yakumo, *Japan* .... **54 C10** 42 15N 140 16 E
Yakutat, *U.S.A.* **100 C6** 59 33N 139 44W
Yakutia = Sakha □,
  Russia .... **53 C13** 66 0N 130 0 E
Yakutsk, *Russia* ...... **53 C13** 62 5N 129 50 E
Yala, *Thailand* .... **65 J3** 6 33N 101 18 E
Yalboroo, *Australia* .... **94 J6** 20 50 S 148 40 E
Yale, *U.S.A.* **116 C2** 43 8N 82 48W
Yalgoo, *Australia* ...... **93 E2** 28 16 S 116 39 E
Yalgorup △, *Australia* .. **93 H2** 24 34 S 115 2 E
Yalinga, *C.A.R.* .... **84 C4** 6 33N 23 10 E
Yalkubul, Punta, Mexico **119 C7** 21 32N 88 37W
Yalleroi, *Australia* ..... **94 C4** 24 3 S 145 42 E
Yalobusha →, *U.S.A.* .. **113 J9** 33 33N 90 10W
Yalong Jiang →, China .. **58 D3** 26 40N 101 55 E
Yalova, *Turkey* .... **45 F13** 40 41N 29 15 E
Yalpuh, Ozero, Ukraine . **29 E13** 45 30N 28 41 E
Yalta, *Ukraine* .... **33 K8** 44 30N 34 10 E
Yalu Jiang →, *China* ... **57 E13** 40 0N 124 22 E
Yalvaç, *Turkey* .... **72 C4** 38 17N 31 10 E
Yam Ha Melah = Dead
  Sea, *Asia* .... **74 D4** 31 30N 35 30 E
Yam Kinneret, *Israel* ... **74 C4** 32 45N 35 35 E
Yamada, *Japan* .... **55 H5** 33 33N 130 49 E
Yamagata, *Japan* ..... **54 E10** 38 15N 140 15 E
Yamagata □, *Japan* .... **54 E10** 38 30N 140 0 E
Yamaguchi, *Japan* .... **55 G5** 34 10N 131 32 E
Yamaguchi □, *Japan* .. **55 G5** 34 20N 131 40 E
Yamal, Poluostrov,
  Russia .... **52 B8** 71 0N 70 0 E
Yamal Pen. = Yamal,
  Poluostrov, *Russia* ... **52 B8** 71 0N 70 0 E
Yamanashi □, *Japan* ... **55 G9** 35 40N 138 40 E
Yamanie Falls △,
  Australia .... **94 B4** 18 29 S 146 9 E
Yamba, *Australia* ..... **95 D5** 29 26 S 153 23 E

Yambarran Ra., *Australia* ... **92 C5** 15 10 S 130 25 E
Yambéring, *Guinea* ... **82 C2** 11 50N 12 18 E
Yâmbiö, *Sudan* ... **81 G2** 4 35N 28 16 E
Yambol, *Bulgaria* ... **45 D10** 42 30N 26 30 E
Yamdena, *Indonesia* ... **63 F8** 7 45 S 131 20 E
Yame, *Japan* ... **55 H5** 33 13N 130 35 E
Yamethin, *Burma* ... **67 J20** 20 29N 96 18 E
Yamma-Yamma, L., *Australia* ... **95 D3** 26 16 S 141 20 E
Yamoussoukro, *Ivory C.* ... **82 D3** 6 49N 5 17W
Yampa →, *U.S.A.* ... **108 F9** 40 32N 108 59W
Yampi Sd., *Australia* ... **92 C3** 16 8 S 123 38 E
Yampil, *Moldova* ... **33 H5** 48 15N 28 15 E
Yampol = Yampil, *Moldova* ... **33 H5** 48 15N 28 15 E
Yamrat, *Nigeria* ... **83 C6** 10 11N 9 55 E
Yamrukchal = Botev, *Bulgaria* ... **45 D8** 42 44N 24 57 E
Yamuna →, *India* ... **69 G9** 25 30N 81 53 E
Yamunanagar, *India* ... **68 D7** 30 7N 77 17 E
Yamzho Yumco, *China* ... **60 D4** 28 48N 90 35 E
Yan, *Nigeria* ... **83 C7** 10 5N 12 11 E
Yana →, *Russia* ... **53 B14** 71 30N 136 0 E
Yanagawa, *Japan* ... **55 H5** 33 10N 130 24 E
Yanai, *Japan* ... **55 H6** 33 58N 132 7 E
Yan'an, *China* ... **56 F5** 36 35N 109 26 E
Yanbian, *China* ... **58 D3** 26 47N 101 31 E
Yanbu 'al Baḥr, *Si. Arabia* ... **70 F3** 24 0N 38 5 E
Yancheng, *Henan, China* ... **56 F6** 36 43N 110 1 E
Yancheng, *Jiangsu, China* ... **56 G7** 33 35N 114 0 E
Yancheng, *Jiangsu, China* ... **57 H11** 33 23N 120 8 E
Yanchep Beach, *Australia* ... **93 F2** 31 33 S 115 37 E
Yanchi, *China* ... **56 F4** 37 48N 107 20 E
Yanchuan, *China* ... **56 F6** 36 51N 110 10 E
Yanco Cr. →, *Australia* ... **95 F4** 35 14 S 145 35 E
Yandoon, *Burma* ... **67 L19** 17 0N 95 40 E
Yanfeng, *China* ... **58 E3** 25 52N 101 8 E
Yanfolila, *Mali* ... **82 C3** 11 11N 8 9W
Yang Xian, *China* ... **56 H4** 33 15N 107 30 E
Yang-Yang, *Senegal* ... **82 B1** 15 30N 15 0W
Yangambi, *Dem. Rep. of the Congo* ... **86 B1** 0 47N 24 24 E
Yangbi, *China* ... **58 E2** 25 41N 99 58 E
Yangcheng, *China* ... **56 G7** 35 28N 112 22 E
Yangch'ü = Taiyuan, *China* ... **56 F7** 37 52N 112 33 E
Yangchun, *China* ... **59 F8** 22 11N 111 48 E
Yanggao, *China* ... **56 D7** 40 21N 113 55 E
Yanggu, *China* ... **56 F8** 36 8N 115 43 E
Yangjiang, *China* ... **59 G8** 21 50N 111 59 E
Yangliuqing, *China* ... **57 E9** 39 2N 117 5 E
Yangon = Rangoon, *Burma* ... **67 L20** 16 45N 96 20 E
Yangping, *China* ... **59 B8** 31 12N 111 25 E
Yangpingguan, *China* ... **56 H4** 32 58N 106 5 E
Yangquan, *China* ... **56 F7** 37 58N 113 31 E
Yangshan, *China* ... **59 E9** 24 30N 112 40 E
Yangshuo, *China* ... **59 E8** 24 48N 110 29 E
Yangtse = Chang Jiang →, *China* ... **59 B13** 31 48N 121 10 E
Yangtze Kiang = Chang Jiang →, *China* ... **59 B13** 31 48N 121 10 E
Yangudi Rassa △, *Ethiopia* ... **81 E5** 10 50N 40 42 E
Yangxin, *China* ... **59 C10** 29 50N 115 12 E
Yangyang, *S. Korea* ... **57 E15** 38 4N 128 38 E
Yangyuan, *China* ... **56 D8** 40 1N 114 10 E
Yangzhong, *China* ... **59 A12** 32 12N 119 22 E
Yangzhou, *China* ... **59 A12** 32 21N 119 26 E
Yanhe, *China* ... **58 C7** 28 31N 108 29 E
Yanji, *China* ... **57 C15** 42 59N 129 30 E
Yanjin, *China* ... **58 C5** 28 5N 104 18 E
Yanjing, *China* ... **58 C2** 29 7N 98 33 E
Yankari △, *Nigeria* ... **83 D7** 9 50N 10 28 E
Yankton, *U.S.A.* ... **112 D6** 42 53N 97 23W
Yanonge, *Dem. Rep. of the Congo* ... **86 B1** 0 35N 24 38 E
Yanqi, *China* ... **60 B3** 42 5N 86 35 E
Yanqing, *China* ... **56 D8** 40 30N 115 58 E
Yanshan, *Hebei, China* ... **57 E9** 38 4N 117 22 E
Yanshan, *Jiangxi, China* ... **59 C11** 28 15N 117 41 E
Yanshan, *Yunnan, China* ... **58 F5** 23 35N 104 20 E
Yanshou, *China* ... **57 B15** 45 28N 128 22 E
Yantabulla, *Australia* ... **95 D4** 29 21 S 145 0 E
Yantai, *China* ... **57 F11** 37 34N 121 22 E
Yantarnyy, *Russia* ... **30 D6** 54 52N 19 57 E
Yanting, *China* ... **58 B5** 31 11N 105 24 E
Yantra →, *Bulgaria* ... **45 C9** 43 40N 25 37 E
Yanwa, *China* ... **58 D2** 27 35N 98 53 E
Yanyuan, *China* ... **58 D3** 27 25N 101 30 E
Yanzhou, *China* ... **56 G9** 35 35N 116 49 E
Yao Noi, Ko, *Thailand* ... **65 a** 8 7N 98 37 E
Yao Xian, *China* ... **56 G5** 34 55N 108 59 E
Yao Yai, Ko, *Thailand* ... **65 a** 8 0N 98 35 E
Yao'an, *China* ... **58 E3** 25 31N 101 18 E
Yaowan, *China* ... **57 G10** 34 15N 118 3 E
Yap, *Pac. Oc.* ... **96 G5** 9 30N 138 10 E
Yapen, *Indonesia* ... **63 E9** 1 50 S 136 0 E
Yapen, Selat, *Indonesia* ... **63 E9** 1 20 S 136 10 E
Yapero, *Indonesia* ... **63 E9** 4 59 S 137 11 E
Yappar →, *Australia* ... **94 B3** 18 22 S 141 16 E
Yaqui →, *Mexico* ... **118 B2** 27 37N 110 39W
Yar-Sale, *Russia* ... **52 C8** 66 50N 70 50 E
Yaraka, *Australia* ... **94 C3** 24 53 S 144 3 E
Yaransk, *Russia* ... **34 B8** 57 22N 47 49 E
Yarbasan, *Turkey* ... **47 C10** 38 59N 28 49 E
Yardımcı Burnu, *Turkey* ... **47 E12** 36 13N 30 25 E
Yare →, *U.K.* ... **15 E9** 52 35N 1 38 E
Yaremcha, *Ukraine* ... **29 B9** 48 27N 24 33 E
Yaremsk, *Russia* ... **52 C5** 62 11N 49 15 E
Yarfa, *Si. Arabia* ... **80 C4** 24 37N 38 35 E
Yari →, *Colombia* ... **124 D4** 0 20 S 72 20W
Yarkand = Shache, *China* ... **60 C2** 38 20N 77 10 E
Yarker, *Canada* ... **117 B8** 44 23N 76 46W
Yarkhun →, *Pakistan* ... **69 A5** 36 17N 72 30 E
Yarlung Zangbo Jiang = Brahmaputra →, *Asia* ... **69 H13** 23 40N 90 35 E
Yarmouth, *Canada* ... **105 D6** 43 50N 66 7W
Yarmūk →, *Syria* ... **74 C4** 32 42N 35 40 E
Yaroslavl, *Russia* ... **32 D10** 57 35N 39 55 E
Yarqa, W. →, *Egypt* ... **74 F2** 30 0N 33 49 E
Yarra Yarra Lakes, *Australia* ... **93 E2** 29 40 S 115 45 E
Yarram, *Australia* ... **95 F4** 38 29 S 146 39 E
Yarraman, *Australia* ... **95 D5** 26 50 S 152 0 E
Yarras, *Australia* ... **95 E5** 31 25 S 152 20 E
Yartsevo, *Sib., Russia* ... **53 C10** 60 20N 90 0 E
Yartsevo, *Smolensk, Russia* ... **32 E7** 55 6N 32 43 E

Yarumal, *Colombia* ... **124 B3** 6 58N 75 24W
Yasawa Group, *Fiji* ... **91 C7** 17 0 S 177 23 E
Yaselda, *Belarus* ... **33 F4** 52 7N 26 28 E
Yasen, *Ukraine* ... **29 B9** 48 45N 24 10 E
Yashi, *Nigeria* ... **83 C6** 12 23N 7 54 E
Yashikera, *Nigeria* ... **83 D5** 9 44N 3 29 E
Yashkul, *Russia* ... **35 G7** 46 11N 45 21 E
Yasin, *Pakistan* ... **69 A5** 36 24N 73 23 E
Yasinovataya, *Ukraine* ... **33 H9** 48 7N 37 57 E
Yasinski, L., *Canada* ... **104 B4** 53 16N 77 35W
Yasinya, *Ukraine* ... **29 B9** 48 16N 24 21 E
Yasothon, *Thailand* ... **64 E5** 15 50N 104 10 E
Yass, *Australia* ... **95 E4** 34 49 S 148 54 E
Yāsūj, *Iran* ... **71 D6** 30 31N 51 31 E
Yatağan, *Turkey* ... **47 D10** 37 20N 28 10 E
Yatakala, *Niger* ... **83 C5** 14 50N 0 22 E
Yates Center, *U.S.A.* ... **113 G7** 37 53N 95 44W
Yathkyed L., *Canada* ... **103 A9** 62 40N 98 0W
Yatsushiro, *Japan* ... **55 H5** 32 30N 130 40 E
Yatta Plateau, *Kenya* ... **86 C4** 2 0 S 38 0 E
Yauco, *Puerto Rico* ... **121 d** 18 2N 66 51W
Yavari →, *Peru* ... **124 D4** 4 21 S 70 2W
Yávaros, *Mexico* ... **118 B3** 26 42N 109 31W
Yavatmal, *India* ... **66 J11** 20 20N 78 15 E
Yavne, *Israel* ... **74 D3** 31 52N 34 45 E
Yavoriv, *Ukraine* ... **31 J10** 49 55N 23 20 E
Yavorov = Yavoriv, *Ukraine* ... **31 J10** 49 55N 23 20 E
Yavuzeli, *Turkey* ... **72 D7** 37 18N 37 24 E
Yawatahama, *Japan* ... **55 H6** 33 27N 132 24 E
Yawri B., *S. Leone* ... **82 D2** 8 22N 13 0W
Yaxi, *China* ... **58 D6** 27 33N 106 41 E
Yazd, *Iran* ... **71 D7** 31 55N 54 27 E
Yazd □, *Iran* ... **71 D7** 32 0N 55 0 E
Yazd-e Khvāst, *Iran* ... **71 D7** 31 31N 52 7 E
Yazıköy, *Turkey* ... **47 E9** 36 40N 27 20 E
Yazman, *Pakistan* ... **68 E4** 29 8N 71 45 E
Yazoo →, *U.S.A.* ... **113 J9** 32 22N 90 54W
Yazoo City, *U.S.A.* ... **113 J9** 32 51N 90 25W
Ybbs, *Austria* ... **26 C8** 48 12N 15 4 E
Ybycuí, *Paraguay* ... **126 B4** 26 5 S 56 46W
Ybytyruzú △, *Paraguay* ... **127 B4** 25 51 S 56 11W
Yding Skovhøj, *Denmark* ... **11 J3** 55 59N 9 46 E
Ye, *Burma* ... **64 E1** 15 15N 97 15 E
Ye Xian, *China* ... **56 H7** 33 35N 113 25 E
Yebyu, *Burma* ... **64 E2** 14 15N 98 13 E
Yecheon, *S. Korea* ... **57 F15** 36 39N 128 27 E
Yecla, *Spain* ... **39 G3** 38 35N 1 5W
Yécora, *Mexico* ... **118 B3** 28 20N 108 58W
Yedebub Biheroch Biheresoboch na Hizboch □, *Ethiopia* ... **81 F4** 12 0N 36 0 E
Yedintsy = Edineţ, *Moldova* ... **29 B12** 48 9N 27 18 E
Yedseram →, *Nigeria* ... **83 C7** 12 30N 14 5 E
Yefremov, *Russia* ... **32 F10** 53 8N 38 3 E
Yeghegnadzor, *Armenia* ... **73 C11** 39 44N 45 19 E
Yegorlyk →, *Russia* ... **35 G5** 46 35N 41 57 E
Yegorlykskaya, *Russia* ... **35 G5** 46 33N 40 35 E
Yegoryevsk, *Russia* ... **32 E10** 55 27N 38 55 E
Yegros, *Paraguay* ... **126 B4** 26 20 S 56 25W
Yehbuah, *Indonesia* ... **63 J17** 8 23 S 114 45 E
Yehuda, Midbar, *Israel* ... **74 D4** 31 35N 35 15 E
Yei, *Sudan* ... **81 G3** 4 9N 30 40 E
Yei, Nahr →, *Sudan* ... **81 F3** 6 15N 30 13 E
Yejmiadzin, *Armenia* ... **35 K7** 40 12N 44 19 E
Yekaterinburg, *Russia* ... **52 D7** 56 50N 60 30 E
Yelabuga, *Russia* ... **34 C11** 55 45N 52 4 E
Yelan, *Russia* ... **34 E6** 50 55N 43 43 E
Yelarbon, *Australia* ... **95 D5** 28 33 S 150 38 E
Yelatma, *Russia* ... **34 C5** 55 0N 41 45 E
Yelets, *Russia* ... **33 F10** 52 40N 38 30 E
Yélimané, *Mali* ... **82 B2** 15 9N 10 34W
Yelizavetgrad = Kirovohrad, *Ukraine* ... **33 H7** 48 35N 32 20 E
Yell, *U.K.* ... **13 A7** 60 35N 1 5W
Yell Sd., *U.K.* ... **13 A7** 60 33N 1 15W
Yellow Sea, *China* ... **57 G12** 35 0N 123 0 E
Yellowhead Pass, *Canada* ... **102 C5** 52 53N 118 25W
Yellowknife, *Canada* ... **102 A6** 62 27N 114 29W
Yellowknife →, *Canada* ... **102 A6** 62 31N 114 19W
Yellowstone △, *U.S.A.* ... **108 D9** 44 40N 110 30W
Yellowstone →, *U.S.A.* ... **112 B3** 47 59N 103 59W
Yellowstone L., *U.S.A.* ... **108 D8** 44 27N 110 22W
Yelnya, *Russia* ... **32 E7** 54 35N 33 15 E
Yelsk, *Belarus* ... **33 G5** 51 50N 29 10 E
Yelwa, *Nigeria* ... **83 C5** 10 49N 4 41 E
Yemen ■, *Asia* ... **75 E3** 15 0N 44 0 E
Yen Bai, *Vietnam* ... **58 G5** 21 42N 104 52 E
Yenagoa, *Nigeria* ... **83 E6** 4 58N 6 16 E
Yenakiyeve, *Ukraine* ... **33 H10** 48 15N 38 15 E
Yenakiyevo = Yenakiyeve, *Ukraine* ... **33 H10** 48 15N 38 15 E
Yenangyaung, *Burma* ... **67 J19** 20 30N 95 0 E
Yenbo = Yanbu 'al Baḥr, *Si. Arabia* ... **70 F3** 24 0N 38 5 E
Yenda, *Australia* ... **95 E4** 34 13 S 146 14 E
Yende Millimou, *Guinea* ... **82 D2** 8 55N 10 10W
Yendéré, *Burkina Faso* ... **82 C4** 10 12N 4 59W
Yendi, *Ghana* ... **83 D4** 9 29N 0 1W
Yenice, *Ankara, Turkey* ... **72 C5** 39 14N 32 42 E
Yenice, *Aydın, Turkey* ... **47 D10** 37 49N 28 15 E
Yenice, *Çanakkale, Turkey* ... **47 B9** 39 55N 27 17 E
Yenice →, *Turkey* ... **45 F10** 40 42N 26 9 E
Yenice →, *Turkey* ... **72 D6** 37 37N 35 33 E
Yenifoça, *Turkey* ... **47 C8** 38 44N 26 51 E
Yenihisar, *Turkey* ... **47 D9** 37 22N 27 16 E
Yeniköy, *Bursa, Turkey* ... **45 F13** 40 31N 29 22 E
Yeniköy, *Çanakkale, Turkey* ... **47 B8** 39 55N 26 10 E
Yeniköy, *Kütahya, Turkey* ... **47 C11** 38 52N 29 17 E
Yenipazar, *Turkey* ... **47 D10** 37 49N 28 11 E
Yenisaía, *Greece* ... **45 E8** 41 1N 24 57 E
Yenişehir, *Turkey* ... **45 F13** 40 16N 29 40 E
Yenisey →, *Russia* ... **52 B9** 71 50N 82 40 E
Yeniseysk, *Russia* ... **53 D10** 58 27N 92 13 E
Yeniseyskiy Zaliv, *Russia* ... **52 B9** 72 20N 81 0 E
Yennádhi, *Greece* ... **49 C9** 36 2N 27 56 E
Yenne, *France* ... **21 C9** 45 43N 5 44 E
Yenotayevka, *Russia* ... **35 G8** 47 15N 47 0 E
Yenyuka, *Russia* ... **53 D13** 57 57N 121 15 E
Yeo →, *U.K.* ... **15 G5** 51 2N 2 49W
Yeo, L., *Australia* ... **93 E3** 28 0 S 124 30 E
Yeo I., *Canada* ... **116 A3** 45 24N 81 48W
Yeola, *India* ... **66 J9** 20 0N 74 30 E
Yeoryioúpolis, *Greece* ... **49 D6** 35 20N 24 15 E
Yeovil, *U.K.* ... **15 G5** 50 57N 2 38W
Yeppoon, *Australia* ... **94 C5** 23 5 S 150 47 E
Yeráki, *Greece* ... **46 D4** 37 0N 22 42 E

Yerbent, *Turkmenistan* ... **52 F6** 39 30N 58 50 E
Yerbogachen, *Russia* ... **53 C11** 61 16N 108 0 E
Yerevan, *Armenia* ... **35 K7** 40 10N 44 31 E
Yerington, *U.S.A.* ... **108 G4** 38 59N 119 10W
Yerkesik, *Turkey* ... **47 D10** 37 7N 28 19 E
Yerköy, *Turkey* ... **72 C6** 39 38N 34 28 E
Yermak, *Kazakhstan* ... **52 D8** 52 2N 76 55 E
Yermo, *U.S.A.* ... **111 L10** 34 54N 116 50W
Yerólakkos, *Cyprus* ... **49 D12** 35 11N 33 15 E
Yeropol, *Russia* ... **53 C17** 65 15N 168 40 E
Yeropótamos →, *Greece* ... **49 D6** 35 3N 24 50 E
Yeroskipos, *Cyprus* ... **49 E11** 34 46N 32 28 E
Yershov, *Russia* ... **34 E9** 51 23N 48 27 E
Yerushalayim = Jerusalem, *Israel* ... **74 D4** 31 47N 35 10 E
Yerville, *France* ... **18 C7** 49 40N 0 53 E
Yes Tor, *U.K.* ... **15 G4** 50 41N 4 0W
Yesan, *S. Korea* ... **57 F14** 36 41N 126 51 E
Yeşilhisar, *Turkey* ... **72 C6** 38 20N 35 5 E
Yeşilırmak →, *Turkey* ... **72 B7** 41 22N 36 37 E
Yeşilkent, *Turkey* ... **72 D7** 36 57N 36 12 E
Yeşilköy, *Turkey* ... **45 F12** 40 57N 28 49 E
Yeşilova, *Turkey* ... **47 D11** 37 31N 29 46 E
Yeşilyurt, *Manisa, Turkey* ... **47 C10** 38 22N 28 40 E
Yeşilyurt, *Muğla, Turkey* ... **47 D11** 37 10N 28 20 E
Yesnogorsk, *Russia* ... **32 E9** 54 32N 37 38 E
Yeso, *U.S.A.* ... **113 H2** 34 26N 104 37W
Yessentuki, *Russia* ... **35 H6** 44 5N 42 53 E
Yessey, *Russia* ... **53 C11** 68 29N 102 10 E
Yhati, *Paraguay* ... **126 B4** 25 45 S 56 35W
Yhú, *Paraguay* ... **127 B4** 25 0 S 56 0W
Yi →, *Uruguay* ... **126 C4** 33 7 S 57 54W
Yi 'Allaq, G., *Egypt* ... **74 E2** 30 22N 33 32 E
Yi He →, *China* ... **57 G10** 34 10N 118 8 E
Yi Xian, *Anhui, China* ... **59 C11** 29 55N 117 57 E
Yi Xian, *Hebei, China* ... **56 E8** 39 20N 115 30 E
Yi Xian, *Liaoning, China* ... **57 D11** 41 30N 121 22 E
Yialí, *Greece* ... **47 E9** 36 41N 27 11 E
Yialiás →, *Cyprus* ... **49 D12** 35 9N 33 44 E
Yi'allaq, G., *Egypt* ... **80 A3** 30 21N 33 31 E
Yialousa, *Cyprus* ... **49 D13** 35 32N 34 10 E
Yiáltra, *Greece* ... **46 C4** 38 51N 22 59 E
Yianisádhes, *Greece* ... **49 D8** 35 20N 26 10 E
Yiannitsa, *Greece* ... **44 F6** 40 46N 22 24 E
Yibin, *China* ... **58 C5** 28 45N 104 32 E
Yichang, *China* ... **59 B8** 30 40N 111 20 E
Yicheng, *Henan, China* ... **59 B9** 31 41N 112 12 E
Yicheng, *Shanxi, China* ... **56 G6** 35 42N 111 40 E
Yichuan, *China* ... **56 F6** 36 2N 110 10 E
Yichun, *Heilongjiang, China* ... **60 B7** 47 44N 128 52 E
Yichun, *Jiangxi, China* ... **59 D10** 27 48N 114 22 E
Yidu, *China* ... **57 F10** 36 43N 118 28 E
Yidun, *China* ... **58 B2** 30 22N 99 21 E
Yifag, *Ethiopia* ... **81 E4** 12 4N 37 46 E
Yifeng, *China* ... **59 C10** 28 21N 114 45 E
Yihuang, *China* ... **59 D11** 27 30N 116 12 E
Yijun, *China* ... **56 G5** 35 28N 109 8 E
Yıldız Dağları, *Turkey* ... **45 E11** 41 48N 27 36 E
Yıldızeli, *Turkey* ... **72 C7** 39 51N 36 36 E
Yiliang, *Yunnan, China* ... **58 D5** 27 38N 104 2 E
Yiliang, *Yunnan, China* ... **58 E4** 24 56N 103 11 E
Yilong, *China* ... **58 B6** 31 34N 106 23 E
Yimen, *China* ... **58 E4** 24 40N 102 10 E
Yimianpo, *China* ... **57 B15** 45 7N 128 2 E
Yinchuan, *China* ... **56 E4** 38 30N 106 15 E
Yindarlgooda, L., *Australia* ... **93 F3** 30 40 S 121 52 E
Ying He →, *China* ... **56 H9** 32 30N 116 30 E
Ying Xian, *China* ... **56 E7** 39 32N 113 10 E
Yingcheng, *China* ... **59 B9** 30 56N 113 35 E
Yingde, *China* ... **59 E9** 24 10N 113 25 E
Yingjiang, *China* ... **58 E1** 24 41N 97 55 E
Yingjing, *China* ... **58 C4** 29 41N 102 52 E
Yingkou, *China* ... **57 D12** 40 37N 122 18 E
Yingshan, *Henan, China* ... **58 C4** 30 57N 114 16 E
Yingshan, *Hubei, China* ... **59 B10** 31 0N 115 32 E
Yingshang, *China* ... **59 A11** 32 38N 116 12 E
Yingtan, *China* ... **59 C11** 28 12N 117 0 E
Yining, *China* ... **52 E9** 43 58N 81 10 E
Yinjiang, *China* ... **58 C7** 28 1N 108 21 E
Yinmabin, *Burma* ... **67 H19** 22 10N 94 55 E
Yiofíros →, *Greece* ... **49 D7** 35 20N 25 6 E
Yioúra, *Nótios Aiyaíon, Greece* ... **46 D6** 37 32N 24 40 E
Yioúra, *Thessalía, Greece* ... **46 B6** 39 23N 24 10 E
Yipinglang, *China* ... **58 E3** 25 10N 101 52 E
Yirba Muda, *Ethiopia* ... **81 F4** 6 12N 38 42 E
Yirga Alem, *Ethiopia* ... **81 F4** 6 48N 38 22 E
Yirol, *Sudan* ... **81 F3** 6 33N 30 30 E
Yirrkala, *Australia* ... **94 A2** 12 14 S 136 56 E
Yishan, *China* ... **58 E7** 24 28N 108 38 E
Yishui, *China* ... **57 G10** 35 47N 118 30 E
Yishun, *Singapore* ... **65 d** 1 26N 103 50 E
Yíthion, *Greece* ... **46 E4** 36 46N 22 34 E
Yitong, *China* ... **57 C13** 43 13N 125 20 E
Yiwu, *China* ... **59 C13** 29 20N 120 3 E
Yixing, *China* ... **59 B12** 31 21N 119 48 E
Yiyang, *Henan, China* ... **56 G7** 34 27N 112 10 E
Yiyang, *Hunan, China* ... **59 C9** 28 35N 112 18 E
Yiyang, *Jiangxi, China* ... **59 C11** 28 22N 117 57 E
Yizhang, *China* ... **59 E9** 25 27N 112 57 E
Yli-Kitka, *Finland* ... **8 C23** 66 8N 28 30 E
Ylitornio, *Finland* ... **8 C20** 66 19N 23 39 E
Ylivieska, *Finland* ... **8 D21** 64 4N 24 28 E
Yngaren, *Sweden* ... **11 F10** 58 50N 16 35 E
Yoakum, *U.S.A.* ... **113 L6** 29 17N 97 9W
Yob →, *Eritrea* ... **81 D4** 17 15N 37 50 E
Yobe □, *Nigeria* ... **83 C7** 12 0N 11 30 E
Yog Pt., *Phil.* ... **63 B6** 14 6N 124 12 E
Yogan, *Togo* ... **83 D5** 6 23N 1 30 E
Yoğuntaş, *Turkey* ... **45 E11** 41 50N 27 4 E
Yogyakarta, *Indonesia* ... **63 G14** 7 49 S 110 22 E
Yoho △, *Canada* ... **102 C5** 51 25N 116 30W
Yojoa, L. de, *Honduras* ... **120 D2** 14 53N 87 50W
Yōju, *S. Korea* ... **57 F14** 37 20N 127 35 E
Yok Don △, *Vietnam* ... **64 F6** 12 50N 107 40 E
Yokadouma, *Cameroon* ... **84 D2** 3 26N 14 55 E
Yokkaichi, *Japan* ... **55 G8** 34 55N 136 38 E

Yoko, *Cameroon* ... **83 D7** 5 32N 12 20 E
Yokohama, *Japan* ... **55 G9** 35 27N 139 28 E
Yokosuka, *Japan* ... **55 G9** 35 20N 139 40 E
Yokote, *Japan* ... **54 E10** 39 20N 140 30 E
Yola, *Nigeria* ... **83 D7** 9 10N 12 29 E
Yolaina, Cordillera de, *Nic.* ... **120 D3** 11 30N 84 0W
Yoloten, *Turkmenistan* ... **71 B9** 37 18N 62 21 E
Yom →, *Thailand* ... **62 A2** 15 35N 100 1 E
Yonago, *Japan* ... **55 G6** 35 25N 133 19 E
Yonaguni-Jima, *Japan* ... **55 M1** 24 27N 123 0 E
Yŏnan, *N. Korea* ... **57 F14** 37 55N 126 11 E
Yonezawa, *Japan* ... **54 F10** 37 57N 140 4 E
Yong Peng, *Malaysia* ... **65 L4** 2 0N 103 3 E
Yong Sata, *Thailand* ... **65 J2** 7 8N 99 41 E
Yong'an, *China* ... **59 E11** 25 59N 117 25 E
Yongcheng, *China* ... **56 H9** 33 55N 116 20 E
Yongch'ŏn, *S. Korea* ... **57 G15** 35 58N 128 56 E
Yongchuan, *China* ... **58 C5** 29 17N 105 55 E
Yongchun, *China* ... **59 E12** 25 16N 118 20 E
Yongde, *China* ... **58 E2** 24 5N 99 25 E
Yongdeng, *China* ... **56 F2** 36 38N 103 25 E
Yongding, *China* ... **59 E11** 24 43N 116 45 E
Yŏngdŏk, *S. Korea* ... **57 F15** 36 24N 129 22 E
Yŏngdŭngpo, *S. Korea* ... **57 F14** 37 31N 126 54 E
Yongfeng, *China* ... **59 D10** 27 20N 115 22 E
Yongfu, *China* ... **58 E7** 24 59N 109 59 E
Yonghe, *China* ... **56 F6** 36 46N 110 38 E
Yŏnghŭng, *N. Korea* ... **57 E14** 39 31N 127 18 E
Yongji, *China* ... **56 G6** 34 52N 110 28 E
Yongjia, *China* ... **59 C13** 28 10N 120 42 E
Yŏngju, *S. Korea* ... **57 F15** 36 50N 128 40 E
Yongkang, *Yunnan, China* ... **58 E2** 24 9N 99 20 E
Yongkang, *Zhejiang, China* ... **59 C13** 28 55N 120 2 E
Yongnian, *China* ... **56 F8** 36 47N 114 29 E
Yongning, *Guangxi Zhuangzu, China* ... **58 F7** 22 44N 108 28 E
Yongning, *Ningxia Huizu, China* ... **56 E4** 38 15N 106 14 E
Yongping, *China* ... **58 E2** 25 27N 99 38 E
Yongqing, *China* ... **56 E9** 39 25N 116 28 E
Yongren, *China* ... **58 D3** 26 4N 101 40 E
Yongshan, *China* ... **58 C4** 28 11N 103 35 E
Yongsheng, *China* ... **58 D3** 26 38N 100 46 E
Yongshun, *China* ... **58 C7** 29 2N 109 51 E
Yongtai, *China* ... **59 E12** 25 49N 118 58 E
Yŏngwŏl, *S. Korea* ... **57 F15** 37 11N 128 28 E
Yongxin, *Jinggangshan, China* ... **59 D10** 26 58N 114 15 E
Yongxing, *China* ... **59 D9** 26 9N 113 8 E
Yongxiu, *China* ... **59 C10** 29 2N 115 42 E
Yongzhou, *China* ... **59 D8** 26 17N 111 37 E
Yonibana, *S. Leone* ... **82 D2** 8 30N 12 19W
Yonkers, *U.S.A.* ... **117 F11** 40 56N 73 54W
Yonne □, *France* ... **19 E10** 47 50N 3 40 E
Yonne →, *France* ... **19 D9** 48 23N 2 58 E
York, *Australia* ... **93 F2** 31 52 S 116 47 E
York, *U.K.* ... **14 D6** 53 58N 1 6W
York, *Ala., U.S.A.* ... **113 J10** 32 29N 88 18W
York, *Nebr., U.S.A.* ... **112 E6** 40 52N 97 36W
York, *Pa., U.S.A.* ... **114 F7** 39 58N 76 44W
York, C., *Australia* ... **94 A3** 10 42 S 142 31 E
York, City of □, *U.K.* ... **14 D6** 53 58N 1 6W
York, Kap, *Greenland* ... **4 B4** 75 55N 66 25W
York, Vale of, *U.K.* ... **14 C6** 54 15N 1 25W
York Haven, *U.S.A.* ... **116 F8** 40 7N 76 46W
York Sd., *Australia* ... **92 C4** 15 0 S 125 5 E
Yorke Pen., *Australia* ... **95 E2** 34 50 S 137 40 E
Yorkshire Dales △, *U.K.* ... **14 C5** 54 12N 2 10W
Yorkshire Wolds, *U.K.* ... **14 C7** 54 8N 0 31W
Yorkton, *Canada* ... **103 C8** 51 11N 102 28W
Yorkville, *U.S.A.* ... **110 G3** 38 52N 123 13W
Yoro, *Honduras* ... **120 C2** 15 9N 87 7W
Yoron-Jima, *Japan* ... **55 L4** 27 2N 128 26 E
Yorosso, *Mali* ... **82 C4** 12 17N 4 55W
Yos Sudarso, Pulau = Dolak, Pulau, *Indonesia* ... **63 F9** 8 0 S 138 30 E
Yosemite △, *U.S.A.* ... **110 H7** 37 45N 119 40W
Yosemite Village, *U.S.A.* ... **110 H7** 37 45N 119 35W
Yoshino-Kumano △, *Japan* ... **55 H8** 34 12N 135 55 E
Yoshkar Ola, *Russia* ... **34 B8** 56 38N 47 55 E
Yŏsu, *S. Korea* ... **57 G14** 34 47N 127 45 E
Yotvata, *Israel* ... **74 F4** 29 55N 35 2 E
You Jiang →, *China* ... **58 F6** 22 50N 108 6 E
You Xian, *China* ... **59 D9** 27 1N 113 17 E
Youbou, *Canada* ... **110 B2** 48 53N 124 13W
Youghal, *Ireland* ... **12 E4** 51 56N 7 52W
Youghal B., *Ireland* ... **12 E4** 51 55N 7 49W
Youkounkoun, *Guinea* ... **82 C2** 12 35N 13 11W
Young, *Australia* ... **95 E4** 34 19 S 148 18 E
Young, *Canada* ... **103 C7** 51 47N 105 45W
Young, *Uruguay* ... **126 C4** 32 44 S 57 36W
Younghusband, L., *Australia* ... **95 E2** 30 50 S 136 5 E
Younghusband Pen., *Australia* ... **95 F2** 36 0 S 139 25 E
Youngstown, *Canada* ... **103 C6** 51 35N 111 10W
Youngstown, *N.Y., U.S.A.* ... **116 C5** 43 15N 79 3W
Youngstown, *Ohio, U.S.A.* ... **116 E4** 41 6N 80 39W
Youngsville, *U.S.A.* ... **116 E5** 41 51N 79 19W
Youngwood, *U.S.A.* ... **116 F5** 40 14N 79 34W
Youxi, *China* ... **59 D12** 26 10N 118 13 E
Youyang, *China* ... **58 C7** 28 47N 108 42 E
Youyu, *China* ... **56 D7** 40 10N 112 20 E
Yozgat, *Turkey* ... **72 C6** 39 51N 34 47 E
Ypacaraí △, *Paraguay* ... **126 B4** 25 18 S 57 19W
Ypané →, *Paraguay* ... **126 A4** 23 29 S 57 19W
Yport, *France* ... **18 C7** 49 45N 0 15 E
Ypres = Ieper, *Belgium* ... **17 D2** 50 51N 2 53 E
Yreka, *U.S.A.* ... **108 F2** 41 44N 122 38W
Yssingeaux, *France* ... **21 C8** 45 9N 4 8 E
Ystad, *Sweden* ... **11 J7** 55 26N 13 50 E
Ysyk-Köl, *Kyrgyzstan* ... **52 E8** 42 25N 77 15 E
Ythan →, *U.K.* ... **13 D7** 57 19N 1 59W
Ytterhogdal, *Sweden* ... **10 B8** 62 12N 14 56 E
Ytyk-Kyuyel, *Russia* ... **53 C14** 62 30N 133 45 E
Yu Jiang →, *China* ... **58 F7** 23 22N 110 3 E
Yu Shan, *Taiwan* ... **59 F13** 23 30N 120 58 E
Yu Xian = Yuzhou, *China* ... **56 G7** 34 10N 113 28 E
Yu Xian, *Hebei, China* ... **56 E8** 39 50N 114 35 E
Yu Xian, *Shanxi, China* ... **56 E7** 38 5N 113 20 E
Yuan Jiang →, *Hunan, China* ... **59 C8** 28 55N 111 50 E
Yuan Jiang →, *Yunnan, China* ... **58 F4** 22 20N 103 59 E
Yuan'an, *China* ... **59 B8** 31 3N 111 34 E
Yuanjiang, *Hunan, China* ... **59 C9** 28 47N 112 21 E

Yuanjiang, *Yunnan, China* ... **58 F4** 23 32N 102 0 E
Yüanli, *Taiwan* ... **59 E13** 24 27N 120 39 E
Yüanlin, *Taiwan* ... **59 F13** 23 58N 120 30 E
Yuanling, *China* ... **59 C8** 28 29N 110 22 E
Yuanmou, *China* ... **58 E3** 25 42N 101 53 E
Yuanqu, *China* ... **56 G6** 35 18N 111 40 E
Yuanyang, *Henan, China* ... **56 G7** 35 3N 113 58 E
Yuanyang, *Yunnan, China* ... **58 F4** 23 10N 102 43 E
Yuba →, *U.S.A.* ... **110 F5** 39 8N 121 36W
Yuba City, *U.S.A.* ... **110 F5** 39 8N 121 37W
Yūbari, *Japan* ... **54 C10** 43 4N 141 59 E
Yubdo, *Ethiopia* ... **81 F4** 8 58N 35 27 E
Yūbetsu, *Japan* ... **54 B11** 44 13N 143 50 E
Yubo, *Sudan* ... **81 F2** 5 23N 27 25 E
Yucatán □, *Mexico* ... **119 C7** 21 30N 86 30W
Yucatán, Canal de, *Caribbean* ... **120 B2** 22 0N 86 30W
Yucatán, Península de, *Mexico* ... **98 H11** 19 30N 89 0W
Yucatan Basin, *Cent. Amer.* ... **98 H11** 19 0N 86 0W
Yucatan Channel = Yucatán, Canal de, *Caribbean* ... **120 B2** 22 0N 86 30W
Yucca, *U.S.A.* ... **111 L12** 34 52N 114 9W
Yucca Valley, *U.S.A.* ... **111 L10** 34 8N 116 27W
Yucheng, *China* ... **56 F9** 36 55N 116 32 E
Yuci, *China* ... **56 F7** 37 42N 112 46 E
Yudu, *China* ... **59 E10** 25 59N 115 30 E
Yuechi, *China* ... **58 B6** 30 34N 106 25 E
Yuendumu, *Australia* ... **92 D5** 22 16 S 131 49 E
Yueqing, *China* ... **59 C13** 28 9N 120 59 E
Yueqing Wan, *China* ... **59 D13** 28 5N 121 12 E
Yuexi, *Anhui, China* ... **59 B11** 30 50N 116 20 E
Yuexi, *Sichuan, China* ... **58 C4** 28 37N 102 26 E
Yueyang, *China* ... **59 C9** 29 21N 113 5 E
Yugan, *China* ... **59 C11** 28 43N 116 37 E
Yugoslavia = Serbia & Montenegro ■, *Europe* ... **44 C4** 43 20N 20 0 E
Yuhuan, *China* ... **59 C13** 28 9N 121 12 E
Yuhuan Dao, *China* ... **59 C13** 28 5N 121 15 E
Yujiang, *China* ... **59 C11** 28 10N 116 43 E
Yukhnov, *Russia* ... **32 E8** 54 44N 35 15 E
Yukon →, *U.S.A.* ... **100 B3** 62 32N 163 54W
Yukon Territory □, *Canada* ... **100 B6** 63 0N 135 0W
Yüksekova, *Turkey* ... **73 D11** 37 34N 44 16 E
Yukta, *Russia* ... **53 C11** 63 26N 105 42 E
Yukuhashi, *Japan* ... **55 H5** 33 44N 130 59 E
Yulara, *Australia* ... **93 E5** 25 10 S 130 55 E
Yule →, *Australia* ... **92 D2** 20 41 S 118 17 E
Yuleba, *Australia* ... **95 D4** 26 37 S 149 24 E
Yuli, *Nigeria* ... **83 D7** 9 44N 10 12 E
Yuli, *Taiwan* ... **59 F13** 23 20N 121 18 E
Yulin, *Guangxi Zhuangzu, China* ... **59 F8** 22 40N 110 8 E
Yulin, *Hainan, China* ... **65 C7** 18 10N 109 31 E
Yulin, *Shaanxi, China* ... **56 E5** 38 20N 109 30 E
Yuma, *Ariz., U.S.A.* ... **111 N12** 32 43N 114 37W
Yuma, *Colo., U.S.A.* ... **112 E3** 40 8N 102 43W
Yuma, B. de, *Dom. Rep.* ... **121 C6** 18 20N 68 35W
Yumbe, *Uganda* ... **86 B3** 3 28N 31 15 E
Yumbi, *Dem. Rep. of the Congo* ... **86 C2** 1 12 S 26 15 E
Yumen, *China* ... **60 C4** 39 50N 97 30 E
Yumurtalık, *Turkey* ... **72 D6** 36 45N 35 43 E
Yun Gui Gaoyuan, *China* ... **58 E3** 26 0N 104 0 E
Yun Ho →, *China* ... **57 E9** 39 10N 117 10 E
Yun Ling, *China* ... **58 D2** 27 0N 99 20 E
Yun Xian, *Hubei, China* ... **59 A8** 32 50N 110 46 E
Yun Xian, *Yunnan, China* ... **58 E3** 24 27N 100 8 E
Yunak, *Turkey* ... **72 C4** 38 49N 31 43 E
Yunan, *China* ... **59 F8** 23 12N 111 30 E
Yuncheng, *Henan, China* ... **56 G8** 35 36N 115 57 E
Yuncheng, *Shanxi, China* ... **56 G6** 35 2N 111 0 E
Yunfu, *China* ... **59 F9** 22 50N 112 5 E
Yungas, *Bolivia* ... **124 G5** 17 0 S 66 0W
Yungay, *Chile* ... **126 D1** 37 10 S 72 5W
Yunhe, *China* ... **59 C12** 28 8N 119 33 E
Yunkai Dashan, *China* ... **59 F8** 22 30N 111 0 E
Yunlin, *Taiwan* ... **59 F13** 23 42N 120 30 E
Yunlong, *China* ... **58 E2** 25 57N 99 13 E
Yunmeng, *China* ... **59 B9** 31 2N 113 43 E
Yunnan □, *China* ... **58 E4** 25 0N 102 0 E
Yunquera de Henares, *Spain* ... **38 E1** 40 47N 3 11W
Yunt Dağı, *Turkey* ... **47 C9** 38 56N 27 13 E
Yunta, *Australia* ... **95 E2** 32 34 S 139 36 E
Yunxiao, *China* ... **59 F11** 23 59N 117 18 E
Yuping, *China* ... **58 D7** 27 13N 108 56 E
Yupyongdong, *N. Korea* ... **57 D15** 41 49N 128 53 E
Yuqing, *China* ... **58 D6** 27 13N 107 53 E
Yuraygir △, *Australia* ... **95 D5** 29 45 S 153 15 E
Yurga, *Russia* ... **52 D9** 55 42N 84 51 E
Yurimaguas, *Peru* ... **124 E3** 5 55 S 76 7W
Yurkivka, *Ukraine* ... **29 B13** 48 42N 28 35 E
Yurubí △, *Venezuela* ... **121 D6** 10 26N 68 42W
Yuryev-Polskiy, *Russia* ... **32 D10** 56 30N 39 40 E
Yuryevets, *Russia* ... **34 B6** 57 25N 43 2 E
Yuscarán, *Honduras* ... **120 D2** 13 58N 86 45W
Yûsef, Baḥr →, *Egypt* ... **80 B3** 28 25N 30 50 E
Yushan, *China* ... **59 C12** 28 42N 118 10 E
Yushanzhen, *China* ... **58 C7** 29 28N 108 22 E
Yushe, *China* ... **56 F7** 37 4N 112 58 E
Yushu, *Jilin, China* ... **57 B14** 44 43N 126 38 E
Yushu, *Qinghai, China* ... **60 C4** 33 5N 96 55 E
Yusufeli, *Turkey* ... **73 B9** 40 50N 41 32 E
Yutai, *China* ... **57 E9** 39 53N 117 45 E
Yuxarı Qarabağ = Nagorno-Karabakh □, *Azerbaijan* ... **70 B5** 39 55N 46 45 E
Yuxi, *China* ... **58 E4** 24 30N 102 35 E
Yuyao, *China* ... **59 B13** 30 3N 121 10 E
Yuzawa, *Japan* ... **54 E10** 39 10N 140 30 E
Yuzha, *Russia* ... **34 B6** 56 34N 42 1 E
Yuzhno-Sakhalinsk, *Russia* ... **53 E15** 46 58N 142 45 E
Yuzhnyy □, *Russia* ... **35 H5** 44 0N 40 0 E
Yuzhou, *China* ... **56 G7** 34 10N 113 28 E
Yvelines □, *France* ... **19 D8** 48 40N 1 45 E
Yverdon-les-Bains, *Switz.* ... **25 J2** 46 47N 6 39 E
Yvetot, *France* ... **18 C7** 49 37N 0 44 E
Yzeure, *France* ... **19 F10** 46 33N 3 22 E

Z

Zaanstad, *Neths.* ...... **17 B4** 52 27N 4 50 E
Zāb al Kabīr →, *Iraq* .. **70 C4** 36 1N 43 24 E
Zāb aş Şaghīr →, *Iraq* .. **70 C4** 35 17N 43 29 E
Zabalj, *Serbia & M.* ... **28 E5** 45 21N 20 5 E
Zabari, *Serbia & M.* .... **44 B5** 44 22N 21 15 E
Zabarjad, *Egypt* ...... **80 C4** 23 40N 36 12 E
Zabaykalsk, *Russia* .... **53 E12** 49 40N 117 25 E
Zabki, *Poland* .... **31 F8** 52 17N 21 7 E
Ząbkowice Śląskie,
  Poland .... **31 H3** 50 35N 16 50 E
Żabludów, *Poland* ..... **31 F9** 53 0N 23 19 E
Zabno, *Poland* .... **31 H7** 50 9N 20 53 E
Zābol, *Iran* .... **71 D9** 31 0N 61 32 E
Zābol □, *Afghan.* ...... **66 D5** 32 0N 67 0 E
Zābolī, *Iran* .... **71 E9** 27 10N 61 35 E
Zabolotiv, *Ukraine* .... **29 B10** 48 28N 25 18 E
Zabolottya, *Ukraine* .. **31 G11** 51 38N 24 16 E
Zabré, *Burkina Faso* ... **83 C4** 11 12N 0 36W
Zábřeh, *Czech Rep.* .... **27 B9** 49 53N 16 52 E
Zabrze, *Poland* .... **31 H5** 50 18N 18 50 E
Zabuzhzhya, *Ukraine* .. **31 G10** 51 21N 23 42 E
Zabzuga, *Ghana* .... **83 D5** 9 20N 0 30 E
Zacapa, *Guatemala* **120 D2** 14 59N 89 31W
Zacapu, *Mexico* **118 D4** 19 50N 101 43W
Zacatecas, *Mexico* **118 C4** 22 49N 102 34W
Zacatecas □, *Mexico* .. **118 C4** 23 30N 103 0W
Zacatecoluca, *El Salv.* . **120 D2** 13 29N 88 51W
Zachary, *U.S.A.* **113 K9** 30 39N 91 9W
Zachodnio-
  Pomorskie □, *Poland* **30 E2** 53 40N 15 50 E
Zacoalco, *Mexico* **118 C4** 20 14N 103 33W
Zacualtipán, *Mexico* .. **119 C5** 20 39N 98 36W
Zadar, *Croatia* .... **41 D12** 44 8N 15 14 E
Zadawa, *Nigeria* .... **83 C7** 11 33N 10 19 E
Zadetkyi Kyun, *Burma* **65 G2** 10 0N 98 25 E
Zadonsk, *Russia* .... **33 F10** 52 25N 38 56 E
Zafarqand, *Iran* .... **71 C7** 33 11N 52 29 E
Zafferana, *Iran* .... **47 E8** 36 5N 26 24 E
Zafra, *Spain* **37 G4** 38 26N 6 30W
Zagań, *Poland* .... **31 G2** 51 39N 15 22 E
Zagaoua, *Chad* .... **79 E10** 15 30N 22 24 E
Zagarė, *Lithuania* ..... **30 B10** 56 21N 23 15 E
Zagazig, *Egypt* .... **80 H7** 30 40N 31 30 E
Zägheh, *Iran* .... **71 C6** 33 30N 48 42 E
Zaglivérion, *Greece* ... **44 F7** 40 36N 23 15 E
Zagnanado, *Benin* ..... **83 D5** 7 18N 2 28 E
Zagorá, *Greece* .... **46 B5** 39 27N 23 6 E
Zagorje, *Slovenia* ..... **41 B11** 46 8N 15 0 E
Zagórów, *Poland* ...... **31 F4** 52 10N 17 54 E
Zagórz, *Poland* .... **31 J9** 49 30N 22 14 E
Zagreb, *Croatia* .... **41 C12** 45 50N 15 58 E
Zagreb ✈ (ZAG),
  Croatia .... **41 C13** 45 45N 16 4 E
Zāgros, Kūhhā-ye, *Iran* **71 C6** 33 45N 48 5 E
Zagros Mts. = Zāgros,
  Kūhhā-ye, *Iran* ..... **71 C6** 33 45N 48 5 E
Žagubica, *Serbia & M.* . **44 B5** 44 15N 21 47 E
Zaguinaso, *Ivory C.* ... **82 C3** 10 1N 6 14W
Zagyva →, *Hungary* .... **28 C5** 47 5N 20 4 E
Zahamena △, *Madag.* . **89 B8** 17 37 S 48 49 E
Zāhedān, *Fārs, Iran* ... **71 D7** 28 46N 53 52 E
Zāhedān,
  Sīstān va Balūchestān,
  Iran .... **71 D9** 29 30N 60 50 E
Zahlah, *Lebanon* ...... **74 B4** 33 52N 35 50 E
Zahna, *Germany* .... **24 D8** 51 55N 12 49 E
Zainsk, *Russia* .... **34 C11** 55 18N 52 4 E
Zaïre = Congo →,
  Africa .... **84 F2** 6 4 S 12 24 E
Zaječar, *Serbia & M.* .. **44 C6** 43 53N 22 18 E
Zaka, *Zimbabwe* ...... **89 C5** 20 20 S 31 29 E
Zakamensk, *Russia* .... **53 D11** 50 23N 103 17 E
Zakarpatska □, *Ukraine* **29 B8** 48 20N 23 0 E
Zakataly = Zaqatala,
  Azerbaijan .... **35 K8** 41 38N 46 35 E
Zakháro, *Greece* ...... **46 D3** 37 30N 21 39 E
Zakhodnaya Dzvina =
  Daugava →, *Latvia* . **9 H21** 57 4N 24 3 E
Zākhū, *Iraq* .... **70 B4** 37 10N 42 50 E
Zákinthos, *Greece* .... **46 D2** 37 47N 20 54 E
Zákinthos □, *Greece* .. **46 D2** 37 47N 20 57 E
Zakopane, *Poland* ..... **31 J6** 49 18N 19 57 E
Zakroczym, *Poland* ... **31 F7** 52 26N 20 38 E
Zákros, *Greece* .... **49 D8** 35 6N 26 10 E
Zala □, *Hungary* ...... **28 D2** 46 42N 16 50 E
Zala →, *Hungary* ...... **28 D2** 46 43N 17 16 E
Zalaegerszeg, *Hungary* . **28 D1** 46 53N 16 47 E
Zalakomár, *Hungary* .. **28 D2** 46 33N 17 10 E
Zalalövő, *Hungary* .... **28 D1** 46 51N 16 35 E
Zalamea de la Serena,
  Spain **37 G5** 38 40N 5 38W
Zalamea la Real, *Spain* **37 H4** 37 41N 6 38W
Zalău, *Romania* .... **28 C8** 47 12N 23 3 E
Žalec, *Slovenia* .... **41 B12** 46 16N 15 10 E
Zaleshchiki =
  Zalishchyky, *Ukraine* **29 B10** 48 45N 25 45 E
Zalesye, *Russia* .... **30 D8** 54 50N 21 31 E
Zalew Wiślany, *Poland* **30 D6** 54 20N 19 50 E
Zalewo, *Poland* .... **30 E6** 53 50N 19 41 E
Zalingei, *Sudan* .... **79 F10** 12 51N 23 29 E
Zalishchyky, *Ukraine* .. **29 B10** 48 45N 25 45 E
Zama L., *Canada* **102 B5** 58 45N 119 5W
Zambeke, *Dem. Rep. of*
  the Congo .... **86 B2** 2 8N 25 17 E
Zambeze →, *Africa* .... **87 F4** 18 35 S 36 20 E
Zambezi = Zambeze →,
  Africa .... **87 F4** 18 35 S 36 20 E
Zambezi, *Zambia* ...... **85 G4** 13 30 S 23 15 E
Zambezi □, *Zimbabwe* **87 F2** 17 54 S 25 41 E
Zambezia □, *Mozam.* .. **87 F4** 16 15 S 37 30 E
Zambia ■, *Africa* ..... **87 F2** 15 0 S 28 0 E
Zamboanga, *Phil.* ..... **61 H5** 6 59N 122 3 E
Zambrów, *Poland* ..... **31 F9** 52 59N 22 14 E
Zametchino, *Russia* ... **34 D6** 53 30N 42 30 E
Zamfara □, *Nigeria* ... **83 C6** 12 10N 6 0 E
Zamfara →, *Nigeria* ... **83 C5** 12 5N 4 2 E
Zamora, *Mexico* **118 D4** 20 0N 102 21W
Zamora, *Spain* **36 D5** 41 30N 5 45W
Zamora □, *Spain* **36 D5** 41 30N 5 46W
Zamość, *Poland* .... **31 H10** 50 43N 23 15 E
Zamtang, *China* .... **58 A3** 32 26N 101 6 E
Zan, *Ghana* **83 D4** 9 26N 0 17W
Záncara →, *Spain* **39 F1** 39 18N 3 18W
Zandvoort, *Neths.* .... **17 B4** 52 22N 4 32 E
Zanesville, *U.S.A.* **116 G2** 39 56N 82 1W
Zangābād, *Iran* .... **70 B5** 38 26N 46 44 E
Zangue →, *Mozam.* .... **87 F4** 17 50 S 35 21 E
Zanjān, *Iran* .... **71 B6** 36 40N 48 35 E
Zanjān □, *Iran* .... **71 B6** 37 20N 49 30 E
Zanjān →, *Iran* .... **71 B6** 37 8N 47 47 E

Zannone, *Italy* .... **42 B6** 40 58N 13 3 E
Zante = Zákinthos,
  Greece .... **46 D2** 37 47N 20 54 E
Zanthus, *Australia* .... **93 F3** 31 2 S 123 34 E
Zanzibar, *Tanzania* ... **86 D4** 6 12 S 39 12 E
Zaouiet El-Kala = Bordj
  Omar Driss, *Algeria* . **78 C7** 28 10N 6 40 E
Zaouiet Reggâne,
  Algeria .... **78 C6** 26 32N 0 3 E
Zaoyang, *China* .... **59 A9** 32 10N 112 45 E
Zaozhuang, *China* ..... **57 G9** 34 50N 117 35 E
Zap Suyu = Zāb al
  Kabīr →, *Iraq* ...... **70 C4** 36 1N 43 24 E
Zapadna Morava →,
  Serbia & M. .... **44 C5** 43 38N 21 30 E
Zapadnaya Dvina =
  Daugava →, *Latvia* . **9 H21** 57 4N 24 3 E
Zapadnaya Dvina,
  Russia .... **32 D7** 56 15N 32 3 E
Západné Beskydy,
  Europe .... **27 B12** 49 30N 19 0 E
Zapadni Rodopi,
  Bulgaria .... **44 E7** 41 50N 24 0 E
Západočeský □,
  Czech Rep. .... **26 B6** 49 35N 13 0 E
Zapala, *Argentina* ..... **128 D2** 39 0 S 70 5W
Zapaleri, Cerro, *Bolivia* **126 A2** 22 49 S 67 11W
Zapata, *U.S.A.* **113 M5** 26 55N 99 16W
Zapatón →, *Spain* **37 F4** 39 0N 6 49W
Zaporizhzhya, *Ukraine* **33 J8** 47 50N 35 10 E
Zaporozhye =
  Zaporizhzhya,
  Ukraine .... **33 J8** 47 50N 35 10 E
Zaqatala, *Azerbaijan* .. **35 K8** 41 38N 46 35 E
Zara, *Turkey* .... **70 B3** 39 58N 37 43 E
Zaragoza, Coahuila,
  Mexico **118 B4** 28 30N 101 0W
Zaragoza, Nuevo León,
  Mexico **119 C5** 24 0N 99 46W
Zaragoza, *Spain* **38 D4** 41 39N 0 53W
Zaragoza □, *Spain* **38 D3** 41 35N 1 0W
Zarand, Kermān, *Iran* . **71 D8** 30 46N 56 34 E
Zarand, Markazī, *Iran* . **71 C6** 35 18N 50 25 E
Zărandului, Munţii,
  Romania .... **28 D7** 46 14N 22 7 E
Zaranj, *Afghan.* .... **66 D2** 30 55N 61 55 E
Zarasai, *Lithuania* .... **9 J22** 55 40N 26 20 E
Zárate, *Argentina* ..... **126 C4** 34 7 S 59 0W
Zarautz, *Spain* **38 B2** 43 17N 2 10W
Zaraysk, *Russia* .... **32 E10** 54 48N 38 53 E
Zard, Kūh-e, *Iran* ..... **71 C6** 32 22N 50 4 E
Zāreh, *Iran* .... **71 C6** 35 7N 49 9 E
Zari, *Nigeria* .... **83 C7** 13 4N 12 45 E
Zaria, *Nigeria* .... **83 C6** 11 0N 7 40 E
Zarki, *Poland* .... **31 H6** 50 38N 19 23 E
Zárkon, *Greece* .... **46 B4** 39 38N 22 6 E
Zarneh, *Iran* .... **70 C5** 33 55N 46 10 E
Zărneşti, *Romania* .... **29 E10** 45 33N 25 18 E
Zárós, *Greece* .... **49 D6** 35 8N 24 54 E
Żarów, *Poland* .... **31 H3** 50 56N 16 29 E
Zarqā', Nahr az →,
  Jordan .... **74 C4** 32 10N 35 37 E
Zarrīn, *Iran* .... **71 C7** 32 46N 54 37 E
Zaruma, *Ecuador* ..... **124 D3** 3 40 S 79 38W
Żary, *Poland* .... **31 G2** 51 37N 15 10 E
Zarza de Granadilla,
  Spain **36 E4** 40 14N 6 3W
Zarzis, *Tunisia* .... **79 B8** 33 31N 11 2 E
Zas, *Spain* **36 B2** 43 4N 8 53W
Zaskar →, *India* ...... **69 B7** 34 13N 77 20 E
Zaskar Mts., *India* .... **69 C7** 33 15N 77 30 E
Zastavna, *Ukraine* .... **29 B10** 48 31N 25 51 E
Zastron, *S. Africa* ..... **88 E4** 30 18 S 27 7 E
Žatec, *Czech Rep.* .... **26 A6** 50 20N 13 32 E
Zaterechnyy, *Russia* ... **35 H7** 44 48N 45 11 E
Zator, *Poland* .... **31 J6** 49 59N 19 28 E
Zatyshshya, *Ukraine* .. **29 C14** 47 20N 29 51 E
Zavala, *Bos.-H.* .... **44 D1** 42 50N 17 59 E
Zavāreh, *Iran* .... **71 C7** 33 29N 52 28 E
Zave, *Zimbabwe* ...... **89 B5** 17 6 S 30 1 E
Zavetnoye, *Russia* .... **35 G6** 47 13N 43 50 E
Zavidovići, *Bos.-H.* ... **28 F3** 44 27N 18 10 E
Zavitinsk, *Russia* ..... **53 D13** 50 10N 129 20 E
Zavodovski, I.,
  Antarctica .... **5 B1** 56 0 S 27 45W
Zavolzhsk, *Russia* ..... **34 B6** 57 30N 42 0 E
Zavolzhye, *Russia* ..... **34 B6** 56 37N 43 26 E
Zawadzkie, *Poland* .... **31 H5** 50 37N 18 28 E
Zawichost, *Poland* .... **31 H8** 50 48N 21 51 E
Zawidów, *Poland* ..... **31 G2** 51 1N 15 1 E
Zawiercie, *Poland* .... **31 H6** 50 30N 19 24 E
Zāwiyat al Baydā = Al
  Baydā, *Libya* .... **79 B10** 32 50N 21 44 E
Zâwyet Shammas, *Egypt* **80 A2** 31 30N 26 37 E
Zâwyet Um el Rakham,
  Egypt .... **80 A2** 31 18N 27 1 E
Zâwyet Ungeîla, *Egypt* **80 A2** 31 30N 26 42 E
Zāyā, *Iraq* .... **70 C5** 33 33N 44 13 E
Zāyandeh →, *Iran* ..... **71 C7** 32 35N 52 0 E
Zaysan, *Kazakhstan* ... **52 E9** 47 28N 84 52 E
Zaysan, Oz., *Kazakhstan* **52 E9** 48 0N 83 0 E
Zayü, *China* .... **58 C1** 28 48N 97 27 E
Zazafotsy, *Madag.* .... **89 C8** 21 11 S 46 21 E
Zázrivá, *Slovak Rep.* .. **27 B12** 49 16N 19 7 E
Zbarazh, *Ukraine* ..... **33 H3** 49 43N 25 44 E
Zbąszyń, *Poland* ...... **31 F2** 52 14N 15 56 E
Zbąszynek, *Poland* .... **31 F2** 52 16N 15 51 E
Zblewo, *Poland* .... **30 E5** 53 56N 18 19 E
Zbruch →, *Ukraine* ... **29 B11** 48 32N 26 27 E
Ždár nad Sázavou,
  Czech Rep. .... **26 B8** 49 34N 15 57 E
Zdolbuniv, *Ukraine* ... **33 G4** 50 30N 26 15 E
Zdrelo, *Serbia & M.* ... **44 B5** 44 16N 21 28 E
Zduńska Wola, *Poland* **31 G5** 51 37N 18 59 E
Zduny, *Poland* .... **31 G4** 51 39N 17 21 E
Zeballos, *Canada* **102 D3** 49 59N 126 50W
Zebediela, *S. Africa* ... **89 C4** 24 20 S 29 17 E
Zebila, *Ghana* **83 C4** 10 55N 0 30W
Zeebrugge, *Belgium* ... **17 C3** 51 19N 3 12 E
Zeehan, *Australia* ..... **95 G4** 41 52 S 145 25 E
Zeeland □, *Neths.* .... **17 C3** 51 30N 3 50 E
Zeerust, *S. Africa* ..... **88 D4** 25 31 S 26 4 E
Zefat, *Israel* .... **74 C4** 32 58N 35 29 E
Zege, *Ethiopia* .... **81 E4** 11 43N 37 18 E
Zeggeuna, Iracher, *Mali* **83 B5** 16 42N 2 5 E
Zégoua, *Mali* **82 C3** 10 32N 5 35W
Zehdenick, *Germany* .. **24 C9** 52 59N 13 20 E
Zeil, Mt., *Australia* ... **92 D5** 23 30 S 132 23 E
Zeila, *Somali Rep.* .... **75 E3** 11 21N 43 30 E
Zeist, *Neths.* .... **17 B5** 52 5N 5 15 E
Zeitz, *Germany* .... **24 D8** 51 2N 12 7 E
Zelechów, *Poland* ..... **31 G8** 51 49N 21 54 E
Zelena, *Ukraine* ...... **29 B9** 48 31N 24 45 E
Zelengora, *Bos.-H.* ... **44 C3** 43 22N 18 30 E
Zelenodolsk, *Russia* .. **34 C9** 55 55N 48 30 E
Zelenogorsk, *Russia* .. **32 B5** 60 12N 29 43 E

Zelenograd, *Russia* .... **32 D9** 56 1N 37 12 E
Zelenogradsk, *Russia* .. **9 J19** 54 53N 20 29 E
Zelenokumsk, *Russia* .. **35 H6** 44 24N 44 0 E
Železná Ruda,
  Czech Rep. .... **26 B6** 49 8N 13 15 E
Železnik, *Serbia & M.* . **44 B4** 44 43N 20 23 E
Zelienople, *U.S.A.* **116 F4** 40 48N 80 8W
Želiezovce, *Slovak Rep.* **27 C11** 48 3N 18 40 E
Zelina, *Croatia* .... **41 C13** 45 57N 16 16 E
Zell, Baden-W.,
  Germany .... **25 H3** 47 42N 7 52 E
Zell, Rhld.-Pfz.,
  Germany .... **25 E3** 50 1N 7 10 E
Zell am See, *Austria* ... **26 D5** 47 19N 12 47 E
Zella-Mehlis, *Germany* **24 E6** 50 39N 10 40 E
Zelów, *Poland* .... **31 G6** 51 28N 19 14 E
Zeltweg, *Austria* ...... **26 D7** 47 11N 14 45 E
Žemaitijos △, *Lithuania* **30 B8** 56 2N 21 55 E
Zémio, *C.A.R.* .... **86 A2** 5 2N 25 5 E
Zemplínska Šírava,
  Slovak Rep. .... **27 C15** 48 48N 22 0 E
Zempoala, *Mexico* **119 D5** 19 22N 96 24W
Zemun, *Serbia & M.* .. **44 B4** 44 51N 20 25 E
Zengbé, *Cameroon* .... **83 D7** 5 46N 13 4 E
Zengcheng, *China* ..... **59 F9** 23 13N 113 32 E
Zenica, *Bos.-H.* .... **28 F2** 44 10N 17 57 E
Žepče, *Bos.-H.* .... **28 F3** 44 28N 18 2 E
Zeraf, Bahr ez →,
  Sudan .... **81 F3** 9 42N 30 52 E
Zerbst, *Germany* ...... **24 D8** 51 58N 12 5 E
Zerków, *Poland* .... **31 F4** 52 4N 17 32 E
Zermatt, *Switz.* .... **25 J3** 46 2N 7 46 E
Zernez, *Switz.* .... **25 J6** 46 42N 10 7 E
Zernograd, *Russia* .... **35 G5** 46 52N 40 19 E
Zerqan, *Albania* ...... **44 E4** 41 27N 20 20 E
Zestaponi, *Georgia* ... **35 J6** 42 6N 43 0 E
Zetel, *Germany* .... **24 B3** 53 25N 7 58 E
Zeulenroda, *Germany* . **24 E7** 50 39N 11 59 E
Zeven, *Germany* ...... **24 B5** 53 17N 9 16 E
Zevenaar, *Neths.* ...... **17 C6** 51 56N 6 5 E
Zévio, *Italy* .... **40 C8** 45 22N 11 8 E
Zeya, *Russia* .... **53 D13** 53 48N 127 14 E
Zeya →, *Russia* .... **53 D13** 51 42N 128 53 E
Zeytinbaği, *Turkey* .... **45 F12** 40 24N 28 47 E
Zeytindağ, *Turkey* .... **47 C9** 38 58N 27 4 E
Zghartā, *Lebanon* ..... **74 A4** 34 21N 35 53 E
Zgierz, *Poland* .... **31 G6** 51 50N 19 27 E
Zgorzelec, *Poland* ..... **31 G2** 51 10N 15 0 E
Zguriţa, *Moldova* ...... **29 B13** 48 8N 28 1 E
Zhabinka, *Belarus* ..... **31 F11** 52 13N 24 2 E
Zhabokrych, *Ukraine* .. **29 B13** 48 23N 28 59 E
Zhailma, *Kazakhstan* .. **52 D7** 51 37N 61 33 E
Zhambyl = Taraz,
  Kazakhstan .... **52 E8** 42 54N 71 22 E
Zhangaly, *Kazakhstan* . **35 G10** 47 1N 50 37 E
Zhangaqazaly,
  Kazakhstan .... **52 E7** 45 48N 62 6 E
Zhangbei, *China* ...... **56 D8** 41 10N 114 45 E
Zhangguangcai Ling,
  China .... **57 B15** 45 0N 129 0 E
Zhangjiakou, *China* ... **56 D8** 40 48N 114 55 E
Zhangping, *China* ..... **59 E11** 25 17N 117 23 E
Zhangpu, *China* .... **59 E11** 24 8N 117 35 E
Zhangshu, *China* ...... **59 C10** 28 4N 115 29 E
Zhangwu, *China* ...... **57 C12** 42 43N 122 52 E
Zhangye, *China* .... **60 C5** 38 50N 100 23 E
Zhangzhou, *China* .... **59 E11** 24 30N 117 35 E
Zhanhua, *China* .... **57 F10** 37 40N 118 8 E
Zhanjiang, *China* ..... **59 G8** 21 15N 110 20 E
Zhannetty, Ostrov,
  Russia .... **53 B16** 76 43N 158 0 E
Zhanyi, *China* .... **58 E4** 25 38N 103 48 E
Zhanyu, *China* .... **57 B12** 44 30N 122 30 E
Zhao Xian, *China* ..... **56 F8** 37 43N 114 45 E
Zhao'an, *China* .... **59 F11** 23 41N 117 10 E
Zhaocheng, *China* .... **56 F6** 36 22N 111 38 E
Zhaojue, *China* .... **58 C4** 28 1N 102 49 E
Zhaoping, *China* ...... **59 E8** 24 11N 110 48 E
Zhaoqing, *China* ...... **59 F9** 23 0N 112 20 E
Zhaotong, *China* ...... **58 D4** 27 20N 103 44 E
Zhaoyuan, Heilongjiang,
  China .... **57 B13** 45 27N 125 0 E
Zhaoyuan, Shandong,
  China .... **57 F11** 37 20N 120 23 E
Zharkovskiy, *Russia* ... **32 E7** 55 56N 32 19 E
Zhashkiv, *Ukraine* .... **33 H6** 49 15N 30 5 E
Zhashui, *China* .... **56 H5** 33 40N 109 8 E
Zhayyq →, *Kazakhstan* **52 E6** 47 0N 51 48 E
Zhdanov = Mariupol,
  Ukraine .... **33 J9** 47 5N 37 31 E
Zhecheng, *China* ...... **56 G8** 34 7N 115 20 E
Zhegao, *China* .... **59 B11** 31 46N 117 44 E
Zhejiang □, *China* ..... **59 C13** 29 0N 120 0 E
Zheleznodorozhnyy,
  Russia .... **30 D8** 54 22N 21 19 E
Zheleznogorsk, *Russia* . **33 F8** 52 22N 35 23 E
Zheleznogorsk-Ilimskiy,
  Russia .... **53 D11** 56 34N 104 8 E
Zheltyye Vody = Zhovti
  Vody, *Ukraine* ...... **33 H7** 48 21N 33 31 E
Zhen'an, *China* .... **56 H5** 33 27N 109 9 E
Zhenba, *China* .... **58 A6** 32 34N 107 58 E
Zhenfeng, *China* ...... **58 E5** 25 24N 105 40 E
Zheng'an, *China* ...... **58 C6** 28 32N 107 27 E
Zhengding, *China* ..... **56 E8** 38 8N 114 32 E
Zhengyang, *China* ..... **59 A10** 32 37N 114 22 E
Zhengyangguan, *China* **59 A11** 32 30N 116 29 E
Zhengzhou, *China* .... **56 G7** 34 45N 113 34 E
Zhenjiang, *China* ..... **59 A12** 32 11N 119 26 E
Zhenkang, *China* ...... **58 F2** 23 58N 99 0 E
Zhenlai, *China* .... **57 B12** 45 50N 123 5 E
Zhenning, *China* ...... **58 D5** 26 4N 105 45 E
Zhenping, Henan, *China* **56 H7** 33 10N 112 16 E
Zhenping, Shaanxi,
  China .... **58 B7** 31 59N 109 31 E
Zhenxiong, *China* ..... **58 D5** 27 27N 104 50 E
Zhenyang, *Gansu, China* **56 G4** 35 35N 107 30 E
Zhenyuan, Guizhou,
  China .... **58 D7** 27 4N 108 21 E
Zherdevka, *Russia* .... **34 E5** 51 56N 41 29 E
Zherebkove, *Ukraine* .. **29 C14** 47 50N 29 52 E
Zherong, *China* .... **59 D12** 27 15N 119 52 E
Zhetiqara, *Kazakhstan* **52 D7** 52 11N 61 12 E
Zhezqazghan,
  Kazakhstan .... **52 E7** 47 44N 67 40 E
Zhicheng, *China* ...... **59 B8** 30 25N 111 27 E
Zhidan, *China* .... **56 F5** 36 48N 108 48 E
Zhigansk, *Russia* ..... **53 C13** 66 48N 123 27 E
Zhigulevsk, *Russia* .... **34 D9** 53 28N 49 30 E
Zhigulevsk, *Russia* .... **34 D9** 53 28N 49 30 E
Zhijiang, Hubei, China .. **59 B8** 30 28N 111 45 E
Zhijiang, Hunan, China . **58 D7** 27 27N 109 42 E
Zhijin, *China* .... **58 D5** 26 37N 105 45 E

Zhilinda, *Russia* ...... **53 C12** 70 0N 114 20 E
Zhilino, *Russia* .... **30 D8** 54 54N 21 54 E
Zhirnovsk, *Russia* ..... **34 E7** 50 57N 44 49 E
Zhitomir = Zhytomyr,
  Ukraine .... **33 G5** 50 20N 28 40 E
Zhizdra, *Russia* .... **32 F8** 53 45N 34 40 E
Zhlobin, *Belarus* ...... **33 F6** 52 55N 30 0 E
Zhmerinka =
  Zhmerynka, *Ukraine* **33 H5** 49 2N 28 2 E
Zhmerynka, *Ukraine* .. **33 H5** 49 2N 28 2 E
Zhob, *Pakistan* .... **68 D3** 31 20N 69 31 E
Zhob →, *Pakistan* ..... **68 C3** 32 4N 69 50 E
Zhodino = Zhodzina,
  Belarus .... **32 E5** 54 5N 28 17 E
Zhodzina, *Belarus* .... **32 E5** 54 5N 28 17 E
Zhokhova, Ostrov,
  Russia .... **53 B16** 76 4N 152 40 E
Zhongdian, *China* ..... **58 D2** 27 48N 99 42 E
Zhongdong, *China* .... **58 F6** 22 48N 107 47 E
Zhongdu, *China* ...... **58 E7** 24 40N 109 40 E
Zhongning, *China* ..... **56 F3** 37 29N 105 40 E
Zhongshan, Guangdong,
  China .... **59 F9** 22 26N 113 20 E
Zhongshan,
  Guangxi Zhuangzu,
  China .... **59 E8** 24 29N 111 18 E
Zhongtiao Shan, *China* **56 G5** 35 0N 111 10 E
Zhongwei, *China* ...... **56 F3** 37 30N 105 12 E
Zhongxiang, *China* .... **59 B9** 31 12N 112 34 E
Zhongyang, *China* ..... **56 F6** 37 20N 111 11 E
Zhorany, *Ukraine* ..... **31 G10** 51 19N 23 58 E
Zhoucun, *China* .... **57 F9** 36 47N 117 48 E
Zhouning, *China* ...... **59 D12** 27 12N 119 20 E
Zhoushan, *China* ...... **59 B14** 30 1N 122 10 E
Zhoushan Dao, *China* . **59 C14** 30 5N 122 10 E
Zhouzhi, *China* .... **56 G5** 34 10N 108 12 E
Zhovti Vody, *Ukraine* . **33 H7** 48 21N 33 31 E
Zhovtneve, *Ukraine* ... **31 H11** 50 42N 24 12 E
Zhovtneve, *Ukraine* ... **33 J7** 46 54N 32 3 E
Zhovtneve =
  Zhovtneve, *Ukraine* . **33 J7** 46 54N 32 3 E
Zhu Jiang →, *China* .. **59 F9** 22 45N 113 37 E
Zhuanghe, *China* ..... **57 E12** 39 40N 123 0 E
Zhucheng, *China* ...... **57 G10** 36 0N 119 27 E
Zhugqu, *China* .... **56 H3** 33 40N 104 30 E
Zhuhai, *China* .... **59 F9** 22 17N 113 34 E
Zhuji, *China* .... **59 C13** 29 40N 120 10 E
Zhukovka, *Russia* ..... **32 F7** 53 35N 33 50 E
Zhumadian, *China* .... **56 H8** 32 59N 114 2 E
Zhuo Xian = Zhuozhou,
  China .... **56 E8** 39 28N 115 58 E
Zhuolu, *China* .... **56 D8** 40 20N 115 12 E
Zhuozhou, *China* ..... **56 E8** 39 28N 115 58 E
Zhuozi, *China* .... **56 D7** 41 0N 112 25 E
Zhushan, *China* .... **59 A8** 32 15N 110 0 E
Zhuzhou, *China* ...... **59 D9** 27 49N 113 12 E
Zhvanets, *Ukraine* .... **29 B11** 48 33N 26 30 E
Zhytomyr, *Ukraine* ... **33 G5** 50 20N 28 40 E
Zi Shui →, *China* ..... **59 C9** 28 40N 112 40 E
Ziar nad Hronom,
  Slovak Rep. .... **27 C11** 48 35N 18 53 E
Ziārān, *Iran* .... **71 B6** 36 7N 50 32 E
Ziarat, *Pakistan* ...... **68 D2** 30 25N 67 49 E
Zibo, *China* .... **57 F10** 36 47N 118 3 E
Zichang, *China* .... **56 F5** 37 18N 109 40 E
Zidarovo, *Bulgaria* .... **45 D11** 42 20N 27 24 E
Zidi = Wandhari,
  Pakistan .... **68 F2** 27 42N 66 48 E
Ziębice, *Poland* .... **31 H4** 50 37N 17 2 E
Zielona Góra, *Poland* . **31 G2** 51 57N 15 31 E
Zierikzee, *Neths.* ..... **17 C3** 51 40N 3 55 E
Ziesar, *Germany* ...... **24 C8** 52 16N 12 17 E
Zifta, *Egypt* .... **80 H7** 30 43N 31 14 E
Zigey, *Chad* .... **79 F9** 14 43N 15 50 E
Zigong, *China* .... **58 C5** 29 15N 104 48 E
Ziguinchor, *Senegal* .. **82 C1** 12 35N 16 20W
Zihuatanejo, *Mexico* .. **118 D4** 17 38N 101 33W
Zijin, *China* .... **59 F10** 23 33N 115 8 E
Zile, *Turkey* .... **72 B6** 40 15N 35 52 E
Žilina, *Slovak Rep.* ... **27 B11** 49 12N 18 42 E
Žilinský □, *Slovak Rep.* **27 B12** 49 10N 19 0 E
Zillah, *Libya* .... **79 C9** 28 30N 17 33 E
Zillertaler Alpen,
  Austria .... **26 D4** 47 6N 11 45 E
Zima, *Russia* .... **53 D11** 54 0N 102 5 E
Zimapán, *Mexico* **119 C5** 20 54N 99 20W
Zimba, *Zambia* .... **87 F2** 17 20 S 26 11 E
Zimbabwe, *Zimbabwe* **87 G3** 20 16 S 30 54 E
Zimbabwe ■, *Africa* .. **87 F3** 19 0 S 30 0 E
Zimi, S. Leone **82 D2** 7 20N 11 20W
Ziminca, *Russia* ...... **29 G10** 43 40N 25 22 E
Zimovniki, *Russia* .... **35 G6** 47 10N 42 0 E
Zinave △, *Mozam.* .... **89 C5** 21 35 S 33 40 E
Zinder, *Niger* .... **83 C6** 13 48N 9 0 E
Zinga, *Tanzania* ...... **87 D4** 9 16 S 38 49 E
Zingst, *Germany* ...... **24 A8** 54 26N 12 39 E
Ziniaré, *Burkina Faso* . **83 C4** 12 35N 1 18W
Zion △, *U.S.A.* **109 H7** 37 15N 113 5W
Zirbitzkogel, *Austria* .. **26 D7** 47 4N 14 34 E
Zirc, *Hungary* .... **28 C3** 47 17N 17 52 E
Žiri, *Slovenia* .... **41 B11** 46 3N 14 5 E
Žirje, *Croatia* .... **41 E12** 43 39N 15 42 E
Zirl, *Austria* .... **26 D4** 47 17N 11 14 E
Zirndorf, *Germany* .... **25 F6** 49 27N 10 58 E
Ziros, *Greece* .... **49 D8** 35 5N 26 8 E
Zirreh, Gowd-e, *Afghan.* **66 E3** 29 45N 62 0 E
Zistersdorf, *Austria* ... **27 C9** 48 33N 16 45 E
Zitácuaro, *Mexico* **118 D4** 19 28N 100 21W
Žitište, *Serbia & M.* ... **28 E5** 45 30N 20 32 E
Žitište, *Serbia & M.* ... **28 B5** 41 37N 105 10 E
Zitsa, *Greece* .... **46 B2** 39 47N 20 40 E
Zittau, *Germany* ...... **24 E10** 50 57N 14 47 E
Zitundo, *Mozam.* ..... **89 D5** 26 48 S 32 47 E
Živinice, *Bos.-H.* ...... **28 F3** 44 27N 18 39 E
Ziwa Magharibi =
  Kagera □, *Tanzania* **86 C3** 2 0 S 31 30 E
Ziway, L., *Ethiopia* .... **81 F4** 8 0N 38 50 E
Zixing, *China* .... **59 D11** 25 59N 113 21 E
Ziyang, Shaanxi, China . **56 H5** 32 32N 108 31 E
Ziyang, Sichuan, China . **58 B5** 30 6N 104 40 E
Ziyun, *China* .... **58 E6** 25 45N 106 5 E
Zizhong, *China* .... **58 C5** 29 48N 104 47 E
Zlarin, *Croatia* .... **41 E12** 43 42N 15 49 E
Zlatar, *Croatia* .... **41 B13** 46 5N 16 3 E
Zlataritsa, *Bulgaria* ... **45 C9** 43 3N 25 55 E

Zlatitsa, *Bulgaria* ..... **45 D8** 42 41N 24 7 E
Zlatna, *Romania* ...... **29 D8** 46 8N 23 11 E
Zlatna Panega, *Bulgaria* **45 C8** 43 5N 24 9 E
Zlatni Pyasŭtsi, *Bulgaria* **45 C11** 43 17N 28 3 E
Zlatograd, *Bulgaria* ... **45 E9** 41 22N 25 7 E
Zlatoust, *Russia* ...... **52 D6** 55 10N 59 40 E
Zletovo, *Macedonia* ... **44 E6** 41 59N 22 17 E
Zlín, *Czech Rep.* ...... **27 B9** 49 14N 17 40 E
Zlínský □, *Czech Rep.* . **27 B10** 49 14N 17 40 E
Złocieniec, *Poland* .... **30 E3** 53 30N 16 1 E
Złoczew, *Poland* ...... **31 G5** 51 24N 18 35 E
Zlot, *Serbia & M.* ..... **44 B5** 44 1N 21 58 E
Złotoryja, *Poland* ..... **31 G2** 51 8N 15 55 E
Złotów, *Poland* .... **30 E4** 53 22N 17 2 E
Zmeinogorsk,
  Kazakhstan .... **52 D9** 51 10N 82 13 E
Żmigród, *Poland* ...... **31 G3** 51 28N 16 53 E
Zmiyev, *Ukraine* ...... **33 H9** 49 39N 36 27 E
Znamenka =
  Znamyanka, *Ukraine* **33 H7** 48 45N 32 30 E
Znamensk, *Russia* .... **30 D8** 54 36N 21 16 E
Znamyanka, *Ukraine* .. **33 H7** 48 45N 32 30 E
Żnin, *Poland* .... **31 F4** 52 51N 17 44 E
Znojmo, *Czech Rep.* .. **26 C9** 48 50N 16 2 E
Zobeyrī, *Iran* .... **70 C5** 34 10N 46 40 E
Zobia, Dem. Rep. of
  the Congo .... **86 B2** 3 0N 25 59 E
Zoetermeer, *Neths.* ... **17 B4** 52 3N 4 30 E
Zogang, *China* .... **58 C1** 29 55N 97 42 E
Zogno, *Italy* .... **40 C6** 45 48N 9 40 E
Zogqên, *China* .... **58 A2** 32 13N 98 47 E
Zolochev = Zolochiv,
  Ukraine .... **33 H3** 49 45N 24 51 E
Zolochiv, *Ukraine* .... **33 H3** 49 45N 24 51 E
Zolotonosha, *Ukraine* . **33 H7** 49 39N 32 5 E
Zolotyy Potik, *Ukraine* **29 B10** 48 54N 25 20 E
Zomba, *Malawi* .... **87 F4** 15 22 S 35 19 E
Zongo, Dem. Rep. of
  the Congo .... **84 D3** 4 20N 18 35 E
Zonguldak, *Turkey* .... **72 B4** 41 28N 31 50 E
Zongyang, *China* ...... **59 B11** 30 42N 117 12 E
Zonqor Pt., *Malta* .... **49 D2** 35 52N 14 34 E
Zonza, *France* .... **21 G13** 41 45N 9 11 E
Zorgo, Burkina Faso ... **83 C4** 12 15N 0 35W
Zorita, *Spain* **37 F5** 39 17N 5 39W
Zorleni, *Romania* ..... **29 D12** 46 14N 27 44 E
Zornitsa, *Bulgaria* .... **45 D10** 42 23N 26 58 E
Zorritos, *Peru* .... **124 D2** 3 43 S 80 40W
Żory, *Poland* .... **31 H5** 50 3N 18 44 E
Zorzor, *Liberia* **82 D3** 7 46N 9 28W
Zossen, *Germany* ..... **24 C9** 52 13N 13 27 E
Zou Xiang, *China* ..... **56 G9** 35 30N 116 58 E
Zouan-Hounien,
  Ivory C. **82 D3** 6 55N 8 15W
Zouar, *Chad* .... **79 D9** 20 30N 16 32 E
Zouérate = Zouîrât,
  Mauritania **78 D3** 22 44N 12 21W
Zouïrât, *Mauritania* .. **78 D3** 22 44N 12 21W
Zourma, Burkina Faso . **83 C4** 12 0N 0 50W
Zoutkamp, *Neths.* .... **17 A6** 53 20N 6 18 E
Zrenjanin, *Serbia & M.* **28 E5** 45 22N 20 23 E
Zuarungu, *Ghana* **83 C4** 10 49N 0 46W
Zuba, *Nigeria* .... **83 D6** 9 11N 7 12 E
Zubayr, *Yemen* .... **81 D5** 15 3N 42 10 E
Zubtsov, *Russia* ...... **32 D8** 56 10N 34 34 E
Zuénoula, *Ivory C.* ... **82 D3** 7 34N 6 3W
Zuera, *Spain* **38 D4** 41 51N 0 49W
Žufār, *Oman* .... **75 D5** 17 40N 54 0 E
Zug, *Switz.* .... **25 H4** 47 9N 8 35 E
Zugdidi, *Georgia* ..... **35 J5** 42 30N 41 30 E
Zugersee, *Switz.* ...... **25 H4** 47 7N 8 35 E
Zugspitze, *Germany* .. **25 H6** 47 25N 10 59 E
Zuid-Holland □, *Neths.* **17 C4** 52 0N 4 35 E
Zuidbeveland, *Neths.* . **17 C3** 51 30N 3 50 E
Zuidhorn, *Neths.* ..... **17 A6** 53 15N 6 23 E
Zújar, *Spain* **37 H8** 37 34N 2 50W
Zújar →, *Spain* **37 G5** 39 1N 5 47W
Żukowo, *Poland* ...... **30 D5** 54 21N 18 22 E
Zula, *Eritrea* .... **81 D4** 15 17N 39 40 E
Zülpich, *Germany* ..... **24 E2** 50 41N 6 39 E
Zumaia, *Spain* **38 B2** 43 19N 2 15W
Zumárraga, *Spain* **38 B2** 43 5N 2 19W
Zumbo, *Mozam.* ...... **87 F3** 15 35 S 30 26 E
Zummo, *Nigeria* ...... **83 D7** 9 51N 12 59 E
Zumpango, *Mexico* ... **119 D5** 19 48N 99 6W
Zungeru, *Nigeria* ..... **83 D6** 9 48N 6 8 E
Zunhua, *China* .... **57 D9** 40 18N 117 58 E
Zuni, *U.S.A.* **109 J9** 35 4N 108 51W
Zunyi, *China* .... **58 D6** 27 42N 106 53 E
Zuo Jiang →, *China* .. **58 F6** 22 42N 107 27 E
Zuozhou, *China* ...... **58 F6** 22 42N 107 27 E
Župa, *Croatia* .... **41 C13** 45 4N 18 43 E
Žur, *Serbia & M.* ..... **44 D4** 42 13N 20 34 E
Zurbāţīyah, *Iraq* ..... **70 C5** 33 9N 46 3 E
Zürich, *Switz.* .... **25 H4** 47 22N 8 32 E
Zürich □, *Switz.* ...... **25 H4** 47 26N 8 40 E
Zürichsee, *Switz.* ..... **25 H4** 47 18N 8 40 E
Zuromin, *Poland* ..... **31 E6** 53 4N 19 51 E
Žut, *Croatia* .... **41 E12** 43 52N 15 17 E
Zutphen, *Neths.* ...... **17 B6** 52 9N 6 12 E
Zuurberg △, *S. Africa* . **88 E4** 33 12 S 25 32 E
Zuwārah, *Libya* ...... **79 B8** 32 58N 12 1 E
Žužan, *Iran* .... **71 C8** 34 22N 59 53 E
Žužemberk, *Slovenia* . **41 C11** 45 52N 14 56 E
Zvenigorodka =
  Zvenyhorodka,
  Ukraine .... **33 H6** 49 4N 30 56 E
Zvenyhorodka, *Ukraine* **33 H6** 49 4N 30 56 E
Zverinogolovskoye,
  Russia .... **52 D7** 54 26N 64 50 E
Zvezdets, *Bulgaria* .... **45 D11** 42 6N 27 26 E
Zvishavane, *Zimbabwe* **87 G3** 20 17 S 30 2 E
Zvolen, *Slovak Rep.* ... **27 C12** 48 33N 19 10 E
Zvonce, *Serbia & M.* .. **44 D6** 42 57N 22 34 E
Zvornik, *Bos.-H.* ..... **28 F4** 44 26N 19 5 E
Zwedru = Tchien,
  Liberia **82 D3** 5 59N 8 15W
Zweibrücken, *Germany* **25 F3** 49 15N 7 21 E
Zwelitsha, *S. Africa* ... **85 L5** 32 55 S 27 22 E
Zwenkau, *Germany* ... **24 D8** 51 13N 12 20 E
Zwettl, *Austria* .... **26 C8** 48 35N 15 9 E
Zwickau, *Germany* .... **24 E8** 50 44N 12 30 E
Zwierzyniec, *Poland* .. **31 H9** 50 36N 22 58 E
Zwiesel, *Germany* ..... **25 F8** 49 1N 13 13 E
Zwoleń, *Poland* .... **31 G8** 51 21N 21 36 E
Zwolle, *Neths.* .... **17 B6** 52 31N 6 6 E
Zwolle, *U.S.A.* **113 K8** 31 38N 93 39W
Zychlin, *Poland* .... **31 F6** 52 15N 19 37 E
Zyrardów, *Poland* ..... **31 F7** 52 3N 20 28 E
Zyryan = Zyryanovsk,
  Kazakhstan .... **52 E9** 49 43N 84 20 E
Zyryanka, *Russia* ..... **53 C16** 65 45N 150 51 E
Zyryanovsk = Zyryan,
  Kazakhstan .... **52 E9** 49 43N 84 20 E
Zywiec, *Poland* .... **31 J6** 49 42N 19 10 E
Zyyi, *Cyprus* .... **49 E12** 34 43N 33 20 E

 AFGHANISTAN
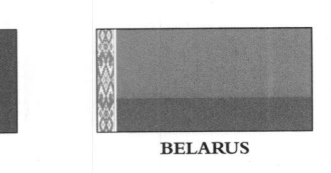 ALBANIA
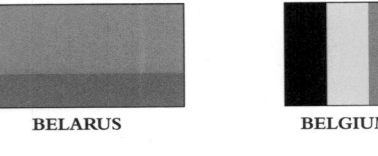 ALGERIA
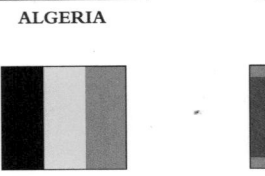 ANDORRA
 ANGOLA
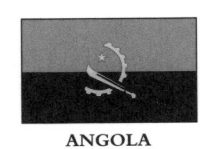 ANTIGUA & BARBUDA
 ARGENTINA

BARBADOS
BELARUS
BELGIUM
BELIZE
BENIN
BHUTAN
BOLIVIA

BURUNDI
CAMBODIA
CAMEROON
CANADA
CAPE VERDE
CENTRAL AFRICAN REP.
CHAD

CROATIA
CUBA
CYPRUS
CZECH REPUBLIC
DENMARK
DJIBOUTI
DOMINICA

ETHIOPIA
FAROE ISLANDS
FIJI
FINLAND
FRANCE
GABON
GAMBIA

GUINEA
GUINEA-BISSAU
GUYANA
HAITI
HONDURAS
HUNGARY
ICELAND

IVORY COAST
JAMAICA
JAPAN
JORDAN
KAZAKHSTAN
KENYA
KIRIBATI

LESOTHO
LIBERIA
LIBYA
LIECHTENSTEIN
LITHUANIA
LUXEMBOURG
MACEDONIA

MARSHALL ISLANDS
MAURITANIA
MAURITIUS
MEXICO
MICRONESIA
MOLDOVA
MONACO

NEW ZEALAND
NICARAGUA
NIGER
NIGERIA
NORTHERN MARIANAS
NORWAY
OMAN

PORTUGAL
PUERTO RICO
QATAR
ROMANIA
RUSSIA
RWANDA
SAMOA

SINGAPORE
SLOVAK REPUBLIC
SLOVENIA
SOLOMON ISLANDS
SOMALIA
SOUTH AFRICA
SPAIN

SWEDEN
SWITZERLAND
SYRIA
TAIWAN
TAJIKISTAN
TANZANIA
THAILAND

UGANDA
UKRAINE
UNITED ARAB EMIRATES
UNITED KINGDOM
UNITED STATES
URUGUAY
UZBEKISTAN